Embark on a voyage of discovery. . .

Your Ship Has Come in . . .
Martin Luther King Jr.
Lessons of War
Communism and the Cold War
Understanding Our World
Historic America
Electronic Field Trips
Jackie Robinson
FDR
Colin Powell
Pocahontas
Biography
A Videodisc Program
MindJogger Videoquiz
The American Journey
SET ON FREEDOM
THE AMERICAN CIVIL RIGHTS MOVEMENT
WORLD WAR II
Testmaker
Chapter Challenger Interactive Review Software
Vocabulary PuzzleMaker
Spanish Resources
Cooperative Learning Activities
Enrichment Activities
Primary Source Readings
Supreme Court Case Studies
GLENCOE VIDEOS
MindJogger Videoquiz
Glencoe Videos
Spanish Section Quizzes
Spanish Vocabulary Activities
Spanish Guided Reading Activities
Spanish Chapter Summaries
Spanish Home Involvement Activities
Spanish Chapter Digest Audiocassettes
Chapter Digest Audiocassettes
Hands-On History Lab Activities
History Simulations
Linking Past and Present Activities
THE AMERICAN REVOLUTION
ENOLA GAY
THE LINCOLN ASSASSINATION
THE AMERICAN INDIAN
A MULTIMEDIA ENCYCLOPEDIA
We the People
LANDMARK DOCUMENTS IN AMERICAN HISTORY
Native Americans
Teacher's Wraparound Edition
Multimedia Connections
Appleby
Brinkley
McPherson
NATIONAL GEOGRAPHIC SOCIETY

A Cargo of Resources Supports Your Journey

Faculty Notes

Take Note of the Valuable Cargo You Will Discover in *The American Journey!*

Read this book! You'll love it!!

"What was it like back then?"

Bringing the people, places, and events of American history to your students is what Glencoe's *The American Journey* video program does best. Students witness the rich history of the United States with the help of such giants as the National Geographic Society, ABCNews InterActive™, A&E Home Video®, The History Channel®, and BIOGRAPHY®.

NATIONAL GEOGRAPHIC SOCIETY

ABC NEWS INTERACTIVE™

A&E HOME VIDEO.

THE HISTORY CHANNEL.

Biography.

Multiple Learning Styles

"Can't We Do Something *Different?*"

Experts say there are multiple learning styles evident in your classroom. Throughout *The American Journey* Teacher's Wraparound Edition, you will find activities for all kinds of learners:

- Verbal/Linguistic Learners
- Logical/Mathematical Learners
- Visual/Spatial Learners
- Auditory/Musical Learners
- Kinesthetic Learners
- Interpersonal Learners
- Intrapersonal Learners

Hands-On HISTORY Lab Activity

Resources available in Glencoe's *The American Journey* guarantee that your classroom will be a multisensory environment, providing multiple paths for student learning.

SKILL BUILDER

Those who care, TEACH!

Performance Assessment

"What's Going to Be On the Test?"

Glencoe's *The American Journey* provides you with two types of assessment. Traditional forms—Chapter and Unit Tests, Section Quizzes, and Testmaker Software—are available. And generously interspersed throughout the text are more authentic forms of assessment—student-directed tasks, teacher-directed tasks, and portfolio activities.

Portfolio Activity

MAPPING America

Go a Step Further

Technology Puts History in Motion

Students are challenged by technology in *The American Journey*. And Glencoe has developed a number of technology programs to accompany the student text.

- **Chapter Challenger Interactive Review Software**
- **Testmaker**
- **Vocabulary PuzzleMaker**
- **MindJogger Videoquiz**

"Browse" through *The American Journey* program to find samples of these technologies.

GLENCOE TECHNOLOGY

NATIONAL GEOGRAPHIC SOCIETY

Multimedia Activities

interNET CONNECTIONS

Block Schedule

Glencoe helps you "get on the block"!

With block scheduling, you can get beyond the "What?" and "When?" questions to delve into the "Why?" and "How?" questions. Glencoe's *The American Journey*—both the Student Edition and the Teacher's Wraparound Edition—provides suggestions for block scheduling instruction in its many cooperative learning activities, team teaching strategies, and interdisciplinary studies.

INTERDISCIPLINARY Activities

Social Studies Connections

Cooperative Learning

Glencoe
McGraw-Hill

New York, New York   Columbus, Ohio   Mission Hills, California   Peoria, Illinois

Teacher's Wraparound Edition

Includes Multimedia Activities

The American Journey

Authors

Joyce Appleby, Ph.D.
Alan Brinkley, Ph.D.
James M. McPherson, Ph.D.

NATIONAL GEOGRAPHIC SOCIETY

Authors

Joyce Appleby, Ph.D. is Professor of History at UCLA. Dr. Appleby's published works include *Capitalism and a New Social Order: The Jeffersonian Vision of the 1790s* and *Ideology and Economic Thought in Seventeenth-Century England,* which won the Berkshire Prize. She served as president of the Organization of American Historians and chaired the Council of the Institute of Early American History and Culture at Williamsburg. Dr. Appleby is currently president of the American Historical Association.

Alan Brinkley, Ph.D. is Professor of American History at Columbia University. His published works include *Voices of Protest: Huey Long, Father Coughlin, and the Great Depression,* which won the 1983 American Book Award, *The End of Reform: New Deal Liberalism in Recession and War,* and *The Unfinished Nation: A Concise History of the American People.* He received the Levenson Memorial Teaching Prize at Harvard University. Dr. Brinkley is a member of the national advisory board for the PBS series "The American Experience."

James M. McPherson, Ph.D. is George Henry Davis Professor of American History at Princeton University. Dr. McPherson is the author of 11 books about the Civil War era. These include *Battle Cry of Freedom: The Civil War Era,* for which he won the Pulitzer Prize in 1989, and *For Cause and Comrades: Why Men Fought in the Civil War.* He is a member of many professional historical associations, including the Association for the Preservation of Civil War Sites and the Civil War Trust.

The **National Geographic Society,** founded in 1888 for the increase and diffusion of geographic knowledge, is the world's largest nonprofit scientific and educational organization. Since its earliest days, the Society has used sophisticated communication technologies and rich historical and archival resources to convey knowledge to a worldwide membership. The Education Products Division supports the Society's mission by developing innovative educational programs—ranging from traditional print materials to multimedia programs including CD-ROMs, videodiscs, and software. "National Geographic Journeys," featured in each unit of this textbook, were designed and developed by the National Geographic Society's Education Products Division.

Glencoe/McGraw-Hill

A Division of The **McGraw-Hill** *Companies*

Design and Production: DECODE, Inc.

Send all inquiries to:
Glencoe/McGraw-Hill, 936 Eastwind Drive, Westerville, Ohio 43081

ISBN 0-02-823218-6 (Student Edition) ISBN 0-02-821787-X (Teacher's Wraparound Edition)

Printed in the United States of America.

1 2 3 4 5 6 7 8 9 027/055 01 00 99 98 97

Academic Consultants

Richard G. Boehm, Ph.D.
Professor of Geography
Southwest Texas State University
San Marcos, Texas

Assad N. Busool, Ph.D.
Professor and Chairman of the Department of Arabic Studies
American Islamic College
Chicago, Illinois

Margo J. Byerly, Ph.D.
Assistant Professor of Social Studies Methods
Ball State University
Muncie, Indiana

Frank de Varona
Region Superintendent
Dade County Public Schools
Miami, Florida

William E. Nelson, Jr., Ph.D.
Research Professor of Black Studies and Professor of Political Science
The Ohio State University
Columbus, Ohio

Bernard Reich, Ph.D.
Professor of Political Science and International Affairs
George Washington University
Washington, D.C.

Donald A. Ritchie, Ph.D.
Associate Historian of the United States Senate Historical Office
Washington, D.C.

Medal with Andrew Jackson's portrait

Teacher Reviewers

John R. Doyle
Director, Division of Social Sciences
Dade County Public Schools
Miami, Florida

David J. Engstrom
American History Teacher
Discovery Junior High School
Fargo, North Dakota

Harry J. Hancock
Social Studies Teacher
Theodore Roosevelt Middle School
Kenner, Louisiana

Elysa E. Toler Robinson, Ed.D.
Program Supervisor
Detroit Public Schools
Detroit, Michigan

Kay R. Selah
Social Studies Teacher
Landmark Middle School
Jacksonville, Florida

Deborah N. Smith
Social Studies Teacher
New Albany Middle School
New Albany, Ohio

Larry John Smith
United States History Teacher
Mt. Savage School
Mt. Savage, Maryland

Cheryl Summers
Clinical Supervisor
Albuquerque Public Schools
Albuquerque, New Mexico

Renée Marie Trufant
Social Studies and Communications Skills Teacher
Brevard Middle School
Brevard, North Carolina

Shaun Kelley Wallace
Social Studies Teacher
Alexander Middle School
Huntersville, North Carolina

Sonya Lou Weaver
Social Studies Teacher
Greencastle–Antrim Middle School
Greencastle, Pennsylvania

Carol Davenport Wood
Social Studies Teacher
Lusher Extension
New Orleans, Louisiana

Table of Contents

Why It's Important xvi

Reference Atlas

- United States Expansion RA2
- United States Facts RA4
- United States (Political) RA6
- United States (Physical) RA8
- Mexico, the Caribbean, and Central America RA10
- Canada RA12
- The World (Political) RA14

Geography HANDBOOK 1

Unit 1

Different Worlds Meet 12

Beginnings to 1625

Chapter 1

The First Americans 16

1 Early Peoples 17
2 Cities and Empires 21
3 North American Peoples 27

Chapter 2

Exploring the Americas 36

1 A Changing World 37
2 Early Exploration 43
3 Spain in America 50
4 Exploring North America 58

Unit 2

Colonial Settlement 66

1587–1770

Chapter 3

Colonial America 70

1 Early English Settlements 71
2 New England Colonies 78
3 Middle Colonies 84
4 Southern Colonies 88
5 Other European Settlements 94

Chest brought from the Netherlands, colonial period

Chapter 4

The Colonies Grow 102

1 Life in the Colonies 103
2 Government, Religion, and Culture 110
3 France and Britain Clash in America 116
4 The French and Indian War 120

Unit 3

Creating a Nation 128

1763–1791

Chapter 5

Road to Independence 132

1 Taxation without Representation 133
2 Building Colonial Unity 138
3 A Call to Arms 142
4 Moving Toward Independence 148

The Declaration of Independence 156

Chapter 6

The American Revolution 162

1 The Early Years 163
2 The War Continues 171
3 The War Moves West and South 176
4 The War Is Won 182

Chapter 7

A More Perfect Union 188

1 The Articles of Confederation 189
2 Convention and Compromise 196
3 A New Plan of Government 204
4 Ratifying the Constitution 209

Civics in Action: A Citizenship Handbook 214

The Constitution of the United States 230

Table of Contents

Unit 4

The New Republic 252
1789–1825

Chapter 8
A New Nation **256**
1 The First President 257
2 Early Challenges 262
3 The First Political Parties 266
4 President John Adams 270

Chapter 9
The Jefferson Era **276**
1 The Republicans Take Power 277
2 The Louisiana Purchase 281
3 A Time of Conflict 289
4 The War of 1812 296

Chapter 10
Growth and Expansion **304**
1 Economic Growth 305
2 Westward Bound 313
3 Unity and Sectionalism 318
4 The Monroe Doctrine 322

Unit 5

The Growing Nation 328
1820–1860

Chapter 11
The Jackson Era **332**
1 From Adams to Jackson 333
2 Jacksonian Democracy 336
3 Conflicts Over Land 342
4 Jackson and the Bank 348

Chapter 12
Manifest Destiny **354**
1 The Oregon Country 355
2 Independence for Texas 362
3 New Mexico and California 368
4 War with Mexico 372
5 New Settlers in California and Utah 376

Chapter 13
North and South **384**
1 The North's Economy 385
2 The North's People 390
3 Southern Cotton Kingdom 396
4 The South's People 401

Chapter 14
The Age of Reform **410**
1 Social Reform 411
2 The Abolitionists 416
3 The Women's Movement 424

Unit 6

Civil War and Reconstruction 432
1846–1896

Chapter 15
Road to Civil War **436**
1 Slavery and the West 437
2 A Nation Dividing 442
3 Challenges to Slavery 448
4 Secession and War 453

The Victory Ball at Fredericksburg, 1781
by Jean L.G. Ferris

Table of Contents

Chapter 16
The Civil War 460

1 The Two Sides 461
2 Early Years of the War 466
3 A Call for Freedom 472
4 Life During the Civil War 476
5 The Way to Victory 482

Chapter 17
Reconstruction and Its Aftermath 494

1 Reconstruction Plans 495
2 Radicals in Control 499
3 The South During Reconstruction 504
4 Reconstruction Ends 508
5 Change in the South 513

Unit 7
Reshaping the Nation 520
1858–1914

Chapter 18
The Western Frontier 524

1 The Mining Booms 525
2 Ranchers and Farmers 531
3 Native American Struggles 538
4 Farmers in Protest 544

Chapter 19
The Growth of Industry 550

1 Railroads Lead the Way 551
2 Inventions 556
3 An Age of Big Business 560
4 Industrial Workers 566

Fan brought to America from China

Chapter 20
Toward an Urban America 574

1 The New Immigrants 575
2 Moving to the City 584
3 A Changing Culture 590

Unit 8
Reform, Expansion, and War 598
1865–1920

Chapter 21
Progressive Reforms 602

1 Progressive Movement 603
2 Women and Progressives 609
3 Progressive Presidents 616
4 Excluded From Reform 622

Chapter 22
Overseas Expansion 630

1 Expanding Horizons 631
2 Imperialism in the Pacific 635
3 Spanish-American War 640
4 Latin American Policies 646

Chapter 23
World War I 654

1 War in Europe 655
2 America's Road to War 660
3 Americans Join the Allies 665
4 The War at Home 670
5 Searching for Peace 674

Unit 9
Turbulent Decades 684
1919–1945

Chapter 24
The Jazz Age 688

1 Time of Turmoil 689
2 Desire for Normalcy 693
3 A Booming Economy 698
4 The Roaring Twenties 702
5 Clashing Cultures 708

Chapter 25
The Depression and FDR 714

1 The Great Depression 715
2 Roosevelt's New Deal 720
3 Life During the Depression 728
4 Effects of the New Deal 733

Chapter 26
World War II 740

1 Road to War 741
2 War Begins 745
3 On the Home Front 750
4 War in Europe and Africa 755
5 War in the Pacific 761

Unit 10
Turning Points 768
1945–1975

Chapter 27
The Cold War Era 772

1 Cold War Origins 773
2 Postwar Politics 780
3 The Korean War 785
4 The Red Scare 789

Chapter 28
America in the Fifties 796

1 Eisenhower's Domestic Policy 797
2 Eisenhower and the Cold War 800
3 1950s Prosperity 807
4 Problems in a Time of Plenty 813

Chapter 29
The Civil Rights Era 820

1 The Civil Rights Movement 821
2 Kennedy and Johnson 826
3 The Struggle Continues 830
4 Other Groups Seek Rights 838

Chapter 30
The Vietnam Era 846

1 Kennedy's Foreign Policy 847
2 War in Vietnam 852
3 The Vietnam Years at Home 858
4 1968—Year of Crises 862
5 Nixon and Vietnam 867

World War II Service Star flag

Unit 11
Modern America 876
1968–Present

Chapter 31
Search for Stability 880

1 Nixon's Foreign Policy 881
2 Nixon and Watergate 886
3 A Time for Healing 892
4 The Carter Presidency 897

Chapter 32
New Challenges 904

1 The Reagan Presidency 905
2 The Bush Presidency 910
3 The Clinton Presidency 918
4 Toward the 21st Century 924

Appendix

Presidents of the United States A1
White House Facts A8
Documents of America's Heritage A9
Gazetteer A21
Glossary A26
Index A36
Spanish Glossary A59
Credits and Acknowledgments A70

Table of Contents

NATIONAL GEOGRAPHIC SOCIETY Journeys

A Missionary's Journey	56
Journey to Jamestown	76
Journey to Independence	154
Lewis & Clark	286
Trail of Tears	340
Underground Railroad	446
An Immigrant's Journey	582
A Suffragist's Journey	614
A Hard Times Road	726
The Freedom Riders	836
Technology's Journey	922

Hands-On HISTORY Lab Activity

Making Soap	100
Go for the Gold	382
Morse Code	492
Retrieving Oil	572
Taffy Pull	682
Recycling Your Own Paper	932

America's Literature

Morning Girl by Michael Dorris	14
The Kidnapped Prince by Olaudah Equiano	68
Johnny Tremain by Esther Forbes	130
Night Flying Woman by Ignatia Broker	254
A Son of the Middle Border by Hamlin Garland	330
The Red Badge of Courage by Stephen Crane	434
Life on the Mississippi by Mark Twain	522
Patriotic Songs: *Over There* by George M. Cohan and *Uncle Sam* by Edward Bushnell	600
The Invisible Thread by Yoshiko Uchida	686
I Know Why the Caged Bird Sings by Maya Angelou	770
Barrio Boy by Ernesto Galarza	878

INTERDISCIPLINARY Activities

Living in the English Colonies	115
The American Revolution	181
Traveling West	371
Inventions of the Late 1800s	565
The Great War	669
All That Jazz	707
The Space Race	806
Our Fragile Planet	896

American Memories

An Aztec Home	51
A Rice Plantation	92
A Colonial Home	111
On the Battlefield	179
America in 1787	207
Building Warships	292
Travel and Fashion	315
Eastern Native American Life	345
Mexican American Cowhand	369
African American Life in the South	404
African American Family Life	506
Life of Plains Native Americans	539
The Gilded Age	562
The New American City	587
Chinese Immigrant Life	623
In the Trenches	667
An American Music	705
A 1930s Kitchen	723
Life in the Suburbs	809
March on Washington, 1963	833
Healing the Wounds	872
Teens of the '70s	894

Social Studies Connections

Economics: Motives for Exploration	42
Geography: A New Frontier	288
Citizenship: Thoreau—The Abolitionist	407
Citizenship: Struggling for Liberty	512
Geography: The Panama Canal Locks	651
Economics: Brother Can You Spare a Dime?	719
World History: The Berlin Wall	917

Table of Contents

TECHNOLOGY AND HISTORY

Spanish Galleon 45
Colonial Printing Press 112
The Conestoga Wagon 294
Textile Mill 308
The Cotton Gin 397
Civil War Camera 479
Steam Locomotive 528
Submarine 662
Henry Ford's Assembly Line 700
Jet Travel 811
Personal Computer 926

Linking PAST & PRESENT

What's In a Name? 31
Astrolabe to Satellite 39
The First Thanksgiving 53
Peddlers to Malls 75
Acadians 123
Boycotts 136
Symbol of a Traitor 149
Women in War 165
Old Allies 174
The Election of Senators 206
The 27th Amendment 219
Mailing a Letter 259
"Modern" Medicine 317
Jeans 377
Ladies' Legwear Creates Scandal 426
From Hardtack to Unmeltable Chocolate 455
The Grange 545
Return of the Train 554
Vaudeville to Virtual Reality 593
Trade With Japan 632
Nationalism 656
The Draft 663
Aerial Warfare 763
German Reunification 777
Political Power 816
Honoring King 834
Women and Sports 839
From War to Tourism 855
China's Leaders 883

Multimedia Activities

Historic America Electronic Field Trips

Cahokia Mounds 33
St. Augustine 97
Lexington and Concord 147
Lowell Factories 312
Frederick Douglass's Home 423
Gettysburg 489
Sutter's Mill 530
Seneca Falls 608
U.S.S. *Arizona* Memorial 760
Vietnam Veterans War Memorial 873

Surfing the "Net"

Modern Explorers 33
Tools of the Trade 97
Modern Inventors 147
E-Mail Your Government Official 312
The Underground Railroad 423
Abraham Lincoln 489
How to Become a Citizen 530
Women and the Progressive Movement 608
The Holocaust 760
The Vietnam War 873

Causes and Effects

Migration to the Americas 18
European Voyages of Exploration 44
Slave Trade Emerges 125
Colonies Declare Independence 143
French-American Alliance in 1778 173
Political Parties Emerge 269
Westward Movement 378
World War I 672
The Cold War 791
Move Toward Equality 824

Table of Contents

America's FLAGS

Spain, 1492 47
Flag of New France 62
Flag of England 81
Continental Colors 1775–77 149
First Stars and Stripes 1777–1795 169
Betsy Ross Flag, 1790 261
The First Star-Spangled Banner, 1779–1818 300
Flag of 1818 319
The Great Star Flag 319
Texas Republic, 1839 366
Confederate Battle Flag, 1861 483
Seventeenth Flag of the Union, 1863 483
The 37-Star Flag 500
Twentieth Flag of the Union, 1876 526
Twenty-fifth Flag, 1912 620
Stars and Stripes Today 799
U.S. Flag Etiquette 934

Footnotes to History

The Land Bridge 18
Preserving Meat 38
It's a Girl! 72
Indentured 113
A Close Call 118
Friendly Persuasion? 135
Tough Defense 140
Midnight Ride 143
Divided Loyalties 151
Worthless Paper? 173
The Cure May Be Worse 179
Two Substitutes Surrender 184

Huron box, 17th century

The State of Franklin 192
Let's Have Quiet! 200
A Man of Many Signatures 201
Long-Term Planning 207
Presidential Design 260
A Hero Passes 265
Modern Political Parties 267
The Laundry Room 271
The White House 319
Native American Alphabet 344
Birth of the Chip 392
Braille 413
Early Freedom Rider 421
Women Physicians 425
A Humble Start 449
Different Names, Same Battle 467
A Soldier's ID 474
No Escaping 487
Your Name is Mud 497
A Fateful Decision 502
Gold Rush Words 526
Rain on the Roof 534
Where the Buffalo Roamed 539
The Price Is Right 576
A Cosmopolitan City 585
The Olympics 594
Teddy Bears 617
Seward's Revenge 633
Hollywood Revolution 650
Holiday Truce 658
Repaying a Debt 667
Silent Cal 695
A Presidential Family 721
Monopoly 731
A Young Scholar 781
Like Father, Like Son 787
"Witch" Trials 790
Bomb Goes Airborne 803
Thurgood Marshall 823
The Prize 832
Peace Prize 870
No More Red 882
Young Leader 885
Watergate Statistics 890
Twenty-fifth Amendment 893
Oldest President 906
The Brady Bill 919
Madeleine Albright 925

SKILL BUILDER

Social Studies Skills

Understanding the Parts of a Map 26
Reading a Time Line 63
Reading a Bar Graph 83
Reading a Military Map 170
Reading a Flowchart 273
Reading a Diagram 325
Understanding Latitude and Longitude 361
Reading a Circle Graph 395
Reading a Special-Purpose Map 537
Reading a Time Zones Map 555
Reading a Line Graph 581
Interpreting a Political Cartoon 621
Analyzing News Media 737

Critical Thinking Skills

Understanding Cause and Effect 125
Distinguishing Fact From Opinion 153
Making Comparisons 203
Recognizing Bias 441
Identifying the Main Idea 517
Making Generalizations 697
Drawing Conclusions 843
Predicting Consequences 901

Technology Skills

Using a Computerized Card Catalog 429
Using a CD-ROM 481
Developing Multimedia Presentations 645
Using E-Mail 793
Using the Internet 817
Building a Database 866
Using an Electronic Spreadsheet 929

Study and Writing Skills

Writing a Journal 301
Analyzing Primary Sources 347
Outlining 679
Writing a Paragraph 765

Maps

United States Expansion RA2
United States (Political) RA6
United States (Physical) RA8
Mexico, the Caribbean, and Central America RA10
Canada RA12
The World (Political) RA14
Continental United States: Physical Profile RA16
Physical Regions of the United States 3
Climate Regions of the United States 5
Natural Resources of the United States 7
Population Shifts, 1980–1995 8
Prehistoric Migrations Through the Americas 19
Empires of the Maya, Aztec, and Inca 26
Native American Cultures Before 1500 30
Selected Sites of the Mound Builders 34
Early Ohio Villages, 1740 35

The Cattle Kingdom

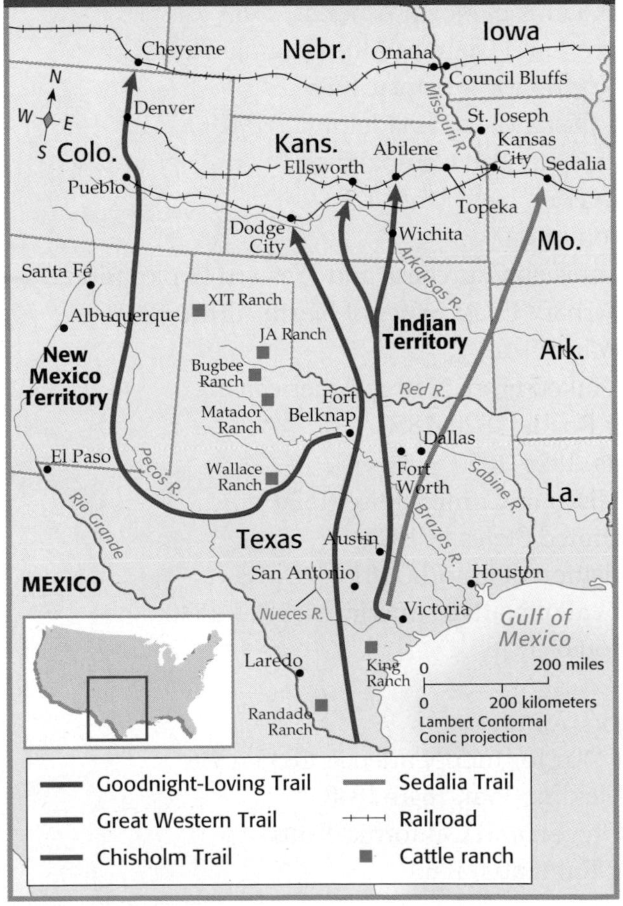

Table of Contents

Maps (continued)

African Trading Kingdoms 40
Motives for Exploration 42
European Voyages of Exploration 48
Spanish Explorers, 1513–1598 52
French Explorers, 1535–1682 60
Missions in New Spain by the 1700s 65
The First English Settlements 73
The New England Colonies 79
The Middle Colonies 85
The Southern Colonies 89
Settlement of the British Colonies 99
Triangular Trade Routes 106
North America in 1753 117
The French and Indian War, 1754–1763 122
National Origins of Colonists, 1760 127
Proclamation of 1763 134
The Battles of Lexington and Concord 144
The Quebec Act, 1774 161
The Revolutionary War, 1776–1777 166
Battle of Bunker Hill, June 17, 1775 170
The Revolutionary War in the West, 1778–1779 177
The Revolutionary War in the South, 1778–1781 178
Land Claims in North America, 1783 187
Western Land Claims of the Original States 191
The Northwest Territory, 1785 193
News Distance to Philadelphia, 1790 213
Native American Campaigns 264
British Forts Held Until 1796 274
Election of 1800 278
The Louisiana Purchase and Western Exploration 283
The Barbary Coast States of North Africa, 1801 290
The War of 1812 298
Land Taken From Native Americans 302
Major Roads, 1820–1850 314
Canals, 1820–1850 316
The Missouri Compromise, 1820 320
The United States in 1824 323
Acquisition of Florida, 1819 326
Removal of Native Americans, 1820–1840 343
Election of 1828 353
Trails West 358
Oregon Country 361
Texas War for Independence, 1835–1836 365
The Mexican War, 1846–1848 374
The Oregon and California Trails 381
Major Railroads, 1860 387
Southern Crops in 1860 400
Northern Products in 1860 408
The Underground Railroad 419
The Compromise of 1850 444
Kansas–Nebraska Act, 1854 444
Seceding States, 1860–1861 456
Election of 1860 459
The Civil War in the East, 1861–1863 468
The Civil War in the West, 1862–1863 484
The Final Battles of the Civil War, 1864–1865 486
Battle of Gettysburg 491
Military Reconstruction Districts, 1867 501
Disputed Election of 1876 510
Western Land Use, 1890 537
Western Native American Lands, 1860–1890 540
Mining in the West 548
The Cattle Kingdom 549
Major Western Railroads Before 1900 553
United States Time Zones 555
Labor's Struggle for Justice, 1880–1920 568
Industrial Expansion 571
Largest Eastern Cities in 1900 597
Voting Rights for Women, 1919 611
Regions of the Federal Reserve System 629
United States Overseas Possessions, 1900 637
The Spanish-American War 642
The Panama Canal 653
Europe in World War I 657
The Western Front 666
Europe After World War I 676
The Eastern Front 681
Dust Bowl Migration 729
The Tennessee Valley Authority 739
World War II in Europe and Africa 756
World War II in the Pacific 762
D-Day Invasion, June 6, 1944 767
Europe After World War II 774
The Election of 1948 782
The Korean War, 1950–53 786
The Occupation of Berlin 795
The Cold War in Europe, 1955 802
The Appalachia Region, 1950s 819
Segregation in United States Schools, 1950 822
Route of the Freedom Rides, 1961 845
The Cuban Missile Crisis: October 14–28, 1962 850
The Vietnam War 868

The Election of 1960 875
The Election of 1968 875
Europe, 1997 912
The Election of 1996 925
Persian Gulf War, 1991 931

Charts, Graphs, and Tables

United States Facts RA4
Geographic Facts About the United States 1
Migration to the Americas 18
European Voyages of Exploration 44
Major European Explorers, 1487–1682 61
Population of Six English Colonies, 1700 83
Founding the Thirteen Colonies 91
Value of American Exports and Imports with England, 1700–1750 98
Slave Trade Emerges 125
Restrictions on Colonial Trade, 1650–1750 139
Colonies Declare Independence 143
French-American Alliance in 1778 173
The Articles of Confederation and the United States Constitution 203
The Federal System 217
The Amendment Process 218
The American System of Checks and Balances 222
How a Bill Becomes a Law 223
The Federal Court System 225
Finances of the New Nation, 1789–1791 260
Differences Between the First Political Parties 268
Political Parties Emerge 269
Conflicts in the Northwest Territory 273
How Banks Work 275
Urban Population Growth in America, 1800–1850 311
Election of 1824 334
Westward Movement 378
Immigration, 1820–1860 394
Agricultural and Nonagricultural Workers, 1840–1870 395
Cotton Production in America, 1800–1860 398
Cotton as a percentage of U.S. exports 398
Populations of the North and South in 1860 409
Resources of the North and South, 1861 463
Final Election Results, 1877 510
Agricultural Production in the South, 1850–1890 514
Native American Population 542
Inventions of the Late 1800s 557
Immigration to the United States, 1860–1920 581
Urban and Rural Population Growth, 1860–1900 586
Length of School Year, 1880–1920 596
World War I 672
World War I Casualties 675
Auto Sales, 1920–1929 699
Families With Radios, 1922–1929 704
Immigration–1921 to 1930 713
Stock Prices, 1920–1932 716
The New Deal 722
The Nation Gears Up for Conflict 747
U.S. Women in the Labor Force, 1900–1950 752
The Cold War 791
Where Americans Lived, 1901–1960 808
Homes With Television Sets 812
Move Toward Equality 824
United States in the Vietnam War 860
Gasoline Consumption and Prices 903
Gross National Debt 907

Finances of the New Nation, 1789–1791

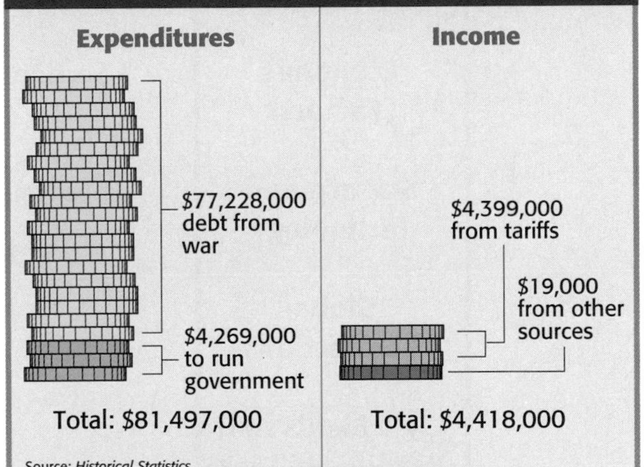

Source: *Historical Statistics of the United States*

Graph Study

Alexander Hamilton, the secretary of the treasury, faced the problem of resolving the national debt.

1. How much money was needed to run the government?
2. **Analyzing Information** How much total income did the government receive?

Scope and Sequence

Themes and Concepts

Each section of *The American Journey* focuses on one central theme, although related themes also appear in each section. The section numbers highlighted here in **red** indicate the central theme that is key to that section. Related themes are listed in black.

Chapter	1	2	3	4
Culture and Traditions	Section 1, 2, 3	Section 1, 4	Section 4, 5	Section 1, 2
Continuity and Change	Section 3	Section 3	Section 1, 5	Section 2, 4
Geography and History	Section 1, 2, 3	Section 1, 2, 3, 4	Section 3	Section 1, 3, 4
Individual Action	Section 2	Section 1, 2, 3, 4	Section 1, 2, 3, 4, 5	Section 1, 2, 3, 4
Groups and Institutions	Section 3	Section 1, 2, 3, 4	Section 1, 3	Section 3
Government and Democracy			Section 1, 2	
Economic Factors	Section 2	Section 1, 4	Section 1, 4	Section 1, 2
Science and Technology	Section 2	Section 1		Section 2
Global Connections		Section 1, 2, 3, 4	Section 5	Section 4
Civic Rights and Responsibilities		Section 3	Section 1, 2	Section 2

Skills

These are the skills taught in the Chapter *SKILL BUILDERS*. Each skill is reinforced in the *Skill Practice Activity* found in the Chapter Reviews and in the ***Chapter Skills Activities*** booklet in the TCR.

Chapter	1	2	3	4
Skill Category	*Social Studies Skill*	*Social Studies Skill*	*Social Studies Skill*	*Critical Thinking Skill*
Specific Skill	Understanding the Parts of a Map	Reading a Time Line	Reading a Bar Graph	Understanding Cause and Effect

	5	6	7	8	9	10
		Section 1	Section 2			Section 3
	Section 1, 4	Section 1, 2	Section 2	Section 1	Section 3	Section 1, 2
		Section 3	Section 1	Section 2	Section 2	Section 1, 2, 4
	Section 1, 2, 3, 4	Section 1, 2, 3, 4	Section 1, 2, 3, 4	Section 1, 2, 3, 4	Section 1, 2, 3, 4	Section 1, 2, 3, 4
	Section 1, 2, 3	Section 1, 2, 3, 4	Section 2, 4	Section 2, 4	Section 3, 4	Section 2, 3
	Section 4		Section 1, 2, 3, 4	Section 1, 3, 4	Section 1, 3	
	Section 1	Section 2	Section 1, 2	Section 1, 3	Section 3	Section 1, 2
			Section 2		Section 2, 3	Section 1, 2
	Section 1, 4	Section 2		Section 2, 4	Section 3	Section 4
	Section 1, 3, 4	Section 2	Section 2, 3, 4	Section 2, 3, 4	Section 1	
	Critical Thinking Skill	*Social Studies Skill*	*Critical Thinking Skill*	*Social Studies Skill*	*Study and Writing Skill*	*Social Studies Skill*
	Distinguishing Fact from Opinion	Reading a Military Map	Making Comparisons	Reading a Flowchart	Writing a Journal	Reading a Diagram

Scope and Sequence

Chapter	11	12	13	14	15
Themes and Concepts					
Culture and Traditions		Section 2, 3, 4	Section 2, 4	Section 1	
Continuity and Change	Section 1			Section 3	Section 3, 4
Geography and History		Section 1, 2, 3, 4, 5	Section 1, 2		Section 2, 4
Individual Action	Section 1, 2, 3, 4	Section 1, 2, 3, 4, 5	Section 1, 3, 4	Section 1, 2, 3	Section 1, 2, 3
Groups and Institutions	Section 1, 3, 4	Section 1, 5	Section 2, 4	Section 1, 2, 3	Section 3
Government and Democracy	Section 2				Section 1, 3
Economic Factors	Section 2, 4	Section 1, 5	Section 1, 3, 4	Section 2	
Science and Technology			Section 1, 3		
Global Connections		Section 4	Section 2	Section 2	
Civic Rights and Responsibilities	Section 1		Section 2, 4	Section 1, 3	Section 2, 3
Skills					
Skill Category	*Study and Writing Skill*	*Social Studies Skill*	*Social Studies Skill*	*Technology Skill*	*Critical Thinking Skill*
Specific Skill	Analyzing Primary Sources	Understanding Latitude and Longitude	Reading a Circle Graph	Using a Computerized Card Catalog	Recognizing Bias

16	17	18	19	20	21
Section 1		Section 2, 3		Section 1	Section 4
Section 1, 2, 3, 4	Section 3	Section 4	Section 1	Section 2, 3	
Section 1, 2		Section 1, 2	Section 1	Section 1, 2	Section 3
Section 2, 3, 4, 5	Section 1, 4	Section 3	Section 2, 3	Section 1, 2, 3	Section 1, 2, 3, 4
Section 3, 4	Section 1, 3, 4	Section 2, 3, 4	Section 4	Section 1, 2, 3	Section 1, 2, 3 4
Section 1	Section 2				Section 1
Section 4	Section 5	Section 1, 2, 4	Section 1, 3, 4	Section 2	Section 1, 3
Section 4		Section 1, 2	Section 1, 2, 3	Section 2	
		Section 1, 2	Section 3	Section 1	Section 4
Section 3	Section 1, 2, 3, 5	Section 3	Section 4		Section 1, 2, 4
Technology Skill	***Critical Thinking Skill***	***Social Studies Skill***	***Social Studies Skill***	***Social Studies Skill***	***Social Studies Skill***
Using a CD-ROM	Identifying the Main Idea	Reading a Special-Purpose Map	Reading a Time Zones Map	Reading a Line Graph	Interpreting a Political Cartoon

Chapter	22	23	24	25	26
Themes and Concepts					
Culture and Traditions	Section 1	Section 2	Section 3, 5	Section 3	
Continuity and Change	Section 1, 3	Section 1, 2	Section 5		Section 1, 2, 5
Geography and History	Section 2	Section 3		Section 3	Section 4, 5
Individual Action	Section 1, 3, 4	Section 2, 3, 5	Section 1, 2, 4, 5	Section 2, 3, 4	Section 1, 2, 4, 5
Groups and Institutions	Section 2, 3, 4	Section 1, 2, 3, 4	Section 1, 4, 5	Section 3	Section 1, 3, 4
Government and Democracy		Section 2, 4, 5		Section 2, 4	
Economic Factors	Section 1, 2, 4	Section 2, 4	Section 1, 3	Section 1, 2, 4	Section 3
Science and Technology	Section 4	Section 1, 2	Section 4		
Global Connections	Section 1, 2, 3, 4	Section 5	Section 2		Section 2, 4, 5
Civic Rights and Responsibilities		Section 2, 4	Section 4		
Skills					
Skill Category	*Technology Skill*	*Study and Writing Skill*	*Critical Thinking Skill*	*Social Studies Skill*	*Study and Writing Skill*
Specific Skill	Developing Multimedia Presentations	Outlining	Making Generalizations	Analyzing News Media	Writing a Paragraph

27	28	29	30	31	32
	Section 3	Section 4			
Section 1	Section 3, 4	Section 3, 4	Section 1, 2, 3	Section 3	Section 2
Section 1, 3			Section 1, 2, 5		
Section 1, 4	Section 1, 2	Section 1, 2, 3	Section 1, 2, 4, 5	Section 1, 2, 3, 4	Section 1, 2
Section 1, 2, 4	Section 3, 4	Section 1, 2, 3, 4	Section 1, 2, 3, 5	Section 2	Section 3
Section 3			Section 2		Section 3, 4
Section 2	Section 1, 3, 4			Section 2, 3	Section 1, 2, 4
	Section 2				Section 4
Section 1, 3	Section 2			Section 1, 3, 4	Section 1, 2, 3
Section 2		Section 1, 2, 3, 4	Section 4	Section 4	Section 2
Technology Skill	*Technology Skill*	*Critical Thinking Skill*	*Technology Skill*	*Critical Thinking Skill*	*Technology Skill*
Using E-Mail	Using the Internet	Drawing Conclusions	Building a Database	Predicting Consequences	Using an Electronic Spreadsheet

Using NCSS Thematic Strands

In *Curriculum Standards for Social Studies: Expectations of Excellence,* the National Council for the Social Studies (NCSS) identified 10 themes that serve as organizing strands for the social studies curriculum at every school level. These themes are interrelated and draw from all of the social science disciplines. The 10 NCSS themes—described below—were the basis for the themes used in *The American Journey.*

The **Scope and Sequence** chart on pages T20–T25 shows where the NCSS social studies themes are incorporated into *The American Journey.*

NCSS Themes

I. Culture Human beings create, learn, and adapt culture. Human cultures are dynamic systems of beliefs, values, and traditions that exhibit both commonalities and differences. Understanding culture helps us understand ourselves and others.

II. Time, Continuity, and Change Human beings seek to understand their historic roots and to locate themselves in time. Such understanding involves knowing what things were like in the past and how things change and develop—allowing us to develop historic perspective and answer important questions about our current condition.

III. People, Places, and Environment Technological advancements have insured that students are aware of the world beyond their personal locations. As students study content related to this theme, they create their spatial views and geographic perspectives of the world; social, cultural, economic, and civic demands mean that students will need such knowledge, skills, and understandings to make informed and critical decisions about the relationship between human beings and their environment.

IV. Individual Development and Identity Personal identity is shaped by one's culture, by groups, and by institutional influences. Examination of various forms of human behavior enhances understanding of the relationships between social norms and emerging personal identities, the social processes that influence identity formation, and the ethical principles underlying individual action.

V. Individuals, Groups, and Institutions Institutions exert enormous influence over us. Institutions are organizational embodiments to further the core social values of those who comprise them. It is important for students to know how institutions are formed, what controls and influences them,

Why It's Important

What Is American History?

American history is people, events, places, documents, art, inventions, literature. In other words—American history is everything about the adventures of all Americans—past and present.

Golden spike commemorating completion of transcontinental railroad

New Deal badge

Why Study American History?

Only by learning about the past can you truly understand the present. Only by learning about your nation's past can you understand what it means to be an American today.

Detail from quilt, mid-1800s

How Can I Remember Everything?

The American Journey helps you learn about your nation's past by organizing its history around 10 themes. A ***theme*** is a concept, or main idea, that happens again and again throughout history. Themes help you understand events in the past and how they affect you today.

Using the Themes in *The American Journey*

To help you learn about your nation's history, the authors have identified major themes for every section of *The American Journey.* You will find these listed under **Chapter Themes** at the beginning of every chapter. You can check your understanding of these themes in every **Section Review.** Finally, in the Reviewing Themes section of every **Chapter Review** you are asked questions that help you put it all together to better understand how ideas are connected across time—and to see why history is important to you today. Read more about these themes on the next page.

What Do the Themes in The American Journey Mean?

1. **Culture and Traditions** Being aware of cultural differences helps us understand ourselves and others.

2. **Continuity and Change** Recognizing our historic roots helps us understand why things are the way they are today.

3. **Geography and History** Understanding geography helps us understand how humans interact with their environment.

4. **Individual Action** Recognizing the contributions of men and women in history helps us see patterns of power, influence, and progress.

5. **Groups and Institutions** Identifying how political and social groups and institutions work helps us work together.

6. **Government and Democracy** Understanding the workings of government helps us become good citizens.

7. **Economic Factors** Understanding production, distribution, and consumption helps us see how economic factors influence our lives.

8. **Science and Technology** Understanding the roles of science and technology helps us see their impact on our society today and the roles they will play in the future.

Twig figure found in Grand Canyon

9. **Global Connections** Being aware of global interdependence helps us make decisions and deal with the difficult issues we will encounter.

10. **Civic Rights and Responsibilities** Recognizing America's democratic principles will help us claim and fulfill our own civic duties.

Continental coin

1950s children's game

how they control and influence individuals and culture, and how institutions can be maintained or changed.

VI. Power, Authority, and Governance Understanding of the historical development of structures of power, authority, and governance and their evolving functions in contemporary society is essential for the emergence of civic competence.

VII. Production, Distribution, and Consumption Decisions about exchange, trade, and economic policy and well-being are global in scope, and the role of government in policy making varies over time and from place to place. The systematic study of an interdependent world economy and the role of technology in economic decision making is essential.

VIII. Science, Technology, and Society Technology is as old as the first crude tool invented by prehistoric humans, and modern life as we know it would be impossible without technology and the science that supports it. Today's technology forms the basis for some of our most difficult social choices.

IX. Global Connections The realities of global interdependence require understanding of the increasingly important and diverse global connections among world societies before there can be analysis leading to the development of possible solutions to persisting and emerging global issues.

X. Civic Ideals and Practices All people have a stake in examining civic ideals and practices across time, in diverse societies, as well as in determining how to close the gap between present practices and the ideals upon which our democratic republic is based. An understanding of civic ideals and practices of citizenship is critical to full participation in society.

What? Where? When? Who?

Internet Connections To receive information and ideas about K-12 social studies education, sponsored by the National Council for the Social Studies, look on the World Wide Web: http://www.ness.org/

UNKNOWN
Mexique
Occident

Reference Atlas

Contents

United States Expansion	RA2
United States Facts	RA4
United States (Political)	RA6
United States (Physical)	RA8
Mexico, the Caribbean, and Central America	RA10
Canada	RA12
The World (Political)	RA14

Atlas Key

SYMBOL KEY

- National capital
- State/province capital
- Major city
- Other city
- International boundary
- Disputed boundary
- Undefined boundary
- State/province/republic boundary
- Non-subject
- Canal/waterway
- Waterfall
- Peak

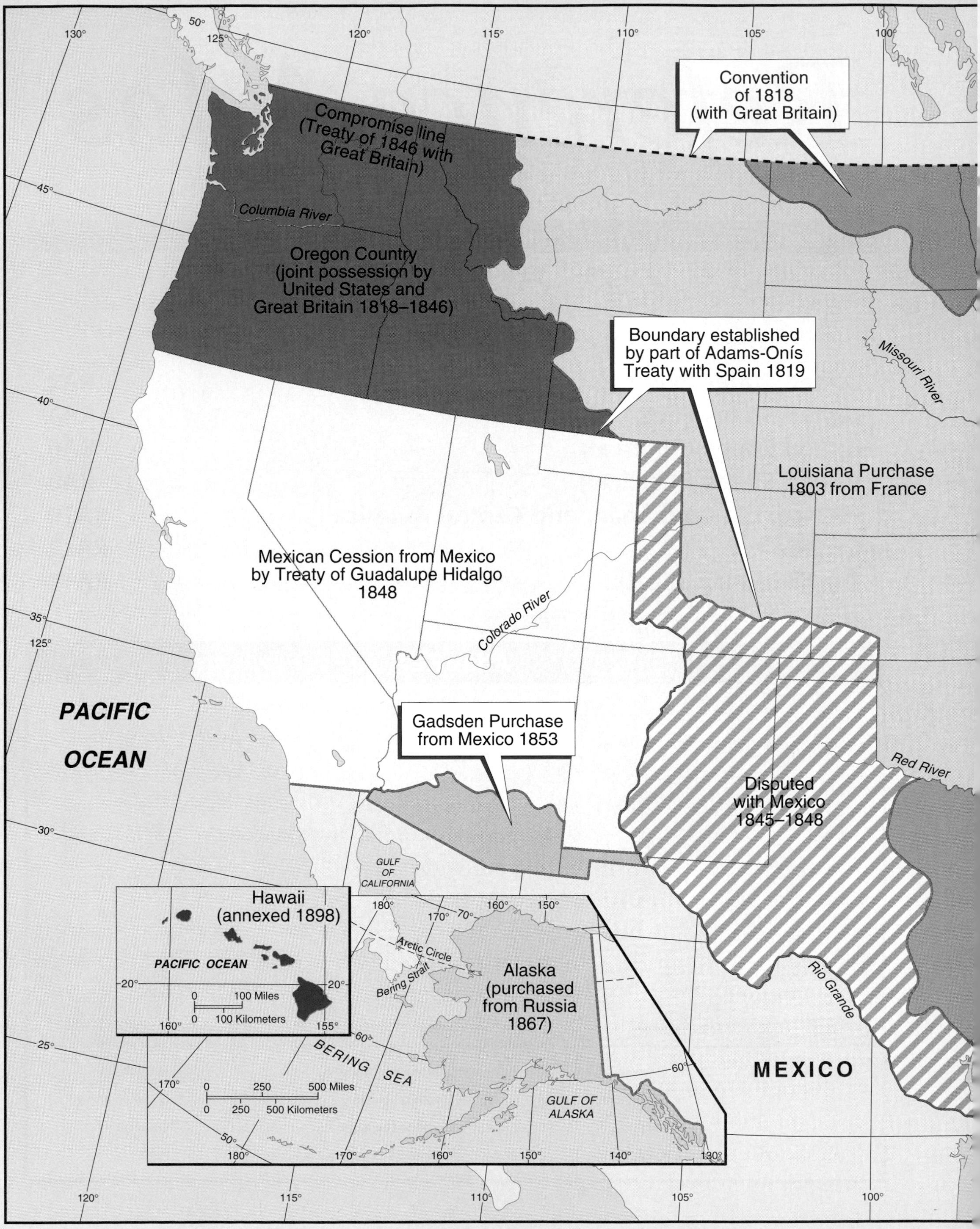
Convention
of 1818
(with Great Britain)
Compromise line
(Treaty of 1846 with
Great Britain)
Columbia River
Oregon Country
(joint possession by
United States and
Great Britain 1818–1846)
Boundary established
by part of Adams-Onís
Treaty with Spain 1819
Missouri River
Louisiana Purchase
1803 from France
Mexican Cession from Mexico
by Treaty of Guadalupe Hidalgo
1848
Colorado River
PACIFIC
OCEAN
Gadsden Purchase
from Mexico 1853
Red River
Disputed
with Mexico
1845–1848
GULF
OF
CALIFORNIA
Hawaii
(annexed 1898)
PACIFIC OCEAN
100 Miles
100 Kilometers
Arctic Circle
Bering Strait
Alaska
(purchased
from Russia
1867)
BERING SEA
250 500 Miles
250 500 Kilometers
GULF OF
ALASKA
Rio Grande
MEXICO

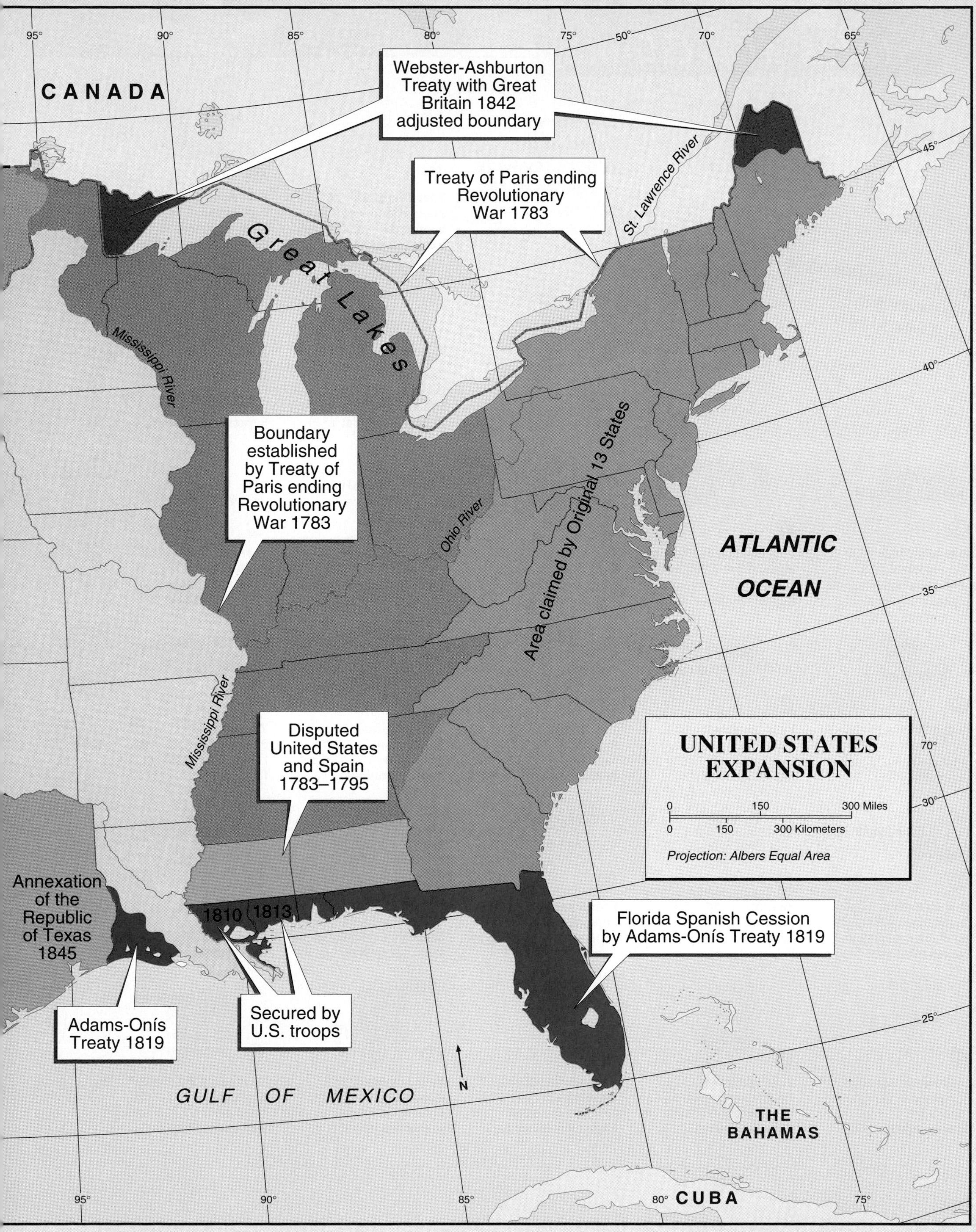
UNITED STATES EXPANSION
0 150 300 Miles
0 150 300 Kilometers
Projection: Albers Equal Area
CANADA
Webster-Ashburton Treaty with Great Britain 1842 adjusted boundary
Treaty of Paris ending Revolutionary War 1783
St. Lawrence River
Great Lakes
Mississippi River
Boundary established by Treaty of Paris ending Revolutionary War 1783
Ohio River
Area claimed by Original 13 States
ATLANTIC OCEAN
Mississippi River
Disputed United States and Spain 1783–1795
Annexation of the Republic of Texas 1845
1810
1813
Florida Spanish Cession by Adams-Onís Treaty 1819
Adams-Onís Treaty 1819
Secured by U.S. troops
N
GULF OF MEXICO
THE BAHAMAS
CUBA
95°
90°
85°
80°
75°
70°
65°
50°
45°
40°
35°
30°
25°

States at a Glance

United States

Population: 266,000,000 (est.)
Land area: 3,539,230 sq. mi.

DISTRICT OF COLUMBIA (Washington, D.C.)
Population: 606,900
Land area: 61 sq. mi.

The states are listed in the order they were admitted to the Union.

1
Year admitted: 1787
Population: 666,168
Land area: 1,954 sq. mi.
Representatives: 1

2
Year admitted: 1787
Population: 11,881,643
Land area: 44,819 sq. mi.
Representatives: 21

3
Year admitted: 1787
Population: 7,730,188
Land area: 7,418 sq. mi.
Representatives: 13

4
Year admitted: 1788
Population: 6,478,216
Land area: 57,918 sq. mi.
Representatives: 11

5
Year admitted: 1788
Population: 3,287,116
Land area: 4,845 sq. mi.
Representatives: 6

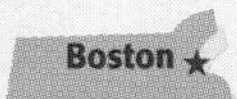

6
Year admitted: 1788
Population: 6,016,425
Land area: 7,838 sq. mi.
Representatives: 10

7
Year admitted: 1788
Population: 4,781,468
Land area: 9,774 sq. mi.
Representatives: 8

8
Year admitted: 1788
Population: 3,486,703
Land area: 30,111 sq. mi.
Representatives: 6

9
Year admitted: 1788
Population: 1,109,252
Land area: 8,969 sq. mi.
Representatives: 2

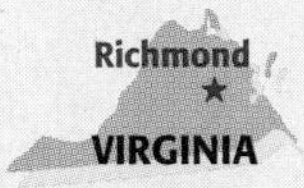

10
Year admitted: 1788
Population: 6,187,358
Land area: 39,597 sq. mi.
Representatives: 11

11
Year admitted: 1788
Population: 17,990,455
Land area: 47,223 sq. mi.
Representatives: 31

12
Year admitted: 1789
Population: 6,628,637
Land area: 48,718 sq. mi.
Representatives: 12

13
Year admitted: 1790
Population: 1,003,464
Land area: 1,212 sq. mi.
Representatives: 2

14
Year admitted: 1791
Population: 562,758
Land area: 9,249 sq. mi.
Representatives: 1

15
Year admitted: 1792
Population: 3,685,296
Land area: 39,732 sq. mi.
Representatives: 6

16
Year admitted: 1796
Population: 4,877,185
Land area: 41,219 sq. mi.
Representatives: 9

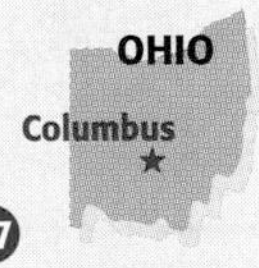

17
Year admitted: 1803
Population: 10,847,115
Land area: 40,952 sq. mi.
Representatives: 19

18
Year admitted: 1812
Population: 4,219,973
Land area: 43,566 sq. mi.
Representatives: 7

19
Year admitted: 1816
Population: 5,544,159
Land area: 35,870 sq. mi.
Representatives: 10

20
Year admitted: 1817
Population: 2,573,216
Land area: 46,913 sq. mi.
Representatives: 5

21
Year admitted: 1818
Population: 11,430,602
Land area: 55,593 sq. mi.
Representatives: 20

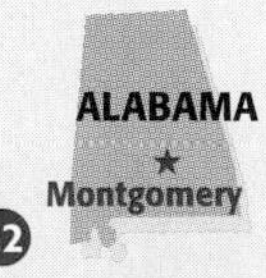

22
Year admitted: 1819
Population: 4,040,587
Land area: 50,750 sq. mi.
Representatives: 7

23
Year admitted: 1820
Population: 1,227,928
Land area: 30,864 sq. mi.
Representatives: 2

24
Year admitted: 1821
Population: 5,117,073
Land area: 68,898 sq. mi.
Representatives: 9

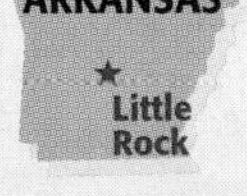

25
Year admitted: 1836
Population: 2,350,725
Land area: 52,075 sq. mi.
Representatives: 4

26

Year admitted: 1837
Population: 9,295,297
Land area: 56,809 sq. mi.
Representatives: 16

27

Year admitted: 1845
Population: 12,937,926
Land area: 53,997 sq. mi.
Representatives: 23

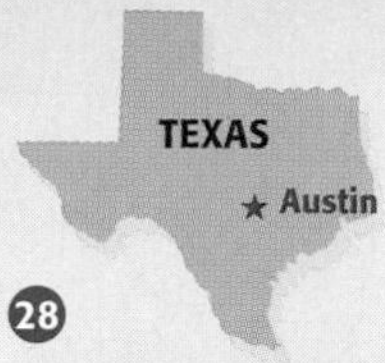

28

Year admitted: 1845
Population: 16,986,510
Land area: 261,194 sq. mi.
Representatives: 30

29

Year admitted: 1846
Population: 2,776,755
Land area: 55,874 sq. mi.
Representatives: 5

30

Year admitted: 1848
Population: 4,891,769
Land area: 54,313 sq. mi.
Representatives: 9

31

Year admitted: 1850
Population: 29,760,021
Land area: 155,973 sq. mi.
Representatives: 52

32

Year admitted: 1858
Population: 4,375,099
Land area: 79,616 sq. mi.
Representatives: 8

33

Year admitted: 1859
Population: 2,853,733
Land area: 96,002 sq. mi.
Representatives: 5

34

Year admitted: 1861
Population: 2,477,574
Land area: 81,823 sq. mi.
Representatives: 4

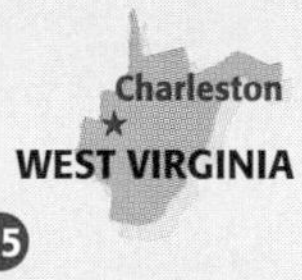

35

Year admitted: 1863
Population: 1,793,477
Land area: 24,086 sq. mi.
Representatives: 3

36

Year admitted: 1864
Population: 1,201,833
Land area: 109,805 sq. mi.
Representatives: 2

37

Year admitted: 1867
Population: 1,578,385
Land area: 76,877 sq. mi.
Representatives: 3

38

Year admitted: 1876
Population: 3,294,394
Land area: 103,729 sq. mi.
Representatives: 6

39

Year admitted: 1889
Population: 638,800
Land area: 68,994 sq. mi.
Representatives: 1

40

Year admitted: 1889
Population: 696,004
Land area: 75,897 sq. mi.
Representatives: 1

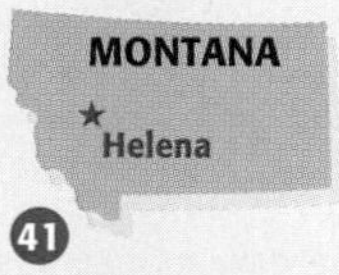

41

Year admitted: 1889
Population: 799,065
Land area: 145,556 sq. mi.
Representatives: 1

42

Year admitted: 1889
Population: 4,887,941
Land area: 66,581 sq. mi.
Representatives: 9

43

Year admitted: 1890
Population: 1,006,749
Land area: 82,750 sq. mi.
Representatives: 2

44

Year admitted: 1890
Population: 455,975
Land area: 97,104 sq. mi.
Representatives: 1

45

Year admitted: 1896
Population: 1,727,784
Land area: 82,168 sq. mi.
Representatives: 3

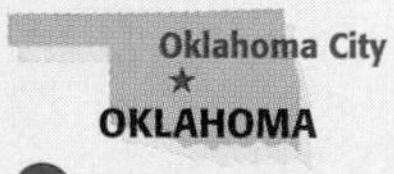

46

Year admitted: 1907
Population: 3,145,585
Land area: 68,678 sq. mi.
Representatives: 6

47

Year admitted: 1912
Population: 1,515,069
Land area: 121,364 sq. mi.
Representatives: 3

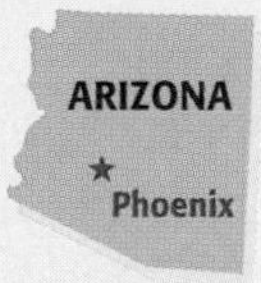

48

Year admitted: 1912
Population: 3,665,228
Land area: 113,642 sq. mi.
Representatives: 6

49

Year admitted: 1959
Population: 550,043
Land area: 591,004 sq. mi.
Representatives: 1

50

Year admitted: 1959
Population: 1,108,229
Land area: 6,432 sq. mi.
Representatives: 2

U.S. Territories

PUERTO RICO
Population: 3,522,037
Land area: 3,459 sq. mi.
Capital: San Juan

U.S. VIRGIN ISLANDS
Population: 101,809
Land area: 132 sq. mi.
Capital: Charlotte Amalie

GUAM
Population: 133,152
Land area: 209 sq. mi.
Capital: Agana

AMERICAN SAMOA
Population: 55,223
Land area: 77 sq. mi.
Capital: Pago Pago

- Population figures and number of members in House of Representatives are from the *1997 Information Please Almanac.*
- States are not drawn to scale.

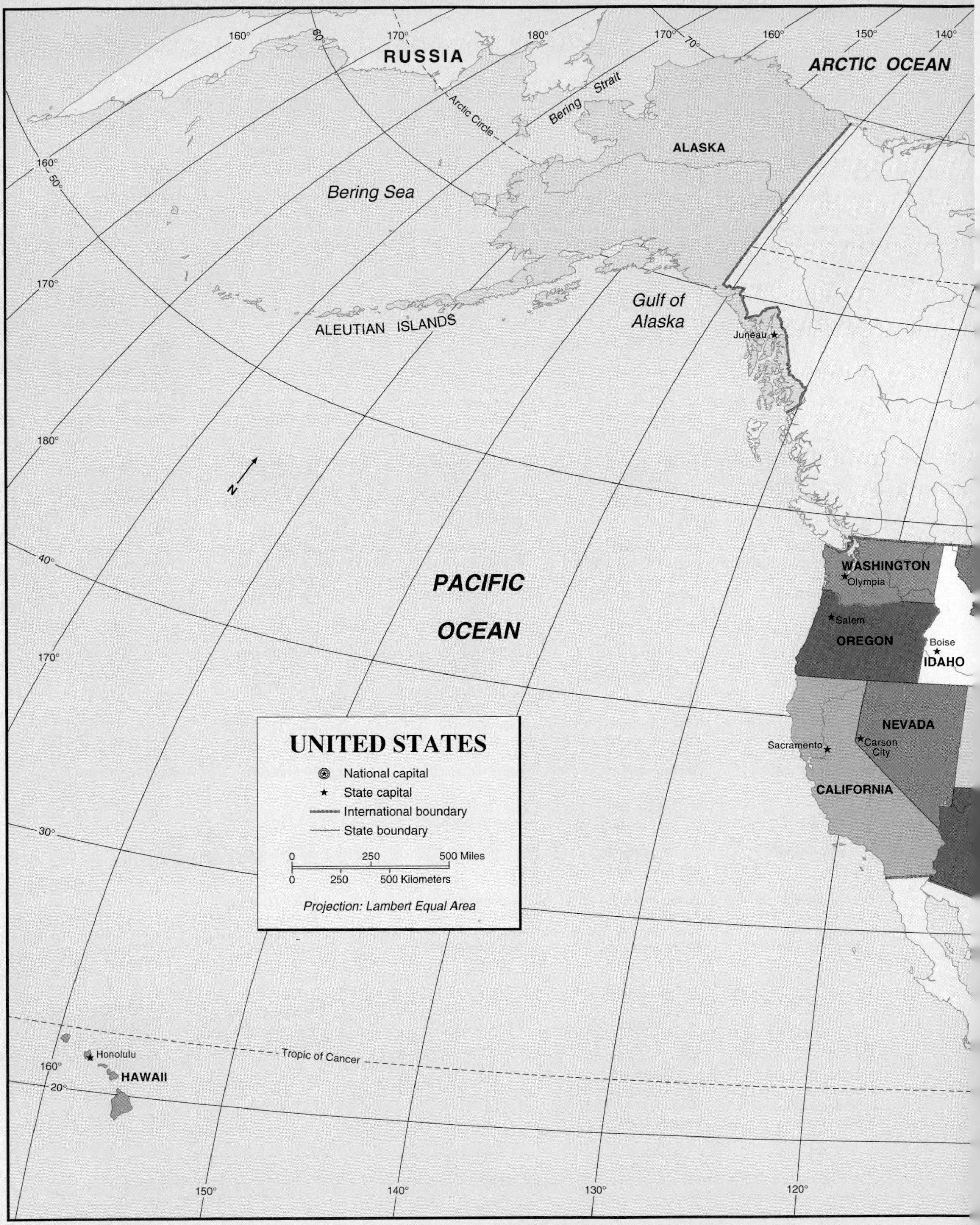

UNITED STATES
National capital
State capital
International boundary
State boundary
0
250
500 Miles
0
250
500 Kilometers
Projection: Lambert Equal Area
RUSSIA
ARCTIC OCEAN
Arctic Circle
Bering Strait
ALASKA
Bering Sea
ALEUTIAN ISLANDS
Gulf of Alaska
Juneau
PACIFIC OCEAN
WASHINGTON
Olympia
Salem
OREGON
Boise
IDAHO
NEVADA
Carson City
Sacramento
CALIFORNIA
Honolulu
HAWAII
Tropic of Cancer
N
160°
170°
180°
170°
160°
150°
140°
60°
70°
50°
40°
30°
20°
150°
140°
130°
120°

Baffin Bay
GREENLAND
ICELAND
Arctic Circle
Labrador Sea
Hudson Bay
CANADA
Lake Superior
Lake Michigan
Lake Huron
Lake Ontario
Lake Erie
MONTANA
Helena
NORTH DAKOTA
Bismarck
MINNESOTA
SOUTH DAKOTA
Pierre
St. Paul
WISCONSIN
Madison
MICHIGAN
Lansing
WYOMING
Cheyenne
NEBRASKA
Lincoln
IOWA
Des Moines
ILLINOIS
Springfield
INDIANA
Indianapolis
OHIO
Columbus
PENNSYLVANIA
Harrisburg
NEW YORK
Albany
MAINE
Augusta
Montpelier
VT.
N.H.
Concord
Boston
MASS.
Hartford
Providence
R.I.
CONN.
Trenton
N.J.
Dover
DEL.
MD.
Annapolis
D.C.
Salt Lake City
UTAH
Denver
COLORADO
Topeka
KANSAS
MISSOURI
Jefferson City
WEST VIRGINIA
Charleston
Frankfort
KENTUCKY
Richmond
VIRGINIA
Nashville
TENNESSEE
NORTH CAROLINA
Raleigh
OKLAHOMA
Oklahoma City
ARKANSAS
Little Rock
ARIZONA
Phoenix
Santa Fe
NEW MEXICO
MISSISSIPPI
Jackson
ALABAMA
Montgomery
Atlanta
GEORGIA
Columbia
SOUTH CAROLINA
TEXAS
Austin
LOUISIANA
Baton Rouge
Tallahassee
FLORIDA
ATLANTIC OCEAN
GULF OF MEXICO
MEXICO
THE BAHAMAS
Tropic of Cancer
CUBA
DOMINICAN REPUBLIC
PUERTO RICO
HAITI
JAMAICA
130°
120°
110°
100°
90°
80°
70°
60°
50°
40°
30°
20°

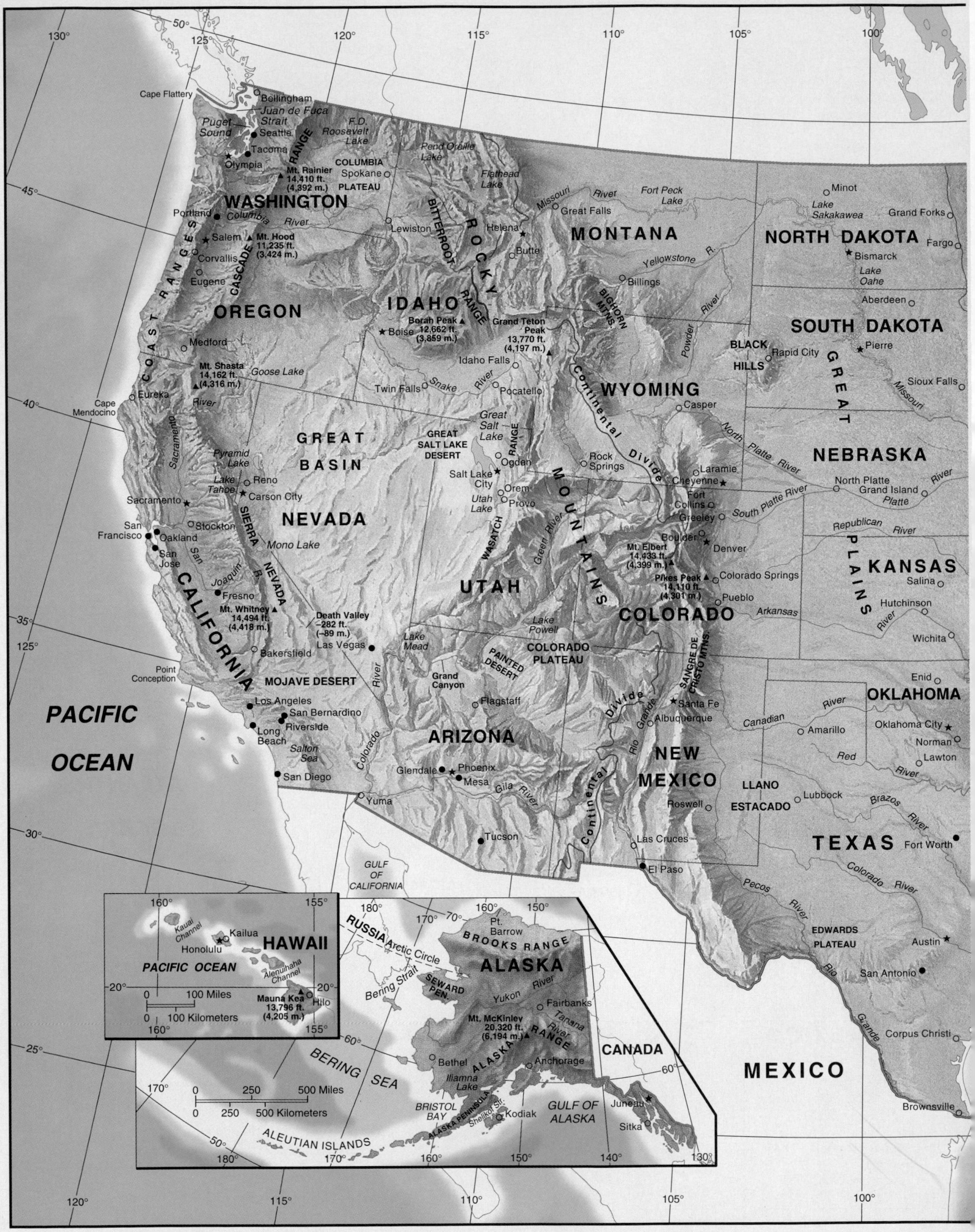
PACIFIC OCEAN
WASHINGTON
OREGON
CALIFORNIA
NEVADA
IDAHO
MONTANA
WYOMING
UTAH
COLORADO
ARIZONA
NEW MEXICO
NORTH DAKOTA
SOUTH DAKOTA
NEBRASKA
KANSAS
OKLAHOMA
TEXAS
MEXICO
Cape Flattery
Bellingham
Juan de Fuca Strait
Puget Sound
Seattle
Tacoma
Olympia
CASCADE RANGE
Mt. Rainier 14,410 ft. (4,392 m.)
F.D. Roosevelt Lake
COLUMBIA PLATEAU
Spokane
Pend Oreille Lake
Flathead Lake
Portland
Columbia River
Salem
Mt. Hood 11,235 ft. (3,424 m.)
Corvallis
Eugene
COAST RANGES
Medford
Mt. Shasta 14,162 ft. (4,316 m.)
Goose Lake
Eureka
Cape Mendocino
Sacramento River
Pyramid Lake
Reno
Lake Tahoe
Carson City
Sacramento
San Francisco
Oakland
San Jose
Stockton
San Joaquin R.
SIERRA NEVADA
Mono Lake
Fresno
Mt. Whitney 14,494 ft. (4,418 m.)
Death Valley −282 ft. (−89 m.)
Las Vegas
Bakersfield
Point Conception
MOJAVE DESERT
Los Angeles
San Bernardino
Riverside
Long Beach
Salton Sea
San Diego
Yuma
GREAT BASIN
Lewiston
BITTERROOT RANGE
ROCKY MOUNTAINS
Helena
Butte
Missouri River
Great Falls
Fort Peck Lake
Yellowstone R.
Billings
BIGHORN MTNS.
Powder River
Borah Peak 12,662 ft. (3,859 m.)
Boise
Grand Teton Peak 13,770 ft. (4,197 m.)
Idaho Falls
Snake River
Twin Falls
Pocatello
Continental Divide
Casper
Great Salt Lake
GREAT SALT LAKE DESERT
WASATCH RANGE
Ogden
Salt Lake City
Orem
Provo
Utah Lake
Rock Springs
Green River
Laramie
Cheyenne
Fort Collins
Greeley
Boulder
Denver
Mt. Elbert 14,433 ft. (4,399 m.)
Pikes Peak 14,110 ft. (4,301 m.)
Colorado Springs
Pueblo
Arkansas
Lake Powell
Lake Mead
COLORADO PLATEAU
PAINTED DESERT
Grand Canyon
Flagstaff
Colorado River
Glendale
Phoenix
Mesa
Gila River
Tucson
SANGRE DE CRISTO MTNS.
Santa Fe
Albuquerque
Rio Grande
Roswell
Las Cruces
El Paso
GULF OF CALIFORNIA
Minot
Lake Sakakawea
Grand Forks
Fargo
Bismarck
Lake Oahe
Aberdeen
BLACK HILLS
Rapid City
Pierre
Sioux Falls
Missouri
GREAT PLAINS
North Platte River
North Platte
Grand Island
Platte
South Platte River
Republican River
Salina
Hutchinson
River
Wichita
Enid
Oklahoma City
Norman
Lawton
Canadian
Amarillo
Red River
LLANO ESTACADO
Lubbock
Brazos River
Fort Worth
Colorado River
Pecos River
EDWARDS PLATEAU
Austin
San Antonio
Rio Grande
Corpus Christi
Brownsville
130° 125° 120° 115° 110° 105° 100°
50° 45° 40° 35° 30° 25°
HAWAII
Kauai Channel
Kailua
Honolulu
PACIFIC OCEAN
Alenuihaha Channel
Mauna Kea 13,796 ft. (4,205 m.)
Hilo
0 100 Miles
0 100 Kilometers
160° 155° 20°
ALASKA
RUSSIA
Arctic Circle
Pt. Barrow
BROOKS RANGE
Bering Strait
SEWARD PEN.
Yukon River
Fairbanks
Tanana River
Mt. McKinley 20,320 ft. (6,194 m.)
ALASKA RANGE
Anchorage
Bethel
Iliamna Lake
BERING SEA
BRISTOL BAY
ALASKA PENINSULA
Shelikof St.
Kodiak
GULF OF ALASKA
CANADA
Juneau
Sitka
ALEUTIAN ISLANDS
0 250 500 Miles
0 250 500 Kilometers
180° 170° 160° 150° 140° 130° 70° 60° 50°

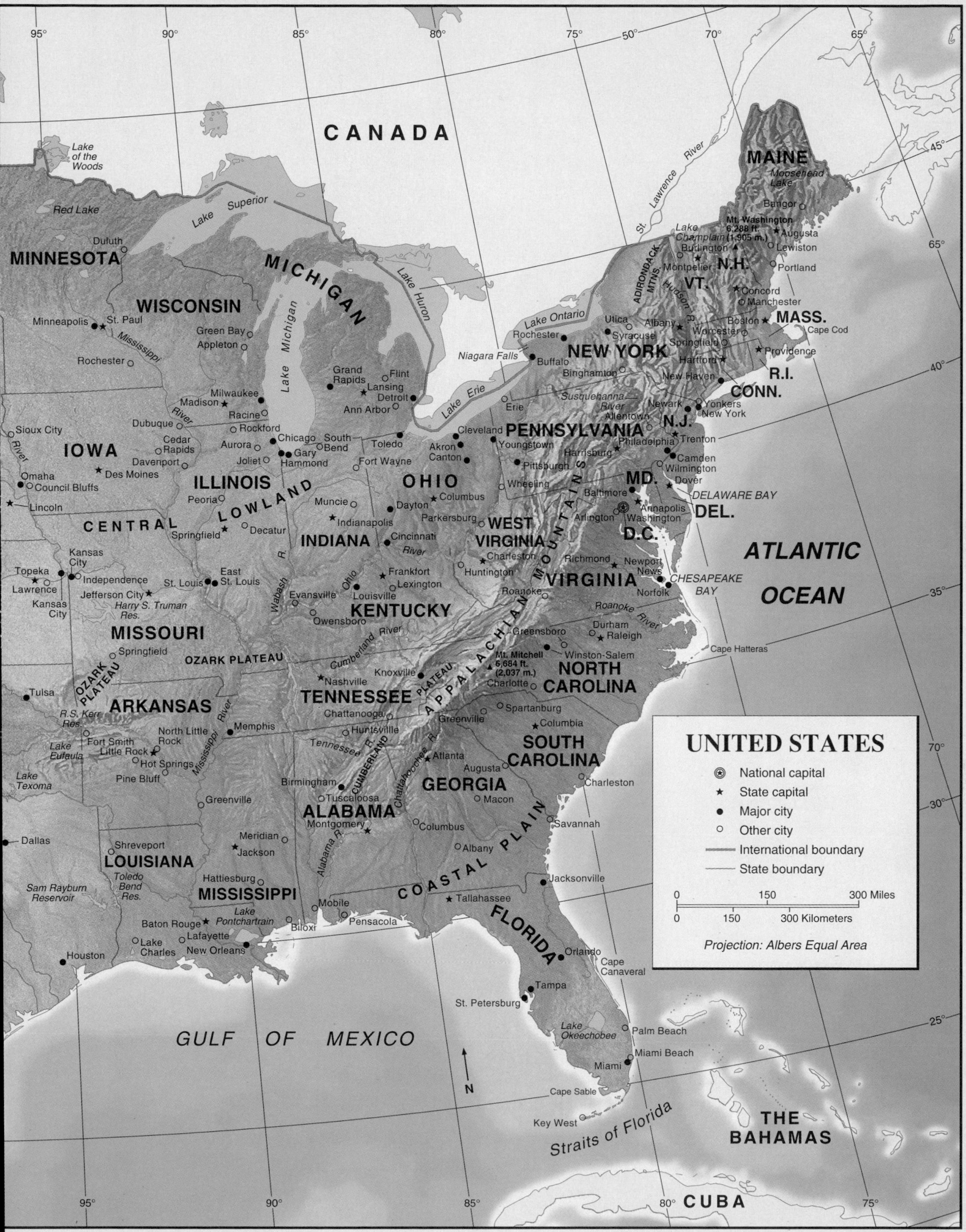
CANADA
MAINE
N.H.
VT.
MASS.
R.I.
CONN.
NEW YORK
N.J.
PENNSYLVANIA
MD.
DEL.
D.C.
WEST VIRGINIA
VIRGINIA
NORTH CAROLINA
SOUTH CAROLINA
GEORGIA
FLORIDA
ALABAMA
MISSISSIPPI
TENNESSEE
KENTUCKY
OHIO
INDIANA
ILLINOIS
MICHIGAN
WISCONSIN
MINNESOTA
IOWA
MISSOURI
ARKANSAS
LOUISIANA
ATLANTIC OCEAN
GULF OF MEXICO
THE BAHAMAS
CUBA
Straits of Florida
CHESAPEAKE BAY
DELAWARE BAY
APPALACHIAN MOUNTAINS
ADIRONDACK MTNS.
CENTRAL LOWLAND
OZARK PLATEAU
COASTAL PLAIN
CUMBERLAND PLATEAU
Lake Superior
Lake Michigan
Lake Huron
Lake Erie
Lake Ontario
Lake of the Woods
Red Lake
Lake Champlain
Moosehead Lake
Lake Okeechobee
Lake Pontchartrain
St. Lawrence River
Mississippi River
Ohio River
Tennessee River
Cumberland River
Wabash R.
Hudson R.
Susquehanna River
Roanoke River
Alabama R.
Chattahoochee R.
Mt. Washington 6,288 ft. (1,905 m.)
Mt. Mitchell 6,684 ft. (2,037 m.)
Cape Cod
Cape Hatteras
Cape Canaveral
Cape Sable
Niagara Falls
Boston
Augusta
Bangor
Lewiston
Portland
Concord
Manchester
Montpelier
Burlington
Providence
Hartford
Worcester
Springfield
New Haven
Albany
Utica
Syracuse
Rochester
Buffalo
Binghamton
Yonkers
New York
Newark
Allentown
Trenton
Philadelphia
Camden
Wilmington
Dover
Harrisburg
Pittsburgh
Erie
Baltimore
Annapolis
Washington
Arlington
Richmond
Newport News
Norfolk
Roanoke
Charleston
Huntington
Wheeling
Parkersburg
Greensboro
Durham
Raleigh
Winston-Salem
Charlotte
Spartanburg
Greenville
Columbia
Charleston
Savannah
Augusta
Atlanta
Macon
Columbus
Albany
Jacksonville
Tallahassee
Orlando
Tampa
St. Petersburg
Palm Beach
Miami Beach
Miami
Key West
Pensacola
Mobile
Montgomery
Birmingham
Tuscaloosa
Huntsville
Chattanooga
Knoxville
Nashville
Memphis
Jackson
Meridian
Hattiesburg
Biloxi
New Orleans
Baton Rouge
Lafayette
Lake Charles
Shreveport
Houston
Dallas
Toledo Bend Res.
Sam Rayburn Reservoir
Little Rock
North Little Rock
Fort Smith
Hot Springs
Pine Bluff
Greenville
Lake Eufaula
R.S. Kerr Res.
Lake Texoma
Tulsa
Springfield
Harry S. Truman Res.
Kansas City
Independence
Topeka
Lawrence
Jefferson City
St. Louis
East St. Louis
Springfield
Decatur
Peoria
Chicago
Joliet
Aurora
Rockford
Gary
Hammond
South Bend
Fort Wayne
Indianapolis
Muncie
Evansville
Owensboro
Louisville
Frankfort
Lexington
Cincinnati
Dayton
Columbus
Toledo
Cleveland
Akron
Canton
Youngstown
Detroit
Ann Arbor
Lansing
Flint
Grand Rapids
Milwaukee
Racine
Madison
Green Bay
Appleton
Dubuque
Davenport
Cedar Rapids
Des Moines
Sioux City
Omaha
Council Bluffs
Lincoln
Minneapolis
St. Paul
Rochester
Duluth
95°
90°
85°
80°
75°
70°
65°
50°
45°
40°
35°
30°
25°
N
UNITED STATES
National capital
State capital
Major city
Other city
International boundary
State boundary
0 150 300 Miles
0 150 300 Kilometers
Projection: Albers Equal Area

MEXICO, the CARIBBEAN, and CENTRAL AMERICA
National capital
Major city
International boundary
0 250 500 Miles
0 250 500 Kilometers
Projection: Azimuthal Equal Area
BAJA CALIFORNIA PENINSULA
GULF OF CALIFORNIA
SIERRA MADRE OCCIDENTAL
SIERRA MADRE ORIENTAL
SIERRA MADRE DEL SUR
MEXICAN PLATEAU
MEXICO
Ciudad Juárez
Chihuahua
Monterrey
Tampico
León
Guadalajara
Mexico City
Puebla
Veracruz
Río Grande
San Pedro River
Balsas River
Tropic of Cancer
GULF OF MEXICO
CAMPECHE BAY
YUCATÁN PENINSULA
Mérida
Belize City
Belmopan
Dolores
BELIZE
GULF OF HONDURAS
GUATEMALA
El Progreso
Guatemala
Quezaltenango
Tegucigalpa
Santa Ana
San Salvador
EL SALVADOR
PACIFIC OCEAN
N
115°
110°
105°
100°
95°
90°
35°
30°
25°
20°
15°
10°
5°

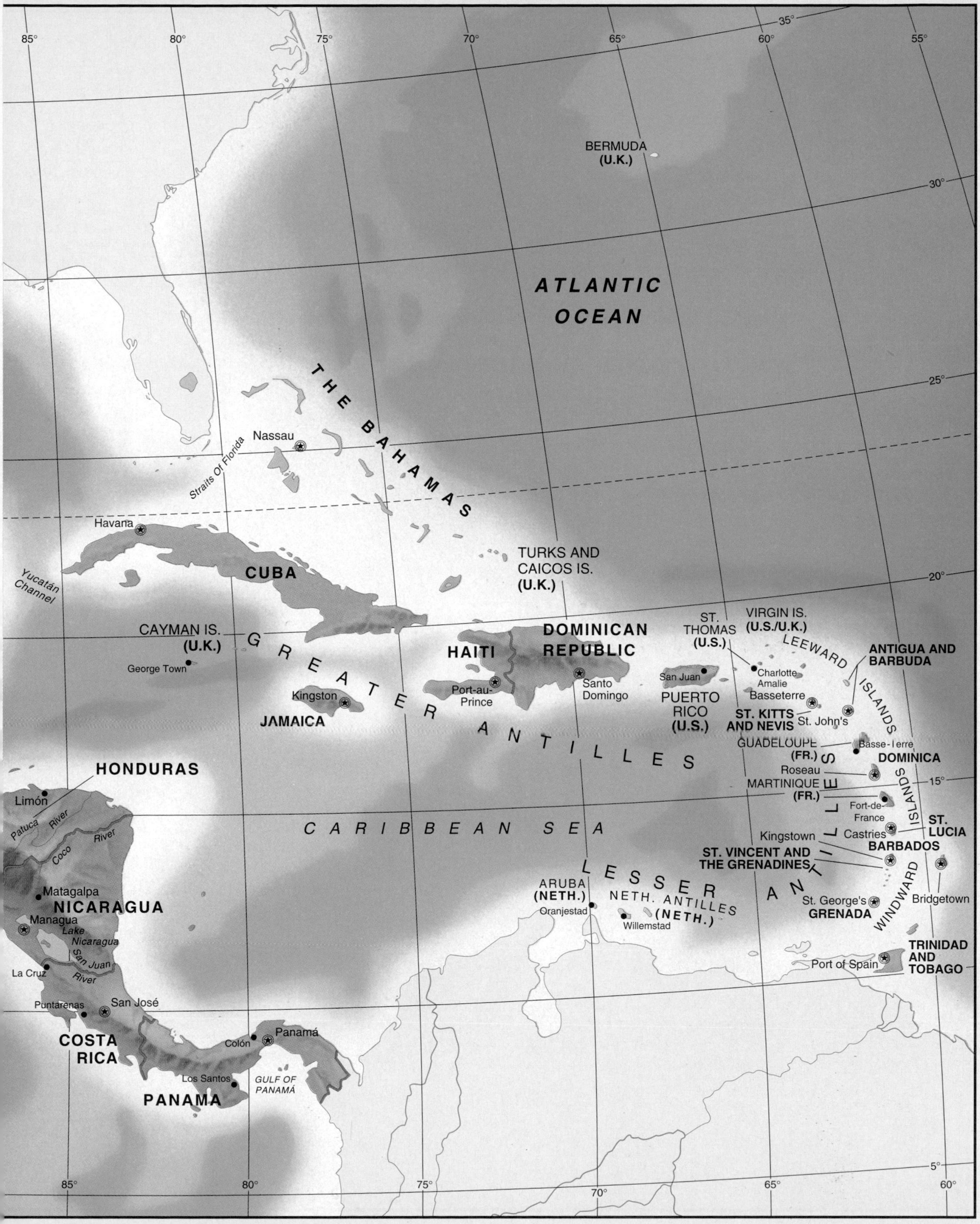
ATLANTIC OCEAN
BERMUDA (U.K.)
THE BAHAMAS
Nassau
Straits Of Florida
Havana
CUBA
Yucatán Channel
TURKS AND CAICOS IS. (U.K.)
CAYMAN IS. (U.K.)
George Town
GREATER ANTILLES
HAITI
Port-au-Prince
DOMINICAN REPUBLIC
Santo Domingo
Kingston
JAMAICA
ST. THOMAS (U.S.)
VIRGIN IS. (U.S./U.K.)
Charlotte Amalie
San Juan
PUERTO RICO (U.S.)
LEEWARD ISLANDS
ANTIGUA AND BARBUDA
Basseterre
ST. KITTS AND NEVIS
St. John's
GUADELOUPE (FR.)
Basse-Terre
DOMINICA
Roseau
MARTINIQUE (FR.)
Fort-de-France
ST. LUCIA
Castries
Kingstown
ST. VINCENT AND THE GRENADINES
BARBADOS
Bridgetown
WINDWARD ISLANDS
St. George's
GRENADA
TRINIDAD AND TOBAGO
Port of Spain
LESSER ANTILLES
ARUBA (NETH.)
Oranjestad
NETH. ANTILLES (NETH.)
Willemstad
CARIBBEAN SEA
HONDURAS
Limón
Patuca River
Coco River
Matagalpa
NICARAGUA
Managua
Lake Nicaragua
San Juan River
La Cruz
Puntarenas
San José
COSTA RICA
Colón
Panamá
Los Santos
GULF OF PANAMÁ
PANAMA
85°
80°
75°
70°
65°
60°
55°
35°
30°
25°
20°
15°
5°

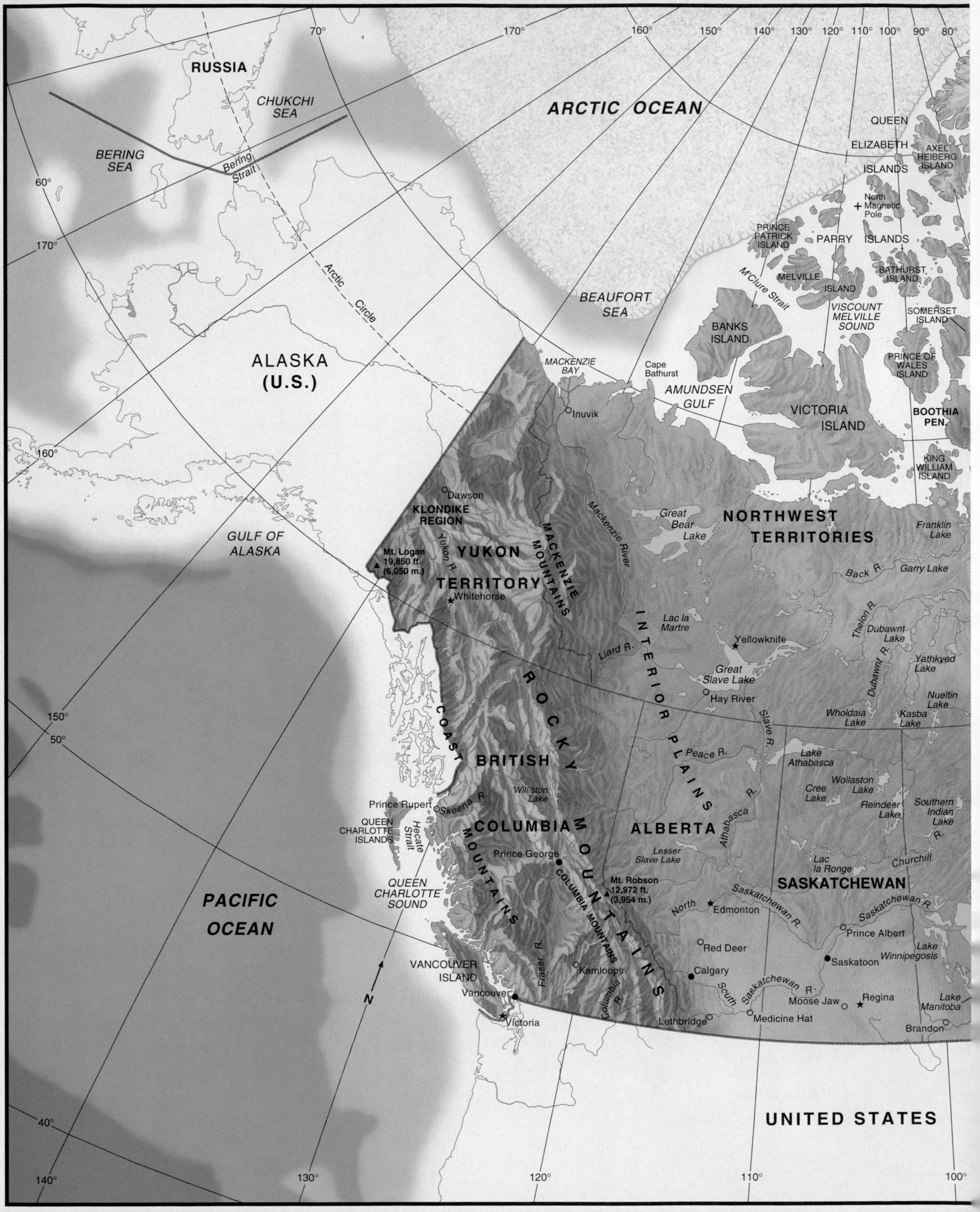

RUSSIA
CHUKCHI SEA
BERING SEA
Bering Strait
ARCTIC OCEAN
Arctic Circle
BEAUFORT SEA
ALASKA (U.S.)
GULF OF ALASKA
PACIFIC OCEAN
QUEEN ELIZABETH ISLANDS
AXEL HEIBERG ISLAND
North Magnetic Pole
PRINCE PATRICK ISLAND
PARRY ISLANDS
M'Clure Strait
MELVILLE ISLAND
BATHURST ISLAND
VISCOUNT MELVILLE SOUND
SOMERSET ISLAND
BANKS ISLAND
PRINCE OF WALES ISLAND
MACKENZIE BAY
Cape Bathurst
AMUNDSEN GULF
VICTORIA ISLAND
BOOTHIA PEN.
KING WILLIAM ISLAND
Inuvik
Dawson
KLONDIKE REGION
Mt. Logan 19,850 ft. (6,050 m.)
Yukon R.
YUKON TERRITORY
Whitehorse
MACKENZIE MOUNTAINS
Mackenzie River
Great Bear Lake
NORTHWEST TERRITORIES
Franklin Lake
Back R.
Garry Lake
Thelon R.
Dubawnt Lake
Dubawnt R.
Yathkyed Lake
Lac la Martre
Yellowknife
Liard R.
INTERIOR PLAINS
Great Slave Lake
Hay River
Slave R.
Nueltin Lake
Wholdaia Lake
Kasba Lake
ROCKY MOUNTAINS
COAST MOUNTAINS
BRITISH COLUMBIA
Peace R.
Lake Athabasca
Williston Lake
Wollaston Lake
Cree Lake
Reindeer Lake
Southern Indian Lake
Prince Rupert
Skeena R.
QUEEN CHARLOTTE ISLANDS
Hecate Strait
ALBERTA
Athabasca R.
Lesser Slave Lake
Lac la Ronge
Churchill R.
Prince George
COLUMBIA MOUNTAINS
Mt. Robson 12,972 ft. (3,954 m.)
SASKATCHEWAN
QUEEN CHARLOTTE SOUND
North Saskatchewan R.
Saskatchewan R.
Edmonton
Prince Albert
Red Deer
Lake Winnipegosis
Saskatoon
VANCOUVER ISLAND
Fraser R.
Kamloops
Calgary
South Saskatchewan R.
Columbia R.
Vancouver
Moose Jaw
Regina
Lake Manitoba
Victoria
Lethbridge
Medicine Hat
Brandon
N
UNITED STATES
170°
160°
150°
140°
130°
120°
110°
100°
90°
80°
70°
60°
50°
40°

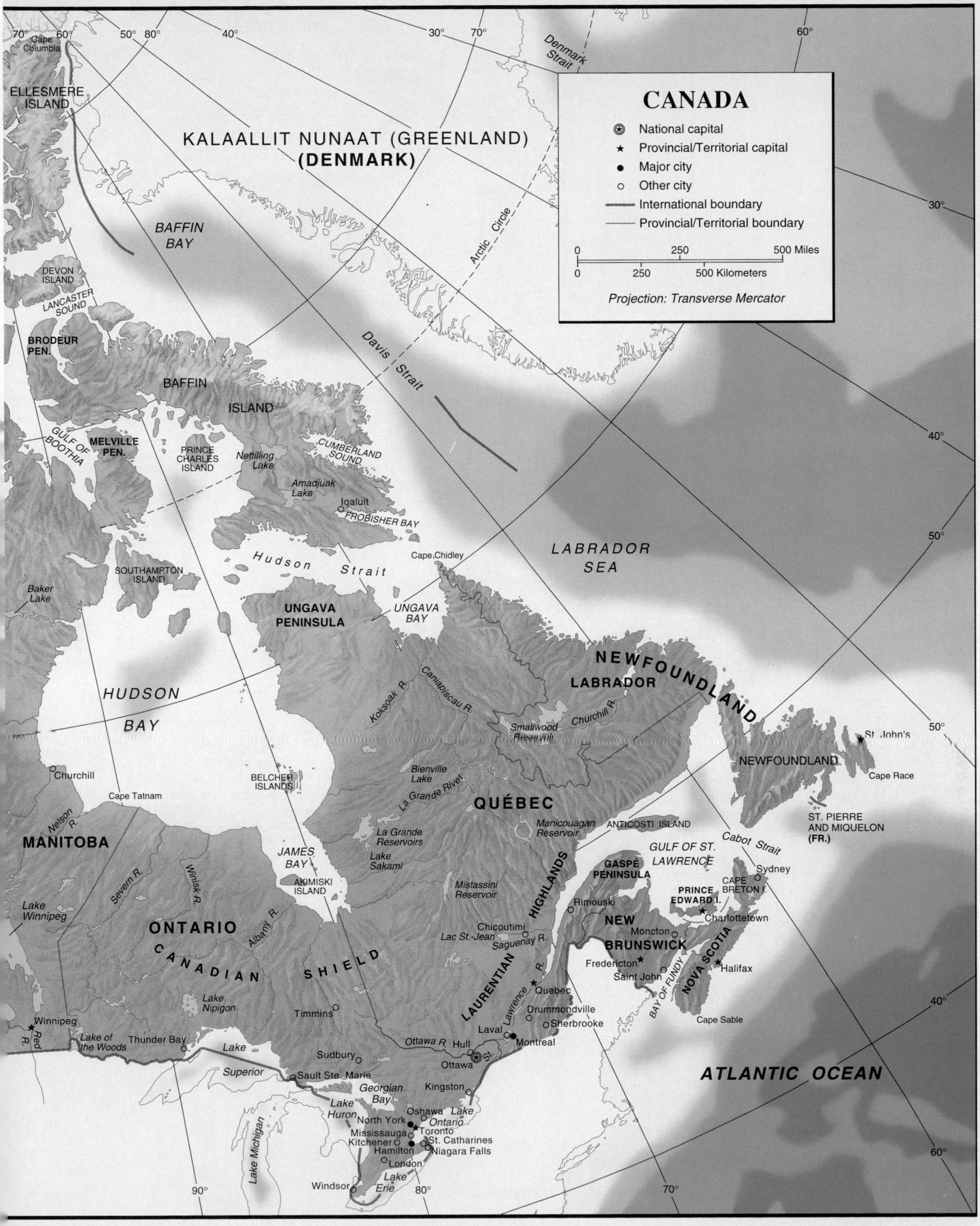
CANADA
National capital
Provincial/Territorial capital
Major city
Other city
International boundary
Provincial/Territorial boundary
0 250 500 Miles
0 250 500 Kilometers
Projection: Transverse Mercator
KALAALLIT NUNAAT (GREENLAND)
(DENMARK)
ELLESMERE ISLAND
Cape Columbia
Denmark Strait
BAFFIN BAY
DEVON ISLAND
LANCASTER SOUND
BRODEUR PEN.
BAFFIN ISLAND
Arctic Circle
Davis Strait
GULF OF BOOTHIA
MELVILLE PEN.
PRINCE CHARLES ISLAND
Nettilling Lake
CUMBERLAND SOUND
Amadjuak Lake
Iqaluit
FROBISHER BAY
LABRADOR SEA
Hudson Strait
Cape Chidley
SOUTHAMPTON ISLAND
Baker Lake
UNGAVA PENINSULA
UNGAVA BAY
HUDSON BAY
NEWFOUNDLAND
LABRADOR
Koksoak R.
Caniapiscau R.
Churchill R.
Smallwood Reservoir
St. John's
NEWFOUNDLAND
Cape Race
Churchill
BELCHER ISLANDS
Bienville Lake
La Grande Rivet
QUÉBEC
Cape Tatnam
Nelson R.
MANITOBA
La Grande Reservoirs
Manicouagan Reservoir
ANTICOSTI ISLAND
Cabot Strait
ST. PIERRE AND MIQUELON (FR.)
JAMES BAY
Lake Sakami
GULF OF ST. LAWRENCE
GASPÉ PENINSULA
Sydney
HIGHLANDS
AKIMISKI ISLAND
Severn R.
Winisk R.
Mistassini Reservoir
PRINCE EDWARD I.
CAPE BRETON I.
Lake Winnipeg
Rimouski
NEW BRUNSWICK
Charlottetown
ONTARIO
Albany R.
Chicoutimi
Lac St.-Jean
Saguenay R.
Moncton
NOVA SCOTIA
CANADIAN SHIELD
Fredericton
Saint John
BAY OF FUNDY
Halifax
LAURENTIAN
St. Lawrence R.
Quebec
Lake Nipigon
Timmins
Drummondville
Sherbrooke
Cape Sable
Winnipeg
Red R.
Lake of the Woods
Thunder Bay
Laval
Montreal
Lake Superior
Sudbury
Ottawa R.
Hull
Ottawa
ATLANTIC OCEAN
Sault Ste. Marie
Georgian Bay
Kingston
Lake Huron
Oshawa
Lake Ontario
North York
Toronto
Mississauga
Kitchener
Hamilton
St. Catharines
Niagara Falls
Lake Michigan
London
Windsor
Lake Erie
70° 60° 50° 80° 40° 30° 70° 60° 30° 40° 50° 50° 40° 90° 80° 70° 60°

THE WORLD
POLITICAL

- • World's most populous cities
- —— International boundary
- - - - Disputed boundary
- ········ Undefined boundary

0 — 1,000 — 2,000 Miles
0 — 1,000 — 2,000 Kilometers

Projection: Robinson

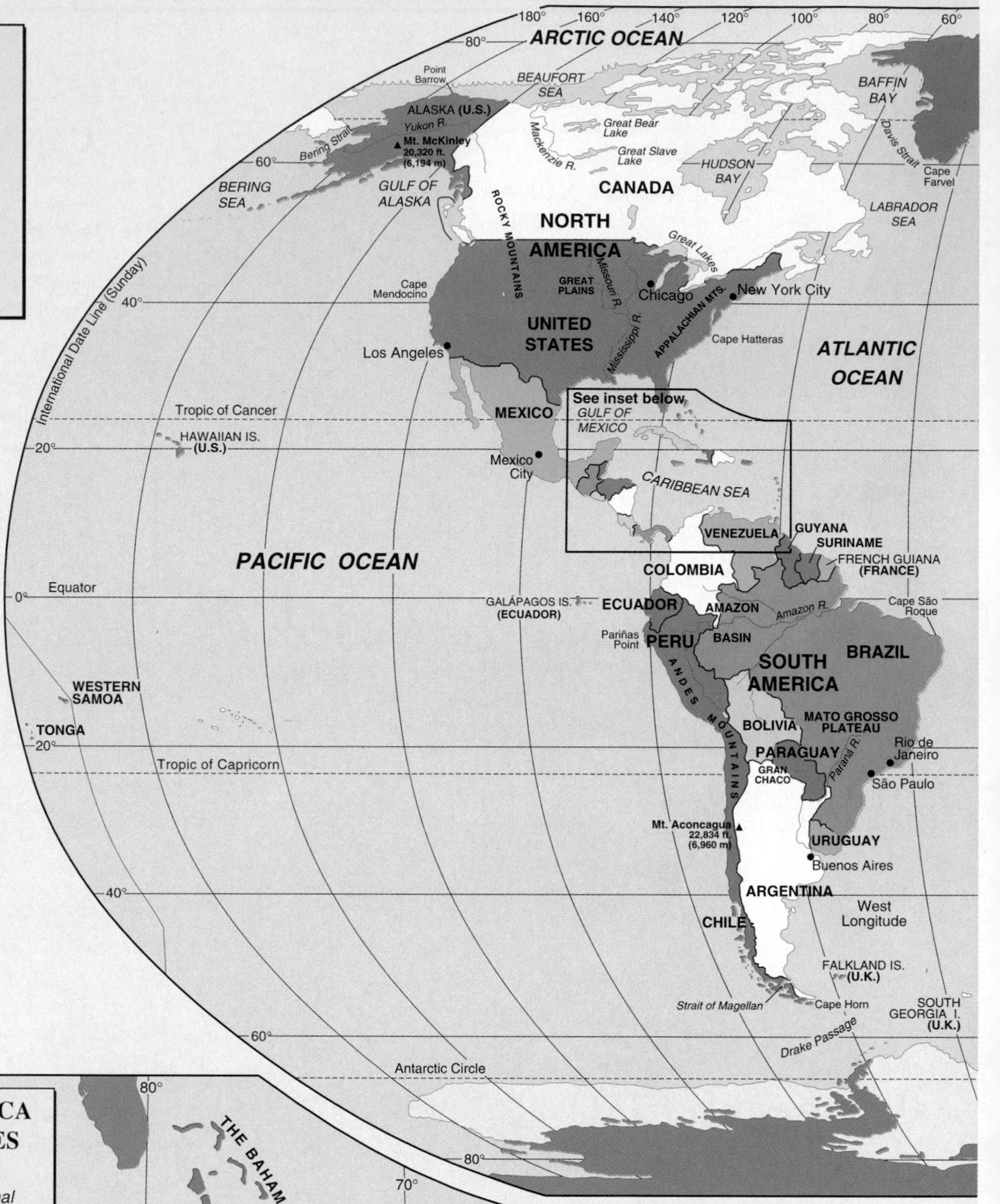

CENTRAL AMERICA AND WEST INDIES

Projection: Bipolar Oblique Conic Conformal

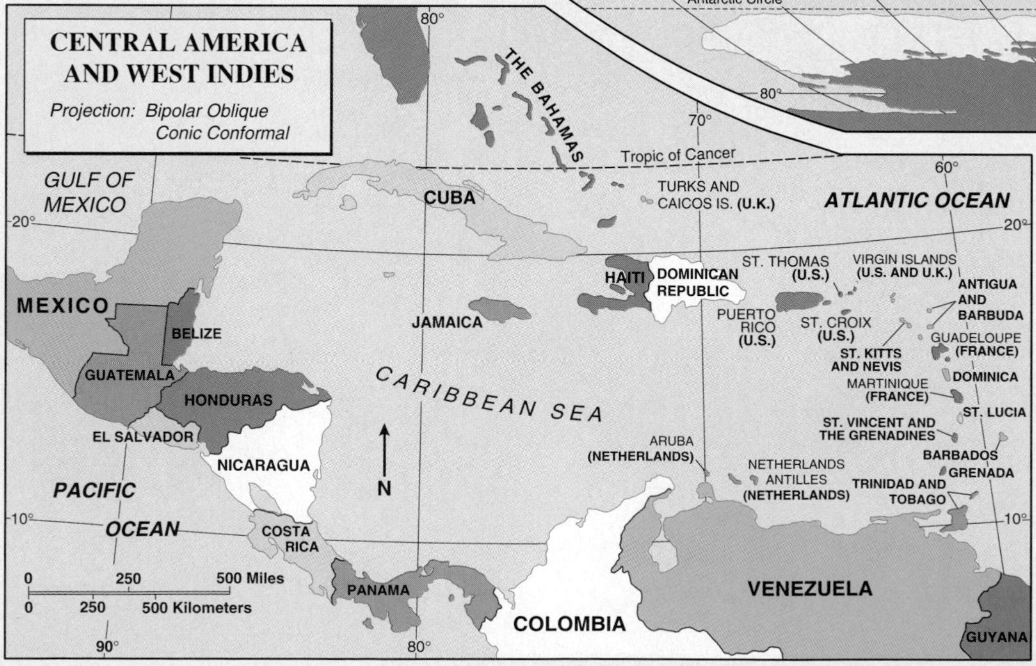

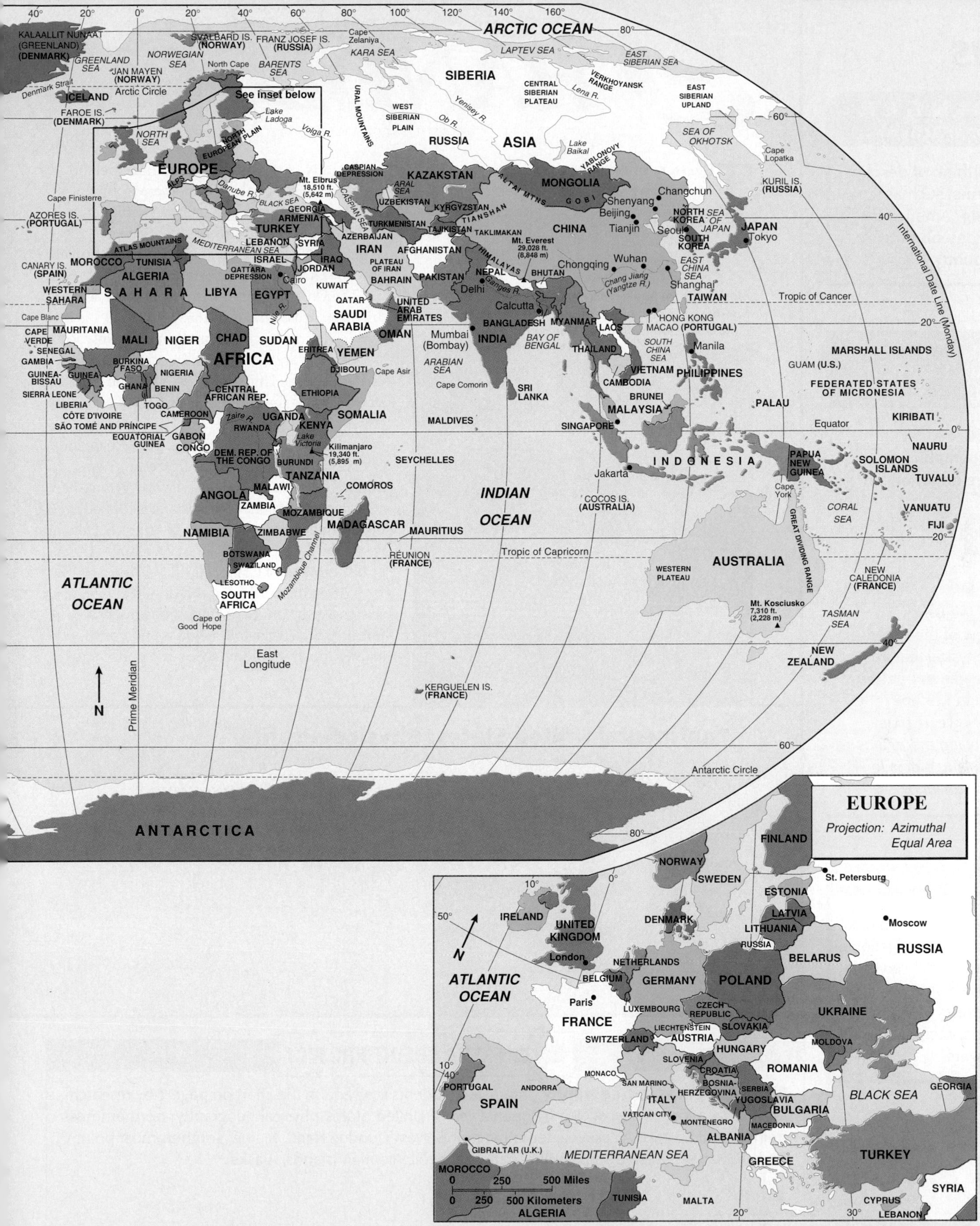
ARCTIC OCEAN
KALAALLIT NUNAAT (GREENLAND) (DENMARK)
GREENLAND SEA
NORWEGIAN SEA
SVALBARD IS. (NORWAY)
FRANZ JOSEF IS. (RUSSIA)
Cape Zelaniya
KARA SEA
LAPTEV SEA
EAST SIBERIAN SEA
BARENTS SEA
North Cape
JAN MAYEN (NORWAY)
Denmark Strait
ICELAND
Arctic Circle
See inset below
FAROE IS. (DENMARK)
NORTH SEA
Lake Ladoga
Volga R.
NORTH EUROPEAN PLAIN
URAL MOUNTAINS
WEST SIBERIAN PLAIN
SIBERIA
CENTRAL SIBERIAN PLATEAU
VERKHOYANSK RANGE
Lena R.
EAST SIBERIAN UPLAND
Yenisey R.
Ob R.
RUSSIA
ASIA
Lake Baikal
YABLONOVY RANGE
SEA OF OKHOTSK
Cape Lopatka
KURIL IS. (RUSSIA)
EUROPE
ALPS
Danube R.
Mt. Elbrus 18,510 ft. (5,642 m)
CASPIAN DEPRESSION
KAZAKSTAN
ARAL SEA
MONGOLIA
ALTAI MTNS.
GOBI
Changchun
Shenyang
Beijing
Tianjin
Seoul
NORTH KOREA
SOUTH KOREA
SEA OF JAPAN
JAPAN
Tokyo
Cape Finisterre
BLACK SEA
GEORGIA
ARMENIA
CASPIAN SEA
UZBEKISTAN
KYRGYZSTAN
TIANSHAN
TURKMENISTAN
TAJIKISTAN
TAKLIMAKAN
CHINA
AZORES IS. (PORTUGAL)
TURKEY
AZERBAIJAN
LEBANON
SYRIA
IRAQ
IRAN
AFGHANISTAN
Mt. Everest 29,028 ft. (8,848 m)
HIMALAYAS
Wuhan
Chongqing
EAST CHINA SEA
ATLAS MOUNTAINS
MEDITERRANEAN SEA
ISRAEL
JORDAN
PLATEAU OF IRAN
NEPAL
BHUTAN
Chang Jiang (Yangtze R.)
Shanghai
International Date Line (Monday)
CANARY IS. (SPAIN)
MOROCCO
TUNISIA
QATTARA DEPRESSION
Cairo
KUWAIT
BAHRAIN
PAKISTAN
Ganges R.
Delhi
TAIWAN
ALGERIA
WESTERN SAHARA
SAHARA
LIBYA
EGYPT
QATAR
UNITED ARAB EMIRATES
SAUDI ARABIA
Calcutta
Tropic of Cancer
Cape Blanc
Nile R.
BANGLADESH
MYANMAR
HONG KONG
MACAO (PORTUGAL)
CAPE VERDE
MAURITANIA
MALI
NIGER
CHAD
SUDAN
OMAN
Mumbai (Bombay)
INDIA
BAY OF BENGAL
LAOS
SOUTH CHINA SEA
Manila
MARSHALL ISLANDS
SENEGAL
GAMBIA
ERITREA
YEMEN
AFRICA
THAILAND
GUAM (U.S.)
BURKINA FASO
GUINEA-BISSAU
GUINEA
NIGERIA
DJIBOUTI
Cape Asir
ARABIAN SEA
VIETNAM
PHILIPPINES
SIERRA LEONE
GHANA
BENIN
CENTRAL AFRICAN REP.
ETHIOPIA
Cape Comorin
SRI LANKA
CAMBODIA
FEDERATED STATES OF MICRONESIA
LIBERIA
TOGO
BRUNEI
PALAU
CÔTE D'IVOIRE
CAMEROON
Zaire R.
UGANDA
SOMALIA
MALDIVES
MALAYSIA
KIRIBATI
SÃO TOMÉ AND PRÍNCIPE
RWANDA
KENYA
SINGAPORE
Equator
EQUATORIAL GUINEA
GABON
CONGO
Lake Victoria
Kilimanjaro 19,340 ft. (5,895 m)
NAURU
DEM. REP. OF THE CONGO
BURUNDI
SEYCHELLES
INDONESIA
PAPUA NEW GUINEA
SOLOMON ISLANDS
Jakarta
TUVALU
TANZANIA
COMOROS
MALAWI
ANGOLA
INDIAN OCEAN
COCOS IS. (AUSTRALIA)
Cape York
ZAMBIA
CORAL SEA
VANUATU
MOZAMBIQUE
MADAGASCAR
GREAT DIVIDING RANGE
FIJI
NAMIBIA
ZIMBABWE
MAURITIUS
BOTSWANA
RÉUNION (FRANCE)
Tropic of Capricorn
SWAZILAND
Mozambique Channel
AUSTRALIA
WESTERN PLATEAU
NEW CALEDONIA (FRANCE)
ATLANTIC OCEAN
LESOTHO
SOUTH AFRICA
Mt. Kosciusko 7,310 ft. (2,228 m)
TASMAN SEA
Cape of Good Hope
NEW ZEALAND
East Longitude
N
Prime Meridian
KERGUELEN IS. (FRANCE)
Antarctic Circle
ANTARCTICA
EUROPE
Projection: Azimuthal Equal Area
FINLAND
NORWAY
SWEDEN
St. Petersburg
ESTONIA
IRELAND
LATVIA
DENMARK
UNITED KINGDOM
LITHUANIA
Moscow
RUSSIA
BELARUS
London
NETHERLANDS
ATLANTIC OCEAN
BELGIUM
GERMANY
POLAND
Paris
LUXEMBOURG
CZECH REPUBLIC
UKRAINE
FRANCE
LIECHTENSTEIN
SLOVAKIA
SWITZERLAND
AUSTRIA
MOLDOVA
HUNGARY
SLOVENIA
ROMANIA
CROATIA
MONACO
SAN MARINO
BOSNIA-HERZEGOVINA
SERBIA
GEORGIA
PORTUGAL
ANDORRA
YUGOSLAVIA
BLACK SEA
SPAIN
ITALY
BULGARIA
VATICAN CITY
MONTENEGRO
MACEDONIA
ALBANIA
GIBRALTAR (U.K.)
MEDITERRANEAN SEA
GREECE
TURKEY
MOROCCO
0 250 500 Miles
0 250 500 Kilometers
ALGERIA
TUNISIA
MALTA
CYPRUS
SYRIA
LEBANON

1 FOCUS

BELLRINGER
Motivational Activity

Ask students to think of descriptive, colorful terms, such as those in the song "America the Beautiful," that describe their region of the country.

NATIONAL GEOGRAPHIC SOCIETY

VIDEODISC
GTV: A Geographic Perspective on American History

Side 1, Chapter 1
Title: *The Lay of the Land*
Subject: Overview of the American landscape and physical features
Ask: **What is the general pattern of the American landscape stretching east to west?** *(flat, coastal land to rolling mountains to flat plains to rolling plains to mountains to coastal land)*

What?Where?When?Who?

Lighthouses In a time when most ships use sophisticated navigational tools, the lighthouse still serves an important purpose. Some 600 lighthouses dot the coasts of the United States and Canada, warning ships of navigational dangers.

Geography HANDBOOK

The story of the United States begins with **geography**—the study of the earth in all of its variety. Geography describes the earth's land, water, and plant and animal life. It is the study of places and the complex relationships between people and their environments.

Mountains frame the eastern and western coasts of the United States; plains span the center. Here, a lighthouse stands on the Maine coast.

The United States is a land of startling physical differences. It is also a nation of diverse groups of people. A study of geography can help explain how the United States acquired its diversity.

The United States—with a total land area of 3,539,230 square miles (9,166,606 sq. km)—is the world's fourth-largest country in size. Only Russia, Canada, and China are larger.

Most of the United States—48 of the 50 states—spans the entire middle part of North America. This group of states touches three major bodies of water—the Atlantic Ocean, the Gulf of Mexico, and the Pacific Ocean. Two states—Alaska and Hawaii—lie apart from the 48 states. Alaska, the largest state, is located in the northwestern part of North America. Hawaii lies in the Pacific Ocean about 2,400 miles (3,862 km) southwest of California.

Within the borders of the United States stretch a rich variety of landscapes—dense forests, hot deserts, rolling grasslands, and snow-capped mountains. Because of its large

Continental United States: Physical Profile

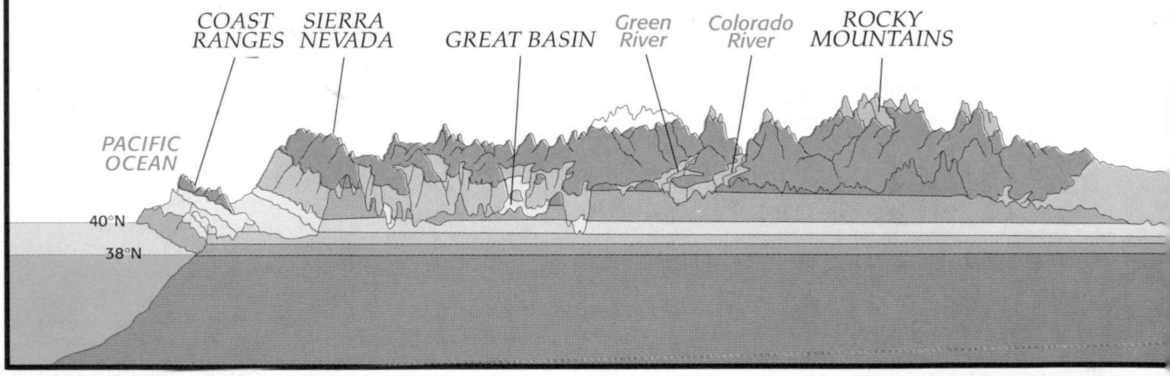

EXTRA CREDIT PROJECT

More Extremes in Geography Interested students may add to the chart on page 1 by researching the location of the following superlatives of United States physical geography: northernmost point—Point Barrow, Alaska; easternmost point—West Quoddy Head, Maine; southernmost point—Ka Lae, Hawaii; westernmost point—Cape Wrangell, Aleutian Islands, Alaska.

Geographic Facts About the United States

Largest state	Alaska	591,004 square miles (1,530,700 sq. km)
Smallest state	Rhode Island	1,212 square miles (3,139 sq. km)
Most populated state	California	31,589,000
Least populated state	Wyoming	480,000
Longest river	Mississippi	2,348 miles (3,778 km)
Highest waterfall	Yosemite Falls (California)	2,425 feet (739 m)
Points farthest apart	Log Point, Elliot Key, Florida and Kure Island, Hawaii	5,859 miles (9,429 km)
Largest lake	Lake Superior*	31,820 square miles (82,414 sq. km)
Deepest lake	Crater Lake (Oregon)	1,932 feet (589 m)
Highest mountain	Mount McKinley (Alaska)	20,320 feet (6,194 m)
Lowest point	Death Valley (California)	282 feet (86 m) below sea level
Rainiest location	Mt. Waialeale (Hawaii)	460 inches (1,168 cm) rainfall per year
Highest recorded temperature	Death Valley (California)	134° Fahrenheit, on July 10, 1913
Lowest recorded temperature	Prospect Creek (Alaska)	-80° Fahrenheit, on January 23, 1971

*Part of Lake Superior is located in Canada

Population source: *1997 Information Please Almanac.*

Chart Study

This chart lists geographic facts about the United States.

1. In what state is the highest mountain?
2. What states have both the highest and lowest of something? Name those highs and lows.

size and diverse environments, the United States throughout its history has offered many opportunities. Many historians believe that thousands of years ago, the first Americans migrated across a land bridge from Asia to the countries we now call the United States and Canada. Over the centuries people from Europe, Africa, Asia, and other parts of the Americas followed. Today more than 266 million people make their homes in the United States. They live in crowded metropolitan areas, in towns and villages, and in rural communities.

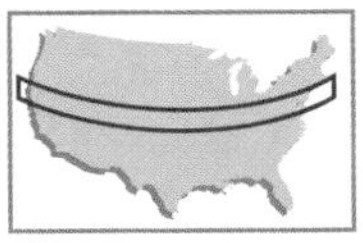

Coast to Coast This diagram shows the proportionate elevation across the continental United States between 38°N and 40°N latitude.

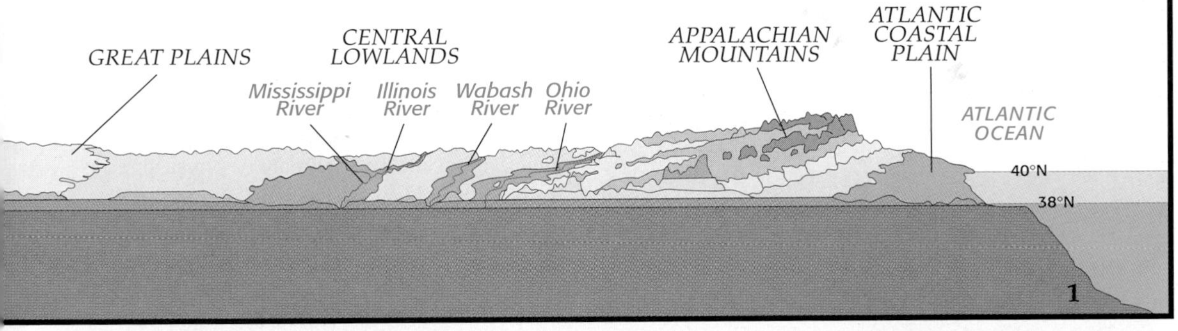

1

2 TEACH

L1, ELL Analyzing Geography's Impact Ask students to think of ways physical geography affects their lives and cultures. Suggest that they consider their types of clothing and homes, leisure activities, and the area's businesses and industries.

L2 Using Geographic Terms Survey the students' knowledge of geographic terms. Create three columns on the chalkboard with the following headings: *Landforms*, *Bodies of water*, and *Climates*. List one term that fits each column, such as "canyon," "bay," and "tropical." Ask students to volunteer as many other terms for each column as they can. Have students turn to pages 10–11 and read the **Geographic Dictionary**. Then have them close their books and continue suggesting terms for each column on the chalkboard.

Chart Study

Answers

1. Alaska
2. California: highest waterfall and lowest point; Alaska: highest mountain and lowest recorded temperature

Chart Skills Practice

Reading a Chart About how much larger is the area of the largest state than the smallest state? *(Alaska is 589,792 square miles larger than Rhode Island.)*

Critical Thinking Activity

Analyzing a Land Profile Point out to students that a land profile (shown above) is a diagram that shows the cross section of a geographic region. Describe a cross section as follows: If you slice a loaf of bread, each slice is a cross section of the whole loaf. Suppose you hold the slice with the flat side facing you and then trace the outline of the top of the slice. Is it flat or curved? Either way, the line formed by the top of the slice shows the profile of the whole loaf. If you slice through a stretch of land as if it were a loaf of bread, each slice would be a cross section, or a land profile. **Ask:** What are the westernmost and easternmost points labeled on the land profile above? *(Coast Ranges; Atlantic Coastal Plain)* What is the latitude of the profile? *(38°N to 40°N latitude)* What is the highest point on the profile? *(Rocky Mountains)* **L2**

L1, ELL Illustrating Themes Write the five themes of geography on the chalkboard. Call on volunteers to provide brief descriptions of each, noting responses on the chalkboard. Then have each student choose one theme to illustrate. Allow students time to display their finished illustrations.

L2 Summarizing Ideas Have students work individually or in pairs to write brief, catchy descriptions of the themes of geography. Offer the following as an example: *Absolute location is a place's global address.*

NATIONAL GEOGRAPHIC SOCIETY

CD-ROM
Picture Atlas of the World

You and your students can learn about the physical features, music, economy, and population of the United States by selecting "North America" on the main menu.

Physical Geography of the World Transparencies

Display and discuss the physical features of the following transparencies:

1. Oregon Coast
2. Sonoran Desert
4. Grand Canyon
6. Mississippi River
7. Lake Superior
9. Appalachian Mountains
10. The Everglades

Five Geography Themes

Geography has shaped the development of the United States. To show the link between history and geography, geographers—the people who study geography—have organized the subject into five broad themes. These themes are location, place, human/environment interaction, movement, and region.

New York City

Location

"Where is it?" Every place has an absolute location and a relative location. **Absolute location** is one exact spot on the earth. To pinpoint places exactly, geographers use numbered lines called latitude and longitude lines.

Relative location tells where a place is, compared with one or more other places. Knowing a place's relative location may give us an understanding of how it was settled and how it developed culturally.

Place

"What is it like?" **Place** describes all the features and characteristics that give an area its own special quality. These can be physical characteristics such as landforms, climate, and plant or animal life. They can also be cultural characteristics —language, religion, music, and architecture.

The Rocky Mountain region shares rugged peaks and swift streams.

Human/Environment Interaction

"How does the relationship between people and their natural surroundings influence the way people live?" This is one of the questions that the theme of **human/environment interaction** answers. This theme also shows how people use the environment and how their actions affect the environment.

Movement

"How do people in one area relate to people in other areas?" Geographers answer this question within the theme of **movement.** People, ideas, goods, and information move from place to place.

The theme of movement shows the connections among different parts of the world. Transportation routes, communication systems, and trade connections linked people and places in the past. They have also helped create a global community today in which the United States plays an important role.

Region

"What common characteristics does a certain area share?" The answer to this question involves the theme of **region.** A region can be an area that has the same climate or physical features. Cultural features such as language, religion, or government can also form a region.

Cooperative Learning Activity

Developing a Lesson Plan Organize students into five groups. Assign each group one of the five geography themes. Direct students to develop a lesson plan they could use to teach their theme to students in a lower grade. Suggest that groups begin by brainstorming what information should be included in the lesson; the order in which they would present these concepts; and what visual materials they might use. Finally, have them create a written plan. If time permits, have each group present its plan to the class.

The Land

Like a patchwork quilt, the United States consists of regional stretches of different landscapes. Look at the map below to find the eight physical regions of the United States.

Coastal Plains

A broad lowland runs along the Atlantic Ocean and the Gulf of Mexico. Geographers divide this lowland into two parts: the **Atlantic Coastal Plain** and the **Gulf Coastal Plain.** These plains begin at sea level along the coasts and rise gradually inland to a height of about 1,000 feet (305 m).

The Atlantic Plain borders the Atlantic coast from Massachusetts to Florida. Many of the region's deepwater ports provided excellent harbors for the first settlers' ships. Today a densely populated area of cities and towns stretches along the Atlantic coast from Boston to Washington, D.C. This area of continuous urbanization is called a **megalopolis.**

Much wider than the Atlantic Plain, the Gulf Plain hugs the Gulf of Mexico from Florida to Texas. The Mississippi River—the longest river in the country—drains much of the Gulf Plain.

Physical Regions of the United States

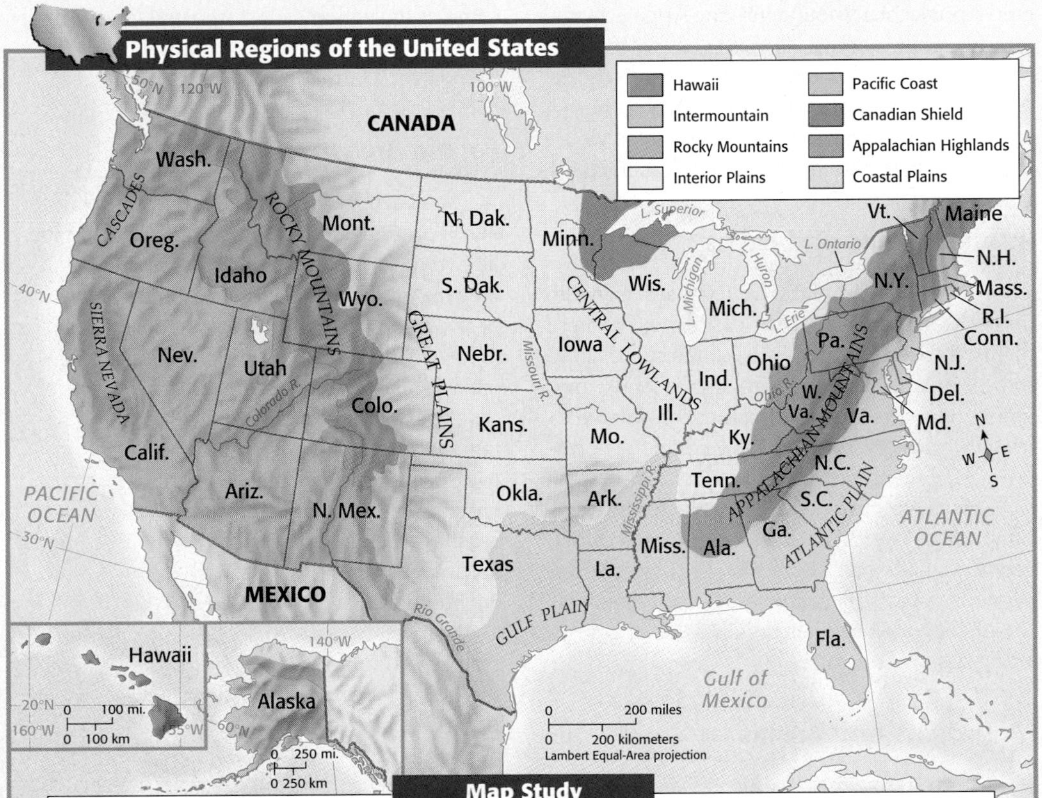

Map Study

The physical features of the United States vary greatly from the Pacific Coast to the Atlantic Coast.

1. **Region** According to the map, in what physical region is Kansas?
2. **Analyzing Information** What physical feature separates the Coastal Plains from the Interior Plains?

L1, ELL Identifying Physical Features Call on volunteers to identify the landforms and bodies of water discussed in the section "The Land." List responses on the chalkboard and have students use the map on pages RA8–RA9 to find examples of the listed responses. If geography textbooks are available, you might have students search them for photographs or other types of illustrations of the landforms and water bodies they listed.

L2 Researching Nicknames Remind students that each state has a nickname or popular name. Have students make a list of these names and determine which ones are related to physical geography.

you don't say...

Megalopolis The term *megalopolis* comes from Greek words meaning "great city." The east coast megalopolis—from Boston to Washington, D.C.—is often referred to as "Boswash."

Map Study

Answers

1. Interior Plains
2. Appalachian Highlands

Map Skills Practice

Reading a Map Have students determine how many physical regions they would pass through if they were to go across the country directly from Delaware to California. *(six)*

Multiple Learning Styles

Visual/Spatial Students having trouble organizing information might benefit from the strategy of combining words and visual materials. Direct them to read the section "The Land" and note the physical regions of the United States. Then have them find the locations of these physical regions on the map above. This strategy will help students visualize information in the text. **L1, ELL**

GEOGRAPHY HANDBOOK

L1 Illustrating Maps Provide students with outline maps of the United States. Have each student use map pencils to mark on the map the physical regions of the United States. Next, have them mark on the map the specific locations mentioned in the text. Then suggest that they include annotations detailing any interesting facts about the United States mentioned in the text. Finally, remind students to title their maps and to provide a map key, if necessary.

L2 Writing Travel Brochures Have students imagine they are writing a travel brochure of the United States. Have them suggest one-sentence descriptions for each of the country's physical regions.

What?Where?When?Who?

The Great Lakes contain about one-fifth of the earth's freshwater supply.

CURRICULUM CONNECTION

LIFE SCIENCE
The saguaro cactus is found only in the Sonoran Desert of the Southwest United States. Well-suited to desert conditions, an average-sized saguaro can store more than 100 gallons of water during the rainy season. Some saguaro grow as high as 60 feet and weigh as much as 10 tons. Desert insects, birds, and bats feed on the nectar of the saguaro's blossoms.

Fields of wheat and other grains span the Interior Plains.

Appalachian Highlands

Curving west along the Atlantic Plain are the **Appalachian** (A•puh•LAY•chuhn) **Highlands.** They stretch about 1,500 miles (2,414 km) from Canada to Alabama and contain the forest-covered Appalachian Mountains. The Appalachians, which average about 6,000 feet (1,829 m) in height, are the oldest mountain range in North America. To the east of the Appalachians, the land descends abruptly to the Piedmont, a well-drained rolling land that meets the Coastal Plains.

Interior Plains and Lakes

The central part of the United States is made up of the Interior Plains. The eastern half of these plains, the **Central Lowlands,** consists of thick forests, broad river valleys, rolling flatlands, and grassy hills. The largest group of freshwater lakes in the world—the Great Lakes—lies in the northern part of the Central Lowlands.

The **Canadian Shield**—a vast expanse of huge rocks, low hills, and lakes—extends from central Canada into Minnesota, Michigan, and Wisconsin. Farther west lie the **Great Plains**—a broad, high area blanketed with fields of grain and grassy pasturelands.

Mountains and Basins

The western part of the Great Plains meets the awesome **Rocky Mountains.** The Rockies are the largest mountain range in North America, stretching all the way from Alaska to Mexico. With some peaks rising more than 14,000 feet (4,267 m), the Rocky Mountains are higher and more rugged than the Appalachians.

A ridge of the Rockies, the **Continental Divide,** separates the rivers and streams that flow west to the Pacific Ocean from those flowing east toward the Mississippi River and Gulf of Mexico. Several important rivers—including the Colorado, Missouri, Arkansas, and Rio Grande—begin in the Rocky Mountains.

West of the Rockies stretches the **Intermountain region,** an area of sparsely populated basins, plateaus, and deserts. The Colorado Plateau—in the southern part of the region—has some of the nation's most unusual landforms, including the Grand Canyon and various flat-topped rock formations.

Pacific Areas

The Pacific Ocean forms the western border of the continental United States. Near the coast lie two major mountain ranges: the **Sierra Nevada** and the **Coast Ranges.** Some of the peaks in these chains tower more than 12,000 feet (3,658 m). West of the Pacific mountain ranges are coastal lowlands and fertile valleys.

Alaska is also part of the Pacific region. Islands, bays, and **glaciers,** or large frozen rivers of slowly moving ice, line Alaska's southern coastline. Central and southern mountain ranges are broken up by lowlands and plateaus. Mount McKinley, North America's highest mountain at 20,320 feet (6,194 m), towers over this area.

The huge saguaro cactus grows only in the desert region of the southwestern United States.

MORE ABOUT . . .

Place-Names The names of certain landforms and bodies of water reflect the multicultural heritage of the United States. For example, the Hudson River, which runs through New York State, is named for Henry Hudson, the English sea captain who explored it. The Mississippi River takes its name from a Native American word meaning "great river" or "big water." The Sierra Nevada is Spanish for "snowy range." Encourage students to locate these features on the United States physical map on pages RA8–RA9 of the Reference Atlas. Have them find names of additional physical features that reflect other cultural groups.

Climate

The United States can be divided into 10 climate regions. **Climate** is the usual pattern of weather events that occurs in an area over a long time period. The United States's climates are determined by distance from the Equator, location near large bodies of water, and changing elevations. The climate map below shows the country's various climates.

Midlatitude Climates

Most of the United States lies in the middle latitudes—midway between the Equator and the North Pole. Climates in the midlatitudes are often moderate. Find the areas on the map that have a **humid continental** climate. Winters in these areas are cold and moist; summers are long and hot. In Chicago, January temperatures hover around 12°F (–11°C), whereas July temperatures may exceed 84°F (29°C).

The southeastern United States has a **humid subtropical** climate. Winters here are mild and cool, while summers are hot and humid. January temperatures in New Orleans rarely dip below 40°F (4°C). The city's July temperatures often soar above 90°F (32°C).

The area along the Pacific coast from northern California to southeastern Alaska has a

Climate Regions of the United States

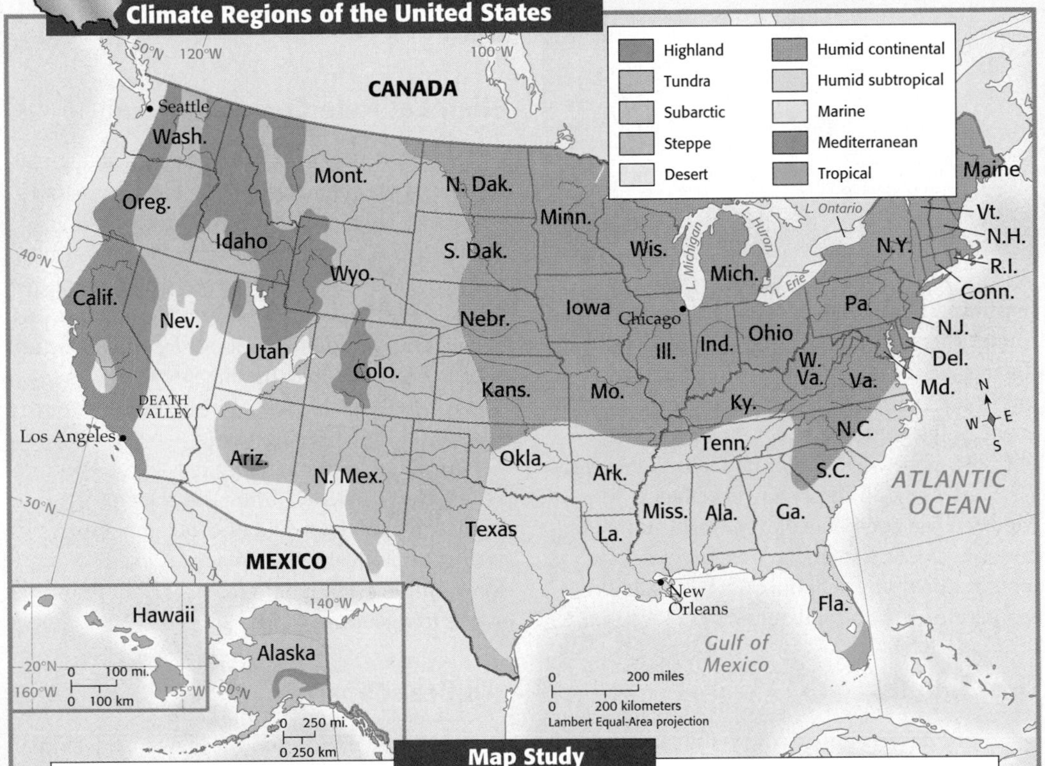

Map Study

Climates in the United States vary as widely as its physical regions do.

1. **Location** What state has a tundra climate region?
2. **Analyzing Information** What state has the most climate regions? What are the regions?

Cooperative Learning Activity

Survival Strategy Organize students into four or more groups. Assign each group a climate type. Encourage group members to imagine that they will be stranded for one year in a remote area that has their assigned climate type. Have groups plan a survival strategy to live in that climate. Each group should identify the following: (1) the type of shelter they need and will be able to make or obtain; (2) the type of clothing they need and will be able to make; and (3) the way they will obtain food and water. Have each group present their survival plan to the class, and have the class challenge each plan with situations or conditions likely to arise in the climate region.

L1, ELL Word Web Write the word *climate* on the chalkboard, then call on students to identify the factors that affect climate. Note responses on the chalkboard as they are offered. Have students use the material on the chalkboard to create a word web explaining the factors that affect climate.

you don't say...

Latitude The word *latitude* comes from the Latin word for "breadth." The word *longitude* comes from the Latin word for "length."

What? Where? When? Who?

Many Climates In 1852, 17-year-old Samuel Clemens—later known as American author Mark Twain—set out to see the United States. Over the next decade, Clemens visited the Atlantic Coast, the Pacific Coast, and the Gulf Coast. "Why, I've counted one hundred and thirty-six different kinds of weather inside of four and twenty hours," boasted Clemens at one point in his travels. Climatologists agree that the United States has the most varied climate on the earth. With its tornadoes, hurricanes, thunderstorms, and blizzards, the climate is also the most unpredictable.

Map Study

Answers

1. Alaska
2. California; Mediterranean, marine, desert, steppe, highland

Map Skills Practice

Reading a Map Have students identify at least two states with the following climates: tropical *(Hawaii, Florida)*; desert *(Arizona, New Mexico)*; marine *(Washington, Oregon)*.

L1, ELL Illustrating a Bulletin Board Have students use newspapers and magazines to find visual images that illustrate the climate types described in this section. Call on volunteers to share their selections with the class. Ask students to explain why their images represent the various climate types. Gather and display the images on a bulletin board titled "Climates of the United States."

you don't say...

Steppe The word *steppe* is from the Russian word *step'*, which means "grassy plain." The world's largest steppe stretches across eastern Europe and western and central Asia.

CURRICULUM CONNECTION

SCIENCE
Ocean water tastes really salty, but it averages only about 3.5 percent salt. Of this, nearly 3 percent is sodium chloride (regular salt). The rest contains almost every chemical element on the earth.

Death Valley (below) has a dry desert climate. Denali National Park (right) in Alaska experiences a subarctic climate.

marine climate. Temperatures here are mild year-round. Pacific winds bring plenty of rainfall to the marine climate region. The northwestern part of Washington State, on the Olympic Peninsula, is one of the wettest areas of the nation. More than 140 inches (356 cm) of rain falls there yearly.

Southern California, however, has a **Mediterranean** climate of dry, warm summers and rainy, mild winters. In Los Angeles, January temperatures stay at about 56°F (13°C). In July, temperatures are a moderate 75°F (24°C).

Dry Climates

A dry **desert** climate covers the plateaus and basins between the Pacific mountain ranges and the Rockies. Hot, dry air gets trapped here when the Pacific ranges block moist ocean winds. This region is dotted with deserts. In California's Death Valley—the hottest place in the United States—summer temperatures often sizzle at 125°F (52°C)!

The western part of the Great Plains, however, has a dry **steppe,** or grasslands, climate. Winters here tend to be very cold, and summers hot and dry.

High Latitude Climates

Some areas of the United States have high latitude, or polar, climates. Alaska has tundra and subarctic climates. The **tundra**—a vast rolling, treeless plain south of the Arctic Circle—has bitterly cold winters in which average temperatures are below –15°F (–26°C). Summer temperatures in the tundra seldom rise above freezing. Farther south, Alaska's **subarctic** climate region has severely cold winters, but temperatures rise above freezing during the summer.

Although mountainous areas in the West are not located near the North Pole, they have a **highland** climate of cold or cool temperatures year-round. The high elevations of the Rockies, for example, cannot hold the heat from the sun, so the temperature drops.

Tropical Climates

Southern Florida and the Hawaiian Islands have **tropical** climates. Humidity and rainfall are high during much of the year. Summers are hot, and winters are warm. In Miami, Florida, January temperatures average more than 67°F (19°C); July temperatures more than 83°F (28°C).

MORE ABOUT . . .

Geographic Information Systems Like all scientists, geographers observe, hypothesize, and collect data to prove or disprove their theories. Aiding them in their tasks are advanced technological tools such as satellites, remote sensors, and computers. Satellites orbiting the earth carry remote sensors, or high-tech cameras and/or radar. These collect information and photographs about such topics as the earth's environment, weather, human settlement patterns, and vegetation. This information is then sent to computers on the earth. Computer programs known as Geographic Information Systems (GIS) process and organize the satellite images with other data collected through censuses, cartographers, and so on. The GIS technology is already invaluable to urban planners, engineers, and geographers, and it may some day help you plan your vacation!

Geography's Impact on United States History

Geographic factors—landforms, waterways, natural resources—have shaped the outcome of America's history. Here are some examples of geography's influences in history that are highlighted in *The American Journey*.

Unit 1 Different Worlds Meet

Native Americans developed various cultures thousands of years ago. Native Americans along the Pacific coast prospered because of the mild climate and the abundance of fish and plants. In the Southwest, Native Americans invented methods of irrigation to farm the dry land. The Great Plains Native Americans depended on herds of buffalo for food, clothing, shelter, and tools. Native Americans living in woodlands hunted a variety of animals and built farming villages.

Unit 2 Colonial Settlement

Europeans settled North America during the 1500s, 1600s, and 1700s. They came seeking land, riches, and the right to live freely. Groups from Spain, France, Great Britain, and other

Natural Resources of the United States

Map Study

Forests, fertile soils, fish, and a wide variety of minerals help give the United States its great wealth of natural resources.

1. Place What mineral resource is most common in Texas?

2. Comparing What natural resources are found in your state?

More About . . .

Cultural Diversity Hispanic Americans make up the fastest-growing ethnic group in the United States, comprising 7 percent of the population. Because the term *Hispanic* is used to describe Spanish-speaking people or people of Latin American descent, the group is diverse. Hispanic Americans include people of Mexican, Puerto Rican, Caribbean, Cuban, Central American, or South American origins. Various Hispanic groups lobby locally in support of issues such as bilingual education or better health care and housing. Invite students to investigate where many of the Spanish-speaking residents of their community originated.

L1 Determining Cause and Effect Forests are considered renewable natural resources, but they are renewable only if people manage them carefully. Depletion of forests causes changes to both ground and climate. **Ask:** What are the possible consequences of deforestation? *(Deforestation causes erosion. It might also cause a change in the world's heating balance or in its water cycle. It could cause many plants and animals to become extinct.)*

NATIONAL GEOGRAPHIC SOCIETY

VIDEODISC
GTV: The American People: Fabric of a Nation

Side 1, Chapter 2
Title: *Kaleidoscope*
Subject: A look at the diversity of Native Americans
Ask: In what ways did Native Americans differ from one another? *(Answers should note the following differences: in diet, in ways of obtaining food, in types of clothing and shelter.)*

Map Study

Answers

1. Oil
2. Answers will vary, depending on your state.

Map Skills Practice

Reading a Map In what states is gold still a natural resource? *(California, Nevada, Oregon, South Dakota, Colorado, New Mexico, Alaska)*

GEOGRAPHY HANDBOOK

When?Who?What?Where?

Prehistory Many students probably believe that the North American environment remained untouched until the arrival of the Europeans. Native Americans, however, had been altering their environment for thousands of years. In the eastern woodlands, for example, Native Americans burned forested areas to make it easier to spot animals and to prepare the land for cultivation.

Map Study

Answers

1. Washington, Idaho, Nevada, Utah, Colorado, Arizona, New Mexico, Alaska
2. Massachusetts, Rhode Island, Connecticut

Map Skills Practice

Reading a Map How many states or partial states are considered part of the Sunbelt (the area below the red line)? *(15)*

L2 Predicting Consequences Have students locate the Sunbelt region on the map of the United States on this page. Then have them note characteristics of the region. Ask students to use the information to predict possible geographic, economic, and political consequences of the continued migration of people to the Sunbelt region. Also have them consider how the loss of population may affect the Northeast and Midwest regions of the United States.

Population Shifts, 1980–1995

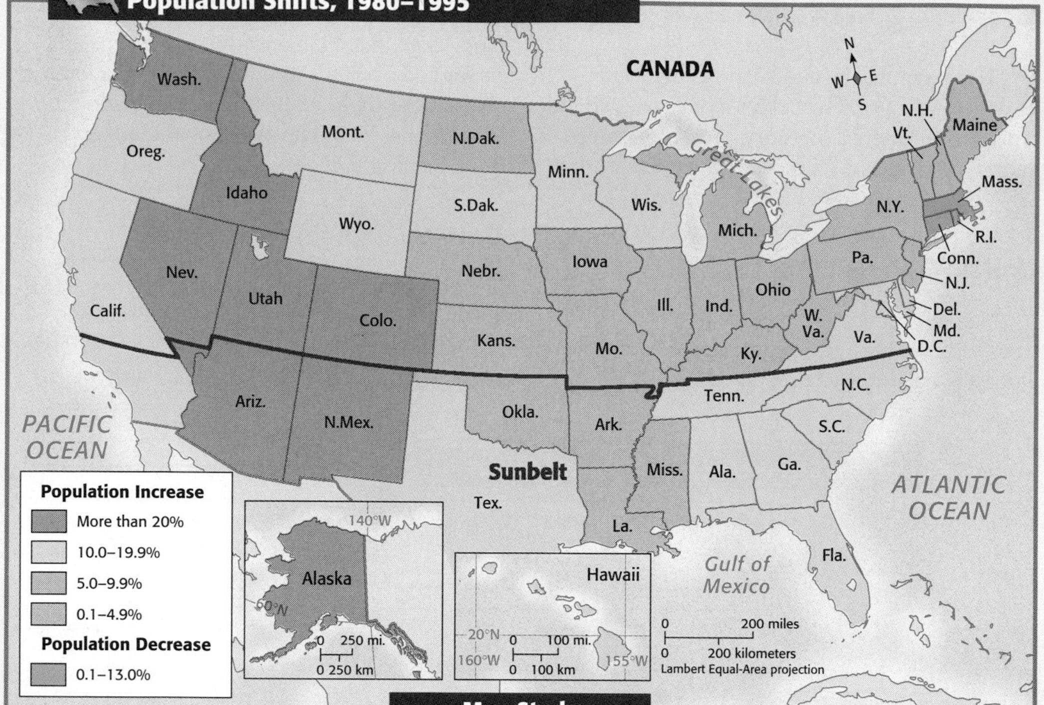

Map Study

In the 1980s many Americans moved to the South and West in search of good jobs and warmer climates.

1. **Region** Which states had the greatest percentage increases (more than 20 percent) in population?
2. **Comparing** Which states had a population decrease?

countries set up colonies along rivers and other waterways. The British colonies along the Atlantic coast were hemmed in by the Appalachian Mountains—the first physical barrier to the West.

Unit 3 Creating a Nation

During the 1700s British colonists began to think of themselves as Americans. They fought to end the Crown's rule in the American colonies. The American soldiers were outnumbered and poorly equipped. Their knowledge of the environment, however, enabled them to use guerrilla tactics to defeat the stronger British troops.

Unit 4 The New Republic

During the early 1800s, New England launched the nation's Industrial Revolution. Factories began using steam-powered machines to make goods. Industry spread as large supplies of coal in Pennsylvania and Ohio made steam power cheap and manufacturing very profitable. Rivers and canals transported goods.

Unit 5 The Growing Nation

Through wars, treaties, and purchases, the United States gained control of the lands west of the Mississippi River. By the mid-1800s, the

CURRICULUM CONNECTION

Economics Early European settlers in North America were stunned by the abundance of trees. Vast tracts of European forest had been cleared to provide raw materials for various commercial activities. The shipbuilding industry was the most voracious consumer of forestland, for it took more than 2,500 trees to construct just one ocean-going ship. By the 1600s, wood was in short supply in most European countries. No such shortage existed in North America. In fact, the harvesting of lumber became an important business for early settlers.

discovery of gold and silver drew thousands of settlers to Western territories. Railroads enabled people to overcome geographic barriers.

Unit 6 Civil War and Reconstruction

In the mid-1800s, the demand for cotton by the textile industry in the North made cotton production highly profitable in the agriculturally rich South. Enslaved Africans provided labor for large-scale farming. In 1861 regional differences and a dispute over slavery sparked the Civil War between the North and the South.

Unit 7 Reshaping the Nation

After the Civil War, transcontinental railroads transported goods from the East to the West and carried food products and beef cattle from the West to the East. Factories used electricity to make goods. The workers who advanced this industrial boom were immigrants and people who moved from farms to the cities.

Unit 8 Reform, Expansion, and War

As industry grew in the United States, foreign trade became more important. During and after World War I and World War II, the vast resources of the United States aided allies around the world. Along with weapons and manufactured goods, American culture also spread overseas and changed the way of life in many places.

Unit 9 Turbulent Decades

Environmental disasters during the first part of the 1900s affected the national economy. During the 1930s winds blew away so much of the soil in the Great Plains that the area became known as the Dust Bowl.

Unit 10 Turning Points

After World War II, high-technology industries helped the United States maintain its leadership role in world manufacturing. As

Across the Continent ***by Currier and Ives, 1868***

computers and robots entered factories, many American workers learned new skills or started new careers.

Unit 11 Modern America

Always a mobile people, Americans during the 1900s continued to move from place to place. As the map on page 8 shows, industrial growth and a pleasant climate drew people to the South and Southwest in the 1980s and 1990s.

In recent years, the economies of the United States and other countries have become more **interdependent,** or reliant on each other. The movement of ideas and products has transformed the world into a global village.

Portfolio Activity **History Journal** As you read *The American Journey,* pay special attention to the ways in which geography has influenced the history of the United States. Also note how geography has shaped the development of your state and local community. Keep a log in your journal describing your findings.

GEOGRAPHY HANDBOOK

NATIONAL GEOGRAPHIC SOCIETY

VIDEODISC
GTV: The American People: Fabric of a Nation

Side 1, Chapter 1
Title: *Living in the Promiseland*
Subject: America's people, promises, problems
Ask: **What is significant about the culture of the United States?** *(The people of the United States are very diverse. They come from a variety of cultural backgrounds but are all Americans.)*

Linking PAST & PRESENT

Environmental Challenges Efforts to preserve a healthy environment date back hundreds of years. In A.D. 1253 the English Parliament placed bans on burning coal. The increasing use of fossil fuels, expanding populations, and the use of chemicals, however, present new challenges.

Portfolio Activity Have students make two columns in their **History Journal** notebook. For each chapter, students should list in the first column any specific physical geography mentioned—including landforms, waterways, climates, and so on. In the second column, students should write one or more historical events that were affected by the specific geography listed in the first column.

MORE ABOUT . . .

The Appalachian Region A plateau called the Piedmont lies at the eastern edge of the Appalachians. The eastern edge of the Piedmont rises sharply from the low-lying Atlantic Coastal Plain. Where fast-moving rivers drop from the plateau to the plains, there are many rapids and waterfalls. The line formed where this drop takes place is called the fall line. Early European settlers were unable to travel beyond the fall line by boat. The waterfalls and rapids, however, later provided water power for industries. Thus, many cities—Macon, Georgia; Columbia, South Carolina; Raleigh, North Carolina; and Richmond, Virginia, for example—developed along the fall line.

GEOGRAPHY HANDBOOK

L1, ELL Constructing a Model Have students use clay to mold a model landscape with all or many of the features mentioned on pages 10 and 11. Suggest that students paint the model after the clay dries to make it look more realistic.

you don't say...

The Geographer's Language

The terms geographers use to describe the earth come from many different languages. To illustrate this, have students locate the term *mesa* on page 11. Point out that geographers use this Spanish word, which means "table," to describe flat-topped, steep-sided hills. Other foreign terms American geographers use include *tsunami*, a Japanese word meaning "overflowing wave," and *fjord*, a Norwegian word meaning "long, narrow bay."

Where?When?Who?What?

The Grand Canyon extends for some 277 miles through northwest Arizona. Parts of the canyon—which was carved by the Colorado River—are 1 mile deep and 18 miles wide.

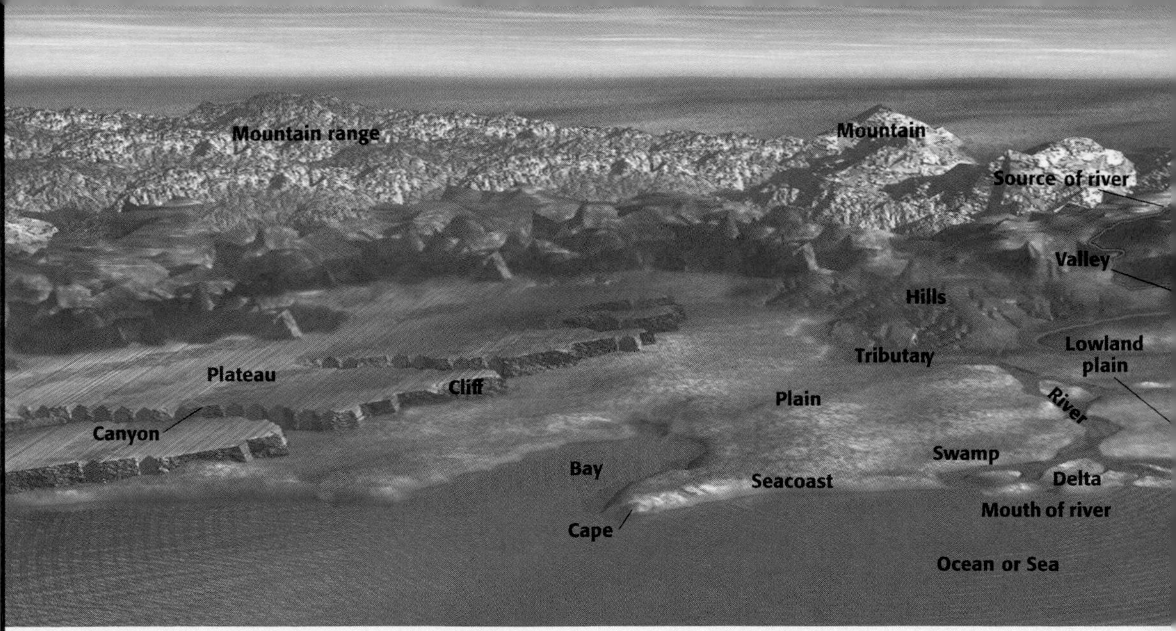

Geographic Dictionary

As you read about America's geography and history, you will encounter most of the terms listed below. Many of the terms are pictured in the diagram above.

absolute location exact location of a place on the earth described by global coordinates

basin area of land drained by a given river and its branches; area of land surrounded by lands of higher elevations

bay part of a large body of water that extends into a shoreline, generally smaller than a gulf

canyon deep and narrow valley with steep walls

cape point of land that extends into a river, lake, or ocean

channel wide strait or waterway between two land-masses that lie close to each other; deep part of a river or other waterway

cliff steep, high wall of rock, earth, or ice

continent one of the seven large landmasses on the earth

cultural feature characteristic that humans have created in a place, such as language, religion, housing, and settlement pattern

delta flat, low-lying land built up from soil carried downstream by a river and deposited at its mouth

divide stretch of high land that separates river systems

downstream direction in which a river or stream flows from its source to its mouth

elevation height of land above sea level

Equator imaginary line that runs around the earth halfway between the North and South Poles; used as the starting point to measure degrees of north and south latitude

glacier large, thick body of slowly moving ice

gulf part of a large body of water that extends into a shoreline, generally larger and more deeply indented than a bay

harbor a sheltered place along a shoreline where ships can anchor safely

highland elevated land area such as a hill, mountain, or plateau

hill elevated land with sloping sides and rounded summit; generally smaller than a mountain

island land area, smaller than a continent, completely surrounded by water

isthmus narrow stretch of land connecting two larger land areas

lake a sizable inland body of water

latitude distance north or south of the Equator, measured in degrees

longitude distance east or west of the Prime Meridian, measured in degrees

lowland land, usually level, at a low elevation

COOPERATIVE LEARNING ACTIVITY

Map Quiz Organize the class into two teams. Provide one team with a map of your county and the other team with a map of your state. Assign each team the following task: Locate every major body of water in your assigned area. Record your findings, including: (1) the name of each major body of water; (2) its relative and/or absolute location; and (3) the type of feature it is—lake, river, bay, and so on. When each team has completed its task, have them create a map quiz based on their work. The teams should then trade maps and challenge each other with their quizzes.

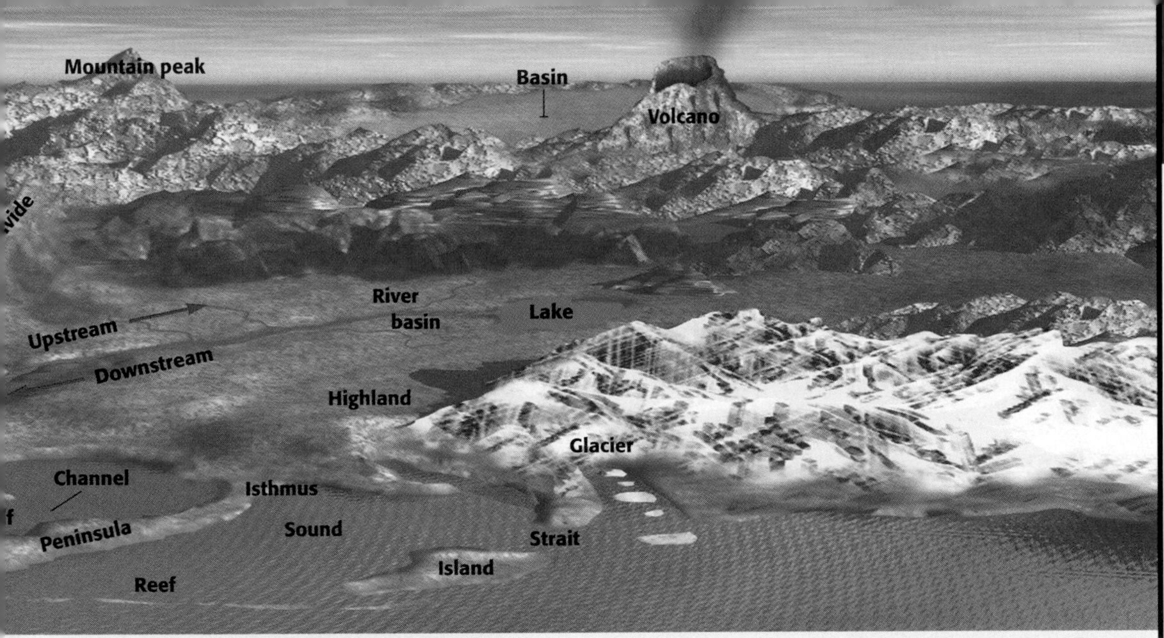

map drawing of the earth shown on a flat surface
meridian one of many lines on the global grid running from the North Pole to the South Pole; used to measure degrees of longitude
mesa broad, flat-topped landform with steep sides; smaller than a plateau
mountain land with steep sides that rises sharply (1,000 feet or more) from surrounding land; generally larger and more rugged than a hill
mountain peak pointed top of a mountain
mountain range a series of connected mountains
mouth (of a river) place where a stream or river flows into a larger body of water
ocean one of the four major bodies of salt water that surround the continents
ocean current stream of either cold or warm water that moves in a definite direction through an ocean
parallel one of many lines on the global grid that circle the earth north or south of the Equator; used to measure degrees of latitude
peninsula body of land jutting into a lake or ocean, surrounded on three sides by water
physical feature characteristic of a place occurring naturally, such as a landform, body of water, climate pattern, or resource
plain area of level land, usually a low elevation and often covered with grasses
plateau area of flat or rolling land at a high elevation, about 300–3,000 feet high
Prime Meridian line of the global grid running from the North Pole to the South Pole at Greenwich, England; starting point for measuring degrees of east and west longitude
relief changes in elevation over a given area of land
river large natural stream of water that runs through the land
sea large body of water completely or partly surrounded by land
seacoast land lying next to a sea or ocean
sea level position on land level with surface of nearby ocean or sea
sound body of water between a coastline and one or more islands off the coast
source (of a river) place where a river or stream begins, often in highlands
strait narrow stretch of water joining two larger bodies of water
tributary small river or stream that flows into a large river or stream; a branch of the river
upstream direction opposite the flow of a river; toward the source of a river or stream
valley area of low land between hills or mountains
volcano mountain created as liquid rock or ash erupt from inside the earth

3 ASSESS

Provide each student with a large sheet of white paper and map pencils. Have students, draw, freehand from memory, a map of the United States with labels for the following: Appalachian Mountains, Great Lakes, Mississippi River, Atlantic Ocean, Pacific Ocean, Rocky Mountains, Sierra Nevada, Gulf of Mexico, Great Plains.

4 CLOSE

Have students create a pictorial essay on the physical region in which they live. **Ask:** **How do you view the future of your local area and the United States?**

CRITICAL THINKING ACTIVITY

Synthesizing Information Have students use atlases and other resources to plan a cross-country trip through the United States. Direct them to choose a definite starting point and destination and plot the route between the two points. Have them calculate the approximate distance of the journey, how long the journey might take, and to list points of interest along the way. Allow time for students to share their itineraries. **L2**

Unit 1 Resource Guide

These Glencoe resources may be used to teach, reteach, or enrich the concepts presented in this unit of study.

Teaching Transparencies

Map Transparency 1 with Overlays A, B, C, D

Cause-and-Effect Transparency 1

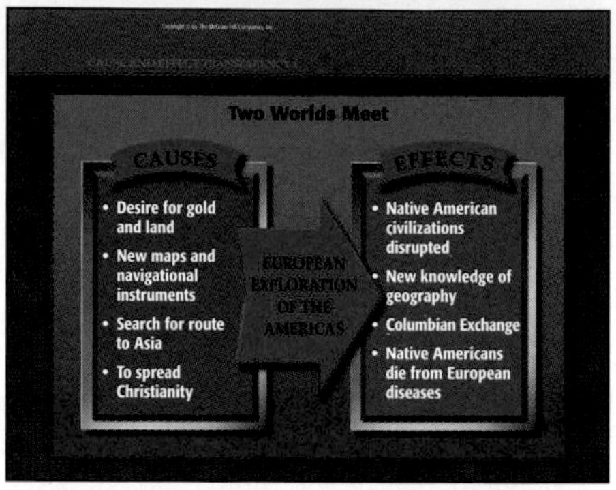

BIBLIOGRAPHY

Readings for the Student

Baquedano, Elizabeth. ***Aztec, Inca & Maya.*** New York: Alfred A. Knopf, 1993. Illustrates cultural aspects of the Aztec, Maya, and Inca.

Scheller, William. ***The World's Greatest Explorers.*** Minneapolis: Oliver Press, 1992. Twelve explorers journey to unknown places.

Reading for the Teacher

Smith-Baranzini, Marlene and Howard Egger-Bovet. ***Book of the American Indian.*** Boston: Little, Brown and Company, 1994. Data and activities on Native North American groups.

Multimedia Resources

Optical Disc. ***Explorers of the New World.*** Nanuet: Future Vision Multimedia, Inc., 1995. Sixty explorers from 1450 to 1600.

Videocassette. ***Lost Kingdoms of the Maya: Unlock the Secrets of an Ancient Civilization.*** Produced by National Geographic Society. Burbank: Tristar Home Video, 1993. One videocassette, 60 minutes. Analysis of artifacts, cities, and hieroglyphics of the Maya.

interNET CONNECTIONS

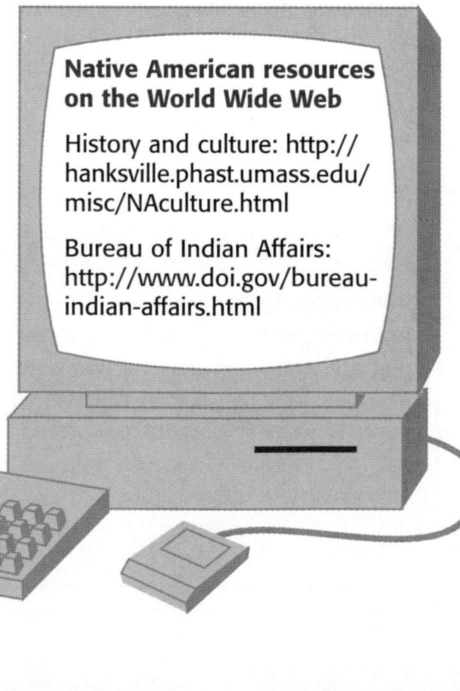

★ ★ ★ ★ ★ ★ ★ ★ ★ ★ ★ ★ ★ Resource Guide Unit 1

Interdisciplinary Activities

American Literature Reading 1

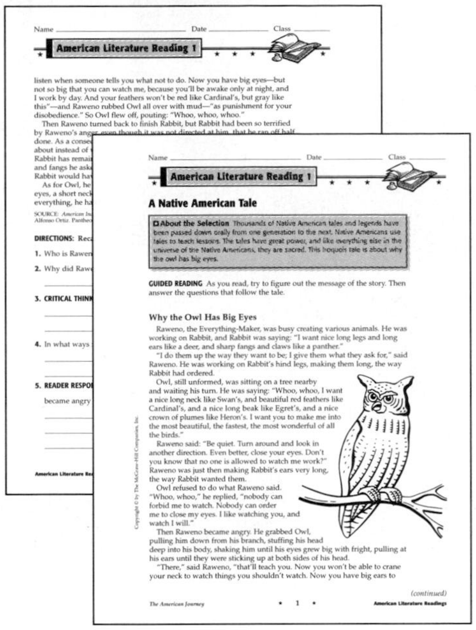

Name ______ Date ______ Class ______

American Literature Reading 1

A Native American Tale

Interdisciplinary Connection 1

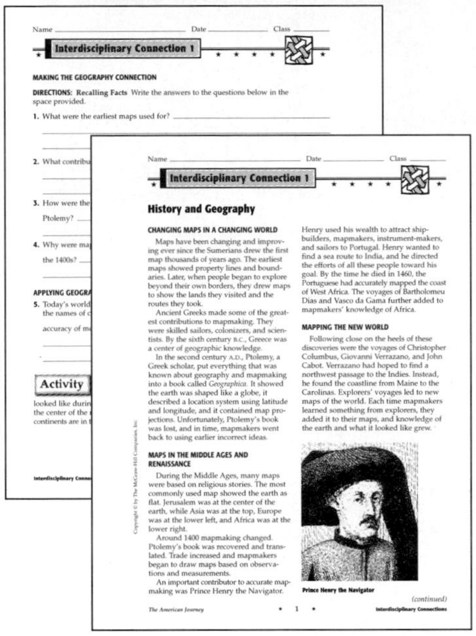

Name ______ Date ______ Class ______

Interdisciplinary Connection 1

History and Geography

Enrichment Activities

Cooperative Learning Activity 1

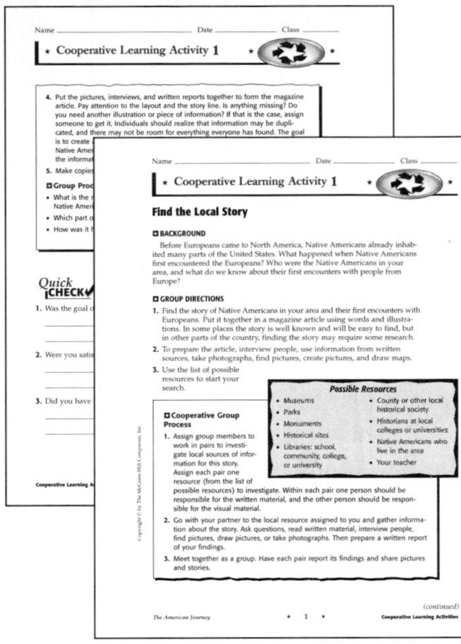

Name ______ Date ______ Class ______

Cooperative Learning Activity 1

Find the Local Story

Hands-On Activities

Hands-On History Lab Activity 1

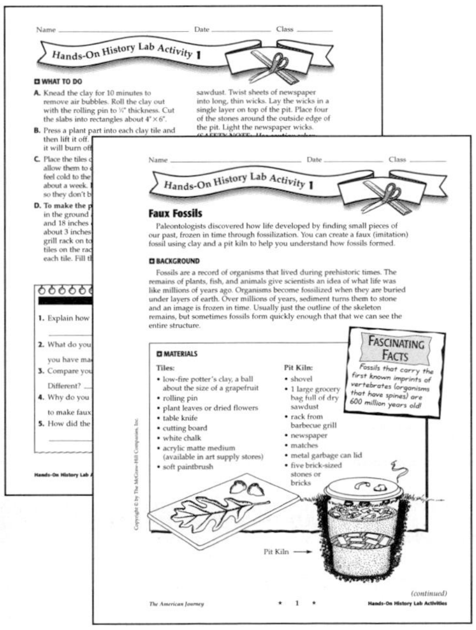

Name ______ Date ______ Class ______

Hands-On History Lab Activity 1

Faux Fossils

History Simulation 1

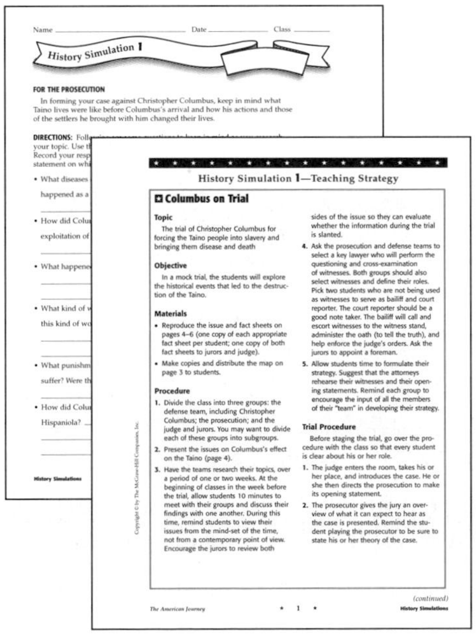

Name ______ Date ______ Class ______

History Simulation 1—Teaching Strategy

Columbus on Trial

Assessment

Unit 1 Test

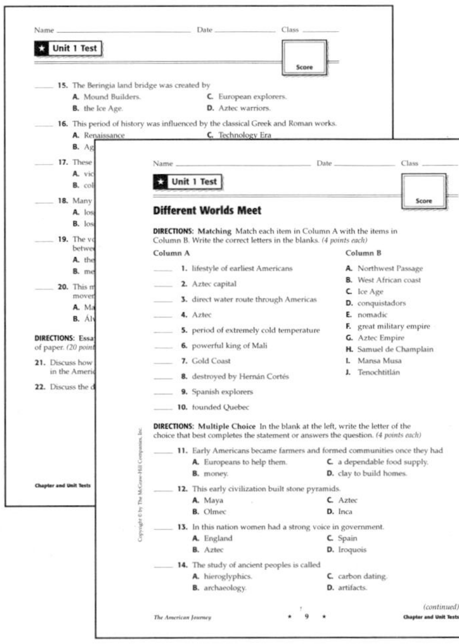

Name ______ Date ______ Class ______

Unit 1 Test

Different Worlds Meet

Introducing
UNIT 1

0:00 OUT OF TIME?

If your teaching time is limited, you may use the *Chapter Summaries* blackline master found in the TCR with the *Chapter Digests Audiocassette Activities and Tests* to condense individual chapters into a one-day lesson.

Introducing the Unit

Activity Invite students to determine the unit's content by studying the graphics on the unit opener. Ask them to speculate about the specifics of the unit. This unit surveys the contributions made by the native peoples living in the Americas before explorers reached the continent. It also describes contributions made by the first explorers who came to the Americas.

Unit Objectives

Upon completing this unit, students will be able to:

1. Explain how people arrived in the Americas.
2. Describe the cultural contributions of the Native Americans.
3. Classify the explorers and their areas of exploration.
4. Evaluate the impact of European exploration on Native American culture.

Hands-On HISTORY

Hands-On History Lab Activity 1, "Faux Fossils," is a high-interest **constructivist approach** activity directly related to the main topic of the unit.

Unit 1

Different Worlds Meet

Beginnings to 1625

"The people of this island [have] such a generosity that they would give away their own hearts."

—Christopher Columbus, 1493

MAPPING *America*

Portfolio Activity Draw a freehand map of North America, Central America, and South America. As you read Unit 1, draw arrows on your map that show how the first Americans traveled throughout the Americas and where they ultimately settled. Also include the European explorers' routes on your map.

Viking carving

Navigator's binoculars and compass

The Americas

c. 28,000 B.C. Asian hunters enter North America

7000 B.C. Farming develops in Mexico

Pre-History

c. 10,000 B.C. Last Ice Age ends

The World

TEAM TEACHING STRATEGIES

Art Pacific Northwest Native Americans made totem poles from red cedar trees. They carved intricate images of real and legendary creatures into these totem poles. Totems, erected in front of houses, symbolized family lineage, power, and prestige. Carvings appeared in order of importance from top to bottom and were painted with bright colors. With the Art teacher, organize the class into groups to create a totem. Hand out the following to each student: empty cylinder, colored paper, tape, scissors, glue, and markers. Instruct each student to draw a design on the colored paper to be glued onto the cylinder. As a group, students should stack and tape each cylinder together in order of importance to create a totem. Display totems and discuss the significance of each.

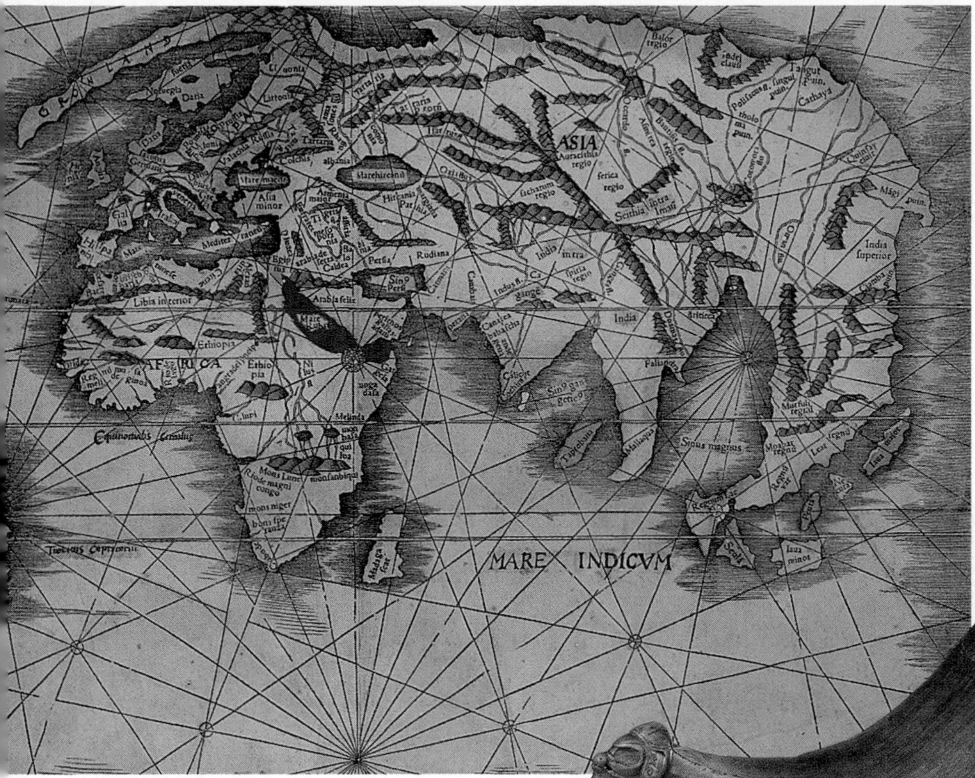

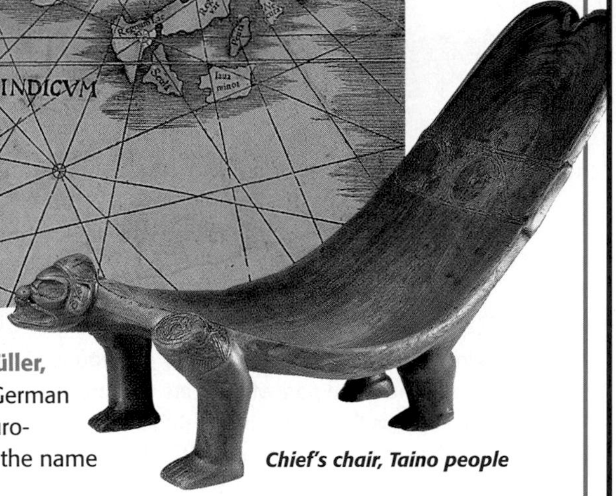

HISTORY AND ART ***World Map* by Martin Waldseemüller, 1507** This hand-drawn map by a German mapmaker gave a view of the world as known by Europeans in the early 1500s. It was the first map to use the name *America* for the lands of the Western Hemisphere.

Chief's chair, Taino people

A.D. 1085 Anasazi build pueblos in North America

A.D. 1295 Italian traveler Marco Polo returns from China

A.D. 1300 Aztec build Tenochtitlán in Mexico

A.D. 1312 Ruler Mansa Musa begins West African kingdom of Mali

A.D. 1400s Inca Empire reaches its height in South America

A.D. 1492 Columbus lands in the Americas

A.D. 1517 Luther starts Protestant Reformation

A.D. 1609 Henry Hudson sails up the Hudson River

1050 — 1250 — 1450 — 1650

TEAM TEACHING STRATEGIES

Science Before printing became possible in the mid-1400s, maps were rare because cartographers drew each map by hand. Early maps provided geographic information and were also works of art. The oldest surviving maps were carved on clay slabs about 500 B.C. by Babylonians. Early maps were based on the best-known information and technology available at that time. Work with the Science teacher to have students gain an appreciation for the amount of work involved in hand-drawn maps. Have the Science teacher explain how to draw and utilize topographic maps. After students have drawn their own topographic maps, ask the Science teacher to explain how modern technology—satellites, remote sensors, radar, computers—do the work of mapmakers today.

NATIONAL GEOGRAPHIC SOCIETY

VIDEODISC
GTV: A Geographic Perspective on American History

Side 1, Chapter 2
Title: *Linking Life and Land*
Subject: The first Americans and the effects of geography on their lives (14,000 years ago to the 1500s)
Ask: How did hunters from Asia reach America? *(They crossed a land bridge.)*

HISTORY AND ART People have relied on maps throughout history. The oldest-known map is in the form of a stone tablet, dating to around 2500 B.C.

Linking PAST & PRESENT

Activity The explorers covered in this unit traveled to places on the earth that were previously unknown to Europeans. Brainstorm with students other places that have yet to be explored on the earth, such as the depths of the ocean floor. Have pairs of students role-play an explorer and a native person from the newly discovered territory.

Block Schedule

Team Teaching This selection from *Morning Girl* may be implemented in a team-teaching context, in conjunction with English/Language Arts.

Reinforcing Vocabulary

Review the **Reader's Dictionary** terms with students to be sure they understand any unfamiliar terms.

Historical Connection

In 1492 Columbus and his crew landed on an island in what is now called the Bahamas. He named it *San Salvador,* which is Spanish for "Holy Savior." He called the native Taino peoples who lived there *Indians* because he believed he had landed in the East Indies.

Background Information

Setting The excerpt takes place in the Bahamas during the landing of Columbus.

Characters The main character in this excerpt is Morning Girl, a young Native American woman.

Plot Morning Girl describes the initial landing of Columbus from her point of view.

America's Literature

Morning Girl

by Michael Dorris

Michael Dorris, a Modoc Native American, has had a distinguished career as an educator, a social activist, and an award-winning author. Morning Girl, *his first book for young adults, portrays the lives of the Taino people of the Bahamas.*

Read to Discover

Morning Girl is the fictional story of a young Native American woman who meets Columbus and his crew as they arrive in the Bahamas in 1492. While reading this passage, think about the ways that Morning Girl's life might change as a result of Columbus's visit.

Reader's Dictionary

canoe: a light, narrow boat
surf: waves
Morning Girl: a young Taino woman
drifting: floating smoothly, without effort

Dawn made a glare on the ocean, so I splashed through the shallow surf and dived without looking. I felt the hair lift from around my head, felt a school of tiny fish glide against my leg as I swam underwater. Then, far in the distance, I heard an unfamiliar and frightening sound. It was like the panting of some giant animal, a steady, slow rhythm, dangerous and hungry. And it was coming closer.

I forgot I was still beneath the surface until I needed air. But when I broke into the sunlight, the water sparkling all around me, the noise turned out to be nothing! Only a canoe! The breathing was the dip of many paddles! It was only *people* coming to visit, and since I could see they hadn't painted themselves to appear fierce, they must be friendly or lost.

I swam closer to get a better look and had to stop myself from laughing. The strangers had wrapped every part of their bodies with colorful leaves and cotton. Some had decorated their faces with fur and wore shiny rocks on their heads. Compared to us, they were very round. Their canoe was short and square, and, in spite of all their dipping and pulling, it moved so slowly. What a backward, distant island they must have come from. But really, to laugh at guests, no matter how odd, would be impolite, especially since I was the first to meet them. If I was foolish, they would think they had arrived at a foolish place. . . .

I kicked toward the canoe and called out the simplest thing.

"Hello!"

One of the people heard me, and he was so startled that he stood up, made his eyes small, as fearful as I had been a moment earlier. . . .

Additional Literary Works About the Period

You may want to refer students to the following:

Jacobs, Francine. ***The Tainos: The People Who Welcomed Columbus.*** New York: The Putnam & Grosset Group, 1992. History, culture, and fate.

Riley, Patricia, ed. ***Growing Up Native American: An Anthology.*** New York: William Morrow & Company, Inc., 1993. About fiction writers.

Wallis, Velma. ***Two Old Women: An Alaskan Legend of Betrayal, Courage and Survival.*** Fairbanks: Epicenter Press, 1993. Based on a legend told from mothers to daughters.

Christopher Columbus and the Taino

The man stared at me as though he'd never seen a girl before, then shouted something to his relatives. They all stopped paddling and looked in my direction.

"Hello," I tried again. "Welcome to home. My name is Morning Girl. My mother is She Wins the Race. My father is Speaks to Birds. My brother is Star Boy. We will feed you and introduce you to everyone."

All the fat people in the canoe began pointing at me and talking at once. In their excitement they almost turned themselves over, and I allowed my body to sink beneath the waves for a moment in order to hide my smile. . . .

When I came up they were still watching, the way babies do: wide eyed and with their mouths uncovered. They had much to learn about how to behave.

"Bring your canoe to the beach," I shouted, saying each word slowly so that they might understand and calm themselves. "I will go to the village and bring back Mother and Father. . . ."

. . . The strangers were drifting in the surf, arguing among themselves, not even paying attention to me any longer. They seemed very worried, very confused, very unsure what to do next. It was clear that they hadn't traveled much before.

Responding to Literature

1. How does Morning Girl treat the unexpected visitors?
2. Why does Morning Girl think the visitors have poor manners?

Activity

Writing a Play Imagine that explorers from another planet landed in your backyard. How would you respond? Write the dialogue you think would occur between you and the aliens. Then ask a classmate to read the dialogue with you in the form of a play.

Answers to Responding to Literature

1. She treats them with respect and is very kind.
2. The visitors stare wide-eyed and with their mouths open. They also point and do not reply to her greeting.

Activity Plays should reflect points raised in the excerpt; for example, communication or language, methods of welcome, polite manners, and so on.

History *and the* Humanities

- American Music Cultural Traditions, Lesson 1: "Rain Dance"
- U.S. History & Art, Transparency 1, *Quilled Buckskin Robe*

Portfolio Activity Ask students to write a short essay describing how their own heritage affected their lives as they were growing up.

At the Movies

The movies *Columbus* and *1492* debuted in 1992 to commemorate the 500th anniversary of Columbus's voyage. They show the contrast of cultures between Native Americans and Europeans at that time. These movies are available on videotape.

What? Where? When? Who?

Food Discoveries Columbus and his crew discovered foods in the Western Hemisphere that were unknown to Europeans: maize (corn), sweet potatoes, peppers, allspice, plantain, pineapples, and turtle meat. Although Europeans did not learn about sweet potatoes until after 1492, the Maori had grown it for almost two centuries on a Pacific island now known as New Zealand.

Chapter 1 Planning Guide

A complete, 1-page lesson plan is provided for each section in the *Reproducible Lesson Plans* booklet.

Section Resources

Daily Objectives	Reproducible Resources	Multimedia Resources
Section 1 Early Peoples Discuss the theories of how people came to the Americas and settled in certain areas.	Reproducible Lesson Plan 1–1 Guided Reading Activity 1–1* Section Quiz 1–1* Reteaching Activity 1–1 Enrichment Activity 1–1	Section Focus Transparency 1–1 Vocabulary PuzzleMaker Chapter Challenger Interactive Review Software Testmaker
Section 2 Cities and Empires Explain how native civilizations in the Americas built powerful empires by making the best use of the environment.	Reproducible Lesson Plan 1–2 Guided Reading Activity 1–2* Section Quiz 1–2* Reteaching Activity 1–2 Enrichment Activity 1–2	Section Focus Transparency 1–2 Vocabulary PuzzleMaker Chapter Challenger Interactive Review Software Testmaker NGS PictureShow: Native Americans, Part 2 Picture Atlas of the World
Section 3 North American Peoples Examine how Native North American groups adapted to their environment.	Reproducible Lesson Plan 1–3 Guided Reading Activity 1–3* Section Quiz 1–3* Reteaching Activity 1–3 Enrichment Activity 1–3	Section Focus Transparency 1–3 U.S. History & Art, Transparency 1, *Quilled Buckskin Robe* Vocabulary PuzzleMaker Chapter Challenger Interactive Review Software Testmaker ABCNews InterActive™ Historic America Electronic Field Trips GTV: A Geographic Perspective on American History GTV: The American People: Fabric of a Nation NGS PictureShow: Native Americans, Part 1 American Music Cultural Traditions, Lesson 1: "Rain Dance"

** Also available in Spanish*

Poster — Transparency — CD-ROM — Software
Blackline Master — Videodisc — Audiocassette — Music Program

0:00 **OUT OF TIME?**
Assign the Chapter 1 Digest and the corresponding Chapter Digests Audiocassettes with activities and tests.

Chapter 1 Planning Guide

Activity

From the Classroom of...

Lorraine O'Neil
MacKinnon Middle School, Wharton, NJ

Create a Disappearing Land Bridge

Organize students into groups of four or five. Using pie tins and modeling clay, have groups make a model of the Beringia land bridge inside the tins. Ask them to leave plenty of room for bodies of water, and allow them to use the map "Prehistoric Migrations Through the Americas" on p. 19 in their textbooks as a guide. After the model land bridges are complete, have students heap finely crushed ice around their bridges. (Make sure they use enough ice so that when it melts, the water covers the bridge.) Have students sprinkle a little cold water on top to help the ice form a sheet. If possible, place the models in a freezer overnight to form the ice sheets.

Remove the models from the freezer and allow them to return to room temperature. As students watch their land bridges submerge, explain that during Ice Ages, ocean levels were low because a large amount of water was frozen in the form of glaciers. As the glaciers melted, water levels rose again and covered the land bridge.

Block Schedule

Block scheduling differs from traditional class scheduling in the amount of time allotted to each period. The extended time frame provided by block scheduling affords you the opportunity to implement a greater number of research-oriented and activity-intense projects to motivate and involve your students. Activities that are particularly suited to use within the block scheduling framework are identified throughout this chapter by the following designation:

NATIONAL GEOGRAPHIC SOCIETY Teacher's Corner

INDEX TO NATIONAL GEOGRAPHIC MAGAZINE

The following articles may be used for research relating to this chapter:

- "The Old Ones of the Southwest," by David Roberts, April 1996.
- "The Timeless Vision of Teotihuacan," by George E. Stuart, December 1995.
- "Maya Masterpiece Revealed at Bonampak," by Mark Miller, February 1995.
- "Powwow," by Michael Parfit, June 1994.
- "Sacred Peaks of the Andes," by Johan Reinhard, March 1992.

NATIONAL GEOGRAPHIC SOCIETY PRODUCTS AVAILABLE FROM GLENCOE

To order the following products for use with this chapter, contact your local Glencoe sales representative, or call Glencoe at 1-800-334-7344:

- *STV: Maya* (Videodisc)
- *GTV: A Geographic Perspective on American History* (Videodisc)
- *GTV: The American People: Fabric of a Nation* (Videodisc)
- *PictureShow: Native Americans, 1 and 2* (CD-ROM, Transparencies)
- *Native Americans* (Poster Set)

ADDITIONAL NATIONAL GEOGRAPHIC SOCIETY PRODUCTS

To order the following products for use with this chapter, call National Geographic Society at 1-800-368-2728:

- *PictureShow: Ancient Civilizations: Middle and South America* (CD-ROM, Transparencies)
- *Lost Kingdoms of the Maya* (Video, Book)
- *Native American Heritage: A Visitor's Guide* (Map)
- *Indians of North America* (Map)
- *The World of the American Indian* (Book)
- *American Indians: A Brief History* (Video)
- *Historical Atlas of the United States* (Atlas)

KEY TO ABILITY LEVELS

Teaching strategies have been coded for varying learning styles and abilities.

L1 **BASIC** activities for all students
L2 **AVERAGE** activities for average to above-average students
L3 **CHALLENGING** activities for above-average students
ELL **ENGLISH LANGUAGE LEARNER** activities

Chapter 1 Resource Guide

Home Involvement

Home Involvement Activity 1

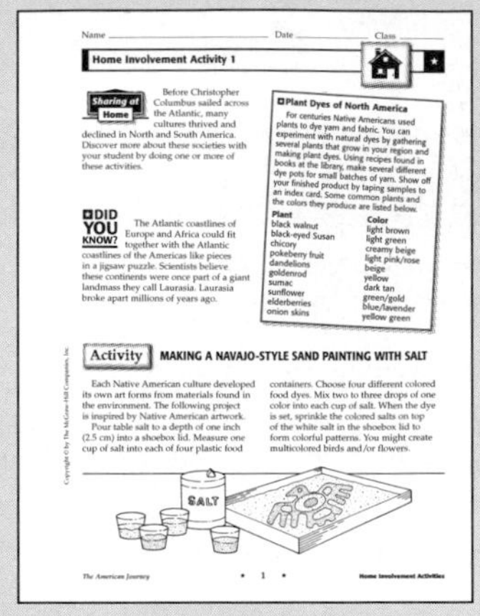
Home Involvement Activity 1

Review Activities

Chapter Summary 1

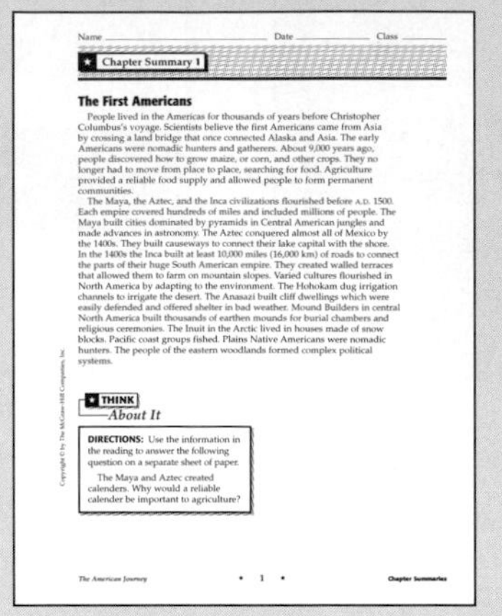
Chapter Summary 1

The First Americans

Workbook Activity 1

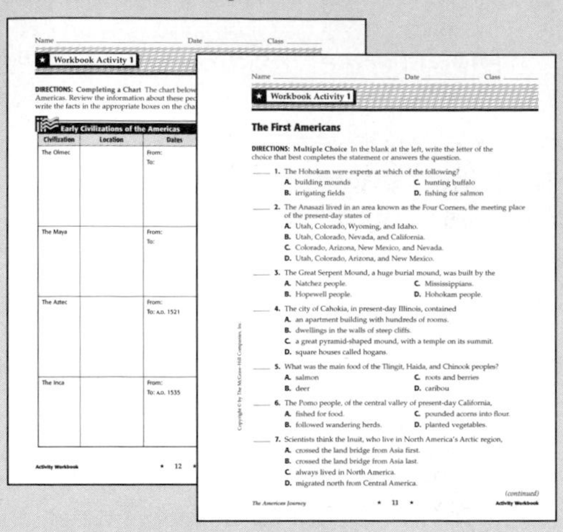
Workbook Activity 1

The First Americans

Reinforcement Activities

Time Line Activity 1

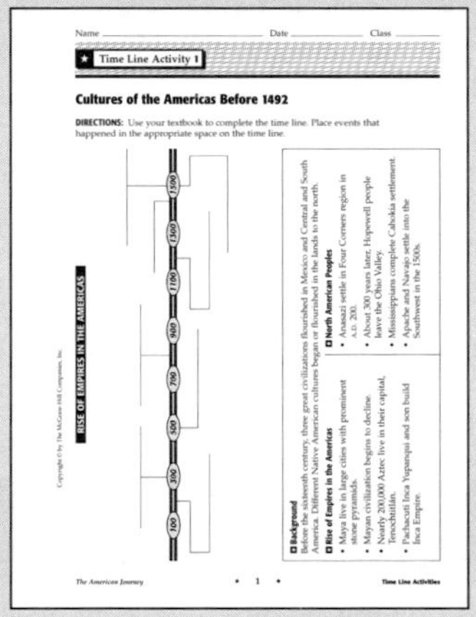
Time Line Activity 1

Cultures of the Americas Before 1492

Vocabulary Activity 1

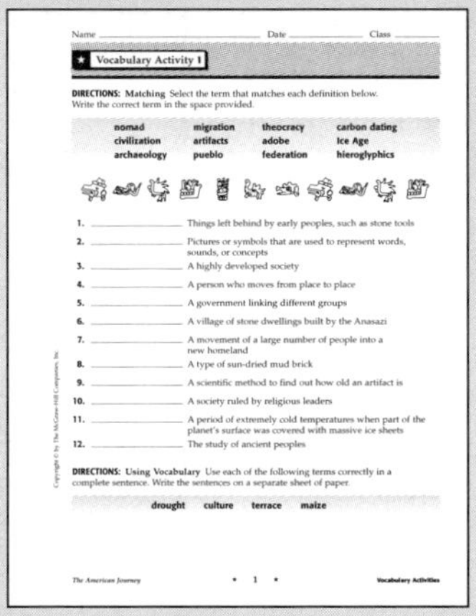
Vocabulary Activity 1

Chapter Skills Activity 1

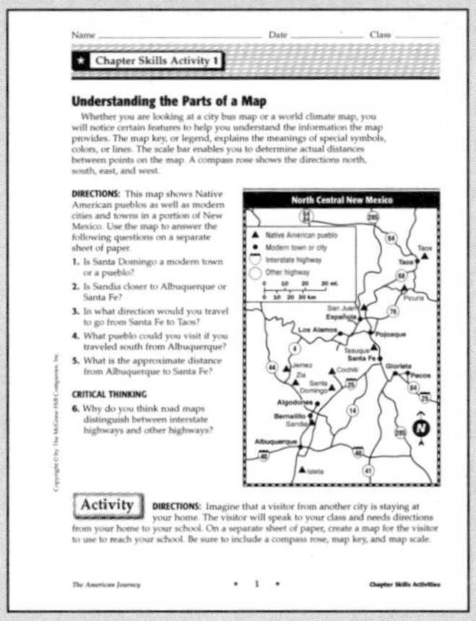
Chapter Skills Activity 1

Understanding the Parts of a Map

Enrichment Activities

Linking Past and Present Activity 1

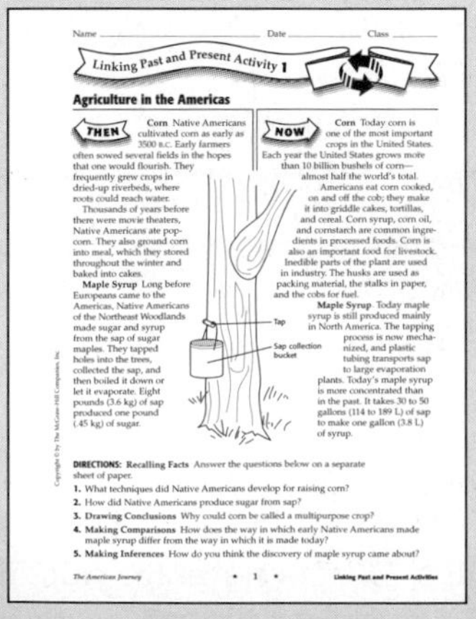
Linking Past and Present Activity 1

Agriculture in the Americas

Primary Source Reading 1

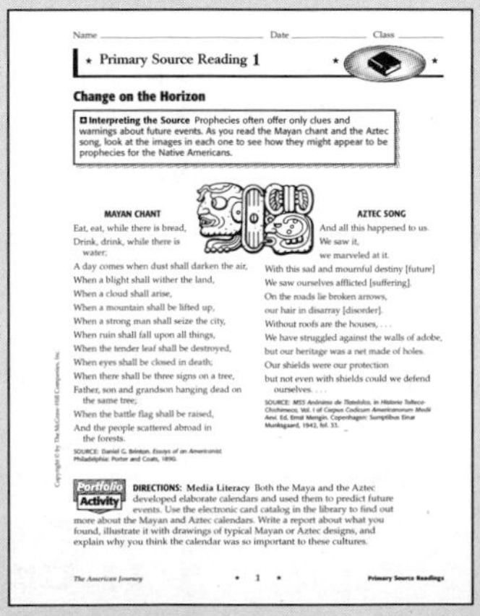
Primary Source Reading 1

Change on the Horizon

Geography Activities

Mapping History Activity 1

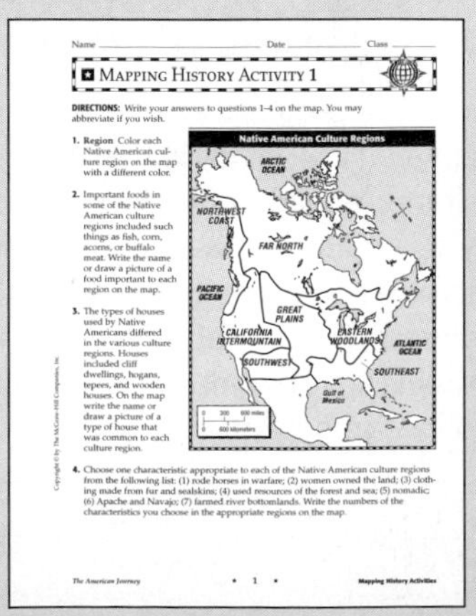
Mapping History Activity 1

Chapter 1 Resource Guide

Assessment

Chapter 1 Test, Form A

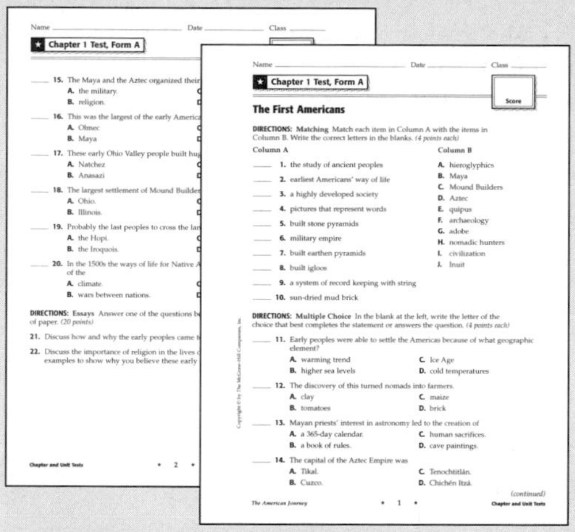
Chapter 1 Test, Form A

The First Americans

Column A

Column B

Chapter 1 Test, Form B

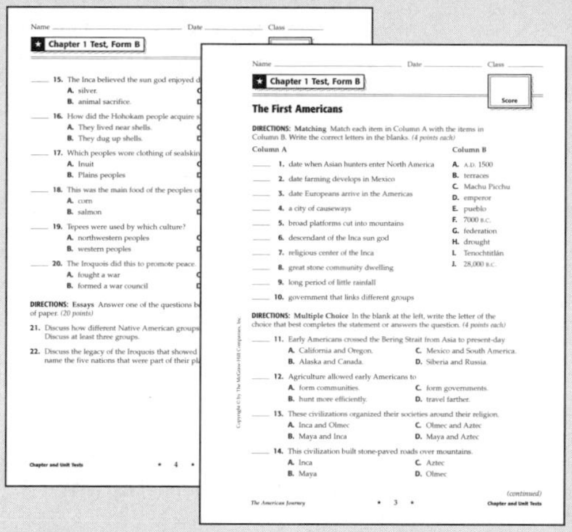
Chapter 1 Test, Form B

The First Americans

Column A

Column B

Performance Assessment Activity 1

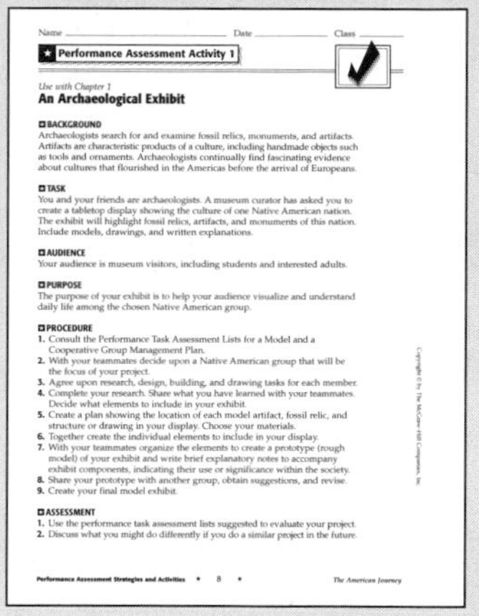
Performance Assessment Activity 1

An Archaeological Exhibit

BACKGROUND

TASK

AUDIENCE

PURPOSE

PROCEDURE

ASSESSMENT

Spanish Resources

The following Spanish language materials are available in the Spanish Resources binder:

- **Spanish Chapter Summary 1**
- **Spanish Vocabulary Activity 1**
- **Spanish Guided Reading Activities, Chapter 1**
- **Spanish Section Quizzes, Chapter 1**
- **Spanish Home Involvement Activity 1**
- **Spanish Chapter 1 Digests Audiocassette Activity and Test**

Activity Manipulatives

Help students learn more about America's cultural history with:

- **American Crafts Hands-On Activities**
- **American Games Hands-On Activities**
- **American History Flash Cards**

Additional Resources From Glencoe

- **U.S. History & Art,** Transparency 1, *Quilled Buckskin Robe*
- **American Music Cultural Traditions,** Lesson 1: *"Rain Dance"*
- **Outline Map Resource Book**
- **U.S. Desk Map**
- **The American History Videodisc and CD-ROM,** *Prehistory to 1680*

A&E HOME VIDEO. Biography™ THE HISTORY CHANNEL.

The following videotape programs are available from Glencoe as supplements to Chapter 1:

- **The Secret Mounds of Prehistoric America** (ISBN 1-56501-681-5)
- **Secrets of the Pueblos** (ISBN 1-56501-811-7)
- **Peru Warriors and Treasure** (ISBN 1-56501-796-X)

To order, call Glencoe at 1-800-334-7344. To find classroom resources to accompany many of these videos, check the following home pages:
A&E Television: http://www.aetv.com
The History Channel: http://www.historychannel.com

Chapter Themes

Chapter Themes are listed by section on this chapter opening page of the Student Edition. A corresponding theme-based activity is available under "FOCUS," and a theme-based question is asked in the Section and Chapter Reviews.

Performance Assessment

Refer to Activity 1 in the *Performance Assessment Strategies and Activities* booklet.

GLENCOE TECHNOLOGY

VIDEODISC
MindJogger Videoquiz

Use MindJogger to preview the Chapter 1 content.

Chapter 1
Disc 1, Side A

Also available in VHS.

HISTORY AND ART Maya wall paintings often included pictographs and phonetic signs called "glyphs" to record historical information. These paintings recorded genealogical information about the hereditary noble class.

Chapter 1

Prehistory to 1492

The First Americans

Why It's Important

Many groups of Native Americans live in the Americas today. Their history is the story of many different peoples, all of whom helped shape the American society we live in today. They are part of the modern world, yet many of them also preserve the ways of life, customs, and traditions developed by their ancestors centuries ago.

Chapter Themes

- *Section 1,* Geography and History
- *Section 2,* Culture and Traditions
- *Section 3,* Groups and Institutions

HISTORY AND ART **Maya Wall Painting** The Maya were one of many Native American peoples living in the Americas before the arrival of Europeans. This wall painting, located at a ceremonial center, shows musicians celebrating a royal birth.

16

EXTRA CREDIT PROJECT

Retelling Origin Myths Origin myths, or creation stories, explain for Native Americans how the world began and how all beings once lived together. They answer the questions: Who are we? Why are we here? What is the purpose of life and death? What is our place in the world, in time, and in space? These accounts have been passed down from generation to generation through oral history. Have interested students research origin myths of several Native American groups and choose one to read aloud to the class. Encourage students to illustrate their stories.

30,000 B.C. — 10,000 B.C. — 5000 B.C. — 1000 B.C.

c. 28,000 B.C. Asian hunters enter North America

c. 10,000 B.C. Last Ice Age ends

c. 7000 B.C. Farming develops in Mexico

c. 3000 B.C. Early villages settled in Mexico

Section 1

Early Peoples

READ TO DISCOVER . . .

- how the first people arrived in the Americas.
- which discovery changed the lives of the early Native Americans.

TERMS TO LEARN

archaeology	migration
artifact	maize
Ice Age	carbon dating
nomad	culture

The Storyteller

No one knows for sure why the first people to settle in North America crossed the land bridge that once connected Asia and North America. With spears poised, small bands of hunters may have pursued a mammoth, a large game animal that is now extinct, or other large animals. Later settlers may have come by boat, hunting seals and whales. Over time, these "native Americans" would inhabit both North and South America.

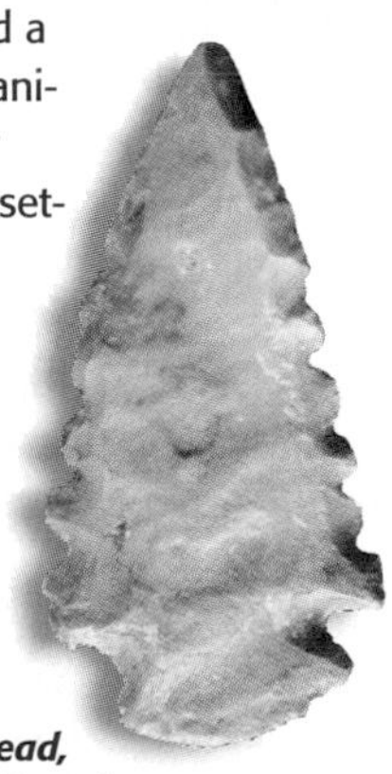

Arrowhead, hand-chipped stone

When Europeans arrived in the Americas in the late 1400s, they found Native Americans living there. The Europeans wondered where these peoples had come from and how they happened to settle in the Americas. Some believed the Native Americans had come from Atlantis, a mythical island that was supposed to have sunk beneath the waves of the Atlantic Ocean.

Modern scientists are still trying to determine when and how the first people appeared in North and South America. The story of the first Americans is still being pieced together by experts in archaeology, the study of ancient peoples. Archaeologists learn about the past from artifacts, things left behind by early people, such as stone tools, weapons, baskets, and carvings. Their most recent discoveries show that the Native Americans *did* come from a land that later sank into the sea. It was not the mythical Atlantis, however, but a stretch of land called **Beringia** that once joined Asia and the Americas.

Geography

The Journey From Asia

During its long history, the earth has passed through several Ice Ages, periods of extremely cold temperatures when part of the planet's surface was covered with massive ice sheets. Much of the water from the oceans was frozen into these ice sheets, or glaciers. For that reason the sea levels were much lower during

SECTION RESOURCES

Reproducible Masters
- Reproducible Lesson Plan 1–1
- Guided Reading Activity 1–1
- Section Quiz 1–1
- Reteaching Activity 1–1
- Enrichment Activity 1–1

Transparencies
- Section Focus Transparency 1–1

Multimedia
- Vocabulary PuzzleMaker
- Chapter Challenger Interactive Review Software
- Testmaker

1 FOCUS

BELLRINGER
Motivational Activity

Before taking roll at the beginning of the class period, project Section Focus Transparency 1–1 and have students answer the questions. Discuss students' responses.

This activity is also available as a blackline master.

Section Focus Transparency 1–1

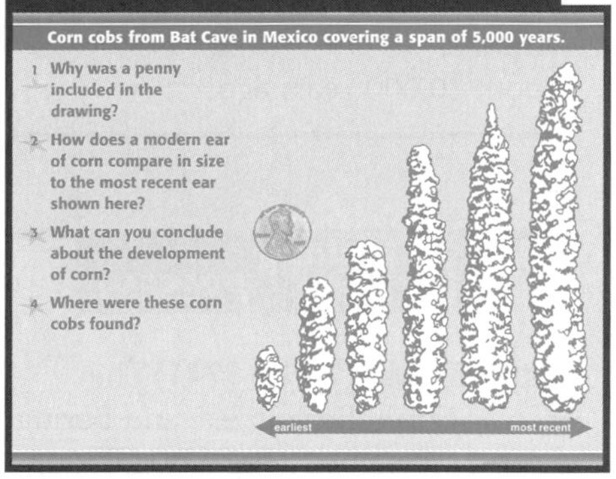

Vocabulary Precheck

Point out that the items under **Terms to Learn** are introduced and defined in this section. These terms are printed in blue type where they first appear.

Use the **Vocabulary PuzzleMaker** to create crossword and word search puzzles.

Section Theme
Geography and History

The Ice Age made it possible for Asian hunters to migrate to the Americas.

Activity Direct students to the map on page 19. Ask them to find evidence showing that the Ice Age made it possible for Asian hunters to migrate to the Americas.

2 TEACH

L1 Reporting Explain the necessary characteristics of a news report (who, what, where, when, why, and how). Ask each student to write a news report describing the peopling of the Americas as outlined in this section. Have students either videotape their news report to play to the class or read their news report aloud.

Chart Study

Answer
about 30,000 years ago

Linking PAST & PRESENT

Vitus Bering (1680–1741) The Bering Strait, Bering Sea, and Bering Island are named after Vitus Bering who was the first to explore these areas. Bad weather prevented him from ever reaching the Alaskan coast. On his return voyage, his ship wrecked on the island where Bering died and which now bears his name.

Guided Reading Activity 1–1

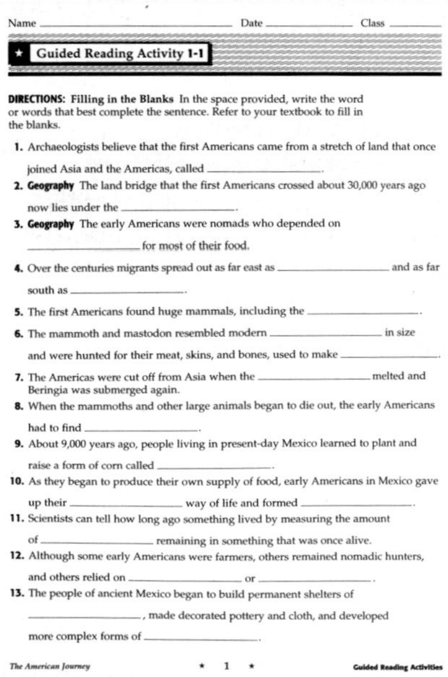
Name ______ Date ______ Class ______

★ Guided Reading Activity 1-1

DIRECTIONS: Filling in the Blanks In the space provided, write the word or words that best complete the sentence. Refer to your textbook to fill in the blanks.

1. Archaeologists believe that the first Americans came from a stretch of land that once joined Asia and the Americas, called ______.
2. **Geography** The land bridge that the first Americans crossed about 30,000 years ago now lies under the ______.
3. **Geography** The early Americans were nomads who depended on ______ for most of their food.
4. Over the centuries migrants spread out as far east as ______ and as far south as ______.
5. The first Americans found huge mammals, including the ______.
6. The mammoth and mastodon resembled modern ______ in size and were hunted for their meat, skins, and bones, used to make ______.
7. The Americas were cut off from Asia when the ______ melted and Beringia was submerged again.
8. When the mammoths and other large animals began to die out, the early Americans had to find ______.
9. About 9,000 years ago, people living in present-day Mexico learned to plant and raise a form of corn called ______.
10. As they began to produce their own supply of food, early Americans in Mexico gave up their ______ way of life and formed ______.
11. Scientists can tell how long ago something lived by measuring the amount of ______ remaining in something that was once alive.
12. Although some early Americans were farmers, others remained nomadic hunters, and others relied on ______ or ______.
13. The people of ancient Mexico began to build permanent shelters of ______, made decorated pottery and cloth, and developed more complex forms of ______.

The American Journey ★ 1 ★ **Guided Reading Activities**

that period than they are today. The lower sea levels exposed large areas of the seabed that would once again be covered with water when the Ice Age ended and the glaciers melted.

Crossing the Land Bridge

The most recent Ice Age began 100,000 years ago and ended about 12,000 years ago. During this period the lower sea level exposed a broad strip of land between Asia and North America. This land bridge ran from **Siberia** in northeastern Asia to present-day **Alaska,** the westernmost part of the Americas. The land bridge, Beringia, now lies under the **Bering Strait.**

Scientists are fairly certain that the first Americans were people from Asia who crossed over Beringia during the last Ice Age. These early peoples probably reached the Americas about 30,000 years ago.

In Search of Hunting Grounds

The early Americans were **nomads,** people who moved from place to place. They gathered wild grains and fruits but depended on hunting for much of their food. While traveling in search of game or following herds of animals, they crossed Beringia into what are now Alaska and Canada.

The crossing of the land bridge was a **migration,** a movement of a large number of people into a new homeland. It did not happen in a single journey. As the centuries passed, many groups of people traveled from Asia, either on foot across the land bridge or in boats along its coast. From the north, the migrants gradually moved into new territory. They spread out across the Americas, going as far east as the Atlantic Ocean and as far south as the tip of South America.

Footnotes to History

The Land Bridge Beringia takes its name from Vitus Bering, a Danish explorer hired by the Russians to explore the Arctic waters of the Bering Strait in the early 1700s.

Causes and Effects

CAUSES

★ The earth enters a long Ice Age.
★ Water from the oceans freezes into glaciers.
★ Sea levels drop, exposing the Beringia land bridge.

Migration to the Americas

EFFECTS

★ Nomadic hunters from Asia cross into North America.
★ People spread into Central America and South America.
★ The early Americans create many new cultures.

Chart Study

The settlement of the Americas can be traced to a geographic element—the earth's climate.
Analyzing Information When did people from Asia first come to the Americas?

Hunting for Food

Native American legends tell of giant beasts that roamed the earth in ancient times. When the first Americans arrived from Asia, they did indeed find huge mammals. There was the saber-toothed tiger—a large, flesh-eating cat—the woolly mammoth, and the mastodon. The mammoth and mastodon resembled modern elephants in size and shape but had shaggy fur and tusks up to 13 feet (4 m) long.

The early Americans were skilled at hunting these beasts. The hunters shaped pieces of stone and bone to make tools for chopping and scrapping. They chipped rocks into extremely sharp points and fastened them on poles to make

COOPERATIVE LEARNING ACTIVITY

Creating a Multimedia Presentation Organize the class into groups of three. Ask each group to create a multimedia presentation illlustrating the scientific theory of migration described in this section. Have group members portray this theory in one of the following ways: draw a storyboard, create a hypermedia stack (if computers are not available, students working on this task can illustrate on paper what would be included in a stack), write a position paper defending or critiquing the theory. Have groups present the completed multimedia presentation to the class. You may wish to discuss other theories of how the first people appeared in the Americas.

spears. Bands of hunters armed with these spears stalked herds of giant bison, mastodons, or mammoths and then charged at the animals, hurling their weapons.

A single mammoth provided tons of meat, enough to feed a group of people for months. The hunters and their families used every part of the animal. They made the skin into clothing, carved the bones into weapons and tools, and may have used the long ribs to build shelters.

About 12,000 years ago the earth's temperatures began to rise. The Ice Age was drawing to an end. As the great glaciers melted, the oceans rose, and Beringia was submerged again. The Americas were cut off from Asia. At the same time, the hunters of America faced a new challenge. The mammoths and other large animals began to die out, either from overhunting or because of changes in the environment. The early Americans had to find other sources of food.

Settling Down

As the large game animals disappeared, the early Americans found new sources of food. They hunted smaller game, such as deer, birds, and rodents. Those who lived along rivers or near the seacoast learned to catch fish with nets and traps—as Native Americans still do today. They continued to gather wild berries and grains.

Prehistoric Migrations Through the Americas

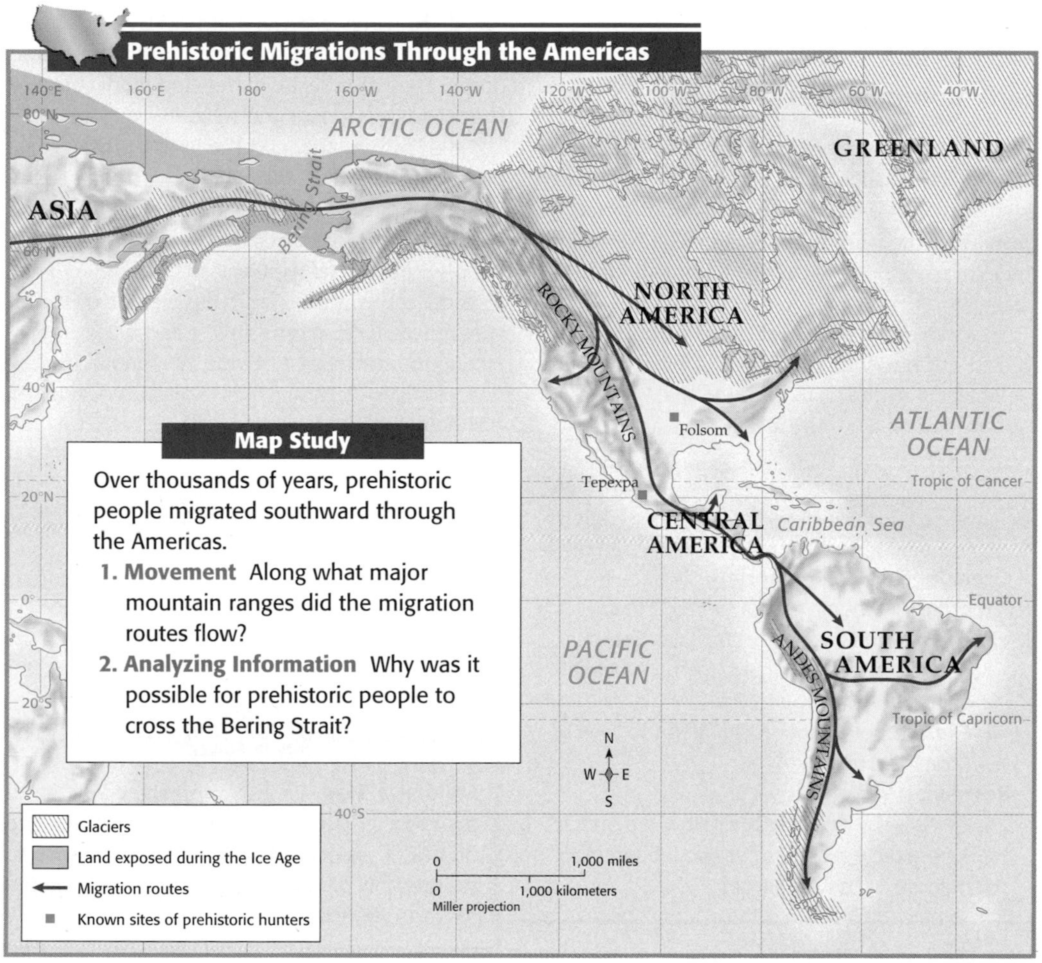

Map Study

Over thousands of years, prehistoric people migrated southward through the Americas.

1. **Movement** Along what major mountain ranges did the migration routes flow?
2. **Analyzing Information** Why was it possible for prehistoric people to cross the Bering Strait?

CHAPTER 1
Section 1, 17–20

3 ASSESS

Assign Section 1 Review as homework or as an in-class activity.

Use **Chapter Challenger Interactive Review Software** to review Section 1.

Sectic n Quiz 1–1

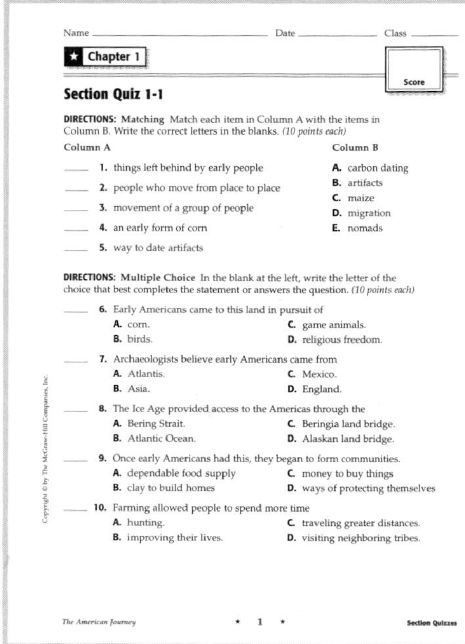
Name ______ Date ______ Class ______

Chapter 1

Score

Section Quiz 1-1

DIRECTIONS: Matching Match each item in Column A with the items in Column B. Write the correct letters in the blanks. *(10 points each)*

Column A	Column B
____ 1. things left behind by early people	A. carbon dating
____ 2. people who move from place to place	B. artifacts
____ 3. movement of a group of people	C. maize
____ 4. an early form of corn	D. migration
____ 5. way to date artifacts	E. nomads

DIRECTIONS: Multiple Choice In the blank at the left, write the letter of the choice that best completes the statement or answers the question. *(10 points each)*

____ 6. Early Americans came to this land in pursuit of
A. corn. C. game animals.
B. birds. D. religious freedom.

____ 7. Archaeologists believe early Americans came from
A. Atlantis. C. Mexico.
B. Asia. D. England.

____ 8. The Ice Age provided access to the Americas through the
A. Bering Strait. C. Beringia land bridge.
B. Atlantic Ocean. D. Alaskan land bridge.

____ 9. Once early Americans had this, they began to form communities.
A. dependable food supply C. money to buy things
B. clay to build homes D. ways of protecting themselves

____ 10. Farming allowed people to spend more time
A. hunting. C. traveling greater distances.
B. improving their lives. D. visiting neighboring tribes.

The American Journey ★ 1 ★ **Section Quizzes**

Map Study

Answers

1. Rocky and Andes Mountains
2. a lowering in sea level exposed a land bridge connecting Alaska and Asia

Map Skills Practice

Reading a Map List the known sites of prehistoric hunters. *(Folsom and Tepexpa)*

Multiple Learning Styles

Logical/Mathematical Discuss with students the difference between "number of years ago" and "years B.C." Explain how to convert "number of years ago" to "years B.C." by subtracting 2000 from the number of years. For example, the most recent Ice Age ended about 12,000 years ago, or 10,000 B.C. Have each student make a double time line listing the events in this section. On the top of the time line use the heading *Number of Years Ago*; on the bottom, use the heading *Years B.C.* This section lists all dates as "years ago." Have students use the conversion equation to complete the time line. **L1**

CHAPTER 1

Section 1, 17–20

Reteaching Activity 1–1

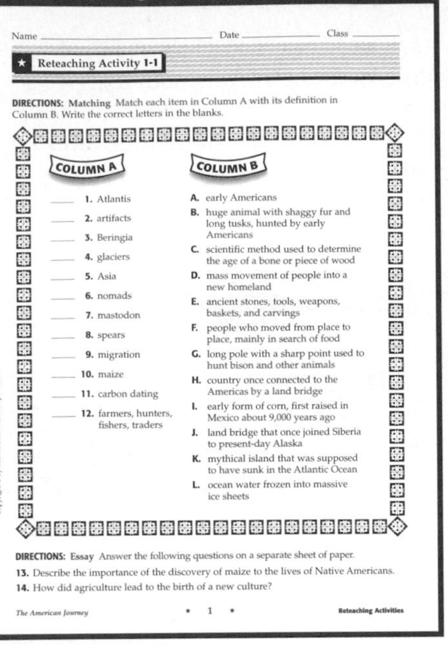

Name ______ Date ______ Class ______

★ Reteaching Activity 1-1

DIRECTIONS: Matching Match each item in Column A with its definition in Column B. Write the correct letters in the blanks.

COLUMN A	COLUMN B
____ 1. Atlantis	A. early Americans
____ 2. artifacts	B. huge animal with shaggy fur and long tusks, hunted by early Americans
____ 3. Beringia	C. scientific method used to determine the age of a bone or piece of wood
____ 4. glaciers	D. mass movement of people into a new homeland
____ 5. Asia	E. ancient stones, tools, weapons, baskets, and carvings
____ 6. nomads	F. people who moved from place to place, mainly in search of food
____ 7. mastodon	G. long pole with a sharp point used to hunt bison and other animals
____ 8. spears	H. country once connected to the Americas by a land bridge
____ 9. migration	I. early form of corn, first raised in Mexico about 9,000 years ago
____ 10. maize	J. land bridge that once joined Siberia to present-day Alaska
____ 11. carbon dating	K. mythical island that was supposed to have sunk in the Atlantic Ocean
____ 12. farmers, hunters, fishers, traders	L. ocean water frozen into massive ice sheets

DIRECTIONS: Essay Answer the following questions on a separate sheet of paper.

13. Describe the importance of the discovery of maize to the lives of Native Americans.

14. How did agriculture lead to the birth of a new culture?

Enrichment Activity 1–1

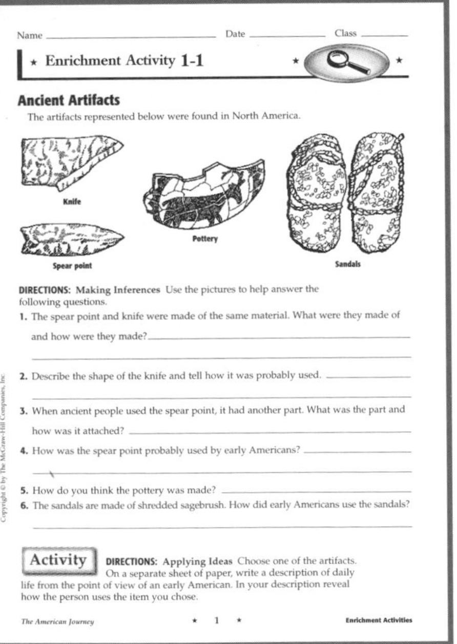

Name ______ Date ______ Class ______

★ Enrichment Activity 1-1 ★ ★

Ancient Artifacts

The artifacts represented below were found in North America.

DIRECTIONS: Making Inferences Use the pictures to help answer the following questions.

1. The spear point and knife were made of the same material. What were they made of and how were they made? ______

2. Describe the shape of the knife and tell how it was probably used. ______

3. When ancient people used the spear point, it had another part. What was the part and how was it attached? ______

4. How was the spear point probably used by early Americans? ______

5. How do you think the pottery was made? ______

6. The sandals are made of shredded sagebrush. How did early Americans use the sandals? ______

Activity **DIRECTIONS: Applying Ideas** Choose one of the artifacts. On a separate sheet of paper, write a description of daily life from the point of view of an early American. In your description reveal how the person uses the item you chose.

Planting Seeds

About 9,000 years ago, people living in present-day **Mexico** made a discovery that would shape the lives of Native Americans for thousands of years. They learned to plant and raise an early form of corn called **maize.** Their harvests of maize provided a steady, reliable source of food. No longer did they have to move from place to place in order to survive.

Early Americans in Mexico also experimented with other kinds of seeds. They planted pumpkins, edible gourds, beans, chili peppers, avocados, and squashes. The people who had once depended on wandering animals for their food were producing more than enough food to feed themselves. The population grew along with the ever-increasing food supply.

Early Communities

With rising numbers of people and a dependable supply of food, early Americans in Mexico gave up their nomadic way of life and started to form stable communities. Scientists have found traces of early villages that date from about 5,000 years ago.

Scientists use a method called **carbon dating** to find out how old an artifact is. By measuring the amount of radioactive carbon that remains in something that was once alive—such as a bone or a piece of wood—they can tell how long ago it lived.

Sometime after the early settlements in Mexico, people began farming in what is now the southwestern United States. Not all the early peoples in the Americas farmed, however. Some remained nomadic hunters, and others relied on fishing or trading instead of agriculture.

The Growth of Cultures

Farming allowed people to spend time on activities other than finding food. Knowing that they would harvest an abundant supply of grains and vegetables, the people of ancient Mexico began to improve their lives in other ways. They built permanent shelters of clay, brick, stone, or wood. They made pottery and cloth and decorated these goods with dyes made from roots and herbs. They also began to develop more complex forms of government and religion.

Agriculture changed the lives of these early people and led to the birth of a new **culture,** a way of life of a particular group of people. Rather than move from place to place in search of food, the people who farmed were able to settle down. They formed communities and developed common customs, beliefs, artistic styles, and ways of protecting themselves. Over time, the many different groups of people living in the Americas developed distinctive cultures.

Section 1 Review

Checking for Understanding

1. ***Identify*** Siberia, Alaska, Bering Strait.
2. ***Define*** archaeology, artifact, Ice Age, nomad, migration, maize, carbon dating, culture.
3. ***Explain*** how farming changed the lives of nomads.

Reviewing Themes

4. **Geography and History** How did an Ice Age make it possible for Asian hunters to migrate to the Americas?

Critical Thinking

5. **Determining Cause and Effect** How do you think the first Americans discovered that they could grow their own plants?

Activity

Making a Map Create an enlarged version of the map on page 19. Label all landmasses and bodies of water. Add illustrations to the map to tell the story of how the first Americans migrated to North America.

4 CLOSE

Ask students to speculate what might have happened in the Americas if the Ice Age had never occurred.

Section 1 Review Answers

1. Siberia, 18; Alaska, 18; Bering Strait, 18
2. The words are defined in the Glossary.
3. Farming provided a reliable food source. It allowed people to spend time doing other things such as creating permanent and more complex communities.
4. Water froze, sea levels dropped, large areas of land such as Beringia were exposed, allowing migration.
5. Answers will vary, but students should refer to the first Americans' observations and experimentation.

Activity Students should create a larger version of the map that appears on page 19 and add illustrations.

1200 B.C. — B.C./A.D. — A.D. 1200 — A.D. 1400

c. 1200 B.C. Rise of Olmec in Mexico

c. A.D. 700 Maya civilization at its height in Central America

A.D. 1325 Aztec establish Tenochtitlán in Mexico

A.D. 1400s Inca Empire at its height in South America

Section 2

Cities and Empires

READ TO DISCOVER . . .

- why powerful empires rose up in the Americas.
- how the people of each empire adapted to their environment and used their resources.

TERMS TO LEARN

civilization
hieroglyphics
theocracy
terrace

The Storyteller

Rumors of a lost city led American historian Hiram Bingham to the mountains of Peru in 1911. Bingham followed a steep mountain trail, pulling himself along by grabbing vines. After many hours of climbing, he reached a clearing. Suddenly he saw acres of huge, crumbling walls and pillars of white stone covered with vines and moss. "It fairly took my breath away," wrote Bingham. He knew that these temples and monuments were the remains of a very advanced people.

A Mayan deity

Long before the arrival of Europeans in the early 1500s, several great **civilizations,** or highly developed societies, arose in present-day Mexico and in Central and South America. These civilizations built enormous cities in dense jungles and on difficult-to-reach mountaintops. They also developed complex systems of writing, counting, and tracking time.

Among the largest and most advanced of these early civilizations were the **Olmec,** the **Maya,** the **Aztec,** and the **Inca.** Each civilization spread out over hundreds of miles, included millions of people, and thrived for centuries.

The Olmec flourished between 1200 B.C. and 400 B.C. along the Gulf Coast of what are now Mexico, Guatemala, and Honduras. Olmec farmers produced enough food to sustain cities containing thousands of people. Olmec workers sculpted large stone monuments and built stone pavements and drainage systems. Their civilization strongly influenced their neighbors.

The Maya

The Maya built their civilization in the dense, steamy rain forests of present-day **Mexico, Guatemala, Honduras,** and **Belize.** Around 1000 B.C. they began clearing the land. They planted maize, beans, sweet potatoes, and other vegetables. They also pulled enormous stones from the earth to build monuments and pyramids that still stand today. Much of this labor was performed by enslaved people, usually prisoners of war.

SECTION RESOURCES

Reproducible Masters
- Reproducible Lesson Plan 1–2
- Guided Reading Activity 1–2
- Section Quiz 1–2
- Reteaching Activity 1–2
- Enrichment Activity 1–2

Transparencies
- Section Focus Transparency 1–2

Multimedia
- Vocabulary PuzzleMaker
- Chapter Challenger Interactive Review Software
- Testmaker
- NGS PictureShow: Native Americans, Part 2
- NGS Picture Atlas of the World

1 FOCUS

BELLRINGER
Motivational Activity

Before taking roll at the beginning of the class period, project Section Focus Transparency 1–2 and have students answer the questions. Discuss students' responses.

This activity is also available as a blackline master.

Section Focus Transparency 1–2

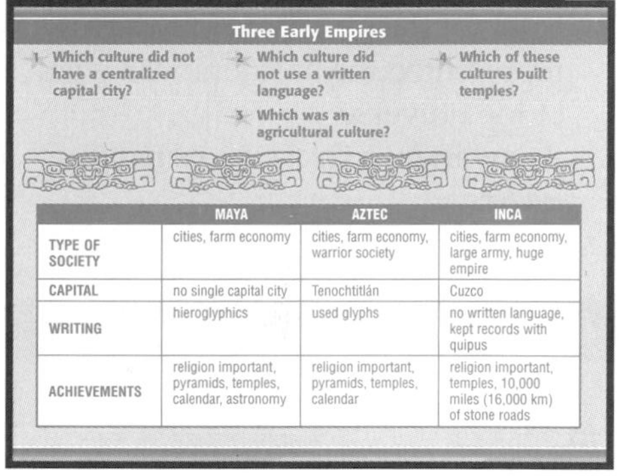

Three Early Empires

1. Which culture did not have a centralized capital city?
2. Which culture did not use a written language?
3. Which was an agricultural culture?
4. Which of these cultures built temples?

	MAYA	AZTEC	INCA
TYPE OF SOCIETY	cities, farm economy	cities, farm economy, warrior society	cities, farm economy, large army, huge empire
CAPITAL	no single capital city	Tenochtitlán	Cuzco
WRITING	hieroglyphics	used glyphs	no written language, kept records with quipus
ACHIEVEMENTS	religion important, pyramids, temples, calendar, astronomy	religion important, pyramids, temples, calendar	religion important, temples, 10,000 miles (16,000 km) of stone roads

Vocabulary Precheck

Ask students to define the word *civilization* using their own, made-up hieroglyphics.

Use the **Vocabulary PuzzleMaker** to create crossword and word search puzzles.

Section Theme
Culture and Traditions

Early civilizations such as the Olmec, the Maya, the Aztec, and the Inca arose in present-day Mexico and in Central and South America. They developed complex cultures long before the arrival of Europeans.

Activity Ask students to scan the photos in this section to make generalizations about each Native American culture portrayed. Discuss how these photos show highly developed civilizations.

CHAPTER 1
Section 2, 21–25

2 TEACH

L1 Creating a Game Organize the class into small groups to create a *Jeopardy!* style game about the Native American civilizations described in this section. Have students in each group identify five categories, then write five answers with correct questions in each category. Pair groups to play the game.

Picturing HISTORY Archaeologists believe the stepped levels of the pyramids may have represented the harmonious layers of the universe.
Answer: *by a theocracy, or religious leaders*

Guided Reading Activity 1–2

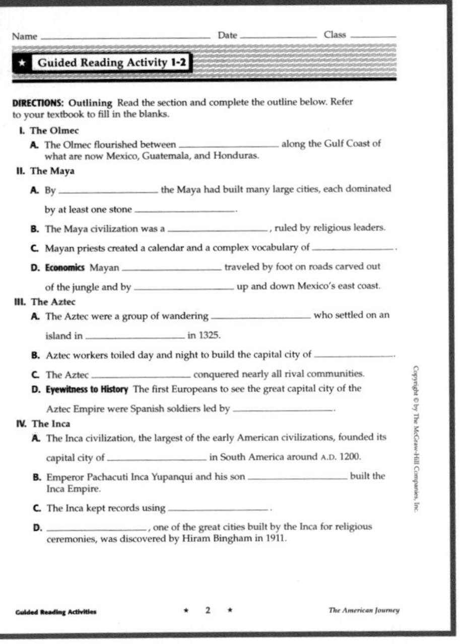
Name ______ Date ______ Class ______

Guided Reading Activity 1-2

DIRECTIONS: Outlining Read the section and complete the outline below. Refer to your textbook to fill in the blanks.

I. The Olmec
- **A.** The Olmec flourished between ______ along the Gulf Coast of what are now Mexico, Guatemala, and Honduras.

II. The Maya
- **A.** By ______ the Maya had built many large cities, each dominated by at least one stone ______.
- **B.** The Maya civilization was a ______, ruled by religious leaders.
- **C.** Mayan priests created a calendar and a complex vocabulary of ______.
- **D.** **Economics** Mayan ______ traveled by foot on roads carved out of the jungle and by ______ up and down Mexico's east coast.

III. The Aztec
- **A.** The Aztec were a group of wandering ______ who settled on an island in ______ in 1325.
- **B.** Aztec workers toiled day and night to build the capital city of ______.
- **C.** The Aztec ______ conquered nearly all rival communities.
- **D.** **Eyewitness to History** The first Europeans to see the great capital city of the Aztec Empire were Spanish soldiers led by ______.

IV. The Inca
- **A.** The Inca civilization, the largest of the early American civilizations, founded its capital city of ______ in South America around A.D. 1200.
- **B.** Emperor Pachacuti Inca Yupanqui and his son ______ built the Inca Empire.
- **C.** The Inca kept records using ______.
- **D.** ______, one of the great cities built by the Inca for religious ceremonies, was discovered by Hiram Bingham in 1911.

NATIONAL GEOGRAPHIC SOCIETY

CD-ROM
NGS PictureShow: Native Americans, Part 2
Expose students to the Maya culture by having them click on the main menu.

Picturing HISTORY In Tikal and other cities, the Maya built huge pyramids where people could gather for ceremonies honoring the deities. A model of a Mayan city is shown (top left). **How were the Maya governed?**

Mayan Cities

By A.D. 300 the Maya had built many large cities. Each city was dominated by at least one stone pyramid. Some pyramids reached about 200 feet (60 m)—the height of a 20-story building. Steps ran up the pyramid sides to a temple on top. The largest Mayan city, **Tikal,** in present-day Guatemala, was surrounded by six pyramids. The pyramid in **Chichén Itzá** (chih•CHEHN iht•SAH), located on Mexico's Yucatán Peninsula, covered an acre of ground.

The temples on top of the pyramids were religious and governmental centers. Wearing gold jewelry and elaborate headdresses, the priests in the temples performed rituals dedicated to the Mayan gods. On special days, the whole city attended religious festivals. Crowds gathered in the plazas to watch masked dancers, drummers, and flute players perform for the gods.

The Maya believed the gods controlled everything that happened on earth. Because only priests knew the gods' wishes, the priests held great power in Mayan society and made most of the important decisions. The civilization of the Maya was a **theocracy,** a society ruled by religious leaders.

Mayan Astronomy

The Mayan priests believed that the gods were visible in the stars, sun, and moon. They thought that studying the night sky would help them understand the gods and predict the future. Their intense interest in the workings of the heavens led to an understanding of astronomy. Their desire to measure time advanced their knowledge of mathematics. The priests created a 365-day calendar by which to schedule plantings, harvests, and religious ceremonies.

COOPERATIVE LEARNING ACTIVITY

Communicating Organize students into groups of three to create a communications system. Use the ideas described in this section about the Maya, Aztec, and Inca communication systems. Have one student create a calendar, another an alphabet, and another a way of counting. Have each group creatively display the completed communication system and use one part of this system to relay a message to the rest of the class. Have other students interpret the message.

Mayan priests recorded the movements of the stars, sun, and moon by carving pictures on stones. These images developed into **hieroglyphics,** pictures or symbols that are used to represent words, sounds, or concepts. The Maya developed a complex vocabulary of hieroglyphics.

$ Economics

Transport and Trade

The Maya did not have wheeled vehicles or horses, so everything they transported overland was carried on human backs. Mayan traders traveled on a network of roads that had been carved out of the jungle. Farmers brought maize and vegetables to outdoor markets in the cities. They exchanged their crops for cotton cloth, pottery, deer meat, and salt.

The Maya also engaged in long-distance trade. At the height of the civilization—from A.D. 300 to A.D. 900—thousands of Mayan canoes traveled up and down Mexico's east coast. The canoes carried jade statues, turquoise jewelry, parrot feathers, cacao beans for making chocolate, and other luxury goods to traders throughout a large area. $

Decline of a Civilization

Around A.D. 800 the Maya civilization began to decline. By A.D. 900 the great cities were almost ghost towns. The jungle crept back across the plazas, roads, and fields. No one knows what caused the decline. Perhaps slaves and farmers revolted against their masters. Perhaps the soil became too exhausted by erosion and fire to produce enough food. The Maya civilization collapsed, but descendants of the Maya still live in parts of Mexico and Central America.

The Aztec

Centuries after the fall of the Maya, a group of hunters called the Aztec wandered through central Mexico, searching for a permanent home. In 1325 they came upon an island in Lake Texcoco, today part of Mexico City. There the Aztec saw a sign: an eagle sitting on a cactus, a snake in its beak. That meant this island was to be their home.

Tenochtitlán

On this island "amidst the water, in the reeds, in the sugar-canes" emerged **Tenochtitlán** (tay•NAWCH•teet•LAHN), one of the greatest cities in the Americas. Its construction was a miracle of engineering and human labor. Directed

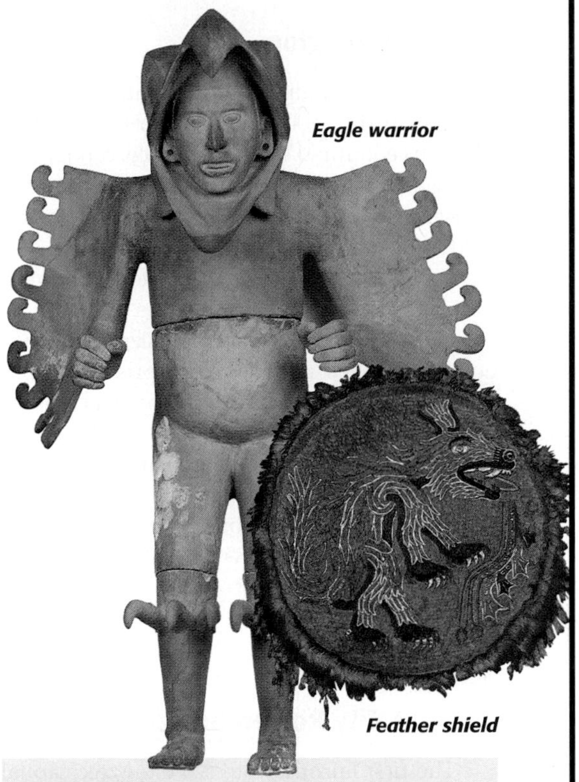

Picturing HISTORY The Aztec were a warrior people, and much of their art reflected military themes. Birds and animals known for their strength and beauty—especially the eagle, jaguar, and coyote—were honored in the Aztec's art and folklore. **How did the Aztec treat the people they conquered?**

CHAPTER 1
Section 2, 21–25

NATIONAL GEOGRAPHIC SOCIETY

CD-ROM
Picture Atlas of the World
To help students understand how geography affected Native American life, have them click on the countries of Central America and South America.

What?Where?When?Who?

Chocolate The word *chocolate* came to English from the Aztec word *xocolatl* meaning "bitter water." The Aztec brewed a ceremonial drink from crushed cocoa beans. This drink was a forerunner of present-day hot chocolate.

Picturing HISTORY Although the Aztec were warriors, they also traded extensively. The market at Tlateloco was the largest in the Americas. About 60,000 people may have visited the market daily.
Answer: *They took their victims' belongings and enslaved them. Some slaves were sacrificed to the Aztec gods.*

MULTIPLE LEARNING STYLES

Verbal/Linguistic After reading Hiram Bingham's description on page 21 of seeing Machu Picchu for the first time, have each student imagine finding remnants of the Aztec, Inca, or Maya civilizations. Ask each student to write a first-person narrative describing what he or she sees and feels. Have students read the account aloud to the class. Have the class name the civilization described. Record the number of correct responses for each description and award the student with the most correct responses the "Creative Writer of the Day Award." **L2**

3 ASSESS

Assign Section 2 Review as homework or as an in-class activity.

Use **Chapter Challenger Interactive Review Software** to review Section 2.

Section Quiz 1–2

Name ______ Date ______ Class ______

★ Chapter 1

Score

Section Quiz 1-2

DIRECTIONS: Matching Match each item in Column A with the items in Column B. Write the correct letters in the blanks. *(10 points each)*

Column A	Column B
____ **1.** largest Mayan city	**A.** Aztec
____ **2.** a warrior people	**B.** Cuzco
____ **3.** builders of stone pyramids	**C.** Tikal
____ **4.** Incan capital city	**D.** Quechua
____ **5.** official Inca language	**E.** Maya

DIRECTIONS: Multiple Choice In the blank at the left, write the letter of the choice that best completes the statement or answers the question. *(10 points each)*

____ **6.** A society ruled by a religious leader is called a
A. democracy. **C.** civilization.
B. theocracy. **D.** quipus.

____ **7.** Mayan temples were used for
A. religious rituals. **C.** food markets.
B. the king's home. **D.** festivals.

____ **8.** One of the greatest cities in the world, the Aztec capital was
A. Mexico City. **C.** Yucatán.
B. Chichén Itzá. **D.** Tenochtitlán.

____ **9.** The largest empire of the early American civilizations was the
A. Aztec. **C.** Inca.
B. Maya. **D.** Olmec.

____ **10.** This is an Inca religious center.
A. Colombia **C.** Pachacuti
B. Machu Picchu **D.** Cuzco

Section Quizzes ★ 2 ★ *The American Journey*

Reteaching Activity 1–2

Name ______ Date ______ Class ______

★ Reteaching Activity 1-2

DIRECTIONS: Organizing Facts The numbered items are characteristics of early American civilizations. Write the number of each item in the appropriate section of the chart. Some items fit more than one group.

Early American Civilizations

Olmec	Maya
______	______
Aztec	**Inca**
______	______

★FACT BANK

1. farmed for food
2. settled in steamy rain forests
3. society ruled by religion
4. largest of early civilizations
5. worshipped a sun god
6. settled an island in Lake Texcoco
7. strong military force
8. developed *quipus* to keep records
9. sculpted stone monuments
10. built system of roads
11. settled in western highlands of South America
12. cut terraces into slopes
13. settled along Gulf coast
14. developed hieroglyphics
15. built Tenochtitlán
16. cities surrounded by pyramids
17. conquered nearly all rivals
18. Priests studied astronomy and created a calendar.
19. Cuzco was its capital city.

Reteaching Activities ★ 2 ★ *The American Journey*

by priests and nobles, workers toiled day and night, sometimes until they died of exhaustion. They pulled soil from the bottom of the lake to make causeways, or bridges of earth, linking the island and the shore. They filled parts of the lake with earth so they could grow crops.

In time the Aztec capital expanded to the mainland around the lake. At its height Tenochtitlán was the largest city in the Americas, perhaps the largest in the world. By A.D. 1500 nearly 200,000 people lived there. Tenochtitlán also served as a center of trade, attracting thousands of merchants to its outdoor marketplaces.

War and Religion

The Aztec civilization grew into a military empire. In the 1400s the Aztec army marched through central and southern Mexico, conquering nearly all rival communities. Aztec warriors took everything they could carry from their victims, including maize, cotton cloth, copper, and weapons. Conquered people were forced to work as slaves in Aztec cities and villages.

Like the Maya, the Aztec organized their society around their religion. Aztec priests studied the stars, moon, and sun and created a complex calendar. At the center of the Aztec religion was the powerful sun god. To make sure that the sun god would rise each morning, the priests offered the blood of humans. Thousands of prisoners of war were sacrificed in ceremonies to the sun god.

Eyewitness to HISTORY

A Great City Remembered

The first Europeans to see the Aztec capital were awed by its splendor. In 1519, 550 Spanish soldiers entered Tenochtitlán, led by Hernán Cortés. He wrote:

> "There are forty towers at least, all of stout construction and very lofty. . . . The workmanship both in wood and stone could not be bettered anywhere."

Bernal Díaz del Castillo, one of the soldiers, marveled at the "great stone towers and temples and buildings that rose straight up out of the water." Tenochtitlán, he explained, was a city of water, and many of the streets were waterways for canoes.

Díaz also admired the gardens, "the diversity of trees and the scents given off by each . . . and the paths choked with roses and other flowers." Some of the Spaniards thought that Tenochtitlán was more magnificent than Rome and other European capitals of the time.

The Inca

Another great American civilization developed in the western highlands of South America. The empire of the Inca was the largest of the early American civilizations.

Empire Builders

The Inca founded their capital city of **Cuzco** (KOOS•koh) around A.D. 1200. In 1438 an emperor named Pachacuti (PAH•chah•KOO•tee) Inca Yupanqui came to the throne and began a campaign of conquest against the neighboring peoples. He and his son, Topa Inca, built an empire that stretched from north to south for more than 3,000 miles (4,800 km), from present-day Colombia to northern Argentina and Chile.

The Incan army was a formidable force. All men between 25 and 50 years old could be drafted to serve in the army for up to five years. Their weapons included clubs, short spears, and spiked copper balls on ropes. Using slings of woven cloth, they could throw stones as far as 30 yards (27 m).

Communication and the Empire

At its height, the Inca Empire had a population of more than 6 million, including many conquered peoples. To control this far-flung empire, the Inca built at least 10,000 miles (16,000 km) of stone-paved roads that ran over mountains, across deserts, and through jungles. Rope bridges, made from grass, crossed canyons and rivers.

Making Connections Activity

Music Percussion instruments were the most important part of Aztec music. The Aztec made two drums—the *huehuetl*, or upright, single-headed drum, and the *teponaztli*, or two-toned wooden drum. They made the drum's body from clay or wood and stretched and tied animal hides or snakeskins around the rim. Have students create the *huehuetl* drum. Use an empty, clean can with one end or both ends removed. Place the open end of the can over heavy plastic or rubber sheeting and trace the outline of the rim. Then draw another circle three inches wider than the rim outline and cut around the wider circle. Tightly stretch this circle around the open end of the can and wrap with cord. Decorate the drum with Aztec symbols. Have students work in groups to create a rhythmic composition to play for the class. **L1, ELL**

CHAPTER 1
Section 2, 21–25

Runners carrying messages to and from the emperor linked remote outposts of the empire to the capital at Cuzco. The Inca language, Quechua (KEH•chuh•wuh), became the official language for all the different peoples in the empire. Although the Inca did not possess paper or writing, they developed a system of record keeping with string called *quipus* (KEE•poos). Using various lengths and colors of string, knotted in special patterns, the *quipus* carried information about resources such as grain supplies.

Inca ceremonial cup

Machu Picchu

Agricultural Achievements

Although mountainous land is not well suited for farming, the Inca devised ways to produce a steady supply of food. They cut **terraces,** or broad platforms, into steep slopes so they could plant crops. They built stone walls on the terraces to hold the soil and plants in place. Incan farmers grew maize, squash, tomatoes, peanuts, chili peppers, melons, cotton, and potatoes.

Religious Beliefs

All land and property within the Inca's domain belonged to the emperor, who was believed to be a descendant of the sun god. Because the Inca thought that the sun god enjoyed displays of gold, they crafted magnificent gold jewelry and temple ornaments. The Inca also built special cities devoted to religious ceremonies. One of these religious centers was **Machu Picchu** (MAH•choo PEE•choo), the mountaintop site discovered by Hiram Bingham in 1911.

The wealth and high achievements of the Inca were remarkable. Inca civilization, however, could not stand up against the Spanish invaders.

Section 2 Review

Checking for Understanding

1. ***Identify*** Olmec, Maya, Aztec, Inca.
2. ***Define*** civilization, theocracy, hieroglyphics, terrace.
3. ***List*** reasons the Maya, Aztec, and Inca were considered advanced civilizations.

Reviewing Themes

4. **Culture and Traditions** What was the connection between religion and astronomy in the Maya civilization?

Critical Thinking

5. **Making Inferences** How does trade help to enrich a civilization? Provide examples in your answer.

Activity

Making a Chart Create a chart that lists some of the accomplishments of the Maya, Aztec, and Inca in the areas of communication, science, and math.

Enrichment Activity 1–2

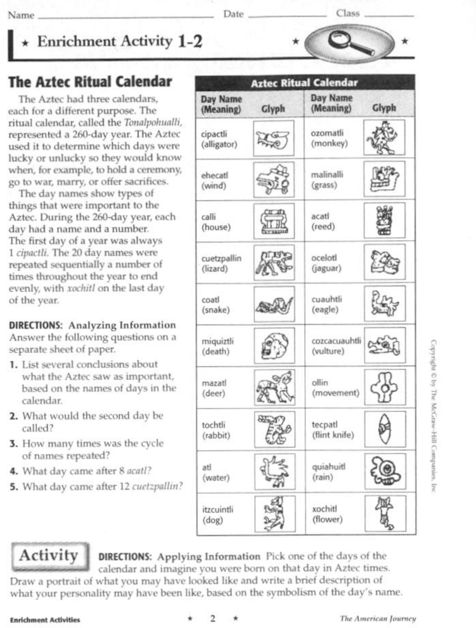

Name ______________ Date ________ Class ________

★ Enrichment Activity 1-2 ★ ★

The Aztec Ritual Calendar

The Aztec had three calendars, each for a different purpose. The ritual calendar, called the *Tonalpohualli,* represented a 260-day year. The Aztec used it to determine which days were lucky or unlucky so they would know when, for example, to hold a ceremony, go to war, marry, or offer sacrifices.

The day names show types of things that were important to the Aztec. During the 260-day year, each day had a name and a number. The first day of a year was always 1 *cipactli.* The 20 day names were repeated sequentially a number of times throughout the year to end evenly, with *xochitl* on the last day of the year.

DIRECTIONS: Analyzing Information Answer the following questions on a separate sheet of paper.

1. List several conclusions about what the Aztec saw as important, based on the names of days in the calendar.
2. What would the second day be called?
3. How many times was the cycle of names repeated?
4. What day came after 8 *acatl?*
5. What day came after 12 *cuetzpallin?*

Aztec Ritual Calendar

Day Name (Meaning)	Glyph	Day Name (Meaning)	Glyph
cipactli (alligator)		ozomatli (monkey)	
ehecatl (wind)		malinalli (grass)	
calli (house)		acatl (reed)	
cuetzpallin (lizard)		ocelotl (jaguar)	
coatl (snake)		cuauhtli (eagle)	
miquiztli (death)		cozcacuauhtli (vulture)	
mazatl (deer)		ollin (movement)	
tochtli (rabbit)		tecpatl (flint knife)	
atl (water)		quiahuitl (rain)	
itzcuintli (dog)		xochitl (flower)	

Activity **DIRECTIONS: Applying Information** Pick one of the days of the calendar and imagine you were born on that day in Aztec times. Draw a portrait of what you may have looked like and write a brief description of what your personality may have been like, based on the symbolism of the day's name.

Enrichment Activities ★ 2 ★ *The American Journey*

4 CLOSE

Ask each student to choose one of the civilizations discussed in this section to write a short description of what life would be like if that civilization had thrived. Encourage students to write from the point of view of someone living in that civilization today.

Section 2 Review Answers

1. Olmec, 21; Maya, 21; Aztec, 21; Inca, 21
2. The words are defined in the Glossary.
3. Answers may include complex systems of writing, counting, and tracking time; complex religions and government; trade; skilled artisans.
4. By studying the sky, the Maya could learn more about the gods and predict the future.
5. Trade fosters the exchange of goods, ideas, technology, and culture. Students should include examples.

Activity Charts should list accomplishments of the Maya, Aztec, and Inca.

Social Studies
SKILL BUILDER

TEACH

Understanding the Parts of a Map

This skill demonstrates how to use the parts of a map, which could include a key, a compass rose, and a scale bar. By using the parts of a map, students will be able to read and understand the information provided on a map.

Invite students to practice using the scale bar. Ask them to first determine the scale on this map before measuring distances. Then have them use a string to measure distances that are not straight lines.

Additional Practice

Chapter Skills Activity 1

School TO WORK

Cartographers Tell students that mapmakers are called cartographers. Have students research the careers available to cartographers in the fields of history, geography, science and technology, sociology, and even economics.

Social Studies
SKILL BUILDER

Understanding the Parts of a Map

Maps can direct you down the street, across the country, or around the world. There are as many different kinds of maps as there are uses for them. Being able to read a map begins with learning about its parts.

Learning the Skill

Maps should always include a key, a compass rose, and a scale bar. The map key explains the meaning of special colors, symbols, and lines used on the map. On a road map, for example, the key tells what map lines stand for paved roads, dirt roads, and interstate highways. A pine tree symbol may represent a park, while an airplane is often the symbol for an airport.

After reading the map key, look for the compass rose. It is the direction marker that shows the cardinal directions of north, south, east, and west. North and south are the directions of the North and South Poles. If you stand facing north, east is the direction to your right—toward the rising sun. West is the direction on your left.

A measuring line, often called a scale bar, helps you estimate distance on a map. The map's scale tells you what distance on the earth is represented by the measurement on the scale bar. For example, 1 inch (2.54 cm) on the map may represent 100 miles (160.9 km) on the earth. Knowing the scale allows you to visualize how large an area is and to measure distances.

Practicing the Skill

The map on this page shows where the ancient Maya, Aztec, and Inca built their empires in North America and South America. Look at the parts of this map, then answer the questions that follow.

Empires of the Maya, Aztec, and Inca

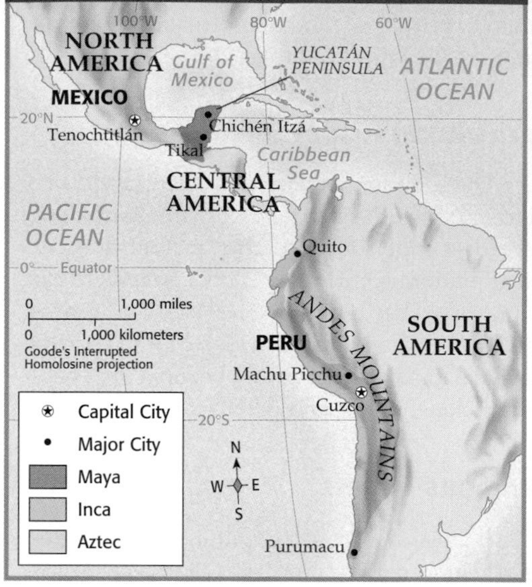

1. What information is given in the key?
2. What color shows the Inca Empire?
3. What direction would you travel to go from Tenochtitlán to Chichén Itzá?
4. About how many miles long was the Inca Empire?
5. What was the capital of the Aztec Empire?

Applying the Skill

Drawing a Map Picture a mental image of your house or room. Draw a map showing the location of various areas. Include a map key explaining any symbols or colors you use. Also include a scale bar explaining the size of your map compared to the real area. Finally, add a compass rose and title to your map.

ANSWERS TO PRACTICING THE SKILL

1. capital city; major cities; location of Maya, Inca, and Aztec civilizations
2. green
3. east
4. about 3,000 miles (4,827 km) long
5. Tenochtitlán

Applying the Skill Students will draw a map of their home or room using a map key, scale bar, and compass rose.

1000 B.C. — B.C./A.D. — A.D. 1000 — A.D. 1100 — A.D. 1200

c. 1000 B.C. First ceremonial mounds built

c. A.D. 1085 Anasazi build pueblos in North America

c. A.D. 1100 City of Cahokia is built in Illinois

A.D. 1200 Hohokam civilization of Southwest begins to decline

Section 3

North American Peoples

Read to Discover . . .

- why Native Americans built cliff dwellings in canyons in the American Southwest.
- how different Native American groups adapted to their environments.

Terms to Learn

pueblo	adobe
drought	federation

The Storyteller

In the summer of 1991, a helicopter passenger made an amazing discovery in Arizona's Coconino National Forest. As the helicopter hovered among the sandstone cliffs, the sun shone into a cave 200 feet (60 m) below the rim of one cliff. Standing in the opening of the cave were three large pottery jars.

Up to that moment, no one even knew the cave existed. It had never been spotted from the ground, and it could not be seen from the cliff top. The three jars had been sitting, untouched and unseen, for more than 700 years.

Hohokam jar

The jars and other objects found in the cave were left there by the Sinagua, Native Americans who lived in present-day Arizona hundreds of years ago. The Sinagua are just one of many Native American peoples who are now being studied by archaeologists and historians.

Early Native Americans

Many Native American cultures rose, flourished, and disappeared in North America long before Europeans arrived in the 1500s. Among the most advanced of these early cultures were the Hohokam and Anasazi of the Southwest and the Mound Builders of the Ohio River valley.

The Hohokam

The dry, hot desert of present-day Arizona was home to the **Hohokam** people. They may have come from Mexico about 300 B.C. The Hohokam culture flourished from about A.D. 300 to A.D. 1200 in an area bordered by the Gila and Salt River valleys.

The Hohokam were experts at squeezing every drop of available water from the sun-baked soil. Their way of life depended on the irrigation channels they dug to carry river water into their fields. In addition to hundreds of miles of irrigation channels, the Hohokam left behind pottery, carved stone, and shells etched with acid. The shells came from trade with coastal peoples.

Section Resources

Reproducible Masters
- Guided Reading Activity 1–3
- Section Quiz 1–3
- Reteaching Activity 1–3
- Enrichment Activity 1–3

Transparencies
- Section Focus Transparency 1–3
- U.S. History & Art, Transparency 1

Multimedia
- GTV: A Geographic Perspective on American History
- GTV: The American People: Fabric of a Nation
- ABCNews InterActive™ Historic America Electronic Field Trips
- NGS PictureShow: Native Americans, Part 1
- American Music Cultural Traditions

1 Focus

BELLRINGER
Motivational Activity

Before taking roll at the beginning of the class period, project Section Focus Transparency 1–3 and have students answer the questions. Discuss students' responses.

This activity is also available as a blackline master.

Section Focus Transparency 1–3

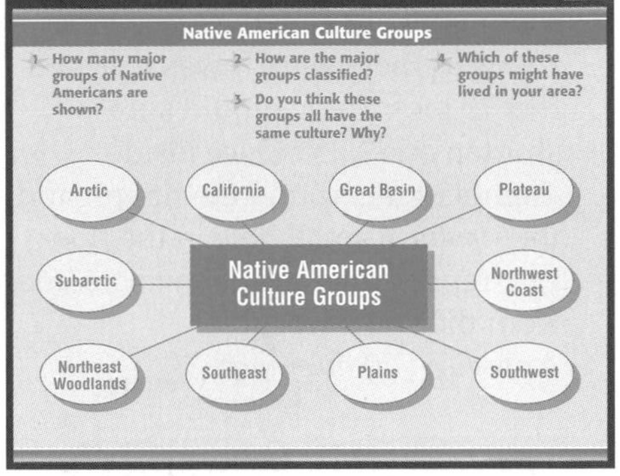

Vocabulary Precheck

Have students use the words *pueblo, drought, adobe,* and *federation* in four different sentences.

Use the **Vocabulary PuzzleMaker** to create crossword and word search puzzles.

Section Theme
Groups and Institutions

Many cultures flourished in North America before the arrival of Europeans in the 1500s. These cultural groups developed diverse societies.

Activity Explain that institutions are groups organized for a social, educational, or religious purpose. Brainstorm to create a list of institutions in your community and their purpose. Ask students to scan the section to describe Native North American institutions.

2 TEACH

L1, ELL Charting Native American Groups Have students work in pairs to create a chart of all Native North American groups described in this section. Headings on the charts should include name of group, location, way of life, type of shelter, and unique cultural achievement.

Picturing HISTORY Kivas were important to the Native Americans. To enter a kiva, one would climb down a ladder into the room, making sure they faced the rungs as they went. It was believed that to look down would surely shorten one's life. Once inside, members sat around the fire pit and the *sipapu,* a small hole in the floor that represented the gateway to and from the spirit world.
Answer: *cliff dwellings*

History *and the* Humanities

American Music Cultural Traditions, Lesson 1: "Rain Dance"

U.S. History & Art, Transparency 1, *Quilled Buckskin Robe*

Guided Reading Activity 1–3

Name ____ Date ____ Class ____

Guided Reading Activity 1-3

DIRECTIONS: Recalling Facts Read the section and answer the questions below. Refer to your textbook to write the answers.

1. Which culture dug irrigation channels to bring water to its fields?
2. What kinds of dwellings were built by the Anasazi?
3. What were two purposes of the mounds built by the Mound Builders?
4. What do the objects, such as pearls, shells, cloth, and copper, found in the mounds indicate?
5. What was the largest settlement of Mound Builders and where was it located?
6. How did the Inuit survive the cold Arctic climate?
7. How did the Tlingit, Haida, and Chinook adapt their way of life to the forest and sea environment of the West Coast?
8. Where did the Nez Perce and Yakima settle?
9. In Native American cultures, who did most of the gathering and flour making?
10. Why did the Ute and Shoshone travel to find food?
11. What groups were formed by the descendants of the Anasazi?
12. How were the Apache and Navajo different from other Southwest peoples?
13. Which Native American peoples rebuilt their culture around the horse?
14. **Citizenship** What five Iroquois nations joined to form the Iroquois League?
15. What happened in the 1500s that changed the Native Americans' way of life?

The American Journey • 3 • **Guided Reading Activities**

Kivas at Pueblo Bonito

Anasazi jar

Picturing HISTORY Pueblo Bonito had more than 800 rooms and 32 kivas, or underground ceremonial chambers. Today, the ruins of Pueblo Bonito are part of Chaco Culture National Historical Park in northwestern New Mexico. **What other kind of dwellings were built by the Anasazi?**

The Anasazi

The **Anasazi** lived around the same time as the Hohokam, roughly A.D. 200 to A.D. 1300, in the area known as the Four Corners (the meeting place of the present-day states of Utah, Colorado, Arizona, and New Mexico). There they built great stone dwellings that the Spanish explorers later called **pueblos** (PWEH•blohs), or villages. **Pueblo Bonito,** one of the most spectacular of the Anasazi pueblos, can still be seen in New Mexico. The huge semicircular structure of stone and sun-dried earth resembles an apartment building. It is four stories high and has hundreds of rooms. Archaeologists have found traces of a complex road system linking Pueblo Bonito with other villages. This suggests that Pueblo Bonito was an important trade or religious center for the Anasazi.

The Anasazi also built dwellings in the walls of steep cliffs. Cliff dwellings were easy to defend and offered protection from winter weather. **Mesa Verde** in Colorado, one of the largest and most elaborate cliff dwellings, held several thousand inhabitants.

In about 1300 the Anasazi began leaving the pueblos and cliff dwellings to settle in smaller communities. Their large villages may have been abandoned because of **droughts,** long periods of little rainfall, during which their crops dried up.

The Mound Builders

The early cultures of Mexico and Central America appear to have influenced people living in lands to the north. In central North America, prehistoric Native Americans built thousands of mounds of earth that look very much like the stone pyramids of the Maya and the Aztec. Some of the mounds contain burial chambers. Some were topped with temples, as in the Mayan and Aztec cultures.

The mounds are dotted across the landscape from present-day Pennsylvania to the Mississippi River valley. They have been found as far north as the Great Lakes and as far south as Florida. Archaeologists think that the first mounds were built about 1000 B.C. They were not the work of a single group but of many different peoples, referred to as the **Mound Builders**.

Among the earliest Mound Builders were the **Adena**, hunters and gatherers who flourished in the Ohio Valley by 800 B.C. They were followed by the **Hopewell** people, who lived between 200 B.C.

COOPERATIVE LEARNING ACTIVITY

Making a Diorama Have students choose a Native American group described in this section that interests them. Ask students to form groups based on this choice. Have each group create a diorama to show the unique characteristics of the Native American culture they selected. Allow each student in the group to choose one part of the culture, such as dwellings, clothing, environment, or crafts that they would like to create for the group's diorama. Encourage groups to use a variety of media. Have each group cooperatively assemble the diorama. Ask students to present completed dioramas to the class, explaining each cultural characteristic shown.

and A.D. 500. Farmers and traders, the Hopewell built huge burial mounds in the shape of birds, bears, and snakes. One of them, the **Great Serpent Mound**, looks like a giant snake winding across the ground. Archaeologists have found freshwater pearls, shells, cloth, and copper in the mounds. The objects indicate a widespread pattern of trade.

Cahokia

The largest settlement of the Mound Builders was **Cahokia** (kuh•HOH•kee•uh) in present-day Illinois. This city, built between A.D. 900 and A.D. 1200 by a people called the Mississippians, may have had 30,000 or more residents. The largest mound in Cahokia, the Monks Mound, rises nearly 100 feet (30 m). When it was built, it was probably the highest structure north of Mexico.

Although nearly 2,000 miles (3,200 km) away from the great cities of Mexico, Cahokia resembled them. The city was dominated by the great pyramid-shaped mound. A temple crowned the summit—perhaps a place where priests studied the movements of the sun and stars or where the priest-ruler of Cahokia lived. A legend of the Natchez people, descendants of the Mississippians, hints of a direct link to Mexico:

> "Before we came into this land we lived yonder under the sun [the speaker pointed southwest toward Mexico]. . . . Our nation extended itself along the great water [the Gulf of Mexico] where this large river [the Mississippi] loses itself."

Other Native North Americans

Although the civilizations of the Hohokam, the Anasazi, and the Mound Builders eventually faded away, other Native American cultures arose to take their place. Around the time that Europeans began arriving, North America was home to dozens of diverse societies.

Peoples of the North

The people who settled in the northernmost part of North America, in the lands around the Arctic Ocean, are called the **Inuit**. Some scientists think that the Inuit were the last migrants to cross the land bridge into North America.

Picturing HISTORY Workshops, dwellings, mounds, and pyramids developed around the central plaza of Cahokia. Farms stretched along the Mississippi River valley. **In what way did Cahokia resemble Native American cities in Mexico?**

MULTIPLE LEARNING STYLES

Intrapersonal The Plains peoples used shields for protection in battle. These shields expressed the personal characteristics of the carrier and reflected the Plains culture. Have each student cut out an 18-inch circle from stiff paper such as cardboard, cardstock, or poster board to use as the shield's base. Encourage students to be creative in using different media such as paints, fabric, colored paper, feathers, and so on to create a design on the front of the shield. The design should reflect students' unique characteristics. Then have them tape or glue a strap of leather or stiff paper about 14 inches long to the back side of the shield. Pair students to interpret one another's shield. **L2**

NATIONAL GEOGRAPHIC SOCIETY

VIDEODISC
GTV: The American People: Fabric of a Nation

Side 1, Chapter 2
Title: *Kaleidoscope*
Subject: A look at the diversity of Native Americans
Ask: **In what ways did the Native American cultures differ from one another?** *(Answers may include diet, ways of obtaining food, clothing, shelter.)*

CURRICULUM CONNECTION

GEOGRAPHY
Complex webs of communication and trade connected the Hopewell culture to other Native American groups. Far-reaching trade is evident by the many different types of raw materials found in Hopewell artifacts. For example, artifacts found east of the Mississippi contained volcanic glass from Yellowstone, silver from Ontario, copper from the Great Lakes, and meteoric iron from Kansas.

Picturing HISTORY Mound Builder burial traditions included the practice of adding artifacts to the grave. High-ranking leaders often were buried with lavish and extravagant items.
Answer: *It was dominated by a great pyramid-shaped mound and a temple, much like Mexican cities.*

you don't say...

Potlatch The word *potlatch* means "to give away" or "a gift giving." The potlatch was an important and festive gathering of the peoples of the northwestern coast. The gatherings marked great events in the life of a leader, his family, and the village. All guests at a potlatch received gifts ranging from food, baskets, and jewelry to canoes and copper tablets. Those who attended a potlatch were expected to give away greater presents at their own potlatches, ensuring the distribution of wealth among the people.

NATIONAL GEOGRAPHIC SOCIETY

VIDEODISC
GTV: A Geographic Perspective on American History

Side 1, Chapter 2
Title: *Linking Life and Land*
Subject: The first Americans and the effects of geography on their lives (14,000 years ago to the 1500s)
Ask: **What three factors served as a barrier between the different groups of Native Americans?** *(distance, landscape, and language)*

Map Study

Answers
1. Southwest
2. longhouses

Map Skills Practice

Reading a Map Which culture was located the farthest north? *(Inupiat)* Farthest south? *(Seminole)*

The Inuit possessed many skills that helped them survive in the cold Arctic climate. They may have brought some of these skills from northern Siberia, probably their original home. In the winter the Inuit built igloos, low-lying structures of snow blocks, which protected them from severe weather. Their clothing of furs and sealskins was both warm and waterproof. The Inuit were hunters and fishers. In the coastal waters, they pursued whales, seals, and walruses in small, skin-covered boats. On land they hunted caribou, large deerlike animals of the far north.

Hopi Kachina doll

Map Study

Early Native Americans spread throughout the continent and adapted their way of life to the terrain and climate where they settled.

1. **Region** To which culture group did the Apache and Hopi belong?
2. **Analyzing Information** What type of dwelling did the Iroquois build?

MAKING CONNECTIONS ACTIVITY

Daily Life For amusement Native North American peoples played guessing games. Most of these games used simple objects such as pebbles or twigs. The moccasin game was one of the most popular guessing games. It was played on a blanket or an animal hide. Two teams of two players each sat in a circle and placed four moccasins in the center. One player from one team took four small stones, one of which was marked, and placed one stone in each moccasin while the teammate distracted the other players by singing, making faces, or using hand tricks. Then the opposing team made one guess to find the marked stone. The team received a point for a correct guess. Teams rotated hiding and guessing until one team made four correct guesses to win. Explain these rules to students and have them play the game. **L1**

The Inuit made clothing from caribou skins and burned seal oil in lamps.

Peoples of the West

The mild climate and dependable food sources of the West Coast created a favorable environment for many different groups.

The peoples of the northwestern coast, such as the **Tlingit** (TLIHNG•kuht), **Haida,** and **Chinook,** developed a way of life that used the resources of the forest and the sea. They built wooden houses and made canoes, cloth, and baskets from tree bark. Using spears and traps, they fished for salmon along the coast and in rivers such as the Columbia. This large fish was the main food of the northwestern people. They preserved the salmon by smoking it over fires.

Salmon was also important for the people of the plateau region, the area between the Cascade Mountains and the Rocky Mountains. The **Nez Perce** (NEHZ PUHRS) and **Yakima** people fished the rivers, hunted deer in forests, and gathered roots and berries. The root of the camas plant, a relative of the lily, was an important part of their diet. The plateau peoples lived in earthen houses.

Present-day California was home to a great variety of cultures. Along the northern coast, Native Americans fished for their food. In the more barren environment of the southern deserts, nomadic groups wandered from place to place collecting roots and seeds. In the central valley, the **Pomo** gathered acorns and pounded them into flour. As in many Indian cultures, the women of the Pomo did most of the gathering and flour making.

In the Great Basin between the Sierra Nevada and the Rocky Mountains, Native Americans found ways to live in the dry climate. The soil was too hard and rocky for farming, so peoples such as the **Ute** (YOOT) and **Shoshone** (shuh•SHOHN) traveled in search of food. They ate small game, pine nuts, juniper berries, roots, and some insects. Instead of making permanent settlements, the Great Basin people created temporary shelters of branches and reeds.

Linking PAST & PRESENT

What's In a Name?

Perhaps the most obvious sign of our country's Native American heritage is the hundreds of place names that dot the map. Some of these names offer a vivid physical description of the place. *Chattanooga,* for example, means "rock rising to a point," while *Nantucket* means "the faraway place."

Peoples of the Southwest

Descendants of the Anasazi formed the **Hopi,** the **Acoma,** and the **Zuni.** They built their homes from a type of sun-dried mud brick called **adobe.** They raised maize, beans, and squash.

In the 1500s two new groups settled in the region—the **Apache** and the **Navajo.** Unlike the other peoples of the Southwest, the Apache and Navajo were hunters. They chased buffalo and other game. Eventually the Navajo settled into stationary communities and built square houses called hogans. Although they grew maize to add to their diet of buffalo meat, they depended primarily on hunting for food.

Peoples of the Plains

The peoples of the Great Plains were nomadic; villages were temporary, lasting only for a growing season or two. When the people moved from place to place, they dragged their homes—cone-shaped skin tents called tepees—behind them. The men hunted antelope, deer, and buffalo. The women tended plots of maize, squash, and beans.

When the Spanish brought horses to Mexico in the 1500s, some got loose. In time horses made their way north, roaming from Texas to the Great Plains. Native Americans captured and tamed the wild horses, and the Apache, the **Dakota,** and other Plains peoples became skilled riders. They learned to use the horses in warfare, attacking their enemies with long spears, and to hunt on horseback.

CRITICAL THINKING ACTIVITY

Drawing Conclusions Have students review the physical map of North America in the Atlas and the map in this section, *Native American Cultures Before 1500.* Ask them to conclude the impact geography had on the development of specific Native American cultures. For example, the map in this section shows dwellings developed by the Southwest, the Plains, and the Woodlands cultures. Ask students to analyze the physical characteristics of each place to conclude how geography influenced these dwellings: forested areas in Eastern Woodlands–trees for longhouses; Plains with hot summers and cold winters–tepees were cool in summer and warm in winter; Southwest desert–adobe mud used for pueblos. **L3**

Linking PAST & PRESENT

State Names Many states have Native American names. *Kentucky* is Iroquois for "meadowland"; *Massachusetts* means "at the big hill" in Algonquian; *Mississippi* is Chippewa for "big river"; and *Utah* means "higher up" in Navajo.

NATIONAL GEOGRAPHIC SOCIETY

CD-ROM
NGS PictureShow: Native Americans, Part 1

Introduce students to the major Native American cultures in the Eastern Woodlands by having them click one group on the main menu. Suggest they research the housing style of one group and report what they find to the class.

3 ASSESS

Assign Section 3 Review as homework or as an in-class activity.

Section Quiz 1–3

Name ______ Date ______ Class ______

★ Chapter 1

Score

Section Quiz 1-3

DIRECTIONS: Matching Match each item in Column A with the items in Column B. Write the correct letters in the blanks. *(10 points each)*

Column A	Column B
____ 1. cliff dwellers	A. Iroquois
____ 2. Mound Builders	B. Plains peoples
____ 3. lived in hogans	C. Hopewell
____ 4. nomads	D. Anasazi
____ 5. peacemakers	E. Navajo

DIRECTIONS: Multiple Choice In the blank at the left, write the letter of the choice that best completes the statement or answers the question. *(10 points each)*

____ 6. These were native peoples who dug hundreds of miles of irrigation channels.
A. Mound Builders C. Hohokam
B. Sinagua D. Anasazi

____ 7. These Native Americans made clothing from sealskins.
A. Nez Perce C. Haida
B. Inuit D. Chinook

____ 8. These native peoples became skilled at riding horses.
A. peoples of the East C. peoples of the Southwest
B. peoples of the Southeast D. peoples of the Plains

____ 9. This constitution shows women had a strong voice in government.
A. Iroquois League C. United States
B. Oneida Nation D. Mohawk Nation

____ 10. The largest settlement of the Mound Builders was
A. Mesa Verde. C. Cahokia.
B. Pueblo Bonito. D. Seneca.

The American Journey ★ 3 ★ **Section Quizzes**

CHAPTER 1
Section 3, 27–32

Use **Chapter Challenger Interactive Review Software** to review Section 3.

Reteaching Activity 1–3

Name ________________ Date ____________ Class ________

★ Reteaching Activity 1-3

DIRECTIONS: Completion In the space provided, write the word or words that best complete the sentence.

Present-day Arizona was home to the **(1)** ________________ people. Their way of life depended on the **(2)** ________________ they dug to carry water to their fields. The **(3)** ________________ lived in the area known as the Four Corners in great stone dwellings called **(4)** ________________, or villages, as well as in cliff dwellings in the walls of steep cliffs.

Several different groups of peoples, known as **(5)** ________________ built thousands of mounds of earth in central North America. Among the earliest of these groups were the **(6)** ________________ who built the Great Serpent Mound. The largest settlement was **(7)** ________________.

The last group of people to cross the Beringia land bridge into North America are called the **(8)** ________________. Their main occupations were **(9)** ________________.

The mild climate and dependable food sources of the **(10)** ________________ created a favorable environment for many different Native American groups including the Tlingit, Haida, and Chinook, who adapted their way of life to the **(11)** ________________; the people of the **(12)** ________________, an area between the Cascade Mountains and the Rocky Mountains; and those who settled in the **(13)** ________________ between the Sierra Nevada and the Rocky Mountains. The peoples of the Great Plains were **(14)** ________________, traveling from place to place in search of food.

Native Americans who lived in eastern North America formed complex political systems to govern their nations. After years of warring, the five Iroquois groups joined an organization called the **(15)** ________________. Among those who settled in the Southeast were the Creek, Chickasaw, and **(16)** ________________, who farmed the mountains of Georgia and Alabama.

Enrichment Activity 1–3

Name ________________ Date ____________ Class ________

★ Enrichment Activity 1-3 ★ ★

Native American Words

English settlers in America borrowed many words from the Native Americans. Over the centuries since Europeans first came to the Americas, many Native American words have become part of the English language. Find out more about some of these words below.

DIRECTIONS: Finding Definitions Use a dictionary to find out what each of the following words means. Write the definition to the left of the word. Then look at the list of Native American words in the box at the bottom of the page and write the Native American word from which the term was borrowed.

Definition		Native American Word
________________	1. mugwump	________________
________________	2. high-muck-a-muck	________________
________________	3. pemmican	________________
________________	4. bayou	________________
________________	5. succotash	________________
________________	6. pone	________________
________________	7. toboggan	________________
________________	8. anorak	________________

msickquatash	annoraaq	hayo makamak	tophagan
pimihkaan	bayuk	poan	mugguomp

4 CLOSE

Discuss the ways in which Native American groups adapted to their environment.

Citizenship

Peoples of the East

The Native Americans who lived in the woodlands of eastern North America formed complex political systems to govern their nations. The **Iroquois** (IHR•uh•KWAWIH) and **Cherokee** had formal law codes. They also formed **federations,** governments that linked different groups.

The Iroquois lived near Canada in what is now northern New York State. There were five Iroquois groups or nations: the **Onondaga,** the **Seneca,** the **Mohawk,** the **Oneida,** and the **Cayuga.** These groups warred with each other until the late 1500s, when they joined in an organization called the Iroquois League.

Iroquois women occupied positions of power and importance in their communities. They owned the land and were responsible for the planting and harvesting of crops. Women also had a strong voice in the community's government. According to the constitution of the Iroquois League, women chose the 50 men who served on the league council.

The Iroquois constitution was written down after the Europeans came to North America. It describes the Iroquois peoples' desire for peace:

> "I am Dekanawidah and with the Five Nations' Confederate Lords I plant the Tree of Great Peace. . . . Roots have spread out from the Tree of the Great Peace, one to the north, one to the east, one to the south and one to the west. The name of these roots is The Great White Roots and their nature is Peace and Strength."

Peoples of the Southeast

The Southeast was also a woodlands area, but with a warmer climate than the eastern woodlands. The Creek, Chickasaw, and Cherokee were among the region's Native American peoples. Many Creek lived in loosely knit farming communities in present-day Georgia and Alabama. There they grew corn, tobacco, squash, and other crops. The Chickasaw, most of whom lived farther west in what is now Mississippi, farmed the river bottomlands. The Cherokee farmed in the mountains of Georgia and the Carolinas.

Wherever they lived in North America, the first Americans developed ways of life that were well suited to their environments. In the 1500s, however, the Native Americans met people whose cultures, beliefs, and ways of life were different from anything they had known or ever seen. These newcomers were the Europeans, and their arrival would change the Native Americans' world forever.

Section 3 Review

Checking for Understanding

1. ***Identify*** Hohokam, Anasazi, Mound Builders, Hopewell, Inuit, Iroquois.
2. ***Define*** pueblo, drought, adobe, federation.
3. ***Identify*** clues that led archaeologists to believe that the Mound Builders were influenced by other cultures.

Reviewing Themes

4. **Groups and Institutions** What organization did the Iroquois form to promote peace among their people?

Critical Thinking

5. **Making Generalizations** Why was the environment of the West Coast favorable for settlement by so many groups of Native Americans?

Activity

Designing a Home Draw a model of a home that a Native American could have built. Use natural materials that exist in the area where you live and label the materials on your diagram. Consider the climate of your area in your design.

Section 3 Review Answers

1. Hohokam, 27; Anasazi, 28; Mound Builders, 28; Hopewell, 28; Inuit, 29; Iroquois, 32
2. The words are defined in the Glossary.
3. Some mounds had temples like Maya and Aztec cultures; artifacts indicate widespread trade.
4. the Iroquois League
5. mild climate; dependable food sources; plentiful forest resources

Activity Home designs should incorporate resources and climate found in the area where the student lives. Label materials.

Multimedia Activities

ABCNEWS INTERACTIVE™ Historic America Electronic Field Trips

Field Trip to Cahokia Mounds

Setting up the Video

Work with a group of your classmates to view "Cahokia Mounds" on the videodisc ***Historic America: Electronic Field Trips***. The community of Cahokia, built about 1,000 years ago, left huge mounds dotting the surrounding landscape. This mound-building civilization, located in present-day Illinois, may have had 30,000 or more residents. The program shows students working with guides to protect the mounds.

Hands-On Activity

Just as the Cahokia mounds revealed details of the Cahokia people, modern monuments and buildings express who we, as Americans, are today. Create a collage of photographs showing American architecture and monuments. Write captions that explain what the buildings reveal about modern American society.

Side 1, Chapter 3

View the video by scanning the bar code or by entering the chapter number on your keypad and pressing Search.

Surfing the "Net"

Modern Explorers

Many European explorers used primitive navigational instruments to help guide them in finding new places. Today, people explore new and exciting places by using the Internet. To become a modern explorer, follow the instructions below.

Getting There

Pick a country you would like to know more about. Follow these steps to gather information about this place.

1. Use a search engine. Type in the name of the country that you want to learn more about.
2. After the country's name, enter words like the following to find more specific information about this place:
   - *geography*
   - *maps*
   - *population*
   - *travel*
   - *culture*
   - *sports*
3. The search engine will provide you with a number of links to follow. Links are "pointers" to different sites on the Internet and commonly appear as blue underlined words.

What to Do When You Are There

Once you are at the country you have chosen, click on the links to navigate through the pages of information. Gather your findings by creating a fact sheet using a word processor. Using the findings, create an illustrated map of the region you explored. Attach your facts to the map.

TEACHER'S NOTES

ABCNEWS INTERACTIVE™

VIDEODISC
Historic America
Electronic Field Trips

Side 1, Chapter 3
Title: *Cahokia Mounds*

If you do not have access to a videodisc player, the **Historic America Electronic Field Trips** are also available in VHS.

Internet Sites

The following are possible sites for completing the "Net" activities:

Virtual Tourist
http://www.vtourist.com/webmap/europe.htm

Fodor's
http://www.fodors.com/

State Department Travel Warnings Consular Information
http://travel.state.gov/travel_warnings.html

Not on the "Net" . . .

If students have limited or no access to the Internet, have them complete the "Modern Explorers" activity by using the electronic card catalog at the school or local library. At the s: prompt, students should type in the name of the country they would like to know more about. They should then use the call numbers to find the books they need to complete their research.

GLENCOE TECHNOLOGY

VIDEODISC
MindJogger Videoquiz

Use MindJogger to review the Chapter 1 content.

Chapter 1
Disc 1, Side A

Also available in VHS.

Reviewing Key Terms

The key terms used in this activity are defined in the textbook glossary on pages A26–A35.

Reviewing Key Facts

1. searching for game or to follow herds of animals
2. maize
3. easy to defend; protection from weather
4. more mobile; more skilled hunters; more skilled warriors

Critical Thinking

1. Answers should refer to at least two of the following: supported larger populations; provided more goods for trade; allowed for more free time to develop a more complex society.
2. Answers will vary but should demonstrate an understanding that the climate of each area was similar, making adaptation easier.

Review and Activities

Reviewing Key Terms

On a sheet of paper, define the following terms:

archaeology	culture
artifact	civilization
Ice Age	hieroglyphics
nomad	pueblo
carbon dating	federation

Reviewing Key Facts

1. Why did Asians cross the land bridge to the Americas?
2. What was the first crop raised by Native Americans in Mexico?
3. What were two advantages of living in cliff dwellings?
4. How did horses change the lives of Native Americans who lived on the Great Plains?

Critical Thinking

Analyzing Information

Over time Native Americans formed unique cultures.

1. In what ways did farming contribute to the growth of large empires in Central and South America?
2. How did living in Siberia help the Inuit adapt to life in the Arctic region?

Time Line Activity

Create a time line on which you place the following events in chronological order.

- Europeans arrive in the Americas
- Asian hunters cross Beringia
- Inca establish their capital at Cuzco
- Maya civilization begins to decline
- Mound Builders begin building mounds
- Native Americans in Mexico learn to grow maize

Reviewing Themes

1. **Geography and History** In what ways did the environment of Native Americans who lived in the Northwest differ from the environment of those who lived in the Southwest?
2. **Culture and Traditions** How do we know that religion was an important part of Native American life?
3. **Groups and Institutions** How did the Inca and Aztec use war to increase their power?

Geography Activity

Study the map below and answer the questions that follow.

Selected Sites of the Mound Builders

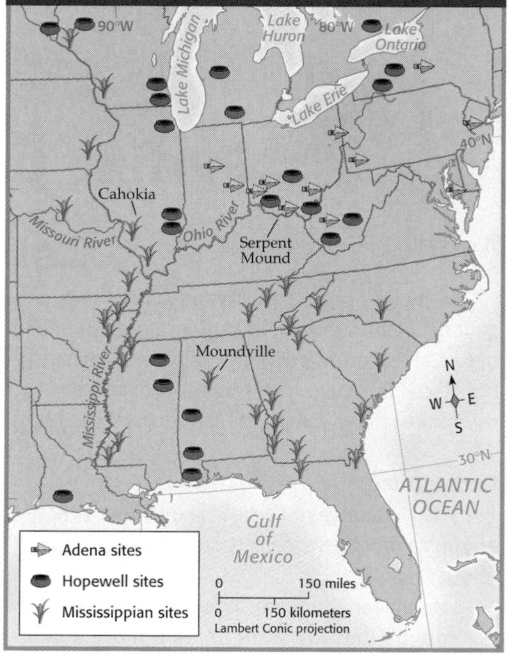

1. **Location** Along what two major rivers did many of the Mound Builders settle?

Time Line Activity

Events should be placed in this order: Asian hunters cross Beringia, Native Americans in Mexico learn to grow maize, Mound Builders begin building mounds, Maya civilization begins to decline, Inca establish their capital at Cuzco, Europeans arrive in the Americas

Reviewing Themes

1. Northwest: plentiful natural resources and a mild climate; Southwest: scarce natural resources and extreme climate
2. Answers will vary but should refer to the following evidence of religious activity: temples and monuments, hieroglyphics, human sacrifices, priests' prominent role in the culture, astronomy, calendars.
3. They conquered others to increase population and land area.

Geography Activity

1. Mississippi and Ohio
2. Ohio
3. Adena

2. **Place** Near which river did the Adena build most of their settlements?
3. **Movement** Of the Adena, Hopewell, and Mississippian cultures, which settled the farthest east?

★ Skill Practice Activity

Understanding the Parts of a Map

Use the key, compass rose, and scale bar on the map of early Ohio villages to answer the questions that follow.

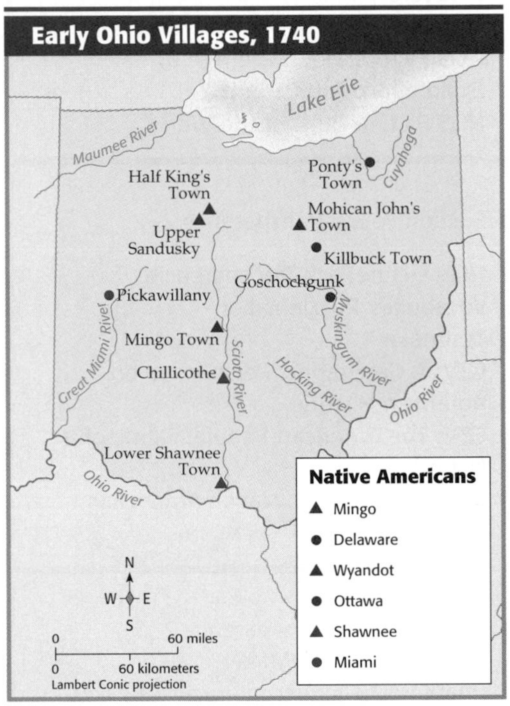

1. What does the map key highlight?
2. About how far from Lake Erie was Mohican John's Town?
3. Which Native Americans settled Goschochgunk?
4. Which town was farther west--Pickawillany or Upper Sandusky?
5. What village is located along the Ohio River?

★ Technology Activity

Using the Internet Search the Internet for a Web site created by a modern Native American organization or group. Based on information you find at the Web site, explain the group's purpose or goals. How do you think this group's activities will help to preserve the culture of Native Americans?

★ Cooperative Activity

History and Art Create a Native American artifact museum for your classroom. With a partner, find an existing photo or illustration (or make your own drawing or model) of a Native American artifact created before 1500. Label your artifact with the name of the Native American group that created it, the approximate date it was made, a description of how it was used, and the materials from which it was made. Mount your artifact on cardboard and display it with other artifacts in a classroom "museum."

Portfolio Activity **History Journal** Scan the chapter to find information describing trade among early Native American groups. Write a shopping list of at least five items that you think would have been most valuable to you if you were living during this time. Next to each item, draw a hieroglyph, or symbol, to represent that item.

Technology Activity

Students should locate one Web site of a Native American group, explain the group's purpose or goals, and explain how that group helps preserve Native American culture.

Cooperative Activity

Pairs should create an artifact display on cardboard for the classroom "museum." The display should include the name of the Native American group that created the artifact, the date it was made, a description of its use, and the materials from which it was made.

Portfolio Activity Students should describe at least five trade items that they would have considered most valuable to them at that time. There should be symbols or hieroglyphs next to each item.

Chapter Bonus Test Question

Ask: **What was the population of Tenochtitlán when Cortés invaded it?** *(300,000 people, perhaps larger than any city in Europe except London)*

Skill Practice Activity

1. Native American culture groups
2. about 40 miles (60 km)
3. Delaware
4. Pickawillany
5. Lower Shawnee Town

Chapter 2 Planning Guide

A complete, 1-page lesson plan is provided for each section in the *Reproducible Lesson Plans* booklet.

Section Resources

Daily Objectives	Reproducible Resources	Multimedia Resources
Section 1 A Changing World Examine how cultural, economic, political, and technological factors led to overseas exploration.	Reproducible Lesson Plan 2–1 Guided Reading Activity 2–1* Section Quiz 2–1* Reteaching Activity 2–1 Enrichment Activity 2–1	Section Focus Transparency 2–1 Vocabulary PuzzleMaker Chapter Challenger Interactive Review Software Testmaker NGS PictureShow: The Age of Exploration, Parts 1 and 2 NGS Picture Atlas of the World
Section 2 Early Exploration Explain Portugal's and Spain's leadership roles in exploration.	Reproducible Lesson Plan 2–2 Guided Reading Activity 2–2* Section Quiz 2–2* Reteaching Activity 2–2 Enrichment Activity 2–2	Section Focus Transparency 2–2 NGS PicturePack Transparencies Vocabulary PuzzleMaker Testmaker GTV: A Geographic Perspective on American History GTV: The American People: Fabric of a Nation NGS PictureShow: Native Americans, Part 2
Section 3 Spain in America Evaluate the decline of the Aztec and Inca Empires and the rise of Spanish rule in the Americas.	Reproducible Lesson Plan 2–3 Guided Reading Activity 2–3* Section Quiz 2–3* Reteaching Activity 2–3 Enrichment Activity 2–3	Section Focus Transparency 2–3 Vocabulary PuzzleMaker Chapter Challenger Interactive Review Software Testmaker ABCNews InterActive™ Historic America Electronic Field Trips GTV: The American People: Fabric of a Nation
Section 4 Exploring North America Summarize the religious and economic reasons for exploration of North America.	Reproducible Lesson Plan 2–4 Guided Reading Activity 2–4* Section Quiz 2–4* Reteaching Activity 2–4 Enrichment Activity 2–4	Section Focus Transparency 2–4 Vocabulary PuzzleMaker Chapter Challenger Interactive Review Software Testmaker GTV: The American People: Fabric of a Nation NGS PictureShow: The Age of Exploration, Part 1

** Also available in Spanish*

Blackline Master · Videodisc · Audiocassette · Music Program · Transparency · CD-ROM · Software

0:00 **OUT OF TIME?**
Assign the Chapter 2 Digest and the corresponding Chapter Digests Audiocassettes with activities and tests.

ACTIVITY

From the Classroom of...

Jane Spivey
J.N. Fries Middle School
Concord, NC

Play a Historical Memory Game

Begin with 50 to 60 large index cards. Number one side of each card consecutively from 1 to 50 or 60. Shuffle the cards thoroughly, and pull two at a time from the pile. On the reverse side of one card write down a historical person's name, a date, a place, or an event. On the reverse side of the second card write down something that links the two cards. For example, label the first card "Columbus's Ships," and label the second card "Niña, Pinta, and Santa María." Use all cards. If possible, illustrate the cards with pictures from old magazines or textbooks.

Organize students into groups of five or six. Appoint a spokesperson, a recorder, and a card turner for each group. The cards should be turned numbered side up on the floor or a large table. Each group takes turns calling a number and trying to match that card's fact with its mate. Groups alternate until one group makes a match. Then the group recorder scores a point for the group, and the next group takes its turn. The group with the most points wins.

Block Schedule

Block scheduling differs from traditional class scheduling in the amount of time allotted to each period. The extended time frame provided by block scheduling affords you the opportunity to implement a greater number of research-oriented and activity-intense projects to motivate and involve your students. Activities that are particularly suited to use within the block scheduling framework are identified throughout this chapter by the following designation:

NATIONAL GEOGRAPHIC SOCIETY Teacher's Corner

INDEX TO NATIONAL GEOGRAPHIC MAGAZINE

The following articles may be used for research relating to this chapter:

- "The Old Ones of the Southwest," by David Roberts, April 1996.
- "New Face for a Desert Mission," by Alice J. Hall, December 1995.
- "The Timeless Vision of Teotihuacán," by George E. Stuart, December 1995.
- "Simón Bolívar: El Libertador," by Brian Hodgson, March 1994.
- "Portugal's Sea Road to the East," by Merle Severy, November 1992.

NATIONAL GEOGRAPHIC SOCIETY PRODUCTS AVAILABLE FROM GLENCOE

To order the following products for use with this chapter, contact your local Glencoe sales representative, or call Glencoe at 1-800-334-7344:

- *GTV: A Geographic Perspective on American History* (Videodisc)
- *GTV: The American People: Fabric of a Nation* (Videodisc)
- *PictureShow: Native Americans, 1 and 2,* (CD-ROM, Transparencies)
- *PictureShow: The Age of Exploration, 1* (CD-ROM, Transparencies)
- *PictureShow: The Renaissance* (CD-ROM, Transparencies)
- *Native Americans* (Poster Set)
- *PictureShow: Ancient Civilizations: Middle and South America* (CD-ROM, Transparencies)

ADDITIONAL NATIONAL GEOGRAPHIC SOCIETY PRODUCTS

To order the following products for use with this chapter, call National Geographic Society at 1-800-368-2728:

- *Native American Heritage: A Visitor's Guide* (Map)
- *Indians of North America* (Map)
- *The World of the American Indian* (Book)
- *American Indians: A Brief History* (Video)
- *Historical Atlas of the United States* (Atlas)

KEY TO ABILITY LEVELS

Teaching strategies have been coded for varying learning styles and abilities.

L1 **BASIC** activities for all students
L2 **AVERAGE** activities for average to above-average students
L3 **CHALLENGING** activities for above-average students
ELL **ENGLISH LANGUAGE LEARNER** activities

Chapter 2 Resource Guide

Home Involvement

Home Involvement Activity 2

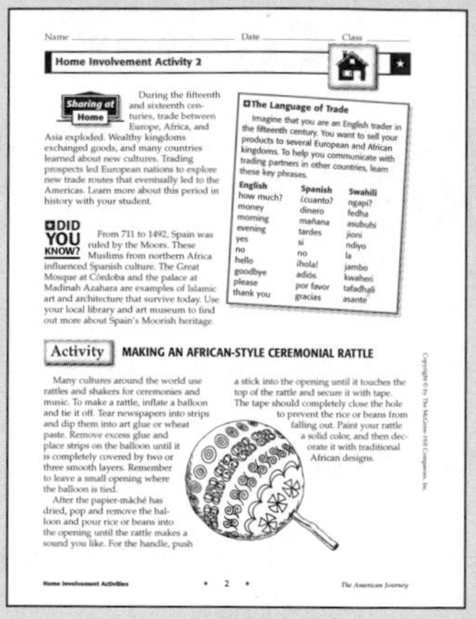

Review Activities

Chapter Summary 2

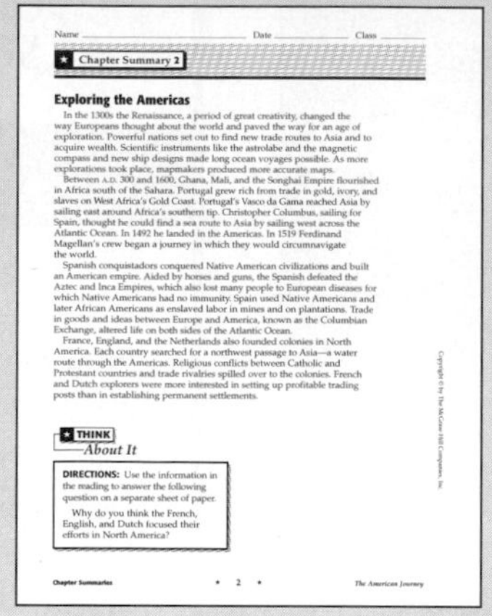

Workbook Activity 2

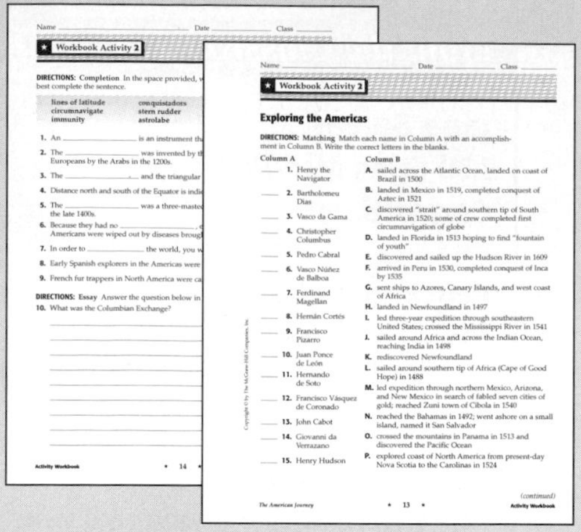

Reinforcement Activities

Time Line Activity 2

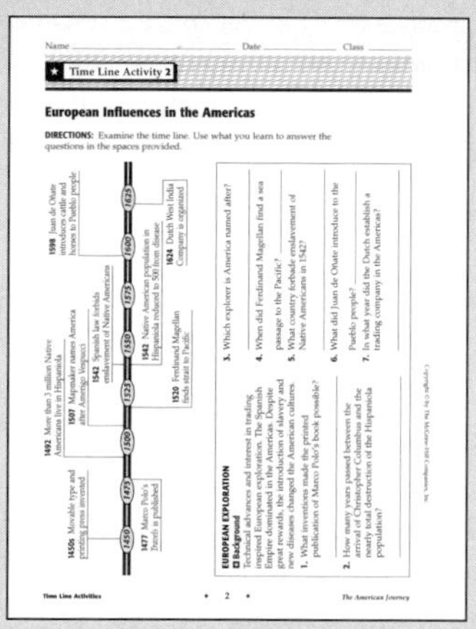

Vocabulary Activity 2

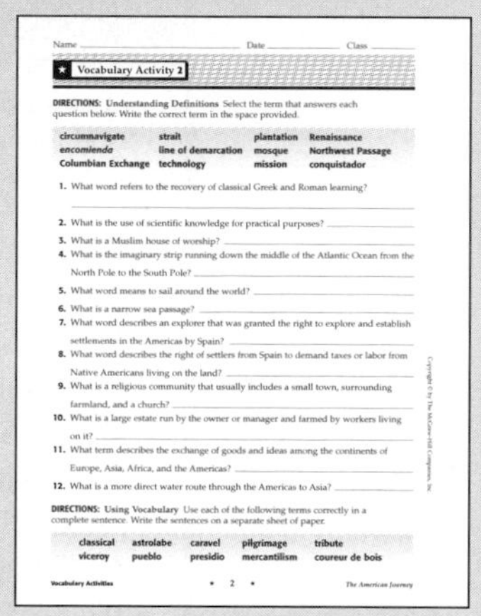

Chapter Skills Activity 2

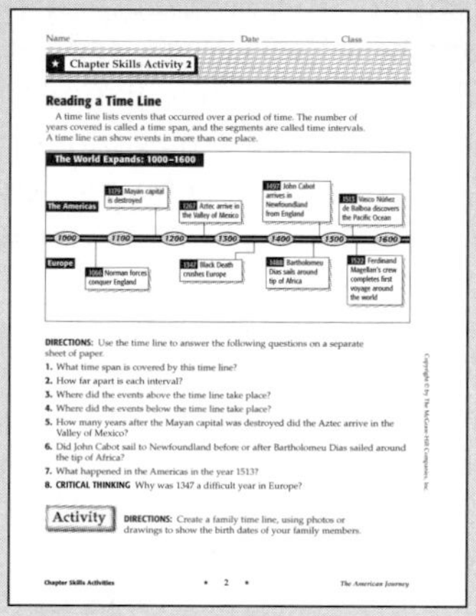

Enrichment Activities

Linking Past and Present Activity 2

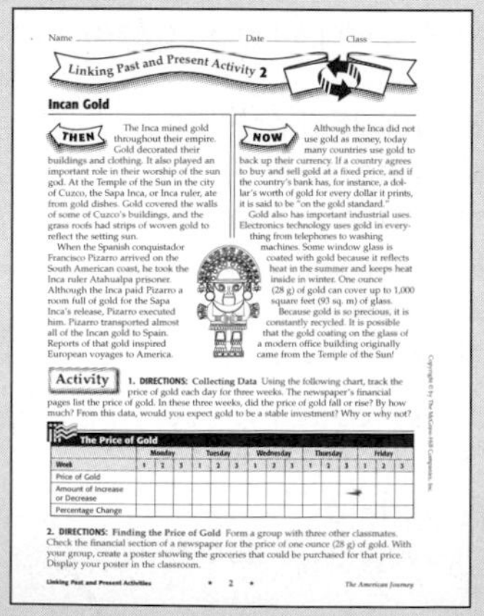

Primary Source Reading 2

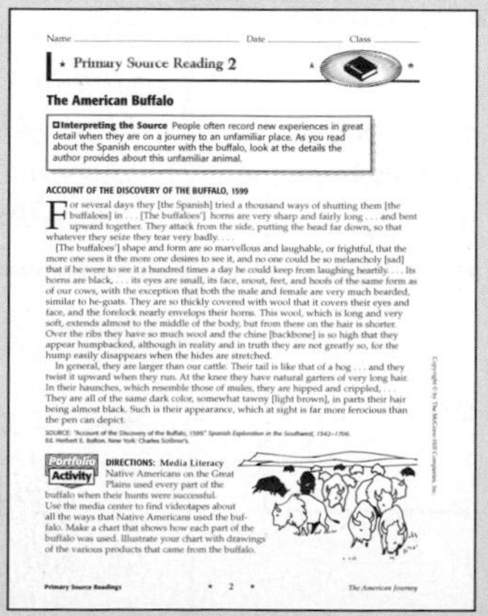

Geography Activities

Mapping History Activity 2

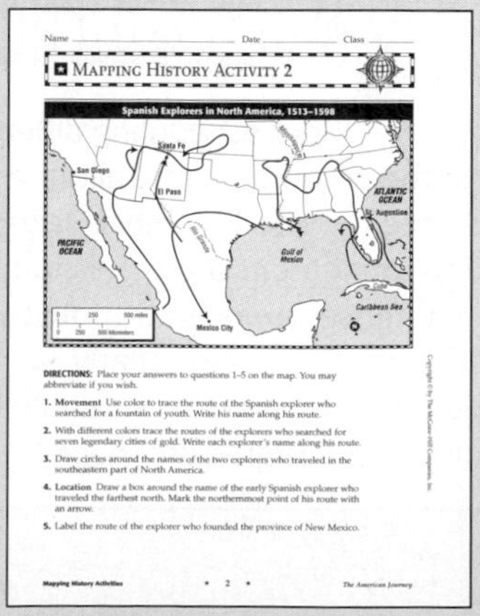

ASSESSMENT

Chapter 2 Test, Form A

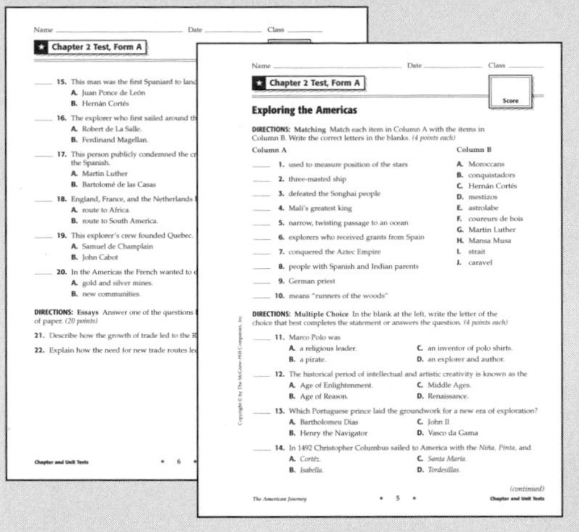

Chapter 2 Test, Form B

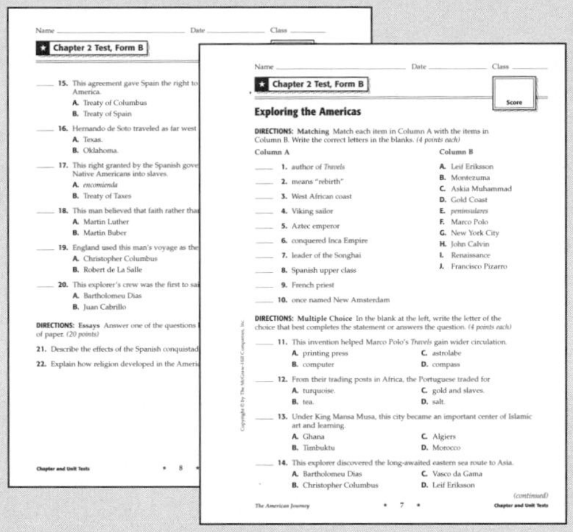

Performance Assessment Activity 2

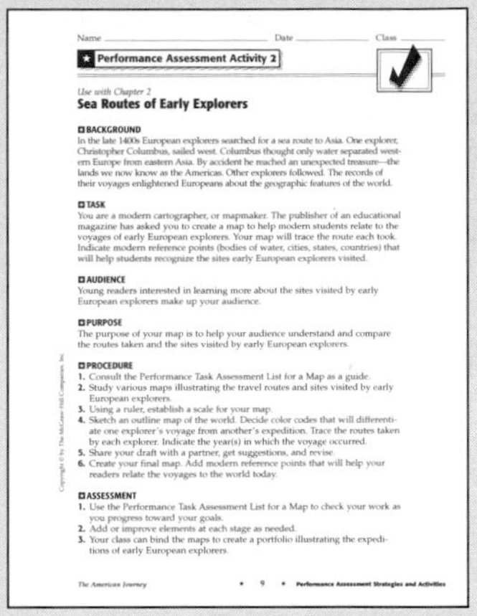

SPANISH RESOURCES

The following Spanish language materials are available in the Spanish Resources binder:

- **Spanish Chapter Summary 2**
- **Spanish Vocabulary Activity 2**
- **Spanish Guided Reading Activities, Chapter 2**
- **Spanish Section Quizzes, Chapter 2**
- **Spanish Home Involvement Activity 2**
- **Spanish Chapter 2 Digests Audiocassette Activity and Test**

ACTIVITY MANIPULATIVES

Help students learn more about America's cultural history with:

- **American Crafts Hands-On Activities**
- **American Games Hands-On Activities**
- **American History Flash Cards**

ADDITIONAL RESOURCES FROM GLENCOE

- **U.S. History & Art,** Transparency 3, *Mission San Xavier del Bac*
- **Political Cartoons,** *Columbus, Then and Now*
- **Outline Map Resource Book**
- **U.S. Desk Map**

A&E HOME VIDEO. Biography THE HISTORY CHANNEL.

The following videotape programs are available from Glencoe as supplements to Chapter 2:

- **The Vikings in North America** (ISBN 1-56501-663-7)
- **Leif Ericson: Voyages of a Viking** (ISBN 1-56501-673-4)
- **Marco Polo: Journey to the East** (ISBN 1-56501-668-8)
- **Christopher Columbus: Explorer of the New World** (ISBN 1-56501-667-X)
- **Ponce de León: The First Conquistador** (ISBN 1-56501-669-6)

To order, call Glencoe at 1-800-334-7344. To find classroom resources to accompany many of these videos, check the following home pages:
A&E Television: http://www.aetv.com
The History Channel: http://www.historychannel.com

Introducing CHAPTER 2

Chapter Themes

Chapter Themes are listed by section on this chapter opening page of the Student Edition. A corresponding theme-based activity is available under "FOCUS," and a theme-based question is asked in the Section and Chapter Reviews.

Performance Assessment

Refer to Activity 2 in the *Performance Assessment Strategies and Activities* booklet.

GLENCOE TECHNOLOGY

VIDEODISC
MindJogger Videoquiz

Use MindJogger to preview the Chapter 2 content.

Chapter 2
Disc 1, Side A

Also available in VHS.

HISTORY AND ART John Vanderlyn's paintings reflect a unique American style that emerged in the 1830s and 1840s. **Ask:** According to Vanderlyn's painting, what did Columbus do when he first landed in the Americas? *(claimed land for Spain by planting a flag)*

Chapter 2

1400–1625

Exploring the Americas

Why It's Important

The Americas today consist of peoples from cultures from around the globe. Although the English have been the dominant influence on United States history, they are only part of the story. The Native Americans, Spanish, Africans, and other peoples who are discussed in this chapter have all played key roles in shaping the culture we now call American.

Chapter Themes

- *Section 1*, Culture and Traditions
- *Section 2*, Geography and History
- *Section 3*, Groups and Institutions
- *Section 4*, Global Connections

HISTORY AND ART ***Landing of Columbus*** **by John Vanderlyn** The European explorations of North America were common subjects for American artists. This painting of Columbus's arrival in the Americas was done by American artist John Vanderlyn in the early 1840s.

EXTRA CREDIT PROJECT

Diagramming Tools of Exploration Have interested students research one technological discovery or improvement mentioned in this chapter. Ask students to draw labeled diagrams on poster board illustrating the technology. Have students present their completed diagrams to the class and explain how the technology works and its impact on exploration.

1200 — 1300 — 1400 — 1500 — 1600

1271 Marco Polo travels to China from Italy

1324 Mansa Musa makes a pilgrimage to Makkah

1400s Renaissance spreads throughout Europe

1500s Songhai Empire rises in Africa

Section 1

A Changing World

Read to Discover . . .

- how the Renaissance and economic and political developments led Europeans to invest in overseas exploration.
- how technology helped make long sea voyages possible.
- how great civilizations flourished in Africa.

Terms to Learn

classical	caravel
Renaissance	pilgrimage
technology	mosque
astrolabe	

The Storyteller

In 1271 Marco Polo set off from the city of Venice on a great trek across Asia to China. Only 17 years old at the time, Polo journeyed with his father and uncle, both Venetian merchants. Traveling on camels for more than 3 years, the merchants crossed almost 7,000 miles (11,263 km) of mountains and deserts. Finally they reached the palace of Kublai Khan (KOO•bluh KAHN), the Mongol emperor of China. There Marco Polo spent 17 years working for the Khan and learning much about China's advanced culture.

Marco Polo

When **Marco Polo** returned to Venice from China in 1295, he wrote an account of the marvels of Asia. He described exotic lands and peoples, great riches, and splendid cities. Polo called the Chinese city of Hangzhou the greatest city in the world, exclaiming that it had "so many pleasures . . . that one fancies himself to be in Paradise." He wrote of things like paper money and coal that filled Europeans with wonder.

Translated into many languages, Polo's *Travels* was eagerly read throughout western Europe. Almost 200 years later, when Columbus set sail from Spain, he hoped to find the golden roofs of Cipangu (Japan) that Marco Polo had described but never seen.

Expanding Horizons

For centuries after the fall of the Roman Empire, the people of western Europe lived in a fairly self-contained world. This world, dominated by the Catholic Church, was divided into many small kingdoms and city-states.

A Growing Interest

Most Europeans knew little about India, China, or the rest of Asia and had no idea that the Western Hemisphere existed. However, as the story of Marco Polo spread and exotic goods from the East appeared in marketplaces in Europe, more people became interested in these distant lands.

Section Resources

Reproducible Masters

- Reproducible Lesson Plan 2–1
- Guided Reading Activity 2–1
- Section Quiz 2–1
- Reteaching Activity 2–1
- Enrichment Activity 2–1

Transparencies

- Section Focus Transparency 2–1

Multimedia

- Vocabulary PuzzleMaker
- Chapter Challenger Interactive Review Software
- Testmaker
- NGS PictureShow: The Age of Exploration, Parts 1 and 2
- NGS Picture Atlas of the World

1 Focus

BELLRINGER
Motivational Activity

Before taking roll at the beginning of the class period, project Section Focus Transparency 2–1 and have students answer the questions. Discuss students' responses.

This activity is also available as a blackline master.

Section Focus Transparency 2–1

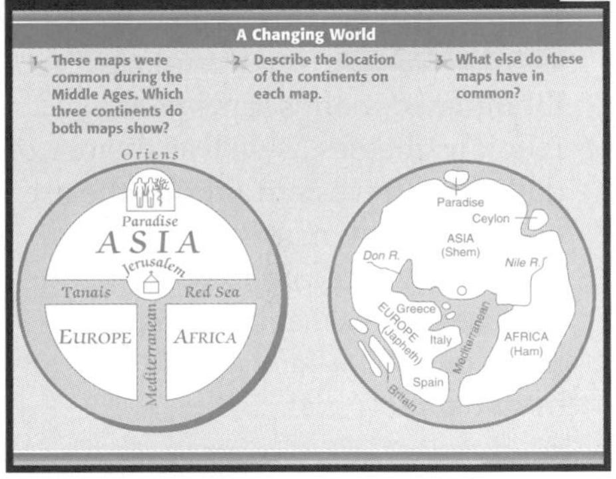

Vocabulary Precheck

Point out that the word *technology* is derived from Greek words meaning "skill" and "theory." Encourage students to define the term based on this information.

Use the **Vocabulary PuzzleMaker** to create crossword and word search puzzles.

Section Theme
Culture and Traditions

The spirit of the Renaissance dramatically changed the way Europeans thought about themselves and the world.

Activity Have students scan the section to list goods that Europeans desired from other lands. Ask students to discuss why Renaissance Europeans valued these items.

CHAPTER 2
Section 1, 37–41

2 TEACH

L1 Categorizing Organize the class into small groups. Have each group review the section to find all the reasons for exploration. Each group should create a chart listing the reasons. To make the chart, have students categorize each reason under the following headings: Cultural, Economic, Political, and Technological. Encourage students to incorporate graphics into their charts.

Picturing HISTORY The brilliantly colored paintings on illuminated manuscripts portrayed religious themes as well as themes of daily life. In western Europe the art of illuminating manuscripts provided a vivid record of daily life between A.D. 300 and the 1200s. **Answer:** *bustling city life, busy canal traffic*

Guided Reading Activity 2–1

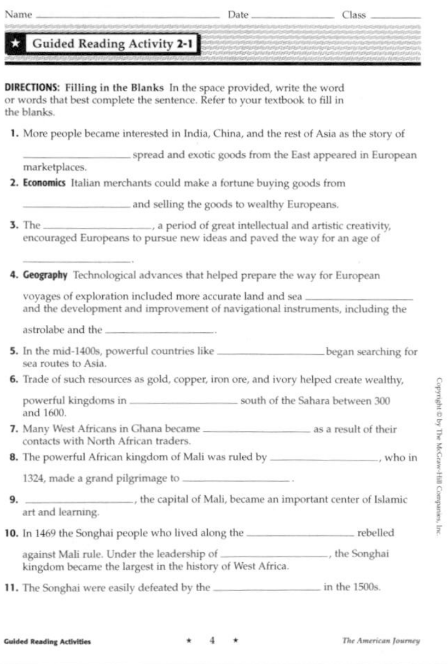
Name ______ Date ______ Class ______

Guided Reading Activity 2-1

DIRECTIONS: Filling in the Blanks In the space provided, write the word or words that best complete the sentence. Refer to your textbook to fill in the blanks.

1. More people became interested in India, China, and the rest of Asia as the story of ______ spread and exotic goods from the East appeared in European marketplaces.
2. **Economics** Italian merchants could make a fortune buying goods from ______ and selling the goods to wealthy Europeans.
3. The ______, a period of great intellectual and artistic creativity, encouraged Europeans to pursue new ideas and paved the way for an age of ______.
4. **Geography** Technological advances that helped prepare the way for European voyages of exploration included more accurate land and sea ______ and the development and improvement of navigational instruments, including the astrolabe and the ______.
5. In the mid-1400s, powerful countries like ______ began searching for sea routes to Asia.
6. Trade of such resources as gold, copper, iron ore, and ivory helped create wealthy, powerful kingdoms in ______ south of the Sahara between 300 and 1600.
7. Many West Africans in Ghana became ______ as a result of their contacts with North African traders.
8. The powerful African kingdom of Mali was ruled by ______, who in 1324, made a grand pilgrimage to ______.
9. ______, the capital of Mali, became an important center of Islamic art and learning.
10. In 1469 the Songhai people who lived along the ______ rebelled against Mali rule. Under the leadership of ______, the Songhai kingdom became the largest in the history of West Africa.
11. The Songhai were easily defeated by the ______ in the 1500s.

Guided Reading Activities ★ 4 ★ *The American Journey*

Picturing HISTORY During the 1200s, Europeans created illuminated manuscripts decorated with beautiful lettering and miniature paintings. As shown in this miniature painting, Marco Polo sets sail from Venice for his journey to China in 1271. **What does the painting reveal about life in Venice during the 1200s?**

Economics

The Growth of Trade

Merchants could make a fortune selling goods from the Orient. Wealthy Europeans clamored for cinnamon, pepper, cloves, and other spices. They also wanted perfumes, silks, and precious stones from India and Persia. Italian merchants obliged.

Buying the goods from Arab traders in the Middle East, the merchants sent them overland by caravan to the **Mediterranean Sea** and then by ship to Italian ports. The cities of Venice, Genoa, and Pisa prospered as centers of the growing East-West trade.

The Growth of Ideas

In the 1300s a powerful new spirit emerged in the Italian city-states and spread throughout Europe. The development of banking and the expansion of trade with Asia enriched Italian merchants. Wealthy citizens were able to pursue an interest in the region's past, to learn more about the glorious civilizations of ancient Rome and Greece.

Because they wanted to improve their knowledge of people and the world, Italians studied the **classical**—ancient Greek and Roman—works with new interest. Scholars translated Greek manuscripts on philosophy, poetry, and science. Many thinkers of this period began to take an experimental approach to science, testing new and old theories and evaluating the results.

Influenced by the classical texts, many authors wrote of the individual and the universe in a secular, or nonreligious, way. Artists studied the sculpture and architecture of the classical world. They particularly admired the harmony and balance in Greek art with its realistic way of portraying people.

The Renaissance

This period of intellectual and artistic creativity became known as the **Renaissance** (REH•nuh•SAHNTS). A French word meaning "rebirth," it refers to the recovery of classical Greek and Roman learning. Over the next two centuries, the Renaissance spread north, south, and west, reaching Spain and northern Europe in the 1400s.

The spirit of the Renaissance dramatically changed the way Europeans thought about themselves and the world. It encouraged them to pursue new ideas and set new goals, paving the way for an age of exploration and discovery.

Footnotes to History

Preserving Meat In the days before refrigeration, salt was used to preserve meats. Europeans wanted pepper and other spices to cover the extremely salty taste or, even worse, the taste of spoiled meat.

COOPERATIVE LEARNING ACTIVITY

Designing a Book Jacket Organize students into groups of four to design a book jacket for Marco Polo's book *Travels.* Have each group use information in this section or outside sources to complete the book cover. Each student in each group should choose one of the following roles: design front cover, write front flap copy about the book, write back flap copy about the author, write back cover endorsements from readers of the period. Display completed jackets on a bulletin board called Travels with Marco Polo.

Powerful Nations Emerge

During the 1400s the population of western Europe began to increase. Merchants and bankers in the growing cities wanted to expand their business through foreign trade. If they could buy spices and silks from the East directly, without going through the Arab and Italian cities, they could reap huge profits. They looked for alternatives to the overland route through the Middle East.

The development of large nation-states in western Europe helped expand trade and interest in overseas exploration. For many years Europe had been a patchwork of small states. Political power was divided among local lords, and few people traveled outside their region.

By the 1400s, however, a new type of centralized state was emerging in western Europe. Strong monarchs came to power in Spain, Portugal, England, and France. They began to establish national laws, courts, taxes, and armies to replace those of local lords. These ambitious kings and queens sought ways to increase trade and make their countries stronger and wealthier.

Technology's Impact

Advances in **technology**—the use of scientific knowledge for practical purposes—prepared the way for European voyages of exploration. In the 1450s the invention of movable type and the printing press revolutionized bookmaking. Now more people could have access to books and to new information. After its publication in print form in 1477, Marco Polo's *Travels* gained much wider circulation in Europe.

Geography

Better Maps

Most early maps were wildly inaccurate, drawn from scattered impressions of travelers and traders. Using the reports of explorers and information from Arab geographers, mapmakers made more accurate land and sea maps. These maps showed the direction of ocean currents. They also showed lines of latitude, which indicated distance north and south of the Equator.

Better instruments were developed for navigating the seas. Sailors could determine their latitude while at sea with an **astrolabe,** an instrument that measured the position of stars. Europeans also improved the magnetic compass, a Chinese invention the Arabs had passed on to Europe in the 1200s. The compass allowed sailors to determine their location when they were far from land.

Linking PAST & PRESENT

Astrolabe to Satellite

"Land ho!" The tools that early explorers used to sail the uncharted seas were much different from the instruments used today. One early navigation tool was the astrolabe. A sailor held the astrolabe vertically, located a star through its sights, and measured the star's elevation above the horizon. A ship's approximate location could be identified this way.

Today navigation satellites do the work of an astrolabe—and more! The NAVSTAR Global Positioning System (GPS) satellites were launched by the United States in 1993. From space the GPS can track the location of a vehicle on the earth to within a few meters of its actual position. **What other inventions aided early explorers?**

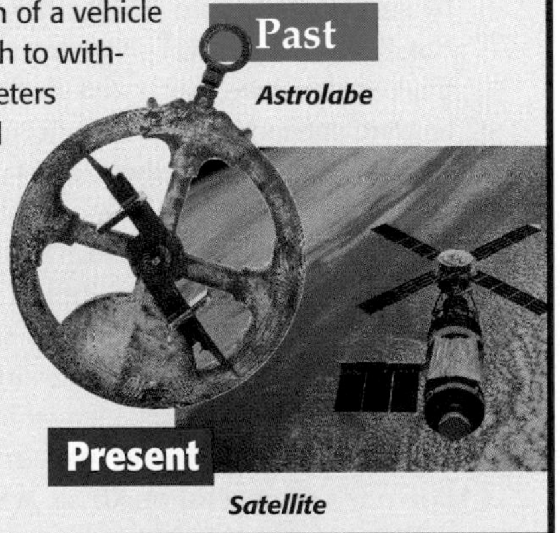

CHAPTER 2
Section 1, 37–41

NATIONAL GEOGRAPHIC SOCIETY

CD-ROM
NGS PictureShow: The Age of Exploration, Parts 1 and 2

Encourage students to explore connections between the development of large nation-states and the expansion of overseas exploration by having them click on the main menu.

CD-ROM
Picture Atlas of the World

To help students understand how geography affected East-West trade, have them click on the photo buttons of countries in western Europe and Asia.

Linking PAST & PRESENT

Astrolabe to Satellite The astrolabe was first used around 1300 by the Arabs. The first explorers used this instrument to determine latitude by suspending the astrolabe from a ring and moving the central rod until it lined up with the North Star or the sun.
Answer: *movable type, printing press, magnetic compass, stern rudder, triangular sail, three-masted caravel, rifles, cannons*

MULTIPLE LEARNING STYLES

Visual/Spatial Organize the class into small groups to create models of buildings typically found in a Renaissance village. The village could include these buildings: observatory, library, palace, theater, craftsperson's workshop, laboratory, home, monastery, chapel, and parliament. Have the groups make signs representing each building. Using the completed models, have other groups match the signs with the buildings. A valuable reference for this activity is:
Howarth, Sarah. *Renaissance Places.* Brookfield: The Millbrook Press, 1992. **L3**

CHAPTER 2
Section 1, 37–41

Map Study

Answers
1. northeast
2. Ghana

Map Skills Practice

Reading a Map To which body of water did most of these trade routes lead? *(Mediterranean Sea)*

3 ASSESS

Assign Section 1 Review as homework or as an in-class activity.

Use **Chapter Challenger Interactive Review Software** to review Section 1.

Section Quiz 2–1

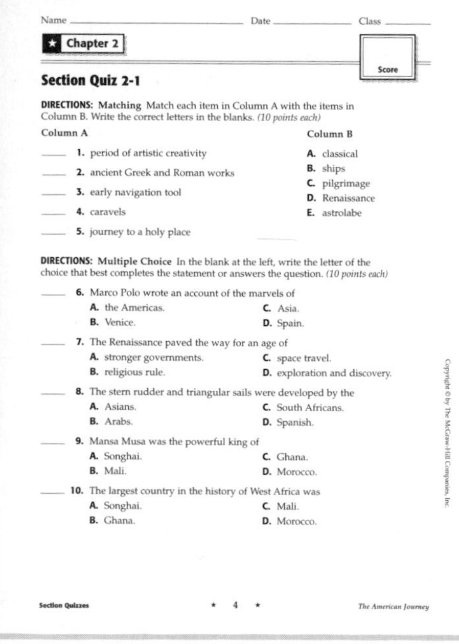
Name ______ Date ______ Class ______

Chapter 2 — Score

Section Quiz 2-1

DIRECTIONS: Matching Match each item in Column A with the items in Column B. Write the correct letters in the blanks. *(10 points each)*

Column A	Column B
____ 1. period of artistic creativity	A. classical
____ 2. ancient Greek and Roman works	B. ships
____ 3. early navigation tool	C. pilgrimage
____ 4. caravels	D. Renaissance
____ 5. journey to a holy place	E. astrolabe

DIRECTIONS: Multiple Choice In the blank at the left, write the letter of the choice that best completes the statement or answers the question. *(10 points each)*

____ 6. Marco Polo wrote an account of the marvels of
A. the Americas. C. Asia.
B. Venice. D. Spain.

____ 7. The Renaissance paved the way for an age of
A. stronger governments. C. space travel.
B. religious rule. D. exploration and discovery.

____ 8. The stern rudder and triangular sails were developed by the
A. Asians. C. South Africans.
B. Arabs. D. Spanish.

____ 9. Mansa Musa was the powerful king of
A. Songhai. C. Ghana.
B. Mali. D. Morocco.

____ 10. The largest country in the history of West Africa was
A. Songhai. C. Mali.
B. Ghana. D. Morocco.

Copyright © by The McGraw-Hill Companies, Inc.

Section Quizzes ★ 4 ★ *The American Journey*

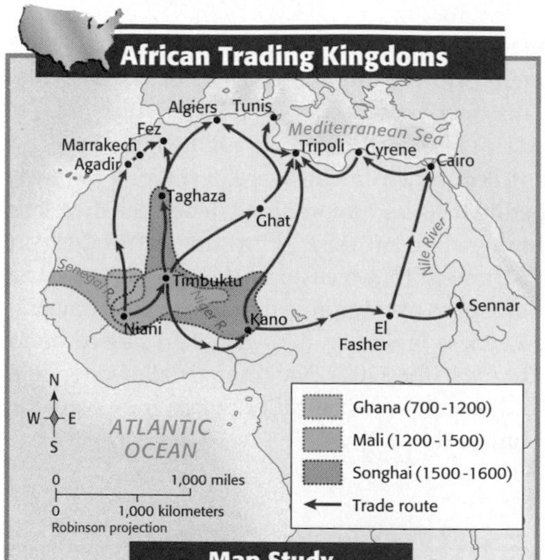

Map Study

Wealthy African trading kingdoms existed long before Europeans sailed west to find riches.

1. **Movement** In which direction would a trading party from Timbuktu travel to reach Ghat?
2. **Comparing** What African kingdom covered the smallest area?

Better Ships

Advances in ship design allowed shipbuilders to construct sailing vessels capable of long ocean voyages. The stern rudder and the triangular sail enabled ships to sail into the wind. Both of these new features came from the Arabs. In the late 1400s, the Portuguese developed the three-masted **caravel.** The caravel sailed faster than earlier ships, navigated shallow harbors better, and carried more cargo and food supplies. A Venetian sailor called the caravels "the best ships that sailed the seas." The caravels also carried new types of weapons—rifles and cannons.

By the mid-1400s the Italian ports faced increased competition for foreign trade. Powerful countries like Portugal and Spain began searching for sea routes to Asia, launching a new era of exploration. These new voyages took sailors down the west coast of Africa, which Europeans had never visited before.

African Kingdoms

Powerful kingdoms flourished in Africa south of the Sahara between 300 and 1600. The region was richly endowed with natural resources. Thus, Africans mined gold, copper, and iron ore. Trade with Islamic societies in North Africa brought wealth and Islamic ideas and customs to the West African kingdoms.

City-states on the east coast of Africa also benefited from trade. There Arab traders from the Middle East brought cotton, silk, and porcelain from India and China to exchange for ivory and metals from the African interior.

The Portuguese started sailing south along the African coastline in the mid-1400s and set up trading posts. From these, they traded for gold and for slaves.

Ghana—A Trading Empire

Between 300 and 1100, a vast trading empire called **Ghana** emerged in West Africa. Well located between the salt mines of the Sahara and the gold mines to the south, Ghana prospered from the taxes its kings imposed on trade.

Caravans with gold, ivory, and slaves from Ghana crossed the Sahara to Morocco. Muslim traders from North Africa loaded caravans with salt, cloth, and brass and headed back to Ghana. As a result of their trading contacts, many West Africans became Muslims.

In 1076 people from North Africa called Almoravids attacked Ghana's trade centers and seized the capital. The Almoravids controlled Ghana for about 10 years. After that Ghana's power declined, and several separate states emerged in the region.

Mali—A Powerful Kingdom

Mali, one of the new states, grew into a powerful kingdom. The people of Mali, under the Almoravids, revived the profitable trade routes with North Africa. By the late 1200s, Mali's expanded territory included the former kingdom of Ghana. The country was mainly agricultural, but well-endowed gold mines enriched the kingdom.

MAKING CONNECTIONS ACTIVITY

Language Arts Ask students to imagine they are writing a television script for a show about European exploration. Students can start by jotting down ideas about what they think would be an interesting scene. Describe the location of the scene, exactly what the scene should look like, and what the characters in the scene would be doing. Direct students to use information from the section to complete the script. **L3**

Mali's greatest king, **Mansa Musa,** ruled from 1307 to 1332. He was described at the time as "the most powerful, the richest, the most fortunate, the most feared by his enemies, and the most able to do good to those around him."

In 1324 Musa, a Muslim, made a grand pilgrimage to **Makkah** (also spelled Mecca). A **pilgrimage** is a journey to a holy place. Arab writers reported that Musa traveled with 12,000 slaves and a huge military escort. Ahead of him marched 500 royal servants who carried staffs of gold to distribute along the way.

Musa returned to Mali with an Arab architect who built great **mosques,** Muslim houses of worship, in the capital of **Timbuktu.** Under Mansa Musa, Timbuktu became an important center of Islamic art and learning.

The Songhai Empire

Some years later the Songhai (SAWNG•hy) people, who lived along the **Niger River,** rose up against Mali rule. They built a navy to control the Niger and in 1469 captured Timbuktu. In the late 1400s, **Askia Muhammad** brought the Songhai empire to the height of its power. Askia strengthened his country and made it the largest in the history of West Africa. He built many schools and encouraged trade with Europe and Asia.

Mansa Musa

Gold pendant, West Africa

In the late 1500s, the North African kingdom of Morocco sent an army across the Sahara to attack Songhai gold-trading centers. Armed with guns and cannons, the Moroccans easily defeated the Songhai.

Section 1 Review

Checking for Understanding

1. ***Identify*** Marco Polo, Ghana, Mali, Mansa Musa, Makkah, Timbuktu, Askia Muhammad.
2. ***Define*** classical, Renaissance, technology, astrolabe, caravel, pilgrimage, mosque.
3. ***Describe*** three technological advances that furthered European exploration.

Reviewing Themes

4. **Culture and Traditions** How did the Islamic religion spread to the early kingdoms of Africa?

Critical Thinking

5. **Drawing Conclusions** Why do you think the Renaissance began in Italy and not in another part of Europe? Provide reasons to support your answer.

Activity

Comparing Paintings Look in a reference book for a painting by an artist of the Renaissance and a painting by an artist of the Middle Ages. Write a paragraph describing the similarities and differences you see in the two paintings.

Section 1 Review Answers

1. Marco Polo, 37; Ghana, 40; Mali, 40; Mansa Musa, 41; Makkah, 41; Timbuktu, 41; Askia Muhammad, 41
2. The words are defined in the Glossary.
3. Answers should include three of the following: movable type and printing press gave people access to information; mapmakers refined their methods and created more accurate maps; the astrolabe and magnetic compass improved navigation; the stern rudder, triangular sail, and three-masted caravel allowed ships to travel farther.
4. through trade between African kingdoms and Arab Muslims in North Africa
5. Answers should refer to Italy's economic and political climate at the time.

Activity Analyses should compare similarities and differences.

Reteaching Activity 2–1

Name ______ Date ______ Class ______

★ Reteaching Activity **2-1**

DIRECTIONS: Recognizing Causes and Effects After each *Cause*, write the letter of its *Effect* from the Fact Bank.

1. **Cause:** Exotic goods from the East appeared in European marketplaces.
   Effect: ______
2. **Cause:** Italians wanted to improve their knowledge of people and the world.
   Effect: ______
3. **Cause:** The spirit of the Renaissance spread in Europe.
   Effect: ______
4. **Cause:** Merchants and bankers in Europe wanted to increase trade profits.
   Effect: ______
5. **Cause:** Movable type and the printing press were invented.
   Effect: ______
6. **Cause:** The astrolabe, which measured the position of the stars, was invented.
   Effect: ______
7. **Cause:** The stern rudder and the triangular sail were invented.
   Effect: ______
8. **Cause:** The kings of Ghana imposed taxes on trade.
   Effect: ______
9. **Cause:** Muslim traders from North Africa came to Ghana.
   Effect: ______
10. **Cause:** Mansa Musa had great mosques built in the capital of Mali.
    Effect: ______

★FACT BANK

- **A.** They looked for an alternative to the overland route through the Middle East.
- **B.** Europeans thought about themselves and the world in a dramatically different way.
- **C.** Timbuktu became an important center of Islamic art and learning.
- **D.** People became interested in India, China, and the rest of Asia.
- **E.** Sailors could determine their latitude at sea.
- **F.** They studied Greek and Roman classical works with new interest.
- **G.** Many West Africans became Muslims.
- **H.** Sailors could sail into the wind.
- **I.** The people of Ghana prospered.
- **J.** Marco Polo's *Travels* was read by more people in Europe.

Reteaching Activities ★ 4 ★ *The American Journey*

Enrichment Activity 2–1

Name ______ Date ______ Class ______

★ Enrichment Activity **2-1** ★ ★

Worth Its Weight in Salt

The gold-for-salt trade made the leaders of the Malinke of West Africa rich. Even though they had no gold or salt mines on their lands, their land lay between the salt mines to the north and the gold mines to the south. The Malinke taxed both products as the traders passed through their lands.

Gold-for-Salt Trade

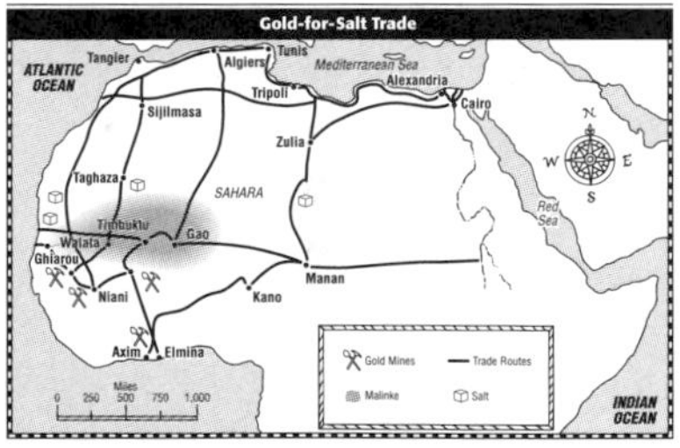

DIRECTIONS: Reading a Map Study the map to answer the questions on a separate sheet of paper.

1. Describe the directions a Muslim salt trader going from Tunis to Algiers to Gao to Timbuktu would travel.
2. Near what location would the trader get salt for trading?
3. Using the map scale provided, determine about how long the trader's trip would be.
4. Are the gold mines located north or south of the Sahara?
5. About how far would you have to travel as a gold trader from Niani to Timbuktu?
6. Would Axim merchants need to import or export salt? Why?

Activity **DIRECTIONS:** Imagine that you are a Muslim salt trader or a West African gold trader. Keep a diary of your journey telling about your trip. Use the information in the exercise and the map to create the details of your diary entry.

Enrichment Activities ★ 4 ★ *The American Journey*

4 CLOSE

Ask students to review the charts they created in the beginning of this section. Ask them to identify the most compelling reason for exploration. They should support their choice with examples from the section.

Social Studies Connections
Economics

TEACH

Motives for Exploration

Discuss with students the concept of supply and demand. *Supply* is the quantity of a good made available for sale. *Demand* is the desire, ability, and willingness of consumers to purchase a product. Discuss the impact supply and demand have on price. Refer to the examples of supply, demand, and price listed in this feature. Brainstorm with students other examples of how supply and demand affect price.

What? Where? When? Who?

Rising Prices The influx of gold and silver into the Spanish economy resulted in a rapid rise in prices of goods and services, or inflation.

Social Studies Connections
Economics
Citizenship | Geography | World History

Motives for Exploration

During the Middle Ages, European merchants journeyed thousands of miles and faced scorching deserts, blinding blizzards, and terrorizing bandits. Why did they do this? They wanted to make a profit.

Europeans of the 1400s wanted to buy fine porcelain, jewels, silk, and spices from East Asia. These items were very expensive, however. Because the Turkish Muslims controlled all the trade routes to Asia, they could also control the prices of goods that traveled along those routes. As Europeans demanded more and more Asian goods, the Muslim merchants raised their prices.

To get these goods for less, the Europeans wanted to find a way to go around the Muslim traders altogether. Their solution was to find their own route to East Asia by sea.

What makes some items more expensive than others? Maybe the product comes from far away and the cost of transporting it is high. Perhaps the item is scarce. For example, gold is expensive because the world supply is limited. Some things are simply much more desirable than others. If many people want to buy the item, the price will probably be high.

Activity

Creating an Advertisement Think of a costly item you have seen in a store. Imagine that you are a merchant who sells the item. Create a newspaper advertisement convincing people to buy the item.

Early Trade Routes

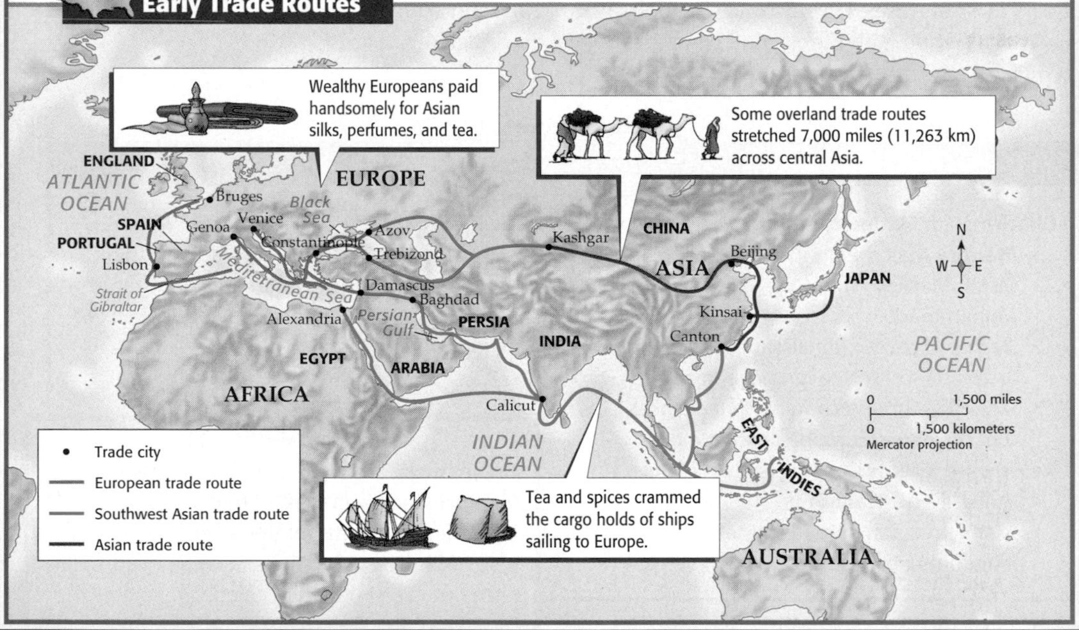

MORE ABOUT . . .

Trade Routes European merchants realized that trade between Europe and Asia was a profitable business. By the fifteenth century, however, the Ottoman Turks had gained control of parts of the major land route through Turkey and Arabia. Ottoman expansion cut off Europeans' easy access to Asian products. By 1450 improvements in navigation enabled European traders to bypass land routes and seek water trade routes.

1000 1200 1400 1600

1000 Leif Eriksson lands in present-day Newfoundland

1488 Bartholomeu Dias sets sail

1492 Columbus lands in the Americas

1498 Vasco da Gama reaches India

1519 Magellan begins circumnavigation of the world

Section 2

Early Exploration

READ TO DISCOVER . . .

- how Portugal led the way in overseas exploration.
- what was Columbus's plan for sailing to Asia.
- why the Europeans explored the Pacific Ocean.

TERMS TO LEARN

line of demarcation circumnavigate
strait

The Storyteller

More than 150 years after Marco Polo's death, a young Italian sea captain–Christopher Columbus–sat down to read Polo's *Travels* with interest. Columbus read what Polo had to say about the islands of Cipangu, or present-day Japan. According to Polo, Cipangu lay some 1,500 miles (2,414 km) off the eastern shore of Asia. Because the earth is round, Columbus reasoned, a person sailing west from Europe should quickly reach Cipangu. It could be much closer than anyone thought.

Unfortunately, Marco Polo–and therefore Columbus–was wrong.

Compass

The maps that the first European explorers used did not include America. They showed three continents—Europe, Asia, and Africa—merged together in a gigantic landmass. This landmass was bound by oceans. Some explorers assumed that the Western (Atlantic) and Eastern (Pacific) Oceans ran together to form the Ocean Sea. At the time, no one realized that another huge landmass was missing from the maps or that the oceans were as large as they are.

Geography

Seeking New Trade Routes

★ Portugal took the lead in exploring the boundaries of the known world. Because Portugal lacked a Mediterranean port, it could not be part of the profitable trade between Asia and Europe. The country's ambitious rulers wanted to find a new route to China and India.

The Portuguese also hoped to find a more direct way to get West African gold. The gold traveled by caravan across the desert to North Africa, then by ship across the Mediterranean. Portuguese traders needed a better route.

Early Portuguese Voyages

Prince Henry of Portugal laid the groundwork for a new era of exploration. He was fascinated by what lay beyond the known boundaries

1 FOCUS

BELLRINGER
Motivational Activity

Before taking roll at the beginning of the class period, project Section Focus Transparency 2–2 and have students answer the questions. Discuss students' responses.

This activity is also available as a blackline master.

Section Focus Transparency 2–2

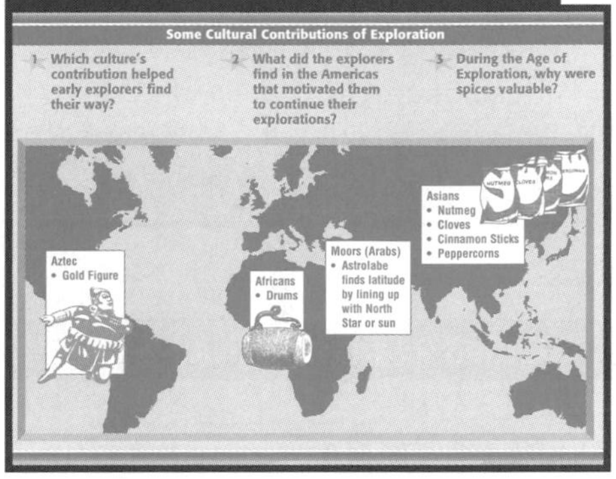

Vocabulary Precheck

Ask students to look up the prefix *circum-* and the verb *navigate* in the dictionary. Encourage students to define the word *circumnavigate* using the information they have found.

Use the **Vocabulary Puzzle-Maker** to create crossword and word search puzzles.

★ Section Theme
Geography and History

In 1400 Europeans had only a limited knowledge of the world. With inaccurate maps and only a few instruments to aid in navigation, many explorers piloted their ships by using the North Star and a compass.

Activity Invite volunteers to tell about situations in which they had inaccurate directions, but still found their way to their destination. Have students describe how they managed to find their way.

SECTION RESOURCES

Reproducible Masters

- Reproducible Lesson Plan 2–2
- Guided Reading Activity 2–2
- Section Quiz 2–2
- Reteaching Activity 2–2
- Enrichment Activity 2–2

Transparencies

- Section Focus Transparency 2–2

Multimedia

- Vocabulary PuzzleMaker
- Chapter Challenger Interactive Review Software
- Testmaker
- GTV: A Geographic Perspective on American History
- GTV: The American People: Fabric of a Nation

CHAPTER 2
Section 2, 43–49

2 TEACH

L1 Creating a Time Line Have each student create a time line of all the explorations described in this section. Use the time lines as the basis of discussion about the success of these explorations.

Chart Study

Answer
Christopher Columbus

Chart Skills Practice

Reading a Chart Was new knowledge about Africa, Asia, and the Americas a cause or an effect of exploration? *(effect)*

Guided Reading Activity 2–2

Name ______ Date ______ Class ______

★ Guided Reading Activity **2-2**

DIRECTIONS: Recording Who, What, When, Where, Why, and **How** Answer the questions below. Refer to your textbook to write the answers.

1. **Geography What** country led exploration in the early 1400s? ______
2. **Geography Why** was Prince Henry called Henry the Navigator? ______
3. **Geography Where** was the Gold Coast? ______
4. **Geography What** did the Portuguese trade and buy on the Gold Coast? ______
5. **Geography Who** led the Portuguese expedition to India in 1497? ______
6. **How** did Christopher Columbus plan to reach Asia? ______
7. **When** did the Viking Leif Eriksson land in Newfoundland? ______
8. **Who** financed Columbus's 1492 voyage? ______
9. **Eyewitness to History What** were the names of Columbus's three ships? ______
10. **Eyewitness to History Why** was Columbus having trouble with his crew? ______
11. **Eyewitness to History Why** are the Caribbean Islands called the West Indies? ______
12. **What** imaginary line down the middle of the Atlantic was established to keep peace between Spain and Portugal? ______
13. **What** gave Spain the right to most of North and South America? ______
14. **Geography Who** claimed the Pacific Ocean and adjoining lands for Spain? ______
15. **Who** was the first to circumnavigate the globe? ______
16. **How** long did the first voyage around the world take? ______

Causes and Effects

CAUSES
- ★ European desire for new trade routes and gold
- ★ New spirit of adventure
- ★ Power and wealth of new European nations
- ★ Competition among European nations
- ★ Missionaries' desire to convert others to Christianity

European Voyages of Exploration

EFFECTS
- ★ New knowledge of Africa, Asia, and the Americas
- ★ Clash of European and Native American cultures
- ★ Enslavement of Africans
- ★ New plants and animals in Europe and the Americas
- ★ Rivalry of European nations in the Americas

Chart Study

The mid-1400s in Europe were a time of adventure, great learning, and curiosity about the world.

Analyzing Information Which explorer sailing for Portugal was the first to land in the Americas?

of the world. In about 1420 he set up a center for exploration on the southwestern tip of Portugal, "where endeth land and where beginneth sea." Known as **Henry the Navigator,** the prince brought astronomers, geographers, and mathematicians to share their knowledge with Portuguese sailors and shipbuilders.

The prince encouraged mariners to explore the west coast of Africa. Up to that time, no ship had gone past Cape Bojador into the "green sea of darkness," an area known for its dangerous currents, fog, and strong coastal winds. The Portuguese maneuvered around this treacherous point by sending their ships farther west into the Atlantic. There they reached the **Azores** and the **Canary Islands.** From the islands the ships could pick up favorable winds and currents that carried them down the African coast.

Bartholomeu Dias

As the Portuguese moved south along the coast of West Africa, they traded for gold and ivory and established trading posts. Because of its abundance of gold, the area came to be known as the **Gold Coast.** In 1441 the Portuguese began buying slaves there as well.

King John II of Portugal launched new efforts to realize the Portuguese dream of a trading empire in Asia. If the Portuguese could find a sea route around Africa, they could trade directly with India and China. In the 1480s the king urged Portuguese sea captains to explore farther and farther south along the African coast.

In 1488 the king sent **Bartholomeu Dias** to explore the southernmost part of Africa. As Dias approached the area, he ran into a terrible storm that carried him off course and around the southern tip of Africa. Dias wrote that he had been around the "Cape of Storms." On learning of Dias's discovery, King John II renamed this southern tip of land the Cape of Good Hope—the passage around Africa might lead to a new route to India.

Vasco da Gama

The first Portuguese expedition to India came years later. In July 1497, after much preparation, **Vasco da Gama** set out from Portugal with four ships. Da Gama sailed down the coast of West Africa, rounded the Cape of Good Hope, and visited cities along the coast of East Africa. He engaged an Arab pilot who knew the Indian Ocean well. With the pilot's help, da Gama sailed on to India. He reached the port of Calicut in 1498, completing the long-awaited eastern sea route to Asia.

Cooperative Learning Activity

Charting Explorers' Routes Organize the class into groups of three. Assign each group one of the explorers mentioned in this section. Allow each group member to choose one of the following tasks: create a map of the explorer's voyage on poster board, write a newspaper-style report describing interesting facts about the voyage and the explorer, or illustrate or cut out graphics of discoveries made on the explorer's voyage. Have each group mount the newspaper report and the graphics on the completed map. Display maps around the classroom.

Columbus Crosses the Atlantic

Christopher Columbus had a different plan for reaching Asia. He thought he could get there by sailing west. Born in Genoa, Italy, in 1451, Columbus became a sailor for Portugal. He had traveled as far north as the Arctic Circle and as far south as the Gold Coast.

In the 1400s most educated people believed the world was round. A more difficult matter was determining its size. Columbus was among those who based their estimates of the earth's size on the work of Ptolemy, an ancient Greek astronomer. Columbus believed Asia was about 2,400 miles (3,800 km) from Europe—a voyage of about two months by ship. Ptolemy, however, had underestimated the size of the world.

The Viking Voyages

Several centuries before Columbus, northern Europeans called **Vikings** had sailed west and

TECHNOLOGY AND HISTORY

Spanish Galleon

In the late 1500s and early 1600s, Spanish galleons carried gold and silver from the West Indies to Spain. That's not all these ships carried, however. The threat of pirates prompted the Spanish galleons to carry weapons as part of their cargo.

What powered the Spanish galleons?

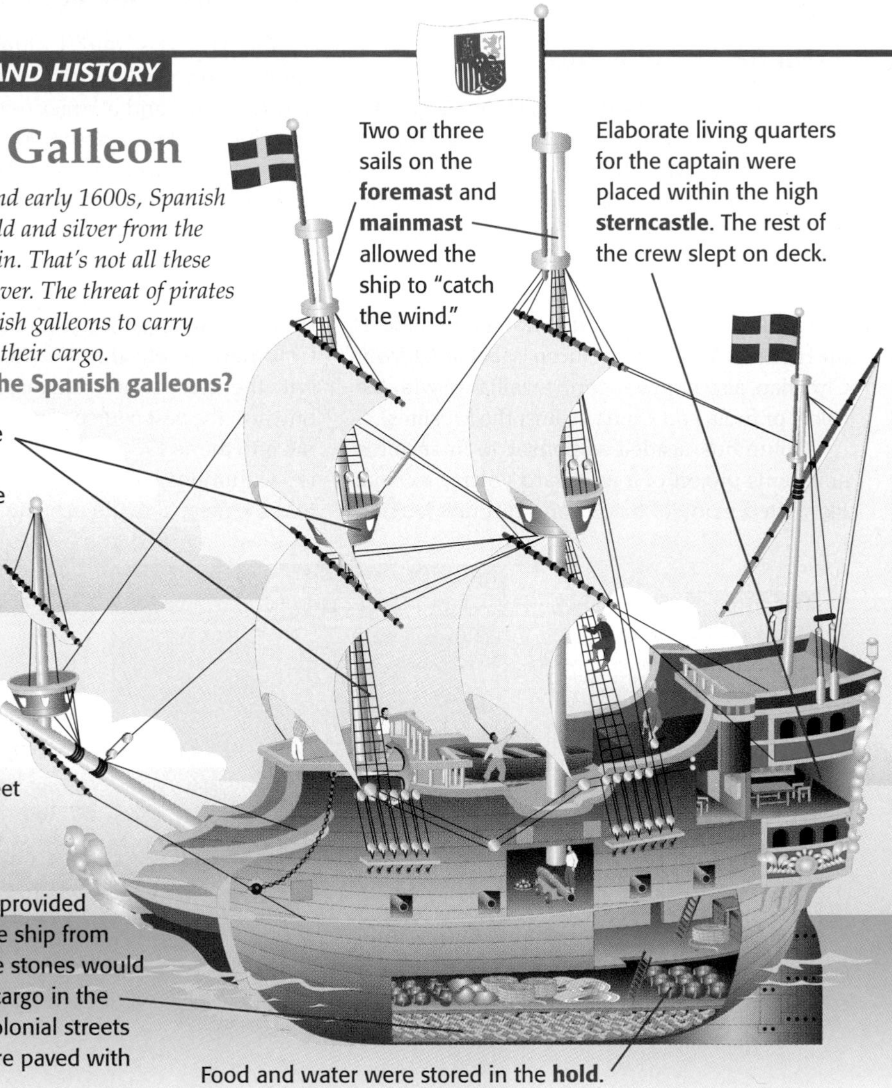

MULTIPLE LEARNING STYLES

Verbal/Linguistic Ask each student to choose an explorer mentioned in this section and write five personal quotations that the explorer might have made. Allow one student to read one quotation, then have the other students guess which explorer the student is portraying until all five quotations have been read. If no one guesses the correct explorer after the student has read the five quotations, the student should reveal the explorer's name. Continue until all students have read their quotations. **L1, ELL**

NATIONAL GEOGRAPHIC SOCIETY

VIDEODISC
GTV: A Geographic Perspective on American History

Side 1, Chapter 4
Title: *Land of Opportunity*
Subject: Europeans gain a foothold in the Americas (1492–1603)
Ask: **What was Christopher Columbus looking for when he found the Americas?** *(Asia)*

TECHNOLOGY AND HISTORY

More About . . .
Spanish Galleons The word "galleon" is often used loosely to describe towering sailing ships of the fifteenth and sixteenth centuries, used for both commerce and war. Properly used, *galleon* refers to a specific type of sailing warship introduced in the mid-sixteenth century. Naval architects slimmed down top-heavy sailing ships of the time to produce the galleon, which had a "galley-like" look. The forecastle—upper deck—of this ship was reduced in size and set well back from the bow, which extended into a beak like a galley (a long, low, single-deck sailing ship).

The first galleons were produced in England. By the early seventeenth century, the galleon had been replaced by a two-deck and a three-deck ship.

Ask students to identify the forecastle and the part of the ship that looks like a galley.

Answer to Caption: *wind*

Who?What?Where?When?

Eric the Red The Vikings told long tales—or sagas—about their adventures. One of the most popular sagas is about Eric the Red, who lived in Iceland. He led a sailing expedition that found a rich and fertile land he called *Greenland.* Eric the Red settled there with his family. While there, his wife gave birth to a son they named Leif. Other Viking sagas call Eric the Red's son "Leif the Lucky" because Leif found a new land he called *Vinland.* Scholars believe Vinland was present-day Newfoundland.

Picturing HISTORY Columbus made four trips to the Americas, each time bringing back to Europe plants and descriptions he claimed proved that the land he had found was part of Asia. Columbus brought back an inedible West Indian nut, *nogal de pais,* that he insisted must be the coconut that Marco Polo described in his accounts of Cathay.
Answer: *because he believed he was in the East Indies*

NATIONAL GEOGRAPHIC SOCIETY

VIDEODISC
GTV: The American People: Fabric of a Nation

Side 1, Chapter 4
Title: *Wealth Enough*
Subject: Europeans in the Americas
Ask: **When the Spanish failed to find gold in New Spain, what did they decide to do instead?** *(convert Native Americans to Christianity)*

reached North America. In the 800s and 900s, Viking ships visited Iceland and Greenland and established settlements. Then in about 1000, a Viking sailor named Leif Eriksson got lost on his way to Greenland and landed in present-day **Newfoundland.** He established a small settlement there, but it did not last.

Although accounts of the Vikings existed in Scandinavian legends, they were unknown in the rest of Europe. Europeans did not "discover" the Americas until Columbus made his great voyage.

Spain Backs Columbus

For most of the 1400s, Spanish monarchs devoted their energy to driving the Muslims out of their country. With the fall of the last Muslim kingdom in southern Spain in 1492, **King Ferdinand** and **Queen Isabella** of Spain could focus on other goals. The Spanish had been watching the seafaring and trading successes of neighboring Portugal with envy. They, too, wanted to share in the riches of Asian trade. Queen Isabella, a devout Christian, also hoped to form an alliance with the rulers of India and China against the Muslims.

Columbus needed a sponsor to finance his ambitious project of a westward voyage to Asia. He visited many of the European courts looking for support. After many years of frustration, he finally found a sponsor in Spain.

Queen Isabella agreed to finance the expedition. She promised Columbus a share of any riches gained from lands he discovered on his way to Asia. At the time, of course, nobody knew that a great landmass blocked his route to Asia.

Eyewitness to HISTORY

Columbus's First Voyage

On August 3, 1492, Columbus set out from Palos, Spain. He had two small ships, the *Niña* and the *Pinta,* and a larger one, the *Santa María,* carrying a total of about 90 sailors. The small fleet stopped at the Canary Islands for repairs and supplies, then sailed westward into the unknown.

The ships had good winds, but after a month at sea the sailors began to worry. Provisions were running low, and they had not sighted any land. Columbus wrote that he was "having trouble with the crew. . . . I am told that if I persist in going onward, the best course of action will be to throw me into the sea."

Columbus, however, was determined. He told the men, "I made this voyage to go to the In-

Picturing HISTORY Financed by Spain's Queen Isabella, the voyages of Columbus led to an exchange of goods and practices between Europe and the Americas. An example is this Taino Native American basket figure that uses European mirrors as earplugs. **Why did Columbus call the local people that he met in the Americas "Indians"?**

MAKING CONNECTIONS ACTIVITY

Daily Life After reading *Eyewitness to History* in this section, have students imagine that they are on Columbus's ship, searching for the Indies. Have each student write five diary entries from a crew member's viewpoint. Encourage students to describe their physical surroundings, feelings about traveling to strange places, feelings about Columbus as a leader, and so on. **L1**

dies, and [I] shall continue until I find them, with God's help." To convince the crew that they had not traveled too far from home, Columbus altered the distances in his ship's log.

"Tierra! Tierra!"

Weeks later, signs of land began to appear—flocks of birds in the air and weeds floating near the ships. On October 12, 1492, at 2:00 in the morning, a lookout shouted, *"Tierra! Tierra!"*—Land! Land! He had spotted a small island, part of the group now called the Bahamas. Columbus went ashore, claimed the island for Spain, and named it San Salvador. He described the island's inhabitants as "all of good stature, a very handsome people." Although he did not know it, Columbus had reached the Americas.

Columbus explored the area for several months, convinced he had reached the East Indies, the islands off the coast of Asia. Today the **Caribbean Islands** are often referred to as the **West Indies.** Columbus called the local people Indians. He noted that they regarded the Europeans with wonder and often touched them to find out "if they were flesh and bones like themselves."

Columbus returned to Spain in triumph in March 1493. Queen Isabella and King Ferdinand received him with great honor and agreed to finance his future voyages. Columbus had earned the title of Admiral of the Ocean Sea.

Columbus's Later Voyages

Columbus made three more voyages from Spain in 1493, 1498, and 1502. He explored the Caribbean islands of Hispaniola (present-day Haiti and the Dominican Republic), Cuba, and Jamaica, and he sailed along the coasts of Central America and northern South America. He claimed the new lands for Spain and established settlements.

Columbus originally thought the lands he had found were in Asia. Later explorations made it clear that Columbus had not reached Asia at all. He had found a part of the globe unknown to Europeans, Asians, and Africans. In the following years, the Spanish explored most of the Caribbean region. In time their voyages led to the establishment of the Spanish Empire in the Americas.

America's FLAGS

Spain, 1492 Christopher Columbus proudly carried the Spanish banner of Castile and Leon to the shores of the Bahamas. The flag's castle represented Queen Isabella. The lion symbolized her husband, King Ferdinand.

The Treaty of Tordesillas

Columbus's voyages fueled the rivalry between Spain and Portugal. The Portuguese king rejected Spanish claims to what Columbus called the Indies. Each country contested the right of the other to explore the new lands.

To keep the peace, Pope Alexander VI worked out an agreement between Spain and Portugal. In 1493 the pope established a **line of demarcation,** an imaginary line running down the middle of the Atlantic from the North Pole to the South Pole. Spain was to have control of all lands to the west of the line, while Portugal was to have control of all lands east of the line. Portugal, however, protested that the division favored Spain. As a result, in 1494 Spain and Portugal signed the **Treaty of Tordesillas** (TAWR•duh•SEE•yuhs), an agreement to move the line of demarcation farther west.

Nobody realized how much land still lay to the west of the line. As it turned out, the Treaty of Tordesillas gave Spain the right to most of North and South America. In 1500 the Portuguese explorer **Pedro Cabral** was blown off course during a storm and landed on the coast of what is now **Brazil.** Because the land lay east of the line of demarcation, Portugal claimed and eventually colonized Brazil.

CURRICULUM CONNECTION

GEOGRAPHY
Drawings of sea monsters appeared on many if not most maps of this era. Tales of bizarre monsters enlivened the study of geography during Columbus's time. For many sailors, these monsters represented real threats and were more than flights of fancy. *Sciapodes* were monsters that had only one giant foot yet could walk amazingly fast. *Monoculars* were giants with a single eye in the middle of their forehead, and they ate only meat and raw fish. The *cynocephalus* were very intelligent and gifted with great intuition.

Who?What?Where?When?

Columbus by another name? Christopher Columbus never referred to himself as Columbus, a name found today on cities and buildings across America. Later in life he preferred to be called Cristóbel Colón.

CRITICAL THINKING ACTIVITY

Formulating Questions Discuss the difference between objective and subjective tests. An *objective test,* such as a multiple-choice test, is one that can be scored with a single answer key. No scorers can disagree as to whether responses are right or wrong. In contrast, a *subjective test,* such as an essay exam, can be scored differently by different scorers. Explain how to construct closed-ended, unambiguous questions from which respondents can choose only one correct answer. Ask individual students to create a 10-question, multiple-choice quiz covering the content in this section. Pair students to take one another's quiz. Have the student who created the quiz grade it and discuss wrong answers with the student who took the quiz. Allow each student to critique the other's questions. **L2**

CHAPTER 2
Section 2, 43–49

3 ASSESS

Assign Section 2 Review as homework or as an in-class activity.

Use **Chapter Challenger Interactive Review Software** to review Section 2.

Section Quiz 2–2

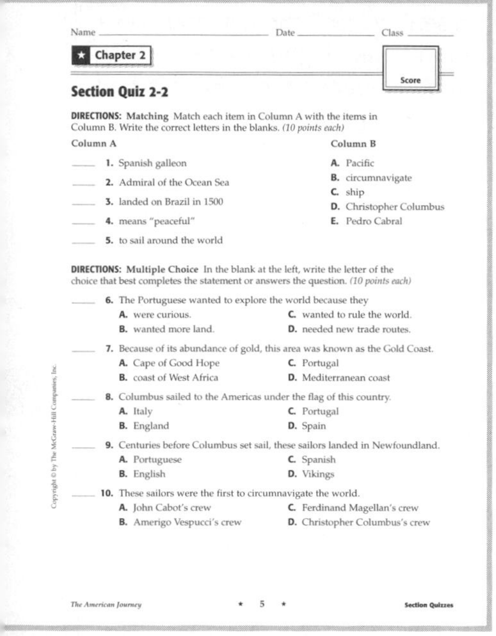
Name ______ Date ______ Class ______

★ Chapter 2

Score

Section Quiz 2-2

DIRECTIONS: Matching Match each item in Column A with the items in Column B. Write the correct letters in the blanks. *(10 points each)*

Column A	Column B
____ **1.** Spanish galleon	**A.** Pacific
____ **2.** Admiral of the Ocean Sea	**B.** circumnavigate
____ **3.** landed on Brazil in 1500	**C.** ship
____ **4.** means "peaceful"	**D.** Christopher Columbus
____ **5.** to sail around the world	**E.** Pedro Cabral

DIRECTIONS: Multiple Choice In the blank at the left, write the letter of the choice that best completes the statement or answers the question. *(10 points each)*

____ **6.** The Portuguese wanted to explore the world because they
A. were curious. **C.** wanted to rule the world.
B. wanted more land. **D.** needed new trade routes.

____ **7.** Because of its abundance of gold, this area was known as the Gold Coast.
A. Cape of Good Hope **C.** Portugal
B. coast of West Africa **D.** Mediterranean coast

____ **8.** Columbus sailed to the Americas under the flag of this country.
A. Italy **C.** Portugal
B. England **D.** Spain

____ **9.** Centuries before Columbus set sail, these sailors landed in Newfoundland.
A. Portuguese **C.** Spanish
B. English **D.** Vikings

____ **10.** These sailors were the first to circumnavigate the world.
A. John Cabot's crew **C.** Ferdinand Magellan's crew
B. Amerigo Vespucci's crew **D.** Christopher Columbus's crew

The American Journey ★ 5 ★ **Section Quizzes**

Map Study

Answers

1. John Cabot

2. The earth's greatest circumference is at the Equator, and sailing north or south of the Equator cuts the traveling distance.

Map Skills Practice

Reading a Map Which explorer landed off the coast of Brazil? Which country did he sail for? *(Pedro Cabral; Portugal)*

Geography

The Vast Pacific

Vasco Núñez de Balboa (bal•BOH•uh), governor of a Spanish town in present-day Panama, had heard stories of the "great waters" beyond the mountains. In 1513 he formed an exploring party and tramped through the steaming jungles. After many days of difficult travel, the Spaniard climbed a hill and saw a vast body of water. When he reached the water's edge, Balboa waded in and claimed the **Pacific Ocean** and adjoining lands for the king and queen of Spain.

A Southern Route to Asia

The Spanish wanted to find a sea route through or around South America that would lead

European Voyages of Exploration

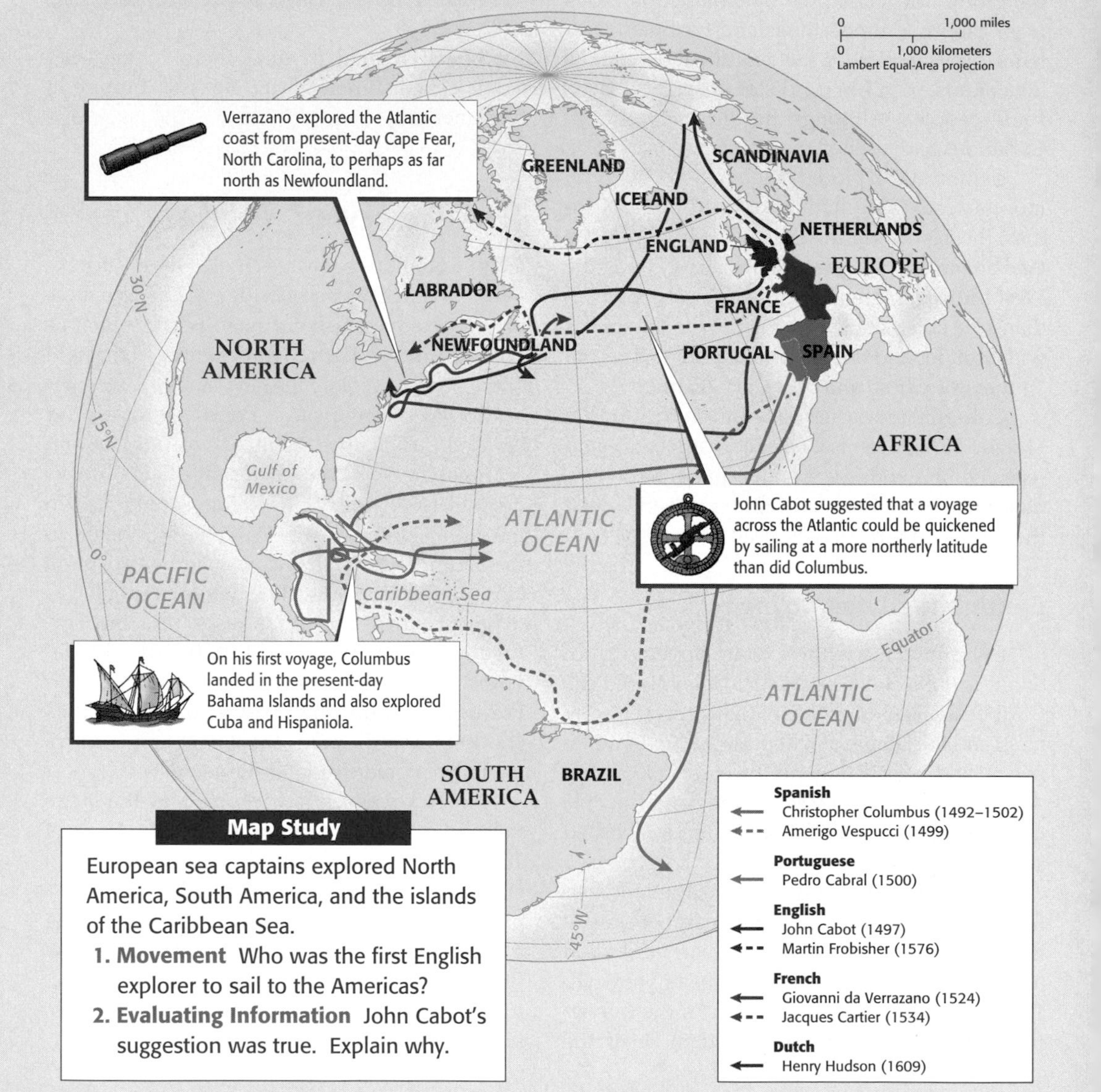

Map Study

European sea captains explored North America, South America, and the islands of the Caribbean Sea.

1. **Movement** Who was the first English explorer to sail to the Americas?
2. **Evaluating Information** John Cabot's suggestion was true. Explain why.

TEACHER'S NOTES

them to Asia. In 1519 they commissioned **Ferdinand Magellan,** a Portuguese mariner, to lead an expedition of five ships. Sailing from Spain, Magellan headed west across the Atlantic and south along the eastern coast of South America.

Searching for a passage that would lead to the Pacific Ocean, the sailors grew restless and rebelled against the long and dangerous journey. Magellan managed to regain command, but one of his ships returned to Spain.

In late November 1520, Magellan finally found and sailed through the narrow, twisting sea passage to the Pacific. This **strait** still bears his name. Looking over the calm waters at the end of the strait, Magellan exclaimed: "We are about to stand [go] into an ocean where no ship has ever sailed before." He named the ocean the Pacific, which means "peaceful."

Sailing Around the World

Magellan expected to reach Asia in just a few weeks after rounding South America, but the voyage across the Pacific lasted four months. The crew ran out of food and ate sawdust, rats, and the leather of the rigging to stay alive. Magellan was killed in the Philippines in a local war, but some of his crew returned to Spain. Their trip had taken almost 3 years. Only 1 of the 5 original ships and 18 of the 250 crew members completed the difficult journey. These men were the first to **circumnavigate,** or sail around, the world.

Ferdinand Magellan

Section 2 Review

Checking for Understanding

1. ***Identify*** Henry the Navigator, Vasco da Gama, Christopher Columbus, Vikings, King Ferdinand, Queen Isabella, Ferdinand Magellan.
2. ***Define*** line of demarcation, strait, circumnavigate.
3. ***Describe*** the accomplishments of Vasco de Balboa and Ferdinand Magellan.

Reviewing Themes

4. **Geography and History** Where did Columbus land on his first voyage?

Critical Thinking

5. **Making Inferences** For many years history books claimed that "Columbus discovered America." Why do you think Native Americans might disagree with the use of the word *discovered* in this statement? What might be a better word choice?

Activity

Drawing a Map Draw a map of the world as you think Columbus might have seen it in 1492. Remember his error in calculating distance.

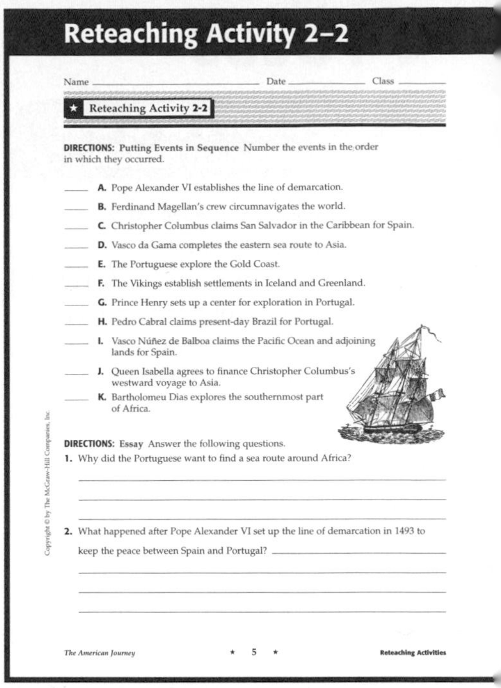

Reteaching Activity 2–2

Name ________ Date ________ Class ________

★ Reteaching Activity 2-2

DIRECTIONS: Putting Events in Sequence Number the events in the order in which they occurred.

____ **A.** Pope Alexander VI establishes the line of demarcation.
____ **B.** Ferdinand Magellan's crew circumnavigates the world.
____ **C.** Christopher Columbus claims San Salvador in the Caribbean for Spain.
____ **D.** Vasco da Gama completes the eastern sea route to Asia.
____ **E.** The Portuguese explore the Gold Coast.
____ **F.** The Vikings establish settlements in Iceland and Greenland.
____ **G.** Prince Henry sets up a center for exploration in Portugal.
____ **H.** Pedro Cabral claims present-day Brazil for Portugal.
____ **I.** Vasco Núñez de Balboa claims the Pacific Ocean and adjoining lands for Spain.
____ **J.** Queen Isabella agrees to finance Christopher Columbus's westward voyage to Asia.
____ **K.** Bartholomeu Dias explores the southernmost part of Africa.

DIRECTIONS: Essay Answer the following questions.

1. Why did the Portuguese want to find a sea route around Africa?
2. What happened after Pope Alexander VI set up the line of demarcation in 1493 to keep the peace between Spain and Portugal?

Copyright © by The McGraw-Hill Companies, Inc.

The American Journey ★ 5 ★ **Reteaching Activities**

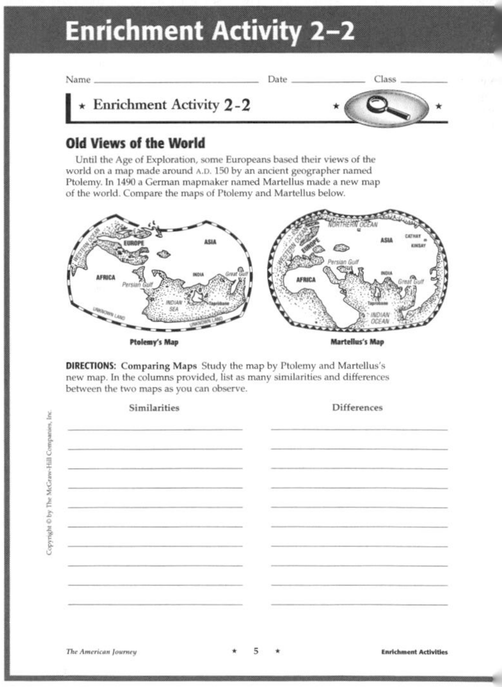

Enrichment Activity 2–2

Name ________ Date ________ Class ________

★ Enrichment Activity 2-2 ★

Old Views of the World

Until the Age of Exploration, some Europeans based their views of the world on a map made around A.D. 150 by an ancient geographer named Ptolemy. In 1490 a German mapmaker named Martellus made a new map of the world. Compare the maps of Ptolemy and Martellus below.

Ptolemy's Map — Martellus's Map

DIRECTIONS: Comparing Maps Study the map by Ptolemy and Martellus's new map. In the columns provided, list as many similarities and differences between the two maps as you can observe.

Similarities	Differences

Copyright © by The McGraw-Hill Companies, Inc.

The American Journey ★ 5 ★ **Enrichment Activities**

Section 2 Review Answers

1. Henry the Navigator, 44; Vasco da Gama, 44; Christopher Columbus, 45; Vikings, 45; King Ferdinand, 46; Queen Isabella, 46; Ferdinand Magellan, 49
2. The words are defined in the Glossary.
3. Balboa claimed the Pacific Ocean for Spain; Magellan's crew made the first circumnavigation of the world.
4. San Salvador, in present-day Bahamas
5. Native Americans lived in the Americas before Columbus arrived; answers will vary, but possible word choices may include: *claimed, found, came upon, reached.*

Activity Students' maps should omit the Americas and the Pacific Ocean. Maps should show Asia about 2,400 miles directly to the west of Europe.

4 CLOSE

Ask students to debate who they think had the most valid claim to the new lands described in this section—the Spaniards, the Portuguese, or the Native Americans. Ask them to debate first as a Spanish explorer, then as a Portuguese king or queen, and finally as a Native American.

CHAPTER 2
Section 3, 50–55

1 FOCUS

BELLRINGER
Motivational Activity

Before taking roll at the beginning of the class period, project Section Focus Transparency 2–3 and have students answer the questions. Discuss students' responses.

This activity is also available as a blackline master.

Section Focus Transparency 2–3

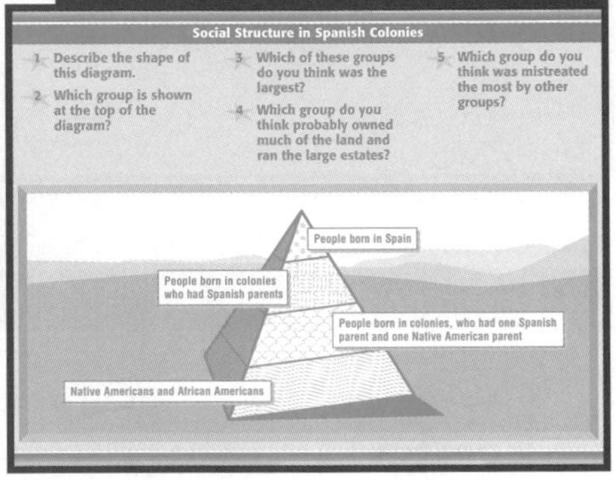

Vocabulary Precheck
Encourage students to write a brief description of the types of settlements in Spain's American empire using the terms *pueblo, mission,* and *presidio.*

Use the **Vocabulary PuzzleMaker** to create crossword and word search puzzles.

Section Theme
Groups and Institutions

The conquistadors, who were fewer in number than the Native Americans, conquered mighty empires in the Americas.

Activity Write the phrase *Gold, Glory, and God* on the board. Have students speculate why these words motivated conquistadors to come to the Americas.

1500 1530 1560 1590

1519 Hernán Cortés lands in Mexico

1532 Francisco Pizarro captures Atahualpa

1541 De Soto crosses the Mississippi River

1565 Spain establishes fort at St. Augustine, Florida

Section 3

Spain in America

READ TO DISCOVER . . .
- how the great Aztec and Inca Empires came to an end.
- how Spain governed its empire in the Americas.
- why the Columbian Exchange was significant.

TERMS TO LEARN

conquistador	presidio
tribute	*encomienda*
viceroy	plantation
pueblo	Columbian Exchange
mission	

The Storyteller

Would you like to visit a place described in the following way? "A river . . . [stretched] two leagues wide, in which there were fishes as big as horses. . . . The lord of the country took his afternoon nap under a great tree on which were hung a great number of little gold bells. . . . The jugs and bowls were [made] of gold."

"[It was] a land rich in gold, silver, and other wealth . . . great cities . . . and civilized people wearing woolen clothes."

Conquistador's armor

Stories of kingdoms wealthy beyond belief greeted the early Spanish explorers in the Americas. The reports led them far and wide in search of fabulous riches.

Spanish Conquistadors

Known as **conquistadors** (kahn•KEES•tuh•dawrs), these explorers received grants from the Spanish rulers. They had the right to explore and establish settlements in the Americas. In exchange they agreed to give the Spanish crown one-fifth of any gold or treasure discovered. This arrangement allowed Spanish rulers to launch expeditions with little risk. If a conquistador failed, he lost his own fortune. If he succeeded, both he and Spain gained wealth and glory.

As one conquistador explained, "We came here to serve God and the king, and also to get rich." The story of how the conquistadors destroyed the most powerful empires of the Americas and went on to build a new Spanish empire is one of the most astonishing in history.

Cortés Conquers the Aztec

When **Hernán Cortés** landed on the east coast of what we now know as Mexico in 1519, he was looking for gold and glory. He came with about 500 soldiers, some horses, and a few cannons. Cortés soon learned about the great Aztec Empire and its capital of Tenochtitlán.

In building their empire, the Aztec had conquered many cities in Mexico. These cities were

SECTION RESOURCES

Reproducible Masters
- Guided Reading Activity 2–3
- Section Quiz 2–3
- Reteaching Activity 2–3
- Enrichment Activity 2–3

Transparencies
- Section Focus Transparency 2–3
- NGS PicturePack Transparencies

Multimedia
- Vocabulary PuzzleMaker
- Chapter Challenger Interactive Review
- Testmaker
- ABCNews Interactive™ Historic America Electronic Field Trips
- GTV: The American People: Fabric of a Nation
- NGS PictureShow: Native Americans, Part 2

forced to give crops, clothing, gold, and precious stones to the Aztec as **tribute.** Cortés used the resentment of the people of these cities to his advantage. With the help of **Doña Marina,** a Mayan woman who acted as his translator, he formed alliances with nearby cities against the Aztec.

Cortés marched into Tenochtitlán in November with his small army and his Native American allies. The Aztec emperor **Montezuma** (MAHN•tuh•ZOO•muh)—also spelled Moctezuma—welcomed Cortés and his soldiers and provided them with food and a fine palace. However, Cortés took advantage of the Aztec's hospitality and made Montezuma his prisoner.

In the spring the Spaniards heard rumors of rebellion. To crush any spark of resistance, they killed Montezuma and many Aztec nobles. The Aztec had had enough. They rose up and drove the Spaniards from Tenochtitlán. Cortés, however, was determined to retake the city. He waited until more Spanish troops arrived, then attacked and destroyed the Aztec capital in 1521. An Aztec lament describes the awful scene:

> “Without roofs are the houses,
> And red are their walls with blood. . . .
> Weep, my friends,
> Know that with these disasters
> We have lost our Mexican nation.”

The Aztec Empire disintegrated, and Spain seized control of the region.

Eyewitness to HISTORY

Pizarro Conquers Peru

In 1530 the conquistador **Francisco Pizarro** sailed down the Pacific coast of South America with about 180 Spanish soldiers. Pizarro had heard tales of the incredibly wealthy Inca Empire in present-day Peru. In 1532 Pizarro captured the Inca ruler, **Atahualpa** (ah•tah•WAHL•pah), and trapped much of the Incan army in a square surrounded by walls. An Incan historian describes what happened:

American Memories — *An Aztec Home*

What Was It Like? Aztec homes were simple and built for usefulness rather than beauty. **How do you think the Aztec used each of the household items shown here?**

Grinding stone

Bowl

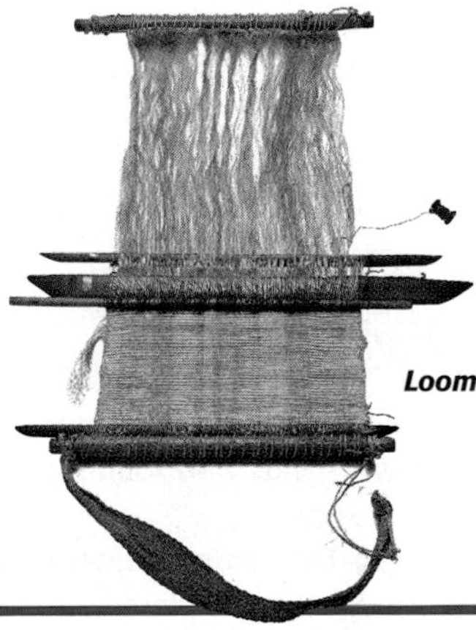

Loom

CHAPTER 2
Section 3, 50–55

2 TEACH

L1 Creating a Graphic Organizer Suggest that students work in pairs to create a graphic organizer with the following information: conquistador's name, areas explored, motivation for exploration, and treatment of Native American groups. Ask students to categorize the motives as either "Gold," "Glory," or "God" and draw a conclusion about the primary motivation for exploration.

American Memories

An Aztec Home
Houses in Tenochtitlán, the Aztec capital, ranged from modest huts to great palaces. The most common dwelling was the stucco house. The house usually included a garden, a yard with a hearth, a bedroom for the entire family, one other small room, and a bathroom. Furniture consisted of mats and cushions. Montezuma's palace contained luxuries such as tables and screens. **Answer:** *Answers will vary but may include storage, cooking, decoration, comfort, and so on.*

Guided Reading Activity 2–3

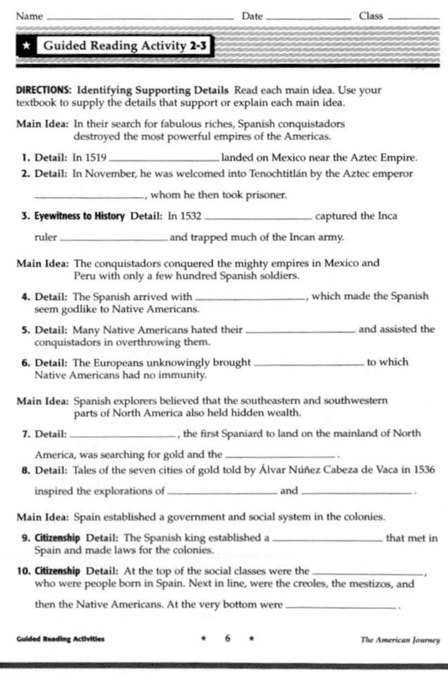

Name ______________ Date ______________ Class ______________

★ Guided Reading Activity **2-3**

DIRECTIONS: Identifying Supporting Details Read each main idea. Use your textbook to supply the details that support or explain each main idea.

Main Idea: In their search for fabulous riches, Spanish conquistadors destroyed the most powerful empires of the Americas.

1. Detail: In 1519 ______________ landed on Mexico near the Aztec Empire.

2. Detail: In November, he was welcomed into Tenochtitlán by the Aztec emperor ______________, whom he then took prisoner.

3. Eyewitness to History Detail: In 1532 ______________ captured the Inca ruler ______________ and trapped much of the Incan army.

Main Idea: The conquistadors conquered the mighty empires in Mexico and Peru with only a few hundred Spanish soldiers.

4. Detail: The Spanish arrived with ______________, which made the Spanish seem godlike to Native Americans.

5. Detail: Many Native Americans hated their ______________ and assisted the conquistadors in overthrowing them.

6. Detail: The Europeans unknowingly brought ______________ to which Native Americans had no immunity.

Main Idea: Spanish explorers believed that the southeastern and southwestern parts of North America also held hidden wealth.

7. Detail: ______________, the first Spaniard to land on the mainland of North America, was searching for gold and the ______________.

8. Detail: Tales of the seven cities of gold told by Álvar Núñez Cabeza de Vaca in 1536 inspired the explorations of ______________ and ______________.

Main Idea: Spain established a government and social system in the colonies.

9. Citizenship Detail: The Spanish king established a ______________ that met in Spain and made laws for the colonies.

10. Citizenship Detail: At the top of the social classes were the ______________, who were people born in Spain. Next in line, were the creoles, the mestizos, and then the Native Americans. At the very bottom were ______________.

Guided Reading Activities ★ 6 ★ *The American Journey*

COOPERATIVE LEARNING ACTIVITY

Creating a News Broadcast Organize the class into groups of four to create a news broadcast about an explorer or a Native American leader mentioned in this section. Assign the following roles: anchorperson to present background information; explorer or leader; reporter to interview the show's guest; art and sound technician to create graphs, maps, props, sound effects, and so on. (If camcorders are available, add a fifth role for a camera operator.) After each group has practiced the newscast, have the group either perform the newscast live or show the videotape to the class.

you don't say...

Florida's Flowers When Ponce de León landed in present-day North America, he saw a beautiful land filled with rivers, lakes, streams, and flowers. He happened to arrive during Easter, which Spaniards also referred to as the Feast of Flowers. He called this land of luxuriant vegetation *Pasqua Florida,* meaning Feast of Flowers. The name was later shortened to Florida.

ABCNEWS INTERACTIVE™

VIDEODISC
Historic America Electronic Field Trips

Side 1, Chapter 4
Title: *St. Augustine*
Subject: The settlement of St. Augustine
Ask: **In Spanish history, what did the city of St. Augustine serve as?** *(a military outpost)*

Also available in VHS.

Map Study

Answers
1. De Soto
2. Cabeza de Vaca

Map Skills Practice

Reading a Map Which two explorers first landed on islands in the Caribbean Sea? *(De Soto and Ponce de León)*

❝All the Indians were inside like llamas. There were a great many of them and they could not get out, nor did they have any weapons. . . . The Spaniards killed them all—with horses, with swords, with guns. . . . From more than 10,000 men there did not escape 200.❞

A few months later, the Spanish falsely accused Atahualpa of crimes and executed him. The Inca were used to obeying commands from their rulers. Without leadership they were not able to fight effectively. By 1535 Pizarro had gained control of most of the vast Inca Empire.

Why Spain Succeeded

The conquistadors' victories in Mexico and Peru were quick and lasting. How could Cortés and Pizarro, with only a few hundred Spanish soldiers, conquer such mighty empires?

First, the Spanish arrived with strange weapons—guns and cannons—and fearsome animals. They rode horses and had huge, ferocious dogs. To the Native Americans, the Spanish seemed almost like gods. Second, many Native Americans hated their Aztec overlords and assisted the conquistadors in overthrowing them.

Finally, disease played an extremely large role in the Spanish conquest. Native Americans had no immunity to the diseases the Europeans had, unknowingly, brought with them. Epidemics of smallpox and other diseases wiped out entire communities in the Americas and did much to weaken the Aztec's and Inca's resistance. In Mexico, a Spanish friar recalled, "More than half the population died. They died in heaps, like bedbugs."

Spanish Explorers, 1513–1598

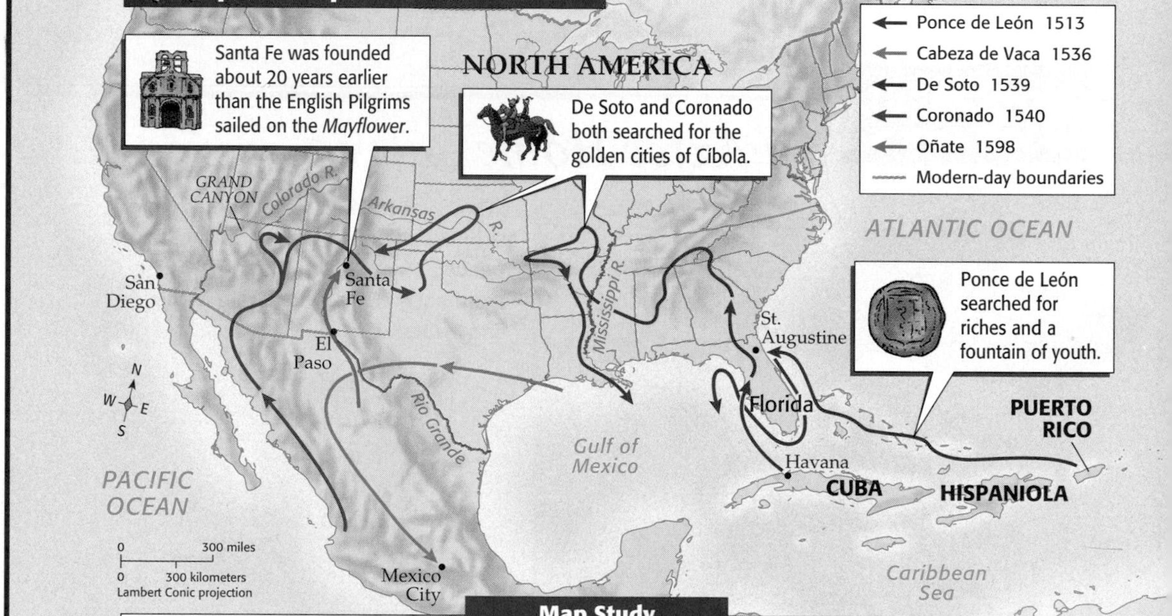

Map Study

Spanish explorers claimed Florida, Caribbean islands, and southwestern North America.

1. **Human/Environment Interaction** Which Spaniard explored areas along the southern half of the Mississippi River?
2. **Analyzing Information** Who was the first explorer to cross the Rio Grande?

MULTIPLE LEARNING STYLES

Visual/Spatial Have each student create a chart of explorers mentioned in this section. Have students include the following categories in the chart: explorer, nationality, country sponsoring explorer, flag of sponsoring country (illustration), dates of exploration, areas of exploration, and discoveries made. **L1, ELL**

Spain in North America

Mexico and Peru were rich in silver and gold. Hoping to find similar wealth to the north, conquistadors explored the southeastern and southwestern parts of North America.

Ponce de León in Florida

Juan Ponce de León made the first Spanish landing on the mainland of North America. He arrived on the east coast of present-day Florida in 1513. Besides gold, Ponce de León hoped to find the legendary fountain of youth, "a spring of running water of such marvelous virtue" that drinking it "makes old men young again." Ponce de León never found the fountain, but his exploration led to the first Spanish settlement in what is now the United States. In 1565 the Spanish established a fort at **St. Augustine,** Florida, to keep out a group of French settlers in the region.

The Seven Cities of Gold

Many other conquistadors searched for quick riches. None ever achieved this goal, and several lost their lives trying. **Álvar Núñez Cabeza de Vaca** (kuh•BAY•suh duh VAH•kuh) was part of a Spanish expedition to Florida in 1528.

The expedition, led by the conquistador **Pánfilo de Narváez,** failed. Stranded, de Narváez and his followers built several boats and sailed along the coast toward Mexico. However, in November 1528, all but two of the boats were lost in a storm. The two boats that survived went aground on an island near present-day Texas. Within a few months, all but a handful of the shipwrecked explorers died from disease and exposure.

Cabeza de Vaca and his companions survived by adopting Native American ways. Cabeza de Vaca and an enslaved African named **Estevanico** became medicine men. Cabeza de Vaca later wrote that their method of healing was "to bless the sick, breathing on them" and to recite Latin prayers. The Spaniards were praying that the patients would recover and be grateful.

In 1533 the Spaniards set off on foot on a great 1,000-mile journey across the Southwest. Arriving in Mexico in 1536, Cabeza de Vaca related tales he had heard of seven cities with walls of emerald and streets of gold.

Linking PAST & PRESENT

The First Thanksgiving

On April 30, 1598, long before the Pilgrims came to North America, Spanish colonists held a thanksgiving feast near present-day El Paso, Texas. Juan de Oñate had led 400 men and their families across the desert from Mexico. After they reached the Rio Grande, Oñate told them to feast and give thanks for the abundance of the new land.

De Soto's Expedition

The stories inspired **Hernando de Soto,** who led an expedition to explore Florida and lands to the west. For three years De Soto and his troops wandered around the southeastern area of the present-day United States, following stories of gold. As the Spaniards traveled, they preyed on the native peoples. Their usual method was to enter a village, take the chief hostage, and demand food and supplies.

De Soto crossed the **Mississippi River** in 1541, describing it as "swift, and very deep." After traveling as far west as present-day Oklahoma, De Soto died of fever. His men buried him in the waters of the Mississippi to keep his death a secret from the Indians.

Coronado and Oñate

Francisco Vásquez de Coronado also wanted to find the fabled seven cities of gold. His expedition included Friar Marcos, who claimed to have seen one of the cities on an earlier trip. After traveling through northern Mexico and present-day Arizona and New Mexico, the expedition reached the Zuni town of Cibola in early summer 1540. They realized at once that the friar's accounts had been false. There was no gold.

MAKING CONNECTIONS ACTIVITY

Cultural Life Invite each student to illustrate social class structure in the Americas under Spanish rule. Tell students to draw a graphic organizer that illustrates the power structure and the number of people in each class. For example, use a triangle to illustrate fewer people at the top holding the most power and more people at the bottom with the least power. **L2**

Linking PAST & PRESENT

Thanksgiving Day In 1863 President Abraham Lincoln declared Thanksgiving a national holiday. Americans celebrate Thanksgiving Day on the fourth Thursday in November.

Who?What?Where?When?

Montezuma Was Cortés's conquering of the Aztec Montezuma's self-fulfilling prophecy? Montezuma's aunt had dreamed of men dressed in black riding antlerless deer into Tenochtitlán to destroy the city. In 1519 Montezuma heard reports of men with black beards and white skin landing on Mexico's coast. He believed his aunt's dream was being fulfilled and that this landing signaled the promised return of Quetzalcoatal, a feathered serpent lord of the morning star. Quetzalcoatal had gone into exile more than 500 years before on a seagoing raft traveling toward the rising sun.

NATIONAL GEOGRAPHIC SOCIETY

VIDEODISC
GTV: The American People: Fabric of a Nation

Side 1, Chapter 5
Title: *When Worlds Collide*
Subject: European and Native American encounters (1500s)
Ask: **What were the early relationships between the Europeans and Native Americans like?** *(They often met in peace. Native Americans showed Europeans how and what to farm. Europeans shared their knowledge of weapons and tools.)*

3 ASSESS

Assign Section 3 Review as homework or as an in-class activity.

Use **Chapter Challenger Interactive Review Software** to review Section 3.

Section Quiz 2–3

Name ______ Date ______ Class ______

★ Chapter 2

Score

Section Quiz 2-3

DIRECTIONS: Matching Match each item in Column A with the items in Column B. Write the correct letters in the blanks. *(10 points each)*

Column A	Column B
____ **1.** conquistadors	**A.** pueblos
____ **2.** king's representative	**B.** Spanish explorers
____ **3.** Spanish towns in the Americas	**C.** missions
____ **4.** Spanish religious communities	**D.** viceroy
____ **5.** Spanish fort	**E.** presidio

DIRECTIONS: Multiple Choice In the blank at the left, write the letter of the choice that best completes the statement or answers the question. *(10 points each)*

____ **6.** Hernán Cortés destroyed the powerful empire of the
A. Inca. **C.** Maya.
B. Aztec. **D.** Olmec.

____ **7.** This man and his army conquered Peru.
A. Francisco Pizarro **C.** Hernán Cortés
B. Atahualpa **D.** Montezuma

____ **8.** Juan Ponce de León landed on the mainland of North America in search of
A. food. **C.** the fountain of youth.
B. his countrymen. **D.** slaves.

____ **9.** This was an essential part of the economy of the Spanish and Portuguese colonies.
A. tobacco **C.** slave labor
B. priests **D.** Native American laws

____ **10.** Nearly 300 million Native Americans on Hispaniola died within 50 years of Christopher Columbus's landing because of
A. overcrowded conditions. **C.** starvation.
B. exposure to heat. **D.** disease.

Section Quizzes ★ 6 ★ *The American Journey*

CURRICULUM CONNECTION

GEOGRAPHY
Columbus's third voyage marked the beginning of the Columbian Exchange, the movement of people, cultures, and ideas between two previously isolated worlds. This exchange grew into a worldwide movement in which whole populations expanded within their homelands or left those lands in mass migrations.

Juana Inés de la Cruz

Juan de Oñate (day ohn•YAH•tay) was sent from Mexico to gain control over lands to the north and to convert the natives. In 1598 Oñate founded the province of New Mexico and introduced cattle and horses to the Pueblo people.

Spain, however, remained much more interested in its colonial empire to the south. The West Indies, Mexico, and South America provided the silver and gold that made Spain wealthy.

Citizenship

Spanish Rule

★ The Spanish governed their colonies the way they governed their own country—from the top down. They divided their new lands into five provinces. The wealthiest were New Spain (Mexico) and Peru. The Spanish king established a Council of the Indies that met in Spain and made laws for the colonies. He also appointed a **viceroy** as his representative in each province.

Spanish law called for three kinds of settlements in the Americas—pueblos, missions, and presidios. **Pueblos,** or towns, were established as centers of trade. **Missions** were religious communities that usually included a small town, surrounding farmland, and a church. A **presidio,** or fort, was usually built near a mission.

Social Classes

A complex class system developed in Spain's empire in the Americas. The upper class consisted of people who had been born in Spain, called *peninsulares.* The *peninsulares* owned the land, served in the Catholic Church, and ran the local government. Below them were the creoles, people born in the Americas to Spanish parents. Lower in the class structure were the mestizos (meh•STEE•zohs), people with Spanish and Indian parents. Still lower were the Native Americans, most of whom lived in great poverty. At the very bottom were enslaved Africans.

Men dominated the society, and a woman's place was in the home. One Mexican woman of the 1600s, however, was different. Juana Inés de la Cruz gained renown as a woman of letters. She wrote plays, poetry, and an essay discussing women's place in society.

Native Americans

In the 1500s the Spanish government granted each conquistador who settled in the Americas an ***encomienda,*** the right to demand taxes or labor from Native Americans living on the land. This system turned the Native Americans into slaves. Grueling labor in the fields and in the gold and silver mines took its toll. Many Native Americans also died from malnutrition and disease.

A Spanish priest named **Bartolomé de las Casas** condemned the cruel treatment of the Native Americans. He reported abuses to the authorities in Spain and pleaded for laws to protect the Native Americans. Las Casas claimed that millions had died because the Spanish "made gold their ultimate aim, seeking to load themselves with riches in the shortest possible time."

CRITICAL THINKING ACTIVITY

Evaluating Information Direct students to the subsection titled *Why Spain Succeeded.* Ask them to analyze the information presented regarding the theories about why the Spaniards were able to conquer the mighty Native American empires. Guide students to scan other parts of the section that contain additional clues. Ask students to outline the pertinent information gathered in the section, make their own judgment about the fall of these empires, and write an essay explaining their theory and supporting it with the information in their outlines. **L3**

Because of Las Casas's reports, in 1542 the Spanish government passed the New Laws, which forbade making slaves of Native Americans. Although not always enforced, the laws did correct the worst abuses.

The Plantation System

Some Spanish settlers made large profits by exporting crops and raw materials back to Spain. In the West Indies, the main exports were tobacco and sugarcane. To raise these crops, the Spanish developed the plantation system. A **plantation** was a large estate run by the owner or a manager and farmed by workers living on it. The Spanish used Native Americans to work their plantations.

In his effort to help the Native Americans, Las Casas suggested replacing them with enslaved Africans—a suggestion he bitterly regretted later. He thought the Africans could endure the labor better than the Native Americans.

The Slave Trade

The Spanish quickly took up Las Casas's idea and began importing enslaved Africans. By the mid-1500s the Spanish were bringing thousands from West Africa to the Americas. The Portuguese did the same in Brazil.

The Africans who survived the brutal ocean voyage were sold to plantation owners. By the late 1500s, plantation slave labor was an essential part of the economy of the Spanish and Portuguese colonies.

The Columbian Exchange

The voyages of Columbus and other explorers brought together two parts of the globe that previously had had no contact: the continents of Europe, Asia, and Africa in one hemisphere and the Americas in the other. The contact led to an exchange of plants, animals, and diseases that altered life on both sides of the Atlantic. Scholars refer to this as the **Columbian Exchange.**

New Ways of Life

Europeans brought horses, cattle, pigs, and chickens. These new animals changed the diet and lifestyle of many Indian cultures. In turn the Americas provided many new foods—such as corn, tomatoes, beans, squash, potatoes, and chocolate—that made the European diet more nutritious and varied.

Recall that Europeans brought many diseases to the Americas that Native Americans had no immunity to. As a result many died of smallpox, influenza, measles, and other diseases. When Columbus landed on Hispaniola in 1492, more than 3 million Native Americans lived there. Fifty years later only about 500 remained.

Section 3 Review

Checking for Understanding

1. ***Identify*** Cortés, Montezuma, Pizarro, Atahualpa, Ponce de León, Las Casas.
2. ***Define*** conquistador, tribute, pueblo, mission, presidio, Columbian Exchange.
3. ***Explain*** how the Spanish, with so few soldiers, were able to conquer empires.

Reviewing Themes

4. **Groups and Institutions** What groups made up the class system in Spanish America?

Critical Thinking

5. **Identifying Assumptions** "We came to serve God and the king, and also to get rich." In what way do you think conquistadors planned to serve "God and the king"?

Activity

Creating a Menu Using cookbooks as your references, create an all-American dinner menu that includes foods introduced to the Europeans by Native Americans.

Section 3 Review Answers

1. Cortés, 50; Montezuma, 51; Pizarro, 51; Atahualpa, 51; Ponce de León, 53; Las Casas, 54
2. The words are defined in the Glossary.
3. through the use of guns, cannons, horses, fear, hatred, disease
4. *peninsulares,* creoles, mestizos, Native Americans, enslaved Africans
5. by spreading religious ideas and claiming land and riches for the king

Activity Menu items should include foods listed in this section.

Reteaching Activity 2–3

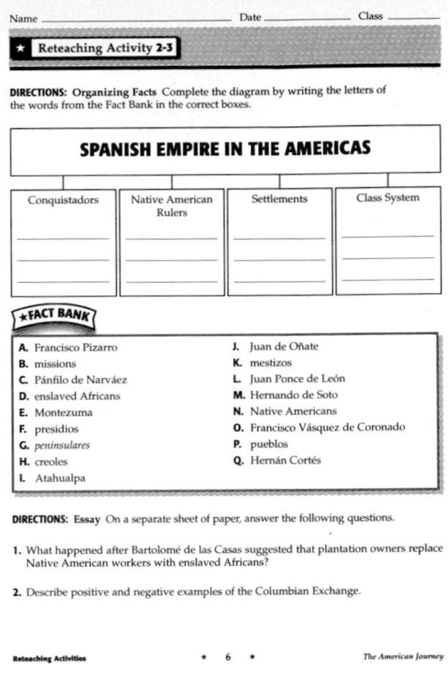
Name ______ Date ______ Class ______

★ Reteaching Activity 2-3

DIRECTIONS: Organizing Facts Complete the diagram by writing the letters of the words from the Fact Bank in the correct boxes.

SPANISH EMPIRE IN THE AMERICAS

Conquistadors	Native American Rulers	Settlements	Class System

★FACT BANK

A. Francisco Pizarro
B. missions
C. Pánfilo de Narváez
D. enslaved Africans
E. Montezuma
F. presidios
G. *peninsulares*
H. creoles
I. Atahualpa
J. Juan de Oñate
K. mestizos
L. Juan Ponce de León
M. Hernando de Soto
N. Native Americans
O. Francisco Vásquez de Coronado
P. pueblos
Q. Hernán Cortés

DIRECTIONS: Essay On a separate sheet of paper, answer the following questions.

1. What happened after Bartolomé de las Casas suggested that plantation owners replace Native American workers with enslaved Africans?
2. Describe positive and negative examples of the Columbian Exchange.

Reteaching Activities ★ 6 ★ *The American Journey*

Copyright © by The McGraw-Hill Companies, Inc.

Enrichment Activity 2–3

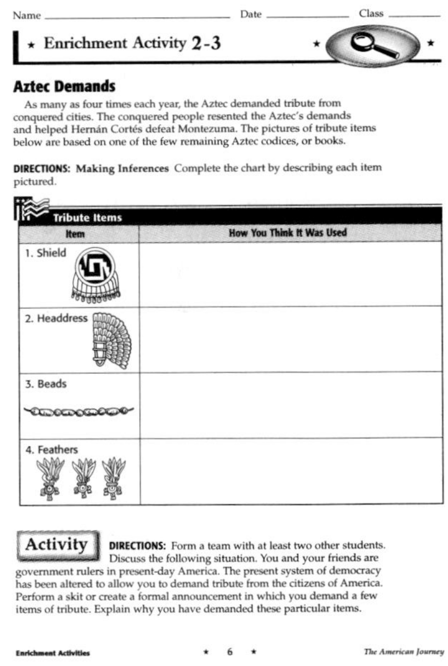
Name ______ Date ______ Class ______

★ Enrichment Activity 2-3

Aztec Demands

As many as four times each year, the Aztec demanded tribute from conquered cities. The conquered people resented the Aztec's demands and helped Hernán Cortés defeat Montezuma. The pictures of tribute items below are based on one of the few remaining Aztec codices, or books.

DIRECTIONS: Making Inferences Complete the chart by describing each item pictured.

Tribute Items

Item	How You Think It Was Used
1. Shield	
2. Headdress	
3. Beads	
4. Feathers	

Activity **DIRECTIONS:** Form a team with at least two other students. Discuss the following situation. You and your friends are government rulers in present-day America. The present system of democracy has been altered to allow you to demand tribute from the citizens of America. Perform a skit or create a formal announcement in which you demand a few items of tribute. Explain why you have demanded these particular items.

Enrichment Activities ★ 6 ★ *The American Journey*

Copyright © by The McGraw-Hill Companies, Inc.

4 CLOSE

Ask students to trace the events of the decline of the mighty empires in the Americas and the conquering of those empires by the Spaniards.

NATIONAL GEOGRAPHIC
Journeys

What? Where? When? Who?

Pima Uprising In 1695 the Piman peoples of the Altar Valley region revolted, killed missionaries, burned public buildings, and drove off livestock. They were protesting the pressure and structure of the mission communities, the encroachment of Spain's frontier onto their lands, and the growing exploitation of Native American labor. Father Kino attempted to reassure the Pima by showing them a document written by the Spanish viceroy. The paper exempted the Pima from forced labor for at least 20 years. Small wonder, then, that the Pima revolted again in the early 1750s.

History *and the* Humanities

U.S. History & Art, Transparency 3, *Mission San Xavier del Bac*

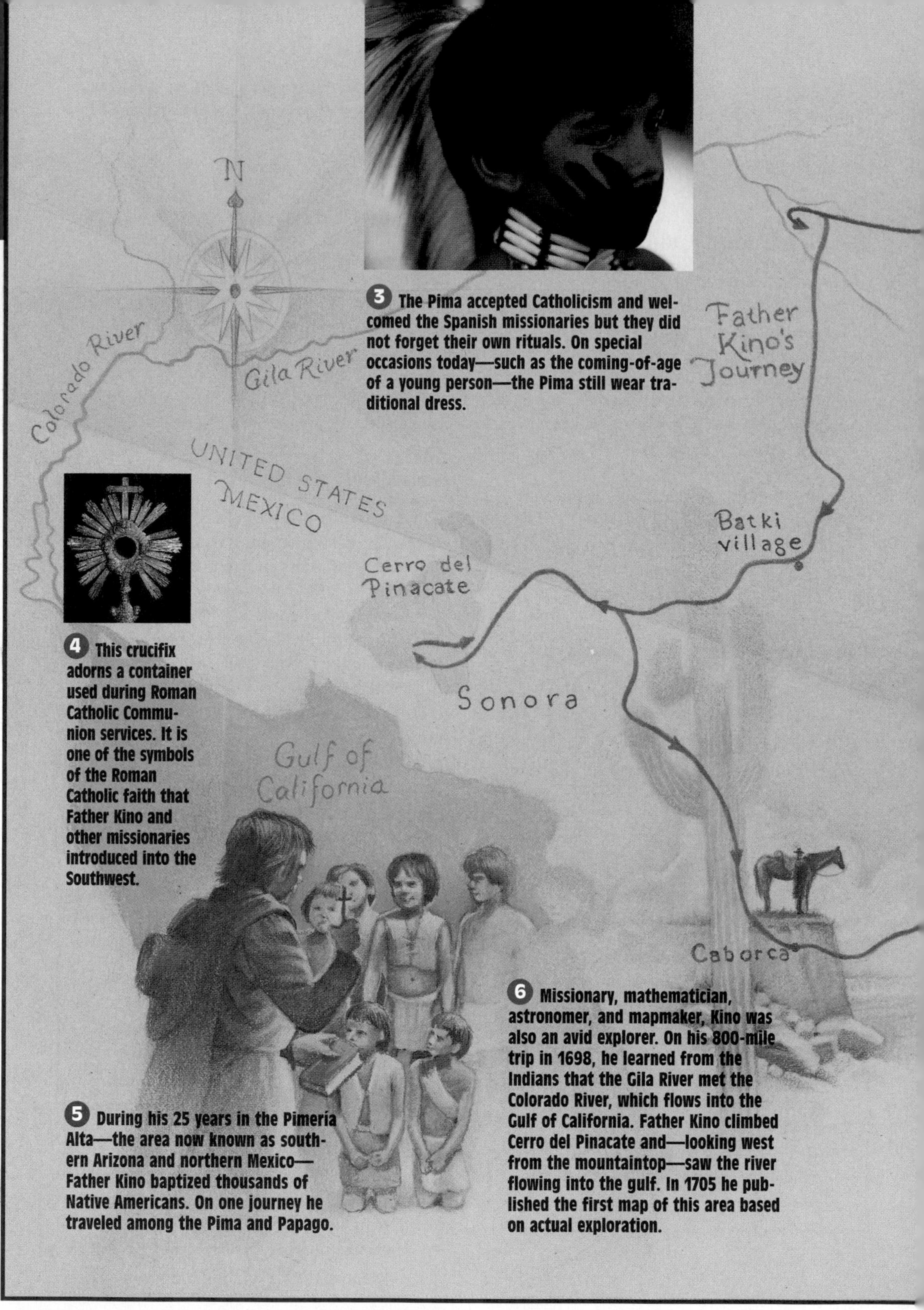

3 The Pima accepted Catholicism and welcomed the Spanish missionaries but they did not forget their own rituals. On special occasions today—such as the coming-of-age of a young person—the Pima still wear traditional dress.

4 This crucifix adorns a container used during Roman Catholic Communion services. It is one of the symbols of the Roman Catholic faith that Father Kino and other missionaries introduced into the Southwest.

5 During his 25 years in the Pimeria Alta—the area now known as southern Arizona and northern Mexico—Father Kino baptized thousands of Native Americans. On one journey he traveled among the Pima and Papago.

6 Missionary, mathematician, astronomer, and mapmaker, Kino was also an avid explorer. On his 800-mile trip in 1698, he learned from the Indians that the Gila River met the Colorado River, which flows into the Gulf of California. Father Kino climbed Cerro del Pinacate and—looking west from the mountaintop—saw the river flowing into the gulf. In 1705 he published the first map of this area based on actual exploration.

TEACHER'S NOTES

NATIONAL GEOGRAPHIC

Journeys

A Missionary's Journey

2 Father Kino established 29 missions, including San Xavier del Bac near Tucson, founded in 1700. Today the mission still serves as a church and school for the Papago Indians.

1 In 1687 Father Francisco Eusebio Kino, a Catholic missionary who came to the Americas with the Spanish, established headquarters at Nuestra Señora de los Dolores Mission in northern Mexico. From there, he set out on more than 50 journeys across Sonora and present-day Arizona. On September 22, 1698, he headed northwest to explore the region and to baptize more than 400 Pima and Papago.

"In this vast and very fertile vineyard of the Indian tribes which they call the Pimas ... I have been able, through the celestial favors of the heavenly saints, to wash about three hundred Indians in the holy water of baptism.... God willing, hundreds, and later, thousands will be gathered into the bosom of our sweet, most holy Mother Church.... In this charge where I am working, a mission [has] been established, and many very suitable rooms of a house [have] been built. We are now occupied in the erection of a new church, with the help of some soldiers, and its walls have ... happily arisen to a height of several feet."

—From a letter written by Father Kino, June 30, 1687.

57

Who?What?Where?When?

Father Kino The tireless efforts of Father Kino proved very fruitful. He introduced cattle, sheep, goats, horses, wheat and other seeds, and trees to the region. Another missionary noted that the San Xavier del Bac mission held 3,000 Native Americans. With its fertile, irrigated farmland and pastures, however, it could support at least 30,000 Native Americans.

NATIONAL GEOGRAPHIC SOCIETY

CD-ROM
NGS PictureShow: Native Americans, Part 2

Have students click on "Southwest" in the main menu to learn more about this culture's ceremonies and rituals and their struggles to preserve their lands and ways of life.

NGS PicturePack Transparencies: Native Americans, Part 2

Display the transparencies relating to the Southwest Native American cultures.

What?Where?When?Who?

Bibliography The excerpt at left was taken from *Rim of Christendom: A Biography of Eusebio Francisco Kino, Pacific Coast Pioneer* by Herbert Eugene Bolton. (Tucson, AZ: University of Arizona Press, 1984)

TEACHER'S NOTES

1 FOCUS

BELLRINGER
Motivational Activity

Before taking roll at the beginning of the class period, project Section Focus Transparency 2–4 and have students answer the questions. Discuss students' responses.

This activity is also available as a blackline master.

Section Focus Transparency 2–4

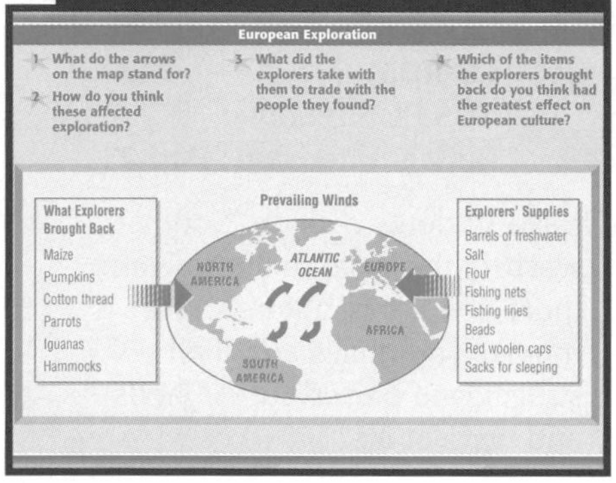

Vocabulary Precheck

Call on a volunteer to define the term *Northwest Passage.* Then have students locate on a map of North America where the Northwest Passage might lie.

Use the **Vocabulary Puzzle-Maker** to create crossword and word search puzzles.

Section Theme
Global Connections

Religion and mercantilism fueled European nations to compete for overseas territory.

Activity Brainstorm with students the motives for the involvement of the United States in the affairs of foreign nations. Compare these motives with the motives that other nations used to claim territory in North America as described in this section.

1450 — 1500 — 1550 — 1600

1497 John Cabot lands in Newfoundland

1517 Martin Luther starts the Protestant Reformation

1535 Jacques Cartier sails up the St. Lawrence River to Montreal

1609 Henry Hudson sails the Hudson River

Section 4

Exploring North America

READ TO DISCOVER . . .

- how the Protestant Reformation affected North America.
- how French, Dutch, and English explorers searched for the Northwest Passage.
- why the activities of early traders encouraged exploration.

TERMS TO LEARN

mercantilism
coureur de bois
Northwest Passage

The Storyteller

In 1517 **Martin Luther,** a German priest, nailed a list of complaints about the Catholic Church on the door of a local church. Luther declared that the Bible was the only true guide for Christians. He rejected many Church practices—even the authority of the pope—because they were not mentioned in the Bible. Luther also believed that faith rather than good deeds was the way to salvation.

Church officials tried to get Luther to take back his statements. "I cannot go against my conscience," he replied. "Here I stand. I cannot do otherwise. God help me."

Martin Luther

Martin Luther's actions led to incredible changes in Europe. Before he voiced his beliefs, the countries of Europe had their differences, but they were bound together by a common church. For centuries, Catholicism had been the main religion of western Europe. In the 1500s, however, Luther's opposition to the policies of the Roman Catholic Church emerged.

A Divided Church

Within a few years, Luther had many followers. They broke away from Catholicism to found their own Christian churches. Martin Luther's protests were the start of a great religious and historical movement known as the **Protestant Reformation.**

Protestantism Spreads in Europe

From Germany Luther's ideas spread rapidly. **John Calvin,** a French priest, also broke away from the Catholic Church. Like Luther, Calvin rejected the idea that good works would ensure an individual's salvation. He believed that God had already chosen those who would be saved.

In England King Henry VIII also left the Catholic Church. A dispute with Pope Clement VII over his marriage led to the break. The pope had refused Henry's request to declare his first marriage invalid. In 1534 the English Parliament denied the authority of the pope and recognized the king as head of the Church of England.

SECTION RESOURCES

Reproducible Masters
- Reproducible Lesson Plan 2–4
- Guided Reading Activity 2–4
- Section Quiz 2–4
- Reteaching Activity 2–4
- Enrichment Activity 2–4

Transparencies
- Section Focus Transparency 2–4

Multimedia
- Vocabulary PuzzleMaker
- Chapter Challenger Interactive Review Software
- Testmaker
- GTV: The American People: Fabric of a Nation
- NGS PictureShow: The Age of Exploration, Part 1

During the rule of Henry's daughter, Queen Elizabeth I, further reforms firmly established England as a Protestant nation.

Religious Rivalries in the Americas

Throughout western Europe, people and nations divided into Catholics and Protestants. When these Europeans crossed the Atlantic, they took along their religious differences.

Spanish and French Catholics worked to spread their faith to the Native Americans. The Spanish settled in the southwestern and southeastern regions of North America, and the French in the northeast. Dutch and English Protestants established colonies in lands along the Atlantic coast between the French and the Spanish settlements. Some of the English settlements were founded by Protestants seeking to practice their beliefs in peace.

Economics

Economic Rivalry

Religion was only one of the factors that pushed European nations across the Atlantic Ocean. The promise of great wealth was equally strong, especially as other Europeans watched Spain draw riches from its colonies.

According to the economic theory of **mercantilism,** a nation's power was based on its wealth. Rulers tried to increase their nation's total wealth by amassing gold and silver and by developing trade. Mercantilism provided great opportunities for individual merchants to make money. It also increased rivalry between nations.

Several countries in Europe competed for overseas territory that could produce wealth. They wanted to acquire colonies in the Americas that could provide valuable resources, such as gold and silver, or raw materials. The colonies also served as a place to sell European products.

A Northwest Passage

The Treaty of Tordesillas had divided the Americas between Spain and Portugal. It did not allow for claims by other nations—but England, France, and the Netherlands ignored the treaty. During the 1500s and early 1600s, these countries sent explorers to chart the coast of North America. The voyage to Asia—either around the southern tip of Africa or South America—was long and difficult. For this reason, the three countries hoped to discover a **Northwest Passage** to Asia—a more direct water route through the Americas.

English and French Explorations

In 1497 England sent **John Cabot,** an Italian, to look for a northern route to Asia. Cabot probably landed on the coast of present-day Newfoundland. England used Cabot's voyage as the basis for its claims to North America.

In 1524 France hired an Italian, **Giovanni da Verrazano,** to look for the northern sea route. Verrazano explored the coast of North America from present-day Nova Scotia to the Carolinas.

Picturing HISTORY In 1676 Kateri Tekakwitha, a 20-year-old Mohawk woman, accepted Christianity from French Catholic missionaries. **What region of North America was settled by the French?**

COOPERATIVE LEARNING ACTIVITY

Creating a Marketing Campaign Organize the class into groups of five to develop a marketing campaign. Ask students to imagine that they are a team working for an advertising company and have been assigned to develop a marketing campaign to promote a journey of exploration. Allow each group to choose the area of exploration, either historical or contemporary. Students in each group should choose from the following roles: designer of stationery and business cards with logo, copywriter for marketing brochure, layout artist to design and lay out brochure (either on paper or with desktop publishing software), writer of radio commercial, designer of a Web page on the Internet, and designer of a magazine advertisement. Then have each group sell the marketing campaign to the class. Have students vote on the most effective campaign.

2 TEACH

L1 Push and Pull Factors Explain to students the difference between push and pull factors. *Push factors* drive away and *pull factors* draw toward. Suggest that students work in small groups to review the section and list all factors that motivated explorers. Then label each factor as *push* or *pull.* As a class, discuss these factors and each group's interpretation of them.

Guided Reading Activity 2–4

Name ________ Date ________ Class ________

★ Guided Reading Activity 2-4

DIRECTIONS: Using Headings and Subheadings Locate each heading in your textbook. Then use the information to help you write each answer.

I. A Divided Church

A. Whose protests started the Protestant Reformation? ________

B. Who was John Calvin? ________

C. What did the English Parliament do in 1534 to turn England into a Protestant nation? ________

D. How did the religious rivalries in western Europe affect the Americas? ________

II. Economic Rivalry

A. Economics What two factors pushed Europeans across the Atlantic Ocean? ________

B. Economics Why did rival European nations want to acquire colonies in the Americas? ________

III. A Northwest Passage

A. How did England, France, and the Netherlands regard the Treaty of Tordesillas? ________

B. Where did John Cabot probably land on his search for a northern route to Asia? ________

C. What countries sent the following explorers to find a northwest passage?

1. Giovanni da Verrazano and Jacques Cartier ________

2. Henry Hudson ________

D. Explorers failed to find a northwest passage to Asia, but their efforts were not wasted. Explain. ________

IV. Early Traders

A. Why did the French settle in Canada? ________

B. Where did the Dutch set up trading posts in the early 1600s? ________

The American Journey ★ 7 ★ **Guided Reading Activities**

Picturing HISTORY The French enjoyed great influence among Native Americans because of their relationships with them. The French forged close ties with Native Americans, and missionaries established some of the first contacts between the peoples. French fur traders formed partnerships with Native Americans, often living among them and, at times, marrying Native American women.

Answer: *Canada*

CURRICULUM CONNECTION

ECONOMICS
During the age of exploration, European nations believed that their power, and ultimately their survival, depended on their acquisition of wealth. This national economic purpose, known as mercantilism, fueled not only exploration but also colonization. European nations considered their colonies as sources of raw materials, which were used to manufacture goods.

NATIONAL GEOGRAPHIC SOCIETY

VIDEODISC
GTV: The American People: Fabric of a Nation

Side 1, Chapter 3
Title: *Change of Scene*
Subject: Why Europeans sought a new home
Ask: **What European countries, discussed in this segment, sent explorers west across the sea?** *(Spain, Portugal, Holland, England, and France)*

CD-ROM
NGS PictureShow: The Age of Exploration, Part 1
Encourage students to explore reasons the explorers headed westward. Have students click on the main menu.

Map Study

Answers
1. Jacques Cartier
2. It was English territory.

Eleven years later Frenchman **Jacques Cartier** (KAR•tyay) sailed up the St. Lawrence River hoping it would lead to the Pacific. He got as far as the Huron Indian village of Hochelaga. From the mountain next to the village, wrote Cartier, "one sees a very great distance." He named the peak Mont-Royal, meaning "royal mountain." This is the site of the city now called **Montreal.** Cartier had heard many stories about gold, but he found neither gold nor a sea route to Asia.

Hudson's Discoveries

The Dutch, too, wanted to find a passage through the Americas. They hired **Henry Hudson,** an English sailor, to explore. In 1609 he discovered the river that now bears his name. In his ship, the *Half Moon,* Hudson sailed north on the Hudson River as far as the site of present-day Albany. Deciding that he had not found a passage to India, he turned back. The following year Hudson tried again, this time sent by England.

French Explorers, 1535–1682

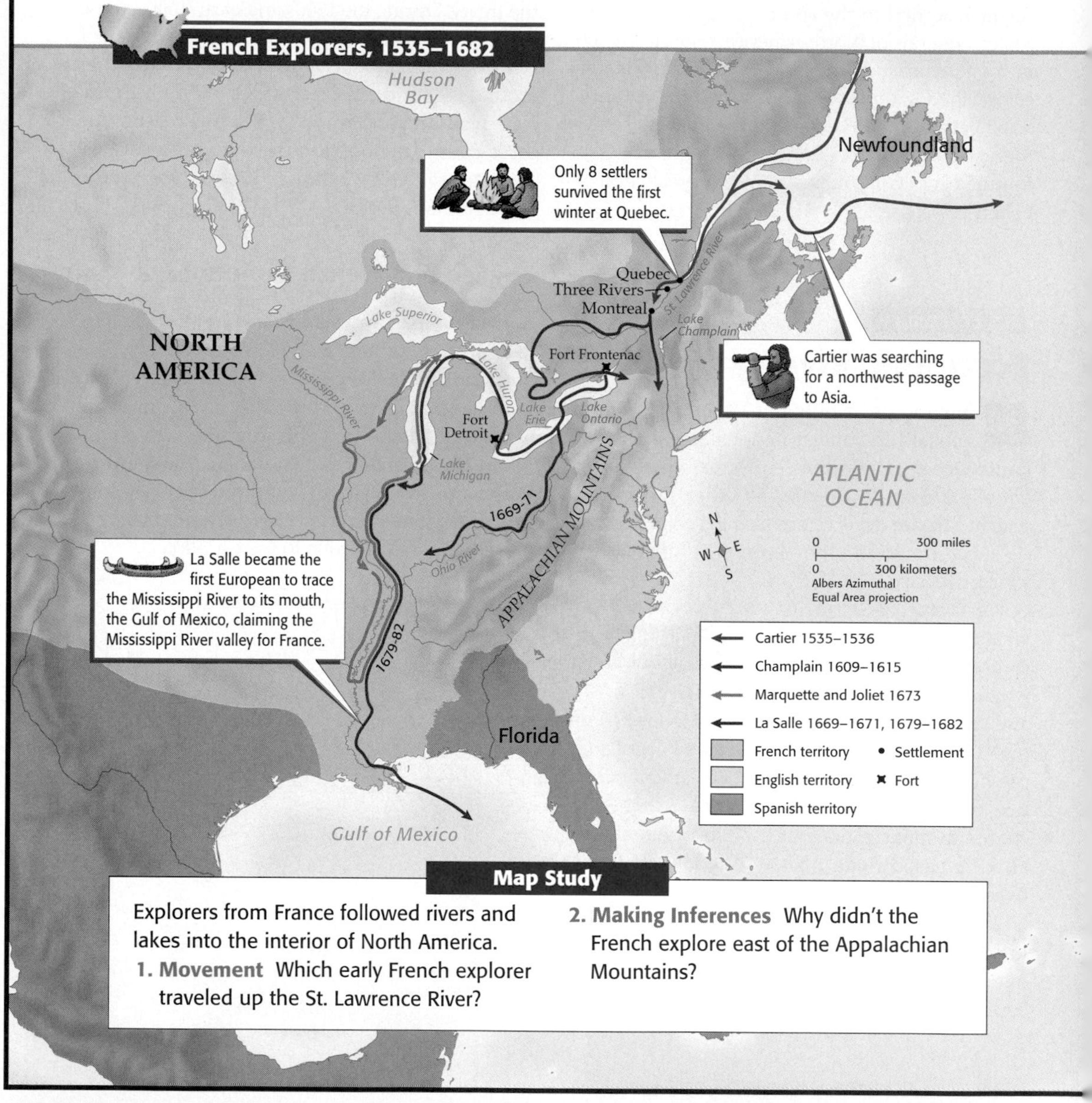

Map Study

Explorers from France followed rivers and lakes into the interior of North America.

1. **Movement** Which early French explorer traveled up the St. Lawrence River?
2. **Making Inferences** Why didn't the French explore east of the Appalachian Mountains?

MULTIPLE LEARNING STYLES

Auditory/Musical Organize the class into three groups, one representing the French, another the English, and the third the Dutch. Have students in each group choose a familiar melody such as "Row Row Row Your Boat" or "Mary Had a Little Lamb." Have groups write words to accompany this melody that describe the cultural contributions brought to the Americas by the group they represent. Encourage students to include names of significant people and settlements, economic activities, and any unique characteristics of that culture. Ask each group to sing the song, and if possible, allow students to play the melody. **L2**

Major European Explorers, 1487-1682

Explorer	Dates of Voyage	Accomplishments
For Portugal		
Bartolomeu Dias	1487–1488	Sailed around the southern tip of Africa
Vasco da Gama	1497–1499	Sailed around Africa to India
Pedro Alvares Cabral	1500	Sailed to Brazil
For Spain		
Christopher Columbus	1492–1504	Explored the islands of the Caribbean Sea
Juan Ponce de León	1508–1509, 1513	Explored Puerto Rico Explored Florida
Ferdinand Magellan	1519–1522	First to sail around the world
Cabeza de Vaca	1530	Explored Spanish northern Mexico and Brazil
Francisco Coronado	1540–1542	Explored southwestern North America
Hernando de Soto	1516–1520, 1539–1543	Explored Central America Led expedition to the Mississippi River
Juan Cabrillo	1542–1543	Explored the west coast of North America
For England		
John Cabot	1497–1501	Rediscovered Newfoundland (east coast of North America)
Henry Hudson	1610–1611	Explored Hudson Strait and Hudson Bay
For the Netherlands		
Henry Hudson	1609	Explored the Hudson River
For France		
Giovanni da Verrazano	1524	Explored the east coast of North America, including New York Harbor
Jacques Cartier	1534–1542	Explored the St. Lawrence River
Samuel de Champlain	1603–1615	Explored the St. Lawrence River Founded Quebec
Jacques Marquette/ Louis Joliet	1673	Explored the Mississippi River
Robert de La Salle	1666–1682	Explored the Great Lakes Founded Louisiana after reaching the mouth of the Mississippi River

Chart Study

Most European explorers reached the Western Hemisphere.

1. Which two countries explored the east coast of North America?
2. **Analyzing Information** Whose expedition was the first to sail around the world?

3 ASSESS

Assign Section 4 Review as homework or as an in-class activity.

Use **Chapter Challenger Interactive Review Software** to review Section 4.

Section Quiz 2–4

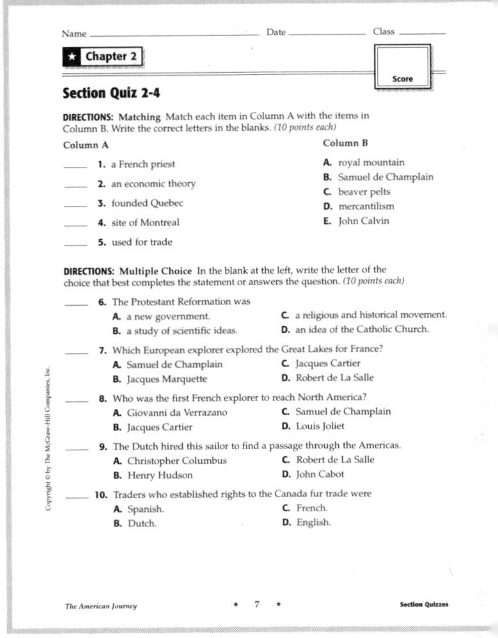

Name ______ Date ______ Class ______

★ Chapter 2

Score

Section Quiz 2-4

DIRECTIONS: Matching Match each item in Column A with the items in Column B. Write the correct letters in the blanks. *(10 points each)*

Column A	Column B
____ **1.** a French priest	**A.** royal mountain
____ **2.** an economic theory	**B.** Samuel de Champlain
____ **3.** founded Quebec	**C.** beaver pelts
____ **4.** site of Montreal	**D.** mercantilism
____ **5.** used for trade	**E.** John Calvin

DIRECTIONS: Multiple Choice In the blank at the left, write the letter of the choice that best completes the statement or answers the question. *(10 points each)*

____ **6.** The Protestant Reformation was
A. a new government. **C.** a religious and historical movement.
B. a study of scientific ideas. **D.** an idea of the Catholic Church.

____ **7.** Which European explorer explored the Great Lakes for France?
A. Samuel de Champlain **C.** Jacques Cartier
B. Jacques Marquette **D.** Robert de La Salle

____ **8.** Who was the first French explorer to reach North America?
A. Giovanni da Verrazano **C.** Samuel de Champlain
B. Jacques Cartier **D.** Louis Joliet

____ **9.** The Dutch hired this sailor to find a passage through the Americas.
A. Christopher Columbus **C.** Robert de La Salle
B. Henry Hudson **D.** John Cabot

____ **10.** Traders who established rights to the Canada fur trade were
A. Spanish. **C.** French.
B. Dutch. **D.** English.

The American Journey ★ 7 ★ **Section Quizzes**

Chart Study

Answers

1. France and England
2. Ferdinand Magellan

Chart Skills Practice

Reading a Chart Which country did not explore what is now North America? *(Portugal)*

Making Connections Activity

Economics Northern Native Americans trapped beaver and traded beaver fur to European settlers in return for blankets and tools. Explain to students that this form of exchange is called bartering. Point out that beaver fur had value because beaver-fur hats were popular in Europe. Blankets and tools had value because Native Americans could use them. Brainstorm items in demand today that could easily be traded among students' peer groups. Consider why the items are popular. Decide what other item or items would be equal in value to trade for the original item. **L2**

CHAPTER 2
Section 4, 58–62

Reteaching Activity 2–4

Name ______ Date ______ Class ______

★ Reteaching Activity 2-4

DIRECTIONS: Matching Match each item in Column A with its corresponding item in Column B. Write the correct letters in the blanks.

COLUMN A

____ **1.** Martin Luther
____ **2.** John Calvin
____ **3.** Henry the VIII
____ **4.** mercantilism
____ **5.** Northwest Passage
____ **6.** John Cabot
____ **7.** Giovanni da Verrazano
____ **8.** Jacques Cartier
____ **9.** *Half Moon*
____ **10.** Samuel de Champlain
____ **11.** coureurs de bois
____ **12.** New Amsterdam

COLUMN B

A. economic theory that a nation's power was based on its wealth
B. fur trappers
C. founded the site of present-day Montreal
D. an Italian whose voyage England used as the basis for its claims to North America
E. French explorer who established a settlement in Quebec, Canada
F. German priest whose protests against the Catholic Church started the Protestant Reformation
G. a direct water route through the Americas
H. present-day New York City
I. left the Catholic Church when the pope refused to grant him a divorce
J. the ship Henry Hudson sailed
K. French priest who believed that God had chosen those who would be saved
L. explored the coast of North America from Nova Scotia to the Carolinas for France

DIRECTIONS: Essay Answer the following questions on a separate sheet of paper.

13. Why did England, France, and the Netherlands hope to discover a northwest passage to Asia?

14. Why did the French settle in Canada?

The American Journey ★ 7 ★ **Reteaching Activities**

Enrichment Activity 2–4

Name ______ Date ______ Class ______

★ Enrichment Activity 2-4 ★ ★

The Habitation of Quebec

Samuel de Champlain established the settlement of Quebec in 1608 as a fur-trading post with 24 settlers. By the end of the first extremely cold winter, only eight of the settlers remained alive. The demand for furs, however, continued to draw new settlers to Quebec.

Quebec

Year	Population
1608	24
1609	8
1629	fewer than 60
1666	547
1690	1,500
1760	7,900

SOURCE: *World Book Encyclopedia*, Vol 3, Chicago, London, Sydney, and Toronto, 1989.

DIRECTIONS: Interpreting a Chart Use the chart to answer the following questions.

1. Between what years did the population of Quebec nearly triple? ______

2. How much did Quebec's population increase in the 70 years between 1690 and 1760? ______

3. When did the population reach its lowest point, and why did it fall so low? ______

4. How many years passed before the population grew to nearly 60 people? ______

5. By how many people did the population increase between 1666 and 1690? ______

Drawing Conclusions

6. Why do you think so many of the first settlers died during the first cold winter in Quebec? ______

7. For the settlement to survive, what steps do you think the settlers needed to take? ______

Activity **DIRECTIONS:** Use the media center to research the population numbers for the early years of your community. Then create a population chart that shows how the population of your community grew over time. Did the first settlers in your community face hardships like those of the early settlers in Quebec?

The American Journey ★ 7 ★ **Enrichment Activities**

America's FLAGS

Flag of New France Settlers in New France flew this French flag, which was based on the French Royal Banner, until 1763. White was the French royal color of the time.

Sailing almost due west from northern England, Henry Hudson and his crew discovered a huge bay, now called **Hudson Bay.** Hudson thought he had reached the Pacific Ocean. After months of searching for an outlet from the bay, however, the crew rebelled. Hudson, his son John, and a few sailors were set adrift in a small boat—and never seen again.

Early Traders

France had shown little interest in building an empire in the Americas. Its rulers were preoccupied by political and religious conflicts at home. The French viewed North America as an opportunity for profits from fishing and fur trading rather than a place to settle.

Furs were popular in Europe, and traders could make large profits from beaver pelts acquired in North America. A group of French traders obtained the rights to the fur trade with Native Americans. In 1608 the group sent **Samuel de Champlain** to establish a settlement in **Quebec** in what is now **Canada.** Champlain made several trips to the region and discovered Lake Champlain. He described the beautiful scenery and abundant wildlife and the Native Americans he met there.

From Quebec the French moved into other parts of Canada, where they built trading posts to collect furs gathered by Native Americans and French trappers. The trappers were called **coureurs de bois** (ku•RUHR duh BWAH), meaning "runners of the woods."

In the early 1600s, the Dutch began to set up trading posts along the Hudson River—first at Fort Orange (later Albany) and then at New Amsterdam (site of present-day New York City). For the Netherlands, England, and France, the 1500s were years of early exploration. In the early 1600s, France and the Netherlands established trading posts in the Americas. More serious efforts to discover and develop the possibilities of North America were to come in the years that followed.

Section 4 Review

Checking for Understanding

1. ***Identify*** Martin Luther, Jacques Cartier, Henry Hudson, Samuel de Champlain.
2. ***Define*** mercantilism, Northwest Passage, coureur de bois.
3. ***Summarize*** the complaints of Protestants who were opposed to the practices of the Roman Catholic Church.

Reviewing Themes

4. **Global Connections** Why did some European nations hope to find raw materials for industry in the Americas?

Critical Thinking

5. **Making Comparisons** How did the goals of the French in the Americas differ from the goals of other European countries?

Activity

Giving Directions Write a letter to one of the explorers who searched for a Northwest Passage. Provide the explorer with specific directions on how to find a water passage through northern Canada to the Pacific Ocean.

4 CLOSE

Ask students to debate which European country discussed in this chapter had the greatest impact on the development of American culture.

Section 4 Review Answers

1. Martin Luther, 58; Jacques Cartier, 60; Henry Hudson, 60; Samuel de Champlain, 62
2. The words are defined in the Glossary.
3. They rejected Catholic practices not listed in the Bible; believed that faith, not good deeds, led to salvation.
4. to supply their industries in Europe
5. The French were interested in making profits from fishing and the fur trade. Other European nations were more interested in claiming and settling land.

Activity Letters should be to one explorer with directions leading from Canada's Atlantic coast to the Pacific coast.

Social Studies
SKILL BUILDER

Reading a Time Line

Knowing the relationship of time to events is important in studying history. A time line is a visual way to show chronological order within a time period. Most time lines are divided into sections representing equal time intervals. For example, a time line showing 1,000 years might be divided into ten 100-year sections. Each event on a time line appears beside the date when the event took place.

Dates at the beginning and the end of a time line mark a time span, or the number of years the time line covers. Events listed on the time line all take place within its time span.

Learning the Skill

To read a time line, follow these steps:

- Find the dates on the opposite ends of the time line to know the time span. Also note the intervals between dates on the time line.
- Study the order of events.
- Analyze relationships among events or look for trends.

Practicing the Skill

Analyze the time line of Magellan's voyage. Use it to answer the questions below.

1. What time span is represented?
2. How many years do each of the sections represent?
3. Did Magellan's voyage to the Spice Islands occur before or after his voyage to the Philippines?
4. About how long after Magellan offered his services to the king of Spain did it take for five ships to sail?
5. How long did the voyage around the world take?

Applying the Skill

Making a Time Line List 10 key events that have occurred in your life and the dates on which these events occurred. Write the events in chronological order on a time line.

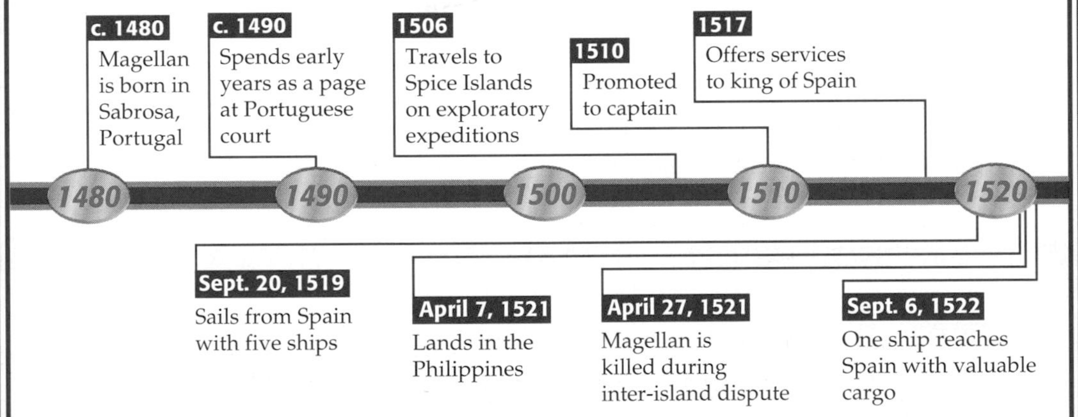

Social Studies
SKILL BUILDER

TEACH

Reading a Time Line

This skill demonstrates how to read a time line and relates the importance of time lines to the study of history. Explain to students that time lines are drawn to scale with each segment measuring a specific length and standing for the same number of years. For example, one inch (2.54 cm) equals 10 years. Ask students to find the scale on the time line on this page *(1 ½ inches [3.81 cm] equals 10 years).* Invite students to find the scales used on the time lines at the beginning of this Unit and each section.

Additional Practice

Chapter Skills Activity 2

you don't say...

Land of Fire As Magellan made his way through the strait at the southern tip of South America, he noticed large fires on land to the south. He named the area *Tierra del Fuego,* or Land of Fire.

ANSWERS TO PRACTICING THE SKILL

1. 1480 to the 1520s
2. 10 years
3. before
4. 2 years
5. 3 years

Applying the Skill Students should design time lines that plot 10 key events in their lives.

GLENCOE TECHNOLOGY

VIDEODISC
MindJogger Videoquiz

Use MindJogger to review the Chapter 2 content.

Chapter 2
Disc 1, Side A

Also available in VHS.

Reviewing Key Terms

The key terms used in this activity are defined in the textbook glossary on pages A26–A35. Students' word search puzzles will vary.

Reviewing Key Facts

1. for trade
2. Ghana, Mali, Songhai
3. Spain
4. Vasco da Gama sailed around the southern tip of Africa; Ponce de León explored Puerto Rico and Florida; John Cabot rediscovered Newfoundland.
5. for their riches, especially gold

Critical Thinking

1. The Portuguese wanted to find an eastern route to Asia by sailing around Africa. Columbus was looking for a western route by sailing across the Atlantic Ocean.
2. England was looking for a Northwest Passage through North America; Spain was interested in wealth found in Mexico and South America.

Time Line Activity

Events should be placed in this order: The Renaissance begins, Dias sails around the tip of Africa, Columbus makes his first voyage to the Americas, Pizarro conquers the Inca, Cartier explores Canada

Chapter 2

Review and Activities

Reviewing Key Terms

On graph paper, create a word search puzzle using the following terms. Crisscross the terms vertically and horizontally, then fill in the remaining squares with extra letters. Use the terms' definitions as clues to find the words in the puzzle. Share your puzzle with a classmate.

Renaissance
astrolabe
caravel
mosque
strait
conquistador
viceroy
pueblo
Columbian Exchange
mercantilism
Northwest Passage

Reviewing Key Facts

1. Why were Europeans interested in Asia?
2. What three large African kingdoms south of the Sahara flourished between 300 and 1600?
3. Which country supported Columbus on his quest to find a water route to Asia?
4. List the major accomplishments of Vasco da Gama, Ponce de León, and John Cabot.
5. What was the main reason the Spanish wanted to conquer the Aztec and Inca?

Critical Thinking

Making Comparisons

European nations had different reasons for exploring overseas.

1. How did Portuguese efforts to reach Asia differ from Columbus's efforts?
2. Why was England more interested in North America than Spain was?

Time Line Activity

Create a time line on which you place the following events in chronological order.

- Columbus makes his first voyage to the Americas
- Pizarro conquers the Inca
- The Renaissance begins
- Dias sails around the tip of Africa
- Cartier explores Canada

Skill Practice Activity

Reading a Time Line

Study the time line below, then answer the following questions.

1. What is the time span covered on this time line?
2. How far apart are the intervals on this time line?
3. Which three events occured in 1492?

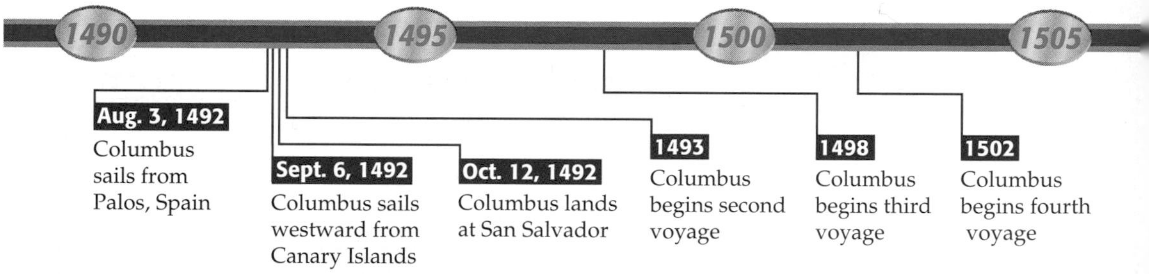

Skill Practice Activity

1. 1490 to 1505
2. 5 years
3. Columbus sailed from Spain and the Canary Islands and landed at San Salvador.

Geography Activity

1. Texas, New Mexico, Arizona, California
2. San Francisco
3. northwest

Geography Activity

Study the map below and answer the questions that follow.

Missions in New Spain by the 1700s

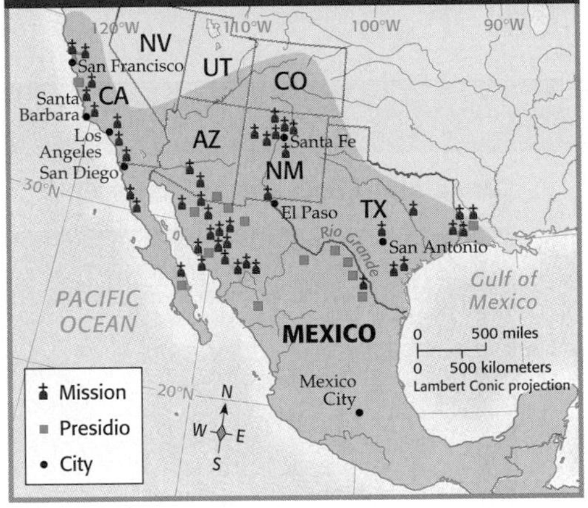

1. **Place** In what present-day states were the Spanish missions located?
2. **Location** Near what city was the northernmost Spanish mission located?
3. **Location** In which direction would a traveler leaving Mexico City journey to reach San Diego?

Reviewing Themes

1. **Culture and Traditions** Give one example of how trade encouraged an exchange of culture.
2. **Geography and History** Why are the Caribbean Islands often referred to as the West Indies?
3. **Groups and Institutions** How did the development of the Spanish *encomienda* system lead to the enslavement of Africans in America?
4. **Global Connections** What factors motivated voyages of exploration?

Technology Activity

Using a Word Processor Search the library for information on boats and sailing. Using a word processor, prepare a report about a navigational instrument that is in use today. Describe how it would have been helpful to an explorer such as Magellan.

Cooperative Activity

History and Language Arts Working in a group, research Spanish influence on American culture. Decide how American words, styles of architecture, and foods were influenced by Spain's presence. Other areas of influence might include clothing styles, traditions, and holidays. Present your findings in an illustrated brochure. Use photos, maps, or sketches to add information to your brochure. Include information about locations in the United States where Spanish influence is particularly strong.

Portfolio Activity **History Journal** Review the chapter for examples of how Spanish explorers treated Native Americans. Then imagine that you have been assigned to a special council of lawmakers in Europe in the 1500s. Make a list of five laws you would pass to ensure that explorers treated the people they encountered in other lands fairly.

CHAPTER 2

Review and Activities

Technology Activity

Students should describe a modern navigational instrument and explain how it could have aided an early explorer.

Cooperative Activity

Students' illustrated brochures should provide an in-depth examination of Spanish influence on American culture. Included in the brochures could be examples of Spanish language, architecture, foods, and customs as well as locations where Spanish influence was greatest.

Portfolio Activity Students should list five laws that would have ensured better treatment of Native Americans by the Spaniards.

Chapter Bonus Test Question

Ask: After what explorer is the Pacific end of the Panama Canal named? *(Vasco Núñez de Balboa)*

Reviewing Themes

1. Answers will vary, but students should provide one of the following examples: Muslim religion, architecture, customs adapted by African kingdoms, or contact through trade brought a rebirth of learning to Europe.
2. Columbus originally believed he had landed in the East Indies near Asia. As a result the islands were later named the West Indies.
3. Spaniards had been using Native Americans as slaves on the *encomienda* system when a Spanish priest, Bartolomé de las Casas, denounced this abusive system. He suggested replacing Native Americans with enslaved Africans.
4. Answers should include: religion, economic wealth, search for Northwest Passage, profits from fishing and fur trading

Unit 2 Resource Guide

These Glencoe resources may be used to teach, reteach, or enrich the concepts presented in this unit of study.

TEACHING TRANSPARENCIES

Map Transparency 2 with Overlays A, B, C

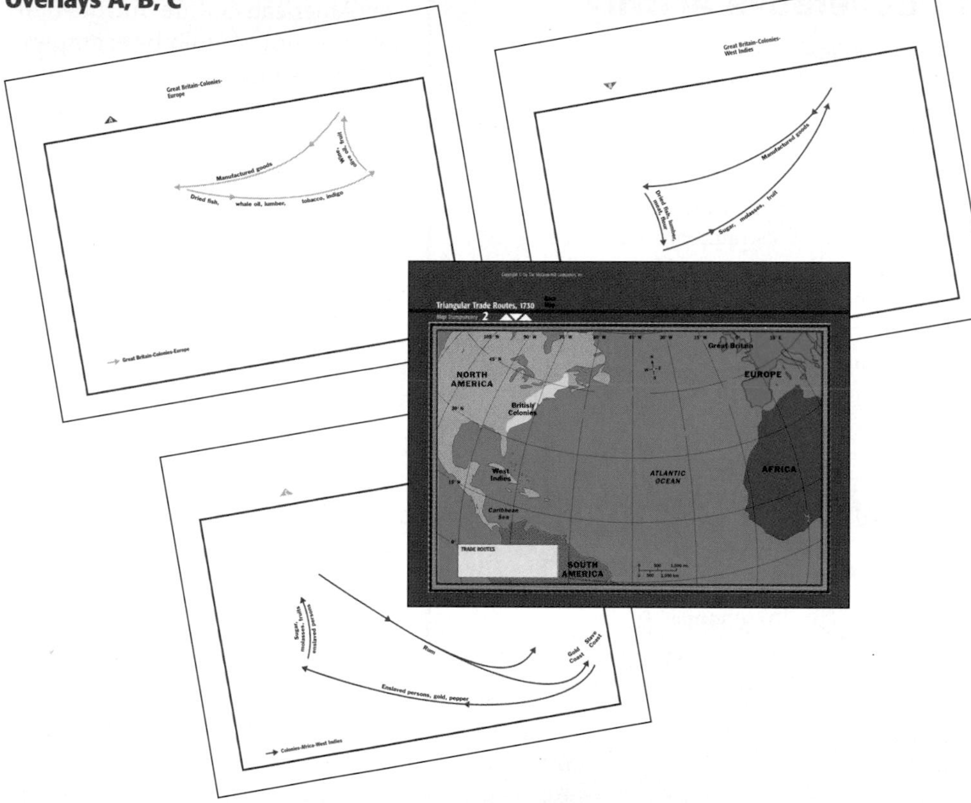

Cause-and-Effect Transparency 2

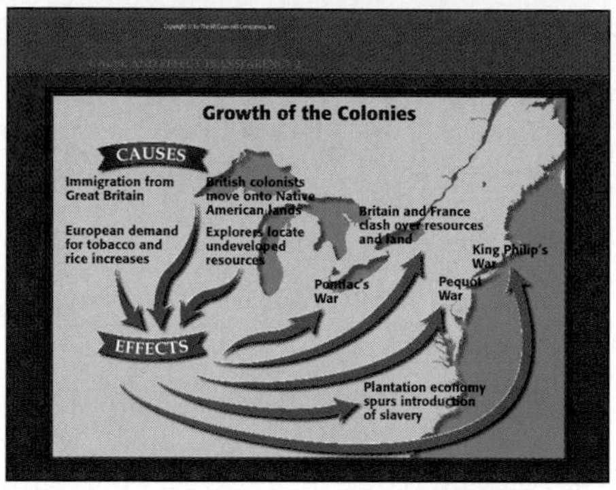

BIBLIOGRAPHY

Readings for the Student

Fleischman, Paul. ***Saturnalia.*** New York: Harper & Row, 1990. An apprentice searches for his relatives.

Warner, John. ***Colonial American Home Life.*** New York: Franklin Watts, 1993. Daily activities of the period.

Reading for the Teacher

Barchers, Suzanne I. and Patricia C. Marden. ***Cooking Up U.S. History: Recipes and Research to Share with Children.*** Englewood, CO: Teacher Ideas Press, 1991. Recipes and information about American foods.

Multimedia Resources

Videocassette. ***Colonial America.*** VHS video. Produced and distributed by Random House Media, 1988. Describes where various ethnic groups settled and the nature of colonial life.

Videocassette. ***The French and Indian War.*** VHS or Beta video. Produced and distributed by Cornet/MTI Film & Video, 1981. Events that led to war.

interNET CONNECTIONS

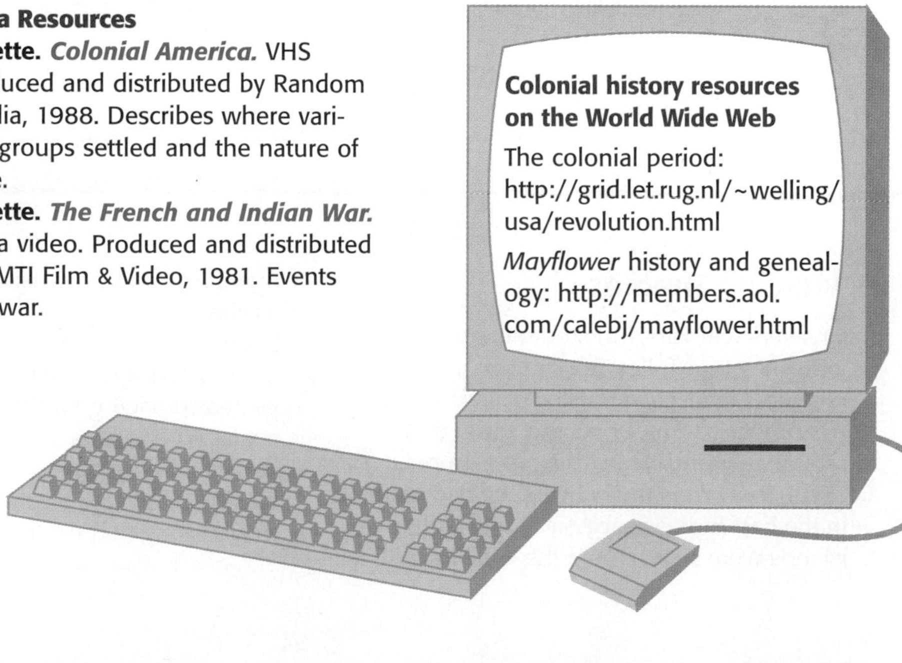

Resource Guide Unit 2

Interdisciplinary Activities

American Literature Reading 2

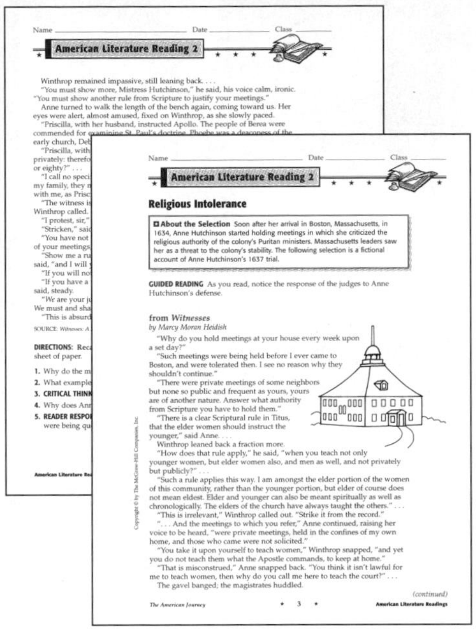

Interdisciplinary Connection 2

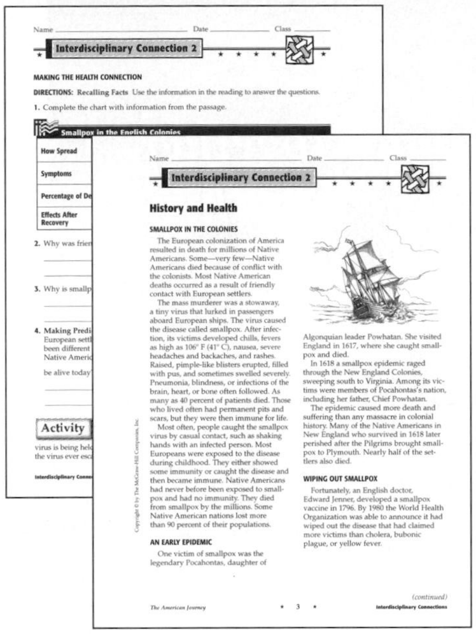

Enrichment Activities

Cooperative Learning Activity 2

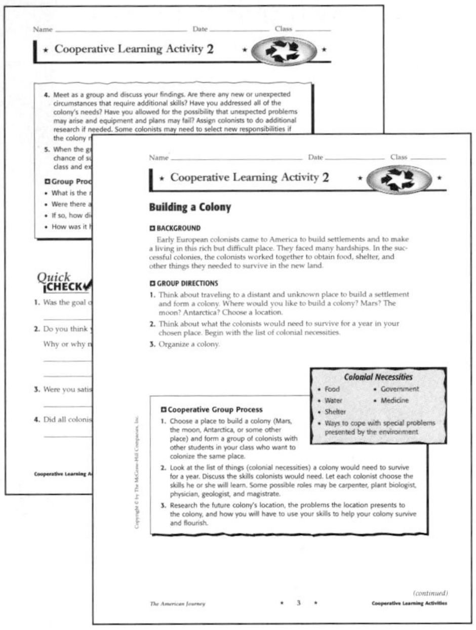

Hands-On Activities

Hands-On History Lab Activity 2

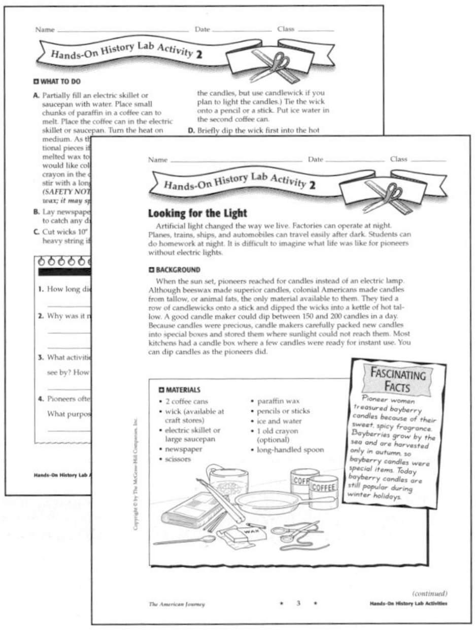

History Simulation 2

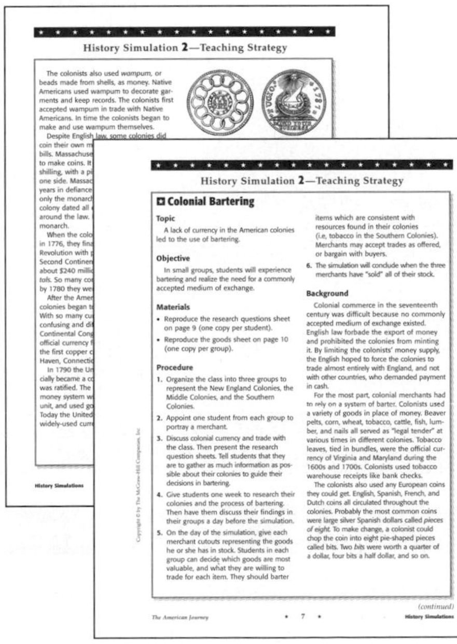

Assessment

Unit 2 Test

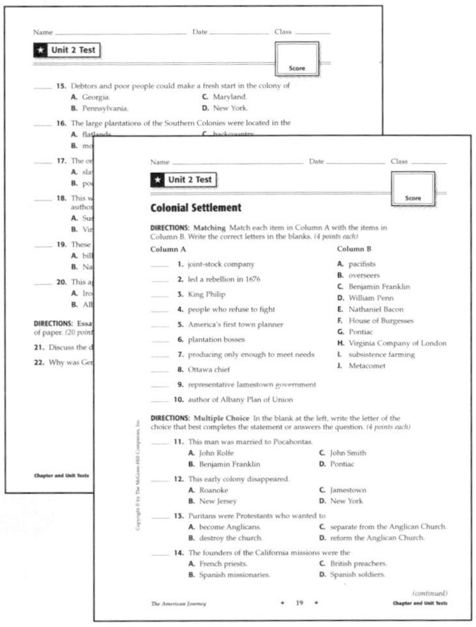

0:00 OUT OF TIME?

If your teaching time is limited, you may use the *Chapter Summaries* blackline master found in the TCR with the *Chapter Digests Audiocassette Activities and Tests* to condense individual chapters into a one-day lesson.

Introducing the Unit

Activity Have students design a chart to fill in as they read the unit. The chart should list each colony and have space for pertinent information, such as date founded, founders, type of colony (royal or proprietary), main religious groups, economic activities, and so on.

Unit Objectives

Upon completing this unit, students will be able to:

1. Describe the founding of the New England, Middle, and Southern Colonies and the other European colonies in America.
2. Discuss economic and cultural aspects of colonial life and explain the causes of the French and Indian War.

Hands-On HISTORY

Hands-On History Lab Activity 2, "Looking for the Light," is a high-interest **constructivist approach** activity directly related to the main topic of the unit.

Unit 2

Colonial Settlement

1587–1770

"Rejoyce together, mourne together, labour and suffer together. . . ."

—John Winthrop, 1630

MAPPING America

Portfolio Activity Draw a freehand outline map of the United States. As you read Unit 2, use map pencils to shade in the various colonial settlements as they are introduced. Plot the important cities on your map, too. Then label the important physical features—mountains, rivers, other bodies of water—on your map.

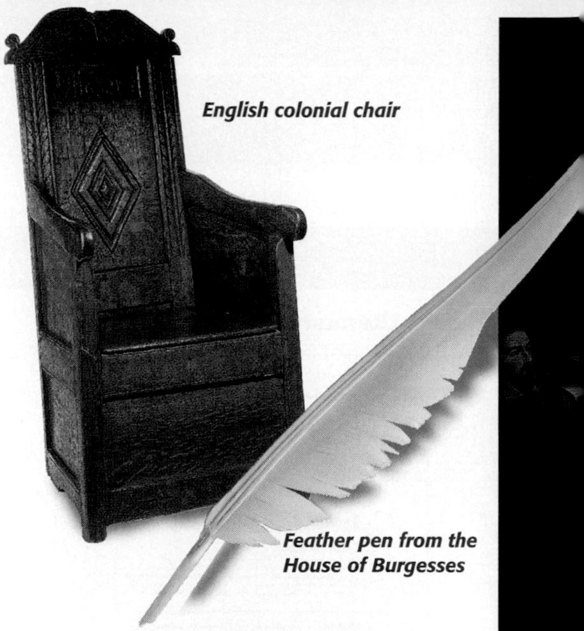

English colonial chair

Feather pen from the House of Burgesses

Algonquin beaver bowl

United States

1607 English establish first permanent settlement at Jamestown

1620 Pilgrims land at Plymouth Rock

1550

1600

1588 England defeats Spanish Armada

World

TEAM TEACHING STRATEGIES

Music Work with the Music teacher to present to students examples of early American vocal music, such as "I Am the Rose of Sharon" by William Billings (1746–1800).

Language Arts For about a decade in the mid-1600s, in an effort to build the population of New France, the French government sent 200 people a year to the colony. Among these people were 40 young, single women selected from orphanages or poor families and sent at the king's expense. Have students work with the Language Arts teacher and write diary entries from the perspective of a single woman sent to New France.

HISTORY AND ART ***Signing the Mayflower Compact* by J.L.G. Ferris** Pilgrims on board the *Mayflower* signed a compact, or agreement, to set up a civil government and obey its laws.

Pewter pitcher, Plymouth Plantation

1630 Puritans begin settling Massachusetts Bay

1649 King Charles I is beheaded in London

1660 King Charles II is restored to the English throne

1670 Alafin Ajagbo founds Oyo Empire in Nigeria

1700s Thousands of Africans are brought to America and enslaved

1701 England and Spain go to war

1718 French establish port of New Orleans

1763 British tighten enforcement of Navigation Acts

1650 — 1700 — 1750 — 1800

Team Teaching Strategies

Art In colonial times, traveling artists painted portraits for a living. Many were self-taught and thus produced rather primitive pieces. Have students work with the Art teacher to find examples of such artists' works. Discuss how the works show the artists' lack of formal training (lack of perspective, problems with proportion, and so on).

NATIONAL GEOGRAPHIC SOCIETY

VIDEODISC
GTV: A Geographic Perspective on American History

Side 1, Chapter 6
Title: *Hoping for the Best in America*
Subject: Trials and triumphs of English settlers (1607–1700)
Ask: **How did Native Americans help the settlers?** *(They taught the settlers how to clear the land and fish with spears, and they introduced new food sources.)*

HISTORY AND ART Jean Léon Gérôme Ferris (1863–1930) lived long after the event shown in the painting, but he made a thorough study of seventeenth-century architecture, customs, and dress. This painting is part of his series of 70 historical paintings. **Ask:** **Do you think women signed the Mayflower Compact?** *(No, only one woman is shown in the painting and she does not seem to be involved in the signing.)*

Linking PAST & PRESENT

Activity In this unit, students will learn how William Penn designed Philadelphia. Most other American cities grew with little or no planning, but in modern times, people have regained interest in city planning. Reston, Virginia, is an example of a modern, planned community. Have students research and compare the plans of Reston and Philadelphia.

Block Schedule

Team Teaching This selection from *The Kidnapped Prince* may be implemented in a team-teaching context, in conjunction with English/ Language Arts.

Reinforcing Vocabulary

Review the **Reader's Dictionary** terms with students to be sure they understand any unfamiliar terms.

Historical Connection

By the time Olaudah Equiano was taken from his home in eastern Nigeria, the slave trade was well established. Equiano survived against great odds. Millions of other Africans were killed during capture or perished aboard the vastly overcrowded and unsanitary ships during the long voyage to the Americas.

Background Information

Setting The excerpt takes place at the end of the horrendous voyage from Africa to America known as the Middle Passage. Unlike most other captives, Equiano eventually bought his freedom, learned to read and write, and published his story.

Characters In this autobiographical account, Equiano is, of course, the main character. Other characters include the captives on the ship with him and the various masters he encounters during his enslavement.

Plot *The Kidnapped Prince* tells Equiano's story from his life in Africa before his capture through the terrifying voyage and slave auction to his eventual purchase of freedom.

America's Literature

The Kidnapped Prince

by Olaudah Equiano

Olaudah Equiano (c. 1745–1797) was an 11-year-old boy when he and his sister were kidnapped and brought to the West Indies, where they were enslaved. His life story includes memories of his childhood in Africa. He wrote his story after receiving the name Gustavus Vassa from one of his masters and buying his freedom. Published during the time of the movement to end slavery, Equiano's work became a best-seller.

Read to Discover

In this selection, Olaudah and his sister have been kidnapped and are forced to endure the terrifying trip across the Atlantic Ocean aboard a slave ship. As you read, think about what life must have been like for Africans who were sold into slavery.

Reader's Dictionary

vessel: ship
Bridgetown: capital of Barbados
parcel: group
lots: groups
toil: work

One day the whites on board gave a great shout, and made many signs of joy to us. We did not know why, but as the vessel drew nearer we plainly saw the island of Barbados and its harbor, and other ships of different kinds and sizes. Soon we anchored among them off Bridgetown.

Many merchants and planters came on board, though it was in the evening. They put us in separate groups, and examined us, and made us jump. They pointed to the land, signifying we were to go there. We thought these ugly men meant they were going to beat us soon. Then we were all put down under the deck again.

There was much dread and trembling among us, and nothing but bitter cries to be heard all night. At last the crew, who heard us, got some old slaves from the land to calm us. They told us no one was going to beat us. We were going to work. Soon we would go on land, and see many of our countrypeople. This report relieved us, and we could sleep. And, sure enough, not long after we landed, Africans of all languages came to talk to us.

Right away we were taken to a merchant's yard, where we were all penned up together like so many sheep. When I looked out at the town, everything was new to me. The houses were built with bricks, in stories, and were completely different from any I had seen in Africa. I was still more astonished at seeing people on horseback. I thought it was more magic, but one of the slaves with me said that the horses were the same kind they had in his country.

Additional Literary Works about the Period

You may want to refer students to the following:

Farber, Norma. ***Mercy Short: A Winter Journal, North Boston, 1692–1693.*** New York: Dutton, 1982. A Salem girl's involvement with witchcraft and her capture by Native Americans.

Koller, Jackie French. ***The Primrose Way.*** Orlando, FL: Harcourt, 1992. In 1633 a young woman chosen to learn the language of the Native Americans begins to understand and respect their culture.

Schurfranz, Vivian. ***Danielle.*** New York: Scholastic, 1984. A young woman chooses between marriage and life as a pirate.

Sullivan, Nancy, ed. ***Treasury of American Poetry.*** New York: Doubleday, 1978. American poetry from Anne Bradstreet's times to the twentieth century.

Between 1600 and 1850, millions of enslaved Africans were brought to the Americas on ships.

We were not many days in the merchant's custody before we were sold—like this:

Someone beat a drum. Then all the buyers rushed at once into the yard where we were penned to choose the parcel of us that they liked best. They rushed from one group of us to another, with tremendous noise and eager faces, terrifying us all.

Three men who were sold were brothers. They were sold in different lots. I still remember how they cried when they were parted. Probably they never saw each other again.

I didn't know it, but this happened all the time in slave sales. Parents lost their children; brothers lost their sisters. Husbands lost their wives.

We had already lost our homes, our countries, and almost everyone we loved. The people who did the selling and buying could have done it without separating us from our very last relatives and friends. They already could live in riches from our misery and toil. What possible advantage did they gain from this refinement of cruelty?

Responding to Literature

1. Where in the Americas was Olaudah Equiano sold into slavery?
2. How were the Africans treated after they landed?

Activity

Writing a Diary Reread the excerpt. Imagine what it must have been like to be separated from family members in the way that Olaudah describes. Write two journal entries as an enslaved person. The first entry should reflect your fears on the day you are sold. The second entry should describe what your life is like one year later.

Answers to Responding to Literature

1. in Bridgetown, on the West Indian island of Barbados
2. They were penned up together like sheep, then sold to the highest bidder with no regard for family groups.

Activity Entries should reflect an understanding of the Africans' fear and sorrow and of the wretchedness and drudgery of life as an enslaved person.

History *and the* Humanities

The Spirit of American Art and Music, *Joshua Johnston*

Portfolio Activity Have students research John Newton, the hard-bitten slave ship captain who experienced a change of heart, became an Anglican minister, and wrote the words to "Amazing Grace," the most popular hymn in the English language. After students present their findings in a format of their choosing, you may wish to show the PBS video *Amazing Grace with Bill Moyers.*

At the Movies

The made-for-TV movie *Roots* is available on videocassette at many libraries. It traces an African American family from capture in Africa to modern times.

Curriculum Connection

GEOGRAPHY

The most popular slave markets in Africa were on the west coast from Senegal south to Angola. So many slaves were exported from the coast along the Bight of Benin (part of the Gulf of Guinea) that the area was called the *Slave Coast.* For European slave traders, timing their arrival on the African coast was crucial. If they arrived during the rainy season, trade proved difficult and the risk of catching malaria greatly increased.

Chapter 3 Planning Guide

A complete, 1-page lesson plan is provided for each section in the *Reproducible Lesson Plans* booklet.

Section Resources

Daily Objectives	Reproducible Resources	Multimedia Resources
Section 1 Early English Settlements Explain why, although England's first attempts at colonizing failed, Jamestown not only survived but also gained the right to representative government.	Reproducible Lesson Plan 3–1 Guided Reading Activity 3–1* Section Quiz 3–1* Reteaching Activity 3–1 Enrichment Activity 3–1	Section Focus Transparency 3–1 Vocabulary PuzzleMaker Chapter Challenger Interactive Review GTV: The American People: Fabric of a Nation NGS PictureShow: Colonial America NGS PictureShow: The Age of Exploration, Part 1
Section 2 New England Colonies Describe the roles of Pilgrims, Puritans, and others in the beginnings of the New England Colonies.	Reproducible Lesson Plan 3–2 Guided Reading Activity 3–2* Section Quiz 3–2* Reteaching Activity 3–2 Enrichment Activity 3–2	Section Focus Transparency 3–2 Vocabulary PuzzleMaker GTV: The American People: Fabric of a Nation Facts On File: Landmark Documents in American History
Section 3 Middle Colonies Explain how the founding of New York City and Penn's Philadelphia helped make the Middle Colonies very diverse.	Reproducible Lesson Plan 3–3 Guided Reading Activity 3–3* Section Quiz 3–3* Reteaching Activity 3–3 Enrichment Activity 3–3	Section Focus Transparency 3–3 Vocabulary PuzzleMaker Chapter Challenger Interactive Review Facts On File: Landmark Documents in American History
Section 4 Southern Colonies Summarize the differences among the Southern Colonies' founding, including ways of life and the role of religion.	Reproducible Lesson Plan 3–4 Guided Reading Activity 3–4* Section Quiz 3–4* Enrichment Activity 3–4 Reteaching Activity 3–4	Section Focus Transparency 3–4 Vocabulary PuzzleMaker GTV: A Geographic Perspective on American History GTV: The American People: Fabric of a Nation NGS PictureShow: Colonial America
Section 5 Other European Settlements Compare French and Spanish settlements in North America with those of the English.	Reproducible Lesson Plan 3–5 Guided Reading Activity 3–5* Section Quiz 3–5* Reteaching Activity 3–5 Enrichment Activity 3–5	Section Focus Transparency 3–5 Vocabulary PuzzleMaker Chapter Challenger Interactive Review Software Testmaker ABCNews InterActive™ Historic America Electronic Field Trips

** Also available in Spanish*

Blackline Master · Videodisc · Audiocassette · Music Program · Transparency · CD-ROM · Software

0:00 **OUT OF TIME?**
Assign the Chapter 3 Digest and the corresponding Chapter Digests Audiocassettes with activities and tests.

ACTIVITY

From the Classroom of...

Steve Burns
Colrain Middle School
Cincinnati, OH

Tracing Steps Toward Representative Government

Organize students into groups of four or five. Ask each group to use their textbooks to create an outline that will list chronologically places, events, individuals or groups, documents, and governing bodies linked to the development of representative types of government. Write the following partial outline on the board as an example:

I. Jamestown 1607
  A. Businesspeople
    1. Captain John Smith served as leader in beginning years.
    2. John Rolfe developed less bitter tobacco.
  B. The House of Burgesses
    1. First assembly of elected lawmakers in colonial America.
    2. People had a say in making their own laws.
II. Plymouth
III. Connecticut

Groups should take turns going to a map at the front of the room and pointing to key locations as they explain facts pertaining to that place.

NATIONAL GEOGRAPHIC SOCIETY Teacher's Corner

INDEX TO NATIONAL GEOGRAPHIC MAGAZINE

The following articles may be used for research relating to this chapter:

- "Treasure from the Silver Bank," by Tracy Bowden, July 1996.
- "Portugal's Sea Road to the East," by Merle Severy, November 1992.

NATIONAL GEOGRAPHIC SOCIETY PRODUCTS AVAILABLE FROM GLENCOE

To order the following products for use with this chapter, contact your local Glencoe sales representative, or call Glencoe at 1-800-334-7344:

- *GTV: The American People: Fabric of a Nation* (Videodisc)
- *GTV: A Geographic Perspective on American History* (Videodisc)
- *PictureShow: Colonial America* (CD-ROM, Transparencies)
- *PictureShow: Native Americans, 1 and 2* (CD-ROM, Transparencies)
- *Native Americans* (Poster Set)

ADDITIONAL NATIONAL GEOGRAPHIC SOCIETY PRODUCTS

To order the following products for use with this chapter, call National Geographic Society at 1-800-368-2728:

- *Native American Heritage: A Visitor's Guide* (Map)
- *Indians of North America* (Map)
- *The World of the American Indian* (Book)
- *American Indians: A Brief History* (Video)
- *Historical Atlas of the United States* (Atlas)

Block Schedule

Block scheduling differs from traditional class scheduling in the amount of time allotted to each period. The extended time frame provided by block scheduling affords you the opportunity to implement a greater number of research-oriented and activity-intense projects to motivate and involve your students. Activities that are particularly suited to use within the block scheduling framework are identified throughout this chapter by the following designation:

KEY TO ABILITY LEVELS

Teaching strategies have been coded for varying learning styles and abilities.

- L1 **BASIC** activities for all students
- L2 **AVERAGE** activities for average to above-average students
- L3 **CHALLENGING** activities for above-average students
- ELL **ENGLISH LANGUAGE LEARNER** activities

Chapter 3 Resource Guide

Home Involvement

Home Involvement Activity 3

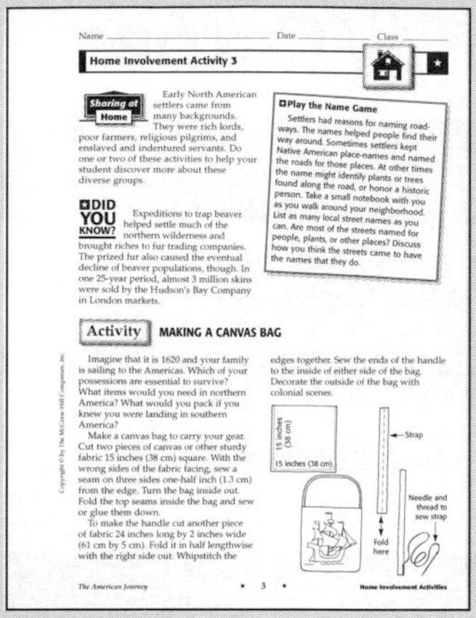

Review Activities

Chapter Summary 3

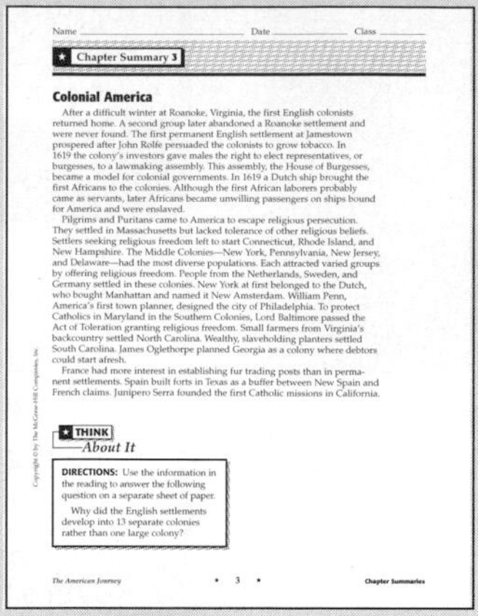

Workbook Activity 3

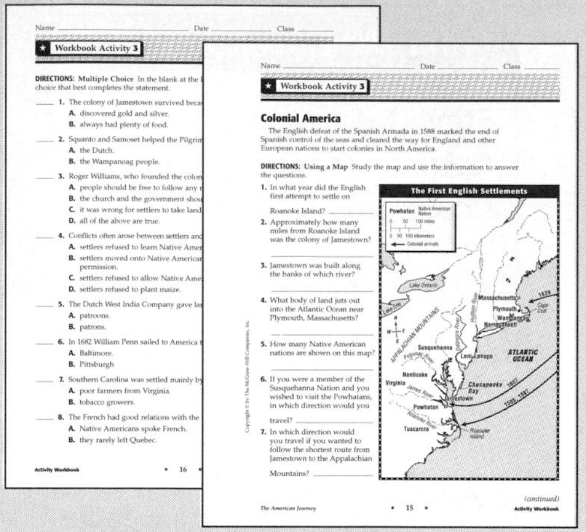

Reinforcement Activities

Time Line Activity 3

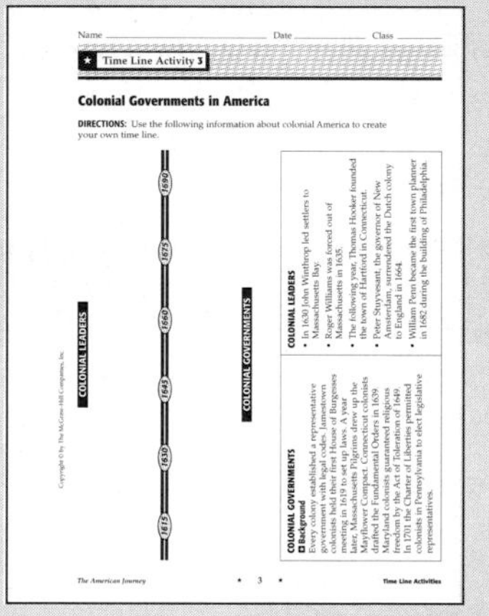

Vocabulary Activity 3

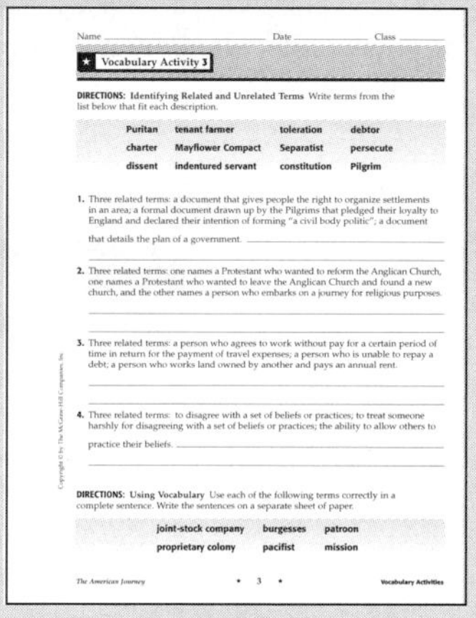

Chapter Skills Activity 3

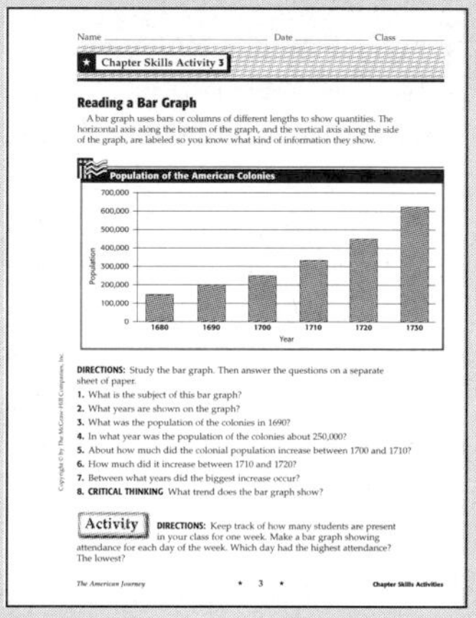

Enrichment Activities

Linking Past and Present Activity 3

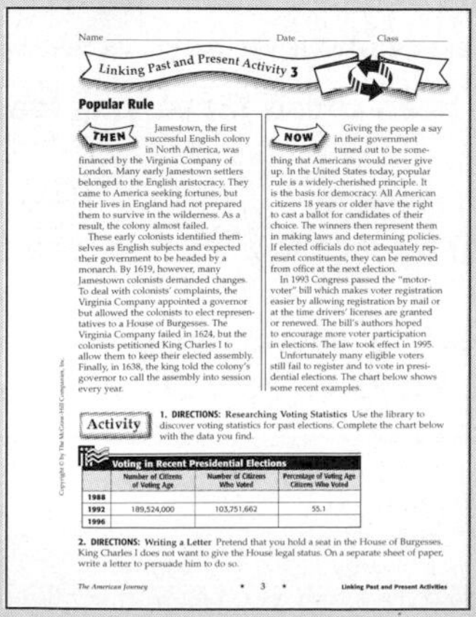

Primary Source Reading 3

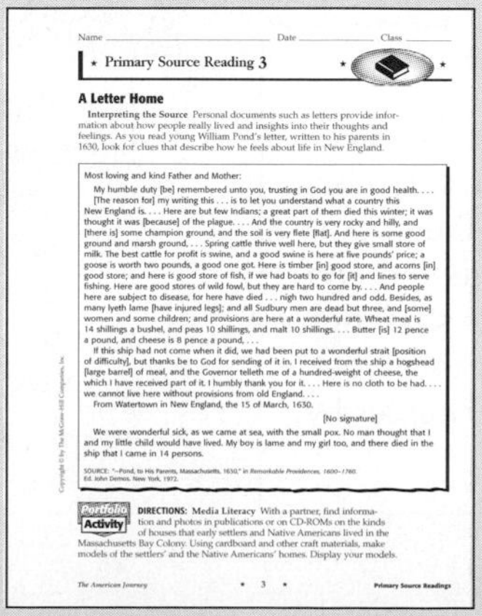

Geography Activities

Mapping History Activity 3

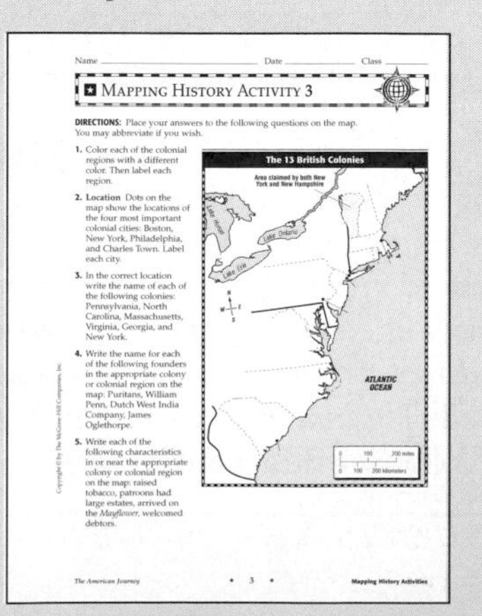

Chapter 3 Resource Guide

ASSESSMENT

Chapter 3 Test, Form A

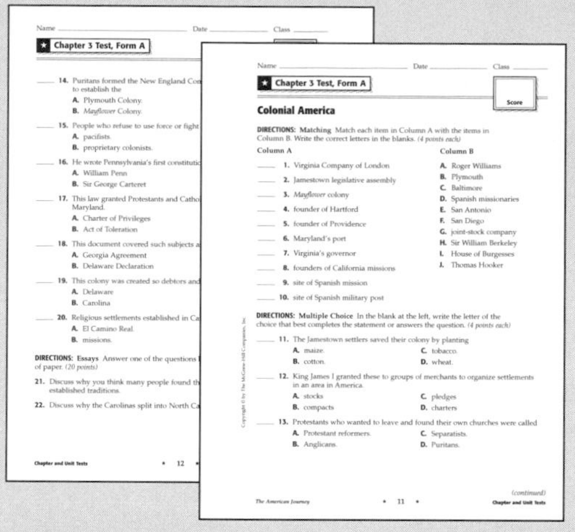

Chapter 3 Test, Form B

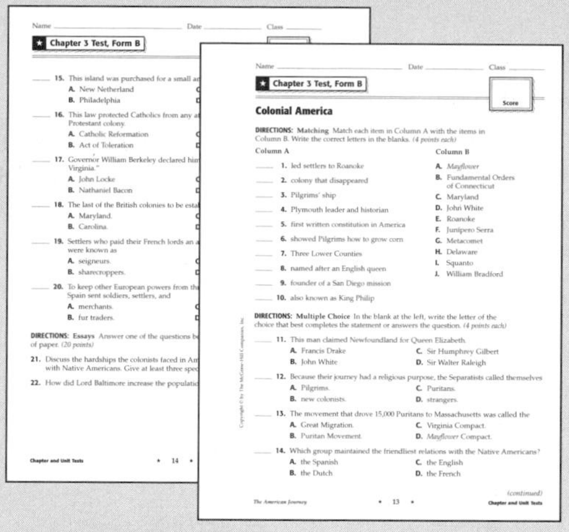

Performance Assessment Activity 3

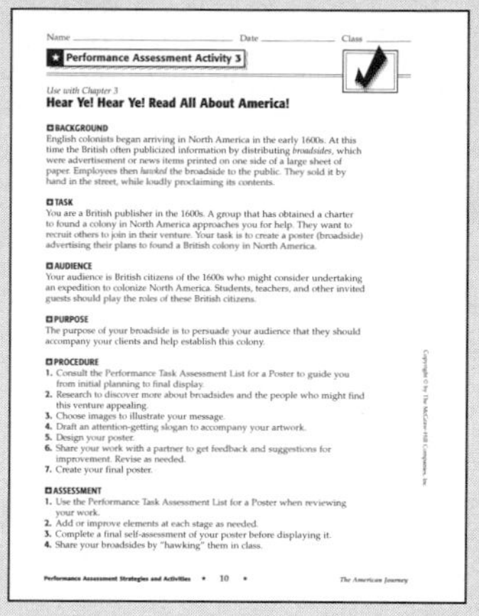

SPANISH RESOURCES

The following Spanish language materials are available in the Spanish Resources binder:

- **Spanish Chapter Summary 3**
- **Spanish Vocabulary Activity 3**
- **Spanish Guided Reading Activities, Chapter 3**
- **Spanish Section Quizzes, Chapter 3**
- **Spanish Home Involvement Activity 3**
- **Spanish Chapter 3 Digests Audiocassette Activity and Test**

ACTIVITY MANIPULATIVES

Help students learn more about America's cultural history with:

- **American Crafts Hands-On Activities**
- **American Games Hands-On Activities**
- **American History Flash Cards**

ADDITIONAL RESOURCES FROM GLENCOE

- **U.S. History & Art,** Transparency 2, *Penn's Treaty With the Indians*
- **Focus on American Art Prints,** *Mrs. Elizabeth Freake and Baby Mary,* by an unknown artist
- **Outline Map Resource Book**
- **U.S. Desk Map**
- **The American History Videodisc and CD-ROM,** *Prehistory to 1680*

A&E HOME VIDEO. Biography™ THE HISTORY CHANNEL.

The following videotape programs are available from Glencoe as supplements to Chapter 3:

- **Pocahontas: Her True Story**
  (ISBN 1-56501-555-X)

To order, call Glencoe at 1-800-334-7344. To find classroom resources to accompany many of these videos, check the following home pages:
A&E Television: http://www.aetv.com
The History Channel: http://www.historychannel.com

Introducing
CHAPTER 3

Chapter Themes

Chapter Themes are listed by section on this chapter opening page of the Student Edition. A corresponding theme-based activity is available under "FOCUS," and a theme-based question is asked in the Section and Chapter Reviews.

Performance Assessment

Refer to Activity 3 in the *Performance Assessment Strategies and Activities* booklet.

GLENCOE TECHNOLOGY

VIDEODISC
MindJogger Videoquiz

Use MindJogger to preview the Chapter 3 content.

Chapter 3
Disc 1, Side A

Also available in VHS.

HISTORY AND ART John Smibert (1688–1751) painted 250 portraits before retiring in 1746. His 1730 art exhibition was the first in the colonies. **Ask:** How can you tell from the painting that Boston was a hub of trade? *(There are many ships in the harbor.)*

Chapter 3

1587–1770

Colonial America

Why It's Important

The early North American colonies were a meeting place of cultures. The Europeans who settled these colonies included Protestants, Catholics, and Jews. Native Americans, the original inhabitants, played an important role in the life of the colonists. Africans were also part of colonial America from the earliest days. The goals and ways of life of these different groups sometimes clashed, ending in conflict. However, America was becoming a place where people of different backgrounds and beliefs could learn to live together peacefully.

Chapter Themes

- *Section 1,* Economic Factors
- *Section 2,* Civic Rights and Responsibilities
- *Section 3,* Individual Action
- *Section 4,* Culture and Traditions
- *Section 5,* Culture and Traditions

HISTORY AND ART ***View of Boston*** **by John Smibert** John Smibert was a prominent artist in Boston, Massachusetts, during the early 1700s. He painted scenes of Boston as well as portraits of the city's wealthy merchant families.

EXTRA CREDIT PROJECT

Diorama Have each student make a diorama using a shoe box. Students' scenes should show a fort or home from an early settlement. Students may paint background scenery on the sides and back of the box. Suggest that students use a variety of materials inside the diorama—clay, twigs, pebbles, craft sticks, paper cutouts, straws, cotton balls, and so on. Each student should write a descriptive paragraph to attach to the finished diorama.

1580 | 1590 | 1600 | 1610 | 1620

1583 Sir Humphrey Gilbert claims Newfoundland for Queen Elizabeth

1590 Settlers of Roanoke Island vanish

1607 Colonists settle at Jamestown

1619 House of Burgesses meets in Jamestown

Section 1

Early English Settlements

Read to Discover . . .

- why England's first two attempts to start a colony failed.
- what crop saved the Jamestown colony.
- how the colonists received political rights.

Terms to Learn

charter
joint-stock company
burgesses

The Storyteller

In the summer of 1588, Spanish warships sailed toward the coast of England. King Philip of Spain had sent the armada, or war fleet, of 132 ships to invade England. With 30,000 troops and 2,400 guns, the Spanish Armada was the mightiest naval force the world had ever seen. Yet the smaller, swifter English ships quickly gained the upper hand. The Spanish Armada fled north to Scotland, where violent storms destroyed and scattered the fleet. Only about one-half of the Spanish ships straggled home.

English soldier's helmet, Jamestown

England and Spain had been heading toward war for years. Trading rivalry and religious differences divided the two countries. Philip II, Spain's Catholic king, wanted to put a Catholic ruler on the throne of England and bring the country back to the Catholic Church. He did not consider Queen Elizabeth, a Protestant, the rightful ruler of England.

Attacks on Spanish ships and ports by such English adventurers as **Sir Francis Drake** infuriated Philip. He thought that Queen Elizabeth should punish Drake for his raids. Instead, she honored Drake with a knighthood. Philip sent the Spanish Armada to conquer England—but it failed.

The English victory had far-reaching consequences. Although war between England and Spain continued until 1604, the defeat of the armada marked the end of Spanish control of the seas. Now the way was clear for England and other European nations to start colonies in North America.

The Lost Colony of Roanoke

The English had made several attempts to establish a base on the other side of the Atlantic before their victory over Spain. In 1583 **Sir Humphrey Gilbert** claimed Newfoundland for Queen Elizabeth. Then he sailed south along the coast looking for a place to establish a colony. Before finding a suitable site, he died at sea.

The following year Queen Elizabeth gave **Sir Walter Raleigh** the right to claim any land in

Section Resources

Reproducible Masters
- Reproducible Lesson Plan 3–1
- Guided Reading Activity 3–1
- Section Quiz 3–1
- Reteaching Activity 3–1
- Enrichment Activity 3–1

Transparencies
- Section Focus Transparency 3–1

Multimedia
- Vocabulary PuzzleMaker
- Chapter Challenger Interactive Review Software
- Testmaker
- GTV: The American People: Fabric of a Nation
- NGS PictureShow: Colonial America; The Age of Exploration, Part 1

1 FOCUS

BELLRINGER
Motivational Activity

Before taking roll at the beginning of the class period, project Section Focus Transparency 3–1 and have students answer the questions. Discuss students' responses.

This activity is also available as a blackline master.

Section Focus Transparency 3–1

Vocabulary Precheck
Point out that the term *burgesses* comes from an Old French word meaning "freeman of a town." Inform students that *bourgeois*—a member of the urban middle class—is derived from the same word.

Use the **Vocabulary Puzzle-Maker** to create crossword and word search puzzles.

Section Theme
Economic Factors

Many Jamestown settlers were gentlemen from wealthy families. The men journeyed to America for adventure and the hope of making a fortune.

Activity Have students skim the text to find out how the hope of striking it rich led to near failure and what economic activity saved Jamestown. *(Colonists searched for gold rather than planting crops; raising tobacco saved the colony.)*

2 TEACH

L1 Identifying Contributions Although the Jamestown site was eventually abandoned, the settlement left its mark on American society. Have students name ways in which it did so. *(Responses should include: established the English as colonists in America, introduced tobacco as a money-making activity, established representative government.)*

Picturing HISTORY The failure of the Roanoke colony caused the English to form joint-stock companies to share the risk of failure.
Answer: *Scouts sent to the area by Sir Walter Raleigh returned with an enthusiastic report.*

Guided Reading Activity 3–1

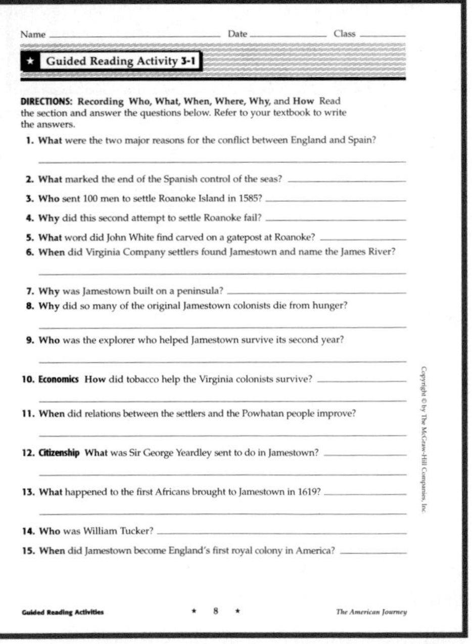
Name ____________ Date ________ Class ______

★ Guided Reading Activity 3-1

DIRECTIONS: Recording Who, What, When, Where, Why, and **How** Read the section and answer the questions below. Refer to your textbook to write the answers.

1. **What** were the two major reasons for the conflict between England and Spain?
2. **What** marked the end of the Spanish control of the seas?
3. **Who** sent 100 men to settle Roanoke Island in 1585?
4. **Why** did this second attempt to settle Roanoke fail?
5. **What** word did John White find carved on a gatepost at Roanoke?
6. **When** did Virginia Company settlers found Jamestown and name the James River?
7. **Why** was Jamestown built on a peninsula?
8. **Why** did so many of the original Jamestown colonists die from hunger?
9. **Who** was the explorer who helped Jamestown survive its second year?
10. **Economics How** did tobacco help the Virginia colonists survive?
11. **When** did relations between the settlers and the Powhatan people improve?
12. **Citizenship What** was Sir George Yeardley sent to do in Jamestown?
13. **What** happened to the first Africans brought to Jamestown in 1619?
14. **Who** was William Tucker?
15. **When** did Jamestown become England's first royal colony in America?

Guided Reading Activities ★ 8 ★ *The American Journey*

Who?What?Where?When?

It's a Boy! Although Virginia Dare was the first English child born in America, she was not the first European child born there. That honor goes to a Viking boy named Snorri who was born in Vinland around A.D. 1009. Before he was three, he and his parents returned to Iceland.

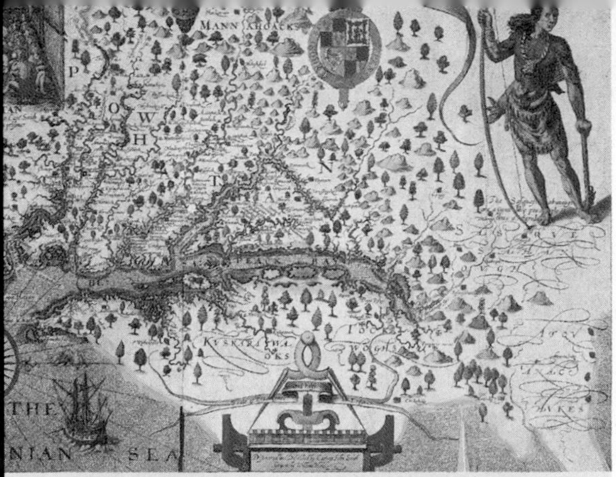

Picturing HISTORY This map of the late 1500s shows an English ship entering a bay near Roanoke Island. Shipwrecks nearby symbolize the dangers of the North Carolina coast at that time. **Why did English colonists settle at Roanoke Island?**

North America not already owned by a Christian monarch. Raleigh sent an expedition to look for a good place to settle. His scouts returned with an enthusiastic report of **Roanoke Island,** off the coast of present-day North Carolina. The land was good for farming, they said, and the local people were "most gentle, loving and faithful."

Roanoke Settlements

In 1585 Raleigh sent about 100 men to settle on Roanoke Island. After a difficult winter on the island, the unhappy colonists returned to England.

Two years later Raleigh tried again, sending 91 men, 17 women, and 9 children to Roanoke. **John White,** a mapmaker and artist, led the group. The new settlers began building a permanent colony. They needed many supplies, however, and White sailed to England for the supplies and to recruit more settlers. Although he had hoped to be back within a few months, the war with Spain delayed his return for three years.

When White finally returned to Roanoke, he found it deserted. The only clue to the fate of the settlers was the word *Croatoan* carved on a gatepost. White thought the colonists must have gone to Croatoan Island, about 100 miles to the south. Bad weather kept White from investigating. The Roanoke colonists were never seen again.

Jamestown Settlement

Roanoke was Sir Walter Raleigh's last attempt to establish a colony. For a time his failure discouraged others from planning English colonies in North America. However, the idea emerged again in 1606. Several groups of merchants sought **charters,** the right to organize settlements in an area, from King James I.

The Virginia Company

One group of merchants, the Virginia Company of London, received a charter to "make habitation . . . into that part of America, commonly called Virginia." The Virginia Company was a **joint-stock company.** Investors bought stock, or part ownership, in the company in return for a share of its future profits.

The company acted quickly. In December 1606, it sent 144 settlers in 3 ships—the *Godspeed,* the *Discovery,* and the *Susan Constant*—to build a new colony in North America. The settlers were to look for gold and attempt to establish trade in fish and furs. Forty of them died during the voyage.

In April 1607, the ships entered **Chesapeake Bay** and then sailed up a river flowing into the bay. The colonists named the river the James and their new settlement **Jamestown** to honor their king.

The settlers built Jamestown on a peninsula so they could defend it from attack. The site had major drawbacks, however. The swampy land teemed with mosquitoes that carried malaria, a disease found in warm, humid climates. Jamestown also lacked good farmland and was surrounded by Native American settlements.

Footnotes to History

It's a Girl! Shortly after arriving on Roanoke Island, John White's daughter gave birth to a baby girl. The baby, named Virginia Dare, was the first English child born in North America.

COOPERATIVE LEARNING ACTIVITY

Radio Programs Organize students into several groups. Tell groups that their task is to develop and present a short radio program titled, "The Roanoke Mystery." Suggest that programs include some background information on the lost colony at Roanoke; interviews with people, such as John White, who had a connection to the colony; and some speculation on what happened to the colonists. Encourage groups to "broadcast" their programs for the rest of the class. Some groups might like to record their programs for use with other history classes.

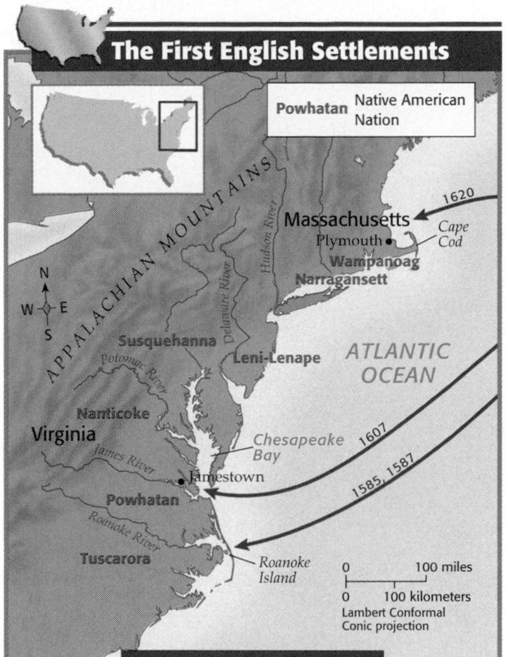

Map Study

The English established colonies along the Atlantic coast in the late 1500s and early 1600s.

1. **Location** Which colony was located farthest north?
2. **Analyzing Information** Which Native American nations lived nearest the Roanoke colonists?

The colonists faced mounting difficulties over the next several months. Many of them were unaccustomed to hard labor. Because the London investors expected a quick profit from their colony, the settlers searched for gold and silver when they should have been growing food. In addition, disease and hunger devastated the colonists. By January 1608, when ships arrived with additional men and supplies, only 38 of the Jamestown colonists remained alive.

Captain John Smith

Governing Jamestown was perhaps the biggest obstacle the colonists faced. The colony survived its second year under the leadership of 27-year-old **Captain John Smith,** a soldier and explorer who arrived in 1608. Smith forced the settlers to work and managed to get corn from the Powhatan people. "It pleased God," he wrote, "to move the Indians to bring us corn . . . when we rather expected they would destroy us."

The Virginia Company replaced Smith with a governor, Lord De La Warr, and a period of strict rule began. The colonists barely survived the winter of 1609–1610, called the "starving time." One settler reported, "Having fed upon horses and other beasts as long as they lasted, we were glad to make shift with [such] vermin as dogs, cats, rats, and mice." Trouble also broke out with the Native Americans, and the 300 desperately hungry colonists had to barricade themselves inside their walls. When new settlers arrived in May, they found only 60 survivors.

Economics

Tobacco Saves the Colony

Although the Virginia colonists found no gold or silver, they did discover another way to make money for the investors. They began to grow tobacco.

Tobacco had become popular in Europe, though some people found smoking unhealthy and disgusting. King James I, for example, called it a "vile and stinking" custom.

One colonist, **John Rolfe,** learned to grow a type of tobacco that was less bitter. The first crop was sold in England in 1614. Soon planters all along the James River were raising tobacco, and the colony of Virginia began to prosper and grow. Relations with the Powhatan also improved after Rolfe married **Pocahontas,** the daughter of Chief Powhatan.

Pocahontas

Multiple Learning Styles

Logical/Mathematical Give students the following information:

Population of Jamestown, 1619–1624

Year	Number of People Arriving	Total Population
1619	—	1,000
1620	100 (est.)	866
1621	1,051	843
1624	4,000	1,277

Have students figure the number of deaths between 1619 and 1620, between 1620 and 1621, and so on. *(234; 1,074; 3,566)* Discuss the possible reasons that settlers continued to come to Jamestown despite such high death rates. Answers may include lure of gold, hope for a better life, perhaps not informed of the dangers, love of adventure. **L3, ELL**

Map Study

Answers

1. Massachusetts or Plymouth
2. Powhatan, Tuscarora

Map Skills Practice

Reading a Map Jamestown was located near the mouth of what large body of water? *(Chesapeake Bay)*

NATIONAL GEOGRAPHIC SOCIETY

VIDEODISC
GTV: The American People: Fabric of a Nation

Side 1, Chapter 3
Title: *Change of Scene*
Subject: Why Europeans sought a new home
Ask: Who was already inhabiting the Americas when the Europeans claimed and settled these lands? *(Native Americans)*

CD-ROM
NGS PictureShow: Colonial America

Have students research the lives of the European colonists in America by having them click on the main menu.

3 *ASSESS*

Assign Section 1 Review as homework or as an in-class activity.

Use **Chapter Challenger Interactive Review Software** to review Section 1.

CHAPTER 3
Section 1, 71–75

Picturing HISTORY Jamestown was burned in 1676 during Bacon's Rebellion. It was rebuilt but suffered permanent decline after 1699 when Williamsburg became the capital.
Answer: *The Jamestown colonists were wealthy adventurers unused to hard labor, disease, and hunger.*

Section Quiz 3–1

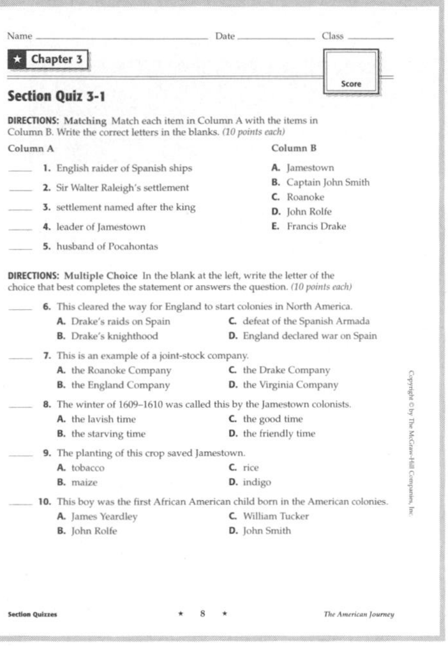
Name ____________ Date ________ Class ______

★ Chapter 3 | Score

Section Quiz 3-1

DIRECTIONS: Matching Match each item in Column A with the items in Column B. Write the correct letters in the blanks. *(10 points each)*

Column A	Column B
____ **1.** English raider of Spanish ships	**A.** Jamestown
____ **2.** Sir Walter Raleigh's settlement	**B.** Captain John Smith
____ **3.** settlement named after the king	**C.** Roanoke
____ **4.** leader of Jamestown	**D.** John Rolfe
____ **5.** husband of Pocahontas	**E.** Francis Drake

DIRECTIONS: Multiple Choice In the blank at the left, write the letter of the choice that best completes the statement or answers the question. *(10 points each)*

____ **6.** This cleared the way for England to start colonies in North America.
A. Drake's raids on Spain **C.** defeat of the Spanish Armada
B. Drake's knighthood **D.** England declared war on Spain

____ **7.** This is an example of a joint-stock company.
A. the Roanoke Company **C.** the Drake Company
B. the England Company **D.** the Virginia Company

____ **8.** The winter of 1609–1610 was called this by the Jamestown colonists.
A. the lavish time **C.** the good time
B. the starving time **D.** the friendly time

____ **9.** The planting of this crop saved Jamestown.
A. tobacco **C.** rice
B. maize **D.** indigo

____ **10.** This boy was the first African American child born in the American colonies.
A. James Yeardley **C.** William Tucker
B. John Rolfe **D.** John Smith

Section Quizzes ★ 8 ★ *The American Journey*

Reteaching Activity 3–1

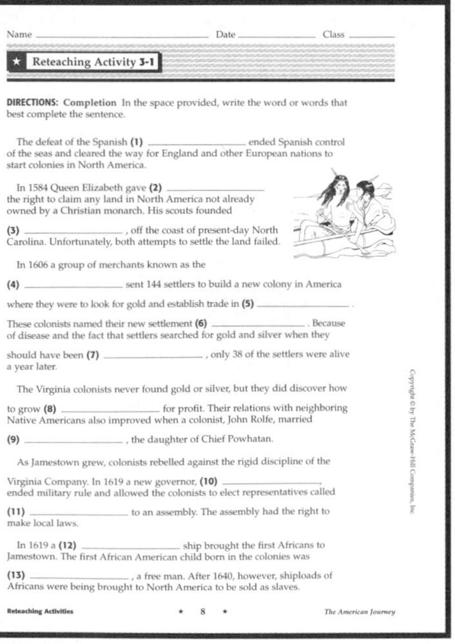
Name ____________ Date ________ Class ______

★ Reteaching Activity 3-1

DIRECTIONS: Completion In the space provided, write the word or words that best complete the sentence.

The defeat of the Spanish **(1)** ____________ ended Spanish control of the seas and cleared the way for England and other European nations to start colonies in North America.

In 1584 Queen Elizabeth gave **(2)** ____________ the right to claim any land in North America not already owned by a Christian monarch. His scouts founded **(3)** ____________, off the coast of present-day North Carolina. Unfortunately, both attempts to settle the land failed.

In 1606 a group of merchants known as the **(4)** ____________ sent 144 settlers to build a new colony in America where they were to look for gold and establish trade in **(5)** ____________. These colonists named their new settlement **(6)** ____________. Because of disease and the fact that settlers searched for gold and silver when they should have been **(7)** ____________, only 38 of the settlers were alive a year later.

The Virginia colonists never found gold or silver, but they did discover how to grow **(8)** ____________ for profit. Their relations with neighboring Native Americans also improved when a colonist, John Rolfe, married **(9)** ____________, the daughter of Chief Powhatan.

As Jamestown grew, colonists rebelled against the rigid discipline of the Virginia Company. In 1619 a new governor, **(10)** ____________, ended military rule and allowed the colonists to elect representatives called **(11)** ____________ to an assembly. The assembly had the right to make local laws.

In 1619 a **(12)** ____________ ship brought the first Africans to Jamestown. The first African American child born in the colonies was **(13)** ____________, a free man. After 1640, however, shiploads of Africans were being brought to North America to be sold as slaves.

Reteaching Activities ★ 8 ★ *The American Journey*

Picturing HISTORY After landing at Jamestown, the English settlers built homes and a meetinghouse, which was used for religious services. **What difficulties did the Jamestown colonists face during their first months of settlement?**

Citizenship

Representative Government

In the early years of the Jamestown colony, nearly all of the settlers were men. They worked for the Virginia Company and lived under strict military rules. The governors imposed rigid discipline and organized the settlers into work gangs.

As the colony grew, the settlers complained about taking orders from the Virginia Company in London. In 1619 the company agreed to let the colonists have some say in their government. It sent a new governor, Sir George Yeardley, to the colony with orders to end military rule.

Yeardley allowed the men of the colony to elect representatives called **burgesses** to an assembly. The assembly had the right to make local laws for the colony. On July 30, 1619, the **House of Burgesses** met for the first time in a church in Jamestown.

New Arrivals in Jamestown

In 1619 the Virginia Company sent 100 women to Jamestown. As a company report noted: "The plantation can never flourish till families be planted, and the respect of wives and children fix the people on the soil." Colonists

MAKING CONNECTIONS ACTIVITY

Economics The modern heirs to the joint-stock company are today's public corporations. Have students choose a number of companies in which they might like to invest $1,000. Have them pick some old reliable corporations and some newcomers. Show students how to read the stock exchange listings in the business section of the local newspaper. Then have them follow their fortunes for several weeks or months, keeping a record of earnings and losses. **L2**

who wanted to marry one of the women had to pay a fee of 120 pounds of tobacco. Men still outnumbered women in the colony, but marriage and children began to be part of life in Virginia.

The First Africans in America

A Dutch ship brought another group of newcomers to Jamestown in 1619—20 Africans who were sold to Virginia planters to labor in the tobacco fields. These first Africans may have come as servants—engaged to work for a set period of time—rather than as slaves.

Until about 1640 some African laborers in Jamestown were free and even owned property. William Tucker, the first African American born in the American colonies, was a free man. In the years to follow, however, many more shiploads of Africans would arrive in North America, and those unwilling passengers would be sold as slaves. Slavery was first recognized in Virginia law in 1661.

In the early 1620s, the Virginia Company faced financial troubles. The company had poured all its money into Jamestown, with little return. The colony also suffered a disastrous attack by the Native Americans. In 1624 King James canceled the company's charter and took control of the colony, making it England's first royal colony in America.

Linking PAST & PRESENT

Peddlers to Malls

During the colonial era, families relied on peddlers, or traveling merchants, for many of their goods. Peddlers journeyed throughout the countryside with such items as clocks, shoes, pans, cloth, and even books. Wherever crowds assembled, a peddler selling wares was usually present. Today, crowds of shoppers still assemble—at malls. Malls often are the focus of community life. They attract shoppers, walkers, and moviegoers. **How are peddlers and malls similar?**

Past

Colonial peddler

Present

Mall of America, Bloomington, Minnesota

Section 1 Review

Checking for Understanding

1. ***Identify*** Sir Francis Drake, Sir Walter Raleigh, Roanoke Island, John White, Jamestown, Captain John Smith, John Rolfe, Pocahontas, House of Burgesses.
2. ***Define*** charter, joint-stock company, burgesses.
3. ***List*** two reasons Jamestown was a poor location for a colony.

Reviewing Themes

4. **Economic Factors** What economic activity helped save the Virginia colony?

Critical Thinking

5. **Making Inferences** Why do you think the king of England was willing to let a group of merchants try to establish a colony in North America?

Activity

Making a Poster Create a poster that might have attracted early colonists to the area where you live. Focus on the location as well as natural features in your area such as good farmland, forests, waterways, and mineral resources.

Section 1 Review Answers

1. Drake, 71; Raleigh, 71; Roanoke, 72; White, 72; Jamestown, 72; Smith, 73; Rolfe, 73; Pocahontas, 73; House of Burgesses, 74.
2. The words are defined in the Glossary.
3. Answers may include: malaria-carrying mosquitoes, poor farmland, surrounded by Native Americans
4. growing tobacco
5. Answers may include: the king wanted political power from having overseas colonies and economic rewards without risking his nation's resources on the venture.

Activity Posters should show that students have an understanding of the geographic conditions in their area, including natural resources.

Linking PAST & PRESENT

Peddlers to Malls The largest mall in the United States is Minnesota's Mall of America. It contains 350 stores, 6 nightclubs, a 14-screen movie theater, an 18-hole miniature golf course, and a 7-acre amusement park.

Answer: *Peddlers provided needed goods as well as a focus for social activity, as do today's malls.*

Enrichment Activity 3–1

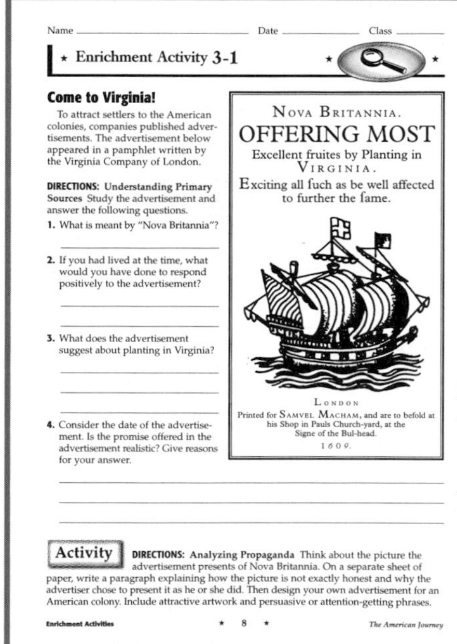

Name ________ Date ________ Class ________

★ Enrichment Activity 3-1

Come to Virginia!

To attract settlers to the American colonies, companies published advertisements. The advertisement below appeared in a pamphlet written by the Virginia Company of London.

DIRECTIONS: Understanding Primary Sources Study the advertisement and answer the following questions.

1. What is meant by "Nova Britannia"?
2. If you had lived at the time, what would you have done to respond positively to the advertisement?
3. What does the advertisement suggest about planting in Virginia?
4. Consider the date of the advertisement. Is the promise offered in the advertisement realistic? Give reasons for your answer.

NOVA BRITANNIA.
OFFERING MOST
Excellent fruites by Planting in VIRGINIA.
Exciting all ſuch as be well affected to further the ſame.

LONDON
Printed for SAMVEL MACHAM, and are to befold at his Shop in Pauls Church-yard, at the Signe of the Bul-head.
1609.

Activity **DIRECTIONS: Analyzing Propaganda** Think about the picture the advertisement presents of Nova Britannia. On a separate sheet of paper, write a paragraph explaining how the picture is not exactly honest and why the advertiser chose to present it as he or she did. Then design your own advertisement for an American colony. Include attractive artwork and persuasive or attention-getting phrases.

Enrichment Activities ★ 8 ★ *The American Journey*

4 CLOSE

Have each student list five important facts from the section.

NATIONAL GEOGRAPHIC *Journeys*

Who? What? Where? When?

Pocahontas After falling in love with John Rolfe, Pocahontas became a Christian and was baptized under the name of Rebecca. She and Rolfe were married in 1614, and about two years later went to England, where she was greeted as a princess by King James I and Queen Anne. Pocahontas became ill and died in England. The Rolfes had one son, Thomas, some of whose descendants include the well-known Randolphs of Virginia.

NATIONAL GEOGRAPHIC SOCIETY

VIDEODISC
GTV: The American People: Fabric of a Nation

Side 1, Chapter 5
Title: *When Worlds Collide*
Subject: European and Native American encounters (1500s)
Ask: **What were the early relationships between the Europeans and Native Americans like?** *(They often met in peace. Native Americans showed Europeans how and what to farm. Europeans shared their knowledge of weapons and tools.)*

CD-ROM
NGS PictureShow: The Age of Exploration, Part 1

Encourage students to explore reasons the explorers headed westward. Have students click on the main menu.

4 This deerskin robe belonged to Powhatan, powerful chief of the Powhatans. The Indians gave the settlers food, taught them to plant yams and corn, and showed them how to survive in the woods. But when the English tried to claim the best land, the Native Americans attacked them.

3 According to John Smith's account, the Powhatan Indians were about to "beat out" his brains when Pocahontas, the chief's daughter, came to his rescue. Pocahontas did repeatedly help the settlers—and eventually married one. But historians have not found reliable evidence to confirm Smith's story.

2 In May the settlers established Jamestown, the first permanent English colony in the Americas. Malaria, bad water, starvation, and Indian attacks took their toll: Only 38 hardy souls survived the first year. Captain John Smith forced the settlers to learn to farm. By 1612 the settlers were growing tobacco, which they traded in Europe, guaranteeing the future of the colony.

TEACHER'S NOTES

NATIONAL GEOGRAPHIC

Journeys

Journey to Jamestown

1 Captain John Smith (above) and more than 100 other men left England and set out for the Americas in December 1606. Three ships under the command of Captain Christopher Newport sailed to the Canary Islands and West Indies, before Cape Henry was sighted at the mouth of the Chesapeake Bay in April 1607. Smith also led later explorations beyond Jamestown and around the Chesapeake Bay.

"From May to September those that escaped [sickness] lived upon sturgeon and sea crabs. Fifty in this time we buried.... Nothing [is] so difficult as to establish a commonwealth so far remote from men and means.... The new [governing council] President ... being little beloved, of weak judgment in dangers and less industry in peace, committed the managing of all things ... to Captain Smith, who by his own example ... set some to mow, others to bind thatch, some to build houses, others to thatch them ... so that in short time he provided most of them lodgings."

—From Captain John Smith's History of Virginia. *This excerpt was written by Thomas Studley, a member of the expedition, in the summer and fall of 1607.*

77

CURRICULUM CONNECTION

GEOGRAPHY
In 1996 archaeologists discovered the exact location and actual foundation of America's first fort. Archaeologists uncovered the remains of Jamestown, proving that it had been built on high ground, away from the shoreline. The Jamestown settlers built their fort on land least likely to erode. Previously the federal government believed that Jamestown had been built right on the riverbank—a site now under the waters of the James River.

NATIONAL GEOGRAPHIC SOCIETY

VIDEODISC
GTV: The American People: Fabric of a Nation

Side 1, Chapter 7
Title: *A Mixed Bag*
Subject: Diversity in the colonies
Ask: **Why were the colonies along the Atlantic coast called the "English colonies"?** *(because they were under the control of English rulers and law)*

What? Where? When? Who?

Bibliography The excerpt on page 77 was taken from *Captain John Smith's History of Virginia,* edited by David Freeman Hawke. Published by Bobbs-Merrill Company, ©1979.

TEACHER'S NOTES

1 FOCUS

BELLRINGER
Motivational Activity

Before taking roll at the beginning of the class period, project Section Focus Transparency 3–2 and have students answer the questions. Discuss students' responses.

This activity is also available as a blackline master.

Section Focus Transparency 3–2

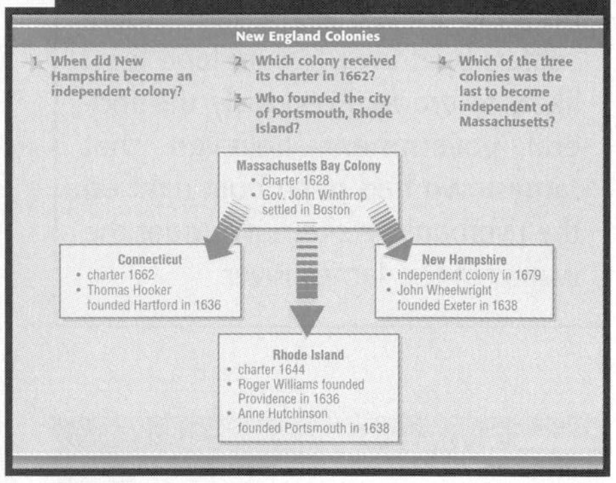

Vocabulary Precheck

Draw students' attention to the terms *Puritan, Separatist,* and *Pilgrim.* Have them demonstrate their understanding of the differences among these terms by using each one correctly in a sentence.

Use the **Vocabulary PuzzleMaker** to create crossword and word search puzzles.

Section Theme
Civic Rights and Responsibilities

Puritan and Pilgrim colonists who settled in America came in search of religious freedom.

Activity Have students skim the section to find the problems the colonists wanted to escape.

1620 — 1630 — 1640

1620 Pilgrims land at Plymouth

1630 Puritans settle the Massachusetts Bay Colony

1636 Thomas Hooker founds Hartford

1638 Anne Hutchinson founds Portsmouth

Section 2

New England Colonies

READ TO DISCOVER . . .

- why the Pilgrims and the Puritans came to America.
- how the Connecticut, Rhode Island, and New Hampshire colonies began.

TERMS TO LEARN

dissent
persecute
Puritan
Separatist
Pilgrim
Mayflower Compact
toleration

The Storyteller

The young man looked around at the other passengers aboard the *Mayflower.* These people had muskets but knew little about shooting. They planned to fish but knew nothing about fishing. They had hoped to settle in Virginia but instead landed in New England without enough supplies to last the winter. The only thing these people had plenty of was courage. They would need it.

Shoes, Plymouth Colony

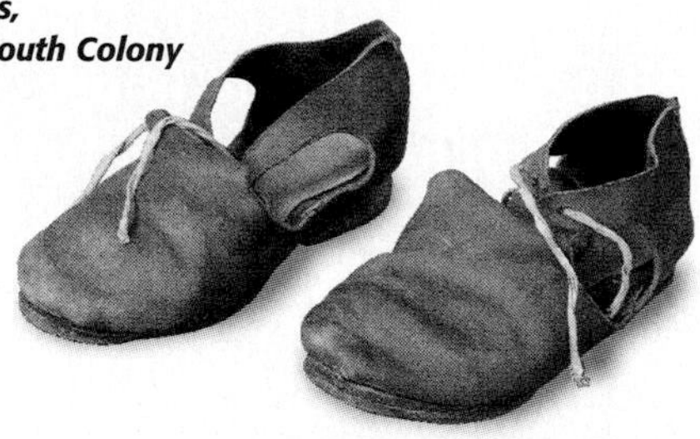

In 1614 Captain John Smith explored and mapped the coast of New England. His map showed a harbor called Patuxet, which was later renamed **Plymouth.** It was here that the next wave of English settlers to America would land. Unlike the Jamestown colonists, many of these settlers did not cross the ocean for riches. They came in search of religious freedom.

Demands for Religious Freedom

In the early 1600s, the Protestant Anglican Church was the official church of England, and the English monarch was head of the church. Many people, however, **dissented**—they disagreed with the beliefs or practices of the Anglicans. English Catholics, for example, still considered the pope the head of the church, and they were often **persecuted,** or treated harshly, for that reason.

At the same time, some Protestants wanted to change—or reform—the Anglican Church, while others wanted to break away from it altogether. The Protestants who wanted to reform the Anglican Church were called **Puritans.** Those who wanted to leave and found their own churches were known as **Separatists.**

The Separatists were persecuted in England, and some fled to the Netherlands. Though they found religious freedom there, the Separatists still had problems. They had difficulty finding work because the local craft guilds did not accept

SECTION RESOURCES

Reproducible Masters
- Reproducible Lesson Plan 3–2
- Guided Reading Activity 3–2
- Section Quiz 3–2
- Reteaching Activity 3–2
- Enrichment Activity 3–2

Transparencies
- Section Focus Transparency 3–2

Multimedia
- Vocabulary PuzzleMaker
- Chapter Challenger Interactive Review Software
- Testmaker
- GTV: The American People: Fabric of a Nation
- Facts On File: Landmark Documents in American History

them. The Separatists also worried that their children would lose their English heritage in the Netherlands.

The Pilgrims' Journey

Some Separatists in the Netherlands made an arrangement with the Virginia Company. The Separatists could settle in Virginia and practice their religion freely. In return they would give the company a share of whatever profits they made.

The Separatists considered themselves **Pilgrims** because their journey had a religious purpose. Only 35 of the 102 passengers who boarded the *Mayflower* in September 1620 were Pilgrims. The others were called "strangers." They were common people—servants, craftspeople, and poor farmers—who hoped to find a better life in America. Because Pilgrim beliefs shaped life in the Plymouth colony, however, all the early settlers are usually called Pilgrims.

The Mayflower Compact

The *Mayflower*'s passengers planned to settle in the Virginia colony. The first land they sighted was **Cape Cod**, well north of their target. Because it was November and winter was fast approaching, the colonists decided to drop anchor in Cape Cod Bay. They went ashore on a cold, bleak day in December at a place called Plymouth. **William Bradford,** their leader and historian, reported that "all things stared upon them with a weather-beaten face."

Plymouth was outside the territory of the Virginia Company and its laws. To provide order in their new colony, the Pilgrims drew up a formal document called the **Mayflower Compact.** The compact pledged their loyalty to England and declared their intention of forming "a civil body politic, for our better ordering and preservation." The signers also promised to obey the laws passed "for the general good of the colony."

Help from the Native Americans

Their first winter in America, almost half the Pilgrims died of malnutrition, disease, and cold. In the spring a few Native Americans approached the settlement. Two of them, **Squanto** and **Samoset,** befriended the colonists. Squanto was a Wampanoag who had been kidnapped by an English ship captain and had learned English.

Squanto and Samoset showed the Pilgrims how to grow corn, beans, and pumpkin and where to hunt and fish. Without this help the Pilgrims might not have survived. Squanto and Samoset also helped the Pilgrims make a treaty with the Wampanoag people who lived in the area.

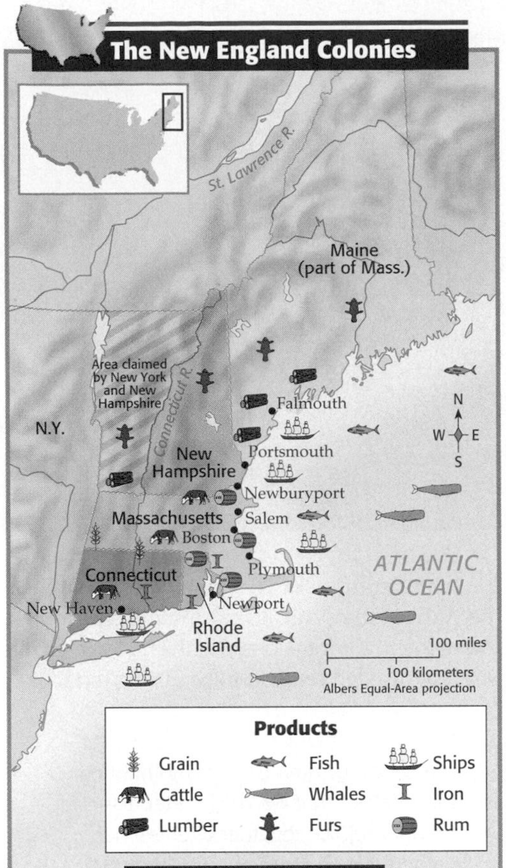

Map Study

The Atlantic waters and thick forests proved valuable for fishing and shipbuilding in New England.

1. **Region** What were the four New England Colonies?
2. **Analyzing Information** What products did Connecticut produce?

COOPERATIVE LEARNING ACTIVITY

Making a Map Have students work together to make a large map of the settlements in the New England Colonies. Some students should draw the map; others should make tags giving pertinent information about founders and reasons for settlement. Other students should use library resources to find the names of settlements not mentioned in the text. Save the map to use for comparing with the Middle and Southern Colonies.

2 TEACH

L1, ELL Identifying Steps to Democracy Three important steps on the road to democracy are discussed in the section. Have students identify them and briefly describe them. *(Mayflower Compact—agreement to form own government; creation of colonial legislature—gave Massachusetts Bay settlers a role in government; Fundamental Orders of Connecticut—first written constitution in America)*

Map Study

Answers

1. Rhode Island, Connecticut, Massachusetts, New Hampshire
2. grain, cattle, ships, iron

Map Skills Practice

Reading a Map Which area that is now a state was a part of the colony of Massachusetts? *(Maine)*

Guided Reading Activity 3–2

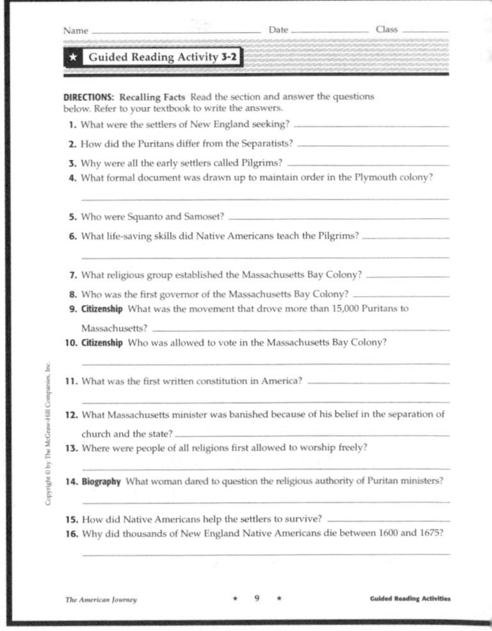
Name ______ Date ______ Class ______

★ Guided Reading Activity 3-2

DIRECTIONS: Recalling Facts Read the section and answer the questions below. Refer to your textbook to write the answers.

1. What were the settlers of New England seeking? ______
2. How did the Puritans differ from the Separatists? ______
3. Why were all the early settlers called Pilgrims? ______
4. What formal document was drawn up to maintain order in the Plymouth colony? ______
5. Who were Squanto and Samoset? ______
6. What life-saving skills did Native Americans teach the Pilgrims? ______
7. What religious group established the Massachusetts Bay Colony? ______
8. Who was the first governor of the Massachusetts Bay Colony? ______
9. **Citizenship** What was the movement that drove more than 15,000 Puritans to Massachusetts? ______
10. **Citizenship** Who was allowed to vote in the Massachusetts Bay Colony? ______
11. What was the first written constitution in America? ______
12. What Massachusetts minister was banished because of his belief in the separation of church and the state? ______
13. Where were people of all religions first allowed to worship freely? ______
14. **Biography** What woman dared to question the religious authority of Puritan ministers? ______
15. How did Native Americans help the settlers to survive? ______
16. Why did thousands of New England Native Americans die between 1600 and 1675? ______

The American Journey ★ 9 ★ **Guided Reading Activities**

CHAPTER 3
Section 2, 78–82

HISTORY AND ART Brownscombe (1850–1936) was born in a log cabin in Pennsylvania. She studied and exhibited her works at home and abroad. This painting is one of her long series on American history. **Ask:** **Why do you think the Pilgrims included Native American guests at their feast?** *(Without their help, Pilgrims would have died.)* **Answer:** *the Wampanoag*

Facts On File

CD-ROM
Landmark Documents in American History

Title: *Mayflower Compact, 1620*
Suggest that students write a one-page paper in answer to this question: What would you change about the Mayflower Compact if you were to write it today?

NATIONAL GEOGRAPHIC SOCIETY

VIDEODISC
GTV: The American People: Fabric of a Nation

Side 1, Chapter 6
Title: *A New England?*
Subject: English ways dominate colonial life
Ask: **Why do you think the English way of life came to dominate the colonies along the Atlantic coast?** *(Answers will vary but should include references to the large number of English settlers versus German, French, Dutch, and so on.)*

HISTORY AND ART
***First Thanksgiving* by Jennie A. Brownscombe** This traditional depiction of the first Thanksgiving shows Pilgrims sharing their bountiful harvest with Native Americans. **What Native American group helped the Pilgrims survive at Plymouth?**

In the autumn of 1621, the Pilgrims invited the Native Americans to celebrate the peace between them. After the losses of the first winter, the Pilgrims also felt relieved to be raising food.

> "Our harvest being gotten in, our Governor sent four men on fowling [hunting for fowl], so that we might after a special manner rejoice together after we had gathered in the fruit of our labors."

During the feast the Pilgrims thanked God for the harvest and for their survival.

Massachusetts Bay

In 1625 the English throne passed to Charles I. Charles objected to the Puritans' calls for reform in the Anglican Church, and persecution of Puritans increased dramatically. Some Puritans looked for a way to leave England.

In 1628 a group of Puritans formed the **New England Company** and received a royal charter to establish the Massachusetts Bay Colony, north of Plymouth. This was the Puritans' chance to create a new society in America—a society based on the Bible and their own beliefs.

The company chose a well-educated Puritan named **John Winthrop** to be the colony's governor. In 1630 Winthrop led 1,000 men, women, and children in 11 ships to **Massachusetts Bay.** Most of them settled in a place they called **Boston.** Winthrop explained that the new colony they were building in the wilderness "shall be as a city upon a hill. The eyes of all the people are upon us." Their settlement would provide a model for other Christian communities to follow.

Citizenship

Growth and Government

During the 1630s religious persecution and economic hard times in England drove more than 15,000 Puritans to journey to Massachusetts. This movement of people became known as the **Great Migration.**

An elected group ran the colony through the General Court of the Massachusetts Bay Company. When the settlers insisted on having a larger role in the government, the company created a colonial legislature. Every adult male who owned property and was a church member could vote for the governor and for representatives to the General Court.

The Puritans had come to America to put their religious beliefs into practice. Yet they were unwilling to allow other religious groups the

MULTIPLE LEARNING STYLES

Kinesthetic American colonists had to make most of what they needed or wanted. Have students use library resources to find out how to make a colonial craft of their choice. Possibilities include decorative work such as quilling (rolled paper strips that form a design) and silhouette making; needlework such as patchwork pillow covers, samplers, hooked or braided rugs; toys such as tops, whirligigs, kites, and rag or cornhusk dolls; apple-with-clove pomander balls (to freshen the air); and miscellaneous items such as gourd rattles and bowls, and cornhusk hot pads, mats, and baskets. **L2, ELL**

freedom to practice their beliefs. The Puritans had litle **toleration**—they criticized or persecuted people who held other religious views. This lack of toleration led to the creation of new colonies.

Connecticut

The fertile Connecticut River valley, south of Massachusetts, was much better for farming than was the stony soil around Boston. In the 1630s colonists began to settle in this area.

A minister named Thomas Hooker became dissatisfied with Massachusetts. He did not like the way that Winthrop and the other Puritan leaders ran the colony. Also, he had heard good reports of the Connecticut farmland. In 1636 Hooker led his congregation through the wilderness to Connecticut, where he founded the town of **Hartford.** Three years later Hartford and two other towns, Windsor and Wethersfield, agreed to form a colony. They adopted a plan of government called the **Fundamental Orders of Connecticut.** The first written constitution in America, it described the organization of government in detail.

Rhode Island

Good land drew colonists to Connecticut, but Rhode Island was settled by colonists who were forced out of Massachusetts. The first of these was **Roger Williams,** a minister. Williams felt that people should be free to follow any religious practices. In his view the church and the government should be completely separate. Williams also believed it was wrong for settlers to take land away from the Native Americans.

The ideas of Roger Williams deeply disturbed the Massachusetts leaders, and in 1635 they decided he should be banished, or forced to leave the colony. Williams left Massachusetts before the authorities could send him back to England and took refuge with the Narragansett people. From them he bought land on Narragansett Bay, the site where he later founded the town of Providence.

Roger Williams received a charter in 1644 for a colony east of Connecticut called **Rhode Island.** With its policy of religious toleration, Rhode Island became a safe place for dissenters. It was the first place in America where people of all faiths—including Jews—could worship freely.

Others followed Williams's example, forming colonies where they could worship as they pleased. In 1638 **John Wheelwright** led a group of dissidents from Massachusetts to the north. They founded the town of Exeter in **New Hampshire.** The same year, a group of Puritans settled Hampton. The colony of New Hampshire became fully independent of Massachusetts in 1679.

Biography

Anne Hutchinson Speaks Out

Anne Hutchinson came to Massachusetts with her husband in 1634 and soon held religious meetings in her Boston home. To the horror of the Massachusetts officials, Hutchinson questioned the religious authority of the colony's ministers. She also believed women should have more power.

Puritans were shocked to hear a woman state her ideas so boldly. As Hutchinson gained followers, she was seen as a danger to the colony's stability. In 1637 the Massachusetts leaders put her on trial for heresy—criticizing church officials.

When Hutchinson defended herself, she showed a remarkable knowledge of religion. Her accusers, however, found her guilty of heresy and ordered her to leave the colony as "a woman

America's FLAGS

Flag of England **Settlers in Jamestown and Massachusetts carried the flag of the British Union. It waved over the colonies until the American Revolution.**

CHAPTER 3
Section 2, 78–82

you don't say...

New England John Smith, the Virginia leader, gave New England its name. In 1614 a group of London merchants hired him to explore the northern coast. As he did so, he found places that looked to him like "old England." Upon his return, he wrote a book about his travels–*A Description of New England*–and the name caught on.

3 ASSESS

Assign Section 2 Review as homework or as an in-class activity.

Use **Chapter Challenger Interactive Review Software** to review Section 2.

Section Quiz 3–2

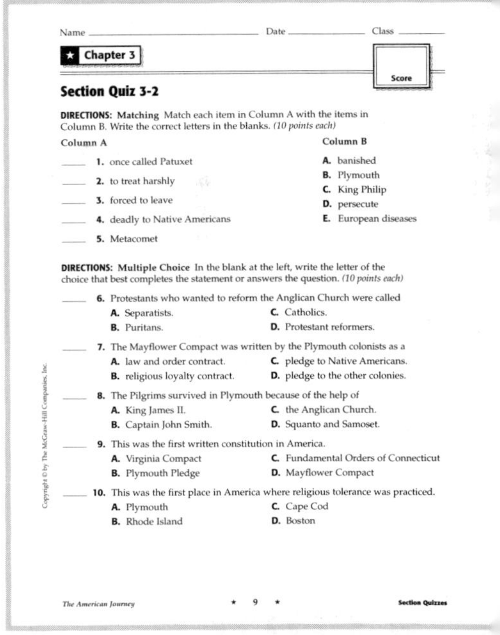

Name ______ Date ______ Class ______

★ Chapter 3

Score

Section Quiz 3-2

DIRECTIONS: Matching Match each item in Column A with the items in Column B. Write the correct letters in the blanks. *(10 points each)*

Column A

____ 1. once called Patuxet
____ 2. to treat harshly
____ 3. forced to leave
____ 4. deadly to Native Americans
____ 5. Metacomet

Column B

A. banished
B. Plymouth
C. King Philip
D. persecute
E. European diseases

DIRECTIONS: Multiple Choice In the blank at the left, write the letter of the choice that best completes the statement or answers the question. *(10 points each)*

____ 6. Protestants who wanted to reform the Anglican Church were called
A. Separatists. C. Catholics.
B. Puritans. D. Protestant reformers.

____ 7. The Mayflower Compact was written by the Plymouth colonists as a
A. law and order contract. C. pledge to Native Americans.
B. religious loyalty contract. D. pledge to the other colonies.

____ 8. The Pilgrims survived in Plymouth because of the help of
A. King James II. C. the Anglican Church.
B. Captain John Smith. D. Squanto and Samoset.

____ 9. This was the first written constitution in America.
A. Virginia Compact C. Fundamental Orders of Connecticut
B. Plymouth Pledge D. Mayflower Compact

____ 10. This was the first place in America where religious tolerance was practiced.
A. Plymouth C. Cape Cod
B. Rhode Island D. Boston

The American Journey ★ 9 ★ Section Quizzes

MAKING CONNECTIONS ACTIVITY

Technology In colonial times most work was done with hand tools. Today people are more likely to use power machinery and equipment. Organize the class into groups to make a bulletin-board display comparing colonial and modern technology. Each group should work on a different category, such as kitchen implements, shop tools, clothmaking equipment, and farm tools. Students should research, then draw the equipment or cut pictures of tools from old magazines. Have students label their work. **L2, ELL**

Reteaching Activity 3–2

Name ________________ Date ________ Class ________

★ Reteaching Activity 3-2

DIRECTIONS: Organizing Facts Complete the diagram by writing the letters of the words from the Fact Bank in the correct boxes.

New England Colonies: ____________________

Protestant Groups Who Broke from the Anglican Church	Native American Peoples	Colonial Leaders	Documents to Establish Order in the Colonies
______	______	______	______
______	______	______	______
______	______	______	______

★FACT BANK

A. John Wheelwright	**J.** Rhode Island
B. Wampanoag	**K.** Mohawks
C. Fundamental Orders of Connecticut	**L.** Mayflower Compact
D. Massachusetts Bay Colony	**M.** Puritans
E. Roger Williams	**N.** Narragansett
F. William Bradford	**O.** John Winthrop
G. Connecticut	**P.** New Hampshire
H. Thomas Hooker	**Q.** Pequot
I. Separatists	

DIRECTIONS: Essay On a separate sheet of paper, answer the following questions.

1. What role did Squanto and Samoset play in the survival of the Pilgrims after their first disastrous winter in America?
2. Why did the Puritans come to America? How did they treat other religious groups?

The American Journey ★ 9 ★ **Reteaching Activities**

Enrichment Activity 3–2

Name ________________ Date ________ Class ________

★ Enrichment Activity 3-2

A Colonial Household

Providence, Rhode Island, founded by Roger Williams, became a prosperous community. What was the household of an average citizen there like? Look at the partial inventory of the items in the estate, or property a deceased person leaves behind, for John Smith, a Providence miller who died in 1682.

An Inventory of the Estate of John Smith, Miller of Providence, Deceased

In the upper room of the dwelling house
- Two bedsteads with the beds and bedding

In the lower room of the dwelling house
- One bedstead with the bed and bedding
- A small piece of homemade cloth
- A frying pan
- Two guns
- A chamber pot
- Two small old pewter platters
- Two basins and three porringers
- Two spinning wheels, & old cards
- An old Bible, some lost & some of it torn
- Four old chairs
- Several wooden dishes
- Four old spoons
- About two pounds of tallow candles
- The corn mill with house over it, and all such other things as do belong to it
- The seventh part of the saw mill adjoining the corn mill . . .

DIRECTIONS: Analyzing Information Answer the following questions.

1. How many floors did John Smith's house have? ________
2. What other building did Smith own besides his house? ________
3. Did the sawmill belong to Smith? Explain. ________

DIRECTIONS: Making Inferences You will find clues to the following questions in the inventory. Use the evidence you find to arrive at answers.

4. How many people lived in the Smith household? What led you to this conclusion?
5. How can you tell that there were women in the Smith household? ________

The American Journey ★ 9 ★ **Enrichment Activities**

not fit for our society." With her family and some followers, Hutchinson left Massachusetts and moved to Rhode Island.

Native Americans

Native Americans helped the settlers adapt to the land. They also traded with the settlers—exchanging furs for goods such as iron pots, blankets, and guns. In Virginia the colonists had frequent dealings with Powhatan's confederacy. In New England the settlers met the Wampanoags, Narragansetts, and other groups.

Conflicts arose, however. Usually settlers moved onto Native American lands without permission or payment. English settlers and Native Americans competed fiercely for control of the land throughout the colonial period.

Decline in Population

For the Native Americans of New England, contact with Europeans was deadly. In 1600 about 100,000 Native Americans lived in New England. By 1675 only 10,000 survived. Most died from disease, not war. Chicken pox, smallpox, measles, and other European illnesses proved fatal to the Native Americans, who had no immunity against them.

Wars with Settlers

In 1637 war broke out in Connecticut between settlers and the Pequot people. The English colonists resented the Pequot trading network, which included Dutch settlers from New Amsterdam. The most savage attack of the **Pequot War** was committed by English soldiers. They surrounded a Pequot village and set fire to it. As the village went up in flames, the English killed those trying to escape.

King Philip

In 1675 the settlers of Massachusetts went to war with the Wampanoag people. **Metacomet,** the chief, was known to the settlers as **King Philip.** To keep the English from advancing into their land, the Wampanoag raided frontier outposts. They killed several thousand settlers in three years.

The settlers found an ally in the Mohawk, rivals of the Wampanoag. The Mohawk attacked Wampanoag villages, finally ambushing and killing Metacomet. **King Philip's War,** as the conflict was called, ended in defeat for the Wampanoag. The colonists were now able to enlarge their settlements in Massachusetts.

Section 2 Review

Checking for Understanding

1. ***Identify*** Great Migration, Roger Williams, Anne Hutchinson, King Philip's War.
2. ***Define*** dissent, persecute, Puritan, Separatist, Pilgrim, Mayflower Compact, toleration.
3. ***Describe*** how Native Americans helped the Plymouth colonists to survive.

Reviewing Themes

4. **Civic Rights and Responsibilities** What freedom did Rhode Island offer that other colonies did not?

Critical Thinking

5. **Making Comparisons** What did the Mayflower Compact and the Fundamental Orders of Connecticut have in common?

Activity

Building a Model Work with a small group to select one event from this section, such as the voyage of the *Mayflower*. Use a small box to create a scene illustrating that event. Use small objects and paint to represent buildings, trees, and other details.

Section 2 Review Answers

1. Great Migration, 80; Roger Williams, 81; Anne Hutchinson, 81; King Philip's War, 82
2. The words are defined in the Glossary.
3. They taught them how to grow corn, beans, and pumpkins; showed them where to hunt and fish; and helped them negotiate a treaty with the Wampanoag.
4. religious freedom
5. Both documents provided for the organization of a government.

Activity Students should use a variety of materials in their models and depict a scene described in this section.

4 CLOSE

Have students look back over the section and find as many examples as they can of the role civic rights played in the founding of the New England colonies. (Example: The Pilgrims' wish to have the right to worship as they pleased led to the founding of Plymouth.)

Social Studies
SKILL BUILDER

Reading a Bar Graph

Population of Six English Colonies, 1700

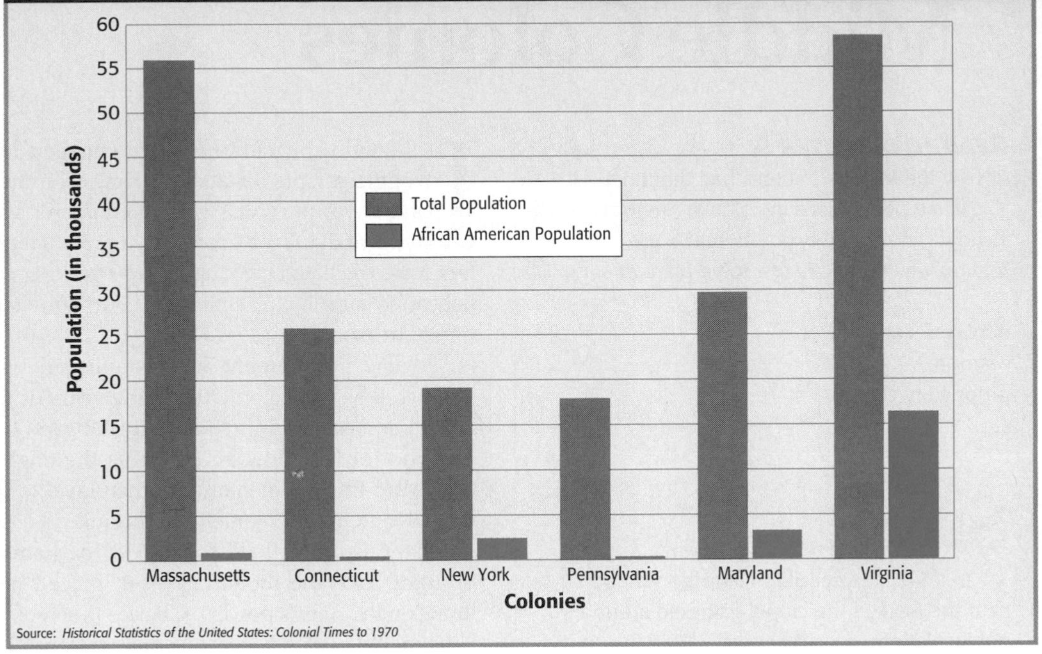

A bar graph presents numerical information in a visual way. Bars of various lengths stand for different quantities. Bars may be drawn vertically—up and down—or horizontally—left to right. Labels along the axes, or the left side and bottom of the graph, explain what the bars represent.

Learning the Skill

To read a bar graph, read the title to learn the subject of the graph. Look at the horizontal and vertical axes to find out what information the graph presents. Then compare the lengths of the bars on the graph.

Practicing the Skill

Study the bar graph on this page and answer the following questions.

1. What do the numbers along the vertical axis represent?
2. Which colony had the highest total population in 1700? The lowest?

Applying the Skill

Reading a Bar Graph Create a bar graph to represent the number of students in each American history class in your school.

ANSWERS TO PRACTICING THE SKILL

1. colonial population in thousands
2. Virginia; Pennsylvania

Applying the Skill Students' bar graphs should include accurately labeled horizontal and vertical axes, a title, a legend, and appropriate data.

Social Studies
SKILL BUILDER

TEACH

Reading a Bar Graph

Have students identify the various parts of the graph—title, horizontal axis, vertical axis, grid lines. **Ask:** Which two colonies had the smallest African American populations? *(Connecticut and Pennsylvania)*

Note that one has to estimate to find the approximate population when the top of a bar falls between grid lines. **Ask:** What was the approximate population of Pennsylvania? *(18,000)* What was the approximate African American population of Massachusetts? *(1,000)*

Additional Practice

Chapter Skills Activity 3

NATIONAL GEOGRAPHIC SOCIETY

VIDEODISC
GTV: The American People: Fabric of a Nation

Side 1, Chapter 8
Title: *The Journey*
Subject: Slavery in early America
Ask: **What one thing, heavily emphasized in this segment, helped unite African Americans?** *(Christianity)*

1 FOCUS

BELLRINGER
Motivational Activity

Before taking roll at the beginning of the class period, project Section Focus Transparency 3–3 and have students answer the questions. Discuss students' responses.

This activity is also available as a blackline master.

Section Focus Transparency 3–3

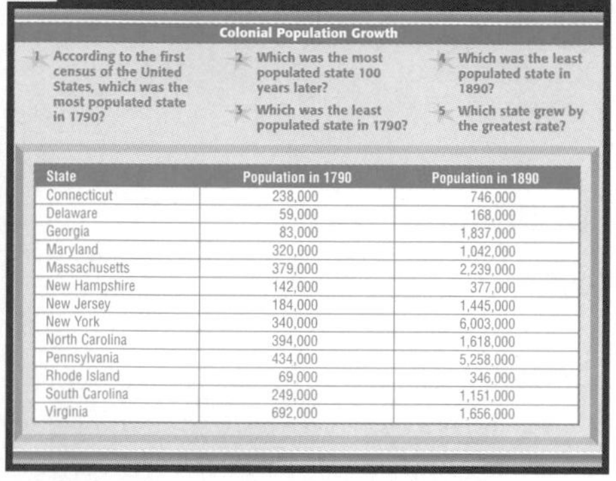

Colonial Population Growth

1. According to the first census of the United States, which was the most populated state in 1790?
2. Which was the most populated state 100 years later?
3. Which was the least populated state in 1790?
4. Which was the least populated state in 1890?
5. Which state grew by the greatest rate?

State	Population in 1790	Population in 1890
Connecticut	238,000	746,000
Delaware	59,000	168,000
Georgia	83,000	1,837,000
Maryland	320,000	1,042,000
Massachusetts	379,000	2,239,000
New Hampshire	142,000	377,000
New Jersey	184,000	1,445,000
New York	340,000	6,003,000
North Carolina	394,000	1,618,000
Pennsylvania	434,000	5,258,000
Rhode Island	69,000	346,000
South Carolina	249,000	1,151,000
Virginia	692,000	1,656,000

Vocabulary Precheck
Ask students to define the words listed under **Terms to Learn.** Have a volunteer consult the dictionary for any unfamiliar words.

Use the **Vocabulary PuzzleMaker** to create crossword and word search puzzles.

Section Theme
Individual Action
In many ways the settlement and development of the Middle Colonies was a direct reflection of the leadership of such people as Peter Stuyvesant, William Penn, and Lord John Berkeley.

Activity Have students skim the section to find what actions of the Duke of York made most of the Dutch colonists decide to remain in New York. *(He promised freedom of religion and allowed the colonists to keep their property.)*

1600 — 1650 — 1700

1626 Manhattan Island purchased from the Manhates people

1664 New York has about 8,000 inhabitants

1681 William Penn founds Pennsylvania

1702 New Jersey becomes a royal colony

Section 3

Middle Colonies

READ TO DISCOVER . . .
- why the Middle Colonies had the most diverse populations in colonial America.
- how New York City got its start.
- who was America's first town planner.

TERMS TO LEARN
patroon
proprietary colony
pacifist

The Storyteller

In 1649, 17-year-old Philip Henry stood near the back of the crowd gathered around a public platform near Whitehall Palace in London. There he watched Charles I, the king of England, prepare to die. The king made a short speech, prayed silently, and then knelt with his head on the block.

With just one blow, the executioner severed the king's head from his body. At that moment, the crowd uttered "such a groan as I never heard before, and desire I may never hear again," Henry wrote in his diary.

Royalty plate

In England the Puritans were engaged in a struggle for power against King Charles I. Soon the country was embroiled in civil war. Led by Puritan Oliver Cromwell, the Parliamentary forces defeated the king. In 1649 the king was beheaded after a parliamentary court convicted him of treason.

A new government was established with Cromwell as Protector. During the years of upheaval and uncertainty, many Puritans left Old England for New England. During the English Civil War, English men and women loyal to the king went to royal colonies like Virginia.

After Cromwell died in 1658, parliament brought back the monarchy—but placed new limits on the ruler's powers. Charles II, son of the beheaded Charles I, became king in 1660. His reign is called the *Restoration* because the monarchy had been restored.

New York

In 1660 England had two clusters of colonies in what is now the United States—Massachusetts, New Hampshire, Connecticut, and Rhode Island in the north and Maryland and Virginia in the south. Between the two groups of English colonies were lands that the Dutch controlled.

In 1624 a group of Dutch merchants had formed the Dutch West India Company to trade in the Americas. Their posts along the Hudson River grew into the colony of New Netherland. The main settlement of the colony was **New Amsterdam,** located on **Manhattan Island.** In 1626

SECTION RESOURCES

Reproducible Masters
- Reproducible Lesson Plan 3–3
- Guided Reading Activity 3–3
- Section Quiz 3–3
- Reteaching Activity 3–3
- Enrichment Activity 3–3

Transparencies
- Section Focus Transparency 3–3

Multimedia
- Vocabulary PuzzleMaker
- Chapter Challenger Interactive Review Software
- Testmaker
- Facts On File: Landmark Documents in American History

the company bought Manhattan from the Manhates people for a small amount of beads and other goods. Blessed with a good natural port, the city of New Amsterdam soon became a center of shipping to and from the Americas.

Peter Stuyvesant

The Patroons

To increase the number of permanent settlers in its colony, the Dutch West India Company sent over families from the Netherlands, Germany, Sweden, and Finland. The company gave a large estate to anyone who brought at least 50 settlers to work the land. The wealthy landowners who acquired these riverfront estates were called **patroons.** The patroons ruled like kings. They could charge whatever rents they wanted to the farmers and other laborers on their estates.

England Takes Over

New Netherland boasted an excellent harbor and thriving river trade. The English wanted to acquire the valuable Dutch colony that lay between England's New England and Southern Colonies. In 1664 the English sent a fleet to attack New Amsterdam.

At the time **Peter Stuyvesant** ruled the colony as governor. His strict rule and heavy taxes turned many of the people in New Netherland against him. When the English ships sailed into New Amsterdam's harbor, the governor was unprepared for a battle and surrendered the colony.

King Charles II gave the colony to his brother, the **Duke of York,** who renamed it **New York.** New York was a **proprietary colony,** a colony in which the owner, or proprietor, owned all the land and controlled the government. It differed from the New England Colonies, which were run by private corporations under a royal charter.

Most of New York's settlers lived in the Hudson River valley. The Duke of York promised the diverse colonists freedom of religion and allowed them to keep their property. As a result, most of the Dutch colonists decided to remain in New York.

The Middle Colonies

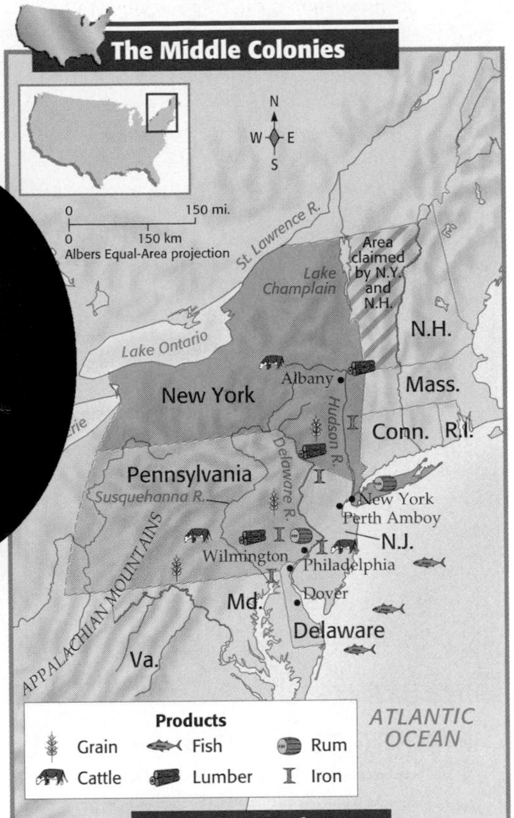

Map Study

The Middle Colonies were settled by people from many different countries.

1. **Region** What were the four Middle Colonies?
2. **Drawing Conclusions** What geographic features made Philadelphia and New York City centers for trade?

The Growth of New York

In 1664 New York had about 8,000 inhabitants. Most were Dutch, but Germans, Swedes, Native Americans, and Puritans from New England lived there as well. The population also included at least 300 enslaved Africans. New

CHAPTER 3
Section 3, 84–87

2 TEACH

L1 Identifying People As students read the section, have them write one or two important facts about each of the following: Charles I, Oliver Cromwell, Charles II, Peter Stuyvesant, the Duke of York, Lord John Berkeley, Sir George Carteret, William Penn. Ask students to use index cards, writing the person's name on one side and the facts on the other. They can then use the index cards as flash cards for review.

Map Study

Answers

1. New York, Pennsylvania, New Jersey, Delaware
2. Philadelphia was on a river with an inlet to the Atlantic Ocean. New York City was on the Atlantic coast with a good harbor. Both were about midway between the New England and Southern Colonies.

Map Skills Practice

Reading a Map Which mountains run through New York and Pennsylvania? *(Appalachian Mountains)*

Guided Reading Activity 3–3

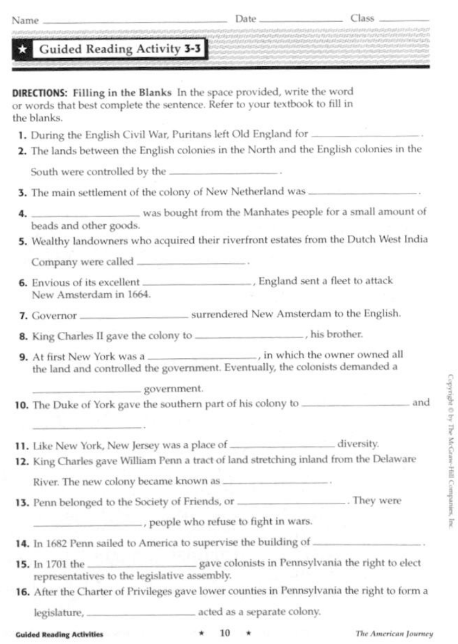

Name ______ Date ______ Class ______

★ Guided Reading Activity 3-3

DIRECTIONS: Filling in the Blanks In the space provided, write the word or words that best complete the sentence. Refer to your textbook to fill in the blanks.

1. During the English Civil War, Puritans left Old England for ______.
2. The lands between the English colonies in the North and the English colonies in the South were controlled by the ______.
3. The main settlement of the colony of New Netherland was ______.
4. ______ was bought from the Manhates people for a small amount of beads and other goods.
5. Wealthy landowners who acquired their riverfront estates from the Dutch West India Company were called ______.
6. Envious of its excellent ______, England sent a fleet to attack New Amsterdam in 1664.
7. Governor ______ surrendered New Amsterdam to the English.
8. King Charles II gave the colony to ______, his brother.
9. At first New York was a ______, in which the owner owned all the land and controlled the government. Eventually, the colonists demanded a ______ government.
10. The Duke of York gave the southern part of his colony to ______ and ______.
11. Like New York, New Jersey was a place of ______ diversity.
12. King Charles gave William Penn a tract of land stretching inland from the Delaware River. The new colony became known as ______.
13. Penn belonged to the Society of Friends, or ______. They were ______, people who refuse to fight in wars.
14. In 1682 Penn sailed to America to supervise the building of ______.
15. In 1701 the ______ gave colonists in Pennsylvania the right to elect representatives to the legislative assembly.
16. After the Charter of Privileges gave lower counties in Pennsylvania the right to form a legislature, ______ acted as a separate colony.

Guided Reading Activities ★ 10 ★ *The American Journey*

COOPERATIVE LEARNING ACTIVITY

Making a Map Have students work together to make a large map of the Middle Colonies, as they did for the New England Colonies. (See the Cooperative Learning Activity on page 79.) As with the New England map, some students should draw the map; others should create tags giving pertinent information about founders and reasons for settlement. Other students should use library resources to find the names of settlements not mentioned in the text. Have students compare the maps of the New England and Middle Colonies in terms of location of settlements and number of settlements.

HISTORY AND ART History painters such as West meant their works to teach a moral, religious, or nationalistic message. The preeminent history painter of his day, West was the first to show people in contemporary dress rather than in the garb of the "nobler" Greeks or Romans.
Answer: *He saw the colony as a chance to put into practice Quaker ideals of toleration and equality.*

3 ASSESS

Assign Section 3 Review as homework or as an in-class activity.

Use **Chapter Challenger Interactive Review Software** to review Section 3.

Section Quiz 3–3

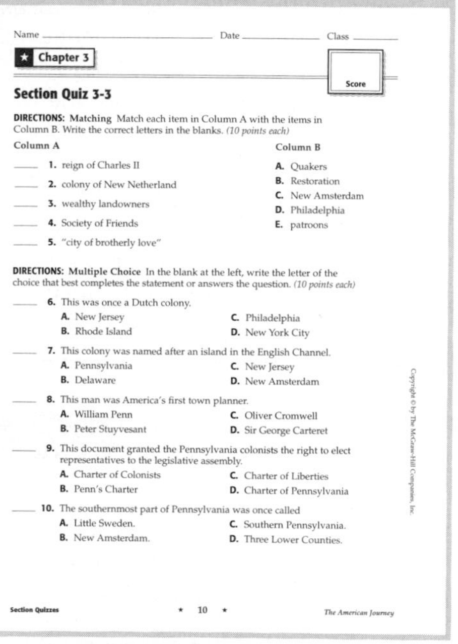
Name ______ Date ______ Class ______

Chapter 3

Score

Section Quiz 3-3

DIRECTIONS: Matching Match each item in Column A with the items in Column B. Write the correct letters in the blanks. *(10 points each)*

Column A

____ **1.** reign of Charles II
____ **2.** colony of New Netherland
____ **3.** wealthy landowners
____ **4.** Society of Friends
____ **5.** "city of brotherly love"

Column B

A. Quakers
B. Restoration
C. New Amsterdam
D. Philadelphia
E. patroons

DIRECTIONS: Multiple Choice In the blank at the left, write the letter of the choice that best completes the statement or answers the question. *(10 points each)*

____ **6.** This was once a Dutch colony.
A. New Jersey **C.** Philadelphia
B. Rhode Island **D.** New York City

____ **7.** This colony was named after an island in the English Channel.
A. Pennsylvania **C.** New Jersey
B. Delaware **D.** New Amsterdam

____ **8.** This man was America's first town planner.
A. William Penn **C.** Oliver Cromwell
B. Peter Stuyvesant **D.** Sir George Carteret

____ **9.** This document granted the Pennsylvania colonists the right to elect representatives to the legislative assembly.
A. Charter of Colonists **C.** Charter of Liberties
B. Penn's Charter **D.** Charter of Pennsylvania

____ **10.** The southernmost part of Pennsylvania was once called
A. Little Sweden. **C.** Southern Pennsylvania.
B. New Amsterdam. **D.** Three Lower Counties.

Section Quizzes ★ 10 ★ *The American Journey*

Facts On File

CD-ROM
Landmark Documents in American History

Title: *Penn's Frame of Government (First Frame of Government of Pennsylvania, William Penn, 1682)* Ask students to outline this document and to highlight aspects that seem to reflect the view of Quakers.

HISTORY AND ART ***Penn's Treaty with the Indians*** **by Benjamin West** In 1682 William Penn made his first treaty with the Delaware people. **Why did Penn see Pennsylvania as a "holy experiment"?**

Amsterdam, now called New York City, was one of the fastest-growing locations in the colony.

By 1683 the colony's population had swelled to about 12,000 people. A governor and council appointed by the Duke of York directed the colony's affairs. The colonists demanded a representative government like the governments of the other English colonies. The duke resisted the idea, but the New Yorkers would not give up. Finally the duke let them form an elected legislature.

New Jersey

The Duke of York gave the southern part of his colony, between the Hudson and Delaware Rivers, to **Lord John Berkeley** and **Sir George Carteret.** The proprietors named their colony New Jersey after the island of Jersey in the English Channel, on which Carteret was born.

Berkeley and Carteret hoped to make money from New Jersey by charging their settlers rent. To attract settlers, they offered large tracts of land and generous terms. They also promised freedom of religion, trial by jury, and a representative assembly. The assembly would make local laws and set tax rates. Every man in the colony would have a vote. The assembly held its first meeting in 1688.

Like New York, New Jersey was a place of ethnic and religious diversity. Because New Jersey had no natural harbors, however, it did not develop a major port or city like New York.

The proprietors of New Jersey did not make the profits they had expected from rents. Berkeley sold his share, West Jersey, in 1674. Carteret's share, East Jersey, was auctioned off in 1680.

By 1702 New Jersey had passed back into the hands of the king, becoming a royal colony. But the colonists continued to make local laws.

MULTIPLE LEARNING STYLES

Intrapersonal Pose the following question and have students answer it orally or in writing: Suppose you were a Quaker threatened with jail for your beliefs. Would you renounce your beliefs? After students have responded individually, discuss the issue as a class. Allow time for students to challenge the decisions of others, who may then defend their decisions. Point out that there is no right answer to such a question; it is a matter of individual choice. **L1**

Pennsylvania

In 1680 **William Penn,** a wealthy English gentleman, presented a plan to King Charles. Penn's father had once lent the king a great deal of money. Penn had inherited the king's promise to repay the loan. Instead of money, however, Penn asked for land in America. Pleased to get rid of his debt so easily, the king gave Penn a tract of land stretching inland from the Delaware River. The new colony, named Pennsylvania, was as large as England.

Penn and the Quakers

William Penn belonged to a Protestant group of dissenters called the Society of Friends, or **Quakers.** The Quakers believed that people had an "inner light" that could guide them to salvation. Each person could experience religious truth directly, which meant that church services and officials were unnecessary. Everybody was equal in God's sight. Though firm in their beliefs, the Quakers were tolerant of the views of others.

Many people found the Quakers' ideas a threat to established traditions. Quakers would not bow or take off their hats to lords and ladies because of their belief that everyone was equal. In addition they were **pacifists,** people who refuse to use force or to fight in wars. Quakers were fined, jailed, and even executed for their beliefs.

The "Holy Experiment"

William Penn saw Pennsylvania as a "holy experiment," a chance to put the Quaker ideals of toleration and equality into practice. In 1682 he sailed to America to supervise the building of **Philadelphia,** the "city of brotherly love."

Penn had designed the city himself, making him America's first town planner. Penn also wrote Pennsylvania's first constitution.

Penn believed that the land belonged to the Native Americans and that settlers should pay for it. Native Americans held Penn in such high regard that some settled in Pennsylvania.

To encourage European settlers to come to Pennsylvania, Penn advertised the colony throughout Europe with pamphlets in several languages. By 1683 more than 3,000 English, Welsh, Irish, Dutch, and German settlers had arrived. In 1701 in the Charter of Liberties, Penn granted the colonists the right to elect representatives to the legislative assembly.

The southernmost part of Pennsylvania was called the Three Lower Counties. Settled by Swedes in 1638, the area had been taken over by the Dutch and the English before becoming part of Pennsylvania. The Charter of Privileges allowed the lower counties to form their own legislature, which they did in 1703. Thereafter Delaware functioned as a separate colony supervised by Pennsylvania's governor.

Section 3 Review

Checking for Understanding

1. ***Identify*** Peter Stuyvesant, William Penn, Quakers.
2. ***Define*** patroon, proprietary colony, pacifist.
3. ***Explain*** why the English wanted the Dutch settlement of New Netherland.

Reviewing Themes

4. **Individual Action** How did William Penn earn the respect of Native Americans?

Critical Thinking

5. **Making Comparisons** How was the Quaker religion different from that of the Puritans?

Activity

Designing a Flag Design a flag for one of the Middle Colonies. Choose one colony, then decide what symbols and colors would be appropriate to represent it.

Section 3 Review Answers

1. Peter Stuyvesant, 85; William Penn, 87; Quakers, 87
2. The words are defined in the Glossary.
3. New Netherland lay between England's New England and Southern Colonies; it had an excellent harbor and a good river trade.
4. He honored their claim to the land and believed settlers should pay for it.
5. Quakers had no formal church services or church officials, were tolerant of other religions, believed all people are equal, and were pacifists. Puritans tried to reform the Anglican Church from within and lacked religious toleration.

Activity Symbols and colors should have some relationship to the history or characteristics of the chosen colony.

CHAPTER 3
Section 3, 84–87

Reteaching Activity 3–3

Name ______ Date ______ Class ______

★ Reteaching Activity 3-3

DIRECTIONS: Organizing Facts The numbered items in the Fact Bank are related to each of the Middle Colonies. Complete the web diagram by writing the number of each item in the correct circle on the chart. Some items fit in more than one group.

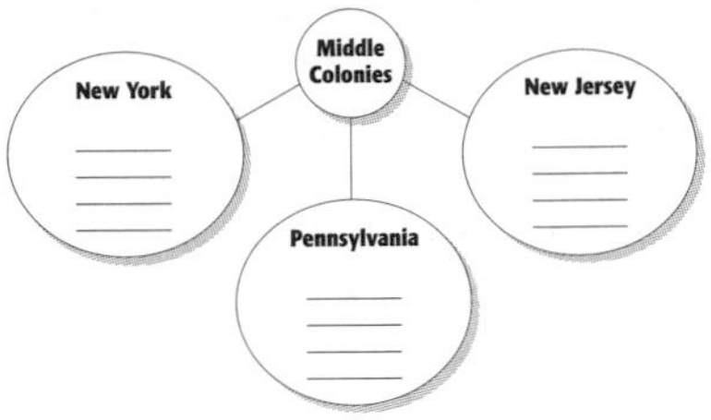

★FACT BANK

1. became a royal colony in 1702
2. Three Lower Counties
3. Manhattan Island
4. Quakers
5. Hudson River valley
6. Dutch West India Company
7. Charter of Privileges
8. Dutch and English settlers
9. promised religious freedom
10. founded in 1681
11. proprietary colony
12. New Amsterdam
13. Lord John Berkeley
14. William Penn
15. charged settlers rent
16. Sir George Carteret
17. excellent harbor
18. Peter Stuyvesant
19. city of brotherly love
20. attracted settlers with pamphlets

Reteaching Activities ★ 10 ★ *The American Journey*

Enrichment Activity 3–3

Name ______ Date ______ Class ______

★ Enrichment Activity 3-3 ★ ★

Across the Appalachians

Early settlers often followed Native American trails. The Mohawk, an eastern nation, used a path across the Appalachian Mountains in what is now New York. Many settlers from eastern settlements used the trail to reach western New York. The map below shows the Mohawk Trail.

The Mohawk Trail

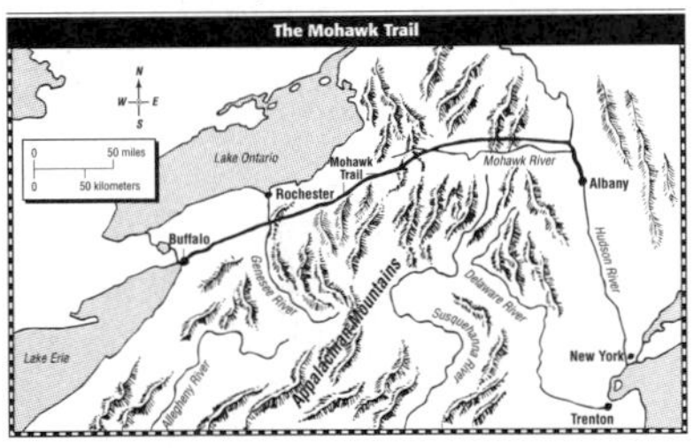

DIRECTIONS: Using a Relief Map Study the map to answer the questions on a separate sheet of paper.

1. On which part of the trail are mountains or foothills most likely to make the trip difficult?
2. Based on this map, would the part of the trail nearing Lake Erie be easier or more difficult than the eastern part for the traveler? Explain.
3. Why might settlers follow rivers after leaving Albany?
4. What is the approximate length of the trail?
5. Along which part of the trail are settlers likely to make better time? Explain.

Activity **DIRECTIONS:** Think of a route you regularly travel, for example, your route to school or to the library. Design a relief map of your route. Remember to include a map title, landmark labels, a distance scale, and markers for hills, if necessary. Exchange maps with a classmate. Determine if the maps are accurate and clear and provide suggestions for improvements.

Enrichment Activities ★ 10 ★ *The American Journey*

4 CLOSE

Have students turn the **Read to Discover** phrases (page 84) into questions and write answers to each.

1 FOCUS

BELLRINGER
Motivational Activity

Before taking roll at the beginning of the class period, project Section Focus Transparency 3–4 and have students answer the questions. Discuss students' responses.

This activity is also available as a blackline master.

Section Focus Transparency 3–4

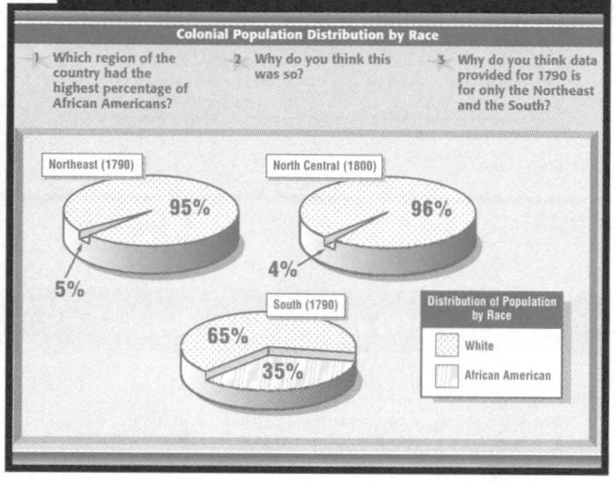

Vocabulary Precheck
Ask several volunteers to use the term *debtor* in a sentence.

Use the **Vocabulary Puzzle-Maker** to create crossword and word search puzzles.

Section Theme
Culture and Traditions
Tensions developed between northern Carolinians, who had small farms and sold forest products, and southern Carolinians, who were largely wealthy planters.

Activity Have students skim the section to find out why the two groups were in conflict. *(Northerners were afraid the powerful southerners would pass laws harmful to the northerners.)*

1600 | 1650 | 1700 | 1750

1632 King Charles I grants Maryland to Lord Baltimore

1676 Bacon's Rebellion occurs

1729 Carolina is divided into two colonies; Baltimore, Maryland, is founded

1733 Georgia is founded

Section 4

Southern Colonies

READ TO DISCOVER . . .
- why the Act of Toleration was passed.
- how North Carolina and South Carolina were different.
- how Georgia was established as a safe place for debtors and the poor.

TERMS TO LEARN
indentured servant
debtor
constitution

The Storyteller

How did it feel to be enslaved on the plantations of the South? In the 1930s, interviewers put this question to African Americans once under slavery. Many of them were approaching 100 years old, and some still carried deep scars on their backs from whippings. To be a slave meant to have no human rights. Elderly Roberta Mason remembered, "Once they whipped my father 'cause he looked at a slave they killed, and cried."

Slave drum, Virginia

Building colonies in North America involved a great deal of work. The settlers had to clear the land, construct homes and churches, plant crops, and tend the fields. As the colonies expanded, the demand for capable workers grew.

Not all people came to work in the colonies of their own free will. Africans were seized and brought over as slaves. English criminals and Scottish and Irish prisoners of war were also shipped to the colonies. They could earn their release by working for a period of time—often seven years. Other colonists complained that their settlements were dumping grounds for "His Majesty's seven-year passengers."

Other men, women, and children came to the colonies as **indentured servants.** In return for the payment of their passage to America, they agreed to work without pay for a certain period of time.

Catholics in Maryland

Maryland was the dream of **Sir George Calvert, Lord Baltimore,** a Catholic. Calvert wanted to establish a safe place for his fellow Catholics, who were being persecuted in England. He also hoped that a colony would bring him a fortune.

Calvert's dream came true in 1632, when King Charles I gave him a proprietary colony north of Virginia. Calvert died before actually receiving the grant. His son Cecilius Calvert took charge of the colony. It was named Maryland after the English queen, Henrietta Maria.

SECTION RESOURCES

Reproducible Masters
- Reproducible Lesson Plan 3–4
- Guided Reading Activity 3–4
- Section Quiz 3–4
- Reteaching Activity 3–4
- Enrichment Activity 3–4

Transparencies
- Section Focus Transparency 3–4

Multimedia
- Vocabulary PuzzleMaker
- Chapter Challenger Interactive Review Software
- GTV: A Geographic Perspective on American History
- GTV: The American People: Fabric of a Nation
- NGS PictureShow: Colonial America

Establishing the Colony

The younger Calvert—the new Lord Baltimore—never lived in Maryland but sent two of his brothers to run the colony. They reached America in 1634 with two ships and more than 200 settlers. Entering the Chesapeake Bay, they sailed up the **Potomac River** through fertile countryside. A priest in the party described the Potomac as "the sweetest and greatest river I have ever seen." The colonists chose a site for their settlement, which they called St. Mary's.

Knowing that tobacco had saved the Virginia colony, the Maryland colonists turned first to tobacco farming. To keep the colony from becoming too dependent on one crop, however, a Maryland law declared that "every person planting tobacco shall plant and tend two acres of corn." In addition to corn, most Maryland tobacco farmers produced wheat, fruit, vegetables, and livestock to feed their families and their workers. **Baltimore,** founded in 1729, was Maryland's port. Before long Baltimore became the colony's largest settlement.

Aristocrats and Farmers

Lord Baltimore gave large estates to his relatives and other English aristocrats. By doing so he created a wealthy and powerful class of landowners in Maryland.

The colony needed people to work in the plantation fields. To bring settlers to the colony, Lord Baltimore promised land—100 acres to each male settler, another 100 for his wife, 100 for each servant, and 50 for each of his children. As the number of plantations increased and additional workers were needed, the colony imported indentured servants and enslaved Africans to supply the needed labor.

Settling Disputes

For years the Calvert family and the Penn family argued over the boundary between Maryland and Pennsylvania. In the 1760s they hired two British astronomers, Charles Mason and Jeremiah Dixon, to map the line dividing the colonies. It took the two scientists five years to lay out the boundary stones. Each stone had the crest of the Penn family on one side and the crest of the Calverts on the other.

Another conflict was harder to resolve. The Calverts had welcomed Protestants as well as Catholics in Maryland. Protestant settlers outnumbered Catholics from the start.

To protect the Catholics from any attempt to make Maryland a Protestant colony, Baltimore passed a law called the **Act of Toleration** in 1649. The act granted Protestants and Catholics the right

The Southern Colonies

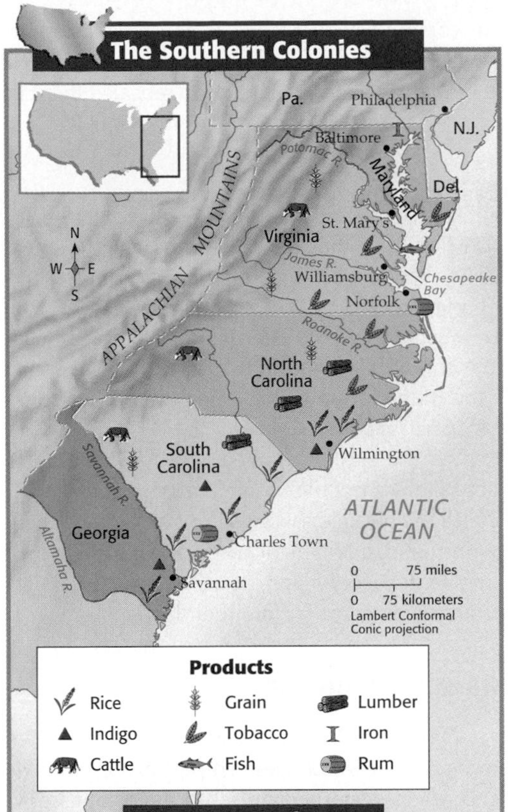

Map Study

The climate in the Southern Colonies allowed colonists to grow rice and tobacco.

1. **Region** What were the five Southern Colonies?
2. **Analyzing Information** What rivers acted as colonial borders in the Southern Colonies?

CHAPTER 3
Section 4, 88–93

2 TEACH

L1, ELL Choosing a Colony After students have read the section, have them choose the colony in which they would have preferred to live if they had been newcomers to America. Have them explain their choice orally or in writing. To extend the activity, have students work in pairs, with each student presenting his or her choice and the other student challenging it. **L1**

Map Study

Answers

1. Maryland, Virginia, North Carolina, South Carolina, Georgia
2. Potomac, Savannah, and Altamaha Rivers

Map Skills Practice

Reading a Map In which three colonies was rice grown? *(North Carolina, South Carolina, Georgia)*

Guided Reading Activity 3–4

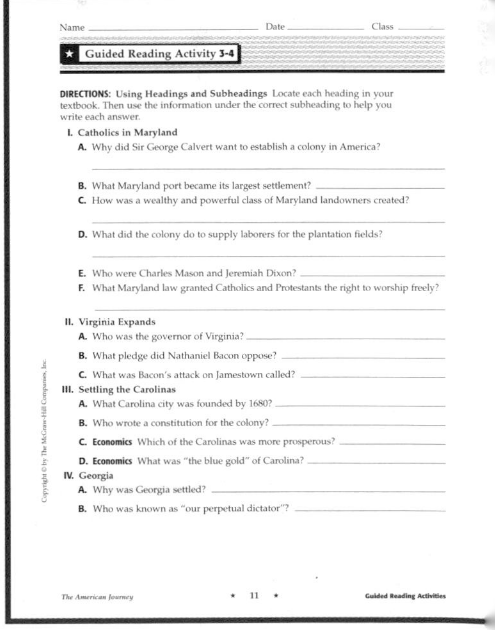
Name ______ Date ______ Class ______

★ Guided Reading Activity 3-4

DIRECTIONS: Using Headings and Subheadings Locate each heading in your textbook. Then use the information under the correct subheading to help you write each answer.

I. Catholics in Maryland
- **A.** Why did Sir George Calvert want to establish a colony in America? ______
- **B.** What Maryland port became its largest settlement? ______
- **C.** How was a wealthy and powerful class of Maryland landowners created? ______
- **D.** What did the colony do to supply laborers for the plantation fields? ______
- **E.** Who were Charles Mason and Jeremiah Dixon? ______
- **F.** What Maryland law granted Catholics and Protestants the right to worship freely? ______

II. Virginia Expands
- **A.** Who was the governor of Virginia? ______
- **B.** What pledge did Nathaniel Bacon oppose? ______
- **C.** What was Bacon's attack on Jamestown called? ______

III. Settling the Carolinas
- **A.** What Carolina city was founded by 1680? ______
- **B.** Who wrote a constitution for the colony? ______
- **C. Economics** Which of the Carolinas was more prosperous? ______
- **D. Economics** What was "the blue gold" of Carolina? ______

IV. Georgia
- **A.** Why was Georgia settled? ______
- **B.** Who was known as "our perpetual dictator"? ______

The American Journey ★ 11 ★ **Guided Reading Activities**

Cooperative Learning Activity

Making a Map Have students work together to make a large map of the Southern Colonies, as they did for the New England and Middle Colonies. (See the Cooperative Learning Activities on pages 79 and 85.) As with the other maps, some students should draw the map; others should create tags giving pertinent information about founders and reasons for settlement. Other students should use library resources to find the names of settlements not mentioned in the text. Have students compare the three maps in terms of location of settlements and number of settlements.

NATIONAL GEOGRAPHIC SOCIETY

VIDEODISC
GTV: A Geographic Perspective on American History

Side 1, Chapter 9
Title: *Settling Down, Moving On*
Subject: Regional differences emerge in the colonies (1650–1750)
Ask: **Where did the most adventurous farmers move?** *(westward)*

VIDEODISC
GTV: The American People: Fabric of a Nation

Side 1, Chapter 9
Title: *The Winds of Warfare!*
Subject: Cultural diversity in the colonies
Ask: **What British action led the colonists to revolution?** *(taxation without representation)*

CURRICULUM CONNECTION

GEOGRAPHY
The coast of North Carolina is protected by long, narrow barrier islands. As one observer remarked, "The coast of North Carolina looks as if it was just coming unglued, with strips of land floating out to sea." These sandy islands shift and change when storms batter the coast. As a result, some of the bridges and roads built over the years have been rendered useless.

to worship freely. It failed to end the tension between Protestants and Catholics, however. In 1692 the colony's Protestant majority repealed the act.

Virginia Expands

While other colonies were being founded, Virginia continued to grow. Wealthy tobacco planters held the best land near the coast, so new settlers pushed inland. Sir William Berkeley, the colony's governor, sent explorers over the Blue Ridge Mountains to open up the backcountry of Virginia to settlement.

As the settlers moved west, they came to lands inhabited by Native Americans. To avoid conflicts, Berkeley worked out an arrangement with the Native Americans in 1644. In exchange for a large piece of land, he agreed to keep settlers from pushing farther into their lands.

Bacon's Rebellion

Nathaniel Bacon, a wealthy young planter, was a leader in the western part of Virginia. He and other westerners opposed the colonial government because it was dominated by easterners. The westerners resented Berkeley's pledge to stay out of Native American territory. Some of them settled in the forbidden lands and then blamed the government in Jamestown for not protecting them from Native American raids.

Nathaniel Bacon

In 1676 Bacon led the angry westerners in attacks on Native American villages. Governor Berkeley declared Bacon "the greatest rebel that ever was in Virginia." Bacon's army marched to Jamestown, set fire to the capital, and drove Berkeley into exile. Only Bacon's sudden illness and death kept him from taking charge of Virginia. British troops helped Berkeley restore order and end the rebellion.

Bacon's Rebellion had shown that the settlers were not willing to be restricted to the coast. In 1677 the colonial government signed a treaty with the Native Americans that opened up more land to settlement.

Settling the Carolinas

In two charters issued in 1663 and 1665, King Charles II created a large proprietary colony south of Virginia. The colony was called Carolina, which means "Charles's land" in Latin. The king gave the colony to a group of eight prominent members of his court.

The Carolina proprietors carved out large estates for themselves and hoped to make money by selling and renting land to settlers. One of the proprietors convinced his partners to provide money to bring colonists over from England. Settlers began arriving in Carolina in 1670. By 1680 they had founded a city, which they called Charles Town after the king. The name later became **Charleston.**

John Locke, an English political philosopher, wrote a constitution for the Carolina colony. This **constitution,** or plan of government, covered such subjects as land distribution and social ranking. Carolina, however, did not develop according to plan. The people of northern and southern Carolina soon went their separate ways, creating two colonies.

Economics

Northern and Southern Carolina

The northern part of Carolina was settled mostly by farmers from Virginia's backcountry. They grew tobacco and sold forest products such as timber and tar. Because the northern Carolina coast offered no good harbor, the farmers relied on Virginia's ports and merchants to conduct their trade.

MULTIPLE LEARNING STYLES

Logical/Mathematical Have students use the figures in the text (page 89) to calculate how much land the following male settlers would have received from Lord Baltimore. (Remind students to include the male settler's allotment.) Settler A has a wife, three children, and two servants. *(550 acres)* Settler B has a wife, six children, and five servants. *(1,000 acres)* Settler C is single, but has three servants. *(400 acres)* **L2**

Founding the Thirteen Colonies

Colony	Date of Charter	Reasons Founded	Founders or Leaders
New England Colonies			
Massachusetts Plymouth Mass. Bay Colony	 1620 1630	 Religious freedom Religious freedom	John Carver, William Bradford, John Winthrop
New Hampshire	1622	Profit from trade and fishing	Ferdinando Gorges, John Mason
Rhode Island	1636	Religious freedom	Roger Williams
Connecticut	1636	Profit from fur trade, farming; religious and political freedom	Thomas Hooker
Middle Colonies			
New York	1624	Expand trade	Dutch settlers
Delaware	1638	Expand trade	Swedish settlers
New Jersey	1664	Profit from selling land	John Berkeley, George Carteret
Pennsylvania	1681	Profit from selling land; religious freedom	William Penn
Southern Colonies			
Virginia	1607	Expand trade	John Smith
Maryland	1632	Profit from selling land; religious freedom	Cecil Calvert
North Carolina	1663	Profit from trade and selling land	Group of eight aristocrats
South Carolina	1663	Profit from trade and selling land	Group of eight aristocrats
Georgia	1732	Religious freedom; protection against Spanish Florida; safe home for debtors	James Oglethorpe

Chart Study

The thirteen colonies were founded over a span of 125 years.

1. What were the two most common reasons for founding these colonies?
2. **Sequencing** What colony was first to be settled? Which was last?

The southern part of the Carolinas was more prosperous, thanks to fertile farmland and a good harbor at Charles Town (later Charleston). Settlements spread, and the trade in corn, lumber, and cattle flourished. In the 1680s planters discovered that rice grew well in the wet coastal lowlands. Rice soon became the colony's leading crop.

In the 1740s a young Englishwoman named Eliza Lucas developed another important Carolina crop—indigo. Indigo, a blue flowering plant, was used to dye textiles. After experimenting with seeds from the West Indies, Lucas succeeded in growing and processing indigo, the "blue gold" of Carolina.

Slave Labor in the Carolinas

Most of the settlers in southern Carolina came from another English colony—the island of Barbados in the West Indies. In Barbados the colonists used enslaved Africans to grow sugar. The colonists brought these workers with them.

Chart Study

Answers

1. religious freedom, trade
2. Virginia; Georgia

Chart Skills Practice

Reading a Chart Which colony was originally settled by the Dutch? *(New York)*

NATIONAL GEOGRAPHIC SOCIETY

CD-ROM
NGS PictureShow: Colonial America

Encourage students to explore the economic activities of the Southern Colonies by having them click on the main menu.

What? Where? When? Who?

Maryland Civil War As Maryland grew, it became more heavily Protestant, with a Puritan governor and a largely Puritan assembly. Fearful that he might lose control of his colony, Cecil Calvert in 1653 ordered that colonists swear allegiance to himself as proprietor. Instead, the assembly rejected his authority, repealed the Act of Toleration, and banned Roman Catholicism. Two years later, civil war broke out between the southern part of the colony (which supported Calvert) and the northern part (which supported the assembly). Puritans won the war and exiled Jesuit missionaries, but the English Parliament returned the colony to Calvert in 1657.

Making Connections Activity

Cultural Life In 1734 James Oglethorpe returned to England with a group of Creek, among them his friend Chief Tomo-Chi-Chi. The Creek, who were formally received by the king and the Archbishop of Canterbury, created a huge sensation in London. Crowds followed them everywhere, even rioting in an attempt to catch a glimpse of the party. On their return, the group praised England so highly that both the Creek and the Cherokee made pacts of friendship with the Georgia colony. Have students speculate on why the Creek were so impressed. **Ask:** **If the chief and his companions could have seen 100 years into the future, do you think they would have promoted friendship? L1, ELL**

CHAPTER 3
Section 4, 88–93

American Memories

A Rice Plantation

South Carolinians had experimented with growing rice very early in the colony's history. Success came only after 1690, however, when new channels for the supply of enslaved African labor were opened. South Carolina's heavy reliance on enslaved African labor coincided closely with the development of rice as a new and profitable staple.

Ask: **Why did rice cultivation increase the demand for enslaved labor?** *(because growing rice required much labor)*

Answer: *rice basket, rice hook*

3 ASSESS

Assign Section 4 Review as homework or as an in-class activity.

Use **Chapter Challenger Interactive Review Software** to review Section 4.

Section Quiz 3–4

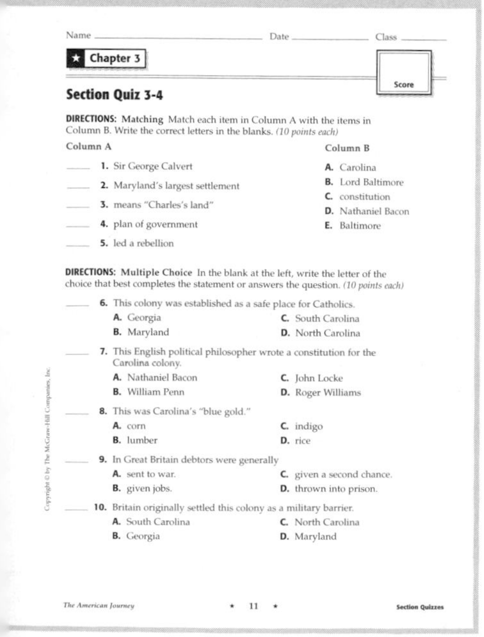
Name ______ Date ______ Class ______

★ Chapter 3

Score

Section Quiz 3-4

DIRECTIONS: Matching Match each item in Column A with the items in Column B. Write the correct letters in the blanks. *(10 points each)*

Column A	Column B
____ **1.** Sir George Calvert	**A.** Carolina
____ **2.** Maryland's largest settlement	**B.** Lord Baltimore
____ **3.** means "Charles's land"	**C.** constitution
____ **4.** plan of government	**D.** Nathaniel Bacon
____ **5.** led a rebellion	**E.** Baltimore

DIRECTIONS: Multiple Choice In the blank at the left, write the letter of the choice that best completes the statement or answers the question. *(10 points each)*

____ **6.** This colony was established as a safe place for Catholics.
A. Georgia **C.** South Carolina
B. Maryland **D.** North Carolina

____ **7.** This English political philosopher wrote a constitution for the Carolina colony.
A. Nathaniel Bacon **C.** John Locke
B. William Penn **D.** Roger Williams

____ **8.** This was Carolina's "blue gold."
A. corn **C.** indigo
B. lumber **D.** rice

____ **9.** In Great Britain debtors were generally
A. sent to war. **C.** given a second chance.
B. given jobs. **D.** thrown into prison.

____ **10.** Britain originally settled this colony as a military barrier.
A. South Carolina **C.** North Carolina
B. Georgia **D.** Maryland

The American Journey ★ 11 ★ **Section Quizzes**

American Memories

A Rice Plantation

What Was It Like? A rice plantation included the owner's large house surrounded by the small dwellings of enslaved Africans. **Of the items shown here, which were used to harvest the rice crop?**

Many enslaved Africans who arrived in the Carolinas worked in the rice fields. Some of them knew a great deal about rice cultivation because they had come from the rice-growing areas of West Africa. Growing rice required much labor, so the demand for slaves increased. By 1700 more than half the people who arrived in Charles Town were enslaved Africans.

Tensions Lead to Division

Tension continued to grow between wealthy planters of southern Carolina and colonists with small farms in the north. In 1719 the settlers seized control of the colony from its proprietors. In 1729 Carolina was formally divided into two colonies—North and South Carolina.

Georgia

Georgia, the last of the British colonies in America to be established, was founded in 1733. A group led by General **James Oglethorpe** received a charter to create a colony where English debtors and poor people could make a fresh start. In Great Britain, **debtors**—those unable to repay their debts—were generally thrown into prison.

The British government had another reason for creating Georgia. This colony could protect the other British colonies from Spanish attack. Great Britain and Spain had been at war in the early 1700s, and new conflicts over territory in North America were always breaking out. Located between Spanish Florida and South Carolina, Georgia could serve as a military barrier.

Oglethorpe's Town

Oglethorpe led the first group of "sober, industrial, and moral persons" to Georgia in 1733. They built a town called **Savannah,** as well as forts to defend themselves from the Spanish.

Oglethorpe wanted the people of Georgia to be hardworking, independent, and Protestant. He

CRITICAL THINKING ACTIVITY

Drawing Conclusions Lead a class discussion on why the Maryland law (mentioned on page 89) that required people to plant corn in addition to tobacco was a good idea. Solicit ideas from students and then add ideas as necessary. *(Possible responses: soil on which only one crop is grown wears out quickly; if a disease attacked the crop, farmers could be wiped out; overproduction of tobacco could produce a glut on the market, prices would fall, and growers would suffer financially.)* **L2**

Picturing HISTORY During the 1700s, Charles Town was the major port in South Carolina. **Why was South Carolina a prosperous colony?**

kept the size of farms small and banned slavery, Catholics, and rum.

Although Georgia had been planned as a debtors' colony, it actually received few debtors. Hundreds of poor people came from Great Britain. Religious refugees from Germany and Switzerland and a small group of Jews also settled there. Georgia soon had a higher percentage of non-British settlers than any other British colony.

The Colony Changes

Many settlers complained about the limits on the size of landholdings and the law banning slave labor. They also objected to the many rules Oglethorpe made regulating their lives. The colonists referred to Oglethorpe as "our perpetual dictator."

Oglethorpe grew frustrated by the colonists' demands and the colony's slow growth. He agreed to let people have larger landholdings and lifted the bans against slavery and rum. In 1751 he gave up altogether and turned the colony back over to the king.

By that time British settlers had been in what is now the eastern United States for almost a century and a half. They had lined the Atlantic coast with colonies. The British were not the only Europeans who were colonizing North America, however. Elsewhere on the continent, the Spanish and the French had built settlements of their own.

Section 4 Review

Checking for Understanding

1. ***Identify*** Sir George Calvert, Lord Baltimore, Act of Toleration, Nathaniel Bacon, Bacon's Rebellion, James Oglethorpe.
2. ***Define*** indentured servant, constitution, debtor.
3. ***Describe*** what the Act of Toleration was supposed to prevent.

Reviewing Themes

4. **Culture and Traditions** How did the need for workers contribute to cultural diversity in Maryland?

Critical Thinking

5. **Analyzing Information** Do you think uprisings such as Bacon's Rebellion were a sign of things to come? Explain your answer.

Activity

Making a Bulletin Board Display Work with a group to create a bulletin board display titled "The Southern Colonies." Include slogans and pictures to show the colonies' origins, climate, land, and products.

Section 4 Review Answers

1. Calvert, 88; Baltimore, 88; Act of Toleration, 89; Bacon, 90; Bacon's Rebellion, 90; Oglethorpe, 92
2. The words are defined in the Glossary.
3. It was supposed to prevent Maryland from becoming a Protestant colony.
4. Landowners brought in indentured servants and enslaved Africans as additional workers were needed on plantations.
5. Answers will vary, but students should recognize that a desire for land and representative government would be likely to continue to cause friction.

Activity In addition to covering the stated topics, displays should be visually attractive.

Picturing HISTORY In 1770 about 62,000 tons of goods passed through South Carolina's harbors. Today Charleston alone handles about 9 million short tons yearly.
Answer: *It had fertile farmland, a good harbor, and important cash crops.*

Reteaching Activity 3–4

Name ______ Date ______ Class ______

★ Reteaching Activity 3-4

DIRECTIONS: Matching Match each item in Column A with its corresponding item in Column B. Write the correct letters in the blanks.

COLUMN A

____ 1. Lord Baltimore
____ 2. Charles Mason and Jeremiah Dixon
____ 3. indentured servants
____ 4. Bacon's Rebellion
____ 5. Baltimore
____ 6. James Oglethorpe
____ 7. Carolina
____ 8. Henrietta Maria
____ 9. Sir William Berkeley
____ 10. John Locke
____ 11. Potomac
____ 12. Charles Town
____ 13. Eliza Lucas
____ 14. Act of Toleration

COLUMN B

A. 1649 law that granted Protestants and Catholics in Maryland religious freedom
B. governor of Virginia
C. queen for whom Maryland was named
D. English political philosopher who wrote the Carolina constitution
E. Maryland river bordered by fertile countryside
F. proprietary colony first settled in 1670
G. Sir George Calvert
H. Carolina city named after the king of England
I. succeeded in growing and processing indigo in Carolina
J. attack on Jamestown that showed that settlers resented being restricted to the coast
K. agreed to work without pay for a certain period of time in return for payment of passage to the colonies
L. mapped the line dividing Maryland and Pennsylvania
M. Maryland port that became its largest settlement
N. Georgia leader known as "our perpetual dictator" because of his many rules and regulations

DIRECTIONS: Essay On a separate sheet of paper, answer the following questions.

15. How did Maryland colonists avoid becoming too dependent on tobacco?
16. How did the cultivation of rice contribute to the growth of slavery in Carolina?

Enrichment Activity 3–4

Name ______ Date ______ Class ______

★ Enrichment Activity 3-4 ★

Savannah

Some American colonial settlements grew in a disorderly way, as people moved in and claimed land. Other settlements were carefully laid out. Study the layout of Savannah, Georgia, founded in 1733.

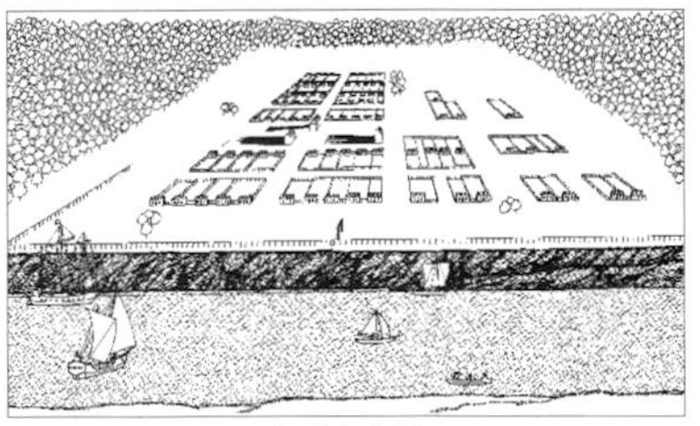

Savannah, Georgia, 1733

DIRECTIONS: Making Inferences Use the picture to help you write a paragraph on a separate sheet of paper. Tell as much as you can about the location, plan, and design of Savannah. Then check to see if your paragraph answers all the Check Questions below. If you need to, revise your paragraph.

✔ **CHECK QUESTIONS**

- What was the land like before settlement?
- How was the land prepared for building?
- How were the buildings designed and laid out?
- Why was a site near water chosen?
- Is the settlement on the ocean, on a river, or in a bay?

4 CLOSE

Have students list the reasons people came to the Southern Colonies.

1 FOCUS

BELLRINGER
Motivational Activity

Before taking roll at the beginning of the class period, project Section Focus Transparency 3–5 and have students answer the questions. Discuss students' responses.

This activity is also available as a blackline master.

Section Focus Transparency 3–5

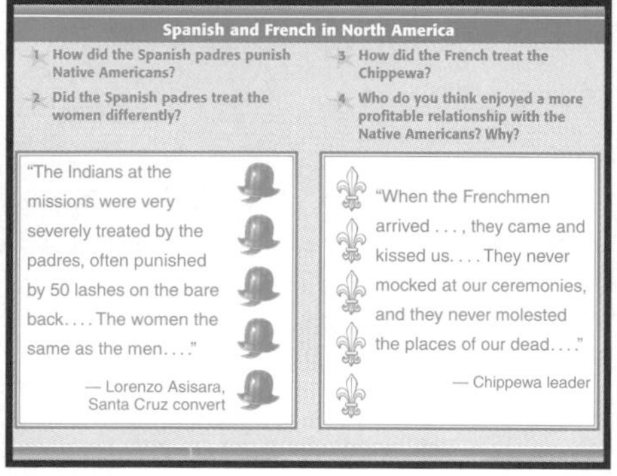

Vocabulary Precheck

Call on students to define *tenant farmer* and *mission.* Ask students to use each of these words in a sentence.

Use the **Vocabulary PuzzleMaker** to create crossword and word search puzzles.

Section Theme
Culture and Traditions

French missionaries respected Native Americans' land and customs, but the Spanish often forced Native Americans to live in missions and work as laborers.

Activity Have students draw conclusions about the relationships Native Americans had with the French and Spanish as a result of this difference in treatment. *(Relations between the French and Native Americans were better than those between the Spaniards and Native Americans.)*

1600 — 1650 — 1700 — 1750

1608 The French settle Quebec

1610 Santa Fe founded by the Spanish

1663 New France becomes a royal colony

1718 French found city of New Orleans

1769 Junípero Serra establishes mission at San Diego

Section 5

Other European Settlements

READ TO DISCOVER . . .

- how France's colony in North America was different from the English colonies.
- why Spain built forts in Texas.
- who founded the first Catholic mission in California.

TERMS TO LEARN

tenant farmer   mission

The Storyteller

Spring had arrived. The French fur trapper and his Native American partner guided their canoe through the huge chunks of ice bobbing in the St. Lawrence River. The canoes behind them carried other fur trappers. All were headed downriver to Montreal after trapping beaver in the snowy wilderness.

The fur trapper looked over his shoulder at the mound of skins in the canoe. The last time he counted, more than 600 beaver skins filled his cargo.

French fur trapper

When French fur trappers reached Montreal every spring, merchants rushed to the river. They set up booths where they traded muskets, blankets, kettles, and other items for the beaver skins the trappers had caught during the winter. The governor greeted the trappers with a speech, and priests offered sermons. Then came several days of trading and celebrations.

New France

The French had founded **Quebec** in 1608. At first they had little interest in large-scale settlement in North America. They were mainly concerned with fishing and furs. French trappers and missionaries went far into the interior of North America. French fur companies built forts and trading posts to protect their profitable trade.

In 1663 **New France** became a royal colony. King Louis XIV limited the privileges of the fur companies. He appointed a royal governor, Jean Talon, who strongly supported new explorations.

Down the Mississippi River

In the 1670s two Frenchmen—a fur trader, **Louis Joliet,** and a priest, **Jacques Marquette**—explored the Mississippi River by canoe. Joliet and Marquette hoped to find gold, silver, or other precious metals. They were also looking for a water passage to the Pacific Ocean. The two explorers reached as far south as the junction of the Arkansas and Mississippi Rivers. When they realized that the Mississippi flowed south into the

SECTION RESOURCES

Reproducible Masters
- Reproducible Lesson Plan 3–5
- Guided Reading Activity 3–5
- Section Quiz 3–5
- Reteaching Activity 3–5
- Enrichment Activity 3–5

Transparencies
- Section Focus Transparency 3–5

Multimedia
- Vocabulary PuzzleMaker
- Chapter Challenger Interactive Review Software
- Testmaker
- ABCNews InterActive™ Historic America Electronic Field Trips

Picturing HISTORY This painting shows French traders receiving furs from Native Americans at a point along the Mississippi River. **Why did the French generally have good relations with the Native Americans?**

Gulf of Mexico rather than west into the Pacific, they turned around and headed back upriver.

A few years later, **Robert Cavelier Sieur de La Salle** followed the Mississippi River all the way to the Gulf of Mexico. La Salle claimed the region around the river for France. He called this territory Louisiana in honor of King Louis XIV. In 1718 the French governor founded the port of **New Orleans** at the mouth of the Mississippi River. Later French explorers, traders, and missionaries traveled west to the Rocky Mountains and southwest to the Rio Grande.

Growth of New France

Settlement in French America advanced very slowly. Settlement in New France consisted of a system of seigneuries (SEHN•yuh•reez), or estates, along the St. Lawrence River. The estates were much like the patroonships of New Netherland. The seigneurs (SEHN•yehrz), or lords, received land in exchange for bringing settlers to the colony. Known as **tenant farmers,** the settlers paid their lord an annual rent and worked for him for a fixed number of days each year.

The French had better relations with the Native Americans than did any other Europeans. French trappers and missionaries traveled deep into Indian lands. They lived among the Native American peoples, learned their languages, and respected their ways.

Although the missionaries had come to convert Native Americans to Catholicism, they did not try to change the Indians' customs. Most important, the French colony grew so slowly that Native Americans were not pushed off their lands.

New Spain

In the early 1600s, England, France, and the Netherlands began their colonization of North America. The Spanish, however, still controlled most of Mexico, the Caribbean, and Central and South America. They also expanded into the western and southern part of what would one day be the United States.

The Southwest and the Pacific Coast

Spain was determined to keep the other European powers from threatening its empire in America. To protect their claims, the Spanish sent soldiers, missionaries, and settlers into the north.

Spanish missionaries, soldiers, and settlers founded **Santa Fe** in present-day New Mexico in

2 TEACH

L1 Creating Concept Webs Help students create two concept webs summarizing the section. The central ovals should be labeled *New France* and *New Spain.* Have students suggest information to place in the surrounding ovals.

Picturing HISTORY Colonial commerce survived despite the absence of currency. Traders relied on barter or money substitutes such as beaver skins.
Answer: *They respected their customs, learned their languages, and did not take their land.*

Guided Reading Activity 3–5

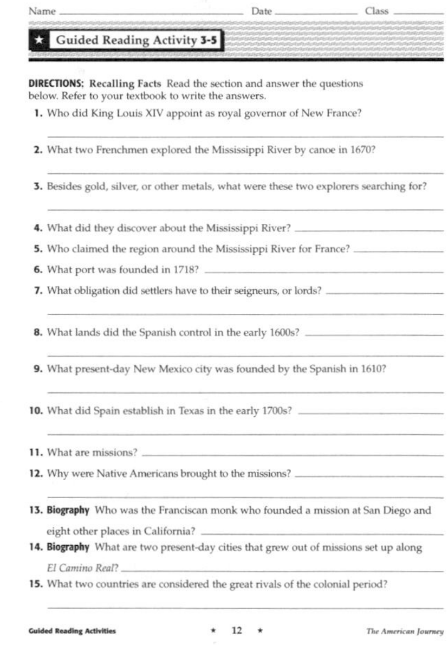

Name ______ Date ______ Class ______

Guided Reading Activity 3-5

DIRECTIONS: Recalling Facts Read the section and answer the questions below. Refer to your textbook to write the answers.

1. Who did King Louis XIV appoint as royal governor of New France?
2. What two Frenchmen explored the Mississippi River by canoe in 1670?
3. Besides gold, silver, or other metals, what were these two explorers searching for?
4. What did they discover about the Mississippi River? ______
5. Who claimed the region around the Mississippi River for France? ______
6. What port was founded in 1718? ______
7. What obligation did settlers have to their seigneurs, or lords? ______
8. What lands did the Spanish control in the early 1600s? ______
9. What present-day New Mexico city was founded by the Spanish in 1610?
10. What did Spain establish in Texas in the early 1700s? ______
11. What are missions? ______
12. Why were Native Americans brought to the missions? ______
13. **Biography** Who was the Franciscan monk who founded a mission at San Diego and eight other places in California? ______
14. **Biography** What are two present-day cities that grew out of missions set up along *El Camino Real*? ______
15. What two countries are considered the great rivals of the colonial period?

Guided Reading Activities ★ 12 ★ *The American Journey*

3 ASSESS

Assign Section 5 Review as homework or as an in-class activity.

Use **Chapter Challenger Interactive Review Software** to review Section 5.

COOPERATIVE LEARNING ACTIVITY

Researching New France Have students research the early history of New France. Organize the class into groups, each of which should, after preliminary research, choose a topic to explore. Work should be divided according to the skills of the group members. Some students may write reports, whereas others may prepare illustrations, maps, or models.

CHAPTER 3
Section 5, 94–96

Section Quiz 3–5

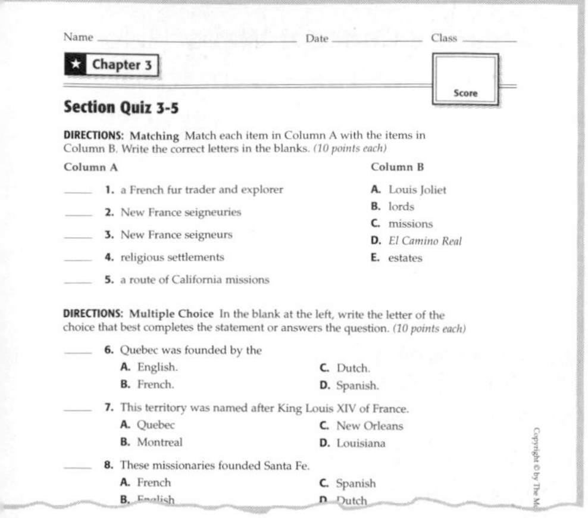
Name ______ Date ______ Class ______

Chapter 3 | Score

Section Quiz 3-5

DIRECTIONS: Matching Match each item in Column A with the items in Column B. Write the correct letters in the blanks. *(10 points each)*

Column A	Column B
___ 1. a French fur trader and explorer	A. Louis Joliet
___ 2. New France seigneuries	B. lords
___ 3. New France seigneurs	C. missions
___ 4. religious settlements	D. *El Camino Real*
___ 5. a route of California missions	E. estates

DIRECTIONS: Multiple Choice In the blank at the left, write the letter of the choice that best completes the statement or answers the question. *(10 points each)*

___ 6. Quebec was founded by the
A. English. C. Dutch.
B. French. D. Spanish.

___ 7. This territory was named after King Louis XIV of France.
A. Quebec C. New Orleans
B. Montreal D. Louisiana

___ 8. These missionaries founded Santa Fe.
A. French C. Spanish

Reteaching Activity 3–5

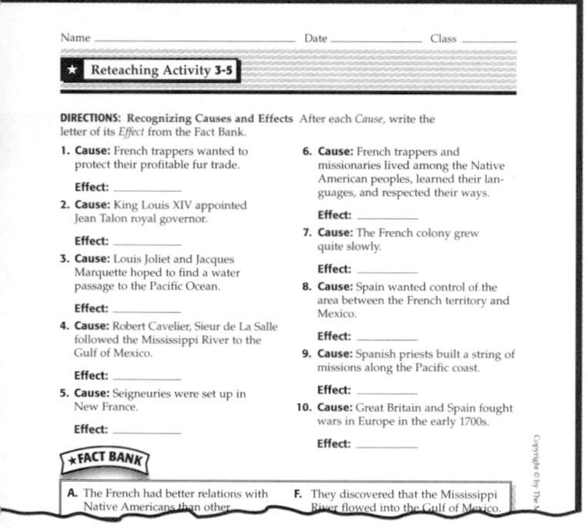
Name ______ Date ______ Class ______

Reteaching Activity 3-5

DIRECTIONS: Recognizing Causes and Effects After each *Cause*, write the letter of its *Effect* from the Fact Bank.

1. **Cause:** French trappers wanted to protect their profitable fur trade.
Effect: ______
2. **Cause:** King Louis XIV appointed Jean Talon royal governor.
Effect: ______
3. **Cause:** Louis Joliet and Jacques Marquette hoped to find a water passage to the Pacific Ocean.
Effect: ______
4. **Cause:** Robert Cavelier, Sieur de La Salle followed the Mississippi River to the Gulf of Mexico.
Effect: ______
5. **Cause:** Seigneuries were set up in New France.
Effect: ______
6. **Cause:** French trappers and missionaries lived among the Native American peoples, learned their languages, and respected their ways.
Effect: ______
7. **Cause:** The French colony grew quite slowly.
Effect: ______
8. **Cause:** Spain wanted control of the area between the French territory and Mexico.
Effect: ______
9. **Cause:** Spanish priests built a string of missions along the Pacific coast.
Effect: ______
10. **Cause:** Great Britain and Spain fought wars in Europe in the early 1700s.
Effect: ______

FACT BANK

A. The French had better relations with Native Americans than other
F. They discovered that the Mississippi River flowed into the Gulf of Mexico.

Enrichment Activity 3–5

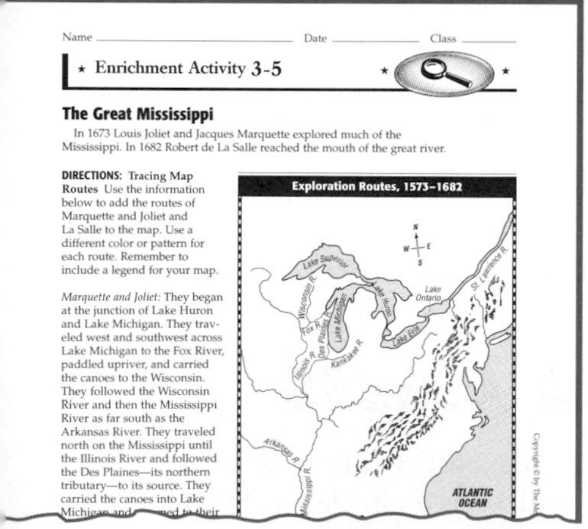
Name ______ Date ______ Class ______

Enrichment Activity 3-5

The Great Mississippi

In 1673 Louis Joliet and Jacques Marquette explored much of the Mississippi. In 1682 Robert de La Salle reached the mouth of the great river.

DIRECTIONS: Tracing Map Routes Use the information below to add the routes of Marquette and Joliet and La Salle to the map. Use a different color or pattern for each route. Remember to include a legend for your map.

Marquette and Joliet: They began at the junction of Lake Huron and Lake Michigan. They traveled west and southwest across Lake Michigan to the Fox River, paddled upriver, and carried the canoes to the Wisconsin. They followed the Wisconsin River and then the Mississippi River as far south as the Arkansas River. They traveled north on the Mississippi until the Illinois River and followed the Des Plaines—its northern tributary—to its source. They carried the canoes into Lake Michigan and

4 CLOSE

Have students speculate on how United States history might have been different if the English had treated the Native Americans the way the French did.

1610. Another group of missionaries and settlers went to present-day Arizona in the late 1600s. When France began exploring and laying claim to lands around the Mississippi River, the Spanish moved into what is now Texas. Spain wanted to control the area between the French territory and their own colony in Mexico. In the early 1700s, Spain established San Antonio and seven other military posts in Texas.

Missions in California

Spanish priests built a string of missions along the Pacific coast. **Missions** are religious settlements established to convert people to a particular faith. The missions enabled the Spanish to lay claim to California.

The Spanish did more than convert Native Americans to Christianity. Spanish missionaries and soldiers also brought the Indians to the missions—often by force—to serve as laborers in fields and workshops.

Junípero Serra

Biography

Father Junípero Serra

In 1769 **Junípero Serra,** a Franciscan monk, founded a mission at **San Diego.** Over the next 15 years, Father Serra set up 8 more missions in California along a route called *El Camino Real* (The King's Highway)—missions that would grow into such cities as Los Angeles and Monterey.

The distance from one mission to the next was usually a day's walk, and Serra traveled on foot to visit each one and advise the missionaries. Serra also championed the rights of the Indians. He worked to prevent Spanish army commanders in the region from mistreating the Native Americans.

European Conflicts in North America

The rivalries between European nations carried over into the Americas. Britain and Spain fought several wars in the early 1700s. When the two countries were at war in Europe, fighting often broke out between British colonists in Georgia and Spanish colonists in Florida.

France and Great Britain were the great rivals of the colonial period. Both nations were expanding their settlements in North America. In the late 1700s and early 1800s, wars in Europe between the British and the French would shape events across the Atlantic even more decisively.

Section 5 Review

Checking for Understanding

1. ***Identify*** Louis Joliet, Jacques Marquette, La Salle, Father Junípero Serra.
2. ***Define*** tenant farmer, mission.
3. ***Explain*** why settlement in French America was slower than in the English colonies.

Reviewing Themes

4. **Culture and Traditions** Why was France's relationship with the Native Americans better than that of other Europeans?

Critical Thinking

5. **Predicting Consequences** What might have happened to Spain's land claims if it had not built military posts in Texas?

Activity

Making a Map Sketch a map of North America and label the areas claimed by the British, French, and Spanish. Then, using a red pencil or marker, indicate border areas that might be potential hot spots between rival nations.

Section 5 Review Answers

1. Joliet, 94; Marquette, 94; La Salle, 95; Serra, 96
2. The words are defined in the Glossary.
3. The French concentrated on fishing and trading furs, not settlement.
4. Unlike other Europeans, the French respected and adapted to Native American culture and did not take Native American lands.
5. Texas was a buffer between the land claims of Spain and France. If Spain had not built forts in Texas, France could have threatened those claims.

Activity Students' maps should highlight the following potential hot spots: borders between English and French areas, English and Spanish areas, and French and Spanish areas.

Multimedia Activities

ABCNEWS INTERACTIVE™ Historic America Electronic Field Trips

Field Trip to St. Augustine

Setting up the Video

With your classmates, view "St. Augustine" on the videodisc ***Historic America: Electronic Field Trips***. St. Augustine is the oldest European settlement in the United States. It was founded as a military outpost in 1565 by the Spanish to protect their ships, which were carrying treasures from Mexico and South America to Spain. This program explains the history of St. Augustine and the influences left behind by the Spanish.

Hands-On Activity

Think of Spanish influences that appear in modern American culture. Organize into five groups, with each group brainstorming several examples of Spanish influences in the areas of: food, language, music, traditions, sports. Hold a "Spanish Legacy Day," with each group bringing samples, artifacts, or videotapes of their topic.

Side 1, Chapter 4

View the video by scanning the bar code or by entering the chapter number on your keypad and pressing Search.

Surfing the "Net"

Tools of the Trade

During the Colonial Era, many remarkable inventions appeared. Benjamin Franklin, one famous inventor of the period, published *Poor Richard's Almanack,* a publication filled with advice on a variety of topics. Many colonists turned to this resource for information. Imagine the Internet was around during Franklin's time. Place yourself in the shoes of a typical colonist and search the Internet for information that is pertinent to your occupation. To assist you on your search, follow the instructions below.

Getting There

Pick a trade that a colonist might have practiced, then research related topics of that trade. For example, if you are a farmer, you might be interested in knowing about the weather and its effect on crop planting.

1. Use a search engine. Type in words that relate to the trade you choose.
2. The search engine will provide you with a number of links to follow. Links are "pointers" to different sites on the Internet and commonly appear as blue underlined words.

What to Do When You Are There

Click on the links to navigate through the pages of information. Print your findings. Using a word processor, create an almanac page that would inform others about your trade and the information you discovered on the Internet.

TEACHER'S NOTES

Multimedia Activities

ABCNEWS INTERACTIVE™

VIDEODISC
Historic America
Electronic Field Trips

Side 1, Chapter 4
Title: *St. Augustine*

If you do not have access to a videodisc player, the **Historic America Electronic Field Trips** are also available in VHS.

Internet Sites

The following are possible sites for completing the "Net" activities:

The Virtual Reference Desk
http://thorplus.lib.purdue.edu/reference/index.html

Better Business Bureau
http://www.bbb.org/

Global Trade Center
http://www.tradezone.com/

United States Bureau of Labor Statistics
http://stats.bls.gov./blshome.html

Not on the "Net" . . .

If students have limited or no access to the Internet, have them complete the "Tools of the Trade" activity by using the electronic card catalog at the school or local library. At the *s:* prompt, students should type in *occupations* or more specific words that relate to the trade they chose. They should then use the call numbers to find the books they need to complete their research.

GLENCOE TECHNOLOGY

VIDEODISC
MindJogger Videoquiz

Use MindJogger to review the Chapter 3 content.

Chapter 3
Disc 1, Side A

Also available in VHS.

Reviewing Key Terms

The key terms used in this activity are defined in the textbook glossary on pages A26–A35.

Reviewing Key Facts

1. Virginia settlers wanted a voice in the government, and the House of Burgesses allowed them to participate in making the laws.
2. Puritans wanted to reform the church from within. Pilgrims wanted to break away and found their own church.
3. Answers will vary but should include any two: offered large tracts of land, religious freedom, trial by jury, the right to participate in government, free passage in exchange for work.
4. He wanted a safe place for Catholics to practice their religion, and he wanted to make money.
5. to convert Native Americans to Christianity and to claim land for Spain

Critical Thinking

1. Settlers were needed to work the land, build towns, and establish businesses.
2. Penn advertised the colony throughout Europe in a variety of languages.

Chapter 3
Review and Activities

Reviewing Key Terms

On a sheet of paper, define the following terms:

charter
joint-stock company
burgesses
dissent
persecute
Puritan
Separatist
Pilgrim
patroon
proprietary colony
pacifist
indentured servant
constitution
debtor
mission

Reviewing Key Facts

1. Why did the Virginia Company create the House of Burgesses?
2. How did the Puritans' and the Pilgrims' view of the Anglican Church differ?
3. Name two things that colonial leaders offered to attract settlers.
4. What were Sir George Calvert's two main reasons for establishing Maryland?
5. Why did Spain send missionaries to the Pacific coast and the Southwest?

Critical Thinking

Identifying Central Issues

For colonies to prosper, they needed a large number of settlers.

1. Why did the success of a colony depend on attracting settlers?
2. In what ways did William Penn try to attract settlers?

Skill Practice Activity

Reading a Bar Graph

Study the bar graph, then answer these questions:

1. What do the numbers on the vertical axis represent?
2. What was the approximate value of exports to England in 1700?
3. In which years were there more exports than imports?

Value of American Exports and Imports with England, 1700–1750

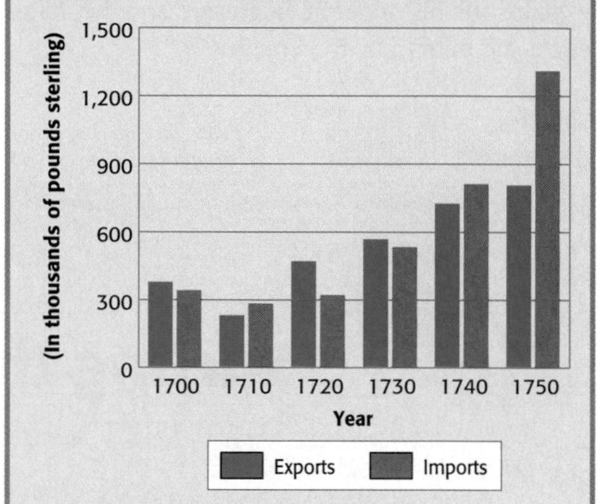

Source: *Historical Statistics of the United States: Colonial Times to 1970*

Time Line Activity

Create a time line on which you place the following events in chronological order.

- *Mayflower* lands at Plymouth
- French found port of New Orleans
- England takes over New Netherland
- Anne Hutchinson founds Portsmouth
- William Penn founds Pennsylvania
- The Spanish settle Santa Fe
- King Philip's War is waged
- Jamestown is established
- Quebec is established

Skill Practice Activity

1. value of American exports and imports with England in thousands of pounds sterling between 1700 and 1750
2. about 400,000 pounds sterling
3. 1700, 1720, 1730

Time Line Activity

Events should be placed in this order: Jamestown is established, Quebec is established, The Spanish settle Santa Fe, *Mayflower* lands at Plymouth, Anne Hutchinson founds Portsmouth, England takes over New Netherland, King Philip's War is waged, William Penn founds Pennsylvania, French found port of New Orleans

Technology Activity

Using a Word Processor Search the library for information about the Canadian cities of Quebec and Montreal. Find historical sites that show the French influence in these cities. Then, on your word processor, create a travel brochure with a brief description of each site.

Geography Activity

Study the map below and answer the questions that follow.

1. **Location** Which colonies had the largest areas of settlement before 1660?
2. **Place** During what time period was Boston settled?

Settlement of the British Colonies

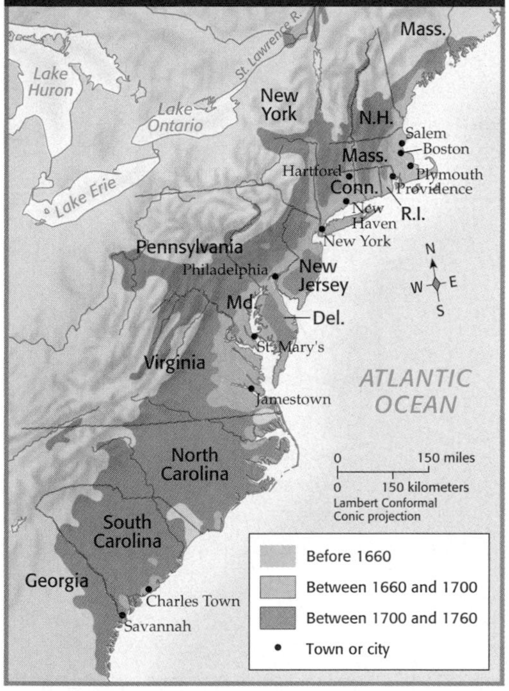

Reviewing Themes

1. **Economic Factors** How did the economic activities of the French differ from those of the English in North America?
2. **Civic Rights and Responsibilities** What role did religious freedom play in the founding of Rhode Island and Pennsylvania?
3. **Individual Action** Why did cooperation turn to conflict between the New England settlers and the Native Americans?
4. **Culture and Traditions** Between what two groups in the Carolinas did tension arise?
5. **Culture and Traditions** How did the treatment of Native Americans by Spanish missionaries differ from their treatment by French missionaries?

Cooperative Activity

History and Math Working in a group, research the populations of the English colonies in 1700. Create a bar graph to compare the populations of each. Use the graph to determine whether the total population of the New England, Middle, or Southern Colonies was largest.

Portfolio Activity **History Journal** Make a list of the New England Colonies. Then assign a number to each, based on where you would have most liked to have settled during the Colonial period. Number 1 should indicate your first choice, number 2 your second choice, and so on. Next to each number, write a brief statement explaining your choices.

CHAPTER 3
Review and Activities

Technology Activity

Students' brochures should reflect information gathered on historical sites that show French influence in Quebec and Montreal.

Geography Activity

1. Virginia and Massachusetts
2. before 1660

Reviewing Themes

1. The French were mainly interested in trade with the Native Americans and in hunting and fishing. The English wanted to build towns and farms.
2. Rhode Island was founded by Roger Williams after Puritans banished him from Massachusetts for his religious beliefs. Rhode Island allowed people of all faiths to worship freely. Pennsylvania was founded by William Penn as a place where Quakers could practice their faith without persecution and as a haven of religious freedom for all people.
3. At first Native Americans helped the English settlers to survive. As settlers began taking more and more land, Native Americans came to view them as a threat.
4. between small farmers of the north and wealthy planters of the south
5. The French missionaries respected their customs and learned their languages. The Spanish missionaries often forced Native Americans to live and work in the missions, and some treated the Indians poorly.

Cooperative Activity

Bar graphs should show the population of each of the English colonies in 1700. The total population of the New England Colonies was largest.

Portfolio Activity Students' rankings and explanations should reflect an understanding of the nature of each colony.

Chapter Bonus Test Question

Ask: **You are traveling through the thirteen colonies and you notice the following things. In which region are you?**

1. Dutch is spoken in some areas.
2. Many Germans have settled here, looking for religious freedom.
3. Peace-loving people called Quakers founded one of the colonies. *(Middle Colonies)*

Hands-On HISTORY Lab Activity

Block Schedule

This activity may be implemented within either a traditional class period or a block scheduling framework.

FOCUS

Have students list the things they need for daily living—food, clothing, shelter, toiletries, medicines, and so on—and think about how they obtain these items.

Point out that pioneers had to make almost everything they needed. If they wanted to make bread they had to raise and harvest the grain and grind it into flour. If they wanted a roast of beef or lamb, they had to raise and butcher livestock. Note that this **Hands-On History Lab Activity** gives them an idea of how long it took to make just one of life's necessities.

TEACH

L1 Bathing and Laundering After students have read **The Way It Was,** discuss the advantages that less frequent bathing and laundering would have (in addition to saving on soap). Possible responses: save on firewood for heating water and making lye, skin would not dry out as much, clothes would last longer.

Note that it is only in modern times—with instant hot water from the tap, readily available soaps and detergents, and washing machines and dryers—that most people can afford the luxury of frequent bathing and laundering. Even in the early 1900s, people commonly took a Saturday night bath in a round tub in the kitchen with water heated in pots on the stove.

Hands-On HISTORY Lab Activity

Making Soap

Early settlers in North America usually made soap once a year from animal fats collected at butchering time. This soap was used for everything— washing dishes, clothes, and people, too! Try making a bar of soap to understand this aspect of colonial life.

The Way It Was

The average American colonist did not have very much need for a large supply of soap. Most colonists washed their clothing only once a month and bathed even less frequently. They thought that baths were bad for their health. Homemade soap—a harsh mixture of wood ashes, water, and animal fat—was often a strong-smelling, soft, jellylike mass. Soap makers made soap in a large pot over an outdoor fire to keep the fumes away from the house. The fat was heated and stirred for hours until it turned into a smooth, thick liquid. The top layer of fat was skimmed off and poured into wooden tubs. Then lye, made from wood ashes and water, was stirred into the melted fat. It took several hours of stirring to combine the fat and lye to make soap. The soap was then poured into small wooden boxes, allowed to cool, and stored.

Believe It Or Not! The basic recipe for homemade soap included 5 to 6 bushels of wood ashes and about 20 to 25 pounds of animal fat. These ingredients would produce one barrel of soap.

1 Materials

- small plastic container
- petroleum jelly
- 1 cup of soap scraps
- cheese grater
- measuring cup
- double boiler, with water in the bottom
- water
- plastic stirring spoon
- small twig

CURRICULUM CONNECTION

Health In addition to a lack of personal cleanliness, the colonists suffered from a lack of public hygiene. When they emptied their chamber pots, for example, they commonly dumped the waste matter directly into the street. Other household wastes, dead animals, wastes from butcher shops, and rubbish were also dumped in the streets. Drains and open sewers carried the mess into harbors, creating an unbearable stench as it rotted in summer at low tide. Runoff also polluted the groundwater, and epidemics caused by drinking such water from village wells were common.

Hands-On HISTORY Lab Activity

2 What To Do

1. Grease the inside of the plastic container with petroleum jelly. Set aside.
2. Grate 1 cup of scraps of soap with the cheese grater until the scraps are about the size of pencil erasers. Put the grated soap into the top of the double boiler.
3. Add 1/2 cup of water.
4. Turn the stove on medium heat. Place the double boiler on the stove and carefully stir the soap and water until the mixture turns into a smooth liquid. Continue stirring and be patient. It may take up to 30 minutes for the soap to melt. SAFETY NOTE: HANDLE HOT MATERIALS CAREFULLY.
5. When the soap is the consistency of honey, stand a small twig in the mixture. If the twig stands up without support, the soap is ready to pour into the plastic container.
6. Allow the soap to cool overnight. After the soap hardens, turn the mold over and slip out the bar of soap.

3 Lab Report

1. What were the main ingredients of the colonists' homemade soap?
2. How was the soap you made different from the soap settlers made?
3. Did you use your soap? How would you compare the soap you made with your usual kind of soap?
4. **Drawing Conclusions** What effect do you think modern soap-making methods have had on the way that we live?

Go a Step Further

Find out more about soap making and soap products of the past. Research the ways that Native Americans, Europeans, Asians, and Africans made soap using the materials found in their environments.

ASSESS

Have students answer the **Lab Report** questions on page 101.

What? Where? When? Who?

The History of Soap No one knows for sure when or where people first made soap. The ancient Romans may have used soap 3,000 years ago. People in France were using a rough soap by about A.D. 100. People in Italy crafted the process of soap-making by about 700, and by 800 Spain became a leading soap-making country. Making soap did not begin in England until 1200. Colonists in America had to make their own soap until the soap industry began in the early 1800s.

CLOSE

Encourage students to complete the **Go a Step Further** research activity. Have students share the results of their research with the class.

ANSWERS

Lab Report

1. animal fat and lye made from wood ashes and water
2. used soap scraps and water instead of animal fat and lye
3. Answers will vary. If students use their soap they may notice that it is somewhat softer than their usual soap. Students may have different experiences with their soap, depending on the kinds of soap scraps they used.
4. Possible answers: modern soap is gentler on the skin than pioneer soap, so people are likely to bathe more often.

Go a Step Further

Students may wish to work in groups, with each group concentrating on a different area of the world.

Chapter 4 Planning Guide

A complete, 1-page lesson plan is provided for each section in the *Reproducible Lesson Plans* booklet.

Section Resources

Daily Objectives	Reproducible Resources	Multimedia Resources
Section 1 **Life in the Colonies** Explain triangular trade and its effect on American society; describe the differences between Tidewater planters and backcountry farmers.	Reproducible Lesson Plan 4–1 Guided Reading Activity 4–1* Section Quiz 4–1* Reteaching Activity 4–1 Enrichment Activity 4–1	Section Focus Transparency 4–1 Vocabulary PuzzleMaker Chapter Challenger Interactive Review Software Testmaker GTV: The American People: Fabric of a Nation GTV: A Geographic Perspective on American History NGS PictureShow: Colonial America
Section 2 **Government, Religion, and Culture** Explain why the Navigation Acts angered the colonists; list the qualifications for voting rights in colonial legislatures.	Reproducible Lesson Plan 4–2 Guided Reading Activity 4–2* Section Quiz 4–2* Reteaching Activity 4–2 Enrichment Activity 4–2	Section Focus Transparency 4–2 Vocabulary PuzzleMaker Chapter Challenger Interactive Review Software Testmaker Facts On File: Landmark Documents in American History Focus on American Art Prints
Section 3 **France and Britain Clash in America** Describe how European wars involved colonists and Native Americans and led to the proposal of the Albany Plan of Union.	Reproducible Lesson Plan 4–3 Guided Reading Activity 4–3* Section Quiz 4–3* Reteaching Activity 4–3 Enrichment Activity 4–3	Section Focus Transparency 4–3 Vocabulary PuzzleMaker Chapter Challenger Interactive Review Software Testmaker NGS PictureShow: Colonial America
Section 4 **The French and Indian War** Describe the roles of William Pitt and Chief Pontiac in the conflicts of the period.	Reproducible Lesson Plan 4–4 Guided Reading Activity 4–4* Section Quiz 4–4* Reteaching Activity 4–4 Enrichment Activity 4–4	Section Focus Transparency 4–4 Chapter Challenger Interactive Review Testmaker GTV: A Geographic Perspective on American History Facts On File: Landmark Documents in American History

** Also available in Spanish*

Poster — Transparency — CD-ROM — Software
Blackline Master — Videodisc — Audiocassette — Music Program

0:00 OUT OF TIME?
Assign the Chapter 4 Digest and the corresponding Chapter Digests Audiocassettes with activities and tests.

ACTIVITY

From the Classroom of...

David Mayo
Galvin Middle School
Wakefield, MA

A Cooperative Chapter Review

Student groups will analyze, review, and creatively present their ideas concerning each of four sections of this chapter. First, organize the class into four groups, and assign each group one of the chapter's four sections to review. Have groups list the main topics and ideas in their sections. Then divide the list so that each group member is responsible for one part of it. For homework, students should write short reports about their items.

Have students share their reports. Each group can decide how to present their material to the class: a play, a lecture, or a "chart show," where they share visual charts and pictures explaining the section.

Allow students time to rehearse their presentations. For homework, students should begin preparing materials that will be needed, such as props, costumes, speeches, or charts.

While groups one and two make presentations, groups three and four should take notes, etc.

Once all groups have made their presentations, review the chapter information.

NATIONAL GEOGRAPHIC SOCIETY — Teacher's Corner

INDEX TO NATIONAL GEOGRAPHIC MAGAZINE

The following articles may be used for research relating to this chapter:

- "Treasure from the Silver Bank," by Tracy Bowden, July 1996.
- "David Thompson," by Priit J. Vesilind, May 1996.
- "The Cruelest Commerce: African Slave Trade," by Colin Palmer, September 1992.

NATIONAL GEOGRAPHIC SOCIETY PRODUCTS AVAILABLE FROM GLENCOE

To order the following products for use with this chapter, contact your local Glencoe sales representative, or call Glencoe at 1-800-334-7344:

- *GTV: The American People: Fabric of a Nation* (Videodisc)
- *GTV: A Geographic Perspective on American History* (Videodisc)
- *PictureShow: Colonial America* (CD-ROM, Transparencies)
- *PictureShow: Native Americans, 1 and 2* (CD-ROM, Transparencies)

ADDITIONAL NATIONAL GEOGRAPHIC SOCIETY PRODUCTS

To order the following products for use with this chapter, call National Geographic Society at 1-800-368-2728:

- *Native American Heritage: A Visitor's Guide* (Map)
- *Indians of North America* (Map)
- *The World of the American Indian* (Book)
- *American Indians: A Brief History* (Video)
- *Historical Atlas of the United States* (Atlas)

Block Schedule

Block scheduling differs from traditional class scheduling in the amount of time allotted to each period. The extended time frame provided by block scheduling affords you the opportunity to implement a greater number of research-oriented and activity-intense projects to motivate and involve your students. Activities that are particularly suited to use within the block scheduling framework are identified throughout this chapter by the following designation:

KEY TO ABILITY LEVELS

Teaching strategies have been coded for varying learning styles and abilities.

L1 **BASIC** activities for all students
L2 **AVERAGE** activities for average to above-average students
L3 **CHALLENGING** activities for above-average students
ELL **ENGLISH LANGUAGE LEARNER** activities

Chapter 4 Resource Guide

Home Involvement

Home Involvement Activity 4

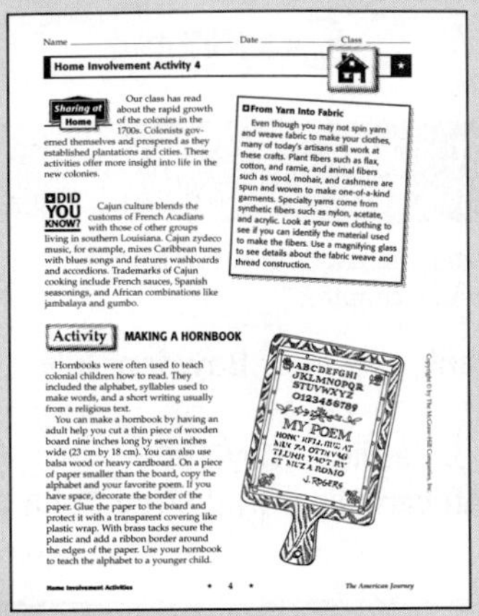

Review Activities

Chapter Summary 4

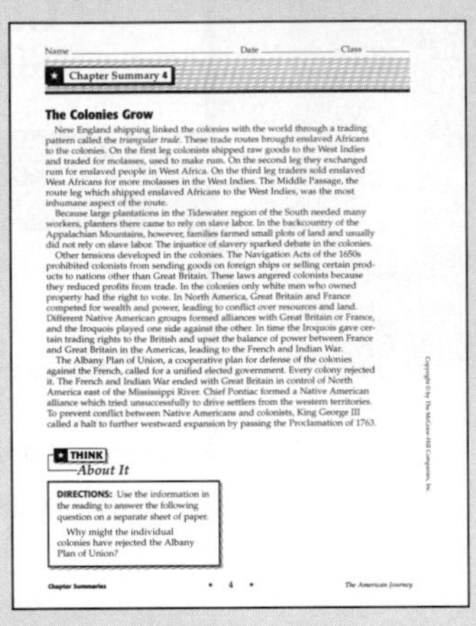

Workbook Activity 4

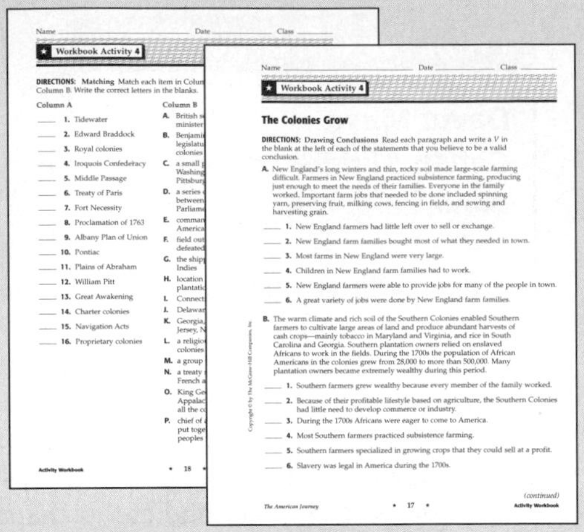

Reinforcement Activities

Time Line Activity 4

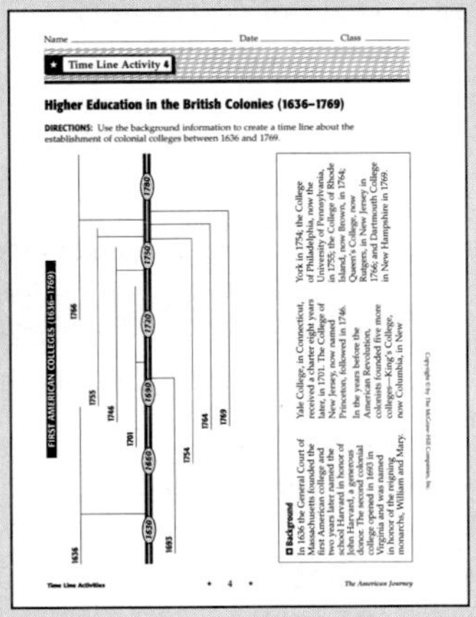

Vocabulary Activity 4

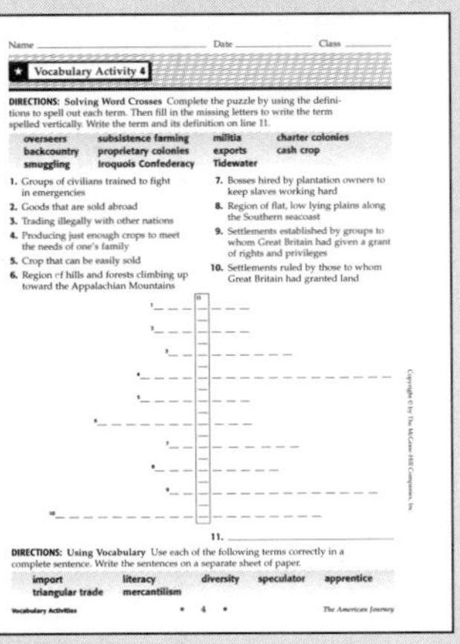

Chapter Skills Activity 4

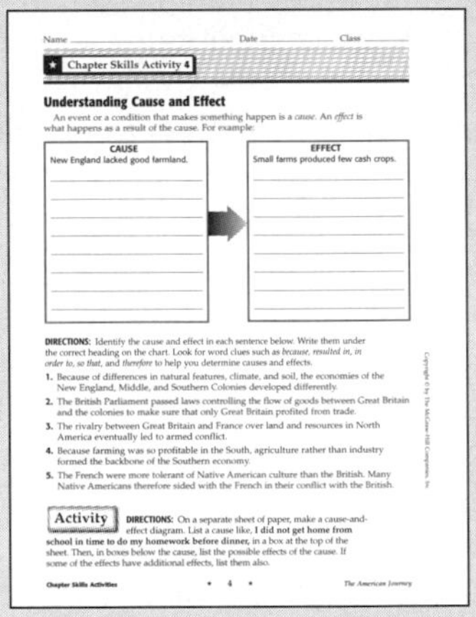

Enrichment Activities

Linking Past and Present Activity 4

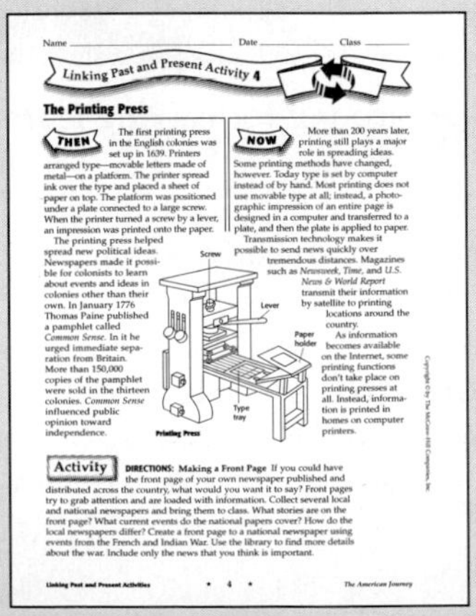

Primary Source Reading 4

Geography Activities

Mapping History Activity 4

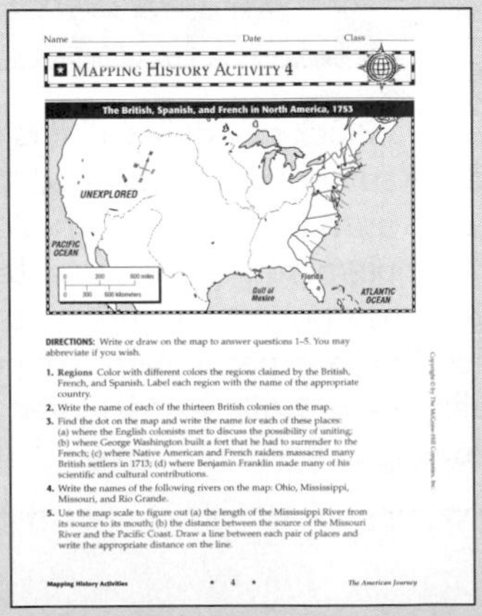

Chapter 4 Resource Guide

ASSESSMENT

Chapter 4 Test, Form A

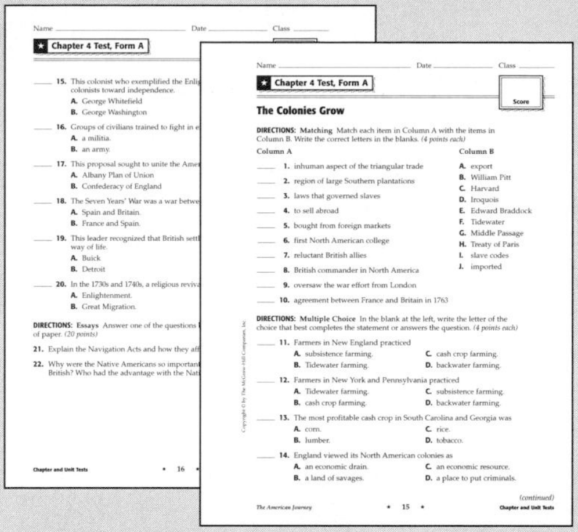
Name ________ Date ________ Class ________

★ Chapter 4 Test, Form A — Score

The Colonies Grow

DIRECTIONS: Matching Match each item in Column A with the items in Column B. Write the correct letters in the blanks. *(4 points each)*

Column A	Column B
____ 1. inhuman aspect of the triangular trade	A. export
____ 2. region of large Southern plantations	B. William Pitt
____ 3. laws that governed slaves	C. Harvard
____ 4. to sell abroad	D. Iroquois
____ 5. bought from foreign markets	E. Edward Braddock
____ 6. first North American college	F. Tidewater
____ 7. reluctant British allies	G. Middle Passage
____ 8. British commander in North America	H. Treaty of Paris
____ 9. oversaw the war effort from London	I. slave codes
____ 10. agreement between France and Britain in 1763	J. imported

DIRECTIONS: Multiple Choice In the blank at the left, write the letter of the choice that best completes the statement or answers the question. *(4 points each)*

____ 11. Farmers in New England practiced
A. subsistence farming. C. cash crop farming.
B. Tidewater farming. D. backwater farming.

____ 12. Farmers in New York and Pennsylvania practiced
A. Tidewater farming. C. subsistence farming.
B. cash crop farming. D. backwater farming.

____ 13. The most profitable cash crop in South Carolina and Georgia was
A. corn. C. rice.
B. lumber. D. tobacco.

____ 14. England viewed its North American colonies as
A. an economic drain. C. an economic resource.
B. a land of savages. D. a place to put criminals.

(continued)

Copyright © by The McGraw-Hill Companies, Inc.

The American Journey • 15 • Chapter and Unit Tests

Chapter 4 Test, Form B

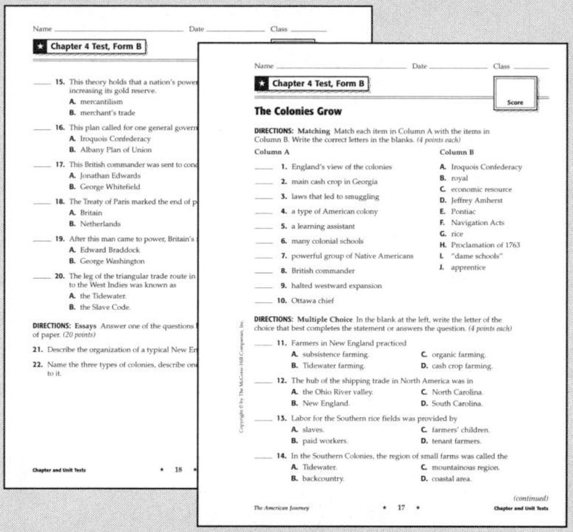
Name ________ Date ________ Class ________

★ Chapter 4 Test, Form B — Score

The Colonies Grow

DIRECTIONS: Matching Match each item in Column A with the items in Column B. Write the correct letters in the blanks. *(4 points each)*

Column A	Column B
____ 1. England's view of the colonies	A. Iroquois Confederacy
____ 2. main cash crop in Georgia	B. royal
____ 3. laws that led to smuggling	C. economic resource
____ 4. a type of American colony	D. Jeffrey Amherst
____ 5. a learning assistant	E. Pontiac
____ 6. many colonial schools	F. Navigation Acts
____ 7. powerful group of Native Americans	G. rice
____ 8. British commander	H. Proclamation of 1763
____ 9. halted westward expansion	I. "dame schools"
____ 10. Ottawa chief	J. apprentice

DIRECTIONS: Multiple Choice In the blank at the left, write the letter of the choice that best completes the statement or answers the question. *(4 points each)*

____ 11. Farmers in New England practiced
A. subsistence farming. C. organic farming.
B. Tidewater farming. D. cash crop farming.

____ 12. The hub of the shipping trade in North America was in
A. the Ohio River valley. C. North Carolina.
B. New England. D. South Carolina.

____ 13. Labor for the Southern rice fields was provided by
A. slaves. C. farmers' children.
B. paid workers. D. tenant farmers.

____ 14. In the Southern Colonies, the region of small farms was called the
A. Tidewater. C. mountainous region.
B. backcountry. D. coastal area.

(continued)

Copyright © by The McGraw-Hill Companies, Inc.

The American Journey • 17 • Chapter and Unit Tests

Performance Assessment Activity 4

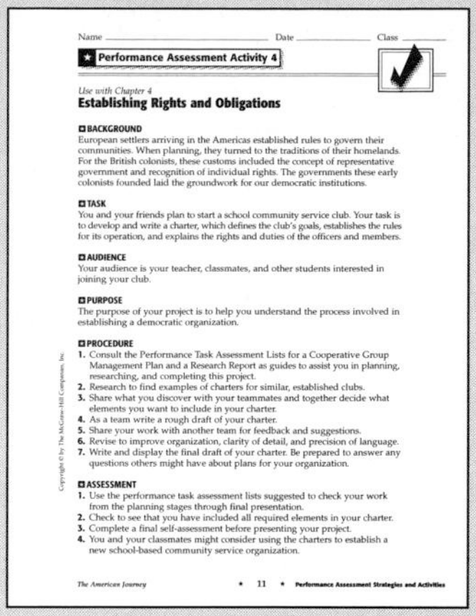
Name ________ Date ________ Class ________

★ Performance Assessment Activity 4

Use with Chapter 4

Establishing Rights and Obligations

BACKGROUND
European settlers arriving in the Americas established rules to govern their communities. When planning, they turned to the traditions of their homelands. For the British colonists, these customs included the concept of representative government and recognition of individual rights. The governments these early colonists founded laid the groundwork for our democratic institutions.

TASK
You and your friends plan to start a school community service club. Your task is to develop and write a charter, which defines the club's goals, establishes the rules for its operation, and explains the rights and duties of the officers and members.

AUDIENCE
Your audience is your teacher, classmates, and other students interested in joining your club.

PURPOSE
The purpose of your project is to help you understand the process involved in establishing a democratic organization.

PROCEDURE
1. Consult the Performance Task Assessment Lists for a Cooperative Group Management Plan and a Research Report as guides to assist you in planning, researching, and completing this project.
2. Research to find examples of charters for similar, established clubs.
3. Share what you discover with your teammates and together decide what elements you want to include in your charter.
4. As a team write a rough draft of your charter.
5. Share your work with another team for feedback and suggestions.
6. Revise to improve organization, clarity of detail, and precision of language.
7. Write and display the final draft of your charter. Be prepared to answer any questions others might have about plans for your organization.

ASSESSMENT
1. Use the performance task assessment lists suggested to check your work from the planning stages through final presentation.
2. Check to see that you have included all required elements in your charter.
3. Complete a final self-assessment before presenting your project.
4. You and your classmates might consider using the charters to establish a new school-based community service organization.

Copyright © by The McGraw-Hill Companies, Inc.

The American Journey • 11 • Performance Assessment Strategies and Activities

SPANISH RESOURCES

The following Spanish language materials are available in the Spanish Resources binder:

- **Spanish Chapter Summary 4**
- **Spanish Vocabulary Activity 4**
- **Spanish Guided Reading Activities, Chapter 4**
- **Spanish Section Quizzes, Chapter 4**
- **Spanish Home Involvement Activity 4**
- **Spanish Chapter 4 Digests Audiocassette Activity and Test**

ACTIVITY MANIPULATIVES

Help students learn more about America's cultural history with:

- **American Crafts Hands-On Activities**
- **American Games Hands-On Activities**
- **American History Flash Cards**

ADDITIONAL RESOURCES FROM GLENCOE

- **Focus on American Art Prints,** *Watson and the Shark* by John Singleton Copley
- **Political Cartoons,** *The Great Awakening; Unity or Division?*
- **American Music Cultural Traditions,** Lesson 1: "Rain Dance"
- **Outline Map Resource Book**
- **U.S. Desk Map**

A&E HOME VIDEO. Biography™ THE HISTORY CHANNEL®

The following videotape programs are available from Glencoe as supplements to Chapter 4:

- **George Washington: Founding Father** (ISBN 1-56501-377-8)
- **Benjamin Franklin: Citizen of the World** (ISBN 1-56501-426-X)

To order, call Glencoe at 1-800-334-7344. To find classroom resources to accompany many of these videos, check the following home pages:
A&E Television: http://www.aetv.com
The History Channel: http://www.historychannel.com

Introducing CHAPTER 4

Chapter Themes

Chapter Themes are listed by section on this chapter opening page of the Student Edition. A corresponding theme-based activity is available under "FOCUS," and a theme-based question is asked in the Section and Chapter Reviews.

Performance Assessment

Refer to Activity 4 in the *Performance Assessment Strategies and Activities* booklet.

GLENCOE TECHNOLOGY

VIDEODISC
MindJogger Videoquiz

Use MindJogger to preview the Chapter 4 content.

Chapter 4
Disc 1, Side A

Also available in VHS.

HISTORY AND ART This painting shows a different side to bustling New York City, which boasted shipyards, refineries, mills, and a slave market in the 1700s. **Ask:** How can you tell that the people of this neighborhood are prosperous? *(large homes, well-dressed people)*

1607–1770

The Colonies Grow

Why It's Important

The settlers who came to the English colonies were English, Scottish, Irish, Ibo, Mandingo, Yoruba, Portuguese, German, Dutch, French, Swedish, and Finnish. They eventually learned English and adapted to the English traditions of the colonies. At the same time, these peoples made their own contributions. Words from a number of languages, foods from many lands, a variety of religious beliefs and holidays—all became part of the emerging culture of colonial America.

Chapter Themes

- *Section 1,* Economic Factors
- *Section 2,* Continuity and Change
- *Section 3,* Groups and Institutions
- *Section 4,* Individual Action

HISTORY AND ART ***The South Side of St. John's Street* by Joseph B. Smith** This colonial-era painting depicts a quiet, middle-class neighborhood in New York City during the late 1760s.

EXTRA CREDIT PROJECT

Diversity In the early years, the Middle Colonies were the most diverse of all the colonies. Today diversity is found in every region of the nation. Have students find at least 10 examples of today's diversity—in place-names, words, customs, foods, and so on. Each example should be from a different national or ethnic group.

1700 | 1750 | 1800

1700s Thousands of enslaved Africans are brought to America

1725 Pennsylvania Quakers speak out against slavery

1750 New England is the center of colonial shipping

1750s South Carolina and Georgia have the fastest-growing colonial economies

Section 1

Life in the Colonies

READ TO DISCOVER . . .

- what the triangular trade was and how it affected American society.
- how the Tidewater planters and backcountry farmers differed.
- why the use of enslaved workers increased in the colonies.

TERMS TO LEARN

subsistence farming
triangular trade
cash crop
diversity
Tidewater
backcountry
overseer

The Storyteller

In 1760 Englishman Andrew Burnaby traveled throughout the North American colonies, observing American life. He could not imagine that these colonies would ever join in union for they were as different from one another as "fire and water," and each colony was jealous of the other. "In short, such is the difference of character, of manners, of religion, of interest, of the different colonies, that I think . . . were they left to themselves, there would soon be a civil war, from one end of the continent to the other."

Colonial spinning wheel

During the 1700s the population of the English colonies grew dramatically. The number of Europeans living in the colonies rose from about 250,000 in 1700 to 2.5 million in 1775—a tenfold increase. The population of African Americans increased at an even faster rate—from 28,000 to more than 500,000.

Colonial Growth

Immigration was a major factor in this growth. Between 1607 and 1790, almost a million people—600,000 Europeans and 300,000 Africans—came to live in the colonies.

Another reason for the increase was that colonial women tended to marry early and have large families. It was not unusual for a woman to have seven or more children. In addition America, especially New England, turned out to be an unusually healthy place to live. Many babies survived the diseases of childhood to become adults, and many adults lived to an old age.

The New England Colonies

Most people in New England lived in well-organized towns. In the center of the town stood the meetinghouse, a building used for both church services and town meetings. The meetinghouse faced a piece of land called the green, where cows grazed and the citizen army trained. Farmers lived in the town and worked in fields on its outskirts.

1 FOCUS

BELLRINGER
Motivational Activity

Before taking roll at the beginning of the class period, project Section Focus Transparency 4–1 and have students answer the questions. Discuss students' responses.

This activity is also available as a blackline master.

Section Focus Transparency 4–1

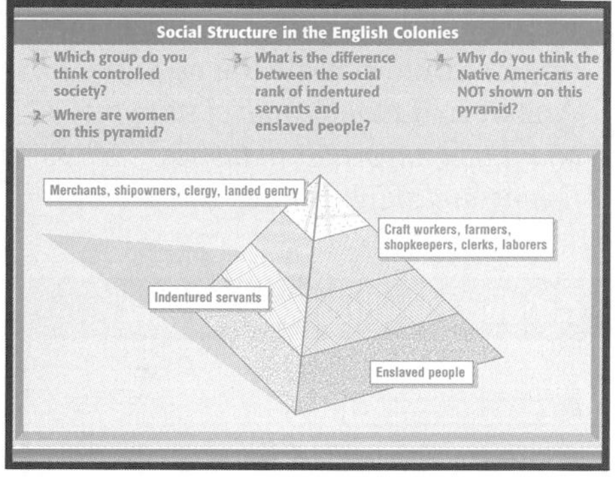

Vocabulary Precheck

Encourage students to speculate about the meaning of the term *triangular trade.* Then have them review the map on page 106 to check the accuracy of their speculations.

Use the **Vocabulary PuzzleMaker** to create crossword and word search puzzles.

Section Theme
Economic Factors

Ways of earning a living varied not only among the three regions of colonial America, but also within each region.

Activity Have students skim the section to identify the various economic activities carried on in the colonies. *(Answers should include shipbuilding, lumbering, fishing, farming, manufacturing, and so on.)*

SECTION RESOURCES

Reproducible Masters

- Reproducible Lesson Plan 4–1
- Guided Reading Activity 4–1
- Section Quiz 4–1
- Reteaching Activity 4–1
- Enrichment Activity 4–1

Transparencies

- Section Focus Transparency 4–1

Multimedia

- Vocabulary PuzzleMaker
- Chapter Challenger Interactive Review Software
- GTV: The American People: Fabric of a Nation
- GTV: A Geographic Perspective on American History
- NGS PictureShow: Colonial America

2 TEACH

L1 Outlining the Section Have students outline the section, filling in appropriate material under these five main headings—Colonial Growth, The New England Colonies, The Middle Colonies, The Southern Colonies, and Slavery. Students may use their outlines for study before doing the section review or taking the section quiz.

HISTORY AND ART Colonial women were expected to be skilled needleworkers, and girls were taught the craft as soon as their fingers could handle the needles. **Answer:** *It was the hub of shipping, and it had important industries such as fishing and shipbuilding.*

Guided Reading Activity 4–1

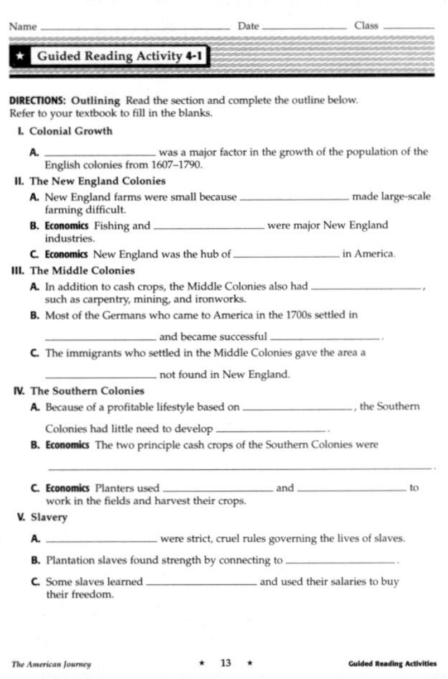

Name ______________ Date ______________ Class ______________

★ Guided Reading Activity 4-1

DIRECTIONS: Outlining Read the section and complete the outline below. Refer to your textbook to fill in the blanks.

I. Colonial Growth

A. ______________ was a major factor in the growth of the population of the English colonies from 1607–1790.

II. The New England Colonies

A. New England farms were small because ______________ made large-scale farming difficult.

B. Economics Fishing and ______________ were major New England industries.

C. Economics New England was the hub of ______________ in America.

III. The Middle Colonies

A. In addition to cash crops, the Middle Colonies also had ______________, such as carpentry, mining, and ironworks.

B. Most of the Germans who came to America in the 1700s settled in ______________ and became successful ______________.

C. The immigrants who settled in the Middle Colonies gave the area a ______________ not found in New England.

IV. The Southern Colonies

A. Because of a profitable lifestyle based on ______________, the Southern Colonies had little need to develop ______________.

B. Economics The two principle cash crops of the Southern Colonies were ______________.

C. Economics Planters used ______________ and ______________ to work in the fields and harvest their crops.

V. Slavery

A. ______________ were strict, cruel rules governing the lives of slaves.

B. Plantation slaves found strength by connecting to ______________.

C. Some slaves learned ______________ and used their salaries to buy their freedom.

The American Journey ★ 13 ★ **Guided Reading Activities**

NATIONAL GEOGRAPHIC SOCIETY

CD-ROM
NGS PictureShow: Colonial America

Encourage students to investigate colonial commerce by having them click on the main menu.

Farming was the main economic activity in all the colonies, but New England farms were smaller than those farther south. Long winters and thin, rocky soil made large-scale farming difficult. Farmers in New England practiced **subsistence farming,** which means that they generally produced just enough to meet the needs of their families, with little left over to sell or exchange. Most Northern farmers relied on their children for labor, and everyone in the family worked—spinning yarn, preserving fruit, milking cows, fencing in fields, and sowing and harvesting grain.

Economics

Commerce in New England

New England also had many small businesses. Some people used the waterpower from the streams on their land to run mills for grinding grain or sawing lumber. Women who made cloth, garments, candles, or soap for their families sometimes produced enough of these products to sell or trade. Large towns attracted skilled craftspeople who set themselves up as blacksmiths, shoemakers, furniture makers, gunsmiths, metalsmiths, and printers.

Shipbuilding was an important local industry. The lumber for building ships came from the forests of New England and was transported down rivers to the shipyards in coastal towns.

Fishing was another major economic activity. New Englanders fished for cod, halibut, crabs, oysters, and lobsters. Some ventured far out to sea to hunt whales for oil and whalebone.

Colonial Trade

As the hub of the shipping trade in America, New England linked the Northern and Southern Colonies and tied America to other parts of the world. New England ships sailed south along the Atlantic coast, trading with the colonies and with islands in the **West Indies.** They crossed the Atlantic carrying fish, furs, and fruit to exchange for manufactured goods in England and Europe.

Triangular Trade

These colonial merchant ships followed many different trading routes. Some ships went directly

HISTORY AND ART ***Needlework* by Hannah Otis** This scene includes John Hancock (on horseback), who later became the first signer of the Declaration of Independence. **Why was New England important for colonial trade?**

COOPERATIVE LEARNING ACTIVITY

Making a Display Have students work in groups to create displays or drawings showing a typical New England village with its green, meetinghouse, and farms; a Middle Colony city (New York or Philadelphia) with shops, docks, and ships; and a Southern plantation with a mansion, workshops, slave cabins, dock, and fields. Assign specific tasks–constructing or drawing, researching, writing labels, preparing a "guided tour"–to each student within a group. ELL

Slaves packed in ship

Picturing HISTORY A deck plan (top left) reveals tightly packed ranks of slaves on a ship bound from Africa to the Americas. Once docked, the ship's human cargo was replaced with rum or molasses. **What does the term *Middle Passage* refer to?**

from the colonies to England and other European ports and back. Others followed routes that came to be called the **triangular trade** because the routes formed a triangle. On one leg of such a route, ships took fish, grain, meat, and lumber to the West Indies. There the ship's captain traded for sugar, molasses—a syrup made from sugarcane—and fruit, which he then took back to New England. Colonists used the molasses to make rum.

The rum, along with manufactured goods, was then shipped to **West Africa.** There these goods were traded for Africans who had been captured and enslaved by slave traders. On another leg of the route, the ships carried the enslaved Africans back to the West Indies, where planters were in need of workers. With the profits made from selling slaves to the planters, the captain bought more molasses and sugar to ship back and sell in the colonies. A later route brought enslaved Africans directly to the American colonies. $

Eyewitness to HISTORY

The Middle Passage

The most inhumane aspect of the triangular trade, shipping enslaved Africans to the West Indies, was known as the **Middle Passage.** Olaudah Equiano, a young African forced onto a ship to America, later described the horror of the voyage across the Atlantic:

> “I was soon put down under the decks, and there I received such . . . [an odor] in my nostrils as I had never experienced in my life. . . . The closeness of the place, and the heat of the climate, added to the number in the ship, which was so crowded that each had scarcely room to turn himself, almost suffocated us. . . . The shrieks of the women, and the groans of the dying, rendered [made] the whole a scene of horror.”

With its trade, shipbuilding, and fishing, New England flourished. Although good farmland

CHAPTER 4
Section 1, 103–109

Picturing HISTORY Between 1768 and 1772, more than 27,000 slaves were brought to the colonies. During this period, the leading colonies involved in the slave trade were South Carolina, Virginia, and Georgia.
Answer: *the leg of the triangular trade in which enslaved Africans were shipped to the West Indies*

NATIONAL GEOGRAPHIC SOCIETY

VIDEODISC
GTV: The American People: Fabric of a Nation

Side 1, Chapter 8
Title: *The Journey*
Subject: Slavery in early America
Ask: **What one thing, heavily emphasized in this segment, helped unite African Americans?** *(Christianity)*

What?Where?When?Who?

Slave Resistance Enslaved Africans found ways to express their anger and resentment at their condition. Individuals might kill an overseer, poison a master, or run away. Some runaways joined bands of other escapees; some joined Native American groups; others went to cities where they could lose themselves in the free African American population. More passive resistance included pretending illness or following orders too literally. Actual revolts were less common, but they did occur. In New York in 1712, a group of about 30 enslaved persons set fire to a building and killed a number of whites. About 100 enslaved Africans staged the Stone Rebellion in 1739 in South Carolina, in which 30 whites were killed.

MULTIPLE LEARNING STYLES

Auditory/Musical Enslaved Africans sang spirituals for comfort and even as a secret means of communicating. Sung in a lively style with strong rhythms and rich harmonies, spirituals usually expressed themes of redemption from sin and slavery and hopes of a better life in the future. Well-known spirituals include "Jacob's Ladder" and "Many a Thousand Gone." Check your local library for recordings of spirituals that you could play for the class. If possible, have students work with the music teacher to learn some spirituals and perform them for other classes. **L2**

Map Study

Answers

1. rum, iron, gunpowder, cloth, tools; enslaved persons
2. lumber, furs, fish, whale oil, iron, gunpowder, rice, tobacco, indigo; manufactured goods, clothes, furniture, luxuries

Map Skills Practice

Reading a Map What did the West Indies export? *(enslaved persons, money, molasses, sugar, fruit)*

NATIONAL GEOGRAPHIC SOCIETY

VIDEODISC
GTV: A Geographic Perspective on American History

Side 1, Chapter 12
Title: *The Rise of Cities*
Subject: Urban life in the colonies (1680–1700)
Ask: **What did all major cities have in common in regard to location?** *(All were built around ports.)*

CURRICULUM CONNECTION

LANGUAGE ARTS
In the seventeenth century, New Englanders spoke with a Southern accent. The Southern accent carried over from England and dominated in America until the eighteenth century, when Americans in New England began speaking much like they do today.

Triangular Trade Routes

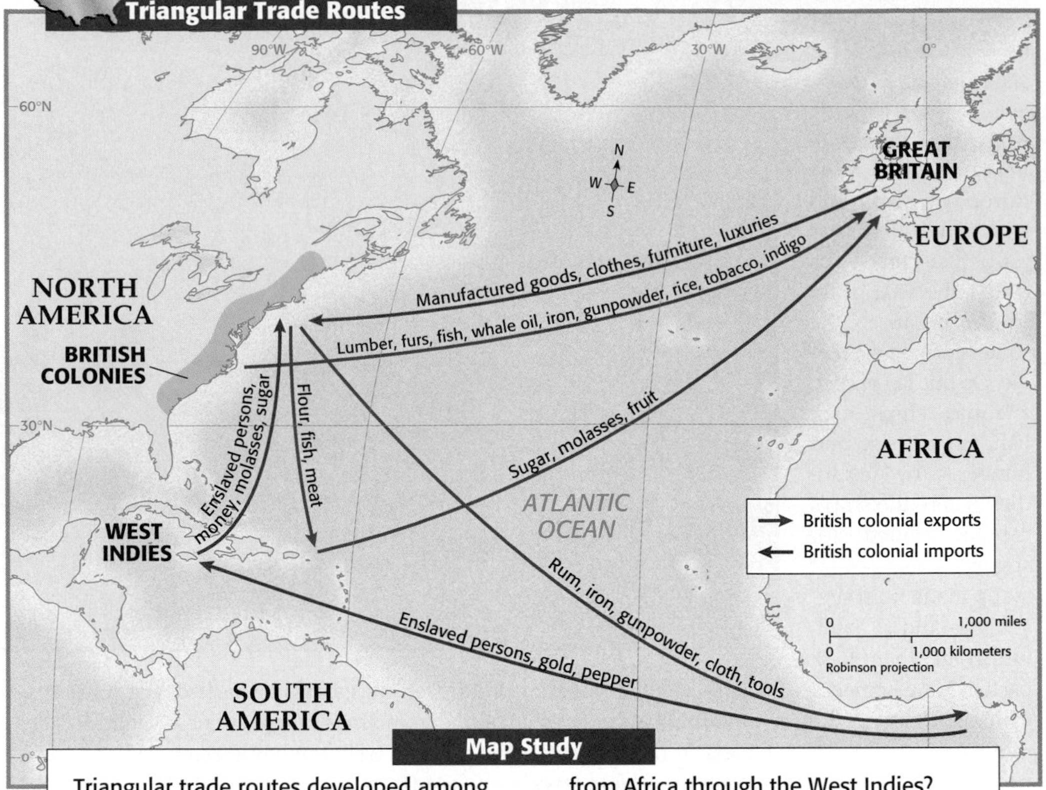

Map Study

Triangular trade routes developed among the British colonies, Great Britain, Africa, and the West Indies.

1. **Movement** What did the colonies export to Africa? What did they import from Africa through the West Indies?
2. **Comparing** What did the colonies export to Great Britain? What did they import from Great Britain?

was lacking in much of the region, New England's population expanded and towns and cities developed.

The Middle Colonies

The Middle Colonies enjoyed fertile soil and a slightly milder climate than that found in New England. Farmers in this region cultivated larger tracts of land and produced bigger harvests than did New Englanders. In New York and Pennsylvania, farmers grew large quantities of wheat and other **cash crops,** crops that could be sold easily in markets in the colonies and overseas.

Farmers sent cargoes of wheat and livestock to New York City and Philadelphia for shipment, and these cities became busy ports. By the 1770s New York, with 25,000 people, and Philadelphia, with 28,000 people, were the largest cities in the American colonies.

Industries of the Middle Colonies

The Middle Colonies—especially New Jersey and Pennsylvania—also had industries. Some were home-based crafts such as carpentry and flour making. Others included commercial ventures such as lumbering, mining, and small-scale manufacturing.

MAKING CONNECTIONS ACTIVITY

Technology Although the colonists did not have electricity, they did use the power of wind and water in their sawmills and grist mills. Windmills were mostly limited to coastal locations where a good breeze could be counted on for much of the time. Using the power of moving water, mills could be located anywhere there was a swift stream. Have students draw diagrams showing how such mills worked. Edwin Tunis's book *Colonial Craftsmen and the Beginning of American Industry* is a good source of information and pictures. **L2, ELL**

One iron mill in northern New Jersey employed several hundred workers, many of them from Germany. Other smaller ironworks operated in New Jersey and Pennsylvania.

German Immigrants

Most of the 100,000 Germans who came to America during the colonial era settled in Pennsylvania. Using agricultural methods developed in Europe, these immigrants became successful farmers.

The Germans belonged to a number of Protestant sects. Together with the Dutch, Swedish, and other non-English immigrants, they gave the Middle Colonies a cultural **diversity,** or variety, not found in New England. With the diversity came tolerance.

The Southern Colonies

With their rich soil and warm climate, the Southern Colonies were well suited to certain kinds of farming. Southern farmers could cultivate large areas of land and produce harvests of cash crops. Because of their profitable lifestyle based on agriculture, the Southern Colonies had little need to develop commerce or industry. For the most part, London merchants rather than local merchants managed Southern trade.

Economics

Tobacco and Rice

Tobacco was the principal cash crop of Maryland and Virginia. Most tobacco was sold in Europe, where the demand for it was strong. Growing tobacco and preparing it for sale required a good deal of labor. At first planters used indentured servants to work in the fields. When indentured servants became scarce and expensive, Southern planters used enslaved Africans instead.

Slaveholders with large properties became rich on tobacco. Sometimes, however, a surplus of tobacco on the market caused prices to fall—and so did the growers' profits. After 1745 some tobacco planters switched to growing corn and wheat.

The main cash crop in South Carolina and Georgia was rice. In low-lying coastal areas, planters built dams to create rice fields called paddies. These fields were flooded when the rice was young and drained when the rice was ready to harvest. Work in the rice paddies involved standing knee-deep in the mud all day with no protection from the blazing sun or the biting insects.

Because rice harvesting required so much strenuous work, rice growers relied on slave labor. Rice proved to be even more profitable than tobacco. As it became popular in southern Europe, the price of rice rose steadily. By the 1750s South Carolina and Georgia had the fastest-growing economies in the colonies.

Tidewater and Backcountry

Most of the large Southern plantations were located in the **Tidewater,** a region of flat, low-lying plains along the seacoast. Plantations, or large farms, were often situated on rivers so crops could be shipped to market by boat.

Each plantation was a self-contained community with fields stretching out around a cluster of buildings. The planter's wife supervised the main

Sugarcane and a rum barrel

CURRICULUM CONNECTION

LITERATURE
Nathaniel Hawthorne (1804–1864) drew on his New England Puritan heritage in writing *The Scarlet Letter* and *The House of Seven Gables,* both of which are set in the colonial period. One ancestor, Major William Hathorne (it was Nathaniel who changed the spelling of the family name), is described in *The Scarlet Letter* as a "grave bearded, sable-cloaked and steeple-crowned progenitor." The major was a magistrate known for his persecution of Quakers. His son John, also a magistrate, presided over the infamous Salem witch trials.

NATIONAL GEOGRAPHIC SOCIETY

VIDEODISC
GTV: The American People: Fabric of a Nation

Side 1, Chapter 7
Title: *A Mixed Bag*
Subject: Diversity in the colonies
Ask: What drew the boundaries of social acceptance in the English colonies? *(the color of people's skin)*

CRITICAL THINKING ACTIVITY

Predicting Consequences Have students formulate hypotheses on the effect the slave trade had on African societies. Before students begin, point out the following: (1) Europeans provided Africans with guns to use in capturing members of other ethnic groups for the slave trade *(promoted violence among African groups).* (2) Most captives were healthy men and women between the ages of 15 and 25 *(robbed African societies of their most economically productive members, as well as those most likely to have children).* (3) African slave traders often received guns, alcohol, and luxury goods in return for captives *(promoted social ills rather than helping develop the economy).* Allow time for class discussion. Then have students use library resources to check their hypotheses. **L2**

When?Who?What?Where?

The Eighteenth Century marked a turning point for African Americans. At that time colonial assemblies made slavery in America legal by passing slave codes. Only one factor determined whether a person was subject to slave codes—color. Any African ancestry was enough to classify a person as black.

CHAPTER 4
Section 1, 103–109

HISTORY AND ART This lively example of folk art shows African heritage in the musical instruments, scarves, and stick ceremony. It may depict a wedding, because jumping over a stick was a custom in some cultures.
Answer: *trades such as carpentry, blacksmithing, and weaving*

3 ASSESS

Assign Section 1 Review as homework or as an in-class activity.

Use **Chapter Challenger Interactive Review Software** to review Section 1.

Section Quiz 4–1

Name ____________ Date ____________ Class ____________

Chapter 4

Score

Section Quiz 4-1

DIRECTIONS: Matching Match each item in Column A with the items in Column B. Write the correct letters in the blanks. *(10 points each)*

Column A	Column B
____ **1.** important New England industry	**A.** cash crops
____ **2.** crops that sold easily	**B.** backcountry
____ **3.** cultural variety	**C.** slave codes
____ **4.** near Appalachian Mountains	**D.** shipbuilding
____ **5.** governed slaves	**E.** diversity

DIRECTIONS: Multiple Choice In the blank at the left, write the letter of the choice that best completes the statement or answers the question. *(10 points each)*

____ **6.** This means producing just enough to meet the families' needs, with little left over to sell or exchange.
A. harvesting **C.** cash crop
B. subsistence farming **D.** Tidewater farming

____ **7.** The most inhuman aspect of the triangular trade was the
A. Southern Route. **C.** Middle Passage.
B. merchant trade route. **D.** fishing trade.

____ **8.** Most of the large Southern plantations were located in the
A. backcountry. **C.** coastal areas.
B. Tidewater. **D.** flatlands.

____ **9.** These plantation bosses kept the slaves working hard.
A. overseers **C.** employers
B. slave enforcers **D.** supervisors

____ **10.** This group controlled the economic and political life of the Southern Colonies.
A. merchants **C.** farmers
B. teachers **D.** plantation owners

The American Journey ★ 13 ★ **Section Quizzes**

HISTORY AND ART ***The Old Plantation* by an unknown artist** This watercolor from the 1700s shows a traditional African celebration on a Southern plantation. **What skills were developed by enslaved Africans on plantations and in towns?**

house and the household servants. A plantation also included slave cabins, barns and stables, and such outbuildings as carpenter and blacksmith shops and storerooms. Even kitchens, which frequently caught fire, were in separate buildings. A large plantation might also have its own chapel and school.

West of the Tidewater lay a region of hills and forests climbing up toward the **Appalachian Mountains.** This region, known as the **backcountry,** was settled in part by hardy newcomers to the colonies. The backcountry settlers grew corn and tobacco on small farms. They usually worked alone or with their families, although some had one or two enslaved Africans to help.

In the Southern Colonies, the independent small farmers of the backcountry outnumbered the large plantation owners. The plantation owners, however, had greater wealth and more influence. They controlled the economic and political life of the region.

Slavery

Most enslaved Africans in North America lived on plantations. Some of the Africans did housework, but most worked in the fields and often suffered great cruelty. The large plantation owners hired **overseers,** or bosses, to keep the slaves working hard.

All the Southern Colonies had **slave codes,** strict rules governing the behavior and punishment of enslaved Africans. Slaves could not leave the plantation without written permission from the master. Enslaved people could not be taught to read or write. They were whipped for minor offenses and hanged or burned to death for serious crimes. Those who ran away were often caught and punished severely.

All white colonists were encouraged to enforce these laws against enslaved Africans. As a result, a person's race determined his or her place in society.

TEACHER'S NOTES

African Traditions

Although the Africans brought to America or born in America had strong family ties, their families were often torn apart. Slaveholders could split up families by selling a spouse, a parent, or a child to another slaveholder. Slaves who worked on plantations found a source of strength in their connection to their African roots. They developed a culture that drew on the languages, customs, and religions of their West African homelands, even as they learned the English ways of the slaveholders.

Some enslaved Africans learned trades such as carpentry, blacksmithing, or weaving. Skilled workers could sometimes set up shops, sharing their profits with the slaveholders. Those lucky enough to be able to buy their freedom joined the small population of free African Americans.

Picturing HISTORY Colonists brought traditions from their homelands and developed new ways of life in America. **Where did most German immigrants settle?**

Criticism of Slavery

Slavery was part of colonial life and one of the main reasons for the economic success of the Southern Colonies. That success, however, was built on a profound injustice: the idea that one human being could own another. Some European colonists did not believe in slavery. Many Puritans refused to hold enslaved people. In Pennsylvania, Quakers and Mennonites—a German religious group—condemned slavery. Eventually the debate over slavery would erupt in a bloody civil war, pitting Northerners against Southerners.

Section 1 Review

Checking for Understanding

1. ***Identify*** West Indies, West Africa, Middle Passage, Appalachian Mountains.
2. ***Define*** subsistence farming, triangular trade, cash crop, diversity, Tidewater, backcountry, overseer.
3. ***Compare*** farming in New England with farming in the Southern Colonies.

Reviewing Themes

4. **Economic Factors** How did New England's natural resources help its commerce?

Critical Thinking

5. **Making Inferences** How do you think plantation owners in the Southern Colonies justified their use of enslaved Africans?

Activity

Writing a Letter Imagine you are from New England and are visiting your cousins on a farm in the Carolinas. Write a letter to a friend at home describing your visit to their farm.

Section 1 Review Answers

1. West Indies, 104; West Africa, 105; Middle Passage, 105; Appalachian Mountains, 108
2. The words are defined in the Glossary.
3. New England had small farms, long winters, poor soil, and subsistence farming; the South had large farms, mild climate, rich soil, cash crops, and slavery.
4. streams and rivers to power mills and transport materials; lumber for shipbuilding; access to rivers and ocean for fishing industry
5. Answers will vary but should indicate that owners felt it was part of life and that it was necessary to keep the economy strong.

Activity Letters should include such regional differences as the importance of agriculture, the use of enslaved Africans, and the lack of commerce and industry.

Picturing HISTORY A unique new civilization developed as a result of the colonists' interaction among the Native Americans as well as other Europeans.
Answer: *in the Middle Colonies*

Reteaching Activity 4–1

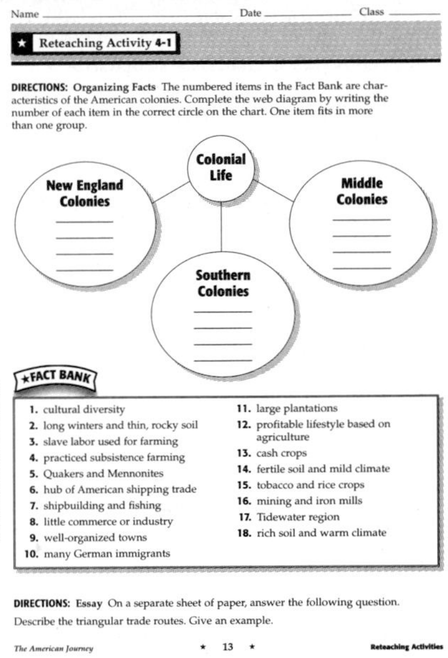

Name ______ Date ______ Class ______

★ Reteaching Activity 4-1

DIRECTIONS: Organizing Facts The numbered items in the Fact Bank are characteristics of the American colonies. Complete the web diagram by writing the number of each item in the correct circle on the chart. One item fits in more than one group.

★FACT BANK

1. cultural diversity
2. long winters and thin, rocky soil
3. slave labor used for farming
4. practiced subsistence farming
5. Quakers and Mennonites
6. hub of American shipping trade
7. shipbuilding and fishing
8. little commerce or industry
9. well-organized towns
10. many German immigrants
11. large plantations
12. profitable lifestyle based on agriculture
13. cash crops
14. fertile soil and mild climate
15. tobacco and rice crops
16. mining and iron mills
17. Tidewater region
18. rich soil and warm climate

DIRECTIONS: Essay On a separate sheet of paper, answer the following question.
Describe the triangular trade routes. Give an example.

The American Journey ★ 13 ★ **Reteaching Activities**

Enrichment Activity 4–1

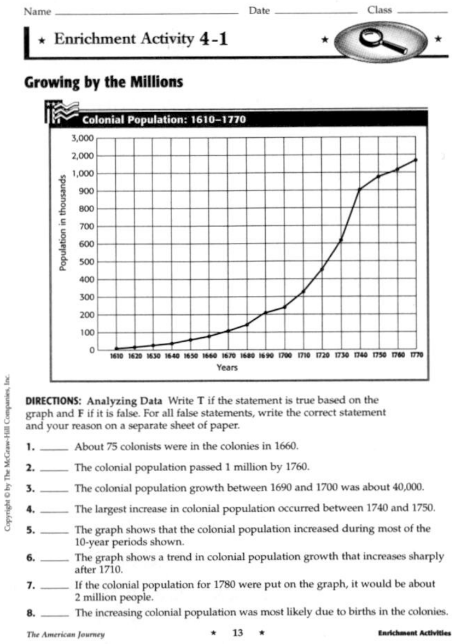

Name ______ Date ______ Class ______

★ Enrichment Activity 4-1

Growing by the Millions

DIRECTIONS: Analyzing Data Write **T** if the statement is true based on the graph and **F** if it is false. For all false statements, write the correct statement and your reason on a separate sheet of paper.

1. ______ About 75 colonists were in the colonies in 1660.
2. ______ The colonial population passed 1 million by 1760.
3. ______ The colonial population growth between 1690 and 1700 was about 40,000.
4. ______ The largest increase in colonial population occurred between 1740 and 1750.
5. ______ The graph shows that the colonial population increased during most of the 10-year periods shown.
6. ______ The graph shows a trend in colonial population growth that increases sharply after 1710.
7. ______ If the colonial population for 1780 were put on the graph, it would be about 2 million people.
8. ______ The increasing colonial population was most likely due to births in the colonies.

The American Journey ★ 13 ★ **Enrichment Activities**

4 CLOSE

Have students speculate on how history might have been different if slavery had not been allowed.

1630	1670	1710	1750

1636 Harvard College is established

1693 William and Mary College is founded

1732 Benjamin Franklin publishes *Poor Richard's Almanack*

1735 Great Awakening sweeps through the colonies

Section 2

Government, Religion, and Culture

READ TO DISCOVER . . .

- what the Navigation Acts were and why they made the colonists angry.
- who had the right to vote in colonial legislatures.

TERMS TO LEARN

mercantilism	charter colony
export	proprietary colony
import	apprentice
smuggling	literacy

The Storyteller

"Fish and Visitors stink after three days."
"Beware of little Expenses: a small Leak will sink a great Ship."
"No gains without pains."

Benjamin Franklin wrote these and other witty sayings for his annual book, *Poor Richard's Almanack*. The last saying—"No gains without pains"—was particularly true in the American colonies in the late 1600s.

***From* Poor Richard's Almanack**

Trouble was brewing in England—and in the colonies—during the mid-1600s. England's monarchy had been restored under Charles II, but many people were not satisfied with his rule. James II, Charles's successor, attempted to seize from Parliament powers that it had won during the English Civil War. He also tried to tighten royal control over the colonies.

In 1688 Parliament took action. It ousted James and placed his daughter Mary and her Dutch husband, William of Orange, on the throne. This change, which showed the power of the elected representatives over the monarch, came to be known as the **Glorious Revolution.**

William and Mary signed an **English Bill of Rights** in 1689 guaranteeing certain basic rights to all citizens. This document became part of the heritage of English law that the American colonists shared. It later inspired the people who created America's own Bill of Rights.

English Colonial Rule

England viewed its North American colonies as an economic resource. The colonies provided England with raw materials. English manufacturers used these materials to produce finished goods, which they sold to the colonists. This process followed an economic theory called **mercantilism**, which held that a nation's power depended on expanding its trade

1 FOCUS

BELLRINGER
Motivational Activity

Before taking roll at the beginning of the class period, project Section Focus Transparency 4–2 and have students answer the questions. Discuss students' responses.

This activity is also available as a blackline master.

Section Focus Transparency 4–2

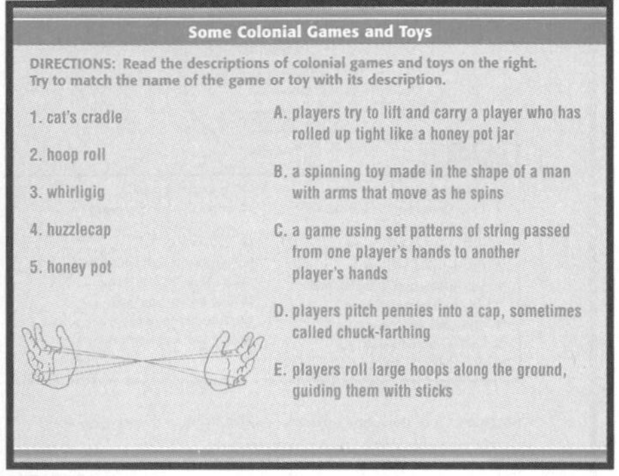

Some Colonial Games and Toys

DIRECTIONS: Read the descriptions of colonial games and toys on the right. Try to match the name of the game or toy with its description.

1. cat's cradle
2. hoop roll
3. whirligig
4. huzzlecap
5. honey pot

A. players try to lift and carry a player who has rolled up tight like a honey pot jar
B. a spinning toy made in the shape of a man with arms that move as he spins
C. a game using set patterns of string passed from one player's hands to another player's hands
D. players pitch pennies into a cap, sometimes called chuck-farthing
E. players roll large hoops along the ground, guiding them with sticks

Vocabulary Precheck

Point out that the term *apprentice* is derived from a Latin word meaning "to grasp." Have students find the definition of the term on page 113. Then have them speculate on the connection between *apprentice* and *grasp. (An apprentice tries to grasp the skills of the craft.)*

Use the **Vocabulary Puzzle-Maker** to create crossword and word search puzzles.

Section Theme
Continuity and Change

The roots of American democracy, freedom of religion, and public education are found in the American colonial experience.

Activity Have students skim the *Colonial Government* section on page 111 to see how the idea of the power of elected representatives carried over into the colonies. *(At least one house of each legislature was elected by colonists.)*

SECTION RESOURCES

Reproducible Masters
- Reproducible Lesson Plan 4–2
- Guided Reading Activity 4–2
- Section Quiz 4–2
- Reteaching Activity 4–2
- Enrichment Activity 4–2

Transparencies
- Section Focus Transparency 4–2

Multimedia
- Vocabulary PuzzleMaker
- Chapter Challenger Interactive Review Software
- Testmaker
- Facts On File: Landmark Documents in American History
- Focus on American Art Prints

and increasing its gold reserves. To make money from its trade, England had to **export,** or sell abroad, more goods than it **imported,** or bought from foreign markets.

To make certain that only England benefited from trade with the colonies, Parliament passed a series of laws in the 1650s called the **Navigation Acts.** These laws directed the flow of goods between England and the colonies. Colonial merchants who had goods to send to England could not use foreign ships—even if those ships offered lower shipping rates. The Navigation Acts also prohibited the colonists from sending certain products, such as sugar or tobacco, outside England's empire.

Some colonists ignored these laws and began **smuggling,** trading illegally with other nations, in Europe or in the West Indies. Restrictions on trade would later cause more conflict between the colonies and England.

Citizenship

Colonial Government

As the colonies grew, they relied more and more on their own governments to make local laws. By the 1760s there were three types of colonies in America--charter colonies, proprietary colonies, and royal colonies.

Charter Colonies

Connecticut and Rhode Island, the **charter colonies,** were established by groups of settlers who had been given a charter, or a grant of rights and privileges. These colonists elected their own governors and the members of both houses of the legislature. Although Great Britain had the right to approve the governor's appointment, the colonial governor could not veto the acts of the legislature.

American Memories

A Colonial Home

What Was It Like? The kitchen was the heart of the early American home. **What items do you see here that are forerunners of items you might find in a modern kitchen?**

Cooperative Learning Activity

Producing a Play Have students work in groups to produce plays about the lives of colonial children. Possible topics include school work, games and toys, and home chores. Divide tasks—writing dialogue, researching, creating props, making costumes, and acting—according to the skills of the group members. As each group presents its play, have the other students write down impressions about what was especially effective as well as ideas for how the play could be improved.

2 TEACH

L1 Identifying the Significance of Events After students have read the section, have them explain the importance of each of the following: Glorious Revolution, English Bill of Rights, Navigation Acts, Great Awakening, Enlightenment. Students may work in pairs to quiz each other with one student giving the explanation and the other trying to identify the term.

American Memories

A Colonial Home

Life in most colonial homes centered around the fireplace. Women cooked there and everyone gathered in front of it to eat, work, and relax. **Answer:** *Answers will vary but should include the kettle and chair.*

Guided Reading Activity 4–2

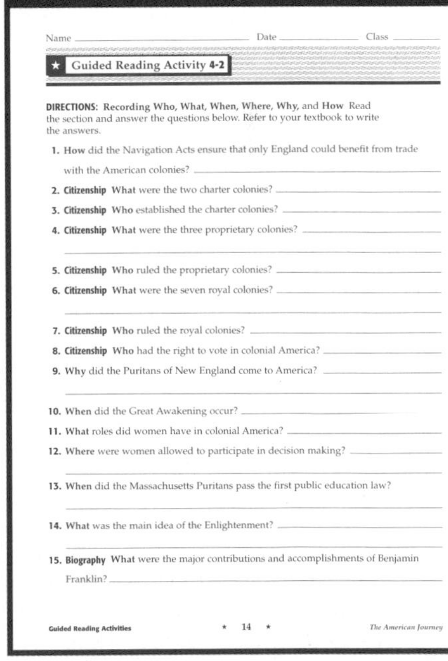
Name ______ Date ______ Class ______

★ Guided Reading Activity 4-2

DIRECTIONS: Recording Who, What, When, Where, Why, and **How** Read the section and answer the questions below. Refer to your textbook to write the answers.

1. **How** did the Navigation Acts ensure that only England could benefit from trade with the American colonies? ______
2. **Citizenship What** were the two charter colonies? ______
3. **Citizenship Who** established the charter colonies? ______
4. **Citizenship What** were the three proprietary colonies? ______
5. **Citizenship Who** ruled the proprietary colonies? ______
6. **Citizenship What** were the seven royal colonies? ______
7. **Citizenship Who** ruled the royal colonies? ______
8. **Citizenship Who** had the right to vote in colonial America? ______
9. **Why** did the Puritans of New England come to America? ______
10. **When** did the Great Awakening occur? ______
11. **What** roles did women have in colonial America? ______
12. **Where** were women allowed to participate in decision making? ______
13. **When** did the Massachusetts Puritans pass the first public education law? ______
14. **What** was the main idea of the Enlightenment? ______
15. **Biography What** were the major contributions and accomplishments of Benjamin Franklin? ______

Guided Reading Activities ★ 14 ★ *The American Journey*

History and the Humanities

Focus on American Art Prints, *Dean George Berkeley and His Party (The Bermuda Group)* by John Smibert; *Isaac Royall and His Family* by Robert Feke

The Spirit of American Art and Music, *Edward Winslow*

TECHNOLOGY AND HISTORY

More About . . .

A Colonial Printing Press Colonial typesetting, or composition, differed very little from the method invented about 300 years earlier by Johannes Gutenberg. It was not until the late 1880s that machines (linotype and monotype) were invented that greatly increased typesetting efficiency. Today those machines have been largely superseded by photocomposition, which does not use metal type at all. Phototypesetting machines involve the use of light to expose the image of the characters on film.

Answer to Caption: *The most time-consuming process was setting the type into the frame, because it had to be done one letter at a time.*

Facts On File

CD-ROM
Landmark Documents in American History

Titles: *First Navigation Act, 1650; Second Navigation Act, 1650; Navigation Act, 1651*
Have students list clauses that might have angered American merchants.

Proprietary Colonies

The proprietary colonies—Delaware, Maryland, and Pennsylvania—were ruled by proprietors, individuals or groups to whom Britain had granted land. Proprietors were generally free to rule as they wished. They appointed the governor and members of the upper house of the legislature, while the people elected the lower house.

Royal Colonies

By the 1760s Georgia, Massachusetts, New Hampshire, New Jersey, New York, North Carolina, and Virginia were royal colonies. Britain directly ruled all royal colonies. In each, Parliament appointed a governor and council, known as the upper house. The colonists elected an assembly, called the lower house. The governor and members of the council usually did what the British leaders told them to do. Often, however, this led to conflict with the colonists in the assembly, especially when officials tried to enforce tax laws and trade restrictions.

Voting Rights

Colonial legislatures gave some people a voice in government. Only white men who owned property had the right to vote. Neither women, nor indentured servants, nor landless and poor people, nor enslaved Africans could vote.

TECHNOLOGY AND HISTORY

Colonial Printing Press

Life in the colonies often revolved around local printers who produced pamphlets, small flyers, books, and newspapers. The first printing press in the American colonies was established by Stephen Daye in 1639. **Which of the processes shown here do you think was most time-consuming?**

MULTIPLE LEARNING STYLES

Verbal/Linguistic Each of the thirteen colonies was divided into counties, as are the 50 states today. (In Louisiana they are called parishes.) In the South, county governments handled jobs that towns and cities handled in New England. Have students find out the name of their county, what the county government does, and how it is organized. Have students present their findings in written form and include an organizational chart. **L2**

Religion in the Colonies

The Puritans of New England came to America to establish their own kind of Christian religion. Because worship was so central to their lives, they built their towns around the church. The Puritans believed that each congregation should be self-governing. All church members could participate in church decisions such as choosing a minister. Everyone was required to attend church services, and people who played or laughed on Sunday could be punished. Later the Puritans were called Congregationalists.

The Great Awakening

In the 1730s and 1740s, a religious revival called the **Great Awakening** swept through the colonies. In New England and the Middle Colonies, ministers called for "a new birth," a return to the strong faith of earlier days. One of the outstanding preachers of the Great Awakening was **Jonathan Edwards** of Massachusetts. People found his sermons powerful and convincing.

The English preacher **George Whitefield,** who arrived in the colonies in 1739, helped spread the religious revival. During a two-year tour, Whitefield electrified worshipers in churches and open fields from New England to Georgia. The Great Awakening led to the formation of many new churches, especially in the Southern backcountry.

Jonathan Edwards

An Emerging Culture

Throughout the colonies, people adapted their traditions to the new conditions of life in America. Religion, education, and the arts all contributed to a new American culture.

Family Roles

A colonial farm was both home and workplace. Women cooked, made butter and cheese, and preserved food. They spun yarn, made clothes, and tended chickens and cows. Men worked in the fields and built barns, houses, and fences. Mothers and fathers cared for their children and taught them to do farming tasks. In the backcountry, women worked in the fields next to their husbands. Women also shared fieldwork in the German areas of Pennsylvania.

Men were the formal heads of the households. They managed the farms and represented the family in community affairs. In church matters, however, women also participated in making decisions. Families often arranged for their adolescent boys to work as indentured servants for farmers or to serve as **apprentices,** or learning assistants, to craft workers who taught them a trade. Married women were considered subject to their husbands' authority and had few rights.

Women in cities and towns sometimes held jobs outside the home. Young unmarried women without income might work for wealthy families as maids, cooks, and nurses. Widows might work as teachers, nurses, and seamstresses. They also opened shops and inns. Widows and women who had never married could run businesses and own property, although they could not vote.

Education

Most colonists placed a high value on education. Children were often taught to read and write at home by their parents, but the daily chores of colonial life left adults little time for giving lessons. In 1647 the Massachusetts Puritans

Footnotes to History

Indentured Servants were termed *indentured* because their contract was indented, or folded, along an irregular line and torn in two. Master and servant each kept half.

CHAPTER 4
Section 2, 110–114

you don't say...

Cooper, Smith, Wright Many proper names come from occupations. For example, a *cooper* was a person who made wooden tubs or barrels. A *smith* was a metalworker. A *wright* was a person who made something (wheelwright, playwright).

3 ASSESS

Assign Section 2 Review as homework or as an in-class activity.

Use **Chapter Challenger Interactive Review Software** to review Section 2.

Section Quiz 4–2

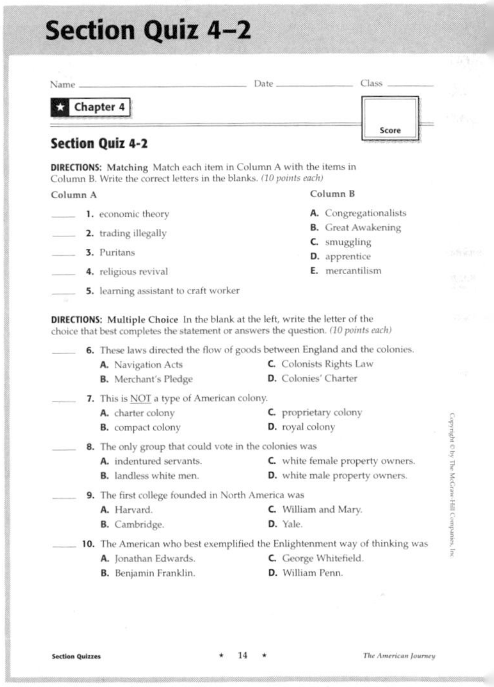

Name ________ Date ________ Class ________

Chapter 4 — Score

Section Quiz 4-2

DIRECTIONS: Matching Match each item in Column A with the items in Column B. Write the correct letters in the blanks. *(10 points each)*

Column A	Column B
____ **1.** economic theory	**A.** Congregationalists
____ **2.** trading illegally	**B.** Great Awakening
____ **3.** Puritans	**C.** smuggling
____ **4.** religious revival	**D.** apprentice
____ **5.** learning assistant to craft worker	**E.** mercantilism

DIRECTIONS: Multiple Choice In the blank at the left, write the letter of the choice that best completes the statement or answers the question. *(10 points each)*

____ **6.** These laws directed the flow of goods between England and the colonies.
A. Navigation Acts **C.** Colonists Rights Law
B. Merchant's Pledge **D.** Colonies' Charter

____ **7.** This is NOT a type of American colony.
A. charter colony **C.** proprietary colony
B. compact colony **D.** royal colony

____ **8.** The only group that could vote in the colonies was
A. indentured servants. **C.** white female property owners.
B. landless white men. **D.** white male property owners.

____ **9.** The first college founded in North America was
A. Harvard. **C.** William and Mary.
B. Cambridge. **D.** Yale.

____ **10.** The American who best exemplified the Enlightenment way of thinking was
A. Jonathan Edwards. **C.** George Whitefield.
B. Benjamin Franklin. **D.** William Penn.

Section Quizzes ★ 14 ★ *The American Journey*

MAKING CONNECTIONS ACTIVITY

Daily Life Point out that Benjamin Franklin made a number of contributions to Philadelphia, including building a library, a fire department, and a college. Have students choose a public service that they can perform. Possibilities include cleaning up a stream, a vacant lot, or graffiti; getting a street light installed on a dark street or parking lot; setting up a book swap; holding a canned goods drive for the needy. Students should write an article for the local paper to announce the event and to ask for community volunteers if needed. **L1, ELL**

Facts On File

CD-ROM
Landmark Documents in American History

Title: *"Sinners in the Hands of an Angry God" sermon, Jonathan Edwards, 1741*
Have students summarize goals promoted by Edwards and list persuasive elements of the sermon.

Reteaching Activity 4–2

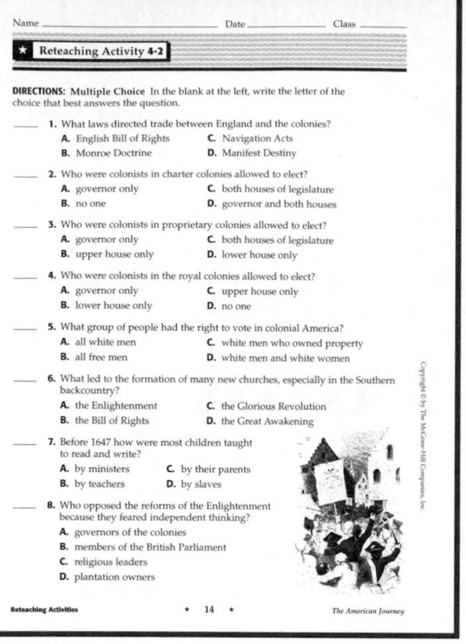

Name ____________ Date ____________ Class ____________

★ Reteaching Activity 4-2

DIRECTIONS: Multiple Choice In the blank at the left, write the letter of the choice that best answers the question.

____ 1. What laws directed trade between England and the colonies?
- **A.** English Bill of Rights
- **B.** Monroe Doctrine
- **C.** Navigation Acts
- **D.** Manifest Destiny

____ 2. Who were colonists in charter colonies allowed to elect?
- **A.** governor only
- **B.** no one
- **C.** both houses of legislature
- **D.** governor and both houses

____ 3. Who were colonists in proprietary colonies allowed to elect?
- **A.** governor only
- **B.** upper house only
- **C.** both houses of legislature
- **D.** lower house only

____ 4. Who were colonists in the royal colonies allowed to elect?
- **A.** governor only
- **B.** lower house only
- **C.** upper house only
- **D.** no one

____ 5. What group of people had the right to vote in colonial America?
- **A.** all white men
- **B.** all free men
- **C.** white men who owned property
- **D.** white men and white women

____ 6. What led to the formation of many new churches, especially in the Southern backcountry?
- **A.** the Enlightenment
- **B.** the Bill of Rights
- **C.** the Glorious Revolution
- **D.** the Great Awakening

____ 7. Before 1647 how were most children taught to read and write?
- **A.** by ministers
- **B.** by teachers
- **C.** by their parents
- **D.** by slaves

____ 8. Who opposed the reforms of the Enlightenment because they feared independent thinking?
- **A.** governors of the colonies
- **B.** members of the British Parliament
- **C.** religious leaders
- **D.** plantation owners

Reteaching Activities ★ 14 ★ *The American Journey*

Enrichment Activity 4–2

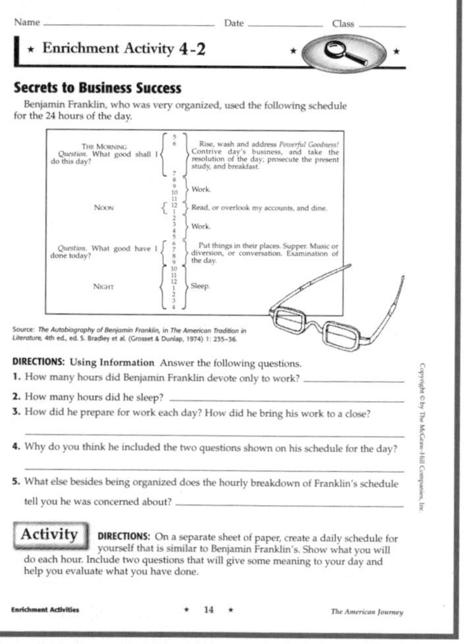

Name ____________ Date ____________ Class ____________

★ Enrichment Activity 4-2 ★

Secrets to Business Success

Benjamin Franklin, who was very organized, used the following schedule for the 24 hours of the day.

	Hours	
THE MORNING *Question.* What good shall I do this day?	5 6 7	Rise, wash and address *Powerful Goodness!* Contrive day's business, and take the resolution of the day; prosecute the present study, and breakfast.
	8 9 10 11	Work.
NOON	12 1	Read, or overlook my accounts, and dine.
	2 3 4 5	Work.
Question. What good have I done today?	6 7 8 9	Put things in their places. Supper. Music or diversion, or conversation. Examination of the day.
NIGHT	10 11 12 1 2 3 4	Sleep.

Source: *The Autobiography of Benjamin Franklin,* in *The American Tradition in Literature,* 4th ed., ed. S. Bradley et al. (Grosset & Dunlap, 1974) 1: 235–36.

DIRECTIONS: Using Information Answer the following questions.
1. How many hours did Benjamin Franklin devote only to work? ____________
2. How many hours did he sleep? ____________
3. How did he prepare for work each day? How did he bring his work to a close? ____________
4. Why do you think he included the two questions shown on his schedule for the day? ____________
5. What else besides being organized does the hourly breakdown of Franklin's schedule tell you he was concerned about? ____________

Activity **DIRECTIONS:** On a separate sheet of paper, create a daily schedule for yourself that is similar to Benjamin Franklin's. Show what you will do each hour. Include two questions that will give some meaning to your day and help you evaluate what you have done.

Enrichment Activities ★ 14 ★ *The American Journey*

passed a public education law. Each community had to have a teacher whose wages would be paid through taxes. Although some communities did not comply, most established schools.

During this period New England had a very high level of **literacy,** the ability to read and write. Perhaps 70 percent of the men and about half of the women could read. *The New England Primer,* first published in 1683, combined lessons in good conduct with reading and writing.

Many colonial schools were "dame schools," run by widows or unmarried women who taught classes in their homes. In the Middle Colonies, some schools were run by Quakers and other religious groups. In the towns and cities, craftspeople set up night schools for their apprentices.

The colonies' early colleges were founded to train ministers. The first was Harvard College, established in 1636 by the Puritans in Cambridge, Massachusetts. Anglicans founded William and Mary College in Virginia in 1693.

The Enlightenment

By the middle of the 1700s, many educated colonists were influenced by **the Enlightenment.** This movement, which began in Europe, spread the idea that knowledge, reason, and science could improve society. Because some religious leaders feared independent thinking, they opposed the reforms proposed under the influence of the Enlightenment. Nevertheless, in colonial cities Enlightenment ideas spread rapidly through newspapers, lectures, and organizations.

Biography

Benjamin Franklin's Contributions

The American who best exemplified the Enlightenment way of thinking was **Benjamin Franklin.** Franklin learned the printer's trade as a young man. By the time he was 23, he owned his own newspaper in Philadelphia. Soon afterward he began publishing *Poor Richard's Almanack,* a calendar filled with advice and wise sayings, such as "Early to bed, early to rise, makes a man healthy, wealthy, and wise."

Franklin was deeply interested in science. His major scientific contribution came from his discoveries about electricity. He invented the lightning rod, bifocal eyeglasses, and the efficient Franklin stove for heating. Energetic and open-minded, Franklin served in the Pennsylvania Assembly for many years. He founded a hospital, a fire department, America's first lending library, and an academy of higher learning that later became the University of Pennsylvania.

Franklin's greatest services to his fellow Americans would come during the 1770s. As a statesman and patriot, Franklin would help guide the colonies toward independence.

Section 2 Review

Checking for Understanding

1. ***Identify*** Jonathan Edwards, George Whitefield, Benjamin Franklin.
2. ***Define*** export, charter colony, proprietary colony, apprentice, literacy.
3. ***Identify*** the only people permitted to vote in the colonies.

Reviewing Themes

4. **Continuity and Change** Why did the Navigation Acts anger the colonists?

Critical Thinking

5. **Making Comparisons** How did the family roles of colonial women and men differ?

Activity

Making an Organizational Chart Draw a chart that shows the structure of a royal colony, a proprietary colony, and a charter colony.

4 CLOSE

A lasting legacy from the Puritans is the tradition of public education. Ask students to list reasons public education is valuable to our society.

Section 2 Review Answers

1. Jonathan Edwards, 113; George Whitefield, 113; Benjamin Franklin, 114
2. The words are defined in the Glossary.
3. white male property owners
4. The acts restricted trade with all nations except England.
5. men: owned property, head of household, managed farms, represented family in community; women: worked in the home, cooked, sewed, and cared for family; helped husbands in fields; participated in church functions; both men and women cared for and taught children farming tasks

Activity Charts should show that students understand the differences in government among the three types of colonies.

INTERDISCIPLINARY

Activities

Living in the English Colonies

Settlers in America brought customs and crafts from home, but they also had to learn new skills. They had to make or grow almost everything they used. How would you get along as a settler in the wilderness? As you complete these activities, imagine how each might have been a part of a colonist's everyday life.

Science

Growing an Herb Garden Herbs and other plants were necessary to colonists as flavorings, preservatives, and medicines. Plant several kinds of herbs in flowerpots and monitor their growth. Many, such as basil and parsley, will sprout from seeds in a few days. Investigate each herb's uses and sample each taste and smell. Then present samples to the class.

School-to-Work

Organizing a Settlement You and other settlers decide to leave Massachusetts Bay Colony and form a new town some miles inland. Make a "business plan" for the settlement: the number of workers and artisans needed (farmers, carpenters, and so on); a list of tools, food, and supplies to take along; and things to look for in a site. Sketch a map of the town plan.

Art

Using Natural Dyes Experiment with plant-based dyes like those used in the 1700s. A yellow-orange dye was made from onion skins or turmeric. Blueberries developed a pink to purple dye. Walnut shells made brown, and apple bark a soft yellow.

Wash wool yarn or pieces of cotton cloth. Simmer the plant material or crushed berries in a gallon of water for a half hour. Strain the liquid; cool it, then put in the clean, wet fibers. Simmer the liquid again, stirring gently. Remove the fibers, rinse, and hang to dry. Make a display of the dyes and dyed fibers.

Music

Learning a Colonial Dance Country dances from England took on an American flavor in the colonies. To learn the Virginia reel, choose a traditional dance tune, such as "Turkey in the Straw." Form a double line with partners facing each other. The lead couple alternately swing each other and the other dancers, moving to the other end of the line. There they form an arch with their arms for other couples to pass through. The next couple repeats the pattern.

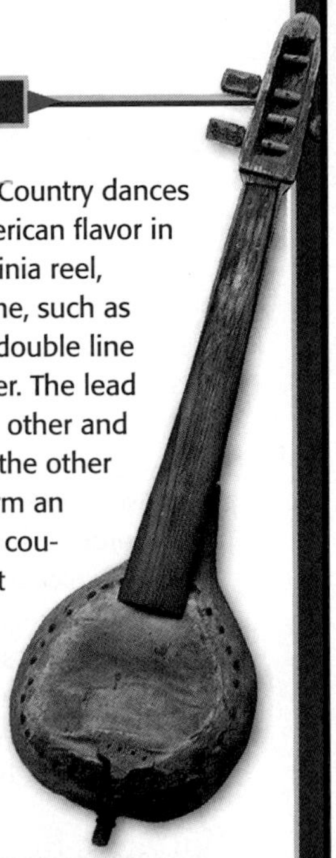

Gourd fiddle played by enslaved Africans

Multiple Learning Styles

The activities included in the feature on this student edition page are ideally suited to meet the different learning styles of your students. These include:

- Science — **Growing an Herb Garden** kinesthetic learners
- School-to-Work — **Organizing a Settlement** logical/mathematical learners
- Art — **Using Natural Dyes** kinesthetic learners
- Music — **Learning a Colonial Dance** kinesthetic and interpersonal learners

INTERDISCIPLINARY

Activities

TEACH

Background

Like other colonial children, Abigail Foote of Colchester, Connecticut, took part in many daily activities. Her diary entry for one day in 1775 included dressmaking, mending, carding wool, making cheese, hatcheling (combing flax fibers), pleating, ironing, spooling, milking, spinning and dyeing thread, broom making, and scouring the pewter. From her diary we learn that she also helped with laundering clothes, cooking, knitting, weeding, picking goose feathers, dipping candles, making soap, and many other tasks.

Team Teaching

These Interdisciplinary Activities provide an excellent opportunity for you to employ Team Teaching and collaboration in your classroom.

Block Schedule

These activities may be implemented within either a traditional class period or a block scheduling framework.

School to WORK

Urban Planners Today, urban planners design residential and commercial areas. Encourage students to research this career. Have them summarize the job of an urban planner and the skills needed to perform that job.

1 FOCUS

BELLRINGER
Motivational Activity

Before taking roll at the beginning of the class period, project Section Focus Transparency 4–3 and have students answer the questions. Discuss students' responses.

This activity is also available as a blackline master.

Section Focus Transparency 4–3

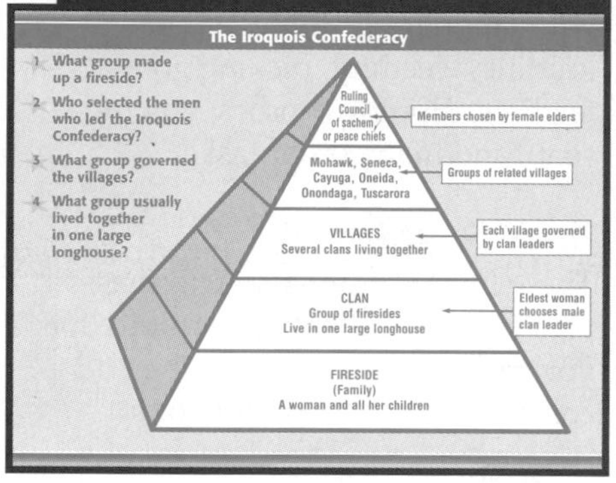

Vocabulary Precheck

List *Iroquois Confederacy* and *militia* on the chalkboard. Have students develop questions for which each term is an answer.

Use the **Vocabulary PuzzleMaker** to create crossword and word search puzzles.

Section Theme
Groups and Institutions

American colonists and Native American groups both became involved in the clash between France and Britain.

Activity Ask students to skim the section to determine the level of involvement of Native Americans and colonists in the clash between Britain and France.

1710 — 1730 — 1750 — 1770

1713 French and Abenaki massacre settlers at Deerfield, Massachusetts

1753 George Washington sent to Ohio country to protest French actions

1754 Washington returns to Ohio and builds Fort Necessity; Benjamin Franklin proposes Albany Plan of Union

Section 3

France and Britain Clash in America

READ TO DISCOVER . . .

- how wars in Europe spread to the American colonies.
- what role the Native Americans played in the conflict between Britain and France.
- what the Albany Plan of Union was.

TERMS TO LEARN

Iroquois Confederacy   militia

The Storyteller

In 1689 England and France began competing to be the richest and most powerful nation in Europe. This contest for power went on for generations with only short intervals of peace. The long rivalry for the control of North America was a drama played against a backdrop of a vast wilderness. In 1758 Nathaniel Ames wrote, "The parts of North America which may be claimed by Great Britain or France are of as much worth as either kingdom. That fertile country to the west of the Appalachian Mountains [is the] 'Garden of the World'!"

Powderhorn, French and Indian War

As the population of the British colonies grew, some land companies wanted to explore opportunities in the **Ohio River valley.** However, the French, who traded throughout the Ohio country, regarded it as their own territory. They had no intention of letting British colonists share in their profitable fur trade with the Native Americans.

In the 1740s British fur traders from Pennsylvania went into the Ohio country. They built a fort deep in the territory of the Miami people at a place called Pickawillany. Acting quickly, the French attacked Pickawillany and drove the British traders back to Pennsylvania. The governor of New France then built a string of forts along the rivers of the upper Ohio Valley, closer to the British colonies than ever before. Two mighty powers—Great Britain and France—were headed for a showdown in North America.

Geography

British-French Rivalry

Britain and France had been competing for wealth for centuries. By 1700 they were the major powers in North America. Their long rivalry aroused hostile feelings between British and French colonists in North America.

Britain had gained control of Nova Scotia, Newfoundland, and the Hudson Bay region in a

SECTION RESOURCES

Reproducible Masters
- Reproducible Lesson Plan 4–3
- Guided Reading Activity 4–3
- Section Quiz 4–3
- Reteaching Activity 4–3
- Enrichment Activity 4–3

Transparencies
- Section Focus Transparency 4–3

Multimedia
- Vocabulary PuzzleMaker
- Chapter Challenger Interactive Review Software
- Testmaker
- NGS PictureShow: Colonial America

treaty in 1713. In the 1740s France attacked Nova Scotia. In response a force of New Englanders went north and captured the important French fortress at **Louisbourg** on Cape Breton Island, north of Nova Scotia. Later Britain returned Louisbourg to France, much to the disgust of the New England colonists.

In North America the French and British fought over resources and land. They clashed over the fur trade and over rights to the rich fishing grounds of the North Atlantic. The French defended the Ohio Valley. The British feared that their colonies would be encircled by French settlements along the lower Mississippi Valley and in Canada.

Native Americans Take Sides

The French traders and the British colonists knew that Native Americans could be a decisive factor in their struggle for North America. The side that received the best trade terms from Native Americans and the most help in war would probably win the contest for control of North America.

The French and the Native Americans

The French had many Native American allies. Unlike the British, the French were interested mainly in trading for furs—not in taking over Native American land. The French were also more tolerant than the British of Native American ways. French trappers and fur traders often married Native American women and followed their customs. French missionaries converted many Native Americans to Catholicism but let them maintain their own cultures.

During the wars between Great Britain and France, Native Americans often helped the French by raiding British settlements. In 1713, for example, the Abenaki people joined the French in an attack on the British frontier outpost at Deerfield, Massachusetts.

North America in 1753

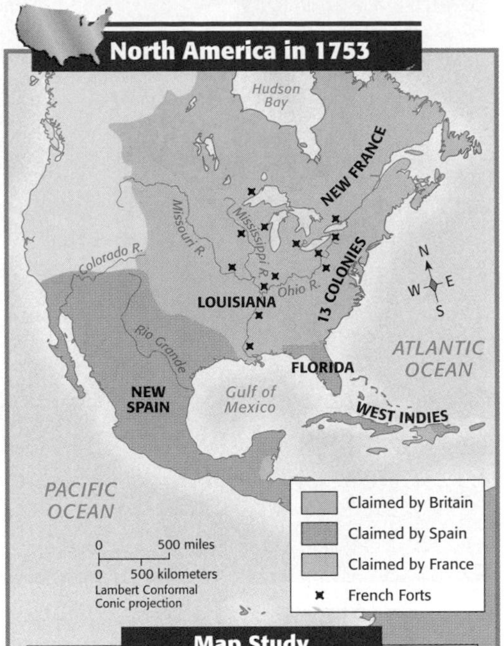

Map Study

In 1753 the British colonies were surrounded by French and Spanish claims in North America.

1. **Region** What power claimed the territory of Florida?
2. **Analyzing Information** What three rivers did France control?

The Iroquois Confederacy

The most powerful group of Native Americans in the East was the **Iroquois Confederacy**, based in New York. When the confederacy was first crafted in about 1570, it included five nations—the Mohawk, Seneca, Cayuga, Onondaga, and Oneida. Other groups later joined or were conquered by the Iroquois.

The Iroquois managed to remain independent by trading with both the British and the French. By skillfully playing the British and French against each other, the Iroquois dominated the area around the Great Lakes.

By the mid-1700s, however, the Iroquois came under increased pressure as the British moved into the Ohio Valley. Eventually the leaders of the

Cooperative Learning Activity

Researching the Iroquois League Have students work in small groups to prepare reports on the Iroquois League and the legends about its formation. Have each student choose his or her own task—researching, writing, drawing illustrations, making a map to show the location of each of the five founding nations, and so on.

2 TEACH

L1 Summarizing Have students use the following words in a summary of the rivalry between the British and French: *power, profit, fur trade, fishing, land. (Students should note that these were all sources of conflict.)*

Map Study

Answers

1. Spain
2. Mississippi, Ohio, Missouri (Although the St. Lawrence River is not labeled, it was also controlled by France.)

Guided Reading Activity 4–3

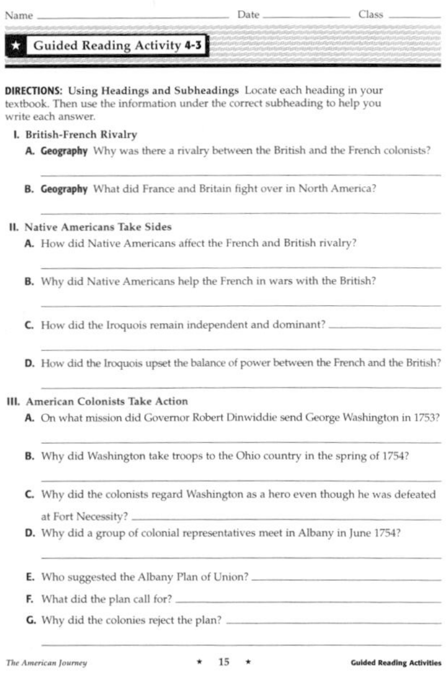
Name ______ Date ______ Class ______

★ Guided Reading Activity **4-3**

DIRECTIONS: Using Headings and Subheadings Locate each heading in your textbook. Then use the information under the correct subheading to help you write each answer.

I. British-French Rivalry

A. Geography Why was there a rivalry between the British and the French colonists?

B. Geography What did France and Britain fight over in North America?

II. Native Americans Take Sides

A. How did Native Americans affect the French and British rivalry?

B. Why did Native Americans help the French in wars with the British?

C. How did the Iroquois remain independent and dominant? ______

D. How did the Iroquois upset the balance of power between the French and the British?

III. American Colonists Take Action

A. On what mission did Governor Robert Dinwiddie send George Washington in 1753?

B. Why did Washington take troops to the Ohio country in the spring of 1754?

C. Why did the colonists regard Washington as a hero even though he was defeated at Fort Necessity? ______

D. Why did a group of colonial representatives meet in Albany in June 1754?

E. Who suggested the Albany Plan of Union? ______

F. What did the plan call for? ______

G. Why did the colonies reject the plan? ______

The American Journey ★ 15 ★ **Guided Reading Activities**

NATIONAL GEOGRAPHIC SOCIETY

CD-ROM
NGS PictureShow: Colonial America

Encourage students to note relationships among Native Americans, American colonists, the French, and the British. Have them start their search at the main menu.

CHAPTER 4
Section 3, 116–119

HISTORY AND ART American artist John Gadsby Chapman (1808–1889) studied art at home and abroad. His *Baptism of Pocahontas* is one of eight large paintings in the Rotunda of the Capitol in Washington, D.C.
Answer: *as a hero who struck the first blow against the French*

What?Where?When?Who?

The Albany Plan Some historians believe that Franklin based the Albany Plan of Union on the organization of the Iroquois League.

3 ASSESS

Assign Section 3 Review as homework or as an in-class activity.

Use **Chapter Challenger Interactive Review Software** to review Section 3.

Section Quiz 4–3

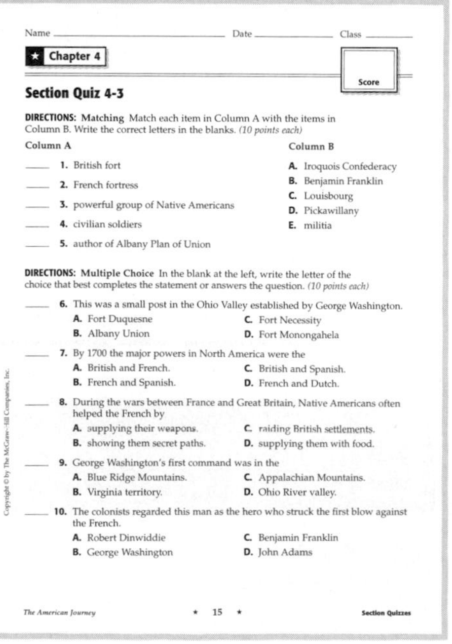
Name ______ Date ______ Class ______

Chapter 4 — Score

Section Quiz 4-3

DIRECTIONS: Matching Match each item in Column A with the items in Column B. Write the correct letters in the blanks. *(10 points each)*

Column A	Column B
____ 1. British fort	A. Iroquois Confederacy
____ 2. French fortress	B. Benjamin Franklin
____ 3. powerful group of Native Americans	C. Louisbourg
____ 4. civilian soldiers	D. Pickawillany
____ 5. author of Albany Plan of Union	E. militia

DIRECTIONS: Multiple Choice In the blank at the left, write the letter of the choice that best completes the statement or answers the question. *(10 points each)*

____ 6. This was a small post in the Ohio Valley established by George Washington.
A. Fort Duquesne C. Fort Necessity
B. Albany Union D. Fort Monongahela

____ 7. By 1700 the major powers in North America were the
A. British and French. C. British and Spanish.
B. French and Spanish. D. French and Dutch.

____ 8. During the wars between France and Great Britain, Native Americans often helped the French by
A. supplying their weapons. C. raiding British settlements.
B. showing them secret paths. D. supplying them with food.

____ 9. George Washington's first command was in the
A. Blue Ridge Mountains. C. Appalachian Mountains.
B. Virginia territory. D. Ohio River valley.

____ 10. The colonists regarded this man as the hero who struck the first blow against the French.
A. Robert Dinwiddie C. Benjamin Franklin
B. George Washington D. John Adams

The American Journey ★ 15 ★ **Section Quizzes**

HISTORY AND ART ***George Washington as a Colonel of Virginia Militia* by John Gadsby Chapman** Washington may have worn this uniform while fighting the French in the Ohio Valley in the mid-1750s. **How was Washington regarded by the colonists after the war?**

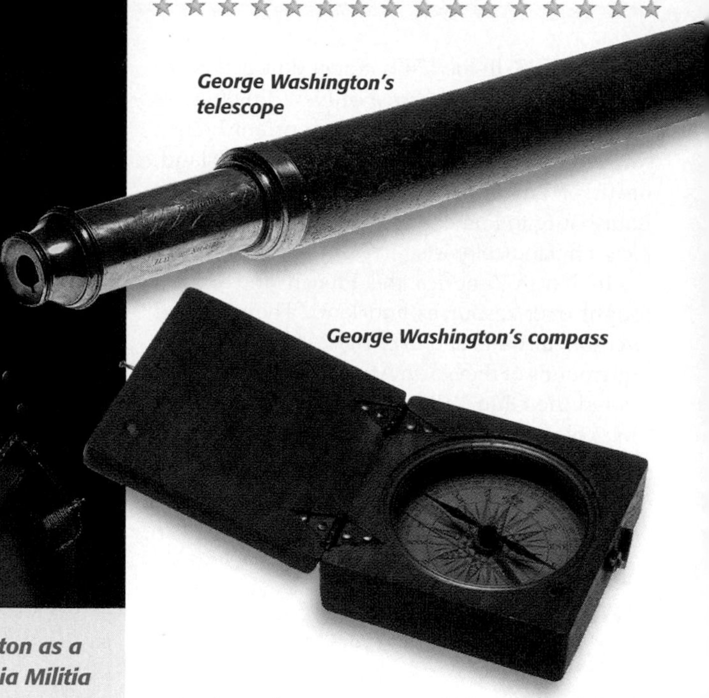

George Washington's telescope

George Washington's compass

Confederacy gave certain trading rights to the British and became their reluctant allies. By taking this step, the Iroquois upset the balance of power between the French and British that they had worked so hard to establish.

American Colonists Take Action

A group of Virginians had plans for settling the Ohio Valley. In the fall of 1753 Governor Robert Dinwiddie of Virginia sent a 21-year-old planter and surveyor named **George Washington** into the Ohio country. Washington's mission was to tell the French that they were trespassing on territory claimed by Great Britain and demand that they leave.

Washington delivered the message, but it did no good. "The French told me," Washington said later, "that it was their absolute design to take possession of the Ohio, and by God they would do it."

Washington's First Command

In the spring of 1754, Dinwiddie made Washington a lieutenant colonel and sent him back to the Ohio country with a **militia**—a group of civilians trained to fight in emergencies—of 150 men. The militia had instructions to build a fort where the Allegheny and Monongahela Rivers meet to form the Ohio River—the site of present-day

Footnotes to History

A Close Call In a skirmish with the French on the way to Fort Duquesne, Washington was nearly killed by his own soldiers. Many years later, Washington said of this incident, "[My life] was in as much jeopardy as it has ever been before or since."

MULTIPLE LEARNING STYLES

Kinesthetic Obtain and bring to class books showing frontier forts of the period. Then have students design an ideal fort, including a location near a cliff or other natural barrier. Have them construct the fort using drinking straws for logs, milk cartons and construction paper for structures, craft sticks for walls, and other available materials. The project should be placed on a large piece of cardboard on which students can show the important features of the fort's location. **L1, ELL**

Pittsburgh. When Washington and his troops arrived, they found the French already building Fort Duquesne on that spot.

Washington established a small post called **Fort Necessity** nearby. Although greatly outnumbered, the forces of the inexperienced Washington attacked a French scouting party. The French surrounded Washington's soldiers and forced them to surrender, but the colonists were later released and returned to Virginia. Washington's account of his experience in the Ohio country was published, and his fame spread throughout the colonies and Europe. In spite of his defeat, the colonists regarded Washington as a hero who struck the first blow against the French.

Editorial cartoon promoting colonial unity, c. 1754

The Albany Plan of Union

While Washington struggled with the French, representatives from New England, New York, Pennsylvania, and Maryland met to discuss the threat of war. In June 1754, the representatives assembled in Albany, New York. They wanted to find a way for the colonies to work together to defend themselves from the French. They also hoped to persuade the Iroquois to take their side against the French.

The representatives adopted a plan suggested by Benjamin Franklin. Known as the **Albany Plan of Union,** Franklin's plan called for "one general government" for all the American colonies. A single elected legislature would govern all the colonies and would have the power to collect taxes, raise troops, and regulate trade.

Not a single colonial assembly approved the plan. None of the colonies was willing to give up any of its power. "Everyone cries, a union is necessary," wrote the disappointed Franklin, "but when they come to the manner and form of the union, their weak noodles [brains] are perfectly distracted."

The Albany meeting failed to unite the colonists to fight the French. Washington's defeat at Fort Necessity marked the beginning of a series of clashes and full-scale war. The colonists called it the French and Indian War because they were fighting two enemies—the French and their Native American allies.

Section 3 Review

Checking for Understanding

1. ***Identify*** George Washington, Fort Necessity, Albany Plan of Union.
2. ***Define*** Iroquois Confederacy, militia.
3. ***List*** two reasons the French felt threatened by British interest in the Ohio River valley.

Reviewing Themes

4. **Groups and Institutions** Why did colonists consider George Washington a hero, even after he was defeated?

Critical Thinking

5. **Analyzing Primary Sources** Based on Benjamin Franklin's quote above, what was his reaction to the colonies' refusal to accept the Albany Plan of Union?

Activity

Preparing an Interview Make a list of three to five questions that a reporter might have wanted to ask Iroquois leaders after they reluctantly sided with the British.

Section 3 Review Answers

1. George Washington, 118; Fort Necessity, 119; Albany Plan of Union, 119
2. The words are defined in the Glossary.
3. tradition of rivalry between the two nations; threat to their profitable fur trade with Native Americans; competition over resources, land, fishing grounds
4. because of his bravery in making the first move against the French
5. Franklin was frustrated that, although the colonies expressed their desire for a union, they were unwilling to give up enough power to form one.

Activity Students' questions should reflect an understanding of the Iroquois position.

Reteaching Activity 4–3

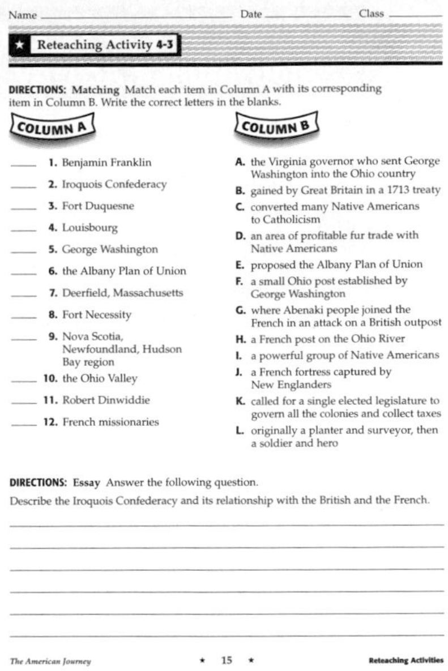
Name ________ Date ________ Class ________

★ Reteaching Activity 4-3

DIRECTIONS: Matching Match each item in Column A with its corresponding item in Column B. Write the correct letters in the blanks.

COLUMN A

____ 1. Benjamin Franklin
____ 2. Iroquois Confederacy
____ 3. Fort Duquesne
____ 4. Louisbourg
____ 5. George Washington
____ 6. the Albany Plan of Union
____ 7. Deerfield, Massachusetts
____ 8. Fort Necessity
____ 9. Nova Scotia, Newfoundland, Hudson Bay region
____ 10. the Ohio Valley
____ 11. Robert Dinwiddie
____ 12. French missionaries

COLUMN B

A. the Virginia governor who sent George Washington into the Ohio country
B. gained by Great Britain in a 1713 treaty
C. converted many Native Americans to Catholicism
D. an area of profitable fur trade with Native Americans
E. proposed the Albany Plan of Union
F. a small Ohio post established by George Washington
G. where Abenaki people joined the French in an attack on a British outpost
H. a French post on the Ohio River
I. a powerful group of Native Americans
J. a French fortress captured by New Englanders
K. called for a single elected legislature to govern all the colonies and collect taxes
L. originally a planter and surveyor, then a soldier and hero

DIRECTIONS: Essay Answer the following question.

Describe the Iroquois Confederacy and its relationship with the British and the French.

The American Journey ★ 15 ★ **Reteaching Activities**

Enrichment Activity 4–3

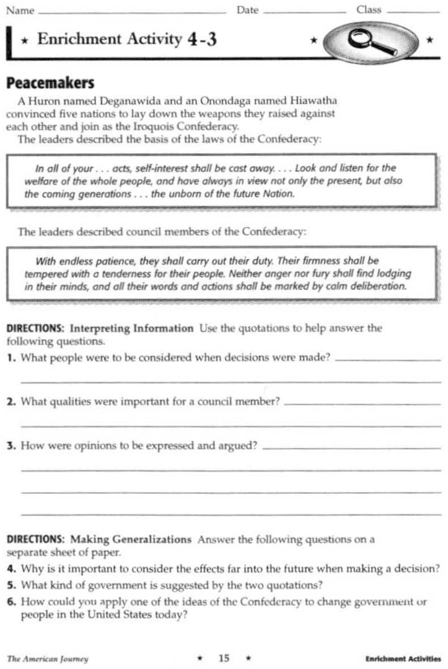
Name ________ Date ________ Class ________

★ Enrichment Activity 4-3 ★

Peacemakers

A Huron named Deganawida and an Onondaga named Hiawatha convinced five nations to lay down the weapons they raised against each other and join as the Iroquois Confederacy.

The leaders described the basis of the laws of the Confederacy:

> *In all of your . . . acts, self-interest shall be cast away. . . . Look and listen for the welfare of the whole people, and have always in view not only the present, but also the coming generations . . . the unborn of the future Nation.*

The leaders described council members of the Confederacy:

> *With endless patience, they shall carry out their duty. Their firmness shall be tempered with a tenderness for their people. Neither anger nor fury shall find lodging in their minds, and all their words and actions shall be marked by calm deliberation.*

DIRECTIONS: Interpreting Information Use the quotations to help answer the following questions.

1. What people were to be considered when decisions were made? ________
2. What qualities were important for a council member? ________
3. How were opinions to be expressed and argued? ________

DIRECTIONS: Making Generalizations Answer the following questions on a separate sheet of paper.

4. Why is it important to consider the effects far into the future when making a decision?
5. What kind of government is suggested by the two quotations?
6. How could you apply one of the ideas of the Confederacy to change government or people in the United States today?

The American Journey ★ 15 ★ **Enrichment Activities**

4 CLOSE

Challenge students to draw a political cartoon mocking those who called for union, yet would not join one.

CHAPTER 4
Section 4, 120–124

1 FOCUS

BELLRINGER
Motivational Activity

Before taking roll at the beginning of the class period, project Section Focus Transparency 4–4 and have students answer the questions. Discuss students' responses.

This activity is also available as a blackline master.

Section Focus Transparency 4–4

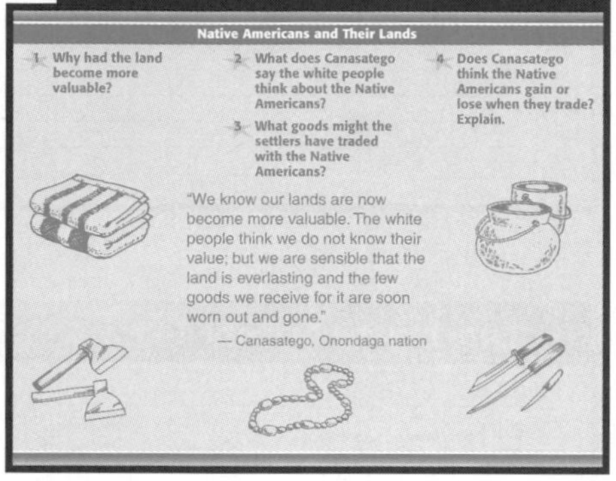

Vocabulary Precheck
Write *speculator* on the chalkboard. Ask students to use the term in a sentence, then have them check their usage of the term with its definition on page 124.

Use the **Vocabulary Puzzle-Maker** to create crossword and word search puzzles.

Section Theme
Individual Action

Victory or loss in war often hinges on the actions (or inaction) of a single leader.

Activity Have students find examples of such leaders and their actions in Section 4. *(Braddock—refusal to change fighting style caused disastrous loss; Pitt—choosing good commanders and avoiding money hassles helped win war; Wolfe—persistence won Battle of Quebec)*

1750 1755 1760 1765

1754 French and Indian War begins

1758 British forces capture Fort Duquesne

1759 British general Wolfe captures Quebec

1763 Proclamation of 1763 forbids colonists to settle west of Appalachians

Section 4

The French and Indian War

READ TO DISCOVER . . .
- how British fortunes improved after William Pitt took over direction of the war.
- how Chief Pontiac united his people to fight for their land.

TERM TO LEARN
speculator

The Storyteller

"These lakes, these woods, and mountains were left us by our ancestors. They are our inheritances, and we will part with them to no one. . . . [Y]ou ought to know that He, the Great Spirit and Master of Life, has provided food for us in these spacious lakes and on the woody mountains. . . ."

These words, spoken by Chief Pontiac, served as a warning to the British colonists who wanted to take Native American lands.

Iroquois mask

In 1754 the governor of Massachusetts fed the fears of that colony's assembly when he announced that the French were on the way to "making themselves masters of this Continent." The British colonists knew that the French were building well-armed forts throughout the Great Lakes region and the Ohio River valley. Their network of alliances with Native Americans allowed the French to control vast interior lands, stretching from the St. Lawrence River all the way south to New Orleans. The French and their Native American allies seemed to be winning control of the American frontier. The final showdown was at hand.

The British Government Takes Action

During the early stages of the French and Indian War, the British colonists fought the French and the Native Americans with little help from Britain. In 1754, however, the government in London decided to intervene in the conflict. It was alarmed by the new forts the French were building and by George Washington's defeat at Fort Necessity. In the fall of 1754, Great Britain appointed **General Edward Braddock** commander in chief of the British forces in America and sent him to drive the French out of the Ohio Valley.

SECTION RESOURCES

Reproducible Masters
- Reproducible Lesson Plan 4–4
- Guided Reading Activity 4–4
- Section Quiz 4–4
- Reteaching Activity 4–4
- Enrichment Activity 4–4

Transparencies
- Section Focus Transparency 4–4

Multimedia
- Vocabulary PuzzleMaker
- Chapter Challenger Interactive Review Software
- Testmaker
- GTV: A Geographic Perspective on American History
- Facts On File: Landmark Documents in American History

Eyewitness to HISTORY

Braddock Marches to Duquesne

In June 1755, Braddock set out from Virginia with 1,400 red-coated British soldiers and a smaller number of blue-coated colonial militia. George Washington served as one of his guides. It took Braddock's army 32 days to trek through the dense forest to **Fort Duquesne.** Washington reported that Braddock "halted to level every mole-hill and to erect bridges over every brook, by which means we were four days in getting twelve miles."

Washington tried to tell Braddock that his army's formal style of marching was not well suited to fighting in frontier country. Lined up in columns and rows, the troops made easy targets for French and Native American sharpshooters. Braddock ignored the advice.

On July 9 the combined force of Native American warriors and French troops ambushed the British. The Indians fired from behind trees, aiming at the bright uniforms. The British, confused and frightened, could not even see their attackers.

One of the survivors of Braddock's army, Captain Orne, later described the "great confusion" that overcame Braddock's troops when they were attacked. Braddock called for an orderly retreat, "but the panic was so great he could not succeed." Braddock was killed, and the battle ended in a bitter defeat for the British, who lost nearly 1,000 soldiers. Washington led the survivors back to Virginia.

Britain Declares War on France

When news of Braddock's defeat reached London, Britain declared war on France, beginning the

Picturing HISTORY Native American warriors and French troops, protected by rocks and trees, fire into General Braddock's army crammed together on a forest trail. **What weakness of the British army contributed to Braddock's defeat?**

COOPERATIVE LEARNING ACTIVITY

Making a TV News Show Have students prepare a TV news show with "live" coverage of the Battle of Quebec. Roles include roving correspondents to interview the generals and troops during the two-month siege and to cover the brief but bloody battle; news anchors to introduce various parts of the show; reporters covering field hospitals and interviewing civilians within the city walls; and actors for commercials. If possible, videotape the show and play it back on a VCR. Tasks for preparing the show include doing any necessary research, preparing maps and other visuals, writing dialogue, and so on. Tasks should be divided according to the strengths of the students.

2 TEACH

L1 Prioritizing Important Events Have students work in pairs or small groups to identify the five most important events in the section and rank their choices in order of importance. Then compare the results and have each group defend its choices and rankings.

Guided Reading Activity 4–4

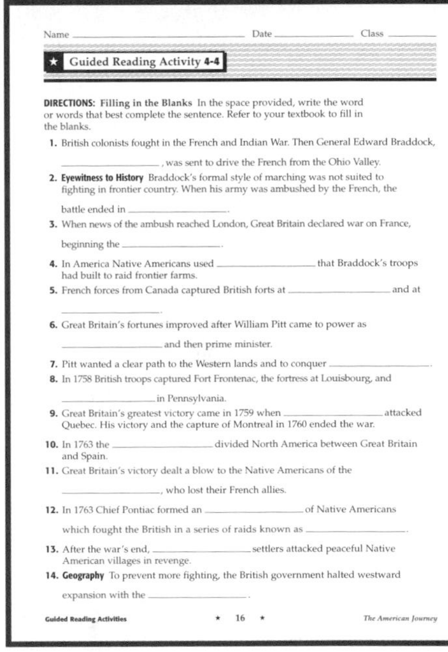

Name ________ Date ________ Class ________

★ Guided Reading Activity 4-4

DIRECTIONS: Filling in the Blanks In the space provided, write the word or words that best complete the sentence. Refer to your textbook to fill in the blanks.

1. British colonists fought in the French and Indian War. Then General Edward Braddock, ________, was sent to drive the French from the Ohio Valley.
2. **Eyewitness to History** Braddock's formal style of marching was not suited to fighting in frontier country. When his army was ambushed by the French, the battle ended in ________.
3. When news of the ambush reached London, Great Britain declared war on France, beginning the ________.
4. In America Native Americans used ________ that Braddock's troops had built to raid frontier farms.
5. French forces from Canada captured British forts at ________ and at ________.
6. Great Britain's fortunes improved after William Pitt came to power as ________ and then prime minister.
7. Pitt wanted a clear path to the Western lands and to conquer ________.
8. In 1758 British troops captured Fort Frontenac, the fortress at Louisbourg, and ________ in Pennsylvania.
9. Great Britain's greatest victory came in 1759 when ________ attacked Quebec. His victory and the capture of Montreal in 1760 ended the war.
10. In 1763 the ________ divided North America between Great Britain and Spain.
11. Great Britain's victory dealt a blow to the Native Americans of the ________, who lost their French allies.
12. In 1763 Chief Pontiac formed an ________ of Native Americans which fought the British in a series of raids known as ________.
13. After the war's end, ________ settlers attacked peaceful Native American villages in revenge.
14. **Geography** To prevent more fighting, the British government halted westward expansion with the ________.

Guided Reading Activities ★ 16 ★ *The American Journey*

Picturing HISTORY As the British army tried to retreat during the fighting on July 9, the baggage train came up the narrow road, blocking it and adding to the confusion. During the battle, Braddock had five horses shot from under him. **Answer:** *A formal style of marching and bright uniforms made the British army an easy target.*

Map Study

Answers
1. St. Lawrence River
2. Edward Braddock

Map Skills Practice

Reading a Map Where did Monckton go after he left Boston? *(to Fort St. John and Fort Beauséjour)*

Who?What?Where?When?

James Wolfe's forces at Quebec included about 200 ships and thousands of soldiers. For two months they sailed along the cliffs looking for a way to get at the seemingly impregnable fortress. Then one day Wolfe noticed women washing clothing in the river and later saw the clothes hanging to dry at the top of the cliff. A scout then found the path the women used. It was attention to detail that solved Wolfe's problem.

NATIONAL GEOGRAPHIC SOCIETY

VIDEODISC
GTV: A Geographic Perspective on American History

Side 1, Chapter 15
Title: *Laying Down the Law*
Subject: The rise of revolutionary feelings (1757–1776)
Ask: **What was established by the Proclamation of 1763 and why did England feel it was necessary?** *(Colonists were not permitted to settle west of the drawn boundary; to keep peace between the colonists and Native Americans)*

The French and Indian War, 1754–1763

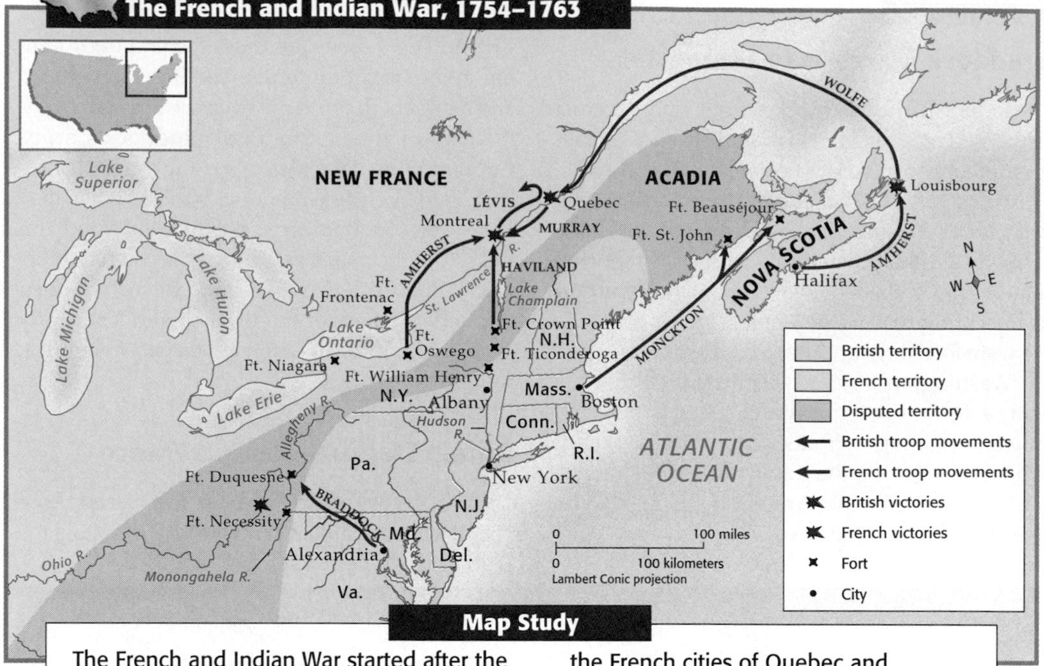

Map Study

The French and Indian War started after the British challenged French control of the Ohio Valley in 1754.

1. **Location** What water route did the British use to make their advances on the French cities of Quebec and Montreal?
2. **Analyzing Information** What British commander led the attack on Fort Duquesne?

Seven Years' War. During the war, French, British, and Spanish forces clashed in Cuba, the West Indies, India, and the Philippines as well as in North America and Europe.

The first years of the war were disastrous for the British and their American colonies. Native Americans used the roads that Braddock's troops cut and the bridges they built to raid frontier farms from Virginia to Pennsylvania. They killed settlers, burned farmhouses and crops, and drove many families back toward the coast. French forces from Canada captured British forts at Lake Ontario and at Lake George.

Pitt Takes Charge

Great Britain's fortunes improved after **William Pitt** came to power as secretary of state and then prime minister. An outstanding military planner, Pitt knew how to pick skilled commanders. He oversaw the war effort from London.

To avoid having to deal with constant arguments from the colonies about the cost of the war, Pitt decided that Great Britain would pay for supplies needed in the war—no matter the cost. In doing so Pitt ran up an enormous debt. After the French and Indian War, the British raised the colonists' taxes to help pay this debt. Pitt had only delayed the moment when the colonists had to pay their share of the bill.

Pitt wanted more than just a clear path to the Western territories. He also intended to conquer French Canada. He sent British troops to North America under the command of such energetic officers as **Jeffrey Amherst** and **James Wolfe.**

In 1758 Amherst and Wolfe led a British assault that recaptured the fortress at Louisbourg. That same year a group of New Englanders, led by

Multiple Learning Styles

Kinesthetic Have students design a statue, plaque, or monument commemorating a person or an event in the section. Possible topics include British soldiers killed under General Braddock's disastrous leadership, George Washington, the Battle of Quebec, William Pitt, Jeffrey Amherst, James Wolfe, the Marquis de Montcalm, or Chief Pontiac. Students may wish to use library resources to find out more about their chosen topics or to find pictures of existing memorials to use for inspiration. Caution students not to just copy such a memorial, but to create their own. **L2, ELL**

British officers, captured Fort Frontenac at Lake Ontario. Still another British force marched across Pennsylvania and captured Fort Duquesne.

The Fall of New France

The year 1759 brought so many British victories that people said the church bells of London wore thin with joyous ringing. The British captured Guadeloupe in the West Indies, the city of Havana in Cuba, defeated the French in India, and destroyed a French fleet that had been sent to reinforce Canada. The greatest victory of the year, though, took place in the heart of New France.

The Battle of Quebec

Perched high atop a cliff overlooking the St. Lawrence River, **Quebec,** the capital of New France, was thought to be impossible to attack. In September 1759, British general James Wolfe found a way.

One of Wolfe's scouts spotted a poorly guarded path up the back of the cliff. Wolfe's soldiers overwhelmed the guards posted on the path and then scrambled up the path during the night. The British troops assembled outside the fortress of Quebec on a field called the **Plains of Abraham.** There they surprised and defeated the French army. James Wolfe died in the battle. The French commander, the Marquis de Montcalm, was mortally wounded and died the next day.

The Treaty of Paris

The fall of Quebec and General Amherst's capture of Montreal the following year brought the fighting in North America between France and Britain to an end. In the **Treaty of Paris** of 1763, France was permitted to keep its sugar-producing islands in the West Indies, but it was forced to give up Canada and its lands east of the Mississippi River to Great Britain. From Spain, France's ally, Great Britain gained Florida. In return, Spain received French lands west of the Mississippi River—the Louisiana Territory—as well as the port of New Orleans.

The Treaty of Paris marked the end of France as a power in North America. The continent was now divided between Great Britain and Spain with the Mississippi River marking the boundary. While the French and British were working out a plan for the future of North America, many Native Americans still lived on the lands covered by the European agreement.

Trouble on the Frontier

The British victory over the French dealt a blow to the Native Americans of the Ohio River valley. They had lost their French allies and trading partners. Although they continued to trade with the British, the Indians regarded them as enemies. The British raised the prices of their goods and, unlike the French, refused to pay rent for their forts. Worst of all, British settlers began moving into the Monongahela and Susquehanna River valleys in western Pennsylvania.

Pontiac's War

Pontiac, chief of an Ottawa village near Detroit, recognized that the British settlers threatened the Native American way of life. Just as Benjamin Franklin had tried to bring the colonies together with the Albany Plan, Pontiac wanted to join Indian groups to fight the British.

In the spring of 1763, Pontiac put together an alliance of Native American peoples. He laid

Linking PAST & PRESENT

Acadians

The French colonists in Nova Scotia were called Acadians. In 1755 the British forced thousands of Acadians to leave Nova Scotia. Some of them made their way to Louisiana. They were the ancestors of today's French-speaking Louisiana Cajuns. The name *Cajun* is derived from the word *Acadian*.

MAKING CONNECTIONS ACTIVITY

Language Arts In class, read aloud all or parts of Henry Wadsworth Longfellow's poem "Evangeline." Allow time for class discussion of the poem. Then have students either write diary entries from the point of view of one of the Acadians or dramatize events in the poem. Included among the many dramatic possibilities are hearing the order for deportation, loading the ships, and Gabriel dying in Evangeline's arms. **L3**

you don't say...

Bury the hatchet comes from a Native American tradition. When smoking the peace pipe, weapons of war must be buried so that all signs of aggression are out of sight. Henry Wadsworth Longfellow references this custom in *The Song of Hiawatha.*

Buried was the bloody hatchet,
Buried was the dreadful war club,
Buried were all warlike weapons,
and the war-cry was forgotten.
There was peace among the nations.

Facts On File

CD-ROM
Landmark Documents in American History

Title: *The Proclamation of 1763*
Have students view the document, then outline its major points.

3 ASSESS

Assign Section 4 Review as homework or as an in-class activity.

Use **Chapter Challenger Interactive Review Software** to review Section 4.

Section Quiz 4–4

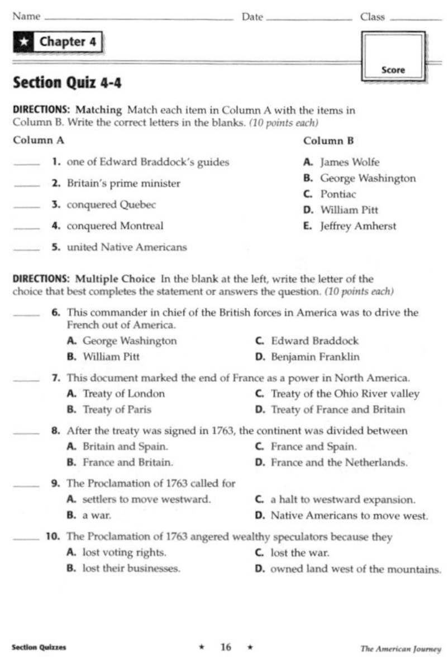
Name ______ Date ______ Class ______

Chapter 4

Score

Section Quiz 4-4

DIRECTIONS: Matching Match each item in Column A with the items in Column B. Write the correct letters in the blanks. *(10 points each)*

Column A	Column B
____ 1. one of Edward Braddock's guides	A. James Wolfe
____ 2. Britain's prime minister	B. George Washington
____ 3. conquered Quebec	C. Pontiac
____ 4. conquered Montreal	D. William Pitt
____ 5. united Native Americans	E. Jeffrey Amherst

DIRECTIONS: Multiple Choice In the blank at the left, write the letter of the choice that best completes the statement or answers the question. *(10 points each)*

____ 6. This commander in chief of the British forces in America was to drive the French out of America.
A. George Washington C. Edward Braddock
B. William Pitt D. Benjamin Franklin

____ 7. This document marked the end of France as a power in North America.
A. Treaty of London C. Treaty of the Ohio River valley
B. Treaty of Paris D. Treaty of France and Britain

____ 8. After the treaty was signed in 1763, the continent was divided between
A. Britain and Spain. C. France and Spain.
B. France and Britain. D. France and the Netherlands.

____ 9. The Proclamation of 1763 called for
A. settlers to move westward. C. a halt to westward expansion.
B. a war. D. Native Americans to move west.

____ 10. The Proclamation of 1763 angered wealthy speculators because they
A. lost voting rights. C. lost the war.
B. lost their businesses. D. owned land west of the mountains.

Section Quizzes ★ 16 ★ *The American Journey*

CHAPTER 4
Section 4, 120–124

Reteaching Activity 4–4

Name ______ Date ______ Class ______

★ Reteaching Activity 4-4

DIRECTIONS: Recognizing Causes and Effects After each *Cause,* write the letter of its *Effect* from the Fact Bank.

1. **Cause:** The French built a number of well-armed forts throughout the Great Lakes region and the Ohio River valley.
   Effect: ______
2. **Cause:** News of Edward Braddock's defeat at Fort Duquesne reached London.
   Effect: ______
3. **Cause:** William Pitt ran up an enormous debt for Great Britain by agreeing to pay for the supplies for the war.
   Effect: ______
4. **Cause:** General James Wolfe's scout spotted a poorly guarded path up to Quebec.
   Effect: ______
5. **Cause:** Quebec and Montreal were captured by British troops.
   Effect: ______
6. **Cause:** The Treaty of Paris was signed in 1763.
   Effect: ______
7. **Cause:** The British settlers mistreated the Native Americans in the Ohio River valley.
   Effect: ______
8. **Cause:** Native Americans and British settlers repeatedly attacked each other throughout 1763.
   Effect: ______

★FACT BANK

A. Fighting in North America between France and Great Britain came to an end.
B. The British government enacted the Proclamation of 1763, which temporarily halted westward expansion beyond the Appalachian Mountains.
C. Following the French and Indian War, the British government raised the colonists' taxes.
D. The British government grew alarmed and decided to intervene in the French and Indian War.
E. France gave Canada and its lands east of the Mississippi River to Great Britain and its lands west of the Mississippi River to Spain. Spain gave Florida to Great Britain.
F. Great Britain declared war on France, beginning the Seven Years' War.
G. British troops defeated French troops on the Plains of Abraham.
H. Chief Pontiac assembled a group of Native Americans and raided a number of British forts and settlements.

Enrichment Activity 4–4

Name ______ Date ______ Class ______

★ Enrichment Activity 4-4 ★

Brave Wolfe

The "Death of General Wolfe," one of the first American broadside ballads, tells of the arrival in 1759 of General James Wolfe at Quebec. It describes a brief meeting between Wolfe and his opponent, the Marquis de Montcalm, before the battle. The following excerpt recounts Wolfe's death.

The drums did loudly beat, colors were flying,
The purple gore did stream, and men lay dying,
When shot off from his horse fell this brave hero,
And we lament his loss in weeds of sorrow.
The French began to break, their ranks were flying,
Wolfe seemed to revive while he lay dying.
He lifted up his head while guns did rattle,
And to his army said, "How goes the battle?"
His aide-de-camp replied, "'Tis in our favor;
Quebec with all her pride, nothing can save her;
She falls into our hands with all her treasure,"
"O then," brave Wolfe replied, "I die with pleasure."

DIRECTIONS: Understanding Information Use the ballad to answer the following questions.

1. What were the "colors" referred to in line 1? ______
2. What does "the purple gore" mean? ______
3. How was Wolfe injured? ______
4. What suggests the French were losing ground? ______

DIRECTIONS: Making Inferences Answer the following questions on a separate sheet of paper.

5. A ballad is a narrative poem, or a poem that tells a story. Explain how this ballad fits the definition.
6. Broadside ballads were printed on large sheets of paper and posted for the public to read. Why would people have been interested in reading a ballad such as this one?
7. Do you think the actual scene was like the death scene described in the poem? Explain your answer.

Chief Pontiac

siege to the British fort at **Detroit** while other war parties captured most of the other British outposts in the Great Lakes region. That summer Native Americans killed settlers along the Pennsylvania and Virginia frontiers in a series of raids called **Pontiac's War.**

The Native Americans, however, failed to capture the important strongholds of Niagara, Fort Pitt, and Detroit. The war ended in late October, when Pontiac learned that the French had signed the Treaty of Paris. He broke off the siege of Detroit. Pennsylvania settlers took their revenge by attacking peaceful Indian villages.

Geography

The Proclamation of 1763

To prevent more fighting, the British government called a halt to the settlers' westward expansion. In the **Proclamation of 1763,** King George III of Great Britain declared that the Appalachian Mountains were the temporary western boundary for all the colonies. Governors were forbidden to grant land west of the Appalachians to settlers without the king's permission.

The proclamation angered many people, especially those who owned shares in land companies, such as the Ohio Company of Virginia. These wealthy **speculators,** or investors, from the East had already bought property west of the mountains. They were furious with Britain for ignoring their land claims.

Although the end of the French and Indian War brought peace for the first time in many years, the Proclamation of 1763 created friction between Britain and the colonies. More conflicts would soon arise between the government in Britain and the colonists in North America.

Section 4 Review

Checking for Understanding

1. ***Identify*** General Edward Braddock, Fort Duquesne, Seven Years' War, William Pitt, Quebec, Treaty of Paris, Pontiac's War, Proclamation of 1763.
2. ***Define*** speculator.
3. ***Name*** the three nations involved in the Seven Years' War and the areas in which the fighting took place.

Reviewing Themes

4. **Individual Action** How did Pontiac plan to protect the people in his village and other Native Americans from British settlers?

Critical Thinking

5. **Identifying Alternatives** What do you think General Braddock could have done to increase his soldiers' chances of defeating the French?

Activity

Making a Map Sketch a map showing the land claims of Great Britain, France, and Spain in North America after the Treaty of Paris.

4 CLOSE

Have students predict the effect of the Proclamation of 1763. **Ask:** Will English colonists obey it? Why or why not?

Section 4 Review Answers

1. Braddock, 120; Fort Duquesne, 121; Seven Years' War, 122; Pitt, 122; Quebec, 123; Treaty of Paris, 123; Pontiac's War, 124; Proclamation of 1763, 124
2. The words are defined in the Glossary.
3. Britain, France, and Spain fought in Cuba, the West Indies, India, the Philippines, mainland North America, and Europe.
4. tried to form alliance; led unified Native American attacks on British outposts and settlers
5. adapted fighting style to American landscape, not halted the troop movement to clear land and build bridges, supplied troops with appropriate clothing

Activity Maps should show approximate territory of each nation as described on page 123.

Critical Thinking
SKILL BUILDER

Understanding Cause and Effect

Causes and Effects

CAUSES

- ★ Colonists need to grow cash crops, such as tobacco and rice.
- ★ European demand for tobacco and rice increases.
- ★ Growing tobacco and rice requires large labor force.

Slave Trade Emerges

EFFECTS

- ★ Africans are robbed of basic human rights.
- ★ African American population grows.
- ★ Slavery creates feelings of injustice and plants seeds of regional conflict.

You know that if you watch television instead of completing your homework, you will receive poor grades. This is an example of a cause-and-effect relationship. The cause—watching television instead of doing homework—leads to an effect—poor grades.

When you look for why or how an event or a chain of events took place, you are developing the skill of understanding causes and effects.

Learning the Skill

A *cause* is any person, event, or condition that makes something happen. What happens as a result of a cause is known as an *effect.* The following guidelines will help you identify cause-and-effect relationships:

- Look for "clue words" that alert you to cause and effect, such as *because, led to, brought about, produced, as a result of, so that, since,* and *therefore.*
- Look for logical relationships between events, such as "She did this, and then that happened."

In a chain of historical events, one effect often becomes the cause of other effects. The chart above shows such a chain of events.

Practicing the Skill

Study the cause-and-effect chart on this page. Then answer the questions below.

1. What were some causes of the development of slavery in the colonies?
2. What were some of the short-term effects of enslaving Africans?
3. What was the long-term effect of the development of slavery?

Applying the Skill

Understanding Cause and Effect Read an account of a recent event or chain of events in your community as reported in a local newspaper. Determine at least one cause and one effect of that event. Show the cause-and-effect relationship in a chart.

ANSWERS TO PRACTICING THE SKILL

1. colonists' need to grow cash crops, increased demand for tobacco and rice, need for large labor force to grow rice and tobacco
2. enslaved Africans robbed of basic human rights, African American population grows
3. created feelings of injustice and sowed seeds of regional conflict

Critical Thinking
SKILL BUILDER

TEACH

Understanding Cause and Effect

Point out that in order to understand history, one must know not only *what* happened, but also *why* it happened. A good way to understand the *whys* of history is to think in terms of cause and effect. Note that most effects have more than one cause, and that causes can have more than one effect.

After students answer the questions in **Practicing the Skill,** have them imagine that the chart has an additional arrow on the right. Ask students to name at least one more effect to place on the new arrow. *(Possible responses: Abolitionist movement develops; Civil War and its destruction and loss of life; Economic and social problems experienced by freed African Americans after the war; Economic disaster for former slaveholders after the war)*

Additional Practice

Chapter Skills Activity 4

NATIONAL GEOGRAPHIC SOCIETY

VIDEODISC
GTV: The American People: Fabric of a Nation

Side 1, Chapter 8
Title: *The Journey*
Subject: Slavery in early America
Ask: **What linked Africans from different backgrounds in America?** *(the burdens of slavery, the struggle for survival)*

GLENCOE TECHNOLOGY

VIDEODISC
MindJogger Videoquiz

Use MindJogger to review the Chapter 4 content.

Chapter 4
Disc 1, Side A

Also available in VHS.

Reviewing Key Terms

The key terms used in this activity are defined in the textbook glossary on pages A26–A35.

Reviewing Key Facts

1. immigration; colonial women often married early and had large families; more children survived; adults lived longer
2. Tidewater planters: large, self-contained plantations that used slave labor; grew large amounts of tobacco and rice; backcountry farmers: many farms, but smaller; grew mostly corn and tobacco; farms usually worked just by family; less political and economic influence
3. to prevent other countries from profiting from trade with the American colonies
4. European movement based on idea that knowledge, reason, and science could improve society
5. all of Canada, lands east and west of the Mississippi including New Orleans
6. It kept colonists from moving west of Appalachians without first acquiring permission from king; speculators had already bought land there and were denied access to it.

Review and Activities

Reviewing Key Terms

On a sheet of paper, define the following terms:

subsistence farming	**smuggling**
triangular trade	**charter colony**
cash crop	**proprietary colony**
diversity	**apprentice**
Tidewater	**literacy**
backcountry	**Iroquois Confederacy**
overseer	**militia**
mercantilism	**speculator**
export	
import	

Reviewing Key Facts

1. Why did the population of the English colonies grow rapidly during the 1700s?
2. What differences existed between the Tidewater planters and the backcountry farmers of the Southern Colonies?
3. What was England's reason for passing the Navigation Acts?
4. What was the Enlightenment?
5. What North American land claims were the French forced to give up in the Treaty of Paris?
6. Why did the Proclamation of 1763 cause friction between Great Britain and the colonies?

Critical Thinking

Identifying Alternatives

The Albany Plan of Union was an effort to unite the colonies in their war against France.

1. Do you think the plan could have been changed to make it more acceptable to the colonies? Explain.
2. What incentives could have been used to interest the colonies in the Albany Plan?

Time Line Activity

Create a time line on which you place the following events in chronological order.

- Puritans found Harvard College
- French and Indian War ends
- England passes Navigation Acts
- French and Indian War begins
- Great Awakening begins

Reviewing Themes

1. **Economic Factors** How did the economies of the Northern Colonies and Southern Colonies differ?
2. **Continuity and Change** In what ways did Benjamin Franklin exemplify the Enlightenment way of thinking?
3. **Groups and Institutions** How did the French relationship with Native Americans help the French in their conflicts with the British?
4. **Individual Action** What was George Washington's role in the French and Indian War?

Skill Practice Activity

Understanding Cause and Effect

Each sentence below illustrates a cause-and-effect relationship. On a separate sheet of paper, identify the cause(s) and the effect(s) in each sentence.

1. During the 1700s the population of the English colonies grew dramatically as a result of high immigration and a high birthrate.
2. To make certain that only England benefited from trade with the colonies, Parliament passed the Navigation Acts.
3. Because worship was so central to the Puritans, they built their towns around the church.

Critical Thinking

1. Students might say that the plan could have been temporary or the colonies could be allowed more input into the details.
2. Students might suggest the following incentives: a share of the French land claims for each colony if the French were defeated, or participation in the treaty process at the end of the war.

Time Line Activity

Events should be placed in this order: Puritans found Harvard College, England passes Navigation Acts, Great Awakening begins, French and Indian War begins, French and Indian War ends

Chapter 4

Geography Activity

People in the American colonies came from many different national and cultural backgrounds. Study the map below, which shows the national origins of colonists. Then answer the questions that follow.

1. **Place** What area is shown on the map?
2. **Movement** What group settled mostly along the Appalachian Mountains?
3. **Region** In what colony did most of the Dutch settle?
4. **Region** Which ethnic group was the most common throughout the colonies in 1760?

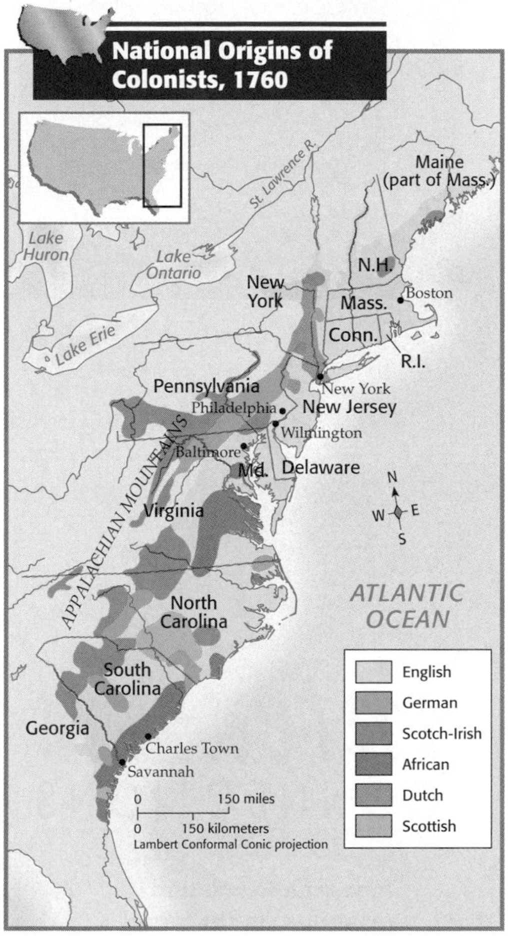

Cooperative Activity

History and Geography Working with a partner, create a map showing a trade route that colonial merchants might use. To get started, examine maps and information from your text and from encyclopedias and historical atlases. Label the approximate points of departure and arrival. Include the physical features that the colonial merchants had to face, including rivers, mountains, lakes, and so on.

Technology Activity

Using an Electronic Card Catalog Search the electronic card catalog of your local or school library for books about Benjamin Franklin. Skim the books to find a little-known fact about Franklin that you think is interesting or unusual. With your class, create a "Believe It or Not" booklet that contains the results of each student's fact-finding mission.

Portfolio Activity **History Journal** Review the chapter for details on the experiences of enslaved Africans and record them in your journal. Use these details to help you write a poem describing the feelings of an enslaved African who is about to board a ship for the Americas.

CHAPTER 4
Review and Activities

Reviewing Themes

1. The North had more commerce and industry; the Southern economy was based on agriculture.
2. He believed in and promoted the value of knowledge, reason, and science and had a wide range of interests and activities, including several inventions. He served in a legislature; founded a hospital, fire department, library, and university. He would later incorporate his Enlightenment philosophy into his work as a statesman.
3. Usually Native Americans sided with the French, who had treated them well and respected them and not tried to take their land as the British had.
4. Although he lost the battle, his attack on Fort Duquesne was the first blow struck against the French. He later served as a guide for General Braddock.

Skill Practice Activity

1. cause: high immigration and birthrate; effect: the population of the English colonies grew dramatically
2. cause: English wish to be only one benefiting from colonial trade; effect: Parliament passed Navigation Acts
3. cause: worship was central to Puritans; effect: built towns around churches

Geography Activity

1. eastern coast of North America, from Maine to Georgia—the English colonies
2. Scotch-Irish
3. New York
4. the English

Cooperative Activity

Each pair of students should create a map showing a trade route, the points of departure and arrival, and various physical features.

Technology Activity

Each student should find at least one interesting or unusual fact about Benjamin Franklin to contribute to the "Believe It or Not" booklet.

Portfolio Activity Poems should include details from the chapter about conditions aboard slave ships and the lives of enslaved Africans in the American colonies.

Chapter Bonus Test Question

Ask: With his dying words, General Marquis de Montcalm seemed to welcome death. What were those words? *("Good. Then I shall not see the surrender of Quebec.")*

These Glencoe resources may be used to teach, reteach, or enrich the concepts presented in this unit of study.

TEACHING TRANSPARENCIES

Map Transparency 3 with Overlays A, B, C, D

Cause-and-Effect Transparency 3

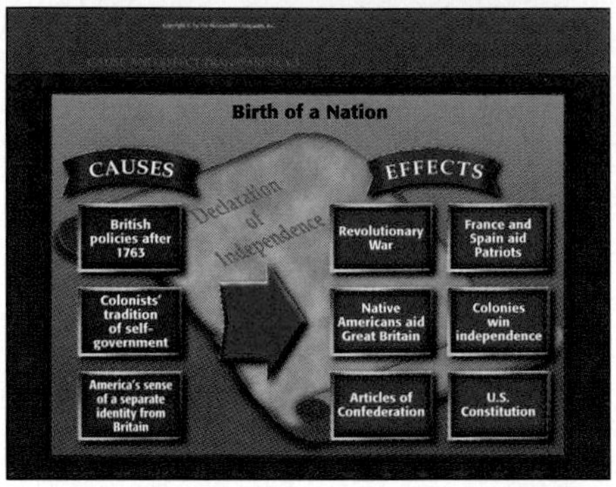

BIBLIOGRAPHY

Readings for the Student

De Pauw, Linda G. ***Founding Mothers: Women of America in the Revolutionary Era.*** New York: Houghton Mifflin, 1975. Stories of women involved in the war as political activists, soldiers, spies, and so on.

Lomask, Milton. ***The Spirit of 1787: The Making of Our Constitution.*** New York: Farrar, Straus Giroux, 1980. Chronicles the United States from the end of the Revolution to the ratification of the Constitution.

Reading for the Teacher

Tuchman, Barbara. ***The First Salute.*** New York: Alfred A. Knopf, 1988. Discusses the American Revolution with emphasis on its place among world events of the era.

Multimedia Resources

Videocassette. ***Independence: Birth of a Free Nation.*** Finley-Holiday Film Corporation. 28 minutes. Summary of the American Revolution.

CD-ROM. ***Origins of the Constitution.*** Fairfield, CT: Queue Inc., 1993 (Macintosh) and 1995 (Windows). Focuses on the people, ideas, and events that brought the Constitution into being.

Resource Guide Unit 3

Interdisciplinary Activities

American Literature Reading 3

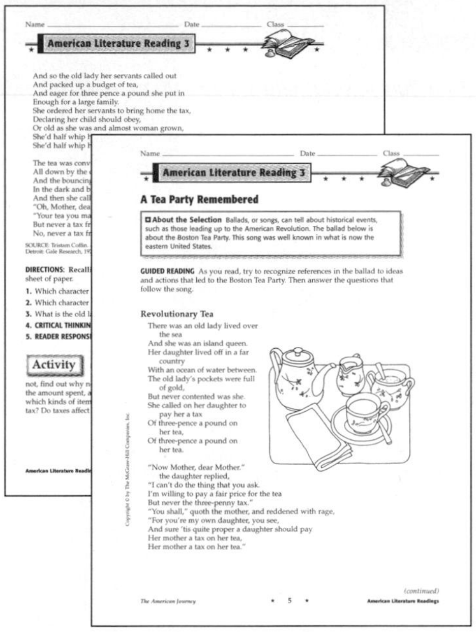

Interdisciplinary Connection 3

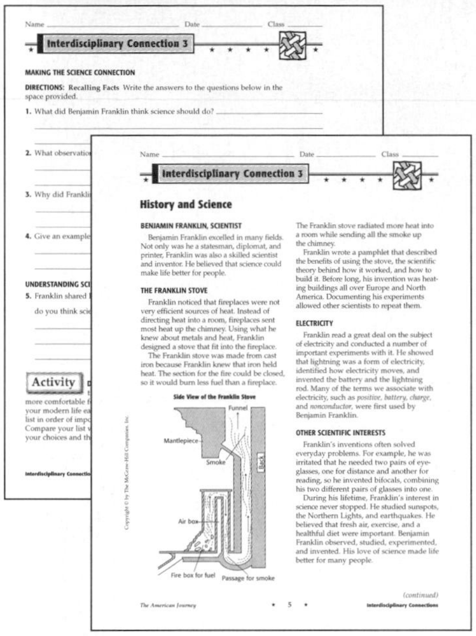

Enrichment Activities

Cooperative Learning Activity 3

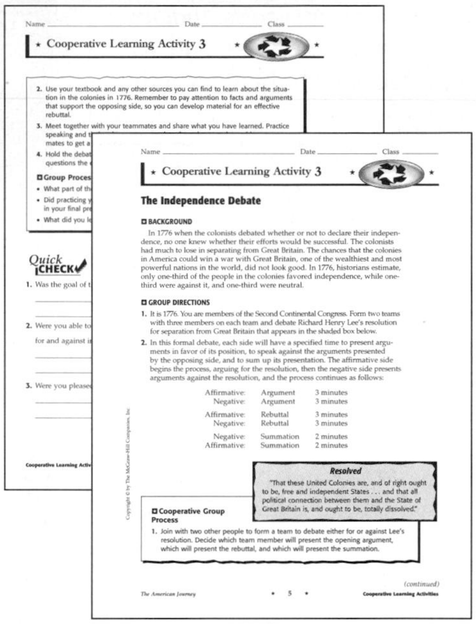

Hands-On Activities

Hands-On History Lab Activity 3

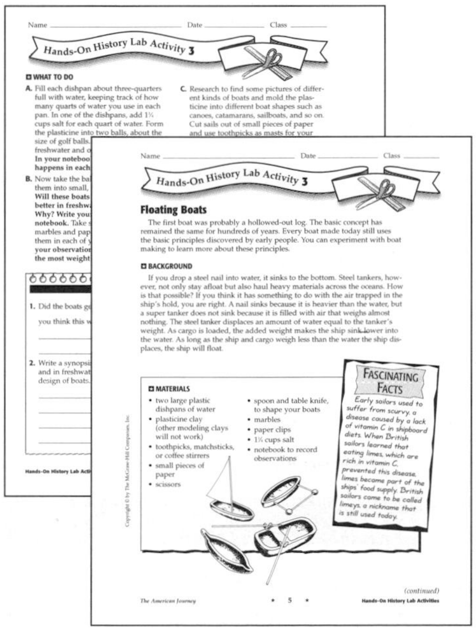

History Simulation 3

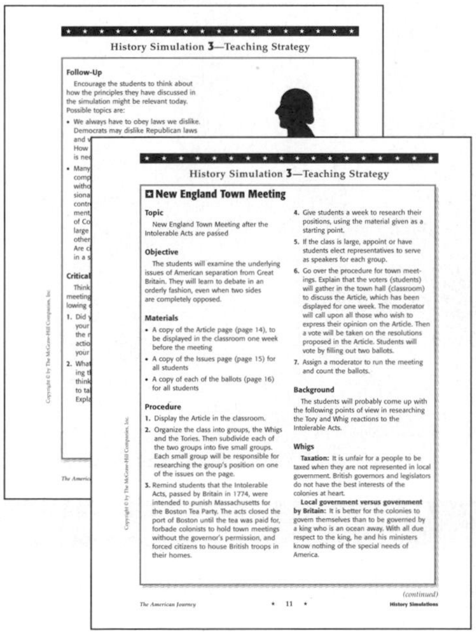

Assessment

Unit 3 Test

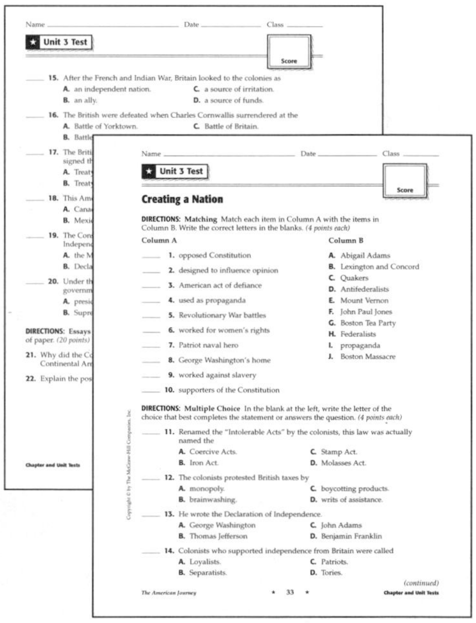

Introducing UNIT 3

0:00 Out of Time?

If your teaching time is limited, you may use the *Chapter Summaries* blackline master found in the TCR with the *Chapter Digests Audiocassette Activities and Tests* to condense individual chapters into a one-day lesson.

Introducing the Unit

Activity Allow students to share things they know or have heard about the Revolutionary era. Then ask: **Why did most Americans of that time rebel against British rule?** *(Expect general answers. You might note some answers and review them in later class discussions.)* Explain that this unit will explore the reasons that the United States declared its independence and the events of the American Revolution.

Unit Objectives

Upon completing this unit, students will be able to:

1. Explain how changes in British policies in North America caused dissatisfaction among colonists.
2. Identify key events that united Patriots.
3. Describe the outbreak of hostilities between Patriot and British forces.
4. Discuss the preparation of and key points in the Declaration of Independence and the Constitution.

Hands-On HISTORY

Hands-On History Lab Activity 3, "Floating Boats," is a high-interest ***constructivist approach*** activity directly related to the main topic of the unit.

Unit 3

Creating a Nation

1763–1791

"Give me liberty, or give me death!"

—Patrick Henry, 1775

MAPPING *America*

Portfolio Activity Draw a freehand outline map of the United States. As you read about events during the Revolutionary War, label their locations on your map. Include battles, confrontations, and important meetings. Illustrate at least three of your labels with sketches.

American flag, Revolutionary War

Liberty Bell

United States

1765 Stamp Act protests erupt

1770 Boston Massacre

1773 Boston Tea Party

1760 — *1770*

1763 Treaty of Paris ends Seven Years' War in Europe

1772 Captain Cook explores the South Pacific

World

128

Team Teaching Strategies

Language Arts Work together with a Language Arts teacher to have students write eyewitness narratives about events described in the unit. Allow students to use the numerous first-person quotations in the text as a springboard for their writing. Compile the results into a class anthology titled "I Was There: Personal Histories of the American Revolution."

Teapot

HISTORY AND ART ***Washington Crossing the Delaware* by Emanuel Gottlieb Leutze** Painted in Germany about 1850, this painting shows General Washington and his troops crossing the Delaware River to launch a surprise attack on British forces at Trenton, New Jersey.

1775 Patriots fight at Lexington and Concord

1776 Declaration of Independence signed

1776 Adam Smith publishes *Wealth of Nations;* James Watt invents the steam engine

1780

1781 British surrender at Yorktown

1787 Turkey declares war on Russia

1788 U.S. Constitution ratified

1789 George Washington inaugurated as first president

1789 French Revolution begins

1790

1791 Bill of Rights ratified

1791 Haitians revolt against French rule

1800

Team Teaching Strategies

Music Work with a music teacher to present the following songs to students (through recording, live performance, or sing-alongs):

Chapter 5: "The Liberty Song" Point out that this song by John Dickinson is considered the first patriotic American ballad. Explain that a ballad is a song or poem that tells a story. Have students summarize the story of "The Liberty Song." (You may want to use or reprise this song to introduce Chapter 7.)

Chapter 6: "An American Frigate" Discuss the meaning of *frigate* (a small, fast war vessel). Explain that this song is about John Paul Jones, commander of the *Bonhomme Richard* and perhaps the best-known Patriot privateer.

NATIONAL GEOGRAPHIC SOCIETY

VIDEODISC
GTV: A Geographic Perspective on American History

Side 1, Chapter 15
Title: *Laying Down the Law*
Subject: The rise of revolutionary feelings (1757–1776)
Ask: **Why did England pass the Proclamation of 1763?** *(to keep peace between colonists and Native Americans)*

HISTORY AND ART Emanuel Gottlieb Leutze was born in Germany and immigrated to Philadelphia with his parents in 1825. After beginning his painting career, Leutze returned to Germany and spent much of the 1850s in that country. In this famous painting, Leutze used the Rhine River as a model for the Delaware. Although his paintings are often full of historical inaccuracies, few modern historical pictures have been more popular in the United States. *Washington Crossing the Delaware* now hangs in the Metropolitan Museum of Art in New York City.

Linking PAST & PRESENT

Activity After World War II, many countries that had been colonies gained independence. As students consider the American independence movement and its aftermath, encourage them to find out how other nations gained independence and met the challenges that followed. Offer these possibilities for research and comparison:

- Barbados
- Bosnia
- Kenya
- Namibia
- Sri Lanka
- Vietnam

Block Schedule

Team Teaching This selection from *Johnny Tremain* may be implemented in a team-teaching context, in conjunction with English/Language Arts.

Reinforcing Vocabulary
Review the **Reader's Dictionary** terms with students to be sure they understand any unfamiliar terms.

Historical Connection
Organized resistance to British colonial policies took many forms. In Boston, the Sons of Liberty defied the Tea Act of 1773 in dramatic fashion. Dumping the tea cargo of three ships made a forceful point and inspired other dissatisfied colonists. This act became known as the Boston Tea Party.

Background Information
Setting The excerpt takes place aboard British ships in Boston Harbor on the night of December 16, 1773.

Characters Johnny Tremain, the teenage hero of the novel, is the main character. He is supported in this excerpt by his friend Rab and by Paul Revere.

Plot Working in an orderly yet determined way, the characters assist in confiscating tea from a British ship and dumping it into Boston Harbor.

America's Literature

Johnny Tremain
by Esther Forbes

Esther Forbes (1891–1967) wrote a number of books, among them the prize-winning biography Paul Revere and the World He Lived In. *As she researched Paul Revere's life, Forbes learned that many young apprentices played a role in the American Revolution.* Johnny Tremain, *a fictional work, tells the story of such an apprentice. Its setting is Massachusetts, where Forbes was born.*

Read to Discover
In this passage from *Johnny Tremain*, 14-year-old Johnny and his friend Rab have covered themselves with soot and disguised themselves as Mohawks. They race toward Griffin's Wharf in Boston Harbor, where three English ships carrying tea are docked and are unable to leave or unload their cargo.

Reader's Dictionary
boatswain: officer on a ship
warped: roped
jargon: strange language
hold: place where cargo is stored on a ship
hoists: lifting mechanisms
winch: machine for hauling

They were running so fast it seemed more like a dream of flying than reality.

The day had started with rain and then there had been clouds, but as they reached Griffin's Wharf the moon, full and white, broke free of the clouds. The three ships, the silent hundreds gathering upon the wharf, all were dipped in the pure white light. The crowds were becoming thousands, and there was not one there but guessed what was to be done, and all approved.

Rab was grunting out of the side of his mouth to a thick-set, active-looking man, whom Johnny would have known anywhere, by his walk and the confident lift of his head, was Mr. Revere. "Me Know You."

"Me Know You," Johnny repeated this countersign and took his place behind Mr. Revere. The other boys . . . began arriving. . . . Many who were now quietly joining one of those three groups were acting on the spur of the moment, seeing what was up. They had blacked their faces, seized axes, and come along. They were behaving as quietly and were as obedient to their leaders as those who had been so carefully picked for this work of destruction.

There was a boatswain's whistle, and in silence one group boarded the *Dartmouth.* The *Eleanor* and the *Beaver* had to be warped in to the wharf. Johnny was close to Mr. Revere's heels. He heard him calling for the captain, promising him, in the jargon everyone talked that night, that not one thing should be damaged on the ship except only the tea, but the captain and all his crew had best stay in the cabin until the work was over.

Additional Literary Works of the Period

You may want to refer students to the following:

Lawrence, Mildred. *Touchmarks.* New York: Harcourt Brace Jovanovich, 1975. Novel about two young people—one a servant girl, the other the disabled daughter of a pewterer, who become involved in the Patriot cause.

Meltzer, Milton, ed. *The American Revolutionaries: A History in Their Own Words.* New York: Thomas Y. Crowell, 1987. Personal narratives that relate to the actions and issues of the American Revolution.

Shields, John, ed. *The Collected Works of Phillis Wheatley.* New York: Oxford University Press, 1988. Presents the works of the African American poet who addressed several of her poems to revolutionary Americans.

The Boston Tea Party

Captain Hall shrugged and did as he was told, leaving his cabin boy to hand over the keys to the hold. The boy was grinning with pleasure. The "tea party" was not unexpected.

"I'll show you," the boy volunteered, "how to work them hoists. I'll fetch lanterns, Mister."

The winches rattled and the heavy chests began to appear—one hundred and fifty of them. As some men worked in the hold, others broke open the chests and flung the tea into the harbor. But one thing made them unexpected difficulty. The tea inside the chests was wrapped in heavy canvas. . . .

Johnny and a parcel of boys brushed the deck until it was clean as a parlor floor. Then Mr. Revere called the captain to come up and inspect. The tea was utterly gone, but Captain Hall agreed that beyond that there had not been the slightest damage.

It was close upon dawn when the work on all three ships was done. And yet the great, silent audience on the wharf, men, women, and children, had not gone home. As the three groups came off the ships, they formed in fours along the wharf, their axes on their shoulders. Then a hurrah went up and a fife began to play. This was almost the first sound Johnny had heard since the tea party started—except only the crash of axes into sea chests, the squeak of hoists, and a few grunted orders.

Responding to Literature

1. Why was the "tea party" expected?
2. Why do you think Mr. Revere asked the captain to inspect the deck of the ship?

Activity

Making a Poster Imagine you lived in Boston during this time. Your town's government will not let the tea ships unload their cargo. Create a poster that either supports this position or opposes it.

Answers to Responding to Literature

1. The ships' captains were aware of the tension between colonists and the British over the Tea Act. This seemed obvious when Captain Hall and other crew members did not resist their visitors.
2. Students may suggest that he wanted to show the captain that he had kept his word and the groups had not harmed anyone or damaged the ships—that they had only ruined the shipments of tea.

Activity Posters should attract attention and make points clearly, but they need not outline reasons for supporting or opposing the position.

History *and the* Humanities

American Music Cultural Traditions, Lesson 2: "Junto Song" and "British Grenadiers"

Portfolio Activity Have students locate and read essays or speeches by key figures in the American Revolution. Ask students to include brief synopses of what they have read in their portfolios. Have them include comments about how the issues relate to what is happening in this excerpt from *Johnny Tremain.*

At the MOVIES

Johnny Tremain & the Sons of Liberty, a 1958 film adaptation of this novel, is available on videocassette. Other films relating to the American Revolution include *Independence* (1976) and *1776* (1972), both of which are also available on videocassette.

CURRICULUM CONNECTION

ECONOMICS

The Boston Tea Party was meant to cause financial inconvenience to Britain. Britain's response, in turn, was meant to cause financial inconvenience to the colonies. The British government closed the port of Boston until Bostonians paid for the tea that had been lost—and for the duty that the Crown would have received if the tea had been unloaded.

Chapter 5 Planning Guide

A complete, 1-page lesson plan is provided for each section in the *Reproducible Lesson Plans* booklet.

Section Resources

Daily Objectives	Reproducible Resources	Multimedia Resources
Section 1 Taxation without Representation Explain how changes in British policies in North America caused dissatisfaction among colonists.	Reproducible Lesson Plan 5–1 Guided Reading Activity 5–1* Political Cartoons, *Two British Views of the Stamp Act* Section Quiz 5–1* Reteaching Activity 5–1 Enrichment Activity 5–1	Section Focus Transparency 5–1 Vocabulary PuzzleMaker Chapter Challenger Interactive Review Software Testmaker GTV: The American People: Fabric of a Nation
Section 2 Building Colonial Unity Identify key events that brought Patriots together.	Reproducible Lesson Plan 5–2 Guided Reading Activity 5–2* Section Quiz 5–2* Reteaching Activity 5–2 Enrichment Activity 5–2	Section Focus Transparency 5–2 Vocabulary PuzzleMaker Chapter Challenger Interactive Review Software Testmaker GTV: A Geographic Perspective on American History Facts On File: Landmark Documents in American History
Section 3 A Call to Arms Describe the outbreak of hostilities between Patriot and British forces.	Reproducible Lesson Plan 5–3 Guided Reading Activity 5–3* Section Quiz 5–3* Reteaching Activity 5–3 Enrichment Activity 5–3	Section Focus Transparency 5–3 Vocabulary PuzzleMaker Chapter Challenger Interactive Review Software Testmaker ABCNews InterActive™ Historic America Electronic Field Trips Facts On File: Landmark Documents in American History
Section 4 Moving Toward Independence Discuss the preparation of and key points in the Declaration of Independence.	Reproducible Lesson Plan 5–4 Guided Reading Activity 5–4* Section Quiz 5–4* Reteaching Activity 5–4 Enrichment Activity 5–4	Section Focus Transparency 5–4 Vocabulary Puzzlemaker Chapter Challenger Interactive Review Software Testmaker GTV: A Geographic Perspective on American History Facts On File: Landmark Documents in American History

** Also available in Spanish*

Blackline Master · Videodisc · Audiocassette · Music Program · Transparency · CD-ROM · Software

0:00 **OUT OF TIME?**
Assign the Chapter 5 Digest and the corresponding Chapter Digests Audiocassettes with activities and tests.

ACTIVITY

From the Classroom of...

Dean Mantz
Lyons Middle School
Sterling, KS

The Stamp Act Revisited

This activity helps students understand how a colonist might have felt during the late 1700s when the Stamp Act was enacted. Students are taxed for their actions (or inactions). Materials needed include play money, which can be taken from a board game, and a box to serve as a treasury. You may also want to give students some type of stamped receipt for taxes paid.

Evenly distribute the play money among students. Have one student serve as the British tax agent, who will collect tax money. Another student can act as an employer who pays students for certain services. (This employer-student will need additional money.) Taxable activities may include turning in an assignment paper, a request for a hall pass to leave the room, not being able to answer a question, and so on. Students can earn money by correctly answering a question, helping another student who has more money, etc.

After about a week of being "taxed" for their actions and inactions, have students discuss their feelings about the tax.

NATIONAL GEOGRAPHIC SOCIETY Teacher's Corner

INDEX TO NATIONAL GEOGRAPHIC MAGAZINE

The following articles may be used for research relating to this chapter:

- "Two Revolutions," by Charles McCarry, July 1989.
- "Yorktown Shipwreck," by John D. Broadwater, June 1988.
- "Thomas Jefferson: Architect of Freedom," by Mike Edwards, February 1976.

NATIONAL GEOGRAPHIC SOCIETY PRODUCTS AVAILABLE FROM GLENCOE

To order the following products for use with this chapter, contact your local Glencoe sales representative, or call Glencoe at 1-800-334-7344:

- *GTV: The American People: Fabric of a Nation* (Videodisc)
- *GTV: A Geographic Perspective on American History* (Videodisc)
- *PictureShow: The American Revolution* (CD-ROM, Transparencies)
- *PictureShow: Colonial America* (CD-ROM, Transparencies)

ADDITIONAL NATIONAL GEOGRAPHIC SOCIETY PRODUCTS

To order the following products for use with this chapter, call National Geographic Society at 1-800-368-2728:

- *Democratic Government Series, "The United States"* (Video)
- *Branches of Government Series* (Video)
- *Historical Atlas of the United States* (Atlas)

Block Schedule

Block scheduling differs from traditional class scheduling in the amount of time allotted to each period. The extended time frame provided by block scheduling affords you the opportunity to implement a greater number of research-oriented and activity-intense projects to motivate and involve your students. Activities that are particularly suited to use within the block scheduling framework are identified throughout this chapter by the following designation:

KEY TO ABILITY LEVELS

Teaching strategies have been coded for varying learning styles and abilities.

- **L1 BASIC** activities for all students
- **L2 AVERAGE** activities for average to above-average students
- **L3 CHALLENGING** activities for above-average students
- **ELL ENGLISH LANGUAGE LEARNER** activities

Chapter 5 Resource Guide

Home Involvement

Home Involvement Activity 5

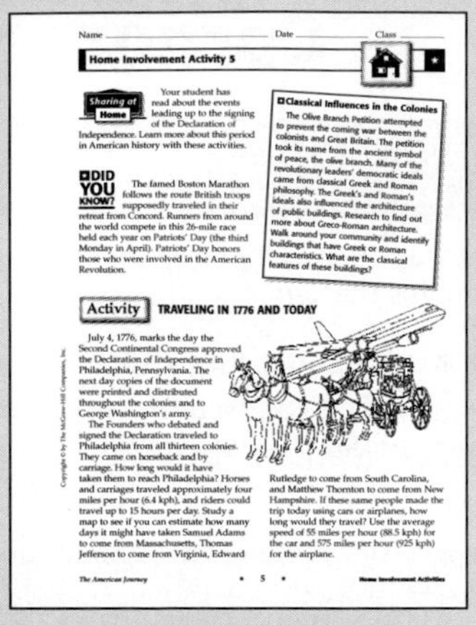

Review Activities

Chapter Summary 5

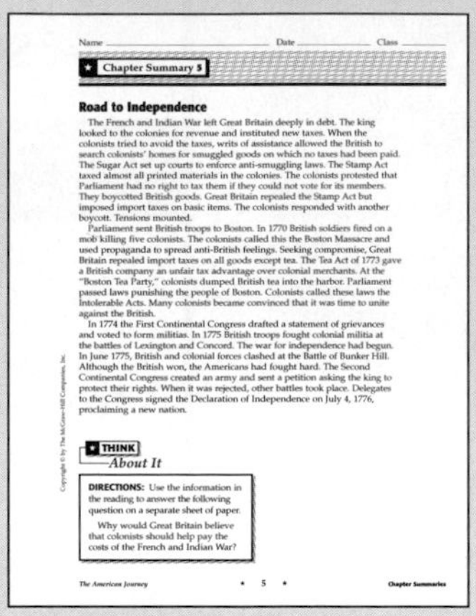

Workbook Activity 5

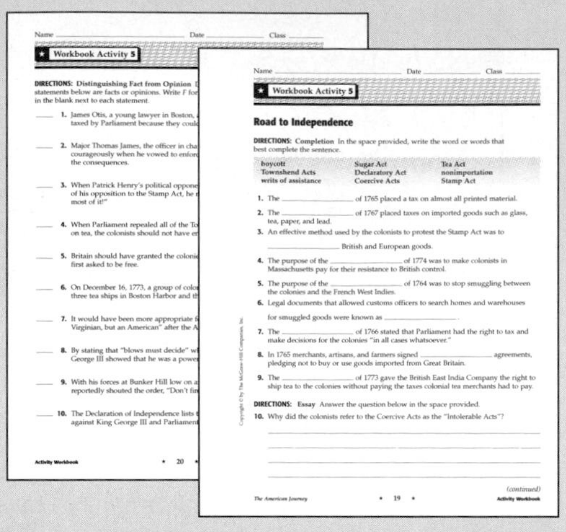

Reinforcement Activities

Time Line Activity 5

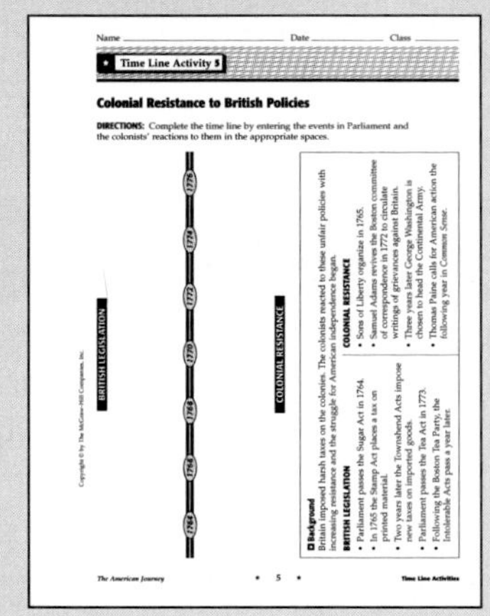

Vocabulary Activity 5

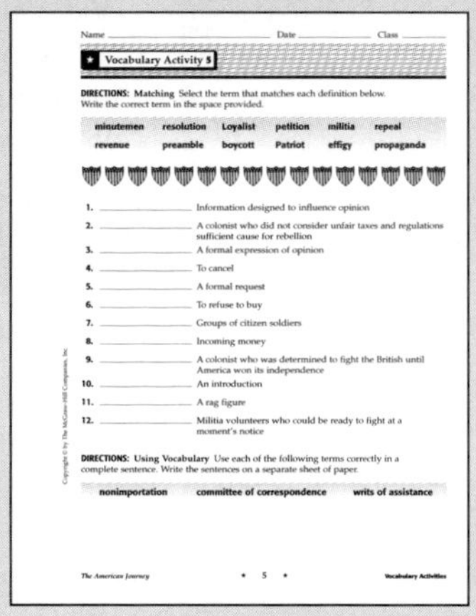

Chapter Skills Activity 5

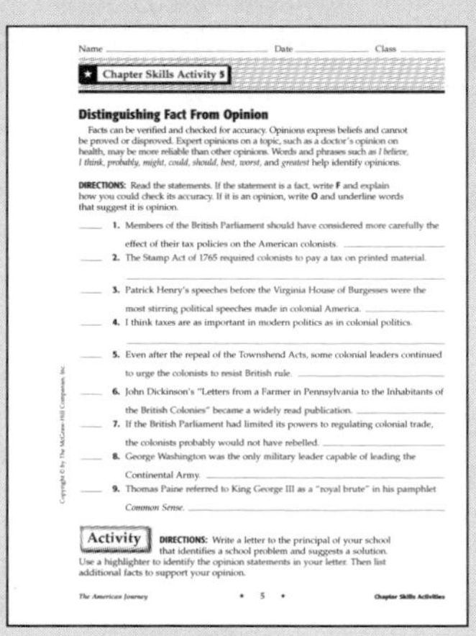

Enrichment Activities

Linking Past and Present Activity 5

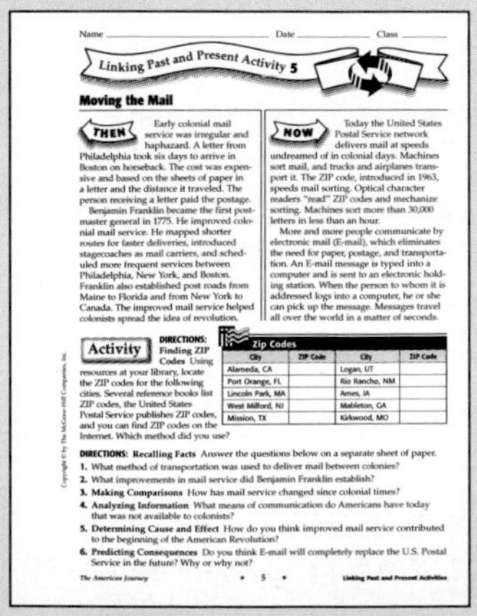

Primary Source Reading 5

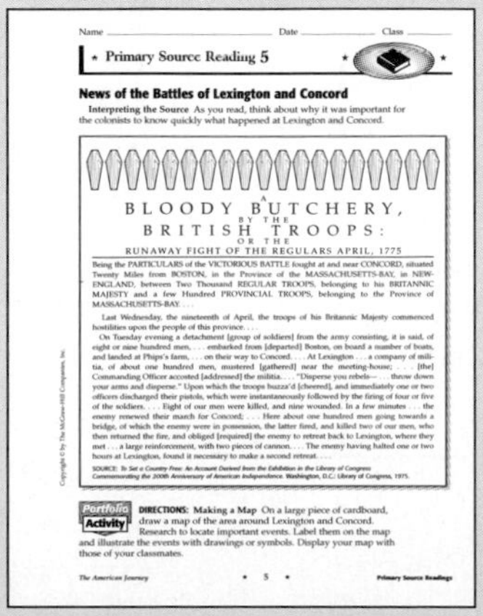

Geography Activities

Mapping History Activity 5

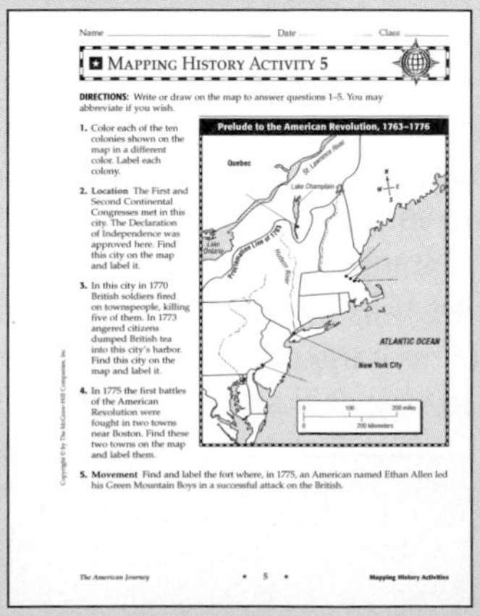

Chapter 5 Resource Guide

Assessment

Chapter 5 Test, Form A

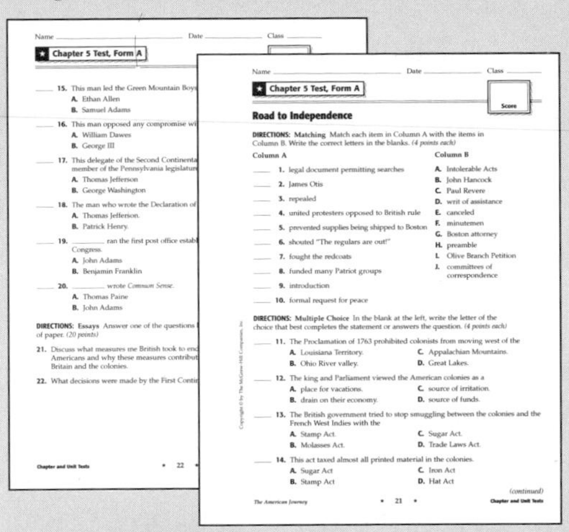

Chapter 5 Test, Form B

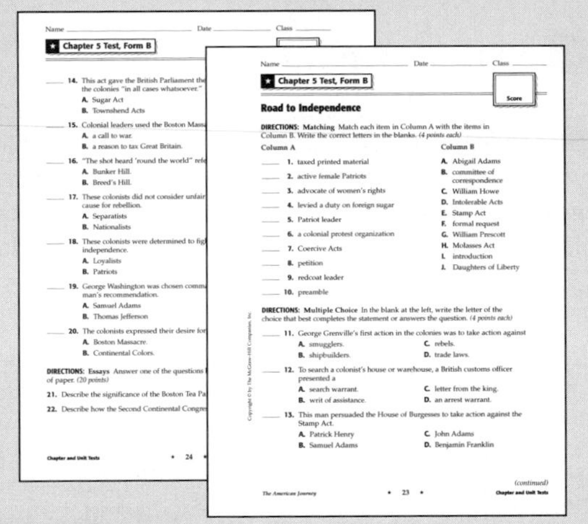

Performance Assessment Activity 5

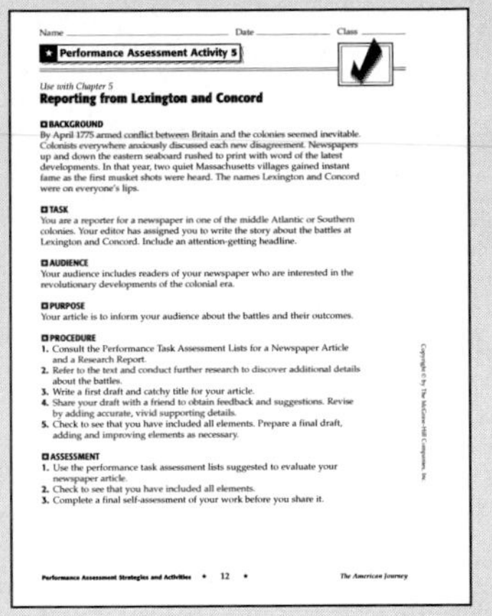

Spanish Resources

The following Spanish language materials are available in the Spanish Resources binder:

- **Spanish Chapter Summary 5**
- **Spanish Vocabulary Activity 5**
- **Spanish Guided Reading Activities, Chapter 5**
- **Spanish Section Quizzes, Chapter 5**
- **Spanish Home Involvement Activity 5**
- **Spanish Chapter 5 Digests Audiocassette Activity and Test**

Activity Manipulatives

Help students learn more about America's cultural history with:

- **American Crafts Hands-On Activities**
- **American Games Hands-On Activities**
- **American History Flash Cards**

Additional Resources From Glencoe

- **U.S. History & Art,** Transparency 4, *The Declaration of Independence, July 4, 1776;* Transparency 10, *Washington Crossing the Delaware*
- **Focus on American Art Prints,** *Watson and the Shark* by John Singleton Copley
- **American Music Cultural Traditions,** Lesson 2: "Junto Song" and "British Grenadiers"
- **Outline Map Resource Book**
- **U.S. Desk Map**
- **The American History Videodisc and CD-ROM,** *The American Revolution and the Early Republic, 1765–1820*

A&E HOME VIDEO. Biography. THE HISTORY CHANNEL.

The following videotape programs are available from Glencoe as supplements to Chapter 5:

- **Thomas Jefferson: Philosopher of Freedom** (ISBN 1-56501-502-9)
- **Benjamin Franklin: Citizen of the World** (ISBN 1-56501-426-X)
- **Patrick Henry: Voice of Liberty** (ISBN 1-56501-645-9)
- **Paul Revere: The Midnight Rider** (ISBN 1-56501-596-7)
- **The American Revolution (Six Video Set)** (ISBN 1-56501-436-7)

To order, call Glencoe at 1-800-334-7344. To find classroom resources to accompany many of these videos, check the following home pages:
A&E Television: http://www.aetv.com
The History Channel: http://www.historychannel.com

Chapter Themes

Chapter Themes are listed by section on this chapter opening page of the Student Edition. A corresponding theme-based activity is available under "FOCUS," and a theme-based question is asked in the Section and Chapter Reviews.

Performance Assessment

Refer to Activity 5 in the *Performance Assessment Strategies and Activities* booklet.

GLENCOE TECHNOLOGY

VIDEODISC
MindJogger Videoquiz

Use MindJogger to preview the Chapter 5 content.

Chapter 5
Disc 1, Side B

Also available in VHS.

HISTORY AND ART Patriots read the Declaration of Independence to some of George Washington's troops before they pulled down this gilded statue on the Bowling Green. Washington told the soldiers that "now the peace and safety of this Country depends [under God] solely on the success of our arms." **Ask: How was this action not merely a kind of vandalism?** *(The statue was "recycled"—melted down and made into bullets for the Patriot cause.)*

Chapter 5

1763–1776

Road to Independence

Why It's Important

Many of the issues that caused the colonists to declare independence remain important today. Americans still protest unfair taxation and attempts to limit the rights of citizens. The ideals and language of revolutionary America still play a major role in shaping the society we live in today.

Chapter Themes

- *Section 1,* Civic Rights and Responsibilities
- *Section 2,* Groups and Institutions
- *Section 3,* Groups and Institutions
- *Section 4,* Government and Democracy

HISTORY AND ART ***Pulling Down the Statue of George III* by William Walcutt** Patriots celebrating independence pulled down the statue of King George III in New York on July 9, 1776. The statue was later melted down into bullets to be used against the king's troops.

EXTRA CREDIT PROJECT

Comparing Plans On page 133, point out the British plan for ending trouble with Native Americans. Ask students to jot down at least two thoughts on how Native American leaders might have felt about this plan. As the chapter unfolds, ask students to add comments about British plans for ending trouble with the American colonists–and about the colonists' responses to those plans. Then have them offer at least one comparison. For example, ask them to discuss how British pride in their military figured into both plans. If students wish, they might respond in a format other than writing–for example, through dramatic monologue or art.

1760 — 1765 — 1770

1763 Proclamation of 1763 forbids settlement west of the Appalachians

1764 Parliament passes Sugar Act

1765 Parliament enacts Stamp Act

1767 Townshend Acts tax colonial imports

Section 1

Taxation without Representation

READ TO DISCOVER . . .

- why the British faced problems in North America after the French and Indian War.
- why the American colonists objected to the new British laws.

TERMS TO LEARN

revenue
writs of assistance
resolution
effigy
boycott
nonimportation
repeal

The Storyteller

Huron and Ottawa warriors silently peered from the woods. They watched about 100 British soldiers camped on Lake Erie's shore. The soldiers—sent by the British Crown—had just stopped to rest on their way to Fort Detroit. They were worried about rumors of Native Americans planning war.

Suddenly the warriors rushed from the forest. The British managed to escape in two boats. War raged on the frontier—and the British were in the thick of it!

St. Edward's crown, worn by George III

After winning the French and Indian War, Great Britain acquired a vast territory in North America. This land was not uninhabited. It was home to nearly 500,000 Native Americans. Conflicts over the use of this territory led to a series of Native American raids on British forts and villages along the western frontier. In attempting to resolve its difficulties with Native Americans, Britain created new problems with its American colonies.

Relations with Britain

The British took two measures to end the troubles with the Native Americans. First they planned to station 10,000 soldiers in the colonies and on the frontier. Then, in the Proclamation of 1763, they prohibited colonists from moving west of the Appalachian Mountains into Native American territory.

Growing Distrust

In 1763 most colonists were satisfied with the government in London. Few wanted or expected any major changes in their relationship with the king or with Parliament. However, these measures by the British alarmed the colonists. Many feared that the large number of British troops in North America might be used to interfere with their liberties. They saw the Proclamation of 1763

SECTION RESOURCES

Reproducible Masters
- Guided Reading Activity 5–1
- Political Cartoons
- Section Quiz 5–1
- Reteaching Activity 5–1
- Enrichment Activity 5–1

Transparencies
- Section Focus Transparency 5–1

Multimedia
- Vocabulary PuzzleMaker
- Chapter Challenger Interactive Review Software
- Testmaker
- GTV: The American People: Fabric of a Nation

1 FOCUS

BELLRINGER
Motivational Activity

Before taking roll at the beginning of the class period, project Section Focus Transparency 5–1 and have students answer the questions. Discuss students' responses.

This activity is also available as a blackline master.

Section Focus Transparency 5–1

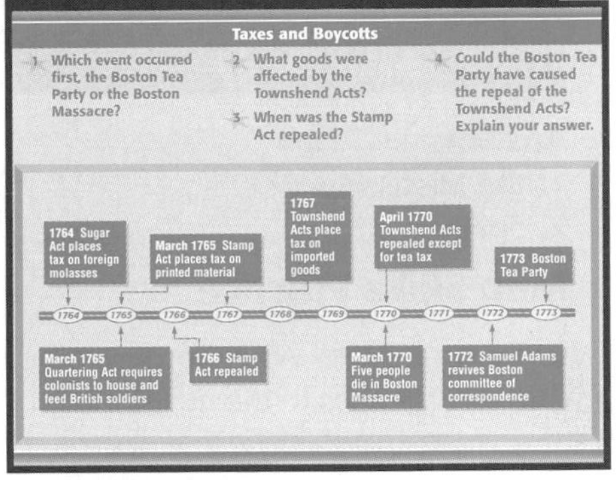

Vocabulary Precheck

Call on a volunteer to define the term *boycott*. Then have students identify examples of boycotts mentioned recently in the news.

Use the **Vocabulary PuzzleMaker** to create crossword and word search puzzles.

Section Theme
Civic Rights and Responsibilities

New British laws caused discontent among colonists who believed that their civic rights were being denied.

Activity Have students name something that they feel they have a right to do. **Ask:** How would you feel if someone tried to limit that right? *(Answers will vary but should suggest unhappiness.)*

CHAPTER 5
Section 1, 133–137

2 TEACH

L1 Charting Laws Ask small groups of students to make charts of the British colonial laws discussed in this section. Have them create three columns for the charts—one each for the Sugar Act, the Stamp Act, and the Townshend Acts. In each column they should summarize the law and note the results of the law.

Political Cartoons, *Two British Views of the Stamp Act*

Map Study

Answers

1. the Mississippi River
2. Spain

Map Skills Practice

Reading a Map What bordered the thirteen colonies to the north, east, and west? *(Nova Scotia to the north, the Atlantic Ocean to the east, and the Appalachian Mountains to the west)*

Guided Reading Activity 5–1

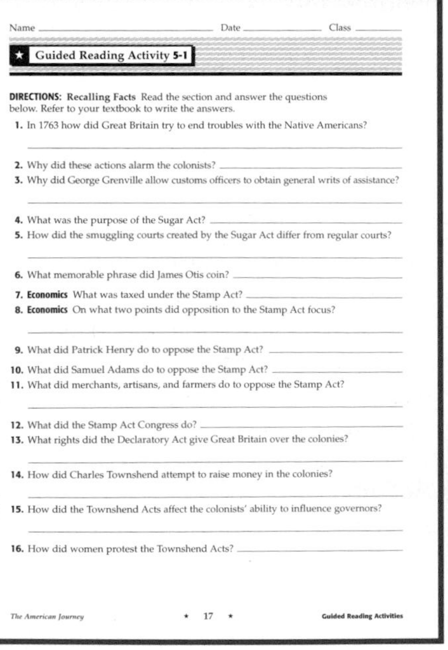

Name ________ Date ________ Class ________

Guided Reading Activity 5-1

DIRECTIONS: Recalling Facts Read the section and answer the questions below. Refer to your textbook to write the answers.

1. In 1763 how did Great Britain try to end troubles with the Native Americans?
2. Why did these actions alarm the colonists? ________
3. Why did George Grenville allow customs officers to obtain general writs of assistance?
4. What was the purpose of the Sugar Act? ________
5. How did the smuggling courts created by the Sugar Act differ from regular courts?
6. What memorable phrase did James Otis coin? ________
7. **Economics** What was taxed under the Stamp Act? ________
8. **Economics** On what two points did opposition to the Stamp Act focus?
9. What did Patrick Henry do to oppose the Stamp Act? ________
10. What did Samuel Adams do to oppose the Stamp Act? ________
11. What did merchants, artisans, and farmers do to oppose the Stamp Act?
12. What did the Stamp Act Congress do? ________
13. What rights did the Declaratory Act give Great Britain over the colonies?
14. How did Charles Townshend attempt to raise money in the colonies?
15. How did the Townshend Acts affect the colonists' ability to influence governors?
16. How did women protest the Townshend Acts? ________

The American Journey ★ 17 ★ Guided Reading Activities

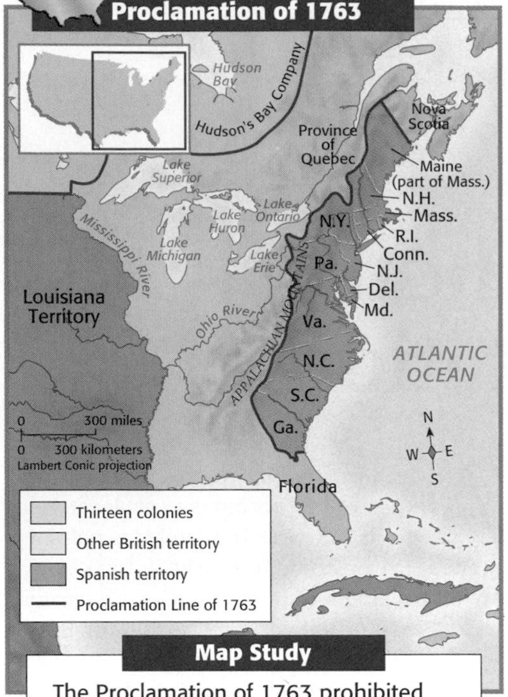

Map Study

The Proclamation of 1763 prohibited colonists from settling west of the Appalachian Mountains.

1. **Location** What natural feature marked the western boundary of British territory?
2. **Analyzing Information** Who controlled Louisiana Territory in 1763?

as a limit on their freedom. These two measures contributed to the feeling of distrust that was growing between Great Britain and its colonies.

Britain Needs Money

The financial problems of Great Britain complicated the situation. The British had amassed a huge public debt fighting the French and Indian War. Desperate for new **revenue,** or incoming money, the king and Parliament began to view their American colonies as a source of funds. They began plans to tax them. This decision set off a chain of events that surprised British authorities and enraged the American colonists.

Britain's Trade Laws

In 1764 **George Grenville,** the British finance minister, decided the American colonists should contribute more toward British expenses in North America. His first step was to take action against smuggling in the colonies. For the British smuggling to avoid import taxes meant lost revenue. Britain intended to monitor colonial trading more closely.

Enforcing Trade Laws

To catch colonists involved in smuggling, Grenville allowed customs officers to obtain general **writs of assistance.** These legal documents enabled the officers to search homes and warehouses for goods that might be smuggled. Many colonists considered Grenville's action as an outrageous abuse of power. They were horrified that government officials could come into their homes without warning.

The Sugar Act

Grenville next turned his attention to tax revenue. In 1764 Parliament passed the **Sugar Act** to stop the smuggling between the colonies and the French West Indies. The act lowered the tax on molasses imported by the colonists. The British hoped the lower tax would encourage colonists to pay the duty on foreign molasses. The British could then collect the tax on molasses and increase their revenues.

The Sugar Act also established special courts to hear smuggling cases. In these courts British-appointed judges, rather than juries, would decide whether accused smugglers were to be jailed. As British citizens, the colonists had enjoyed the right to a jury trial. But now, in the eyes of the colonists, the Sugar Act would take away this basic right.

These measures alarmed the colonists. Never before had their taxes been used to raise money for the British treasury. Leaders of New York's legislature declared, "There can be no liberty, no happiness, no security" with this interference in colonial life.

COOPERATIVE LEARNING ACTIVITY

Round-robin Brainstorming Organize the class into groups of five to seven students each. Ask one student in each group to write the following statement on a sheet of paper: *We must protest British taxes because* ____. Explain that everyone in the group should provide one answer—and that students should try not to be influenced by other responses on the page. Then have each group circulate the page with each member completing the statement as quickly as possible. Assign a secretary in each group to present the responses to the class. Afterward, discuss these questions:

- Which responses were based on fact? Which were more emotional?
- Which responses might you have heard most often from colonial Americans?

James Otis, a young lawyer in **Boston,** argued that colonists should not be taxed by Parliament because they could not vote for members of Parliament. Otis coined a memorable slogan for colonial protesters: "Taxation without representation is tyranny."

Economics

The Stamp Act

In 1765 Parliament passed another, even more disturbing, law in an effort to raise money for Britain. This law, the **Stamp Act,** placed a tax on almost all printed material in the colonies—everything from newspapers and pamphlets to wills and playing cards. All printed material had to have a stamp, which was applied by British colonial officials. Because the tax pertained to so many items, it affected everyone in the colonial cities. The Stamp Act was a terrible nuisance, but it also convinced many colonists of the need for united action.

Opposition to the Stamp Act focused on two points. Parliament had interfered in colonial affairs by taxing the colonies directly. In addition, it taxed the colonists without their consent. In passing the Stamp Act without consulting the colonial legislatures, Parliament ignored the colonial tradition of self-government.

Protesting the Stamp Act

A young member of the **Virginia** House of Burgesses, **Patrick Henry,** persuaded the burgesses to take action against the Stamp Act. When opponents accused him of treason, Henry replied, "If this be treason, make the most of it!" The Virginia assembly passed a resolution—a formal expression of opinion—declaring it had "the only and sole exclusive right and power to lay taxes" on its citizens.

Protest mounted in Boston as well. **Samuel Adams** helped start an organization called the **Sons of Liberty.** Members took to the streets to protest the Stamp Act. People in other cities also organized Sons of Liberty groups. Throughout the summer of 1765, protesters burned effigies—rag figures—representing unpopular tax collectors. They also ransacked and destroyed houses belonging to royal officials and marched through the streets shouting that only Americans had the right to tax Americans.

Revenue stamp

In the colonial cities, people refused to use the stamps. They urged merchants to boycott—refuse to buy—British and European goods in protest. Thousands of merchants, artisans, and farmers signed nonimportation agreements. In these agreements, they pledged not to import or use goods imported from Great Britain. As the boycott spread, British merchants lost so much business that they begged Parliament to repeal, or cancel, the Stamp Act.

In **New York** Major Thomas James, the officer in charge of the stamps, vowed to enforce the Stamp Act no matter what the consequences. The

Footnotes to History

Friendly Persuasion? The Sons of Liberty had an effective way of getting what they wanted from British officials. They merely sent a note asking: "What think you of . . . ten gallons of liquid tar [poured] on your [head]—with the feathers of a dozen wild geese laid over that to enliven your appearance? Your friends . . . THE COMMITTEE OF TARRING AND FEATHERING."

CHAPTER 5
Section 1, 133–137

NATIONAL GEOGRAPHIC SOCIETY

VIDEODISC
GTV: The American People: Fabric of a Nation

Side 1, Chapter 6
Title: *A New England?*
Subject: English ways dominate colonial life
Ask: **Why do you think the English way of life came to dominate the colonies?** *(Answers will vary but should reference the great number of English settlers versus French, German, Dutch, and so on.)*

Linking PAST & PRESENT

Friendly Persuasion? A threatening note such as the one from the Sons of Liberty might be handled differently today. It could be seen as terrorism, a crime to be prosecuted. Extra security forces might be assigned to the buildings and targets of the threats, and the police would probably investigate.

What?Where?When?Who?

The Liberty Tree In Boston the first effigy that protested the Stamp Act hung from an elm tree that was officially named *The Tree of Liberty* on August 14, 1765. The tree served as a rallying site for protesting Bostonians. Even after it was cut down, its remains were known as *The Liberty Stump.*

MULTIPLE LEARNING STYLES

Kinesthetic Between 1765 and 1767, British taxes affected many items that colonists used every day. Ask students to collect and display a variety of items that would have been taxed, first under the Stamp Act (for example, newspapers, stationery, and a deck of playing cards) and then under the Townshend Acts (for example, a glass pitcher and a tin of tea). Call on volunteers to pick up various items from the display. Have each volunteer describe the item and explain its importance. Have the student explain, as a protesting colonist might, why a tax on the item is unfair. **L1**

HISTORY AND ART Peter Rothermel also turned out paintings based on religious and literary themes. This work illustrates Rothermel's technique of combining sharp details with shadowy forms in a single painting. **Answer:** *Henry wanted the burgesses to formally oppose the Stamp Act.*

you don't say...

Boycott derives from Captain Charles C. Boycott, an English land agent in County Mayo, Ireland. His methods of collecting rent from the Irish tenants of the land were so harsh that in 1880 the Irish Land League decreed that Boycott be shunned, "isolated from his kind."

3 ASSESS

Assign Section 1 Review as homework or as an in-class activity.

Use **Chapter Challenger Interactive Review Software** to review Section 1.

Section Quiz 5-1

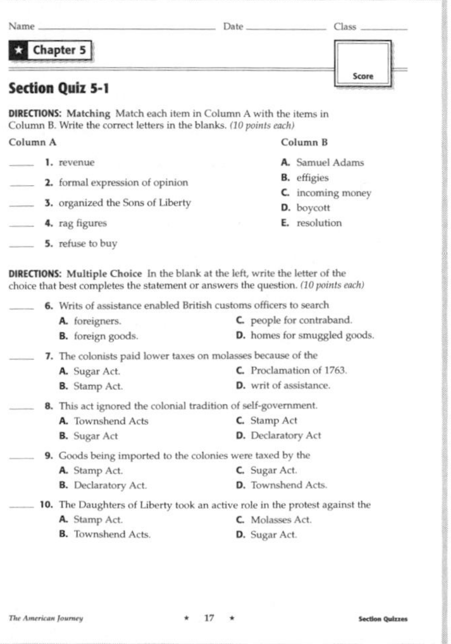

Name ______ Date ______ Class ______

Chapter 5 Score

Section Quiz 5-1

DIRECTIONS: Matching Match each item in Column A with the items in Column B. Write the correct letters in the blanks. *(10 points each)*

Column A	Column B
____ 1. revenue	A. Samuel Adams
____ 2. formal expression of opinion	B. effigies
____ 3. organized the Sons of Liberty	C. incoming money
____ 4. rag figures	D. boycott
____ 5. refuse to buy	E. resolution

DIRECTIONS: Multiple Choice In the blank at the left, write the letter of the choice that best completes the statement or answers the question. *(10 points each)*

____ 6. Writs of assistance enabled British customs officers to search
A. foreigners. C. people for contraband.
B. foreign goods. D. homes for smuggled goods.

____ 7. The colonists paid lower taxes on molasses because of the
A. Sugar Act. C. Proclamation of 1763.
B. Stamp Act. D. writ of assistance.

____ 8. This act ignored the colonial tradition of self-government.
A. Townshend Acts C. Stamp Act
B. Sugar Act D. Declaratory Act

____ 9. Goods being imported to the colonies were taxed by the
A. Stamp Act. C. Sugar Act.
B. Declaratory Act. D. Townshend Acts.

____ 10. The Daughters of Liberty took an active role in the protest against the
A. Stamp Act. C. Molasses Act.
B. Townshend Acts. D. Sugar Act.

The American Journey • 17 • Section Quizzes

HISTORY AND ART ***Patrick Henry Before the Virginia House of Burgesses* by Peter F. Rothermel** Patrick Henry gave a fiery speech before the Virginia House of Burgesses in 1765. **Why did Henry deliver the speech?**

consequences turned out to be a rampaging mob that raided his home. An observer reported:

> "The multitude burst open the doors, proceeded to destroy every individual article the house contained: the beds they cut open, and threw the feathers abroad; broke all the glasses, china, tables, chairs, desks, trunks, chests; made a large fire, [and] threw in everything that would burn."

Linking PAST & PRESENT

Boycotts

The boycott has served as a form of protest throughout our country's history. One successful boycott in the twentieth century was the 1955–56 bus boycott in Montgomery, Alabama. African Americans—40,000 a day—refused to ride the city-owned buses until the bus company stopped segregated seating.

In October delegates from nine colonies met in New York at the **Stamp Act Congress.** They drafted a petition to the king and Parliament declaring that the colonies could not be taxed except by their own assemblies.

Britain Repeals the Stamp Act

In February 1766, Parliament gave in to the colonists' demands and repealed the Stamp Act. Yet the colonists' trust in the king and Parliament was never fully restored.

While the colonists celebrated their victory over the Stamp Act, Parliament passed another act with far-reaching consequences. The **Declaratory Act** of 1766 stated that Parliament had the right to tax and make decisions for the British colonies "in all cases whatsoever." The colonists might have won one battle, but the war over making decisions for the colonies had just begun.

New Taxes

Soon after the Stamp Act crisis, a new British finance minister, **Charles Townshend,** made another attempt to raise money in the colonies. He thought he knew how to do this without creating another crisis.

The Townshend Acts

Under Townshend's leadership Parliament passed a set of laws in 1767 that came to be known as the **Townshend Acts.** In these acts the British leaders tried to avoid some of the problems the Stamp Act caused. They understood that the colonists would not tolerate internal taxes—those levied or paid inside the colonies. As a result the new taxes applied only to imported goods, with the tax being paid at the port of entry. The goods taxed, however, included basic items—such as

MAKING CONNECTIONS ACTIVITY

Politics The Sugar Act, the Stamp Act, and the Townshend Acts show the power of the British Parliament in making laws. Ask students to find out more about this governing body. The following questions can guide research:

- If Britain has a monarchy, why does it also have a parliament?
- How can a person become a member of Parliament?
- What is the difference between the House of Lords and the House of Commons?
- How does parliament work with the monarchy to make laws for Britain?

Provide classroom time to share information. **L2**

glass, tea, paper, and lead—that the colonists had to import because they did not produce them.

New courts were set up to try cases under the Townshend Acts. Some of the tax revenue was to go to pay for these courts. The British authorities planned also to use this revenue to pay the British governors in the colonies. In the past, the governors had been paid by the colonial local assemblies, supported by various taxes paid by the colonists. Under the new plan, the British, not the local assemblies, would pay the governors. The colonists would lose this means of controlling the British officials.

By this time the colonists were outraged by *any* taxes Parliament imposed. They believed that only their own representatives had the right to levy taxes on them. The colonists responded by reviving the boycott that had worked so well against the Stamp Act. The boycott proved to be even more widespread this time.

Picturing HISTORY To protest the Stamp Act, angry colonists burned stamps in the streets. **What group formed in Boston to lead opposition to the act?**

Colonial Women Organize Protests

Women took an active role in the protest against the Townshend Acts. In towns throughout the colonies, women organized groups to support the boycott of British goods, sometimes calling themselves the **Daughters of Liberty.** They urged Americans to wear homemade fabrics and produce other goods that were previously available only from Britain. In this way, they believed, the American colonies could become economically independent.

Section 1 Review

Checking for Understanding

1. ***Identify*** George Grenville, Sugar Act, Boston, Stamp Act, Virginia, Patrick Henry, Samuel Adams, Sons of Liberty, New York, Townshend Acts, Daughters of Liberty.
2. ***Define*** revenue, writs of assistance, resolution, effigy, boycott, nonimportation, repeal.
3. ***State*** two reasons that relations between the British and the colonists began to deteriorate.

Reviewing Themes

4. **Civic Rights and Responsibilities** Why did the colonists think the writs of assistance infringed on their rights?

Critical Thinking

5. **Identifying Cause and Effect** Why did the British think the colonists would tolerate the Townshend Acts when they did not tolerate the Stamp Act?

Activity

Making a Poster Design a poster that encourages colonists to boycott British goods.

Section 1 Review Answers

1. Grenville, Sugar Act, 134; Boston, Stamp Act, Virginia, Henry, Adams, Sons of Liberty, New York, 135; Townshend Acts, 136; Daughters of Liberty, 137
2. The words are defined in the Glossary.
3. Colonists felt the Proclamation of 1763 restricted freedom; they did not want to pay for French and Indian War, did not believe in taxation without representation, and were alarmed by British troops stationed in the colonies
4. They thought it was an abuse of power for government officials to be allowed to enter their homes without warning.
5. Townshend Acts taxed only imported goods, but the Stamp Act taxed products made and used in the colonies.

Activity Posters should encourage boycotts.

CHAPTER 5
Section 1, 133–137

Picturing HISTORY Because there was no guarantee that violent actions would be stopped, protests such as this persuaded many stamp agents to resign.
Answer: *the Sons of Liberty*

Reteaching Activity 5–1

Name ______ Date ______ Class ______

★ Reteaching Activity 5-1

DIRECTIONS: Putting Events in Sequence Number the events in the order in which they occurred. Write the same number for the three events that occurred simultaneously.

____ **A.** Parliament passes the Townshend Acts.
____ **B.** Samuel Adams helps start the Sons of Liberty.
____ **C.** Parliament passes the Sugar Act.
____ **D.** Parliament passes the Declaratory Act.
____ **E.** George Grenville takes action against colonial smuggling.
____ **F.** Thousands of merchants, artisans, and farmers sign nonimportation agreements.
____ **G.** Parliament passes the Stamp Act.
____ **H.** Patrick Henry persuades the Virginia assembly to pass a resolution declaring the state has the exclusive right to tax its citizens.
____ **I.** Britain passes a proclamation that limits westward expansion.
____ **J.** Women organize groups called the Daughters of Liberty.
____ **K.** Delegates from nine colonies meet at the Stamp Act Congress.

DIRECTIONS: Essay Answer the following questions.

1. What was the main reason Great Britain enacted the Sugar Act, the Stamp Act, the Declaratory Act, and the Townshend Acts, and what was the main reason the colonists opposed the acts? ______
2. How did the colonists force the British government to repeal the various taxation acts enacted between 1764 and 1767? ______

The American Journey ★ 17 ★ **Reteaching Activities**

Enrichment Activity 5–1

Name ______ Date ______ Class ______

★ Enrichment Activity 5-1

Call to Action

ADVERTISEMENT

THE Members of the Affociation of the Sons of Liberty, are requefted to meet at the City-Hall, at one o'Clock, To-morrow, (being Friday) on Bufinefs of the utmoft Importance;—And every other Friend to the Liberties, and Trade of America, are hereby moft cordially invited, to meet at the fame Time and Place. *The Committee of the Affociation.*

Thurfday, NEW-YORK, 16th December, 1773.

DIRECTIONS: Using Information Answer the following questions.

1. Who signed the advertisement? (Remember that the colonial letter *s* sometimes looks like the letter *f*.) ______
2. Why do you think the announcement is called an advertisement? ______
3. What does the advertisement request? ______
4. Why is the phrase "(being Friday)" included? ______
5. Who is invited besides the members of the Sons of Liberty? ______
6. What is the time, date, and place of the meeting? ______

Activity **DIRECTIONS:** The style of posters has changed since 1773. Using the poster or advertisement above as a starting point, update the poster to appeal to today's audiences. Use color, illustrations, and modern language in your poster.

The American Journey ★ 17 ★ **Enrichment Activities**

4 CLOSE

Ask students which British taxation law they consider the most objectionable and why.

CHAPTER 5
Section 2, 138–141

1 FOCUS

BELLRINGER
Motivational Activity

Before taking roll at the beginning of the class period, project Section Focus Transparency 5–2 and have students answer the questions. Discuss students' responses.

This activity is also available as a blackline master.

Section Focus Transparency 5–2

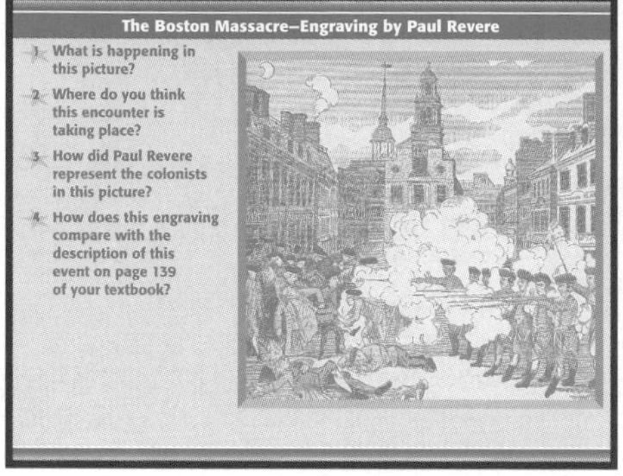

Vocabulary Precheck
Ask a student to read aloud the definition of the term *propaganda* from the textbook glossary. Have another student use the term in a sentence.

Use the **Vocabulary Puzzle-Maker** to create crossword and word search puzzles.

Section Theme
Groups and Institutions
Colonists banded together to protest increasingly strict methods of control by Great Britain.

Activity Have students jot down some things they would be willing to give up for the sake of freedom. Volunteers may share examples of material or other kinds of sacrifices they feel most people would be willing to make.

1770 — 1773 — 1776

1770 Boston Massacre takes place

1772 Samuel Adams sets up committee of correspondence

1773 Boston Tea Party occurs

1774 Parliament passes the Intolerable Acts

Section 2

Building Colonial Unity

READ TO DISCOVER . . .
- why Boston colonists and British soldiers clashed in the Boston Massacre.
- how the British government tried to maintain its control over the colonies.

TERMS TO LEARN
propaganda
committee of correspondence

The Storyteller

In the summer of 1768, British customs officials in Boston seized the *Liberty,* a ship belonging to John Hancock, a prominent merchant and protest leader. The ship had docked in Boston Harbor to unload a shipment of wine and take on new supplies. The customs officials, however, charged that Hancock was using the ship for smuggling. As news of the ship's seizure spread through Boston, angry townspeople filled the streets. They shouted against Parliament and the taxes it had imposed on them.

The *Liberty* affair became one of the events that united the colonists against British policies.

American protest banner

In the summer of 1768, nervous customs officers sent word back to Britain that the colonies were on the brink of rebellion. Parliament responded by ordering two regiments of troops to Boston. On October 1, 1768, a fleet of British ships sailed into **Boston Harbor** and docked. Seven hundred soldiers in red uniforms filed out of the ships with "muskets charged, bayonets fixed, colours flying, drums beating and fifes playing." As angry Bostonians jeered, the "redcoats" marched right into the center of the city and set up camp.

Trouble in Boston

Many colonists, especially those living in Boston, felt that the British had pushed them too far. First the British had passed a series of laws that violated colonial rights. Now they sent an army to occupy colonial cities.

Tension Grows

To make matters worse, the soldiers who were stationed in Boston acted rudely and sometimes even violently toward the colonists. Mostly poor men from Ireland, Scotland, and rural England, the redcoats earned little pay. Some of them stole goods from local shops or scuffled with boys who taunted them in the streets. The soldiers competed off-hours for jobs that Bostonians wanted. Fights broke out between redcoats and Bostonians. The townspeople's hatred for the soldiers grew every day.

SECTION RESOURCES

Reproducible Masters
- Reproducible Lesson Plan 5–2
- Guided Reading Activity 5–2
- Section Quiz 5–2
- Reteaching Activity 5–2
- Enrichment Activity 5–2

Transparencies
- Section Focus Transparency 5–2

Multimedia
- Vocabulary PuzzleMaker
- Chapter Challenger Interactive Review Software
- Testmaker
- GTV: A Geographic Perspective on American History
- Facts On File: Landmark Documents in American History

Eyewitness to HISTORY

The Boston Massacre

Throughout the next year, the tense atmosphere between the redcoats and the Boston colonists grew. On March 5, 1770, the tension finally reached a peak.

That day a fight broke out between townspeople and soldiers. This spurred the crowd on. While some British officers tried to calm the crowd, a man shouted, "We did not send for you. We will not have you here. We'll get rid of you, we'll drive you away!"

The angry townspeople moved on through the streets, picking up sticks, stones, shovels, and clubs—any weapon they could find. They pushed forward toward the customshouse on King Street.

As the crowd approached, the sentry on duty panicked and called for help. Seven soldiers stationed nearby rushed into the street to confront the raging crowd. The crowd responded by throwing stones, snowballs, oyster shells, and pieces of wood at the soldiers. "Fire, you bloodybacks, you lobsters," the crowd screamed. "You dare not fire."

After one of the soldiers was knocked down, the nervous and confused redcoats did fire. Seven shots rang out, killing five colonists. One Bostonian cried out: "Are the inhabitants to be knocked down in the streets? Are they to be murdered in this manner?" Among the dead was **Crispus Attucks,** an African American dockworker who some said was the leader of the crowd. The colonists called the tragic encounter the **Boston Massacre.**

The Word Spreads

Colonial leaders used the killings as **propaganda**—information designed to influence opinion—against the British. Samuel Adams put up posters describing the "Boston Massacre" as a slaughter of innocent Americans by bloodthirsty redcoats. An engraving by **Paul Revere** showed a British officer giving the order to open fire on an orderly crowd. Nearly every colonist in Boston saw copies of the engraving. The powerful image inflamed anti-British feeling.

The Boston Massacre led many colonists to call for stronger boycotts on British goods. Aware of the growing opposition to its policies, Parliament repealed all the Townshend Acts taxes except the one on tea. Many colonists believed they had won another victory. They ended their boycotts, except on the taxed tea, and started to trade with British merchants again.

Some colonial leaders, however, continued to call for resistance to British rule. In 1772 Samuel Adams revived the Boston **committee of correspondence,** an organization used in earlier protests. The committee circulated writings about colonists' grievances against Britain. Soon other

Restrictions on Colonial Trade, 1650–1750

Acts	Restrictions
Navigation Acts 1650, 1651, 1660–1661, 1696	Only English-owned and -crewed ships could carry on colonial trade. Tobacco, cotton, indigo, and other colonial products could be sent only to England. Colonial trade laws had to agree with the Navigation Acts.
Woolen Act 1699	Prohibited the colonial exports of wool or wool products.
Hat Act 1732	Prohibited the exporting of hats from one colony to another.
Molasses Act 1733	Levied a large duty on foreign sugar, molasses, and rum.
Iron Act 1750	Prohibited building of new colonial iron plants. Prohibited colonial import duties on iron bought from Britain.

Chart Study

British trade acts affected many American products.

1. Which trade act dealt with food products?
2. **Drawing Conclusions** Which trade act was passed to protect the British sheep-farming industry?

CHAPTER 5

Section 2, 138–141

2 TEACH

L1, ELL Interpreting Symbols Direct students' attention to the flag on page 138. **Ask:** **Why wouldn't you want to step on a snake?** *(It could bite you.)* **Why might this flag be a warning to Britain?** *(It might be telling Britain to leave the colonies alone or risk some sort of violent response.)*

Chart Study

Answers

1. the Molasses Act
2. the Woolen Act

Chart Skills Practice

Reading a Chart Which act tried to restrict trade between the colonies? *(the Hat Act)*

Guided Reading Activity 5–2

Name ____ Date ____ Class ____

★ Guided Reading Activity 5-2

DIRECTIONS: Outlining Read the section and complete the outline below. Refer to your textbook to fill in the blanks.

I. Trouble in Boston

- **A.** When ____ set up camp in Boston in 1768, the colonists were angry because it seemed a foreign army had invaded Boston.
- **B. Eyewitness to History** The tension exploded on ____ when a fight broke out. An angry crowd threw items at the soldiers.
- **C. Eyewitness to History** The nervous soldiers fired into the crowd. Five colonists were killed, including ____, an African American dockworker.
- **D. Eyewitness to History** The colonists called the encounter ____.
- **E.** An engraving by ____ showed a British officer giving the order to open fire on an orderly crowd.
- **F.** Parliament repealed all the ____ except the one on tea.
- **G.** In 1772 Samuel Adams revived the ____.

II. A Crisis over Tea

- **A.** In 1773 Parliament passed ____, which gave the East India Company a ____.
- **B.** Colonists vowed to stop the East India Company's ships from ____.
- **C.** In every port except ____, colonists forced the ships' captains to turn around and go back to Great Britain.
- **D.** On December 16 a group of colonists, disguised as Mohawks, boarded the ships docked in Boston and threw 342 chests of ____ overboard.

III. The Intolerable Acts

- **A.** King ____ and Parliament vowed to ____.
- **B.** Parliament passed the ____ in 1774, which closed Boston Harbor until the colonists paid for the ____. The laws also prohibited most ____ and forced Bostonians to shelter soldiers in their homes.
- **C.** Other colonies sent ____ to show support.

COOPERATIVE LEARNING ACTIVITY

Preparing a News Report Have students imagine themselves as television reporters covering the Boston Massacre. Student reports should focus on differentiating between facts and propaganda. Coverage could include the following:

- A report about how the event came to happen, including eyewitness accounts
- An interview with a friend of Crispus Attucks's
- Use of Paul Revere's engraving of the event
- Two editorials—one by a British officer, the other by Samuel Adams

Various roles to be assigned or selected by students include writers, interviewers, illustrator, program host, and so on.

you don't say...

Redcoats was the name Patriots used to describe British soldiers. Patriots also called the British "bloodybacks" and "lobsters" to ridicule their bright red uniforms.

CHAPTER 5
Section 2, 138–141

NATIONAL GEOGRAPHIC SOCIETY

VIDEODISC
GTV: A Geographic Perspective on American History

Side 1, Chapter 15
Title: *Laying Down the Law*
Subject: The rise of revolutionary feelings (1757–1776)
Ask: **Why did colonists object to British taxes?** *(because they had no voice in the government that taxed them)*

3 ASSESS

Assign Section 2 Review as homework or as an in-class activity.

Use **Chapter Challenger Interactive Review Software** to review Section 2.

Section Quiz 5–2

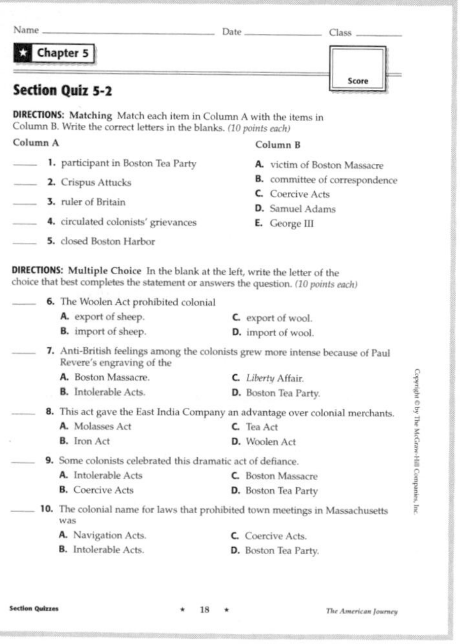

Name ______ Date ______ Class ______

Chapter 5 Score

Section Quiz 5-2

DIRECTIONS: Matching Match each item in Column A with the items in Column B. Write the correct letters in the blanks. *(10 points each)*

Column A	Column B
____ 1. participant in Boston Tea Party	A. victim of Boston Massacre
____ 2. Crispus Attucks	B. committee of correspondence
____ 3. ruler of Britain	C. Coercive Acts
____ 4. circulated colonists' grievances	D. Samuel Adams
____ 5. closed Boston Harbor	E. George III

DIRECTIONS: Multiple Choice In the blank at the left, write the letter of the choice that best completes the statement or answers the question. *(10 points each)*

____ 6. The Woolen Act prohibited colonial
A. export of sheep. C. export of wool.
B. import of sheep. D. import of wool.

____ 7. Anti-British feelings among the colonists grew more intense because of Paul Revere's engraving of the
A. Boston Massacre. C. *Liberty* Affair.
B. Intolerable Acts. D. Boston Tea Party.

____ 8. This act gave the East India Company an advantage over colonial merchants.
A. Molasses Act C. Tea Act
B. Iron Act D. Woolen Act

____ 9. Some colonists celebrated this dramatic act of defiance.
A. Intolerable Acts C. Boston Massacre
B. Coercive Acts D. Boston Tea Party

____ 10. The colonial name for laws that prohibited town meetings in Massachusetts was
A. Navigation Acts. C. Coercive Acts.
B. Intolerable Acts. D. Boston Tea Party.

Section Quizzes ★ 18 ★ *The American Journey*

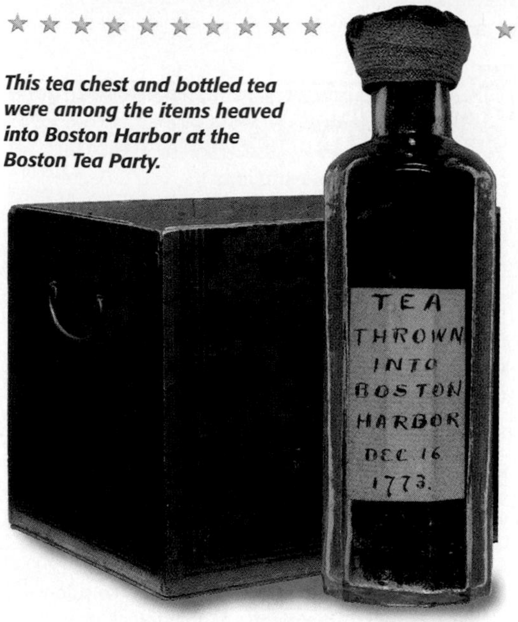

This tea chest and bottled tea were among the items heaved into Boston Harbor at the Boston Tea Party.

committees of correspondence sprang up throughout the colonies, bringing together protesters opposed to British measures.

A Crisis over Tea

In the early 1770s, some Americans considered British colonial policy a "conspiracy against liberty." The British government's actions in 1773 seemed to confirm that view.

The British East India Company had acquired much more tea than it could sell in Great Britain. If it could not sell the extra tea, it faced ruin. For both economic and political reasons, the British government wanted to keep the company in business.

To save the East India Company, Parliament passed the **Tea Act** of 1773. This measure gave the company the right to ship tea to the colonies without paying the taxes colonial tea merchants had to pay. This would allow the company to sell its tea very cheaply and eventually lure the colonists to pay the tea tax. The Tea Act gave the East India Company a very favorable advantage over colonial merchants.

Colonial Demands

Colonial merchants immediately called for a new boycott on British goods. Samuel Adams and others denounced the British monopoly. The Tea Act, they exclaimed, was just another attempt to crush the colonists' liberty.

At mass meetings in Boston and Philadelphia, colonists vowed to stop the East India Company's ships from unloading. The Daughters of Liberty issued a pamphlet declaring that rather than part with freedom, "we'll part with our tea." Women in Wilmington, North Carolina, marched solemnly through town and burned their tea.

Although some British politicians warned of another crisis with the colonies, Parliament ignored the warnings. The East India Company loaded its ships with the tea and set sail for America. In all colonial ports except Boston, colonists forced the ships' captains to turn around and go back to Great Britain.

The Boston Tea Party

Three tea ships docked in Boston Harbor in December 1773. The royal governor, whose house had been destroyed by Stamp Act protesters, refused to let the ships turn back. When he ordered the tea unloaded, Adams and the Boston Sons of Liberty acted swiftly. On December 16 a group of men disguised as Mohawks and armed with hatchets marched to the wharves. At midnight they boarded the ships and threw 342 chests of tea overboard, an event that became known as the **Boston Tea Party.**

Word of this dramatic act of defiance spread throughout the colonies. Men and women poured into the streets to celebrate the Boston Sons of Liberty for boldly championing the colonial cause. Yet no one spoke of challenging British rule, and colonial leaders continued to press their claims as members of the British empire.

Footnotes to History

Tough Defense John Adams, who would become America's second president, served as a defense attorney for the British soldiers accused in the Boston Massacre.

MULTIPLE LEARNING STYLES

Interpersonal Colonists persuaded the captains of almost all of the East India Company ships that arrived in American ports loaded with tea to turn back. Ask students with strong interpersonal skills to write or speak what they think a colonist might have said to influence one of these ship's captains. You might offer this first statement to get students thinking: "Captain, you may not realize what this tea means to us in the colonies. . . ." You also may wish to have the class vote for the most persuasive argument. Interested students might enjoy turning this activity into a skit for classroom performance. **L2**

The Intolerable Acts

When news of the Boston Tea Party reached London, the reaction was quite different. King **George III** realized that Britain was losing control of the colonies. "We must master them or leave them to themselves." Not prepared to give up, the king and Parliament vowed to punish Boston.

Lord North, the British prime minister, decided to make an example of Massachusetts. In the spring of 1774, Parliament passed the **Coercive Acts,** very harsh laws intended to make Massachusetts pay for its resistance.

Punishing Boston

The Coercive Acts closed Boston Harbor until the Massachusetts colonists paid for the ruined tea. This action prevented the arrival of food and other supplies that normally came by ship. Even worse the laws took away many of the rights of the Massachusetts colonists. For example, the laws prohibited most town meetings, an important form of self-government in New England.

As a final insult, the Coercive Acts forced Bostonians to shelter soldiers in their own homes. The British Parliament wished to isolate Boston with these acts. Instead the other colonies sent food and clothing to demonstrate their support for Boston. The feelings of the colonists were made clear by *their* name for the new laws—the Intolerable Acts.

HISTORY AND ART ***King George III* by Johann Zoffany** An energetic leader, George III strongly opposed any compromise with the American colonists. **How did George III and Parliament respond to news of the Boston Tea Party?**

Section 2 Review

Checking for Understanding

1. ***Identify*** Boston Harbor, Crispus Attucks, Boston Massacre, Paul Revere, Boston Tea Party, George III, Coercive Acts.
2. ***Define*** propaganda, committee of correspondence.
3. ***Explain*** how colonial leaders used the Boston Massacre to their advantage.

Reviewing Themes

4. **Groups and Institutions** Why were the committees of correspondence powerful?

Critical Thinking

5. **Drawing Conclusions** Why do you think some saw the Boston Tea Party as a turning point in the relationship between the British and the colonists?

Activity

Drawing a Cartoon Draw a cartoon strip showing the story of the Boston Tea Party. Use at least four cartoon frames to tell the story from your point of view.

Section 2 Review Answers

1. Boston Harbor, 138; Crispus Attucks, 139; Boston Massacre, 139; Paul Revere, 139; Boston Tea Party, 140; George III, 141; Coercive Acts, 141
2. The words are defined in the Glossary.
3. The event was used as propaganda to drum up support against the British.
4. They spread political ideas and united opponents to British rule.
5. Students should mention that the Boston Tea Party represented a dramatic act of defiance by the colonists. Many colonists celebrated this bold move and pressed their claims as British citizens.

Activity Cartoon strips should show the sequence of events during the Boston Tea Party and present a clearly pro-Patriot or pro-British point of view.

HISTORY AND ART The German-born Zoffany (1733–1810) gained fame in England by painting scenes from plays. **Answer:** *They vowed to punish the rebels and passed the Coercive Acts.*

Reteaching Activity 5–2

Name ______ Date ______ Class ______

★ Reteaching Activity 5-2

DIRECTIONS: Matching Match each item in Column A with its corresponding item in Column B. Write the correct letters in the blanks.

COLUMN A	COLUMN B
____ 1. Daughters of Liberty	A. inflamed anti-British feelings with an engraving of the Boston Massacre
____ 2. March 5, 1770	B. passed by Parliament in 1773, it excused East India Company from paying tea taxes
____ 3. Lord North	C. vowed to punish Boston
____ 4. the Intolerable Acts	D. revived in 1772 by Samuel Adams
____ 5. Samuel Adams	E. acted rudely and sometimes violently toward the colonists
____ 6. the Tea Act	F. colonists' name for the laws passed in 1774 that took away many of the Massachusetts colonists' rights
____ 7. Boston committee of correspondence	G. put up posters describing the Boston Massacre as a slaughter
____ 8. King George III	H. passed by Parliament in 1774, it closed Boston Harbor, prohibited town meetings, and forced Bostonians to shelter soldiers in their homes
____ 9. the Coercive Acts	I. the Boston Massacre
____ 10. Paul Revere	J. urged American women to give up tea
____ 11. redcoats	K. British prime minister
____ 12. December 16, 1773	L. the Boston Tea Party

DIRECTIONS: Essay Answer the following question.

How did many colonists react to the Boston Tea Party? ______

Reteaching Activities ★ 18 ★ *The American Journey*

Enrichment Activity 5–2

Name ______ Date ______ Class ______

★ Enrichment Activity 5-2 ★ ★

A Young Poet

Phillis Wheatley, born in about 1753, gained fame for her poetry when she was just a teenager. Wheatley sent this poem to William Legge, secretary of state for North America.

DIRECTIONS: Interpreting a Historical Poem Read the excerpt and answer the following questions.

Should you, my lord, while you peruse my song,
Wonder from whence my love of freedom sprung, . . .
I, young in life, by seeming cruel fate
Was snatch'd from Afric's fancied happy seat:
What pangs excruciating must molest,
What sorrow labour in my parent's breast?
Steeled was that soul and by no misery moved,
That from a father seized his babe beloved:
Such, such my case. And can I then but pray
Others may never feel tyrannic sway?

1. To whom does "my lord" refer? ______
2. Where is Wheatley from and what was her life like there? ______
3. How, when, and under what circumstances did she come to America? ______
4. What disturbed her most about coming to America? ______
5. Who had a "steeled soul" that was not moved by misery? ______
6. In the poem how did she connect her experience with her view of life? ______

Activity **DIRECTIONS: Applying Ideas** Write a poem or personal narrative to present to your class as a dramatic reading. Use issues that may have appealed to Phillis Wheatley such as freedom, equality, and separation from home and family, but give these ideas your own interpretation.

Enrichment Activities ★ 18 ★ *The American Journey*

4 CLOSE

Discuss how Britain tried to control the colonies by isolating them.

1 FOCUS

BELLRINGER
Motivational Activity

Before taking roll at the beginning of the class period, project Section Focus Transparency 5–3 and have students answer the questions. Discuss students' responses.

This activity is also available as a blackline master.

Section Focus Transparency 5–3

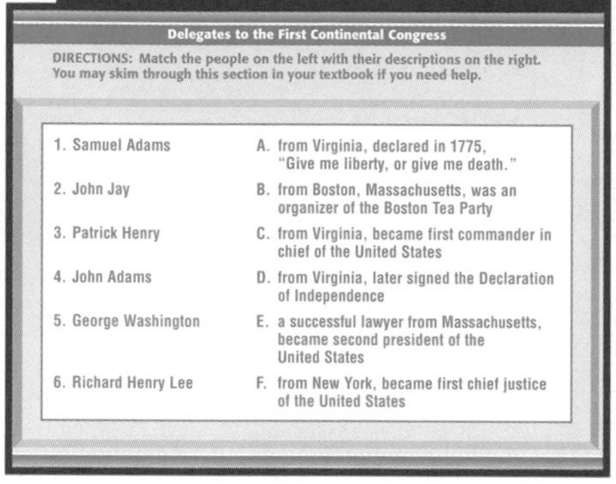

Delegates to the First Continental Congress

DIRECTIONS: Match the people on the left with their descriptions on the right. You may skim through this section in your textbook if you need help.

1. Samuel Adams	A. from Virginia, declared in 1775, "Give me liberty, or give me death."
2. John Jay	B. from Boston, Massachusetts, was an organizer of the Boston Tea Party
3. Patrick Henry	C. from Virginia, became first commander in chief of the United States
4. John Adams	D. from Virginia, later signed the Declaration of Independence
5. George Washington	E. a successful lawyer from Massachusetts, became second president of the United States
6. Richard Henry Lee	F. from New York, became first chief justice of the United States

Vocabulary Precheck
Have students demonstrate their understanding of the terms *Loyalist* and *Patriot* by using each term in a sentence about that group's beliefs or actions.

Use the **Vocabulary Puzzle-Maker** to create crossword and word search puzzles.

Section Theme
Groups and Institutions
With the establishment of the Continental Congress, the colonies continued to protest. At the same time, they prepared for war.

Activity Have students think about British policies in the colonies. **Ask:** How could the colonists avoid a war? *(Answers should include the idea of accepting the current British policies.)* Discuss the responses.

1774 — 1775 — 1776

1774 First Continental Congress meets

April 19, 1775 Battles of Lexington and Concord are fought

May 10, 1775 Ethan Allen captures Fort Ticonderoga

June 17, 1775 Battle of Bunker Hill is fought

Section 3

A Call to Arms

READ TO DISCOVER . . .
- what happened at the Continental Congress in Philadelphia.
- how the colonists met British soldiers in the first resort to arms.

TERMS TO LEARN
militia
minutemen
Loyalist
Patriot

The Storyteller

At first few colonists wanted a complete break with Britain. One of the most popular songs of the time, "The Bold Americans," called for *both* liberty and continued loyalty to the British king:

We'll honor George, our sovereign, while he sits on the throne.
If he grants us liberty, no other king we'll own.
If he will grant us liberty, so plainly shall you see,
We are the boys that fear no noise! Success to liberty.

As tensions mounted, however, a peaceful compromise no longer was possible.

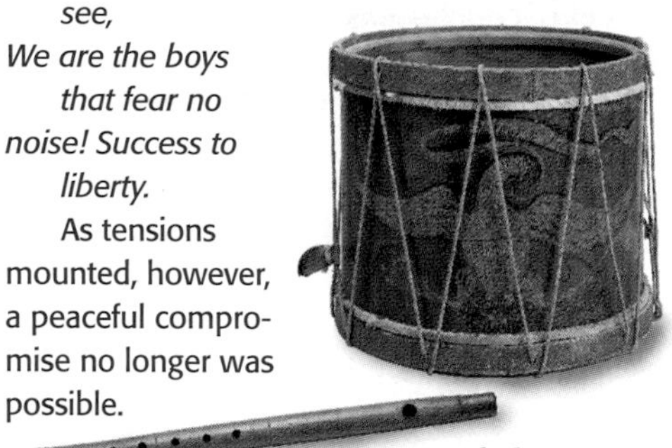

Revolutionary War drum and fife

With the passage of the Intolerable Acts, the colonial leaders realized that they must be more vigorous in protesting the abuses from their British rulers. The outpouring of sympathy for Bostonians demonstrated that the people wanted them to continue resisting new taxes. Bostonians vowed to boycott all British goods, but something new was needed—a gathering of the colonial leaders. From Massachusetts to Virginia, word spread through the committees of correspondence: the colonies must unite in protest or lose their liberties.

Citizenship

The Continental Congress

In September 1774, 56 men arrived in Philadelphia. Sent as delegates from all the colonies except Georgia, these men had come to establish a political body to represent the American interests. They called the new organization the **Continental Congress.**

Delegates to the Congress

Major political leaders from all the colonies attended the Congress. Massachusetts sent fiery Samuel Adams and his younger cousin **John Adams,** a successful lawyer. New York sent **John Jay,** another lawyer. From Virginia came **Richard Henry Lee** and **Patrick Henry,** two of the most outspoken defenders of colonial rights, as well as **George Washington.**

SECTION RESOURCES

Reproducible Masters
- Reproducible Lesson Plan 5–3
- Guided Reading Activity 5–3
- Section Quiz 5–3
- Reteaching Activity 5–3
- Enrichment Activity 5–3

Transparencies
- Section Focus Transparency 5–3

Multimedia
- Vocabulary PuzzleMaker
- Chapter Challenger Interactive Review Software
- Testmaker
- ABCNews InterActive™ Historic America Electronic Field Trips
- Facts On File: Landmark Documents in American History

Patrick Henry summed up the meaning of the gathering. "The distinctions between Virginians, Pennsylvanians, New Yorkers, and New Englanders are no more," he said. "I am not a Virginian, but an American."

Decisions of the Congress

Although the delegates were hardly united in their views, they managed to work together in behalf of their common interests. First they drafted a statement of grievances calling for the repeal of 13 acts of Parliament passed since 1763. They declared that these laws violated the colonists' rights. Their rights were based on the "laws of nature, the principles of the English constitution, and the several charters" of the colonies. The delegates also voted to boycott all British goods and trade. No British products could be brought into or consumed in the colonies, and no colonial goods could be shipped to Britain.

Perhaps the most important decision the Congress made concerned armed opposition to Britain. After much debate the delegates passed a resolution to form **militias,** groups of citizen soldiers. If fighting broke out, the colonies would be ready with their own armed forces. People in the colonies and in Britain wondered whether this meant war. The answer came soon after the Continental Congress adjourned in October.

Causes and Effects

CAUSES

★ Colonists' tradition of self-government
★ Americans' desire for a separate identity from Britain
★ Proclamation of 1763
★ British policies toward North America after 1763

Colonies Declare Independence

EFFECTS

★ A long war with Great Britain
★ Self-government for the United States
★ World recognition of United States independence

Chart Study

The conflict between Britain and America worsened after passage of the Intolerable Acts of 1774.
Analyzing Information What did the British learn after the Battle of Bunker Hill?

The First Battles

★ Colonists expected that if fighting against the British broke out, it would begin in New England. Militia companies in Massachusetts held frequent training sessions, made bullets, and stockpiled rifles and muskets. Some companies, known as **minutemen,** boasted they would be ready to fight on a minute's notice. In the winter of 1774–1775, a British officer stationed in Boston noted in his diary: "The people are evidently making every preparation for resistance. They are taking every means to provide themselves with arms."

Footnotes to History

Midnight Ride In 1861 poet Henry Wadsworth Longfellow described Paul Revere's ride: *"Listen, my children, and you shall hear/ Of the midnight ride of Paul Revere."* For Longfellow, the ride marked a momentous event in the nation's history. *"The fate of a nation was riding that night;/ And the spark struck out by that steed in his flight,/ Kindled the land into flame with its heat."*

CHAPTER 5
Section 3, 142–146

2 TEACH

L1, ELL Responding to a Quote Have a volunteer read aloud the comment from Patrick Henry at the top of page 143. Discuss why it would be important for his opinion to be widely held if the Patriot cause were to succeed.

Chart Study

Answer
The British learned that defeating the Americans would not be quick or easy.

Chart Skills Practice

Reading a Chart Which cause do you think was the most persuasive in motivating the colonists to declare their independence? *(Students may suggest that the desire for a separate identity was more powerful than any particular event.)*

Guided Reading Activity 5–3

Name ______ Date ______ Class ______

★ Guided Reading Activity **5-3**

DIRECTIONS: Filling in the Blanks In the space provided, write the word or words that best complete the sentence. Refer to your textbook to fill in the blanks.

1. **Citizenship** Delegates from every colony except ______ attended the Continental Congress in September 1774.
2. **Citizenship** The most important decision delegates made concerned armed opposition to Great Britain. A resolution was passed to form ______.
3. Well-prepared militia companies in Massachusetts were known as ______.
4. General Thomas Gage ordered ______ and his troops to ______ to destroy all the artillery and ammunition.
5. When Dr. Joseph Warren saw British troops march out of Boston on ______, he rushed to alert ______ and William Dawes.
6. Revere and Dawes then rode to Lexington to warn Samuel Adams and ______.
7. **Eyewitness to History** In Lexington the redcoats came across a group of ______, and the fight for independence began.
8. **Eyewitness to History** Along the road from Concord to ______, colonists fired at the British, wounding 200 and killing 73.
9. On May 10, 1775, a small group of New Englanders, known as ______, led by ______ captured the British ______ at Lake Champlain.
10. Committees of correspondence sent out calls for ______ to join the militias.
11. In June 1775 redcoats charged militia members on ______. The colonists ran out of ______ and withdrew, but the British suffered heavy losses.
12. The ______ did not consider unfair taxes and regulations sufficient cause for rebellion.
13. The ______ were determined to fight for independence.

The American Journey ★ 19 ★ **Guided Reading Activities**

Cooperative Learning Activity

Reviewing the Sides Organize the class into two teams—one to represent the First Continental Congress, the other to represent Parliament. Have students in both groups choose one of the following tasks:

- Summarize the group's feelings about the conflict
- Identify the basis for those feelings
- Outline the group's plan of action
- Explain how they demonstrated the plan at Lexington, Concord, and Bunker Hill

Students should divide work according to their skills and abilities. Students can research, write, prepare speeches, or illustrate concepts. Have them present their findings as a section review.

When?Who?What?Where?

Patriots' Day, a public holiday in Massachusetts, marks the defeat of the British at Lexington and Concord in 1775. First held on April 19—the day of the battles—Patriots' Day is now celebrated on the third Monday in April. Since 1897 the Boston Marathon, a race that attracts runners from all over the world, has been a major part of the celebrations. The route of the race generally follows the route taken by the British in their retreat.

Facts On File

CD-ROM
Landmark Documents in American History

Title: *"Give Me Liberty" Speech, Patrick Henry, 1775*
Ask students to imagine they are burgesses listening to Henry's speech. Have them summarize their reactions to Henry's powerful words.

Map Study

Answers
1. Lexington
2. about 6–7 miles

Map Skills Practice

Reading a Map From which town did both Revere and Dawes head northwest toward Lexington? *(Menotomy)*

Who?What?Where?When?

The Green Mountain Boys Best known for their capture of Fort Ticonderoga, the Green Mountain Boys first gained fame in 1770. In that year, under the leadership of Ethan and Levi Allen, they fought the settlement of Green Mountain land by settlers from New York.

Britain Sends Troops

The British, also, prepared for conflict. George III announced to Parliament that the New England colonies were "in a state of rebellion" and said that "blows must decide" who would control America. By April 1775, British general Sir Thomas Gage had 3,000 soldiers under his command in and around Boston, with many more on the way. Gage had instructions to take away the weapons of the Massachusetts militia and arrest the leaders of the colony's resistance movement.

Gage learned that the militia was storing arms and ammunition at **Concord,** a town 20 miles northwest of Boston. He ordered 700 troops under Major John Pitcairn to move out of Boston "to Concord, where you will seize and destroy all the artillery and ammunition you can find."

Alerting the Colonists

On the night of April 18, 1775, Dr. Joseph Warren walked the streets of Boston, looking for any unusual activity by the British army. He saw a regiment form ranks in Boston Common and then begin to march out of the city.

Warren rushed to alert **Paul Revere** and **William Dawes,** leading members of the Sons of Liberty. Revere and Dawes rode to **Lexington,** a town east of Concord, to warn **Samuel Adams** and **John Hancock** that the British were coming.

Revere galloped off across the moonlit countryside, shouting, "The regulars are out!" to the people and houses he passed along the way. When he reached Lexington, he raced to tell Adams and Hancock his news. Adams could barely control his excitement. "What a glorious morning this is!" Adams was ready to fight for American independence.

Eyewitness to HISTORY

Fighting at Lexington and Concord

At dawn the redcoats under Major Pitcairn approached Lexington. When they reached the center of the town, they came across a group of

The Battles of Lexington and Concord

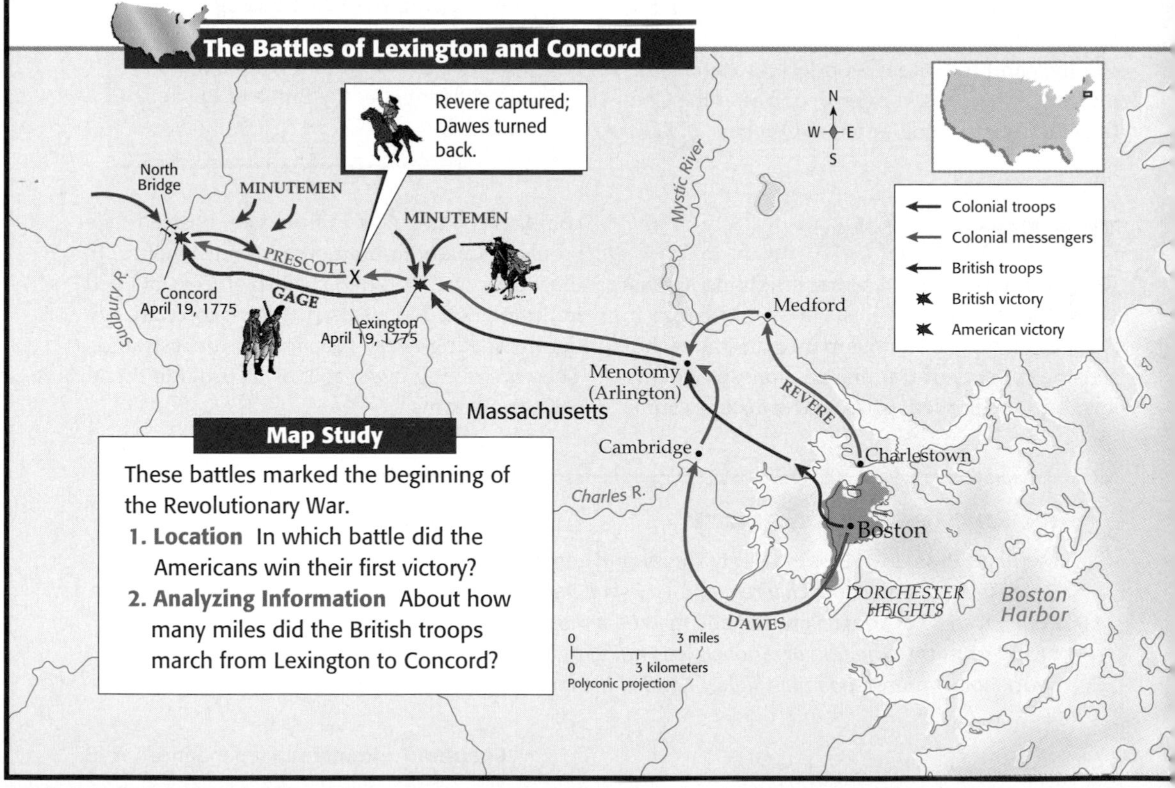

Map Study

These battles marked the beginning of the Revolutionary War.

1. **Location** In which battle did the Americans win their first victory?
2. **Analyzing Information** About how many miles did the British troops march from Lexington to Concord?

Multiple Learning Styles

Verbal/Linguistic Patrick Henry's statement: "I am not a Virginian, but an American" reflects a new point of view shared by many delegates to the First Continental Congress. Invite students to imagine themselves as delegates from various colonies. Have them, in character, write diary entries kept during the meeting in Philadelphia. The entries should show how their attitudes change—from seeking the best for their own colonies to promoting the good of the colonies as a whole—and why. **L2**

HISTORY AND ART ***A View of the Town of Concord, 1775* by an unknown artist** Two British officers (left) search for fleeing minutemen, while British troops march through Concord. **What happened to British forces after destroying militia supplies at Concord?**

about 70 minutemen who had been alerted by Revere and Dawes. Led by Captain John Parker, the minutemen had positioned themselves on the town common with muskets in hand.

A minuteman reported, "There suddenly appeared a number of the King's troops, about a thousand . . . the foremost of which cried, 'Throw down your arms, ye villains, ye rebels.'" A shot was fired, and then both sides let loose with a barrage. When the fighting was over, eight minutemen lay dead.

The British troops continued their march to Concord. When they arrived there, they discovered that most of the militia's gunpowder had already been removed. They destroyed the remaining supplies, turned around, and headed back to Boston. Now the minutemen were waiting for them.

Messengers on horseback had spread word of the British movements. All along the road from Concord to Boston, farmers, blacksmiths, saddle makers, and clerks hid behind trees, rocks, and stone fences. As the British marched down the road, the militia fired. A British officer wrote, "These fellows were generally good marksmen, and many of them used long guns made for duck shooting." By the time the redcoats reached Boston, more than 200 were wounded and 73 were dead.

Looking back, the poet Ralph Waldo Emerson wrote in "The Concord Hymn" that the Americans at Lexington and Concord had fired the "shot heard 'round the world." The battle for America's independence from Great Britain had begun.

More Military Action

A few weeks later, on May 10, more fighting broke out. Leading a small group of New Englanders known as the **Green Mountain Boys, Ethan Allen** captured the British **Fort Ticonderoga** on Lake Champlain. The British were caught by surprise. When Allen called for them to surrender "in the name of . . . the Continental Congress," the British commander obeyed.

Building Forces

Following the battles of Lexington and Concord, the committees of correspondence sent out calls for volunteers to join the militias. Soon the colonial militia assembled around Boston was 20,000 strong. For several weeks, the American and British armies waited nervously for the other to make the next move.

HISTORY AND ART The British officers shown are Colonel Francis Smith of the 10th Lincolnshires, who commanded the march to Lexington and Concord, and Major John Pitcairn of the Royal Marines, second in command. **Answer:** *On their march back to Boston, many of their soldiers were wounded or killed by Patriots who shot at them from hiding places.*

3 ASSESS

Assign Section 3 Review as homework or as an in-class activity.

Use **Chapter Challenger Interactive Review Software** to review Section 3.

Section Quiz 5–3

Name ______ Date ______ Class ______

★ Chapter 5 Score

Section Quiz 5-3

DIRECTIONS: Matching Match each item in Column A with the items in Column B. Write the correct letters in the blanks. *(10 points each)*

Column A	Column B
____ 1. citizen soldiers	A. Major John Pitcairn
____ 2. storage place for arms	B. militias
____ 3. redcoat leader	C. Ralph Waldo Emerson
____ 4. leader of minutemen	D. Concord
____ 5. writer of "The Concord Hymn"	E. Captain John Parker

DIRECTIONS: Multiple Choice In the blank at the left, write the letter of the choice that best completes the statement or answers the question. *(10 points each)*

____ 6. This king said that "blows must decide" who would rule America.
A. George III C. Philip III
B. Edward III D. James III

____ 7. This man had orders to take away the weapons of the Massachusetts militia.
A. George Washington C. Thomas Gage
B. William Dawes D. Paul Revere

____ 8. Paul Revere and this man warned John Hancock and Samuel Adams that the British were coming.
A. John Adams C. George Washington
B. Thomas Gage D. William Dawes

____ 9. The Green Mountain Boys, who captured the British-held Fort Ticonderoga, were led by
A. Paul Revere. C. George Washington.
B. Ethan Allen. D. Ralph Waldo Emerson.

____ 10. Although the British won this battle, they learned that defeating the Americans would not be easy.
A. Battle of Bunker Hill C. Battle of Concord
B. Battle of Boston D. Battle of Lexington

The American Journey ★ 19 ★ Section Quizzes

MAKING CONNECTIONS ACTIVITY

Daily Life The First Continental Congress drafted a list of grievances toward British policies and actions. As a review, ask students to list anything they have read in the unit thus far that they think colonists would have considered a "grievance." You might prompt students by giving them the option of imagining themselves as delegates to the Congress. Conclude by discussing how people express political grievances today; mention such formats as editorials, demonstrations, and talk radio. **L1**

Who? What? Where? When?

David Lamson, an African American who had fought in the French and Indian War, commanded the forces defending Concord. After the warning at Boston, all the young men of Concord had been pressed into service as minutemen, so the defense of the town fell to older citizens.

CHAPTER 5
Section 3, 142–146

HISTORY AND ART Almost half of the British troops in this battle died over the course of three attacks.
Answer: *across the harbor from Boston*

Reteaching Activity 5–3

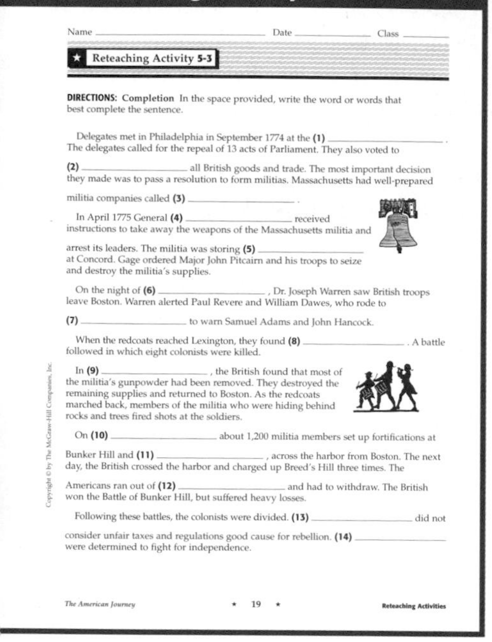
Name ______ Date ______ Class ______

★ Reteaching Activity 5-3

DIRECTIONS: Completion In the space provided, write the word or words that best complete the sentence.

Delegates met in Philadelphia in September 1774 at the **(1)** ______. The delegates called for the repeal of 13 acts of Parliament. They also voted to **(2)** ______ all British goods and trade. The most important decision they made was to pass a resolution to form militias. Massachusetts had well-prepared militia companies called **(3)** ______.

In April 1775 General **(4)** ______ received instructions to take away the weapons of the Massachusetts militia and arrest its leaders. The militia was storing **(5)** ______ at Concord. Gage ordered Major John Pitcairn and his troops to seize and destroy the militia's supplies.

On the night of **(6)** ______, Dr. Joseph Warren saw British troops leave Boston. Warren alerted Paul Revere and William Dawes, who rode to **(7)** ______ to warn Samuel Adams and John Hancock.

When the redcoats reached Lexington, they found **(8)** ______. A battle followed in which eight colonists were killed.

In **(9)** ______, the British found that most of the militia's gunpowder had been removed. They destroyed the remaining supplies and returned to Boston. As the redcoats marched back, members of the militia who were hiding behind rocks and trees fired shots at the soldiers.

On **(10)** ______ about 1,200 militia members set up fortifications at Bunker Hill and **(11)** ______, across the harbor from Boston. The next day, the British crossed the harbor and charged up Breed's Hill three times. The Americans ran out of **(12)** ______ and had to withdraw. The British won the Battle of Bunker Hill, but suffered heavy losses.

Following these battles, the colonists were divided. **(13)** ______ did not consider unfair taxes and regulations good cause for rebellion. **(14)** ______ were determined to fight for independence.

Copyright © by The McGraw-Hill Companies, Inc.

The American Journey ★ 19 ★ **Reteaching Activities**

Enrichment Activity 5–3

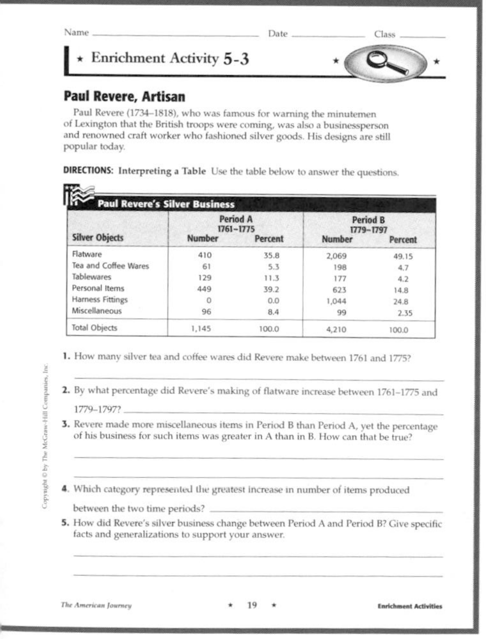
Name ______ Date ______ Class ______

★ Enrichment Activity 5-3

Paul Revere, Artisan

Paul Revere (1734–1818), who was famous for warning the minutemen of Lexington that the British troops were coming, was also a businessperson and renowned craft worker who fashioned silver goods. His designs are still popular today.

DIRECTIONS: Interpreting a Table Use the table below to answer the questions.

Paul Revere's Silver Business

Silver Objects	Period A 1761–1775 Number	Period A 1761–1775 Percent	Period B 1779–1797 Number	Period B 1779–1797 Percent
Flatware	410	35.8	2,069	49.15
Tea and Coffee Wares	61	5.3	198	4.7
Tablewares	129	11.3	177	4.2
Personal Items	449	39.2	623	14.8
Harness Fittings	0	0.0	1,044	24.8
Miscellaneous	96	8.4	99	2.35
Total Objects	1,145	100.0	4,210	100.0

1. How many silver tea and coffee wares did Revere make between 1761 and 1775? ______
2. By what percentage did Revere's making of flatware increase between 1761–1775 and 1779–1797? ______
3. Revere made more miscellaneous items in Period B than Period A, yet the percentage of his business for such items was greater in A than in B. How can that be true? ______
4. Which category represented the greatest increase in number of items produced between the two time periods? ______
5. How did Revere's silver business change between Period A and Period B? Give specific facts and generalizations to support your answer. ______

Copyright © by The McGraw-Hill Companies, Inc.

The American Journey ★ 19 ★ **Enrichment Activities**

4 CLOSE

Review the chart on page 143. Have students defend their choice of the greatest cause for declaring independence.

HISTORY AND ART ***Battle of Bunker Hill* by Alonzo Chappel** The Battle of Bunker Hill showed that the untrained American militia could match the professional British army. **Where is Bunker Hill located?**

The Battle of Bunker Hill

On June 16, 1775, about 1,200 militiamen under the command of Colonel William Prescott set up fortifications at Bunker Hill and nearby Breed's Hill, across the harbor from Boston.

The British decided to drive the Americans from their strategic locations overlooking the city. The next day redcoats crossed the harbor and assembled at the bottom of Breed's Hill. Bayonets drawn, they charged up the hill. With his forces low on ammunition, Colonel Prescott reportedly shouted the order, "Don't fire until you see the whites of their eyes." The Americans opened fire, forcing the British to retreat. The redcoats charged two more times, receiving furious fire. In the end the Americans ran out of gunpowder and had to withdraw.

The British won the **Battle of Bunker Hill** but suffered heavy losses—more than 1,000 dead and wounded. As one British officer wrote in his diary, "A dear bought victory, another such would have ruined us." The British had learned that defeating the Americans on the battlefield would not be quick or easy.

Choosing Sides

As American colonists heard about these battles, they faced a major decision. Should they join the rebels or remain loyal to Britain? Those who chose to stay with Britain, the **Loyalists,** did not consider unfair taxes and regulations sufficient cause for rebellion. The **Patriots,** on the other hand, were determined to fight the British to the end—until American independence was won.

Section 3 Review

Checking for Understanding

1. ***Identify*** Continental Congress, John Adams, John Jay, Richard Henry Lee, George Washington, Concord, Paul Revere, Lexington, Ethan Allen, Fort Ticonderoga, Battle of Bunker Hill.
2. ***Define*** militia, minutemen, Loyalist, Patriot.
3. ***Explain*** why the British sent troops to Concord.

Reviewing Themes

4. **Groups and Institutions** Which action by the Continental Congress made it obvious that the colonies were preparing for war?

Critical Thinking

5. **Analyzing Ideas** What reasons might Loyalists have had to support Great Britain?

Activity

Writing a Poem Write a poem about one of the events described in this section.

Section 3 Review Answers

1. Continental Congress, 142; John Adams, 142; John Jay, 142; Richard Henry Lee, 142; George Washington, 142; Concord, 144; Paul Revere, 144; Lexington, 144; Ethan Allen, 145; Fort Ticonderoga, 145; Battle of Bunker Hill, 146
2. The words are defined in the Glossary.
3. Concord was a storehouse for the militia's arms and ammunition; British troops were sent to destroy the supplies.
4. the resolution to form a militia
5. Students may suggest that Britain seemed stronger. Loyalists thought that a Patriot victory would mean upheaval. Loyalists did not consider unfair taxes and regulations sufficient cause for rebellion.

Activity Poems should describe an event that occurs in this section.

ABC NEWS INTERACTIVE™

Historic America Electronic Field Trips

Field Trip to Lexington and Concord

Setting up the Video

Work with a group of your classmates to view "Lexington and Concord" on the videodisc ***Historic America: Electronic Field Trips***. The Battles of Lexington and Concord were the first armed conflicts of the American Revolution. Although the idea of independence from Great Britain was growing popular, some colonists remained unsure. This program reenacts the events during the Battles of Lexington and Concord.

Hands-On Activity

Organize into groups. Imagine you are colonists faced with making the decision of whether to fight for independence. As a group, decide whether you are pro-independence or wish to remain loyal to the British Crown. Then write and videotape a propaganda commercial designed to influence public opinion in your favor.

Side 1, Chapter 6

View the video by scanning the bar code or by entering the chapter number on your keypad and pressing Search.

Surfing the "Net"

Modern Inventors

Although he is known primarily for writing the Declaration of Independence, Thomas Jefferson was accomplished in many other ways. He was recognized for inventing the moldboard of least resistance (otherwise known as the plow), the cipher wheel, and the spherical sundial. Americans continue to design new innovations to make their lives easier. Information about many of these innovations can be found on the Internet.

Getting There

Pick a subject that you would like to know more about and research recent innovations that are related to that subject. Follow these steps to gather your information.

1. Use a search engine. Type in the subject that you are searching for.
2. Enter words like the following to find specific information about the newest technology: *inventions, innovations, patents, licenses.*
3. The search engine will provide you with a number of links to follow. Links are "pointers" to different sites on the Internet.

What to Do When You Are There

Click on the links to navigate through the pages of information. Gather your findings. Using the findings, create a consumer report highlighting five inventions. Evaluate each invention for its innovation and usability.

Multimedia Activities

ABC NEWS INTERACTIVE™

VIDEODISC
Historic America Electronic Field Trips

Side 1, Chapter 6
Title: *Lexington and Concord*

If you do not have access to a videodisc player, the **Historic America Electronic Field Trips** are also available in VHS.

Internet Sites

The following are possible sites for completing the "Net" activities:

United States Patent and Trademark Office:
http://www.uspto.gov/

National Inventors Hall of Fame:
http://www.invent.org

Not on the "Net" . . .

If students have limited or no access to the Internet, have them complete the "Modern Inventors" activity by using the electronic card catalog at their school or local library. At the *s:* prompt, students should type in the name of the product or invention they would like to know more about. They should then use the call numbers to find the books they need to complete their consumer reports.

The "How Things Work" series (New York: Kingfisher Books, Grisewood & Dempsey Inc.) and *How Science Works* (London: Dorling Kindersley Limited, Reader's Digest) can be used to help students in their invention evaluations.

TEACHER'S NOTES

CHAPTER 5
Section 4, 148–152

1 FOCUS

BELLRINGER
Motivational Activity

Before taking roll at the beginning of the class period, project Section Focus Transparency 5–4 and have students answer the questions. Discuss students' responses.

This activity is also available as a blackline master.

Section Focus Transparency 5–4

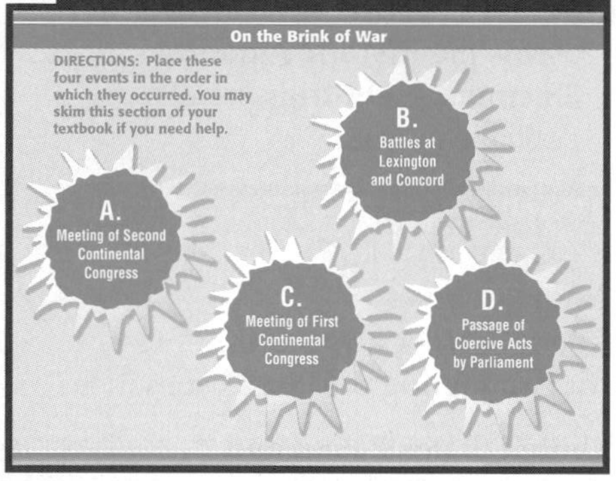

Vocabulary Precheck
Point out that the prefix *pre-* means "before," "in front of," or "prior to" and that *amble* means "to walk." A preamble, then, "walks before" or introduces a document.

Use the **Vocabulary PuzzleMaker** to create crossword and word search puzzles.

Section Theme
Government and Democracy
The Declaration of Independence outlined the Patriots' grievances and proclaimed the United States to be a self-governing democracy.

Activity Have students share what they know about the Declaration of Independence and explain why they think this document is important.

1775 — 1776 — 1777

May 10, 1775 Second Continental Congress meets

July 1775 The Congress sends Olive Branch Petition to George III

March 1776 George Washington takes Boston from the British

July 4, 1776 Declaration of Independence is approved

Section 4

Moving Toward Independence

READ TO DISCOVER . . .
- what happened at the Second Continental Congress.
- why the colonists drafted the Declaration of Independence.

TERMS TO LEARN
petition
preamble

The Storyteller

In June 1776, delegates to the Second Continental Congress came to a momentous decision. They agreed to have a committee draw up a document declaring America's independence from Great Britain. Many years later John Adams recalled a conversation with Thomas Jefferson about the writing of the document.

Jefferson: You should do it.
Adams: Oh! no.
Jefferson: Why will you not? You ought to do it. . . .
Adams: You can write ten times better than I can.
Jefferson: Well, if you are decided, I will do as well as I can.

Lap desk invented by Jefferson

Declaring independence was still a long way off when the **Second Continental Congress** assembled for the first time in **Philadelphia.** The Congress held its first meeting on May 10, 1775, just three weeks after the battles at Lexington and Concord. All 13 colonies sent delegates to the Congress.

Biography

Colonial Leaders Emerge

The delegates to the Second Continental Congress included some of the greatest political leaders in America. Among those attending were John and Samuel Adams, Patrick Henry, Richard Henry Lee, and George Washington—all delegates to the First Continental Congress held in 1774. Several distinguished new delegates came as well.

Benjamin Franklin, one of the most accomplished and respected individuals in the colonies, had been an influential member of the Pennsylvania legislature. In 1765, during the Stamp Act crisis, he had acted as a colonial spokesman in London.

John Hancock of Massachusetts, 38 years old, was one of the wealthiest colonists. He funded many of the Patriot groups, including the Sons of Liberty. The delegates chose Hancock as president of the Second Continental Congress.

SECTION RESOURCES

Reproducible Masters
- Reproducible Lesson Plan 5–4
- Guided Reading Activity 5–4
- Section Quiz 5–4
- Reteaching Activity 5–4
- Enrichment Activity 5–4

Transparencies
- Section Focus Transparency 5–4

Multimedia
- Vocabulary PuzzleMaker
- Chapter Challenger Interactive Review Software
- Testmaker
- GTV: A Geographic Perspective on American History
- Facts On File: Landmark Documents in American History

America's FLAGS

Continental Colors, 1775–77 **The Continental Colors, or Grand Union flag, was the first to represent all the colonies. Its 13 stripes stood for the thirteen colonies. The crosses represented the British flag and symbolized the colonists' loyalty to Great Britain at that time.**

Thomas Jefferson, only 32 years old when the Second Continental Congress met, had already acquired a reputation as a brilliant thinker and writer. As a member of the Virginia House of Burgesses, Jefferson had become associated with the movement for independence.

The Congress Becomes a Government

The Second Continental Congress began to govern the colonies. It authorized the printing of money and set up a post office with Franklin in charge. It established committees to communicate with Native Americans and with other countries. Most important, the Congress created the **Continental Army** to fight against Britain in a more organized way than the colonial militias could.

The new army needed a commander. On John Adams's recommendation, the Congress unanimously chose George Washington. Washington had more military experience than any other American, and the delegates admired and trusted him. Washington offered to serve without pay.

The Olive Branch Petition

After Washington left to take charge of the colonial forces in Boston, the delegates offered Britain one last chance to avoid all-out war. In July the Congress sent a petition, or formal request, to George III. Called the **Olive Branch Petition,** it assured the king of the colonists' desire for peace. It asked the king to protect the colonists' rights, which Parliament seemed determined to destroy.

George III refused to receive the Olive Branch Petition. Instead he prepared for war, hiring more than 30,000 German troops to send to America.

The Colonies Take the Offensive

Washington reached Boston in July 1775, a few weeks after the Battle of Bunker Hill. He found the members of the militia growing in number every day, but lacking discipline, organization, and leadership. He began the hard work of shaping these armed civilians into an army.

By March 1776, Washington judged the Continental Army ready to fight. He positioned the army in a semicircle around Boston and gave the order for its cannons to bombard the British forces. The redcoats, under Sir William Howe, hurriedly withdrew from the city and boarded their ships. On March 17 Washington led his jubilant troops into Boston. The British troops sailed to Halifax, Nova Scotia.

Meanwhile the Congress learned that British troops stationed in present-day Canada were planning to invade New York. The Americans decided to strike first. Marching north from Fort Ticonderoga, a Patriot force captured Montreal in November. An American attack on Quebec led by **Benedict Arnold** failed, however. The American

Linking PAST & PRESENT

Symbol of a Traitor

In 1780 Patriot general Benedict Arnold was in debt and beginning to doubt that the Americans could win the war. Papers found on a British spy indicated that Arnold plotted to surrender West Point to the British. In America today, the name *Benedict Arnold* has come to mean "traitor."

2 TEACH

L1 Supporting Key Ideas Write the following statement on the chalkboard: *By the spring of 1776, the colonies had started to resemble an independent nation.* Have students work together to locate details that support this statement (for example, the Second Continental Congress was meeting; the Continental Army was established).

you don't say...

Militia From the Latin *miles*—which means "soldier"—comes *militia.* During the Revolutionary War, the term referred to all able-bodied men between the ages of 16 and 60 (who were potential soldiers).

Guided Reading Activity 5–4

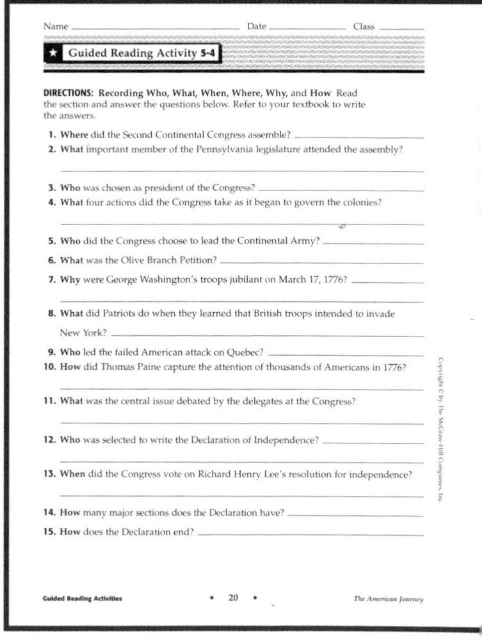

Name ______ Date ______ Class ______

Guided Reading Activity 5-4

DIRECTIONS: Recording Who, What, When, Where, Why, and **How** Read the section and answer the questions below. Refer to your textbook to write the answers.

1. **Where** did the Second Continental Congress assemble? ______
2. **What** important member of the Pennsylvania legislature attended the assembly? ______
3. **Who** was chosen as president of the Congress? ______
4. **What** four actions did the Congress take as it began to govern the colonies? ______
5. **Who** did the Congress choose to lead the Continental Army? ______
6. **What** was the Olive Branch Petition? ______
7. **Why** were George Washington's troops jubilant on March 17, 1776? ______
8. **What** did Patriots do when they learned that British troops intended to invade New York? ______
9. **Who** led the failed American attack on Quebec? ______
10. **How** did Thomas Paine capture the attention of thousands of Americans in 1776? ______
11. **What** was the central issue debated by the delegates at the Congress? ______
12. **Who** was selected to write the Declaration of Independence? ______
13. **When** did the Congress vote on Richard Henry Lee's resolution for independence? ______
14. **How** many major sections does the Declaration have? ______
15. **How** does the Declaration end? ______

Guided Reading Activities • 20 • *The American Journey*

COOPERATIVE LEARNING ACTIVITY

Enacting a Historic Moment The Second Continental Congress witnessed several moments of historic impact. Have students prepare and present skits on any of the following events:

- The choice of John Hancock as president of the meetings
- The choice of George Washington as commander of the new Continental Army
- Debate over the wisdom of declaring independence
- Approval of Thomas Jefferson's Declaration of Independence draft

Each group should choose a director. Other roles include actors, propmaster, costume designer, and makeup artists. Encourage actors to try different roles in the skit before choosing characters to portray.

CURRICULUM CONNECTION

LITERATURE
As Jefferson drafted the Declaration of Independence, he was greatly influenced by other literary works. Six months earlier Thomas Paine, in *Common Sense,* had outlined the steps needed to declare independence. Jefferson also drew many ideas from John Locke's *Two Treatises of Government.*

Congress began to edit Jefferson's draft on July 2. As Jefferson witnessed the revisions, he commented that Benjamin Franklin, "who perceived that I was not insensitive to these mutilations," leaned over from his adjacent seat and tried to divert him with a story.

HISTORY AND ART Delegates from New England and the South favored independence. Some delegates from the Middle Colonies, though, still desired strong ties with Great Britain at this time.
Answer: *Samuel Adams, Patrick Henry, Richard Henry Lee, George Washington, John Hancock*

forces stayed outside the city of Quebec through the long winter and returned to Fort Ticonderoga in 1776.

Moving Toward Independence

Throughout the colonies in late 1775 and early 1776, some Americans still hoped to avoid a total break with Britain. Support for the position of complete independence was growing, however.

In January 1776, **Thomas Paine** published a pamphlet that captured the attention of the American colonists. Called ***Common Sense,*** it sold 120,000 copies within three months of publication. In bold language, Paine called for complete independence from Britain. He argued that it was simply "common sense" to stop following the "royal brute," King George III. Paine told the colonists their cause was not just a squabble over taxes but a struggle for freedom—"in great measure the cause of all mankind." *Common Sense* inspired thousands of Americans.

HISTORY AND ART ***Drafting the Declaration of Independence* by J. L. G. Ferris** Thomas Jefferson prepared the draft of the Declaration of Independence, while Benjamin Franklin and John Adams made suggestions. **What other leaders were involved in the Second Continental Congress?**

Eyewitness to HISTORY

The Colonies Declare Independence

At the Second Continental Congress in Philadelphia, the meeting hall was filled with spirited debate. One central issue occupied the delegates: Should the colonies declare themselves an independent nation, or should they stay under British rule?

In April 1776, North Carolina instructed its delegates to support independence. On June 7 Virginia's Richard Henry Lee proposed a bold resolution:

> "That these United Colonies are, and of right ought to be, free and independent States . . . and that all political connection between them and the State of Great Britain is, and ought to be, totally dissolved."

The Congress debated the resolution. Some delegates still thought the colonies were not ready to form a separate nation. Others argued that war already had begun and a large portion of the American population wanted to separate from Great Britain. Still others feared Great Britain's power to hold down the rebellion.

Drafting a Declaration

While the delegates debated the issue, the Congress chose a committee to draft a **Declaration of Independence.** The committee included Jefferson, Franklin, John Adams, Roger Sherman of Connecticut, and Robert Livingston of New York. Jefferson was selected to write the document.

MULTIPLE LEARNING STYLES

Auditory/Musical The musical play *1776,* by Peter Stone and Sherman Edwards, ran on Broadway and was made into a film in 1972. It celebrates the events leading up to the signing of the Declaration of Independence. The musical offers characterizations of Thomas Jefferson, Benjamin Franklin, and other Patriot leaders. Invite students to view the film (available on videocassette) or listen to the cast album. Afterward, have students discuss the characters they found most interesting. Ask them to explain how hearing the story of the Declaration of Independence affected their understanding of revolutionary events. **L2**

Jefferson spent about two weeks writing the document. He later recalled the goal was

> **"**. . . to place before mankind the common sense of the subject, in terms so plain and firm as to command their assent. . . . Neither aiming at originality of principle or sentiment, nor yet copied from any particular and previous writing, it was intended to be an expression of the American mind.**"**

Picturing HISTORY Abigail Adams was an advocate for women's rights. **What request did Abigail Adams make in a letter to her husband, John Adams?**

While the Congress considered a declaration of independence, John Adams received a letter from his wife, **Abigail Adams.** She told Adams the delegates should

> **"**. . . remember all men would be tyrants if they could. If particular care and attention is not paid to the ladies, we are determined to foment a rebellion, and will not hold ourselves bound by any laws in which we have no voice or representation.**"**

John Adams did not circulate Abigail's letter at the Congress.

Congress Votes for Independence

On July 2, 1776, the Congress finally voted on Lee's resolution for independence. Twelve colonies voted for it. New York did not vote but later announced its support. Next the delegates took up Jefferson's draft of the Declaration of Independence. After making some changes, they approved the document on July 4, 1776.

John Hancock, the president of the Congress, was the first to sign the Declaration of Independence. Hancock remarked that he wrote his name large enough for King George to read it without his glasses. Hancock's bold signature stands out on the original document. Eventually 55 delegates signed the paper announcing the birth of the United States.

Copies of the Declaration went out to the newly declared states. Washington had it read to his troops on July 9. In New York American soldiers tore down a statue of George III in celebration. In Worcester, Massachusetts, the reading of the Declaration of Independence was followed by "repeated huzzas [cheers], firing of musketry and cannon, bonfires, and other demonstrations of joy."

Footnotes to History

Divided Loyalties Many colonial families were divided over the issue of loyalty to the Crown. Benjamin Franklin, one of the strongest voices for independence, experienced this division firsthand. Franklin's son William, who was governor of New Jersey, remained loyal to Britain, causing a lifelong rift between father and son.

CHAPTER 5
Section 4, 148–152

Picturing HISTORY Writing to her husband about the public reading of the Declaration of Independence in Boston, Abigail Adams later said, "Thus ends royal Authority in this State, and all the people shall say 'Amen.'"
Answer: *that women be represented in the new government*

3 ASSESS

Assign Section 4 Review as homework or as an in-class activity.

Use **Chapter Challenger Interactive Review Software** to review Section 4.

Section Quiz 5–4

Name ______ Date ______ Class ______

★ Chapter 5

Score

Section Quiz 5-4

DIRECTIONS: Matching Match each item in Column A with the items in Column B. Write the correct letters in the blanks. *(10 points each)*

Column A	Column B
____ 1. home of the Continental Congress	A. Thomas Paine
____ 2. governed the colonies	B. Abigail Adams
____ 3. wrote *Common Sense*	C. Second Continental Congress
____ 4. crusader for women's rights	D. Thomas Jefferson
____ 5. wrote the Declaration of Independence	E. Philadelphia

DIRECTIONS: Multiple Choice In the blank at the left, write the letter of the choice that best completes the statement or answers the question. *(10 points each)*

____ 6. The colonies organized this group to fight against Great Britain.
A. Continental Army C. Continental Congress
B. Colonial Army D. Redcoat Army

____ 7. The first commander of the Continental Army was
A. George Washington. C. John Adams.
B. Benjamin Franklin. D. Thomas Jefferson.

____ 8. The Olive Branch Petition asked the king to
A. protect the colonists' rights. C. start another war.
B. leave America. D. stop taxation.

____ 9. The American attack on Quebec was led by
A. William Howe. C. Benedict Arnold.
B. John Hancock. D. George Washington.

____ 10. The first man to sign the Declaration of Independence was
A. Benjamin Franklin. C. Thomas Jefferson.
B. John Adams. D. John Hancock.

Section Quizzes ★ 20 ★ *The American Journey*

MAKING CONNECTIONS ACTIVITY

Daily Life The Declaration of Independence ends with this promise from those who signed it: ". . . we mutually pledge to each other our lives, our fortunes, and our sacred honor." Have students investigate (using such sources as *Signers of the Declaration,* by John Bakeless) what happened during the course of the war to the people who made this pledge. Which delegates lost their lives, their fortunes, or their reputations (political or personal) in defense of independence—and how? Encourage students to choose a variety of formats for presenting their information. Follow up with a class discussion of the presentations. **L2**

CHAPTER 5
Section 4, 148–152

Reteaching Activity 5–4

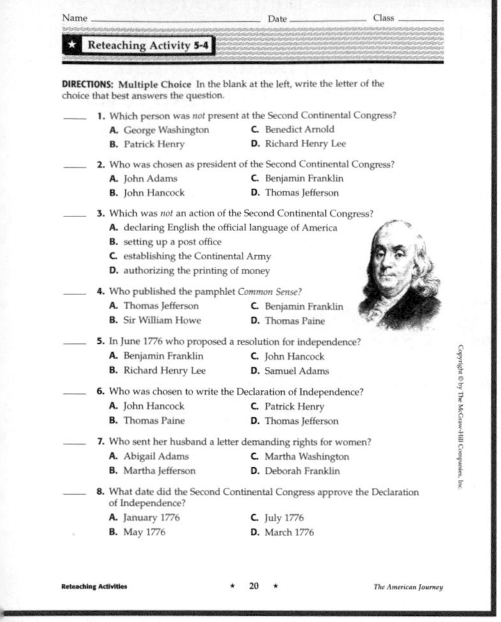

Name ______ Date ______ Class ______

★ Reteaching Activity 5-4

DIRECTIONS: Multiple Choice In the blank at the left, write the letter of the choice that best answers the question.

____ 1. Which person was *not* present at the Second Continental Congress?
A. George Washington — C. Benedict Arnold
B. Patrick Henry — D. Richard Henry Lee

____ 2. Who was chosen as president of the Second Continental Congress?
A. John Adams — C. Benjamin Franklin
B. John Hancock — D. Thomas Jefferson

____ 3. Which was *not* an action of the Second Continental Congress?
A. declaring English the official language of America
B. setting up a post office
C. establishing the Continental Army
D. authorizing the printing of money

____ 4. Who published the pamphlet *Common Sense?*
A. Thomas Jefferson — C. Benjamin Franklin
B. Sir William Howe — D. Thomas Paine

____ 5. In June 1776 who proposed a resolution for independence?
A. Benjamin Franklin — C. John Hancock
B. Richard Henry Lee — D. Samuel Adams

____ 6. Who was chosen to write the Declaration of Independence?
A. John Hancock — C. Patrick Henry
B. Thomas Paine — D. Thomas Jefferson

____ 7. Who sent her husband a letter demanding rights for women?
A. Abigail Adams — C. Martha Washington
B. Martha Jefferson — D. Deborah Franklin

____ 8. What date did the Second Continental Congress approve the Declaration of Independence?
A. January 1776 — C. July 1776
B. May 1776 — D. March 1776

Copyright © by The McGraw-Hill Companies, Inc.

Reteaching Activities ★ 20 ★ The American Journey

Enrichment Activity 5–4

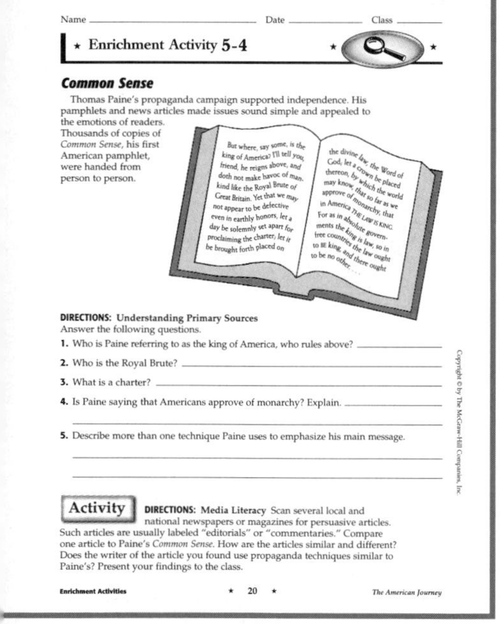

Name ______ Date ______ Class ______

★ Enrichment Activity 5-4 ★

Common Sense

Thomas Paine's propaganda campaign supported independence. His pamphlets and news articles made issues sound simple and appealed to the emotions of readers. Thousands of copies of *Common Sense,* his first American pamphlet, were handed from person to person.

But where, say some, is the king of America? I'll tell you, friend, he reigns above, and doth not make havoc of mankind like the Royal Brute of Great Britain. Yet that we may not appear to be defective even in earthly honors, let a day be solemnly set apart for proclaiming the charter; let it be brought forth placed on the divine law, the Word of God; let a crown be placed thereon, by which the world may know, that so far as we approve of monarchy, that in America THE LAW IS KING. For as in absolute governments the king is law, so in free countries the law ought to BE king; and there ought to be no other. . . .

DIRECTIONS: Understanding Primary Sources
Answer the following questions.

1. Who is Paine referring to as the king of America, who rules above? ______
2. Who is the Royal Brute? ______
3. What is a charter? ______
4. Is Paine saying that Americans approve of monarchy? Explain. ______
5. Describe more than one technique Paine uses to emphasize his main message. ______

Activity DIRECTIONS: Media Literacy Scan several local and national newspapers or magazines for persuasive articles. Such articles are usually labeled "editorials" or "commentaries." Compare one article to Paine's *Common Sense.* How are the articles similar and different? Does the writer of the article you found use propaganda techniques similar to Paine's? Present your findings to the class.

Copyright © by The McGraw-Hill Companies, Inc.

Enrichment Activities ★ 20 ★ The American Journey

4 CLOSE

Call on volunteers to suggest reasons for (PROS) and reasons against (CONS) a formal declaration of independence.

The Declaration of Independence

The Declaration has four major sections. The **preamble,** or introduction, states that people who wish to form a new country should explain their reasons for doing so. The next two sections list the rights the colonists believed they should have and their complaints against Britain. The final section proclaims the existence of the new nation.

Continental infantryman

Demanding Basic Rights

The Declaration of Independence states what Jefferson and many Americans thought were universal principles. It begins with a description of basic human rights.

> "We hold these truths to be self-evident, that all men are created equal, that they are endowed by their Creator with certain unalienable Rights, that among these are Life, Liberty, and the pursuit of Happiness."

Government exists to protect these rights. If it does not, the Declaration states that "it is the Right of the People to alter or to abolish it and to institute new Government."

Listing British Abuses

The Declaration goes on to list the many grievances Americans held against the king and Parliament. The crimes of George III included "cutting off our trade with all parts of the world" and "imposing taxes on us without our consent." Americans, the Declaration says, had "Petitioned for Redress" of these grievances. These petitions, however, were rejected by Britain.

Declaring Independence

The Declaration ends by announcing America's new status. Now pledging "to each other our Lives, our Fortunes, and our sacred Honor," the Americans declared themselves a new nation. The struggle for American independence—the American Revolution—had begun.

Section 4 Review

Checking for Understanding

1. ***Identify*** Second Continental Congress, Philadelphia, Benjamin Franklin, Thomas Jefferson, Thomas Paine, *Common Sense,* Declaration of Independence, Abigail Adams.
2. ***Define*** petition, preamble.
3. ***Describe*** George III's response to the Olive Branch Petition.

Reviewing Themes

4. **Government and Democracy** Why was the Second Continental Congress more like a government than the First?

Critical Thinking

5. **Analyzing Primary Sources** Based on the letter that appears on page 151, what do you think Abigail Adams was asking her husband to include in the Declaration of Independence?

Activity

Writing an Advertisement Prepare a help-wanted ad to locate a qualified person to write the Declaration of Independence. Describe the responsibilities of the job as well as the experience and character traits needed.

Section 4 Review Answers

1. Second Continental Congress, 148; Philadelphia, 148; Benjamin Franklin, 148; Thomas Jefferson, 149; Thomas Paine, 150; *Common Sense,* 150; Declaration of Independence, 150; Abigail Adams, 151
2. The words are defined in the Glossary.
3. He refused it and began to prepare for war.
4. It began to govern the colonies. It authorized the printing of money, set up a post office, established committees to communicate with Native Americans and with other countries, and created the Continental Army.
5. women's rights

Activity Ads will vary but might include the following: ability to write and express complex ideas clearly, patriotism and belief in the colonists' goal of independence, and so on.

Critical Thinking
SKILL BUILDER

Distinguishing Fact From Opinion

Suppose a friend says, "Our school's basketball team is awesome. That's a fact." Actually, it's not a fact; it is an opinion. Can you tell the difference?

Learning the Skill

A **fact** answers a specific question such as: What happened? Who did it? When and where did it happen? Why did it happen? Statements of fact can be checked for accuracy and proven. If your friend had said, "We have the highest-ranking team in the state," that could be a fact. We can look up the rankings of state teams and determine whether the statement is a fact.

An **opinion,** on the other hand, expresses beliefs and feelings. Although it may reflect someone's thoughts, we cannot prove or disprove it. An opinion often begins with phrases such as *I believe, I think, probably, it seems to me,* or *in my opinion.* It often contains words such as *might, could, should,* and *ought* and superlatives such as *best, worst,* and *greatest.*

To distinguish between facts and opinions, ask yourself these questions:

- Does this statement give specific information about an event?
- Can I check the accuracy of this statement?
- Does this statement express someone's feelings or beliefs?
- Does it include words such as *I believe* or superlatives such as *the greatest?*

Practicing the Skill

Read each numbered statement below. Tell whether each is a fact or an opinion, and explain how you arrived at your answer.

Applying the Skill

Distinguishing Fact from Opinion Analyze 10 newspaper advertisements or television commercials. List at least 3 facts and 3 opinions presented in the ads.

1. *The Second Continental Congress held its first meeting on May 10, 1775.*
2. *The delegates to the Second Continental Congress included the greatest men in America.*
3. *The Continental Army fought against the British.*
4. *George Washington should have been paid for his services as commander.*
5. *King George III was a foolish king.*

Critical Thinking
SKILL BUILDER

TEACH

Distinguishing Fact From Opinion

In schoolwork and in daily life, students need to recognize the difference between verifiable statements (facts) and statements of personal belief (opinions). This ability is especially important when opinions, stated with conviction, seem to be facts. By evaluating statements according to a checklist, students will be able to classify specific statements as facts or as opinions.

Ask students to rephrase *We have the highest-ranking team in the state* as an opinion. (Answers include: *We have the best team in the state.)*

Call on volunteers to make statements about popular TV shows. Have the class identify each statement as a fact or an opinion.

Additional Practice

Chapter Skills Activity 5

Facts On File

CD-ROM
Landmark Documents in American History

Title: *Autobiography, Benjamin Franklin, 1771–88*
Have students skim a section of the document and list two facts and two opinions presented by Franklin.

ANSWERS TO PRACTICING THE SKILL

1. Fact; the accuracy of this statement can be verified.
2. Opinion; the idea that the delegates were great men reflects a personal belief. The superlative *greatest* also gives it away.
3. Fact; the accuracy of this statement can be verified.
4. Opinion; the expression *should have been* indicates someone's feeling.
5. Opinion; the idea that George III was foolish reflects a personal belief.

Applying the Skill Opinions should be easy to locate; facts may be a little more difficult. Ask students how easy it would be to check some of the facts for accuracy and why ads seem to be based on opinions.

NATIONAL GEOGRAPHIC *Journeys*

you don't say...

Stagecoaches Horse-drawn coaches carried passengers between towns and cities. Many journeys lasted two days or more. The coaches stopped at inns at night and completed trips in stages. As a result, people called the coaches "stagecoaches."

The first stagecoach service between Boston and New York City began in 1772. The journey took about six days.

What? Where? When? Who?

Tough Travel Before and during the Revolution, travel by land meant roadways clogged with ruts, tree roots, rocks, fallen trees, and mud. After the war, Americans made their first hard-surfaced roads out of crushed stone or wood planks. Private citizens built most of the roads and charged travelers a fee for using them. By 1789 land travel had improved enough that a New York publisher printed the nation's first road maps.

NATIONAL GEOGRAPHIC SOCIETY

VIDEODISC
GTV: The American People: Fabric of a Nation

Side 1, Chapter 9
Title: *The Winds of Warfare!*
Subject: Events leading to revolution
Ask: **What is one action taken by the British that led the colonists to revolt?** *(taxation without representation)*

2 **Jefferson traveled for seven days. Colonial inns along the way offered food and a chance to exchange news. And what news there was! General George Washington had chased British troops from Boston in March, and Thomas Paine had called King George III "the Royal Brute of Great Britain" in a pamphlet titled *Common Sense*.**

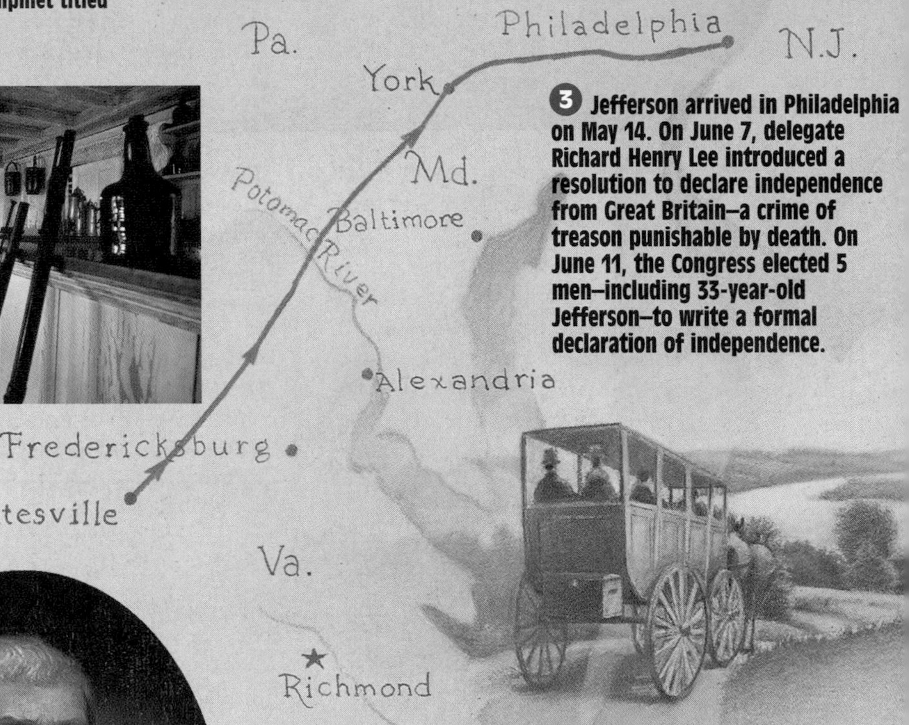

3 **Jefferson arrived in Philadelphia on May 14. On June 7, delegate Richard Henry Lee introduced a resolution to declare independence from Great Britain—a crime of treason punishable by death. On June 11, the Congress elected 5 men—including 33-year-old Jefferson—to write a formal declaration of independence.**

1 **On May 7, 1776, Virginia delegate Thomas Jefferson embarked from his home, Monticello, near Charlottesville, Virginia. He headed toward Philadelphia to join other delegates at the Second Continental Congress. Since May 1775 the delegates had debated the issue of self-rule as a colony versus total independence from Britain. That issue would soon be resolved.**

TEACHER'S NOTES

4 Jefferson asked John Adams to write the document, but Adams refused, saying, "Reason 1st–You are a Virginian, and a Virginian ought to appear at the head of this business. Reason 2d. I am obnoxious, suspected, and unpopular. You are very much otherwise. Reason 3d. You can write ten times better than I can."

5 On July 2, 1776, the delegates formally voted to accept the first draft of the document. John Adams later wrote to his wife: "The Second Day of July 1776 . . . ought to be solemnized with Pomp and Parade, with Shews, Games, Sports, Guns, Bells, Bonfires, and Illuminations from one End of this Continent to the other from this Time forward forever more." The final draft of the Declaration was adopted on July 4, 1776.

ATLANTIC OCEAN

NATIONAL GEOGRAPHIC

Journeys

Journey to Independence

"You inquire why so young a man as Mr. Jefferson was placed at the head of the Committee for preparing a Declaration of Independence? I answer: . . . to place Virginia at the head of every thing. . . . Mr. Jefferson came into Congress, in June 1775, and brought with him a reputation for literature, science, and a happy talent of composition. Writings of his were handed about, remarkable for the peculiar felicity [happiness] of expression. Though a silent member in Congress, he was so prompt, frank, explicit, and decisive upon committees and in conversation . . . that he soon seized upon my heart and upon this occasion I gave him my vote. . . ."

—From a letter written by John Adams to Timothy Pickering, August 22, 1822

Facts On File

CD-ROM
Landmark Documents in American History

Title: *The Declaration of Independence*
Suggest that students write a one-page paper in answer to this question: Do you consider the truths that were listed by Thomas Jefferson in the Declaration of Independence to be self-evident? Explain.

History *and the* Humanities

American Music Cultural Traditions, Lesson 2: "Tunes from Colonial America & The President's March"

you don't say...

Federal The term *federal* comes from the Latin word *foedus,* meaning "compact" or "league."

What? Where? When? Who?

Bibliography The excerpt at left was taken from *Autobiography of Thomas Jefferson, 1743–1790* (New York and London: G.P. Putnam's Sons, The Knickerbocker Press, 1914).

Jefferson's seven-day journey to Philadelphia took him through Culpepper, Fauquier, and Leesburg, Virginia; Frederick and Tannytown, Maryland; and McAlister's Town, York, Lancaster, and Chester, Pennsylvania. He crossed two rivers—the Potomac and Susquehanna—on ferries. This information, detailed in Thomas Jefferson's Memorandum Books, was provided by the Monticello Research Department.

Teacher's Notes

1 FOCUS

BELLRINGER
Motivational Activity

Inform students that at the signing of the Declaration of Independence, Benjamin Franklin remarked to John Hancock, "We must indeed all hang together, or, most assuredly, we shall all hang separately." Have students suggest what Franklin meant by this comment. *(that if the colonists did not work together for independence, they would all be hanged for treason)* Then have students consider if they would readily risk their lives for a cause.

What?Where?When?Who?

Earlier Attempt Thomas Jefferson had already addressed most of the issues discussed in the Declaration in *A Summary of the Rights of British America,* a pamphlet he published in 1774.

ABCNEWS INTERACTIVE™

VIDEODISC
Historic America
Electronic Field Trips

Side 1, Chapter 7
Title: *Independence Hall*
Subject: Historical Philadelphia, Pennsylvania
Ask: **When did Congress approve the Declaration of Independence?** *(July 4, 1776)*

Also available in VHS.

The Declaration of Independence

Delegates at the Second Continental Congress faced an enormous task. The war against Great Britain had begun, but to many colonists the purpose for fighting was unclear. As sentiment increased for a complete break with Britain, Congress decided to act. A committee was appointed to prepare a document that declared the thirteen colonies free and independent from Britain. More important, the committee needed to explain why separation was the only fitting solution to long-standing disputes with Parliament and the British Crown. Thomas Jefferson was assigned to write a working draft of this document, which was then revised. It was officially adopted on July 4, 1776. More than any other action of Congress, the Declaration of Independence served to make the American colonists one people.

The printed text of the document shows the spelling and punctuation of the parchment original. To aid in comprehension, selected words and their definitions appear in the side margin, along with other explanatory notes.

In Congress, July 4, 1776. The unanimous Declaration of the thirteen united States of America,

Preamble

When in the Course of human events, it becomes necessary for one people to dissolve the political bands which have connected them with another, and to assume among the powers of the earth, the separate and equal station to which the Laws of Nature and Nature's God entitle them, a decent respect to the opinions of mankind requires that they should declare the causes which impel them to the separation.—

impel *force*

Declaration of Natural Rights

We hold these truths to be self-evident, that all men are created equal, that they are endowed by their Creator with certain unalienable Rights, that among these are Life, Liberty, and the pursuit of Happiness.—

endowed *provided*

That to secure these rights, Governments are instituted among Men, deriving their just powers from the consent of the governed,—

People create governments to ensure that their natural rights are protected.

That whenever any Form of Government becomes destructive of these ends, it is the Right of the People to alter or to abolish it, and to institute new Government, laying its foundation on such principles and organizing its powers in such form, as to them shall seem most likely to effect their Safety and Happiness. Prudence, indeed, will dictate that Governments long established should not be changed for light and transient causes; and accordingly all experience hath shewn, that mankind are more disposed to suffer, while evils are sufferable, than to right themselves by abolishing the forms to which they are accustomed. But when a long train of abuses and usurpations, pursuing invariably the same Object evinces a design to reduce them under absolute Despotism, it is their right, it is their duty, to throw off such Government, and to provide new Guards for their future security.—

If a government does not serve its purpose, the people have a right to abolish it. Then the people have the right and duty to create a new government that will safeguard their security.

Despotism *unlimited power*

MORE ABOUT . . .

The Declaration of Independence The Continental Congress had copies of the Declaration of Independence made, and messengers rushed them to leaders in each of the thirteen colonies. The leaders then had the Declaration read aloud in public places. The first such reading was given on July 8, 1776, from the steps of the Philadelphia Statehouse—the building where the Continental Congress had debated the document. Philadelphians were summoned to the reading by the ringing of the Liberty Bell.

List of Grievances

Such has been the patient sufferance of these Colonies; and such is now the necessity which constrains them to alter their former Systems of Government. The history of the present King of Great Britain is a history of repeated injuries and usurpations, all having in direct object the establishment of an absolute Tyranny over these States. To prove this, let Facts be submitted to a candid world.—

He has refused his Assent to Laws, the most wholesome and necessary for the public good.—

He has forbidden his Governors to pass Laws of immediate and pressing importance, unless suspended in their operation till his Assent should be obtained; and when so suspended, he has utterly neglected to attend to them.—

He has refused to pass other Laws for the accommodation of large districts of people, unless those people would relinquish the right of Representation in the Legislature, a right inestimable to them and formidable to tyrants only.—

He has called together legislative bodies at places unusual, uncomfortable, and distant from the depository of their public Records, for the sole purpose of fatiguing them into compliance with his measures.—

He has dissolved Representative Houses repeatedly, for opposing with manly firmness his invasions on the rights of the people.—

He has refused for a long time, after such dissolutions, to cause others to be elected; whereby the Legislative powers, incapable of Annihilation, have returned to the People at large for their exercise; the State remaining in the meantime exposed to all the dangers of invasion from without, and convulsions within.—

He has endeavoured to prevent the population of these States; for that

usurpations ***unjust uses of power***

Each paragraph lists alleged injustices of George III.

relinquish ***give up***
inestimable ***priceless***

Annihilation ***destruction***

convulsions ***violent disturbances***

Eagle and crossed flags

The Second Continental Congress **by Edward Savage**

THE DECLARATION OF INDEPENDENCE

2 TEACH

L1 Analyzing Information Inform students that statements in the Declaration of Natural Rights proclaim some of the most important ideas on which democratic government is based. Then have students identify these statements in the Declaration of Independence. *(Most students will note the following: All people are created equal; all people possess certain basic rights; the purpose of governments is to secure these rights for the people; the power and authority of governments are derived from the people.)*

What?Where?When?Who?

Serious Editing Congress did not adopt the Declaration of Independence with just a few minor changes in Jefferson's work. Congress cut about a quarter of the document, most notably a scathing attack on slaveholding and the slave trade.

CURRICULUM CONNECTION

World History The Declaration of Independence proved very influential, inspiring the struggle for freedom in other parts of the world. The Marquis de Lafayette, who fought for the colonists in the American Revolution and became a key figure in the French Revolution, hung a copy of the Declaration on his dining room wall. He looked forward to the day when a copy of a French Declaration of Human Rights would hang beside it. The leaders of the Latin American independence movements of the early 1800s also were spurred to take action by the democratic sentiments expressed in the Declaration.

L2 Determining Cause and Effect Write *Declaration of Independence* on the chalkboard and tell students that this is the event in a cause-effect-cause chain. Ask students to complete the chain by noting the causes and effects of the Declaration of Independence. Suggest that they add annotations explaining which cause they think made the passage of the Declaration inevitable and which outcome they think was the most important.

Who?What?Where?When?

Only George III Although Parliament was the body that drafted the laws that so upset the colonists, Parliament is not mentioned once in the Declaration of Independence. The List of Grievances singles out George III for blame.

Naturalization of Foreigners *process by which foreign-born persons become citizens*

purpose obstructing the Laws for Naturalization of Foreigners; refusing to pass others to encourage their migrations hither, and raising the conditions of new Appropriations of Lands.—

He has obstructed the Administration of Justice, by refusing his Assent to Laws for establishing Judiciary powers.—

tenure *term*

He has made Judges dependent on his Will alone, for the tenure of their offices, and the amount and payment of their salaries.—

Refers to the British troops sent to the colonies after the French and Indian War.

He has erected a multitude of New Offices, and sent hither swarms of Officers to harass our people, and eat out their substance.—

He has kept among us, in times of peace, Standing Armies without the Consent of our legislatures.—

He has affected to render the Military independent of and superior to the Civil power.—

Refers to the 1766 Declaratory Act.

He has combined with others to subject us to a jurisdiction foreign to our constitution, and unacknowledged by our laws; giving his Assent to their Acts of pretended Legislation:—

quartering *lodging*

For quartering large bodies of troops among us:—

For protecting them, by a mock Trial, from punishment for any Murders which they should commit on the Inhabitants of these States:—

For cutting off our Trade with all parts of the world:—

For imposing Taxes on us without our Consent:—

For depriving us in many cases, of the benefits of Trial by Jury:—

For transporting us beyond Seas to be tried for pretended offences:—

Refers to the 1774 Quebec Act.

render *make*

For abolishing the free System of English Laws in a neighbouring Province, establishing therein an Arbitrary government, and enlarging its Boundaries so as to render it at once an example and fit instrument for introducing the same absolute rule into these Colonies:—

For taking away our Charters, abolishing our most valuable Laws, and altering fundamentally the Forms of our Governments:—

For suspending our own Legislatures, and declaring themselves invested with power to legislate for us in all cases whatsoever.—

abdicated *given up*

He has abdicated Government here, by declaring us out of his Protection and waging War against us.—

He has plundered our seas, ravaged our Coasts, burnt our towns, and destroyed the Lives of our people.—

perfidy *violation of trust*

He is at this time transporting large Armies of foreign Mercenaries to compleat the works of death, desolation and tyranny, already begun with circumstances of Cruelty & perfidy scarcely paralleled in the most barbarous ages, and totally unworthy the Head of a civilized nation.—

He has constrained our fellow Citizens taken Captive on the high Seas to bear Arms against their Country, to become the executioners of their friends and Brethren, or to fall themselves by their Hands.—

insurrections *rebellions*

He has excited domestic insurrections amongst us, and has endeavoured to bring on the inhabitants of our frontiers, the merciless Indian Savages, whose known rule of warfare, is an undistinguished destruction of all ages, sexes and conditions.

Petitioned for Redress *asked formally for a correction of wrongs*

In every stage of these Oppressions We have Petitioned for Redress in the most humble terms: Our repeated Petitions have been answered only by repeated injury. A Prince, whose character is thus marked by every act which may define a Tyrant, is unfit to be the ruler of a free people.

Cooperative Learning Activity

Research Report Inform students that the Declaration of Independence has been a force for change in the United States. Americans have used its ideas to promote such measures as the abolition of slavery and equal rights for women. Then organize students into several small groups. Have groups conduct research to find three examples of individuals or groups using the Declaration of Independence to promote reform. Have groups present their findings in an illustrated report.

Nor have We been wanting in attentions to our British brethren. We have warned them from time to time of attempts by their legislature to extend an unwarrantable jurisdiction over us. We have reminded them of the circumstances of our emigration and settlement here. We have appealed to their native justice and magnanimity, and we have conjured them by the ties of our common kindred to disavow these usurpations, which would inevitably interrupt our connections and correspondence. They too have been deaf to the voice of justice and of consanguinity. We must, therefore, acquiesce in the necessity, which denounces our Separation, and hold them, as we hold the rest of mankind, Enemies in War, in Peace Friends.—

unwarrantable jurisdiction ***unjustified authority***

consanguinity ***originating from the same ancestor***

Resolution of Independence by the United States

We, therefore, the Representatives of the united States of America, in General Congress, Assembled, appealing to the Supreme Judge of the world for the rectitude of our intentions, do, in the Name, and by Authority of the good People of these Colonies, solemnly publish and declare, That these United Colonies are, and of Right ought to be Free and Independent States; that they are Absolved from all Allegiance to the British Crown, and that all political connection between them and the State of Great Britain, is and ought to be totally dissolved; and that as Free and Independent States, they have full Power to levy War, conclude Peace, contract Alliances, establish Commerce, and to do all other Acts and Things which Independent States may of right do.—

And for the support of this Declaration, with a firm reliance on the protection of divine Providence, we mutually pledge to each other our Lives, our Fortunes and our sacred Honour.

rectitude ***rightness***

The signers, as representatives of the American people, declared the colonies independent from Great Britain. Most members signed the document on August 2, 1776.

John Hancock
President from Massachusetts

Georgia
Button Gwinnett
Lyman Hall
George Walton

North Carolina
William Hooper
Joseph Hewes
John Penn

South Carolina
Edward Rutledge
Thomas Heyward, Jr.
Thomas Lynch, Jr.
Arthur Middleton

Maryland
Samuel Chase
William Paca
Thomas Stone
Charles Carroll of Carrollton

Virginia
George Wythe
Richard Henry Lee
Thomas Jefferson
Benjamin Harrison
Thomas Nelson Jr.
Francis Lightfoot Lee
Carter Braxton

Pennsylvania
Robert Morris
Benjamin Rush
Benjamin Franklin
John Morton
George Clymer
James Smith
George Taylor
James Wilson
George Ross

Delaware
Caesar Rodney
George Read
Thomas McKean

New York
William Floyd
Philip Livingston
Francis Lewis
Lewis Morris

New Jersey
Richard Stockton
John Witherspoon
Francis Hopkinson
John Hart
Abraham Clark

New Hampshire
Josiah Bartlett
William Whipple
Matthew Thornton

Massachusetts
Samuel Adams
John Adams
Robert Treat Paine
Elbridge Gerry

Rhode Island
Stephen Hopkins
William Ellery

Connecticut
Samuel Huntington
William Williams
Oliver Wolcott
Roger Sherman

Who? What? Where? When?

Two Lees Richard Henry Lee and Francis Lightfoot Lee, two Virginians who signed the Declaration of Independence, were brothers. Their cousin, Henry "Lighthorse Harry" Lee, served with considerable distinction in the Continental Army.

Linking PAST & PRESENT

Democratic Ideas The ideas expressed in the Declaration of Independence still reverberate in the twentieth century. When Ho Chi Minh declared Vietnam free of its French colonial rulers in 1945, he quoted freely from the Declaration. And Jawaharlal Nehru, a leader of the struggle for independence in India, considered the Declaration a "landmark in human freedom."

MULTIPLE LEARNING STYLES

Verbal/Linguistic Learners Students who have difficulty decoding unfamiliar words sometimes skip over them. The Declaration of Independence is reproduced in its original language and, therefore, contains a number of words that probably are unfamiliar. Point out to students that many of these words are defined in the margin notes. Suggest that students substitute the definitions for the unfamiliar words as they read through the document. Ask volunteers to paraphrase various sections of the document in everyday language. ELL

GLENCOE TECHNOLOGY

VIDEODISC
MindJogger Videoquiz

Use MindJogger to review the Chapter 5 content.

Chapter 5
Disc 1, Side B

Also available in VHS.

Chapter 5 Review and Activities

Reviewing Key Terms

On a sheet of paper, define the following terms:

revenue
writs of assistance
resolution
effigy
boycott
nonimportation
repeal
propaganda
committee of correspondence
militia
minutemen
Loyalist
Patriot
petition
preamble

Reviewing Key Facts

1. What did the British do to keep colonists from expanding westward?
2. How did the British government use the colonies to raise revenue?
3. What incident caused the British Parliament to pass the Coercive Acts?
4. What was the purpose of the first Continental Congress?
5. If government does not protect the basic rights of the people it governs, what did the Declaration of Independence say that people had the right to do?

Critical Thinking

Drawing Conclusions

Colonists created many documents to rouse anti-British feelings and to support the move for independence.

1. Why did the Boston Massacre present a good opportunity for the colonists to use propaganda against the British?
2. Why do you think Thomas Paine chose the title *Common Sense* for his pamphlet? How did the pamphlet encourage the colonists' move toward freedom from Great Britain?

Time Line Activity

Create a time line on which you place the following events in chronological order.

- Declaration of Independence written
- Battle of Bunker Hill begins
- Britain passes Stamp Act
- First Continental Congress meets
- The Boston Massacre occurs
- Colonists throw tea into Boston Harbor

Reviewing Themes

1. **Civic Rights and Responsibilities** Why did colonists think that the Stamp Act ignored the colonial tradition of self-government?
2. **Groups and Institutions** Give two examples of how colonies gained strength against the British by working in groups.
3. **Groups and Institutions** What did Patrick Henry mean when he said, "I am not a Virginian, but an American"?
4. **Government and Democracy** According to the Declaration of Independence, what are the three basic freedoms to which every person is entitled?

Skill Practice Activity

Distinguishing Fact from Opinion

Read the following statements. Tell whether each is a fact or an opinion.

1. Great Britain should not have tried to stop the colonists from settling west of the Appalachians.
2. The Stamp Act placed a tax on almost all printed material in the colonies.
3. The Daughters of Liberty urged Americans to wear homemade fabrics.
4. Thomas Jefferson was a better writer than John Adams was.

Reviewing Key Terms

The key terms used in this activity are defined in the textbook glossary on pages A26–A35.

Reviewing Key Facts

1. issued the Proclamation of 1763
2. imposed taxes such as the Stamp Act and Townshend Acts
3. Boston Tea Party
4. It was a political body formed to unite all the American colonies in protest of British taxes.
5. alter or abolish the government and create a new government

Critical Thinking

1. Because the British fired the first shots, the colonists could portray themselves as innocent victims of the "bloodthirsty redcoats."
2. Students may suggest that Paine wanted to convey that it was only "common sense" to want independence from a "brute" of a king. The pamphlet clearly spelled out reasons to seek independence; it also appealed to the hearts as well as the minds of readers.

Time Line Activity

Events should be placed in this order: Britain passes Stamp Act, The Boston Massacre occurs, Colonists throw tea into Boston Harbor, First Continental Congress meets, Battle of Bunker Hill begins, Declaration of Independence written

Reviewing Themes

1. It taxed the colonies directly without the colonists' consent.
2. any two: boycotts; Sons of Liberty; Daughters of Liberty; committees of correspondence; militias; Boston Tea Party; Continental Army, Continental Congress, or any other acceptable colonial group
3. His loyalty to his home colony was replaced by his new loyalty to the colonies as a whole.
4. life, liberty, and the pursuit of happiness

Geography Activity

Study the map below and answer the questions that follow.

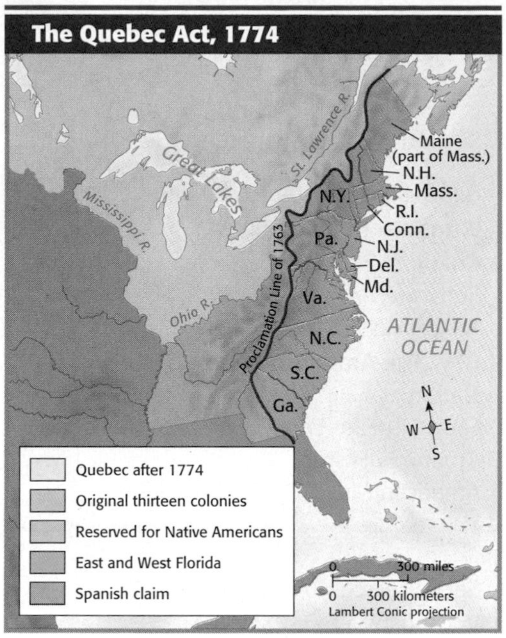

1. **Place** What bodies of water were part of Quebec after the Quebec Act?
2. **Location** What country claimed the land west of Quebec?
3. **Movement** What inland waterways marked the southern and western boundaries of Quebec's new territory?
4. **Region** For whom was land reserved just west of the Appalachian Mountains?

Cooperative Activity

History and Citizenship Work with a group of classmates to create your own "Declaration of Independence." Use the original Declaration of Independence on pages 156-159 as a guide to create your document. Outline the basic freedoms that you expect to have as a citizen and describe why these freedoms are important to you. Then write at least three responsibilities and/or sacrifices that citizens should be willing to make to enjoy the freedoms you listed. After your group has completed its Declaration of Independence, have the groups come together as a class. Share all the groups' documents and decide which group best represented the needs of the whole class.

Technology Activity

Using the Internet On the Internet, locate the computer address for the National Archives or the Library of Congress in Washington, D.C. Search each site for documents concerning the drafting of the Declaration of Independence and/or photos of pamphlets produced by the colonies in the 1700s. Print a copy of what you find or sketch a likeness to share with the class.

Portfolio Activity

History Journal Review the chapter for details about the Boston Massacre, the Battle of Bunker Hill, and the writing of the Declaration of Independence. Record the details in your journal. Use your information to create three headlines for articles that might have run in a colonial newspaper when these events occurred.

Cooperative Activity

Students' declarations should reflect thoughtful and respectful insight about some of the independence issues that teenagers face. These issues might include curfews, household or school responsibilities, use of free time, or discipline. Each student should take a copy of the declaration home to share and discuss with an adult in his or her household. Encourage students to make it a "living" document by revising it as their situations change.

Technology Activity

Students should locate at least one photo or document at the National Archives or Library of Congress Internet sites and present what they find to the class.

Portfolio Activity Students should write three headlines relevant to these events: the Boston Massacre, the Battle of Bunker Hill, and the writing of the Declaration of Independence.

Chapter Bonus Test Question

Ask: **What kind of work had George Washington done before he began his military service?** *(surveying)*

Skill Practice Activity

1. opinion
2. fact
3. fact
4. opinion

Geography Activity

1. the Great Lakes and the St. Lawrence River
2. Spain
3. Mississippi and Ohio Rivers
4. Native Americans

Chapter 6 Planning Guide

A complete, 1-page lesson plan is provided for each section in the *Reproducible Lesson Plans* booklet.

Section Resources

Daily Objectives	Reproducible Resources	Multimedia Resources
Section 1 The Early Years Recognize the comparative strengths and weaknesses of the Patriot and British forces during the first year and a half of the war.	Reproducible Lesson Plan 6–1 Guided Reading Activity 6–1* Section Quiz 6–1* Reteaching Activity 6–1 Enrichment Activity 6–1	Section Focus Transparency 6–1 U.S. History and Art, Transparency 10 Vocabulary PuzzleMaker Chapter Challenger Interactive Review Software Testmaker GTV: The American People: Fabric of a Nation Facts On File: Landmark Documents in American History American Music Cultural Traditions
Section 2 The War Continues Discuss the Patriots' search for support, both abroad and at home.	Reproducible Lesson Plan 6–2 Guided Reading Activity 6–2* Section Quiz 6–2* Reteaching Activity 6–2 Enrichment Activity 6–2	Section Focus Transparency 6–2 Vocabulary PuzzleMaker Chapter Challenger Interactive Review Software Testmaker GTV: A Geographic Perspective on American History
Section 3 The War Moves West and South Describe key battles west of the Appalachian Mountains, in the Southern states, and at sea.	Reproducible Lesson Plan 6–3 Guided Reading Activity 6–3* Section Quiz 6–3* Reteaching Activity 6–3 Enrichment Activity 6–3	Section Focus Transparency 6–3 Vocabulary PuzzleMaker Chapter Challenger Interactive Review Software Testmaker NGS PictureShow: Native Americans, Part 1 American Music Cultural Traditions
Section 4 The War Is Won Explain how the Revolutionary War ended and why the Patriots won.	Reproducible Lesson Plan 6–4 Guided Reading Activity 6–4* Section Quiz 6–4* Reteaching Activity 6–4 Enrichment Activity 6–4	Section Focus Transparency 6–4 Vocabulary PuzzleMaker Chapter Challenger Interactive Review Software Testmaker Facts On File: Landmark Documents in American History

** Also available in Spanish*

Blackline Master · Transparency · Videodisc · CD-ROM · Music Program · Audiocassette · Software

0:00 **OUT OF TIME?**
Assign the Chapter 6 Digest and the corresponding Chapter Digests Audiocassettes with activities and tests.

Activity

From the Classroom of...

Edward McKinney
Hugh Hartman Middle School
Redmond, OR

Covering the Revolution in a Classroom Newspaper

Students will publish a newspaper to further develop the material covered in this chapter. Organize the class into groups, and make each group responsible for one of these topics: (1) biographies and fictional interviews of famous people, (2) coverage of specific battles, (3) recipes of the types of food prepared during the Revolutionary era, (4) articles about weapons used, and so on.

Each student will research and submit a short story on the group's topic. Stories should be typed using narrow margins so they can be pasted onto 11" X 17" pieces of paper. Each group then decides which one of its stories it wants on the front page. The groups' other stories will be placed on the inside pages.

Assign one member from each group to work together on designing the newspaper's front page. The rest of the groups should design their own pages. Remind them to include art, illustrations, advertisements, and so on.

Block Schedule

Block scheduling differs from traditional class scheduling in the amount of time allotted to each period. The extended time frame provided by block scheduling affords you the opportunity to implement a greater number of research-oriented and activity-intense projects to motivate and involve your students. Activities that are particularly suited to use within the block scheduling framework are identified throughout this chapter by the following designation:

NATIONAL GEOGRAPHIC SOCIETY Teacher's Corner

INDEX TO NATIONAL GEOGRAPHIC MAGAZINE

The following articles may be used for research relating to this chapter:

- "Two Revolutions," by Charles McCarry, July 1989.
- "Yorktown Shipwreck," by John D. Broadwater, June 1988.

NATIONAL GEOGRAPHIC SOCIETY PRODUCTS AVAILABLE FROM GLENCOE

To order the following products for use with this chapter, contact your local Glencoe sales representative, or call Glencoe at 1-800-334-7344:

- *GTV: A Geographic Perspective on American History* (Videodisc)
- *GTV: The American People: Fabric of a Nation* (Videodisc)
- *PictureShow: The American Revolution* (CD-ROM)
- *PictureShow: The American Revolution* (Transparencies)
- *PictureShow: Colonial America* (CD-ROM)
- *PictureShow: Colonial America* (Transparencies)

ADDITIONAL NATIONAL GEOGRAPHIC SOCIETY PRODUCTS

To order the following products for use with this chapter, call National Geographic Society at 1-800-368-2728:

- *Democratic Government Series, "The United States"* (Video)
- *Branches of Government Series* (Video)
- *Historical Atlas of the United States* (Atlas)

KEY TO ABILITY LEVELS

Teaching strategies have been coded for varying learning styles and abilities.

L1 **BASIC** activities for all students
L2 **AVERAGE** activities for average to above-average students
L3 **CHALLENGING** activities for above-average students
ELL **ENGLISH LANGUAGE LEARNER** activities

Chapter 6 Resource Guide

Home Involvement

Home Involvement Activity 6

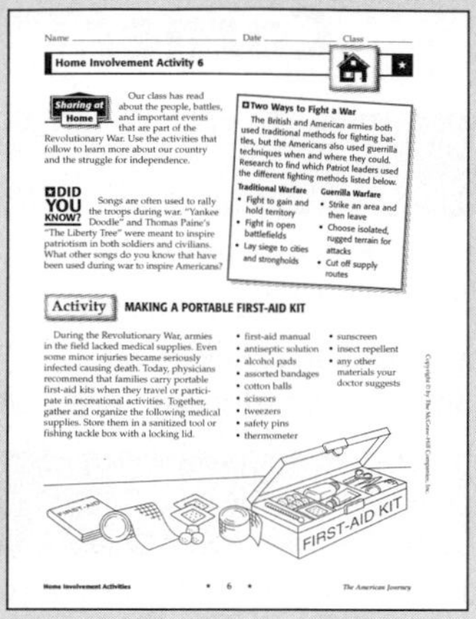

Review Activities

Chapter Summary 6

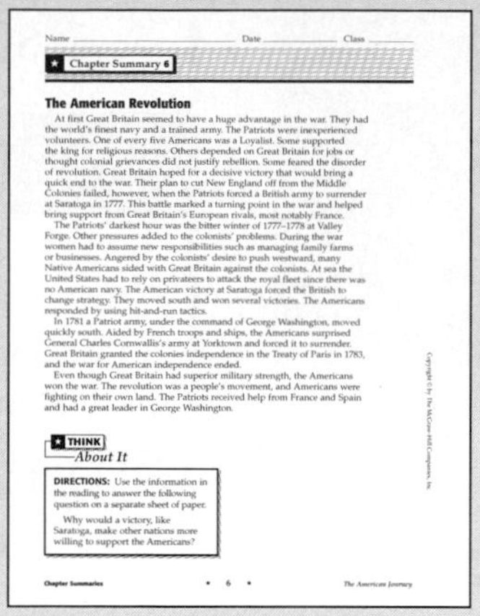

Workbook Activity 6

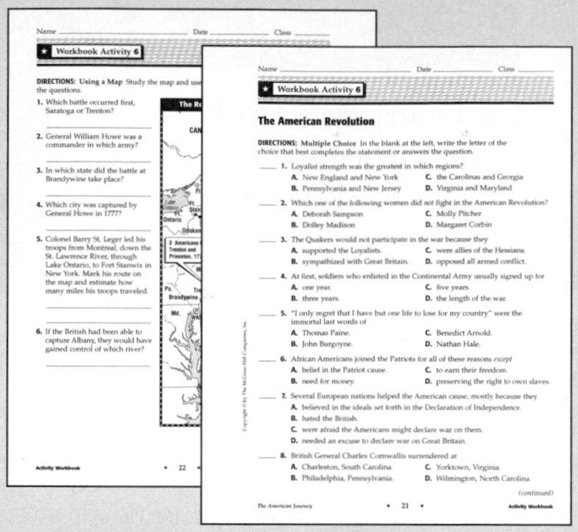

Reinforcement Activities

Time Line Activity 6

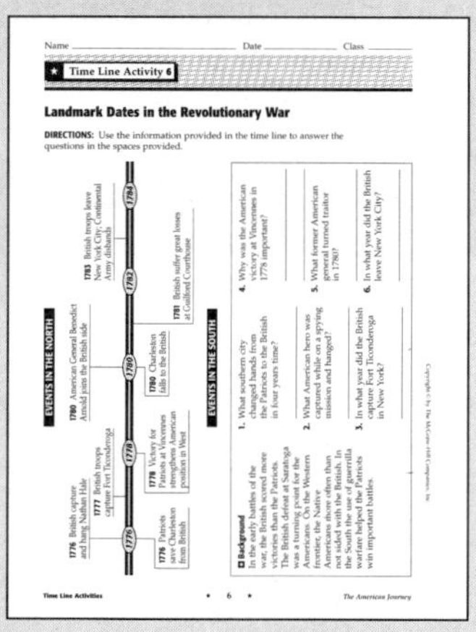

Vocabulary Activity 6

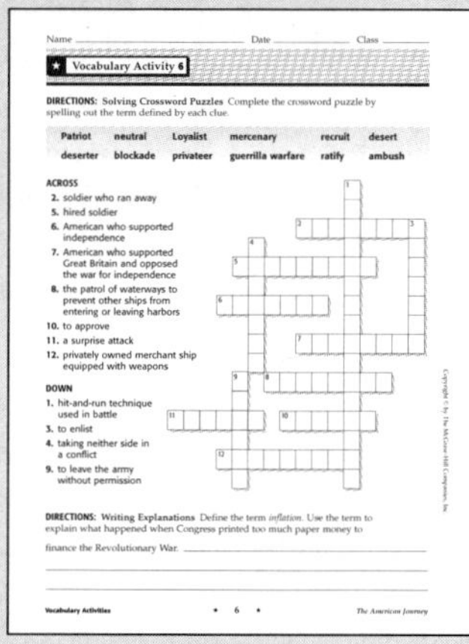

Chapter Skills Activity 6

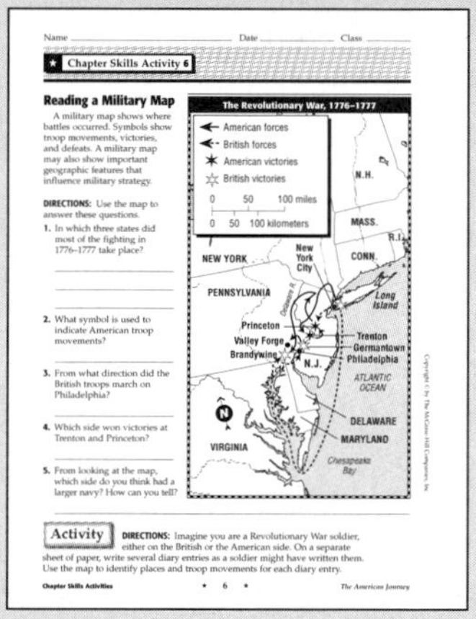

Enrichment Activities

Linking Past and Present Activity 6

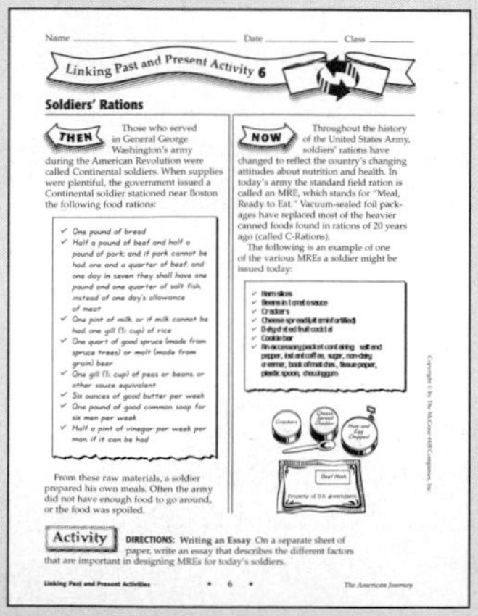

Primary Source Reading 6

Geography Activities

Mapping History Activity 6

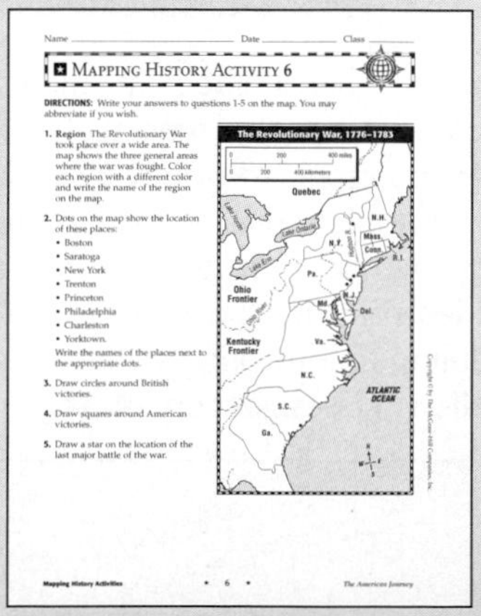

Chapter 6 Resource Guide

Assessment

Chapter 6 Test, Form A

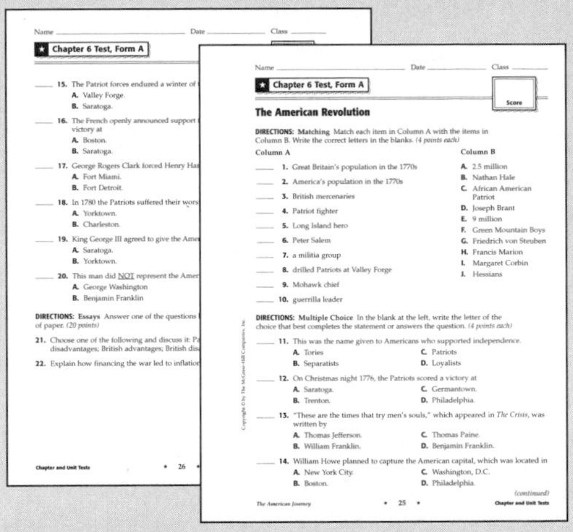

Chapter 6 Test, Form B

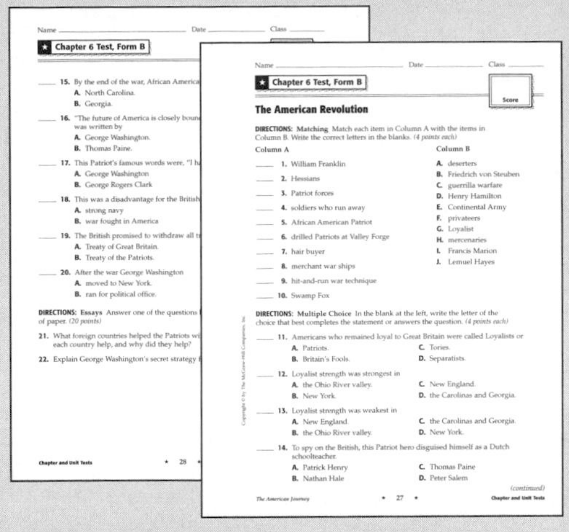

Performance Assessment Activity 6

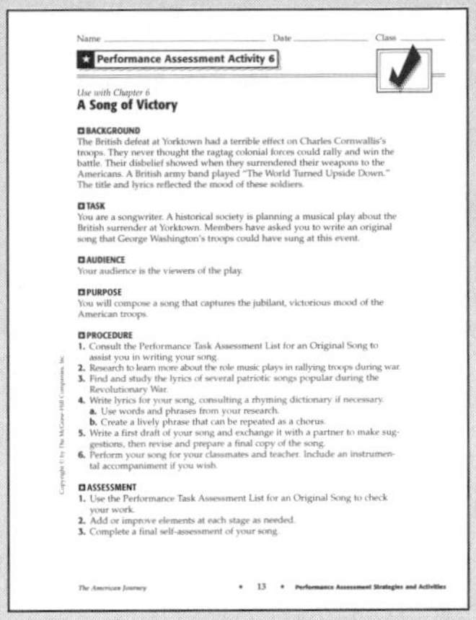

Spanish Resources

The following Spanish language materials are available in the Spanish Resources binder:

- **Spanish Chapter Summary 6**
- **Spanish Vocabulary Activity 6**
- **Spanish Guided Reading Activities, Chapter 6**
- **Spanish Section Quizzes, Chapter 6**
- **Spanish Home Involvement Activity 6**
- **Spanish Chapter 6 Digests Audiocassette Activity and Test**

Activity Manipulatives

Help students learn more about America's cultural history with:

- **American Crafts Hands-On Activities**
- **American Games Hands-On Activities**
- **American History Flash Cards**

Additional Resources From Glencoe

- **U.S. History & Art,** Transparency 10, *Washington Crossing the Delaware*
- **Focus on American Art Prints,** *Watson and the Shark* by John Singleton Copley
- **American Music Cultural Traditions,** Lesson 2: "Junto Song"
- **The Spirit of American Art and Music,** Benjamin West
- **Outline Map Resource Book**
- **U.S. Desk Map**
- **The American History Videodisc and CD-ROM,** *The American Revolution and the Early Republic*

A&E HOME VIDEO. Biography THE HISTORY CHANNEL.

The following videotape programs are available from Glencoe as supplements to Chapter 6:

- **John Paul Jones: Captain of the High Seas** (ISBN 1-56501-875-3)
- **The American Revolution (Six Video Set)** (ISBN 1-56501-436-7)
- **Benedict Arnold** (ISBN 1-56501-594-0)

To order, call Glencoe at 1-800-334-7344. To find classroom resources to accompany many of these videos, check the following home pages:
A&E Television: http://www.aetv.com
The History Channel: http://www.historychannel.com

Chapter Themes

Chapter Themes are listed by section on this chapter opening page of the Student Edition. A corresponding theme-based activity is available under "FOCUS," and a theme-based question is asked in the Section and Chapter Reviews.

Performance Assessment

Refer to Activity 6 in the *Performance Assessment Strategies and Activities* booklet.

GLENCOE TECHNOLOGY

VIDEODISC
MindJogger Videoquiz

Use MindJogger to preview the Chapter 6 content.

Chapter 6
Disc 1, Side B

Also available in VHS.

HISTORY AND ART For a little more than two years after the Battle of Yorktown—and for seven months after Congress had ratified the Treaty of Paris—New York remained securely under the control of Sir Guy Carleton and his British forces.

Chapter 6

1776–1783

The American Revolution

Why It's Important

Although the United States declared its independence in 1776, no country recognized it as an independent nation at that time. It took a war and the efforts of American diplomats to win this recognition from Britain, France, Spain, and other European countries. In fighting for the principles set forth in the Declaration, the American Patriots laid the foundation for the United States of America we know today.

Chapter Themes

- *Section 1,* Groups and Institutions
- *Section 2,* Groups and Institutions
- *Section 3,* Geography and History
- *Section 4,* Groups and Institutions

HISTORY AND ART ***Washington's Triumphant Entrance*** **by an unknown artist** George Washington, commander of the Continental Army, entered New York in triumph after the departure of British troops from the city in November 1783.

162

EXTRA CREDIT PROJECT

Depicting a Revolution This chapter is filled with dramatic moments. Invite students to select one such moment to depict artistically. Here are a few ideas:
- Margaret Corbin or Deborah Sampson on the battlefield
- An African American enlisting in the Continental Army
- Washington's arrival at Trenton
- Winter camp at Valley Forge
- The battle between the *Bonhomme Richard* and the *Serapis*
- The surrender at Yorktown

You may wish to work with students to prepare a classroom display of the individual works.

1776 — 1777 — 1778

April 1776
Battle of Lexington

December 1776
Patriots capture Hessians at Trenton

October 1777
Burgoyne surrenders at Saratoga

1778
African American regiment forms in Rhode Island

Section 1

The Early Years

READ TO DISCOVER . . .

- why some Americans supported the British.
- how the British planned to win the war.
- how the Battle of Saratoga marked a turning point of the war.

TERMS TO LEARN

Patriot	mercenary
neutral	recruit
Loyalist	deserter

The Storyteller

The mighty British troops sailed to America, confident that they would quickly and easily crush the rebellious colonists. A British officer wrote to his friend, describing a military skirmish:

September 3, 1776

We landed on Long-Island. . . . [I]t was a fine sight to see with what [eagerness] they dispatched the Rebels with their bayonets after we had surrounded them so that they could not resist. . . . The island is all ours, and we shall soon take New-York, for the Rebels dare not look us in the face. I expect the affair will be over [after] this campaign. . . .

British cannon

Both the British and the Americans expected the war for independence to be short. The British planned to crush the rebellious colonists by force. Most of the **Patriots**—Americans who supported independence—believed the British would give up after losing one or two major battles. Few Patriots believed John Adams when he predicted in April 1776: "We shall have a long, obstinate, and bloody war to go through."

The Opposing Sides

At first glance the British had an overwhelming advantage in the war. They had the strongest navy in the world; an experienced, well-trained army; and the wealth of a worldwide empire. Britain also had a much larger population than the United States—9 million people in Britain compared to only 2.5 million in the United States.

The colonists suffered serious disadvantages. They lacked a regular army and a strong navy. American soldiers also lacked military experience, and weapons and ammunition were in short supply. Many Patriots belonged to militia groups—local forces—but they were volunteer soldiers who fought for short periods of time before returning home to tend their farms.

The Patriots faced another obstacle. Not all Americans supported the struggle for independence. Some people were **neutral,** taking neither side in the conflict. The Quakers, for example, would not participate in the war because they opposed all armed conflict. Still other Americans remained loyal to Britain.

SECTION RESOURCES

Reproducible Masters
- Guided Reading Activity 6–1
- Section Quiz 6–1
- Reteaching Activity 6–1
- Enrichment Activity 6–1

Transparencies
- Section Focus Transparency 6–1
- U.S. History and Art, Transparency 10

Multimedia
- Vocabulary PuzzleMaker
- Chapter Challenger Interactive Review Software
- GTV: The American People: Fabric of a Nation
- Facts On File: Landmark Documents in American History
- American Music Cultural Traditions

1 FOCUS

BELLRINGER
Motivational Activity

Before taking roll at the beginning of the class period, project Section Focus Transparency 6–1 and have students answer the questions. Discuss students' responses.

This activity is also available as a blackline master.

Section Focus Transparency 6–1

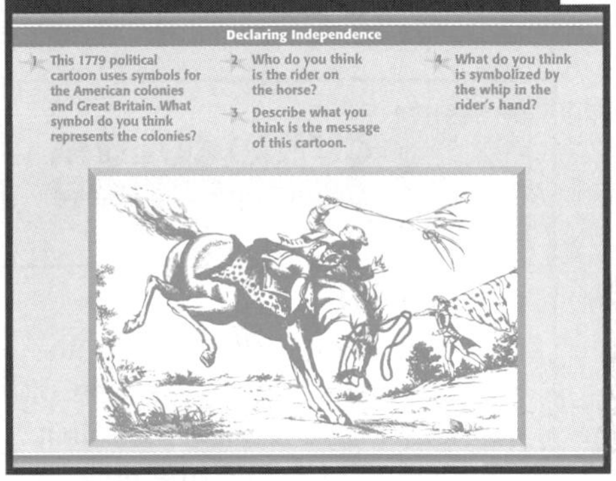

Vocabulary Precheck

Before students begin their study of this section, quiz them on the meanings of the **Terms to Learn.** Assist them in understanding any terms that may be unfamiliar.

Use the **Vocabulary PuzzleMaker** to create crossword and word search puzzles.

Section Theme
Groups and Institutions

Although British forces won several battles at the beginning of the war, Patriot victories slowed their progress.

Activity Ask students to complete these sentences in as many ways as they can. Discuss the results.
- The British will win the war because _____.
- The Patriots will win the war because _____.

2 TEACH

L1 Discussing Reasons Ask pairs of students: **Why might you have wanted to support Britain in the war?** Discuss responses that partners present to the class (for example, *I work for the British and don't want to lose my job; I don't think the colonies can work together).*

Picturing HISTORY Many colonists took neither a pro-British nor pro-American stance. They waited to see what would happen. **Answer:** *the Carolinas and Georgia*

CURRICULUM CONNECTION

LITERATURE
Benjamin Franklin satirized the Hessians by writing "The Sale of the Hessians," a fictional letter. In it, the Count de Schaumbergh tells the commander of the Hessian troops not to worry about losing soldiers in battle. Since the count is paid for Hessians who die, he urges the commander to "exhort them to seek glory in the midst of dangers."

Guided Reading Activity 6–1

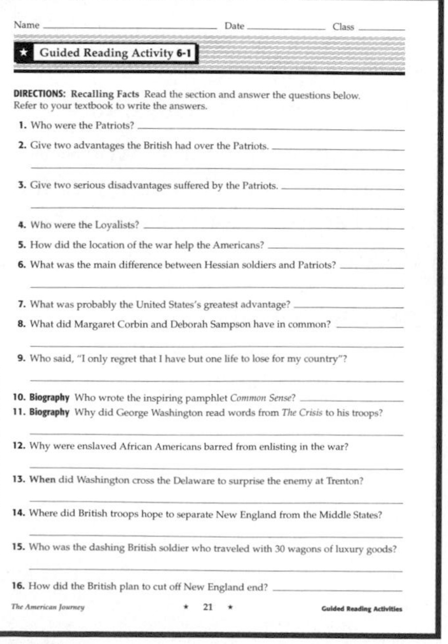
Name ________ Date ________ Class ________

★ Guided Reading Activity 6-1

DIRECTIONS: Recalling Facts Read the section and answer the questions below. Refer to your textbook to write the answers.

1. Who were the Patriots? ________
2. Give two advantages the British had over the Patriots. ________
3. Give two serious disadvantages suffered by the Patriots. ________
4. Who were the Loyalists? ________
5. How did the location of the war help the Americans? ________
6. What was the main difference between Hessian soldiers and Patriots? ________
7. What was probably the United States's greatest advantage? ________
8. What did Margaret Corbin and Deborah Sampson have in common? ________
9. Who said, "I only regret that I have but one life to lose for my country"? ________
10. **Biography** Who wrote the inspiring pamphlet *Common Sense*? ________
11. **Biography** Why did George Washington read words from *The Crisis* to his troops? ________
12. Why were enslaved African Americans barred from enlisting in the war? ________
13. **When** did Washington cross the Delaware to surprise the enemy at Trenton? ________
14. Where did British troops hope to separate New England from the Middle States? ________
15. Who was the dashing British soldier who traveled with 30 wagons of luxury goods? ________
16. How did the British plan to cut off New England end? ________

The American Journey ★ 21 ★ Guided Reading Activities

Picturing HISTORY Some Americans used force against British sympathizers. **In what regions was Loyalist strength the greatest?**

The Loyalists

Those who remained loyal to Britain and opposed the war for independence were called **Loyalists** or Tories. Perhaps one American in five was a Loyalist. Some people changed sides during the war, depending on which army was closer. Loyalist strength varied from region to region. In general it was strongest in the Carolinas and Georgia and weakest in New England.

Loyalists supported Britain for different reasons. Some remained loyal because they were members of the Anglican Church, headed by the British king. Some depended on the British for their jobs. Many feared the disorder that would come from challenging the established government. Others simply could not understand what all the commotion was about. No other country, one Loyalist complained, "faced a rebellion arising from such trivial causes."

The issue of independence disrupted normal relations. Friends and families were divided over loyalty to Britain. For example, William Franklin, son of Patriot Benjamin Franklin, was a Loyalist. He had served as the royal governor of New Jersey. As one Connecticut Loyalist observed:

> "Neighbor was against neighbor, father against son and son against father. He that would not thrust his own blade through his brother's heart was called an infamous villain."

African Americans in the War

Some African Americans also sided with the Loyalists. At the start of the war, the British appealed to enslaved Africans to join them. Lord Dunmore, the royal governor of Virginia, announced that slaves who fought on the British side would be freed, and many men answered his call. Eventually some of them ended up free in Canada, and others settled the British colony of Sierra Leone in Africa.

Patriot Advantages

The Americans possessed some advantages. They were fighting on their own ground and fought with great determination to protect it. The British, on the other hand, had to wage war in a faraway land and were forced to transport soldiers and supplies 3,000 miles across the Atlantic Ocean.

The nature of the British army in America also helped the Patriots. The British relied on **mercenaries**—hired soldiers—to fight. The Americans called the mercenaries **Hessians,** after the region in Germany where most of them lived. To gain support for the war effort, Patriots compared their own troops, who were fighting for the freedom of their own land, to the Hessians, who fought for money. The Patriots had a much greater stake in winning the war than the hired soldiers did. This determination to succeed gave the Americans an edge over the Hessians in battle.

Probably the Americans' greatest advantage was their leader, George Washington. Few individuals could match him for courage, honesty,

COOPERATIVE LEARNING ACTIVITY

Creating a Board Game Organize the class into groups. Explain that each group will create a board game of Revolutionary War battles. Have each group choose a name for the game and discuss how it will be played. Make sure that each group assigns the following tasks to individual group members: drawing a map of the colonies on poster board as a gameboard; illustrating the gameboard; writing the rules of the game; creating playing pieces; and designing playing cards. After each group has completed its game, have groups swap games and play another group's game.

and determination. The war might have taken a different turn without Washington steering its course.

Raising an Army

The Americans placed great value on liberty and personal freedom. After throwing off the rule of the British Parliament, they hesitated to transfer power to their own Continental Congress. In some ways the American Revolution was really 13 separate wars, with each state pursuing its own interests. As a result Congress experienced difficulty enlisting soldiers and raising money to fight the war.

Although the militia played an essential role in the Patriots' forces, the Americans also needed a regular army—well-trained soldiers who could fight anywhere in the colonies. The Congress established the Continental Army but depended on the states to recruit, or enlist, soldiers.

At first soldiers signed up for one year of army service. General Washington appealed for longer terms. "If we ever hope for success," he said, "we must have men enlisted for the whole term of the war." Eventually the Continental Congress offered enlistments for three years or for the length of the war. Most soldiers, however, still signed up for only a year.

Women also fought with the Patriot forces. Margaret Corbin of Pennsylvania accompanied her husband when he joined the Continental Army. After he died in battle, she took his place. Deborah Sampson of Massachusetts disguised herself as a man so she could fight. When she was wounded, she treated the wounds herself so no one would discover that she was a woman.

Fighting in New York

Most of the early battles involved few troops. At Bunker Hill, for example, about 2,000 British soldiers fought 1,200 Americans. The British had not yet won a decisive victory over the Patriots, however, and they realized they would need more troops to end the war quickly.

During the summer of 1776, Britain sent 32,000 troops across the Atlantic to New York. The British commander, **General William Howe,** hoped the sheer size of his army would convince the Patriots to give up. He was soon disappointed.

Defeat on Long Island

Although Washington and the Patriots had fewer than 20,000 troops, they were determined to fight. In late August the two sides clashed in the **Battle of Long Island.** Outnumbered and

Linking PAST & PRESENT

Women in War

Molly Pitcher and Deborah Sampson were two of the few women who actually fought in the Revolution. Other colonial women, along with their families, followed the armies to cook and clean for their husbands. Today women make up about 12 percent of the armed forces of the United States. Women soldiers fought in Panama in 1989 and in the Persian Gulf War of 1991. **How do modern female soldiers differ from Patriot female volunteers?**

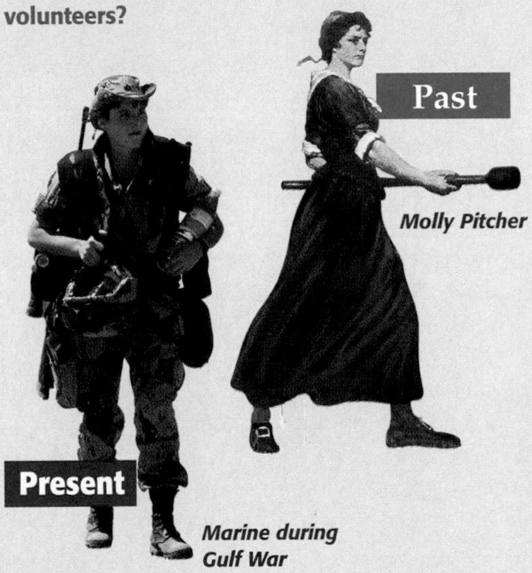

Past

Molly Pitcher

Present

Marine during Gulf War

CHAPTER 6
Section 1, 163–169

NATIONAL GEOGRAPHIC SOCIETY

VIDEODISC
GTV: The American People: Fabric of a Nation

Side 1, Chapter 9
Title: *The Winds of Warfare!*
Subject: Cultural diversity in the colonies
Ask: **What is one action taken by the British that brought the colonists together and led them to revolution?** *(taxation without representation)*

Linking PAST & PRESENT

Women in War The Women's Army Corps began in 1942 (as the Women's Auxiliary Army Corps), as did its Navy counterpart, Women Accepted for Voluntary Emergency Service. During World War II there were also women's corps for the Marines, the Coast Guard, and the Air Force. Approximately 350,000 women served in the United States military during that war.
Answer: *Modern women make a formal commitment to serve in the armed forces, receive the same military training as male soldiers, and have the same responsibilities.*

MULTIPLE LEARNING STYLES

Visual/Spatial Although the Continental forces had some factors in their favor, they also had several needs. Some students may grasp this concept better if they draw representations of what the Continental Army lacked, especially in the early days of the war—a well-trained force, greater numbers of soldiers, and blankets and other supplies. Encourage students to consider their drawings as they explain how these needs gave the early advantage to the British. ELL

History *and the* Humanities

U.S. History & Art, Transparency 10, *Washington Crossing the Delaware*

American Music Cultural Traditions, Lesson 2: "Junto Song"

Who?What?Where?When?

George Washington actually lost more battles than he won. However, he met his goal of keeping the army in the field.

Map Study

Answers

1. American forces
2. Burgoyne surrendered to the Patriot forces.

Map Skills Practice

Reading a Map How did Howe travel from Nova Scotia to New York? *(by ship)*

NATIONAL GEOGRAPHIC SOCIETY

CD-ROM
NGS PictureShow: The American Revolution

After students have viewed the CD-ROM, have half the class write cause-and-effect charts outlining the steps leading up to the Revolutionary War. Then have the other half of the class write two paragraphs summarizing the outcome of the war.

outmaneuvered, the Continental Army suffered a serious defeat at the hands of the British forces.

One Patriot, **Nathan Hale,** proved himself a hero at Long Island. A teacher from Connecticut, Hale volunteered to spy on British troops and disguised himself as a Dutch schoolteacher. The British discovered his true identity, however, and hanged him. Hale's immortal last words were, "I only regret that I have but one life to lose for my country."

Although the Americans showed no lack of bravery, they ran short of supplies for the army. In the autumn of 1776, a British officer wrote that many of the Patriot soldiers killed on Long Island had not been wearing shoes, socks, or jackets. "They are also in great want of blankets," he said, predicting that "the Rebel Army must suffer greatly as soon as the severe weather sets in."

After their defeat on Long Island, Washington retreated to Manhattan, pursued by the British. By late November, the Continental Army had retreated across New Jersey into Pennsylvania.

A Low Point

In the winter of 1776 to 1777, the Patriots' cause was near collapse. The size of the Continental Army had dwindled. Some soldiers

The Revolutionary War, 1776–1777

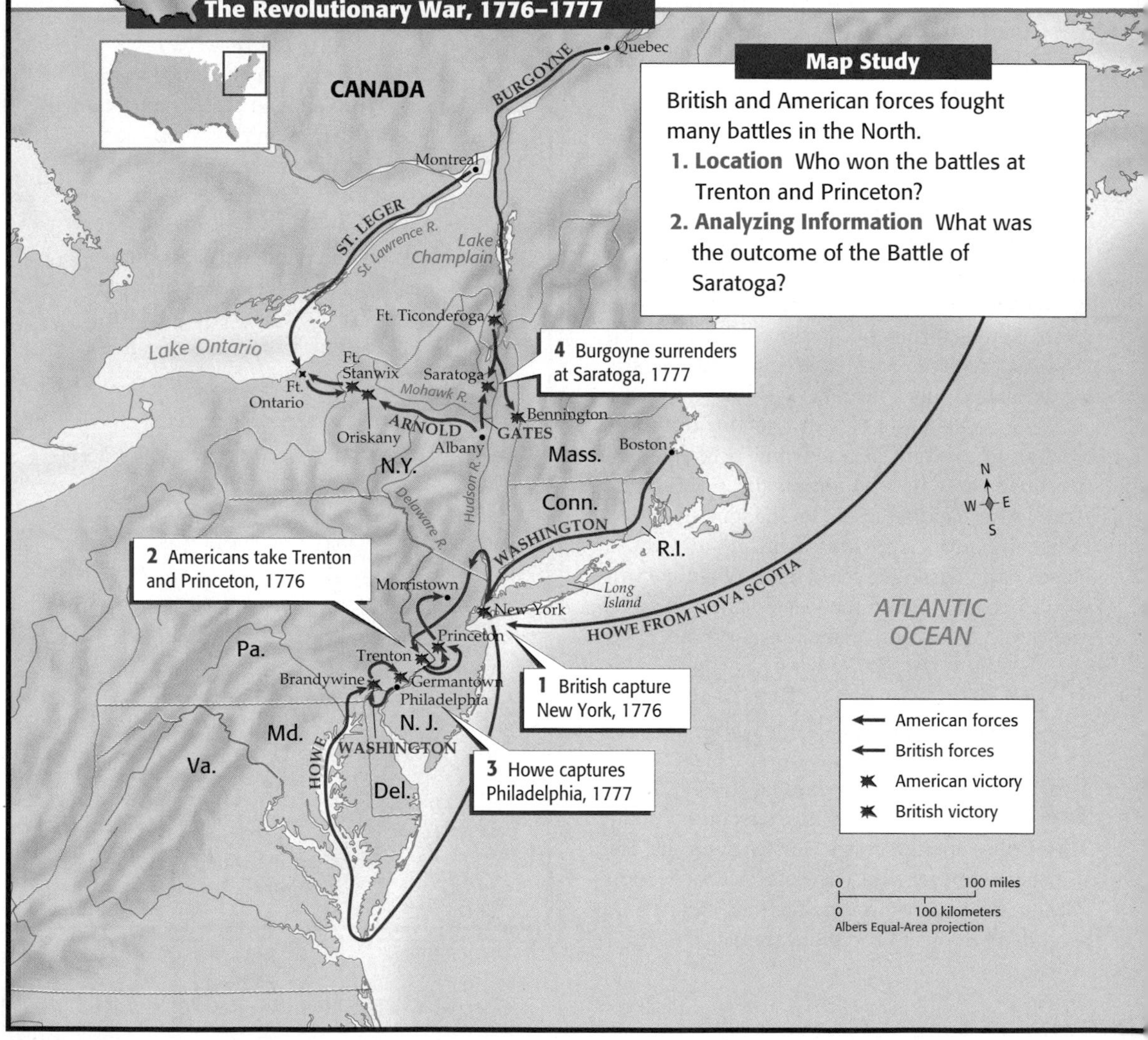

Map Study

British and American forces fought many battles in the North.

1. **Location** Who won the battles at Trenton and Princeton?
2. **Analyzing Information** What was the outcome of the Battle of Saratoga?

Making Connections Activity

Literature As the text points out, George Washington found Thomas Paine's *The Crisis* so empowering that he had it read to his troops. Secure a few copies of *The Crisis* and have students work in small groups to analyze it. Ask them to find and share 8 to 10 statements by Paine that they think would inspire the Continental soldiers. Encourage them to choose their own format for the presentation but to be prepared to explain why they consider each statement inspirational. **L3**

completed their terms of service and went home. Others were **deserters,** soldiers who ran away.

Washington wrote his brother that if new soldiers were not recruited soon, "I think the game is pretty near up." Still, Washington could not believe that the fight for liberty would truly fail.

Biography

Thomas Paine and *The Crisis*

In early 1776 **Thomas Paine** wrote a pamphlet, *Common Sense,* that moved many American colonists toward independence. After taking part in the retreat across New York and New Jersey, Paine published another pamphlet to help boost Americans' lagging spirits. In *The Crisis* he reminded Americans that "the harder the conflict, the more glorious the triumph."

> "These are the times that try men's souls. The summer soldier and the sunshine patriot will in this crisis shrink from the service of their country; but he that stands it now deserves the love and thanks of man and woman."

Washington had Paine's encouraging words read to his troops to inspire them to continue the fight. Throughout the colonies people passed copies of *The Crisis* from hand to hand and discussed Paine's stirring ideas.

Patriot Gains

Washington pleaded with the Continental Congress for more troops. He asked the Congress to enlist free African Americans. Early in the war, the Southern states had persuaded the Congress to bar African American soldiers from the Continental Army. Many white people in the Southern states felt uncomfortable about giving guns to African Americans and allowing them to serve as soldiers. In Southern states with large enslaved populations, whites feared revolts.

Picturing HISTORY About 5,000 African Americans fought for the Americans. **Why did many African Americans support the Americans' cause?**

African Americans Join the Fight

As the need for soldiers grew, some states ignored the ban and enlisted African Americans. Rhode Island raised an all–African American regiment in 1778. By war's end, every state except South Carolina enlisted African Americans to fight.

Historians estimate that as many as 5,000 African Americans joined the Patriots. Among them were **Lemuel Hayes** and **Peter Salem,** who fought at Concord. African Americans fought for the same reasons as other Americans. They believed in the Patriot cause or they needed the money. Some soldiers were enslaved Africans who had run away from slaveholders. Others fought to earn their freedom.

American Victories in New Jersey

The British army settled in New York for the winter of 1776 to 1777, leaving some troops in New Jersey at **Trenton** and **Princeton.** Armies

CHAPTER 6
Section 1, 163–169

Picturing HISTORY The British also made an appeal to African Americans, offering freedom and grants of land in Canada for fighting on their side. In response, thousands of African Americans, including a group called the Black Pioneers, took up arms against the Patriots.
Answer: *support for the Patriot cause, the need for money, the desire for freedom*

Facts On File

CD-ROM
Landmark Documents in American History

Title: *Common Sense, Thomas Paine, 1776*
After students have viewed the document, ask how they would react to *Common Sense* today.

3 ASSESS

Assign Section 1 Review as homework or as an in-class activity.

Use **Chapter Challenger Interactive Review Software** to review Section 1.

CRITICAL THINKING ACTIVITY

Recognizing Ideologies Organize the class into three groups—Patriots, Loyalists, and Neutrals. Have each group discuss its views on the friction between Britain and America and then write three position statements. Have a representative from each group read the group's statements, one at a time. After each statement is read, have the groups discuss the statement. Encourage students to include comments about how the position was reflected in the behavior of those who held it. Students may switch groups to support or protest a statement. Continue until all statements have been read. How have the groups changed? How might that change be explained? **L2**

CHAPTER 6

Section 1, 163–169

HISTORY AND ART Holding New York City gave Britain an excellent harbor (especially important after the loss of Boston). It also put control of the Hudson River into British hands, allowing much freer shipping to and from Canada and greater possibilities of blocking trade between the northern and southern colonies. **Answer:** *The Continental Army reached a low point as a result of a string of defeats and finally retreated into Pennsylvania.*

Section Quiz 6–1

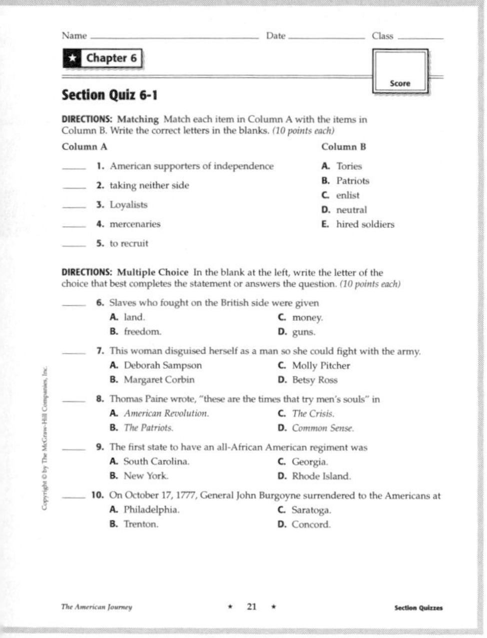

Name ______________ Date ______________ Class ______________

Chapter 6 Score

Section Quiz 6-1

DIRECTIONS: Matching Match each item in Column A with the items in Column B. Write the correct letters in the blanks. *(10 points each)*

Column A	Column B
____ 1. American supporters of independence	A. Tories
____ 2. taking neither side	B. Patriots
____ 3. Loyalists	C. enlist
____ 4. mercenaries	D. neutral
____ 5. to recruit	E. hired soldiers

DIRECTIONS: Multiple Choice In the blank at the left, write the letter of the choice that best completes the statement or answers the question. *(10 points each)*

____ 6. Slaves who fought on the British side were given
A. land. C. money.
B. freedom. D. guns.

____ 7. This woman disguised herself as a man so she could fight with the army.
A. Deborah Sampson C. Molly Pitcher
B. Margaret Corbin D. Betsy Ross

____ 8. Thomas Paine wrote, "these are the times that try men's souls" in
A. *American Revolution.* C. *The Crisis.*
B. *The Patriots.* D. *Common Sense.*

____ 9. The first state to have an all-African American regiment was
A. South Carolina. C. Georgia.
B. New York. D. Rhode Island.

____ 10. On October 17, 1777, General John Burgoyne surrendered to the Americans at
A. Philadelphia. C. Saratoga.
B. Trenton. D. Concord.

you don't say...

Yankee Many scholars believe the word *Yankee* comes from the Dutch *Jan Kees*, or "John Cheese"—a term that other Europeans used to ridicule the Dutch. The Dutch used the term to ridicule the English settlers of Connecticut, and the English later used it to ridicule the Patriots.

HISTORY AND ART ***Hut Camp of the 17th Regiment*** **by John W. Dunsmore** A British military camp guards New York City against American attack. **What happened to the Continental Army during the New York campaign of 1776?**

usually called a halt to their wars during the winter, and the British did not expect to fight.

Stationed across the Delaware River from the British camp in New Jersey, Washington saw a chance to catch the British off guard. On Christmas night 1776, Washington took 2,400 troops across the icy river and surprised the enemy at Trenton the next day.

The Americans captured 900 Hessians at Trenton. Washington called the victory "glorious." The British sent reinforcements under Lord Charles Cornwallis, but Washington led his troops away from Cornwallis's men. Washington then marched the army to Princeton, where they drove away the British. One discouraged British soldier wrote in his diary, "A few days ago [the Americans] had given up the cause for lost. Their late successes have turned the scale and now they are all liberty mad again."

A British Plan for Victory

The British worked out a battle plan for 1777. They would take **Albany,** New York, and gain control of the Hudson River. This would separate New England from the Middle States.

The plan involved a three-pronged attack. **General John Burgoyne** would lead 8,000 troops south from Canada. A second force, under Lieutenant Colonel Barry St. Leger (leh•ZHAY), would move east from Lake Ontario. A third group, under General Howe, would move north from New York City. The three British forces would meet at Albany and destroy the Patriot troops.

The British Capture Philadelphia

Howe planned to take Philadelphia, the American capital, before marching to Albany. After winning battles in September 1777 at Brandywine and Paoli near Philadelphia, Howe's troops captured the city itself without much of a fight. The Continental Congress fled to the Pennsylvania countryside. In early October Washington attacked the main British camp at nearby Germantown, but he was forced to withdraw. Postponing the move north to Albany, Howe decided to spend the winter in Philadelphia.

Patriots Slow the British

Meanwhile the British plans for moving toward Albany were not going well. In August American soldiers halted St. Leger's advance at Fort Stanwix, New York. Led by **Benedict Arnold,** the Americans forced the British to retreat.

TEACHER'S NOTES

General Burgoyne's army was not making much progress toward Albany either. In July Burgoyne captured Fort Ticonderoga, but his army had trouble advancing after that. Burgoyne, a dashing general who enjoyed good food and drink and fine clothes, traveled with 30 wagons of luxury goods. Loaded down with this heavy baggage, Burgoyne's army moved slowly through the dense forests. To make matters worse, the Americans blocked the British at every opportunity by felling trees across their path.

In need of food and supplies, Burgoyne sent 700 British and Hessian soldiers to capture the military stores at Bennington, Vermont. The British troops' brightly colored uniforms made the soldiers easy targets in the woods. A local militia group, the **Green Mountain Boys,** attacked and defeated them. Having lost part of his army and desperately short of supplies, Burgoyne retreated in October to the town of **Saratoga** in New York.

America's FLAGS

First Stars and Stripes, 1777–1795 On June 14, 1777, the Continental Congress designed the first Stars and Stripes. The Congress determined that "the Flag of the United States be 13 stripes, alternate red and white; that the Union be 13 stars, white in a blue field representing a new constellation." For Americans past and present, the color red symbolizes courage; white, purity of ideals; and blue, strength and unity of the states.

The Battle of Saratoga

At Saratoga Burgoyne faced serious trouble. He expected British forces from the west and south to join him, but they had not arrived. The Americans had stopped St. Leger's army at Fort Stanwix, and Howe's forces were still in Philadelphia. In addition American troops under the command of **General Horatio Gates** blocked his path to the south. Burgoyne found himself surrounded by an army about three times as large as his own. Burgoyne made a last desperate attack on October 7, but the Americans held firm. The British were trapped. They had no food, and wounded soldiers lay all around.

On October 17, 1777, General Burgoyne surrendered. As a Patriot band played "Yankee Doodle," 5,700 British soldiers handed their weapons to the Americans. At dinner with Gates, Burgoyne offered a toast to George Washington. The British plan to cut off New England had failed.

Section 1 Review

Checking for Understanding

1. ***Identify*** Hessians, Nathan Hale, Thomas Paine, Benedict Arnold, Saratoga.
2. ***Define*** Patriot, neutral, Loyalist, mercenary, recruit, deserter.
3. ***Compare*** the strengths of the British and American military forces.

Reviewing Themes

4. **Groups and Institutions** What problems did the Continental Congress face in raising an army to fight during the American Revolution?

Critical Thinking

5. **Making Critical Judgments** Provide reasons to explain why African Americans wanted to enlist in the Continental Army.

Activity

Making a Recruitment Poster Design a poster that encourages colonists to join the war effort on the side of the Americans.

Section 1 Review Answers

1. Hessians, 164; Hale, 166; Paine, 167; Arnold, 168; Saratoga, 169
2. The words are defined in the Glossary.
3. British: strongest navy in world, larger population, more experienced; American: fighting on own land, fighting for freedom, Washington was a skilled military leader
4. They were afraid that the Continental Congress, if given too much power, would control the colonies just as the British Parliament had. They wanted each state to retain its independence.
5. African Americans saw hope for their personal freedom in a move for national independence.

Activity Posters should list reasons colonists should support the Americans.

CHAPTER 6
Section 1, 163–169

Reteaching Activity 6–1

Name ______ Date ______ Class ______

★ Reteaching Activity **6-1**

DIRECTIONS: Completing a Chart Write the number of the names and terms from the Fact Bank in the section of the chart where they belong.

The Early Years of the Revolutionary War

	Patriots	British
Advantages	______	______
Disadvantages	______	______
People	______	______
Victory Sites	______	______

★FACT BANK

1. at home
2. Long Island
3. Lemuel Hayes
4. Saratoga
5. Loyalists
6. volunteer militia
7. Thomas Paine
8. Hessians
9. Brandywine
10. wealth
11. Trenton
12. Deborah Sampson
13. far from home
14. Bennington
15. weak navy
16. Nathan Hale
17. fighting for freedom
18. shortage of supplies
19. General John Burgoyne
20. strong army and navy
21. determination to succeed
22. reliance on mercenaries
23. George Washington

The American Journey ★ 21 ★ **Reteaching Activities**

Enrichment Activity 6–1

Name ______ Date ______ Class ______

★ Enrichment Activity **6-1** ★

A Soldier's Story

"The Dying Redcoat" tells the story of a British soldier from the time he left Great Britain in December 1773 to his death in the New York campaign during the Revolutionary War in September 1776. Read the stanzas below.

. . . And when to Boston we did come,
We thought by the aid of our British guns,
To drive the rebels from that place,
To fill their hearts with sore disgrace.
But to our sorrow and surprise,
We saw men like grasshoppers rise;
They fought like heroes much enraged,
Which did affright old General Gage.

Like lions roaring for their prey,
They feared no danger or dismay;
Bold British blood runs through their veins,
And still with courage they sustain.
We saw those bold Columbia's sons
Spread death and slaughter from their guns:
Freedom or death! these heroes cry,
They did not seem afraid to die.

We sailed to York, as you've been told
With the loss of many a Briton bold,
For to make those rebels own our King,
And daily tribute to him bring.
They said it was a garden place,
And that our armies could, with ease,
Pull down their town, lay waste their lands,
In spite of all their boasted bands.

. . . Now I've received my mortal wound,
I bid farewell to Old England's ground;
My wife and children will mourn for me,
Whilst I lie cold in America.
Fight on America's noble sons,
Fear not Britannia's thundering guns;
Maintain your cause from year to year,
God's on your side, you need not fear.

DIRECTIONS: Analyzing Information Answer the following questions.

1. Compare what the British soldier expected to happen in Boston to what really happened. ______
2. Describe the British soldier's view of American soldiers. ______
3. What had the British soldier been told to expect in New York and who probably told him? ______
4. What is unexpected about his view of the revolution? ______

Activity **DIRECTIONS: Visualizing a Scene** Imagine what one of the scenes in the poem looked like and create an illustration that might accompany this poem.

The American Journey ★ 21 ★ **Enrichment Activities**

4 CLOSE

Work with students to brainstorm a list of reasons the Patriots might have felt optimistic about the war in the fall of 1777.

Social Studies
SKILL BUILDER

TEACH

Reading a Military Map

Military maps are an excellent way to condense information in a highly visual fashion. Students who know how to read details on such a map can gain a clearer understanding of troop movements, battle strategy, and more.

Have students apply the directions provided in "Learning the Skill" to the map of Bunker Hill.

Invite students to suggest symbols that they might expect to see on a more recent military map. *(Answers may include air routes, missile locations, tank movements, and so on.)*

Additional Practice

Chapter Skills Activity 6

Social Studies
SKILL BUILDER

Reading a Military Map

In your study of American history, you often use maps. A military map shows the area where battles occur, where victories are won, routes soldiers take, and who controls various sites.

Learning the Skill

Military maps use colors, symbols, and arrows to show major battles, troop movements, and defensive positions during a particular battle or over a period of time.

When reading a military map, follow these steps:

- Read the map title. This will indicate the location and time period covered on the map.
- Read the map key. This tells what the symbols on the map represent. For example, battle sites may be symbolized by crossed swords, a burst shell, or a star.
- Study the map itself. This will reveal the actual events or sequence of events that took place. Notice the geography of the area and try to determine how it could affect military strategy.

Battle of Bunker Hill, June 17, 1775

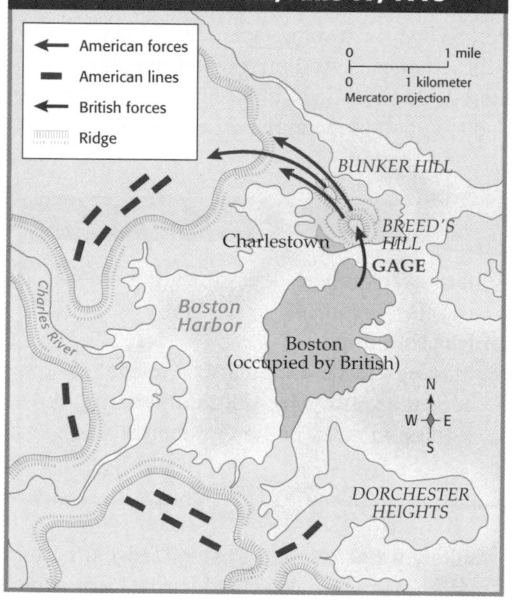

Practicing the Skill

Analyze the information on the map on this page, then answer the following questions.

1. What is the title of this map?
2. What troops surrounded Boston Harbor? How do you know this?
3. Which commander led the British troops to Breed's Hill?
4. What action did the American forces take after fighting on Bunker Hill?
5. In which direction did the British forces move when they left Boston? What parts of the map help you find this information?
6. What type of physical feature generally surrounds Boston Harbor? Explain how you know this.

Applying the Skill

Reading a Military Map Find a map of a specific battle of the American Revolution in an encyclopedia or other reference book. Create a three-dimensional model of the battle and use moveable pieces to represent troops. Then demonstrate troop movements over the course of the battle.

ANSWERS TO PRACTICING THE SKILL

1. Battle of Bunker Hill, June 17, 1775
2. American; the symbol that depicts American forces appears around the harbor.
3. Gage
4. They retreated.
5. They moved, counterclockwise, to the northwest; the compass rose and the arrows.
6. A ridge; it snakes around most of the harbor, except at the city of Boston itself. The map key points out the ridge symbol.

Applying the Skill Students may wish to work in groups, with some students in each group doing the research, others building the model, and the rest using it to demonstrate troop movements.

1777 — 1778 — 1779

October 1777
Americans win Battle of Saratoga

Winter 1777-1778
Patriot troops suffer at Valley Forge

February 1778
France and U.S. form an alliance

1779
Spain declares war on Britain

Section 2

The War Continues

READ TO DISCOVER . . .
- how the Patriots received help from other nations.
- how Washington's troops survived the winter at Valley Forge.
- what challenges Americans faced at home as a result of the war.

TERMS TO LEARN
desert
inflation

The Storyteller

The Continental Congress sent Jonathan Austin of Boston to France to deliver the news of the American victory at Saratoga. Benjamin Franklin was already in France trying to get that country to help the Americans against the British. As soon as Austin arrived, Franklin nervously inquired, "Is Philadelphia taken?" Austin answered, "It is, sir. But, sir, I have greater news than that. General Burgoyne and his whole army are prisoners of war."

The news prompted France to agree to an alliance with America.

French medal showing Benjamin Franklin

The American victory at Saratoga in October 1777 marked a turning point in the war. The European nations, especially France, realized that the United States might actually win its war against Great Britain. Now was the time for the Americans to seek support from Great Britain's rivals.

Gaining Allies

By late 1777 Benjamin Franklin had been in Paris for a year, trying to get the French to support the Americans' fight for independence. With his skill and charm, Franklin gained many friends for the United States. The French gave the Americans money secretly, but they would not commit to an alliance.

France

News of the American victory at Saratoga caused a shift in France's policy. Realizing that the Americans had a chance of defeating Britain, the French announced support for the United States openly. In February 1778, the French and the Americans worked out a trade agreement and an alliance. France declared war on Britain and sent money, equipment, and troops to aid the American Patriots.

Spain and the Netherlands

Other European nations also helped the American cause, mostly because they hated the

SECTION RESOURCES

Reproducible Masters
- Reproducible Lesson Plan 6–2
- Guided Reading Activity 6–2
- Section Quiz 6–2
- Reteaching Activity 6–2
- Enrichment Activity 6–2

Transparencies
- Section Focus Transparency 6–2

Multimedia
- Vocabulary PuzzleMaker
- Chapter Challenger Interactive Review Software
- Testmaker
- GTV: A Geographic Perspective on American History

1 FOCUS

BELLRINGER
Motivational Activity

Before taking roll at the beginning of the class period, project Section Focus Transparency 6–2 and have students answer the questions. Discuss students' responses.

This activity is also available as a blackline master.

Section Focus Transparency 6–2

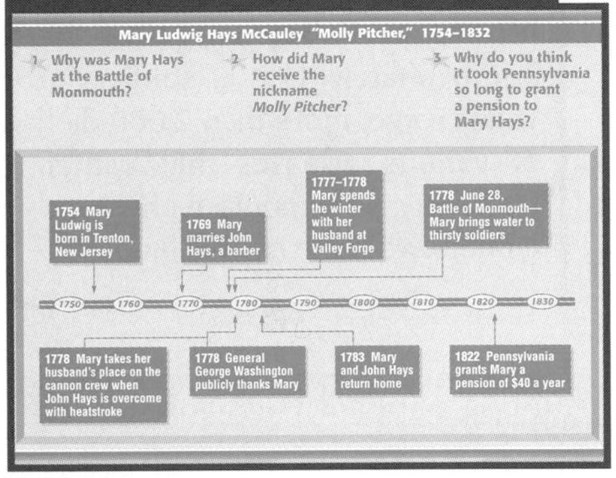

Vocabulary Precheck

Point out that *inflation* is the noun form of *inflate,* a verb that comes from Latin and literally means "to blow into." Have students speculate about how this meaning relates to the idea of economic inflation.

Use the **Vocabulary PuzzleMaker** to create crossword and word search puzzles.

Section Theme
Groups and Institutions

Patriots faced hardships at the front and at home but were encouraged by help from Europeans.

Activity Ask students: What are some things that an army needs? *(Answers may include food, clothing, training, and so on.)* Discuss the problems that would arise from a lack of these things.

2 TEACH

L1 Solving Problems Have groups of students create a problem/solution chart. In the left-hand column, they should list problems that the Americans faced (such as the need for allies and financing the war); in the right-hand column, they should note how each problem was handled. Students may use the completed charts as study guides.

What?Where?When?Who?

Illness at Valley Forge Of the approximately 12,000 soldiers at Valley Forge, more than 2,000 died of various diseases that winter. Dysentery, pneumonia, typhus, and typhoid were the chief killers.

Guided Reading Activity 6–2

Name ________________ Date ____________ Class ______

★ Guided Reading Activity **6-2**

DIRECTIONS: Identifying Supporting Details Read each main idea. Use your textbook to supply the details that support or explain each main idea.

Main Idea: After the Saratoga victory, America obtained support from Great Britain's rivals.

1. **Detail:** In 1778 Americans worked out an agreement with ________________.
2. **Detail:** ________________ declared war on Great Britain in 1779.
3. **Detail:** ________________, the Spanish governor of Louisiana, sent money, rifles, and supplies to American troops, and Dutch bankers lent money.

Main Idea: During the winter of 1777 to 1778, American troops endured terrible hardships.

4. **Detail:** George Washington and his troops set up camp at ________________, where they lacked decent food, clothing, and shelter.
5. **Eyewitness to History Detail:** Volunteers, including Washington's wife ________________, made clothes for the troops and cared for the sick.

Main Idea: Several Europeans worked for the Patriot cause.

6. **Detail:** French nobleman ________________ rushed to join the battle for freedom in the United States.
7. **Detail:** Polish cavalry officer ________________ died in 1780, fighting for the Continental Army in the South.
8. **Detail:** Friedrich von Steuben, from Germany, taught the Patriot troops military discipline, and ________________, of Spain, lent Patriot leaders money.

Main Idea: Getting money to finance the war was a major concern.

9. **Economics Detail:** The ________________ had no power to levy taxes.
10. **Economics Detail:** Congress printed hundreds of millions of dollars worth of paper money. The money soon lost its value because there was not enough ________________ to back it.

Main Idea: The war had a major impact on the lives of all Americans.

11. **Detail:** The ideals of liberty and freedom caused some ________________ to question their place in society.
12. **Citizenship Detail:** The Revolutionary War inspired some Americans to question the morality of ________________.

Guided Reading Activities ★ 22 ★ *The American Journey*

HISTORY AND ART Washington's troops built an encampment of wooden huts. It was not until the soldiers had packed up their tents that Washington moved out of his own tent and into a nearby house.

Answer: *The soldiers lacked proper clothing; supplies were scarce.*

British. Although Spain did not recognize American independence until after the Revolution, Spain declared war on Britain in 1779. The Spanish governor of Louisiana, **Bernardo de Gálvez** (GAHL•vez), sent money, rifles, and other supplies to American armies in Virginia and the Ohio Valley. Spanish troops under Gálvez captured five British forts in the Mississippi Valley. The Netherlands also went to war with Britain, and Dutch bankers lent money to the Americans.

A Difficult Winter

Word of the French-American alliance did not reach the United States until the spring of 1778. Meanwhile British general Howe and his forces spent the winter in comfort in Philadelphia. Washington set up camp at **Valley Forge,** 20 miles to the west of the British. Washington and his troops endured a winter of terrible suffering, lacking decent food, clothing, and shelter. Washington's greatest challenge at Valley Forge was keeping the Continental Army together.

Eyewitness to HISTORY

Winter at Valley Forge

Joseph Martin, a 17-year-old private from Connecticut, spent the winter at Valley Forge. "We had a hard duty to perform," he wrote years later, "and little or no strength to perform it with." Most of the men lacked blankets, shoes, and shirts. Martin made a rough pair of moccasins for himself out of a scrap of cowhide. Although the moccasins hurt his feet, they were better than going barefoot, "as hundreds of my companions had to do, till they might be tracked by their blood upon the rough, frozen snow."

Not surprisingly, many men **deserted,** or left without permission, the Continental Army while it was camped at Valley Forge. Some officers resigned. The army seemed to be falling apart.

Yet somehow, with enormous determination and effort, the Continental Army survived the winter, and conditions gradually improved. The troops built huts and gathered supplies from the countryside, often by force. Volunteers—including

HISTORY AND ART ***The March to Valley Forge* by William B.J. Trego** While waiting for French aid, American soldiers spent a brutal winter at Valley Forge, Pennsylvania. **What were the soldiers' living conditions at Valley Forge?**

COOPERATIVE LEARNING ACTIVITY

Creating Concept Webs This section focuses on the idea of freedom—not only political freedom for a country seeking independence, but also the lack of freedom of opportunity for women and African Americans. Organize students into three teams; supply each team with poster board and markers. Within each team have some students specialize in political meanings of freedom, others focus on the status of women, and still others consider the status of African Americans. Then ask each team to create a concept web relating to this section. Have teams begin with the word *freedom* in the center of the page, then branch out to show the kinds of or lack of freedom discussed, and note a few details about each one. Encourage teams to compare and discuss their webs.

Washington's wife, Martha—made clothes for the troops and cared for the sick. Washington declared that no army had ever suffered "such uncommon hardships" with such "patience and fortitude." New soldiers joined the ranks in the spring. "The army grows stronger every day," one officer wrote. "There is a spirit of discipline among the troops that is better than numbers."

In April 1778 Washington told his troops of the Patriots' alliance with France. Everyone's spirits rose at the thought of help from overseas. The Continental Army celebrated with a religious service and a parade.

Help From Overseas

Among the hardy soldiers who spent the winter at Valley Forge was a French nobleman, the **Marquis de Lafayette** (LAH•fee•EHT). Filled with enthusiasm for the ideas expressed in the Declaration of Independence, Lafayette had bought a ship and set sail for America. He rushed to join the battle for freedom despite a prohibition by King Louis XIV of France.

To his wife and children in France, Lafayette wrote, "The future of America is closely bound up with the future of all mankind." Upon his arrival in Philadelphia, Lafayette offered his services and those of his followers to General Washington. Lafayette became a trusted aide to Washington.

Other Europeans also volunteered to work for the Patriot cause. Two Poles—Thaddeus Kościuszko (kawsh•CHUSH•KOH), an engineer, and **Casimir Pulaski,** a cavalry officer—contributed to the American efforts. Pulaski died in 1780, fighting for the Continental Army in the South.

Friedrich von Steuben (STOO•buhn), a former army officer from Germany, also came to help Washington. Steuben drilled the Patriot troops at Valley Forge, teaching them military discipline. He turned the ragged Continental Army into a more effective fighting force.

Juan de Miralles (mee•RAH•yays) arrived in Philadelphia in 1778 as a representative of Spain. At his urging, Spain, Cuba, and Mexico sent financial aid to the colonies. Miralles befriended many Patriot leaders and lent them money for their cause.

Causes and Effects

CAUSES

- ★ Long-standing hostility between Britain and France
- ★ Conflict between Britain and France during French and Indian War
- ★ Victory at Saratoga boosts French confidence in Patriots

French-American Alliance in 1778

EFFECTS

- ★ France lends money to the Continental Congress
- ★ France sends soldiers and ships to help Patriot forces
- ★ Patriots win the American Revolution

Chart Study

In 1777 Benjamin Franklin negotiated with French leaders for money and support for the American cause. **Drawing Conclusions** Why was it important for France to recognize the independence of the American colonies?

Footnotes to History

Worthless Paper? The paper dollar bills that the Congress issued were called *Continentals.* People used the expression "not worth a Continental" to describe something of little value.

Chart Study

Answer
With France's recognition came much-needed supplies, food, and reinforcements.

Chart Skills Practice

Reading a Chart How did France hope that its relationship with Britain would change as a result of the alliance with the Americans? *(Students may suggest that France wanted to be victorious over Britain—or at least to humiliate the British government in some way.)*

NATIONAL GEOGRAPHIC SOCIETY

VIDEODISC
GTV: A Geographic Perspective on American History

Side 1, Chapter 17
Title: *The American Revolution*
Subject: The impact of geography and aid from France on the American Revolution
Ask: **Who allied with the Americans during the Revolution?** *(France)*

Linking PAST & PRESENT

The Value of a Dollar The Coinage Act of 1792 reinforced the security of America's paper money by backing it with gold and silver. In 1900 the gold standard became the official way of defining the worth of a dollar, but the United States went off the gold standard in 1933.

MULTIPLE LEARNING STYLES

Logical/Mathematical Why would a European nation want to become involved in the Americans' war for independence? Encourage students who enjoy analytical questions to make up a list of pro and con statements that a European leader might consider before committing to the Patriot cause. (You might ask students to do additional research to learn what various nations stood to gain or lose by siding against Britain.) Interested students might use this activity as a springboard for a debate on involvement in the war. **L3**

Linking PAST & PRESENT

Old Allies NATO was founded in 1949, largely as a means of protection from possible aggression by nations under Soviet control. Since the end of the cold war, NATO has focused on preparedness for local conflicts. Ironically, France withdrew its military participation in NATO in 1966.

3 ASSESS

Assign Section 2 Review as homework or as an in-class activity.

Use **Chapter Challenger Interactive Review Software** to review Section 2.

Section Quiz 6–2

Name ______ Date ______ Class ______

Chapter 6

Score

Section Quiz 6-2

DIRECTIONS: Matching Match each item in Column A with the items in Column B. Write the correct letters in the blanks. *(10 points each)*

Column A	Column B
____ 1. William Howe's winter camp	A. Valley Forge
____ 2. George Washington's winter camp	B. Judith Sargeant Murray
____ 3. French noble at Valley Forge	C. Loyalists
____ 4. fled the colonies for England	D. Marquis de Lafayette
____ 5. essay writer for women's education	E. Philadelphia

DIRECTIONS: Multiple Choice In the blank at the left, write the letter of the choice that best completes the statement or answers the question. *(10 points each)*

____ 6. George Washington's greatest challenge at Valley Forge was keeping
A. the British away. C. his army together.
B. his spirits up. D. entertainment for his army.

____ 7. This problem caused Congress to stop issuing paper money.
A. cold winter C. slavery
B. inflation D. soldiers

____ 8. This woman made clothes for the troops and cared for the sick at Valley Forge.
A. Abigail Adams C. Martha Washington
B. Judith Sargeant Murray D. Betsy Ross

____ 9. This man turned the ragged Continental Army into a more efficient fighting force.
A. Casimir Pulaski C. Thaddeus Kościuszko
B. Friedrich von Steuben D. Juan de Miralles

____ 10. The nation who signed a treaty of alliance with the revolutionary United States in 1778 was
A. Spain. C. Great Britain.
B. France. D. Canada.

Section Quizzes ★ 22 ★ *The American Journey*

Picturing HISTORY This bill is a good example of what Americans of the time called a *soft dollar* or *soft currency.* Both terms referred to paper money, especially paper money that was not backed by silver or gold.
Answer: *There were more bills in circulation than the available gold and silver could back.*

Linking PAST & PRESENT

Old Allies

France was the first nation to sign a treaty of alliance with the revolutionary United States. France and the United States were allies in the twentieth century, too. They fought on the same side in World War I and World War II. They remain allies today in the North Atlantic Treaty Organization (NATO), an organization formed to defend its members from aggression.

Economics

Money Problems

Getting money to finance the war was a major concern. The Continental Congress had no power to raise money through taxes. Although the Congress received some contributions from the states and from foreign countries, much more money was needed.

To pay for the war, the Congress and the states printed hundreds of millions of dollars worth of paper money. These bills quickly lost their value, however, because the amount of bills in circulation grew faster than the supply of gold and silver backing them. This led to **inflation,** which means that it took more and more money to buy the same amount of goods. The Congress stopped issuing the paper money because no one would use it. However, the Americans had no other way to finance fighting their war for independence.

Life on the Home Front

The war had a major impact on the lives of all Americans, even those who stayed at home. With thousands of men away in military service, women took over the duties that had once been the responsibility of their husbands or fathers. **Abigail Adams** was just one of many women who managed the family farm while her husband was away.

Other women ran their husband's or their own businesses. According to popular legend, **Betsy Ross**, a seamstress in Philadelphia, made the first American flag for George Washington. Although the story cannot be verified, it is known that a Philadelphia woman named Elizabeth Ross sewed flags for a living.

Changing Attitudes

The ideals of liberty and freedom that inspired the American Revolution caused some women to question their place in society. In an essay on education, **Judith Sargeant Murray** of Massachusetts argued that women's minds are as good as men's. Girls, therefore, should get as good an education as boys. At a time when most girls received little schooling, this was a radical idea.

Abigail Adams also championed women's interests. She wrote to her husband, John Adams, who was a member of the Second Continental Congress:

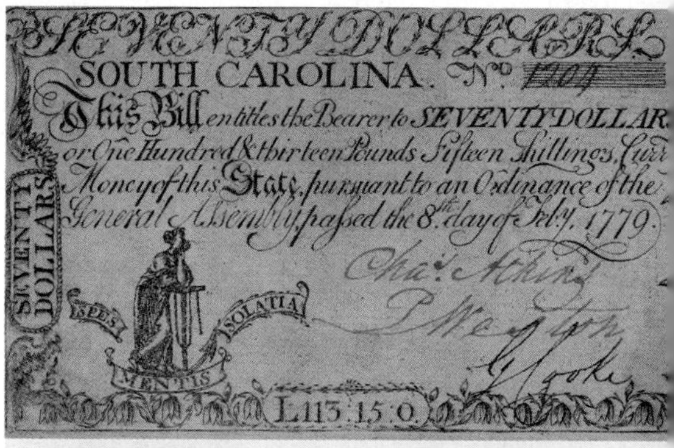

Picturing HISTORY Paper notes issued by the Congress and the states rapidly declined in value. By the time these South Carolina bills were printed, their real value was only 10 percent of their face value. **Why did American notes quickly decline in value?**

MAKING CONNECTIONS ACTIVITY

Drama Call on volunteers to assume the persona of George Washington. Have them improvise dramatic monologues that reflect what they think the general might have said about the following topics:

- The progress of the war thus far
- Conditions at Valley Forge
- Alliances with European nations
- Military experts who have arrived recently from Europe
- The army's financial needs **L1**

"I cannot say that I think you are very generous to the ladies, for, whilst you are proclaiming peace and good will to men, emancipating all nations, you insist upon retaining an absolute power over wives."

Treatment of Loyalists

Every state had some Loyalists. Thousands of them fought with the British against the Patriots. To prove their loyalty to Britain, some Loyalists spied and informed on the Patriots.

Many Loyalists, however, fled the American colonies during the Revolutionary War. They packed their belongings and sold whatever they could. Some left hurriedly for England. Others took off for Spanish-owned Florida. Still others journeyed to the frontier beyond the Appalachian Mountains.

Loyalists who remained in the United States faced difficult times. Their neighbors often shunned them. Some became victims of mob violence. Loyalists who actively helped the British could be arrested and tried as traitors. Patriots executed a few Loyalists, but such extreme measures were unusual.

Citizenship

Hopes for Equality

The Revolutionary War ideals of freedom and liberty inspired some white Americans to question the morality of the institution of slavery. As early as the Stamp Act crisis, the Boston town meeting had voted to condemn slavery. In 1778 Governor William Livingston of New Jersey asked the legislature to free all enslaved people in the state. Slavery, Livingston said, was "utterly inconsistent with the principles of Christianity and humanity."

African Americans made similar arguments. In New Hampshire enslaved Africans asked the legislature for their freedom "so that the name of *slave* may not be heard in a land gloriously contending for the sweets of freedom."

From the beginning of the war—at Lexington, Concord, and Bunker Hill—African American soldiers fought for the American cause. To some fighting for freedom, both African American and white, the Revolution seemed to bring nearer the day when slavery would be abolished. Vermont, New Hampshire, Massachusetts, and Pennsylvania attempted to end slavery in their states. The issue of slavery would remain unsettled for many years, however.

Section 2 Review

Checking for Understanding

1. ***Identify*** Bernardo de Gálvez, Valley Forge, Marquis de Lafayette, Friedrich von Steuben, Abigail Adams, Betsy Ross, Judith Sargeant Murray.
2. ***Define*** desert, inflation.
3. ***Explain*** why the French did not publicly support the Americans until after the Battle of Saratoga.

Reviewing Themes

4. **Groups and Institutions** How were the Loyalists treated by the Patriots during the war?

Critical Thinking

5. **Determining Cause and Effect** The Americans claimed they were fighting for the ideals of liberty and freedom. How did these ideals make women and enslaved Americans question their position in society?

Activity

Making a Survival Package Imagine you had friends among the troops at Valley Forge during the winter of 1777–1778. Make a list of five items you would send to them to help them get through the winter.

Section 2 Review Answers

1. Bernardo de Gálvez, 172; Valley Forge, 172; Marquis de Lafayette, 173; Friedrich von Steuben, 173; Abigail Adams, 174; Betsy Ross, 174; Judith Sargeant Murray, 174
2. The words are defined in the Glossary.
3. Not until then did the French believe that the Americans truly had a chance of defeating Britain.
4. shunned by neighbors and occasionally victims of mob violence; some were arrested and tried as traitors; a few were executed
5. Women and enslaved Americans did not have equal rights or the same freedoms and opportunities that white American males had at the time.

Activity Lists should include such things as shoes, blankets, warm clothing, and food.

Reteaching Activity 6–2

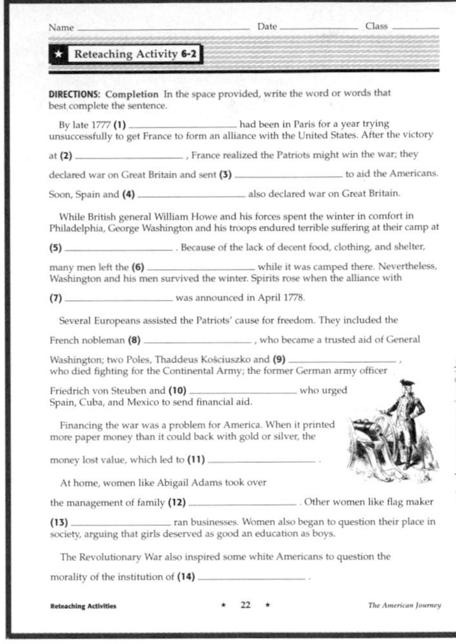

Name ______ Date ______ Class ______

★ Reteaching Activity 6-2

DIRECTIONS: Completion In the space provided, write the word or words that best complete the sentence.

By late 1777 **(1)** ______ had been in Paris for a year trying unsuccessfully to get France to form an alliance with the United States. After the victory at **(2)** ______, France realized the Patriots might win the war; they declared war on Great Britain and sent **(3)** ______ to aid the Americans. Soon, Spain and **(4)** ______ also declared war on Great Britain.

While British general William Howe and his forces spent the winter in comfort in Philadelphia, George Washington and his troops endured terrible suffering at their camp at **(5)** ______. Because of the lack of decent food, clothing, and shelter, many men left the **(6)** ______ while it was camped there. Nevertheless, Washington and his men survived the winter. Spirits rose when the alliance with **(7)** ______ was announced in April 1778.

Several Europeans assisted the Patriots' cause for freedom. They included the French nobleman **(8)** ______, who became a trusted aid of General Washington; two Poles, Thaddeus Kościuszko and **(9)** ______, who died fighting for the Continental Army; the former German army officer Friedrich von Steuben and **(10)** ______ who urged Spain, Cuba, and Mexico to send financial aid.

Financing the war was a problem for America. When it printed more paper money than it could back with gold or silver, the money lost value, which led to **(11)** ______.

At home, women like Abigail Adams took over the management of family **(12)** ______. Other women like flag maker **(13)** ______ ran businesses. Women also began to question their place in society, arguing that girls deserved as good an education as boys.

The Revolutionary War also inspired some white Americans to question the morality of the institution of **(14)** ______.

Reteaching Activities ★ 22 ★ *The American Journey*

Enrichment Activity 6–2

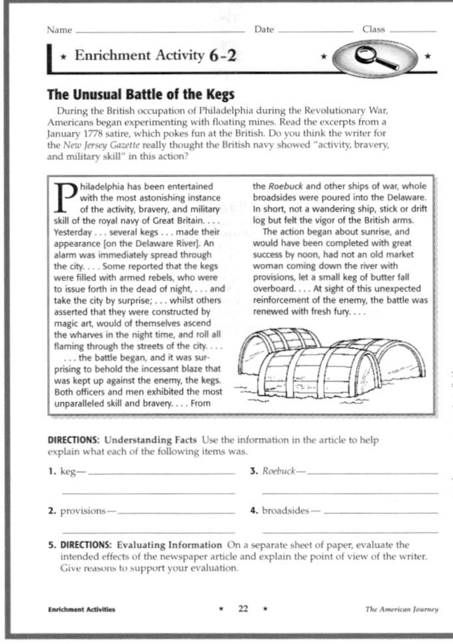

Name ______ Date ______ Class ______

★ Enrichment Activity 6-2 ★

The Unusual Battle of the Kegs

During the British occupation of Philadelphia during the Revolutionary War, Americans began experimenting with floating mines. Read the excerpts from a January 1778 satire, which pokes fun at the British. Do you think the writer for the *New Jersey Gazette* really thought the British navy showed "activity, bravery, and military skill" in this action?

Philadelphia has been entertained with the most astonishing instance of the activity, bravery, and military skill of the royal navy of Great Britain. . . . Yesterday . . . several kegs . . . made their appearance [on the Delaware River]. An alarm was immediately spread through the city. . . . Some reported that the kegs were filled with armed rebels, who were to issue forth in the dead of night, . . . and take the city by surprise; . . . whilst others asserted that they were constructed by magic art, would of themselves ascend the wharves in the night time, and roll all flaming through the streets of the city. . . .

. . . the battle began, and it was surprising to behold the incessant blaze that was kept up against the enemy, the kegs. Both officers and men exhibited the most unparalleled skill and bravery. . . . From the *Roebuck* and other ships of war, whole broadsides were poured into the Delaware. In short, not a wandering ship, stick or drift log but felt the vigor of the British arms.

The action began about sunrise, and would have been completed with great success by noon, had not an old market woman coming down the river with provisions, let a small keg of butter fall overboard. . . . At sight of this unexpected reinforcement of the enemy, the battle was renewed with fresh fury. . . .

DIRECTIONS: Understanding Facts Use the information in the article to help explain what each of the following items was.

1. keg— ______
2. provisions— ______
3. *Roebuck*— ______
4. broadsides— ______

5. **DIRECTIONS: Evaluating Information** On a separate sheet of paper, evaluate the intended effects of the newspaper article and explain the point of view of the writer. Give reasons to support your evaluation.

Enrichment Activities ★ 22 ★ *The American Journey*

4 CLOSE

Ask students how the Continental Army's experience at Valley Forge reflected problems that many of the Patriots—both military and civilian—faced.

1 FOCUS

BELLRINGER
Motivational Activity

Before taking roll at the beginning of the class period, project Section Focus Transparency 6–3 and have students answer the questions. Discuss students' responses.

This activity is also available as a blackline master.

Section Focus Transparency 6–3

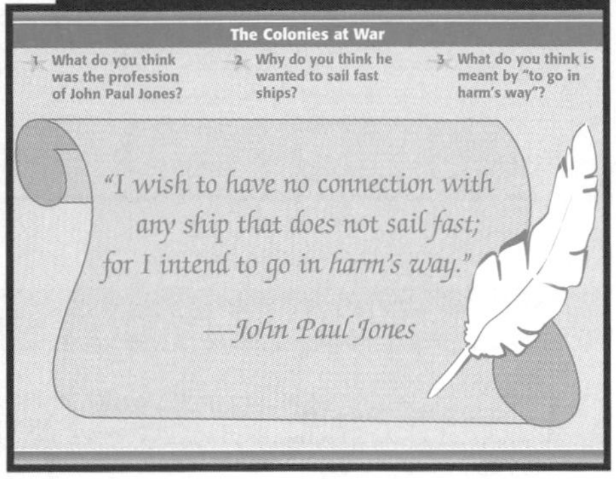

Vocabulary Precheck

Call on volunteers to explain the terms *blockade* and *privateer.* Then have students write a sentence that shows the connection between these two terms.

Use the **Vocabulary PuzzleMaker** to create crossword and word search puzzles.

Section Theme
Geography and History

As the war continued, Patriot victories were won in the west, in the south, and at sea.

Activity Have students look at the map on page 178 and comment on how the war expanded beyond what either side had envisioned at first. Discuss why each side was willing to continue its commitment to the struggle.

1778	1779	1780	1781

June 1778 George Rogers Clark captures Vincennes

September 1779 The *Serapis* surrenders to John Paul Jones

May 1780 British troops take Charleston

January 1781 Patriots defeat British at Cowpens

Section 3

The War Moves West and South

READ TO DISCOVER . . .
- how the war involved Native Americans.
- how the Americans and British waged a war at sea.
- how a new kind of fighting helped the Patriots win battles in the South.

TERMS TO LEARN

blockade
privateer
guerrilla warfare

The Storyteller

On June 28, 1778, one of the hottest days of the summer, General Washington pursued the British and attacked at Monmouth, New Jersey. The battle raged as the heat robbed the Patriots of their energy. Dodging shots, Mary Hays ran back and forth from a nearby spring to her husband's station with water to quench the soldiers' thirst. When her husband collapsed from heatstroke, Mary helped the crew fire the cannon. The British escaped, but the Patriots had fought well—especially with the help of Mary, who earned the nickname Molly Pitcher.

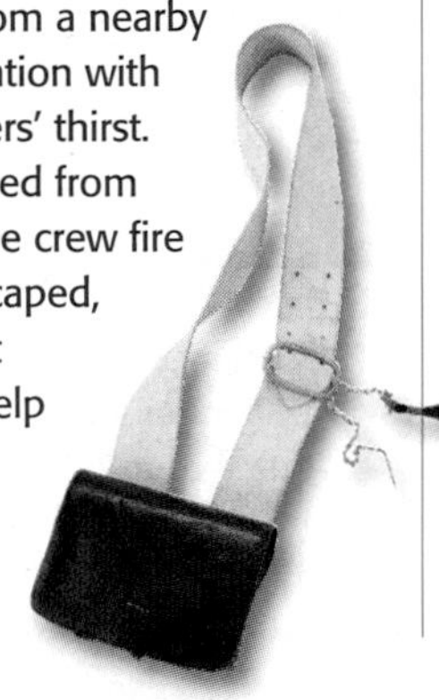

Pack for carrying ammunition

Important battles of the Revolutionary War took place along the western frontier. Much of this fighting involved Native Americans. Although some Indians helped the Patriots, more of them sided with the British. For the Native Americans, the British seemed to present less of a threat than the Americans did. American settlers continued to push westward, threatening the Native Americans' way of life.

Settlement Raids

West of the Appalachian Mountains, the British and their Indian allies were raiding American settlements. Mohawk chief **Joseph Brant** led a number of brutal attacks in southwestern New York and northern Pennsylvania.

Henry Hamilton commanded the main British base in the west, Detroit. Some called Hamilton the "hair buyer" because of rumors that he paid Native Americans for the scalps of settlers.

Geography

Victory at Vincennes

George Rogers Clark, a lieutenant colonel in the Virginia militia, set out to end the British attacks on western settlers. In June 1778, Clark and 175 soldiers sailed down the Ohio River to the mouth of the Tennessee River. After marching 120

SECTION RESOURCES

Reproducible Masters
- Reproducible Lesson Plan 6–3
- Guided Reading Activity 6–3
- Section Quiz 6–3
- Reteaching Activity 6–3
- Enrichment Activity 6–3

Transparencies
- Section Focus Transparency 6–3

Multimedia
- Vocabulary PuzzleMaker
- Chapter Challenger Interactive Review Software
- Testmaker
- NGS PictureShow: Native Americans, Part 1
- American Music Cultural Traditions

miles, the Patriots seized the British post at Kaskaskia (ka•SKAS•kee•uh) in present-day Illinois. Then they captured the town of **Vincennes** (vihn•SEHNZ), in present-day Indiana, from the British.

During Clark's absence in December, British troops under Henry Hamilton's command recaptured Vincennes. Clark vowed to get it back. In February, after marching for days through countrysides flooded with icy waters, Clark and his troops surprised the British, forcing Hamilton to surrender. George Rogers Clark's victory at Vincennes strengthened the American position in the West.

The Revolutionary War in the West, 1778–1779

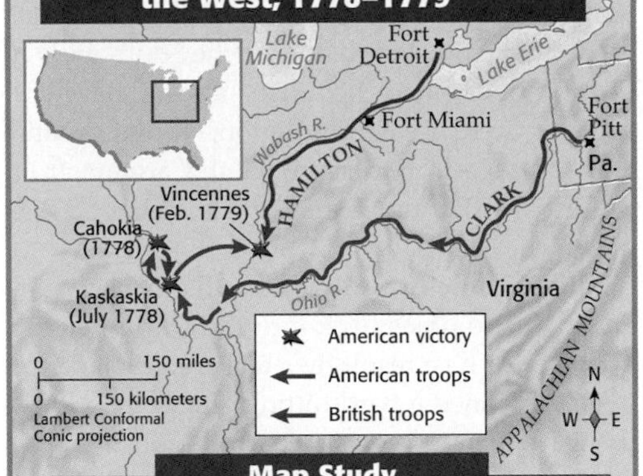

Map Study

The Revolutionary War spread west of the Appalachian Mountains.

1. **Region** What victories did the American forces win in the West?
2. **Analyzing Information** From what fort did Clark's troops set out?

Glory at Sea

As fighting continued on the western frontier, other battles raged at sea. Great Britain used its powerful navy to patrol American waterways, keeping the ships of the Patriots and their allies from entering or leaving American harbors. This British **blockade** prevented supplies and reinforcements from reaching the Continental Army.

Privateers

To break the British naval blockade, the Second Continental Congress ordered the construction of 13 American warships. Few of these, however, sailed to sea. The Americans destroyed 4 of their own ships to keep them out of British hands. Others were quickly captured by the British. Several states maintained their own small fleets, but the American navy was too weak to operate effectively.

American privateers captured more British vessels at sea than did the American navy. The **privateers** were privately owned merchant ships equipped with weapons. The Congress authorized more than 1,000 ships to sail as privateers and attack enemy shipping. Finding crews for these ships was not difficult. Sailors from the whaling and fishing ports of New England signed on eagerly for the profitable privateering trade.

Biography

John Paul Jones

One of the most daring privateer commanders, **John Paul Jones,** raided British ports beginning in 1777. He sailed in an old French ship that Benjamin Franklin had obtained for him. Jones gave the ship a French name, *Bonhomme Richard,* in honor of Franklin's *Poor Richard's Almanack.*

Sailing near the coast of Great Britain in September 1779, the *Bonhomme Richard* met a large fleet of British merchant ships escorted by the warship *Serapis.* The *Bonhomme Richard* moved close to the *Serapis* before attacking. The two ships fought for more than three hours. At one point Jones's ship was so badly damaged that the British captain asked whether Jones wished to surrender. Jones is said to have answered, "I have not yet begun to fight."

In the end the *Serapis* surrendered, but the *Bonhomme Richard* sank not long after the battle. Still, his victory made John Paul Jones a naval hero to the American Patriots.

CHAPTER 6

Section 3, 176–180

2 TEACH

L1 Reviewing Facts Ask students to recall details of the war's beginning in the northern colonies. **Ask:** **By early 1778, was the war going well for Britain in that area?** *(No)* Use that answer to introduce the new fronts of the war.

Map Study

Answers

1. Vincennes, Cahokia, and Kaskaskia
2. Fort Pitt

Map Skills Practice

Reading a Map What waterway did Hamilton's troops follow for part of their trip from Fort Detroit to Vincennes? *(the Wabash River)*

Guided Reading Activity 6–3

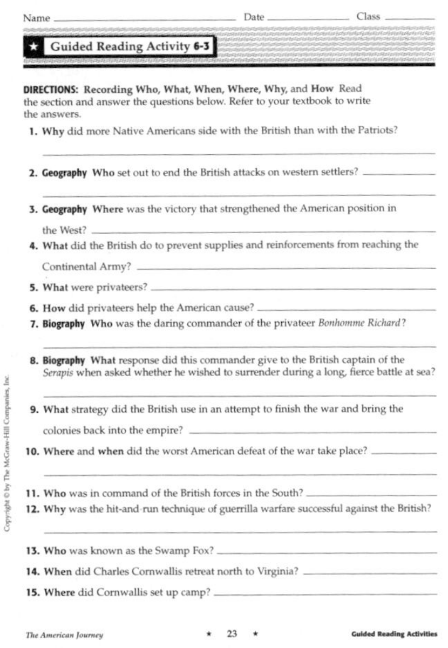
Name ______ Date ______ Class ______

★ Guided Reading Activity 6-3

DIRECTIONS: Recording Who, What, When, Where, Why, and **How** Read the section and answer the questions below. Refer to your textbook to write the answers.

1. **Why** did more Native Americans side with the British than with the Patriots? ______
2. **Geography Who** set out to end the British attacks on western settlers? ______
3. **Geography Where** was the victory that strengthened the American position in the West? ______
4. **What** did the British do to prevent supplies and reinforcements from reaching the Continental Army? ______
5. **What** were privateers? ______
6. **How** did privateers help the American cause? ______
7. **Biography Who** was the daring commander of the privateer *Bonhomme Richard*? ______
8. **Biography What** response did this commander give to the British captain of the *Serapis* when asked whether he wished to surrender during a long, fierce battle at sea? ______
9. **What** strategy did the British use in an attempt to finish the war and bring the colonies back into the empire? ______
10. **Where** and **when** did the worst American defeat of the war take place? ______
11. **Who** was in command of the British forces in the South? ______
12. **Why** was the hit-and-run technique of guerrilla warfare successful against the British? ______
13. **Who** was known as the Swamp Fox? ______
14. **When** did Charles Cornwallis retreat north to Virginia? ______
15. **Where** did Cornwallis set up camp? ______

The American Journey ★ 23 ★ Guided Reading Activities

Cooperative Learning Activity

Organizing a Battle Chart Students may find it hard to distinguish the various battles discussed in this section. To aid their memories, organize the class into groups representing battles at Monmouth, along the western frontier (including Vincennes), in South Carolina (including Camden and Cowpens), and in North Carolina (including Kings Mountain and Guilford Courthouse). You also might designate a group to document the naval battle between the *Bonhomme Richard* and the *Serapis.* Have each group complete a column in a classroom battle chart noting dates, giving details of the battles, and relating the battles to the war's progress. Assign students to create a detailed time line of the battle, research important people in the battle, and illustrate the crucial turning point in the battle.

NATIONAL GEOGRAPHIC SOCIETY

CD-ROM
NGS PictureShow: Native Americans, Part 1

Students can learn more about Native Americans at the time of the Revolution by selecting the Northeast regional groups. Suggest that students focus on Native Americans of the Ohio Valley.

History *and the* Humanities

- American Music Cultural Traditions, Lesson 2: "Junto Song"
- The Spirit of American Art and Music, Benjamin West

Map Study

Answers

1. Lafayette, Washington, and Rochambeau
2. It kept British fleets from reaching Yorktown and Cornwallis's troops from escaping by sea; also cut off supplies and reinforcements.

Map Skills Practice

Reading a Map Describe the route that Cornwallis took to reach Yorktown from Wilmington. *(He traveled north, through North Carolina and into Virginia, and then he headed east.)*

you don't say...

Guerrilla is a Spanish word meaning "little war."

Struggles in the South

In the early years of the war, the Americans had won some battles in the South. In 1776 they had crushed Loyalists at the Battle of Moore's Creek, near Wilmington, North Carolina, and had saved **Charleston,** South Carolina, from the British. Although a small battle, its impact was great.

By 1778 the British realized that bringing the American colonies back into the empire would not be easy. As a result they changed their strategy and planned a hard-hitting offensive to finish the war.

The British concentrated their efforts in the South, where there were many Loyalists. They hoped to use British sea power and the support of the Loyalists to win decisive victories in the Southern states. Initially the strategy worked.

British Victories

In late 1778 General Henry Clinton sent 3,500 British troops from New York to take Savannah, on the coast of Georgia. The British occupied the city and overran most of the state.

Clinton himself headed south with a large army in early 1780 to attack the port of Charleston, South Carolina. Charleston surrendered in May, and the British took thousands of prisoners. It marked the worst American defeat of the war. A member of Britain's Parliament gloated, "We look on America as at our feet."

Clinton returned to New York, leaving **General Charles Cornwallis** in command of British forces in the South. The Continental Congress sent forces under General Horatio Gates to face Cornwallis. The two armies met at **Camden,** South Carolina, in August 1780. Although the British won,

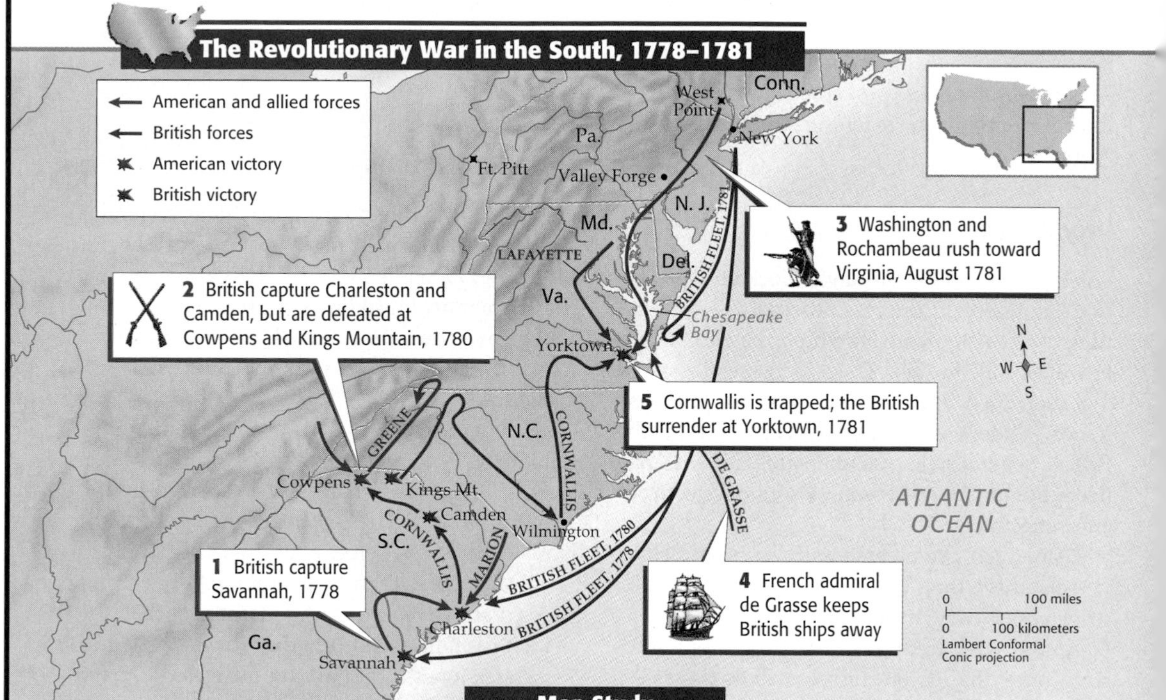

Map Study

Most of the fighting took place in the South during the latter years of the Revolutionary War.

1. **Movement** Who led American land forces at Yorktown, Virginia?
2. **Drawing Conclusions** How did the French navy help the Americans win the war?

MULTIPLE LEARNING STYLES

Kinesthetic As evidenced by the forces led by Francis Marion, guerrilla warfare was a Patriot tactic. Ask students to use clay and a cardboard or wooden surface to make a natural setting. Use figures created from clothespins to represent colonial guerrilla soldiers and British redcoats. Students should demonstrate how this type of warfare affected the British. As time permits, follow up with a discussion of these topics:

- How guerrilla warfare might be used in the woods of the North
- How privateering was a sort of naval guerrilla warfare ELL

American Memories

On the Battlefield

What Was It Like? Both sides fought furiously, as shown in William T. Ranney's *Tarleton's Cavalrymen in a Skirmish After the Battle of Cowpens.* **Describe the Patriots' clothing and weapons.**

Cornwallis soon found that he could not control the area he had conquered. He and his troops faced a new kind of warfare.

Guerrilla Warfare

The British received less help than they had expected from Loyalists in Southern states. Instead, as British troops moved through the countryside, small forces of Patriots attacked them. These bands of soldiers appeared suddenly, struck their blows, and then disappeared. This hit-and-run technique of **guerrilla warfare** caught the British off guard.

One successful guerrilla leader, **Francis Marion,** operated out of the swamps of eastern South Carolina. Known as the Swamp Fox, Marion was quick and smart. One British colonel grumbled that "the devil himself" could not catch Marion.

Patriot Victories

The British tried to invade central North Carolina in September 1780. At **Kings Mountain** a British officer and more than 1,000 Loyalists defended an outpost against the attack of Patriot sharpshooters. The Patriots forced the British to retreat. The victory brought new support for

Footnotes to History

The Cure May Be Worse For every Patriot soldier killed by the British, about nine died from disease or poor medical practices. In some cases, doctors drained about three-fourths of a soldier's blood. Then the soldier might be given calomel—a medicine sometimes used as an insecticide—which was sure to kill the already weakened patient.

CHAPTER 6

Section 3, 176–180

American Memories

On the Battlefield

Answer: *Most Patriots wore their own clothing—breeches, vests, hose, and tricorner hats—rather than uniforms. They carried muskets and knives into battle.*

Linking PAST & PRESENT

Bled to Death Draining "sick" blood to spur the production of "healthy" blood later proved fatal to the Patriots' commander. In 1799 the ailing George Washington gave his permission to be bled three times—and died shortly afterward. James Craik, his doctor, later wrote that if they had "taken no more blood from him, our good friend might have been alive now. But we were governed by the best light we had."

3 ASSESS

Assign Section 3 Review as homework or as an in-class activity.

Use **Chapter Challenger Interactive Review Software** to review Section 3.

Section Quiz 6–3

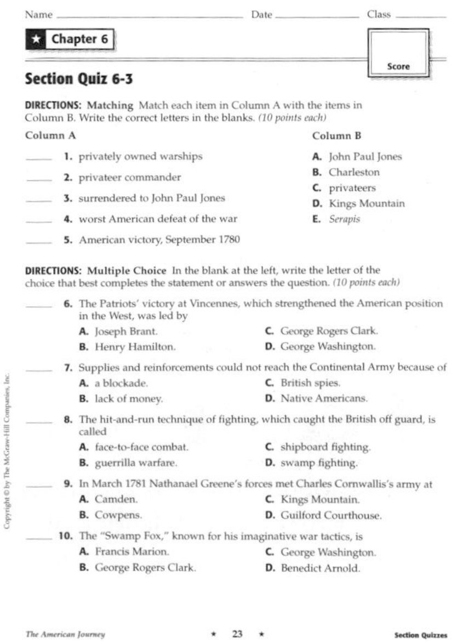

Name ______ Date ______ Class ______

Chapter 6

Score

Section Quiz 6-3

DIRECTIONS: Matching Match each item in Column A with the items in Column B. Write the correct letters in the blanks. *(10 points each)*

Column A

____ **1.** privately owned warships
____ **2.** privateer commander
____ **3.** surrendered to John Paul Jones
____ **4.** worst American defeat of the war
____ **5.** American victory, September 1780

Column B

A. John Paul Jones
B. Charleston
C. privateers
D. Kings Mountain
E. *Serapis*

DIRECTIONS: Multiple Choice In the blank at the left, write the letter of the choice that best completes the statement or answers the question. *(10 points each)*

____ **6.** The Patriots' victory at Vincennes, which strengthened the American position in the West, was led by
A. Joseph Brant. **C.** George Rogers Clark.
B. Henry Hamilton. **D.** George Washington.

____ **7.** Supplies and reinforcements could not reach the Continental Army because of
A. a blockade. **C.** British spies.
B. lack of money. **D.** Native Americans.

____ **8.** The hit-and-run technique of fighting, which caught the British off guard, is called
A. face-to-face combat. **C.** shipboard fighting.
B. guerrilla warfare. **D.** swamp fighting.

____ **9.** In March 1781 Nathanael Greene's forces met Charles Cornwallis's army at
A. Camden. **C.** Kings Mountain.
B. Cowpens. **D.** Guilford Courthouse.

____ **10.** The "Swamp Fox," known for his imaginative war tactics, is
A. Francis Marion. **C.** George Washington.
B. George Rogers Clark. **D.** Benedict Arnold.

The American Journey ★ 23 ★ **Section Quizzes**

MAKING CONNECTIONS ACTIVITY

Politics As the text points out, many Native Americans of this era sided with the British, but some did support the Patriot cause. How political was their reasoning? Students may work independently or in small groups to chart some reasons for supporting either side. Have them discuss questions such as the following as they consider the issues:

- How had each side treated Native Americans before the war?
- Which side seemed more likely to win?
- What might Native Americans have to gain from a British victory? From a Patriot victory? **L2**

CHAPTER 6
Section 3, 176–180

HISTORY AND ART A guerrilla band's purpose is not to capture territory. Rather, it tries to weaken an opponent's strength by picking off its members. **Answer:** *guerrilla warfare*

Reteaching Activity 6–3

Name ______ Date ______ Class ______

★ Reteaching Activity 6-3

DIRECTIONS: Putting Events in Sequence Number the events in the order in which they occurred.

____ **A.** General Henry Clinton sends 3,500 British troops to Savannah.
____ **B.** The British attempt to invade central North Carolina.
____ **C.** General Clinton attacks the port of Charleston, South Carolina.
____ **D.** General Cornwallis retreats to Virginia.
____ **E.** George Rogers Clark sails down the Ohio River in an attempt to end the British attacks on western settlers.
____ **F.** The armies of General Charles Cornwallis and General Horatio Gates meet at Camden, South Carolina.
____ **G.** The British ship *Serapis* surrenders to the privateer *Bonhomme Richard* and its commander John Paul Jones.
____ **H.** General Cornwallis sets up camp at Yorktown.
____ **I.** Nathanael Greene becomes commander of the Continental forces in the South.
____ **J.** Clark and his troops are victorious at Vincennes.
____ **K.** General Cornwallis takes over command of British forces in the South.

DIRECTIONS: Essay Answer the following questions.

1. Describe the British blockade and America's response to it.

2. How was guerrilla warfare used in the Revolution?

The American Journey ★ 23 ★ **Reteaching Activities**

Enrichment Activity 6–3

Name ______ Date ______ Class ______

★ Enrichment Activity 6-3

Science and Humanity

In 1780 Benjamin Franklin wrote the letter, excerpted below, to Joseph Priestley, a British chemist who supported the American Revolution.

Dear Sir,
. . . I always rejoice to hear of your being still employed in experimental researches into nature. . . . The rapid Progress true Science now makes, occasions my regretting sometimes that I was born so soon. . . . [I]n a thousand years . . . [we] may perhaps learn to deprive large masses of their gravity, and give them absolute levity, for the sake of easy transport. Agriculture may diminish its labour and double its produce: all diseases may by sure means be prevented or cured, not excepting even that of old age, and our lives lengthened. . . . O that moral science were in as fair a way of improvement, that men would cease to be wolves to one another . . .

DIRECTIONS: Interpreting Information In the chart, list four areas of concern Franklin discusses and solutions he believes science may provide. Then list a change or invention that has been made like the one Franklin predicted.

Scientific Solutions

Problem	Result	Change/Invention
1. ______	______	______
2. ______	______	______
3. ______	______	______
4. ______	______	______

Activity **DIRECTIONS:** Imagine that you and a partner are able to travel back in time to interview Benjamin Franklin. Pick a modern invention, explain it to Franklin, and record his reaction. Then create a skit with one of you playing the role of Franklin and one of you playing the role of the reporter. Present the interview to the class.

The American Journey ★ 23 ★ **Enrichment Activities**

4 CLOSE

Ask students to speculate about how British military leaders justified their losses to the Patriots at this point in the war.

HISTORY AND ART ***The "Swamp Fox" and His Men* by William Ranney, c. 1850** Francis Marion, known as the "Swamp Fox," led his troops in quick, surprise strikes. **What is this type of warfare called?**

independence from Americans in the Southern states. They wanted to see an end to the war that was destroying their homes and farms.

In October 1780, **Nathanael Greene** replaced Gates as commander of the Continental forces in the South. Greene split his army in two. In January 1781, one section of the army, led by General Daniel Morgan, defeated the British at **Cowpens,** South Carolina. Another section joined Marion's guerrilla raids. In March Greene reunited his forces to meet Cornwallis's army at **Guilford Courthouse,** in present-day Greensboro, North Carolina. Greene's army was forced to retreat, but the British sustained great losses. General Cornwallis abandoned the Carolina campaign.

British Retreat

Cornwallis retreated north to Virginia in April 1781. His troops carried out raids throughout the state, nearly capturing Governor Thomas Jefferson and the Virginia legislature in June. Jefferson fled on horseback, just ahead of the advancing British troops.

General Washington sent Lafayette and von Steuben south to fight Cornwallis. Meanwhile Cornwallis set up camp at Yorktown, which was located on the Virginia coast, and awaited further orders from Clinton in New York. The battle for control of the South was entering its final phase.

Section 3 Review

Checking for Understanding

1. ***Identify*** George Rogers Clark, John Paul Jones, Charleston, General Charles Cornwallis, Francis Marion, Kings Mountain, Nathanael Greene, Cowpens.
2. ***Define*** blockade, privateer, guerrilla warfare.
3. ***Explain*** why most Native Americans sided with the British in the conflict.

Reviewing Themes

4. **Geography and History** How did the location of the colonies aid the British navy?

Critical Thinking

5. **Drawing Conclusions** Why was guerrilla warfare effective against the British?

Activity

Creating a Symbol Design a symbol or emblem that captures the spirit of the Patriot soldiers.

Section 3 Review Answers

1. Clark, 176; Jones, 177; Charleston, 178; Cornwallis, 178; Marion, 179; Kings Mountain, 179; Greene, 180; Cowpens, 180
2. The words are defined in the Glossary.
3. The British seemed less of a threat than the Americans did. They knew the Americans wanted to expand onto their lands.
4. The colonies bordered the Atlantic, which gave the British access to important harbors and ports.
5. Students may suggest that the British, more formal in their fighting style, were unused to guerrilla hit-and-run tactics. The British also were unfamiliar with the terrain, giving the guerrillas an added advantage.

Activity Symbols should represent the spirit of Patriots during the war.

INTERDISCIPLINARY

Activities

The American Revolution

The American Revolution was a time of danger and drama for American colonists. Experience some of the excitement of this period by completing these activities in which you or your group will personally play a role in the Revolutionary Era.

Language Arts

Interviewing the Patriots As a newspaper reporter, you have been assigned to interview delegates to the Second Continental Congress. Choose one or two delegates who interest you. Write a dialogue in which you interview each delegate and record the answers. With a classmate taking the delegate's role, record your interviews to present in class.

Art

Creating a Poster Choose one of the following events of the Revolutionary War period and make a poster that will win people's support for it: the Boston Tea Party, the boycott of British goods, opposition to the Stamp Act, or the recruitment of troops to serve in the Continental Army.

Design the poster with your own artwork or a collage of cut-out letters and images. Arrange a classroom display of all the posters.

Drama

Writing a Play Write a one-act play in which a small group of ordinary men, women, and children in a small town react to the news of the Declaration of Independence. Remember that reactions varied from colony to colony and that not all colonists wanted independence from Great Britain. Practice with a group of classmates and present the play in class.

School-to-Work

Making a Banner Use fabric and your imagination to make a banner or flag honoring an event in the new United States–such as the Declaration of Independence or Paul Revere's ride. Sketch your design. Then use graph paper to draw the patterns you will use for cutting letters, numbers, and symbols from scraps of colorful cloth. Glue or sew the designs on your banner. Attach it to a pole or cord for display in class.

Paul Revere galloped to Lexington with the urgent news that the British redcoats were coming.

Multiple Learning Styles

The activities included in the feature on this student edition page are ideally suited to meet the different learning styles of your students. These include:

- Language Arts — **Interviewing the Patriots** verbal/linguistic learners
- Art — **Creating a Poster** visual/spatial learners
- Drama — **Writing a Play** interpersonal learners
- School-to-Work — **Making a Banner** kinesthetic learners

INTERDISCIPLINARY

Activities

TEACH

Background

Explain to students that Patriot leaders clearly saw both the drama and the danger of the American Revolution. Writing about the Boston Tea Party, for example, John Adams commented, "The people should never rise without doing something to be remembered—something notable and striking." And Josiah Quincy, responding to the Intolerable Acts that soon followed, wrote, "Under God we are determined that wheresoever, whensoever, or howsoever we shall be called to make our exit, we will die free men." Suggest that students include quotes such as these in their interviews, posters, or plays.

Team Teaching

These Interdisciplinary Activities provide an excellent opportunity for you to employ Team Teaching and collaboration in your classroom.

Block Schedule

These activities may be implemented within either a traditional class period or a block scheduling framework.

School to WORK

Journalist In most democracies, people depend on newspapers for fair and accurate reporting of current events. An excellent way to learn more about journalism would be to volunteer to work on your school newspaper or join the yearbook staff. Such experience will help you find out about the many jobs available in journalism.

1 FOCUS

BELLRINGER
Motivational Activity

Before taking roll at the beginning of the class period, project Section Focus Transparency 6–4 and have students answer the questions. Discuss students' responses.

This activity is also available as a blackline master.

Section Focus Transparency 6–4

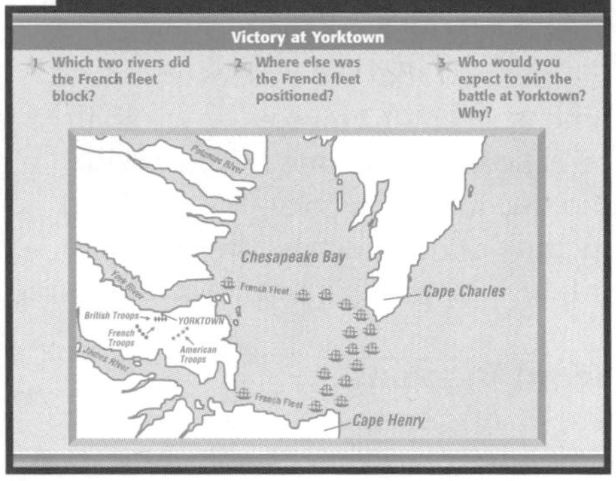

Vocabulary Precheck
Encourage students to think of a symbol or other visual to illustrate the word *ratify*, such as a "thumbs up" sign.

Use the **Vocabulary PuzzleMaker** to create crossword and word search puzzles.

Section Theme
Groups and Institutions
At Yorktown a combined Patriot force secured final victory in the Revolutionary War, ensuring an independent United States.

Activity Have students look at the four major headings in this section. **Ask:** Without reading ahead, why do you think the Americans won? *(Answers may include strong leadership and devotion to the Patriot cause.)*

1780 — 1782 — 1784

July 1780 French troops arrive in colonies

August 1781 Washington advances toward British at Yorktown

October 1781 Cornwallis surrenders at Yorktown

September 1783 Treaty of Paris is signed

Section 4

The War Is Won

READ TO DISCOVER . . .
- how George Washington changed his military strategy.
- why the Americans won the Revolutionary War despite many disadvantages.

TERMS TO LEARN
ratify
ambush

The Storyteller

A popular children's tune in eighteenth-century Britain went like this:

"If ponies rode men and if grass ate the cows,
And cats should be chased into holes by the mouse . . .
If summer were spring and the other way 'round,
Then all the world would be upside down."

This song would hold special meaning for the British troops in America as the Revolution reached its peak.

General Jean Baptiste de Rochambeau, French commander

In July 1780, French troopships appeared in the waters off **Newport,** Rhode Island. The ships carried more than 5,000 soldiers under the command of **General Jean Baptiste de Rochambeau** (ROH•SHAM•BOH). Cheering crowds greeted the French soldiers who were well armed and clad in colorful uniforms and plumed caps. The promised French aid had arrived at last. Unfortunately the British fleet arrived soon afterward and trapped the French ships in Newport.

Victory at Yorktown

In the autumn of 1780, Washington camped north of New York City waiting for a second fleet of French ships. From this position he could keep a close eye on the British army based in New York that General Clinton commanded. Washington planned to attack Clinton's army as soon as this second French fleet arrived from the West Indies. He had to wait a year to put his plan into action, however, because the fleet did not set sail for America until the summer of 1781.

Change in Plans

Washington had followed reports of the fighting in the South during 1780 and 1781. He knew that the British army commanded by Cornwallis was camped in **Yorktown,** Virginia. Washington also knew that Patriot forces under the Marquis de Lafayette were keeping Cornwallis and his troops bottled up on the Yorktown peninsula.

SECTION RESOURCES

Reproducible Masters
- Reproducible Lesson Plan 6–4
- Guided Reading Activity 6–4
- Section Quiz 6–4
- Reteaching Activity 6–4
- Enrichment Activity 6–4

Transparencies
- Section Focus Transparency 6–4

Multimedia
- Vocabulary PuzzleMaker
- Chapter Challenger Interactive Review Software
- Testmaker
- Facts On File: Landmark Documents in American History

In August 1781, Washington learned that **Admiral François de Grasse,** the French naval commander, was heading toward Chesapeake Bay instead of New York. Washington quickly changed his plans. He would advance on the British at Yorktown rather than at New York City.

Gathering of Forces

Washington took steps to ensure that the new American strategy stayed secret. He wanted Clinton to think the Patriots still planned to attack New York. This, he hoped, would keep Clinton from sending aid to Cornwallis.

General Rochambeau had marched his troops from Newport to join General Washington in July. Washington and Rochambeau then rushed south with their armies. The secrecy was so strict that most of the soldiers did not know where they were going. One soldier wrote, "We do not know the object of our march, and are in perfect ignorance whether we are going against New York, or . . . Virginia."

Washington also ordered Patriot soldiers from the western territories, under the command of **Anthony Wayne,** to march toward Virginia. Three groups—Wayne's troops, Washington's and Rochambeau's main American-French army, and the French fleet under Admiral de Grasse—would meet at Yorktown.

The Siege of Yorktown

Washington wondered whether his complicated plan had fooled Clinton, and whether the French fleet would reach Yorktown in time. On September 5, to his great relief, Washington received news that Admiral de Grasse's ships were nearing Yorktown.

The plan worked perfectly, and the British were thoroughly confused. By the end of September, 17,000 American and French troops had trapped Cornwallis's 8,000 British and Hessian troops at Yorktown. Meanwhile, Admiral de Grasse's fleet kept Cornwallis from escaping by sea. General Clinton and the rest of the British army waited in New York, unable to help the besieged Cornwallis.

Picturing HISTORY The Marquis de Lafayette (left) relied on James Armistead (right), an enslaved African American, to gather military information about the British. Armistead was later freed and took the name James Armistead Lafayette. **How did the French help the Patriots win the war?**

Cornwallis's Defeat

On October 11 the Americans and French began a tremendous bombardment. A Hessian soldier described the dreadful scene in his diary:

> "One saw men lying nearly everywhere who were mortally wounded and whose heads, arms, and legs had been shot off. . . . Likewise on watch and on post in the lines, on trench and work details, they were wounded by the fearfully heavy fire."

British supplies began running low, and many soldiers were sick. Cornwallis realized the hopelessness of his situation. On October 19 he surrendered. The Patriots had won the **Battle of Yorktown.**

CHAPTER 6
Section 4, 182–185

2 TEACH

L1 Making Inferences Read aloud the first two paragraphs on page 182. **Ask:** **What do you suppose Washington was thinking about as he waited for the arrival of the next group of French ships?** Discuss students' answers and how Washington might lead the Patriots to victory.

Picturing HISTORY James Armistead was a courier and spy for the Patriots. He even worked as a servant—gathering military information as he did so—in the headquarters of General Cornwallis.

Answer: *They contributed ships, troops, leaders, and money to the Patriot cause.*

Facts On File

CD-ROM
Landmark Documents in American History

Title: *Treaty of Paris of 1783*
Have students use this document in conjunction with the "Cooperative Learning Activity" below.

Guided Reading Activity 6–4

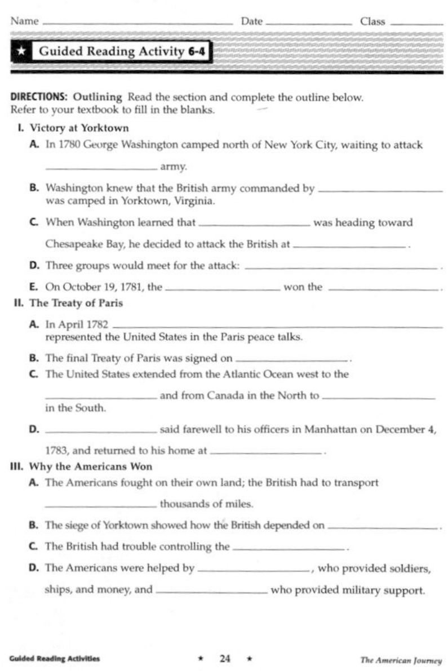

Name ______ Date ______ Class ______

★ Guided Reading Activity **6-4**

DIRECTIONS: Outlining Read the section and complete the outline below. Refer to your textbook to fill in the blanks.

I. Victory at Yorktown
- **A.** In 1780 George Washington camped north of New York City, waiting to attack ______ army.
- **B.** Washington knew that the British army commanded by ______ was camped in Yorktown, Virginia.
- **C.** When Washington learned that ______ was heading toward Chesapeake Bay, he decided to attack the British at ______.
- **D.** Three groups would meet for the attack: ______.
- **E.** On October 19, 1781, the ______ won the ______.

II. The Treaty of Paris
- **A.** In April 1782 ______ represented the United States in the Paris peace talks.
- **B.** The final Treaty of Paris was signed on ______.
- **C.** The United States extended from the Atlantic Ocean west to the ______ and from Canada in the North to ______ in the South.
- **D.** ______ said farewell to his officers in Manhattan on December 4, 1783, and returned to his home at ______.

III. Why the Americans Won
- **A.** The Americans fought on their own land; the British had to transport ______ thousands of miles.
- **B.** The siege of Yorktown showed how the British depended on ______.
- **C.** The British had trouble controlling the ______.
- **D.** The Americans were helped by ______, who provided soldiers, ships, and money, and ______ who provided military support.

Guided Reading Activities ★ 24 ★ *The American Journey*

COOPERATIVE LEARNING ACTIVITY

Discussing the Revolution Use a press-conference format to help students focus on the conclusion of the American Revolution. Call on volunteers (male or female) to portray Jean Baptiste de Rochambeau, Anthony Wayne, Charles Cornwallis, Lord North, and John Adams. Have the remainder of the class portray reporters and ask questions about the end of the war. Encourage questions that elicit details about battles. Also encourage discussion of the Treaty of Paris and the significance of a newly independent United States.

CHAPTER 6
Section 4, 182–185

HISTORY AND ART Among John Trumbull's other well-known historical paintings are *The Battle of Bunker Hill* and *The Declaration of Independence.* **Answer:** *Britain recognized America's independence and withdrew its troops.*

What?Where?When?Who?

A Military Ruse To keep the American strategy secret, the French built large bread ovens in New Jersey. General Rochambeau explained that doing so could "make Clinton believe that we were seriously considering an attack on New York, and that the army would remain encamped in that region."

3 ASSESS

Assign Section 4 Review as homework or as an in-class activity.

Use **Chapter Challenger Interactive Review Software** to review Section 4.

Section Quiz 6–4

Name ______ Date ______ Class ______

Chapter 6 — Score

Section Quiz 6-4

DIRECTIONS: Matching Match each item in Column A with the items in Column B. Write the correct letters in the blanks. *(10 points each)*

Column A	Column B
____ 1. French commander	A. Treaty of Paris
____ 2. British commander at Yorktown	B. Jean Baptiste de Rochambeau
____ 3. September 3, 1783	C. George Washington bid farewell to his troops
____ 4. Patriot commander in western territories	D. Charles Cornwallis
____ 5. December 4, 1783	E. Anthony Wayne

DIRECTIONS: Multiple Choice In the blank at the left, write the letter of the choice that best completes the statement or answers the question. *(10 points each)*

____ 6. Due to George Washington's strategy, Charles Cornwallis was defeated at the
A. Battle of Boston. C. Battle of New York.
B. Battle of Yorktown. D. Battle of Chesapeake.

____ 7. This Patriot victory convinced the British that the war was too difficult and costly to pursue.
A. Battle of Chesapeake C. Battle of Yorktown
B. Battle of New York D. Battle of Boston

____ 8. The British recognized the United States as an independent nation in the
A. Treaty of Paris. C. Treaty of Great Britain.
B. Treaty of the United States. D. Treaty of America.

____ 9. These foreign troops helped defeat Charles Cornwallis.
A. Spanish C. French
B. African D. German

____ 10. The British were attacked in the Mississippi Valley and along the Gulf of Mexico by forces from
A. France. C. Germany.
B. Africa. D. Spain.

Section Quizzes • 24 • *The American Journey*

HISTORY AND ART

***Surrender of Lord Cornwallis at Yorktown* by John Trumbull** Trapped by American and French forces, General Charles Cornwallis surrendered at Yorktown. The victory would guarantee America's independence. **What were the two major terms of the Treaty of Paris?**

Handing over their weapons, the British marched between rows of French and American troops—the French in fancy white uniforms on one side and the raggedly clothed Continental Army on the other. A French band played "Yankee Doodle," and a British band responded with a children's tune called "The World Turned Upside Down." Indeed it had.

The Treaty of Paris

The fighting did not really end with Yorktown. The British still held Savannah, Charleston, and New York, and a few more clashes took place on land and sea. The Patriot victory at Yorktown, however, convinced the British that the war was too costly to pursue. In March 1782, King George III appointed new ministers who were prepared to give Americans their independence.

Footnotes to History

Two Substitutes Surrender At Yorktown, Washington waited to accept Cornwallis's sword in the gesture of surrender. Cornwallis was not there, instead naming General Charles O'Hara to act in his place. Washington, therefore, selected General Benjamin Lincoln to represent the Americans. Lincoln accepted O'Hara's sword.

The two sides sent delegates to Paris to work out a treaty. **Benjamin Franklin, John Adams,** and **John Jay** represented the United States. The talks began in April 1782, and the British accepted a preliminary agreement written by the Americans six months later. The American Congress **ratified,** or approved, the preliminary treaty in April 1783. The final **Treaty of Paris** was signed on September 3, 1783. By that time Britain had also made peace with France, Spain, and the Netherlands.

Terms of the Treaty

The Treaty of Paris was a triumph for the Americans. Great Britain recognized the United States as an independent nation. The territory that the new nation claimed extended from the Atlantic Ocean west to the Mississippi River and from Canada in the north to Spanish Florida in the south. The British promised to withdraw all their troops from this expanded American territory. They also agreed to give Americans the right to fish in the waters off the coast of Canada.

The United States, in turn, agreed that British merchants could collect debts owed by Americans. The treaty also stated that the Congress would "earnestly recommend" to the states that property taken from Loyalists be returned to them. Most of this property was never returned, however.

MULTIPLE LEARNING STYLES

Visual/Spatial Have students research and draw uniforms worn by Continental and British forces. (Before offering this activity, you may wish to ask the school librarian to reserve a few relevant books for student research.) Remind students to color the uniforms correctly; have them provide labeling as well. Work with students to create a classroom display of the uniforms. Then lead a discussion of why the uniforms were different and in what ways the uniforms might symbolize the two sides of the conflict. Use the display as a visual prompt to lead an end-of-unit review. **L1, ELL**

Washington's Farewell

British troops left New York City in late November 1783. The war had truly ended, and George Washington could at last give up his command. On December 4 Washington said farewell to his officers at Fraunces' Tavern in Manhattan. "With a heart full of love and gratitude, I now take my leave of you."

Two weeks later Washington formally resigned from the army at a meeting of the Second Continental Congress in Annapolis, Maryland. A witness described the scene: "The spectators all wept, and there was hardly a member of Congress who did not drop tears." Washington said,

> "Having now finished the work assigned me I retire . . . and take my leave of all the employments of public life."

He returned to his home, Mount Vernon, in time for Christmas. There he planned to live quietly with his family.

Why the Americans Won

How had the Americans managed to win the Revolutionary War? How had they defeated Britain, the strongest military power in the world?

Fighting on Home Ground

The Americans had several advantages in the war. They fought on their own land, while the British had to bring troops and supplies from thousands of miles away. The siege of Yorktown showed how the British depended on support from the sea. When their ships were blocked, the troops faced American forces without support.

The British succeeded in occupying cities—they held New York for almost the entire war—but had difficulty controlling the countryside. They had not been successful at Saratoga or in the Carolinas. The Patriots, however, knew the local terrain and where to lay an **ambush**—surprise attack—or what route to take through a forest.

Help from other nations contributed to the American victory. The success at Yorktown would not have been possible without French soldiers and ships. Loans from France helped the Americans win the war. The Spanish also aided the Patriots by attacking the British in the Mississippi Valley and along the Gulf of Mexico.

Washington and the Patriots

George Washington's leadership skills played a critical role in the American victory. Perhaps most important, the American Revolution was a people's movement. Its outcome depended not on any one battle or event but on the determination and spirit of all the Patriots.

Section 4 Review

Checking for Understanding

1. ***Identify*** General Jean Baptiste de Rochambeau, Yorktown, Admiral François de Grasse, Treaty of Paris of 1783.
2. ***Define*** ratify, ambush.
3. ***Describe*** how the French navy helped Washington at Yorktown.

Reviewing Themes

4. **Groups and Institutions** What did the British agree to do in the Treaty of Paris?

Critical Thinking

5. **Analyzing Information** What qualities do you think Washington must have had to generate such loyalty in his soldiers?

Activity

Selecting an Appropriate Gift Draw a picture of a gift that you think the Continental Congress might have sent to the French government in appreciation for its help in ending the war.

Section 4 Review Answers

1. De Rochambeau, 182; Yorktown, 182; De Grasse, 183; Treaty of Paris of 1783, 184
2. The words are defined in the Glossary.
3. helped to trap Cornwallis and his soldiers and kept them from escaping by sea
4. recognize the United States as an independent nation; withdraw troops; turn over the British territory that extended from the Atlantic Ocean west to the Mississippi River and from Canada in the north to Spanish Florida in the south; grant fishing rights in Canadian waters
5. Answers may include a willingness to endure hardship along with his soldiers; skill as a military strategist and leader; respect for others; dignity; and honesty.

Activity Gifts might symbolize the independent status of the United States.

CHAPTER 6
Section 4, 182–185

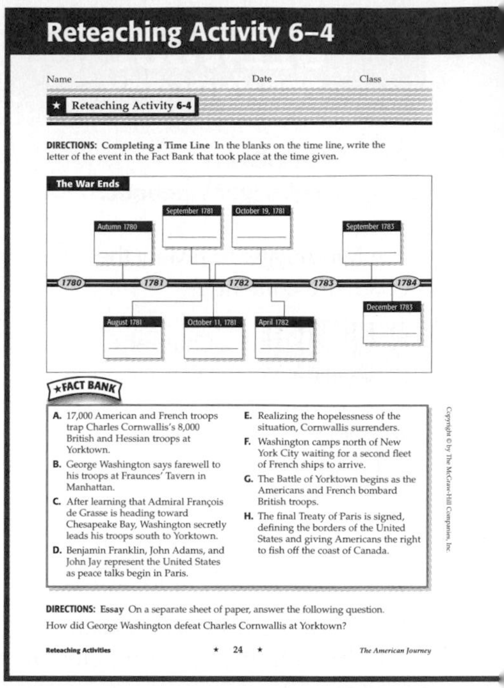
Reteaching Activity 6–4

Name ______ Date ______ Class ______

Reteaching Activity 6-4

DIRECTIONS: Completing a Time Line In the blanks on the time line, write the letter of the event in the Fact Bank that took place at the time given.

FACT BANK

- **A.** 17,000 American and French troops trap Charles Cornwallis's 8,000 British and Hessian troops at Yorktown.
- **B.** George Washington says farewell to his troops at Fraunces' Tavern in Manhattan.
- **C.** After learning that Admiral François de Grasse is heading toward Chesapeake Bay, Washington secretly leads his troops south to Yorktown.
- **D.** Benjamin Franklin, John Adams, and John Jay represent the United States as peace talks begin in Paris.
- **E.** Realizing the hopelessness of the situation, Cornwallis surrenders.
- **F.** Washington camps north of New York City waiting for a second fleet of French ships to arrive.
- **G.** The Battle of Yorktown begins as the Americans and French bombard British troops.
- **H.** The final Treaty of Paris is signed, defining the borders of the United States and giving Americans the right to fish off the coast of Canada.

DIRECTIONS: Essay On a separate sheet of paper, answer the following question.
How did George Washington defeat Charles Cornwallis at Yorktown?

Reteaching Activities ★ 24 ★ *The American Journey*

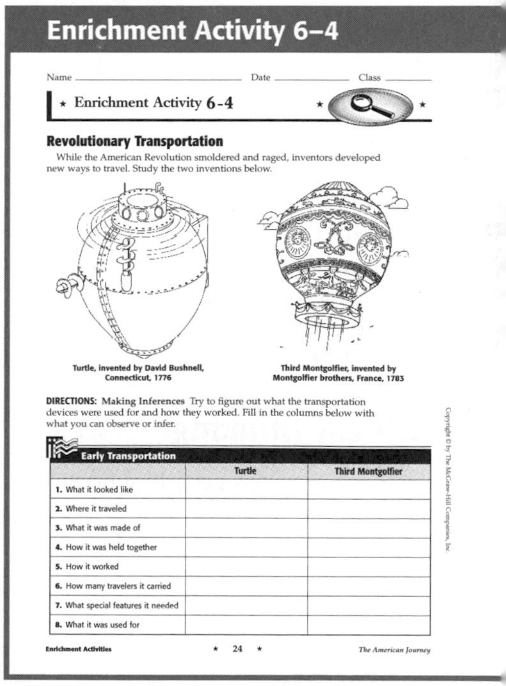
Enrichment Activity 6–4

Name ______ Date ______ Class ______

Enrichment Activity 6-4

Revolutionary Transportation

While the American Revolution smoldered and raged, inventors developed new ways to travel. Study the two inventions below.

Turtle, invented by David Bushnell, Connecticut, 1776

Third Montgolfier, invented by Montgolfier brothers, France, 1783

DIRECTIONS: Making Inferences Try to figure out what the transportation devices were used for and how they worked. Fill in the columns below with what you can observe or infer.

Early Transportation

	Turtle	Third Montgolfier
1. What it looked like		
2. Where it traveled		
3. What it was made of		
4. How it was held together		
5. How it worked		
6. How many travelers it carried		
7. What special features it needed		
8. What it was used for		

Enrichment Activities ★ 24 ★ *The American Journey*

4 CLOSE

Ask students to explain why the end of the Revolutionary War meant a "world turned upside-down" for the British.

GLENCOE TECHNOLOGY

VIDEODISC
MindJogger Videoquiz

Use MindJogger to review the Chapter 6 content.

Chapter 6
Disc 1, Side B

Also available in VHS.

Reviewing Key Terms

The key terms used in this activity are defined in the textbook glossary on pages A26–A35.

Reviewing Key Facts

1. Its forces were larger and more experienced; Britain had the most powerful navy in the world.
2. France, Spain, and the Netherlands
3. They knew that many Americans wanted to take their land.
4. guerrilla warfare
5. the Battle of Yorktown

Critical Thinking

1. the American people who sided with the Patriots
2. Students may suggest that he recognized the Patriots' determination to win and their dedication to the ideals of independence.

Time Line Activity

Events should be placed in this order: American Revolution begins, British are defeated at Saratoga, British capture Philadelphia, France openly supports the Patriots, Patriots suffer at Valley Forge, John Paul Jones attacks British warship, The British capture Charleston, Americans win at Yorktown, American Revolution ends

Review and Activities

Reviewing Key Terms

On a sheet of paper, define the following terms:

Patriot
neutral
Loyalist
mercenary
recruit
deserter
inflation
blockade
privateer
guerrilla warfare
ratify

Reviewing Key Facts

1. Why did the British think its military forces were superior to those of the Americans?
2. What European nations supported the Americans in the war?
3. Why did many Native Americans give their support to the British?
4. What fighting method did the Americans use to keep the British from taking the Southern Colonies?
5. Which battle convinced the British that they could not defeat the Americans?

Critical Thinking

Analyzing Primary Sources

When George Washington marched from New York to Yorktown with his soldiers, he pointed to the cheering crowds and said, "We may be beaten by the English . . . but here is an army they will never conquer."

1. To what "army" was George Washington referring?
2. Why did he think they could never be conquered?

Time Line Activity

Create a time line on which you place the following events in chronological order.

- France openly supports the Patriots
- The British capture Charleston
- American Revolution begins
- Americans win at Yorktown
- John Paul Jones attacks British warship
- American Revolution ends
- British are defeated at Saratoga
- Patriots suffer at Valley Forge
- British capture Philadelphia

Reviewing Themes

1. **Groups and Institutions** What advantage did the Patriots have over the British mercenaries?
2. **Groups and Institutions** How did women help in the war effort?
3. **Geography and History** Why do you think the British found it easier to capture American cities than to take over the American countryside?
4. **Groups and Institutions** Why were the Americans able to defeat the British in the war?

Skill Practice Activity

Reading a Military Map

Study the military map on page 178, then answer the questions that follow.

1. What color symbolizes British troop movement?
2. What symbol represents battles?
3. When did the British capture the city of Savannah?
4. Who was victorious at the Battle of Cowpens?

Reviewing Themes

1. The Patriots had a personal interest in the outcome of the war; the mercenaries were fighting for money.
2. They took over the management of farms and businesses, made clothes for the troops, and accompanied the troops into battle to cook and care for the sick and injured.
3. Patriots had an advantage in rural areas because they were more familiar with the terrain. Guerrilla warfare used this advantage.
4. Americans were fighting on their own land; they received help from other nations; George Washington was an effective military leader; they were more motivated because they were fighting for their freedom.

Geography Activity

The Treaty of Paris in 1783 established the boundaries of the new United States. The newly independent nation shared land claims on the North American continent with several nations. Study the map below and answer the questions that follow.

Land Claims in North America, 1783

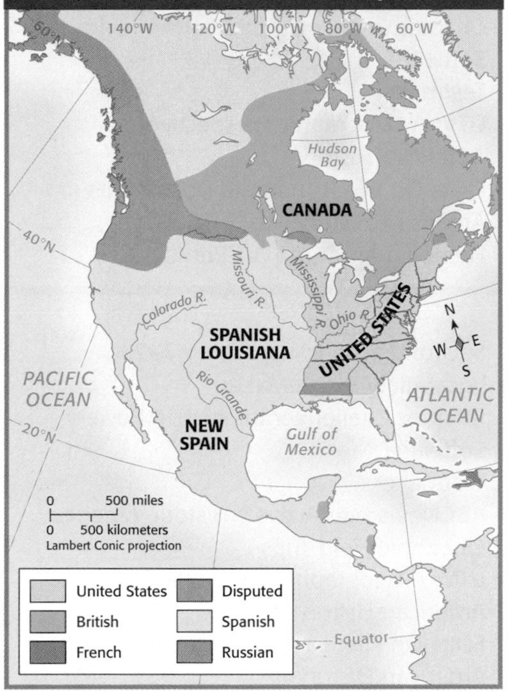

1. **Location** What natural landmark formed the new western boundary of the United States?
2. **Region** Which country claimed the most land in North America in 1783? The least land?
3. **Location** Which country claimed the land north of the United States?
4. **Location** Which country's land claims lay farthest north?
5. **Region** What nations claimed territory along the Pacific Ocean?

Cooperative Activity

History and Language Arts Conduct library research to learn more about the lives of American soldiers during the Revolutionary War. Select either an American soldier or an American regiment. Then organize your group into two smaller groups. One group will write a biography of an American soldier or a description of an American regiment. The other group will make a poster-sized, illustrated map displaying the names and geographic locations where your soldier or regiment fought.

Technology Activity

Using a Word Processor Search resources in your library for quotes made by at least five of the people mentioned in the chapter. Then retype and enlarge the quotes on a word processor. Post your quotes on a bulletin board display entitled "What Did They Say?" Add your own drawings of the people quoted.

Portfolio Activity **History Journal** Scan the chapter for details about people who came to the United States from other countries to help in the war effort. Record the names in your journal. Then create a chart that shows the peoples' names, their home countries, and what they did to aid the Americans.

CHAPTER 6
Review and Activities

Cooperative Activity

Before forming two smaller groups, students should research to find the name of an American soldier or regiment. Then one group should produce a written biography of that soldier or regiment and the other should create a poster-sized map showing the movements of that person or regiment during the war.

Technology Activity

Students should locate at least one quotation from a person mentioned in the chapter and combine their quotations in a bulletin-board display.

Portfolio Activity Students' charts should include information about the following people: Bernardo de Gálvez, Marquis de Lafayette, Thaddeus Kosciuszko, Casimir Pulaski, Friedrich von Steuben, Juan de Miralles, General Jean Baptiste de Rochambeau, and Admiral François de Grasse.

Chapter Bonus Test Question

Ask: By what nickname was Anthony Wayne known, and why? *(He was called "Mad" Anthony Wayne, because of his eagerness for battle.)*

Skill Practice Activity

1. red
2. a star burst
3. 1778
4. American and allied forces

Geography Activity

1. the Mississippi River
2. Spain; Russia
3. Great Britain
4. Russia
5. Spain and Russia

Chapter 7 Planning Guide

A complete, 1-page lesson plan is provided for each section in the ***Reproducible Lesson Plans*** **booklet.**

Section Resources

Daily Objectives	Reproducible Resources	Multimedia Resources
Section 1 **The Articles of Confederation** Evaluate the effectiveness of the Articles of Confederation in dealing with the challenges faced by the new nation.	Reproducible Lesson Plan 7–1 Guided Reading Activity 7–1* Section Quiz 7–1* Reteaching Activity 7–1 Enrichment Activity 7–1	Section Focus Transparency 7–1 Vocabulary PuzzleMaker Chapter Challenger Interactive Review Software Testmaker GTV: A Geographic Perspective on American History Facts On File: Landmark Documents in American History Focus on American Art Prints
Section 2 **Convention and Compromise** Discuss the compromises that enabled the Constitutional Convention to draft a new constitution for the country.	Reproducible Lesson Plan 7–2 Guided Reading Activity 7–2* Political Cartoons, *Foundations of Our Government* Section Quiz 7–2* Reteaching Activity 7–2 Enrichment Activity 7–2	Section Focus Transparency 7–2 Vocabulary PuzzleMaker Chapter Challenger Interactive Review Software Testmaker ABCNews InterActive™ Historic America Electronic Field Trips GTV: A Geographic Perspective on American History Facts On File: Landmark Documents in American History
Section 3 **A New Plan of Government** Explain key concepts in the Constitution and, where appropriate, their origin.	Reproducible Lesson Plan 7-3 Guided Reading Activity 7–3* Political Cartoons, *Federalism Then and Now* Section Quiz 7–3* Reteaching Activity 7–3 Enrichment Activity 7–3	Section Focus Transparency 7–3 Vocabulary PuzzleMaker Chapter Challenger Interactive Review Software Testmaker GTV: A Geographic Perspective on American History
Section 4 **Ratifying the Constitution** Contrast the views held by Federalists and Antifederalists regarding the Constitution.	Reproducible Lesson Plan 7–4 Guided Reading Activity 7–4* Section Quiz 7–4* Reteaching Activity 7–4 Enrichment Activity 7–4	Section Focus Transparency 7–4 Vocabulary PuzzleMaker Chapter Challenger Interactive Review Software Testmaker

** Also available in Spanish*

Poster — Transparency — CD-ROM — Software
Blackline Master — Videodisc — Audiocassette — Music Program

0:00 **OUT OF TIME?**
Assign the Chapter 7 Digest and the corresponding Chapter Digests Audiocassettes with activities and tests.

Activity

From the Classroom of...

Gary Chinn
Rooftop K-8 School
San Francisco, CA

Compromise—
My Rights or Yours?

Have students research both sides of the following debate, which formed the basis of the Federalist and Antifederalist stand-off: The United States needs a strong central government versus individual states' rights. After researching, students should choose either a "for" or "against" stance toward the statement. Then have them produce posters, advertisements, flyers, or political cartoons to promote either the cause of the Federalists or the cause of the Antifederalists. Each student is responsible for a one-minute presentation, explaining his or her artwork and viewpoint.

When presentations are completed, have a group of students collate the artwork into a portfolio that can be used during a class discussion or debate concerning the pros and cons of ratifying the Constitution.

Block Schedule

Block scheduling differs from traditional class scheduling in the amount of time allotted to each period. The extended time frame provided by block scheduling affords you the opportunity to implement a greater number of research-oriented and activity-intense projects to motivate and involve your students. Activities that are particularly suited to use within the block scheduling framework are identified throughout this chapter by the following designation:

NATIONAL GEOGRAPHIC SOCIETY — Teacher's Corner

INDEX TO NATIONAL GEOGRAPHIC MAGAZINE

The following articles may be used for research relating to this chapter:

- "L'Enfant's Washington," by Alice J. Hall, August 1991.
- "The Peales: America's First Family of Art," by Otto Friedrich, December 1990.
- "James Madison, Architect of the Constitution," by Alice J. Hall, September 1987.
- "George Washington's Patowmack Canal," by Wilbur E. Garrett, June 1987.

NATIONAL GEOGRAPHIC SOCIETY PRODUCTS AVAILABLE FROM GLENCOE

To order the following products for use with this chapter, contact your local Glencoe sales representative, or call Glencoe at 1-800-334-7344:

- *GTV: The American People: Fabric of a Nation* (Videodisc)
- *GTV: A Geographic Perspective on American History* (Videodisc)
- *The Presidents: A Picture History of Our Nation* (CD-ROM)

ADDITIONAL NATIONAL GEOGRAPHIC SOCIETY PRODUCTS

To order the following products for use with this chapter, call National Geographic Society at 1-800-368-2728:

- *Democratic Government Series, "The United States"* (Video)
- *Branches of Government Series* (Video)
- *Washington, D.C.* (Video)
- *Historical Atlas of the United States* (Atlas)

KEY TO ABILITY LEVELS

Teaching strategies have been coded for varying learning styles and abilities.

L1 **BASIC** activities for all students
L2 **AVERAGE** activities for average to above-average students
L3 **CHALLENGING** activities for above-average students
ELL **ENGLISH LANGUAGE LEARNER** activities

Chapter 7 Resource Guide

HOME INVOLVEMENT

Home Involvement Activity 7

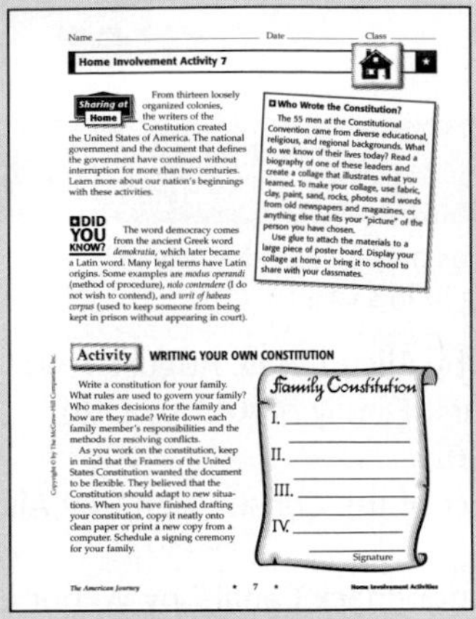

REVIEW ACTIVITIES

Chapter Summary 7

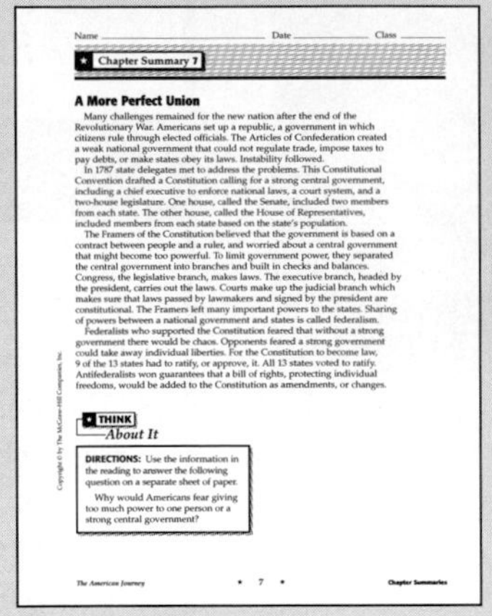

Workbook Activity 7

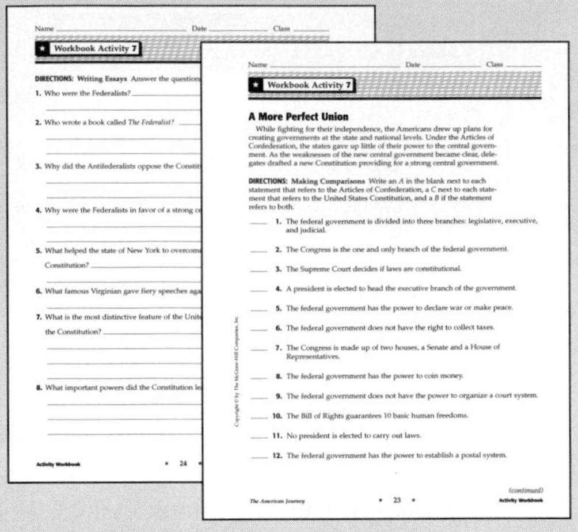

REINFORCEMENT ACTIVITIES

Time Line Activity 7

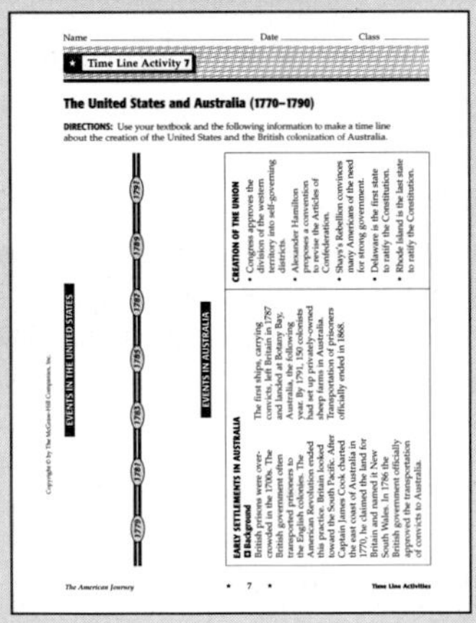

Vocabulary Activity 7

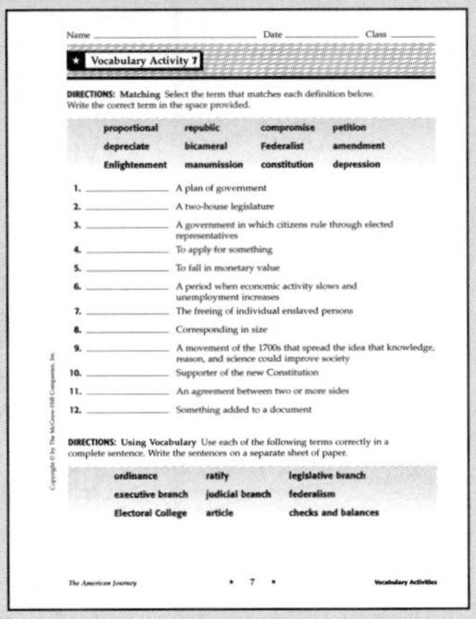

Chapter Skills Activity 7

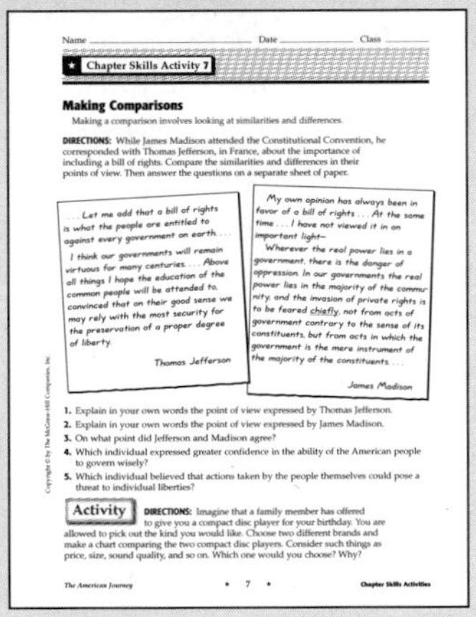

ENRICHMENT ACTIVITIES

Linking Past and Present Activity 7

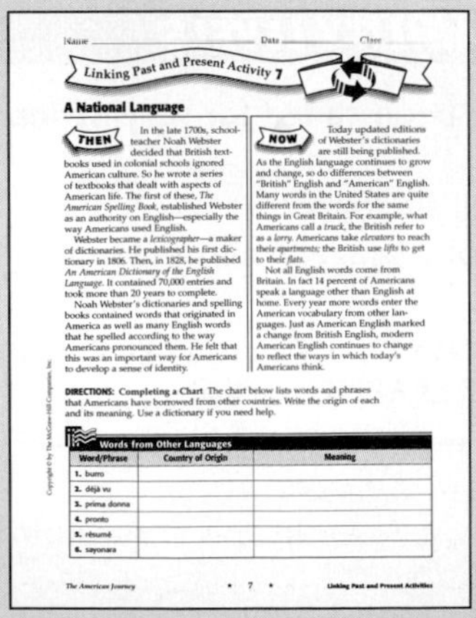

Primary Source Reading 7

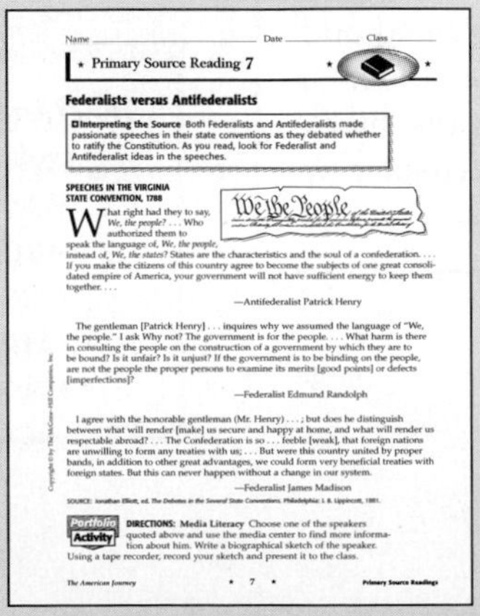

GEOGRAPHY ACTIVITIES

Mapping History Activity 7

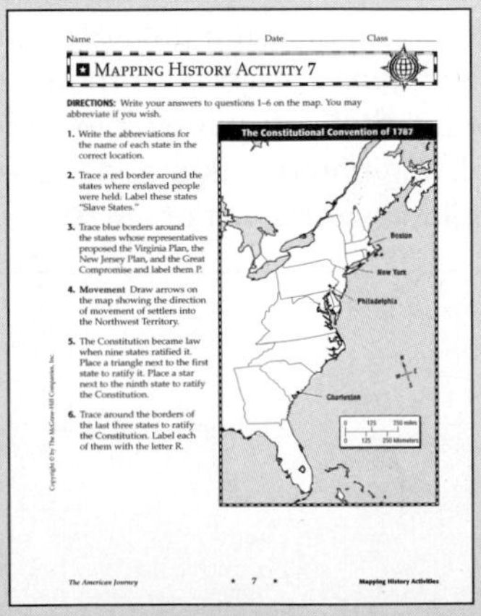

Chapter 7 Resource Guide

Assessment

Chapter 7 Test, Form A

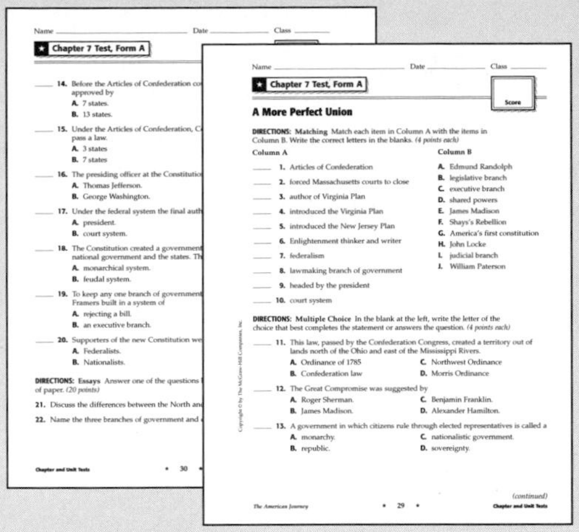

Chapter 7 Test, Form B

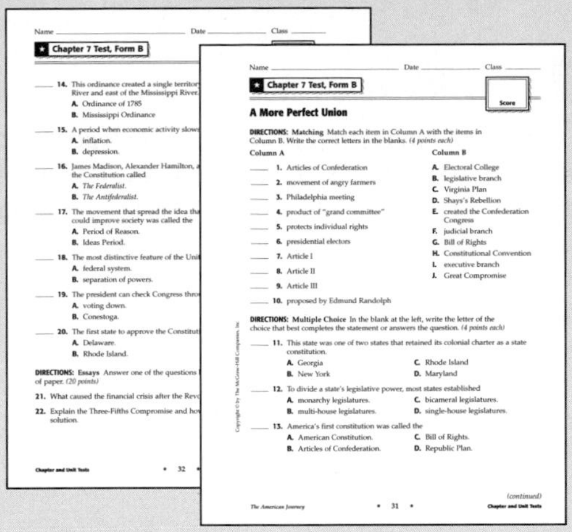

Performance Assessment Activity 7

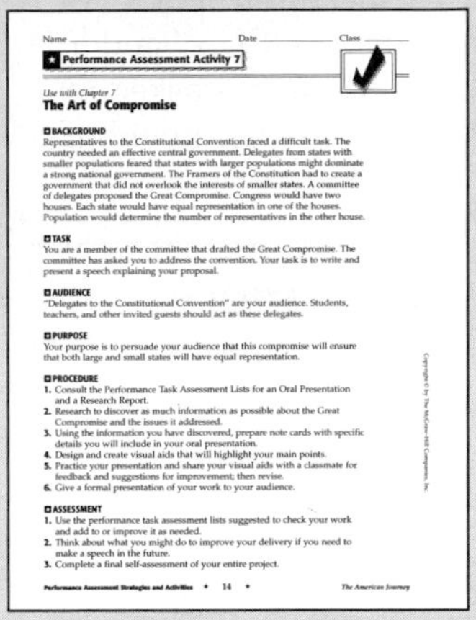

Spanish Resources

The following Spanish language materials are available in the Spanish Resources binder:

- **Spanish Chapter Summary 7**
- **Spanish Vocabulary Activity 7**
- **Spanish Guided Reading Activities, Chapter 7**
- **Spanish Section Quizzes, Chapter 7**
- **Spanish Home Involvement Activity 7**
- **Spanish Chapter 7 Digests Audiocassette Activity and Test**

Activity Manipulatives

Help students learn more about America's cultural history with:

- ***American Crafts Hands-On Activities***
- ***American Games Hands-On Activities***
- ***American History Flash Cards***

Additional Resources From Glencoe

- **U.S. History & Art,** Transparency 5, *University of Virginia, Charlottesville*
- **Focus on American Art Prints,** *The Staircase Group* by Charles Willson Peale
- **American Music Cultural Traditions,** Lesson 2: "Tunes from Colonial America & The President's March"
- **Outline Map Resource Book**
- **U.S. Desk Map**
- **The American History Videodisc and CD-ROM,** *The American Revolution and the Early Republic, 1765–1820*

A&E HOME VIDEO. Biography THE HISTORY CHANNEL.

The following videotape programs are available from Glencoe as supplements to Chapter 7:

- **George Washington: Founding Father** (ISBN 1-56501-377-8)
- **Thomas Jefferson: Philosopher of Freedom** (ISBN 1-56501-502-9)
- **Benjamin Franklin: Citizen of the World** (ISBN 1-56501-426-X)
- **Patrick Henry: Voice of Liberty** (ISBN 1-56501-645-9)

To order, call Glencoe at 1-800-334-7344. To find classroom resources to accompany many of these videos, check the following home pages:
A&E Television: http://www.aetv.com
The History Channel: http://www.historychannel.com

Introducing
CHAPTER 7

Chapter Themes

Chapter Themes are listed by section on this chapter opening page of the Student Edition. A corresponding theme-based activity is available under "FOCUS," and a theme-based question is asked in the Section and Chapter Reviews.

Performance Assessment

Refer to Activity 7 in the *Performance Assessment Strategies and Activities* booklet.

GLENCOE TECHNOLOGY

VIDEODISC
MindJogger Videoquiz

Use MindJogger to preview the Chapter 7 content.

Chapter 7
Disc 1, Side B

Also available in VHS.

HISTORY AND ART Mixed feelings about the new Constitution were expressed by many, including Benjamin Franklin, who ultimately supported it by saying, "The older I grow, the more apt I am to doubt my own judgment and pay more respect to the judgment of others."

Chapter 7

1777–1790

A More Perfect Union

Why It's Important

When the American colonies broke their political ties with Great Britain, they were faced with the task of forming independent governments at both the state and national levels. In 1788 the Constitution became the official plan of American government. Created to meet the growing needs of a changing nation, the Constitution has been the fundamental law of the United States for more than 200 years. Of all the written national constitutions in the world, the United States Constitution is the oldest that is still operating. It has served as a model for many other countries in the world.

Chapter Themes

- *Section 1,* Government and Democracy
- *Section 2,* Groups and Institutions
- *Section 3,* Civic Rights and Responsibilities
- *Section 4,* Groups and Institutions

HISTORY AND ART ***Signing the Constitution of the United States* by Thomas P. Rossiter** The delegates sign the final draft of the Constitution in Philadelphia's Independence Hall. Despite mixed feelings, most of those present were hopeful about the future.

188

EXTRA CREDIT PROJECT

Creating Headlines Students can trace the events in this chapter by writing imaginary newspaper headlines. If possible, bring newspapers to class for students to examine. Then ask them to write a few headlines that point out the new nation's problems. Have them write headlines about the adoption of the Articles of Confederation and the problems that continued. Finally, ask students to write a few headlines about drafting and ratifying the Constitution and the need for a bill of rights. Use the headlines as an outline for chapter review.

1775 1780 1785 1790

1777 Articles of Confederation are written

1781 All states approve Confederation government

1783 Treaty of Paris officially ends American Revolution

1787 Northwest Ordinance is passed

Section 1

The Articles of Confederation

READ TO DISCOVER . . .

- how the weaknesses of the Articles of Confederation created instability in the new United States.
- how the Confederation Congress dealt with the western lands.

TERMS TO LEARN

constitution
bicameral
republic
petition
ordinance
depreciate

The Storyteller

The Revolutionary War had officially ended, but British troops continued to occupy American lands. George Rogers Clark had personally led many attacks against British-backed Native Americans. He boasted in his journal that he and his troops had left five Shawnee villages in Ohio, as well as a British trading post, "in ashes."

Powder horn and sash

Although the Americans won their independence from Britain, they had trouble winning Britain's respect. Ignoring the terms of the Treaty of Paris, the British kept troops at frontier posts within the United States. The British knew the new American government was weak and ineffective. In the years following the Revolution, Britain did not even bother to send a representative to the United States.

Thirteen Independent States

While Americans were fighting for their independence on the battlefield, they were also creating new governments. After rejecting British rule, they needed to establish their own political institutions at both the state and national levels.

State Constitutions

In May 1776 the Continental Congress asked the states to organize their governments, and each moved quickly to adopt a state **constitution**, or plan of government. By the end of 1776, eight states had drafted constitutions. New York and Georgia followed suit in 1777, and Massachusetts in 1780. Connecticut and Rhode Island retained their colonial charters as state constitutions.

1 FOCUS

BELLRINGER
Motivational Activity

Before taking roll at the beginning of the class period, project Section Focus Transparency 7–1 and have students answer the questions. Discuss students' responses.

This activity is also available as a blackline master.

Section Focus Transparency 7–1

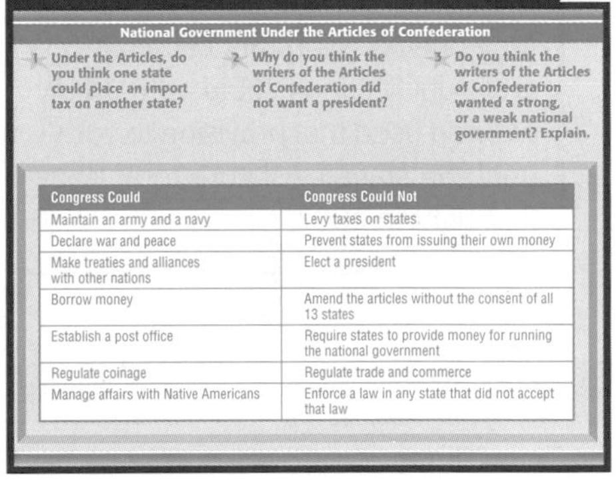

National Government Under the Articles of Confederation

1 Under the Articles, do you think one state could place an import tax on another state?

2 Why do you think the writers of the Articles of Confederation did not want a president?

3 Do you think the writers of the Articles of Confederation wanted a strong, or a weak national government? Explain.

Congress Could	Congress Could Not
Maintain an army and a navy	Levy taxes on states
Declare war and peace	Prevent states from issuing their own money
Make treaties and alliances with other nations	Elect a president
Borrow money	Amend the articles without the consent of all 13 states
Establish a post office	Require states to provide money for running the national government
Regulate coinage	Regulate trade and commerce
Manage affairs with Native Americans	Enforce a law in any state that did not accept that law

Vocabulary Precheck

Call on volunteers to define each of the entries in **Terms to Learn.** Ask students to use the textbook glossary to check the accuracy of the definitions.

Use the **Vocabulary PuzzleMaker** to create crossword and word search puzzles.

Section Theme
Government and Democracy

At both state and national levels, the government of the new United States sought to define its function and powers.

Activity Ask students to imagine that they are leaders of a new country. Have them list several powers they think their government should have. Then have them vote for the power they consider most important.

SECTION RESOURCES

Reproducible Masters

- Reproducible Lesson Plan 7–1
- Guided Reading Activity 7–1
- Section Quiz 7–1
- Reteaching Activity 7–1
- Enrichment Activity 7–1

Transparencies

- Section Focus Transparency 7–1

Multimedia

- Vocabulary PuzzleMaker
- Chapter Challenger Interactive Review Software
- GTV: A Geographic Perspective on American History
- Facts On File: Landmark Documents in American History
- Focus on American Art Prints

2 TEACH

L1, ELL Discussing Reasons Ask pairs of students: **Why is a government important? Why can't people just do what they feel is right?** Discuss responses that partners present to the class *(for example, not everyone agrees about what is right; some people purposely will do wrong).*

What?Where?When?Who?

Voting in New Jersey In New Jersey under that state's constitution, "any person" who met certain property qualifications could vote. Many women used that provision to vote—until the state legislature took away that right in 1807.

Guided Reading Activity 7–1

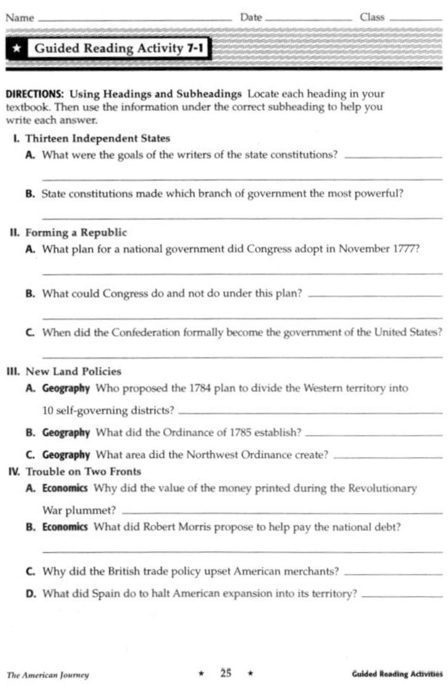
Name ______ Date ______ Class ______

Guided Reading Activity 7-1

DIRECTIONS: Using Headings and Subheadings Locate each heading in your textbook. Then use the information under the correct subheading to help you write each answer.

I. Thirteen Independent States
A. What were the goals of the writers of the state constitutions? ______
B. State constitutions made which branch of government the most powerful? ______

II. Forming a Republic
A. What plan for a national government did Congress adopt in November 1777? ______
B. What could Congress do and not do under this plan? ______
C. When did the Confederation formally become the government of the United States? ______

III. New Land Policies
A. **Geography** Who proposed the 1784 plan to divide the Western territory into 10 self-governing districts? ______
B. **Geography** What did the Ordinance of 1785 establish? ______
C. **Geography** What area did the Northwest Ordinance create? ______

IV. Trouble on Two Fronts
A. **Economics** Why did the value of the money printed during the Revolutionary War plummet? ______
B. **Economics** What did Robert Morris propose to help pay the national debt? ______
C. Why did the British trade policy upset American merchants? ______
D. What did Spain do to halt American expansion into its territory? ______

Copyright © by The McGraw-Hill Companies, Inc.

The American Journey • 25 • Guided Reading Activities

Their experience with British rule made Americans cautious about placing too much power in the hands of a single ruler. For that reason the states adopted constitutions that limited the power of the governor. Pennsylvania even replaced the office of governor with an elected council of 12 members.

The states took further precautions against concentration of power. They divided government functions between the governor (or Pennsylvania's council) and the legislature. Most states established two-house, or **bicameral,** legislatures to divide the power even further.

The writers of the constitutions not only wanted to stop the abuses of power in the states, but they also wanted to keep power in the hands of the people. State legislators were popularly elected, and elections were frequent.

In most states, only white males over the age of 21 could vote. To qualify as a voter, these citizens also had to own a certain amount of property or pay a certain amount of taxes. Some states allowed free African American males to vote.

Popular Politics

The state constitutions restricted the powers of the governors, which made the legislatures the most powerful branch of government. Western parts of the states got more seats in legislatures, with many more farmers and common men elected than in the Colonial Era. The state legislatures struggled to make taxes more fair, but there were many squabbles between those who represented poor debtors and the wealthier state legislators. Going from dependent colonies to self-governing states brought many new challenges.

The Articles of Confederation

Forming a Republic

For Americans, establishing separate state governments was a much easier task than creating a single national government. They agreed that their nation should be a **republic,** a government in which citizens rule through elected representatives. They could not agree, however, on the organization and powers of their new republic.

At first most Americans favored a weak central government. They assumed the states would be very much like small, independent countries—similar to the way that the colonies had been set up. The states would act independently on most issues, working together through a central government only to wage war and handle relations with other nations.

Planning a New Government

In 1776 the Second Continental Congress appointed a committee to draw up a plan for a new national government. The delegates in the Congress realized they needed a central government to coordinate the war effort against Britain. After much debate the Congress adopted the committee's plan, the **Articles of Confederation,** in November 1777.

The Articles, America's first constitution, provided for a new central government to which the states gave little of their power. For the states the Confederation was "a firm league of friendship" in which each state retained "its sovereignty, freedom and independence."

Under the Articles of Confederation, the national government—consisting of the Confederation

COOPERATIVE LEARNING ACTIVITY

Reviewing Problems This jigsaw activity can reinforce discussion of early problems the United States faced. Organize students into groups and assign each group one of the following problems: preparing a plan for a national government; establishing new land policies; paying off war debts; establishing relationships with other nations. Each member of the group should become an "expert" on the group's topic. Students should summarize the text's discussion of the topic, exchanging and answering questions within the group, considering "What if . . . " situations, and so on. Then form new groups, making sure that at least one representative from each "problem" topic is in each new group. Have the "experts" teach their topics to fellow group members.

Western Land Claims of the Original States

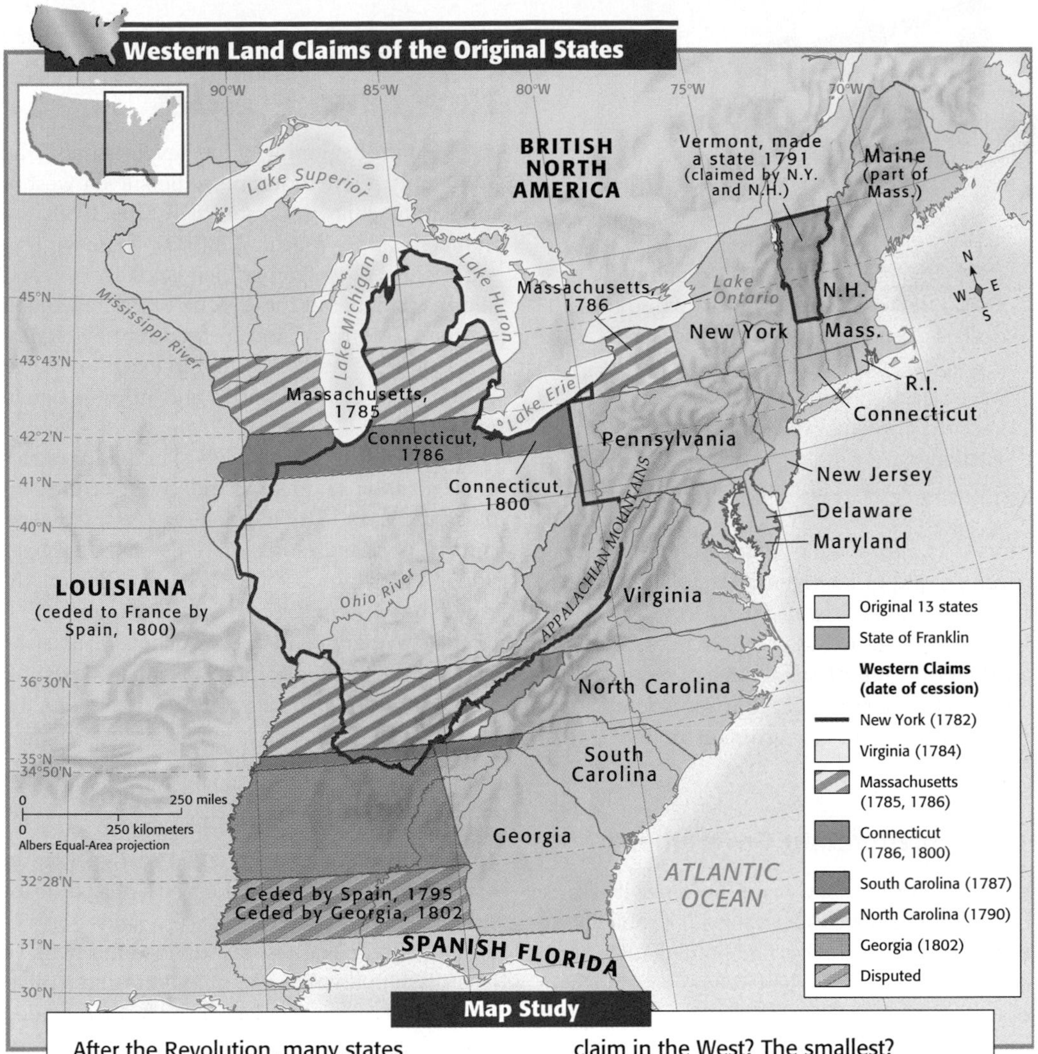

Map Study

After the Revolution, many states extended their boundaries west of the Appalachian Mountains.

1. **Region** Which state had the largest claim in the West? The smallest?
2. **Analyzing Information** Who claimed land west of the Mississippi River in 1800?

Congress—had the authority to conduct foreign affairs, maintain armed forces, borrow money, and issue currency. Yet it could not regulate trade, force soldiers to join the army, or impose taxes. If the Confederation Congress needed to raise money or troops, it had to ask the state legislatures—but the states were not required to contribute. In addition the new national government lacked a chief executive to enforce its laws.

Approving the Articles

All 13 states had to approve the Articles of Confederation before they could go into effect. Under the new plan, each state had one vote in the Confederation Congress. However, the large states thought they should have more votes because of their size and population. The states also argued about rights to western lands. Maryland

MULTIPLE LEARNING STYLES

Verbal/Linguistic Encourage students to consider the new nation's name: *United States.* Have them work individually or with partners to brainstorm for words and images they associate with (1) a union that sought to take its place among the nations of the world *(United)* and (2) the individuality of the former colonies *(States).* Call on volunteers to share responses as you introduce or review this section. **L2**

CHAPTER 7
Section 1, 189–195

NATIONAL GEOGRAPHIC SOCIETY

VIDEODISC
GTV: A Geographic Perspective on American History

Side 2, Chapter 3
Title: *Map Rap*
Subject: The growth of the United States (1776–1867)
Ask: **How many states did the United States include in 1776?** *(13)*

Map Study

Answers

1. Virginia; South Carolina
2. France

Facts On File

CD-ROM
Landmark Documents in American History

Title: *Letters from an American Farmer, Hector St. John Crèvecoeur, 1782*
Ask students what they think might have resulted from this document.

What?Where?When?Who?

The bald eagle became America's national symbol in 1872. Benjamin Franklin suggested the turkey as the national bird. The American bald eagle, Franklin claimed, was "a bird of bad moral character . . . and often [full of lice]." Franklin stated, "The turkey is . . . a much more respectable bird, withal a true original native of America."

Picturing HISTORY At this time many foreign coins were still being used, as well as coins that were struck privately. The only way to determine the value of a coin was to determine the weight of the gold used in making the coin. **Answer:** *at least a dollar an acre, or at least 640 dollars a section*

NATIONAL GEOGRAPHIC SOCIETY

VIDEODISC
GTV: A Geographic Perspective on American History

Side 2, Chapter 6
Title: *The Advancing Frontier: The Near West*
Subject: Settlement between the Appalachians and the Mississippi (1820–1850)
Ask: **What kinds of policies did the government take in regard to the Native Americans who occupied western lands?** *(The government chased them off their land by "any means possible.")*

Linking PAST & PRESENT

Where's Franklin? *Franklin* continues to be a popular place-name today. Dozens of cities, towns, and counties in the United States bear the name of this Framer of the Constitution.

you don't say...

Land Speculator The Latin *specula*—"watchtower"—is part of the word history of *speculator.* It could be said that a speculator's attempts to second-guess the future are like trying to see far away from the top of a watchtower.

Picturing HISTORY In the 1780s, American bankers, merchants, and dealers often used weighing devices such as this fold-up pocket scale to determine the value of coins. **For how much was each section of western township land sold at auction?**

refused to approve the Articles until New York, Virginia, and other states abandoned claims to lands west of the Appalachian Mountains. Finally the states settled their differences, and with Maryland's ratification, all 13 had approved the Articles. On March 1, 1781, the Confederation formally became the government of the United States.

The Confederation Government

Within the next few years, however, it became clear that the Articles had serious problems. To begin with, the Congress had limited authority. It could not pass a law unless 9 states voted in favor of it. Any attempt to change the Articles required the consent of all 13 states. These strict voting requirements made it difficult for the Congress to pass laws when there was any opposition.

Despite its weaknesses, the Confederation did accomplish some important things. Its major accomplishment was winning the war, but it also provided for new states in the West.

Geography

New Land Policies

At the beginning of the Revolutionary War, only a few thousand settlers lived west of the Appalachian Mountains. By the 1780s the number was approaching 100,000. These western settlers hoped to organize their lands as states and join the nation, but the Articles of Confederation contained no provision for adding new states. The Congress realized it had to extend national authority over the frontier and bring order to this territory.

During the 1780s and 1790s, individual states gave up their claims to lands west of the Appalachians, and the national government took control of these lands. In 1784 the Congress, under a plan proposed by Thomas Jefferson, divided the western territory into 10 self-governing districts. When the number of people in a district reached the population of the smallest existing state, that district could **petition**, or apply to, the Congress for statehood.

The Ordinance of 1785

In 1785 the Confederation Congress passed an **ordinance**, or law, that established a procedure for surveying and selling the western lands north of the Ohio River. The new law divided this massive territory into townships 6 miles long and 6 miles wide. These townships were to be further divided into 36 sections of 640 acres each that would be sold at auction for at least a dollar an acre.

Land speculators viewed the law as an opportunity to cheaply accumulate large tracts of land. Concerned about lawless people moving into western lands, Richard Henry Lee, the president of the Congress, urged that "the rights of

Footnotes to History

The State of Franklin In 1784 three counties from the western territory of North Carolina formed their own state—Franklin. Named for Benjamin Franklin, the new "state" never met the requirements for admission to the Union. Franklin eventually became part of Tennessee.

MAKING CONNECTIONS ACTIVITY

Politics Part of the work of founding an independent United States was defining the governments of individual states. Ask students to find pictures and information about the legislative buildings of the states that arose from the thirteen colonies (especially if your state is among them). Have students discuss the following questions: What style elements do some of the capitols share? Do the structures suggest the kind of state government that was instituted? Do they suggest the political ideals that were important to that state? Although it may be confusing, point out to students that the seat of government is known as the state *capital,* but the building where the government conducts its business is called the state *capitol.* **L2**

The Northwest Territory, 1785

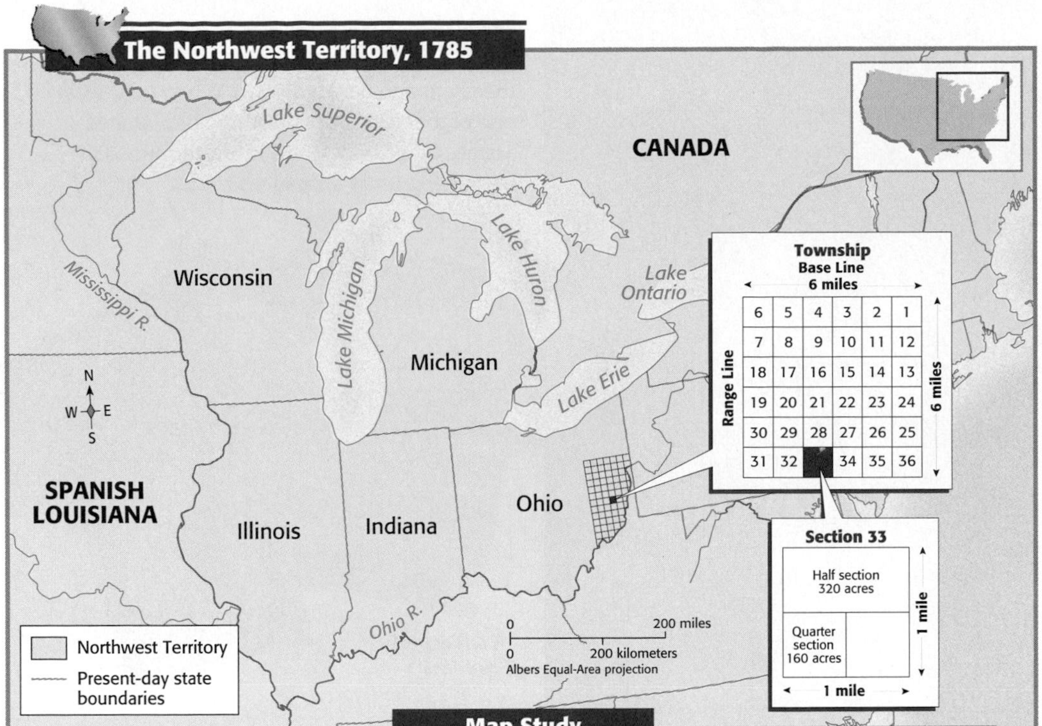

Map Study

The Northwest Territory was divided into townships, each with 36 sections. Section 16 was reserved to support public schools.

1. Region What present-day states were created from the Northwest Territory?

2. Analyzing Information How many miles long and wide was a township? A section?

property be clearly defined" by the government. The Congress drafted another ordinance to protect the interests of hard-working settlers.

The Northwest Ordinance

The Northwest Ordinance, passed in 1787, created a single **Northwest Territory** out of the lands north of the Ohio River and east of the Mississippi River. The lands were to be divided into three to five smaller territories. When the population of a territory reached 60,000, the people could apply for statehood. Each new state would come into the Union on "an equal footing" with the original 13 states.

The Northwest Ordinance included a bill of rights for the settlers, guaranteeing freedom of religion and trial by jury. It also stated, "There shall be neither slavery nor involuntary servitude in said territory." This clause marked the national government's first attempt to stop the spread of slavery.

The Confederation's western ordinances had enormous significance for American expansion and development. These policies opened the way for settlement of the Northwest Territory in a stable and orderly manner.

Trouble on Two Fronts

Despite its accomplishments in dealing with western lands, the Confederation government had so little power that it could not

CRITICAL THINKING ACTIVITY

Recognizing Bias Many details in this section suggest opinions that might have weakened the effectiveness of the early state and federal governments. Have students comment upon biased thinking and its effects in the following areas:

- Qualifications for voting, under state constitutions
- The establishment of a national government
- Status of land west of the Appalachians
- Relations with Britain and Spain

Help students summarize their comments. **L3**

Facts On File

CD-ROM
Landmark Documents in American History

Title: *Land Ordinance of 1785; Northwest Ordinance, 1787*
Have students examine the documents, then imagine they are reporters covering the passage of the Land Ordinance of 1785 and the Northwest Ordinance of 1787. Have them write an article outlining the provisions of the two ordinances and suggest what effects the new laws will have on settlement northwest of the Ohio River.

Map Study

Answers

1. Illinois, Indiana, Michigan, Ohio, and Wisconsin
2. 6 miles by 6 miles; 1 mile by 1 mile

Map Skills Practice

Reading a Map Which state borders two of the Great Lakes? *(Wisconsin)* Which state borders three of the Great Lakes? *(Michigan)*

Who?What?Where?When?

Richard Henry Lee (1732–1794) influenced the United States in important ways. Before the war, one of his proposals resulted in the creation of the committees of correspondence; another was a key factor in drafting the Declaration of Independence; and still another called for a colonial confederation.

CHAPTER 7
Section 1, 189–195

HISTORY AND ART Peale (1741–1827) was perhaps the most popular portrait painter of his time. He served the Patriot cause as a colonel during the Revolutionary War. In 1782 he opened the first art gallery in the United States, in Philadelphia. His first display consisted of portraits of major war figures. **Answer:** *a five percent tax on imported goods to help pay off the national debt*

History *and the* Humanities

Focus on American Art Prints, *The Staircase Group* by Charles Willson Peale

3 ASSESS

Assign Section 1 Review as homework or as an in-class activity.

Use **Chapter Challenger Interactive Review Software** to review Section 1.

Section Quiz 7–1

Name ______ Date ______ Class ______

Chapter 7 — Score

Section Quiz 7-1

DIRECTIONS: Matching Match each item in Column A with the items in Column B. Write the correct letters in the blanks. *(10 points each)*

Column A	Column B
____ 1. plan of government	A. Articles of Confederation
____ 2. two-house legislatures	B. constitution
____ 3. America's first constitution	C. ordinance
____ 4. law	D. depreciated
____ 5. fallen in value	E. bicameral

DIRECTIONS: Multiple Choice In the blank at the left, write the letter of the choice that best completes the statement or answers the question. *(10 points each)*

____ 6. The states adopted constitutions that limited the power of the
A. state senator. C. governor.
B. state representative. D. president.

____ 7. The Americans formed a republic, a government in which citizens rule through
A. elected representatives. C. kingships.
B. monarchies. D. appointed representatives.

____ 8. One of the Confederation's accomplishments was an arrangement for handling
A. currency. C. the military.
B. new states in the West. D. foreign troops.

____ 9. The single territory that was created out of the lands north of the Ohio River and east of the Mississippi River was called the
A. Mississippi Territory. C. Northwest Territory.
B. Western Territory. D. Ohio River valley Territory.

____ 10. One major weakness of the Confederation was it could not deal with
A. drawing maps C. Native Americans
B. new states D. the nation's finances

The American Journey ★ 25 ★ Section Quizzes

HISTORY AND ART ***Robert Morris*** **by Charles Willson Peale** Pennsylvania merchant and banker Robert Morris (left) was one of the richest people in the new United States. **What reform did Morris propose to help the country's finances?**

Continental currency

deal with the nation's pressing financial problems. It also failed to resolve problems over land holdings and trade with Britain and Spain.

Economics

Financial Problems

By 1781 the money printed during the Revolutionary War had **depreciated,** or fallen in value, so much that it was almost completely worthless. Unable to collect taxes, both the Continental Congress and the states had printed their own paper money. No gold or silver backed up these bills. For this reason the value of the bills plummeted, while the prices of food and other goods soared. Between 1779 and 1781, the number of Continental dollars required to buy one Spanish silver dollar rose from 40 to 146. In Boston and some other areas, the resulting high prices led to food riots.

Fighting the war left the Confederation Congress with a large debt. The Congress had borrowed money from American citizens and foreign governments during the war. It still owed the Revolutionary soldiers their pay for military service. Lacking the power to tax, the Confederation could not pay its debts. It requested funds from the states, but the states contributed only about one-sixth of the money needed.

Robert Morris's Import Tax

Faced with a total collapse of the country's finances, the Confederation created a department of finance under Philadelphia merchant **Robert Morris.** He proposed collecting a 5 percent tax on imported goods to help pay the national debt.

The plan required that the Articles of Confederation be changed to give the Congress the power to tax. Although 12 states approved the plan, the opposition of Rhode Island killed the measure. A second effort five years later also failed to win approval by all the states. The financial crisis worsened.

TEACHER'S NOTES

Problems with Britain

As the weaknesses of the new American government became clear, the United States developed problems with other countries. In the Treaty of Paris of 1783, Britain had promised to withdraw from the lands east of the Mississippi River. Yet British troops continued to occupy several strategic forts in the Great Lakes region.

British trade policy was another problem. American merchants complained that the British were keeping Americans out of the West Indies and other profitable British markets.

In 1784 the Confederation Congress sent **John Adams** to London to discuss these problems. The British, however, were not willing to talk. They pointed to the failure of the United States to honor *its* promises made in the Treaty of Paris. The British claimed that Americans had agreed to pay Loyalists for the property taken from them during the Revolutionary War. The Congress had, in fact, recommended that the states pay the Loyalists, but the states refused.

Problems with Spain

If American relations with Great Britain were poor, affairs with Spain were worse. Spain, which held Florida as well as lands west of the Mississippi River, was anxious to halt American expansion into the territory it claimed. As a result, Spain closed the lower Mississippi River to American shipping in 1784.

American settlers west of the Appalachian Mountains protested vigorously because this new policy deprived westerners of their major avenue of trade. As **John Jay**, the American secretary of foreign affairs, had noted a few years earlier: "The Americans, almost to a man, believed that God Almighty had made that river a highway for the people of the upper country to go to sea by."

In 1786 American diplomats reached an agreement with Spain to limit American shipping on the Mississippi. In exchange Spain promised to accept the border between Georgia and Spanish Florida proposed by the Americans. The people living in the Southern states, however, rejected the agreement because it would have forced them to give up their right to use the Mississippi River.

The weakness of the Confederation and its inability to deal with problems worried many national leaders. George Washington described the government as "little more than the shadow without the substance." Many Americans began to agree that the country needed a stronger national government.

Section 1 Review

Checking for Understanding

1. ***Identify*** Articles of Confederation, Northwest Territory, Robert Morris, John Adams, John Jay.
2. ***Define*** constitution, bicameral, republic, petition, ordinance, depreciate.
3. ***List*** two weaknesses of the government under the Articles of Confederation.

Reviewing Themes

4. **Government and Democracy** Why did most states limit the power of their governors and divide their legislatures into two bodies?

Critical Thinking

5. **Predicting Consequences** What effects do you think the Northwest Ordinance had on Native Americans?

Activity

Making a Poster Imagine you are a United States citizen in the 1780s. Create a poster that defends the Articles. Be sure to include reasons the Confederation Congress is needed.

CHAPTER 7
Section 1, 189–195

Reteaching Activity 7–1

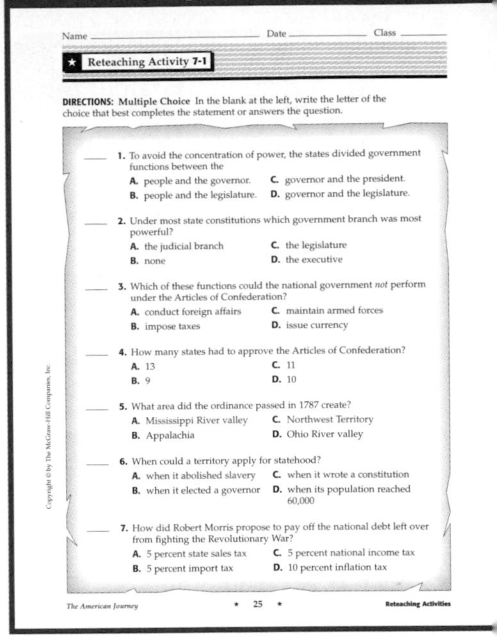
Name ____ Date ____ Class ____

★ Reteaching Activity 7-1

DIRECTIONS: Multiple Choice In the blank at the left, write the letter of the choice that best completes the statement or answers the question.

____ 1. To avoid the concentration of power, the states divided government functions between the
A. people and the governor. C. governor and the president.
B. people and the legislature. D. governor and the legislature.

____ 2. Under most state constitutions which government branch was most powerful?
A. the judicial branch C. the legislature
B. none D. the executive

____ 3. Which of these functions could the national government *not* perform under the Articles of Confederation?
A. conduct foreign affairs C. maintain armed forces
B. impose taxes D. issue currency

____ 4. How many states had to approve the Articles of Confederation?
A. 13 C. 11
B. 9 D. 10

____ 5. What area did the ordinance passed in 1787 create?
A. Mississippi River valley C. Northwest Territory
B. Appalachia D. Ohio River valley

____ 6. When could a territory apply for statehood?
A. when it abolished slavery C. when it wrote a constitution
B. when it elected a governor D. when its population reached 60,000

____ 7. How did Robert Morris propose to pay off the national debt left over from fighting the Revolutionary War?
A. 5 percent state sales tax C. 5 percent national income tax
B. 5 percent import tax D. 10 percent inflation tax

Copyright © by The McGraw-Hill Companies, Inc.

The American Journey ★ 25 ★ Reteaching Activities

Enrichment Activity 7–1

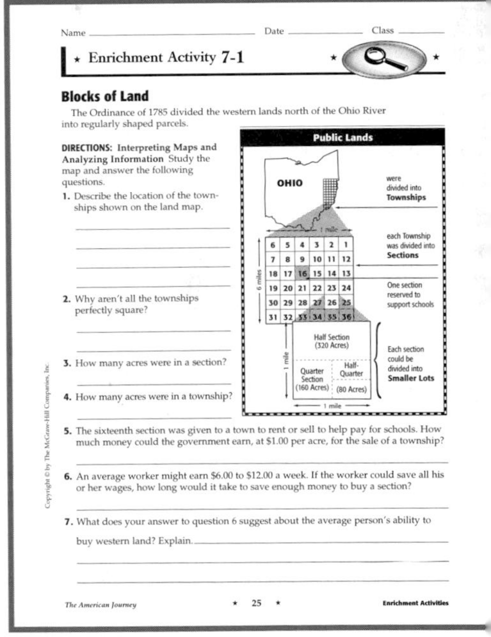
Name ____ Date ____ Class ____

★ Enrichment Activity 7-1

Blocks of Land

The Ordinance of 1785 divided the western lands north of the Ohio River into regularly shaped parcels.

DIRECTIONS: Interpreting Maps and Analyzing Information Study the map and answer the following questions.

1. Describe the location of the townships shown on the land map.
2. Why aren't all the townships perfectly square?
3. How many acres were in a section?
4. How many acres were in a township?
5. The sixteenth section was given to a town to rent or sell to help pay for schools. How much money could the government earn, at $1.00 per acre, for the sale of a township?
6. An average worker might earn $6.00 to $12.00 a week. If the worker could save all his or her wages, how long would it take to save enough money to buy a section?
7. What does your answer to question 6 suggest about the average person's ability to buy western land? Explain.

Copyright © by The McGraw-Hill Companies, Inc.

The American Journey ★ 25 ★ Enrichment Activities

Section 1 Review Answers

1. Articles of Confederation, 190; Northwest Territory, 193; Robert Morris, 194; John Adams, 195; John Jay, 195
2. The words are defined in the Glossary.
3. Any two: Congress could not pass a law unless nine states voted in favor of it; it could not add states; it could not regulate trade; it could not force soldiers to join the army; it could not impose taxes or enforce laws.
4. British rule made them cautious about placing too much power in the hands of a single ruler or political body.
5. Students should predict that Native Americans once again would be forced to fight or give up their lands and move farther west.

Activity Posters should cite reasons to keep the existing government.

4 CLOSE

Have students name strengths and weaknesses of the Articles of Confederation. Ask them to explain why a weak government plan could cause problems for a growing country.

1 FOCUS

BELLRINGER
Motivational Activity

Before taking roll at the beginning of the class period, project Section Focus Transparency 7–2 and have students answer the questions. Discuss students' responses.

This activity is also available as a blackline master.

Section Focus Transparency 7–2

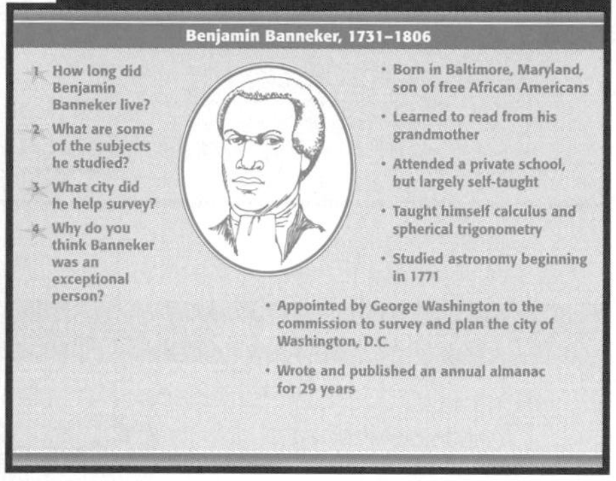

Vocabulary Precheck

Point out that in the context of this section, *compromise* is a noun. Add that it also can be used as a verb. Have students write two sentences, one using *compromise* as a noun, the other using it as a verb.

Use the **Vocabulary Puzzle-Maker** to create crossword and word search puzzles.

Section Theme
Groups and Institutions

Flaws in the Articles of Confederation brought national leaders together. Ultimately their work produced a new constitution for the United States.

Activity Have students discuss how a government might find out that some of its decisions are not working. *(Answers may include a rise in crime, formal protests from groups of citizens, and so on.)*

1783 1785 1787 1789

1783 Massachusetts court rules slavery illegal

January 1787 Daniel Shays leads rebellion

May 1787 Delegates meet to revise Articles of Confederation

September 1787 Delegates sign draft of Constitution

Section 2

Convention and Compromise

READ TO DISCOVER . . .

- how the Constitutional Convention broke the deadlock over the form of the new government.
- how the delegates resolved the issue of representation.

TERMS TO LEARN

depression
manumission
proportional
compromise

The Storyteller

By 1786 many Americans observed that the Confederation government was not working. George Washington himself agreed that the United States was really "thirteen Sovereignties [independent nations] pulling against each other."

In the summer of 1787, Washington joined delegates from Virginia and 11 other states in Philadelphia. Rhode Island decided not to participate. The delegates came "for the sole and express purpose of revising the Articles of Confederation."

George Washington

The young nation faced difficult problems. An economic slowdown led to hardships and unrest among the people. Slavery became an issue as some states took action to limit or abolish it. Many Americans believed that the Confederation government was too weak to deal with the tough challenges facing the United States.

Economic Depression

After the Revolutionary War ended, the United States went through a **depression,** a period when economic activity slows and unemployment increases. Southern plantations had been damaged during the war, and rice exports dropped sharply. Trade also fell off as the British closed the profitable West Indian market to American merchants. What little money there was went to pay foreign debts, and a serious currency shortage resulted.

Difficult Times for Farmers

American farmers suffered because they could not sell their goods. They had problems paying the taxes that the states levied to meet Revolutionary War debts. As a result state officials seized farmers' lands to pay their debts and threw many farmers into jail. Grumblings of protest soon grew into revolt.

SECTION RESOURCES

Reproducible Masters
- Reproducible Lesson Plan 7–2
- Guided Reading Activity 7–2
- Political Cartoons
- Section Quiz 7–2
- Reteaching Activity 7–2
- Enrichment Activity 7–2

Transparencies
- Section Focus Transparency 7–2

Multimedia
- Vocabulary PuzzleMaker
- Chapter Challenger Interactive Review
- ABCNews InterActive™ Historic America Electronic Field Trips
- GTV: A Geographic Perspective on American History
- Facts On File: Landmark Documents in American History

Eyewitness to HISTORY

Shays's Rebellion

Resentment grew especially strong in Massachusetts. Farmers viewed the new government as just another form of tyranny. They wanted the government to issue paper money and make new policies to relieve debtors. In a letter to state officials, some farmers proclaimed: "Surely your honours are not strangers to the distresses [problems] of the people but . . . know that many of our good inhabitants are now confined in [jail] for debt and taxes." In 1786 angry farmers took the law into their own hands. Led by **Daniel Shays,** a former Continental Army captain, they forced courts in western Massachusetts to close so judges could not confiscate farmers' lands.

In January 1787 Shays led more than 1,000 farmers toward the federal arsenal in **Springfield,** Massachusetts, for arms and ammunition. The state militia ordered the advancing farmers to halt, then fired over their heads. The farmers did not stop, and the militia fired again, killing four rebels. Shays and his followers scattered, and the uprising was over.

Shays's Rebellion frightened many Americans. They worried whether the government could control unrest and prevent violence. On hearing of the rebellion, George Washington wondered whether "mankind, when left to themselves, are unfit for their own government." Thomas Jefferson, minister to France at the time, had a different view. "A little rebellion, now and then," he wrote, "is a good thing."

The Issue of Slavery

The Revolutionary War had brought into focus the contradiction between the American battle for liberty and the practice of slavery. Between 1776 and 1786, 11 states—all except South Carolina and Georgia—outlawed or heavily taxed the importing of slaves.

Although slavery was not a major source of labor in the North, it existed and was legal in all the Northern states. However, many individuals and groups worked to end the institution of slavery. In 1775 Quakers in Pennsylvania organized the first American antislavery society. Five years later Pennsylvania passed a law that provided for the gradual freeing of enslaved people.

In 1783 the Massachusetts high court ruled slavery illegal because the state constitution declared that "all men are born free and equal." Between 1784 and 1804, New Hampshire, Connecticut, Rhode Island, New York, and New Jersey also abolished slavery. To help the free African Americans make their way in society, two ministers formed the Free African Society in Philadelphia in 1787.

The states south of Pennsylvania, however, clung to the institution of slavery. The plantation system of the South had been built on the backs of slaves, and many Southerners feared that their economy could not survive without slavery. Nonetheless an increasing number of

Picturing HISTORY Only through donations was Massachusetts able to raise a militia to defeat Shays. **Why did Shays's Rebellion frighten many Americans?**

COOPERATIVE LEARNING ACTIVITY

Writing Editorials Direct students' attention to the statements made by George Washington and Thomas Jefferson in response to Shays's Rebellion. Invite two groups of students to create editorials that expand upon those statements. To help shape the editorials, distribute the following questions among group members:

- Why did Shays feel justified in leading the revolt?
- Did these farmers have no other option?
- How did the rebellion symbolize a major problem in the new government?

Have an editorial director lead the writing and a representative from each group present it to the class for discussion.

2 TEACH

L1 Making Inferences Direct students' attention to the time line of events on page 196. Invite students to speculate about the relationship between Shays's Rebellion and the move to replace the Articles of Confederation with the Constitution. *(Students may suggest that the rebellion made it clear that the Articles of Confederation were not working.)*

Guided Reading Activity 7–2

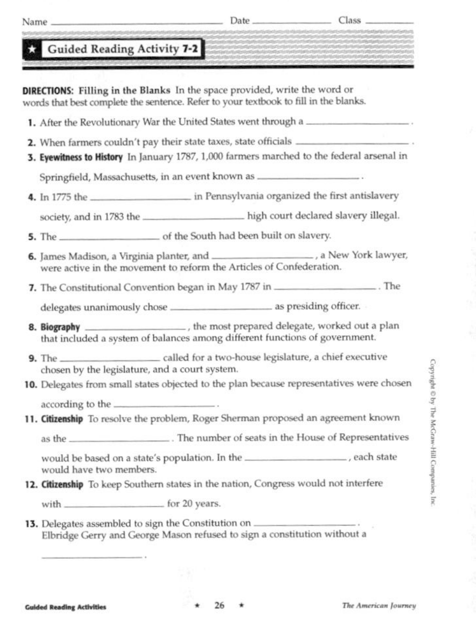

Name ______ Date ______ Class ______

Guided Reading Activity 7-2

DIRECTIONS: Filling in the Blanks In the space provided, write the word or words that best complete the sentence. Refer to your textbook to fill in the blanks.

1. After the Revolutionary War the United States went through a ______.
2. When farmers couldn't pay their state taxes, state officials ______.
3. **Eyewitness to History** In January 1787, 1,000 farmers marched to the federal arsenal in Springfield, Massachusetts, in an event known as ______.
4. In 1775 the ______ in Pennsylvania organized the first antislavery society, and in 1783 the ______ high court declared slavery illegal.
5. The ______ of the South had been built on slavery.
6. James Madison, a Virginia planter, and ______, a New York lawyer, were active in the movement to reform the Articles of Confederation.
7. The Constitutional Convention began in May 1787 in ______. The delegates unanimously chose ______ as presiding officer.
8. **Biography** ______, the most prepared delegate, worked out a plan that included a system of balances among different functions of government.
9. The ______ called for a two-house legislature, a chief executive chosen by the legislature, and a court system.
10. Delegates from small states objected to the plan because representatives were chosen according to the ______.
11. **Citizenship** To resolve the problem, Roger Sherman proposed an agreement known as the ______. The number of seats in the House of Representatives would be based on a state's population. In the ______, each state would have two members.
12. **Citizenship** To keep Southern states in the nation, Congress would not interfere with ______ for 20 years.
13. Delegates assembled to sign the Constitution on ______. Elbridge Gerry and George Mason refused to sign a constitution without a ______.

Guided Reading Activities ★ 26 ★ *The American Journey*

Picturing HISTORY Donations for the militia did not come from average citizens because many of them sympathized with the farmers. Instead, Boston merchants paid for the force that put down Shays's Rebellion.
Answer: *It made them wonder how well the government could control the country.*

Picturing HISTORY In the early 1800s, some African American movements encouraged immigration to Africa. Allen and Jones opposed this idea, stating that since "our ancestors (not of choice) were the first successful cultivators of the wilds of America, we their descendants feel ourselves entitled to participate in the blessings of her soil. . . . "
Answer: *to help free African Americans function and succeed in society*

ABCNEWS INTERACTIVE™

VIDEODISC
Historic America Electronic Field Trips

Side 1, Chapter 7
Title: *Independence Hall*
Subject: Tour Philadelphia's Independence Hall
Ask: **Why is Independence Hall so important in American history?** *(Both the Declaration of Independence and the Constitution were written there.)*

Also available in VHS.

Who?What?Where?When?

James Madison (1751–1836) argued passionately for ideas contained in the Constitution. Despite his zealous support for the Constitution, later in his life he felt awkward about being called the "Father of the Constitution." After one especially fiery speech, Madison complained to a friend, "Why didn't you pull me when you heard me going like that?" His friend replied, "I would rather have laid a finger on the lightning."

Picturing HISTORY Philadelphia preachers Absalom Jones (left) and Richard Allen (right) founded the Free African Society and later set up the first African American churches. **Why was the Free African Society formed?**

slaveholders began freeing their slaves after the war. Virginia passed a law that encouraged **manumission,** the freeing of individual enslaved persons, and the state's free African American population grew rapidly.

The abolition of slavery in the North divided the states on the critical issue of whether people should be allowed to hold slaves. This division came at the time when many American leaders had decided that the Articles of Confederation needed strengthening. In the summer of 1787, when state representatives assembled to plan a new government, they compromised on this issue. It would take years of debate, bloodshed, and ultimately a war to settle the slavery question.

A Call for Change

The American Revolution had led to a union of 13 states; it had not yet created a nation. Some leaders were satisfied with a system of independent state governments that resembled the old colonial governments. Others saw a strong national government as the solution to America's problems. They demanded a reform of the Articles of Confederation.

Significant Voices

Two Americans active in the movement for change were **James Madison,** a Virginia planter, and **Alexander Hamilton,** a New York lawyer. In September 1786, Hamilton proposed calling a convention in **Philadelphia** to discuss trade issues. He also suggested that this convention consider what possible changes were needed to make "the Constitution of the Federal Government adequate to the exigencies [needs] of the Union."

At first George Washington was not enthusiastic about the movement to revise the Articles of Confederation. When he heard the news of Shays's Rebellion, however, Washington changed his mind. He observed, "There are combustibles in every State which a spark might set fire to." After Washington agreed to travel to Philadelphia, the meeting took on greater significance.

MULTIPLE LEARNING STYLES

Kinesthetic The makeup of the nation's legislature caused one of the greatest areas of dispute among convention delegates. Call on volunteers to use manipulatives to illustrate the differences between the Virginia Plan and the New Jersey Plan. (Have on hand such items as shoe boxes to indicate the number of houses in the proposed legislature and paper clips to indicate the number of members that would represent a state's population, but allow students to choose creative alternatives.) Try to have a volunteer-created model of each plan on display as the class discusses the two plans and the compromise that resulted. **L1, ELL**

The Constitutional Convention

The Philadelphia meeting began in May 1787 and continued through one of the hottest summers in years. The 55 delegates included planters, merchants, lawyers, college presidents, physicians, generals, and governors. Three of the delegates were under 30 years of age, and one, America's elder statesman Benjamin Franklin, was over 80. Many were well educated. In a time when only one white man in 1,000 went to college, 26 of the delegates had college degrees. Native Americans, African Americans, and women were not considered part of the political process, so none attended.

Virginia's distinguished delegation included **Edmund Randolph**, former governor of Virginia; George Mason, author of the state's bill of rights; Madison, who kept a detailed journal of the convention; and Washington, the nation's hero. Pennsylvania sent the highly regarded Benjamin Franklin, as well as Gouverneur Morris, Robert Morris, and James Wilson. Alexander Hamilton was one of the representatives sent from New York.

The delegates unanimously chose Washington as presiding officer of the convention. Then they decided to close their doors to the public and to keep the proceedings secret. This would allow the delegates to speak freely and change their minds. Each state delegation had only a single vote, and a simple majority vote would be sufficient to make decisions.

Biography

James Madison and the Constitution

James Madison, only 36 at the time, was the best prepared of the delegates. In the months before the convention, he had made a detailed study of government, reading hundreds of books on history, politics, and economics. He also had corresponded with Thomas Jefferson, who was serving as the United States minister to France.

Madison looked for ways to build a strong but fair system of government for the new republic. He knew that republics were considered weaker than monarchies because kings or queens could use their authority to act quickly and decisively. Who would provide the same leadership in a republic? At the same time, Madison was concerned about protecting the people from the misuse of power. As he searched for solutions to these questions, Madison worked out a new plan that included a system of balances among different functions of government. The delegates adopted many of Madison's ideas in what would become the Virginia Plan.

James Madison

Picturing HISTORY The Pennsylvania State House, later known as Independence Hall, was the site of the signing of the Declaration of Independence and of the Constitutional Convention. **What were some characteristics of the Convention delegates?**

CURRICULUM CONNECTION

ECONOMICS
A few years before the Constitutional Convention met, Gouverneur Morris and Thomas Jefferson had worked together to propose a monetary system for the United States. Based on the decimal system, it used dollars and cents. The Second Continental Congress approved their proposal in 1785.

Linking PAST & PRESENT

Public Scrutiny of Political Figures
Today many political commentators and reporters comment on the personal lives and personalities of government officials. During the Constitutional Convention, William Pierce, a delegate from Georgia, recorded vivid impressions of his colleagues. Pierce described Roger Sherman as "the oddest-shaped character I ever remember to have met with. He is awkward, un-meaning and unaccountably strange in his manner . . . and yet he deserves infinite praise,—no Man has a better heart or a clearer Head." Pierce characterized Robert Morris as a man "who never once spoke on any point" and who later wound up in debtors' prison. Pierce praised Benjamin Franklin as "the greatest philosopher of the present age."

MAKING CONNECTIONS ACTIVITY

Daily Life James Madison worked out a personal system of shorthand and then wrote a full account from these notes immediately following each session of the Constitutional Convention. Madison carefully kept his notes out of the public eye. His notes were finally published in 1840. Ask each student to create his or her own shorthand system for taking notes. Have them discuss symbols they used to shorten the time it takes them to write notes. You may even want to develop a classroom shorthand booklet that all students can use. **L1**

Picturing HISTORY The Pennsylvania State House is a historical treasure, but it is not the original meeting place of the First Continental Congress. That honor belongs to Carpenters' Hall, where the Declaration of Rights and Grievances was drafted.
Answer: *They were a varied group, but all of them were white males.*

Picturing HISTORY Alexander Hamilton was born on the West Indian island of Nevis in 1755. His father, James Hamilton, was a Scottish trader.
Answer: *They feared that without a bill of rights the new national government might abuse its power.*

NATIONAL GEOGRAPHIC SOCIETY

VIDEODISC
GTV: A Geographic Perspective on American History

Side 2, Chapter 1
Title: *A Fresh Start*
Subject: The Constitution (1781–1800)
Ask: **Why did the location of the capital make both the North and the South happy?** *(It was in the South, but very close to the North.)*

CURRICULUM CONNECTION

SCIENCE
As the Constitutional Convention drew to a close, delegates saw the demonstration of a possible new form of transportation. Meeting at the Delaware River on August 11, they boarded a steam-powered boat built by John Fitch and rode along at three miles per hour (4.8 kph).

What?Where?When?Who?

One Signature More Roger Sherman also signed the earlier Articles of Association (1774), a response to the Quebec Act and the Coercive Acts.

Picturing HISTORY Delegate Alexander Hamilton emphasized the need for a stronger central government. **Why did some delegates worry that the Constitution lacked a bill of rights?**

The Virginia Plan

Edmund Randolph proposed that the delegates create a strong national government instead of revising the Articles of Confederation. He introduced the **Virginia Plan,** which was largely the work of Madison. The plan called for a two-house legislature, a chief executive chosen by the legislature, and a court system. The members of the lower house of the legislature would be elected by the people. The members of the upper house would be chosen by the lower house. In both houses the number of representatives would be **proportional,** or corresponding in size, to the population of each state. This would give Virginia many more delegates than Delaware, the state with the smallest population.

Delegates from Delaware, New Jersey, and other small states immediately objected to the plan. They preferred the Confederation Congress in which all states were represented equally.

The New Jersey Plan

Delegates unhappy with the Virginia Plan rallied around **William Paterson** of New Jersey. On June 15 he presented an alternative plan that modified—but did not completely discard—the Articles of Confederation. His proposal, the **New Jersey Plan**, kept the Confederation's one-house Congress with equal representation. However, Paterson proposed to give the Congress expanded powers to tax and regulate trade.

Compromise Wins Out

The convention delegates had to decide whether they were simply revising the Articles or writing a constitution for a new national government. On June 19 the states voted to work toward a national government based on the Virginia Plan. However, they still had to resolve the thorny issue of representation that divided the large and small states.

Discussion and Disagreement

As the convention delegates struggled to deal with difficult questions, tempers and temperatures grew hotter. How were the members of Congress to be elected? How would state representation be determined in the upper and lower houses? Were enslaved Africans to be counted as part of the population on which representation was based?

By the end of June, the disagreements grew so intense that the convention was in danger of falling apart. Benjamin Franklin suggested that each session be opened with a prayer asking for divine guidance. Otherwise, Franklin believed, "We shall be divided by our little partial local interests" and fail to reach agreement.

Footnotes to History

Let's Have Quiet! Philadelphia took great efforts to give the delegates a quiet atmosphere during the convention. The city went so far as to cover the paved road around the hall with dirt to reduce noise.

CRITICAL THINKING ACTIVITY

Analyzing Generalizations Write the following generalization on the chalkboard: "The Constitution shows more of what the delegates did not want than what they did want." Have students skim the section to locate facts and details that either support or challenge this generalization. Ask for volunteers to write their answers on the chalkboard. **L2**

★ ★ ★ ★ ★ ★ ★ ★ ★ ★ ★ ★ ★ ★ ★ ★

Citizenship

The Great Compromise

Under Franklin's leadership, the convention appointed a "grand committee" to try to resolve their disagreements. **Roger Sherman** of Connecticut suggested what came to be known as the **Great Compromise.** A **compromise** is an agreement between two or more sides in which each side gives up some of what it wants.

Sherman proposed a two-house legislature. In the lower house—the House of Representatives—the number of seats for each state would vary according to the state's population. In the upper house—the Senate—each state would have two members.

The Three-Fifths Compromise

A second part of the Great Compromise dealt with counting slaves. Southern states wanted to include enslaved Africans in their population counts to gain delegates in the House of Representatives. Northern states objected to this idea because enslaved people were legally considered property. Some delegates from Northern states argued that slaves, as property, should be counted for the purpose of taxation but not representation. However, neither side considered giving enslaved African Americans the right to vote.

The committee's solution, known as the **Three-Fifths Compromise,** was to count each enslaved person as three-fifths of a free person for both taxation and representation. In other words, every five slaves would equal three "people." On July 16 the convention delegates voted to approve the Great Compromise, breaking the deadlock between large and small states.

Footnotes to History

A Man of Many Signatures Roger Sherman was the only man to sign all three major documents of the Revolutionary period. He signed the Declaration of Independence, the Articles of Confederation, and the United States Constitution.

Picturing HISTORY Connecticut's Roger Sherman proposed what became known as the Great Compromise. **How did the Great Compromise deal with slavery?**

Slave Trade

The convention needed to resolve another difficult issue that divided the Northern and Southern states. Having banned the slave trade within their borders, Northern states wanted to prohibit it throughout the nation. Southern states considered slavery and the slave trade essential to their economies. To keep the Southern states in the nation, Northerners agreed to a compromise. The Congress would not interfere with the slave trade for 20 years. After that, the Congress could limit the slave trade if it chose to.

Bill of Rights

One important issue that the convention did not deal with was that of individual rights. The new state constitutions included sections listing rights of individuals—such as freedom of religion and trial by jury—that government could not take away. Some delegates worried that without the protection of a bill of rights the new national government might abuse its power. However, most of the delegates believed that the Constitution, with its carefully defined listing of government powers, provided adequate protection of individual rights.

CHAPTER 7

Section 2, 196–202

Picturing HISTORY Roger Sherman was born in Newton, Massachusetts, in 1721. He served on the Committee of Five appointed to prepare a draft of the Declaration of Independence. In 1787 he became a member of the Constitutional Convention, where he proposed his "Great Compromise." From 1784 to his death in 1793, he served as mayor of New Haven, Connecticut.
Answer: *It counted each enslaved person as three-fifths of a free person for both taxation and representation.*

Political Cartoons, *Foundations of Our Government*

3 ASSESS

Assign Section 2 Review as homework or as an in-class activity.

Use **Chapter Challenger Interactive Review Software** to review Section 2.

Section Quiz 7–2

Name ______ Date ______ Class ______

★ Chapter 7 — Score

Section Quiz 7-2

DIRECTIONS: Matching Match each item in Column A with the items in Column B. Write the correct letters in the blanks. *(10 points each)*

Column A	Column B
____ 1. led a rebellion	A. manumission
____ 2. antislavery society	B. Roger Sherman
____ 3. freeing of individual enslaved persons	C. James Madison
____ 4. author of Virginia Plan	D. Daniel Shays
____ 5. proposed Great Compromise	E. Quakers

DIRECTIONS: Multiple Choice In the blank at the left, write the letter of the choice that best completes the statement or answers the question. *(10 points each)*

____ 6. Shays's Rebellion forced courts to close so judges could not confiscate
A. tax money. C. smuggled goods.
B. farmers' land. D. criminals' homes.

____ 7. The Revolutionary War brought into focus the contradiction between the American battle for liberty and the
A. need to raise money. C. practice of slavery.
B. right to rebellion. D. right for women to vote.

____ 8. Constitutional Convention delegates voted for a national government based on the
A. New Jersey Plan. C. New York Plan.
B. Virginia Plan. D. Northwest Territory Plan.

____ 9. Convention delegates broke the deadlock between large and small states when they approved the
A. Two-thirds Compromise. C. Three-fifths Compromise.
B. Washington's Compromise. D. Great Compromise.

____ 10. Convention delegates agreed the Constitution must be approved by how many states?
A. 3 states C. 12 states
B. all states D. 9 states

Section Quizzes ★ 26 ★ *The American Journey*

TEACHER'S NOTES

CHAPTER 7
Section 2, 196–202

Picturing HISTORY Independence Hall is also known as the Old State House. It stands only a block from the site of Carpenters' Hall, where the First Continental Congress had met in 1774.
Answer: *nine*

Reteaching Activity 7–2

Name ______________ Date __________ Class ________

★ Reteaching Activity 7-2

DIRECTIONS: Recognizing Causes and Effects After each *Cause*, write the letter of its *Effect* from the Fact Bank.

1. **Cause:** Rice exports dropped sharply; trade fell off when Great Britain closed the West Indian market to Americans; the little bit of money available went to pay foreign debt.
   Effect: ________
2. **Cause:** American farmers could not pay the taxes levied by the states.
   Effect: ________
3. **Cause:** Daniel Shays led Shays's Rebellion, during which four rebels were killed by the state militia.
   Effect: ________
4. **Cause:** Virginia passed a law that encouraged manumission.
   Effect: ________
5. **Cause:** George Washington agreed to travel to the Constitutional Convention.
   Effect: ________
6. **Cause:** The proceedings of the convention were kept secret.
   Effect: ________
7. **Cause:** In the Virginia Plan, the number of representatives in the legislature would correspond to a state's population.
   Effect: ________
8. **Cause:** Southern states refused to abolish slavery.
   Effect: ________
9. **Cause:** The Constitution did not contain a bill of rights.
   Effect: ________
10. **Cause:** The Articles of Confederation required unanimous approval of the states, a slow and frustrating process.
   Effect: ________

★FACT BANK

A. The state's free African American population grew rapidly.
B. The approval process for the Constitution was 9 of the 13 states.
C. State officials seized farmers' lands to pay their debts.
D. The meeting took on a greater significance.
E. Elbridge Gerry and George Mason would not sign the Constitution.
F. Congress agreed not to interfere with the slave trade for 20 years.
G. Some delegates rallied around William Paterson's proposal for a one-house Congress with equal representation.
H. A depression occurred.
I. Delegates were allowed to speak freely and change their minds.
J. Americans worried whether the government could control unrest and prevent violence.

Enrichment Activity 7–2

Name ______________ Date __________ Class ________

★ Enrichment Activity 7-2 ★

The Founders

When the Constitutional Convention met, a young delegate from Georgia, William Pierce, wrote brief character sketches of his fellow delegates. Below are selections from these sketches.

Alexander Hamilton
"Colo. [Colonel] Hamilton is deservedly celebrated for his talents. . . . [He] requires time to think,—he enquires into every part of his subject with the searchings of philosophy. . . . His manners are tinctured [touched] with stiffness, and sometimes with a degree of vanity that is highly disagreeable."

James Madison
"Mr. Madison is a character who has long been in public life; and what is very remarkable every Person seems to acknowledge his greatness. . . . [He] is . . . a Gentleman of great modesty [simplicity],—with a remarkable sweet temper. He is easy and unreserved among his acquaintance, and has a most agreeable style of conversation."

Benjamin Franklin
"Dr. Franklin is well-known to be the greatest philosopher of the present age. . . . He is . . . a most extraordinary Man and tells a story in a style more engaging than anything I have ever heard. . . . He is 82 years old, and possesses an activity of mind equal to a youth of 25 years of age."

DIRECTIONS: Analyzing Information Read the selections from Pierce's sketches. Then use Pierce's observations and what you have learned about the delegates in Chapter 7 to answer the following questions.

1. How does Pierce describe the quality of Franklin's mind? ________________
2. Which delegate does Pierce suggest is easier to approach, Hamilton or Madison?
   Explain. ________________
3. What negative characteristics does Pierce say Hamilton has? ________________
4. From the descriptions, which of these men would you most like to meet? Explain your answer. ________________
5. Why must historians exercise caution in using Pierce's sketches? ________________

4 CLOSE

Call on volunteers to name as many ways as they can in which the Constitution reflects compromise.

Picturing HISTORY Delegates to the Constitutional Convention met in this room at Independence Hall. **How many states had to ratify the Constitution before it went into effect?**

Approving the Constitution

The committees finished their work on the Constitution in late summer, and on September 17, 1787, the delegates assembled in the Philadelphia State House to sign the document. Franklin made a final plea for approval: "I consent to this Constitution because I expect no better, and because I am not sure, that it is not the best." Three delegates refused to sign—Elbridge Gerry of Massachusetts and Edmund Randolph and George Mason of Virginia. Gerry and Mason would not sign a constitution without a bill of rights.

The convention then sent the approved draft of the Constitution to the states for consideration. The Articles of Confederation had required unanimous approval of the states for the government to act. Getting a unanimous vote had proved slow and frustrating. Therefore, the delegates agreed to change the approval process for the Constitution. When 9 of the 13 states had approved, the new government of the United States would come into existence.

Section 2 Review

Checking for Understanding

1. ***Identify*** Daniel Shays, Springfield, James Madison, Alexander Hamilton, Philadelphia, Edmund Randolph, Virginia Plan, William Paterson, Roger Sherman, Great Compromise, Three-Fifths Compromise.
2. ***Define*** depression, manumission, proportional, compromise.
3. ***Explain*** what caused Shays's Rebellion to erupt.

Reviewing Themes

4. **Groups and Institutions** How did the Great Compromise satisfy the small and large states on the question of representation?

Critical Thinking

5. **Media Literacy** You are asked to write a 30-second news broadcast to announce the agreement made in the Great Compromise. What would you include in the broadcast?

Activity

Drawing a Political Cartoon Create a political cartoon that illustrates either the Northern states' view or the Southern states' view on how enslaved African Americans should be counted for representation.

Section 2 Review Answers

1. Shays, 197; Springfield, 197; Madison, 198; Hamilton, 198; Philadelphia, 198; Randolph, 199; Virginia Plan, 200; Paterson, 200; Sherman, 201; Great Compromise, 201; Three-Fifths Compromise, 201
2. The words are defined in the Glossary.
3. Farmers could not sell their products and pay their taxes. Many lost their farms or went to jail. They wanted the government to make policies to help farmers.
4. It created a two-house legislature. The seats of the lower house were based on each state's population; in the upper house, each state had two members.
5. Answers will vary but should include the role of Roger Sherman, a discussion of the two-house legislature, and an explanation of the Three-Fifths Compromise.

Critical Thinking
SKILL BUILDER

Making Comparisons

Suppose you want to buy a portable compact disc (CD) player, and you must choose among three models. To make this decision, you would probably compare various characteristics of the three models, such as price, sound quality, size, and so on. By making comparisons, you will figure out which model is best for you. In the study of American history, you often compare people or events from one time period with those from a different time period.

Learning the Skill

When making comparisons, you examine two or more groups, situations, events, or documents. Then you identify any similarities (ways they are alike) and differences (ways they are different). For example, the chart on this page compares two documents in regard to the powers they gave the federal government. The Articles of Confederation were passed and implemented before the United States Constitution, which took their place.

When making comparisons, apply the following steps:

- Decide what items will be compared.
- Determine which characteristics you will use to compare them.
- Identify similarities and differences in these characteristics.

Practicing the Skill

Analyze the information on the chart on this page. Then answer the questions.

1. What items are being compared in this chart?

The Articles of Confederation and the United States Constitution

Powers of Federal Government	Articles of Confederation	United States Constitution
Declare war; make peace	✔	✔
Coin money	✔	✔
Manage foreign affairs	✔	✔
Establish a postal system	✔	✔
Impose taxes		✔
Regulate trade		✔
Organize a court system		✔
Call state militia for service		✔
Protect copyrights		✔
Take other necessary actions to run the federal government		✔

2. In what ways are the two documents different?
3. In what ways are the two documents similar?
4. Which document allowed the government to organize state militias?

Applying the Skill

Making Comparisons On the editorial page of your local newspaper, find two letters to the editor that express different viewpoints on the same issue. Read the letters and identify the similarities and differences between the two points of view.

Critical Thinking
SKILL BUILDER

TEACH

Making Comparisons

Making comparisons is an important skill in all academic areas. In science one might compare various forms of life. In a literature class, two or more pieces of literature might be compared.

Making comparisons is also a life skill that we utilize in everyday transactions. We employ this skill when choosing between two or more products or services. Making comparisons might also come into play when establishing priorities.

In this chapter, students compare the views of the Federalists and Antifederalists. Students will see that, whatever the topic, charting is a valuable way to record details for easy comparison.

As students examine the chart on this page, call on volunteers to locate the various items in their text. Be sure students understand the importance of stating each item as succinctly as possible.

Students might extend this activity by creating a comparison chart about two professional sports teams, two entertainers, two automobiles, and so on.

Additional Practice

Chapter Skills Activity 7

Facts On File

CD-ROM
Landmark Documents in American History

Title: *For the Constitution, James Madison, 1787; Against the Constitution, Patrick Henry, 1788*
Encourage students to practice the skill by viewing both documents, then creating a comparison chart that lists similarities and differences of the opposing viewpoints.

Answers to Practicing the Skill

1. the powers of the federal government as spelled out in the Articles of Confederation and the United States Constitution
2. The Constitution specifies powers that are not named in the Articles—impose taxes, regulate trade, organize a court system, call state militias into service, protect copyrights, and take other actions deemed necessary to run the federal government.
3. Both documents give the federal government the power to declare war and make peace, to coin money, to manage foreign affairs, and to establish a postal system.
4. the United States Constitution

Applying the Skill Ask students how they chose the characteristics for comparison and which letter they think did a better job overall of presenting its case.

1 FOCUS

BELLRINGER
Motivational Activity

Before taking roll at the beginning of the class period, project Section Focus Transparency 7–3 and have students answer the questions. Discuss students' responses.

This activity is also available as a blackline master.

Section Focus Transparency 7–3

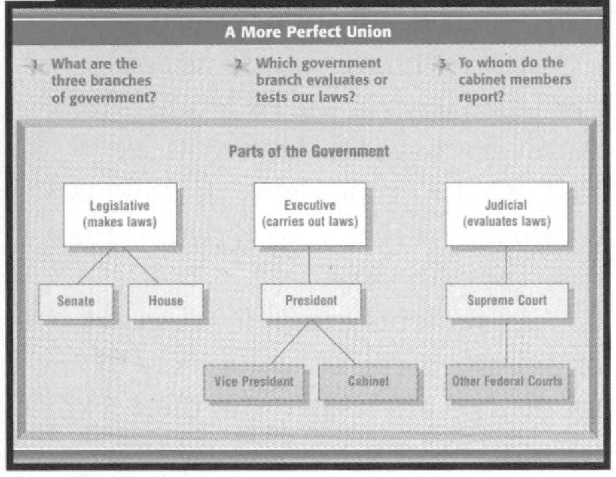

Vocabulary Precheck

Have students read the textbook glossary definition of each term listed in **Terms to Learn.** Then call on volunteers to restate each definition in their own words.

Use the **Vocabulary Puzzle-Maker** to create crossword and word search puzzles.

Section Theme
Civic Rights and Responsibilities

The Constitution outlined the responsibilities and the limits of the three branches of the national government.

Activity Have students complete these sentences with responses that suggest the national government's powers. Discuss the results.

- The president can _____.
- Congress can _____.
- Judges can _____.

1680 1720 1760 1800

1689 English Bill of Rights established

1690 Locke writes *Two Treatises on Civil Government*

1748 Montesquieu writes *The Spirit of Laws*

1787 Constitutional Convention meets in Philadelphia

Section 3

A New Plan of Government

READ TO DISCOVER . . .

- how European ideas influenced the Constitution.
- how the Constitution limits the power of government.

TERMS TO LEARN

Enlightenment
federalism
article
legislative branch
executive branch
Electoral College
judicial branch
checks and balances

The Storyteller

As the delegates hammered out the Constitution, Benjamin Franklin looked toward the president's chair, at the back of which a rising sun happened to be painted. "I have," said he, "often and often in the course of the Session . . . looked at that [sun] behind the President without being able to tell whether it was rising or setting; but now, at length I have the happiness to know it is a rising and not a setting Sun."

Rising Sun chair, Constitutional Convention

After four long and difficult months, the delegates in **Philadelphia** had produced a new constitution. The document provided the framework for a strong central government for the United States.

Although a uniquely American document, the Constitution had roots in many civilizations. The delegates had studied and discussed the history of political development at length—starting with ancient Greece—so that their new government could avoid the mistakes of the past.

Roots of the Constitution

Many ideas embedded in the Constitution came from the study of European political institutions and political writers. British ideas and institutions particularly influenced the delegates.

The Framers who shaped the document were familiar with the parliamentary system of Britain, and many had participated in the colonial assemblies or the state assemblies that followed. They valued the individual rights guaranteed by the British judicial system. Although the Americans had broken away from Britain, they wanted to continue many British traditions.

British System of Government

Beginning in the 1200s, the English had found ways to limit the power of the monarch. England's

SECTION RESOURCES

Reproducible Masters
- Reproducible Lesson Plan 7–3
- Guided Reading Activity 7–3
- Political Cartoons
- Section Quiz 7–3
- Reteaching Activity 7–3
- Enrichment Activity 7–3

Transparencies
- Section Focus Transparency 7–3

Multimedia
- Vocabulary PuzzleMaker
- Chapter Challenger Interactive Review Software
- Testmaker
- GTV: A Geographic Perspective on American History

lawmaking body, Parliament, emerged as a force that the king had to depend on to pay for wars and to finance the royal government. Like Parliament, the colonial assemblies controlled their colony's funds. For that reason the assemblies had some control over colonial governors.

The English Bill of Rights of 1689 provided another important model for Americans. Many Americans felt that the Constitution also needed a bill of rights.

The Enlightenment

Framers of the Constitution got many ideas on the nature of people and government from European writers of the Enlightenment. The **Enlightenment** was a movement of the 1700s that spread the idea that knowledge, reason, and science could improve society. James Madison and other architects of the Constitution were familiar with the work of **John Locke** and **Baron de Montesquieu** (MAHN•tuhs•KYOO), two important thinkers who influenced the debate of the Enlightenment period.

John Locke, English political thinker, late 1600s

Locke, an English philosopher, believed that all people have a natural right to life, liberty, and property. In his *Two Treatises on Civil Government* (1690), he wrote that government is based on an agreement, or contract, between the people and the ruler. The Framers viewed the Constitution as a contract between the American people and their government. The contract protected the people's natural rights by limiting the government's power.

In *The Spirit of Laws* (1748), the French writer Montesquieu declared that the powers of government should be separated and balanced against each other. This separation would keep any one person or group from gaining too much power. The powers of government should also be clearly defined and limited to prevent misuse. Following the ideas of Montesquieu, the Framers of the Constitution carefully described and divided the powers of government.

The Federal System

The Constitution created a federal system of government that divided powers between the national, or federal, government and the states. Under the Articles of Confederation, the states were much stronger than the national Congress. Under the Constitution the states gave up some of their powers to the federal government while keeping others.

Shared Powers

Federalism, or sharing power between the federal and state governments, is one of the distinctive features of the United States government. Under the Constitution, the federal government gained broad powers to tax, regulate trade, control the currency, raise an army, and declare war. It could also pass laws that were "necessary and proper" for carrying out its responsibilities.

However, the Constitution left important powers in the hands of the states. The states had the power to pass and enforce laws and regulate trade within their borders. They could also establish local governments, schools, and other institutions affecting the welfare of their citizens. Both federal and state governments also had the power to tax and build roads.

The Constitution Becomes Supreme Law of the Land

The Constitution and the laws that Congress passed were to be "the supreme law of the land." No state could make laws or take actions that went against the Constitution. Any dispute between the federal government and the states was to be settled by the federal courts on the basis of the Constitution. Under the new federal system, the Constitution became the final authority.

Cooperative Learning Activity

Painting the Past Organize the class into groups of four or five students. Ask each group to create a mural that illustrates the sources from which the Framers of the Constitution drew their ideas. Allow students to decide how to distribute work in each group. Students can illustrate part of the mural, provide additional research, gather supplies, sketch scene outlines, color sketches, and so on. Prepare a "gallery walk" in which the artists explain the completed mural to onlookers.

2 TEACH

L1, ELL Applying Information Brainstorm with students a list of current topics in the national news. Have partners or small groups of students choose various topics and decide which branch of government is most directly involved in each topic.

Political Cartoons, *Federalism Then and Now*

CURRICULUM CONNECTION

TECHNOLOGY
Modern technology has helped preserve the Constitution document. It is scanned by electronic scanners frequently to detect any minor changes in the ink or parchment. These periodic measurements enable curators to detect if any deterioration has taken place that is invisible to the human eye.

Guided Reading Activity 7–3

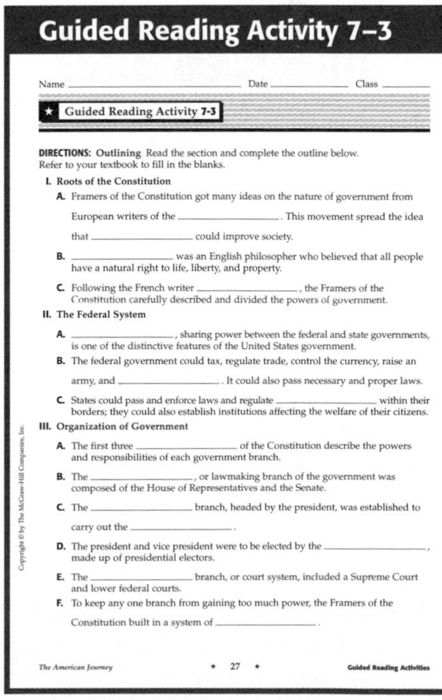

Name ______ Date ______ Class ______

Guided Reading Activity 7-3

DIRECTIONS: Outlining Read the section and complete the outline below. Refer to your textbook to fill in the blanks.

I. Roots of the Constitution
- **A.** Framers of the Constitution got many ideas on the nature of government from European writers of the ______. This movement spread the idea that ______ could improve society.
- **B.** ______ was an English philosopher who believed that all people have a natural right to life, liberty, and property.
- **C.** Following the French writer ______, the Framers of the Constitution carefully described and divided the powers of government.

II. The Federal System
- **A.** ______, sharing power between the federal and state governments, is one of the distinctive features of the United States government.
- **B.** The federal government could tax, regulate trade, control the currency, raise an army, and ______. It could also pass necessary and proper laws.
- **C.** States could pass and enforce laws and regulate ______ within their borders; they could also establish institutions affecting the welfare of their citizens.

III. Organization of Government
- **A.** The first three ______ of the Constitution describe the powers and responsibilities of each government branch.
- **B.** The ______, or lawmaking branch of the government was composed of the House of Representatives and the Senate.
- **C.** The ______ branch, headed by the president, was established to carry out the ______.
- **D.** The president and vice president were to be elected by the ______, made up of presidential electors.
- **E.** The ______ branch, or court system, included a Supreme Court and lower federal courts.
- **F.** To keep any one branch from gaining too much power, the Framers of the Constitution built in a system of ______.

The American Journey ★ 27 ★ **Guided Reading Activities**

CHAPTER 7
Section 3, 204–208

Picturing HISTORY The Senate wing of the Capitol once was home to the Senate, the House of Representatives, and the Supreme Court.
Answer: *the legislative branch*

NATIONAL GEOGRAPHIC SOCIETY

VIDEODISC
GTV: A Geographic Perspective on American History

Side 2, Chapter 1
Title: *A Fresh Start*
Subject: The Constitution (1781–1800)
Ask: **Describe the Framers of the Constitution.** *(The Framers were from different regions and had varied interests. They came from small states, large states, cities, farms, plantations, the North, and the South.)*

Linking PAST & PRESENT

Senatorial Terms The people now elect senators, but unlike the president, there is no limit on the number of terms they can serve. In recent years citizens have debated setting term limits for senators. Some people feel that having a limited term of activity would encourage senators to work harder for the people they represent.

Picturing HISTORY Now restored as a museum, the Old Senate Chamber was used from 1810 to 1859. **What branch of government is the Senate a part of?**

The Organization of Government

Influenced by Montesquieu's idea of a division of powers, the Framers divided the federal government into three branches—legislative, executive, and judicial. The first three **articles,** or parts, of the Constitution describe the powers and responsibilities of each branch.

The Legislative Branch

Article I of the Constitution established Congress, the **legislative,** or lawmaking, **branch** of the government. Congress was composed of the House of Representatives and the Senate. As a result of the Great Compromise between large and small states, each state's representation in the House would be proportional to its population. Representation in the Senate would be equal—two senators for each state.

The powers of Congress would include collecting taxes, coining money, and regulating trade. Congress also could declare war and "raise and support armies." Finally it could make all laws needed to fulfill the functions given to it by the Constitution.

The Executive Branch

Memories of King George III's rule made some delegates reluctant to establish a powerful executive, or ruler. Others believed that the Confederation had failed, in part, because it lacked an executive. They argued that a strong executive would serve as a check on Congress.

Article II of the Constitution established the **executive branch,** headed by the president, to carry out the nation's laws and policies. The president was to serve as commander in chief of the armed forces and to conduct relations with foreign countries.

The president and a vice president were to be elected indirectly by a special group called the **Electoral College,** made up of presidential electors. State legislatures would select electors to cast their votes for the president and vice president. Each state was to have as many electors as it had senators and representatives in Congress. The president and vice president chosen by the electors would serve a four-year term.

The Judicial Branch

Article III of the Constitution dealt with the **judicial branch,** or court system, of the United States. The nation's judicial power was to reside in

Linking PAST & PRESENT

The Election of Senators

The Seventeenth Amendment, adopted in 1913, changed the way senators are elected. Today members of the Senate, like those of the House, are elected directly by the people instead of by state legislatures.

MULTIPLE LEARNING STYLES

Auditory/Musical Challenge students to write a rap song, a spoken poem with strong and varying rhythms. The song should describe the powers of each branch of the federal government, as outlined by the Constitution. Offer this example to stimulate thinking:

Legislative *means the making of the law;*
And a two-part branch is what they all foresaw. . . .

Students can include a chorus that recalls the need for a federal government. Encourage students to perform the results; if possible, videotape the performances for a permanent record. **L3**

American Memories: America in 1787

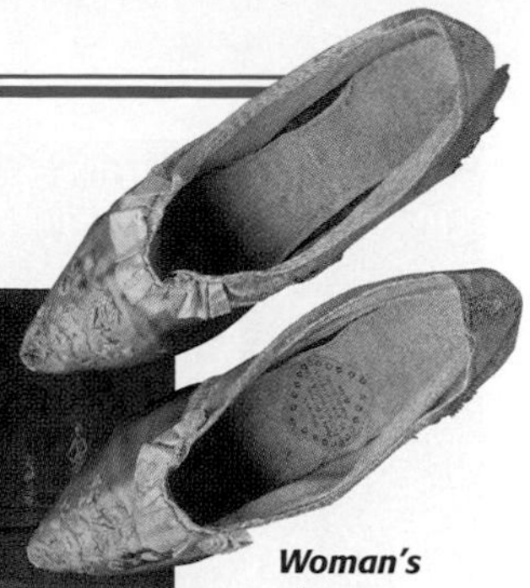

Woman's shoes

Hepplewhite chair

Boy's homespun woolen suit

What Was It Like? Some American families bought imported goods from Europe. For others, however, everyday items were homemade. **What do these photos reveal about life in America in 1787?**

"one supreme Court" and any other lower federal courts that Congress might establish. The Supreme Court and the federal courts were to hear cases involving the Constitution, laws passed by Congress, and disputes between states.

System of Checks and Balances

The most distinctive feature of the United States government is the separation of powers. The Constitution divides government power among the legislative, executive, and judicial branches. To keep any one branch from gaining too much power, the Framers built in a system of **checks and balances.** The three branches have roles that check, or limit, the others so that no single branch can dominate the government.

Both the House and the Senate must pass a bill for it to become law. The president can check Congress by vetoing, or rejecting, the bill. However, Congress can then check the president by overriding, or voting down, the veto. To override a veto, two-thirds of the members of both houses of Congress must vote for the bill.

The system of checks and balances also applies to the Supreme Court. The president appoints Supreme Court justices, and the Senate must approve the appointments.

Footnotes to History

Long-Term Planning When the delegates at the Constitutional Convention established the executive branch, they debated about the number of years a presidential term should be. One suggestion promoted a 15-year term!

American Memories

America in 1787
It was not until 1789 that Samuel Slater left England for the United States. Therefore a great deal of clothing was still being imported from Europe in 1787.
Answers: *Wealthy Americans enjoyed imported luxuries, but most Americans made their own things from available natural resources.*

Linking PAST & PRESENT

The Longest Term President Franklin D. Roosevelt, who took office in 1933 and died in office in 1945, came the closest to fulfilling the 15-year-term idea.

3 ASSESS

Assign Section 3 Review as homework or as an in-class activity.

Use **Chapter Challenger Interactive Review Software** to review Section 3.

Section Quiz 7–3

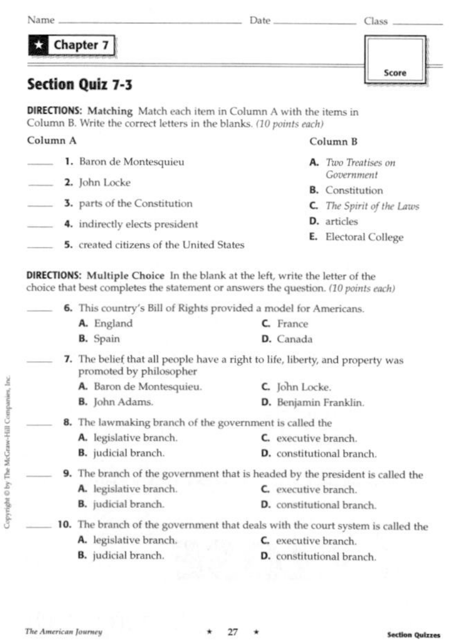

Name ________ Date ________ Class ________

★ Chapter 7

Score

Section Quiz 7-3

DIRECTIONS: Matching Match each item in Column A with the items in Column B. Write the correct letters in the blanks. *(10 points each)*

Column A	Column B
____ **1.** Baron de Montesquieu	**A.** *Two Treatises on Government*
____ **2.** John Locke	**B.** Constitution
____ **3.** parts of the Constitution	**C.** *The Spirit of the Laws*
____ **4.** indirectly elects president	**D.** articles
____ **5.** created citizens of the United States	**E.** Electoral College

DIRECTIONS: Multiple Choice In the blank at the left, write the letter of the choice that best completes the statement or answers the question. *(10 points each)*

____ **6.** This country's Bill of Rights provided a model for Americans.
A. England **C.** France
B. Spain **D.** Canada

____ **7.** The belief that all people have a right to life, liberty, and property was promoted by philosopher
A. Baron de Montesquieu. **C.** John Locke.
B. John Adams. **D.** Benjamin Franklin.

____ **8.** The lawmaking branch of the government is called the
A. legislative branch. **C.** executive branch.
B. judicial branch. **D.** constitutional branch.

____ **9.** The branch of the government that is headed by the president is called the
A. legislative branch. **C.** executive branch.
B. judicial branch. **D.** constitutional branch.

____ **10.** The branch of the government that deals with the court system is called the
A. legislative branch. **C.** executive branch.
B. judicial branch. **D.** constitutional branch.

The American Journey ★ 27 ★ **Section Quizzes**

MAKING CONNECTIONS ACTIVITY

Politics Irish playwright George Bernard Shaw described the Constitution as "one of the few modern political documents drawn up by men who were forced by the sternest circumstances to think about what they really had to face, instead of chopping logic in a university classroom." In a class brainstorming session, ask students to recall the history of the American Revolution and of the early nation. Have them suggest some of the practical issues reflected in the Constitution (for example, currency problems resulting in giving Congress the sole power to coin money; differences in the states' populations leading to two kinds of representation in the federal legislature). Ask students if they agree with Shaw. **L2**

CHAPTER 7

Section 3, 204–208

Picturing HISTORY Justice Charles Evans Hughes said in 1907, "[T]he judiciary is the safeguard of our liberty."

Answer: *cases that involve the Constitution, laws passed by Congress, and disputes between states*

Reteaching Activity 7–3

Name ______ Date ______ Class ______

★ Reteaching Activity 7-3

DIRECTIONS: Matching Match each item in Column A with its corresponding item in Column B. Write the correct letters in the blanks.

COLUMN A	COLUMN B
____ 1. Framers	A. lawmaking branch of the government that includes the House of Representatives and the Senate
____ 2. Enlightenment	B. sharing power between the federal and state governments
____ 3. John Locke	C. a special group responsible for electing the president and vice president
____ 4. Baron de Montesquieu	D. a movement in the 1700s that spread the idea that knowledge, reason, and science could improve society
____ 5. federalism	E. French writer who declared that powers of government should be separated and balanced against each other
____ 6. articles	F. court system that includes the Supreme Court
____ 7. legislative branch	G. parts of the Constitution
____ 8. executive branch	H. men who shaped the Constitution
____ 9. Electoral College	I. headed by the president
____ 10. judicial branch	J. rejecting a bill or proposal
____ 11. Supreme Court	K. English philosopher who believed that all people have a right to life, liberty, and property
____ 12. veto	L. hears cases involving the Constitution

DIRECTIONS: Essay Answer the following questions on a separate sheet of paper.

13. Describe the powers that the federal and state governments gained under the Constitution.

14. How is the system of checks and balances applied to pass a law?

The American Journey ★ 27 ★ **Reteaching Activities**

Enrichment Activity 7–3

Name ______ Date ______ Class ______

★ Enrichment Activity 7-3 ★ ★

Checks and Balances

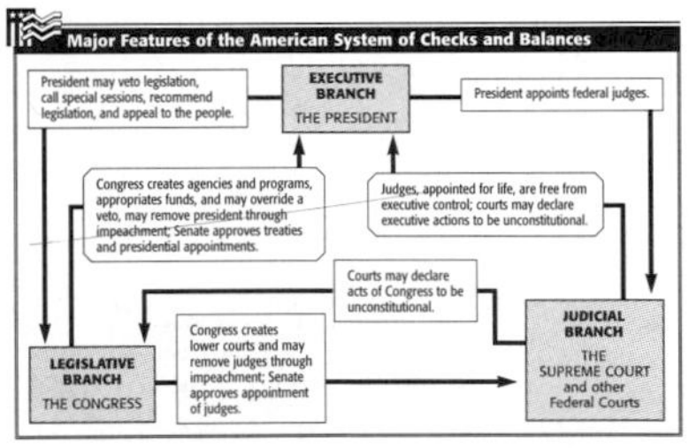

DIRECTIONS: Interpreting a Flow Chart Use the flow chart to answer the questions.

1. What control does the executive branch exert over the judicial branch? ______

2. How is the control in question 1 checked by the legislative branch? ______

3. Which branch or branches can declare acts or actions to be unconstitutional? ______

4. Which branch or branches can remove members of government, and which members can be removed? ______

5. Suppose Congress makes a law that the president vetoes. Can that law be passed by Congress? Explain. ______

The American Journey ★ 27 ★ **Enrichment Activities**

4 CLOSE

Have students explain in which branch of government they would like to work.

Picturing HISTORY The Supreme Court has the final say in deciding what the Constitution means. **What types of cases does the Supreme Court hear?**

Sometimes this system of checks and balances prevents the federal government from acting quickly and decisively. Yet for the most part, the system has been successful in maintaining a balance of power among the branches of the federal government and limiting abuses of power.

National Citizens

The Constitution created citizens of the United States. It set up a government in which the people would choose their officials—directly or indirectly. Officials would answer to the people rather than to the states. The new government pledged to protect the personal freedoms of its citizens.

With these revolutionary changes, Americans had shown the world that it was possible for a people to change its form of government through discussion and choice—rather than through chaos, force, or war. The rest of the world regarded the new nation with interest to see whether its experiment in self-government would really work.

Section 3 Review

Checking for Understanding

1. ***Identify*** Philadelphia, John Locke, Baron de Montesquieu.
2. ***Define*** Enlightenment, federalism, article, legislative branch, executive branch, Electoral College, judicial branch, checks and balances.
3. ***Compare*** the powers of the national government under the Articles of Confederation and under the Constitution.

Reviewing Themes

4. **Civic Rights and Responsibilities** Why did the Framers of the Constitution believe that a division of powers and a system of checks and balances were necessary in a government?

Critical Thinking

5. **Identifying Central Issues** Why was a powerful national government needed to unite the states?

Activity

Compiling Newspaper Reports Clip three newspaper articles that discuss the three different branches of our national government. Read the articles and discuss them with a classmate.

Section 3 Review Answers

1. Philadelphia, 204; John Locke, 205; Baron de Montesquieu, 205
2. The words are defined in the Glossary.
3. The Constitution granted the federal government much more power—to tax, regulate trade, control currency, raise an army, declare war, and pass laws.
4. to keep any one branch from gaining too much power
5. Without a strong national government, it would have been difficult to get all the states to agree on issues and to take action on matters that involved the nation as a whole.

Activity Each student should provide three newspaper articles. One should focus on the legislative branch, one on the executive branch, and one on the judicial branch.

1787 **1788** **1789**

September 1787
Delegates sign draft of Constitution

December 1787
Delaware is first state to ratify Constitution

June 1788
Constitution is ratified by nine states and goes into effect

Section 4

Ratifying the Constitution

READ TO DISCOVER . . .
- how the Federalists and Antifederalists differed in their views on government.
- how the arguments for and against a bill of rights affected the vote for ratification.

TERMS TO LEARN
ratify
Federalist
amendment

The Storyteller

Some voices rang out loud and clear in favor of the Constitution. Merchants shouted for better trade agreements with Britain. Frontier settlers cheered, hoping for more protection from attacks by Native Americans. Others, however, fiercely opposed the Constitution. Why revolt, people asked, simply to fall under a new kind of tyranny? Patrick Henry, one of the most popular leaders in Virginia, was deeply suspicious of centralized power. He warned Americans to "be extremely cautious, watchful, jealous of your liberty; for instead of securing your rights, you may lose them forever."

Desk used by Patrick Henry

Gaining approval of the Constitution with its radical new plan of government was not going to be easy. Supporters and opponents prepared to defend their positions.

Citizenship

The Constitutional Debate

The Confederation Congress sent the Constitution to the states. Before the Constitution could go into effect, nine states needed to ratify, or approve, it. State legislatures set up special ratifying conventions to consider the document. By late 1787 these conventions started to meet. **Rhode Island** stood apart. Its leaders opposed the Constitution from the beginning and therefore did not call a convention to approve it.

At the same time, a great debate took place throughout the nation. In newspapers, public meetings, and in ordinary conversations, Americans discussed the arguments for and against the new Constitution.

Federalists

Supporters of the new Constitution were called Federalists. Better organized than their opponents, Federalists enjoyed the support of two of the most famous and respected men in America—George Washington and Benjamin Franklin. Three of the nation's most gifted political thinkers—James Madison, Alexander Hamilton, and **John Jay**—also backed the Federalists.

SECTION RESOURCES

Reproducible Masters
- Reproducible Lesson Plan 7–4
- Guided Reading Activity 7–4
- Section Quiz 7–4
- Reteaching Activity 7–4
- Enrichment Activity 7–4

Transparencies
- Section Focus Transparency 7–4

Multimedia
- Vocabulary PuzzleMaker
- Chapter Challenger Interactive Review Software
- Testmaker

1 FOCUS

BELLRINGER
Motivational Activity

Before taking roll at the beginning of the class period, project Section Focus Transparency 7–4 and have students answer the questions. Discuss students' responses.

This activity is also available as a blackline master.

Section Focus Transparency 7–4

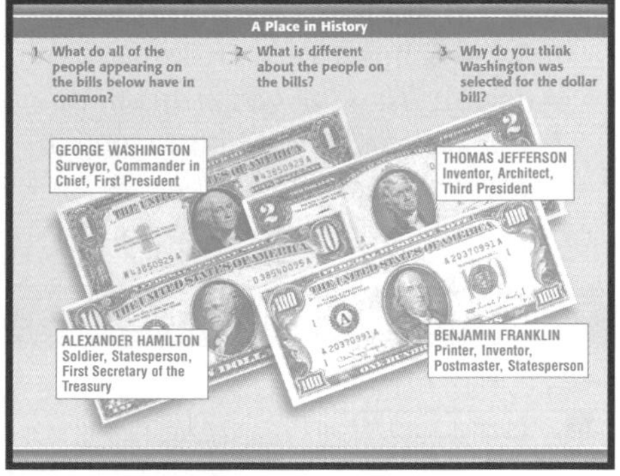

Vocabulary Precheck
Write the entries listed in **Terms to Learn** on the chalkboard. Have volunteers skim the section to find each term and paraphrase its meaning for the class.

Use the **Vocabulary Puzzle-Maker** to create crossword and word search puzzles.

Section Theme
Groups and Institutions

Federalist and Antifederalist groups debated the Constitution, and the document was eventually ratified.

Activity Have students look at the picture on page 211. **Ask:** Why would a ratified Constitution be a cause for celebration? *(Students should suggest that the nation needed a better plan for government, and now it had one.)*

CHAPTER 7
Section 4, 209–211

2 TEACH

L1 Noting Viewpoints Write on the chalkboard the words *Federalist* and *Antifederalist.* As students discuss this section, have them suggest key points to remember about each viewpoint.

Picturing HISTORY Mercy Otis Warren was not afraid to criticize the government. Before the American Revolution, she wrote plays that ridiculed Tories and their policies. Several of her satirical dramas were published in Massachusetts.
Answer: *The strongest criticism was that it lacked a bill of rights to protect individual freedoms.*

Guided Reading Activity 7–4

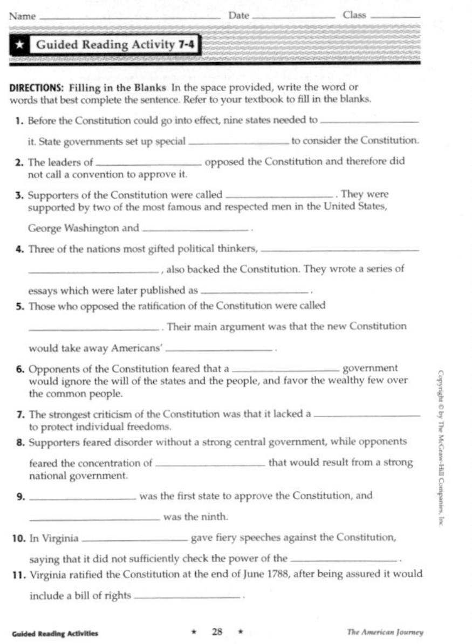

Name ________ Date ________ Class ________

Guided Reading Activity 7-4

DIRECTIONS: Filling in the Blanks In the space provided, write the word or words that best complete the sentence. Refer to your textbook to fill in the blanks.

1. Before the Constitution could go into effect, nine states needed to ________ it. State governments set up special ________ to consider the Constitution.
2. The leaders of ________ opposed the Constitution and therefore did not call a convention to approve it.
3. Supporters of the Constitution were called ________. They were supported by two of the most famous and respected men in the United States, George Washington and ________.
4. Three of the nations most gifted political thinkers, ________ ________, also backed the Constitution. They wrote a series of essays which were later published as ________.
5. Those who opposed the ratification of the Constitution were called ________. Their main argument was that the new Constitution would take away Americans' ________.
6. Opponents of the Constitution feared that a ________ government would ignore the will of the states and the people, and favor the wealthy few over the common people.
7. The strongest criticism of the Constitution was that it lacked a ________ to protect individual freedoms.
8. Supporters feared disorder without a strong central government, while opponents feared the concentration of ________ that would result from a strong national government.
9. ________ was the first state to approve the Constitution, and ________ was the ninth.
10. In Virginia ________ gave fiery speeches against the Constitution, saying that it did not sufficiently check the power of the ________.
11. Virginia ratified the Constitution at the end of June 1788, after being assured it would include a bill of rights ________.

Guided Reading Activities ★ 28 ★ *The American Journey*

3 ASSESS

Assign Section 4 Review as homework or as an in-class activity.

Use **Chapter Challenger Interactive Review Software** to review Section 4.

Picturing HISTORY Antifederalist Mercy Otis Warren feared that the Constitution would make the central government too powerful. **What was the biggest criticism of the Constitution by Antifederalists?**

Madison, Hamilton, and Jay teamed up to write a series of essays explaining and defending the Constitution. These essays appeared in newspapers around the country and were widely read by colonists. They were later published as a book called ***The Federalist.*** Jefferson described the series of essays as "the best commentary on the principles of government which was ever written."

Antifederalists

The Federalists called those who opposed ratification Antifederalists. Although not as well organized as the Federalists, the Antifederalists had some dedicated supporters. Their main argument was that the new Constitution would take away the liberties Americans had fought to win from Great Britain. The Constitution would create a strong central government, ignore the will of the states and the people, and favor the wealthy few over the common people. Antifederalists preferred local government close to the people. Central government, they feared, would be government by a small, educated group of individuals. They agreed with Thomas Paine, who had said, "That government is best which governs least."

Protecting Rights

Perhaps the strongest criticism of the Constitution was that it lacked a bill of rights to protect individual freedoms. Antifederalists believed that no government can be trusted to protect the freedom of its citizens. Several state conventions took a stand and announced that they would not ratify the Constitution without the addition of a bill of rights.

Mercy Otis Warren, a Massachusetts opponent of the Constitution, expressed the problem faced by many Antifederalists. She admitted the need for a strong government but feared it.

> "We have struggled for liberty and made costly sacrifices . . . and there are still many among us who [value liberty] too much to relinquish . . . the rights of man for the dignity of government."

In many ways the debate between Federalists and Antifederalists came down to their different fears. Federalists feared disorder without a strong central government and that more uprisings like Shays's Rebellion would occur. They looked to the Constitution to create a national government capable of maintaining order.

The Antifederalists feared government more than disorder. They worried about the concentration of power that would result from a strong national government.

Adopting the Constitution

Despite Antifederalist opposition the ratification of the Constitution proceeded fairly rapidly. On December 7, 1787, Delaware became

COOPERATIVE LEARNING ACTIVITY

Debating a Position Write the following statement on the chalkboard: *Without this new constitution, the United States would not have survived as a nation.* Organize the class into two teams—one to support the statement, the other to argue against it. Within each team, designate a discussion leader, students to do research, at least one person to record important details, and two or three students to argue the position. Then conduct an informal debate. Which position does the class feel is stronger?

the first state to approve the Constitution. On June 21, 1788, the ninth state—New Hampshire—ratified. In theory that meant that the new government could go into effect. Without the support of the two largest states—New York and Virginia—however, the future of the new government was not promising. Neither state had ratified yet, and both had strong Antifederalist groups.

In Virginia, **Patrick Henry** gave fiery speeches against the proposed Constitution. It did not, he charged, sufficiently check the power of the federal government. Nevertheless, Washington, Madison, Randolph, and the other Virginia Federalists carried the day. Virginia ratified the Constitution at the end of June 1788, after being assured that the Constitution would include a bill of rights amendment. An **amendment** is something added to a document.

That left three states—New York, North Carolina, and Rhode Island—to ratify. In July 1788, New York finally ratified by a narrow margin. One reason for its approval was New York City's threat to leave the state and join the Union on its own. North Carolina approved in November 1789 and Rhode Island in May 1790.

Picturing HISTORY Ratification of the Constitution set off a wave of celebration. This flag was carried by artisans in a New York City parade in July 1788. **Who were the most well-known Federalists supporting ratification of the Constitution?**

Americans Celebrate

After ratification came the celebrations. Boston, New York, and Philadelphia held big parades accompanied by cannon salutes and pealing church bells. Smaller celebrations took place in hundreds of American towns.

The task of creating the Constitution had ended with its ratification by the state conventions. The Bill of Rights would be added in 1791, after the new government took office. Now it was time for the nation to elect leaders and begin the work of government.

Section 4 Review

Checking for Understanding

1. ***Identify*** Rhode Island, John Jay, *The Federalist,* Patrick Henry.
2. ***Define*** ratify, Federalist, amendment.
3. ***List*** three reasons the Antifederalists opposed the Constitution.

Reviewing Themes

4. **Groups and Institutions** Why were the Federalists effective at getting their message across to the public?

Critical Thinking

5. **Predicting Consequences** Although the government could have gone into effect earlier, why was it important for *all* the states to ratify it?

Activity

Creating a Poster Collect photographs from newspapers or magazines that show the freedoms guaranteed in the Bill of Rights. Put your photos on a poster entitled "The Face of Liberty."

Section 4 Review Answers

1. Rhode Island, 209; John Jay, 209; *The Federalist,* 210; Patrick Henry, 211
2. The words are defined in the Glossary.
3. Any three: It would take away liberties that Americans had won from Britain; it called for a strong central government; it would ignore the will of people and the states; it would favor the wealthy over common people; it did not have a bill of rights.
4. Federalists were better organized and were supported by respected leaders; they also offered a clear defense of the Constitution in a series of newspaper essays.
5. Without the cooperation of all the states (especially the two largest), the government would be less able to act for a unified nation.

Activity Posters should depict scenes that illustrate the rights granted in the Bill of Rights.

CHAPTER 7

Section 4, 209–211

Picturing HISTORY New York may have celebrated ratification of the Constitution on July 26, but it was not until November 1 that the Articles of Confederation Congress, meeting in New York, officially adjourned.
Answer: *George Washington and Benjamin Franklin*

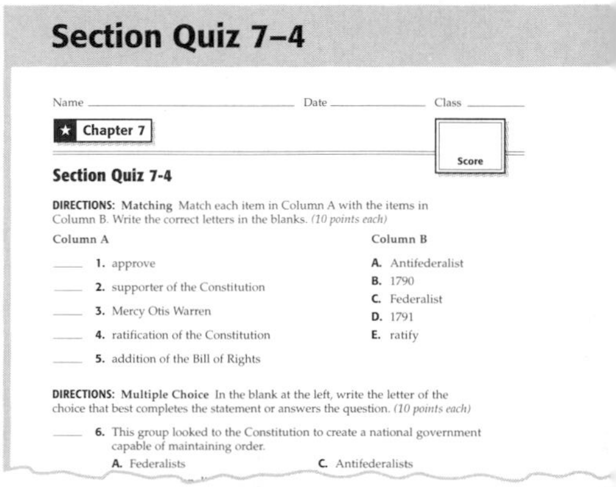

Section Quiz 7–4

Name ______ Date ______ Class ______

Chapter 7 — Score

Section Quiz 7-4

DIRECTIONS: Matching Match each item in Column A with the items in Column B. Write the correct letters in the blanks. *(10 points each)*

Column A	Column B
____ 1. approve	A. Antifederalist
____ 2. supporter of the Constitution	B. 1790
____ 3. Mercy Otis Warren	C. Federalist
____ 4. ratification of the Constitution	D. 1791
____ 5. addition of the Bill of Rights	E. ratify

DIRECTIONS: Multiple Choice In the blank at the left, write the letter of the choice that best completes the statement or answers the question. *(10 points each)*

____ 6. This group looked to the Constitution to create a national government capable of maintaining order.
A. Federalists C. Antifederalists

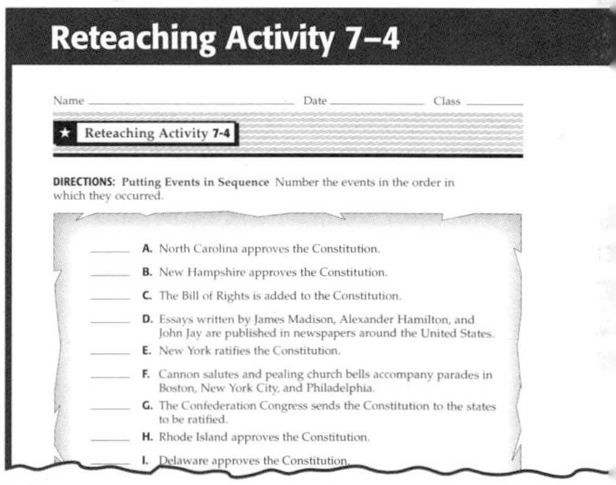

Reteaching Activity 7–4

Name ______ Date ______ Class ______

Reteaching Activity 7-4

DIRECTIONS: Putting Events in Sequence Number the events in the order in which they occurred.

____ A. North Carolina approves the Constitution.
____ B. New Hampshire approves the Constitution.
____ C. The Bill of Rights is added to the Constitution.
____ D. Essays written by James Madison, Alexander Hamilton, and John Jay are published in newspapers around the United States.
____ E. New York ratifies the Constitution.
____ F. Cannon salutes and pealing church bells accompany parades in Boston, New York City, and Philadelphia.
____ G. The Confederation Congress sends the Constitution to the states to be ratified.
____ H. Rhode Island approves the Constitution.
____ I. Delaware approves the Constitution.

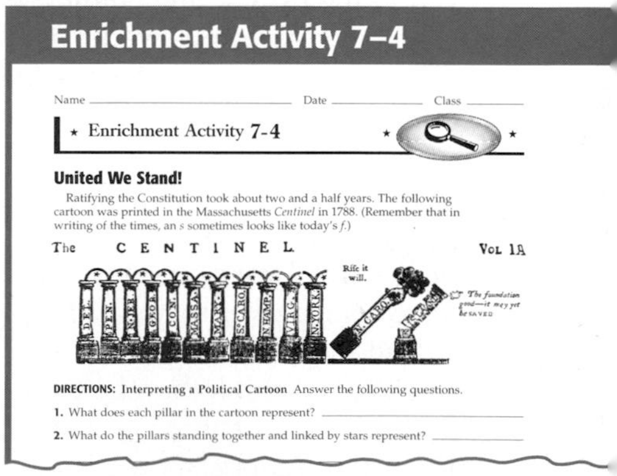

Enrichment Activity 7–4

Name ______ Date ______ Class ______

Enrichment Activity 7-4

United We Stand!

Ratifying the Constitution took about two and a half years. The following cartoon was printed in the Massachusetts *Centinel* in 1788. (Remember that in writing of the times, an *s* sometimes looks like today's *f*.)

DIRECTIONS: Interpreting a Political Cartoon Answer the following questions.

1. What does each pillar in the cartoon represent? ______
2. What do the pillars standing together and linked by stars represent? ______

4 CLOSE

Ask pairs of students to prepare one-sentence summaries of the Federalist and Antifederalist viewpoints.

CHAPTER 7
Review and Activities

GLENCOE TECHNOLOGY

VIDEODISC
MindJogger Videoquiz

Use MindJogger to review the Chapter 7 content.

Chapter 7
Disc 1, Side B

Also available in VHS.

Reviewing Key Terms

The key terms used in this activity are defined in the textbook glossary on pages A26–A35.

Reviewing Key Facts

1. Answers will vary but may include winning the war or establishing a policy to provide for new states in the West.
2. Damage to plantations cut rice exports; trade slowed when Britain closed the West Indies to American merchants; foreign debts had to be paid; there was a currency shortage; higher taxes forced farmers out of business.
3. Locke said that government is based on a contract between people and their ruler. The Framers of the Constitution viewed it as a contract between the American people and their government. The contract protected people's natural rights by limiting the government's power.
4. Answers will vary but may include the power to tax and the building of roads.
5. They did not think that the Constitution, as written, protected individual rights.

Reviewing Themes

1. State governments; each state wanted to keep "its sovereignty, freedom and independence," the federal government needed the states' approval on many matters and lacked a chief executive and the power to impose taxes.
2. No; they were mostly wealthy, educated white male landowners. Women, African Americans, and Native Americans were not included.
3. to keep any one branch from dominating the government
4. the addition of the Bill of Rights

Critical Thinking

1. to help regulate trade among states and with other nations, and to solve trading problems with Britain
2. The government would need money to support its activities.

Review and Activities

Reviewing Key Terms

On a sheet of paper, define the following terms:

constitution, **bicameral**, **republic**, **ordinance**, **depreciate**, **depression**, **proportional**, **compromise**, **Enlightenment**, **federalism**, **legislative branch**, **executive branch**, **judicial branch**, **checks and balances**, **ratify**, **amendment**

Reviewing Key Facts

1. What was one achievement under the Articles of Confederation?
2. What caused the depression after the Revolutionary War?
3. How were John Locke's ideas incorporated into the Constitution?
4. What are two powers shared by federal and state governments?
5. Why did some states want a bill of rights added to the Constitution?

Reviewing Themes

1. **Government and Democracy** Did the state governments or the national government hold most of the power under the Articles of Confederation? Explain.
2. **Groups and Institutions** Were the people who attended the Constitutional Convention representative of the American public? Explain.
3. **Civic Rights and Responsibilities** Why was a system of checks and balances built into the Constitution?
4. **Groups and Institutions** What compromise was needed for Virginia to ratify the Constitution?

Critical Thinking

Determining Cause and Effect

The state of the economy had a great effect on people's desire to replace the Articles of Confederation.

1. Why did merchants and manufacturers want a stronger national government?
2. Why was it important for a national government to have the power to tax?

Skill Practice Activity

Making Comparisons

The two statements below reflect the opinions of an Antifederalist and a Federalist toward the Constitution. Read the opinions, then answer the questions that follow.

"These lawyers, and men of learning, and moneyed men . . . make us poor illiterate people swallow down the pill, expect to get into Congress themselves; they expect to be the managers of this Constitution, and get all the power and all the money into their own hands, and then they will swallow up all us little folks. . . . This is what I am afraid of."

—Amos Singletary, farmer

"I am a plain man, and get my living by the plough. . . . I did not go to any lawyer, to ask his opinion; I formed my own opinion, and was pleased with this Constitution. . . . I don't think the worse of the Constitution because lawyers, and men of learning, and moneyed men, are fond of it."

—Jonathan Smith, farmer

1. Who is the Antifederalist? How do you know?
2. How are the two opinions similar? How are they different?

Geography Activity

By 1790 Philadelphia was one of the information capitals of the United States. The map below shows the number of days it took for newspapers in Philadelphia to publish events that occurred elsewhere. Study the map and answer the questions that follow.

News Distance to Philadelphia, 1790

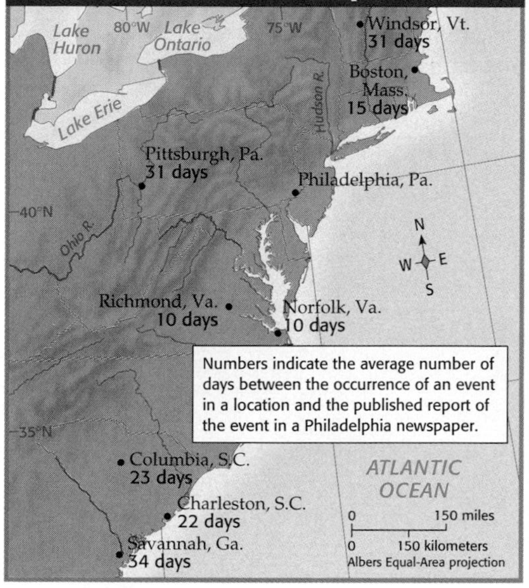

1. **Movement** How long, on average, did it take information from Pittsburgh to reach Philadelphia? From Savannah? From Windsor?
2. **Region** What effect do you think this information time lag had on different regions of the country?

Cooperative Activity

History and Global Issues Working in a small group, select a nation that has emerged in the last 25 years. Write a report that describes this nation's quest for independence.

Time Line Activity

Create a time line on which you place the following events in chronological order.

- Ninth state ratifies Constitution
- Articles of Confederation adopted
- Constitutional Convention begins
- Daniel Shays leads rebellion
- Congress passes first law regarding settlement of western lands
- Bill of Rights added to Constitution

Technology Activity

Using E-Mail Search the Internet for the names of your state's representatives in the United States Senate and House of Representatives. Find the E-mail address of one representative. Then write and send an electronic letter to the representative suggesting action on a national issue you feel strongly about.

Portfolio Activity **History Journal** Review the Bill of Rights to the Constitution (first 10 amendments). Summarize each in your journal. Then, knowing what you know about today's society, write a short description of a right you think the Framers of the Constitution should have included.

Skill Practice Activity

1. Amos Singletary; he opposed the Constitution, fearing that it would give the government too much power.
2. The opinions are similar in that both express distrust of lawyers, the highly educated, and the wealthy. The opinions differ in that one basically has confidence in the Constitution; whereas, the other fears that it would be used to increase the wealth and power of the country's leaders.

Geography Activity

1. 31 days; 34 days; 31 days
2. Students may suggest that people would not learn about an event from another colony until long after it happened. This would encourage parts of the country to think of themselves as separate and thus discouraged national unity.

Cooperative Activity

Each group should produce a written report that compares its nation's quest for independence and form of government to that of the United States in its early years.

Time Line Activity

Events should be placed in this order: Articles of Confederation adopted, Congress passes first law regarding settlement of western lands, Daniel Shays leads rebellion, Constitutional Convention begins, Ninth state ratifies Constitution, Bill of Rights added to Constitution

Technology Activity

Students should locate the names of their two United States senators and the congressional representatives who represent the districts where students live. They should then write, address, and send a letter to one of these people, expressing an opinion about an issue of national importance.

Portfolio Activity Students should suggest one right that they think the Framers of the Constitution should have included in the Bill of Rights.

Chapter Bonus Test Question

Ask: How many total essays were included in *The Federalist?* (85)

Beginning the Handbook

Inform students that when members of the first Congress gathered in New York in 1789, a bill of rights had not been added to the Constitution. These amendments were important because a number of states made their ratification conditional on such an addition. Other states had threatened to revoke their ratification if the bill of rights proved too radical. Have students speculate why Congress moved so quickly to inaugurate the new government. *(The country was eager for a new government; Congress perhaps felt that if the process of government had begun, it would be harder for wavering states to leave the new union.)*

Vocabulary Precheck

Ask students to write definitions of each of the entries listed in **Terms to Learn.** Have them check the accuracy of their definitions as they read each section.

Picturing HISTORY The Constitution is on permanent display at the National Archives in Washington, D.C. The Bill of Rights and the Declaration of Independence can be seen there as well.

Civics in Action
A Citizenship Handbook

READ TO DISCOVER . . .

- what goals shape the Constitution.
- the functions of the legislative, executive, and judicial branches.
- what the responsibilities of American citizens are.

TERMS TO LEARN

preamble
domestic tranquility
popular sovereignty
enumerated powers
reserved powers
concurrent powers
amendment
implied powers
judicial review
appropriate
impeach
constituent
warrant
due process of law

Picturing HISTORY The Constitution—on display in the National Archives—is the nation's most important document. Written in 1787, it set up a system of government that has weathered crisis and change for more than 200 years.

EXTRA CREDIT PROJECT

Making International Connections The United States Constitution is the oldest written national constitution still in operation. Compared to other written constitutions from around the world, it might be characterized as succinct. (The average federal constitution contains about 26,500 words, whereas the United States Constitution with its 27 amendments has fewer than 7,500 words.) Have students research and write a brief report comparing the United States Constitution with the constitutions of other nations. Suggest that students focus on such points as length, time in effective use, and political values espoused.

Section 1

The Constitution

In the summer of 1787, delegates from 12 states assembled in Philadelphia. They had come to address some of the weaknesses in the Articles of Confederation. Instead of changing the Articles, however, the delegates proposed an entirely new system of national government—in the Constitution of the United States. For more than 200 years, the Constitution has provided the framework for the United States government and has helped preserve American citizens' basic rights.

Silver inkwell used in the signing of the Constitution

Goals of the Constitution

The **Preamble,** or introduction, to the Constitution reflects the basic principle of American government—the right of the people to govern themselves. It also lists six goals for the United States government:

> ". . . to form a more perfect Union, establish Justice, insure domestic Tranquility, provide for the common defence [defense], promote the general Welfare, and secure the Blessings of Liberty to ourselves and our Posterity."

These goals guided the Constitution's Framers as they created a new government. They remain as important today as they were when the Constitution was written.

To Form a More Perfect Union

Under the Articles of Confederation, the states functioned almost like independent nations. For the most part, they did not work together on important matters such as defense and finances. This lack of unity could have been dangerous for the nation during times of crisis. To form "a more perfect Union" the Framers believed the states needed to agree to operate as a single country and cooperate on major issues, for the benefit of all.

To Establish Justice

For the Framers, treating each citizen equally was a fundamental principle on which to build the new nation. The Constitution provides a national system of courts to protect the people's rights and to hear cases involving violations of federal law and disputes between the states.

To Insure Domestic Tranquility

Shays's Rebellion in 1787 shocked Americans. The United States had become a self-governing nation, yet a group of people had resorted to violence to express their anger over government policies. The Constitution provides a strong central government "to insure **domestic Tranquility**"—that is, to keep peace among the people.

To Provide for the Common Defense

The Articles of Confederation did not provide an army or navy to defend the nation's borders. Its only defense system was the poorly trained militia of individual states. The Constitution

COOPERATIVE LEARNING ACTIVITY

Exploring Key Concepts Organize the class into groups of four students, one group for each of the Constitution's underlying principles—popular sovereignty, limited government, federalism, and separation of powers. Have each group delegate the following tasks among its members:

- Define the principle
- Locate at least one part of the Constitution that addresses that principle
- Prepare a skit that shows that principle at work in the lives of Americans today (This task can be divided further with student writers, director, and actors).

Allow time for presentation of each group's work; follow up with a class vote about which principle they think affects their lives the most right now.

1 FOCUS

BELLRINGER
Motivational Activity

Provide pairs of students with board games, such as chess or checkers. Have each pair play the game, but tell them there are no rules—they are to make up their own rules as they go along. After a few minutes, initiate a discussion about the need for rules and organization. Conclude by asking students to consider why the Constitution might be regarded as a rule book for government.

CURRICULUM CONNECTION

CIVICS
Though only a single sentence, the Preamble expresses the most important idea behind our system of government—that the people have the right and power to govern themselves.

Linking PAST & PRESENT

An Enduring Document Not many governments have had the stability that the U.S. Constitution has provided. France, for example, has had 16 constitutions since 1789. Peru, independent since 1821, has had 11.

The Constitution is amazing in another aspect. It was conceived as a governmental plan for an eighteenth-century agrarian nation of less than 4 million people. Today, though, that same document functions as the supreme law in a twentieth-century industrial nation of more than 260 million people.

2 TEACH

L1, ELL Discussing Precedents Have groups of students recall aspects of self-government with which American colonists had experimented. *(Answers include the Mayflower Compact, the Articles of Confederation, and organizations such as the Virginia House of Burgesses and the Continental Congresses.)* Explain that this handbook will help them see how those experiments helped shape the American system of government.

you don't say...

Popular Students may hear so much grumbling about governmental issues today that they may wonder why we say that the government is empowered by *popular* sovereignty. Point out that the word comes from the Latin word *populus* meaning "the people" and that *popular,* in the sense of "liked by most people," is just one of its meanings. The same Latin word also gives us *population* and *populate.*

What?Where?When?Who?

The power to award titles of nobility is denied to Congress. This clause was written into the Constitution to prevent the development of a noble class in the United States.

gives the federal government the power to maintain armed forces to protect the country and its citizens from attack.

To Promote the General Welfare

The Declaration of Independence states that the purpose of government is to promote "Life, Liberty, and the pursuit of Happiness" for the people of the nation. The Constitution includes measures that promote the general welfare—or well-being—of the people by maintaining order, protecting individual liberties, and by using its laws and resources to ensure, as much as possible, that citizens will be free from poverty, hunger, and disease.

To Secure the Blessings of Liberty

The American colonists fought the Revolutionary War to gain their liberty from Great Britain. The Framers believed that preserving liberty should also be a major goal of the Constitution. The Constitution guarantees that no American's basic rights will be taken away now or for posterity. (Posterity means generations not yet born.)

Underlying Principles

The Constitution's Framers struggled to create a balance between a strong government and the liberties of the people. To achieve this, they adopted four ideas, or principles: popular sovereignty, limited government, federalism, and separation of powers.

Popular Sovereignty

The Declaration of Independence states that governments derive their powers from "the consent of the governed." The opening words of the Constitution, "We the people," reinforce this idea of **popular sovereignty**—or "authority of the people." In the Constitution the people of America not only consent to be governed, but they also specify the powers and rules by which they shall be governed.

The Constitution allows the people to hold the final authority, or ruling power, in government. The people grant the government limited powers to act on their behalf, however. They choose representatives who understand and agree with their views to make laws and government policies.

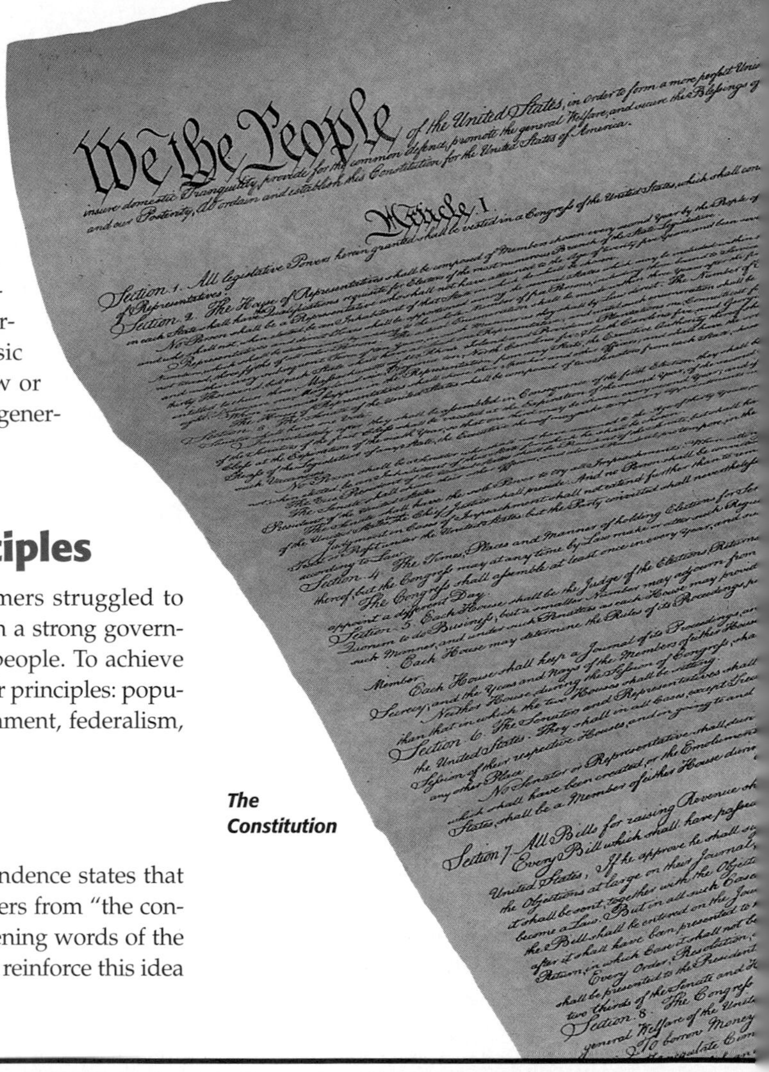

The Constitution

MULTIPLE LEARNING STYLES

Verbal/Linguistic Committing the Preamble of the Constitution to memory provides a useful language model for students whose spoken language development is slow. To aid in this memory task, structure the activity by asking students to write the words "who," "why," and "what" in their notebooks. Have students write the various phrases of the Preamble under the words to which they are most closely related. **L2**

The Federal System

Powers of the National Government	Powers shared by National and State Governments	Powers reserved for State Governments
• Regulate interstate and foreign trade • Raise/support armed forces • Declare war/make peace • Coin and print money • Grant patents/copyrights • Establish federal courts • Govern territories and admit new states • Set weights/measures • Establish a postal system • Regulate immigration	• Collect taxes • Borrow money • Make and enforce laws • Establish and maintain courts • Charter banks • Provide for public welfare	• Regulate trade within the state • Write business/corporation laws • Establish and maintain public schools • Set up local governments • Pass marriage/divorce laws • Conduct elections • Ratify constitutional amendments

Chart Study

The Constitution divides power between state and national levels.

1. Are public universities supported by the national or state government?
2. **Synthesizing Information** What powers shared by national and state governments deal with money?

Limited Government

The Framers saw both benefits and risks in creating a powerful national government. Although they agreed that the nation needed a stronger central authority, they feared misuse of power. They wanted to prevent the government from using its power to give one group special advantages or deprive another group of its rights. By creating a limited government, they restricted the government's authority to specific powers granted by the people.

Article I of the Constitution states the powers that the government has and the powers that it does not have. Other limits on government appear in the Bill of Rights, which guarantees certain rights and liberties to the people.

Limited government can be described as the "rule of law." No people or groups are above the law. Government officials must obey the law.

Federalism

In establishing a strong central government, the Framers did not deprive states of all authority. The states would give up some powers to the national government while retaining others. This principle of shared power is **federalism.**

Types of Powers

The Constitution defines three types of government powers. Certain powers belong only to the federal government. These **enumerated powers** include the power to coin money, regulate interstate and foreign trade, maintain the armed forces, and create federal courts (Article I, Section 8).

The second kind of powers are those retained by the states, known as **reserved powers.** They

Making Connections Activity

Politics Federalism can be graphically illustrated in many ways. After reading the section on federalism, ask students to graphically represent federalism. Encourage them to reflect shared powers as well as independent powers in their graphics. **L1**

L2 Comparing Governments
Have students find out what a unitary system of government is and report briefly to the class. Discuss who would control such groups as schools or police under a unitary system. Ask students how a unitary system differs from our system. *(In a unitary system, the national government has ultimate legal authority. The national government—not the state constitution—grants power to local government units.)*

Chart Study

Answers

1. state governments
2. collecting taxes, borrowing money, and chartering banks

Chart Skills Practice

Reading a Chart What types of trade cannot be regulated by state governments? *(trade between states or with another country)*

Facts On File

CD-ROM
Landmark Documents in American History

Title: *On the Constitution, Benjamin Franklin, 1787*
Encourage students to read the document and outline Franklin's opinions of the Constitution and his recommendations about it. Ask students to discuss why Franklin might have written such a paper. *(Known for his skills in politics and compromise, Franklin wrote this piece to launch the new charter as successfully as possible. He realized that the Constitution would require much support to be accepted by all the states.)*

CURRICULUM CONNECTION

CIVICS
"Administering criminal justice" is a controversial shared power. The Framers regarded execution by beheading and drawing and quartering as "cruel and unusual punishments." More recently, opponents of the death penalty have argued that any form of capital punishment is "cruel and unusual." The Supreme Court has not upheld that view. As a result some states impose a death penalty; others do not.

Chart Study

Answers
1. States can request a national convention at which an amendment can be proposed; states must ratify amendments.
2. Congressional proposals occur more often; the states have never called a special convention.

Chart Skills Practice

Reading a Chart Why do you think a higher degree of approval is needed to ratify an amendment than to propose one? *(Students may suggest that this is one more way in which the Framers sought to discourage minor or frequent changes in the Constitution.)*

Who?What?Where?When?

James Madison, who has been called "the father of the Constitution," believed that the Constitution would have to be altered as new situations arose but that this had to depend on the majority. He wrote: "If the will of the majority cannot be trusted where there are diversified and conflicting interests, it can be trusted nowhere."

include such rights as the power to establish schools, pass marriage and divorce laws, and regulate trade within a state. Although reserved powers are not listed specifically in the Constitution, the Tenth Amendment says that all powers not specifically granted to the federal government "are reserved to the States."

The third set of powers defined by the Constitution are **concurrent powers**—powers shared by the state and federal governments. Among these powers are the right to raise taxes, borrow money, provide for public welfare, and administer criminal justice.

When conflicts arise between state law and federal law, the Constitution declares that the Constitution is "the supreme Law of the Land." Such conflicts must be settled in a federal court.

Separation of Powers

To prevent any single group or institution in government from gaining too much authority, the Framers divided the federal government into three branches: **legislative, executive,** and **judicial.** Each branch has its own functions and powers. The legislative branch, Congress, makes the laws. The executive branch, headed by the president, carries out the laws. The judicial branch, consisting of the Supreme Court and other federal courts, interprets and applies the laws.

As an additional safeguard, the Framers established a system of **checks and balances** in which each branch of government can check, or limit, the power of the other branches. This system helps maintain a balance in the power of the three branches. For example, Congress can pass a law. Then the president can reject the law by vetoing it. However, Congress can override, or reverse, the president's veto if two-thirds of the members of both houses vote again to approve the law.

Over the years, the Supreme Court has acquired the power to determine the meaning of the Constitution and to declare that a law or a

The Amendment Process

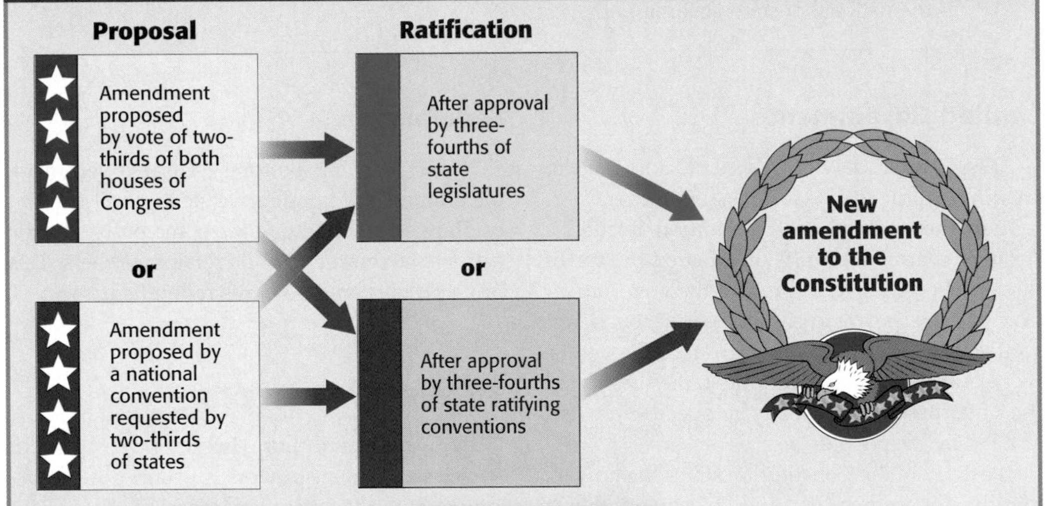

Chart Study

Amending the Constitution helps it adapt to changing times.

1. What role do the states play in the amendment process?
2. **Evaluating Information** Which method of proposal do you think is used more often? Explain.

CRITICAL THINKING ACTIVITY

Analyzing Information As the text notes, more than 9,000 amendments to the Constitution have been proposed, but only 27 have become part of the Constitution. Using this numerical information, ask students to calculate the odds of a proposed amendment being approved. Remind students that 10 of the 27 amendments were proposed by the original Framers of the Constitution. Have students figure the odds based on only 17 of the 9,000 proposed amendments having been approved. Ask them to discuss the wisdom of making the amendment process such a difficult one. **L3**

government policy goes against the Constitution. In doing so, the Court provides a check on the powers of Congress and the president. Judicial decisions—those made by the courts—can be overruled by amending the Constitution. The president and the Senate provide a check on the judicial branch through their power to appoint and approve federal judges.

A Living Constitution

Two years after the Constitutional Convention, Benjamin Franklin wrote to a friend: "Our Constitution is in actual operation; everything appears to promise that it will last; but in this world nothing is certain but death and taxes."

Despite Franklin's uncertainty about the Constitution's future, it is still very much alive today. The Constitution has survived because the Framers wrote a document that the nation could alter and adapt to meet changing needs. They accomplished this by making the wording of the Constitution general rather than specific. The result is a flexible document that can be interpreted in different ways in keeping with conditions and thinking of a particular time. The Constitution's flexibility allows the government to deal with matters the Framers never anticipated—such as regulating nuclear power plants or developing a space program. In addition the Constitution contains a provision for amending—changing or adding to—the document.

Amending the Constitution

The Framers made the amendment process difficult to discourage minor or frequent changes being made in the Constitution. Although more than 9,000 **amendments**—changes to the Constitution—have been proposed since 1788, only 27 have actually become part of the Constitution.

An amendment to the Constitution may be proposed in two ways: by the vote of two-thirds of both houses of Congress or by two-thirds of the state legislatures asking for a special convention on the amendment. The second method has never been used.

Linking PAST & PRESENT

The 27th Amendment

The most recent amendment to the Constitution was the Twenty-seventh Amendment. It was proposed on September 25, 1789, but not ratified until May 7, 1992. This amendment prevents Congress from passing immediate salary increases for itself. It delays congressional pay raises until after the next election. Congress passed the amendment in 1789 and sent it to the states for ratification. Because no time limit was set for its ratification, the proposal did not become part of the Constitution until Michigan became the 38th state to ratify it, 202 years later.

Ratification of an amendment requires approval by three-fourths of the states. The Constitution can be ratified by the approval of state legislatures or by special state conventions.

Only the Twenty-first Amendment—which repealed the Eighteenth Amendment, banning the sale of alcoholic beverages—was ratified by state conventions. Voters in each state chose the delegates to the special conventions. Congress chose this method to give the people a direct voice in the decision.

The Bill of Rights and Other Amendments

The Bill of Rights became part of the Constitution in 1791. These first 10 amendments protect basic liberties and rights that you may take for granted—including freedom of speech, freedom of the press, freedom of assembly, freedom of religion, and the right to a trial by jury.

The 17 amendments that follow the Bill of Rights expand the rights of Americans and adjust certain provisions of the Constitution. Included among them are amendments that abolish slavery, define citizenship, guarantee the right to vote to all citizens, authorize an income tax, and set a two-term limit on the presidency.

you don't say...

Check The verb *check* comes from Persian and is related to the royal title *shah.* It is a sports term, relating to a blocking action in chess. (The term also is used for a blocking action in hockey.)

Linking PAST & PRESENT

Financial Reform The final ratification of the Twenty-seventh Amendment was only one of several 1992 financial reforms directed at Congress. That same year also saw public anger over the revelation that representatives owed about $300,000 in unpaid bills at the House restaurant. Outcry also led to the closure of the House bank when it became known that in one year the bank had covered more than 8,000 overdrawn checks.

When?Who?What?Where?

Not until 1939 did three states ratify the Bill of Rights. Although the required 11 states ratified the Bill of Rights by 1791, Connecticut, Georgia, and Massachusetts waited until 1939 to grant their approval.

MAKING CONNECTIONS ACTIVITY

Foreign Affairs One of the enumerated powers of the federal government is to maintain the nation's armed forces. Briefly discuss students' familiarity with present-day recruitment techniques. Then ask them to create an advertisement or poster that encourages Americans of the late eighteenth century to join the army or navy of the United States. The recruitment message should touch on the desirability of defending the nation as a whole instead of the need to defend just one state. As students share their advertisements and posters, invite comments about how ready they think Americans of that day might have been to join a federally controlled military force. **L1**

Facts On File

CD-ROM
Landmark Documents in American History

Title: *Marbury* v. *Madison, 1803*
Ask students to view the document and detail how this case established the principle of judicial review.

Who?What?Where?When?

William Marbury had been appointed a judge by President John Adams on the night before Thomas Jefferson became president. When Secretary of State James Madison denied Marbury's commission, Marbury petitioned and won a favorable ruling from the Supreme Court.

Supreme Court Case Studies, *Marbury* v. *Madison* (1803)

3 ASSESS

Assign Section 1 Activity as homework or as an in-class activity.

4 CLOSE

Have students offer one-sentence definitions of the terms *legislative, executive, judicial, checks and balances,* and *amendment.*

Medal of Washington

Interpreting the Constitution

The Constitution includes two provisions that give Congress the power to act as needed to meet changing conditions. The first of these provisions is what is known as the "elastic clause" (Article I, Section 8). It directs Congress to "make all Laws which shall be necessary and proper" for executing all the powers of government. Congress has interpreted this clause to mean that it has certain **implied powers,** powers not specifically defined in the Constitution. Over the years, Congress has drawn on its implied power to pass laws to deal with the needs of a changing society. When Congress created the United States Air Force in 1947, for example, it used the power implied in its authority to maintain an army and navy and to declare war.

The second provision used to expand congressional authority, the "commerce clause" (Article I, Section 8), gives Congress the power to "regulate Commerce with foreign Nations, and among the several States." Congress has used this clause to expand its powers into a number of areas, such as regulation of the airline industry, radio and television, and nuclear energy.

Power of the Presidency

The Constitution describes the role and the powers of the president in general terms. This has allowed the executive branch to extend its powers. In 1803, for example, President Thomas Jefferson approved a treaty with France that enabled the United States to buy an enormous tract of land. The treaty made the people living in the Louisiana Territory citizens of the United States. Although the Constitution gives the president the power to make treaties, it contains no provision granting the president the power to grant citizenship through a treaty.

The Courts

The role of the judicial branch has also grown as powers implied in the Constitution have been put into practice. In 1803 Chief Justice John Marshall expanded the powers of the Supreme Court by striking down an act of Congress in the case of *Marbury* v. *Madison.* In the Court's decision, Marshall wrote: "It is emphatically the province and duty of the judicial department to say what the law is." In that decision the Court defined its right to determine whether a law violates the Constitution. Although not mentioned in the Constitution, **judicial review** has become a major power of the judicial branch.

The process of amending the Constitution and applying its principles in new areas helps keep our government functioning well. In 1974 Barbara Jordan, an African American member of Congress and a constitutional scholar, spoke in ringing tones of her faith in the Constitution:

> "I felt somehow for many years that George Washington and Alexander Hamilton just left me out by mistake. But through the process of amendment, interpretation, and court decision I have finally been included in 'We, the people.'"

Activity

Analyzing Information The Bill of Rights guarantees certain basic rights to all Americans. Select one of the 10 amendments that make up the Bill of Rights (see pages 242–243) and research its history. Present your findings in a one-page essay.

Section 1 Activity Answers

Essays should focus on how one of the first 10 amendments has been interpreted since it became law in 1791 and perhaps how it affects the lives of Americans today. Encourage students to work together to plan a format to present their information.

Section 2

The Federal Government

The government of the United States has three branches: the legislative branch, the executive branch, and the judicial branch. Each branch has specific powers that it uses to create, enforce, and interpret the nation's laws.

The presidential seal

The Legislative Branch

Congress, the legislative branch of the government, makes the nation's laws. It also has the power to "lay and collect taxes" and to declare war. Congress has two houses, the House of Representatives and the Senate.

The House and Senate

Today the House of Representatives has 435 voting members and 5 nonvoting delegates from the District of Columbia, Puerto Rico, Guam, American Samoa, and the Virgin Islands. The number of representatives from each state is determined by the state's population. Representatives, who must be at least 25 years old, serve 2-year terms.

The Senate consists of 100 senators, 2 from each state. Senators, who must be at least 30 years old, serve 6-year terms. The senators' terms are staggered, which means that one-third of the Senate seats come up for election every 2 years.

The Role of Congress

Congress has two primary functions: to make the nation's laws and to control government spending. The government cannot spend any money unless Congress **appropriates,** or sets aside, funds. All tax and spending bills must originate in the House of Representatives and gain approval in both the House and the Senate before going to the president for signature.

Congress also serves as a watchdog over the executive branch, monitoring its actions and investigating possible abuses of power. The House of Representatives can **impeach,** or bring formal charges against, any federal official it suspects of wrongdoing or misconduct. If an official is impeached, the Senate acts as a court and tries the accused official. Officials who are found guilty may be removed from office.

The Senate also holds certain special powers. Only the Senate can ratify treaties made by the president and confirm presidential appointments of federal officials such as department heads, ambassadors, and federal judges.

All members of Congress have the responsibility of representing their **constituents,** the people of their home states and districts. As a constituent you can expect your senators and representative to promote and protect your state's interests as well as those of the nation.

Congress at Work

Thousands of **bills**—proposed laws—are introduced in Congress every year. Because individual members of Congress could not

1 FOCUS

BELLRINGER
Motivational Activity

Ask students to consider how our government would be different if we did not have a division of responsibility among the three parts of our government. How would the government function if one group conducted all legislative, executive, and judicial functions?

CURRICULUM CONNECTION

CIVICS
In speaking of the Senate to Thomas Jefferson, George Washington is believed to have said, "We pour legislation into the senatorial saucer to cool it." He was referring to the view that the Senate (whose members serve for six years) would be a more deliberative body than the House of Representatives (whose members serve for only two years).

Linking PAST & *PRESENT*

The People's Choice Since January 1789, Americans have voted every other year on persons to represent them in their national government. This has not stopped despite a civil war, two world wars, and an economic depression. The American people reaffirm in every election James Madison's belief in the people's right to choose the government we would live by.

COOPERATIVE LEARNING ACTIVITY

Applying Ideas Have students work together to develop a set of 5 to 10 rules to use in the classroom. Offer the following as an example of such rules: During class discussion, students should not talk unless they raise their hands and the teacher recognizes them. Point out that rules should be acceptable to a two-thirds majority of the class. After students have completed the task, ask them to discuss the most difficult problems they faced in developing the rules.

2 *TEACH*

L1 Charting Powers Have partners or small groups of students make charts of the federal government's powers. Ask them to create three columns for the charts—one each for the legislative, the executive, and the judicial branches of government—noting the powers of each in the appropriate column. Students can share their charts during class discussion and use them for review.

Chart Study

Answers

1. by appointing federal judges and by granting pardons to federal offenders
2. Answers will vary, but students may cite evidence of how the system of checks and balances keeps any one branch from gaining too much power. Encourage students to defend their views.

Chart Skills Practice

Reading a Chart What power allows Congress to remove a judge or president from office? *(the power to impeach)*

L2 Examining Checks and Balances Organize the class into three groups—executive branch, legislative branch, and judicial branch. Use the situations below and have each group determine how it could check the power of another branch.

1. The president makes an unwise appointment of a Supreme Court justice. *(Senate refuses to confirm.)*
2. The Supreme Court makes several decisions that Congress determines are detrimental to public welfare. *(Congress proposes an amendment.)*
3. Congress passes a law that the president opposes. *(presidential veto)*

The American System of Checks and Balances

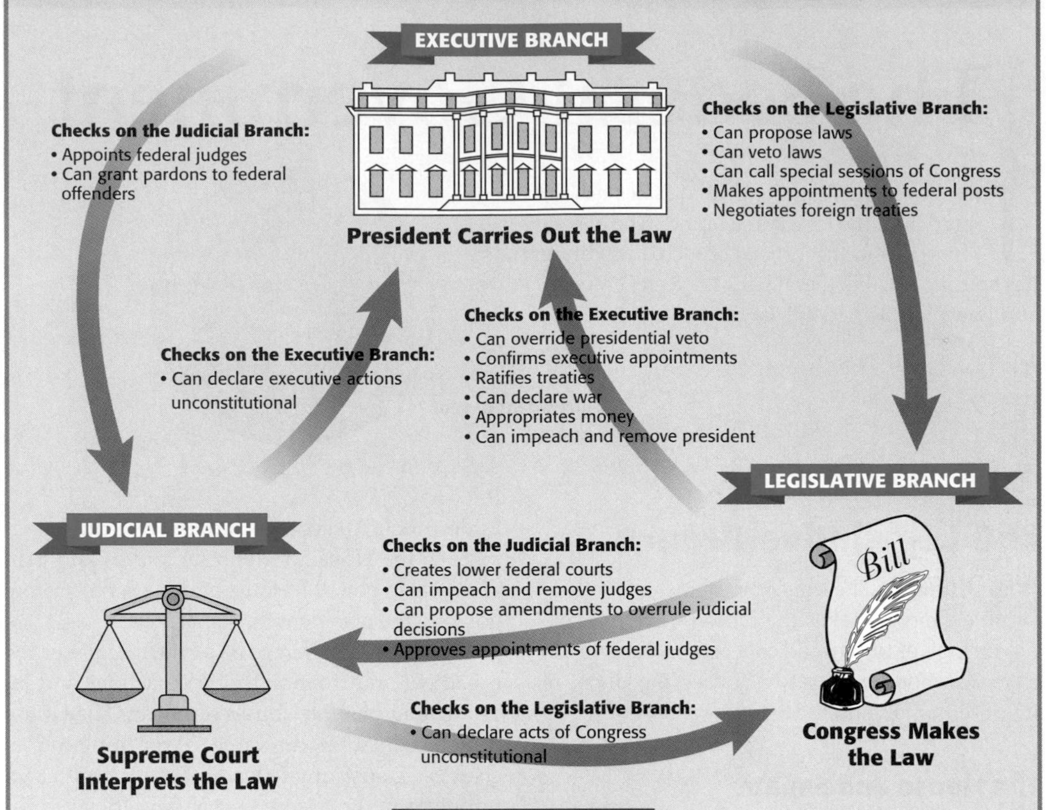

Chart Study

"You must first enable the government to control the governed," wrote Madison, "and in the next place, oblige it to control itself." The control Madison meant is found in the system of checks and balances in the Constitution.

1. How does the executive branch check the judicial branch?
2. **Making Generalizations** Do you think this system of checks and balances works? Explain.

possibly study all these bills carefully, both houses use committees of selected members to evaluate proposed legislation.

Standing committees are permanent committees in both the House and the Senate that specialize in a particular topic, such as agriculture, commerce, or veterans' affairs. These committees usually are broken down into **subcommittees** that focus on a particular aspect of a problem or issue.

The House and the Senate sometimes form temporary **select committees** to deal with issues requiring special attention. These committees meet only until they complete their task.

Occasionally the House and the Senate form **joint committees** with members from both houses. These committees meet to consider specific issues, such as the system of federal taxation. One type of joint committee, a **conference committee,** has a special function. If the House and the Senate pass different versions of the same bill, a conference committee tries to work out a compromise bill acceptable to both houses.

MULTIPLE LEARNING STYLES

Interpersonal *Committee, office, department, agency, cabinet*—all of these words from Section 2 suggest the need for effective interaction among group members. Brainstorm with students for a list of characteristics of effective group work. The following ideas can prompt their thinking:

- In an effective group, everyone has the chance to participate.
- Group members respect each other's ideas.
- The group works for the benefit of all, not for the promotion of any individual.

Discuss how each characteristic can benefit the work of a committee, agency, and so on. **L1**

When it receives a bill, a committee can kill it by rejecting it outright, "pigeonhole" it by setting it aside without reviewing it, or prepare it for consideration by the full House or Senate. While preparing bills committees hold public hearings at which citizens can present arguments and documents supporting or opposing the bills.

Once a bill is approved by a committee in either house of Congress, it is sent to the full Senate or House for debate. After debate the bill may be passed, rejected, or returned to committee for further changes.

When both houses pass a bill, the bill goes to the president. If the president approves the bill and signs it, it becomes law. If the president vetoes the bill, it does not become law. Congress, however, may **override**—cancel—the presidential veto by a vote of two-thirds of the members in each house.

The Executive Branch

The executive branch of government includes the president, the vice president, and various executive offices, departments, and agencies. The executive branch carries out the laws that Congress passes.

Chief Executive

The president plays a number of different roles in government, each of which has specific powers and responsibilities. These roles include the nation's chief executive, chief diplomat, commander in chief, chief of state, and legislative leader.

As chief executive the president is responsible for carrying out the nation's laws. Many executive departments and agencies assist the president in this job.

How a Bill Becomes a Law

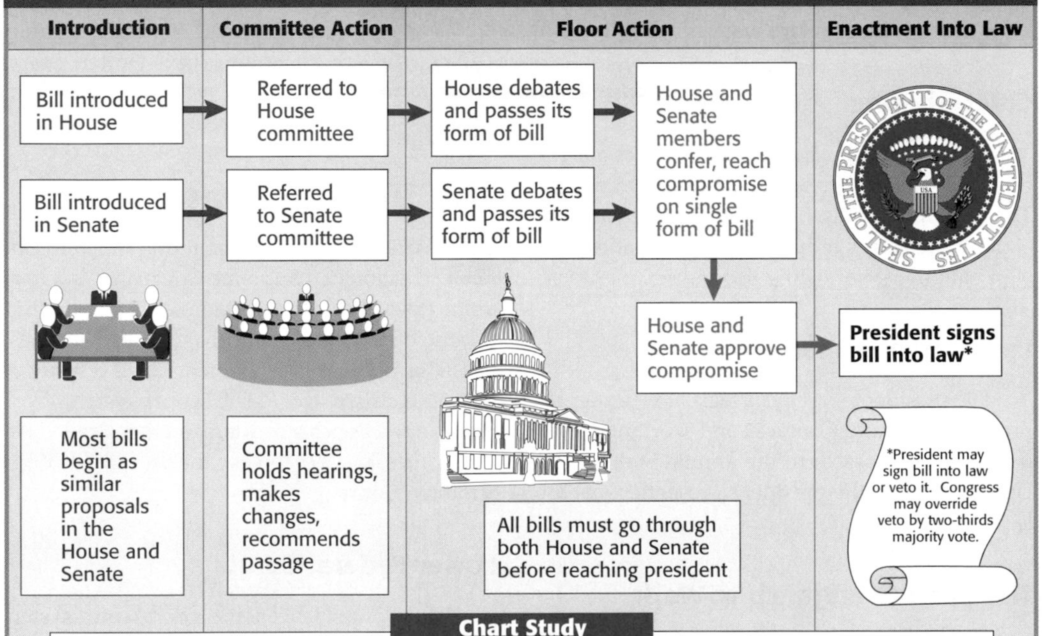

Chart Study

A bill introduced in Congress goes through many steps before it becomes a law.

1. What role does the president play in the passage of a new law?
2. **Evaluating Information** What happens immediately after the House and Senate have both passed their own forms of a bill?

MAKING CONNECTIONS ACTIVITY

Politics Bring home the idea of representation in Congress by asking students to list 10 states of their choice. Have them use almanacs, encyclopedias, and other reference books to rank their choices in order of geographic size. Then have them find out how many members of the House of Representatives each state sends to Washington, D.C. Ask students to reorder their lists accordingly; then discuss the differences between the lists. Also ask students how this activity helps them see the value of two kinds of representation—one based on population (for the House of Representatives), the other a set number (for the Senate). **L2**

CURRICULUM CONNECTION

CIVICS
Some presidents have used the veto sparingly; others have used it often. Franklin D. Roosevelt, for example, vetoed 635 pieces of legislation (only 9 of which were overridden). On the other hand, Richard M. Nixon vetoed 42 bills (with 5 overrides), and John F. Kennedy vetoed 21 (with no overrides).

you don't say...

Veto is a Latin word meaning "I forbid." It originated in the Senate of ancient Rome to protect the rights of commoners.

Chart Study

Answers

1. The president may sign a passed bill into law or may try to keep it from becoming law by vetoing it.
2. They confer and compromise upon a single form of the bill.

What? Where? When? Who?

What's That Name? When George Washington became the nation's first president, no one knew how to address him. John Adams suggested "His Highness, the President of the United States and Protector of the Rights of the Same." The House of Representatives finally settled on "President of the United States."

Facts On File

CD-ROM
Landmark Documents in American History

Title: *Judiciary Act, 1789*
Have students work together to complete an outline of the judicial branch as established by Article III of the Constitution (see pages 238–239 of the textbook) and the Judiciary Act of 1789. Students may add to their outline by researching changes in the judicial branch that Congress has made since 1789.

you don't say...

Cabinet is French in origin; it is an old word referring to a small room for private meetings. Today the media covers cabinet meetings, but the term retains the idea of a close, private talk with trusted advisers.

3 ASSESS

Assign Section 2 Activity as homework or as an in-class activity.

Chief Diplomat

As chief diplomat, the president directs foreign policy, appoints ambassadors, and negotiates treaties with other nations. Treaties must be approved by a two-thirds vote of the Senate before they go into effect.

Commander in Chief

As commander in chief of the armed forces, the president can use the military to intervene or offer assistance in crises at home and around the world. The president cannot declare war; only Congress holds this power. The president can send troops to other parts of the world for up to 60 days but must notify Congress when doing so. The troops may remain longer only if Congress gives approval or declares war.

President Clinton and Israeli prime minister Yitzhak Rabin

Chief of State

As chief of state, the president serves a symbolic role as the representative of all Americans. The president fulfills this role when receiving foreign ambassadors or heads of state, visiting foreign nations, or bestowing honors on Americans.

Legislative Leader

The president serves as a legislative leader by proposing laws to Congress and working to see that they are passed. In the annual State of the Union address, the president presents goals for legislation.

The Executive Branch at Work

Many executive offices, departments, and independent agencies help the president carry out and enforce the nation's laws. The Executive Office of the President (EOP) is made up of individuals and agencies that directly assist the president. Presidents rely heavily on the EOP for advice and for gathering information needed for decision making.

The executive branch also includes 14 executive departments, each responsible for a different area of government. For example, the Department of State plans and carries out foreign policy, and the Department of the Interior manages and protects the nation's public lands and natural resources. The heads, or secretaries, of these departments are members of the president's **cabinet,** a group that helps the president make decisions and set government policy.

The independent agencies manage federal programs in many fields. These include aeronautics and space, banking, communications, farm credit, and trade. Government corporations are government agencies that are run like privately owned businesses. One government corporation whose services you may use often is the United States Postal Service.

The Judicial Branch

Article III of the Constitution called for the creation of a Supreme Court and "such inferior [lower] courts as Congress may from time to time ordain and establish." In 1789 Congress passed a **Judiciary Act,** which added a series of district courts to the federal court system. Congress added appeals courts, sometimes called circuit courts, in 1891 to ease the workload of the Supreme Court.

Lower Federal Courts

At the lowest level of the federal court system are the United States **district courts.** These courts consider criminal and civil cases that come under federal, rather than state, authority. The criminal cases include such offenses as kidnapping and federal tax evasion. Civil cases cover claims against the federal government and cases

CRITICAL THINKING ACTIVITY

Making Comparisons Organize students into three groups of equal size. Have the first group focus on the local courts, the second on state courts, and the third on federal courts. Within each group designate students to be responsible for one of the following investigations: finding the nearest location of the group's court; identifying the kinds of cases that the court hears (with examples); outlining the options that the court has in dealing with those cases. Give students time to share their information with their groups. Then divide the class into groups of three, with each group containing a representative from each of the previous groups. Have group members share what they know about their courts. **L3**

The Federal Court System

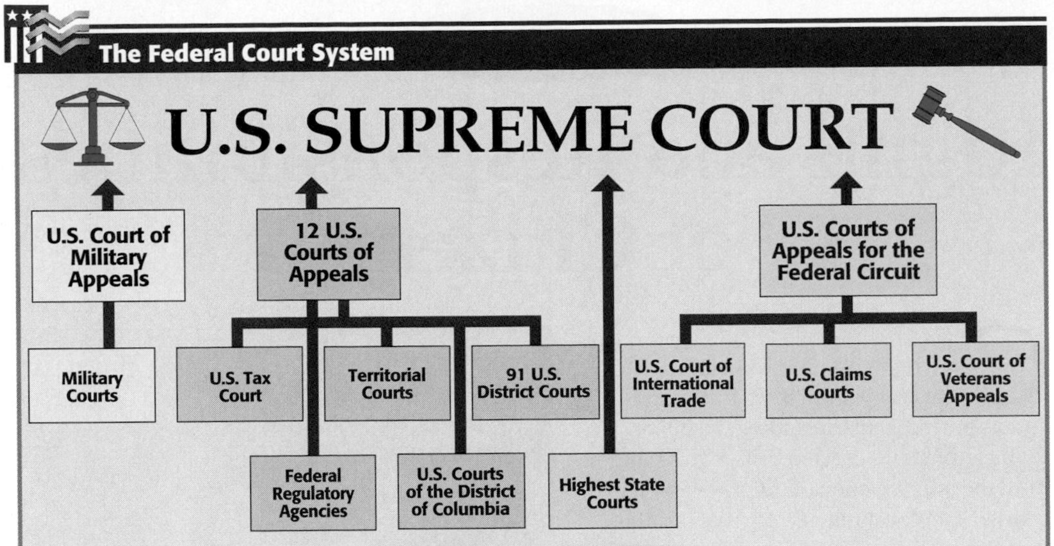

Chart Study

Federal courts of appeals may review cases tried by district courts or other courts at the district level.

1. At what higher level might cases from an appeals court be heard?
2. **Synthesizing Information** At what type of court do you think cases involving tax fraud would be heard?

involving constitutional rights, such as free speech. There are 91 district courts in the nation, with at least 1 in every state.

The next level of federal courts, the **appeals courts,** considers district court decisions in which the losing side has asked for a review of the verdict. If an appeals court disagrees with the lower court's decision, it can either overturn the verdict or order a retrial. There are 14 appeals courts in the United States.

The Supreme Court

The **Supreme Court,** the highest court in the federal court system, consists of a chief justice and eight associate justices. Most of the Supreme Court's cases come from appeals of lower-court decisions. Only cases involving foreign ambassadors or disputes between states can begin in the Supreme Court. The Supreme Court hears only about 150 cases each year.

The Supreme Court has the power of judicial review; that is, it can review laws and decide whether they are constitutional—in agreement with the Constitution. Over the years, the Supreme Court has interpreted the Constitution in different ways, sometimes reaching decisions that overturned earlier ones. Supreme Court decisions cannot be appealed, but Congress can modify a law to make it constitutional or propose an amendment to the Constitution.

Activity

Reading a Flowchart Flowcharts are meant to show the steps in a certain process. The flowchart on page 223 shows the movement of a bill through Congress. Use that chart to answer the following questions.

1. In what two places can a bill be introduced?
2. What is used to show the direction in which the bill is moving?
3. Where does a bill go after receiving approval by the House and the Senate?

Chart Study

Answers

1. at the Supreme Court
2. United States Tax Court

Chart Skills Practice

Reading a Chart Aside from the appeals courts, from which type of court can one appeal directly to the Supreme Court? *(from the highest court in a state)*

CURRICULUM CONNECTION

CIVICS
The Constitution does not specify any requirements for a Supreme Court justice—not even a law degree. So far, however, all the justices have been lawyers, and most have served as judges.

Who?What?Where?When?

Sandra Day O'Connor became the first female Supreme Court justice in 1981. President Ronald Reagan appointed her, saying, "She is truly a person for all seasons, possessing those unique qualities of temperament, fairness, intellectual capacity, and devotion to the public good which had characterized the 101 brethren who had preceded her." Ruth Bader Ginsburg joined O'Connor on the Court in 1993. President Bill Clinton appointed Ginsburg.

4 CLOSE

Ask students to suggest a scenario in which all three branches of government would become involved in making and administering a law.

Section 2 Activity Answers

1. in the House or in the Senate
2. arrows
3. to the president for signing into law

1 FOCUS

BELLRINGER
Motivational Activity

Ask students to list the rights they possess as American citizens. *(Most students will mention the right to speak their minds, right to worship their religion, right to vote, right to a fair trial, right to be treated equally regardless of race or religion.)* Point out that we "pay" for American citizenship by performing certain duties and responsibilities.

2 TEACH

L1 Discussing Key Terms Ask students to speculate about the difference between a freedom, a right, and a responsibility. Call on volunteers to give examples to support their ideas. As students read and discuss this section, encourage them to modify their ideas.

L2 Comparing Citizenship Have students research and write a report about the rights, duties, and responsibilities of citizenship in another country, comparing them with those in the United States.

Section 3

Rights and Responsibilities of Citizens

Citizens of the United States have both rights and responsibilities. The rights come from the Constitution and its amendments, including the Bill of Rights; from laws enacted by Congress; and from the interpretation of those laws by the courts. State constitutions also confer rights on citizens. The responsibilities derive from each American's role as a member of society.

Citizens taking part in a town meeting

The Rights of American Citizens

> "We hold these truths to be self-evident, that all men are created equal, that they are endowed by their Creator with certain unalienable Rights, that among these are Life, Liberty, and the pursuit of Happiness."

These words from the Declaration of Independence have inspired Americans. They have encouraged Americans to pursue the ideals expressed in the Declaration and to create a Constitution and Bill of Rights that protect these rights.

Types of Rights

The rights of Americans fall into three broad categories: the right to be protected from unfair actions of the government, to have equal treatment under the law, and to have basic freedoms.

Parts of the Constitution and the Bill of Rights protect all Americans from abuse, or unfair treatment, by the government or the law. Among these rights are the right to a lawyer when accused of a crime and the right to trial by jury when charged with a crime. In addition the Fourth Amendment to the Constitution offers protection from unreasonable searches and seizures. This provision requires police to have a **warrant** before searching a person's home for criminal evidence. To obtain the search warrant, the police must have a very strong reason to suspect the person of committing a crime.

Due Process

The Fifth Amendment states that no person shall "be deprived of life, liberty, or property, without due process of law." **Due process of law** means that the government must follow procedures established by law and guaranteed by the Constitution, treating all people according to these principles.

COOPERATIVE LEARNING ACTIVITY

Depicting Citizenship Ask groups of students to create collages that illustrate the broad theme "Citizenship in Action." Each collage should depict Americans exercising the rights, the duties, and/or the responsibilities of their citizenship. Each group should choose a slogan as a basis for selecting that group's illustrations. Tasks could include gathering used magazines and newspapers to clip pictures; working on layout; providing necessary lettering; and selecting and pasting pictures. As group representatives explain their finished collages, invite comments from the class about their own citizenship.

Equal Protection

All Americans, regardless of race, religion, or political beliefs, have the right to be treated the same under the law. The Fourteenth Amendment requires every state to grant its citizens "equal protection of the laws."

Basic Freedoms

The basic freedoms involve the fundamental liberties outlined in the First Amendment—freedom of speech, freedom of religion, freedom of the press, freedom of assembly, and the right to petition. In addition the Ninth Amendment states that the rights of Americans are not limited to those mentioned in the Constitution. This has allowed basic freedoms to expand over the years through the passage of other amendments and laws. The Twenty-sixth Amendment, for example, extends the right to vote to American citizens 18 to 20 years of age.

Limits on Rights

The rights of Americans are limited, based on the principle of respecting everyone's rights equally.

Consider this situation. Many cities and towns require groups to obtain a permit to march on city streets. You might feel that this restricts your right to freedom of speech and assembly. However, the permit also protects the community by allowing the police to make provisions so that the march will not disturb the lives of other people. A law banning all marches would be unreasonable and in conflict with the First Amendment rights of free speech and assembly. Similarly, a law preventing only certain groups from marching would be unfair because it would not apply equally to everyone.

In this and other cases, the government applies the principle of limiting an individual's rights to protect the rights of others and the community's health and safety. Most Americans are willing to accept some limitations on their rights to gain these protections as long as the restrictions are reasonable and apply equally to all.

Citizens' Responsibilities

★ Participation in a democratic society involves certain duties and responsibilities. **Duties** are actions required by law. **Responsibilities** are voluntary actions. No law requires you to fulfill responsibilities in the community. Fulfilling both your duties and your responsibilities, however, helps ensure good government and the protection of your rights.

Duties

One of the fundamental duties of all Americans is to obey the law. Laws serve three important functions. They help maintain order; they protect the health, safety, and property of all citizens; and they make it possible for people to live together peacefully. If you disobey laws, for example, you endanger others and interfere with the smooth functioning of society. If you believe a law needs to be changed, you can work through your representatives to improve it.

Americans also have a duty to pay taxes. The government uses tax money to defend the nation, provide health insurance for people over 65, and build roads and bridges. Americans benefit from services provided by the government.

Upon Becoming 18 Years Old

Another duty of citizens is to defend the nation. All males aged 18 and older must register with the government in case the nation needs to call on them for military service. The nation no longer has a **draft,** or required military service, but a war could make the draft necessary again.

The Constitution guarantees all Americans the right to a trial by a jury of their peers. For this reason you should be prepared to serve on a jury when you become eligible at the age of 18. Having a large group of jurors on hand is necessary to guarantee the right to a fair trial. You also have a duty to serve as a witness at a trial if called to do so.

Most states require you to attend school until a certain age. School is where you gain the knowledge and skills needed to be a good citizen. In school you learn to think more clearly, to express

Multiple Learning Styles

Auditory/Musical Ask students to prepare a choral reading about the responsibilities of American citizens. Have them begin by listing responsibilities from the text and points about how to accomplish each one. Offer this example:
KNOW WHAT'S GOING ON–
Find out the issues in your community.
Read about the issues in your newspaper.
Learn what local politicians think about the issues.
Talk about the issues with your friends.
Give students time to practice and present their reading. **L2**

Facts On File

CD-ROM
Landmark Documents in American History

Title: *Schenck* v. *United States, 1919*
This case is one of the nation's most famous free speech cases. The *Schenck* case presented the idea that First Amendment freedoms are not unlimited. The government does not tolerate actions that threaten the safety of other people. Encourage students to summarize the case and its outcome, explaining why this was a landmark case. Then discuss with students whether they agree with the decision in the case.

What? Where? When? Who?

The Draft *Conscription* is another word that refers to the draft. The first official conscription legislation passed in the United States was the Militia Act of 1792. That act made service in the militia obligatory for all free, white male citizens, 18 to 45 years old. Various conscription laws resulted in drafting men for military service for the Civil War, World War I, and so on. In 1973, however, the last conscription law expired, and our military became an all-volunteer force.

you don't say...

Draft This use of the noun *draft* comes from Old English and refers to a drawing or pulling—for example, as draftees' names or numbers might be drawn from a container.

3 ASSESS

Assign Section 3 Activity as homework or as an in-class activity.

Where?When?Who?What?

Polling places are located in each precinct in the United States. Polls may be set up in a firehouse, a public school, a private home, a barbershop, the lobby of a hotel, or any place convenient to all voters in the precinct. Polling places, though, cannot be located where alcoholic beverages are served. Laws in most states prohibit the distribution or display of campaign literature within a certain distance of the polling place, usually 100 feet.

Linking PAST & PRESENT

The Secret Ballot Today we recognize the secret ballot as a protection of our right to make our electoral choices unhindered and without fear. When it was first introduced, however, some Southern states used it to deny voting rights to African Americans. Illiteracy rates were high among African Americans at the time, and to cast a secret ballot a voter had to be able to read.

CURRICULUM CONNECTION

ECONOMICS
Income taxes account for nearly half the money collected by the federal government, whereas sales taxes are the source of about half of the revenue of state governments.

4 CLOSE

Have students brainstorm a list of what they consider to be their rights as American citizens.

Citizens' demonstration

your opinions more accurately, and to analyze the statements and ideas of others. These skills will help you make informed choices when voting.

Responsibilities

The responsibilities of citizens are not as clear-cut as their duties. Responsibilities are as important as duties, however, because they help maintain the quality of government and society.

One important responsibility is to become well informed. You need to know what is happening in your community, your state, your country, and the world. Knowing what your government representatives are doing and expressing your feelings about their actions can help keep the government responsive to the wishes of the people. You can gain information about public issues and government activities by reading books, newspapers, and magazines and by listening to the news on radio or television. Discussing issues and events with others is another important way of gaining information and understanding.

You also need to be informed about your rights and to exercise them when necessary. Knowing your rights helps preserve them.

Vote, Vote, Vote!

Perhaps your most important responsibility as an American citizen will be to vote when you reach the age of 18. Voting allows you to participate in government and guide its direction. When you vote for people to represent you in government, you will be exercising your right of self-government. If you disapprove of the job your representatives are doing, it will be your responsibility to help elect other people in the next election. You can also let your representatives know how you feel about issues through letters, telephone calls, and petitions and by taking part in public meetings or political rallies.

While not everyone holds public office, everyone can participate in government in other ways. Working on a political campaign, volunteering to help in a hospital or a library, and participating in a local park cleanup are all ways to take responsibility and make a contribution to good government and a well-run community.

To enjoy your rights to the fullest, you must be prepared to respect the rights of others. Respecting the rights of others also means respecting the rights of people with whom you disagree. Respecting and accepting others regardless of race, religion, beliefs, or other differences is essential in a democracy. All Americans are entitled to the same respect and treatment.

Activity

Making a Poster One responsibility of being an American citizen is to become involved in the democratic system. Make a poster showing how students can get involved in their community's democracy. Display your poster in a prominent place in the school.

Section 3 Activity Answers

Posters should demonstrate a clear understanding of the concepts presented in this section. Work with students to plan the display for the finished posters.

Handbook Review and Activities

Reviewing Key Terms

On a sheet of paper, define the following terms:

preamble	**implied powers**
domestic tranquility	**judicial review**
popular sovereignty	**appropriate**
enumerated powers	**impeach**
reserved powers	**constituent**
concurrent powers	**warrant**
amendment	**due process of law**

Reviewing Key Facts

Section 1

1. *List* the six goals of government stated in the Preamble.
2. *Name* the three types of powers found in the Constitution.
3. *Explain* why the amendment process is so difficult.

Section 2

4. *Name* the three branches of government.
5. *Explain* how a bill becomes a law.
6. *Identify* the roles of the president of the United States.

Section 3

7. *List* the basic freedoms outlined in the First Amendment.
8. *State* three of the duties and three of the responsibilities of an American citizen.

Understanding Themes

1. **Government and Democracy** Why did the Framers of the Constitution provide for the separation of powers?
2. **Government and Democracy** What is the power of judicial review?
3. **Civic Rights and Responsibilities** How does due process of law protect individual rights?

Critical Thinking

1. **Analyzing Information** Review the six goals of the United States government in the Preamble. List them in order of importance as you think they should be carried out. Why did you select your first listed goal as most important? What goal would you eliminate if you had to? Why?
2. **Predicting Consequences** What might have happened to the U.S. republic if the Framers had not provided for a system of checks and balances?
3. **Evaluating Information** Some people have argued that there should be a limit on the number of terms a senator or representative can serve. What are some of the advantages of the present system, which does not limit these terms? What are some of the disadvantages?

Cooperative Activity

History and Citizenship Working with a partner, draw scenes from your community that show the freedoms guaranteed in the Bill of Rights. Put your drawings on a poster titled "The Face of Liberty."

Technology Activity

Using a Word Processor Part of your responsibility as an American citizen is to be informed about what the government is doing and to voice your opinion about its actions. On your word processor, compose a letter to the editor of your local newspaper. In your letter, express your opinion about an issue in your community.

Reviewing Key Terms

The key terms used in this activity are defined in the textbook glossary on pages A26–A35.

Reviewing Key Facts

1. to form a more perfect union, to establish justice, to insure domestic tranquility, to provide for the common defense, to promote the general welfare, and to secure the blessings of liberty
2. enumerated, reserved, concurrent
3. The Framers wanted to discourage frequent or trivial changes to the Constitution.
4. legislative, executive, judicial
5. A bill is introduced in either the House or the Senate and is referred to a committee. If the committee recommends its passage, it is put to a vote. If it passes, House and Senate members work together to prepare a single form of the bill. If the House and Senate approve that bill, it goes to the president. If the president signs it, or if a presidential veto is overridden by Congress, the bill becomes law.
6. chief executive, chief diplomat, commander in chief, chief of state, and legislative leader
7. freedom of speech, religion, press, assembly, and the right to petition
8. Duties: obeying the law, paying taxes, defending the nation, serving on a jury or as a witness in a trial, attending school
   Responsibilities: being well informed, voting, participating in government, respecting the rights of others

Understanding Themes

1. to keep any governmental group from becoming too powerful
2. the Supreme Court's power to determine whether a law is constitutional
3. Government must follow legal procedures for everyone.

Critical Thinking

1. Have students defend their ratings.
2. A despotic president, an opportunistic Congress, or a corrupt judicial system may have emerged.
3. Students may suggest that under the current system, the nation benefits from the experience of legislators who have served several terms; on the other hand, legislators who serve term after term may become set in their ways, less willing to consider new ideas, and less responsive to the needs of constituents.

Cooperative Activity

Work with students to create a display of the finished posters.

Technology Activity

Letters should demonstrate awareness of a community issue.

UNITED STATES CONSTITUTION

1 FOCUS

BELLRINGER
Motivational Activity

Ask students to read the Preamble to the Constitution. Have them identify which purpose of the Constitution is most important to them personally.

Who?What?Where?When?

Committee of Style The final draft of the Constitution was written by the members of the Committee of Style—William Samuel Johnson, Alexander Hamilton, Gouverneur Morris, James Madison, and Rufus King.

ABCNEWS INTERACTIVE™

VIDEODISC
Powers of the Congress

Side 1, Chapter 5
Title: *Preamble to the Constitution*
Subject: Montage of students reading the preamble
Ask: **What reasons are given for establishing the Constitution?** *(to form a more perfect union, to establish justice, to insure domestic tranquility, to provide for the common defense, to promote the general welfare, and to secure the blessings of liberty)*

The Constitution of the United States

The Constitution of the United States is truly a remarkable document. It was one of the first written constitutions in modern history. The Framers wanted to devise a plan for a strong central government that would unify the country, as well as preserve the ideals of the Declaration of Independence. The document they wrote created a representative legislature, the office of president, a system of courts, and a process for adding amendments. For over 200 years, the flexibility and strength of the Constitution has guided the nation's political leaders. The document has become a symbol of pride and a force for national unity.

The entire text of the Constitution and its amendments follows. For easier study, those passages that have been set aside or changed by the adoption of amendments are printed in blue. Also included are explanatory notes that will help clarify the meaning of each article and section.

The Capitol, Washington, D.C.

MULTIPLE LEARNING STYLES

Verbal/Linguistic The Constitution, like the Declaration of Independence, is reproduced in its original language and contains a number of unfamiliar words. Point out to students that many of these words are defined in the margin notes. Suggest that students substitute the definitions for the unfamiliar words as they read through the document. **L1, ELL**

Preamble

We, the people of the United States, in Order to form a more perfect Union, establish Justice, insure domestic Tranquility, provide for the common defence, promote the general Welfare, and secure the Blessings of Liberty to ourselves and our Posterity, do ordain and establish this Constitution for the United States of America.

The Preamble introduces the Constitution and sets forth the general purposes for which the government was established. The Preamble also declares that the power of the government comes from the people.

The printed text of the document shows the spelling and punctuation of the parchment original.

Article I

Section 1

All legislative Powers herein granted shall be vested in a Congress of the United States, which shall consist of a Senate and House of Representatives.

Section 2

1. The House of Representatives shall be composed of Members chosen every second Year by the People of the several States, and the Electors in each State shall have the Qualifications requisite for Electors of the most numerous Branch of the State Legislature.

2. No Person shall be a Representative who shall not have attained to the Age of twenty-five Years, and been seven Years a Citizen of the United States, and who shall not, when elected, be an Inhabitant of that State in which he shall be chosen.

3. Representatives and direct Taxes shall be apportioned among the several states which may be included within this Union, according to the respective Numbers, which shall be determined by adding to the whole Number of free Persons, including those bound to Service for a Term of Years, and excluding Indians not taxed, three-fifths of all other Persons. The actual Enumeration shall be made within three Years after the first Meeting of the Congress of the United States, and within every subsequent Term of ten Years, in such Manner as they shall by Law direct. The Number of Representatives shall not exceed one for every thirty Thousand, but each state shall have at Least one Representative; and until such enumeration shall be made, the State of New Hampshire shall be entitled to chuse three; Massachusetts eight, Rhode Island and Providence Plantations one, Connecticut five, New York six, New Jersey four, Pennsylvania eight, Delaware one, Maryland six, Virginia ten; North Carolina five, South Carolina five, and Georgia three.

4. When vacancies happen in the Representation from any State, the Executive Authority thereof shall issue Writs of Election to fill such Vacancies.

5. The House of Representatives shall chuse their Speaker and other Officers; and shall have the sole Power of Impeachment.

Article I. The Legislative Branch

Section 1. Congress

The power to make laws is given to a Congress made up of two chambers to represent different interests: the Senate to represent the states; the House to be more responsive to the people's will.

Section 2. House of Representatives

1. Election and Term of Office

"Electors" means voters. Every two years the voters choose new Congress members to serve in the House of Representatives. The Constitution states that each state may specify who can vote. But the 15th, 19th, 24th, and 26th Amendments have established guidelines that all states must follow regarding the right to vote.

2. Qualifications

Representatives must be 25 years old, citizens of the United States for 7 years, and residents of the state they represent.

3. Division of Representatives Among the States

The number of representatives from each state is based on the size of the state's population. Each state is divided into congressional districts, with each district required to be equal in population. Each state is entitled to at least one representative. The number of representatives in the House was set at 435 in 1929. Since then, there has been a reapportionment of seats based on population shifts rather than on addition of seats.

Only three-fifths of a state's slave population was to be counted in determining the number of representatives elected by the state. Native Americans were not counted at all.

The "enumeration" referred to is the census, the population count taken every 10 years since 1790.

4. Vacancies

Vacancies in the House are filled through special elections called by the state's governor.

5. Officers

The Speaker is the leader of the majority party in the House and is responsible for choosing the heads of various House committees. "Impeachment" means indictment, or bringing charges against an official.

ARTICLE I

The Legislative Branch

Facts On File

CD-ROM
Landmark Documents in American History

Title: *U.S. Constitution, 1787*
Ask students to think about how the Constitution established guidelines for American government.

ABCNEWS INTERACTIVE™

VIDEODISC
Powers of the Congress

Side 1, Chapter 3
Title: *Constitutional Government*
Subject: Overview of constitutional government
Ask: **What are the three branches of the United States government?** *(legislative, executive, and judicial)*

ABCNEWS INTERACTIVE™

VIDEODISC
Historic America Electronic Field Trips

Side 1, Chapter 7
Title: *Independence Hall*
Subject: Tour of historic Independence Hall
Ask: **What is the message of this video segment?** *(We use our constitutional rights every day.)*

Also available in VHS.

TEACHER'S NOTES

ARTICLE I
The Legislative Branch

2 TEACH

L1 Analyzing Information Write on the chalkboard the following, which George Washington supposedly said to Thomas Jefferson in defense of the Senate: "We pour legislation into the senatorial saucer to cool it." Have students speculate on what Washington meant by this. *(The Senate was seen as the more deliberative of the two houses of Congress.)*

Who?What?Where?When?

Senior Senator The *oldest* senator from each state is not known as the senior senator. It is the senator who has served the longest time in the upper house who is known as the senior senator.

Section 3. The Senate

1. Number of Members, Terms of Office, and Voting Procedure
Originally, senators were chosen by the state legislators of their own states. The 17th Amendment changed this, so that senators are now elected directly by the people. There are 100 senators, 2 from each state.

2. Staggered Elections; Vacancies
One-third of the Senate is elected every two years. The terms of the first Senate's membership was staggered: one group served two years, one four, and one six. All senators now serve a six-year term.
The 17th Amendment changed the method of filling vacancies in the Senate.

3. Qualifications
Qualifications for the Senate are more restrictive than those for the House. Senators must be at least 30 years old and they must have been citizens of the United States for at least 9 years. The Framers of the Constitution made the Senate a more elite body in order to produce a further check on the powers of the House of Representatives.

4. President of the Senate
The vice president's only duty listed in the Constitution is to preside over the Senate. The only real power the vice president has is to cast the deciding vote when there is a tie. However, modern presidents have given their vice presidents new responsibilities.

5. Other Officers
The Senate selects its other officers, including a presiding officer (president pro tempore) who serves when the vice president is absent or has become president of the United States.

6. Trial of Impeachments
When trying a case of impeachment brought by the House, the Senate convenes as a court. The chief justice of the United States acts as the presiding judge, and the Senate acts as the jury. A two-thirds vote of the members present is necessary to convict officials under impeachment charges.

7. Penalty for Conviction
If the Senate convicts an official, it may only remove the official from office and prevent that person from holding another federal position. However, the convicted official may still be tried for the same offense in a regular court of law.

Section 3

1. The Senate of the United States shall be composed of two Senators from each State, chosen by the Legislature thereof; for six Years; and each Senator shall have one Vote.

2. Immediately after they shall be assembled in Consequence of the first Election, they shall be divided as equally as may be into three Classes. The Seats of the Senators of the first Class shall be vacated at the Expiration of the second Year, of the second Class at the Expiration of the fourth Year, and of the third Class at the Expiration of the sixth Year, so that one-third may be chosen every second Year; and if Vacancies happen by Resignations, or otherwise, during the Recess of the Legislature of any State, the Executive thereof may make temporary Appointments until the next Meeting of the Legislature, which shall then fill such Vacancies.

3. No person shall be a Senator who shall not have attained the Age of thirty Years, and been nine Years a Citizen of the United States, and who shall not, when elected, be an Inhabitant of that State in which he shall be chosen.

4. The Vice President of the United States shall be President of the Senate, but shall have no vote, unless they be equally divided.

5. The Senate shall chuse their Officers, and also a President pro tempore, in the absence of the Vice-President or when he shall exercise the Office of the President of the United States.

6. The Senate shall have the sole Power to try all impeachments. When sitting for that purpose they shall be on Oath or Affirmation. When the President of the United States is tried, the Chief Justice shall preside: And no person shall be convicted without the Concurrence of two-thirds of the Members present.

7. Judgment in Cases of Impeachment shall not extend further than to removal from Office, and disqualification to hold and enjoy any Office of Honor, Trust or Profit under the United States: but the Party convicted shall nevertheless be liable and subject to Indictment, Trial, Judgment and Punishment, according to Law.

Section 4. Elections and Meetings

1. Holding Elections
In 1842 Congress required members of the House to be elected from districts in states having more than one representative rather than at large. In 1845 it set the first Tuesday after the first Monday in November as the day for selecting presidential electors.

2. Meetings
The 20th Amendment, ratified in 1933, has changed the date of the opening of the regular session of Congress to January 3.

Section 4

1. The Times, Places, and Manner of holding Elections for Senators and Representatives, shall be prescribed in each state by the Legislature thereof; but the Congress may at any time by Law make or alter such Regulations, except as to the Places of Chusing Senators.

2. The Congress shall assemble at least once in every Year, and such Meeting shall be on the first Monday in December, unless they shall by Law appoint a different Day.

CRITICAL THINKING ACTIVITY

Analyzing Information Remind students that representation in the House of Representatives is based on each state's population. Then have students ascertain the number of members in the House currently representing your state, and also the numbers in 1990 and 1985. This information is readily available in many almanacs. Ask students to discuss how a change in the number of House seats might affect a state. **L2**

Section 5

1. Each House shall be the Judge of the Elections, Returns and Qualifications of its own Members, and a Majority of each shall constitute a Quorum to do Business; but a smaller Number may adjourn from day to day, and may be authorized to compel the Attendance of absent Members, in such Manner, and under such Penalties as each House may provide.

2. Each House may determine the Rules of its Proceedings, punish its Members for disorderly Behaviour, and, with the Concurrence of two-thirds, expel a Member.

3. Each House shall keep a Journal of its Proceedings, and from time to time publish the same, excepting such Parts as may in their Judgment require Secrecy; and the Yeas and Nays of the Members of either House on any question shall, at the desire of one-fifth of those Present, be entered on the Journal.

4. Neither House during the Session of Congress, shall, without the Consent of the other, adjourn for more than three days, nor to any other Place than that in which the two Houses shall be sitting.

Section 6

1. The Senators and Representatives shall receive a Compensation for their Services, to be ascertained by Law, and paid out of the Treasury of the United States. They shall in all Cases, except Treason, Felony and Breach of the Peace be privileged from Arrest during their attendance at the Session of their respective Houses, and in going to and returning from the same; and for any Speech or Debate in either House, they shall not be questioned in any other place.

2. No Senator or Representative shall, during the Time for which he was elected, be appointed to any civil Office under the Authority of the United States, which shall have been created, or the Emoluments whereof shall have been encreased, during such time; and no Person holding any Office under the United States, shall be a Member of either House during his continuance in Office.

Section 7

1. All Bills for raising Revenue shall originate in the House of Representatives; but the Senate may propose or concur with Amendments as on other bills.

2. Every Bill which shall have passed the House of Representatives and the Senate, shall, before it become a Law, be presented to the President of the United States; If he approve he shall sign it, but if not he shall return it, with his Objections, to that House in which it shall have originated, who shall enter the Objections at large on their Journal, and proceed to reconsider it. If after such Reconsideration two-thirds of that House shall agree to pass the bill, it shall be sent, together with the objections, to the other House, by which it shall likewise be reconsidered, and if approved by two-thirds of that House, it shall

Section 5. Organization and Rules of Procedure

1. Organization

Until 1969 Congress acted as the sole judge of qualifications of its own members. In that year, the Supreme Court ruled that Congress could not legally exclude victorious candidates who met all the requirements listed in Article I, Section 2.

A "quorum" is the minimum number of members that must be present for the House or Senate to conduct sessions. For a regular House session, a quorum consists of the majority of the House, or 218 of the 435 members.

2. Rules

Each house sets its own rules, can punish its members for disorderly behavior, and can expel a member by a two-thirds vote.

3. Journals

In addition to the journals, a complete official record of everything said on the floor, as well as the roll call votes on all bills or issues, is available in the *Congressional Record*, published daily by the Government Printing Office.

4. Adjournment

Neither house may adjourn for more than three days or move to another location without the approval of the other house.

Section 6. Privileges and Restrictions

1. Pay and Privileges

To strengthen the federal government, the Founders set congressional salaries to be paid by the United States Treasury rather than by members' respective states. Originally, members were paid $6 per day. Salaries for senators and representatives are $133,600.

The "immunity" privilege means members cannot be sued or be prosecuted for anything they say in Congress. They cannot be arrested while Congress is in session, except for treason, major crimes, or breaking the peace.

2. Restrictions

"Emoluments" means salaries. The purpose of this clause is to prevent members of Congress from passing laws that would benefit them personally. It also prevents the president from promising them jobs in other branches of the federal government.

Section 7. Passing Laws

1. Revenue Bills

"Revenue" is income raised by the government. The chief source of government revenue is taxes. All tax laws must originate in the House of Representatives. This ensures that the branch of Congress which is elected by the people every two years has the major role in determining taxes. This clause does not prevent the Senate from amending tax bills.

2. How Bills Become Laws

A bill may become a law only by passing both houses of Congress and by being signed by the president. If the president disapproves, or vetoes, the bill, it is returned to the house where it originated, along with a written statement of the president's objections. If two-thirds of each house

ARTICLE I

The Legislative Branch

L1 Constructing a Chart Have students construct a chart categorizing the legislative powers of Congress. Suggest that they list powers under the following categories: *Monetary, Commerce, Regulatory, Judicial, War, Implied.*

ABCNEWS INTERACTIVE™

VIDEODISC
Powers of the Congress

Side 1, Chapter 8
Title: *Making Laws*
Subject: The Clerk of the House reads the purpose of a bill being considered by Congress
Ask: **In which house of Congress must bills dealing with money originate?** *(House of Representatives)*

COOPERATIVE LEARNING ACTIVITY

Understanding Ideas Organize students into groups of five to consider one of the expressed powers of Congress–taxing and spending; regulating commerce, foreign policy and national defense; providing for the nation's growth, and so on. Have each group discuss why the power it selected was delegated to Congress rather than to the executive branch.

ARTICLE I
The Legislative Branch

L2 Writing Letters Point out that because of the heavy volume of legislation, both houses of Congress have committees that do much of the work in preparing bills. Each committee deals with a particular issue, such as banking, foreign affairs, or natural resources. Encourage students to write letters asking representatives and senators from your state about the committees they serve on. Invite volunteers to share the replies they receive.

When?Who?What?Where?

A Late Start When the first Congress was called to assemble in New York City in 1789, it took nearly a month for enough members to arrive to make a quorum.

approves the bill after the president has vetoed it, it becomes law. In voting to override a president's veto, the votes of all members of Congress must be recorded in the journals or official records. If the president does not sign or veto a bill within 10 days (excluding Sundays), it becomes law. However, if Congress has adjourned during this 10-day period, the bill does not become law. This is known as a "pocket veto."

3. Presidential Approval or Veto
The Framers included this paragraph to prevent Congress from passing joint resolutions instead of bills to avoid the possibility of a presidential veto. A bill is a draft of a proposed law, whereas a resolution is the legislature's formal expression of opinion or intent on a matter.

become a Law. But in all such Cases the Votes of both Houses shall be determined by Yeas and Nays, and the Names of the Persons voting for and against the Bill shall be entered on the Journal of each House respectively. If any Bill shall not be returned by the President within ten Days (Sundays excepted) after it shall have been presented to him, the Same shall be a Law, in like Manner as if he had signed it, unless the Congress by their Adjournment prevent its Return, in which Case it shall not be a Law.

3. Every Order, Resolution, or Vote to which the Concurrence of the Senate and House of Representatives may be necessary (except on a question of Adjournment) shall be presented to the President of the United States; and before the Same shall take Effect, shall be approved by him, or, being disapproved by him, shall be repassed by two-thirds of the Senate and House of Representatives, according to the Rules and Limitations prescribed in the case of a Bill.

Section 8. Powers Granted to Congress

1. Revenue
This clause gives Congress the power to raise and spend revenue. Taxes must be levied at the same rate throughout the nation.

2. Borrowing
The federal government borrows money by issuing bonds.

3. Commerce
The exact meaning of "commerce" has caused controversy. The trend has been to expand its meaning and, consequently, the extent of Congress's powers.

4. Naturalization and Bankruptcy
"Naturalization" refers to the procedure by which a citizen of a foreign nation becomes a citizen of the United States.

5. Currency
Control over money is an exclusive federal power; the states are forbidden to issue currency.

6. Counterfeiting
"Counterfeiting" means illegally imitating or forging.

7. Post Office
In 1970 the United States Postal Service replaced the Post Office Department.

8. Copyrights and Patents
Under this provision, Congress has passed copyright and patent laws.

9. Courts
This provision allows Congress to establish a federal court system.

10. Piracy
Congress has the power to protect American ships on the high seas.

11. Declare War
While the Constitution gives Congress the right to declare war, the United States has sent troops into combat without a congressional declaration.

Section 8

The Congress shall have the Power

1. To lay and collect Taxes, Duties, Imposts and Excises, to pay the Debts and provide for the common Defence and general Welfare of the United States; but all Duties, Imposts and Excises shall be uniform throughout the United States;

2. To borrow money on the credit of the United States;

3. To regulate Commerce with foreign Nations, and among the several States, and with the Indian Tribes;

4. To establish an uniform Rule of Naturalization, and uniform Laws on the subject of Bankruptcies throughout the United States.

5. To coin Money, regulate the Value thereof, and of foreign Coin, and fix the Standard of Weights and Measures;

6. To provide for the Punishment of counterfeiting the Securities and current Coin of the United States;

7. To establish Post Offices and post Roads;

8. To promote the Progress of Science and useful Arts, by securing for limited Times to Authors and Inventors the exclusive Right to their respective Writings and Discoveries;

9. To constitute Tribunals inferior to the Supreme Court;

10. To define and punish Piracies and Felonies committed on the high Seas, and Offenses against the Law of Nations.

11. To declare War, grant Letters of Marque and Reprisal, and make Rules concerning Captures on Land and Water;

CRITICAL THINKING ACTIVITY

Synthesizing Information Call on students to list the qualifications for serving in Congress as set forth in the Constitution. Then ask students what other qualifications, if any, they think should be applied to members of Congress. Discuss with students whether they would like to serve in Congress. **L1**

12. To raise and support Armies, but no Appropriation of Money to that Use shall be for a longer Term than two Years;
13. To provide and maintain a Navy;
14. To make Rules for the Government and Regulation of the land and naval forces;
15. To provide for calling forth the Militia to execute the Laws of the Union, suppress Insurrections, and repel Invasions;
16. To provide for organizing, arming, and disciplining, the Militia, and for governing such Part of them as may be employed in the Service of the United States, reserving to the States respectively, the Appointment of the Officers, and the Authority of training the Militia according to the discipline prescribed by Congress;
17. To exercise exclusive Legislation in all Cases whatsoever, over such District (not exceeding ten Miles square) as may, by Cession of particular States, and the acceptance of Congress, become the Seat of Government of the United States, and to exercise like Authority over all Places purchased by the Consent of the Legislature of the State in which the Same shall be, for the Erection of Forts, Magazines, Arsenals, dock-Yards, and other needful Buildings;—And
18. To make all Laws which shall be necessary and proper for carrying into Execution the foregoing Powers, and all other Powers vested by this Constitution in the Government of the United States, or in any Department or Officer thereof.

Section 9

1. The Migration or Importation of such Persons as any of the States now existing shall think proper to admit, shall not be prohibited by the Congress prior to the Year one thousand eight hundred and eight, but a tax or duty may be imposed on such importation, not exceeding ten dollars for each Person.
2. The privilege of the Writ of Habeas Corpus shall not be suspended, unless when in Cases of Rebellion or Invasion the public Safety may require it.
3. No Bill of Attainder or ex post facto Law shall be passed.
4. No capitation, or other direct, Tax shall be laid unless in Proportion to the Census or Enumeration herein before directed to be taken.
5. No Tax or Duty shall be laid on Articles exported from any State.
6. No Preference shall be given by any Regulation of Commerce or Revenue to the Ports of one State over those of another: nor shall Vessels bound to, or from, one State, be obliged to enter, clear, or pay Duties in another.

12. Army
This provision reveals the Framers' fears of a standing army.

13. Navy
This clause allows Congress to establish a navy.

14. Rules for Armed Forces
Congress may pass regulations that deal with military discipline.

15. Militia
The "militia" is now called the National Guard. It is organized by the states.

16. National Guard
Even though the National Guard is organized by the states, Congress has the authority to pass rules for governing its behavior.

17. Nation's Capital
This clause grants Congress the right to make laws for Washington, D.C.

18. Elastic Clause
This is the so-called "elastic clause" of the Constitution and one of its most important provisions. The "necessary and proper" laws must be related to one of the 17 enumerated powers.

Section 9. Powers Denied to the Federal Government

1. Slave Trade
This paragraph contains the compromise the Framers reached regarding regulation of the slave trade in exchange for Congress's exclusive control over interstate commerce.

2. Habeas Corpus
Habeas corpus is a Latin term meaning "you may have the body." A writ of habeas corpus issued by a judge requires a law official to bring a prisoner to court and show cause for holding the prisoner. The writ may be suspended only during wartime.

3. Bills of Attainder
A "bill of attainder" is a bill that punishes a person without a jury trial. An "ex post facto" law is one that makes an act a crime after the act has been committed.

4. Direct Taxes
The 16th Amendment allowed Congress to pass an income tax.

5. Tax on Exports
Congress may not tax goods that move from one state to another.

6. Uniformity of Treatment
This prohibition prevents Congress from favoring one state or region over another in the regulation of trade.

ARTICLE I
The Legislative Branch

L2 Evaluating Issues Article I, Section 9, prohibits the suspension of the writ of habeas corpus. Discuss with students the protection this offers. Ask students if they think this is an outdated principle today, or still necessary to the Constitution. *(Most students will see this is a major principle of our legal system.)*

Linking PAST & PRESENT

Undeclared Wars On many occasions when the United States has intervened militarily, Congress has not issued a declaration of war. These "undeclared wars" of the twentieth century include the conflicts in Korea and Vietnam. Both wars were fought on the president's authority to support governments against external aggression.

MORE ABOUT . . .

The Capitol The interior of the Capitol is a combination of new and old. Many of the furnishings and works of art date from the mid-1800s. However, signs of modern technology are everywhere. Roll-call votes are counted electronically. In addition, members of both houses have access to computers and other electronic information services. There are even electric subways connecting many of the office buildings on Capitol Hill.

ARTICLE II
The Executive Branch

1 FOCUS

BELLRINGER
Motivational Activity

Point out that one of the difficult questions for the Framers of the Constitution concerned the Chief Executive—exactly how much power should the president have? Have students discuss why the Framers set up an office of president with limited powers. *(Discussion should focus on the Framers' fear of a single leader with uncontrolled powers.)*

ABC NEWS INTERACTIVE™

VIDEODISC
Powers of the President

Side 1, Chapter 3
Title: *Constitution and the President*
Subject: The basic duties of the president
Ask: **How have the president's duties changed over the last 200 years?** *(They have increased through laws that Congress has passed.)*

7. Appropriation Law
This clause protects against the misuse of funds. All of the president's expenditures must be made with the permission of Congress.

8. Titles of Nobility
This clause prevents the development of a nobility in the United States.

7. No Money shall be drawn from the Treasury, but in Consequence of Appropriations made by Law; and a regular Statement and Account of the Receipts and Expenditures of all public Money shall be published from time to time.

8. No Title of Nobility shall be granted by the United States:—And no Person holding any Office of Profit or Trust under them, shall, without the Consent of the Congress, accept of any present, Emolument, Office, or Title, of any kind whatever, from any King, Prince, or foreign State.

Section 10. Powers Denied to the States

1. Limitations on Power
The states are prohibited from conducting foreign affairs, carrying on a war, or controlling interstate and foreign commerce. States are also not allowed to pass laws that the federal government is prohibited from passing, such as enacting ex post facto laws or bills of attainder. These restrictions on the states were designed, in part, to prevent an overlapping in functions and authority with the federal government that could create conflict and chaos.

2. Export and Import Taxes
This clause prevents states from levying duties on exports and imports. If states were permitted to tax imports and exports, they could use their taxing power in a way that weakens or destroys Congress's power to control interstate and foreign commerce.

3. Duties, Armed Forces, War
This clause prohibits states from maintaining an army or navy and from going to war, except in cases where a state is directly attacked. It also forbids states from collecting fees from foreign vessels or from making treaties with other nations. All of these powers are reserved for the federal government.

Section 10

1. No State shall enter into any Treaty, Alliance, or Confederation; grant Letters of Marque and Reprisal; coin Money; emit Bills of Credit; make any Thing but gold and silver Coin a Tender in Payment of Debts; pass any Bill of Attainder; ex post facto Law, or Law impairing the Obligation of Contracts, or grant any Title of Nobility.

2. No State shall, without the Consent of the Congress, lay any Imposts or Duties on Imports or Exports, except what may be absolutely necessary for executing its inspection Laws: and the net Produce of all Duties and Imposts, laid by any State on Imports and Exports, shall be for the Use of the Treasury of the United States; and all such Laws shall be subject to the Revision and Controul of the Congress.

3. No State shall, without the Consent of Congress, lay any duty on Tonnage, keep Troops, or Ships of War in time of Peace, enter into any Agreement or Compact with another State, or with a foreign Power, or engage in War, unless actually invaded, or in such imminent Danger as will not admit of delay.

Article II. The Executive Branch

Section 1. President and Vice President

1. Term of Office
The president is given power to enforce the laws passed by Congress. Both the president and the vice president serve four-year terms. The 22nd Amendment limits the number of terms the president may serve to two.

2. Election
The Philadelphia Convention had trouble deciding how the president was to be chosen. The system finally agreed upon was indirect election by "electors" chosen for that purpose. The president and vice president are not directly elected. Instead, the president and vice president are elected by presidential electors from each state who form the electoral college. Each state has the number of presidential electors equal to the total number of its senators and representatives. State legislatures determine how the electors are chosen. Originally, the state legislatures chose the electors, but today they are nominated by political parties and elected by the voters. No senator, representative, or any other federal officeholder can serve as an elector.

Article II

Section 1

1. The executive Power shall be vested in a President of the United States of America. He shall hold his Office during the Term of four years, and together with the Vice-President chosen for the same Term, be elected, as follows:

2. Each State shall appoint, in such Manner as the Legislature thereof may direct, a Number of Electors, equal to the whole Number of Senators and Representatives to which the State may be entitled in the Congress: but no Senator or Representative, or Person holding an Office of Trust or Profit under the United States, shall be appointed an Elector.

MORE ABOUT . . .

Two-term Limits The Constitution originally did not limit the number of terms the Chief Executive could serve. George Washington served two terms, as did all presidents until Franklin D. Roosevelt. Many people opposed Roosevelt's four terms in office. This opposition eventually led to the ratification of the Twenty-second Amendment in 1951, which limited presidents to two terms.

3. The Electors shall meet in their respective States, and vote by Ballot for two Persons, of whom one at least shall not be an Inhabitant of the same State with themselves. And they shall make a List of all the Persons voted for and of the Number of Votes for each; which List they shall sign and certify, and transmit sealed to the Seat of the Government of the United States, directed to the President of the Senate. The President of the Senate shall, in the Presence of the Senate and House of Representatives, open all the Certificates, and the Votes shall then be counted. The Person having the greatest Number of Votes shall be the President, if such Number be a Majority of the whole Number of Electors appointed; and if there be more than one who have such Majority, and have an equal Number of Votes, then the House of Representatives shall immediately chuse by Ballot one of them for President; and if no Person have a Majority, then from the five highest on the List the said House shall in like Manner chuse the President. But in chusing the President, the Votes shall be taken by States, the Representation from each State having one Vote; a quorum for this Purpose shall consist of a Member or Members from two-thirds of the States, and a Majority of all the States shall be necessary to a Choice. In every Case, after the Choice of the President, the Person having the greatest Number of Votes of the Electors shall be the Vice-President. But if there should remain two or more who have equal votes, the Senate shall chuse from them by Ballot the Vice President.

4. The Congress may determine the Time of chusing the Electors, and the Day on which they shall give their Votes; which Day shall be the same throughout the United States.

5. No person except a natural born Citizen, or a Citizen of the United States, at the time of the Adoption of this Constitution, shall be eligible to the Office of President; neither shall any Person be eligible to that Office who shall not have attained to the Age of thirty-five years, and been fourteen Years a Resident within the United States.

6. In Case of the Removal of the President from Office, or of his Death, Resignation, or Inability to discharge the Powers and Duties of the said Office, the same shall devolve on the Vice-President, and the Congress may by Law provide for the Case of Removal, Death, Resignation or Inability, both of the President and Vice-President, declaring what Officer shall then act as President, and such Officer shall act accordingly, until the disability be removed, or a President shall be elected.

7. The President shall, at stated Times, receive for his Services a Compensation, which shall neither be encreased nor diminished during the Period for which he shall have been elected, and he shall not receive within that Period any other Emolument from the United States, or any of them.

8. Before he enter on the execution of his office, he shall take the following Oath or Affirmation "I do solemnly swear (or affirm) that I will faithfully execute the Office of President of the United States, and will to the best of my Ability, preserve, protect and defend the Constitution of the United States.

3. Former Method of Election

This clause describes the original method of electing the president and vice president. According to this method, each elector voted for two candidates. The candidate with the most votes (as long as it was a majority) became president. The candidate with the second highest number of votes became vice president. In the election of 1800, the two top candidates received the same number of votes, making it necessary for the House of Representatives to decide the election. To prevent such a situation from recurring, the 12th Amendment was added in 1804.

4. Date of Elections

Congress selects the date when the presidential electors are chosen and when they vote for president and vice president. All electors must vote on the same day. The first Tuesday after the first Monday in November has been set as the date for presidential elections. Electors cast their votes on the Monday after the second Wednesday in December.

5. Qualifications

The president must be a citizen of the United States by birth, at least 35 years old, and a resident of the United States for 14 years. See Amendment 22.

6. Vacancies

If the president dies, resigns, is removed from office by impeachment, or is unable to carry out the duties of the office, the vice president becomes president. (Amendment 25 deals with presidential disability.) If both the president and vice president are unable to serve, Congress has the power to declare by law who acts as president. Congress set the line of succession in the Presidential Succession Act of 1947.

7. Salary

Originally, the president's salary was $25,000 per year. The president's current salary of $200,000 plus a $50,000 taxable expense account per year was enacted in 1969. The president also receives numerous fringe benefits including a $120,000 nontaxable allowance for travel and entertainment, and living accommodations in two residences—the White House and Camp David. However, the president cannot receive any other income from the United States government or state governments while in office.

8. Oath of Office

The oath of office is generally administered by the chief justice, but can be administered by any official authorized to administer oaths. All presidents-elect except Washington have been sworn into office by the chief justice. Only Vice Presidents John Tyler, Calvin Coolidge, and Lyndon Johnson in succeeding to the office have been sworn in by someone else.

ARTICLE II
The Executive Branch

2 TEACH

L1 Classifying Information Have students read Article II to find the powers of the president. Suggest that they classify these powers under the headings *Executive, Legislative, Diplomatic, Military, Judicial*.

L2 Making Judgments Ask students to discuss why the Framers of the Constitution made the president commander in chief of the armed forces and any state militias called to serve the United States. *(The Framers wanted to ensure civilian control of the military.)*

ABCNEWS INTERACTIVE™

VIDEODISC
Powers of the President

Side 1, Chapter 5
Title: *The White House*
Subject: The historic and symbolic importance of the White House
Ask: **Who was the first president to reside in the White House?** *(John Adams)*

Critical Thinking Activity

Determining Cause and Effect Write the following statement on the chalkboard: "The increase in presidential power during this century has been largely related to crises, whether domestic or foreign." Then ask students to discuss the following question: Do you think this is the true cause of the increase in presidential power? Why or why not? If not, what—in your opinion—did cause the increase? **L3**

ARTICLE III
The Judicial Branch

1 FOCUS

BELLRINGER
Motivational Activity

Ask students to consider the meaning of the phrase "respect for the law." Guide their discussion by asking the following questions: What is the law? How can the law affect individuals and society? Why is respect for the law necessary to good government?

ABCNEWS INTERACTIVE™

VIDEODISC
Powers of the Supreme Court

Side 1, Chapter 3
Title: *Constitution and the Court*
Subject: Review of the separation of powers and checks and balances
Ask: **What is the purpose in having separation of powers?** *(Separation allows power to be distributed and prevents one branch of government from holding all of the power.)*

Section 2. Powers of the President

1. Military, Cabinet, Pardons

Mention of "the principal officer in each of the executive departments" is the only suggestion of the president's cabinet to be found in the Constitution. The cabinet is a purely advisory body, and its power depends on the president. Each cabinet member is appointed by the president and must be confirmed by the Senate. This clause also makes the president, a civilian, the head of the armed services. This established the principle of civilian control of the military.

2. Treaties and Appointments

The president is the chief architect of American foreign policy. He or she is responsible for the conduct of foreign relations, or dealings with other countries. All treaties, however, require approval of two-thirds of the senators present. Most federal positions today are filled under the rules and regulations of the civil service system. Most presidential appointees serve at the pleasure of the president. Removal of an official by the president is not subject to congressional approval. But the power can be restricted by conditions set in creating the office.

3. Vacancies in Offices

The president can temporarily appoint officials to fill vacancies when the Senate is not in session.

Section 3. Duties of the President

Under this provision the president delivers annual State of the Union messages. On occasion, presidents have called Congress into special session to consider particular problems.

The president's duty to receive foreign diplomats also includes the power to ask a foreign country to withdraw its diplomatic officials from this country. This is called "breaking diplomatic relations" and often carries with it the implied threat of more drastic action, even war. The president likewise has the power of deciding whether or not to recognize foreign governments.

Section 4. Impeachment

This section states the reasons for which the president and vice president may be impeached and removed from office. (See annotations of Article I, Section 3, Clauses 6 and 7.)

Article III. The Judicial Branch

Section 1. Federal Courts

The term *judicial* refers to courts. The Constitution set up only the Supreme Court but provided for the establishment of other federal courts. There are presently nine justices on the Supreme Court. Congress has created a system of federal district courts and courts of appeals, which review certain district court cases. Judges of these courts serve during "good behavior," which means that they usually serve for life or until they choose to retire.

Section 2

1. The President shall be Commander in Chief of the Army and Navy of the United States, and of the Militia of the several States, when called into the actual Service of the United States; he may require the Opinion, in writing, of the principal Officer in each of the executive Departments, upon any subject relating to the Duties of their respective Offices, and he shall have Power to Grant Reprieves and Pardons for Offences against the United States, except in Cases of Impeachment.

2. He shall have Power, by and with the Advice and Consent of the Senate, to make Treaties, provided two-thirds of the Senators present concur; and he shall nominate, and by and with the Advice and Consent of the Senate, shall appoint Ambassadors, other public Ministers and Consuls, Judges of the supreme Court, and all other Officers of the United States, whose Appointments are not herein otherwise provided for, and which shall be established by Law. But the Congress may by Law vest the Appointment of such inferior Officers, as they think proper, in the President alone, in the Courts of Law, or in the Heads of Departments.

3. The President shall have Power to fill up all Vacancies that may happen during the Recess of the Senate, by granting Commissions which shall expire at the End of their next Session.

Section 3

He shall from time to time give to Congress Information of the State of the Union, and recommend to their Consideration such Measures as he shall judge necessary and expedient; he may, on extraordinary occasions, convene both Houses, or either of them, and in Case of Disagreement between them, with respect to the Time of Adjournment, he may adjourn them to such Time as he shall think proper; he shall receive Ambassadors and other public Ministers; he shall take Care that the Laws be faithfully executed, and shall Commission all the Officers of the United States.

Section 4

The President, Vice-President and all civil Officers of the United States, shall be removed from Office on Impeachment for, and Conviction of, Treason, Bribery, or other high Crimes and Misdemeanors.

Article III

Section 1

The Judicial Power of the United States, shall be vested in one supreme Court, and in such inferior Courts as the Congress may from time to time ordain and establish. The judges, both of the supreme and inferior Courts, shall hold their Offices during good Behaviour, and shall, at stated Times, receive for their Services, a Compensation, which shall not be diminished during their Continuance in Office.

MORE ABOUT . . .

Minorities and the Supreme Court Until the late 1900s all Supreme Court justices were white males. The first African American justice, Thurgood Marshall, was named to the Court by President Lyndon Johnson in 1967. President Ronald Reagan nominated the first woman justice, Sandra Day O'Connor, in 1981.

Section 2

1. The judicial Power shall extend to all Cases, in Law and Equity, arising under this Constitution, the Laws of the United States, and treaties made, or which shall be made, under their Authority; to all Cases affecting ambassadors, other public ministers and consuls; to all cases of admiralty and maritime Jurisdiction; to Controversies to which the United States shall be a party; to Controversies between two or more states; between a State and Citizens of another State; between Citizens of different States; between Citizens of the same State claiming Lands under Grants of different States, and between a State, or the Citizens thereof, and foreign States, Citizens or Subjects.

2. In all Cases affecting Ambassadors, other public Ministers and Consuls, and those in which a State shall be Party, the supreme Court shall have original Jurisdiction. In all the other Cases before mentioned, the supreme Court shall have appellate Jurisdiction, both as to Law and Fact, with such Exceptions, and under such Regulations as the Congress shall make.

3. The trial of all Crimes, except in Cases of Impeachment, shall be by Jury; and such Trial shall be held in the State where the said Crimes shall have been committed; but when not committed within any State, the Trial shall be at such Place or Places as the Congress may by Law have directed.

Section 3

1. Treason against the United States, shall consist only in levying War against them, or in adhering to their Enemies, giving them Aid and Comfort. No Person shall be convicted of Treason unless on the Testimony of two Witnesses to the same overt Act, or on Confession in open Court.

2. The Congress shall have power to declare the Punishment of Treason, but no Attainder of Treason shall work Corruption of Blood, or Forfeiture except during the Life of the Person attainted.

Article IV

Section 1

Full Faith and Credit shall be given in each State to the public Acts, Records, and judicial Proceedings of every other State. And the Congress may by general Laws prescribe the Manner in which such Acts, Records, and Proceedings shall be proved, and the Effect thereof.

Section 2. Jurisdiction

1. General Jurisdiction

Use of the words *in law and equity* reflects the fact that American courts took over two kinds of traditional law from Great Britain. The basic law was the "common law," which was based on over five centuries of judicial decisions. "Equity" was a special branch of British law developed to handle cases where common law did not apply.

Federal courts deal mostly with "statute law," or laws passed by Congress, treaties, and cases involving the Constitution itself. "Admiralty and maritime jurisdiction" covers all sorts of cases involving ships and shipping on the high seas and on rivers, canals, and lakes.

2. The Supreme Court

When a court has "original jurisdiction" over certain kinds of cases, it means that the court has the authority to be the first court to hear a case. A court with "appellate jurisdiction" hears cases that have been appealed from lower courts. Most Supreme Court cases are heard on appeal from lower courts.

3. Jury Trials

Except in cases of impeachment, anyone accused of a crime has the right to a trial by jury. The trial must be held in the state where the crime was committed. Jury trial guarantees were strengthened in the 6th, 7th, 8th, and 9th Amendments.

Section 3. Treason

1. Definition

Knowing that the charge of treason often had been used by monarchs to get rid of people who opposed them, the Framers of the Constitution defined treason carefully, requiring that at least two witnesses be present to testify in court that a treasonable act was committed.

2. Punishment

Congress is given the power to determine the punishment for treason. The children of a person convicted of treason may not be punished nor may the convicted person's property be taken away from the children. Convictions for treason have been relatively rare in the nation's history.

Article IV. Relations Among the States

Section 1. Official Acts

This provision ensures that each state recognizes the laws, court decisions, and records of all other states. For example, a marriage license or corporation charter issued by one state must be accepted in other states.

ARTICLE III
The Judicial Branch

2 TEACH

L2 Analyzing Ideas Point out that federal judges are appointed for life and can be removed only by their death, resignation, or impeachment. Ask students why they think the Framers of the Constitution made judgeships lifetime appointments. *(The Framers believed that judges who felt secure in their positions would be more likely to make unpopular, but correct, decisions.)*

L2 Writing Reports Encourage students to listen to excerpts from *May It Please the Court*—recordings of the Supreme Court in session. Have them write a brief report on the case or cases they listened to.

What?Where?When?Who?

The Court System The judiciary is only briefly described in the Constitution. The federal court system was established by the Judiciary Act of 1789.

CRITICAL THINKING ACTIVITY

Predicting Outcomes Have students discuss the pros and cons of federal judges being elected rather than appointed. Direct them to list the possible outcomes they foresee if the federal judiciary were subject to the electoral process. Encourage students to share and compare their lists. **L3**

1 FOCUS

BELLRINGER
Motivational Activity

Inform students that one political scientist has called the supremacy clause—Article VI, Section 2—"the most important single provision of the Constitution." Ask students to think about why this might be so. *(This clause made it clear that the national Constitution and laws are supreme over state constitutions.)*

2 TEACH

L2 Expressing Viewpoints Have students speculate on why the Framers of the Constitution established the amendment process as they did. *(The Framers wanted to make the Constitution flexible, but not so easy to amend that it would not be respected.)* Then have students discuss the following: Should the amendment process be made easier? Why or why not?

Section 2. Mutual Duties of States

1. Privileges

The "privileges and immunities," or rights of citizens, guarantee each state's citizens equal treatment in all states.

2. Extradition

"Extradition" means that a person convicted of a crime or a person accused of a crime must be returned to the state where the crime was committed. Thus, a person cannot flee to another state hoping to escape the law.

3. Fugitive-Slave Clause

Formerly this clause meant that slaves could not become free persons by escaping to free states.

Section 2

1. The Citizens of each State shall be entitled to all Privileges and Immunities of Citizens in the several States.

2. A Person charged in any State with Treason, Felony, or other Crime, who shall flee from Justice, and be found in another State, shall on demand of the executive Authority of the State from which he fled, be delivered up, to be removed to the State having Jurisdiction of the crime.

3. No Person held to Service of Labour in one State, under the Laws thereof, escaping into another, shall, in Consequence of any Law or Regulation therein, be discharged from such Service or Labour, but shall be delivered up on Claim of the Party to whom such Service or Labour may be due.

Section 3. New States and Territories

1. New States

Congress has the power to admit new states. It also determines the basic guidelines for applying for statehood. One state, Maine, was created within the original boundaries of another state (Massachusetts) with the consent of Congress and the state.

2. Territories

Congress has power over federal land. But neither in this clause nor anywhere else in the Constitution is the federal government explicitly empowered to acquire new territory.

Section 3

1. New States may be admitted by the Congress into this Union; but no new State shall be formed or erected within the Jurisdiction of any other State; nor any State be formed by the Junction of two or more States, or parts of States, without the Consent of the Legislatures of the States concerned as well as of the Congress.

2. The Congress shall have Power to dispose of and make all needful Rules and Regulations respecting the Territory or other Property belonging to the United States; and nothing in this Constitution shall be so construed as to Prejudice any Claims of the United States, or of any particular State.

Section 4. Federal Protection for States

This section allows the federal government to send troops into a state to guarantee law and order. The president may send in troops even without the consent of the state government involved.

Section 4

The United States shall guarantee to every State in this Union a Republican Form of Government, and shall protect each of them against Invasion; and on Application of the Legislature, or of the Executive (when the Legislature cannot be convened) against domestic Violence.

Article V. The Amending Process

There are now 27 amendments to the Constitution. The Framers of the Constitution deliberately made it difficult to amend or change the Constitution. Two methods of proposing and ratifying amendments are provided for. A two-thirds majority is needed in Congress to propose an amendment, and at least three-fourths of the states (38 states) must accept the amendment before it can become law. No amendment has yet been proposed by a national convention called by the states, though in the 1980s a convention to propose an amendment requiring a balanced budget had been approved by 32 states.

Article V

The Congress, whenever two-thirds of both Houses shall deem it necessary, shall propose Amendments to this Constitution, or, on the Application of the Legislatures of two-thirds of the several States, shall call a Convention for proposing Amendments, which, in either Case, shall be valid to all Intents and Purposes, as part of this Constitution, when ratified by the Legislatures of three-fourths of the several States, or by Conventions in three-fourths thereof, as the one or the other Mode of Ratification may be proposed by the Congress; Provided that no Amendment which may be made prior to the Year One thousand eight hundred and eight shall in any Manner affect the first and fourth clauses in the Ninth Section of the first Article; and that no State, without its Consent, shall be deprived of its equal Suffrage in the Senate.

COOPERATIVE LEARNING ACTIVITY

Writing Reports Organize students into four groups and assign to each group one of the four sections of Article I—sections 2, 3, 4, or 9—that has been modified by amendment. Have each group research how, why, and when the amendment to its assigned section was made. Encourage groups to present their findings to the rest of the class in brief written reports.

Article VI

1. All Debts contracted and Engagements entered into, before the Adoption of this Constitution, shall be as valid against the United States under this Constitution as under the Confederation.

2. This Constitution, and the Laws of the United States which shall be made in Pursuance thereof; and all Treaties made, or which shall be made, under the Authority of the United States, shall be the supreme Law of the Land; and the Judges in every State shall be bound thereby, any Thing in the Constitution or Laws of any State to the Contrary notwithstanding.

3. The Senators and Representatives before mentioned, and the Members of the several State Legislatures, and all executive and judicial Officers, both of the United States and of the several States, shall be bound by Oath or Affirmation, to support this Constitution; but no religious Test shall ever be required as a Qualification to any Office or public Trust under the United States.

Article VI. National Supremacy

1. Public Debts and Treaties
This section promised that all debts the colonies had incurred during the Revolution and under the Articles of Confederation would be honored by the new United States government.

2. The Supreme Law
The "supremacy clause" recognized the Constitution and federal laws as supreme when in conflict with those of the states. It was largely based on this clause that Chief Justice John Marshall wrote his historic decision in *McCulloch* v. *Maryland*. The 14th Amendment reinforced the supremacy of federal law over state laws.

3. Oaths of Office
This clause also declares that no religious test shall be required as a qualification for holding public office. This principle is also asserted in the First Amendment, which forbids Congress to set up an established church or to interfere with the religious freedom of Americans.

Article VII

The Ratification of the Conventions of nine States shall be sufficient for the Establishment of this Constitution between the States so ratifying the same.

Done in Convention, by the Unanimous Consent of the States present, the Seventeenth Day of September, in the Year of our Lord one thousand seven hundred and Eighty-seven, and of the Independence of the United States of America the Twelfth. In Witness whereof We have hereunto subscribed our Names.

Article VII. Ratification of the Constitution

Unlike the Articles of Confederation, which required approval of all thirteen states for adoption, the Constitution required approval of only nine of thirteen states. Thirty-nine of the 55 delegates at the Constitutional Convention signed the Constitution. The Constitution went into effect in June 1788.

Signers

George Washington, **President and Deputy from Virginia**

New Hampshire
John Langdon
Nicholas Gilman

Massachusetts
Nathaniel Gorham
Rufus King

Connecticut
William Samuel Johnson
Roger Sherman

New York
Alexander Hamilton

New Jersey
William Livingston
David Brearley
William Paterson
Jonathan Dayton

Pennsylvania
Benjamin Franklin
Thomas Mifflin
Robert Morris
George Clymer
Thomas FitzSimons
Jared Ingersoll
James Wilson
Gouverneur Morris

Delaware
George Read
Gunning Bedford, Jr.
John Dickinson
Richard Bassett
Jacob Broom

Maryland
James McHenry
Daniel of St. Thomas Jenifer
Daniel Carroll

Virginia
John Blair
James Madison, Jr.

North Carolina
William Blount
Richard Dobbs Spaight
Hugh Williamson

South Carolina
John Rutledge
Charles Cotesworth Pinckney
Charles Pinckney
Pierce Butler

Georgia
William Few
Abraham Baldwin

Attest: William Jackson, **Secretary**

L2 Biographical Sketches Ask students to research and write a brief biographical sketch of one of the signers of the Constitution. Suggest that students focus on such factors as background, education, family life, and so on, that might reveal their subjects' motivation in taking part in the Constitutional Convention.

When?Who?What?Where?

Ratification The first five states to ratify the Constitution—Delaware, Pennsylvania, New Jersey, Georgia, and Connecticut—did so quickly and by large majorities.

MORE ABOUT . . .

Signers of the Constitution Of the 55 delegates who attended the Constitutional Convention, only 38 signed the document. A thirty-ninth signature—that of John Dickinson—was written by George Read at Dickinson's request. Elbridge Gerry of Massachusetts and Edmund Randolph and George Mason of Virginia refused to sign, while 13 other delegates left the Convention early.

THE AMENDMENTS

1 FOCUS

BELLRINGER
Motivational Activity

Write the word *change* on the chalkboard. Have students discuss why the Framers included a process for changing the Constitution. *(They realized that the needs of the people would eventually change.)*

What?Where?When?Who?

Freedom of speech, as guaranteed by the First Amendment, has limits. Among other things, the First Amendment does not protect slander (a spoken lie meant to damage another person's reputation) or libel (slander that is published).

ABCNEWS INTERACTIVE™

VIDEODISC
Powers of the Supreme Court

Side 1, Chapter 6
Title: *The Bill of Rights*
Subject: Discussion of the importance of the Bill of Rights
Ask: **Why is the Bill of Rights necessary?** *(It contains individual rights, which are guaranteed to citizens of the United States.)*

Amendment 1.
Freedom of Religion, Speech, Press, and Assembly (1791)
The 1st Amendment protects the civil liberties of individuals in the United States. The 1st Amendment freedoms are not absolute, however. They are limited by the rights of other individuals.

Amendment I

Congress shall make no law respecting an establishment of religion, or prohibiting the free exercise thereof; or abridging the freedom of speech, or of the press; or the right of the people peaceably to assemble, and to petition the Government for a redress of grievances.

Amendment 2.
Right to Bear Arms (1791)
The purpose of this amendment is to guarantee states the right to keep a militia.

Amendment II

A well-regulated Militia, being necessary to the security of a free State, the right of the people to keep and bear Arms, shall not be infringed.

Amendment 3.
Quartering Troops (1791)
This amendment is based on the principle that people have a right to privacy in their own homes. It also reflects the colonists' grievances against the British government before the Revolution. Britain had angered Americans by quartering (housing) troops in private homes.

Amendment III

No soldier shall, in time of peace be quartered in any house, without the consent of the Owner, nor in time of war, but in a manner to be prescribed by law.

Amendment 4.
Searches and Seizures (1791)
Like the 3rd Amendment, the 4th Amendment reflects the colonists' desire to protect their privacy. Britain had used writs of assistance (general search warrants) to seek out smuggled goods. Americans wanted to make sure that such searches and seizures would be conducted only when a judge felt that there was "reasonable cause" to conduct them. The Supreme Court has ruled that evidence seized illegally without a search warrant may not be used in court.

Amendment IV

The right of the people to be secure in their persons, houses, papers, and effects, against unreasonable searches and seizures, shall not be violated, and no Warrants shall issue, but upon probable cause, supported by Oath or affirmation, and particularly describing the place to be searched, and the persons or things to be seized.

Amendment 5.
Rights of Accused Persons (1791)
To bring a "presentment" or "indictment" means to formally charge a person with committing a crime. It is the function of a grand jury to see whether there is enough evidence to bring the accused person to trial. A person may not be tried more than once for the same crime (double jeopardy).

Members of the armed services are subject to military law. They may be tried in a court martial. In times of war or a natural disaster, civilians may also be put under martial law.

The 5th Amendment also guarantees that persons may not be forced in any criminal case to be a witness against themselves. That is, accused persons may refuse to answer questions on the ground that the answers might tend to incriminate them.

Amendment V

No person shall be held to answer for a capital, or otherwise infamous crime, unless on a presentment or indictment of a Grand Jury, except in cases arising in the land or naval forces, or in the Militia, when in actual service in time of War or public danger; nor shall any person be subject for the same offence to be twice put in jeopardy of life or limb; nor shall be compelled in any criminal case to be a witness against himself, nor be deprived of life, liberty, or property, without due process of law; nor shall private property be taken for public use, without just compensation.

MORE ABOUT . . .

The Bill of Rights Critics of the Constitution felt that it did not go far enough in protecting individual rights and liberties. To answer these objections, supporters of the Constitution promised to introduce a series of amendments listing the rights of individuals. On September 25, 1789, James Madison kept this promise by proposing 14 amendments to the Constitution, 10 of which were adopted and are now known as the Bill of Rights. One amendment not adopted concerned pay raises for members of Congress. It eventually became part of the Constitution as the Twenty-seventh Amendment.

Amendment VI

In all criminal prosecutions, the accused shall enjoy the right to a speedy and public trial, by an impartial jury of the State and district wherein the crime shall have been committed, which district shall have been previously ascertained by law, and to be informed of the nature and cause of the accusation; to be confronted with the witnesses against him; to have compulsory process for obtaining witnesses in his favor, and to have the Assistance of Counsel for his defence.

Amendment 6.
Right to Speedy, Fair Trial (1791)

The requirement of a "speedy" trial ensures that an accused person will not be held in jail for a lengthy period as a means of punishing the accused without a trial. A "fair" trial means that the trial must be open to the public and that a jury must hear witnesses and evidence on both sides before deciding the guilt or innocence of a person charged with a crime. This amendment also provides that legal counsel must be provided to a defendant. In 1963, the Supreme Court ruled, in *Gideon* v. *Wainwright*, that if a defendant cannot afford a lawyer, the government must provide one to defend him or her.

Amendment VII

In suits at common law, where the value in controversy shall exceed twenty dollars, the right of trial by jury shall be preserved, and no fact tried by a jury, shall be otherwise reexamined in any Courts of the United States, than according to the rules of common law.

Amendment 7.
Civil Suits (1791)

"Common law" means the law established by previous court decisions. In civil cases where one person sues another for more than $20, a jury trial is provided for. But customarily, federal courts do not hear civil cases unless they involve a good deal more money.

Amendment VIII

Excessive bail shall not be required, nor excessive fines imposed, nor cruel and unusual punishments inflicted.

Amendment 8.
Bail and Punishment (1791)

"Bail" is money that an accused person provides to the court as a guarantee that he or she will be present for a trial. This amendment ensures that neither bail nor punishment for a crime shall be unreasonably severe.

Amendment IX

The enumeration in the Constitution, of certain rights, shall not be construed to deny or disparage others retained by the people.

Amendment 9.
Powers Reserved to the People (1791)

This amendment provides that the people's rights are not limited to those mentioned in the Constitution.

Amendment X

The powers not delegated to the United States by the Constitution, nor prohibited by it to the States, are reserved to the States respectively, or to the people.

Amendment 10.
Powers Reserved to the States (1791)

This amendment protects the states and the people from an all-powerful federal government. It provides that the states or the people retain all powers except those denied them or those specifically granted to the federal government. This "reserved powers" provision is a check on the "necessary and proper" power of the federal government provided in the "elastic clause" in Article I, Section 8, Clause 18.

Amendment XI

The Judicial power of the United States shall not be construed to extend to any suit in law or equity, commenced or prosecuted against one of the United States by Citizens of another State, or by Citizens or Subjects of any Foreign State.

Amendment 11.
Suits Against States (1795)

This amendment provides that a lawsuit brought by a citizen of the United States or a foreign nation against a state must be tried in a state court, not in a federal court. This amendment was passed after the Supreme Court ruled that a federal court could try a lawsuit brought by citizens of South Carolina against a citizen of Georgia. This case, *Chisholm* v. *Georgia*, decided in 1793, was protested by many Americans, who insisted states would lose authority if they could be sued in federal courts.

2 TEACH

L2, ELL Analyzing Ideas Ask students to identify areas of concern that they would like to see addressed by a constitutional amendment. Write suggestions on the chalkboard and have students discuss each in terms of the following questions: Why is an amendment needed? Would it be better for Congress to pass laws or the courts to establish precedents on this issue?

What?Where?When?Who?

Mass Media Some lawyers feel that the mass media threaten a defendant's Sixth Amendment rights. Extensive coverage of a crime on television and in the newspapers, these lawyers argue, makes it difficult to find jurors who are truly impartial.

CRITICAL THINKING ACTIVITY

Expressing Problems Clearly Point out that the Fifth Amendment protects the right of people charged with crimes to remain silent. In some countries, however, silence is equated with an admittance of guilt. Ask students to write a paragraph that supports or challenges the following statement: The Fifth Amendment is little more than a shield for the guilty. **L3**

THE AMENDMENTS

L3 Identifying Alternatives Point out that the electoral college has been criticized as being obsolete, and various reforms have been suggested for changing it or abolishing it altogether. Ask students to discuss and assess alternatives to the electoral college.

What?Where?When?Who?

Political Parties The Constitution did not provide for the existence of political parties, which today play a major role in the election of the president and vice president.

ABCNEWS INTERACTIVE™

VIDEODISC
Powers of the Supreme Court

Side 1, Chapter 20
Title: *Amendment 13 (1865): Abolition of Slavery*
Subject: Historical images of the abolition of slavery
Ask: **What is depicted in this video segment?** *(slavery and the Emancipation Proclamation)*

Amendment 12. Election of President and Vice President (1804)

This amendment changes the procedure for electing the president and vice president as outlined in Article II, Section 1, Clause 3.

To prevent the recurrence of the election of 1800 whereby a candidate running for vice president (Aaron Burr) could tie a candidate running for president (Thomas Jefferson) and thus force the election into the House of Representatives, the 12th Amendment specifies that the electors are to cast separate ballots for each office. The votes for each office are counted and listed separately. The results are signed, sealed, and sent to the president of the Senate. At a joint session of Congress, the votes are counted. The candidate who receives the most votes, providing it is a majority, is elected president. Other changes include: (1) a reduction from the five to three candidates receiving the most votes among whom the House is to choose if no candidate receives a majority of the electoral votes, and (2) provision for the Senate to choose the vice president from the two highest candidates if neither has received a majority of the electoral votes.

The 12th Amendment does place one restriction on electors. It prohibits electors from voting for two candidates (president and vice president) from their home state.

United States coins

Amendment 13. Abolition of Slavery (1865)

This amendment was the final act in ending slavery in the United States. It also prohibits the binding of a person to perform a personal service due to debt. In addition to imprisonment for crime, the Supreme Court has held that the draft is not a violation of the amendment.

This amendment is the first adopted to be divided into sections. It is also the first to contain specifically a provision granting Congress power to enforce it by appropriate legislation.

Amendment XII

The Electors shall meet in their respective States and vote by ballot for President and Vice-President, one of whom, at least, shall not be an inhabitant of the same State with themselves; they shall name in their ballots the person voted for as President, and in distinct ballots the person voted for as Vice-President, and they shall make distinct lists of all persons voted for as President, and of all persons voted for as Vice-President, and of the number of votes for each, which lists they shall sign and certify, and transmit sealed to the seat of the government of the United States, directed to the President of the Senate;—The President of the Senate shall, in the presence of the Senate and House of Representatives, open all the certificates and the votes shall then be counted;—The person having the greatest number of votes for President, shall be the President, if such number be a majority of the whole number of Electors appointed; and if no person have such majority, then from the persons having the highest numbers not exceeding three on the list of those voted for as President, the House of Representatives shall choose immediately, by ballot, the President. But in choosing the President, the votes shall be taken by states, the representation from each state having one vote; a quorum for this purpose shall consist of a member or members from two-thirds of the states, and a majority of all the states shall be necessary to a choice. And if the House of Representatives shall not choose a President whenever the right of choice shall devolve upon them, before the fourth day of March next following, then the Vice-President shall act as President, as in the case of the death or other constitutional disability of the President.—The person having the greatest number of votes as Vice-President, shall be the Vice-President, if such number be a majority of the whole number of Electors appointed, and if no person have a majority, then from the two highest numbers on the list, the Senate shall choose the Vice-President; a quorum for the purpose shall consist of two-thirds of the whole number of Senators, and a majority of the whole number shall be necessary to a choice. But no person constitutionally ineligible to the office of President shall be eligible to that of Vice-President of the United States.

Amendment XIII

Section 1

Neither slavery nor involuntary servitude, except as a punishment for crime whereof the party shall have been duly convicted, shall exist within the United States, or any place subject to their jurisdiction.

Section 2

Congress shall have power to enforce this article by appropriate legislation.

MORE ABOUT . . .

Racial Discrimination and the Constitution The Thirteenth, Fourteenth, and Fifteenth Amendments represent attempts to use the Constitution to end slavery, to extend citizenship to former enslaved persons, and to guarantee African Americans the right to vote. Literacy tests, poll taxes, and grandfather clauses, however, continued to keep large numbers of African Americans from voting in many Southern states even after Reconstruction.

Amendment XIV

Section 1

All persons born or naturalized in the United States, and subject to the jurisdiction thereof, are citizens of the United States and of the State wherein they reside. No State shall make or enforce any law which shall abridge the privileges or immunities of citizens of the United States; nor shall any State deprive any person of life, liberty, or property, without due process of law, nor deny to any person within its jurisdiction the equal protection of the laws.

Section 2

Representatives shall be apportioned among the several States according to their respective numbers, counting the whole number of persons in each State, excluding Indians not taxed. But when the right to vote at any election for the choice of electors for President and Vice-President of the United States, Representatives in Congress, the Executive and Judicial officers of a State, or the members of the Legislature thereof, is denied to any of the male inhabitants of such State, being twenty-one years of age, and citizens of the United States, or in any way abridged, except for participation in rebellion, or other crime, the basis of representation therein shall be reduced in the proportion which the number of such male citizens shall bear to the whole number of male citizens twenty-one years of age in such State.

Section 3

No person shall be a Senator or Representative in Congress, or elector of President and Vice-President, or hold any office, civil or military, under the United States, or under any State, who, having previously taken an oath, as a member of Congress, or as an officer of the United States, or as a member of any State legislature, or as an executive or judicial officer of any State, to support the Constitution of the United States, shall have engaged in insurrection or rebellion against the same, or given aid or comfort to the enemies thereof. But Congress may by a vote of two-thirds of each House, remove such disability.

Section 4

The validity of the public debt of the United States incurred for payment of pensions and bounties for service, authorized by law, including debts in suppressing insurrections or rebellion, shall not be questioned. But neither the United States nor any State shall assume or pay any debt or obligation incurred in aid of insurrection or rebellion against the United States, or any claim for the loss or emancipation of any slave; but all such debts, obligations and claims shall be held illegal and void.

Amendment 14.
Rights of Citizens (1868)

The clauses of this amendment were intended (1) to penalize Southern states that refused to grant African Americans the vote, (2) to keep former Confederate leaders from serving in government, (3) to forbid payment of the Confederacy's debt by the federal government, and (4) to ensure payment of the war debts owed the federal government.

Section 1. Citizenship Defined By granting citizenship to all persons born in the United States, this amendment granted citizenship to former slaves. The amendment also guaranteed "due process of law." By the 1950s, Supreme Court rulings used the due process clause to protect civil liberties. The last part of Section 1 establishes the doctrine that all citizens are entitled to equal protection of the laws. In 1954 the Supreme Court ruled, in *Brown* v. *Board of Education of Topeka,* that segregation in public schools was unconstitutional because it denied equal protection.

Section 2. Representation in Congress This section reduced the number of members a state had in the House of Representatives if it denied its citizens the right to vote. This section was not implemented, however. Later civil rights laws and the 24th Amendment guaranteed the vote to African Americans.

Section 3. Penalty for Engaging in Insurrection The leaders of the Confederacy were barred from state or federal offices unless Congress agreed to revoke this ban. By the end of Reconstruction all but a few Confederate leaders were allowed to return to public life.

Section 4. Public Debt The public debt incurred by the federal government during the Civil War was valid and could not be questioned by the South. However, the debts of the Confederacy were declared to be illegal. And former slaveholders could not collect compensation for the loss of their slaves.

THE AMENDMENTS

L2 Time Lines Have students make a time line that includes each of the amendments, the year of ratification, and significant concurrent political, economic, and social events. Encourage students to display and compare their time lines.

Who?What?Where?When?

American Citizens Section 1 of the Fourteenth Amendment sets out two of the three basic requirements of American citizenship—birth on American soil and naturalization. The third basic requirement is birth to a parent who is an American citizen.

MORE ABOUT . . .

Due Process of Law References to due process of law are made in the Fifth and Fourteenth Amendments. As a result of Supreme Court rulings, two types of due process have developed: procedural and substantive. Procedural due process requires that government use fair procedures in enforcing the law. Substantive due process requires that the laws under which the government acts be fair.

THE AMENDMENTS

L1, ELL Making Reasoned Judgments Inform students that, at times, the constitutional provisions protecting personal liberties have been sorely tested. One such test occurred during World War II, when more than 100,000 Japanese Americans were put into relocation camps as security risks. Ask students to discuss the following question: **In times of crisis, is the government justified in suspending personal liberties? Why or why not?**

Linking PAST & PRESENT

Political Reforms Direct election of senators was one of the many political reforms advanced by the Progressive movement.

Section 5. Enforcement Congress was empowered to pass civil rights bills to guarantee the provisions of the amendment.

Section 5

The Congress shall have power to enforce, by appropriate legislation, the provisions of this article.

Amendment 15.
The Right to Vote (1870)
Section 1. Suffrage for African Americans The 15th Amendment replaced Section 2 of the 14th Amendment in guaranteeing African Americans the right to vote; that is, the right of African Americans to vote was not to be left to the states. Yet, despite this prohibition, African Americans were denied the right to vote by many states by such means as poll taxes, literacy tests, and white primaries.
Section 2. Enforcement Congress was given the power to enforce this amendment. During the 1950s and 1960s, it passed successively stronger laws to end racial discrimination in voting rights.

Amendment XV

Section 1

The right of citizens of the United States to vote shall not be denied or abridged by the United States or by any State on account of race, color, or previous condition of servitude.

Section 2

The Congress shall have power to enforce this article by appropriate legislation.

Amendment 16.
Income Tax (1913)
The origins of this amendment went back to 1895, when the Supreme Court declared a federal income tax unconstitutional. To overcome this Supreme Court decision, this amendment authorized an income tax that was levied on a direct basis.

Amendment XVI

The Congress shall have power to lay and collect taxes on incomes, from whatever source derived, without apportionment among several States, and without regard to any census or enumeration.

Amendment 17.
Direct Election of Senators (1913)

Section 1. Method of Election The right to elect senators was given directly to the people of each state. It replaced Article I, Section 3, Clause 1, which empowered state legislatures to elect senators. This amendment was designed not only to make the choice of senators more democratic but also to cut down on corruption and to improve state government.

Section 2. Vacancies A state must order an election to fill a Senate vacancy. A state may empower its governor to appoint a person to fill a Senate seat if a vacancy occurs until an election can be held.

Section 3. Time in Effect This amendment was not to affect any Senate election or temporary appointment until it was in effect.

Amendment XVII

Section 1

The Senate of the United States shall be composed of two Senators from each State, elected by the people thereof, for six years; and each Senator shall have one vote. The electors in each state shall have the qualifications requisite for electors of the most numerous branch of the state legislatures.

Section 2

When vacancies happen in the representation of any State in the Senate, the executive authority of such State shall issue writs of election to fill such vacancies: *Provided*, that the legislature of any State may empower the executive thereof to make temporary appointments until the people fill the vacancies by election as the legislature may direct.

Section 3

This amendment shall not be so construed as to affect the election or term of any Senator chosen before it becomes valid as part of the Constitution.

MORE ABOUT . . .

The Poll Tax After the Civil War, poll taxes were levied in many Southern states. Although the poll tax kept many low-income white males from voting, its major purpose was to keep African Americans away from the polls. Not until the 1960s did Congress take firm action to enforce the guarantee of the Fifteenth Amendment and end this kind of racial discrimination.

Amendment XVIII

Section 1

After one year from ratification of this article the manufacture, sale, or transportation of intoxicating liquors within, the importation thereof into, or the exportation thereof from the United States and all territory subject to the jurisdiction thereof for beverage purposes is hereby prohibited.

Section 2

The Congress and the several states shall have concurrent power to enforce this article by appropriate legislation.

Section 3

This article shall be inoperative unless it shall have been ratified as an amendment to the Constitution by the legislatures of the several States, as provided in the Constitution, within seven years from the date of the submission hereof to the states of the Congress.

Amendment XIX

Section 1

The right of citizens of the United States to vote shall not be denied or abridged by the United States or by any state on account of sex.

Section 2

Congress shall have power to enforce this article by appropriate legislation.

Amendment XX

Section 1

The terms of the President and Vice President shall end at noon on the 20th day of January, and the terms of the Senators and Representatives at noon on the 3rd day of January, of the years in which such terms would have ended if this article had not been ratified; and the terms of their successors shall then begin.

Section 2

The Congress shall assemble at least once in every year, and such meeting shall begin at noon on the 3rd day of January, unless they shall by law appoint a different day.

Amendment 18.
Prohibition of Alcoholic Beverages (1919)

This amendment prohibited the production, sale, or transportation of alcoholic beverages in the United States. Prohibition proved to be difficult to enforce, especially in states with large urban populations. This amendment was later repealed by the 21st Amendment.

Amendment 19.
Woman Suffrage (1920)

This amendment, extending the vote to all qualified women in federal and state elections, was a landmark victory for the woman suffrage movement, which had worked to achieve this goal for many years. The women's movement had earlier gained full voting rights for women in four Western states in the late nineteenth century.

Amendment 20.
"Lame-Duck" Amendment (1933)

Section 1. New Dates of Terms This amendment had two major purposes: (1) to shorten the time between the president's and vice president's election and inauguration, and (2) to end "lame-duck" sessions of Congress.

When the Constitution first went into effect, transportation and communication were slow and uncertain. It often took many months after the election in November for the president and vice president to travel to Washington, D.C., and prepare for their inauguration on March 4. This amendment ended this long wait for a new administration by fixing January 20 as Inauguration Day.

Section 2. Meeting Time of Congress "Lame-duck" sessions occurred every two years, after the November congressional election. That is, the Congress that held its session in December of an election year was not the newly elected Congress but the old Congress that had been elected two years earlier. This Congress continued to serve for several more months, usually until March of the next year. Often many of its members had failed to be reelected and were called "lame-ducks." The 20th Amendment abolished this lame-duck session, and provided that the new Congress hold its first session soon after the November election, on January 3.

THE AMENDMENTS

L2 Writing Reports Point out that a number of states preceded the national government in giving women the vote. Encourage students to research the fight for woman suffrage in these states. Ask them to present their findings in written reports.

ABCNEWS INTERACTIVE™

VIDEODISC
Powers of the Supreme Court

Side 1, Chapter 26
Title: *Amendment 19 (1920): Woman Suffrage*
Subject: Brief history of woman suffrage
Ask: **Who was given the right to vote with the passage of the Nineteenth Amendment?** *(women)*

CRITICAL THINKING ACTIVITY

Analyzing Information Make sure that students understand the "lame-duck" issue by reminding them that lame ducks are presidents and members of Congress waiting to leave office after retiring or failing to gain reelection. Since lame ducks often were members of the defeated party, they were in a position to affect legislation even though they no longer spoke for the majority of voters. Then ask students to note how the Twentieth Amendment addressed this problem. *(It shortened the waiting period between Election Day and the beginning of a new term.)* **L1**

THE AMENDMENTS

L1 Categorizing Information Have students categorize on a chart the amendments according to the following headings: *Personal freedoms, Relations among states, Process of government, Citizenship.* They should keep in mind the substance of the amendment and its affect on American life. Remind students that some amendments might fit in more than one category.

What?Where?When?Who?

Prohibition Although Prohibition caused many problems, it did succeed in reducing the consumption of alcohol in the United States, thus decreasing the number of alcohol-related deaths and accidents.

Section 3. Succession of President and Vice President This amendment provides that if the president-elect dies before taking office, the vice president-elect becomes president. In the cases described, Congress will decide on a temporary president.

Section 3

If, at the time fixed for the beginning of the term of the President, the President elect shall have died, the Vice President elect shall become President. If a President shall not have been chosen before the time fixed for the beginning of his term, or if the President elect shall have failed to qualify, then the Vice President elect shall act as President until a President shall have qualified; and the Congress may by law provide for the case wherein neither a President elect nor a Vice President elect shall have qualified, declaring who shall then act as President, or the manner in which one who is to act shall be selected, and such person shall act accordingly until a President or Vice President shall have qualified.

Section 4. Filling Presidential Vacancy If a presidential candidate dies while an election is being decided in the House, Congress may pass legislation to deal with the situation. Congress has similar power if this occurs when the Senate is deciding a vice-presidential election.

Section 4

The Congress may by law provide for the case of the death of any of the persons from whom the House of Representatives may choose a President whenever the right of choice shall have devolved upon them, and for the case of the death of any of the persons from whom the Senate may choose a Vice President whenever the right of choice shall have devolved upon them.

Section 5. Beginning the New Dates Sections 1 and 2 affected the Congress elected in 1934 and President Roosevelt, elected in 1936.

Section 5

Sections 1 and 2 shall take effect on the 15th day of October following the ratification of this article.

Section 6. Time Limit on Ratification The period for ratification by the states was limited to seven years.

Section 6

This article shall be inoperative unless it shall have been ratified as an amendment to the Constitution by the legislatures of three-fourths of the several States within seven years from the date of its submission.

Amendment 21. Repeal of Prohibition Amendment (1933)

This amendment nullified the 18th Amendment. It is the only amendment ever passed to overturn an earlier amendment. It remained unlawful to transport alcoholic beverages into states that forbade their use. It is the only amendment ratified by special state conventions instead of state legislatures.

Amendment XXI

Section 1

The eighteenth article of amendment to the Constitution of the United States is hereby repealed.

Section 2

The transportation or importation into any State, Territory, or possession of the United States for delivery or use therein of intoxicating liquors, in violation of the laws thereof, is hereby prohibited.

Section 3

This article shall be inoperative unless it shall have been ratified as an amendment to the Constitution by conventions in the several States, as provided in the Constitution, within seven years from the date of the submission hereof to the States by the Congress.

COOPERATIVE LEARNING ACTIVITY

Debate Form groups of students to debate the pros and cons of Prohibition. Give groups time to prepare their arguments and encourage each group member to be responsible for a different part of the research. As each group presents its argument, note major points on the chalkboard. When groups have completed the debate, lead the class in a discussion of the following question: Is Prohibition an issue that should have been addressed in a constitutional amendment? Why or why not?

Amendment XXII

Section 1

No person shall be elected to the office of the President more than twice, and no person who had held the office of President, or acted as President, for more than two years of a term to which some other person was elected President shall be elected to the office of the President more than once.

But this Article shall not apply to any person holding the office of President when this Article was proposed by the Congress, and shall not prevent any person who may be holding the office of President, or acting as President, during the term within which this Article becomes operative from holding the office of President or acting as President during the remainder of such term.

Section 2

This article shall be inoperative unless it shall have been ratified as an amendment to the Constitution by the legislatures of three-fourths of the several States within seven years from the date of its submission to the States by the Congress.

Amendment XXIII

Section 1

The District constituting the seat of Government of the United States shall appoint in such manner as the Congress may direct:

A number of electors of President and Vice President equal to the whole number of Senators and Representatives in Congress to which the District would be entitled if it were a State, but in no event more than the least populous State; they shall be in addition to those appointed by the States, but they shall be considered, for the purposes of the election of President and Vice President, to be electors appointed by a State; and they shall meet in the District and perform such duties as provided by the twelfth article of amendment.

Section 2

The Congress shall have power to enforce this article by appropriate legislation.

Amendment 22.
Limit on Presidential Terms (1951)

This amendment wrote into the Constitution a custom started by Washington, Jefferson, and Madison, whereby presidents limited themselves to two terms in office. Although both Ulysses S. Grant and Theodore Roosevelt sought third terms, the two-term precedent was not broken until Franklin D. Roosevelt was elected to a third term in 1940 and then a fourth term in 1944. The passage of the 22nd Amendment ensures that no president is to be considered indispensable. It also provides that anyone who succeeds to the presidency and serves for more than two years of the term may not be elected more than one more time.

Presidential campaign button

Amendment 23.
Presidential Electors for the District of Columbia (1961)

This amendment granted people living in the District of Columbia the right to vote in presidential elections. The District casts three electoral votes. The people of Washington, D.C., still are without representation in Congress.

THE AMENDMENTS

L2 Expressing Viewpoints Write the following statement on the chalkboard: That the people of Washington, D.C., have no representation in Congress is a violation of their democratic rights. Call on volunteers to express their views on this statement.

ABCNEWS INTERACTIVE™

VIDEODISC
Powers of the Supreme Court

Side 1, Chapter 27
Title: *Amendment 21 (1933): Repeal of Prohibition*
Subject: Roosevelt's signing of the Twenty-first Amendment
Ask: **Which amendment did the Twenty-first Amendment repeal?** *(It repealed the Eighteenth Amendment, which prohibited the manufacture, sale, and purchase of alcoholic beverages.)*

CRITICAL THINKING ACTIVITY

Evaluating Information Have students list the advantages and disadvantages of the two-term limit for presidents. Ask volunteers to present and defend their lists. Then have students discuss the following: Should there be presidential term limits? If so, how many terms should the president be limited to? Should members of Congress have term limits? Why or why not? **L2**

THE AMENDMENTS

Who?What?Where?When?

Disabled Presidents The United States has had a disabled president several times in its history. In the 1880s James Garfield lingered 80 days in a coma before succumbing to an assassin's bullet. In this century Woodrow Wilson suffered a stroke that incapacitated him for the last several months of his presidency.

NATIONAL GEOGRAPHIC SOCIETY

CD-ROM
The Presidents: A Picture History of Our Nation

Have students choose Garfield or Wilson from the main menu. Suggest that students search for information about how the presidents' disabilities may have affected the presidency of each.

Amendment 24.
Abolition of the Poll Tax (1964)

A "poll tax" was a fee that persons were required to pay in order to vote in a number of Southern states. This amendment ended poll taxes as a requirement to vote in any presidential or congressional election. In 1966 the Supreme Court voided poll taxes in state elections as well.

Amendment 25.
Presidential Disability and Succession (1967)

Section 1. Replacing the President The vice president becomes president if the president dies, resigns, or is removed from office.

Section 2. Replacing the Vice President The president is to appoint a new vice president in case of a vacancy in that office, with the approval of the Congress.

The 25th Amendment is unusually precise and explicit because it was intended to solve a serious constitutional problem. Sixteen times in American history, before passage of this amendment, the office of vice president was vacant, but fortunately in none of these cases did the president die or resign.

This amendment was used in 1973, when Vice President Spiro Agnew resigned from office after being charged with accepting bribes. President Richard Nixon then appointed Gerald R. Ford as vice president in accordance with the provisions of the 25th Amendment. A year later, President Nixon resigned during the Watergate scandal, and Ford became president. President Ford then had to fill the vice presidency, which he had left vacant upon assuming the presidency. He named Nelson A. Rockefeller as vice president. Thus both the presidency and vice presidency were held by men who had not been elected to their offices.

Section 3. Replacing the President With Consent If the president informs Congress, in writing, that he or she cannot carry out the duties of the office of president, the vice president becomes acting president.

Section 4. Replacing the President Without Consent If the president is unable to carry out the duties of the office but is unable or unwilling to so notify Congress, the cabinet and the vice president are to inform Congress of this fact. The vice president then becomes acting president. The procedure by which the president may regain the office if he or she recovers is also spelled out in this amendment.

Amendment XXIV

Section 1

The right of citizens of the United States to vote in any primary or other election for President or Vice President, for electors for President or Vice President, or for Senator or Representative in Congress, shall not be denied or abridged by the United States or any State by reason of failure to pay any poll tax or other tax.

Section 2

The Congress shall have power to enforce this article by appropriate legislation.

Amendment XXV

Section 1

In case of the removal of the President from office or his death or resignation, the Vice President shall become President.

Section 2

Whenever there is a vacancy in the office of the Vice President, the President shall nominate a Vice President who shall take the office upon confirmation by a majority vote of both houses of Congress.

Section 3

Whenever the President transmits to the President pro tempore of the Senate and the Speaker of the House of Representatives his written declaration that he is unable to discharge the powers and duties of his office, and until he transmits to them a written declaration to the contrary, such powers and duties shall be discharged by the Vice President as Acting President.

Section 4

Whenever the Vice President and a majority of either the principal officers of the executive departments or of such other body as Congress may by law provide, transmit to the President pro tempore of the Senate and the Speaker of the House of Representatives their written declaration that the President is unable to discharge the powers and duties of his office, the Vice President shall immediately assume the power and duties of the office of Acting President.

Thereafter, when the President transmits to the President pro tempore of the Senate and the Speaker of the House of Representatives his written declaration that no inability exists, he shall resume the powers and duties of his office unless the Vice President and a majority of either the principal officers of the executive departments or of such other body as Congress may by law provide, transmit within four days to the President pro tempore of the Senate and the Speaker of the House of Representatives their written declaration that the President is unable

MORE ABOUT . . .

The Twenty-fifth Amendment The assassination of President John F. Kennedy made the need for a constitutional amendment on presidential disability apparent. Kennedy's successor, Lyndon Johnson, had once suffered a heart attack, and the two men in line of succession after Johnson were both over 70 years old. Congress quickly passed the Twenty-fifth Amendment, which was submitted to the states in mid-1965 and was ratified early in 1967.

to discharge the powers and duties of his office. Thereupon Congress shall decide the issue, assembling within forty-eight hours for that purpose if not in session. If the Congress within twenty-one days after receipt of the latter written declaration, or, if Congress is not in session, within twenty-one days after Congress is required to assemble, determines by two-thirds vote of both houses that the President is unable to discharge the powers and duties of his office, the Vice President shall continue to discharge the same as Acting President; otherwise, the President shall resume the power and duties of his office.

Amendment XXVI

Section 1

The right of citizens of the United States, who are eighteen years of age or older, to vote shall not be denied or abridged by the United States or by any State on account of age.

Section 2

The Congress shall have power to enforce this article by appropriate legislation.

Amendment 26.
Eighteen-Year-Old Vote (1971)
This amendment made 18-year-olds eligible to vote in all federal, state, and local elections. Until then, the minimum age had been 21 in most states.

Amendment XXVII

No law, varying the compensation for the services of Senators and Representatives, shall take effect, until an election of Representatives shall have intervened.

Amendment 27.
Restraint on Congressional Salaries (1992)
Any increase in the salaries of members of Congress will take effect in the subsequent session of Congress.

Joint meeting of Congress

THE AMENDMENTS

What?Where?When?Who?

The Twenty-sixth Amendment Many people used the Vietnam War to justify the adoption of the Twenty-sixth Amendment. These people argued that those old enough to fight and die for their country were also old enough to vote.

ABCNEWS INTERACTIVE™

VIDEODISC
Powers of the Supreme Court

Side 1, Chapter 30
Title: *Amendment 26 (1971): Suffrage for 18-year-olds*
Subject: Testimony during congressional hearings
Ask: **What was suggested as the reason for protests and riots in the 1970s by young people?**
(It was suggested that, because young people could not vote, protests were the only way they could express unhappiness with the government.)

COOPERATIVE LEARNING ACTIVITY

Writing a School Constitution Have students form a group to write a constitution for your school. Students should begin the document with a preamble that lists goals for school government. Each group member should write an article describing one branch of the school government. Be certain groups list the functions of each branch. Then, as a group, have students decide if they think some powers should be denied to the school government and list these in another article. Finally, decide if a bill of rights is necessary. If so, have students list the rights they think should be added. **L1**

Unit 4 Resource Guide

These Glencoe resources may be used to teach, reteach, or enrich the concepts presented in this unit of study.

TEACHING TRANSPARENCIES

Map Transparency 4 with Overlays A, B, C, D

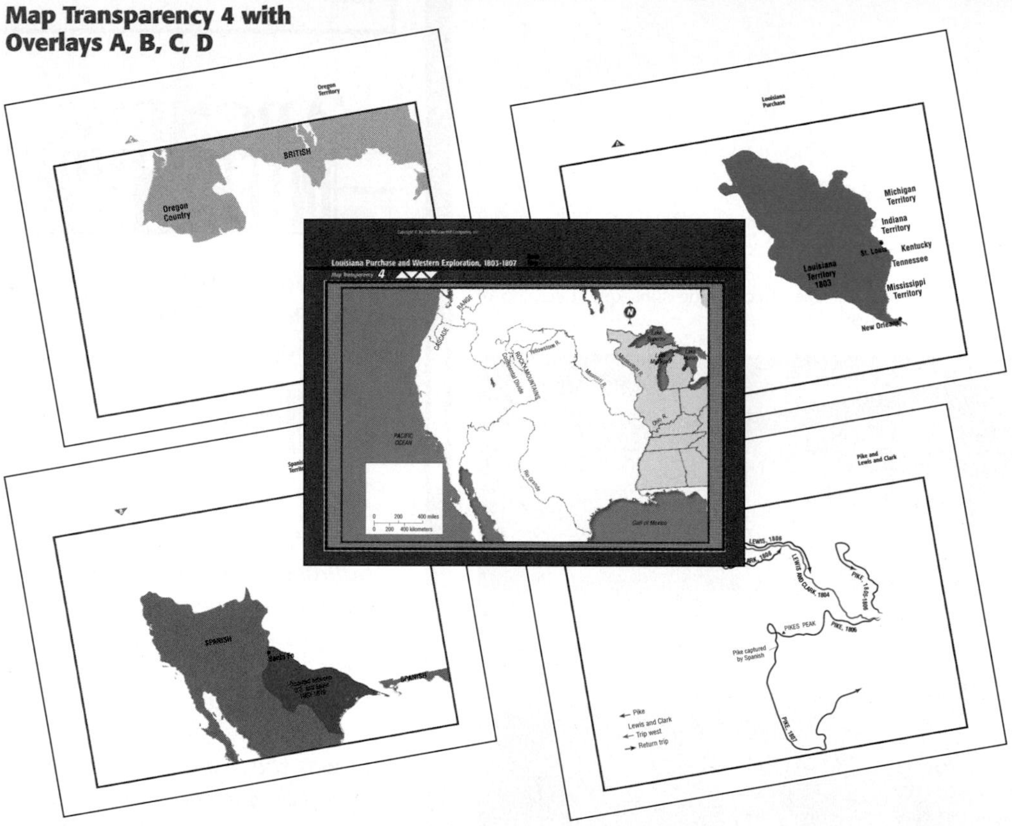

Cause-and-Effect Transparency 4

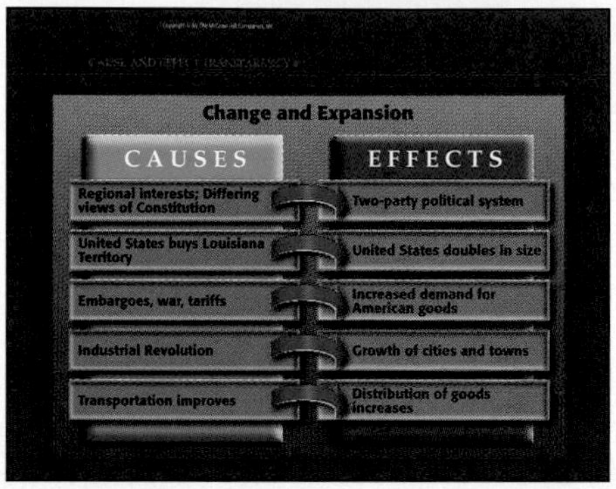

BIBLIOGRAPHY

Readings for the Student

O'Dell, Scott. ***Streams to the River, River to the Sea: A Novel of Sacagawea.*** Boston: Houghton Mifflin, 1986. Told as a first-person narrative.

Tunis, Edwin. ***The Young United States, 1783 to 1830.*** New York: World Publishing, 1969. Well-illustrated social history.

Reading for the Teacher

Boorstin, Daniel J. ***The Americans: The Democratic Experience.*** New York: Random House, 1973. Social history.

Multimedia Resources

Videocassette. ***The Adams Chronicles.*** American Film Foundation. VHS or Beta video. Produced by WNET New York. Distributed by Films Inc. Video. 1976. Series. The story of the Adams family from pre-Revolutionary times to the Industrial Revolution.

Videocassette. ***City Out of Wilderness: Washington.*** VHS or Beta video. Produced by U.S. Capitol Historical Society. Distributed by Films Inc. Video. 1975. Documents, photographs tell the story of the capital.

Videocassette. ***In Search of Justice.*** VHS or Beta video. Produced by Terry Sanders, American Film Foundation. Distributed by Barr Films, Irwindale, CA. 1979. Survey of the United States judicial system.

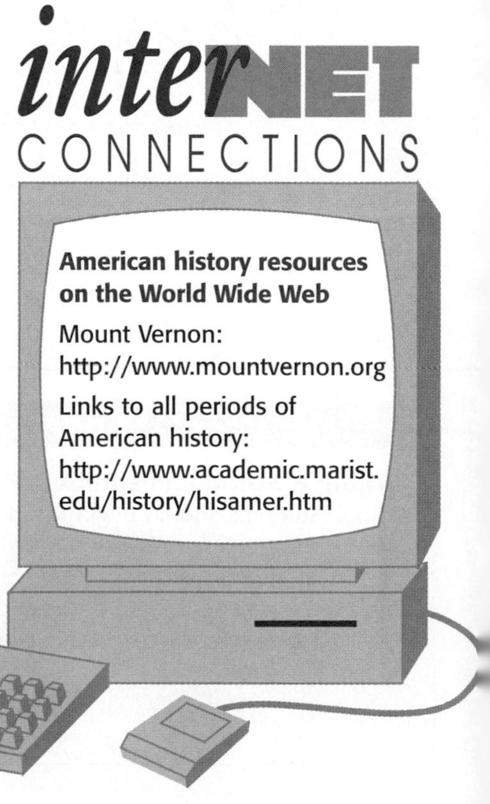

Resource Guide Unit 4

INTERDISCIPLINARY ACTIVITIES

American Literature Reading 4

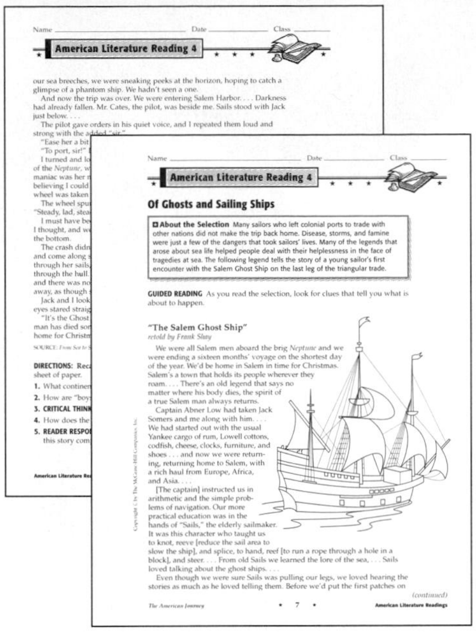

Interdisciplinary Connection 4

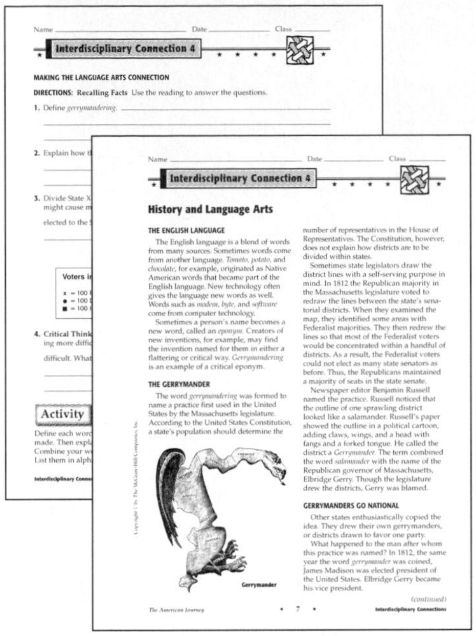

ENRICHMENT ACTIVITIES

Cooperative Learning Activity 4

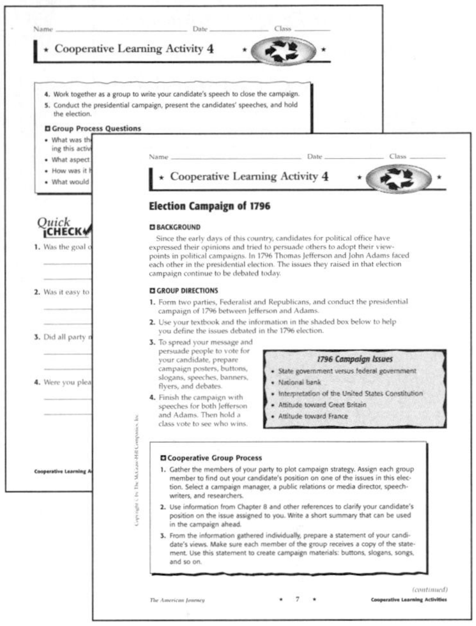

HANDS-ON ACTIVITIES

Hands-On History Lab Activity 4

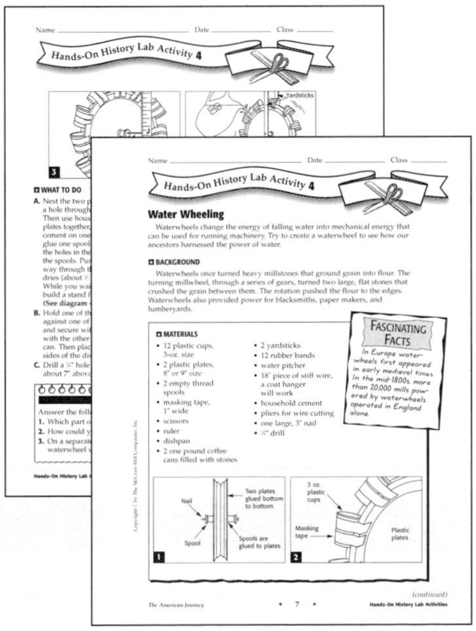

History Simulation 4

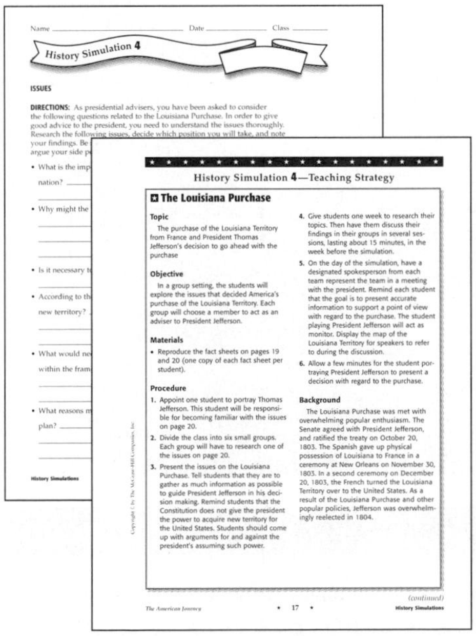

ASSESSMENT

Unit 4 Test

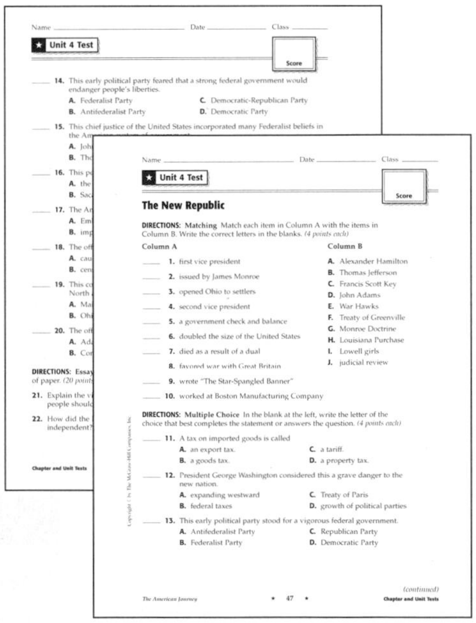

0:00 OUT OF TIME?

If your teaching time is limited, you may use the *Chapter Summaries* blackline master found in the TCR with the *Chapter Digests Audiocassette Activities and Tests* to condense individual chapters into a one-day lesson.

Introducing the Unit

Activity Have students skim the chapters in the unit, looking at headings and photographs. Tell them that as they do so, they should be thinking about questions they hope to have answered by the time they finish the unit. Make a class list of about 10 questions. Use the list in reviewing the unit.

Unit Objectives

Upon completing this unit, students will be able to:

1. List highlights of the new government, including economic, political, and foreign affairs.
2. Identify and discuss the importance of various aspects of the Jefferson era, including strengthening the Supreme Court, acquisition of the Louisiana Territory, and conflicts with Native Americans, Barbary pirates, and Great Britain.
3. Discuss the Industrial Revolution and its effects; explain how sectionalism developed; summarize the Monroe Doctrine and the independence movement in Latin America.

Hands-On HISTORY

Hands-On History Lab Activity 4, "Water Wheeling," is a high-interest **constructivist approach** activity directly related to the main topic of the unit.

Unit 4

The New Republic

1789–1825

"I walk on untrodden ground."

—GEORGE WASHINGTON, 1789

MAPPING *America*

Portfolio Activity Draw a freehand outline map of the United States. As you read about the expansion of the United States's borders in this unit, note this expansion on your map. Include the boundaries of the Louisiana Purchase, the 10 states admitted to the Union between 1791 and 1821, and the movement of settlers into western lands.

252

Compass used in Lewis and Clark expedition, 1804–1805

Factory spool

United States

1789 George Washington sworn in as first president

1791 Bill of Rights is ratified

1793 Eli Whitney invents cotton gin

1796 John Adams is elected president

1785 — *1795*

1791 Toussaint-Louverture leads revolt in Haiti

1789 French Revolution begins

World

TEAM TEACHING STRATEGIES

Science Have the class work with the Science or Health teacher (or the school nurse) to investigate how diseases such as cholera and yellow fever—a deadly threat in early cities—have been brought under control in the developing world. Cholera—which is spread by fecal-contaminated food and water—is still prevalent in parts of Asia, Africa, and South America where public sanitation is poor. Yellow fever, caused by a virus carried by mosquitoes, has been largely eliminated.

HISTORY AND ART ***Election Day in Philadelphia*** **by John Krimmel** An Election Day crowd gathers in front of the Pennsylvania State House (Independence Hall) in Philadelphia. With the ratification of the Constitution, the United States set out to establish a new government.

Pitcher honoring Washington's inauguration, 1789

- **1801** Thomas Jefferson becomes president
- **1803** United States buys Louisiana Territory
- **1804** Napoleon Bonaparte becomes emperor of France
- **1805**
- **1807** Slave trade is abolished in British Empire
- **1811** Native Americans defeated at Battle of Tippecanoe
- **1814** Treaty of Ghent ends War of 1812
- **1815**
- **1819** Simón Bolívar elected president of Greater Colombia
- **1820** Missouri Compromise is reached
- **1820** Liberia is founded in Africa
- **1821** Mexico declares independence from Spain
- **1825** Erie Canal opens

Team Teaching Strategies

Music Have the class work with the Music teacher to learn the song "The Erie Canal," which became very popular in the canal-building era. **Ask:** **What lyrics in the song explain why canal craft could not be very tall?** *(Low bridge, everybody down)* **Why was the worker's mule (Sal) important?** *(Canal craft were pulled by mules.)* Students might be interested to know that steam-powered boats could not be used at first for fear of damage to the earthen sides of the canals. They were used later, after the sides of the canals had been reinforced with stone.

NATIONAL GEOGRAPHIC SOCIETY

VIDEODISC
GTV: The American People: Fabric of a Nation

Side 2, Chapter 1
Title: *Picture This*
Subject: America's first century, people by people
Ask: **What factors determined the role a person took in the nation's growth?** *(who you were, what color you were, how long your family had lived in America)*

HISTORY AND ART John Krimmel (1786–1821), who was born in Germany and emigrated to the United States in 1810, began the American tradition of genre painting (showing ordinary people doing ordinary things).

Linking PAST & *PRESENT*

Activity The first documented bicycle was made in France in the late 1700s. Called a *celerifere* (swift footed), it had no pedals but was propelled by the rider's feet pushing the ground. By 1813 a celerifere had appeared in America. Have students read about changes in bicycle design that have taken place over the years and make labeled drawings showing those changes. One good source is *Two Hundred Years of Bicycles* by Jim Murphy (New York: Lippincott, 1983).

Block Schedule

Team Teaching This selection from *Night Flying Woman* may be implemented in a team-teaching context with English/Language Arts.

Reinforcing Vocabulary

Review the **Reader's Dictionary** terms with students to be sure they understand any unfamiliar terms.

Historical Connection

In the early 1800s the Ojibway occupied areas around the Great Lakes, stretching from Canada through the present-day states of Michigan, Ohio, Indiana, Wisconsin, Minnesota, and North Dakota. Their communities usually were in remote, forested regions far from white settlements. By the 1830s, however, the westward movement of the United States's frontier had begun to encroach on Ojibway lands.

Background Information

Setting This excerpt describes part of the experiences of eight Ojibway families during their trip from their native home to a new home where they will not be in conflict with new strangers (white people).

Characters The major character in *Night Flying Woman* is Ni-bo-wi-se-gwe, which means "Night Flying Woman." *Oona* is the nickname given to Ni-bo-wi-se-gwe by her family. Other major characters are A-wa-sa-si (storyteller); Oona's father Me-ow-ga-bo (Outstanding); Oona's mother Wa-wi-e-cu-mig-go-gwe (Round Earth); Oona's friend E-quay (Lady); and her grandparents.

Plot This book is a story about the traditions of the Ojibway people, and their desire to pass their culture on to future generations of Ojibway. The book is also about the impact on Ojibway culture by contact with white people.

Night Flying Woman

by Ignatia Broker

Born on the White Earth Ojibway Reservation in Minnesota, Ignatia Broker (1919–1987) grew up hearing the stories of her people. She decided that one day she would tell others about Ojibway traditions. Through her writing, Broker passed on many Ojibway tales about "the purity of man and nature and keeping them in balance."

Read to Discover

Night Flying Woman tells the story of Oona, Ignatia Broker's great-great-grandmother. Oona was still a child when the Ojibway were forced to leave their land and find a new home. As you read, look for the ways in which Oona overcomes her fears. What gives the Ojibway people faith that they will continue as a people?

Reader's Dictionary

Gitchi Manito: Great Spirit

Anishinabe: Ojibway name for "people"

On this, the fifth night of their travels, after the people had given thanks and eaten the evening meal, there was a firelight council. The people decided to stay on this small lake for two days while three of the men went deep into the forest to look for the new place.

The next morning, very early, Grandfather, Oldest Uncle, and Father walked into the thick forest. Oona did not see them leave, for she was sleeping soundly. When Mother told her that they were gone, Oona looked at the forest fearfully. It seemed very unfriendly. She thought, "It has swallowed up my grandfather and father." She became fretful.

Mother said, "Daughter, look at the forest again but do not look and see only the dark and shadows. Instead, look at the trees, each one, as many as you can. Then tell me what you think."

Oona looked at the trees. Then she walked to the forest's edge to see them better. There were many, many kinds of trees. Some were tall, so tall that they must surely touch the sky, thought Oona. Instead of leaves they had needles that were long and pointed like porcupine quills. Beneath these tall trees smaller ones reached up, as if in friendship. As Oona looked at the trees, she heard the si-si-gwa-d—the murmuring that the trees do when they brush their branches together. It was a friendly sound, and the sun sent sparkles through the si-si-gwa-d that chased the shadows. Suddenly the forest seemed different to Oona, and she knew that Grandfather, Oldest Uncle, and Father had gone into a friendly place.

"Mother," said Oona, "I have the feeling now that the trees are glad we are

Additional Literary Works of the Period

You may refer students to the following:

Collier, James Lincoln, and Christopher Collier. ***The Clock.*** New York: Delacorte Press, 1992. Fictional account of a girl's life in a textile mill.

Cooper, James Fenimore. ***The Pioneers.*** New York: Bantam, 1993. Natty Bumppo struggles against the encroachments of civilization on the New York State frontier.

Emrich, Duncan, ed. ***American Folk Poetry: An Anthology.*** New York: Little, Brown, 1974. Folk song lyrics, ballads, and poems.

Fritz, Jean. ***The Great Little Madison.*** New York: Putnam, 1989. Interesting biography.

Longfellow, Henry Wadsworth. ***The Poetical Works of Longfellow.*** Boston: Houghton Mifflin, 1975. Works from one of the most popular writers of the nineteenth century.

Pine forest, northern Minnesota

here. The forest is happy and I know that we will be happy, too."

"That is good, my daughter, for I also have the feeling that this will be a good and happy place." A-wa-sa-si and Grandmother, who had been listening, nodded their heads in agreement.

A-wa-sa-si said, "The forests have never failed the Ojibway. The trees are the glory of the Gitchi Manito. The trees, for as long as they shall stand, will give shelter and life to the Anishinabe and the Animal Brothers. They are a gift. As long as the Ojibway are beneath, the trees will murmur with contentment. When the Ojibway and the Animal Brothers are gone, the forest will weep and this will be reflected in the sound of the si-si-gwa-d. My grandmother told me this is so, and her grandmother told her. When the forest weeps, the Anishinabe who listen will look back at the years. In each generation of Ojibway there will be a person who will hear the si-si-gwa-d, who will listen and remember and pass it on to the children. Remembering our past and acting accordingly will ensure that we, the Ojibway, will always people the earth. The trees have patience and so they have stood and have seen many generations of Ojibway. Yet will there be more, and yet will they see more."

Responding to Literature

1. Why did Oona's father, uncle, and grandfather go into the forest?
2. What sound did Oona hear in the forest? How did the sound affect Oona's feelings about the forest?

Activity

Making an Illustration Create a painting or drawing that shows the forest as Oona saw it. Use symbols to hint at the coming of the Europeans.

Answers to Responding to Literature

1. They were looking for a new place to settle.
2. si-si-gwa-d, the sound of the leaves brushing together; It made her feel that the forest was friendly, not threatening.

Activity Drawings should reflect Oona's feeling that the forest was a friendly place. Drawings should also depict the coming of the Europeans in some way.

History *and the* Humanities

U.S. History & Art, Transparency 6, *The Great Blue Heron;* Transparency 7, *The Buffalo Chase, Mouth of the Yellowstone*

Political Cartoons, *Native Americans and a Nation of Immigrants*

Portfolio Activity

Have students write a description of a family tradition in their own family or something they value that they would like to pass on to future generations. Descriptions should include an explanation of why the tradition is important to them.

At the Movies

There are hundreds of movies dealing with Native Americans. *Dances With Wolves* portrays Native Americans in a positive light. Other movies that might be appropriate are any of the four versions (1920, 1936, 1977, and 1992) of the action-filled *Last of the Mohicans.*

Curriculum Connection

GEOGRAPHY

In the 1600s, the Ojibway (or Ojibwa) lived along Lake Superior. They drove the Sioux away from the region to gain control of the lands where wild rice grew. Some Ojibway migrated west as far as the plains of North Dakota. Today the descendants of the Ojibway (also known as the Chippewa) live mainly in Canada, Minnesota, and Michigan and make up one of the largest Native American groups north of Mexico.

Chapter 8 Planning Guide

A complete, 1-page lesson plan is provided for each section in the *Reproducible Lesson Plans* booklet.

Section Resources

Daily Objectives	Reproducible Resources	Multimedia Resources
Section 1 **The First President** Explain the roles of Congress, Washington, and Hamilton in launching the new government and strengthening the nation's credit and economy.	Reproducible Lesson Plan 8–1 Guided Reading Activity 8–1* Section Quiz 8–1* Reteaching Activity 8–1 Enrichment Activity 8–1	Section Focus Transparency 8–1 Vocabulary PuzzleMaker Chapter Challenger Interactive Review Software Testmaker Facts On File: Landmark Documents in American History The Presidents: A Picture History of Our Nation
Section 2 **Early Challenges** Describe how the new government exerted its power domestically, but tried to avoid foreign involvement.	Reproducible Lesson Plan 8–2 Guided Reading Activity 8–2* Section Quiz 8–2* Reteaching Activity 8–2 Enrichment Activity 8–2	Section Focus Transparency 8–2 Vocabulary PuzzleMaker Chapter Challenger Interactive Review Software Testmaker GTV: The American People: Fabric of a Nation
Section 3 **The First Political Parties** Summarize the formation of political parties and their positions, including the candidates of the election of 1796.	Reproducible Lesson Plan 8–3 Guided Reading Activity 8–3* Section Quiz 8–3* Reteaching Activity 8–3 Enrichment Activity 8–3	Section Focus Transparency 8–3 U.S. History & Art, Transparency 8, *George Washington* Vocabulary PuzzleMaker Chapter Challenger Interactive Review Software Testmaker Focus on American Art Prints, *Athenaeum Portrait of George Washington* by Gilbert Stuart
Section 4 **President John Adams** Explain the relationship between the undeclared war with France and the Alien and Sedition acts.	Reproducible Lesson Plan 8–4 Guided Reading Activity 8–4* Political Cartoons, *The XYZ Affair* Section Quiz 8–4* Reteaching Activity 8–4 Enrichment Activity 8–4	Section Focus Transparency 8–4 Vocabulary PuzzleMaker Chapter Challenger Interactive Review Software Testmaker Facts On File: Landmark Documents in American History

** Also available in Spanish*

Poster · Transparency · CD-ROM · Software
Blackline Master · Videodisc · Audiocassette · Music Program

0:00 OUT OF TIME?
Assign the Chapter 8 Digest and the corresponding Chapter Digests Audiocassettes with activities and tests.

Activity

From the Classroom of...

Carolyn Steinbrink
Shenandoah Middle School
Shenandoah, IA

Illustrating Reading Assignments

Students will illustrate the main ideas of the chapter. They will need several sheets of plain paper and colored pens and pencils for this activity. First, have students write a list of the main ideas and topics they encountered in their reading assignment, such as Washington's actions as president, the Whiskey Rebellion, the rise of political parties, and so on. As students read, have them create a design incorporating these topics.

The design itself should relate to the main ideas of the reading—for example, Washington's accomplishments as president could be listed on branches of a cherry tree or within the pillars of the White House. The finished product could be as simple as a sketch of a road with the topics arranged on "highway" signs in chronological order. As you discuss the chapter in class, have students share their artwork and explain their topics.

Block Schedule

Block scheduling differs from traditional class scheduling in the amount of time allotted to each period. The extended time frame provided by block scheduling affords you the opportunity to implement a greater number of research-oriented and activity-intense projects to motivate and involve your students. Activities that are particularly suited to use within the block scheduling framework are identified throughout this chapter by the following designation:

NATIONAL GEOGRAPHIC SOCIETY Teacher's Corner

INDEX TO NATIONAL GEOGRAPHIC MAGAZINE

The following articles may be used for research relating to this chapter:

- "L'Enfant's Washington," by Alice J. Hall, August 1991.
- "The Peales: America's First Family of Art," by Otto Friedrich, December 1990.

NATIONAL GEOGRAPHIC SOCIETY PRODUCTS AVAILABLE FROM GLENCOE

To order the following products for use with this chapter, contact your local Glencoe sales representative, or call Glencoe at 1-800-334-7344:

- *GTV: The American People: Fabric of a Nation* (Videodisc)
- *GTV: A Geographic Perspective on American History* (Videodisc)
- *The Presidents: A Picture History of Our Nation* (CD-ROM)

ADDITIONAL NATIONAL GEOGRAPHIC SOCIETY PRODUCTS

To order the following products for use with this chapter, call National Geographic Society at 1-800-368-2728:

- *Washington, D.C.* (Video)
- *Historical Atlas of the United States* (Atlas)

KEY TO ABILITY LEVELS

Teaching strategies have been coded for varying learning styles and abilities.

L1 **BASIC** activities for all students
L2 **AVERAGE** activities for average to above-average students
L3 **CHALLENGING** activities for above-average students
ELL **ENGLISH LANGUAGE LEARNER** activities

Chapter 8 Resource Guide

Home Involvement

Home Involvement Activity 8

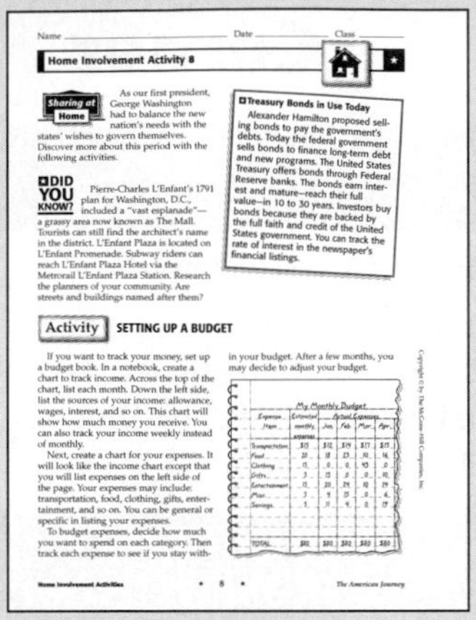

Review Activities

Chapter Summary 8

Workbook Activity 8

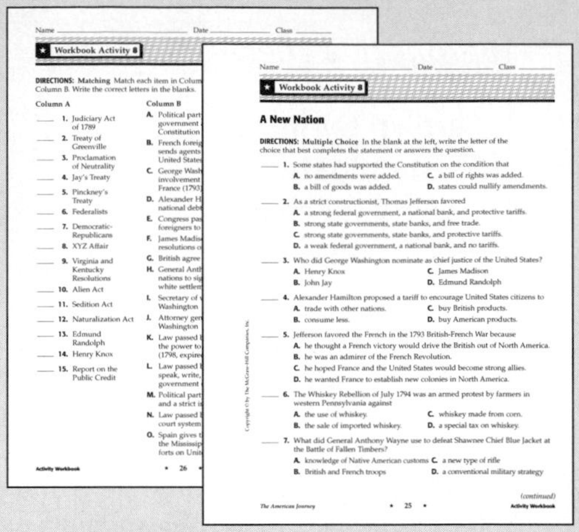

Reinforcement Activities

Time Line Activity 8

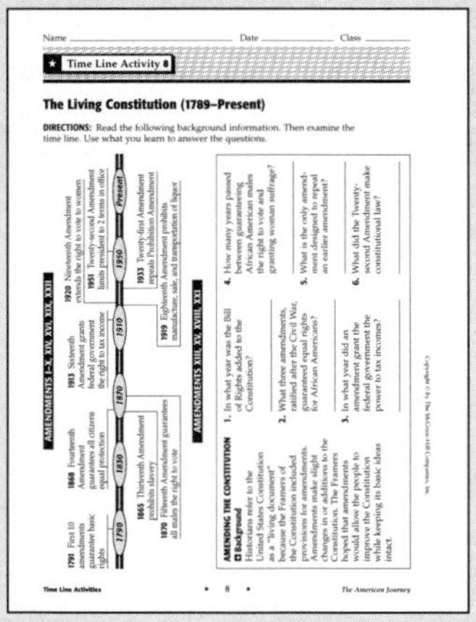

Vocabulary Activity 8

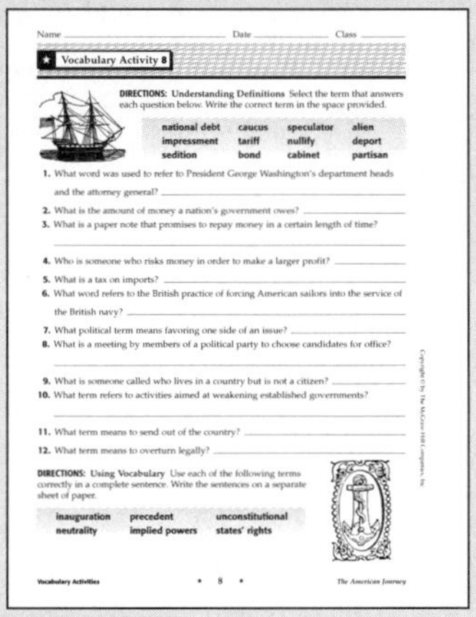

Chapter Skills Activity 8

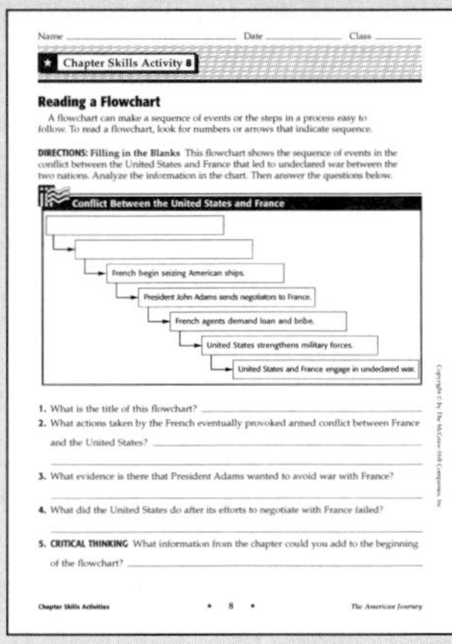

Enrichment Activities

Linking Past and Present Activity 8

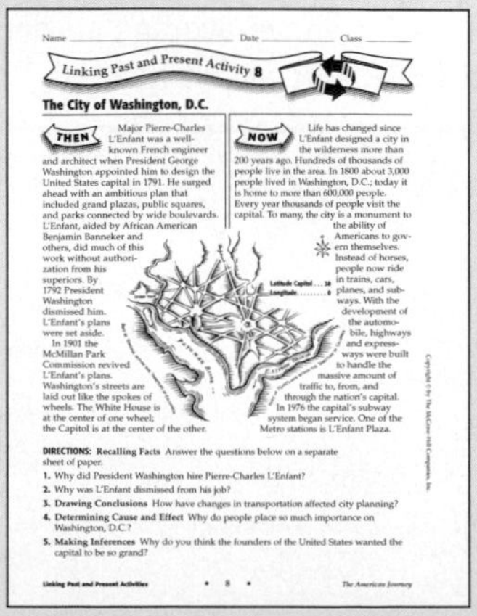

Primary Source Reading 8

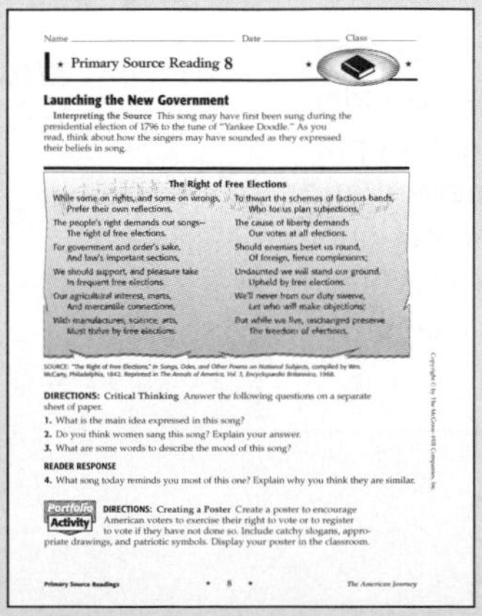

Geography Activities

Mapping History Activity 8

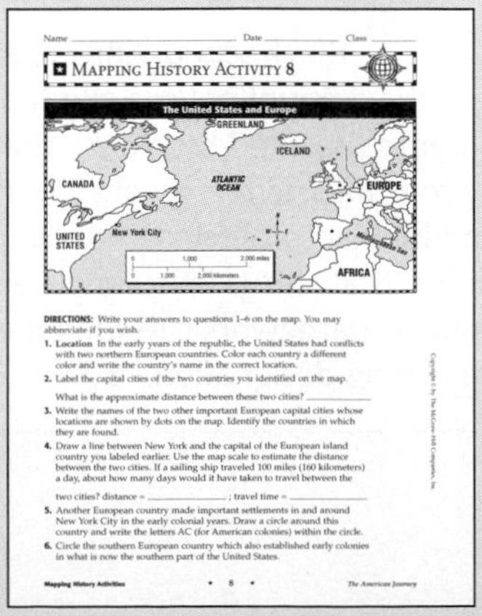

Assessment

Chapter 8 Test, Form A

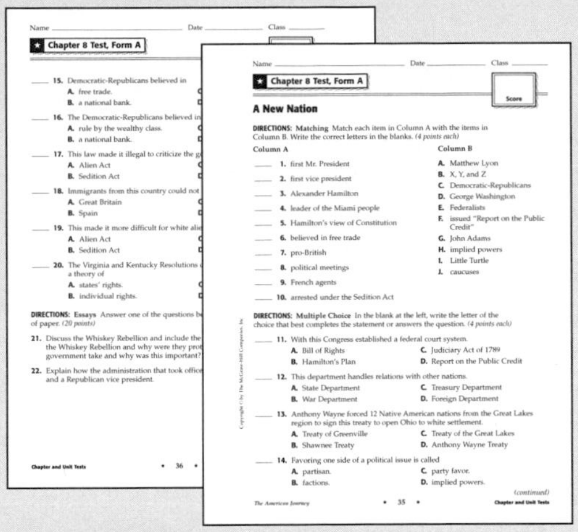

Chapter 8 Test, Form B

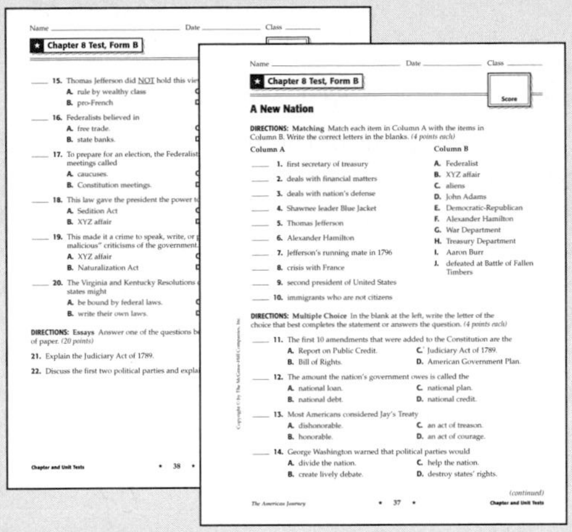

Performance Assessment Activity 8

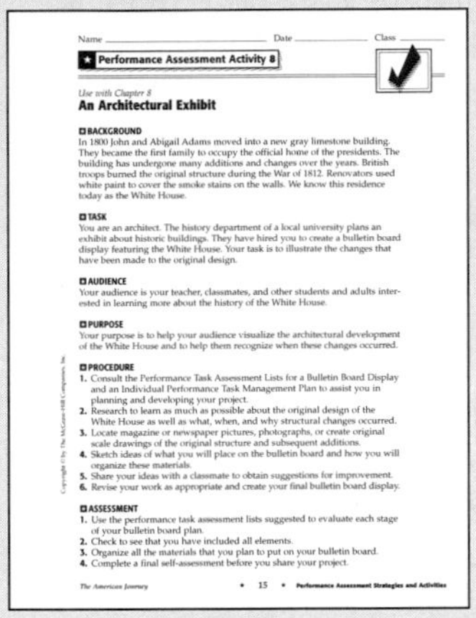

Spanish Resources

The following Spanish language materials are available in the Spanish Resources binder:

- **Spanish Chapter Summary 8**
- **Spanish Vocabulary Activity 8**
- **Spanish Guided Reading Activities, Chapter 8**
- **Spanish Section Quizzes, Chapter 8**
- **Spanish Home Involvement Activity 8**
- **Spanish Chapter 8 Digests Audiocassette Activity and Test**

Activity Manipulatives

Help students learn more about America's cultural history with:

- **American Crafts Hands-On Activities**
- **American Games Hands-On Activities**
- **American History Flash Cards**

Additional Resources From Glencoe

- **Focus on American Art Prints,** *The Staircase Group* by Charles Willson Peale
- **The Spirit of American Art and Music,** Joshua Johnston; Edward Hicks
- **American Music Cultural Traditions,** Lesson 3: "The Rose Tree"
- **Outline Map Resource Book**
- **U.S. Desk Map**
- **The American History Videodisc and CD-ROM,** *The American Revolution and the Early Republic, 1765-1820*

A&E HOME VIDEO. Biography™ THE HISTORY CHANNEL.

The following videotape programs are available from Glencoe as supplements to Chapter 8:

- **George Washington: Founding Father** (ISBN 1-56501-377-8)
- **Thomas Jefferson: Philosopher of Freedom** (ISBN 1-56501-502-9)

To order, call Glencoe at 1-800-334-7344. To find classroom resources to accompany many of these videos, check the following home pages:
A&E Television: http://www.aetv.com
The History Channel: http://www.historychannel.com

Chapter Themes

Chapter Themes are listed by section on this chapter opening page of the Student Edition. A corresponding theme-based activity is available under "FOCUS," and a theme-based question is asked in the Section and Chapter Reviews.

Performance Assessment

Refer to Activity 8 in the *Performance Assessment Strategies and Activities* booklet.

GLENCOE TECHNOLOGY

VIDEODISC
MindJogger Videoquiz

Use MindJogger to preview the Chapter 8 content.

Chapter 8
Disc 1, Side B

Also available in VHS.

HISTORY AND ART Martha Washington stands on a platform (at left) during a reception in her honor in 1789. **Ask:** **Why do you think the artist called the reception a court?** *(because it was similar to a royal court in formality and lavishness)*

Chapter 8

1789–1800

A New Nation

Why It's Important

The Washington administration faced the huge task of establishing a new government. The Constitution had created the office of the presidency, but it was Washington who established the procedures and customs that succeeding presidents would follow. He tried also to set a precedent for not getting involved in the political affairs of foreign nations. In the 1790s revolution and war raged throughout Europe. Despite the efforts of Washington and of John Adams, who followed him, the United States did become involved in disputes with European powers.

Chapter Themes

- *Section 1*, Government and Democracy
- *Section 2*, Civic Rights and Responsibilities
- *Section 3*, Economic Factors
- *Section 4*, Groups and Institutions

HISTORY AND ART ***The Republican Court*** **by Daniel Huntington** President George Washington and his wife, Martha, entertained guests at formal receptions.

EXTRA CREDIT PROJECT

Flags of the United States Have each student research the changes in the United States flag and make drawings of the various flags. Students should also find out about the present code of etiquette for the flag and summarize the main points. The code covers the following topics: when to display the flag, flying it at half-staff, how to fly it, church and platform use of the flag, how to dispose of worn flags, how to salute the flag, and prohibited uses of the flag. Some students might want to investigate the various constitutional amendments to protect the flag that have been proposed in recent years. Refer students to page 934 for a summary of proper flag etiquette.

1789 1790 1791 1792

April 6, 1789 George Washington is elected president

April 30, 1789 Washington takes the oath of office

September 1789 Judiciary Act sets up federal court system

December 1791 Bill of Rights added to the Constitution

Section 1

The First President

READ TO DISCOVER . . .
- what actions Washington and Congress took to launch the new government.
- how Hamilton proposed to strengthen the nation's credit and economy.

TERMS TO LEARN

inauguration
precedent
cabinet
national debt
bond
speculator
unconstitutional
tariff

The Storyteller

Celebrations erupted in the streets of Philadelphia, New York, Boston, and Charleston in 1789. News about the Constitution's ratification was greeted with relief and enthusiasm. All that was needed now was a leader to guide the new nation.

On April 6 the new Senate counted the presidential ballots. To no one's surprise, the votes were unanimous. Senator John Langdon wrote to General George Washington: "Sir, I have the honor to transmit to Your Excellency the information of your unanimous election to the office of President of the United States of America."

Washington banner

The 57-year-old president-elect made his way slowly toward **New York City,** the nation's temporary capital, and the job he had never wanted. After the Constitutional Convention, **George Washington** had looked forward to the peace and quiet of retirement at his beloved estate of Mount Vernon. Instead his fellow citizens summoned him to assume the highest office in the land. On April 30, 1789, Washington took the oath of office as the first president of the United States. **John Adams** became vice president. This inauguration ceremony took place at Federal Hall on the island of Manhattan.

Biography

President Washington

Perhaps no office in the new government created more suspicion among the people than the office of president. Although many Americans feared that a president would try to become king, they trusted Washington. They believed that his leadership had brought them through the Revolutionary War to victory. Most political leaders agreed with Alexander Hamilton's assessment of the new president: "He consulted much, pondered much, resolved slowly, resolved surely."

Washington was aware of the "ocean of difficulties" he faced. He knew that the precedents, or traditions, he established as the nation's first president would shape the future of the United States. "No slip will pass unnoticed," he remarked. One precedent he established concerned the way

SECTION RESOURCES

Reproducible Masters
- Reproducible Lesson Plan 8–1
- Guided Reading Activity 8–1
- Section Quiz 8–1
- Reteaching Activity 8–1
- Enrichment Activity 8–1

Transparencies
- Section Focus Transparency 8–1

Multimedia
- Vocabulary PuzzleMaker
- Chapter Challenger Interactive Review Software
- Testmaker
- Facts On File: Landmark Documents in American History
- The Presidents: A Picture History of Our Nation

1 FOCUS

BELLRINGER
Motivational Activity

Before taking roll at the beginning of the class period, project Section Focus Transparency 8–1 and have students answer the questions. Discuss students' responses.

This activity is also available as a blackline master.

Section Focus Transparency 8–1

Electoral Vote for the Presidential Election of 1792

1. Who won the election of 1792? How many votes did he receive?
2. How many states were there at the time?
3. Who received the second largest number of votes?

State	George Washington	John Adams	George Clinton	Thomas Jefferson	Aaron Burr
N.H.	6	6			
Mass.	16	16			
R.I.	4	4			
Conn.	9	9			
Vt.	3	3			
N.Y.	12		12		
N.J.	7	7			
Pa.	15	14	1		
Del.	3	3			
Md.	8	8			
Va.	21		21		
Ky.	4			4	
N.C.	12		12		
S.C.	8	7			1
Ga.	4		4		
TOTAL	132	77	50	4	1

Vocabulary Precheck

Point out to the students that the term *inauguration* contains the root *augur* which means "to give promise of" or "to predict the future." Encourage students to discuss the meaning of *inauguration* and how that meaning relates to the root *augur.*

Use the **Vocabulary Puzzle-Maker** to create crossword and word search puzzles.

Section Theme
Government and Democracy

During George Washington's two terms as president, precedents were established by the president and Congress that would shape the future of government in our nation.

Activity Ask students to identify some of the precedents established during this period. *(manner of addressing the president; presidential authority to dismiss cabinet officers; establishment of federal court system)*

2 TEACH

L1 Finding Main Points Have students turn the "Read to Discover" items into questions. After students have read the section, have them go back over it listing the main points that answer those questions.

Picturing HISTORY In 1947 the War Department was renamed the Department of the Army and became a part of the Department of Defense. **Ask: Why might people prefer the name *Defense* to *War*?** *(People may prefer to think of themselves as defending their homes and lives rather than being the aggressors.)*
Answer: *Thomas Jefferson*

Facts On File

CD-ROM
Landmark Documents in American History

Title: *First Inaugural Address, George Washington, 1789*
Encourage students to review the document and outline Washington's hopes and plans for the new government.

Guided Reading Activity 8–1

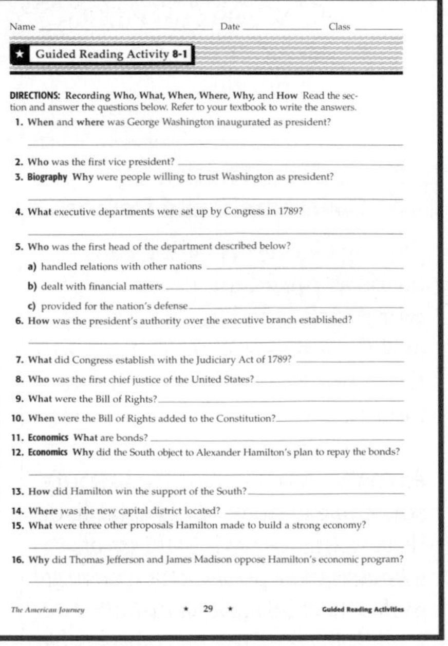
Name ______ Date ______ Class ______

★ Guided Reading Activity 8-1

DIRECTIONS: Recording Who, What, When, Where, Why, and **How** Read the section and answer the questions below. Refer to your textbook to write the answers.

1. **When** and **where** was George Washington inaugurated as president?
2. **Who** was the first vice president?
3. **Biography Why** were people willing to trust Washington as president?
4. **What** executive departments were set up by Congress in 1789?
5. **Who** was the first head of the department described below?
   a) handled relations with other nations
   b) dealt with financial matters
   c) provided for the nation's defense
6. **How** was the president's authority over the executive branch established?
7. **What** did Congress establish with the Judiciary Act of 1789?
8. **Who** was the first chief justice of the United States?
9. **What** were the Bill of Rights?
10. **When** were the Bill of Rights added to the Constitution?
11. **Economics What** are bonds?
12. **Economics Why** did the South object to Alexander Hamilton's plan to repay the bonds?
13. **How** did Hamilton win the support of the South?
14. **Where** was the new capital district located?
15. **What** were three other proposals Hamilton made to build a strong economy?
16. **Why** did Thomas Jefferson and James Madison oppose Hamilton's economic program?

Copyright © by The McGraw-Hill Companies, Inc.

The American Journey ★ 29 ★ Guided Reading Activities

Picturing HISTORY President Washington relied on the expert advice of his cabinet. Henry Knox is seated at left. Next to him are Thomas Jefferson, Edmund Randolph (back turned), Alexander Hamilton, and Washington himself. **Who was the first secretary of state?**

people should address him. Vice President Adams suggested "His Highness the President of the United States," but Washington decided that "Mr. President" would be appropriate.

Washington and the new Congress also had many decisions to make about the structure of government. For example, the Constitution gave Congress the power to establish departments, but it did not specify whether the department heads would report to the president or to Congress.

Washington's Cabinet

During the summer of 1789, Congress set up three departments in the executive branch of government. The State Department would handle relations with other nations, the Treasury Department would deal with financial matters, and the War Department would provide for the nation's defense. Congress also created the office of attorney general to handle the government's legal affairs and the office of postmaster general to oversee the postal service.

To head the departments, Washington chose leading political figures of the day—**Thomas Jefferson** as secretary of state, **Alexander Hamilton** as secretary of the treasury, and **Henry Knox** as secretary of war. He appointed **Edmund Randolph** as attorney general. Washington met regularly with the three department heads and the attorney general, who together became known as the **cabinet.**

The First Congress

★ Congress created the executive departments; however, opinion was divided on how much power the president should have over them. For example, should the president be able to replace an official he had appointed and the Senate had confirmed? Senators were evenly divided in voting on the issue.

Vice President Adams broke the tie by voting to allow the president the authority to dismiss cabinet officers without the Senate's approval. This decision strengthened the president's position. It also helped create a greater separation between the legislative and executive branches of government by establishing the president's authority over the executive branch.

Judiciary Act

The first Congress also had to decide how to set up the nation's court system. The Constitution briefly mentioned a supreme court but had left further details about the courts to Congress.

A dispute arose between those favoring a uniform, national legal system and those favoring state laws. The two groups reached a compromise in the **Judiciary Act of 1789.** With this act, Congress established a federal court system with 13 district courts and 3 circuit courts in the nation.

COOPERATIVE LEARNING ACTIVITY

Presenting the National Capital Organize the class into small groups. Each group should choose an important building or monument in Washington, D.C. Have each group find or draw a picture of its building or make a model of it. Each group should also write a paragraph about it. Some groups may choose to draw a diagram of the interior of the building. One group might choose to draw a map of the capital marking the location of various points of interest. Tasks within groups should be divided according to the skills of the members.

State laws would remain, but the federal courts would have the power to reverse state decisions.

The Supreme Court would be the final authority on many issues. Washington nominated **John Jay** to lead the Supreme Court as chief justice, and the Senate approved Jay's nomination. With the Judiciary Act, Congress had taken the first steps toward creating a strong and independent judiciary.

The Bill of Rights

Americans had long feared strong central governments. They had fought a revolution to throw off one and did not want to replace it with another. Some people thought the best protection lay in stronger state governments. Others insisted the Constitution needed to include specific statements guaranteeing personal liberties. Some states had supported the Constitution on the condition that a bill of rights be added.

John Jay, first chief justice of the United States

After studying hundreds of proposals for protecting "essential rights," James Madison presented a list of possible constitutional amendments to Congress. Congress passed 12 amendments, and the states ratified 10 of them. In December 1791, these 10 amendments were added to the Constitution and became known as the Bill of Rights.

Among the liberties guaranteed in the Bill of Rights are freedom of speech, press, and religion. The Tenth Amendment protects the rights of states and individuals by saying that powers not specifically given to the federal government "are reserved to the States respectively, or to the people."

Economics

Financial Problems

The first president rarely proposed laws, and he almost always approved the bills that were passed by Congress. Washington focused his attention on foreign affairs and military matters and left the government's economic policies to his dynamic secretary of the treasury, Alexander Hamilton.

The new nation faced serious financial problems. The national debt—the amount the nation's government owed—was growing. Hamilton tried to find a way to improve the government's financial reputation and to strengthen the nation at the same time.

Hamilton's Plan

In 1790 Hamilton issued a "Report on the Public Credit." He proposed that the new government pay off the millions of dollars in debts owed by the Confederation government to other countries and to individual American citizens.

The states had fought for the nation's independence, Hamilton argued, so the national government should pay for the cost of their help. Hamilton also believed that federal payment of state debts would give the states a strong interest in the success of the national government.

Opposition to the Plan

Congress agreed to pay money owed to other nations. However, Hamilton's plan to pay off the debt to American citizens unleashed a storm of protest. When the government had borrowed money during the American Revolution, it had issued bonds—paper notes promising to repay

Linking PAST & PRESENT

Mailing a Letter

Samuel Osgood, the first postmaster general, ran the nation's postal service from a one-room office with two assistants. Today the United States Postal Service employs more than 850,000 people.

CHAPTER 8
Section 1, 257–261

Facts On File

CD-ROM
Landmark Documents in American History

Title: *First Report on the Public Credit,* Alexander Hamilton, 1790
Ask students to review the document and list the goals of Hamilton's fiscal program. *(Hamilton wished to establish public credit domestically and abroad, and to strengthen the central government at the expense of the states.)*

NATIONAL GEOGRAPHIC SOCIETY

CD-ROM
The Presidents: A Picture History of Our Nation

Have students select President Washington from the main menu. Suggest that they note important events in his administration.

What?Where?When?Who?

The Election of 1789 George Washington was chosen by the electors from just 10 states. Election problems prevented New York from casting its ballot, and Rhode Island and North Carolina had not yet ratified the Constitution.

MULTIPLE LEARNING STYLES

Logical/Mathematical Speculators bought the old state war bonds at 10 to 20 cents on the dollar and later sold them at full value, making huge profits. Have students solve word problems to calculate possible profits. For example: Person A buys a bond worth $50. At 10 cents per dollar, how much did he/she pay for the bond? *($5.00)* Ignoring interest, what was the profit? *($45.00)* If person A bought 100 bonds, what was the profit? *($4,500.00)* **L2**

CURRICULUM CONNECTION

ECONOMICS
Washington was one of the richest men in America. At his death his assets were worth about a half million dollars. His holdings included: 33,000 acres of land; $25,000 worth of stocks; 640 sheep; 329 cows; 42 mules; and 20 workhorses.

CHAPTER 8
Section 1, 257–261

Graph Study

Answers
1. $4,269,000
2. $4,418,000

Graph Skills Practice

Reading a Graph What was the difference between expenditures and income? *($77,079,000)*

3 ASSESS

Assign Section 1 Review as homework or as an in-class activity.

Use **Chapter Challenger Interactive Review Software** to review Section 1.

Section Quiz 8–1

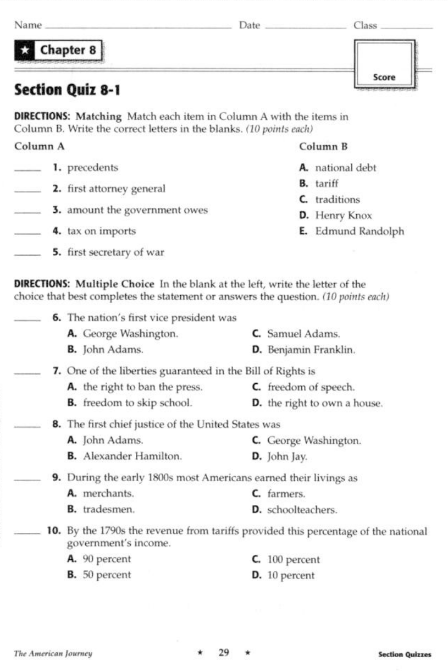

Name ____________ Date ________ Class ________

★ Chapter 8

Score

Section Quiz 8-1

DIRECTIONS: Matching Match each item in Column A with the items in Column B. Write the correct letters in the blanks. *(10 points each)*

Column A	Column B
____ 1. precedents	A. national debt
____ 2. first attorney general	B. tariff
____ 3. amount the government owes	C. traditions
____ 4. tax on imports	D. Henry Knox
____ 5. first secretary of war	E. Edmund Randolph

DIRECTIONS: Multiple Choice In the blank at the left, write the letter of the choice that best completes the statement or answers the question. *(10 points each)*

____ 6. The nation's first vice president was
A. George Washington. C. Samuel Adams.
B. John Adams. D. Benjamin Franklin.

____ 7. One of the liberties guaranteed in the Bill of Rights is
A. the right to ban the press. C. freedom of speech.
B. freedom to skip school. D. the right to own a house.

____ 8. The first chief justice of the United States was
A. John Adams. C. George Washington.
B. Alexander Hamilton. D. John Jay.

____ 9. During the early 1800s most Americans earned their livings as
A. merchants. C. farmers.
B. tradesmen. D. schoolteachers.

____ 10. By the 1790s the revenue from tariffs provided this percentage of the national government's income.
A. 90 percent C. 100 percent
B. 50 percent D. 10 percent

The American Journey ★ 29 ★ **Section Quizzes**

Finances of the New Nation, 1789–1791

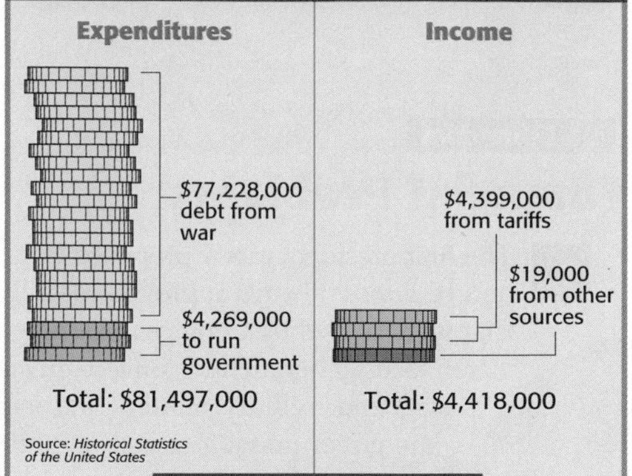

Graph Study

Alexander Hamilton, the secretary of the treasury, faced the problem of resolving the national debt.
1. How much money was needed to run the government?
2. **Analyzing Information** How much total income did the government receive?

money in a certain length of time. During hard times, many of the original bond owners—shopkeepers, farmers, and soldiers—had sold the bonds for less than their value. They were purchased by **speculators,** people who risk money in order to make a larger profit. Hamilton proposed that these bonds be paid off at their original value. Opponents believed that Hamilton's plan would make speculators rich at the expense of average Americans.

Opposition to the plan went beyond political leaders. In the view of one Pennsylvania farmer, Hamilton's plan was "established at the expense of national justice, gratitude, and humanity." The original bond owners felt betrayed by the government because they had lost money on their bonds while new bond owners profited.

Even stronger opposition came from the Southern states, which had accumulated much less debt than the Northern states. Southern states complained that they would have to pay more than their share under Hamilton's plan.

Compromise Results in a Capital

To win support for his plan, Hamilton compromised. He agreed to a proposal from Virginia and Maryland to locate the new nation's capital in the South. A special district would be laid out along the banks of the Potomac River. This district became **Washington, D.C.** In return, Southerners supported his plan to pay off the state debts. Congress approved Hamilton's plan 36 to 13.

Building the Economy

Hamilton made other proposals for building a strong national economy. He asked Congress to create a national bank, the Bank of the United States. Both private investors and the national government would own the Bank's stock.

The Fight Over the Bank

Until this time only three banks existed in the nation—in Boston, New York City, and Philadelphia. All three had been established by state governments. Madison and Jefferson opposed the idea of a national bank. They believed it would benefit the wealthy. They also charged that the Bank was **unconstitutional**—that the Constitution had no provision for creating such

Footnotes to History

Presidential Design Pierre-Charles L'Enfant of France planned the city of Washington. Helping L'Enfant lay out the boundaries of the new capital was Benjamin Banneker, the son of free African Americans. Recommended by Thomas Jefferson, Banneker was a mathematician and inventor and also published an almanac.

What?Where?When?Who?

A competition for the design of the new executive mansion (White House) was sponsored by the government. One design, although not chosen, was submitted by a mysterious Mr. A.Z.—who later turned out to be Thomas Jefferson.

MAKING CONNECTIONS ACTIVITY

Politics Have students find out about the 14 departments that are now part of the cabinet (State, Treasury, Defense, Justice, Interior, Agriculture, Commerce, Labor, Housing and Urban Development, Transportation, Energy, Education, Health and Human Services, Veterans Affairs). Ask students to write a paragraph or two about each department and to use an almanac to find the names of the current secretaries. (The head of the Department of Justice is called the attorney general, not secretary.) **L2**

an institution. Hamilton argued that although the Constitution did not specifically say that Congress could create a bank, Congress still had the power to do so.

Washington asked Hamilton and Jefferson to write opinions on the question. In the end the president agreed with Hamilton and signed the bill creating the national bank.

Tariffs and Taxes

At the time, most Americans earned their living by farming. Hamilton thought the development of manufacturing industries would make America stronger. He proposed a tariff—a tax on imports—to encourage people to buy American products. This **protective tariff** would protect American industry from foreign competition.

The South, having little industry to protect, opposed protective tariffs. Hamilton did win support in Congress for some low tariffs to raise money rather than to protect industries. By the 1790s the revenue from tariffs provided 90 percent of the national government's income.

The final portion of Hamilton's economic program concerned the creation of national taxes. The government needed additional funds to operate and to make interest payments on the national debt. At Hamilton's request Congress approved a variety of taxes, including one on whiskey distilled in the United States.

Hamilton's economic program gave the national government new financial powers and protected the investments and interests of well-to-do Americans. However, his proposals split Congress and the nation. The opponents—including Jefferson and Madison—feared a national government with strong economic powers dominated by the wealthy class. They had a very different vision of what America should become.

America's FLAGS

Betsy Ross Flag, 1790 Legend holds that Philadelphia seamstress Betsy Ross stitched the first Stars and Stripes. Historical record does not support this account, however. The popular "Betsy Ross flag," with 13 stars arranged in a circle, did not appear until the early 1790s.

Section 1 Review

Checking for Understanding

1. ***Identify*** George Washington, John Adams, Alexander Hamilton, Judiciary Act of 1789.
2. ***Define*** inauguration, precedent, cabinet, national debt, bond, speculator, unconstitutional, tariff.
3. ***Name*** three things that Hamilton wanted to do to strengthen the economy.

Reviewing Themes

4. **Government and Democracy** How did Congress try to balance power between the state and federal courts?

Critical Thinking

5. **Analyzing Primary Sources** About Washington, Hamilton said: "He consulted much, pondered much, resolved slowly, resolved surely." Did this make Washington a good first president? Explain.

Activity

Mock Interview Imagine that you must choose the first cabinet members. Write a job description for the secretary of state, treasury, or war. Then interview a classmate to see if he or she would be good for the position.

Section 1 Review Answers

1. Washington, 257; Adams, 257; Hamilton, 258; Judiciary Act of 1789, 258
2. The words are defined in the Glossary.
3. Any three: pay off bonds issued during the American Revolution, pay off states' debts, form a national bank, tariffs, taxes
4. It kept state laws in place, but gave federal courts power to reverse state decisions with Supreme Court as final authority.
5. Answers should show that students understand that the first president was setting precedents. It was important to consult others, think carefully about his actions, and once he took action to do it firmly and with confidence.

Activity Job descriptions should list personal characteristics and experiences that would make a person suitable for these positions.

Reteaching Activity 8–1

Name ______ Date ______ Class ______

★ Reteaching Activity 8-1

DIRECTIONS: Matching Match each item in Column A with its corresponding item in Column B. Write the correct letters in the blanks.

COLUMN A

____ 1. New York City
____ 2. John Adams
____ 3. Thomas Jefferson
____ 4. Alexander Hamilton
____ 5. Henry Knox
____ 6. Edmund Randolph
____ 7. cabinet
____ 8. Judiciary Act of 1789
____ 9. John Jay
____ 10. Bill of Rights
____ 11. "Report on the Public Credit"
____ 12. bonds
____ 13. speculators
____ 14. Washington, D.C.
____ 15. tariffs

COLUMN B

A. first secretary of war
B. executive branch department heads and the attorney general
C. first 10 amendments to the Constitution guaranteeing personal liberties
D. people who risk money to make a larger profit
E. the temporary capital of the United States in 1789
F. outlined Hamilton's proposal to pay off the national debt
G. first secretary of state
H. special district designated to be the new nation's capital
I. first attorney general
J. first vice president of the United States
K. taxes on imports
L. first secretary of the treasury
M. established federal court system
N. paper notes promising to repay money in a certain length of time
O. first chief justice of the United States

DIRECTIONS: Essay Answer the following questions on a separate sheet of paper.

16. What three departments of the executive branch were set up by Congress in 1789 and what responsibility was given to each department?
17. What happened to the bonds issued to American citizens by the American government during the Revolutionary War? Why did people oppose Alexander Hamilton's plan to pay off the bonds?

Enrichment Activity 8–1

Name ______ Date ______ Class ______

★ Enrichment Activity 8-1 ★ ★

What Is an American?

In the late 1700s St. Jean de Crèvecoeur, a Frenchman who had lived for many years in the United States, published essays about being an American. Read these excerpts from his essay "What Is an American?"

> . . . We have no princes, for whom we toil, starve, and bleed: we are the most perfect society now existing in the world. Here man is free as he ought to be; nor is this pleasing equality so transitory as many others are. Many ages will not see the shores of our great lakes replenished with inland nations, nor the unknown bounds of North America entirely peopled. Who can tell how far it extends? Who can tell the millions of men whom it will feed and contain? . . .
>
> . . . I could point out to you a family whose grandfather was an Englishman, whose wife was Dutch, whose son married a French woman, and whose present four sons have now four wives of different nations. *He* is an American, who, leaving behind him all his ancient prejudices and manners, receives new ones from the new mode of life he has embraced. . . . The American is a new man, who acts upon new principles; he must therefore entertain new ideas, and form new opinions. From involuntary idleness, servile [lowly] dependence, penury [poverty], and useless labour, he has passed to toils of a very different nature, rewarded by ample subsistence—this is an American.
>
> SOURCE: *The American Tradition in Literature*, Sculley Bradley, Richard Coom Beatty, and E. Hudson Long, ed. W. W. Norton & Co., Inc. New York.

DIRECTIONS: Interpreting and Classifying Information Write one or more sentences to explain what St. Jean de Crèvecoeur states or suggests about each topic listed below.

1. Government in the United States ______
2. Land in the United States ______
3. Work in the United States ______
4. Ethnic Backgrounds of Americans ______
5. The Injustices Left Behind in Europe ______
6. The Duration of Freedom in the United States ______

Activity **DIRECTIONS:** Pick one of the topics that Crèvecoeur discusses in his essay. Think about how today's Americans are similar to or different from those that Crèvecoeur described in the 1700s. Then prepare a short speech for your class in which you define what an American is today.

4 CLOSE

A member of the House of Representatives reacted to the job ahead—launching the new government—by exclaiming, "We are in a wilderness!" Have students explain the statement, giving specific examples from the section.

1 FOCUS

BELLRINGER
Motivational Activity

Before taking roll at the beginning of the class period, project Section Focus Transparency 8–2 and have students answer the questions. Discuss students' responses.

This activity is also available as a blackline master.

Section Focus Transparency 8–2

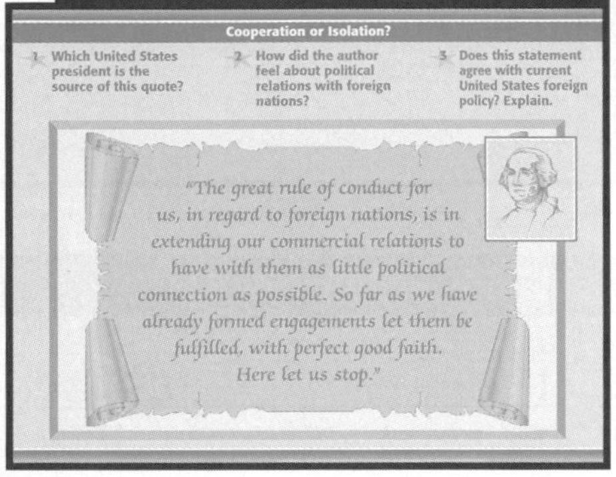

Vocabulary Precheck

Explain that the term *neutrality* comes from a Latin word meaning "neither." Have students explain the relationship between the two terms.

Use the **Vocabulary PuzzleMaker** to create crossword and word search puzzles.

Section Theme
Civic Rights and Responsibilities

The farmers in western Pennsylvania used violent means to protest what they felt was an unfair tax.

Activity Have students discuss what rights the farmers were exercising. *(right to protest, right to freedom from unfair or oppressive taxation)*
Ask: How did the farmers violate their civic responsibilities? *(by using violence)*

1790 — 1792 — 1794 — 1796

November 1791 Little Turtle defeats St. Clair's forces

April 1793 Washington issues Proclamation of Neutrality

July 1794 Western farmers revolt in Whiskey Rebellion

August 1794 Battle of Fallen Timbers occurs

October 1795 Spain opens Mississippi River to American shipping

Section 2

Early Challenges

READ TO DISCOVER . . .

- how the federal government asserted its power in the West.
- how the United States tried to stay out of European conflicts.

TERMS TO LEARN

neutrality
impressment

The Storyteller

Far removed from the bustle of trade and shipping along the Atlantic coast, farmers on the western frontier moved at a slower pace. In fact, western ways seemed almost primitive to travelers from the East. They seemed to notice only the poor roads and the boring diet of corn and salted pork. Living in scattered, isolated homesteads, frontier farmers were proud of their self-reliance. They wanted no "eastern" tax collectors heading their way.

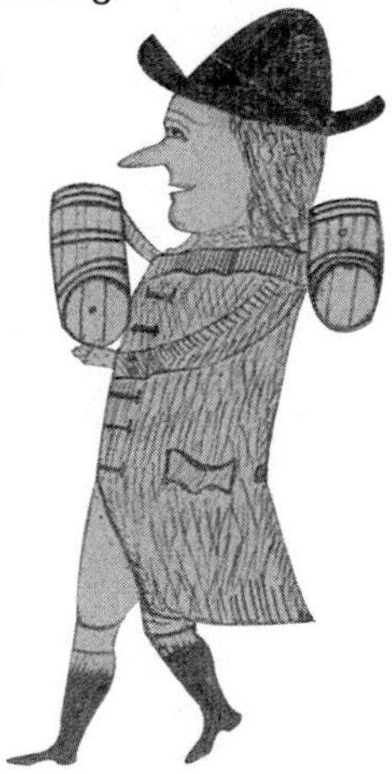

Tax collector

Hamilton's taxes led to rebellion in western Pennsylvania. The farmers were in an uproar over paying a special tax on the whiskey they made from surplus corn. In the backcountry most farmers lived by bartering—exchanging whiskey and other items they produced for goods they needed. They rarely had cash. How could they pay a tax on whiskey?

The Whiskey Rebellion

The farmers' resistance was mostly peaceful until July 1794, when federal officers stepped up efforts to collect the tax. Then a mob of about 500 people armed with swords, guns, and pitchforks attacked tax collectors and burned down buildings. Some chanted a slogan from the French Revolution—"Liberty, Equality, Fraternity"—and waved a flag symbolizing an independent "country" in western Pennsylvania.

The armed protest, called the **Whiskey Rebellion,** alarmed government leaders. President Washington personally led an army of about 13,000 soldiers to crush the challenge. The rebellion collapsed as soon as the army crossed the **Appalachian Mountains.**

The Whiskey Rebellion set a milestone in determining how far people could go in protesting the laws of the new nation. By his action, Washington served notice on those who opposed government actions. If citizens wished to change the law, they had to do so peacefully, through constitutional means. Government would meet with force any threats to disturb the social order.

SECTION RESOURCES

Reproducible Masters
- Reproducible Lesson Plan 8–2
- Guided Reading Activity 8–2
- Section Quiz 8–2
- Reteaching Activity 8–2
- Enrichment Activity 8–2

Transparencies
- Section Focus Transparency 8–2

Multimedia
- Vocabulary PuzzleMaker
- Chapter Challenger Interactive Review Software
- Testmaker
- GTV: The American People: Fabric of a Nation

Geography

Struggle Over the West

The new government faced problems in the West that were not easy to resolve. The Native Americans who lived between the Appalachian Mountains and the Mississippi River denied that the United States had any authority over them. On many occasions Native Americans turned to Britain and Spain to help them in their cause. Both countries welcomed the opportunity to prevent American settlement of the region.

Foreign Powers in the West

Washington worried about European ambitions in the Northwest Territory. His goal was to remove that threat, "in peace if I can, and to be prepared for war if I cannot." He hoped that signing treaties with Native Americans would lessen the influence of the British and Spanish.

American settlers, however, ignored the treaties and continued to move onto lands promised to the Indians. Fighting broke out between the settlers and Native Americans.

Washington sent a large military expedition under General Arthur St. Clair to restore order in the Northwest Territory. In November 1791, St. Clair's forces were badly beaten by Little Turtle, chief of the Miami people. More than 600 American troops died in a battle by the Wabash River.

Many Americans believed that an alliance with France would enable them to defeat the combined forces of the British, Spanish, and Native Americans in the West. The British, who still had forts in the region, wanted to hold on to the profitable fur trade. The possibility of French involvement in the region pushed the British to make a bold bid for control of the West. In 1794 the British governor of Canada urged Indians to destroy American settlements west of the Appalachians. The British also began building a new fort in **Ohio.**

American Victories in the West

Washington sent John Jay to Britain to try to halt the nation's slide toward war. He also instructed **General Anthony Wayne** to gain control over the Native Americans in the Ohio River valley. Wayne used his knowledge of Native American customs to gain an important advantage. Aware that Indians usually fasted before a battle, he spread rumors that he planned to attack on August 17. Then he delayed his attack. Expecting the battle to begin at any moment, the Native Americans continued to fast. Finally on August 20, 1794, Wayne attacked and defeated Shawnee chief Blue Jacket and his warriors—weakened by hunger—at the **Battle of Fallen Timbers.**

A year later Wayne forced 12 Indian nations in the Great Lakes region to sign the **Treaty of Greenville.** The treaty opened most of Ohio to white settlement.

Picturing HISTORY Upon signing the Treaty of Greenville, 12 Indian nations received $20,000 worth of goods to share. **What did white settlers receive?**

COOPERATIVE LEARNING ACTIVITY

Making Matching Games Organize the class into small groups to invent matching games using information in the section, such as key terms, names of people and places, events, and treaties. Suggest that extra points be awarded for students who can not only match items but also explain how they are related. Divide tasks, such as writing rules, creating cards, and monitoring play, according to the skills of group members.

CHAPTER 8
Section 2, 262–265

2 TEACH

L1, ELL Taking Notes Have students write a one-paragraph summary of each of the four main parts of the section. Challenge students to answer the review questions, referring only to their paragraphs.

Guided Reading Activity 8–2

Name ______ Date ______ Class ______

★ Guided Reading Activity 8-2

DIRECTIONS: Identifying Supporting Details Read each main idea. Use your textbook to supply the details that support or explain each main idea.

Main Idea: Alexander Hamilton's taxes led to unrest in western Pennsylvania.

1. **Detail:** The ______ in western Pennsylvania objected to paying a special tax on ______.
2. **Detail:** An armed protest called the ______ was crushed by an army led by ______.

Main Idea: America faced problems in the West that were not easily resolved.

3. **Geography Detail:** George Washington hoped that treaties with Native Americans would lessen the influence of the ______ and the ______.
4. **Detail:** More than 600 American troops died in a battle by the ______.
5. **Detail:** In 1794 the British governor of Canada urged Native Americans to ______.
6. **Detail:** On August 20, 1794, General Anthony Wayne defeated Shawnee leader Blue Jacket and his warriors at the ______.
7. **Detail:** Wayne forced 12 Native American nations to sign the ______, which opened most of Ohio to white settlement.

Main Idea: The war between France and Great Britain in 1793 led to problems in America.

8. **Detail:** Americans in the ______ tended to side with France, while ______ who traded with Great Britain, favored Great Britain.
9. **Detail:** On April 22, 1793, Washington issued a ______ that prohibited American citizens from fighting in the war between Great Britain and France.
10. **Detail:** Few Americans supported ______ with the British because it did not deal with ______.

Main Idea: When Washington left office, he had concerns about the nation's health.

11. **Detail:** Washington considered the ______ a danger to the country.
12. **Detail:** In his "Farewell Address," he attacked entanglements in ______.

Guided Reading Activities ★ 30 ★ *The American Journey*

Picturing HISTORY After the Battle of Fallen Timbers, the Shawnee lost any hope of keeping their land.
Answer: *the opportunity to settle in most of Ohio*

NATIONAL GEOGRAPHIC SOCIETY

VIDEODISC
GTV: The American People: Fabric of a Nation

Side 2, Chapter 2
Title: *Between Worlds*
Subject: For Native Americans, a shrinking realm
Ask: **What did the "Indian agents" want the Native Americans to become?** *(farmers)*

CHAPTER 8

Section 2, 262–265

What? Where? When? Who?

The Death of Louis XVI An observer described the American reaction to the king's death as follows: "Never was the memory of any man so cruelly insulted as that of this mild and humane monarch. He was guillotined in effigy, in [Philadelphia], twenty or thirty times every day, during one whole winter and part of the summer. Men, women and children flocked to the tragical exhibition, and not a single paragraph appeared in the papers to shame them from it."

Map Study

Answers

1. by the Wabash River near Fort Recovery in 1791
2. 1794

3 ASSESS

Assign Section 2 Review as homework or as an in-class activity.

Use **Chapter Challenger Interactive Review Software** to review Section 2.

Section Quiz 8–2

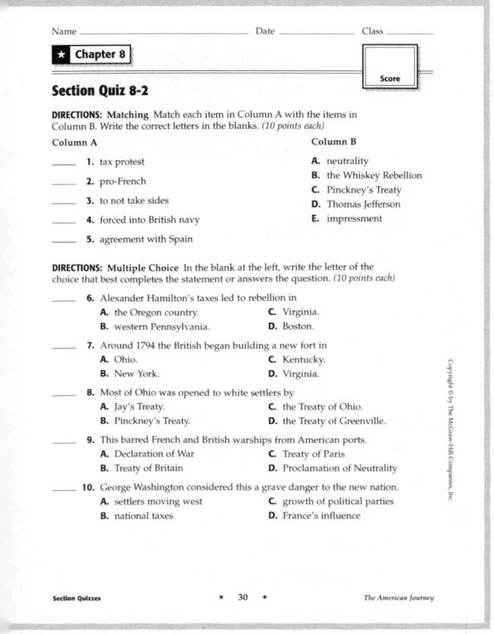

Name ______ Date ______ Class ______

★ Chapter 8

Score

Section Quiz 8-2

DIRECTIONS: Matching Match each item in Column A with the items in Column B. Write the correct letters in the blanks. *(10 points each)*

Column A	Column B
____ **1.** tax protest	**A.** neutrality
____ **2.** pro-French	**B.** the Whiskey Rebellion
____ **3.** to not take sides	**C.** Pinckney's Treaty
____ **4.** forced into British navy	**D.** Thomas Jefferson
____ **5.** agreement with Spain	**E.** impressment

DIRECTIONS: Multiple Choice In the blank at the left, write the letter of the choice that best completes the statement or answers the question. *(10 points each)*

____ **6.** Alexander Hamilton's taxes led to rebellion in
A. the Oregon country. **C.** Virginia.
B. western Pennsylvania. **D.** Boston.

____ **7.** Around 1794 the British began building a new fort in
A. Ohio. **C.** Kentucky.
B. New York. **D.** Virginia.

____ **8.** Most of Ohio was opened to white settlers by
A. Jay's Treaty. **C.** the Treaty of Ohio.
B. Pinckney's Treaty. **D.** the Treaty of Greenville.

____ **9.** This barred French and British warships from American ports.
A. Declaration of War **C.** Treaty of Paris
B. Treaty of Britain **D.** Proclamation of Neutrality

____ **10.** George Washington considered this a grave danger to the new nation.
A. settlers moving west **C.** growth of political parties
B. national taxes **D.** France's influence

Section Quizzes ★ 30 ★ *The American Journey*

Native American Campaigns

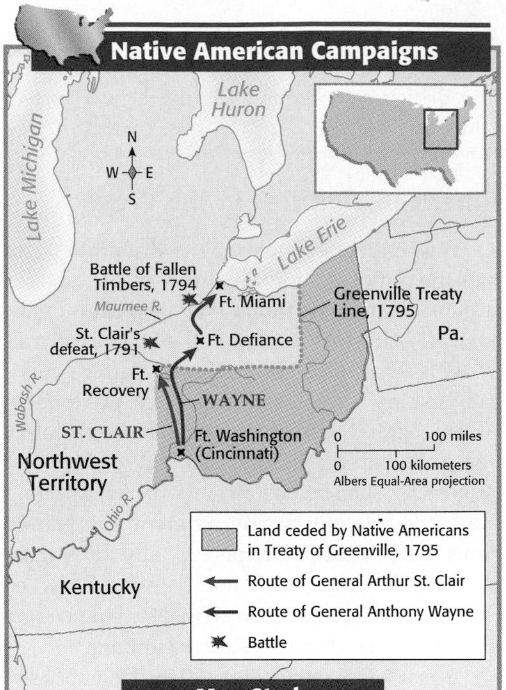

Map Study

General Anthony Wayne's forces marched north from Fort Washington to fight the Shawnee chief Blue Jacket.

1. **Location** When and where was St. Clair defeated?
2. **Analyzing Information** When was the Battle of Fallen Timbers fought?

The French Revolution

In 1789 the French rebelled against their king, Louis XVI, and overthrew the government. At first most Americans cheered the news. The French had helped the Americans in their struggle for independence, and their revolution seemed to embody many of the ideals of the American Revolution.

By 1793, however, the French Revolution had turned bloody. The leaders had executed the king and queen of France and thousands of French citizens. Public opinion in the United States started to divide. The violence of the French Revolution, as well as its attack on religion and disregard of individual liberties, offended many Americans.

In 1793 Britain and France went to war. Some Americans, particularly in the South, sympathized with France. Others, especially manufacturers and merchants who traded with the British, favored Britain. Hamilton, Adams, and their supporters generally sided with the British. Jefferson was pro-French. A French victory, Jefferson reasoned, would help drive the British out of North America.

Washington hoped that the nation could maintain its **neutrality**—that is, that it would not take sides in the conflict between France and Britain. As time went on, however, neutrality became increasingly difficult.

Washington Proclaims Neutrality

The French tried to involve the United States in their conflict with Britain. In April 1793, they sent diplomat **Edmond Genêt** (zhuh•NAY) to the United States. His mission was to recruit American volunteers to attack British shipping.

President Washington took action to discourage American involvement. On April 22 he issued a **Proclamation of Neutrality.** It prohibited American citizens from fighting in the war and barred French and British warships from American ports. Genêt's plans eventually failed, but he did manage to sign up a few hundred Americans to serve on French ships. These ships seized British vessels and stole their cargoes before Washington ended their adventures by closing American ports.

Outraged by the French attacks at sea, the British began seizing American ships that traded with the French. The British also stopped American merchant ships and forced their crews into the British navy. This practice, known as **impressment,** infuriated the American government and people. British attacks on American ships and sailors, along with the challenge in the West, pushed the nation closer toward war with Great Britain.

A Controversial Treaty

General Wayne's victory at the Battle of Fallen Timbers persuaded the British in November 1794 to accept many of the American demands

MULTIPLE LEARNING STYLES

Visual/Spatial Have students draw a political cartoon dealing with some aspect of the section. Possibilities include the whiskey tax or the Whiskey Rebellion from the point of view of farmers in western Pennsylvania, treaties with Native Americans from the point of view of the Native Americans, and Jay's Treaty from the point of view of those who opposed it. **L3, ELL**

presented by the negotiator, John Jay. In **Jay's Treaty** the British agreed to withdraw from American soil, to pay damages for ships they had seized, and to allow some American ships to trade with British colonies in the Caribbean. The treaty also provided for settlement of debts from before 1776.

Despite these gains few Americans approved of Jay's Treaty. Most considered it dishonorable. They protested that the treaty did not deal with the issue of impressment and did not mention British interference with American trade.

Crowds marched in the streets and burned images of John Jay. When Hamilton tried to speak in support of the treaty, people threw stones at him. Although Washington found fault with the treaty, he realized it would end an explosive crisis with Great Britain. He sent the treaty to the Senate, which narrowly approved it after a fierce debate.

Success with Spain

In 1795 the United States signed an agreement with Spain known as **Pinckney's Treaty.** American victories west of the Appalachians had convinced the Spanish to make peace. The Spanish gave the Americans unrestricted access to the Mississippi River and promised to dismantle all forts on American territory.

Washington's Farewell

In the spring of 1796, Washington announced he would not seek a third term. By choosing to serve only two terms, Washington set a precedent that later presidents would follow.

Plagued with a variety of ailments, the 64-year-old president looked forward to retirement at Mount Vernon. He also felt troubled over the divisions in American politics and with what he considered a grave danger to the new nation—the growth of political parties.

Washington's "Farewell Address" was published in a Philadelphia newspaper. In it he attacked the evils of political parties and entanglement in foreign affairs. He also urged his fellow citizens to "observe good faith and justice toward all nations" while avoiding "passionate attachment" and "permanent alliances" with any. Washington's parting words had great influence on the nation's foreign policy for more than 100 years. The text is still read aloud in the U.S. Senate each year on Washington's birthday.

Footnotes to History

A Hero Passes Washington died on December 14, 1799. He became ill with what was probably pneumonia.

Section 2 Review

Checking for Understanding

1. ***Identify*** Whiskey Rebellion, Anthony Wayne, Treaty of Greenville.
2. ***Define*** neutrality, impressment.
3. ***Explain*** the message that Washington was sending to the American people by using force to stop the Whiskey Rebellion.

Reviewing Themes

4. **Civic Rights and Responsibilities** How did the Treaty of Greenville affect the rights of Native Americans?

Critical Thinking

5. **Predicting Consequences** What did the United States have to gain by remaining neutral?

Activity

Writing a Tribute A tribute is a speech showing respect and gratitude. Write a one-paragraph tribute that you might have delivered if you had been asked to speak at President George Washington's funeral.

Section 2 Review Answers

1. Whiskey Rebellion, 262; Anthony Wayne, 263; Treaty of Greenville, 263
2. The words are defined in the Glossary.
3. The government would not tolerate violent protests. Laws had to be changed peacefully, through constitutional means.
4. It allowed settlers to take Native Americans' land.
5. Americans would not be killed in battle; less money and property loss; better relations with other nations; support of many United States citizens

Activity Tributes should cite some of Washington's achievements and his strengths as a leader.

CHAPTER 8
Section 2, 262–265

Reteaching Activity 8–2

Name ______ Date ______ Class ______

★ Reteaching Activity 8-2

DIRECTIONS: Organizing Facts Complete the diagram by writing the letters of the words from the Fact Bank in the correct boxes.

The New Nation Faces Early Challenges

Whiskey Rebellion	Western United States	French and British relations	Washington's Farewell

★ FACT BANK

- **A.** Edmond Genêt
- **B.** influenced American foreign policy
- **C.** Battle of Fallen Timbers
- **D.** Treaty of Greenville
- **E.** Jay's Treaty
- **F.** attacks on tax collectors
- **G.** avoid "permanent alliances"
- **H.** impressment of American citizens
- **I.** General Arthur St. Clair
- **J.** government responds with show of force
- **K.** "observe good faith and justice toward all nations"
- **L.** Proclamation of Neutrality
- **M.** Shawnee chief Blue Jacket

DIRECTIONS: Essay Answer the following questions on a separate sheet of paper.

1. Why was Pinckney's Treaty significant to the United States?
2. Why were some Americans unhappy with Jay's Treaty?

Reteaching Activities ★ 30 ★ *The American Journey*

Enrichment Activity 8–2

Name ______ Date ______ Class ______

★ Enrichment Activity 8-2 ★

Give Me Liberty!

Since *liberty* is an abstract noun, it can mean different things to people. As shown by the American Revolution and the French Revolution, the way to gain liberty can vary too.

DIRECTIONS: Interpreting Symbols Study the two political cartoons. List all the items and actions used as symbols in each cartoon and what you think each one stands for.

Interpreting Symbols

American Liberty		French Liberty	
Symbol	What it stands for	Symbol	What it stands for

Activity **DIRECTIONS:** Think about what liberty means to you. Then create a flag that symbolizes liberty. Include a key with a brief explanation to help others understand the symbols on your flag. Display the flags and keys in your classroom. In what ways are the symbols similar? Different? Discuss the flags with your teacher and classmates.

Enrichment Activities ★ 30 ★ *The American Journey*

4 CLOSE

General Henry Lee, who had fought with Washington in the Revolution, had this tribute upon the president's death: "First in war, first in peace, first in the hearts of his countrymen." Have students cite examples supporting the statement.

1 FOCUS

BELLRINGER
Motivational Activity

Before taking roll at the beginning of the class period, project Section Focus Transparency 8–3 and have students answer the questions. Discuss students' responses.

This activity is also available as a blackline master.

Section Focus Transparency 8–3

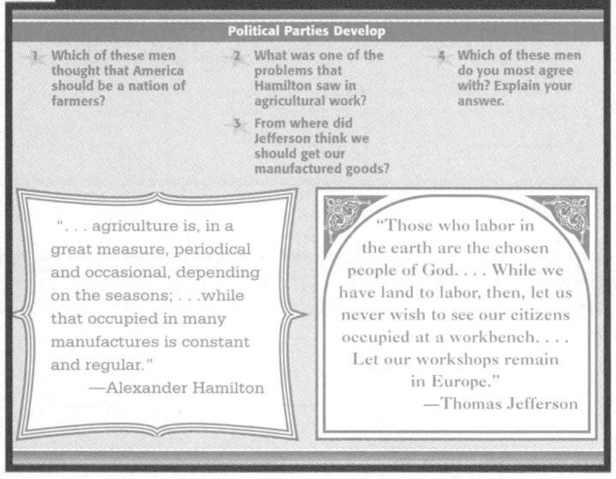

Political Parties Develop

1. Which of these men thought that America should be a nation of farmers?
2. What was one of the problems that Hamilton saw in agricultural work?
3. From where did Jefferson think we should get our manufactured goods?
4. Which of these men do you most agree with? Explain your answer.

". . . agriculture is, in a great measure, periodical and occasional, depending on the seasons; . . .while that occupied in many manufactures is constant and regular."
—Alexander Hamilton

"Those who labor in the earth are the chosen people of God. . . . While we have land to labor, then, let us never wish to see our citizens occupied at a workbench. . . . Let our workshops remain in Europe."
—Thomas Jefferson

Vocabulary Precheck
Call attention to the words *partisan* and *caucus* in **Terms to Learn.** Have students write a sentence or two showing how the terms relate to political parties.

Use the **Vocabulary Puzzle-Maker** to create crossword and word search puzzles.

Section Theme
Economic Factors
Federalists and Republicans disagreed on economic policy, foreign relations, the power of the federal government, interpretation of the Constitution, and the role ordinary people should play in government.

Activity Have students skim the section to determine different positions taken on these subjects.

1795 — 1796 — 1797

1796
Federalists nominate John Adams for president; Democratic-Republicans nominate Jefferson for president

1797
John Adams takes the office of president

Section 3

The First Political Parties

READ TO DISCOVER . . .
- how political parties got started and what positions they supported.
- how John Adams and Thomas Jefferson became candidates of opposing parties in the election of 1796.

TERMS TO LEARN
partisan
implied powers
caucus

The Storyteller

The Washington presidency was known for its dignity and elegance. The president rode in a coach drawn by horses and accompanied by mounted attendants. He and his wife, Martha, lived in the finest house in Philadelphia, the new nation's capital. They entertained a great deal, holding weekly receptions. Each year a ball was held on Washington's birthday. The president wore a black velvet suit with gold buckles, yellow gloves, powdered hair, an ostrich plume in his hat, and a sword in a white leather sheath. Despite these extravagances, Washington's character and military record were admired by most Americans.

Pennsylvania ballot box

Although hailed by Americans as the nation's greatest leader, George Washington did not escape criticism during his two terms as president. From time to time, harsh attacks on his policies and on his personality appeared in newspapers. One paper even called Washington "the scourge and the misfortune of his country."

Opposing Views

The attacks on Washington had come from supporters of Thomas Jefferson. They were trying to discredit the policies of Washington and Hamilton by attacking the president. By 1796 Americans were beginning to divide into opposing groups and to form political parties.

Distrust of Political Parties

Most Americans of the late 1700s considered political parties harmful. Parties—or "factions" as they were called—were as much to be avoided as strong central government. The nation's founders did not even mention political parties in the Constitution.

Washington had denounced political parties and warned that they would divide the nation. Nevertheless as various issues arose in the new republic, it was only natural that people would disagree about them and that people of similar views would band together.

In Washington's cabinet Hamilton and Jefferson increasingly took opposing sides on issues.

SECTION RESOURCES

Reproducible Masters
- Guided Reading Activity 8–3
- Section Quiz 8–3
- Reteaching Activity 8–3
- Enrichment Activity 8–3

Transparencies
- Section Focus Transparency 8–3
- U.S. History & Art, Transparency 8

Multimedia
- Vocabulary PuzzleMaker
- Chapter Challenger Interactive Review Software
- Testmaker
- Focus on American Art Prints, *Athenaeum Portrait of George Washington* by Gilbert Stuart

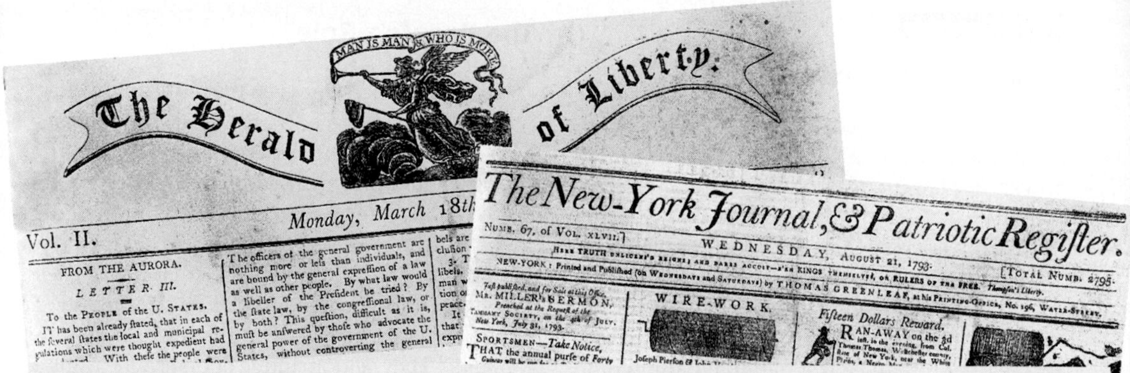

Picturing HISTORY Both Federalists and Republicans used newspaper articles, editorials, and cartoons to influence public opinion. **What were the major differences between Federalists and Republicans?**

They disagreed on economic policy and foreign relations, on the power of the federal government, and on interpreting the Constitution. Even Washington had been partisan—favoring one side of an issue. Although he believed he stood above politics, Washington usually supported Hamilton's positions.

Political Parties Emerge

In Congress and the nation at large, similar differences existed. By the mid-1790s, two distinct political parties had taken shape.

The name **Federalist** had first described someone who supported ratification of the Constitution. By the 1790s the word was applied to a group of people who generally supported the policies of Alexander Hamilton. One man who called himself a Federalist declared he was a "friend of order, of government, and of the present administration."

Generally Federalists stood for a vigorous federal government. They admired Britain, because of its stability, and distrusted France, because of the violent changes following the French Revolution. Federalist policies tended to favor banking and shipping interests. Federalists received the strongest support in the Northeast, especially in New England, and from wealthy plantation owners in the South.

Efforts to turn public opinion against Federalist policies began seriously in late 1791 when Philip Freneau began publishing the *National Gazette* in **Philadelphia.** Jefferson, then secretary of state, helped the newspaper get started. Later he and Madison began to organize people who disagreed with Hamilton's policies. They called their party the **Republicans**, or the **Democratic-Republicans.**

The Republicans wanted to leave as much power as possible to the state governments. They feared that a strong federal government would endanger people's liberties. They supported the French and condemned what they regarded as the Washington administration's pro-British policies. Republican policies appealed to small farmers and urban workers, especially in the Middle Atlantic states and the South.

Footnotes to History

Modern Political Parties Today's Democratic Party traces its roots to Jefferson's Democratic-Republicans. The modern Republican Party, however, was not founded until 1854.

Cooperative Learning Activity

Holding a Panel Discussion Organize the class into small groups with half of each group representing the Federalists and the other half the Democratic-Republicans. Have each group present a panel discussion in which students try to recruit people to their own party. Remind students that to be effective recruiters, they cannot just disparage the beliefs of the other party; they must offer some attractive inducements for people to join their party. Students should prepare their arguments together before presenting the discussion.

2 TEACH

L1 Choosing a Party Have students select the political party they would have joined and defend their choice, orally or in writing.

Picturing HISTORY By 1790, the United States had 92 newspapers. Of that number, 8 were dailies, the first of which was the *Pennsylvania Evening Post,* founded in 1783. **Ask:** **Are newspapers as important to politics today as they were in the 1790s?** *(Students will probably argue that they are not, because TV plays such a large role today.)*

Answer: *Federalists: preferred strong central government, admired Britain, distrusted France, tended to favor wealthy interests, loose interpretation of Constitution. Republicans: preferred strong state governments over strong federal government, supported French, distrusted pro-British policies, favored small farmers and urban workers, strict interpretation of Constitution.*

Guided Reading Activity 8–3

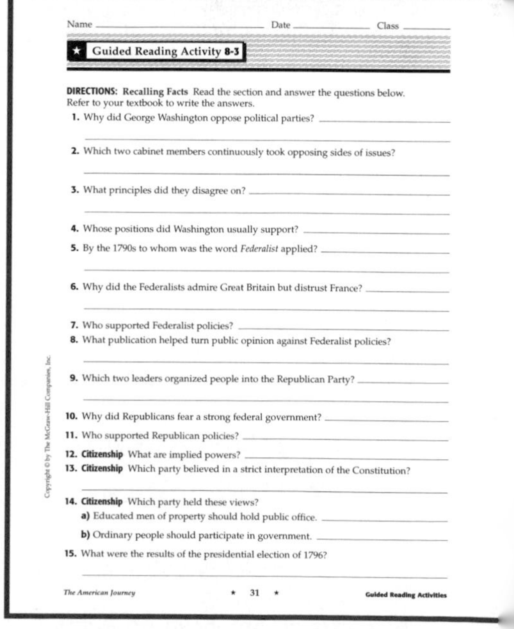
Name ______ Date ______ Class ______

Guided Reading Activity 8-3

DIRECTIONS: Recalling Facts Read the section and answer the questions below. Refer to your textbook to write the answers.

1. Why did George Washington oppose political parties? ______
2. Which two cabinet members continuously took opposing sides of issues? ______
3. What principles did they disagree on? ______
4. Whose positions did Washington usually support? ______
5. By the 1790s to whom was the word *Federalist* applied? ______
6. Why did the Federalists admire Great Britain but distrust France? ______
7. Who supported Federalist policies? ______
8. What publication helped turn public opinion against Federalist policies? ______
9. Which two leaders organized people into the Republican Party? ______
10. Why did Republicans fear a strong federal government? ______
11. Who supported Republican policies? ______
12. **Citizenship** What are implied powers? ______
13. **Citizenship** Which party believed in a strict interpretation of the Constitution? ______
14. **Citizenship** Which party held these views?
    a) Educated men of property should hold public office. ______
    b) Ordinary people should participate in government. ______
15. What were the results of the presidential election of 1796? ______

The American Journey ★ 31 ★ **Guided Reading Activities**

3 ASSESS

Assign Section 3 Review as homework or as an in-class activity.

Use **Chapter Challenger Interactive Review Software** to review Section 3.

Section Quiz 8–3

Name ______ Date ______ Class ______

Chapter 8 — Score

Section Quiz 8-3

DIRECTIONS: Matching Match each item in Column A with the items in Column B. Write the correct letters in the blanks. *(10 points each)*

Column A	Column B
____ 1. political parties	A. Alexander Hamilton
____ 2. favoring one side of an issue	B. Philip Freneau
____ 3. published the *National Gazette*	C. partisan
____ 4. Federalist	D. Thomas Jefferson
____ 5. Democratic-Republican	E. factions

DIRECTIONS: Multiple Choice In the blank at the left, write the letter of the choice that best completes the statement or answers the question. *(10 points each)*

____ 6. This political party stood for a vigorous federal government.
A. Federalist C. Democratic-Republican
B. Antifederalist D. Democratic

____ 7. This party feared that a strong central government would endanger people's liberties.
A. Federalist C. Republican
B. Antifederalist D. Democratic

____ 8. This was NOT a view held by Alexander Hamilton.
A. rule by the wealthy class C. strong federal government
B. British alliance D. free trade

____ 9. This was NOT a view held by Thomas Jefferson.
A. rule by the people C. state banks
B. national bank D. French alliance

____ 10. The second president of the United States was
A. Thomas Jefferson. C. John Adams.
B. Aaron Burr. D. Charles Pinckney.

The American Journey ★ 31 ★ Section Quizzes

Chart Study

Answers
1. Jefferson
2. Hamilton

Chart Skills Practice

Reading a Chart Which party would appeal to someone who favored states' rights? *(Democratic-Republican Party)*

History *and the* Humanities

U.S. History & Art, Transparency 8, *George Washington*

Focus on American Art Prints, *Athenaeum Portrait of George Washington* by Gilbert Stuart

Citizenship

Views of the Constitution

One difference between Federalists and Republicans concerned the basis of government power. In Hamilton's view the federal government had **implied powers,** powers that were not specifically mentioned in the Constitution.

Hamilton used the idea of implied powers to justify a national bank. He argued that the Constitution gave Congress the power to issue money and regulate trade, and a national bank would clearly help the government carry out these responsibilities. Therefore, creating a bank was within the constitutional power of Congress.

Jefferson and Madison disagreed. They believed in a strict interpretation of the Constitution. In their view, unless the Constitution specifically mentioned government powers in a particular area, the government had no authority to act.

Differences Between the First Political Parties

Federalists	Democratic-Republicans
Leader: Alexander Hamilton	**Leader:** Thomas Jefferson
Favored:	**Favored:**
★ Rule by the wealthy class	★ Rule by the people
★ Strong federal government	★ Strong state governments
★ Emphasis on manufactured products	★ Emphasis on agricultural products
★ Loose interpretation of the Constitution	★ Strict interpretation of the Constitution
★ British alliance	★ French alliance
★ National bank	★ State banks
★ Protective tariffs	★ Free trade

Chart Study

Hamilton and Jefferson represented the beliefs of opposition parties.

1. Which leader would have encouraged trade with France? Explain.
2. **Analyzing Information** Which leader would American business owners be more likely to favor?

The People's Role

The differences between the parties, however, went even deeper. Federalists and Republicans had sharply opposing views on the role ordinary people should play in government.

Federalists supported representative government, in which elected officials ruled in the people's name. They did not believe that it was wise to let the public become too involved in politics. "The people are turbulent and changing," Hamilton said. "They seldom judge or determine right."

Public office, Federalists thought, should be held by honest and educated men of property who would protect everyone's rights. Ordinary people were too likely to be swayed by agitators.

In contrast, the Republicans feared a strong central government controlled by a few people. They believed that liberty would be safe only if ordinary people participated in government. As Jefferson explained: "I am not among those who fear the people; they, and not the rich, are our dependence [what we depend on] for continued freedom."

Washington's Dilemma

Washington tried to get his two advisers to work out their differences. Knowing Jefferson was discontented, Washington wrote:

> "I have a great sincere esteem and regard for you both, and ardently wish that some line could be marked out by which both [of] you could walk."

Nevertheless, by 1793 Jefferson was so unhappy that he resigned as secretary of state. Alexander Hamilton resigned, too. The rival groups and their points of view moved further apart.

The Election of 1796

In the presidential election of 1796, candidates sought office for the first time as members of a party rather than as individuals. To

MULTIPLE LEARNING STYLES

Verbal/Linguistic Write this saying on the chalkboard: *"Liberty for the whale means death for the minnow."* Have students explain its meaning. Then have them relate it to each political party. **Ask:** How could Federalists have used it to justify their policies? *(Some sacrifices must be made for the sake of the greater good of the nation.)* How might Democratic-Republicans have refuted it? *(People are not minnows, and so a way must be found for both the wealthy and the common folk to enjoy liberty.)* **L1, ELL**

Causes and Effects

CAUSES

- ★ Different philosophies of government
- ★ Conflicting interpretations of the Constitution
- ★ Different economic and regional interests
- ★ Disagreement over foreign affairs

Political Parties Emerge

EFFECTS

- ★ Federalists and Democratic-Republicans propose different solutions
- ★ The two parties nominate candidates
- ★ Political parties become a way of American life

Chart Study

Thomas Jefferson and Alexander Hamilton emerged as the leaders of the two opposing parties.

Analyzing Information Which political party favored rule by the wealthy and educated class?

prepare for the election, the Federalists and the Republicans held meetings called **caucuses.** At the caucuses members of Congress and other leaders chose their party's candidates for office.

The Federalists nominated Vice President Adams as their candidate for president and Charles Pinckney for vice president. The Republicans put forth former secretary of state Jefferson for president and Aaron Burr for vice president. Adams and Jefferson, who had been good friends, became rivals. The Federalists expected to carry New England. The Republicans' strength lay in the South, which would give most of its votes to Jefferson.

In the end Adams received 71 electoral votes, winning the election. Jefferson finished second with 68 votes. Under the provisions of the Constitution at that time, the person with the second-highest number of electoral votes became vice president. Jefferson therefore became the new vice president even though he represented a different party from the elected president. The administration that took office on March 4, 1797, had a Federalist president and a Republican vice president.

Section 3 Review

Checking for Understanding

1. ***Identify*** Federalist, Philadelphia, Democratic-Republican.
2. ***Define*** partisan, implied powers, caucus.
3. ***Compare*** the Federalists' and Republicans' views of the Constitution.

Reviewing Themes

4. **Economic Factors** Which party was most popular with middle-class urban workers and farmers? Explain.

Critical Thinking

5. **Synthesizing Information** Do you think the development of political parties was necessary? Why or why not?

Activity

Making a Campaign Poster Choose the candidate that you would have voted for in the election of 1796 and make a campaign poster using words and illustrations to promote your candidate.

Section 3 Review Answers

1. Federalist, 267; Philadelphia, 267; Democratic-Republican, 267
2. The words are defined in the Glossary.
3. Federalists believed government had implied powers not mentioned in the Constitution. Republicans believed that unless powers were mentioned in the Constitution, government had no authority to act.
4. Democratic-Republican; it allowed them more say in government.
5. Answers may include: *Yes,* because people will always disagree on some issues and there must be a way for them to act as a group to represent their point of view. *No,* because parties divide the nation.

Activity Posters should accurately represent the beliefs of each party and candidate.

Chart Study

Answer Federalists

Reteaching Activity 8–3

Name ______ Date ______ Class ______

★ Reteaching Activity 8-3

DIRECTIONS: Organizing Facts The numbered items are characteristics of the first political parties. Write the number of each item in the appropriate section of the chart.

The First Political Parties

	Federalist	Republican
Political Leaders		
Policies		
Public Supporters		

★FACT BANK

1. small Southern farmers
2. Alexander Hamilton
3. strict interpretation of the Constitution
4. British alliance
5. French alliance
6. New Englanders
7. Thomas Jefferson
8. implied powers of the federal government
9. rule by educated property owners
10. strong state governments
11. rule by ordinary citizens
12. favored banking and shipping interests
13. James Madison
14. wealthy Southern plantation owners
15. strong central government
16. urban workers in Mid-Atlantic states

DIRECTIONS: Essay Answer the following question on a separate sheet of paper. Explain why the administration that took office on March 4, 1797, had a Federalist president and a Republican vice president.

The American Journey ★ 31 ★ **Reteaching Activities**

Enrichment Activity 8–3

Name ______ Date ______ Class ______

★ Enrichment Activity 8-3

Monticello

Thomas Jefferson spent more than 50 years designing and redesigning Monticello, which had three stories, Greek columns, and the first dome in an American home. The drawing to the right shows Jefferson's original first-floor plan and the additions to the first floor made over the years.

DIRECTIONS: Interpreting a Floor Plan Study the floor plan and answer the following questions.

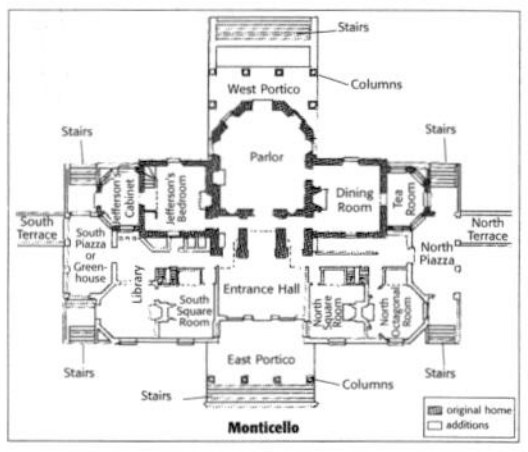

1. What direction or directions did the building face? ______
2. What was unique about the room sizes, shapes, and functions? ______
3. What exterior, or outside, design features are suggested? ______
4. In what ways is the design of the first floor symmetrical (balanced)? Describe one design feature that is not symmetrical. ______
5. What features were added to the design after 1771? ______
6. Jefferson's bed was placed between his bedroom and his cabinet. What does that suggest about the use of Jefferson's cabinet? ______
7. Why do the west and east porticos show large stairways, but the north and south entrances do not? ______

Activity **DIRECTIONS:** Imagine that you and a partner are able to design and build a home that is similar in size to Monticello. Think about how houses and their uses have changed since Thomas Jefferson designed Monticello—the need for a garage or a television viewing area, for example. Then draw a design for your modern-day Monticello.

The American Journey ★ 31 ★ **Enrichment Activities**

4 CLOSE

Have students think of one reason to support Hamilton's idea of implied powers and one reason to support Jefferson's strict interpretation of the Constitution.

1 FOCUS

BELLRINGER
Motivational Activity

Before taking roll at the beginning of the class period, project Section Focus Transparency 8–4 and have students answer the questions. Discuss students' responses.

This activity is also available as a blackline master.

Section Focus Transparency 8–4

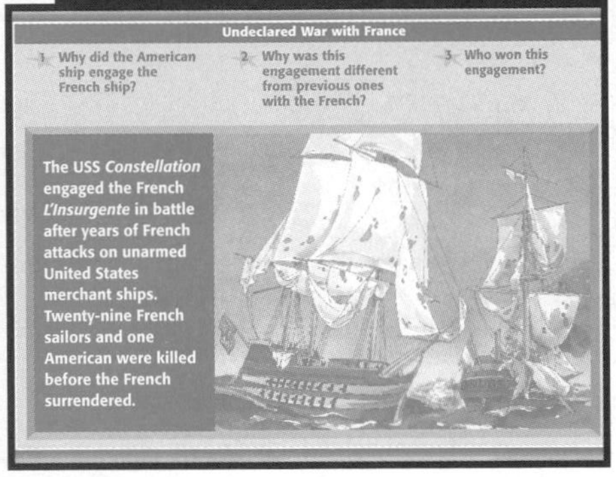

Vocabulary Precheck

Point out that the term *alien* comes from a Latin word meaning "other." Have students speculate on how *alien* and *other* are connected.

Use the **Vocabulary PuzzleMaker** to create crossword and word search puzzles.

Section Theme
Groups and Institutions

In 1798 the Federalist-controlled Congress passed the Alien and Sedition acts.

Activity Have students discuss why these acts were an abuse of power on the part of Congress. *(The acts were aimed at weakening and harassing the opposition, rather than strengthening or helping the nation.)*

1797 — 1798 — 1799 — 1800

March 1797 John Adams becomes president

1798 Congress passes Alien and Sedition acts

May 1798 Congress establishes the Navy Department

1800 France makes peace with the United States

Section 4

President John Adams

READ TO DISCOVER . . .
- why the United States fought an undeclared war with France.
- why the Alien and Sedition acts divided the country.

TERMS TO LEARN

alien
sedition
deport
states' rights
nullify

The Storyteller

Before John Adams was inaugurated, he had been widely criticized in the newspapers. At one time he had worked on the idea of titles for high government officials. Perhaps the president should be called "His Mightiness," Adams offered. This suggestion earned Adams great ridicule, including being rudely dubbed "His Rotundity"—a comment on his stout figure.

Pitcher honoring John Adams, 1797

John Adams became the second president of the United States on March 4, 1797. The new president was a man of great intelligence and ability. Reserved and somewhat rigid, he felt more comfortable with ideas than with people. In the emotionally charged political atmosphere of the day, the nation needed a strong leader.

The XYZ Affair

Early in his administration, Adams faced a crisis with France. The French regarded Jay's Treaty, signed in 1794, as an American attempt to help the British in their war with France. To punish the United States, the French seized American ships that carried cargo to Britain.

Adams wanted to avoid war with France. In the fall of 1797, he sent a delegation to Paris to try to resolve the dispute. French foreign minister **Charles de Talleyrand,** however, refused to meet with the Americans. Instead, Talleyrand sent three agents who demanded a bribe and a loan for France from the Americans. "Not a sixpence," the Americans replied and sent a report of the incident to the United States. Adams was furious. Referring to the three French agents as X, Y, and Z, the president urged Congress to prepare for war. The incident became known as the **XYZ affair.**

Undeclared War With France

Congress responded with a program to strengthen the armed forces. It established the Navy Department in May 1798 and set aside

SECTION RESOURCES

Reproducible Masters
- Reproducible Lesson Plan 8–4
- Guided Reading Activity 8–4
- Political Cartoons, *The XYZ Affair*
- Section Quiz 8–4
- Reteaching Activity 8–4
- Enrichment Activity 8–4

Transparencies
- Section Focus Transparency 8–4

Multimedia
- Vocabulary PuzzleMaker
- Chapter Challenger Interactive Review
- Testmaker
- Facts On File: Landmark Documents in American History

money for building warships. Congress also increased the size of the army. George Washington was appointed commanding general.

Between 1798 and 1800, American and French naval forces fought an undeclared war. The Americans seized more than 90 French armed ships. No fighting took place on land.

For most Americans France had become an enemy. The Republican Party, friendly toward France in the past, hesitated to turn around and condemn France. As a result, in the 1798 elections, Americans voted many Republicans out of office.

Alien and Sedition Acts

The threat of war with France made Americans more suspicious of **aliens,** immigrants living in the country who were not citizens. Many Europeans who came to the United States in the 1790s endorsed the ideals of the French Revolution. Some became active supporters of the Republican Party. Some Americans questioned whether these aliens would remain loyal in the event of a war with France.

Federalists in Congress responded with strict laws to protect the nation's security. In 1798 they passed a group of measures known as the **Alien and Sedition acts. Sedition** refers to activities aimed at weakening established government. Adams had not asked for these laws, but he went along with the Federalist majority in Congress.

The Alien Act

The Alien Act gave the president the power to **deport,** or send out of the country, aliens he considered dangerous. Another law, the **Naturalization Act,** made it difficult for white aliens—African Americans could not even apply—to become citizens. Individuals would have to live in the country for 14 years—instead of 5 years—before applying for citizenship. This law was aimed at preventing foreigners, who were likely to join the Republicans, from becoming citizens.

Picturing HISTORY In Congress, Federalist Roger Griswold, wielding a cane, fights with Republican Matthew Lyon, a victim of the Sedition Act of 1798. **What was the aim of the Sedition Act?**

The Sedition Act

The Sedition Act made it a crime to speak, write, or publish "false, scandalous and malicious" criticisms of the government, Congress, or the president. The Federalists, who controlled Congress, pointedly omitted mention of the vice president in the law because Thomas Jefferson—a Republican—held the office.

Nobody was deported under the Alien Act, which expired in 1802. The government did use the Sedition Act, however, to prosecute a number

Footnotes to History

The Laundry Room When John and Abigail Adams moved into the White House in 1800, the house was largely unfinished. Because there was no place to dry the family laundry, Mrs. Adams strung up a clothesline in the East Room.

Cooperative Learning Activity

Researching the U.S.S. *Constitution* The U.S.S. *Constitution* was built in response to the French threat. The frigate is still afloat and open to the public at Charlestown, Massachusetts. Organize the class into groups to do research on "Old Ironsides," as it was called, and to present their findings in an illustrated report. Have students in each group choose their own tasks, such as doing research, drawing a diagram of the ship, writing the report, making maps of the ship's voyages, and making a time line showing its battles. One or two students might like to present to the class the Oliver Wendell Holmes poem "Old Ironsides."

2 TEACH

L1 Explaining Relationships
Have students explain the relationship between each of the following pairs: XYZ affair—undeclared war on France; Alien Act—Republicans; Sedition Act—Matthew Lyon; Virginia and Kentucky Resolutions—federal laws.

Picturing HISTORY Lyon had earlier earned the nickname the "Spitting Lion" for spitting in the face of a Federalist. His offense under the Sedition Act was writing that President Adams had an "unbounded thirst for ridiculous pomp, foolish adulation, and selfish avarice." **Ask:** **Which amendment to the Constitution did the Sedition Act violate?** *(First Amendment, freedom of speech)*
Answer: *It provided a way for the Federalists to harass Republicans and prohibited people from criticizing the government.)*

Political Cartoons, *The XYZ Affair*

Guided Reading Activity 8–4

Name ______ Date ______ Class ______

Guided Reading Activity 8-4

DIRECTIONS: Using Headings and Subheadings Locate each heading in your textbook. Then use the information under the correct subheading to help you write each answer.

I. The XYZ Affair
A. How did France punish the United States for signing Jay's Treaty with Great Britain?
B. What French foreign minister refused to negotiate with the American delegation sent to Paris in 1797 to resolve the dispute?
C. How did John Adams respond to the story about three French agents who demanded a bribe and a loan for France?
D. How did Congress prepare for the war with France?
E. In the undeclared war with France, where did all of the fighting take place?

II. Alien and Sedition Acts
A. What power did the Alien Act grant the president?
B. How did the Naturalization Act make it difficult for foreigners to become citizens?
C. What did the Sedition Act make a crime?

III. States' Rights
A. **Citizenship** Which states endorsed the resolutions on states' rights written by Republican leaders James Madison and Thomas Jefferson?
B. **Citizenship** According to the resolutions, what rights did the states have?

IV. Peace with France
A. Who urged Adams to step up the war with France?
B. What were the political results of Adams's decision to seek peace with France?

Guided Reading Activities • 32 • *The American Journey*

3 ASSESS

Assign Section 4 Review as homework or as an in-class activity.

Use **Chapter Challenger Interactive Review Software** to review Section 4.

Section Quiz 8–4

Name ______ Date ______ Class ______

Chapter 8 — Score

Section Quiz 8-4

DIRECTIONS: Matching Match each item in Column A with the items in Column B. Write the correct letters in the blanks. *(10 points each)*

Column A	Column B
____ 1. French foreign minister	A. XYZ affair
____ 2. led to undeclared war with France	B. nullify
____ 3. activities aimed at weakening government	C. Alien Act
____ 4. gave president power to deport	D. Charles de Talleyrand
____ 5. legally overturn	E. sedition

DIRECTIONS: Multiple Choice In the blank at the left, write the letter of the choice that best completes the statement or answers the question. *(10 points each)*

____ 6. This law was aimed at preventing foreigners from becoming citizens.
A. Republican Act C. Sedition Act
B. Naturalization Act D. Alien Act

Enrichment Activity 8–4

Name ______ Date ______ Class ______

Enrichment Activity 8-4

The New American Navy

In 1797 Americans finished construction of three frigates to fight French ships harassing Americans at sea. One of these ships was the *Constitution*, shown to the right.

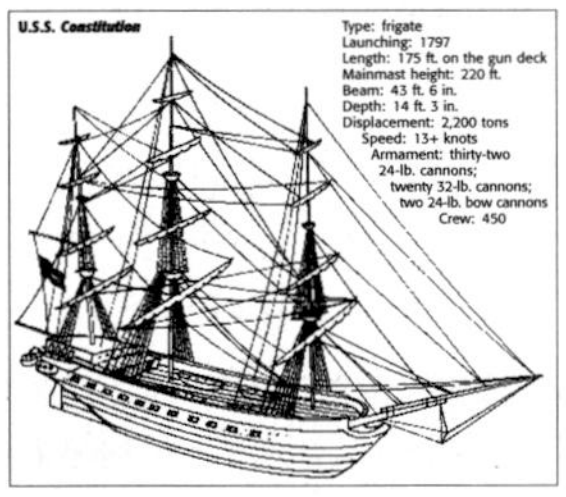

DIRECTIONS: Interpreting Information Use the picture to answer the following questions.

1. How many masts did the ship have?
2. How many cannons were on the ship?

Reteaching Activity 8–4

Name ______ Date ______ Class ______

Reteaching Activity 8-4

DIRECTIONS: Putting Events in Sequence Number the events in the order in which they occurred.

____ A. The Alien Act expires.
____ B. Great Britain and the United States sign Jay's Treaty.
____ C. The Virginia legislature endorses the Virginia Resolution.
____ D. Congress passes the Alien and Sedition acts.
____ E. French ships stop attacking American ships.
____ F. President John Adams sends a diplomatic delegation to France.
____ G. The Kentucky legislature endorses the Kentucky Resolution.
____ H. Congress establishes the Navy department.

DIRECTIONS: Essay Answer the following questions.
1. Why did Republicans lose many elections in 1798?

4 CLOSE

Ask: Why did Federalists want to step up the war with France? Why did Adams refuse to do so? *(to stir up patriotic fervor in their favor; he felt it was dishonorable)*

of people—mostly Republican newspaper editors. One Republican representative, Matthew Lyon of Vermont, even went to jail for criticizing Adams. In all, 25 people were arrested and 10 convicted of violating the law.

Citizenship

States' Rights

For some Americans, fears of a strong central government abusing its power seemed to be coming true. The Republicans looked to the states to preserve the people's liberties and stand up to what they regarded as Federalist tyranny. Madison and Jefferson wrote two resolutions on the rights of states that were endorsed by the legislatures of **Virginia** and **Kentucky**.

The **Virginia** and **Kentucky Resolutions** of 1798 and 1799 spelled out a theory of states' rights. According to the resolutions, states had the right to judge the constitutionality of federal laws. The Kentucky Resolutions further suggested that states might nullify—that is, legally overturn—federal laws considered unconstitutional.

The Virginia and Kentucky Resolutions posed a direct challenge to the constitutional authority of the national government. The prospect of state militias fighting with federal army troops seemed real at the time to many people. Although no other states adopted similar resolutions, the Resolutions revealed the extent of people's fears about a strong federal government interfering with their rights. The issue of states' rights would arise again and again in the nation's early history, leading in time to a division of the states into opposing camps and to civil war.

Peace With France

As the election of 1800 approached, the Federalists found themselves under attack. They urged Adams to step up the war with France. They hoped to benefit politically from the patriotic feelings that war would unleash.

Adams refused to rush to war, especially for his own political gain. Instead he appointed a new commission to seek peace with France. In 1800 the French agreed to a treaty and stopped attacks on American ships.

Although the agreement with France was in the best interest of the United States, it divided the Federalists and hurt Adams's chance for reelection. Rather than benefiting from a conflict with France, Hamilton and his supporters were now in open opposition to their own president.

With the Federalists split, the Republican prospects for capturing the presidency improved. The way was prepared for Thomas Jefferson in the election of 1800.

Section 4 Review

Checking for Understanding

1. ***Identify*** John Adams, XYZ affair, Alien and Sedition acts, Kentucky Resolution.
2. ***Define*** alien, sedition, deport, states' rights, nullify.
3. ***Explain*** why the Federalists passed the Alien and Sedition acts.

Reviewing Themes

4. **Groups and Institutions** What did the Virginia and Kentucky Resolutions uphold?

Critical Thinking

5. **Determining Cause and Effect** How did President Adams's decision to avoid a war with France divide the Federalists and help the Republicans?

Activity

Drawing a Political Cartoon Draw a political cartoon that criticizes the Alien and Sedition acts of 1798.

Section 4 Review Answers

1. John Adams, 270; XYZ affair, 270; Alien and Sedition acts, 271; Kentucky Resolution, 272
2. The words are defined in the Glossary.
3. to protect national security at a time when war with France was a possibility and to weaken the Republican Party
4. They upheld states' rights over the constitutional authority of the national government.
5. When Adams refused to go to war for political gain, it pitted Federalist leaders against their own president, dividing the party and improving Republican chances of gaining the presidency.

Activity Cartoons should illustrate some of the negative sentiments created by the Alien and Sedition acts.

Social Studies
SKILL BUILDER

Reading a Flowchart

Sometimes determining a sequence of events can confuse us, particularly when many events are occurring at the same time. Reading a flowchart can help you understand what is going on.

Learning the Skill

Flowcharts show the steps in a process or a sequence of events. A flowchart could be used to show the movement of goods through a factory, of people through a training program, or of a bill through Congress.

The following steps explain how to read a flowchart:

- Read the title or caption of the flowchart to find out what you are studying.
- Read all of the labels or sentences on the flowchart.
- Look for numbers indicating a sequence of steps, or arrows showing the direction of movement.
- Evaluate the information in the flowchart.

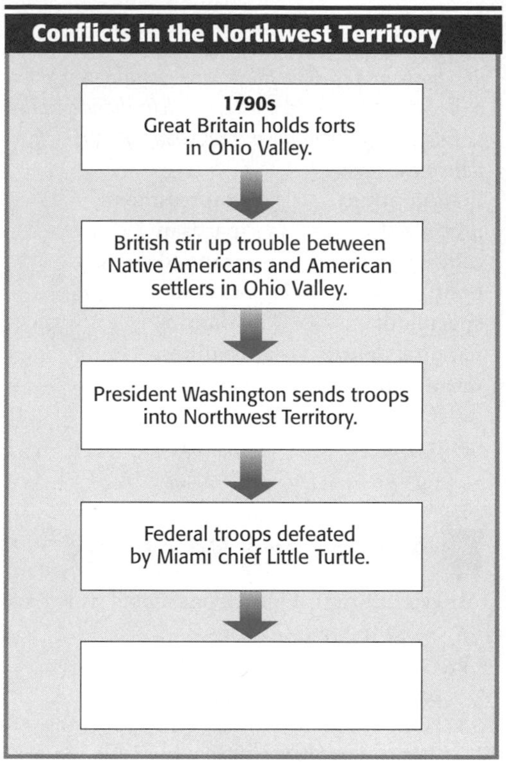

Practicing the Skill

Read the flowchart on this page. It shows a sequence of events that took place in the Northwest Territory. Analyze the information in the flowchart, then answer the following questions.

1. What is the title of this flowchart?
2. What symbol is used to show the direction in which the events are moving?
3. What actions taken by the British set off the sequence of events that are reflected in the title of the chart?
4. What action did President Washington take in response to trouble in the Ohio Valley?
5. What information from the chapter could you add to the flowchart to show a further sequence of events?

Applying the Skill

Making a Flowchart Imagine that a student who is new to your school asks you how to sign up for a sport or social club. Draw a flowchart outlining the steps the student should follow.

Social Studies
SKILL BUILDER

TEACH

Reading a Flowchart

This skill teaches students how to read a flowchart, a kind of diagram that is useful in showing a process or a sequence of events. Point out that this flowchart reads from top to bottom, but that others may go from side to side. A more complicated one might go in more than one direction.

Have students think of everyday things they do that might be explained in a flowchart. *(doing laundry, washing dishes, caring for a pet, and so forth)*

Additional Practice

Chapter Skills Activity 8

Facts On File

CD-ROM
Landmark Documents in American History

Title: *Chisholm* v. *Georgia, 1793*
Have students practice the skill by reviewing the document and outlining—in a flowchart—the sequence of events occurring before, during, and after this Supreme Court decision. *(Students' flowcharts will vary, but should include: Confiscation of Chisholm's land by Georgians; Chisholm's heirs sue state of Georgia for compensation; Georgia refuses to appear in Court; Court rules in favor of Chisholm; State protests against decision; Passage of Eleventh Amendment.)*

ANSWERS TO PRACTICING THE SKILL

1. Conflicts in the Northwest Territory
2. arrow
3. The British took control of forts and stirred up trouble between Native Americans and American settlers in the Ohio Valley.
4. He sent troops into the Northwest Territory.
5. General Anthony Wayne sent to gain control of Ohio River valley; Shawnee defeated at Battle of Fallen Timbers; Native Americans forced to sign treaty opening Ohio to white settlement

Applying the Skill Students' flowcharts should outline a logical sequence of events associated with joining a school club.

GLENCOE TECHNOLOGY

VIDEODISC
MindJogger Videoquiz

Use MindJogger to review the Chapter 8 content.

Chapter 8
Disc 1, Side B

Also available in VHS.

Reviewing Key Terms

The key terms used in this activity are defined in the textbook glossary on pages A26–A35. Students' word search puzzles will vary.

Reviewing Key Facts

1. State Department, Treasury Department, War Department
2. Many people had already sold their bonds at a loss; speculators would get rich; Southern states did not want the debt accumulated by Northern states.
3. At first Americans supported the French Revolution because the French had offered aid during the Revolutionary War and their revolution seemed to embody the ideals of the American Revolution. Later, when the French Revolution turned bloody, many Americans opposed its violence as well as its attack on religion and its disregard for individual liberties.
4. People disagreed about many issues, so people of similar views banded together in political parties.
5. The French began seizing American ships that carried cargo to British ports; the XYZ affair

Chapter 8
Review and Activities

Reviewing Key Terms

On graph paper, create a word search puzzle using the following terms. Crisscross the terms vertically and horizontally, then fill in the remaining squares with extra letters. Use the terms' definitions as clues to find the words in the puzzle. Share your puzzle with a classmate.

inauguration	**impressment**
precedent	**partisan**
cabinet	**implied powers**
bond	**caucus**
speculator	**alien**
national debt	**sedition**
unconstitutional	**deport**
tariff	**states' rights**
neutrality	**nullify**

Reviewing Key Facts

1. What three cabinet departments were created by the first Congress?
2. Why did many people think Hamilton's proposal to sell bonds was unfair?
3. Why did many Americans support the French Revolution at first but later oppose it?
4. What was the main reason for the formation of political parties?
5. What actions by France led to an undeclared war with the United States?

Critical Thinking

Identifying Assumptions

The issue of states' rights versus national rights was a problem that would plague the new nation for many years.

1. Why did some Americans fear a strong central government?
2. How did the Alien and Sedition acts increase these fears?

Time Line Activity

Create a time line on which you place the following events in chronological order.

- John Adams is elected president
- Twelve Native American nations sign the Treaty of Greenville
- Bill of Rights is added to the Constitution
- Congress passes Alien and Sedition acts
- George Washington becomes the first president of the United States
- Undeclared war between America and France ends

Geography Activity

The British held on to their frontier outposts until the Jay Treaty. Study the map below, then answer the questions that follow.

British Forts Held Until 1796

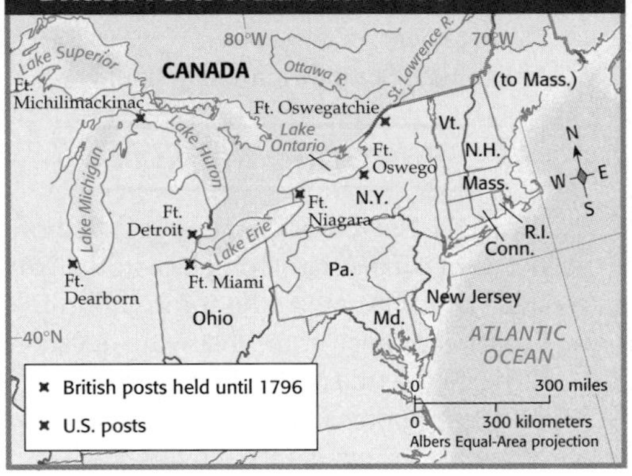

1. **Location** What two British forts were located in New York?
2. **Movement** Along what natural transportation route were British forts located?
3. **Location** About how many miles apart were the easternmost and westernmost U.S. posts?

Critical Thinking

1. They thought it would abuse its power and infringe on individual and states' rights.
2. These acts took away individual rights, such as freedom of expression.

Time Line Activity

Events should be placed in this order: George Washington becomes the first president of the United States, Bill of Rights is added to the Constitution, Twelve Native American nations sign the Treaty of Greenville, John Adams is elected president, Congress passes Alien and Sedition acts, Undeclared war between America and France ends

Skill Practice Activity

Reading a Flowchart

Alexander Hamilton promoted the creation of a national bank. Study the flowchart below, then answer the questions that follow.

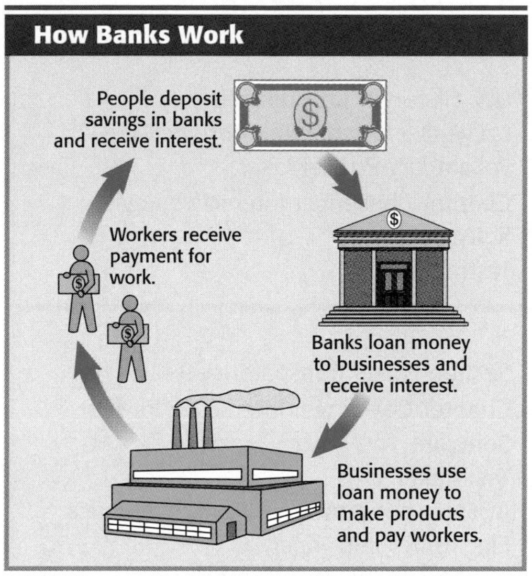

1. What is the title of this flowchart?
2. What is used to show the direction in which the events are moving?
3. What happens after workers receive payment for their work?
4. What two parts on this flowchart show who receives interest on their money?

Cooperative Activity

History and Journalism Working in pairs, scan newspapers to find five articles that, as written, would have been considered a violation of the Sedition Act in 1798. Clip each article and highlight the information you think would have violated the Sedition Act.

Reviewing Themes

1. **Government and Democracy** How did the Tenth Amendment strengthen the rights of individual states?
2. **Civic Rights and Responsibilities** What advice did President Washington give Americans in his Farewell Address?
3. **Economic Factors** How did Federalists justify Congress's creation of a national bank?
4. **Groups and Institutions** How did the XYZ affair increase bad feelings between France and the United States?

Technology Activity

Using a Computerized Card Catalog Search your local library's computerized card catalog for sources on Mount Vernon, George Washington's home. Find the sources on the library shelves, then use the information you find to write a two-paragraph description that Washington might have written if he had ever wanted to sell his home.

Portfolio Activity History Journal Review the chapter and make a list of the differences between the Federalist and Republican parties. Based on your list, create a symbol to represent each of the parties.

CHAPTER 8
Review and Activities

Reviewing Themes

1. Any powers not granted to the federal government were granted to the states or to individuals.
2. Washington encouraged Americans to avoid the formation of political parties and entanglement in foreign affairs.
3. Hamilton argued that the Constitution gave Congress the power to issue money and regulate trade and that a national bank would help the government carry out these responsibilities—implied powers.
4. The French foreign minister refused to negotiate with American representatives and demanded a bribe and a loan. This action infuriated President Adams and moved the two countries toward war.

Technology Activity

Students' paragraphs should reflect knowledge gained about Mount Vernon.

Portfolio Activity Students should sketch a symbol that represents one or more of the stands taken by either the Republican or Federalist parties.

Chapter Bonus Test Question

Ask: What salary did George Washington receive as president? *($25,000)* What does the president receive today? *($200,000 plus expenses for transportation, staff, entertainment)*

Geography Activity

1. Oswego, Niagara
2. Great Lakes
3. about 750 miles

Skill Practice Activity

1. How Banks Work
2. arrows
3. People deposit savings in banks and receive interest.
4. Banks receive interest on loans and people receive interest on savings.

Cooperative Activity

Students' choices should reflect an understanding of the Sedition Act.

Chapter 9 Resource Guide

A complete, 1-page lesson plan is provided for each section in the *Reproducible Lesson Plans* booklet.

Section Resources

Daily Objectives	Reproducible Resources	Multimedia Resources
Section 1 **The Republicans Take Power** Explain how the election deadlock of 1800 was resolved and how John Marshall strengthened the Supreme Court.	Reproducible Lesson Plan 9–1 Guided Reading Activity 9–1* Section Quiz 9–1* Reteaching Activity 9–1 Enrichment Activity 9–1	Section Focus Transparency 9–1 U.S. History & Art, Transparency 5, *University of Virginia, Charlottesville* Vocabulary PuzzleMaker Chapter Challenger Interactive Review Software Testmaker
Section 2 **The Louisiana Purchase** Discuss the acquisition and exploration of the Louisiana Territory.	Reproducible Lesson Plan 9–2 Guided Reading Activity 9–2* Section Quiz 9–2* Reteaching Activity 9–2 Enrichment Activity 9–2	Section Focus Transparency 9–2 Chapter Challenger Interactive Review Software Testmaker ABCNews InterActive™ Historic America Electronic Field Trips GTV: A Geographic Perspective on American History
Section 3 **A Time of Conflict** Summarize the results of Jefferson's actions in sending ships against the Barbary pirates and in promoting a trade ban, and explain why Tecumseh wanted a confederation and the War Hawks wanted war.	Reproducible Lesson Plan 9–3 Guided Reading Activity 9–3* Political Cartoons, *The Embargo Act of 1807* Section Quiz 9–3* Reteaching Activity 9–3 Enrichment Activity 9–3	Section Focus Transparency 9–3 Vocabulary PuzzleMaker Chapter Challenger Interactive Review Software Testmaker GTV: A Geographic Perspective on American History GTV: The American People: Fabric of a Nation The Presidents: A Picture History of Our Nation
Section 4 **The War of 1812** Summarize the course of the war from the failed invasion of Canada to the unnecessary Battle of New Orleans.	Reproducible Lesson Plan 9–4 Guided Reading Activity 9–4* Section Quiz 9–4* Reteaching Activity 9–4 Enrichment Activity 9–4	Section Focus Transparency 9–4 Vocabulary PuzzleMaker Chapter Challenger Interactive Review Software Testmaker ABCNews InterActive™ Historic America Electronic Field Trips Facts On File: Landmark Documents in American History

** Also available in Spanish*

Blackline Master · Videodisc · Audiocassette · Transparency · CD-ROM · Software

0:00 **OUT OF TIME?**
Assign the Chapter 9 Digest and the corresponding Chapter Digests Audiocassettes with activities and tests.

Activity

From the Classroom of...

Rick Wilson
Brunswick Jr. High School
Brunswick, ME

"Who Has?" "I Have."
(Around-the-World Chapter Review)

Students will identify the major people and events in Chapter 9 by playing a game using index cards. First, write a "Who has. . . ?" question—such as, "Who has the name of the man inaugurated as president on March 4, 1801?"—on the front of an index card. Then write the answer to that question *on the back of a different card:* "I have Thomas Jefferson." Continue this process of writing a "Who has. . . ?" question on the front of one card and the "I have . . . " answer on the back of a different card—one card for every student. The last step involves writing your last "I have . . . " answer on the back of the very first card, completing the circle "around the world." You may want to play the game several times, redistributing the cards and seeing how much faster the class can complete it a second or third time.

National Geographic Society Teacher's Corner

INDEX TO NATIONAL GEOGRAPHIC MAGAZINE

The following articles may be used for research relating to this chapter:

- "L'Enfant's Washington," by Alice J. Hall, August 1991.
- "The Peales: America's First Family of Art," by Otto Friedrich, December 1990.
- "Thomas Jefferson: Architect of Freedom," by Mike Edwards, February 1976

NATIONAL GEOGRAPHIC SOCIETY PRODUCTS AVAILABLE FROM GLENCOE

To order the following products for use with this chapter, contact your local Glencoe sales representative, or call Glencoe at 1-800-334-7344:

- *GTV: The American People: Fabric of a Nation* (Videodisc).
- *GTV: A Geographic Perspective on American History* (Videodisc)
- *The Presidents: A Picture History of Our Nation* (CD-ROM)
- *PictureShow: The Westward Movement* (CD-ROM)
- *PictureShow: The Westward Movement* (Transparencies)

ADDITIONAL NATIONAL GEOGRAPHIC SOCIETY PRODUCTS

To order the following products for use with this chapter, call National Geographic Society at 1-800-368-2728:

- *Washington, D.C.* (Video)
- *Historical Atlas of the United States* (Atlas)

Block Schedule

Block scheduling differs from traditional class scheduling in the amount of time allotted to each period. The extended time frame provided by block scheduling affords you the opportunity to implement a greater number of research-oriented and activity-intense projects to motivate and involve your students. Activities that are particularly suited to use within the block scheduling framework are identified throughout this chapter by the following designation:

KEY TO ABILITY LEVELS

Teaching strategies have been coded for varying learning styles and abilities.

- **L1 BASIC** activities for all students
- **L2 AVERAGE** activities for average to above-average students
- **L3 CHALLENGING** activities for above-average students
- **ELL ENGLISH LANGUAGE LEARNER** activities

Chapter 9 Resource Guide

Home Involvement

Home Involvement Activity 9

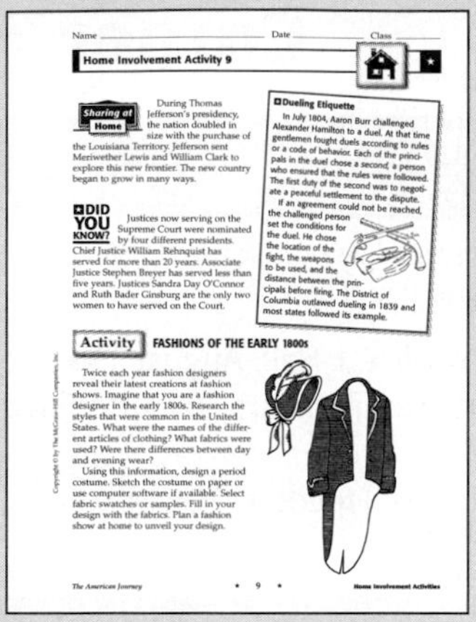
Home Involvement Activity 9

Activity FASHIONS OF THE EARLY 1800s

Review Activities

Chapter Summary 9

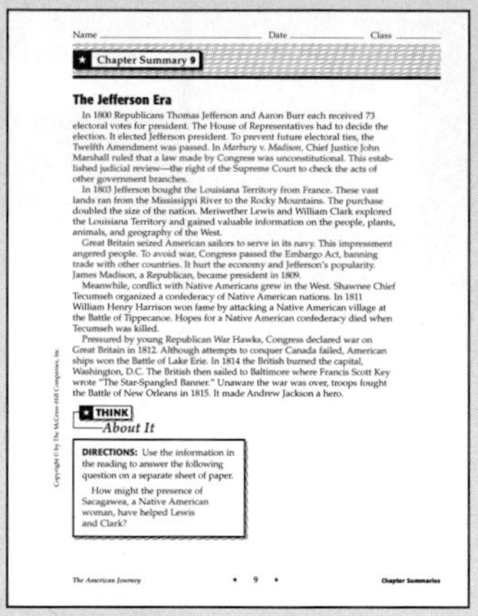
Chapter Summary 9

The Jefferson Era

Workbook Activity 9

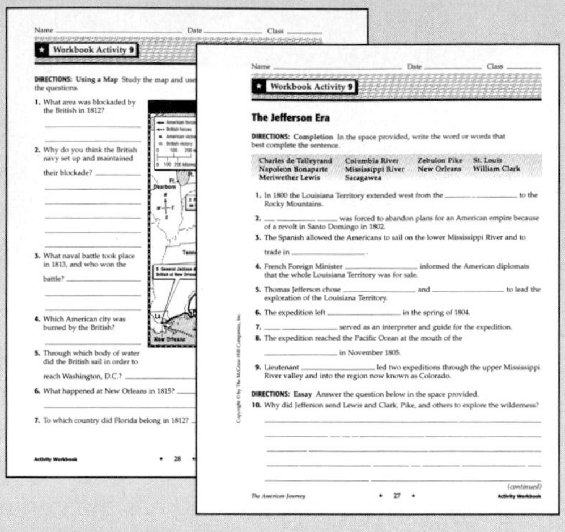
Workbook Activity 9

The Jefferson Era

Reinforcement Activities

Time Line Activity 9

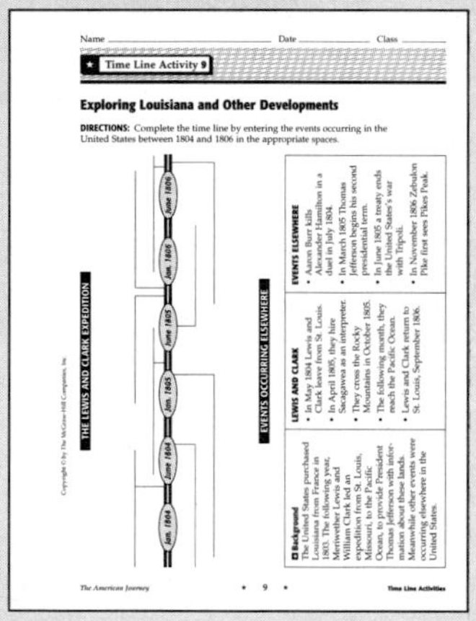
Time Line Activity 9

Exploring Louisiana and Other Developments

Vocabulary Activity 9

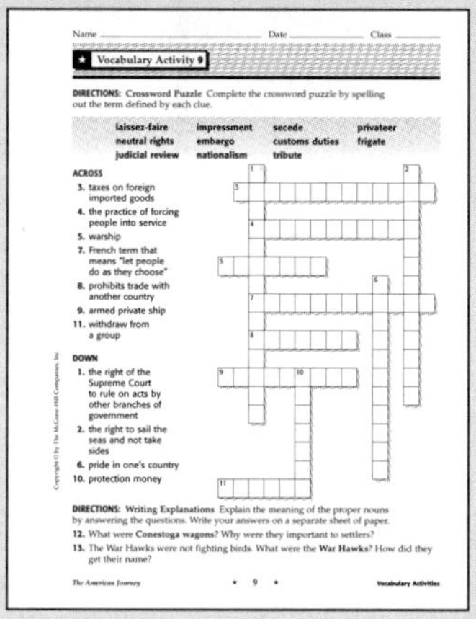
Vocabulary Activity 9

Chapter Skills Activity 9

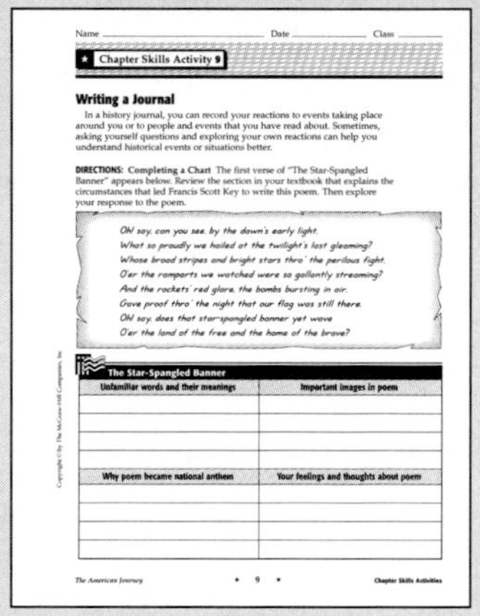
Chapter Skills Activity 9

Writing a Journal

Enrichment Activities

Linking Past and Present Activity 9

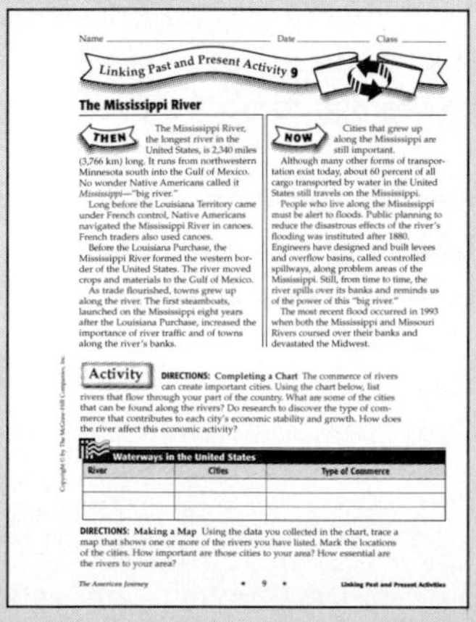
Linking Past and Present Activity 9

The Mississippi River

Primary Source Reading 9

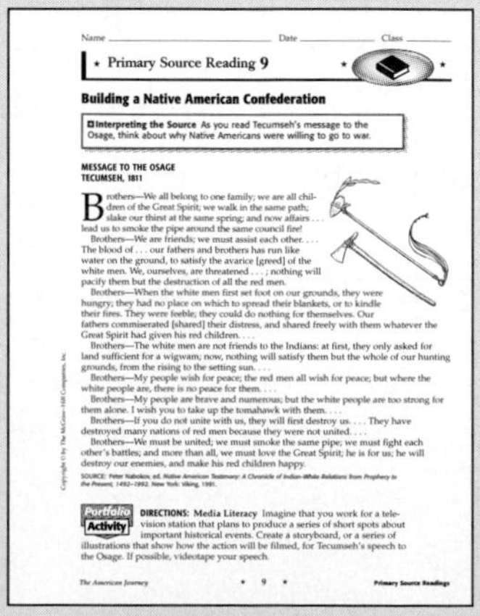
Primary Source Reading 9

Building a Native American Confederation

Geography Activities

Mapping History Activity 9

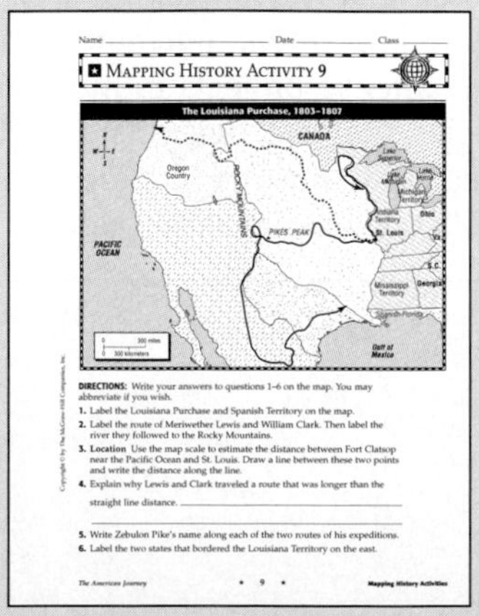
Mapping History Activity 9

The Louisiana Purchase, 1803–1807

Chapter 9 Resource Guide

Assessment

Chapter 9 Test, Form A

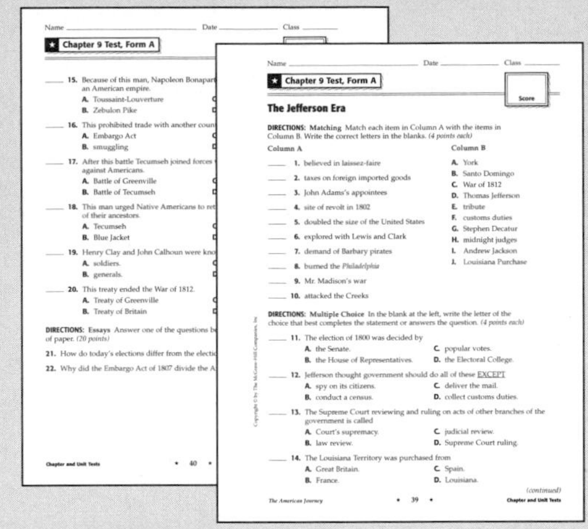
Chapter 9 Test, Form A

The Jefferson Era

Chapter 9 Test, Form B

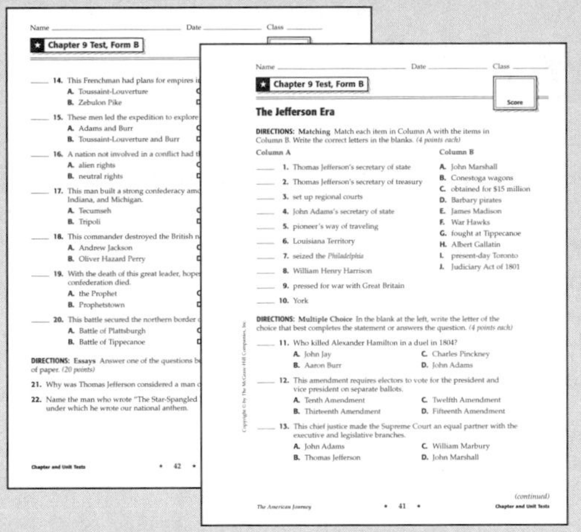
Chapter 9 Test, Form B

The Jefferson Era

Performance Assessment Activity 9

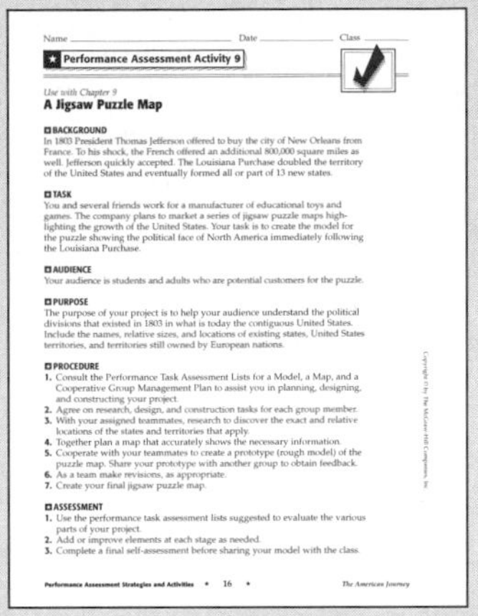
Performance Assessment Activity 9

A Jigsaw Puzzle Map

Spanish Resources

The following Spanish language materials are available in the Spanish Resources binder:

- **Spanish Chapter Summary 9**
- **Spanish Vocabulary Activity 9**
- **Spanish Guided Reading Activities, Chapter 9**
- **Spanish Section Quizzes, Chapter 9**
- **Spanish Home Involvement Activity 9**
- **Spanish Chapter 9 Digests Audiocassette Activity and Test**

Activity Manipulatives

Help students learn more about America's cultural history with:

- **American Crafts Hands-On Activities**
- **American Games Hands-On Activities**
- **American History Flash Cards**

Additional Resources From Glencoe

- **Focus on American Art Prints,** *The Staircase Group* by Charles Willson Peale
- **Supreme Court Case 1,** *Marbury* v. *Madison (1803)*
- **American Music Cultural Traditions,** Lesson 3: "Hull's Victory" and "Hunters of Kentucky"
- **Outline Map Resource Book**
- **U.S. Desk Map**
- **The American History Videodisc and CD-ROM,** *The American Revolution and the Early Republic, 1765–1820*

A&E HOME VIDEO. Biography™ THE HISTORY CHANNEL.

The following videotape programs are available from Glencoe as supplements to Chapter 9:

- **Thomas Jefferson: Philosopher of Freedom** (ISBN 1-56501-502-9)
- **Lewis & Clark** (ISBN 1-56501-592-4)

To order, call Glencoe at 1-800-334-7344. To find classroom resources to accompany many of these videos, check the following home pages:
A&E Television: http://www.aetv.com
The History Channel: http://www.historychannel.com

Introducing CHAPTER 9

Chapter Themes

Chapter Themes are listed by section on this chapter opening page of the Student Edition. A corresponding theme-based activity is available under "FOCUS," and a theme-based question is asked in the Section and Chapter Reviews.

Performance Assessment

Refer to Activity 9 in the *Performance Assessment Strategies and Activities* booklet.

GLENCOE TECHNOLOGY

VIDEODISC
MindJogger Videoquiz

Use MindJogger to preview the Chapter 9 content.

Chapter 9
Disc 2, Side A

Also available in VHS.

HISTORY AND ART On April 30, 1798, Congress established the Department of the Navy. Between 1798 and 1800 Congress expanded the navy to more than 30 ships. **Ask: Did the launching of this ship seem to be an important event?** *(Yes, a crowd has gathered.)*

Chapter 9

1800–1816

The Jefferson Era

Why It's Important

In 1801 the Democratic-Republican Party took control of the nation's government. The Federalists—the party of George Washington, Alexander Hamilton, and John Adams—were now on the sidelines and played the role of critics to the Republican administration. Today politicians operate within the party system that took shape at that time. While the two main parties have changed, each still works to win votes and gain power. If the people vote to change the party in power, the newly elected representatives take office peacefully and the government continues.

Chapter Themes

- *Section 1,* Government and Democracy
- *Section 2,* Geography and History
- *Section 3,* Global Connections
- *Section 4,* Groups and Institutions

HISTORY AND ART ***Launching of the Ship* Fame by George Ropes** During Jefferson's term, the United States experienced rapid expansion. The launching of this ship in 1802 symbolized growth of the nation's naval forces.

276

EXTRA CREDIT PROJECT

"Don't Give Up the Ship" This saying originated during the War of 1812. Have students find out the story behind this famous motto and prepare a brief report on it. Students may illustrate their reports for added interest. *(The originator of the saying is James Lawrence [1781–1813]. His actual words were, "Tell the men to fire faster and not to give up the ship; fight her till she sinks." It was his final order as captain of the American vessel* Chesapeake, *uttered as he was being carried below, fatally wounded, on June 1, 1813.)*

1800 | 1801 | 1802 | 1803

1800 Thomas Jefferson and John Adams contend for presidency

1801 Judiciary Act expands court system

March 1801 Jefferson is inaugurated

1803 *Marbury* v. *Madison* sets precedent for judicial review

Section 1

The Republicans Take Power

READ TO DISCOVER . . .

- how the election deadlock of 1800 was resolved.
- how John Marshall strengthened the Supreme Court of the United States.

TERMS TO LEARN

laissez-faire
customs duties
judicial review

The Storyteller

In 1801 Washington, D.C., was slowly rising from a swampy site on the Potomac River. The nation's new capital had only two noteworthy buildings—the president's mansion (later called the White House) and the still-unfinished Capitol. Between them stretched a mile and a half of muddy streets on which pigs and chickens roamed freely.

Very few people liked being in Washington. It was hot and steamy in the summer, and mosquitoes carried the dreaded disease malaria. Abigail Adams called the new capital "the very dirtiest Hole."

Surveyor's tools

The Federalist and Republican parties fought a bitter election campaign in 1800. Federalists supported President Adams for a second term and Charles Pinckney of South Carolina for vice president. Republicans nominated **Thomas Jefferson** for president and **Aaron Burr** of New York as his running mate.

The Election of 1800

The election campaign of 1800 differed greatly from campaigns of today. Neither Adams nor Jefferson traveled around the country making speeches about why he should be elected. That would have been considered in bad taste. Instead the candidates and their allies wrote hundreds of letters to leading citizens and friendly newspapers to publicize their views. The letter-writing campaign, however, was not polite.

Federalists charged the Republican Jefferson, who believed in freedom of religion, as being "godless." Republicans warned that the Federalists would bring back the monarchy. Federalists, they claimed, represented the interests of wealthy people with property.

Election Deadlock

When members of the Electoral College voted, Jefferson and Burr each received 73 votes. Because of this tie, the House of Representatives

SECTION RESOURCES

Reproducible Masters
- Guided Reading Activity 9–1
- Section Quiz 9–1
- Reteaching Activity 9–1
- Enrichment Activity 9–1

Transparencies
- Section Focus Transparency 9–1
- U.S. History & Art, Transparency 5

Multimedia
- Vocabulary PuzzleMaker
- Chapter Challenger Interactive Review Software
- Testmaker

1 FOCUS

BELLRINGER
Motivational Activity

Before taking roll at the beginning of the class period, project Section Focus Transparency 9–1 and have students answer the questions. Discuss students' responses.

This activity is also available as a blackline master.

Section Focus Transparency 9–1

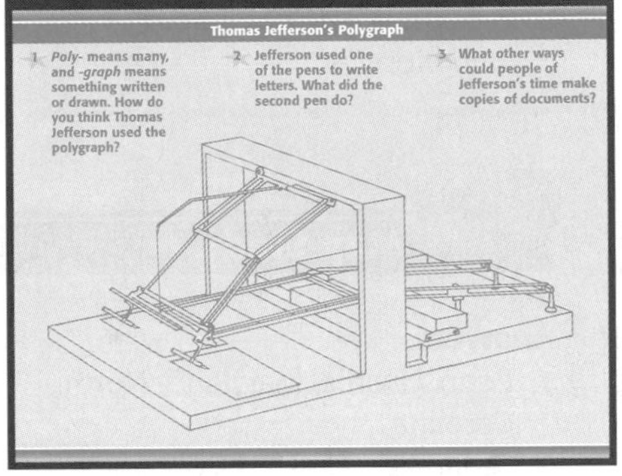

Vocabulary Precheck
Refer students to **Terms to Learn.** Have students write questions for which each term is an answer.

Use the **Vocabulary PuzzleMaker** to create crossword and word search puzzles.

Section Theme
Government and Democracy

Jefferson and the Republicans believed that a large federal government threatened liberty and that strong states could best protect freedom. They also believed that government should play only a small part in the economic concerns of the country.

Activity Jefferson considered himself a revolutionary. Have students write a brief essay discussing what, if anything, was revolutionary about Jefferson's first actions as president.

CHAPTER 9
Section 1, 277–280

2 TEACH

L1, ELL Ranking Events Have each student choose three events from the section and rank them in order of importance. Call on volunteers to read their lists. Then have a class discussion in which students decide whether they agree or disagree with the volunteers' rankings.

History *and the* Humanities

U.S. History & Art, Transparency 5, *University of Virginia, Charlottesville*

Map Study

Answers

1. Pennsylvania, Maryland, North Carolina
2. Federalist

Map Skills Practice

Reading a Map Which state had the most electors? *(Virginia)*

Guided Reading Activity 9–1

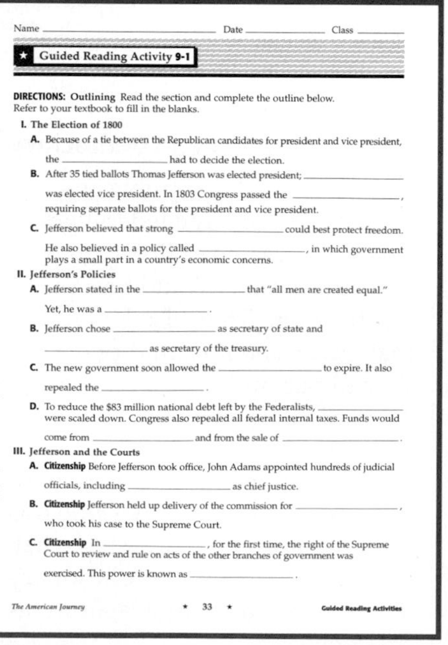
Name ______ Date ______ Class ______

★ Guided Reading Activity 9-1

DIRECTIONS: Outlining Read the section and complete the outline below. Refer to your textbook to fill in the blanks.

I. The Election of 1800

A. Because of a tie between the Republican candidates for president and vice president, the ______ had to decide the election.

B. After 35 tied ballots Thomas Jefferson was elected president; ______ was elected vice president. In 1803 Congress passed the ______, requiring separate ballots for the president and vice president.

C. Jefferson believed that strong ______ could best protect freedom. He also believed in a policy called ______, in which government plays a small part in a country's economic concerns.

II. Jefferson's Policies

A. Jefferson stated in the ______ that "all men are created equal." Yet, he was a ______.

B. Jefferson chose ______ as secretary of state and ______ as secretary of the treasury.

C. The new government soon allowed the ______ to expire. It also repealed the ______.

D. To reduce the $83 million national debt left by the Federalists, ______ were scaled down. Congress also repealed all federal internal taxes. Funds would come from ______ and from the sale of ______.

III. Jefferson and the Courts

A. Citizenship Before Jefferson took office, John Adams appointed hundreds of judicial officials, including ______ as chief justice.

B. Citizenship Jefferson held up delivery of the commission for ______, who took his case to the Supreme Court.

C. Citizenship In ______, for the first time, the right of the Supreme Court to review and rule on acts of the other branches of government was exercised. This power is known as ______.

The American Journey ★ 33 ★ **Guided Reading Activities**

Election of 1800

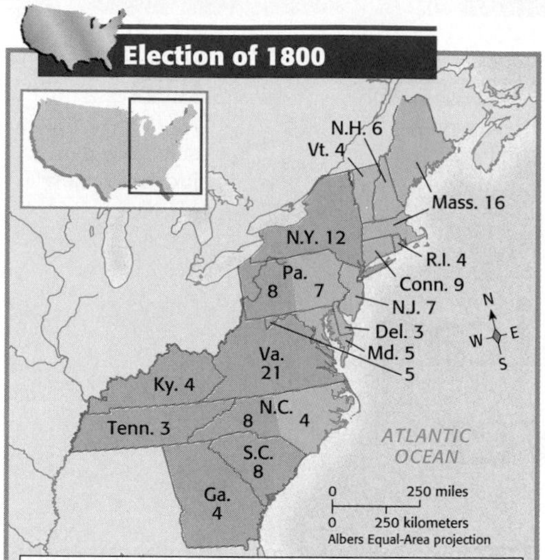

Numbers on map indicate number of state's electors.

Candidate	Electoral Votes	Party
Jefferson	73	Democratic-Republican
Burr	73	Democratic-Republican
Adams	65	Federalist
Pinckney	64	Federalist
Jay	1	Federalist
	276 Total number of electoral votes	

Map Study

Although the Democratic-Republicans won the election of 1800, there was no clear presidential winner.

1. **Region** Which three states split their electoral votes?
2. **Drawing Conclusions** Which political party did the former New England Colonies support?

had to decide the election. At the time the electors voted for each presidential and vice-presidential candidate individually rather than voting for a party's candidates as a team.

In the House, Federalists saw a chance to prevent the election of Jefferson by supporting Burr. For 35 ballots, the election remained tied. Finally, at Alexander Hamilton's urging, one Federalist decided not to vote for Burr. Although he was no friend of Jefferson's, Hamilton greatly distrusted Burr. Jefferson became president and Burr became vice president.

To prevent another showdown between a presidential and a vice-presidential candidate, Congress passed the Twelfth Amendment to the Constitution in 1803. This amendment, ratified in 1804, requires electors to vote for the president and vice president on separate ballots.

Jefferson's Inauguration

On March 4, 1801, the day of the inauguration, Jefferson dressed in everyday clothes. He left his boardinghouse and walked to the Senate to be sworn in as president. President Adams did not attend the ceremony. He had slipped out of the presidential mansion at 4:00 A.M. and left the city so he would not have to watch Thomas Jefferson become president.

In his Inaugural Address, Jefferson tried to bridge the gap between the developing political parties and reach out to Federalists with healing words. "We are all Republicans, we are all Federalists," he said. Then he outlined some of his goals, which included "a wise and frugal government," and "the support of state governments in all their rights." Jefferson had long been a supporter of states' rights. He believed that a large federal government threatened liberty and that strong states could best protect freedom.

Jefferson also believed in a policy called **laissez-faire** (LEH•SAY FEHR). This French term means "let (people) do (as they choose)." A laissez-faire government plays only a small part in the economic concerns of a country.

Jefferson's Policies

Thomas Jefferson was a man of contradictions. He had proclaimed in the Declaration of Independence that "all men are created equal"—but he was a slaveholder. He thought the United States should be a nation of small farmers—but he himself was a wealthy landowner with a huge estate at Monticello, Virginia. A political philosopher, he excelled as a practical politician. In addition he designed buildings and loved to tinker with gadgets and with his own inventions.

COOPERATIVE LEARNING ACTIVITY

Presenting Jefferson: Inventor/Architect Organize the class into small groups and have each group use library resources to find examples of some of Jefferson's inventions and of buildings he designed. Have each group prepare a coffee table-style book containing drawings of inventions and buildings with descriptive captions. Tasks such as drawing, writing, and finding resources should be assigned according to the skills of group members.

Jefferson's Cabinet

When Jefferson entered office, he surrounded himself with men who shared his Republican principles. His secretary of state was his friend and fellow Virginian James Madison. For secretary of the treasury, he chose **Albert Gallatin.** This Pennsylvanian had a grasp of financial matters that equaled Alexander Hamilton's.

The new government soon ended two unpopular Federalist measures. It allowed the Alien and Sedition acts to expire and repealed the Naturalization Act. For Republicans both acts were symbols of a big federal government that threatened individual liberties.

Cutting Costs

Jefferson and Gallatin aimed to reduce the huge national debt of $83 million that the Federalists had left. They scaled down military expenses. They cut the army by one-third and reduced the navy from 25 to 7 ships. By slashing spending Jefferson and Gallatin significantly lowered the national debt within a few years.

Jefferson and Gallatin also persuaded Congress to repeal all federal internal taxes, including the hated whiskey tax. At that point government funds would come only from **customs duties**—taxes on foreign imported goods—and from the sale of western lands.

The entire federal government in 1801 consisted of only a few hundred people, and some of these were part-time workers. This was exactly how Jefferson thought it should be. In his view the responsibilities of government should be limited to delivering the mail, collecting customs duties, and conducting a census every 10 years.

Jefferson and the Courts

Jefferson hoped that some Federalists would support his policies. However, bitter feelings between the parties continued during his administration. Much of the ill will resulted from a fight over control of the federal courts.

Citizenship

Judiciary Act of 1801

Before Jefferson took office, the Federalists passed the Judiciary Act of 1801. The act set up regional courts for the United States with 16 judges and many other judicial officials. In his last days as president, John Adams made hundreds of appointments to these positions, and the Federalist-controlled Congress approved them. Adams also asked **John Marshall,** his secretary of state, to serve as chief justice of the United States after

HISTORY AND ART

***Washington, D.C., 1803* by Nicholas King**
Washington, D.C., at the time of Jefferson's presidency, did not resemble the capital city familiar to citizens today. **How did Abigail Adams describe the city?**

CHAPTER 9
Section 1, 277–280

Who?What?Where?When?

John Marshall's decision in *Marbury* v. *Madison* was a brilliant solution to a difficult problem. If the Court had issued a writ ordering delivery of the commission, Jefferson and Madison could have ignored it, thus diminishing the power of the Court. Without a writ, the Republicans would have won by default. By declaring the Judiciary Act of 1789 unconstitutional, Marshall did limit the original jurisdiction of the Court, but expanded its power to include judicial review.

3 ASSESS

Assign Section 1 Review as homework or as an in-class activity.

Use **Chapter Challenger Interactive Review Software** to review Section 1.

HISTORY AND ART President Washington chose the specific location for the capital at the head of navigation of the Potomac River.
Answer: *as "the very dirtiest Hole"*

Section Quiz 9–1

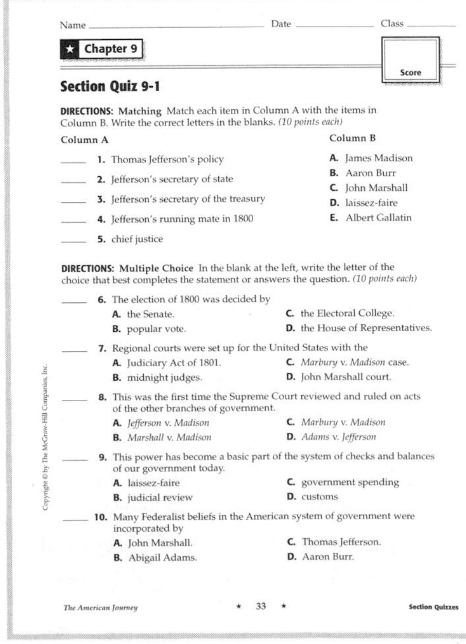

Name ______ Date ______ Class ______

Chapter 9

Score

Section Quiz 9-1

DIRECTIONS: Matching Match each item in Column A with the items in Column B. Write the correct letters in the blanks. *(10 points each)*

Column A

____ 1. Thomas Jefferson's policy
____ 2. Jefferson's secretary of state
____ 3. Jefferson's secretary of the treasury
____ 4. Jefferson's running mate in 1800
____ 5. chief justice

Column B

A. James Madison
B. Aaron Burr
C. John Marshall
D. laissez-faire
E. Albert Gallatin

DIRECTIONS: Multiple Choice In the blank at the left, write the letter of the choice that best completes the statement or answers the question. *(10 points each)*

____ 6. The election of 1800 was decided by
A. the Senate. C. the Electoral College.
B. popular vote. D. the House of Representatives.

____ 7. Regional courts were set up for the United States with the
A. Judiciary Act of 1801. C. *Marbury* v. *Madison* case.
B. midnight judges. D. John Marshall court.

____ 8. This was the first time the Supreme Court reviewed and ruled on acts of the other branches of government.
A. *Jefferson* v. *Madison* C. *Marbury* v. *Madison*
B. *Marshall* v. *Madison* D. *Adams* v. *Jefferson*

____ 9. This power has become a basic part of the system of checks and balances of our government today.
A. laissez-faire C. government spending
B. judicial review D. customs

____ 10. Many Federalist beliefs in the American system of government were incorporated by
A. John Marshall. C. Thomas Jefferson.
B. Abigail Adams. D. Aaron Burr.

Copyright © by The McGraw-Hill Companies, Inc.

The American Journey ★ 33 ★ Section Quizzes

MULTIPLE LEARNING STYLES

Logical/Mathematical Have students use *Historical Statistics of the United States* or other library references to find the value of United States imports and exports from 1800 to 1820. Have them make a line graph showing this information. Review proper procedures for drawing line graphs before students begin (dollar amounts on vertical axis, years on the horizontal axis, equal space between numbers and between years). Have students use different colors for the two lines and provide a key to show which is which. **L2**

CHAPTER 9
Section 1, 277–280

Reteaching Activity 9–1

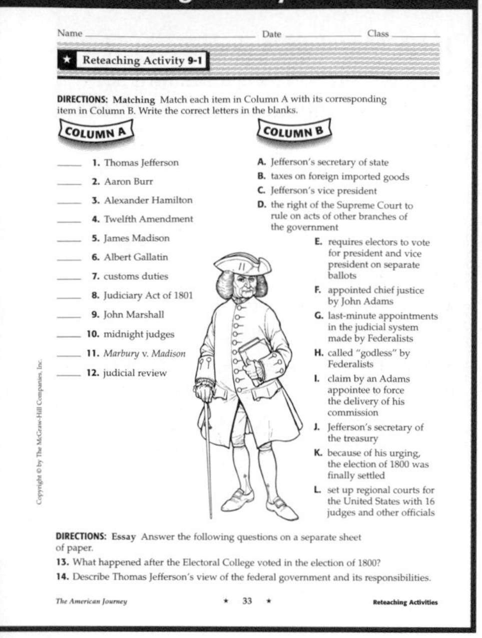
Name ______ Date ______ Class ______

★ Reteaching Activity 9-1

DIRECTIONS: Matching Match each item in Column A with its corresponding item in Column B. Write the correct letters in the blanks.

COLUMN A

____ 1. Thomas Jefferson
____ 2. Aaron Burr
____ 3. Alexander Hamilton
____ 4. Twelfth Amendment
____ 5. James Madison
____ 6. Albert Gallatin
____ 7. customs duties
____ 8. Judiciary Act of 1801
____ 9. John Marshall
____ 10. midnight judges
____ 11. *Marbury* v. *Madison*
____ 12. judicial review

COLUMN B

A. Jefferson's secretary of state
B. taxes on foreign imported goods
C. Jefferson's vice president
D. the right of the Supreme Court to rule on acts of other branches of the government
E. requires electors to vote for president and vice president on separate ballots
F. appointed chief justice by John Adams
G. last-minute appointments in the judicial system made by Federalists
H. called "godless" by Federalists
I. claim by an Adams appointee to force the delivery of his commission
J. Jefferson's secretary of the treasury
K. because of his urging, the election of 1800 was finally settled
L. set up regional courts for the United States with 16 judges and other officials

DIRECTIONS: Essay Answer the following questions on a separate sheet of paper.

13. What happened after the Electoral College voted in the election of 1800?
14. Describe Thomas Jefferson's view of the federal government and its responsibilities.

Enrichment Activity 9–1

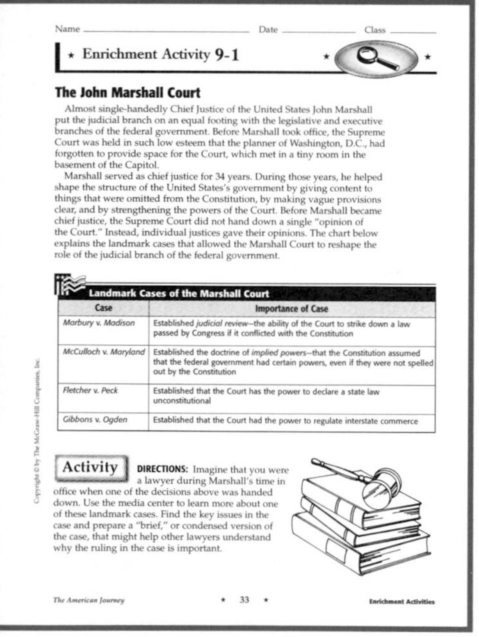
Name ______ Date ______ Class ______

★ Enrichment Activity 9-1 ★ ★

The John Marshall Court

Almost single-handedly Chief Justice of the United States John Marshall put the judicial branch on an equal footing with the legislative and executive branches of the federal government. Before Marshall took office, the Supreme Court was held in such low esteem that the planner of Washington, D.C., had forgotten to provide space for the Court, which met in a tiny room in the basement of the Capitol.

Marshall served as chief justice for 34 years. During those years, he helped shape the structure of the United States's government by giving content to things that were omitted from the Constitution, by making vague provisions clear, and by strengthening the powers of the Court. Before Marshall became chief justice, the Supreme Court did not hand down a single "opinion of the Court." Instead, individual justices gave their opinions. The chart below explains the landmark cases that allowed the Marshall Court to reshape the role of the judicial branch of the federal government.

Landmark Cases of the Marshall Court

Case	Importance of Case
Marbury v. *Madison*	Established *judicial review*—the ability of the Court to strike down a law passed by Congress if it conflicted with the Constitution
McCulloch v. *Maryland*	Established the doctrine of *implied powers*—that the Constitution assumed that the federal government had certain powers, even if they were not spelled out by the Constitution
Fletcher v. *Peck*	Established that the Court has the power to declare a state law unconstitutional
Gibbons v. *Ogden*	Established that the Court had the power to regulate interstate commerce

Activity **DIRECTIONS:** Imagine that you were a lawyer during Marshall's time in office when one of the decisions above was handed down. Use the media center to learn more about one of these landmark cases. Find the key issues in the case and prepare a "brief," or condensed version of the case, that might help other lawyers understand why the ruling in the case is important.

4 CLOSE

Ask students to describe Jefferson's probable reaction to today's federal government. *(possible answer: appalled at number of people employed by government, at size of national debt, and at extent of government regulation)*

Chief Justice Oliver Ellsworth resigned. By these actions Adams shut President-elect Jefferson out of the appointment process and ensured that Federalists would control the courts.

"Midnight Judges"

Adams and Marshall worked around the clock in the final hours of the Federalist government, processing the papers for these judicial appointments. The appointments could not take effect, however, until the papers (commissions) for these last-minute "midnight judges" were delivered. When Jefferson became president on March 4, a few of the commissions had not been delivered. He told Secretary of State Madison not to send them out. One commission was addressed to William Marbury.

Chief Justice John Marshall

Marbury v. *Madison*

To force the delivery of his commission, Marbury took his case directly to the Supreme Court, which he claimed had jurisdiction as a result of the Judiciary Act of 1789. Chief Justice John Marshall, a Federalist, wrote an opinion turning down Marbury's claim. He noted that the Constitution did not give the Court jurisdiction to decide Marbury's case.

In ***Marbury* v. *Madison*** Justice Marshall had for the first time exercised the right of the Supreme Court to review and rule on acts of the other branches of government. Known as **judicial review,** this power has become a basic part of the system of checks and balances of our government today.

The Marshall Court

John Marshall served as chief justice until 1835. He made the Supreme Court an equal partner in government with the executive and legislative branches by declaring the Court's right to review the actions of the other branches.

Under Marshall the Court usually upheld the power of the national government over the rights of states. The Federalists had lost the presidency and Congress, but the Marshall Supreme Court incorporated many Federalist beliefs in the American system of government.

Section 1 Review

Checking for Understanding

1. ***Identify*** Washington, D.C., Thomas Jefferson, Aaron Burr, Albert Gallatin, John Marshall, *Marbury* v. *Madison*.
2. ***Define*** laissez-faire, customs duties, judicial review.
3. ***Explain*** how Jefferson cut government spending.

Reviewing Themes

4. **Government and Democracy** How did the judicial branch under Jefferson serve as a check on the executive and legislative branches?

Critical Thinking

5. **Identifying Central Issues** How was the deadlock in the presidential election of 1800 finally resolved?

Activity

Turning Words into Pictures Draw a picture of what you think the city of Washington, D.C., might have looked like on the day of Jefferson's inauguration.

Section 1 Review Answers

1. Washington, D.C., 277; Thomas Jefferson, 277; Aaron Burr, 277; Albert Gallatin, 279; John Marshall, 279; *Marbury* v. *Madison,* 280
2. The words are defined in the Glossary.
3. reduced the size of the army and navy
4. With the establishment of judicial review, the Supreme Court could review and rule on acts of the other branches of government.
5. The House of Representatives decided the election. Hamilton swayed the vote in Jefferson's favor.

Activity Pictures should contain most of the following details: swampy land, White House, partially finished Capitol, muddy streets, pigs, chickens, crowds of people

1804 1805 1806 1807

December 1803
United States buys Louisiana Territory

May 1804
Lewis and Clark expedition sets off from St. Louis

September 1806
Lewis and Clark return to St. Louis

November 1806
Zebulon Pike sights Pikes Peak

Section 2

The Louisiana Purchase

READ TO DISCOVER . . .

- how the United States expanded in the early 1800s.
- how Lewis and Clark led an expedition to explore the Louisiana Territory.

TERMS TO LEARN

Conestoga wagon   secede

The Storyteller

Why did Americans risk everything they had to travel west? An English visitor, Harriet Martineau, observed: "The pride and delight of Americans is in their quantity of land. . . . The possession of land is the aim of all action . . . and the cure for all social evils. . . . If a man is disappointed in politics or love, he goes and buys land. If he disgraces himself, he betakes himself to a lot in the West. . . ."

Conestoga wagon

American pioneers in search of land and adventure headed over the mountains into Kentucky and Tennessee and the less settled areas of the Northwest Territory. Most of these pioneers were farmers. They made a long and exhausting journey over the Appalachian Mountains. Pioneers had to trudge along crude, muddy roads or cut their way through dense forests.

Settlers loaded their household goods in **Conestoga wagons,** sturdy vehicles topped with white canvas. For these westward-bound pioneers, their two most valued possessions were a rifle for protection and hunting and an ax to hack their way through the dense forests.

Western Territory

In 1800 the territory of the United States extended only as far west as the Mississippi River. The area to the west of the river—known as the **Louisiana Territory**—belonged to Spain. It was an enormous area of land, anchored to the south by the city of New Orleans and extending west to the Rocky Mountains. Its northern boundaries remained undefined.

Many of the pioneers settled down and established farms along rivers that fed into the upper Mississippi River. They needed the river to ship their crops to markets. The Spanish allowed the Americans to sail on the lower Mississippi and trade in **New Orleans.** For the western farmers, this right was vital. The goods they sent downriver were unloaded in New Orleans and sent by ship to markets on the East Coast.

SECTION RESOURCES

Reproducible Masters
- Reproducible Lesson Plan 9–2
- Guided Reading Activity 9–2
- Section Quiz 9–2
- Reteaching Activity 9–2
- Enrichment Activity 9–2

Transparencies
- Section Focus Transparency 9–2

Multimedia
- Vocabulary PuzzleMaker
- Chapter Challenger Interactive Review Software
- Testmaker
- ABCNews InterActive™ Historic America Electronic Field Trips
- GTV: A Geographic Perspective on American History

1 FOCUS

BELLRINGER
Motivational Activity

Before taking roll at the beginning of the class period, project Section Focus Transparency 9–2 and have students answer the questions. Discuss students' responses.

This activity is also available as a blackline master.

Section Focus Transparency 9–2

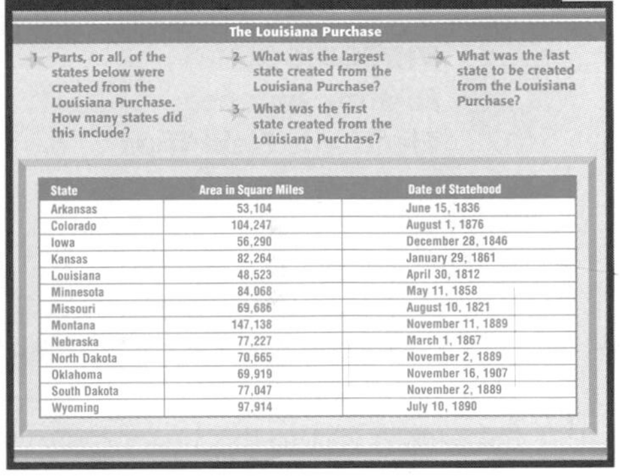

The Louisiana Purchase

1 Parts, or all, of the states below were created from the Louisiana Purchase. How many states did this include?

2 What was the largest state created from the Louisiana Purchase?

3 What was the first state created from the Louisiana Purchase?

4 What was the last state to be created from the Louisiana Purchase?

State	Area in Square Miles	Date of Statehood
Arkansas	53,104	June 15, 1836
Colorado	104,247	August 1, 1876
Iowa	56,290	December 28, 1846
Kansas	82,264	January 29, 1861
Louisiana	48,523	April 30, 1812
Minnesota	84,068	May 11, 1858
Missouri	69,686	August 10, 1821
Montana	147,138	November 11, 1889
Nebraska	77,227	March 1, 1867
North Dakota	70,665	November 2, 1889
Oklahoma	69,919	November 16, 1907
South Dakota	77,047	November 2, 1889
Wyoming	97,914	July 10, 1890

Vocabulary Precheck

Inform students that the word *secede* comes from a Latin word meaning "to go away." Encourage volunteers to use *secede* correctly in a sentence.

Use the **Vocabulary PuzzleMaker** to create crossword and word search puzzles.

Section Theme
Geography and History

In 1803 the United States doubled its size with the purchase of the Louisiana Territory from France for $15 million.

Activity Have students skim the section to find at least one effect of that purchase. *(possible responses: Americans gained access to the port at New Orleans; prevented French empire from expanding in America; provided plenty of land for generations of farmers; doubled size of United States)*

2 TEACH

L1 Finding Answers As students read the section, have them find answers to the following questions: (1) Why did Jefferson want to buy New Orleans? (2) Why did the French want to sell the Louisiana Territory? (3) What did the Lewis and Clark expedition achieve?

ABCNEWS INTERACTiVE™

VIDEODISC
Historic America Electronic Field Trips

Side 1, Chapter 5
Title: *New Orleans*
Subject: A visit to this historic city
Ask: **Who owned New Orleans before France?** *(Spain)*

Also available in VHS.

Guided Reading Activity 9–2

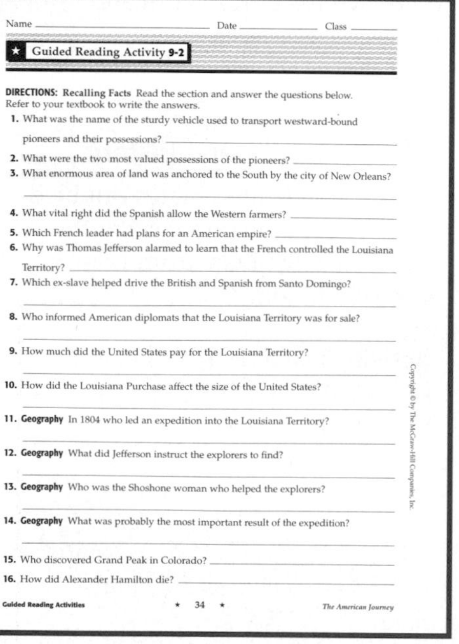

Name ______ Date ______ Class ______

★ Guided Reading Activity 9-2

DIRECTIONS: Recalling Facts Read the section and answer the questions below. Refer to your textbook to write the answers.

1. What was the name of the sturdy vehicle used to transport westward-bound pioneers and their possessions? ______
2. What were the two most valued possessions of the pioneers? ______
3. What enormous area of land was anchored to the South by the city of New Orleans? ______
4. What vital right did the Spanish allow the Western farmers? ______
5. Which French leader had plans for an American empire? ______
6. Why was Thomas Jefferson alarmed to learn that the French controlled the Louisiana Territory? ______
7. Which ex-slave helped drive the British and Spanish from Santo Domingo? ______
8. Who informed American diplomats that the Louisiana Territory was for sale? ______
9. How much did the United States pay for the Louisiana Territory? ______
10. How did the Louisiana Purchase affect the size of the United States? ______
11. **Geography** In 1804 who led an expedition into the Louisiana Territory? ______
12. **Geography** What did Jefferson instruct the explorers to find? ______
13. **Geography** Who was the Shoshone woman who helped the explorers? ______
14. **Geography** What was probably the most important result of the expedition? ______
15. Who discovered Grand Peak in Colorado? ______
16. How did Alexander Hamilton die? ______

Guided Reading Activities ★ 34 ★ *The American Journey*

The French Threat

In 1802 the Spanish suddenly changed their policy. They refused to allow American goods to move into or past New Orleans. Representatives in Washington muttered about taking New Orleans by force. That same year, President Jefferson learned that Spain and France had made a secret agreement that transferred the Louisiana Territory to France. This agreement posed a serious threat for the United States. France's leader, **Napoleon Bonaparte,** had plans for empires in Europe and the Americas.

Jefferson was alarmed. He believed French control would jeopardize American trade on the Mississippi River. Jefferson sent James Monroe to France as his special representative. In a letter to **Robert Livingston,** U.S. ambassador to France, Jefferson declared:

> "There is on this globe one single spot, the possessor of which is our natural . . . enemy. It is New Orleans."

Jefferson authorized American diplomats to offer as much as $10 million for New Orleans and West Florida. Jefferson believed that France had gained Florida as well as Louisiana in its secret agreement with Spain.

Toussaint-Louverture

Revolt in Santo Domingo

Napoleon was forced to abandon his plans for an American empire. In 1802 Napoleon sent troops to the Caribbean island of Santo Domingo (now Haiti and the Dominican Republic) to crush a major revolt against French rule. The leader of the revolt, **Toussaint-Louverture** (TOO•SAN LOO•vuhr•TYUR), was the grandson of an African chief and a fiercely determined ex-slave. He had helped drive the British and Spanish from the island and end slavery. The French captured Toussaint-Louverture but could not regain control of the island. Thousands of French troops died in the effort, many from disease.

The Nation Expands

The situation in Santo Domingo helped the United States. Stunned by their losses, the French feared that Britain might persuade the United States to join forces against them. Also, the French needed money to finance Napoleon's plans for war against Britain. The French believed they had something for sale that the United States might want to buy.

French foreign minister Charles de Talleyrand informed the American diplomats that the whole Louisiana Territory was for sale. Monroe and Livingston were taken completely by surprise. Accepting the offer went far beyond what they were authorized to do, but the deal was too good to pass up. After a few days of negotiation, the parties agreed on a price of $15 million.

Legality of the Purchase

The Louisiana Purchase pleased Jefferson. The new territory would provide cheap and abundant land for farmers for generations to come. He worried, however, whether the purchase was legal. The Constitution said nothing about acquiring new territory. By what authority could he justify the purchase? Livingston wrote from Paris, urging Jefferson to accept the deal before Napoleon changed his mind. Jefferson decided the government's treaty-making powers allowed the purchase of the new territory. The Senate gave its approval in October 1803. With the signing of the treaty, the size of the United States doubled.

COOPERATIVE LEARNING ACTIVITY

Creating a Lewis and Clark Board Game Organize the class into small groups and have each group create a board game based on the journeys of Lewis and Clark. For example, players might lose a turn or points when they encounter a hazard such as a large uprooted tree floating in the river. They might gain spaces when they meet Sacagawea. Assign tasks—making tokens, cards, playing board; finding out about the events of the journey; making rules; monitoring play—according to the skills of individual group members.

★ ★

Geography

Lewis and Clark

Jefferson wanted to know more about the mysterious lands west of the Mississippi. Even before the Louisiana Purchase was complete, he persuaded Congress to sponsor an expedition to explore the new territory. Jefferson was particularly interested in the expedition as a scientific venture. Congress was interested in commercial possibilities and in sites for future forts.

To head the expedition, Jefferson chose his private secretary, 28-year-old **Meriwether Lewis.** Lewis was well qualified to lead this journey of exploration. He had joined the militia during the Whiskey Rebellion and had been in the army since that time. The expedition's coleader was **William Clark,** 32, a friend of Lewis's from military service. Both Lewis and Clark were knowledgeable amateur scientists and had conducted business with Native Americans. Together they assembled a crew that included expert river men, gunsmiths, carpenters, scouts, and a cook. Two men of mixed Native American and French heritage served as interpreters. An African American named York rounded out the group.

Who? What? Where? When?

Aaron Burr fled to the West to avoid standing trial for murder. There he took part in arranging conspiracies, sometimes for the secession of the western territories, sometimes for the conquest of Mexico with himself as emperor. Whatever his goal, he collected arms, bought flatboats, and floated downriver toward New Orleans with some 80 to 100 followers. His movements became widely known, however, and President Jefferson ordered his arrest. Burr fled again, this time into Spanish Florida. In 1807 he was captured and tried for treason. He was acquitted on a technicality and went into exile.

For the next five years, Burr tried unsuccessfully to sell his schemes of empire to Europeans. Burr returned to New York in 1812 and practiced law until his death in 1836.

The Louisiana Purchase and Western Exploration

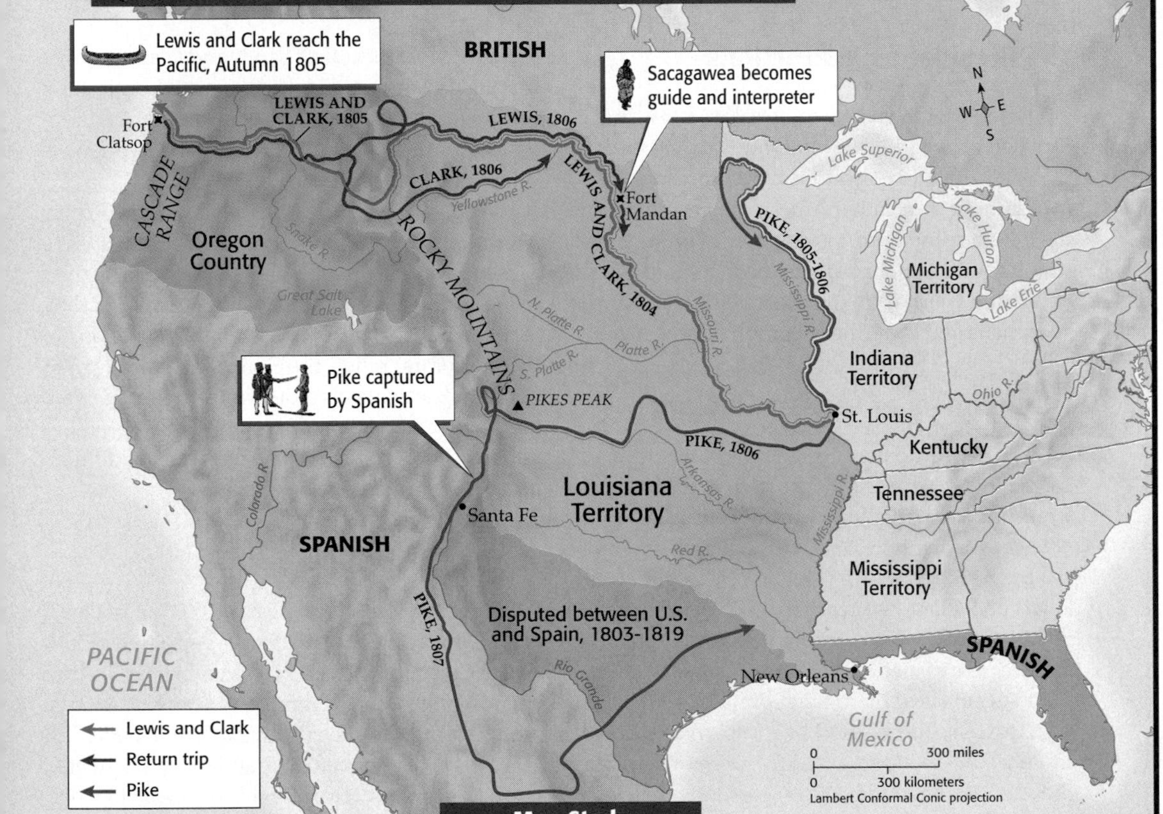

Map Study

The purchase of the Louisiana Territory doubled the size of the United States. Americans quickly set out to explore the region and lands farther west.

1. **Location** What natural feature is named after Zebulon Pike?
2. **Analyzing Information** What rivers flowed through the Louisiana Territory?

Map Study

Answers

1. Pikes Peak
2. (Mississippi and Rio Grande on borders) Missouri, North and South Platte, Arkansas, Red, Yellowstone, Snake

Map Skills Practice

Reading a Map What is the straight-line distance between St. Louis and Santa Fe? *(about 900 miles; 1,500 km)*

Multiple Learning Styles

Kinesthetic Have students make a relief map of the area explored by Lewis and Clark. Materials needed are plywood for the base, tempera paints or watercolors, and modeling clay made from salt, flour, and water. (Clay recipe: 2 cups salt, 1 cup flour, 1 cup water. Mix ingredients until smooth and pliable.) Spread base layer of clay no more than 1/4 inch deep. Depress clay for rivers and lakes and add more for mountains. Allow to dry for at least a week before painting. You may find it is easier to make paper labels than try to paint them. **L1, ELL**

CURRICULUM CONNECTION

ECONOMICS
The Louisiana Territory consisted of about 828,000 square miles. At a purchase price of $15 million, that calculates to about $18.12 per square mile, a bargain even in 1803.

CHAPTER 9

Section 2, 281–285

HISTORY AND ART Boqueta de Woiseri, an engraver and painter, worked six years preparing the plates for this New Orleans aquatint. He dedicated the plates for it to Thomas Jefferson. **Ask:** What does the eagle in the picture stand for? *(the United States)* **Answer:** *He decided that the government's treaty-making powers allowed the purchase.*

3 ASSESS

Assign Section 2 Review as homework or as an in-class activity.

Use **Chapter Challenger Interactive Review Software** to review Section 2.

Section Quiz 9–2

Name ______ Date ______ Class ______

Chapter 9

Score

Section Quiz 9-2

DIRECTIONS: Matching Match each item in Column A with the items in Column B. Write the correct letters in the blanks. *(10 points each)*

Column A	Column B
____ 1. area west of the Mississippi River	A. Toussaint-Louverture
____ 2. trade center	B. Napoleon Bonaparte
____ 3. France's leader	C. Louisiana Territory
____ 4. revolt leader	D. New Orleans
____ 5. Lewis and Clark guide	E. Sacagawea

DIRECTIONS: Multiple Choice In the blank at the left, write the letter of the choice that best completes the statement or answers the question. *(10 points each)*

____ **6.** Before it was transferred in 1802, the Louisiana Territory belonged to
A. Louisiana. **C.** the United States.
B. Spain. **D.** France.

____ **7.** After it was transferred, the Louisiana Territory belonged to
A. Louisiana. **C.** the United States.
B. Spain. **D.** France.

____ **8.** The size of the United States was doubled with
A. the adoption of New Orleans. **C.** the expedition of Lewis and Clark.
B. Zebulon Pike's expedition. **D.** the Louisiana Purchase.

____ **9.** The Grand Peak was named after the explorer
A. Meriwether Lewis. **C.** Zebulon Pike.
B. Sacagawea. **D.** William Clark.

____ **10.** This politician died as a result of a duel.
A. Thomas Jefferson **C.** John Adams
B. Alexander Hamilton **D.** Aaron Burr

Section Quizzes • 34 • *The American Journey*

HISTORY AND ART

***A View of New Orleans* by John L. Boqueta de Woiseri** This painting celebrates the purchase of the Louisiana Territory from France in 1803. **How did Jefferson justify the purchase?**

The President's Instructions

Jefferson instructed the explorers to find a route across the Rocky Mountains to the Pacific Ocean. They were also to learn as much as they could about the Native Americans who lived in the new territory and to treat them "in the most friendly and conciliatory manner." In addition Lewis and Clark were to collect plant and animal specimens and chart the geography of the region.

The Journals of Lewis and Clark

The expedition left **St. Louis** in the spring of 1804, slowly working its way up the **Missouri River.** Lewis and Clark kept a journal of their voyage, making notes on what they saw and did.

By the time the cold weather of October came, Lewis and Clark had reached a site near present-day **Bismarck, North Dakota.** There they camped for the winter with the Mandan people. The Mandan survived by hunting buffalo and raising corn, squash, and beans. Long known as shrewd traders, the Mandan acted as go-betweens for the fur traders and other Native American peoples.

Before Lewis and Clark began the next leg of their journey, they hired a French trapper as a guide. The trapper was married to a young Shoshone woman named **Sacagawea** (SA•kuh•juh•WEE•uh). At first Lewis and Clark thought that having a woman and her infant son in their party would be a burden. As it turned out, Sacagawea proved invaluable. She served as an interpreter and helped the explorers survive.

When Lewis and Clark reached the **Rocky Mountains** in the summer of 1805, Sacagawea's presence was essential. This was the land she had come from. At first the Shoshone warriors they met reacted to the white men with suspicion. To the explorers' relief, the Shoshone chief turned out to be Sacagawea's older brother, Cameahwait. He helped Lewis and Clark secure horses and supplies and provided directions for the difficult journey over the Rockies.

To the Pacific and Back

After 18 months and nearly 4,000 miles, Lewis and Clark reached the Pacific Ocean at the mouth of the **Columbia River** in November 1805. After spending the winter there, they headed back east along separate routes. Both explorers arrived in St. Louis in September 1806, and Jefferson greeted the news of their return "with unspeakable joy." The expedition collected valuable information on people, plants, animals, and the geography of the West. Perhaps most important, the journey provided inspiration to a nation of people eager to move westward.

MAKING CONNECTIONS ACTIVITY

Foreign Affairs After France outlawed slavery, ex-slaves in Santo Domingo, the French colony on Hispaniola, formed outlaw bands that raided and burned towns and farms. Toussaint-Louverture organized the bands into an army that eventually won independence for the colony. Have students propose qualities that made Toussaint a natural leader and brainstorm some arguments he might have used to get the bands to work together. For a follow-up, show a video or make biographies of Toussaint available. **L1, ELL**

Pike's Expedition

Even before Lewis and Clark returned, Jefferson sent others to explore the wilderness. Lieutenant **Zebulon Pike** led two expeditions between 1805 and 1807, traveling through the upper Mississippi River valley and into the region that now is **Colorado.** In Colorado he found a snow-capped mountain he called Grand Peak. Today this mountain is known as Pikes Peak. During his expedition Pike was captured by the Spanish but was eventually released.

Federalists Plan to Secede

Many Federalists opposed the Louisiana Purchase. They feared that the agricultural states carved out of the new territory would become Republican, reducing the Federalists' power. A group of Federalists in Massachusetts plotted to **secede**—withdraw—from the Union. They wanted New England to form a separate "Northern Confederacy."

Aaron Burr

The plotters realized that to have any chance of success, the Northern Confederacy would have to include New York. The Massachusetts Federalists needed a powerful friend in that state who would back their plan. They turned to Aaron Burr, who had been cast aside by the Republicans for his refusal to withdraw from the 1800 election. The Federalists gave Burr their support in 1804, when he ran for governor of New York.

The Hamilton-Burr Feud

Alexander Hamilton had never trusted Aaron Burr. Now Hamilton was concerned about rumors that Burr had secretly agreed to lead New York out of the Union. Hamilton accused Burr of plotting treason. When Burr lost the election for governor, he blamed Hamilton and challenged him to a duel. In July 1804, the two men—armed with pistols—met in Weehawken, New Jersey. Hamilton fired first and missed Burr, probably deliberately. Burr, however, aimed to hit. Seriously wounded, Hamilton died the next day. Burr fled to avoid arrest.

Section 2 Review

Checking for Understanding

1. ***Identify*** Louisiana Territory, New Orleans, Toussaint-Louverture, Meriwether Lewis, William Clark, Sacagawea, Zebulon Pike.
2. ***Define*** Conestoga wagon, secede.
3. ***Explain*** why France agreed to sell the Louisiana Territory to the United States.

Reviewing Themes

4. **Geography and History** Why was the Mississippi River and New Orleans important to the United States?

Critical Thinking

5. **Determining Cause and Effect** How do you think the Lewis and Clark expedition helped to prepare people who wanted to move west?

Activity

Recording Details Accurate descriptions and drawings in their journals made Lewis and Clark's observations valuable. Find an example of plants or animals nearby. Carefully draw and describe what you see.

Section 2 Review Answers

1. Louisiana Territory, 281; New Orleans, 281; Toussaint-Louverture, 282; Lewis, 283; Clark, 283; Sacagawea, 284; Pike, 285
2. The words are defined in the Glossary.
3. France was overextended by fighting in Santo Domingo, needed cash for war against Britain, and did not want the United States to ally with Britain against it.
4. Farmers needed to ship their goods down the Mississippi River to New Orleans to get them to markets on the East Coast.
5. Answers will vary but may include: provided maps, descriptions and locations of landforms, locations and information about Native American groups, distribution of animals and plants

Activity Students' drawings and descriptions of an animal or a plant should be detailed.

Reteaching Activity 9–2

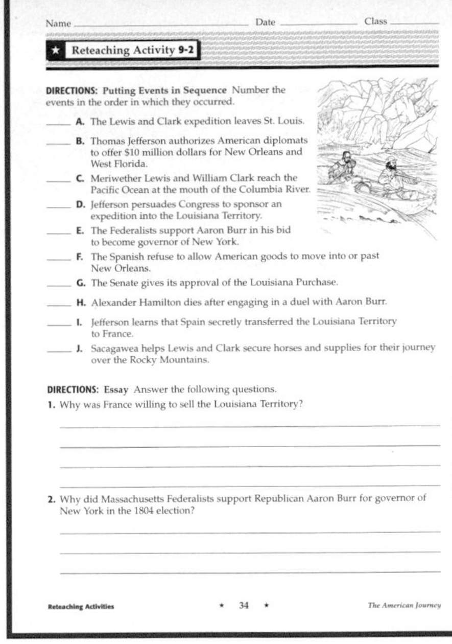

Name ______ Date ______ Class ______

★ Reteaching Activity 9-2

DIRECTIONS: Putting Events in Sequence Number the events in the order in which they occurred.

____ **A.** The Lewis and Clark expedition leaves St. Louis.
____ **B.** Thomas Jefferson authorizes American diplomats to offer $10 million dollars for New Orleans and West Florida.
____ **C.** Meriwether Lewis and William Clark reach the Pacific Ocean at the mouth of the Columbia River.
____ **D.** Jefferson persuades Congress to sponsor an expedition into the Louisiana Territory.
____ **E.** The Federalists support Aaron Burr in his bid to become governor of New York.
____ **F.** The Spanish refuse to allow American goods to move into or past New Orleans.
____ **G.** The Senate gives its approval of the Louisiana Purchase.
____ **H.** Alexander Hamilton dies after engaging in a duel with Aaron Burr.
____ **I.** Jefferson learns that Spain secretly transferred the Louisiana Territory to France.
____ **J.** Sacagawea helps Lewis and Clark secure horses and supplies for their journey over the Rocky Mountains.

DIRECTIONS: Essay Answer the following questions.

1. Why was France willing to sell the Louisiana Territory?
2. Why did Massachusetts Federalists support Republican Aaron Burr for governor of New York in the 1804 election?

Reteaching Activities ★ 34 ★ *The American Journey*

Enrichment Activity 9–2

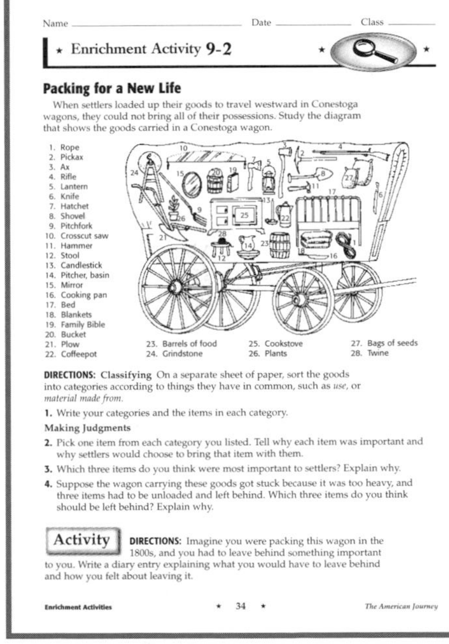

Name ______ Date ______ Class ______

★ Enrichment Activity 9-2 ★

Packing for a New Life

When settlers loaded up their goods to travel westward in Conestoga wagons, they could not bring all of their possessions. Study the diagram that shows the goods carried in a Conestoga wagon.

1. Rope
2. Pickax
3. Ax
4. Rifle
5. Lantern
6. Knife
7. Hatchet
8. Shovel
9. Pitchfork
10. Crosscut saw
11. Hammer
12. Stool
13. Candlestick
14. Pitcher, basin
15. Mirror
16. Cooking pan
17. Bed
18. Blankets
19. Family Bible
20. Bucket
21. Plow
22. Coffeepot
23. Barrels of food
24. Grindstone
25. Cookstove
26. Plants
27. Bags of seeds
28. Twine

DIRECTIONS: Classifying On a separate sheet of paper, sort the goods into categories according to things they have in common, such as *use*, or *material made from.*

1. Write your categories and the items in each category.

Making Judgments

2. Pick one item from each category you listed. Tell why each item was important and why settlers would choose to bring that item with them.
3. Which three items do you think were most important to settlers? Explain why.
4. Suppose the wagon carrying these goods got stuck because it was too heavy, and three items had to be unloaded and left behind. Which three items do you think should be left behind? Explain why.

Activity **DIRECTIONS:** Imagine you were packing this wagon in the 1800s, and you had to leave behind something important to you. Write a diary entry explaining what you would have to leave behind and how you felt about leaving it.

Enrichment Activities ★ 34 ★ *The American Journey*

4 CLOSE

Some historians consider Jefferson's purchase of the Louisiana Territory his greatest accomplishment. Ask students whether they agree with this assessment, and why.

NATIONAL GEOGRAPHIC *Journeys*

NATIONAL GEOGRAPHIC SOCIETY

VIDEODISC
GTV: A Geographic Perspective on American History

Side 2, Chapter 3
Title: *Lewis and Clark*
Subject: The Lewis and Clark expedition (1804–1806)
Ask: **What did President Jefferson hope to find in the Louisiana Territory?** *(a water route to the Pacific Ocean)*

Linking PAST & PRESENT

Wise and Foolish Finances In 1803 Barings Brothers, a British bank, wisely financed the purchase of the Louisiana Territory. Barings later became one of the world's most powerful banks. In the mid-1990s, however, a Barings official in Singapore caused the bank to collapse when he invested heavily in stock futures on Asian stock markets.

What?Where?When?Who?

Against the Deal The Boston newspaper *Columbian Centennial* strongly criticized the Louisiana Purchase, arguing that "we are to give money of which we have too little, for land of which we already have too much."

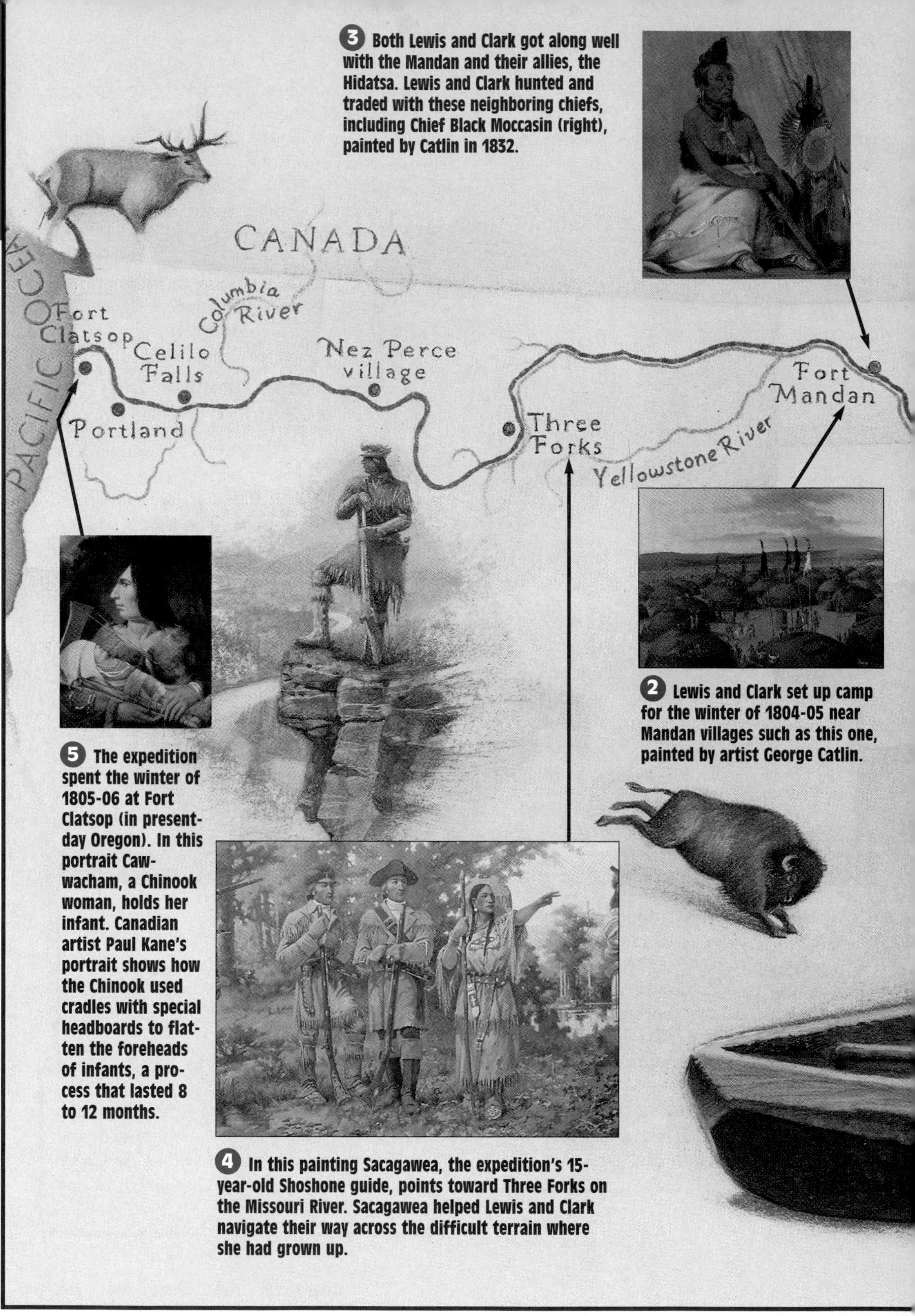

3 Both Lewis and Clark got along well with the Mandan and their allies, the Hidatsa. Lewis and Clark hunted and traded with these neighboring chiefs, including Chief Black Moccasin (right), painted by Catlin in 1832.

2 Lewis and Clark set up camp for the winter of 1804-05 near Mandan villages such as this one, painted by artist George Catlin.

5 The expedition spent the winter of 1805-06 at Fort Clatsop (in present-day Oregon). In this portrait Caw-wacham, a Chinook woman, holds her infant. Canadian artist Paul Kane's portrait shows how the Chinook used cradles with special headboards to flatten the foreheads of infants, a process that lasted 8 to 12 months.

4 In this painting Sacagawea, the expedition's 15-year-old Shoshone guide, points toward Three Forks on the Missouri River. Sacagawea helped Lewis and Clark navigate their way across the difficult terrain where she had grown up.

TEACHER'S NOTES

NATIONAL GEOGRAPHIC

Journeys

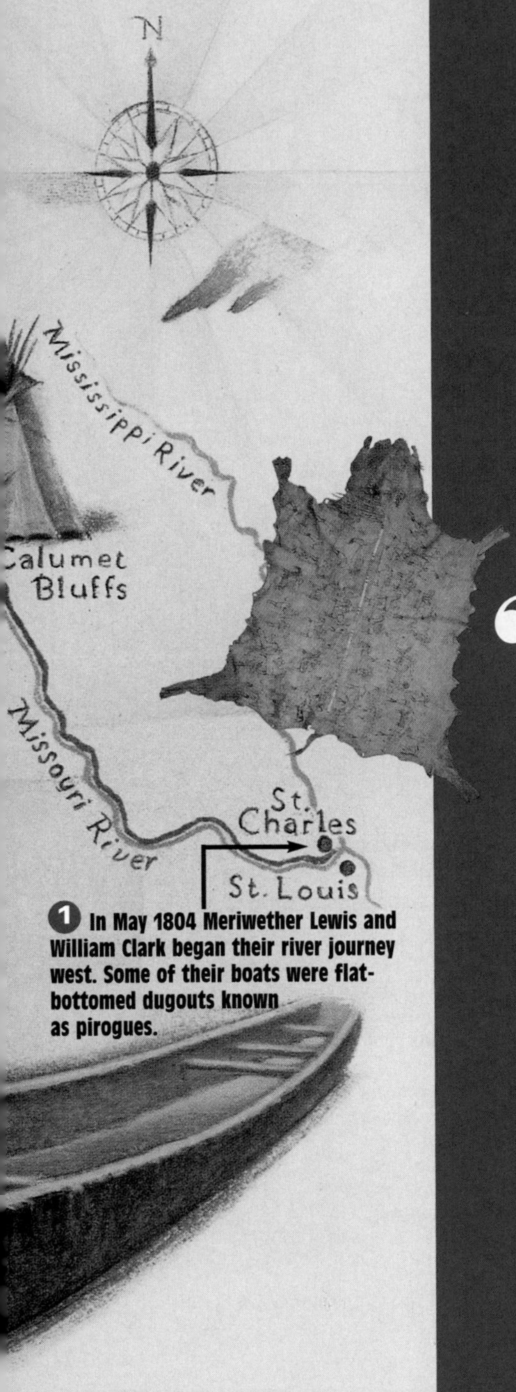

1 In May 1804 Meriwether Lewis and William Clark began their river journey west. Some of their boats were flat-bottomed dugouts known as pirogues.

Lewis & Clark

"Our vessels consisted of six small canoes and two large pirogues. This little fleet, altho' not quite so respectable as those of Columbus or Capt. Cook, was still viewed by us with much pleasure.... We were about to penetrate a country at least two thousand miles in width, on which the foot of civilized man had never trodden; the good or evil it had in store ... was for experiment yet to determine.... The picture which now presented itself to me was a most pleasing one.... I could but esteem this moment of ... departure as among the most happy of my life."

— From an April 1805 entry in the journal of Meriwether Lewis, as he prepares to leave Fort Mandan.

Who?What?Where?When?

York An African American servant named York accompanied Lewis and Clark on the expedition to the western frontier. York played an important role in the success of the expedition, and he made many friends among the Native Americans whom Lewis and Clark encountered. Although the Native Americans were familiar with white people because of their contacts with traders and fur trappers, few had ever seen an African American. York, therefore, became something of a celebrity among the western Native American nations.

What?Where?When?Who?

Bibliography The paragraph at left was excerpted from *Undaunted Courage: Meriwether Lewis, Thomas Jefferson, and the Opening of the American West* by Stephen Ambrose (New York: Simon & Schuster, ©1996).

TEACHER'S NOTES

Social Studies Connections

Geography

TEACH

A New Frontier

Tell students that part of Lewis and Clark's mission was to find a water route across the continent. Have them compare the map on page 283 with a physical map of the United States and ask whether the expedition was successful in that mission. *(no)* Ask students to name the mountains through which the expedition passed as it followed the Columbia River to the ocean. *(Cascade Range, Coast Ranges)*

Who?What?Where?When?

Alexander Mackenzie, not Lewis and Clark, became the first non-native to travel overland to the Pacific Ocean. In 1793 the Scottish fur trader reached the Pacific across barren and trackless northwest Canada. Mackenzie kept a journal, which President Jefferson read. In part, it was Mackenzie's account of his trek that inspired the Lewis and Clark expedition.

Social Studies Connections | Geography | World History | Economics | Citizenship

A New Frontier

What lay in the vast Louisiana Territory? How far was it to the Pacific Ocean? Certainly the members of the Lewis and Clark expedition had little idea of what distances and difficulties they would face on their trek. Nor could they imagine that they would come face-to-face with unknown species of flora (plants) and fauna (animals).

The two explorers carefully mapped the entire trip, which covered about 8,000 miles (12,900 km). William Clark constructed 60 maps—some eight feet in length—depicting the expedition's route. The maps included the latitude and longitude of natural features such as rapids and islands. Both Lewis and Clark packed their journals with descriptions and sketches of all they saw.

Many of the local animals and plants were new to Lewis and Clark. They collected and preserved specimens such as a prairie dog, jackrabbit, black-tailed deer, pronghorn, and mountain sheep. Huge grizzly bears were a frequent threat to the party. The annoyed explorers gave the bear its scientific name: *Ursus arctos horribilis,* or "terrible bear." They also found some huge bones that may have been those of a dinosaur.

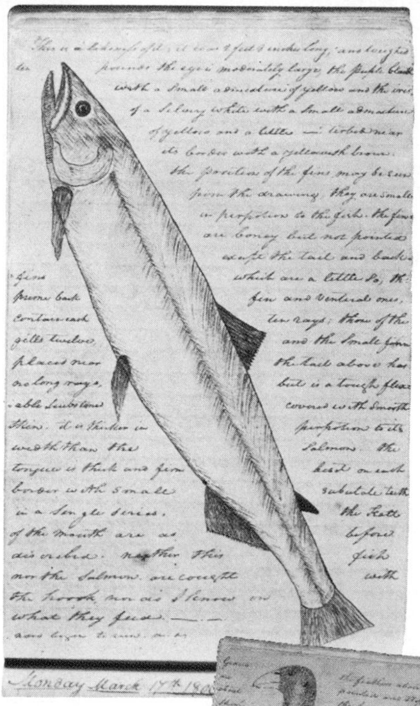

White salmon trout

While exploring the Louisiana Territory with Meriwether Lewis, William Clark recorded his observations in a journal. The pages of Clark's journal also include drawings of the animals found in the area.

Heath cock

Activity

Writing a Journal Entry Imagine you are a member of the Lewis and Clark expedition. Write a day's journal entry that details the route you take and what you see.

More About . . .

Jefferson's Instructions President Jefferson had very detailed instructions for Lewis and Clark. "The object of your mission is to explore the Missouri River . . . and [find] the water of the Pacific Ocean. Beginning at the mouth of the Missouri, you will take observations of latitude and longitude at all remarkable points on the river. . . . Your observations are to be taken with great pains and accuracy, to be entered distinctly and intelligibly for others as well as yourself to comprehend.

"Other objects worthy of notice will be: the soil and face of the country, its growth and vegetable productions . . . the animals . . . especially those not known in the U. S.; the remains . . . which may be . . . rare or extinct; the mineral productions of every kind . . . the dates at which particular plants put forth or lose their flowers, or leaf; times of appearance of particular birds, reptiles, or insects. . . ."

1804 | 1808 | 1812

1804 Barbary pirates seize the U.S. warship *Philadelphia*

1807 The British navy attacks the American vessel *Chesapeake*; Congress passes the Embargo Act

1811 Harrison defeats the Prophet at Tippecanoe

1812 Madison asks Congress to declare war on Britain

Section 3

A Time of Conflict

READ TO DISCOVER . . .

- why Jefferson sent American ships to the Mediterranean Sea.
- why the Embargo Act of 1807 proved to be a disaster.
- why Tecumseh built a confederacy among tribes in Indiana, Ohio, and Michigan.
- why the War Hawks wanted to go to war with Britain.

TERMS TO LEARN

tribute
neutral rights
impressment
embargo
War Hawks
nationalism

The Storyteller

The floors of the oceans are littered with the remains of once mighty ships and the unmarked graves of unlucky sailors who sank with them in the 1700s. Seafarer Francis Rogers described the terror of a storm in this journal entry: "The sky seemed all on fire and [all around] were such swift darting rays of lightning, flying in long bright veins, with inexpressible fury as was very frightful."

Shipbuilder's tool bag and tools

In 1785 the American ship *Empress of China* returned to New York from China with a highly prized cargo of tea and silk. The goods sold for a fabulous profit. Soon ships from New York, Philadelphia, and especially New England were sailing regularly to China and India carrying furs and other goods. In the following years, American merchant ships sailed far and wide, making calls in South America, Africa, and lands along the Mediterranean Sea.

Americans in Foreign Seas

War between the French and British in the mid-1790s gave an additional boost to American shipping. Rather than risk capture or destruction by the enemy, many French and British merchant ships remained at home. American shippers profited from the situation and increased their trade. By 1800 the United States was second only to Great Britain in the number of merchant ships trading around the world.

Barbary Pirates

Sailing in foreign seas was not without danger. In the Mediterranean, for example, ships had to be on guard for pirates from Tripoli and the other **Barbary Coast states** of North Africa. For years these Barbary pirates had been terrorizing the Mediterranean. They demanded **tribute**, or protection money, from European governments to let their ships pass safely. The United States, too, had paid tribute—but not enough.

SECTION RESOURCES

Reproducible Masters
- Guided Reading Activity 9–3
- Political Cartoons, *The Embargo Act of 1807*
- Section Quiz 9–3
- Reteaching Activity 9–3
- Enrichment Activity 9–3

Transparencies
- Section Focus Transparency 9–3

Multimedia
- Vocabulary PuzzleMaker
- Testmaker
- GTV: A Geographic Perspective on American History
- GTV: The American People: Fabric of a Nation
- The Presidents: A Picture History of Our Nation

1 FOCUS

BELLRINGER
Motivational Activity

Before taking roll at the beginning of the class period, project Section Focus Transparency 9–3 and have students answer the questions. Discuss students' responses.

This activity is also available as a blackline master.

Section Focus Transparency 9–3

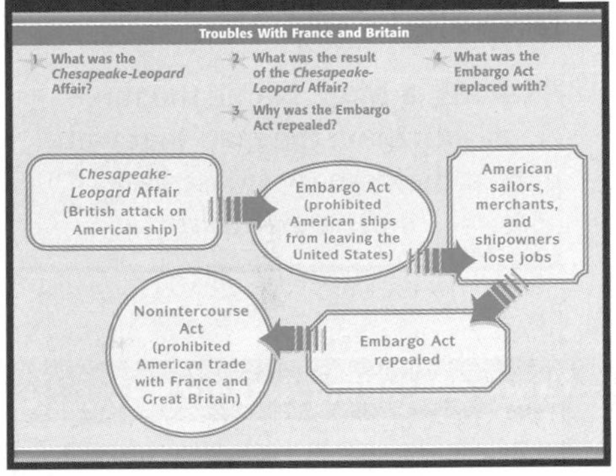

Vocabulary Precheck

Point out that a hawk is a bird of prey. Then have students suggest why supporters of war are called hawks.

Use the **Vocabulary PuzzleMaker** to create crossword and word search puzzles.

Section Theme
Global Connections

In December 1807, Congress passed the Embargo Act banning imports and exports from all foreign countries.

Activity Have students find out how the Embargo Act proved that the United States was dependent on foreign nations. *(Unemployment rose; goods meant for export were not sold at home, rather they rotted in warehouses or remained unharvested.)*

CHAPTER 9
Section 3, 289–295

2 TEACH

L1 Writing Headlines Have students compose a newspaper headline for each major part of the section. Remind them that dramatic events, such as Decatur's burning of the *Philadelphia*, sell newspapers.

Map Study

Answers

1. Atlantic Ocean, Mediterranean Sea
2. about 400 miles

Map Skills Practice

Reading a Map Name the three cities shown on the map that were part of the Barbary Coast states. *(Algiers, Tunis, and Tripoli)*

Guided Reading Activity 9–3

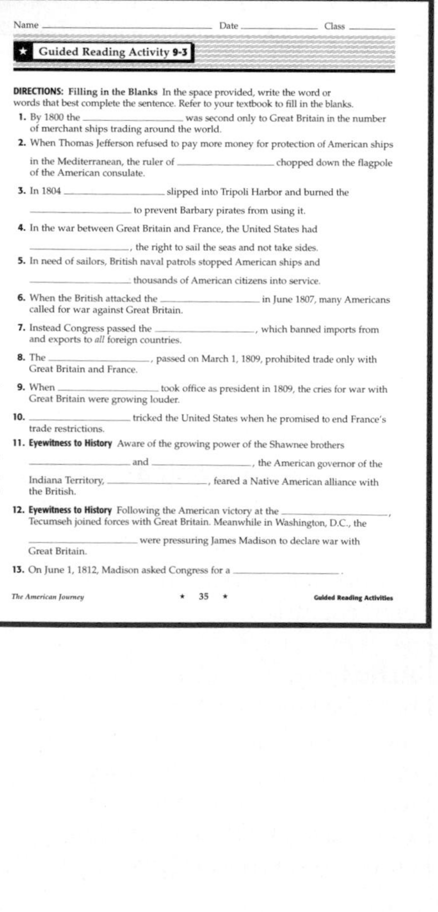

Name ______ Date ______ Class ______

★ Guided Reading Activity 9-3

DIRECTIONS: Filling in the Blanks In the space provided, write the word or words that best complete the sentence. Refer to your textbook to fill in the blanks.

1. By 1800 the ______ was second only to Great Britain in the number of merchant ships trading around the world.
2. When Thomas Jefferson refused to pay more money for protection of American ships in the Mediterranean, the ruler of ______ chopped down the flagpole of the American consulate.
3. In 1804 ______ slipped into Tripoli Harbor and burned the ______ to prevent Barbary pirates from using it.
4. In the war between Great Britain and France, the United States had ______, the right to sail the seas and not take sides.
5. In need of sailors, British naval patrols stopped American ships and ______ thousands of American citizens into service.
6. When the British attacked the ______ in June 1807, many Americans called for war against Great Britain.
7. Instead Congress passed the ______, which banned imports from and exports to *all* foreign countries.
8. The ______, passed on March 1, 1809, prohibited trade only with Great Britain and France.
9. When ______ took office as president in 1809, the cries for war with Great Britain were growing louder.
10. ______ tricked the United States when he promised to end France's trade restrictions.
11. **Eyewitness to History** Aware of the growing power of the Shawnee brothers ______ and ______, the American governor of the Indiana Territory, ______, feared a Native American alliance with the British.
12. **Eyewitness to History** Following the American victory at the ______, Tecumseh joined forces with Great Britain. Meanwhile in Washington, D.C., the ______ were pressuring James Madison to declare war with Great Britain.
13. On June 1, 1812, Madison asked Congress for a ______.

The American Journey ★ 35 ★ **Guided Reading Activities**

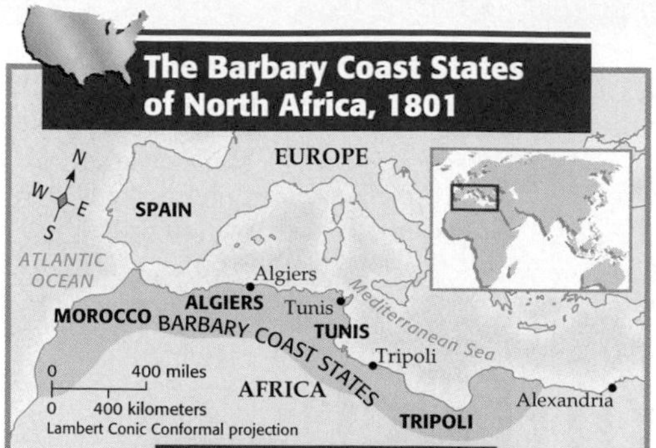

Map Study

To protect United States ships, the American government paid a yearly bribe to the rulers of the Barbary States.

1. **Location** What bodies of water bordered the Barbary Coast states?
2. **Analyzing Information** About how many miles is it from the port of Algiers to the port of Tunis?

War With Tripoli

In 1801 the ruler of Tripoli asked for more money from the United States. When President Jefferson refused, the ruler chopped down the flagpole of the American consulate—a declaration of war. Jefferson sent ships to the Mediterranean and blockaded, or closed off, Tripoli. The American fleet, however, was not powerful enough to defeat the Barbary pirates, and the conflict continued.

In 1804 the pirates seized the U.S. warship *Philadelphia* and towed it into Tripoli Harbor. They threw the captain and crew into jail. Then **Stephen Decatur,** a 25-year-old United States Navy captain, took action. Slipping into the heavily guarded harbor with a small raiding party, Decatur burned the captured ship to prevent the pirates from using it. A British admiral praised the deed as the "most bold and daring act of the age."

Negotiations finally ended the conflict with Tripoli in June 1805. Tripoli agreed to stop demanding tribute, but the United States had to pay a ransom of $60,000 for the release of the American prisoners.

Freedom of the Seas

Riding the wave of four successful years as president, Jefferson won reelection easily in 1804. Jefferson received 162 electoral votes to only 14 for his Federalist opponent, Charles Pinckney. His second term began with the nation at peace. Across the sea, however, Great Britain and France were already involved in a war that threatened to interfere with American trade.

The thriving foreign trade of the United States depended on being able to sail the seas freely. The nation had resolved the threat from the Barbary pirates. Now it was challenged at sea by the two most powerful nations in Europe.

Neutral Rights Violated

When Britain and France went to war in 1803, America enjoyed a prosperous commerce with both countries. As long as the United States remained neutral, shippers could continue doing business. A nation not involved in a conflict had **neutral rights**—the right to sail the seas and not take sides.

For two years American shipping continued to prosper. By 1805, however, the warring nations had lost patience with American "neutrality." Britain blockaded the French coast and threatened to search all ships trading with France. France announced that it would search and seize ships caught trading with Britain.

American Sailors Kidnapped

The British needed sailors for their naval war. However, conditions in the British navy were terrible. Sailors were poorly paid, poorly fed, and badly treated. Many of them deserted. Desperately in need of sailors, the British often used force to get them. British naval patrols claimed the right to stop American ships at sea. They seized any sailors on board suspected of being deserters from the British navy and forced them into service.

This practice, known as **impressment,** was a clear violation of neutral rights. While some of those taken were deserters from the British navy, the British also impressed thousands of native-born and naturalized American citizens.

Cooperative Learning Activity

Protesting the Embargo Have students work in small groups to prepare a campaign to convince President Jefferson that the trade embargo is a bad idea. Have each student choose a specific role in the project–writing a petition, preparing and designing posters, preparing a brief argument to get people to sign the petition, designing T-shirts and buttons, and writing and delivering speeches.

Attack on the *Chesapeake*

Quite often the British would lie in wait for American ships outside an American harbor. This happened in June 1807 off the coast of **Virginia.** A British warship intercepted the American vessel *Chesapeake* and demanded to search the ship for British deserters. When the *Chesapeake*'s captain refused, the British opened fire, killing 3, wounding 18, and crippling the American ship.

As news of the attack spread, Americans reacted with an anti-British fury not seen since the Revolutionary War. Secretary of State **James Madison** called the attack an outrage. Many demanded war against Britain. Although President Jefferson did not intend to let Great Britain's actions go unanswered, he sought a course of action other than war.

Picturing HISTORY Americans resented the British method of recruiting for their navy by impressment. **How did the United States respond when the British ship *Leopard* attacked the American frigate *Chesapeake*?**

President Bans Trade

Britain's practice of impressment and its violation of America's neutral rights had led Jefferson to ban some trade with Britain. The attack on the *Chesapeake,* however, triggered even stronger measures.

A Disastrous Trade Ban

In December 1807, the Republican Congress passed the **Embargo Act.** An **embargo** prohibits trade with another country. Although Great Britain was the target of this act, the embargo banned imports from and exports to *all* foreign countries. Jefferson wanted to prevent Americans from using other countries as go-betweens in the forbidden trade.

By using the embargo, Jefferson and Madison hoped to hurt Britain but avoid war. They believed the British depended on American agricultural products. As it turned out, the embargo of 1807 was a disaster. The measure wiped out all American commerce with other nations. Worse, it proved ineffective against Britain. The British simply traded with South America for its agricultural goods. Even worse, the embargo divided the American people.

Opposition to the Trade Ban

Federalist New England, the heart of the American shipping industry, complained the loudest about the embargo. With ships stuck in their ports, unemployment began to rise, and protests flooded Washington. The feeling of frustration was summed up in a bitter poem:

> Our ships all in motion,
> Once whiten'd the ocean;
> They sail'd and return'd with a Cargo;
> Now doom'd to decay
> They are fallen a prey,
> To Jefferson, worms, and EMBARGO.

New England was not the only region hurt by the embargo. In the South tobacco meant for Europe rotted on the docks, and cotton went unpicked. In the West the price of wheat declined, and river traffic came to a halt. At first, however, these Republican regions continued to support Jefferson.

The embargo proved difficult to enforce also. Before long American shippers began smuggling

When?Who?What?Where?

No Tribute? At the time of the XYZ affair, when Americans were chanting, "Millions for defense, but not one cent for tribute," a United States warship was on its way to Algiers, carrying 26 barrels of silver dollars to pay the Barbary pirates for their "protection."

Picturing HISTORY It is estimated that about 6,000 United States citizens were impressed by the British between 1808 and 1811. **Answer:** *with outrage and calls for war and an embargo on foreign trade*

you don't say...

Embargo Americans enraged by the embargo made anagrams of the word *embargo* that reflected their anger: "O Grab Me," "Go Bar 'Em," and "Mobrage." One cartoon of the time shows a snapping turtle (the embargo) clenching a merchant's trousers in its jaws, preventing the man from loading his cargo. The merchant's speech balloon reads, "Oh! this cursed Ograbme."

Political Cartoons, *The Embargo Act of 1807*

Linking PAST & PRESENT

Embargoes Throughout its history, the United States has used the embargo as a political weapon. In 1980 President Jimmy Carter placed an embargo on the sale of American grain to the Soviet Union because the country's troops had invaded Afghanistan. The embargo was meant to put pressure on the Soviet Union to withdraw its troops.

MULTIPLE LEARNING STYLES

Intrapersonal Have each student choose a person from the section and write several diary entries that the person might have made. In addition to the named people—Tecumseh, the Prophet, William Henry Harrison, and so on—students may choose the role of an unnamed Shawnee, soldier, or settler. Before they write their entries, encourage students to think about how their chosen character might have felt, and how they themselves would have felt in the same situation. **L1**

American Memories

Building Warships
Plans to build a large American battle fleet were doomed by the election of President Thomas Jefferson in 1800. Jefferson, though, effectively utilized the existing fleet by not limiting its use to patrolling and escorting. Rather, he used American ships to blockade and bombard Tripoli.
Answer: plane, saw, hammer

NATIONAL GEOGRAPHIC SOCIETY

VIDEODISC
GTV: A Geographic Perspective on American History

Side 2, Chapter 6
Title: *The Advancing Frontier: The Near West*
Subject: Settlement between the Appalachians and the Mississippi (1820–1850)
Ask: **How did the northwestern and southwestern frontiers mirror the North and the South of the eastern United States?** *(Northwest frontiers relied on industry while the Southwest frontier relied on slave labor)*

CD-ROM
The Presidents: A Picture History of Our Nation

Have students select Thomas Jefferson from the main menu. Ask them to look for important elements of Jefferson's domestic policies.

American Memories — *Building Warships*

What Was It Like? During the early 1800s, shipbuilding was a major economic activity and was important for national defense. **What were some of the tools used to build early ships?**

their goods—as they had done in the days of the Revolutionary War. Public opinion started to turn against the president and the Republicans. Having suffered a disastrous setback in the 1804 elections, the Federalists now gained support from the surge of feeling against the embargo.

Jefferson Leaves Office

Following Washington's precedent, Jefferson made it clear in mid-1808 that he would not be a candidate for a third term. With Jefferson's approval the Republicans chose James Madison as their candidate for president. The Federalists nominated Charles Pinckney and hoped that anger over the embargo would gain support for their party. Pinckney carried most of New England, but the Federalist ticket collected little support from the other regions. Madison won with 122 electoral votes to Pinckney's 47 votes.

The embargo clearly had not worked. On March 1, 1809, Congress repealed it. In its place Congress enacted the much weaker **Nonintercourse Act.** The new act prohibited trade only with Britain and France and their colonial possessions. It was no more popular or successful than the Embargo Act.

War Fever

James Madison did not take office as president under the most favorable conditions. Called "Little Jemmy" by his enemies—he stood only 5 feet 4 inches tall—Madison had to follow in the imposing footsteps of Thomas Jefferson. At home and abroad, the nation was mired in the embargo crisis. Meanwhile Britain continued to claim the right to halt American ships, and cries for war with Britain grew louder and louder.

Closer to War

In 1810 the Nonintercourse Act expired and Congress replaced it with a complicated new law. This law permitted direct trade with either France

MORE ABOUT . . .

Tecumseh is believed to have been born at Old Piqua, a Shawnee village on the Mad River, northeast of present-day Dayton. His father and two brothers lost their lives battling American colonists.

Besides forging a Native American confederacy in Ohio, Indiana, and Michigan, Tecumseh also stirred up the Creek Nation, who rose up against colonists throughout Alabama, Georgia, and Mississippi. Although a force led by Andrew Jackson broke the power of the Creek in 1814, the Seminole, a southern branch of the Creek in Florida, continued to fight, which led to the Seminole Wars.

Many colonists, including William Henry Harrison, held Tecumseh in high regard. In a private report to the War Department, Harrison described him as "one of those uncommon geniuses which spring up occasionally to produce revolutions and overturn the established order of things."

or Britain, depending on which country first lifted its trade restrictions against America. Napoleon seized the opportunity and promised to end France's restrictions.

Unfortunately for Madison, Napoleon had tricked the American administration. The French continued to seize American ships, selling them and pocketing the proceeds. Americans were deeply divided. To some it seemed as if the nation was on the verge of war—but it was hard to decide if the enemy should be Britain or France. Madison knew that France had tricked him, but he continued to see Britain as the bigger threat.

Frontier Conflicts

While Madison was trying to decide how to resolve the difficulties with European powers, news arrived about problems in the West. **Ohio** had become a state in 1803. Between 1801 and 1810, white settlers continued to press for more land in the Ohio Valley. Native Americans had given up some 100 million acres. Now the settlers were moving onto lands that had been guaranteed to Native Americans by treaty.

Tecumseh and the Prophet

As tensions increased, some Native Americans began renewing their contacts with British agents and fur traders in Canada. Others pursued a new strategy. A powerful Shawnee chief named **Tecumseh** (tuh•KUHM•suh) built a confederacy among Native American nations in Indiana, Ohio, and Michigan. Tecumseh believed that a strong alliance—with the backing of the British in Canada—could put a halt to white movement onto Native American lands.

A commanding speaker, Tecumseh possessed great political skills. In his view the United States government treaties with individual nations were worthless. "The Great Spirit gave this great island to his red children," he said. No one nation had the right to give it away.

Tecumseh had a powerful ally—his brother, known as **the Prophet.** The Prophet urged Native Americans everywhere to return to the customs of their ancestors. They should, he said, give up practices learned from the white invaders—wearing western dress, using plows and firearms and, especially, drinking alcohol. The Prophet attracted a huge following. He founded a village at a site in northern Indiana, near present-day Lafayette, where the Tippecanoe and Wabash Rivers meet. It was called Prophetstown.

Eyewitness to HISTORY

A Meeting With Harrison

The American governor of the Indiana Territory, **General William Henry Harrison,** became alarmed by the growing power of the two Shawnee brothers. He feared they would form an alliance with the British.

In a letter to Tecumseh, Harrison warned that the United States had many more warriors than all the Indian nations could put together. "Do not think that the redcoats can protect you; they are not able to protect themselves." Tecumseh sent word that he would reply in person.

A few weeks later, Tecumseh arrived at the river across from Fort Knox, accompanied by 400 armed warriors in canoes. He spoke to the white people assembled there:

> "Brothers: Since the peace was made, you have killed some of the Shawnees, Winnebagoes, Delawares, and Miamis, and you have taken our land from us; and I do not see how we can remain at peace if you continue to do so. You try to force the red people to do some injury; it is you who are pushing them on to do mischief. You try to keep the tribes apart, and make distinctions among them. You wish to prevent the Indians from uniting."

The Battle of Tippecanoe

In 1811 while Tecumseh was in the South trying to expand his confederacy, Harrison decided to attack Prophetstown on the Tippecanoe River.

CHAPTER 9
Section 3, 289–295

NATIONAL GEOGRAPHIC SOCIETY

VIDEODISC
GTV: The American People: Fabric of a Nation

Side 2, Chapter 2
Title: *Between Worlds*
Subject: For Native Americans, a shrinking realm
Ask: **What did the bison provide for the Native Americans?** *(food, clothing, shelter, and tools)*

you don't say...

Tecumseh is the anglicized version of *Tek-am-thi*, which is Shawnee for the "Panther Passing Across." His father chose that name because Tecumseh was born just as a shooting star of great brilliance passed overhead. According to Shawnee legend, shooting stars were panthers looking for a deep hole or cave in which to sleep.

CURRICULUM CONNECTION

LANGUAGE ARTS
The plight of the sailors thrown into unemployment by the embargo prompted a 13-year-old Massachusetts boy to write a poem in 1808. The writer, William Cullen Bryant, went on to become one of America's leading poets and newspaper editors. He was editor of the *New York Evening Post* from 1829 until his death in 1878.

CRITICAL THINKING ACTIVITY

Rewriting History Have students work in small groups to brainstorm how history might have been different had Tecumseh succeeded in uniting the Native Americans and had thus been present with a large force at the Battle of Tippecanoe. Have each group present its ideas in a format chosen by the group—written report, skit, mural, and so on. Tasks in preparing the presentation should be divided according to the skills of individual group members. **L1**

CHAPTER 9
Section 3, 289–295

you don't say...

Conestoga is the name of a Native American group whose population was reduced by epidemics from about 5,000 in 1600 to 20 people in 1763. These last few were massacred by white settlers.

TECHNOLOGY AND HISTORY

More About . . .

The Conestoga Wagon The wagons were later called prairie schooners. Seen from a distance across the plains, the white canvas covers looked like sails. The custom of driving on the right side derives from the days of the Conestoga wagon.

Answer to Caption: *to keep goods from falling out when the wagon was going uphill or downhill*

3 ASSESS

Assign Section 3 Review as homework or as an in-class activity.

Use **Chapter Challenger Interactive Review** Software to review Section 3.

Section Quiz 9–3

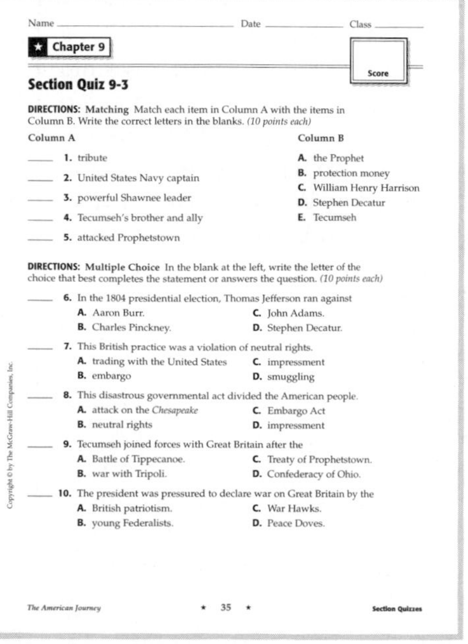

Name ______ Date ______ Class ______

★ Chapter 9

Score

Section Quiz 9-3

DIRECTIONS: Matching Match each item in Column A with the items in Column B. Write the correct letters in the blanks. *(10 points each)*

Column A	Column B
____ 1. tribute	A. the Prophet
____ 2. United States Navy captain	B. protection money
____ 3. powerful Shawnee leader	C. William Henry Harrison
____ 4. Tecumseh's brother and ally	D. Stephen Decatur
____ 5. attacked Prophetstown	E. Tecumseh

DIRECTIONS: Multiple Choice In the blank at the left, write the letter of the choice that best completes the statement or answers the question. *(10 points each)*

____ 6. In the 1804 presidential election, Thomas Jefferson ran against
A. Aaron Burr. C. John Adams.
B. Charles Pinckney. D. Stephen Decatur.

____ 7. This British practice was a violation of neutral rights.
A. trading with the United States C. impressment
B. embargo D. smuggling

____ 8. This disastrous governmental act divided the American people.
A. attack on the *Chesapeake* C. Embargo Act
B. neutral rights D. impressment

____ 9. Tecumseh joined forces with Great Britain after the
A. Battle of Tippecanoe. C. Treaty of Prophetstown.
B. war with Tripoli. D. Confederacy of Ohio.

____ 10. The president was pressured to declare war on Great Britain by the
A. British patriotism. C. War Hawks.
B. young Federalists. D. Peace Doves.

After a two-hour battle, the Prophet's forces fled the area in defeat. The **Battle of Tippecanoe** was proclaimed a glorious victory for the Americans. Harrison acquired the nickname "Tippecanoe" and used it as a patriotic rallying cry when he ran for president in 1840.

The American victory at the Battle of Tippecanoe, however, resulted in something the American people had hoped to prevent. Tecumseh now joined forces with the British troops. White settlers in the region claimed that the British had supplied Tecumseh's confederacy with guns. As a result, the rallying cry of the settlers became "On to Canada!"

War Hawks

Back in the nation's capital, President Madison faced demands for a more aggressive policy toward the British. The most insistent voices came from a group of young Republicans elected to Congress in 1810. Known as the **War Hawks,** they came from the South and the West. The War Hawks pressured the president to declare war with Britain.

While the War Hawks wanted to avenge British actions against Americans, they were also eager to expand the nation's power. Their **nationalism** appealed to a renewed sense of

TECHNOLOGY AND HISTORY

The Conestoga Wagon

By the mid-1700s, sturdy Conestoga wagons transported settlers and their freight over the Appalachian Mountains. These wagons were first built in the Conestoga Creek region of Lancaster, Pennsylvania. As people pushed even farther westward, the Conestoga was seen rolling across the plains toward Oregon and California. **Why did Conestoga wagons have a high front and back?**

TEACHER'S NOTES

Picturing HISTORY The Battle of Tippecanoe began a series of conflicts between Native Americans and white settlers. **How did Harrison's victory at Tippecanoe affect Tecumseh (right) and his Native American forces?**

American patriotism. The leading War Hawks were **Henry Clay** from Kentucky and **John Calhoun** from South Carolina, both in their 30s.

Preparing for War

With the support of the other War Hawks, Clay was elected Speaker of the House of Representatives in 1811. This was an extraordinary step in view of his youth and lack of experience. The War Hawks urged major spending to strengthen the United States military. Through their efforts Congress quadrupled the army's size. During all these preparations, the Federalists in the Northeast remained strongly opposed to war.

Declaring War

By the spring of 1812, Madison concluded that war with Britain was inevitable. In a message to Congress on June 1, he cited "the spectacle of injuries and indignities which have been heaped on our country" and asked for a declaration of war.

In the meantime the British had decided to end their policy of search and seizure of American ships. Unfortunately, because of the amount of time it took for news to travel across the Atlantic, this change in policy was not known in Washington. Word of the breakthrough arrived too late. Once set in motion, the war machine could not be stopped.

Section 3 Review

Checking for Understanding

1. ***Identify*** James Madison, Embargo Act, Tecumseh, the Prophet, Henry Clay.
2. ***Define*** tribute, neutral rights, impressment, embargo, War Hawks, nationalism.
3. ***Describe*** the negotiations that ended the war with Tripoli.

Reviewing Themes

4. **Global Connections** How did conflict in Europe help American shipping prosper?

Critical Thinking

5. **Identifying Cause and Effect** How did battles on the frontier with Native Americans intensify Americans' anti-British feelings?

Activity

Drawing a Political Cartoon Choose a side in the argument about war with Great Britain. Draw a political cartoon supporting your point of view.

Section 3 Review Answers

1. James Madison, 291; Embargo Act, 291; Tecumseh, 293; the Prophet, 293; Henry Clay, 295
2. The words are defined in the Glossary.
3. Tripoli agreed to stop demanding tribute, but the United States had to pay a $60,000 ransom for the release of American prisoners.
4. By remaining neutral, the United States could trade with both France and Britain. Both countries kept most of their trading ships in port to avoid capture, so Americans increased their trade.
5. The British sided with Native Americans against Americans; this interference angered many Americans.

Activity Political cartoons should encourage support for or opposition to a war with Britain.

Picturing HISTORY The Battle of Tippecanoe was fought near Battle Ground, Indiana. **Answer:** *His forces joined the British.*

Reteaching Activity 9–3

Name ______ Date ______ Class ______

★ Reteaching Activity 9-3

DIRECTIONS: Organizing Facts Complete the diagram by writing the numbers of the words from the Fact Bank in the correct boxes.

A Time of Conflicts

The Barbary Coast	Acts Against the United States by Great Britain

The Trade Ban	The American Frontier

★FACT BANK

1. the Battle of Tippecanoe
2. Pirates demand tribute.
3. impressment
4. Prophetstown
5. Americans smuggle goods.
6. the attack of the *Chesapeake*
7. the Embargo Act
8. the blockade of Tripoli
9. Unemployment rises in New England.
10. Tobacco rots on Southern docks.
11. Tecumseh builds a confederacy of Native American nations.
12. Wheat prices decline in the West.
13. Settlers move onto lands guaranteed to Native Americans.
14. search and seizure of American ships
15. Stephen Decatur burns the *Philadelphia.*

DIRECTIONS: Essay Answer the following question on a separate sheet of paper.

Why was the embargo of 1807 considered a disaster?

The American Journey ★ 35 ★ **Reteaching Activities**

Enrichment Activity 9–3

Name ______ Date ______ Class ______

★ Enrichment Activity 9-3

Pirates of North Africa

Thomas Jefferson expected to reduce military spending, but by 1801 he had to send the navy to face North African pirates.

The Barbary Coast States of North Africa, 1801

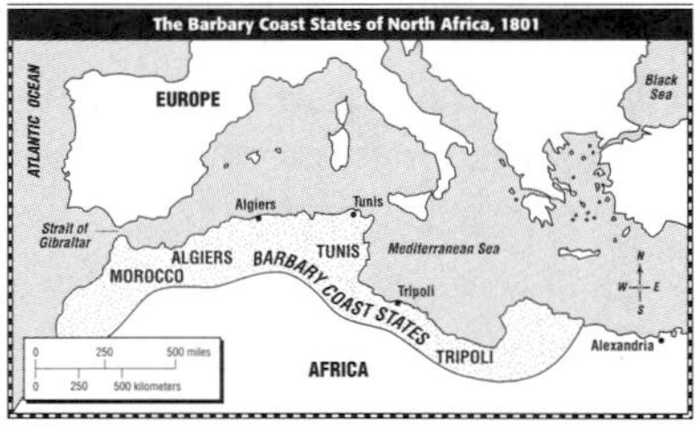

DIRECTIONS: Locating Places Use the map to answer the following questions.

1. Thomas Jefferson sent ships to blockade Tripoli Harbor. In what body of water were these ships stationed? ______
2. Which Barbary state was located farthest to the west? ______
3. At what strait do Africa and Europe almost touch? ______
4. What Barbary state was Tripoli located in? ______

Activity **DIRECTIONS:** Use an atlas or other reference books to locate a modern-day map of the Barbary Coast region. Then create and complete a chart that compares the region today with the region in the 1800s. What modern-day countries occupy the region? What important cities are located there? Are the relationships between these countries and the United States similar or different from those in the 1800s?

The American Journey ★ 35 ★ **Enrichment Activities**

4 CLOSE

President Jefferson wrote, "Never did a prisoner, released from his chains, feel such relief as I shall on shaking off the shackles of power." Have students explain Jefferson's relief at leaving the presidency.

CHAPTER 9
Section 4, 296–300

1 FOCUS

BELLRINGER
Motivational Activity

Before taking roll at the beginning of the class period, project Section Focus Transparency 9–4 and have students answer the questions. Discuss students' responses.

This activity is also available as a blackline master.

Section Focus Transparency 9–4

Native American Unity

1 Tecumseh, a Shawnee chief, was born in 1768 in what is now Ohio. What was Tecumseh trying to do?

2 What do you think he meant when he said, "we walk in the same path; slake our thirst at the same spring"?

3 What was the significance of smoking the same pipe?

"Brothers—We all belong to one family; we are all children of the Great Spirit; we walk in the same path; slake our thirst at the same spring; and now affairs of the greatest concern lead us to smoke the pipe around the same council fire! . . . They have destroyed many nations of red men because they were not united, because they were not friends to each other. . . . We must be united; we must smoke the same pipe; we must fight each other's battles; . . ." —Tecumseh

Vocabulary Precheck

Ask students to speculate on the meaning of each term. Then have them check their guesses by finding the definitions in the text.

Use the **Vocabulary PuzzleMaker** to create crossword and word search puzzles.

Section Theme
Groups and Institutions

The decision to fight the War of 1812 was a political victory for the War Hawks. At the conclusion of the war, Americans felt a new spirit of nationalism and pride in their new and more equal relationship with their former homeland.

Activity How did Prevost's defeat contribute to the ending of the war? *(British leaders decided the war was too costly.)*

1812 — 1813 — 1814 — 1815

June 1812 United States declares war on Britain

September 1813 Perry defeats the British navy on Lake Erie

August 1814 The British burn Washington, D.C.

January 1815 American forces win the Battle of New Orleans

Section 4

The War of 1812

READ TO DISCOVER . . .

- how the American plan to invade Canada failed.
- how the British seized Washington, D.C.
- why Andrew Jackson fought a battle after the war was over.

TERMS TO LEARN

frigate
privateer

The Storyteller

While President Madison awarded peace medals to Native Americans who supported the United States against the British, Congressional War Hawks could be heard singing:

Ye Parliaments of England,
Ye lords and commons, too,
Consider well what you're
about,
And what you're
goin' to do;
You're now at war
with Yankees,
And I'm sure you'll rue
the day
Ye roused the sons of
liberty,
In North Americay.

Madison peace medal

The War Hawks predicted that the war with Great Britain would last no more than 30 days. Their plan was to invade Canada and keep the fighting on land; the Royal Navy was too powerful to challenge at sea.

In following this course of action, the Americans committed a series of blunders that showed how unprepared they were for war. The regular army now consisted of fewer than 7,000 troops. The states had nearly 700,000 militia, but the units were poorly trained, and many states opposed "Mr. Madison's war." The military commanders, veterans of the American Revolution, were too old for warfare, and the government in Washington provided no leadership. In addition the Americans underestimated the strength of the British and their Native American allies.

The Canadian Campaign

The war started in July 1812, when **General William Hull** led the American army from **Detroit** into Canada. Hull was met by Tecumseh and his warriors. Fearing a massacre by the Native Americans, Hull retreated and surrendered Detroit to a small British force.

The Americans made three more attempts at invasion. One ended in defeat. The second never got off the ground because some of the state militia troops refused to cross the border into Canada. A third attempt by General William Henry Harrison had no more success. Harrison decided that the Americans could make no headway in Canada as long as the British controlled Lake Erie.

SECTION RESOURCES

Reproducible Masters
- Reproducible Lesson Plan 9–4
- Guided Reading Activity 9–4
- Section Quiz 9–4
- Reteaching Activity 9–4
- Enrichment Activity 9–4

Transparencies
- Section Focus Transparency 9–4

Multimedia
- Vocabulary PuzzleMaker
- Chapter Challenger Interactive Review Software
- Testmaker
- ABCNews InterActive™ Historic America Electronic Field Trips
- Facts On File: Landmark Documents in American History

Lake Erie

Oliver Hazard Perry, commander of the **Lake Erie** naval forces, had his orders. He was to assemble a fleet and seize the lake from the British. From his headquarters in Put-in-Bay, Ohio, Perry could watch the movements of the enemy ships. The showdown came on September 10, 1813, when the British ships sailed out to face the Americans. In the bloody battle that followed, Perry and his ships destroyed the British naval force. "We have met the enemy, and they are ours," Perry reported.

Thames and Toronto

With Lake Erie in American hands, the British and their Native American allies tried to pull back from the Detroit area. Harrison and his troops cut them off. In the fierce **Battle of the Thames** on October 5, the great leader Tecumseh was killed.

The Americans also attacked the town of York (present-day **Toronto,** Canada), burning the parliament buildings. Canada remained unconquered, but by the end of 1813 the Americans had won some victories on land and at sea.

Naval Battles

To lower the national debt, the Republicans had reduced the size of the navy. However, the navy still boasted three of the fastest **frigates,** or warships, afloat. Americans exulted when the *Constitution,* one of these frigates, destroyed two British vessels—the *Guerrière* in August 1812 and the *Java* four months later. After seeing a shot bounce off the *Constitution*'s hull during battle, a sailor nicknamed the ship "Old Ironsides."

American **privateers,** armed private ships, also staged spectacular attacks on British shipping and captured numerous vessels. These victories were more important for morale than for their strategic value.

The British hit back with a devastating blockade of the American coast from the Chesapeake Bay to New York Harbor. In a divide-and-conquer strategy, the British left the New England coast open. They were well aware of the war's unpopularity in Federalist New England. Madison fumed about Federalist disloyalty, but the New Englanders did not join the British. Finally in 1814 the British extended the blockade to New England as well.

Setbacks for Native Americans

With the death of Tecumseh at the Battle of the Thames in 1813, hopes for an Indian confederation died. In his travels two years before his death, Tecumseh had discussed plans for a confederation with the Creeks in the Mississippi Territory.

In March 1814, a lanky Tennessee planter named **Andrew Jackson** attacked the Creeks. Jackson's forces slaughtered more than 550 men, women, and children. Known as the **Battle of Horseshoe Bend,** the defeat broke the Creeks' resistance and forced them to give up most of their lands to the United States.

HISTORY AND ART ***Perry's Victory on Lake Erie* by William Birch**
During the War of 1812, Oliver Hazard Perry led 10 small ships on an attack against the British. **What was the result of the Battle of Lake Erie?**

CHAPTER 9
Section 4, 296–300

2 TEACH

L1 Making a Chart Have students work in pairs to make a chart showing the major events and people in the War of 1812. Charts should include Perry's victory on Lake Erie, the Battle of the Thames, the British blockade, and so on. If any students are interested in learning more about the war, a well-written, involving account is *1812: The War Nobody Won* by Albert Marrin (New York: Atheneum, 1985).

Guided Reading Activity 9–4

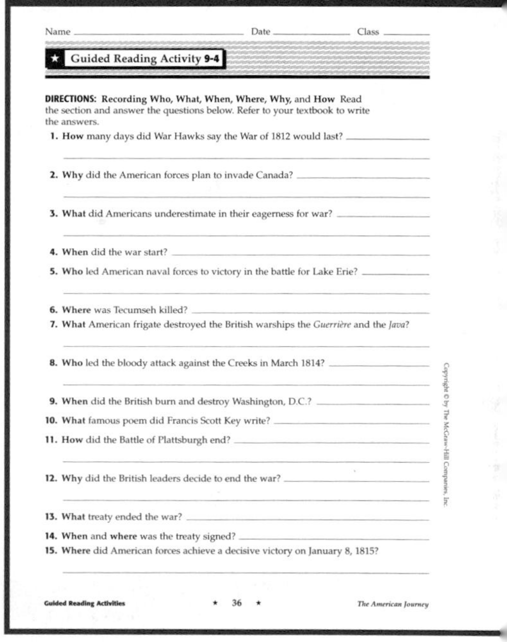

Name ______ Date ______ Class ______

★ Guided Reading Activity **9-4**

DIRECTIONS: Recording Who, What, When, Where, Why, and **How** Read the section and answer the questions below. Refer to your textbook to write the answers.

1. **How** many days did War Hawks say the War of 1812 would last? ______
2. **Why** did the American forces plan to invade Canada? ______
3. **What** did Americans underestimate in their eagerness for war? ______
4. **When** did the war start? ______
5. **Who** led American naval forces to victory in the battle for Lake Erie? ______
6. **Where** was Tecumseh killed? ______
7. **What** American frigate destroyed the British warships the *Guerrière* and the *Java*? ______
8. **Who** led the bloody attack against the Creeks in March 1814? ______
9. **When** did the British burn and destroy Washington, D.C.? ______
10. **What** famous poem did Francis Scott Key write? ______
11. **How** did the Battle of Plattsburgh end? ______
12. **Why** did the British leaders decide to end the war? ______
13. **What** treaty ended the war? ______
14. **When** and **where** was the treaty signed? ______
15. **Where** did American forces achieve a decisive victory on January 8, 1815? ______

Guided Reading Activities ★ 36 ★ *The American Journey*

HISTORY AND ART William Birch (1755–1834) was an English engraver who came to America in 1794. His son Thomas was also an artist, and William did engravings of his works as well as of his own drawings. **Ask:** **Why were battles often the subject of paintings?** *(Possible response: Artists wanted to stir patriotic feelings.)*
Answer: *Perry destroyed the British forces. The British and their Native American allies tried to retreat but were cut off by Harrison's troops in the Battle of the Thames in which Tecumseh was killed.*

COOPERATIVE LEARNING ACTIVITY

Making a Mural Have students work together in small groups to create a mural showing various dramatic events from the War of 1812. Each group should be responsible for a different section of the mural. Students may use events from the text or do further research on other events of the period. Among the many good possibilities are the shelling of the *Chesapeake,* Dolley Madison saving the famous Gilbert Stuart painting of George Washington, the burning of the capital, the attack on Fort McHenry, and the voyage of the *Essex.*

ABCNEWS INTERACTIVE™

VIDEODISC
Historic America
Electronic Field Trips

Side 1, Chapter 5

Title: *New Orleans*
Subject: Tour this historic city
Ask: **Where is New Orleans located?** *(New Orleans is located in Louisiana, between Lake Pontchartrain and the Mississippi River.)*

Also available in VHS.

Facts On File

CD-ROM
Landmark Documents in American History

Title: *War Message, James Madison, 1812*
Ask students to think about how Americans felt about this war.

Map Study

Answers
1. by blockading the coast
2. Americans under Jackson

you don't say...

Uncle Sam During the War of 1812, Samuel Wilson, an army meat inspector from Troy, New York, stamped *U.S.* for *United States* on the barrels of salted meat he approved. One day government inspectors asked a meat packer what the initials stood for. The worker did not know, so he said that the initials represented his boss, "Uncle Sam." "Uncle" Samuel Wilson soon became a symbol of the federal government.

The British Offensive

British military fortunes improved in the spring of 1814. They had been fighting a war with Napoleon and had finally won. Now they were free to concentrate their forces against the United States. The British soon discovered, however, that American forces had been toughened by their earlier defeats.

In August 1814, the British sailed into Chesapeake Bay. Their destination was Washington, D.C. **Dolley Madison** waited at the president's mansion on August 24 for word from her husband. "We have had a battle, or skirmish, near Bladensburg [Maryland], and I am still here within sound of the cannon!" she wrote her sister.

A messenger arrived with news that the British were fast approaching. The First Lady refused to leave. First, she insisted, she must see that the portrait of George Washington was removed from the wall and sent to safety.

The War of 1812

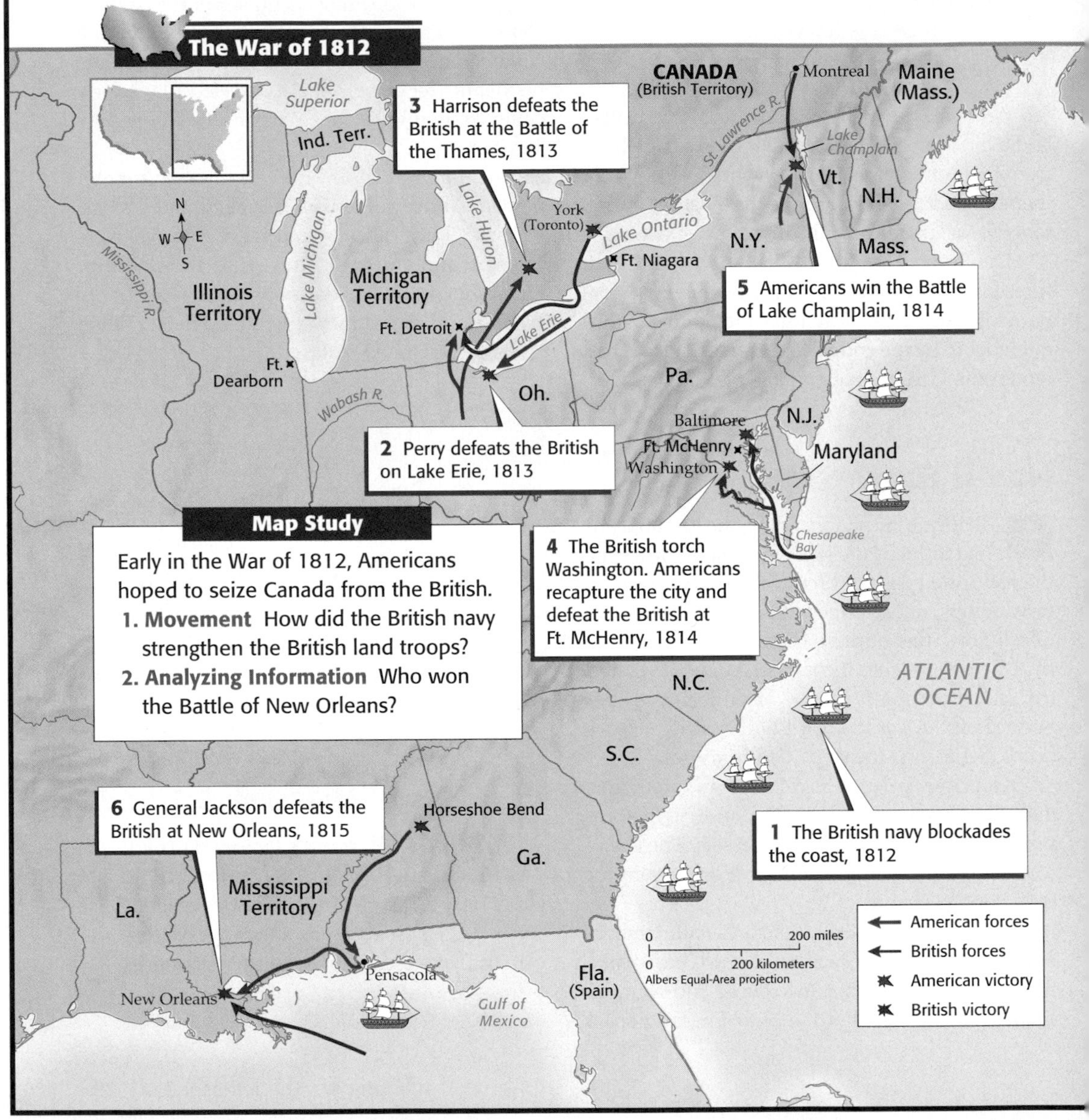

Map Study

Early in the War of 1812, Americans hoped to seize Canada from the British.
1. **Movement** How did the British navy strengthen the British land troops?
2. **Analyzing Information** Who won the Battle of New Orleans?

MULTIPLE LEARNING STYLES

Auditory/Musical In addition to the "Star-Spangled Banner," a number of patriotic songs came out during the War of 1812. Many songs are listed in Chapter 6 of *Music for Patriots, Politicians, and Presidents* by Vera Brodsky Lawrence (New York: Macmillan, 1975). Have student volunteers read some of them aloud. Or ask the Music teacher to teach one or more songs to the class. Some students might try to compose tunes to go with the words for which no musical score has survived. **L1**

Attack on Washington

Meanwhile on the outskirts of Washington, D.C., the British troops quickly overpowered the American militia and then marched into the city. "They proceeded, without a moment's delay, to burn and destroy everything in the most distant degree connected with government," reported a British officer.

The Capitol and the president's mansion were among the buildings burned. Watching from outside the city, President Madison and his cabinet saw the night sky turn orange. Fortunately a violent thunderstorm put out the fires before they could do more damage. August 24, 1814, was a low point for the American side.

Baltimore Holds Firm

Much to everyone's surprise, the British did not try to hold Washington. They left the city and sailed north to Baltimore. Baltimore, however, was ready and waiting—with barricaded roads, a blocked harbor, and some 13,000 militiamen. The British attacked in mid-September. They were kept from entering the town by a determined defense and ferocious bombardment from Fort McHenry in the harbor.

During the night of September 13–14, a young attorney named **Francis Scott Key** watched as the bombs burst over Fort McHenry. Finally "by the dawn's early light," Key was able to see that the American flag still flew over the fort. Deeply moved by patriotic feeling, Key wrote a poem called "The Star-Spangled Banner."

Defeat at Plattsburgh

Meanwhile in the north, **General Sir George Prevost** led more than 10,000 British troops into New York State from Canada. The British had every advantage—trained soldiers, superior firepower, cavalry, and professional leaders. Nevertheless in September 1814, the British suffered a humiliating defeat in the **Battle of Plattsburgh.** Demoralized by this unexpected loss, Prevost abandoned the campaign. The American victory secured the northern border of the United States.

Picturing HISTORY After sailing up Chesapeake Bay, British troops captured and burned Washington, D.C. **How did Dolley Madison, as First Lady, respond to the British attack?**

After Plattsburgh, British leaders in London came to the conclusion that the war in North America was too costly and unnecessary. They had achieved their goal in Europe with the removal of Napoleon. To continue a minor war in America with little to gain no longer seemed worth the effort.

The War Ends

American and British representatives signed a peace agreement in December 1814 in Ghent, Belgium. The **Treaty of Ghent** did not change any existing borders. Nothing was mentioned about the impressment of sailors, but with Napoleon's defeat, neutral rights had become a dead issue.

The Battle of New Orleans

Before word of the treaty had reached the United States, one final—and ferocious—battle occurred at New Orleans. In December 1814, a British army under **General Sir Edward Pakenham** moved toward New Orleans, located between Lake Ponchartrain and the Mississippi River. Awaiting them behind earthen fortifications was an American army led by Andrew Jackson.

CHAPTER 9
Section 4, 296–300

Picturing HISTORY The Library of Congress was destroyed during the burning of Washington, D.C. To start a new library, Thomas Jefferson sold the government more than 6,000 books at a bargain price.
Answer: *She refused to leave until George Washington's portrait was safely removed from the president's mansion.*

you don't say...

The White House After the war, the president's mansion was painted white to cover the scorch marks acquired during the torching of the city. It was then that people started calling the building the White House.

3 ASSESS

Assign Section 4 Review as homework or as an in-class activity.

Use **Chapter Challenger Interactive Review Software** to review Section 4.

Section Quiz 9–4

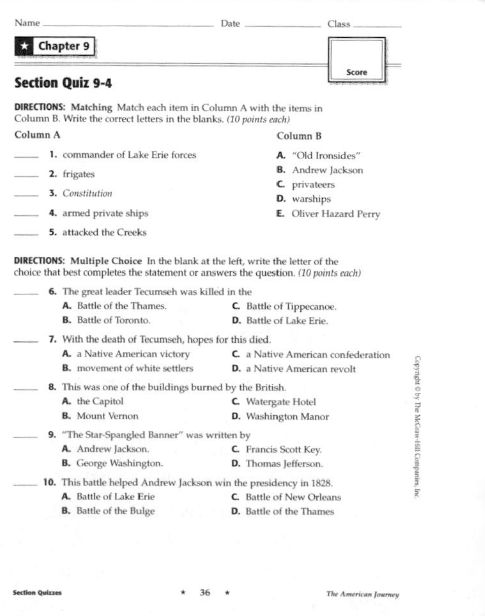

Name ______ Date ______ Class ______

★ Chapter 9 — Score

Section Quiz 9-4

DIRECTIONS: Matching Match each item in Column A with the items in Column B. Write the correct letters in the blanks. *(10 points each)*

Column A

____ **1.** commander of Lake Erie forces
____ **2.** frigates
____ **3.** *Constitution*
____ **4.** armed private ships
____ **5.** attacked the Creeks

Column B

A. "Old Ironsides"
B. Andrew Jackson
C. privateers
D. warships
E. Oliver Hazard Perry

DIRECTIONS: Multiple Choice In the blank at the left, write the letter of the choice that best completes the statement or answers the question. *(10 points each)*

____ **6.** The great leader Tecumseh was killed in the
A. Battle of the Thames. **C.** Battle of Tippecanoe.
B. Battle of Toronto. **D.** Battle of Lake Erie.

____ **7.** With the death of Tecumseh, hopes for this died.
A. a Native American victory **C.** a Native American confederation
B. movement of white settlers **D.** a Native American revolt

____ **8.** This was one of the buildings burned by the British.
A. the Capitol **C.** Watergate Hotel
B. Mount Vernon **D.** Washington Manor

____ **9.** "The Star-Spangled Banner" was written by
A. Andrew Jackson. **C.** Francis Scott Key.
B. George Washington. **D.** Thomas Jefferson.

____ **10.** This battle helped Andrew Jackson win the presidency in 1828.
A. Battle of Lake Erie **C.** Battle of New Orleans
B. Battle of the Bulge **D.** Battle of the Thames

Section Quizzes ★ 36 ★ *The American Journey*

MORE ABOUT . . .

Daily Life On July 4, 1826, Thomas Jefferson died at the age of 83. A few hours later on the same day, John Adams (then 91) passed away. Ironically, or perhaps metaphysically, his last words were, "Thomas Jefferson still survives."

Have students research the lives of Thomas Jefferson, John Adams, James Madison, Dolley Madison, or Andrew Jackson. Each student should then make a poster, collage, stained-glass window (using a construction paper "frame" and multi-colored tissue paper "glass"), or a three-dimensional art form to portray an achievement of one of these extraordinary Americans. **L2, ELL**

Reteaching Activity 9–4

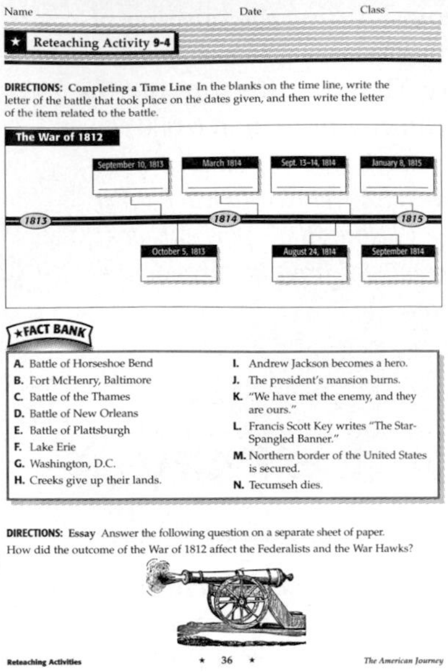
Name ____________ Date ________ Class ________

★ Reteaching Activity 9-4

DIRECTIONS: Completing a Time Line In the blanks on the time line, write the letter of the battle that took place on the dates given, and then write the letter of the item related to the battle.

The War of 1812

1813 — 1814 — 1815

September 10, 1813 ______
October 5, 1813 ______
March 1814 ______
August 24, 1814 ______
Sept. 13–14, 1814 ______
September 1814 ______
January 8, 1815 ______

★FACT BANK

A. Battle of Horseshoe Bend
B. Fort McHenry, Baltimore
C. Battle of the Thames
D. Battle of New Orleans
E. Battle of Plattsburgh
F. Lake Erie
G. Washington, D.C.
H. Creeks give up their lands.
I. Andrew Jackson becomes a hero.
J. The president's mansion burns.
K. "We have met the enemy, and they are ours."
L. Francis Scott Key writes "The Star-Spangled Banner."
M. Northern border of the United States is secured.
N. Tecumseh dies.

DIRECTIONS: Essay Answer the following question on a separate sheet of paper.
How did the outcome of the War of 1812 affect the Federalists and the War Hawks?

Reteaching Activities ★ 36 ★ *The American Journey*

Copyright © by The McGraw-Hill Companies, Inc.

Enrichment Activity 9–4

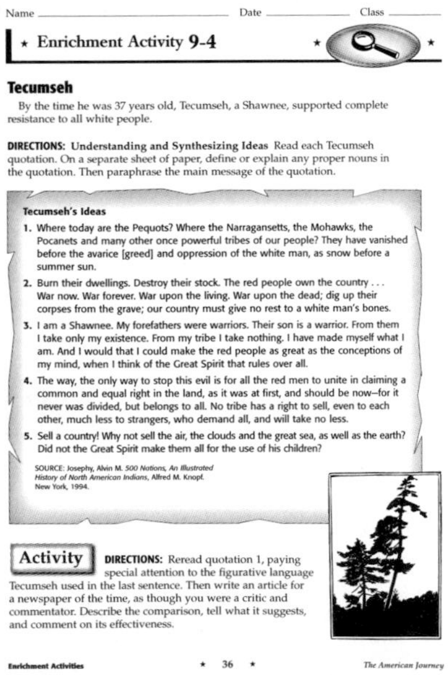
Name ____________ Date ________ Class ________

★ Enrichment Activity 9-4

Tecumseh

By the time he was 37 years old, Tecumseh, a Shawnee, supported complete resistance to all white people.

DIRECTIONS: Understanding and Synthesizing Ideas Read each Tecumseh quotation. On a separate sheet of paper, define or explain any proper nouns in the quotation. Then paraphrase the main message of the quotation.

Tecumseh's Ideas

1. Where today are the Pequots? Where the Narragansetts, the Mohawks, the Pocanets and many other once powerful tribes of our people? They have vanished before the avarice [greed] and oppression of the white man, as snow before a summer sun.
2. Burn their dwellings. Destroy their stock. The red people own the country . . . War now. War forever. War upon the living. War upon the dead; dig up their corpses from the grave; our country must give no rest to a white man's bones.
3. I am a Shawnee. My forefathers were warriors. Their son is a warrior. From them I take only my existence. From my tribe I take nothing. I have made myself what I am. And I would that I could make the red people as great as the conceptions of my mind, when I think of the Great Spirit that rules over all.
4. The way, the only way to stop this evil is for all the red men to unite in claiming a common and equal right in the land, as it was at first, and should be now—for it never was divided, but belongs to all. No tribe has a right to sell, even to each other, much less to strangers, who demand all, and will take no less.
5. Sell a country! Why not sell the air, the clouds and the great sea, as well as the earth? Did not the Great Spirit make them all for the use of his children?

SOURCE: Josephy, Alvin M. *500 Nations, An Illustrated History of North American Indians*, Alfred M. Knopf. New York, 1994.

Activity **DIRECTIONS:** Reread quotation 1, paying special attention to the figurative language Tecumseh used in the last sentence. Then write an article for a newspaper of the time, as though you were a critic and commentator. Describe the comparison, tell what it suggests, and comment on its effectiveness.

Enrichment Activities ★ 36 ★ *The American Journey*

Copyright © by The McGraw-Hill Companies, Inc.

4 CLOSE

When the Madisons returned to the capital, Dolley said, "We shall rebuild Washington. The enemy cannot frighten a free people." Have students explain her statement.

America's FLAGS

The First Star-Spangled Banner, 1779–1818
The Stars and Stripes flag gained two more stars and two more stripes in 1795, after Kentucky and Vermont had joined the Union. This flag flew over Fort McHenry during the War of 1812 and inspired Francis Scott Key to write "The Star-Spangled Banner."

Congress realized that the flag would become too large if a stripe were added for every new state. It decided to keep the stripes at 13—for the thirteen original colonies—and to add a star for each new state.

On January 8, 1815, Pakenham's troops advanced. The redcoats were no match for Jackson's soldiers, who shot from behind bales of cotton. In an hour of gruesome bloodshed, about 700 British soldiers, including Pakenham, were killed. At the **Battle of New Orleans,** Americans achieved a decisive victory in the War of 1812. Andrew Jackson became a hero, and his fame helped him win the presidency in 1828.

Federalist Disgrace

New England Federalists had opposed "Mr. Madison's war" from the start. In December 1814, disgruntled New England Federalists gathered in Connecticut at the **Hartford Convention.** A few favored secession. Most wanted to remain within the Union, however. To protect their interests, they drew up a list of proposed amendments to the Constitution.

After the convention broke up, word came of Jackson's spectacular victory at New Orleans, followed by news of the peace treaty. In this moment of triumph, the Federalist grievances seemed unpatriotic. The party lost respect.

American Triumph

Americans celebrated the end of the War of 1812 with candlelight parades, fireworks, and public prayers. The war brought a new spirit of nationalism throughout the country, even in New England. Americans felt pride in their new and more equal relationship with their former homeland.

Perhaps the biggest winners were the War Hawks, who took up the banner of the Republican party and carried it in new directions. These young Republicans favored trade, western expansion, the energetic development of the economy, and a strong army and navy.

Section 4 Review

Checking for Understanding

1. ***Identify*** Lake Erie, Toronto, Andrew Jackson, Dolley Madison, Treaty of Ghent, Battle of New Orleans.
2. ***Define*** frigate, privateer.
3. ***State*** the importance of the Battle of Plattsburgh.

Reviewing Themes

4. **Groups and Institutions** Why did Americans consider the War of 1812 a glorious victory?

Critical Thinking

5. **Determining Relevance** What impact did the Battle of New Orleans have on the outcome of the war?

Activity

Writing a Song Imagine that Francis Scott Key had been at the Battle of New Orleans instead of in Baltimore. Rewrite the first verse of "The Star-Spangled Banner" based on what occurred in that battle.

Section 4 Review Answers

1. Lake Erie, 297; Toronto, 297; Andrew Jackson, 297; Dolley Madison, 298; Treaty of Ghent, 299; Battle of New Orleans, 300
2. The words are defined in the Glossary.
3. It secured the northern border of the United States and convinced Britain that the war was unnecessary and too costly to continue.
4. They had prevailed against a much stronger enemy and were on a more equal footing with their former homeland. The war brought a new spirit of nationalism and boosted the popularity of the Republican Party.
5. Although it was a decisive American victory, it did not impact the war's outcome—the war had already ended.

Activity Words to songs should reflect what occurred at the Battle of New Orleans.

Study and Writing
SKILL BUILDER

Writing a Journal

As you can see from William Clark's journal, journal writing is personal writing with a casual style. What you write *on* is not as important as what you write *about*—your experiences, interests, and even your feelings.

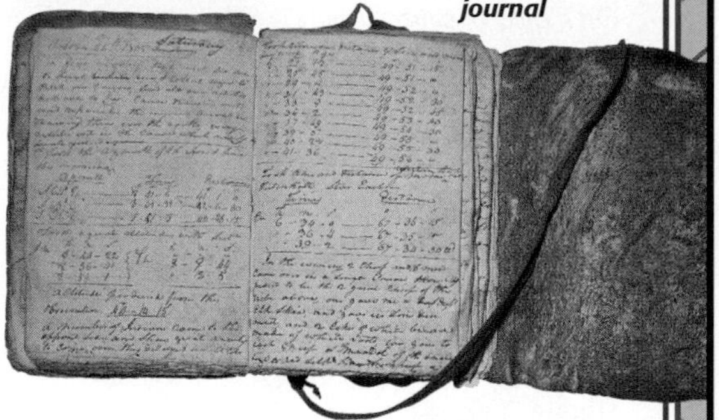

William Clark's journal

Learning the Skill

A journal is a written account that records what you have learned or experienced. In the journal you can express your feelings about a subject, summarize key topics, describe difficulties or successes in solving particular problems, and draw maps or other visuals. To help you get started writing in your journal, follow these steps:

- As you read your textbook, jot down notes or questions about a specific topic or event. Then look for details and answers about it as you continue reading.
- Describe your feelings as you read a selection or look at a photograph. Are you angry, happy, frustrated, sad? Explain why.
- Ask yourself if drawing a map or flowchart would help you understand a topic or an event better. If so, draw in your journal.

Practicing the Skill

The following excerpt is a description of the burning of Washington, D.C., during the War of 1812. Read the excerpt, then use the following questions to help you write entries in your own journal.

"... [T]his was a night of dismay to the inhabitants of Washington. They were taken completely by surprise. . . . The first impulse of course tempted them to fly. . . . [T]he streets were . . . crowded with soldiers and senators, men, women, and children, horses, carriages, and carts loaded with household furniture, all hastening towards a wooden bridge which crosses the Potomac. The confusion . . . was terrible, and the crowd upon the bridge was such to endanger its giving way."

1. What is particularly interesting about this description?
2. What are your feelings as you read the excerpt?
3. Draw a map or other visual to help you understand the situation described in the excerpt.

Applying the Skill

Writing a Journal Imagine that you have had the chance to take part in an American adventure—for instance, accompanying Lewis and Clark, or fighting Barbary pirates. Make notes for a journal entry describing what you have done and seen.

Study and Writing
SKILL BUILDER

TEACH

Writing a Journal

This skill explains the purpose of keeping a journal. Make sure students realize that entries in personal journals may be about anything that interests them. Point out that much of what we know about history, especially social history, comes from diaries and journals of the men, women, and even children of the past. Discuss the kinds of information included in social history (ways of everyday living—work, school, home life, religion, community events, and so forth, as opposed to political or military events).

Call on volunteers to share the notes they wrote for Applying the Skill. Discuss whether the notes are more appropriate for journal writing or narratives, and if the latter, what would make them more suitable for a journal.

Additional Practice

Chapter Skills Activity 9

Answers to Practicing the Skill

1. Accept any reasonable answer.
2. Accept any reasonable answer.
3. Drawings should show that students understand the excerpt.

Applying the Skill Students' notes should be based on information from the chapter regarding a specific American adventure. Although the notes should be based on factual information, students' notes may be creative and imaginative.

GLENCOE TECHNOLOGY

VIDEODISC
MindJogger Videoquiz

Use MindJogger to review the Chapter 9 content.

Chapter 9
Disc 2, Side A

Also available in VHS.

Reviewing Key Terms

The key terms used in this activity can be found in the textbook glossary on pages A26–A35.

Reviewing Key Facts

1. passed the Twelfth Amendment which requires electors to vote for the president and vice president on separate ballots
2. Jefferson knew that Napoleon had plans to create an empire in the United States; he feared that United States trade on the Mississippi would be jeopardized.
3. It stopped all American commerce with other nations, proved ineffective against Britain, divided the American people, increased unemployment, and turned public opinion against the president and the Republicans.
4. a group of young Republicans in Congress from the South and West who urged war with Britain as a part of their plan to expand the power of the United States
5. The Americans were trying to gain control of British land in Canada, but could not make any headway until they won control of Lake Erie.

Critical Thinking

1. Adams greatly distrusted Aaron Burr, who would become president if Jefferson lost.

Review and Activities

Reviewing Key Terms

On a sheet of paper, define the following terms:
laissez-faire
judicial review
secede
tribute
impressment
neutral rights
embargo
War Hawks
nationalism
frigate
privateer

Reviewing Key Facts

1. What did Congress do to prevent an election deadlock between a presidential and vice-presidential candidate?
2. Why was Jefferson alarmed by the secret agreement that Spain made with France regarding the Louisiana Territory?
3. How did the Embargo Act of 1807 hurt the United States?
4. Who were the War Hawks?
5. Why was the Battle of Lake Erie fought?

Critical Thinking

Analyzing Information

The Republicans were in power for the first time with Jefferson's election to the presidency in 1801.

1. Why did Alexander Hamilton help his political foe, Thomas Jefferson, win the presidential election of 1800?
2. Why was *Marbury* v. *Madison* a victory for the Federalists over the Republicans?

Time Line Activity

Create a time line on which you place the following events in chronological order.

- Lewis and Clark begin their expedition
- Treaty of Ghent ends War of 1812
- United States purchases Louisiana
- Thomas Jefferson becomes president
- Tecumseh is killed
- James Madison is elected president

Geography Activity

Study the map below and answer the following questions.

1. **Region** During which of the three time periods was the largest amount of land taken along the Atlantic coast?
2. **Movement** During what years was land taken from the Iroquois?
3. **Location** Which Native American nations still held on to their land after 1810?

Land Taken From Native Americans

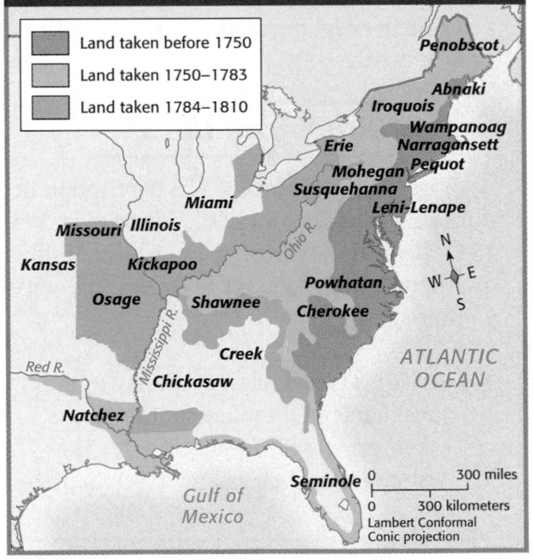

2. As a result of the decision, the Supreme Court became an equal partner with the legislative and executive branches. Using the power of judicial review, Chief Justice John Marshall upheld the power of the national government over the states and incorporated many Federalist beliefs in the American government.

Time Line Activity

Events should be placed in this order: Thomas Jefferson becomes president, United States purchases Louisiana, Lewis and Clark begin their expedition, James Madison is elected president, Tecumseh is killed, Treaty of Ghent ends War of 1812

Chapter 9

Reviewing Themes

1. **Government and Democracy** What was the importance of the *Marbury* v. *Madison* decision?
2. **Geography and History** What were the boundaries of the Louisiana Territory?
3. **Global Connections** Why were American merchants eager to trade with countries in Asia?
4. **Groups and Institutions** How did the War Hawks and Federalists differ in their views of war?

Skill Practice Activity

Writing a Journal

By the late 1700s, more than 55,000 Americans had crossed the mountains into Kentucky and Tennessee. They endured terrible hardships in their trek to the "Promised Land." One person wrote the following excerpt about the journey. Read the excerpt, then in your journal answer the questions that follow.

> "Women and Children in the Month of [December], Travelling a Wilderness through Ice and Snow, passing large rivers and Creeks without Shoe or Stocking, and barely as many raggs as covers their Nakedness. . . . Here is Hundreds Travelling hundreds of Miles, they know not what for Nor Whither, except its to Kentucky . . . the Land of Milk and Honey."

1. What questions do you have about the excerpt?
2. What are your feelings as you read the excerpt?
3. Why do you think settlers would endure such hardships to move to new land? Explain your reasoning.
4. Draw a visual to illustrate the situation described in the excerpt.

Cooperative Activity

History and Geography Work in small groups to prepare an international trade map. Your map should show United States imports during the early 1800s from each of the major continents. What major ports were merchants sailing to during this time? What products were they bringing back to the United States? Your map should include the names of important ports, the countries where they were located, symbols to represent the different products, a map key to explain the symbols, and other information such as distances or major shipping routes.

Technology Activity

Using a Spreadsheet Search the library for information about the modern city of New Orleans. Make a spreadsheet with the following headings: Spanish Street Names, French Street Names, Spanish Buildings, French Buildings, Spanish Foods, French Foods, and other sites that reflect Spanish and French influences in the area.

Portfolio Activity **History Journal** Review the chapter for information about the expedition of Lewis and Clark. Imagine that you had the chance to accompany them on their adventure. Write a letter home describing what you have done and seen.

CHAPTER 9

Review and Activities

Skill Practice Activity

1. Answers will vary, but students might want to know who wrote the journal, why the pioneers were traveling in December, or why they were so poorly clothed.
2. Feelings might include sympathy for the travelers.
3. Accept answers that reflect moving to improve their lives such as moving to more open spaces, getting a better job, excitement of a new life, and so on.
4. Skill in drawing is not the important point, rather the visual should reflect understanding of the excerpt.

Cooperative Activity

Maps should include all the major continents, important ports and the countries where they were located, symbols for products, and other pertinent information discovered in student research.

Technology Activity

Students should locate information about New Orleans that reflects Spanish and French influence in that city and present that information in spreadsheet form.

Portfolio Activity Students' letters should include accurate information about the Lewis and Clark expedition as presented in the chapter.

Geography Activity

1. land taken before 1750
2. 1750–1783
3. Miami, Illinois, Creek, Chickasaw, Seminole, Kansas, Natchez

Reviewing Themes

1. It gave the Supreme Court the power of judicial review, making the judicial branch equal to the legislative and executive branches.
2. all the land west of the Mississippi River to the Rocky Mountains; south to New Orleans; northern boundaries were not defined
3. Goods from Asia generated very high profits.
4. War Hawks strongly favored war; Federalists strongly opposed it.

Chapter Bonus Test Question

Ask: **As Lewis and Clark traveled down the Columbia River, they knew they were getting close to the ocean when they saw salmon in the river. Why?** *(Salmon are an ocean-dwelling fish and travel only in freshwater to lay their eggs.)*

Chapter 10 Planning Guide

A complete, 1-page lesson plan is provided for each section in the *Reproducible Lesson Plans* booklet.

Section Resources

Daily Objectives	Reproducible Resources	Multimedia Resources
Section 1 Economic Growth Describe the beginning of the Industrial Revolution in the United States and how it affected American society and the economy.	Reproducible Lesson Plan 10–1 Guided Reading Activity 10–1* Political Cartoons, *The Embargo Act of 1807* Section Quiz 10–1* Reteaching Activity 10–1 Enrichment Activity 10–1	Section Focus Transparency 10–1 Focus on American Art Prints Vocabulary PuzzleMaker Chapter Challenger Interactive Review Testmaker ABCNews InterActive™ Historic America Electronic Field Trips Facts on File: Landmark Documents in American History American Music Cultural Traditions
Section 2 Westward Bound List transportation improvements in the early 1800s and describe their effects on demographics, the economy, and the establishment of new states.	Reproducible Lesson Plan 10–2 Guided Reading Activity 10–2* Section Quiz 10–2* Reteaching Activity 10–2 Enrichment Activity 10–2	Section Focus Transparency 10–2 Vocabulary PuzzleMaker Chapter Challenger Interactive Review Software Testmaker GTV: A Geographic Perspective on American History
Section 3 Unity and Sectionalism Explain why the period of Monroe's presidency was called the Era of Good Feelings and—by summarizing the positions of Webster, Calhoun, and Clay—describe the sectional differences that intensified in the 1820s.	Reproducible Lesson Plan 10–3 Guided Reading Activity 10–3* Section Quiz 10–3* Reteaching Activity 10–3 Enrichment Activity 10–3	Section Focus Transparency 10–3 Vocabulary PuzzleMaker Chapter Challenger Interactive Review Software Testmaker The Presidents: A Picture History of Our Nation Facts On File: Landmark Documents in American History
Section 4 The Monroe Doctrine Give examples of John Quincy Adams's influence and the effect of the Monroe Doctrine on American foreign policy.	Reproducible Lesson Plan 10–4 Guided Reading Activity 10–4* Section Quiz 10–4* Reteaching Activity 10–4 Enrichment Activity 10–4	Section Focus Transparency 10–4 Vocabulary PuzzleMaker Chapter Challenger Interactive Review Software Testmaker

** Also available in Spanish*

Poster · Transparency · CD-ROM · Software
Blackline Master · Videodisc · Audiocassette · Music Program

0:00 **OUT OF TIME?**
Assign the Chapter 10 Digest and the corresponding Chapter Digests Audiocassettes with activities and tests.

Activity

From the Classroom of...

Michael Branch
Van Devender Junior High
Parkersburg, WV

Westward Journey

Organize students into groups and give them the following scenario: You and your spouse are part of a small caravan of wagons traveling west. Because your wagon is falling behind, you must eliminate eight of the following items to reduce your load. Remind students that they do not know where they will be settling, so they must keep what is important. **1.** two barrels of bacon; **2.** pans you received as a wedding present; **3.** four bolts of cloth; **4.** small Franklin metal stove; **5.** crate of lead and gunpowder; **6.** 100 feet of heavy rope; **7.** barrel of flour; **8.** spare tools; **9.** case of salted dried beef; **10.** trunk of winter clothing; **11.** small anvil and hammer; **12.** spare wheel rim; **13.** plow; **14.** heirloom table and chairs; **15.** set of axes; **16.** set of books; **17.** two cows; **18.** spinning wheel; **19.** barrel of molasses. When the small groups come to a consensus on which items to discard, put group decisions on the chalkboard. Ask: What were the reasons you discarded these items? What were the two most important items you kept? Convene the whole class to arrive at a class consensus if possible.

National Geographic Society Teacher's Corner

INDEX TO NATIONAL GEOGRAPHIC MAGAZINE

The following articles may be used for research relating to this chapter:

- "The Cherokee," by Geoffrey Norman, May 1995.
- "The Cruelest Commerce: African Slave Trade," by Colin Palmer, September 1992.
- "Erie Canal: Living Link to Our Past," by Joel L. Swerdlow, November 1990.
- "Philadelphia's African Americans," by Roland L. Freeman, August 1990.

NATIONAL GEOGRAPHIC SOCIETY PRODUCTS AVAILABLE FROM GLENCOE

To order the following products for use with this chapter, contact your local Glencoe sales representative, or call Glencoe at 1-800-334-7344:

- *GTV: A Geographic Perspective on American History* (Videodisc)
- *GTV: The American People: Fabric of a Nation* (Videodisc)
- *The Presidents: A Picture History of Our Nation* (CD-ROM)
- *The Westward Movement* (CD-ROM, Transparencies)
- *PictureShow: Native Americans, 1* (CD-ROM)
- *Native Americans: Eastern Woodlands and Plains* (Transparencies)

ADDITIONAL NATIONAL GEOGRAPHIC SOCIETY PRODUCTS

To order the following products for use with this chapter, call National Geographic Society at 1-800-368-2728:

- *Washington, D.C.* (Video)
- *Historical Atlas of the United States* (Atlas)

Block Schedule

Block scheduling differs from traditional class scheduling in the amount of time allotted to each period. The extended time frame provided by block scheduling affords you the opportunity to implement a greater number of research-oriented and activity-intense projects to motivate and involve your students. Activities that are particularly suited to use within the block scheduling framework are identified throughout this chapter by the following designation:

KEY TO ABILITY LEVELS

Teaching strategies have been coded for varying learning styles and abilities.

L1 **BASIC** activities for all students
L2 **AVERAGE** activities for average to above-average students
L3 **CHALLENGING** activities for above-average students
ELL **ENGLISH LANGUAGE LEARNER** activities

Chapter 10 Resource Guide

Home Involvement

Home Involvement Activity 10

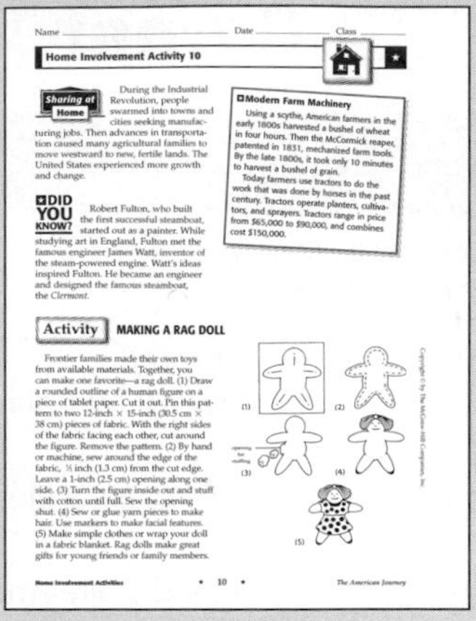

Review Activities

Chapter Summary 10

Workbook Activity 10

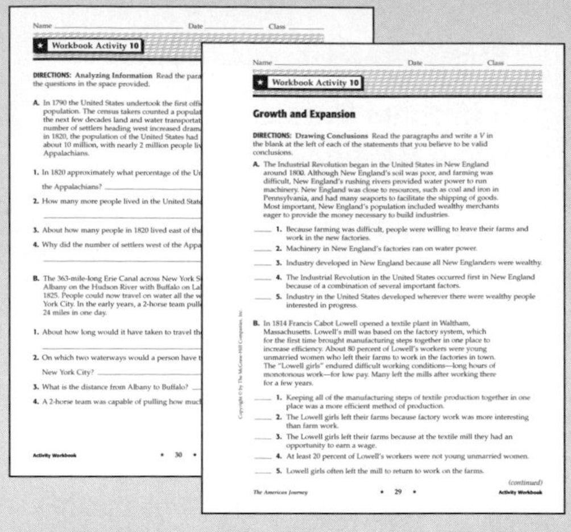

Reinforcement Activities

Time Line Activity 10

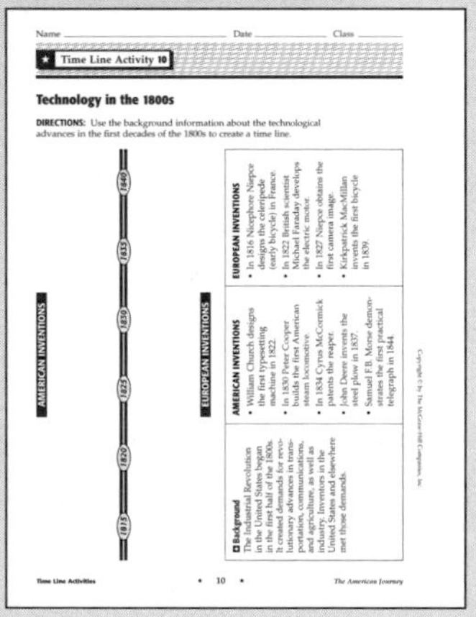

Vocabulary Activity 10

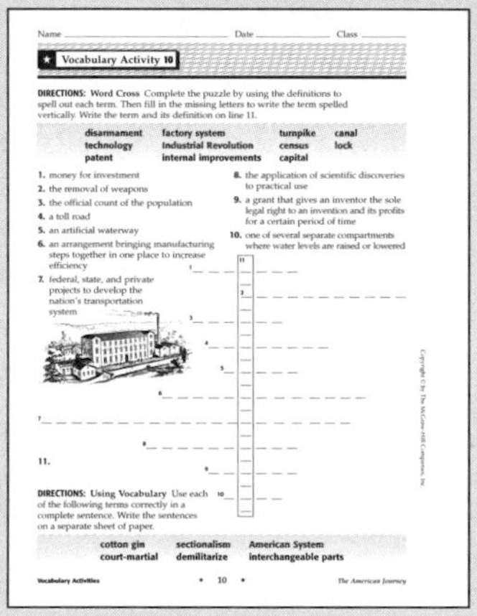

Chapter Skills Activity 10

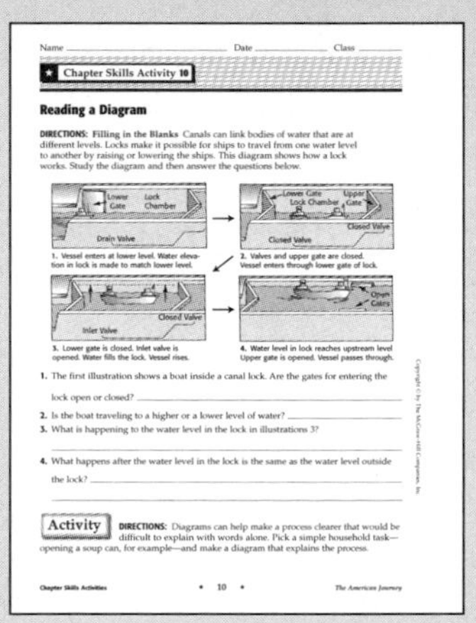

Enrichment Activities

Linking Past and Present Activity 10

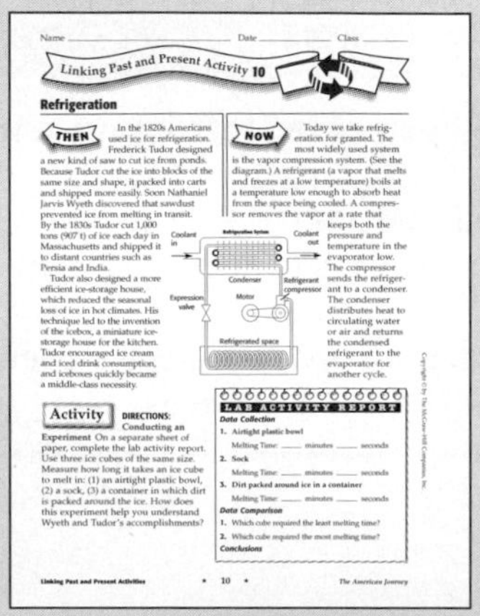

Primary Source Reading 10

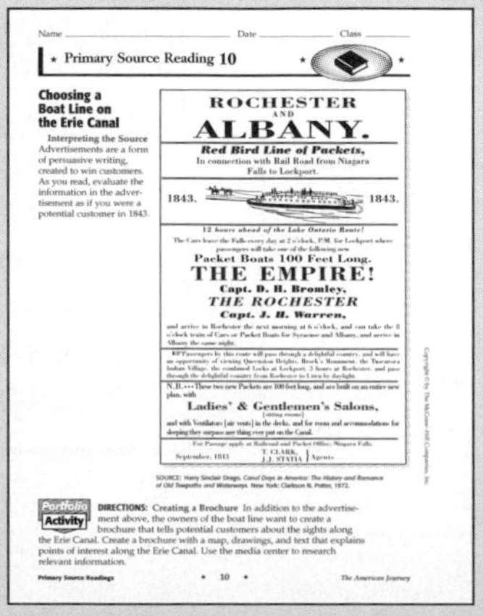

Geography Activities

Mapping History Activity 10

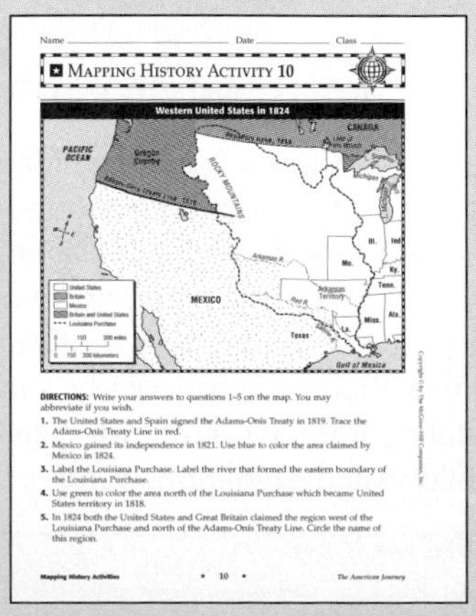

Chapter 10 Resource Guide

ASSESSMENT

Chapter 10 Test, Form A

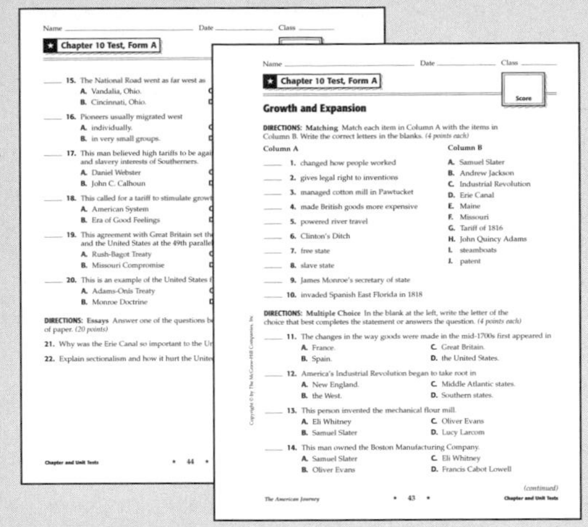

Chapter 10 Test, Form B

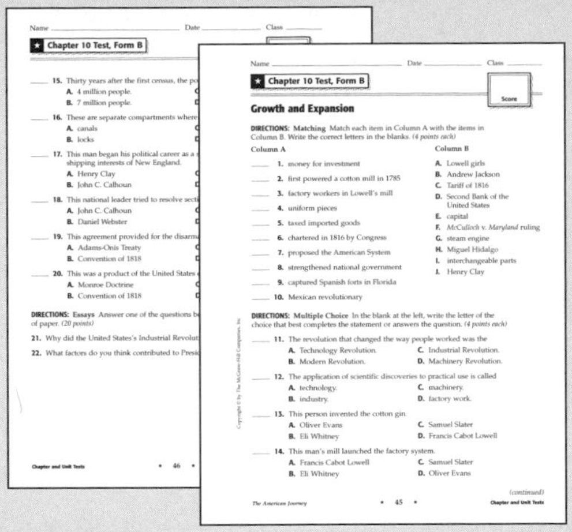

Performance Assessment Activity 10

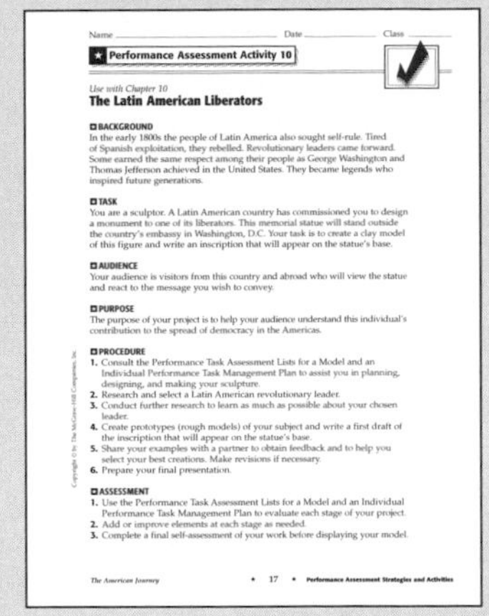

SPANISH RESOURCES

The following Spanish language materials are available in the Spanish Resources binder:

- **Spanish Chapter Summary 10**
- **Spanish Vocabulary Activity 10**
- **Spanish Guided Reading Activities, Chapter 10**
- **Spanish Section Quizzes, Chapter 10**
- **Spanish Home Involvement Activity 10**
- **Spanish Chapter 10 Digests Audiocassette Activity and Test**

ACTIVITY MANIPULATIVES

Help students learn more about America's cultural history with:

- **American Crafts Hands-On Activities**
- **American Games Hands-On Activities**
- **American History Flash Cards**

ADDITIONAL RESOURCES FROM GLENCOE

- **U.S. History & Art,** Transparency 6, *The Great Blue Heron*
- **Focus on American Art Prints,** *The Staircase Group* by Charles Willson Peale
- **American Music Cultural Traditions,** Lesson 3 : "Hunters of Kentucky"
- **The Spirit of American Art and Music,** Joshua Johnston
- **Political Cartoons,** *The Embargo Act of 1807*
- **Supreme Court Case 1,** *Marbury* v. *Madison* (1803); **Supreme Court Case 2,** *McCulloch* v. *Maryland* (1819)
- **Outline Map Resource Book**
- **U.S. Desk Map**
- **The American History Videodisc and CD-ROM,** *The American Revolution and the Early Republic*

A&E HOME VIDEO. Biography™ THE HISTORY CHANNEL.

The following videotape programs are available from Glencoe as supplements to Chapter 10:

- **The Best of the Real West (Set)**
  (ISBN 1-56501-352-2)

To order, call Glencoe at 1-800-334-7344. To find classroom resources to accompany many of these videos, check the following home pages:
A&E Television: http://www.aetv.com
The History Channel: http://www.historychannel.com

Introducing
CHAPTER 10

Chapter Themes

Chapter Themes are listed by section on this chapter opening page of the Student Edition. A corresponding theme-based activity is available under "FOCUS," and a theme-based question is asked in the Section and Chapter Reviews.

Performance Assessment

Refer to Activity 10 in the *Performance Assessment Strategies and Activities* booklet.

GLENCOE TECHNOLOGY

VIDEODISC
MindJogger Videoquiz

Use MindJogger to preview the Chapter 10 content.

Chapter 10
Disc 2, Side A

Also available in VHS.

HISTORY AND ART Francis Alexander (1800–1880) had a studio in Boston, where he executed many portraits. **Ask:** Why was it important to build factories near rivers? *(to provide waterpower for machinery and a route for trade)*

Chapter 10

1790–1825

Growth and Expansion

Why It's Important

Between 1790 and 1825, manufacturing took on an important role in the American economy. During the same period, people moved westward across the continent in larger and larger numbers. In 1823 the United States proclaimed its dominant role in the Americas with the Monroe Doctrine. These three developments were major factors in shaping the nation. Today the United States is one of the leading economic and military powers in the world.

Chapter Themes

- *Section 1,* Economic Factors
- *Section 2,* Science and Technology
- *Section 3,* Individual Action
- *Section 4,* Global Connections

HISTORY AND ART **Globe Village by Francis Alexander** Changes in the countryside came during the Industrial Revolution of the early 1800s. In New England, factories were built along the falls and rapids of rivers.

EXTRA CREDIT PROJECT

Inventions Challenge each student to come up with a new invention and make a working model of it. Tell students it can be something to help people, or to make the home or school environment safer, or to provide fun and entertainment. You may want to provide some library books on the subject. One that might stimulate students' thinking is *Brainstorm! (The Stories of Twenty American Kid Inventors)* by Tom Tucker. Students are sure to enjoy two books by Jim Murphy: *Weird and Wacky Inventions* and *Guess Again: More Weird and Wacky Inventions.*

1790 — 1800 — 1810 — 1820

1793 Eli Whitney invents the cotton gin

1807 Congress passes the Embargo Act

1814 Francis Lowell opens textile plant in Massachusetts

1816 Second National Bank is chartered

Section 1

Economic Growth

READ TO DISCOVER . . .

- how the Industrial Revolution began in the United States and what its effects were.
- how the United States changed as it became more economically independent.

TERMS TO LEARN

Industrial Revolution	patent
capital	factory system
technology	interchangeable parts
cotton gin	

The Storyteller

Both men and women in the early 1800s valued hard work. An English journalist described the farmers of Long Island in 1818: "Every man can use an axe, a saw, and a hammer. Scarcely one who cannot do any job at rough carpentering, and mend a plough and wagon. . . ." Another European noted the daily activities of American women in 1823: "They take care of everything pertaining to the domestic economy, for example making candles, boiling soap, preparing starch, canning berries, fruit and cucumbers, baking, and spinning, sewing, and milking the cows."

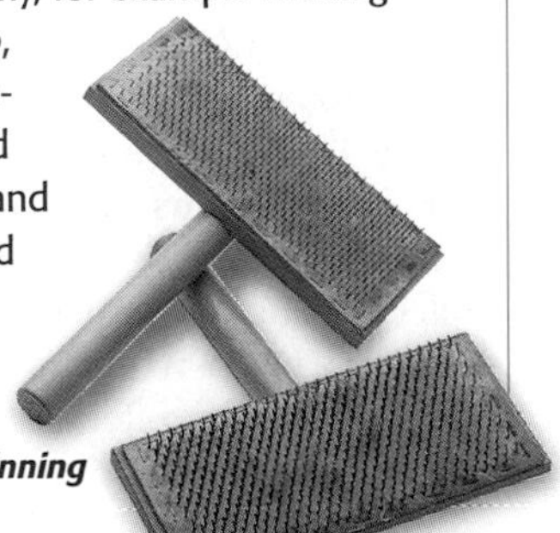

Paddles used to prepare cotton for spinning

During the colonial era, workers were in short supply. Americans learned to develop tools that made work easier and more efficient. American methods and inventions won the admiration of Europeans. One observer exclaimed:

> "The axe here [in America] . . . is a combination axe, wedge, and sledgehammer; what an accomplished woodchopper can do with this instrument! There are some among them who can chop and split five and one-half loads of wood a day, including stacking them."

Economics

The Growth of Industry

People working in their homes or in workshops made cloth and most other goods. Using hand tools, they produced furniture, farm equipment, household items, and clothing.

In the mid-1700s, however, the way goods were made began to change. These changes appeared first in Great Britain. British inventors created machinery to perform some of the work involved in cloth making, such as spinning. The machines ran on waterpower, so British cloth makers built mills along rivers and installed the machines in these mills.

People left their homes and farms to work in the mills and earn wages. This meant a new way

SECTION RESOURCES

Reproducible Masters
- Guided Reading Activity 10–1
- Political Cartoons, *The Embargo Act of 1807*
- Section Quiz 10–1
- Reteaching Activity 10–1
- Enrichment Activity 10–1

Transparencies
- Section Focus Transparency 10–1

Multimedia
- Focus on American Art Prints
- Chapter Challenger Interactive Review
- Testmaker
- ABCNews InterActive™ Historic America Electronic Field Trips
- Landmark Documents in American History
- American Music Cultural Traditions

1 FOCUS

BELLRINGER
Motivational Activity

Before taking roll at the beginning of the class period, project Section Focus Transparency 10–1 and have students answer the questions. Discuss students' responses.

This activity is also available as a blackline master.

Section Focus Transparency 10–1

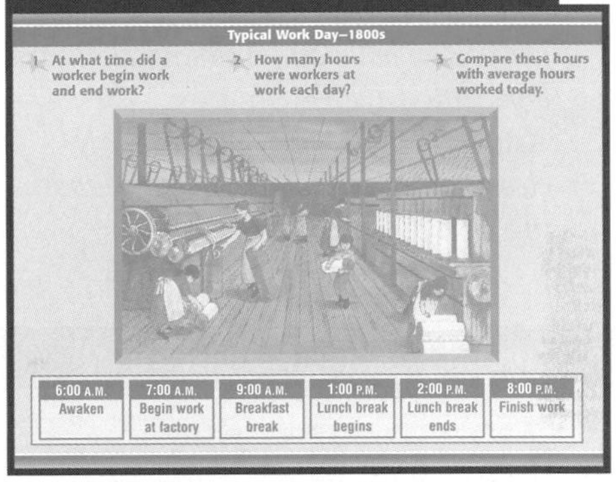

Vocabulary Precheck

Have students look up *revolution* in a dictionary and choose the meaning they think will fit best in the term *Industrial Revolution. ("momentous or radical change")*

Use the **Vocabulary PuzzleMaker** to create crossword and word search puzzles.

Section Theme
Economic Factors

The Industrial Revolution, which began in America in New England, changed forever the way goods were made. It also changed the way people lived.

Activity Have students skim the section to find out why the Industrial Revolution began in New England. *(farming difficult, rivers to provide power, location near resources, many ports, capital available)*

2 TEACH

L1, ELL Finding Changes Among the several umbrella terms that could characterize this section is the term *change*. Write the term on the board and have students brainstorm as many changes discussed in the section as they can.

Picturing HISTORY Before the advent of the cotton gin and textile factories, only the wealthy could afford cotton. **Ask: Why do you think this was so?** *(Cotton was expensive because cleaning cotton bolls and weaving cloth was labor intensive.)*
Answer: *It allowed one worker to clean cotton as fast as 50 people working by hand.*

Guided Reading Activity 10–1

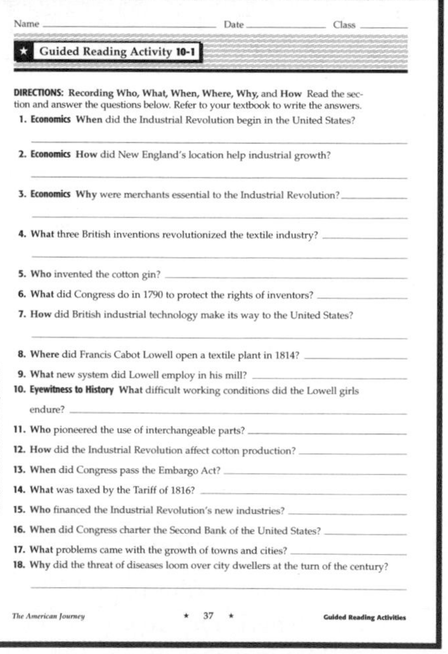
Name ________ Date ________ Class ________

★ Guided Reading Activity 10-1

DIRECTIONS: Recording Who, What, When, Where, Why, and **How** Read the section and answer the questions below. Refer to your textbook to write the answers.

1. **Economics When** did the Industrial Revolution begin in the United States?
2. **Economics How** did New England's location help industrial growth?
3. **Economics Why** were merchants essential to the Industrial Revolution?
4. **What** three British inventions revolutionized the textile industry?
5. **Who** invented the cotton gin?
6. **What** did Congress do in 1790 to protect the rights of inventors?
7. **How** did British industrial technology make its way to the United States?
8. **Where** did Francis Cabot Lowell open a textile plant in 1814?
9. **What** new system did Lowell employ in his mill?
10. **Eyewitness to History What** difficult working conditions did the Lowell girls endure?
11. **Who** pioneered the use of interchangeable parts?
12. **How** did the Industrial Revolution affect cotton production?
13. **When** did Congress pass the Embargo Act?
14. **What** was taxed by the Tariff of 1816?
15. **Who** financed the Industrial Revolution's new industries?
16. **When** did Congress charter the Second Bank of the United States?
17. **What** problems came with the growth of towns and cities?
18. **Why** did the threat of diseases loom over city dwellers at the turn of the century?

The American Journey ★ 37 ★ **Guided Reading Activities**

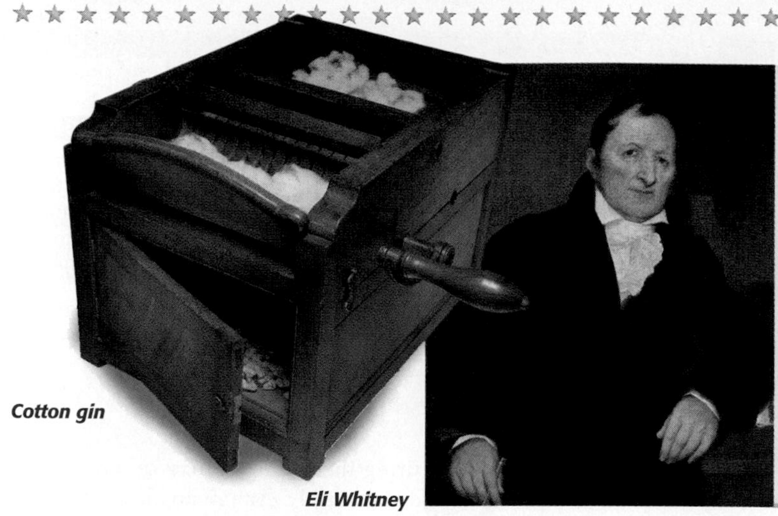
Cotton gin

Eli Whitney

Picturing HISTORY The cotton gin's crank turned a cylinder that drew cotton fibers, but not cotton seeds, through small slots. **How did the cotton gin transform the production of cotton?**

of working as well as a new way of producing goods. The changes this system brought about were so great that this time in history is known as the **Industrial Revolution.**

The Industrial Revolution in New England

The Industrial Revolution began to take root in the United States around 1800, appearing first in **New England.** The New England states—Massachusetts, Rhode Island, Connecticut, Vermont, and New Hampshire—offered ideal conditions for the development of factories. New England's soil was poor, and farming was difficult. As a result, people were willing to leave their farms to find work elsewhere. Also, New England had many rushing rivers and streams. These provided the waterpower necessary to run the machinery in the new factories.

New England's geographic location also proved to be an advantage. It was close to other resources, including coal and iron from nearby Pennsylvania. Equally important, New England had many ports. Through these ports passed the cotton shipped from Southern states to New England factories as well as the finished cloth bound for markets throughout the nation.

Most important of all, merchants in New England had **capital**—money for investment. The merchants of Boston and Providence had grown wealthy as American shipping thrived in the 1790s and early 1800s. Their capital was essential for developing needed machinery and building industries.

New Technology

Workers, waterpower, location, and capital all played key roles in New England's Industrial Revolution. Yet without the invention of new machines and new **technology**—the application of scientific discoveries to practical use—the Industrial Revolution could not have taken place.

In Great Britain inventors devised new machinery and methods that revolutionized the textile industry, totally changing the way cloth was manufactured. Inventions such as the spinning jenny and the water frame—which spun thread—and the power loom—which wove the thread into cloth—made it possible to perform many steps in making cloth by machine, saving time and money.

Because these new machines ran on waterpower, most mills were built near rivers. In 1785, for the first time, a steam engine provided power for a cotton mill.

The United States also had its share of inventors. **Oliver Evans** of Delaware improved the steam engine and developed a mechanical flour mill. His flour mill needed only two workers: one to empty a bag of wheat into it and another to roll away the barrels of flour. In 1793 **Eli Whitney** of Massachusetts invented the **cotton gin,** a simple

COOPERATIVE LEARNING ACTIVITY

Making a Flowchart Note that one invention often creates a need for another. Have students do research as needed on the following six inventions and then create an illustrated flowchart explaining the relationships among them: flying shuttle, spinning jenny, water frame, spinning mule, power loom, cotton gin. Have students choose their own role in the project—researching, making the chart, drawing the illustrations, or writing descriptive paragraphs.

machine that quickly and efficiently removed the cotton seeds from the fiber. The cotton gin enabled one worker to clean cotton as fast as 50 people working by hand.

In 1790 Congress passed a patent law to protect the rights of those who developed "useful and important inventions." A **patent** gives an inventor the sole legal right to the invention and its profits for a certain period of time. One of the first patents went to Jacob Perkins for a machine to make nails.

New England Factories

★ The British tried to keep their new industrial technology a secret. They even passed laws prohibiting their machinery as well as their skilled mechanics from leaving the country. However, a few enterprising workers managed to slip away to the United States.

In Britain **Samuel Slater** had worked in a factory that used machines invented by Richard Arkwright for spinning cotton threads. Slater memorized the design of Arkwright's machines and slipped out of Britain in 1789.

Once in the United States, Slater took over the management of a cotton mill in Pawtucket, Rhode Island. There he duplicated all of Arkwright's machines. Using these machines the mill made cotton thread. Women working in their homes wove the thread into cloth.

The establishment of Slater's mill marked an important step in the Industrial Revolution in America. In 1790 Slater had 10 people working for him. By 1800 his Pawtucket factory employed more than 100 workers, mostly women and young children.

Lowell's Mills

In 1811 **Francis Cabot Lowell,** a wealthy New Englander, traveled to Great Britain, where he visited many textile mills. At night in his hotel room, he made detailed drawings of the factories and machines. After returning home, Lowell borrowed $400,000 to start the Boston Manufacturing Company. Lowell improved on the design of the British power looms and made plans to put his design to use.

In 1814 Francis Lowell's company opened a textile plant in Waltham, Massachusetts. The plan he implemented went several steps beyond Slater's mill. As one of Lowell's partners explained, the factory used "an entirely new arrangement, in order to save labor, in passing from one process to another." For the first time, all the stages of cloth making were performed under one roof. Lowell's mill launched the **factory system,** a system bringing manufacturing steps together in one place to increase efficiency. The factory system was a significant development in the way goods were made—and an important part of the Industrial Revolution.

★ Picturing HISTORY As the Industrial Revolution spread, factories sprang up in many New England towns. **How did the factory system differ from earlier methods of production?**

Lunch pail

MULTIPLE LEARNING STYLES

Visual/Spatial Have students think about the inventions that make their lives easier or that provide entertainment (lightbulb, CDs, VCRs, microwaves, zippers, Velcro, and so on). Then have students choose one and come up with an improvement or a new invention that can do more than the one chosen. Have students draw a picture or diagram showing and explaining how it works. **L2**

What?Where?When?Who?

Nothing New? In 1838 the clerk of the patent office resigned because he felt that all worthwhile inventions had been discovered.

you don't say...

Cotton Gin The word *gin* is a shortened form of *engine.*

Who?What?Where?When?

The Lowell Girls In an effort to avoid the horrible working and living conditions of factories in England, The Boston Associates decided to hire young, unmarried women from New England and to provide well-kept and supervised company boardinghouses. Girls living in these company houses were not allowed to drink or play cards. They were required to be in bed by ten o'clock and to attend church every Sunday. The girls were encouraged to read books, to write letters, and to listen to lectures. The Lowell Girls received weekly wages of about $3.00, about half of which went for room and board.

★ Picturing HISTORY The Industrial Revolution had an unpleasant side effect on the environment. Because early factories relied on waterpower, many New England rivers became polluted.
Ask: **What were the probable sources of such pollution?** *(chemicals and dyes used in manufacturing, human wastes from workers)*
Answer: *All stages of production were under one roof, rather than in individual shops or homes.*

CHAPTER 10
Section 1, 305–311

History *and the* Humanities

- Focus on American Art Prints, *The Staircase Group* by Charles Willson Peale
- American Music Cultural Traditions, Lesson 3: "The Rose Tree"
- The Spirit of American Art and Music, Joshua Johnston
- Political Cartoons, *The Embargo Act of 1807*

TECHNOLOGY AND HISTORY

More About . . .
Textile Mills In addition to being monotonous and mind-dulling, factory jobs were hazardous to one's health and safety. Some workers lost their hearing from the din of the machinery. Tiny particles of fiber filled the air and people's lungs, causing lung cancer and other respiratory diseases. The huge and powerful machines had no safety devices, so the workers had to be careful. One slip could cost a hand or an arm.
Answer to Caption: *waterpower*

Eyewitness to HISTORY

Lowell Girls

Lowell's mills drew about 80 percent of their workers from unmarried women between the ages of 15 and 30—and some were even younger. Known as the "Lowell girls," they left their farms and headed to the factories in towns for the opportunity to earn a wage and the adventure of working on their own.

The company built boardinghouses for the Lowell girls and tried to ensure their safety. These young women were carefully supervised and were expected to attend church regularly and to observe curfews. Most of them worked for a few years in the mill and either sent their pay home to their parents or saved their wages for the day when they would marry. After marrying, many left the mill to care for their families.

The young women who worked in Lowell's mills endured difficult working conditions. They put in long hours—from sunrise to sunset—for low wages. The volume of the factory machinery was earsplitting, and the work was monotonous and required little skill. The women usually performed one task over and over again. Sometimes the only skill necessary was the ability to tie a knot in thread that had broken.

Lucy Larcom started working in the mills when she was 11 years old. She later recalled her life at Waltham:

TECHNOLOGY AND HISTORY

Textile Mill

The Lowell factory system was designed to bring work and workers together. A typical Lowell textile mill in 1830 housed 4,500 spindles, 120 power looms, and more than 200 employees under one roof. **What type of energy powered the mills?**

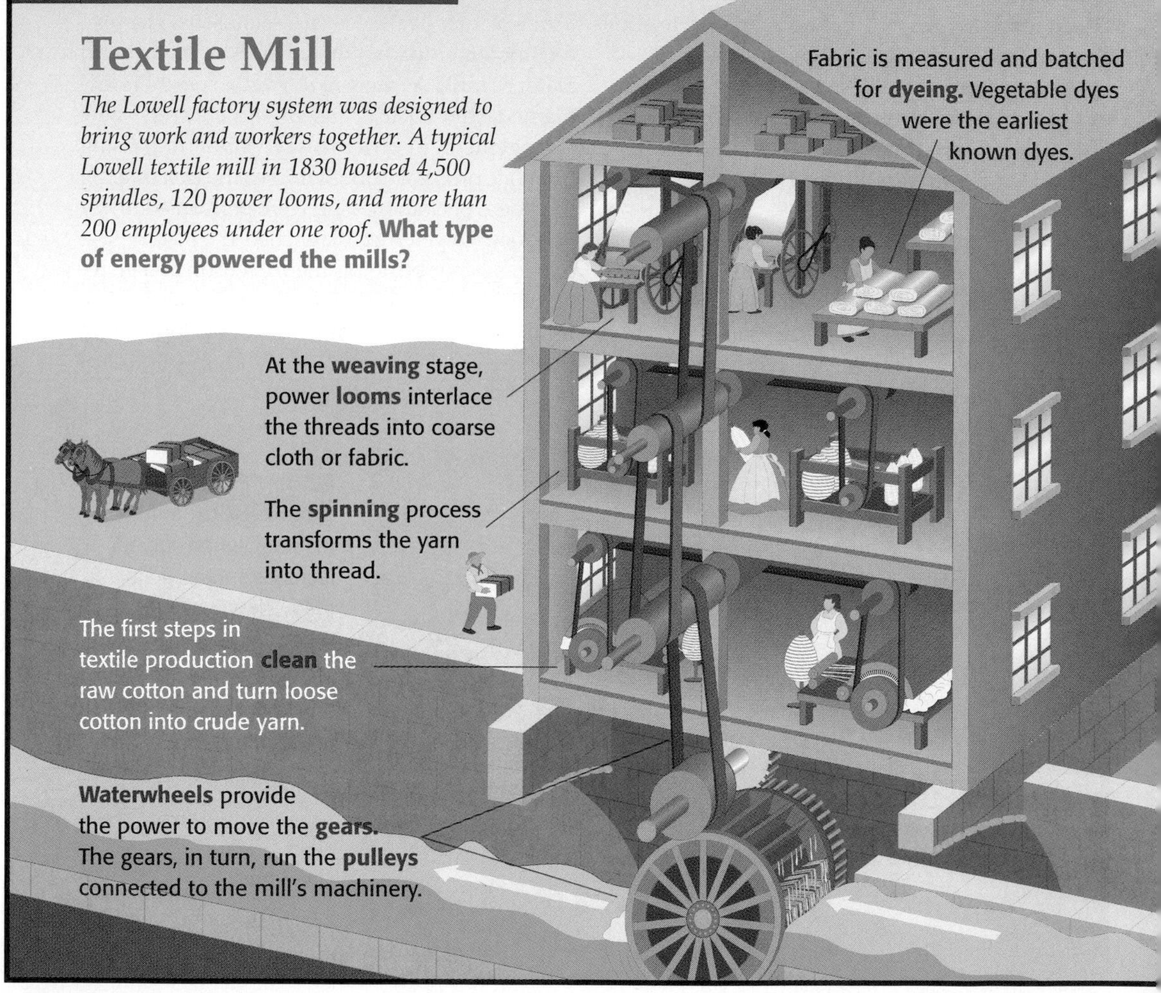

MAKING CONNECTIONS ACTIVITY

Economics Pay for factory workers depended not on the job, but on the worker's age and gender. Lowell girls (among the best paid) made from $2.50 to $3.00 per week; men earned $4.00 for the same job. Have students propose theories as to why this was accepted practice. Note that despite modern legislation, women still struggle for equal pay. Interested students should research the current gender gap in earnings. **L2**

HISTORY AND ART ***Ralph Weelock's Farm*** **by Francis Alexander** Farmers benefited from improved transportation that brought their produce to the cities. **What percentage of Americans earned their living from agriculture during the 1820s?**

"We did not call ourselves ladies. We did not forget that we were working girls, wearing aprons suitable to our work, and that there was some danger of our becoming drudges."

When the noisy machinery got to her, Lucy would

". . . lean far out of the window, and try not to hear the unceasing clash of sound inside."

To many visitors, the mills seemed a promising opportunity for the women who worked there. For the women themselves, however, the daily drudgery of the mills was not so wonderful. Many eventually abandoned their work there and sought jobs as teachers or maids. By the 1830s and 1840s, factory workers—often immigrants—labored under even harsher conditions at textile mills and other factories.

Interchangeable Parts

Revolutionary changes occurred in other industries beyond cloth making. In 1798 Eli Whitney received a contract from the United States government to make 10,000 rifles in 28 months. To produce this enormous quantity in such a short time, Whitney devised a manufacturing method that would produce **interchangeable parts.** The idea was to make large quantities of uniform pieces that could replace any other identical pieces.

Whitney made a mold for each part of the rifle, and the pieces that came out of the molds were supposed to be identical and interchangeable. The pieces were fairly crude, however, and had to be finished by hand.

For Whitney, the new system had its flaws. It took 10 years to complete the government's order. Later, the development of more precise machines that could turn out uniform pieces made interchangeable parts a reality. Interchangeable parts opened the way for producing many different kinds of goods on a mass scale and for reducing the price of the goods.

Agriculture Expands

Although many New Englanders went to work in factories, most Americans still lived and worked on farms. In the 1820s more than 65 percent of Americans were farmers.

In the Northeast, farms tended to be small, and the produce was usually marketed locally. In the South, cotton production increased dramatically. The demand for cotton had grown steadily with the development of the textile industries of New England and Europe. Southern plantation owners used enslaved workers to plant, tend, and pick the cotton. The cotton gin—which made it possible to clean the cotton much faster and more cheaply than by hand—encouraged the planters to raise larger crops. Between 1790 and 1820, cotton production soared from 3,000 to more than 300,000 bales a year.

HISTORY AND ART Francis Alexander (1800–1880) was influenced by the works of Gilbert Stuart. Alexander spent much of his later life in Italy. **Ask:** **How can you tell that Ralph Weelock was a prosperous farmer?** *(by the size of the main house and the number of workers)* **Answer:** *65 percent*

you don't say...

New expressions from the early 1800s reflect the nation's rapid growth—"like greased lightning," "quick as a wink," "like a house afire," "shake a leg," and "lickety-split."

Who?What?Where?When?

Eli Whitney After graduating from Yale in 1792, Eli Whitney set out for an expected job in Savannah, Georgia. When this job did not materialize, he gratefully accepted an invitation from Catherine Greene to live on one of her plantations. While there he worked as a handyman. Mrs. Greene asked him to make a machine that could strip seeds from cotton. Within 10 days he invented his first version of the cotton gin. Six months later, on March 14, 1794, he received a patent for an improved version of his cotton gin.

CRITICAL THINKING ACTIVITY

Cause and Effect Whitney's cotton gin (and others like it) made it profitable to grow more cotton, and production increased dramatically. While some planters did grow rich, social and economic problems resulted from the cotton boom. First, slavery—which had been declining because of economic problems in the South—rebounded. Second, reliance on cotton meant a lack of economic diversity for the region. Ask students to propose at least one possible effect that resulted from each problem. **L2**

Facts On File

CD-ROM
Landmark Documents in American History

Title: *War Message, James Madison, 1812*
Ask students to think about how Americans felt about this war.

3 ASSESS

Assign Section 1 Review as homework or as an in-class activity.

Use **Chapter Challenger Interactive Review Software** to review Section 1.

Section Quiz 10–1

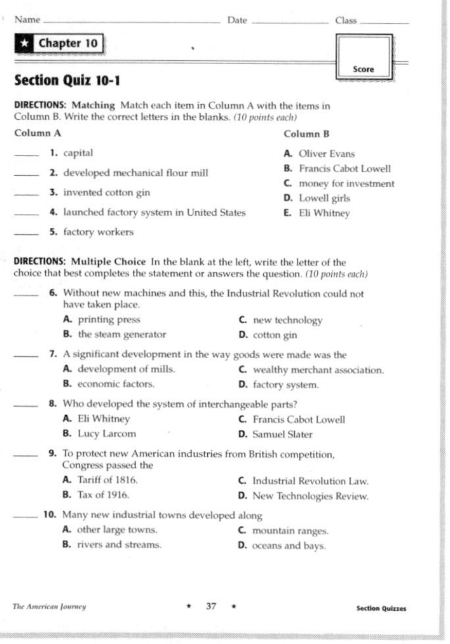
Name ______ Date ______ Class ______

Chapter 10 — Score

Section Quiz 10-1

DIRECTIONS: Matching Match each item in Column A with the items in Column B. Write the correct letters in the blanks. *(10 points each)*

Column A	Column B
____ 1. capital	A. Oliver Evans
____ 2. developed mechanical flour mill	B. Francis Cabot Lowell
____ 3. invented cotton gin	C. money for investment
____ 4. launched factory system in United States	D. Lowell girls
____ 5. factory workers	E. Eli Whitney

DIRECTIONS: Multiple Choice In the blank at the left, write the letter of the choice that best completes the statement or answers the question. *(10 points each)*

____ 6. Without new machines and this, the Industrial Revolution could not have taken place.
A. printing press C. new technology
B. the steam generator D. cotton gin

____ 7. A significant development in the way goods were made was the
A. development of mills. C. wealthy merchant association.
B. economic factors. D. factory system.

____ 8. Who developed the system of interchangeable parts?
A. Eli Whitney C. Francis Cabot Lowell
B. Lucy Larcom D. Samuel Slater

____ 9. To protect new American industries from British competition, Congress passed the
A. Tariff of 1816. C. Industrial Revolution Law.
B. Tax of 1916. D. New Technologies Review.

____ 10. Many new industrial towns developed along
A. other large towns. C. mountain ranges.
B. rivers and streams. D. oceans and bays.

The American Journey ★ 37 ★ Section Quizzes

Picturing HISTORY Early attempts at correcting problems in cities include Boston implementing a sewer system in 1823 and New York abandoning wells and cisterns for a piped-in water supply. **Ask:** **Which diseases would a sewer system help eliminate?** *(cholera and yellow fever)* **Answer:** *overcrowding, unsanitary conditions, disease, threat of fire*

In the West, agriculture also expanded. Southern farmers seeking new land moved west to plant cotton. Western farmers north of the Ohio River concentrated on raising pork and cash crops such as corn and wheat.

Economic Independence

As more cotton and wool factories went into operation, Americans came to rely less on British-made cloth. The Industrial Revolution helped make the United States more independent economically. In the early 1800s, foreign relations also affected the American economy.

Embargo, War, and Tariffs

In 1807 Congress passed the Embargo Act, which cut off all foreign trade for two years. In 1812 the United States went to war with Great Britain. During the war the British blockaded American ports.

The embargo and the blockades sharply reduced America's overseas trade. At the same time, these factors contributed to the nation's quickly growing economic independence. With foreign goods difficult to acquire, new American industries emerged to meet local needs. Some New England merchants put the money they made before the embargo into building new factories and machinery to increase production.

As soon as the War of 1812 ended, British goods began to pour into the United States. British manufacturers often sold these goods at very low prices to take business away from American manufacturers. To protect the new American industries from British competition, Congress passed the **Tariff of 1816.** The new law placed a tax on imported goods, making the ironware, paper, and woolen and cotton goods from Britain more expensive than products made in the United States.

Fire bucket

Picturing HISTORY As industry grew, Philadelphia, shown here in the early 1800s, increased its population from about 91,000 in 1810 to about 161,000 in 1830. **What problems did Northeast cities face as a result of the growth of industry?**

The Second National Bank

Most new industries were financed by small investors—merchants, shopkeepers, and farmers. These people invested some of their money in the hope of earning profits if the new businesses succeeded.

Businesses that needed a larger amount of capital had to obtain it from banks. The charter of the First Bank of the United States had expired in 1811. The Bank had faced fierce opposition from Republicans when it was established 20 years earlier, and some people still believed Congress had no authority to create such a bank. However, Republican president Madison came to accept the Federalist view of national economic development and supported a new bank.

In 1816 Congress chartered the **Second Bank of the United States.** The Bank had the power to establish a national currency and to make large loans to businesses. It, too, helped strengthen the economic independence of the nation.

Cities Come of Age

The growth of factories and trade spurred the growth of towns and cities, especially in the Northeast. Along with this development, however, came new problems: overcrowding, unsanitary conditions, disease, and the threat of fire.

TEACHER'S NOTES

Urban Growth

The new industrial towns grew quickest. Many developed along rivers and streams because of waterpower. Older cities like New York, Boston, and Baltimore also grew as centers of commerce and trade. In the West, towns like Pittsburgh, Cincinnati, and Louisville profited from their locations on major rivers. As farmers in the West shipped more and more of their products by water, these towns grew rapidly.

City Life

Cities and towns looked quite different from modern urban areas. Buildings were made of wood or brick. Streets and sidewalks were unpaved, and barnyard animals often roamed freely. No sewers carried waste and dirty water away, and as a result, the threat of such diseases as cholera and yellow fever always loomed over city dwellers. In 1793, for example, a yellow fever epidemic in Philadelphia killed thousands of people.

Fire posed another threat to cities. Sparks from a fireplace or chimney could easily ignite a wooden building and spread to others. Few towns or cities had organized fire companies, and fires could be disastrous.

Cities and towns of the period also had advantages, however. Some people left farming because cities and towns offered a variety of jobs and steady wages. As cities grew they added libraries, museums, and shops that were unavailable in the countryside. For many, the jobs and attractions of city life outweighed any dangers.

Urban Population Growth in America, 1800-1850

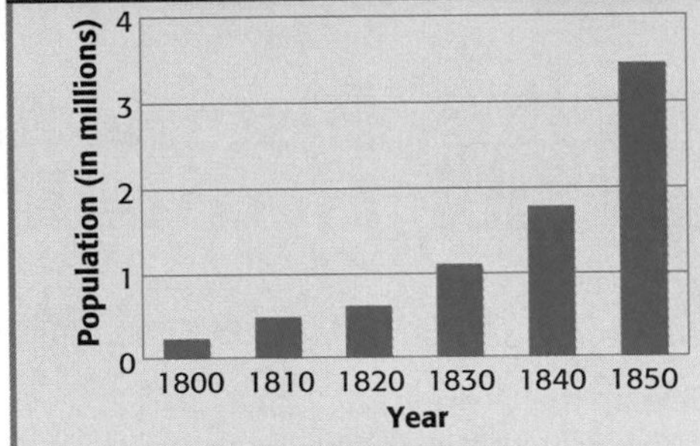

Source: *Historical Statistics of the United States.*

Graph Study

Urban population began to increase quickly by the mid-1800s.

1. By what year had the number of people living in cities first reached more than 1 million?
2. **Analyzing Information** What was the urban population of the United States in 1850?

Section 1 Review

Checking for Understanding

1. ***Identify*** Eli Whitney, Samuel Slater.
2. ***Define*** Industrial Revolution, capital, technology, cotton gin, patent, factory system, interchangeable parts.
3. ***List*** three reasons New England was ideal for the development of factories.

Reviewing Themes

4. **Economic Factors** How did the cotton gin affect production?

Critical Thinking

5. **Determining Cause and Effect** Was new technology necessary for the Industrial Revolution to take place? Explain your point of view.

Activity

Making a State Map Make an outline map of your state showing the three largest cities and the geographic features you think might have contributed to their growth.

Section 1 Review Answers

1. Eli Whitney, 306; Samuel Slater, 307
2. The words are defined in the Glossary.
3. Any three: workers, waterpower, location, capital
4. It made the cleaning of cotton quicker and more efficient.
5. Yes; without new technology people would have continued to produce goods at home as they had done in the past.

Activity Maps should show at least three of your state's major cities and geographic features, such as rivers or mountain passes, that could have contributed to cities' growth.

Graph Study

Answers

1. 1830
2. about 3½ million

Reteaching Activity 10–1

Name ______ Date ______ Class ______

★ Reteaching Activity **10-1**

DIRECTIONS: Matching Match each item in Column A with its corresponding item in Column B. Write the correct letters in the blanks.

COLUMN A

____ **1.** technology
____ **2.** New England
____ **3.** Oliver Evans
____ **4.** Eli Whitney
____ **5.** Samuel Slater
____ **6.** Francis Cabot Lowell
____ **7.** factory system
____ **8.** Lowell girls
____ **9.** interchangeable parts
____ **10.** Embargo Act of 1807
____ **11.** Tariff of 1816
____ **12.** Second Bank of the United States
____ **13.** New York, Boston, Baltimore
____ **14.** Pittsburgh, Cincinnati, Louisville

COLUMN B

A. memorized designs of British machinery then duplicated them in the United States
B. cut off foreign trade for two years
C. profited from location on major rivers
D. opened a textile plant in Waltham, Massachusetts, in 1814
E. strengthened the nation's economic independence
F. Massachusetts, Rhode Island, Connecticut, Vermont, New Hampshire
G. application of scientific discoveries to practical use
H. invented the cotton gin
I. made imported goods more expensive than products made in the United States
J. brought manufacturing steps together in one place to increase efficiency
K. centers of commerce and trade
L. 80 percent of workers in Lowell's mills
M. developed a mechanical flour mill
N. uniform pieces that could replace any other identical pieces

DIRECTIONS: Essay Answer the following question on a separate sheet of paper.
How were Eli Whitney's inventions important to the Industrial Revolution?

Enrichment Activity 10–1

Name ______ Date ______ Class ______

★ Enrichment Activity **10-1** ★ ★

A Home Away from Home

During the Industrial Revolution young women became factory workers and had to obey strict rules, such as those from the Middlesex Woolen Mills boardinghouse.

Regulations for the Boarding Houses of the Middlesex Company

The [keepers] of the Boarding Houses are not to board, or permit any part of their houses to be occupied by any person except those in the employ of the Company.

They will be considered answerable for any improper conduct in their houses, and are not to permit their boarders to have company at unseasonable hours.

The doors must be closed at ten o'clock in the evening, and no one admitted after that time without some reasonable excuse.

The keepers of the Boarding Houses must give an account of the number, names, and employment of their boarders, when required; and report the names of such as are guilty of any improper conduct, or are not in the regular habit of attending public worship. . .

It is indispensable that all persons in the employ of the Middlesex Company should be vaccinated who have not been, as also the families with whom they board; which will be done at the expense of the Company.

SAMUEL LAWRENCE, Agent

DIRECTIONS: Recalling Facts Answer the questions on a separate sheet of paper.

1. Who could live in the boardinghouses besides the keepers and their families?
2. What happened if boarders did not go to church regularly?
3. How did the textile company contribute to the health care of its workers?

CRITICAL THINKING

4. Why do you think the company imposed such strict rules on their employees?
5. What do you think would happen today if employers tried to enforce rules like these for their employees?

Activity **DIRECTIONS:** Think about how you would feel about these rules if you were a mill worker. Write a letter to the owner of the mill about a rule that you find unfair. Then put yourself in the mill owner's place and write a letter in response.

4 CLOSE

Ask students if they would have chosen to stay on the family farm or move to a city if they had been alive in the early 1800s. **Why?**

ABCNEWS INTERACTIVE™

VIDEODISC
Historic America
Electronic Field Trips

Side 2, Chapter 4
Title: *The Lowell Factories*

If you do not have access to a videodisc player, the **Historic America Electronic Field Trips** are also available in VHS.

Internet Sites
The following are possible sites for completing the "Net" activities:

The White House home page
http://www2.whitehouse.gov/WH/Welcome.html

Youth Central: E-mail Government Officials
http://www.youthcentral.apple.com/the village/speakers/default.html

Not on the "Net" . . .
If students have limited or no access to the Internet, have them complete the activity "E-Mail Your Government Officials" by going to the library. There, students can use the *Congressional Directory* to find out who their state representatives in Congress are. After recording the representatives' names and office addresses in Washington, D.C., students should compose their letters and mail them. Students can share any responses they receive with the rest of the class.

Multimedia Activities

ABCNEWS INTERACTIVE™ Historic America Electronic Field Trips

Field Trip to the Lowell Factories

Setting up the Video

Work with a group of your classmates to view "Lowell Factories" on the videodisc ***Historic America: Electronic Field Trips***.

The Lowell textile mill was one of the first mechanized factories in the country. The program reveals a letter written by a young woman named Mary who experienced the hardships of factory work firsthand.

Hands-On Activity

Call your local chamber of commerce for a list of manufacturing companies in your area. Find out how many employees each company employs. Create a circle graph to show the percentage of people from your community that depend on factories for their livelihood.

Side 2,
Chapter 4

View the video by scanning the bar code or by entering the chapter number on your keypad and pressing Search.

Surfing the "Net"

E-Mail Your Government Officials

The legislative branch of the U.S. government consists of the House of Representatives and the Senate. With the Internet, constituents can communicate with their representatives quickly. To find out how you can E-mail your representatives, follow the instructions below.

Getting There

Find out who your representatives are in Congress. Think of any issues, concerns, or questions you might like to discuss with one of your elected representatives.

1. Use a search engine. Type in the word *Congress.*
2. After typing in *Congress,* enter words like the following to focus your search: *E-mail address, state's name, representative's name.*
3. The search engine will provide you with a number of links to follow.

What to Do When You Are There

Click on the links to navigate through the pages to find your representative's E-mail address. Using your E-mail service, compose and send a letter to your representative that expresses your interests or concerns. When you receive your response, share your news with your class.

TEACHER'S NOTES

1800 · 1810 · 1820 · 1830

1806 Congress approves funds for a national road

1807 Robert Fulton's *Clermont* steams to Albany

1820 The U.S. population stands at 10 million

1825 The Erie Canal is completed

Section 2

Westward Bound

READ TO DISCOVER . . .

- how land and water transportation improved in the early 1800s.
- how settlements in the West affected economic and political developments in the nation.

TERMS TO LEARN

census | canal
turnpike | lock

The Storyteller

During the early 1800s, settlers poured into the frontier west of the Appalachians. The typical frontier family moved from place to place as the frontier pushed ever westward. Their home often consisted of a three-sided shack or a log cabin with a dirt floor and no windows or door. A pile of leaves in the loft of the cabin often served as a bed. Loneliness, poverty, and an almost primitive lifestyle were daily companions to many frontier people.

Mug honoring the first census

The first census—the official count of the population—of the United States in 1790 revealed a population of nearly 4 million. Most of the Americans counted lived east of the Appalachian Mountains and within a few hundred miles of the Atlantic coast.

Within a few decades this changed. The number of settlers heading west increased by leaps and bounds. In 1811 a Pennsylvania resident reported seeing 236 wagons filled with people and their possessions on the road to Pittsburgh. A man in Newburgh, New York, counted 60 wagons rolling by in a single day. In 1820, just 30 years after the first census, the population of the United States had more than doubled to about 10 million people, with nearly 2 million living west of the Appalachians.

Geography

Moving West

Traveling west was not easy in the late 1790s and early 1800s. The 370-mile trip from **New York City** to **Buffalo** could take as long as three weeks. A pioneer family heading west with a wagonload of household goods faced hardship and danger along the way.

Roads and Turnpikes

The nation needed good inland roads for travel and for the shipment of goods to and from seaports. Private companies built many roads as

1 FOCUS

BELLRINGER
Motivational Activity

Before taking roll at the beginning of the class period, project Section Focus Transparency 10–2 and have students answer the questions. Discuss students' responses.

This activity is also available as a blackline master.

Section Focus Transparency 10–2

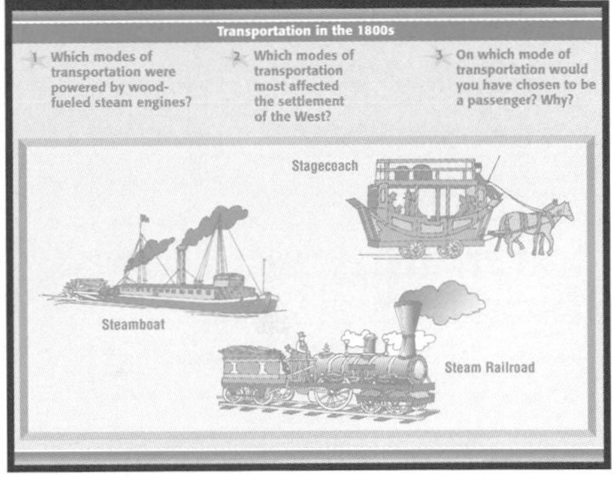

Vocabulary Precheck

Ask students which three of the terms have to do with transportation. *(turnpike, canal, lock)*

Use the **Vocabulary PuzzleMaker** to create crossword and word search puzzles.

Section Theme
Science and Technology

During the 1800s settlers poured into the frontier west of the Appalachians. The expansion of canal systems allowed these settlers to live farther away from rivers.

Activity Have students skim the section to find the purpose of canal locks. *(to raise or lower boats from one elevation to another)*

SECTION RESOURCES

Reproducible Masters
- Reproducible Lesson Plan 10–2
- Guided Reading Activity 10–2
- Section Quiz 10–2
- Reteaching Activity 10–2
- Enrichment Activity 10–2

Transparencies
- Section Focus Transparency 10–2

Multimedia
- Vocabulary PuzzleMaker
- Chapter Challenger Interactive Review Software
- Testmaker
- GTV: A Geographic Perspective on American History

2 TEACH

L1, ELL Making Concept Webs After students have read the section, work with them to make a concept web for each major part. The first web, for example, might consist of a central oval called "land travel." Surrounding balloons might consist of "turnpikes," "crushed stone," and so on.

Guided Reading Activity 10–2

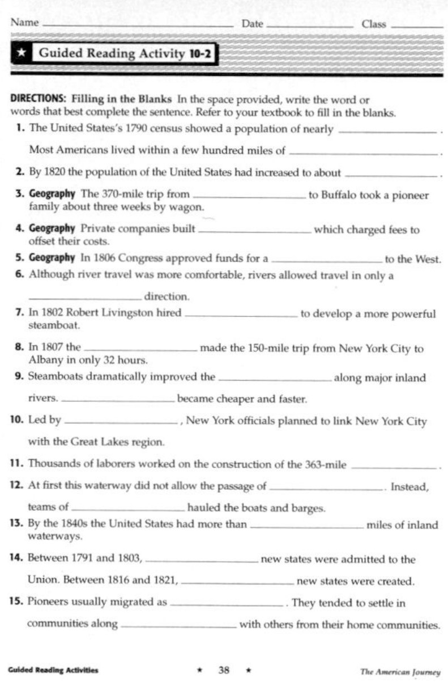
Name ________ Date ________ Class ________

★ Guided Reading Activity **10-2**

DIRECTIONS: Filling in the Blanks In the space provided, write the word or words that best complete the sentence. Refer to your textbook to fill in the blanks.

1. The United States's 1790 census showed a population of nearly ________. Most Americans lived within a few hundred miles of ________.
2. By 1820 the population of the United States had increased to about ________.
3. **Geography** The 370-mile trip from ________ to Buffalo took a pioneer family about three weeks by wagon.
4. **Geography** Private companies built ________ which charged fees to offset their costs.
5. **Geography** In 1806 Congress approved funds for a ________ to the West.
6. Although river travel was more comfortable, rivers allowed travel in only a ________ direction.
7. In 1802 Robert Livingston hired ________ to develop a more powerful steamboat.
8. In 1807 the ________ made the 150-mile trip from New York City to Albany in only 32 hours.
9. Steamboats dramatically improved the ________ along major inland rivers. ________ became cheaper and faster.
10. Led by ________, New York officials planned to link New York City with the Great Lakes region.
11. Thousands of laborers worked on the construction of the 363-mile ________.
12. At first this waterway did not allow the passage of ________. Instead, teams of ________ hauled the boats and barges.
13. By the 1840s the United States had more than ________ miles of inland waterways.
14. Between 1791 and 1803, ________ new states were admitted to the Union. Between 1816 and 1821, ________ new states were created.
15. Pioneers usually migrated as ________. They tended to settle in communities along ________ with others from their home communities.

Guided Reading Activities ★ 38 ★ *The American Journey*

Map Study

Answers

1. Vandalia, Illinois
2. Maryland, Pennsylvania, Virginia, Ohio, Indiana, Illinois

Map Skills Practice

Reading a Map Which road connected Albany and Buffalo? *(Mohawk Turnpike)*

turnpikes, or toll roads. The fees travelers paid to use those roads helped offset construction costs. Many of the roads had a base of crushed stone. In areas where the land was often muddy, companies built "corduroy roads," consisting of logs laid side by side like the ridges of corduroy cloth.

Many pioneers from New York and Philadelphia began their trip west on the Lancaster Turnpike, built in the 1790s from Philadelphia to Lancaster, Pennsylvania. From there they could continue west on rough dirt roads to Pittsburgh and then switch to a barge and sail down the **Ohio River** toward Ohio and Kentucky.

When Ohio joined the Union in 1803, the new state asked the federal government to build a road to connect it with the East. In 1806 Congress approved funds for a **National Road** to the West and agreed on the route five years later. Because work on the road stopped during the War of 1812, the first section, from Maryland to western Virginia, did not open until 1818. In later years the National Road reached Ohio and continued on to Vandalia, Illinois. Congress viewed the National Road as a military necessity, but it did not undertake other road-building projects.

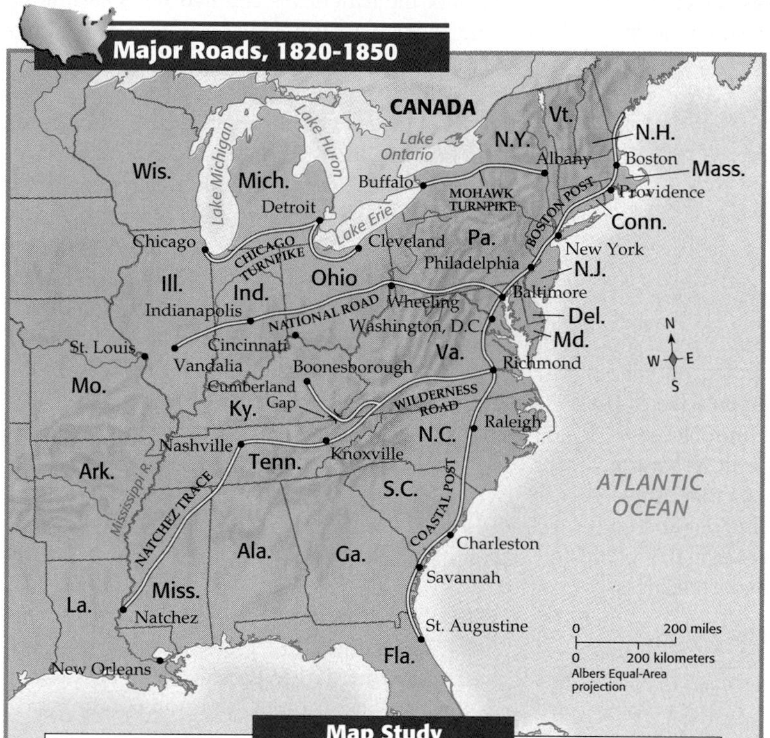

Map Study

By the mid-1800s, the United States had a number of roads west of the Appalachian Mountains.

1. **Location** According to the map, what was the westernmost city travelers could reach by road?
2. **Analyzing Information** Through what states did the National Road run?

River Travel

River travel had definite advantages over wagon and horse travel. It was far more comfortable than travel over the bumpy roads, and pioneers could load all their goods on river barges—if they were heading downstream in the direction of the current.

River travel had two problems, however. The first related to the geography of the eastern United States. Most major rivers in the region flowed in a north-south direction, not east to west, where most people and goods were headed. Second, traveling upstream by barge against the current was extremely difficult and slow.

Steamboats

Steam engines were already being used in the 1780s and 1790s to power boats in quiet waters. Inventor James Rumsey equipped a small boat on the Potomac River with a steam engine, and David

COOPERATIVE LEARNING ACTIVITY

Planning a Pioneer Living Day Have students work together in small groups to plan a Pioneer Living Day. Have each group choose a different part of pioneer life to demonstrate—recreation for adults and children, foods, crafts, tools, and so forth. Allow students to choose the task or tasks they would like to do, such as researching; writing; making drawings, models, or actual items; or speaking. Invite parents or other classes to view the results of students' work.

American Memories

Travel and Fashion

Man's overcoat

Cotton and wool dress

Children's shoes

What Was It Like? The lavish clothing and elegant carriages of wealthy Americans in the early 1800s may not seem comfortable by modern standards. **What problems did travelers face during this period?**

Fitch, another inventor, built a steamboat that navigated the Delaware River. Neither of these boats, however, had enough power to withstand the strong currents and shifting winds found in large rivers or open bodies of water.

In 1802 Robert Livingston, a political and business leader, hired **Robert Fulton** to develop a steamboat with a powerful engine. Livingston wanted the steamboat to carry cargo and passengers up the **Hudson River** from New York City to **Albany.**

In 1807 Fulton had his steamboat, the ***Clermont***, ready for a trial. Powered by a newly designed engine, the *Clermont* made the 150-mile trip from New York to Albany in the unheard-of time of 32 hours. Using only sails, the trip would have taken four days.

About 140 feet long and 14 feet wide, the *Clermont* offered great comforts to its passengers. They could sit or stroll about on deck, and at night they could relax in the sleeping compartments below deck. The engine was noisy, but its power provided a fairly smooth ride.

Steamboats ushered in a new age in river travel. They dramatically improved the transport of goods and passengers along major inland rivers. Shipping goods became cheaper and faster. Steamboats also contributed to the growth of river cities like Cincinnati and St. Louis.

Canals

★ Although steamboats represented a great improvement in transportation, their routes depended on the existing river system. Steamboats could not effectively tie the eastern and western parts of the country together.

In New York business and government officials led by **De Witt Clinton** came up with a plan to link New York City with the Great Lakes region. They would build a **canal**—an artificial waterway—across New York State, connecting Albany on the Hudson River with Buffalo on **Lake Erie.** Clinton declared the canal would "create the greatest inland trade ever witnessed."

American Memories

Travel and Fashion
Many communities in our nation began as nothing more than stagecoach stops.
Answer: *poor roads, few bridges*

What?Where?When?Who?

Transportation and Daily Life
Roads, canals, steamboats, and railroads had created a truly national economy by the mid-1800s. People could now buy goods produced in distant places. Rural Americans could have glass windows in their homes and hang curtains sewn from cloth manufactured in the mills of New England. All citizens could enjoy the same foods, fashions, and household furnishings.

NATIONAL GEOGRAPHIC SOCIETY

VIDEODISC
GTV: A Geographic Perspective on American History

Side 2, Chapter 9
Title: *Getting Up to Speed*
Subject: Transportation and a growing nation
Ask: **What new methods of transportation were invented that helped transport trade from the east to the west?** *(canals, railroads, and national roads)*

MULTIPLE LEARNING STYLES

Visual/Spatial Have students make labeled diagrams showing how canal locks or steamboats work. Students should be able to explain their diagrams orally or in writing. Explanations should include the reason that locks are necessary. Students should not have trouble finding diagrams to use for reference; the subject is covered in most, if not all, general encyclopedias. Challenge students to find the name of a canal built between 1859 and 1869 that has no locks. *(Suez)* **L1**

CHAPTER 10
Section 2, 313–317

Map Study

Answers
1. Lake Erie, Ohio River
2. 300

Linking PAST & PRESENT

Federal Road Building Another federal road project was completed much later than the National Road. In the 1950s, truckers asked Congress for modern high-speed highways. Increased car and truck use on such highways would benefit the construction, oil, auto, and auto supply industries. To justify financing the interstate highway system with federal funds, Congress decided that interstates were necessary for defense.

3 ASSESS

Assign Section 2 Review as homework or as an in-class activity.

Use **Chapter Challenger Interactive Review Software** to review Section 2.

Section Quiz 10–2

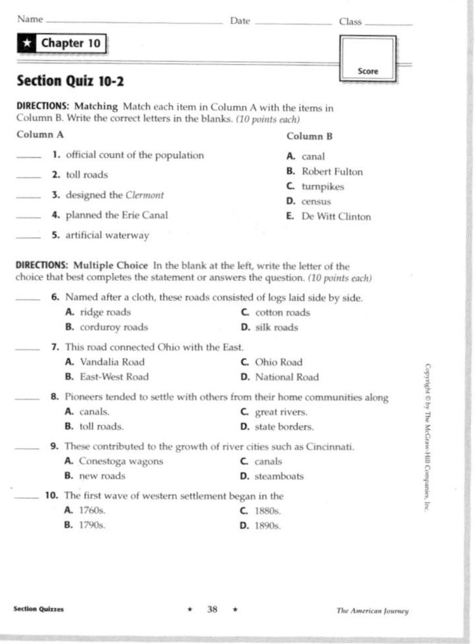
Name ______ Date ______ Class ______

★ Chapter 10 | Score

Section Quiz 10-2

DIRECTIONS: Matching Match each item in Column A with the items in Column B. Write the correct letters in the blanks. *(10 points each)*

Column A	Column B
____ 1. official count of the population	A. canal
____ 2. toll roads	B. Robert Fulton
____ 3. designed the *Clermont*	C. turnpikes
____ 4. planned the Erie Canal	D. census
____ 5. artificial waterway	E. De Witt Clinton

DIRECTIONS: Multiple Choice In the blank at the left, write the letter of the choice that best completes the statement or answers the question. *(10 points each)*

____ 6. Named after a cloth, these roads consisted of logs laid side by side.
A. ridge roads C. cotton roads
B. corduroy roads D. silk roads

____ 7. This road connected Ohio with the East.
A. Vandalia Road C. Ohio Road
B. East-West Road D. National Road

____ 8. Pioneers tended to settle with others from their home communities along
A. canals. C. great rivers.
B. toll roads. D. state borders.

____ 9. These contributed to the growth of river cities such as Cincinnati.
A. Conestoga wagons C. canals
B. new roads D. steamboats

____ 10. The first wave of western settlement began in the
A. 1760s. C. 1880s.
B. 1790s. D. 1890s.

Section Quizzes ★ 38 ★ *The American Journey*

Canals, 1820-1850

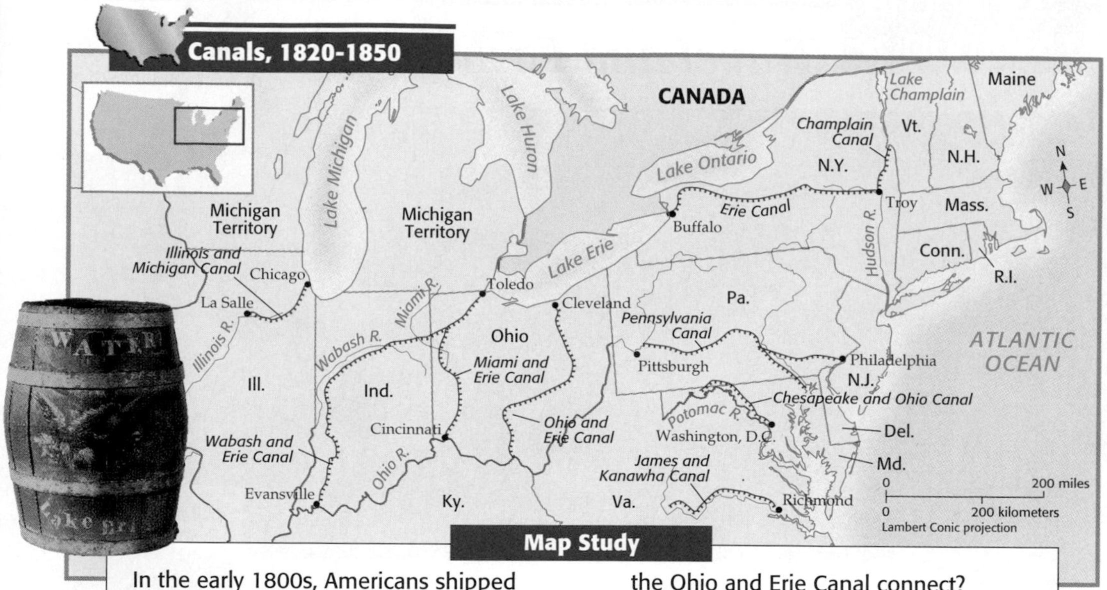

Map Study

In the early 1800s, Americans shipped many goods along canals.

1. **Location** What two water bodies did the Ohio and Erie Canal connect?
2. **Analyzing Information** About how many miles long was the Erie Canal?

Building the Erie Canal

Thousands of laborers, many of them Irish immigrants, worked on the construction of the 363-mile **Erie Canal.** Along the canal they built a series of **locks**—separate compartments where water levels were raised or lowered. Locks provided a way to raise and lower boats where canal levels changed significantly. Many people made fun of the canal, calling it Clinton's Ditch.

In 1825 Clinton boarded a barge in Buffalo and journeyed on the canal to New York City. Officials poured water from Lake Erie into the Atlantic Ocean. The East and Midwest were joined.

In its early years, the canal did not allow steamboats because their powerful engines could damage the earthen embankments along the canal. Instead teams of mules or horses hauled the boats and barges. A 2-horse team pulled a 100-ton barge about 24 miles in one day—astonishingly fast compared to travel by wagon. In the 1840s the canal banks were reinforced to accommodate steam tugboats pulling barges.

The success of the Erie Canal led to an explosion in canal building. By 1840 the United States had more than 3,300 miles of canals, 20 times more than it had in 1817. Canals lowered the cost of shipping goods. They brought prosperity to the towns along their routes. Perhaps most important, they helped unite the growing country.

Western Settlement

Americans moved westward in waves. The first wave began before the 1790s and led to the admission of four new states between 1791 and 1803—Vermont, Kentucky, Tennessee, and Ohio. During the next 13 years, only one new state, Louisiana, entered the Union. The westward movement slowed during the War of 1812. After the war, however, a second wave of westward growth began. Between 1816 and 1821, five new western states were created—Indiana, Illinois, Mississippi, Alabama, and Missouri.

The new states reflected the dramatic population growth of the region west of the Appalachians. Ohio, for example, had only 45,000 Americans in 1800. By 1820 the population had soared to 581,000.

MAKING CONNECTIONS ACTIVITY

Cultural Life Several colorful characters lived in the late 1700s and early 1800s; among them were John Chapman (Johnny Appleseed), Davy Crockett, Mike Fink, and Jean Lafitte. Have students, working in small groups, choose a character, read about him or her, and decide on a way to present their findings to the class–skits, drawings, written reports, or a combination of forms. Groups should include factual information and tall tales in their presentations. Tasks should be divided according to the skills of group members. **L1, ELL**

Building Communities

Pioneers usually migrated as families rather than as individuals. They tended to settle in communities along the great rivers, such as the Ohio and the Mississippi, so that they could ship their crops to market. The expansion of canals, which crisscrossed the land in the 1820s and 1830s, allowed people to live farther away from the rivers.

People also tended to settle with others from their home communities. Indiana, for example, was settled mainly by Southerners moving north from Kentucky and Tennessee, while Michigan's pioneers came mostly from New England.

Life in the West

Western families often gathered together for social events. Men took part in sports such as wrestling and pole jumping, a sport similar to present-day pole vaulting. Women met for quilting and sewing parties. Both men and women participated in cornhuskings—gatherings where farm families shared the work of stripping the husks from ears of corn.

Life in the West did not include the conveniences of Eastern town life. The pioneers, however, had not come west to be pampered. They wanted to make a new life for themselves and their families. America's population continued to travel westward in the years ahead.

Linking PAST & PRESENT

"Modern" Medicine

In the mid-1800s, a visit to the doctor's office was viewed with suspicion. Faced with "cures" that were often fatal, people started using patent medicines—those they could buy in stores. One popular remedy, Snake Oil, was a mixture of wintergreen and white gasoline.

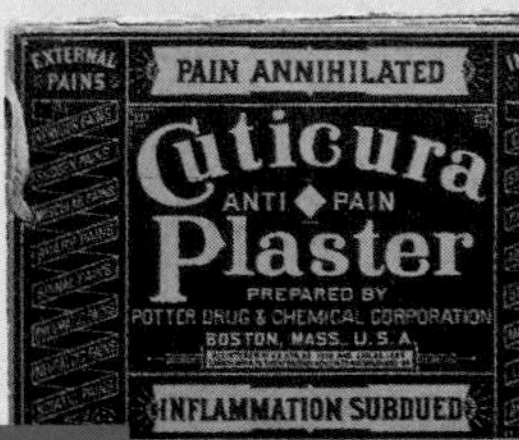

Past

Patent medicine

Today artificial hearts, cameras that move through veins, and other products have greatly improved Americans' health. **Why did settlers turn to patent medicines to cure their ills?**

Present

Genetic engineer

Section 2 Review

Checking for Understanding

1. ***Identify*** National Road, Robert Fulton, *Clermont,* De Witt Clinton, Erie Canal.
2. ***Define*** census, turnpike, canal, lock.
3. ***Describe*** the improvements in transportation in the early 1800s.

Reviewing Themes

4. **Science and Technology** How did steam-powered boats improve river travel?

Critical Thinking

5. **Drawing Conclusions** How did better transportation affect westward expansion?

Activity

Making a Chart Create a chart that lists the major means of transportation that helped the United States grow. Include the advantages and disadvantages of each type of transportation.

Section 2 Review Answers

1. National Road, 314; Robert Fulton, 315; *Clermont,* 315; DeWitt Clinton, 315; Erie Canal, 316
2. The words are defined in the Glossary.
3. steamboat, turnpike, National Road, canals
4. increased speed of transporting goods and passengers; shipping goods was cheaper; the more powerful steamboats could withstand currents and winds
5. shortened the time and made travel more comfortable, which made western travel more attractive

Activity Charts should include steamboat, turnpikes, corduroy roads, the National Road, and canals. At least one advantage and one disadvantage should be listed under each type of transportation.

CHAPTER 10

Section 2, 313–317

Linking PAST & PRESENT

"Modern" Medicine Alternative remedies today are acupuncture, herbalism, and chiropractic healing. **Answer:** *because doctors' "remedies" were often fatal*

Reteaching Activity 10–2

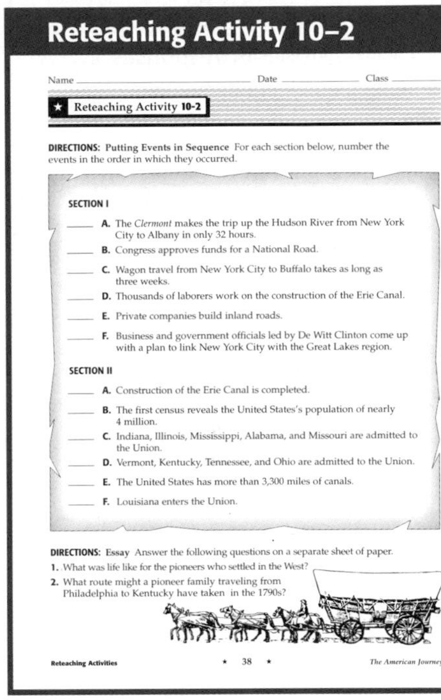

Name ______ Date ______ Class ______

Reteaching Activity **10-2**

DIRECTIONS: Putting Events in Sequence For each section below, number the events in the order in which they occurred.

SECTION I

____ **A.** The *Clermont* makes the trip up the Hudson River from New York City to Albany in only 32 hours.
____ **B.** Congress approves funds for a National Road.
____ **C.** Wagon travel from New York City to Buffalo takes as long as three weeks.
____ **D.** Thousands of laborers work on the construction of the Erie Canal.
____ **E.** Private companies build inland roads.
____ **F.** Business and government officials led by De Witt Clinton come up with a plan to link New York City with the Great Lakes region.

SECTION II

____ **A.** Construction of the Erie Canal is completed.
____ **B.** The first census reveals the United States's population of nearly 4 million.
____ **C.** Indiana, Illinois, Mississippi, Alabama, and Missouri are admitted to the Union.
____ **D.** Vermont, Kentucky, Tennessee, and Ohio are admitted to the Union.
____ **E.** The United States has more than 3,300 miles of canals.
____ **F.** Louisiana enters the Union.

DIRECTIONS: Essay Answer the following questions on a separate sheet of paper.

1. What was life like for the pioneers who settled in the West?
2. What route might a pioneer family traveling from Philadelphia to Kentucky have taken in the 1790s?

Reteaching Activities ★ 38 ★ *The American Journey*

Enrichment Activity 10–2

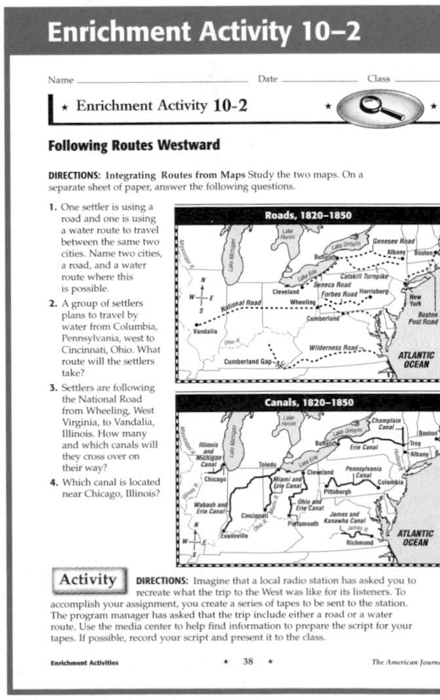

Name ______ Date ______ Class ______

Enrichment Activity **10-2**

Following Routes Westward

DIRECTIONS: Integrating Routes from Maps Study the two maps. On a separate sheet of paper, answer the following questions.

1. One settler is using a road and one is using a water route to travel between the same two cities. Name two cities, a road, and a water route where this is possible.
2. A group of settlers plans to travel by water from Columbia, Pennsylvania, west to Cincinnati, Ohio. What route will the settlers take?
3. Settlers are following the National Road from Wheeling, West Virginia, to Vandalia, Illinois. How many and which canals will they cross over on their way?
4. Which canal is located near Chicago, Illinois?

Activity **DIRECTIONS:** Imagine that a local radio station has asked you to recreate what the trip to the West was like for its listeners. To accomplish your assignment, you create a series of tapes to be sent to the station. The program manager has asked that the trip include either a road or a water route. Use the media center to help find information to prepare the script for your tapes. If possible, record your script and present it to the class.

Enrichment Activities ★ 38 ★ *The American Journey*

4 CLOSE

Ask students to explain why it could be said that Fulton "reversed the rivers."

1 FOCUS

BELLRINGER
Motivational Activity

Before taking roll at the beginning of the class period, project Section Focus Transparency 10–3 and have students answer the questions. Discuss students' responses.

This activity is also available as a blackline master.

Section Focus Transparency 10–3

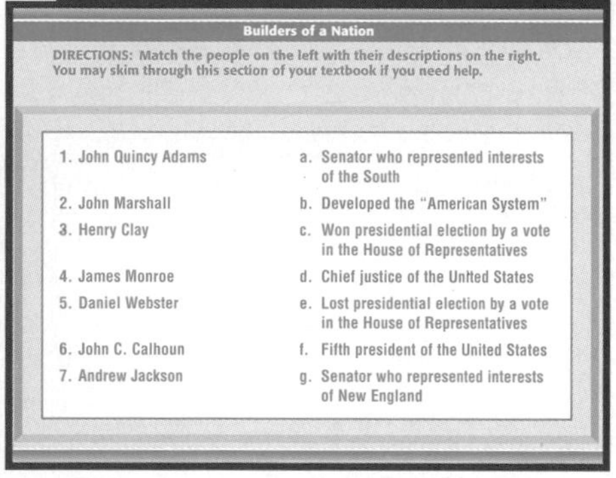

Builders of a Nation

DIRECTIONS: Match the people on the left with their descriptions on the right. You may skim through this section of your textbook if you need help.

1. John Quincy Adams	a. Senator who represented interests of the South
2. John Marshall	b. Developed the "American System"
3. Henry Clay	c. Won presidential election by a vote in the House of Representatives
4. James Monroe	d. Chief justice of the United States
5. Daniel Webster	e. Lost presidential election by a vote in the House of Representatives
6. John C. Calhoun	f. Fifth president of the United States
7. Andrew Jackson	g. Senator who represented interests of New England

Vocabulary Precheck

Ask students to guess the meaning of *internal improvements.* Then have them check their accuracy by finding the definition in the Glossary.

Use the **Vocabulary PuzzleMaker** to create crossword and word search puzzles.

Section Theme
Individual Action

Following the Era of Good Feelings, regional differences as represented by Senators John C. Calhoun, Daniel Webster, and Henry Clay came to the surface, ending the period of national harmony.

Activity After reading the section, have students make a list of how Henry Clay's work on the Compromise preserved a balance between North and South. *(allowed Maine into Union as a free state and Missouri as a slave state, thus keeping number of slave and free states equal; fixed 36°30′ as dividing line between future slave states and free states)*

1815 — 1820 — 1825

1816 James Monroe is elected president

1819 *McCulloch* v. *Maryland* strengthens national government

1820 Missouri Compromise passed

1824 Henry Clay promotes the American System

Section 3

Unity and Sectionalism

READ TO DISCOVER . . .

- why the period of James Monroe's presidency was called the Era of Good Feelings.
- why sectional differences intensified in the 1820s.
- what roles Daniel Webster, John Calhoun, and Henry Clay played in 1820s politics.

TERMS TO LEARN

sectionalism
internal improvements
American System

The Storyteller

Following the War of 1812, Americans felt buoyed by a new sense of pride and faith in the United States. In his Inaugural Address on March 4, 1817, President James Monroe expressed this feeling of proud nationalism: "If we look to the history of other nations, ancient or modern, we find no example of a growth so rapid, so gigantic, of a people so prosperous and happy."

James Monroe pocket watch

The absence of major political divisions after the War of 1812 helped forge a sense of national unity. In the 1816 presidential election, Republican candidate **James Monroe** faced almost no opposition. The Federalists, weakened by doubts of their loyalty during the War of 1812, barely existed as a national party. Monroe won the election by an overwhelming margin.

The Era of Good Feelings

Although the Federalist Party had almost disappeared, many of its programs gained support. Republican president James Madison, Monroe's predecessor, had called for tariffs to protect new industries, for a national bank, and for some national development programs.

Political differences seemed to fade away, causing a Boston newspaper to call these years the **Era of Good Feelings.** The president himself symbolized these good feelings.

Eyewitness to HISTORY

Monroe Tours the Nation

Monroe had been involved in national politics since the American Revolution. He wore breeches and powdered wigs—dress no longer in fashion. With his sense of dignity, Monroe represented a united America free of political strife.

Early in his presidency, Monroe toured the nation. No president since George Washington

SECTION RESOURCES

Reproducible Masters
- Reproducible Lesson Plan 10–3
- Guided Reading Activity 10–3
- Section Quiz 10–3
- Reteaching Activity 10–3
- Enrichment Activity 10–3

Transparencies
- Section Focus Transparency 10–3

Multimedia
- Vocabulary PuzzleMaker
- Chapter Challenger Interactive Review Software
- Testmaker
- The Presidents: A Picture History of Our Nation
- Facts On File: Landmark Documents in American History

had done this. He paid his own expenses and tried to travel without an official escort. Everywhere Monroe went, local officials greeted him and celebrated his visit.

Monroe arrived in Boston, the former Federalist stronghold, in the summer of 1817. About 40,000 well-wishers cheered him, and John Adams, the second president, invited Monroe to his home. Abigail Adams commended the new president's "unassuming manner."

Monroe did not think the demonstrations were meant for him personally. He wrote Madison that they revealed a "desire in the body of the people to show their attachment to the union."

Two years later Monroe continued his tour, traveling as far south as Savannah and as far west as Detroit. In 1820 President Monroe won reelection, winning all but one electoral vote.

Sectionalism Grows

The Era of Good Feelings did not last very long. Regional differences came to the surface, ending the period of national harmony.

Most Americans felt a strong allegiance to the region where they lived. They thought of themselves as Westerners or Southerners or Northerners. This **sectionalism,** or loyalty to their region, became more intense as differences arose over national policies.

The conflict over slavery, for example, always simmered beneath the surface. Most Southerners believed in the necessity and value of slavery. Northerners increasingly opposed it. To protect slavery, Southerners stressed the importance of states' rights, defending the powers of the states over the power of the federal government.

Footnotes to History

The White House Because the British had burned the president's mansion during the War of 1812, the sooty exterior had been painted white. People began calling the building "the White House," although that name did not become official until 1901.

America's FLAGS

Flag of 1818 By 1818 the number of states had reached 20. In April President Monroe signed a bill that set the basic design of the flag. Each newly admitted state added a star to the field of blue. The addition of a new star took place on the Fourth of July following the state's year of entry.

The Great Star Flag Congress did not state how the stars should be arranged, so flagmakers used various designs. The Great Star Flag placed the stars in the form of a five-pointed star.

The different regions also disagreed on the need for tariffs, a national bank, and internal improvements. **Internal improvements** were federal, state, and privately funded projects, such as canals and roads, to develop the nation's transportation system. Three powerful voices emerged in Congress in the early 1800s as spokespersons for their regions: John C. Calhoun, Daniel Webster, and Henry Clay.

John C. Calhoun

John C. Calhoun, a planter from South Carolina, was one of the War Hawks who had called for war with Great Britain in 1812. Calhoun remained a nationalist for some time after the war. He favored support for internal improvements and developing industries and backed a national bank. At the time, he believed these programs would benefit the South.

In the 1820s, however, Calhoun's views started to change, and he emerged as one of the

COOPERATIVE LEARNING ACTIVITY

Presenting the Great Statesmen Have students work in small groups and study Calhoun, Webster, or Clay. Each group should write a short biography of its statesman, write a description of an important event in his life or make a drawing of it, and recite aloud a portion of one of his speeches. (You may want to refer students to the Facts On File CD-ROM "Landmark Documents in American History" in order to locate documents associated with these individuals.) Assign the various tasks according to the skills of group members.

2 TEACH

L1 Writing Questions Have students each write five questions that can be answered with information in the section. Then have students work in pairs and use their questions to quiz each other on content knowledge.

Guided Reading Activity 10–3

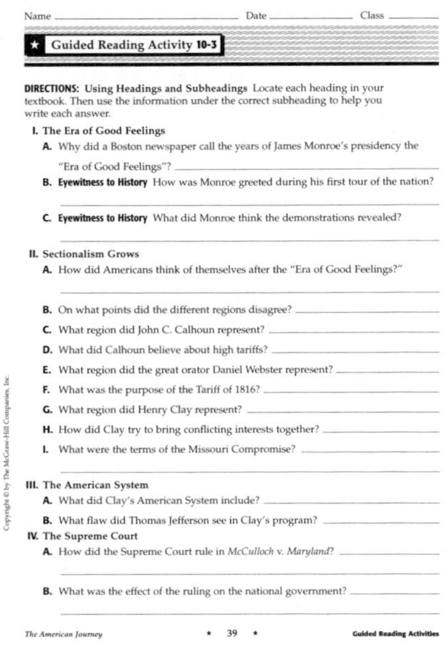
Name ______ Date ______ Class ______

Guided Reading Activity 10-3

DIRECTIONS: Using Headings and Subheadings Locate each heading in your textbook. Then use the information under the correct subheading to help you write each answer.

I. The Era of Good Feelings
- **A.** Why did a Boston newspaper call the years of James Monroe's presidency the "Era of Good Feelings"? ______
- **B. Eyewitness to History** How was Monroe greeted during his first tour of the nation? ______
- **C. Eyewitness to History** What did Monroe think the demonstrations revealed? ______

II. Sectionalism Grows
- **A.** How did Americans think of themselves after the "Era of Good Feelings?" ______
- **B.** On what points did the different regions disagree? ______
- **C.** What region did John C. Calhoun represent? ______
- **D.** What did Calhoun believe about high tariffs? ______
- **E.** What region did the great orator Daniel Webster represent? ______
- **F.** What was the purpose of the Tariff of 1816? ______
- **G.** What region did Henry Clay represent? ______
- **H.** How did Clay try to bring conflicting interests together? ______
- **I.** What were the terms of the Missouri Compromise? ______

III. The American System
- **A.** What did Clay's American System include? ______
- **B.** What flaw did Thomas Jefferson see in Clay's program? ______

IV. The Supreme Court
- **A.** How did the Supreme Court rule in *McCulloch* v. *Maryland*? ______
- **B.** What was the effect of the ruling on the national government? ______

The American Journey ★ 39 ★ **Guided Reading Activities**

Who? What? Where? When?

Henry Clay first won election to the House of Representatives in 1811. When the session began, the other representatives disregarded his lack of experience and elected him Speaker of the House.

NATIONAL GEOGRAPHIC SOCIETY

CD-ROM
The Presidents: A Picture History of Our Nation

Have students learn more about James Monroe's presidency by choosing him from the main menu.

CHAPTER 10
Section 3, 318–321

Map Study

Answers
1. slave state
2. free state

Map Skills Practice

Reading a Map Which parallel did the Missouri Compromise Line follow? *(36°30′N)*

Facts On File

CD-ROM
Landmark Documents in American History

Title: *McCulloch* v. *Maryland, 1819*
Ask students to think about the importance of this Supreme Court decision as they view the document on-screen.

3 ASSESS

Assign Section 3 Review as homework or as an in-class activity.

Use **Chapter Challenger Interactive Review Software** to review Section 3.

Section Quiz 10–3

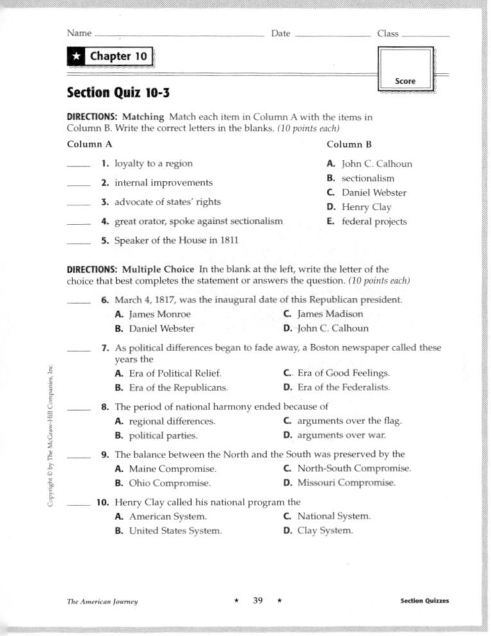
Name ______ Date ______ Class ______

Chapter 10

Score

Section Quiz 10-3

DIRECTIONS: Matching Match each item in Column A with the items in Column B. Write the correct letters in the blanks. *(10 points each)*

Column A	Column B
____ **1.** loyalty to a region	**A.** John C. Calhoun
____ **2.** internal improvements	**B.** sectionalism
____ **3.** advocate of states' rights	**C.** Daniel Webster
____ **4.** great orator, spoke against sectionalism	**D.** Henry Clay
____ **5.** Speaker of the House in 1811	**E.** federal projects

DIRECTIONS: Multiple Choice In the blank at the left, write the letter of the choice that best completes the statement or answers the question. *(10 points each)*

____ **6.** March 4, 1817, was the inaugural date of this Republican president.
A. James Monroe **C.** James Madison
B. Daniel Webster **D.** John C. Calhoun

____ **7.** As political differences began to fade away, a Boston newspaper called these years the
A. Era of Political Relief. **C.** Era of Good Feelings.
B. Era of the Republicans. **D.** Era of the Federalists.

____ **8.** The period of national harmony ended because of
A. regional differences. **C.** arguments over the flag.
B. political parties. **D.** arguments over war.

____ **9.** The balance between the North and the South was preserved by the
A. Maine Compromise. **C.** North-South Compromise.
B. Ohio Compromise. **D.** Missouri Compromise.

____ **10.** Henry Clay called his national program the
A. American System. **C.** National System.
B. United States System. **D.** Clay System.

The American Journey ★ 39 ★ **Section Quizzes**

The Missouri Compromise, 1820

Map Study

After 1820 all new states north of 36°30′N were to join as free states.

1. **Region** Did Missouri enter the Union as a free state or a slave state?
2. **Analyzing Information** Was Maine a slave state or a free state in 1820?

foremost advocates of states' rights. Calhoun became a strong opponent of nationalist programs such as high tariffs. He believed them to be against the agricultural and slavery interests of Southerners.

Daniel Webster

First elected to Congress in 1812 to represent his native New Hampshire, **Daniel Webster** later served in both the House and Senate representing Massachusetts. Webster began his political career as a supporter of free trade and the shipping interests of New England. In time, however, Webster came to favor the **Tariff of 1816**—which protected American industries from foreign competition—and other policies that he thought would strengthen the nation and help the North.

Webster gained fame as one of the greatest orators of his time. As a United States senator, he spoke eloquently in defense of the nation as a whole against sectional interests. In one memorable speech Webster declared: "Liberty and Union, now and forever, one and inseparable."

Henry Clay

Another leading War Hawk, **Henry Clay** of Kentucky, became Speaker of the House of Representatives in 1811 and a leader who represented the interests of the western states. He also served as a member of the delegation that negotiated the Treaty of Ghent ending the War of 1812. Above all, Henry Clay became known as the national leader who tried to resolve sectional disputes and bring conflicting interests together through compromise.

The Missouri Compromise

Sectional tension reached new heights in 1820 over the issue of admitting new states to the Union. The problem revolved around slavery. The South wanted **Missouri,** part of the Louisiana Purchase, admitted as a slave state. Northerners wanted Missouri to be free of slavery. The issue became the subject of debate throughout the country, exposing bitter regional divisions that would plague national politics for decades.

While Congress considered the Missouri question, Maine—still part of Massachusetts—also applied for statehood. The discussions about Missouri now broadened to include Maine.

Some observers feared for the future of the Union. Eventually Henry Clay helped work out a compromise that preserved the balance between North and South. The **Missouri Compromise,** reached in March 1820, provided for the admission of Missouri as a slave state and Maine as a free state. The agreement banned slavery in the remainder of the Louisiana Territory north of the 36°30′ parallel.

The American System

Though he was a spokesperson for the West, Henry Clay believed his policies would benefit *all* sections of the nation. In an 1824 speech, he called his program the American System. The American System included a protective tariff to stimulate the growth of the nation's industries; a program of internal improvements,

MULTIPLE LEARNING STYLES

Logical/Mathematical Although Congress had passed the Mint Act of 1792, foreign and state currencies continued to circulate. Henry Clay (and others after him) called for standardization to avoid mixed currency. Standardization, when it eventually took place, included many of the coins provided for in the Mint Act. Those were coins valued at \$10.00, \$5.00, \$2.50, \$1.00, 50¢, 25¢, 10¢, 5¢, 1¢, and ½¢. Note that our currency system is a decimal one, based on the dollar. Present the list of coins, expressed in words, and have students express each as a decimal. **L2**

especially the building of roads and canals, to stimulate trade; and a national bank to promote one currency throughout the nation and to lend money to build developing industries.

Clay believed that the three parts of his plan would work together. The tariff would protect American industries but would also provide the government with money to build roads and canals. Healthy businesses could use their profits to buy more agricultural goods from the South, then ship these goods northward along the nation's efficient new transportation system.

Henry Clay

Not everyone, however, saw Clay's program in such positive terms. Former president Jefferson believed the American System favored the wealthy manufacturing classes in New England. Many people in the South agreed with Jefferson. They saw no benefits to the South from the tariff or internal improvements.

In the end little of Clay's American System went into effect. Congress eventually adopted some internal improvements, though not on the scale Clay had hoped for. Congress had created the Second National Bank in 1816, but it remained an object of controversy.

The Supreme Court

★ The Supreme Court also became involved in sectional and states' rights issues at this time. The state of Maryland imposed a tax on the Baltimore branch of the Second Bank of the United States—a federal institution. The Bank refused to pay the state tax, and the case, ***McCulloch* v. *Maryland*,** reached the Court in 1819.

Speaking for the Court, Chief Justice **John Marshall** ruled that Maryland had no right to tax the Bank because it was a federal institution. He argued that the Constitution and the federal government received their authority directly from the people, not by way of the state governments. The Bank was a legal creation of the federal government because the Constitution gave Congress the power to issue and borrow money. The states therefore had no right to interfere with the Bank.

The Supreme Court's ruling strengthened the national government. It also contributed to the debate over sectional issues. People who supported states' rights believed the decision was a threat to individual liberties. Strong nationalists welcomed the decision's support for national power.

Section 3 Review

Checking for Understanding

1. ***Identify*** James Monroe, John C. Calhoun, Daniel Webster, Henry Clay, *McCulloch* v. *Maryland,* John Marshall.
2. ***Define*** sectionalism, internal improvements, American System.
3. ***Summarize*** the disagreement between the North and South that resulted in the Missouri Compromise.

Reviewing Themes

4. **Individual Action** What action did Daniel Webster take that shows he placed his concerns for the nation above his sectional interests?

Critical Thinking

5. **Analyzing Information** How did sectionalism destroy the Era of Good Feelings?

Activity

Creating a Flag Design a flag to represent either the North, South, or West during the early 1800s. Use photos, symbols, or mottoes that might have been popular with the people who lived in these regions.

Section 3 Review Answers

1. James Monroe, 318; John C. Calhoun, 319; Daniel Webster, 320; Henry Clay, 320; *McCulloch* v. *Maryland,* 321; John Marshall, 321
2. The words are defined in the Glossary.
3. The South wanted Missouri to be admitted to the Union as a slave state; the North wanted Missouri to be a free state.
4. He supported policies, such as the Tariff of 1816, that he thought would strengthen the United States as a whole, not just the North. He used his skills as an orator to defend the nation against sectional interests.
5. Disputes over national policies—such as tariffs, banks, and slavery—created major political divisions among the regions.

Activity Flags should have elements that make them unique to one of the regions.

Reteaching Activity 10–3

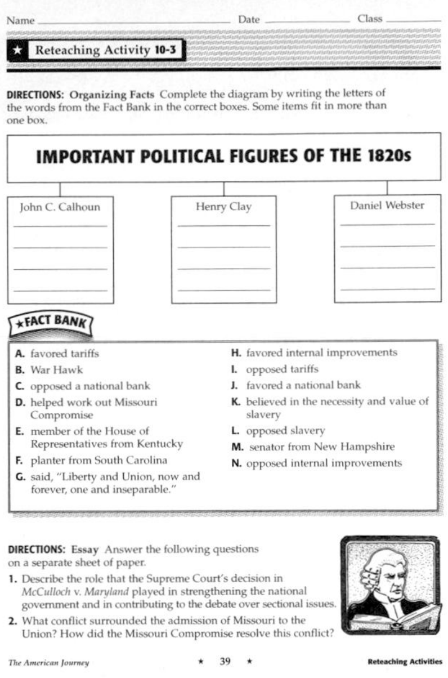

Name ________ Date ________ Class ________

★ Reteaching Activity 10-3

DIRECTIONS: Organizing Facts Complete the diagram by writing the letters of the words from the Fact Bank in the correct boxes. Some items fit in more than one box.

IMPORTANT POLITICAL FIGURES OF THE 1820s

John C. Calhoun | Henry Clay | Daniel Webster

★FACT BANK

- **A.** favored tariffs
- **B.** War Hawk
- **C.** opposed a national bank
- **D.** helped work out Missouri Compromise
- **E.** member of the House of Representatives from Kentucky
- **F.** planter from South Carolina
- **G.** said, "Liberty and Union, now and forever, one and inseparable."
- **H.** favored internal improvements
- **I.** opposed tariffs
- **J.** favored a national bank
- **K.** believed in the necessity and value of slavery
- **L.** opposed slavery
- **M.** senator from New Hampshire
- **N.** opposed internal improvements

DIRECTIONS: Essay Answer the following questions on a separate sheet of paper.

1. Describe the role that the Supreme Court's decision in *McCulloch* v. *Maryland* played in strengthening the national government and in contributing to the debate over sectional issues.
2. What conflict surrounded the admission of Missouri to the Union? How did the Missouri Compromise resolve this conflict?

The American Journey ★ 39 ★ **Reteaching Activities**

Enrichment Activity 10–3

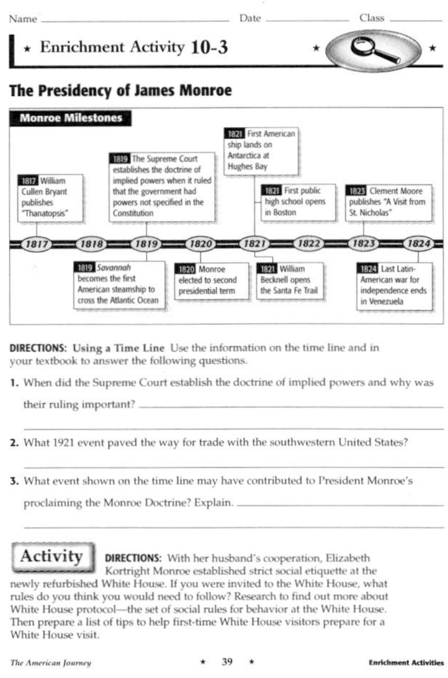

Name ________ Date ________ Class ________

★ Enrichment Activity 10-3

The Presidency of James Monroe

DIRECTIONS: Using a Time Line Use the information on the time line and in your textbook to answer the following questions.

1. When did the Supreme Court establish the doctrine of implied powers and why was their ruling important? ________
2. What 1921 event paved the way for trade with the southwestern United States? ________
3. What event shown on the time line may have contributed to President Monroe's proclaiming the Monroe Doctrine? Explain. ________

Activity **DIRECTIONS:** With her husband's cooperation, Elizabeth Kortright Monroe established strict social etiquette at the newly refurbished White House. If you were invited to the White House, what rules do you think you would need to follow? Research to find out more about White House protocol—the set of social rules for behavior at the White House. Then prepare a list of tips to help first-time White House visitors prepare for a White House visit.

The American Journey ★ 39 ★ **Enrichment Activities**

4 CLOSE

Discuss with students the following quote from Edmund Burke, an Irish member of Parliament: "All government—indeed, every human benefit and enjoyment, every virtue and prudent act—is founded on compromise and barter." *(Burke was calling for reconciliation with the colonies in 1775, but his words apply to many situations in history and to students' personal lives.)*

1 FOCUS

BELLRINGER
Motivational Activity

Before taking roll at the beginning of the class period, project Section Focus Transparency 10–4 and have students answer the questions. Discuss students' responses.

This activity is also available as a blackline master.

Section Focus Transparency 10–4

Latin American Independence

1. Who led enslaved Africans to independence in 1803?
2. What countries did José San Martín lead to freedom?
3. When did Mexico gain independence?
4. Who led Bolivia to freedom?

UPRISINGS IN SPANISH LATIN AMERICA

	REVOLUTIONARIES	LEADER(S)	RESULTS
Haiti	Enslaved Africans	François Toussaint-Louverture	Independence 1803
Mexico	Native Americans and mestizos	Miguel Hidalgo and José Morelos	Independence 1821
Northern S. America	Volunteer army	Simón Bolívar	Freed Venezuela, Panama, Bolivia, and Ecuador
Southern S. America	Creole army	José de San Martín	Freed Chile and Peru

Vocabulary Precheck

Ask students the meaning of the prefixes *dis-* and *de-* (reverse, undo, negate, and so on). Then have students speculate on the meaning of *disarmament* and *demilitarize.*

Use the **Vocabulary PuzzleMaker** to create crossword and word search puzzles.

Section Theme
Global Connections

Three agreements between 1817 and 1819 helped the United States settle disputes with Europeans.

Activity Have students find the names of those agreements and the European nation involved with each. *(Rush-Bagot Treaty, Britain; Convention of 1818, Britain; Adams-Onís Treaty, Spain)*

1815 — 1820 — 1825

1817 Rush-Bagot Treaty limits ships in Great Lakes

1818 Convention of 1818 fixes U.S.–Canada boundary

1819 Adams-Onís Treaty cedes Florida to the U.S.

1823 Monroe Doctrine prohibits European colonization

Section 4

The Monroe Doctrine

READ TO DISCOVER . . .

- how John Quincy Adams influenced American foreign policy.
- what effect the Monroe Doctrine had on foreign policy.

TERMS TO LEARN

disarmament
demilitarize
court-martial

The Storyteller

The War of 1812 heightened Americans' pride in their country. Abigail Adams, wife of John Adams, wrote from England to her sister back in Massachusetts: "Do you know that European birds have not half the melody of ours? Nor is their fruit half so sweet, nor their flowers half so fragrant, nor their manners half so pure, nor their people half so virtuous."

At the same time, many Americans realized that the United States needed peace with Britain to grow and develop. It had to put differences aside and establish a new relationship with the "Old World."

Brass eagle mounted on tortoiseshell box

In the years following the War of 1812, President Monroe and his secretary of state, John Quincy Adams, moved to resolve long-standing disputes with Great Britain and Spain.

Relations With Britain

In 1817, in the **Rush-Bagot Treaty,** the two nations agreed to set limits on the number of naval vessels each could have on the Great Lakes. The treaty provided for the disarmament—the removal of weapons—along an important part of the border between the United States and British **Canada.**

The second agreement with Britain, the **Convention of 1818,** set the official boundary between the United States and Canada at the 49th parallel. The convention created a secure and demilitarized border—one without armed forces. Through Adams's efforts, Americans also gained the right to settle in the **Oregon Country.**

Relations With Spain

Spain owned East Florida and also claimed West Florida. The United States contended that West Florida was part of the Louisiana Purchase. In 1810 and 1812, Americans simply added parts of West Florida to the states of Louisiana and Mississippi. Spain objected but took no action.

In April 1818, General **Andrew Jackson** invaded Spanish East **Florida,** seizing control of two Spanish forts. Jackson had been ordered to

SECTION RESOURCES

Reproducible Masters
- Reproducible Lesson Plan 10–4
- Guided Reading Activity 10–4
- Section Quiz 10–4
- Reteaching Activity 10–4
- Enrichment Activity 10–4

Transparencies
- Section Focus Transparency 10–4

Multimedia
- Vocabulary PuzzleMaker
- Chapter Challenger Interactive Review Software
- Testmaker

The United States in 1824

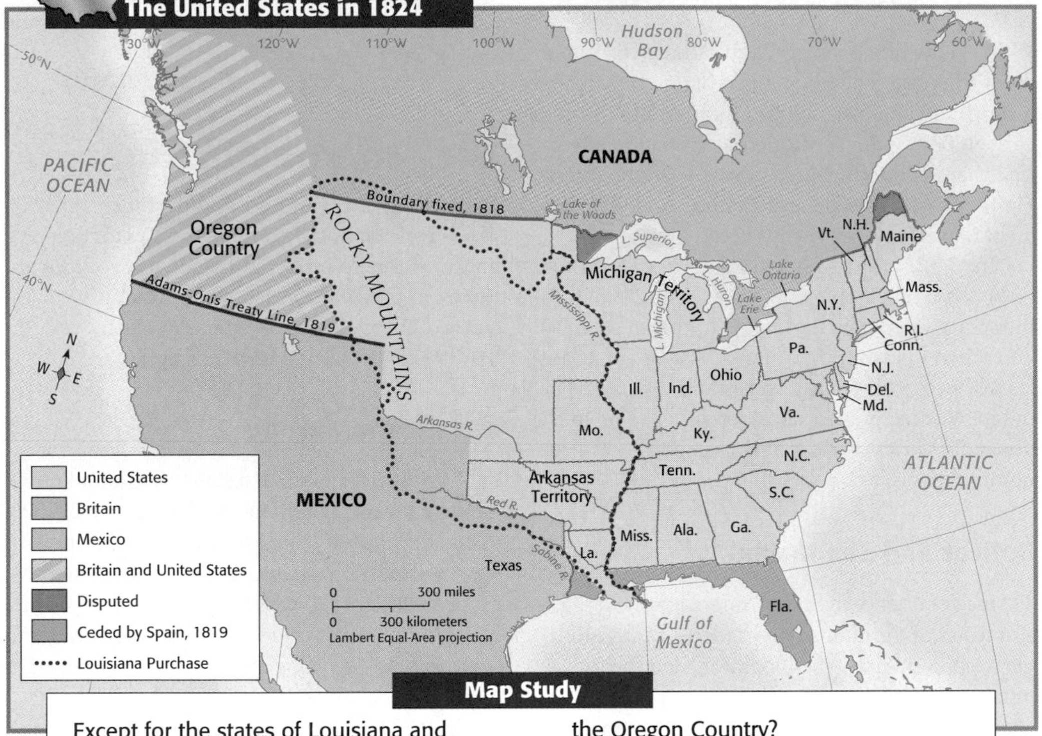

Map Study

Except for the states of Louisiana and Missouri, the Louisiana Purchase was still unorganized by 1824.

1. Location Which two countries occupied the Oregon Country?

2. Analyzing Information To what country did the territory of Texas belong in 1824?

stop Seminole raids on American territory from Florida. In capturing the Spanish forts, however, Jackson went beyond his instructions.

Luis de Onís, the Spanish minister to the United States, protested forcefully and demanded the punishment of Jackson and his officers. Secretary of War Calhoun said that Jackson should be court-martialed—tried by a military court—for overstepping instructions. Secretary of State John Quincy Adams disagreed.

Geography

Adams-Onís Treaty

Although Secretary of State Adams had not authorized Jackson's raid, he did nothing to stop it. Adams guessed that the Spanish did not want war and that they might be ready to settle the Florida dispute. He was right. For the Spanish the raid had demonstrated the military strength of the United States.

Already troubled by rebellions in **Mexico** and South America, Spain signed the **Adams-Onís Treaty** in 1819. Spain gave East Florida to the United States and abandoned all claims to West Florida. In return the United States gave up its claims to Spanish Texas and took over responsibility for paying the $5 million that American citizens claimed Spain owed them for damages.

The two countries also agreed on a border between the United States and Spanish possessions in the West. The border extended northwest from the Gulf of Mexico to the 42nd parallel and then west to the Pacific, giving the United States a large piece of territory in the Pacific Northwest. America had become a transcontinental power.

Cooperative Learning Activity

Presenting Heroes of Independence The independence movement in Latin America had many colorful heroes and dramatic events. Have students work in small groups to present skits or murals of such an event. Figures to investigate in addition to those in the text include Agustín de Iturbide and José Maria Morelos of Mexico, Francisco Miranda and José Antonio Páez of Venezuela, and Antonio José de Sucre, a colleague of Bolívar. Tasks—writing, researching, acting, drawing—should be divided according to the skills of group members.

CHAPTER 10

Section 4, 322–324

2 TEACH

L1 Making Summaries Have students include these terms in a brief summary of the section: *disarmament, borders, Florida, transcontinental power, independence,* and *colonization.*

Map Study

Answers

1. Britain, United States
2. Mexico

Guided Reading Activity 10–4

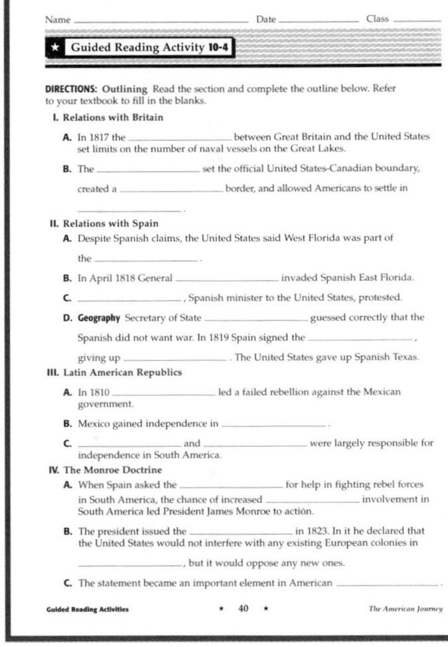
Name ______ Date ______ Class ______

Guided Reading Activity 10-4

DIRECTIONS: Outlining Read the section and complete the outline below. Refer to your textbook to fill in the blanks.

I. Relations with Britain

A. In 1817 the ______ between Great Britain and the United States set limits on the number of naval vessels on the Great Lakes.

B. The ______ set the official United States-Canadian boundary, created a ______ border, and allowed Americans to settle in ______.

II. Relations with Spain

A. Despite Spanish claims, the United States said West Florida was part of the ______.

B. In April 1818 General ______ invaded Spanish East Florida.

C. ______, Spanish minister to the United States, protested.

D. Geography Secretary of State ______ guessed correctly that the Spanish did not want war. In 1819 Spain signed the ______, giving up ______. The United States gave up Spanish Texas.

III. Latin American Republics

A. In 1810 ______ led a failed rebellion against the Mexican government.

B. Mexico gained independence in ______.

C. ______ and ______ were largely responsible for independence in South America.

IV. The Monroe Doctrine

A. When Spain asked the ______ for help in fighting rebel forces in South America, the chance of increased ______ involvement in South America led President James Monroe to action.

B. The president issued the ______ in 1823. In it he declared that the United States would not interfere with any existing European colonies in ______, but it would oppose any new ones.

C. The statement became an important element in American ______.

Guided Reading Activities ★ 40 ★ *The American Journey*

3 ASSESS

Assign Section 4 Review as homework or as an in-class activity.

Use **Chapter Challenger Interactive Review Software** to review Section 4.

CHAPTER 10
Section 4, 322–324

Section Quiz 10–4

Name ______ Date ______ Class ______

★ Chapter 10

Score

Section Quiz 10-4

DIRECTIONS: Matching Match each item in Column A with the items in Column B. Write the correct letters in the blanks. *(10 points each)*

Column A	Column B
____ 1. liberated Chile and Peru	A. disarmament
____ 2. removal of weapons	B. Adams-Onís Treaty
____ 3. tried by a military court	C. Simón Bolívar
____ 4. agreement with Spain	D. José de San Martín
____ 5. "the Liberator"	E. court-martialed

DIRECTIONS: Multiple Choice In the blank at the left, write the letter of the choice that best completes the statement or answers the question. *(10 points each)*

____ 6. James Monroe's able secretary of state was
A. Andrew Jackson. C. John Quincy Adams.
B. Miguel Hidalgo. D. Abigail Adams.

____ 7. This agreement set limits on the number of naval vessels Great Britain and the United States could have on the Great Lakes.
A. Convention of 1818 C. Monroe Doctrine
B. Adams-Onís Treaty D. Rush-Bagot Treaty

____ 8. This agreement set the official boundary between the United States and Canada.
A. Convention of 1818 C. Monroe Doctrine
B. Adams-Onís Treaty D. Rush-Bagot Treaty

Reteaching Activity 10–4

Name ______ Date ______ Class ______

★ Reteaching Activity 10-4

DIRECTIONS: Organizing Facts Following the War of 1812, the United States settled many outstanding territorial issues with Great Britain and Spain. Complete the diagram by writing the letters of the words from the Fact Bank in the correct boxes.

Territorial Disputes

Great Britain	Spain

★FACT BANK

A. The United States gives up its claims in Texas.
B. border set at the 49th parallel
C. Rush-Bagot Treaty limits the number of naval vessels on the Great Lakes.
D. border runs northwest from the Gulf
E. disarmament along the northern border
F. Andrew Jackson seizes two forts in Florida.
G. East Florida becomes United States territory.

Enrichment Activity 10–4

Name ______ Date ______ Class ______

★ Enrichment Activity 10-4

Independence in South America

Study the map and chart that provide information about the independence of South American countries.

From Spanish Colonies to Independent Countries

Spanish Colony	Independent Country	Date of Independence
New Granada	Colombia Ecuador Venezuela	1830 1830 1830
Peru	Chile Peru	1818 1824
Río de la Plata	Argentina Paraguay Bolivia Uruguay	1810 1811 1825 1828

DIRECTIONS: Integrating Information Follow the directions below.

1. Color the countries in blue that made up the colony known as Río de la Plata.
2. Color in red the South American countries that were never under Spanish rule.
3. Circle the name of the country that is still held by France.
4. What countries made up New Granada? ______
5. What colony eventually became Chile ______?

4 CLOSE

Have students explain why it was in the nation's best interest to make peace with European powers.

Latin American Republics

While the Spanish were settling territorial disputes with the United States, they faced a series of challenges within their empire. In the early 1800s, Spain controlled a vast colonial empire that included what is now the southwestern United States, Mexico and Central America, and all of South America except Brazil.

In 1810 a priest, Miguel Hidalgo (ee• DAHL• goh), led a rebellion against the Spanish government of Mexico. Hidalgo called for racial equality and the redistribution of land. The Spanish defeated the revolutionary forces and executed Hidalgo. Mexico gained its independence in 1821, but independence did not bring social and economic change.

Bolívar and San Martín

Independence in South America came largely as a result of the efforts of two men—**Simón Bolívar,** also known as "the Liberator," led the movement that won freedom for the present-day countries of Venezuela, Colombia, Panama, Bolivia, and Ecuador. **José de San Martín** successfully achieved independence for Chile and Peru. By 1824 the revolutionaries' military victory was complete, and most of South America had liberated itself from Spain. Portugal's large colony of Brazil gained its independence peacefully in 1822. Spain's empire in the Americas had shrunk to Cuba, Puerto Rico, and a few other islands in the Caribbean.

The Monroe Doctrine

In 1822 Spain had asked France, Austria, Russia, and Prussia—the Quadruple Alliance—for help in its fight against revolutionary forces in South America. The possibility of increased European involvement in North America led President Monroe to take action.

A Notice to Europe

The president issued a statement, later known as the **Monroe Doctrine,** on December 2, 1823. While the United States would not interfere with any existing European colonies in the Americas, Monroe declared, it would oppose any new ones. North and South America "are henceforth not to be considered as subjects for future colonization by any European powers."

In 1823 the United States did not have the military power to enforce the Monroe Doctrine. The Monroe Doctrine nevertheless became an important element in American foreign policy and has remained so for more than 170 years. It was another example of America flexing its muscles and expressing its nationalistic feelings.

Section 4 Review

Checking for Understanding

1. ***Identify*** Convention of 1818, Andrew Jackson, Adams-Onís Treaty, Monroe Doctrine.
2. ***Define*** disarmament, demilitarize, court-martial.
3. ***Explain*** how Adams helped solve border disputes with Canada.

Reviewing Themes

4. **Global Connections** What warning was issued in the Monroe Doctrine?

Critical Thinking

5. **Synthesizing Information** Explain the following statement: The Monroe Doctrine was a product of United States nationalism.

Activity

Writing an Editorial Write a newspaper editorial supporting or rejecting the ideas of the Monroe Doctrine.

Section 4 Review Answers

1. Convention of 1818, 322; Andrew Jackson, 322; Adams-Onís Treaty, 323; Monroe Doctrine, 324
2. The words are defined in the Glossary.
3. Secretary of State Adams helped develop Rush-Bagot Treaty limiting the number of naval vessels each country could have on the Great Lakes; Convention of 1818 set boundary at the 49th parallel and created a demilitarized border; Americans also gained the right to settle in the Oregon area.
4. that the United States would oppose any new European colonies in the Americas
5. By opposing further European colonization, the United States sent the message that it was a strong, independent nation.

Activity Students' editorials should be based on information in the chapter.

Social Studies
SKILL BUILDER

Reading a Diagram

Suppose you buy a new bicycle and discover that you must assemble the parts before you can ride it. A *diagram,* or drawing that shows how the parts fit together, would make this job much easier.

Learning the Skill

To read a diagram, follow these steps:

- Read the title or caption to find out what the diagram shows.
- Read all labels carefully to determine their meanings.
- Read the legend and identify symbols and colors used in the diagram.
- Look for numbers indicating a sequence of steps, or arrows showing movement.

Practicing the Skill

Analyze the diagram of the *Clermont,* then answer the following questions.

1. How long did the *Clermont*'s round-trip between New York City and Albany take?
2. What type of energy was used to power this ship?

Applying the Skill

Making a Diagram Draw a diagram showing either how to make macaroni and cheese or how to tie a pair of shoes. Use clear drawings and labels in your diagram.

The *Clermont* Steamboat

On August 17, 1807, the Clermont *steamed up the Hudson River from New York City on its way to Albany, New York. It returned to New York City 62 hours later—a commercial success!*

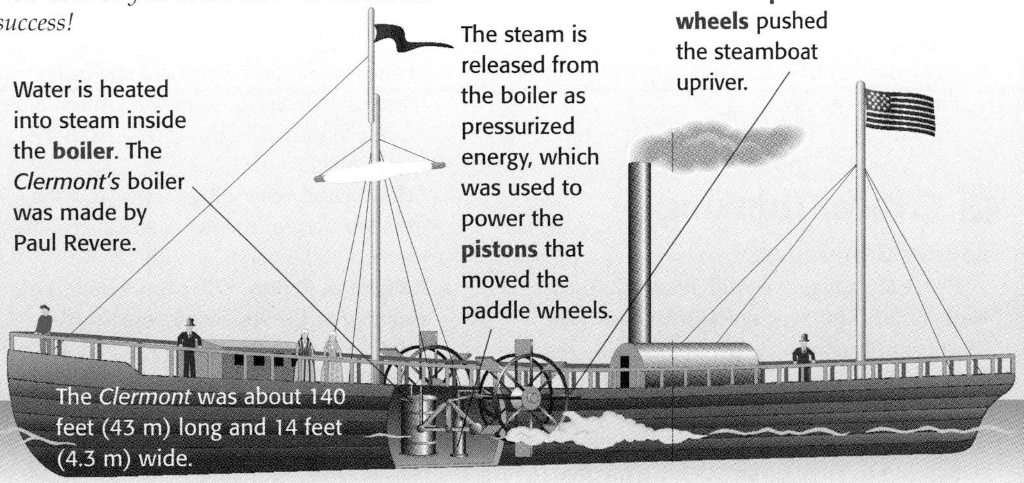

Answers to Practicing the Skill

1. 62 hours
2. steam (pressurized energy)

Applying the Skill Students will draw and label a diagram of either how to make macaroni and cheese or how to tie a pair of shoes.

Social Studies
SKILL BUILDER

TEACH

Reading a Diagram

This skill teaches students what to look for in interpreting a diagram. After they have answered the questions in **Practicing the Skill**, challenge students to think of another question that could be asked about the diagram. *(Possible responses: What was the* Clermont's *width and length? Who made the* Clermont's *boiler? What was the function of the boiler?)*

Additional Practice

Chapter Skills Activity 10

you don't say...

Diagram comes to us from the Latin *diagramma,* which came from the Greek *diagraphein* (to mark out), from *dia-* (apart) and *graphein* (write).

GLENCOE TECHNOLOGY

VIDEODISC
MindJogger Videoquiz

Use MindJogger to review the Chapter 10 content.

Chapter 10
Disc 2, Side A

Also available in VHS.

Review and Activities

Reviewing Key Terms

On a sheet of paper, create a crossword puzzle using the following terms. Use the terms' definitions as your crossword clues.

Industrial Revolution
factory system
interchangeable parts
sectionalism
internal improvements
American System
disarmament
demilitarize
court-martial

Reviewing Key Facts

1. What problems faced cities as a result of their rapid growth during the Industrial Revolution?
2. How did canals boost the economy of the Great Lakes region?
3. Why did people who migrated to the West usually settle near rivers?
4. What had happened to the Federalist Party by the time James Monroe became president?
5. How did Andrew Jackson help to secure Florida from Spain?

Critical Thinking

Making Generalizations

Political and regional differences in the North, South, and West brought an end to the Era of Good Feelings.

1. How did the economy of the North and South differ?
2. Why do you think many people who were moving to the West might have favored states' rights?

Geography Activity

Study the map below and answer the questions that follow.

Acquisition of Florida, 1819

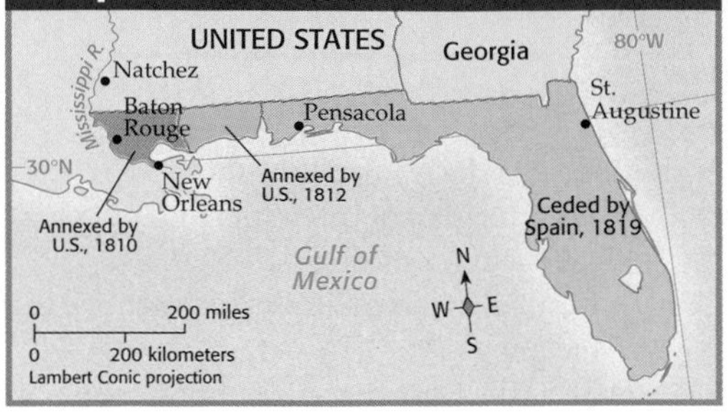

1. **Region** When was the largest portion of Florida acquired from Spain?
2. **Movement** In what direction did the United States acquire the various parts of Florida?
3. **Location** What body of water blocked further expansion of Florida to the west?

Reviewing Themes

1. **Economic Factors** How did the Industrial Revolution help to make the United States more economically independent in the early 1800s?
2. **Science and Technology** How did the development of roads boost the growth of the United States?
3. **Individual Action** What three men were considered the spokespersons for the North, South, and West regions in the early 1800s?
4. **Global Connections** Why did Secretary of State John Adams do nothing to stop General Andrew Jackson's invasion into Spanish East Florida in 1818?

Reviewing Key Terms

The key terms used in this activity can be found in the textbook glossary on pages A26–A35. Students' crossword puzzles will vary.

Reviewing Key Facts

1. overcrowding, unsanitary conditions, disease, threat of fire
2. linked the Great Lakes to the Atlantic coast and allowed people to ship their goods at a lower cost
3. to be able to ship their crops to market
4. It had almost disappeared. Republicans adopted many Federalist proposals such as federal support for tariffs and a national bank.
5. Although it was unauthorized, Jackson's raid on Spanish forts demonstrated the strength of the United States. Spain had rebellions to deal with in Mexico and South America, so it gave Florida to the United States peacefully.

Critical Thinking

1. The North was mostly industrial and the South was mostly agricultural.
2. Answers will vary but might include: people moving to the West were generally more independent and did not want a distant national government making decisions for them; one reason that people moved west was to gain the freedom to determine their own fates without government interference.

Geography Activity

1. 1819
2. west to east
3. Mississippi River

Time Line Activity

Create a time line on which you place the following events in chronological order.

- Spain gives Florida to the United States
- Erie Canal opens
- President Monroe issues Monroe Doctrine
- Samuel Slater starts textile mill using British technology
- Eli Whitney invents cotton gin
- Francis Lowell opens textile plant
- Congress charters the Second Bank of the United States

Skill Practice Activity

Reading a Diagram

Study the diagram of the textile mill on page 308. Use the diagram to answer the questions below.

1. What is the first step in the production of textiles?
2. At what stage does the thread become cloth?
3. What process turns the yarn into thread?
4. When would a cotton gin be necessary in this process?

Now choose one of the inventions mentioned in the chapter. Prepare a diagram that traces the development of that invention to a similar device in use today. For example, you might diagram the development of a modern cruise ship showing all the improvements made from start to finish. Use illustrations, short descriptions, and dates to diagram the improvements.

Technology Activity

Using the Internet Search the Internet for information about how to apply for a patent for an invention. Create a step-by-step list of directions describing the process.

Cooperative Activity

History and Language Arts Organize into a group to produce a song about traveling and living in the West during this time. Part of your group can write the lyrics. Another part can write the melody and decide on the instruments. Be sure to include a chorus, which is repeated between each stanza. Record the song and play it for the class.

The following song was popular after the Erie Canal opened. You may want to follow its style when your group writes its own song.

I've got a mule, her name is Sal,
Fifteen miles on the Erie Canal.
She's a good old worker and a good old pal,
Fifteen miles on the Erie Canal.
We've hauled some barges in our day,
Filled with lumber, coal, and hay,
And we know every inch of the way
From Albany to Buffalo.

CHORUS
Low bridge, everybody down!
Low bridge, for we're going through a town;
And you'll always know your neighbor,
You'll always know your pal,
If you ever navigated on the Erie Canal.

Portfolio Activity History Journal Review Section 2 of the chapter for information about what it was like to live in the West. Record your notes in your journal. Use your notes to write a postcard to a friend describing your social life.

CHAPTER 10
Review and Activities

Time Line Activity

Events should be placed in this order: Samuel Slater starts textile mill using British technology, Eli Whitney invents cotton gin, Francis Lowell opens textile plant, Congress charters the Second Bank of the United States, Spain gives Florida to the United States, President Monroe issues Monroe Doctrine, Erie Canal opens

Skill Practice Activity

1. clean cotton, turn loose cotton into yarn
2. weaving
3. spinning
4. cleaning stage

Students' diagrams should reflect their research.

Technology Activity

Students should gather information to prepare step-by-step directions on how to apply for a patent.

Cooperative Activity

Students' songs should show that they have researched the period.

Portfolio Activity Students' postcards should include information presented in Section 2 of the chapter.

Chapter Bonus Test Question

Ask: Which American inventor of the early 1800s invented a torpedo-firing submarine? *(Robert Fulton)*

Reviewing Themes

1. Since the United States could produce more of its own goods, it did not have to rely on other countries to provide them as they previously had.
2. made it easier for people to move west, allowed for better transportation of goods
3. North: Daniel Webster; South: John C. Calhoun; West: Henry Clay
4. He guessed correctly that the Spanish did not want war and were ready to settle the Florida dispute.

Unit 5 Resource Guide ★ ★ ★ ★ ★ ★ ★ ★ ★ ★ ★ ★ ★ ★ ★

These Glencoe resources may be used to teach, reteach, or enrich the concepts presented in this unit of study.

TEACHING TRANSPARENCIES

Map Transparency 5 with Overlays A, B, C, D

Cause-and-Effect Transparency 5

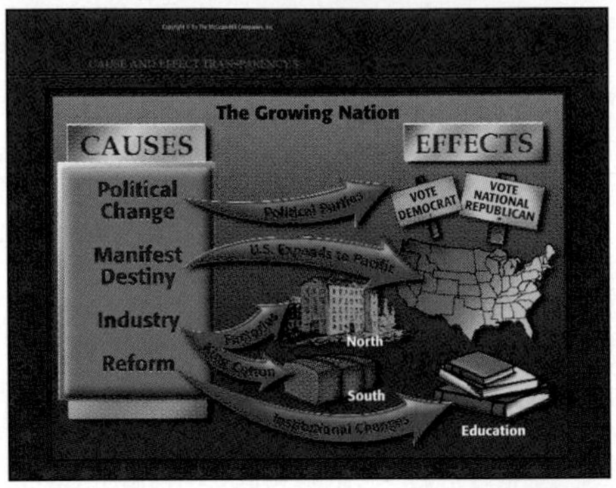

BIBLIOGRAPHY

Readings for the Student

Avi. ***The True Confessions of Charlotte Doyle.*** New York: Avon, 1992. Exciting adventures of a young Englishwoman on a ship bound for America in 1832.

Katz, William Loren. ***Black People Who Made the Old West.*** New York: Thomas Y. Crowell, 1977. Short biographical sketches of 35 men and women.

Readings for the Teacher

Schlesinger, Arthur, Jr. ***The Age of Jackson.*** Boston: Little, Brown, 1988. This Pulitzer Prize-winning book stimulated reconsideration of the Jackson era.

Walters, Ronald G. ***American Reformers: 1815–1860.*** New York: 1978. Describes some of America's early reformers.

Multimedia Resources

Videocassette. ***As the Wind Rocks the Wagon.*** VHS. Distributed by Great Plains National, New Orleans. Life on the Oregon Trail.

Videocassette. ***Across the Great Divide.*** VHS. Distributed by Media Home Entertainment, Los Angeles. Two orphans cross the Rockies to claim their 400-acre inheritance.

interNET CONNECTIONS

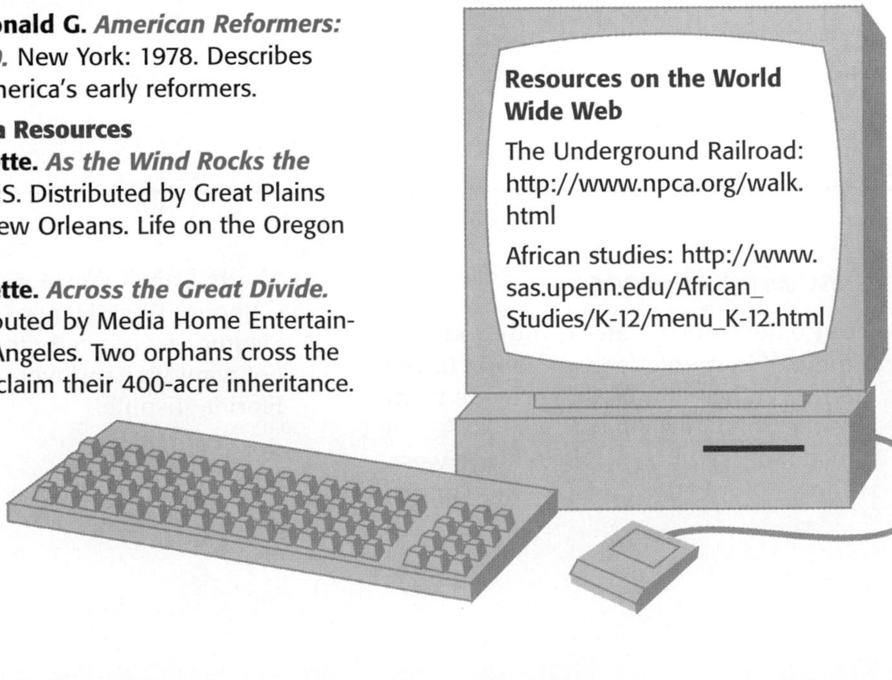

Resource Guide Unit 5

Interdisciplinary Activities

American Literature Reading 5

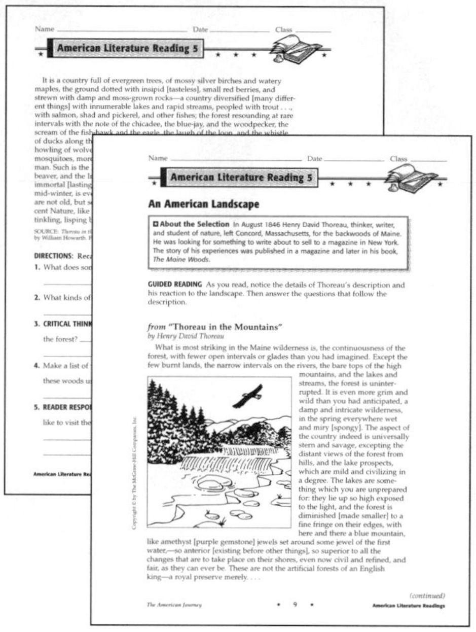

Interdisciplinary Connection 5

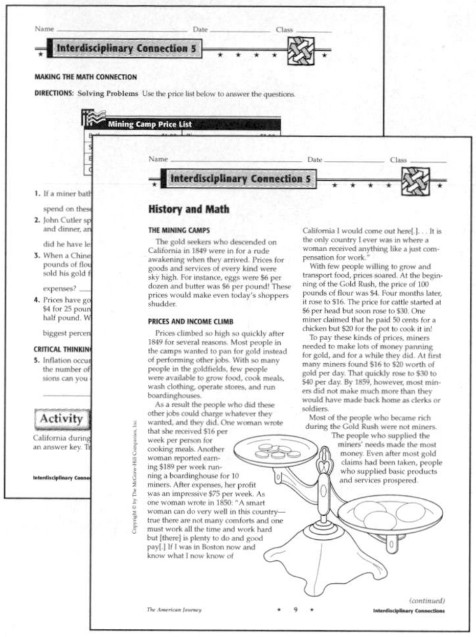

Enrichment Activities

Cooperative Learning Activity 5

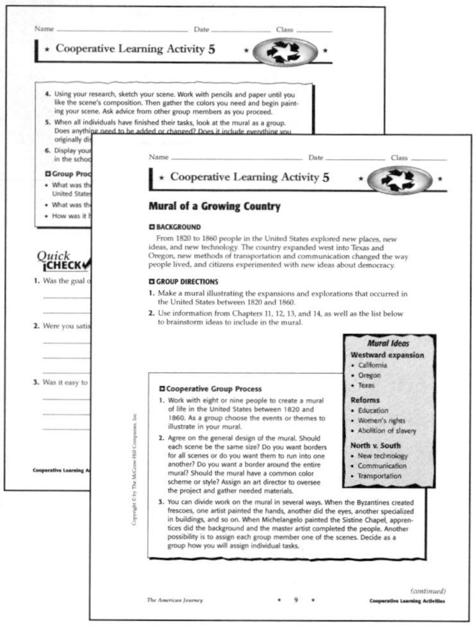

Hands-On Activities

Hands-On History Lab Activity 5

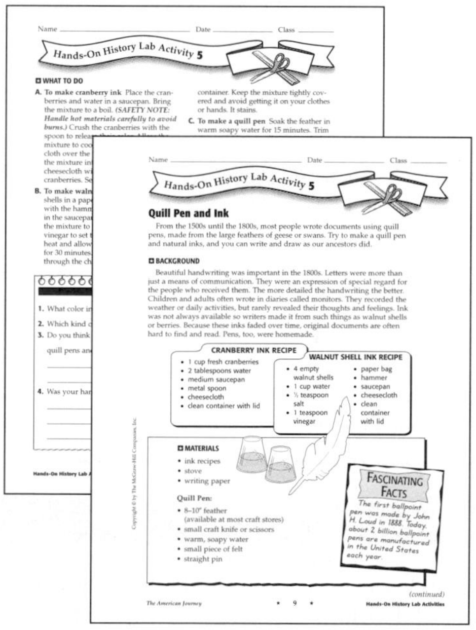

History Simulation 5

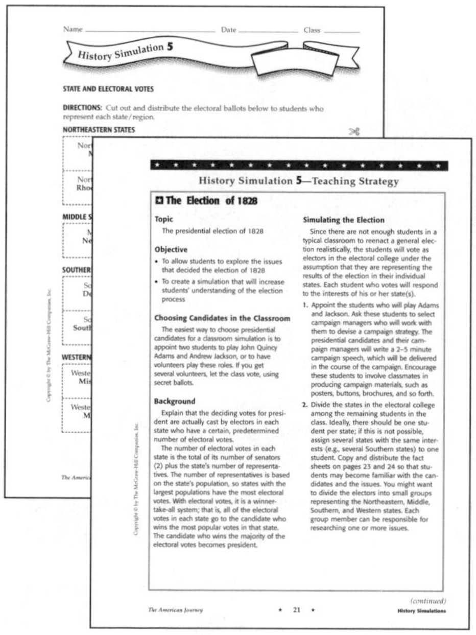

Assessment

Unit 5 Test

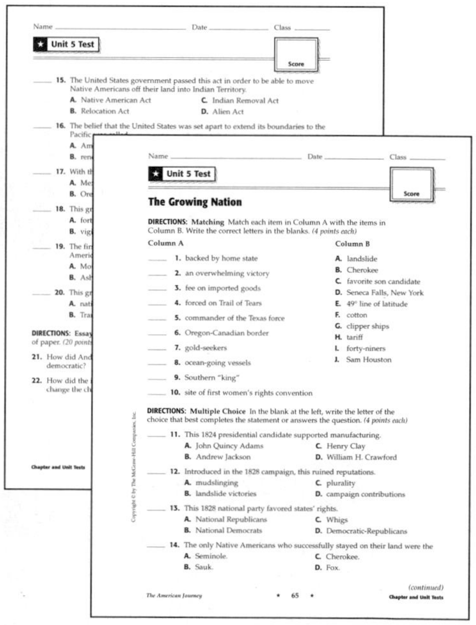

0:00 OUT OF TIME?

If your teaching time is limited, you may use the *Chapter Summaries* blackline master found in the TCR with the *Chapter Digests Audiocassette Activities and Tests* to condense individual chapters into a one-day lesson.

Introducing the Unit

Activity The towns of St. Louis, Independence, and St. Joseph were starting points for pioneers heading to California or Oregon. Have students look at the map on page 358 and speculate on why so many pioneers started their journeys here. *(location in the westernmost state of the time and on the Missouri River)*

Unit Objectives

Upon completing this unit, students will be able to:

1. Describe key political and social events of the Jackson era.
2. Summarize the ways in which California, Texas, Oregon, Utah, and New Mexico became part of the United States, including the roles of Manifest Destiny and the Mexican War.
3. Compare and contrast the economy and people of the North with those of the South.
4. Discuss the social history of the early and mid-1800s with regard to artists and writers and various reform movements.

Hands-On HISTORY

Hands-On History Lab Activity 5, "Quill Pen and Ink," is a high-interest **constructivist approach** activity directly related to the main topic of the unit.

Unit 5

The Growing Nation

1820–1860

"It is an extraordinary era in which we live."
—DANIEL WEBSTER, 1847

MAPPING *America*

Portfolio Activity Draw an outline map of the United States. As you read this unit, draw and label the new territories that were added to the Union. Add symbols to your map showing what economic activities took place in the new areas. Include a key to explain your symbols.

Rifle and leather shooting bag

United States

1823 Monroe Doctrine is issued

1825 Erie Canal opens

1833 American Antislavery Society is established

1820 — *1830*

1821 Mexico proclaims independence from Spain

1822 Liberia is founded in West Africa

World

328

TEAM TEACHING STRATEGIES

Science Have students work with the Science teacher to make a simple device that can be used to send "telegraph" messages using Morse code. Materials needed include wire, nails, screws, one or two dry cell batteries, a block of wood, and small pieces of flexible metal. Two books that have copies of the code and directions for building a transmitter are *Table Top Science,* by S.H. Fisher (Garden City, N.Y.: The Natural History Press, 1972) and *Science in Action: The World of Numbers,* edited by Sue Lyon (New York: Marshall Cavendish Corporation, 1988). Pages 492–493 of this student edition also list the steps involved in making a Morse-code transmitter.

Slave identification tags

HISTORY AND ART ***St. Louis in 1846*** **by Henry Lewis** During this era, the United States was a nation of change, a nation on the move—socially, economically, and politically.

1836 Cherokee people are forced to move west

1837 Victoria becomes queen of Great Britain

1840

1840 Upper and Lower Canada united

1843 Dorothea Dix works to help persons with mental illness

1845 United States annexes Texas

1848 Revolutions break out in Europe

1848 Women rally for rights at Seneca Falls; California Gold Rush begins

1850

1850 Taiping Rebellion begins in China

1854 Henry David Thoreau publishes *Walden*

1857 Soldiers in India revolt against British rule

1860

TEAM TEACHING STRATEGIES

Science Some scientists of the nineteenth century actually contended that women were less intelligent than men because their brains were physically smaller than those of men. Today we know that this is nonsense. The average human brain is about 1,360 cubic centimeters (83 cubic inches). There is a fairly large range in brain size among humans, but it doesn't seem to affect intelligence. Ivan Turgenev's brain was 2,000 cubic centimeters (122 cubic inches); Anatole France's was 1,000 cubic centimeters (61 cubic inches). Have students work with the Science teacher to learn more about the source of intelligence. If brain size does not govern intelligence, what *does?*

Introducing
UNIT 5

NATIONAL GEOGRAPHIC SOCIETY

VIDEODISC
GTV: A Geographic Perspective on American History

Side 2, Chapter 6
Title: *The Advancing Frontier: The Near West*
Subject: Settlement between the Appalachians and the Mississippi (1820–1850)
Ask: **What issue was a source of conflict as new states formed out of western territories?** *(whether slavery would be allowed in the new states)*

HISTORY AND ART For Henry Lewis, expressing the spirit of the westward movement called for extraordinary dimensions. To show the beauty of western rivers, he created a panorama 12 feet (3.7 m) high and 1,200 yards (1,097 m) long. **Ask: How does this painting suggest movement?** *(boats on river, wagon in foreground)*

Linking PAST & PRESENT

Activity St. Louis today has a famous monument commemorating its role as a starting point for pioneers. Have students find the name of the monument and write a brief description of it. *(Gateway Arch, made of steel and stands 630 feet [192 m] high; elevators carry visitors to an observation platform at top; below arch, underground museum houses exhibits on United States history)*

Block Schedule

Team Teaching This selection from *A Son of the Middle Border* may be implemented in a team-teaching context, in conjunction with English/Language Arts.

Reinforcing Vocabulary
Review the **Reader's Dictionary** terms with students to be sure they understand any unfamiliar terms.

Historical Connection
At first considered uninhabitable, the Great Plains was the last section of the nation to be settled. Farming on the plains presented special challenges, including the unpredictability of rain.

Background Information
Setting This excerpt takes place on the vast and magnificent plains of South Dakota.

Characters The main characters are Garland and his father, mother, brother, and sisters.

Plot Garland remembers his family's move westward to the plains in the late 1800s.

America's Literature

A Son of the Middle Border

by Hamlin Garland

Hamlin Garland (1860–1940) was born in rural Wisconsin and grew up on farms in Iowa and South Dakota. At the age of 24, he moved to Boston to begin his writing career. Although he gave up the life of a prairie farmer, Garland's work—fiction and nonfiction—reflects his background and his concern for the hard, lonely lives of pioneer men and women.

Read to Discover

A Son of the Middle Border is Garland's autobiography. The following excerpt describes one of the many westward moves that the Garland family made. As you read, pay attention to the emotions that the author expresses when he sees the plains for the first time.

Reader's Dictionary

middle border: the advancing frontier across the Mississippi River
habitation: residence
blue-joint: type of prairie grass
primeval: ancient or primitive
clarion: brilliantly clear
poker: metal rod for stirring a fire
sod: grass-covered surface of the ground
billow: to rise or roll in waves
russet: reddish-brown
fleck: mark

Late in August my father again loaded our household goods into wagons, and with our small herd of cattle following, set out toward the west, bound once again to overtake the actual line of the middle border.

This journey has an unforgettable epic charm as I look back upon it. Each mile took us farther and farther into the unsettled prairie until in the afternoon of the second day, we came to a meadow so wide that its western rim touched the sky without revealing a sign of man's habitation other than the road in which we travelled.

The plain was covered with grass tall as ripe wheat and when my father stopped his team and came back to us and said, "Well, children, here we are on The Big Prairie," we looked about us with awe, so endless seemed this spread of wild oats and waving blue-joint.

Far away dim clumps of trees showed, but no chimney was in sight, and no living thing moved save our own cattle and the hawks lazily wheeling in the air. My heart filled with awe as well as wonder. The majesty of this primeval world exalted me. I felt for the first time the poetry of the unplowed spaces. It seemed that the "herds of deer and buffalo" of our song might, at any moment, present themselves—but they did not, and my father took no account even of the marsh fowl.

"Forward march!" he shouted, and on we went.

Hour after hour he pushed into the west, the heads of his tired horses hanging ever lower, and on my mother's face the shadow deepened, but her chieftain's voice cheerily urging his team lost

Additional Literary Works of the Period

You may want to refer to students to the following:

Alcott, Louisa May. ***Little Women.*** New York: Knopf, 1988. A classic.

Dickinson, Emily. ***The Complete Poems of Emily Dickinson.*** Boston: Little, Brown, 1960. Works of the "recluse of Amherst."

Poe, Edgar Allan. ***The Complete Tales and Poems of Edgar Allan Poe.*** New York: Modern Library, 1983. A master of gothic tales.

Powell, Laurence C., ed. ***Poems of Walt Whitman: Leaves of Grass.*** New York: Harper Collins, 1986. Collection of poems in *Leaves of Grass* most suited for young people.

Whittier, John Greenleaf. ***The Poetical Works of Whittier.*** Boston: Houghton Mifflin, 1975. This poet was a pacifist, abolitionist, and champion of human rights.

Pioneer families on the prairies built their homes using squares of hard sod—the dense top layer of earth.

nothing of its clarion resolution. He was in his element. He loved this shelterless sweep of prairie. This westward march entranced him, I think he would have gladly kept on until the snowy wall of the Rocky Mountains met his eyes, for he was a natural explorer.

Sunset came at last, but still he drove steadily on through the sparse settlements. Just at nightfall we came to a beautiful little stream, and stopped to let the horses drink. I heard its rippling, reassuring song on the pebbles. Thereafter all is dim and vague to me until my mother called out sharply, "Wake up, children! Here we are!"

Struggling to my feet I looked about me. Nothing could be seen but the dim form of a small house.—On every side the land melted into blackness, silent and without boundary.

Driving into the yard, father hastily unloaded one of the wagons and taking mother and Harriet and Jessie drove away to spend the night with Uncle David who had preceded us, as I now learned, and was living on a farm not far away. My brother and I were left to camp as best we could with the hired man.

Spreading a rude bed on the floor, he told us to "hop in" and in ten minutes we were all fast asleep.

The sound of a clattering poker awakened me next morning and when I opened my sleepy eyes and looked out a new world displayed itself before me.

The cabin faced a level plain with no tree in sight. A mile away to the west stood a low stone house and immediately in front of us opened a half-section of unfenced sod. To the north, as far as I could see, the land billowed like a russet ocean with scarcely a roof to fleck its lonely spread. . . .

Once more and for the sixth time since her marriage, [my mother] Belle Garland adjusted herself to a pioneer environment. . . . No doubt she also congratulated herself on the fact that she had not been carried beyond the Missouri River. . . .

Responding to Literature

1. Give two details that Garland uses to describe "The Big Prairie" at the beginning of the selection.
2. How do Garland's parents feel about moving west?

Activity

Writing a Poem The vast prairie fills Garland with awe because the land is empty and untouched. Write a poem about a vast empty place that you know, or base your poem on a place about which you have read.

Answers to Responding to Literature

1. any two: "so wide that its western rim touched the sky," no sign of habitation, "covered with grass tall as ripe wheat," "wild oats and waving blue joint," "dim clumps of trees, . . . but no chimney," "hawks lazily wheeling."
2. His father loved it; his mother was worried, but adjusted to it.

Activity Students' poems should use expressive language.

History *and the* Humanities

Focus on American Art Prints, *The Long Story* by William Sidney Mount; *Fur Traders Descending the Missouri* by George Caleb Bingham

Portfolio Activity Have students describe a scene that filled them with awe or excitement. It might be a vast empty place like Garland's prairie or something as small as a spider or a flower. Descriptions may be in a format of the student's choosing—written, taped, or drawn.

At the Movies

Ken Burns's series *The West* (available on VHS) chronicles the expansion of the United States and its effect on Native Americans, Californios, and the environment.

Curriculum Connection

GEOGRAPHY

Farmers who settled on the Great Plains faced a stern land and climate. Summer temperatures reached 110°F (43°C), and rains were unreliable. Winters brought fierce snowstorms with white-out conditions. Every few years swarms of crop-stripping grasshoppers arrived in such numbers as to darken the sky. There was no wood for buildings, fencing, and fuel, and the tough sod could not be plowed with the wooden plows eastern farmers used.

Chapter 11 Planning Guide

A complete, 1-page lesson plan is provided for each section in the *Reproducible Lesson Plans* booklet.

Section Resources

Daily Objectives	Reproducible Resources	Multimedia Resources
Section 1 From Adams to Jackson Describe the main political events of the 1820s.	Reproducible Lesson Plan 11–1 Guided Reading Activity 11–1* Section Quiz 11–1* Reteaching Activity 11–1 Enrichment Activity 11–1	Section Focus Transparency 11–1 Vocabulary PuzzleMaker Chapter Challenger Interactive Review Software Testmaker The Presidents: A Picture History of Our Nation
Section 2 Jacksonian Democracy Characterize Jackson the man and summarize the changes he made and the challenges he faced as president.	Reproducible Lesson Plan 11–2 Guided Reading Activity 11–2* Section Quiz 11–2* Reteaching Activity 11–2 Enrichment Activity 11–2	Section Focus Transparency 11–2 Vocabulary PuzzleMaker Chapter Challenger Interactive Review Software Testmaker GTV: The American People: Fabric of a Nation NGS PictureShow: Native Americans, Part 1 Facts On File: Landmark Documents in American History Facts On File: The American Indian
Section 3 Conflicts Over Land Summarize the ways in which Native Americans of the Southeast were forced off their lands; explain why the Supreme Court decision in favor of the Cherokee did not help them keep their lands.	Reproducible Lesson Plan 11–3 Guided Reading Activity 11–3* Section Quiz 11–3* Reteaching Activity 11–3 Enrichment Activity 11–3	Section Focus Transparency 11–3 Vocabulary PuzzleMaker Chapter Challenger Interactive Review Software Testmaker Facts On File: Landmark Documents in American History
Section 4 Jackson and the Bank Describe the role of the Bank of the United States and explain how the Whigs came to power in 1840.	Reproducible Lesson Plan 11–4 Guided Reading Activity 11–4* Political Cartoons, *Andrew Jackson and the Second Bank of the United States* Section Quiz 11–4* Reteaching Activity 11–4 Enrichment Activity 11–4	Section Focus Transparency 11–4 Vocabulary PuzzleMaker Chapter Challenger Interactive Review Software Testmaker The Presidents: A Picture History of Our Nation

* *Also available in Spanish*

Blackline Master · Videodisc · Audiocassette · Music Program · Transparency · CD-ROM · Software

0:00 **OUT OF TIME?**
Assign the Chapter 11 Digest and the corresponding Chapter Digests Audiocassettes with activities and tests.

Activity

From the Classroom of...

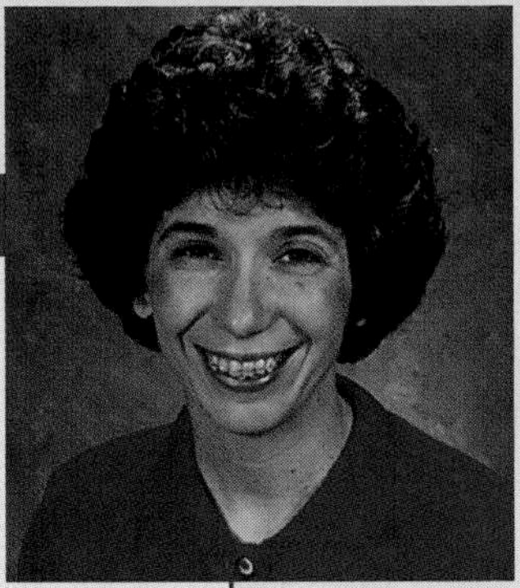

Winnie Cohran
Drakes Creek Middle School
Bowling Green, KY

Create an Andrew Jackson Mural

To help students review the main issues and events of the chapter, have them make a mural using a large sheet of paper and colored pencils or pens. Students can work individually or in pairs. First, have students cut the paper into five irregularly shaped pieces (similar to puzzle pieces). On each piece of paper, have students label an issue or event and then illustrate it. For example, a student might write "Indian Removal Act" and then draw pictures of footsteps, or "Jackson Attacks Bank of United States" illustrated with dollar bill signs. Have students use different colors for each piece. Each student or group should present their mural to the class and explain it. Murals can be taped together and displayed in class.

Block Schedule

Block scheduling differs from traditional class scheduling in the amount of time allotted to each period. The extended time frame provided by block scheduling affords you the opportunity to implement a greater number of research-oriented and activity-intense projects to motivate and involve your students. Activities that are particularly suited to use within the block scheduling framework are identified throughout this chapter by the following designation:

NATIONAL GEOGRAPHIC SOCIETY

Teacher's Corner

INDEX TO NATIONAL GEOGRAPHIC MAGAZINE

The following articles may be used for research relating to this chapter:

- "The Cherokee," by Geoffrey Norman, May 1995.
- "The Cruelest Commerce: African Slave Trade," by Colin Palmer, September 1992.
- "Erie Canal: Living Link to Our Past," by Joel L. Swerdlow, November 1990.
- "Philadelphia's African Americans," by Roland L. Freeman, August 1990.

NATIONAL GEOGRAPHIC SOCIETY PRODUCTS AVAILABLE FROM GLENCOE

To order the following products for use with this chapter, contact your local Glencoe sales representative, or call Glencoe at 1-800-334-7344:

- *GTV: The American People: Fabric of a Nation* (Videodisc)
- *GTV: A Geographic Perspective on American History* (Videodisc)
- *PictureShow: Native Americans, 1* (CD-ROM)
- *Native Americans: Eastern Woodlands and Plains* (Transparencies)
- *The Presidents: A Picture History of Our Nation* (CD-ROM)
- *PictureShow: The Westward Movement* (CD-ROM, Transparencies)

ADDITIONAL NATIONAL GEOGRAPHIC SOCIETY PRODUCTS

To order the following products for use with this chapter, call National Geographic Society at 1-800-368-2728:

- *Historical Atlas of the United States* (Atlas)
- *Mark Twain: When I Was a Boy* (Video)

KEY TO ABILITY LEVELS

Teaching strategies have been coded for varying learning styles and abilities.

L1 **BASIC** activities for all students
L2 **AVERAGE** activities for average to above-average students
L3 **CHALLENGING** activities for above-average students
ELL **ENGLISH LANGUAGE LEARNER** activities

Chapter 11 Resource Guide

Home Involvement

Home Involvement Activity 11

Review Activities

Chapter Summary 11

Workbook Activity 11

Reinforcement Activities

Time Line Activity 11

Vocabulary Activity 11

Chapter Skills Activity 11

Enrichment Activities

Linking Past and Present Activity 11

Primary Source Reading 11

Geography Activities

Mapping History Activity 11

Chapter 11 Resource Guide

ASSESSMENT

Chapter 11 Test, Form A

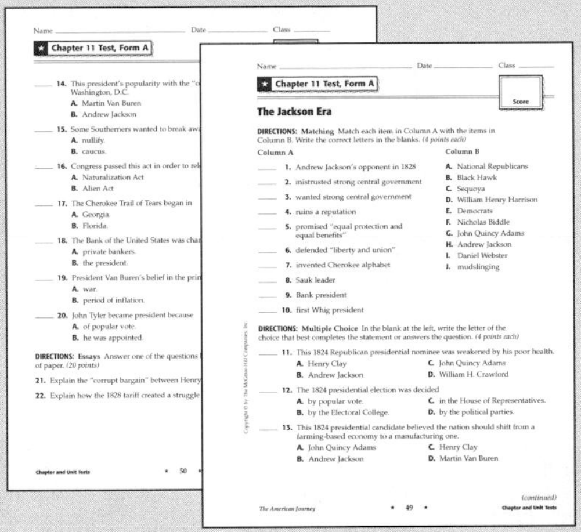

Name ________ Date ________ Class ________

Chapter 11 Test, Form A

Score

The Jackson Era

DIRECTIONS: Matching Match each item in Column A with the items in Column B. Write the correct letters in the blanks. *(4 points each)*

Column A	Column B
____ 1. Andrew Jackson's opponent in 1828	A. National Republicans
____ 2. mistrusted strong central government	B. Black Hawk
____ 3. wanted strong central government	C. Sequoya
____ 4. ruins a reputation	D. William Henry Harrison
____ 5. promised "equal protection and equal benefits"	E. Democrats
____ 6. defended "liberty and union"	F. Nicholas Biddle
____ 7. invented Cherokee alphabet	G. John Quincy Adams
____ 8. Sauk leader	H. Andrew Jackson
____ 9. Bank president	I. Daniel Webster
____ 10. first Whig president	J. mudslinging

DIRECTIONS: Multiple Choice In the blank at the left, write the letter of the choice that best completes the statement or answers the question. *(4 points each)*

____ 11. This 1824 Republican presidential nominee was weakened by his poor health.
A. Henry Clay C. John Quincy Adams
B. Andrew Jackson D. William H. Crawford

____ 12. The 1824 presidential election was decided
A. by popular vote. C. in the House of Representatives.
B. by the Electoral College. D. by the political parties.

____ 13. This 1824 presidential candidate believed the nation should shift from a farming-based economy to a manufacturing one.
A. John Quincy Adams C. Henry Clay
B. Andrew Jackson D. Martin Van Buren

(continued)

The American Journey • 49 • Chapter and Unit Tests

Chapter 11 Test, Form B

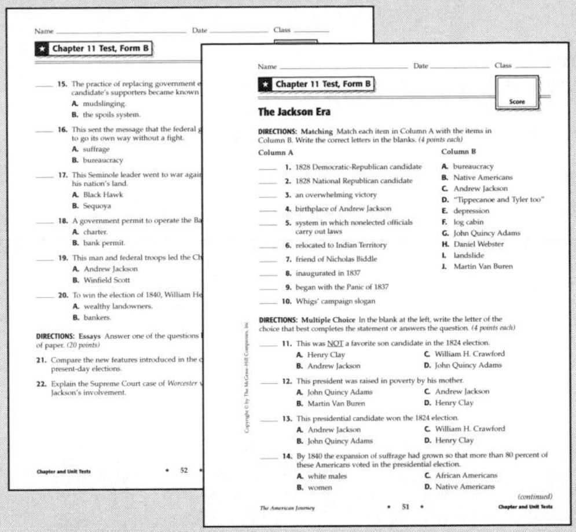

Name ________ Date ________ Class ________

Chapter 11 Test, Form B

Score

The Jackson Era

DIRECTIONS: Matching Match each item in Column A with the items in Column B. Write the correct letters in the blanks. *(4 points each)*

Column A	Column B
____ 1. 1828 Democratic-Republican candidate	A. bureaucracy
____ 2. 1828 National Republican candidate	B. Native Americans
____ 3. an overwhelming victory	C. Andrew Jackson
____ 4. birthplace of Andrew Jackson	D. "Tippecanoe and Tyler too"
____ 5. system in which nonelected officials carry out laws	E. depression
____ 6. relocated to Indian Territory	F. log cabin
____ 7. friend of Nicholas Biddle	G. John Quincy Adams
____ 8. inaugurated in 1837	H. Daniel Webster
____ 9. began with the Panic of 1837	I. landslide
____ 10. Whigs' campaign slogan	J. Martin Van Buren

DIRECTIONS: Multiple Choice In the blank at the left, write the letter of the choice that best completes the statement or answers the question. *(4 points each)*

____ 11. This was NOT a favorite son candidate in the 1824 election.
A. Henry Clay C. William H. Crawford
B. Andrew Jackson D. John Quincy Adams

____ 12. This president was raised in poverty by his mother.
A. John Quincy Adams C. Andrew Jackson
B. Martin Van Buren D. Henry Clay

____ 13. This presidential candidate won the 1824 election.
A. Andrew Jackson C. William H. Crawford
B. John Quincy Adams D. Henry Clay

____ 14. By 1840 the expansion of suffrage had grown so that more than 80 percent of these Americans voted in the presidential election.
A. white males C. African Americans
B. women D. Native Americans

(continued)

The American Journey • 51 • Chapter and Unit Tests

Performance Assessment Activity 11

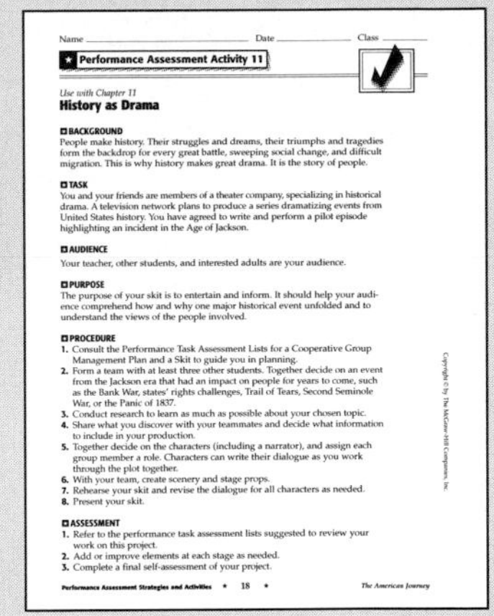

Name ________ Date ________ Class ________

Performance Assessment Activity 11

Use with Chapter 11
History as Drama

BACKGROUND
People make history. Their struggles and dreams, their triumphs and tragedies form the backdrop for every great battle, sweeping social change, and difficult migration. This is why history makes great drama. It is the story of people.

TASK
You and your friends are members of a theater company, specializing in historical drama. A television network plans to produce a series dramatizing events from United States history. You have agreed to write and perform a pilot episode highlighting an incident in the Age of Jackson.

AUDIENCE
Your teacher, other students, and interested adults are your audience.

PURPOSE
The purpose of your skit is to entertain and inform. It should help your audience comprehend how and why one major historical event unfolded and to understand the views of the people involved.

PROCEDURE
1. Consult the Performance Task Assessment Lists for a Cooperative Group Management Plan and a Skit to guide you in planning.
2. Form a team with at least three other students. Together decide on an event from the Jackson era that had an impact on people for years to come, such as the Bank War, states' rights challenges, Trail of Tears, Second Seminole War, or the Panic of 1837.
3. Conduct research to learn as much as possible about your chosen topic.
4. Share what you discover with your teammates and decide which information to include in your production.
5. Together decide on the characters (including a narrator), and assign each group member a role. Characters can write their dialogue as you work through the plot together.
6. With your team, create scenery and stage props.
7. Rehearse your skit and revise the dialogue for all characters as needed.
8. Present your skit.

ASSESSMENT
1. Refer to the performance task assessment lists suggested to review your work on this project.
2. Add or improve elements at each stage as needed.
3. Complete a final self-assessment of your project.

Performance Assessment Strategies and Activities • 18 • The American Journey

SPANISH RESOURCES

The following Spanish language materials are available in the Spanish Resources binder:

- **Spanish Chapter Summary 11**
- **Spanish Vocabulary Activity 11**
- **Spanish Guided Reading Activities, Chapter 11**
- **Spanish Section Quizzes, Chapter 11**
- **Spanish Home Involvement Activity 11**
- **Spanish Chapter 11 Digests Audiocassette Activity and Test**

ACTIVITY MANIPULATIVES

Help students learn more about America's cultural history with:

- **American Crafts Hands-On Activities**
- **American Games Hands-On Activities**
- **American History Flash Cards**

ADDITIONAL RESOURCES FROM GLENCOE

- **U.S. History & Art,** Transparency 9, *Shooting for the Beef*
- **Focus on American Art Prints,** *Pat Lyon at the Forge* by John Neagle
- **American Music Cultural Traditions,** Lesson 4: "Kneebone Bend" and "The Monongahela Waltz"
- **Outline Map Resource Book**
- **U.S. Desk Map**
- **The American History Videodisc and CD-ROM,** *Expansion, Development, Sectionalism and Division, 1820–1860*

A&E HOME VIDEO. Biography™ THE HISTORY CHANNEL.

The following videotape programs are available from Glencoe as supplements to Chapter 11:

- **Andrew Jackson: A Man for the People** (ISBN 1-56501-647-5)

To order, call Glencoe at 1-800-334-7344. To find classroom resources to accompany many of these videos, check the following home pages:
A&E Television: http://www.aetv.com
The History Channel: http://www.historychannel.com

Introducing CHAPTER 11

Chapter Themes

Chapter Themes are listed by section on this chapter opening page of the Student Edition. A corresponding theme-based activity is available under "FOCUS," and a theme-based question is asked in the Section and Chapter Reviews.

Performance Assessment

Refer to Activity 11 in the *Performance Assessment Strategies and Activities* booklet.

GLENCOE TECHNOLOGY

VIDEODISC
MindJogger Videoquiz

Use MindJogger to preview the Chapter 11 content.

Chapter 11
Disc 2, Side A

Also available in VHS.

HISTORY AND ART George Caleb Bingham (1811–1879), a chronicler of the frontier, received his inspiration from the spirited life along the Missouri and Mississippi Rivers. **Ask:** **Why are there no women in the painting?** *(Women did not have the right to vote.)*

Chapter 11

1824–1845

The Jackson Era

Why It's Important

The struggle for political rights took shape in the 1820s and 1830s, when many people questioned the limits of American democracy. In the years since the Jackson era, women, African Americans, and other minorities have won the right to vote and to participate in the political process. Today every United States citizen aged 18 or older, regardless of gender, race, or wealth, has the right to vote.

Chapter Themes

- *Section 1,* Continuity and Change
- *Section 2,* Government and Democracy
- *Section 3,* Groups and Institutions
- *Section 4,* Economic Factors

HISTORY AND ART ***Stump Speaking* by George Caleb Bingham** Bingham's series of election paintings in the 1850s expressed faith in the growth of democracy.

EXTRA CREDIT PROJECT

Presidential Nicknames Many presidents have been given nicknames, sometimes more than one. Some, such as Old Hickory, were complimentary. Others, such as King Andrew, were not. (Both of those nicknames applied to Andrew Jackson, the nation's seventh president.) Have students do research to find nicknames for presidents. In their reports, students should briefly explain the reason for each nickname.

1820 1825 1830 1835

1825 John Quincy Adams wins presidency in House election

1826 Adams attends the first congress of American nations in Panama

1828 Andrew Jackson is elected president

1834 National Republicans change their name to Whigs

Section 1

From Adams to Jackson

READ TO DISCOVER . . .

- why the nation's sixth president was chosen by the House of Representatives.
- why the Republican Party split into two parties.

TERMS TO LEARN

favorite son
majority
plurality
mudslinging
landslide

The Storyteller

The presidential campaign of 1828 was one of the most vicious in American history. Supporters of John Quincy Adams in Philadelphia distributed a pamphlet titled "An Account of Some of the Bloody Deeds of General Jackson." One illustration in the pamphlet showed a ferocious-looking Andrew Jackson plunging his sword through the body of a helpless civilian. Meanwhile Jackson's supporters falsely accused John Quincy Adams of kidnapping a young American girl and selling her to the ruler of Russia.

Jackson sewing box

From 1816 to 1824, the United States had only one political party—the Jeffersonian Republicans. However, within the party differences arose among various groups with their own views and interests.

In 1824 James Monroe was finishing his second term as president. Following the example of earlier presidents, Monroe declined to run for a third term. Four candidates from the Republican Party competed for the presidency.

The Election of 1824

The four candidates' opinions differed on the role of the federal government. They also spoke for different areas of the country. The Republican Party nominated **William H. Crawford,** a former congressman from Georgia. He called for a limited federal government and strong state powers. He also defended slavery. However, Crawford's poor health weakened him as a candidate.

The other three Republicans in the presidential race were favorite son candidates, meaning they received the backing of their home states rather than that of the national party. Two of these candidates—**Andrew Jackson** and **Henry Clay**—came from the West. Clay of Kentucky was Speaker of the House of Representatives. Clay fought for his program of internal improvements, high tariffs, and a stronger national bank.

General Andrew Jackson of Tennessee was not a Washington politician but a hero of the War of 1812. Raised in poverty by his widowed mother,

SECTION RESOURCES

Reproducible Masters
- Reproducible Lesson Plan 11–1
- Guided Reading Activity 11–1
- Section Quiz 11–1
- Reteaching Activity 11–1
- Enrichment Activity 11–1

Transparencies
- Section Focus Transparency 11–1

Multimedia
- Vocabulary PuzzleMaker
- Chapter Challenger Interactive Review Software
- Testmaker
- The Presidents: A Picture History of Our Nation

1 FOCUS

BELLRINGER
Motivational Activity

Before taking roll at the beginning of the class period, project Section Focus Transparency 11–1 and have students answer the questions. Discuss students' responses.

This activity is also available as a blackline master.

Section Focus Transparency 11–1

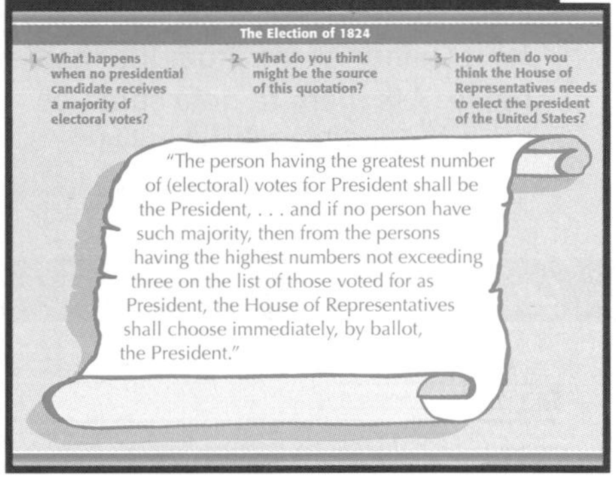

Vocabulary Precheck

Have students find the difference between *majority* and *plurality.* (majority: *more than half;* plurality: *largest share)*

Use the **Vocabulary Puzzle-Maker** to create crossword and word search puzzles.

Section Theme
Continuity and Change

In the 1820s James Monroe's decision not to run for a third term was followed by two hotly contested elections.

Activity Have students find as many examples of continuity and of change in the section as they can. (Continuity: *Monroe followed precedent in declining third term; election of 1824, though unusual, followed Constitution;* Change: *Republican Party split; new campaign tactics in 1828 election)*

2 TEACH

L1 Using Vocabulary Have students use each of the words in **Terms to Learn** plus *Democratic-Republicans* and *National Republicans* in writing a summary of the section.

NATIONAL GEOGRAPHIC SOCIETY

CD-ROM
The Presidents: A Picture History of Our Nation

Have students select President John Quincy Adams from the main menu. Ask them to note some of this president's political beliefs.

Guided Reading Activity 11–1

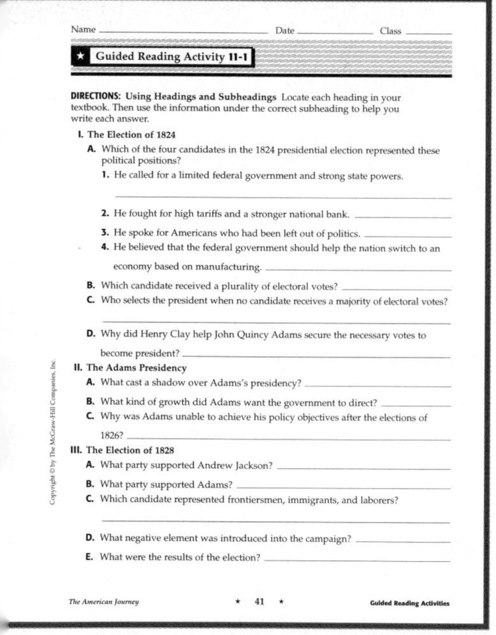
Name ______ Date ______ Class ______

★ Guided Reading Activity 11-1

DIRECTIONS: Using Headings and Subheadings Locate each heading in your textbook. Then use the information under the correct subheading to help you write each answer.

I. The Election of 1824
A. Which of the four candidates in the 1824 presidential election represented these political positions?
1. He called for a limited federal government and strong state powers. ______
2. He fought for high tariffs and a stronger national bank. ______
3. He spoke for Americans who had been left out of politics. ______
4. He believed that the federal government should help the nation switch to an economy based on manufacturing. ______
B. Which candidate received a plurality of electoral votes? ______
C. Who selects the president when no candidate receives a majority of electoral votes? ______
D. Why did Henry Clay help John Quincy Adams secure the necessary votes to become president? ______

II. The Adams Presidency
A. What cast a shadow over Adams's presidency? ______
B. What kind of growth did Adams want the government to direct? ______
C. Why was Adams unable to achieve his policy objectives after the elections of 1826? ______

III. The Election of 1828
A. What party supported Andrew Jackson? ______
B. What party supported Adams? ______
C. Which candidate represented frontiersmen, immigrants, and laborers? ______
D. What negative element was introduced into the campaign? ______
E. What were the results of the election? ______

The American Journey ★ 41 ★ **Guided Reading Activities**

Chart Study

Answers
1. 44,804
2. Jackson; Clay

Chart Skills Practice

Reading a Chart How many votes would a candidate have needed to receive a majority of the electoral votes in 1824? *(131)*

President John Quincy Adams

Jackson claimed to speak for the Americans who had been left out of politics. His supporters included farmers in the hill country of the South, settlers trying to carve out a life in the West, and struggling laborers in the cities of the East.

John Quincy Adams of Massachusetts, son of former president John Adams, received support from merchants of the Northeast. Adams believed that the federal government should actively help the nation shift from an economy based on farming to one based on manufacturing.

Striking a Bargain

In the election Jackson received the largest number of popular votes. However, no candidate received a **majority,** or more than half, of the electoral votes. Jackson won 99 electoral votes, which gave him a **plurality,** or largest single share. Under the terms of the Twelfth Amendment to the Constitution, when no candidate receives a majority of electoral votes, the House of Representatives selects the president.

While the House was preparing to vote on the next president, Henry Clay met with Adams. Clay agreed to use his influence as Speaker of the House to defeat Jackson. In return Clay may have hoped to gain the position of secretary of state.

With Clay's help Adams received enough votes in the House to become president. Adams quickly named Clay as secretary of state, traditionally the stepping-stone to the presidency. Jackson's followers accused the two men of making a **"corrupt bargain"** and stealing the election.

The Adams Presidency

In **Washington, D.C.,** the "corrupt bargain" had cast a shadow over Adams's presidency. Outside the capital Adams's policies ran against popular opinion. Adams wanted a stronger navy and government funds for scientific expeditions. Adams also wanted the federal government to direct economic growth.

Such ideas horrified those who desired a more limited role for the federal government, and Congress turned down many of Adams's proposals. This was especially true after the congressional elections of 1826, when Adams's enemies controlled both the House and Senate.

The Election of 1828

In 1828 Andrew Jackson tried again for the presidency. He ran against John Quincy Adams in a bitter election campaign.

In 1824 all four presidential candidates had run as Republicans. By the time of the election of 1828, the party had divided into two separate parties: the **Democratic-Republicans,** who supported Jackson, and the **National Republicans,** who supported Adams. Jackson's Democratic-Republicans, or Democrats, favored states' rights and mistrusted strong central government. Many Democrats were individualists from the frontier, immigrants, or laborers in the big cities.

Election of 1824

Candidate	Electoral Vote	Popular Vote	House Vote
Jackson	99	153,544	7
Adams	84	108,740	13
Crawford	41	46,618	4
Clay	37	47,136	–

Chart Study

The presidential election of 1824 was decided in the House of Representatives.
1. How many more popular votes did Jackson have than Adams?
2. **Analyzing Information** Which candidate received the most electoral votes? The least?

COOPERATIVE LEARNING ACTIVITY

Campaigning for Office Organize the class into groups to run campaigns for class or school president. Have each group choose a candidate; decide on the issues; and make posters, campaign buttons, and other paraphernalia. Candidates should each give a short speech. At the end of the campaign hold an election; then discuss why the winner's campaign was most effective and how other campaigns might have been improved.

The National Republicans wanted a strong central government. They supported federal measures, such as road building and the Bank of the United States, that would shape the nation's economy. Many were merchants or successful farmers.

A Vicious Campaign

During the campaign both parties resorted to **mudslinging,** attempts to ruin their opponent's reputation with insults. The Democratic-Republicans accused Adams of betraying the interests of the people. They put out a handbill calling the election a contest "between an honest patriotism, on the one side, and an unholy and selfish ambition, on the other."

The National Republicans fought back. They created a vicious campaign song to play up embarrassing incidents in Jackson's life. One involved Jackson's order in the War of 1812 to execute several soldiers who had deserted. Adams himself referred to Jackson as "a barbarian and a savage."

Mudslinging was not the only new element introduced in the 1828 campaign. Election slogans, rallies, buttons, and events such as barbecues were also used to arouse enthusiasm, mostly by Jackson's supporters. All of these new features became a permanent part of American political life.

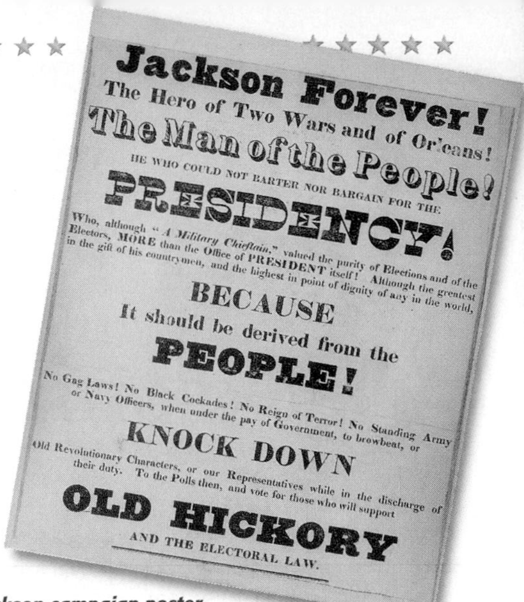

Jackson campaign poster

Jackson Triumphs

In the election of 1828, Jackson received most of the votes cast by voters of the new frontier states. He also received many votes in the South, where his support for states' rights was popular. **John C. Calhoun** of South Carolina, who had served as Adams's vice president, switched parties to run with Jackson. Calhoun also championed states' rights. Jackson won the election in a **landslide,** an overwhelming victory, with 56 percent of the popular vote and 178 electoral votes.

Section 1 Review

Checking for Understanding

1. ***Identify*** Andrew Jackson, Henry Clay, John Quincy Adams, Democratic-Republicans, National Republicans.
2. ***Define*** favorite son, majority, plurality, mudslinging, landslide.
3. ***Compare*** and contrast the Democratic-Republicans and the National Republicans.

Reviewing Themes

4. **Continuity and Change** What election practices used in the 1828 presidential campaign are still in use today?

Critical Thinking

5. **Identifying Central Issues** What was the main reason President Adams was not popular with the Democratic-Republicans?

Activity

Drawing a Political Cartoon Draw a political cartoon to illustrate your opinion of the "corrupt bargain."

Section 1 Review Answers

1. Andrew Jackson, 333; Henry Clay, 333; John Quincy Adams, 334; Democratic-Republicans, 334; National Republicans, 334
2. The words are defined in the Glossary.
3. Democratic-Republicans: supported Jackson, favored states' rights, mistrusted strong central government, were frontier people, immigrants, or laborers. National Republicans: supported Adams, a strong central government, and the Bank of the United States. Many were merchants or successful farmers.
4. mudslinging, election slogans, rallies, buttons, staged events to arouse enthusiasm
5. He tried to make the federal government too powerful.

Activity Cartoons should show that students understand the "corrupt bargain."

3 ASSESS

Assign Section 1 Review as homework or as an in-class activity.

Use **Chapter Challenger Interactive Review Software** to review Section 1.

Section Quiz 11–1

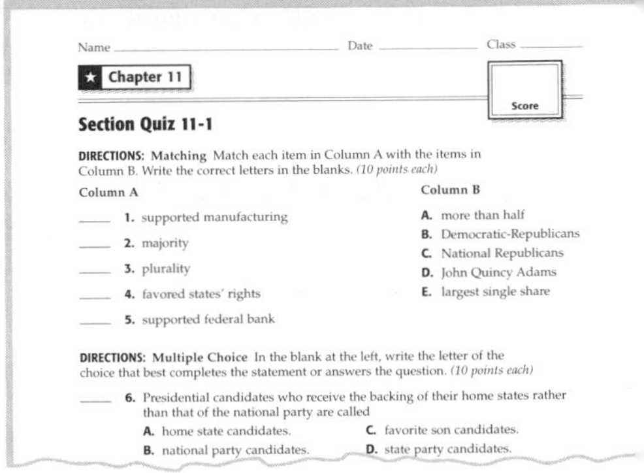

Reteaching Activity 11–1

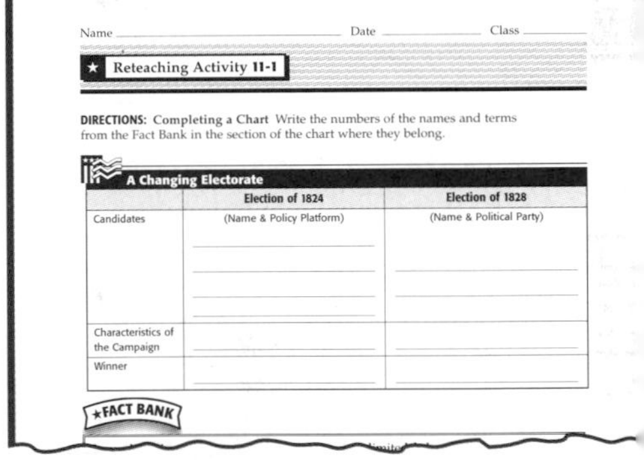

Enrichment Activity 11–1

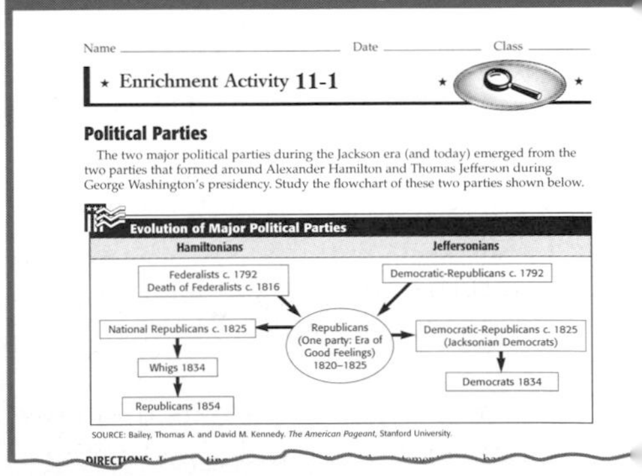

4 CLOSE

Have students choose the candidate they would have voted for in the elections of 1824 and 1828 and defend their choice.

CHAPTER 11
Section 2, 336–339

1 FOCUS

BELLRINGER
Motivational Activity

Before taking roll at the beginning of the class period, project Section Focus Transparency 11–2 and have students answer the questions. Discuss students' responses.

This activity is also available as a blackline master.

Section Focus Transparency 11–2

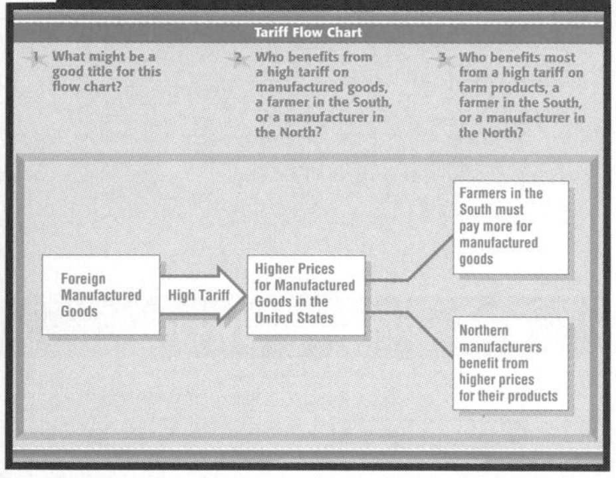

Vocabulary Precheck
Point out that the term *nullify* is derived from Latin *nullus,* which means "none." Have students speculate on the connection between *nullify* and *none.*

Use the **Vocabulary Puzzle-Maker** to create crossword and word search puzzles.

Section Theme
Government and Democracy
During Jackson's presidency democracy expanded, the candidate selection process changed, and the government faced a crisis over states' rights.

Activity Have students find how democracy expanded, what the change in candidate selection was, and the outcome of the states' rights crisis. *(Easing of property requirement increased suffrage; nominating conventions replaced caucuses; South Carolina accepted compromise rather than face military action.)*

1828 1830 1832 1834

1828 Congress passes the Tariff of Abominations

1830 Webster and Hayne debate

1832 South Carolina threatens to secede

1833 Congress passes the Force Bill

Section 2

Jacksonian Democracy

READ TO DISCOVER . . .
- why Andrew Jackson was a popular leader.
- what changes President Jackson brought to the American political system.
- why South Carolina threatened to withdraw from the United States in 1832.

TERMS TO LEARN
suffrage	tariff
bureaucracy	nullify
spoils system	secede
caucus	states' rights
nominating convention	

The Storyteller

Andrew Jackson was everything most Americans admired—a patriot, a self-made man, and a war hero. On March 4, 1829, thousands of farmers, laborers, and other ordinary Americans crowded into the nation's capital to hear Jackson's Inaugural Address. After Jackson's speech a crowd joined him at a White House reception. They filled the elegant rooms of the mansion, trampling on the carpets with muddy shoes, spilling food on sofas and chairs. They were there to shake the hand of the general who seemed just like them.

Goblet showing Jackson's log cabin

Like many of his supporters, Andrew Jackson had been born in a log cabin. His parents, poor farmers, died before he was 15. As a teenager Jackson fought with the Patriots in the American Revolution. Before he was 30, he was elected to Congress from Tennessee.

Jackson gained fame during the War of 1812. He defeated the Creek Nation in the Battle of Horseshoe Bend and led the Americans to victory at New Orleans. His troops called him "Old Hickory" because he was as tough as a hickory stick.

Small farmers, craft workers, and others who felt left out of the expanding American economy loved Jackson. They felt that his rise from a log cabin to the White House demonstrated the American success story. His popularity with the common man changed politics in Washington, D.C.

A New Era in Politics

President Andrew Jackson promised "equal protection and equal benefits" for all Americans—at least for all white American men. During his first term, a spirit of equality spread through American politics.

Citizenship

New Voters

In the nation's early years, most states had limited suffrage, or the right to vote, to men who owned property or paid taxes. Starting in 1815

SECTION RESOURCES

Reproducible Masters
- Reproducible Lesson Plan 11–2
- Guided Reading Activity 11–2
- Section Quiz 11–2
- Reteaching Activity 11–2
- Enrichment Activity 11–2

Transparencies
- Section Focus Transparency 11–2

Multimedia
- Vocabulary PuzzleMaker
- Testmaker
- GTV: The American People: Fabric of a Nation
- NGS PictureShow: Native Americans, Part 1
- Facts On File: The American Indian; Landmark Documents in American History

Western and Eastern states alike loosened the property requirements for voting. In the 1820s democracy expanded as people who had not been allowed to vote voted for the first time. Between 1824 and 1828, the percentage of white males voting in presidential elections increased from 36.9 to 57.6 percent. For the first time, white male sharecroppers, factory workers, and many others were brought into the political process.

The expansion of suffrage continued, and by 1840 more than 80 percent of white males voted in the presidential election. However, women still could not vote, and African Americans and Native Americans had few rights of any kind.

Another important development in the broadening of democracy involved presidential electors. By 1828, 22 of the 24 states changed their constitutions to allow the people, rather than the state legislatures, to choose presidential electors.

The Spoils System

Democrats carried the spirit of democracy into government. They wanted to open up government jobs to people from all walks of life. They were disturbed that the federal government had become a **bureaucracy,** a system in which nonelected officials carry out laws. Democrats argued that ordinary citizens could handle any government job.

President Jackson fired many federal workers and replaced them with his supporters. The discharged employees protested vehemently. They charged that Jackson was acting like a tyrant, hiring and firing people at will. Jackson responded that a new set of federal employees would be good for democracy.

One Jackson supporter explained it another way: "To the victors belong the spoils." In other words, because the Jacksonians had won the election, they had the right to the spoils—benefits of victory—such as handing out government jobs to supporters. The practice of replacing government employees with the winning candidate's supporters became known as the **spoils system.**

Electoral Changes

Jackson's supporters worked to make the political system more democratic as well. They abandoned the unpopular **caucus** system. In this system major political candidates were chosen by committees made up of members of Congress. The caucuses were replaced by **nominating conventions** in which delegates from the states selected the party's presidential candidate.

The Democrats held their first national party convention in 1832 in **Baltimore, Maryland.** The convention drew delegates from each state in the Union. The delegates decided to nominate the candidate who could gather two-thirds of the vote, and Jackson won the nomination. This system allowed many people to participate in the selection of political candidates.

Picturing HISTORY Carriages, wagons, and thousands of people followed Jackson to the White House for his inauguration reception. **What change in politics did Jackson's presidency represent?**

Cooperative Learning Activity

Covering Jackson's Inauguration Have students work together to do a TV broadcast covering Jackson's inauguration and the reception that followed. Roles include reporters to cover the inauguration and reception, news anchors to introduce various parts of the show, and actors to stage the inauguration, reception, and commercials. If possible, videotape the show and play it back on a VCR. Have students choose the tasks they would like to do to prepare for the show—researching facts, preparing visuals, writing dialogue, and so on.

2 TEACH

L1 Finding Supporting Details Have students find the three main heads in the section *(A New Era in Politics, The Tariff Debate, The Nullification Crisis).* Then have students find for each head at least two supporting details that explain the head.

Guided Reading Activity 11–2

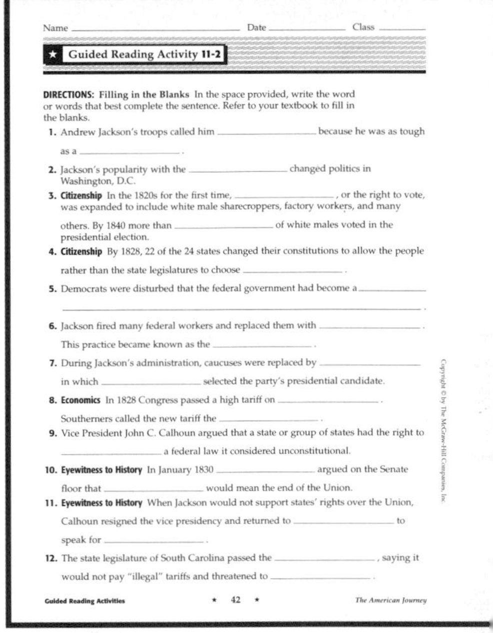

Name ______ Date ______ Class ______

★ Guided Reading Activity **11-2**

DIRECTIONS: Filling in the Blanks In the space provided, write the word or words that best complete the sentence. Refer to your textbook to fill in the blanks.

1. Andrew Jackson's troops called him ______ because he was as tough as a ______.
2. Jackson's popularity with the ______ changed politics in Washington, D.C.
3. **Citizenship** In the 1820s for the first time, ______, or the right to vote, was expanded to include white male sharecroppers, factory workers, and many others. By 1840 more than ______ of white males voted in the presidential election.
4. **Citizenship** By 1828, 22 of the 24 states changed their constitutions to allow the people rather than the state legislatures to choose ______.
5. Democrats were disturbed that the federal government had become a ______.
6. Jackson fired many federal workers and replaced them with ______. This practice became known as the ______.
7. During Jackson's administration, caucuses were replaced by ______ in which ______ selected the party's presidential candidate.
8. **Economics** In 1828 Congress passed a high tariff on ______. Southerners called the new tariff the ______.
9. Vice President John C. Calhoun argued that a state or group of states had the right to ______ a federal law it considered unconstitutional.
10. **Eyewitness to History** In January 1830 ______ argued on the Senate floor that ______ would mean the end of the Union.
11. **Eyewitness to History** When Jackson would not support states' rights over the Union, Calhoun resigned the vice presidency and returned to ______ to speak for ______.
12. The state legislature of South Carolina passed the ______, saying it would not pay "illegal" tariffs and threatened to ______.

Guided Reading Activities ★ 42 ★ *The American Journey*

Picturing HISTORY During the reception, Jackson had to leave the White House by a side door to avoid being crushed by the overly enthusiastic mob. **Ask: Why did the common people think of Jackson as one of them?** *(because he came from humble origins)*
Answer: *Jackson's first term brought a spirit of equality to American politics.*

you don't say...

Caucus probably derives from the Algonquin word *caucauasu,* which means "counselor" or "adviser." The first recorded use of the word to mean a meeting of political leaders came in the 1770s.

CHAPTER 11
Section 2, 336–339

Picturing HISTORY Discuss how politics is like a card game—one tries to figure out the opponent's strengths and to devise strategies for winning despite those strengths.
Answer: *tariffs (and states' rights)*

Linking PAST & PRESENT

Meeting in the Kitchen During his presidency Andrew Jackson surrounded himself with a group of trusted advisers. Because they met in the White House kitchen, Jackson's critics referred to the group as the "kitchen cabinet." Martin Van Buren was the only member of this influential group who also belonged to the president's official cabinet.

Like Jackson, many later presidents—often mistakenly—put their trust in their kitchen cabinet of friends rather than in officially appointed cabinet members.

3 ASSESS

Assign Section 2 Review as homework or as an in-class activity.

Use **Chapter Challenger Interactive Review Software** to review Section 2.

Section Quiz 11-2

Name ______________ Date ________ Class ________

Chapter 11 Score

Section Quiz 11-2

DIRECTIONS: Matching Match each item in Column A with the items in Column B. Write the correct letters in the blanks. *(10 points each)*

Column A	Column B
____ **1.** Old Hickory	**A.** spoils
____ **2.** suffrage	**B.** Andrew Jackson
____ **3.** benefits of victory	**C.** to break away
____ **4.** nullify	**D.** the right to vote
____ **5.** secede	**E.** cancel

DIRECTIONS: Multiple Choice In the blank at the left, write the letter of the choice that best completes the statement or answers the question. *(10 points each)*

____ **6.** These were the only Americans allowed to vote in 1824 and 1828.
A. African Americans **C.** Native Americans
B. white men **D.** white women

____ **7.** Andrew Jackson's supporters replaced the caucuses with
A. selection meetings. **C.** nominating conventions.
B. state conventions. **D.** delegate conventions.

____ **8.** A fee paid by merchants who imported goods was called a
A. tariff. **C.** bureaucracy.
B. spoils system. **D.** caucus.

____ **9.** This state passed the Nullification Act.
A. North Carolina **C.** South Carolina
B. Georgia **D.** Maryland

____ **10.** This allowed the president to use the United States military to enforce acts of Congress.
A. Military Act **C.** Congressional Bill
B. Presidential Act **D.** Force Bill

Section Quizzes • 42 • *The American Journey*

Picturing HISTORY In an 1832 political cartoon, Andrew Jackson (right) plays a card game with his political enemies. **What major issue divided Jackson and his opponents in 1832?**

Economics

The Tariff Debate

Americans from different parts of the country disagreed strongly on some issues. One such issue was the **tariff,** a fee paid by merchants who imported goods. While president, Jackson faced a tariff crisis that tested the national government's powers.

In 1828 Congress passed a very high tariff on manufactured goods from Europe. Manufacturers in the United States—mostly in the Northeast—welcomed the tariff. Because tariffs made European goods more expensive, American consumers were more likely to buy American-made goods.

Southerners, however, hated the new tariff. They called it the Tariff of Abominations—something detestable. The South traded cotton to Europe for manufactured goods, and the new tariff would make these items more expensive.

The South Protests

Southern politicians and plantation owners were outraged over the high tariff. Vice President John C. Calhoun argued that a state or group of states had the right to **nullify,** or cancel, a federal law it considered unconstitutional.

Some Southerners called for the Southern states to **secede,** or break away, from the United States and form their own government. When Calhoun explored this idea, troubling questions arose. The United States had been a nation for nearly 50 years. What if a state disagreed with the federal government? Did a state have the right to go its own way?

Calhoun said yes. In his view the states had created the federal government, so they should have the last word on decisions affecting them. Calhoun's argument grew out of the broad idea of **states' rights**—that the states have many rights and powers that are independent of the federal government. Many Northerners disagreed with Calhoun.

Eyewitness to HISTORY

The Webster–Hayne Debate

In January 1830, Senator **Daniel Webster** delivered a stinging attack on states' rights. Webster stood on the floor of the Senate to challenge a speech given by Robert Hayne, a young senator from South Carolina. Hayne had defended the idea that the states had a right to nullify acts of the federal government, and even to secede.

In his response, Webster defended the Constitution and the Union. He argued that nullification could only mean the end of the Union. Webster closed with the ringing statement, "Liberty and union, now and forever, one and inseparable!"

MULTIPLE LEARNING STYLES

Auditory/Musical Challenge students to compose limericks that Jackson's critics might have written about (a) the reception following his inauguration, (b) the spoils system, (c) the kitchen cabinet, or (d) the Force Bill. If necessary, review the limerick form with students: it is a 5-line poem in which the longer lines (1, 2, and 5) rhyme with one another as do the shorter lines (3 and 4). **L3**

Jackson Takes a Stand

Nobody knew exactly where President Jackson stood on the issue of states' rights. Many Southerners hoped that Jackson might side with them. In April 1830 supporters of states' rights invited the president to speak at a dinner. The guests, including Calhoun, waited anxiously for Jackson to speak. Finally, the president rose to his feet and spoke directly to Calhoun. "Our federal union . . . must be preserved!"

The states' rights supporters were shocked and disappointed, but Calhoun answered the president's challenge. He raised his glass and said, "The Union—next to our liberty, most dear." He meant that the fate of the Union must take second place to a state's liberty to make its own laws.

Calhoun realized that Jackson would not change his views. Wishing to return to Congress to speak for Southern interests, Calhoun won election to the Senate in December 1832. Two weeks later he resigned the vice presidency.

The Nullification Crisis

★ Southern anger over the tariff continued to build. The Union seemed on the verge of splitting apart. In 1832 Congress passed a new, lower tariff, hoping that the protest in the South would die down. It did not.

South Carolina, Calhoun's home state, had led the fight against the so-called Tariff of Abominations. Now South Carolina took the battle one step further. The state legislature passed the **Nullification Act,** declaring that it would not pay the "illegal" tariffs of 1828 and 1832. The South Carolina legislators threatened to secede from the Union if the federal government tried to interfere with their actions.

The Crisis Passes

"The Nullifiers of the South have run mad," Jackson said. "It leads directly to civil war and bloodshed." To ease the crisis, Jackson supported a compromise bill proposed by Henry Clay that would greatly lower the tariff. At the same time, Jackson made sure that the South would accept Clay's compromise. Early in 1833 he persuaded Congress to pass the **Force Bill,** which allowed the president to use the United States military to enforce acts of Congress. The message was clear: If South Carolina did not give in, it would face the army.

South Carolina quickly accepted the compromise tariff and agreed to set aside the Nullification Act. For the time being, the crisis between a state and the federal government was over. Yet South Carolina and the rest of the South would remember the lesson of the nullification crisis—that the federal government would not allow a state to go its own way without a fight.

Section 2 Review

Checking for Understanding

1. ***Identify*** Nullification Act, Force Bill.
2. ***Define*** suffrage, bureaucracy, spoils system, caucus, nominating convention, tariff, nullify, secede, states' rights.
3. ***Explain*** why President Jackson was popular with the average citizen.

Reviewing Themes

4. **Government and Democracy** How did the method of choosing electors change during Jackson's administration?

Critical Thinking

5. **Demonstrating Reasoned Judgment** Do you agree or disagree with Calhoun's statement, "The Union–next to our liberty, most dear"? Explain your answer.

Activity

Formulating Questions Prepare a list of five questions that you might have asked President Jackson if you were able to interview him.

Section 2 Review Answers

1. Nullification Act, 339; Force Bill, 339
2. The words are defined in the Glossary.
3. Average citizens identified with the president and felt they had a role in the government and the economy because Jackson came from humble beginnings.
4. States began to allow the people, rather than the state legislatures, to choose presidential electors.
5. Answers will vary, but students should decide whether they would have placed more value on the rights of individual states or on a strong federal government.

Activity Questions should take into account Jackson's personality and activities as described in the section.

CHAPTER 11

Section 2, 336–339

Reteaching Activity 11–2

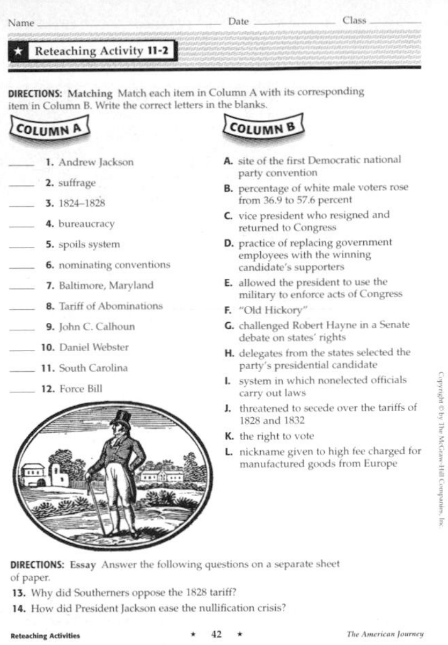

Name ______ Date ______ Class ______

★ Reteaching Activity 11-2

DIRECTIONS: Matching Match each item in Column A with its corresponding item in Column B. Write the correct letters in the blanks.

COLUMN A

____ 1. Andrew Jackson
____ 2. suffrage
____ 3. 1824–1828
____ 4. bureaucracy
____ 5. spoils system
____ 6. nominating conventions
____ 7. Baltimore, Maryland
____ 8. Tariff of Abominations
____ 9. John C. Calhoun
____ 10. Daniel Webster
____ 11. South Carolina
____ 12. Force Bill

COLUMN B

A. site of the first Democratic national party convention
B. percentage of white male voters rose from 36.9 to 57.6 percent
C. vice president who resigned and returned to Congress
D. practice of replacing government employees with the winning candidate's supporters
E. allowed the president to use the military to enforce acts of Congress
F. "Old Hickory"
G. challenged Robert Hayne in a Senate debate on states' rights
H. delegates from the states selected the party's presidential candidate
I. system in which nonelected officials carry out laws
J. threatened to secede over the tariffs of 1828 and 1832
K. the right to vote
L. nickname given to high fee charged for manufactured goods from Europe

DIRECTIONS: Essay Answer the following questions on a separate sheet of paper.

13. Why did Southerners oppose the 1828 tariff?
14. How did President Jackson ease the nullification crisis?

Reteaching Activities ★ 42 ★ *The American Journey*

Copyright © by The McGraw-Hill Companies, Inc.

Enrichment Activity 11–2

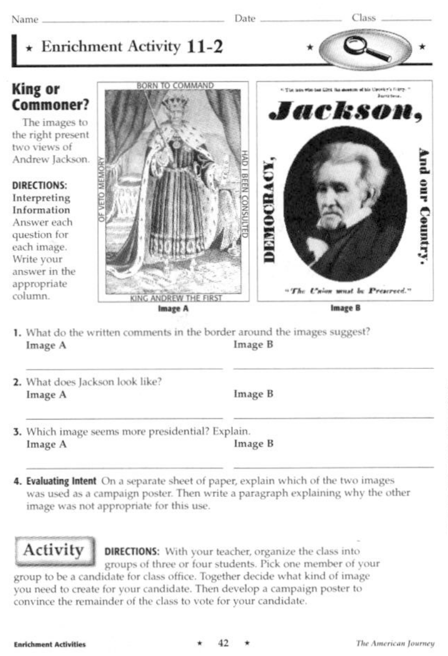

Name ______ Date ______ Class ______

★ Enrichment Activity 11-2

King or Commoner?

The images to the right present two views of Andrew Jackson.

DIRECTIONS: Interpreting Information Answer each question for each image. Write your answer in the appropriate column.

Image A

Image B

1. What do the written comments in the border around the images suggest?
   Image A ______ Image B ______
2. What does Jackson look like?
   Image A ______ Image B ______
3. Which image seems more presidential? Explain.
   Image A ______ Image B ______
4. **Evaluating Intent** On a separate sheet of paper, explain which of the two images was used as a campaign poster. Then write a paragraph explaining why the other image was not appropriate for this use.

Activity **DIRECTIONS:** With your teacher, organize the class into groups of three or four students. Pick one member of your group to be a candidate for class office. Together decide what kind of image you need to create for your candidate. Then develop a campaign poster to convince the remainder of the class to vote for your candidate.

Enrichment Activities ★ 42 ★ *The American Journey*

Copyright © by The McGraw-Hill Companies, Inc.

4 CLOSE

The spoils system has become an accepted part of American politics. Have students speculate on the possible negative and positive aspects of the system. (positive: *smoothes job of president to have loyal workers;* negative: *people could be given jobs on the basis of their support rather than on their qualifications)*

NATIONAL GEOGRAPHIC

Journeys

NATIONAL GEOGRAPHIC SOCIETY

CD-ROM
NGS PictureShow: Native Americans, Part 1

Have students view the program, then compare Native Americans' lives before resettlement and after forced relocation.

Facts On File

CD-ROM
Landmark Documents in American History

Title: *Indian Removal Act, 1830; Cherokee Nation* v. *Georgia, 1831* Have students outline the main provisions of the Indian Removal Act and then review the Cherokee Nation's case against Georgia by listing the Cherokee arguments against forced relocation.

CD-ROM
The American Indian

Students can learn more about the Trail of Tears by selecting the categories HISTORY and TRIBES from the main menu.

Linking PAST & PRESENT

Oklahoma The state of Oklahoma entered the Union in 1907. It was created from the Indian and Oklahoma territories. The state seal displays a large circle in whose center is a five-pointed star. Within the points of the star are five symbols, one for each seal of the "Five Civilized Tribes."

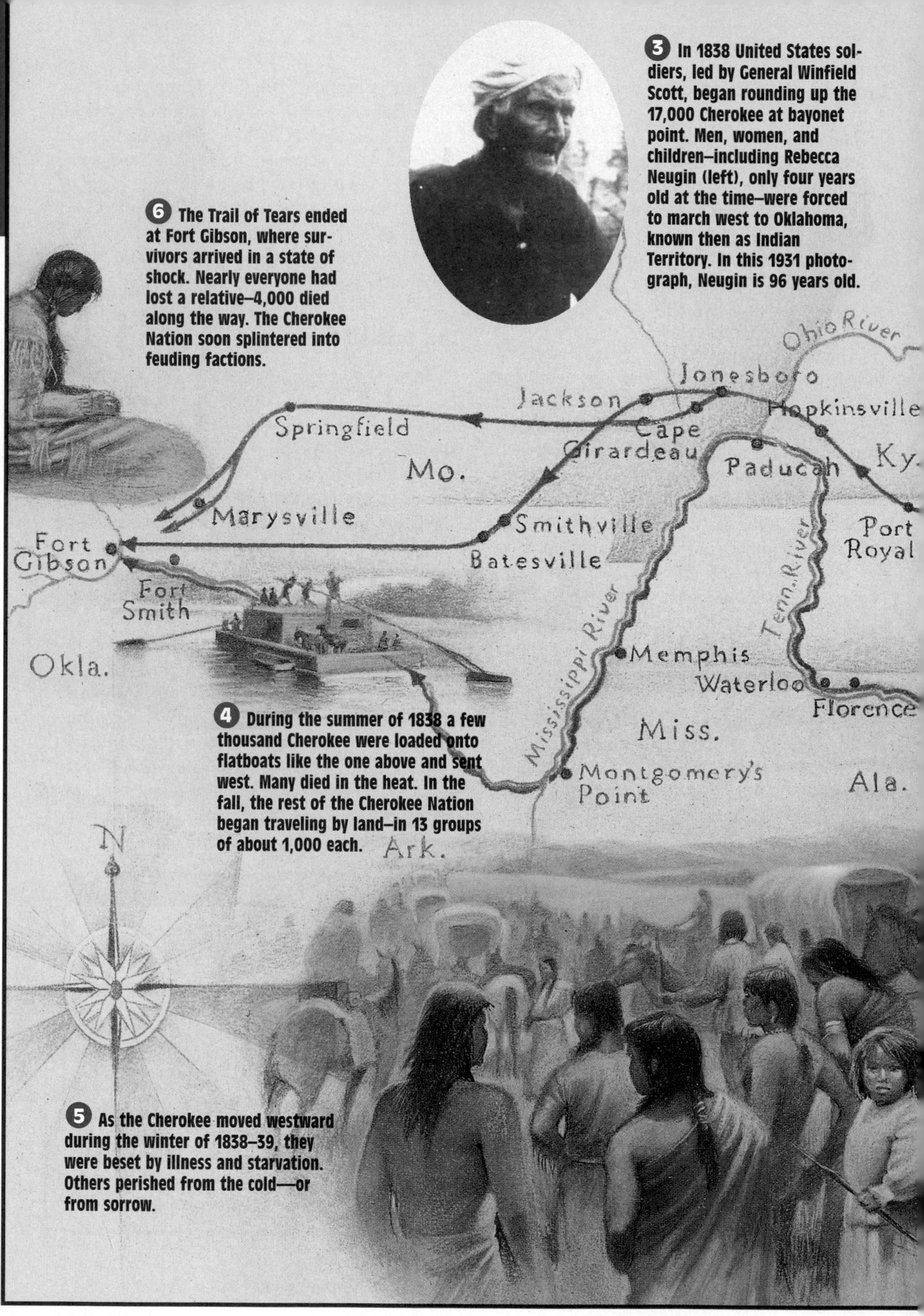

TEACHER'S NOTES

2 John Ross (right), the principal chief of the Cherokee, was a well-educated, wealthy planter. He opposed the policy of President Andrew Jackson (above left) to remove Cherokee from their homes in the Southeast and relocate them west of the Mississippi River. By 1838 Ross had lost the battle, and the Cherokee were forced off their lands.

1 In the early 19th century the Cherokee began adapting their ways to the lifestyles of Southern whites. The Cherokee lived in log cabins, kept cattle, and tended fields of grain. A few even grew rich and kept slaves.

NATIONAL GEOGRAPHIC

Journeys

Trail of Tears

"When [the] soldier came to our house, my father wanted to fight, but my mother told him that the soldiers would kill him if he did, and we surrendered without a fight. They drove us out of our house to join other prisoners in a stockade.... The people got so tired of salt pork on the journey that my father would walk through the woods as we traveled [in the wagon], hunting for turkeys and deer, which he brought into camp to feed us.... There was much sickness among the emigrants and a great many little children died of whooping cough."

— From the recollections of Rebecca Neugin, as told to historian Grant Foreman in the 1930s

Who? What? Where? When?

John Ross, the leader of the Cherokee Nation, had a Scots-Cherokee heritage but chose to put his Cherokee identity first. His Cherokee name was Cooweecoowee (white bird). Ross's wife was among those who died on the Trail of Tears. When he reached Indian Territory, he tried unsuccessfully to unite the various groups that had been relocated there.

NATIONAL GEOGRAPHIC SOCIETY

VIDEODISC
GTV: The American People: Fabric of a Nation

Side 2, Chapter 2
Title: *Between Worlds*
Subject: For Native Americans, a shrinking realm
Ask: **What did the "Indian agents" want the Native Americans to become?** *(farmers)*

Linking PAST & PRESENT

A Nation Remembers In 1987, nearly 150 years after the forced removal of the Cherokee, the Trail of Tears was designated a national monument.

TEACHER'S NOTES

CHAPTER 11
Section 3, 342–346

1 FOCUS

BELLRINGER
Motivational Activity

Before taking roll at the beginning of the class period, project Section Focus Transparency 11–3 and have students answer the questions. Discuss students' responses.

This activity is also available as a blackline master.

Section Focus Transparency 11–3

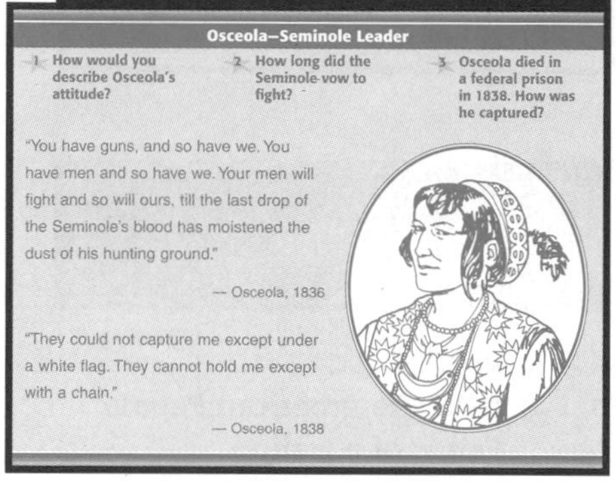

Vocabulary Precheck

Have students give a homonym for *guerrilla* and ask what the difference is between the two. *(gorilla; a gorilla is a kind of ape; a guerrilla is a kind of [human] fighter. The two words are not related.)*

Use the **Vocabulary PuzzleMaker** to create crossword and word search puzzles.

Section Theme
Groups and Institutions

In the 1830s many Native American peoples were forced to relocate. The Cherokee were among those peoples relocated despite a Supreme Court ruling in their favor.

Activity Have students find out why the Supreme Court's ruling did not prevent the forced removal of the Cherokee. *(President Jackson refused to enforce the ruling.)*

1830 | 1833 | 1836 | 1839

1830 Congress passes the Indian Removal Act

1832 Black Hawk leads Sauk and Fox people to Illinois

1835 Seminole refuse to leave Florida

1838 Cherokee driven from their homelands on the Trail of Tears

Section 3

Conflicts Over Land

READ TO DISCOVER . . .
- how Native American peoples were forced off their lands in the Southeast.
- how President Jackson defied the Supreme Court.

TERMS TO LEARN

relocate
guerrilla

The Storyteller

Following the defeat of his forces, Sauk and Fox leader Black Hawk said: "We always had plenty; our children never cried from hunger, neither were our people in want. . . . The rapids of Rock River furnished us with an abundance of excellent fish, and the land being very fertile, never failed to produce good crops of corn, beans, pumpkin, and squash. . . . If a prophet had come to our village in those days and told us that the things were to take place which have since come to pass, none of our people would have believed him."

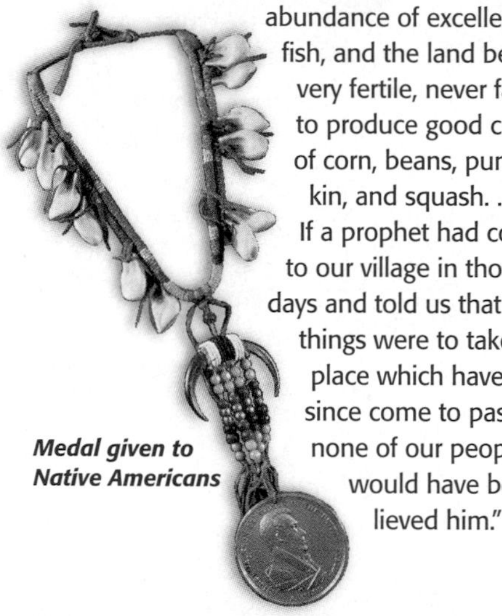

Medal given to Native Americans

While the United States had expanded westward by the 1830s, large numbers of Native Americans still lived in the eastern part of the country. In Georgia, Alabama, Mississippi, and Florida, the Cherokee, Creek, Choctaw, Chickasaw, and Seminole held valuable lands.

Moving Native Americans

Because the area west of the Mississippi was dry and seemed unsuitable for farming, few white Americans lived there. Many settlers wanted the federal government to **relocate** Native Americans living in the Southeast, to force them to leave their land and move west of the Mississippi River. President Andrew Jackson, a man of the frontier himself, supported the settlers' demand for Native American land. In his presidential campaign he had promised to back white settlers who wanted Native American lands.

Indian Removal Act

Congress responded by passing the **Indian Removal Act** in 1830. The act allowed the federal government to pay Native Americans to move west. Jackson then sent federal officials to negotiate treaties with Indians of the Southeast. Most accepted payment for their lands and agreed to move. In 1834 Congress created the **Indian Territory,** an area in present-day Oklahoma, for Native Americans from the Southeast.

SECTION RESOURCES

Reproducible Masters
- Reproducible Lesson Plan 11–3
- Guided Reading Activity 11–3
- Section Quiz 11–3
- Reteaching Activity 11–3
- Enrichment Activity 11–3

Transparencies
- Section Focus Transparency 11–3

Multimedia
- Vocabulary PuzzleMaker
- Chapter Challenger Interactive Review Software
- Testmaker
- Facts On File: Landmark Documents in American History

The Cherokee Nation

The Cherokee Nation, however, refused to give up its land. In treaties of the 1790s, the federal government had recognized the Cherokee people in the state of Georgia as a separate nation with its own laws. Georgia, however, refused to recognize Cherokee laws.

The Cherokee sued the state government and eventually took their case to the Supreme Court. In *Worcester* v. *Georgia* (1832), Chief Justice John Marshall ruled that Georgia had no right to interfere with the Cherokee. The Native Americans, he said, were protected by the federal government and the Constitution.

President Jackson had supported Georgia's efforts to remove the Cherokee. He vowed to ignore the Supreme Court's ruling. "John Marshall has made his decision," Jackson reportedly said. "Now let him enforce it."

Removal of Native Americans, 1820-1840

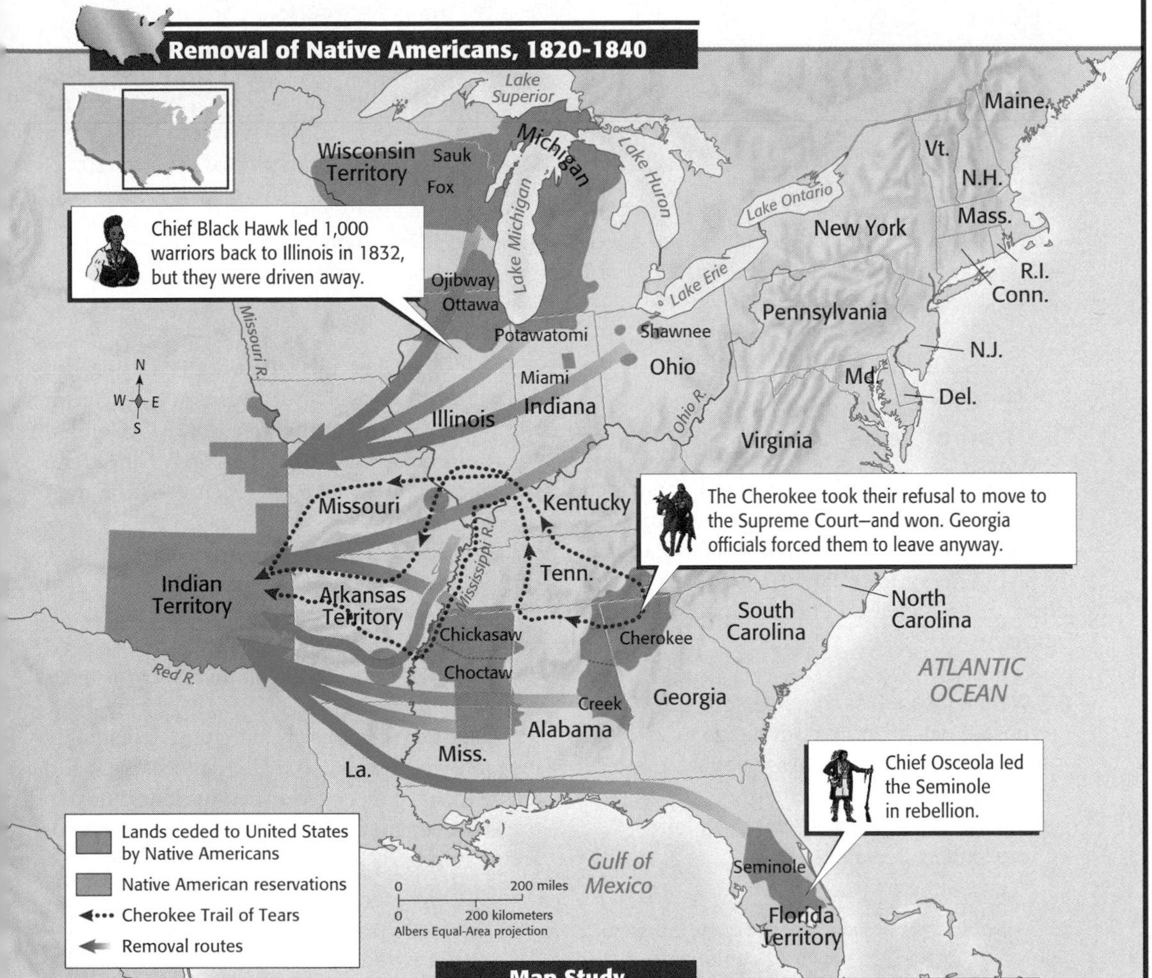

Map Study

The U.S. government moved about 120,000 Native Americans to reservations.

1. **Movement** What group was taken farthest from its homeland?
2. **Analyzing Information** Which groups were forced from Mississippi?

COOPERATIVE LEARNING ACTIVITY

Making an Illustrated Booklet Have students work in small groups to make an illustrated booklet on one of the topics in the section, such as Osceola and the Seminole Wars. Tasks—researching, writing, illustrating—should be divided according to the strengths of group members. Students might be especially moved by the description of Osceola's deathbed scene on page 127 of *The New Nation,* by Joy Hakim (New York: Oxford University Press, 1993).

2 TEACH

L1 Classifying Responses Have students review the section and list the three main ways Native Americans responded to the Indian Removal Act. *(accepted payment and agreed to move; sued the government; resisted forcefully)* **Ask: How were the outcomes of each response alike?** *(All ended with relocation of the Native Americans.)*

Guided Reading Activity 11–3

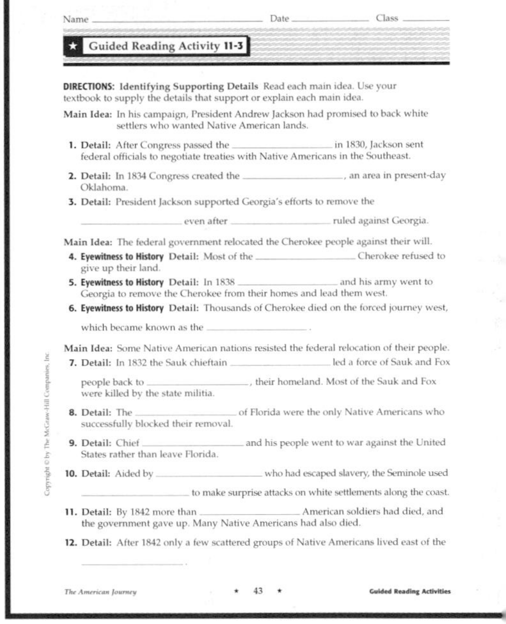
Name ______ Date ______ Class ______

★ Guided Reading Activity **11-3**

DIRECTIONS: Identifying Supporting Details Read each main idea. Use your textbook to supply the details that support or explain each main idea.

Main Idea: In his campaign, President Andrew Jackson had promised to back white settlers who wanted Native American lands.

1. **Detail:** After Congress passed the ______ in 1830, Jackson sent federal officials to negotiate treaties with Native Americans in the Southeast.
2. **Detail:** In 1834 Congress created the ______, an area in present-day Oklahoma.
3. **Detail:** President Jackson supported Georgia's efforts to remove the ______ even after ______ ruled against Georgia.

Main Idea: The federal government relocated the Cherokee people against their will.

4. **Eyewitness to History Detail:** Most of the ______ Cherokee refused to give up their land.
5. **Eyewitness to History Detail:** In 1838 ______ and his army went to Georgia to remove the Cherokee from their homes and lead them west.
6. **Eyewitness to History Detail:** Thousands of Cherokee died on the forced journey west, which became known as the ______.

Main Idea: Some Native American nations resisted the federal relocation of their people.

7. **Detail:** In 1832 the Sauk chieftain ______ led a force of Sauk and Fox people back to ______, their homeland. Most of the Sauk and Fox were killed by the state militia.
8. **Detail:** The ______ of Florida were the only Native Americans who successfully blocked their removal.
9. **Detail:** Chief ______ and his people went to war against the United States rather than leave Florida.
10. **Detail:** Aided by ______ who had escaped slavery, the Seminole used ______ to make surprise attacks on white settlements along the coast.
11. **Detail:** By 1842 more than ______ American soldiers had died, and the government gave up. Many Native Americans had also died.
12. **Detail:** After 1842 only a few scattered groups of Native Americans lived east of the ______.

Copyright © by The McGraw-Hill Companies, Inc.

The American Journey ★ 43 ★ **Guided Reading Activities**

Map Study

Answers

1. Seminole
2. Choctaw, Chickasaw

Map Skills Practice

Reading a Map Where were Native Americans sent? *(to reservations or to Indian Territory)*

HISTORY AND ART Although created a century after the event, John Lindeaux's painting captures the defeat and sadness of the Cherokee people. **Ask:** **What details in the painting show that the Cherokee followed some practices that were similar to those of whites?** *(using wagons pulled by domesticated animals, plow in lead wagon)*
Answer: *because they were forced to leave their homes, and thousands died on the march*

At the MOVIES

The film *Trail of Death* is a movie on VHS video that tells the story of the forced removal of the Potawatomi from north-central Indiana in 1838. It is distributed by Cambridge Educational, Charleston, WV.

CURRICULUM CONNECTION

ECONOMICS
The Cherokee Nation in Georgia enjoyed economic success. The nation owned 22,000 head of cattle, 2,000 spinning wheels, 700 looms, 31 gristmills, 10 sawmills, and 18 schools and held 1,300 enslaved persons.

HISTORY AND ART ***Trail of Tears* by Robert Lindeaux** Native Americans who were forced from their land traveled west in the 1830s. **Why did the Cherokee call the forced march the "Trail of Tears"?**

Eyewitness to HISTORY

The Trail of Tears

In 1835 the federal government persuaded a few Cherokee to sign a treaty giving up their people's land. Yet most of the 17,000 Cherokee refused to honor the treaty. They wrote a protest letter to the government and people of the United States.

> "We are aware that some persons suppose it will be for our advantage to [re]move beyond the Mississippi. . . . Our people universally think otherwise. . . . We wish to remain on the land of our fathers."

The Cherokee plea for understanding did not soften the resolve of President Jackson or the white settlers of the area. In 1838 **General Winfield Scott** and an army of 7,000 federal troops came to remove the Cherokee from their homes and lead them west.

Scott threatened to use force if the Cherokee did not leave. He told them he had positioned troops all around the country so that resistance and escape were both hopeless. "Chiefs, head men, and warriors—Will you then, by resistance, compel us to resort to arms?"

The Cherokee knew that fighting would only lead to their destruction. Filled with sadness and anger, their leaders gave in, and the long march to the West began. One man in Kentucky wrote of seeing hundreds of Cherokee marching by:

Footnotes to History

Native American Alphabet In 1821 Sequoya (sih•KWAWIH•uh), a Cherokee, invented an alphabet based on the spoken language of his people. Once they had a written language, many Cherokee learned to read. The Cherokee were the first Native Americans to publish a newspaper.

MULTIPLE LEARNING STYLES

Intrapersonal Have each student choose an event discussed in the section (such as the Trail of Tears), imagine what it would have been like to live through the event, and write a first-person narrative describing his or her experiences. Students may do additional research and read firsthand accounts of the period to lend additional authenticity to their narratives. Encourage them to share their narratives with the rest of the class. **L2**

“Even [the] aged . . . nearly ready to drop in the grave, were traveling with heavy burdens attached to their backs, sometimes on frozen ground and sometimes on muddy streets, with no covering for their feet.”

The brutal weather of the Great Plains claimed thousands of Cherokee lives along the way. Their forced journey west became known to the Cherokee people as the Trail Where They Cried. Historians call it the **Trail of Tears.**

Native American Resistance

In 1832 the Sauk chieftain, **Black Hawk,** led a force of Sauk and Fox people back to **Illinois,** their homeland. They wanted to recapture this area, which had been given up in a treaty. The Illinois state militia and federal troops responded with force, killing hundreds of Sauk and Fox and chasing the survivors over the border into present-day **Iowa.** The troops pursued the retreating Indians and slaughtered most of them.

Seminole leader Osceola

The Seminole Wars

The Seminole people of Florida were the only Native Americans who successfully blocked their removal. Although they were pressured in the early 1830s to sign treaties giving up their land, the Seminole chief, **Osceola,** and some

American Memories

Eastern Native American Life

Clothes

Blanket

Cooking kettle

What Was It Like? Eastern Native American men did most of the hunting and fishing, while the women farmed and gathered berries and nuts. **What do these items reveal about how eastern Native Americans met their other needs?**

MAKING CONNECTIONS ACTIVITY

Cultural Life The Cherokee and Seminole were not the only Southern Native Americans to be removed from lands east of the Mississippi River during the 1830s. The Choctaw, Chickasaw, and Creek peoples—who with the Cherokee and Seminole were known as the Five Civilized Tribes—were also driven from their lands. Have students do research for a report on one of these groups or on the Sauk or Fox of the Old Northwest. Students may describe the culture as a whole or the circumstances of the group's removal, or they may choose to do a biographical sketch of one of the leaders. **L2**

3 ASSESS

Assign Section 3 Review as homework or as an in-class activity.

Use **Chapter Challenger Interactive Review Software** to review Section 3.

Section Quiz 11–3

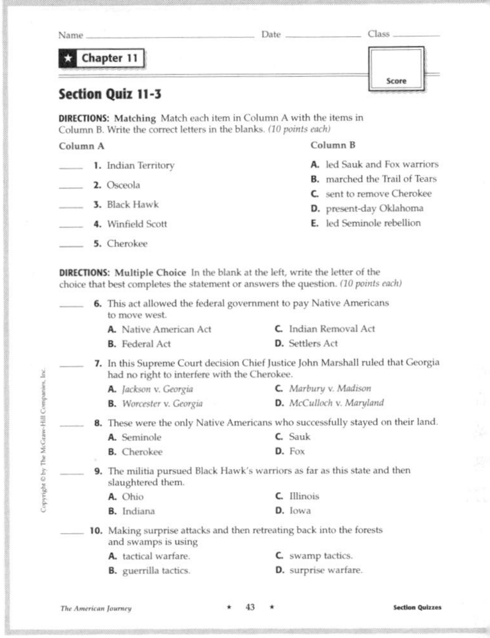

Name ______ Date ______ Class ______

★ Chapter 11

Score

Section Quiz 11-3

DIRECTIONS: Matching Match each item in Column A with the items in Column B. Write the correct letters in the blanks. *(10 points each)*

Column A	Column B
____ 1. Indian Territory	A. led Sauk and Fox warriors
____ 2. Osceola	B. marched the Trail of Tears
____ 3. Black Hawk	C. sent to remove Cherokee
____ 4. Winfield Scott	D. present-day Oklahoma
____ 5. Cherokee	E. led Seminole rebellion

DIRECTIONS: Multiple Choice In the blank at the left, write the letter of the choice that best completes the statement or answers the question. *(10 points each)*

____ 6. This act allowed the federal government to pay Native Americans to move west.
A. Native American Act C. Indian Removal Act
B. Federal Act D. Settlers Act

____ 7. In this Supreme Court decision Chief Justice John Marshall ruled that Georgia had no right to interfere with the Cherokee.
A. *Jackson v. Georgia* C. *Marbury v. Madison*
B. *Worcester v. Georgia* D. *McCulloch v. Maryland*

____ 8. These were the only Native Americans who successfully stayed on their land.
A. Seminole C. Sauk
B. Cherokee D. Fox

____ 9. The militia pursued Black Hawk's warriors as far as this state and then slaughtered them.
A. Ohio C. Illinois
B. Indiana D. Iowa

____ 10. Making surprise attacks and then retreating back into the forests and swamps is using
A. tactical warfare. C. swamp tactics.
B. guerrilla tactics. D. surprise warfare.

The American Journey ★ 43 ★ Section Quizzes

American Memories

Eastern Native American Life

People of the Iroquois nations built their villages along riverbanks, moving the villages from one location to another when the soil in which they grew crops became worn out. Rather than living in separate houses, several families lived together in longhouses that were 50 to 100 feet (15–30 meters) long. About 50 to 60 people lived in each longhouse. A village might contain as many as 40 longhouses enclosed in a stockade-style fence that surrounded the village. **Answer:** *They wove cloth for clothing and blankets; used kettle to cook food.*

CHAPTER 11
Section 3, 342–346

HISTORY AND ART This painting was done after the subjects had been taken captive. **Answer:** *to repel the attempt of the Sauk and Fox people to recapture their lost homeland*

Reteaching Activity 11–3

Name ____________ Date ________ Class ________

★ Reteaching Activity **11-3**

DIRECTIONS: Recalling Facts In the space provided, write the words or sentence that answer the questions.

1. What did the Indian Removal Act allow? ____________
2. What area did Congress create in 1834? ____________
3. How did Chief Justice John Marshall rule in *Worcester* v. *Georgia*? ____________
4. Whom did President Andrew Jackson support in the same case? ____________
5. Who was sent to remove the Cherokee from their land? ____________
6. What was the Trail of Tears? How did it get its name? ____________
7. Who was the Sauk chieftain who led a force of Sauk and Fox people back to their homeland in Illinois? ____________
8. How were the Seminole people different from other Native American groups? ____________
9. What Seminole chief went to war rather than leave Florida? ____________
10. Who aided the Seminole people in their war against white settlers? ____________
11. What fighting tactics did the Seminole use? ____________
12. Who won the Seminole wars? ____________

Osceola

Enrichment Activity 11–3

Name ____________ Date ________ Class ________

★ Enrichment Activity **11-3** ★

The Voice of a Nation

Native Americans struggled to keep their cultures alive. Sequoya of the Cherokee Nation, developed an alphabet that made the Cherokee the first Native American people who could read and write. Sequoya's system was a syllabary (a system where symbols stand for sounds in the language).

DIRECTIONS: Applying Information The message below came from the *Cherokee Phoenix*, first published in 1828 and named for a mythical bird that burned and then rose again from the ashes. Use Sequoya's syllabary to write each syllable's pronunciation.

Pronunciation of Cherokee Language

Letter	Pronunciation
1. Ꮆ	
2. Ꮃ	
3. Ꭹ	
4. Ꮷ	
5. Ꮄ	
6. Ꭿ	
7. Ꮜ	
8. Ꮼ	
9. Ꭿ	

Cherokee Pronunciation Chart

10. The vertical message translates, "Cherokee will rise again." How does the message connect to the name of the newspaper and the life of the Cherokee? ____________

Activity **DIRECTIONS:** Imagine that you are a writer for the *Cherokee Phoenix*. Prepare a short article for the paper explaining why it is important for the readers to learn to read and write their language as well as speak it.

4 CLOSE

Seminole leader Osceola was finally seized—under a flag of truce. Ask students how that act symbolizes white–Native American relations.

HISTORY AND ART

***Black Hawk and Whirling Thunder* by John Wesley Jarvis** This portrait of the 66-year-old Sauk leader Black Hawk (left) with his son was painted in 1833. **Why did Illinois settlers and militia use force against Black Hawk?**

of his people refused to leave Florida. The Seminole decided to go to war against the United States instead.

In 1835 the Seminole joined forces with a group of African Americans who had run away to escape slavery. Together they attacked white settlements along the Florida coast. They used **guerrilla** tactics, making surprise attacks and then retreating back into the forests and swamps.

By 1842 more than 1,500 of the 10,000 American soldiers who fought in the Seminole wars had died, mostly from disease. The government gave up and allowed the Seminole to remain in Florida. Many Seminole, however, had died in the long war, and many more were captured and forced to move westward. After 1842 only a few scattered groups of Native Americans lived east of the Mississippi.

Section 3 Review

Checking for Understanding

1. ***Identify*** Indian Removal Act, General Winfield Scott, Trail of Tears, Black Hawk, Osceola.
2. ***Define*** relocate, guerrilla.
3. ***Describe*** how President Jackson reacted to the Supreme Court decision regarding the Cherokee.

Reviewing Themes

4. **Groups and Institutions** How were the Seminole able to resist relocation?

Critical Thinking

5. **Drawing Conclusions** Do you think it was fair for white Americans to force Native Americans to relocate? Why or why not?

Activity

Writing a Letter Imagine that you were a member of the Cherokee Nation. Write a letter to Andrew Jackson telling him why you should be allowed to stay in your homeland.

Section 3 Review Answers

1. Indian Removal Act, 342; General Winfield Scott, 344; Trail of Tears, 345; Black Hawk, 345; Osceola, 345
2. The words are defined in the Glossary.
3. He ignored the ruling and sided with Georgia in its efforts to remove the Cherokee.
4. They waged a guerrilla war until the United States gave in and let the Seminole survivors stay in Florida.
5. Answers will vary. Most students will probably argue that it was unfair because Native Americans occupied the land first, many had demonstrated they could coexist peacefully with whites, and the Supreme Court ruling should've been upheld.

Activity Letters will vary, but should explain why Native Americans had a right to stay in their homelands.

Study and Writing
SKILL BUILDER

Analyzing Primary Sources

How do historians determine what happened in the past? They do some detective work. They comb through bits of evidence from the past to reconstruct events. These bits of historical evidence—both written and illustrated—are called *primary sources.*

Learning the Skill

Primary sources are records of events made by the people who witnessed them. They include letters, diaries, photographs and pictures, news articles, and legal documents. A primary source is considered more valid if it was written at the time of the event instead of years later, when the author's perspective may have changed.

Primary sources yield several important kinds of information. Often they give detailed accounts of events. However, the account reflects only one perspective. For this reason, you must examine as many perspectives as possible before drawing any conclusions. To analyze primary sources, follow these steps:

- Identify the author of the document.
- Identify when and where the document was written.
- Read the document for its content and try to answer the five "W" questions: Who is it about? What is it about? When did it happen? Where did it happen? Why did it happen?
- Identify the author's opinions.
- Determine what kind of information may be missing from the primary source.

Practicing the Skill

The primary source that follows comes from Speckled Snake, an elder of the Creek Nation, in 1829. He was more than 100 years old at the time he said these words. Read the quote, then answer the questions that follow.

> "Brothers! I have listened to many talks from our Great Father. When he first came over the wide waters, he was but a little man. . . . But when the white man had warmed himself before the Indians' fire and filled himself with their hominy, he became very large. With a step he bestrode the mountains and his feet covered the plains and the valleys. His hand grasped the eastern and the western sea, and his head rested on the moon. Then he became our Great Father. He loved his red children, and he said, 'Get a little further, lest I tread on thee. . . .' Brothers, I have listened to a great many talks from our Great Father. But they always began and ended in this—'Get a little further; you are too near me.'"

1. When was this document written?
2. What events are described?
3. Who was affected by these events?
4. Where did these events take place?
5. What is the general feeling of the person who stated this opinion?

Applying the Skill

Analyzing Primary Sources Find a primary source from your past—a photo, a report card, an old newspaper clipping, or your first baseball card. Bring this source to class and explain what it shows about that time in your life.

Study and Writing
SKILL BUILDER

TEACH

Analyzing Primary Sources

This skill teaches students to identify and evaluate primary sources. Point out that primary sources include not only written materials but also paintings, photographs, and artifacts. Ask students whether their textbook is a primary source. *(no, although it contains many primary sources)* Ask students why two eyewitness accounts of the same event might be very different. *(People have different biases; one person might be intentionally trying to deceive; one person might be better at remembering details; and so on.)*

Additional Practice

Chapter Skills Activity 11

Facts On File

CD-ROM
Landmark Documents in American History

Title: *Message on Removal of Southern Indians (Seventh Annual Message to Congress), Andrew Jackson, 1835*
Encourage students to practice the skill by reviewing this primary document and answering the five "W" questions.

ANSWERS TO PRACTICING THE SKILL

1. 1829
2. the coming of white people and the forcing of Native Americans from their land
3. Native Americans
4. North America
5. The writer feels disgust, anger, distrust, and resentment because the white settlers have overpowered the Native Americans and taken their lands, pushing them farther and farther west.

Applying the Skill Students should use a primary source from their past and explain what it shows about that time in their lives.

1 FOCUS

BELLRINGER
Motivational Activity

Before taking roll at the beginning of the class period, project Section Focus Transparency 11–4 and have students answer the questions. Discuss students' responses.

This activity is also available as a blackline master.

Section Focus Transparency 11–4

Presidential Elections of 1836 and 1840

1. Who were the two major presidential candidates in 1836 and 1840?
2. Who won the presidential election in 1836? In 1840?
3. Give two possible explanations for the significant increase in popular votes and electoral votes in 1840.

	Election of 1836		Election of 1840	
	Popular Vote	Electoral Vote	Popular Vote	Electoral Vote
Martin Van Buren	726,676	170	1,128,702	60
William Henry Harrison	548,007	73	1,275,017	234

(Source: *1994 World Almanac*, page 614)

Vocabulary Precheck

Ask students to speculate on the meaning of each term. Then have them check their guesses by finding the definitions in the text.

Use the **Vocabulary PuzzleMaker** to create crossword and word search puzzles.

Section Theme
Economic Factors

The Bank of the United States and a depression each played a role in the presidential elections of 1832 and 1840, respectively.

Activity Have students find the role that each played. *(Jackson's veto of the Bank charter helped him gain support. The depression caused people to turn away from Van Buren.)*

1830 — 1835 — 1840 — 1845

1832 Andrew Jackson challenges the Bank of the United States

1836 Martin Van Buren is elected president

1837 Panic of 1837 strikes the nation

1841 Vice President John Tyler becomes president

Section 4

Jackson and the Bank

READ TO DISCOVER . . .

- why Jackson wanted to destroy the Bank of the United States.
- why the Whigs came to power in 1840.

TERMS TO LEARN

veto
depression
laissez-faire
log cabin campaign

The Storyteller

President Andrew Jackson made many enemies. His most outspoken rivals, the Whigs, were strong in Congress. They accused "King Andrew" of increasing his power and spreading corruption with the spoils system. In response, Jackson declared that the president was responsible for the protection of "the liberties and rights of the people and the integrity of the Constitution against the Senate, or the House of Representatives, or both together."

Bank note issued in the mid-1800s

Jackson had another great battle during his presidency. For years, he had attacked the Bank of the United States as being an organization of wealthy Easterners over which ordinary citizens had no control. The Bank of the United States was a powerful institution. It held the federal government's money and controlled much of the country's money supply. Although the Bank had been chartered by Congress, it was run by private bankers rather than elected officials.

The Bank's president, **Nicholas Biddle,** represented everything Jackson disliked. Jackson prided himself on being a self-made man who started with nothing. Biddle, on the other hand, came from a wealthy family and had a fine education and social standing.

War against the Bank

In 1832 Jackson's opponents gave him the chance to take action against the Bank. Senators **Henry Clay** and **Daniel Webster,** friends of Biddle, planned to use the Bank to defeat Jackson in the 1832 presidential election. They persuaded Biddle to apply early for a new charter—a government permit to operate the Bank—even though the Bank's current charter did not expire until 1836.

Clay and Webster believed the Bank had popular support. They thought that an attempt by Jackson to veto its charter would lead to his defeat and allow Henry Clay to be elected president.

When the bill to renew the Bank's charter came to Jackson for signature, he was sick in bed.

SECTION RESOURCES

Reproducible Masters
- Guided Reading Activity 11–4
- Political Cartoons
- Section Quiz 11–4
- Reteaching Activity 11–4
- Enrichment Activity 11–4

Transparencies
- Section Focus Transparency 11–4

Multimedia
- Vocabulary PuzzleMaker
- Chapter Challenger Interactive Review Software
- Testmaker
- The Presidents: A Picture History of Our Nation

Jackson told his friend **Martin Van Buren,** "The bank, Mr. Van Buren, is trying to kill me. But I will kill it!" Jackson **vetoed,** or rejected, the bill.

In a message to Congress, Jackson angrily denounced the Bank for favoring the rich and hurting the poor. Jackson argued that

> "... when laws ... make the rich richer and the potent more powerful, the humble members of society—the farmers, mechanics, and laborers—who have neither the time nor the means of securing like favors to themselves, have a right to complain of the injustice of their Government."

The Election of 1832

Webster and Clay were right about one thing. The Bank of the United States did play a large part in the campaign of 1832. Their strategy for gaining support for Clay as president, however, backfired. Most people supported Jackson's veto of the bank charter bill. Jackson was reelected, receiving 55 percent of the popular vote and collecting 219 electoral votes to Clay's 49. Martin Van Buren was elected vice president.

Once reelected, Jackson decided on a plan to "kill" the Bank ahead of the 1836 schedule. He ordered the withdrawal of all government deposits from the Bank and placed the funds in smaller state banks. By 1836 Nicholas Biddle was forced to close the Bank.

Politics after Jackson

When Jackson decided not to run for a third term in 1836, the Democrats selected Martin Van Buren of **New York,** Jackson's friend and vice president, as their candidate. Van Buren faced bitter opposition from the **Whigs,** a new political party that included former National Republicans and other anti-Jackson forces. Jackson's great popularity and his personal support of Van Buren helped Van Buren easily defeat several Whig opponents. Van Buren was inaugurated in 1837.

Picturing HISTORY Nicholas Biddle was a noted writer, legislator, and diplomat as well as a brilliant financier. **What major institution did Nicholas Biddle head?**

Economics

The Panic of 1837

Two months after Van Buren took office, the country entered a severe economic **depression,** a period in which business and employment fall to a very low level. The depression began with the **Panic of 1837,** a time when land values dropped sharply, investments declined suddenly, banks failed, and people lost confidence in the economic system.

Within a few weeks, thousands of businesses had closed and hundreds of thousands of people lost their jobs. Prices rose so high that poor people could not afford food or rent. In February 1837, people in New York put up signs voicing their anger:

2 TEACH

L1, ELL Matching Have each student create a matching quiz using the people and terms in the section and a brief definition or identification of each. Then have pairs of students swap quizzes and try to complete one another's quiz.

Political Cartoons, *Andrew Jackson and the Second Bank of the United States*

Picturing HISTORY Jackson may have disliked Biddle for his wealthy origins, but by the time he became president, Jackson himself was a wealthy plantation owner. **Answer:** *the Bank of the United States*

NATIONAL GEOGRAPHIC SOCIETY

CD-ROM
The Presidents: A Picture History of Our Nation

Have students select Andrew Jackson from the main menu. Have them note major events in Jackson's presidency.

Guided Reading Activity 11–4

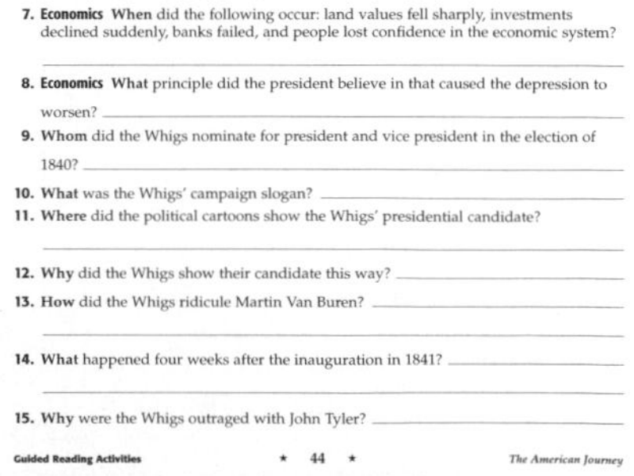

Name ______ Date ______ Class ______

★ Guided Reading Activity 11-4

DIRECTIONS: Recording Who, What, When, Where, Why, and **How** Read the section and answer the questions below. Refer to your textbook to write the answers.

1. **Why** did President Andrew Jackson attack the Bank of the United States? ______
2. **Who** was president of the Bank? ______
3. **What** did Jackson do when the bill to renew the Bank's charter came to him for his signature? ______
4. **How** did Jackson "kill" the Bank once he was reelected? ______
5. **Whom** did the Democrats select to succeed Jackson as president in 1836? ______
6. **What** new political party participated in the election of 1836? ______
7. **Economics When** did the following occur: land values fell sharply, investments declined suddenly, banks failed, and people lost confidence in the economic system? ______
8. **Economics What** principle did the president believe in that caused the depression to worsen? ______
9. **Whom** did the Whigs nominate for president and vice president in the election of 1840? ______
10. **What** was the Whigs' campaign slogan? ______
11. **Where** did the political cartoons show the Whigs' presidential candidate? ______
12. **Why** did the Whigs show their candidate this way? ______
13. **How** did the Whigs ridicule Martin Van Buren? ______
14. **What** happened four weeks after the inauguration in 1841? ______
15. **Why** were the Whigs outraged with John Tyler? ______

Guided Reading Activities ★ 44 ★ *The American Journey*

Copyright © by The McGraw-Hill Companies, Inc.

COOPERATIVE LEARNING ACTIVITY

Studying the Presidents Organize the class into small groups to make a large chart listing the presidents up to Andrew Jackson. Have students give at least one interesting or fun-to-know fact about each and at least one important accomplishment of each. When available, add information about presidential wives and number of children. Each group should research different presidents. Assign some students to do the actual research, others to write the information on the chart, and others to illustrate some of the fun facts. You may wish to extend this project over several units, so that students will be researching presidents of the period under study.

CHAPTER 11
Section 4, 348–351

Who?What?Where?When?

William Henry Harrison was not born in a log cabin as his supporters claimed. He was actually born in a two-and-a-half-story mansion made of red brick, located on a large plantation on the James River.

Picturing HISTORY In addition to showing him fighting the monster representing the Bank of the United States, this cartoonist suggested that the public was weary of the conflict between Jackson and the Bank. He showed this by representing the public as the person pulling on Jackson's suspenders, trying to get him back into bed. **Answer:** *felt it favored the rich and hurt the poor*

3 ASSESS

Assign Section 4 Review as homework or as an in-class activity.

Use **Chapter Challenger Interactive Review Software** to review Section 4.

Section Quiz 11–4

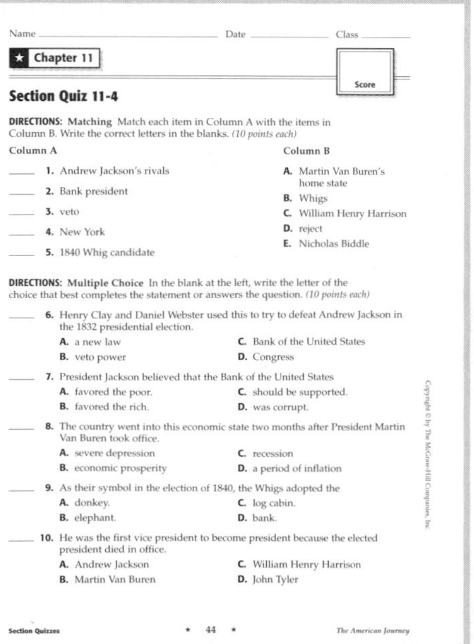

Name ______ Date ______ Class ______

★ Chapter 11 | Score

Section Quiz 11-4

DIRECTIONS: Matching Match each item in Column A with the items in Column B. Write the correct letters in the blanks. *(10 points each)*

Column A

____ 1. Andrew Jackson's rivals
____ 2. Bank president
____ 3. veto
____ 4. New York
____ 5. 1840 Whig candidate

Column B

A. Martin Van Buren's home state
B. Whigs
C. William Henry Harrison
D. reject
E. Nicholas Biddle

DIRECTIONS: Multiple Choice In the blank at the left, write the letter of the choice that best completes the statement or answers the question. *(10 points each)*

____ 6. Henry Clay and Daniel Webster used this to try to defeat Andrew Jackson in the 1832 presidential election.
A. a new law C. Bank of the United States
B. veto power D. Congress

____ 7. President Jackson believed that the Bank of the United States
A. favored the poor. C. should be supported.
B. favored the rich. D. was corrupt.

____ 8. The country went into this economic state two months after President Martin Van Buren took office.
A. severe depression C. recession
B. economic prosperity D. a period of inflation

____ 9. As their symbol in the election of 1840, the Whigs adopted the
A. donkey. C. log cabin.
B. elephant. D. bank.

____ 10. He was the first vice president to become president because the elected president died in office.
A. Andrew Jackson C. William Henry Harrison
B. Martin Van Buren D. John Tyler

Section Quizzes ★ 44 ★ *The American Journey*

“Bread, Meat, Rent, and Fuel!
Their prices must come down!
The Voice of the People shall be heard
and will prevail!”

The Depression Continues

President Van Buren did little to solve the economic problems causing the depression. He believed in the principle of **laissez-faire**—that government should interfere as little as possible in the nation's economy. As the situation worsened, the administration did take a few steps, such as borrowing money to pay off government debts. These steps had little effect on the economic crisis, however. The depression lasted for about six years. The laborers, farmers, and small businesspeople who had enthusiastically supported Jackson now turned against President Van Buren.

The Whigs Come to Power

The Democrats had controlled the presidency for 12 years. However, with the country still in the depths of depression, the Whigs thought they had a chance to win the election in 1840. They nominated **William Henry Harrison,** a hero of the War of 1812, to run against President Van Buren. **John Tyler,** a planter from Virginia, was Harrison's running mate. Because Harrison had gained national fame defeating Tecumseh's followers in the Battle of Tippecanoe, the Whigs' campaign slogan was “Tippecanoe and Tyler too.”

The Election of 1840

To win the election, Harrison had to gain the support of the laborers and farmers who had voted for Jackson. The Whigs adopted a log cabin as their symbol. Political cartoons appeared in newspapers showing Harrison, a wealthy man from an upper-class Virginia family, in front of a log cabin. The Whigs wanted to show that their candidate was a “man of the people.”

The Whigs also ridiculed Van Buren as “King Martin,” a wealthy snob who had spent the people's money on fancy furniture for the White House. The **log cabin campaign** seemed to work, and Harrison went on to defeat Van Buren by a wide margin.

Disappointment in Office

William Henry Harrison was inaugurated in 1841 as the first Whig president. The Whigs were still celebrating their victory four weeks later, when Harrison died of pneumonia. John Tyler of Virginia became the first vice president to gain the presidency because the elected president died in office.

Picturing HISTORY In this political cartoon, President Jackson tries to kill the bank-serpent before it destroys him. **Why did Jackson oppose the Bank of the United States?**

MULTIPLE LEARNING STYLES

Logical/Mathematical Under Jackson the United States paid off the national debt. Today's national debt is about $5 trillion ($5,000,000,000,000), and our population is about 260 million (260,000,000). Have students express both figures in numerals. Then have them figure out how much every man, woman, and child in the United States would have to contribute to pay off the debt if it were distributed equally. *(about $20,000)* Ask students to calculate how much their own family would have to contribute. *($20,000 times the number of family members)* Have each student make a pictograph showing the amount his or her family would have to contribute. **L2, ELL**

Picturing HISTORY In the 1840 election campaign, the Whigs marched in street parades, often carrying miniature log cabins on poles. **Why did Harrison's supporters make the log cabin their symbol?**

Although Tyler had been elected vice president as a Whig, he had once been a Democrat. As president, Tyler disagreed with many Whig policies. A strong supporter of states' rights and an independent thinker, Tyler quickly vetoed several bills sponsored by Whigs in Congress, including a bill to recharter the Bank of the United States. His lack of party loyalty outraged Whigs. Most of Tyler's cabinet resigned, and Whig leaders in Congress expelled Tyler from the party.

It seemed that the Whigs could not agree on their party's goals. Increasingly, Whigs voted according to sectional ties—North, South, and West—not party ties. This division may explain why the Whig candidate, Henry Clay, lost the election of 1844 to Democratic candidate **James Polk.** After only four years, the Whigs were out of power again.

Section 4 Review

Checking for Understanding

1. ***Identify*** Nicholas Biddle, Henry Clay, Daniel Webster, Martin Van Buren, Whigs, Panic of 1837, William Henry Harrison, James Polk.
2. ***Define*** veto, depression, laissez-faire, log cabin campaign.
3. ***List*** Jackson's reasons for wanting to "kill" the Bank of the United States.

Reviewing Themes

4. **Economic Factors** Why did President Van Buren do little to solve the nation's economic problems caused by the depression?

Critical Thinking

5. **Evaluating Information** What tactics did the Whigs borrow from Jackson's campaign to win the election of 1840?

Activity

Designing a Campaign Button Write a campaign slogan for Van Buren or Harrison in the election of 1840. Then design a campaign button that incorporates your slogan.

Section 4 Review Answers

1. Biddle, 348; Clay, 348; Webster, 348; Van Buren, 349; Whigs, 349; Panic of 1837, 349; Harrison, 350; Polk, 351
2. The words are defined in the Glossary.
3. He believed it favored the rich and hurt the poor and that it had too much power.
4. He believed in the principle of laissez-faire—that government should interfere as little as possible in the nation's economy.
5. Like Jackson, they tried to appeal to the "common man" by portraying Harrison as a humble man of the people. They ridiculed Van Buren, calling him King Martin to suggest that he was interested only in the welfare of the rich.

Activity Students' slogans and buttons should show an understanding of each candidate's platform.

Picturing HISTORY "Keep the ball rolling" comes from Harrison's campaign. Supporters made a huge ball covered with slogans and pushed it from city to city. **Answer:** *to show he was a man of the people*

Reteaching Activity 11–4

Name ______ Date ______ Class ______

★ Reteaching Activity **11-4**

DIRECTIONS: Organizing Facts The numbered items in the Fact Bank are characteristics of United States presidents in the mid-1800s. Write the number of each item in the appropriate section of the chart.

Presidents in the Mid-1800s

Andrew Jackson	Martin Van Buren	William Henry Harrison	John Tyler	James Polk

★FACT BANK

1. used "Tippecanoe and Tyler too" as campaign slogan
2. vetoed bills sponsored by his own political party
3. took a laissez-faire approach to the economy
4. elected president in 1844 as a Democrat
5. received 55 percent of the popular vote in 1832 election
6. hero of the War of 1812
7. After his inauguration, the Panic of 1837 struck the economy.
8. vetoed bill to renew Bank of the United States in 1832
9. first president to take office following the death of an elected president
10. first Whig candidate to be elected president
11. withdrew government deposits from the Bank of the United States
12. died four weeks after his inauguration

Reteaching Activities ★ 44 ★ *The American Journey*

Enrichment Activity 11–4

Name ______ Date ______ Class ______

★ Enrichment Activity **11-4** ★ ★

Political Slogans

By 1840 slogans had been part of the American election scene for almost half a century. Identify and explain the slogans below from the campaigns of 1824, 1828, 1832, 1836, and 1840, using what you have learned in the chapter.

DIRECTIONS: Recalling Facts Name the candidate and/or the election year for each slogan below.

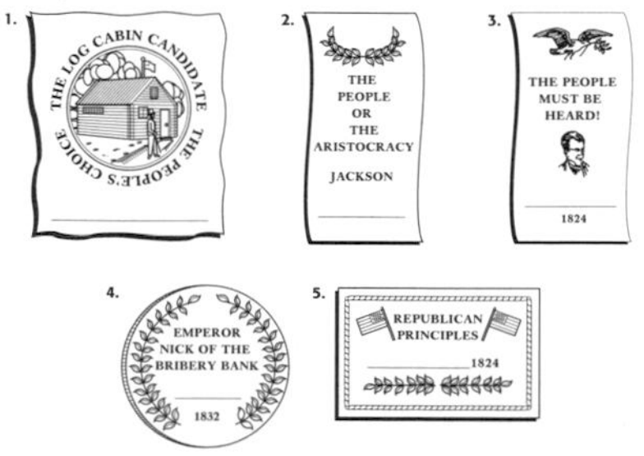

DIRECTIONS: Interpreting Sayings Explain each of the following slogans.

6. Democrats, 1824: The Glorious Principles of Seventy-Six ______
7. Whigs, 1836: Our Country, Not Our Party ______
8. Democrats, 1836: Firm Friend of the South ______
9. Whigs, 1840: He Leaves the Plough to Save His Country ______

Enrichment Activities ★ 44 ★ *The American Journey*

4 CLOSE

Ask students which of Jackson's nicknames they think is more fitting: King Andrew or Old Hickory. **Why?**

GLENCOE TECHNOLOGY

VIDEODISC
MindJogger Videoquiz

Use MindJogger to review the Chapter 11 content.

Chapter 11
Disc 2, Side A

Also available in VHS.

Reviewing Key Terms

The key terms used in this activity are defined in the textbook glossary on pages A26–A35.

Reviewing Key Facts

1. Jackson's supporters: favored states' rights, suspicious of a strong central government; Adams's suporters: supported a strong central government, supported federal measures such as road building and a national bank
2. Women, African Americans, and Native Americans were still excluded from voting. Only white male property owners could vote before the 1800s.
3. Nominating conventions replaced caucuses, which were made up of members of Congress. Delegates from the states selected the party's presidential candidate at nominating conventions, allowing more people to participate.
4. money and a place to relocate
5. By focusing on the "common man," it appealed to the same voters that were attracted to Jackson.

Critical Thinking

1. white males
2. No; he supported their relocation, showing that he did not consider them to have the same rights as other Americans.

Review and Activities

Reviewing Key Terms

On a sheet of paper, use each of the following terms in a sentence:

favorite son
majority
plurality
mudslinging
landslide
suffrage
spoils system
nominating convention
nullify
secede
states' rights
depression
laissez-faire

Reviewing Key Facts

1. How did the supporters of Jackson and Adams differ in their beliefs?
2. Which Americans were prohibited from voting in most states before the 1800s?
3. How did nominating conventions make the selection of political candidates more democratic?
4. What did the government promise Native Americans in exchange for their land?
5. Why was Harrison's log cabin campaign successful?

Critical Thinking

Recognizing Bias

President Andrew Jackson promised "equal protection and equal benefits" for all Americans.

1. Who were the "Americans" that he was referring to?
2. Do you think he considered Indians to be Americans? Why or why not?

Reviewing Themes

1. **Continuity and Change** How have United States voters' rights been expanded since the 1800s?
2. **Government and Democracy** How did President Jackson justify his use of the spoils system?
3. **Groups and Institutions** What agreement did the Cherokee Nation make with the federal government that Georgia refused to recognize?
4. **Economic Factors** What did Andrew Jackson do after he was elected president in 1832 to "kill" the Bank of the United States?

Skill Practice Activity

Analyzing Primary Sources

In an annual message to Congress in 1835, President Andrew Jackson spoke the words below. Read the excerpt, then answer the questions that follow.

> "All preceding experiments for the improvement of the Indians have failed. It seems now to be an established fact that they cannot live in contact with a civilized community and prosper. . . . A country West of Missouri and Arkansas has been assigned to them, into which the white settlements are not to be pushed."

1. Whose opinion is stated in the excerpt?
2. When and on what occasion were these words spoken?
3. What is the speaker's attitude toward the Indians?
4. According to the speaker, why should the Indians be assigned to a country west of Missouri and Arkansas?

Reviewing Themes

1. Today women and African Americans, Native Americans, and other minorities can vote and participate in national decision making.
2. He wanted to open up government jobs to more people. He rationalized that a new set of federal employees would be good for democracy. A Jackson supporter explained that since Jackson had won the election, he had the right to the benefits of victory.
3. In treaties of the 1790s, the federal government acknowledged the Cherokee in Georgia as a separate nation with its own laws.
4. He ordered all government deposits to be withdrawn and placed the money in state banks; by 1836 the Bank was forced to close.

Geography Activity

Study the map below and answer the questions that follow.

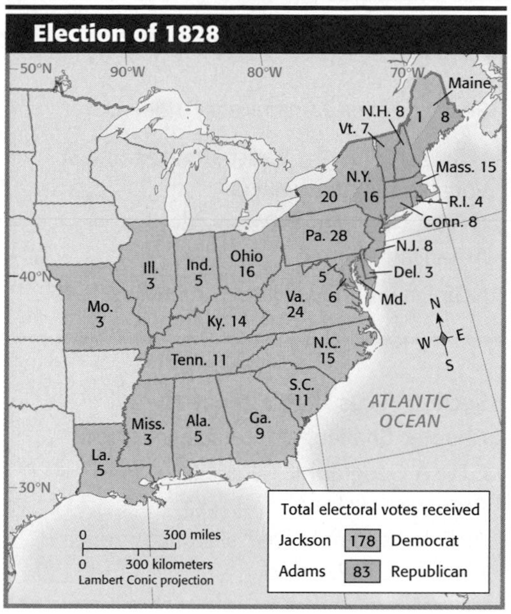

1. **Region** Which general areas of the United States voted for Andrew Jackson in the election of 1828?
2. **Location** Which candidate won more votes in Adams's home state of Massachusetts?
3. **Place** Which three states divided their total electoral count between the two candidates?

Cooperative Activity

History and Geography With the members of your group, research and compare the geography of the southeastern United States to that of Oklahoma—the Indian Territory. Use your research to create a how-to booklet that will tell the Cherokee and other Native Americans who were forced from their homes what they will find in this new region.

Technology Activity

Using a Word Processor Search historical references to find an event that occurred in another part of the world during the time Andrew Jackson was president of the United States. On your word processor, write a headline that might have appeared at the time to describe the event. Then in a paragraph, answer the five "W" questions about the event: Who is it about? What is it about? When did it happen? Where did it happen? Why did it happen?

Time Line Activity

Create a time line on which you place the following events in chronological order.

- Congress passes the Indian Removal Act
- Harrison is elected president
- Andrew Jackson is elected president
- John Quincy Adams becomes president
- Cherokee walk the Trail of Tears
- South Carolina threatens to secede

Portfolio Activity History Journal In your journal make a list of Andrew Jackson's personality traits and characteristics. As you read your list, decide whether you would have voted for Jackson if you had lived during the early 1800s.

Cooperative Activity

Students' booklets should show the differences between the geography of the southeastern states and that of Oklahoma. Students might mention average temperatures and rainfall as well as landforms, plants, and animals. Booklets should be presented in a how-to fashion with information that will help the Cherokee prepare for a different way of life.

Technology Activity

Students should locate historical reference materials on the Internet to help them find an event that occurred in another country between 1829 and 1837. Paragraphs should address the five "W" questions about the headline event.

Time Line Activity

Events should be placed in this order: John Quincy Adams becomes president, Andrew Jackson is elected president, Congress passes the Indian Removal Act, South Carolina threatens to secede, Cherokee walk the Trail of Tears, Harrison is elected president

Portfolio Activity Students' decisions should reveal a knowledge of the kind of person Jackson was.

Chapter Bonus Test Question

Ask: **Who was the first president to be born a United States citizen?** *(Martin Van Buren)*

Skill Practice Activity

1. Jackson's
2. an annual message to Congress in 1835
3. negative, considers them uncivilized and less important than the whites
4. Whites would not move to that country and Native Americans could not prosper if they lived among whites.

Geography Activity

1. the West and the South
2. Adams
3. Maine, New York, Maryland

Chapter 12 Planning Guide

A complete, 1-page lesson plan is provided for each section in the *Reproducible Lesson Plans* booklet.

Section Resources

Daily Objectives	Reproducible Resources	Multimedia Resources
Section 1 The Oregon Country Summarize the reasons people moved to the Oregon country and explain the role of Manifest Destiny in territorial growth of the United States.	Reproducible Lesson Plan 12–1 Guided Reading Activity 12–1* Section Quiz 12–1* Reteaching Activity 12–1 Enrichment Activity 12–1	Section Focus Transparency 12–1 U.S. History & Art, Transparencies 6, 7, 9 Vocabulary PuzzleMaker GTV: A Geographic Perspective on American History NGS PictureShow: Native Americans, Part 2
Section 2 Independence for Texas Explain how conflicts between American settlers and the Mexican government led to independence and eventually statehood for Texas.	Reproducible Lesson Plan 12–2 Guided Reading Activity 12–2* Section Quiz 12–2* Reteaching Activity 12–2 Enrichment Activity 12–2	Section Focus Transparency 12–2 Chapter Challenger Interactive Review GTV: A Geographic Perspective on American History ABCNews InterActive™ Historic America Electronic Field Trips
Section 3 New Mexico and California Describe the roles of economics and Manifest Destiny in the American settlement of New Mexico and California.	Reproducible Lesson Plan 12–3 Guided Reading Activity 12–3* Section Quiz 12–3* Reteaching Activity 12–3 Enrichment Activity 12–3	Section Focus Transparency 12–3 Vocabulary PuzzleMaker Chapter Challenger Interactive Review Software Testmaker
Section 4 War with Mexico Describe the causes and effects of the Mexican War.	Reproducible Lesson Plan 12–4 Guided Reading Activity 12–4* Section Quiz 12–4* Reteaching Activity 12–4 Enrichment Activity 12–4	Section Focus Transparency 12–4 Vocabulary PuzzleMaker Chapter Challenger Interactive Review Testmaker The Presidents: A Picture History of Our Nation
Section 5 New Settlers in California and Utah Compare the reasons that drew people to California with those that drew them to Utah.	Reproducible Lesson Plan 12–5 Guided Reading Activity 12–5* Section Quiz 12–5* Reteaching Activity 12–5 Enrichment Activity 12–5	Section Focus Transparency 12–5 Vocabulary PuzzleMaker Chapter Challenger Interactive Review Software Testmaker GTV: The American People: Fabric of a Nation

** Also available in Spanish*

Blackline Master · Videodisc · Audiocassette · Transparency · CD-ROM · Software

0:00 **OUT OF TIME?**
Assign the Chapter 12 Digest and the corresponding Chapter Digests Audiocassettes with activities and tests.

Activity

From the Classroom of...

Sharon Owens
Westerville School District
Westerville, OH

Manifest Destiny Road Trip

Organize students into groups of four or five. Have them consult modern road maps and plan a trip out west that duplicates, as closely as possible, one of the trails presented on maps in this chapter, such as the Oregon or California Trails. Each student is responsible for researching at least one location along the route and making a short report on how the pioneers might have seen it versus how it appears today. For example, one student might research Fort Boise and compare it to present-day Boise, Idaho. Another student might research the Columbia River, examining how much more developed it is today than it was in the 1840s. Groups can present their trips to the class. Have them use visual aids, such as a drawing of their trail that includes those points of interest they have researched.

Block Schedule

Block scheduling differs from traditional class scheduling in the amount of time allotted to each period. The extended time frame provided by block scheduling affords you the opportunity to implement a greater number of research-oriented and activity-intense projects to motivate and involve your students. Activities that are particularly suited to use within the block scheduling framework are identified throughout this chapter by the following designation:

NATIONAL GEOGRAPHIC SOCIETY Teacher's Corner

INDEX TO NATIONAL GEOGRAPHIC MAGAZINE

The following articles may be used for research relating to this chapter:

- "Tex-Mex Border," by Richard Conniff, February 1996.
- "The Cherokee," by Geoffrey Norman, May 1995.
- "The American Prairie: Roots of the Sky," by Douglas H. Chadwick, October 1993.
- "Along the Santa Fe Trail," by Rowe Findley, February 1989.
- "Life and Death on the Oregon Trail: The Itch to Move West," by Boyd Gibbons, August 1986.
- "Sam Houston: A Man Too Big for Texas," by Bart McDowell, March 1986.

NATIONAL GEOGRAPHIC SOCIETY PRODUCTS AVAILABLE FROM GLENCOE

To order the following products for use with this chapter, contact your local Glencoe sales representative, or call Glencoe at 1-800-334-7344:

- *GTV: A Geographic Perspective on American History* (Videodisc)
- *GTV: The American People: Fabric of a Nation* (Videodisc)
- *The Presidents: A Picture History of Our Nation* (CD-ROM)
- *PictureShow: Native Americans, 1 and 2* (CD-ROM, Transparencies)
- *PictureShow: The Westward Movement* (CD-ROM, Transparencies)

ADDITIONAL NATIONAL GEOGRAPHIC SOCIETY PRODUCTS

To order the following products for use with this chapter, call National Geographic Society at 1-800-368-2728:

- *American Indians: A Brief History* (Video)
- *Historical Atlas of the United States* (Atlas)

KEY TO ABILITY LEVELS

Teaching strategies have been coded for varying learning styles and abilities.

L1 **BASIC** activities for all students
L2 **AVERAGE** activities for average to above-average students
L3 **CHALLENGING** activities for above-average students
ELL **ENGLISH LANGUAGE LEARNER** activities

Chapter 12 Resource Guide

Home Involvement

Home Involvement Activity 12

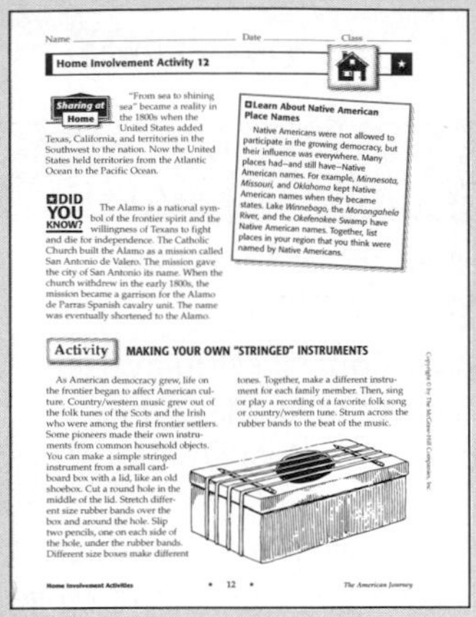
Home Involvement Activity 12

Making Your Own "Stringed" Instruments

Review Activities

Chapter Summary 12

Chapter Summary 12

Manifest Destiny

Workbook Activity 12

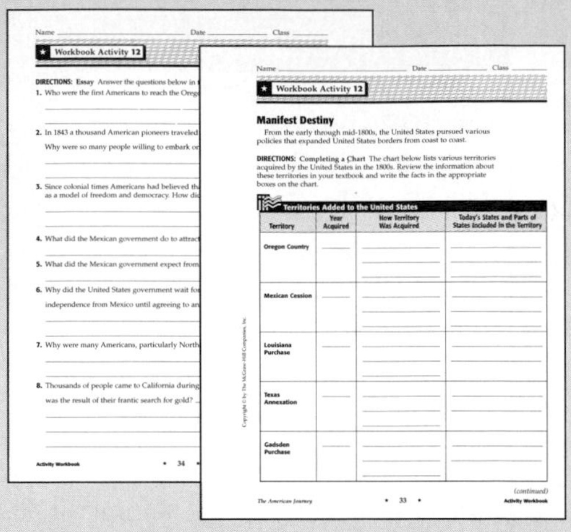
Workbook Activity 12

Manifest Destiny

Reinforcement Activities

Time Line Activity 12

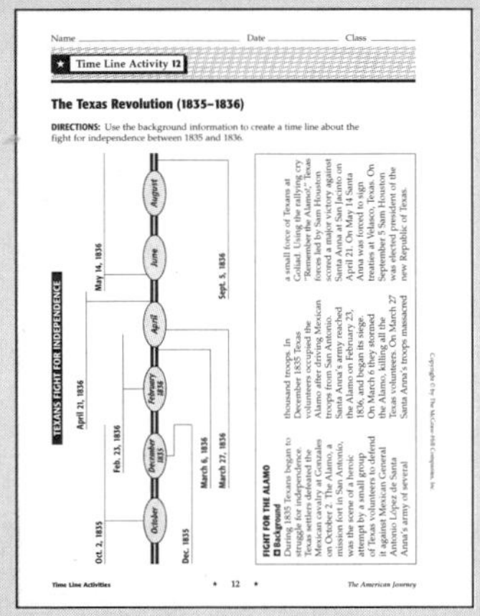
Time Line Activity 12

The Texas Revolution (1835–1836)

Vocabulary Activity 12

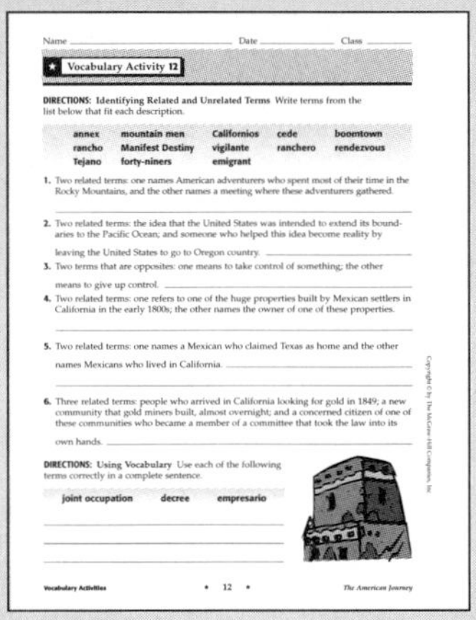
Vocabulary Activity 12

Chapter Skills Activity 12

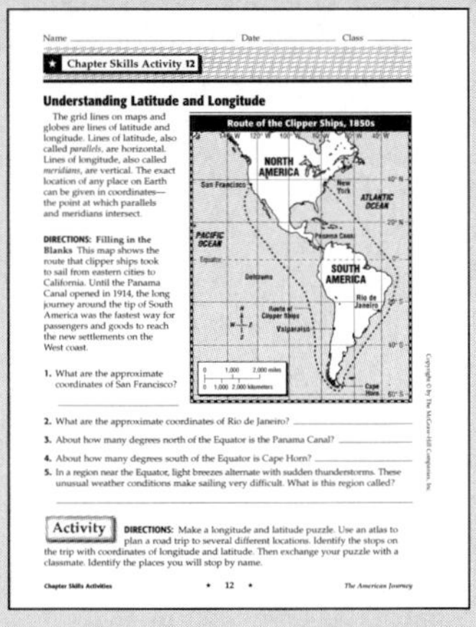
Chapter Skills Activity 12

Understanding Latitude and Longitude

Enrichment Activities

Linking Past and Present Activity 12

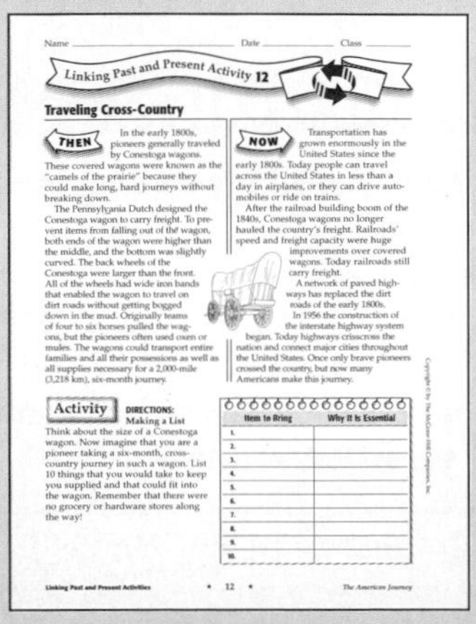
Linking Past and Present Activity 12

Traveling Cross-Country

Primary Source Reading 12

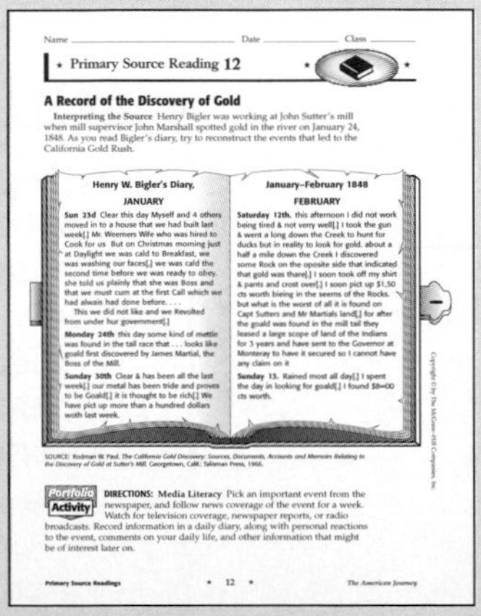
Primary Source Reading 12

A Record of the Discovery of Gold

Geography Activities

Mapping History Activity 12

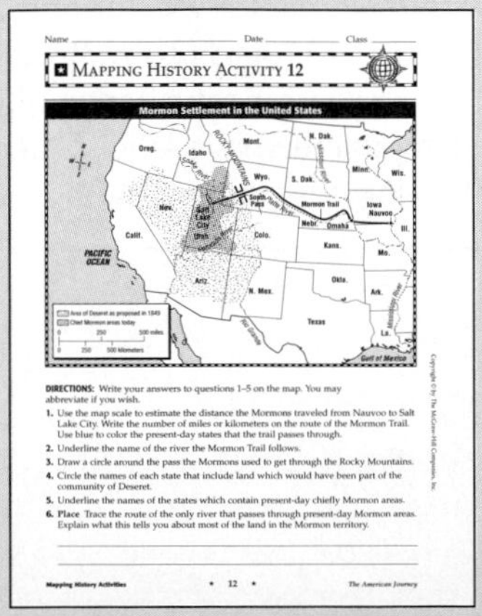
Mapping History Activity 12

Mormon Settlement in the United States

Chapter 12 Resource Guide

ASSESSMENT

Chapter 12 Test, Form A

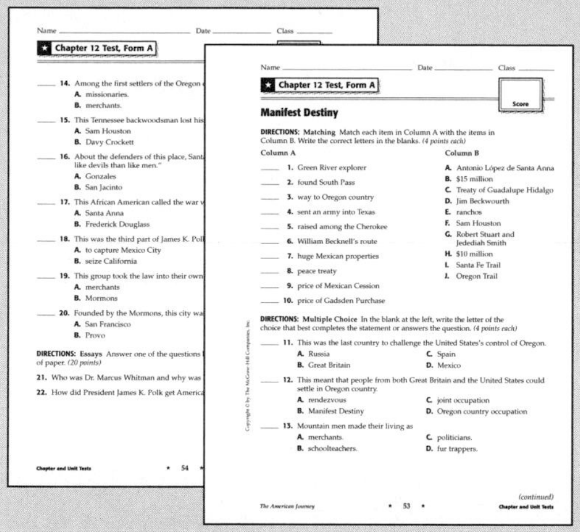
Chapter 12 Test, Form A

Manifest Destiny

DIRECTIONS: Matching Match each item in Column A with the items in Column B. Write the correct letters in the blanks. (4 points each)

Column A	Column B
1. Green River explorer	A. Antonio López de Santa Anna
2. found South Pass	B. $15 million
3. way to Oregon country	C. Treaty of Guadalupe Hidalgo
4. sent an army into Texas	D. Jim Beckwourth
5. raised among the Cherokee	E. ranchos
6. William Becknell's route	F. Sam Houston
7. huge Mexican properties	G. Robert Stuart and Jedediah Smith
8. peace treaty	H. $10 million
9. price of Mexican Cession	I. Santa Fe Trail
10. price of Gadsden Purchase	J. Oregon Trail

DIRECTIONS: Multiple Choice In the blank at the left, write the letter of the choice that best completes the statement or answers the question. (4 points each)

11. This was the last country to challenge the United States's control of Oregon.
A. Russia C. Spain
B. Great Britain D. Mexico

12. This meant that people from both Great Britain and the United States could settle in Oregon country.
A. rendezvous C. joint occupation
B. Manifest Destiny D. Oregon country occupation

13. Mountain men made their living as
A. merchants. C. politicians.
B. schoolteachers. D. fur trappers.

(continued)

Chapter 12 Test, Form B

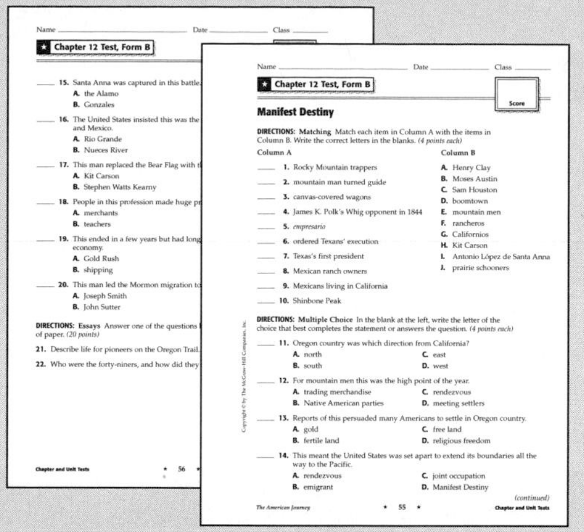
Chapter 12 Test, Form B

Manifest Destiny

DIRECTIONS: Matching Match each item in Column A with the items in Column B. Write the correct letters in the blanks. (4 points each)

Column A	Column B
1. Rocky Mountain trappers	A. Henry Clay
2. mountain man turned guide	B. Moses Austin
3. canvas-covered wagons	C. Sam Houston
4. James K. Polk's Whig opponent in 1844	D. boomtown
5. *empresario*	E. mountain men
6. ordered Texans' execution	F. rancheros
7. Texas's first president	G. Californios
8. Mexican ranch owners	H. Kit Carson
9. Mexicans living in California	I. Antonio López de Santa Anna
10. Shinbone Peak	J. prairie schooners

DIRECTIONS: Multiple Choice In the blank at the left, write the letter of the choice that best completes the statement or answers the question. (4 points each)

11. Oregon country was which direction from California?
A. north C. east
B. south D. west

12. For mountain men this was the high point of the year.
A. trading merchandise C. rendezvous
B. Native American parties D. meeting settlers

13. Reports of this persuaded many Americans to settle in Oregon country.
A. gold C. free land
B. fertile land D. religious freedom

14. This meant the United States was set apart to extend its boundaries all the way to the Pacific.
A. rendezvous C. joint occupation
B. emigrant D. Manifest Destiny

(continued)

Performance Assessment Activity 12

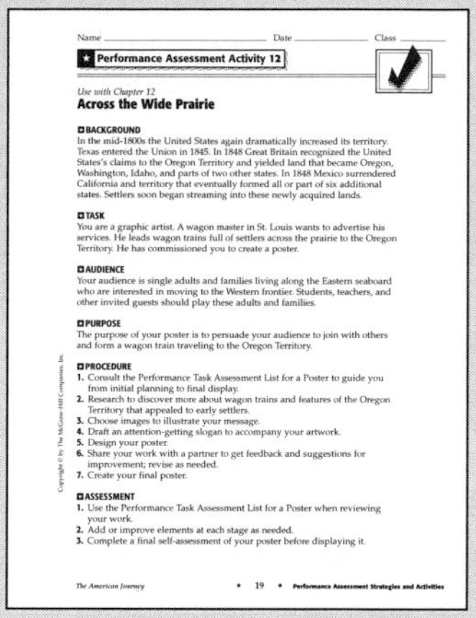
Performance Assessment Activity 12

Use with Chapter 12
Across the Wide Prairie

BACKGROUND
In the mid-1800s the United States again dramatically increased its territory. Texas entered the Union in 1845. In 1848 Great Britain recognized the United States's claims to the Oregon Territory and yielded land that became Oregon, Washington, Idaho, and parts of two other states. In 1848 Mexico surrendered California and territory that eventually formed all or part of six additional states. Settlers soon began streaming into these newly acquired lands.

TASK
You are a graphic artist. A wagon master in St. Louis wants to advertise his services. He leads wagon trains full of settlers across the prairie to the Oregon Territory. He has commissioned you to create a poster.

AUDIENCE
Your audience is single adults and families living along the Eastern seaboard who are interested in moving to the Western frontier. Students, teachers, and other invited guests should play these adults and families.

PURPOSE
The purpose of your poster is to persuade your audience to join with others and form a wagon train traveling to the Oregon Territory.

PROCEDURE
1. Consult the Performance Task Assessment List for a Poster to guide you from initial planning to final display.
2. Research to discover more about wagon trains and features of the Oregon Territory that appealed to early settlers.
3. Choose images to illustrate your message.
4. Draft an attention-getting slogan to accompany your artwork.
5. Design your poster.
6. Share your work with a partner to get feedback and suggestions for improvement; revise as needed.
7. Create your final poster.

ASSESSMENT
1. Use the Performance Task Assessment List for a Poster when reviewing your work.
2. Add or improve elements at each stage as needed.
3. Complete a final self-assessment of your poster before displaying it.

SPANISH RESOURCES

The following Spanish language materials are available in the Spanish Resources binder:

- **Spanish Chapter Summary 12**
- **Spanish Vocabulary Activity 12**
- **Spanish Guided Reading Activities, Chapter 12**
- **Spanish Section Quizzes, Chapter 12**
- **Spanish Home Involvement Activity 12**
- **Spanish Chapter 12 Digests Audiocassette Activity and Test**

ACTIVITY MANIPULATIVES

Help students learn more about America's cultural history with:

- **American Crafts Hands-On Activities**
- **American Games Hands-On Activities**
- **American History Flash Cards**

ADDITIONAL RESOURCES FROM GLENCOE

- **U.S. History & Art,** Transparency 6, *The Great Blue Heron;* Transparency 7, *The Buffalo Chase, Mouth of the Yellowstone;* Transparency 9, *Shooting for the Beef*
- **Focus on American Art Prints,** *Pat Lyon at the Forge* by John Neagle; *The Long Story* by William Sidney Mount; *Fur Traders Descending the Missouri* by George Caleb Bingham
- **American Music Cultural Traditions,** Lesson 4: "Kneebone Bend" and "Come Life, Shaker Life"
- **The Spirit of American Art and Music,** Edward Hicks; Nathaniel Currier and James Ives
- **Outline Map Resource Book**
- **U.S. Desk Map**
- **The American History Videodisc and CD-ROM,** *Expansion, Development, Sectionalism and Division*

A&E HOME VIDEO. Biography. THE HISTORY CHANNEL.

The following videotape programs are available from Glencoe as supplements to Chapter 12:

- **Davy Crockett: American Frontier Legend** (ISBN 1-56501-392-1)
- **Brigham Young: Architect of Faith** (ISBN 1-56501-666-1)
- **The Alamo** (1-56501-784-6)
- **The Best of the Real West (Set)** (1-56501-352-2)

To order, call Glencoe at 1-800-334-7344. To find classroom resources to accompany many of these videos, check the following home pages:
A&E Television: http://www.aetv.com
The History Channel: http://www.historychannel.com

Chapter Themes

Chapter Themes are listed by section on this chapter opening page of the Student Edition. A corresponding theme-based activity is available under "FOCUS," and a theme-based question is asked in the Section and Chapter Reviews.

Performance Assessment

Refer to Activity 12 in the *Performance Assessment Strategies and Activities* booklet.

GLENCOE TECHNOLOGY

VIDEODISC
MindJogger Videoquiz

Use MindJogger to preview the Chapter 12 content.

Chapter 12
Disc 2, Side A

Also available in VHS.

HISTORY AND ART William T. Ranney (1813–1857) is one of the artists whose work Currier and Ives used for their lithographs. **Ask:** What five items do you think would be the most important on a journey across the Great Plains? *(Students may debate answers.)*

Chapter 12

1818–1853

Manifest Destiny

Why It's Important

The tremendous expansion during the first half of the 1800s left a lasting imprint on the United States. It transformed the shape of the nation—and the national character. Thousands of pioneers moved west, adding their struggles and triumphs to the American story. At the same time, the Native Americans and Spanish-speaking peoples of the West became part of the United States. They made their own contributions to the American character.

Chapter Themes

- *Section 1,* Economic Factors
- *Section 2,* Geography and History
- *Section 3,* Culture and Traditions
- *Section 4,* Global Connections
- *Section 5,* Groups and Institutions

HISTORY AND ART *Advice on the Prairie* **by William T. Ranney** Ranney was a leading painter of the American frontier during the mid-1800s. Many of his works show pioneers crossing the vast, empty West.

EXTRA CREDIT PROJECT

Conestoga Wagons Have students use library resources to find drawings of Conestoga wagons to use for reference in building a model wagon. Note that the back and front were tilted up so that goods would shift toward the center rather than spilling out when the wagon was traveling up or down hills. Materials needed include a shoe box or other similar box, cardboard, dowels or pencils for axles, craft sticks, paints, scissors, tape, glue, and fabric.

1820 1830 1840 1850

1819 Adams-Onís Treaty is signed

1836 Marcus Whitman builds mission in Oregon

1840s "Oregon fever" sweeps through Mississippi Valley

1846 U.S. and Britain set the Oregon boundary at 49°N

Section 1

The Oregon Country

READ TO DISCOVER . . .

- why large numbers of settlers headed for the Oregon country.
- how the idea of Manifest Destiny contributed to the growth of the United States.

TERMS TO LEARN

joint occupation
mountain man
rendezvous
emigrant
Manifest Destiny

The Storyteller

On an April morning in 1851, 13-year-old Martha Gay said good-bye to her friends, her home, and the familiar world of Springfield, Missouri. She and her family were beginning a long, hazardous journey. The townsfolk watched as the Gays left in four big wagons pulled by teams of oxen. "Farewell sermons were preached and prayers offered for our safety," Martha wrote years later. "All places of business and the school were closed . . . and everybody came to say good-bye to us." This same scene occurred many times in the 1840s and 1850s as thousands of families set out for the Oregon country.

Doll owned by a young pioneer

The **Oregon country** was the huge area that lay between the Pacific Ocean and the Rocky Mountains north of **California.** It included all of what is now Oregon, Washington, and Idaho plus parts of Montana and Wyoming. The region also contained about half of what became the Canadian province of British Columbia.

Geography

Rivalry in the Northwest

In the early 1800s, four nations laid claim to the vast, rugged land known as the Oregon country. The United States based its claim on Robert Gray's discovery of the **Columbia River** in 1792 and on the Lewis and Clark expedition. Great Britain based its claim on British explorations of the Columbia River. Spain, which had also explored the Pacific coast in the late 1700s, controlled California to the south. Russia had settlements that stretched south from **Alaska** into Oregon.

Many Americans wanted control of the Oregon country to gain access to the Pacific Ocean. Secretary of State **John Quincy Adams** played a key role in promoting this goal. In 1819 he negotiated the **Adams-Onís Treaty** with Spain. In the treaty the Spanish agreed to set the limits of their territory at what is now California's northern border and gave up any claim to Oregon. In 1824 Russia also surrendered its claim to the land south of Alaska. Only Britain remained to challenge American control of Oregon.

SECTION RESOURCES

Reproducible Masters
- Guided Reading Activity 12–1
- Section Quiz 12–1
- Reteaching Activity 12–1
- Enrichment Activity 12–1

Transparencies
- Section Focus Transparency 12–1
- U.S. History & Art, Transparencies 6, 7, 9

Multimedia
- Vocabulary PuzzleMaker
- Chapter Challenger Interactive Review Software
- Testmaker
- GTV: A Geographic Perspective on American History
- NGS PictureShow: Native Americans, Part 2

1 FOCUS

BELLRINGER
Motivational Activity

Before taking roll at the beginning of the class period, project Section Focus Transparency 12–1 and have students answer the questions. Discuss students' responses.

This activity is also available as a blackline master.

Section Focus Transparency 12–1

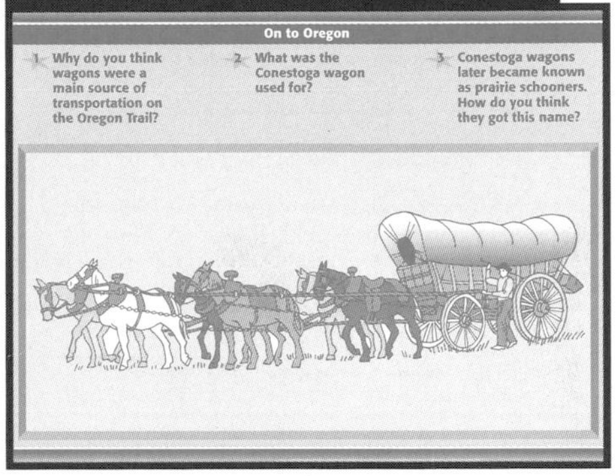

Vocabulary Precheck

Point out that *rendezvous* is a French word that literally means "present yourselves." Have students suggest how this meaning is connected to today's meaning of the word.

Use the **Vocabulary Puzzle-Maker** to create crossword and word search puzzles.

Section Theme
Economic Factors

Economics played a part in drawing fur traders, mountain men, and pioneers to Oregon.

Activity Have students name the role economics played in each case. *(good money to be made from sale of furs for both traders and mountain men; later mountain men earned a living as guides; hard times in East made Oregon more attractive)*

2 TEACH

L1, ELL Describing Characteristics Mountain men and pioneers alike were independent, resourceful, hardworking, and determined—characteristics that people often attribute to Americans in general. Write those traits on the board and ask students to find examples of each in the section.

Guided Reading Activity 12–1

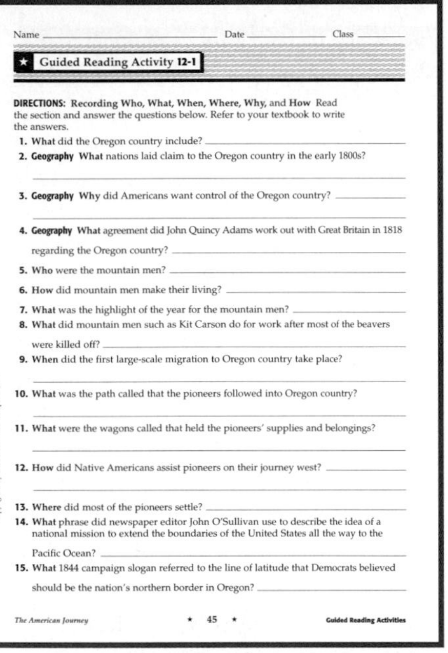
Name ____ Date ____ Class ____

★ Guided Reading Activity **12-1**

DIRECTIONS: Recording Who, What, When, Where, Why, and How Read the section and answer the questions below. Refer to your textbook to write the answers.

1. **What** did the Oregon country include? ____
2. **Geography What** nations laid claim to the Oregon country in the early 1800s? ____
3. **Geography Why** did Americans want control of the Oregon country? ____
4. **Geography What** agreement did John Quincy Adams work out with Great Britain in 1818 regarding the Oregon country? ____
5. **Who** were the mountain men? ____
6. **How** did mountain men make their living? ____
7. **What** was the highlight of the year for the mountain men? ____
8. **What** did mountain men such as Kit Carson do for work after most of the beavers were killed off? ____
9. **When** did the first large-scale migration to Oregon country take place? ____
10. **What** was the path called that the pioneers followed into Oregon country? ____
11. **What** were the wagons called that held the pioneers' supplies and belongings? ____
12. **How** did Native Americans assist pioneers on their journey west? ____
13. **Where** did most of the pioneers settle? ____
14. **What** phrase did newspaper editor John O'Sullivan use to describe the idea of a national mission to extend the boundaries of the United States all the way to the Pacific Ocean? ____
15. **What** 1844 campaign slogan referred to the line of latitude that Democrats believed should be the nation's northern border in Oregon? ____

Copyright © by The McGraw-Hill Companies, Inc.

The American Journey ★ 45 ★ **Guided Reading Activities**

NATIONAL GEOGRAPHIC SOCIETY

VIDEODISC
GTV: A Geographic Perspective on American History

Side 2, Chapter 11
Title: *Going to Extremes: The Far West*
Subject: Settlement in the Far West, 1820–1850
Ask: **What group of Americans ventured into the Rockies to make a living?** *(trappers and traders)*

In 1818 Adams had worked out an agreement with Britain for **joint occupation** of the area. This meant that people from both the United States and Great Britain could settle there. When Adams became president in 1825, he proposed that the two nations divide Oregon along the 49° line of latitude. Britain refused, insisting on a larger share of the territory. Unable to resolve their dispute, the two countries agreed to extend the joint occupation. In the following years, thousands of Americans streamed into Oregon, and they pushed the issue toward settlement.

Mountain Men

The first Americans to reach the Oregon country were not farmers but fur traders. They had come to trap beaver, whose skins were in great demand in the eastern United States and in Europe. The British established several trading posts in the region, as did American merchant **John Jacob Astor.**

At first the merchants traded for furs that the Native Americans supplied. Gradually American adventurers joined the trade. These people, who spent most of their time in the Rocky Mountains, came to be known as **mountain men.**

Traders and Trappers

The tough, independent mountain men made their living by trapping beaver. Many had Native American wives and adopted Native American ways. They lived in buffalo-skin lodges and dressed in fringed buckskin pants, moccasins, and beads.

Some mountain men worked for fur-trading companies; others sold their furs to the highest bidder. Whatever the arrangement, they spent most of the year alone in the wild. Throughout the spring and early summer, they ranged across the mountains, setting traps and then collecting the beaver pelts. In late summer they gathered for a **rendezvous** (RAHN•dih•VOO), or meeting.

For the mountain men, the annual rendezvous was the high point of the year. They met with the trading companies to exchange their "hairy banknotes"—beaver skins—for traps, guns, coffee, and other goods. They spent what cash they received on food and drink or on ornaments for their wives and children. They met old friends and exchanged news. They relaxed by competing in races and other contests—including swapping stories about who had the most exciting adventures.

Buckskin jacket
Beaded pouch

From Trappers to Guides

As they roamed far and wide searching for beaver, the mountain men explored the mountains, valleys, and trails of the West. **Jim Beckwourth,** an African American from Virginia, explored Wyoming's Green River. Robert Stuart and Jedediah Smith both found the **South Pass,** a broad break through the Rockies. South Pass later became the main route that settlers took to Oregon.

To survive in the wilderness, a mountain man had to be skillful and resourceful. Trapper Joe Meek told how, when faced with starvation, he once held his hands "in an anthill until they were covered with ants, then greedily licked them off." The mountain men took pride in joking about the dangers they faced.

In time the mountain men killed off most of the beaver and could no longer trap. Some went to settle on farms in Oregon. With their knowledge of the western lands, though, some mountain men found new work. Jim Bridger, Kit Carson, and others acted as guides to lead the parties of settlers now streaming west.

COOPERATIVE LEARNING ACTIVITY

Advertising the Oregon Country Organize the class into small groups, each of which is to design and make two or three posters encouraging people to move to the Oregon country. Students should find many of Oregon's attractions in the section, but may do additional research if time permits. Suggest that each poster concentrate on one main attraction. Each group should choose one member to be the artist and another to do any lettering on each poster, while the group as a whole should decide on the themes. Some groups may want to make their posters historically accurate, others may decide to use modern techniques and ideas.

HISTORY AND ART ***Encampment on Green River*** **by Alfred Jacob Miller** Miller's painting shows a rendezvous on the Green River in Wyoming. **What was the purpose of a rendezvous?**

Settling Oregon

Americans began traveling to the Oregon country to settle in the 1830s. Reports of the fertile land persuaded many to make the journey. Economic troubles at home made new opportunities in the West look attractive.

The Whitman Mission

Among the first settlers of the Oregon country were missionaries who wanted to bring Christianity to the Native Americans. Dr. Marcus Whitman and his wife, Narcissa, went to Oregon in 1836 and built a mission among the Cayuse people near the present site of Walla Walla, Washington.

New settlers unknowingly brought measles to the mission. An epidemic killed many of the Indian children. Blaming the Whitmans for the sickness, the Cayuse attacked the mission in November 1847 and killed them and 12 others. Despite this tragedy the flood of settlers continued.

The Oregon Trail

In the early 1840s, "Oregon fever" began to sweep through the towns of the Mississippi Valley. People formed societies to gather information about Oregon and to plan and make the long journey.

The first large-scale migration took place in 1843, when 120 wagons carrying more than 1,000 pioneers left Independence, Missouri, for Oregon. In the years that followed, tens of thousands of Americans made the trip. These pioneers were called **emigrants** because they left the United States to go to Oregon.

To reach Oregon these pioneers undertook a difficult 2,000-mile journey. Gathering in Independence or other towns in Missouri, they followed the **Oregon Trail** across the Great Plains along the Platte River and through the South Pass of the Rocky Mountains. On the other side, they took the trail north and west along the Snake and Columbia Rivers into the Oregon country.

MULTIPLE LEARNING STYLES

Logical/Mathematical Travel on the 2,000-mile (3,200-km) Oregon Trail was slow—wagons went from 1 to 2 miles an hour (1.6 to 3.2 kph) and averaged about 100 miles (160 km) a week. The whole trip took about five months. Today the same trip could be completed easily in less than a week, traveling by car for just five or six hours a day and averaging 60 miles per hour (97 kph). Have students create a pictograph comparing the pioneers' trip with a modern trip by automobile. **L2, ELL**

HISTORY AND ART Fur traders placed ads in newspapers to recruit men for trapping. One ad called for a hundred men to work for one, two, or three years under the leadership of an army major. **Ask: Would you have liked the life of a mountain man? Why?** *(Answers will vary but should reveal an understanding of the kind of life mountain men lived.)*
Answer: *to exchange beaver skins for other goods; talk to friends*

Where? When? Who? What?

Oregon The following quote from a Missouri farmer gives one man's reasons to pack up and head to Oregon: "Out in Oregon I can get me a square mile of land. And a quarter section for each of you all. Dad burn me, I am done with this country. Winters it's frost and snow to freeze a body; summers the overflow from Old Muddy drowns half my acres; taxes take the yield of them that are left. What say, Maw, it's God's country."

NATIONAL GEOGRAPHIC SOCIETY

CD-ROM
NGS PictureShow:
Native Americans, Part 2

Have students learn more about how Native Americans helped westward travelers.

CD-ROM
NGS PictureShow:
The Westward Movement

Have students view the CD-ROM to learn more about American settlers' harrowing journeys to the West. Ask students to briefly summarize how each territory was acquired and how westward expansion led to conflict with Native Americans.

CHAPTER 12
Section 1, 355–360

Map Study

Answers
1. Rockies, Cascades, Sierra Nevada
2. Oregon, Santa Fe

Map Skills Practice

Reading a Map Which trail ended in Los Angeles? *(Old Spanish Trail)*

Who?What?Where?When?

Janette Riker One of the many stories of endurance on the way west to Oregon is that of a young woman named Janette Riker. In Montana in September 1849, she was left alone with the wagon by her father and two brothers who went hunting and never came back. To survive the coming winter, Janette built a hut, which she heated with the family stove and firewood that she chopped. To add to the provisions from the wagon, she butchered an ox and salted the meat. The threat of hungry wolves and mountain lions kept her in the hut until the spring thaw forced her to move back to the wagon. Finally Native Americans discovered her. They were so impressed that she had made it through the winter alone that they agreed to take her where she wanted to go.

History *and the* Humanities

U.S. History & Art, Transparency 6, *The Great Blue Heron;* Transparency 7, *The Buffalo Chase, Mouth of the Yellowstone;* Transparency 9, *Shooting for the Beef*

American Music Cultural Traditions, Lesson 4: "Kneebone Bend" and "Come Life, Shaker Life"

Woman's bonnet

Trails West

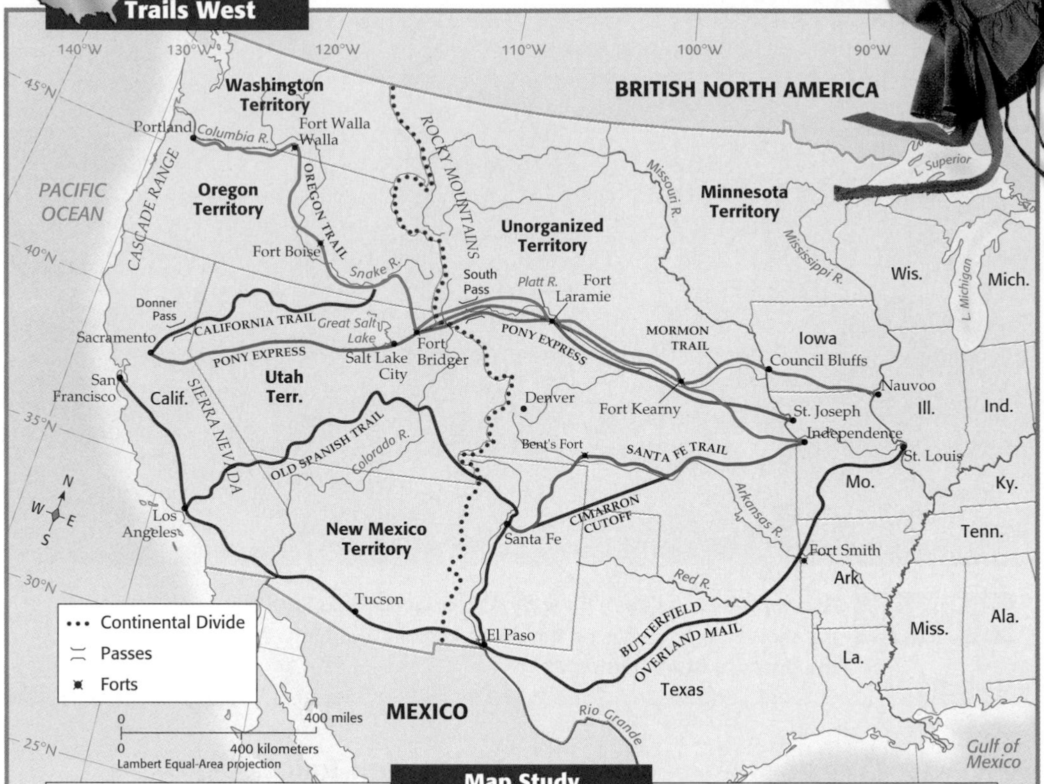

Map Study

By the late 1840s, thousands of Americans had settled large amounts of new territory.

1. **Movement** What major mountains did travelers to the Pacific Coast cross?
2. **Analyzing Information** What two trails began in Independence, Missouri?

Life on the Trail

The journey lasted five or six months. The pioneers had to start in the spring and complete the trip before winter snows blocked the mountain passes. They usually traveled in large groups, often of related families. They stuffed their canvas-covered wagons, called **prairie schooners,** with supplies and everything they owned. From a distance, these wagons looked like schooners (ships) at sea. Most people walked alongside the wagons. Only pregnant women, sick people, and very old or very young people rode in the wagons.

The trail crossed difficult terrain. The pioneers walked across seemingly endless plains, forded swift rivers, and labored up high mountains. One man described crossing the Platte River in Nebraska:

> "A more foaming mad[d]ening river I never saw . . . and the water the color of soapsuds you cannot see the bottom where it is not more than six inches deep."

If families fell behind on the trail or faced a very steep climb, they sometimes decided to lighten their wagons. They would unload a piece of furniture or a family treasure and sadly abandon it at the side of the trail.

MAKING CONNECTIONS ACTIVITY

Biography Have each student find a biography of someone from the period, read it, and write a book report. Subjects may include the following people, among others: Jim Beckwourth, Jim Bridger, Kit Carson, John J. Astor, Jedediah Smith, Marcus and Narcissa Whitman, and John Sager and his family. John and his brothers and sisters were orphaned on the Oregon Trail and were taken to the Whitman mission by members of their wagon train. (At least one book has 13-year-old John and his younger siblings—one a baby and one with a broken leg—proceeding alone to the mission, which makes a dramatic story but is not true.) **L2**

Everyone worked hard. Men drove the wagons, tended the animals, and hunted. Women, after walking all day, had more work to do at night. They cared for the children and cooked the meals. They carried on with their chores in all kinds of weather. Making bread in the rain, a woman kneaded her dough, then "watched and nursed the fire and held an umbrella over the fire and her skill[e]t . . . for near two hours."

The pioneers' food supplies often ran low. Fresh water always had to be conserved. The pioneers might not launder their clothes more than two or three times during the entire trip.

At night the travelers arranged their wagons in a square or circle for protection, with the people and horses on the inside. Although the pioneers feared attacks by Native Americans, such attacks rarely occurred. More often Native Americans assisted the pioneers, serving as guides and trading necessary food and supplies. Most of the emigrants who died on the trail perished from disease, overwork, hunger, or accidents.

The Division of Oregon

Most pioneers headed for the fertile **Willamette Valley** south of the Columbia River. Between 1840 and 1845, the number of American settlers in the area increased from 500 to 5,000, while the British population remained at about 700. The question of ownership of Oregon arose again.

Expansion of Freedom

Since colonial times many Americans had believed their nation had a special role to fulfill. For years people thought the nation's mission should be to serve as a model of freedom and democracy.

In the 1800s that vision changed. Many believed that the United States's mission was to spread freedom by occupying the entire continent. In 1819 John Quincy Adams expressed what many Americans were thinking when he called expansion to the Pacific a "law of nature," saying it was as inevitable "as that the Mississippi should flow to the sea."

Manifest Destiny

In the 1840s New York newspaper editor John O'Sullivan put the idea of a national mission in more specific words. O'Sullivan declared it was America's "**manifest destiny** to overspread and to possess the whole of the continent which Providence has given us." O'Sullivan meant that the United States was clearly destined—set apart for

HISTORY AND ART ***The Pioneers* by William T. Ranney** Emigrants in search of a better life headed west in large numbers during the mid-1800s. **Why were emigrants attracted to Oregon?**

Chest of clothing

CRITICAL THINKING ACTIVITY

Recognizing Bias Ask each student to write several sentences expressing his or her point of view about the United States expansion westward for each of the following people: a young American settler emigrating to Oregon, a frontiersman living in the Rocky Mountains, a Native American living on the Great Plains, a Mexican citizen farming in Texas, and a British shipowner operating off the Oregon coast. Have volunteers read their sentences aloud. Allow class time for students to evaluate and challenge one another's sentences. **L2**

3 ASSESS

Assign Section 1 Review as homework or as an in-class activity.

Use **Chapter Challenger Interactive Review Software** to review Section 1.

Section Quiz 12–1

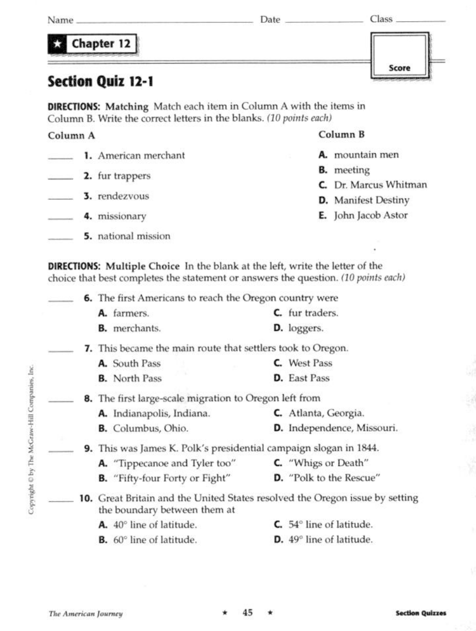

Name ________ Date ________ Class ________

★ Chapter 12

Score

Section Quiz 12-1

DIRECTIONS: Matching Match each item in Column A with the items in Column B. Write the correct letters in the blanks. *(10 points each)*

Column A	Column B
____ 1. American merchant	A. mountain men
____ 2. fur trappers	B. meeting
____ 3. rendezvous	C. Dr. Marcus Whitman
____ 4. missionary	D. Manifest Destiny
____ 5. national mission	E. John Jacob Astor

DIRECTIONS: Multiple Choice In the blank at the left, write the letter of the choice that best completes the statement or answers the question. *(10 points each)*

____ 6. The first Americans to reach the Oregon country were
A. farmers. C. fur traders.
B. merchants. D. loggers.

____ 7. This became the main route that settlers took to Oregon.
A. South Pass C. West Pass
B. North Pass D. East Pass

____ 8. The first large-scale migration to Oregon left from
A. Indianapolis, Indiana. C. Atlanta, Georgia.
B. Columbus, Ohio. D. Independence, Missouri.

____ 9. This was James K. Polk's presidential campaign slogan in 1844.
A. "Tippecanoe and Tyler too" C. "Whigs or Death"
B. "Fifty-four Forty or Fight" D. "Polk to the Rescue"

____ 10. Great Britain and the United States resolved the Oregon issue by setting the boundary between them at
A. 40° line of latitude. C. 54° line of latitude.
B. 60° line of latitude. D. 49° line of latitude.

The American Journey ★ 45 ★ **Section Quizzes**

HISTORY AND ART William T. Ranney, who also created the painting on page 354, was elected an associate of the National Academy in 1850. One of his works *(Duck-Shooting)* hangs in the Corcoran Gallery in Washington, D.C. **Ask:** **Why were pioneers to Oregon called emigrants?** *(because they had left the United States)* **Answer:** *reports of fertile land; economic troubles at home*

CHAPTER 12

Section 1, 355–360

Reteaching Activity 12–1

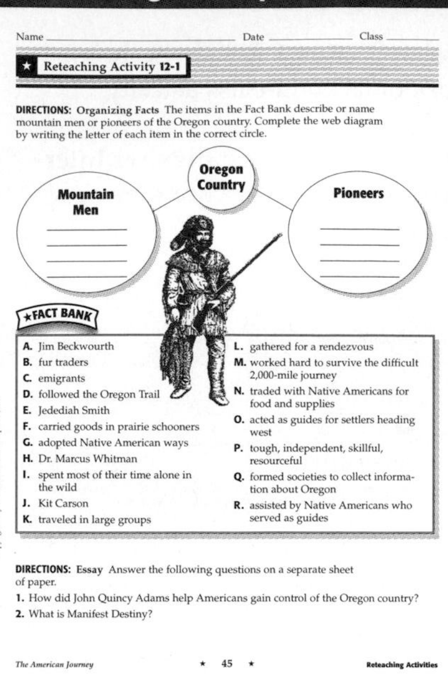

Name __________ Date ________ Class _______

★ Reteaching Activity **12-1**

DIRECTIONS: Organizing Facts The items in the Fact Bank describe or name mountain men or pioneers of the Oregon country. Complete the web diagram by writing the letter of each item in the correct circle.

★FACT BANK

A. Jim Beckwourth
B. fur traders
C. emigrants
D. followed the Oregon Trail
E. Jedediah Smith
F. carried goods in prairie schooners
G. adopted Native American ways
H. Dr. Marcus Whitman
I. spent most of their time alone in the wild
J. Kit Carson
K. traveled in large groups
L. gathered for a rendezvous
M. worked hard to survive the difficult 2,000-mile journey
N. traded with Native Americans for food and supplies
O. acted as guides for settlers heading west
P. tough, independent, skillful, resourceful
Q. formed societies to collect information about Oregon
R. assisted by Native Americans who served as guides

DIRECTIONS: Essay Answer the following questions on a separate sheet of paper.

1. How did John Quincy Adams help Americans gain control of the Oregon country?
2. What is Manifest Destiny?

Enrichment Activity 12–1

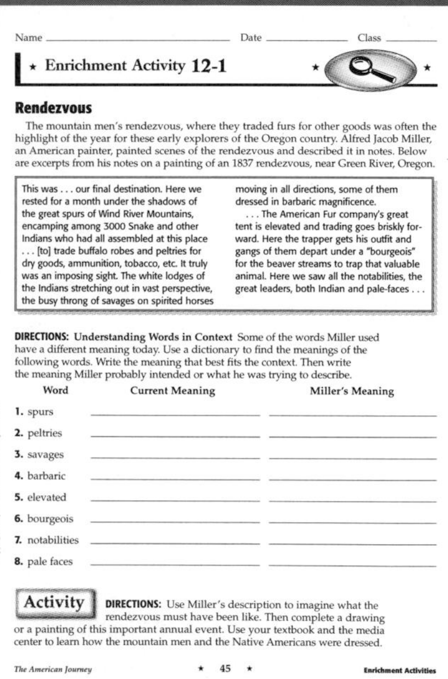

Name __________ Date ________ Class _______

★ Enrichment Activity **12-1** ★ ★

Rendezvous

The mountain men's rendezvous, where they traded furs for other goods was often the highlight of the year for these early explorers of the Oregon country. Alfred Jacob Miller, an American painter, painted scenes of the rendezvous and described it in notes. Below are excerpts from his notes on a painting of an 1837 rendezvous, near Green River, Oregon.

> This was . . . our final destination. Here we rested for a month under the shadows of the great spurs of Wind River Mountains, encamping among 3000 Snake and other Indians who had all assembled at this place . . . [to] trade buffalo robes and peltries for dry goods, ammunition, tobacco, etc. It truly was an imposing sight. The white lodges of the Indians stretching out in vast perspective, the busy throng of savages on spirited horses moving in all directions, some of them dressed in barbaric magnificence.
>
> . . . The American Fur company's great tent is elevated and trading goes briskly forward. Here the trapper gets his outfit and gangs of them depart under a "bourgeois" for the beaver streams to trap that valuable animal. Here we saw all the notabilities, the great leaders, both Indian and pale-faces . . .

DIRECTIONS: Understanding Words in Context Some of the words Miller used have a different meaning today. Use a dictionary to find the meanings of the following words. Write the meaning that best fits the context. Then write the meaning Miller probably intended or what he was trying to describe.

Word	Current Meaning	Miller's Meaning
1. spurs		
2. peltries		
3. savages		
4. barbaric		
5. elevated		
6. bourgeois		
7. notabilities		
8. pale faces		

Activity **DIRECTIONS:** Use Miller's description to imagine what the rendezvous must have been like. Then complete a drawing or a painting of this important annual event. Use your textbook and the media center to learn how the mountain men and the Native Americans were dressed.

James K. Polk

Henry Clay

a special purpose—to extend its boundaries all the way to the Pacific. This idea of a national mission gained widespread support by 1844 and played a role in that year's presidential election.

"Fifty-four Forty or Fight"

The settlers in Oregon insisted that the United States should have sole ownership of the area. More and more Americans agreed. As a result Oregon became an issue in the 1844 presidential election.

James K. Polk received the Democratic Party's nomination for president, partly because he supported American claims for sole ownership of Oregon. Democrats campaigned using the slogan "Fifty-four Forty or Fight." The slogan referred to the line of latitude that Democrats believed should be the nation's northern border in Oregon.

Henry Clay of the Whig Party, Polk's principal opponent, did not take a strong position on the Oregon issue. Polk won 50 percent of the popular vote and 170 electoral votes to Clay's 48 percent and 105 electoral votes.

Reaching a Settlement

Filled with the spirit of Manifest Destiny, President Polk was determined to make Oregon part of the United States. Britain would not accept a border at "Fifty-four Forty," however. To do so would have meant giving up its claim entirely. Instead, in June 1846, the two countries compromised, setting the boundary between the American and British portions of Oregon at latitude 49°. The two nations had finally resolved the Oregon issue.

During the 1830s Americans sought to fulfill their Manifest Destiny by looking much closer to home than Oregon. Much attention at that time also focused on Texas.

Section 1 Review

Checking for Understanding

1. ***Identify*** John Quincy Adams, Oregon Trail, James K. Polk, Henry Clay.
2. ***Define*** joint occupation, mountain man, rendezvous, emigrant, Manifest Destiny.
3. ***Name*** the four countries that laid claim to the Oregon country.

Reviewing Themes

4. **Economic Factors** How did the fur trade in Oregon aid Americans who began settling there?

Critical Thinking

5. **Analyzing Information** How did the notion of Manifest Destiny help Americans justify their desire to extend the United States to the Pacific Ocean?

Activity

Writing a Letter Imagine you are traveling with your family to the Oregon country in the 1840s. A friend will be making the same trip soon. Write a letter telling your friend what to expect on the journey.

4 CLOSE

Have students evaluate John Quincy Adams's statement that American expansion to the Pacific was a "law of Nature."

Section 1 Review Answers

1. John Quincy Adams, 355; Oregon Trail, 357; James K. Polk, 360; Henry Clay, 360
2. The words are defined in the Glossary.
3. United States, Great Britain, Spain, Russia
4. Fur trappers and traders served as guides to settlers because they were so familiar with the land; many had also established relationships with some of the Native Americans in the area.
5. Many Americans believed that it was the United States's destiny or mission to spread freedom by occupying all the territory of North America.

Activity Students should refer to some of the hardships of travel over the Oregon Trail.

Social Studies
SKILL BUILDER

Understanding Latitude and Longitude

For more than 17 centuries, mapmakers have used lines of latitude and longitude from the global grid to pinpoint locations on maps and globes.

Learning the Skill

The imaginary horizontal lines that circle the globe from east to west are called lines of **latitude.** Because the distance between the lines of latitude is always the same, they are also called *parallels.* The imaginary vertical lines that intersect the parallels are lines of **longitude,** also called *meridians.*

Parallels and meridians are numbered in degrees. The Equator, located halfway between the North and South Poles, is at 0°. Moving north or south of the Equator, the number of degrees increases until reaching 90°N or S latitude at the poles.

The Prime Meridian is 0° longitude. Moving east or west of the Prime Meridian, the number of degrees east or west increases up to 180°. The 180° line of longitude is located on the opposite side of the globe from the Prime Meridian and is called the *International Date Line.*

The point at which parallels and meridians intersect is the grid address, or coordinates, of an exact location. The coordinates for Salt Lake City, for example, are 41°N and 112°W.

Oregon Country

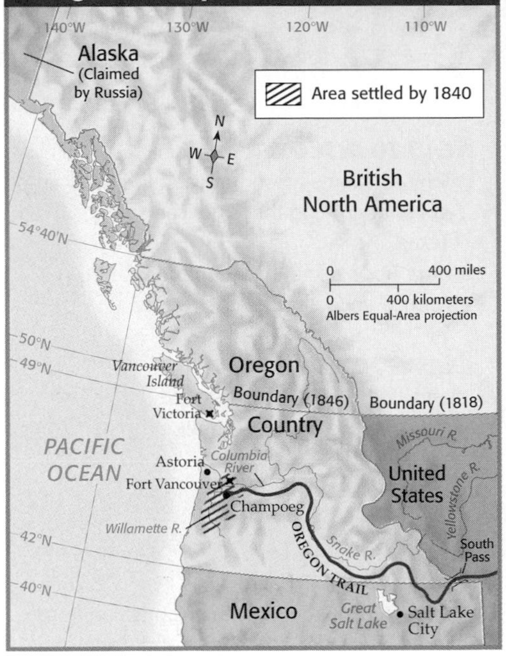

Practicing the Skill

Analyze the information on the map on this page, then answer the following questions.

1. What are the approximate coordinates of Fort Victoria?
2. Is Vancouver Island located at about 40°N or 50°N?
3. At what line of latitude was the Oregon country divided between the United States and Britain?
4. What geographic feature lies at about 42°N and 109°W?

Applying the Skill

Understanding Latitude and Longitude Turn to the Atlas map of the United States on pages RA6 and RA7. Find your city or the city closest to it. What are its coordinates? Now list the coordinates of five other cities and ask a classmate to find the cities based on your coordinates.

Social Studies
SKILL BUILDER

TEACH

Understanding Latitude and Longitude

This skill teaches students how to use latitude and longitude to locate places. Point out that 0° latitude (Equator), 0° longitude (Prime Meridian), and 180° are not labeled north, south, east, or west because they are lines of reference. Note also that not all the lines of latitude or longitude are labeled. To find coordinates, students will have to estimate distance between lines. Astoria, for example, is a little less than halfway between 120°W and 130°W, so it is a little less than 125°W, or about 124°W. **Ask:** **Is the boundary of 1846 a parallel or a meridian?** *(parallel)*

You may wish to introduce the idea that latitude and longitude lines may be further divided into minutes and seconds. A degree of latitude or longitude equals 60 minutes, so a place that is exactly halfway between 49°N and 50°N is at 49°30'N. The line at which Americans wanted to divide the Oregon Territory (49°40'N) is two-thirds of the way between 49°N and 50°N. In the same way, a minute of latitude or longitude equals 60 seconds. So a place that is halfway between 49°40'N and 49°41'N is at 49°40'30"N.

Additional Practice

Chapter Skills Activity 12

ANSWERS TO PRACTICING THE SKILL

1. 48°N, 129°W
2. 50°N
3. 49°N
4. South Pass

Applying the Skill Students should find the coordinates of their city or the city closest to it and have a partner find other cities based on their coordinates.

1 FOCUS

BELLRINGER
Motivational Activity

Before taking roll at the beginning of the class period, project Section Focus Transparency 12–2 and have students answer the questions. Discuss students' responses.

This activity is also available as a blackline master.

Section Focus Transparency 12–2

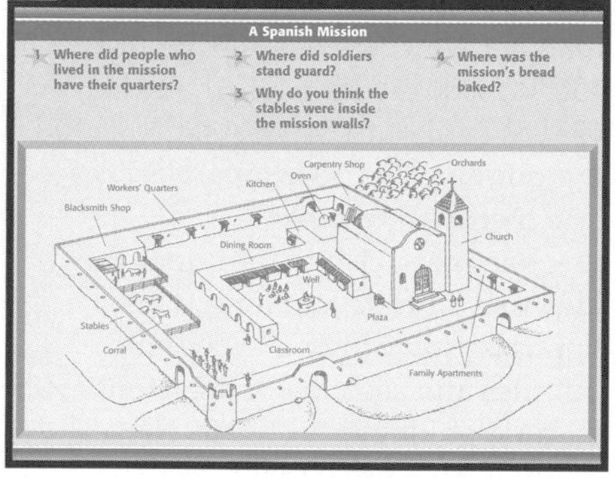

Vocabulary Precheck
Write *empresario* on the board. Then have a volunteer skim the section to find the term and read it in context.

Use the **Vocabulary PuzzleMaker** to create crossword and word search puzzles.

Section Theme
Geography and History
Mexico's offer of huge tracts of fertile land brought American settlers to Texas, which eventually became a state in the United States, much to Mexico's dismay.

Activity Have students skim the section to find the roles played by Moses and Stephen Austin and the Old Three Hundred in the settling of Texas. *(Moses received a grant which, upon his death, passed to Stephen. The Old Three Hundred were the settlers carefully chosen by Stephen.)*

1820 — 1830 — 1840

1821 Moses Austin receives land grant in Texas

1833 Santa Anna becomes president of Mexico

March 1836 The Alamo falls to Mexican troops

September 1836 Sam Houston is elected president of Texas

Section 2

Independence for Texas

READ TO DISCOVER . . .
- why problems arose between the Mexican government and the American settlers in Texas.
- how Texas achieved independence from Mexico and later became a state.

TERMS TO LEARN

Tejano	decree
empresario	annex

The Storyteller

Davy Crockett was a backwoodsman from Tennessee. His skill as a hunter and storyteller helped get him elected to three terms in Congress. But when he started his first political campaign, Crockett was doubtful about his chances of winning. "The thought of having to make a speech made my knees feel mighty weak and set my heart to fluttering." Fortunately for Crockett, the other candidates spoke all day and tired out the audience. "When they were all done," Crockett boasted, "I got up and told some laughable story, and quit. . . . I went home, and didn't go back again till after the election was over." In the end, Crockett won the election by a wide margin.

Davy Crockett

Davy Crockett of Tennessee won notice for his frontier skills, his sense of humor, and the shrewd common sense he often displayed in politics. When he lost his seat in Congress in 1835, he did not return to Tennessee. Instead he went southwest to Texas.

Crockett thought he could get a new start there. He also wanted to give the Texans "a helping hand on the high road to freedom"—winning their independence from Mexico. Little did he know his deeds in Texas would bring him greater fame than his adventures on the frontier or his years in Congress.

A Clash of Cultures

Conflict over Texas began in 1803, when the United States bought the Louisiana Territory from France. Americans claimed that the land in present-day Texas was part of the purchase. Spain protested. In 1819, in the **Adams-Onís Treaty**, the United States agreed to drop any further claim to the region.

Land Grants

At the time, few people lived in Texas. Some settlers came from the United States. Most residents—about 3,000—were **Tejanos** (teh•HAH•nohs), or Mexicans who claimed Texas as their home. Native Americans from the North also ventured into the area.

Because the Spanish wanted to promote the growth of Texas, they offered vast tracts of land to

SECTION RESOURCES

Reproducible Masters
- Reproducible Lesson Plan 12–2
- Guided Reading Activity 12–2
- Section Quiz 12–2
- Reteaching Activity 12–2
- Enrichment Activity 12–2

Transparencies
- Section Focus Transparency 12–2

Multimedia
- Vocabulary PuzzleMaker
- Chapter Challenger Interactive Review Software
- Testmaker
- GTV: A Geographic Perspective on American History
- ABCNews Interactive™ Historic America Electronic Field Trips

people who agreed to bring families to settle on the land. The people who arranged for these settlements were called **empresarios.**

Moses Austin heard about the Spanish plan. Austin, who had made a fortune in lead mining in Missouri, applied for and received the first land grant in 1821.

Americans Move In

Before Moses Austin could establish his colony, however, Mexico declared its independence from Spain. Austin died while waiting for the new Mexican government to confirm his land grant. The confirmation went instead to his son, **Stephen F. Austin,** who began to organize the colony.

Stephen F. Austin recruited 300 American families to settle the fertile land along the **Brazos River** and the **Colorado River** of Texas. He picked his settlers carefully, and they came to be called the **Old Three Hundred.** These first families received 960 acres, with additional acres for each child. Austin's success made him a leader among the American settlers in Texas.

From 1823 to 1825, Mexico passed three colonization laws. All these laws offered new settlers large tracts of land at extremely low prices and no taxes for four years. In return the colonists agreed to learn Spanish, convert to Catholicism—the religion of Mexico—and obey Mexican law.

Mexican leaders hoped to attract settlers from all over, including other parts of Mexico. Most Texas settlers, however, came from the United States.

Growing Tension

By 1830 Americans in Texas far outnumbered Mexicans. Further, these American colonists had not adopted Mexican ways. In the meantime the United States had twice offered to buy Texas from Mexico.

The Mexican government viewed the growing American influence in Texas with alarm. In 1830 the Mexican government issued a **decree,** or official order, that stopped all immigration from the United States. At the same time, the decree encouraged the immigration of Mexican and European families with generous land grants. Trade between Texas and the United States was discouraged by placing a tax on goods imported from the United States.

These new policies angered the Texans. The prosperity of many citizens depended on trade with the United States. Many had friends and relatives who wanted to come to Texas. In addition, those colonists who held slaves were uneasy about the Mexican government's plans to end slavery.

Stephen F. Austin

Attempt at Reconciliation

Some of the American settlers called for independence. Others hoped to stay within Mexico but on better terms. In 1833 **General Antonio López de Santa Anna** became president of Mexico. Stephen F. Austin traveled to Mexico City with the Texans' demands—to remove the ban on American settlers and to make Texas a separate state.

Santa Anna agreed to the first request but refused the second. Austin sent a letter back to Texas, suggesting that plans for independence get under way. The Mexican government intercepted the letter and arrested Austin.

While Austin was in jail, Santa Anna named himself dictator and overthrew Mexico's constitution of 1824. Without a constitution to protect their rights, Texans felt betrayed. Santa Anna reorganized the government, placing greater central control over the regions—including Texas. This loss of local power dismayed many people.

The Struggle for Independence

★ During 1835 unrest grew among Texans and occasionally resulted in open conflict. Santa Anna sent an army into Texas late that year

Cooperative Learning Activity

Making an Illustrated Time Line Have students work together to make a large, illustrated time line for this section for the bulletin board. As a class, students should decide which events to include. Assign some students to make the actual time line. Then organize the remainder of the class into small groups, each working on one event. In each group some students may do any necessary research; others should make the illustrations; others should write brief captions describing the event.

2 TEACH

L1 Finding Answers Have students find the answers to the following questions as they read the section. What was the significance of the Battle of San Jacinto? *(Texan victory led to independence.)* When did Texas become a state? *(December 29, 1845)*

Guided Reading Activity 12–2

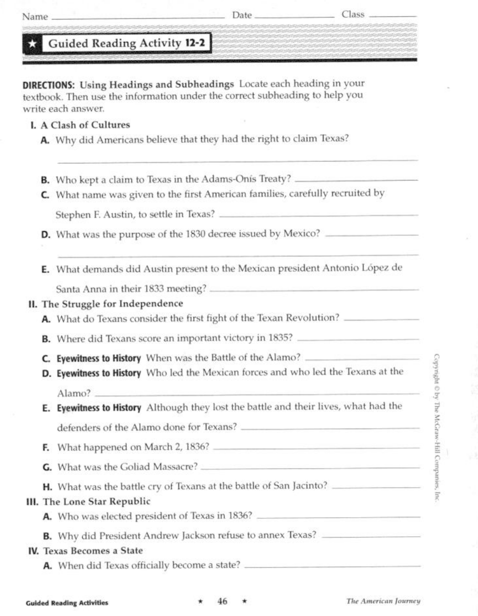

Name ______ Date ______ Class ______

★ Guided Reading Activity **12-2**

DIRECTIONS: Using Headings and Subheadings Locate each heading in your textbook. Then use the information under the correct subheading to help you write each answer.

I. A Clash of Cultures

A. Why did Americans believe that they had the right to claim Texas? ______

B. Who kept a claim to Texas in the Adams-Onís Treaty? ______

C. What name was given to the first American families, carefully recruited by Stephen F. Austin, to settle in Texas? ______

D. What was the purpose of the 1830 decree issued by Mexico? ______

E. What demands did Austin present to the Mexican president Antonio López de Santa Anna in their 1833 meeting? ______

II. The Struggle for Independence

A. What do Texans consider the first fight of the Texan Revolution? ______

B. Where did Texans score an important victory in 1835? ______

C. Eyewitness to History When was the Battle of the Alamo? ______

D. Eyewitness to History Who led the Mexican forces and who led the Texans at the Alamo? ______

E. Eyewitness to History Although they lost the battle and their lives, what had the defenders of the Alamo done for Texans? ______

F. What happened on March 2, 1836? ______

G. What was the Goliad Massacre? ______

H. What was the battle cry of Texans at the battle of San Jacinto? ______

III. The Lone Star Republic

A. Who was elected president of Texas in 1836? ______

B. Why did President Andrew Jackson refuse to annex Texas? ______

IV. Texas Becomes a State

A. When did Texas officially become a state? ______

Guided Reading Activities ★ 46 ★ *The American Journey*

NATIONAL GEOGRAPHIC SOCIETY

VIDEODISC
GTV: A Geographic Perspective on American History

Side 2, Chapter 11
Title: *Going to Extremes: The Far West*
Subject: Settlement in the Far West, 1820–1850
Ask: Why did many people settle in Texas? *(Land was cheap.)*

Picturing HISTORY Though dramatic, this painting is inaccurate—the Texans' last stand took place inside the Alamo. **Ask: Why was the battle at the Alamo helpful to Texans even though they lost the battle?** *(gained time for them to organize)*
Answer: *Davy Crockett, Jim Bowie, William B. Travis*

Where? When? Who? What?

Gone to Texas As an additional incentive for American settlers in Texas, the Mexican government promised protection from lawsuits filed in the United States for failure to pay debts. So many bankrupted families decided to take the opportunity to start over that vacated homes with signs reading "Gone to Texas" became a familiar sight throughout the South.

you don't say...

Texas The name Texas comes from a Native American word, *texía,* meaning "friends" or "allies." Spanish speakers changed it to *tejas* and English speakers to *Texas.*

Picturing HISTORY This painting depicts the last moments of the Battle of the Alamo, before the remaining Texans were finally forced to surrender. **What three noted Western leaders fought for Texas at the Alamo?**

to punish the rebels. Some Mexican troops tried in October to seize a cannon held by Texans at the town of **Gonzales.** During the battle the Texans decorated the front of the cannon with a white flag that bore the words "Come and Take It." After a brief struggle, Texans drove back the Mexican troops. Texans consider this the first fight of the Texan Revolution.

Early Victories

The Texans called on volunteers to join their fight. They offered free land to anyone who would help. Davy Crockett and many others—including a number of African Americans and Tejanos—answered that call.

In December 1835, the Texans scored an important victory. They liberated **San Antonio** from the control of a larger Mexican force. The Mexicans retreated to the other side of the Rio Grande.

Despite these victories, the Texans encountered problems. With the Mexican withdrawal, some Texans left San Antonio, thinking the war was won. Various groups argued over who was in charge and what course of action to follow. In early 1836, when Texas should have been making preparations to face Santa Anna, nothing was being done.

Eyewitness to HISTORY

The Battle of the Alamo

Santa Anna marched north, furious at the loss of San Antonio. When his army reached San Antonio in late February 1836, it found a small Texan force barricaded inside a nearby mission called **the Alamo.**

Although the Texans had cannons, they lacked gunpowder. Worse, they had only about 150 soldiers to face Santa Anna's army of several thousand. The Texans did have brave leaders, though, including Davy Crockett, who had arrived with a band of sharpshooters from Tennessee, and a tough Texan named Jim Bowie. The commander, William B. Travis, was only 25 years old, but he was determined to hold his position.

Travis managed to send messages out through Mexican lines. In a now famous letter of February 24, 1836, Travis wrote:

> "The enemy has demanded surrender. . . . I have answered that demand with a cannon shot, and our flag still waves proudly from the walls. *I shall never surrender or retreat. . . . Victory or Death!*"

MULTIPLE LEARNING STYLES

Verbal/Linguistic Quite naturally we tend to think of historical events from the American point of view. Have students list the quarrels between the two sides–Americans' failure to learn Spanish, convert to Catholicism, and obey Mexican law; Mexico's forbidding further American settlement and taxing of goods imported from the United States; Mexico's plan to end slavery. Then have students write a letter to a newspaper editor describing the quarrels from the Mexican point of view. **L2**

For 12 long days, the defenders of the Alamo kept Santa Anna's army at bay with rifle fire. The Mexicans launched two assaults but had to break them off. During the siege, 32 volunteers from Gonzales slipped through the Mexican lines to join the Alamo's defenders.

They were too few, however. Davy Crockett's journal entry for March 3 read:

> "We have given over all hopes of receiving assistance. . . . Colonel Travis harangued [commanded] the garrison . . . to fight to the last gasp. . . . This was followed by three cheers."

On March 6, 1836, Mexican cannon fire smashed the Alamo's walls, and the Mexicans launched an all-out attack. The Alamo defenders killed many Mexican soldiers as they crossed open land and tried to mount the Alamo's walls. The Mexicans were too numerous to hold back, however, and they finally entered the fortress, killing William Travis, Davy Crockett, Jim Bowie, and all the other defenders. Only a few women and children and some servants survived to tell of the battle.

In the words of Santa Anna's aide, "The Texans fought more like devils than like men." The defenders of the Alamo had killed hundreds of Mexican soldiers. But more important, they had bought Texans some much needed time.

Texas Declares Its Independence

During the siege of the Alamo, Texan leaders were meeting at Washington-on-the-Brazos, where they were drawing up a new constitution. There, on March 2, 1836—four days before the fall of the Alamo—American settlers and Tejanos firmly declared the independence of the Republic of Texas.

Sam Houston Leads the Fight

The provisional government of the new republic named **Sam Houston** as commander in chief of the Texas forces. Houston had come to Texas in 1833. Raised among the Cherokee people, he became a soldier, fighting with Andrew Jackson against the Creek people. A politician as well, Houston had served in Congress and as governor of Tennessee.

Houston wanted to prevent other forts from being overrun by the Mexicans. He ordered the troops at **Goliad** to abandon their position. As they retreated, however, they came face to face with Mexican troops. After a fierce fight, several hundred Texans surrendered. On Santa Anna's orders, the Texans were executed a few days later. This action outraged Texans, who called it the "Goliad Massacre."

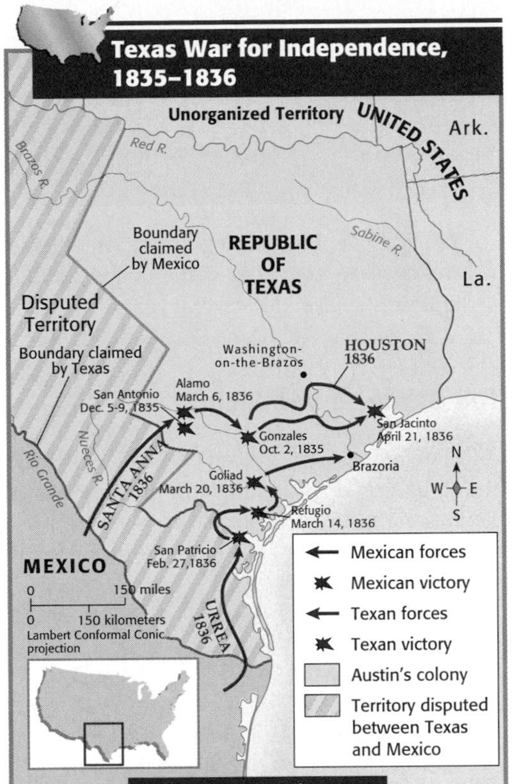

Map Study

In 1836 General Santa Anna led Mexico's main forces across the Rio Grande into Texas.

1. **Location** At which places did Texans win victories?
2. **Analyzing Information** What battle immediately followed the Alamo?

Making Connections Activity

Drama Santa Anna, one of Latin America's first dictators, was frequently in and out of power between 1833 and 1855. A colorful figure, he was an expert at rewriting events to cast himself in a favorable light. During a battle with the French at Veracruz, his leg was shattered by an artillery shell. Believing he was dying, he arranged a dramatic deathbed scene. While his officers stood grieving, he dictated a 15-page farewell message to the Mexican people. Anticlimactically, Santa Anna survived the injury, although his lower leg did not. He had the amputated leg enshrined in an elaborate tomb, and later had it brought to the military cemetery at Mexico City, where it was ceremoniously placed in an urn. Have students read about Santa Anna's exploits and prepare a skit dramatizing one of the events described above or some other event that they discover in their research. **L2**

ABCNEWS INTERACTIVE™

VIDEODISC
Historic America Electronic Field Trips

Side 1, Chapter 10

Title: *The Alamo*
Subject: Tour of this historic site
Ask: **How did Mexico view Texas?** *(as part of their country)*

Also available in VHS.

you don't say...

Bronco, corral, **and** ***rodeo*** all came to us via Mexican vaqueros, or cowhands. The Alamo was named after cottonwood trees that grew nearby.

Map Study

Answers

1. San Antonio, Gonzales, San Jacinto
2. Refugio

Map Skills Practice

Reading a Map Which is the last battle shown on the map? *(San Jacinto)*

Who?What?Where?When?

Santa Anna tried to escape after his defeat at San Jacinto by dressing in an ordinary soldier's uniform and hiding in a marsh. He was captured the day after the battle by Texan soldiers who did not recognize him. When they brought Santa Anna back to camp, his identity was revealed by Mexican prisoners who saluted "El Presidente."

CHAPTER 12
Section 2, 362–367

Picturing HISTORY Before the Texas Revolution, San Antonio was the capital of the territory. The Governor's Palace was the center of a bright social life. Today the palace has been restored and is open to visitors. **Ask: What is the capital of Texas today?** *(Austin)* **Answer:** *Southerners favored annexation, but Northerners did not want another slave state.*

Who?What?Where?When?

Sam Houston aided his country well. He was elected governor of Tennessee and was a U.S. senator from Texas for 14 years. Serving later as governor of Texas, he is the only man ever elected governor of two different states of the Union.

3 ASSESS

Assign Section 2 Review as homework or as an in-class activity.

Use **Chapter Challenger Interactive Review Software** to review Section 2.

Section Quiz 12–2

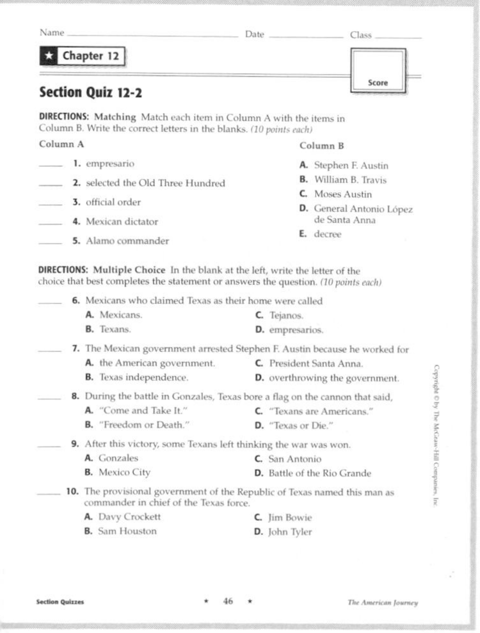

Name ________ Date ________ Class ________

★ Chapter 12

Score

Section Quiz 12-2

DIRECTIONS: Matching Match each item in Column A with the items in Column B. Write the correct letters in the blanks. *(10 points each)*

Column A

____ **1.** empresario
____ **2.** selected the Old Three Hundred
____ **3.** official order
____ **4.** Mexican dictator
____ **5.** Alamo commander

Column B

A. Stephen F. Austin
B. William B. Travis
C. Moses Austin
D. General Antonio López de Santa Anna
E. decree

DIRECTIONS: Multiple Choice In the blank at the left, write the letter of the choice that best completes the statement or answers the question. *(10 points each)*

____ **6.** Mexicans who claimed Texas as their home were called
A. Mexicans. **C.** Tejanos.
B. Texans. **D.** empresarios.

____ **7.** The Mexican government arrested Stephen F. Austin because he worked for
A. the American government. **C.** President Santa Anna.
B. Texas independence. **D.** overthrowing the government.

____ **8.** During the battle in Gonzales, Texas bore a flag on the cannon that said,
A. "Come and Take It." **C.** "Texans are Americans."
B. "Freedom or Death." **D.** "Texas or Die."

____ **9.** After this victory, some Texans left thinking the war was won.
A. Gonzales **C.** San Antonio
B. Mexico City **D.** Battle of the Rio Grande

____ **10.** The provisional government of the Republic of Texas named this man as commander in chief of the Texas force.
A. Davy Crockett **C.** Jim Bowie
B. Sam Houston **D.** John Tyler

Section Quizzes ★ 46 ★ *The American Journey*

Picturing HISTORY This painting shows San Antonio in the late 1840s, after Texas had become part of the United States. **Why was the admission of Texas to the Union delayed for several years?**

The Battle of San Jacinto

Houston moved his small army eastward about 100 miles, watching the movements of Santa Anna and waiting for a chance to strike. Six weeks after the Alamo, he found the opportunity.

America's FLAGS

Texas Republic, 1839 For its first six years, this Lone Star flag symbolized the independent nation of the Republic of Texas. Texans kept the Lone Star banner as their official state flag after joining the Union in 1845.

After adding some new troops, Houston gathered an army of about 800 at **San Jacinto** (SAN huh•SIN•tuh), near the site of present-day Houston. Santa Anna was camped nearby with an army of more than 1,300. On April 21 the Texans launched a surprise attack on the Mexican camp, shouting, "Remember the Alamo! Remember Goliad!" They killed more than 600 soldiers and captured about 700 more—including Santa Anna. On May 14, 1836, Santa Anna signed a treaty that recognized the independence of Texas.

The Lone Star Republic

Texans elected Sam Houston as their president in September 1836. He sent a delegation to Washington, D.C., asking the United States to **annex**—take control of—Texas. President Andrew Jackson refused, however, because the addition of another slave state would upset the balance of slave and free states in Congress.

CRITICAL THINKING ACTIVITY

Evaluating Information During the controversy over the admission of Texas as a state, some Northerners claimed that the move to bring Texas into the Union was a conspiracy by the Southern "slavocracy" to expand slavery. Have students consider that theory in light of Texas's geographic location. *(Students should note that Texas is near the Southern states and that it is more probable that a majority of the American settlers in Texas were from states in which slavery was widespread and merely continued the practice in their new homes.)* Ask students why people would come up with such a theory, which, though possible, is not probable. *(People sometimes exaggerate and make wild claims in the heat of promoting or defending a cause.)* **L1, ELL**

For the moment Texas would remain an independent country.

Despite rapid population growth, the new republic faced political and financial difficulties. The Mexican government refused to honor Santa Anna's recognition of independence, and fighting continued between Texas and Mexico. In addition Texas had an enormous debt of $7 million and no money to repay it.

The Annexation Debate

Many Texans still hoped to join the United States. Southerners favored the annexation of Texas, but Northerners objected that Texas would add another slave state to the Union. President Martin Van Buren, like Jackson, did not want to inflame the slavery issue or risk war with Mexico. He put off the question of annexing Texas.

John Tyler, who became president in 1841, supported adding Texas to the Union and persuaded Texas to reapply for annexation. However, the Senate was divided over slavery and failed to ratify the annexation treaty.

Texas Becomes a State

The situation changed with the 1844 presidential campaign. The feeling of Manifest Destiny was growing throughout the country.

General Sam Houston

The South favored annexation of Texas. The North demanded that the United States gain control of the Oregon country from Britain. The Democratic candidate, James K. Polk, supported both actions. The Whig candidate, Henry Clay, initially opposed adding Texas to the Union. When he finally came out for annexation, it lost him votes in the North—and the election.

After Polk's victory, supporters of annexation pressed the issue in Congress. They proposed and passed a resolution to annex Texas. On December 29, 1845, Texas officially became a state of the United States.

Section 2 Review

Checking for Understanding

1. ***Identify*** Davy Crockett, Stephen F. Austin, the Alamo, Sam Houston, John Tyler.
2. ***Define*** Tejano, empresario, decree, annex.
3. ***Name*** the three things that American settlers agreed to do in exchange for receiving land in Texas.

Reviewing Themes

4. **Geography and History** Why did Northerners and Southerners disagree on the annexation of Texas?

Critical Thinking

5. **Predicting Consequences** Why did Mexico's plan to colonize Texas backfire?

Activity

Creating an Advertisement Imagine you are Stephen Austin and you are recruiting settlers to colonize Texas. Draw an advertisement that would attract American settlers.

CHAPTER 12
Section 2, 362–367

Reteaching Activity 12–2

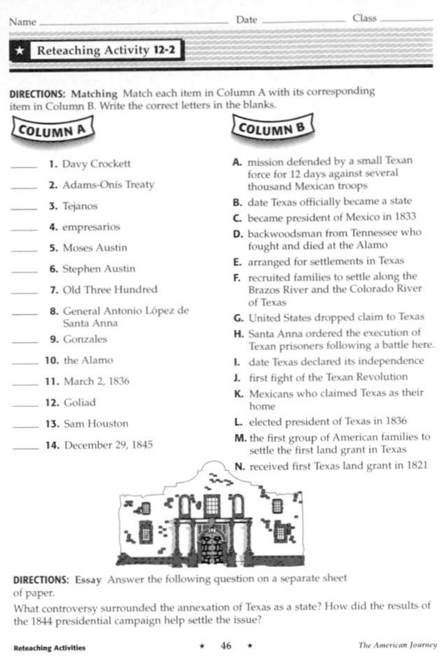

Name ______ Date ______ Class ______

★ Reteaching Activity 12-2

DIRECTIONS: Matching Match each item in Column A with its corresponding item in Column B. Write the correct letters in the blanks.

COLUMN A

____ 1. Davy Crockett
____ 2. Adams-Onís Treaty
____ 3. Tejanos
____ 4. empresarios
____ 5. Moses Austin
____ 6. Stephen Austin
____ 7. Old Three Hundred
____ 8. General Antonio López de Santa Anna
____ 9. Gonzales
____ 10. the Alamo
____ 11. March 2, 1836
____ 12. Goliad
____ 13. Sam Houston
____ 14. December 29, 1845

COLUMN B

A. mission defended by a small Texan force for 12 days against several thousand Mexican troops
B. date Texas officially became a state
C. became president of Mexico in 1833
D. backwoodsman from Tennessee who fought and died at the Alamo
E. arranged for settlements in Texas
F. recruited families to settle along the Brazos River and the Colorado River of Texas
G. United States dropped claim to Texas
H. Santa Anna ordered the execution of Texan prisoners following a battle here.
I. date Texas declared its independence
J. first fight of the Texan Revolution
K. Mexicans who claimed Texas as their home
L. elected president of Texas in 1836
M. the first group of American families to settle the first land grant in Texas
N. received first Texas land grant in 1821

DIRECTIONS: Essay Answer the following question on a separate sheet of paper.

What controversy surrounded the annexation of Texas as a state? How did the results of the 1844 presidential campaign help settle the issue?

Reteaching Activities ★ 46 ★ *The American Journey*

Copyright © by The McGraw-Hill Companies, Inc.

Enrichment Activity 12–2

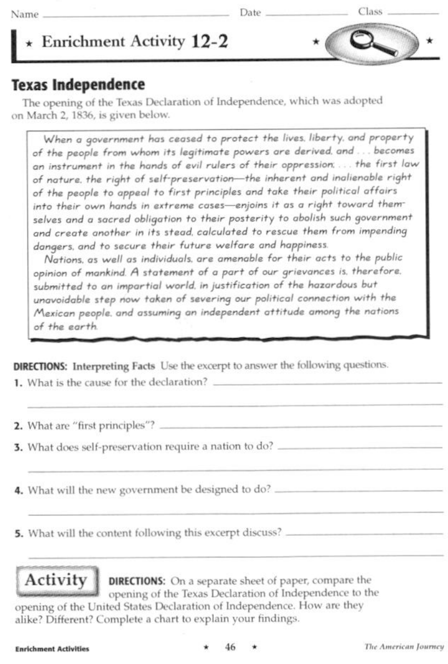

Name ______ Date ______ Class ______

★ Enrichment Activity 12-2

Texas Independence

The opening of the Texas Declaration of Independence, which was adopted on March 2, 1836, is given below.

When a government has ceased to protect the lives, liberty, and property of the people from whom its legitimate powers are derived, and . . . becomes an instrument in the hands of evil rulers of their oppression; . . . the first law of nature, the right of self-preservation—the inherent and inalienable right of the people to appeal to first principles and take their political affairs into their own hands in extreme cases—enjoins it as a right toward themselves and a sacred obligation to their posterity to abolish such government and create another in its stead, calculated to rescue them from impending dangers, and to secure their future welfare and happiness.

Nations, as well as individuals, are amenable for their acts to the public opinion of mankind. A statement of a part of our grievances is, therefore, submitted to an impartial world, in justification of the hazardous but unavoidable step now taken of severing our political connection with the Mexican people, and assuming an independent attitude among the nations of the earth.

DIRECTIONS: Interpreting Facts Use the excerpt to answer the following questions.

1. What is the cause for the declaration? ______
2. What are "first principles"? ______
3. What does self-preservation require a nation to do? ______
4. What will the new government be designed to do? ______
5. What will the content following this excerpt discuss? ______

Activity **DIRECTIONS:** On a separate sheet of paper, compare the opening of the Texas Declaration of Independence to the opening of the United States Declaration of Independence. How are they alike? Different? Complete a chart to explain your findings.

Enrichment Activities ★ 46 ★ *The American Journey*

Copyright © by The McGraw-Hill Companies, Inc.

Section 2 Review Answers

1. Davy Crockett, 362; Stephen F. Austin, 363; the Alamo, 364; Sam Houston, 365; John Tyler, 367
2. The words are defined in the Glossary.
3. learn Spanish, convert to Catholicism, obey Mexican laws
4. Northerners objected because it would add another slave state to the Union; Southerners favored it for the same reason.
5. So many American settlers came that Americans far outnumbered Mexican settlers. This gave Americans more leverage in making demands from Mexico and eventually led to the Texas fight for independence.

Activity Advertisements should make Texas and the benefits of settling there sound very attractive.

4 CLOSE

Ask students why Houston's troops shouted "Remember the Alamo" and "Remember Goliad." *(Texans who died at those places were considered martyrs and heroes; troops were inspired to avenge their deaths.)*

1 FOCUS

BELLRINGER
Motivational Activity

Before taking roll at the beginning of the class period, project Section Focus Transparency 12–3 and have students answer the questions. Discuss students' responses.

This activity is also available as a blackline master.

Section Focus Transparency 12–3

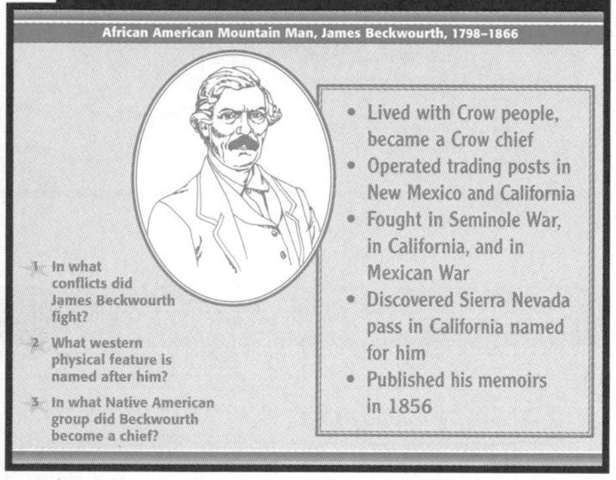

Vocabulary Precheck

Point out that the word *rancho* means not only "ranch" but "a hut or group of huts for ranch workers." Have students look up the etymology of the word and speculate on the links between the various roots.

Use the **Vocabulary Puzzle-Maker** to create crossword and word search puzzles.

Section Theme
Culture and Traditions

Both New Mexico and California were former Spanish lands with Spanish culture and traditions.

Activity Have students speculate on some of the different ways of life that Americans would bring to those lands. *(spirit of independence, democratic form of government, Protestant and other non-Catholic religions, and so on)*

1820 — 1830 — 1840 — 1850

1820 Twenty-one missions exist in California

1821 William Becknell reaches Santa Fe

1840s Americans settle in California

1845 President Polk offers to buy California and New Mexico

Section 3

New Mexico and California

READ TO DISCOVER . . .
- why Americans began to settle in the Southwest after Mexican independence.
- why California became a source of conflict between the United States and Mexico.

TERMS TO LEARN
rancho
ranchero

The Storyteller

Long lines of covered wagons stretched as far as the eye could see. "All's set!" a driver called out. "All's set!" everyone shouted in reply.

"Then the 'Heps!' of drivers—the cracking of whips—the trampling of feet—the occasional creak of wheels—the rumbling of wagons—form a new scene of [intense] confusion," reported Josiah Gregg. Gregg was one of the traders who traveled west on the Santa Fe Trail in the 1830s to sell cloth, knives, and other goods in New Mexico.

Wagon wheel

In the early 1800s, **New Mexico** was the name of a vast region sandwiched between the Texas and California territories. It included all of present-day New Mexico, Arizona, and Nevada and parts of Colorado and Utah.

The New Mexico Territory

Native American peoples had lived in the area for thousands of years. Spanish conquistadors began exploring there in the late 1500s and made it part of Spain's colony of Mexico. In 1609 the Spanish founded the settlement of **Santa Fe.** Missionaries followed soon after.

When Mexico won its independence in 1821, it inherited the New Mexico province from Spain. The Mexicans, however, had little control over the distant province. The inhabitants of New Mexico mostly governed themselves.

The Spanish had tried to keep Americans away from Santa Fe, fearing that Americans would want to take over the area. The Mexican government changed this policy, welcoming American traders into New Mexico. It hoped that the trade would boost the economy of the province.

Geography

The Santa Fe Trail

William Becknell, the first American trader to reach Santa Fe, arrived in 1821 with a pack of mules laden with goods. Becknell sold the

SECTION RESOURCES

Reproducible Masters
- Reproducible Lesson Plan 12–3
- Guided Reading Activity 12–3
- Section Quiz 12–3
- Reteaching Activity 12–3
- Enrichment Activity 12–3

Transparencies
- Section Focus Transparency 12–3

Multimedia
- Vocabulary PuzzleMaker
- Chapter Challenger Interactive Review Software
- Testmaker

American Memories
Mexican American Cowhand

Silver-inlaid spurs

Vaquero's hat

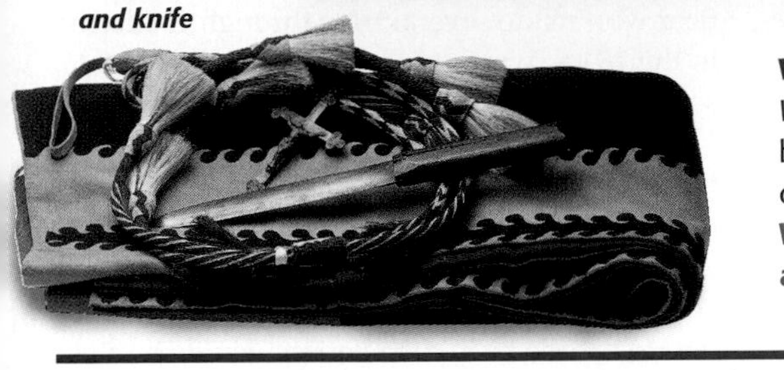

Riding whip, religious medal, blanket, and knife

What Was It Like?
Vaqueros in a Horse Corral by James Walker shows a typical day on a ranch in the Southwest. **What do the objects shown here reveal about the kind of work vaqueros did?**

merchandise he brought for many times what he would have received for it in St. Louis.

Becknell's route came to be known as the **Santa Fe Trail.** The trail left the Missouri River near Independence, Missouri, and crossed the prairies to the Arkansas River. It followed the river west toward the Rocky Mountains before turning south into New Mexico Territory. Because the trail was mostly flat, Becknell used wagons to carry his merchandise on later trips.

Other traders followed Becknell, and the Santa Fe Trail became a busy trade route for hundreds of wagons. Americans brought textiles and firearms, which they exchanged in Santa Fe for silver, furs, and mules. The trail remained in use until the arrival of the railroad in 1880.

As trade with New Mexico increased, Americans began settling in the region. In the United States, the idea of Manifest Destiny captured the popular imagination, and many people saw New Mexico as territory worth acquiring. At the same time, they eyed another prize—the Mexican territory of California, which would provide access to the Pacific.

California's Spanish Culture

Spanish explorers and missionaries from Mexico had been the first Europeans to settle in California. In the 1760s Captain Gaspar de Portolá and Father Junípero Serra began building a string of missions that eventually extended from San Diego to San Francisco.

The Mission System

The mission system was a key part of Spain's plan to colonize California. The Spanish used the missions to convert Native Americans to Christianity. By 1820, 21 missions dotted California, with about 20,000 Native Americans living in them.

In 1820 American mountain man Jedediah Smith visited the San Gabriel Mission east of present-day Los Angeles. Smith reported that the Indians farmed thousands of acres and worked at weaving and other crafts. He described the missions as "large farming and grazing establishments." Another American in Smith's party, called the Indians "slaves in every sense of the word."

Cooperative Learning Activity

Mapping Missions Have students use library resources to find the information they need to prepare a map showing the missions established by Father Junípero Serra. Have them also prepare biographical information on Father Serra and anecdotes about his travels. (Serra was the leader of five missionaries who accompanied Gaspar de Portola's expedition, which began exploring California in 1769. During Serra's lifetime, 9 missions were built; eventually there were 21. They stretched from San Diego to San Francisco and were each about a day's walk apart.) Students may work in pairs with one student drawing the map and the other preparing the written material. Students may also work in groups of 3 with the third student making a diagram of a typical mission.

American Memories

Mexican American Cowhand
Cattle on Mexican ranches were raised mainly for their hides and for their fat, which was used in candlemaking.
Answer: *Objects suggest that they rode horses, worked under the hot sun, and sometimes slept in the open.*

2 TEACH

L1 Finding Similarities Have students list similarities between New Mexico and California and in the way Americans settled in the two places.

Guided Reading Activity 12–3

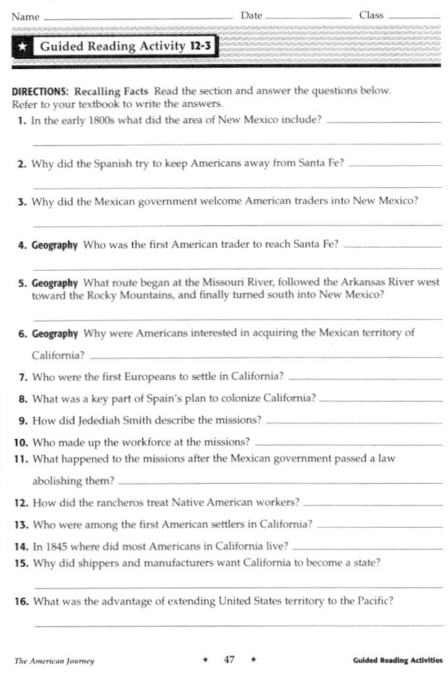
Name ______ Date ______ Class ______

Guided Reading Activity 12-3

DIRECTIONS: Recalling Facts Read the section and answer the questions below. Refer to your textbook to write the answers.

1. In the early 1800s what did the area of New Mexico include?
2. Why did the Spanish try to keep Americans away from Santa Fe?
3. Why did the Mexican government welcome American traders into New Mexico?
4. **Geography** Who was the first American trader to reach Santa Fe?
5. **Geography** What route began at the Missouri River, followed the Arkansas River west toward the Rocky Mountains, and finally turned south into New Mexico?
6. **Geography** Why were Americans interested in acquiring the Mexican territory of California?
7. Who were the first Europeans to settle in California?
8. What was a key part of Spain's plan to colonize California?
9. How did Jedediah Smith describe the missions?
10. Who made up the workforce at the missions?
11. What happened to the missions after the Mexican government passed a law abolishing them?
12. How did the rancheros treat Native American workers?
13. Who were among the first American settlers in California?
14. In 1845 where did most Americans in California live?
15. Why did shippers and manufacturers want California to become a state?
16. What was the advantage of extending United States territory to the Pacific?

The American Journey • 47 • Guided Reading Activities

3 ASSESS

Assign Section 3 Review as homework or as an in-class activity.

Use **Chapter Challenger Interactive Review Software** to review Section 3.

CHAPTER 12
Section 3, 368–370

Section Quiz 12–3

Name ______ Date ______ Class ______

★ Chapter 12

Score

Section Quiz 12-3

DIRECTIONS: Matching Match each item in Column A with the items in Column B. Write the correct letters in the blanks. *(10 points each)*

Column A	Column B
____ 1. founded by the Spanish	A. Santa Fe Trail
____ 2. American trader	B. rancheros
____ 3. busy trade route	C. William Becknell
____ 4. mission slaves	D. Santa Fe
____ 5. ranch owners	E. Native Americans

DIRECTIONS: Multiple Choice In the blank at the left, write the letter of the choice that best completes the statement or answers the question. *(10 points each)*

____ 6. This trail left the Missouri River near Independence, Missouri, and crossed the prairies to the Arkansas River.
A. Missouri Trail C. Independence Trail
B. Santa Fe Trail D. Arkansas River Trail

____ 7. Americans wanted this Mexican territory because it provided access to the Pacific.
A. New Mexico C. California
B. Oregon D. Washington

Reteaching Activity 12–3

Name ______ Date ______ Class ______

★ Reteaching Activity 12-3

DIRECTIONS: Making Comparisons and Contrasts After each statement of fact, write the letter of a fact from the Fact Bank that makes a comparison or contrast.

1. **Fact:** The Spanish tried to keep Americans away from Santa Fe, fearing that Americans would want to take over the area.
Comparison or Contrast: ______
2. **Fact:** Not knowing the conditions of the route he would be traveling, William Becknell used a pack of mules to transport goods to Santa Fe.
Comparison or Contrast: ______
3. **Fact:** Many Americans saw New Mexico as a territory worth acquiring.
Comparison or Contrast: ______
4. **Fact:** Jedediah Smith described the missions as "large farming and grazing establishments" where Native Americans farmed and worked at weaving and other crafts.
Comparison or Contrast: ______
5. **Fact:** Plantation owners depended on African American slaves to work their plantations.
Comparison or Contrast: ______
6. **Fact:** Early travelers to California arrived on trading or whaling ships.
Comparison or Contrast: ______

★FACT BANK

A. Rancheros persuaded Native Americans to work their lands and tend their cattle in return for food and shelter.
B. Americans also eyed California as
D. In the 1840s families made the long journey from Missouri over land in wagons.
E. One American called the Native Americans at the missions "slaves

Enrichment Activity 12–3

Name ______ Date ______ Class ______

★ Enrichment Activity 12-3 ★

The Santa Fe Trail

Although the Santa Fe Trail, opened in 1821, was one of the longest commercial trails in the United States, its use was short-lived. In the late 1860s more than 5,000 wagons used the trail each year. Then railroads took over the movement of freight and use of the busy trail dwindled.

Santa Fe Trail Opens, 1821

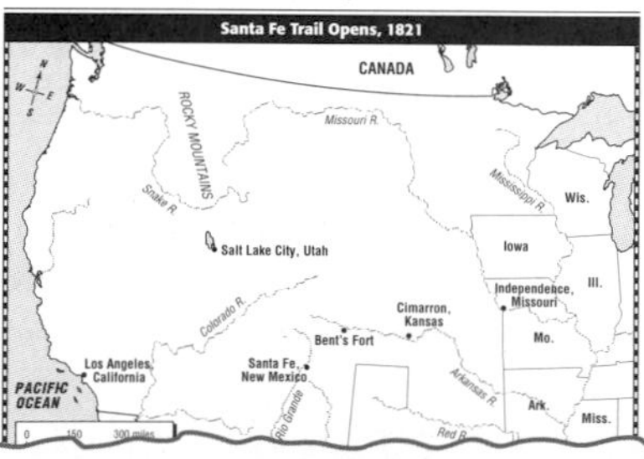

California after 1821

After Mexico gained its independence from Spain in 1821, **California** became a state in the new Mexican nation. At the time only a few hundred Spanish settlers lived in California, but emigrants began arriving from Mexico. The wealthier settlers lived on ranches devoted to raising cattle and horses.

In 1833 the Mexican government passed a law abolishing the missions. The government gave some of the lands to Native Americans and sold the remainder. Mexican settlers bought these lands and built huge properties called **ranchos**.

The Mexican settlers persuaded Native Americans to work their lands and tend their cattle in return for food and shelter. The California ranchos were similar to the plantations of the South, and the **rancheros**—ranch owners—treated Native American workers almost like slaves.

Americans Eye California

Americans had been visiting California for years. Most arrived on trading or whaling ships, although a few hardy travelers like Jedediah Smith came overland from the East. Soon more began to arrive.

At first the Mexican authorities welcomed Americans in California. The newcomers included agents for American shipping companies, fur traders from Oregon, and merchants from New Mexico. In the 1840s families began to arrive in California to settle. They made the long journey from Missouri on the Oregon Trail and then turned south after crossing the Rocky Mountains. Still, by 1845 the American population of California numbered only about 700. Most Americans lived in the Sacramento River valley.

Manifest Destiny and California

Some American travelers wrote glowing reports of California. **John C. Frémont,** an army officer who made several trips through California in the 1840s, wrote of the region's mild climate, scenic beauty, and abundant resources.

Americans began to talk about adding California to the nation. Shippers and manufacturers hoped to build ports on the Pacific coast for trade with China and Japan. Many Americans saw the advantage of extending United States territory to the Pacific. That way the nation would be safely bordered by the sea instead of by a foreign power.

In 1845 Secretary of War William Marcy wrote that "if the people [of California] should desire to unite their destiny with ours, they would be received as brethren [brothers]." Polk twice offered to buy California and New Mexico from Mexico, but Mexico refused. Before long the United States would take over both regions by force.

Section 3 Review

Checking for Understanding

1. ***Identify*** William Becknell, Santa Fe Trail, John C. Frémont.
2. ***Define*** rancho, ranchero.
3. ***Explain*** why Mexico, at first, welcomed Americans to New Mexico.

Reviewing Themes

4. **Culture and Traditions** Why did the Spanish establish missions in the Southwest?

Critical Thinking

5. **Identifying Assumptions** State the hidden message in this statement: "If the people [of California] should desire to unite their destiny with ours, they would be received as brethren."

Activity

Creating a Picture Map Create an enlarged version of the map on page 358. Then add illustrations to tell the story of the Santa Fe Trail.

Section 3 Review Answers

1. William Becknell, 368; Santa Fe Trail, 369; John C. Frémont, 370
2. The words are defined in the Glossary.
3. Mexico hoped that American traders would boost the province's economy.
4. to convert Native Americans to Christianity and spread Spanish culture
5. that the United States intended to take over California

Activity Picture maps might show traders and settlers using the trail, Spanish and Native American settlements, or some of the goods that were transported along the trail.

4 CLOSE

The Santa Fe Trail passed through rugged country that included deserts, mountains, mosquitoes, and rattlesnakes. **Ask: Why would traders put up with these conditions?** *(love of adventure, curiosity about new lands, and profits to be made)*

INTERDISCIPLINARY

Activities

Traveling West

In the early 1800s many Americans believed that they would find their fortune on the frontier, even though the way west was long and dangerous. Imagine yourself as a pioneer as you complete these activities about traveling west.

Art

Picturing the West Painters and photographers were amazed by the spectacular scenery of the West. Research the work of painters such as Albert Bierstadt and Frederic Remington or photographers such as William H. Jackson or Ansel Adams. Then create your own painting or photograph that conveys the majestic scenery of the West.

Science

Keeping a Science Log Settlers traveling west encountered new wildlife, vegetation, and landforms. Some, like Lewis and Clark, wrote careful descriptions, drew sketches, and collected samples—feathers, bones, rocks. Choose one region of the West and investigate it as a traveling scientist would. List plants and animals you would see there. Draw sketches of characteristics such as leaves or pawprints. If possible, collect samples for your log. Write a "naturalist's report" to the class, summarizing what you have observed.

Music

Learning a Western Song Many classic American folk songs come from the Old West. Organize a group of classmates who sing or play guitar, banjo, or another instrument. Then learn the words and music to a traditional song such as "Red River Valley," "Shenandoah," or "Home on the Range." Plan a performance for your class.

School-to-Work

Building a Western Town Set designers for movies and television have made the typical Western town a familiar scene—a dusty main street with general store, saloon, corral, and a few houses. Imagine you are a set designer. Plan and build a model of a Western town to be used for constructing scenery for an upcoming movie. First design the layout of the town, then assemble small buildings out of wood or cardboard. Add shutters and colorful signboards. Paint the streets brown and sprinkle sand on the wet paint. Set up your town on a table in the classroom.

Miner with tools of the trade

INTERDISCIPLINARY

Activities

TEACH

Background

Francis Parkman (1823–1893) was an American historian who traveled west to Wyoming to study Native Americans. He described his travels in *The Oregon Trail* (1849):

"Before sunrise in the morning the snow-covered mountains were beautifully tinged with a delicate rose-color. A noble spectacle awaited us as we moved forward. . . . For one instant some snowy peak, towering in awful solitude, would be disclosed to view. As the clouds broke along the mountain, we could see the dreary forests, the tremendous precipices, the white patches of snow, the gulfs and chasms as black as night, all revealed for an instant, and then disappearing from the view."

Ask students to imagine the various emotions such a sight must have inspired in the travelers. *(awe, fear, wonder, weariness, and so on)*

Team Teaching

These Interdisciplinary Activities provide an excellent opportunity for you to employ Team Teaching and collaboration in your classroom.

Block Schedule

These activities may be implemented within either a traditional class period or a block scheduling framework.

School to WORK

Architect Use library resources, Internet sources, or a community theater to find information on building sets for a theater or the movie or television industries. Use the information to create a resume or cover letter that you would send to employers.

MULTIPLE LEARNING STYLES

The activities included in the feature on this student edition page are ideally suited to meet the different learning styles of your students. These include:

- **Art** — **Picturing the West** visual/spatial learners
- **Science** — **Keeping a Science Log** logical/mathematical learners
- **Music** — **Learning a Western Song** auditory/musical learners
- **School-to-Work** — **Building a Western Town** kinesthetic learners

CHAPTER 12
Section 4, 372–375

1 FOCUS

BELLRINGER
Motivational Activity

Before taking roll at the beginning of the class period, project Section Focus Transparency 12–4 and have students answer the questions. Discuss students' responses.

This activity is also available as a blackline master.

Section Focus Transparency 12–4

The Mexican War at Home

1. What future president was against the war?
2. On what side were most Democrats?
3. How do you think feelings about slavery affected feelings about the war?

For the Mexican War	Against the Mexican War
President John Polk	Abraham Lincoln
Most Democrats	Frederick Douglass
Many Southerners	Many Whigs
Most newspapers	Many Northerners
Most Texans	Abolitionists

Vocabulary Precheck

Tell students that *cede* comes from the same root as *secede,* which they encountered in Chapter 9, Section 2. Do students recall what the root was? (Latin *cedere,* "to withdraw" or "to yield")

Use the **Vocabulary PuzzleMaker** to create crossword and word search puzzles.

Section Theme
Global Connections

After attempts to purchase New Mexico and California failed, President Polk gave General Zachary Taylor orders that he hoped would provoke war with Mexico. His hope was fulfilled.

Activity Have students find out how the American people reacted to the declaration of war with Mexico. *(mixed; some favored war, some were outraged and disgusted)*

1845 The United States annexes Texas

1846 Congress declares war on Mexico

1847 General Winfield Scott reaches Mexico City

1848 Treaty of Guadalupe Hidalgo signed

Section 4

War with Mexico

READ TO DISCOVER . . .
- how the idea of Manifest Destiny contributed to the outbreak of war.
- how the United States acquired New Mexico and California.

TERMS TO LEARN
Californios
cede

The Storyteller

John Kenly from Maryland had volunteered to fight in the Mexican War. He and other soldiers led by General Zachary Taylor attacked the Mexican city of Monterrey. Bright cannon fire lit up nearby mountains. As he advanced with the other troops, Kenly saw heavy fighting near the bishop's palace. In his diary, Kenly later wrote: "How my heart beat! For I felt that if they could carry the palace, the town was ours." The Americans pushed forward and entered the palace. The Mexican flag was lowered, and a mighty cheer erupted from American forces remaining on the plain below.

Case showing General Zachary Taylor

After Mexico refused to sell California and New Mexico, President **James K. Polk** plotted to pull the Mexican provinces into the Union through war. He wanted, however, to provoke Mexico into taking military action first. This way Polk could justify the war to Congress and the American people.

The Outbreak of the War

Polk was determined to get the California and New Mexico territories from Mexico. Their possession would guarantee that the United States had clear passage to the Pacific Ocean—an important consideration because the British still occupied part of Oregon. Polk's main reason, though, involved fulfilling the nation's Manifest Destiny. Like many Americans, Polk saw California and New Mexico as rightfully belonging to the United States.

Geography

Rising Tensions

Relations between Mexico and the United States had been strained for some years. When the United States annexed Texas in 1845, the situation worsened. Mexico, which had never recognized the independence of Texas, charged that the annexation was illegal.

Another dispute concerned the Texas-Mexico border. The United States insisted that the **Rio**

SECTION RESOURCES

Reproducible Masters
- Reproducible Lesson Plan 12–4
- Guided Reading Activity 12–4
- Section Quiz 12–4
- Reteaching Activity 12–4
- Enrichment Activity 12–4

Transparencies
- Section Focus Transparency 12–4

Multimedia
- Vocabulary PuzzleMaker
- Chapter Challenger Interactive Review Software
- Testmaker
- The Presidents: A Picture History of Our Nation

Grande formed the border. Mexico claimed that the border lay along the **Nueces** (nu•AY•suhs) **River**, 150 miles farther north. Because of this dispute, Mexico had stopped payments on the more than $2 million it owed to American citizens for losses suffered during outbreaks of fighting in Mexico.

Polk sent an agent, John Slidell, to Mexico to propose a deal. Slidell was authorized to offer $30 million for California and New Mexico in return for Mexico's acceptance of the Rio Grande as the Texas boundary. In addition, the United States would take over payment of Mexico's debts to American citizens.

The Mexican government refused to discuss the offer and announced its intention to reclaim Texas for Mexico. In response Polk ordered General **Zachary Taylor** to march his soldiers across the disputed borderland between the Nueces River and the Rio Grande. Taylor did so and built a fort there on his arrival. A month later, on April 24, Mexican soldiers attacked a small force of Taylor's soldiers. Taylor sent the report the president wanted to hear: "Hostilities may now be considered as commenced."

Polk called an emergency meeting of his cabinet, and the cabinet agreed that the attack was grounds for war with Mexico. On May 11, 1846, the president told Congress that Mexico had "invaded our territory and shed American blood upon the American soil." Congress passed a declaration of war against Mexico.

American Attitudes toward the War

The American people were divided over the Mexican War. Polk's party, the Democrats, generally supported the war. Many Whigs opposed it, calling Polk's actions aggressive and unjust. Northerners accused Democrats of waging the war to spread slavery.

Illinois congressman Abraham Lincoln demanded to know the exact spot where the first attack against American troops had occurred. Lincoln, like many who opposed the war, claimed that the spot was clearly in Mexico and that Polk therefore had no grounds for blaming the war on Mexico.

Frederick Douglass, an African American leader in the antislavery movement, called the war "disgraceful" and "cruel." Douglass shared the belief that if the United States expanded into the West, the Southern states would carry slavery into the new territories.

American soldier, Mexican War

Newspapers generally supported the war, and volunteers quickly signed up for military service. As time went on, however, antiwar feeling grew, particularly in the North.

Polk's War Plan

President Polk had a three-part plan for the war with Mexico. First, American troops would drive Mexican forces out of the disputed border region in Texas and make the border secure. Second, the United States would seize New Mexico and California. Finally, American forces would take **Mexico City,** the capital of Mexico.

Zachary Taylor accomplished the first goal. Crossing the Rio Grande in September 1846, Taylor's army captured the town of **Monterrey.** In February 1847, Taylor defeated the Mexicans again at Buena Vista. The Texas border was secure.

Conquering New Mexico and California

While Taylor made progress in northern Mexico, American forces also advanced farther west. General **Stephen Watts Kearny** led his troops to New Mexico and California.

The Fall of New Mexico

In the summer of 1846, Kearny led about 1,500 cavalry soldiers along the Santa Fe Trail from Missouri to New Mexico. The Mexican

Cooperative Learning Activity

Arguing a Position Organize the class into small groups. Have two students in each group take the Mexican view (and that of many Americans) that the war was the result of deliberate provocation and that it was wrong to take land by force. The other two students should take the point of view of President Polk. Each side should attempt to convince the other of its position. Students may do additional research to add force to their arguments. Divide the tasks of writing, researching, and speaking according to the strengths of group members.

2 TEACH

L1 Outlining the Section Have students outline the section, using the three main heads *(The Outbreak of the War, Conquering New Mexico and California, The End of the War)* as Roman numerals I, II, and III. Have students use their outlines to help them complete the Section Review.

Guided Reading Activity 12–4

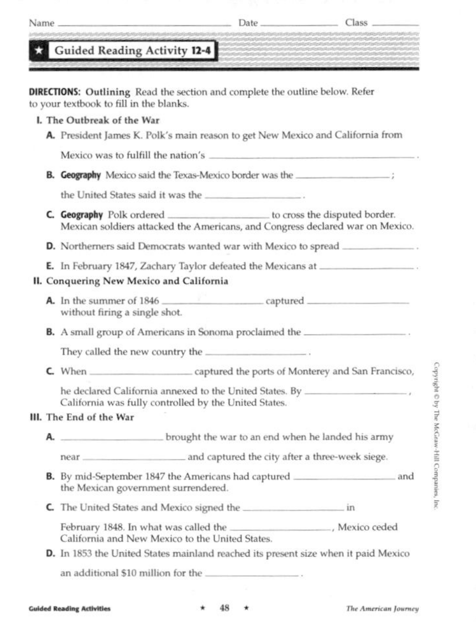

Name ______ Date ______ Class ______

Guided Reading Activity 12-4

DIRECTIONS: Outlining Read the section and complete the outline below. Refer to your textbook to fill in the blanks.

I. The Outbreak of the War
- **A.** President James K. Polk's main reason to get New Mexico and California from Mexico was to fulfill the nation's ______.
- **B. Geography** Mexico said the Texas-Mexico border was the ______; the United States said it was the ______.
- **C. Geography** Polk ordered ______ to cross the disputed border. Mexican soldiers attacked the Americans, and Congress declared war on Mexico.
- **D.** Northerners said Democrats wanted war with Mexico to spread ______.
- **E.** In February 1847, Zachary Taylor defeated the Mexicans at ______.

II. Conquering New Mexico and California
- **A.** In the summer of 1846 ______ captured ______ without firing a single shot.
- **B.** A small group of Americans in Sonoma proclaimed the ______. They called the new country the ______.
- **C.** When ______ captured the ports of Monterey and San Francisco, he declared California annexed to the United States. By ______, California was fully controlled by the United States.

III. The End of the War
- **A.** ______ brought the war to an end when he landed his army near ______ and captured the city after a three-week siege.
- **B.** By mid-September 1847 the Americans had captured ______ and the Mexican government surrendered.
- **C.** The United States and Mexico signed the ______ in February 1848. In what was called the ______, Mexico ceded California and New Mexico to the United States.
- **D.** In 1853 the United States mainland reached its present size when it paid Mexico an additional $10 million for the ______.

Guided Reading Activities ★ 48 ★ *The American Journey*

Linking PAST & PRESENT

Provoking War In 1845 American forces provoked Mexico into an attack, which allowed President Polk to demand and obtain from Congress a declaration of war. A similar event occurred 119 years later when United States ships may have provoked a North Vietnamese attack. This event led President Lyndon Johnson to demand and obtain quickly from Congress a resolution permitting the United States to fight without the constitutionally required declaration of war. To prevent this from ever happening again, Congress passed the War Powers Act in 1973.

CHAPTER 12
Section 4, 372–375

Map Study

Answers
1. Bear Flag Revolt
2. Mexico City

NATIONAL GEOGRAPHIC SOCIETY

CD-ROM
The Presidents: A Picture History of Our Nation

Have students learn more about Polk's handling of the Mexican War by selecting James K. Polk from the main menu.

3 ASSESS

Assign Section 4 Review as homework or as an in-class activity.

Use **Chapter Challenger Interactive Review Software** to review Section 4.

Section Quiz 12–4

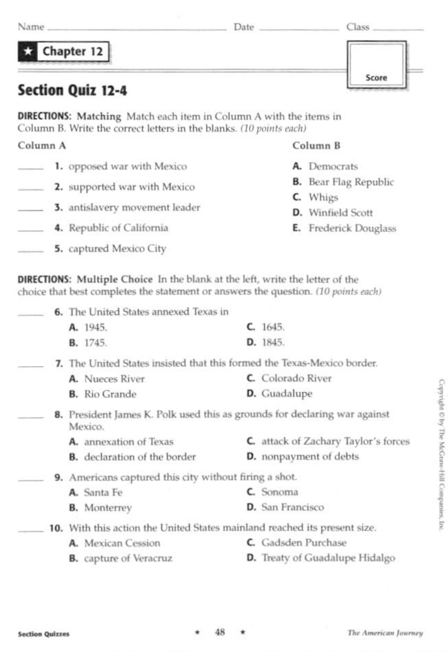

Name ____ Date ____ Class ____

Chapter 12

Score

Section Quiz 12-4

DIRECTIONS: Matching Match each item in Column A with the items in Column B. Write the correct letters in the blanks. *(10 points each)*

Column A	Column B
____ 1. opposed war with Mexico	A. Democrats
____ 2. supported war with Mexico	B. Bear Flag Republic
____ 3. antislavery movement leader	C. Whigs
____ 4. Republic of California	D. Winfield Scott
____ 5. captured Mexico City	E. Frederick Douglass

DIRECTIONS: Multiple Choice In the blank at the left, write the letter of the choice that best completes the statement or answers the question. *(10 points each)*

____ 6. The United States annexed Texas in
A. 1945. C. 1645.
B. 1745. D. 1845.

____ 7. The United States insisted that this formed the Texas-Mexico border.
A. Nueces River C. Colorado River
B. Rio Grande D. Guadalupe

____ 8. President James K. Polk used this as grounds for declaring war against Mexico.
A. annexation of Texas C. attack of Zachary Taylor's forces
B. declaration of the border D. nonpayment of debts

____ 9. Americans captured this city without firing a shot.
A. Santa Fe C. Sonoma
B. Monterrey D. San Francisco

____ 10. With this action the United States mainland reached its present size.
A. Mexican Cession C. Gadsden Purchase
B. capture of Veracruz D. Treaty of Guadalupe Hidalgo

Section Quizzes ★ 48 ★ *The American Journey*

Copyright © by The McGraw-Hill Companies, Inc.

Map Study

War between the United States and Mexico broke out in 1846 near the Rio Grande.

1. **Location** Which battle occurred farthest north?
2. **Analyzing Information** Where was the last battle fought?

were already out West on an American military expedition in California, joined the Americans in Sonoma.

Though unaware of the outbreak of war with Mexico, Frémont declared that he would conquer California. Frémont's actions outraged many **Californios,** the Mexicans who lived in California. They might have supported a revolt for local control of government, but they opposed what looked like an attempt by a band of Americans to seize land.

Naval Intervention

In July 1846, a United States Navy squadron under Commodore John Sloat captured the ports of Monterey and San Francisco. Sloat declared California annexed to the United States, and the American flag replaced the Bear Flag in California.

Commodore Sloat's fleet sailed for **San Diego,** carrying Frémont and Carson. The Americans captured San Diego and moved north to Los Angeles. Carson headed east with the news of California's annexation. On his way he met and joined Kearny's force, marching west from Santa Fe.

After Sloat's ships left, many Californios in San Diego rose up in arms against the Americans who had taken over the city. General Kearny and his troops arrived in the midst of the rebellion. Exhausted from their journey across the desert, they faced a stiff fight but eventually won. By January 1847, California was fully controlled by the United States.

governor fled, allowing the Americans to capture New Mexico's capital, Santa Fe, on August 18, 1846, without firing a shot. Kearny and his army then headed across the deserts of New Mexico and Arizona to California.

California and the Bear Flag Republic

In June 1846, a small group of Americans had seized the town of Sonoma north of San Francisco and proclaimed the independent Republic of California. They called the new country the **Bear Flag Republic** because their flag showed a bear and a star on a white background. **John C. Frémont** and mountain man **Kit Carson,** who

MULTIPLE LEARNING STYLES

Visual/Spatial Have students make a map showing the growth of the United States through 1853. The map should show the states that existed in 1783, the various sections of Florida, the Louisiana Purchase, the annexation of Texas, Oregon country, cessions granted by Britain in 1818 and 1842, the Mexican Cession, and the Gadsden Purchase. Each section should be labeled and dated. Have students consult a historical atlas of the United States for the information they need. Some students may wish to make a map large enough for display on the bulletin board. **L2,** ELL

The End of the War

With their victories in New Mexico and California, the Americans met their original goals in the war. President Polk then launched the third part of his war plan—an attack on Mexico City.

The Capture of Mexico City

Polk gave the task of capturing Mexico City to General **Winfield Scott.** Scott devised a brilliant campaign that brought the Mexican War to a speedy conclusion. In March 1847, Scott's army landed on the coast of the Gulf of Mexico, near the Mexican port of **Veracruz.** Scott captured Veracruz after a 3-week siege and then set out to march the 300 miles to Mexico City.

The Americans had to fight their way toward Mexico City, battling not only the Mexican army but also bands of armed peasants. Scott reached the outskirts of Mexico City with his troops at the end of August 1847.

The Mexican high command was in disorder, but a few divisions of the Mexican army—and a group of boys from the Mexican Military College—fought heroically to defend the capital. Scott's forces overcame the Mexican resistance, however, and by mid-September the Americans had taken Mexico City. The Mexican government surrendered.

California Bear Flag

The United States lost 1,721 men to battle and more than 11,000 to disease in the Mexican War. Mexico's losses were far greater. The war cost the United States nearly $100 million, but here, too, Mexico paid a higher price. The war would cost Mexico half its territory.

The Peace Treaty

Peace talks between the United States and Mexico began in January 1848. The **Treaty of Guadalupe Hidalgo** (GWAH•duhl•OOP hih•DAL•goh) was signed in February 1848.

In the treaty Mexico gave up all claims to Texas and agreed to the Rio Grande as the border between Texas and Mexico. Furthermore, in what was called the **Mexican Cession,** Mexico **ceded**—gave—its provinces of California and New Mexico to the United States. In return the United States gave Mexico $15 million.

In 1853 the United States paid Mexico an additional $10 million for the **Gadsden Purchase,** a strip of land along the southern edge of the present-day states of Arizona and New Mexico. With the Gadsden Purchase, the United States mainland reached its present size. All that remained was to settle the newly acquired territories.

Section 4 Review

Checking for Understanding

1. ***Identify*** James K. Polk, Zachary Taylor, John C. Frémont, Winfield Scott, Mexican Cession, Gadsden Purchase.
2. ***Define*** Californios, cede.
3. ***Summarize*** President Polk's three-part plan in the war with Mexico.

Reviewing Themes

4. **Global Connections** What were the terms of the Treaty of Guadalupe Hidalgo?

Critical Thinking

5. **Drawing Conclusions** Why do you think President Polk wanted to make it seem as if Mexico had started the war?

Activity

Writing a Diary Entry Imagine you are a Mexican living on lands acquired in the Mexican Cession. Write a diary entry in which you record your feelings on learning the terms of the Treaty of Guadalupe Hidalgo.

Section 4 Review Answers

1. James K. Polk, 372; Zachary Taylor, 373; John C. Frémont, 374; Winfield Scott, 375; Mexican Cession, 375; Gadsden Purchase, 375
2. The words are defined in the Glossary.
3. (a) drive Mexican forces out of Texas border region and secure border, (b) seize New Mexico and California, (c) take Mexico City
4. Mexico gave up claims to Texas; accepted Rio Grande as border; ceded California and New Mexico for $15 million.
5. to gain the support of those who opposed war

Activity Students' diaries might express emotions such as fear, regret, sadness, or anger.

Reteaching Activity 12–4

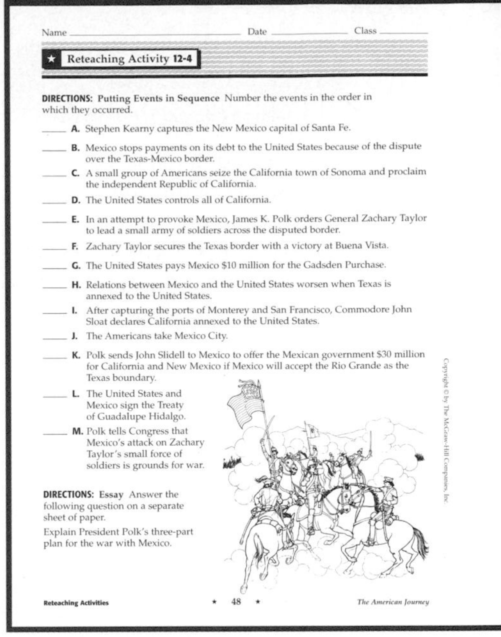
Name ________ Date ________ Class ________

★ Reteaching Activity 12-4

DIRECTIONS: Putting Events in Sequence Number the events in the order in which they occurred.

_____ **A.** Stephen Kearny captures the New Mexico capital of Santa Fe.
_____ **B.** Mexico stops payments on its debt to the United States because of the dispute over the Texas-Mexico border.
_____ **C.** A small group of Americans seize the California town of Sonoma and proclaim the independent Republic of California.
_____ **D.** The United States controls all of California.
_____ **E.** In an attempt to provoke Mexico, James K. Polk orders General Zachary Taylor to lead a small army of soldiers across the disputed border.
_____ **F.** Zachary Taylor secures the Texas border with a victory at Buena Vista.
_____ **G.** The United States pays Mexico $10 million for the Gadsden Purchase.
_____ **H.** Relations between Mexico and the United States worsen when Texas is annexed to the United States.
_____ **I.** After capturing the ports of Monterey and San Francisco, Commodore John Sloat declares California annexed to the United States.
_____ **J.** The Americans take Mexico City.
_____ **K.** Polk sends John Slidell to Mexico to offer the Mexican government $30 million for California and New Mexico if Mexico will accept the Rio Grande as the Texas boundary.
_____ **L.** The United States and Mexico sign the Treaty of Guadalupe Hidalgo.
_____ **M.** Polk tells Congress that Mexico's attack on Zachary Taylor's small force of soldiers is grounds for war.

DIRECTIONS: Essay Answer the following question on a separate sheet of paper.

Explain President Polk's three-part plan for the war with Mexico.

Copyright © by The McGraw-Hill Companies, Inc.

Reteaching Activities ★ 48 ★ *The American Journey*

Enrichment Activity 12–4

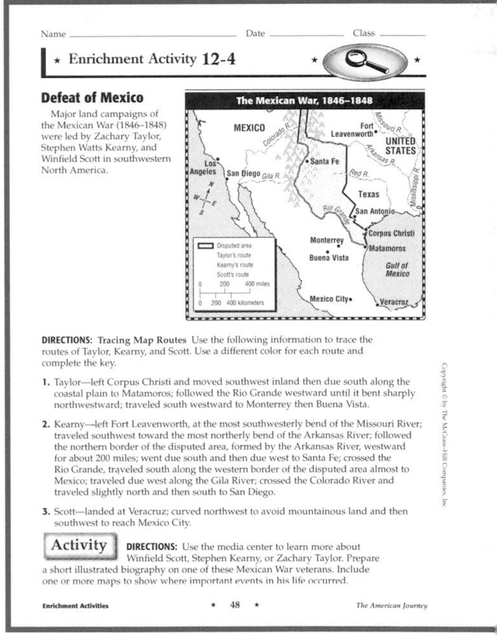
Name ________ Date ________ Class ________

★ Enrichment Activity 12-4 ★ ★

Defeat of Mexico

Major land campaigns of the Mexican War (1846–1848) were led by Zachary Taylor, Stephen Watts Kearny, and Winfield Scott in southwestern North America.

DIRECTIONS: Tracing Map Routes Use the following information to trace the routes of Taylor, Kearny, and Scott. Use a different color for each route and complete the key.

1. Taylor—left Corpus Christi and moved southwest inland then due south along the coastal plain to Matamoros; followed the Rio Grande westward until it bent sharply northwestward; traveled south westward to Monterrey then Buena Vista.
2. Kearny—left Fort Leavenworth, at the most southwesterly bend of the Missouri River; traveled southwest toward the most northerly bend of the Arkansas River; followed the northern border of the disputed area, formed by the Arkansas River, westward for about 200 miles; went due south and then due west to Santa Fe; crossed the Rio Grande, traveled south along the western border of the disputed area almost to Mexico; traveled due west along the Gila River; crossed the Colorado River and traveled slightly north and then south to San Diego.
3. Scott—landed at Veracruz; curved northwest to avoid mountainous land and then southwest to reach Mexico City.

Activity **DIRECTIONS:** Use the media center to learn more about Winfield Scott, Stephen Kearny, or Zachary Taylor. Prepare a short illustrated biography on one of these Mexican War veterans. Include one or more maps to show where important events in his life occurred.

Copyright © by The McGraw-Hill Companies, Inc.

Enrichment Activities ★ 48 ★ *The American Journey*

4 CLOSE

After the war, Frederick Douglass wrote, ". . . we are not the people to rejoice; we ought rather to blush and hang our heads for shame." Have students explain what he meant.

CHAPTER 12
Section 5, 376–379

1 FOCUS

BELLRINGER
Motivational Activity

Before taking roll at the beginning of the class period, project Section Focus Transparency 12–5 and have students answer the questions. Discuss students' responses.

This activity is also available as a blackline master.

Section Focus Transparency 12–5

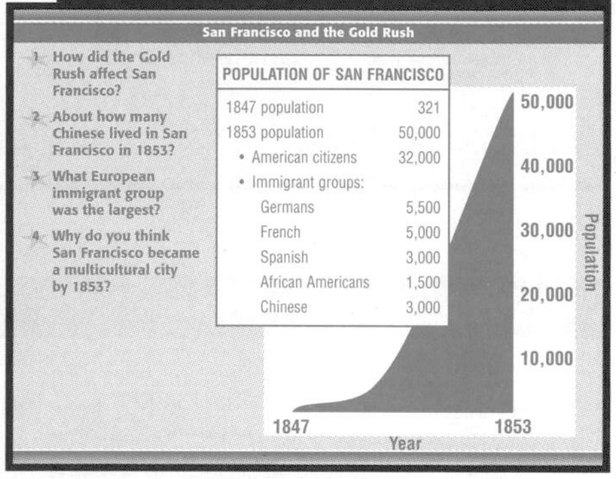

Vocabulary Precheck
Note that *vigilante* is a Spanish word that comes from the Latin *vigilans,* meaning "alert" or "watchful." Have students skim the section to find what vigilantes were watchful of or alert to. *(criminals)*

Use the **Vocabulary Puzzle-Maker** to create crossword and word search puzzles.

Section Theme
Groups and Institutions

In the mid-1800s, people from all over the world came to California in search of gold. Mormons came to Utah in search of religious freedom.

Activity Have students skim the section to find how these people fared in California and Utah.

1846 Mormons migrate to the Great Salt Lake area

1848 Gold is discovered at Sutter's Mill

1850 California applies for statehood

Section 5

New Settlers in California and Utah

READ TO DISCOVER . . .
- how the hope of getting rich quick drew thousands of people to California.
- how the search for religious freedom led to the settlement of Utah.

TERMS TO LEARN
forty-niners
boomtown
vigilante

The Storyteller

James Marshall was building a sawmill on the South Fork of the American River in California. He worked for John Sutter, who owned a vast tract of land about 40 miles from present-day Sacramento. On January 24, 1848, Marshall saw something shining in a ditch. "I reached my hand down and picked it up," he wrote later. "It made my heart thump, for I was certain it was gold." Looking around, he found other shiny pieces. Marshall rushed to show the glittering pieces to Sutter, who determined that they were gold. Sutter tried to keep the discovery a secret, but word soon leaked out. The great California Gold Rush was under way!

Gold miner's cradle

People from all over the world flocked to California in search of quick riches. An official in Monterey reported that "the farmers have thrown aside their plows, the lawyers their briefs, the doctors their pills, the priests their prayer books, and all are now digging gold." By the end of 1848, these farmers, lawyers, doctors, and priests had taken $6 million in gold from the American River.

Geography

California Gold Rush

Nearly 100,000 people came to California looking for gold in 1848 and 1849. Those who arrived in 1849 were called **forty-niners.**

Many came by sea. In February 1849 alone, 130 ships left the East Coast for San Francisco. Other forty-niners came overland, traveling on the Oregon Trail or the Sante Fe Trail and then pushing westward through California's **Sierra Nevada** mountain range.

Americans made up more than half of the forty-niners. Others came from Mexico, South America, Europe, and Australia. About 300 men arrived from China, the first large group of Asian immigrants to come to America. Although some eventually returned to China, others remained, establishing California's Chinese American community.

SECTION RESOURCES

Reproducible Masters
- Reproducible Lesson Plan 12–5
- Guided Reading Activity 12–5
- Section Quiz 12–5
- Reteaching Activity 12–5
- Enrichment Activity 12–5

Transparencies
- Section Focus Transparency 12–5

Multimedia
- Vocabulary PuzzleMaker
- Chapter Challenger Interactive Review Software
- Testmaker
- GTV: The American People: Fabric of a Nation

Boomtowns

As people rushed to a new area to look for gold, they built new communities, called **boomtowns,** almost overnight. At one site on the Yuba River where only two houses stood in September 1849, a miner arrived the next year to find a town of 1,000 people "with a large number of hotels, stores, groceries, bakeries, and . . . gambling houses." The miners gave some of the boomtowns colorful names such as Shinbone Peak, Murderers' Gulch, and Whiskey Diggings.

Cities also flourished during the Gold Rush. As ships arrived daily with gold seekers and adventurers, **San Francisco** grew from a tiny village to a city of about 20,000 people.

A Hard Life

Miners found gold along a 150-mile stretch of the western slope of the Sierra Nevada. Any stream or canyon might contain the precious metal. Most of the hopeful forty-niners had no experience in mining. Rushing furiously from place to place, they attacked hillsides with pickaxes and shovels and spent hours bent over streambeds, "washing" or "panning" the water to seek gold dust and nuggets.

The California Gold Rush more than doubled the world's supply of gold. For all their effort, however, very few of the forty-niners achieved lasting wealth. Most of the miners found little or no gold. Many of those who did lost their riches through gambling or wild spending.

Merchants, however, made huge profits. They could charge whatever they liked because the miners had no place else to go to buy food and other essential items. Eggs sold for $10 a dozen. A Jewish immigrant named **Levi Strauss** sold the miners sturdy pants made of denim. His "Levi's" made him rich.

Gold Rush Society

Very few women lived in the mining camps, which were populated by men of all races and walks of life. Lonely and suffering from the hardships of mining, many men spent their free hours drinking, gambling, and fighting. Songs such as "O Susanna" and "Sweet Betsy from Pike" reminded them of the women they missed.

> "Oh, don't you remember sweet Betsy
> from Pike,
> Who crossed the wide mountains with her
> lover Ike,
> With two yoke of cattle, a large yellow dog,
> A tall shanghai rooster and a one-spotted
> hog."

The camps lacked law and order. One miner wrote, "Robberies and murders were of daily occurrence. Organized bands of thieves existed in the towns and in the mountains." Concerned citizens formed vigilance committees for security. The **vigilantes** (VIH•juh•LAN•tees) took the law into their own hands, acting as police, judge, jury, and sometimes executioner.

Linking PAST & PRESENT

Jeans

Levi Strauss listened as miners complained about how fast their clothes wore out. He stitched up a pair of pants made from a tough fabric called denim. Then Strauss folded the seams and reinforced the corners with small copper tacks called rivets. He had a fashion hit. **Why do you think jeans have remained a popular item of clothing?**

Today's look

Early Levi pants ad

COOPERATIVE LEARNING ACTIVITY

Making a Cause-and-Effect Chart Have students work together in small groups to make illustrated charts showing the effects of the discovery of gold in California. One student in each group should design the chart and another student should make a list of all the effects cited in the section. A third student should do the labeling, and the remaining group members can do the illustrating.

2 TEACH

L1, ELL Making a Graph Have students make a bar graph showing California's population in 1848 (20,000) and in 1852 (220,000). Ask them to list effects of that huge increase.

Linking PAST & PRESENT

Jeans People today call Levis by a variety of names. Regardless, miners' pants are the top sportswear choice of people around the world.
Answer: *sturdiness, comfort, good looks*

Guided Reading Activity 12–5

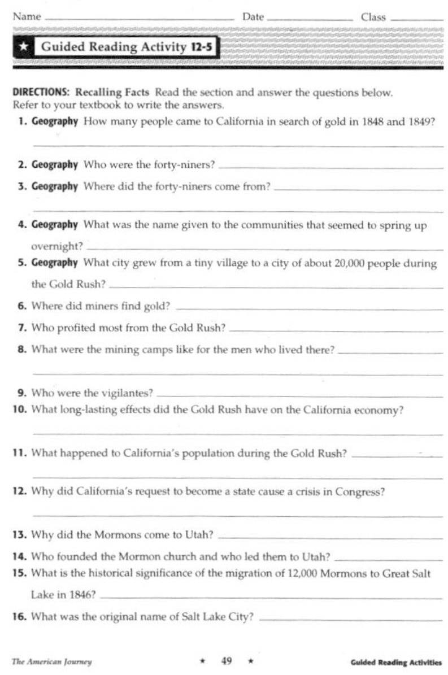

Name ______ Date ______ Class ______

★ Guided Reading Activity 12-5

DIRECTIONS: Recalling Facts Read the section and answer the questions below. Refer to your textbook to write the answers.

1. **Geography** How many people came to California in search of gold in 1848 and 1849?
2. **Geography** Who were the forty-niners?
3. **Geography** Where did the forty-niners come from?
4. **Geography** What was the name given to the communities that seemed to spring up overnight?
5. **Geography** What city grew from a tiny village to a city of about 20,000 people during the Gold Rush?
6. Where did miners find gold?
7. Who profited most from the Gold Rush?
8. What were the mining camps like for the men who lived there?
9. Who were the vigilantes?
10. What long-lasting effects did the Gold Rush have on the California economy?
11. What happened to California's population during the Gold Rush?
12. Why did California's request to become a state cause a crisis in Congress?
13. Why did the Mormons come to Utah?
14. Who founded the Mormon church and who led them to Utah?
15. What is the historical significance of the migration of 12,000 Mormons to Great Salt Lake in 1846?
16. What was the original name of Salt Lake City?

The American Journey ★ 49 ★ **Guided Reading Activities**

NATIONAL GEOGRAPHIC SOCIETY

VIDEODISC
GTV: The American People: Fabric of a Nation

Side 2, Chapter 5
Title: *Close-up U.S.A.*
Subject: the Gold Rush
Ask: **Where and when did the Gold Rush take place?** *(California, 1848)*

CHAPTER 12
Section 5, 376–379

Chart Study

Answer
discovery of gold

3 ASSESS

Assign Section 5 Review as homework or as an in-class activity.

Use **Chapter Challenger Interactive Review Software** to review Section 5.

Section Quiz 12–5

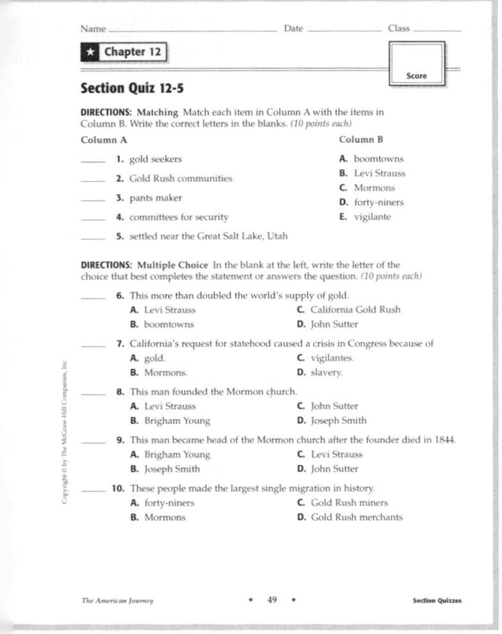

Name ______ Date ______ Class ______

★ Chapter 12

Score

Section Quiz 12-5

DIRECTIONS: Matching Match each item in Column A with the items in Column B. Write the correct letters in the blanks. *(10 points each)*

Column A	Column B
____ 1. gold seekers	A. boomtowns
____ 2. Gold Rush communities	B. Levi Strauss
____ 3. pants maker	C. Mormons
____ 4. committees for security	D. forty-niners
____ 5. settled near the Great Salt Lake, Utah	E. vigilante

DIRECTIONS: Multiple Choice In the blank at the left, write the letter of the choice that best completes the statement or answers the question. *(10 points each)*

____ 6. This more than doubled the world's supply of gold.
A. Levi Strauss C. California Gold Rush
B. boomtowns D. John Sutter

____ 7. California's request for statehood caused a crisis in Congress because of
A. gold. C. vigilantes.
B. Mormons. D. slavery.

____ 8. This man founded the Mormon church.
A. Levi Strauss C. John Sutter
B. Brigham Young D. Joseph Smith

____ 9. This man became head of the Mormon church after the founder died in 1844.
A. Brigham Young C. Levi Strauss
B. Joseph Smith D. John Sutter

____ 10. These people made the largest single migration in history.
A. forty-niners C. Gold Rush miners
B. Mormons D. Gold Rush merchants

The American Journey ★ 49 ★ **Section Quizzes**

Picturing HISTORY Joseph Smith claimed he was led by an angel to find a holy book inscribed on gold tablets—the Book of Mormon.
Answer: *Brigham Young*

Causes and Effects

CAUSES

★ Americans accept Manifest Destiny.
★ As the East becomes crowded, Americans want more land.
★ The West contains furs, lumber, and precious metals.

Westward Movement

EFFECTS

★ Native Americans are forced off lands.
★ The United States wars with Mexico.
★ America extends from sea to sea.

Chart Study

Americans believed the United States had the right to expand to the Pacific Ocean.
Analyzing Information What event drew settlers to California?

Economic and Political Progress

The Gold Rush ended within a few years but had long-lasting effects on California's economy. Agriculture, shipping, and trade expanded to meet the miners' needs for food and other goods. Many people who had come looking for gold stayed in the area to farm or run a business. California's population soared, increasing from about 20,000 in 1848 to more than 220,000 only 4 years later.

Such rapid growth brought the need for more effective government. Zachary Taylor, the Mexican War hero and now president, urged the people of California to apply for statehood. They did so, choosing representatives to write a constitution in September 1849. Once their constitution was approved, Californians elected a governor and state legislators.

California applied to Congress for statehood in March 1850. Because California's constitution banned slavery, however, the request caused a crisis in Congress. The Southern states objected to making California a state because it would upset the balance of free and slave states. California did not become a state until Congress worked out a compromise six months later.

A Religious Refuge in Utah

A visitor to the Utah Territory in the 1850s wrote admiringly: "The whole of this small nation occupy themselves as usefully as the working bees of a hive." This account described the **Mormons,** or members of the Church of Jesus Christ of Latter-day Saints. Mormons had come to Utah to fulfill their vision of the godly life.

Picturing HISTORY Mormon pioneers traveled across the country and from other parts of the world to settle in the Great Salt Lake area. **Who was the Mormon leader who brought the first Mormon settlers to Utah?**

MULTIPLE LEARNING STYLES

Interpersonal The Mormons under Brigham Young did not just pack their bags one day and leave Illinois for Utah. They did a great deal of advance planning. Have students brainstorm the preparations needed to get thousands of people across the Mississippi River, through the plains, and over the Rocky Mountains to their new desert homes. Then have students check their ideas in library resources. A brief but interesting account appears on pages 43–47 of *Liberty for All?* by Joy Hakim (New York: Oxford University Press, 1994). **L2**

The First Mormons

Joseph Smith founded the Mormon church in 1830 in New York State. He had visions that led him to launch a new Christian church. He hoped to use these visions to build an ideal society.

Smith formed a community in New York, but unsympathetic neighbors disapproved of the Mormons' religion. They forced the Mormons to move on. From New York the Mormons went to Ohio, then to Missouri, and then Illinois.

In 1844 a mob in Illinois killed Smith, and **Brigham Young** took over as head of the Mormons. Young decided the Mormons should move again, this time near the **Great Salt Lake** in Utah. Although part of Mexico, no Mexicans had settled in the region because of its harsh terrain.

Picturing HISTORY Mormon settlers brought their possessions overland to Utah in covered wagons. By the end of the 1860s, more than 51,000 Mormons had journeyed to the Salt Lake Valley. **How did the Mormons make their Salt Lake settlements flourish?**

A Haven in the Desert

The Mormon migration to the Great Salt Lake area started in 1846. About 12,000 Mormons made the journey—the largest single migration in American history. In the midst of the desert, they founded a community they called **Deseret.** Later they changed the name to **Salt Lake City.**

With hard work and determination, the Mormons made Deseret flourish. They planned their towns carefully and built irrigation canals to water their farms. They also founded industries so they could be self-sufficient. Mormon merchants sold supplies to the forty-niners who passed through Utah on their way to California.

Utah Joins the United States

In 1848 the United States acquired the Salt Lake area as part of the settlement of the Mexican War. Two years later Congress established the Utah Territory, and President Millard Fillmore made Brigham Young its governor.

Utah was not easily incorporated into the United States. The Mormons wanted to be left alone and resisted federal authority. In 1857 and 1858, war almost broke out between the Mormons and the United States Army. Utah did not become a state until 1896.

Section 5 Review

Checking for Understanding

1. ***Identify*** Levi Strauss, Mormons, Joseph Smith, Brigham Young.
2. ***Define*** forty-niners, boomtown, vigilante.
3. ***Describe*** how the Gold Rush helped California's economy grow.

Reviewing Themes

4. **Groups and Institutions** What was the goal of Mormons who migrated to Utah?

Critical Thinking

5. **Identifying Alternatives** How might the history of California have been different if the Gold Rush had not occurred?

Activity

Drawing a Historical Scene Draw a scene that might have existed in a mining boomtown.

Section 5 Review Answers

1. Levi Strauss, 377; Mormons, 378; Joseph Smith, 379; Brigham Young, 379
2. The words are defined in the Glossary.
3. It increased the population, which resulted in the expansion of agriculture, shipping, and trade to serve the needs of the miners.
4. to create a self-sufficient community in which they could practice their religion freely
5. Without the surge in population, California probably would not have become a state as early as it did. Fewer people would have settled there, so the economy would not have received the boost that it did from the onslaught of miners.

Activity Illustrations should incorporate descriptions of boomtowns presented in the section.

Picturing HISTORY Today there are more than 8 million Mormons in the world. **Answer:** *carefully planned towns, irrigation canals for farms, built workshops*

Reteaching Activity 12–5

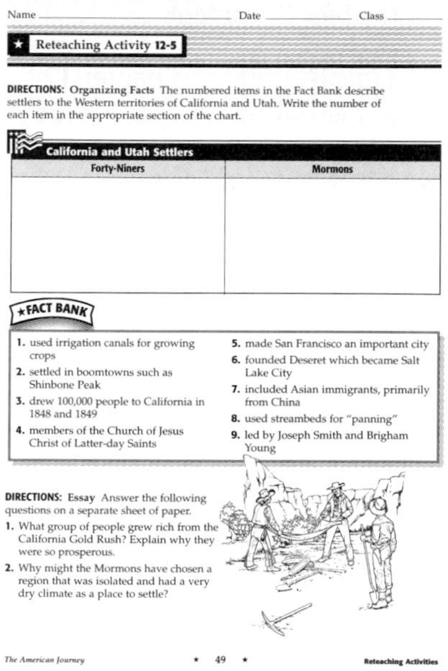
Name ________ Date ________ Class ________

Reteaching Activity 12-5

DIRECTIONS: Organizing Facts The numbered items in the Fact Bank describe settlers to the Western territories of California and Utah. Write the number of each item in the appropriate section of the chart.

California and Utah Settlers

Forty-Niners	Mormons

FACT BANK

1. used irrigation canals for growing crops
2. settled in boomtowns such as Shinbone Peak
3. drew 100,000 people to California in 1848 and 1849
4. members of the Church of Jesus Christ of Latter-day Saints
5. made San Francisco an important city
6. founded Deseret which became Salt Lake City
7. included Asian immigrants, primarily from China
8. used streambeds for "panning"
9. led by Joseph Smith and Brigham Young

DIRECTIONS: Essay Answer the following questions on a separate sheet of paper.

1. What group of people grew rich from the California Gold Rush? Explain why they were so prosperous.
2. Why might the Mormons have chosen a region that was isolated and had a very dry climate as a place to settle?

Enrichment Activity 12–5

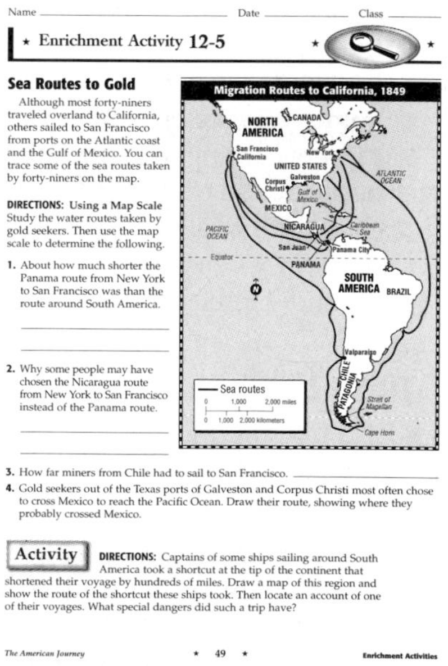
Name ________ Date ________ Class ________

Enrichment Activity 12-5

Sea Routes to Gold

Although most forty-niners traveled overland to California, others sailed to San Francisco from ports on the Atlantic coast and the Gulf of Mexico. You can trace some of the sea routes taken by forty-niners on the map.

Migration Routes to California, 1849

DIRECTIONS: Using a Map Scale Study the water routes taken by gold seekers. Then use the map scale to determine the following.

1. About how much shorter the Panama route from New York to San Francisco was than the route around South America.
2. Why some people may have chosen the Nicaragua route from New York to San Francisco instead of the Panama route.
3. How far miners from Chile had to sail to San Francisco. ________
4. Gold seekers out of the Texas ports of Galveston and Corpus Christi most often chose to cross Mexico to reach the Pacific Ocean. Draw their route, showing where they probably crossed Mexico.

Activity **DIRECTIONS:** Captains of some ships sailing around South America took a shortcut at the tip of the continent that shortened their voyage by hundreds of miles. Draw a map of this region and show the route of the shortcut these ships took. Then locate an account of one of their voyages. What special dangers did such a trip have?

4 CLOSE

Have students find out why there is a monument to seagulls in Salt Lake City. *(In 1848 the Mormons' crops were attacked by crickets; seagulls arrived and ate the insects in the nick of time.)*

GLENCOE TECHNOLOGY

VIDEODISC
MindJogger Videoquiz

Use MindJogger to review the Chapter 12 content.

Chapter 12
Disc 2, Side A

Also available in VHS.

Reviewing Key Terms

The key terms used in this activity are defined in the textbook glossary on pages A26–A35.

Reviewing Key Facts

1. Both agreed to set the boundary at the 49th parallel.
2. He did not want to upset the balance of slave and free states.
3. If the United States was bordered by the Pacific Ocean rather than by a foreign power, the threat to security would be lessened.
4. border disputes; Manifest Destiny
5. Miners coming to California needed food and supplies. Merchants could sell these goods for high prices, because the miners had nowhere else to buy them.

Time Line Activity

Events should be placed in this order: Mexico gains independence from Spain, Texas declares independence from Mexico, Mexican War begins, California Gold Rush begins, California becomes a state, Gadsden Purchase sets present-day boundaries of mainland United States

Critical Thinking

1. Students may mention that these areas had many valuable natural resources, that having these lands would enhance the United States as a world power, or that these areas would help to accommodate an expanding population.
2. Students may say that these two countries had probably used the same justification at some time in history to gain land; these countries might have thought that this notion was a potential threat to them; or they might have seen it as an excuse to justify expansion at any cost—even war.
3. Students may say they probably would not have paid much attention to it unless they had hopes of moving to the West, and gaining new land, in which case they would have agreed with it.
4. Students should realize that most Native Americans would not have favored it because it would eventually mean displacement and death for their people.

Chapter 12 Review and Activities

Reviewing Key Terms

On a sheet of paper, define the following terms:

joint occupation
mountain man
rendezvous
emigrant
Manifest Destiny
Tejano
empresario
annex
ranchero
cede
forty-niners
vigilante

Reviewing Key Facts

1. What agreement did the United States and Canada reach about the Oregon Territory?
2. Why did President Jackson refuse to annex Texas?
3. Why did some Americans think that making California part of the United States would strengthen its security?
4. Summarize the two main causes of the United States's war with Mexico.
5. Why did merchants earn such large profits during the Gold Rush?

Time Line Activity

Create a time line on which you place the following events in chronological order.

- California Gold Rush begins
- Gadsden Purchase sets present-day boundaries of mainland United States
- Texas declares independence from Mexico
- Mexico gains independence from Spain
- Mexican War begins
- California becomes a state

Critical Thinking

Recognizing Bias

The belief in Manifest Destiny helped the American government and people to justify many of their actions during the 1830s and 1840s.

1. Do you think the United States would have been interested in the Oregon country, New Mexico, and California if the notion of Manifest Destiny had not existed? Explain your answer.
2. What reactions do you think the governments of Canada and Mexico had to the American idea of Manifest Destiny?
3. What do you think your attitude toward Manifest Destiny would have been if you were a farmer in Virginia in the early 1800s?
4. What do you think your attitude toward Manifest Destiny would have been if you were a Native American in the early 1800s?

Reviewing Themes

1. **Economic Factors** How did economic troubles in the East affect settlement in the Oregon area?
2. **Geography and History** Before Stephen Austin established a colony in Texas, who inhabited the area?
3. **Culture and Traditions** What work did Native Americans perform at the Spanish missions?
4. **Global Connections** How did the negotiations between the United States and Britain over the Oregon Territory differ from those between the United States and Mexico over the Southwest?
5. **Groups and Institutions** Why did rapid growth create the need for a more effective government in California?

Geography Activity

Study the routes of the western trails shown on the map below. Then answer the questions that follow.

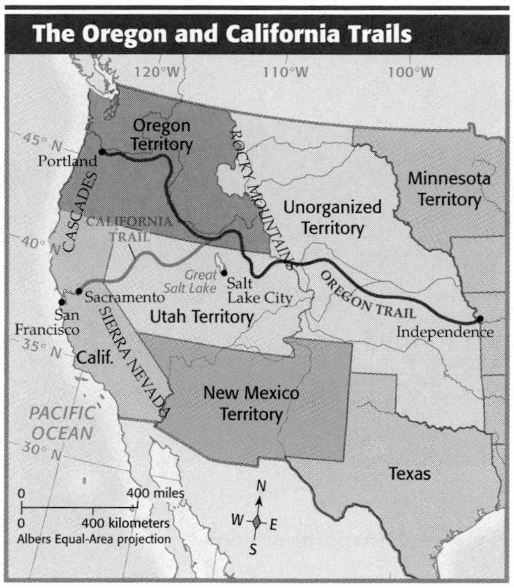

1. **Region** Which mountains did settlers have to cross to reach Oregon's Pacific coast? To reach California's Pacific coast?
2. **Location** In what city did the Oregon Trail begin? In what city did it end?

Cooperative Activity

History and Economics Imagine that a large deposit of gold has been discovered in the area where you live. You and a partner have decided to open a business to serve miners. Create a business plan detailing what type of product, store, or service might be most profitable. Then write a letter to a local bank describing the business, how much money you think you will need to borrow, and a list of what you will use the money for. Explain why you think your enterprise is sure to make money.

Skill Practice Activity

Understanding Latitude and Longitude

Turn to the map on page 358. Use it to answer the following questions.

1. What are the latitude and longitude coordinates of Fort Laramie in Unorganized Territory?
2. In general, between what lines of longitude did the Pony Express run?
3. What city lies at about 37°N, 90°W?

Technology Activity

Using an Electronic Card Catalog

Search your library's card catalog for books containing information about Salt Lake City and the state of Utah. Use this information to make an alphabetical directory of historic sites that someone who is a Mormon might like to visit. Your list might include museums, sites of Mormon activities, Mormon businesses, or other places of interest.

Portfolio Activity **History Journal** If you were asked to make a film about one event described in this chapter, what would it be? In your journal describe the event and make a list of at least three historical characters (real or imagined) who would be in your movie. Then suggest the names of modern movie or TV stars you think would be suitable for these roles.

Reviewing Themes

1. made the West look more attractive
2. mostly Tejanos, a few settlers from the United States, and Native Americans
3. farming, ranching, weaving, carpentry, soap making, and other crafts
4. The Oregon boundary dispute was settled peacefully; the United States, after offering to buy the Southwest from Mexico, resorted to war to get the land that it wanted.
5. Government was needed to maintain law and order and to serve the needs of the large number of people who were now living and working there.

Geography Activity

1. Rockies, Cascades; Rockies, Sierra Nevada
2. Independence; Portland

Cooperative Activity

Responses should clearly and thoroughly describe plans for a business that will serve miners. Students can base their proposals on the economies of the mid-1800s, or they can create a modern business based on today's economy. Plans should include a specific loan amount, an itemized list of start-up expenses, and a convincing description of the business and why it should be profitable.

Skill Practice Activity

1. 42°N, 105°W
2. 95°W and 130°W
3. St. Louis

Technology Activity

Students should locate information about Salt Lake City and Utah and compile a directory on Mormon points of interest.

Portfolio Activity Movies should be based on an event discussed in this chapter. Students should list at least three characters and cast modern movie or television actors to play their roles.

Chapter Bonus Test Question

Ask: Which defender of the Alamo designed a knife that still carries his name? *(Jim Bowie, bowie knife)*

Hands-On HISTORY Lab Activity

Block Schedule

This activity may be implemented within either a traditional class period or a block scheduling framework.

FOCUS

Have students look at a map of North and South America. Note that there were three main ways of getting to California from the East Coast. Ask students to speculate on what they were. *(overland, which was cheapest, hence most popular route; by ship around the tip of South America; or by ship to Panama, then overland to the Pacific coast and by another ship to California)* Remind students that very few of the thousands who made the trip struck it rich, except those who went as merchants.

TEACH

L2 Population Ask volunteers to create a bar graph on the chalkboard comparing the increase in the population of California and Florida between 1850 and 1900. Provide the following figures for California:

1850—93,000	1880—865,000
1860—380,000	1890—1,213,000
1870—560,000	1900—1,485,000

Provide the following figures for Florida:

1850—87,000	1880—269,000
1860—140,000	1890—391,000
1870—188,000	1900—529,000

Discuss with students the possible reasons California grew so much faster than Florida.

Hands-On HISTORY Lab Activity

Go for the Gold

You're off to the gold fields! It's 1849 and the California Gold Rush is on. Will you find your fortune? Make your own sluice box to see how some California forty-niners searched for gold nearly 150 years ago.

California gold miners

The Way It Was

In the mid-1800s, a call echoed across the United States. "There's gold in California!" Prospectors and adventurers by the thousands headed west hoping to make their fortunes. Teachers, farmers, businesspeople, and merchants armed themselves with picks and shovels. They attacked streambeds and gravel beds, searching for shiny gold dust, flakes, and nuggets. Because much of this valuable mineral washed down from California's mountains, panning for gold in rivers became a common choice for prospecting.

Believe It Or Not! Stories of gold in California were not new in 1849. In 1842 a rancher in southern California found gold dust on the roots of a wild onion he dug up for lunch. No one paid much attention until James Marshall found gold while building a sawmill on John Sutter's property in 1848.

1 Materials

- 1/2 gallon empty milk or juice carton
- sand, dirt, gravel, with 3 or 4 heavy metal screw nuts (gold nuggets)
- 3 small dowel rods about 6 inches long
- modeling clay
- large baking pan
- water
- scissors

CURRICULUM CONNECTION

Geography As settlers turned their sights toward the West, the country's population center began to shift. In 1790 the center of population was located approximately 23 miles (376 km) east of Baltimore, Maryland. By 1800 the center had moved all the way to Chillicothe, Ohio. Today the center is just northwest of Steelville, Missouri, which is nearly 820 miles (1,319 km) from the 1790 population center. Since 1900 the population of the United States has been growing by about 2.8 million people per year. Almost 80 percent of the people live in metropolitan areas. More than half of the total population (56.4 percent) lives in the South and West.

2 What To Do

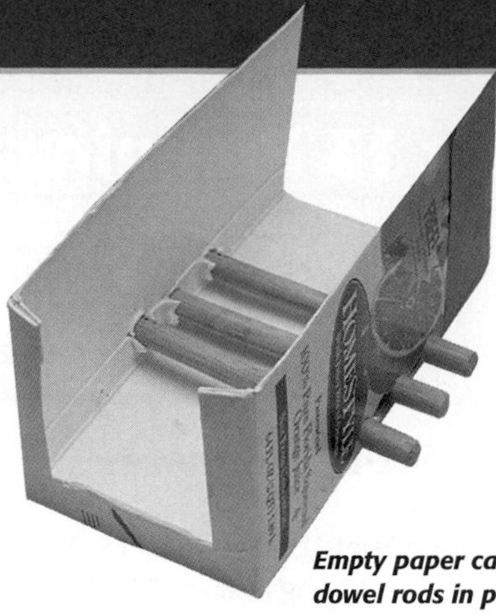

Empty paper carton with dowel rods in place

1. Use the modeling clay to form a ridge about 1 inch high at one end of the baking pan. Cut off the top end and one side of the milk or juice carton.
2. At the bottom end of the carton, cut a U-shaped opening. Leave about 1/2 inch around 3 sides. Turn the carton so that the cut-away side is up, forming a trough.
3. Insert the 3 dowel rods through two sides of the trough, close to the bottom of the trough. (Use the trough on this page as a model.) Make 2 small holes near the bottom of the trough about 2 inches away from the U-shaped end for the water to drain.
4. Place the trough in the cake pan with the open end on the clay ridge.
5. Place a handful of sand, dirt, gravel, and metal screw nuts at the upper end of your trough. Pour water down your trough and look for "gold nuggets."
6. Repeat the process in step 5 several times. Now you are sluicing for "gold."

3 Lab Report

1. Which materials tended to wash all the way down the trough?
2. What happened to the heavier "gold nuggets"?
3. How efficient do you think sluicing was as a mining method?
4. **Drawing Conclusions** How much mining experience and money for equipment do you think the average forty-niner brought to the gold fields?

Go a Step Further

Find out more about the discovery of gold at Sutter's Mill near Sacramento in 1848. Write a series of diary entries that you think John Sutter might have made about the discovery of gold and the arrival of miners.

Hands-On HISTORY Lab Activity

ASSESS

Have students answer the **Lab Report** questions on this page.

ABCNEWS INTERACTIVE™

VIDEODISC
Historic America Electronic Field Trips

Side 1, Chapter 11
Title: *Sutter's Mill*
Subject: Tour of the site where gold was discovered
Ask: **What groups were treated with violence by other miners?** *(ethnic minority groups and especially Native Americans)*

Also available in VHS.

CLOSE

Encourage students to complete the **Go a Step Further** writing activity. Ask volunteers to read their diary entries to the class. Initiate a discussion on the impact of the Gold Rush on California.

ANSWERS

Lab Report

1. sand and dirt
2. sank to the bottom
3. Answers will vary. Students might mention that the smaller nuggets would probably get washed away.
4. Answers will vary, but most students will point out that the miners did not need much money to get started.

Go a Step Further

Responses should include entries on the actual discovery as well as Sutter's dismay at the arrival of huge numbers of prospectors within a relatively short time.

Chapter 13 Planning Guide

A complete, 1-page lesson plan is provided for each section in the *Reproducible Lesson Plans* booklet.

Section Resources

Daily Objectives	Reproducible Resources	Multimedia Resources
Section 1 **The North's Economy** Summarize ways that advances in technology, transportation, and communication spurred economic growth.	Reproducible Lesson Plan 13–1 Guided Reading Activity 13–1* Section Quiz 13–1* Reteaching Activity 13–1 Enrichment Activity 13–1	Section Focus Transparency 13–1 Vocabulary PuzzleMaker Chapter Challenger Interactive Review Software Testmaker GTV: A Geographic Perspective on American History
Section 2 **The North's People** Describe the nature of work in the North and how immigration shaped American life.	Reproducible Lesson Plan 13–2 Guided Reading Activity 13–2* Political Cartoons, *Native Americans and a Nation of Immigrants* Section Quiz 13–2* Reteaching Activity 13–2 Enrichment Activity 13–2	Section Focus Transparency 13–2 Vocabulary PuzzleMaker Chapter Challenger Interactive Review Software Testmaker GTV: The American People: Fabric of a Nation
Section 3 **Southern Cotton Kingdom** Describe the economy of the pre-Civil War South.	Reproducible Lesson Plan 13–3 Guided Reading Activity 13–3* Section Quiz 13–3* Reteaching Activity 13–3 Enrichment Activity 13–3	Section Focus Transparency 13–3 Vocabulary PuzzleMaker Chapter Challenger Interactive Review Software Testmaker GTV: The American People: Fabric of a Nation
Section 4 **The South's People** Summarize the different lifestyles of the South's people.	Reproducible Lesson Plan 13–4 Guided Reading Activity 13–4* Section Quiz 13–4* Reteaching Activity 13–4 Enrichment Activity 13–4	Section Focus Transparency 13–4 Vocabulary PuzzleMaker Chapter Challenger Interactive Review Software Testmaker GTV: A Geographic Perspective on American History Facts On File: Landmark Documents in American History

** Also available in Spanish*

Poster · Transparency · CD-ROM · Software
Blackline Master · Videodisc · Audiocassette · Music Program

0:00 OUT OF TIME?
Assign the Chapter 13 Digest and the corresponding Chapter Digests Audiocassettes with activities and tests.

Activity

From the Classroom of...

Gerald Schuchard
Flandreau Indian School
Flandreau, SD

Immigration and Geography —Regional Comparisons

Remind students that one of the major themes of geography is regional comparison, and that we can learn a great deal about how geography affects people by comparing regions of the world. Review the chapter's content regarding immigration to the United States between 1840–1860. Explain that many immigrants—at least those who had the money to choose where they lived—selected certain regions of this country to live in partly because of the similarities of those regions to regions in their home countries.

To illustrate this concept, have students consult encyclopedias, weather-related Internet sites, or use other resource materials to collect information on climatic conditions found in Germany. Then have them compare this data to information they find on climatic regions in the United States. Many German immigrants settled in New York and Pennsylvania. Ask students to compare the climatic data of these two states to the climate found in Germany. Ask students, "If you were moving to another land, how important would climate be to you?"

Block Schedule

Block scheduling differs from traditional class scheduling in the amount of time allotted to each period. The extended time frame provided by block scheduling affords you the opportunity to implement a greater number of research-oriented and activity-intense projects to motivate and involve your students. Activities that are particularly suited to use within the block scheduling framework are identified throughout this chapter by the following designation:

NATIONAL GEOGRAPHIC SOCIETY

Teacher's Corner

INDEX TO NATIONAL GEOGRAPHIC MAGAZINE

The following articles may be used for research relating to this chapter:

- "America's Poet: Walt Whitman," by Joel L. Swerdlow, December 1994.
- "C.S.S. *Alabama,*" by Max Guerout, December 1994.
- "The Cruelest Commerce: African Slave Trade," by Colin Palmer, September 1992.
- "Philadelphia's African Americans," by Roland L. Freeman, August 1990.

NATIONAL GEOGRAPHIC SOCIETY PRODUCTS AVAILABLE FROM GLENCOE

To order the following products for use with this chapter, contact your local Glencoe sales representative, or call Glencoe at 1-800-334-7344:

- *GTV: The American People: Fabric of a Nation* (Videodisc)
- *GTV: A Geographic Perspective on American History* (Videodisc)
- *The Presidents: A Picture History of Our Nation* (CD-ROM)
- *PictureShow: The Civil War* (CD-ROM, Transparencies)
- *PictureShow: The Westward Movement* (CD-ROM, Transparencies)

ADDITIONAL NATIONAL GEOGRAPHIC SOCIETY PRODUCTS

To order the following products for use with this chapter, call National Geographic Society at 1-800-368-2728:

- *Immigration: The Triumph of Hope* (Video)
- *Steal Away: The Harriet Tubman Story* (Video)
- *Historical Atlas of the United States* (Atlas)

KEY TO ABILITY LEVELS

Teaching strategies have been coded for varying learning styles and abilities.

- L1 **BASIC** activities for all students
- L2 **AVERAGE** activities for average to above-average students
- L3 **CHALLENGING** activities for above-average students
- ELL **ENGLISH LANGUAGE LEARNER** activities

Chapter 13 Resource Guide

Home Involvement

Home Involvement Activity 13

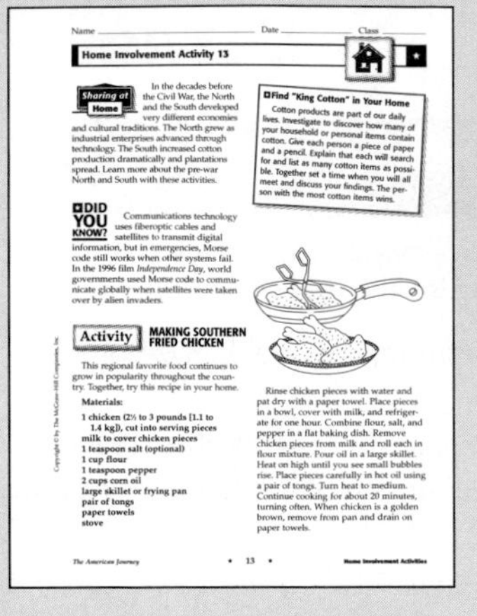

Review Activities

Chapter Summary 13

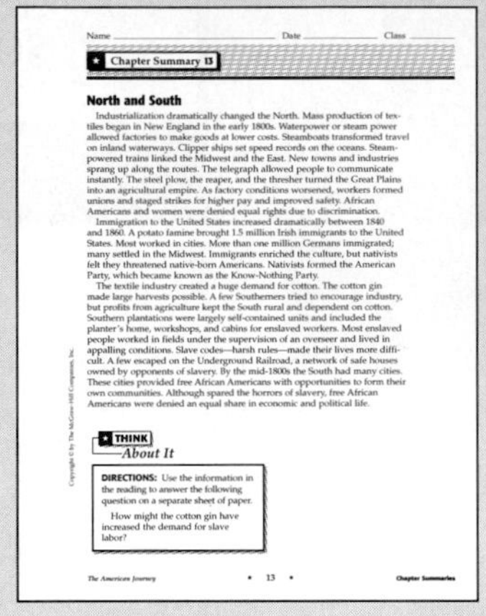

Workbook Activity 13

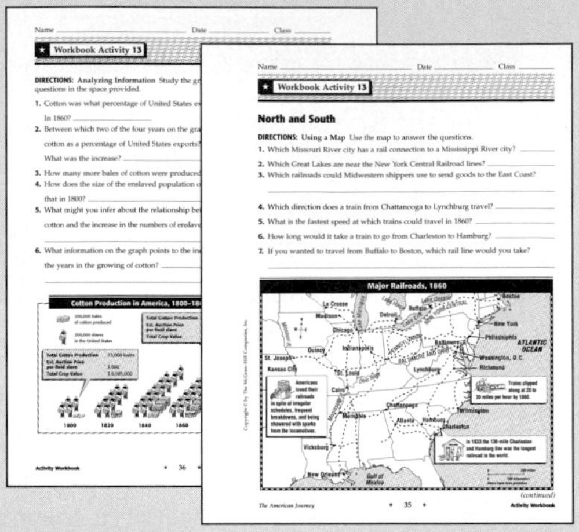

Reinforcement Activities

Time Line Activity 13

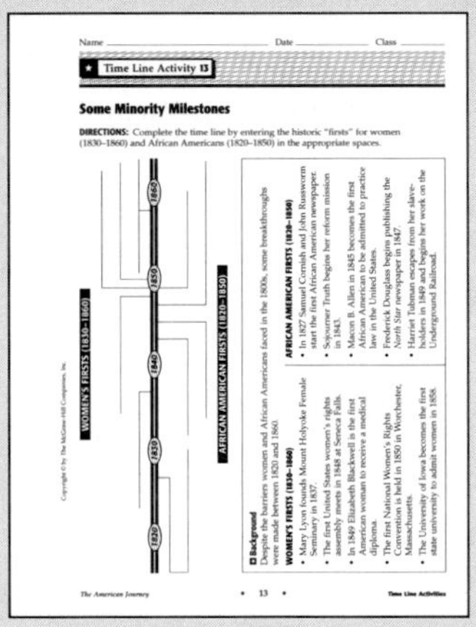

Vocabulary Activity 13

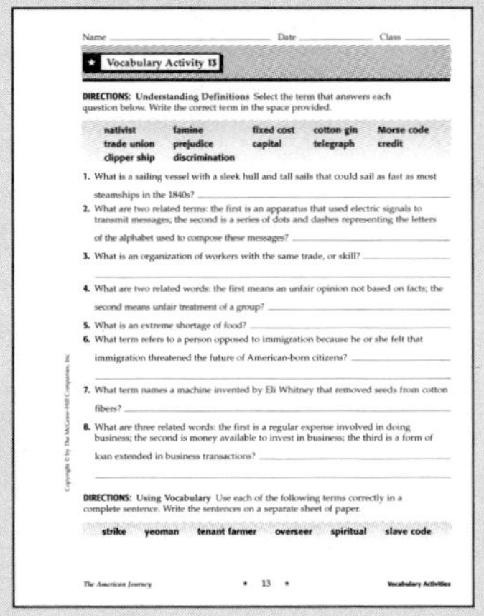

Chapter Skills Activity 13

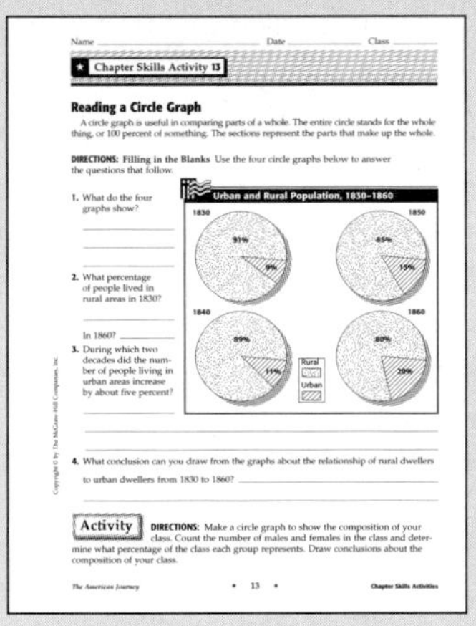

Enrichment Activities

Linking Past and Present Activity 13

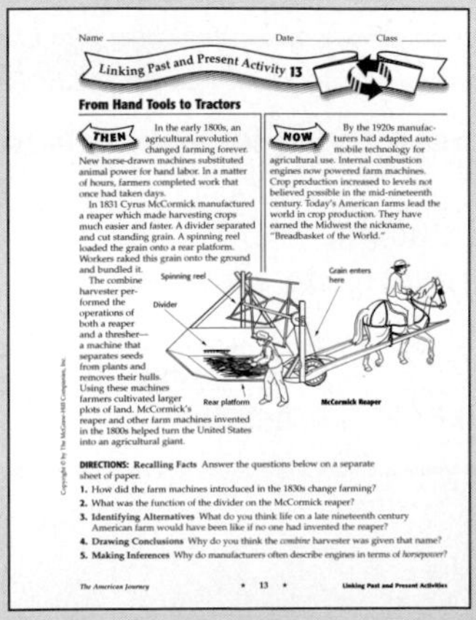

Primary Source Reading 13

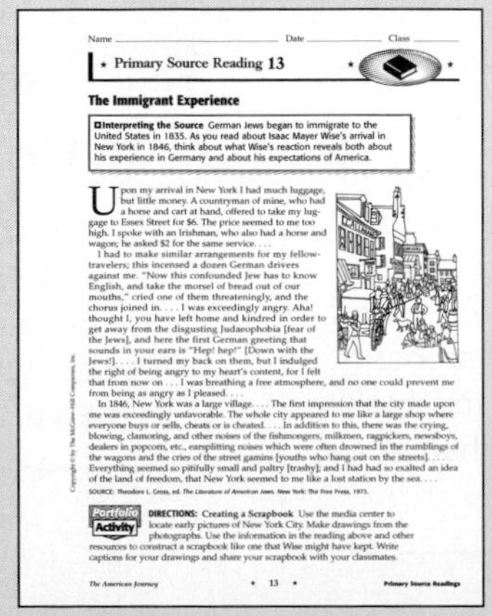

Geography Activities

Mapping History Activity 13

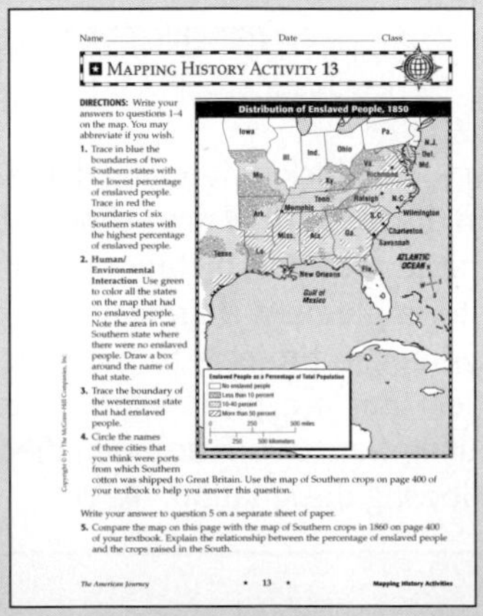

Assessment

Chapter 13 Test, Form A

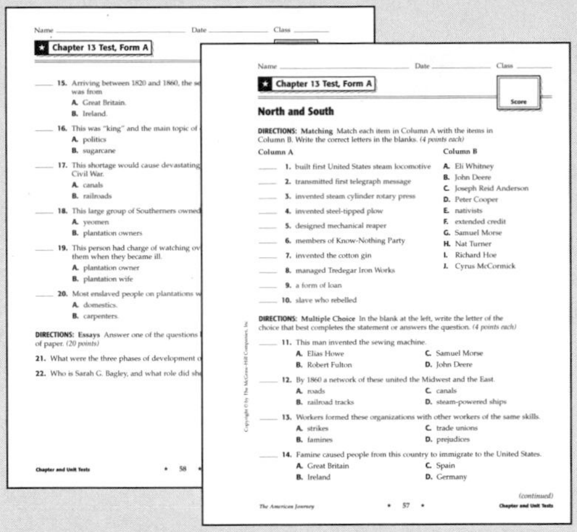

Chapter 13 Test, Form B

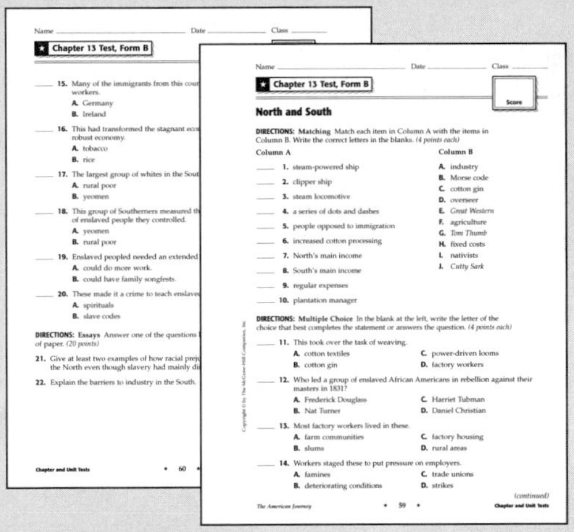

Performance Assessment Activity 13

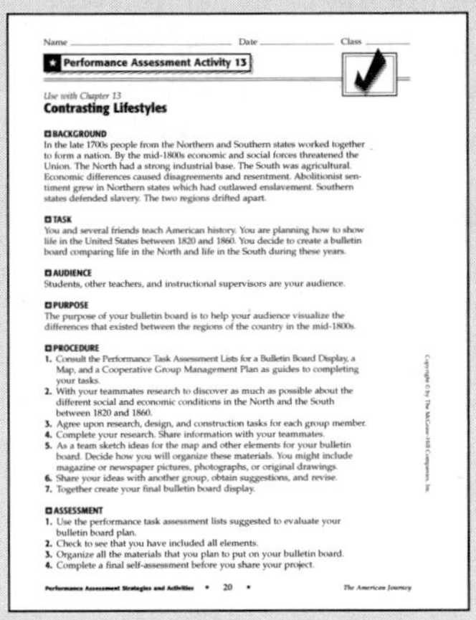

Spanish Resources

The following Spanish language materials are available in the Spanish Resources binder:

- **Spanish Chapter Summary 13**
- **Spanish Vocabulary Activity 13**
- **Spanish Guided Reading Activities, Chapter 13**
- **Spanish Section Quizzes, Chapter 13**
- **Spanish Home Involvement Activity 13**
- **Spanish Chapter 13 Digests Audiocassette Activity and Test**

Activity Manipulatives

Help students learn more about America's cultural history with:

- **American Crafts Hands-On Activities**
- **American Games Hands-On Activities**
- **American History Flash Cards**

Additional Resources From Glencoe

- **U.S. History & Art,** Transparency 9, *Shooting for the Beef*
- **Focus on American Art Prints,** *Pat Lyon at the Forge* by John Neagle
- **The Spirit of American Art and Music,** Joshua Johnston
- **American Music Cultural Traditions,** Lesson 4: "Kneebone Bend" and "The Monongahela Waltz"; Lesson 5: "Get Off the Track!" and "Roll, Jordan, Roll"
- **Outline Map Resource Book**
- **U.S. Desk Map**
- **The American History Videodisc and CD-ROM,** *Expansion, Development, Sectionalism and Division, 1820–1860*

A&E HOME VIDEO. Biography. THE HISTORY CHANNEL.

The following videotape programs are available from Glencoe as supplements to Chapter 13:

- **Civil War Journal (Set 1)** (ISBN 1-56501-200-3)

To order, call Glencoe at 1-800-334-7344. To find classroom resources to accompany many of these videos, check the following home pages:
A&E Television: http://www.aetv.com
The History Channel: http://www.historychannel.com

Introducing CHAPTER 13

Chapter Themes

Chapter Themes are listed by section on this chapter opening page of the Student Edition. A corresponding theme-based activity is available under "FOCUS," and a theme-based question is asked in the Section and Chapter Reviews.

Performance Assessment

Refer to Activity 13 in the *Performance Assessment Strategies and Activities* booklet.

GLENCOE TECHNOLOGY

VIDEODISC
MindJogger Videoquiz

Use MindJogger to preview the Chapter 13 content.

Chapter 13
Disc 2, Side B

Also available in VHS.

HISTORY AND ART John Bunyan Bristol was a member of the National Academy. His landscapes received medals in the exhibitions in Philadelphia in 1876 and in Paris in 1889. **Ask: What details from the painting tell you this is the property of a poor farmer?** *(small house, few crops, no living quarters for servants or slaves, and so on)*

Chapter 13

1820–1860

North and South

Why It's Important

Many of the differences between the North and the South have disappeared since the 1800s. Differences still exist, but no longer are there sharp economic and cultural distinctions between the two regions. The South now has many industries, while many cities in the North now have fewer factories than they did in the 1800s. Mass communication and the migration of people from one region to another have also erased regional differences.

Chapter Themes

- *Section 1,* Economic Factors
- *Section 2,* Geography and History
- *Section 3,* Science and Technology
- *Section 4,* Culture and Traditions

HISTORY AND ART ***On the Saint Johns River* by John Bunyan Bristol** Most Southerners did not own plantations. Many were poor farmers, living off the crops they raised.

EXTRA CREDIT PROJECT

Pony Express Have interested students read about the Pony Express and prepare a report on this colorful element of our history. (For a short time, the Pony Express was the fastest way of getting mail and news across the country. In just 10 days riders could carry mailbags from St. Joseph, Missouri, to Sacramento, California. The 190 Pony Express stations were 10 to 15 miles [16–24 km] apart. The service employed 80 riders and 500 horses. Horses were changed at every station; riders about every eight stations. William [Buffalo Bill] Cody is probably the most famous Pony Express rider. Though glamorous, the Pony Express was a financial failure, and it was put out of business after just 18 months by the telegraph.)

1830 — 1840 — 1850 — 1860

1834 Cyrus McCormick patents reaper

1844 Samuel Morse sends first telegraph message

1847 Elias Howe introduces the sewing machine

1860 About 3,000 steamboats are operating

Section 1

The North's Economy

READ TO DISCOVER . . .

- how advances in technology shaped the economy of the North.
- how new kinds of transportation and communication spurred economic growth.

TERMS TO LEARN

clipper ship
telegraph
Morse code

The Storyteller

In the 1840s, telegraph wires and railroads began to cross the nation. But traveling by rail had its discomforts, as writer Charles Dickens describes: "[T]here is a great deal of jolting, a great deal of noise, a great deal of wall, not much window, a locomotive engine, a shriek, and a bell. . . . In the center of the carriage there is usually a stove . . . which is for the most part red-hot. It is insufferably close; and you see the hot air fluttering between yourself and any other object you may happen to look at, like the ghost of smoke. . . ."

Samuel Morse's telegraph key

In the Northern states, technology changed the way Americans worked, traveled, and communicated. By the mid-1800s, power-driven machinery performed many tasks that were once done by hand, and factories had largely replaced cottage industries.

Technology and Industry

The industrialization of the North developed in three phases. In the first, manufacturers made products by dividing the tasks involved among the workers. One worker would spin thread all day and another would weave cloth—instead of having one person spinning and then weaving. During the second phase, manufacturers built factories to bring specialized workers together. This allowed products to be made more quickly than before.

In the third phase, factory workers used machinery to perform some of their work. Many of the new machines ran on waterpower or steam power. For example, power-driven looms took over the task of weaving. The worker's job was no longer to weave but to tend the machine, which produced more products in less time.

Mass Production

Mass production of cotton textiles began in New England in the early 1800s. After **Elias Howe** invented the sewing machine in 1843, machine operators could produce clothing on a large scale from textiles made by machine. Other types

SECTION RESOURCES

Reproducible Masters

- Reproducible Lesson Plan 13–1
- Guided Reading Activity 13–1
- Section Quiz 13–1
- Reteaching Activity 13–1
- Enrichment Activity 13–1

Transparencies

- Section Focus Transparency 13–1

Multimedia

- Vocabulary PuzzleMaker
- Chapter Challenger Interactive Review Software
- Testmaker
- GTV: A Geographic Perspective on American History

1 FOCUS

BELLRINGER
Motivational Activity

Before taking roll at the beginning of the class period, project Section Focus Transparency 13–1 and have students answer the questions. Discuss students' responses.

This activity is also available as a blackline master.

Section Focus Transparency 13–1

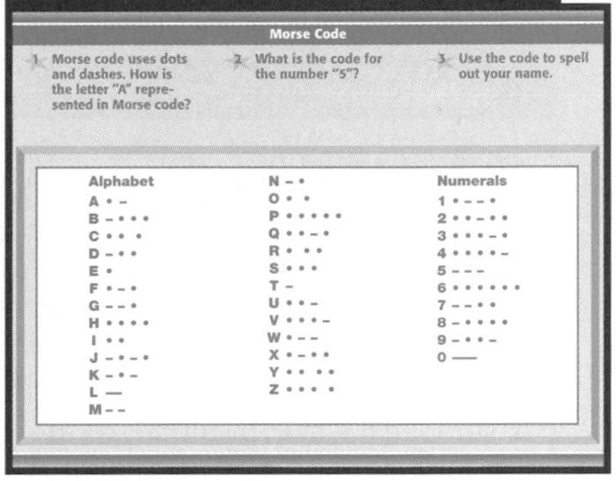

Vocabulary Precheck

Point out that the word *telegraph* comes from the Greek words *tele* (at a distance, far off) and *graphein* (to write). Encourage students to define *telegraph* based on this information.

Use the **Vocabulary Puzzle-Maker** to create crossword and word search puzzles.

Section Theme
Economic Factors

During the 1800s advances in technology, transportation, and communication shaped the North's economy.

Activity Have students skim the section to find examples of such advances. *(sewing machine, ocean-going steamboat, clipper ship, steam locomotive, growth of canals and railroads, telegraph, rotary press, steel-tipped plow, mechanical reaper, and thresher)*

CHAPTER 13
Section 1, 385–389

2 TEACH

L1 Creating a Concept Web Work with students to create on the chalkboard a concept web showing the interrelationships of developments discussed in the section. The central oval should be labeled *Industrialized Economy of the North.*

Picturing HISTORY Merchants used clipper ships in the tea trade between the United States and China.
Answer: *They clipped time from the length of voyages.*

What? Where? When? Who?

Air brakes to stop locomotives were not invented until the 1860s. Before George Westinghouse invented them, brakemen had to stop railcars by hand. Standing on the roof of a car, the brakeman slowed or stopped the train by turning a cast-iron wheel connected to a shaft that ran down to the brakes. Many a brakeman lost his life falling from the top of a fast freight on an icy winter's night as he wrestled with the wheel while the train sped around dangerous curves.

Guided Reading Activity 13–1

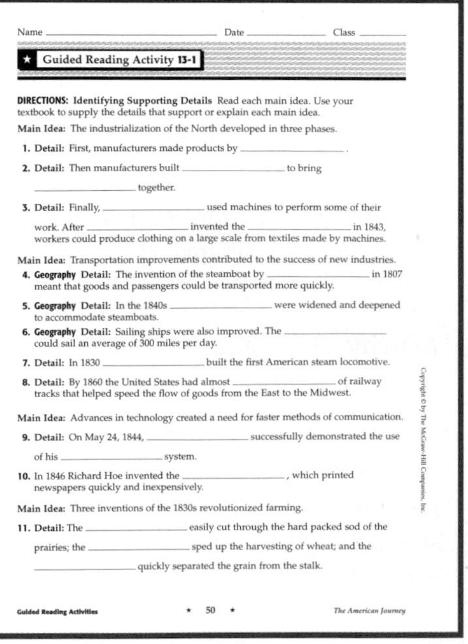
Name ____________ Date ________ Class ______

★ Guided Reading Activity 13-1

DIRECTIONS: Identifying Supporting Details Read each main idea. Use your textbook to supply the details that support or explain each main idea.

Main Idea: The industrialization of the North developed in three phases.

1. **Detail:** First, manufacturers made products by ____________.
2. **Detail:** Then manufacturers built ____________ to bring ____________ together.
3. **Detail:** Finally, ____________ used machines to perform some of their work. After ____________ invented the ____________ in 1843, workers could produce clothing on a large scale from textiles made by machines.

Main Idea: Transportation improvements contributed to the success of new industries.

4. **Geography Detail:** The invention of the steamboat by ____________ in 1807 meant that goods and passengers could be transported more quickly.
5. **Geography Detail:** In the 1840s ____________ were widened and deepened to accommodate steamboats.
6. **Geography Detail:** Sailing ships were also improved. The ____________ could sail an average of 300 miles per day.
7. **Detail:** In 1830 ____________ built the first American steam locomotive.
8. **Detail:** By 1860 the United States had almost ____________ of railway tracks that helped speed the flow of goods from the East to the Midwest.

Main Idea: Advances in technology created a need for faster methods of communication.

9. **Detail:** On May 24, 1844, ____________ successfully demonstrated the use of his ____________ system.
10. In 1846 Richard Hoe invented the ____________, which printed newspapers quickly and inexpensively.

Main Idea: Three inventions of the 1830s revolutionized farming.

11. **Detail:** The ____________ easily cut through the hard packed sod of the prairies; the ____________ sped up the harvesting of wheat; and the ____________ quickly separated the grain from the stalk.

Guided Reading Activities ★ 50 ★ *The American Journey*

Picturing HISTORY A clipper ship, the *Flying Cloud*, set a new record by sailing from New York to California in less than 90 days. **How did clipper ships get their name?**

of industries developed during the same period. By 1860 the Northeast's 74,000 factories produced about two-thirds of the country's manufactured goods.

Improved Transportation

★ Improvements in transportation contributed to the success of many of America's new industries. Between 1800 and 1850, construction crews built thousands of miles of roads and canals. The canals opened new shipping routes by connecting many lakes and rivers. The growth of railroads in the 1840s and 1850s produced another means to speed the flow of goods.

Geography

Steamboats and Steamships

Inventor **Robert Fulton** changed river travel in 1807 with his steamboat. Steamboats carried goods and passengers more cheaply and quickly along inland waterways than flatboats or sail-powered vessels could do.

In the 1840s canal builders began to widen and deepen canals to accommodate steamboats. By 1860 about 3,000 steamboats traveled the major rivers and canals of the country as well as the Great Lakes. Steamboats spurred the development of cities such as Cincinnati, Buffalo, and Chicago.

Before long, steam also powered ships across the ocean. One of the first steam-powered oceangoing vessels was an iron ship called the *Great Western.* On its first voyages between the United States and Great Britain in 1838, the *Great Western* carried a supply of sails in case the steam engine broke down in midocean.

Clipper Ships

In the 1840s sailing ships were improved. The **clipper ships**—with their sleek hulls and tall sails—were the pride of the open seas. They could sail an average of 300 miles per day, as fast as most steamships of the day. The ships got their name because they "clipped" time from long journeys. Before the clippers, the voyage from New York to Great Britain took about 21 to 28 days. A clipper ship could usually make that trip in half the time.

Famous clipper ships included the *Flying Cloud,* the *Sea Witch,* and the *Cutty Sark.* In 1853 the *Champion of the Seas* set a new record, sailing 465 miles in 24 hours. No steamship matched this speed for more than 25 years.

Locomotives

The development of railroads in the United States began with short stretches of tracks that connected mines with nearby rivers. Early trains were drawn by horses rather than by locomotives. The first steam-powered locomotive, the *Rocket,* began operating in Britain in 1829.

Peter Cooper designed and built the first American steam locomotive in 1830. Called the *Tom Thumb,* it got off to a bad start. In a race against a horse-drawn train in **Baltimore,** the *Tom Thumb*'s engine failed. Engineers soon improved the engine, and within 10 years steam locomotives were pulling trains in the United States.

COOPERATIVE LEARNING ACTIVITY

Illustrating Relationships Have students work together in small groups to create a mural illustrating the concept web they created (See Teach, above). Each group should choose a different aspect to illustrate—steamboats, clipper ships, trains, telegraph and printing press, agricultural technology, and so on. If necessary, have some students do research. Others can be responsible for making drawings, while still others can write captions and labels.

A Railway Network

In 1840 the United States had some 3,000 miles of railroad track. By 1860 it had almost 31,000 miles, mostly in the North and the **Midwest.** One railway linked New York City and Buffalo. Another connected Philadelphia and Pittsburgh. Still another linked Baltimore with Wheeling, Virginia (now West Virginia).

Railway builders tied these eastern lines to lines being built farther west in Ohio, Indiana, and Illinois. By 1860 a network of railroad track united the Midwest and the East.

Moving Goods and People

Along with canals, the railways transformed trade in the nation's interior. The changes began with the opening of the Erie Canal in 1825 and the first railroads of the 1830s. Before this time agricultural goods were carried down the Mississippi River to New Orleans and then shipped to other countries or to the East Coast of the United States.

The development of the east-west canal and the rail network allowed grain, livestock, and dairy products to move directly from the Midwest to the East. Because goods now traveled

Major Railroads, 1860

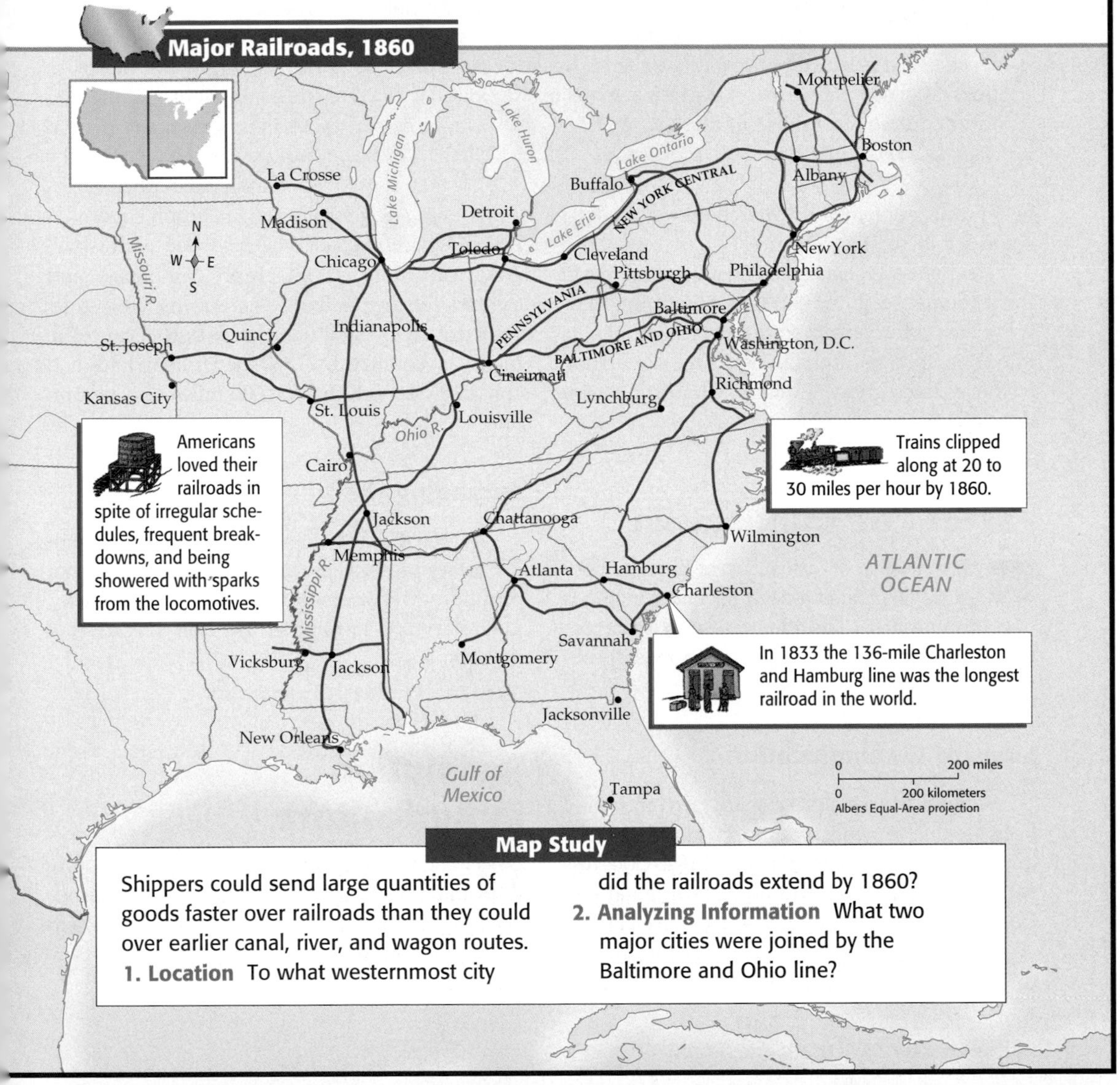

Americans loved their railroads in spite of irregular schedules, frequent breakdowns, and being showered with sparks from the locomotives.

Trains clipped along at 20 to 30 miles per hour by 1860.

In 1833 the 136-mile Charleston and Hamburg line was the longest railroad in the world.

Map Study

Shippers could send large quantities of goods faster over railroads than they could over earlier canal, river, and wagon routes.

1. **Location** To what westernmost city did the railroads extend by 1860?
2. **Analyzing Information** What two major cities were joined by the Baltimore and Ohio line?

CHAPTER 13

Section 1, 385–389

What?Where?When?Who?

News Syndicates In the same year that Hoe invented the rotary press, newspaper publishers formed the Associated Press, an organization that provided news stories to scores of newspapers. The Associated Press sent its news dispatches by telegraph. For the first time, large numbers of Americans could read about national and world events almost as soon as they occurred, making newspapers an increasingly important part of American life.

NATIONAL GEOGRAPHIC SOCIETY

VIDEODISC

GTV: A Geographic Perspective on American History

Side 2, Chapter 9

Title: *Getting Up to Speed*

Subject: Transportation and the growing nation (1825–1850)

Ask: **How were the new transportation methods effective?** *(The new methods of transportation made travel easier, faster, and cheaper. These methods helped connect the growing nation.)*

Map Study

Answers

1. St. Joseph
2. Baltimore and Cincinnati

Map Skills Practice

Reading a Map What town could you visit on a railroad trip from Louisville to Chicago? *(Indianapolis)*

MULTIPLE LEARNING STYLES

Kinesthetic Sailors on whaling ships filled idle hours by making scrimshaw, an art form consisting of designs or pictures carved on the teeth or jawbone of the sperm whale. Students can make their own version of this art form. Materials needed are pencil, carbon paper, tape, black crayon, paper towel, soft plastic jug, scissors, large needle, and paper. Directions: (1) Cut a smooth piece of plastic that has no writing or design on it. (2) Draw a design or picture on a sheet of paper and tape the drawing to the back of the carbon paper. (3) Place the carbon paper on the plastic so the picture is facing you. Trace the drawing onto the plastic with the pencil. (4) Use the needle to etch the drawing onto the plastic. (5) Darken the scratched lines by rubbing them lightly with the crayon. Clean off excess crayon by wiping the drawing with the paper towel. **L2,** ELL

CHAPTER 13
Section 1, 385–389

Picturing HISTORY Early railroads were expensive to build and maintain. Although state governments funded canal building, private enterprise provided the money for early railroads. **Ask:** **What kind of engine has replaced the steam engine in today's locomotives?** *(diesel-powered internal combustion engine)*
Answer: *East and Midwest*

Linking PAST & PRESENT

Fiber-optic Cables In the 1840s people began sending messages over telegraph wires. Today fiber-optic cables—composed of microscopically thin strands of glass or plastic that transmit light—are used in advanced communication systems that send electronic information in the form of pictures, voices, and words.

3 ASSESS

Assign Section 1 Review as homework or as an in-class activity.

Use **Chapter Challenger Interactive Review Software** to review Section 1.

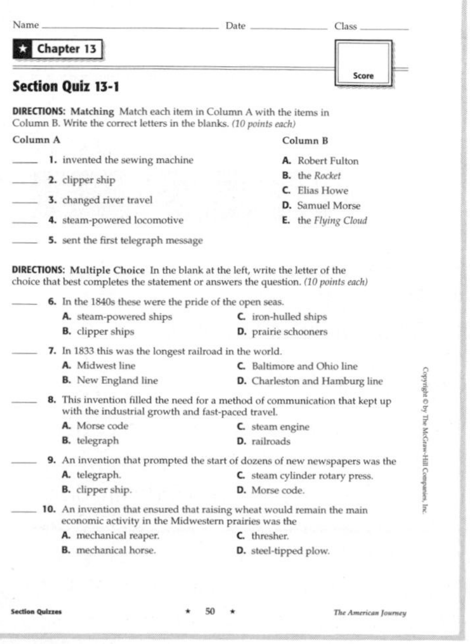

Section Quiz 13–1

Name ________ Date ________ Class ________

Chapter 13

Score

Section Quiz 13-1

DIRECTIONS: Matching Match each item in Column A with the items in Column B. Write the correct letters in the blanks. *(10 points each)*

Column A	Column B
____ 1. invented the sewing machine	A. Robert Fulton
____ 2. clipper ship	B. the *Rocket*
____ 3. changed river travel	C. Elias Howe
____ 4. steam-powered locomotive	D. Samuel Morse
____ 5. sent the first telegraph message	E. the *Flying Cloud*

DIRECTIONS: Multiple Choice In the blank at the left, write the letter of the choice that best completes the statement or answers the question. *(10 points each)*

____ 6. In the 1840s these were the pride of the open seas.
A. steam-powered ships C. iron-hulled ships
B. clipper ships D. prairie schooners

____ 7. In 1833 this was the longest railroad in the world.
A. Midwest line C. Baltimore and Ohio line
B. New England line D. Charleston and Hamburg line

____ 8. This invention filled the need for a method of communication that kept up with the industrial growth and fast-paced travel.
A. Morse code C. steam engine
B. telegraph D. railroads

____ 9. An invention that prompted the start of dozens of new newspapers was the
A. telegraph. C. steam cylinder rotary press.
B. clipper ship. D. Morse code.

____ 10. An invention that ensured that raising wheat would remain the main economic activity in the Midwestern prairies was the
A. mechanical reaper. C. thresher.
B. mechanical horse. D. steel-tipped plow.

Section Quizzes ★ 50 ★ *The American Journey*

Picturing HISTORY The defeat of the train *Tom Thumb* in 1830 did not mean the end of the steam engine. The first successful use of a steam locomotive in the United States took place in South Carolina in 1831. **In 1860 which regions of the United States had the most miles of railroad track?**

faster and more cheaply, merchants in the East could sell them at lower prices.

The railroads also played an important role in the settlement and industrialization of the Midwest. Fast, affordable train travel brought people into Ohio, Indiana, and Illinois. As the population of these states grew, new towns and industries developed.

Faster Communication

The growth of industry and the new pace of travel created a need for faster methods of communication. The **telegraph**—an apparatus that used electric signals to transmit messages—filled that need.

Lines of Communication

Samuel Morse, an American inventor, had been seeking to win support for a system of telegraph lines for five years. Finally, in 1843 Congress set aside $30,000 to build an experimental line from Baltimore, Maryland, to Washington, D.C.

On May 24, 1844, Morse got the chance to demonstrate that he could send messages instantly along wires. As a crowd in the U.S. capital watched, Morse tapped in the words, "What hath God wrought!" A few moments later, the telegraph operator in Baltimore sent the same message back in reply. The telegraph worked! Soon telegraph messages were flashing back and forth between Washington and Baltimore.

Morse transmitted his message in **Morse code,** a series of dots and dashes representing the letters of the alphabet. A skilled Morse code operator could rapidly tap out words in the dot-and-dash alphabet.

Americans adopted the telegraph eagerly. A British visitor marveled at the speed with which Americans formed telegraph companies and erected telegraph lines. Americans, he wrote, were driven to "annihilate [wipe out] distance" in their vast country. By 1860 the United States had constructed more than 50,000 miles of telegraph lines.

Spreading the News

In 1846 Richard Hoe invented the steam cylinder rotary press, a new kind of printing press that printed newspapers quickly and inexpensively. The rotary press prompted the start of dozens of newspapers.

Revolution in Agriculture

The railroads gave farmers access to new markets where they could sell their products. Advances in technology allowed farmers to greatly increase the size of the crops they produced.

MAKING CONNECTIONS ACTIVITY

Technology The first successful transatlantic telegraph cable was laid in 1858. Financed by a wealthy New York paper manufacturer named Cyrus Field, it stretched from Newfoundland to Ireland. Field had previously tried four times to lay a cable and had gained nothing but mockery for his efforts. His success in 1858, however, was greeted with great celebration, including a two-day cable carnival in New York City. That first cable lasted only three weeks, but in 1866 after the Civil War, he laid a heavier cable that did continue to work. Reviled after the failure of the 1858 cable, Field once again became a hero. Have students read about the laying of the cable, or watch a video about it if one is available, and write a description of some of the story's highlights. **L2**

Farm Technology

Very few farmers ventured into the treeless **Great Plains** west of Missouri, Iowa, and Minnesota in the early 1800s. Even areas of mixed forest and prairie west of Ohio and Kentucky seemed too difficult for farming. Settlers worried that their wooden plows could not break the prairie's matted sod and that the soil was not fertile.

Three revolutionary inventions of the 1830s changed farming methods and encouraged settlers to cultivate larger areas of the West. One was the **steel-tipped plow** that **John Deere** invented in 1837. Far sturdier than the wooden plow, Deere's plow easily cut through the hard-packed sod of the prairies. Equally important were the **mechanical reaper,** which sped up the harvesting of wheat, and the **thresher,** which quickly separated the grain from the stalk.

Biography

McCormick's Reaper

Born on a Virginia farm, **Cyrus McCormick** became interested in machines that would ease the burden of farmwork. After years of tinkering, McCormick designed and constructed the mechanical reaper and made a fortune manufacturing and selling it. After patenting the reaper in 1834, McCormick opened a factory in Chicago in 1847 to mass-produce the machine. By 1860 he had sold 100,000 reapers.

For hundreds of years, farmers had harvested grain with handheld sickles. McCormick's reaper could harvest grain four times faster than the sickle. Because farmers could harvest wheat so quickly, they began planting more of it. Growing wheat became profitable. McCormick's reaper ensured that raising wheat would remain the main economic activity in the Midwestern prairies.

Cash Crops

American farmers had always kept some of their crops for themselves and sold some for cash. New agricultural machines and railroads helped farmers plant more acres in cash crops and sell those crops in distant markets. Midwestern farmers began growing wheat in large quantities and shipping it east by train and canal barge. Farmers in the Northeast and the Middle Atlantic states also increased their production of cash crops, concentrating on the fruits and vegetables that grew well in Eastern soils.

Despite improvements in agriculture, however, the North turned increasingly toward industry. It was difficult making a living farming the rocky soil of New England, but industry flourished in the area. The number of people who worked in factories continued to rise—and so did problems connected with factory labor.

Section 1 Review

Checking for Understanding

1. ***Identify*** Robert Fulton, Samuel Morse, John Deere, Cyrus McCormick.
2. ***Define*** clipper ship, telegraph, Morse code.
3. ***Identify*** the three phases of industrialization in the North.

Reviewing Themes

4. **Economic Factors** How did improvements in transportation affect the price of goods?

Critical Thinking

5. **Determining Cause and Effect** How did the steel-tipped plow aid settlers on the Great Plains?

Activity

Making a Graph Research the number of acres of wheat harvested in the United States before and after McCormick introduced his reaper. Then create a chart or graph to illustrate your findings.

Section 1 Review Answers

1. Robert Fulton, 386; Samuel Morse, 388; John Deere, 389; Cyrus McCormick, 389
2. The words are defined in the Glossary.
3. (a) division of tasks among workers, (b) building factories to bring specialized workers together, (c) use of machinery by factory workers
4. reduced prices because goods traveled faster and more cheaply
5. Farmers originally stayed away from this area, because wooden plows could not break through the tough sod. When the steel plow was invented, it solved this problem—the sturdy plow easily cut through hard-packed sod.

Activity Graphs should compare wheat production before and after the invention of the McCormick reaper.

CHAPTER 13
Section 1, 385–389

Reteaching Activity 13–1

Name ____________ Date ________ Class ________

Reteaching Activity 13-1

DIRECTIONS: Recognizing Causes and Effects After each *Cause*, write the letter of its *Effect* from the Fact Bank.

1. **Cause:** Factory workers use machinery to perform some of their work.
   Effect: ________
2. **Cause:** Elias Howe invents the sewing machine in 1843.
   Effect: ________
3. **Cause:** Robert Fulton invents the steamboat in 1807.
   Effect: ________
4. **Cause:** Clipper ships with sleek hulls and tall sails are built.
   Effect: ________
5. **Cause:** Almost 31,000 miles of railroad tracks are installed in the North and the Midwest and an east-west canal system is developed.
   Effect: ________
6. **Cause:** Samuel Morse demonstrates the use of the telegraph on May 24, 1844.
   Effect: ________
7. **Cause:** Richard Hoe invents the steam cylinder rotary press in 1846.
   Effect: ________
8. **Cause:** Revolutionary agricultural equipment, such as the steel-tipped plow and the thresher, is invented.
   Effect: ________
9. **Cause:** Cyrus McCormick designs and constructs the mechanical reaper.
   Effect: ________
10. **Cause:** People find it difficult to make a living farming the rocky soil of New England.
    Effect: ________

★FACT BANK

- **A.** People can communicate with friends and relatives in distant cities instantly.
- **B.** The trip from New York to Great Britain takes about 10 to 14 days.
- **C.** Farming methods change and settlers cultivate larger fields.
- **D.** Industry flourishes in the North.
- **E.** More products can be produced in less time.
- **F.** The flow of goods from east to west speeds up and becomes less expensive.
- **G.** Dozens of new newspapers start up.
- **H.** Workers can produce clothing on a large scale from textiles made by machine.
- **I.** Raising wheat is guaranteed to remain the main economic activity in the Midwestern prairies.
- **J.** Cities such as Cincinnati, Buffalo, and Chicago develop.

Reteaching Activities ★ 50 ★ *The American Journey*

Enrichment Activity 13–1

Name ____________ Date ________ Class ________

★ Enrichment Activity 13-1 ★

Communicating in Code

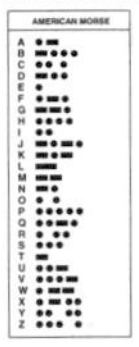

Samuel F.B. Morse and Alfred Vail developed a code to make it easy to communicate on the telegraph. Morse code uses a combination of dots and dashes to represent letters, numbers, and punctuation.

The message STAND BY looks like this in American Morse code:

The message WHAT HATH GOD WROUGHT looks like this in American Morse code:

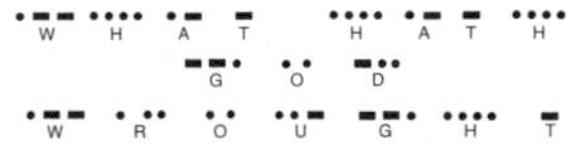

Activity **DIRECTIONS: Applying Information** Study the American Morse code. Then put the following in American Morse code.

1. The first message sent by telegraph ____________
2. Your name and address ____________
3. An imaginary SOS or distress call from a ship at sea ____________
4. An imaginary dialogue between two people ____________
5. A message to a friend ____________

Enrichment Activities ★ 50 ★ *The American Journey*

4 CLOSE

Although railroads boosted the economy and were a boon to many people, they were rightly viewed as a threat to business by turnpike investors and canal backers. **Ask: Who else might have lost income because of the railroads?** *(innkeepers along roads and canals; farmers who raised horses and hay; wagon makers, saddle makers, wheelwrights, and so on)*

CHAPTER 13
Section 2, 390–394

1 FOCUS

BELLRINGER
Motivational Activity

Before taking roll at the beginning of the class period, project Section Focus Transparency 13–2 and have students answer the questions. Discuss students' responses.

This activity is also available as a blackline master.

Section Focus Transparency 13–2

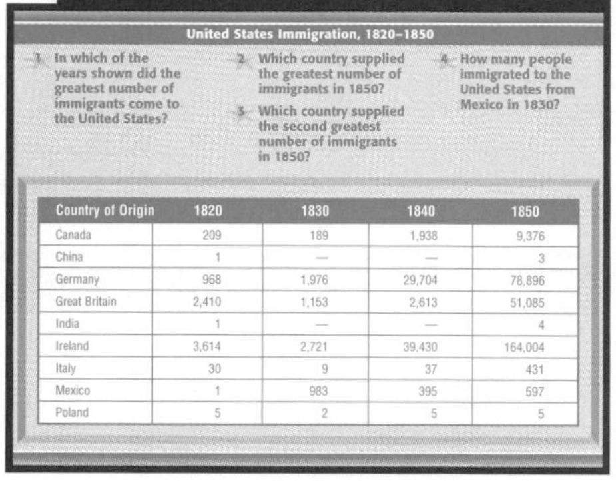
United States Immigration, 1820–1850

1. In which of the years shown did the greatest number of immigrants come to the United States?
2. Which country supplied the greatest number of immigrants in 1850?
3. Which country supplied the second greatest number of immigrants in 1850?
4. How many people immigrated to the United States from Mexico in 1830?

Country of Origin	1820	1830	1840	1850
Canada	209	189	1,938	9,376
China	1	—	—	3
Germany	968	1,976	29,704	78,896
Great Britain	2,410	1,153	2,613	51,085
India	1	—	—	4
Ireland	3,614	2,721	39,430	164,004
Italy	30	9	37	431
Mexico	1	983	395	597
Poland	5	2	5	5

Vocabulary Precheck

Point out that the term *strike* was first used in a labor context in 1768 when British sailors protested by striking, or taking down, the sails. Encourage students to describe what they think happens when a strike occurs.

Use the **Vocabulary Puzzle-Maker** to create crossword and word search puzzles.

Section Theme
Geography and History

The growth of both industry and immigration impacted the demographics of the North.

Activity Have students skim the section to find out what effect industry and immigration had on where Northerners lived. *(Between 1840 and 1860 the percentage of Northern city dwellers almost doubled—from 14 percent to 26 percent.)*

1820 — 1840 — 1860

1827 *Freedom's Journal*, first African American newspaper, is published

1834 The General Trades Union of New York is formed

1853 Know-Nothing Party is formed

1860 Population of New York City reaches 1 million

Section 2

The North's People

READ TO DISCOVER . . .
- how working conditions in industries changed.
- why workers began forming trade unions.
- how immigration affected American economic, political, and cultural life.

TERMS TO LEARN

trade union	discrimination
strike	famine
prejudice	nativist

The Storyteller

"At first the hours seemed very long, but I was so interested in learning that I endured it very well; when I went out at night the sound of the mill was in my ears," a Northern mill worker wrote in 1844. The worker compared the noise of the cotton mill to the ceaseless, deafening roar of Niagara Falls. The roar of machinery was only one feature of factory life workers had to adjust to. Industrialization created new challenges for the men, women, and children who worked in the nation's factories.

12-year-old factory worker

Between 1820 and 1860, more and more of America's manufacturing shifted to mills and factories. Machines took over many of the production tasks.

Northern Factories

In the early 1800s, in the mills established in **Lowell, Massachusetts,** the entire production process was brought together under one roof—setting up the factory system. In addition to textiles and clothing, factories now produced such items as shoes, watches, guns, sewing machines, and agricultural machinery.

Working Conditions

As the factory system developed, working conditions worsened. Factory owners wanted their employees to work longer hours in order to produce more goods. As the workday grew longer—by 1840 factory workers averaged 11.4 hours a day—on-the-job accidents became more common.

Factory work involved some dangerous conditions. For example, the long leather belts that connected the machines to the factory's water-powered driveshaft had no protective shields. Workers often suffered injuries such as lost fingers and broken bones from the rapidly spinning belts. Young children working on machines with powerful moving parts were especially at risk.

Workers often labored under unpleasant conditions. In the summer factories were miserably

SECTION RESOURCES

Reproducible Masters
- Guided Reading Activity 13–2
- Political Cartoons
- Section Quiz 13–2
- Reteaching Activity 13–2
- Enrichment Activity 13–2

Transparencies
- Section Focus Transparency 13–2

Multimedia
- Vocabulary PuzzleMaker
- Chapter Challenger Interactive Review Software
- Testmaker
- GTV: The American People: Fabric of a Nation

hot and stifling. The machines gave off heat, and air-conditioning had not yet been invented. In the winter workers suffered because most factories had no heating.

Factory owners showed more concern for profits than for the comfort and safety of their employees. They knew that they could easily replace an unhappy worker with someone else eager for a job. No laws existed to regulate working conditions or to protect workers.

The owners of the Lowell mills had built simple but clean lodging for employees in an effort to attract young women workers to the new industry. By the 1840s, however, factory owners no longer provided this benefit. Workers had to find their own lodging. Because of low wages, most workers ended up living in slums near the factories.

Attempts to Organize

By the 1830s workers began organizing to improve working conditions. Fearing the growth of the factory system, skilled workers had formed **trade unions**—organizations of workers with the same trade, or skill. Steadily deteriorating conditions led unskilled workers to organize as well.

In the mid-1830s skilled workers in New York City staged a series of **strikes**, refusing to work to put pressure on employers. Workers struck to get higher wages and to limit their workday to 10 hours. In 1834 groups of skilled workers formed the General Trades Union of New York.

The Right to Strike

In the early 1800s, going on strike was illegal. Striking workers could be punished by the law, or they could be fired from their jobs. In 1842 a Massachusetts court ruled that workers did have the right to strike. It would be many years, however, before workers received other legal rights.

African American Workers

Slavery had largely disappeared from the North by 1820. However, racial **prejudice**—an unfair opinion not based on facts—and **discrimination**—unfair treatment of a group—remained in Northern states. For example, in 1821 New York eliminated the requirement that white men had to own property in order to vote—yet few African Americans were allowed to vote. Both Rhode Island and Pennsylvania passed laws prohibiting free African Americans from voting.

Most communities would not allow free African Americans to attend public schools and barred them from public facilities as well. Often African Americans were forced into segregated, or separate, schools and hospitals.

Another damaging effect of prejudice in the North was that African Americans had to take the lowest-paying jobs. William J. Brown, a free African American who lived in Rhode Island in the 1830s, later wrote:

> "To drive carriages, carry a market basket after the boss, and brush his boots . . . was as high as a colored man could rise."

HISTORY AND ART

***Young Man in White Apron* by John Mackie Falconer** The artist of this painting was known for his watercolors depicting New York City workers such as this African American clerk. **How did prejudice affect the lives of African Americans in the North?**

CHAPTER 13
Section 2, 390–394

2 TEACH

L1 Synthesizing Information As students read the section, have them answer the following questions. (1) Why could workers of the mid-1800s be called wage slaves? *(poor conditions in factories, no laws protecting safety or limiting hours, little or no choice but to accept their lot)* (2) What similar experiences did women, African Americans, and immigrants face? *(discrimination and prejudice)* (3) What was the agenda of the Know-Nothing Party? *(anti-Catholic and anti-immigrant)*

Guided Reading Activity 13–2

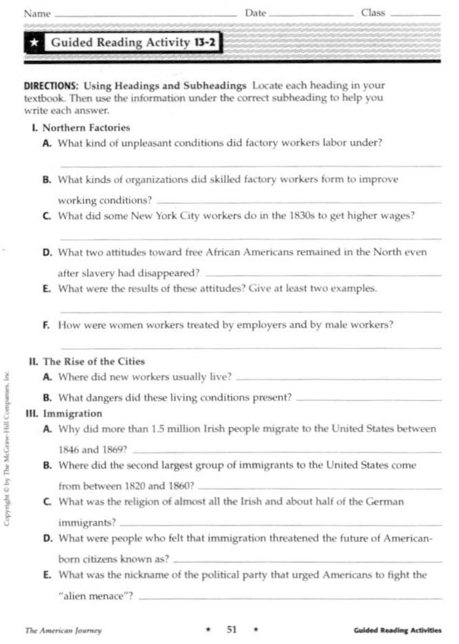

Name ______ Date ______ Class ______

★ Guided Reading Activity 13-2

DIRECTIONS: Using Headings and Subheadings Locate each heading in your textbook. Then use the information under the correct subheading to help you write each answer.

I. Northern Factories
- **A.** What kind of unpleasant conditions did factory workers labor under? ______
- **B.** What kinds of organizations did skilled factory workers form to improve working conditions? ______
- **C.** What did some New York City workers do in the 1830s to get higher wages? ______
- **D.** What two attitudes toward free African Americans remained in the North even after slavery had disappeared? ______
- **E.** What were the results of these attitudes? Give at least two examples. ______
- **F.** How were women workers treated by employers and by male workers? ______

II. The Rise of the Cities
- **A.** Where did new workers usually live? ______
- **B.** What dangers did these living conditions present? ______

III. Immigration
- **A.** Why did more than 1.5 million Irish people migrate to the United States between 1846 and 1869? ______
- **B.** Where did the second largest group of immigrants to the United States come from between 1820 and 1860? ______
- **C.** What was the religion of almost all the Irish and about half of the German immigrants? ______
- **D.** What were people who felt that immigration threatened the future of American-born citizens known as? ______
- **E.** What was the nickname of the political party that urged Americans to fight the "alien menace"? ______

The American Journey ★ 51 ★ **Guided Reading Activities**

HISTORY AND ART John Falconer (1820–1903) was born in Scotland and emigrated to the United States in 1836. He worked in oils as well as watercolors and made etchings of his own works and of those of other artists.
Answer: *Most African Americans could not vote or attend public schools, they were barred from other public facilities, forced to use segregated schools and hospitals, and could get only low-paying jobs.*

COOPERATIVE LEARNING ACTIVITY

Writing Letters to the Editor Organize the class into small groups, each of which is to write a letter to the editor describing the problems facing one of the groups discussed in the section—factory workers, African Americans, women, city dwellers, and immigrants. The letters should be written from the standpoint of one imaginary family or individual, and should make suggestions for ways to improve conditions. Before the letter is written, group members should brainstorm ideas for making the letters realistic and persuasive. One group member should act as recorder and another can use the group's ideas in writing the letter. Before presenting the letter to the class, the group should critique it and revise it as necessary.

CHAPTER 13
Section 2, 390–394

NATIONAL GEOGRAPHIC SOCIETY

VIDEODISC
GTV: The American People: Fabric of a Nation

Side 2, Chapter 3
Title: *At Home in America*
Subject: The immigrant experience of the Irish
Ask: **According to the narrator, what are the only kinds of jobs Irish men could get?** *(laying rails and building roads)*

Linking PAST & PRESENT

Women in the Labor Force The women who worked in New England's textile mills were the first American women to work in factories. Today women make up 46 percent of the total labor force. Inequality still exists, however. On average, women earn about 76 cents for every dollar men earn.

What?Where?When?Who?

City Life Despite the problems, urban life had much to offer. Perhaps the biggest attraction was the prospect of finding work. To many people from rural America and Europe, even a low-paying factory job seemed like an opportunity to move ahead. Cities were also exciting places where a newcomer could meet all kinds of people and be part of the urban hustle and bustle.

A few African Americans in the North became well-to-do businesspeople. Henry Boyd owned a furniture manufacturing company in Cincinnati, Ohio. In 1827 Samuel Cornish and John B. Russwurm founded *Freedom's Journal,* the first African American newspaper, in New York City. In 1845 Macon B. Allen became the first African American licensed to practice law in the United States. The overwhelming majority of African Americans, however, were extremely poor. Although better off than the enslaved people of the South, Northern African Americans still suffered the cruel and lasting effects of discrimination.

Women Workers

Women had played a major role in the developing mill and factory systems. However, employers discriminated against women, paying them less than male workers. When men began to form unions, they excluded women. Male workers wanted women kept out of the workplace so that more jobs would be available for men.

Some female workers attempted to organize in the 1830s and 1840s. In Massachusetts the Lowell Female Labor Reform Organization, founded by a weaver named **Sarah G. Bagley,** petitioned the state legislature for a 10-hour day in 1845. Because most of the petition's signers were women, the legislature did not consider the petition.

Most of the early efforts by women to achieve equality and justice in the workplace failed. They paved the way, however, for later movements to correct the injustices against female workers.

The Rise of Cities

The growth of factories went hand in hand with the growth of Northern cities. People looking for work flocked to the cities, where most of the factories were located. In 1840, 14 percent of the population of the Northern states lived in cities. By 1860 that figure had grown to 26 percent. The population of New York City, the nation's largest city, reached 1 million, and Philadelphia, more than 500,000 in 1860.

City life could be difficult and dangerous. Unable to afford decent housing, new workers usually lived in overcrowded, run-down buildings with no plumbing or heat. Disease spread quickly in such conditions. Fire was also a constant danger in the closely spaced wooden buildings.

Immigration

Immigration—the movement of people into a country—to the United States increased dramatically between 1840 and 1860. American manufacturers welcomed the tide of immigrants, many of whom were willing to work for long hours and for low pay.

Newcomers From Ireland

The largest group of immigrants to the United States at this time traveled across the Atlantic from Ireland. Between 1846 and 1860, more than 1.5 million Irish immigrants arrived in the country, settling mostly in the Northeast.

The Irish migration to the United States was brought on by a terrible potato famine. A **famine** is an extreme shortage of food. Potatoes were the mainstay of the Irish diet, eaten for breakfast, lunch, and dinner. When a devastating blight, or disease, destroyed Irish potato crops in the 1840s, starvation struck the country. More than 1 million people died.

Although most of the immigrants had been farmers in Ireland, they were too poor to buy land

Footnotes to History

Birth of the Chip In 1853 a diner at an elegant resort in Sarasota Springs, New York, refused an order of potatoes that were "too thick." The chef, Native American George Crum, sliced and fried a batch so thin that they could not be picked up with a fork. The guest loved the crisp potatoes, and the "potato chip" was born!

MULTIPLE LEARNING STYLES

Visual/Spatial Make library resources available to students to use for reference in creating collages showing living and working conditions discussed in the section. Materials needed are a piece of cardboard 9" X 12" or larger, newspapers, magazines, tissue paper, foil, gift wrap, white glue, paintbrush, waxed paper, and scissors. Have students experiment with cutting and tearing shapes out of the various materials (for example, tear a shape of a factory from the newspaper). Have students arrange the shapes on the cardboard until they are satisfied with the colors and positions. Thin the white glue with water and tell students to use the paintbrush to spread it on the pieces of the collage. Cover the completed and glued collage with waxed paper and weigh it down with books to keep the shapes flat as they dry. **L1,** ELL

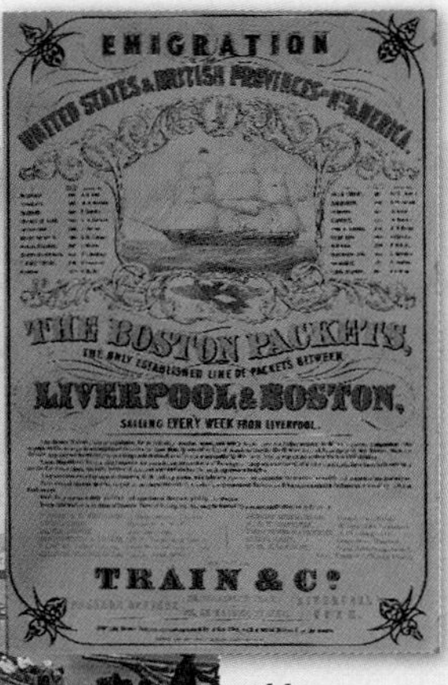

Ship advertisement

Picturing HISTORY

Immigrants land at New York Harbor after a long ocean voyage from Ireland. **Why did many Irish immigrants come to the United States during the mid-1800s?**

in the United States. For this reason many Irish immigrants took low-paying factory jobs in Northern cities. The men who came from Ireland worked in factories or performed manual labor, such as digging ditches and working on the railroads. The women, who accounted for almost half of the immigrants, became servants and factory workers. By 1850 one-third of all workers in Boston were Irish.

German Immigrants

The second-largest group of immigrants in the United States between 1820 and 1860 came from Germany. Some sought work and opportunity. Others had left their homes because of the failure of a democratic revolution in Germany in 1848.

Between 1848 and 1860, more than 1 million German immigrants—mostly men—settled in the United States. Many arrived with enough money to buy farms or open their own businesses. They prospered in many parts of the country, founding their own communities and self-help organizations. Some German immigrants settled in New York and Pennsylvania, but many moved to the Midwest and the western territories.

The Impact of Immigration

The immigrants who came to the United States between 1820 and 1860 changed the character of the country. These people brought their languages, customs, religions, and ways of life with them. Various features soon filtered into American culture.

Before the early 1800s, the majority of immigrants to America had been either Protestants from Great Britain or Africans brought forcibly to America as slaves. At the time, the country had relatively few Catholics, and most of these lived around Baltimore, New Orleans, and St. Augustine. Most of the Irish immigrants and about one-half of the German immigrants were Roman Catholics.

Many Catholic immigrants settled in cities of the Northeast. The church gave the newcomers more than a source of spiritual guidance. It also provided a center for the community life of the immigrants.

The German immigrants brought their language as well as their religion. When they settled, they lived in their own communities, founded German-language publications, and established musical societies.

Immigrants Face Prejudice

In the 1830s and 1840s, anti-immigrant feelings rose. Some Americans feared that immigrants were changing the character of the United States too much.

People opposed to immigration were known as **nativists** because they felt that immigration threatened the future of "native"—American-

Making Connections Activity

Daily Life When the first census was taken in 1790, 95 percent of Americans lived on farms. By 1850 the population was 85 percent rural. Today our population is largely urban and suburban. Have students find the information they need to create a graph showing the changing nature of the United States population from 1790 to the present. One likely source is *Historical Statistics of the United States,* a two-volume reference work available in most libraries. Students may work in small groups, each taking a different block of time to show on a graph. Have each group use the same scale, so that changes are apparent when the graphs are placed side by side. **L2**

Picturing HISTORY So many Irish people immigrated to New York that it soon became the city with the largest Irish population in the world. In just a few decades, more Irish people lived in America than lived in Ireland. **Ask: Why did most Irish immigrants live in cities?** *(They were too poor to buy land for farming.)*
Answer: *to avoid starvation caused by the potato blight in Ireland*

Political Cartoons, *Native Americans and a Nation of Immigrants*

3 ASSESS

Assign Section 2 Review as homework or as an in-class activity.

Use **Chapter Challenger Interactive Review Software** to review Section 2.

Section Quiz 13–2

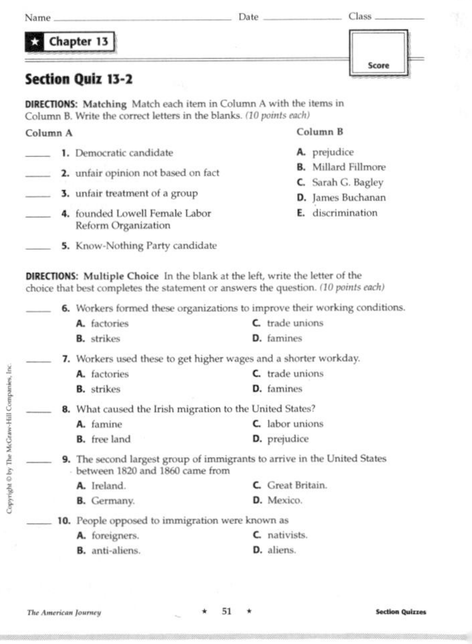

Name ________ Date ________ Class ________

Chapter 13

Score

Section Quiz 13-2

DIRECTIONS: Matching Match each item in Column A with the items in Column B. Write the correct letters in the blanks. *(10 points each)*

Column A	Column B
____ 1. Democratic candidate	A. prejudice
____ 2. unfair opinion not based on fact	B. Millard Fillmore
____ 3. unfair treatment of a group	C. Sarah G. Bagley
____ 4. founded Lowell Female Labor Reform Organization	D. James Buchanan
____ 5. Know-Nothing Party candidate	E. discrimination

DIRECTIONS: Multiple Choice In the blank at the left, write the letter of the choice that best completes the statement or answers the question. *(10 points each)*

____ 6. Workers formed these organizations to improve their working conditions.
A. factories C. trade unions
B. strikes D. famines

____ 7. Workers used these to get higher wages and a shorter workday.
A. factories C. trade unions
B. strikes D. famines

____ 8. What caused the Irish migration to the United States?
A. famine C. labor unions
B. free land D. prejudice

____ 9. The second largest group of immigrants to arrive in the United States between 1820 and 1860 came from
A. Ireland. C. Great Britain.
B. Germany. D. Mexico.

____ 10. People opposed to immigration were known as
A. foreigners. C. nativists.
B. anti-aliens. D. aliens.

The American Journey ★ 51 ★ **Section Quizzes**

CHAPTER 13
Section 2, 390–394

Graph Study

Answers
1. Ireland
2. about 220,000

Reteaching Activity 13–2

Name ______ Date ______ Class ______

★ Reteaching Activity 13-2

DIRECTIONS: Organizing Facts Write the letter of each item in the Fact Bank in the appropriate section of the chart. Some items fit in more than one category.

The North's People

Factory Working Conditions	Trade Unions	African American Workers
Women Workers	**City Life**	**Immigrants**

★FACT BANK

A. groups of skilled workers who feared the growth of factory system
B. overcrowded buildings
C. suffered discrimination
D. forced into segregated schools
E. stifling hot in summer
F. constant danger of fire
G. 1.5 million Irish people
H. petitioned for a 10-hour day in 1845
I. staged strikes for higher wages and to limit workday
J. risk of quick spread of disease
K. average workdays of 11.4 hours
L. more than 1 million Germans
M. were not allowed to vote
N. freezing cold in winter
O. paid less than white males
P. brought their languages, customs, religions, and ways of life

DIRECTIONS: Essay Answer the following questions on a separate sheet of paper.
1. How did the factory system change the way Americans worked?
2. Discrimination affected many groups of Americans during the first half of the 1800s. Who were these groups and how were they discriminated against?

The American Journey ★ 51 ★ **Reteaching Activities**

Enrichment Activity 13–2

Name ______ Date ______ Class ______

★ Enrichment Activity 13-2

Immigration

In the decades before 1820, about 60,000 immigrants had been arriving each year to the United States. Between 1820 and 1830, a total of about 152,000 immigrants arrived. Study the graph of immigration from 1831 to 1860.

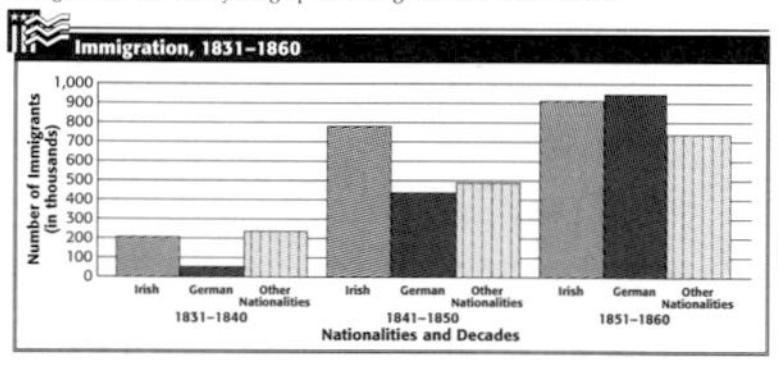

DIRECTIONS: Interpreting a Graph Answer the following questions.
1. About how many Irish immigrants arrived between 1841 and 1850? ______
2. In which decade did German immigration exceed Irish immigration? ______
3. Approximately what was the total number of immigrants who arrived between 1841 and 1850? ______
4. In which decade was the total immigration about eight times that of the average in the decades before 1820? ______
5. About how many more people of Irish descent arrived in 1851 to 1860 than people of all other nationalities? ______
6. Describe the trends in immigration during this time period as shown by the graph.

Activity **DIRECTIONS:** Use the media center to learn more about immigrants. How many immigrants came to the United States in recent years? Where did they come from? Use the electronic card catalog, a statistical abstract, or atlas to find more information about immigration statistics. Then prepare a graph to illustrate modern immigration to the United States.

The American Journey ★ 51 ★ **Enrichment Activities**

4 CLOSE

Ask students to explain why nativists could be said to have forgotten their own origins.

Immigration, 1820-1860

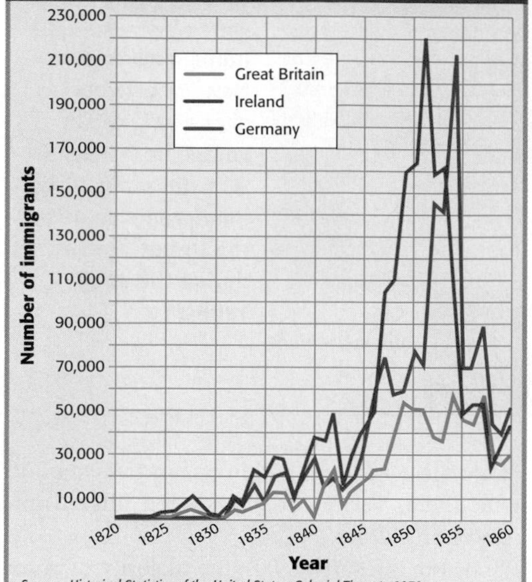

Source: *Historical Statistics of the United States: Colonial Times to 1970.*

Graph Study

Immigration to the United States increased dramatically between 1820 and 1860.
1. Which country provided the most immigrants?
2. **Analyzing Information** What was the highest number of German immigrants before 1855?

born—citizens. Some nativists accused immigrants of taking jobs from "real" Americans and were angry that immigrants would work for lower wages. Others accused the newcomers of bringing crime and disease to American cities. Immigrants who lived in crowded slums served as likely targets of this kind of prejudice.

A New Political Party

The nativists formed secret anti-Catholic societies, and in the 1850s they joined to form a new political party: the American Party. Because members of nativist groups often answered questions about their organization with the statement "I know nothing," their party came to be known as the **Know-Nothing Party.**

The Know-Nothings urged Americans to fight the "alien menace." They called for stricter citizenship laws—extending the immigrants' waiting period for citizenship from 5 to 14 years—and wanted to ban foreign-born citizens from holding office. In 1856 the Know-Nothings supported former president **Millard Fillmore** as their presidential candidate. He lost to the Democratic candidate, **James Buchanan.**

In the mid-1850s the Know-Nothing movement split into a Northern branch and a Southern branch over the question of slavery. At this time the slavery issue was also dividing the Northern and Southern states of the nation.

Section 2 Review

Checking for Understanding
1. ***Identify*** Sarah G. Bagley, Know-Nothing Party.
2. ***Define*** trade union, strike, prejudice, discrimination, famine, nativist.
3. ***List*** three reasons workers formed unions in the 1830s.

Reviewing Themes
4. **Geography and History** How did German and Irish immigrants differ in where they settled?

Critical Thinking
5. **Making Inferences** How do you think nativists would have defined a "real" American?

Activity

Making a Poster Design a campaign poster for a Know-Nothing Party candidate.

Section 2 Review Answers

1. Sarah G. Bagley, 392; Know-Nothing Party, 394
2. The words are defined in the Glossary.
3. Any three: to protest unsafe working conditions, long hours, and unfair wages and to protect themselves from the ramifications of a growing factory system
4. Irish immigrants settled mostly in cities in the Northeast. They were too poor to buy land, so they took factory jobs. German immigrants settled in New York, Pennsylvania, the Midwest, and the western territories. Many arrived with money to buy farms and open businesses.
5. a Protestant born in the United States

Activity Posters should reflect the nativist views of the party.

Social Studies
SKILL BUILDER

Reading a Circle Graph

Have you ever watched someone dish out pieces of pie? When the pie is cut evenly, everybody gets the same size slice. If one slice is cut a little larger, however, someone else gets a smaller piece. A **circle graph** is like a pie cut in slices. Often, a circle graph is called a *pie chart*.

Learning the Skill

In a circle graph, the complete circle represents a whole group—or 100 percent. The circle is divided into "slices," or wedge-shaped sections representing parts of the whole.

Suppose, for example, that 25 percent of your friends watch five hours of television per day. On a circle graph representing hours of TV watching, 25 percent of the circle would represent friends who watch five hours.

To read a circle graph, follow these steps:

- Read the title of the graph to find out what the subject is.
- Study the labels or key to determine what the parts or "slices" represent.
- Compare the parts of the graph to draw conclusions about the subject.
- When two or more circle graphs appear together, read their titles and labels. Then compare the graphs for similarities and differences.

Practicing the Skill

Read the graphs on this page, then answer the following questions.

1. What do the four graphs represent?
2. What percentage of workers were in agriculture in 1840? In 1870?

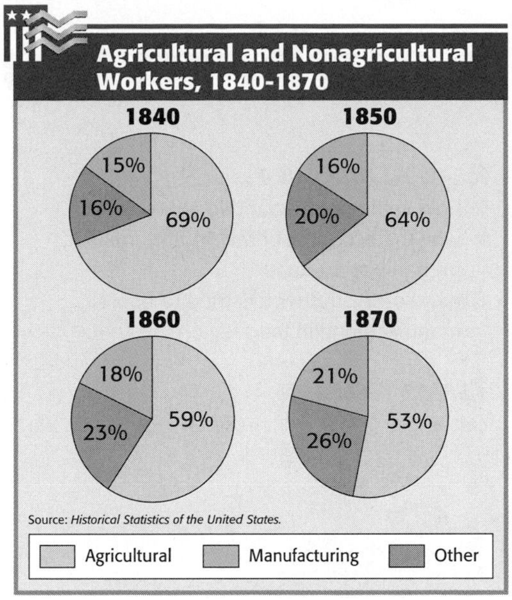

3. During what decade did the percentage of workers in manufacturing increase the most?
4. In what year did manufacturing workers surpass 20 percent?
5. In what year did agricultural workers make up 59 percent of all workers?
6. What can you conclude from the graphs about the relationship between manufacturing and agricultural workers from 1840 to 1870?

Applying the Skill

Reading a Circle Graph Find a circle graph related to the economy in a newspaper or magazine. Compare its sections. Then draw a conclusion about the economy.

Social Studies
SKILL BUILDER

TEACH

Reading a Circle Graph

This skill teaches students how to read a circle graph. A circle graph is most useful for showing parts of a whole, rather than a progression or changes over time. When you have several graphs together, as on this page, you can do both.

If you would like students to make their own circle graphs, you may wish to review the use of a protractor. To find the size of the angle of a wedge, students must multiply the part number by 360 and divide that figure by the total. For example, suppose students were to make a graph showing hair color in a class of 30, in which 6 students have black hair, 14 have brown hair, 8 have blonde hair, and 2 are redheads. To find the angle for black-haired students, multiply 6 by 360 (2,160) and divide that figure by 30, the total number of students (2,160 ÷ 30 = 72). The angle should be 72°.

Additional Practice

Chapter Skills Activity 13

ANSWERS TO PRACTICING THE SKILL

1. agricultural and non-agricultural workers in 1840, 1850, 1860, and 1870
2. 69 percent, 53 percent
3. 1860s
4. 1870
5. 1860
6. number of manufacturing workers increased, number of agricultural workers decreased (or agricultural workers made up a larger, though decreasing, percentage of workers than non-agricultural workers)

Applying the Skill Students should correctly analyze an economic circle graph using the steps outlined in "Learning the Skill."

1 FOCUS

BELLRINGER
Motivational Activity

Before taking roll at the beginning of the class period, project Section Focus Transparency 13–3 and have students answer the questions. Discuss students' responses.

This activity is also available as a blackline master.

Section Focus Transparency 13–3

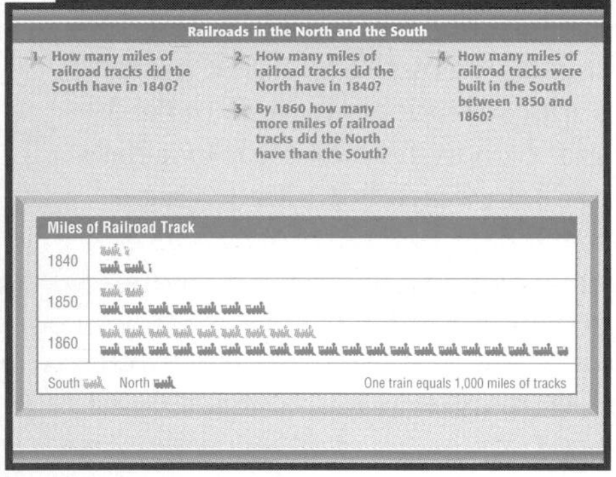

Vocabulary Precheck

Have students define *capital* in their own words.

Use the **Vocabulary PuzzleMaker** to create crossword and word search puzzles.

Section Theme
Science and Technology

A combination of new technology, favorable climate, high demand, and drawbacks from other cash crops led to the cotton boom in the Deep South.

Activity Have students find what the favorable climate was, what the new technology was, and what the drawbacks were for other crops. *(wet springs and summers, dry autumns; cotton gin; tobacco had varying demand and wore out soil quickly; rice needed wet climate; sugarcane needed large investment in irrigation canals and machinery)*

1780 — 1820 — 1860

1793 Eli Whitney invents cotton gin

1800s Removal of Native Americans spurs expansion of cotton production

1860 The South remains largely rural and dependent on cotton

Section 3

Southern Cotton Kingdom

READ TO DISCOVER . . .
- how settlement expanded in the South.
- why the economy of the South remained primarily agricultural.
- why some Southerners tried to boost manufacturing in their region.

TERMS TO LEARN

cotton gin   capital

The Storyteller

Cotton was "king" in the South before 1860. "Look which way you will, you see it; and see it moving," wrote a visitor to Mobile, Alabama. "Keel boats, ships, brigs, schooners, wharves, stores, and press-houses, all appeared to be full." Cotton was also the main topic of conversation: "I believe that in the three days that I was there . . . I must have heard the word *cotton* pronounced more than 3,000 times."

Stem of cotton

In 1790 the South seemed to be an underdeveloped agricultural region with little prospect for future growth. Most Southerners lived along the Atlantic coast in Maryland, Virginia, and North Carolina in what came to be known as the **Upper South.**

By 1850 the South had changed. Its population had spread inland into the **Deep South**—a band of states spreading from Georgia through South Carolina, Alabama, Mississippi, Louisiana, Missouri, Arkansas, and Texas. The economy of the South was thriving. Slavery, which was disappearing from the North, grew stronger than ever in the South. Cotton had transformed the stagnant economy of the South into a prosperous, robust economy.

Rise of the Cotton Kingdom

Cotton had not always been the South's leading cash crop. In colonial times tobacco was the most profitable crop in Virginia. Georgia and South Carolina produced ever-increasing quantities of rice and indigo.

Both tobacco and rice had drawbacks. Tobacco depended on foreign markets, so its price varied wildly. Tobacco also wore out land quickly because it stripped the soil of important nutrients. Rice could not be grown in the dry climate of inland areas.

Sugarcane, another Southern crop, was raised in southeastern Louisiana. To grow sugarcane,

SECTION RESOURCES

Reproducible Masters
- Reproducible Lesson Plan 13–3
- Guided Reading Activity 13–3
- Section Quiz 13–3
- Reteaching Activity 13–3
- Enrichment Activity 13–3

Transparencies
- Section Focus Transparency 13–3

Multimedia
- Vocabulary PuzzleMaker
- Chapter Challenger Interactive Review Software
- Testmaker
- GTV: The American People: Fabric of a Nation

farmers needed to invest large sums of money in irrigation canals and machinery. Sugarcane was therefore considered a "rich man's crop."

The Cotton Gin

The growth of the British textile industry in the late 1700s had created a huge demand for cotton. Unfortunately cotton was difficult to process. After harvest, workers had to painstakingly separate the plant's sticky seeds from the cotton fibers.

Cotton production was revolutionized when **Eli Whitney** invented the cotton gin in 1793. The **cotton gin** was a machine that removed seeds from cotton fibers, dramatically increasing the amount of cotton that could be processed. A worker could clean 50 pounds of cotton a day with the machine—instead of 1 pound by hand. Furthermore the gin was small enough for one person to carry from place to place.

Whitney's invention had far-reaching consequences for the South. The cotton gin led to the demand for more slaves. Because the cotton gin processed cotton fibers so quickly, farmers wanted to grow more cotton. Many Southern planters relied on slave labor to perform these tasks.

New Lands for Cotton

The removal of Native Americans from the Southeast in the early 1800s opened the way for expanding cotton production across the Deep

TECHNOLOGY AND HISTORY

The Cotton Gin

In 1793 Eli Whitney visited Catherine Greene, a Georgia plantation owner. She asked him to build a device that removed the seeds from cotton pods. Whitney called the machine the cotton gin—"gin" being short for engine. **How did the invention of the cotton gin affect slavery?**

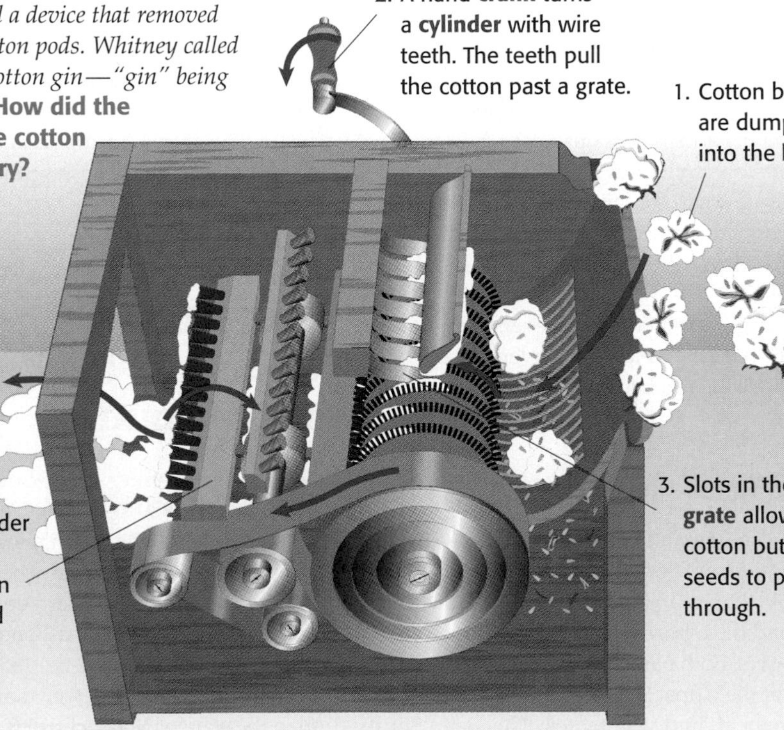

COOPERATIVE LEARNING ACTIVITY

Researching Developments Form four or five classroom groups with the goal of having each group research and provide written and oral reports on subjects such as the development of the cotton gin, Eli Whitney, growing cotton today, products made from cotton, and so on. Students should divide tasks, such as organizing, researching, illustrating, and presenting, according to the skills of group members.

CHAPTER 13
Section 3, 396–400

2 TEACH

L1 Finding Main Points Have students turn the "Read to Discover" items into questions and find the main points that answer those questions.

TECHNOLOGY AND HISTORY

More About . . .

The Cotton Gin The hand-cranked model of the cotton gin that Eli Whitney made increased productivity from one pound (0.5 kg) of cotton cleaned per day to 50 pounds (23 kg). A gin operated by waterpower increased the total to 1,000 pounds (454 kg) a day.

Cotton production proved to be ideally suited to the use of enslaved labor. The planting, hoeing, picking, and ginning all required manual labor, and enslaved persons provided a cheap source. Furthermore, most of the field work was done in groups and could thus be easily supervised. ***Answer to Caption:*** *increased the amount of cotton that could be processed, so people wanted to grow more cotton and wanted more slaves to plant and harvest it*

Guided Reading Activity 13–3

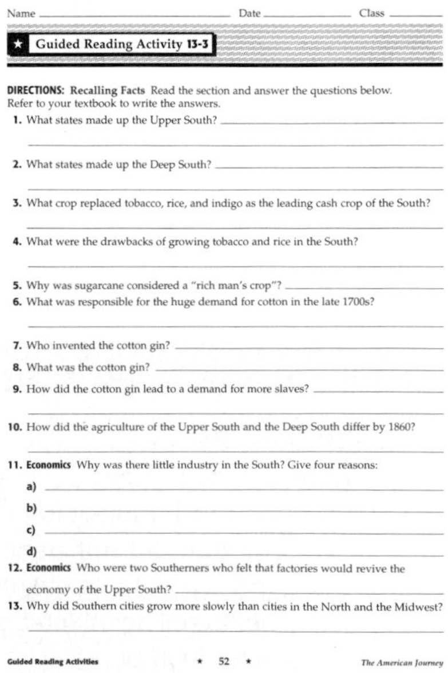
Name ________ Date ________ Class ________

★ Guided Reading Activity 13-3

DIRECTIONS: Recalling Facts Read the section and answer the questions below. Refer to your textbook to write the answers.

1. What states made up the Upper South?
2. What states made up the Deep South?
3. What crop replaced tobacco, rice, and indigo as the leading cash crop of the South?
4. What were the drawbacks of growing tobacco and rice in the South?
5. Why was sugarcane considered a "rich man's crop"?
6. What was responsible for the huge demand for cotton in the late 1700s?
7. Who invented the cotton gin?
8. What was the cotton gin?
9. How did the cotton gin lead to a demand for more slaves?
10. How did the agriculture of the Upper South and the Deep South differ by 1860?
11. **Economics** Why was there little industry in the South? Give four reasons:
    a)
    b)
    c)
    d)
12. **Economics** Who were two Southerners who felt that factories would revive the economy of the Upper South?
13. Why did Southern cities grow more slowly than cities in the North and the Midwest?

Copyright © by The McGraw-Hill Companies, Inc.

Guided Reading Activities ★ 52 ★ *The American Journey*

Graph Study

Answers

1. 3,841,000 bales
2. 4 million

Graph Skills Practice

Reading a Graph What happened to the price of a field slave between 1800 and 1860? *(tripled, went from $600 to $1,800)*

What?Where?When?Who?

Illegal Slave Trade Although the legal slave trade ended on January 1, 1808, the illegal trade in slaves continued to flourish. As many as 250,000 enslaved Africans entered the United States from abroad between 1808 and 1860. They were smuggled in by Northern shipowners.

NATIONAL GEOGRAPHIC SOCIETY

VIDEODISC
GTV: The American People: Fabric of a Nation

Side 1, Chapter 8
Title: *The Journey*
Subject: Slavery in early America
Ask: **What linked Africans from different backgrounds in America?** *(the burdens of slavery and the struggle for survival)*

Who?What?Where?When?

Eli Whitney Because he delayed patenting the cotton gin, Whitney did not make much money from it. Catherine Greene did not benefit either. Financial problems eventually forced her to sell her plantation, Mulberry Grove, in 1800.

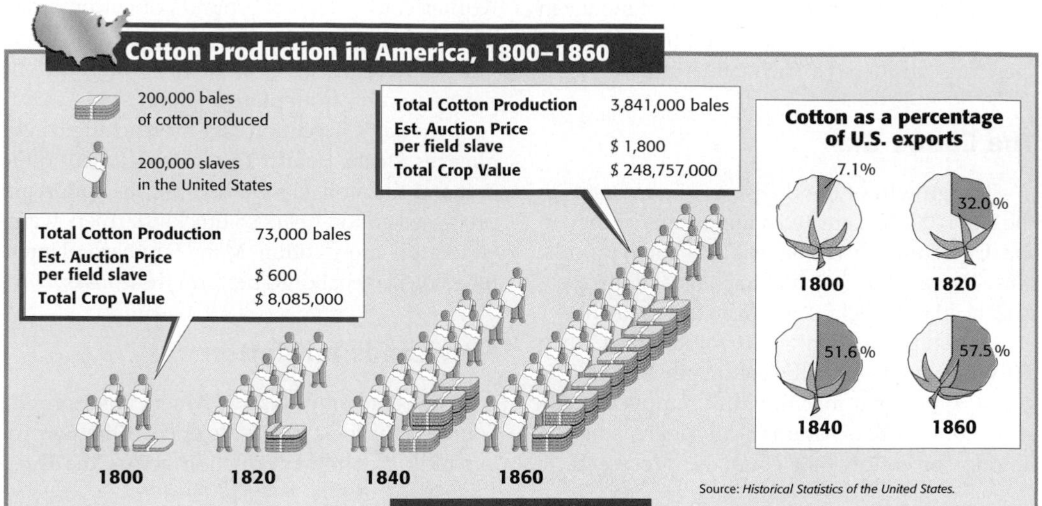

Graph Study

As cotton increased in value, the number of slaves grew dramatically.

1. About how many bales of cotton were produced in 1860?
2. **Analyzing Information** About how many slaves lived in the United States in 1860?

South. Settlers swept into the regions of Alabama and Mississippi after 1815.

With wet springs and summers and dry autumns, the Deep South was well suited for cotton production. Farmers without cotton gins or slaves could make a profit growing cotton even on small farms. They could succeed without actually owning a cotton gin because gins could be rented, and enslaved African Americans could be hired from slaveholders.

On large plantations, however, cotton growing went hand in hand with slavery. Using slave labor, the planters could plant and tend vast fields of cotton.

Cotton Rules the Deep South

Intense demand for cotton in Great Britain kept the price of cotton high in the years before 1860. By that year the economies of the Deep South and the Upper South had developed in different ways. Both parts of the South were agricultural, but the Upper South still produced tobacco, hemp, wheat, and vegetables. The Deep South was committed to cotton and, in some areas, to rice and sugarcane.

The value of enslaved people increased because of their key role in producing cotton and sugar. The Upper South became a center for the sale and transport of enslaved people throughout the region.

Economics

Industry's Limited Role in the South

The economy of the South prospered between 1820 and 1860. Unlike the industrial North, however, the South remained overwhelmingly rural, and its economy became increasingly different from the Northern economy. The South accounted for only a small percentage of the nation's manufacturing in the 1850s. In fact, the entire South produced fewer manufactured goods than the state of Massachusetts.

MULTIPLE LEARNING STYLES

Verbal/Linguistic The expansion of cotton growing and slavery into new states in the Deep South caused great hardship for enslaved African Americans. Planters there bought slaves from slaveholders in older slave states, since they could no longer legally import slaves from Africa or the West Indies. Between 1810 and 1860 more than 2 million African Americans were forced to move from North Carolina and the Chesapeake—areas that were ill-suited for growing cotton—to the new slave states along the Gulf of Mexico and the Mississippi River. That forced migration separated family members and caused untold suffering among African Americans. Have students imagine themselves in the position of an African American of the time and write a poem or diary entry expressing their pain at being separated from friends and family. **L2**

Barriers to Industry

Why was there little industry in the South? One reason was the boom in cotton sales. Because agriculture was so profitable, Southerners remained committed to farming rather than starting new businesses.

Another stumbling block was the lack of **capital**—money to invest in businesses—in the South. To develop industries required money, but many Southerners had their wealth invested in land and slaves. Planters would have had to sell slaves to raise the money to build factories. Most wealthy Southerners were unwilling to do this. They believed that an economy based on cotton and slavery would continue to prosper, and they saw no reason to risk their resources in new industrial ventures.

In addition the market for manufactured goods in the South was smaller than it was in the North. A large portion of the Southern population consisted of enslaved people with no money to buy merchandise. So the limited local market discouraged industries from developing.

Yet another reason for the lack of industry in the South is that some Southerners simply did not want industry to flourish there. One Alabama politician summed up the Southerners' point of view this way:

> "We want no manufactures; we desire no trading, no mechanical or manufacturing classes. As long as we have our rice, our sugar, our tobacco and our cotton, we can command wealth to purchase all we want."

Southern Factories

While most Southerners felt confident about the future of the cotton economy, some leaders wanted to develop industry in the region. These promoters of industry believed that, by remaining rural and committed to cotton production, the South was becoming dependent on the North for manufactured goods. These Southerners also argued that factories would revive the economy of the Upper South, which was less prosperous than the cotton states.

One Southerner who shared this view was **William Gregg,** a merchant from Charleston, South Carolina. After touring New England's

HISTORY AND ART

***Slave Market in Richmond, Virginia* by Eyre Crowe** A British observer, Crowe showed the dignity of enslaved people. His work, however, fails to show the inhumanity of the slave market. **What role did the Upper South play in promoting slavery?**

Making Connections Activity

Music One of the most popular composers of the times was Stephen Foster, who became famous for his songs idealizing the South. Foster used African American melodies to create lively songs. He wrote mostly for the popular minstrel shows, which incorporated the songs, dances, and instruments of African Americans (although the shows used white actors in black facepaint and depicted African Americans in a way that we consider demeaning today). Present some of his songs for the class to listen to. Then discuss how the songs paint a rosy picture of the South that was in stark contrast with the actual conditions. **L1, ELL**

3 ASSESS

Assign Section 3 Review as homework or as an in-class activity.

Use **Chapter Challenger Interactive Review Software** to review Section 3.

Section Quiz 13–3

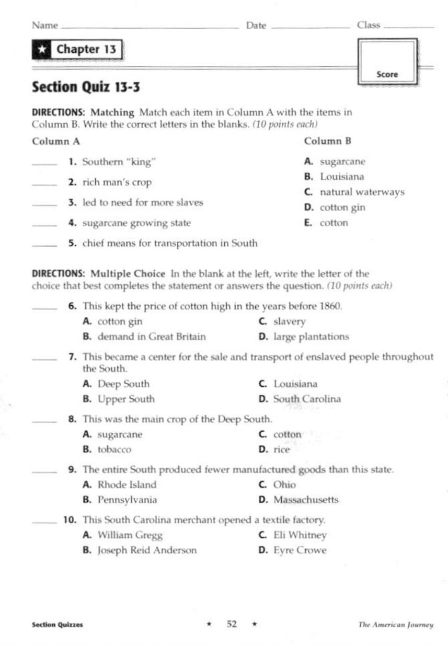

Name ______ Date ______ Class ______

Chapter 13

Score

Section Quiz 13-3

DIRECTIONS: Matching Match each item in Column A with the items in Column B. Write the correct letters in the blanks. *(10 points each)*

Column A	Column B
____ 1. Southern "king"	A. sugarcane
____ 2. rich man's crop	B. Louisiana
____ 3. led to need for more slaves	C. natural waterways
____ 4. sugarcane growing state	D. cotton gin
____ 5. chief means for transportation in South	E. cotton

DIRECTIONS: Multiple Choice In the blank at the left, write the letter of the choice that best completes the statement or answers the question. *(10 points each)*

____ 6. This kept the price of cotton high in the years before 1860.
A. cotton gin C. slavery
B. demand in Great Britain D. large plantations

____ 7. This became a center for the sale and transport of enslaved people throughout the South.
A. Deep South C. Louisiana
B. Upper South D. South Carolina

____ 8. This was the main crop of the Deep South.
A. sugarcane C. cotton
B. tobacco D. rice

____ 9. The entire South produced fewer manufactured goods than this state.
A. Rhode Island C. Ohio
B. Pennsylvania D. Massachusetts

____ 10. This South Carolina merchant opened a textile factory.
A. William Gregg C. Eli Whitney
B. Joseph Reid Anderson D. Eyre Crowe

Section Quizzes ★ 52 ★ *The American Journey*

HISTORY AND ART Although slaves, especially field hands, worked long hours and suffered harsh punishments, most masters did not make a practice of mistreating their slaves. **Why?** *(Even if masters were not moved by empathy, it made poor economic sense to harm someone who was so valuable as property.)* **Answer:** *It became the center for sale and transportation of enslaved people.*

CURRICULUM CONNECTION

WORLD HISTORY

The first government to pass a law ending slavery was Great Britain in 1772. Other countries soon followed. By the early 1860s, only two countries in the Western Hemisphere besides the United States maintained slaveholding—Brazil and Cuba.

CHAPTER 13
Section 3, 396–400

Map Study

Answers
1. Louisiana **2.** Cotton

Reteaching Activity 13–3

Name ______ Date ______ Class ______

★ Reteaching Activity 13-3

DIRECTIONS: Making Comparisons and Contrasts After each statement of fact, write the letter of a fact from the Fact Bank that makes a comparison or contrast.

1. **Fact:** In 1790 the South seemed to be an underdeveloped agricultural region with little prospect for future growth.
   Comparison or Contrast: ______
2. **Fact:** In the colonial period, tobacco was the most profitable crop in Virginia; Georgia and South Carolina produced rice and indigo.
   Comparison or Contrast: ______
3. **Fact:** In the late 1700s a worker painstakingly separated the cotton plant's sticky seeds from the cotton fibers by hand, processing about one pound of cotton a day.
   Comparison or Contrast: ______
4. **Fact:** By 1860 the Upper South still produced tobacco, hemp, wheat, and vegetables.
   Comparison or Contrast: ______
5. **Fact:** In the industrial North, large numbers of people moved to the cities to be near factories and work.
   Comparison or Contrast: ______
6. **Fact:** In the 1840s and 1850s, the North experienced a railroad boom that connected cities from the Northeast to the Midwest.
   Comparison or Contrast: ______

★FACT BANK

A. In the 1800s with the use of a cotton gin a worker could clean 50 pounds of cotton a day.
B. The South remained overwhelmingly rural with only a small percentage of the nation's industry.
C. In the mid-1800s cotton became the South's leading cash crop.
D. Southern rail lines were short and local and did not connect all parts of the region in a network.
E. At the same time, the Deep South was committed to cotton, and in some areas, rice and sugarcane.
F. By 1850 the stagnant economy of the South had been transformed into a prosperous, robust economy.

DIRECTIONS: Essay Answer the following question on a separate sheet of paper.
How did the lack of capital become a stumbling block to the growth of industry in the South?

Enrichment Activity 13–3

Name ______ Date ______ Class ______

★ Enrichment Activity 13-3

The Decade That Cotton Became King

The graph below shows cotton production for 1850 in states of the cotton belt.

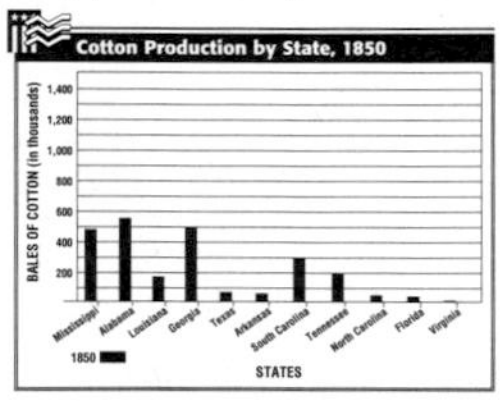

Bales of Cotton Produced, 1860	
Mississippi	1,202,507
Alabama	989,955
Louisiana	777,738
Georgia	701,840
Texas	431,463
Arkansas	367,393
South Carolina	353,412
Tennessee	296,464
North Carolina	1,455,514
Florida	65,153
Virginia	12,727

DIRECTIONS: Comparing Data The chart on the right shows cotton production for states in 1860. Add the bars for 1860 to the graph above for each state—be sure to add the new data to the map key. Compare the 1850 and 1860 data. Then answer the questions on a separate sheet of paper.

1. About how many times more cotton was produced in Virginia in 1860 than in 1850?
2. By about how much did cotton production in Mississippi increase between 1850 and 1860?
3. Did North Carolina or South Carolina show the smaller increase in production between 1850 and 1860?
4. Which states produced the most cotton in 1850 and in 1860?
5. How did cotton production in South Carolina in 1860 compare with cotton production in Georgia that year?

Activity **DIRECTIONS:** Imagine that you are a market analyst in the cotton industry. Study each state's pattern of growth in cotton production from 1850 to 1860. Then make a prediction on the basis of what you see. Explain your reasoning in a report that recommends either investing or not investing in cotton. If possible include a graph to explain your predictions. What historic event will affect your report?

4 CLOSE

The text states that cotton demand was high. It does not say that this boom will come to an end, yet you can sense that it will. **Why?**

Southern Crops in 1860

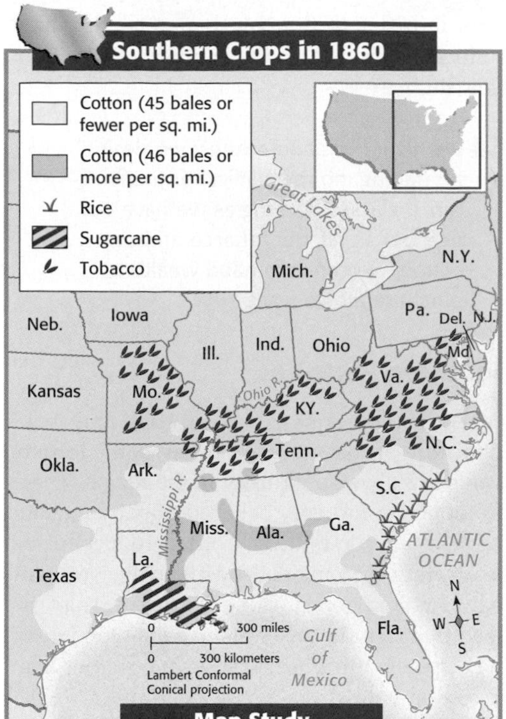

Map Study

In 1860 the Southern states were more agricultural than industrial.

1. **Location** In what state was the most sugarcane grown?
2. **Analyzing Information** What crop was grown most extensively throughout the South?

textile mills in 1844, Gregg opened his own textile factory in South Carolina.

In Richmond, Virginia, **Joseph Reid Anderson** took over the Tredegar Iron Works in the 1840s and made it one of the nation's leading producers of iron. Years later during the Civil War, Tredegar provided artillery and other iron products for the Southern forces.

The industries that Gregg and Anderson built stood as the exception rather than the rule in the South. In 1860 the region remained largely rural and dependent on cotton.

Southern Transportation

Natural waterways provided the chief means for transporting goods in the South. Most towns were located on the seacoast or along rivers. There were few canals, and roads were poor.

The railroad boom that the North experienced in the 1840s and 1850s did not take hold in the South until late in the period. Southern rail lines were short and local and did not connect all parts of the region in a network. As a result Southern cities grew more slowly than cities in the North and Midwest, where railways provided the major routes of commerce and settlement.

By 1860 only about one-third of the nation's rail lines lay within the South. The railway shortage would have devastating consequences for the South during the Civil War.

Section 3 Review

Checking for Understanding

1. ***Identify*** Eli Whitney, William Gregg, Joseph Reid Anderson.
2. ***Define*** cotton gin, capital.
3. ***Compare*** agriculture in the Upper South and Deep South.

Reviewing Themes

4. **Science and Technology** Why did the invention of the cotton gin increase the demand for enslaved Africans?

Critical Thinking

5. **Predicting Consequences** If slavery had been outlawed, how do you think it would have affected the South's economy?

Activity

Creating an Advertisement Design an advertisement to sell the newly invented cotton gin.

Section 3 Review Answers

1. Eli Whitney, 397; William Gregg, 399; Joseph Reid Anderson, 400
2. The words are defined in the Glossary.
3. Upper South produced tobacco, hemp, wheat, vegetables; Deep South dominated by cotton, also rice and sugarcane
4. Because farmers could process their cotton more quickly, they wanted to grow more. As a result, they wanted more slaves to plant and harvest the crop.
5. Paid workers would increase the price of cotton, or lower profits. More Southerners might have turned to other means to make money, such as developing businesses and industries.

Activity Ads should appeal to cotton farmers and tout the advantages of the cotton gin.

1800 — 1820 — 1840 — 1860

1808 Congress outlaws the slave trade

1831 Nat Turner leads rebellion in Virginia

1859 Arkansas orders free blacks to leave

1860 Population of Baltimore reaches 212,000

Section 4

The South's People

READ TO DISCOVER . . .

- how people lived on Southern plantations.
- what roles different people played on plantations.
- how enslaved African Americans maintained strong family and cultural ties.

TERMS TO LEARN

yeoman	overseer
tenant farmer	spiritual
fixed cost	slave code
credit	

The Storyteller

Planters gathered in the bright Savannah sunshine. They were asked to bid on a strong slave who could plow their fields. Fear and grief clouded the enslaved man's face because he had been forced to leave his wife and children. Later, he wrote this letter: "My Dear wife I [write] . . . with much regret to inform you that I am Sold to a man by the name of Peterson. . . . Give my love to my father and mother and tell them good Bye for me. And if we Shall not meet in this world, I hope to meet in heaven. My Dear wife for you and my Children my pen cannot express the [grief] I feel to be parted from you all."

Plow

Popular novels and films often portray the South before 1860 as a land of stately plantations owned by rich white slaveholders. In reality most white Southerners were either small farmers without slaves or planters with a handful of slaves. Only a few planters could afford the many enslaved Africans and the lavish mansions shown in fictional accounts of the Old South. Most white Southerners fit into one of four categories: yeomen, tenant farmers, the rural poor, or plantation owners.

Small Farmers and the Rural Poor

The farmers who did not have slaves—**yeomen**—made up the largest group of whites in the South. Most yeomen owned land. Although they lived throughout the region, they were most numerous in the Upper South and in the hilly rural areas of the Deep South, where the land was unsuited to large plantations.

A yeoman's farm usually ranged from 50 to 200 acres. Yeomen grew crops both for their own use and to sell, and they often traded their produce to local merchants and workers for goods and services.

Not all Southern whites owned land. Some rented land or worked as **tenant farmers** on landlords' estates. Others—the rural poor—lived in crude cabins in wooded areas where they could clear a few trees, plant some corn, and keep a hog or a cow. They also fished and hunted for food.

SECTION RESOURCES

Reproducible Masters
- Reproducible Lesson Plan 13–4
- Guided Reading Activity 13–4
- Section Quiz 13–4
- Reteaching Activity 13–4
- Enrichment Activity 13–4

Transparencies
- Section Focus Transparency 13–4

Multimedia
- Vocabulary PuzzleMaker
- Chapter Challenger Interactive Review Software
- Testmaker
- GTV: A Geographic Perspective on American History
- Facts On File: Landmark Documents in American History

1 FOCUS

BELLRINGER
Motivational Activity

Before taking roll at the beginning of the class period, project Section Focus Transparency 13–4 and have students answer the questions. Discuss students' responses.

This activity is also available as a blackline master.

Section Focus Transparency 13–4

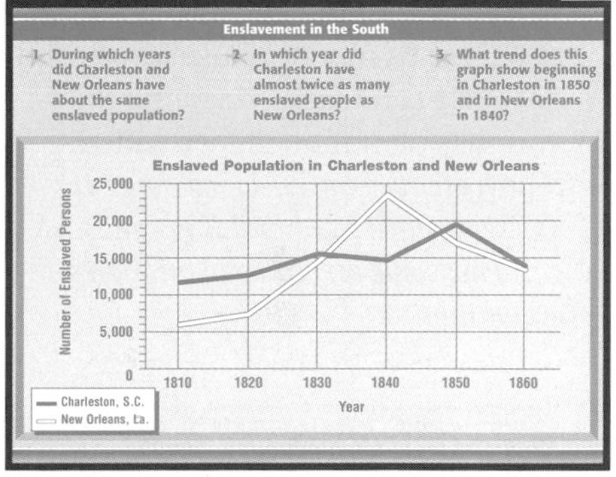

Vocabulary Precheck

Note that in medieval England, yeomen were not part of the gentry. Inform students that the word probably comes from the Middle English *yengman,* meaning "young man." Encourage students to describe *yeomen.*

Use the **Vocabulary PuzzleMaker** to create crossword and word search puzzles.

Section Theme
Culture and Traditions

The people of the pre-war South could be classified by their situation in life.

Activity Have students find the different categories into which the South's people could be placed. *(plantation owners, yeomen, tenant farmers, rural poor, enslaved African Americans, free African Americans)*

2 TEACH

L1 Comparing Lifestyles Have students compare and contrast the lifestyles of the various types of Southerners—plantation owners, yeomen, tenant farmers, rural poor, enslaved African Americans, free African Americans. Students may wish to present this information in chart form.

Picturing HISTORY Plantations were far apart and travel was slow; so when a planter held a party, most of the guests would stay at the host's manor house for several days or even weeks, enjoying the various entertainments provided. **Answer:** *oversaw enslaved domestic workers; supervised buildings and gardens; some served as plantation's accountant*

When?Who?What?Where?

In the early 1850s, Indiana, Iowa, and Illinois bordered slave states. All three had laws that banned African Americans, whether free or enslaved, from entering their states.

Guided Reading Activity 13–4

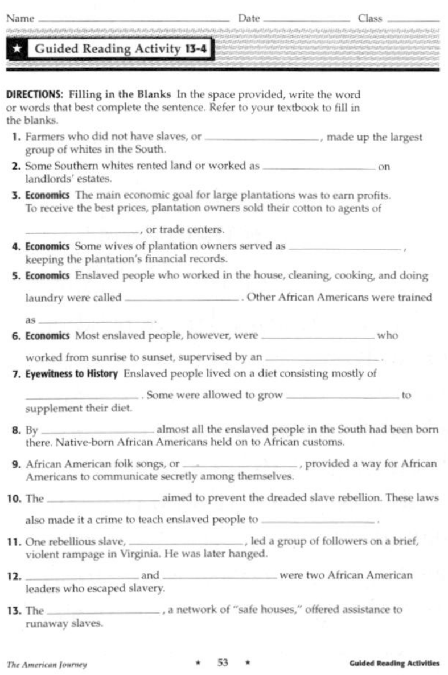

Name ____________ Date ________ Class ________

Guided Reading Activity 13-4

DIRECTIONS: Filling in the Blanks In the space provided, write the word or words that best complete the sentence. Refer to your textbook to fill in the blanks.

1. Farmers who did not have slaves, or ____________, made up the largest group of whites in the South.
2. Some Southern whites rented land or worked as ____________ on landlords' estates.
3. **Economics** The main economic goal for large plantations was to earn profits. To receive the best prices, plantation owners sold their cotton to agents of ____________, or trade centers.
4. **Economics** Some wives of plantation owners served as ____________, keeping the plantation's financial records.
5. **Economics** Enslaved people who worked in the house, cleaning, cooking, and doing laundry were called ____________. Other African Americans were trained as ____________.
6. **Economics** Most enslaved people, however, were ____________ who worked from sunrise to sunset, supervised by an ____________.
7. **Eyewitness to History** Enslaved people lived on a diet consisting mostly of ____________. Some were allowed to grow ____________ to supplement their diet.
8. By ____________ almost all the enslaved people in the South had been born there. Native-born African Americans held on to African customs.
9. African American folk songs, or ____________, provided a way for African Americans to communicate secretly among themselves.
10. The ____________ aimed to prevent the dreaded slave rebellion. These laws also made it a crime to teach enslaved people to ____________.
11. One rebellious slave, ____________, led a group of followers on a brief, violent rampage in Virginia. He was later hanged.
12. ____________ and ____________ were two African American leaders who escaped slavery.
13. The ____________, a network of "safe houses," offered assistance to runaway slaves.

The American Journey • 53 • **Guided Reading Activities**

Picturing HISTORY Wealthy Southerners pose for the camera in front of an elegant plantation home. **What were the duties of the wife of a plantation owner?**

The poor people of the rural South were stubbornly independent. They refused to take any job that resembled the work of enslaved people. Although looked down on by other whites, the rural poor were proud of being self-sufficient.

Plantations

A large plantation might cover several thousand acres. Well-to-do plantation owners usually lived in comfortable but not luxurious farmhouses. They measured their wealth partly by the number of enslaved people they controlled and partly by such possessions as homes, furnishings, and clothing. A small group of plantation owners—about 12 percent—held more than half of the slaves. About half of the planters held fewer than five enslaved workers.

Economics

Plantation Owners

The main economic goal for large plantation owners was to earn profits. Such plantations had **fixed costs**—regular expenses such as housing and feeding workers and maintaining cotton gins and other equipment. Fixed costs remained about the same year after year.

Cotton prices, however, varied from season to season, depending on the market. To receive the best prices, planters sold their cotton to agents in cities such as **New Orleans, Charleston,** Mobile, and Savannah. The cotton exchanges, or trade centers, in Southern cities were of vital importance to those involved in the cotton economy. The agents of the exchanges extended **credit**—a form of loan—to the planters and held the cotton for several months until the price rose. Then the agents sold the cotton. This system kept the planters always in debt because they did not receive payment for their cotton until the agents sold it.

Plantation Wives

The wife of a plantation owner generally had charge of watching over the enslaved workers who toiled in her home and tending to them when they became ill. Her responsibilities also included supervising the plantation's buildings and the fruit and vegetable gardens. Some wives served as accountants, keeping the plantation's financial records.

Cooperative Learning Activity

Creating a Documentary Organize the class into small groups, each of which is to plan a segment for a documentary on Southern life. Since making an actual film would be time-consuming and probably impractical, groups may present their ideas in the form of storyboards, which are a series of sketches representing the scenes intended to be shown in the final product. Students may use library resources as well as the information presented in the text. Two recently published books recommended by the magazine *Social Education* may be helpful to students. They are *Escape from Slavery: The Boyhood of Frederick Douglass in His Own Words* (Michael McCurdy, editor. New York: Knopf, 1994) and *Our Song, Our Toil: The Story of American Slavery as Told by Slaves* (Michael Stepto, editor. Highland, Park, N.J.: Mill Brook Press, 1994).

Women often led a difficult and lonely life on the plantation. When plantation agriculture spread westward into Alabama and Mississippi, many planters' wives felt they were moving into a hostile, uncivilized region. Planters traveled frequently to look at new land or to deal with agents in New Orleans or **Memphis.** Their wives spent long periods alone at the plantation.

Work on the Plantation

Large plantations needed many different kinds of workers. Some enslaved people worked in the house, cleaning, cooking, doing laundry, sewing, and serving meals. They were called domestic slaves. Other African Americans were trained as blacksmiths, carpenters, shoemakers, or weavers. Still others worked in the pastures, tending the horses, cows, sheep, and pigs.

Most of the enslaved African Americans, however, were field hands. They worked from sunrise to sunset planting, cultivating, and picking cotton and other crops. They were supervised by an overseer—a plantation manager.

Life Under Slavery

Enslaved African Americans endured appalling hardship and misery. They worked hard, earned no money, and had little hope of freedom. One of their worst fears was being resold to another planter and separated from their loved ones. In the face of these brutal conditions, enslaved African Americans maintained their family life as best they could and developed a culture all their own. They resisted slavery through a variety of ingenious methods, and they looked to the day when they would be liberated.

Enslaved Workers

Overseers rang the wake-up bell or horn well before dawn. The enslaved workers reached the fields before the sun came up, and they stayed there until after sundown.

Planters wanted to keep the slaves busy all the time, which meant long and grueling days in the fields. Enslaved women as well as men were required to do heavy fieldwork. Young children carried buckets of water. By the age of 10, they were considered ready for fieldwork. Enslaved people who reached old age—60 or older—performed lighter chores such as weaving or caring for children.

Eyewitness to HISTORY

Life in the Slave Cabins

Enslaved people had few comforts beyond the bare necessities. Josiah Henson, an African American who escaped from slavery, described the quarters where he had lived.

> "We lodged in log huts and on the bare ground. Wooden floors were an unknown luxury. In a single room were huddled, like cattle, ten or a dozen persons, men, women and children. . . . Our beds were collections of straw and

Picturing HISTORY A family of enslaved workers gathers in front of their cabin on a plantation near Savannah, Georgia. **How did enslaved people cope with the injustices in their lives?**

CHAPTER 13
Section 4, 401–406

NATIONAL GEOGRAPHIC SOCIETY

VIDEODISC
GTV: A Geographic Perspective on American History

Side 2, Chapter 13
Title: *One Nation, Still?*
Subject: Regional differences deepen (1850-1860)
Ask: **Compare the different sources of trade in New York and New Orleans.** *(People in New York engaged in manufacturing and banking, while residents of New Orleans traded cotton and slaves.)*

Picturing HISTORY In *Twelve Years a Slave,* Solomon Northup described the life of a field hand on a Southern plantation: "The hands are required to be in the cotton fields as soon as it is light in the morning, and, with the exception of ten or fifteen minutes, which is given them at noon to swallow their allowance of cold bacon, they are not permitted to be a moment idle until it is too dark to see, and when the moon is full, they often times labor till the middle of night."
Answer: *maintained family and culture as well as they could; resisted in various ways; found comfort and hope of freedom in their religious beliefs*

Multiple Learning Styles

Auditory/Musical Students may enjoy reading aloud some African or African American folktales. There are many versions of the Brer Rabbit stories available. (Brer Rabbit's roots come from the East African stories of Kalulu the Rabbit, whose wit alternately gets him into trouble and rescues him.) In addition, these recently published folktale collections are recommended by *Social Education: The Headless Haunt and Other African-American Ghost Stories* (collected and retold by James Haskins. New York: Harper Trophy, 1994) and *Misoso: Once Upon a Time Tales from Africa* (retold by Verna Aardema. New York: Knopf, 1994). **L1**

What? Where? When? Who?

Spirituals African American spirituals, still popular today, influenced other forms of music. For example, the sorrowful songs that were related to spirituals, such as "Nobody Knows the Trouble I've Seen," developed into blues music. The more joyous spirituals, such as "Roll, Jordan, Roll," influenced gospel music.

American Memories

African American Life in the South
In North America, whites attempted to wipe out African culture. Slaveholders deliberately mixed the population groups to prevent a sense of ethnic identity from fostering a unified rebellion.
Answer: *The cotton kerchief is similar to colorful cloths that some African peoples wore on their heads.*

Who?What?Where?When?

Several African Americans had slaves. For example, Andrew Durnford, a free African American planter in Louisiana, had a labor force of about 75 slaves.

Facts On File

CD-ROM
Landmark Documents in American History

Title: *American Slavery, Frederick Douglass, 1850*
Have students write a brief outline of the major points Douglass makes.

CURRICULUM CONNECTION

ECONOMICS
The economies of the North and the South were interconnected. The South depended on the North for most manufactured goods. The North relied on the South for raw materials. For example, the Northern textile industry could not operate without Southern cotton. Further, Southern cotton, indigo, and rice accounted for about 60 percent of all American exports. But most of these exports were carried overseas by Northern merchant ships.

American Memories

African American Life in the South

What Was It Like? Although enslaved people had few personal possessions, their lives were marked by a strong shared spirit. **Which of the items shown here reflect the African traditions of enslaved people?**

old rags, thrown down in the corners and boxed in with boards, a single blanket the only covering. . . . The wind whistled and the rain and snow blew in through the cracks, and the damp earth soaked in the moisture till the floor was miry [filthy] as a pigsty. ❞

Enslaved people lived on a diet consisting mostly of cornmeal, pork fat, and molasses. Many plantation owners allowed enslaved people to have their own gardens. The slaves grew greens and yams to supplement their diet. They usually had enough to eat, but their diet often was not well balanced or nutritious.

Family Life

Enslaved people faced constant uncertainty and danger. American law in the early 1800s did not protect enslaved families. At any given time a husband or wife could be sold away, or a slaveholder's death could lead to the breakup of an enslaved family. Although marriage between enslaved people was not recognized by law, many couples did marry. Their marriage ceremonies included the phrase "until death or separation do us part"—recognizing the possibility that a marriage might end with the sale of one spouse.

To provide some measure of stability in their lives, enslaved African Americans established a network of relatives and friends, who made up their extended family. If a husband or wife were sold away, an aunt, uncle, or close friend could raise the children left behind. Large, close-knit extended families became a vital feature of African American culture.

African American Culture

Enslaved African Americans endured their hardships by extending their own culture, fellowship, and community. They fused African and American elements into a new and distinctive culture.

MAKING CONNECTIONS ACTIVITY

Music African music, with its polyrhythms, liveliness, and inventiveness, influenced many new musical forms that developed outside of Africa. Among these are jazz, blues, be-bop, soul, mambo, and reggae. Jazz drumming in particular is based on the drumming style typical of the southern Guineas on the coast of Africa. Have students research to find out more about this influence and present to the class examples of both African music and the music that is derived from or influenced by African music. **L2, ELL**

The growth of the African American population came mainly from children born in the United States. In 1808 Congress had outlawed the slave trade. Although slavery remained legal in the South, no new slaves could enter the United States. By 1860 almost all the enslaved people in the South had been born there.

These native-born African Americans held on to their African customs. They continued to practice African music and dance. They passed traditional African folk stories and proverbs on to their children. Some wrapped colored cloths around their heads in the African style. Although a large number of enslaved African Americans accepted Christianity, they often followed the religious beliefs and practices of their African ancestors as well.

African American Christianity

For many enslaved African Americans, Christianity became a religion of hope and resistance. They prayed fervently for the day when they would be free from bondage.

The passionate beliefs of the Southern slaves found expression in the **spiritual**, an African American religious folk song. Spirituals provided a way for the enslaved African Americans to communicate secretly among themselves. Many spirituals combined Christian faith with laments about earthly suffering. The song "Didn't My Lord Deliver Daniel," for example, refers to the biblical tale of Daniel who was saved from the lions' den.

> "Didn't my Lord deliver Daniel,
> deliver Daniel, deliver Daniel,
> Didn't my Lord deliver Daniel,
> An' why not every man?"

Slave Codes

Between 1830 and 1860, life under slavery became even more difficult because the **slave codes**—the laws in the Southern states that controlled enslaved people—became more severe. In existence since the 1700s, slave codes aimed to prevent the event white Southerners dreaded most—the slave rebellion. For this reason slave codes prohibited slaves from assembling in large groups and from leaving their master's property without a written pass.

Slave codes also made it a crime to teach enslaved people to read or write. White Southerners feared that a literate slave might lead other African Americans in rebellion. A slave who did not know how to read and write, whites believed, was less likely to rebel.

Resistance to Slavery

Some enslaved African Americans did rebel openly against their masters. One was **Nat Turner,** a popular religious leader among his fellow slaves. Turner had taught himself to read and write. In 1831 Turner led a group of followers on a brief, violent rampage in Southhampton County, Virginia. Before being captured Turner and his followers killed at least 55 whites. Nat Turner was hanged, but his rebellion frightened white Southerners and led them to the passage of more severe slave codes.

Armed rebellions were rare, however. African Americans in the South knew that they would only lose in an armed uprising. For the most part, enslaved people resisted slavery by working slowly or by pretending to be ill. Occasionally resistance took more active forms, such as setting fire to a plantation building or breaking tools. Resistance helped enslaved African Americans endure their lives by striking back at white masters—and perhaps establishing boundaries that white people would respect.

Escaping Slavery

Some enslaved African Americans tried to run away to the North. A few succeeded. **Harriet Tubman** and **Frederick Douglass,** two African American leaders who were born in slavery, gained their freedom when they fled to the North.

Yet for most enslaved people, getting to the North was almost impossible, especially from the Deep South. Most slaves who succeeded in running away escaped from the Upper South. The **Underground Railroad**—a network of "safe

CRITICAL THINKING ACTIVITY

Analyzing Information Another side of slavery is revealed in this quote from historian Thomas A. Bailey. "The dark taint of slavery also left its mark on whites. It fostered the brutality of the whip, the bloodhound, and the branding iron. White southerners increasingly lived in a state of imagined siege, surrounded by potentially rebellious blacks inflamed by abolitionist propaganda. . . . Their fears bolstered an intoxicating theory of biological superiority and turned the South into a reactionary backwater in an era of progress—one of the last bastions of slavery in the Western world. The defenders of slavery were forced to degrade themselves along with their victims. As Booker T. Washington . . . later observed, whites could not hold blacks in a ditch without getting down there with them." Discuss this quote with students and ask them to explain it in their own words. **L2**

3 ASSESS

Assign Section 4 Review as homework or as an in-class activity.

Use **Chapter Challenger Interactive Review Software** to review Section 4.

Section Quiz 13–4

Name ______ Date ______ Class ______

★ Chapter 13 — Score

Section Quiz 13-4

DIRECTIONS: Matching Match each item in Column A with the items in Column B. Write the correct letters in the blanks. *(10 points each)*

Column A	Column B
____ 1. owned small farm	A. tenant farmers
____ 2. farmed landlords' estates	B. credit
____ 3. lived in crude cabins	C. yeoman
____ 4. form of loan	D. overseer
____ 5. plantation manager	E. rural poor

DIRECTIONS: Multiple Choice In the blank at the left, write the letter of the choice that best completes the statement or answers the question. *(10 points each)*

____ 6. This made up the largest group of whites in the South.
A. yeomen C. tenant farmers
B. plantation owners D. rural poor

____ 7. The main goal of large plantation owners was to
A. enslave people. C. earn a profit.
B. produce more cotton. D. build a larger plantation.

____ 8. This religious leader led a slave revolt in 1831.
A. Harriet Tubman C. Frederick Douglass
B. Nat Turner D. Eli Whitney

____ 9. These African American folk songs expressed the passionate beliefs of the South's enslaved workers.
A. overseers C. slave codes
B. yeomen D. spirituals

____ 10. This network of safe houses assisted runaway enslaved persons.
A. slave houses C. Underground Railroad
B. runaway houses D. slave codes

The American Journey ★ 53 ★ **Section Quizzes**

Facts On File

CD-ROM
Landmark Documents in American History

Title: *Trial of Mrs. Douglass For Teaching Colored Children to Read, 1853*

After students read the document ask them the following questions: **Who was Mrs. Douglass?** *(a Norfolk, Virginia, Sunday school teacher arrested for teaching African American children to read)* **What laws did Mrs. Douglass violate?** *(slave codes forbidding whites from teaching slaves to read)* **How did Mrs. Douglass defend herself at the trial?** *(She claimed that the slave codes were unjust laws.)* **What were the results of the trial?** *(The court found her guilty and sentenced her to one month in jail.)*

CHAPTER 13
Section 4, 401–406

Reteaching Activity 13–4

Name ______________ Date ________ Class ________

★ Reteaching Activity 13-4

DIRECTIONS: Matching Match each item in Column A with its corresponding item in Column B. Write the correct letters in the blanks.

COLUMN A

____ 1. yeoman
____ 2. tenant farmers
____ 3. rural poor
____ 4. fixed costs
____ 5. cotton exchange
____ 6. plantation wives
____ 7. domestic slaves
____ 8. field hands
____ 9. overseer
____ 10. slave cabin
____ 11. spirituals
____ 12. slave codes
____ 13. Nat Turner
____ 14. Harriet Tubman
____ 15. Underground Railroad

COLUMN B

A. regular expenses such as housing and feeding workers and maintaining equipment
B. enslaved workers who planted, cultivated, and picked cotton and other crops
C. worked on landlords' estates
D. one-room log hut with dirt floor
E. watched over enslaved workers and tended to them when they were ill
F. Southern laws that controlled enslaved people
G. farmers who did not have slaves
H. African American leader who fled to the North to escape slavery
I. African American religious folk song
J. led a violent rampage in Southhampton County, Virginia, in 1831
K. self-sufficient Southerners who lived in crude cabins in wooded areas
L. plantation manager
M. a network of safe houses that assisted runaway slaves
N. trade centers where planters sold their cotton to agents
O. enslaved people who worked in the plantation houses

DIRECTIONS: Essay Answer the following question on a separate sheet of paper.
How did enslaved people resist slavery? How did resistance help enslaved people?

The American Journey ★ 53 ★ Reteaching Activities

Enrichment Activity 13–4

Name ______________ Date ________ Class ________

★ Enrichment Activity 13-4 ★ ★

New Orleans, City of Music

In New Orleans African Americans have a long history of contributions to American music. Free African Americans established an opera company in New Orleans before the Emancipation Proclamation. They created moving spirituals in their churches and later developed jazz, a musical form that is often called the only truly original American music.

DIRECTIONS: Use the words in the Word Bank to complete the musical crossword puzzle. You may use your dictionary if you wish.

spiritual	aria	libretto	score	improvisation
syncopation	New Orleans	ragtime	Dixieland	swing

Across:
1. jazz term describing a shift of an accent to a normally unaccented beat
2. music with happy, relaxed jazz beat
3. moving religious song
4. the text of an opera
5. home of early African American opera company and "the cradle of jazz"

Down:
1. written or printed music for an opera
2. in opera, an emotional vocal solo
3. spontaneously created
4. kind of music created by Scott Joplin
5. the first kind of jazz band to make records

Activity **DIRECTIONS:** What musical forms are popular today? Do these forms have a special vocabulary? With a partner brainstorm to find terms used in today's musical forms. Then create your own crossword puzzle and exchange it with another partnership and work the puzzles.

The American Journey ★ 53 ★ Enrichment Activities

Frederick Douglass

houses" owned by free blacks and whites who opposed slavery—offered assistance to runaways.

Some slaves ran away to find relatives on nearby plantations or to escape punishment. Rarely did they plan to make a run for the North. Most runaways were captured and returned to their masters. Discipline was severe; the most common punishment was whipping.

Life in the Cities

Although the South was primarily agricultural, it was the site of several large cities by the mid-1800s. By 1860 the population of **Baltimore** had reached 212,000 and that of New Orleans 168,000. Other cities on the rise included Charleston, **Richmond,** and Memphis. The population of Southern cities included white city dwellers, some enslaved workers, and a large share—about 250,000—of the South's free African Americans.

Free African Americans

The cities provided free African Americans with opportunities to form their own communities. African American barbers, carpenters, and small traders offered their services throughout their communities. Free African Americans founded their own churches and institutions. In New Orleans they formed an opera company.

Although some free African Americans prospered in the cities, their lives were far from secure. Between 1830 and 1860, Southern states passed laws that limited the rights of free African Americans. Most states would not allow them to migrate from other states. In 1859 Arkansas ordered all free African Americans out of the state. Although spared the horrors of slavery, free African Americans were denied an equal share in economic and political life.

Section 4 Review

Checking for Understanding

1. ***Identify*** Nat Turner, Harriet Tubman, Frederick Douglass, Underground Railroad.
2. ***Define*** yeoman, tenant farmer, fixed cost, credit, overseer, spiritual, slave code.
3. ***List*** two differences between yeomen and plantation owners.

Reviewing Themes

4. **Culture and Traditions** Why were extended families vital to African American culture?

Critical Thinking

5. **Making Generalizations** If you were a plantation owner, what would you tell your son or daughter if they asked why you held slaves?

Activity

Illustrating Differences Draw scenes that illustrate differences between planters and enslaved people in the 1800s.

4 CLOSE

Ask students why marriage vows of enslaved persons sometimes included the phrase "until death *or distance* do you part."

Section 4 Review Answers

1. Turner, 405; Tubman, 405; Douglass, 405; Underground Railroad, 405
2. The words are defined in the Glossary.
3. Yeomen: lived in Upper South and backcountry of Deep South, did not have slaves, farms smaller than plantations; Plantation owners: lived in Deep South, held slaves, much larger farms, wealthier
4. They provided some stability. For example, if a husband or wife was sold, the extended family would raise the children left behind.
5. Answers will vary but might include to earn bigger profits to support the family; because it is acceptable in the South.

Activity Students should create drawings that show the dramatic differences between the lives of planters and enslaved people.

Social Studies Connections Citizenship

Geography World History Economics

Thoreau—The Abolitionist

"If a man does not keep pace with his companions, perhaps it is because he hears a different drummer. Let him step to the music he hears, however measured and far away." These are the words of a man who believed strongly in personal freedom. He believed that if a government, company, or society interferes with a person's life, that person has a right to protest.

This man was Henry David Thoreau (1817–1862). While living in a small cabin on Walden Pond near Concord, Massachusetts, Thoreau devoted himself to the study of nature and to writing about social issues. When he saw something in society that he thought was unjust, he spoke out.

In the mid-1800s, Thoreau became very active in the abolitionist movement. He helped fugitive slaves who were following the Underground Railroad. Horrified by slavery, Thoreau never missed an opportunity to speak out against the government that allowed slavery to continue.

"How does . . . a man behave toward this American government today? I answer that he cannot without disgrace be associated with it. I cannot for an instant recognize that political organization as *my* government which is the *slave's* government also.

. . . [W]hen a sixth of the population of a nation which has undertaken to be the refuge of liberty are slaves . . . I think that it is not too soon for honest men to rebel and revolutionize.

. . . There are thousands who are *in opinion* opposed to slavery and to the [Mexican] war, who yet in effect do nothing to put an end to them; who, esteeming themselves children of Washington and Franklin, sit down with their hands in their pockets, and say that they know not what to do, and do nothing. . . ."

Henry David Thoreau

Walden Pond

Thoreau wrote these ideas in an essay called "Civil Disobedience." His powerful message later influenced Martin Luther King, Jr., and Indian leader Mohandas Gandhi.

Activity

Designing a Poster What is there in your community that needs changing? Perhaps homeless people need help or litter needs cleaning up. Design a poster to convince people in your community to take action.

MORE ABOUT . . .

Thoreau Henry David Thoreau was one of the most influential philosophers and writers in American history. For two years he lived in solitude in a small cabin by Walden Pond near Concord, Massachusetts. There he lived out his philosophy of freedom of the individual. He observed nature, walked, read, and expanded his Transcendental ideas. The journal he kept during that time became his most famous book, *Walden,* published in 1854. Not only a philosopher, Thoreau was also a dedicated naturalist. His first book, *A Week on the Concord and Merrimack Rivers,* and later works, *Excursions* and *Cape Cod,* grew out of his Walden journal as well. They express his observations and ideas about nature.

Social Studies Connections Citizenship

TEACH

Thoreau—The Abolitionist
Ask students what duty Thoreau believed people have when they see injustice. *(to protest it)* **Ask: Why did Thoreau feel that association with the American government was a disgrace?** *(The government allowed slavery.)* **To what nation was he referring when he said, "a nation which has undertaken to be the refuge of liberty"?** *(United States)* **To what besides slavery did Thoreau object in the last quoted paragraph?** *(Mexican War)* **What did he mean by "the children of Washington and Franklin"?** *(people who feel that they are the heirs of freedom as represented by those two men)*

Linking PAST & PRESENT

Civil Disobedience In encouraging civil disobedience, Thoreau was echoing the ideas and practices of the Patriots who refused to pay taxes to the British government. This nonviolent approach has been employed frequently in the late twentieth century by protesters to denounce what they see as the country's social ills.

Facts On File

CD-ROM
Landmark Documents in American History

Title: *"Civil Disobedience," Henry David Thoreau, 1849*
Encourage students to review Thoreau's work and outline his main points. Ask students how they might use Thoreau's ideas to protest what they see as society's ills today.

GLENCOE TECHNOLOGY

VIDEODISC
MindJogger Videoquiz

Use MindJogger to review the Chapter 13 content.

Chapter 13
Disc 2, Side B

Also available in VHS.

Review and Activities

Reviewing Key Terms

On graph paper, create a word search puzzle using the following terms. Crisscross the terms vertically and horizontally, then fill in the remaining squares with extra letters. Use the terms' definitions as clues to find the words in the puzzle. Share your puzzle with a classmate.

telegraph
Morse code
trade union
prejudice
nativist
cotton gin
yeoman
credit
overseer
slave code

Reviewing Key Facts

1. How did the development of the canal and rail network alter the trade route between the Midwest and the East Coast?
2. How did the the telegraph influence long-distance communication?
3. In what ways were women in the workforce discriminated against?
4. Why was there little industry in the South?
5. What was the purpose of the slave codes?

Critical Thinking

Comparing and Contrasting

The difference in the economies of the North and South was reflected in the way people lived.

1. Why did the North have more large cities than the South?
2. How did the lives of Northern African Americans differ from those of Southern African Americans?

Reviewing Themes

1. **Economic Factors** How did improvements in transportation affect the economy in the North?
2. **Geography and History** Discuss one advantage and one disadvantage of city life in the North.
3. **Science and Technology** Compare the use of railroads in the North and South before 1860.
4. **Culture and Traditions** Describe ways in which enslaved African Americans held on to their African customs.

Geography Activity

Study the map below and answer the questions that follow.

Northern Products in 1860

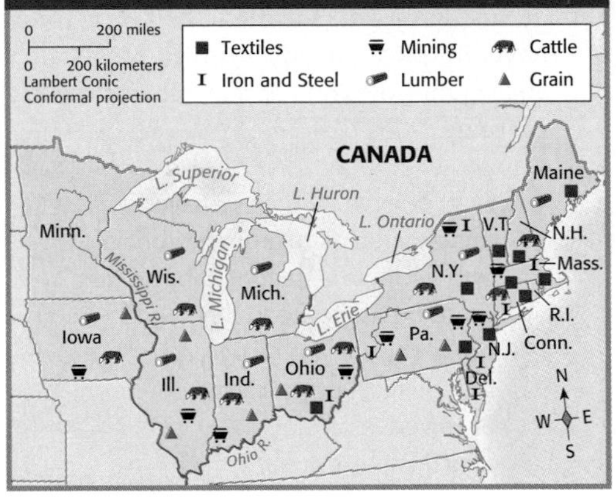

1. **Place** What products were developed in Ohio?
2. **Location** In general, where were most textile mills located?
3. **Region** How do the products shown here differ from the South's products as shown on the map on page 400?

Reviewing Key Terms

Students' word search puzzles will vary. The key terms used in this activity are defined in the textbook glossary on pages A26–A35.

Reviewing Key Facts

1. Before canals and railroads were in use, agricultural goods were transported down the Mississippi to New Orleans and then shipped to other countries or to the East Coast. After canals and railroads, products were transported directly from the Midwest to the East.
2. News of national and world events could be transmitted as soon as they occurred.
3. Women were paid less and excluded from joining male unions and jobs; legislative appeals ignored
4. agriculture was very profitable, lack of capital to invest in businesses, market for manufactured goods was small, some Southerners did not want industry to flourish in the South
5. to prevent slave rebellions and control slaves

Critical Thinking

1. In the North, people flocked to the cities to work in the factories; in the South, most people earned a living by farming, which was done in rural areas.
2. Both were targets of discrimination and prejudice, but Northern African Americans were not enslaved. Northern African Americans were usually barred from public facilities and could get only low-paying jobs. Southern enslaved African Americans lived lives of hardship and misery.

Reviewing Themes

1. Goods could be transported more quickly and cheaply, which meant profits were higher; railroads and canals provided an important link between farmers and industries and markets in the East.
2. Advantages: find work, social center; disadvantages: overcrowded, expensive, rundown housing, threat of disease and fire

Skill Practice Activity

Reading a Circle Graph

Study the circle graphs below, then answer the questions that follow.

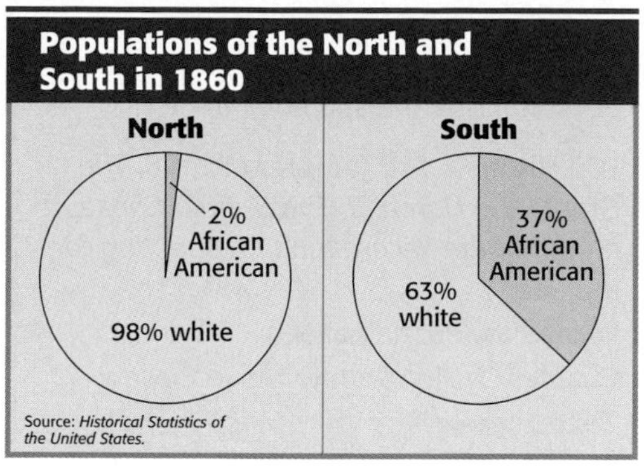

1. What does the information in the two graphs represent?
2. What percentage of the population in the North was white in 1860?
3. In which part of the country did African Americans make up more than one-third of the population?
4. What can you conclude from the graphs about the total population of the North and South?

Cooperative Activity

History and Art With members of your group, create a model of what you think a Southern plantation might have looked like. Your model should include a planter's home, slave quarters, farm fields, a cookhouse, barns for the horses, and other details. Research to find illustrations to help you construct your model. Draw a design of your plantation on grid paper. Then gather scrap materials from home to construct your model. You will also need markers, glue, tape, and a large piece of stiff cardboard on which to build your model.

Technology Activity

Using a Word Processor Search encyclopedias and other library resources for information about the world's cotton industry today. Find out the countries that grow cotton, quantities grown, and the types of fertilizer used, if any. Gather this information and create a minireport of interesting cotton facts on your word processor. Share your report with the rest of the class.

Time Line Activity

Create a time line on which you place the following events in chronological order.

- Nat Turner leads a rebellion
- Elias Howe invents the sewing machine
- Samuel Morse sends the first telegraph message
- First steam-powered locomotive operates
- Cyrus McCormick patents the mechanical reaper
- Know-Nothing Party is formed

Portfolio Activity History Journal Write a conversation between a Southerner and Northerner who meet on a train in the mid-1800s. Have them talk about the differences between their lives. Use the notes from your journal in the script.

CHAPTER 13
Review and Activities

Skill Practice Activity

1. white and African American populations of the North and South in 1860
2. 98 percent
3. South
4. More African Americans lived in the South than in the North.

Cooperative Activity

Students should do research so that they can build accurate models.

Technology Activity

Students should locate information on the world's cotton industry and prepare a report of interesting facts about cotton.

Time Line Activity

Events should be placed in this order: First steam-powered locomotive operates, Nat Turner leads a rebellion, Cyrus McCormick patents the mechanical reaper, Elias Howe invents the sewing machine, Samuel Morse sends the first telegraph message, Know-Nothing Party is formed

Portfolio Activity Scripts should reflect students' understanding of the differences between the lives of Northerners and Southerners.

Chapter Bonus Test Question

Ask: Who wrote *The New American Practical Navigator,* a book that revolutionized ship navigation in the 1800s? *(Nathaniel Bowditch)*

3. The North relied heavily on railroads for commerce and settlement. The South mainly used natural waterways to transport goods. Southern rail lines were usually short and local. By 1860 the South had only about one-third of the nation's rail lines.
4. They merged African and American elements into a new culture, practiced African music and dance, passed African folk stories and proverbs on to their children, dressed in African styles, and followed religious beliefs and practices of African ancestors.

Geography Activity

1. grain, textiles, iron and steel, mining, cattle, lumber
2. New England
3. more manufactured products than farm products

Chapter 14 Planning Guide

A complete, 1-page lesson plan is provided for each section in the *Reproducible Lesson Plans* booklet.

Section Resources

Daily Objectives	Reproducible Resources	Multimedia Resources
Section 1 **Social Reform** Describe the various reform movements of the mid-1800s and the development of American artists and writers.	Reproducible Lesson Plan 14–1 Guided Reading Activity 14–1* Section Quiz 14–1* Reteaching Activity 14–1 Enrichment Activity 14–1	Section Focus Transparency 14–1 U.S. History & Art, Transparencies 6, *The Great Blue Heron;* 7, *The Buffalo Chase, Mouth of the Yellowstone;* 9, *Shooting for the Beef* Vocabulary PuzzleMaker Chapter Challenger Interactive Review Testmaker Facts On File: Landmark Documents in American History Focus on American Art Prints, *Fur Traders Descending the Missouri*
Section 2 **The Abolitionists** List important abolitionists and summarize the arguments of those who supported slavery and those who fought against it.	Reproducible Lesson Plan 14–2 Guided Reading Activity 14–2* Section Quiz 14–2* Reteaching Activity 14–2 Enrichment Activity 14–2	Section Focus Transparency 14–2 Vocabulary PuzzleMaker Chapter Challenger Interactive Review Testmaker Facts On File: Landmark Documents in American History ABCNews InterActive™ Historic America Electronic Field Trips GTV: A Geographic Perspective on American History American Music Cultural Traditions, Lesson 4: "Kneebone Bend," "The Monongahela Waltz"; Lesson 5: "Roll, Jordan, Roll," "Get Off the Track!"
Section 3 **The Women's Movement** Describe the relationship between the antislavery movement and the women's movement and summarize the progress of women in the 1800s.	Reproducible Lesson Plan 14–3 Guided Reading Activity 14–3* Section Quiz 14–3* Reteaching Activity 14–3 Enrichment Activity 14–3	Section Focus Transparency 14–3 Vocabulary PuzzleMaker Chapter Challenger Interactive Review Testmaker ABCNews InterActive™ Historic America Electronic Field Trips Facts On File: Landmark Documents in American History

** Also available in Spanish*

Poster · Transparency · CD-ROM · Software
Blackline Master · Videodisc · Audiocassette · Music Program

0:00 **OUT OF TIME?**
Assign the Chapter 14 Digest and the corresponding Chapter Digests Audiocassettes with activities and tests.

ACTIVITY

From the Classroom of...

Debbie Behling
Angleton Middle School East
Angleton, TX

Who Am I?

Introduce this chapter by going around the room and asking each student these questions: "If you could change anything in the world today, what would you change? Why?" Give students some time to think of several answers to avoid duplicate responses.

Then assign each student an individual reformer from this chapter. After students have read the chapter, have them write on an index card a "Who Am I?" question about their reformer. Remind students of the types of things that they and their classmates said needed reform today and include those issues in their questions when possible. Collect the cards and save them. As a review at the end of the chapter, organize the class into teams and have a quiz show. Use the cards to see which teams can answer the "Who Am I?" questions correctly, and award points based on the responses.

Block Schedule

Block scheduling differs from traditional class scheduling in the amount of time allotted to each period. The extended time frame provided by block scheduling affords you the opportunity to implement a greater number of research-oriented and activity-intense projects to motivate and involve your students. Activities that are particularly suited to use within the block scheduling framework are identified throughout this chapter by the following designation:

NATIONAL GEOGRAPHIC SOCIETY Teacher's Corner

INDEX TO NATIONAL GEOGRAPHIC MAGAZINE

The following articles may be used for research relating to this chapter:

- "The Cherokee," by Geoffrey Norman, May 1995.
- "America's Poet: Walt Whitman," by Joel L. Swerdlow, December 1994.
- "The Cruelest Commerce: African Slave Trade," by Colin Palmer, September 1992.
- "Erie Canal: Living Link to Our Past," Joel L. Swerdlow, November 1990.
- "Philadelphia's African Americans," by Roland L. Freeman, August 1990.
- "The Underground Railroad," by Charles L. Blockson, July 1984.

NATIONAL GEOGRAPHIC SOCIETY PRODUCTS AVAILABLE FROM GLENCOE

To order the following products for use with this chapter, contact your local Glencoe sales representative, or call Glencoe at 1-800-334-7344:

- *GTV: A Geographic Perspective on American History* (Videodisc)
- *GTV: The American People: Fabric of a Nation* (Videodisc)
- *The Presidents: A Picture History of Our Nation* (CD-ROM)
- *PictureShow: Native Americans, 1* (CD-ROM)
- *Native Americans: Eastern Woodlands and Plains* (Transparencies)
- *PictureShow: The Civil War* (CD-ROM, Transparencies)

ADDITIONAL NATIONAL GEOGRAPHIC SOCIETY PRODUCTS

To order the following products for use with this chapter, call National Geographic Society at 1-800-368-2728:

- *Steal Away: The Harriet Tubman Story* (Video)
- *Immigration: The Triumph of Hope* (Video)
- *Historical Atlas of the United States* (Atlas)

KEY TO ABILITY LEVELS

Teaching strategies have been coded for varying learning styles and abilities.

L1 **BASIC** activities for all students
L2 **AVERAGE** activities for average to above-average students
L3 **CHALLENGING** activities for above-average students
ELL **ENGLISH LANGUAGE LEARNER** activities

Chapter 14 Resource Guide

Home Involvement

Home Involvement Activity 14

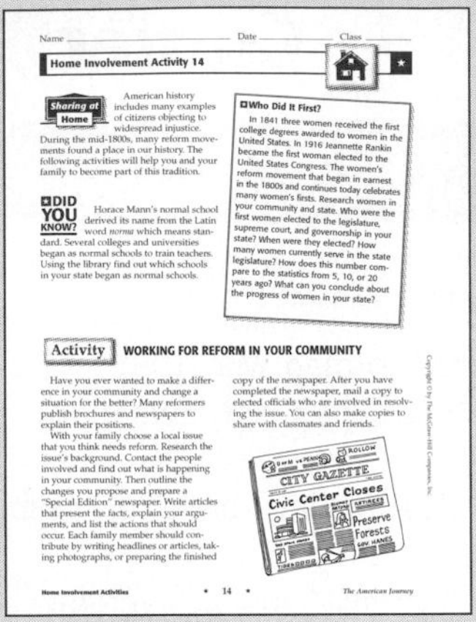

Review Activities

Chapter Summary 14

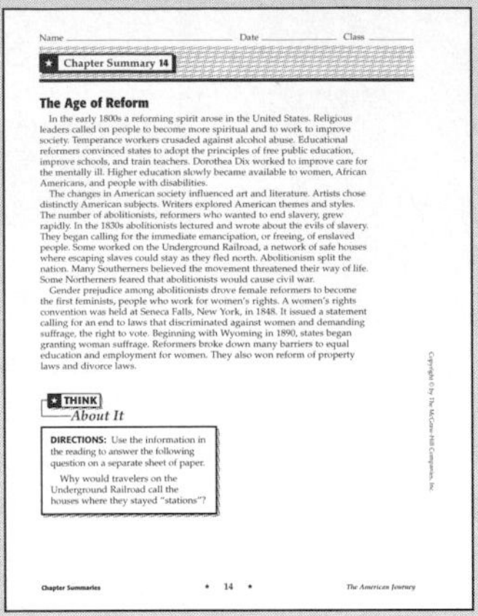

Workbook Activity 14

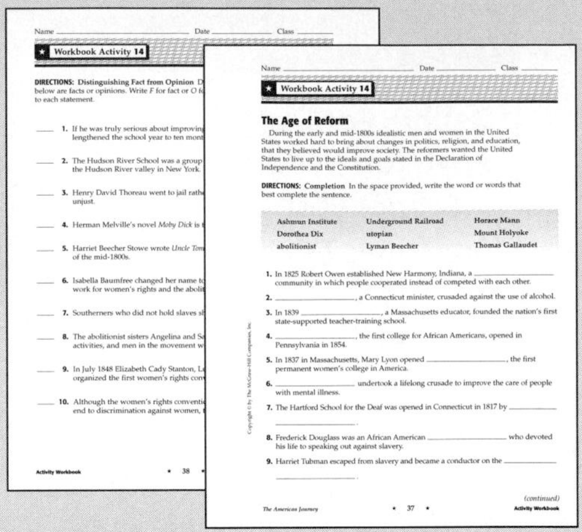

Reinforcement Activities

Time Line Activity 14

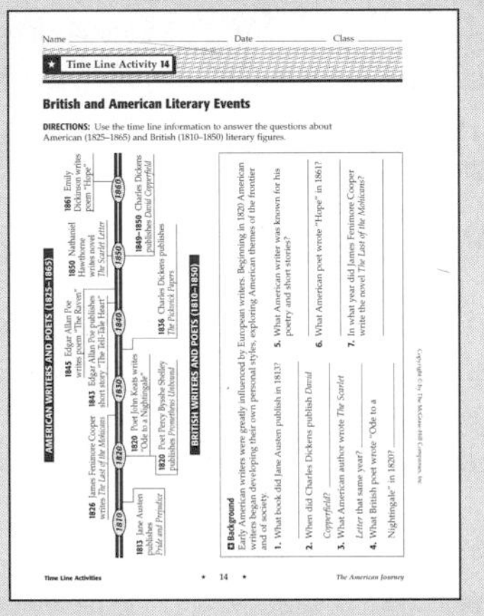

Vocabulary Activity 14

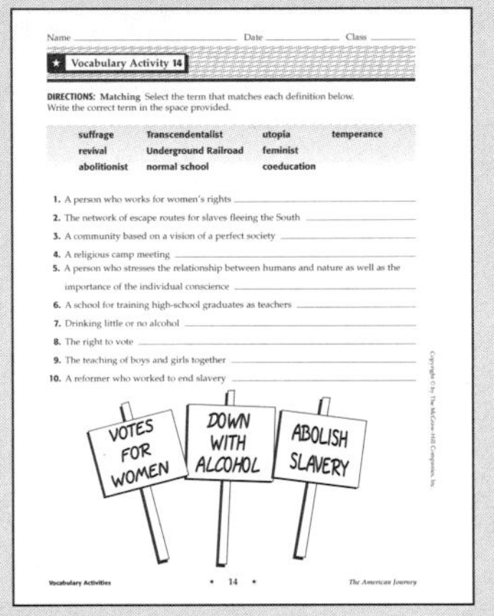

Chapter Skills Activity 14

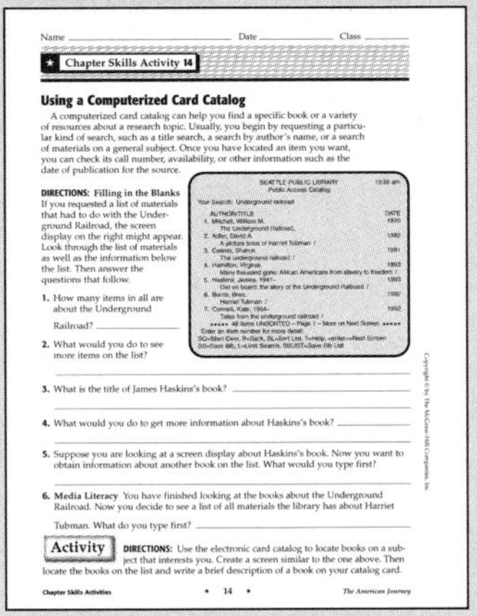

Enrichment Activities

Linking Past and Present Activity 14

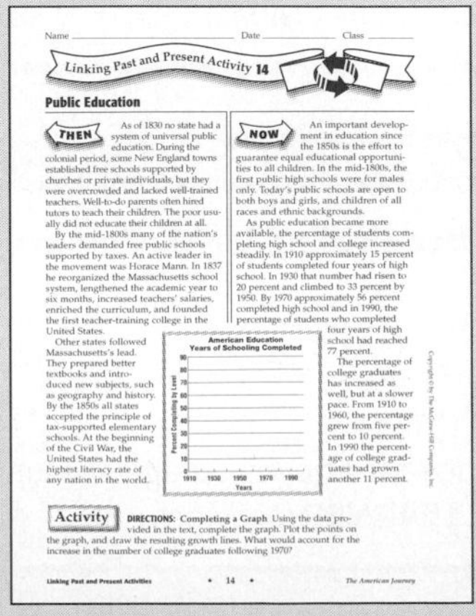

Primary Source Reading 14

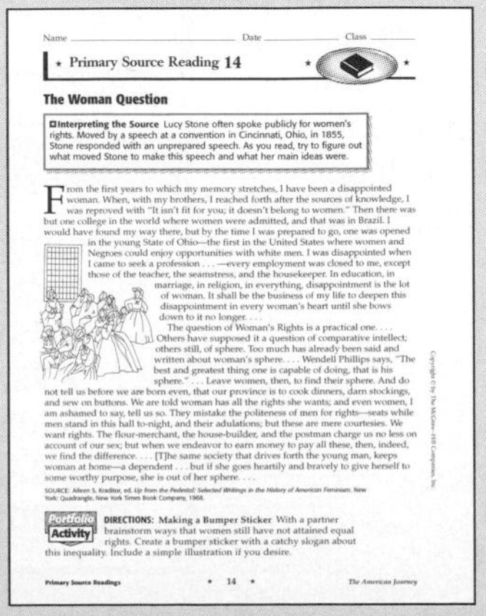

Geography Activities

Mapping History Activity 14

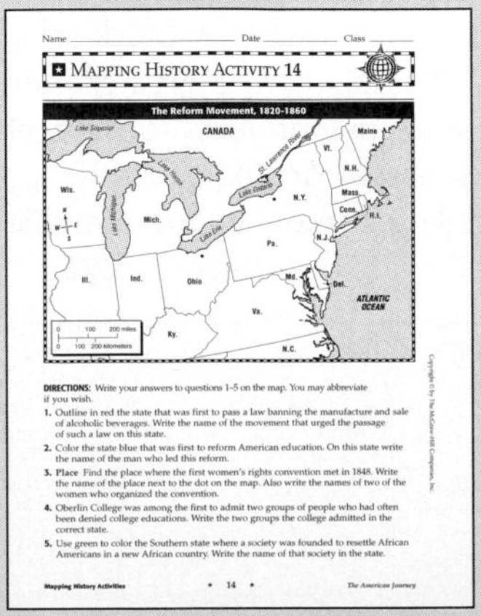

Chapter 14 Resource Guide

Assessment

Chapter 14 Test, Form A

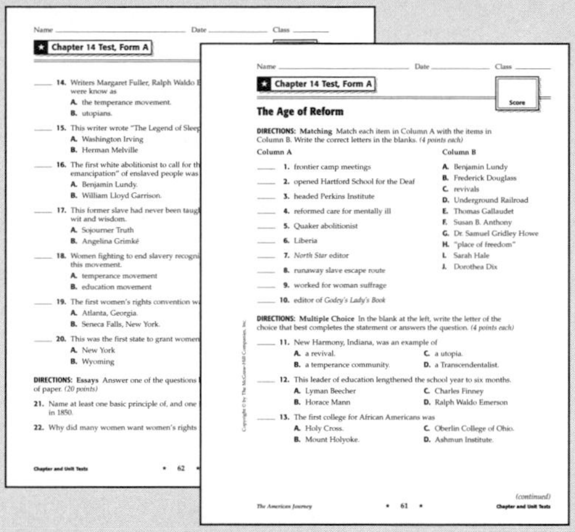
Chapter 14 Test, Form A
The Age of Reform

Chapter 14 Test, Form B

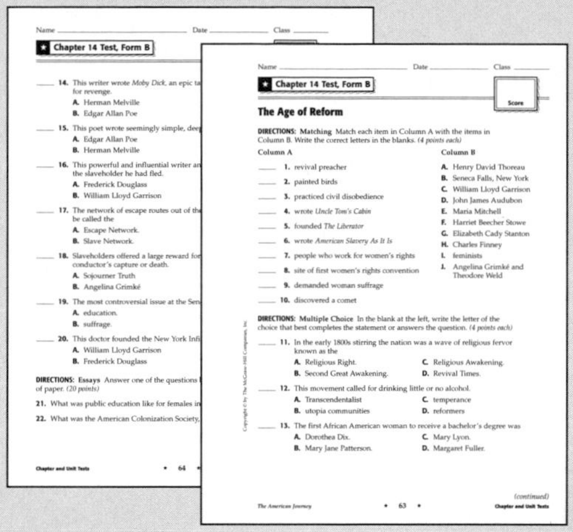
Chapter 14 Test, Form B
The Age of Reform

Performance Assessment Activity 14

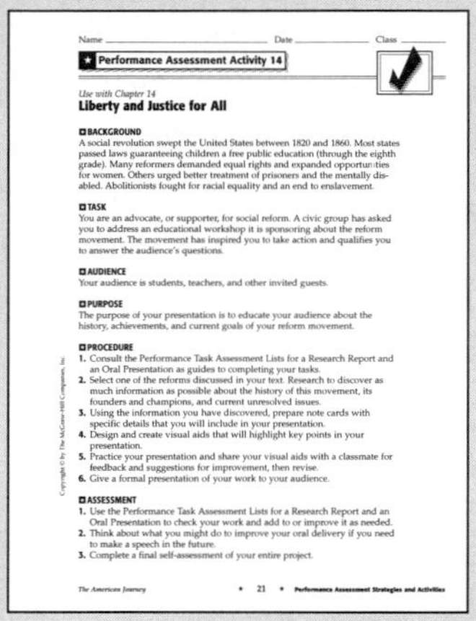
Performance Assessment Activity 14
Liberty and Justice for All

Spanish Resources

The following Spanish language materials are available in the Spanish Resources binder:

- **Spanish Chapter Summary 14**
- **Spanish Vocabulary Activity 14**
- **Spanish Guided Reading Activities, Chapter 14**
- **Spanish Section Quizzes, Chapter 14**
- **Spanish Home Involvement Activity 14**
- **Spanish Chapter 14 Digests Audiocassette Activity and Test**

Activity Manipulatives

Help students learn more about America's cultural history with:

- **American Crafts Hands-On Activities**
- **American Games Hands-On Activities**
- **American History Flash Cards**

Additional Resources From Glencoe

- **U.S. History & Art,** Transparency 6, *The Great Blue Heron;* Transparency 7, *The Buffalo Chase, Mouth of the Yellowstone;* Transparency 9, *Shooting for the Beef*
- **Focus on American Art Prints,** *Fur Traders Descending the Missouri* by George Caleb Bingham
- **American Music Cultural Traditions,** Lesson 4: "Kneebone Bend," "The Monongahela Waltz"; Lesson 5: "Roll, Jordan, Roll," "Get Off the Track!"
- **Outline Map Resource Book**
- **U.S. Desk Map**

A&E HOME VIDEO. Biography. THE HISTORY CHANNEL.

The following videotape programs are available from Glencoe as supplements to Chapter 14:

- **Susan B. Anthony: Rebel for the Cause** (ISBN 1-56501-646-7)

To order, call Glencoe at 1-800-334-7344. To find classroom resources to accompany many of these videos, check the following home pages:
A&E Television: http://www.aetv.com
The History Channel: http://www.historychannel.com

Introducing CHAPTER 14

Chapter Themes

Chapter Themes are listed by section on this chapter opening page of the Student Edition. A corresponding theme-based activity is available under "FOCUS," and a theme-based question is asked in the Section and Chapter Reviews.

Performance Assessment

Refer to Activity 14 in the *Performance Assessment Strategies and Activities* booklet.

GLENCOE TECHNOLOGY

VIDEODISC
MindJogger Videoquiz

Use MindJogger to preview the Chapter 14 content.

Chapter 14
Disc 2, Side B

Also available in VHS.

HISTORY AND ART Early in his career, Winslow Homer (1836–1910) focused on everyday life, such as this schoolroom scene, rather than the high drama of his marine paintings, which were created after 1880. **Ask:** How does this classroom compare to your classroom?

Chapter 14

1820–1860

The Age of Reform

Why It's Important

The idea of reform—the drive to improve society and the lives of individuals—runs like a continuous thread through American history. During the mid-1800s, American reformers attacked such social problems as cruelty toward people with mental illness. They worked to make education available to more young people. Many also crusaded against slavery or for women's rights. These movements paved the way for later social changes.

Chapter Themes

- *Section 1,* Civic Rights and Responsibilities
- *Section 2,* Individual Action
- *Section 3,* Groups and Institutions

HISTORY AND ART ***The Country School* by Winslow Homer** Homer painted scenes of rural American life in the 1800s. This painting shows a classroom in a rural public school.

410

EXTRA CREDIT PROJECT

Artists of the Hudson River School The artists of this school were the first to develop a uniquely American school of landscape painting. The school began in the late 1820s and 1830s along the Hudson River in New York but soon spread to the West. Whereas European artists painted scenes of peaceful countrysides, the Hudson River School painters showed the wild beauty of America. Have students compare the works of these artists with those of European artists of the period. Students could also state ways the paintings are like the spirit of Americans of the time.

1820 1830 1840 1850

1825 Robert Owen establishes New Harmony, Indiana

1835 Oberlin College admits African Americans

1837 Horace Mann initiates education reform

1843 Dorothea Dix reveals abuses of mentally ill

Section 1

Social Reform

READ TO DISCOVER . . .

- how religious and philosophical ideas inspired various reform movements.
- why educational reformers thought all citizens should go to school.
- how a new American style developed in art and literature.

TERMS TO LEARN

utopia
revival
temperance
normal school
Transcendentalist

The Storyteller

Henry David Thoreau sat on the hard, wooden bench in the jail cell, but he did not complain about its stiffness. He felt proud that he had stood up for his beliefs. Thoreau had refused to pay a one-dollar tax to vote, not wanting his money to support the Mexican War. As he looked through the cell bars, he heard a voice. "Why are you here?" asked his friend Ralph Waldo Emerson. Thoreau replied, "Why are you *not* here?" He would later write, "Under a government which imprisons any unjustly, the true place for a just man is also a prison."

Ralph Waldo Emerson

A new reforming spirit arose in America in the early 1800s. The men and women who led the reform movement wanted to extend the nation's ideals of liberty and equality to all Americans. They believed the nation should live up to the noble goals stated in the Declaration of Independence and the Constitution.

The Reforming Spirit

The spirit of reform brought changes to American religion, politics, education, art, and literature. Some reformers sought to improve society by forming **utopias,** communities based on a vision of a perfect society. In 1825 **Robert Owen** established **New Harmony, Indiana,** a village dedicated to cooperation rather than competition among its members.

The Shakers, the Mormons, and other religious groups also built their own communities. Founded on high hopes and sometimes impractical ideas, few of the utopian communities lasted more than a few years. Only the Mormons established a stable, enduring community.

The Religious Influence

In the early 1800s, a wave of religious fervor—known as the **Second Great Awakening**—stirred the nation. The first Great Awakening had spread through the colonies in the mid-1700s.

The new religious movement began with frontier camp meetings called **revivals.** People came from miles around to hear eloquent preach-

SECTION RESOURCES

Reproducible Masters
- Guided Reading Activity 14–1
- Section Quiz 14–1
- Reteaching Activity 14–1
- Enrichment Activity 14–1

Transparencies
- Section Focus Transparency 14–1
- U.S. History & Art, Transparencies 6, 7, 9

Multimedia
- Vocabulary PuzzleMaker
- Chapter Challenger Interactive Review Software
- Testmaker
- Facts On File: Landmark Documents in American History
- Focus on American Art Prints, *Fur Traders Descending the Missouri*

1 FOCUS

BELLRINGER
Motivational Activity

Before taking roll at the beginning of the class period, project Section Focus Transparency 14–1 and have students answer the questions. Discuss students' responses.

This activity is also available as a blackline master.

Section Focus Transparency 14–1

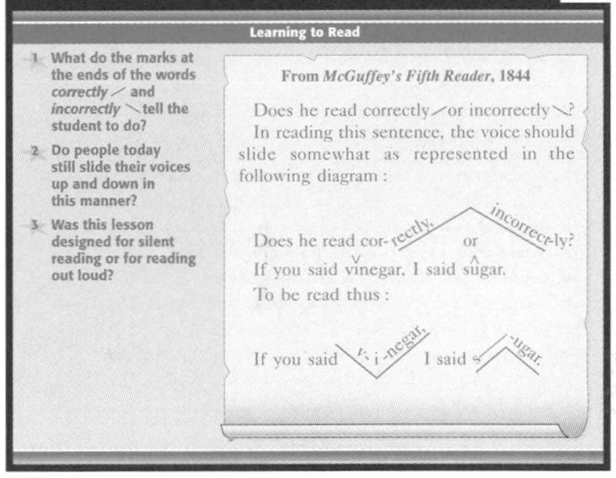
Learning to Read

1. What do the marks at the ends of the words *correctly* ⁄ and *incorrectly* ⁊ tell the student to do?
2. Do people today still slide their voices up and down in this manner?
3. Was this lesson designed for silent reading or for reading out loud?

From *McGuffey's Fifth Reader,* 1844

Does he read correctly or incorrectly? In reading this sentence, the voice should slide somewhat as represented in the following diagram:

Does he read correctly or incorrectly?
If you said vinegar, I said sugar.
To be read thus:
If you said vinegar, I said sugar.

Vocabulary Precheck

Revival comes from the Latin *re* meaning "again" and *vivificare,* meaning "to bring life to." Have students research the origins of the other **Terms to Learn.**

Use the **Vocabulary PuzzleMaker** to create crossword and word search puzzles.

Section Theme
Civic Rights and Responsibilities

Reforms in the 1800s covered a wide variety of areas, including religion, education, mental illness, special needs, and use of alcohol.

Activity Have students skim the section to find areas addressed by reformers.

2 TEACH

L1 Matching Have students write matching-style quizzes using the vocabulary words and people, places, and movements discussed in the section. Students may then swap quizzes and try to answer one another's quizzes.

Guided Reading Activity 14–1

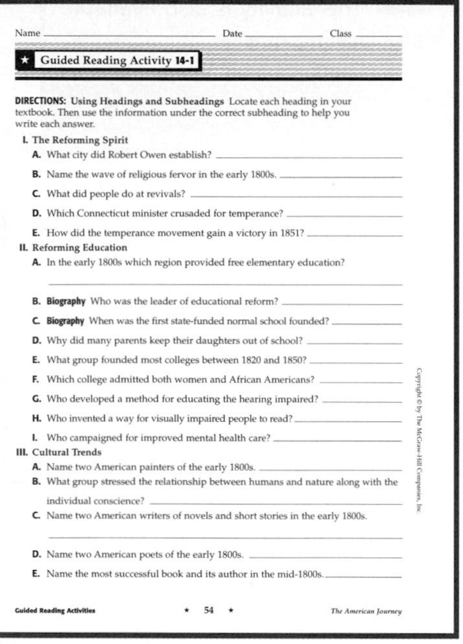

Name ______ Date ______ Class ______

Guided Reading Activity 14-1

DIRECTIONS: Using Headings and Subheadings Locate each heading in your textbook. Then use the information under the correct subheading to help you write each answer.

I. The Reforming Spirit
- **A.** What city did Robert Owen establish? ______
- **B.** Name the wave of religious fervor in the early 1800s. ______
- **C.** What did people do at revivals? ______
- **D.** Which Connecticut minister crusaded for temperance? ______
- **E.** How did the temperance movement gain a victory in 1851? ______

II. Reforming Education
- **A.** In the early 1800s which region provided free elementary education? ______
- **B. Biography** Who was the leader of educational reform? ______
- **C. Biography** When was the first state-funded normal school founded? ______
- **D.** Why did many parents keep their daughters out of school? ______
- **E.** What group founded most colleges between 1820 and 1850? ______
- **F.** Which college admitted both women and African Americans? ______
- **G.** Who developed a method for educating the hearing impaired? ______
- **H.** Who invented a way for visually impaired people to read? ______
- **I.** Who campaigned for improved mental health care? ______

III. Cultural Trends
- **A.** Name two American painters of the early 1800s. ______
- **B.** What group stressed the relationship between humans and nature along with the individual conscience? ______
- **C.** Name two American writers of novels and short stories in the early 1800s. ______
- **D.** Name two American poets of the early 1800s. ______
- **E.** Name the most successful book and its author in the mid-1800s. ______

Guided Reading Activities ★ 54 ★ *The American Journey*

Picturing HISTORY Unlike the revival of the 1700s, which stressed human weakness in the face of the Almighty, the Second Great Awakening taught that people's good works could make a difference in their world, thereby earning them a place in heaven.
Ask: **Why did some people inspired by the camp meetings go on to fight alcohol abuse?** *(possible response: Alcoholism often prevents a person from being a useful member of the community.)*
Answer: *Methodists and Baptists*

ers, such as **Charles Finney,** and to pray, sing, weep, and shout. The experience often made men and women eager to reform both their own lives and the world. The Second Great Awakening increased church membership, especially among Methodists and Baptists. It also inspired people to become involved in missionary work and social reform movements.

War Against Alcohol

Religious leaders stood at the forefront of the war against alcohol. Public drunkenness was common in the early 1800s. Alcohol abuse was widespread, especially in the West and among urban workers. **Lyman Beecher,** a Connecticut minister and crusader against the use of alcohol, wanted to protect society against "rum-selling, tippling folk, infidels and ruff-scruff."

Reformers blamed alcohol for poverty, the breakup of families, crime, and even insanity. They called for **temperance,** drinking little or no alcohol. The movement gathered momentum in 1826 when the American Society for the Promotion of Temperance was formed.

Beecher and other temperance crusaders used lectures, pamphlets, and revival-style rallies to warn people of the dangers of liquor. The **temperance movement** gained a major victory in 1851, when Maine passed a law banning the manufacture and sale of alcoholic beverages. Other states passed similar laws. Many Americans resented these laws, however, and most were later repealed, or canceled.

The temperance movement would reemerge in the early 1900s and lead to a constitutional amendment banning alcohol. You will read about this amendment and its repeal in Chapter 21.

Reforming Education

Reformers also focused on education. They argued that the poor state of education threatened the nation's well-being. Thomas Jefferson had stated that a democracy could not survive without educated citizens.

In the early 1800s, only New England provided free elementary education. In other areas parents had to pay fees or send their children to schools for the poor—a choice some parents refused out of pride. Some communities had no schools at all.

Biography

Horace Mann

The leader of educational reform was **Horace Mann,** a lawyer who became the head of the Massachusetts board of education in 1837. During his term Mann lengthened the school year to six months, made improvements in the school curriculum, doubled teachers' salaries, and developed better ways of training teachers.

Mann shared Jefferson's belief that education was vital to democracy:

Picturing HISTORY During the 1800s, many Americans on the frontier attended religious camp meetings. At these gatherings, preachers gave rousing messages that stirred the listeners' emotions. **What two religious groups gained members as a result of the camp meetings?**

COOPERATIVE LEARNING ACTIVITY

Making a Newspaper Point out that newspapers were the primary means of mass communication in the 1800s. List on the chalkboard the reformers discussed in the section—Lyman Beecher, Horace Mann, Dorothea Dix, Thomas Gallaudet, Samuel Gridley Howe, Harriet Beecher Stowe, and the Transcendentalists—Margaret Fuller, Ralph Waldo Emerson, and Henry David Thoreau. Organize the class into small groups, each of which is to create a human rights newspaper. Have some students in each group select one of the people listed on the board and write an article for the newspaper in the character of that person. Other students may create cartoons, draw pictures, write letters to the editor, or create advertisements for the paper. Remind students that their paper needs an appropriate name.

“If we do not prepare our children to be good citizens, then our republic must go down to destruction, as others have gone before it.”

Partly due to Mann's efforts, Massachusetts in 1839 founded the nation's first state-supported **normal school,** a school for training high-school graduates as teachers. Other states soon adopted the reforms that Mann had pioneered.

Education for Some

By the 1850s all states had accepted three basic principles of public education—that schools should be free and supported by taxes, that teachers should be trained, and that children should be required to attend school.

These principles did not immediately go into effect. Opposition to compulsory education slowed the development of public schools in many places. In addition schools were poorly funded, and many teachers lacked training.

Most females received a limited education. Parents often kept their daughters from school because of the belief that a woman's primary role was to become a wife and mother and that this role did not require an education. When girls did go to school, they often studied music or needlework rather than science, mathematics, and history—considered "men's" subjects.

In the West, where settlers lived far apart, many children had no school to attend. And African Americans in all parts of the country had few opportunities to go to school.

Higher Education

Dozens of new colleges and universities were created during the age of reform. Most admitted only men. Religious groups founded many colleges between 1820 and 1850, including Amherst and Holy Cross in Massachusetts and Trinity and Wesleyan in Connecticut.

Slowly, higher education became available to groups who were previously denied the opportunity. Oberlin College of Ohio, founded in 1833, admitted both women and African Americans to the student body. In 1837 a teacher named Mary Lyon in Massachusetts opened Mount Holyoke, the first permanent women's college in America. The first college for African Americans—Ashmun Institute, which later became Lincoln University—opened in Pennsylvania in 1854.

Picturing HISTORY In 1862 Mary Jane Patterson, the first African American woman to receive a bachelor's degree, graduated from Oberlin College in Ohio. **Why were educational opportunities limited for women during the mid-1800s?**

People with Special Needs

Some reformers focused on the problem of teaching people with disabilities. **Thomas Gallaudet** (ga•luh•DEHT), who developed a method of educating people who were hearing impaired, opened the Hartford School for the Deaf in Connecticut in 1817.

At about the same time, Dr. **Samuel Gridley Howe** advanced the cause of those who were visually impaired. He developed books with large raised letters that people with sight impairments could "read" with their fingers. Howe headed the Perkins Institute, a school for the blind, in Boston.

Footnotes to History

Braille Howe's raised-letter system was later replaced by Braille, a method invented by Louis Braille of France, in which raised dots represent letters.

Picturing HISTORY Unlike many of the new colleges and universities founded during the reform era, Oberlin was nonsectarian, although its founders were Quakers and Presbyterians.
Answer: *Many, if not most, people did not think a woman needed to be educated in anything other than domestic arts.*

Where? When? Who? What?

Brook Farm George Ripley, a Unitarian minister, founded the Utopian community Brook Farm near Boston in 1841 "to insure a more natural union between intellectual and manual labor." Leading New England writers and thinkers spent their days at Brook Farm discussing music, art, and literature and doing farm chores. Members became disillusioned, however, because of the time, energy, and hard work required by farm labor. Nathaniel Hawthorne, who was persuaded to live there for a time, found it difficult to write because of the hard work. He wrote to his fiancée, "It is my opinion . . . that a man's soul may be buried under a dungheap, or in a furrow of the field, just as well as under a pile of money."

History *and the* Humanities

U.S. History & Art, Transparency 6, *The Great Blue Heron;* Transparency 7, *The Buffalo Chase, Mouth of the Yellowstone;* Transparency 9, *Shooting for the Beef*

Focus on American Art Prints, *Fur Traders Descending the Missouri* by George Caleb Bingham

Multiple Learning Styles

Kinesthetic People throughout the world have developed ways of communicating manually. In the United States, hearing impaired people are often taught a system that combines sign language and fingerspelling. Sign language uses hand signs to represent ideas or things, whereas fingerspelling uses hand positions to represent the letters of the alphabet. Since sign language was brought to the United States in the 1800s, some of the signs reflect the daily life of the period. For example, the sign for *toast* mimics the action of a person placing a fork into bread to hold it over a flame. The sign for *female* represents a bonnet string. Have students learn enough signs or fingerspelling letters to convey simple messages. **L2, ELL**

Picturing HISTORY Herman Melville so admired Hawthorne's work that he compared Hawthorne to Shakespeare.
Answer: *Edgar Allan Poe*

Facts On File

CD-ROM
Landmark Documents in American History

Title: *"The American Scholar," speech, Ralph Waldo Emerson, 1837*
Ask students to note the sections in Emerson's speech that clearly show his philosophy of intellectual independence.

3 ASSESS

Assign Section 1 Review as homework or as an in-class activity.

Use **Chapter Challenger Interactive Review Software** to review Section 1.

Section Quiz 14–1

Name ________ Date ________ Class ________

Chapter 14

Score

Section Quiz 14-1

DIRECTIONS: Matching Match each item in Column A with the items in Column B. Write the correct letters in the blanks. *(10 points each)*

Column A	Column B
____ 1. utopia	A. The Great Awakening
____ 2. wave of religious fervor	B. Horace Mann
____ 3. preached at revivals	C. New Harmony, Indiana
____ 4. leader of educational reform	D. Walt Whitman
____ 5. poet	E. Charles Finney

DIRECTIONS: Multiple Choice In the blank at the left, write the letter of the choice that best completes the statement or answers the question. *(10 points each)*

____ 6. By the 1850s, when girls did go to school, they often studied
A. mathematics. C. music or needlework.
B. history. D. science.

____ 7. This was the first college in the United States to admit women and African Americans.
A. Harvard C. Mount Holyoke
B. Ashmun Institute D. Oberlin College of Ohio

____ 8. This schoolteacher helped reform attitudes toward the mentally ill.
A. Dorothea Dix C. George Catlin
B. Dr. Samuel Gridley Howe D. Thomas Gallaudet

____ 9. People who stressed the relationship between humans and nature and the importance of the individual conscience were called
A. Naturalists. C. Reformers.
B. Transcendentalists. D. Conscience-raisers.

____ 10. This writer wrote about the clash between the values of the white settlers on the frontier and those of the Native Americans.
A. Nathaniel Hawthorne C. James Fenimore Cooper
B. Herman Melville D. Washington Irving

Section Quizzes • 54 • *The American Journey*

Picturing HISTORY Puritan author Nathaniel Hawthorne explored themes of guilt and innocence, and good and evil. **What American writer of the mid-1800s focused on the supernatural?**

New Attitudes Toward Mental Illness

When schoolteacher **Dorothea Dix** visited a women's jail in Cambridge, Massachusetts, she found that some women confined there had committed no crime. They were mentally ill. These "lunatics," as the jailers called them, were locked up in the back of the jail in cold, dark cells.

Dix spent 18 months visiting the jails, poorhouses, and asylums of Massachusetts. She took notes on what she saw and made a report to the Massachusetts legislature. People were shocked by her vivid description of mentally ill people kept in pens, cellars, and cages, "chained, naked, beaten with rods and lashed into obedience."

Massachusetts lawmakers agreed to spend the money needed to provide better care for the mentally ill. Dix then began a lifelong crusade to improve the care of people with mental illness—one of many reforms dedicated to transforming American society in the mid-1800s.

Cultural Trends

The changes in American society influenced art and literature. Earlier generations of American painters and writers looked to Europe for their inspiration and models. Beginning in the 1820s American artists developed their own style and explored American themes.

Painters

American painters started choosing subjects that were specifically American. One group of painters, known as the Hudson River School, painted landscapes of the Hudson River valley in New York.

George Catlin painted hundreds of pictures of Native American life in the West. George Caleb Bingham of Missouri celebrated contemporary river and frontier life. In a series of elegant paintings and sketches, **John James Audubon** portrayed the birds of America.

Transcendentalists

The American spirit of reform influenced **Transcendentalists.** Transcendentalists stressed the relationship between humans and nature as well as the importance of the individual conscience. Writers such as **Margaret Fuller, Ralph Waldo Emerson,** and **Henry David Thoreau** were leading Transcendentalists. Through her life and writings, Fuller supported rights for women. In his poems and essays, Emerson urged people to listen to the inner voice of conscience and to break the bonds of prejudice. Thoreau put his beliefs into practice through **civil disobedience**—refusing to obey laws he thought were unjust. In 1846 Thoreau went to jail rather than pay a tax to support the Mexican War.

Other Writers

The Transcendentalists were not the only important writers of the period. Two of the most popular authors of the early 1800s were **James Fenimore Cooper** and **Washington Irving.** In novels such as *The Deerslayer* and *The Last of the Mohicans,* James Fenimore Cooper wrote of the clash between the values of the white settlers on the frontier and those of Native Americans. Washington Irving wrote tales, such as "The Legend of Sleepy Hollow" and "Rip Van Winkle," set in the Hudson River valley of New York.

Nathaniel Hawthorne, a descendant of early Massachusetts colonists, wrote of moral struggles in Puritan New England in *The Scarlet Letter.*

MAKING CONNECTIONS ACTIVITY

The Arts John James Audubon (1785–1851) was born in Santo Domingo (now Haiti), but grew up in France. He came to America in 1803 to avoid fighting for Napoleon. Eventually he decided to put his childhood pastime—drawing wildlife, especially birds—to work. He spent hours outdoors watching and sketching birds engaged in their daily activities. Unable to find an American publisher that met his standards, he went to London where he found a brilliant craftsman to do the engravings for *Birds of America,* a classic reference work. Have students research the life of this important scientist and artist and make a brief report on his works. Then ask students to render their own drawing of wildlife. **L2, ELL**

Using his experiences at sea, **Herman Melville** wrote *Moby Dick,* an epic tale of a whaling captain's search for revenge. In stories such as "The Tell-Tale Heart," **Edgar Allan Poe** explored the world of the supernatural. Poe perfected the modern detective story and has been called the "father of the modern short story."

American Poets

Many poets created impressive works during this period. **Henry Wadsworth Longfellow** wrote narrative, or story, poems, such as *The Song of Hiawatha,* on American themes. **Walt Whitman** captured the American impulse for self-improvement and equality in *Leaves of Grass* and other poetry. He wrote of a growing, confident people.

Emily Dickinson wrote simple, deeply personal poems. In a poem called "Hope," written in 1861, she compares hope with a bird:

> "'Hope' is the thing with feathers—
> That perches in the soul—
> And sings the tune without the words—
> And never stops—at all—"

Women writers of the period were generally not taken seriously, yet they were the authors of the most popular fiction. **Harriet Beecher Stowe** wrote the most successful best-seller of the mid-1800s, *Uncle Tom's Cabin.* Stowe's novel explores the injustice of slavery—an issue that took on new urgency during the age of reform.

Picturing HISTORY First printed as a series in a newspaper, Harriet Beecher Stowe's *Uncle Tom's Cabin* came out as a book in 1852. **What was the major topic of *Uncle Tom's Cabin?***

Section 1 Review

Checking for Understanding

1. ***Identify*** Horace Mann, Dorothea Dix, Ralph Waldo Emerson, Henry David Thoreau, Emily Dickinson, Harriet Beecher Stowe.
2. ***Define*** utopia, revival, temperance, normal school, Transcendentalist.
3. ***Explain*** the link between religion and reform in the early 1800s.

Reviewing Themes

4. **Civic Rights and Responsibilities** How did Thoreau act on his beliefs?

Critical Thinking

5. **Drawing Conclusions** What did Thomas Jefferson mean when he said that the United States could not survive as a democracy without educated and well-informed citizens?

Activity

Conducting an Interview Interview your grandparents or other adults who are more than 50 years old to find out what they remember about their public school days.

Section 1 Review Answers

1. Mann, 412; Dix, 414; Emerson, 414; Thoreau, 414; Dickinson, 415; Stowe, 415
2. The words are defined in the Glossary.
3. The Second Great Awakening inspired many people to renew their faith. As a result they tried to reform their own lives and the world.
4. He believed individuals must decide for themselves what is right and wrong, so he refused to obey laws that he thought were unjust. He went to jail for refusing to pay a tax to support the Mexican War.
5. Democracy is based on citizen involvement in government. Uneducated people cannot effectively and intelligently make decisions about governing themselves.

Activity Encourage students to share the results of their interviews with the class.

CHAPTER 14

Section 1, 411–415

Picturing HISTORY *Uncle Tom's Cabin* sold 300,000 copies in 1852, its first year of publication. **Answer:** *the injustice of slavery*

Reteaching Activity 14–1

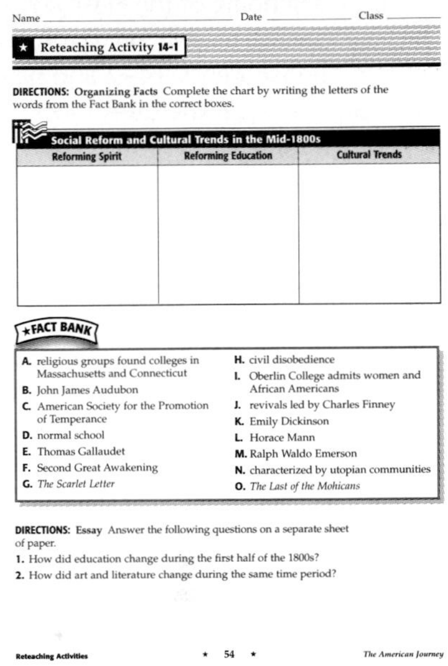

Name ______ Date ______ Class ______

★ Reteaching Activity 14-1

DIRECTIONS: Organizing Facts Complete the chart by writing the letters of the words from the Fact Bank in the correct boxes.

Social Reform and Cultural Trends in the Mid-1800s

Reforming Spirit	Reforming Education	Cultural Trends

★FACT BANK

- **A.** religious groups found colleges in Massachusetts and Connecticut
- **B.** John James Audubon
- **C.** American Society for the Promotion of Temperance
- **D.** normal school
- **E.** Thomas Gallaudet
- **F.** Second Great Awakening
- **G.** *The Scarlet Letter*
- **H.** civil disobedience
- **I.** Oberlin College admits women and African Americans
- **J.** revivals led by Charles Finney
- **K.** Emily Dickinson
- **L.** Horace Mann
- **M.** Ralph Waldo Emerson
- **N.** characterized by utopian communities
- **O.** *The Last of the Mohicans*

DIRECTIONS: Essay Answer the following questions on a separate sheet of paper.

1. How did education change during the first half of the 1800s?
2. How did art and literature change during the same time period?

Reteaching Activities ★ 54 ★ *The American Journey*

Enrichment Activity 14–1

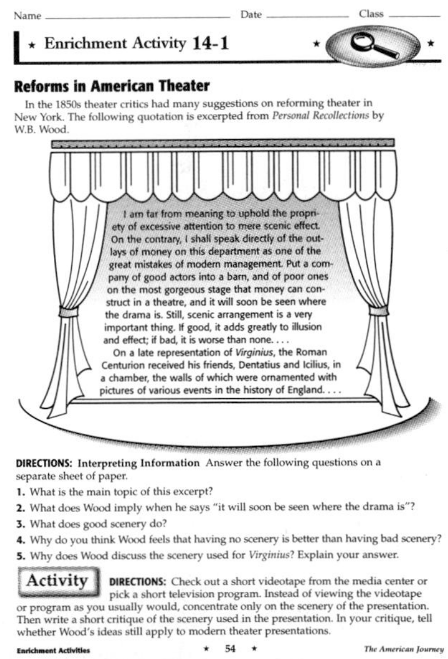

Name ______ Date ______ Class ______

★ Enrichment Activity 14-1

Reforms in American Theater

In the 1850s theater critics had many suggestions on reforming theater in New York. The following quotation is excerpted from *Personal Recollections* by W.B. Wood.

> I am far from meaning to uphold the propriety of excessive attention to mere scenic effect. On the contrary, I shall speak directly of the outlays of money on this department as one of the great mistakes of modern management. Put a company of good actors into a barn, and of poor ones on the most gorgeous stage that money can construct in a theatre, and it will soon be seen where the drama is. Still, scenic arrangement is a very important thing. If good, it adds greatly to illusion and effect; if bad, it is worse than none. . . .
> On a late representation of *Virginius*, the Roman Centurion received his friends, Dentatius and Icilius, in a chamber, the walls of which were ornamented with pictures of various events in the history of England. . . .

DIRECTIONS: Interpreting Information Answer the following questions on a separate sheet of paper.

1. What is the main topic of this excerpt?
2. What does Wood imply when he says "it will soon be seen where the drama is"?
3. What does good scenery do?
4. Why do you think Wood feels that having no scenery is better than having bad scenery?
5. Why does Wood discuss the scenery used for *Virginius*? Explain your answer.

Activity **DIRECTIONS:** Check out a short videotape from the media center or pick a short television program. Instead of viewing the videotape or program as you usually would, concentrate only on the scenery of the presentation. Then write a short critique of the scenery used in the presentation. In your critique, tell whether Wood's ideas still apply to modern theater presentations.

Enrichment Activities ★ 54 ★ *The American Journey*

4 CLOSE

When Abraham Lincoln met Harriet Beecher Stowe, he said, "So this is the little lady who wrote the book that made this great war." **Ask: In what sense was his comment true?**

1 FOCUS

BELLRINGER
Motivational Activity

Before taking roll at the beginning of the class period, project Section Focus Transparency 14–2 and have students answer the questions. Discuss students' responses.

This activity is also available as a blackline master.

Section Focus Transparency 14–2

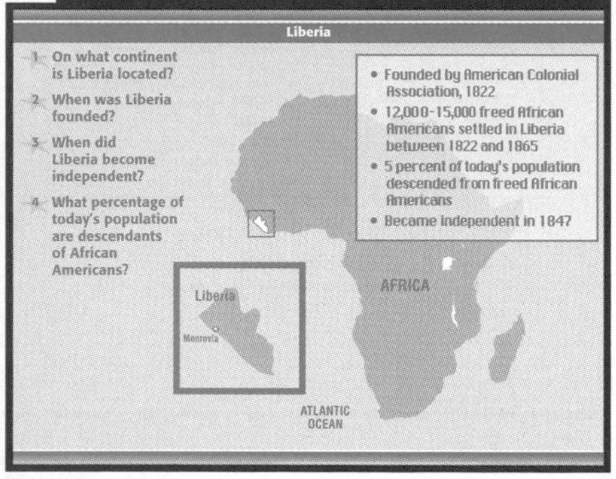

Vocabulary Precheck

List this section's **Terms to Learn** on the chalkboard. Have students develop questions for which each term is an answer.

Use the **Vocabulary PuzzleMaker** to create crossword and word search puzzles.

Section Theme
Individual Action

The abolitionist movement gained great momentum during the early and mid-1800s.

Activity Have students skim the section for the names of individuals involved in the movement. *(Benjamin Lundy, William Lloyd Garrison, Sarah and Angelina Grimké, David Walker, Frederick Douglass, Sojourner Truth, Harriet Tubman, Elijah Lovejoy)*

1815 — 1830 — 1845 — 1860

1817 American Colonization Society is formed

1822 First African Americans settle in Liberia

1831 William Lloyd Garrison founds *The Liberator*

1847 Liberia becomes an independent country

Section 2

The Abolitionists

READ TO DISCOVER . . .

- how some Americans—African Americans and whites—fought to eliminate slavery.
- why many Southerners and some Northerners feared the end of slavery.

TERMS TO LEARN

abolitionist
Underground Railroad

The Storyteller

William Lloyd Garrison, a dramatic and spirited man, fought strongly for the right of African Americans to be free. On one occasion Garrison was present when Frederick Douglass, an African American who had escaped from slavery, spoke to a white audience about life as a slave. Douglass electrified his listeners with a powerful speech. Suddenly Garrison leaped to his feet. "Is this a man," he demanded of the audience, "or a thing?" Garrison shared Douglass's outrage at the notion that people could be bought and sold like objects.

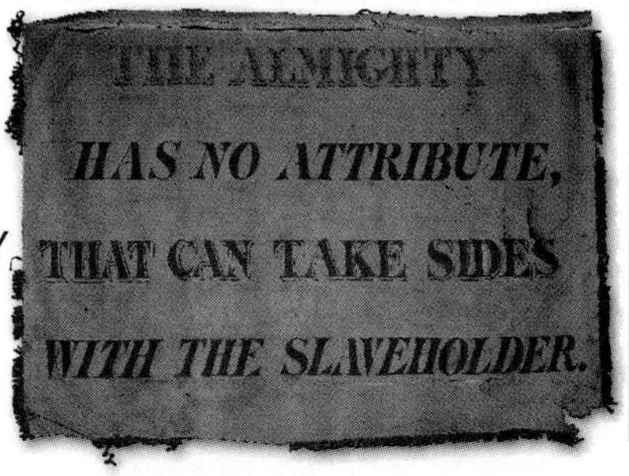

Antislavery banner

The spirit of reform that swept the United States in the early 1800s was not limited to improving education and expanding the arts. It also included the efforts of **abolitionists**—members of the growing band of reformers who worked to abolish, or end, slavery.

Early Efforts to End Slavery

Even before the American Revolution, some Americans had tried to limit or end slavery. At the Constitutional Convention in 1787, the delegates had reached a compromise on the difficult issue, agreeing to let each state decide whether to allow slavery. By the early 1800s, Northern states had ended slavery, but it continued in the South. The North and the South then engaged in a heated debate over the issue of slavery.

The religious revival and the reform movement of the early and mid-1800s gave new life to the antislavery movement. Many Americans came to believe that slavery was wrong. Yet not all Northerners shared this view. The conflict over slavery continued to build.

Quakers for Freedom

Many of the men and women who led the antislavery movement came from the Quaker faith. One Quaker, **Benjamin Lundy** of New Jersey, founded a newspaper in 1815 to spread the

SECTION RESOURCES

Reproducible Masters
- Reproducible Lesson Plan 14–2
- Guided Reading Activity 14–2
- Section Quiz 14–2
- Reteaching Activity 14–2
- Enrichment Activity 14–2

Transparencies
- Section Focus Transparency 14–2

Multimedia
- Vocabulary PuzzleMaker
- Chapter Challenger Interactive Review
- Testmaker
- Facts On File: Landmark Documents in American History
- GTV: A Geographic Perspective on American History
- American Music Cultural Traditions

abolitionist message. Lundy wrote, "I heard the wail of the captive. I felt his pang of distress, and the iron entered my soul."

American Colonization Society

The first large-scale antislavery effort was not aimed at abolishing slavery but at resettling African Americans in Africa or the Caribbean. The **American Colonization Society,** formed in 1817 by a group of white Virginians, worked to free enslaved workers gradually by buying them from slaveholders and sending them abroad to start new lives.

The society raised enough money from private donors, Congress, and the Virginia and Maryland legislatures to send several groups of African Americans out of the country. Some went to the west coast of Africa, where the society had acquired land for a colony. In 1822 the first African American settlers arrived in this colony, called **Liberia,** Latin for "place of freedom."

In 1847 Liberia became an independent country. American emigration to Liberia continued until the Civil War. Some 12,000 to 15,000 African Americans settled in the new country between 1822 and 1865.

Problems With Resettlement

The American Colonization Society did not halt the growth of slavery. The number of enslaved people continued to increase at a steady pace, and the society could only resettle a small number of African Americans. Furthermore, most African Americans did not want to go to Africa. Many were from families that had lived in America for several generations. They simply wanted to be free in American society. African Americans feared that the society aimed to strengthen slavery.

The Movement Changes

Reformers realized that the gradual approach to ending slavery had failed. Moreover, the numbers of enslaved persons had sharply increased because the cotton boom in the Deep South made planters increasingly dependent on slave labor. Beginning in about 1830, the American antislavery movement took on new life. Soon it became the most pressing social issue for reformers.

William Lloyd Garrison, 1825

Biography

William Lloyd Garrison

Abolitionist **William Lloyd Garrison** stimulated the growth of the antislavery movement. In 1829 Garrison left Massachusetts to work for the country's leading antislavery paper in Baltimore. Impatient with the paper's moderate position, Garrison returned to Boston in 1831 to found his own newspaper, *The Liberator.*

Garrison was the first white abolitionist to call for the "immediate and complete emancipation [freeing]" of enslaved people. Promising to be "as harsh as truth, and as uncompromising as justice," he denounced the slow, gradual approach of other reformers. In the first issue of his paper he wrote: "I will not retreat a single inch—AND I WILL BE HEARD."

COOPERATIVE LEARNING ACTIVITY

Dramatizing Escape Organize the class into small groups for this activity. Have each group first research to find out more about what it was like to be an enslaved African American on the run, and then choose an escape episode to dramatize. Stories can be those of people using the Underground Railroad or of those attempting escape on their own. Some students should do the research, while others write dialogue, make props and costumes, or play a role in the dramatization.

2 TEACH

L1 Identifying People and Movements Write the following on the chalkboard: Benjamin Lundy, American Colonization Society, William Lloyd Garrison, Sarah and Angelina Grimké, David Walker, Frederick Douglass, Sojourner Truth, Underground Railroad, Harriet Tubman, Elijah Lovejoy. Have students write a sentence or two identifying each one.

Guided Reading Activity 14–2

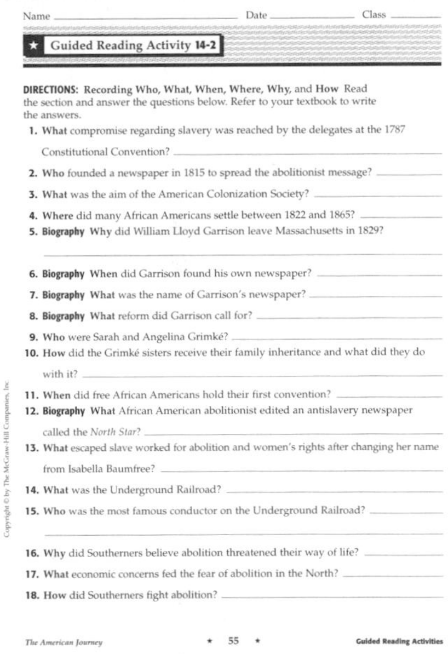

Name ______ Date ______ Class ______

★ Guided Reading Activity 14-2

DIRECTIONS: Recording Who, What, When, Where, Why, and **How** Read the section and answer the questions below. Refer to your textbook to write the answers.

1. **What** compromise regarding slavery was reached by the delegates at the 1787 Constitutional Convention? ______
2. **Who** founded a newspaper in 1815 to spread the abolitionist message? ______
3. **What** was the aim of the American Colonization Society? ______
4. **Where** did many African Americans settle between 1822 and 1865? ______
5. **Biography Why** did William Lloyd Garrison leave Massachusetts in 1829? ______
6. **Biography When** did Garrison found his own newspaper? ______
7. **Biography What** was the name of Garrison's newspaper? ______
8. **Biography What** reform did Garrison call for? ______
9. **Who** were Sarah and Angelina Grimké? ______
10. **How** did the Grimké sisters receive their family inheritance and what did they do with it? ______
11. **When** did free African Americans hold their first convention? ______
12. **Biography What** African American abolitionist edited an antislavery newspaper called the *North Star*? ______
13. **What** escaped slave worked for abolition and women's rights after changing her name from Isabella Baumfree? ______
14. **What** was the Underground Railroad? ______
15. **Who** was the most famous conductor on the Underground Railroad? ______
16. **Why** did Southerners believe abolition threatened their way of life? ______
17. **What** economic concerns fed the fear of abolition in the North? ______
18. **How** did Southerners fight abolition? ______

The American Journey ★ 55 ★ **Guided Reading Activities**

NATIONAL GEOGRAPHIC SOCIETY

VIDEODISC
GTV: A Geographic Perspective on American History

Side 2, Chapter 13
Title: *One Nation, Still?*
Subject: Regional differences deepen (1850–1860)
Ask: **In what ways did the North prosper in the 1850s?** *(growth of industries, number of workers, and cities; improved farming tools; faster transportation such as the railroad)*

CHAPTER 14
Section 2, 416–422

Picturing HISTORY After the Civil War, Douglass was a leading supporter of the women's rights movement, fought against racial segregation laws and practices, and held important government posts such as United States minister and consul general to Haiti. *My Bondage and My Freedom,* published in 1855, was the second volume of Frederick Douglass's autobiography. Douglass felt the need to tell his life story because white abolitionists could never quite give a complete picture of slavery. Although they could detail slavery's history and depict its horrors, Douglass noted, "they cannot speak from experience as I can."
Answer: *He spoke at abolitionist meetings and edited an antislavery newspaper, the* North Star. *He was the most widely known abolitionist.*

Where?When?Who?What?

Monrovia Liberia's main port and capital city, Monrovia, was named after James Monroe, president of the United States at the time of the first settlement.

you don't say...

Simon Legree was the cruel white overseer in *Uncle Tom's Cabin.* Today the name is still used occasionally to describe an overbearing person, particularly a boss who works employees hard with no regard for their welfare.

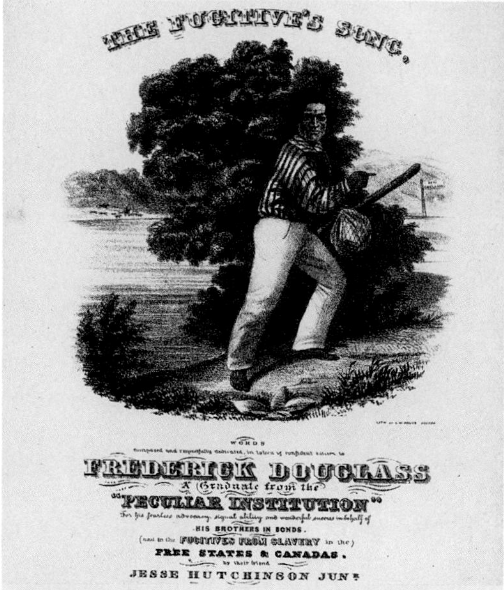

Picturing HISTORY This song sheet commemorates Frederick Douglass's 1838 escape from slavery. **What role did Frederick Douglass play in the abolitionist movement?**

Garrison *was* heard. He attracted enough followers to start the New England Antislavery Society in 1832 and the American Antislavery Society a year later. The **abolitionist movement** grew rapidly. By 1838 the antislavery societies Garrison started had more than 1,000 chapters, or local branches.

Americans Against Slavery

Among the first women who spoke out publicly against slavery were **Sarah** and **Angelina Grimké.** Born in South Carolina to a wealthy slaveholding family, the sisters moved to Philadelphia in 1832.

In the North the Grimké sisters lectured and wrote against slavery. At the National Anti-Slavery Convention in Philadelphia in 1838, Angelina Grimké exclaimed, "As a Southerner, I feel that it is my duty to stand up . . . against slavery. I have seen it! I have seen it!"

The Grimkés persuaded their mother to give them their share of the family inheritance. Instead of money or land, the sisters asked for several of the enslaved workers, whom they immediately freed.

Angelina Grimké and her husband, abolitionist Theodore Weld, wrote *American Slavery As It Is* in 1839. This collection of firsthand accounts of life under slavery was one of the most influential abolitionist publications of its time.

African American Abolitionists

Although white abolitionists drew public attention to the cause, African Americans themselves played a major role in the abolitionist movement from the start. The abolition of slavery was an especially important goal to the free African Americans of the North, who numbered about 250,000 in 1850.

Most African Americans in the North lived in poverty in cities. Excluded from most jobs and often attacked by white mobs, a great many of these African Americans were nevertheless intensely proud of their freedom and wanted to help those who were still enslaved.

Fighting Slavery

African Americans took active part in organizing and directing the American Antislavery Society, and they subscribed in large numbers to William Lloyd Garrison's *The Liberator.* In 1827 Samuel Cornish and John Russwurm started the country's first African American newspaper, *Freedom's Journal.* Most of the other newspapers that African Americans founded before the Civil War also promoted abolition.

Born a free man in North Carolina, writer **David Walker** of Boston published an impassioned argument against slavery, challenging African Americans to rebel and overthrow slavery by force. "America is more our country than it is the whites'—we have enriched it with our blood and tears," he wrote.

MULTIPLE LEARNING STYLES

Kinesthetic Have students choose an event or a person discussed in the section (or one about which they have learned through independent reading) and create a monument honoring that person or event. Monuments should show some symbolic relationship to the subject and may include inscriptions. Students may execute their work in clay, pâpier maché, soap, or whatever medium they prefer. You may wish to have each student give a brief oral presentation of his or her monument. **L2**, ELL

In 1830 free African American leaders held their first convention in Philadelphia. Delegates met "to devise ways and means for the bettering of our condition." They discussed starting an African American college and encouraging free African Americans to emigrate to Canada.

Biography

Frederick Douglass

Frederick Douglass, the most widely known African American abolitionist, was born enslaved in Maryland. After teaching himself to read and write, he escaped from slavery in Maryland in 1838 and settled first in Massachusetts and then in New York.

As a runaway, Douglass could have been captured and returned to slavery. Nevertheless he joined the Massachusetts Antislavery Society and traveled widely to address abolitionist meetings. A powerful speaker, Douglass often moved listeners to tears with his message. At an Independence Day gathering he told the audience:

> "What, to the American slave, is your Fourth of July? I answer: a day that reveals to him, more than all other days in the year, the gross injustice and cruelty to which he is the constant victim. To him, your celebration is a sham . . . your national greatness, swelling vanity; your sounds of rejoicing are empty and heartless . . . your shouts of liberty and equality, hollow mockery."

The Underground Railroad

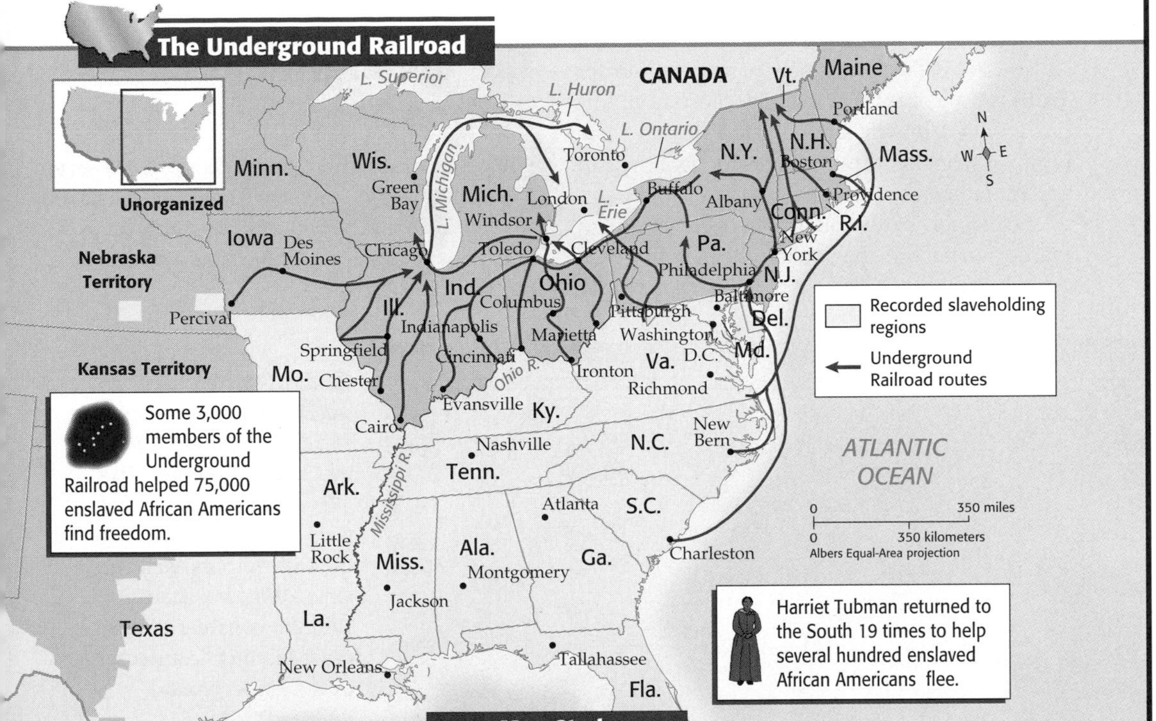

Map Study

Many enslaved African Americans escaped to freedom with the help of the Underground Railroad.

1. **Movement** Which river did enslaved persons cross before reaching Indiana and Ohio?
2. **Analyzing Information** About how many miles did an enslaved person travel from Montgomery, Alabama, to Windsor, Canada?

MAKING CONNECTIONS ACTIVITY

Literature Have each student choose a book and read it for a book report. Subjects may include groups and people discussed in the section, historical fiction about the period, or accounts of other people and events of the time. One or more of your better readers might like to read *Uncle Tom's Cabin.* Caution anyone who does decide to read it that, although it was considered radical in its time, by today's standards the book is guilty of racism and stereotyping. **L2**

CHAPTER 14
Section 2, 416–422

What? Where? When? Who?

The Liberator Despite its influence, *The Liberator* was a small newspaper with a low circulation. In its first year, the four-page weekly had only six subscribers. Its greatest circulation was only about 5,000.

History *and the* Humanities

American Music Cultural Traditions, Lesson 4: "Kneebone Bend," "The Monongahela Waltz"; Lesson 5: "Roll, Jordan, Roll," "Get Off the Track!"

What? Where? When? Who?

The Gag Resolution Southerners grew very sensitive to criticisms of slavery, so much so that Southern congressmen pushed a resolution through the House—the so-called Gag Resolution. It required that the piles of antislavery petitions that Congress received be tabled without debate. It took him eight years, but an outraged John Quincy Adams, representative and former president, managed to get the resolution repealed.

Map Study

Answers

1. Ohio River
2. about 790 miles (1,260 km)

Map Skills Practice

Reading a Map Through what city did the Underground Railroad route from Marietta to Windsor pass? *(Cleveland, Ohio)*

CHAPTER 14
Section 2, 416–422

Facts On File

CD-ROM
Landmark Documents in American History

Title: *"Ain't I a Woman" speech, Sojourner Truth, 1852*
Have students describe their reaction to this speech.

Who?What?Where?When?

Truly the Weaker Sex? One of Sojourner Truth's most often quoted speeches was given in response to a man who claimed that men needed to protect women because they were the weaker sex. "The man over there says women need to be helped into carriages and over ditches, and to have the best place everywhere. Nobody ever helps me into carriages, or over puddles, or gives me the best place. And ain't I a woman? I have ploughed and planted and gathered into barns and no man could head [do better than] me. And ain't I a woman? I could work as much and eat as much as a man—when I could get it—and bear the lash as well. And ain't I a woman?"

HISTORY AND ART The painting shows the farm of Levi Coffin in Newport, Indiana.
Ask: From which states did most passengers on the Underground Railroad come? *(border states)*
Answer: *because she risked her freedom and probably her life making so many trips back into the South to guide people out*

For 16 years, Douglass edited an antislavery newspaper called the *North Star.* Douglass won admiration as a powerful and influential speaker and writer. He traveled abroad, speaking to huge antislavery audiences in London and the West Indies. Douglass returned to the United States believing abolitionists must fight slavery at its source. He insisted that African Americans receive not just their freedom but full equality with whites as well. In 1847 friends helped Douglass purchase his freedom from the slaveholder he had fled in Maryland.

Sojourner Truth

"I was born a slave in Ulster County, New York," Isabella Baumfree began when she told her story to audiences. Called "Belle," she lived in the cellar of her master's house. When New York banned slavery in 1827, her owner insisted she stay a year longer. Instead, she fled.

In 1843 Belle chose a new name. "**Sojourner Truth** is my name," she said, "because from this day I will walk in the light of [God's] truth." She began to work in the movements for abolitionism and for women's rights.

Sojourner Truth had never been taught to read or write, but she spoke with wit and wisdom. In 1852 at a gathering of Ohioans, a rowdy farmer challenged her: The Constitution did not oppose slavery. Was she against the Constitution?

In answer, Sojourner used an example the farmer could understand. She knew that insects called weevils had eaten that year's wheat crop in Ohio. So she described walking near a wheat field and touching the tall, healthy-looking stalks but finding no grain there. "I says, 'God, what's the matter with this wheat?' And he says to me, 'Sojourner, there's a little weevil in it.'"

The farmer started to interrupt, but Sojourner continued to speak: "I hears talk about the Constitution and rights of man. I come up and I takes hold of this Constitution. It looks mighty big. And I feels for my rights. But they not there. Then I says, 'God, what ails this Constitution?' And you know what he says to me? . . . 'Sojourner, there's a little weevil in it.'"

The Underground Railroad

Some abolitionists risked prison—even death—by secretly helping enslaved Africans escape. The network of escape routes out of the South came to be called the **Underground Railroad.**

HISTORY AND ART
***The Underground Railroad* by Charles T. Weber** This 1850s painting shows fugitives arriving at a station of the Underground Railroad in Ohio. **Why was Harriet Tubman considered the most famous "conductor" of the Underground Railroad?**

CRITICAL THINKING ACTIVITY

Identifying Alternatives Abolitionists such as William Lloyd Garrison, Frederick Douglass, and others did not agree on how to end slavery. Most rejected the American Colonization Society's answer of shipping African Americans off to Liberia. Some called for an immediate end to slavery, others hoped for a more gradual approach to eliminate what they considered the scourge of American society. Have students brainstorm ideas for a way that slavery could have been ended peacefully. Then have each student use the ideas in writing a plan for a peaceful solution. **L2**

The Underground Railroad had no trains or tracks. Instead, passengers on this "railroad" traveled through the night, often on foot, and went north—guided by the North Star. The runaway slaves followed rivers and mountain chains, or felt for moss growing on the north sides of trees.

Songs such as "Follow the Drinkin' Gourd" encouraged runaways on their way to freedom. A hollowed-out gourd was used to dip water for drinking. Its shape resembled the Big Dipper, which pointed to the North Star.

> "When the river ends in between two
> hills,
> Follow the drinkin' gourd,
> For the Ole Man's waitin' for to carry you
> to freedom.
> Follow the drinkin' gourd."

During the day passengers rested at "stations"—barns, attics, church basements, or other places where fugitives could rest, eat, and hide until the next night's journey. The railroad's "conductors" were whites and African Americans who helped guide the escaping slaves to freedom in the North.

In the early days, many people made the journey north on foot. Later they traveled in wagons, sometimes equipped with secret compartments. One runaway, Henry "Box" Brown, traveled from Richmond, Virginia, to Philadelphia, Pennsylvania, hidden in a crate.

African Americans on the Underground Railroad hoped to settle in a free state in the North or to move on to Canada. Once in the North, however, fugitives still feared capture. Henry Bibb, a runaway who reached Ohio, arrived at "the place where I was directed to call on an Abolitionist, but I made no stop: so great were my fears of being pursued."

Harriet Tubman

Harriet Tubman

Harriet Tubman escaped from slavery to become the most famous conductor on the Underground Railroad. She made many dangerous trips into the South and guided hundreds of enslaved people, including her parents, to freedom.

Slaveholders offered a large reward for Tubman's capture or death. "There was one of two things I had a right to, liberty or death," she said. "If I could not have one, I would have the other; for no man should take me alive." Tubman was never captured and lived to an old age.

The Underground Railroad helped only a tiny fraction of the enslaved population. Most who used it as a route to freedom came from the border states, not the Deep South. Still the Underground Railroad gave hope to those who suffered in slavery. It also provided abolitionists with a way to help some enslaved people to freedom.

Clashes over Abolitionism

★ The antislavery movement led to an intense reaction against abolitionism. Southern slaveholders—and many Southerners who did not have slaves—opposed abolitionism because they believed it threatened the South's way

Footnotes to History

Early Freedom Rider During the Civil War, Sojourner Truth tried to desegregate public transportation. Desegregated public transportation would not exist until almost 100 years later, in the 1950s.

More About . . .

Harriet Tubman had to be quick-witted to avoid capture. Once, she noticed slave catchers approaching as she and her group were about to get on a northbound train. Quickly she herded everyone onto a southbound train, knowing that no one would expect to find runaways heading south. Another time, when she was disguised as an old woman, she saw her old master coming toward her. Instantly she dropped the live chickens she happened to be carrying and went rushing after them. The man laughed and called, "Go get them, Granny," and Tubman once again escaped.

Using her experiences as a conductor on the Underground Railroad, Tubman became a valuable scout and spy for the Union Army during the Civil War. After the war she lived in Auburn, New York, where she established a home for elderly African Americans.

3 ASSESS

Assign Section 2 Review as homework or as an in-class activity.

Use **Chapter Challenger Interactive Review Software** to review Section 2.

Section Quiz 14–2

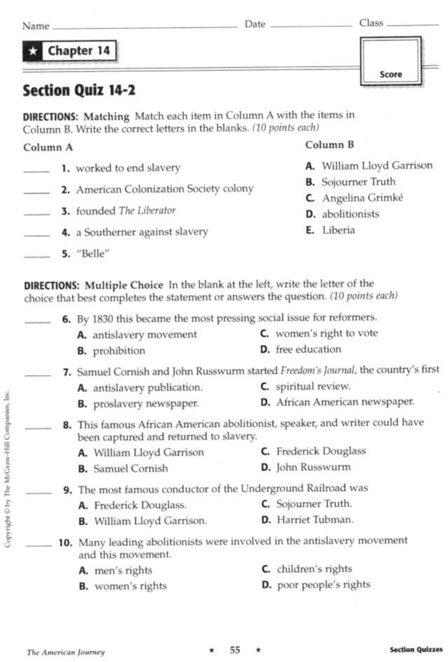

Name ______ Date ______ Class ______

★ Chapter 14

Score

Section Quiz 14-2

DIRECTIONS: Matching Match each item in Column A with the items in Column B. Write the correct letters in the blanks. *(10 points each)*

Column A	Column B
____ 1. worked to end slavery	A. William Lloyd Garrison
____ 2. American Colonization Society colony	B. Sojourner Truth
____ 3. founded *The Liberator*	C. Angelina Grimké
____ 4. a Southerner against slavery	D. abolitionists
____ 5. "Belle"	E. Liberia

DIRECTIONS: Multiple Choice In the blank at the left, write the letter of the choice that best completes the statement or answers the question. *(10 points each)*

____ 6. By 1830 this became the most pressing social issue for reformers.
A. antislavery movement C. women's right to vote
B. prohibition D. free education

____ 7. Samuel Cornish and John Russwurm started *Freedom's Journal*, the country's first
A. antislavery publication. C. spiritual review.
B. proslavery newspaper. D. African American newspaper.

____ 8. This famous African American abolitionist, speaker, and writer could have been captured and returned to slavery.
A. William Lloyd Garrison C. Frederick Douglass
B. Samuel Cornish D. John Russwurm

____ 9. The most famous conductor of the Underground Railroad was
A. Frederick Douglass. C. Sojourner Truth.
B. William Lloyd Garrison. D. Harriet Tubman.

____ 10. Many leading abolitionists were involved in the antislavery movement and this movement.
A. men's rights C. children's rights
B. women's rights D. poor people's rights

The American Journey ★ 55 ★ **Section Quizzes**

Linking PAST & PRESENT

Bus desegregation came about in Montgomery, Alabama, because of the efforts of another African American woman, Rosa Parks. Her refusal to sit at the back of a bus led to her arrest and a subsequent successful boycott of the city's buses by African Americans, who constituted the majority of the city's bus riders.

Reteaching Activity 14–2

Name ______ Date ______ Class ______

★ Reteaching Activity 14-2

DIRECTIONS: Matching Match each item in Column A with its corresponding item in Column B. Write the correct letters in the blanks.

COLUMN A

____ 1. Benjamin Lundy
____ 2. William Lloyd Garrison
____ 3. David Walker
____ 4. Frederick Douglass
____ 5. Sojourner Truth
____ 6. Harriet Tubman
____ 7. Elijah Lovejoy
____ 8. American Colonization Society
____ 9. *Freedom's Journal*
____ 10. the Underground Railroad
____ 11. *American Slavery As It Is*

COLUMN B

A. the United States first African American newspaper
B. abolitionist newspaper editor who was killed by angry proslavery whites
C. bought slaves then sent them abroad to start new lives
D. guided hundreds of slaves to freedom
E. edited an antislavery newspaper, the *North Star*
F. founded a newspaper in 1815 to spread the abolitionist message
G. founded *The Liberator* in 1831
H. escape network for slaves
I. former slave from Ulster County, New York, who worked for abolition and the women's movement
J. African American writer who challenged African Americans to rebel and overthrow slavery by force
K. collection of firsthand accounts of life under slavery

DIRECTIONS: Essay Answer the following questions on a separate sheet of paper.

12. Describe the journey many slaves made on the Underground Railroad, including the methods they used to find their way north.
13. How did Southerners defend slavery?

The American Journey ★ 55 ★ **Reteaching Activities**

Enrichment Activity 14–2

Name ______ Date ______ Class ______

★ Enrichment Activity 14-2 ★ ★

Liberia for a New Life

The American Colonization Society, founded in 1817, worked to send thousands of African Americans to settle Liberia.

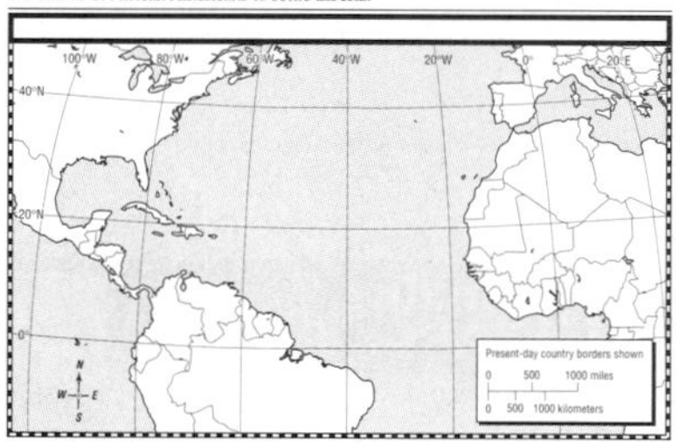

DIRECTIONS: Locating Places Follow the directions to complete the map.

1. Label North America and Africa and title the map.
2. Many enslaved Africans were originally captured in West Africa, and were loaded on ships on the Gulf of Guinea. The gulf is at a point where the Equator and the Prime Meridian cross. Label West Africa, the Gulf of Guinea, the Equator, and the Prime Meridian.
3. Many enslaved Africans were unloaded from ships at the West Indies. Label the West Indies, the Gulf of Mexico, and the Caribbean Sea.
4. The American Colonization Society was formed in Virginia. Virginia is located at about 37°N latitude along the Chesapeake Bay. Label Virginia and the Chesapeake Bay.
5. Name and label the ocean African Americans who decided to return to Africa had to cross.
6. Find and label Liberia and Cape Palmas, which lie along Africa's southern coast.

Activity **DIRECTIONS:** Imagine you are leaving Virginia to settle in Liberia in 1825. You are keeping a journal of your journey. Write a passage describing your trip and comparing your feelings with those of an ancestor of yours who was taken from Africa to be sold as a slave in the 1700s.

The American Journey ★ 55 ★ **Enrichment Activities**

of life, which depended on enslaved labor. Many people in the North also opposed the abolitionist movement.

Opposition in the North

Even in the North, abolitionists never numbered more than a small fraction of the population. Many Northerners saw the antislavery movement as a threat to the nation's social order. They feared the abolitionists could bring on a destructive war between the North and the South. They also claimed that, if the enslaved African Americans were freed, they could never blend into American society.

Economic fears further fed the backlash against abolitionism. Northern workers worried that freed slaves would flood the North and take jobs away from whites by agreeing to work for lower pay.

Violence against Abolitionists

Opposition to abolitionism sometimes erupted into violence against the abolitionists themselves. In the 1830s a Philadelphia mob burned the city's antislavery headquarters to the ground and set off a bloody race riot. In Boston a mob attacked abolitionist William Lloyd Garrison and threatened to hang him. Authorities saved his life by locking him in jail.

Elijah Lovejoy was not so lucky. Lovejoy edited an abolitionist newspaper in Illinois. Three times angry whites invaded his offices and wrecked his presses. Each time Lovejoy installed new presses and resumed publication. The fourth time the mob set fire to the building. When Lovejoy came out of the blazing building, he was shot and killed.

The South Reacts

Southerners fought abolitionism by mounting arguments in defense of slavery. They claimed that slavery was essential to economic progress and prosperity in the South. Slave labor, they said, had allowed Southern whites to reach a high level of culture and civilization. Southerners also argued that they treated enslaved people well, and that for African Americans slavery was preferable to factory work in the North.

Other defenses of slavery were based on racism. Many whites believed that African Americans were better off under white care than on their own. "Providence has placed [the slave] in our hands for his own good," declared one Southern governor.

The conflict between proslavery and antislavery groups continued to mount. At the same time, a new women's rights movement was growing, and many leading abolitionists were involved in that movement as well.

Section 2 Review

Checking for Understanding

1. ***Identify*** Liberia, William Lloyd Garrison, Sarah and Angelina Grimké, Frederick Douglass, Sojourner Truth, Harriet Tubman.
2. ***Define*** abolitionist, Underground Railroad.
3. ***Discuss*** the American Colonization Society's solution to slavery.

Reviewing Themes

4. **Individual Action** What role did Harriet Tubman play in the antislavery movement?

Critical Thinking

5. **Making Comparisons** Compare the arguments of Northerners and Southerners who opposed abolitionism.

Activity

Creating a Political Cartoon Find a political cartoon that depicts abolitionists or expresses an abolitionist sentiment. Use it as a model to create your own cartoon about the antislavery movement.

Section 2 Review Answers

1. Liberia, 417; Garrison, 417; Sarah and Angelina Grimké, 418; Douglass, 419; Sojourner Truth, 420; Harriet Tubman, 421
2. The words are defined in the Glossary.
3. It wanted to resettle African Americans in Africa or the Caribbean.
4. She risked her life leading slaves to freedom on the Underground Railroad.
5. Northerners: saw it as a threat that could lead to war; said African Americans could not "fit in" to society and feared they would take jobs from whites; Southerners: said slavery was essential to economy, that African Americans were treated better in the South, that they were better off under white care

Activity Cartoons should show abolitionist views.

4 CLOSE

It was against the law to help a runaway slave. In fact the law said that those who did not return slaves to their owners could be arrested, fined, and jailed as criminals. Ask students what they would do if they had to decide whether to help a runaway.

Multimedia Activities

ABCNEWS INTERACTIVE™ Historic America Electronic Field Trips

Field Trip to Frederick Douglass's Home

Setting up the Video

With a group of your classmates, view "Frederick Douglass's Home" on the videodisc ***Historic America: Electronic Field Trips***. Frederick Douglass's efforts to abolish slavery make him one of America's greatest civil rights leaders. This program focuses on different aspects of Douglass's life and contributions he made during his lifetime.

Hands-On Activity

Create a map of the United States. Include its borders as they appeared just before the Civil War. Color-code the map to reflect both free and slave states. Draw symbols for the agricultural and economic resources of each state. Include these symbols in your map key.

Side 1, Chapter 9

View the video by scanning the bar code or by entering the chapter number on your keypad and pressing Search.

Surfing the "Net"

The Underground Railroad

The Underground Railroad was a secret, widespread network of people and places that helped enslaved people reach freedom in the North. Many conductors of the Underground Railroad, such as Harriet Tubman, used Polaris—the fixed star in the northern sky—to guide them to the North. To find out more about the Underground Railroad's famous history, travel the Internet.

Getting There

Follow these steps to gather information about the Underground Railroad.

1. Use a search engine. Type in the phrase *Underground Railroad.*
2. After typing in the phrase, enter words like the following to focus your search: *maps, stations, fugitives, slaves.*
3. The search engine should provide you with a number of links to follow. Links are "pointers" to different sites on the Internet.

What to Do When You Are There

Click on the links to navigate through the pages of information. Locate information about escape routes and stations that fugitive slaves used. Then use a large wall map of North America and trace the various routes that fugitive slaves used to reach freedom in the North. Place pins on the map to represent the location of stations.

TEACHER'S NOTES

Multimedia Activities

ABCNEWS INTERACTIVE™

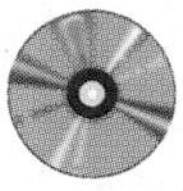

VIDEODISC
Historic America Electronic Field Trips

Side 1, Chapter 9
Title: *Frederick Douglass's Home*

If you do not have access to a videodisc player, the **Historic America Electronic Field Trips** are also available in VHS.

Internet Sites

The following are possible sites for completing the "Net" activities:

African American History
http://www.msstate.edu/Archives/History/USA/Afro-Amer/afro.html

The Walk to Canada—Tracing the Underground Railroad
http://www.npca.org/walk.html

Not on the "Net" . . .

If students have limited or no access to the Internet, have them complete "The Underground Railroad" activity by using the electronic card catalog at the school or local library. At the *s:* prompt, students should type in *slavery, Underground Railroad,* or *abolitionists.* They should then use the call numbers to find the books they need to complete their wall maps.

CHAPTER 14
Section 3, 424–428

1 FOCUS

BELLRINGER
Motivational Activity

Before taking roll at the beginning of the class period, project Section Focus Transparency 14–3 and have students answer the questions. Discuss students' responses.

This activity is also available as a blackline master.

Section Focus Transparency 14–3

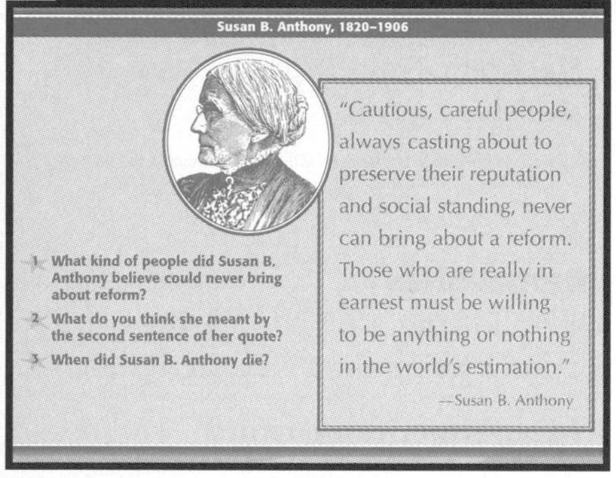

Vocabulary Precheck
Call on a volunteer to find the definition of *suffrage* in the Glossary and read it aloud.

Use the **Vocabulary PuzzleMaker** to create crossword and word search puzzles.

Section Theme
Groups and Institutions

While working to end slavery, women realized that they themselves had very limited freedom. Working individually and in groups, women in the 1800s made some progress toward equality.

Activity Have students skim the section to find the name of the first female doctor in the United States. *(Elizabeth Blackwell)*

1830 · 1860 · 1890

1837 Mary Lyon establishes Mount Holyoke Female Seminary

1848 First women's rights convention held in Seneca Falls, New York

1857 Elizabeth Blackwell founds the New York Infirmary for Women and Children

1890 Wyoming grants women the right to vote

Section 3

The Women's Movement

READ TO DISCOVER . . .
- how the antislavery and the women's rights movements were related.
- what progress women made toward equality during the 1800s.

TERMS TO LEARN
feminist
suffrage
coeducation

The Storyteller

Women who fought to end slavery began to recognize their own bondage. On April 19, 1850, about 400 women met at a Quaker meetinghouse in the small town of Salem, Ohio. They came together "to assert their rights as independent human beings." One speaker stated: "I use the term *Woman's Rights,* because it is a technical phrase. I like not the expression. It is not Woman's *Rights* of which I design to speak, but of Woman's *Wrongs*. I shall claim nothing for ourselves because of our sex. . . . [W]e should demand *our* recognition as equal members of the human family. . . ."

Antislavery drawstring purses

In the early 1800s, American women lacked many of the rights that men enjoyed. The British system of law, which the American states had adopted after independence, made men the guardians of women. The law treated women like children who needed to be looked after and cared for. Unmarried women came under the authority of their fathers or nearest male relatives. Married women came under their husbands' authority. Widows and single women could own property and make wills. When they married, however, control of their property and earnings passed to their husbands.

Women and Reform

Women played a major role in all the American reform movements of the 1800s, but they were especially active in the campaign to end slavery. The female abolitionists, however, were often pushed aside or excluded by the men in the movement.

Some men believed that women should not speak in public or publish their writings. When American women attended a world antislavery meeting in London in 1840, they had to sit behind a curtain that separated them from the all-male meeting.

The Birth of the Movement

Gender prejudice turned many female abolitionists into champions of women's rights. "We have good cause to be grateful to the slave,"

SECTION RESOURCES

Reproducible Masters
- Reproducible Lesson Plan 14–3
- Guided Reading Activity 14–3
- Section Quiz 14–3
- Reteaching Activity 14–3
- Enrichment Activity 14–3

Transparencies
- Section Focus Transparency 14–3

Multimedia
- Vocabulary PuzzleMaker
- Chapter Challenger Interactive Review Software
- Testmaker
- ABCNews InterActive™ Historic America Electronic Field Trips
- Facts On File: Landmark Documents in American History

wrote reformer Abby Kelley. "In striving to strike his irons off, we found most surely, that we were manacled [chained] *ourselves*."

Women abolitionists became the first American **feminists,** people who work for women's rights. Seeking to improve women's lives and win equal rights, they launched a continuing struggle.

Like many of the women reformers, **Lucretia Mott** was a Quaker. Quaker women, who enjoyed a certain amount of equality in their own communities, were particularly disturbed by the sexism in the antislavery movement. Mott gave lectures in Philadelphia calling for temperance, peace, workers' rights, and abolition. Mott also helped fugitive slaves and organized the Philadelphia Female Anti-Slavery Society.

At the world antislavery convention in London, Mott met **Elizabeth Cady Stanton.** There the two female abolitionists joined forces to work for women's rights.

Feminists Meet Opposition

The abolitionist sisters **Angelina** and **Sarah Grimké** were early supporters of women's rights. Some men in the movement criticized the Grimkés for engaging in "unfeminine" activities, but the sisters continued their work. "Men and women were CREATED EQUAL," they declared, ". . . and whatever is right for man to do, is right for woman to do."

Sojourner Truth also met opposition as she traveled throughout the North speaking about women's rights and slavery. When she addressed a women's meeting in New York City, a hostile crowd forced its way into the hall to jeer at the women. Truth told the mob,

"We'll have our rights; see if we don't; and you can't stop us from them; see if you can. You may hiss as much as you like, but it is comin'."

Sojourner Truth

Eyewitness to HISTORY

The Seneca Falls Convention

In July 1848, Elizabeth Cady Stanton, Lucretia Mott, and a few other women organized the first women's rights convention in **Seneca Falls, New York.** About 200 women and 40 men attended.

The convention issued a Declaration of Sentiments and Resolutions modeled on the Declaration of Independence. The women's document declared: "We hold these truths to be self-evident: that all men and women are created equal."

Just as the Declaration of Independence had listed Americans' complaints against King George III, the Seneca Falls declaration listed women's grievances against men. It read,

"He [man] has endeavored, in every way he could, to destroy her [woman's] confidence in her own powers, to lessen her self-respect, and to make her willing to lead a dependent and . . . [miserable] life."

Footnotes to History

Women Physicians The first American medical school for women, the Boston Female Medical School, opened in 1848 with an enrollment of 12 students.

Cooperative Learning Activity

Making Position Statements Organize the class into small groups. Have each group write on a sheet of paper the question, "Why should women and men be treated equally?" Ask each group to circulate the paper among members with each member providing a response to the question. Continue circulating the paper until each member has given at least two responses. Then have each group select a writer/editor to summarize and compile the group's arguments into a position statement to be read aloud to the class.

2 TEACH

L1 Finding Inequalities As students read the section, have them list (a) the inequalities or problems women faced, (b) the names of the feminists discussed and (c) the "firsts" mentioned in the section.

Guided Reading Activity 14–3

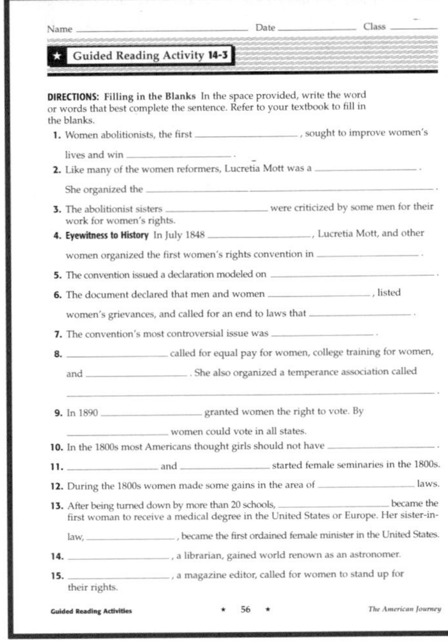

Name ______ Date ______ Class ______

★ Guided Reading Activity 14-3

DIRECTIONS: Filling in the Blanks In the space provided, write the word or words that best complete the sentence. Refer to your textbook to fill in the blanks.

1. Women abolitionists, the first ______, sought to improve women's lives and win ______.
2. Like many of the women reformers, Lucretia Mott was a ______. She organized the ______.
3. The abolitionist sisters ______ were criticized by some men for their work for women's rights.
4. **Eyewitness to History** In July 1848 ______, Lucretia Mott, and other women organized the first women's rights convention in ______.
5. The convention issued a declaration modeled on ______.
6. The document declared that men and women ______, listed women's grievances, and called for an end to laws that ______.
7. The convention's most controversial issue was ______.
8. ______ called for equal pay for women, college training for women, and ______. She also organized a temperance association called ______.
9. In 1890 ______ granted women the right to vote. By ______ women could vote in all states.
10. In the 1800s most Americans thought girls should not have ______.
11. ______ and ______ started female seminaries in the 1800s.
12. During the 1800s women made some gains in the area of ______ laws.
13. After being turned down by more than 20 schools, ______ became the first woman to receive a medical degree in the United States or Europe. Her sister-in-law, ______, became the first ordained female minister in the United States.
14. ______, a librarian, gained world renown as an astronomer.
15. ______, a magazine editor, called for women to stand up for their rights.

Guided Reading Activities ★ 56 ★ *The American Journey*

ABCNEWS INTERACTIVE™

VIDEODISC
Historic America Electronic Field Trips

Side 2, Chapter 6

Title: *Seneca Falls*
Subject: Women's rights
Ask: **What restrictions did women experience during the 1840s?** *(usually did not go to college, few jobs, could not own property if married, could not vote)*
Turn to page 608 for a Multimedia Activity dealing with the Seneca Falls Convention.

Also available in VHS.

Picturing HISTORY At a meeting of the New York Teachers' Association in which more than two-thirds of the members were women, a panel of male speakers began to discuss the topic "Why the profession of a teacher is not as much respected as that of lawyer, doctor, or minister." After some debate Susan B. Anthony was granted her request to give her opinion. "Do you not see," she said, "that so long as society says a woman is incompetent to be a lawyer, minister, or doctor, but has ample ability to be a teacher, every man of you who chooses this profession tacitly acknowledges that he has no more brains than a woman?"

Answer: *an end to laws that discriminated against women, admittance into various occupations, suffrage*

What?Where?When?Who?

Bloomers Many people attended Amelia Bloomer's lectures just to see her unusual costume. She finally decided that her bloomers were distracting people's attention from her message and returned to more traditional garb.

you don't say...

Suzy Bs Susan B. Anthony became so well known that progressive women everywhere were known as "Suzy Bs."

Linking PAST & PRESENT

Women Physicians In 1994 women made up only 19 percent of all United States physicians. The numbers are changing, however. Women constitute 32 percent of doctors under age 35.

Picturing HISTORY Lucretia Mott (left) and Susan B. Anthony were leaders in the effort to allow women a greater role in American society. **What changes did the Seneca Falls declaration demand?**

The women's declaration called for an end to all laws that discriminated against women. It demanded that women be allowed to enter the all-male world of trades, professions, and businesses. The most controversial issue at the Seneca Falls Convention concerned **suffrage,** or the right to vote.

Elizabeth Stanton insisted that the declaration include a demand for **woman suffrage,** but delegates thought the idea of women voting was too radical. Lucretia Mott told her friend, "Lizzie, thee will make us ridiculous." After a heated debate, however, the convention voted to include the demand for woman suffrage in the United States. As Stanton later reasoned:

> "Having decided to petition for a redress of grievances, the question is *for what shall you first petition*? For the exercise of your right to elective franchise [vote]—nothing short of this. The grant to you of this right will secure all others, and the granting of every other right, whilst this is denied, is a mockery. For instance: What is the right to property, without the right to protect it?"

The Movement Grows

The Seneca Falls Convention paved the way for the growth of the **women's rights movement.** During the 1800s women held several national conventions. Many reformers—including William Lloyd Garrison—joined the movement.

Susan B. Anthony, the daughter of a Quaker abolitionist in rural New York, worked for women's rights, temperance, and the reform of New York property and divorce laws. She called for equal pay for women, college training for girls, and **coeducation**—the teaching of boys and girls together. Excluded from a group called the Sons of Temperance, Anthony organized the country's first women's temperance association, the Daughters of Temperance.

Susan B. Anthony met Elizabeth Cady Stanton at a temperance meeting in 1851. They became lifelong friends and partners in the struggle for women's rights. For the rest of the century, Anthony and Stanton led the women's movement. They worked with other women to win the right to vote. Beginning with Wyoming in 1890,

Linking PAST & PRESENT

Ladies' Legwear Creates Scandal

In the early 1850s, women's rights worker Amelia Jenks Bloomer thought that huge hoops and long skirts kept women from moving about easily and naturally. She began wearing a pair of loose trousers gathered at the ankles. The trousers—invented by Elizabeth Miller but commonly called "bloomers"—caused quite a scandal. Some men shouted taunts, while others hurled sticks. Eighty years later, in the 1930s, wearing pants became commonplace for women.

MULTIPLE LEARNING STYLES

Intrapersonal Point out that the women who worked for women's rights were ridiculed, taunted, and shouted at. They were pelted with garbage and rotten eggs. On occasion they were even arrested. Ask students to think about problems or injustices in today's world. Is there a cause with which students are deeply concerned? After discussing the question, ask them to write or tape a description of the cause and the actions they would take to promote the cause. Have students also consider how much risk they would be willing to take or how much abuse they would be willing to endure in supporting the cause. **L2,** ELL several states granted women the right to vote. It was not until 1920, however, that woman suffrage became a reality everywhere in the United States.

Progress by American Women

In the 1800s most Americans believed that girls should not have advanced education. Some even questioned whether girls should be taught to read and write. Education, people feared, might make young women dissatisfied with their lives.

Without institutions that would offer them advanced education degrees, women were stopped from expanding their professional horizons. Before the 1830s no university or college in the United States would accept female students. Many men and women alike believed that it was useless and even dangerous for women to learn such subjects as mathematics. The stress of studying such subjects, some felt, might cause delicate women to have nervous breakdowns.

The only schools for women beyond elementary schools at that time offered courses for women on how to be good wives and mothers. Some young women, however, began to make their own opportunities. They broke barriers to female education and helped other women do the same.

Education

After her marriage **Emma Willard** educated herself in subjects considered suitable only for boys, such as science and mathematics. In 1821 Willard established the Troy Female Seminary in upstate New York. Catharine Beecher, the daughter of temperance crusader Lyman Beecher, founded schools to teach women about homemaking in Connecticut and Ohio. **Mary Lyon** established Mount Holyoke Female Seminary (later Mount Holyoke College) in Massachusetts in 1837. She modeled its curriculum on that of nearby Amherst College.

Marriage and Family Laws

During the 1800s women made some gains in the area of marriage and property laws. New York, Pennsylvania, Indiana, Wisconsin, Mississippi, and the new state of California recognized the right of women to own property after their marriage.

Some states passed laws permitting women to share the guardianship of their children jointly with their husbands. Indiana was the first of several states that allowed women to seek divorce if their husbands were chronic abusers of alcohol.

Breaking Barriers

In the 1800s women had few career choices. They could become elementary teachers—although school boards often paid much lower salaries to women than to men. Breaking into fields such as medicine and the ministry was far more difficult. Some strong-minded women, however, succeeded in entering these all-male professions.

Hoping to study medicine, **Elizabeth Blackwell** applied to—and was turned down

Picturing HISTORY Mary Lyon was a gifted teacher and a pioneer in the cause of higher education for women. **What institution did Mary Lyon found?**

CHAPTER 14
Section 3, 424–428

3 ASSESS

Assign Section 3 Review as homework or as an in-class activity.

Use **Chapter Challenger Interactive Review Software** to review Section 3.

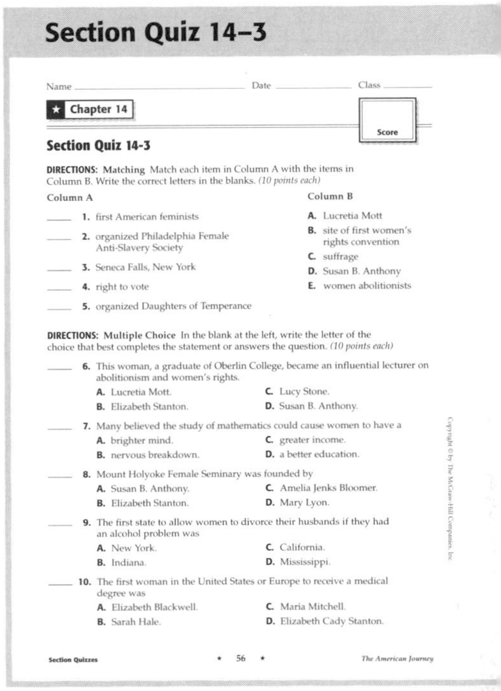

Section Quiz 14–3

Name ______ Date ______ Class ______

Chapter 14 — Score

Section Quiz 14-3

DIRECTIONS: Matching Match each item in Column A with the items in Column B. Write the correct letters in the blanks. *(10 points each)*

Column A	Column B
____ 1. first American feminists	A. Lucretia Mott
____ 2. organized Philadelphia Female Anti-Slavery Society	B. site of first women's rights convention
____ 3. Seneca Falls, New York	C. suffrage
____ 4. right to vote	D. Susan B. Anthony
____ 5. organized Daughters of Temperance	E. women abolitionists

DIRECTIONS: Multiple Choice In the blank at the left, write the letter of the choice that best completes the statement or answers the question. *(10 points each)*

____ 6. This woman, a graduate of Oberlin College, became an influential lecturer on abolitionism and women's rights.
A. Lucretia Mott. C. Lucy Stone.
B. Elizabeth Stanton. D. Susan B. Anthony.

____ 7. Many believed the study of mathematics could cause women to have a
A. brighter mind. C. greater income.
B. nervous breakdown. D. a better education.

____ 8. Mount Holyoke Female Seminary was founded by
A. Susan B. Anthony. C. Amelia Jenks Bloomer.
B. Elizabeth Stanton. D. Mary Lyon.

____ 9. The first state to allow women to divorce their husbands if they had an alcohol problem was
A. New York. C. California.
B. Indiana. D. Mississippi.

____ 10. The first woman in the United States or Europe to receive a medical degree was
A. Elizabeth Blackwell. C. Maria Mitchell.
B. Sarah Hale. D. Elizabeth Cady Stanton.

Section Quizzes ★ 56 ★ *The American Journey*

Picturing HISTORY At Mount Holyoke the students did their own cooking and cleaning, which helped keep tuition low.
Ask: **Why would Lyon have wanted to keep tuition low?** *(so that as many women as possible could receive an education)*
Answer: *Mount Holyoke Female Seminary (Mount Holyoke College)*

MAKING CONNECTIONS ACTIVITY

Foreign Affairs The women's rights movement was not limited to the United States. Nevertheless, woman suffrage was slow in coming to most places. Only a handful of countries allowed women to vote before World War I. (New Zealand–1893, Australia–1902, Finland–1906, Norway–1913) Have students research the suffrage movement and make a table showing countries and the date that women gained suffrage in each. Ask students to find out whether there are still countries in which women do not have the vote. **L2**

Facts On File

CD-ROM
Landmark Documents in American History

Title: *New York Married Women's Property Acts, 1848*
After viewing the document, have students write a paragraph explaining how this act changed the lives of American women.

CHAPTER 14
Section 3, 424–428

Picturing HISTORY Mitchell also discovered several groups of distant stars and studied Jupiter and Saturn.
Answer: *Elizabeth Blackwell, Antoinette Brown, Sarah Hale*

Reteaching Activity 14–3

Name ________ Date ________ Class ________

★ Reteaching Activity 14-3

DIRECTIONS: Organizing Facts The items in the Fact Bank list the achievements, beliefs, and characteristics of women who played major roles in the women's movement during the 1800s. Write the appropriate letters on the line next to each name. Some letters will be used more than once.

Lucretia Mott ________	Mary Lyon ________
Elizabeth Cady Stanton ________	Elizabeth Blackwell ________
Angelina and Sarah Grimké ________	Antoinette Brown ________
Sojourner Truth ________	Lucy Stone ________
Susan B. Anthony ________	Maria Mitchell ________
Emma Willard ________	Sarah Hale ________

★FACT BANK

A. New York Infirmary for Women and Children	K. Seneca Falls Convention
B. suffrage for women	L. the Daughters of Temperance
C. Mount Holyoke Female Seminary	M. discovered a comet in 1847
D. abolitionist	N. first ordained female minister in the United States
E. magazine editor	O. Philadelphia Female Anti-Slavery Society
F. first woman to receive medical degree in the United States or Europe	P. first woman elected to the American Academy of Arts and Sciences
G. Quaker	Q. improvements in women's education
H. librarian	R. Troy Female Seminary
I. reform of property and marriage laws	S. criticized by men for speaking out publicly against discrimination
J. kept her maiden name after she married	

DIRECTIONS: Essay Answer the following questions on a separate sheet of paper.

1. Describe the differences in educational and employment opportunities for women in the early 1800s.
2. What arguments did men give against equal educational opportunities for women?

Enrichment Activity 14–3

Name ________ Date ________ Class ________

★ Enrichment Activity 14-3 ★

Women's Right to Vote

The *Declaration of Sentiments and Resolutions* was approved by the Seneca Falls Convention in 1848. Read the excerpts below.

1. The history of mankind is a history of repeated injuries and usurpations [unlawful seizing] on the part of man toward woman. . . . To prove this, let facts be submitted to a candid world.
2. He has never permitted her to exercise her inalienable right to the elective franchise.
3. He has compelled her to submit to laws in the formation of which she has no voice. . . .
4. He has made her, if married, in the eye of the law, civilly dead. . . .
5. He has taken from her all right of property, even to the wages she earns. . . .
6. He has denied her the facilities for obtaining a thorough education. . . .
7. Now in view of this denial of the rights of one half the people of this country . . . we insist that they have immediate admission to all the rights and privileges which belong to them as citizens of the United States.

DIRECTIONS: Analyzing and Paraphrasing Information For each of the underlined passages in the *Declaration of Sentiments and Resolutions,* rewrite the sentence in your own words.

1. ________
2. ________
3. ________
4. ________
5. ________
6. ________
7. ________
8. Place the number of each statement in the appropriate box.

Definition of Problem	Examples of Problem	Solution to Problem

Activity **DIRECTIONS:** The women's movement has had a number of prominent spokespersons over the years. Use the media center to find important people in the women's movement. Pick one and prepare a creative presentation to tell your class more about your choice. You might present a dramatic reading, prepare a portrait and a picture history of the person, write a song or poem, or create a short skit with a partner.

4 CLOSE

Have students write essays responding to the following: **In what ways were women like slaves? How was their condition different?**

Picturing HISTORY Maria Mitchell won worldwide recognition for her achievements in astronomy. **What other notable women made contributions in fields once closed to women?**

by—more than 20 schools. Finally accepted by Geneva College in New York, Blackwell graduated at the head of her class. She went on to become the first woman to receive a medical degree in the United States or Europe. In 1857 she founded the New York Infirmary for Women and Children, staffed entirely by women.

One of Blackwell's sisters-in-law, Antoinette Brown, became the first ordained female minister in the United States. Blackwell's other sister-in-law, **Lucy Stone,** an Oberlin College graduate, became an influential lecturer on abolitionism and women's rights. To symbolize her equality with her husband, Stone kept her maiden name after she married and encouraged other women to do the same.

Maria Mitchell, a librarian, taught herself astronomy. Mitchell gained world renown when she discovered a comet in 1847. She became a professor of astronomy at Vassar College and the first woman elected to the American Academy of Arts and Sciences.

Sarah Hale, editor of a popular magazine called *Godey's Lady's Book,* influenced thousands of American women. Hale mixed articles on fashions and other traditional female subjects with a call for women to stand up for their rights.

Despite the accomplishments of notable women, some gains in education, and changes in state laws, women in the 1800s remained limited by social customs and expectations. The early feminists—like the abolitionists, temperance workers, and other activists of the age of reform—had just begun the long struggle to achieve their goals.

Section 3 Review

Checking for Understanding

1. ***Identify*** Lucretia Mott, Elizabeth Cady Stanton, Susan B. Anthony, Mary Lyon, Elizabeth Blackwell, Maria Mitchell.
2. ***Define*** feminist, suffrage, coeducation.
3. ***Summarize*** how the fight to end slavery helped to spark the women's movement.

Reviewing Themes

4. **Groups and Institutions** Discuss three specific goals of the women's rights movement.

Critical Thinking

5. **Making Generalizations** What qualities do you think women such as Sojourner Truth, Susan B. Anthony, Elizabeth Cady Stanton, and Elizabeth Blackwell shared?

Activity

Composing a Song Write and record a song designed to win supporters for the women's rights movement. Include lyrics that will draw both men and women supporters.

Section 3 Review Answers

1. Mott, 425; Stanton, 425; Anthony, 426; Lyon, 427; Blackwell, 427; Mitchell, 428
2. The words are defined in the Glossary.
3. Many women working for the abolitionist cause became aware of the inequality and discrimination in their own lives.
4. Any three: freedom to enter all-male professions; suffrage; improved property rights; marriage and divorce laws; equal pay; college training; coeducation
5. Answers will vary but may include self-confidence, intelligence, perseverance, patience, commitment, and so on.

Activity Songs should express some of the goals of the women's movement.

Technology
SKILL BUILDER

Using a Computerized Card Catalog

How many times have you had to go to the library to research a report or paper? Skill in using a computerized card catalog will help you find the information you need.

Learning the Skill

Go to the card catalog computer in your school or local library. What do you want to know about? Type in the name of an author or performer; the title of a book, videotape, audiocassette, or CD; or a subject heading. You will access the on-line, or computerized, card catalog that lists all the library's resources for that topic. The computer will list on screen the titles, authors, or whatever you requested.

The "card" that appears on screen will provide other information as well, including the year the work was published, who published it, what media type it is, and the language it is written or recorded in. Use this information to determine if the material meets your needs. Then check to see if the item is available. In addition, find the classification (biography, travel, etc.) and call number under which it is shelved.

Practicing the Skill

This chapter discusses abolitionists. These steps will help you use the computerized card catalog to find additional information on the subject "abolitionists":

1. Type "s/abolitionists."
2. From the list of subjects that appears on the screen, determine which might apply to abolitionists in the United States during the years between 1820 and 1860.
3. Follow the instructions on the computer screen to display all the titles under each subject you selected. For example, the instructions might be to type the line number next to the subject and press RETURN.
4. Determine which of the books, videos, audiocassettes, and CDs now on the screen you want to learn more about.
5. What do the instructions on the screen tell you to do to find more details?
6. What do the instructions on the screen tell you to do if you want to find out how many copies of the title the library owns and if and where a copy is available?

In antislavery newspapers, abolitionists showed the horrors of a slave auction.

Applying the Skill

Using a Computerized Card Catalog Use the computerized card catalog in your school or local library to identify four resources—books, videotapes, CDs, or audiocassettes—you can use to write two reports, one on Elizabeth Cady Stanton and the other on public education in the 1800s.

Technology
SKILL BUILDER

TEACH

Using a Computerized Card Catalog

This skill introduces the use of the computer in finding library materials. After students have read **Learning the Skill,** have them use the library computer to follow the instructions in **Practicing the Skill.** If the school library does not have a computerized card catalog, make arrangements with the public library to work with students. You might arrange a class field trip to the library for that purpose.

Point out to students the advantage of a computerized card catalog—the ability of the computer to narrow the student's search for information. If the student does not know or remember the name of a specific book or author, the subject heading can guide the student in the right direction.

Additional Practice

Chapter Skills Activity 14

Answers to Practicing the Skill

Answers will vary depending on the computer program in use and the resources available in the library system.

Applying the Skill Students' resources should focus on Elizabeth Cady Stanton and public education in the 1800s. Make sure the students include a book, videotape, CD-ROM, and audiocassettes among their resources.

GLENCOE TECHNOLOGY

VIDEODISC
MindJogger Videoquiz

Use MindJogger to review the Chapter 14 content.

Chapter 14
Disc 2, Side B

Also available in VHS.

Reviewing Key Terms

Students' word search puzzles will vary. The key terms used in this activity are defined in the textbook glossary on pages A26–A35.

Reviewing Key Facts

1. a perfect society
2. poverty, breakup of families, crime, insanity
3. Schools should be free and supported by taxes; teachers should be trained; children should be required to attend school.
4. They no longer looked to Europe for inspiration and models. They began developing their own style and exploring American themes.
5. He called for "immediate and complete emancipation" of enslaved people and denounced the gradual approach of other reformers. He drew more people to the antislavery movement.
6. It gave hope to enslaved African Americans and gave abolitionists a way to help them to freedom.
7. They were considered to be the weaker sex, incapable of managing their own affairs. Men—fathers, other male relatives, or husbands—were considered their guardians.

Chapter 14

Review and Activities

Reviewing Key Terms

On graph paper, create a word search puzzle using the following terms. Crisscross the terms vertically and horizontally, then fill in the remaining squares with extra letters. Use the terms' definitions as clues to find the words in the puzzle. Share your puzzle with a classmate.

utopia
revival
temperance
normal school
Transcendentalist
civil disobedience
abolitionist
Underground Railroad
feminist
suffrage
women's rights movement
coeducation

Reviewing Key Facts

1. What were the founders of utopias hoping to achieve?
2. What problems in society did leading reformers in the temperance movement blame on the manufacture and sale of alcoholic beverages?
3. What were the three basic principles of public education?
4. What was unique about the subject matter that American artists and writers of the mid-1800s used?
5. How did William Lloyd Garrison's demands make him effective in the antislavery movement?
6. What purposes did the Underground Railroad serve besides helping runaway slaves?
7. How were women viewed under the American system of law in the early 1800s?

Time Line Activity

Create a time line on which you place the following events in chronological order.

- Oberlin College admits women and African Americans
- William Lloyd Garrison founds abolitionist newspaper
- Horace Mann introduces major changes in schools
- Seneca Falls Convention held in New York
- First African American settlers arrive in Liberia
- Dorothea Dix files report revealing abuses of people with mental illness

Reviewing Themes

1. **Civic Rights and Responsibilities** How did Dorothea Dix win rights for people with mental illness?
2. **Individual Action** Summarize Frederick Douglass's role in the abolitionist movement.
3. **Groups and Institutions** What was the significance of the Seneca Falls Convention?

Skill Practice Activity

Using a Computerized Card Catalog

Use the card catalog computer in your school or local library to find out more about American poets of the early 1800s.

1. Type "s/poetry."
2. From the list of subjects that appears on the screen, determine which might apply to the United States during the years 1820 to 1860.
3. Follow the instructions on the computer screen to display all the titles under each subject you selected.
4. Which of the books on the screen do you want to learn more about?

Time Line Activity

Events should be placed in this order: First African American settlers arrive in Liberia, William Lloyd Garrison founds abolitionist newspaper, Oberlin College admits women and African Americans, Horace Mann introduces major changes in schools, Dorothea Dix files report revealing abuses of people with mental illness, Seneca Falls Convention held in New York

Reviewing Themes

1. After visiting facilities for the mentally ill, she submitted a detailed report to the Massachusetts legislature revealing the terrible conditions. The legislature agreed to spend the money needed to provide better care for the mentally ill.
2. A powerful abolitionist speaker, he founded an antislavery newspaper and

Chapter 14

Critical Thinking

Analyzing Information

Emily Dickinson's special talent was to write about great subjects—life, death, nature—using concrete images from everyday experience. Read the poem below, then answer the questions that follow.

> **"'Nature' is what we see"**
>
> "Nature" is what we see—
> The Hill—the Afternoon—
> Squirrel—Eclipse—the Bumble bee—
> Nay—Nature is Heaven—
> Nay—Nature is what we hear—
> The Bobolink—the Sea—
> Thunder—the Cricket—
> Nay—Nature is Harmony—
> Nature is what we know—
> Yet have no art to say—
> So impotent [weak] our Wisdom is
> To her Simplicity.

1. What does the poet say nature is in line 1? In line 4?
2. In your own words explain what the last four lines suggest about nature.
3. Write your own poem describing "What Nature Is."

Geography Activity

Use the map on page 419 to answer the following questions.

1. **Movement** About how many enslaved African Americans found freedom through the Underground Railroad?
2. **Location** From what Southern ports did African Americans flee by ship?
3. **Location** What "stations" of the Underground Railroad were situated on the Ohio River?
4. **Movement** How many times did Harriet Tubman risk her life to help slaves escape?

Technology Activity

Using the Internet Search the Internet for a modern organization whose goal is to support women's rights. Write a brief description of the organization, including its name, location, and a description of its purpose or activities.

Cooperative Activity

History and Language Arts Work in small groups to create a deck of "author cards" for your class. With members of your group, create a card for each of the 11 writers and poets discussed in the chapter. The front of each card should show a sketch of the author and a memorable line from one of that author's works. The back of each card should contain biographical information, a list of some of the author's titles, and other interesting facts about the author's life or writing style. Combine the cards of all the groups. Then work with your group to come up with a set of rules to play a game using your cards.

Portfolio Activity History Journal Review the chapter and make a list of the major reform movements of this period. Create a graphic organizer that links the reform movements to the names of the people who participated in each.

CHAPTER 14

Review and Activities

Critical Thinking

1. what we see; Heaven
2. Students may say that the poet means we know what nature is, but we cannot adequately describe it.
3. Poems will vary.

Geography Activity

1. 75,000
2. Charleston, New Bern
3. Pittsburgh, Marietta, Ironton, Cincinnati, Evansville
4. 19

Technology Activity

Students should write a brief description of a modern organization that supports women's rights.

Cooperative Activity

Students should work in groups to create a deck of author cards, which include information about the 11 authors in this chapter. After the deck is complete, have each group create a set of rules for an "authors" card game.

Portfolio Activity Graphic organizers can be of any design, but should accurately and clearly depict the major movements of the period and the people who participated in them.

? Chapter Bonus Test Question

Ask: Who said, "A foolish consistency is the hobgoblin of little minds"? *(Ralph Waldo Emerson)*

took a stand that African Americans should not only have freedom but also full equality with whites.

3. It was the first women's rights convention in the United States and served as a platform calling for an end to discrimination against women.

Skill Practice Activity

Students' lists of poets will vary. Encourage students to read some of the poems they found in their search.

Unit 6 Resource Guide

These Glencoe resources may be used to teach, reteach, or enrich the concepts presented in this unit of study.

Teaching Transparencies

Map Transparency 6 with Overlays A, B, C, D

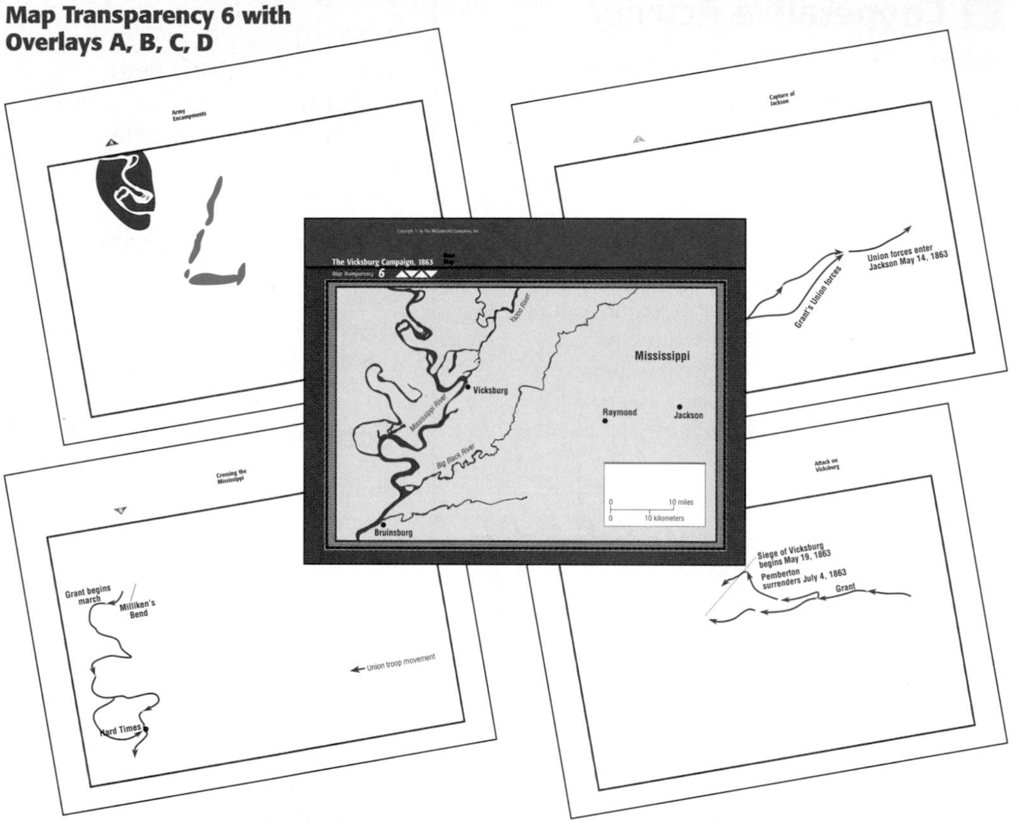

Cause-and-Effect Transparency 6

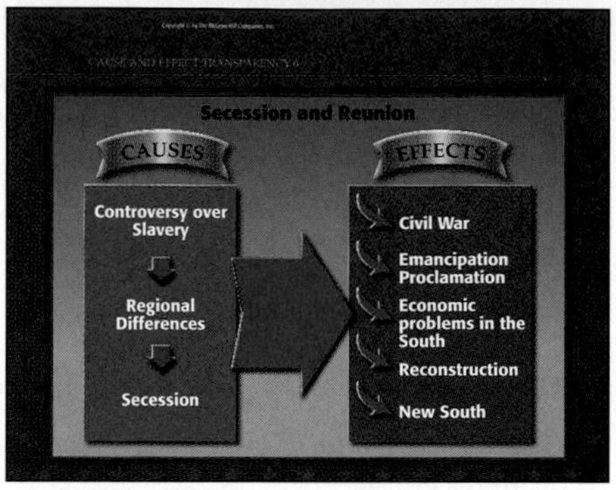

BIBLIOGRAPHY

Readings for the Student

Young, Robert. ***The Emancipation Proclamation: Why Lincoln Really Freed the Slaves.*** New York: Dillion Press, 1994. Provides information for critical thinking about the Emancipation Proclamation.

Haskins, Jim. ***Get on Board: The Story of the Underground Railroad.*** New York: Scholastic, 1993. History of the Underground Railroad, including stories of slaves.

Readings for the Teacher

Katcher, Philip. ***The Civil War Source Book.*** New York: Facts On File, 1992. Illustrated reference to battles, armies, technology.

Stalcup, Brenda. ***Reconstruction: Opposing Viewpoints.*** San Diego: Greenhaven Press, 1995. Collection of primary source articles from people of various classes.

Multimedia Resources

Optical disc. Foote, Shelby. ***Gettysburg Multimedia Battle Simulation.*** Atlanta: Turner Publishing, 1993. Windows 3.1 or higher. Historic battle as presented through an interactive, game-like medium.

CD-ROM. ***America's Civil War: A Nation Divided.*** Phoenix: Software Marketing Corporation, 1994. Windows 3.1 or higher. More than 2,300 Civil War events.

*inter*NET CONNECTIONS

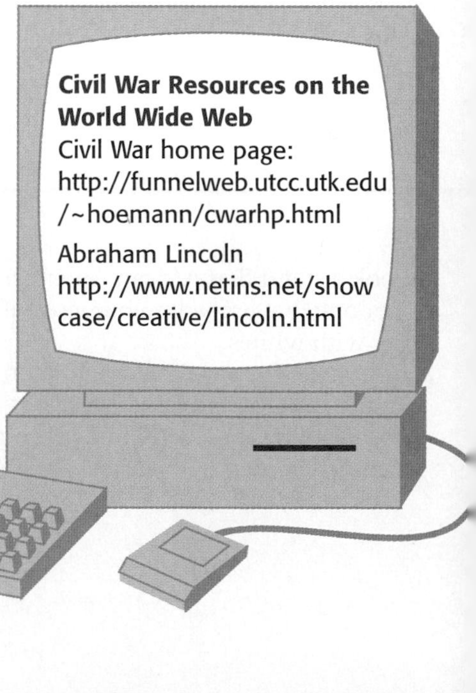

Civil War Resources on the World Wide Web

Civil War home page:
http://funnelweb.utcc.utk.edu/~hoemann/cwarhp.html

Abraham Lincoln
http://www.netins.net/showcase/creative/lincoln.html

Resource Guide Unit 6

Interdisciplinary Activities

American Literature Reading 6

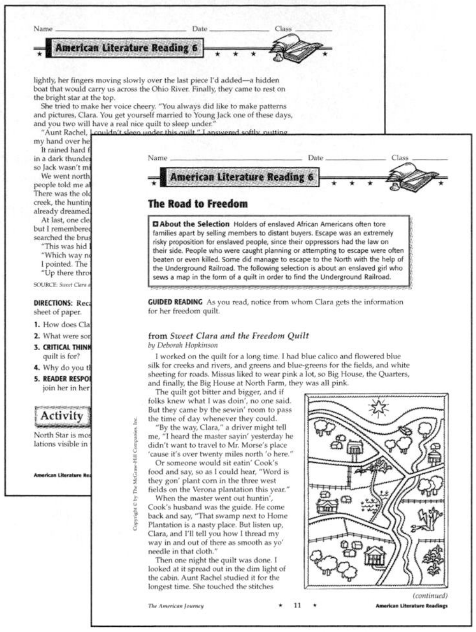

Interdisciplinary Connection 6

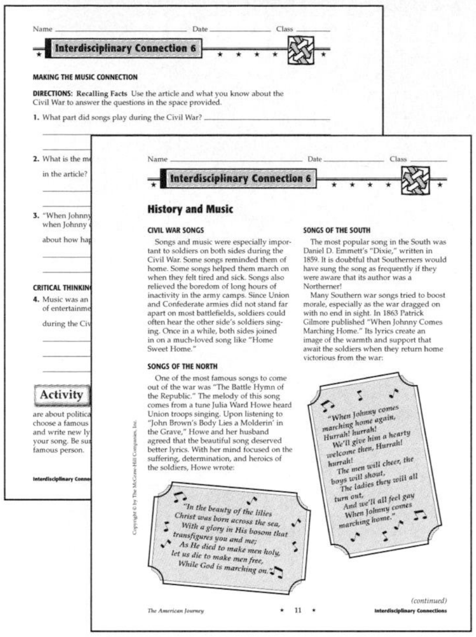

Enrichment Activities

Cooperative Learning Activity 6

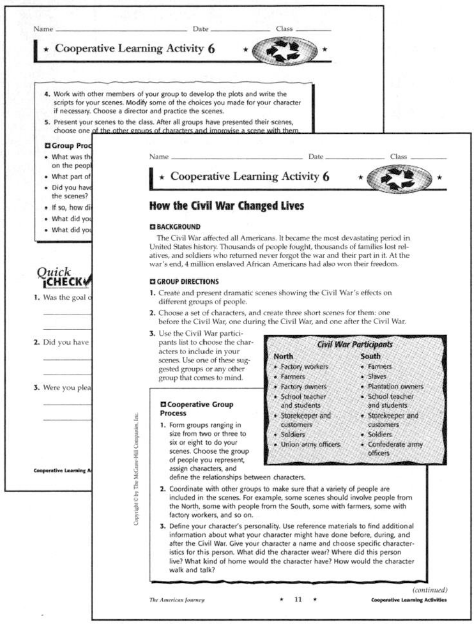

Hands-On Activities

Hands-On History Lab Activity 6

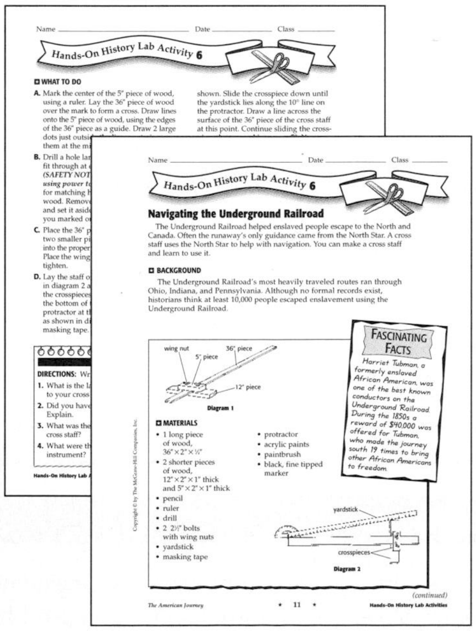

History Simulation 6

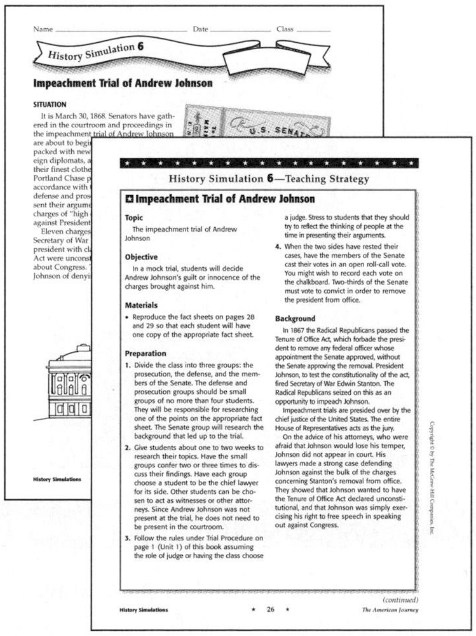

Assessment

Unit 6 Test

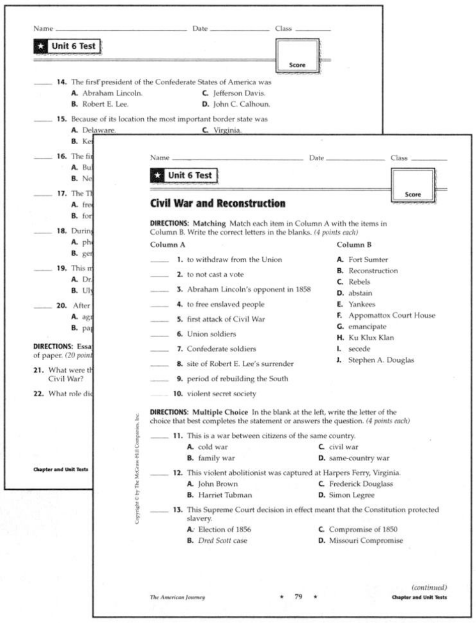

0:00 OUT OF TIME?

If your teaching time is limited, you may use the *Chapter Summaries* blackline master found in the TCR with the *Chapter Digests Audiocassette Activities and Tests* to condense individual chapters into a one-day lesson.

Introducing the Unit

Activity To dispel students' preconceived ideas about the causes of the Civil War, ask them to list in their notebooks the major cause of the Civil War. Then have them evaluate that cause at the end of this unit. Explain that this unit analyzes the increasing differences between the North and the South that led to the outbreak of the Civil War in 1861. It also details the major campaigns of the war and concludes with a discussion of Reconstruction and its lasting effects on both the North and the South.

Unit Objectives

Upon completing this unit, students will be able to:

1. Explain how differences between the North and the South led to the secession of most slave states from the United States.
2. Detail the major campaigns and strategies of the Civil War.
3. Describe Reconstruction policies and their effects on the former Confederacy.
4. Examine educational and social reforms, as well as the early women's movement.

Hands-On HISTORY

Hands-On History Lab Activity 6, "Navigating the Underground Railroad," is a high-interest **constructivist approach** activity directly related to the main topic of the unit.

Unit 6

Civil War and Reconstruction

1846–1896

"A house divided against itself cannot stand."
—ABRAHAM LINCOLN, 1858

MAPPING *America*

Portfolio Activity Draw a freehand outline map of the United States as it existed in 1850. As you read the unit about the Civil War and Reconstruction, note important events such as battles, government actions, or even cultural events. Plot the location of these events on your map and label them.

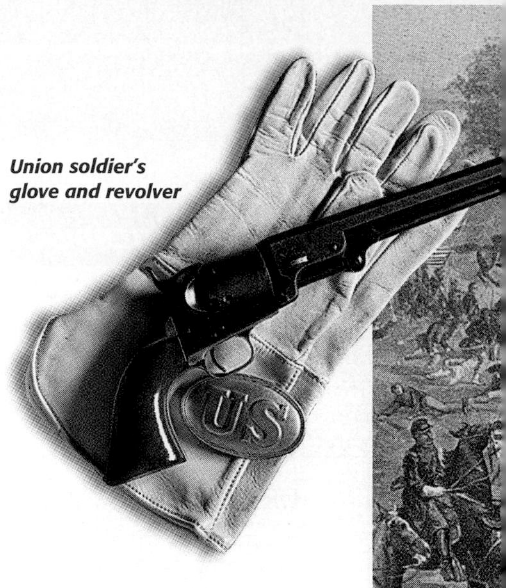

Union soldier's glove and revolver

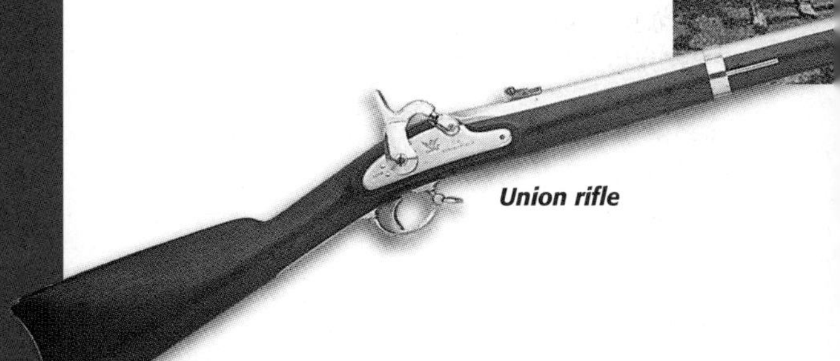

Union rifle

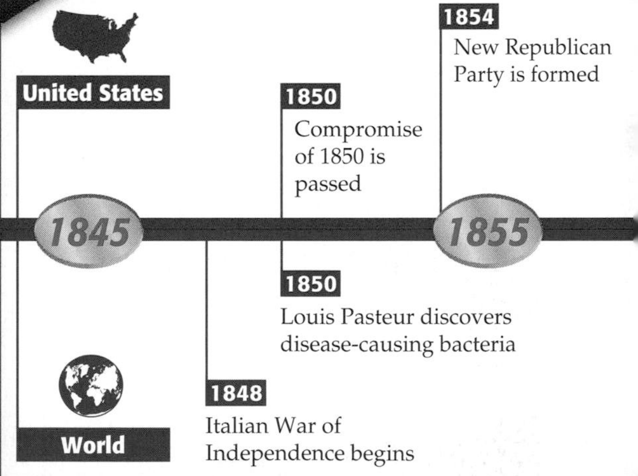

432

TEAM TEACHING STRATEGIES

Science The importance of sanitary procedures in medicine, particularly surgery, were just beginning to be developed during the Civil War era. As a result, many soldiers died from infections caused by unsanitary procedures. Work with the Science teacher to coordinate the study of medical discoveries during this era. For example, Louis Pasteur's work with bacteria led to more sanitary operating room procedures and to the first use of antiseptics in surgical procedures. Students may also document the unsanitary conditions of field hospitals during the Civil War.

HISTORY AND ART ***Battle of Gettysburg* by an unknown artist** An accidental clash between troops near a small Pennsylvania town developed into three of the bloodiest days of fighting in the Civil War.

Confederate soldier's cap (above) and Union soldier's cap (right)

1860 Abraham Lincoln is elected president

1861 Civil War begins

1865 Civil War ends

1867 Congressional Reconstruction begins in the South

1877 Reconstruction ends

1865 — 1875 — 1885

1861 Czar Alexander II frees Russian serfs

1868 Japan begins to modernize

1871 Germany is unified as a nation

1876 Great Britain makes elementary school compulsory

Introducing UNIT 6

NATIONAL GEOGRAPHIC SOCIETY

VIDEODISC
GTV: A Geographic Perspective on American History

Side 2, Chapter 16
Title: *The Civil War*
Ask: **What advantages did the North have in the Civil War?** *(more people, more industry, better transportation)*

Facts On File

CD-ROM
Landmark Documents in American History

Title: *Lincoln-Douglas Debates, 1858*
Ask students to determine who was probably considered the winner of the debates.

HISTORY AND ART The Battle of Gettysburg marked the turning point of the Civil War. After 3 days of fighting, nearly 23,000 Union soldiers and 22,000 Confederates were killed or wounded.

Linking PAST & PRESENT

Activity Discuss the definition of civil war as an armed conflict between geographical regions or political groups of the same nation. Ask students to identify places where civil wars are currently taking place. Evaluate whether a civil war could occur in the present-day United States.

TEAM TEACHING STRATEGIES

Music Ask the Music teacher to discuss the role of spirituals during the period covered in this unit. Spirituals were sometimes called the plantation grapevine. The lyrics often had double meanings that allowed enslaved persons to safely pass along warnings, to share ways of enduring sufferings, and to tell about pathways to freedom. Play the following spirituals to the class: "Go Down Moses," the song from which Harriet Tubman earned her nickname *Moses;* "Follow the Drinking Gourd"; and "Wade in the Water." Discuss the hidden meanings in each song. Then ask students to write a three-verse spiritual (one for each chapter in the unit). Each verse should tell how African Americans felt about changing conditions of daily life during the specific time period covered in each chapter.

Block Schedule

Team Teaching This selection from *The Red Badge of Courage* may be implemented in a team-teaching context, in conjunction with English/Language Arts.

Reinforcing Vocabulary

Review the **Reader's Dictionary** terms with students to be sure they understand any unfamiliar terms.

Historical Connection

In 1861 sectional differences in the United States burst into open warfare. The bloodiest conflict in the nation's history, the Civil War, lasted four years and claimed the lives of more than 600,000 soldiers—equal to 2 percent of the population.

Background Information

Setting The excerpt takes place on the battlefields of the Civil War. A young recruit is reflecting on what his first battle might be like.

Characters The major character in the excerpt is Henry Fleming, the young recruit who is the hero of the book.

Plot As young Fleming faces the rigors of combat for the first time, he learns the meaning of heroism.

America's Literature

The Red Badge of Courage

by Stephen Crane

Stephen Crane (1871–1900) began his career in journalism while still in his teens. Later, as a reporter, Crane covered several wars in the late 1890s. He had not yet seen a battlefield, however, when he wrote The Red Badge of Courage. *Even so, he described the experience of war so realistically that even combat veterans admired his work. Critics still consider his novel* The Red Badge of Courage *a masterpiece.*

Read to Discover

What is it like to be a soldier facing battle for the first time? Henry Fleming, the young recruit in *The Red Badge of Courage,* offers some answers as he thinks about his role in the war. What battle does Henry fight with himself before he fights in an actual Civil War battle?

Reader's Dictionary

veterans: experienced soldiers
valor: bravery
Huns: soldiers known for their fierce fighting
despondent: sad
haversack: bag soldiers used to carry personal items
tumult: uproar

Various veterans had told him tales. Some talked of gray, bewhiskered hordes who were advancing with relentless curses, and chewing tobacco with unspeakable valor—tremendous bodies of fierce soldiery who were sweeping along like the Huns. Others spoke of tattered and eternally hungry men who fired despondent powders. "They'll charge through hell's fire an' brimstone t' git a holt on a haversack, an' sech stomachs ain't a-lastin' long," he was told. From the stories, the youth imagined the red, live bones sticking out through slits in the faded uniforms.

Still, he could not put a whole faith in veterans' tales, for recruits were their prey. They talked much of smoke, fire, and blood, but he could not tell how much might be lies. They persistently yelled "Fresh fish!" at him, and were in no wise to be trusted.

However, he perceived now that it did not greatly matter what kind of soldiers he was going to fight, so long as they fought, which fact no one disputed. There was a more serious problem. He lay in his bunk pondering upon it. He tried to mathematically prove to himself that he would not run from a battle.

Previously he had never felt obliged to wrestle too seriously with this question. In his life he had taken certain things for granted, never challenging his belief in ultimate success, and bothering little about means and roads. But here he was confronted with a thing of moment. It had suddenly appeared to him that perhaps in a battle he might run. He was forced to admit that as far as war was concerned he knew nothing of himself.

Additional Literary Works of the Period

You may want to refer students to the following:

Alcott, Louisa May. ***Little Women.*** New York: Collins, 1969. A heart-warming novel about family life in the 1800s.

Sinclair, Upton. ***The Jungle.*** New York: Doubleday, 1906. Depicts the squalor of early industrial America.

Stowe, Harriet Beecher. ***Uncle Tom's Cabin.*** New York: P. S. Eriksson, 1964. The annotated version with biographical references of the original work that exposed the cruelty of slavery.

Twain, Mark. ***The Adventures of Tom Sawyer.*** New York: Grosset & Dunlap, 1946. The adventures and pranks of a mischievous boy growing up in a Mississippi town in the early 1800s.

Military engineers of Company K, 8th New York State Militia

A sufficient time before he would have allowed the problem to kick its heels at the outer portals of his mind, but now he felt compelled to give serious attention to it.

A little panic-fear grew in his mind. As his imagination went forward to a fight, he saw hideous possibilities. He contemplated the lurking menaces of the future, and failed in an effort to see himself standing stoutly in the midst of them. He recalled his visions of broken-bladed glory, but in the shadow of the impending tumult he suspected them to be impossible pictures.

He sprang from the bunk and began to pace nervously to and fro. "Good Lord, what's th' matter with me?" he said aloud.

He felt that in this crisis his laws of life were useless. Whatever he had learned of himself was here of no avail. He was an unknown quantity. He saw that he would again be obliged to experiment as he had in early youth. He must accumulate information of himself, and meanwhile he resolved to remain close upon his guard lest those qualities of which he knew nothing should everlastingly disgrace him. "Good Lord!" he repeated in dismay.

Responding to Literature

1. How did Henry view the veterans and their war tales?
2. Why did Henry express doubts about his belief in himself?
3. What feelings do you think you might have just before going to battle?

Activity

Drawing Draw a picture showing items you think a young Civil War recruit would carry in a soldier's haversack. Include an item that might give the soldier courage.

Answers to Responding to Literature

1. He knew veterans told tales to young recruits that could be lies. He thought veterans were not to be trusted.
2. He felt that during this wartime situation, his laws of life were useless and that he was an unknown quantity.
3. Students should describe their feelings about going to battle.

Activity Call on volunteers to display and explain what they thought a soldier would have carried in a haversack.

History *and the* Humanities

- American Music Cultural Traditions, Lesson 5: "Bonnie Blue Flag," "Glory! Glory! Glory! Hallelujah!"
- The Spirit of American Art and Music, Mathew B. Brady
- U.S. History & Art, Transparency 11, *A Rainy Day at Camp*

Portfolio Activity Have students write in their portfolios about a personal experience they had involving fear. Ask them to describe how they handled the situation. Then have them predict how Henry Fleming would handle his situation.

At the Movies

John Huston directed the 1951 film version of *The Red Badge of Courage,* starring Audie Murphy. It is available as a 70-minute, black-and-white movie on videotape. Victor Fleming's Civil War movie classic, *Gone With the Wind,* is based on the 1936 novel by Margaret Mitchell. It premiered on December 15, 1939, and ran 222 minutes, requiring an intermission. This movie is available on videotape.

Curriculum Connection

MUSIC

Army of the Potomac chief of staff General Daniel Butterfield composed the notes for the bugle call "Taps" early in July 1862. He wrote the bugle call to be played at lights-out and at funerals.

Chapter 15 Planning Guide

A complete, 1-page lesson plan is provided for each section in the *Reproducible Lesson Plans* booklet.

Section Resources

Daily Objectives	Reproducible Resources	Multimedia Resources
Section 1 Slavery and the West Examine how the debate over slavery and the admission of new states to the Union fueled sectionalism.	Reproducible Lesson Plan 15–1 Guided Reading Activity 15–1* Section Quiz 15–1* Reteaching Activity 15–1 Enrichment Activity 15–1	Section Focus Transparency 15–1 Vocabulary PuzzleMaker Chapter Challenger Interactive Review Testmaker GTV: A Geographic Perspective on American History Facts On File: Landmark Documents in American History
Section 2 A Nation Dividing Investigate how federal laws about slavery led to violence.	Reproducible Lesson Plan 15–2 Guided Reading Activity 15–2* Political Cartoons, *Bloody Kansas* Section Quiz 15–2* Reteaching Activity 15–2 Enrichment Activity 15–2	Section Focus Transparency 15–2 Vocabulary PuzzleMaker Chapter Challenger Interactive Review Testmaker GTV: A Geographic Perspective on American History GTV: The American People: Fabric of a Nation
Section 3 Challenges to Slavery Summarize how political and social events affected Americans in the North and the South.	Reproducible Lesson Plan 15–3 Guided Reading Activity 15–3* Section Quiz 15–3* Reteaching Activity 15–3 Enrichment Activity 15–3	Section Focus Transparency 15–3 Vocabulary PuzzleMaker Chapter Challenger Interactive Review Software Testmaker GTV: The American People: Fabric of a Nation Facts On File: Landmark Documents in American History
Section 4 Secession and War Evaluate the impact of the 1860 election and how secession led to the Civil War.	Reproducible Lesson Plan 15–4 Guided Reading Activity 15–4* Section Quiz 15–4* Reteaching Activity 15–4 Enrichment Activity 15–4	Section Focus Transparency 15–4 Vocabulary PuzzleMaker Chapter Challenger Interactive Review Software Testmaker GTV: A Geographic Perspective on American History American Music Cultural Traditions, Lesson 5: "Get Off the Track!"

** Also available in Spanish*

Blackline Master · Videodisc · Audiocassette · Music Program · Transparency · CD-ROM · Software

0:00 OUT OF TIME?
Assign the Chapter 15 Digest and the corresponding Chapter Digests Audiocassettes with activities and tests.

Activity

From the Classroom of...

John Deluca
Drexel Hill Middle School
Drexel Hill, Pennsylvania

A Mock Trial of John Brown—American Martyr or Radical?

A "mock" trial of John Brown will enable students to scrutinize the events that led to the Civil War. Students can examine the viewpoints of both the North and South concerning issues that divided the nation. First, organize the class into four groups. Assign each group a topic to research, such as the Compromise of 1850, the *Dred Scott* Decision, the Kansas-Nebraska Act, or the Fugitive Slave law of 1850.

Have students role-play real people they find in their research. For example, a student could play the role of Stephen Douglas explaining the Kansas-Nebraska Act or Robert E. Lee discussing the capture of Brown. Some fictional characters could also be developed for the trial scene. Have characters take the stand one-by-one and let the rest of the class question them on activities that led to Brown's raid and eventually to the outbreak of the Civil War. Encourage students to examine different sides to all the issues discussed.

National Geographic Society Teacher's Corner

INDEX TO NATIONAL GEOGRAPHIC MAGAZINE

The following articles may be used for research relating to this chapter:

- "America's Poet: Walt Whitman," by Joel L. Swerdlow, December 1994.
- "C.S.S. *Alabama*" by Max Guerout, December 1994.
- "The Cruelest Commerce: African Slave Trade," by Colin Palmer, September 1992.
- "The Underground Railroad," by Charles L. Blockson, July 1984.

NATIONAL GEOGRAPHIC SOCIETY PRODUCTS AVAILABLE FROM GLENCOE

To order the following products for use with this chapter, contact your local Glencoe sales representative, or call Glencoe at 1-800-334-7344:

- *GTV: A Geographic Perspective on American History* (Videodisc)
- *GTV: The American People: Fabric of a Nation* (Videodisc)
- *The Presidents: A Picture History of Our Nation* (CD-ROM)
- *PictureShow: The Civil War* (CD-ROM, Transparencies)

ADDITIONAL NATIONAL GEOGRAPHIC SOCIETY PRODUCTS

To order the following products for use with this chapter, call National Geographic Society at 1-800-368-2728:

- *Steal Away: The Harriet Tubman Story* (Video)
- *Immigration: The Triumph of Hope* (Video)
- *The Blue and the Gray* (Book)
- *Historical Atlas of the United States* (Atlas)

Block Schedule

Block scheduling differs from traditional class scheduling in the amount of time allotted to each period. The extended time frame provided by block scheduling affords you the opportunity to implement a greater number of research-oriented and activity-intense projects to motivate and involve your students. Activities that are particularly suited to use within the block scheduling framework are identified throughout this chapter by the following designation:

KEY TO ABILITY LEVELS

Teaching strategies have been coded for varying learning styles and abilities.

L1 **BASIC** activities for all students
L2 **AVERAGE** activities for average to above-average students
L3 **CHALLENGING** activities for above-average students
ELL **ENGLISH LANGUAGE LEARNER** activities

Chapter 15 Resource Guide

Home Involvement

Home Involvement Activity 15

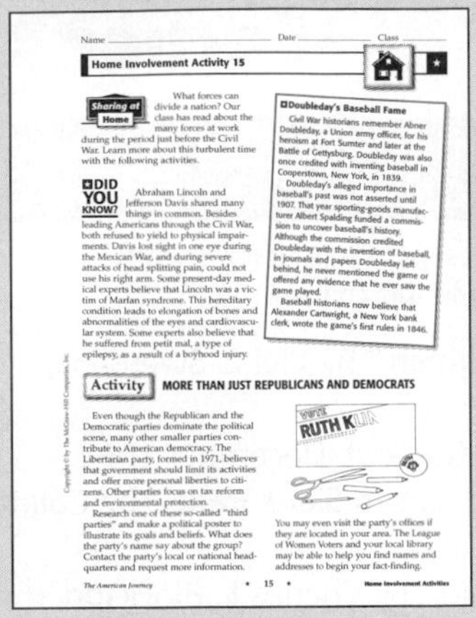

Review Activities

Chapter Summary 15

Workbook Activity 15

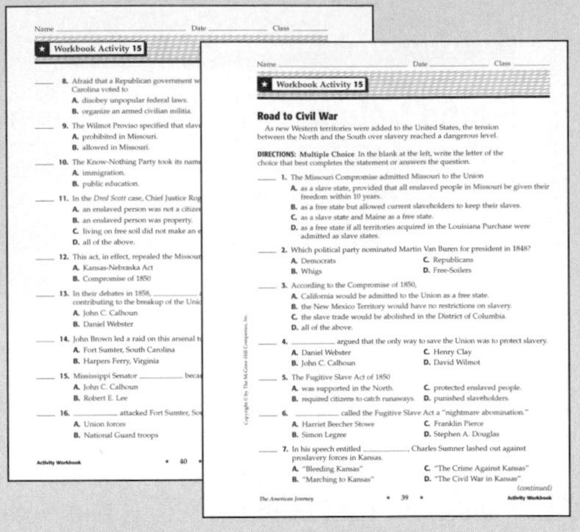

Reinforcement Activities

Time Line Activity 15

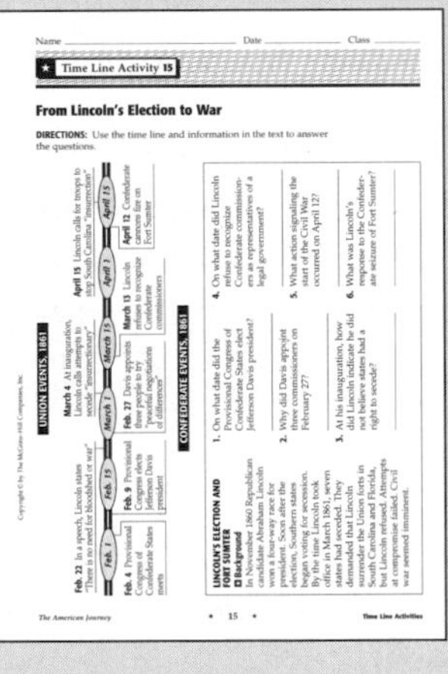

Vocabulary Activity 15

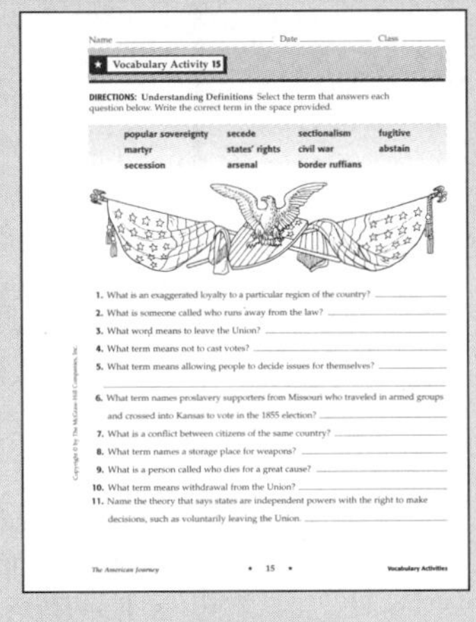

Chapter Skills Activity 15

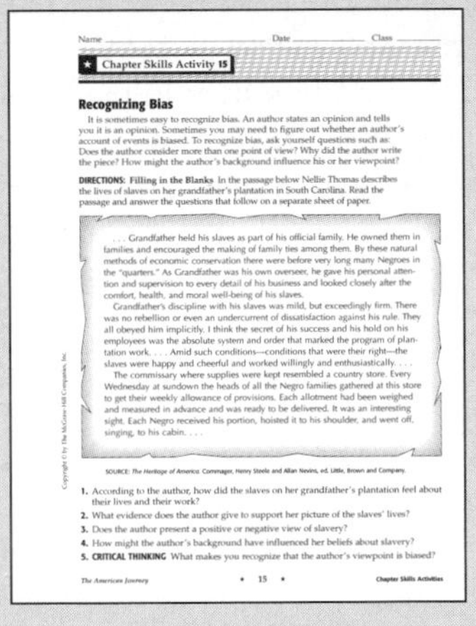

Enrichment Activities

Linking Past and Present Activity 15

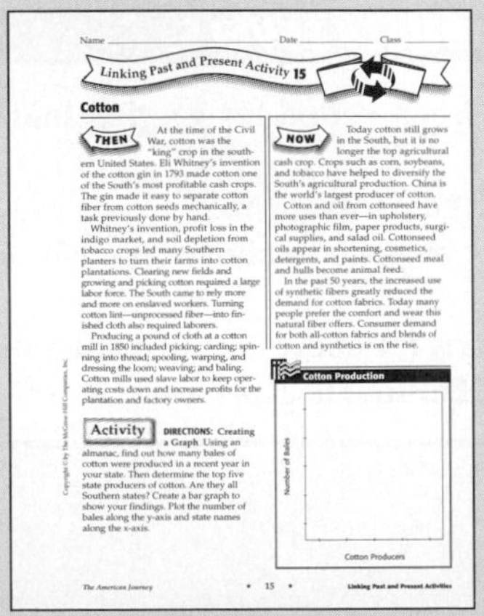

Primary Source Reading 15

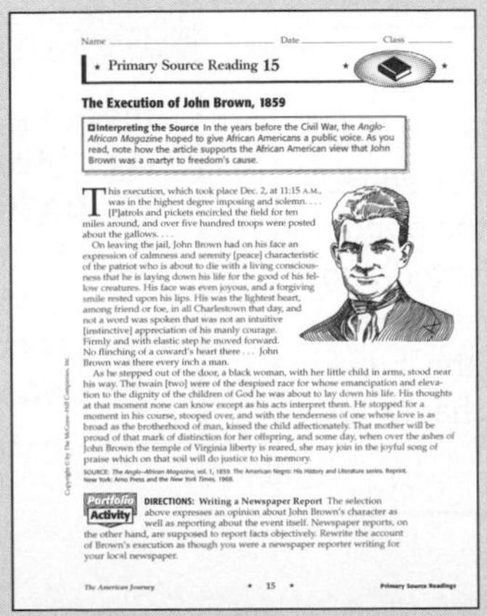

Geography Activities

Mapping History Activity 15

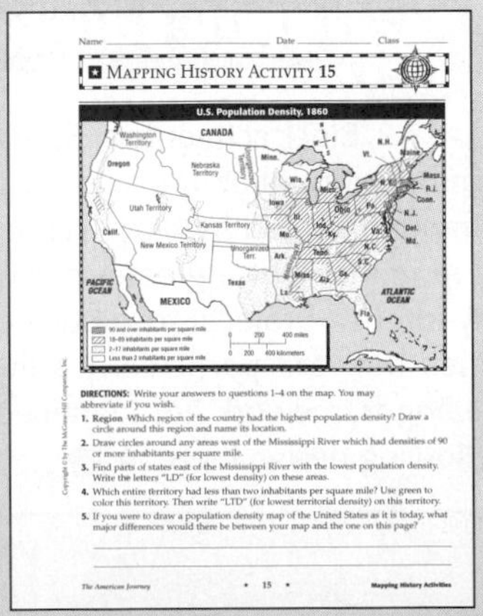

Chapter 15 Resource Guide

Assessment

Chapter 15 Test, Form A

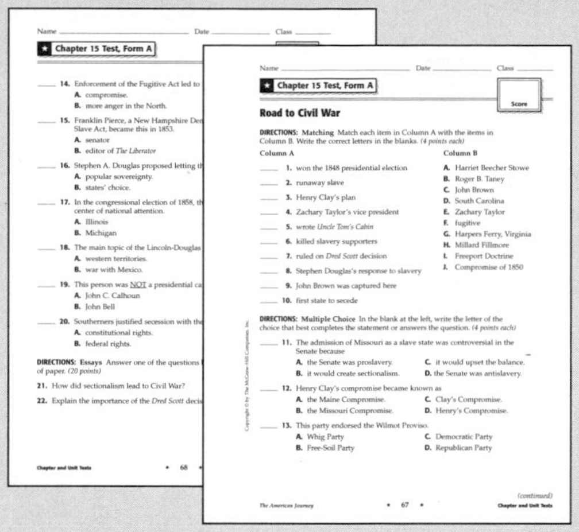

Chapter 15 Test, Form B

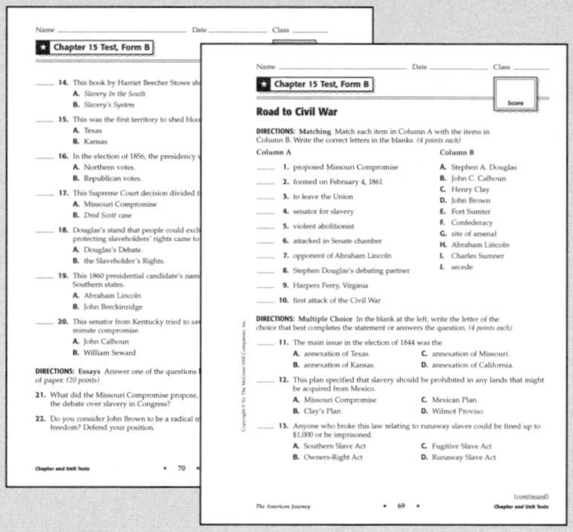

Performance Assessment Activity 15

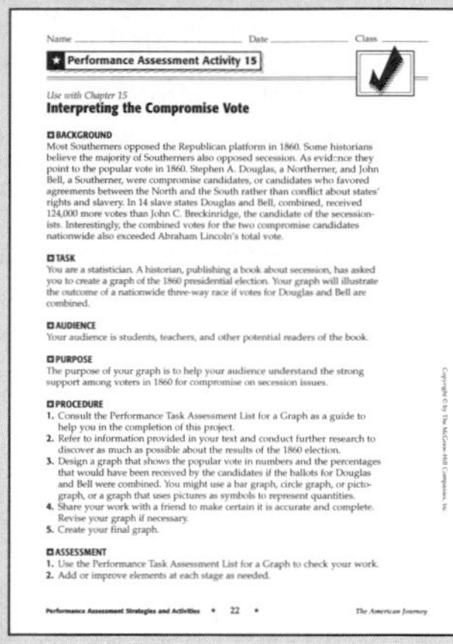

Spanish Resources

The following Spanish language materials are available in the Spanish Resources binder:

- **Spanish Chapter Summary 15**
- **Spanish Vocabulary Activity 15**
- **Spanish Guided Reading Activities, Chapter 15**
- **Spanish Section Quizzes, Chapter 15**
- **Spanish Home Involvement Activity 15**
- **Spanish Chapter 15 Digests Audiocassette Activity and Test**

Activity Manipulatives

Help students learn more about America's cultural history with:

- **American Crafts Hands-On Activities**
- **American Games Hands-On Activities**
- **American History Flash Cards**

Additional Resources From Glencoe

- **Focus on American Art Prints,** *Pat Lyon at the Forge* by John Neagle; *The Long Story* by William Sidney Mount
- **American Music Cultural Traditions,** Lesson 5: "Get Off the Track!"
- **The Spirit of American Art and Music,** Edward Hicks; Nathaniel Currier and James Ives; Mathew B. Brady
- **Outline Map Resource Book**
- **U.S. Desk Map**
- **The American History Videodisc and CD-ROM,** *Expansion, Development, Sectionalism and Division*
- **Political Cartoons,** *Bloody Kansas*

A&E HOME VIDEO. Biography™ THE HISTORY CHANNEL.

The following videotape programs are available from Glencoe as supplements to Chapter 15:

- **Civil War Journal (Set 1)** (ISBN 1-56501-200-3)
- **Cartoons Go to War** (ISBN 1-56501-625-4)

To order, call Glencoe at 1-800-334-7344. To find classroom resources to accompany many of these videos, check the following home pages:
A&E Television: http://www.aetv.com
The History Channel: http://www.historychannel.com

Introducing CHAPTER 15

Chapter Themes

Chapter Themes are listed by section on this chapter opening page of the Student Edition. A corresponding theme-based activity is available under "FOCUS," and a theme-based question is asked in the Section and Chapter Reviews.

Performance Assessment

Refer to Activity 15 in the *Performance Assessment Strategies and Activities* booklet.

GLENCOE TECHNOLOGY

VIDEODISC
MindJogger Videoquiz

Use MindJogger to preview the Chapter 15 content.

Chapter 15
Disc 2, Side B

Also available in VHS.

HISTORY AND ART Harpers Ferry, Virginia, established in 1794, was one of the first United States national arsenals. The Civil War battle at Harpers Ferry took place September 12–15, 1862. The Confederacy was victorious over the Union.

Chapter 15

1820–1861

Road to Civil War

Why It's Important

Slavery was a major cause of the worsening division between the North and the South in the decades preceding the Civil War. The struggle between the North and South turned more hostile, and there was talk of disunion and civil war. Americans today are still struggling with the legacy of slavery.

Chapter Themes

- *Section 1,* Government and Democracy
- *Section 2,* Civic Rights and Responsibilities
- *Section 3,* Continuity and Change
- *Section 4,* Geography and History

HISTORY AND ART ***View of Harpers Ferry*** **by Ferdinand Richardt** Danish artist Ferdinand Richardt captured a peaceful view of Harpers Ferry, Virginia (now West Virginia). The town was the location of the arsenal targeted for attack by abolitionist John Brown in 1859.

436

EXTRA CREDIT PROJECT

Storytelling Invite interested students to research accounts of fugitive enslaved persons who made their way to freedom on the Underground Railroad. Ask students to select one account to retell as if they were the original storyteller. Possible sources include: Blockson, Charles L. *The Underground Railroad: Dramatic First-Hand Accounts of Daring Escapes to Freedom.* New York: The Berkley Publishing Group, 1987; Blockson, Charles L. "Escape from Slavery: The Underground Railroad." *National Geographic,* July 1984, pp. 3–39; Blassingame, John W. *Slave Testimony.* Baton Rouge: Louisiana State University Press, 1977.

1820 | 1830 | 1840 | 1850

1820 Missouri Compromise is passed

1845 Texas becomes a state

1848 Free-Soil Party nominates Martin Van Buren

1850 Compromise of 1850 diverts war

Section 1

Slavery and the West

READ TO DISCOVER . . .

- how the debate over slavery was related to the admission of new states.
- what the Compromise of 1850 accomplished.

TERMS TO LEARN

sectionalism	secede
fugitive	abstain

The Storyteller

"The deed is done. The . . . chains of slavery are forged for [many] yet unborn. Humble yourselves in the dust, ye high-minded citizens of Connecticut. Let your cheeks be red as crimson. On *your* representatives rests the stigma of this foul disgrace." These biting, fiery words were published in a Connecticut newspaper in 1820. They were in response to members of Congress who had helped pave the way for the admission of Missouri as a slaveholding state.

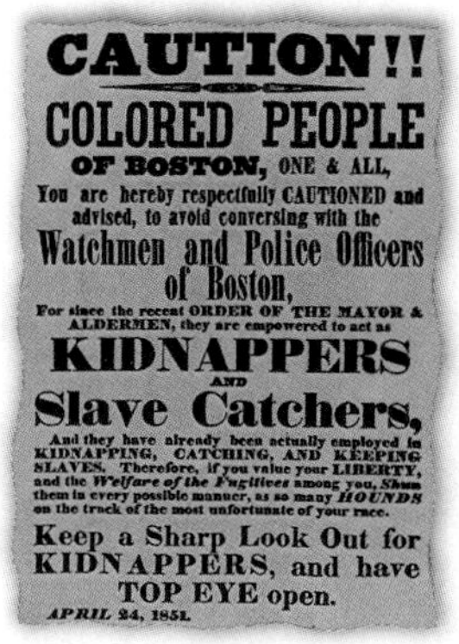

Warning to African Americans

The request by slaveholding **Missouri** to join the Union in 1819 caused an angry debate that worried former president Thomas Jefferson and Secretary of State John Quincy Adams. Jefferson called the dispute "a fire-bell in the night" that "awakened and filled me with terror." Adams accurately predicted that the bitter debate was "a mere preamble—a title-page to a great tragic volume."

The Missouri Compromise

Many Missouri settlers had brought enslaved African Americans into the territory with them. By 1819 the Missouri Territory included about 50,000 whites and 10,000 slaves. When Missouri applied to Congress for admission as a state, its constitution allowed slavery.

In 1819, 11 states in the Union permitted slavery and 11 did not. The Senate—with two members from each state—was therefore evenly balanced between slave and free states. The admission of a new state would upset that balance.

In addition, the North and the South, with their different economic systems, were competing for new lands in the western territories. At the same time, a growing number of Northerners wanted to restrict or ban slavery. Southerners, even those who disliked slavery, opposed these antislavery efforts. They resented the interference by outsiders in Southerners' affairs. These differences between the North and the South grew into **sectionalism**—an exaggerated loyalty to a particular region of the country.

SECTION RESOURCES

Reproducible Masters
- Reproducible Lesson Plan 15–1
- Guided Reading Activity 15–1
- Section Quiz 15–1
- Reteaching Activity 15–1
- Enrichment Activity 15–1

Transparencies
- Section Focus Transparency 15–1

Multimedia
- Vocabulary PuzzleMaker
- Chapter Challenger Interactive Review Software
- Testmaker
- GTV: A Geographic Perspective on American History
- Facts On File: Landmark Documents in American History

1 FOCUS

BELLRINGER
Motivational Activity

Before taking roll at the beginning of the class period, project Section Focus Transparency 15–1 and have students answer the questions. Discuss students' responses.

This activity is also available as a blackline master.

Section Focus Transparency 15–1

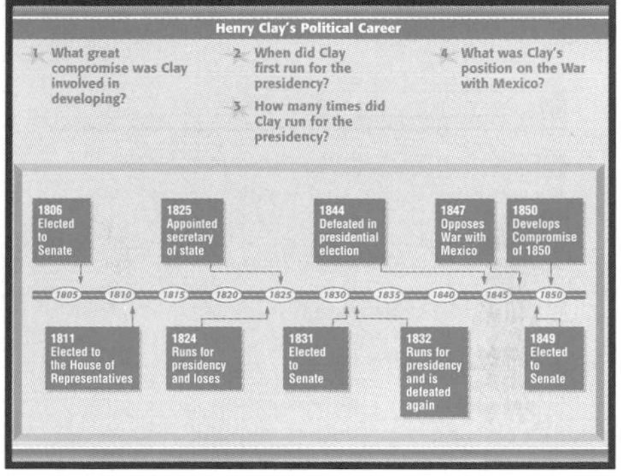

Vocabulary Precheck

Ask students to read the definition of *sectionalism* on page 437. Compare this to the definition of *nationalism,* a feeling of loyalty and devotion to one's country, honoring that nation above all others. Discuss with students how each of these feelings can help to unite or divide a nation.

Use the **Vocabulary PuzzleMaker** to create crossword and word search puzzles.

Section Theme
Government and Democracy

As new states were admitted to the Union, the question of whether to admit them as free or slave states fueled sectionalism.

Activity Review with students the concept of balance of power. **Ask: Why did slavery become a volatile issue when the balance of slave and free states was upset?** *(Answers should refer to the Senate's structure and how states are represented.)*

CHAPTER 15
Section 1, 437–440

2 TEACH

L1 Compromising Discuss the definition of compromise, pointing out that an effective compromise satisfies all parties involved. Pair students to make a graphic organizer for each compromise mentioned in this section. Have each pair show the following on the graphic organizer: name of the compromise, parties involved, what each party gave up, what each party received, the features of the final compromise.

Guided Reading Activity 15–1

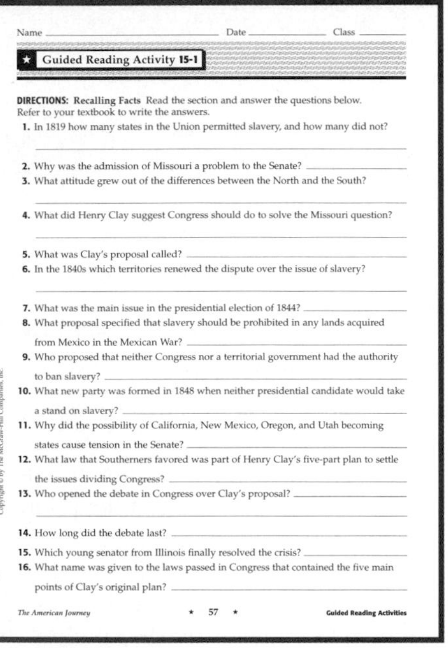
Name ______ Date ______ Class ______

★ Guided Reading Activity 15-1

DIRECTIONS: Recalling Facts Read the section and answer the questions below. Refer to your textbook to write the answers.

1. In 1819 how many states in the Union permitted slavery, and how many did not?
2. Why was the admission of Missouri a problem to the Senate?
3. What attitude grew out of the differences between the North and the South?
4. What did Henry Clay suggest Congress should do to solve the Missouri question?
5. What was Clay's proposal called?
6. In the 1840s which territories renewed the dispute over the issue of slavery?
7. What was the main issue in the presidential election of 1844?
8. What proposal specified that slavery should be prohibited in any lands acquired from Mexico in the Mexican War?
9. Who proposed that neither Congress nor a territorial government had the authority to ban slavery?
10. What new party was formed in 1848 when neither presidential candidate would take a stand on slavery?
11. Why did the possibility of California, New Mexico, Oregon, and Utah becoming states cause tension in the Senate?
12. What law that Southerners favored was part of Henry Clay's five-part plan to settle the issues dividing Congress?
13. Who opened the debate in Congress over Clay's proposal?
14. How long did the debate last?
15. Which young senator from Illinois finally resolved the crisis?
16. What name was given to the laws passed in Congress that contained the five main points of Clay's original plan?

The American Journey ★ 57 ★ **Guided Reading Activities**

NATIONAL GEOGRAPHIC SOCIETY

VIDEODISC
GTV: A Geographic Perspective on American History

Side 2, Chapter 13
Title: *One Nation, Still?*
Subject: Regional differences
Ask: **Identify the sources which the South and the North relied upon for their livelihood.** *(The South relied upon agriculture and slave labor, while the North relied upon industry.)*

Clay's Proposal

Henry Clay of Kentucky, then Speaker of the House of Representatives, proposed a solution to the Missouri question. Clay suggested that Congress admit Missouri as a slave state and Maine as a free state. Maine, formerly part of Massachusetts, had also applied for admission to the Union. Clay also sought to settle the issue of slavery in the territories for good. His proposal would prohibit slavery from any territory acquired in the Louisiana Purchase that was north of 36°30'N latitude—except Missouri.

This proposal, known as the **Missouri Compromise,** passed in 1820. It preserved the balance between slave and free states in the Senate and brought about a lull in the bitter debate in Congress over slavery.

New Western Lands

For the next 25 years, Congress managed to keep the slavery issue in the background. In the 1840s, however, this heated debate moved back into Congress. Once again the cause of the dispute was the issue of slavery in new territories. The territories involved were **Texas,** which had won its independence from Mexico in 1836, and **New Mexico** and **California,** which were still part of Mexico.

Many Southerners hoped to see Texas, where slavery already existed, join the Union. As a result the annexation of Texas became the main issue in the presidential election of 1844. Democrat **James Polk** of Tennessee won the election and pressed forward on acquiring Texas, and Texas became a state in 1845. At the same time, support for taking over New Mexico and California also grew in the South. The federal government's actions on these lands led to war with Mexico.

Conflicting Views

Just months after the Mexican War began, Representative David Wilmot of Pennsylvania introduced a proposal in Congress. Called the **Wilmot Proviso,** it specified that slavery should be prohibited in any lands that might be acquired from Mexico. Southerners protested furiously. They wanted to keep open the possibility of introducing slavery to California and New Mexico.

Senator **John C. Calhoun** of South Carolina countered with another proposal. It stated that neither Congress nor any territorial government had the authority to ban slavery from a territory or regulate it in any way.

Neither Wilmot's nor Calhoun's proposal passed, but both caused bitter debate. By the time of the 1848 presidential election, the United States had gained the territories of California and New Mexico from Mexico but had taken no action on the issue of slavery in those areas.

Polk campaign banner

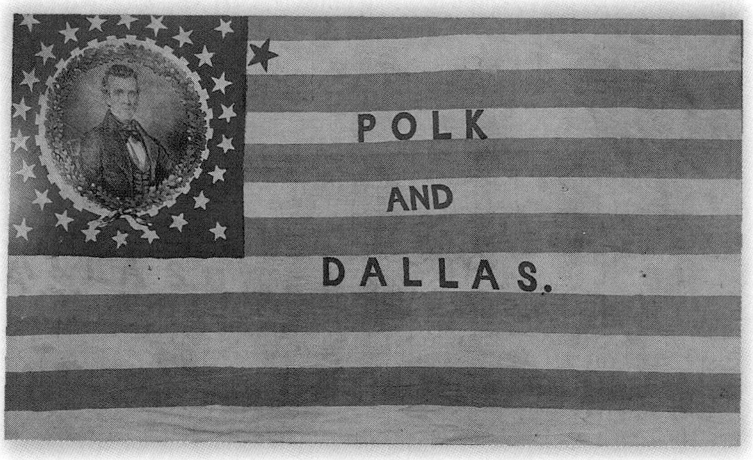

The Free-Soil Party

The debate over slavery led to the formation of a new political party. In 1848 the Whigs chose **Zachary Taylor,** a Southerner and a hero of the Mexican War, as their presidential candidate. The Democrats selected Senator Lewis Cass of Michigan. Neither candidate took a stand on slavery in the territories.

COOPERATIVE LEARNING ACTIVITY

Illustrating Loyalties Review the definitions of sectionalism and nationalism. Discuss the different levels of loyalty to areas of a country. Lead students to define the differences among loyalty to nation, region, state, county, city, and neighborhood. Organize the class into groups of six to create a booklet illustrating the six different levels of loyalty mentioned above. Have one student in each group create a page for the booklet illustrating one of the six loyalties, making sure all six are covered. Each page should be a collage showing examples, either text or illustrations, of the particular loyalty. Have each group assemble the pages into a booklet from the largest area of loyalty to the smallest and create a cover including title and authors.

Picturing HISTORY This engraving shows the great Senate debate in 1850 about Clay's compromise bill. **What did Clay's plan propose about slavery?**

This failure to take a position angered voters. Many antislavery Democrats and Whigs left their parties and joined with members of the old Liberty Party to form the **Free-Soil Party.** The new party proclaimed "Free Soil, Free Speech, Free Labor, and Free Men," and endorsed the Wilmot Proviso. The party nominated former president **Martin Van Buren** as its presidential candidate.

Whig candidate Zachary Taylor won the election by successfully appealing to both slave and free states. Taylor defeated Cass 163 to 127 in electoral votes. Van Buren captured only 14 percent of the popular vote in the North, but 13 candidates of the Free-Soil Party won seats in Congress.

California

Once in office President Taylor hoped to avoid congressional debate on the slavery question in California and New Mexico. He urged leaders in the two territories to apply for statehood immediately. Once these lands had become states, he reasoned, their citizens could decide whether to allow slavery. New Mexico did not apply for statehood, but California did in 1849.

Taylor's plan ran into trouble when California's statehood became tangled up with other issues before Congress. Antislavery forces wanted to abolish slavery in the District of Columbia, the nation's capital. Southerners wanted a strong national law requiring states to return **fugitive,** or runaway, slaves to their masters. Another dispute involved the New Mexico–Texas border.

The greatest obstacle to Taylor's plan, however, was renewed Southern concern over the balance of power in the Senate. In 1849 the nation included 15 slave states and 15 free states. If California entered as a free state—and New Mexico, Oregon, and Utah followed as free states, which seemed likely—the South would be hopelessly outvoted in the Senate. As tension reached a dangerous level, some Southerners began talking about having their states **secede** from, or leave, the United States.

A New Compromise

★ In January 1850, Henry Clay, now a senator, presented a five-part plan to settle all the issues dividing Congress. First, California would be admitted as a free state. Second, the New Mexico Territory would have no restrictions on slavery. Third, the New Mexico–Texas border dispute would be settled in favor of New Mexico. Fourth, the slave trade, but not slavery

CHAPTER 15
Section 1, 437–440

Picturing HISTORY Henry Clay was more than 70 years old and in poor health when he argued forcefully for his plan.
Answer: *California would be admitted as a free state; New Mexico Territory would have no restrictions on slavery; slave trade, but not slavery itself, would be abolished in the District of Columbia; stronger Fugitive Slave Law*

Facts On File

CD-ROM
Landmark Documents in American History

Title: *Compromise of 1850*
Ask students to outline the provisions of this compromise.

3 ASSESS

Assign Section 1 Review as homework or as an in-class activity.

Use **Chapter Challenger Interactive Review Software** to review Section 1.

Section Quiz 15–1

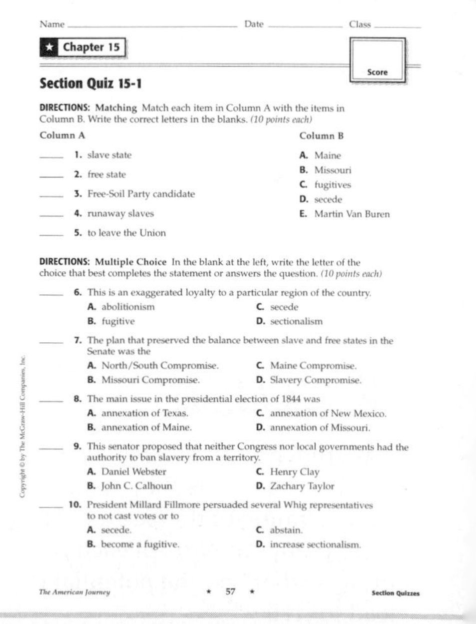

Name ______ Date ______ Class ______

★ Chapter 15

Score

Section Quiz 15-1

DIRECTIONS: Matching Match each item in Column A with the items in Column B. Write the correct letters in the blanks. *(10 points each)*

Column A	Column B
____ 1. slave state	A. Maine
____ 2. free state	B. Missouri
____ 3. Free-Soil Party candidate	C. fugitives
____ 4. runaway slaves	D. secede
____ 5. to leave the Union	E. Martin Van Buren

DIRECTIONS: Multiple Choice In the blank at the left, write the letter of the choice that best completes the statement or answers the question. *(10 points each)*

____ 6. This is an exaggerated loyalty to a particular region of the country.
A. abolitionism C. secede
B. fugitive D. sectionalism

____ 7. The plan that preserved the balance between slave and free states in the Senate was the
A. North/South Compromise. C. Maine Compromise.
B. Missouri Compromise. D. Slavery Compromise.

____ 8. The main issue in the presidential election of 1844 was
A. annexation of Texas. C. annexation of New Mexico.
B. annexation of Maine. D. annexation of Missouri.

____ 9. This senator proposed that neither Congress nor local governments had the authority to ban slavery from a territory.
A. Daniel Webster C. Henry Clay
B. John C. Calhoun D. Zachary Taylor

____ 10. President Millard Fillmore persuaded several Whig representatives to not cast votes or to
A. secede. C. abstain.
B. become a fugitive. D. increase sectionalism.

The American Journey ★ 57 ★ **Section Quizzes**

MULTIPLE LEARNING STYLES

Kinesthetic Actively involve students in the issues and candidates of the 1848 presidential election by having each student create a campaign platform for one of the candidates. Make sure the platforms include the important issues of each party's objectives and personal information about each candidate. Remind students that campaign platforms are used to persuade voters. **L2**

CHAPTER 15
Section 1, 437–440

Reteaching Activity 15–1

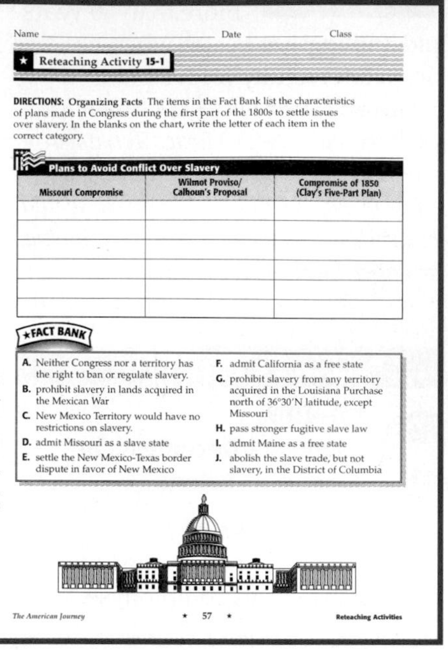

Name ______________ Date ______________ Class ______________

★ Reteaching Activity 15-1

DIRECTIONS: Organizing Facts The items in the Fact Bank list the characteristics of plans made in Congress during the first part of the 1800s to settle issues over slavery. In the blanks on the chart, write the letter of each item in the correct category.

Plans to Avoid Conflict Over Slavery

Missouri Compromise	Wilmot Proviso/ Calhoun's Proposal	Compromise of 1850 (Clay's Five-Part Plan)

★FACT BANK

A. Neither Congress nor a territory has the right to ban or regulate slavery.
B. prohibit slavery in lands acquired in the Mexican War
C. New Mexico Territory would have no restrictions on slavery.
D. admit Missouri as a slave state
E. settle the New Mexico-Texas border dispute in favor of New Mexico
F. admit California as a free state
G. prohibit slavery from any territory acquired in the Louisiana Purchase north of 36°30'N latitude, except Missouri
H. pass stronger fugitive slave law
I. admit Maine as a free state
J. abolish the slave trade, but not slavery, in the District of Columbia

Copyright © by The McGraw-Hill Companies, Inc.

The American Journey ★ 57 ★ Reteaching Activities

Enrichment Activity 15–1

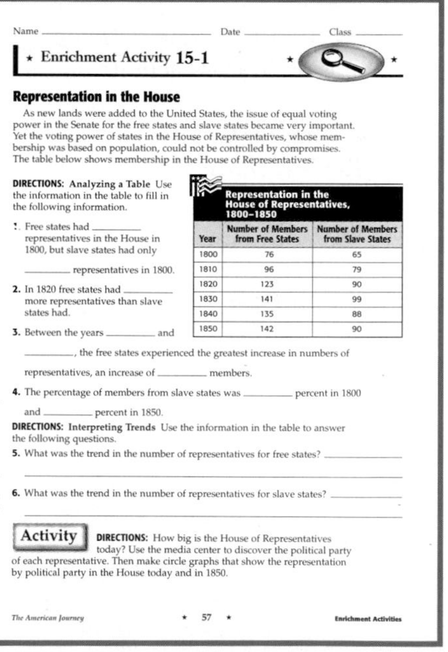

Name ______________ Date ______________ Class ______________

★ Enrichment Activity 15-1

Representation in the House

As new lands were added to the United States, the issue of equal voting power in the Senate for the free states and slave states became very important. Yet the voting power of states in the House of Representatives, whose membership was based on population, could not be controlled by compromises. The table below shows membership in the House of Representatives.

DIRECTIONS: Analyzing a Table Use the information in the table to fill in the following information.

Representation in the House of Representatives, 1800–1850

Year	Number of Members from Free States	Number of Members from Slave States
1800	76	65
1810	96	79
1820	123	90
1830	141	99
1840	135	88
1850	142	90

1. Free states had ________ representatives in the House in 1800, but slave states had only ________ representatives in 1800.
2. In 1820 free states had ________ more representatives than slave states had.
3. Between the years ________ and ________, the free states experienced the greatest increase in numbers of representatives, an increase of ________ members.
4. The percentage of members from slave states was ________ percent in 1800 and ________ percent in 1850.

DIRECTIONS: Interpreting Trends Use the information in the table to answer the following questions.

5. What was the trend in the number of representatives for free states? ________
6. What was the trend in the number of representatives for slave states? ________

Activity **DIRECTIONS:** How big is the House of Representatives today? Use the media center to discover the political party of each representative. Then make circle graphs that show the representation by political party in the House today and in 1850.

Copyright © by The McGraw-Hill Companies, Inc.

The American Journey ★ 57 ★ Enrichment Activities

4 CLOSE

Ask students to reexamine the graphic organizers they created at the beginning of this section. Have them point out parts of each compromise that had the potential to lead to civil war.

itself, would be abolished in the District of Columbia. Finally, Clay pushed for a stronger fugitive slave law.

The Great Debate

Clay's proposal launched an extremely emotional debate in Congress that raged for seven months. Opening that debate were Clay and two other distinguished Senators—John C. Calhoun of South Carolina and **Daniel Webster** of Massachusetts.

Calhoun opposed Clay's plan. Almost 70 and too ill to deliver his own speech, he asked Senator James Mason of Virginia to read it for him. Calhoun believed that the only way to save the Union was to protect slavery. If Congress admitted California as a free state, Calhoun warned, the Southern states had to leave the Union.

Three days later Webster gave an eloquent speech in support of Clay's plan. He claimed to speak "not as a Massachusetts man, nor as a Northern man, but as an American." What was most important was to preserve the Union.

> "I would rather hear of natural blasts and mildews, war, pestilence, and famine, than to hear gentlemen talk of secession."

The Compromise of 1850

Clay's plan could not pass as a complete package. Too many members of Congress objected to one part of it or another. President Taylor also opposed the plan and threatened to use force against the South if states tried to secede.

Then in July President Taylor suddenly died, the second president to die in office. The new president and Taylor's vice president, **Millard Fillmore,** supported some form of compromise. At the same time, **Stephen A. Douglas,** a young senator from Illinois, took charge of efforts to resolve the crisis. Douglas divided Clay's plan into a series of measures that Congress could vote on separately. In this way members of Congress would not have to support proposals they bitterly opposed.

During months of complicated bargaining, President Fillmore persuaded several Whig representatives to **abstain**—not to cast votes—on measures they opposed. Congress finally passed a series of five separate bills in August and September of 1850. Taken together these laws, known as the **Compromise of 1850,** contained the five main points of Clay's original plan. Fillmore called the compromise a "final settlement" of the conflict between North and South. The president would soon be proved wrong.

Section 1 Review

Checking for Understanding

1. ***Identify*** Henry Clay, Wilmot Proviso, John C. Calhoun, Zachary Taylor, Free-Soil Party, Daniel Webster, Stephen A. Douglas.
2. ***Define*** sectionalism, fugitive, secede, abstain.
3. ***List*** the provisions of the Missouri Compromise.

Reviewing Themes

4. **Government and Democracy** Why was the Free-Soil Party created?

Critical Thinking

5. **Media Literacy** Use the computerized card catalog in your library to list three subject headings you could investigate to learn more about the Missouri Compromise.

Activity

Designing a Campaign Poster Create a campaign poster for the Free-Soil Party presidential candidate. Include slogans or symbols to gain popular support.

Section 1 Review Answers

1. Henry Clay, 438; Wilmot Proviso, 438; John C. Calhoun, 438; Zachary Taylor, 438; Free-Soil Party, 439; Daniel Webster, 440; Stephen A. Douglas, 440
2. The words are defined in the Glossary.
3. Missouri admitted as slave state and Maine as free; prohibited slavery in Louisiana Purchase territory in areas north of 36°30' N latitude except Missouri
4. to take a stand opposing the extension of slavery
5. any three of the following subject headings: Missouri Compromise; Henry Clay; slavery; Civil War; Missouri; Maine

Activity Poster should address the importance of slavery as a campaign issue.

Critical Thinking
SKILL BUILDER

Recognizing Bias

Cats make better pets than dogs. If you say this—without ever having owned a dog—then you are stating a bias. A bias is a prejudice. It prevents one from looking at a situation in a reasonable or truthful way.

Learning the Skill

Most people have feelings and ideas that affect their point of view. This viewpoint, or *bias,* influences the way they interpret events. For this reason, an idea that is stated as a fact may really be only an opinion. Recognizing bias will help you judge the accuracy of what you read.

To recognize bias, follow these steps:

- Identify the author of the statement and examine his or her views and possible reasons for writing the material.
- Look for language that reflects an emotion or opinion—words such as *all, never, best, worst, might,* or *should.*
- Examine the writing for imbalances—leaning only to one viewpoint and failing to provide equal coverage of other possible viewpoints.
- Identify statements of fact. Factual statements usually answer the Who? What? Where? and When? questions.
- Determine how the author's bias is reflected in the work.

Practicing the Skill

Read the excerpts on this page. The first excerpt is from a speech by Senator John C. Calhoun of South Carolina. The second is from an 1858 newspaper editorial. Then answer the five questions that follow.

"... [T]he two great divisions of society are not rich and poor, but white and black; and all the former, the poor as well as the rich, belong to the upper classes, and are respected and treated as such."

—Senator Calhoun

"Popular sovereignty for the territories will never work. Under this system, each territory would decide whether or not to legalize slavery. This method was tried in the territory of Kansas and all it produced was bloodshed and violence."

—*The Republican Leader,* 1858

1. Is Senator Calhoun expressing a proslavery or antislavery bias?
2. What statements indicate the racism in Calhoun's bias?
3. What evidence does Calhoun offer to support his viewpoint?
4. What political party's view does the editorial represent?
5. What biases or beliefs are expressed in the editorial?

Applying the Skill

Recognizing Bias Look through the letters to the editor in your local newspaper. Write a short report analyzing one of the letters for evidence of bias.

Critical Thinking
SKILL BUILDER

TEACH

Recognizing Bias
This skill illustrates how bias prevents someone from looking at a situation in a reasonable and truthful way. By analyzing two excerpts, students apply the steps to recognizing bias.

Have students work in pairs to apply these steps to the quotations in Section 1 to determine each speaker's bias. Discuss the quotations and the biases. Point out to students how their own biases can influence their interpretation of bias.

Additional Practice

Chapter Skills Activity 15

ANSWERS TO PRACTICING THE SKILL

1. proslavery
2. by saying that rich and poor whites are of the upper class and that the divisions of society are black and white
3. none
4. Republican
5. Popular sovereignty does not work.

Applying the Skill
Students should write a short report analyzing a letter to the editor for evidence of bias.

CHAPTER 15
Section 2, 442–445

1 FOCUS

BELLRINGER
Motivational Activity

Before taking roll at the beginning of the class period, project Section Focus Transparency 15–2 and have students answer the questions. Discuss students' responses.

This activity is also available as a blackline master.

Section Focus Transparency 15–2

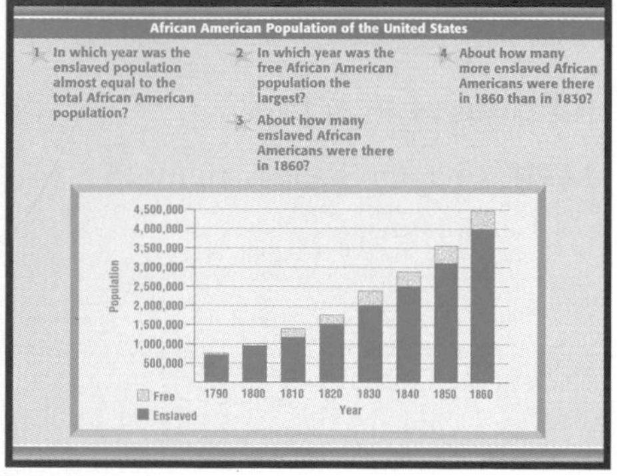

Vocabulary Precheck
Write the words *popular* and *sovereignty* on the chalkboard. Lead students to understand that *popular* means "of or carried on by the common people" and *sovereignty* means "supreme, independent political authority." Combining the two meanings, *popular sovereignty* means "let the people decide."

Section Theme
Civic Rights and Responsibilities
Most of the compromises made in the early to mid-1800s did not work because Northerners and Southerners differed about whether it was a civic responsibility to obey them or a civic right to disobey them.

Activity Have students read *The Storyteller* and the information about the Fugitive Slave Act on this page. **Ask:** **Do you think it was the Northerners' civic duty to follow the Fugitive Slave Act or their civic right to disobey it?**

1850 — 1853 — 1856

1850 Fugitive Slave Act is passed
1852 *Uncle Tom's Cabin* is published
1854 Kansas-Nebraska Act is passed
1856 "Bleeding Kansas" erupts in violence

Section 2

A Nation Dividing

READ TO DISCOVER . . .
- why the Fugitive Slave Act and the Kansas-Nebraska Act made the division between North and South worse.
- how popular sovereignty led to violence.

TERMS TO LEARN
popular sovereignty
border ruffians
civil war

The Storyteller

On May 24, 1854, the people of Boston erupted in outrage. Federal officers had seized Anthony Burns, a runaway slave who lived in Boston, to send him back to slavery. Abolitionists tried to rescue Burns from the federal courthouse, and city leaders attempted to buy his freedom. All efforts failed. More than 1,000 militia joined the marines and cavalry in Boston to keep order. Federal troops escorted Burns to a ship that would carry him back to Virginia and slavery. In a gesture of bitter protest, Bostonians draped buildings in black and hung the American flag upside down.

Anthony Burns

The calm that followed passage of the Compromise of 1850 did not last long. Many in the North could not accept the Fugitive Slave Act, a key part of the compromise.

The Fugitive Slave Act

The **Fugitive Slave Act** of 1850 required all citizens to help catch runaways. Anyone who aided a fugitive could be fined—up to $1,000—or imprisoned. People in the South believed the law would force Northerners to recognize the rights of Southerners. Instead enforcement of the law led to mounting anger in the North, convincing more people of the evils of slavery.

Resistance to the Law

After passage of the Fugitive Slave Act, slaveholders stepped up their efforts to catch runaway slaves. They even tried to capture runaways who had lived in freedom in the North for years. Sometimes they seized African Americans who were not runaways and forced them into slavery.

In spite of the penalties, many Northerners refused to cooperate with the law's enforcement. The **Underground Railroad,** a network of free African Americans and whites, helped runaways make their way to freedom. Antislavery groups tried to rescue African Americans who were being pursued or to free those who were captured. In Boston members of one such group followed federal agents shouting, "Slave hunters—there go the slave hunters." People contributed funds to

SECTION RESOURCES

Reproducible Masters
- Guided Reading Activity 15–2
- Political Cartoons, *Bloody Kansas*
- Section Quiz 15–2
- Reteaching Activity 15–2
- Enrichment Activity 15–2

Transparencies
- Section Focus Transparency 15–2

Multimedia
- Vocabulary PuzzleMaker
- Chapter Challenger Interactive Review Software
- Testmaker
- GTV: A Geographic Perspective on American History
- GTV: The American People: Fabric of A Nation

buy the freedom of African Americans. Northern juries refused to convict those accused of breaking the Fugitive Slave Law.

Biography

Uncle Tom's Cabin

Writer **Harriet Beecher Stowe** called the Fugitive Slave Act a "nightmare abomination." The daughter of a New England minister and wife of a religion professor, Stowe was active in antislavery work for much of her life. She wrote a novel about the evils of slavery. Her book, ***Uncle Tom's Cabin,*** was published in 1852. Packed with dramatic incidents and vivid characters, the novel shows slavery as a brutal, cruel system. In one scene Simon Legree, a slaveholder, tries to justify why Tom is a slave.

Harriet Beecher Stowe

> "Didn't I pay down $1,200 cash. . . ? An't yer mine, now, body and soul?" he said, giving Tom a violent kick with his heavy boot. "Tell me!" . . . "No! no! no! my soul an't yours . . . [Tom replied]. You haven't bought it—ye can't buy it!"

Uncle Tom's Cabin quickly became a sensation, selling more than 300,000 copies within its first year.

Proslavery writers responded with works that defended slavery. They argued that enslaved African Americans in the South lived better than free factory workers in the North. These books had little effect on the growing antislavery sentiment in the North.

The Kansas–Nebraska Act

Franklin Pierce, a New Hampshire Democrat who supported the Fugitive Slave Law, became president in 1853. Pierce intended to enforce the Fugitive Slave Law, and his actions hardened the opposition.

In 1854 the dispute over slavery erupted in Congress again. The cause was a bill introduced by Stephen A. Douglas, the Illinois senator who had forged the Compromise of 1850.

Hoping to encourage settlement of the West and open the way for a transcontinental railroad, Douglas proposed organizing the region west of Missouri and Iowa as the territories of **Kansas** and **Nebraska.** Douglas was trying to work out a way for the nation to expand that both the North and the South would accept, but his bill reopened the conflict about slavery in the territories. In this new sectional crisis, violence began to infect the political debate.

Repeal of the Missouri Compromise

Because of their location, Kansas and Nebraska seemed likely to become free states. Both lay north of 36°30'N latitude, the line established in the Missouri Compromise as the boundary of slavery. Douglas knew that Southerners would object to having Kansas and Nebraska become free states because it would give the North an advantage in the Senate. As a result Douglas proposed abandoning the Missouri Compromise and letting the settlers in each territory vote on whether to allow slavery. He called this **popular sovereignty**—allowing the people to decide.

Passage of the Act

Many Northerners protested strongly. Douglas's plan to repeal the Missouri Compromise would allow slavery into areas that had been free for more than 30 years. Opponents of the bill demanded that Congress vote down the bill.

Southerners in Congress, however, provided solid support for the bill. They expected that Kansas would be settled in large part by

Cooperative Learning Activity

Mediating Conflict Organize the class into groups of four to devise alternate compromises that might have avoided the bloodshed following the Kansas-Nebraska Act. Ask each group to role-play a debate over an alternative compromise. Assign the following roles: Stephen A. Douglas, who proposed the Kansas-Nebraska Act and was for popular sovereignty; Charles Sumner, who was an adamant abolitionist; Andrew P. Butler, a proslavery senator; a mediator. Make sure students accurately represent the point of view of the person whose role they are playing. If the sides cannot agree on an alternate plan with the help of the mediator, then the mediator should assume the role of binding arbitrator, who evaluates the different positions and imposes a decision. Have each group analyze the process of compromise and binding arbitration.

2 TEACH

L1 Creating a Graphic Organizer
Ask students to create a cause-and-effect graphic organizer showing the effects of the Fugitive Slave Act and the Kansas-Nebraska Act. Encourage students to illustrate their graphic organizers. Use the organizers as the basis for discussing why the nation was dividing.

Guided Reading Activity 15–2

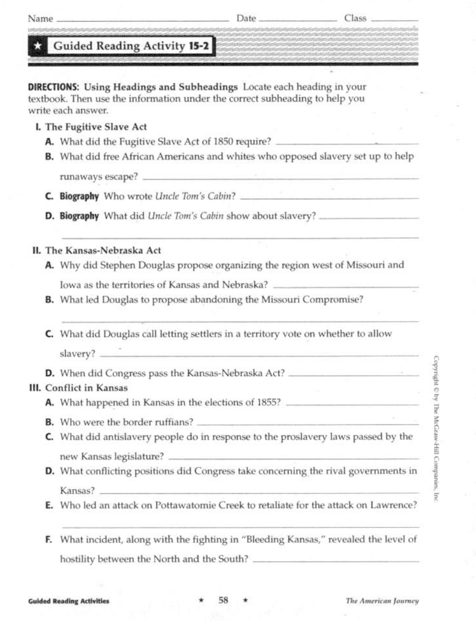
Name ______ Date ______ Class ______

Guided Reading Activity 15-2

DIRECTIONS: Using Headings and Subheadings Locate each heading in your textbook. Then use the information under the correct subheading to help you write each answer.

I. The Fugitive Slave Act
- **A.** What did the Fugitive Slave Act of 1850 require? ______
- **B.** What did free African Americans and whites who opposed slavery set up to help runaways escape? ______
- **C. Biography** Who wrote *Uncle Tom's Cabin*? ______
- **D. Biography** What did *Uncle Tom's Cabin* show about slavery? ______

II. The Kansas-Nebraska Act
- **A.** Why did Stephen Douglas propose organizing the region west of Missouri and Iowa as the territories of Kansas and Nebraska? ______
- **B.** What led Douglas to propose abandoning the Missouri Compromise? ______
- **C.** What did Douglas call letting settlers in a territory vote on whether to allow slavery? ______
- **D.** When did Congress pass the Kansas-Nebraska Act? ______

III. Conflict in Kansas
- **A.** What happened in Kansas in the elections of 1855? ______
- **B.** Who were the border ruffians? ______
- **C.** What did antislavery people do in response to the proslavery laws passed by the new Kansas legislature? ______
- **D.** What conflicting positions did Congress take concerning the rival governments in Kansas? ______
- **E.** Who led an attack on Pottawatomie Creek to retaliate for the attack on Lawrence? ______
- **F.** What incident, along with the fighting in "Bleeding Kansas," revealed the level of hostility between the North and the South? ______

Copyright © by The McGraw-Hill Companies, Inc.

Guided Reading Activities ★ 58 ★ *The American Journey*

NATIONAL GEOGRAPHIC SOCIETY

VIDEODISC
GTV: A Geographic Perspective on American History

Side 2, Chapter 15
Title: *The Gathering Storm*
Subject: Conflict and compromise before the Civil War
Ask: **How did Congress attempt to settle the question of whether Kansas and Nebraska would become free or slave states?**
(to let the people of Kansas and Nebraska decide for themselves)

Map Study

Answers

1. repealed it
2. Washington, Oregon, and Minnesota

Map Skills Practice

Reading a Map From which territory or territories were the Nebraska and Kansas Territories formed? *(Unorganized Territory)*

Who? What? Where? When?

John Brown made the fight against slavery his life's work. In 1837, at a memorial service for murdered abolitionist Elijah Lovejoy, Brown had pledged to spend the rest of his life battling slavery.

3 ASSESS

Assign Section 2 Review as homework or as an in-class activity.

Use **Chapter Challenger Interactive Review Software** to review Section 2.

Section Quiz 15–2

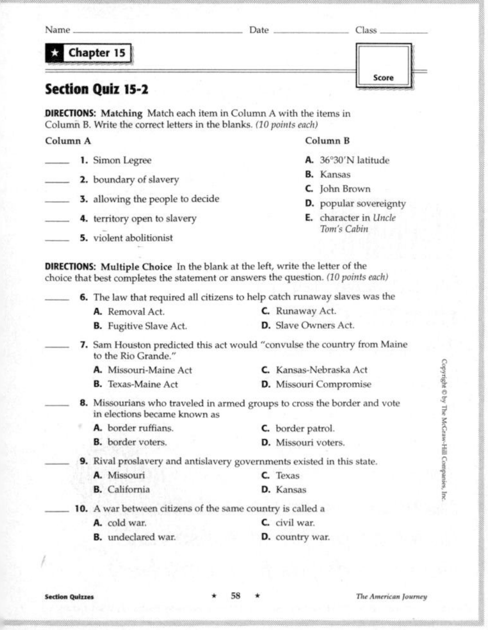
Name ______ Date ______ Class ______

★ Chapter 15

Score

Section Quiz 15-2

DIRECTIONS: Matching Match each item in Column A with the items in Column B. Write the correct letters in the blanks. *(10 points each)*

Column A	Column B
____ 1. Simon Legree	A. 36°30′N latitude
____ 2. boundary of slavery	B. Kansas
____ 3. allowing the people to decide	C. John Brown
____ 4. territory open to slavery	D. popular sovereignty
____ 5. violent abolitionist	E. character in *Uncle Tom's Cabin*

DIRECTIONS: Multiple Choice In the blank at the left, write the letter of the choice that best completes the statement or answers the question. *(10 points each)*

____ 6. The law that required all citizens to help catch runaway slaves was the
- A. Removal Act.
- B. Fugitive Slave Act.
- C. Runaway Act.
- D. Slave Owners Act.

____ 7. Sam Houston predicted this act would "convulse the country from Maine to the Rio Grande."
- A. Missouri-Maine Act
- B. Texas-Maine Act
- C. Kansas-Nebraska Act
- D. Missouri Compromise

____ 8. Missourians who traveled in armed groups to cross the border and vote in elections became known as
- A. border ruffians.
- B. border voters.
- C. border patrol.
- D. Missouri voters.

____ 9. Rival proslavery and antislavery governments existed in this state.
- A. Missouri
- B. California
- C. Texas
- D. Kansas

____ 10. A war between citizens of the same country is called a
- A. cold war.
- B. undeclared war.
- C. civil war.
- D. country war.

Copyright © by The McGraw-Hill Companies, Inc.

Section Quizzes ★ 58 ★ *The American Journey*

Map Study

The Compromise of 1850 closed the area of Kansas and Nebraska Territories to slaveholding.

1. **Region** How did the Kansas-Nebraska Act affect the agreement reached in the Compromise of 1850?
2. **Analyzing Information** What territories were nonslaveholding in 1854?

slaveholders from Missouri who would vote to keep slavery legal. With some support from Northern Democrats and the backing of President Pierce, Congress passed the **Kansas–Nebraska Act** in May 1854.

Northern Democrats in the House split evenly on the vote, revealing deep divisions in the party. Many Northerners became convinced that compromise with the South was no longer possible. Sam Houston, senator from Texas, predicted that the bill "will convulse [upset] the country from Maine to the Rio Grande."

Conflict in Kansas

Right after passage of the Kansas–Nebraska Act, proslavery and antislavery groups rushed supporters into Kansas. In the spring of 1855, when elections took place in Kansas, a proslavery legislature was elected.

Although only about 1,500 voters lived in Kansas at the time, more than 6,000 people cast ballots in the elections. Thousands of proslavery supporters from Missouri had crossed the border just to vote in the election. These Missourians traveled in armed groups and became known as **border ruffians.**

Soon after the election, the new Kansas legislature passed laws supporting slavery. One law even restricted political office to proslavery candidates. The antislavery people refused to accept these laws. Instead they armed themselves, held their own elections, and adopted a constitution that banned slavery.

By January 1856, rival governments existed in Kansas, one for and one against slavery. Each asked Congress for recognition. To confuse matters further, the president and the Senate favored the proslavery government, while the House backed the forces opposed to slavery.

"Bleeding Kansas"

With proslavery and antislavery forces in Kansas arming themselves, the outbreak of violence became inevitable. In May 1856, 800 slavery supporters attacked the town of Lawrence, the antislavery capital. They sacked the town, burned the hotel and the home of the governor, and destroyed two newspaper offices. Soon after, forces opposed to slavery retaliated.

John Brown, a fervent abolitionist, believed God had chosen him to end slavery. Brown had recently come to Kansas from Ohio with six sons and a son-in-law. When he heard of the attack on

MULTIPLE LEARNING STYLES

Visual/Spatial Harriet Beecher Stowe's novel, *Uncle Tom's Cabin,* did much to rally Northern public opinion against slavery. The novel was first published on June 5, 1851, as a 10-month serial in the abolitionist newspaper, *National Era.* When it was published as a novel in 1852, George Aiken (without Stowe's consent) dramatized the story into a play. Countless stage versions of this story were enacted before the Civil War, but most versions sensationalized the plot and the characters. Detailed posters were commonly used to announce the play. Have each student create a poster to announce the opening of *Uncle Tom's Cabin.* **L1,** ELL

Lawrence, Brown went into a rage. He vowed to "strike terror in the hearts of the proslavery people." One night Brown led four of his sons and two other men along Pottawatomie Creek, where they seized and killed five supporters of slavery.

More violence followed as armed bands roamed the territory. Newspapers began referring to "Bleeding Kansas" and "the Civil War in Kansas." A **civil war** is a conflict between citizens of the same country. Not until the fall of 1856 could the United States Army stop the bloodshed in Kansas. By then more than 200 people had been killed.

John Brown Calls Down the Storm of the Civil War, ***a painting by John Steuart Curry***

Violence in Congress

The violence that erupted in Kansas spread to Congress as well. Abolitionist senator **Charles Sumner** of Massachusetts delivered a speech entitled "The Crime Against Kansas." Sumner lashed out against proslavery forces in Kansas. He also criticized proslavery senators, repeatedly attacking Andrew P. Butler of South Carolina.

Two days after the speech, Butler's distant cousin, Representative **Preston Brooks,** walked into the Senate chamber. He hit Sumner again and again over the head and shoulders with a cane. Sumner fell to the floor, unconscious and bleeding. He suffered injuries so severe that he did not return to the Senate for several years. The Brooks-Sumner incident and the fighting in "Bleeding Kansas" revealed the rising level of hostility between North and South.

Section 2 Review

Checking for Understanding

1. ***Identify*** Fugitive Slave Act, *Uncle Tom's Cabin,* John Brown, Charles Sumner.
2. ***Define*** popular sovereignty, border ruffians, civil war.
3. ***Describe*** how the Northern abolitionists reacted to the Fugitive Slave Act.

Reviewing Themes

4. **Civic Rights and Responsibilities** How did popular sovereignty lead to violence in Kansas?

Critical Thinking

5. **Predicting Consequences** Do you think the violence in Kansas could have been prevented if Congress had not abandoned the Missouri Compromise? Explain your answer.

Activity

Producing a Play With members of your class, choose a scene from *Uncle Tom's Cabin* to portray in a one-act play. Write a short script, assign roles, and present it to the class.

Section 2 Review Answers

1. Fugitive Slave Act, 442; *Uncle Tom's Cabin,* 443; John Brown, 444; Charles Sumner, 445
2. The words are defined in the Glossary.
3. refused to accept the terms, refused to enforce it, aided escaping slaves, refused to convict those who helped
4. Outsiders corrupted the election and fighting broke out over the results.
5. Students should state *yes* or *no* and use evidence to support their answers.

Activity Students should write a script for a one-act play based on *Uncle Tom's Cabin.*

CHAPTER 15
Section 2, 442–445

Reteaching Activity 15–2

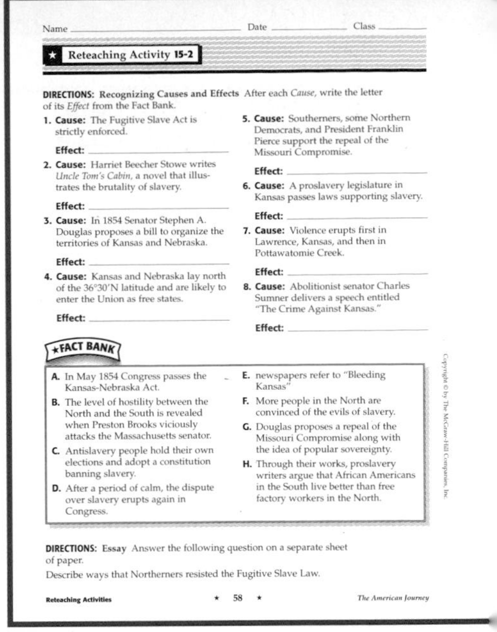

Name ______ Date ______ Class ______

★ Reteaching Activity **15-2**

DIRECTIONS: Recognizing Causes and Effects After each *Cause,* write the letter of its *Effect* from the Fact Bank.

1. **Cause:** The Fugitive Slave Act is strictly enforced.
   Effect: ______
2. **Cause:** Harriet Beecher Stowe writes *Uncle Tom's Cabin,* a novel that illustrates the brutality of slavery.
   Effect: ______
3. **Cause:** In 1854 Senator Stephen A. Douglas proposes a bill to organize the territories of Kansas and Nebraska.
   Effect: ______
4. **Cause:** Kansas and Nebraska lay north of the 36°30'N latitude and are likely to enter the Union as free states.
   Effect: ______
5. **Cause:** Southerners, some Northern Democrats, and President Franklin Pierce support the repeal of the Missouri Compromise.
   Effect: ______
6. **Cause:** A proslavery legislature in Kansas passes laws supporting slavery.
   Effect: ______
7. **Cause:** Violence erupts first in Lawrence, Kansas, and then in Pottawatomie Creek.
   Effect: ______
8. **Cause:** Abolitionist senator Charles Sumner delivers a speech entitled "The Crime Against Kansas."
   Effect: ______

★FACT BANK

A. In May 1854 Congress passes the Kansas-Nebraska Act.
B. The level of hostility between the North and the South is revealed when Preston Brooks viciously attacks the Massachusetts senator.
C. Antislavery people hold their own elections and adopt a constitution banning slavery.
D. After a period of calm, the dispute over slavery erupts again in Congress.
E. newspapers refer to "Bleeding Kansas"
F. More people in the North are convinced of the evils of slavery.
G. Douglas proposes a repeal of the Missouri Compromise along with the idea of popular sovereignty.
H. Through their works, proslavery writers argue that African Americans in the South live better than free factory workers in the North.

DIRECTIONS: Essay Answer the following question on a separate sheet of paper.
Describe ways that Northerners resisted the Fugitive Slave Law.

Reteaching Activities ★ 58 ★ *The American Journey*

Copyright © by The McGraw-Hill Companies, Inc.

Enrichment Activity 15–2

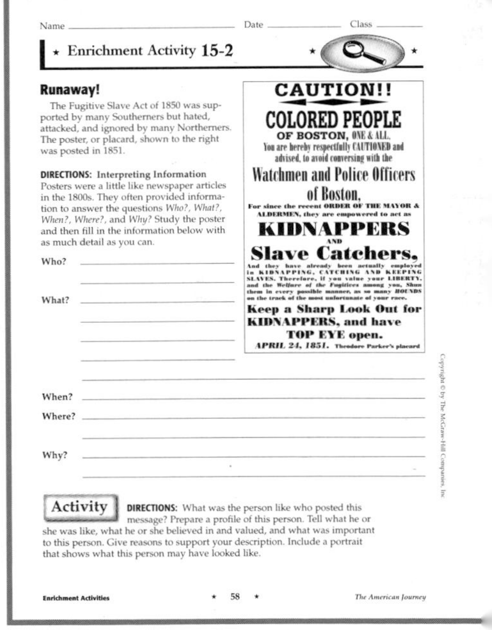

Name ______ Date ______ Class ______

★ Enrichment Activity **15-2**

Runaway!

The Fugitive Slave Act of 1850 was supported by many Southerners but hated, attacked, and ignored by many Northerners. The poster, or placard, shown to the right was posted in 1851.

DIRECTIONS: Interpreting Information Posters were a little like newspaper articles in the 1800s. They often provided information to answer the questions *Who?, What?, When?, Where?,* and *Why?* Study the poster and then fill in the information below with as much detail as you can.

CAUTION!!
COLORED PEOPLE
OF BOSTON, ONE & ALL,
You are hereby respectfully CAUTIONED and advised, to avoid conversing with the
Watchmen and Police Officers of Boston,
For since the recent ORDER OF THE MAYOR & ALDERMEN, they are empowered to act as
KIDNAPPERS
AND
Slave Catchers,
And they have already been actually employed in KIDNAPPING, CATCHING AND KEEPING SLAVES. Therefore, if you value your LIBERTY, and the Welfare of the Fugitives among you, Shun them in every possible manner, as so many HOUNDS on the track of the most unfortunate of your race.
Keep a Sharp Look Out for KIDNAPPERS, and have TOP EYE open.
APRIL 24, 1851. Theodore Parker's placard

Who? ______

What? ______

When? ______

Where? ______

Why? ______

Activity **DIRECTIONS:** What was the person like who posted this message? Prepare a profile of this person. Tell what he or she was like, what he or she believed in and valued, and what was important to this person. Give reasons to support your description. Include a portrait that shows what this person may have looked like.

Enrichment Activities ★ 58 ★ *The American Journey*

Copyright © by The McGraw-Hill Companies, Inc.

4 CLOSE

Ask students to speculate about what the federal government could have done, if anything, to prevent the violence that erupted over the Kansas-Nebraska Act.

NATIONAL GEOGRAPHIC *Journeys*

Linking PAST & PRESENT

Harriet Tubman, abolitionist and author, on February 1, 1978, became the first black woman to be honored on a United States postage stamp.

History *and the* Humanities

American Music Cultural Traditions, Lesson 5: "Get Off the Track!"

What? Where? When? Who?

Freedom Packages Many Northerners defied the Fugitive Slave Act and helped enslaved people escape. Henry Brown, an enslaved person in Richmond, Virginia, had a friend build a box to send through the mail. Brown poked three breathing holes in it and placed himself inside. The trip to freedom was rough. At one point the box was thrown so hard that Brown's neck was almost broken. Brown reached Philadelphia, though, and when his Northern friends opened the box, the former slave stood up and fainted.

you don't say...

Station was a code word in the Underground Railroad for "hiding place," while *conductor* was the term for the person who was helping the runaways to escape.

Harriet Tubman's Journey

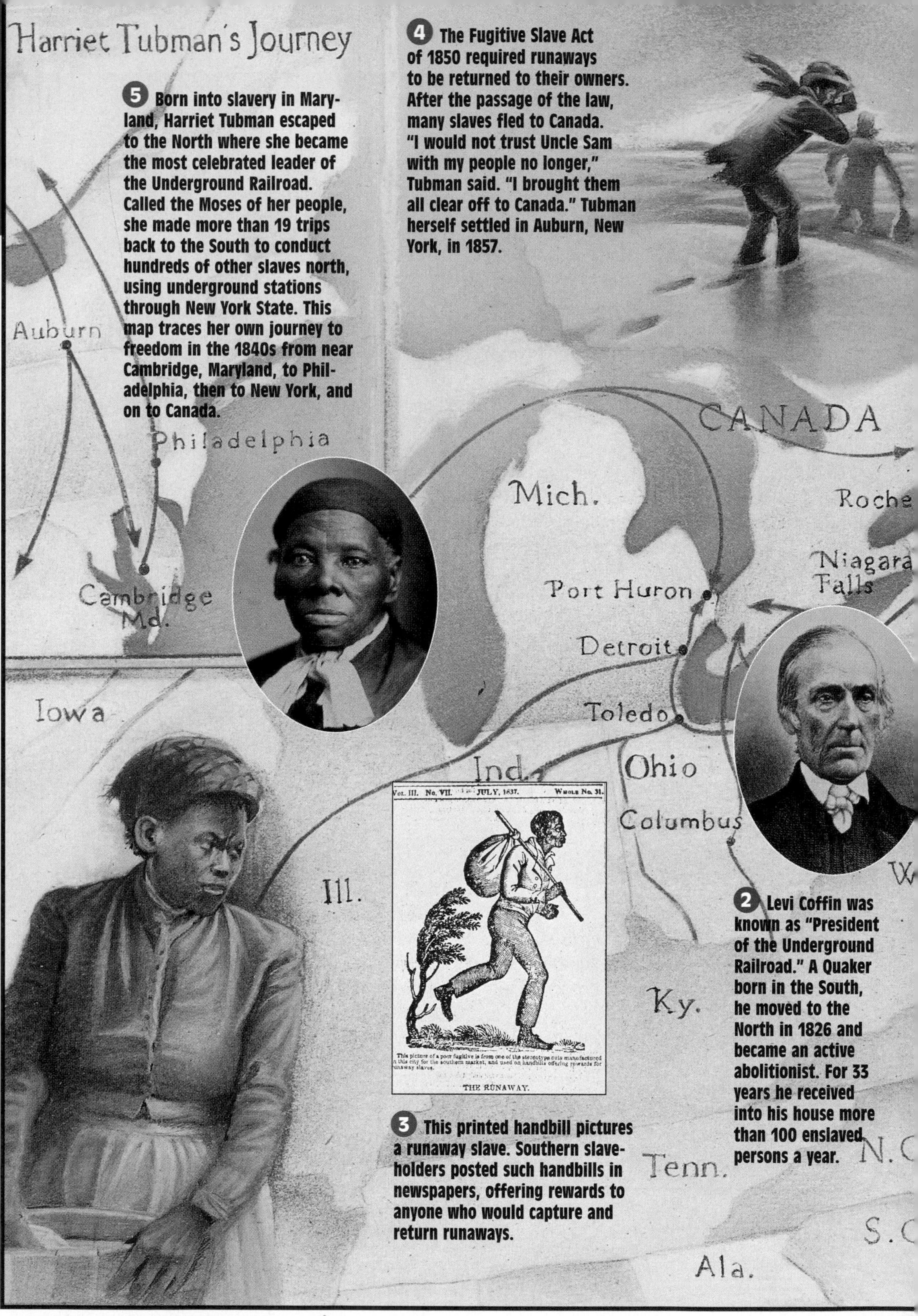

5 **Born into slavery in Maryland, Harriet Tubman escaped to the North where she became the most celebrated leader of the Underground Railroad. Called the Moses of her people, she made more than 19 trips back to the South to conduct hundreds of other slaves north, using underground stations through New York State. This map traces her own journey to freedom in the 1840s from near Cambridge, Maryland, to Philadelphia, then to New York, and on to Canada.**

4 **The Fugitive Slave Act of 1850 required runaways to be returned to their owners. After the passage of the law, many slaves fled to Canada. "I would not trust Uncle Sam with my people no longer," Tubman said. "I brought them all clear off to Canada." Tubman herself settled in Auburn, New York, in 1857.**

3 **This printed handbill pictures a runaway slave. Southern slaveholders posted such handbills in newspapers, offering rewards to anyone who would capture and return runaways.**

2 **Levi Coffin was known as "President of the Underground Railroad." A Quaker born in the South, he moved to the North in 1826 and became an active abolitionist. For 33 years he received into his house more than 100 enslaved persons a year.**

TEACHER'S NOTES

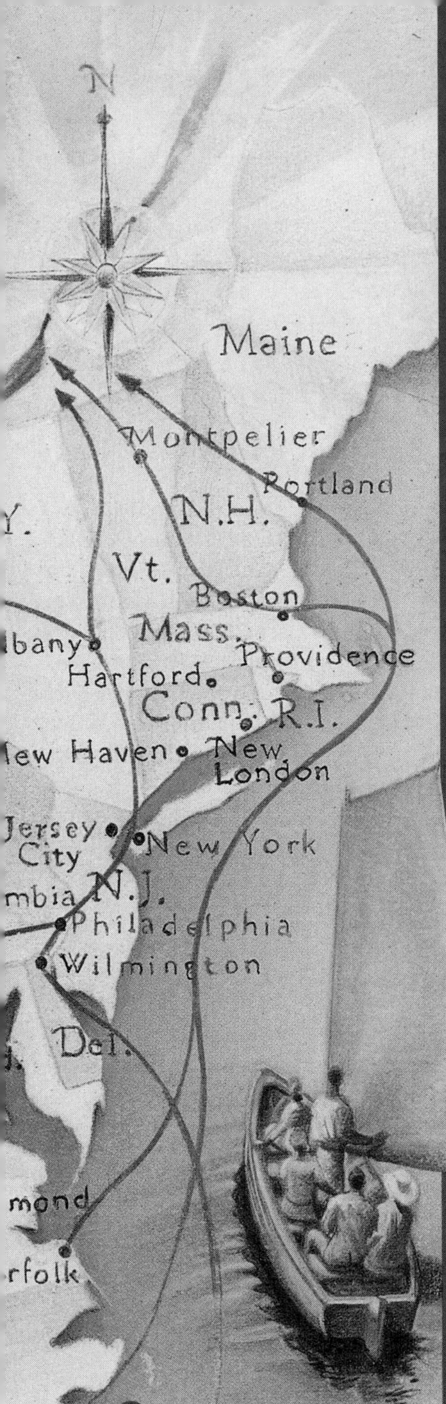

1 Many slaves fled north by water. Some seized small sailing boats; others were taken by ferry operators. Most stowed away on ships bound for Northern ports.

NATIONAL GEOGRAPHIC

Journeys

Underground Railroad

"We knew not what night or what hour of the night we would be roused from slumber by a gentle rap at the door.... Outside in the cold or rain ... would be a two-horse wagon loaded with fugitives.... I would invite them, in a low tone, to come in, and they would follow me into the house without a word.... When they were all safely inside and the door fastened, I would cover the windows, strike a light, and build a good fire.... The fugitives would rest on pallets before the fire the rest of the night."

— *From* Reminiscence *by Levi Coffin, published 1876*

447

TEACHER'S NOTES

NATIONAL GEOGRAPHIC SOCIETY

VIDEODISC
GTV: The American People: Fabric of a Nation

Side 1, Chapter 8
Title: *The Journey*
Subject: Slavery in early America
Ask: What provided a common link for Africans in America who came from different African cultures? *(the burdens of slavery and the struggle for survival)*

CURRICULUM CONNECTION

WORLD HISTORY
Uncle Tom's Cabin had a tremendous impact on British politicians. Lord Palmerston, who served as prime minister in the late 1850s, read the book three times.

Who?What?Where?When?

Free African Americans, despite being carefully watched, helped many enslaved African Americans escape. Their homes and stores were frequently stations of the Underground Railroad. Others contributed money, food, clothing, directions, or forged passes to help enslaved people escape. Formerly enslaved Samuel Martin of Mississippi became wealthy, bought six enslaved people, and, in 1844, led them to the free state of Pennsylvania.

1 FOCUS

BELLRINGER
Motivational Activity

Before taking roll at the beginning of the class period, project Section Focus Transparency 15–3 and have students answer the questions. Discuss students' responses.

This activity is also available as a blackline master.

Section Focus Transparency 15–3

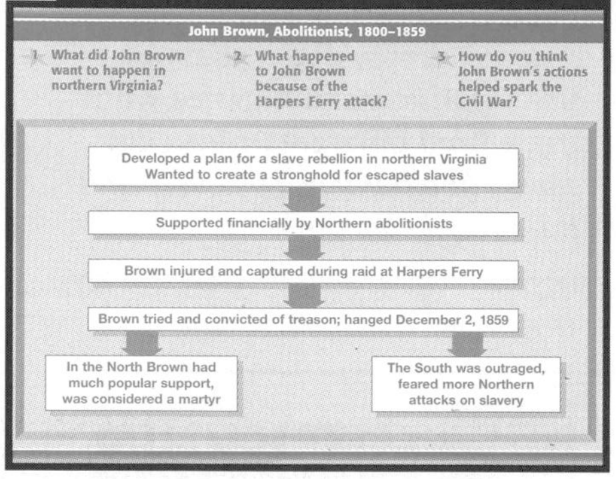

Vocabulary Precheck

Encourage students to write definitions of the terms *arsenal* and *martyr.* Then have them find the terms in the text to check the accuracy of their definitions.

Use the **Vocabulary PuzzleMaker** to create crossword and word search puzzles.

Section Theme
Continuity and Change

The effects of the popular sovereignty aspect of the Kansas-Nebraska Act transformed American political party structure.

Activity Discuss the two-party system of the United States. Compare this to multiparty systems of other countries. Brainstorm the advantages and disadvantages of a two-party system.

1854 | 1856 | 1858 | 1860

1854 Republican Party is formed

1856 James Buchanan is elected president

1857 *Dred Scott* decision states that all slaves are property

1859 John Brown raids Harpers Ferry, Virginia

Section 3

Challenges to Slavery

READ TO DISCOVER . . .
- why the Republican Party was formed.
- how the *Dred Scott* decision, the Lincoln-Douglas debates, and John Brown's raid affected Americans in the North and the South.

TERMS TO LEARN
arsenal
martyr

The Storyteller

Many people considered John Brown to be a radical murderer, while others viewed him as a fighter for the cause of freedom. When he was executed in 1859, the *Anglo-African Magazine* wrote: "On leaving the jail, John Brown had on his face an expression of calmness and serenity characteristic of the patriot who is about to die with a living consciousness that he is laying down his life for the good of his fellow creatures. . . . As he stepped out of the door, a black woman, with a little child in her arms, stood near his way. . . . He stopped for a moment in his course, stooped over, and with the tenderness of one whose love is as broad as the brotherhood of man, kissed the child affectionately."

Kansas Free-Soil poster

Anger over the Kansas–Nebraska Act changed the structure of American politics. The Democratic Party began to divide along sectional lines, with Northern Democrats leaving the party. The death of Whig leaders Henry Clay and Daniel Webster in 1852 had discouraged the party. Differing views over the slavery issue destroyed the party.

In 1854 antislavery Whigs and Democrats joined forces with Free-Soilers to form the **Republican Party.** The new party was determined to "rally as one man for the establishment of liberty and the overthrow of the Slave Power."

The Republican Party

The Republicans began to challenge the proslavery Whigs and Democrats, choosing candidates to run in the state and congressional elections of 1854. Their main message was that the government should ban slavery from new territories.

Gaining Ground in 1854

The Republican Party quietly showed its strength in the North. In the election, the Republicans won control of the House of Representatives and of several state governments. In the South the Republicans had almost no support.

Northern Democrats suffered a beating. Almost three-fourths of the Democratic candidates from free states lost in 1854. The party was increasingly becoming a Southern party.

SECTION RESOURCES

Reproducible Masters
- Reproducible Lesson Plan 15–3
- Guided Reading Activity 15–3
- Section Quiz 15–3
- Reteaching Activity 15–3
- Enrichment Activity 15–3

Transparencies
- Section Focus Transparency 15–3

Multimedia
- Vocabulary PuzzleMaker
- Chapter Challenger Interactive Review Software
- Testmaker
- GTV: The American People: Fabric of a Nation
- Facts On File: Landmark Documents in American History

The Election of 1856

Democrats and Republicans met again in the presidential election of 1856. The Whig Party, disintegrating over the slavery issue, did not offer a candidate of its own.

The Republicans chose **John C. Frémont** of California as their candidate for president. Frémont had gained fame as an explorer in the West and a champion of free California. Party strategists considered Frémont's lack of a political record an asset and hoped that "the romance of his life" would win votes.

The Democrats decided not to nominate President Franklin Pierce because of Pierce's role in the Kansas troubles. Instead the Democrats chose **James Buchanan** of Pennsylvania, who had been minister to Great Britain at the time and was not tainted by Kansas. The Democrats supported popular sovereignty. They attacked the Republicans as a sectional party and accused them of being abolitionists.

A third party, the **American Party** or Know-Nothings, supported former president Millard Fillmore as their candidate in 1856. The party took its name from an organization that opposed immigration. Its members, when questioned about their organization, replied, "I know nothing." The Know-Nothing Party appealed to voters who disliked the growing number of immigrants, but it was divided on the subject of slavery.

Southern votes secured the presidency for Buchanan. Frémont won about one-third of the popular vote even though he received almost no votes in the South. Fillmore carried only the state of Maryland. Soon after this election, the Know-Nothings who opposed slavery joined forces with the Republicans.

Picturing HISTORY James Buchanan and John Frémont campaigned for the 1856 presidential election. **Whose support enabled Buchanan to win the election?**

Footnotes to History

A Humble Start Two presidents, Millard Fillmore and Andrew Johnson, were once indentured as apprentices. Andrew Johnson ran away from his master. Fillmore bought his freedom for $30.

The *Dred Scott* Decision

President Buchanan took office on March 4, 1857. Two days later the Supreme Court announced a decision about slavery and the territories that shook the nation.

The *Dred Scott* Case

Dred Scott was an enslaved African American bought by an army doctor in Missouri, a slave state. In the 1830s the doctor moved his household to **Illinois,** a free state, and then to the Wisconsin Territory, where slavery was banned by the Northwest Ordinance of 1787. Later the family returned to Missouri, where the doctor died. In 1846, with the help of antislavery lawyers, Scott sued for his freedom. He claimed he should be free because he had once lived on free soil. Eleven years later, in the midst of growing anger over the slavery issue, the case reached the Supreme Court.

The case attracted enormous attention. While the immediate issue was Dred Scott's status, the Court also had the opportunity to rule on the question of slavery in territories. Many Americans hoped that the Court would resolve the issue for good.

CHAPTER 15
Section 3, 448–452

2 TEACH

L1, ELL Creating a Diagram Discuss the reasons why a third party could develop in a two-party political system, such as the United States. Explain that the Kansas-Nebraska Act changed the United States political parties. Ask students to work in small groups to create a poster-size diagram of the changes in the political parties outlined in this section. Post the diagrams on the bulletin board to be used in the "CLOSE" activity.

Picturing HISTORY John C. Frémont, who explored the West, stood firmly against expansion of slavery into that region. His campaign slogan was "Free Soil, Free Speech, Freemen, and Frémont."
Answer: *Southern voters*

Guided Reading Activity 15–3

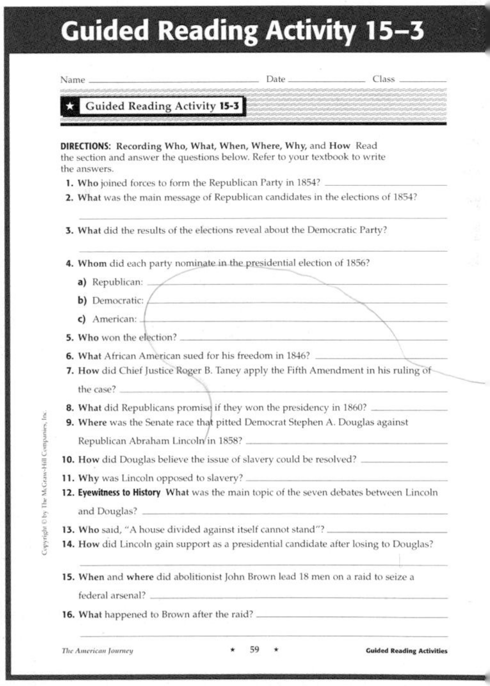
Name ______ Date ______ Class ______

★ Guided Reading Activity **15-3**

DIRECTIONS: Recording Who, What, When, Where, Why, and **How** Read the section and answer the questions below. Refer to your textbook to write the answers.

1. **Who** joined forces to form the Republican Party in 1854? ______
2. **What** was the main message of Republican candidates in the elections of 1854? ______
3. **What** did the results of the elections reveal about the Democratic Party? ______
4. **Whom** did each party nominate in the presidential election of 1856?
   - **a)** Republican: ______
   - **b)** Democratic: ______
   - **c)** American: ______
5. **Who** won the election? ______
6. **What** African American sued for his freedom in 1846? ______
7. **How** did Chief Justice Roger B. Taney apply the Fifth Amendment in his ruling of the case? ______
8. **What** did Republicans promise if they won the presidency in 1860? ______
9. **Where** was the Senate race that pitted Democrat Stephen A. Douglas against Republican Abraham Lincoln in 1858? ______
10. **How** did Douglas believe the issue of slavery could be resolved? ______
11. **Why** was Lincoln opposed to slavery? ______
12. **Eyewitness to History What** was the main topic of the seven debates between Lincoln and Douglas? ______
13. **Who** said, "A house divided against itself cannot stand"? ______
14. **How** did Lincoln gain support as a presidential candidate after losing to Douglas? ______
15. **When** and **where** did abolitionist John Brown lead 18 men on a raid to seize a federal arsenal? ______
16. **What** happened to Brown after the raid? ______

The American Journey ★ 59 ★ **Guided Reading Activities**

COOPERATIVE LEARNING ACTIVITY

Campaigning Organize students into groups of four to create a political campaign for the 1856 presidential election. Allow each group to choose a candidate. Have students in each group choose from the following roles: write party platform, write campaign speech, design button and write slogan, design poster. After all groups have completed their campaigns, have them present their campaigns to the class. Then have the class vote for president based on the campaigns.

Picturing HISTORY President James Buchanan's followers saw the *Dred Scott* decision as the final answer to sectional controversy. Republicans, however, believed that the *Dred Scott* decision was a bad ruling and that it would not last long. They pointed out that seven of the nine judges on the Supreme Court were Democrats and that five of the seven were from the South.
Answer: *the Missouri Compromise*

NATIONAL GEOGRAPHIC SOCIETY

VIDEODISC
GTV: The American People: Fabric of A Nation

Side 2, Chapter 7
Title: *Justice is Blind*
Subject: The *Dred Scott* decision
Ask: **What did the United States Supreme Court rule in the *Dred Scott* case?** *(that slaves were not citizens and had no political rights)*

What?Where?When?Who?

The Lincoln-Douglas debates were held in the Illinois cities of Ottawa, Freeport, Quincy, Jonesboro, Charleston, Galesburh, and Alton. The seven counties surrounding these cities turned out 30,736 voters in the election of 1858.

Picturing HISTORY The Supreme Court ruled that Dred Scott had no right to sue for his freedom in the federal courts because he was not a citizen. **What did the Supreme Court rule unconstitutional in the *Dred Scott* case?**

The Court's Decision

The Court's decision electrified the nation. Chief Justice **Roger B. Taney** (TAW•nee) said that Dred Scott was still a slave. As a slave, Scott was not a citizen and had no right to bring a lawsuit. Taney could have stopped there, but he decided to address the broader issues.

Taney wrote that Scott's residence on free soil did not make him free. An enslaved person was property, and the Fifth Amendment prohibits Congress from taking away property without "due process of law."

Finally, Taney wrote that Congress had no power to prohibit slavery in any territory. The Missouri Compromise—which had banned slavery north of 36°30'N latitude—was unconstitutional. For that matter, so was popular sovereignty. Not even the voters in a territory could prohibit slavery because that would amount to taking away a person's property. In effect, the decision meant that the Constitution protected slavery.

Reaction to the Decision

Rather than settling the issue, the Supreme Court's decision divided the country even more. Many Southerners were elated. The Court had reaffirmed what many in the South had always maintained: Nothing could legally prevent the spread of slavery. Northern Democrats were pleased that the Republicans' main issue—restricting the spread of slavery—had been ruled unconstitutional.

Republicans and other antislavery groups were outraged, calling the *Dred Scott* decision "a wicked and false judgment" and "the greatest crime" ever committed in the nation's courts. Several state legislatures passed resolutions declaring that the decision was "not binding in law and conscience." Republicans promised that if they won the presidency in 1860 they would change the Supreme Court—by appointing new justices—and reverse the decision.

African American abolitionist **Frederick Douglass** looked to the future. He hoped that the decision would begin a "chain of events" that would produce a "complete overthrow of the whole slave system."

Lincoln and Douglas

In the congressional election of 1858, the Senate race in Illinois was the center of national attention. The contest pitted the current senator, Democrat Stephen A. Douglas, against Republican challenger **Abraham Lincoln.** People considered Douglas a likely candidate for president in 1860. Lincoln was nearly an unknown.

The Candidates

Douglas, a successful lawyer, had joined the Democratic Party and won election to the House in 1842 and to the Senate in 1846. Short, stocky, and powerful, Douglas was called "the Little Giant." He disliked slavery but thought that the controversy over it would interfere with the nation's growth. He believed the issue could be resolved through popular sovereignty.

MULTIPLE LEARNING STYLES

Intrapersonal Discuss the effects of the *Dred Scott* decision, the Lincoln-Douglas debates, and John Brown's raid. Have students imagine that they are living in the North or the South during the time period covered in this section. Have each student decide which event would have had the most impact on his or her life. Then write a poem or short story describing the event and its personal impact. **L2**

Born in the poor backcountry of Kentucky, Abraham Lincoln moved to Indiana as a child and later moved to Illinois. Like Douglas, Lincoln was intelligent, ambitious, and a successful lawyer. He had little formal education—but excellent political instincts. Although Lincoln saw slavery as morally wrong, he admitted there was no easy way to eliminate slavery where it already existed. He was certain, though, that slavery should not be allowed to spread.

Eyewitness to HISTORY

The Lincoln–Douglas Debates

Not as well known as Douglas, Lincoln challenged the senator to a series of debates. Douglas reluctantly agreed. The two met seven times in August, September, and October of 1858 at locations all over Illinois. Thousands came to these debates. The main topic, of course, was slavery.

Lincoln had launched his campaign in June with a memorable speech, in which he declared:

> “'A house divided against itself cannot stand.' I believe this Government cannot endure permanently half *slave* and half *free.*”

In the debates, Douglas accused Lincoln of contributing to the breakup of the Union.

> “[If the states] cannot endure thus divided, then [he] must strive to make them all free or all slave, which will inevitably bring about a dissolution of the Union.”

During the debate at Freeport, Lincoln pressed Douglas about his views on popular sovereignty. Could the people of a territory legally exclude slavery before achieving statehood? Douglas replied that the people could exclude slavery by refusing to pass laws protecting slaveholders' rights. Douglas's response, which satisfied antislavery followers but lost him support in the South, became known as the **Freeport Doctrine.**

Douglas claimed that Lincoln wanted African Americans to be fully equal to whites. Lincoln denied this. Still, Lincoln said, "in the right to eat the bread . . . which his own hand earns, [an African American] is *my equal and the equal of [Senator] Douglas, and the equal of every living man.*" The real issue, Lincoln said, is "between the men who think slavery a wrong and those who do not think it wrong. The Republican Party thinks it wrong."

Picturing HISTORY Thousands attended the Lincoln-Douglas debates. Douglas sits to Lincoln's right in the debate at Charleston, Illinois, in September 1858. **What was the Freeport Doctrine?**

Making Connections Activity

Politics Thomas Nast, the famous political cartoonist, was called "a crusader with pen and ink." In his political cartoons, Nast reduced complex issues to simple but inspiring images depicting strong feelings about the issues of the time. Have each student draw a political cartoon of an issue described in this section that evokes strong feelings. **L2, ELL**

Facts On File

CD-ROM
Landmark Documents in American History

Title: *Lincoln-Douglas Debates, 1858*
Ask students to determine who was probably the winner of the debates.

3 ASSESS

Assign Section 3 Review as homework or as an in-class activity.

Use **Chapter Challenger Interactive Review Software** to review Section 3.

Section Quiz 15–3

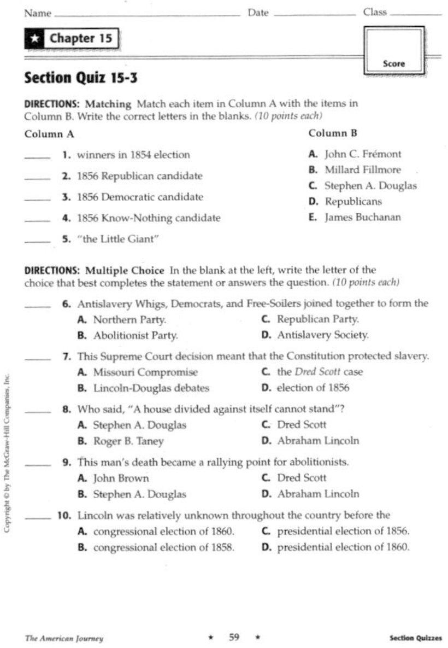

Name ______ Date ______ Class ______

Chapter 15 Score

Section Quiz 15-3

DIRECTIONS: Matching Match each item in Column A with the items in Column B. Write the correct letters in the blanks. *(10 points each)*

Column A

____ **1.** winners in 1854 election
____ **2.** 1856 Republican candidate
____ **3.** 1856 Democratic candidate
____ **4.** 1856 Know-Nothing candidate
____ **5.** "the Little Giant"

Column B

A. John C. Frémont
B. Millard Fillmore
C. Stephen A. Douglas
D. Republicans
E. James Buchanan

DIRECTIONS: Multiple Choice In the blank at the left, write the letter of the choice that best completes the statement or answers the question. *(10 points each)*

____ **6.** Antislavery Whigs, Democrats, and Free-Soilers joined together to form the
A. Northern Party. **C.** Republican Party.
B. Abolitionist Party. **D.** Antislavery Society.

____ **7.** This Supreme Court decision meant that the Constitution protected slavery.
A. Missouri Compromise **C.** the *Dred Scott* case
B. Lincoln-Douglas debates **D.** election of 1856

____ **8.** Who said, "A house divided against itself cannot stand"?
A. Stephen A. Douglas **C.** Dred Scott
B. Roger B. Taney **D.** Abraham Lincoln

____ **9.** This man's death became a rallying point for abolitionists.
A. John Brown **C.** Dred Scott
B. Stephen A. Douglas **D.** Abraham Lincoln

____ **10.** Lincoln was relatively unknown throughout the country before the
A. congressional election of 1860. **C.** presidential election of 1856.
B. congressional election of 1858. **D.** presidential election of 1860.

The American Journey • 59 • **Section Quizzes**

Picturing HISTORY Through the Lincoln-Douglas debates, Abraham Lincoln and Stephen Douglas took their arguments directly to the people even though at that time senators were elected by the state legislators. It was not until 1913 with the passage of the Seventeenth Amendment to the Constitution that senators were elected directly by the people.
Answer: *Douglas's statement that people could exclude slavery from a territory by refusing to pass laws protecting slaveholders' rights*

CHAPTER 15
Section 3, 448–452

Reteaching Activity 15–3

Name ______________ Date ______ Class ______

★ Reteaching Activity 15-3

DIRECTIONS: Organizing Facts The items in the Fact Bank describe Stephen Douglas and Abraham Lincoln before the 1858 congressional election. Complete the chart by writing the letter of each item in the correct place on the chart.

Lincoln-Douglas Debates

Abraham Lincoln	Stephen Douglas

★FACT BANK

A. "Little Giant"
B. believed that slavery was morally wrong
C. Democrat
D. promoted popular sovereignty
E. Republican
F. born in Kentucky
G. incumbent senator
H. relatively unknown in political circles

DIRECTIONS: Essay Answer the following questions on a separate sheet of paper.

1. How did the Supreme Court's decision in the *Dred Scott* case affect the Missouri Compromise?
2. What political groups joined to form the Republican Party in 1854?
3. What were the goals of the Republican Party?

The American Journey ★ 59 ★ Reteaching Activities

Enrichment Activity 15–3

Name ______________ Date ______ Class ______

★ Enrichment Activity 15-3 ★

Dred Scott

The Supreme Court decision on the case of *Dred Scott* v. *Sanford* caused an uproar. Eventually, it became one of only four Supreme Court decisions that were overturned by a constitutional amendment. Study the poster below that appeared in 1857.

DIRECTIONS:
Understanding Information
Answer the following questions.

1. What is the poster announcing? ______
2. At what point in the case was this announcement made? ______
3. Exactly when and where is the meeting to be held? ______
4. Who will speak at the meeting? Who else of note will attend? ______
5. Who is invited? ______
6. What is the cost? ______

A PUBLIC MEETING
WILL BE HELD ON
THURSDAY EVENING, 2D INSTANT.
7 o'clock in ISRAEL CHURCH, to consider atrocious decision of the Supreme Court in the
DRED SCOTT CASE
and other outrages to which the colored people are subject under the Justices of the United States.
C.L. REMOND,
ROBERT PURVIS,
and others will be speakers on the occasion. Mrs. MOTT, Mr. M'KIM and B.S. JONES of Ohio, have also accepted invitations to be present.
All persons are invited to attend. Admittance is free.

Activity **DIRECTIONS:** Imagine that you are C.L. Remond. Prepare a speech that you will use in today's meeting. Include visual aids where appropriate. Then present your speech to a group of classmates.

The American Journey ★ 59 ★ Enrichment Activities

Lincoln Emerges as a Leader

Following the debates Douglas won reelection to the Senate in 1858. However, he lost support in other areas. By saying that voters could keep slavery out of a territory, Douglas further angered the South. In 1860 he lost Southern support in the presidential election. Lincoln, by contrast, lost the Senate race, but his performance in the Illinois debates catapulted him into the national spotlight. He campaigned for Republican candidates in other states and gained support as a candidate for president.

The Raid on Harpers Ferry

Political tensions heightened after the election of 1858. Southerners felt threatened by growing Republican power. In October 1859, an act of violence further fed their fears.

John Brown's Raid

On October 16 the abolitionist John Brown led 18 men, both whites and free African Americans, on a raid on **Harpers Ferry, Virginia.** His target was an **arsenal,** a storage place for weapons and ammunition. Brown—who had killed 5 proslavery Kansans in 1856—was encouraged and financed by some abolitionists to carry out his plan.

Brown had the idea to seize the federal arsenal and spark an uprising of enslaved people, whom he would arm with the weapons he captured. The plan failed. No slaves rebelled, and United States Marines under the command of Colonel Robert E. Lee captured Brown and several of his followers. During Brown's raid, which lasted only 36 hours, 10 of his men—including 2 of Brown's sons—were killed. The raiders killed 4 civilians, 1 marine, and 2 slaves.

Brown was tried and found guilty of murder and treason and was sentenced to hang on December 2, 1859. Six of his followers met the same fate over the next few months.

Sectional Response

Brown's trial and execution created an uproar in the North. Some antislavery Northerners, including Republican leaders, denounced Brown for promoting violence. To some Northerners, though, Brown was a great hero. Writer Ralph Waldo Emerson called Brown a **martyr**—a person who dies for a great cause—who would "make the gallows as glorious as the cross."

John Brown's death became a rallying point for abolitionists. When Southerners learned of Brown's connection to abolitionists, their fears of a great Northern conspiracy against them seemed to be confirmed. The nation was on the brink of disaster.

Section 3 Review

Checking for Understanding

1. ***Identify*** Republican Party, John C. Frémont, James Buchanan, Dred Scott, Roger B. Taney, Abraham Lincoln.
2. ***Define*** arsenal, martyr.
3. ***Discuss*** the stages in the development of the Republican Party.

Reviewing Themes

4. **Continuity and Change** How did the *Dred Scott* decision reverse a previous decision made by Congress?

Critical Thinking

5. **Making Inferences** Why did Lincoln emerge as a leader after the Douglas–Lincoln debates?

Activity

Creating a Political Cartoon Draw a political cartoon that illustrates Lincoln's statement "A house divided against itself cannot stand."

Section 3 Review Answers

1. Republican Party, 448; John C. Frémont, 449; James Buchanan, 449; Dred Scott, 449; Roger B. Taney, 450; Abraham Lincoln, 450
2. The words are defined in the Glossary.
3. Northern Democrats left the party; Whig Party dissolved; antislavery Whigs and Democrats joined Free-Soilers to form Republican Party
4. ruled Missouri Compromise unconstitutional
5. He performed well.

Activity Students should draw a political cartoon illustrating the statement.

4 CLOSE

Ask students to form the same groups as in the "TEACH" activity to complete their diagrams of the political parties. Tell students to add the following to their diagrams for each political party: party platform, major party leaders, and party supporters.

1860 — 1861 — 1862

1860
Abraham Lincoln is elected president; South Carolina secedes

February 1861
Southern states form the Confederate States of America

April 1861
Confederate forces attack Fort Sumter; the Civil War begins

Section 4

Secession and War

READ TO DISCOVER . . .

- how the 1860 election led to the breakup of the Union.
- why secession led to the outbreak of the Civil War.

TERMS TO LEARN

secession
states' rights

The Storyteller

In April 1861, Emma Holmes witnessed the Confederates' attack on Fort Sumter. About 4:30 in the afternoon—just 12 hours after the first shot was fired—she observed that bullets and shells were still "pouring into Fort Sumter from Fort Stevens where our 'Palmetto boys' [South Carolina soldiers] have won the highest praise. . . . Though every shot is distinctly heard and shakes our house, I feel calm and composed. . . . The great body of the citizens seem to be so impressed with the justice of our Cause that they place entire confidence on the God of Battles. . . ."

Secessionist ribbon

Would the Union break up? That was the burning question in the months before the presidential election of 1860. Tensions between the North and the South had risen to dangerous levels. In the North antislavery sentiment took on new strength. In the South the Alabama legislature declared that the state would secede if a Republican became president.

The Election of 1860

Despite heightening tensions, efforts to save the Union continued. "One after another," wrote a Mississippian, "the links which have bound the North and South together have been severed . . . [but] the Democratic Party looms gradually up . . . and waves the olive branch over the troubled waters of politics." The party tried to make peace between the two sides but, like the nation, the Democrats were deeply divided.

The Candidates

The Democrats met in Charleston, South Carolina, in April 1860 to choose their presidential candidate. Many Democrats supported Stephen A. Douglas, but Southern delegates insisted that the party promise to protect slavery in the territories. When Douglas and most Northern delegates refused, many Southern delegates walked out. The convention adjourned.

The Democrats met again in Baltimore in June. Northern and Southern factions still could not agree on the slavery issue. When anti-Douglas

SECTION RESOURCES

Reproducible Masters

- Reproducible Lesson Plan 15–4
- Guided Reading Activity 15–4
- Section Quiz 15–4
- Reteaching Activity 15–4
- Enrichment Activity 15–4

Transparencies

- Section Focus Transparency 15–4

Multimedia

- Vocabulary PuzzleMaker
- Chapter Challenger Interactive Review
- Testmaker
- GTV: A Geographic Perspective on American History
- American Music Cultural Traditions

1 FOCUS

BELLRINGER
Motivational Activity

Before taking roll at the beginning of the class period, project Section Focus Transparency 15–4 and have students answer the questions. Discuss students' responses.

This activity is also available as a blackline master.

Section Focus Transparency 15–4

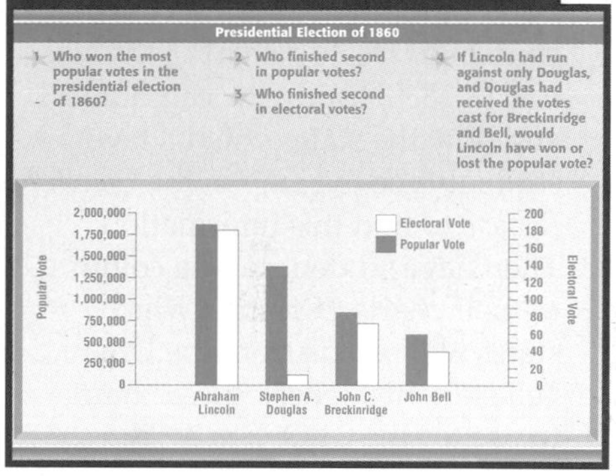

Vocabulary Precheck

Call on volunteers to speculate on the relationship between *states' rights* and *secession* in the period leading up to the Civil War. Have other students check the accuracy of their speculations by scanning the text for evidence.

Use the **Vocabulary Puzzle-Maker** to create crossword and word search puzzles.

Section Theme
Geography and History

The election of 1860 clearly divided the nation along sectional lines.

Activity Ask students to read the quote on this page made by a Mississippian about the Democratic Party. **Ask: What had split the Democratic Party by 1860?** *(differences between the North and the South)*

CHAPTER 15
Section 4, 453–457

Picturing HISTORY Mathew B. Brady photographed celebrities and, by doing so, became a celebrity himself. His own picture-taking, however, was limited because of his bad eyesight. Through a corps of assistant photographers, he captured the images of many of the era's leading political figures, such as Abraham Lincoln and Stephen A. Douglas.
Answer: *John Breckinridge, John Bell*

2 TEACH

L1 Predicting Outcomes Ask each student to create a chart of the election of 1860, listing the candidates and how the states voted. Have students use the map in the *Chapter Review* to find this information. Then have students add a column to their charts to predict which states will secede from the Union. Tell students to keep these charts to use for the CLOSE activity.

Guided Reading Activity 15–4

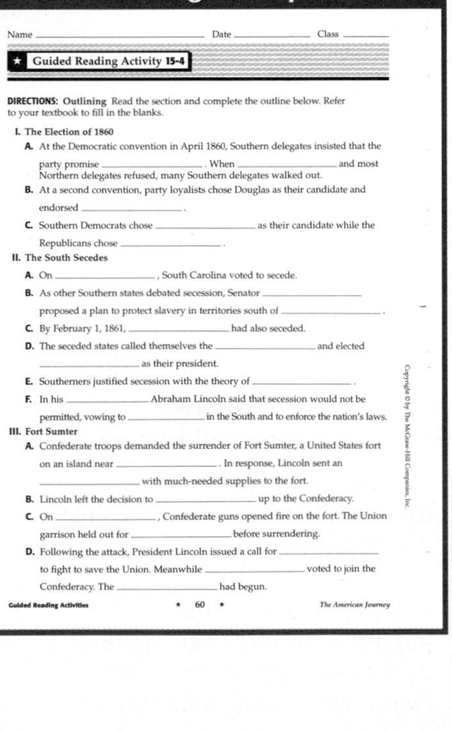

Name ____________ Date ________ Class ________

Guided Reading Activity 15-4

DIRECTIONS: Outlining Read the section and complete the outline below. Refer to your textbook to fill in the blanks.

I. The Election of 1860
- **A.** At the Democratic convention in April 1860, Southern delegates insisted that the party promise ____________. When ____________ and most Northern delegates refused, many Southern delegates walked out.
- **B.** At a second convention, party loyalists chose Douglas as their candidate and endorsed ____________.
- **C.** Southern Democrats chose ____________ as their candidate while the Republicans chose ____________.

II. The South Secedes
- **A.** On ____________, South Carolina voted to secede.
- **B.** As other Southern states debated secession, Senator ____________ proposed a plan to protect slavery in territories south of ____________.
- **C.** By February 1, 1861, ____________ had also seceded.
- **D.** The seceded states called themselves the ____________ and elected ____________ as their president.
- **E.** Southerners justified secession with the theory of ____________.
- **F.** In his ____________ Abraham Lincoln said that secession would not be permitted, vowing to ____________ in the South and to enforce the nation's laws.

III. Fort Sumter
- **A.** Confederate troops demanded the surrender of Fort Sumter, a United States fort on an island near ____________. In response, Lincoln sent an ____________ with much-needed supplies to the fort.
- **B.** Lincoln left the decision to ____________ up to the Confederacy.
- **C.** On ____________, Confederate guns opened fire on the fort. The Union garrison held out for ____________ before surrendering.
- **D.** Following the attack, President Lincoln issued a call for ____________ to fight to save the Union. Meanwhile ____________ voted to join the Confederacy. The ____________ had begun.

Guided Reading Activities ★ 60 ★ *The American Journey*

Picturing HISTORY The portraits of Lincoln and Douglas on these 1860 campaign ribbons were photographed by Mathew Brady. **What other candidates participated in the 1860 presidential election?**

Southerners walked out again, the party loyalists who remained chose Douglas and endorsed popular sovereignty.

Southern Democrats met in Richmond, Virginia, and Baltimore, Maryland. They nominated **John Breckinridge** of Kentucky, the current vice president, as their candidate. They adopted the position that neither Congress nor territorial legislatures could prevent citizens from taking "their property"—enslaved people—into a territory.

The Republicans, meanwhile, met in Chicago in May to choose their candidate. The leading contenders for the nomination were Senator **William Seward** of New York and **Abraham Lincoln** of Illinois. Although Seward had long been a leader in the Republican Party, the Republicans chose Lincoln because of his more moderate views. The party did, however, declare its opposition to the "legal existence of Slavery in any Territory."

A fourth candidate entered the campaign. **John Bell** of Tennessee was nominated by moderates from both the North and the South who had formed the Constitutional Union Party. This party took no position on slavery.

The campaign stirred political forces in both the South and the North. Many Southerners feared that a Republican victory would encourage abolitionist radicals—inspired by John Brown—to start slave revolts. Douglas campaigned tirelessly, urging moderation.

The Election Outcome

With the Democrats divided, Lincoln won a clear majority of the electoral votes—180 out of 303. He received only 40 percent of the popular vote, but this was more than any other candidate. Douglas was second with 30 percent of the popular vote.

The vote was along purely sectional lines. Lincoln's name did not even appear on the ballot in most Southern states, but he won every Northern state. Breckinridge swept the South, and Bell took most border states. Douglas won only the state of Missouri and three of New Jersey's seven electoral votes.

In effect, the more populous North had outvoted the South. The victory for Lincoln was a short-lived one, however, for the nation Lincoln was to lead would soon disintegrate.

The South Secedes

Lincoln and the Republicans had promised not to disturb slavery where it already existed. Nevertheless, many people in the South mistrusted the party, fearing that the Republican government would not protect Southern rights and liberties. On December 20, 1860, the South's long-standing threat to leave the Union became a reality when South Carolina held a special convention and voted to secede.

Attempt at Compromise

Even after South Carolina's action, many people still wished to preserve the Union. The question was *how.* As other Southern states debated secession—withdrawal from the Union—leaders in Washington, D.C., worked frantically to fashion a last-minute compromise. Senator **John Crittenden** of Kentucky proposed a series of amendments to the Constitution. Central to Crittenden's plan was a provision to protect slavery south of 36°30'N latitude—the line set by the Missouri Compromise—in all territories "now held or hereafter acquired."

Republicans considered this unacceptable. They had just won an election on the principle

COOPERATIVE LEARNING ACTIVITY

Creating an Illustrated Time Line Organize the class into groups of six to create a bulletin board time line illustrating factors leading to the Civil War. Have each group scan the chapter to determine what factors to include on the time line. Have students in each group choose the following roles: identify dates; draw time line listing dates, people, and events; illustrate the people; illustrate the events; write short descriptions of people; write short descriptions of events. Have each group construct the time line on the bulletin board.

that slavery would not be extended in any territories. "Now we are told," Lincoln said, "the government shall be broken up, unless we surrender to those we have beaten."

Leaders in the South also rejected the plan. "We spit upon every plan to compromise," exclaimed one Southern leader. "No human power can save the Union," wrote another.

The Confederacy

By the first of February 1861, Texas, Louisiana, Mississippi, Alabama, Florida, and Georgia had joined South Carolina and also seceded. Delegates from these states and South Carolina met in Montgomery, Alabama, on February 4 to form a new nation and government. Calling themselves the **Confederate States of America,** they chose **Jefferson Davis,** a senator from Mississippi, as president.

Southerners justified secession with the theory of **states' rights.** The states, they argued, had voluntarily chosen to enter the Union. They defined the Constitution as a contract among the independent states. Now because the national government had violated that contract—by refusing to enforce the Fugitive Slave Act and by denying the Southern states equal rights in the territories—the states were justified in leaving the Union.

Reactions to Secession

Many Southerners welcomed secession. In Charleston, South Carolina, people rang church bells, fired cannons, and celebrated in the streets. A newspaper in Atlanta, Georgia, said the South "will never submit" and would defend its liberties no matter what the cost.

Other Southerners, however, were alarmed. A South Carolinian wrote, "My heart has been rent [torn] by . . . the destruction of my country—the dismemberment of that great and glorious Union." Virginian Robert E. Lee expressed concern about the future. "I see only that a fearful calamity is upon us," he wrote.

In the North some abolitionists preferred allowing the Southern states to leave. If the Union could be kept together only by compromising on slavery, they declared, then let the Union be destroyed. One Republican newspaper wrote of the Southern states, "Let the erring sisters depart in peace."

Most Northerners, however, believed that the Union must be preserved. For Lincoln the issue was "whether in a free government the minority have the right to break up the government whenever they choose."

Linking PAST & *PRESENT*

From Hardtack to Unmeltable Chocolate

Feeding troops has always been a problem of warfare. During the Civil War, rations typically consisted of dried salt pork, hardtack (a saltless, hard flour biscuit) or cornmeal, and coffee.

Soldier's hardtack

Past

With age, hardtack could become infested with weevils. Some soldiers thought it better to eat it in the dark. Rations for today's soldier are far different. Meals Ready to Eat (MREs) were distributed to soldiers during the Persian Gulf War. MREs are dehydrated foods in airtight containers. Soldiers add hot water to make them edible. The military even found a way to make unmeltable chocolate! **Why is it important for modern soldiers to have dehydrated foods?**

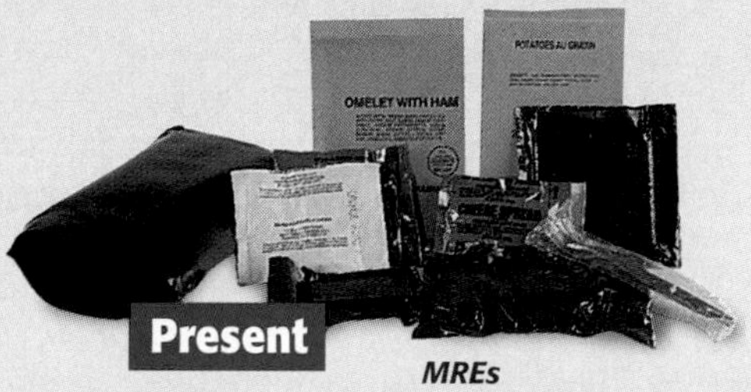

Present

MREs

MULTIPLE LEARNING STYLES

Auditory/Musical Play to the class at least one of the following songs that were used as rallying cries at the beginning of the Civil War: "The Bonnie Blue Flag" by Harry Macarthy (South), "Battle Cry of Freedom" by George F. Root (North), and "The Battle Hymn of the Republic" by Julia Ward Howe (North). Have students decide whether each song rallied the North or the South. Assign individual students to write the lyrics of a patriotic song favoring either the North or the South. Ask volunteers to read aloud their lyrics to the class and allow the class to decide whether the song best represents the North or the South. **L2**

Linking PAST & *PRESENT*

From Hardtack to Unmeltable Chocolate Hardtack could be modified by breaking each cracker into a tin cup of coffee and suspending it over an open fire. This enabled soldiers to skim dead weevils off the top. It could also be crumbled into soup for thickening, or it could be stuck on the end of a stick and toasted over an open fire. Crumbled hardtack in water could be fried in animal fat. The present-day MREs, however, are dehydrated foods, which require the addition of water to be edible. During the Persian Gulf War, some soldiers fighting in the desert where water was in short supply found themselves with inedible food!

Answer: *to preserve the food and to minimize its size and weight*

NATIONAL GEOGRAPHIC SOCIETY

VIDEODISC
GTV: A Geographic Perspective on American History

Side 2, Chapter 15
Title: *The Gathering Storm*
Subject: Conflict and compromise before the Civil War (1850–1860)
Ask: **What was the final straw that led the South to secede from the Union? Why?** *(Abraham Lincoln was elected president; he opposed the extension of slavery into new territories.)*

CHAPTER 15

Section 4, 453–457

History *and the* Humanities

American Music Cultural Traditions, Lesson 5: "Get Off the Track!"

The Spirit of American Art and Music, Mathew B. Brady

3 ASSESS

Assign Section 4 Review as homework or as an in-class activity.

Use **Chapter Challenger Interactive Review Software** to review Section 4.

Section Quiz 15–4

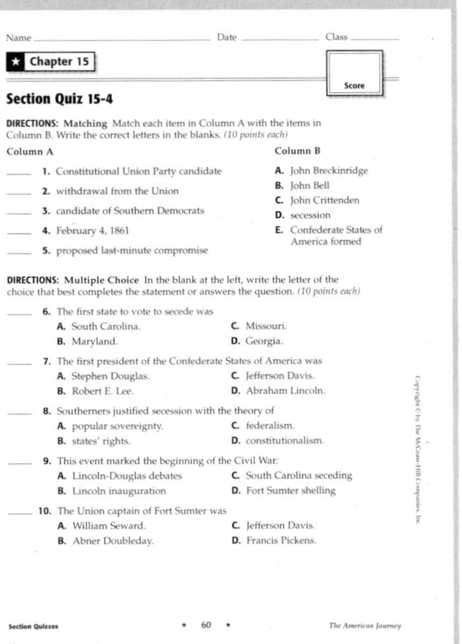

Name ______ Date ______ Class ______

Chapter 15 | Score

Section Quiz 15-4

DIRECTIONS: Matching Match each item in Column A with the items in Column B. Write the correct letters in the blanks. *(10 points each)*

Column A	Column B
____ 1. Constitutional Union Party candidate	A. John Breckinridge
____ 2. withdrawal from the Union	B. John Bell
____ 3. candidate of Southern Democrats	C. John Crittenden
____ 4. February 4, 1861	D. secession
____ 5. proposed last-minute compromise	E. Confederate States of America formed

DIRECTIONS: Multiple Choice In the blank at the left, write the letter of the choice that best completes the statement or answers the question. *(10 points each)*

____ 6. The first state to vote to secede was
A. South Carolina. C. Missouri.
B. Maryland. D. Georgia.

____ 7. The first president of the Confederate States of America was
A. Stephen Douglas. C. Jefferson Davis.
B. Robert E. Lee. D. Abraham Lincoln.

____ 8. Southerners justified secession with the theory of
A. popular sovereignty. C. federalism.
B. states' rights. D. constitutionalism.

____ 9. This event marked the beginning of the Civil War.
A. Lincoln-Douglas debates C. South Carolina seceding
B. Lincoln inauguration D. Fort Sumter shelling

____ 10. The Union captain of Fort Sumter was
A. William Seward. C. Jefferson Davis.
B. Abner Doubleday. D. Francis Pickens.

Copyright © by The McGraw-Hill Companies, Inc.

Section Quizzes • 60 • The American Journey

Map Study

Answers

1. Missouri, Kentucky, Maryland, Delaware (West Virginia became part of the Union in 1863 when it seceded from Virginia.)
2. Virginia, North Carolina, Tennessee, Arkansas

Presidential Responses

Lincoln had won the election, but he was not yet president. James Buchanan's term ran until March 4, 1861. In December 1860, Buchanan sent a message to Congress saying that the Southern states had no right to secede. Then he added that he had no power to stop them from doing so.

Lincoln disagreed. He believed it was the president's duty to enforce the laws of the United States. That meant preserving the government. He warned that "no state . . . can lawfully get out of the Union."

As Lincoln prepared for his inauguration on March 4, 1861, people in both the North and the South wondered what he would say and do. They wondered, too, what would happen in Virginia, North Carolina, Kentucky, Tennessee, Missouri, and Arkansas. These slave states had chosen to remain in the Union, but the decision was not final. If the United States used force against the Confederate States of America, the remaining slave states also might secede.

In his Inaugural Address, the new president mixed toughness and words of peace. He said that secession would not be permitted, vowing to hold federal property in the South and to enforce the laws of the United States. At the same time, Lincoln pleaded with the South for reconciliation:

> "We are not enemies, but friends. We must not be enemies. Though passion may have strained, it must not break our bonds of affection."

Seceding States, 1860–1861

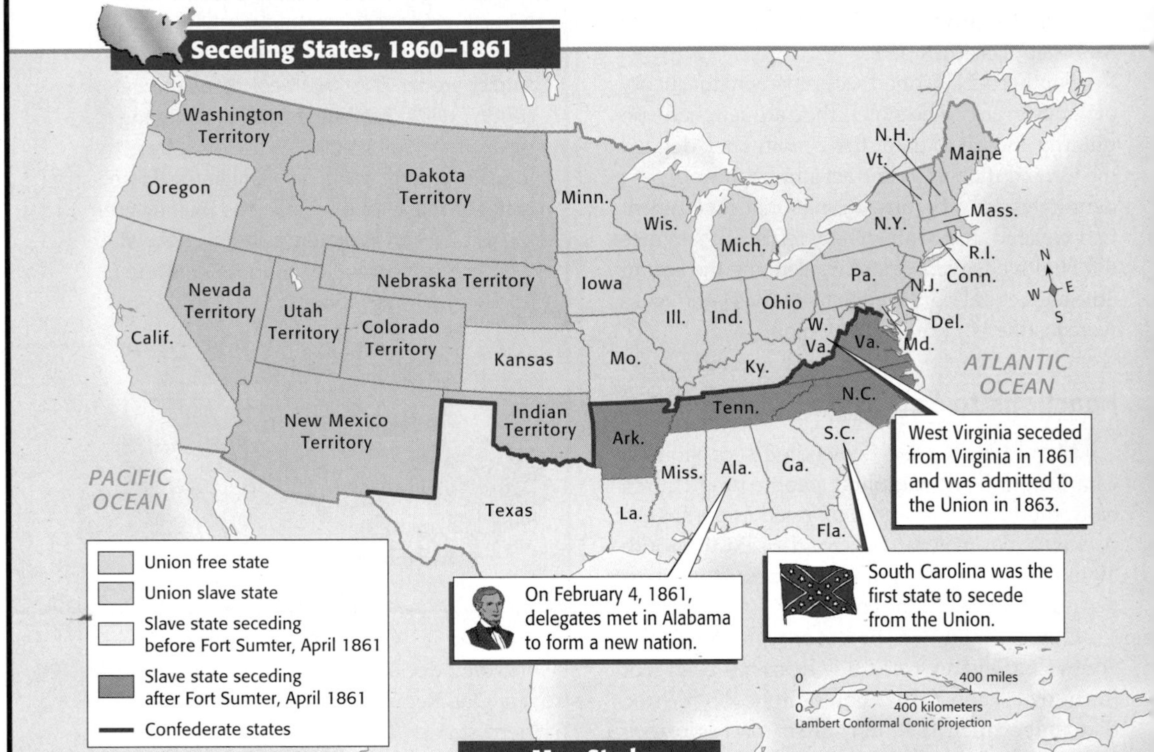

Map Study

After the attack on Fort Sumter, four more Southern states joined the seven that had already seceded from the Union.

1. **Region** Which slave states remained in the Union after the Fort Sumter attack?
2. **Analyzing Information** Which states did not secede until after the Fort Sumter attack?

MAKING CONNECTIONS ACTIVITY

Health More soldiers died from sickness during the Civil War than from bullets. Improper food and sanitation caused diarrhea, dysentery, measles, smallpox, typhoid, gangrene, and chicken pox, killing more than 400,000 of the 618,000 who died. Have students investigate the causes, symptoms, and cures for the sicknesses noted above. **L2**

Fort Sumter

The South soon tested President Lincoln's vow to hold federal property. Confederate forces had already seized some United States forts within their states. Although Lincoln did not want to start a war by trying to take the forts back, allowing the Confederates to keep them would amount to admitting their right to secede.

On the day of his inauguration, Lincoln received a dispatch from the commander of **Fort Sumter,** a United States fort on an island guarding Charleston Harbor. The message warned that the fort was low on supplies and that the Confederates demanded its surrender.

The War Begins

Lincoln responded by sending a message to Governor **Francis Pickens** of South Carolina. He informed Pickens that he was sending an unarmed expedition with supplies to Fort Sumter. Lincoln promised that Union forces would not "throw in men, arms, or ammunition" unless they were fired upon. The president thus left the decision to start shooting up to the Confederates.

Confederate president Jefferson Davis and his advisers made a fateful choice. They ordered their forces to attack Fort Sumter before the Union supplies could arrive. Confederate guns opened fire on the fort on April 12, 1861. Union captain Abner Doubleday witnessed the attack from inside the fort:

Jefferson Davis

> "Showers of balls . . . and shells . . . poured into the fort in one incessant stream, causing great flakes of masonry to fall in all directions."

High seas had prevented Union relief ships from reaching the besieged fort. The Union garrison held out for 33 hours before surrendering on April 14. Thousands of shots were exchanged during the siege, but there was no loss of life on either side.

News of the attack galvanized the North. President Lincoln issued a call for 75,000 troops to fight to save the Union, and volunteers quickly signed up. Meanwhile, Virginia, North Carolina, Tennessee, and Arkansas voted to join the Confederacy. The Civil War had begun.

Section 4 Review

Checking for Understanding

1. ***Identify*** John Breckinridge, William Seward, John Bell, John Crittenden, Jefferson Davis, Fort Sumter.
2. ***Define*** secession, states' rights.
3. ***Explain*** how Southern states used the theory of states' rights to justify secession.

Reviewing Themes

4. **Geography and History** What role did sectionalism play in Lincoln's winning the 1860 election?

Critical Thinking

5. **Identifying Assumptions** Do you think either Northerners or Southerners believed that secession would not lead to war? Explain.

Activity

Creating a Political Slogan Make up a campaign slogan or song for Abraham Lincoln, Stephen A. Douglas, John C. Breckinridge, or John Bell in the 1860 presidential election.

Section 4 Review Answers

1. John Breckinridge, 454; William Seward, 454; John Bell, 454; John Crittenden, 454; Jefferson Davis, 455; Fort Sumter, 457
2. The words are defined in the Glossary.
3. States had voluntarily chosen to enter the Union. The national government violated that contract, so the states were justified in leaving.
4. He won in every Northern state; votes in the South were divided among three other candidates.
5. Students should state *yes* or *no* and support their answers.

Activity Students' slogans or songs should accurately depict each party's stand.

Reteaching Activity 15–4

Name ____ Date ____ Class ____

★ Reteaching Activity **15-4**

DIRECTIONS: Recalling Facts In the space provided, write the words or sentence that answer the question.

1. Who was the Democratic presidential candidate in the election of 1860?
2. What position did the Southern Democrats adopt and who was their candidate?
3. Why did the Republicans choose Abraham Lincoln as their candidate over William Seward?
4. How did the population of the North affect the outcome of the election?
5. What happened on December 20, 1860?
6. Why did Republicans consider Senator John Crittenden's plan to protect slavery south of 36°30′N latitude unacceptable?
7. Which states met on February 4, 1861, to form a new nation, known as the Confederate States of America?
8. According to the Confederacy, how had the national government violated the contract among the states?
9. How did the South test President Lincoln's vow to hold federal property?
10. What fateful choice did Confederate President Jefferson Davis and his advisers make on April 12, 1861?

Reteaching Activities ★ 60 ★ *The American Journey*

Enrichment Activity 15–4

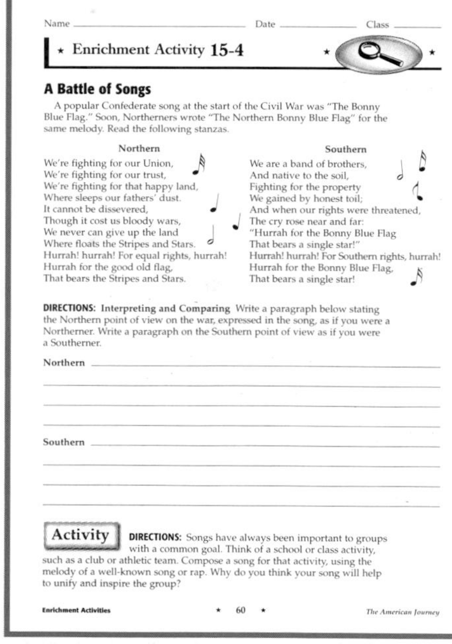
Name ____ Date ____ Class ____

★ Enrichment Activity **15-4** ★

A Battle of Songs

A popular Confederate song at the start of the Civil War was "The Bonny Blue Flag." Soon, Northerners wrote "The Northern Bonny Blue Flag" for the same melody. Read the following stanzas.

Northern

We're fighting for our Union,
We're fighting for our trust,
We're fighting for that happy land,
Where sleeps our fathers' dust.
It cannot be dissevered,
Though it cost us bloody wars,
We never can give up the land
Where floats the Stripes and Stars.
Hurrah! hurrah! For equal rights, hurrah!
Hurrah for the good old flag,
That bears the Stripes and Stars.

Southern

We are a band of brothers,
And native to the soil,
Fighting for the property
We gained by honest toil;
And when our rights were threatened,
The cry rose near and far:
"Hurrah for the Bonny Blue Flag
That bears a single star!"
Hurrah! hurrah! For Southern rights, hurrah!
Hurrah for the Bonny Blue Flag,
That bears a single star!

DIRECTIONS: Interpreting and Comparing Write a paragraph below stating the Northern point of view on the war, expressed in the song, as if you were a Northerner. Write a paragraph on the Southern point of view as if you were a Southerner.

Northern ____

Southern ____

Activity **DIRECTIONS:** Songs have always been important to groups with a common goal. Think of a school or class activity, such as a club or athletic team. Compose a song for that activity, using the melody of a well-known song or rap. Why do you think your song will help to unify and inspire the group?

Enrichment Activities ★ 60 ★ *The American Journey*

4 CLOSE

Have students correct the charts they created in the "TEACH" activity to accurately show which states seceded from the Union. Have them use the map on page 456 as a guide. Ask volunteers to discuss the accuracy of their predictions.

GLENCOE TECHNOLOGY

VIDEODISC
MindJogger Videoquiz

Use MindJogger to review the Chapter 15 content.

Chapter 15
Disc 2, Side B

Also available in VHS.

Reviewing Key Terms

The key terms used in this activity are defined in the textbook glossary on pages A26–A35.

Reviewing Key Facts

1. to ease tension between North and South by preserving the balance between slave and free states in the Senate
2. California admitted as free state; no restrictions on slavery in New Mexico Territory; New Mexico–Texas border dispute resolved in favor of New Mexico; slave trade abolished in District of Columbia; Fugitive Slave Law was strengthened
3. to abandon the Missouri Compromise and let settlers in each territory decide by popular sovereignty
4. a Supreme Court decision that considered slaves not to be free just because they lived on free soil, declared slaves as property, neither Congress nor voters could prohibit slavery in any territory
5. He vowed to hold federal property in the South and enforce the laws of the United States.

Critical Thinking

1. They had won the election based on their principles of not extending slavery and refused to give in.
2. Many Southerners had accepted the idea of secession and were ready to let the new Confederate government handle the issue of slavery.

Time Line Activity

Events should be placed in this order: Missouri Compromise passes, *Uncle Tom's Cabin* is published, Kansas-Nebraska Act is passed, *Dred Scott* decision, Lincoln is elected president, Civil War begins

Skill Practice Activity

1. Dr. Martin R. Delany
2. He is against slavery.
3. language used to describe what he would do if someone came looking for a fugitive slave in his house
4. He believed it was wrong.

Chapter 15

Review and Activities

Reviewing Key Terms

On a sheet of paper, define the following terms:

sectionalism
fugitive
secede
popular sovereignty
border ruffians
civil war
arsenal
martyr
secession
states' rights

Reviewing Key Facts

1. What was the purpose of the Missouri Compromise?
2. List the five parts of the Compromise of 1850.
3. What was Stephen Douglas's solution to the slavery issue in the Kansas and Nebraska territories?
4. What was the *Dred Scott* decision?
5. How did Lincoln plan to prevent secession?

Critical Thinking

Drawing Conclusions

Even after South Carolina seceded, the nation's leaders worked hard to come up with a last-minute compromise to save the Union.

1. Why did newly elected Republicans refuse to compromise any further on the slavery issue?
2. Why do you think people in the South rejected compromise efforts altogether by saying "We spit upon every plan to compromise"?

Time Line Activity

Create a time line on which you place the following events in chronological order.

- Civil War begins
- *Dred Scott* decision
- Missouri Compromise passes
- Lincoln is elected president
- *Uncle Tom's Cabin* is published
- Kansas–Nebraska Act is passed

Skill Practice Activity

Recognizing Bias

The excerpt below was written by Dr. Martin R. Delany, an abolitionist, to the mayor of Pittsburgh about his opinion of the Fugitive Slave Law of 1850. Read the excerpt, then answer the questions.

"Honorable mayor, whatever ideas of liberty I may have, have been received from reading the lives of your revolutionary fathers. I have therein learned that a man has a right to defend his castle with his life, even unto the taking of life. Sir, my house is my castle. . . . If any man approaches that house in search of a slave—I care not who he may be, whether constable or sheriff, magistrate or even judge of the Supreme Court . . . with the Declaration of Independence waving above his head as his banner . . . —if he crosses the threshold of my door, and I do not lay him a lifeless corpse at my feet. . . . O, no! he cannot enter that house and we both live."

1. Who is the author?
2. What is his view toward slavery?
3. What language reflects emotion or opinion?
4. What is the author's bias toward the Fugitive Slave Law?

Geography Activity

Study the map below, then answer the questions that follow.

Election of 1860

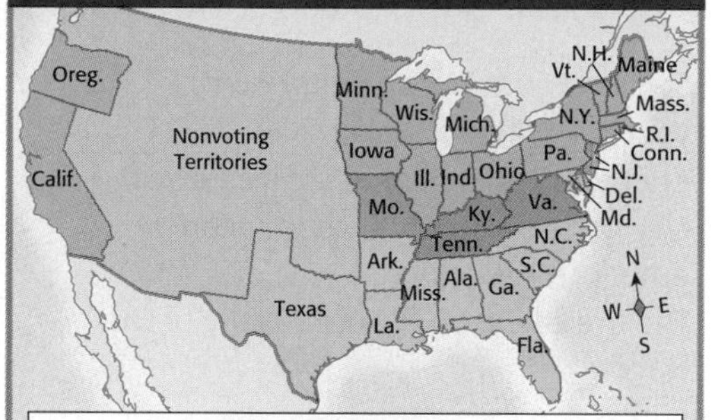

	Popular vote: 4,689,568	Electoral vote: 303	
Lincoln	1,865,593	180	Republican
Breckinridge	848,356	72	Southern Democrat
Bell	592,906	39	Constitutional Union
Douglas	1,382,713	12	Northern Democrat

1. **Location** Which states supported Douglas?
2. **Region** In what region(s) was the Republican Party strongest?
3. **Region** In what region did Breckinridge find support?

Reviewing Themes

1. **Government and Democracy** Why was the balance of free and slave states in the Senate such an important issue?
2. **Civic Rights and Responsibilities** Why did Northerners protest Douglas's plan to repeal the Missouri Compromise?
3. **Continuity and Change** How did pro- and antislavery groups change the structure of political parties in the 1850s?
4. **Geography and History** How did the North's larger population give it an edge over the South in the 1860 election?

Technology Activity

Using a Word Processor Search the Internet or your library for a list of political parties in existence today. Using your word processor, make a table that briefly summarizes each party's current goals. Then research to find the date that the party was founded and who its first and prominent party leaders have been. Include this information on your table, too. Then compare your table to the political parties discussed in Chapter 15.

Cooperative Activity

History and Citizenship With a partner, think of a controversial issue that is a source of disagreement today. Take opposite sides on the issue, then work together to come up with a list of three compromises that would make the solution to this problem acceptable to both sides. Share the issue and your compromises with the class.

Portfolio Activity **History Journal** Imagine what it was like for President Lincoln after his election when South Carolina seceded and other states were likely to follow. Write a diary entry that expresses Lincoln's fears and hopes for the nation.

CHAPTER 15
Review and Activities

Geography Activity

1. Missouri (also received three of New Jersey's seven electoral votes)
2. North and West Coast
3. South

Reviewing Themes

1. If the balance were upset, one section of the country would have more decision-making power than the other.
2. because it would allow slavery into areas that had been free for more than 30 years
3. The Democratic Party divided along sectional lines, and the Whig Party dissolved. The antislavery Whigs and Democrats joined the Free-Soil Party members to form the Republican Party.
4. The North had more electoral votes even if the South had not been divided among three candidates.

Technology Activity

Students' tables should contain a list of the major political parties as well as some of the small, lesser-known parties and provide a brief description of their platforms, the date the party was founded, its first and prominent party leaders, and the laws the party helped pass.

Cooperative Activity

Students should choose a controversial issue and find three compromises that would be acceptable to both sides.

Portfolio Activity Diary entries should convey some of the emotions that Lincoln might have felt upon hearing about the secession.

Chapter Bonus Test Question

Ask: What was Frederick Douglass's last name before he changed it to Douglass when he escaped to the North? *(Bailey)*

Chapter 16 Planning Guide

A complete, 1-page lesson plan is provided for each section in the *Reproducible Lesson Plans* booklet.

Section Resources

Daily Objectives	Reproducible Resources	Multimedia Resources
Section 1 The Two Sides Compare the political, economic, social, and military characteristics of the North and the South.	Reproducible Lesson Plan 16–1 Guided Reading Activity 16–1* Section Quiz 16–1* Reteaching Activity 16–1 Enrichment Activity 16–1	Section Focus Transparency 16–1 Vocabulary PuzzleMaker Chapter Challenger Interactive Review GTV: A Geographic Perspective on American History The Presidents: A Picture History of Our Nation
Section 2 Early Years of the War Identify the early successes and failures of the North and the South on land and on sea.	Reproducible Lesson Plan 16–2 Guided Reading Activity 16–2* Section Quiz 16–2* Reteaching Activity 16–2 Enrichment Activity 16–2	Section Focus Transparency 16–2 Vocabulary PuzzleMaker Chapter Challenger Interactive Review NGS PictureShow: The Civil War Facts On File: Landmark Documents in American History American Music Cultural Traditions
Section 3 A Call for Freedom Explain why Lincoln issued the Emancipation Proclamation.	Reproducible Lesson Plan 16–3 Guided Reading Activity 16–3* Section Quiz 16–3* Reteaching Activity 16–3 Enrichment Activity 16–3	Section Focus Transparency 16–3 Vocabulary PuzzleMaker Chapter Challenger Interactive Review Facts On File: Landmark Documents in American History
Section 4 Life During the Civil War Describe the life of soldiers and the role of women in the Civil War.	Reproducible Lesson Plan 16–4 Guided Reading Activity 16–4* Section Quiz 16–4* Reteaching Activity 16–4 Enrichment Activity 16–4	Section Focus Transparency 16–4 U.S. History & Art, Transparency 11 Vocabulary PuzzleMaker Chapter Challenger Interactive Review Testmaker
Section 5 The Way to Victory Evaluate the battles that were turning points in the war.	Reproducible Lesson Plan 16–5 Guided Reading Activity 16–5* Section Quiz 16–5* Reteaching Activity 16–5 Enrichment Activity 16–5	Section Focus Transparency 16–5 Vocabulary PuzzleMaker Chapter Challenger Interactive Review Testmaker NGS PictureShow: The Civil War Facts On File: Landmark Documents in American History ABCNews InterActive™ Historic America Electronic Field Trips

** Also available in Spanish*

Blackline Master · Videodisc · Audiocassette · Music Program · Transparency · CD-ROM · Software

0:00 **OUT OF TIME?**
Assign the Chapter 16 Digest and the corresponding Chapter Digests Audiocassettes with activities and tests.

Activity

From the Classroom of...

Terri Cook
Carthage Junior High School
Carthage, MO

Write a Wartime Letter

Explain to students that a majority of Civil War soldiers were very literate. Letters between soldiers on the battlefields and their friends back home were widespread. If possible, find Civil War resources showing several letters and share them with the class. Then have students choose a character—soldier, doctor, nurse, spy, soldier's mother, soldier's father, friend back home, and so on. Have students, in character, write a letter to a fictional friend, relative, or sweetheart. They may research a particular battle or life in the mid-1800s to add more details to their letters. Have them use pencils and unlined paper, explaining that ball-point pens were not yet invented, and that ink was hard to transport. By showing students facsimiles of envelopes, stamps, and stationery from the period, you can also ask them to imitate the designs and styles of these in their own correspondences. Have students share their letters with the rest of the class.

NATIONAL GEOGRAPHIC SOCIETY

Teacher's Corner

INDEX TO NATIONAL GEOGRAPHIC MAGAZINE

The following articles may be used for research relating to this chapter:

- "America's Poet: Walt Whitman," by Joel L. Swerdlow, December 1994.
- "C.S.S. Alabama," by Max Guerout, December 1994.
- "The Cruelest Commerce: African Slave Trade," by Colin Palmer, September 1992.
- "The Underground Railroad," by Charles L. Blockson, July 1984.

NATIONAL GEOGRAPHIC SOCIETY PRODUCTS AVAILABLE FROM GLENCOE

To order the following products for use with this chapter, contact your local Glencoe sales representative, or call Glencoe at 1-800-334-7344:

- *GTV: A Geographic Perspective on American History* (Videodisc)
- *GTV: The American People: Fabric of a Nation* (Videodisc)
- *PictureShow: The Civil War* (CD-ROM, Transparencies)
- *The Presidents: A Picture History of Our Nation* (CD-ROM)

ADDITIONAL NATIONAL GEOGRAPHIC SOCIETY PRODUCTS

To order the following products for use with this chapter, call National Geographic Society at 1-800-368-2728:

- *Battlefields of the Civil War* (Map)
- *Field of Battle: The Civil War Letters of Major Thomas J. Halsey* (Book)
- *The Blue and the Gray* (Book)
- *Historical Atlas of the United States* (Atlas)

Block Schedule

Block scheduling differs from traditional class scheduling in the amount of time allotted to each period. The extended time frame provided by block scheduling affords you the opportunity to implement a greater number of research-oriented and activity-intense projects to motivate and involve your students. Activities that are particularly suited to use within the block scheduling framework are identified throughout this chapter by the following designation:

KEY TO ABILITY LEVELS

Teaching strategies have been coded for varying learning styles and abilities.

L1 BASIC activities for all students
L2 AVERAGE activities for average to above-average students
L3 CHALLENGING activities for above-average students
ELL ENGLISH LANGUAGE LEARNER activities

Chapter 16 Resource Guide

Home Involvement

Home Involvement Activity 16

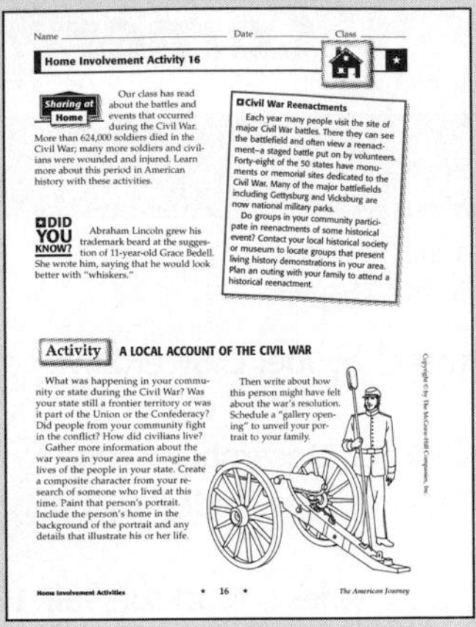

Review Activities

Chapter Summary 16

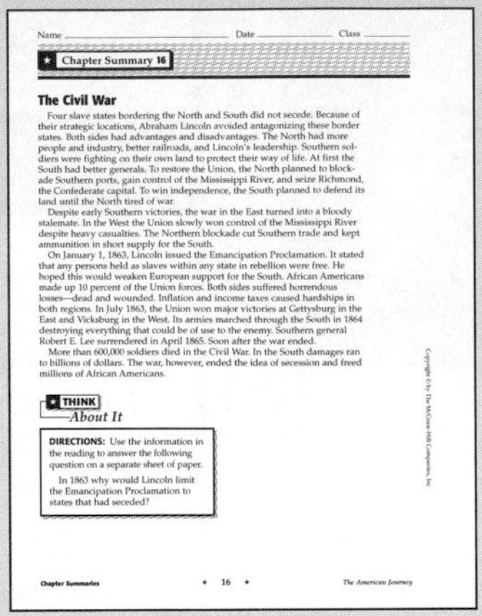

Workbook Activity 16

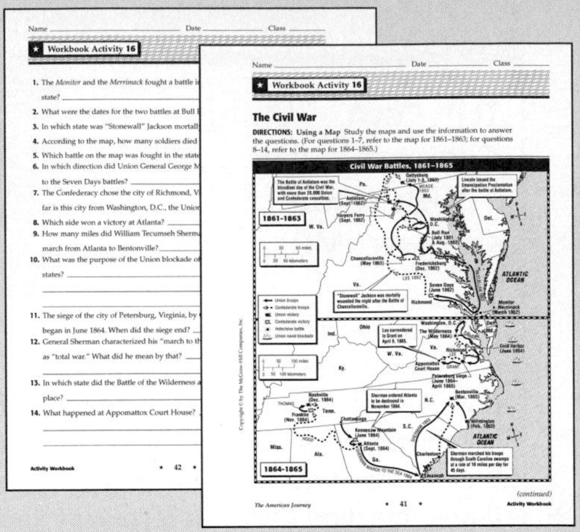

Reinforcement Activities

Time Line Activity 16

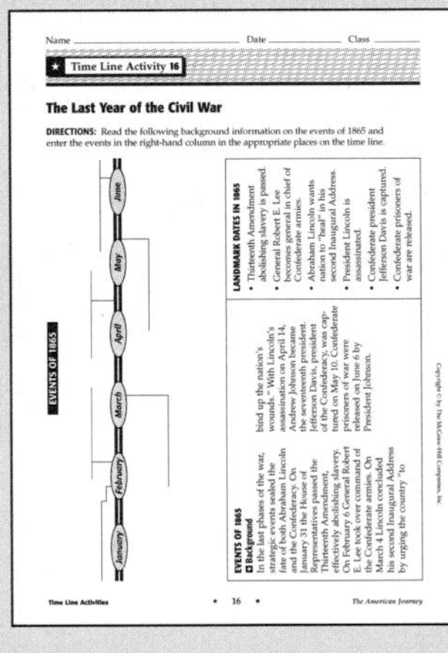

Vocabulary Activity 16

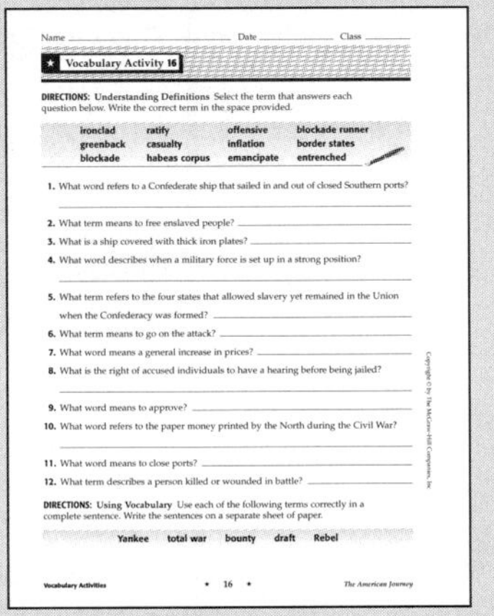

Chapter Skills Activity 16

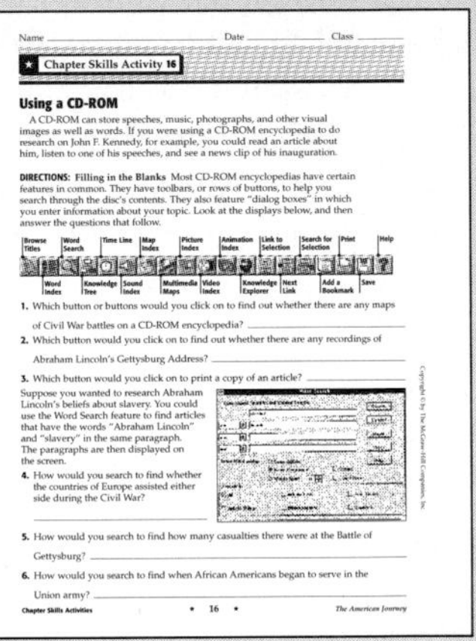

Enrichment Activities

Linking Past and Present Activity 16

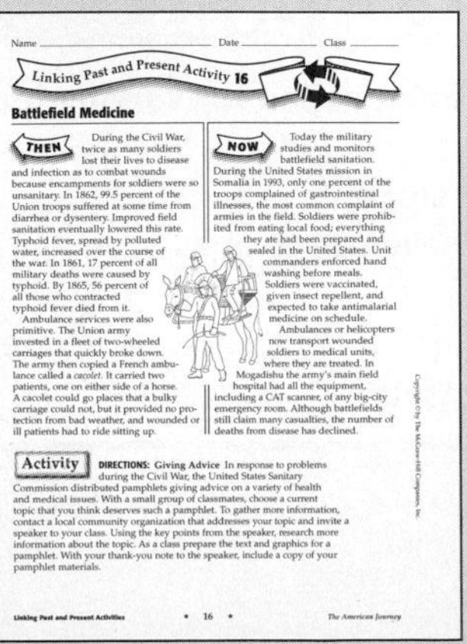

Primary Source Reading 16

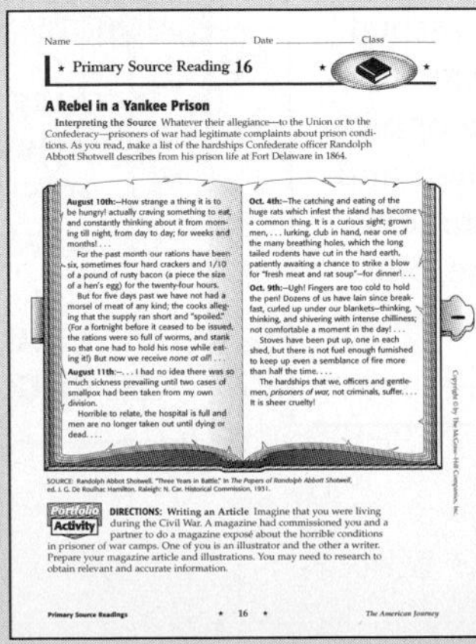

Geography Activities

Mapping History Activity 16

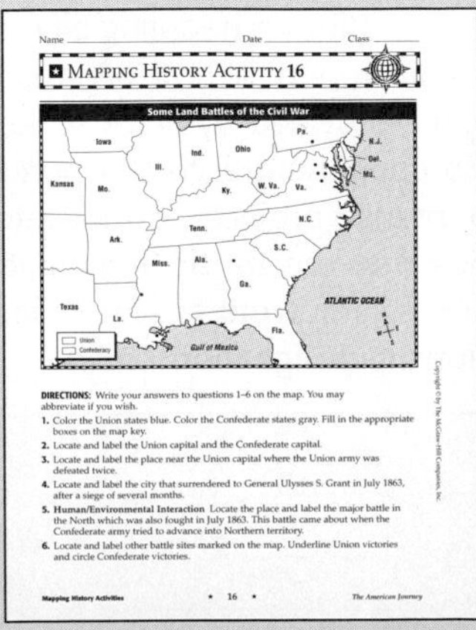

Chapter 16 Resource Guide

Assessment

Chapter 16 Test, Form A

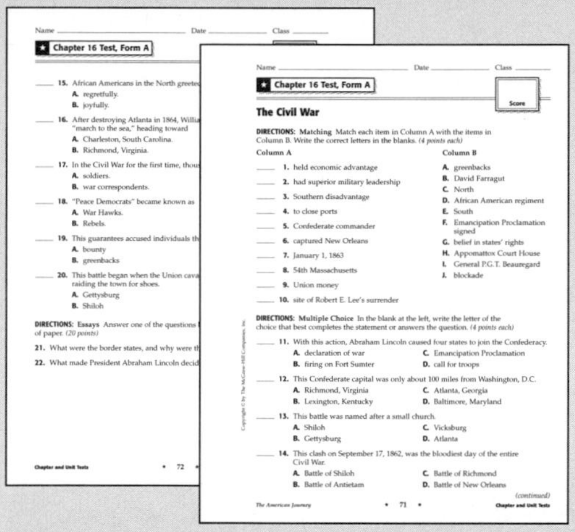

Chapter 16 Test, Form B

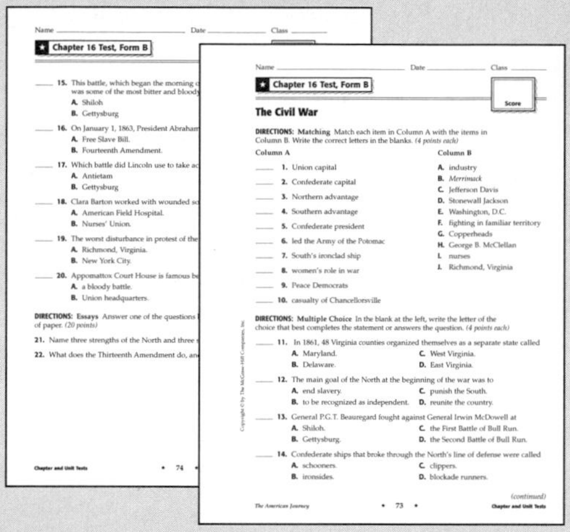

Performance Assessment Activity 16

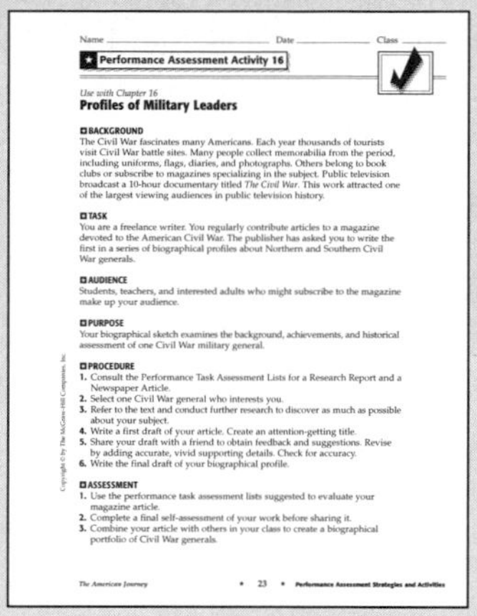

Spanish Resources

The following Spanish language materials are available in the Spanish Resources binder:

- **Spanish Chapter Summary 16**
- **Spanish Vocabulary Activity 16**
- **Spanish Guided Reading Activities, Chapter 16**
- **Spanish Section Quizzes, Chapter 16**
- **Spanish Home Involvement Activity 16**
- **Spanish Chapter 16 Digests Audiocassette Activity and Test**

Activity Manipulatives

Help students learn more about America's cultural history with:

- ***American Crafts Hands-On Activities***
- ***American Games Hands-On Activities***
- ***American History Flash Cards***

Additional Resources From Glencoe

- **American Music Cultural Traditions,** Lesson 5: "Bonnie Blue Flag" and "Glory! Glory! Glory! Hallelujah!"
- **U.S. History & Art,** Transparency 11, *A Rainy Day in Camp*
- **Outline Map Resource Book**
- **U.S. Desk Map**
- **The American History Videodisc and CD-ROM:** *The Civil War and Reconstruction*

A&E HOME VIDEO. Biography™ THE HISTORY CHANNEL.

The following videotape programs are available from Glencoe as supplements to Chapter 16:

- **Civil War Journal (Set 1)** (ISBN 1-56501-200-3)
- **Civil War Journal (Set 2)** (ISBN 1-56501-326-3)

To order, call Glencoe at 1-800-334-7344. To find classroom resources to accompany many of these videos, check the following home pages:
A&E Television: http://www.aetv.com
The History Channel: http://www.historychannel.com

Introducing
CHAPTER 16

Chapter Themes

Chapter Themes are listed by section on this chapter opening page of the Student Edition. A corresponding theme-based activity is available under "FOCUS," and a theme-based question is asked in the Section and Chapter Reviews.

Performance Assessment

Refer to Activity 16 in the *Performance Assessment Strategies and Activities* booklet.

GLENCOE TECHNOLOGY

VIDEODISC
MindJogger Videoquiz

Use MindJogger to preview the Chapter 16 content.

Chapter 16
Disc 2, Side B

Also available in VHS.

HISTORY AND ART Much of the fighting during the devastating Battle of Gettysburg took place at Evergreen Cemetery. A sign near the arched gateway to the graveyard read: "All persons found using firearms in these grounds will be prosecuted with the utmost rigor of the law."

1861–1865

The Civil War

Why It's Important

The Civil War—a war in which Americans fought other Americans—transformed the United States. It devastated the economy of the South while contributing to the rapid economic growth of the North and the West. African Americans gained freedom as slavery was abolished, but the war left a legacy of bitterness between North and South that lasted for generations. In addition the war established the power of the federal government over the states.

Chapter Themes

- *Section 1,* Government and Democracy
- *Section 2,* Geography and History
- *Section 3,* Groups and Institutions
- *Section 4,* Economic Factors
- *Section 5,* Individual Action

HISTORY AND ART ***Fight for the Colors* by Don Troiani** Troiani has painted several dramatic Civil War scenes, such as this one of the Battle of Gettysburg.

EXTRA CREDIT PROJECT

Categorizing Information Invite each student to create a computerized database of Civil War battles. Remind students of the essential parts of a database: a file, records, fields, and entries. Make sure students carefully select and define fields. The fields should be as specific as possible to allow researchers to write queries or filters to search for information easily. Possible fields for this database may include: Name of Battle, Date of Battle, Place of Battle, Northern Leader, Southern Leader, Victor, and so on. If no computers are available, encourage students to create a paper database of this information.

1861 — 1862 — 1863

February 1861
The Confederacy is formed

April 1861
Four more states join the Confederacy

Summer 1861
Rebel soldiers total about 112,000; Yankees number about 187,000

1863
West Virginia is admitted to the Union

Section 1

The Two Sides

READ TO DISCOVER . . .
- why the border states played an important role in the war.
- how the North and the South compared in terms of population, industry, resources, and war aims.

TERMS TO LEARN

border state	Rebel
blockade	Yankee
offensive	

The Storyteller

Union sergeant Driscoll led his troops up Malvern Hill on July 1, 1862. The enemy fought fiercely, especially one young Confederate soldier. Driscoll raised his rifle, took aim, and shot the boy. As he passed the spot where the boy had fallen, Driscoll turned the daring soldier over to see what he looked like. The boy opened his eyes and faintly murmured, "Father," then his eyes fluttered shut, never to open again. A Union captain later wrote, "I will forever recollect the frantic grief of Driscoll; it was harrowing to witness. He [had killed] his son, who had gone South before the war."

Union cavalry cap

By February 1861, seven states had left the Union and formed the Confederacy. After the Confederate bombardment of Fort Sumter, President **Abraham Lincoln** issued a call for troops to save the Union. His action caused Virginia, North Carolina, Tennessee, and Arkansas to join the Confederacy. These four states brought needed soldiers, animals, industry, and food to the Confederacy, greatly increasing its chances of winning independence. For its capital, the Confederacy chose **Richmond,** Virginia, a city only about 100 miles from the Union capital of **Washington, D.C.**

Geography

Choosing Sides

Four states that allowed slavery—Missouri, Kentucky, Maryland, and Delaware—remained in the Union. The people of these border states were divided over whether to support the Union or join the Confederacy. Missouri, Kentucky, and Maryland had such strong support for the South that the three states teetered on the brink of secession.

Losing the border states would seriously damage the North. All had strategic locations. Missouri could control parts of the **Mississippi River** and major routes to the West. Kentucky controlled the Ohio River. Delaware was close to the important Northern city of Philadelphia.

Maryland, perhaps the most important of the border states, was close to Richmond. Vital

SECTION RESOURCES

Reproducible Masters
- Reproducible Lesson Plan 16–1
- Guided Reading Activity 16–1
- Section Quiz 16–1
- Reteaching Activity 16–1
- Enrichment Activity 16–1

Transparencies
- Section Focus Transparency 16–1

Multimedia
- Vocabulary PuzzleMaker
- Chapter Challenger Interactive Review Software
- Testmaker
- GTV: A Geographic Perspective on American History
- The Presidents: A Picture History of Our Nation

1 FOCUS

BELLRINGER
Motivational Activity

Before taking roll at the beginning of the class period, project Section Focus Transparency 16–1 and have students answer the questions. Discuss students' responses.

This activity is also available as a blackline master.

Section Focus Transparency 16–1

Food Prices in Richmond, Virginia, 1860–1863

1. About how many times more did these supplies cost in 1863 than in 1860?
2. In 1860 how many pounds of butter could be bought for the price of one pound in 1863?
3. Why do you think prices rose so much in three years?

1860 pre-war prices		1863 war prices	
Bacon, 10 lb. at 12½ cents*	$1.25	Bacon, 10 lb. at $1*	$10.00
Flour, 30 lb. at 5 cents*	1.50	Flour, 30 lb. at 12½ cents*	3.75
Sugar, 5 lb. at 8 cents*	.40	Sugar, 5 lb. at $1.15*	5.75
Coffee, 4 lb. at 12½ cents*	.50	Coffee, 4 lb. at $5*	20.00
Butter, 3 lb. at 25 cents*	.75	Butter, 3 lb. at $1.75*	5.25
	$4.40		$44.75

*price per pound

Vocabulary Precheck

Use the map on page 456 to point out the *border states.* Ask students to determine the characteristics of border states and determine their importance to the North.

Use the **Vocabulary PuzzleMaker** to create crossword and word search puzzles.

Section Theme
Government and Democracy

The Southern states seceded from the Union to protect states' rights. Preservation of this principle led to the downfall of the Confederacy. Individual states refused to give the Confederate government enough power to fight the war effectively.

Activity Remind students of the definitions of the words *confederacy* and *federalism.* Have them draw Venn diagrams showing the similarities and differences between the two.

2 TEACH

L1 Writing a Newspaper Article Ask groups of students to design and create the front page of a newspaper announcing the beginning of the Civil War. Recommend that each group include on their front pages a banner headline, some form of illustration, a story that includes eyewitness accounts, and announcements from the Union and Confederate governments about the outbreak of war.

Guided Reading Activity 16–1

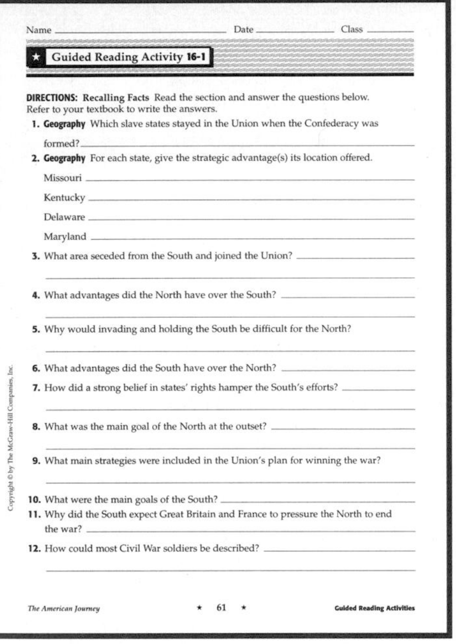

Name ______ Date ______ Class ______

★ Guided Reading Activity **16-1**

DIRECTIONS: Recalling Facts Read the section and answer the questions below. Refer to your textbook to write the answers.

1. **Geography** Which slave states stayed in the Union when the Confederacy was formed? ______
2. **Geography** For each state, give the strategic advantage(s) its location offered.
   Missouri ______
   Kentucky ______
   Delaware ______
   Maryland ______
3. What area seceded from the South and joined the Union? ______
4. What advantages did the North have over the South? ______
5. Why would invading and holding the South be difficult for the North? ______
6. What advantages did the South have over the North? ______
7. How did a strong belief in states' rights hamper the South's efforts? ______
8. What was the main goal of the North at the outset? ______
9. What main strategies were included in the Union's plan for winning the war? ______
10. What were the main goals of the South? ______
11. Why did the South expect Great Britain and France to pressure the North to end the war? ______
12. How could most Civil War soldiers be described? ______

The American Journey ★ 61 ★ **Guided Reading Activities**

HISTORY AND ART Virginia's secession resulted in Washington, D.C., being surrounded by Virginia on the south and the slave state of Maryland on the north. Only a week after the fall of Fort Sumter, 16 people were killed in Baltimore as a result of Confederate sympathizers attacking Northern troops in the city. Lincoln responded by placing Baltimore under martial law. **Ask:** What is martial law? *(a form of military rule that includes suspending Bill of Rights freedoms)* **Answer:** *to protect Washington, D.C., and vital railroad lines passing through Maryland, and to prevent Maryland from leaving the Union*

railroad lines passed through Maryland. Most significantly, Washington, D.C., lay within the state. If Maryland seceded, the North's government would be surrounded.

Maryland's key role became clear in April 1861—just a month after Lincoln's inauguration as president. A mob in Baltimore attacked Northern troops marching through the city. Then, Confederate sympathizers burned railroad bridges and cut the telegraph line to Washington, isolating the capital from the rest of the North. Northern troops soon arrived, but the nation's capital had suffered some anxious days.

Remaining With the Union

Lincoln had to move cautiously to avoid antagonizing people in the border states. If he announced that he aimed to end slavery, for instance, groups supporting the Confederacy might take their states out of the Union. If he ordered Northern troops into Kentucky, Confederate sympathizers there would claim the state had been invaded and swing it to the South.

In some ways Lincoln acted boldly. He suspended some constitutional rights and used his power to arrest people for active support of secession. Lincoln supported rebellion against Missouri's pro-Confederate state government. In the end Lincoln's approach worked. The four border states stayed in the Union—although thousands of their citizens left to join the armies of the South.

A Secession from the South

Most white Southerners favored secession. Still, pockets of Union support existed in eastern Tennessee and western Virginia. People in the Appalachian region generally opposed secession.

In western Virginia a movement to secede from the state and rejoin the Union grew. In 1861, 48 Virginia counties organized themselves as a separate state called **West Virginia.** Congress admitted this state to the Union in 1863.

Comparing North and South

When the war began, both sides had advantages and disadvantages. How they would use those strengths and weaknesses would determine the war's outcome.

Northern Strengths and Weaknesses

The North enjoyed the advantages of a larger population to support the war effort, more industry, and more abundant resources than the South. It had a better banking system, which helped in raising money for the war. The North also possessed more ships, though most of them were old, and almost all the members of the regular navy remained loyal to the Union. Finally, the North had a larger and more efficient railway network.

HISTORY AND ART

***7th New York Militia at Jersey City on April 19, 1861* by E.L. Henry.** The 7th New York Militia was one of the first fully equipped and trained units at war's outbreak. **Why were troops ordered to the nation's capital in early 1861?**

COOPERATIVE LEARNING ACTIVITY

Creating a Graphic Organizer Explain to students that a graphic organizer is a visual tool that helps them to organize their thinking and to remember information they read. A graphic organizer can be a chart, diagram, table, map, web, Venn diagram, fishbone map, and so on. Have students work in groups of four to create a graphic organizer about the strengths and weaknesses of the North and South. They should scan the section for information on strengths and weaknesses and cooperatively categorize each strength and weakness into the following categories: cultural, social, economic, and political factors. As a group, students should decide which type of graphic organizer they want to use. Then have each student decide which category to depict on the graphic organizer. Finally, each student should illustrate the information in their specific category on the graphic organizer.

The North also faced disadvantages. Bringing the Southern states back into the Union would be a difficult task. The North would have to invade and hold the South—a large area filled with a hostile population. Furthermore, public opinion in the North was divided over the war, and support for the war remained shaky until very near the end. Recalling the example of the American Revolution, when the smaller, weaker colonies had won independence from wealthy Great Britain, many people believed the South had a good chance of winning.

One Northern advantage was not obvious until later. Both sides greatly underestimated Abraham Lincoln. His dedication, intelligence, skill, and humanity led the North to victory.

Southern Strengths and Weaknesses

One of the main advantages of the South was the strong support its white population gave the war. Southerners also had the advantage of fighting in familiar territory—defending their land, their homes, and their way of life.

The military leadership of the South, at least at first, was superior to the North's. Southern families had a strong tradition of military training and service, and military college graduates provided the South with a large pool of officers. Overseeing the Southern effort was Confederate president **Jefferson Davis,** a West Point graduate and experienced soldier who took a keen interest in the activities of his War Department.

The South faced material disadvantages. It had a smaller population of free men to draw upon in building an army. It also possessed very few factories to manufacture weapons and other supplies, and it produced less than half as much food as the North. With less than half the miles of railroad tracks and vastly fewer trains than the North, the Confederate government had difficulty delivering food, weapons, and other supplies to its troops.

The belief in **states' rights**—a founding principle of the Confederacy—also hampered the South's efforts. The individual states refused to give the Confederate government enough power to fight the war effectively.

Resources of the North and South, 1861

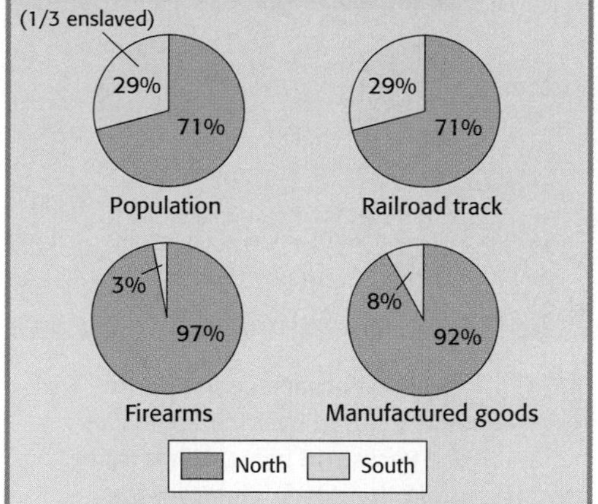

Source: *Encyclopedia Americana*, 1994; *Historical Statistics of the United States.*

Graph Study

The North had an economic advantage at the start of the Civil War.

1. By how much did Northern manufactured goods exceed Southern manufactured goods?
2. **Analyzing Information** What percentage of all firearms were manufactured in the North?

War Aims and Strategy

The North and the South entered the Civil War with different war aims. To achieve these aims and win the war, each side devised its own strategy.

Northern Aims and Strategies

The main goal of the North at the outset was to win the war and bring the Southern states back into the Union. Ending slavery was not a major Northern goal at first, but this changed as the war continued.

The Union's plan for winning the war included three main strategies. First, using its superior navy, the North would **blockade,** or close, Southern ports to prevent supplies from reaching the South—and to prevent the South from earning

Multiple Learning Styles

Verbal/Linguistic Review the definition of *personification* with students. Have each student choose a border state to personify. Then ask each student to write a short paragraph describing how the state feels being a border state. Encourage students to describe their feelings geographically, emotionally, historically, socially, and politically. Allow students to read their paragraph aloud to the class and have the rest of the students guess which border state is being described. **L2**

Graph Study

Answers

1. 84 percent
2. 97 percent

Graph Skills Practice

Reading a Graph In which resource shown on the graph did the North hold the greatest advantage? *(firearms)*

At the MOVIES

The film *The Civil War Soldier: The Infantryman* (American Historical Productions, Gaithersburg, MD) portrays the daily life of the common soldier of the North and the South.

NATIONAL GEOGRAPHIC SOCIETY

VIDEODISC
GTV: A Geographic Perspective on American History

Side 2, Chapter 16
Title: *The Civil War*
Subject: Summary of the Civil War and how geography played a role in the outcome (1861–1865)
Ask: **What advantages did the North have in the Civil War?** *(more people, more industry, better transportation)*

CD-ROM
The Presidents: A Picture History of Our Nation

Suggest that students research the issues facing Abraham Lincoln when he took office.

Picturing HISTORY The railroad was an integral part of the movement and the preservation of field armies during the Civil War. A railcar mounted with a heavy cannon for bombardment of forts was first used during the Civil War. **Answer:** *larger population, more firearms, more manufactured goods, more resources, better banking system, more ships*

3 ASSESS

Assign Section 1 Review as homework or as an in-class activity.

Use **Chapter Challenger Interactive Review Software** to review Section 1.

Section Quiz 16–1

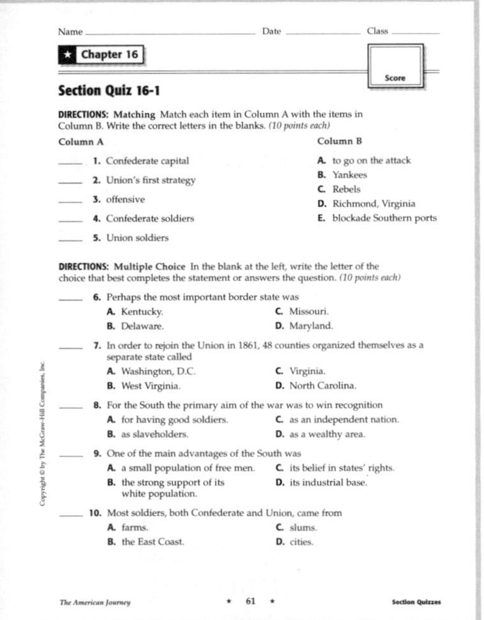

Name ______ Date ______ Class ______

Chapter 16 Score

Section Quiz 16-1

DIRECTIONS: Matching Match each item in Column A with the items in Column B. Write the correct letters in the blanks. *(10 points each)*

Column A	Column B
____ 1. Confederate capital	A. to go on the attack
____ 2. Union's first strategy	B. Yankees
____ 3. offensive	C. Rebels
____ 4. Confederate soldiers	D. Richmond, Virginia
____ 5. Union soldiers	E. blockade Southern ports

DIRECTIONS: Multiple Choice In the blank at the left, write the letter of the choice that best completes the statement or answers the question. *(10 points each)*

____ 6. Perhaps the most important border state was
A. Kentucky. C. Missouri.
B. Delaware. D. Maryland.

____ 7. In order to rejoin the Union in 1861, 48 counties organized themselves as a separate state called
A. Washington, D.C. C. Virginia.
B. West Virginia. D. North Carolina.

____ 8. For the South the primary aim of the war was to win recognition
A. for having good soldiers. C. as an independent nation.
B. as slaveholders. D. as a wealthy area.

____ 9. One of the main advantages of the South was
A. a small population of free men. C. its belief in states' rights.
B. the strong support of its white population. D. its industrial base.

____ 10. Most soldiers, both Confederate and Union, came from
A. farms. C. slums.
B. the East Coast. D. cities.

The American Journey ★ 61 ★ **Section Quizzes**

Picturing HISTORY One advantage the North enjoyed over the South was better railroad tracks and trains. **What other advantages did the North have over the South?**

money by exporting cotton. Second, the Union intended to gain control of the Mississippi River to cut Southern supply lines and to split the Confederacy. Third, the North planned to capture Richmond, the Confederate capital.

Southern Aims and Strategies

For the South the primary aim of the war was to win recognition as an independent nation. Independence would allow Southerners to preserve their traditional way of life—a way of life that included slavery.

To achieve this goal, the South devised a defensive strategy. It planned to defend its homeland, holding on to as much territory as possible until the North tired of fighting and agreed to recognize the independence of the Confederacy. The South expected that Britain and France, which imported large quantities of Southern cotton, would pressure the North to end the war so that their cotton supply would be restored.

During the war Southern leaders sometimes changed strategy and took the **offensive**—went on the attack. They would move their armies northward to threaten Washington and other Northern cities, hoping to persuade the North that it could not win the war.

American People at War

Both North and South had to contend with conflicting loyalties that split families and divided friends. The Civil War was more than a war between the states. It often pitted brother against brother, parents against their children, and neighbor against neighbor.

American Against American

The leaders from both North and South—and their families—felt these divisions. President Lincoln's wife, Mary Todd Lincoln, had a brother, three half brothers, and three brothers-in-law who fought in the Confederate army. John Crittenden, a senator from Kentucky, had two sons who became generals in the war—one for the Confederacy and one for the Union. Officers on both sides—including Confederate president Davis, Confederate general Robert E. Lee, and Union generals George McClellan and William Tecumseh Sherman—had attended the United States Military Academy at West Point, never dreaming that they would one day command forces against each other.

Sometimes, family members actually faced each other in combat. In one battle a Union regiment commanded by a man from West Virginia attacked a Confederate regiment from Virginia commanded by his cousin.

Who Were the Soldiers?

Most of the solders were inexperienced, and many were young. The average age of a recruit was about 25 years, but about 40 percent were 21 years or younger. Ted Upson of Indiana was only 16 when he begged his father to let him join the Union army. "This Union your ancestors and mine helped to make must be saved from destruction," he said.

William Stone from Louisiana rushed to join the Confederate army after the attack on Fort Sumter. His sister Kate wrote that he was

> ". . . wild to be off to Virginia. He so fears that the fighting will be over before he can get there."

MAKING CONNECTIONS ACTIVITY

Politics Pair students to research and create a series of circle graphs showing the differences between the North and the South in 1861. Have them use the graphs on page 463 as examples. Encourage students to compare as many categories as possible, such as number of enslaved persons, number of factories, types of exports and imports, acreage devoted to agriculture, and so on. Display completed graphs on a bulletin board called *Sectionalism in 1861.* **L2**

you don't say...

Johnny Reb and Billy Yank
Northern troops called the Southern soldier *Johnny Reb* or *Reb,* after the term rebel. Southerners called the Northerners *Billy Yank, Yank,* or *Yankees.*

Soldiers came from all parts of both sections of the country and all walks of life. Most, though, came from farms. Almost half of the North's troops and more than 60 percent of the South's had owned or worked on farms. The Union army did not permit African Americans to join at first, but they did serve later.

Early terms of enlistment were short. After the shelling of Fort Sumter, Lincoln asked state governors to supply soldiers for 90 days. When the conflict did not end quickly, soldiers' terms became longer. In the first year of the war, leaders in both the North and the South asked volunteers to sign up for 3 years of service.

By the summer of 1861, the Confederate army had about 112,000 soldiers, who were sometimes called **Rebels.** The Union had about 187,000 soldiers, or **Yankees** as they were also known. By the end of the war, about 850,000 men fought for the Confederacy and about 2.1 million men fought for the Union. The Union number included just under 200,000 African Americans. Approximately 10,000 Hispanic soldiers fought in the conflict.

Confederate soldier

False Hopes

When the war began, each side expected a brief conflict and an early victory. Many Southerners believed that Northern soldiers lacked the conviction needed to win the war. A Confederate soldier from Alabama expected the war to be over within a year because "we are going to kill the last Yankee before that time if there is any fight in them still." Northerners were just as confident that they would beat the South quickly—"in thirty days," according to one newspaper.

Some leaders saw the situation more clearly. Northern general William Tecumseh Sherman wrote, "I think it is to be a long war—very long—much longer than any politician thinks." The first spring of the war proved that Sherman's prediction was accurate.

Section 1 Review

Checking for Understanding

1. ***Identify*** Abraham Lincoln, states' rights.
2. ***Define*** border state, blockade, offensive, Rebel, Yankee.
3. ***List*** the North's three main strategies for winning the war.

Reviewing Themes

4. **Government and Democracy** How did a belief in states' rights hamper the South during the war?

Critical Thinking

5. **Predicting Consequences** What do you think would be the South's greatest advantage in the war? Explain your answer.

Activity

Keeping a Journal Imagine that you are a Southerner or a Northerner in 1861. Write a journal entry that explains your reasons for joining the Confederate or Union army.

CHAPTER 16

Section 1, 461–465

Reteaching Activity 16–1

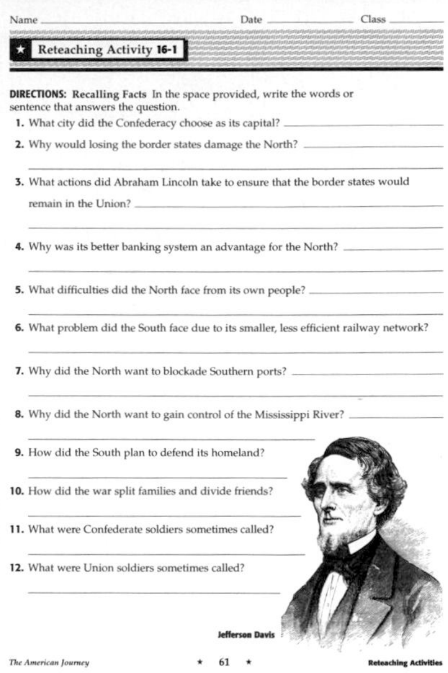
Name ______ Date ______ Class ______

★ Reteaching Activity 16-1

DIRECTIONS: Recalling Facts In the space provided, write the words or sentence that answers the question.

1. What city did the Confederacy choose as its capital?
2. Why would losing the border states damage the North?
3. What actions did Abraham Lincoln take to ensure that the border states would remain in the Union?
4. Why was its better banking system an advantage for the North?
5. What difficulties did the North face from its own people?
6. What problem did the South face due to its smaller, less efficient railway network?
7. Why did the North want to blockade Southern ports?
8. Why did the North want to gain control of the Mississippi River?
9. How did the South plan to defend its homeland?
10. How did the war split families and divide friends?
11. What were Confederate soldiers sometimes called?
12. What were Union soldiers sometimes called?

Jefferson Davis

Copyright © by The McGraw-Hill Companies, Inc.

The American Journey ★ 61 ★ Reteaching Activities

Enrichment Activity 16–1

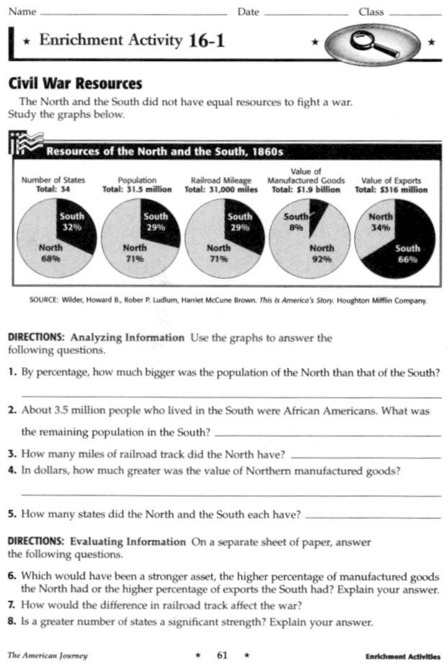
Name ______ Date ______ Class ______

★ Enrichment Activity 16-1 ★ ★

Civil War Resources

The North and the South did not have equal resources to fight a war. Study the graphs below.

Resources of the North and the South, 1860s

Number of States Total: 34	Population Total: 31.5 million	Railroad Mileage Total: 31,000 miles	Value of Manufactured Goods Total: $1.9 billion	Value of Exports Total: $316 million
South 32%	South 29%	South 29%	South 8%	North 34%
North 68%	North 71%	North 71%	North 92%	South 66%

SOURCE: Wilder, Howard B., Rober P. Ludlum, Harriet McCune Brown. *This Is America's Story.* Houghton Mifflin Company.

DIRECTIONS: Analyzing Information Use the graphs to answer the following questions.

1. By percentage, how much bigger was the population of the North than that of the South?
2. About 3.5 million people who lived in the South were African Americans. What was the remaining population in the South?
3. How many miles of railroad track did the North have?
4. In dollars, how much greater was the value of Northern manufactured goods?
5. How many states did the North and the South each have?

DIRECTIONS: Evaluating Information On a separate sheet of paper, answer the following questions.

6. Which would have been a stronger asset, the higher percentage of manufactured goods the North had or the higher percentage of exports the South had? Explain your answer.
7. How would the difference in railroad track affect the war?
8. Is a greater number of states a significant strength? Explain your answer.

Copyright © by The McGraw-Hill Companies, Inc.

The American Journey ★ 61 ★ Enrichment Activities

Section 1 Review Answers

1. Abraham Lincoln, 461; states' rights, 463
2. The words are defined in the Glossary.
3. blockade Southern ports, gain control of Mississippi River, capture Richmond
4. State governments refused to give the Confederate government the power it needed to fight the war.
5. Students' answers may vary, but most likely will include knowledge of the land and fighting for a cause.

Activity Journal entries should be written from the point of view of a Confederate or Union recruit and explain reasons for joining.

4 CLOSE

Ask students to review the newspaper articles they created in the "TEACH" activity. Have them compare their articles with information learned from the section.

1 FOCUS

BELLRINGER
Motivational Activity

Before taking roll at the beginning of the class period, project Section Focus Transparency 16–2 and have students answer the questions. Discuss students' responses.

This activity is also available as a blackline master.

Section Focus Transparency 16–2

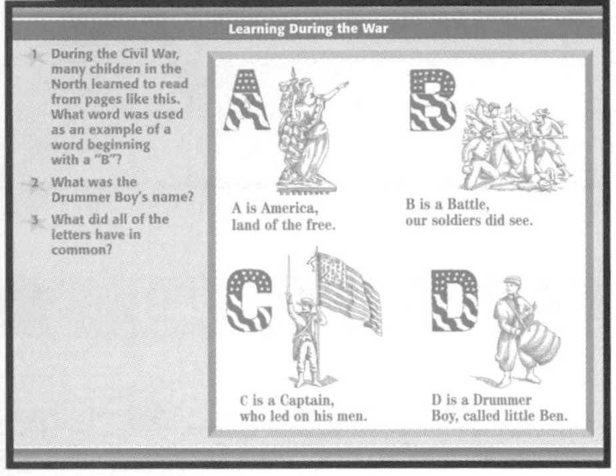

Vocabulary Precheck

Ask students to identify each of the **Terms to Learn** as a liability or an asset in fighting a war.

Use the **Vocabulary PuzzleMaker** to create crossword and word search puzzles.

Section Theme
Geography and History

The North and the South fought the Civil War differently in different geographic regions, applying strategies to match the geography.

Activity Explain to students that the South held the geographic advantage of fighting on their own land. Ask students to identify reasons why this would be an advantage.

1861 — 1862 — 1863

July 1861 Confederates win First Battle of Bull Run

February 1862 Grant captures Fort Henry and Fort Donelson

April 1862 Union wins Battle of Shiloh

September 1862 Battle of Antietam boosts Union morale

Section 2

Early Years of the War

READ TO DISCOVER . . .
- what successes and failures the North and the South had in the early years of the Civil War.
- how the North's naval blockade hurt the South.

TERMS TO LEARN
blockade runner
casualty
ironclad

The Storyteller

Sunday, July 21, 1861, was a pleasant, sunny day in Washington, D.C. Hundreds of cheerful residents, food baskets in hand, left the city and crossed the Potomac River to spend the day in Virginia. They planned to picnic while watching the first battle between the Union and the Confederate armies. Expecting to see the Union troops crush the Rebels, they looked forward to a quick victory. The Confederate soldiers also expected a quick victory. They "carried dress suits with them, and any quantity of fine linen. Every soldier, nearly, had a servant with him, and a whole lot of spoons and forks, so as to live comfortably and elegantly in camp. . . ."

1st Virginia Infantry flag

The first major battle of the Civil War was fought in northern Virginia, about 5 miles from a town called Manassas Junction near Bull Run— a small river in the area. Usually called the **First Battle of Bull Run,** it began when about 30,000 inexperienced Union troops commanded by General Irvin McDowell attacked a slightly smaller, equally inexperienced Confederate force led by General **P. G.T. Beauregard.**

Eyewitness to HISTORY

First Battle of Bull Run

The Yankees drove the Confederates back at first. Then the Rebels rallied, inspired by reinforcements under General Thomas Jackson. Jackson, who was seen holding out "like a stone wall," became known thereafter as **"Stonewall" Jackson.** The Confederates unleashed a savage counterattack that forced the Union lines to break.

The Confederates surged forward with a strange, unearthly scream that came to be known as the Rebel yell. Terrified, the Northern soldiers began to drop their guns and packs and run. One observer, Representative Albert Riddle, reported:

> "A cruel, crazy, mad, hopeless panic possessed them. . . . The heat was awful . . . the men were exhausted—their mouths gaped, their lips cracked and blackened with the powder of the cartridges they had bitten off in the battle, their eyes staring in frenzy."

SECTION RESOURCES

Reproducible Masters
- Reproducible Lesson Plan 16–2
- Guided Reading Activity 16–2
- Section Quiz 16–2
- Reteaching Activity 16–2
- Enrichment Activity 16–2

Transparencies
- Section Focus Transparency 16–2

Multimedia
- Vocabulary PuzzleMaker
- Chapter Challenger Interactive Review
- Testmaker
- NGS PictureShow: The Civil War
- Facts On File: Landmark Documents in American History
- American Music Cultural Traditions

General Thomas "Stonewall" Jackson

Picturing HISTORY Union troops fled in panic from Bull Run (Manassas) after a fierce Confederate counterattack led by General Thomas "Stonewall" Jackson. **What Confederate action on the battlefield frightened Union forces into fleeing?**

The Union army began an orderly retreat that quickly became a mad stampede when the retreating Union troops collided with the civilians, fleeing in panic back to Washington.

The Confederates, though victorious, were too disorganized and weakened to pursue the retreating Yankees. Regardless, the South rejoiced. Edmund Ruffin of Virginia thought it meant "the close of the war."

A Shock for the North

The outcome of the battle shocked the North. Northerners began to understand that the war could be a long, difficult, and costly struggle. Although discouraged by the results, President Abraham Lincoln was also determined. Within days he issued a call for more volunteers for the army. This time he requested 1 million soldiers who would serve for 3 years. Volunteers soon crowded into recruiting offices. Lincoln also appointed a new general, **George B. McClellan,** to head the Union army of the East—called the **Army of the Potomac**—and organize the troops.

War at Sea

Even before Bull Run, Lincoln had ordered a planned naval blockade of Southern ports. An effective blockade would prevent the South from exporting its cotton and importing the supplies necessary to continue the war.

Enforcing the Blockade

When the war began, the North did not have enough ships to blockade the South's entire 3,500-mile coastline. Many Confederate ships, called **blockade runners,** could sail in and out of Southern ports. In time, the North built more ships and became better able to enforce the blockade.

The blockade caused serious problems for the South. Although the blockade could never close off all Southern trade, it did reduce the trade by two-thirds. Goods such as coffee, shoes, nails, and salt—as well as guns and ammunition—were in short supply throughout the war.

Footnotes to History

Different Names, Same Battle Many Civil War battles have two names. The Union named battles after the nearest body of water. The Confederacy named them after the nearest settlement. Therefore, the battle called the Battle of Bull Run (a river) in the North was known as the Battle of Manassas (a settlement) in the South.

2 TEACH

L1 Outlining Ask students to make an outline of this section using the subheads. Then have them complete the outlines by listing the strategies used by the North and the South.

Picturing HISTORY Before the war General Thomas "Stonewall" Jackson was an instructor at the Virginia Military Institute. In 1859 he commanded a contingent of V.M.I. cadets serving as guards at John Brown's execution.

The Confederates' Rebel yell might have sounded like a fox-hunt yip mixed with a banshee squall. The Yankees had a sort of "hurrah," which was identified by one soldier as "the deep generous manly shout of the Northern soldier."

Answer: *Rebel yell*

Guided Reading Activity 16–2

Name ________ Date ________ Class ________

★ Guided Reading Activity **16-2**

DIRECTIONS: Recording Who, What, When, Where, Why, and **How** Read the section and answer the questions below. Refer to your textbook to write the answers.

1. **Where** was the first major battle of the Civil War? ________
2. **Eyewitness to History** **Who** were the two generals who led the South in this battle? ________
3. **Who** won this battle? ________
4. **What** was the Union army of the East called? ________
5. **Who** headed the Union army of the East? ________
6. **Why** did Abraham Lincoln order a blockade of Southern ports? ________
7. **How** did the South challenge the blockade? ________
8. **What** was the North's first strategic goal in the West? ________
9. **Geography** **How** long did the Battle of Shiloh last? ________
10. **Geography** **Who** was victorious in the Battle of Shiloh? ________
11. **Why** was David Farragut's capture of New Orleans significant? ________
12. **What** was George McClellan's goal in March of 1862? ________
13. **What** was McClellan's operation known as? ________
14. **How** did McClellan's delays benefit the Confederates? ________
15. **Who** commanded the South's army for the Seven Days battles? ________
16. **What** was the outcome of McClellan's offensive? ________
17. **What** took place on August 29, 1862? ________
18. **Who** was victorious? ________
19. **What** advantage over the South did the North have when it launched an offensive into Maryland in September 1862? ________
20. **When** was the single bloodiest day of the war? ________
21. **How** did Lincoln react to McClellan's repeated hesitance? ________

Guided Reading Activities ★ 62 ★ *The American Journey*

Cooperative Learning Activity

Creating a Civil War Trivia Game Organize the class into groups of three. As a group, have students create and write the rules of a Civil War trivia game using information in this section. Have students choose from the following roles: design question cards, design playing pieces and any other game pieces described in the rules, and design game board. As a group, determine the trivia questions and answers to be used in the game and write them on the question cards. Have groups trade and play the completed games.

CHAPTER 16
Section 2, 466–471

What?Where?When?Who?

The *Monitor* The Swedish-born inventor John Ericsson invented the *Monitor.* He built this first entirely iron ship in 101 days. The *Monitor* contained 47 patented devices. It housed two guns to the *Merrimack's* 10, but they were mounted on a revolving turret.

History *and the* Humanities

American Music Cultural Traditions, Lesson 5: "Bonnie Blue Flag" and "Glory! Glory! Glory! Hallelujah!"

Facts On File

CD-ROM
Landmark Documents in American History

Title: *Constitution of the Confederate States of America, 1861*
Have students list some distinguishing characteristics of the Confederate constitution.

Title: *Confederate States of America Presidential Inaugural Address, Jefferson Davis, 1862*
Have students note the key points in Davis's address.

Map Study

Answers
1. Seven Days Battle
2. Union

Map Skills Practice

Reading a Map Which battle was fought on water? *(Monitor v. Merrimack)*

The *Monitor* Versus the *Merrimack*

The South did not intend to let the blockade go unchallenged. Southerners salvaged the ***Merrimack,*** a Union warship that Northern forces had abandoned when Confederate forces seized the naval shipyard in **Norfolk, Virginia.** The Confederates rebuilt the wooden ship, covered it with thick iron plates, and renamed it the *Virginia.*

On March 8, 1862, this **ironclad** warship attacked a group of Union ships off the coast of Virginia. The North's wooden warships could not damage the Confederate ship—shells simply bounced off its sides.

Some Northern leaders feared the South would use the ironclad warship to destroy much of the Union navy, steam up the Potomac River, and bombard Washington, D.C. However, the North had already built an ironclad ship of its own, the ***Monitor.*** Described as looking like a "tin can on a shingle," the *Monitor* rushed south to engage the Confederate ship in battle.

On March 9, the two ironclads exchanged fire, but neither ship could sink the other. The Union succeeded in keeping the *Merrimack* in the harbor, so it never again threatened Northern ships. The battle marked a new age in naval warfare—the first battle between two metal-covered ships.

The Civil War in the East, 1861–1863

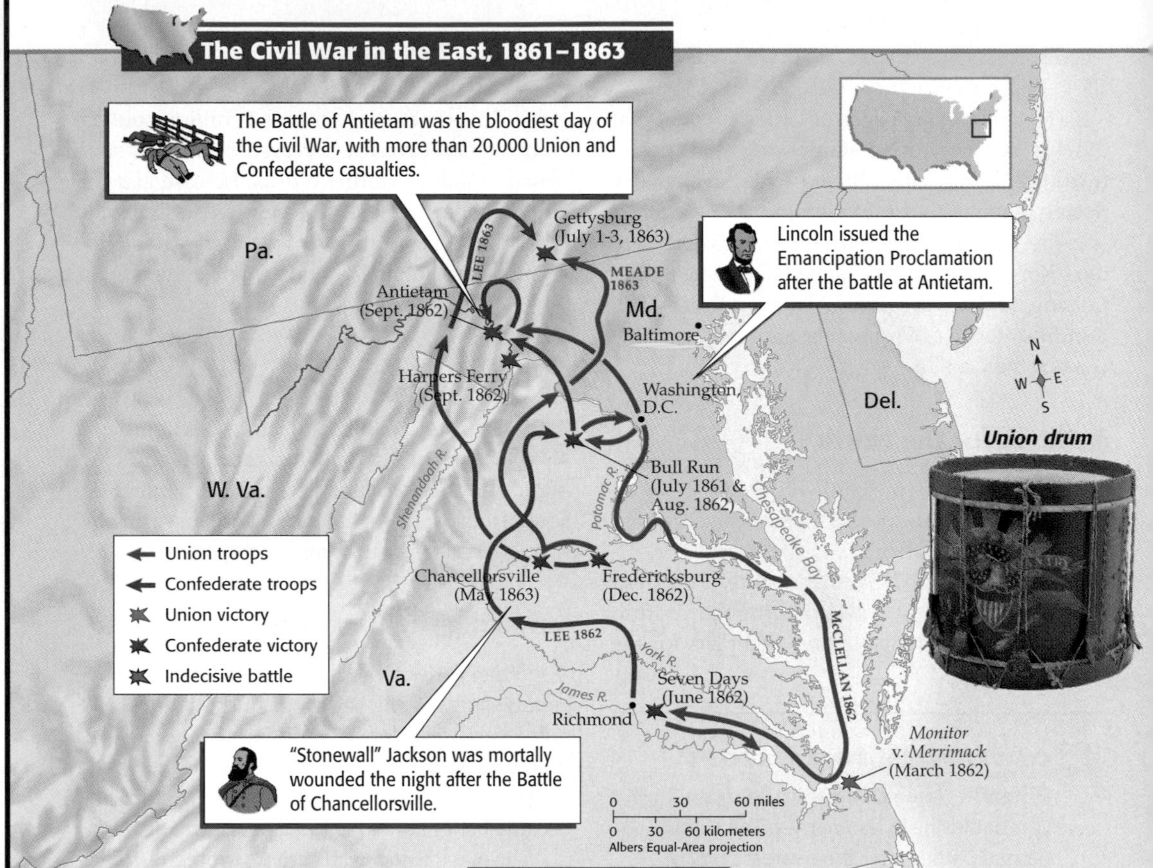

Map Study

The North struggled to capture the city of Richmond, but Confederate general Robert E. Lee held off all Union advances in northern Virginia.

1. **Location** What battle was fought near Richmond, Virginia?
2. **Analyzing Information** Who claimed victory at Antietam?

MULTIPLE LEARNING STYLES

Visual/Spatial Have each student scan this section to find the successes and failures of the North and the South in the early years of the Civil War. Ask them to illustrate this information as a poster-size graphic organizer. Encourage students to use both type and graphics as they create their organizers. **L1, ELL**

War in the West

After the First Battle of Bull Run in July 1861, military operations in the East settled into a long stalemate as each side built up its strength. Generals focused on training their raw recruits, trying to turn civilians into disciplined soldiers. For a while the action shifted to the West.

Early Victories for the North

One of the North's primary goals in the West was to gain control of the Mississippi and Tennessee Rivers. This would split the Confederacy and hinder Southern efforts to transport goods.

In February 1862, Union forces under General **Ulysses S. Grant** captured Fort Henry on the **Tennessee River** and Fort Donelson on the **Cumberland River,** both in northern Tennessee. Grant's victories helped secure the lower Tennessee River. They also opened a path for Union troops to march into Tennessee, Mississippi, and Alabama. The victories drove the Confederates out of Kentucky, where the South had been attempting to persuade Kentuckians to secede.

Union drummer boy at Shiloh

Geography

The Battle of Shiloh

General Grant and about 40,000 troops then headed south along the Tennessee River toward Corinth, Mississippi, an important railroad junction. In early April the Union army camped at Pittsburg Landing, 20 miles from Corinth. Nearby was a small church named Shiloh. Additional Union forces started from Nashville to join Grant.

Confederate leaders decided to strike first before the reinforcements arrived. Early in the morning of April 6, Confederate forces led by Albert Sidney Johnston and P. G. T. Beauregard launched a surprise attack on the Union troops. The **Battle of Shiloh** lasted 2 days, with some of the most bitter and bloody fighting of the war. On the first day of battle, the Confederates drove Grant and his troops back to the Tennessee River. On the second day, the Union forces recovered. Aided by the 25,000 troops from Nashville and shelling by gunboats on the river, they defeated the Confederates, who withdrew to Corinth.

The losses in the Battle of Shiloh were enormous. Together the two armies suffered 20,000 casualties—people killed or wounded. Confederate general Johnston also died in the bloodbath. One Confederate soldier lamented that the battle "was too shocking [and] too horrible."

After their narrow victory at Shiloh, Union forces gained control of Corinth on May 30. Memphis, Tennessee, fell to Union armies on June 6. The North seemed well on its way to controlling the Mississippi River.

New Orleans Falls

A few weeks after Shiloh, the North won another important victory. On April 25, 1862, Union naval forces under **David Farragut** captured **New Orleans,** Louisiana, the largest city in the South. Farragut, who was of Spanish descent, had grown up in the South but remained loyal to the Union.

His capture of New Orleans, near the mouth of the Mississippi River, meant that the Confederacy could no longer use the river to carry its crops to sea. Coupled with Grant's victories to the north, Farragut's capture of New Orleans gave Union forces control of almost all the Mississippi River.

War in the East

In the East General McClellan was training the Army of the Potomac to be an effective fighting force. An expert at training soldiers, McClellan showed great caution when faced with

CHAPTER 16
Section 2, 466–471

Who?What?Where?When?

Mathew Brady In late September 1862, Mathew Brady held a photographic exhibition at his New York gallery called "The Dead of Antietam." No one had ever seen photographs like these in America before. A *New York Times* reporter described the exhibition as follows: "Mr. Brady has done something to bring to us the terrible reality and earnestness of the war. If he has not brought bodies and laid them in our door-yards and along [our] streets, he has done something very like it."

CURRICULUM CONNECTION

SCIENCE
The single most-important invention used by McClellan's army was an inch-long slug that expanded into the barrel's rifled grooves and spun at great speed from the muzzle. The spin allowed the ball to travel farther and more accurately than musket balls fired from smooth-barreled weapons. The ball was accurate at 250 yards (229 m), five times as far as any other one-person weapon.

NATIONAL GEOGRAPHIC SOCIETY

CD-ROM
NGS PictureShow: The Civil War

Have students view the main battles of the Civil War.

MAKING CONNECTIONS ACTIVITY

Daily Life Ask students to create a time line from the following information on a day in the life of a Civil War soldier (who was not engaged in battle).

5:00 AM Reveille played
5:15 AM Roll call and special orders
5:30–8:00 AM Breakfast, tend horses, infirmary calls, cleanup duty, and necessary chores
8:00 AM–2:00 PM Two hours of sentry-duty out of six hours
8:00 AM–12:00 PM Drill if not on sentry-duty
12:00 PM Dinner followed by more drill
4:30 PM Polish weapons and care for uniforms
5:45 PM Retreat ceremony with roll call, inspection, and dress parade
7:30 PM Supper
8:30 PM Assembly and last roll call
9:00 PM Taps sounded and lights out **L2,** ELL

Picturing HISTORY Robert Edward Lee was born on January 19, 1807, in Stratford, Virginia. In 1829 he graduated second in his class at West Point. Prior to the start of the Civil War, Abraham Lincoln offered Lee the field command of the Union forces, but Lee declined. **Answer:** *McClellan*

3 ASSESS

Assign Section 2 Review as homework or as an in-class activity.

Use **Chapter Challenger Interactive Review Software** to review Section 2.

Section Quiz 16–2

Name ______ Date ______ Class ______

Chapter 16 Score

Section Quiz 16-2

DIRECTIONS: Matching Match each item in Column A with the items in Column B. Write the correct letters in the blanks. *(10 points each)*

Column A	Column B
____ 1. General Thomas Jackson	A. casualties
____ 2. *Merrimack*	B. "Stonewall" Jackson
____ 3. people killed or wounded	C. *Virginia*
____ 4. Union general at Shiloh	D. Seven Days battles
____ 5. Peninsula Campaign	E. Ulysses S. Grant

DIRECTIONS: Multiple Choice In the blank at the left, write the letter of the choice that best completes the statement or answers the question. *(10 points each)*

____ 6. The first major battle of the Civil War was at
A. Shiloh. C. Bull Run (Manassas).
B. Antietam Creek. D. Richmond.

____ 7. This Union general captured New Orleans.
A. Ulysses S. Grant C. Robert E. Lee
B. David Farragut D. George B. McClellan

____ 8. President Abraham Lincoln became disgusted with George B. McClellan's performance and replaced him with
A. David Farragut. C. George Meade.
B. Ulysses S. Grant. D. Ambrose Burnside.

____ 9. The second battle here left the victorious Confederate army only 20 miles from Washington, D.C.
A. Shiloh C. Bull Run (Manassas)
B. Antietam Creek D. Richmond

____ 10. The single bloodiest day of the entire Civil War took place at
A. Shiloh. C. Bull Run (Manassas).
B. Antietam. D. Richmond.

Section Quizzes ★ 62 ★ *The American Journey*

When?Who?What?Where?

September 16, 1862 During the Battle of Antietam on September 16, 1862—the bloodiest single day of the war—Union losses included 2,108 dead and 10,293 more wounded or missing. This total was double the casualties of D-Day during World War II, which occurred 82 years later. The Confederacy lost fewer men (10,318) but they represented a quarter of Lee's army.

Picturing HISTORY While Lincoln searched desperately for a general who could win in the East, the Confederates remained under the able command of General Robert E. Lee. **Which Union general did Lee oppose in the Seven Days battles?**

the prospect of battle, and he worried continually that his troops were not ready. He also hesitated to fight because of reports that overestimated the size of the Rebel forces. Finally, in March 1862, the Army of the Potomac was ready for action. Its goal was to capture Richmond, the Confederate capital.

Union Defeat at Richmond

Instead of advancing directly overland to Richmond as Lincoln wished, McClellan moved his huge army by ship to a peninsula between the York and the James Rivers southeast of the city. From there he began a major offensive known as the **Peninsula Campaign.** The operation took many weeks.

Time passed and opportunities to attack slipped away as General McClellan readied his troops and tried to evaluate the enemy's strength. Lincoln, constantly prodding McClellan to fight, ended one message with an urgent plea: *"You must act."* Complaining of his difficult situation, McClellan did not attack. His delays allowed the Confederates to prepare their defense of Richmond.

McClellan and his army inched slowly toward Richmond, getting so close that the troops could hear the city's church bells ringing. At the end of June, the Union forces finally met the Confederates in a series of encounters known as the **Seven Days battles.**

In these battles Confederate general **Robert E. Lee** took command of the army opposing McClellan. Before the battles began, Lee's cavalry leader, **James E.B. (J.E.B.) Stuart,** performed a daring tactic. He led his 1,200 troopers in a circle around the Union army, gathering vital information about Union positions and boosting Southern morale. Stuart lost only one man in the action. General Lee then boldly countered Union advances and eventually drove the Yankees back to the James River. The Union troops had failed to capture Richmond.

Gloom in the North

Reports from Richmond disheartened the North. Despite the good news in the West, failure to take the Confederate capital left Northerners with little hope. There was another call for volunteers—300,000 this time—but few people signed up. The Southern strategy of making the North weary of war seemed to be working.

The defeat had not been complete, however. McClellan's army had been pushed back, but it was still larger than Lee's and still only 25 miles from Richmond. When McClellan failed to renew the attack, President Lincoln ordered him to move his army back to northern Virginia and join the troops led by Major General **John Pope.**

The bold Lee sent Stonewall Jackson's forces north to attack Pope's supply base at Manassas. Jackson's troops marched 50 miles in 2 days and were then joined by the rest of Lee's army. On

CRITICAL THINKING ACTIVITY

Recognizing Bias Organize the class into small groups to write 10 statements about the battles and the people discussed in this section. Review with students the steps for recognizing bias learned in Chapter 15 *Skill Builder.* Ask students to write some statements that are factual and some that are biased. Have each group read the statements to the class. Then have the other groups decide whether each statement is factual or biased. **L2**

August 29 Pope attacked the approaching Confederates and started the **Second Battle of Bull Run.** This battle, like the first, ended in a Confederate victory. Richmond was no longer threatened. Indeed the situation of the 2 sides was completely reversed. Lee and the Confederates now stood only 20 miles from Washington, D.C.

The Battle of Antietam

Following these Southern victories, Confederate president **Jefferson Davis** ordered Lee to launch an offensive into Maryland northwest of Washington. He hoped another victory would win aid from Great Britain and France. Davis also issued a proclamation urging the people of Maryland to join the Confederacy, but he received no response.

As Lee's army marched into Maryland in September 1862, McClellan and 80,000 Union troops moved slowly after them. On September 13 the North had an extraordinary piece of good luck. In a field near Frederick, Maryland, 2 Union soldiers found a copy of Lee's orders for his army wrapped around 3 cigars. The small bundle had probably been dropped by a careless Southern officer. Now McClellan knew exactly what Lee planned to do. He also learned that Lee's army was divided into 5 parts, providing McClellan with an opportunity to overwhelm Lee's army one piece at a time.

Once again, however, McClellan was overly cautious. He waited four days before he decided to attack the Confederates. This enabled Lee to gather most of his forces together near Sharpsburg, Maryland, along the Antietam Creek.

The Union and the Confederate armies clashed on September 17 in the **Battle of Antietam.** It was the single bloodiest day of the entire war. A Union officer wrote that "the slain lay in rows precisely as they had stood in their ranks a few minutes before." By the time the fighting ended, close to 6,000 soldiers lay dead or dying, and another 17,000 were seriously wounded. Although both armies suffered heavy losses, neither was destroyed.

The day after the battle, Lee withdrew to Virginia. The Confederate retreat allowed the Union troops to claim victory. However, McClellan, who had been ordered by President Lincoln to "destroy the rebel army," did not pursue the Confederate troops. The president, disgusted with McClellan's failure to follow up his victory, removed McClellan from his command in November. Lincoln placed General **Ambrose Burnside** in command of the Army of the Potomac.

Antietam had a profound impact on the war. The Army of the Potomac finally gained some confidence, having forced Lee and his soldiers back south. More important, the battle marked a major change in Northern war aims. President Lincoln used the battle to take action against slavery.

Section 2 Review

Checking for Understanding

1. ***Identify*** George B. McClellan, *Monitor* and *Merrimack*, Ulysses S. Grant, David Farragut, Robert E. Lee.
2. ***Define*** blockade runner, ironclad, casualty.
3. ***Explain*** why the North wanted to blockade Southern ports.

Reviewing Themes

4. **Geography and History** What were the North's main goals in the West?

Critical Thinking

5. **Analyzing Information** Why was Union general McClellan not effective as a military commander?

Activity

Drawing a Cartoon Draw a cartoon that would accompany a front-page story describing the battle between the *Merrimack* and *Monitor.*

CHAPTER 16
Section 2, 466–471

Reteaching Activity 16–2

Name ______ Date ______ Class ______

★ Reteaching Activity 16-2

DIRECTIONS: Putting Events in Sequence Number the events in the order in which they occurred.

____ **A.** George McClellan moves the Army of the Potomac by ship to begin the Peninsula Campaign.
____ **B.** The first battle between ironclad ships takes place.
____ **C.** Robert E. Lee sends Stonewall Jackson's troops to attack a Union supply base at Manassas.
____ **D.** Jefferson Davis orders Lee to launch an offensive into Maryland.
____ **E.** Confederate cavalry leader J.E.B. Stuart leads his men in a circle around the Union army to gather tactical information.
____ **F.** Union General Irwin McDowell attacks Confederate troops led by General P.G.T. Beauregard near Bull Run.
____ **G.** Ulysses S. Grant's troops narrowly defeat Confederate troops led by General Albert Sidney Johnston and Beauregard in the Battle of Shiloh.
____ **H.** Union troops claim victory in the Battle of Antietam.
____ **I.** McClellan's troops fight General Lee's troops in the Seven Days battles, which end in defeat for McClellan.
____ **J.** General McClellan becomes head of the Army of the Potomac.
____ **K.** Abraham Lincoln places General Ambrose Burnside in command of the Army of the Potomac.
____ **L.** Union naval forces under David Farragut capture New Orleans.
____ **M.** Rebel troops, with reinforcements under General Stonewall Jackson, defeat Union soldiers in Virginia.
____ **N.** The Second Battle of Bull Run begins.
____ **O.** Union forces capture the Confederate Forts Henry and Donelson.
____ **P.** Lincoln orders McClellan to join troops led by Major General John Pope.
____ **Q.** Union soldiers find a copy of Lee's orders for his army.

Enrichment Activity 16–2

Name ______ Date ______ Class ______

★ Enrichment Activity 16-2 ★

A Clash of Iron

In the spring of 1862 the first battle between ironclad ships took place off the Virginia coast. The Union sent its newly-built USS *Monitor* to attack the Confederate ship CSS *Virginia*, a ship that had been captured from the Union, fortified with iron, and renamed. The *Virginia* was the Confederate name for the *Merrimack*. The picture below shows the ships at war.

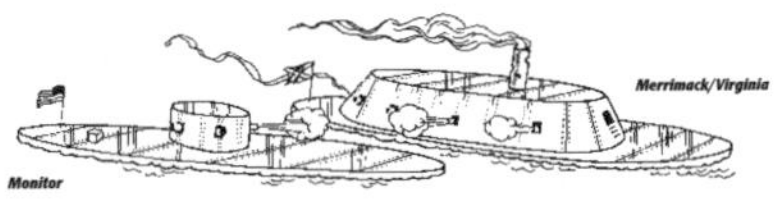

DIRECTIONS: Comparing and Contrasting Use the drawings and the information on the table to answer the questions.

Ironclad Ships

	Monitor	*Merrimack/Virginia*
Approximate relative size	smaller	larger
Source of power	steam	steam
General design	flat; sat low in water; round turret	flat base with slanted sides; triangular peak; high smokestack
Offensive weapons	cannons; main gun in turret	cannons; guns forward and to side of peaked area
Defenses	iron-covered deck; cannon balls roll off flat deck	iron-covered deck; slanted sides of turret deflect cannon balls

DIRECTIONS: Drawing Conclusions Based on the designs, which ship do you think was better prepared for attack? Which was better prepared for defense? Give reasons for your answers.

Activity **DIRECTIONS:** What do you think it would have been like inside one of these ships? Imagine that you are assigned to the *Monitor* or the *Merrimack*. Write a letter to your family at home telling about your experiences. Include specific details to give a feeling of having been there.

Section 2 Review Answers

1. George B. McClellan, 467; *Monitor* and *Merrimack*, 468; Ulysses S. Grant, 469; David Farragut, 469; Robert E. Lee, 470
2. The words are defined in the Glossary.
3. to prevent exports from getting out and imports from getting in
4. gain control of Mississippi and Tennessee Rivers
5. McClellan's goal to be perfect gave Confederacy time to prepare for attacks.

Activity Cartoons should illustrate the battle between the *Monitor* and the *Merrimack.*

4 CLOSE

Ask students to refer to the outlines they created in the "TEACH" activity to determine which side, the North or the South, had the greatest geographic advantage.

1 FOCUS

BELLRINGER
Motivational Activity

Before taking roll at the beginning of the class period, project Section Focus Transparency 16–3 and have students answer the questions. Discuss students' responses.

This activity is also available as a blackline master.

Section Focus Transparency 16–3

Vocabulary Precheck
Have students read the definition of *emancipate* on page 473. Ask them to speculate about the purpose of the Emancipation Proclamation.

Use the **Vocabulary PuzzleMaker** to create crossword and word search puzzles.

Section Theme
Groups and Institutions

The Northerners' main goal from the start of the war was to preserve the Union, not to abolish the institution of slavery. As the war continued, more and more Northerners turned against slavery.

Activity Have students read the excerpt from the Emancipation Proclamation on page 473. **Ask:** How does this excerpt show that Lincoln was very careful not to alienate the border states? *(freed only those slaves in states in rebellion against the United States)*

1862 | 1863 | 1864 | 1865

1862 African Americans allowed to serve in the Union army

January 1863 Lincoln signs the Emancipation Proclamation

July 1863 Half of the 54th Massachusetts Regiment is wiped out

1865 Thirteenth Amendment is ratified by the Union

Section 3

A Call for Freedom

READ TO DISCOVER . . .
- why Lincoln issued the Emancipation Proclamation.
- what role African Americans played in the Civil War.

TERMS TO LEARN
emancipate
ratify

The Storyteller

The rain poured on the little cabin in South Carolina. Inside, old and young slaves filled the room, sitting around a large, wooden table. One held a watch in his hand, staring at it intently. A young boy held a lit torch so a Yankee officer could see to read the president's Proclamation of Freedom. As the watch ticked closer to midnight, a deep silence fell. The holder of the watch counted: five, four, three, two, . . . Just then a loud strain of a banjo was heard. Free! They were free Americans at last!

Lincoln portrait by artist Peter Baumgras

From the start of the war through the brutal Battle of Antietam, the Northerners' main goal was to preserve the Union rather than to destroy slavery. Abolitionists did not control the North, or even the Republican Party. Abraham Lincoln and other Republican leaders insisted on many occasions that they would act only to prevent the expansion of slavery.

Although Lincoln considered slavery immoral, he hesitated to move against slavery because of the border states. Lincoln knew that making an issue of slavery would divide the people—both in the border states and in the North—and make the war less popular.

In August 1862, Abraham Lincoln responded to pressure to declare an end to slavery with a public letter stating his views.

> "If I could save the Union without freeing *any* slave, I would do it; and if I could save it by freeing *all* the slaves, I would do it; and if I could save it by freeing some and leaving others alone, I would also do that."

That was, Lincoln added, his official position. His personal wish was "that all men everywhere could be free."

Emancipation

As the war went on, attitudes toward slavery began to change. More and more Northerners believed that slavery was helping

SECTION RESOURCES

Reproducible Masters
- Reproducible Lesson Plan 16–3
- Guided Reading Activity 16–3
- Section Quiz 16–3
- Reteaching Activity 16–3
- Enrichment Activity 16–3

Transparencies
- Section Focus Transparency 16–3

Multimedia
- Vocabulary PuzzleMaker
- Chapter Challenger Interactive Review Software
- Testmaker
- Facts On File: Landmark Documents in American History

the war effort in the South. The 3.5 million slaves in the Confederacy formed the backbone of the Southern economy. They raised much of the crops used to feed the armies, and they did the heavy work in the trenches at the army camps. In their view anything that weakened slavery struck a blow against the Confederacy.

As early as May 1861, some African Americans in the South escaped slavery by going into territory held by the Union army. In 1861 and 1862, Congress passed laws that freed enslaved people who were used to support the Confederate war effort or held by people active in the rebellion against the Union.

Citizenship

The Emancipation Proclamation

Lincoln was keenly aware of the shifts in public opinion. He also knew that striking a blow against slavery would make Britain and France less likely to aid the South. Moreover, Lincoln became convinced that slavery helped the South continue fighting. Every enslaved person who worked enabled a white Southerner to fight in the Confederate army.

Lincoln had political reasons as well for taking action on slavery. He believed it was important that the president rather than the antislavery Republicans in Congress make the decision on ending slavery. Lincoln told his cabinet, "I must do the best I can, and bear the responsibility."

By the summer of 1862, Lincoln had decided to **emancipate,** or free, all enslaved African Americans in the South. He waited, however, for the right moment. He did not want to appear to be acting in desperation when the North seemed to be losing the war.

After the Union forces turned back the Confederate troops at the Battle of Antietam, Lincoln decided to act. Five days after that battle, on September 22, 1862, he announced his plan to issue an order freeing all enslaved people in the Confederacy. On January 1, 1863, Lincoln formally signed the **Emancipation Proclamation,** which said that

> "... all persons held as slaves within any state ... in rebellion against the United States, shall be then, thenceforward, and forever free."

Effects of the Proclamation

Because the Emancipation Proclamation applied only to areas that the Confederacy controlled, it did not actually free anyone. Lincoln knew, however, that many enslaved people would hear about the proclamation. He hoped that knowledge of it would encourage them to run away from their slaveholders. Even before the Emancipation Proclamation, some 100,000 African Americans had left slavery for the safety of Union lines.

Despite the limitations of the Emancipation Proclamation, African Americans in the North greeted it joyfully. On the day it was signed, a crowd of African Americans gathered at the White House to cheer the president. Frederick

HISTORY AND ART ***First Reading of the Emancipation Proclamation*** **by Francis Bicknell Carpenter** After the Union victory at Antietam, President Lincoln issued the Emancipation Proclamation. **What amendment to the Constitution ended slavery?**

Cooperative Learning Activity

Creating a Battle Diorama Organize the class into groups of four to create a diorama of the all-African American 54th Massachusetts' attack on Fort Wagner. Describe this fort to students as a Confederate, earthen fort made out of piled-up sand with timber and sandbags that sat at the entrance to Charleston Harbor. The fort mounted 11 heavy guns and numerous mobile field pieces that could be run into position when needed. The only possible approach was up the beach from the south. Allow students to choose from the following roles: create three-dimensional battlefield with fort, create the battle figures, create the artillery and weapons, and create labels for all items displayed. Have each group assemble their diorama.

2 TEACH

L1 Developing a Story Map Have students work in small groups to create a story map detailing the story leading up to the Emancipation Proclamation. Review with students the four steps of plot development in story maps: 1) introduction of the problem, 2) roadblocks, 3) climax or high point, and 4) solution. Ask groups to present their completed story maps to the class. Discuss how the "plot thickened" to enable President Lincoln to issue the Emancipation Proclamation.

Guided Reading Activity 16–3

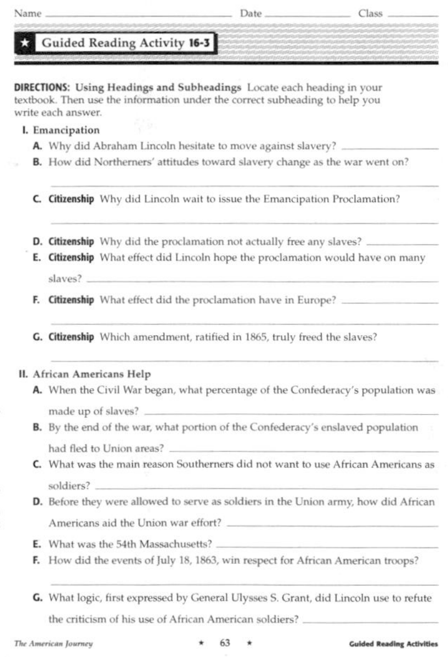

Name ______ Date ______ Class ______

★ Guided Reading Activity **16-3**

DIRECTIONS: Using Headings and Subheadings Locate each heading in your textbook. Then use the information under the correct subheading to help you write each answer.

I. Emancipation

A. Why did Abraham Lincoln hesitate to move against slavery? ______

B. How did Northerners' attitudes toward slavery change as the war went on? ______

C. Citizenship Why did Lincoln wait to issue the Emancipation Proclamation? ______

D. Citizenship Why did the proclamation not actually free any slaves? ______

E. Citizenship What effect did Lincoln hope the proclamation would have on many slaves? ______

F. Citizenship What effect did the proclamation have in Europe? ______

G. Citizenship Which amendment, ratified in 1865, truly freed the slaves? ______

II. African Americans Help

A. When the Civil War began, what percentage of the Confederacy's population was made up of slaves? ______

B. By the end of the war, what portion of the Confederacy's enslaved population had fled to Union areas? ______

C. What was the main reason Southerners did not want to use African Americans as soldiers? ______

D. Before they were allowed to serve as soldiers in the Union army, how did African Americans aid the Union war effort? ______

E. What was the 54th Massachusetts? ______

F. How did the events of July 18, 1863, win respect for African American troops? ______

G. What logic, first expressed by General Ulysses S. Grant, did Lincoln use to refute the criticism of his use of African American soldiers? ______

Copyright © by The McGraw-Hill Companies, Inc.

The American Journey ★ 63 ★ **Guided Reading Activities**

HISTORY AND ART Before President Lincoln began to read his draft of the Proclamation to his cabinet, he said, "I have got you together to hear what I have written down. I do not wish your advice about the main matter, for that I have determined for myself. . . . I must do the best I can and bear the responsibility of taking the course which I feel I ought to take." **Ask: How are Lincoln's Cabinet members shown responding to Lincoln's reading?** *(Answers should describe facial expressions and body language.)* **Answer:** *Thirteenth Amendment*

CHAPTER 16
Section 3, 472–475

What?Where?When?Who?

Emancipation Proclamation The Emancipation Proclamation not only freed the slaves in states in rebellion but also authorized the recruitment of freed slaves and free blacks as Union soldiers. During the two years after the Proclamation, 180,000 African Americans fought in the Union army and 10,000 in the navy.

Facts On File

CD-ROM
Landmark Documents in American History

Title: *Emancipation Proclamation, Abraham Lincoln, 1863*
Have students review the document and then discuss the impact it might have had on Americans.

3 ASSESS

Assign Section 3 Review as homework or as an in-class activity.

Use **Chapter Challenger Interactive Review Software** to review Section 3.

Section Quiz 16–3

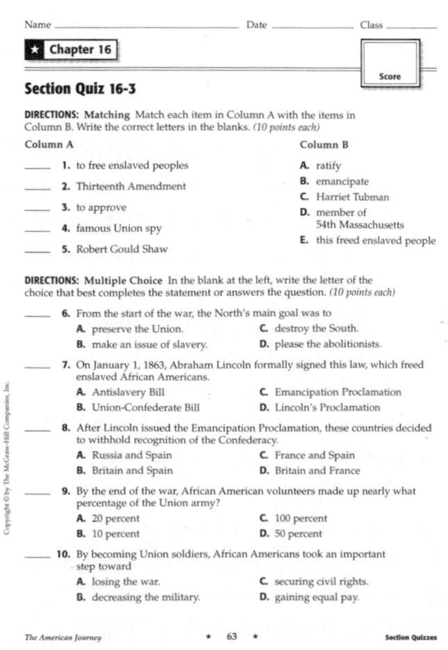
Name ________ Date ________ Class ________

Chapter 16 Score

Section Quiz 16-3

DIRECTIONS: Matching Match each item in Column A with the items in Column B. Write the correct letters in the blanks. *(10 points each)*

Column A	Column B
____ 1. to free enslaved peoples	A. ratify
____ 2. Thirteenth Amendment	B. emancipate
____ 3. to approve	C. Harriet Tubman
____ 4. famous Union spy	D. member of 54th Massachusetts
____ 5. Robert Gould Shaw	E. this freed enslaved people

DIRECTIONS: Multiple Choice In the blank at the left, write the letter of the choice that best completes the statement or answers the question. *(10 points each)*

____ 6. From the start of the war, the North's main goal was to
A. preserve the Union. C. destroy the South.
B. make an issue of slavery. D. please the abolitionists.

____ 7. On January 1, 1863, Abraham Lincoln formally signed this law, which freed enslaved African Americans.
A. Antislavery Bill C. Emancipation Proclamation
B. Union-Confederate Bill D. Lincoln's Proclamation

____ 8. After Lincoln issued the Emancipation Proclamation, these countries decided to withhold recognition of the Confederacy.
A. Russia and Spain C. France and Spain
B. Britain and Spain D. Britain and France

____ 9. By the end of the war, African American volunteers made up nearly what percentage of the Union army?
A. 20 percent C. 100 percent
B. 10 percent D. 50 percent

____ 10. By becoming Union soldiers, African Americans took an important step toward
A. losing the war. C. securing civil rights.
B. decreasing the military. D. gaining equal pay.

The American Journey ★ 63 ★ **Section Quizzes**

Frederick Douglass's son, Charles, was a member of the 54th Massachusetts Regiment.

Douglass wrote, "We shout for joy that we live to record this righteous decree."

The proclamation had the desired effect in Europe as well. The Confederacy had been seeking support from its longtime trading partners, Britain and France. However, the British took a strong position against slavery. Once Lincoln proclaimed emancipation, Britain—and France as well—decided to withhold recognition of the Confederacy.

In 1864 Republican leaders in Congress prepared a constitutional amendment to abolish slavery everywhere in the United States. In 1865 Congress passed the **Thirteenth Amendment,** which was **ratified,** or approved, the same year by states loyal to the Union. It was this amendment that truly freed the slaves in the United States.

African Americans Help

The Emancipation Proclamation and the Thirteenth Amendment changed the status of enslaved African Americans. Meanwhile, in both the South and the North, the war changed the lives of all African Americans.

In the South

When the Civil War began, about 3.5 million enslaved people lived in the Confederacy. Making up almost 40 percent of the region's population and the bulk of its workforce, slaves labored on plantations and in the vital iron, salt, and lead mines. Some also worked as nurses in military hospitals and cooks in the army. By the end of the war, about one-fourth of the enslaved population had fled to areas controlled by Union armies.

The possibility of a slave rebellion terrified white Southerners. For this reason most Southerners refused to consider using African Americans as soldiers—for then they would be given weapons.

Near the end of the war, however, the military situation of the Confederacy became desperate. Robert E. Lee and some other leaders supported using African Americans as soldiers and believed that those who fought should be freed. The Confederate Congress passed a law in 1865 to enlist enslaved people, although the law did not include automatic freedom. The war ended before any regiments could be organized.

Helping the North

The story was different in the North. At the start of the war, African Americans were not permitted to serve as soldiers in the Union army. This was a bitter disappointment to thousands of free African Americans living in the North who volunteered to fight for the Union.

Yet African Americans who wished to help the war effort found ways to do so. Although the army would not accept African American volunteers, the Union navy did. African Americans who had escaped slavery often proved to be especially useful to the North as guides and spies because of their knowledge of the South. Some women helped in this way as well. **Harriet Tubman,** who had helped hundreds escape slavery by way of the Underground Railroad, repeatedly spied behind Confederate lines.

In 1862 Congress passed a law allowing African Americans to serve in the Union army. As a result both free African Americans and those who had escaped slavery began enlisting. In the Emancipation Proclamation, Lincoln supported

Footnotes to History

A Soldier's ID Heavy death tolls in battle led Civil War soldiers to devise the first dog tags for identification if they were killed. Soldiers printed their names and addresses on handkerchiefs or paper, which they pinned to their clothing before going into battle.

MULTIPLE LEARNING STYLES

Auditory/Musical Make available to students a copy of the Emancipation Proclamation. Working in pairs, students should choose a part of the proclamation they think is the most important and rewrite it in their own words. Then have each pair write a rap song using these words to rap to the class. **L2**

the use of African American soldiers, and this helped increase the movement of African Americans into the military.

By the end of the war, African American volunteers made up nearly 10 percent of the Union army and 20 percent of the navy. In all, more than 200,000 African Americans served. About 37,000 lost their lives defending the Union.

By becoming soldiers, African Americans were taking an important step toward securing civil rights. Abolitionist Frederick Douglass, himself an escaped slave, understood the point well:

> "[Just] once let the black man get upon his person the brass letters, *U.S.;* let him get an eagle on his button, and a musket on his shoulder and bullets in his pocket, and there is no power on earth which can deny that he has earned the right to citizenship."

African American Soldiers

African American soldiers were organized into regiments separate from the rest of the Union army. Most commanding officers of these regiments were white. African Americans received lower pay than white soldiers at first, but protests led to equal pay in 1864.

One of the most famous African American regiments was the **54th Massachusetts,** led by white abolitionists. On July 18, 1863, the 54th spearheaded a dramatic attack on a Confederate fortification near Charleston, South Carolina. With Colonel Robert Gould Shaw shouting, "Forward Fifty-Fourth!" the troops charged ahead and battled their way to the top of the fort. The Confederates drove them back with heavy fire. Nearly half of the soldiers in the 54th were wounded, captured, or killed. Their bravery under fire won respect for African American troops.

Lincoln's political opponents criticized the use of African American soldiers. Lincoln replied by quoting General Grant. Grant had written him that African Americans "will make good soldiers and taking them from the enemy weakens him in the same proportion they strengthen us."

Many white Southerners, outraged by the African American soldiers, threatened to execute any that they captured. In a few instances, this threat was carried out. However, slaves were overjoyed when they saw that the Union army included African American soldiers. As one African American regiment entered Wilmington, North Carolina, a soldier wrote, "Men and women, old and young, were running throughout the streets, shouting and praising God. We could then truly see what we have been fighting for."

Section 3 Review

Checking for Understanding

1. ***Identify*** Emancipation Proclamation, Thirteenth Amendment, Harriet Tubman.
2. ***Define*** emancipate, ratify.
3. ***Summarize*** President Lincoln's reasons for issuing the Emancipation Proclamation.

Reviewing Themes

4. **Groups and Institutions** Why did abolitionist Frederick Douglass think it was important for African Americans to be allowed to fight in the Civil War?

Critical Thinking

5. **Making Comparisons** How did President Lincoln's political and personal stands on slavery differ during the war?

Activity

Sewing a Banner Imagine that you are an enslaved African American and you learn about the passage of the Thirteenth Amendment. Using material, thread, beads, and/or felt letters, sew a banner that you anticipate carrying in a parade after the Civil War is over.

Section 3 Review Answers

1. Emancipation Proclamation, 473; Thirteenth Amendment, 474; Harriet Tubman, 474
2. The words are defined in the Glossary.
3. to weaken the South by encouraging slaves to run away, to encourage Britain and France to stop supporting the South, to earn public support by ending slavery
4. to give African Americans equal footing to other citizens
5. political: first priority to restore Union; personal: opposed slavery

Activity Banners should reflect enslaved persons' happiness about their freedom and the end of the war.

CHAPTER 16
Section 3, 472–475

Reteaching Activity 16–3

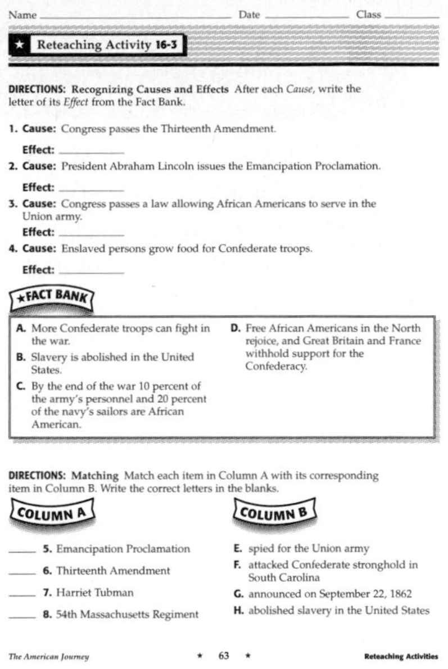
Name ______ Date ______ Class ______

Reteaching Activity 16-3

DIRECTIONS: Recognizing Causes and Effects After each *Cause,* write the letter of its *Effect* from the Fact Bank.

1. Cause: Congress passes the Thirteenth Amendment.
   Effect: ______
2. Cause: President Abraham Lincoln issues the Emancipation Proclamation.
   Effect: ______
3. Cause: Congress passes a law allowing African Americans to serve in the Union army.
   Effect: ______
4. Cause: Enslaved persons grow food for Confederate troops.
   Effect: ______

FACT BANK

A. More Confederate troops can fight in the war.
B. Slavery is abolished in the United States.
C. By the end of the war 10 percent of the army's personnel and 20 percent of the navy's sailors are African American.
D. Free African Americans in the North rejoice, and Great Britain and France withhold support for the Confederacy.

DIRECTIONS: Matching Match each item in Column A with its corresponding item in Column B. Write the correct letters in the blanks.

COLUMN A	COLUMN B
____ 5. Emancipation Proclamation	E. spied for the Union army
____ 6. Thirteenth Amendment	F. attacked Confederate stronghold in South Carolina
____ 7. Harriet Tubman	G. announced on September 22, 1862
____ 8. 54th Massachusetts Regiment	H. abolished slavery in the United States

The American Journey ★ 63 ★ Reteaching Activities

Enrichment Activity 16–3

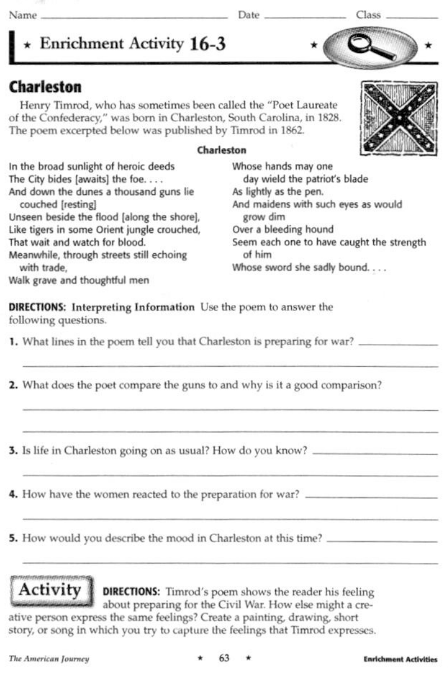
Name ______ Date ______ Class ______

Enrichment Activity 16-3

Charleston

Henry Timrod, who has sometimes been called the "Poet Laureate of the Confederacy," was born in Charleston, South Carolina, in 1828. The poem excerpted below was published by Timrod in 1862.

Charleston

In the broad sunlight of heroic deeds
The City bides [awaits] the foe. . . .
And down the dunes a thousand guns lie
couched [resting]
Unseen beside the flood [along the shore],
Like tigers in some Orient jungle crouched,
That wait and watch for blood.
Meanwhile, through streets still echoing
with trade,
Walk grave and thoughtful men
Whose hands may one
day wield the patriot's blade
As lightly as the pen.
And maidens with such eyes as would
grow dim
Over a bleeding hound
Seem each one to have caught the strength
of him
Whose sword she sadly bound. . . .

DIRECTIONS: Interpreting Information Use the poem to answer the following questions.

1. What lines in the poem tell you that Charleston is preparing for war? ______
2. What does the poet compare the guns to and why is it a good comparison? ______
3. Is life in Charleston going on as usual? How do you know? ______
4. How have the women reacted to the preparation for war? ______
5. How would you describe the mood in Charleston at this time? ______

Activity DIRECTIONS: Timrod's poem shows the reader his feeling about preparing for the Civil War. How else might a creative person express the same feelings? Create a painting, drawing, short story, or song in which you try to capture the feelings that Timrod expresses.

The American Journey ★ 63 ★ Enrichment Activities

4 CLOSE

Discuss the following quotation made by American historian Henry Adams while he was in London: "The Emancipation Proclamation has done more for us here than all our former victories and all our diplomacy. It is creating an almost convulsive reaction in our favor."

1 FOCUS

BELLRINGER
Motivational Activity

Before taking roll at the beginning of the class period, project Section Focus Transparency 16–4 and have students answer the questions. Discuss students' responses.

This activity is also available as a blackline master.

Section Focus Transparency 16–4

Vocabulary Precheck

Write the entries listed under **Terms to Learn** on the chalkboard. Have volunteers skim the section to find each term and paraphrase its meaning for the class.

Use the **Vocabulary PuzzleMaker** to create crossword and word search puzzles.

Section Theme
Economic Factors

The Civil War strained the Northern and Southern economies. The North, with its greater resources, was better able to cope with wartime demands.

Activity Have students imagine that they are factory owners or transportation specialists in either the North or the South. Ask them to provide a plan showing how they would convert their peacetime industries to provide needed military supplies and means of transportation.

1861 1862 1863 1864

1861 Union Congress passes income tax

April 1862 Confederate Congress passes draft law

March 1863 The Union passes draft law

July 1863 Angry mobs oppose the draft in New York City

Section 4

Life During the Civil War

READ TO DISCOVER . . .
- what life was like for soldiers in the Civil War.
- what role women played in the war.
- how the war affected the economies of the North and the South.

TERMS TO LEARN
habeas corpus
draft
bounty
greenback
inflation

The Storyteller

A soldier's life was not easy—whether in battle or in the mess tent! A Louisiana soldier wrote, "No soldier will forget his first horsemeat breakfast. It was comical to see the facial expression as they viewed the platters of hot steak fried in its own grease or the 'chunk' of boiled mule as it floated in a bucket of 'stew.' However, there seemed to be perfect good humor as they one after the other 'tackled the job.' . . . Occasionally would some stalwart fellow throw back his head and utter a long and loud 'Ye-ha, ye-ha, ye-haw!' in imitation of a . . . mule."

Union soldier and family

In both the North and the South, civilians and soldiers suffered terrible hardships and faced new challenges. In touching letters to their families and friends at home, soldiers described what they saw and how they felt—their boredom, discomfort, sickness, fear, and horror.

The Lives of Soldiers

At the start of the war, men in both the North and the South rushed to volunteer for the armies. Their enthusiasm did not last.

Most of the time, the soldiers lived in camps. Camp life had its pleasant moments of songs, stories, letters from home, and baseball games. Often, however, a soldier's life was dull, a routine of drills, bad food, marches, and rain.

During lulls between battles, Confederate and Union soldiers sometimes forgot that they were enemies. A Southern private described a Fourth of July on the front lines in 1862:

> "Our boys and Yanks made a bargain not to fire at each other . . . and talked over the fight, and traded tobacco and coffee and newspaper as peacefully and kindly as if they had not been engaged . . . in butchering one another."

The Reality of War

In spite of the fleeting moments of calm, the reality of war was never far away. Both sides suffered terrible losses in the fighting. The new rifles

SECTION RESOURCES

Reproducible Masters
- Guided Reading Activity 16–4
- Section Quiz 16–4
- Reteaching Activity 16–4
- Enrichment Activity 16–4

Transparencies
- Section Focus Transparency 16–4
- U.S. History & Art, Transparency 11

Multimedia
- Vocabulary PuzzleMaker
- Chapter Challenger Interactive Review Software
- Testmaker

used during the Civil War fired with greater accuracy than the muskets of earlier wars.

Both sides used trench warfare. Soldiers dug trenches in the ground to hold their positions; they often inflicted great damage on attackers. Some generals, however, continued to launch charge after charge toward the trenches, resulting in thousands of casualties.

Medical facilities were overwhelmed by the thousands of casualties in each battle. After the Battle of Shiloh, many wounded soldiers lay in the rain for more than 24 hours waiting for treatment. A Union soldier reported, "Many had died there, and others were in the last agonies as we passed. Their groans and cries were heart-rending."

Faced with such horrors, many men deserted. About one of every 11 Union soldiers and one of every 8 Confederates ran away because of fear, hunger, or sickness.

Rebel soldiers suffered from a lack of food and supplies that worsened during the war. One reason for Lee's invasion of Maryland in 1862 was to allow his hungry army to feed off Maryland crops. A woman who saw the Confederates march to Antietam recalled the "gaunt starvation that looked from their cavernous eyes."

Women and the War

★ Many Northern and Southern women took on new responsibilities during the war. They became teachers, office workers, salesclerks, and government workers. They worked in factories and managed farms. They also suffered the loss of husbands, fathers, sons, and brothers. As Southerner **Mary Chesnut** wrote:

> "Does anyone wonder [why] so many women die? Grief and constant anxiety kill nearly as many women at home as men are killed on the battle-field."

Aiding the Troops

Women performed many jobs that helped the soldiers and the armies. They rolled bandages, wove blankets, and made ammunition. Many women collected food, clothing, and medicine for distribution to the troops. They also raised money to buy needed supplies.

Some women served as spies. While Harriet Tubman spied for the North, **Rose O'Neal Greenhow** entertained Union leaders in Washington, D.C., picking up information about Union plans that she passed to the South. Greenhow was caught, convicted of treason, and exiled, eventually going to Britain. **Belle Boyd** of Front Royal, Virginia, kept Confederate generals informed of Union army movements in the Shenandoah Valley. A few women even disguised themselves as men and became soldiers. **Loretta Janeta Velázquez** fought for the South at the First Battle of Bull Run and at Shiloh. Later the Havana, Cuba, native became a spy for the Confederacy.

Treating the Sick and Wounded

In the Civil War, for the first time, thousands of women served as nurses. At first many doctors did not want women nurses on the grounds that women were too delicate for such work. Men also

Picturing HISTORY This 1862 photo shows a Union soldier with his family at the front near Washington, D.C. Most soldiers on both sides, however, faced long separations from their families. **What other hardships did Civil War soldiers face?**

CHAPTER 16
Section 4, 476–480

2 TEACH

L1, ELL Making a Chart Have students work in small groups to make a chart of economic advantages and disadvantages of the North and the South. Ask a volunteer from each group to share the chart with the class. Use each group's information to make a class chart on the bulletin board titled *The Economics of War.*

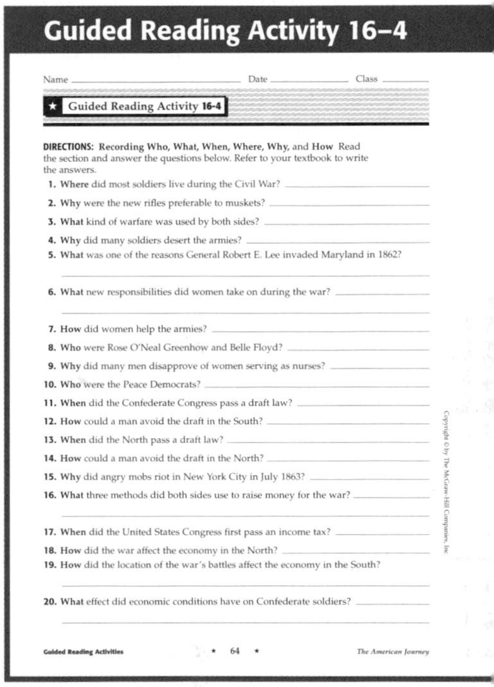

Guided Reading Activity 16–4

Name ______ Date ______ Class ______

★ Guided Reading Activity **16-4**

DIRECTIONS: Recording Who, What, When, Where, Why, and **How** Read the section and answer the questions below. Refer to your textbook to write the answers.

1. **Where** did most soldiers live during the Civil War? ______
2. **Why** were the new rifles preferable to muskets? ______
3. **What** kind of warfare was used by both sides? ______
4. **Why** did many soldiers desert the armies? ______
5. **What** was one of the reasons General Robert E. Lee invaded Maryland in 1862? ______
6. **What** new responsibilities did women take on during the war? ______
7. **How** did women help the armies? ______
8. **Who** were Rose O'Neal Greenhow and Belle Floyd? ______
9. **Why** did many men disapprove of women serving as nurses? ______
10. **Who** were the Peace Democrats? ______
11. **When** did the Confederate Congress pass a draft law? ______
12. **How** could a man avoid the draft in the South? ______
13. **When** did the North pass a draft law? ______
14. **How** could a man avoid the draft in the North? ______
15. **Why** did angry mobs riot in New York City in July 1863? ______
16. **What** three methods did both sides use to raise money for the war? ______
17. **When** did the United States Congress first pass an income tax? ______
18. **How** did the war affect the economy in the North? ______
19. **How** did the location of the war's battles affect the economy in the South? ______
20. **What** effect did economic conditions have on Confederate soldiers? ______

Copyright © by The McGraw-Hill Companies, Inc.

Guided Reading Activities ★ 64 ★ *The American Journey*

Picturing HISTORY The army hired its own photographers to produce pictures of such things as field fortifications, bridges, and major buildings. Civilian photographers also photographed the war.
Answer: *lack of food and supplies, pain, casualties, boredom, sickness, discomfort, fear, horror, bad weather*

COOPERATIVE LEARNING ACTIVITY

Designing a Newspaper Page Organize the class into groups of four to create a newspaper page highlighting selected topics about the Civil War. Have each group choose whether to describe a Northern or Southern newspaper and decide on a name for the newspaper. Then allow group members to choose from the following roles: draw a political cartoon, design an advertisement to raise money for the war effort, write an article on women's roles in the war, and write an interview with a person living at that time. Have each group either paste up the completed pieces of the newspaper page onto newsprint or compose the page on the computer using desktop publishing software.

HISTORY AND ART Some artists such as William L. Sheppard, a second lieutenant in the Richmond Howitzers and later in the Confederate Engineers, accompanied the armies to produce paintings. After the war Sheppard studied in Paris and produced watercolors. His watercolors of individual Confederate soldiers are in the Museum of the Confederacy. **Ask:** **Why do you think Sheppard chose to paint this scene?** *(Answers may address the importance of women in the war, the trials of the wounded, and so on.)* **Answer:** *rolled bandages; wove blankets; made ammunition; collected food, clothing, medicine for troops; raised money; took over jobs and responsibilities of men; and aided troops as nurses and spies*

CURRICULUM CONNECTION

ART
Artists during the Civil War produced drawings in the field that were sent back to their studios to be redrawn on hardwood blocks and printed as linecuts. These illustrations were produced and printed several weeks after an event so that everyone would have an opportunity to view the event.

History *and the* Humanities

- U.S. History & Art, Transparency 11, *A Rainy Day in Camp*
- The Spirit of American Art and Music, Mathew B. Brady

HISTORY AND ART ***In The Hospital, 1861* by William Sheppard**
Soldier-artist William Sheppard portrays a fashionably dressed Southern woman visiting a wounded soldier after the Battle of Bull Run (Manassas). **In what other ways did women help in the war effort?**

disapproved of women doing what was considered male work, and they felt it was improper for women to tend the bodies of unknown men.

Strong-minded women disregarded these objections. In the North **Dorothea Dix** organized large numbers of women to serve as military nurses. Another Northerner, **Clara Barton,** became famous for her work with wounded soldiers. Barton later founded the American Red Cross. In the South **Sally Tompkins** established a hospital for soldiers in Richmond, Virginia.

Nursing was not easy work. Kate Cummings of Alabama, who nursed the wounded in Corinth after the Battle of Shiloh, wrote, "Nothing that I had ever heard or read had given me the faintest idea of the horrors witnessed here." Yet women did a remarkable job in the war.

Opposition to the War

The war efforts of the Union and the Confederate governments faced opposition. Politicians objected to wartime policies, and ordinary citizens protested the way the war affected their lives.

Opposition in the North

When the war began, Northern Democrats split into two groups. One group supported most of Lincoln's wartime policies. The other, the "Peace Democrats," opposed the president and favored negotiating with the Confederacy. The Peace Democrats warned that continuing the war would lead to "terrible social change and revolution." They also appealed to racist feelings among Northern whites. Republican newspapers likened the Peace Democrats to poisonous snakes, calling them **Copperheads.** When Union armies fared poorly, support for the Copperheads rose.

Some Republicans suspected Copperheads of actively aiding the Confederates. The president ordered the arrest of anyone who interfered with the war effort—such as discouraging men from enlisting in the army. Several times Lincoln suspended the right of **habeas corpus,** which guarantees accused individuals the right to a hearing before being jailed. Lincoln defended his actions by asking, "Must I shoot a simple-minded soldier boy who deserts while I must not touch a hair of a wily agitator who induces him to desert?"

Enlistments Decline

As the war dragged on, the numbers of volunteers declined in both the North and the South. Enlisting enough soldiers became a problem, and both sides tried new measures.

In April 1862, the Confederate Congress passed a **draft** law that required men between ages 18 and 35 to serve in the army for three years. A person could avoid the draft by hiring a substitute. Later, certain groups—including slaveholders with 20 or more slaves—were exempted from the draft. This led ordinary people to complain of "a rich man's war but a poor man's fight." In

MULTIPLE LEARNING STYLES

Logical/Mathematical Write the following organizational structure of Civil War armies on the board:

Armies of the Civil War

Company = 100 soldiers	Division = 3 brigades
Regiment = 10 companies	Corps = 3 divisions
Brigade = 5 regiments	

Have students copy this information onto a sheet of paper. Ask each student to calculate and record how many soldiers made up each unit (regiment, brigade, division, corps) using *company* as a base. Continue posing calculations that require mathematical skills such as: How many companies in a brigade? How many regiments in a division? How many companies in a corps? and so on. **L2** reality people from all levels of society served in the Confederate and Union armies.

Union states encouraged enlistment by offering **bounties**—payments of $100 or more—to volunteers. In March 1863, when this system failed, the North turned to a draft. All men over 20 and under 45 had to register, and the army drew the soldiers it needed from this pool of names. A person could avoid the draft by hiring a substitute or by paying the government $300.

Resistance to the Draft

Draft laws aroused opposition in both the North and the South, with protests erupting into riots in several Northern cities. The worst disturbance took place in **New York City** in July 1863. Angry mobs opposed to the draft and to fighting to free African Americans went on a rampage of burning, looting, and killing. After 4 days of terror, more than 100 people, including about 15 African Americans, were dead. Troops from the Army of the Potomac had to be rushed in to end the rioting.

No disturbance as severe took place in the South, but many opposed the draft. The strong opposition led the president of the Confederacy, Jefferson Davis, to proclaim military law and suspend habeas corpus as Lincoln had done early in the war. Davis's action outraged Southerners who feared that they would lose the liberties for which they had gone to war.

TECHNOLOGY AND HISTORY

Civil War Camera

Mathew Brady and his many assistants recorded the camps, lives, and deaths of Union soldiers in more than 10,000 photos. **What is the biggest difference between this camera and a modern one?**

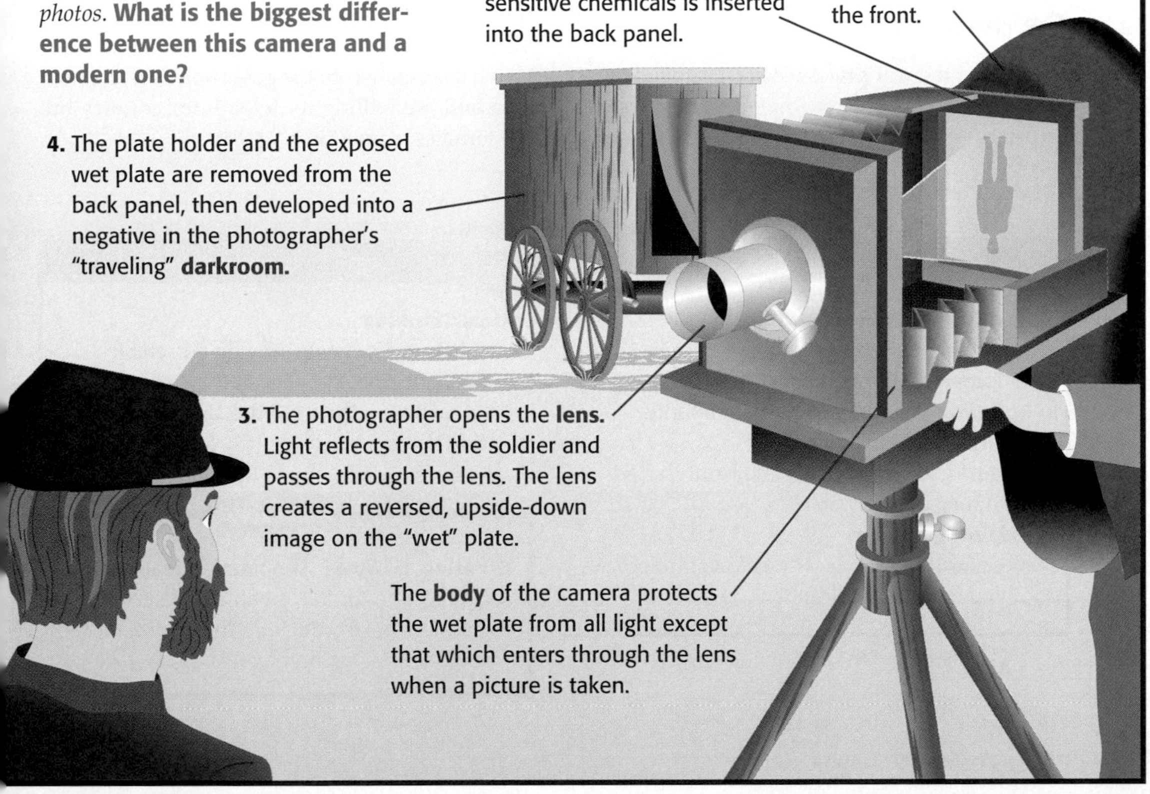

Making Connections Activity

The Arts Ask students to select a family, school, or community event and to illustrate that event with a series of photographs. Students that do not own cameras can be paired with students that do own cameras. Another alternative is to give students the choice of illustrating an event with photographs or by making a series of drawings. Ask students to present their photographic essays with and without captions. **L1, ELL**

CHAPTER 16
Section 4, 476–480

What? Where? When? Who?

The Draft The United States government also used the draft in World War I and World War II. The government drafted soldiers for the Korean and Vietnam Wars as well. Congress ended the draft in 1973. Since then the nation has relied on all-volunteer armed services.

3 ASSESS

Assign Section 4 Review as homework or as an in-class activity.

Use **Chapter Challenger Interactive Review Software** to review Section 4.

Section Quiz 16–4

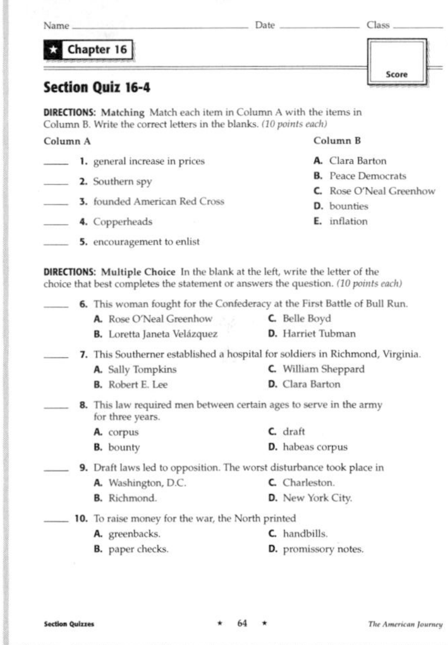
Name ______ Date ______ Class ______

★ Chapter 16 — Score

Section Quiz 16-4

DIRECTIONS: Matching Match each item in Column A with the items in Column B. Write the correct letters in the blanks. *(10 points each)*

Column A	Column B
____ 1. general increase in prices	A. Clara Barton
____ 2. Southern spy	B. Peace Democrats
____ 3. founded American Red Cross	C. Rose O'Neal Greenhow
____ 4. Copperheads	D. bounties
____ 5. encouragement to enlist	E. inflation

DIRECTIONS: Multiple Choice In the blank at the left, write the letter of the choice that best completes the statement or answers the question. *(10 points each)*

____ 6. This woman fought for the Confederacy at the First Battle of Bull Run.
A. Rose O'Neal Greenhow C. Belle Boyd
B. Loretta Janeta Velázquez D. Harriet Tubman

____ 7. This Southerner established a hospital for soldiers in Richmond, Virginia.
A. Sally Tompkins C. William Sheppard
B. Robert E. Lee D. Clara Barton

____ 8. This law required men between certain ages to serve in the army for three years.
A. corpus C. draft
B. bounty D. habeas corpus

____ 9. Draft laws led to opposition. The worst disturbance took place in
A. Washington, D.C. C. Charleston.
B. Richmond. D. New York City.

____ 10. To raise money for the war, the North printed
A. greenbacks. C. handbills.
B. paper checks. D. promissory notes.

Section Quizzes ★ 64 ★ *The American Journey*

TECHNOLOGY AND HISTORY

More About . . .

Civil War Camera Photographic methods were first invented in 1839 in England and France. Americans produced some of the first war photographs during the Mexican War. By 1861 the camera was common throughout the United States.

Answer to Caption: *Answers will vary but should note the changes in technology such as size, automation, processing film, and so on.*

CHAPTER 16
Section 4, 476–480

Reteaching Activity 16–4

Name ______ Date ______ Class ______

★ Reteaching Activity **16-4**

DIRECTIONS: Completing a Chart Write the number of the names and terms from the Fact Bank in the section of the chart where they belong. Some numbers will be used twice.

The Civil War

	Union	Confederacy
Soldiers		
Spies		
Nurses		
Economics		

★FACT BANK

EMANCIPATION PROCLAMATION

1. farmland overrun
2. sold government bonds to finance the war
3. borrowed more than $700 million to finance the war
4. draft law passed in March 1863
5. farmers prospered
6. Loretta Janeta Velázquez
7. increase in railroad construction
8. 9,000 percent rise in prices
9. one in 11 desertion rate
10. Sally Tompkins
11. draft law passed in April 1862
12. passed an income tax to finance the war
13. Dorothea Dix
14. one in 8 desertion rate
15. 80 percent rise in prices
16. Rose O'Neal Greenhow
17. borrowed more than $2 billion to finance the war
18. Harriet Tubman
19. rail lines torn up
20. Clara Barton
21. printed greenbacks to finance the war
22. Belle Boyd

DIRECTIONS: Essay Answer the following questions on a separate sheet of paper.

1. What role did women play in the Civil War?
2. Who were the "Peace Democrats"?

Reteaching Activities ★ 64 ★ *The American Journey*

Enrichment Activity 16–4

Name ______ Date ______ Class ______

★ Enrichment Activity **16-4** ★ ★

Arriving in America

Even as the Civil War raged and news of fighting spread throughout the world, immigrants, hoping for better, more peaceful lives, continued to arrive in the United States. Study the table of immigration during the war years.

Immigration to the United States, 1860–1866

Year	Great Britain	Ireland	Germany	All Other Places
1860	29,737	48,637	54,491	20,775
1861	19,675	23,797	31,661	16,785
1862	24,639	23,351	27,529	16,466
1863	66,882	55,916	33,162	20,322
1864	53,428	63,523	57,276	19,191
1865	82,465	29,772	83,424	52,459
1866	94,924	36,690	115,892	71,062

SOURCE: Bailey, Thomas A. and David M. Kennedy. *The American Pageant*. Stanford University.

DIRECTIONS: Analyzing Information Use the table to help answer the following questions.

1. Which country had the highest immigration figure for a single year? ______
   Which year? ______
2. What was the total number of immigrants who arrived in 1860? ______
   In what following year was the total number of immigrants first greater than in 1860, and by how much? ______
3. Which country had the largest total number of immigrants to the United States for 1863 to 1864? ______
   How many more immigrants arrived from that country than the country with the next largest number for 1863 to 1864? ______
4. During which two consecutive years was total immigration almost the same?
   ______
5. What percentage of all immigrants for 1865 were from Great Britain? ______

Activity **DIRECTIONS:** Make a series of bar graphs showing immigration from the different countries for three consecutive years. Then compare your graphs and write conclusions.

Enrichment Activities ★ 64 ★ *The American Journey*

4 CLOSE

Ask students to explain the following quote made by a colonel of a New York regiment: "We started out in the spring . . . smart, well provided with everything. . . . And we were returning before the autumn, sad, weary, covered with mud, with uniforms in rags."

Economics

War and the Economy

The Civil War strained the Northern and the Southern economies. The North, with its greater resources, was better able to cope with wartime demands.

Both the Union and the Confederacy financed the war by borrowing money, increasing taxes, and printing paper money. The North borrowed more than $2 billion, mainly by selling war bonds that promised high interest. The South borrowed more than $700 million. It issued so many bonds that people stopped buying them.

Both sides imposed new taxes as well. The Union passed an income tax in 1861. When Southern states did not provide sufficient funds, the Confederacy also imposed an income tax.

Because neither borrowing nor taxes raised enough money to pay for the war, both sides simply began printing paper money. Northern money was called **greenbacks** because of its color. The Confederacy also issued paper money, several times the amount printed in the North.

The North Prospers

During the war prices rose faster than wages in the North. This **inflation**—general increase in prices—caused great hardship for working people. Overall, however, the Northern economy boomed. Railroad traffic increased, as did the production of coal, iron, and clothing. The need for a steady supply of food for Union troops helped farmers prosper. Industry and agriculture responded to wartime needs by adopting new, more efficient methods of production.

Economic Troubles in the South

The economy of the South suffered far more than that of the North. Because most fighting occurred in the South, Southern farmland was overrun and rail lines were torn up. By the end of the war, large portions of the South lay in ruins, thousands of people were homeless, and many Southern cities were burned.

The North's blockade of Southern ports caused severe shortages of essential goods. A scarcity of food led to riots in Atlanta, Richmond, and other cities. Inflation, too, was much worse in the South. During the course of the war, prices rose 9,000 percent—compared to a rise of 80 percent in the North.

These conditions affected soldiers. Worries about their families caused many men to desert. A Mississippi soldier who overstayed his leave to help his family wrote the governor: "We are poor men and are willing to defend our country but our families [come] first."

Section 4 Review

Checking for Understanding

1. ***Identify*** Dorothea Dix, Clara Barton, Sally Tompkins, Copperheads.
2. ***Define*** habeas corpus, draft, bounty, greenback, inflation.
3. ***Name*** three ways that the North raised money for the war.

Reviewing Themes

4. **Economic Factors** How did war affect the economy of the South?

Critical Thinking

5. **Making Inferences** Why do you think President Lincoln believed the Copperheads were a threat to the Union war effort?

Activity

Creating a Travel Brochure Create a travel brochure of a Civil War battlefield site that you would like to visit. Include the name, location, and other activities in the area.

Section 4 Review Answers

1. Dorothea Dix, 478; Clara Barton, 478; Sally Tompkins, 478; Copperheads, 478
2. The words are defined in the Glossary.
3. borrowed money, increased taxes, printed money
4. inflation, infrastructure and land destroyed, shortage of essential goods
5. By splitting Union loyalties, Copperheads could give the Confederacy an edge. The Copperheads also appealed to racist feelings and encouraged disloyalty among Union soldiers.

Activity Call on volunteers to display and explain their travel brochures.

Technology
SKILL BUILDER

Using a CD-ROM

You have probably listened to your favorite music on compact discs. There is another type of compact disc, called a CD-ROM, that holds information. Learning how to use a CD-ROM can help you research information without spending a long time or using many resources.

Learning the Skill

CD-ROM stands for Compact Disc, Read-Only Memory. A CD-ROM stores huge amounts of information that a computer equipped with a CD-ROM drive can access in both audio and video form. This makes a CD-ROM a perfect storage place for games, simulations, dictionaries, encyclopedias, and other reference books. Using a CD-ROM disc or software loaded on your computer, you can "view" the information on your computer screen in many forms—words, pictures, video images, and even sounds.

Practicing the Skill

Follow these steps to use a CD-ROM to get information about the Civil War:

1. Check out a CD-ROM encyclopedia at your local library, and insert it into your CD-ROM drive.
2. Find your topic by using the mouse to click on the Search button in the main toolbar, typing in "Civil War," and clicking on the word *Search.* (If there is no Search button, click the Help button to learn what features are available and how to use them.)
3. Use the arrow key to scroll—move up, down, left, or right—through the list of article titles on the screen. If you double-click while pointing to an article title, the article will appear on the screen. Click the Print button on the toolbar to print the article.
4. To find out what photos are available on the Civil War, click the Picture Index button on the toolbar. When the list of picture titles appears, double-click the title of the picture you want to see. Click the Caption button to read the picture's caption.
5. Each encyclopedia is different. Check the Help menu to see how to access sound clips, videos, animations, outlines, or any other features that may be available to give you information on the Civil War.

Applying the Skill

Using a CD-ROM Using the steps just described and a CD-ROM encyclopedia, find enough information about Abraham Lincoln to tell a classmate where and when he was born, what he looked like, what his role was during the Civil War, and what he said in one of his speeches.

Technology
SKILL BUILDER

TEACH

Using a CD-ROM

This skill demonstrates how to use a CD-ROM to find information. By searching a CD-ROM database, students will find how quickly and easily specific information can be found on a CD-ROM. They will also discover how much information can be stored on a CD-ROM.

Have students work in small groups to create questions and answers that can be found on the National Geographic Society's CD-ROM *PictureShow: The Civil War.* Then have groups exchange questions and CD-ROMs and answer the questions. Have the group that created the questions check the other group's answers.

Additional Practice

Chapter Skills Activity 16

Answers to Practicing the Skill

1. Students should check out a CD-ROM about the Civil War from the library.
2. Students should search the CD-ROM for information about the Civil War.
3. Students should scroll through the information and print an article.
4. Students should find photos and read the captions.
5. Students should access the multimedia options available on the CD-ROM.

Applying the Skill Students should use the CD-ROM to find Abraham Lincoln's birth date and birthplace, details about his appearance, his role during the Civil War, and the contents of one of his speeches.

CHAPTER 16
Section 5, 482–488

1 FOCUS

BELLRINGER
Motivational Activity

Before taking roll at the beginning of the class period, project Section Focus Transparency 16–5 and have students answer the questions. Discuss students' responses.

This activity is also available as a blackline master.

Section Focus Transparency 16–5

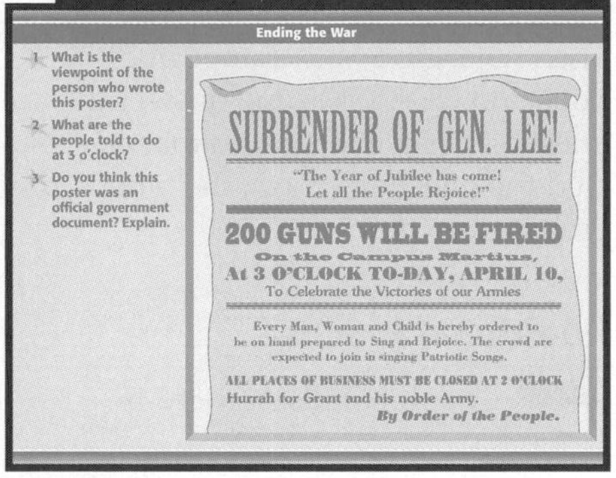
Ending the War

1. What is the viewpoint of the person who wrote this poster?
2. What are the people told to do at 3 o'clock?
3. Do you think this poster was an official government document? Explain.

SURRENDER OF GEN. LEE!

"The Year of Jubilee has come! Let all the People Rejoice!"

200 GUNS WILL BE FIRED

On the Campus Martius,

At 3 O'CLOCK TO-DAY, APRIL 10,

To Celebrate the Victories of our Armies

Every Man, Woman and Child is hereby ordered to be on hand prepared to Sing and Rejoice. The crowd are expected to join in singing Patriotic Songs.

ALL PLACES OF BUSINESS MUST BE CLOSED AT 2 O'CLOCK

Hurrah for Grant and his noble Army.

By Order of the People.

Vocabulary Precheck
Ask students to read the definition of *total war* and Sherman's quote on page 487. Ask students to interpret Sherman's quote by applying their understanding of *total war.*

Use the **Vocabulary Puzzle-Maker** to create crossword and word search puzzles.

Section Theme
Individual Action

Strong leaders from both the North and the South fought gallantly during the Civil War.

Activity Discuss the impact individual actions can have within a large group of people. Ask students whether they think one person can change the course of history.

1862 · 1863 · 1864 · 1865

December 1862 Lee wins the Battle of Fredericksburg

July 1863 Battle of Gettysburg crushes Lee's troops

March 1864 Grant takes over Union command

April 1865 Lee surrenders to Grant

Section 5

The Way to Victory

READ TO DISCOVER . . .
- what great battles turned the tide of the war in 1863.
- what events led the South to surrender in 1865.

TERMS TO LEARN

entrenched
total war

The Storyteller

"My shoes are gone; my clothes are almost gone. I'm weary, I'm sick, I'm hungry. My family have been killed or scattered, and may be now wandering helpless and unprotected in a strange country. And I have suffered all this for my country. I love my country. I would die—yes, I would die willingly because I love my country. But if this war is ever over, I'll . . . [n]ever love another country!" So wrote a Confederate soldier in 1863.

Cannon at Bull Run (Manassas) battlefield

Gone were the parades and masses of volunteers, the fancy uniforms and arrogance of the first years of the war. From 1862 until 1865, the soldiers and civilians faced a grim and grinding conflict marked by death, destruction, and wrenching change. Hopes were raised and dashed. What endured on each side was a fierce dedication to the cause for which it fought.

Southern Victories

The winter of 1862–1863 saw gloom in the North and hope in the South as Robert E. Lee's **Army of Northern Virginia** seemed unbeatable. With bold plans, quick movements, and knowledge of the countryside, Lee managed to surprise and defeat weak Union generals.

Fredericksburg and Chancellorsville

Lee needed little skill to win the **Battle of Fredericksburg.** On December 13, 1862, Union general **Ambrose Burnside** clashed with Lee near the Virginia town. Burnside had the larger army, but the Confederates were **entrenched,** or set up in a strong position, on a number of hills south of the town. Repeated attacks failed to overcome Lee's troops as thousands of Union soldiers fell on the hillside. A newspaper report concluded, "It can hardly be in human nature for men to show more valor [bravery], or generals to manifest less judgment." Devastated by his failure, Burnside resigned his command and was replaced by General **Joseph Hooker.**

SECTION RESOURCES

Reproducible Masters
- Reproducible Lesson Plan 16–5
- Guided Reading Activity 16–5
- Section Quiz 16–5
- Reteaching Activity 16–5
- Enrichment Activity 16–5

Transparencies
- Section Focus Transparency 16–5

Multimedia
- Vocabulary PuzzleMaker
- Chapter Challenger Interactive Review
- Testmaker
- NGS PictureShow: The Civil War
- Facts On File: Landmark Documents in American History
- ABCNews InterActive™ Historic America Electronic Field Trips

Hooker rebuilt the army and then, in early May 1863, launched a campaign against Lee. Before Hooker could mount a major attack, Lee struck at **Chancellorsville,** Virginia, a few miles west of Fredericksburg.

Boldly dividing his troops for an assault on the Union forces, Lee won another victory—but it proved costly. The battle's heavy casualties included General **Stonewall Jackson.** On May 2 Jackson and his troops attacked Union troops just before dark. One of the Confederate companies fired on Jackson's party by mistake, wounding the general in the left arm. Jackson's arm had to be amputated and he died a week later.

The Tide of War Turns

★ Despite his own heavy losses, Lee decided to invade the North. Another victory—one on Northern soil—might persuade Britain and France to aid the Confederacy and convince the North to give up.

The Battle of Gettysburg

In June Lee began moving north with an army of 75,000. Confederate spirits were high. A Richmond newspaper wrote, "We can . . . carry our armies far into the enemy's country, exacting peace by blows leveled at his vitals."

Union general Hooker wanted to advance against Richmond, but Lincoln told him, "I think Lee's Army, and not Richmond, is your true objective." When Hooker started to make excuses for not attacking the Confederate forces, Lincoln replaced him with General **George Meade.** Meade's mission was to find and fight Lee's forces and, at the same time, to protect Washington and Baltimore from Confederate attack. Meade began moving his army to meet the enemy.

The two armies met by accident on July 1, 1863, near the small town of Gettysburg, Pennsylvania. The three-day **Battle of Gettysburg** began when Union cavalry surprised Rebel infantry raiding the town for shoes. Outnumbered, the Northerners fought desperately to hold the town before retreating to Cemetery Ridge, a line of hills south of Gettysburg. They established strong positions along the ridge and prepared to defend it. The following day the Rebels launched another major assault and almost overran part of the Yankee line, but a counterattack saved the Union position.

America's FLAGS

Confederate Battle Flag, 1861 **During Civil War battles, soldiers had difficulty distinguishing between the Confederate and Union flags. As a result, Southern soldiers began to carry this battle flag. It had 13 stars, although there were only 11 states in the Confederacy. The other two stars represented the border states of Kentucky and Missouri, whose pro-Confederate minority governments had been admitted to the Confederacy.**

Seventeenth Flag of the Union, 1863 **The Union flag of 1863 held 35 stars. Like all the union flags of the Civil War, it retained stars for the seceded Southern states. Thus it supported Lincoln and the North's claim that the Union could not be broken.**

Eyewitness to HISTORY

Pickett's Charge

On the third and final day of battle, Lee's boldness proved his undoing. He decided to launch one more attack, determined to "create a panic and virtually destroy the [Union] army."

2 TEACH

L1 Describing Leaders Ask students to scan the section to choose one Union leader and one Confederate leader they believe had the most significant effect on the outcome of the Civil War. Then have them write a paragraph on each one, describing the outstanding leadership characteristics and the specific role each leader played during the Civil War. Ask volunteers to share their paragraphs with the class.

Guided Reading Activity 16–5

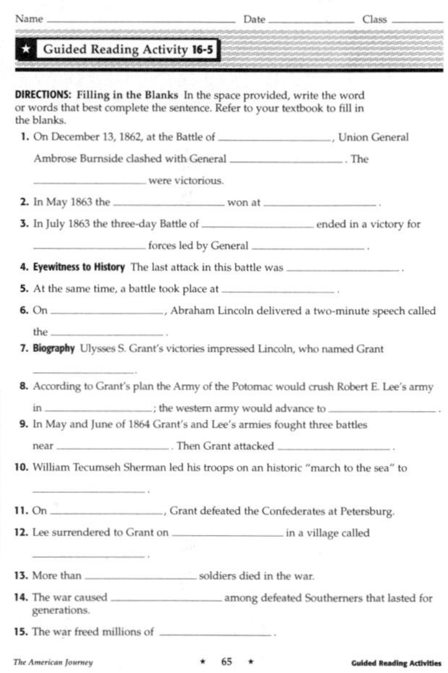

Name ________ Date ________ Class ________

★ Guided Reading Activity **16-5**

DIRECTIONS: Filling in the Blanks In the space provided, write the word or words that best complete the sentence. Refer to your textbook to fill in the blanks.

1. On December 13, 1862, at the Battle of ________, Union General Ambrose Burnside clashed with General ________. The ________ were victorious.
2. In May 1863 the ________ won at ________.
3. In July 1863 the three-day Battle of ________ ended in a victory for ________ forces led by General ________.
4. **Eyewitness to History** The last attack in this battle was ________.
5. At the same time, a battle took place at ________.
6. On ________, Abraham Lincoln delivered a two-minute speech called the ________.
7. **Biography** Ulysses S. Grant's victories impressed Lincoln, who named Grant ________.
8. According to Grant's plan the Army of the Potomac would crush Robert E. Lee's army in ________; the western army would advance to ________.
9. In May and June of 1864 Grant's and Lee's armies fought three battles near ________. Then Grant attacked ________.
10. William Tecumseh Sherman led his troops on an historic "march to the sea" to ________.
11. On ________, Grant defeated the Confederates at Petersburg.
12. Lee surrendered to Grant on ________ in a village called ________.
13. More than ________ soldiers died in the war.
14. The war caused ________ among defeated Southerners that lasted for generations.
15. The war freed millions of ________.

The American Journey ★ 65 ★ **Guided Reading Activities**

you don't say...

Sideburns are named for the Union commander Ambrose E. Burnside. His distinctive muttonchop whiskers inspired a fashion, which became known as burnsides. Within 10 years the two syllables had been transposed.

COOPERATIVE LEARNING ACTIVITY

Illustrating a Time Line of Battles Assign each group of four students a battle described in this section that led to the South's surrender. Have students in each group choose one of these roles: draw a map locating the battle site, write a description of the most colorful leader of the battle, write a description of the battle events, and illustrate a part of the battle. As a class create a bulletin board-sized time line of the dates of the assigned battles. Have each group post the completed battle information on the appropriate place on the time line.

you don't say...

Civil War Terms The Civil War was the first war in which strictly military terms were passed into wider usage. Many of these terms still used in common speech today are *K.P.* (kitchen police), *AWOL* (absent without leave), *pup tents* (originally known as dog tents), *grapevine* (medium for transmission of rumors), and *shoddy* (uniforms poorly made from recycled woolen fibers known as shoddy, which came to denote any article of inferior quality).

Who?What?Where?When?

Hero of Little Round Top The extreme left flank of the Union lines at Gettysburg—a hill called Little Round Top—was commanded by Colonel Joshua Lawrence Chamberlain, a college professor who had taken a leave from teaching to fight in the war. Chamberlain knew that if the Confederates took Little Round Top, they would have a view of the whole Union line. Although greatly outnumbered, Chamberlain's forces withstood numerous attacks. Finally, Chamberlain led his troops in a bayonet charge that drove the Confederates from the hill. Chamberlain received the Medal of Honor for his bravery at Gettysburg.

Map Study

Answers
1. Chickamauga
2. Grant

Map Skills Practice

Reading a Map Who led troops from the Gulf of Mexico? *(Farragut)*

This last attack, led by General George Pickett, is remembered as **Pickett's Charge.** About 13,000 Confederate soldiers advanced across about one-half mile of open ground toward the Union lines. Faced with this bold attack, the Union soldiers rushed to defend their position.

Confederate soldiers made easy targets for Union fire as they marched across the open fields. Few of the Rebels reached the center of the Union lines, and barely half returned from the charge. The next day a Union officer said:

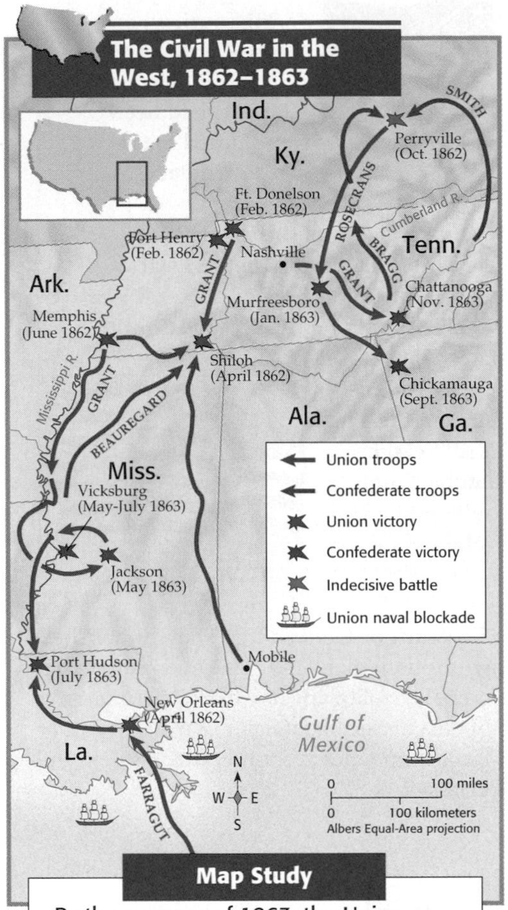

Map Study

By the summer of 1863, the Union controlled the lower Mississippi River.

1. **Location** What battle in Georgia did Union forces lose?
2. **Analyzing Information** Who led the Union troops at Shiloh, Tennessee?

> "I tried to ride over the field but could not, for dead and wounded lay too thick to guide a horse through them."

Lee knew the battle was lost. "It's all my fault," he told his troops. He waited one day for a counterattack that never came and then painfully retreated to Virginia.

General Meade was proud of the victory, but Lincoln was disappointed. Upset that the Union army had once again allowed Lee and his soldiers to get away, Lincoln exclaimed,"We had them in our grasp. We had only to stretch forth our hands and they were ours."

Victory at Vicksburg

While Confederate and Union troops were fighting at Gettysburg, a great battle was also taking place at **Vicksburg, Mississippi.** Vicksburg stood on a high bluff above the Mississippi River. To gain control of the river, one of the North's major war goals, the Union needed to seize Vicksburg. For several months, Union forces under Ulysses S. Grant had laid siege to the town. Finally, on July 4, 1863, Vicksburg surrendered.

With the surrender of Vicksburg and then Port Hudson—another Confederate fort in Louisiana—the Union now held the entire Mississippi River. Texas, Louisiana, and Arkansas were sealed off from the rest of the Confederacy.

The Union victories at Gettysburg and Vicksburg marked a turning point in the war. They drove Lee's army out of Pennsylvania, secured the Mississippi as a Union highway, and cut the South in two. Nevertheless, the South still had troops and a will to fight. The war would continue for two more terrible years.

Lincoln at Gettysburg

On November 19, 1863, at a ceremony dedicating a cemetery at Gettysburg, Edward Everett, a prominent scholar, gave a two-hour address. Then President Lincoln rose to speak. In a two-minute speech, called the **Gettysburg Address,** Lincoln beautifully expressed what the war had come to mean:

MULTIPLE LEARNING STYLES

Intrapersonal Ask students to imagine what it would have been like to be at General Lee's surrender at Appomattox Court House. Then have each student choose to describe a Northern or a Southern viewpoint of this surrender by writing a first-person account of the personal and emotional impact of the surrender. **L2**

Picturing HISTORY The Union won an important victory at the Battle of Chattanooga when forces under General Ulysses S. Grant (right) drove the Confederates from the high ground around the city. **To what military position did Lincoln name Grant after Chattanooga?**

> "It is for us the living . . . to be here dedicated to the great task remaining before us . . . that these dead shall not have died in vain—that this nation, under God, shall have a new birth of freedom—and that government of the people, by the people, for the people shall not perish from the earth."

The speech helped war-weary Americans look beyond the images of the battlefield and focus on their shared ideals.

Final Phases of the War

In November 1863, Grant and General **William Tecumseh Sherman** won an important victory at Chattanooga, Tennessee. Following the Northern triumphs at Vicksburg and Gettysburg, Chattanooga further weakened the Confederates. The following March, President Lincoln turned to Grant for help.

Biography

Grant Takes Command

Ulysses S. Grant was small and unimpressive in appearance. His early army career was not impressive either, and in 1854 he had been forced to resign because of a drinking problem. When the Civil War broke out, he rejoined the army. Grant's victories in the West and his willingness to attack hard and keep fighting impressed President Lincoln. "I can't spare this man," the president said. "He fights." After the victory at Chattanooga, Lincoln named Grant commander of all the Union armies.

Grant devised a plan to attack the Confederacy on all fronts at once. The Army of the Potomac would try to crush Lee's army in Virginia. The western army, under Sherman, would advance to **Atlanta, Georgia,** and crush the Confederate forces in the Deep South. If the plan succeeded, they would destroy the Confederacy.

Virginia Battles

Grant soon put his strategy into effect. In May and June of 1864, his army of 115,000 men smashed into Lee's 65,000 troops in a series of 3 battles near Richmond—the Battles of the Wilderness, Spotsylvania Courthouse, and Cold Harbor. Each time, Confederate lines held, but each time, Grant quickly resumed the attack.

The battles were vicious, costing the North more than 60,000 men. Critics called Grant a butcher, but he said, "I propose to fight it out on

Picturing HISTORY Chattanooga guarded the gateway to the eastern Confederacy and the Southern war industries in Georgia. From this city the Confederate army could mount expeditions into Tennessee and Kentucky. The Union could use the city to mount raids into Georgia and further divide the South.
Answer: *commander of all the Union armies*

Facts On File

CD-ROM
Landmark Documents in American History

Title: *Gettysburg Address, Abraham Lincoln, 1863*
Have students read the entirety of the address, then rewrite the speech in their own words. (NOTE: The *Gettysburg Address* can also be found in the Appendix of this textbook.)

NATIONAL GEOGRAPHIC SOCIETY

CD-ROM
NGS PictureShow: The Civil War

Have students research the three battles that took place near Richmond in May and June, 1864—The Battles of the Wilderness, Spotsylvania Courthouse, and Cold Harbor.

MAKING CONNECTIONS ACTIVITY

The Arts Although Mathew Brady revolutionized the artistic documentation of the Civil War through his photography, many artists of the time captured this historic event through fine art. For example, Winslow Homer's paintings *Veteran in a New Field* and *Prisoners from the Front* were completed from sketches he drew from the field. Conrad Chapman took his sketchbook, pencils, and brushes to the actual battlefield or viewed the scene from a telescope. Using either the Student Edition or the media center, have each student research a fine art piece that stirs personal feelings about the Civil War. Then have each student present the fine art piece to the class. **L2, ELL**

Who?What?Where?When?

Ulysses S. Grant Grant's given names were Hiram Ulysses. However, his commission to West Point mistakenly identified him as "Ulysses S. Grant." Since he hated the name Hiram, he never bothered to correct the mistake.

Grant did not seem much like a general. He freely admitted that the military life did not particularly appeal to him. To begin with, he did not like to wear uniforms! But he had proven to be a brave and able officer in the Mexican War. Confederates who had known Grant in Mexico did not underestimate his capabilities. General James Longstreet, for example, warned a colleague "that man will fight us every day and every hour till the end of this war."

Who?What?Where?When?

General Sherman Civil War historian Shelby Foote said of Sherman: "[He] was maybe the first truly modern general. He was the first one to understand that civilians were the backers-up of things and that if you went against civilians, you'd deprive the army of what kept it going."

Map Study

Answers
1. Sherman
2. Appomattox Court House

Map Skills Practice

Reading a Map Where did Grant and Lee fight a battle before Appomattox? *(Petersburg)*

this line if it takes all summer." Lincoln supported him, knowing that Lee could not afford the continuing casualties in his army.

After Cold Harbor, Grant swung south of Richmond to attack **Petersburg,** an important railroad center. If it fell, Richmond would be cut off from the rest of the Confederacy. Petersburg, however, had strong defenses. Grant's assault turned into a nine-month siege.

The Election of 1864

To the war-weary North, the events of the first half of 1864 looked like yet another stalled offensive. Grant was stuck outside Richmond and Petersburg, and Sherman was stuck outside Atlanta. Sentiment for a negotiated peace grew.

The Democrats wanted to make peace with the South, even though that might result in Confederate independence. Lincoln was determined to push for restoring the Union and ending slavery. In the summer of 1864, Lincoln's chances for reelection did not look good. "I am going to be beaten and unless some great change takes place, badly beaten," he said.

Great changes did take place. In August David Farragut, now an admiral, led a Union fleet into **Mobile Bay,** braving the Confederate defenses. Union control over the Gulf of Mexico was now complete. Then, in early September, news arrived

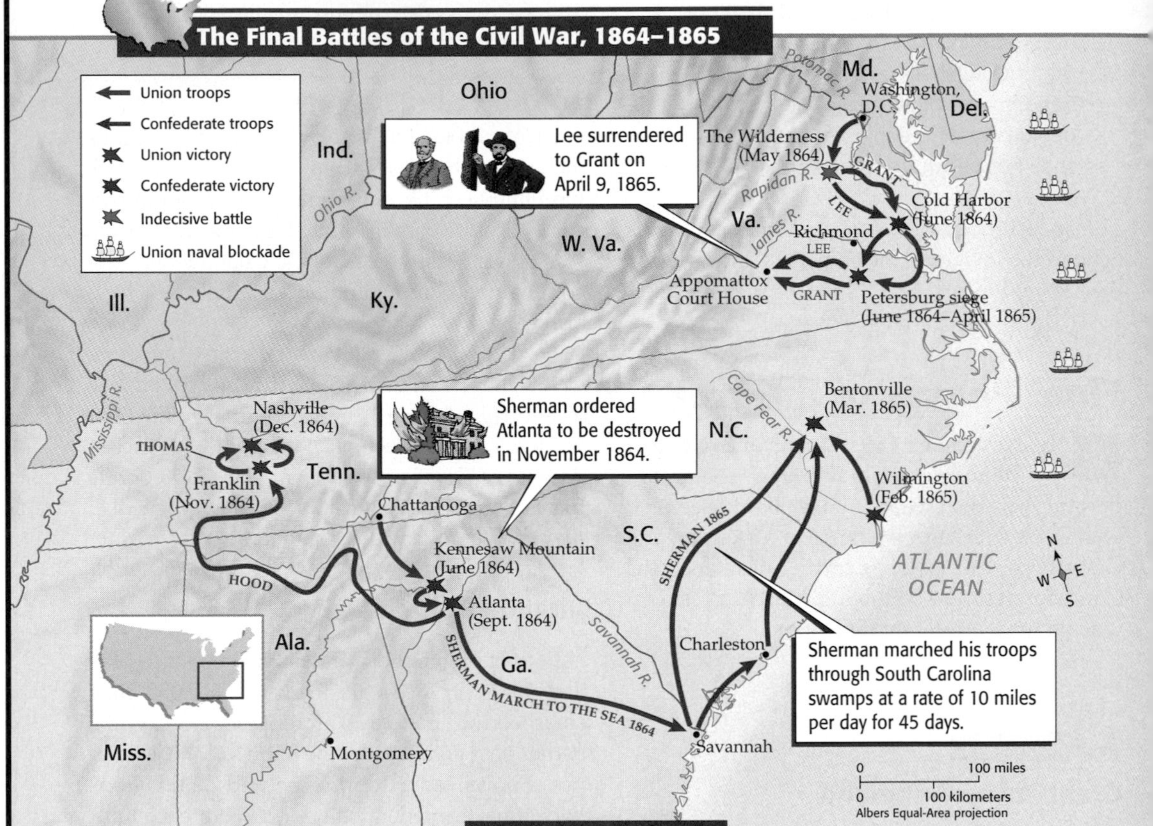

Map Study

The final battles of the Civil War caused heavy troop losses for both sides.

1. **Movement** Which Union general took Atlanta and later marched to the sea?
2. **Analyzing Information** Where did Lee surrender to Grant?

CRITICAL THINKING ACTIVITY

Formulating Questions Pair students to work together to calculate distance and time. Have each pair use the map *The Final Battles of the Civil War, 1864-1865* above to practice math skills. Review with students how to find time of travel (divide total number of miles traveled by rate of speed). Tell students that a person walks an average of 3 mph (4.8 kmph) and a horse walks an average of 4 mph (6.4 kmph). Have one student make up two questions from the map about rate of travel using the two different rates. The other student should answer the questions. Then have each pair change roles. **L2**

that Sherman had captured Atlanta. More news followed in October, when General Sheridan's Union force completed a campaign that drove the Rebels out of the Shenandoah Valley in Virginia. The North's mood changed. With the end of the war in sight, Lincoln easily won reelection, taking 55 percent of the popular vote.

The fall of Atlanta created a deep sense of gloom in the South. "Since Atlanta I have felt as if all were dead within me, forever," Mary Chesnut wrote. "We are going to be wiped off the earth."

Total War

Leaving Atlanta in ruins, Sherman convinced Grant to let him try a bold plan. Sherman's army began a historic "march to the sea" to **Savannah, Georgia.** As the army advanced, it abandoned its supply lines and lived off the land it passed through. Union troops took what food they needed, tore up railroad lines and fields, and killed animals in an effort to destroy anything useful to the South. They cut a path of destruction 50 miles wide. This method of waging war is known as **total war.** Sherman said:

> "We are not only fighting hostile armies, but a hostile people, and must make old and young, rich and poor, feel the hard hand of war."

After capturing Savannah in December, Sherman turned north. The army marched through South Carolina, devastating the state. Sherman planned to join Grant's forces in Virginia.

Victory for the North

In his second Inaugural Address on March 4, 1865, Lincoln spoke of the coming peace:

> "With malice toward none, with charity for all . . . let us strive on to finish the work we are in, to bind up the nation's wounds . . . to do all which may achieve and cherish a just and lasting peace among ourselves and with all nations."

Richmond, Virginia, April 1865

Richmond Falls

Throughout the fall and winter of 1864, Grant continued the siege of Petersburg. Lee and his troops desperately defended the town, but sickness, hunger, casualties, and desertion weakened them. Finally, on April 2, 1865, the Confederate lines broke and Petersburg fell to the Union.

Richmond fell the same day. Rebel troops, government officials, and many residents fled the Confederate capital. They set fire to much of the city to keep it from falling into Union hands.

On April 4 Lincoln visited Richmond. As he walked its streets, African Americans crowded around him. One elderly man approached the president, took off his hat, and bowed. With tears rolling down his cheeks, he said, "May God bless you." Lincoln removed his own hat and bowed in return.

Footnotes to History

No Escaping Wilmer McLean could not escape the Civil War, which started in his front yard and ended in his front parlor! The First Battle of Bull Run was fought on his property, and his home became headquarters for several Confederate generals. McLean tried to escape the devastation of war by moving to Appomattox Court House, Virginia. On April 9, 1865, Grant and Lee discussed the terms of surrender in his parlor.

TEACHER'S NOTES

CHAPTER 16
Section 5, 482–488

3 ASSESS

Assign Section 5 Review as homework or as an in-class activity.

Use **Chapter Challenger Interactive Review Software** to review Section 5.

Section Quiz 16–5

Name ______ Date ______ Class ______

★ Chapter 16

Score

Section Quiz 16-5

DIRECTIONS: Matching Match each item in Column A with the items in Column B. Write the correct letters in the blanks. *(10 points each)*

Column A

____ **1.** Robert E. Lee's opponent at Fredericksburg
____ **2.** set up in a strong position
____ **3.** site of Pickett's Charge
____ **4.** commander of the Union armies
____ **5.** took place on July 4, 1863

Column B

A. Battle of Gettysburg
B. Ulysses S. Grant
C. entrenched
D. surrender of Vicksburg
E. Ambrose Burnside

DIRECTIONS: Multiple Choice In the blank at the left, write the letter of the choice that best completes the statement or answers the question. *(10 points each)*

____ **6.** President Abraham Lincoln's address at this battlefield helped war-weary Americans focus on their shared ideals.
A. Vicksburg **C.** Shiloh
B. Chancellorsville **D.** Gettysburg

____ **7.** Ulysses S. Grant's assault on this railroad center turned into a nine-month siege.
A. Petersburg **C.** Vicksburg
B. Richmond **D.** Shiloh

____ **8.** This helped Lincoln win the 1864 election.
A. Lee's surrender **C.** William T. Sherman's capture of Atlanta
B. winning at Gettysburg **D.** promotion of Grant

____ **9.** Sherman's march to Savannah was called
A. cold war. **C.** total war.
B. undeclared war. **D.** malicious war.

____ **10.** General Robert E. Lee surrendered to General Ulysses S. Grant in a small Virginia village called
A. Richmond. **C.** Vicksburg.
B. Appomattox Court House. **D.** Gettysburg.

Reteaching Activity 16–5

Name ______ Date ______ Class ______

★ Reteaching Activity **16-5**

DIRECTIONS: Completing a Time Line In the Fact Bank are battle sites, military leaders, and other events of the Civil War. Complete the time line by writing the correct letters in each box.

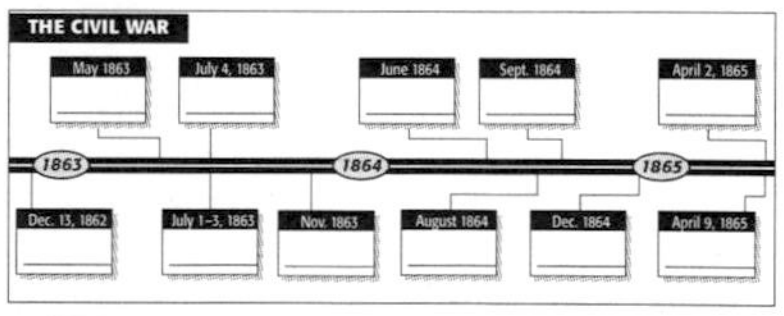

★FACT BANK

A. William Tecumseh Sherman
B. Spotsylvania Courthouse
C. Atlanta
D. George Meade
E. Chancellorsville
F. Petersburg
G. Stonewall Jackson
H. Gettysburg
I. Robert E. Lee
J. Fredericksburg
K. Ulysses S. Grant
L. Pickett's Charge
M. Appomattox Court House
N. David Farragut
O. Chattanooga
P. Savannah
Q. Ambrose Burnside
R. Vicksburg
S. Mobile Bay
T. Cold Harbor
U. Joseph Hooker
V. Richmond
W. the Wilderness

DIRECTIONS: Essay Answer the following question on a separate sheet of paper.

Discuss the presidential election of 1864. Explain the change in public opinion of Abraham Lincoln from the beginning of the campaign to the end.

HISTORY AND ART A crowd of weeping soldiers stood in front of Lee's tent at Appomattox. "Boys," he told them, "I have done the best I could for you. Go home now, and if you make as good citizens as you have soldiers, you will do well, and I shall always be proud of you. Good-bye, and God bless you all."

Answer: *Generous. Confederate soldiers had to lay down their arms but then were free to go home. He allowed them to keep their horses, and gave them three days' worth of food.*

Who? What? Where? When?

Jefferson Davis After his capture Jefferson Davis was charged with treason and imprisoned. He was never put on trial, and after two years he was released. He remained a rebel for another 100 years, however. In 1978 Congress finally restored his American citizenship.

Enrichment Activity 16–5

Name ______ Date ______ Class ______

★ Enrichment Activity **16-5**

Deaths in Battles

Hundreds of thousands of people died as a result of the Civil War. Deaths from diseases greatly exceeded combat deaths. The table below shows financial costs and battle deaths of major United States wars.

Battle Deaths and Costs of Major Wars Fought by the United States (estimated)

	Number of Battle Deaths	Total Costs (Millions of Dollars)	Original Costs (Millions of Dollars)
Vietnam Conflict (1959–1983)	47,318	352,000	140,600
Korean Conflict	33,629	164,000	54,000
World War II	291,557	664,000	288,000
World War I	53,402	112,000	26,000
Spanish-American War	385	6,460	400
Civil War: Union only	140,414	12,952	3,200
Civil War: Confederacy (est.)	94,000	NA	1,000
Mexican War	1,733	147	73
War of 1812	2,260	158	93
American Revolution	6,824	190	100

DIRECTIONS: Analyzing Information Use the table to complete the fact list.

1. Total number of battle deaths in the Civil War ______
2. The North's percentage of Civil War battle deaths ______
3. The war with the highest total cost ______
4. The war whose total cost least exceeded its original cost ______
5. The war with the highest number of battle deaths ______
6. The difference between the number of battle deaths in the American Revolution and the Civil War ______

Activity **DIRECTIONS:** In addition to the costs in money and health, wars have emotional costs. With your classmates prepare an oral history book of Americans' war experiences. Pick one of the wars for which the United States still has living veterans, such as World War II, the Korean Conflict, the Vietnam Conflict, or the Gulf War. Interview a veteran and ask about the emotional costs of the war. Share your findings with the class.

The American Journey ★ 65 ★ Enrichment Activities

4 CLOSE

Ask students to speculate about how the outcome of the war would have been different if the two leaders they chose in the "TEACH" activity had not been involved in the war.

HISTORY AND ART ***Surrender of the Confederate Flag at Appomattox* by Richard Norris Brooke** At Appomattox Court House Confederate troops sadly and carefully folded their battle-torn flag and laid it on the ground. **What kind of surrender terms did Grant make to Lee's troops?**

Surrender at Appomattox

Lee moved his army west of Richmond, hoping to link up with the small Confederate force that was trying to stop Sherman's advance. But the Union army blocked his escape route. Realizing that the situation was hopeless, Lee said:

> "There is nothing left for me to do but go and see General Grant, and I would rather die a thousand deaths."

On April 9 Lee and his troops surrendered to Grant in a small Virginia village called **Appomattox Court House.** Grant's terms were generous. The Confederate soldiers had to lay down their arms but then were free to go home. Grant allowed them to keep their horses so that they could, as he said, "put in a crop to carry themselves and their families through the next winter." Grant also ordered three days' worth of food to be sent to Lee's hungry troops.

Several days after Lee's surrender, the Confederate forces in North Carolina surrendered to General Sherman. Jefferson Davis, the president of the Confederacy, was captured in Georgia on May 10. The Civil War was over at last.

Results of the War

The Civil War was the most devastating conflict in American history. More than 600,000 soldiers died, and the war caused billions of dollars of damage, most of it in the South. The war also created bitter feelings among defeated Southerners that lasted for generations.

The war had other consequences as well. The North's victory saved the Union. The federal government was strengthened and was now clearly more powerful than the states. Finally, the war freed millions of African Americans. How the nation would treat these new citizens remained to be seen.

Section 5 Review

Checking for Understanding

1. ***Identify*** Gettysburg Address, William Tecumseh Sherman, Appomattox Court House.
2. ***Define*** entrenched, total war.
3. ***Identify*** the reasons that Gettysburg and Vicksburg were important battles.

Reviewing Themes

4. **Individual Action** Why did President Lincoln name Ulysses S. Grant commander of all the Union armies?

Critical Thinking

5. **Drawing Conclusions** How did the Union victory in the war strengthen the federal government?

Activity

Composing a Poem Write a poem that a Civil War soldier might have written after hearing that the war was over.

Section 5 Review Answers

1. Gettysburg Address, 484; William Tecumseh Sherman, 485; Appomattox Court House, 488
2. The words are defined in the Glossary.
3. Both were turning points in the war. Lee's army was driven from Pennsylvania, the Mississippi River was secured as a Union highway, and the South was cut in two.
4. Grant's victories in the West and his will to fight and continue fighting
5. The war demonstrated that the federal government would not tolerate states acting on their own.

Activity Poems should reflect the feelings of a Civil War soldier at the end of the war.

ABCNEWS INTERACTIVE Historic America Electronic Field Trips

Field Trip to Gettysburg

Setting up the Video

With a group of your classmates, view "Gettysburg" on the videodisc ***Historic America: Electronic Field Trips***.

During the Civil War, one of the most devastating battles was the battle at Gettysburg, Pennsylvania. The battle lasted 3 days, and about 40,000 soldiers died or were wounded. The program gives different perspectives of the battle and its results.

Hands-On Activity

Civil War soldiers and prisoners of war played chess and card games while stationed in military camps. Some soldiers made their own chess sets. Make your own Civil War chess set labeled with the names of presidents, generals, spies, doctors, drummers, and foot soldiers from both the Union and the Confederacy.

Side 1, Chapter 8

View the video by scanning the bar code or by entering the chapter number on your keypad and pressing Search.

Surfing the "Net"

Abraham Lincoln

Abraham Lincoln was the nation's sixteenth president. During his presidency, he had the task of guiding our country through one of the most difficult experiences in its history—the Civil War. Many historians regard him as one of our greatest presidents. To research more about Lincoln's presidency, look on the Internet.

Getting There

Follow these steps to gather information about Abraham Lincoln's presidency.

1. Use a search engine. Type in the phrase *Abraham Lincoln.*
2. After typing in the subject *Abraham Lincoln,* enter words like the following to focus your search: *Civil War, Library of Congress, history, presidency.*
3. The search engine will provide you with a number of links to follow. Links are "pointers" to different sites on the Internet and commonly appear as blue underlined words.

What to Do When You Are There

Use the Internet to research Abraham Lincoln and his presidency. Click on the links to navigate through the pages of information. Gather your findings. Then, using a word processor, write a research report on the presidency of Abraham Lincoln. Be sure to cite the various web page sources.

Teacher's Notes

Multimedia Activities

ABCNEWS INTERACTIVE

VIDEODISC
Historic America
Electronic Field Trips

Side 1, Chapter 8
Title: *Gettysburg*

If you do not have access to a videodisc player, the **Historic America Electronic Field Trips** are also available in VHS.

Internet Sites

The following are possible sites for completing the "Net" activities:

Abraham Lincoln Online
http://www.netins.net/showcase/creative/lincoln.html

The Library of Congress Home Page
http://lcweb.loc.gov/

American Civil War Home Page
http://funnelweb.utcc.utk.edu/~hoemann/cwarhp.html

Not on the "Net" . . .

If students have limited or no access to the Internet, have them complete the activity on "Abraham Lincoln" by using the electronic card catalog at the school or local library. At the *s:* prompt, students should type in *Abraham Lincoln.* They should then use the call numbers to find the books they need to complete their research reports on the presidency of Lincoln.

Chapter 16

Review and Activities

Reviewing Key Terms

On a sheet of paper, define the following terms:

border state
blockade
offensive
Rebel
Yankee
blockade runner
ironclad
casualty
emancipate
habeas corpus
draft
bounty
greenback

Reviewing Key Facts

1. What three advantages did the South have in the Civil War?
2. What did most Northerners expect to happen at the First Battle of Bull Run?
3. Why did Lincoln hesitate to make a move against slavery in the early stages of the war?
4. What roles did women play in the war?
5. How did the war help to strengthen the economy of the North?

Critical Thinking

Analyzing Information

Sherman's "march to the sea" left a wide path of destruction in the South.

1. Do you think waging total war at this stage of the fighting was necessary? Why or why not?
2. How do you think Sherman's actions would affect the South's ability to rebuild its economy after the war?

Time Line Activity

Create a time line on which you place the following events in chronological order.

- Lincoln elected to second term as president
- Battle between the *Monitor* and *Merrimack*
- Jefferson Davis is captured
- First Battle of Bull Run
- Confederate army surrenders at Appomattox Court House
- Lincoln issues Emancipation Proclamation
- Battle of Gettysburg

Skill Practice Activity

Using a CD-ROM

Using the steps described on page 481 and a CD-ROM encyclopedia, find enough information about the Battle of Shiloh to tell a classmate where and when it took place, who were the generals involved, what their role was during the battle, and what was the outcome of the battle. Compare what you find to the details shown in this painting. Is the art accurate? Explain.

Battle of Shiloh

GLENCOE TECHNOLOGY

VIDEODISC
MindJogger Videoquiz

Use MindJogger to review the Chapter 16 content.

Chapter 16
Disc 2, Side B

Also available in VHS.

Reviewing Key Terms

The key terms used in this activity are defined in the textbook glossary on pages A26–A35.

Reviewing Key Facts

1. strong support of white population, fighting defensive war, strong military leadership
2. thought Union would win and end the war
3. did not want to alienate border states
4. took over jobs and responsibilities of men, aided troops as nurses and spies, gathered supplies, raised money
5. encouraged growth of industry and growth of the railroad

Critical Thinking

1. Answers will vary. Yes, it was a way to convince the South that war was indeed terrible and that it was time to end the fighting. No, Sherman did not need to destroy so much property along the way. He could have accomplished as much by confining his fighting to the battlefields.
2. It would take a long time and large amounts of money for the South to rebuild.

Time Line Activity

Events should be placed in this order: First Battle of Bull Run, Battle between the *Monitor* and *Merrimack,* Lincoln issues Emancipation Proclamation, Battle of Gettysburg, Lincoln elected to second term as president, Confederate army surrenders at Appomattox Court House, Jefferson Davis is captured

Skill Practice Activity

Students should follow the steps on page 481 for using a CD-ROM to find information about the Battle of Shiloh and to answer the question about the accuracy of the painting.

CHAPTER 16
Review and Activities

Geography Activity

Study the map below and answer the questions that follow.

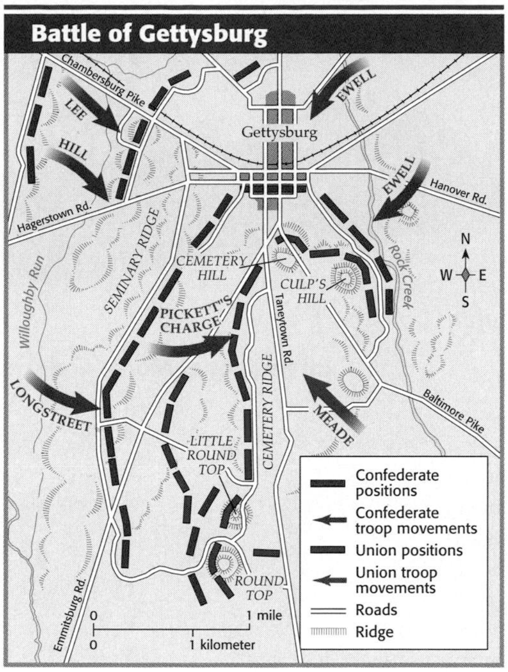

1. **Location** Along what ridge were the Union troops positioned? The Confederate troops?
2. **Movement** Who led the attack on Union troops at Little Round Top?
3. **Movement** What five Confederate commanders are shown on the map?

Cooperative Activity

History and Geography Work with members of your group to create a three-dimensional relief map of one of the battle sites described in the chapter. Do research to find out the geography of the area and use clay, cardboard, or other materials to construct your map. Then use different colored objects to demonstrate troop movements.

Technology Activity

Using the Internet Search the Internet for a list of museums that have Civil War artifact and photo collections. Make a map to show the names and locations of the museums.

Reviewing Themes

1. **Government and Democracy** How did the people of western Virginia respond to Virginia's secession from the Union?
2. **Geography and History** Why was controlling the Mississippi River vital to both the North and the South?
3. **Groups and Institutions** What two government orders changed the status of enslaved African Americans during the war?
4. **Economic Factors** How did inflation affect the lives of people during the war?
5. **Individual Action** Why was General Lee such an effective military leader?

Portfolio Activity History Journal Review the chapter to make a list of the major battles of the war. Make a "scoreboard" that shows at a glance which side won each battle, where it was fought, and the names of important military leaders who were involved.

Reviewing Themes

1. They seceded from Virginia and formed their own state of West Virginia in 1863.
2. It was the main north-south water transportation route.
3. Emancipation Proclamation and Thirteenth Amendment
4. It caused a dramatic rise in prices, which made it difficult to purchase necessities—especially in the South.
5. He implemented bold plans, made quick movements, and had knowledge of Southern geography.

Portfolio Activity Students' portfolios should include a scoreboard-type chart listing battles, including who won, battle location, and the names of any major leaders involved.

Chapter Bonus Test Question

Ask: **How was Jefferson Davis transported to prison?**
(He was driven in a horse-drawn ambulance.)

Geography Activity

1. Cemetery Ridge; Seminary Ridge
2. Longstreet
3. Lee, Hill, Ewell, Pickett, Longstreet

Cooperative Activity

Relief maps should accurately portray the geography of the region and relevant troop movements.

Technology Activity

Maps should include names and locations of museums that house Civil War collections.

Hands-On HISTORY Lab Activity

Block Schedule

This activity may be implemented within either a traditional class period or a block scheduling framework.

FOCUS

Ask students to look at the chart on international Morse code. Have them determine the two symbols used in Morse code. **Ask:** How did Morse code change the communication system used in the Civil War? *(Answers will vary but should address the increased speed of communication.)* Compare communicating with the telegraph and Morse code with today's use of E-mail. Make sure students address the equipment, how it works, and how it is used.

TEACH

L2 Practicing the Code Ask students to imagine they are a new recruit in the Civil War. Have them write a message home in Morse code telling about a battle they recently fought. Then have students exchange messages and decode them.

Hands-On HISTORY Lab Activity

Morse Code

"What hath God wrought!" On May 24, 1844, Samuel Morse tapped this message on his telegraph and sent it across wire from Washington, D.C., to Baltimore, Maryland. A few seconds later the operator in Baltimore tapped back the same message. Americans were astonished. Astonish yourself by building your own simple telegraph.

Early telegraph

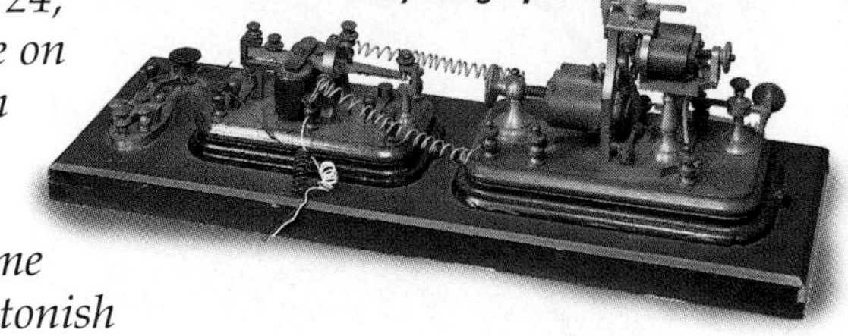

The Way It Was

Armies in the Civil War made use of the newest communication system—the telegraph. Inventor Samuel Morse sent the first long-distance message in 1844, using a code of short and long (dot-dash) electrical signals invented by Morse and Alfred Vail. Telegraph operators throughout the world began using this Morse code to send messages. By 1846 more than 5,000 miles (8,045 km) of telegraph wire had been strung, and 3,000 more miles (4,827 km) were under construction.

International Morse Code

a ._	n _.
b _...	o ___
c _._.	p .__.
d _..	q __._
e .	r ._.
f .._.	s ...
g __.	t _
h	u .._
I ..	v ..._
j .___	w .__
k _._	x _.._
l ._..	y _.__
m __	z __..

1 Materials

- Size D battery
- tape
- 2 feet of insulated wire, cut into 3 pieces
- 1 metal paper clip
- 2 metal thumbtacks
- flashlight-sized lightbulb and holder
- piece of thick cardboard about 1 foot square

Believe It Or Not!

The fastest speed recorded for a hand-key transmission of Morse code is 175 symbols a minute. A member of the United States Army Signal Corps accomplished this feat in 1942.

CURRICULUM CONNECTION

Civics In 1837 Samuel F. B. Morse publicly demonstrated his magnetic telegraph. On September 23 of that year, he was granted a United States patent. Morse's assistant Alfred Lewis Vail devised the Morse code system of dots and dashes, replacing the early system that assigned numbers to letters. In 1843 Congress appropriated $30,000 to enable Morse to build an experimental telegraph line between Washington, D.C., and Baltimore, Maryland. With additional private funding, he proceeded to construct the world's first long-distance telephone line. The telegraph revolutionized American life. Just 10 years after the first line opened, 23,000 miles of telegraph cable crisscrossed the United States.

2 What To Do

1. Push one thumbtack into the cardboard.
2. Trap the end of one piece of wire under the thumbtack and tape the other end to one terminal of the battery.
3. Tape another piece of wire to the other battery terminal and connect it to the lightbulb holder.
4. Connect a third piece of wire to the lightbulb holder and to a second tack about 1 inch from the first tack.
5. Trap a paper clip under the first thumbtack and bend the end up at an angle. The paper clip will act as a telegraph key. Tap the bent paper clip down on the second thumbtack and observe what happens.

3 Lab Report

1. What happened when you touched the paper clip to the thumbtack in Step 5?
2. Was it easy or difficult to send a coded message with your paper clip? Explain why.
3. **Drawing Conclusions** How do you think the use of the telegraph might have affected the outcome of the Civil War?

Go a Step Further

Use the Morse code dot-dash symbols listed on page 492 to tap a message to a friend. Then have someone tap you a message. For easier translation, write down the dot-dashes as the light flashes. Decipher the message after you have written down the entire code of dots and dashes.

Hands-On HISTORY Lab Activity

Who? What? Where? When?

Samuel Morse was a very successful portrait painter and sculptor. He was also a professor of painting and sculpture at New York University.

CURRICULUM CONNECTION

JOURNALISM
During the Civil War, newspapers often held one page open until just before press time. This allowed them to include any last-minute telegraph dispatches from the battlefront.

ASSESS

Have students answer the **Lab Report** questions on page 493.

CLOSE

Encourage students to complete the **Go a Step Further** writing activity. Ask volunteers to tap out the message they wrote in the "TEACH" activity. Initiate a discussion on the advantages and disadvantages of telegraphy.

ANSWERS

Lab Report

1. light bulb lights up
2. Answers will vary but should address the advantages and disadvantages in sending messages in this manner.
3. Answers should include references to the advantages and disadvantages of using the telegraph during the Civil War.

Go a Step Further

Students should use the Morse code to tap a message to a friend and then receive a message.

Chapter 17 Planning Guide

A complete, 1-page lesson plan is provided for each section in the *Reproducible Lesson Plans* booklet.

Section Resources

Daily Objectives	Reproducible Resources	Multimedia Resources
Section 1 **Reconstruction Plans** Compare Lincoln's, the Radical Republicans', and Johnson's Reconstruction plans.	Reproducible Lesson Plan 17–1 Guided Reading Activity 17–1* Section Quiz 17–1* Reteaching Activity 17–1 Enrichment Activity 17–1	Section Focus Transparency 17–1 Vocabulary PuzzleMaker Chapter Challenger Interactive Review Facts On File: Landmark Documents in American History
Section 2 **Radicals in Control** Discuss the main features of Radical Reconstruction.	Reproducible Lesson Plan 17–2 Guided Reading Activity 17–2* Section Quiz 17–2* Reteaching Activity 17–2 Enrichment Activity 17–2	Section Focus Transparency 17–2 Vocabulary PuzzleMaker Chapter Challenger Interactive Review GTV: The American People: Fabric of a Nation Facts On File: Landmark Documents in American History The Presidents: A Picture History of Our Nation American Music Cultural Traditions
Section 3 **The South During Reconstruction** Identify how Southern life changed during Reconstruction.	Reproducible Lesson Plan 17–3 Guided Reading Activity 17–3* Political Cartoons Section Quiz 17–3* Reteaching Activity 17–3 Enrichment Activity 17–3	Section Focus Transparency 17–3 Vocabulary PuzzleMaker Chapter Challenger Interactive Review Software Testmaker
Section 4 **Reconstruction Ends** Describe the decline and virtual end of Reconstruction.	Reproducible Lesson Plan 17–4 Guided Reading Activity 17–4* Section Quiz 17–4* Reteaching Activity 17–4 Enrichment Activity 17–4	Section Focus Transparency 17–4 Vocabulary PuzzleMaker Chapter Challenger Interactive Review GTV: A Geographic Perspective on American History Historic America Electronic Field Trips
Section 5 **Change in the South** Examine the advantages and disadvantages of the New South.	Reproducible Lesson Plan 17–5 Guided Reading Activity 17–5* Section Quiz 17–5* Reteaching Activity 17–5 Enrichment Activity 17–5	Section Focus Transparency 17–5 Vocabulary PuzzleMaker Chapter Challenger Interactive Review Software Testmaker

** Also available in Spanish*

Blackline Master · Transparency · Videodisc · CD-ROM · Audiocassette · Software · Music Program

0:00 **OUT OF TIME?**
Assign the Chapter 17 Digest and the corresponding Chapter Digests Audiocassettes with activities and tests.

Activity

From the Classroom of…

Phil Trotter
San Diego School District
San Diego, California

A State of the Union Address on the Fourteenth Amendment—Then and Now

Organize the class into an equal number of groups. Have half of the groups research the legal rights of people—particularly African Americans—just prior to the passage of the Fourteenth Amendment. The other half of the class should research how the amendment protects African Americans and other minorities today. Using as many specific examples as they can find, have each group write a State of the Union Address for either "then" or "now."

Before having groups present their addresses to the class, ask all students to find articles in newspapers or magazines that deal with the rights and freedoms covered by the Fourteenth Amendment. These articles can be shared during class discussion after each group's State of the Union presentation.

Block Schedule

Block scheduling differs from traditional class scheduling in the amount of time allotted to each period. The extended time frame provided by block scheduling affords you the opportunity to implement a greater number of research-oriented and activity-intense projects to motivate and involve your students. Activities that are particularly suited to use within the block scheduling framework are identified throughout this chapter by the following designation:

National Geographic Society — Teacher's Corner

NATIONAL GEOGRAPHIC SOCIETY PRODUCTS AVAILABLE FROM GLENCOE

To order the following products for use with this chapter, contact your local Glencoe sales representative, or call Glencoe at 1-800-334-7344:

- *GTV: A Geographic Perspective on American History* (Videodisc)
- *GTV: The American People: Fabric of a Nation* (Videodisc)
- *The Presidents: A Picture History of Our Nation* (CD-ROM)
- *PictureShow: The Civil War* (CD-ROM)
- *PictureShow: The Civil War* (Transparencies)
- *PictureShow: The Westward Movement* (CD-ROM)
- *PictureShow: The Westward Movement* (Transparencies)
- *Picture Atlas of the World* (CD-ROM)

ADDITIONAL NATIONAL GEOGRAPHIC SOCIETY PRODUCTS

To order the following products for use with this chapter, call National Geographic Society at 1-800-368-2728:

- *Heritage of the Black West* (Video)
- *Historical Atlas of the United States* (Atlas)

KEY TO ABILITY LEVELS

Teaching strategies have been coded for varying learning styles and abilities.

L1 **BASIC** activities for all students
L2 **AVERAGE** activities for average to above-average students
L3 **CHALLENGING** activities for above-average students
ELL **ENGLISH LANGUAGE LEARNER** activities

Chapter 17 Resource Guide

Home Involvement

Home Involvement Activity 17

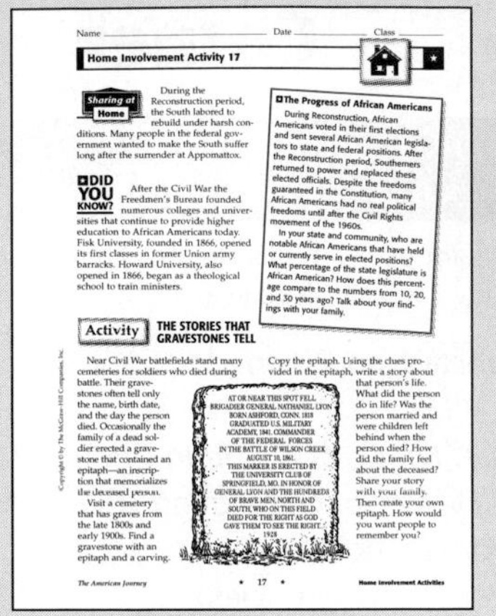

Review Activities

Chapter Summary 17

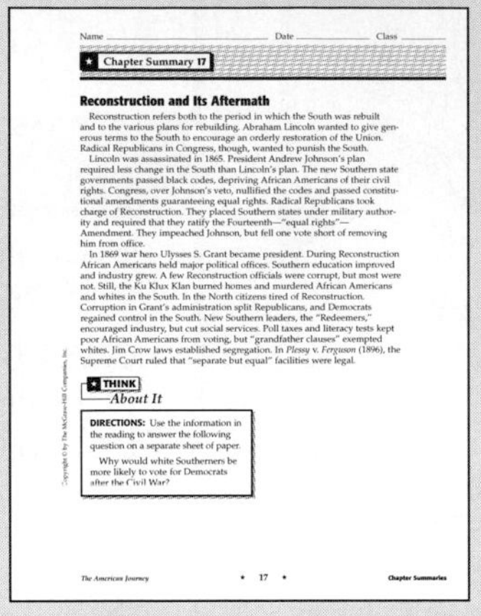

Workbook Activity 17

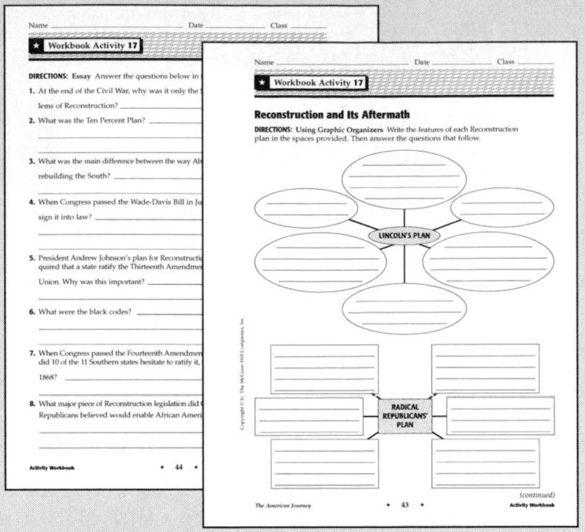

Reinforcement Activities

Time Line Activity 17

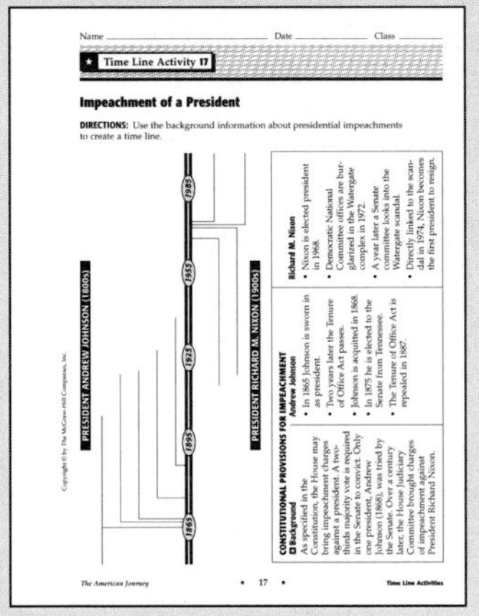

Vocabulary Activity 17

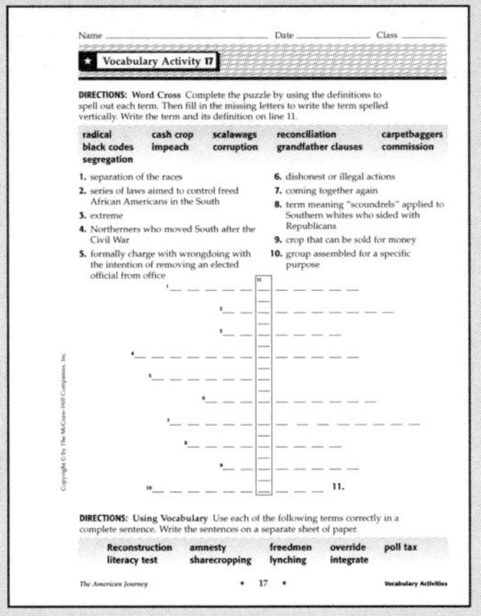

Chapter Skills Activity 17

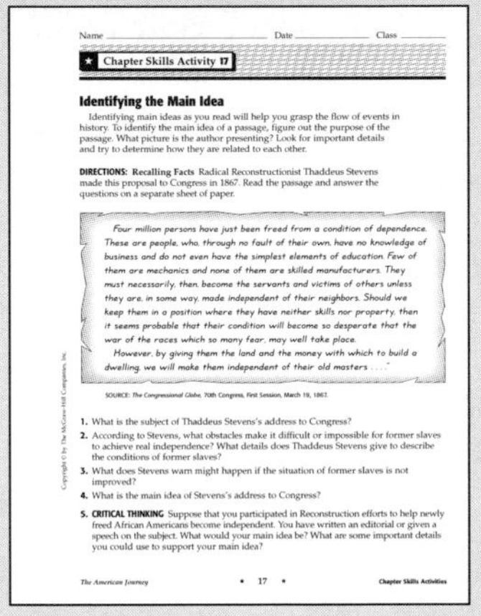

Enrichment Activities

Linking Past and Present Activity 17

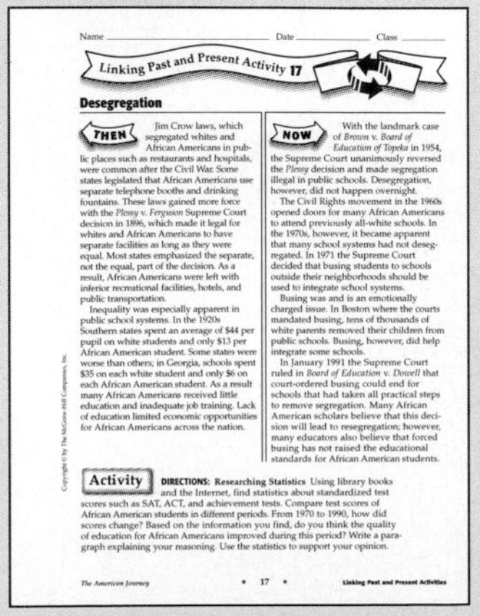

Primary Source Reading 17

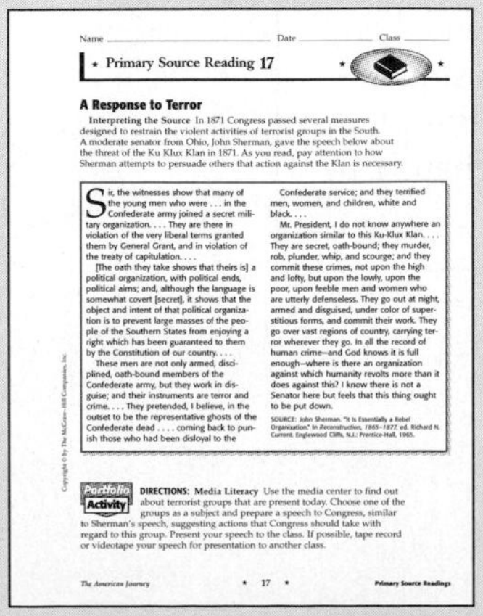

Geography Activities

Mapping History Activity 17

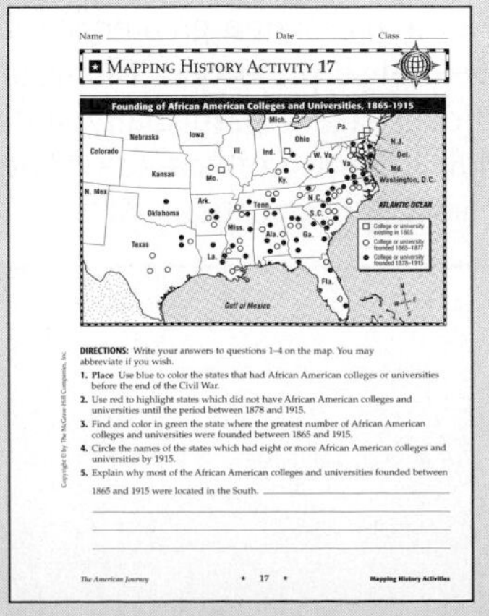

Chapter 17 Resource Guide

ASSESSMENT

Chapter 17 Test, Form A

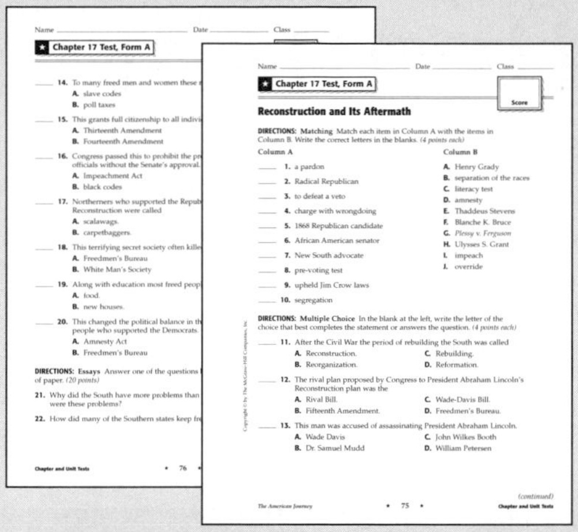

Chapter 17 Test, Form B

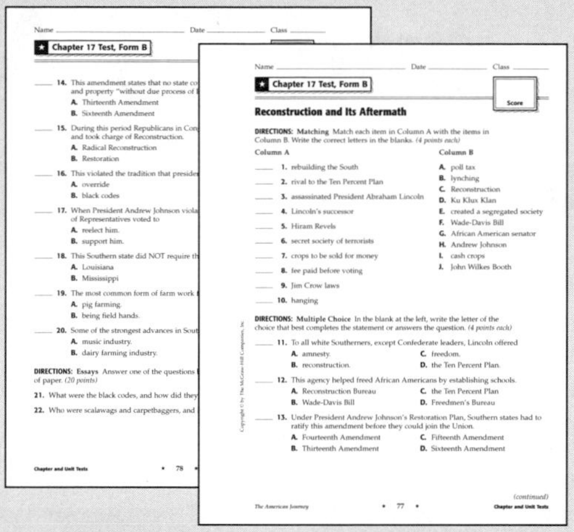

Performance Assessment Activity 17

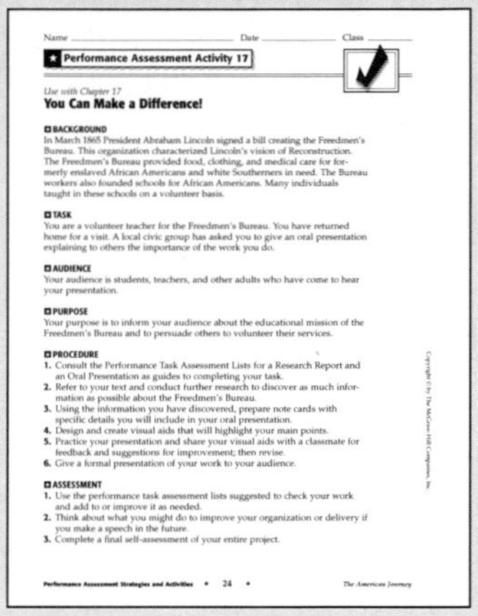

SPANISH RESOURCES

The following Spanish language materials are available in the Spanish Resources binder:

- **Spanish Chapter Summary 17**
- **Spanish Vocabulary Activity 17**
- **Spanish Guided Reading Activities, Chapter 17**
- **Spanish Section Quizzes, Chapter 17**
- **Spanish Home Involvement Activity 17**
- **Spanish Chapter 17 Digests Audiocassette Activity and Test**

ACTIVITY MANIPULATIVES

Help students learn more about America's cultural history with:

- **American Crafts Hands-On Activities**
- **American Games Hands-On Activities**
- **American History Flash Cards**

ADDITIONAL RESOURCES FROM GLENCOE

- **Political Cartoons,** *Reconstruction and Carpetbaggers*
- **American Music Cultural Traditions,** Lesson 5: "Roll, Jordan, Roll"
- **The American History Videodisc and CD-ROM,** *The Civil War and Reconstruction*
- **Outline Map Resource Book**
- **U.S. Desk Map**

A&E HOME VIDEO. Biography. THE HISTORY CHANNEL.

The following videotape programs are available from Glencoe as supplements to Chapter 17:

- **The Lincoln Assassination (Set)** (ISBN 1-56501-568-1)
- **John Wilkes Booth** (ISBN 1-56501-715-3)

To order, call Glencoe at 1-800-334-7344. To find classroom resources to accompany many of these videos, check the following home pages:
A&E Television: http://www.aetv.com
The History Channel: http://www.historychannel.com

Introducing
CHAPTER 17

Chapter Themes

Chapter Themes are listed by section on this chapter opening page of the Student Edition. A corresponding theme-based activity is available under "FOCUS," and a theme-based question is asked in the Section and Chapter Reviews.

Performance Assessment

Refer to Activity 17 in the *Performance Assessment Strategies and Activities* booklet.

GLENCOE TECHNOLOGY

VIDEODISC
MindJogger Videoquiz

Use MindJogger to preview the Chapter 17 content.

Chapter 17
Disc 3, Side A

Also available in VHS.

HISTORY AND ART Winslow Homer, noted for his oil paintings such as the one shown here, originally started as an artist for *Harper's Weekly*. This painting suggests Homer's admiration for African Americans who enrolled in schools to learn new skills after the Civil War.

Chapter 17

1865–1896

Reconstruction and Its Aftermath

Why It's Important

Reconstruction raised questions about government and the rights of citizens that remained long after it ended. Debate over the rightful power of the federal government and the states continues to this day. Americans continue to wrestle with the problem of providing civil rights and equal opportunity to all American citizens.

Chapter Themes

- *Section 1,* Groups and Institutions
- *Section 2,* Civic Rights and Responsibilities
- *Section 3,* Continuity and Change
- *Section 4,* Individual Action
- *Section 5,* Economic Factors

HISTORY AND ART ***Sunday Morning in Virginia* by Winslow Homer** Artist Winslow Homer skillfully painted everyday scenes in the lives of rural Southerners during Reconstruction. This African American family shares a reading from the Bible.

494

EXTRA CREDIT PROJECT

Reconstruction Policy Interested students can imagine they are federal officials touring the South immediately after the Civil War. Ask them to report on geographic conditions; the changing social status of white planters, merchants, poor whites, African Americans; and the changes in labor. Then have students make recommendations to the president for a harsher or more lenient Reconstruction policy. Have students share their reports with the class.

1864 · 1865 · 1866

July 1864 Congress passes Wade-Davis Bill

March 1865 Freedmen's Bureau is established

April 9, 1865 Lee surrenders

April 14, 1865 President Lincoln is assassinated

Section 1

Reconstruction Plans

Read to Discover . . .

- how the Reconstruction plans of Lincoln and the Radical Republicans differed.
- what were Johnson's Reconstruction plans.

Terms to Learn

Reconstruction
amnesty
radical
freedmen

The Storyteller

About a month after President Lincoln began his second term of office, the Civil War ended, and the soldiers returned to their homes. One Illinois veteran wrote upon reaching the family farm, "The morning after my arrival, September 29th, I [took off] my uniform of first lieutenant, put on some of my father's old clothes, and proceeded to wage war on the standing corn. The feeling I had while engaged in this work was sort of [odd]. It almost seemed, sometimes, as if I had been away only a day or two, and had just taken up the farm work where I had left off."

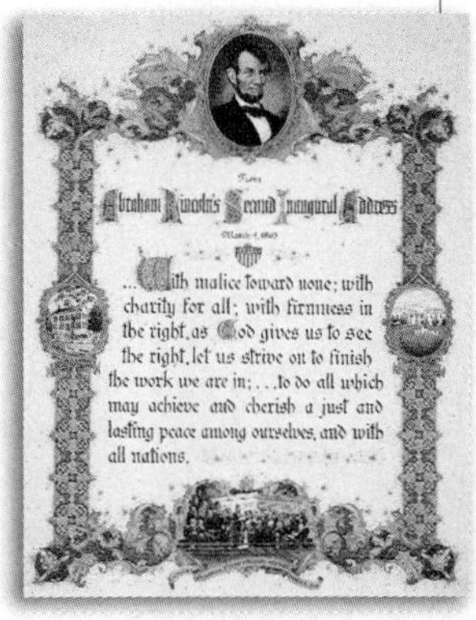

Lincoln's second Inaugural Address

The end of the Civil War raised many difficult questions. For example, should the slaveholding Southerners be punished or forgiven? What rights should be granted to the freed African Americans? How could the war-torn nation be brought back together?

Reconstruction Debate

The war had left the South with enormous problems. Most of the major fighting had taken place in the South. Towns and cities were in ruin, plantations burned, and roads, bridges, and railroads destroyed.

More than 258,000 Confederate soldiers had died in the war, and illness and wounds weakened thousands more. Many Southern families faced the task of rebuilding their lives with few resources and without the help of adult males.

People in all parts of the nation agreed that the devastated Southern economy and society needed rebuilding. They disagreed bitterly, however, over how to accomplish this. This period of rebuilding is called **Reconstruction.** This term also refers to the various plans for accomplishing the rebuilding.

Lincoln's Plan

President Lincoln offered the first plan for accepting the Southern states back into the Union. In December 1863, during the Civil War, the president announced what came to be known as the **Ten Percent Plan.** When 10 percent of the voters of a state took an oath of loyalty to the Union, the

Section Resources

Reproducible Masters
- Reproducible Lesson Plan 17–1
- Guided Reading Activity 17–1
- Section Quiz 17–1
- Reteaching Activity 17–1
- Enrichment Activity 17–1

Transparencies
- Section Focus Transparency 17–1

Multimedia
- Vocabulary PuzzleMaker
- Chapter Challenger Interactive Review Software
- Testmaker
- Facts On File: Landmark Documents in American History

1 FOCUS

BELLRINGER
Motivational Activity

Before taking roll at the beginning of the class period, project Section Focus Transparency 17–1 and have students answer the questions. Discuss students' responses.

This activity is also available as a blackline master.

Section Focus Transparency 17–1

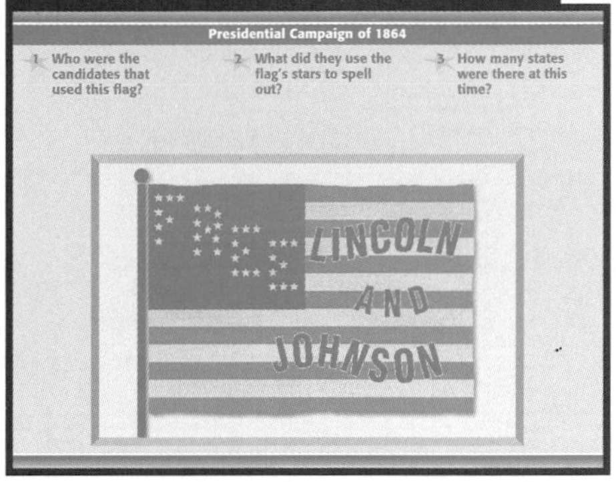

Vocabulary Precheck

Have students brainstorm nouns commonly associated with the adjective *radical.* Discuss the meaning and application of *radical* in this section.

Use the **Vocabulary PuzzleMaker** to create crossword and word search puzzles.

Section Theme
Groups and Institutions

People in all parts of the nation agreed that the devastated Southern economy and society needed rebuilding. They disagreed, however, over how to accomplish this reconstruction.

Activity Discuss what Reconstruction involved. Point out to students the social, political, economic, physical, and psychological factors involved.

2 TEACH

L1 Debating Viewpoints Have students scan the section to find the opposing viewpoints on Reconstruction. Have them choose between the Radical Republicans' and Lincoln's plans for Reconstruction. Organize the class into two groups to debate the advantages and disadvantages of each plan.

Guided Reading Activity 17–1

Name ____________ Date ________ Class ______

★ Guided Reading Activity 17-1

DIRECTIONS: Identifying Supporting Details Read each main idea. Use your textbook to supply the details that support or explain each main idea.

Main Idea: President Abraham Lincoln proposed the first plan for Reconstruction of the South.

1. **Detail:** In December 1863, during the Civil War, Lincoln announced the ____________ which offered Southern states a way back into the Union.
2. **Detail:** The president offered ____________ to all white Southerners, except ____________, who were willing to swear loyalty to the Union.
3. **Detail:** Lincoln also supported granting African Americans ____________.

Main Idea: A group of Republicans presented a rival plan for Reconstruction.

4. **Detail:** Some Republicans favored a more ____________ approach.
5. **Detail:** In July 1864, Congress passed the ____________ which said that ____________ of a state's white males had to swear loyalty to the Union.
6. **Detail:** Only white males who swore that ____________ could vote for state constitutional convention delegates and the new constitution had to ____________.

Main Idea: The Freedmen's Bureau helped freed African Americans.

7. **Detail:** The agency reached its greatest success in the area of ____________.
8. **Detail:** The bureau helped freed people acquire land and free transportation to work sites, and it helped them obtain ____________.

Main Idea: Lincoln's assassination changed the plans for Reconstruction.

9. **Detail:** President Lincoln was shot by ____________ while he was watching a play at Ford's Theater.
10. **Detail:** President Andrew Johnson revealed his plan, which he preferred to call ____________.
11. **Detail:** Johnson opposed granting ____________ equal rights.
12. **Detail:** By the end of ____________ all the former Confederate states were ready to rejoin the Union.

Guided Reading Activities ★ 66 ★ *The American Journey*

HISTORY AND ART The Battle of Fredericksburg was fought in and near Fredericksburg, Virginia, December 13–15, 1862. The Union Army of the Potomac under the command of Ambrose Everett Burnside had 122,000 troops and 312 guns. The Confederate Army of Northern Virginia under the command of Robert E. Lee consisted of about 79,000 men and 270 guns. About 1,300 Union soldiers and 600 Confederate soldiers were killed during this battle. An additional 15,000 soldiers were reported wounded or missing. **Answer:** *because they were likely killed during the Civil War*

state could form a new government and adopt a new constitution that had to ban slavery.

Lincoln wanted to encourage Southerners who supported the Union to take charge of the state governments. He believed that punishing the South would serve no useful purpose and would only delay healing the torn nation.

The president offered **amnesty**—a pardon—to all white Southerners, except Confederate leaders, who were willing to swear loyalty to the Union. Lincoln also supported granting the right to vote to African Americans who were educated or had served in the Union army. He would not force the Southern states to give rights held by white Americans to African Americans.

In 1864 three states that the Union army occupied—**Louisiana, Arkansas,** and **Tennessee**—established governments under Lincoln's plan. These states then became caught in a struggle between the president and Congress when Congress refused to seat the states' representatives.

A Rival Plan

A group of Republicans in Congress considered Lincoln's plan too mild. They argued that Congress, not the president, should control Reconstruction policy. Because these Republicans favored a tougher and more **radical,** or extreme, approach to Reconstruction, they were called **Radical Republicans.** A leading Radical Republican, **Thaddeus Stevens,** declared that Southern institutions "must be broken up and relaid, or all our blood and treasure have been spent in vain."

Controlled by the Radical Republicans, Congress voted to deny seats to representatives from any state reconstructed under Lincoln's plan. Then Congress began to create its own plan.

The Wade-Davis Bill

In July 1864, Congress passed the **Wade-Davis Bill.** The bill offered a plan much harsher than Lincoln's. First, 50 percent of the white males in a state had to swear loyalty to the Union. Second, a state constitutional convention could be held, but only white males who swore they had never taken up arms against the Union could vote for delegates to this convention. Former Confederates were also denied the right to hold public office. Finally, the convention had to adopt a new state constitution that abolished slavery. Only then could a state be readmitted to the Union.

Lincoln refused to sign the bill into law. He wanted to encourage the formation of new state governments so that order could be restored quickly. Lincoln realized that he would have to compromise with the Radical Republicans.

The Freedmen's Bureau

More progress was made on the other great issue of Reconstruction—helping African Americans freed from slavery. In March 1865, during the

HISTORY AND ART

***The Return to Fredericksburg After the Battle* by David English Henderson** A Virginia family returns to its home in war-shattered Fredericksburg. **Why do you think the painting shows no men of military age?**

COOPERATIVE LEARNING ACTIVITY

Writing Plays Organize students into groups of four. Encourage groups to imagine that they are members of the United States Congress during the time period covered in this section. Have each group write a play involving a debate in Congress that might have taken place between the supporters of President Lincoln's approach to Reconstruction and the Radical Republicans' approach. Have students in each group choose one of the following writing roles: dialogue from Lincoln's point of view; dialogue from the Radical Republicans' point of view; description of the setting; historical and critical asides. Ask groups to perform their plays for the rest of the class.

final weeks of the war, Congress and the president established a new government agency to help former enslaved persons, or **freedmen.** Called the **Freedmen's Bureau,** this agency was actually part of the army.

In the years following the war, the Freedmen's Bureau played an important role in helping African Americans make the transition to freedom. The agency distributed food and clothing and also provided medical services that lowered the death rate among freed men and women.

The Freedmen's Bureau achieved one of its greatest successes in the area of education. The bureau established schools, staffed mostly by teachers from the North. It also gave aid to new institutions of higher learning, such as Atlanta University, Howard University, and Fisk University.

The bureau helped freed people acquire land that had been abandoned by owners or seized by Union armies. It offered African Americans free transportation to the countryside where laborers were needed, and it helped them obtain fair wages. Although its main goal was to aid African Americans, the bureau also helped Southerners who had supported the Union.

Lincoln Assassinated!

A terrible event soon threw the debates over Reconstruction into confusion. On the evening of April 14, 1865, President and Mrs. Lincoln attended the play *Our American Cousin* at Ford's Theater in **Washington, D.C.** It was just five days after the surrender of Lee's army and four years to the day after the fall of Fort Sumter.

As the Lincolns watched the play from a private box in the balcony, **John Wilkes Booth,** an actor and Confederate sympathizer, entered the box without anyone seeing him. Booth shot the president in the back of the head, then leaped to the stage and escaped during the chaos that followed the shooting. Aides carried the wounded president to the nearby house of William Petersen, a tailor. Lincoln died there a few hours later, without ever regaining consciousness.

After escaping from Ford's Theater, Booth fled on horseback to Virginia. Union troops tracked him down and on April 26 cornered him in a barn near Port Royal, Virginia. When Booth refused to surrender, he was shot to death.

Booth was part of a small group that plotted to kill high officials of the United States government. On the night of Lincoln's assassination, a fellow conspirator attacked Secretary of State William Seward, wounding him seriously. Another conspirator went to kill Vice President Andrew Johnson but failed to carry out the assignment. A military court convicted eight people of taking part in the plot. Four were hanged and the others imprisoned for life.

News of Lincoln's assassination shocked the nation. African Americans mourned the death of

Picturing HISTORY

Actor John Wilkes Booth used this pistol to shoot Lincoln at Ford's Theater. The wanted poster promises a large reward for help in capturing Booth. **How was Booth finally captured?**

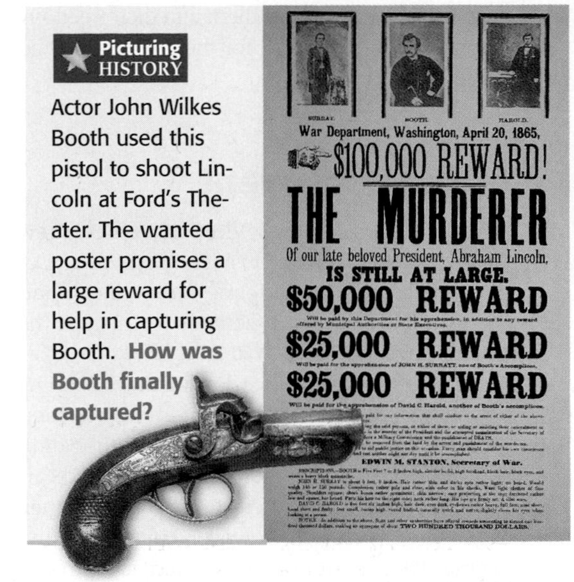

Footnotes to History

Your Name Is *Mud* During his escape, John Wilkes Booth broke his leg and was treated by Dr. Samuel Mudd. The doctor was later imprisoned for giving aid to the president's assassin. "Your name is mud" came to mean having a damaged reputation.

MULTIPLE LEARNING STYLES

Interpersonal President Andrew Johnson was raised in North Carolina. He had no formal schooling and remained illiterate until he was 18 years old. After Johnson married, his wife taught him to write. Quick to learn and devoted to hard work, Johnson prospered and decided to enter politics. Have students work in pairs to analyze President Johnson's background and write a personality profile that reflects how his life of struggle was reflected in his plans for Reconstruction. Include in the profile examples of Johnson's conflict with Congress over Reconstruction plans and how his personality played a major role in this conflict. **L3**

CHAPTER 17
Section 1, 495–498

Picturing HISTORY John Wilkes Booth's original plan was to kidnap President Lincoln and exchange him for Confederate prisoners of war.
Answer: *Union troops tracked Booth down and, on April 26, cornered him in a barn near Port Royal, Virginia. When Booth refused to surrender, he was shot to death.*

Facts On File

CD-ROM
Landmark Documents in American History

Title: *Freedmen's Bureau Act, 1865*
Have students list the objectives of the Freedmen's Bureau.

3 ASSESS

Assign Section 1 Review as homework or as an in-class activity.

Use **Chapter Challenger Interactive Review Software** to review Section 1.

Section Quiz 17–1

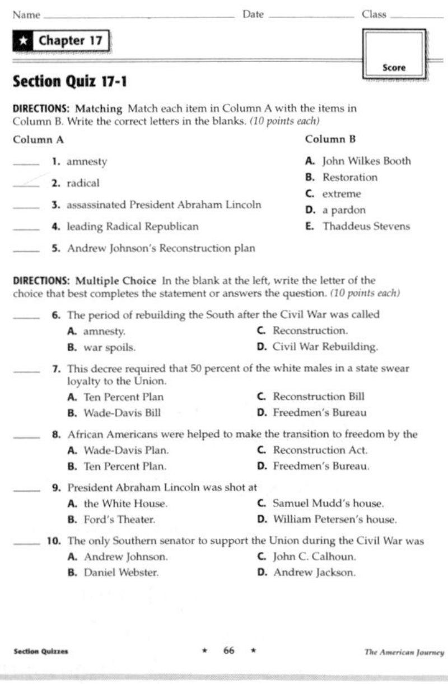
Name ______ Date ______ Class ______

Chapter 17 Score

Section Quiz 17-1

DIRECTIONS: Matching Match each item in Column A with the items in Column B. Write the correct letters in the blanks. *(10 points each)*

Column A

____ 1. amnesty
____ 2. radical
____ 3. assassinated President Abraham Lincoln
____ 4. leading Radical Republican
____ 5. Andrew Johnson's Reconstruction plan

Column B

A. John Wilkes Booth
B. Restoration
C. extreme
D. a pardon
E. Thaddeus Stevens

DIRECTIONS: Multiple Choice In the blank at the left, write the letter of the choice that best completes the statement or answers the question. *(10 points each)*

____ 6. The period of rebuilding the South after the Civil War was called
A. amnesty. C. Reconstruction.
B. war spoils. D. Civil War Rebuilding.

____ 7. This decree required that 50 percent of the white males in a state swear loyalty to the Union.
A. Ten Percent Plan C. Reconstruction Bill
B. Wade-Davis Bill D. Freedmen's Bureau

____ 8. African Americans were helped to make the transition to freedom by the
A. Wade-Davis Plan. C. Reconstruction Act.
B. Ten Percent Plan. D. Freedmen's Bureau.

____ 9. President Abraham Lincoln was shot at
A. the White House. C. Samuel Mudd's house.
B. Ford's Theater. D. William Petersen's house.

____ 10. The only Southern senator to support the Union during the Civil War was
A. Andrew Johnson. C. John C. Calhoun.
B. Daniel Webster. D. Andrew Jackson.

Reteaching Activity 17–1

Name ______ Date ______ Class ______

★ Reteaching Activity 17-1

DIRECTIONS: Organizing Facts The numbered items in the Fact Bank describe characteristics of three Reconstruction plans. Complete the diagram by writing the number of each item in the correct box on the diagram. One item fits more than one category.

RECONSTRUCTION PLANS FOR THE SOUTH

Abraham Lincoln's Plan	Wade-Davis Bill	Andrew Johnson's Plan
______	______	______
______	______	______
______	______	______

★FACT BANK

1. Only white males who had never fought against the Union could vote at a state's convention.
2. States had to ratify the Thirteenth Amendment.
3. The state constitution had to ban slavery.
4. did not punish the South
5. Former Confederates could not hold public office.
6. Fifty percent of white males in a state had to swear loyalty to the Union.
7. opposed to giving African Americans equal rights
8. Ten Percent Plan
9. Wealthy landowners had to apply to the president personally for a pardon.
10. offered amnesty to all white Southerners, except Confederate leaders
11. Restoration
12. Only whites who had been pardoned could vote at the state's convention.
13. granted the right to vote for some African Americans

DIRECTIONS: Essay Answer the following question on a separate sheet of paper.
How did the Freedmen's Bureau help African Americans after the war?

Reteaching Activities ★ 66 ★ *The American Journey*

Enrichment Activity 17–1

Name ______ Date ______ Class ______

★ Enrichment Activity 17-1 ★ ★

The Death of Lincoln

William Cullen Bryant wrote the following poem for the New York funeral ceremony for Abraham Lincoln. The poem was later published in the *Atlantic Monthly.*

The Death of Lincoln

Oh, slow to smite and swift to spare,
Gentle and merciful and just!
Who, in the fear of God, didst bear
The sword of power, a nation's trust!
In sorrow by thy bier we stand,
Amid the awe that hushes all,
And speak the anguish of a land
That shook with horror at thy fall.

Thy task is done; the bond are free:
We bear thee to an honored grave,
Whose proudest monument shall be
The broken fetters of the slave.
Pure was thy life; its bloody close
Hath placed thee with the sons of light,
Among the noble host of those
Who perished in the cause of Right.

DIRECTIONS: Interpreting Information Think what the poem reveals about the poet. Was Bryant a Northerner or Southerner? What political beliefs did he hold? Describe what you can tell about the poet and explain how you know.

______

Activity **DIRECTIONS:** Pick a prominent person who died within your lifetime. Use the media center to find out more about that person. Then write a poem that might have been read at the funeral of the person you chose.

Enrichment Activities ★ 66 ★ *The American Journey*

the man who had helped them win their freedom. Northern whites grieved for the leader who had saved the Union.

A New President

When Lincoln died, Vice President **Andrew Johnson** became president. Formerly a Democratic senator from Tennessee, Johnson had been the only Southern senator to support the Union during the Civil War.

Soon after taking office, President Johnson revealed his plan for Reconstruction. He resented the slaveholders who had dominated the South and wished to punish them. As a result Radicals thought Johnson would create a harsh plan they could accept. Johnson, however, believed in giving the states control over many decisions, and he had no desire to help African Americans.

"Restoration"

Johnson announced his plan, which he preferred to call "Restoration," in the summer of 1865—while Congress was in recess. Under his plan, most Southerners would be granted amnesty once they swore an oath of loyalty to the Union. High-ranking Confederate officials and wealthy landowners, however, could be pardoned only by applying personally to the president. This provision was Johnson's attack on the wealthy leaders who he believed had tricked the average people of the South into seceding.

Johnson also appointed governors to Southern states and required them to hold elections for state constitutional conventions. Only whites who had sworn their loyalty and been pardoned would be allowed to vote. Johnson opposed granting freed African Americans equal rights or letting them vote. He believed that each Southern state should decide what to do about freed people, saying, "White men alone must manage the South."

Before a state could reenter the Union, its constitutional convention had to denounce secession and abolish slavery. States also had to ratify the **Thirteenth Amendment** to the Constitution, which Congress had passed in January 1865. This amendment abolished slavery in all parts of the United States.

By the end of 1865, all the former Confederate states had formed new governments under Johnson's plan and were ready to rejoin the Union. President Johnson declared that "Restoration" was almost complete.

Section 1 Review

Checking for Understanding

1. ***Identify*** Radical Republicans, Wade-Davis Bill, John Wilkes Booth, Andrew Johnson, Thirteenth Amendment.
2. ***Define*** Reconstruction, amnesty, radical, freedmen.
3. ***Compare*** Lincoln's Ten Percent Plan to the Radical Republicans' Wade-Davis Bill.

Reviewing Themes

4. **Groups and Institutions** Why do you think both Lincoln and the Radical Republicans excluded former Confederate officials from their Reconstruction plans?

Critical Thinking

5. **Recognizing Bias** Do you think President Johnson's early ties to the South influenced his treatment of African Americans in his Reconstruction plans? Explain your answer.

Activity

Creating a Table of Contents What would it have been like for an enslaved African American to be in control of his or her life for the first time? Prepare a table of contents for a booklet to help African Americans make an easier transition to freedom.

4 CLOSE

Pose the following questions to students: **What if President Lincoln had not been assassinated? How would Reconstruction have been different?** *(Answers should show an understanding of Lincoln's contributions and beliefs.)*

Section 1 Review Answers

1. Radical Republicans, 496; Wade-Davis Bill, 496; John Wilkes Booth, 497; Andrew Johnson, 498; Thirteenth Amendment, 498
2. The words are defined in the Glossary.
3. Ten Percent Plan: required 10 percent of voters in state to pledge loyalty to Union and accept a constitution banning slavery; Wade-Davis Bill: required 50 percent of white males to swear loyalty to Union, former Confederates could not hold public office, new state constitutions had to abolish slavery
4. as punishment for traitors
5. Yes, his attitudes reflected views similar to many Southerners.

Activity Table of contents could include how to register for school, how to buy land, methods of finding a job.

1865 1867 1869 1871

1865 First black codes passed

March 1867 Radical Reconstruction begins

1868 Ulysses S. Grant is elected president

February 1870 Fifteenth Amendment extends voting rights

Section 2

Radicals in Control

READ TO DISCOVER . . .

- what some Southerners did to deprive freed people of their rights and how Congress responded.
- what the main features of Radical Reconstruction were.

TERMS TO LEARN

black codes
impeach
override

The Storyteller

For three days in May 1866, white mobs in Memphis, Tennessee, burned African American churches, schools, and homes. Forty-eight people, all but two of them African American, were killed in the rioting. Many Northerners saw the rampage as an attempt by whites to terrorize African Americans and keep them from exercising their new freedoms. This incident and similar riots in other Southern cities helped convince Radical Republicans that President Johnson's Reconstruction plans were not strong enough.

Ku Klux Klan flag

During the fall of 1865, the Southern states created new governments that met the rules President Johnson laid down, and Southern voters elected new representatives to Congress. More than two dozen of these representatives had been high-ranking officials in the Confederacy—including the Confederacy's vice president, Alexander H. Stephens. When the newly elected Southern representatives arrived in Washington, D.C., Congress refused to seat them. Many Republicans refused to readmit the Southern states on such easy terms and rejected Johnson's claim that Reconstruction was complete.

African Americans' Rights

To many in the North, it seemed that Johnson's plan for Reconstruction was robbing the Union of its hard-won victory. In addition Northerners realized that the treatment of African Americans in Southern states was not improving.

Black Codes

In 1865 and early 1866, the new Southern state legislatures passed a series of laws called **black codes.** Key parts of these laws aimed to control freed men and women and to enable plantation owners to exploit African American workers.

Modeled on laws that had regulated free African Americans before the Civil War, the black codes of each Southern state trampled the rights of African Americans. Some laws allowed local officials to arrest and fine unemployed African

SECTION RESOURCES

Reproducible Masters
- Reproducible Lesson Plan 17–2
- Guided Reading Activity 17–2
- Section Quiz 17–2
- Reteaching Activity 17–2
- Enrichment Activity 17–2

Transparencies
- Section Focus Transparency 17–2

Multimedia
- Chapter Challenger Interactive Review
- Testmaker
- GTV: American People: Fabric of a Nation
- Facts On File: Landmark Documents in American History
- The Presidents: A Picture History of Our Nation
- American Music Cultural Traditions

1 FOCUS

BELLRINGER
Motivational Activity

Before taking roll at the beginning of the class period, project Section Focus Transparency 17–2 and have students answer the questions. Discuss students' responses.

This activity is also available as a blackline master.

Section Focus Transparency 17–2

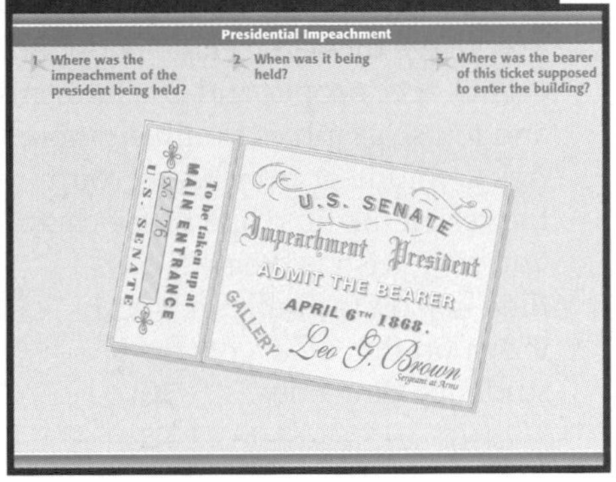

Vocabulary Precheck

Ask students to read the definition of *impeach* on page 502. Explain that to impeach is to bring charges against. After a formal charge is made, then, according to the Constitution, the impeachment trial takes place in the Senate.

Section Theme
Civic Rights and Responsibilities

In the beginning of Reconstruction, Southern states created new governments and elected new representatives to Congress. Many Republicans refused to recognize these leaders.

Activity Discuss with students the opinions of the Radical Republicans who controlled Congress. Ask students whether they think it was the Radical Republicans' civic responsibility to recognize new Southern governments and leaders or whether it was their right to reject them.

HISTORY AND ART The Fifteenth Amendment is the last of three Reconstruction amendments. The Thirteenth and Fifteenth Amendments were meant to guard the people against the misuse of state power.
Answer: *The passage of the Fifteenth Amendment gave African American males the right to vote.*

2 TEACH

L1 Creating a Time Line Ask students to work in small groups to create a time line of Reconstruction. Encourage them to include important events, acts, people, and amendments and to use graphics for illustration. Ask a volunteer from each group to present the time line to the class. You may wish to create a class time line on the bulletin board incorporating all events from students' time lines.

Guided Reading Activity 17–2

Name ____________ Date ____________ Class ____________

★ Guided Reading Activity 17-2

DIRECTIONS: Recalling Facts Read the section and answer the questions below. Refer to your textbook to write the answers.

1. What series of laws did the new Southern state legislatures pass in 1865 and early 1866? ____________
2. What did key parts of these laws aim to do? ____________
3. What authority did Congress give to the Freedmen's Bureau in early 1866? ____________
4. What did Congress pass in 1866 that granted full citizenship to African Americans? ____________
5. What did this law overturn and contradict? ____________
6. Why did President Andrew Johnson veto the Freedmen's Bureau Bill and the Civil Rights Act? ____________
7. How did Congress respond to Johnson's vetoes? ____________
8. **Citizenship** What did Congress do to avoid having the Civil Rights Act overturned? ____________
9. **Citizenship** Which was the only Southern state to ratify the Fourteenth Amendment? ____________
10. What signal did Republican victories in the elections of 1866 send to Congress? ____________
11. How did the First Reconstruction Act divide the 10 Southern states? ____________
12. What did this act guarantee African American males? ____________
13. What law did Congress pass in March 1867 to limit the president's power? ____________
14. How did President Johnson violate this act? ____________
15. What did the House of Representatives do in response? ____________
16. When did African American men win the right to vote? ____________

The American Journey ★ 67 ★ **Guided Reading Activities**

HISTORY AND ART
***Black Voter* by Thomas Waterman Wood** Wood's oil painting emphasized the importance of the ballot to African American voters. **How did African American males gain the right to vote?**

Americans and make them work for white employers to pay off their fines. Other laws banned African Americans from owning or renting farms. One law allowed whites to take orphaned African American children as unpaid apprentices. To freed men and women and many Northerners, the black codes reestablished slavery in disguise.

Challenging the Black Codes

In early 1866 Congress extended the life of the Freedmen's Bureau and granted it new powers. The Freedmen's Bureau now had authority to set up special courts to prosecute individuals charged with violating the rights of African Americans. These courts provided African Americans with a form of justice where they could serve on juries.

Congress also passed the **Civil Rights Act of 1866.** This act granted full citizenship to African Americans and gave the federal government the power to intervene in state affairs to protect their rights. The law overturned the black codes. It also contradicted the 1857 *Dred Scott* decision of the Supreme Court, which had ruled that African Americans were not citizens.

President Johnson vetoed both the Freedmen's Bureau bill and the Civil Rights Act, arguing that the federal government was overstepping its proper authority. He also said that the laws were unconstitutional because they were passed by a Congress that did not include representatives from all the states. By raising the issue of representation, Johnson indirectly threatened to veto any law passed by this Congress.

Republicans in Congress had enough votes to **override**, or defeat, both vetoes, and the bills became law. As the split between Congress and the president grew, the possibility of their working together faded. The Radical Republicans abandoned the idea of compromise and drafted a new Reconstruction plan—one led by Congress.

Citizenship

The Fourteenth Amendment

Congress wanted to ensure that African Americans would not lose the rights that the Civil Rights Act granted. Fearing the Civil Rights Act might be overturned in court, Congress in June 1866 passed a new amendment to the Constitution.

The **Fourteenth Amendment** granted full citizenship to all individuals born in the United States. Because most African Americans in the United States had been born there, they became full citizens. The amendment also stated that no state could take away a citizen's life, liberty, and property "without due process of law," and that every citizen was entitled to "equal protection of the laws." States that prevented any adult male citizen from voting could lose part of their representation in Congress.

The amendment did not include voting rights for African Americans—a right granted only in a

America's FLAGS

The 37-Star Flag By 1866 Nebraskans had ratified their state's constitution. The state was admitted into the Union on March 1, 1867.

COOPERATIVE LEARNING ACTIVITY

Creating a Reconstruction Graphic Organizer Discuss with students the different viewpoints of major groups affected by Reconstruction. Organize students into groups of four to choose from the following roles: Radical Republican, freed African American, white Southerner, and white Northerner. Each student should make a list of Reconstruction needs from that person's point of view and create a graphic organizer illustrating the most important needs. Then have each group discuss the needs shown on the organizer and cooperatively develop a plan for Reconstruction that incorporates these needs. Have each group create a large graphic organizer that illustrates this cooperative Reconstruction plan.

few Northern states. The amendment also barred prominent former Confederates from holding national or state office unless pardoned by a vote of two-thirds of Congress.

Congress declared that Southern states had to ratify the amendment to be readmitted to the Union. Of the 11 Southern states, only Tennessee ratified the Fourteenth Amendment. The refusal of the other states to ratify the amendment delayed its adoption until 1868.

Republican Victory

The Fourteenth Amendment became a major issue in the congressional elections of 1866. Johnson urged Northern and Southern state legislatures to reject it. He also campaigned vigorously against Republican candidates. Many Northerners were disturbed by the nastiness of Johnson's campaign. They also worried about violent clashes between whites and African Americans, such as the riots that erupted in Memphis, Tennessee, and New Orleans, Louisiana.

The Republicans won a decisive victory, increasing their majorities in both houses of Congress. The Republicans also gained control of the governments in every Northern state. The election gave Congress the signal to take Reconstruction into its own hands.

Radical Reconstruction

The Republicans in Congress quickly took charge of Reconstruction. President Johnson could do little to stop them because Congress could easily override his vetoes. Thus began a period known as Radical Reconstruction.

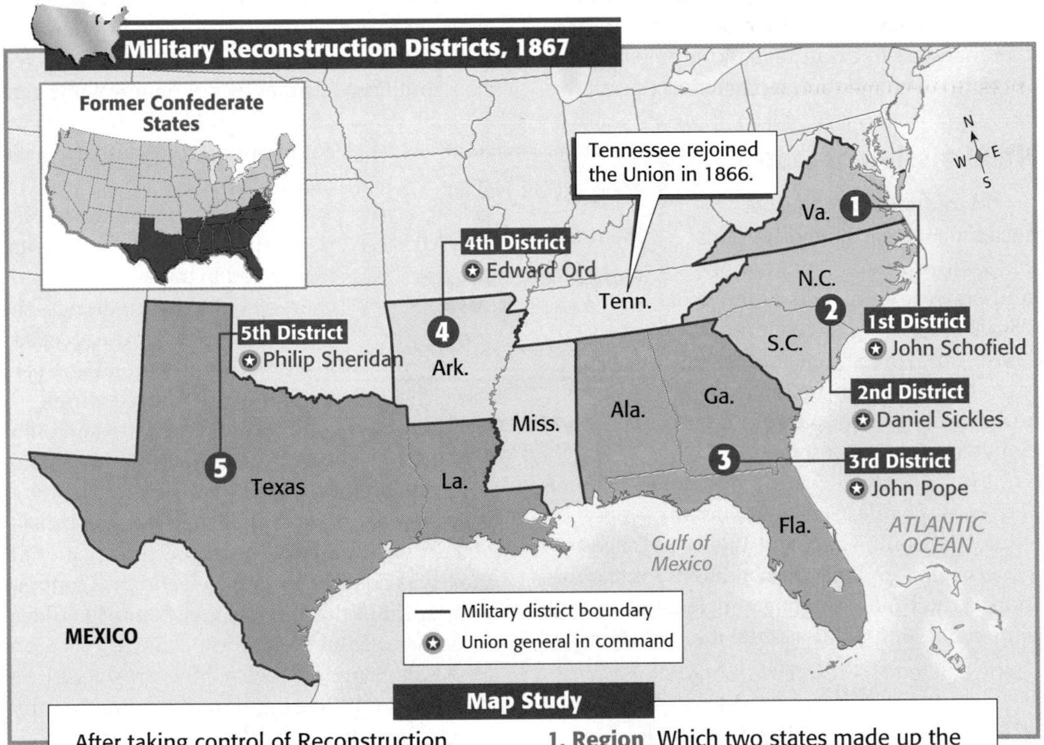

Map Study

After taking control of Reconstruction, Congress divided the South into five districts under the command of military officers.

1. **Region** Which two states made up the largest district?
2. **Analyzing Information** Why did no Union troops occupy Tennessee?

Multiple Learning Styles

Verbal/Linguistic Congress passed many acts and amendments during Reconstruction to guarantee the rights of newly freed peoples and to restore the Union. Have students scan this section to list these laws, acts, and amendments. Then have them write in their own words what was granted by each. Organize students into pairs to create a mnemonic device (a combination of letters or words that are easy to remember) that can be used to memorize each law, act, or amendment. Ask volunteers to share a mnemonic device with the class without revealing what it stands for and have other students guess which law, act, or amendment it represents. **L1**

History *and the* Humanities

American Music Cultural Traditions, Lesson 5: "Roll, Jordan, Roll"

Facts On File

CD-ROM
Landmark Documents in American History

Title: *Reconstruction Acts, 1867–68*
Have students summarize the goals of the Reconstruction Acts.

NATIONAL GEOGRAPHIC SOCIETY

VIDEODISC
GTV: The American People: Fabric of a Nation

Side 2, Chapter 8
Title: *The Dream Deferred*
Subject: African Americans and equal rights
Ask: What three goals did Congress have after the Civil War? *(abolish slavery, extend citizenship to all African Americans, and protect the right to vote for black males)* **What amendments did Congress pass to achieve these goals?** *(Thirteenth, Fourteenth, and Fifteenth Amendments)*

Map Study

Answers

1. Texas and Louisiana
2. because Tennessee had rejoined the Union in 1866, before Radical Reconstruction began

Map Skills Practice

Reading a Map Which district did John Pope command? *(third)*

CHAPTER 17

Section 2, 499–503

NATIONAL GEOGRAPHIC SOCIETY

CD-ROM
The Presidents: A Picture History of Our Nation

Have students select Andrew Johnson from the main menu. Ask them to note some of Johnson's challenges as president.

3 ASSESS

Assign Section 2 Review as homework or as an in-class activity.

Use **Chapter Challenger Interactive Review Software** to review Section 2.

Section Quiz 17–2

Name ______ Date ______ Class ______

Chapter 17 — Score

Section Quiz 17-2

DIRECTIONS: Matching Match each item in Column A with the items in Column B. Write the correct letters in the blanks. *(10 points each)*

Column A	Column B
____ 1. to defeat a president's veto	A. Ulysses S. Grant
____ 2. divided South into military districts	B. Horatio Seymour
____ 3. Tenure of Office Act	C. override
____ 4. 1868 Republican presidential candidate	D. First Reconstruction Act
____ 5. Ulysses S. Grant's opponent	E. threatened president's power

DIRECTIONS: Multiple Choice In the blank at the left, write the letter of the choice that best completes the statement or answers the question. *(10 points each)*

____ 6. This law granted full citizenship to African Americans.
A. Thirteenth Amendment C. Civil Rights Act of 1866
B. Ten Percent Law D. black codes

____ 7. This law granted full citizenship to all individuals born in the United States.
A. Thirteenth Amendment C. Civil Rights Act of 1866
B. black codes D. Fourteenth Amendment

____ 8. The only Southern state to immediately ratify the Fourteenth Amendment was
A. Maryland. C. Kentucky.
B. Tennessee. D. North Carolina.

____ 9. When President Andrew Johnson violated the Tenure of Office Act, the House of Representatives voted to
A. impeach. C. abstain.
B. applaud him. D. override.

____ 10. This amendment gave African American men the right to vote.
A. Thirteenth Amendment C. Fifteenth Amendment
B. Fourteenth Amendment D. Sixteenth Amendment

The American Journey ★ 67 ★ **Section Quizzes**

Reconstruction Act of 1867

On March 2, 1867, Congress passed the **First Reconstruction Act.** The act called for the creation of new governments in the 10 Southern states that had not ratified the Fourteenth Amendment. Tennessee, which had ratified the amendment, kept its government, and the state was quickly readmitted to the Union.

The act divided the 10 Southern states into 5 military districts and placed each under the authority of a military commander until new governments were formed. The act also guaranteed African American males the right to vote in state elections, and it prevented former Confederate leaders from holding political office.

To gain readmission to the Union, the states had to ratify the Fourteenth Amendment and submit their new state constitutions to Congress for approval. A **Second Reconstruction Act,** passed a few weeks later, required the military commanders to begin registering voters and to prepare for new state constitutional conventions.

Readmission of States

Many white Southerners refused to take part in the elections for constitutional conventions and state governments. Almost 750,000 newly registered African American voters did use their right to vote. In the elections, Republicans gained control of Southern state governments.

Ticket to Johnson's impeachment trial

By 1868 seven Southern states—Alabama, Arkansas, Florida, Georgia, Louisiana, North Carolina, and South Carolina—had established new governments and met the conditions for readmission to the Union. Virginia and Texas were readmitted in 1869 and Mississippi the year after.

Challenge to Johnson

Strongly opposed to Radical Reconstruction, President Johnson had the power as commander in chief of the army to direct the actions of the military governors. For this reason Congress passed several laws to limit the president's power.

One of these laws, the **Tenure of Office Act** of March 1867, was a deliberate challenge. It prohibited the president from removing government officials, including members of his own cabinet, without the Senate's approval. The act violated the tradition that presidents controlled their cabinets, and it threatened presidential power.

Impeaching the President

The conflict between Johnson and the Radicals grew more intense. In August 1867—when Congress was not in session—Johnson suspended Secretary of War **Edwin Stanton** without the Senate's approval. When the Senate met again and refused to approve the suspension, Johnson removed Stanton from office—a deliberate violation of the Tenure of Office Act. Johnson angered the Republicans further by appointing some generals the Radicals opposed as commanders of Southern military districts.

Outraged by Johnson's actions, the House of Representatives voted to **impeach**—formally charge with wrongdoing—the president. The House accused Johnson of misconduct and sent the case to the Senate for trial.

The trial began in March 1868 and lasted three months. Johnson's defenders claimed that the president was exercising his right to challenge laws he considered unconstitutional. The impeachment, they argued, was politically motivated and thus contrary to the spirit of the Constitution. Samuel J. Tilden, a Democrat from New York, claimed that Congress was trying to remove the president from office without accusing him of a crime "or anything more than a mere difference of opinion."

Johnson's accusers argued that Congress should retain the supreme power to make the laws. Senator Charles Sumner of Massachusetts declared that Johnson had turned "the veto

MAKING CONNECTIONS ACTIVITY

Music Newly freed African Americans used songs to express their feelings about the difficulties they endured under the black codes. The Civil Rights Act of 1866 outlawed the black codes. Have students imagine that they are a newly freed person living in 1866 after the passage of the Civil Rights Act. Ask them to write the words to a song to express their feelings about the act and its elimination of the black codes. Have volunteers share their completed songs with the class. **L2**

power conferred by the Constitution as a remedy for ill-considered legislation . . . into a weapon of offense against Congress."

In May, as the nation waited anxiously, the senators cast their votes. The result was 35 to 19 votes to convict the president—one vote short of the two-thirds majority required by the Constitution for conviction. Several moderate Republicans voted for a verdict of not guilty, because they did not believe a president should be removed from office for political differences. As a result, Johnson stayed in office until the end of his term in March 1869.

Picturing HISTORY

A cloth banner from the 1868 election shows presidential candidate Ulysses S. Grant. **How many electoral votes did Grant receive?**

Election of 1868

By the presidential election of 1868, most Southern states had rejoined the Union. Many Americans hoped that conflicts over Reconstruction and sectional divisions were behind them.

Abandoning Johnson, the Republicans chose General **Ulysses S. Grant,** the Civil War hero, as their presidential candidate. The Democrats nominated Horatio Seymour, a former governor of New York.

Grant won the election, gaining 214 of 294 electoral votes. He also received most of the 500,000 votes of African Americans in the South. The 1868 election was a vote on Reconstruction, and the voters supported the Republican approach to the issue.

The Fifteenth Amendment

After the election Republicans added their last major piece of Reconstruction legislation. In February 1869, Congress passed the **Fifteenth Amendment**. It prohibited the state and federal governments from denying the right to vote to any male citizen because of "race, color, or previous condition of servitude."

African American men won the right to vote when the Fifteenth Amendment was ratified and became law in February 1870. Republicans thought that the power of the ballot would enable African Americans to protect themselves. That belief, it turned out, was too optimistic.

Section 2 Review

Checking for Understanding

1. ***Identify*** Fourteenth Amendment, First Reconstruction Act, Edwin Stanton, Ulysses S. Grant, Fifteenth Amendment.
2. ***Define*** black codes, override, impeach.
3. ***Discuss*** two ways Southerners violated Lincoln's plan for Reconstruction.

Reviewing Themes

4. **Civic Rights and Responsibilities** How did Congress challenge the black codes set up by Southern states?

Critical Thinking

5. **Distinguishing Fact from Opinion** If you had been a member of the Senate, would you have voted for or against convicting President Andrew Johnson? Explain your decision.

Activity

Creating a Political Cartoon Imagine you are an African American during Reconstruction. Draw a political cartoon critical of the black codes.

Section 2 Review Answers

1. Fourteenth Amendment, 500; First Reconstruction Act, 502; Edwin Stanton, 502; Ulysses S. Grant, 503; Fifteenth Amendment, 503
2. The words are defined in the Glossary.
3. Former Confederate officials were chosen for congressional representatives, and treatment of African Americans did not improve.
4. granted power to Freedmen's Bureau to prosecute those who violated rights of African Americans, passed Civil Rights Act of 1866
5. Students should choose to convict or not and include reasons why.

Activity Political cartoons should criticize black codes.

CHAPTER 17
Section 2, 499–503

Picturing HISTORY Grant's two terms were marred by corruption. He redeemed his place in history by writing his *Personal Memoirs* at Mark Twain's suggestion.
Answer: *214*

Reteaching Activity 17–2

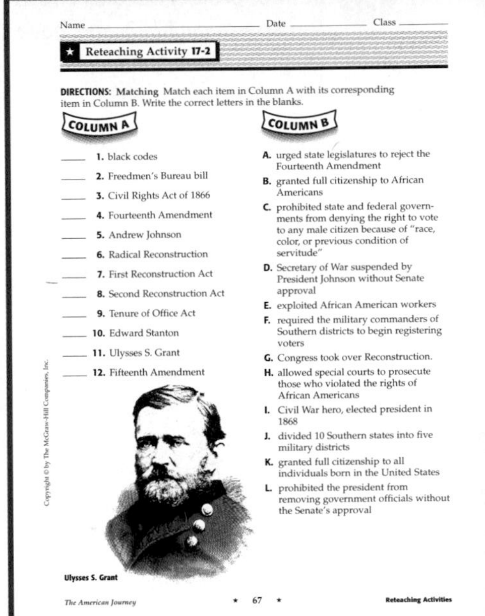

Name ______ Date ______ Class ______

★ Reteaching Activity 17-2

DIRECTIONS: Matching Match each item in Column A with its corresponding item in Column B. Write the correct letters in the blanks.

COLUMN A

____ 1. black codes
____ 2. Freedmen's Bureau bill
____ 3. Civil Rights Act of 1866
____ 4. Fourteenth Amendment
____ 5. Andrew Johnson
____ 6. Radical Reconstruction
____ 7. First Reconstruction Act
____ 8. Second Reconstruction Act
____ 9. Tenure of Office Act
____ 10. Edward Stanton
____ 11. Ulysses S. Grant
____ 12. Fifteenth Amendment

COLUMN B

A. urged state legislatures to reject the Fourteenth Amendment
B. granted full citizenship to African Americans
C. prohibited state and federal governments from denying the right to vote to any male citizen because of "race, color, or previous condition of servitude"
D. Secretary of War suspended by President Johnson without Senate approval
E. exploited African American workers
F. required the military commanders of Southern districts to begin registering voters
G. Congress took over Reconstruction.
H. allowed special courts to prosecute those who violated the rights of African Americans
I. Civil War hero, elected president in 1868
J. divided 10 Southern states into five military districts
K. granted full citizenship to all individuals born in the United States
L. prohibited the president from removing government officials without the Senate's approval

Ulysses S. Grant

Copyright © by The McGraw-Hill Companies, Inc.

The American Journey ★ 67 ★ Reteaching Activities

Enrichment Activity 17–2

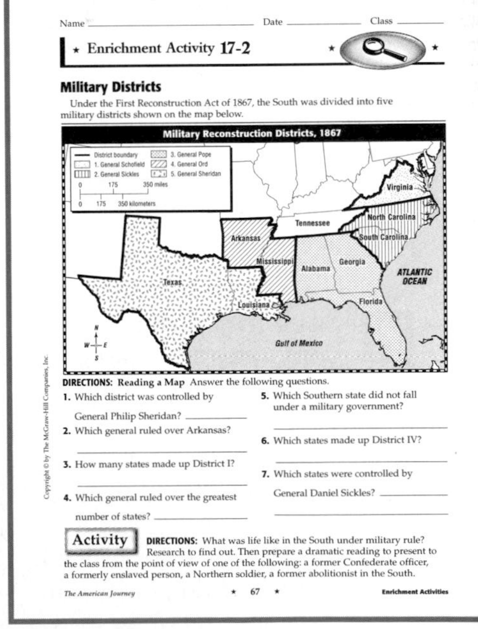

Name ______ Date ______ Class ______

★ Enrichment Activity 17-2

Military Districts

Under the First Reconstruction Act of 1867, the South was divided into five military districts shown on the map below.

DIRECTIONS: Reading a Map Answer the following questions.

1. Which district was controlled by General Philip Sheridan? ______
2. Which general ruled over Arkansas? ______
3. How many states made up District I? ______
4. Which general ruled over the greatest number of states? ______
5. Which Southern state did not fall under a military government? ______
6. Which states made up District IV? ______
7. Which states were controlled by General Daniel Sickles? ______

Activity **DIRECTIONS:** What was life like in the South under military rule? Research to find out. Then prepare a dramatic reading to present to the class from the point of view of one of the following: a former Confederate officer, a formerly enslaved person, a Northern soldier, a former abolitionist in the South.

Copyright © by The McGraw-Hill Companies, Inc.

The American Journey ★ 67 ★ Enrichment Activities

4 CLOSE

Discuss the purposes of the Thirteenth, Fourteenth, and Fifteenth Amendments. Include the difficulties in implementing these amendments.

CHAPTER 17
Section 3, 504–507

1 FOCUS

BELLRINGER
Motivational Activity

Before taking roll at the beginning of the class period, project Section Focus Transparency 17–3 and have students answer the questions. Discuss students' responses.

This activity is also available as a blackline master.

Section Focus Transparency 17–3

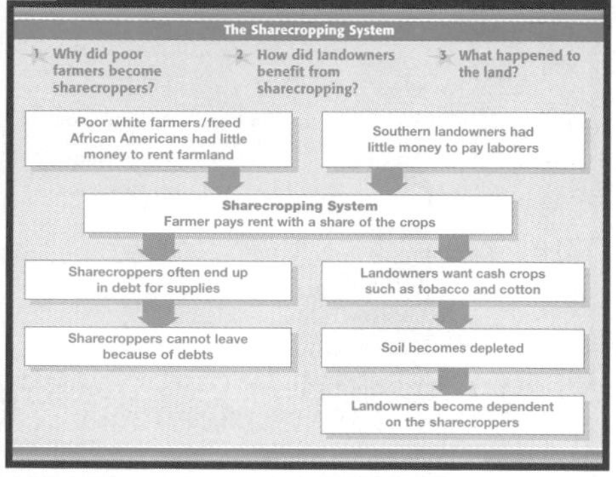

Vocabulary Precheck

Have students read the subsection *Scalawags and Carpetbaggers* on page 505. Ask them to draw a cartoon illustrating the origins of one of these words.

Use the **Vocabulary PuzzleMaker** to create crossword and word search puzzles.

Section Theme
Continuity and Change

During Reconstruction the Republicans who dominated Southern politics did their best to change and rebuild the South.

Activity Discuss the role of education in rebuilding the South.

1865 1867 1869 1871

1865 Freedmen's Bank is established

1866 Ku Klux Klan is formed

1869 African Americans serve in House of Representatives

1870 First African American is elected to the Senate

Section 3

The South During Reconstruction

READ TO DISCOVER . . .
- what groups participated in Reconstruction in the South.
- how Southern life changed during Reconstruction.

TERMS TO LEARN
- scalawag
- carpetbagger
- corruption
- integrate
- sharecropping

The Storyteller

"The dust of our fathers mingles with yours in the same graveyards. . . . This is your country, but it is ours too." So spoke an emancipated African American after the Civil War. Most former slaves did not seek revenge or power over whites, only respect and equality. The petition of an African American convention in 1865 stated: "We simply ask that we shall be recognized as *men;* . . . that the same laws which govern *white men* shall govern *black men;* . . . that, in short, we be dealt with as others are—in equity and justice."

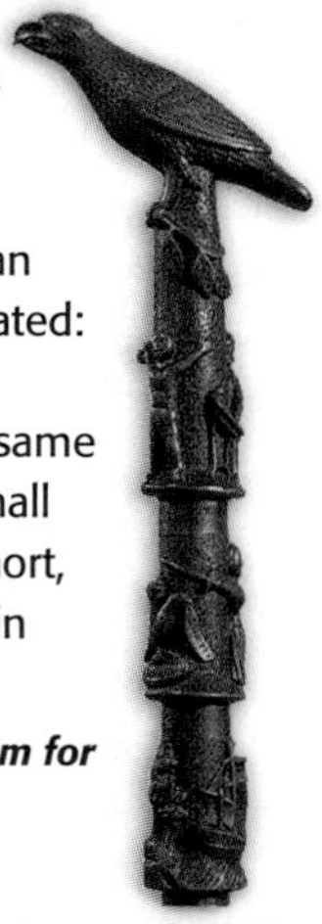

Cane honoring freedom for African Americans

The Republicans who controlled Southern state governments did their best to change and rebuild the South. However, former Confederates resisted, urging white Southerners to take back "their" governments and to restore their "birthright" [heritage].

New Groups Take Charge

During Reconstruction the Republican Party came to dominate Southern politics. The party consisted mainly of three groups—African Americans, white Southerners who supported Republican policies, and white settlers from the North. These groups dominated the state constitutional conventions and state governments.

African Americans in Government

African Americans played an important role in Reconstruction politics both as voters and as elected officials. In states where African American voters were the majority, they contributed heavily to Republican victories.

African Americans did not control the government of any state, although they briefly held a majority in the lower house of the South Carolina legislature. In other Southern states, they held important positions but never in proportion to their numbers.

SECTION RESOURCES

Reproducible Masters
- Reproducible Lesson Plan 17–3
- Guided Reading Activity 17–3
- Political Cartoons, *Reconstruction and Carpetbaggers*
- Section Quiz 17–3
- Reteaching Activity 17–3
- Enrichment Activity 17–3

Transparencies
- Section Focus Transparency 17–3

Multimedia
- Vocabulary PuzzleMaker
- Chapter Challenger Interactive Review Software
- Testmaker

Revels and Bruce

At the national level, 16 African Americans served in the House of Representatives and 2 in the Senate between 1869 and 1880. **Hiram Revels,** one of the African American senators, was an ordained minister. During the Civil War, he had recruited African Americans for the Union army, started a school for freed African Americans in St. Louis, Missouri, and served as chaplain of an African American regiment in Mississippi. Revels remained in Mississippi after the war and was elected to the Senate in 1870. He served a year in the Senate, where he declared he received "fair treatment."

Blanche K. Bruce, the other African American senator, also came from Mississippi. A former runaway slave, Bruce had established a school for African Americans in Missouri when the war began. In 1869 he went to Mississippi, entered politics, and became a superintendent of schools. He was elected to the Senate in 1874, serving there for six years.

Picturing HISTORY The first African American United States senators were Blanche K. Bruce (left) and Hiram R. Revels (right), shown here with Frederick Douglass. **What political party did most African Americans support during Reconstruction?**

Scalawags and Carpetbaggers

Some Southern whites supported Republican policy throughout Reconstruction. Many were nonslaveholding farmers or business leaders who had opposed secession in the first place. Former Confederates despised them for siding with the Republicans and called them **scalawags,** a term meaning "scoundrel" or "worthless rascal."

Many Northern whites who moved South after the war also supported the Republicans and served as Republican leaders during Reconstruction. Critics called these Northerners **carpetbaggers** because they arrived with all their belongings in cheap suitcases made of carpet fabric. Although some of the carpetbaggers were greedy and took advantage of the situation in the South, most did not. Many carpetbaggers were former Union army soldiers or members of the Freedmen's Bureau who liked the South and wanted to settle there. Others were reformers from the North—including lawyers, doctors, and teachers—who wanted to help reshape Southern society.

Government Corruption

Many Southerners ridiculed the Reconstruction governments and accused them of **corruption**—dishonest or illegal actions—and financial mismanagement. While some officials made money illegally, the practice was hardly widespread. Indeed, there was probably less corruption in the South than in the North.

Resistance to Reconstruction

Most white Southerners opposed efforts to expand African Americans' rights. Carl Schurz, a Republican from Missouri who toured the South right after the war, reported:

> "Wherever I go—the street, the shop, the house, the hotel, or the steamboat—I hear the people talk in such a way as to indicate that they are yet unable to conceive of the Negro as possessing any rights at all."

CHAPTER 17
Section 3, 504–507

2 TEACH

L1 Making a Chart Have students scan the section to create a two-column chart. One column should list how the South changed during Reconstruction, and the other should list how it stayed the same.

Political Cartoons, *Reconstruction and Carpetbaggers*

Picturing HISTORY In addition to the 2 United States senators, the Southern states sent 20 African Americans to the House of Representatives. South Carolina alone elected 8 African Americans to Congress. Revels took over the seat vacated by Jefferson Davis in 1861 when Davis resigned to become president of the Confederacy.
Answer: *Republican*

Guided Reading Activity 17–3

Name ________ Date ________ Class ________

Guided Reading Activity 17-3

DIRECTIONS: Outlining Read the section and complete the outline below. Refer to your textbook to fill in the blanks.

I. African Americans in Government
- **A.** At the national level 16 African Americans served in the ________ and two in the Senate between ________.
- **B.** Senator ________ was an ordained minister. The other African American senator was ________, a former runaway slave.

II. Scalawags and Carpetbaggers
- **A.** Former ________ despised Southern whites who supported Reconstruction, calling them ________.
- **B.** Northerners who moved South after the war were called carpetbaggers because ________.

III. Resistance to Reconstruction
- **A.** Plantation owners refused to ________ to freedmen. Store owners denied them ________, and employers refused to hire them.
- **B.** The most terrifying of the secret societies, organized to prevent freed men and women from ________, was the ________.
- **C.** Wearing ________, members of this group launched ________ against African Americans.

IV. Some Improvements
- **A.** ________ improved for both African Americans and whites during Reconstruction.
- **B.** The ________ and private charities played a major role in spreading education. By 1870 about ________ schools had been established.
- **C.** After the Civil War, more than half of the white children and about 40 percent of African American children were enrolled in ________.
- **D.** Only Louisiana, South Carolina, and Florida required that schools be ________, but the laws were not enforced.
- **E.** Freed individuals usually worked as ________.

Guided Reading Activities ★ 68 ★ *The American Journey*

COOPERATIVE LEARNING ACTIVITY

Making a Collage Organize students into groups of three to create a collage illustrating the changes that took place in the South during Reconstruction. Have each student in each group choose one of the following areas to be covered on the collage: educational changes, agricultural changes, and industrial changes. Have groups use poster board divided into three equal sections to create the collage. Each student should use drawings, words, photographs, and so on to show the changes on the designated section of the collage. As a group, have students decide which items to use for each section and assemble the collage. Encourage groups to title their collage and display it in the classroom. Ask for volunteers to explain their collages to the rest of the class.

Who?What?Where?When?

Robert Smalls Born a slave, Robert Smalls became a Civil War hero when he seized a Confederate ship *(Planter)* for the Union navy. He was later elected to the United States House of Representatives.

American Memories

African American Family Life

A powerful sense of family was the most important characteristic that African Americans carried with them out of slavery. Families had been torn apart by the sale of their members. Two decades after the war, newspapers were still full of queries from formerly enslaved persons seeking their family members. **Answer:** *Bible: spiritual guidance and to record family names, births, deaths, and marriages; bowl: family gatherings; banjo: music to celebrate*

3 ASSESS

Assign Section 3 Review as homework or as an in-class activity.

Use **Chapter Challenger Interactive Review Software** to review Section 3.

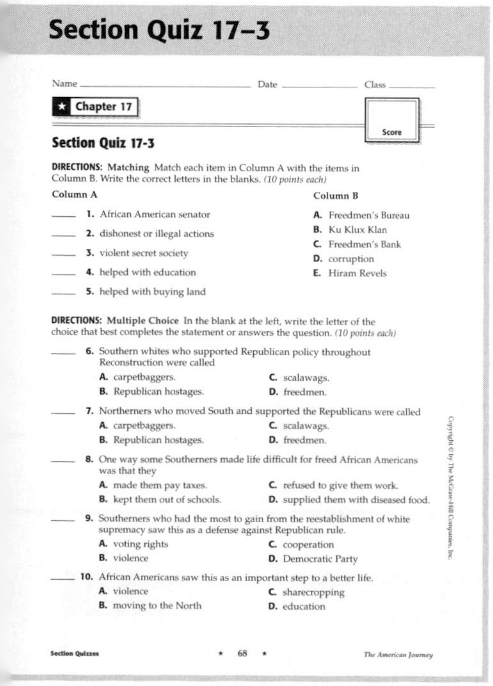

Section Quiz 17–3

Name ______ Date ______ Class ______

★ Chapter 17 | Score

Section Quiz 17-3

DIRECTIONS: Matching Match each item in Column A with the items in Column B. Write the correct letters in the blanks. *(10 points each)*

Column A	Column B
____ **1.** African American senator	**A.** Freedmen's Bureau
____ **2.** dishonest or illegal actions	**B.** Ku Klux Klan
____ **3.** violent secret society	**C.** Freedmen's Bank
____ **4.** helped with education	**D.** corruption
____ **5.** helped with buying land	**E.** Hiram Revels

DIRECTIONS: Multiple Choice In the blank at the left, write the letter of the choice that best completes the statement or answers the question. *(10 points each)*

____ **6.** Southern whites who supported Republican policy throughout Reconstruction were called
A. carpetbaggers. **C.** scalawags.
B. Republican hostages. **D.** freedmen.

____ **7.** Northerners who moved South and supported the Republicans were called
A. carpetbaggers. **C.** scalawags.
B. Republican hostages. **D.** freedmen.

____ **8.** One way some Southerners made life difficult for freed African Americans was that they
A. made them pay taxes. **C.** refused to give them work.
B. kept them out of schools. **D.** supplied them with diseased food.

____ **9.** Southerners who had the most to gain from the reestablishment of white supremacy saw this as a defense against Republican rule.
A. voting rights **C.** cooperation
B. violence **D.** Democratic Party

____ **10.** African Americans saw this as an important step to a better life.
A. violence **C.** sharecropping
B. moving to the North **D.** education

Section Quizzes ★ 68 ★ *The American Journey*

American Memories

African American Family Life

What Was It Like? As Reconstruction brought changes, many African Americans found strength and support in their families. **What part did each of these items play in the life of an African American family during this period?**

Plantation owners tried to maintain control over freed people in any way they could. Many told African Americans they could not leave the plantations. Most refused to rent land to freedmen.

Other white Southerners also made life difficult for African Americans. Store owners refused them credit, and employers refused to give them work. As in the days of slavery, some whites also used fear and force to keep freedmen in line.

The Ku Klux Klan

Violence against African Americans and their white supporters became commonplace during Reconstruction. Much of this violence was committed by secret societies organized to prevent freed men and women from exercising their rights and to help whites regain power.

The most terrifying of these societies, the **Ku Klux Klan,** was formed in 1866. Wearing white sheets and hoods, members of the Klan launched "midnight rides" against African Americans, burning their homes, churches, and schools. The Klan killed as well. In Jackson County, Florida, the Klan murdered more than 150 people over a 3-year period. Klan violence increased before elections, as the group tried to scare African Americans to keep them from voting.

The tactics of the Klan and other violent groups had the support of many Southerners, especially planters and Democrats. These Southerners, who had the most to gain from the reestablishment of white supremacy, saw violence as a defense against Republican rule.

Taking Action against Violence

Southerners opposed to terrorism appealed to the federal government to do something. In 1870 and 1871, Congress passed several laws to try to stop the growing violence of the Klan. These laws had limited success. Most white Southerners refused to testify against those who attacked African Americans and their white supporters. Still, enough arrests were made to restore order for the 1872 presidential election.

Making Connections Activity

Cultural Life Despite slavery's hardships, many African Americans clung to family as a source of strength and identity. Many families separated by slavery sought to reunite after their emancipation and the war's end. A Freedmen's Bureau agent reported in 1865 that it was like "every mother in search of her children." African Americans used a family record to keep track of births, deaths, and marriages after emancipation. Ask students to create their own family record with the following information: Name, Born, Married, Died. Discuss the difficulties in trying to recreate this information from memory. **L2**

Some Improvements

Despite the violence, Reconstruction brought important changes throughout the South. This was especially true in education.

Education improved for both African Americans and whites. African Americans saw education as an important step to a better life. In many regions they created their own schools, contributing both labor and money to build the schools.

The Freedmen's Bureau and private charities played a major role in spreading education. Northern women and free African Americans came South to teach in these schools. By 1870 about 4,000 schools had been established with 200,000 students. More than half the teachers in these schools were African American.

Mother and daughter reading

Public Schools

In the 1870s Reconstruction governments began creating public school systems, which had not existed in the South before the Civil War. Within a few years, more than 50 percent of the white children and about 40 percent of African American children in the South were enrolled in public schools. Northern missionary societies also established academies offering advanced education for African Americans. Over time these academies developed into colleges and universities, such as Morehouse College and Atlanta University.

Generally African American and white students attended different schools. Only three states—Louisiana, South Carolina, and Florida—required that schools be **integrated**—include whites and African Americans—but the laws were not enforced.

Farming the Land

Along with education, most freed people wanted land. Some African Americans were able to buy land with the assistance of the Freedmen's Bank, established in 1865. Most, however, failed to get their own land.

The most common form of farmwork for freed individuals was **sharecropping.** In this system a landowner rented a plot of land to a sharecropper, or farmer, along with a crude shack, some seeds and tools, and perhaps a mule. In return sharecroppers shared a percentage of their crop with the landowner.

After paying the landowners, sharecroppers often had little or nothing left to sell. Sometimes there was barely enough to feed their families. For many sharecropping was little better than slavery.

Section 3 Review

Checking for Understanding

1. ***Identify*** Hiram Revels, Blanche K. Bruce, Ku Klux Klan.
2. ***Define*** scalawag, carpetbagger, corruption, integrate, sharecropping.
3. ***Name*** the three groups that made up the Southern Republican Party.

Reviewing Themes

4. **Continuity and Change** What two groups spread education in the South?

Critical Thinking

5. **Determining Relevance** Why was voting and holding political office so important to newly freed African Americans?

Activity

Planning a Speech Imagine you have been asked to discuss changes you would like to see in the South's new public schools during the late 1860s. Write an outline of the speech that you would make.

Section 3 Review Answers

1. Hiram Revels, 505; Blanche K. Bruce, 505; Ku Klux Klan, 506
2. The words are defined in the Glossary.
3. African Americans, white Southerners who supported Republican policies, white settlers from the North
4. Freedmen's Bureau, private charities
5. gave them a voice in government and made them fully participating citizens

Activity Outlines should emphasize the link between education and opportunities for African Americans.

CHAPTER 17

Section 3, 504–507

Reteaching Activity 17–3

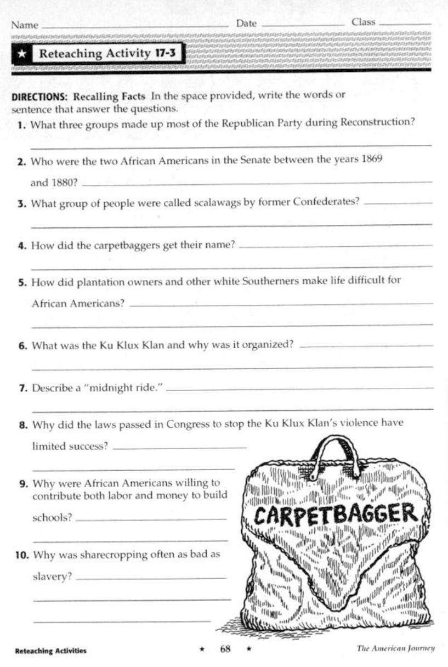

Name ______ Date ______ Class ______

Reteaching Activity 17-3

DIRECTIONS: Recalling Facts In the space provided, write the words or sentence that answer the questions.

1. What three groups made up most of the Republican Party during Reconstruction?
2. Who were the two African Americans in the Senate between the years 1869 and 1880?
3. What group of people were called scalawags by former Confederates?
4. How did the carpetbaggers get their name?
5. How did plantation owners and other white Southerners make life difficult for African Americans?
6. What was the Ku Klux Klan and why was it organized?
7. Describe a "midnight ride."
8. Why did the laws passed in Congress to stop the Ku Klux Klan's violence have limited success?
9. Why were African Americans willing to contribute both labor and money to build schools?
10. Why was sharecropping often as bad as slavery?

Reteaching Activities ★ 68 ★ *The American Journey*

Copyright © by The McGraw-Hill Companies, Inc.

Enrichment Activity 17–3

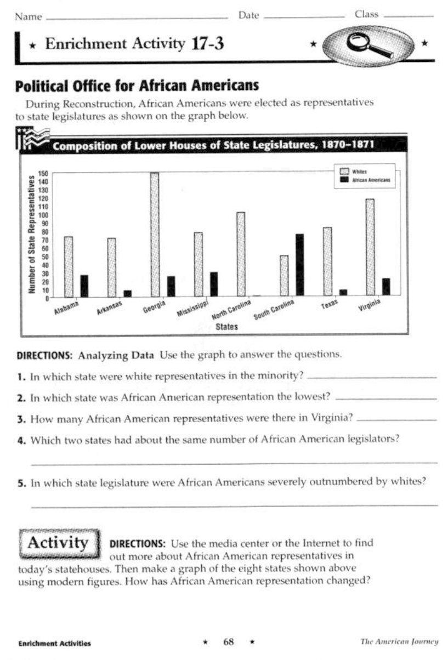

Name ______ Date ______ Class ______

★ Enrichment Activity 17-3

Political Office for African Americans

During Reconstruction, African Americans were elected as representatives to state legislatures as shown on the graph below.

DIRECTIONS: Analyzing Data Use the graph to answer the questions.

1. In which state were white representatives in the minority?
2. In which state was African American representation the lowest?
3. How many African American representatives were there in Virginia?
4. Which two states had about the same number of African American legislators?
5. In which state legislature were African Americans severely outnumbered by whites?

Activity **DIRECTIONS:** Use the media center or the Internet to find out more about African American representatives in today's statehouses. Then make a graph of the eight states shown above using modern figures. How has African American representation changed?

Enrichment Activities ★ 68 ★ *The American Journey*

Copyright © by The McGraw-Hill Companies, Inc.

4 CLOSE

Have students review the charts they made in the "TEACH" activity. Ask them to add another column to the chart to list the changes *they* would have made in the South during Reconstruction.

CHAPTER 17
Section 4, 508–511

1 FOCUS

BELLRINGER
Motivational Activity

Before taking roll at the beginning of the class period, project Section Focus Transparency 17–4 and have students answer the questions. Discuss students' responses.

This activity is also available as a blackline master.

Section Focus Transparency 17–4

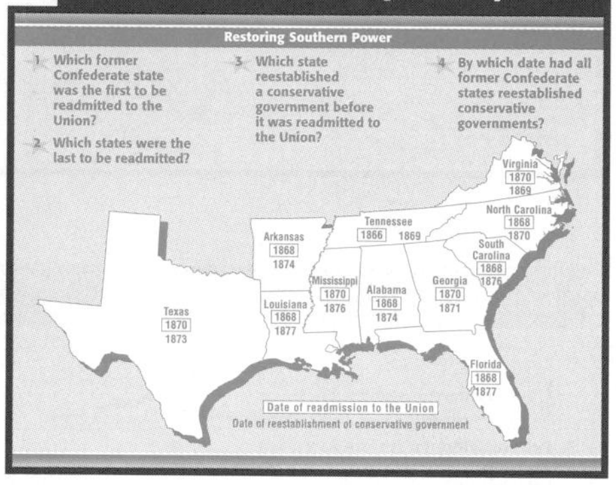

Vocabulary Precheck
Ask students to give an example of *reconciliation*. Then have them apply the term to Reconstruction.

Use the **Vocabulary PuzzleMaker** to create crossword and word search puzzles.

Section Theme
Individual Action

During the Grant administration, Northerners began losing interest in Reconstruction. Many believed it was time for the South to solve its own problems.

Activity Ask students to imagine they are citizens living in a Northern state 10 or 12 years after the end of the Civil War. Have them describe how they might feel about the South and its impact on the nation.

1870 — 1875 — 1880

May 1872 The Amnesty Act pardons most former Confederates

1872 President Grant wins reelection

March 1877 Electoral committee names Hayes president

1877 Reconstruction ends

Section 4

Reconstruction Ends

READ TO DISCOVER . . .
- why interest in Reconstruction declined.
- what changes occurred in the South during the last years of Reconstruction.
- how Reconstruction ended.

TERMS TO LEARN
reconciliation
commission

The Storyteller

In 1875 the carpetbag governor of Mississippi faced growing violence between whites and African Americans in his state. He appealed to President Grant for troops to restore order. The president's attorney general responded: "The whole public are tired out with these . . . outbreaks in the South, and the great majority are now ready to condemn any interference on the part of the government. . . . Preserve the peace by the forces in your own state. . . ." Sharp in tone, the attorney general's letter reflected the government's desire to end Reconstruction.

Badge worn by freed African Americans

By 1876 Southern Democrats were regaining political and economic control in the South. Some freed men and women went back to work for landholders because they had no other way to make a living.

Reconstruction Declines

During the Grant administration, Northerners began losing interest in Reconstruction. Many believed it was time for the South to solve its own problems.

Business leaders in the North wanted to end Reconstruction because they believed it was holding back Southern economic expansion. Some conservative Republicans saw the federal actions as a violation of states' rights. In addition the continuing violence in the South disturbed Northerners.

Southerners protested what they called "bayonet rule"—the use of federal troops to support Reconstruction governments. President Grant had sent federal troops to the South to stop violence or to enforce the law only when absolutely necessary. Generally, though, he tried to avoid any clashes with the South. The troops remained to protect African Americans and white Republicans.

Republican Revolt

President Grant had difficulties enough within his own party. In the early 1870s, reports of corruption in his administration and in Reconstruction governments spread throughout the nation. Some Republicans split with the party

SECTION RESOURCES

Reproducible Masters
- Reproducible Lesson Plan 17–4
- Guided Reading Activity 17–4
- Section Quiz 17–4
- Reteaching Activity 17–4
- Enrichment Activity 17–4

Transparencies
- Section Focus Transparency 17–4

Multimedia
- Vocabulary PuzzleMaker
- Chapter Challenger Interactive Review Software
- Testmaker
- GTV: A Geographic Perspective on American History
- ABCNews InterActive™ Historic America Electronic Field Trips

over the issue of corruption. Another group of Republicans broke with the party over Reconstruction, proposing peaceful reconciliation—coming together again—with Southern whites. Calling themselves Liberal Republicans, these two groups nominated **Horace Greeley,** a newspaper editor from New York, to run against Grant in the 1872 presidential election.

The Democrats also supported Greeley for president—despite his long opposition to their party—because he offered a chance to defeat the Republicans. Despite the division in the Republican ranks, however, Grant won a decisive victory in the election.

The Amnesty Act

During the 1872 election campaign, Liberal Republicans had called for expanding amnesty for white Southerners. In May 1872, Congress passed the **Amnesty Act,** which pardoned most former Confederates. All white Southerners could vote and hold office again. The amnesty changed the political balance in the South by restoring full rights to people who supported the Democratic Party.

Democrats Regain Power

In Southern states such as **Virginia** and **North Carolina,** where a majority of voters were white, Democrats soon regained control of state governments. In states where African Americans held a majority or where white and African American populations were nearly equal, the Ku Klux Klan and other violent groups helped the Democrats take power by terrorizing Republican voters.

In an election in Mississippi in 1875, Democrats won by a 30,000 majority, although the Republicans had held a 30,000 majority in the previous election. The Democrats used threats to pressure white Republicans to become Democrats. As one Republican put it:

> "No white man can live in the South in the future and act with any other than the Democratic Party unless he is willing and prepared to live a life of social isolation."

The Democrats also used violence to persuade African Americans not to vote. By 1876 Republicans held only three Southern states—Florida, South Carolina, and Louisiana.

Republican Decline

During these years the Republicans had other problems they could not blame on the Democrats. In 1873 a series of political scandals came to light. Investigations uncovered top government officials making unfair business deals, scheming to withhold public tax money, and accepting bribes. One scandal involved the vice president, and another the secretary of war. These scandals shocked the public and further damaged the Grant administration and the Republicans. At the same time, the nation suffered an economic depression. Blame for the hard times fell on the Republicans.

By the time of the congressional elections in 1874, charges of corruption and economic mismanagement had badly weakened the Republican

Picturing HISTORY Problems in the Grant administration hurt the Republican Party. **What happened in 1873 to make Republicans focus on the economy?**

CHAPTER 17
Section 4, 508–511

2 TEACH

L1 Writing an Essay Have each student write an essay outlining the successes of the Democratic Party and the failures of the Republican Party that led to increased Democratic popularity. Have students volunteer information from their essays.

Guided Reading Activity 17–4

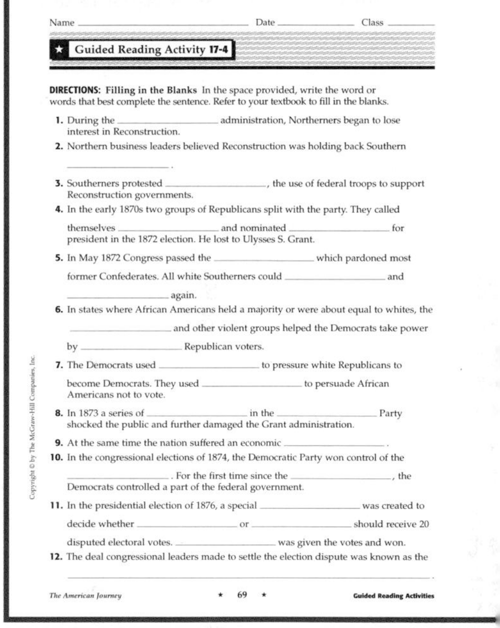
Name ______ Date ______ Class ______

★ Guided Reading Activity 17-4

DIRECTIONS: Filling in the Blanks In the space provided, write the word or words that best complete the sentence. Refer to your textbook to fill in the blanks.

1. During the ______ administration, Northerners began to lose interest in Reconstruction.
2. Northern business leaders believed Reconstruction was holding back Southern ______.
3. Southerners protested ______, the use of federal troops to support Reconstruction governments.
4. In the early 1870s two groups of Republicans split with the party. They called themselves ______ and nominated ______ for president in the 1872 election. He lost to Ulysses S. Grant.
5. In May 1872 Congress passed the ______ which pardoned most former Confederates. All white Southerners could ______ and ______ again.
6. In states where African Americans held a majority or were about equal to whites, the ______ and other violent groups helped the Democrats take power by ______ Republican voters.
7. The Democrats used ______ to pressure white Republicans to become Democrats. They used ______ to persuade African Americans not to vote.
8. In 1873 a series of ______ in the ______ Party shocked the public and further damaged the Grant administration.
9. At the same time the nation suffered an economic ______.
10. In the congressional elections of 1874, the Democratic Party won control of the ______. For the first time since the ______, the Democrats controlled a part of the federal government.
11. In the presidential election of 1876, a special ______ was created to decide whether ______ or ______ should receive 20 disputed electoral votes. ______ was given the votes and won.
12. The deal congressional leaders made to settle the election dispute was known as the ______.

Copyright © by The McGraw-Hill Companies, Inc.

The American Journey ★ 69 ★ **Guided Reading Activities**

Picturing HISTORY President Grant expressed his personal feelings about the corruption associated with his administration: ". . . from my candidacy for my present office in 1868 to the close of the last presidential campaign I have been the subject of abuse and slander scarcely ever equaled in political history, which today I feel that I can afford to disregard in view of your verdict, which I gratefully accept as my vindication."
Answer: *an economic depression*

COOPERATIVE LEARNING ACTIVITY

Illustrating the End of Reconstruction Organize the class into groups of three to scan the section for dates, events, and people that played a significant role in the end of Reconstruction. Have each group choose a type of graphic organizer to display this information. Then ask each group member to choose one of the following to illustrate on the graphic organizer: events, dates, people. Encourage students to draw their own illustrations or use pictures, drawings, clip art, and so on. Have each group create and assemble the graphic organizer.

CHAPTER 17

Section 4, 508–511

NATIONAL GEOGRAPHIC SOCIETY

VIDEODISC
GTV: A Geographic Perspective on American History

Side 3, Chapter 1
Title: *1876: The State of the Union*
Subject: The end of Reconstruction
Ask: **How did the speaker view the United States as a nation in 1876?** *(as three nations: North, South, and West)*

3 ASSESS

Assign Section 4 Review as homework or as an in-class activity.

Use **Chapter Challenger Interactive Review Software** to review Section 4.

Section Quiz 17–4

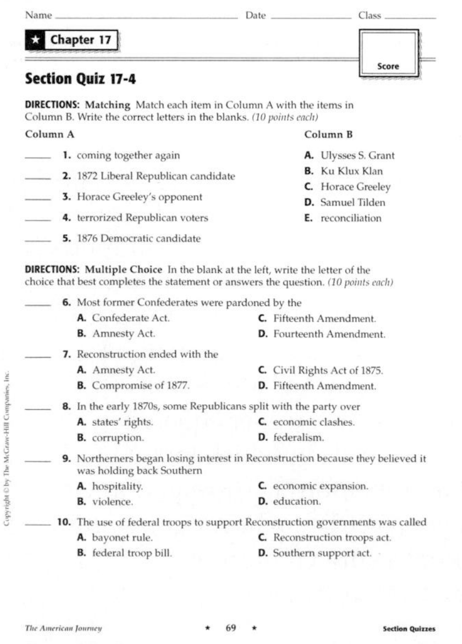
Name ______ Date ______ Class ______

Chapter 17

Score

Section Quiz 17-4

DIRECTIONS: Matching Match each item in Column A with the items in Column B. Write the correct letters in the blanks. *(10 points each)*

Column A

____ **1.** coming together again
____ **2.** 1872 Liberal Republican candidate
____ **3.** Horace Greeley's opponent
____ **4.** terrorized Republican voters
____ **5.** 1876 Democratic candidate

Column B

A. Ulysses S. Grant
B. Ku Klux Klan
C. Horace Greeley
D. Samuel Tilden
E. reconciliation

DIRECTIONS: Multiple Choice In the blank at the left, write the letter of the choice that best completes the statement or answers the question. *(10 points each)*

____ **6.** Most former Confederates were pardoned by the
A. Confederate Act. **C.** Fifteenth Amendment.
B. Amnesty Act. **D.** Fourteenth Amendment.

____ **7.** Reconstruction ended with the
A. Amnesty Act. **C.** Civil Rights Act of 1875.
B. Compromise of 1877. **D.** Fifteenth Amendment.

____ **8.** In the early 1870s, some Republicans split with the party over
A. states' rights. **C.** economic clashes.
B. corruption. **D.** federalism.

____ **9.** Northerners began losing interest in Reconstruction because they believed it was holding back Southern
A. hospitality. **C.** economic expansion.
B. violence. **D.** education.

____ **10.** The use of federal troops to support Reconstruction governments was called
A. bayonet rule. **C.** Reconstruction troops act.
B. federal troop bill. **D.** Southern support act.

Copyright © by The McGraw-Hill Companies, Inc.

The American Journey ★ 69 ★ Section Quizzes

Map Study

Answers

1. Florida, Louisiana, South Carolina
2. one

Party. Democrats gained seats in the Senate and won control of the House. For the first time since the Civil War, the Democratic Party controlled a part of the federal government. This situation further weakened Congress's commitment to Reconstruction and protecting the rights of newly freed African Americans. Although Congress would pass a Civil Rights Act in 1875, many people evaded the law.

The End of Reconstruction

President Grant considered running for reelection in 1876. Most Republican leaders preferred a new candidate—one who could win back the Liberal Republicans and unite the party.

The Election of 1876

The Republicans nominated **Rutherford B. Hayes,** a former member of Congress and governor of Ohio, for president. A champion of political reform, Hayes had a reputation for honesty, and he held moderate views on Reconstruction. The Democrats nominated New York governor **Samuel Tilden.** Tilden had gained national fame for fighting political corruption in New York City.

After the election, Tilden appeared to be the winner, receiving almost 250,000 more votes than Hayes. However, disputed returns from Florida, Louisiana, and South Carolina—representing 20 electoral votes—kept the outcome in doubt. Tilden had 184 electoral votes, only one short of what he needed to win. Yet if Hayes received all

Disputed Election of 1876

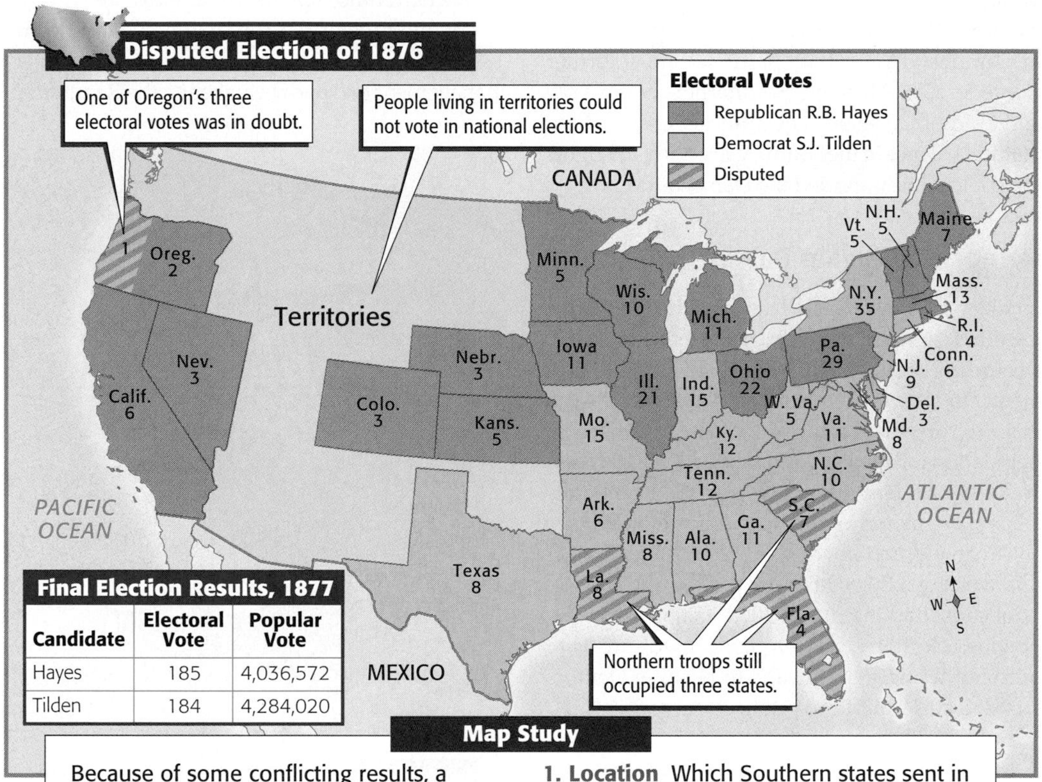

Final Election Results, 1877

Candidate	Electoral Vote	Popular Vote
Hayes	185	4,036,572
Tilden	184	4,284,020

Map Study

Because of some conflicting results, a committee of 15 members from Congress and the Supreme Court decided the final count in the 1876 election.

1. **Location** Which Southern states sent in disputed election returns?
2. **Analyzing Information** By how many electoral votes did Hayes finally win?

MULTIPLE LEARNING STYLES

Logical/Mathematical Using current population figures and electoral college votes for each state, ask students to create scenarios in which a candidate for the presidency today could lose the popular vote, but win the electoral college vote. For example, a presidential candidate in 1996 could have won by only one popular vote in each of the following states: California, New York, Texas, Florida, Pennsylvania, Illinois, Ohio, Michigan, New Jersey, North Carolina, and Georgia; and lost by a large number of popular votes in all of the remaining 39 states. The candidate would have won the election but would have lost the popular vote by a wide margin. **L2**

★ ★ ★ ★ ★ ★ ★ ★ ★ ★ ★ ★ ★ ★ ★

20 of the disputed votes, he would have the 185 electoral votes required for victory.

Americans worried that the dispute would upset the political stability of the nation. In January Congress created a special **commission**, or group, of seven Republicans, seven Democrats, and one independent to review the election results. But the independent resigned, and a Republican took his place. After examining the reports of state review boards, the commission voted 8 to 7 to award all 20 disputed votes to Hayes. The vote followed party lines.

Democrats in Congress threatened to fight the verdict. Republican and Southern Democratic leaders met secretly to work out an agreement that would allow the Democrats to accept Hayes as president. On March 2, 1877—almost four months after the election—Congress confirmed the verdict of the commission and declared Hayes the winner. He was inaugurated president two days later.

Compromise of 1877

The deal congressional leaders made to settle the election dispute, the **Compromise of 1877,** included various favors to the South. The new government would give more aid to the region and withdraw all remaining troops from Southern states. The Democrats, in turn, promised to maintain African Americans' rights.

In his Inaugural Address, Hayes declared that what the South needed most was the restoration of "wise, honest, and peaceful local self-government." During a goodwill trip to the South, Hayes announced his intention of letting Southerners handle racial issues. In Atlanta he told an African American audience:

> "... your rights and interests would be safer if this great mass of intelligent white men were left alone by the general government."

Hayes's message was clear. The federal government would no longer attempt to reshape Southern society or help Southern African Americans. Reconstruction was over.

★ Picturing HISTORY

The Republicans nominated Rutherford B. Hayes of Ohio, and the Democrats selected Samuel J. Tilden of New York for president in 1876. **What were the results of the election?**

Hayes paper lantern

Section 4 Review

Checking for Understanding

1. ***Identify*** Horace Greeley, Rutherford B. Hayes, Samuel Tilden, Compromise of 1877.
2. ***Define*** reconciliation, commission.
3. ***Explain*** how the Amnesty Act helped the Democratic Party regain its strength.

Reviewing Themes

4. **Individual Action** Why did the Republicans choose Hayes as a presidential candidate?

Critical Thinking

5. **Identifying the Main Idea** Why was Reconstruction largely unsuccessful?

Activity

Illustrating a Quote Create a drawing to illustrate the meaning of the quote by the Republican on page 509.

Section 4 Review Answers

1. Horace Greeley, 509; Rutherford B. Hayes, 510; Samuel Tilden, 510; Compromise of 1877, 511
2. The words are defined in the Glossary.
3. allowed all white Southerners to vote and hold office again; Southern Democrats gradually began to regain control of the state governments
4. Grant's administration was corrupt, and Hayes had a reputation for reform, honesty, and moderate views on Reconstruction.
5. Answers should address the bitterness of South toward North, use of military force, refusal to accept abolition of slavery, problem of trying to legislate attitudes.

Activity Drawings should reflect Democratic Party using threats and violence.

CHAPTER 17
Section 4, 508–511

★ Picturing HISTORY Republicans held a private swearing in for Hayes on the evening before the official inauguration ceremony. **Answer:** *A special commission declared Hayes the winner.*

Reteaching Activity 17–4

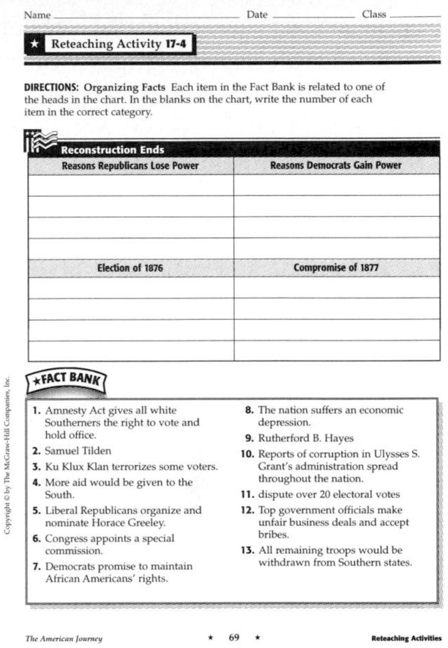

Name ________ Date ________ Class ________

★ Reteaching Activity 17-4

DIRECTIONS: Organizing Facts Each item in the Fact Bank is related to one of the heads in the chart. In the blanks on the chart, write the number of each item in the correct category.

Reconstruction Ends

Reasons Republicans Lose Power	Reasons Democrats Gain Power
Election of 1876	**Compromise of 1877**

★FACT BANK

1. Amnesty Act gives all white Southerners the right to vote and hold office.
2. Samuel Tilden
3. Ku Klux Klan terrorizes some voters.
4. More aid would be given to the South.
5. Liberal Republicans organize and nominate Horace Greeley.
6. Congress appoints a special commission.
7. Democrats promise to maintain African Americans' rights.
8. The nation suffers an economic depression.
9. Rutherford B. Hayes
10. Reports of corruption in Ulysses S. Grant's administration spread throughout the nation.
11. dispute over 20 electoral votes
12. Top government officials make unfair business deals and accept bribes.
13. All remaining troops would be withdrawn from Southern states.

The American Journey ★ 69 ★ **Reteaching Activities**

Enrichment Activity 17–4

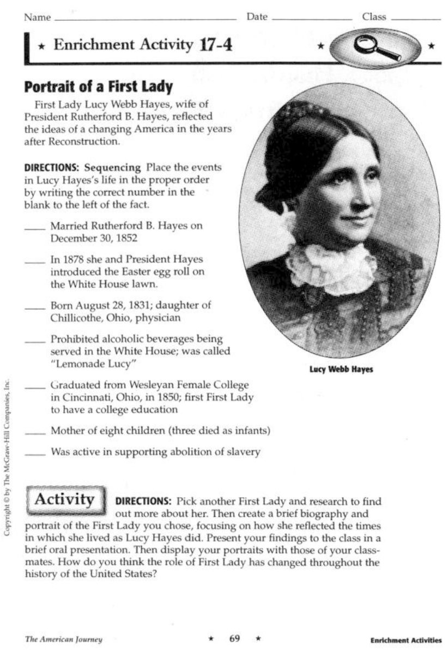

Name ________ Date ________ Class ________

★ Enrichment Activity 17-4

Portrait of a First Lady

First Lady Lucy Webb Hayes, wife of President Rutherford B. Hayes, reflected the ideas of a changing America in the years after Reconstruction.

DIRECTIONS: Sequencing Place the events in Lucy Hayes's life in the proper order by writing the correct number in the blank to the left of the fact.

____ Married Rutherford B. Hayes on December 30, 1852

____ In 1878 she and President Hayes introduced the Easter egg roll on the White House lawn.

____ Born August 28, 1831; daughter of Chillicothe, Ohio, physician

____ Prohibited alcoholic beverages being served in the White House; was called "Lemonade Lucy"

____ Graduated from Wesleyan Female College in Cincinnati, Ohio, in 1850; first First Lady to have a college education

____ Mother of eight children (three died as infants)

____ Was active in supporting abolition of slavery

Lucy Webb Hayes

Activity **DIRECTIONS:** Pick another First Lady and research to find out more about her. Then create a brief biography and portrait of the First Lady you chose, focusing on how she reflected the times in which she lived as Lucy Hayes did. Present your findings to the class in a brief oral presentation. Then display your portraits with those of your classmates. How do you think the role of First Lady has changed throughout the history of the United States?

The American Journey ★ 69 ★ **Enrichment Activities**

4 CLOSE

Ask students to work in small groups to devise their own Compromise of 1877.

Social Studies Connections — Citizenship

TEACH

Struggling for Liberty

Before students read the excerpt by Frederick Douglass, discuss the concept of liberty. Point out the struggle for liberty throughout world history and United States history. Compare African Americans' struggle for liberty with the colonists' struggle, which led to the American Revolution. Ask students to define what liberty means to them as citizens of the United States. Call on volunteers to share their definitions of liberty with the class.

As a prereading activity, have students scan the excerpt to list unfamiliar terms. Ask students to define these terms using context clues. Call on students to read their lists and their definitions.

ABC NEWS INTERACTIVE™

VIDEODISC
Historic America Electronic Field Trips

Side 1, Chapter 9
Title: *Frederick Douglass's Home*
Subject: A tour of the famous abolitionist's home
Ask: What were some of Frederick Douglass's accomplishments? *(public speaker, advocate for abolitionist cause, recruited African American soldiers, supported women's rights, and writer)*

Also available in VHS.

Social Studies Connections — Citizenship | Geography | World History | Economics

Struggling for Liberty

This 1892 political cartoon shows how African Americans were denied the right to vote.

After the Civil War the Thirteenth, Fourteenth, and Fifteenth Amendments were ratified. These amendments prohibited slavery, gave citizenship to African Americans, and guaranteed them the right to vote. But most African Americans continued to be extremely poor and to suffer discrimination, including violent prejudice.

In 1883 Frederick Douglass, the great abolitionist, spoke to the National Convention of Colored Men in Louisville, Kentucky. He explained that African Americans needed to continue to fight for their liberty.

> "With apparent surprise, astonishment and impatience we have been asked: 'What more can the colored people of this country want than they now have, and what more is possible to them?' It is said they were once slaves, they are now free . . . they were once outside of all American institutions, they are now inside of all and are a recognized part of the whole American people. . . .
>
> If the six millions of colored people of this country, armed with the Constitution of the United States . . . have not sufficient spirit and wisdom to organize and combine to defend themselves from outrage, discrimination and oppression, it will be idle for them to expect that the Republican Party or any other political party will . . . care what becomes of them. . . . [W]e are men and must speak for ourselves, or we shall not be spoken for at all.
>
> [African American voters] have marched to the ballot-box in face of gleaming weapons, wounds and death. They have been abandoned by the Government and left to the laws of nature. So far as they are concerned, there is no Government or Constitution of the United States."

Activity

Analyzing Current Events Bring newspapers to class and search for stories that show groups of people struggling for their rights throughout the United States and the world. After reading the articles aloud in class, post the items on the bulletin board with the heading "Let Freedom Ring."

MORE ABOUT . . .

Frederick Douglass As a skilled orator, Frederick Douglass was a master of irony. In his famous Fourth of July speech in 1852, he stated, "This Fourth of July is *yours,* not *mine. You* may rejoice, *I* must mourn." There are few better sources of insight into the deepest contradictions in American history than Douglass's speeches. In addition, there are few better starting points for understanding prejudice than his timeless definition of racism as a "diseased imagination." In the 1870s Douglass moved to Washington, D.C., and became a stalwart Republican. He was appointed marshal (1877–1881) and recorder of deeds (1881–1886) for the District of Columbia and *chargé d'affaires* for Santo Domingo and minister to Haiti (1889–1891).

1885 — 1890 — 1895 — 1900

1889 Poll taxes and literacy tests are initiated

1890s Southern mills produce nearly 20 percent of nation's iron and steel

1896 *Plessy* v. *Ferguson* rules segregation constitutional

Section 5

Change in the South

READ TO DISCOVER . . .
- how the economy changed in the "New South."
- what policies the "Redeemers" supported.
- how Southern states denied African Americans their rights.

TERMS TO LEARN

cash crop
poll tax
literacy test
grandfather clause
segregation
lynching

The Storyteller

"I am treated, not as an American citizen, but as a brute. . . . [A]nd for what? Not that I am unable or unwilling to pay my way; not that I am obnoxious in my personal appearance or disrespectful in my conduct; but simply because I happen to be of a darker complexion." These words were spoken by John Lynch, a member of Congress who had once been enslaved. At the end of Reconstruction, many African Americans faced lives of poverty, indignity, and despair.

Sharecropper's plow

Many Southern whites hated Republicans because of their role in the Civil War and in Reconstruction. When Reconstruction ended, political power in the South shifted to the Democrats.

A New Ruling Party

In some regions, the ruling Democrats were the large landowners and other groups that had held power before the Civil War. In most areas, however, a new ruling class took charge. Among their ranks were merchants, bankers, industrialists, and other business leaders who supported economic development and opposed Northern interference. These Democrats called themselves **"Redeemers"** because they had "redeemed," or saved, the South from Republican rule.

The Redeemers adopted conservative policies such as lower taxes, less public spending, and reduced government services. They drastically cut, or even eliminated, many social services started during Reconstruction, including public education. Their one-party rule and conservative policies dominated Southern politics well into the 1900s.

The Southern Economy

For many years after the Civil War ended, the South continued to lag behind the rest of the nation economically. Despite efforts to industrialize, it remained a poor, rural economy.

SECTION RESOURCES

Reproducible Masters
- Reproducible Lesson Plan 17–5
- Guided Reading Activity 17–5
- Section Quiz 17–5
- Reteaching Activity 17–5
- Enrichment Activity 17–5

Transparencies
- Section Focus Transparency 17–5

Multimedia
- Vocabulary PuzzleMaker
- Chapter Challenger Interactive Review Software
- Testmaker

1 FOCUS

BELLRINGER
Motivational Activity

Before taking roll at the beginning of the class period, project Section Focus Transparency 17–5 and have students answer the questions. Discuss students' responses.

This activity is also available as a blackline master.

Section Focus Transparency 17–5

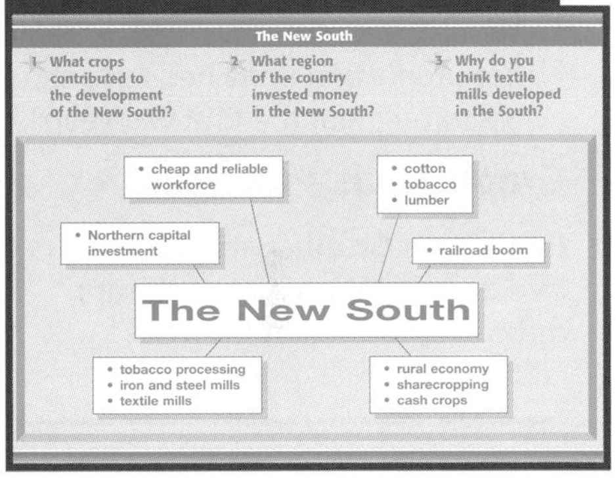

Vocabulary Precheck

Ask students to scan the chapter to identify which vocabulary words are associated with voting rights *(poll tax, literacy tax, grandfather clause)*. Discuss how each term was used to discriminate against African Americans.

Use the **Vocabulary Puzzle-Maker** to create crossword and word search puzzles.

Section Theme
Economic Factors

After the Civil War ended, the South continued to lag behind the rest of the nation economically. Despite efforts to industrialize, it remained an agricultural economy for many years.

Activity Discuss the advantages and disadvantages of an agricultural economy. Ask students to evaluate whether a diversified agricultural economy can compete effectively with an industrialized economy.

CHAPTER 17
Section 5, 513–516

2 TEACH

L1, ELL Creating a Poster Organize students into small groups to create posters illustrating the economies of the North and the South during the late 1800s. Encourage students to use maps, graphs, illustrations, and so on to illustrate their posters. Ask volunteers from each group to present the posters to the class.

Graph Study

Answers

1. 1880
2. rice production remained fairly stable throughout the Civil War years

Graph Skills Practice

Reading a Graph Between which two decades shown on the graph did corn production drop? *(1860–1870)*

Guided Reading Activity 17–5

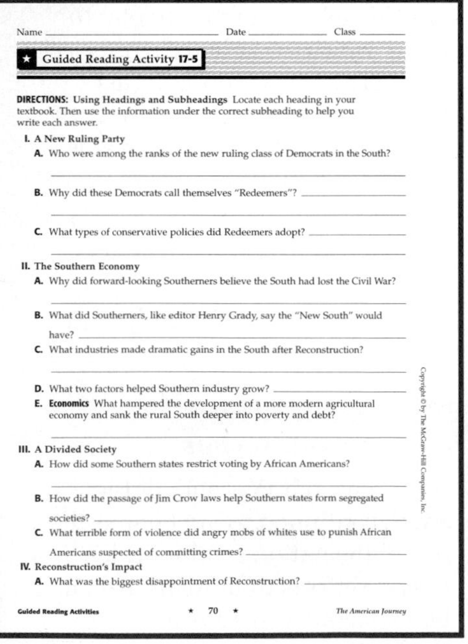

Name ______ Date ______ Class ______

★ Guided Reading Activity 17-5

DIRECTIONS: Using Headings and Subheadings Locate each heading in your textbook. Then use the information under the correct subheading to help you write each answer.

I. A New Ruling Party
- A. Who were among the ranks of the new ruling class of Democrats in the South? ______
- B. Why did these Democrats call themselves "Redeemers"? ______
- C. What types of conservative policies did Redeemers adopt? ______

II. The Southern Economy
- A. Why did forward-looking Southerners believe the South had lost the Civil War? ______
- B. What did Southerners, like editor Henry Grady, say the "New South" would have? ______
- C. What industries made dramatic gains in the South after Reconstruction? ______
- D. What two factors helped Southern industry grow? ______
- E. **Economics** What hampered the development of a more modern agricultural economy and sank the rural South deeper into poverty and debt? ______

III. A Divided Society
- A. How did some Southern states restrict voting by African Americans? ______
- B. How did the passage of Jim Crow laws help Southern states form segregated societies? ______
- C. What terrible form of violence did angry mobs of whites use to punish African Americans suspected of committing crimes? ______

IV. Reconstruction's Impact
- A. What was the biggest disappointment of Reconstruction? ______

Guided Reading Activities ★ 70 ★ *The American Journey*

Agricultural Production in the South, 1850–1890

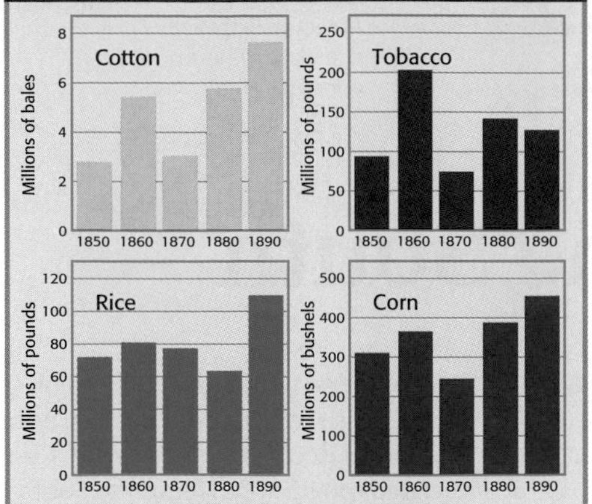

Source: *Historical Statistics of the South.*

Graph Study

Southern farm production decreased during the war years of the 1860s.

1. By what year did cotton production levels again equal production levels of 1860?
2. **Analyzing Information** Which crop's production remained highest during the Civil War years?

Rise of the "New South"

By the 1880s forward-looking Southerners were convinced that their region must develop a strong industrial economy. They argued that the South had lost the Civil War because its industry and manufacturing did not match the North's. **Henry Grady,** editor of the *Atlanta Constitution,* headed a group that urged Southerners to "out-Yankee the Yankees" and build a "New South." This New South would have industries based on coal, iron, tobacco, cotton, lumber, and the region's other abundant resources. Southerners would create this new economy by embracing a spirit of hard work and regional pride. In 1886 Grady told a Boston audience that industrial development would allow the New South to match the North in a peaceful competition.

Southern Industries

Industry in the South made dramatic gains after Reconstruction. Some of the strongest advances were in the textile industry. Before the Civil War, Southern planters had shipped cotton to textile mills in the North or in Europe. In the 1880s textile mills sprang up throughout the South. Many Northern mills would later close as companies built new plants in the South.

Other important industries were lumbering and tobacco processing. The tobacco industry was developed largely through the efforts of **James Duke** of North Carolina. Duke's American Tobacco Company eventually controlled almost all tobacco manufacturing in the nation.

The iron and steel industry also grew rapidly. By 1890 Southern mills produced nearly 20 percent of the nation's iron and steel. Much of the industry was in Alabama near deposits of iron ore.

Factors in Growth

A cheap and reliable workforce helped Southern industry grow. Most factory workers put in long hours for low wages. Sometimes whole families, including children, worked in factories. African Americans got few opportunities in industry except in the lowest-paying jobs.

A railroad-building boom also aided industrial development. By 1870 the Southern railroad system, which had been destroyed during the war, was largely rebuilt. Track mileage more than doubled between 1880 and 1890.

Still, the South did not develop an industrial economy as strong as the North's. The North was still industrializing more rapidly. The South remained primarily agricultural.

Economics

Rural Economy

Henry Grady and other New South advocates hoped to change Southern agriculture as well as industry. They pictured small, profitable farms raising a variety of crops rather than large plantations devoted to growing cotton.

COOPERATIVE LEARNING ACTIVITY

Presenting Information on Transparencies Organize the class into groups of four to create overhead transparency presentations on the ways in which African Americans' rights were denied during Reconstruction. Ask groups to create a set of four overhead transparencies that can be layered on top of each other to show each of the following terms: poll tax, literacy test, grandfather clause, Jim Crow laws. Have group members decide how each transparency will be layered to show all four terms together. Then have each member choose a term and illustrate it on a transparency. Have groups present their overheads to the class with each member presenting his or her transparency to complete the layered presentation.

A different economy emerged, however. Some plantations were broken up, but many large landowners kept control of their property. When estates were divided, much of the land went to sharecropping and tenant farming, neither of which was profitable.

Debt caused problems as well. Poor farmers had to buy on credit to get the food and supplies they needed. The merchants who sold on credit charged high prices for their goods, increasing the farmers' debt. The quickest way for farmers to repay that debt, they thought, was to grow **cash crops**—crops that could be sold for money. As in the past, the biggest cash crop was cotton. An oversupply of cotton forced prices down, however. The farmers then had to grow even more cotton to try to recover their losses.

Sharecropping and reliance on a single cash crop hampered the development of a more modern agricultural economy. Instead, the rural South sank deeper into poverty and debt.

A Divided Society

As Reconstruction ended, African Americans' dreams for freedom faded. In the last 20 years of the 1800s, racism became firmly entrenched, and individuals took steps to keep African Americans separated from whites and to deny them basic rights.

Voting Restrictions

The Fifteenth Amendment prohibited any state from denying an individual the right to vote because of race. Southern leaders, however, found ways to get around the amendment and prevent African Americans from voting.

Many Southern states required a **poll tax**, a fee that people had to pay before voting. Because many African Americans could not afford the tax, they could not vote. The tax also prevented many poor whites from voting. Another approach was to make prospective voters take a **literacy test**, in which they had to read and explain difficult parts of state constitutions or the federal Constitution. Because most African Americans had little education, literacy tests prevented many from voting.

Literacy tests could also keep some whites from voting. For this reason some states passed **grandfather clauses**. These laws allowed individuals who did not pass the literacy test to vote if their fathers or grandfathers had voted before Reconstruction. Because African Americans could not vote until 1867, they were excluded.

Georgia enacted a poll tax and other limits as early as 1870, but such laws did not become widespread until after 1889. African Americans continued to vote in some states until the end of the 1800s. Because of restrictive voting laws and the constant threat of violence, however, African American voting drastically declined.

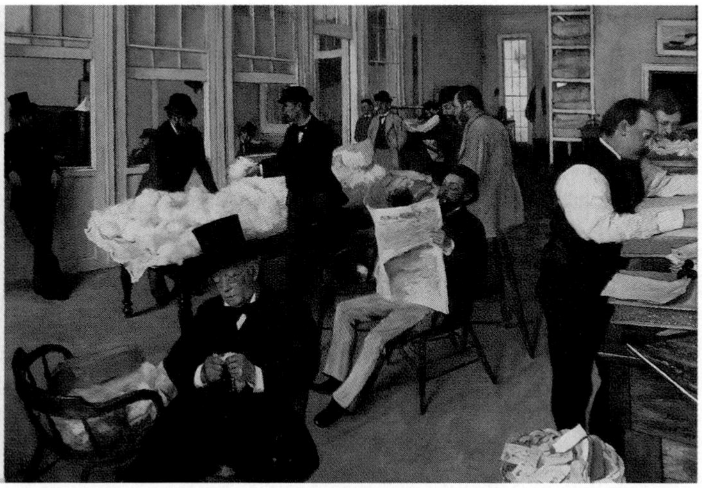

HISTORY AND ART ***Portrait in an Office (New Orleans)* by Edgar Degas** French painter Edgar Degas shows employees in a business office in New Orleans, one of the South's major ports. **What major change did many Southerners of the 1880s favor for their region?**

MULTIPLE LEARNING STYLES

Visual/Spatial Have students scan the section to create a chart showing the changes in the economy of the New South. Have them first list the major cities of the New South mentioned in this section. Then, in another column, have them describe the major economic bases of the New South. Have students scan this and other sections of this chapter to describe in a third column the economic bases of the South before the Civil War. Finally, have students research the present economic bases of some major cities in the South and list this information in a fourth column. **L1**

3 ASSESS

Assign Section 5 Review as homework or as an in-class activity.

Use **Chapter Challenger Interactive Review Software** to review Section 5.

Section Quiz 17–5

Name ______ Date ______ Class ______

Chapter 17 Score

Section Quiz 17-5

DIRECTIONS: Matching Match each item in Column A with the items in Column B. Write the correct letters in the blanks. *(10 points each)*

Column A	Column B
____ 1. Southern Democrats	A. W.E.B. DuBois
____ 2. *Atlanta Constitution* editor	B. Redeemers
____ 3. court decision upholding segregation	C. *Plessy v. Ferguson*
____ 4. African American civil rights leader	D. New Orleans
____ 5. major Southern port	E. Henry Grady

DIRECTIONS: Multiple Choice In the blank at the left, write the letter of the choice that best completes the statement or answers the question. *(10 points each)*

____ 6. Some of the strongest industrial gains in the New South were in
A. the textile industry. C. the chemical industry.
B. the coal industry. D. the publishing industry.

____ 7. After Reconstruction the South's economy was based on
A. industry. C. agriculture.
B. textiles. D. paper mills.

____ 8. Farmers thought that the quickest way to repay debt was to grow
A. sugarcane. C. tobacco.
B. cash crops. D. corn.

____ 9. Many Southern states required this as a means of keeping poor people and African Americans from voting.
A. crop tax C. Reconstruction laws
B. Jim Crow laws D. poll tax

____ 10. By passing the Jim Crow laws, Southern states formed this type of society.
A. an integrated society C. a segregated society
B. a healthy society D. an economic society

Section Quizzes ★ 70 ★ *The American Journey*

HISTORY AND ART Edgar Degas belonged to a group of artists called Impressionists. These artists were more interested in the fleeting light and color reflected from an object than form or content. They had little interest in storytelling. **Answer:** *to develop a strong industrial economy*

you don't say...

Jim Crow comes from the song "Jim Crow" by Thomas D. Rice popularized in the mid-1830s. The song portrayed African Americans as happy-go-lucky, childlike people who wanted nothing more from life than something good to eat and a chance to sing and dance.

Reteaching Activity 17–5

Name ______ Date ______ Class ______

★ Reteaching Activity 17-5

DIRECTIONS: Crossword Puzzle Complete the crossword puzzle by writing the term that matches each clue.

Redeemers	New South	Henry Grady	industry
agricultural	cotton	sharecropping	poll tax
literacy test	textile	Jim Crow laws	W.E.B. DuBois
James Duke			

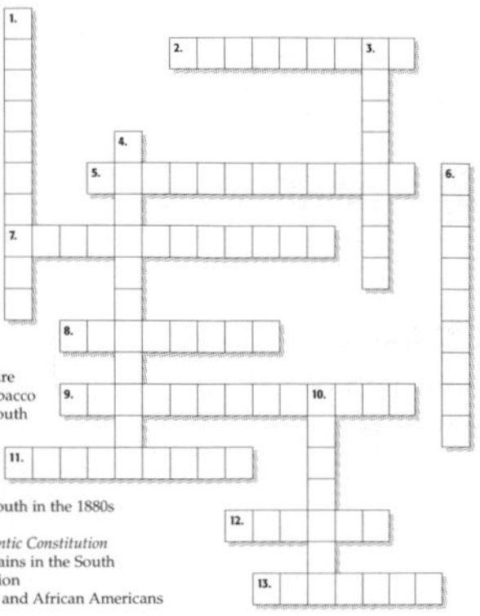

Across
2. African American writer and civil rights leader
5. Prospective voters had to read and explain difficult parts of the Constitution.
7. kind of Southern economy
8. Southern economy with industries based on coal, iron, tobacco, and so on
9. hampered the development of modern agriculture
11. developed the tobacco industry in the South
12. South's biggest cash crop
13. strongest advancing industry in the South in the 1880s

Down
1. editor of the *Atlantic Constitution*
3. made dramatic gains in the South after Reconstruction
4. separated whites and African Americans in public places
6. name for Democrats who "saved" the South from Republican rule
10. fee people had to pay before voting

Reteaching Activities ★ 70 ★ *The American Journey*

Enrichment Activity 17–5

Name ______ Date ______ Class ______

★ Enrichment Activity 17-5 ★ ★

Growing Links

Industry grew during the post-Civil War period in the South, helped by the rebuilding and expansion of railroads that provided the transportation industries needed for profitable operation. Moreover, the transcontinental railroad, completed in 1869, linked the East with the West.

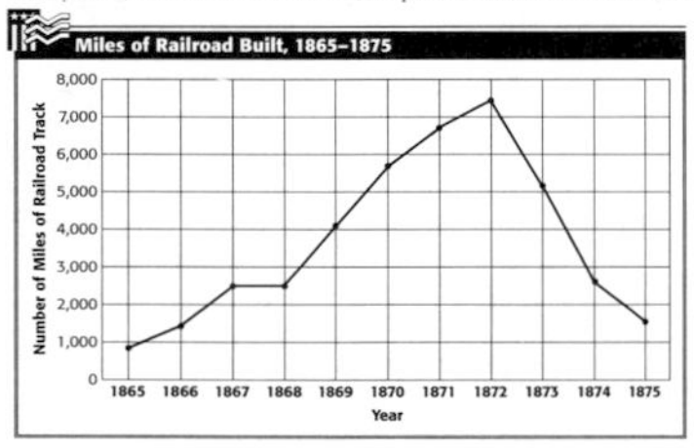

DIRECTIONS: Reading a Line Graph Study the line graph, which shows miles of railroad built in the country between 1865 and 1875, to answer the following questions.

1. About how many miles of track were built in 1870? ______
2. In which two successive years was the number of miles of track built almost the same? ______
3. Between which pair or pairs of years did the mileage-per-year increase by less than 1,000 miles of track? ______
4. For how many years were the miles laid greater than 3,000? ______
5. Which year represented the largest boom in railroad building? ______
6. What was the highest total miles laid in any three successive years? ______

Activity **DIRECTIONS:** Are railroads still important to the United States's transportation system? Use the media center to find if more new railroad lines are being built in the United States or if more old lines are being abandoned. Prepare a graph to show your findings.

Enrichment Activities ★ 70 ★ *The American Journey*

Jim Crow Laws

Another set of laws hurt African Americans. By the 1890s **segregation**, or the separation of the races, was a prominent feature of life in the South.

The Southern states formed a segregated society by passing so-called **Jim Crow laws.** Taking their name from a character in a song, Jim Crow laws required African Americans and whites to be separated in almost every public place where they might come in contact with each other.

In 1896 the Supreme Court upheld Jim Crow laws and segregation in ***Plessy* v. *Ferguson*.** The case involved a Louisiana law requiring separate sections on trains for African Americans. The Court ruled that segregation was legal as long as African Americans had access to public facilities or accommodations equal to those of whites.

The problem, however, was that the facilities were separate but in no way equal. Southern states spent much more money on schools and other facilities for whites than on those for African Americans. This "separate but equal" doctrine provided a legal foundation for segregation in the South that lasted for more than 50 years.

Violence against African Americans

Along with restrictions on voting rights and laws passed to segregate society, white violence against African Americans increased. This violence took many terrible forms, including **lynching,** in which an angry mob killed a person by hanging. African Americans were lynched because they were suspected of committing crimes—or because they did not behave as whites thought they should.

Reconstruction's Impact

★ Reconstruction was both a success and a failure. It helped the South recover from the war and begin rebuilding its economy. Yet economic recovery was far from complete. Although Southern agriculture took a new form, the South was still a rural economy, and that economy was still very poor.

Under Reconstruction African Americans gained greater equality and began creating their own institutions. They joined with whites in new governments, fairer and more democratic than the South had ever seen. This improvement for African Americans did not last long, however.

The biggest disappointment of Reconstruction was that it did not make good on the promise of true freedom for freed African Americans. The South soon created a segregated society. In the words of African American writer and civil rights leader **W.E.B. Du Bois,** "The slave went free; stood a brief moment in the sun; then moved back again toward slavery."

Section 5 Review

Checking for Understanding

1. ***Identify*** "Redeemers," *Plessy* v. *Ferguson*.
2. ***Define*** cash crop, poll tax, literacy test, grandfather clause, segregation, lynching.
3. ***State*** how some Southern states' efforts to keep African Americans from voting violated the Fifteenth Amendment.

Reviewing Themes

4. **Economic Factors** In what industries did the South make great gains after Reconstruction?

Critical Thinking

5. **Determining Cause and Effect** How did the Redeemers' efforts to cut government services affect freed African Americans?

Activity

Researching Statistics Research to find out how many African Americans hold seats in Congress today. Make a list of their names and states of residence.

Section 5 Review Answers

1. "Redeemers," 513; *Plessy* v. *Ferguson*, 516
2. The words are defined in the Glossary.
3. The Fifteenth Amendment stated no one could be denied the vote because of race, but poll taxes and literacy tests kept African Americans from voting.
4. textiles, lumber, tobacco processing, iron and steel
5. made it more difficult for African Americans to get ahead

Activity Lists should contain the names and states of residence of current African American members of Congress.

4 CLOSE

Ask students to interpret the following quote from the section, "Reconstruction was both a success and a failure."

Critical Thinking
SKILL BUILDER

Identifying the Main Idea

As you read about American history, you come across historical dates, events, and names. These details are easier to understand and remember when they are connected to one main idea. Understanding the main ideas allows you to grasp the whole picture or story. The details then become more easily understood.

Poor Southern farmers struggled to make a living during Reconstruction.

Learning the Skill

To understand the main idea, follow these steps:

- Before you read the material, find out the setting of the article or document: the time, the place, and who the writer is. Also find out what events occurred there.
- Read the material and ask, "What is the purpose of this information?"
- Study any photographs or illustrations that accompany the material.
- Ask, "What are the most forceful statements in this material?"
- Identify supporting details.
- Identify the main idea, or central issue.

Practicing the Skill

The passage that follows is from a history of Reconstruction by W.E.B. Du Bois, an African American scholar. In it he describes the attitudes of people in Charleston, South Carolina, just after the Civil War. Read the passage and answer the questions that follow.

"The economic loss which came through war was great, but not nearly as influential as the psychological change, the change in habit and thought. . . .

The hatred of the Yankee was increased. The defeated Southern leaders were popular heroes. Numbers of Southerners planned to leave the country, and go to South America or Mexico. . . .

The labor situation, the prospect of free Negroes, caused great apprehension. It was accepted as absolutely true by most planters that the Negro could not and would not work without a white master."

1. Du Bois begins by naming two kinds of losses from the war. What are they? Which does he say was greater?
2. What points in the passage are stated most forcefully?
3. What is the main idea of this passage?
4. What details are provided that support the main idea?
5. How does the photograph support or negate Du Bois's main idea?

Applying the Skill

Identifying the Main Idea Bring a news article about a current event to class. Identify the main idea and supporting details in the article.

Critical Thinking
SKILL BUILDER

TEACH

Identifying the Main Idea

This skill demonstrates how to read for the main idea. By reading a quote from W.E.B. Du Bois, students will practice how to find the main idea using a primary source.

Have students work in pairs to apply the steps on this page to identify the main idea of *The Storyteller* on page 513. The main idea deals with the question of equality for an African American.

Additional Practice

Chapter Skills Activity 17

Who? What? Where? When?

W.E.B. Du Bois was the first African American to earn a Ph.D. from Harvard University. He edited the NAACP journal, *The Crisis,* for more than 20 years.

ANSWERS TO PRACTICING THE SKILL

1. economic and psychological; psychological
2. Southerners' hatred of Yankees and belief that African Americans could not and would not work without a white master
3. Psychological changes had the greatest impact on the South after the Civil War.
4. hatred of Yankees increased, defeated Southern leaders were heroes, many Southerners planned to leave country, African American labor situation caused apprehension
5. Answers may point out that the painting supports Du Bois's idea that economic loss in the South was great during Reconstruction.

Applying the Skill Students should identify the main idea and supporting details in a news article.

GLENCOE TECHNOLOGY

VIDEODISC
MindJogger Videoquiz

Use MindJogger to review the Chapter 17 content.

Chapter 17
Disc 3, Side A

Also available in VHS.

Chapter 17

Review and Activities

Reviewing Key Terms

On a sheet of paper, define the following terms:

Reconstruction
amnesty
freedmen
black codes
impeach
scalawag
carpetbagger
sharecropping
poll tax
literacy test
grandfather clause
segregation
lynching

Reviewing Key Facts

1. What services did the Freedmen's Bureau provide?
2. How was the Fourteenth Amendment supposed to help African Americans?
3. What role did African Americans play in early Reconstruction politics in the South?
4. What tactic did the Ku Klux Klan use to influence elections in the South?
5. What conservative policies did the Redeemers adopt in the South?

Critical Thinking

Analyzing Illustrations

The Freedmen's Bureau set up hundreds of schools attended by African American adults and children. Analyze the painting to the right, then answer the questions below.

1. What ages do the students in this school appear to be?
2. How would you characterize the attitude toward learning of the students in this school?

Time Line Activity

Create a time line on which you place the following events in chronological order.

- Civil Rights Act passed
- President Johnson's impeachment trial held
- Radical Republicans pass Wade-Davis Bill
- Reconstruction ends
- Fifteenth Amendment passed
- Lincoln assassinated

Reviewing Themes

1. **Groups and Institutions** Why did the Freedmen's Bureau consider education to be so important for freed African Americans?
2. **Civic Rights and Responsibilities** How did the black codes deny rights?
3. **Continuity and Change** Explain the following quote as it applies to Reconstruction: "The slave went free; stood a brief moment in the sun; then moved back again toward slavery."
4. **Individual Action** What president brought an end to Reconstruction?
5. **Economic Factors** Why did growing cotton after the Civil War send many Southern farmers into debt?

Freedmen's Bureau school

Reviewing Key Terms

The key terms used in this activity are defined in the textbook glossary on pages A26–A35.

Reviewing Key Facts

1. distributed food and clothing, provided medical services, established schools, helped people acquire land, provided transportation to jobs, helped workers obtain fair wages
2. granted full citizenship to all individuals born in the U.S. and prohibited states from denying citizens "constitutional privileges and immunities" without "due process of law"
3. voted and served as elected officials in some Southern states
4. terrorized African Americans and other Republican voters to keep them from casting their votes
5. lowered taxes, reduced public spending and government services

Critical Thinking

1. all ages, children and adults
2. They are involved and attentive.

Time Line Activity

Events should be placed in this order: Radical Republicans pass Wade-Davis Bill, Lincoln assassinated, Civil Rights Act passed, President Johnson's impeachment trial held, Fifteenth Amendment passed, Reconstruction ends

Reviewing Themes

1. would put them on an equal level with other citizens
2. made it illegal for African Americans to do certain things such as own or rent farms
3. It describes the brief period after the war when African Americans gained dignity and greater equality as a result of the abolition of slavery. As interest in Reconstruction faded, much of the South went back to its old ways by creating a segregated society and denying rights to African Americans.
4. Rutherford B. Hayes
5. Farmers grew more cotton as a cash crop, which forced prices down and plunged farmers deeper into debt.

Skill Practice Activity

Identifying the Main Idea

The excerpt below was written by Charlotte Forten, one of many African American teachers who went south to teach freed individuals during the period of Reconstruction. Read the excerpt, which describes her first days of teaching school, then answer the questions that follow.

> "... I never before saw children so eager to learn, although I had had several years' experience in New England schools. Coming to school is a constant delight and recreation to them. They come here as other children go to play. The older ones, during the summer, work in the fields from early morning until eleven or twelve o'clock, and then come to school, after their hard toil in the hot sun, as bright and as anxious to learn as ever.
>
> ... The majority learn with wonderful rapidity. Many of the grown people [want to learn] to read. It is wonderful how a people who have been so long crushed to the earth ... can have so great a desire for knowledge, and such a capacity for attaining it. ..."

1. What points in this passage are stated most forcefully?
2. What is the main idea of this passage?
3. What details support the main idea of this passage?

Cooperative Activity

History and Citizenship Laws about voter registration vary from place to place. Working with a partner, contact your local election board to find out what the requirements for voter registration are in your community. Then design a brochure that encourages citizens to register to vote.

Technology Activity

Using a Word Processor Search your library for information about Lincoln and the assassination. Then, using a word processor, write a brief radio announcement about the event that might have been broadcast if radio had been invented by that time.

Geography Activity

Turn to the map on page 510 to answer the following questions.

1. **Location** Electoral votes are based on population. What were the six most populous states in 1876?
2. **Region** Which political party gained the most votes in the western states?
3. **Place** How many electoral votes were in dispute?

Portfolio Activity History Journal Review the chapter to make a list of specific ways that Southern states tried to deny equal rights to African Americans after the war. Then decide which amendment(s)—Thirteenth, Fourteenth, or Fifteenth—should have prevented each action.

CHAPTER 17
Review and Activities

Technology Activity

Radio announcements should include details about Lincoln's assassination.

Geography Activity

1. New York, Pennsylvania, Ohio, Illinois, Missouri, Indiana
2. Republican
3. 20

Portfolio Activity Students' lists should include the actions taken in Southern states to limit African Americans' freedoms and should note whether the Thirteenth, Fourteenth, or Fifteenth Amendment was passed to prevent these types of actions.

Chapter Bonus Test Question

Ask: **Which president mentioned in this chapter served as an indentured servant to a tailor?** *(Andrew Johnson hated his indenture and ran away. The tailor took out an ad in the Raleigh, North Carolina, Gazette, offering a reward of $10 to anyone who would capture Johnson. No one volunteered.)*

Skill Practice Activity

1. that the children were so eager to learn, school is a constant delight to them, so great a desire for learning, such a capacity for attaining [education]
2. African Americans had a great hunger for knowledge and to learn how to read.
3. They come to school anxious to learn after working hard all morning. The children want to go to school instead of playing. The majority learn quickly.

Cooperative Activity

Students should use information acquired from the board of elections to design a brochure that encourages citizens to register to vote.

Unit 7 Resource Guide

These Glencoe resources may be used to teach, reteach, or enrich the concepts presented in this unit of study.

TEACHING TRANSPARENCIES

Map Transparency 7 with Overlays A, B, C

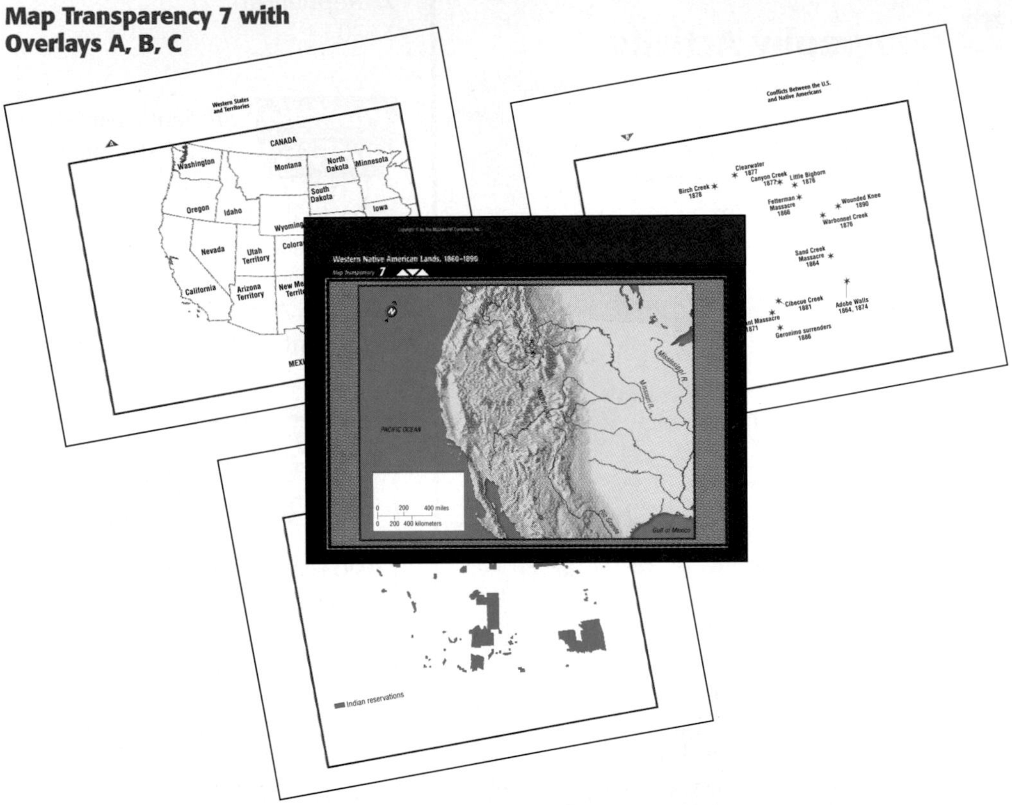

Cause-and-Effect Transparency 7

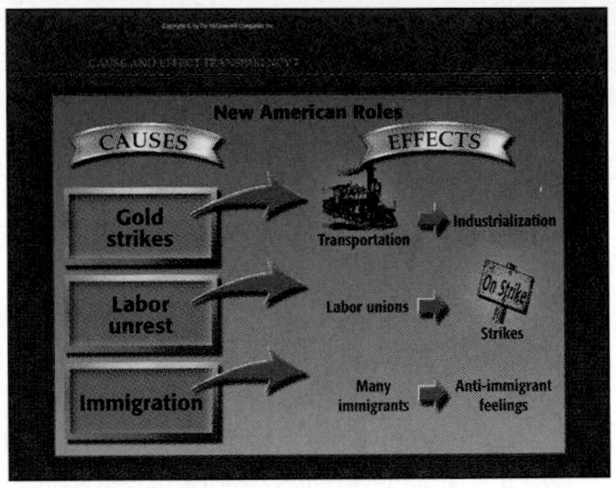

BIBLIOGRAPHY

Readings for the Student

Hafen, Lyman. ***Over the Joshua Slope.*** New York: Bradbury Press, 1994. A 12-year-old learns about life while on a cattle drive with his father.

Swanson, Gloria B. ***I've Got an Idea: The Story of Frederick McKinley Jones.*** Minneapolis: Runestone Press, 1994. Biography of the African American who invented refrigeration units for trucks and railroads, portable X-ray units, and more.

Readings for the Teacher

Jackson, Helen Hunt. ***A Century of Dishonor.*** Available in several modern editions. Classic work on whites' treatment of Native Americans.

Webb, Walter Prescott. ***The Great Plains.*** Lincoln, NE: University of Nebraska Press, 1981. The classic work on the Great Plains.

Multimedia Resources

Videocassette. ***How the West Was Lost.*** VHS. 3 vols., 300 minutes. Distributed by Discovery Home Entertainment, Bethesda, MD. The story of Native American–white conflict.

Videocassette. ***I Will Fight No More Forever.*** VHS, 109 minutes. Distributed by Cambridge Educational, Charleston, WV. Re-enacts the 1,700-mile fighting retreat of the Nez Perce.

interNET CONNECTIONS

Inventions and Immigration on the World Wide Web

National Inventors Hall of Fame: http://www.invent.org/

U.S. Immigration and Naturalization Service: http://www.usdoj.gov/ins/index.html

Resource Guide Unit 7

Interdisciplinary Activities

American Literature Reading 7

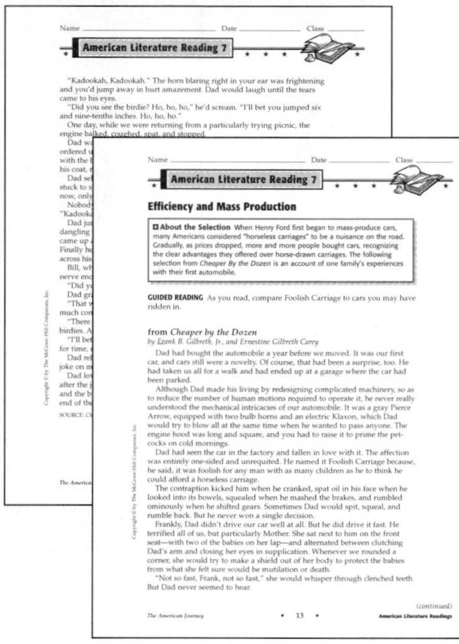
American Literature Reading 7

Efficiency and Mass Production

from *Cheaper by the Dozen*

Interdisciplinary Connection 7

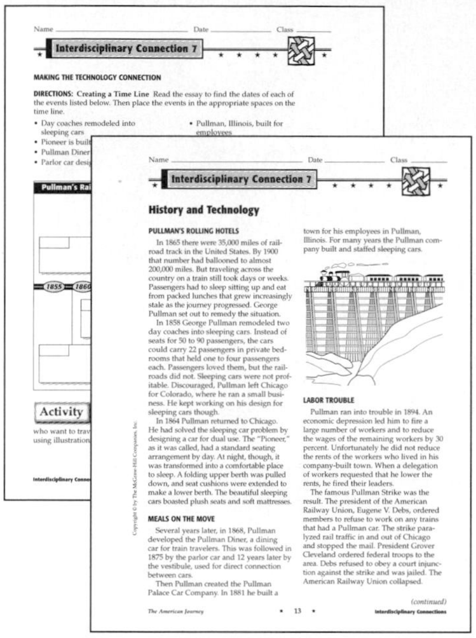
Interdisciplinary Connection 7

History and Technology

Enrichment Activities

Cooperative Learning Activity 7

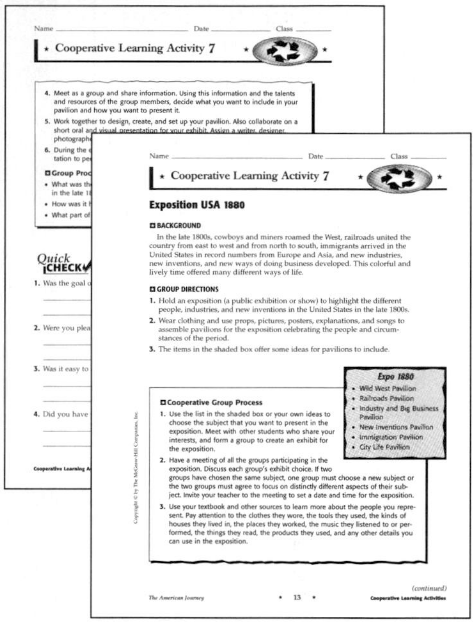
Cooperative Learning Activity 7

Exposition USA 1880

Hands-On Activities

Hands-On History Lab Activity 7

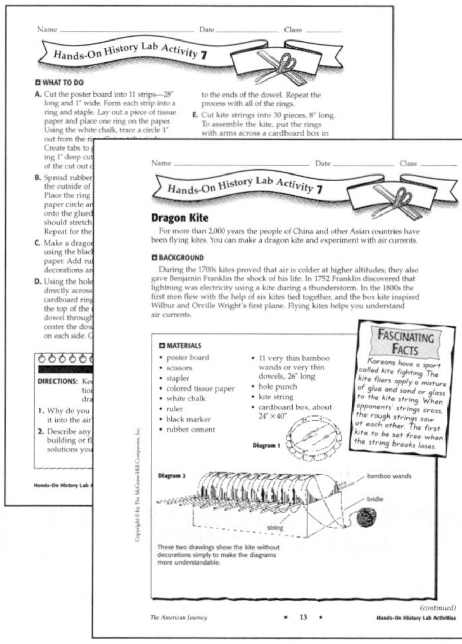
Hands-On History Lab Activity 7

Dragon Kite

History Simulation 7

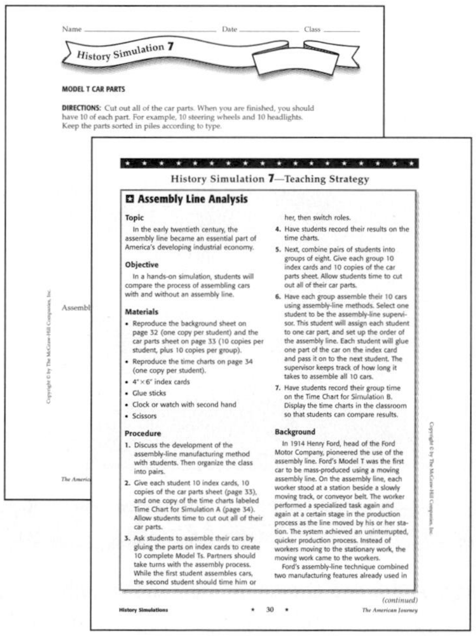
History Simulation 7—Teaching Strategy

Assembly Line Analysis

Assessment

Unit 7 Test

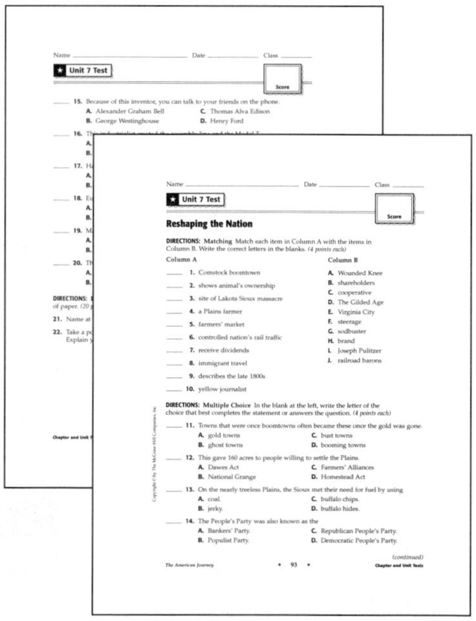
Unit 7 Test

Reshaping the Nation

0:00 OUT OF TIME?

If your teaching time is limited, you may use the *Chapter Summaries* blackline master found in the TCR with the *Chapter Digests Audiocassette Activities and Tests* to condense individual chapters into a one-day lesson.

Introducing the Unit

Activity Have students look at the time line on this spread. Do they understand the meaning of the words *czar, Sino,* and *transatlantic?* What are the subjects of the Sixteenth and Seventeenth Amendments? *(national income tax, direct election of senators)*

Next have students survey the photographs on these pages and in the rest of the unit and make a list of topics that they think will be covered.

Unit Objectives

Upon completing this unit, students will be able to:

1. Discuss the role of mining booms, railroads, ranching, and farming in the development of the West; the final conflicts between Native Americans and whites; and the plight of farmers in the late 1800s.
2. Explain the role of railroad barons, inventions, corporations, and labor in America in the late 1800s and early 1900s.
3. Describe the social history of the late 1800s and early 1900s, including the impact of immigration, city growth, and developments in education, literature, and leisure activities.

Hands-On HISTORY

Hands-On History Lab Activity 7, "Dragon Kite," is a high-interest **constructivist approach** activity directly related to the main topic of the unit.

Unit 7

Reshaping the Nation

1858 – 1914

"America! America! . . . From sea to shining sea!"

—KATHERINE LEE BATES, 1893

MAPPING *America*

Portfolio Activity Draw a freehand outline map of the United States. Include state and territorial borders. As you read this unit about the settlement of the West and the growth of industries and cities, highlight major events on your map. Plot the location of these events on your map and label them. You may want to include mining and ranching areas, routes of the railroads, and the journeys of immigrants.

Plains Native American war shirt

Cattle branding iron

United States

1876 Alexander Graham Bell invents the telephone

1878 First electric light company is established

1870 — *1880*

World

1871 Germany unifies under Bismarck

1881 Czar Alexander II of Russia is assassinated

TEAM TEACHING STRATEGIES

Language Arts Ask the Language Arts teacher to present to the class Emily Dickinson's poem "I Like to See It Lap the Miles." Students should enjoy discovering that the subject of the poem is a train, although it is written using only animal imagery.

Music Ask the Music teacher to teach students some of the many songs about working on railroads. "I've Been Working on the Railroad" and "Drill, Ye Tarriers, Drill" are two of the best-known songs.

Traveler's trunk

HISTORY AND ART ***New York* by George Bellows** As pioneers continued to spread across the continent and immigrants flocked to the cities, Americans adapted to their rapidly changing environment.

1890 Sherman Antitrust Act passed

1894 Sino–Japanese War begins

1895 Cubans revolt against Spanish rule

1896 Henry Ford builds his first automobile

1901 Theodore Roosevelt becomes president

1901 First transatlantic wireless message sent

1907 Oklahoma becomes forty-sixth state

1911 China becomes a republic

1913 Sixteenth and Seventeenth Amendments are ratified

1914 World War I begins

1890 — 1900 — 1910 — 1920

Team Teaching Strategies

Math Have the Math teacher work with students to create a bar graph comparing immigration from the leading nations of the old immigration (England, Ireland, Germany) and the new immigration (Italy, Austria-Hungary, and Russia). The following figures may be used:

Years	Old	New
1871–1880	1,593,000	181,000
1881–1890	2,753,000	926,000
1891–1900	1,110,000	1,847,000
1901–1910	1,069,000	5,789,000
1911–1920	540,000	2,928,000

NATIONAL GEOGRAPHIC SOCIETY

VIDEODISC
GTV: A Geographic Perspective on American History

Side 2, Chapter 11
Title: *Going to Extremes: The Far West*
Subject: Settlement in the Far West (1820–1850)
Ask: **What prevented most Americans from moving west until the 1840s?** *(fear of Native Americans and the trip across the plains and mountains)* **What drew settlers to California in the late 1840s?** *(gold)*

HISTORY AND ART George Bellows (1882–1925) was a student of Robert Henri, the artist whose work began the realist tradition in America. Bellows, like other realists, showed grim urban scenes, but he also painted high society.

Linking PAST & PRESENT

Activity In the mid-1880s the pattern of immigration to the United States began to change. Where most previous immigrants were from northern and western Europe, the new immigrants came from eastern and southern Europe. Today the pattern has again changed. Have students use an almanac to find out where most of today's immigrants come from. *(Mexico, China, Philippines, Vietnam, former Soviet Union, Dominican Republic, India, and Poland)*

Block Schedule

Team Teaching This selection from *Life on the Mississippi* may be implemented in a team-teaching context, in conjunction with English/Language Arts.

Reinforcing Vocabulary

Review the **Reader's Dictionary** terms with students to be sure they understand any unfamiliar terms.

Historical Connection

By the time Twain was born, steamboats were well established on the Mississippi, carrying passengers and freight on day trips and week-long voyages. Steamboats contributed greatly to the growth of such towns as Cincinnati, St. Louis, Louisville, Memphis, and Natchez. Although commercial steamboat traffic was disrupted by the Civil War, it quickly resumed after hostilities ended. Steamboats dominated travel on inland waterways well into the twentieth century, only declining in the 1930s.

Background Information

Setting The setting is Hannibal, Missouri, in the mid-1800s.

Plot There is no central plot. Rather, the book is made up of often humorous stories and anecdotes about riverboat life, including Twain's experiences as an apprentice pilot. Twain was 17 years old when he persuaded an experienced pilot to teach him the skill of navigating the 1,200–1,300 miles of river, with its various landmarks (points), bends, islands, and often shifting shoals and sandbars. *Life on the Mississippi* originally appeared as a series in the magazine *Atlantic Monthly* under the title "Old Times on the Mississippi."

America's Literature

Life on the Mississippi

by Mark Twain

Mark Twain, who was born Samuel Langhorne Clemens in 1835, spent his early life in Hannibal, Missouri. There he became a printer and later a riverboat pilot. So much did he love life on the Mississippi River that he later chose a pen name that would link him with the river forever. "Mark twain!" was a river call meaning "two fathoms," or that the water was deep enough for safe passage.

Read to Discover

Mark Twain's boyhood dreams and memories are the sources of *Life on the Mississippi.* The work begins with a vivid description of the arrival of a riverboat. As you read this excerpt, think about the importance of the riverboat's arrival to the town and to young Twain.

Reader's Dictionary

packet: boat that carries mail, passengers, and freight at fixed times over a fixed route
Keokuk: town at the southeastern tip of Iowa
drayman: driver of a dray—a low sturdy cart with removable sides
texas deck: the deck adjoining the officers' cabins was called *texas* because the cabins there were the largest on the ship
forecastle: upper deck
stage: plank for loading and unloading cargo and passengers
gauge-cock: measuring instrument

Once a day a cheap, gaudy packet arrived upward from St. Louis, and another downward from Keokuk. Before these events, the day was glorious with expectancy; after them, the day was a dead and empty thing. Not only the boys, but the whole village, felt this. After all these years I can picture that old time to myself now, just as it was then: the white town drowsing in the sunshine of a summer's morning; the streets empty, or pretty nearly so; one or two clerks sitting in front of the Water Street stores, . . . the great Mississippi, the majestic, the magnificent Mississippi, rolling its mile-wide tide along, shining in the sun; the dense forest away on the other side; the "point" above the town, and the "point" below. . . . Presently a film of dark smoke appears above one of those remote "points"; instantly a . . . drayman, famous for his quick eye and prodigious voice, lifts up the cry, "S-t-e-a-m-boat a-comin'!" and the scene changes! The . . . clerks wake up, a furious clatter of drays follows, every house and store pours out a human contribution, and all in a twinkling the dead town is alive and moving. Drays, carts, men, boys, all go hurrying from many quarters to a common center, the wharf. Assembled there, the people fasten their eyes upon the coming boat as upon a wonder they are seeing for the first time. And the boat *is* rather a handsome sight, too. She is long and sharp and trim and pretty; she has two tall, fancy-topped chimneys, with a gilded device of some kind swung between them; a fanciful pilot-house, all glass and "gingerbread," perched on top of the "texas" deck behind them; the paddle-boxes are gorgeous with a picture

Additional Literary Works of the Period

You may want to refer students to the following:

Harris, Joel Chandler. ***Complete Tales of Uncle Remus.*** Boston: Houghton Mifflin, 1995. Stories the author learned as a boy visiting slave quarters for evening storytelling.

Harte, Bret. ***The Luck of Roaring Camp and Other Short Stories.*** Mineola, NY: Dover, 1992. Often humorous stories of Gold Rush era.

Jewett, Sarah Orne. ***The Country of the Pointed Firs and Other Stories.*** Magnolia, MA: Peter Smith, 1990. Realistic stories that focus on lives of women in small-town Maine.

London, Jack. ***The Call of the Wild.*** Available in various editions. Buck, a sled dog, returns to the wild after his master is killed. Also ***White Fang;*** a dog sacrifices his life to save his owner.

George Catlin's painting On the River *shows one of the steamboats that traveled on the Mississippi River during the 1800s.*

or with gilded rays above the boat's name; the boiler-deck, the hurricane-deck, and the texas deck are fenced and ornamented with clean white railings; there is a flag gallantly flying from the jack-staff; the furnace doors are open and the fires glaring bravely; the upper decks are black with passengers; the captain stands by the big bell, calm, imposing, the envy of all; great volumes of the blackest smoke are rolling and tumbling out of the chimneys; . . . the crew are grouped on the forecastle; the broad stage is run far out over the port box, and an envied deck-hand stands picturesquely on the end of it with a coil of rope in his hand; the pent steam is screaming through the gauge-cocks; the captain lifts his hand, a bell rings, the wheels stop; then they turn back, churning the water to foam, and the steamer is at rest. Then such a scramble as there is to get aboard, and to get ashore, and to take in freight and to discharge freight, all at one and the same time; and such a yelling! . . .

Ten minutes later the steamer is under way again, with no flag on the jack-staff and no black smoke issuing from the chimneys. After ten more minutes the town is dead again.

Responding to Literature

1. What adjectives does Twain use to describe the Mississippi River?
2. What major event transpires once a day? Why is the event so important?

Activity

"Painting" Literature Reread Twain's descriptions of the Mississippi River, a steamboat, or the crowd rushing to the wharf. Then draw a picture of one of the scenes. Be sure to add details that reflect Twain's words.

America's Literature

Portfolio Activity Have students describe an exciting event in their own lives. The event should include the kind of expressive language and wealth of detail that make Twain's scene come alive. If some students prefer, they can describe an imagined event.

At the Movies

The movie *The Adventures of Huckleberry Finn* was originally made for PBS television. Produced by Great Amwell Company and distributed by MCA/Universal Home Video, Universal City, CA.

Curriculum Connection

GEOGRAPHY

The Mississippi River is 2,340 miles (3,766 km) long and drains an area of 1,234,700 square miles (3,197,873 square km). Its source is in Lake Itasca in northwestern Minnesota. The Mississippi River's waters flow into the Gulf of Mexico through several mouths in the delta area. These mouths are known locally as passes—the Main, North, South, and Southwest Passes.

Answers to Responding to Literature

1. great, majestic, magnificent
2. One packet arrives from upstream, another arrives from downstream. Answers will vary, but students may note that it is about the only interesting thing that happens in the sleepy little town.

Activity Drawings should reflect the description provided of the steamboat and excitement on the part of town inhabitants.

Chapter 18 Planning Guide

A complete, 1-page lesson plan is provided for each section in the *Reproducible Lesson Plans* booklet.

Section Resources

Daily Objectives	Reproducible Resources	Multimedia Resources
Section 1 **The Mining Booms** Describe how the discovery of gold and silver affected the development of the West and the nation, including the expansion of railroads.	Reproducible Lesson Plan 18–1 Guided Reading Activity 18–1* Section Quiz 18–1* Reteaching Activity 18–1 Enrichment Activity 18–1	Section Focus Transparency 18–1 U.S. History & Art, Transparency 12 Vocabulary PuzzleMaker Chapter Challenger Interactive Review GTV: A Geographic Perspective on American History ABCNews InterActive™ Historic America Electronic Field Trips
Section 2 **Ranchers and Farmers** Explain the relationship among the railroads, the Cattle Kingdom, and farmers.	Reproducible Lesson Plan 18–2 Guided Reading Activity 18–2* Section Quiz 18–2* Reteaching Activity 18–2 Enrichment Activity 18–2	Section Focus Transparency 18–2 Vocabulary PuzzleMaker Chapter Challenger Interactive Review GTV: A Geographic Perspective on American History Facts On File: Landmark Documents in American History American Music Cultural Traditions
Section 3 **Native American Struggles** Explain why whites and Native Americans of the Plains were in conflict and summarize the results of the conflict.	Reproducible Lesson Plan 18–3 Guided Reading Activity 18–3* Political Cartoons, *Thomas Nast: America's Well-Known Political Cartoonist* Section Quiz 18–3* Reteaching Activity 18–3 Enrichment Activity 18–3	Section Focus Transparency 18–3 U.S. History & Art, Transparency 13 Vocabulary PuzzleMaker Chapter Challenger Interactive Review Testmaker GTV: A Geographic Perspective on American History GTV: The American People: Fabric of a Nation ABCNews InterActive™ Historic America Electronic Field Trips NGS PictureShow: Native Americans, Parts 1 and 2 Facts On File: The American Indian
Section 4 **Farmers in Protest** Summarize the plight of farmers in the late 1800s and explain how they tried to help themselves.	Reproducible Lesson Plan 18–4 Guided Reading Activity 18–4* Section Quiz 18–4* Reteaching Activity 18–4 Enrichment Activity 18–4	Section Focus Transparency 18–4 Vocabulary PuzzleMaker Chapter Challenger Interactive Review Testmaker American Music Cultural Traditions

** Also available in Spanish*

Blackline Master · Videodisc · Audiocassette · Music Program · Transparency · CD-ROM · Software

0:00 **OUT OF TIME?**
Assign the Chapter 18 Digest and the corresponding Chapter Digests Audiocassettes with activities and tests.

Chapter 18 Planning Guide

Activity

From the Classroom of...

Harold J. Washington
St. Edwards School
Seattle, WA

Adopt a State

Organize your class into at least four groups. Place the names of western states into a container and have students select one. Each group will be responsible for researching that state. Research will include the date when the territory became a state and its major resources and industries. If students find there is a major industry or agricultural product that is often associated with the state, have them research that topic as fully as possible. For example, students could collect data on the apple industry of Washington state and show how Washington compares to other regions of the country and the world in apple production.

Encourage groups to make charts, graphs, or drawings to accompany their state's report. Groups should then present their information to the class. To keep information closely linked to the chapter, have students pay particular attention to the early development and early histories of their respective states.

Block Schedule

Block scheduling differs from traditional class scheduling in the amount of time allotted to each period. The extended time frame provided by block scheduling affords you the opportunity to implement a greater number of research-oriented and activity-intense projects to motivate and involve your students. Activities that are particularly suited to use within the block scheduling framework are identified throughout this chapter by the following designation:

NATIONAL GEOGRAPHIC SOCIETY Teacher's Corner

INDEX TO NATIONAL GEOGRAPHIC MAGAZINE

The following articles may be used for research relating to this chapter:

- "Buffalo: Back Home on the Range," by Bryan Hodgson, November 1994.
- "John Wesley Powell," by Peter Miller, April 1994.
- "Federal Lands," by Richard Conniff, February 1994.
- "The American Prairie: Roots of the Sky," by Douglas H. Chadwick, October 1993.
- "Wide Open Wyoming," by Thomas J. Abercrombie, January 1993.
- "Geronimo," by David Roberts, October 1992.
- "The Life and Times of William Henry Jackson," by Rowe Findley, February 1989.
- "Along the Santa Fe Trail," by Rowe Findley, February 1989.

NATIONAL GEOGRAPHIC SOCIETY PRODUCTS AVAILABLE FROM GLENCOE

To order the following products for use with this chapter, contact your local Glencoe sales representative, or call Glencoe at 1-800-334-7344:

- *GTV: A Geographic Perspective on American History* (Videodisc)
- *GTV: The American People: Fabric of a Nation* (Videodisc)
- *The Presidents: A Picture History of Our Nation* (CD-ROM)
- *PictureShow: Native Americans, 1 and 2* (CD-ROM, Transparencies)
- *PictureShow: The Westward Movement* (CD-ROM, Transparencies)

ADDITIONAL NATIONAL GEOGRAPHIC SOCIETY PRODUCTS

To order the following products for use with this chapter, call National Geographic Society at 1-800-368-2728:

- *Heritage of the Black West* (Video)
- *American Indians: A Brief History* (Video)
- *Immigration: The Triumph of Hope* (Video)
- *Historical Atlas of the United States* (Atlas)

KEY TO ABILITY LEVELS

Teaching strategies have been coded for varying learning styles and abilities.

L1 **BASIC** activities for all students
L2 **AVERAGE** activities for average to above-average students
L3 **CHALLENGING** activities for above-average students
ELL **ENGLISH LANGUAGE LEARNER** activities

Chapter 18 Resource Guide

Home Involvement

Home Involvement Activity 18

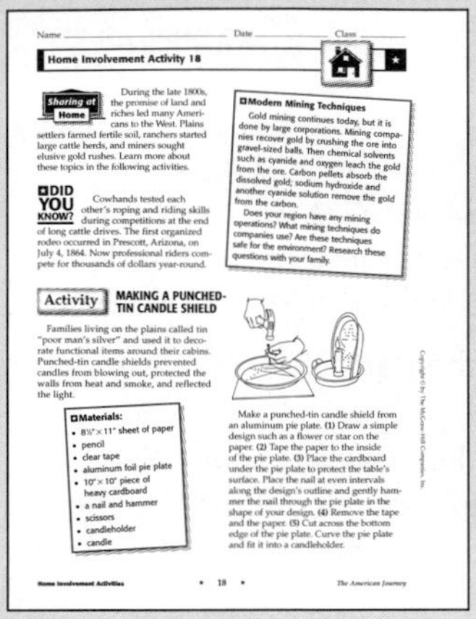

Review Activities

Chapter Summary 18

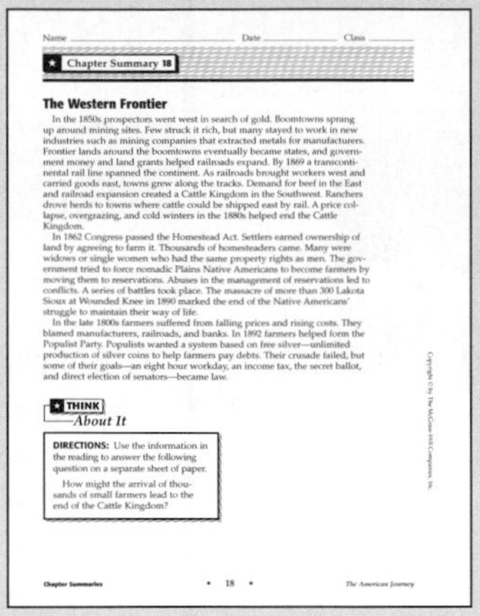

Workbook Activity 18

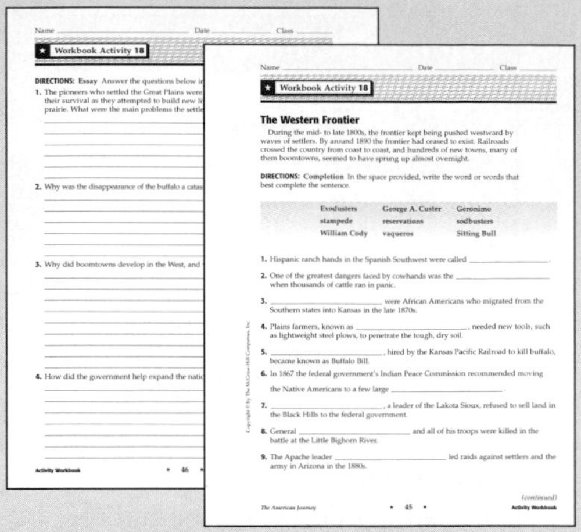

Reinforcement Activities

Time Line Activity 18

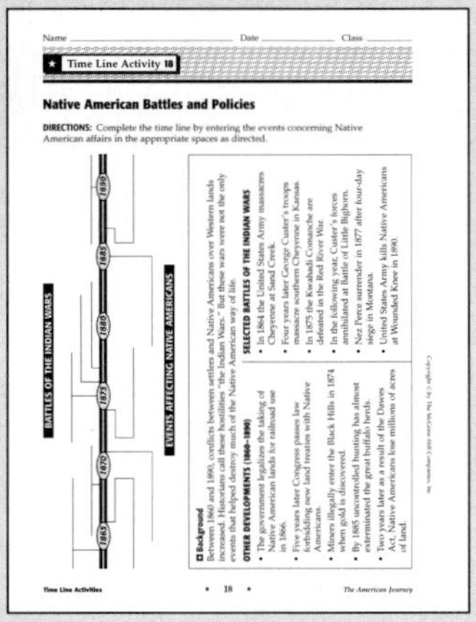

Vocabulary Activity 18

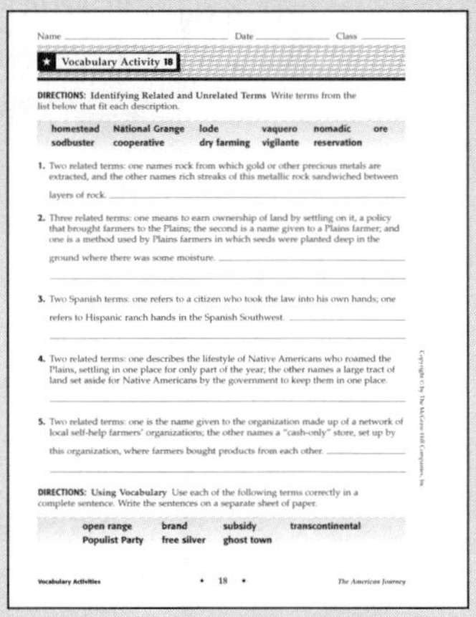

Chapter Skills Activity 18

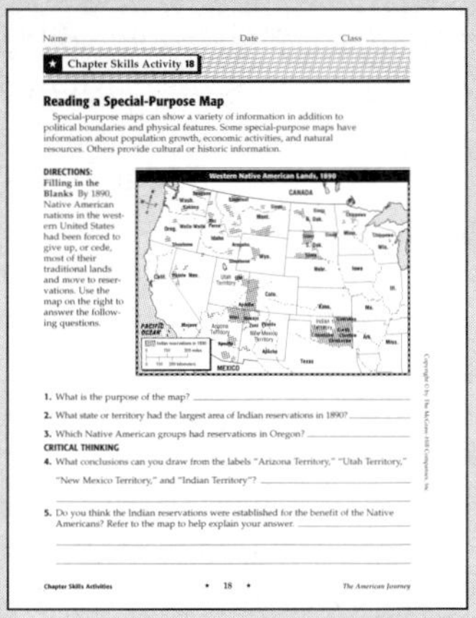

Enrichment Activities

Linking Past and Present Activity 18

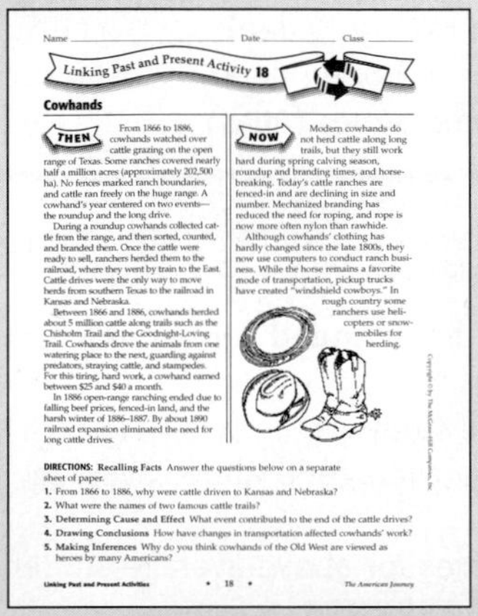

Primary Source Reading 18

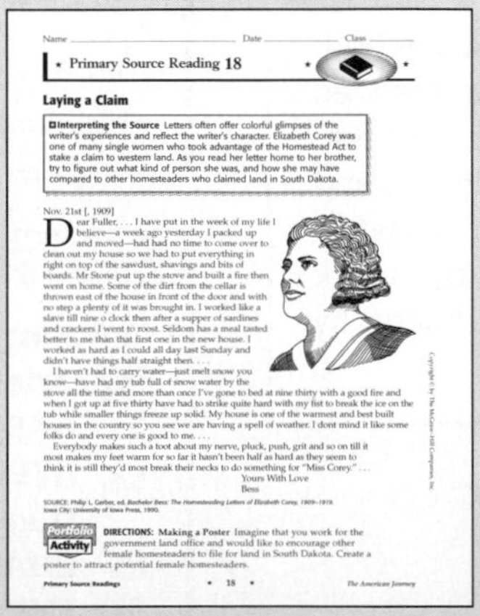

Geography Activities

Mapping History Activity 18

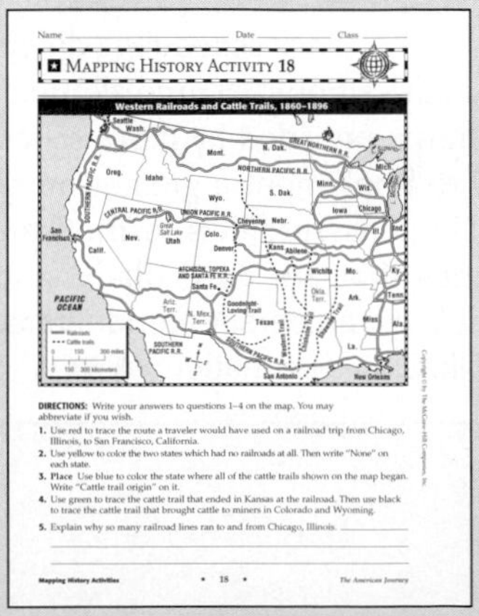

Chapter 18 Resource Guide

Assessment

Chapter 18 Test, Form A

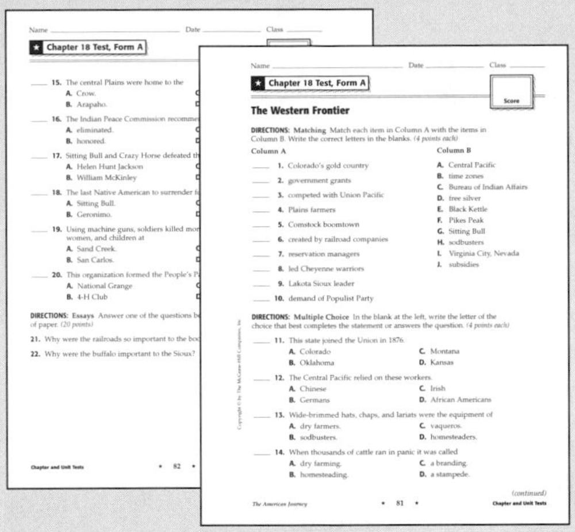

Chapter 18 Test, Form B

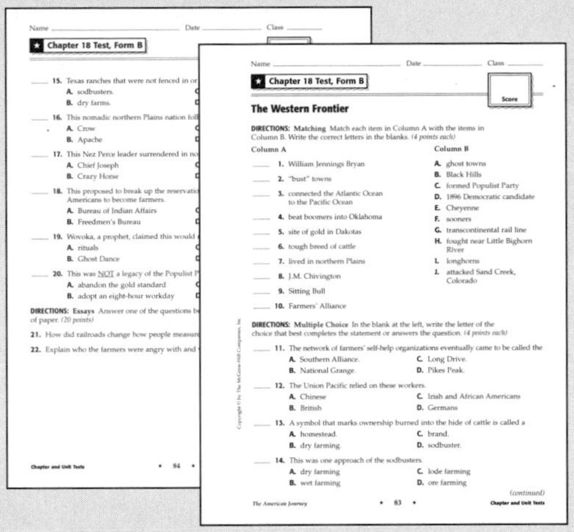

Performance Assessment Activity 18

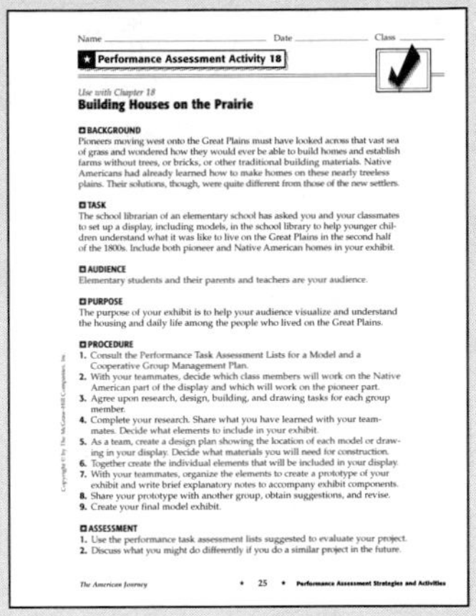

Spanish Resources

The following Spanish language materials are available in the Spanish Resources binder:

- **Spanish Chapter Summary 18**
- **Spanish Vocabulary Activity 18**
- **Spanish Guided Reading Activities, Chapter 18**
- **Spanish Section Quizzes, Chapter 18**
- **Spanish Home Involvement Activity 18**
- **Spanish Chapter 18 Digests Audiocassette Activity and Test**

Activity Manipulatives

Help students learn more about America's cultural history with:

- **American Crafts Hands-On Activities**
- **American Games Hands-On Activities**
- **American History Flash Cards**

Additional Resources From Glencoe

- **U.S. History & Art,** Transparency 12, *Merced River, Yosemite Valley;* Transparency 13, *Chief Joseph*
- **American Music Cultural Traditions,** Lesson 6: "Little Old Sod Shanty" and "The Farmer Is the Man that Feeds Them All"
- **The Spirit of American Art and Music,** Edmonia Lewis
- **Political Cartoons,** *Thomas Nast: America's Well-Known Political Cartoonist*
- **U.S. Desk Map**
- **Outline Map Resource Book**
- **The American History Videodisc and CD-ROM,** *Post–Civil War Expansion and Change, 1865–1900*

A&E HOME VIDEO. Biography™ THE HISTORY CHANNEL.

The following videotape programs are available from Glencoe as supplements to Chapter 18:

- **George Custer: Showdown at Little Bighorn** (ISBN 1-56501-683-1)
- **Sitting Bull: Chief of the Lakota Nation** (ISBN 1-56501-684-X)
- **Crazy Horse** (ISBN 1-56501-597-5)
- **The Best of the Real West (Set)** (ISBN 1-56501-352-2)
- **Transcontinental Railroads** (ISBN 1-56501-731-5)

To order, call Glencoe at 1-800-334-7344. To find classroom resources to accompany many of these videos, check the following home pages:
A&E Television: http://www.aetv.com
The History Channel: http://www.historychannel.com

Introducing
CHAPTER 18

Chapter Themes

Chapter Themes are listed by section on this chapter opening page of the Student Edition. A corresponding theme-based activity is available under "FOCUS," and a theme-based question is asked in the Section and Chapter Reviews.

Performance Assessment

Refer to Activity 18 in the *Performance Assessment Strategies and Activities* booklet.

GLENCOE TECHNOLOGY

VIDEODISC
MindJogger Videoquiz

Use MindJogger to preview the Chapter 18 content.

Chapter 18
Disc 3, Side A

Also available in VHS.

HISTORY AND ART The works of Thomas Moran (1837–1926) reflect a changing approach among landscape painters. He was more concerned with "the aesthetic qualities of pigment, light, color, air, and brushwork" than with nature worship.

Chapter 18

1858–1896

The Western Frontier

Why It's Important

Although Native Americans on the Plains tried to resist the advance of American settlers, the newcomers came in overwhelming numbers. With the 1890 census, the government declared that no line could be drawn that clearly marked the end of settlement. For the first time in the nation's history, there was no western frontier. With the settlement of the Great Plains and the closing of this last frontier, the United States fulfilled the dream of Manifest Destiny.

Chapter Themes

- *Section 1,* Geography and History
- *Section 2,* Economic Factors
- *Section 3,* Culture and Traditions
- *Section 4,* Groups and Institutions

HISTORY AND ART ***The Mirage*** **by Thomas Moran** Moran painted the mountains, canyons, and plains of the West during the late 1800s. Many of his scenes show the magnificence and vastness of the region.

EXTRA CREDIT PROJECT

Famous Native Americans Have students choose a famous Native American chief of the late 1800s and read a biography of that leader. They may choose one of the people named in the text (Crazy Horse, Black Kettle, Chief Joseph, Sitting Bull, Geronimo) or any other appropriate person, such as Cochise or Quanah Parker. Among the many biographies available are those of the series *North American Indians of Achievement* published in the 1990s by Chelsea House of New York (various authors). Have each student prepare a book report, either in writing or on tape, and ask volunteers to share their reports with the class.

1855 1865 1875 1885

1858 Gold is discovered at Pikes Peak

1869 Transcontinental railroad links East and West

1876 Colorado joins the Union

1883 Nation is divided into four time zones

Section 1

The Mining Booms

READ TO DISCOVER . . .

- how the rush to find gold and silver created new communities in the West.
- how the railroad network expanded.
- how the development of railroads affected the nation.

TERMS TO LEARN

lode	ghost town
ore	subsidy
vigilante	transcontinental

The Storyteller

"We'll cross the bold Missouri, and we'll steer
for the West,
And we'll take the road we think is the
shortest and the best,
We'll travel over plains where the wind is
blowing bleak,
And the sandy wastes shall echo with—
Hurrah for Pikes Peak."

—"The Gold Seeker's Song"

Miners sang this hopeful song in 1859 as they headed for Pikes Peak, Colorado, where gold had been discovered.

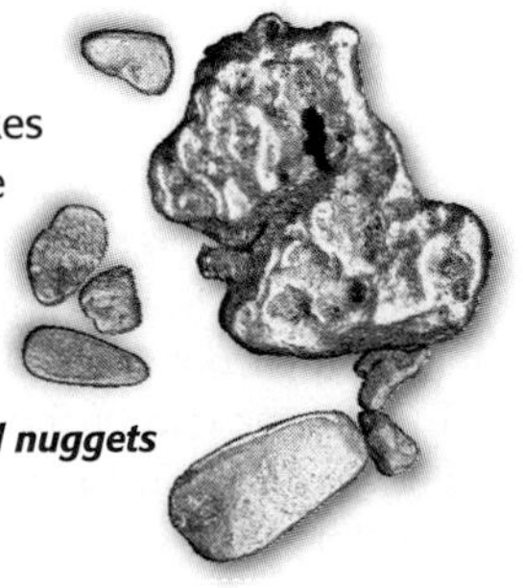

Gold nuggets

By the mid-1850s the California Gold Rush had ended. Disappointed miners, still hoping to strike it rich, began prospecting in other parts of the West.

In 1858 a mining expedition found gold on the slopes of **Pikes Peak** in the Colorado Rockies. Newspapers claimed that miners were making $20 a day panning for gold—a large sum at a time when servants made less than a dollar a day. By the spring of 1859, about 50,000 prospectors had flocked to Colorado. Their slogan was "Pikes Peak or Bust." Most went home no richer than when they had arrived.

Economics

Mining Is Big Business

Prospectors skimmed gold dust from streams or scratched particles of gold from the surface of the land. Most of the gold, however, was deep in underground **lodes**, rich streaks of ore sandwiched between layers of rock. Mining this rock, or **ore**, and then extracting the gold required expensive machinery, many workers, and business organization. Companies made up of several investors had a better chance of getting rich in the goldfields than individual miners did. At most gold rush sites, mining companies soon replaced the lone miner.

Gold and silver mining attracted foreign as well as American investors. The British, for example, invested heavily in the American mining industry.

SECTION RESOURCES

Reproducible Masters
- Guided Reading Activity 18–1
- Section Quiz 18–1
- Enrichment Activity 18–1
- Reteaching Activity 18–1

Transparencies
- Section Focus Transparency 18–1
- U.S. History & Art, Transparency 12

Multimedia
- Vocabulary PuzzleMaker
- Chapter Challenger Interactive Review Software
- Testmaker
- GTV: A Geographic Perspective on American History
- ABCNews InterActive™ Historic America Electronic Field Trips

1 FOCUS

BELLRINGER
Motivational Activity

Before taking roll at the beginning of the class period, project Section Focus Transparency 18–1 and have students answer the questions. Discuss students' responses.

This activity is also available as a blackline master.

Section Focus Transparency 18–1

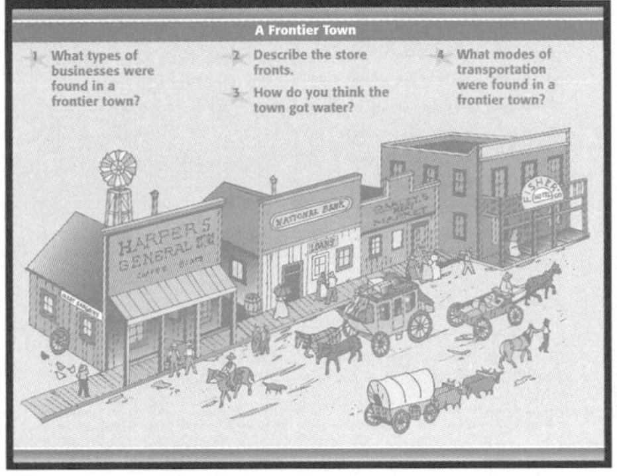

Vocabulary Precheck

Have students look up unfamiliar words listed under **Terms to Learn** and then use each term in a sentence.

Use the **Vocabulary PuzzleMaker** to create crossword and word search puzzles.

Section Theme
Geography and History

Prospectors, businesspeople, traders, and others rushed into rugged mountain and desert regions, braving hardships in hopes of getting rich. Few did, but the mining boom encouraged completion of the transcontinental rail line.

Activity Have students skim the section to identify an important by-product of the mining boom. *(expansion of the railroads to span the continent)*

CHAPTER 18
Section 1, 525–529

2 TEACH

LI Making a Cause-and-Effect Chart Work with students to create a cause-and-effect chart on the chalkboard showing the results of the discovery of gold and other metals in the West.

Guided Reading Activity 18–1

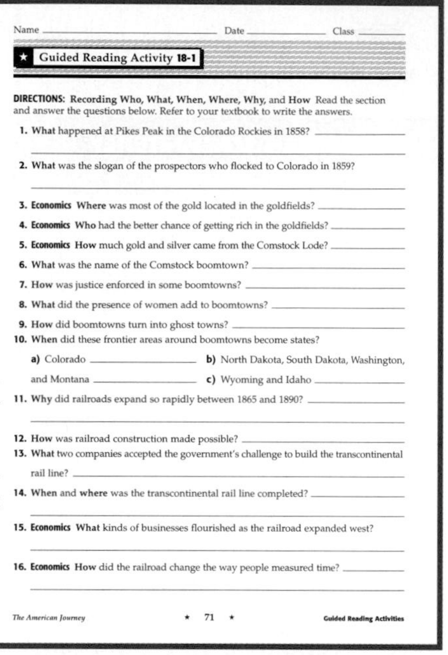
Name ______ Date ______ Class ______

Guided Reading Activity 18-1

DIRECTIONS: Recording Who, What, When, Where, Why, and How Read the section and answer the questions below. Refer to your textbook to write the answers.

1. **What** happened at Pikes Peak in the Colorado Rockies in 1858? ______
2. **What** was the slogan of the prospectors who flocked to Colorado in 1859? ______
3. **Economics Where** was most of the gold located in the goldfields? ______
4. **Economics Who** had the better chance of getting rich in the goldfields? ______
5. **Economics How** much gold and silver came from the Comstock Lode? ______
6. **What** was the name of the Comstock boomtown? ______
7. **How** was justice enforced in some boomtowns? ______
8. **What** did the presence of women add to boomtowns? ______
9. **How** did boomtowns turn into ghost towns? ______
10. **When** did these frontier areas around boomtowns become states?
    a) Colorado ______ **b)** North Dakota, South Dakota, Washington, and Montana ______ **c)** Wyoming and Idaho ______
11. **Why** did railroads expand so rapidly between 1865 and 1890? ______
12. **How** was railroad construction made possible? ______
13. **What** two companies accepted the government's challenge to build the transcontinental rail line? ______
14. **When** and **where** was the transcontinental rail line completed? ______
15. **Economics What** kinds of businesses flourished as the railroad expanded west? ______
16. **Economics How** did the railroad change the way people measured time? ______

The American Journey ★ 71 ★ **Guided Reading Activities**

NATIONAL GEOGRAPHIC SOCIETY

VIDEODISC
GTV: A Geographic Perspective on American History

Side 3, Chapter 3
Title: *A World of Change*
Subject: Settlement on the Great Plains
Ask: **What made the Great Plains and the West "more accessible"?** *(the railroad)*

America's FLAGS

Twentieth Flag of the Union, 1876
Statehood for Colorado in 1876 brought the number of stars in the flag to 38. This was the Twentieth Flag.

The Comstock Lode

In 1858 several prospectors found a rich lode of gold-bearing ore on the banks of the Carson River in Nevada. The discovery was called the **Comstock Lode** after Henry Comstock, who owned a share of the claim.

Thousands of mines opened near the site, but only a few were profitable. Mining companies reaped the largest share of the profits. When Comstock sold his share of the claim, he received $11,000 and two mules—a huge sum at the time. It was, however, just a tiny fraction of the $300 million worth of gold and silver pulled from the Comstock Lode strike.

The Mining Frontier

The gold strikes created **boomtowns**—towns that grew up almost overnight around mining sites. The Comstock boomtown was **Virginia City, Nevada.** In 1859 the town was a mining camp. Two years later it had a stock exchange, hotels, banks, an opera company, and five newspapers.

Footnotes to History

Gold Rush Words Many of the terms used during the gold rush found their way into our daily language. These include *pay dirt, pan out, to stake a claim,* and *to strike it rich.*

Boomtowns were lively, untamed places filled with people from far-off regions. Gold and silver strikes attracted eager prospectors from Mexico, China, and other countries.

Money came quickly—and was often lost just as quickly through extravagant living and gambling. A fortunate miner could earn as much as $2,000 a year, about four times the annual salary of a teacher at that time. Still food, lodging, clothing, and other goods cost dearly in the boomtowns, draining the miners' earnings.

Violence was part of everyday life in boomtowns, where many people carried large amounts of cash and guns. Cheating and stealing were common. Few boomtowns had police or prisons so citizens sometimes took the law into their own hands. These **vigilantes** dealt out their own brand of justice without benefit of judge or jury, often hanging the accused person from the nearest tree.

Women in the Boomtowns

Boomtowns were largely men's towns in the early days. Men outnumbered women by two to one in Virginia City, and children made up less than 10 percent of the population.

Eager to share in the riches of the boomtowns, some women opened businesses. Others worked as laundresses, cooks, or dance-hall entertainers. Women added stability to the boomtowns, founding schools and churches and working to make the communities safer and more orderly.

Boom and Bust

Many mining "booms" were followed by "busts." When the mines no longer yielded ore, people left the towns. At its peak in the 1870s, Virginia City had about 30,000 inhabitants. By 1900 its population had dropped below 4,000.

Many boomtowns turned into **ghost towns**—deserted as prospectors moved on to more promising sites or returned home. Some can still be seen in the West today, relics of the glory days of the mining frontier.

Toward the end of the rush, gold and silver mining gave way in some sites to the mining of other metals. Copper became the key metal found

COOPERATIVE LEARNING ACTIVITY

Making a Mural Organize students into small groups to create a mural of the Old West, illustrating scenes applying to this section as well as to Sections 2 and 3. Have students use library resources and information from the Internet to find additional information and illustrations for inspiration. Groups should choose different sections to illustrate: a cross-section of a mine, a boomtown, a map showing railroads and the location of mines, a diagram of how mining equipment worked, and so on. It might be a good idea to have delegates from each group meet to make an overall plan for the mural, bearing in mind that they will also need space for material pertaining to the next two sections. ELL in Montana, New Mexico, and Arizona in the 1870s. In the 1890s people began mining lead and zinc in some former silver-mining towns of Colorado. In its final stage, the mining frontier became part of American industry, providing raw materials for manufacturers.

Many people who went west to seek their fortunes in gold or silver settled there permanently. Frontier areas around the boomtowns eventually became states. Colorado joined the United States in 1876. North Dakota, South Dakota, Washington, and Montana became states in 1889. Wyoming and Idaho were admitted to the Union in 1890.

Railroads Connect East and West

The western mines operated far from the industrial centers of the East and Midwest. For this reason transportation played a vital role in the survival of mining communities. Gold and silver had little value unless they could reach factories, ports, and markets. At the same time, the miners and others in the boomtowns needed shipments of food and other supplies.

Wagon trains and stagecoach lines could not move people and goods fast enough to meet these demands. Railroads could—and did. The nation's railroad network expanded rapidly between 1865 and 1890. In that period the miles of track in the United States soared from about 35,000 to more than 190,000.

Government and the Railroads

Railroad construction was made possible by large government **subsidies**—financial aid and land grants from the government. Railroad executives argued that their companies should receive free public land on which to lay track because a rail network would benefit the entire nation.

The national government—and states, too—agreed. In all, the federal government granted more than 130 million acres of land to the railroad companies. Much of the land was purchased or obtained by treaty from Native Americans.

The government grants included the land for the tracks plus strips of land along the railway, 20 to 80 miles wide. Railroad companies sold those strips of land to raise additional money for construction costs.

States and local communities also helped the railroads. Towns offered cash subsidies to make sure that the railroads came to their communities. For example, Los Angeles gave the Southern Pacific Railroad money and paid for a passenger terminal to ensure that the railroad would come to the town.

Spanning the Continent

The search for a route for a **transcontinental** rail line—one that would span the continent and connect the Atlantic and Pacific coasts—began in the 1850s. Southerners wanted the route to run through the South, and Northerners through the North. During the Civil War, the Union government chose a northerly route. The government offered land grants to railroad companies willing to build the transcontinental line.

The challenge was enormous—laying track for more than 1,700 miles across hot plains and

Picturing HISTORY The boomtown of Leadville, Colorado, surrounds a settler's cabin that sits in the middle of the main street. **Why did boomtowns develop almost overnight in the West after 1850?**

Multiple Learning Styles

Logical/Mathematical Have students make a pictograph entitled *Growth of the Railroads, 1860–1900,* showing the approximate miles of railroad track in the United States during that period. Give them the following figures: 1860–40,000 miles; 1870–50,000; 1880–80,000; 1890–170,000; 1900–220,000. Have students list the years on the vertical axis. Suggest that they pick a symbol, such as a locomotive or a length of track, to represent 10,000 or 20,000 miles of track. Note that the symbol may be divided to show smaller amounts. Have students each write three math problems based on their graph, then exchange papers with a partner to solve one another's problems. **L3**

you don't say...

"Asleep at the switch" is an American expression describing someone who is not alert or is unaware of danger. It refers to moving trains from one set of rails to another by flipping a switch. Failure to flip the switch could place two trains on the same track.

History *and the* Humanities

U.S. History & Art, Transparency 12, *Merced River, Yosemite Valley*

Picturing HISTORY Today, Leadville is the county seat of Lake County in central Colorado. Located in the Rocky Mountains near the headwaters of the Arkansas River, it lies at an altitude of about 10,200 feet (3,110 m). The town began as a gold mining camp in 1859. In the 1870s Leadville became a major silver mining center as well. **Answer:** *because of the discovery in 1858 of gold near Pikes Peak and the Comstock Lode in Nevada*

CURRICULUM CONNECTION

SCIENCE
Many prospectors mistook pyrite—fool's gold—for the real thing. Cautious miners could perform simple experiments to test the malleability, durability, tarnish resistance, and density that identified real gold. Real gold does not break when it is hammered, and gold placed on a shovel and thrust into a campfire will not melt. Heat and acid will not affect real gold.

3 ASSESS

Assign Section 1 Review as homework or as an in-class activity.

Use **Chapter Challenger Interactive Review Software** to review Section 1.

TECHNOLOGY AND HISTORY

More About . . .
Locomotives and Railroads The first public railroad in the world opened in Great Britain in 1825 and ran for 20 miles (32 km). The first public railroad in the United States began operations in 1830. Known as the Baltimore and Ohio Railroad, it ran on 13 miles (21 km) of track in Maryland. Railroads were so successful that the first transcontinental line was finished in 1869. Railroads remained the nation's chief form of long-distance transportation until passenger airplanes took over in the late twentieth century.

Answer to Caption: *Answers will vary, but students might suggest that steam power was the first form of machine power of the Industrial Revolution. It was therefore logical that steam be used for locomotives.*

Section Quiz 18–1

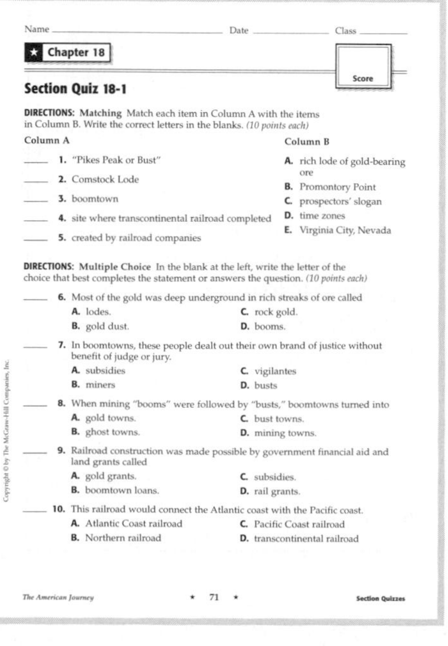

Name ______ Date ______ Class ______

★ Chapter 18 — Score

Section Quiz 18-1

DIRECTIONS: Matching Match each item in Column A with the items in Column B. Write the correct letters in the blanks. *(10 points each)*

Column A	Column B
____ 1. "Pikes Peak or Bust"	A. rich lode of gold-bearing ore
____ 2. Comstock Lode	B. Promontory Point
____ 3. boomtown	C. prospectors' slogan
____ 4. site where transcontinental railroad completed	D. time zones
____ 5. created by railroad companies	E. Virginia City, Nevada

DIRECTIONS: Multiple Choice In the blank at the left, write the letter of the choice that best completes the statement or answers the question. *(10 points each)*

____ 6. Most of the gold was deep underground in rich streaks of ore called
A. lodes. C. rock gold.
B. gold dust. D. booms.

____ 7. In boomtowns, these people dealt out their own brand of justice without benefit of judge or jury.
A. subsidies C. vigilantes
B. miners D. busts

____ 8. When mining "booms" were followed by "busts," boomtowns turned into
A. gold towns. C. bust towns.
B. ghost towns. D. mining towns.

____ 9. Railroad construction was made possible by government financial aid and land grants called
A. gold grants. C. subsidies.
B. boomtown loans. D. rail grants.

____ 10. This railroad would connect the Atlantic coast with the Pacific coast.
A. Atlantic Coast railroad C. Pacific Coast railroad
B. Northern railroad D. transcontinental railroad

The American Journey ★ 71 ★ **Section Quizzes**

through rugged mountains. Two companies accepted the challenge. The Union Pacific Company began laying track westward from **Omaha, Nebraska,** while the Central Pacific Company worked eastward from **Sacramento, California.**

The two companies competed fiercely. Each wanted to cover a greater distance in order to receive more of the government subsidies.

The Central Pacific hired about 10,000 Chinese laborers to work on its tracks. The Union Pacific relied on Irish and African American workers. All workers toiled for low wages in harsh conditions. In the choking heat of summer and the icy winds of winter, they cleared forests, blasted tunnels through mountains, and laid hundreds of miles of track. In the end the Union Pacific workers laid 1,038 miles of track, and the Central Pacific workers laid 742 miles. However, the Central Pacific covered a much harsher terrain.

The Transcontinental Railway

On May 10, 1869, construction was completed. The two sets of track met at **Promontory Point** in Utah Territory. **Leland Stanford,** governor of

TECHNOLOGY AND HISTORY

Steam Locomotive

Since 1825, when the first steam locomotive was built in the United States, trains have crisscrossed the country. As America's transportation needs increased, so did the miles of railroad track linking its people.

Why do you think steam power was the first power source for locomotives?

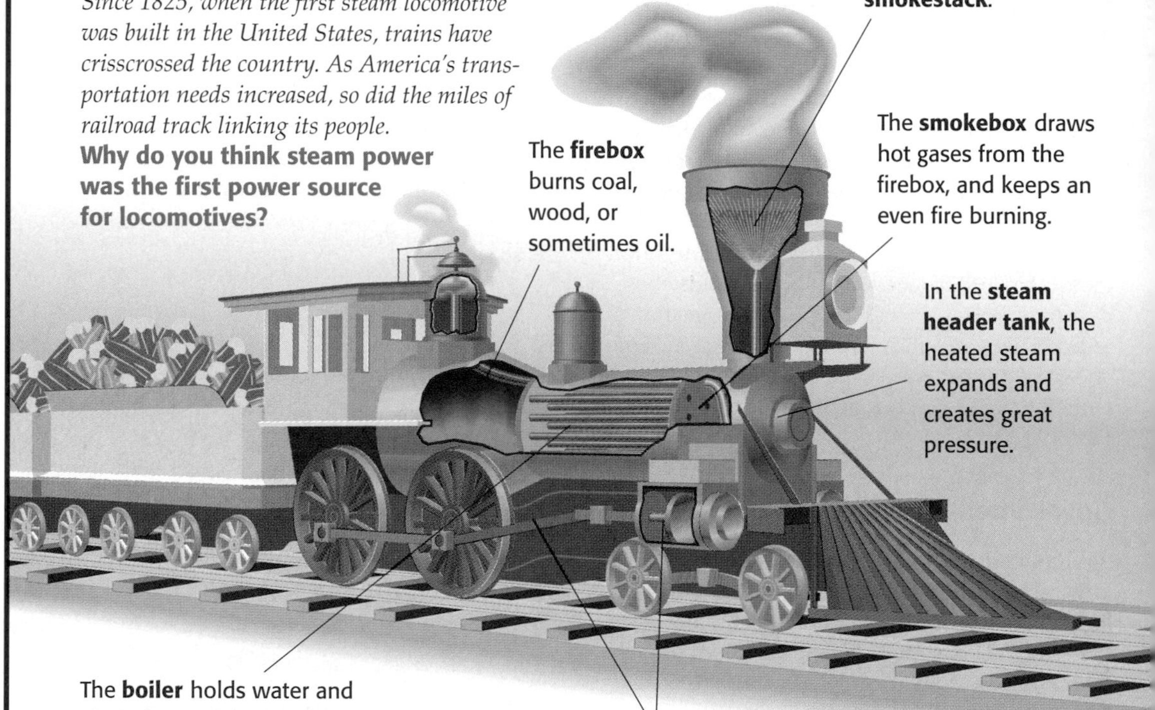

MAKING CONNECTIONS ACTIVITY

Global Issues Have students research and report on gold rushes in other parts of the world—especially Alaska, Australia, South Africa, West Africa, Siberia, and Mexico. Students may do a summary report that either includes all those areas or focuses on one particular region. Encourage them to explain how frontier prospectors overcame the difficulties they faced and to note any similarities to the gold rushes in the western United States. Students' reports should include a map showing where the largest deposits of gold have been found. Some students may wish to illustrate their reports with other visuals as well. **L2**

★ ★ ★ ★ ★ ★ ★ ★ ★ ★ ★ ★

California, drove a final golden spike into a tie to join the two railroads. Almost as the event occurred, telegraph lines flashed the news across the country: "The last rail is laid . . . the last spike driven. . . . The Pacific Railroad is completed."

Picturing HISTORY A Union Pacific work train approaches a bridge being built over the Green River in Wyoming Territory in 1868. **Which railroad companies helped build the first transcontinental railroad?**

Economics

Effects of the Railroads

By 1883 two more transcontinental lines and dozens of shorter lines connected cities in the West with the rest of the nation. The economic consequences were enormous. The railroads brought thousands of workers to the West. Trains carried metals and produce east and manufactured goods west. As more tracks were laid, more steel was needed, and the demand boosted the nation's steel industry. Coal producers, railroad car manufacturers, and construction companies also flourished as the railroads spread across the West.

Towns sprang up along the rail lines that carried the settlers' agricultural goods to market. Some of these towns eventually became large cities. The railroads also brought the next wave of new settlers to the West—cattle ranchers and farmers.

Railroads even changed how people measured time. Before railroads, each community kept its own time. Clocks in Boston, for example, were 11 minutes ahead of clocks in New York. The demand for sensible train schedules, however, changed that. In 1883 the railroad companies divided the country into four **time zones.** All communities in each zone would share the same time, and each zone was exactly one hour apart from the zones on either side of it. Congress passed a law making this practice official in 1918.

Section 1 Review

Checking for Understanding

1. ***Identify*** Pikes Peak, Promontory Point, Leland Stanford.
2. ***Define*** lode, ore, vigilante, ghost town, subsidy, transcontinental.
3. ***Describe*** life in a typical boomtown.

Reviewing Themes

4. **Geography and History** What physical features and climate made building the transcontinental railroad difficult?

Critical Thinking

5. **Determining Cause and Effect** How did the construction of the transcontinental railroad influence settlement of the Great Plains?

Activity

Making a Map Draw a map of what you think a boomtown would look like. Be sure to label all the buildings in the town.

Section 1 Review Answers

1. Pikes Peak, 525; Promontory Point, 528; Leland Stanford, 528
2. The words are defined in the Glossary.
3. lively, often violent; made up mostly of men from many different places; extravagant living and gambling; few police or prisons
4. extreme heat of plains and deserts in summer, icy winds of winter, mountainous terrain that had to be cleared of forest and through which tunnels had to be dug
5. attracted more settlers and a new type of settlers—cattle ranchers and farmers

Activity Students may base their maps on the text on page 526 and the picture on page 527, or they may look in library resources for more ideas.

Picturing HISTORY Have students estimate the distance from the Green River in Wyoming to Promontory Point to see how much farther the railroad crew pictured had to go. *(about 160 miles)*
Answer: *Central Pacific, Union Pacific*

Reteaching Activity 18–1

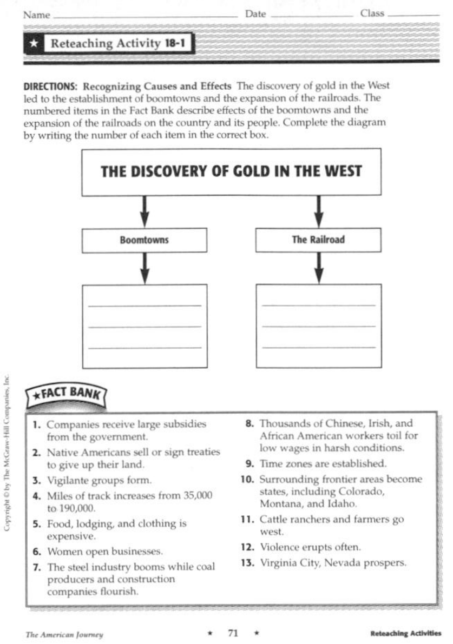

Name ______ Date ______ Class ______

★ Reteaching Activity 18-1

DIRECTIONS: Recognizing Causes and Effects The discovery of gold in the West led to the establishment of boomtowns and the expansion of the railroads. The numbered items in the Fact Bank describe effects of the boomtowns and the expansion of the railroads on the country and its people. Complete the diagram by writing the number of each item in the correct box.

★FACT BANK

1. Companies receive large subsidies from the government.
2. Native Americans sell or sign treaties to give up their land.
3. Vigilante groups form.
4. Miles of track increases from 35,000 to 190,000.
5. Food, lodging, and clothing is expensive.
6. Women open businesses.
7. The steel industry booms while coal producers and construction companies flourish.
8. Thousands of Chinese, Irish, and African American workers toil for low wages in harsh conditions.
9. Time zones are established.
10. Surrounding frontier areas become states, including Colorado, Montana, and Idaho.
11. Cattle ranchers and farmers go west.
12. Violence erupts often.
13. Virginia City, Nevada prospers.

The American Journey ★ 71 ★ Reteaching Activities

Enrichment Activity 18–1

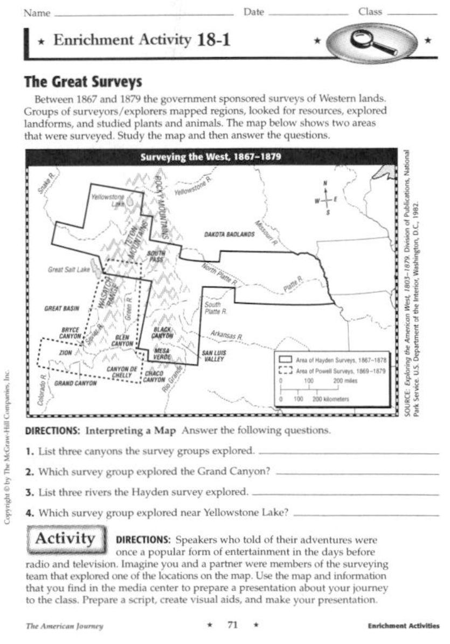

Name ______ Date ______ Class ______

★ Enrichment Activity 18-1 ★

The Great Surveys

Between 1867 and 1879 the government sponsored surveys of Western lands. Groups of surveyors/explorers mapped regions, looked for resources, explored landforms, and studied plants and animals. The map below shows two areas that were surveyed. Study the map and then answer the questions.

SOURCE: *Exploring the American West, 1803–1879.* Division of Publications, National Park Service. U.S. Department of the Interior, Washington, D.C., 1982.

DIRECTIONS: Interpreting a Map Answer the following questions.

1. List three canyons the survey groups explored. ______
2. Which survey group explored the Grand Canyon? ______
3. List three rivers the Hayden survey explored. ______
4. Which survey group explored near Yellowstone Lake? ______

Activity **DIRECTIONS:** Speakers who told of their adventures were once a popular form of entertainment in the days before radio and television. Imagine you and a partner were members of the surveying team that explored one of the locations on the map. Use the map and information that you find in the media center to prepare a presentation about your journey to the class. Prepare a script, create visual aids, and make your presentation.

The American Journey ★ 71 ★ Enrichment Activities

4 CLOSE

Ask: **If gold were discovered in a remote part of North America, would you want to go? Why?**

ABCNEWS INTERACTIVE™

VIDEODISC
Historic America
Electronic Field Trips

Side 1, Chapter 11
Title: *Sutter's Mill*

If you do not have access to a videodisc player, the **Historic America Electronic Field Trips** are also available in VHS.

Internet Sites
The following is a possible site for completing the "Net" activities:

The United States Immigration and Naturalization Service Home Page
http://www.usdoj.gov/ins/index.html

Not on the "Net" . . .
If students have limited or no access to the Internet, have them complete the activity "How to Become a Citizen" by contacting the nearest Immigration and Naturalization Service listed in a phone directory under "U.S. Government Justice Department." Students should request information about becoming a United States citizen. From the literature students receive, have them write their own pamphlet on becoming a citizen through the naturalization process.

Multimedia Activities

ABCNEWS INTERACTIVE™ Historic America Electronic Field Trips

Field Trip to Sutter's Mill

Setting up the Video

Work with a group of your classmates to view "Sutter's Mill" on the videodisc ***Historic America: Electronic Field Trips***. Gold was discovered on John Sutter's land near Sacramento, California, in 1848. Thousands of people rushed westward to try their luck at getting rich. This program explains how the discovery of gold helped California obtain statehood.

Hands-On Activity

Create a poster advertising the discovery of gold in 1848. Think of a colorful name for a boomtown, and advertise how one can become rich quick there! Use a word processor to create letters of different sizes and font styles on your poster.

Side 1, Chapter 11

View the video by scanning the bar code or by entering the chapter number on your keypad and pressing Search.

Surfing the "Net"

How to Become a Citizen

Between 1865 and 1914, the United States experienced a massive influx of immigrants. Today immigrants enter the country on a limited basis. People who legally reside in the United States but are not citizens are called *aliens.* The process by which aliens become citizens is called *naturalization.* Learn more about this process on the Internet.

Getting There

Follow these steps to gather information about the naturalization process.

1. Use a search engine. Type in the word *naturalization.*
2. Enter words like the following to focus your search: *immigration, citizenship skills, alien, INS* (Immigration and Naturalization Service).
3. The search engine will provide you with a number of links to follow. Links are "pointers" to different sites on the Internet.

What to Do When You Are There

Click on the links to navigate through the pages of information. Gather your findings. Using a word processor, create an information pamphlet on how to become a citizen through the naturalization process. Include sample questions asked of immigrants by immigration examiners. These questions determine knowledge about the United States.

TEACHER'S NOTES

1860 1870 1880 1890

1862 Homestead Act gives free land to settlers

1866 Missouri Pacific Railroad reaches Missouri

1867 Abilene, Kansas, is founded

1889 Oklahoma land rush occurs

Section 2

Ranchers and Farmers

READ TO DISCOVER . . .

- how the railroads helped create a "Cattle Kingdom" in the Southwest.
- how women contributed to the settling of the Great Plains.

TERMS TO LEARN

open range
brand
vaquero
homestead
sodbuster
dry farming

The Storyteller

An old Texas cowhand, E. C. Abbott, recalled the early days of riding the trail:

"Here [were] all these cheap long-horned steers overrunning Texas; here was the rest of the country crying for beef—and no railroads to get them out. So we trailed them out, across hundreds of miles of wild country that was thick with Indians. . . . In 1867 the town of Abilene was founded at the end of the Kansas Pacific Railroad and that was when the trail really started."

Cattle ranching book, 1880s

When the Spanish settled Mexico and Texas, they brought a tough breed of cattle with them. Called **longhorns** because of their prominent horns, these cattle gradually spread across Texas. By 1865 the longhorns numbered about 5 million.

Cattle on the Plains

At this time much of Texas was **open range**—not fenced or divided into lots. Huge ranches covered other areas of the state. Ranchers added to their own herds by rounding up wild cattle. The ranchers burned a **brand,** or symbol, into the animals' hides to show who owned the cattle.

Railroads and Cow Towns

Although Texas ranchers had plenty of cattle, the markets were in the North and the East. In 1866 the Missouri Pacific Railroad reached Missouri, and Texas cattle suddenly increased in value. The cattle could be loaded on trains in Missouri for shipment north and east. Some Texans drove their combined herds—about 260,000 head of cattle—north to **Sedalia, Missouri,** the nearest rail point. Longhorns that had formerly been worth $3 each quickly rose in value to $40.

Cattle drives to **cow towns**—railroad towns for marketing and shipping cattle—turned into a yearly event. Over the next decade, cow towns such as **Abilene** and **Dodge City, Kansas,** and **Cheyenne, Wyoming,** became important stations.

SECTION RESOURCES

Reproducible Masters
- Reproducible Lesson Plan 18–2
- Guided Reading Activity 18–2
- Section Quiz 18–2
- Enrichment Activity 18–2
- Reteaching Activity 18–2

Transparencies
- Section Focus Transparency 18–2

Multimedia
- Vocabulary PuzzleMaker
- Chapter Challenger Interactive Review
- Testmaker
- GTV: A Geographic Perspective on American History
- Facts On File: Landmark Documents in American History
- American Music Cultural Traditions

1 FOCUS

BELLRINGER
Motivational Activity

Before taking roll at the beginning of the class period, project Section Focus Transparency 18–2 and have students answer the questions. Discuss students' responses.

This activity is also available as a blackline master.

Section Focus Transparency 18–2

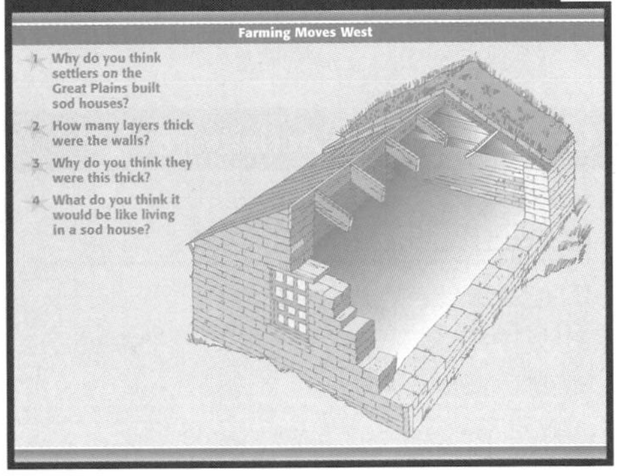

Vocabulary Precheck

"Dry farming" seems contrary to the need for water to grow crops. Have students find out what the term means. Was it really dry?

Use the **Vocabulary PuzzleMaker** to create crossword and word search puzzles.

Section Theme
Economic Factors

Economics played a role in the success or failure for both ranchers and farmers.

Activity Have students list economic factors that created the cattle boom and bust and factors that led to farm failure. (*Cattle—railroads allowed ranchers to sell to the East where there was a big market; overproduction and weather conditions led to bust. Farms—land grants too small to make a living, climate was unpredictable, grasshoppers stripped crops)*

2 TEACH

L1 Outlining the Section Work with students to create an outline of the section. Use the main heads for Roman numerals I to V, and have students provide details to fill in the subheads.

HISTORY AND ART Charles Russell (1864–1926) was a self-taught painter, sculptor, illustrator, and writer. He produced more than 100 bronze sculptures and thousands of paintings.
Answer: *with Hispanic ranch hands in Spanish Southwest*

Guided Reading Activity 18–2

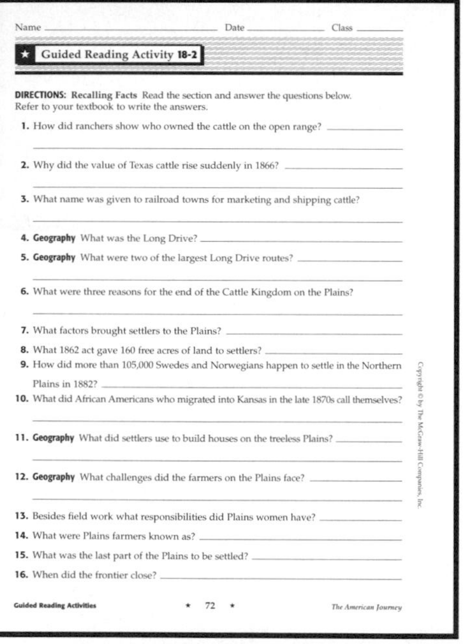
Name ______ Date ______ Class ______

★ Guided Reading Activity **18-2**

DIRECTIONS: Recalling Facts Read the section and answer the questions below. Refer to your textbook to write the answers.

1. How did ranchers show who owned the cattle on the open range? ______
2. Why did the value of Texas cattle rise suddenly in 1866? ______
3. What name was given to railroad towns for marketing and shipping cattle? ______
4. **Geography** What was the Long Drive? ______
5. **Geography** What were two of the largest Long Drive routes? ______
6. What were three reasons for the end of the Cattle Kingdom on the Plains? ______
7. What factors brought settlers to the Plains? ______
8. What 1862 act gave 160 free acres of land to settlers? ______
9. How did more than 105,000 Swedes and Norwegians happen to settle in the Northern Plains in 1882? ______
10. What did African Americans who migrated into Kansas in the late 1870s call themselves? ______
11. **Geography** What did settlers use to build houses on the treeless Plains? ______
12. **Geography** What challenges did the farmers on the Plains face? ______
13. Besides field work what responsibilities did Plains women have? ______
14. What were Plains farmers known as? ______
15. What was the last part of the Plains to be settled? ______
16. When did the frontier close? ______

Guided Reading Activities ★ 72 ★ *The American Journey*

Who?What?Where?When?

Dime Novels and Nat Love The popular image of the "Wild West" was fueled by dime novels—exaggerated tales of daring that sold for a dime. One author, Edward Wheeler, wrote a series of books about Deadwood Dick—based on a cowhand whose real name was Nat Love. Love was born an enslaved person in Tennessee in 1854. He became a cowhand at the age of 15 and remained one until 1890. Later he became a rodeo celebrity.

HISTORY AND ART ***Jerked Down* by Charles Russell** Celebrated for his detailed and dramatic scenes of Western life, Charles Russell depicts cowhands on their surefooted horses lassoing cattle. **Where did the traditions of cattle herding begin?**

Geography

The Long Drive

The sudden increase in the longhorns' value set off what became known as the **Long Drive**—the herding of cattle 1,000 miles or more to meet the railroads. The drives left Texas in the spring, when there was enough grass along the way to feed the cattle. The longhorns had to remain well fed because underweight cattle could not be sold.

Some of the largest Long Drives led from central Texas to Abilene on the **Chisholm Trail.** The **Goodnight-Loving Trail,** named for ranchers Charlie Goodnight and Oliver Loving, swung west through New Mexico Territory and then turned north. During the heyday of the "Cattle Kingdom," from the late 1860s to the mid-1880s, the trails carried more than 5 million cattle north.

Life on the Trail

The cattle drives and the cowhands who worked on them captured the imagination of the nation. Contrary to the popular view, however, cattle driving was hard work. Cowhands rode in the saddle up to 15 hours every day, in driving rain, dust storms, and blazing sun. The life was lonely too. Cowhands saw few outsiders.

Spanish Influence

Many cowhands were veterans of the Confederate army. Some were African Americans who moved west in search of a better life after the Civil War. Others were Hispanics. In fact, the traditions of cattle herding began with Hispanic ranch hands in the Spanish Southwest. These **vaqueros** developed many of the skills—riding, roping, and branding—that cowhands used on the drives. Much of the language of the rancher today is derived from Spanish words used by vaqueros for centuries. Even the word *ranch* comes from the Spanish word *rancho.*

The cowhand's gear was based on the vaquero's equipment too. Cowhands wore wide-brimmed hats to protect themselves from the sun and leather leggings, called **chaps,** to shield their legs from brush and mishaps with cattle. They used ropes called **lariats** to lasso cattle that strayed from the herd.

Hazards on the Trail

On the trail for many months, the cowhands faced violent storms, "rustlers" who tried to steal cattle, and many other dangers. They had to drive the herds across swift-flowing rivers, where cattle could be lost.

COOPERATIVE LEARNING ACTIVITY

Continuing the Mural Have students work in small groups to continue the mural begun in Section 1 (see Cooperative Learning Activity on page 526). Students should now add scenes from the open range, cattle towns, sod homes, and so forth. Page 549 of the Chapter Review provides a map showing the cattle trails, which students may wish to include. Group members could make labels or extended captions for the mural. ELL

One of the greatest dangers on the trail was the **stampede,** when thousands of cattle ran in panic. Any sudden sound—a roar of thunder or the crack of a gunshot—could set off the cattle. The cowhands had to race on horseback with the stampeding cattle and bring them under control.

The "Wild West"

African American, Native American, Hispanic, and Anglo cowhands all met and worked together. Yet discrimination existed in the West just as it did elsewhere. Members of minorities rarely became trail bosses and often received less pay for their work. Some towns discriminated against Hispanics, segregated African Americans, and excluded Chinese cowhands altogether.

After many tiring weeks on the trail, the cowhands delivered their cattle and enjoyed some time off in cow towns. Cowhands drank and gambled and got involved in fistfights and gunplay. Places such as Dodge City and Abilene were rowdy, lawless, and violent. Eventually, though, they grew into settled, businesslike communities.

The Cattle Kingdom Ends

As profits from cattle increased, cattle ranching spread north from Texas. On the northern Plains, ranchers crossbred longhorns with fatter Hereford and Angus cattle to produce hardy, plumper new breeds.

Ranching on the northern Plains began to replace the Long Drive. The sturdy crossbred cattle multiplied on open-range ranches. When cattle prices "boomed" in the early 1880s, ranchers became rich. The boom, however, was soon followed by a bust. Overgrazing depleted the grasslands. In addition, too many cattle glutted the market and prices fell. Then came the bitterly cold winters of 1885 and 1886, which killed large numbers of cattle.

The price collapse of the mid-1880s marked the end of the "Cattle Kingdom." Ranchers built fences and grew hay to feed their cattle during the harsh winters. Another group of settlers would rise on the Plains—the farmers.

Farmers Settle the Plains

The early pioneers who reached the Great Plains did not believe they could farm the dry, treeless area. In the late 1860s, however, farmers began settling there and planting crops. In a surprisingly short time, the Plains changed from "wilderness" to farmland. In 1872 a Nebraska settler wrote,

> "One year ago this was a vast houseless, uninhabited prairie. . . . Today I can see more than thirty dwellings from my door."

Several factors brought settlers to the Plains. The railroads made the journey west easier and cheaper. New laws offered free land. Finally, above-average rainfall in the late 1870s made the Plains better suited to farming.

Picturing HISTORY European immigrants on a flatcar view land open for settlement on the Great Plains. In moving to the area, settlers were often influenced by advertising. **Which groups used advertising to promote settlement of the Great Plains?**

Multiple Learning Styles

Auditory/Musical Students may enjoy learning or listening to cowhand songs such as "Git Along Little Dogies" or "Cowboy's Lament." One source for such music is *Cowboy Songs and Other Frontier Ballads*, by John A. and Alan Lomax, which was originally published in 1910 but has been reissued since then. Your library probably has some recordings of cowhand songs, as well as other songbooks that might be useful. **L1, ELL**

NATIONAL GEOGRAPHIC SOCIETY

VIDEODISC
GTV: A Geographic Perspective on American History

Side 2, Chapter 11
Title: *Going to Extremes: The Far West*
Subject: Settling the West
Ask: **Why did many people settle in Texas?** *(Land was cheap.)*

Side 3, Chapter 3
Title: *A World of Change*
Subject: Settlement on the Great Plains
Ask: **What technologies helped settlers to adapt to life on the Great Plains?** *(barbed wire fences, steel plows, windmills, well-digging machines, steam-powered farm machinery, railroads)*

Picturing HISTORY Land-grant railroads had Bureaus of Immigration to persuade farmers to settle along their lines. They maintained offices in the principal European cities and agents in Eastern seaports to meet immigrants as they left the boat.
Answer: *railroads, steamship companies, land speculators, western states and territories*

you don't say...

Dogie At roundup time there were usually some motherless calves, who were called "dough-guts," which later became *dogie*. Being prematurely weaned, their stomachs could not digest grass and swelled as a result.

Picturing HISTORY In April 1879, Benjamin "Pap" Singleton led a vast migration of former enslaved persons from the South to Kansas. By the end of autumn, approximately 15,000 African Americans had arrived in Kansas. **Ask: Describe the material possessions of these Exodusters.** *(They had very few possessions.)* **Answer:** *They feared for their safety if they stayed in former slaveholding regions.*

Facts On File

CD-ROM
Landmark Documents in American History

Title: *Homestead Act, 1862*
After reading the document, ask students if they think they could have carried out the act's terms in order to gain free land.

History *and the* Humanities

American Music Cultural Traditions, Lesson 6: "Little Old Sod Shanty"

you don't say...

Maverick Today a *maverick* is a rover or a person who goes his or her own way. The term comes from a Texas cattle raiser, Samuel A. Maverick, who did not bother to brand his cattle. As a result, cowhands began to call any unbranded calf a maverick. In time, the usage extended to other animals and to people.

Picturing HISTORY A group of "Exodusters" wait along a Southern waterway for a steamboat to carry them westward. **Why did the "Exodusters" move west?**

The Homestead Act

In 1862 Congress passed the **Homestead Act,** which gave 160 free acres of land to a settler who paid a filing fee and lived on the land for 5 years. This federal land policy brought farmers to the Plains to **homestead**—earn ownership of land by settling on it.

Homesteading lured thousands of new settlers to the Great Plains. Some were immigrants who had begun the process of becoming American citizens and were eligible to file for land. Others were women. Although married women could not claim land, single women and widows had the same rights as men—and they took advantage of the Homestead Act to acquire property. In Colorado and Wyoming, 12 percent of all those who filed homestead claims were women.

Promoting the Plains

Homesteaders came to the Plains to own land and be independent. They were also swayed by advertising paid for by railroads, steamship companies, land speculators, and western states and territories.

Railroad companies wanted to sell the strips of land alongside the rail lines to raise cash. Steamship companies went to great lengths to advertise the Plains in Scandinavia. In 1882 alone more than 105,000 Swedes and Norwegians settled in the northern Plains—Minnesota and the Dakotas—where the Scandinavian influence remains strong today.

African American Settlers

Thousands of African Americans also migrated from the Southern states into Kansas in the late 1870s. They called themselves **"Exodusters,"** from the biblical book of Exodus, which describes the Jews' escape from slavery in Egypt.

The end of Reconstruction in 1877 had meant the end of federal protection for African Americans. Fearing for their safety in former slave regions, freed people sought land farther west. By 1881 more than 40,000 African Americans had migrated to Kansas. Some, however, had to return to the South because they lacked the money to start new farms or businesses.

The Farmers' Frontier

A pioneer woman on the Great Plains described her surroundings as "a new world, reaching to the far horizon without break of tree or chimney stack; just sky and grass and grass and sky." Farmers wondered how they could survive in such an environment.

Geography

The "Soddie"

To survive on the Plains, settlers needed to find new ways of doing things. To begin with, they had to build houses that did not require lumber on this treeless land. The pioneers carved

Footnotes to History

Rain on the Roof Sod roofs often leaked after rains. Even during dry periods, dirt and grass fell like raindrops from the roof.

MAKING CONNECTIONS ACTIVITY

Technology Plains farmers faced many challenges, some of which were solved by new technology, among them barbed wire, the chilled iron plow, and the mechanical seed drill. Have students find out about each invention and explain what problem it solved. *(barbed wire—farmers needed to fence in land to keep cattle and sheep from ruining crops, but wood for fencing was prohibitively expensive; plow—extra strong, so it could cut through the tough sod; seed drill—saved farmers the backbreaking labor of planting seed by hand)* **L2**

dugouts in the sides of hills, over which they built houses made of sod. The **sod,** densely packed soil held together by grass roots, was cut into rectangles resembling bricks. It made a useful building material. A Plains family's first home was usually a sod house, called a "soddie." Some sod houses lasted for years, until farmers could afford to buy lumber, which was scarce and expensive.

Other Challenges

The climate of the Plains presented farmers with their greatest challenge. Generally there was little rainfall, but in some years rain came down in torrents, destroying crops and flooding homesteads. The other extreme—drought—also threatened crops and lives. Fire was another enemy. In times of drought, brushfires swept rapidly through a region, destroying crops, livestock, and homes.

Summer might bring plagues of grasshoppers. Several times during the 1870s, swarms of the insects swept over the Plains. Thousands of grasshoppers would land on a field of corn. When they left, not a stalk would remain.

Winters presented even greater dangers. Winds howled across the open Plains, and deep snow could bury animals and trap families in their homes. Farm families had to plan ahead and store food for the winter.

Farm Families

Farming on the Great Plains was a family affair. Men labored hard in the fields. Women often did the same work, but they also cared for the children. A farm wife sewed clothing, made candles, and cooked and preserved food. In the absence of doctors and teachers, she also tended to the children's health and education. When her husband was away—taking the harvest to town or buying supplies—she bore all responsibility for keeping the farm running. She also had to endure the isolation of the Plains.

When children grew old enough, they too worked the farm. Children helped in the fields, tended animals, and did chores around the house. Farmwork often kept children from attending school.

Although separated by great distances, farm families socialized whenever they could. People took great pleasure in getting together for weddings, church services, picnics, and other occasions.

New Farming Methods

The Plains could not be farmed by the usual methods of the 1860s. Most parts of the region had little rainfall and too few streams for irrigation. The Plains farmers, known as **sodbusters,** needed new methods and tools.

One approach, called **dry farming,** was to plant seeds deep in the ground where there was some moisture. Wooden plows could not penetrate the tough layer of sod, but farmers could use the lightweight steel plows invented in the late 1870s to do the job.

The sodbusters had other tools to help them conquer the Plains—windmills to pump water

Picturing HISTORY Evelyn Cameron moved from England to the plains of eastern Montana where she photographed the settlers. This 1904 photo shows Cameron kneading dough. **What kind of life did most women experience on the Great Plains?**

CHAPTER 18
Section 2, 531–536

What?Where?When?Who?

Grasshoppers One Kansas woman tried to keep the hordes of grasshoppers out of her house by putting mosquito netting over the windows. The grasshoppers ate the netting as well as the crops.

3 ASSESS

Assign Section 2 Review as homework or as an in-class activity.

Use **Chapter Challenger Interactive Review Software** to review Section 2.

Section Quiz 18–2

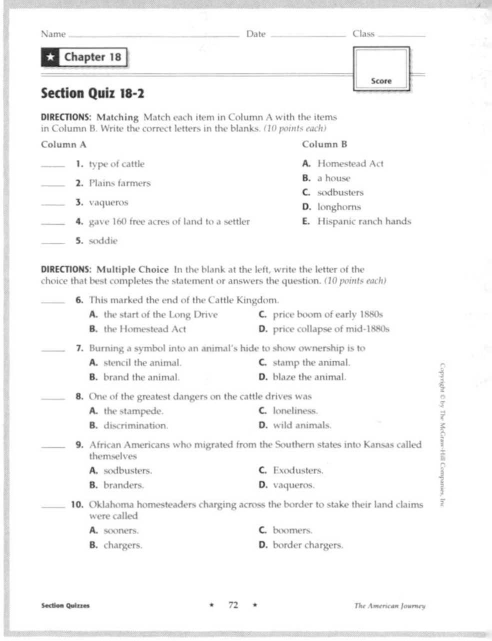

Name ________ Date ________ Class ________

★ Chapter 18 — Score

Section Quiz 18-2

DIRECTIONS: Matching Match each item in Column A with the items in Column B. Write the correct letters in the blanks. *(10 points each)*

Column A	Column B
____ 1. type of cattle	A. Homestead Act
____ 2. Plains farmers	B. a house
____ 3. vaqueros	C. sodbusters
____ 4. gave 160 free acres of land to a settler	D. longhorns
____ 5. soddie	E. Hispanic ranch hands

DIRECTIONS: Multiple Choice In the blank at the left, write the letter of the choice that best completes the statement or answers the question. *(10 points each)*

____ 6. This marked the end of the Cattle Kingdom.
A. the start of the Long Drive
B. the Homestead Act
C. price boom of early 1880s
D. price collapse of mid-1880s

____ 7. Burning a symbol into an animal's hide to show ownership is to
A. stencil the animal.
B. brand the animal.
C. stamp the animal.
D. blaze the animal.

____ 8. One of the greatest dangers on the cattle drives was
A. the stampede.
B. discrimination.
C. loneliness.
D. wild animals.

____ 9. African Americans who migrated from the Southern states into Kansas called themselves
A. sodbusters.
B. branders.
C. Exodusters.
D. vaqueros.

____ 10. Oklahoma homesteaders charging across the border to stake their land claims were called
A. sooners.
B. chargers.
C. boomers.
D. border chargers.

Section Quizzes ★ 72 ★ *The American Journey*

Picturing HISTORY The high walls and floor in the photograph show that this was not a sod house, which would have had a low ceiling and an earthen floor. Direct students to page 331 to see a photograph of a sod house.
Answer: *one filled with hard work and isolation*

Critical Thinking Activity

Identifying Alternatives In addition to the conflict between ranchers and farmers, there was the conflict between cattle ranchers and sheep ranchers (although both at times joined together against the farmers). One source of the range wars centered around the eating habits of sheep, who crop grass closely, leaving little for cattle to eat. In dry years, sheep ate grass roots, which made the land vulnerable to erosion. Have students read about the conflict between sheep raisers and cattle raisers on the Plains and then propose peaceful ways the conflict might have been resolved. **L2**

CHAPTER 18
Section 2, 531–536

Picturing HISTORY Settlers who arrived early in Oklahoma on April 22 worked their horses hard. Tired horses proved settlers had ridden fast to get there early.
Answer: *the frontier no longer existed*

Reteaching Activity 18–2

Name ______ Date ______ Class ______

★ Reteaching Activity 18-2

DIRECTIONS: Organizing Facts In the blanks on the chart, write the letter of each item below in the correct category. One item fits in two categories.

Cattle on the Plains

Cow Towns	Cowhands	End of Cattle Kingdom

Farming on the Plains

People	Challenges	Methods and Tools

★FACT BANK

A. harsh climate
B. barbed wire
C. severe winters of 1885 and 1886
D. Swedes and Norwegians
E. Abilene, Dodge City, Cheyenne
F. faced rustlers and stampedes
G. plagues of grasshoppers
H. a glut of cattle
I. windmills
J. rode in saddle for 15 hours a day
K. overgrazing
L. sodbusters
M. lonely, isolated
N. Exodusters
O. rowdy, lawless, and violent
P. treeless land
Q. homesteaders
R. wore wide-brimmed hats, chaps, and lariats
S. dry farming

DIRECTIONS: Essay On a separate sheet of paper, answer the questions below.
1. What was the Long Drive? Describe the routes of two Long Drives.
2. Describe the Oklahoma Land Rush. Include an explanation of boomers and sooners.

Reteaching Activities ★ 72 ★ *The American Journey*

Enrichment Activity 18–2

Name ______ Date ______ Class ______

★ Enrichment Activity 18-2 ★ ★

Building a House

When Easterners moved west to live on the Great Plains, they left many things behind, including styles of building homes that did not work on the almost treeless prairie. Because they lacked lumber to build homes, the pioneers built houses of sod—the most abundant material on the Plains. Some carved dugouts in the sides of hills and covered the dugouts with brick-like rectangles made of packed soil and grass roots. Others used sod "bricks." Study the picture of an Eastern home.

DIRECTIONS: Creating a Chart For each category below, list the features of the two kinds of houses.

Pioneer Housing

	Eastern House	Western House
Materials needed:		
Method of construction:		
Major advantages:		
Major disadvantages:		

Activity **DIRECTIONS:** On a separate sheet of paper, draw a diagram of the inside and outside of a modern home. Then pretend that you are a pioneer living in a sod home. Label those features of the modern home that you think a pioneer would most appreciate. Be ready to explain the reasons for your choices to the class.

Enrichment Activities ★ 72 ★ *The American Journey*

4 CLOSE

Assume you are a cowhand or a homesteader from the East. Write a letter back home, describing some aspect of your new life.

Picturing HISTORY Wagons line up just before the start of the largest—and last—Oklahoma land rush in 1893. **What important development did the federal government announce soon after the Oklahoma land rushes?**

from deep in the ground and a new fencing called **barbed wire.** With no wood to build fences, farmers used these wire fences to protect their land.

Dry farming, however, did not produce large crop yields, and the 160-acre grants were too small to make a living. Most farmers needed at least 300 acres as well as advanced machinery to make a Plains farm profitable. Many farmers went into debt. Others lost ownership of their farms and then had to rent the land.

The Oklahoma Land Rush

The last part of the Plains to be settled was the Oklahoma Territory, which Congress had designated as "Indian Territory" in the 1830s. In 1889, after years of pressure from land dealers and settlers' groups, the federal government opened Oklahoma to homesteaders.

On the morning of April 22, 1889—the official opening day—more than 10,000 people lined up on the edge of this land. At the sound of a bugle, the homesteaders charged across the border to stake their claims. The eager **boomers,** as the homesteaders were called, discovered to their dismay that some settlers had already slipped into Oklahoma. These so-called **sooners** had already claimed most of the best land. Within a few years, all of Oklahoma was opened to settlement.

Closing the Frontier

Not long after the Oklahoma land rush, the government announced in the 1890 census that the frontier no longer existed. Settlement had changed the Plains dramatically. No one felt these changes more keenly than the Native Americans who had lived on the Plains for centuries.

Section 2 Review

Checking for Understanding

1. ***Identify*** Long Drive, Chisholm Trail, Goodnight-Loving Trail, Homestead Act, "Exodusters."
2. ***Define*** open range, brand, vaquero, homestead, sodbuster, dry farming.
3. ***Explain*** why cow towns developed.

Reviewing Themes

4. **Economic Factors** Discuss two developments that contributed to the collapse of cattle prices during the mid-1880s.

Critical Thinking

5. **Analyzing Information** What opportunities did settlement on the Plains provide for women and African Americans?

Activity

Making a Poster Create a poster that the United States government might have used to encourage farmers to move west.

Section 2 Review Answers

1. Long Drive, 532; Chisholm Trail, 532; Goodnight-Loving Trail, 532; Homestead Act, 534; Exodusters, 534
2. The words are defined in the Glossary.
3. Ranchers had to get their cattle to markets in the East; so they took them to places where the cattle could be loaded onto trains. Towns grew up around these cattle shipping centers.
4. any two: overgrazing; too many cattle glutted the market; bitterly cold winters killed cattle; farmers took grazing land
5. Single and widowed women could own land; African Americans could own land and be assured of freedom.

Activity Posters should give vivid descriptions and encourage people to move west.

Social Studies
SKILL BUILDER

Reading a Special-Purpose Map

Maps that show information on specialized subjects, or themes, are called special-purpose maps. They differ from general-purpose maps in that they show more than basic physical features or political boundaries. Special-purpose maps can contain physical, economic, climatic, historic, or cultural information—almost anything that can be expressed geographically.

Western Land Use, 1890

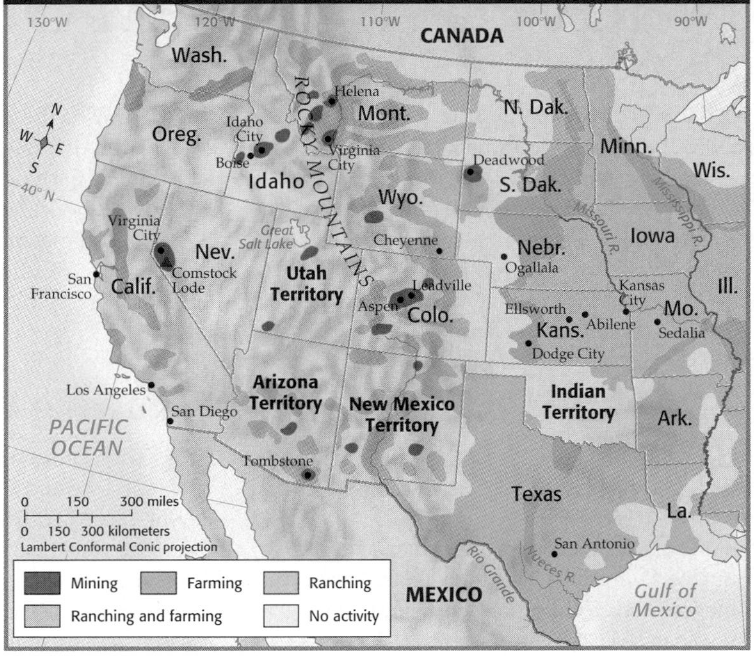

Learning the Skill

To interpret a special-purpose map, apply the following steps:

- Read the map title to determine the subject and purpose of the map.
- Read all the labels to identify the geographic region and other information displayed on the map.
- Study the map key to find out what information it gives. Identify each symbol and color shown in the key.
- Locate and study each symbol and color on the map.
- Look for similarities and differences in the region shown on the map.

Practicing the Skill

1. What is the subject of the map above?
2. What do the colors represent?
3. What is the most common use of land in Texas?

Applying the Skill

Reading a Special-Purpose Map Look at the map on page 540. Where were Indian reservations placed in relation to productive ranching and farming land in 1890?

Social Studies
SKILL BUILDER

TEACH

Reading a Special-Purpose Map

This skill teaches students to read special-purpose maps. Review with students the steps described in **Learning the Skill.** Then have students name states west of 95°W in which no mining activity is shown. *(Washington, Oregon, California, North Dakota, Nebraska, Kansas, Texas)* Have students look in atlases to find other types of special-purpose maps. *(vegetation, population density, languages, and so on)*

Additional Practice

Chapter Skills Activity 18

What? Where? When? Who?

The Comstock Lode was discovered by Henry T.P. Comstock, but not in the way he claimed. Comstock rode past two prospectors hard at work. Noticing that they had found some gold, he informed them that they were working on his land and offered them partnership with him. His partners eventually discovered that the land taken by Comstock was rich in gold.

ANSWERS TO PRACTICING THE SKILL

1. use of land in the West in 1890
2. the different types of activity—orange represents mining, blue represents farming, green represents ranching, pink represents ranching and farming, yellow represents no activity
3. ranching

Applying the Skill Students should recognize that Indian reservations were placed well out of the areas that contained productive ranching and farming land in 1890.

1 FOCUS

BELLRINGER
Motivational Activity

Before taking roll at the beginning of the class period, project Section Focus Transparency 18–3 and have students answer the questions. Discuss students' responses.

This activity is also available as a blackline master.

Section Focus Transparency 18–3

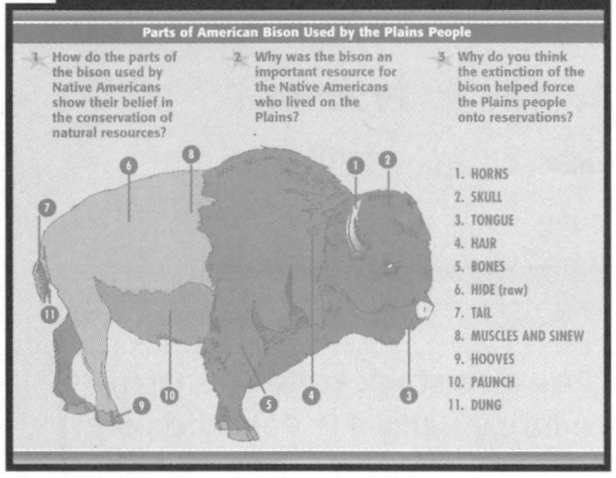

Vocabulary Precheck

Call on volunteers to define each of the **Terms to Learn.**

Use the **Vocabulary PuzzleMaker** to create crossword and word search puzzles.

Section Theme
Culture and Traditions

The culture and traditions of the nomadic Plains Indians were very different from those of the whites.

Activity Have students skim the section to find out how whites wanted Native Americans to live. *(as settled farmers, like most whites)*

Linking PAST & PRESENT

Buffalo The buffalo (or more properly, bison) population has grown from a low of about 500 animals at the end of the nineteenth century to about 35,000 to 50,000 today.

1860 — 1870 — 1880 — 1890

1864 Sand Creek massacre occurs

1876 Sioux victorious at Little Bighorn

1886 Geronimo surrenders to the army

1890 300 Lakota Sioux killed at Wounded Knee

Section 3

Native American Struggles

READ TO DISCOVER . . .

- why the federal government forced Native Americans to move to reservations.
- how conflict between Native Americans and whites led to a series of battles on the Plains.

TERMS TO LEARN

nomadic   reservation

The Storyteller

In May 1876, George Crook led an army from the North Platte River to round up Native American bands. Chief Crazy Horse urged on his warriors with the cry, "Come on Dakotas, it's a good day to die." The two sides fought until midafternoon. Then the Native Americans began to drift away. "They were tired and hungry, so they went home," one warrior later explained. . . . The Native Americans retired to a large camp on the Little Bighorn River. Great leaders were there—Sitting Bull, Gall, Crazy Horse. A vast pony herd grazed nearby; the grass was green; there was dancing at night. . . .

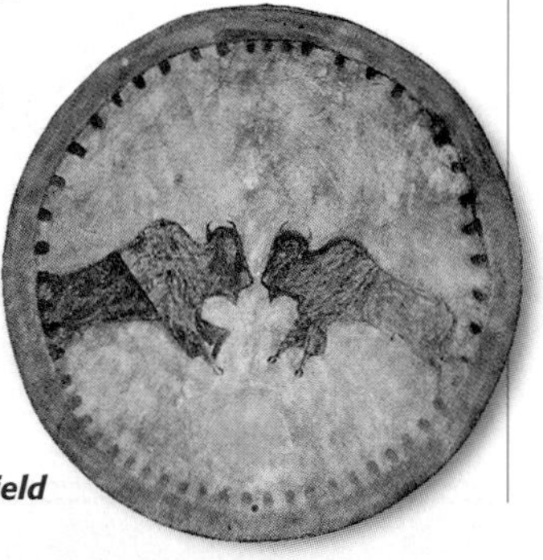

Sioux buffalo shield

Starting in the mid-1850s, miners, railroads, cattle drives, and farmers came to the Plains. Each new group dealt another blow to Native Americans living there. The Sioux chief Red Cloud lamented, "The white children [settlers] have surrounded me and left me nothing but an island."

Following the Buffalo

The southern Plains were home to the Apache and Comanche. The Arapaho and Pawnee lived in the central Plains. The Crow, Cheyenne, and Sioux lived in the northern Plains.

The Sioux led a lifestyle typical of the Plains Indians. The Sioux adopted horses from the Spanish and used them to hunt the huge buffalo herds that roamed the Plains. They lived a **nomadic** life, settling in one place for only part of the year—although they generally returned to traditional grounds. Most of the time, they followed the buffalo across the vast Plains region north of the Arkansas River. Their culture depended on the horse, the buffalo, and open land.

Village and Family Life

The buffalo provided most of the essentials of Sioux life. The Sioux used buffalo skin to make tepees, clothes, and bags for carrying food. They dried the meat into **jerky** for winter food. They shaped the bones into tools such as hoes, knives, and fishhooks. They used dried manure, called **buffalo chips,** for fuel.

SECTION RESOURCES

Reproducible Masters
- Political Cartoons
- Section Quiz 18–3
- Enrichment Activity 18–3
- Reteaching Activity 18–3

Transparencies
- Section Focus Transparency 18–3
- U.S. History & Art, Transparency 13

Multimedia
- Vocabulary PuzzleMaker
- Testmaker
- GTV: A Geographic Perspective on American History
- GTV: American People: Fabric of a Nation
- Historic America Electronic Field Trips
- NGS PictureShow: Native Americans, 1 & 2
- Facts On File: The American Indian

American Memories Life of Plains Native Americans

Arapaho adult's and child's moccasins

Sioux bow case with bow and arrows

Sioux beaded robe

What Was It like? Native Americans of the Great Plains settled in one place for only part of the year. **What do the images reveal about how the Plains Native Americans obtained their food?**

The Sioux were also traders, exchanging buffalo and beaver skins for food farmed by more settled Plains Indians. With white people, the Sioux traded for pots, knives, and firearms.

Life for the Sioux, as for other Plains groups, revolved around extended families and community ties. Families joined forces to hunt and plant. Extended families set up large camps near hunting grounds in the summer and established small villages in sheltered areas for the winter months.

Indian women had many responsibilities. They raised the children and taught them their people's traditions. They also prepared food and made clothing and tools. Women rarely joined in the hunt, however.

Threats to the Buffalo

The Plains Indians had millions of buffalo to supply their needs. After the Civil War, though, American hunters hired by the railroads began slaughtering the animals to feed the crews building the railroad. The railroad companies also wanted to prevent huge herds of buffalo from blocking the trains. William Cody, hired by the Kansas Pacific Railroad, boasted that he had killed 4,280 buffalo in less than 18 months. He became known as Buffalo Bill.

Some people traveled west to kill buffalo for the sport of hunting, often shooting from the windows of trains. Starting in 1872 hunters targeted buffalo to sell the hides to the East, where tanneries made them into leather goods.

Between 1872 and 1875, whites killed more than 9 million buffalo for their hides, often leaving the carcasses to rot on the Plains. Government officials encouraged the slaughter. By destroying the buffalo, they thought, they could change the way the Plains Indians lived. The Native Americans wanted to preserve their nomadic life, but the government wanted them to become farmers. A clash seemed inevitable.

Footnotes to History

Where the Buffalo Roamed Between 1830 and 1895, the millions of buffalo on the Great Plains were reduced to just 800.

Cooperative Learning Activity

Continuing the Mural Have students work in small groups to continue the mural begun in Sections 1 and 2 (see Cooperative Learning Activities on pages 526 and 532) with scenes from Native American life—buffalo hunts, teepees and encampments, traveling with families from one site to another, and so forth. As they did with the other sections, students may wish to use library resources for additional information and illustrations. ELL

American Memories

Life of Plains Native Americans
For generations the nomadic peoples of the Plains had only dogs to haul their possessions as they traveled from one hunting area to another. Then in the 1600s, horses—either traded or stolen from Spanish settlers in the Southwest—changed the Plains peoples' way of life. By the mid-1700s, almost every Plains group rode on horseback.
Answer to Caption: *by chasing and shooting arrows at the buffalo while on horseback*

2 TEACH

L1 Making a Chart Have students make a chart showing each of the people mentioned in the section and a phrase or two identifying each person.

Guided Reading Activity 18–3

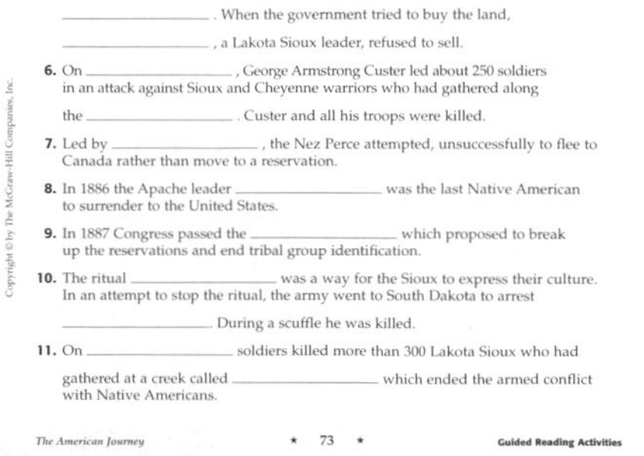

Name ______ Date ______ Class ______

★ Guided Reading Activity **18-3**

DIRECTIONS: Filling in the Blanks In the space provided, write the word or words that best complete the sentence. Refer to your textbook to fill in the blanks.

1. The Sioux were typical of the Plains Native Americans. Their culture depended on the ______. The ______ provided most essentials.
2. American hunters, hired by the railroads, killed thousands of buffalo, and more than ______ buffalo were killed by whites for their hides between 1872 and 1875.
3. In 1867 the federal government appointed the ______ which recommended moving Native Americans to ______.
4. In November 1864 the American militia massacred 100 Cheyenne who resisted moving from their land. Enraged, ______ led Cheyenne warriors to battle. In November 1868 ______ killed the Cheyenne chief and most of his followers, ending the resistance.
5. Conflict with the Sioux erupted over the rumor that there was gold in the ______. When the government tried to buy the land, ______, a Lakota Sioux leader, refused to sell.
6. On ______, George Armstrong Custer led about 250 soldiers in an attack against Sioux and Cheyenne warriors who had gathered along the ______. Custer and all his troops were killed.
7. Led by ______, the Nez Perce attempted, unsuccessfully to flee to Canada rather than move to a reservation.
8. In 1886 the Apache leader ______ was the last Native American to surrender to the United States.
9. In 1887 Congress passed the ______ which proposed to break up the reservations and end tribal group identification.
10. The ritual ______ was a way for the Sioux to express their culture. In an attempt to stop the ritual, the army went to South Dakota to arrest ______. During a scuffle he was killed.
11. On ______ soldiers killed more than 300 Lakota Sioux who had gathered at a creek called ______ which ended the armed conflict with Native Americans.

The American Journey ★ 73 ★ **Guided Reading Activities**

Linking PAST & PRESENT

Reservations Approximately 755,000 Native Americans live on reservations in the United States today. Some 300 nations remain, but many of their languages are lost. No native Lakota speaker could be found to act as adviser during the filming of *Dances with Wolves*.

NATIONAL GEOGRAPHIC SOCIETY

VIDEODISC
GTV: A Geographic Perspective on American History

Side 3, Chapter 3
Title: *A World of Change*
Subject: Violent settlement
Ask: **How were new weapons used in the settlements of the Great Plains?** *(The army used guns to kill Native Americans or force them to leave their homes.)*

VIDEODISC
GTV: The American People: Fabric of a Nation

Side 2, Chapter 2
Title: *Between Worlds*
Subject: A shrinking world for Native Americans
Ask: **What did the "Indian agents" want the Native Americans to become?** *(farmers)*

Map Study

Answers
1. Montana
2. Cherokee, Creek, Choctaw, Chickasaw, Comanche

Government Policy

As long as white people regarded the Plains as the "Great American Desert," they left the Native Americans who lived there more or less alone. When whites began settling the Plains, the situation changed. In the late 1860s, the government tried a new Indian policy.

Reservation Policy

In 1867 the federal government appointed the Indian Peace Commission to develop a new policy toward Native Americans. The commission recommended moving the Native Americans to a few large **reservations**—tracts of land set aside for them. Moving Native Americans to reservations was not a new policy, but the government now increased its efforts in that direction.

One large reservation was in **Oklahoma,** the "Indian Territory" that Congress had created in the 1830s for Native Americans relocated from the Southeast. Another one, meant for the Sioux people, was in the **Dakota Territory.** Managing the reservations would be the job of the federal Bureau of Indian Affairs.

Government agents often used trickery to persuade Native American groups to move to the

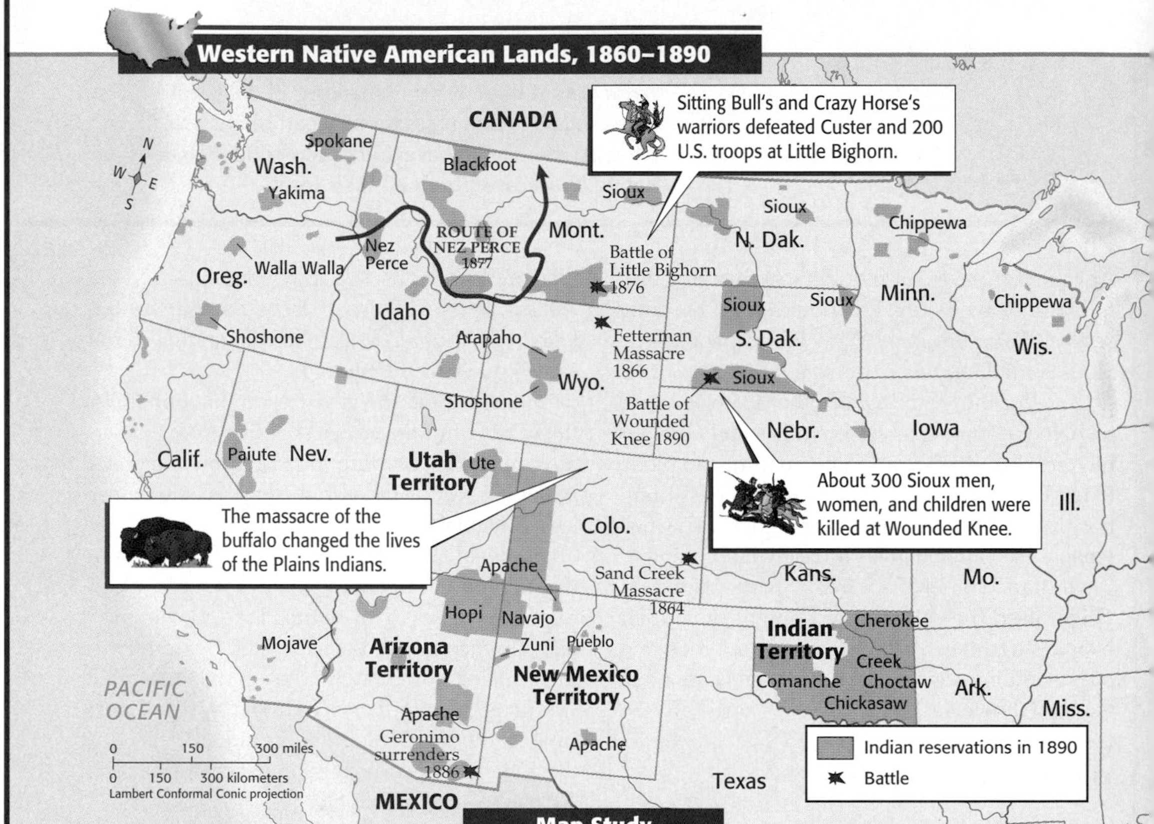

Map Study

During the late 1800s, Native Americans and the United States Army fought many battles over land.

1. **Location** In what state did the Battle of Little Bighorn occur?
2. **Analyzing Information** Which Native American nations resettled in the Indian Territory?

MULTIPLE LEARNING STYLES

Kinesthetic Some museums, particularly children's museums, have kits that they lend to schools. The kits consist of collections of artifacts on various subjects and are intended to give students hands-on experience. A local museum might have such a kit with items pertaining to Plains Indians. If no kits are available, most libraries have many books dealing with Native Americans, which students may use for reference or for instructions in creating replicas of Native American homes, clothing, tools, and so forth. Have students create a three-dimensional aspect of Plains Native American culture. **L1,** ELL reservations. Many reservations were located on poor land—land that white settlers did not want. In addition the government often failed to deliver promised food and supplies, and the goods that were delivered were of poor quality.

A great many Native Americans accepted the reservation policy at first. Many southern Kiowa, Comanche, Cheyenne, and Arapaho agreed to stay on the Oklahoma reservation. Thousands of Sioux agreed to move onto the Dakota reservation in the north.

Pockets of resistance remained, however. Some Native Americans refused to make the move, and some who tried reservation life abandoned it. The stage was set for conflict.

Chief Joseph of the Nez Perce (left) and Sitting Bull

The Indian Wars

Armed clashes between Native Americans and whites had taken place since the 1850s. Congress had appointed the Indian Peace Commission in the hope of ending the fighting, but Native American resistance grew stronger after the reservation policy took effect. The Cheyenne and the Sioux were among the most determined opponents.

Tragedy at Sand Creek

The fighting with the Cheyenne began in the mid-1860s, when a group of Cheyenne refused to move to a reservation. In November 1864, Colonel **J.M. Chivington** swooped down on a Cheyenne camp near **Sand Creek, Colorado,** with a group of volunteer militia. Although the Cheyenne tried to surrender, the militia killed more than 100 men, women, and children.

Enraged by the Chivington massacre, **Chief Black Kettle** led Cheyenne warriors to battle. Fearing another massacre, most Cheyenne moved to a reservation in 1867. Black Kettle, however, continued to fight. In November 1868 Cheyenne resistance came to an end when troops led by Civil War veteran **George Armstrong Custer** defeated Black Kettle along the Washita River in Indian Territory, killing him and most of his followers.

Little Bighorn

The Sioux also began to fight in the 1860s. Although an 1868 treaty was supposed to bring peace, tensions remained and erupted in more fighting a few years later.

This time the conflict arose over the **Black Hills** of the Dakotas. The government had promised that "No white person or persons shall be permitted to settle upon or occupy" or even "to pass through" these hills. However, the hills were rumored to contain gold. In 1874 Custer led an army expedition to check on the rumors and confirmed that there was gold, "from the grass roots down." Prospectors swarmed into the area.

The Sioux protested against the trespassers. Instead of protecting the Sioux's rights, the government tried to buy the hills. **Sitting Bull,** an important leader of the Lakota Sioux, refused. "I do not want to sell any land. Not even this much," he said, holding a pinch of dust.

Sitting Bull gathered Sioux and Cheyenne warriors along the **Little Bighorn River** in present-day Montana. They were joined by **Crazy Horse,** another Sioux chief, and his forces. The United States Army planned a three-pronged attack. One force, the Seventh Cavalry, was led by Custer, who was ordered to scout the Native American encampment.

CHAPTER 18
Section 3, 538–543

you don't say...

Nez Perce is French for "pierced nose." The name was given to the group by an interpreter who saw some Nez Perce with decorative shells in their noses. The words have been anglicized, but were originally pronounced NAY PURSAY.

History *and the* Humanities

- U.S. History & Art, Transparency 13, *Chief Joseph*
- The Spirit of American Art and Music, Edmonia Lewis
- Political Cartoons, *Thomas Nast: America's Well-Known Political Cartoonist*

ABCNEWS INTERACTIVE™

VIDEODISC
Historic America Electronic Field Trips

Side 2, Chapter 3

Title: *Little Bighorn*
Subject: Site of 1876 battle
Ask: **What was the outcome of the battle?** *(Native American forces surrounded and killed Custer and his troops.)*

Also available in VHS.

MAKING CONNECTIONS ACTIVITY

Politics The American Indian Movement, an activist group, was established in 1968 to promote Native American civil rights. Members of the group briefly occupied the Bureau of Indian Affairs in 1973, then led 200 Sioux in a 71-day takeover of Wounded Knee. The takeover was an effort to demand a review of 300 treaties with the United States government. Have students research the activities of this group and other Native American efforts to gain an equal footing in the American political structure. Students may present their findings in writing or on tape. **L2**

Facts On File

CD-ROM
The American Indian

Have students research the Ghost Dance and other spiritual beliefs of the Sioux.

CHAPTER 18
Section 3, 538–543

Graph Study

Answer 1870–1880

NATIONAL GEOGRAPHIC SOCIETY

CD-ROM NGS PictureShow: Native Americans, Parts 1 and 2

Have students view the effects of the buffalo massacres on Plains Indian culture.

3 ASSESS

Assign Section 3 Review as homework or as an in-class activity.

Use **Chapter Challenger Interactive Review Software** to review Section 3.

Section Quiz 18–3

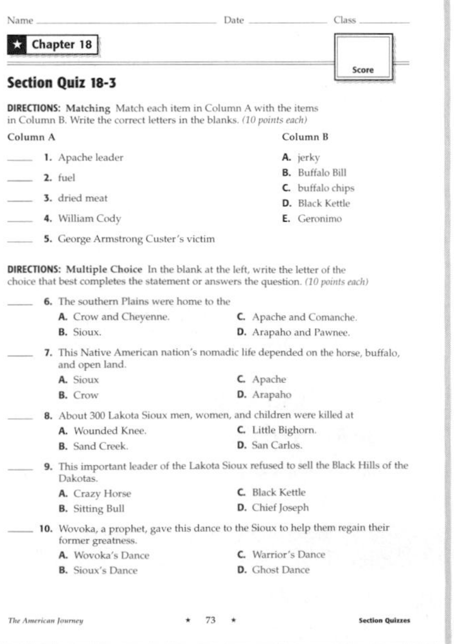

Name ______ Date ______ Class ______

★ Chapter 18

Score

Section Quiz 18-3

DIRECTIONS: Matching Match each item in Column A with the items in Column B. Write the correct letters in the blanks. *(10 points each)*

Column A	Column B
____ 1. Apache leader	A. jerky
____ 2. fuel	B. Buffalo Bill
____ 3. dried meat	C. buffalo chips
____ 4. William Cody	D. Black Kettle
____ 5. George Armstrong Custer's victim	E. Geronimo

DIRECTIONS: Multiple Choice In the blank at the left, write the letter of the choice that best completes the statement or answers the question. *(10 points each)*

____ 6. The southern Plains were home to the
A. Crow and Cheyenne. C. Apache and Comanche.
B. Sioux. D. Arapaho and Pawnee.

____ 7. This Native American nation's nomadic life depended on the horse, buffalo, and open land.
A. Sioux C. Apache
B. Crow D. Arapaho

____ 8. About 300 Lakota Sioux men, women, and children were killed at
A. Wounded Knee. C. Little Bighorn.
B. Sand Creek. D. San Carlos.

____ 9. This important leader of the Lakota Sioux refused to sell the Black Hills of the Dakotas.
A. Crazy Horse C. Black Kettle
B. Sitting Bull D. Chief Joseph

____ 10. Wovoka, a prophet, gave this dance to the Sioux to help them regain their former greatness.
A. Wovoka's Dance C. Warrior's Dance
B. Sioux's Dance D. Ghost Dance

The American Journey ★ 73 ★ **Section Quizzes**

Native American Population

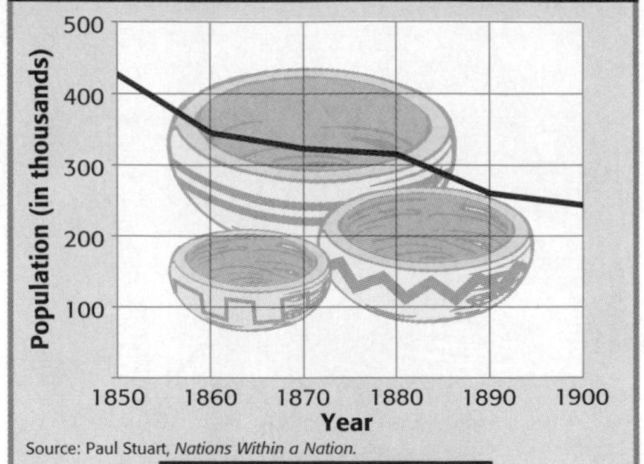

Source: Paul Stuart, *Nations Within a Nation.*

Graph Study

Census figures show a declining Native American population before 1900.

1. **Analyzing Information** During what decade did the Native American population decline the least?

Custer wanted the glory of leading a major victory. He divided his regiment and attacked the Indians on June 25, 1876. He had seriously underestimated their strength, however. With about 250 soldiers, Custer faced a Sioux and Cheyenne force of thousands. He and all his troops were killed. News of the army's defeat shocked the nation.

The Indians' triumph at Little Bighorn was short-lived. The army, with its greater firepower, soon crushed the uprising, sending most of the Native Americans to reservations. Sitting Bull and his followers fled north to Canada. By 1881, exhausted and starving, the Lakota and Cheyenne agreed to live on a reservation.

The Nez Perce

The **Nez Perce** Indians, who lived in present-day Idaho, Oregon, and Washington, raised horses and hunted buffalo. They also fished and planted crops. By the late 1870s, all but one group of the Nez Perce had yielded their lands and were living on reservations.

In 1877 the army ordered this last group to the reservation. Under their leader, **Chief Joseph,** they began to move. However, a few young warriors, bitterly angry about the relocation, attacked and killed several white settlers. The army came to punish the Nez Perce.

Fearing for the safety of his people, Chief Joseph told them—men, women, and children—to set out for Canada. With the army in close pursuit, the Nez Perce traveled through rugged mountains and lush valleys. They fought, and won, four battles along the way. Then, in northern Montana, just 30 miles short of the Canadian border, they were surrounded by an overwhelming force. Chief Joseph finally surrendered, saying:

> "I am tired of fighting. . . . Hear me, my chiefs. I am tired: my heart is sick and sad. From where the sun now stands, I will fight no more forever."

The Apache Wars

Trouble also broke out in the Southwest. The Chiracahua Apache had been moved from their homeland to the San Carlos reservation in Arizona in the mid-1870s. Many Apache resented confinement to this reservation. The Apache leader, **Geronimo,** escaped from San Carlos and fled to Mexico with a small band of followers. During the 1880s he led raids against settlers and the army in Arizona.

Thousands of troops pursued Geronimo and his warriors. Several times he went back to the reservation. "Once I moved about like the wind. Now I surrender to you," Geronimo said, but again he left the reservation. In 1886 Geronimo finally gave up—the last Native American to surrender formally to the United States.

A Changing Culture

Many things contributed to changing the traditional Native American way of life—the movement of whites onto Indian lands, the slaughter of the buffalo, United States Army attacks, and the reservation policy. More change came from well-meaning reformers who wanted to abolish reservations and absorb the Indians into American life.

CRITICAL THINKING ACTIVITY

Synthesizing Information In 1879 Chief Joseph of the Nez Perce, in an appeal to President Rutherford B. Hayes, said:

"Let me be a freeman—free to travel, free to stop, free to work, free to trade where I choose, free to choose my own teachers, free to follow the religion of my fathers, free to think and talk and act for myself—and I will obey every law or submit to the penalty."

Ask students which of these requests are guaranteed by the Bill of Rights. *(all)* Also ask them to tell how these rights were denied to Native Americans. *(They were forced to live on reservations.)* **L2**

CHAPTER 18
Section 3, 538–543

The Dawes Act

American reformers such as **Helen Hunt Jackson** were horrified by the massacres of Native Americans and by the cruelty of the reservation system. Describing the whites' treatment of Native Americans in her 1881 book, *A Century of Dishonor,* Jackson wrote:

> "It makes little difference . . . where one opens the record of the history of the Indians; every page and every year has its dark stain."

Congress changed government policy in the **Dawes Act** in 1887. The law aimed to eliminate what Americans regarded as the two weaknesses of Native American life: the lack of private property and the nomadic tradition.

The Dawes Act proposed to break up the reservations and to end Indian identification with a tribal group. Each Native American would receive a plot of reservation land. The goal was to encourage the Indians to become farmers. Eventually they would become American citizens. Native American children would be sent to white-run boarding schools. Some of the reservation lands would be sold to support this schooling.

Over the next 50 years, the government divided up the reservations. Speculators acquired most of the valuable land. Indians got dry, gravelly plots that were not suited to farming.

Ghost Dance

The Dawes Act changed forever the Native American way of life and weakened Indian cultural traditions. In their despair the Sioux turned in 1890 to **Wovoka,** a prophet. Wovoka claimed that the Sioux could regain their former greatness if they performed a ritual known as the **Ghost Dance.**

The Ghost Dance was a way for the Sioux to express their culture that was being destroyed. As the ritual spread, reservation officials became alarmed and decided to ban the dance. Believing that Sitting Bull was the leader of the movement, police went to his camp to arrest him. During a scuffle, they shot and killed Sitting Bull.

Wounded Knee

Several hundred Lakota Sioux fled in fear after Sitting Bull's death. They gathered at a creek called **Wounded Knee** in southwestern South Dakota. On December 29, 1890, the army went there to collect the Sioux's weapons. The Indians were starving and freezing in the December winter. No one knows how the fighting started, but when a pistol shot rang out, the army responded with fire. Using machine guns, soldiers killed more than 300 Lakota.

Wounded Knee marked the end of armed conflict between Americans and Indians. The Native Americans had lost their long struggle.

Section 3 Review

Checking for Understanding

1. ***Identify*** Sitting Bull, Crazy Horse, Chief Joseph, Geronimo, Dawes Act, Wovoka.
2. ***Define*** nomadic, reservation.
3. ***Describe*** the lifestyle of Native Americans on the Plains.

Reviewing Themes

4. **Culture and Traditions** What two weaknesses of Native American life was the Dawes Act supposed to eliminate?

Critical Thinking

5. **Identifying Central Issues** In what ways did the government reservation policy ignore the needs of Native Americans?

Activity

Making a Graphic Organizer With the buffalo at the center, create a graphic organizer that shows the importance of this animal in the everyday life and culture of the Plains Indians.

Section 3 Review Answers

1. Sitting Bull, 541; Crazy Horse, 541; Chief Joseph, 542; Geronimo, 542; Dawes Act, 543; Wovoka, 543
2. The words are defined in the Glossary.
3. They lived a nomadic life, mostly following the buffalo; their culture depended on horses, buffalo, and open land.
4. lack of private property, the nomadic tradition
5. Answers may include: prevented them from following buffalo herds; many reservations were located on poor land; government failed to deliver promised supplies.

Activity Graphic organizers should reveal students' knowledge of the role of the buffalo in the lives of the Plains Indians.

Reteaching Activity 18–3

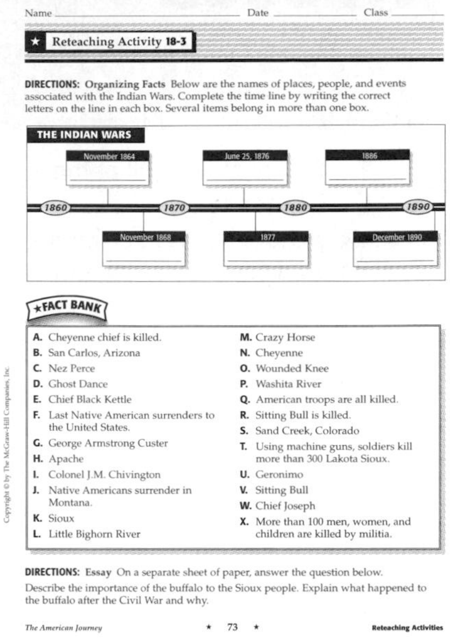
Name ______ Date ______ Class ______

★ Reteaching Activity 18-3

DIRECTIONS: Organizing Facts Below are the names of places, people, and events associated with the Indian Wars. Complete the time line by writing the correct letters on the line in each box. Several items belong in more than one box.

★FACT BANK

A. Cheyenne chief is killed.
B. San Carlos, Arizona
C. Nez Perce
D. Ghost Dance
E. Chief Black Kettle
F. Last Native American surrenders to the United States.
G. George Armstrong Custer
H. Apache
I. Colonel J.M. Chivington
J. Native Americans surrender in Montana.
K. Sioux
L. Little Bighorn River
M. Crazy Horse
N. Cheyenne
O. Wounded Knee
P. Washita River
Q. American troops are all killed.
R. Sitting Bull is killed.
S. Sand Creek, Colorado
T. Using machine guns, soldiers kill more than 300 Lakota Sioux.
U. Geronimo
V. Sitting Bull
W. Chief Joseph
X. More than 100 men, women, and children are killed by militia.

DIRECTIONS: Essay On a separate sheet of paper, answer the question below.
Describe the importance of the buffalo to the Sioux people. Explain what happened to the buffalo after the Civil War and why.

The American Journey ★ 73 ★ Reteaching Activities

Copyright © by The McGraw-Hill Companies, Inc.

Enrichment Activity 18–3

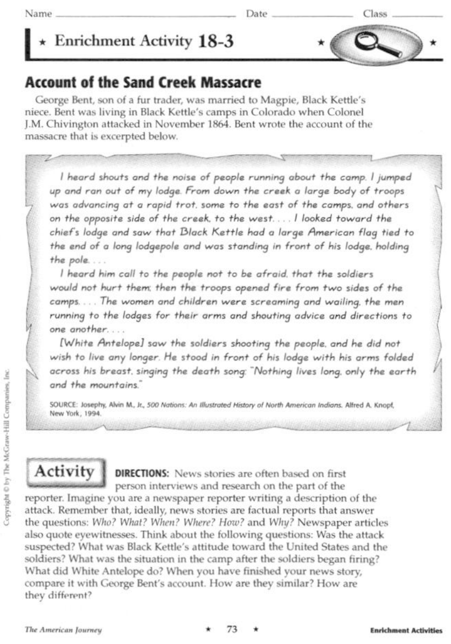
Name ______ Date ______ Class ______

★ Enrichment Activity 18-3

Account of the Sand Creek Massacre

George Bent, son of a fur trader, was married to Magpie, Black Kettle's niece. Bent was living in Black Kettle's camps in Colorado when Colonel J.M. Chivington attacked in November 1864. Bent wrote the account of the massacre that is excerpted below.

I heard shouts and the noise of people running about the camp. I jumped up and ran out of my lodge. From down the creek a large body of troops was advancing at a rapid trot, some to the east of the camps, and others on the opposite side of the creek, to the west. . . . I looked toward the chief's lodge and saw that Black Kettle had a large American flag tied to the end of a long lodgepole and was standing in front of his lodge, holding the pole. . . .

I heard him call to the people not to be afraid, that the soldiers would not hurt them; then the troops opened fire from two sides of the camps. . . . The women and children were screaming and wailing, the men running to the lodges for their arms and shouting advice and directions to one another. . . .

[White Antelope] saw the soldiers shooting the people, and he did not wish to live any longer. He stood in front of his lodge with his arms folded across his breast, singing the death song: "Nothing lives long, only the earth and the mountains."

SOURCE: Josephy, Alvin M., Jr., *500 Nations: An Illustrated History of North American Indians.* Alfred A. Knopf, New York, 1994.

Activity **DIRECTIONS:** News stories are often based on first person interviews and research on the part of the reporter. Imagine you are a newspaper reporter writing a description of the attack. Remember that, ideally, news stories are factual reports that answer the questions: *Who? What? When? Where? How?* and *Why?* Newspaper articles also quote eyewitnesses. Think about the following questions: Was the attack suspected? What was Black Kettle's attitude toward the United States and the soldiers? What was the situation in the camp after the soldiers began firing? What did White Antelope do? When you have finished your news story, compare it with George Bent's account. How are they similar? How are they different?

The American Journey ★ 73 ★ Enrichment Activities

Copyright © by The McGraw-Hill Companies, Inc.

4 CLOSE

A Standing Rock Sioux named Vine Deloria, Jr., wrote a book called *Bury My Heart at Wounded Knee.* Ask students how that title summarizes the Plains Indians' struggles for freedom.

CHAPTER 18
Section 4, 544–547

1 FOCUS

BELLRINGER
Motivational Activity

Before taking roll at the beginning of the class period, project Section Focus Transparency 18–4 and have students answer the questions. Discuss students' responses.

This activity is also available as a blackline master.

Section Focus Transparency 18–4

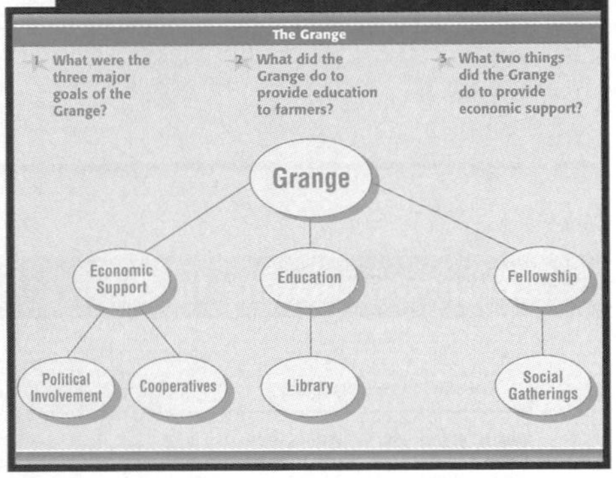

Vocabulary Precheck

Note that *Populist* comes from the Latin word *populus,* meaning "people." Ask students to define each of the **Terms to Learn.** Have a volunteer consult the dictionary for any unfamiliar words.

Use the **Vocabulary PuzzleMaker** to create crossword and word search puzzles.

Section Theme
Groups and Institutions

During the late 1800s farmers worked together to try to better their situation.

Activity Have students skim the section to find the groups formed by farmers. *(Grange, Farmers' Alliances)*

1870 · 1880 · 1890 · 1900

1870s The Grange works to reduce shipping costs

1880s Farmers' Alliances seek federal support

1892 Alliance members form the Populist Party

1896 William McKinley is elected president

Section 4

Farmers in Protest

READ TO DISCOVER . . .
- why farmers were suffering in the late 1800s.
- how new organizations and political parties tried to solve farmers' problems.

TERMS TO LEARN

National Grange
cooperative
Populist Party
free silver

The Storyteller

In the last decades of the 1800s, farmers suffered from falling prices and rising costs. They expressed their frustration in a popular song:

"When the banker says he's broke
And the merchant's up in smoke
They forget that it's the farmer feeds
them all. . . .
The farmer is the man,
Lives on credit till the fall;
With the interest
rates so high,
It's a wonder he
don't die,
For the mortgage
man's the one
who gets it all."

Poster celebrating the farmer, 1876

After the Civil War, farming expanded in the West and the South, and more land came under cultivation. The supply of crops grew faster than the demand for them, however, and prices fell steadily. In 1866 a bushel of wheat sold for $1.45. By the mid-1880s the price had dropped to 80 cents and by the mid-1890s to 49 cents. At the same time, farmers' expenses—for transporting their goods to market, for seed, and for equipment and other manufactured goods—remained high.

Farmers' Problems

The farmers' plight gave rise to bitter feelings. Farmers blamed their troubles on three groups in particular. They resented the railroad companies, which charged farmers more to ship crops than they charged manufacturers to ship goods. They were angry at the Eastern manufacturers, who charged high prices for their products. They also disliked bankers.

Farmers needed to borrow money to buy seed, equipment, and other goods. After they sold their crops, they had to pay the high interest rates set by bankers. When crops failed and farmers could not repay the loans, they were in danger of losing their farms.

Farmers with small and middle-sized holdings struggled to survive. Senator William A. Peffer of Kansas summed up the farmers' plight when he noted that the railroad companies "took possession of the land" and the bankers "took possession of the farmer."

SECTION RESOURCES

Reproducible Masters
- Reproducible Lesson Plan 18–4
- Guided Reading Activity 18–4
- Section Quiz 18–4
- Enrichment Activity 18–4
- Reteaching Activity 18–4

Transparencies
- Section Focus Transparency 18–4

Multimedia
- Vocabulary PuzzleMaker
- Chapter Challenger Interactive Review Software
- Testmaker
- American Music Cultural Traditions, Lesson 6: "The Farmer Is the Man that Feeds Them All"

The Farmers Organize

Farmers began to organize in an effort to solve their problems. Within a short time, they had created a mass political movement.

The Grange

The first farmers' organization of this period was a network of local self-help organizations that eventually came to be called the **National Grange**. The Grange offered farmers education, fellowship, and support. For inexperienced farmers, the Grange provided a library with books on planting and livestock raising. For lonely farm families, it organized social gatherings.

Above all, the Grange tried to encourage economic self-sufficiency. It set up "cash-only" **cooperatives,** stores where farmers bought products from each other. The cooperatives charged lower prices than regular stores and provided an outlet for farmers' crops. The purpose of the "cash-only" policy was to remove the burden of credit buying that threatened farmers.

In the 1870s the Grange tried to cut farmers' costs by getting state legislatures to limit railroad shipping rates. Many Midwestern states did pass such laws. By 1878, however, the railroads had put so much pressure on state legislatures that these states repealed the rate regulations.

The Grange cooperatives also failed. Farmers were always short of cash and had to borrow money until their next crop was sold. The cash-only cooperative could not work if borrowing was necessary.

By the late 1870s, the Grange had declined. Rural reformers tried to help farmers through the Farmers' Alliances.

The Farmers' Alliances

The **Farmers' Alliances** were networks of organizations that sprang up in the West and the South in the 1880s. The Southern Alliance was founded in Texas when farmers rallied against the railroads and against "money power."

Alliance leaders extended the movement to other states. By 1890 the Southern Alliance had more than 3 million members, and the Colored Farmers' National Alliance, a separate organization of African American farmers, had 1 million members. An Alliance movement developed in the Plains states as well.

Like the Grange, the Farmers' Alliances sponsored education and cooperative buying and selling. The Alliances also proposed a plan in which the federal government would store farmers' crops in warehouses and lend money to the farmers. When the stored crops were sold, the farmers would pay back the government loans. Such a plan would reduce the power that railroads, banks, and merchants had over farmers and would offer farmers some federal protection.

If the Alliances had remained united, they would have been a powerful political force. Regional differences and personality clashes kept the groups apart, however.

Picturing HISTORY The Grange worked to promote better agricultural methods and to improve farmers' lives. **What did state legislatures do to help the Grange?**

Linking PAST & PRESENT

The Grange

More than 350,000 farmers in 37 states belong to the Grange today. The organization still pursues its original goals of providing educational and social support to farmers.

CHAPTER 18
Section 4, 544–547

Picturing HISTORY The Grange was the common name of the Patrons of Husbandry founded in 1867 by Oliver Hudson Kelley, a clerk in the Department of Agriculture.
Answer: *passed laws limiting railroad freight rates for farmers*

2 TEACH

L1 Answering a Job Ad Present the following job description to students: "Wanted: Person to own and manage small business. Applicant must be willing to do physical labor for long hours (12–14), especially during spring and summer. Wages based on current market price of product minus cost of shipment to customers. Payment for services made at point of sale of product." Tell students that the job describes the work of a farmer in the late 1800s. Discuss the pros and cons of choosing such a job.

you don't say...

Grange comes from the Middle Latin word *granica*, which is from Latin *granum*, or "grain." The grange was the farm of a monastery, where grain was stored.

Guided Reading Activity 18–4

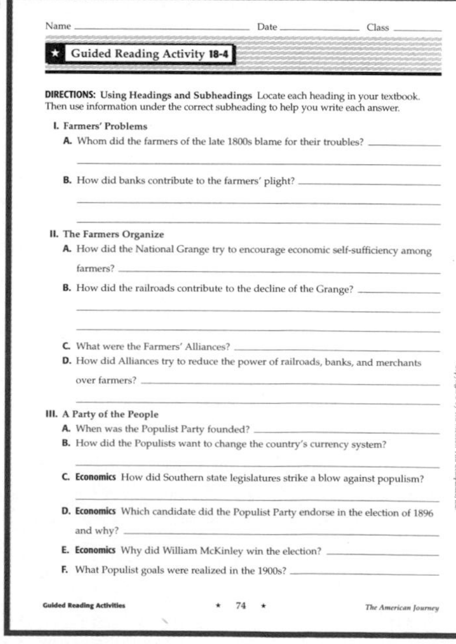
Name ______ Date ______ Class ______

Guided Reading Activity 18-4

DIRECTIONS: Using Headings and Subheadings Locate each heading in your textbook. Then use information under the correct subheading to help you write each answer.

I. Farmers' Problems
A. Whom did the farmers of the late 1800s blame for their troubles? ______
B. How did banks contribute to the farmers' plight? ______

II. The Farmers Organize
A. How did the National Grange try to encourage economic self-sufficiency among farmers? ______
B. How did the railroads contribute to the decline of the Grange? ______
C. What were the Farmers' Alliances? ______
D. How did Alliances try to reduce the power of railroads, banks, and merchants over farmers? ______

III. A Party of the People
A. When was the Populist Party founded? ______
B. How did the Populists want to change the country's currency system? ______
C. **Economics** How did Southern state legislatures strike a blow against populism? ______
D. **Economics** Which candidate did the Populist Party endorse in the election of 1896 and why? ______
E. **Economics** Why did William McKinley win the election? ______
F. What Populist goals were realized in the 1900s? ______

Guided Reading Activities ★ 74 ★ *The American Journey*

Copyright © by The McGraw-Hill Companies, Inc.

COOPERATIVE LEARNING ACTIVITY

Brainstorming Organize students into groups of four or five. Give each group the topic of the Grange, the Farmers' Alliances, or the Populist Party. Using one piece of paper per group, have each student write a statement about the history of their topic during the late 1800s. Have them pass the paper around several times until they have written down all they know about their topic. Then have students review the statements and add any information that is missing. Have each group share their statements with the class.

Picturing HISTORY Among Populist demands were a graduated income tax, election of senators directly by the people, the secret ballot, and a shorter working day. **Ask:** **Which constitutional amendments address two of these concerns?** *(Sixteenth—income tax; Seventeenth—election of senators)*
Answer: *They believed that putting more silver coins into circulation would give farmers more money to pay debts.*

History *and the* Humanities

American Music Cultural Traditions, Lesson 6: "The Farmer Is the Man that Feeds Them All"

3 ASSESS

Assign Section 4 Review as homework or as an in-class activity.

Use **Chapter Challenger Interactive Review Software** to review Section 4.

Section Quiz 18–4

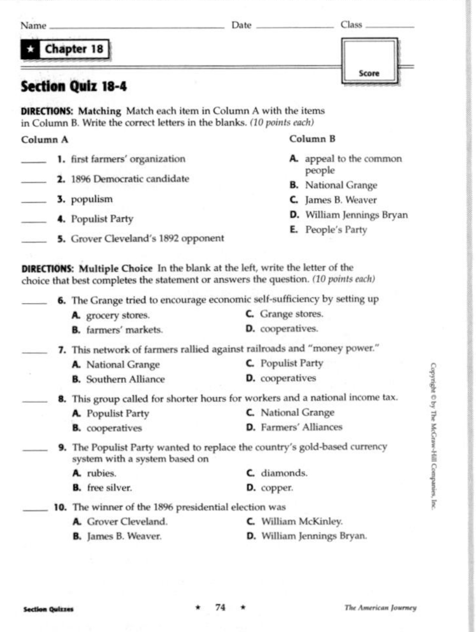
Name ______ Date ______ Class ______

Chapter 18 | Score

Section Quiz 18-4

DIRECTIONS: Matching Match each item in Column A with the items in Column B. Write the correct letters in the blanks. *(10 points each)*

Column A	Column B
____ 1. first farmers' organization	A. appeal to the common people
____ 2. 1896 Democratic candidate	B. National Grange
____ 3. populism	C. James B. Weaver
____ 4. Populist Party	D. William Jennings Bryan
____ 5. Grover Cleveland's 1892 opponent	E. People's Party

DIRECTIONS: Multiple Choice In the blank at the left, write the letter of the choice that best completes the statement or answers the question. *(10 points each)*

____ 6. The Grange tried to encourage economic self-sufficiency by setting up
A. grocery stores. C. Grange stores.
B. farmers' markets. D. cooperatives.

____ 7. This network of farmers rallied against railroads and "money power."
A. National Grange C. Populist Party
B. Southern Alliance D. cooperatives

____ 8. This group called for shorter hours for workers and a national income tax.
A. Populist Party C. National Grange
B. cooperatives D. Farmers' Alliances

____ 9. The Populist Party wanted to replace the country's gold-based currency system with a system based on
A. rubies. C. diamonds.
B. free silver. D. copper.

____ 10. The winner of the 1896 presidential election was
A. Grover Cleveland. C. William McKinley.
B. James B. Weaver. D. William Jennings Bryan.

Section Quizzes • 74 • The American Journey

Populist Party ribbon

Picturing HISTORY For many farmers in isolated areas, Populist meetings like this one in Dickinson County, Kansas, provided fellowship and a chance to promote political ideas. **Why did Populists favor a flexible currency system based on free silver?**

A Party of the People

In the 1890 election, the Alliances became active in political campaigns. Candidates they supported won 6 governorships, 3 seats in the United States Senate, and 50 seats in the House of Representatives.

The Populist Party

Pleased with such successes, Alliance leaders worked to turn the movement into a national political party. In February 1892, Alliance members formed the People's Party of the U.S.A., also known as the Populist Party. Its goals were rooted in **populism,** or appeal to the common people.

The new party claimed that the government, not private companies, should own the railroads and telegraph lines. The Populists also wanted to replace the country's gold-based currency system with a flexible currency system that was based on free silver—the unlimited production of silver coins. They believed that putting more silver coins into the economy would give farmers more money to pay their debts.

The Populist Party supported a number of political and labor reforms. They wanted election reforms such as limiting the president and vice president to a single term, electing senators directly, and introducing the use of secret ballots. They also called for shorter hours for workers and the creation of a national income tax.

Populist Gains and Problems

At a convention in **Omaha, Nebraska,** in July 1892, the Populist Party nominated **James B. Weaver** of Iowa to run for president. In the election Weaver received more than 1 million votes—8.5 percent of the total—and 22 electoral votes. **Grover Cleveland,** the Democratic candidate, won the election, but the Populists had done well for a third party.

The Populists made a strong showing in the state and local elections of 1894 and had high hopes for the presidential election of 1896. The party nominated a number of energetic candidates, but it lacked money and organization.

Economics

Free Silver

To make matters worse, antagonism between the North and the South plagued the Populist Party. In addition many white Southerners could not bring themselves to join forces with African American Populists.

Another blow against populism was struck by the Democratic Party in the South. In the 1890s Democrat-controlled Southern state legislatures placed strict limits on the rights of African Americans to vote. Many freedmen—who might have supported the Populists—were unable to vote.

MULTIPLE LEARNING STYLES

Verbal/Linguistic Farm families of the late 1800s bought many of the things they needed through mail-order catalogs. Have pairs of students find reproductions of Sears or Montgomery Ward catalogs of the late 1800s and choose two sections for study. Have them list the types of goods sold in the sections they chose. Ask students to compare the early listings with those of present-day catalogs to find out how items, descriptions, prices, and illustrations differ. Then ask students to make generalizations about the needs of families of the late nineteenth century with the needs of families today. L2

The Populist crusade for free silver and against the "money power" continued, however. Banking and business interests warned that coining unlimited amounts of new currency would lead to inflation and ruin the economy.

Farmers were joined by debtors in supporting free silver, hoping that loans could be repaid more cheaply. Silver-mining companies in the West also supported the cause. If the government coined large quantities of silver, they had a place to sell their metal.

In the mid-1890s Democrats from farm and silver-producing states took up the free silver issue. This created a problem for Populists. Should they ally themselves with these Democrats? Or should they remain a separate party and risk dividing the free-silver vote?

The Election of 1896

President Grover Cleveland, a Democrat, opposed free silver. At their 1896 convention, however, the Democrats chose a candidate for president who supported free silver and other Populist goals. He was 36-year-old **William Jennings Bryan,** known as the Great Commoner because of his appeal to average Americans. Bryan passionately believed in the farmers' causes.

The Populists decided to endorse Bryan as their candidate for president and to nominate their own candidate, Tom Watson of Georgia, for vice president. The Republicans nominated **William McKinley** of Ohio for president. A former representative and governor of Ohio, McKinley was a shrewd politician who opposed free silver.

A fiery speaker, Bryan proved to be an outstanding campaigner. He crossed the nation giving one dynamic speech after another, attacking bankers and other money interests.

Bryan's strenuous campaigning was in vain. By the time of the election, an economic depression that had slowed business in the early 1890s was nearly over. Voters believed that good times were returning, and they put their trust in McKinley, who represented stability. Even the economic situation of the farmers was improving. The Populists' message no longer seemed urgent. McKinley won 271 electoral votes to Bryan's 176. The Populist ticket received only 222,600 popular votes and won no electoral votes. $

The Populist Legacy

In one sense, however, the Populists were victorious. Reformers adopted many Populist ideas and succeeded in getting many new laws passed. In the 1900s, the United States abandoned the gold standard, adopted an eight-hour workday, and introduced an income tax. Election reforms brought in the secret ballot and direct election of senators. These were Populist goals.

Section 4 Review

Checking for Understanding

1. ***Identify*** Farmers' Alliances, James B. Weaver, Grover Cleveland, William Jennings Bryan, William McKinley.
2. ***Define*** National Grange, cooperative, Populist Party, free silver.
3. ***Name*** the groups on which farmers of the late 1800s blamed their problems.

Reviewing Themes

4. **Groups and Institutions** Why were granges and alliances formed?

Critical Thinking

5. **Making Inferences** Why do you think the Populists considered themselves to be a party of the people?

Activity

Creating a Bumper Sticker Write a campaign slogan for a Populist candidate who is running for office, and make a bumper sticker displaying your slogan.

Section 4 Review Answers

1. Farmers' Alliances, 545; James B. Weaver, 546; Grover Cleveland, 546; William Jennings Bryan, 547; William McKinley, 547
2. The words are defined in the Glossary.
3. railroad companies, Eastern manufacturers, bankers
4. to encourage farmers to organize and solve their problems; to offer farmers education, fellowship, and support; to encourage self-sufficiency; to influence political and labor policies
5. Answers may include: promoted the needs of people over the needs of private businesses and government; called for reform to improve people's lives and give them more political influence.

Activity Slogans should indicate that students understand Populist Party goals.

CHAPTER 18
Section 4, 544–547

Reteaching Activity 18–4

Name ______ Date ______ Class ______

★ Reteaching Activity 18-4

DIRECTIONS: Completing a Flowchart The flowchart shows how the farmers' problems in the late 1800s led to the formation of new groups and a new political party. Write the number of each item in the section of the chart where it belongs. One item fits in two categories.

★FACT BANK

1. claimed that the government should own the railroads
2. proposed a plan in which the federal government would store farmers' crops and make loans to farmers
3. sponsored education and cooperative buying and selling
4. Expenses for seed, shipping, and manufactured goods remained high.
5. groups separated by regional differences and personality clashes
6. organized social gatherings
7. wanted election reforms, shorter hours for workers, and a national income tax
8. tried to get state legislatures to limit railroad shipping rates
9. formed in February 1892
10. Crop prices fell steadily.
11. encouraged economic self-sufficiency
12. supported a currency system based on free silver
13. Supply of crops grew faster than demand.
14. endorsed William Jennings Bryan in the election of 1896

Farmers' Problems ______

(led to the formation of)

The Grange ______

(which eventually led to the formation of)

The Farmers' Alliances ______

(which led to the formation of)

The Populist Party ______

DIRECTIONS: Essay On a separate sheet of paper, answer the question below.

Why did the farmers in the late 1880s blame the railroad companies, Eastern manufacturers, and bankers for their problems?

Reteaching Activities ★ 74 ★ *The American Journey*

Enrichment Activity 18–4

Name ______ Date ______ Class ______

★ Enrichment Activity 18-4

The Farmer Is the Man

During the late 1800s farmers faced great difficulties. Prices for crops such as wheat and cotton fell, while machinery, shipping, and other operating costs continued to climb. Farmers became frustrated with their situation. They felt that everyone depended on them to provide necessities and then made more money than they did on the crops they grew. Read the excerpt from the late 1800s song "The Farmer Is the Man."

The Farmer Is the Man

. . . When the lawyer hangs around,
While the butcher cuts a pound,
Oh, the farmer is the man who feeds them all.
When the preacher and the cook
Go strolling by the brook
Oh, the farmer is the man who feeds them all.
The farmer is the man,
The farmer is the man,
Lives on credit till the fall;
Then they take him by the hand,
And they lead him from the land,
And the middleman's the one who gets it all.

SOURCE: Scott, John Anthony. *The Ballad of America: The History of the United States in Song and Story.* Bantam Books, Inc., New York.

DIRECTIONS: Interpreting Lyrics Answer each question about the song.

1. What is meant by ". . . the farmer is the man who feeds them all"? ______
2. Who could be the "middleman" who gets it all? ______

Activity **DIRECTIONS:** Do research to find out the current financial situation of farmers and to answer some of the following questions: Are farmers better off today than when the song was written? Are they able to make money and pay their bills today? What is the government doing to help farmers? How are people trying to help farmers? Then choose a favorite tune and compose your own song lyrics about the current plight of farmers. If possible, perform your song with some of your classmates.

Enrichment Activities ★ 74 ★ *The American Journey*

4 CLOSE

Present these lyrics from a late 1800s farm protest song and challenge students to write lyrics of their own.

The bankers followed us
 out west;
And did in mortgages invest;
They looked ahead and
 shrewdly planned,
And soon they'll have our
 Kansas land.

GLENCOE TECHNOLOGY

VIDEODISC
MindJogger Videoquiz

Use MindJogger to review the Chapter 18 content.

Chapter 18
Disc 3, Side A

Also available in VHS.

Reviewing Key Terms

The key terms used in this activity are found in the textbook glossary on pages A26–A35.

Reviewing Key Facts

1. brought workers to the West; transported goods to and from the East; need for steel tracks and other supplies gave boost to steel and other industries; towns grew up around the railroad; attracted settlers to the area
2. railroads made journey easier and cheaper; Homestead Act offered free land; above average rainfall in late 1870s; advertising
3. railroads hired hunters to kill buffalo to feed railroad workers and to prevent the animals from blocking trains; hunting for sport; selling hides for profit
4. to encourage Native Americans to give up their nomadic way of life and become farmers
5. limiting presidential and vice presidential terms; electing senators directly; using secret ballots

Critical Thinking

1. The Native American way of life depended on access to the land, which would be limited by an invasion of white settlers.
2. Transcontinental railroad made travel easier and cheaper; new agricultural methods made it easier to farm the Great Plains.

Chapter 18
Review and Activities

Reviewing Key Terms

On a sheet of paper, define the following terms:

lode	**cooperative**
ore	**Populist Party**
vigilante	**free silver**
subsidy	**dry farming**
transcontinental	**nomadic**
open range	**reservation**

Reviewing Key Facts

1. In what ways did the transcontinental railroad help to boost the American economy?
2. What attracted farmers to the Great Plains?
3. What actions by whites destroyed the buffalo population?
4. What was the goal of the Dawes Act?
5. What political reforms did the Populists support?

Critical Thinking

Drawing Conclusions

Many Americans in the 1800s viewed the West as free, open land awaiting civilization by white people.

1. Why was this attitude a threat to the Native Americans?
2. How did new technology encourage settlement of the West?

Time Line Activity

Create a time line on which you place the following events in chronological order.

- First transcontinental railroad completed
- Comstock Lode discovered in Nevada
- Congress passes Homestead Act
- Custer defeated at Little Bighorn

Technology Activity

Using E-mail Use an on-line address book to locate a modern farming organization. Copy the E-mail address of this organization and contact it through E-mail. Explain that you would like to know more about the organization. Ask what services or support the organization provides to farmers today.

Geography Activity

Study the map below, then answer the questions.

Mining in the West

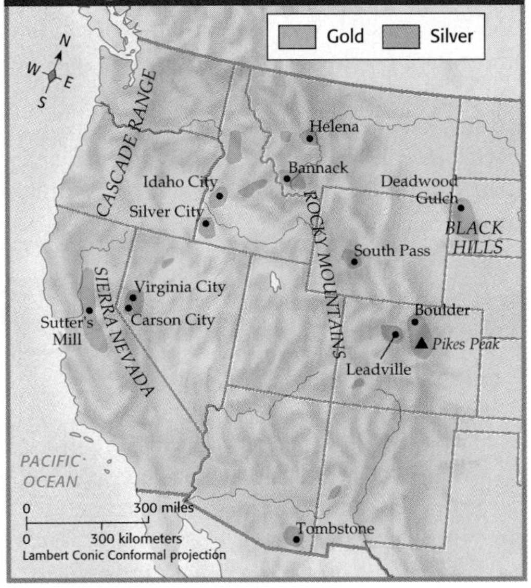

1. **Region** What is the topic of this map?
2. **Place** What minerals were mined near the Black Hills?
3. **Location** Near what mountain range was Sutter's Mill located?

Time Line Activity

Events should be placed in this order: Comstock Lode discovered in Nevada, Congress passes Homestead Act, First transcontinental railroad completed, Custer defeated at Little Bighorn

Technology Activity

Students should locate a farming organization that caters to modern farmers and describe the services and support that the organization provides.

Skill Practice Activity

Reading a Special-Purpose Map

Study the special-purpose map below, then answer the questions that follow it.

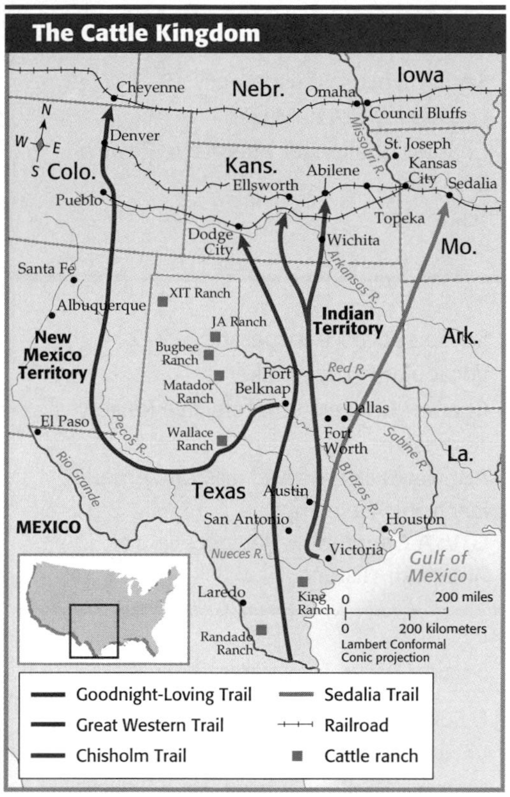

1. What is the subject of the map?
2. What geographic region is shown?
3. What do the different colored lines represent?
4. In what part of Texas were most of the large cattle ranches found?
5. Along which two trails did several major Texas cities develop?
6. Where did a majority of the trails end? Explain why.
7. In which state did the Chisholm Trail end?

Reviewing Themes

1. **Geography and History** How did the rush to find gold and silver spark the creation of new communities in the West?
2. **Economic Factors** Why was the "Cattle Kingdom" dependent on the railroads?
3. **Culture and Traditions** What actions by the United States government and white settlers brought an end to the traditional Native American way of life?
4. **Groups and Institutions** What problems led farmers to organize granges and alliances?

Cooperative Activity

History and Economics Today many Native Americans still live on reservations. Some reservations have developed their own businesses and industries to help make them more self-sufficient. With a partner research to find information about a reservation in the United States today. Write a report describing one of the major businesses on that reservation.

Portfolio Activity **History Journal** Reread and take notes on the section of the chapter that discusses the chores of a farm woman. Use your notes to create an hour-by-hour schedule to show one day's typical activities for a farm wife who lived on the Great Plains.

CHAPTER 18
Review and Activities

Reviewing Themes

1. Communities were formed to serve the needs of miners in the area. Although some towns were abandoned, others thrived when people settled permanently in the area.
2. Ranchers could get their cattle to markets in the East only by shipping them on railroads.
3. reservation policy; white settlers trespassing on Native American land; sale of Native American land; slaughter of buffalo; the Dawes Act
4. falling prices, rising costs, relationship with banks in regard to loans

Cooperative Activity

Students should research information on a modern Native American reservation. Their reports should describe a particular business or industry that exists on that reservation.

Portfolio Activity Students should refer to the description of women on the Great Plains in Section 2 to create a schedule of daily activities.

Chapter Bonus Test Question

Ask: **What was the name of the woman with a powerful speaking voice who made an estimated 160 speeches on behalf of the Populist farmers' cause in 1890?** *(Mary Elizabeth Lease)*

Geography Activity

1. mining in the West
2. gold
3. Sierra Nevada range

Skill Practice Activity

1. The Cattle Kingdom
2. Students' answers should include the American Southwest.
3. cattle trails
4. the northern part near New Mexico Territory and Indian Territory (the Panhandle)
5. Sedalia, Chisholm
6. at towns along railroads; so the cattle could be shipped to markets in the East
7. Kansas

Chapter 19 Planning Guide

A complete, 1-page lesson plan is provided for each section in the *Reproducible Lesson Plans* booklet.

Section Resources

Daily Objectives	Reproducible Resources	Multimedia Resources
Section 1 Railroads Lead the Way Describe the ways railroad barons made their fortunes and how the railroads changed the national economy.	Reproducible Lesson Plan 19–1 Guided Reading Activity 19–1* Section Quiz 19–1* Reteaching Activity 19–1 Enrichment Activity 19–1	Section Focus Transparency 19–1 Vocabulary PuzzleMaker Chapter Challenger Interactive Review Software Testmaker
Section 2 Inventions List inventions and improvements that transformed American transportation, communication, and daily life.	Reproducible Lesson Plan 19–2 Guided Reading Activity 19–2* Section Quiz 19–2* Reteaching Activity 19–2 Enrichment Activity 19–2	Section Focus Transparency 19–2 Vocabulary PuzzleMaker Chapter Challenger Interactive Review Testmaker ABCNews InterActive™ Historic America Electronic Field Trips GTV: A Geographic Perspective on American History
Section 3 An Age of Big Business Describe the growth of large corporations and the benefits and problems that developed with that growth.	Reproducible Lesson Plan 19–3 Guided Reading Activity 19–3* Political Cartoons, *Battle Against the Trusts* Section Quiz 19–3* Reteaching Activity 19–3 Enrichment Activity 19–3	Section Focus Transparency 19–3 U.S. History & Art, Transparency 14 Vocabulary PuzzleMaker Chapter Challenger Interactive Review Software Testmaker GTV: A Geographic Perspective on American History Facts On File: Landmark Documents in American History
Section 4 Industrial Workers Summarize the reasons workers demanded improvements in working conditions and wages and explain how unions helped workers gain power.	Reproducible Lesson Plan 19–4 Guided Reading Activity 19–4* Section Quiz 19–4* Reteaching Activity 19–4 Enrichment Activity 19–4	Section Focus Transparency 19–4 Vocabulary PuzzleMaker Chapter Challenger Interactive Review Software Testmaker Facts On File: Landmark Documents in American History

** Also available in Spanish*

Blackline Master · Videodisc · Audiocassette · Music Program · Transparency · CD-ROM · Software

0:00 **OUT OF TIME?**
Assign the Chapter 19 Digest and the corresponding Chapter Digests Audiocassettes with activities and tests.

Activity

From the Classroom of…

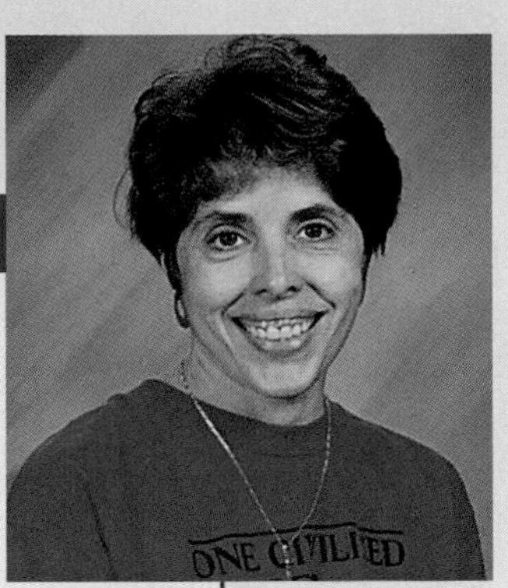

Debbie Dumler
Lyons Middle School
Sterling, KS

A Classroom Industry

Set up a small in-class industry. First, have students select a simple product to produce—for example, spirit ribbons to support an athletic team (students can wear these or put them on their lockers before a big game or tournament) or bookmarks. Next, help students organize the class into divisions of labor. There will need to be managers, production workers, and a sales force (if you would like to distribute your product throughout the school). You can also sell shares in the company to acquire working capital.

Students should set up their industry based on information in the chapter and what they already know about companies and how they work. If you have a school newsletter or newspaper, some students could act as an advertising team, designing ads. Posters and flyers could also be used as advertising materials. Any profits could go toward a classroom party or be given to a local charity.

Block Schedule

Block scheduling differs from traditional class scheduling in the amount of time allotted to each period. The extended time frame provided by block scheduling affords you the opportunity to implement a greater number of research-oriented and activity-intense projects to motivate and involve your students. Activities that are particularly suited to use within the block scheduling framework are identified throughout this chapter by the following designation:

NATIONAL GEOGRAPHIC SOCIETY — Teacher's Corner

INDEX TO NATIONAL GEOGRAPHIC MAGAZINE

The following articles may be used for research relating to this chapter:

- "Buffalo: Back Home on the Range," by Bryan Hodgson, November 1994.
- "John Wesley Powell," by Peter Miller, April 1994.
- "The American Prairie: Roots of the Sky," by Douglas H. Chadwick, October 1993.
- "Geronimo," by David Roberts, October 1992.
- "New Life for Ellis Island," by Alice J. Hall, September 1990.
- "The Life and Times of William Henry Jackson," by Rowe Findley, February 1989.
- "Alexander Graham Bell," by Robert V. Bruce, September 1988.

NATIONAL GEOGRAPHIC SOCIETY PRODUCTS AVAILABLE FROM GLENCOE

To order the following products for use with this chapter, contact your local Glencoe sales representative, or call Glencoe at 1-800-334-7344:

- *GTV: A Geographic Perspective on American History* (Videodisc)
- *GTV: The American People: Fabric of a Nation* (Videodisc)
- *The Presidents: A Picture History of Our Nation* (CD-ROM)
- *PictureShow: Native Americans, 1 and 2* (CD-ROM, Transparencies)
- *PictureShow: The Westward Movement* (CD-ROM, Transparencies)

ADDITIONAL NATIONAL GEOGRAPHIC SOCIETY PRODUCTS

To order the following products for use with this chapter, call National Geographic Society at 1-800-368-2728:

- *Full Steam Ahead: The Race to Build a Transcontinental Railroad* (Book)
- *Native Americans* (Poster Set)
- *Historical Atlas of the United States* (Atlas)

KEY TO ABILITY LEVELS

Teaching strategies have been coded for varying learning styles and abilities.

L1 **BASIC** activities for all students
L2 **AVERAGE** activities for average to above-average students
L3 **CHALLENGING** activities for above-average students
ELL **ENGLISH LANGUAGE LEARNER** activities

Chapter 19 Resource Guide

Home Involvement

Home Involvement Activity 19

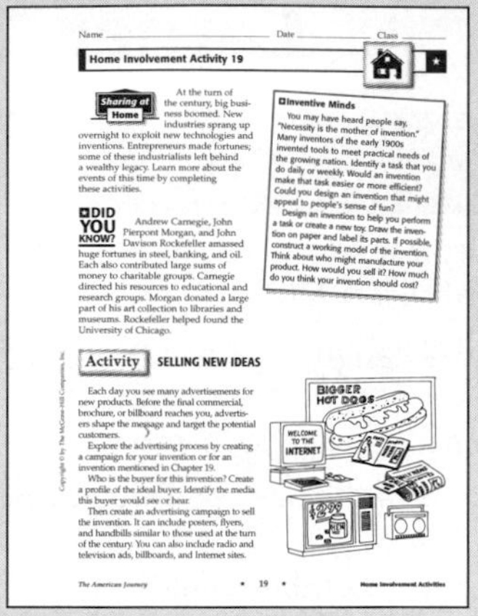
Home Involvement Activity 19

Review Activities

Chapter Summary 19

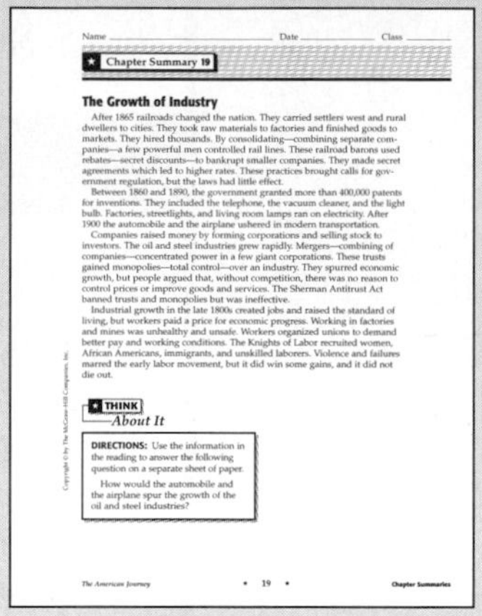
Chapter Summary 19

The Growth of Industry

Workbook Activity 19

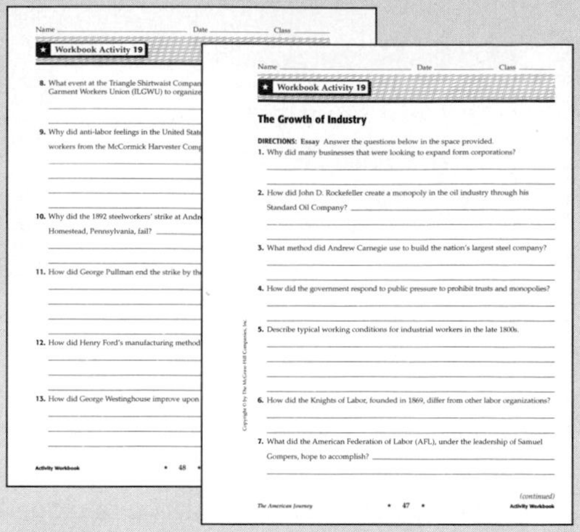
Workbook Activity 19

The Growth of Industry

Reinforcement Activities

Time Line Activity 19

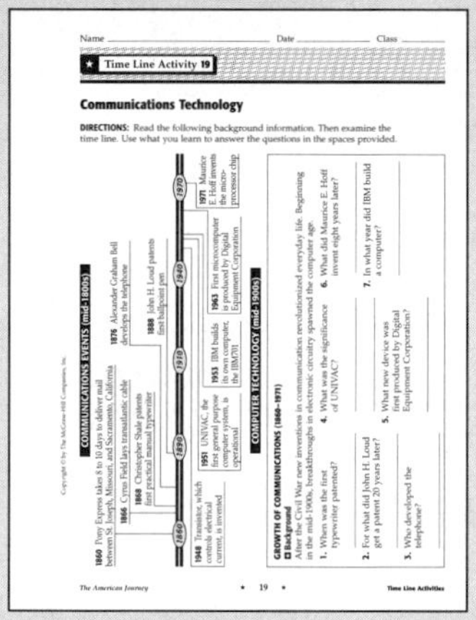
Time Line Activity 19

Communications Technology

Vocabulary Activity 19

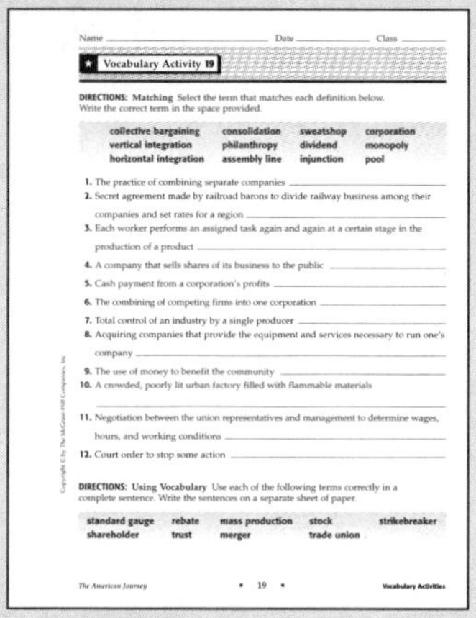
Vocabulary Activity 19

Chapter Skills Activity 19

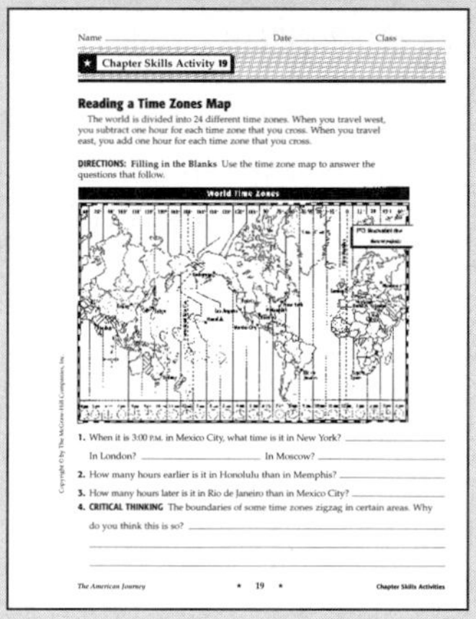
Chapter Skills Activity 19

Reading a Time Zones Map

Enrichment Activities

Linking Past and Present Activity 19

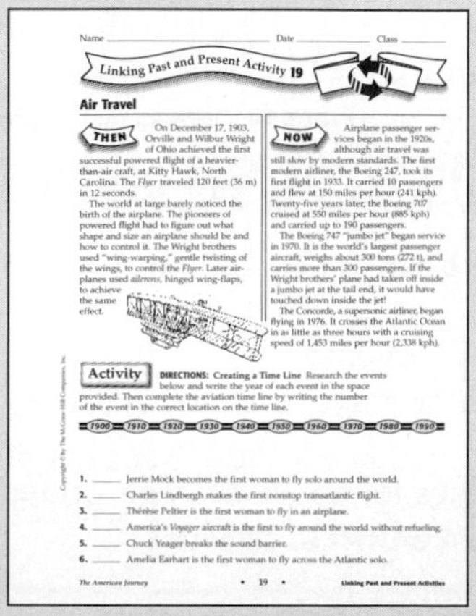
Linking Past and Present Activity 19

Air Travel

Primary Source Reading 19

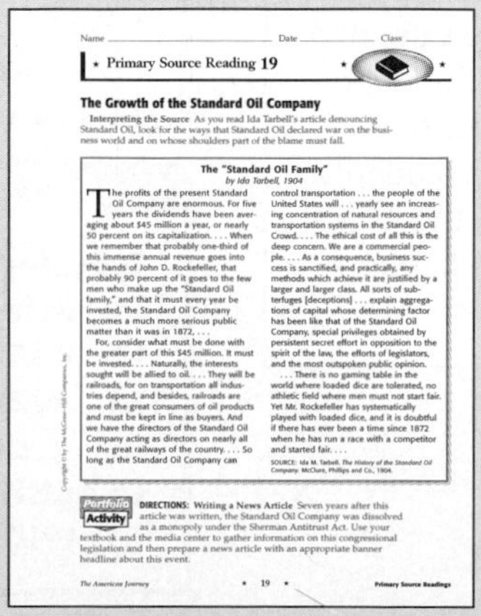
Primary Source Reading 19

The Growth of the Standard Oil Company

Geography Activities

Mapping History Activity 19

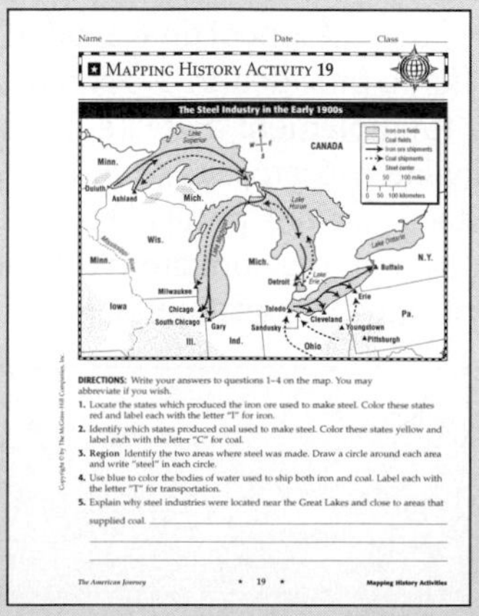
Mapping History Activity 19

The Steel Industry in the Early 1900s

Chapter 19 Resource Guide

ASSESSMENT

Chapter 19 Test, Form A

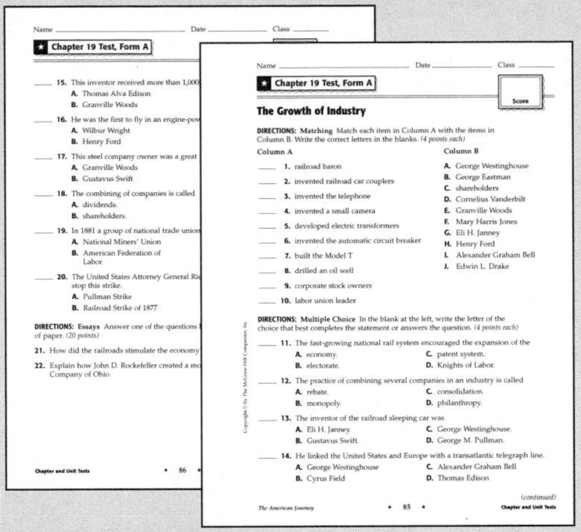

Name ______ Date ______ Class ______

Chapter 19 Test, Form A

____ 15. This inventor received more than 1,000
A. Thomas Alva Edison
B. Granville Woods

____ 16. He was the first to fly in an engine-pow
A. Wilbur Wright
B. Henry Ford

____ 17. This steel company owner was a great
A. Granville Woods
B. Gustavus Swift

____ 18. The combining of companies is called
A. dividends.
B. shareholders.

____ 19. In 1881 a group of national trade union
A. National Miners' Union
B. American Federation of Labor

____ 20. The United States Attorney General Ri
stop this strike.
A. Pullman Strike
B. Railroad Strike of 1877

DIRECTIONS: Essays Answer one of the questions
of paper. *(20 points)*

21. How did the railroads stimulate the economy
22. Explain how John D. Rockefeller created a mo
Company of Ohio.

Chapter and Unit Tests • 86 •

Name ______ Date ______ Class ______

Chapter 19 Test, Form A

Score

The Growth of Industry

DIRECTIONS: Matching Match each item in Column A with the items in Column B. Write the correct letters in the blanks. *(4 points each)*

Column A	Column B
____ 1. railroad baron	A. George Westinghouse
____ 2. invented railroad car couplers	B. George Eastman
____ 3. invented the telephone	C. shareholders
____ 4. invented a small camera	D. Cornelius Vanderbilt
____ 5. developed electric transformers	E. Granville Woods
____ 6. invented the automatic circuit breaker	F. Mary Harris Jones
____ 7. built the Model T	G. Eli H. Janney
____ 8. drilled an oil well	H. Henry Ford
____ 9. corporate stock owners	I. Alexander Graham Bell
____ 10. labor union leader	J. Edwin L. Drake

DIRECTIONS: Multiple Choice In the blank at the left, write the letter of the choice that best completes the statement or answers the question. *(4 points each)*

____ 11. The fast-growing national rail system encouraged the expansion of the
A. economy. C. patent system.
B. electorate. D. Knights of Labor.

____ 12. The practice of combining several companies in an industry is called
A. rebate. C. consolidation.
B. monopoly. D. philanthropy.

____ 13. The inventor of the railroad sleeping car was
A. Eli H. Janney. C. George Westinghouse.
B. Gustavus Swift. D. George M. Pullman.

____ 14. He linked the United States and Europe with a transatlantic telegraph line.
A. George Westinghouse C. Alexander Graham Bell
B. Cyrus Field D. Thomas Edison

(continued)

Copyright © by The McGraw-Hill Companies, Inc.

The American Journey • 85 • Chapter and Unit Tests

Chapter 19 Test, Form B

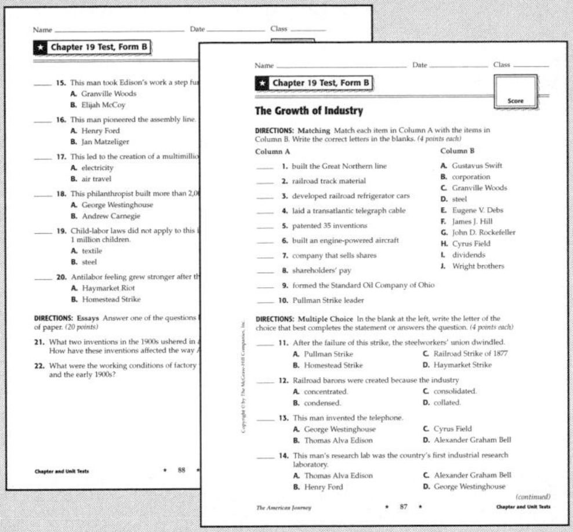

Name ______ Date ______ Class ______

Chapter 19 Test, Form B

____ 15. This man took Edison's work a step fu
A. Granville Woods
B. Elijah McCoy

____ 16. This man pioneered the assembly line.
A. Henry Ford
B. Jan Matzeliger

____ 17. This led to the creation of a multimillio
A. electricity
B. air travel

____ 18. This philanthropist built more than 2,0
A. George Westinghouse
B. Andrew Carnegie

____ 19. Child-labor laws did not apply to this i
1 million children.
A. textile
B. steel

____ 20. Antilabor feeling grew stronger after th
A. Haymarket Riot
B. Homestead Strike

DIRECTIONS: Essays Answer one of the questions
of paper. *(20 points)*

21. What two inventions in the 1900s ushered in
How have these inventions affected the way
22. What were the working conditions of factory
and the early 1900s?

Chapter and Unit Tests • 88 •

Name ______ Date ______ Class ______

Chapter 19 Test, Form B

Score

The Growth of Industry

DIRECTIONS: Matching Match each item in Column A with the items in Column B. Write the correct letters in the blanks. *(4 points each)*

Column A	Column B
____ 1. built the Great Northern line	A. Gustavus Swift
____ 2. railroad track material	B. corporation
____ 3. developed railroad refrigerator cars	C. Granville Woods
____ 4. laid a transatlantic telegraph cable	D. steel
____ 5. patented 35 inventions	E. Eugene V. Debs
____ 6. built an engine-powered aircraft	F. James J. Hill
____ 7. company that sells shares	G. John D. Rockefeller
____ 8. shareholders' pay	H. Cyrus Field
____ 9. formed the Standard Oil Company of Ohio	I. dividends
____ 10. Pullman Strike leader	J. Wright brothers

DIRECTIONS: Multiple Choice In the blank at the left, write the letter of the choice that best completes the statement or answers the question. *(4 points each)*

____ 11. After the failure of this strike, the steelworkers' union dwindled.
A. Pullman Strike C. Railroad Strike of 1877
B. Homestead Strike D. Haymarket Strike

____ 12. Railroad barons were created because the industry
A. concentrated. C. consolidated.
B. condensed. D. collated.

____ 13. This man invented the telephone.
A. George Westinghouse C. Cyrus Field
B. Thomas Alva Edison D. Alexander Graham Bell

____ 14. This man's research lab was the country's first industrial research laboratory.
A. Thomas Alva Edison C. Alexander Graham Bell
B. Henry Ford D. George Westinghouse

(continued)

Copyright © by The McGraw-Hill Companies, Inc.

The American Journey • 87 • Chapter and Unit Tests

Performance Assessment Activity 19

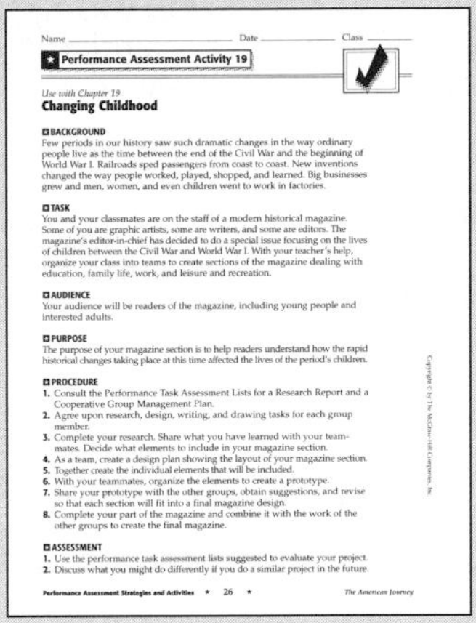

Name ______ Date ______ Class ______

Performance Assessment Activity 19

Use with Chapter 19

Changing Childhood

BACKGROUND
Few periods in our history saw such dramatic changes in the way ordinary people live as the time between the end of the Civil War and the beginning of World War I. Railroads sped passengers from coast to coast. New inventions changed the way people worked, played, shopped, and learned. Big businesses grew and men, women, and even children went to work in factories.

TASK
You and your classmates are on the staff of a modern historical magazine. Some of you are graphic artists, some are writers, and some are editors. The magazine's editor-in-chief has decided to do a special issue focusing on the lives of children between the Civil War and World War I. With your teacher's help, organize your class into teams to create sections of the magazine dealing with education, family life, work, and leisure and recreation.

AUDIENCE
Your audience will be readers of the magazine, including young people and interested adults.

PURPOSE
The purpose of your magazine section is to help readers understand how the rapid historical changes taking place at this time affected the lives of the period's children.

PROCEDURE
1. Consult the Performance Task Assessment Lists for a Research Report and a Cooperative Group Management Plan.
2. Agree upon research, design, writing, and drawing tasks for each group member.
3. Complete your research. Share what you have learned with your teammates. Decide what elements to include in your magazine section.
4. As a team, create a design plan showing the layout of your magazine section.
5. Together create the individual elements that will be included.
6. With your teammates, organize the elements to create a prototype.
7. Share your prototype with the other groups, obtain suggestions, and revise so that each section will fit into a final magazine design.
8. Complete your part of the magazine and combine it with the work of the other groups to create the final magazine.

ASSESSMENT
1. Use the performance task assessment lists suggested to evaluate your project.
2. Discuss what you might do differently if you do a similar project in the future.

Copyright © by The McGraw-Hill Companies, Inc.

Performance Assessment Strategies and Activities • 26 • *The American Journey*

SPANISH RESOURCES

The following Spanish language materials are available in the Spanish Resources binder:

- **Spanish Chapter Summary 19**
- **Spanish Vocabulary Activity 19**
- **Spanish Guided Reading Activities, Chapter 19**
- **Spanish Section Quizzes, Chapter 19**
- **Spanish Home Involvement Activity 19**
- **Spanish Chapter 19 Digests Audiocassette Activity and Test**

ACTIVITY MANIPULATIVES

Help students learn more about America's cultural history with:

- **American Crafts Hands-On Activities**
- **American Games Hands-On Activities**
- **American History Flash Cards**

ADDITIONAL RESOURCES FROM GLENCOE

- **The Spirit of American Art and Music,** Henry Jackson, Thomas Eakins, Richard Morris Hunt
- **U.S. History & Art,** Transparency 14, *Smoking Room*
- **Political Cartoons,** *Battle Against the Trusts*
- **Outline Map Resource Book**
- **U.S. Desk Map**
- **The American History Videodisc and CD-ROM,** *Post–Civil War Expansion and Change, 1865–1900*

A&E HOME VIDEO. Biography. THE HISTORY CHANNEL.

The following videotape programs are available from Glencoe as supplements to Chapter 19:

- **Andrew Carnegie** (ISBN 1-56501-741-2)
- **Du Ponts: America's Wealthiest Family** (ISBN 1-56501-860-5)
- **Henry Ford: Tin Lizzy Tycoon** (ISBN 1-56501-380-8)
- **Wilbur & Orville: Dreams of Flying** (ISBN 1-56501-386-7)
- **Locomotion: The Amazing World of Trains** (ISBN 1-56501-286-0)
- **Transcontinental Railroads** (ISBN 1-56501-731-5)

To order, call Glencoe at 1-800-334-7344. To find classroom resources to accompany many of these videos, check the following home pages:
A&E Television: http://www.aetv.com
The History Channel: http://www.historychannel.com

Introducing CHAPTER 19

Chapter Themes

Chapter Themes are listed by section on this chapter opening page of the Student Edition. A corresponding theme-based activity is available under "FOCUS," and a theme-based question is asked in the Section and Chapter Reviews.

Performance Assessment

Refer to Activity 19 in the *Performance Assessment Strategies and Activities* booklet.

GLENCOE TECHNOLOGY

VIDEODISC
MindJogger Videoquiz

Use MindJogger to preview the Chapter 19 content.

Chapter 19
Disc 3, Side A

Also available in VHS.

HISTORY AND ART Between 1866 and 1876, the production of American steel jumped from 20,000 to 600,000 tons a year. By 1897 it had skyrocketed to more than 7 million tons. **Ask: What does your eye focus on first in this painting?** *(Students' eyes should be drawn toward the chimney stacks.)*

Chapter 19

1865–1914

The Growth of Industry

Why It's Important

By the early 1900s, many changes had taken place in the nation's economy. Large, powerful corporations had developed, and labor had organized into unions to protect workers' interests. Business owners and employees struggled to establish new ways of working together. The years also brought change to everyday life. Inventions such as the telephone and the automobile revolutionized society in the United States and around the world.

Chapter Themes

- *Section 1,* Geography and History
- *Section 2,* Science and Technology
- *Section 3,* Economic Factors
- *Section 4,* Groups and Institutions

HISTORY AND ART ***Steel Mills At Night* by Aaron Henry Gorson** Gorson's painting depicts the changes that industrial growth brought to America's landscape during the late 1800s.

EXTRA CREDIT PROJECT

Inventions Have interested students research a modern-day invention of their choice, such as computers, fax machines, lasers, or fiber-optic cables. Ask students to prepare an oral report in which they present information about the invention and the inventor. Their reports should be accompanied by visuals and include information on how the invention has changed people's lives.

1860 — 1870 — 1880 — 1890

1869 First transcontinental railroad completed

1880s Standard width for railroad tracks adopted

1883 Northern Pacific Railroad opens

1890s Five railway lines cross the country

Section 1

Railroads Lead the Way

READ TO DISCOVER . . .

- how the railroad barons made fortunes.
- how the national railroad system changed the American economy.

TERMS TO LEARN

consolidation
standard gauge
rebate
pool

The Storyteller

Rugged construction gangs labored on the Union Pacific and other railways during the transportation boom of the late 1800s. A favorite song was:

Well, every morning at seven o'clock
There were 20 tarriers [drillers] a-workin' at the rock,
And the boss comes around and he says "Kape still!"
And come down heavy on the cast iron drill,
And drill, ye tarriers, drill!"
Drill, ye tarriers, drill!
For it's work all day for sugar in your tay,
Down behind of the railway and,
Drill, ye tarriers, drill!
And blast!
And fire!

Train song sheet

During the Civil War, trains carried troops, weapons, and supplies to the front. The superior railroad system of the North played an important role in its victory over the South. In the decades after the war, railroads became a driving force behind America's economic growth.

Railroad Expansion

The first transcontinental railroad, completed in 1869, was soon followed by others. By the 1890s five railway lines crossed the country, and hundreds of smaller lines branched off from them. The railroad system grew rapidly. In 1860 the United States had about 30,000 miles of railroad track. By 1900, 163,000 more miles of track had been laid.

Work songs such as "John Henry" and "I've Been Working on the Railroad" were popular among those who labored to build these miles of track. They sang:

> "I've been working on the railroad,
> All the live-long day,
> I've been working on the railroad,
> Just to pass the time away."

The expansion of the railroad system was accompanied by **consolidation**—the practice of combining separate companies—in the industry. Large railroad companies expanded by buying smaller companies or by driving them out of business. Consolidation made the large companies

SECTION RESOURCES

Reproducible Masters
- Reproducible Lesson Plan 19–1
- Guided Reading Activity 19–1
- Section Quiz 19–1
- Reteaching Activity 19–1
- Enrichment Activity 19–1

Transparencies
- Section Focus Transparency 19–1

Multimedia
- Vocabulary PuzzleMaker
- Chapter Challenger Interactive Review Software
- Testmaker

1 FOCUS

BELLRINGER
Motivational Activity

Before taking roll at the beginning of the class period, project Section Focus Transparency 19–1 and have students answer the questions. Discuss students' responses.

This activity is also available as a blackline master.

Section Focus Transparency 19–1

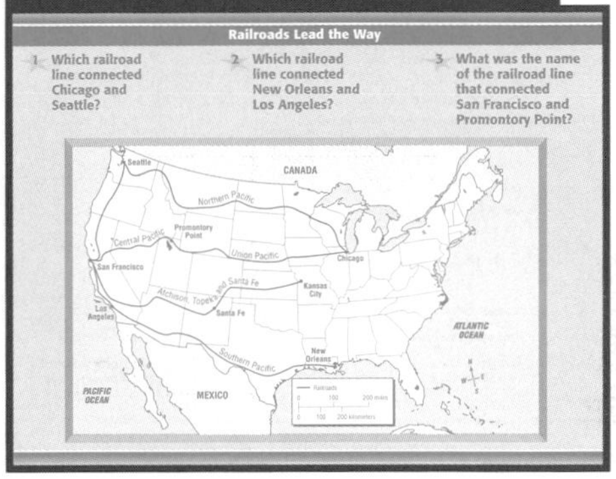

Vocabulary Precheck

Point out that the word *pool* has several meanings. Ask students to name some of them and then find which way the word is used in the section.

Use the **Vocabulary PuzzleMaker** to create crossword and word search puzzles.

Section Theme
Geography and History

As the railroads expanded, the centers of certain industries shifted.

Activity Have students skim the section to find how these centers shifted. *(Flour milling centers and the manufacturing of agricultural equipment moved westward.)*

2 TEACH

L1 Making a Graphic Organizer Work with students to create a graphic organizer that reflects the main ideas of the section—consolidation creates railroad barons, growth of railroads spurs industrial growth, and so on.

Guided Reading Activity 19–1

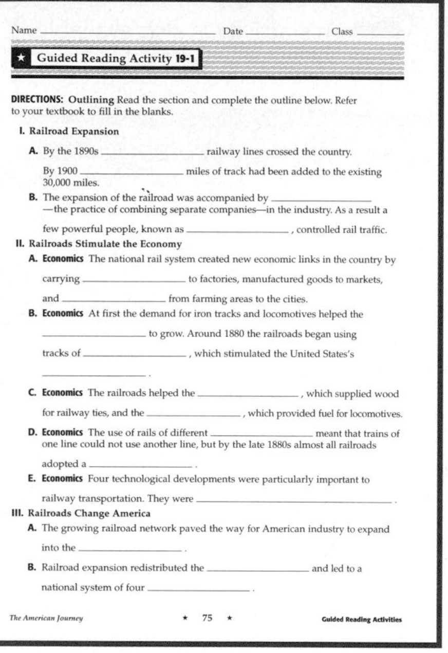

Name ______________ Date ______________ Class ______________

★ Guided Reading Activity **19-1**

DIRECTIONS: Outlining Read the section and complete the outline below. Refer to your textbook to fill in the blanks.

I. Railroad Expansion

A. By the 1890s ______________ railway lines crossed the country.

By 1900 ______________ miles of track had been added to the existing 30,000 miles.

B. The expansion of the railroad was accompanied by ______________ —the practice of combining separate companies—in the industry. As a result a few powerful people, known as ______________, controlled rail traffic.

II. Railroads Stimulate the Economy

A. Economics The national rail system created new economic links in the country by carrying ______________ to factories, manufactured goods to markets, and ______________ from farming areas to the cities.

B. Economics At first the demand for iron tracks and locomotives helped the ______________ to grow. Around 1880 the railroads began using tracks of ______________, which stimulated the United States's ______________.

C. Economics The railroads helped the ______________, which supplied wood for railway ties, and the ______________, which provided fuel for locomotives.

D. Economics The use of rails of different ______________ meant that trains of one line could not use another line, but by the late 1880s almost all railroads adopted a ______________.

E. Economics Four technological developments were particularly important to railway transportation. They were ______________.

III. Railroads Change America

A. The growing railroad network paved the way for American industry to expand into the ______________.

B. Railroad expansion redistributed the ______________ and led to a national system of four ______________.

The American Journey ★ 75 ★ **Guided Reading Activities**

History *and the* Humanities

The Spirit of American Art and Music, Henry Jackson

CURRICULUM CONNECTION

ECONOMICS
In the late 1800s, railroads were the nation's largest industry, employing the largest number of workers and surpassing all others as a buyer of iron, steel, and coal. By 1910 there were 1.7 million railroad workers.

A coal train steams through a Rocky Mountain pass on its way to California.

more efficient. After consolidating the railroad industry, a few powerful individuals known as **railroad barons** controlled the nation's rail traffic.

Railroad Barons

New Yorker **Cornelius Vanderbilt,** one of the first railroad barons, gained control of the New York Central line and then made a fortune by consolidating several companies. His railroad empire stretched from **New York City** to the Great Lakes. To Vanderbilt, having money was a source of great power.

Another railroad baron, **James J. Hill,** built the Great Northern line between **Minnesota** and **Washington State. Collis P. Huntington, Leland Stanford,** and two other partners founded the Central Pacific, which connected California and Utah.

Economics

Railroads Stimulate the Economy

★ The fast-growing national rail system created new economic links in the country. The railroads carried raw materials such as iron ore, coal, and timber to factories. They also carried manufactured goods from factories to markets and transported produce from farming areas to the cities.

The national railroad system encouraged the expanding economy in many other ways. At first the demand for iron tracks and locomotives helped the iron mining and processing industries grow. Around 1880 railroad companies began using tracks of **steel**—a stronger metal made by adding carbon and other elements to refined iron. The use of steel in railroad tracks stimulated America's steel industry.

The railroads also helped other industries to thrive. The lumber industry, which supplied wood for railway ties, and the coal industry, which provided fuel for locomotives, saw extraordinary growth. In addition railroad companies provided work for thousands of people who laid tracks and built stations and for those who manufactured railway cars and equipment.

Improving the Railroads

Increased use made it necessary for railroads to expand and unify their systems. While railroads were being built across the country, different lines used rails of different gauges, or widths. As a result trains of one line could not use another line's tracks. Many early local lines carried goods for short distances and did not even connect with other lines. The gaps in service between the various lines made long-distance railroad travel slow and inefficient.

As the railroad companies consolidated, railroad barons saw the advantages of being part of a national railroad network. By the late 1880s, almost all companies had adopted a standard gauge of 4 feet, 8.5 inches as the width of the railroad track. A standard gauge allowed faster shipment of goods at a reduced cost. It was no longer necessary to load and unload goods from one train to another. One train could make the entire journey.

CRITICAL THINKING ACTIVITY

Analyzing Information Read to students the following excerpts about entrepreneurs of the late 1800s. Have students decide with which opinion they agree, and write a paragraph explaining their reasons.

"These new Americans were primitive souls, ruthless, predatory, capable, single-minded men; rogues and rascals often, but never feeble, never hindered by petty scruples. . . . They fought their way encased in rhinoceros hides."—Historian Vernon L. Parrington

"It is cruel to slander the rich because they have been successful. . . . They are not scoundrels because they have gotten money. They have gone into great enterprises that have enriched the nation and the nation has enriched them."—Reverend Russell H. Conwell **L1**

Railroad Technology

Railway transportation also improved with the introduction of new technology. Four developments were particularly important. Inventor **George Westinghouse** devised air brakes that improved the system for stopping trains, making train travel safer. Janney car couplers, named after inventor **Eli H. Janney,** made it easier for railroad workers to link cars. Refrigerated cars, developed by **Gustavus Swift,** enabled the railroads to ship meat and other perishable goods over long distances. Finally, **George M. Pullman** developed the Pullman sleeping car—a luxury railway car with seats that converted into beds for overnight journeys. Pullman also introduced improved dining cars, raising train travel to a new level of comfort.

Competing for Customers

As the railroad network expanded, the railroad companies competed fiercely with one another to keep old customers and to win new ones. Large railroads offered secret discounts called **rebates** to their biggest customers. Smaller

Major Western Railroads Before 1900

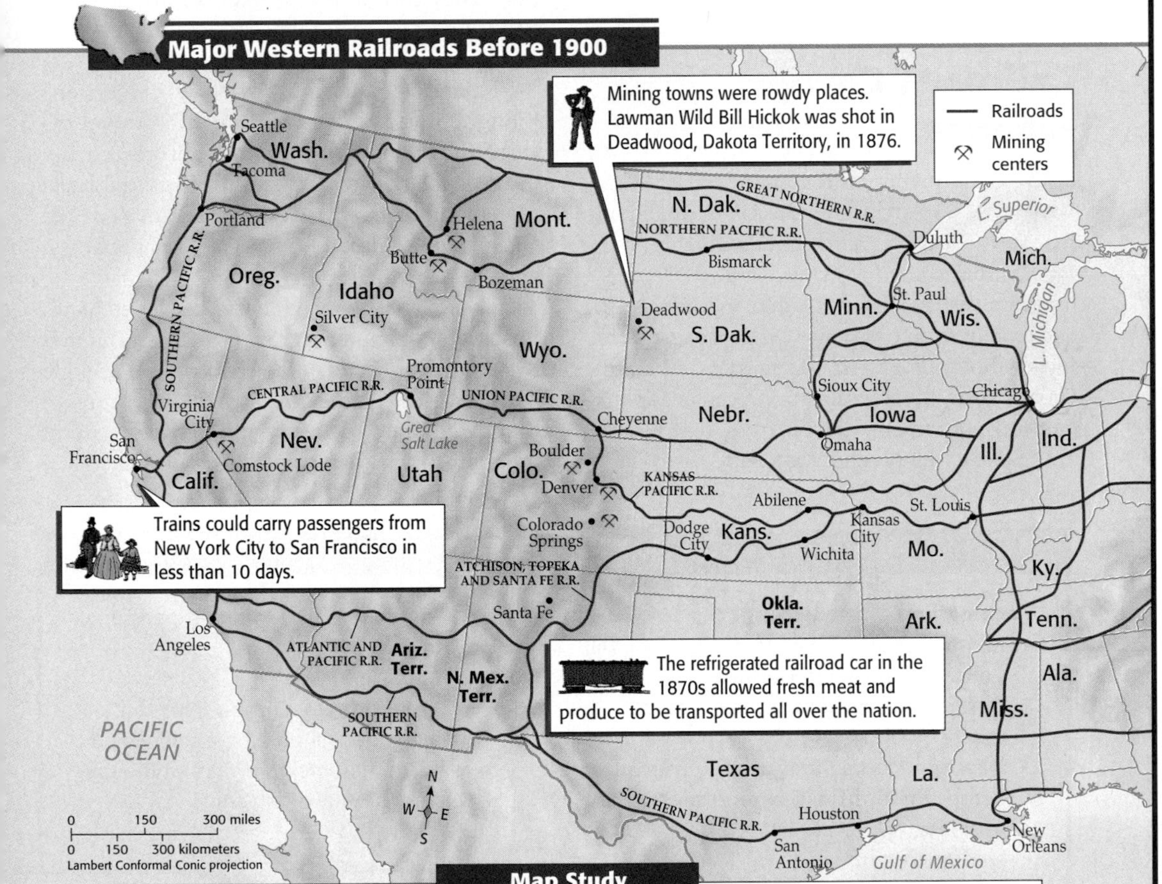

Map Study

By the 1890s more than 150,000 miles (241,350 km) of tracks had been laid.

1. **Movement** Which railroad connected Los Angeles to New Orleans?
2. **Analyzing Information** Which railroads would a miner have traveled from St. Louis to the Comstock Lode?

MULTIPLE LEARNING STYLES

Visual/Spatial Have students look into the history of trains from the early days of railroading to the present, focusing on the changes in locomotives and power sources. Students should present their findings as a series of captioned drawings, possibly using a time line as a base. A possible source of information on the railroad's early days is the book *Tracks Across America: The Story of the American Railroad, 1825–1900* (New York: Holiday House, 1992). **L2, ELL**

3 ASSESS

Assign Section 1 Review as homework or as an in-class activity.

Use **Chapter Challenger Interactive Review Software** to review Section 1.

Section Quiz 19–1

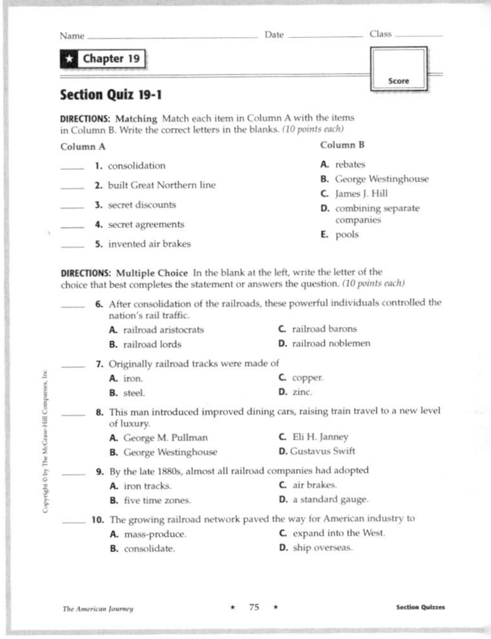
Name ______ Date ______ Class ______

★ Chapter 19

Score

Section Quiz 19-1

DIRECTIONS: Matching Match each item in Column A with the items in Column B. Write the correct letters in the blanks. *(10 points each)*

Column A

____ 1. consolidation
____ 2. built Great Northern line
____ 3. secret discounts
____ 4. secret agreements
____ 5. invented air brakes

Column B

A. rebates
B. George Westinghouse
C. James J. Hill
D. combining separate companies
E. pools

DIRECTIONS: Multiple Choice In the blank at the left, write the letter of the choice that best completes the statement or answers the question. *(10 points each)*

____ 6. After consolidation of the railroads, these powerful individuals controlled the nation's rail traffic.
A. railroad aristocrats C. railroad barons
B. railroad lords D. railroad noblemen

____ 7. Originally railroad tracks were made of
A. iron. C. copper.
B. steel. D. zinc.

____ 8. This man introduced improved dining cars, raising train travel to a new level of luxury.
A. George M. Pullman C. Eli H. Janney
B. George Westinghouse D. Gustavus Swift

____ 9. By the late 1880s, almost all railroad companies had adopted
A. iron tracks. C. air brakes.
B. five time zones. D. a standard gauge.

____ 10. The growing railroad network paved the way for American industry to
A. mass-produce. C. expand into the West.
B. consolidate. D. ship overseas.

Copyright © by The McGraw-Hill Companies, Inc.

The American Journey ★ 75 ★ Section Quizzes

Map Study

Answers

1. Southern Pacific
2. Kansas Pacific, Union Pacific, Central Pacific

Map Skills Practice

Reading a Map Which is the northernmost railroad shown? *(Great Northern)*

Where? When? Who? What?

Tourist Destinations Railroads brought Eastern tourists to places that once were remote and inaccessible—like the Grand Tetons in Wyoming. The Chicago, Burlington, and Quincy railroads, for example, conducted escorted tour groups.

CHAPTER 19
Section 1, 551–554

Reteaching Activity 19–1

Name ______ Date ______ Class ______

★ Reteaching Activity 19-1

DIRECTIONS: Organizing Facts The numbered items are associated with the different aspects of railroad expansion. Write the number of each item in the correct box on the chart. Some items may be used more than once.

United States Railroad Expansion in the Late 1800s
- Railroad Barons ______
- Economic Growth ______
- Competitive Practices ______
- Improvements and Technology ______
- Changes for Americans ______

★FACT BANK

1. The population is redistributed.	11. pools
2. Collis P. Huntington	12. construction companies
3. Gustavus Swift develops refrigerated cars.	13. George M. Pullman develops a luxury sleeping car.
4. iron mining and processing	14. Cornelius Vanderbilt
5. Industry shifts to the West.	15. The standard gauge is adopted.
6. railway equipment manufacturers	16. steel industry
7. Leland Stanford	17. George Westinghouse devises air brakes.
8. People move from rural areas to the cities more easily.	18. Eli H. Janney invents car couplers.
9. a national system of four time zones	19. lumber and coal industries
10. James J. Hill	20. rebates

DIRECTIONS: Essay On a separate sheet of paper, answer the question below. Define consolidation and explain how the railroad system was consolidated.

The American Journey ★ 75 ★ Reteaching Activities

Enrichment Activity 19–1

Name ______ Date ______ Class ______

★ Enrichment Activity 19-1 ★ ★

Trains

After the Civil War economic growth spread to the West and gradually to the South. The growing economy helped support new inventions and create new industries. Economic growth was evident in the railroad industry. With the influence of developing technology, the design of steam trains changed during the 1800s and early 1900s. Study the pictures of the steam trains.

Steam Train of the 1870s

Steam Train of the 1930s

DIRECTIONS: Comparing and Contrasting Complete the chart with the similarities and differences you can observe between the two trains.

Development of Steam Locomotives

Similarities	Differences
Ran on tracks	The 1930s train was streamlined.
Had headlights	The 1870s train was ornate.

Activity **DIRECTIONS:** Diesel trains of today are much different than those of the 1800s and 1900s. Research to find out more about modern trains such as the high speed trains of Europe and Japan. Should the United States invest in high speed passenger trains? Would such trains be good for the environment? Would they help conserve energy? Use what you learn to prepare a presentation that might be used to convince Congress to help fund the development of high speed trains. Then design materials to accompany your presentation and share them with your class.

The American Journey ★ 75 ★ Enrichment Activities

4 CLOSE

Point out that in medieval Europe, barons were nobles who usually had large estates with many serfs and to whom a number of knights owed allegiance. **Ask:** Why were men such as Hill and Vanderbilt called railroad barons?

---

railroads that could not match these rebates were often forced out of business. Giving discounts to big customers raised freight rates for farmers and other customers who shipped small amounts of goods.

The railroad barons also made secret agreements among themselves, known as **pools**. They divided the railway business among their companies and set rates for a region. With no other competition in its region, a railroad could charge higher rates and earn greater profits. Although Congress and some states passed laws to regulate the railroads, these laws did little to curb the railroad barons.

> **Linking PAST & PRESENT**
>
> **Return of the Train**
>
> Rising fuel costs and environmental concerns have revived interest in trains. Trains use less energy per passenger than do cars, airplanes, and buses. As a result, trains help conserve energy as more passengers use them.

Railroads Change America

The growing railroad network paved the way for American industry to expand into the West. The center of the flour milling industry, for example, shifted westward in the 1800s, moving from the East Coast to Ohio, to Minneapolis, and finally to Kansas City. Other industries followed the same pattern. As farmers settled the Great Plains, the manufacturing center for agricultural equipment moved from central New York State to Illinois and Wisconsin.

Railroads also touched the lives of thousands of Americans. Trains redistributed the population. They carried homesteaders into the Great Plains and the West. Trains also made it easy for people to move from rural areas to the cities.

Railroads affected the way Americans thought about time as well. As train travel became more common, people began measuring distances by how many hours the trip would take rather than by the number of miles traveled. The spread of the railroad system led to a national system of time with four time zones.

The railroads opened the entire United States to settlement and economic growth and united the different regions of the country into a single network. At the same time, inventions that revolutionized transportation and communication brought Americans together in new ways.

Section 1 Review

Checking for Understanding

1. ***Identify*** Cornelius Vanderbilt, James J. Hill, Collis P. Huntington, Gustavus Swift.
2. ***Define*** consolidation, standard gauge, rebate, pool.
3. ***Describe*** the methods used by railroad barons to drive smaller companies out of business.

Reviewing Themes

4. **Geography and History** How did the railroad pave the way for the expansion of industry in the West?

Critical Thinking

5. **Making Inferences** Do you think the federal government should have intervened to regulate the unfair practices of the railroad barons? Why or why not?

Activity

Designing an Advertisement Create an ad with words and pictures to announce the development of the new Pullman sleeping car.

Section 1 Review Answers

1. Cornelius Vanderbilt, 552; James J. Hill, 552; Collis P. Huntington, 552; Gustavus Swift, 553
2. The words are defined in the Glossary.
3. They bought smaller companies and used rebates, pools, and other unfair business practices.
4. It was easier to ship raw materials to factories and manufactured goods to markets.
5. Answers will vary. *Yes,* their practices made it difficult for small businesses to survive. *No,* the government should not be involved in regulating businesses. Our system of free enterprise should regulate itself.

Activity Ads should make people eager to try the new Pullman sleeping car.

Social Studies
SKILL BUILDER

Reading a Time Zones Map

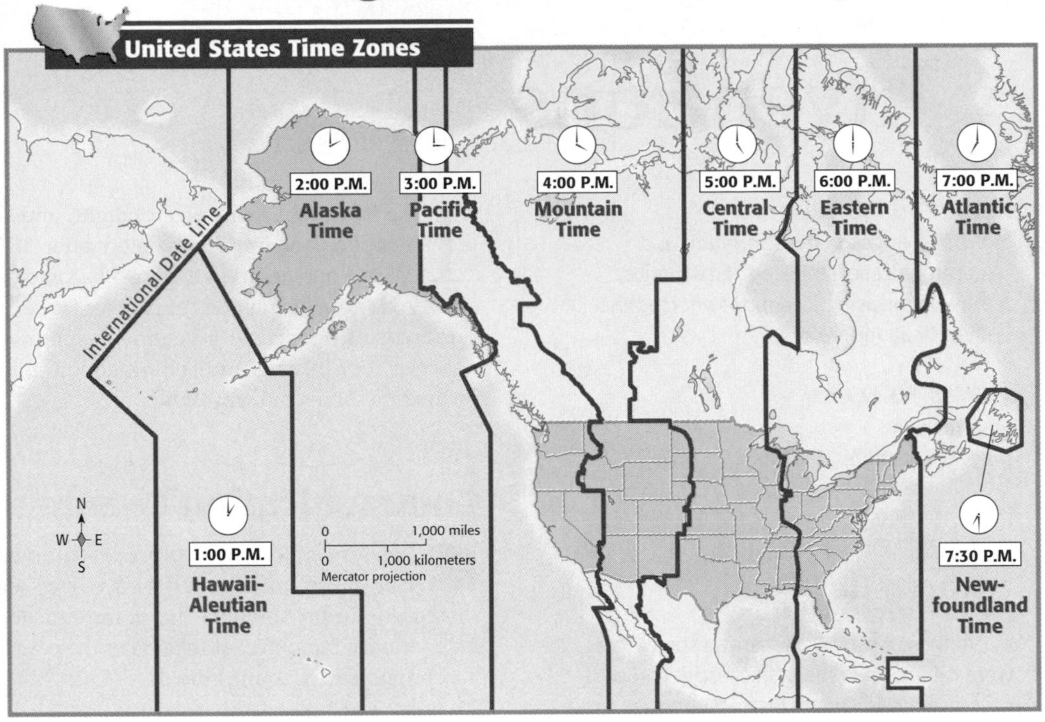

Learning the Skill

Earth's surface is divided into 24 time zones. The 0° line of longitude—the Prime Meridian—is the starting point for figuring time around the world. To read a time zones map, follow these steps:

- Locate a place where you know what time it is and select another place where you wish to know the time.
- Notice the time zones you cross between these places.
- If the second place lies east of the first, add an hour for each time zone. If it lies west, subtract an hour for each zone.

Practicing the Skill

1. What U.S. time zone lies farthest west?
2. If it is 6:00 P.M. in Washington, D.C., what time is it in San Diego, California?

Applying the Skill

Reading a Time Zones Map It takes two hours to fly from Denver, Colorado, to Chicago, Illinois. If you leave Denver at 2:00 A.M. Friday, what time will it be in Chicago when you arrive?

ANSWERS TO PRACTICING THE SKILL

1. Hawaii-Aleutian Time
2. 3:00 P.M.

Applying the Skill: 5:00 A.M.

Social Studies
SKILL BUILDER

TEACH

Reading a Time Zones Map

This skill teaches students how to read and use maps that provide time zone information. Point out that time zones are needed because the earth makes one complete rotation every 24 hours. As the earth spins, dawn comes to each part of the earth in turn, about one hour apart for every 15 degrees of longitude ($24 \times 15 = 360°$). **Ask:** **What would happen if everyone on the earth had their clocks set to the same time?**

Point out to students that most of the 180° line of longitude is called the International Date Line. If you travel east across this line, you add one day. If you travel west across this line, you subtract one day.

Additional Practice

Chapter Skills Activity 19

CHAPTER 19
Section 2, 556–559

1 FOCUS

BELLRINGER
Motivational Activity

Before taking roll at the beginning of the class period, project Section Focus Transparency 19–2 and have students answer the questions. Discuss students' responses.

This activity is also available as a blackline master.

Section Focus Transparency 19–2

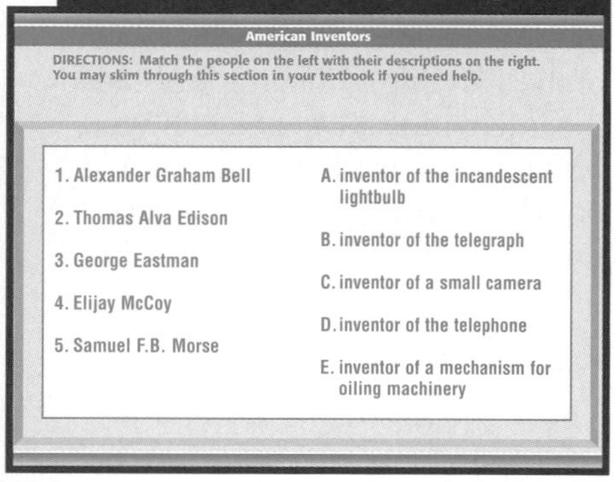
American Inventors

DIRECTIONS: Match the people on the left with their descriptions on the right. You may skim through this section in your textbook if you need help.

1. Alexander Graham Bell	A. inventor of the incandescent lightbulb
2. Thomas Alva Edison	B. inventor of the telegraph
3. George Eastman	C. inventor of a small camera
4. Elijay McCoy	D. inventor of the telephone
5. Samuel F.B. Morse	E. inventor of a mechanism for oiling machinery

Vocabulary Precheck
Have students explain how *assembly line* and *mass production* are related.

Use the **Vocabulary PuzzleMaker** to create crossword and word search puzzles.

Section Theme
Science and Technology

New inventions helped unify the different regions of the country and promoted economic growth.

Activity Have students find in the section an invention or improvement that changed transportation, communication, and daily life.

History *and the* Humanities

The Spirit of American Art and Music, Thomas Eakins

1870 — 1890 — 1910

1868 Christopher Sholes invents the typewriter

1876 Alexander Bell develops the telephone

1879 Edison develops first practical lightbulb

1903 The Wright brothers fly at Kitty Hawk

1908 Henry Ford introduces the Model T

Section 2

Inventions

READ TO DISCOVER . . .
- what changes in transportation and communication transformed America.
- how laborsaving inventions affected the lives of all Americans.

TERMS TO LEARN
assembly line
mass production

The Storyteller

In the early 1900s, American songwriters were caught up in the public fascination with new inventions. One of the most popular songs of 1905, "In My Merry Oldsmobile," celebrated the automobile:

"Come away with me Lucile,
In my merry Oldsmobile.
Down the road of life we'll fly,
Automobubbling you and I.
To the church we'll swiftly
steal,
Then our wedding
bells will peal;
You can go as far
as you like, . . .
In my merry
Oldsmobile."

Hood ornament

The automobile, the electric light, and the telephone were all invented after 1870. Within a generation they had become part of everyday life for millions of people. These and hundreds of other new inventions, along with new ways of buying and selling goods, transformed the American way of life.

Communication Changes

New inventions helped people communicate more quickly and easily over long distances. Improvements in communication helped unify the different regions of the country and promoted economic growth.

The Telegraph

Samuel F.B. Morse had introduced the telegraph in 1844. By 1860 the United States had thousands of miles of telegraph lines, controlled for the most part by the Western Union Telegraph Company. At telegraph offices, trained operators transmitted people's messages in Morse code. Telegrams offered almost instant communication and had many uses. Shopkeepers relied on telegrams to order goods, and reporters used them to transmit stories to their newspapers. Americans also began sending personal messages by telegram.

The telegraph soon linked the United States and Europe. In the 1860s news from Europe traveled to this country by ship and took several weeks. **Cyrus Field** wanted to speed up the

SECTION RESOURCES

Reproducible Masters
- Reproducible Lesson Plan 19–2
- Guided Reading Activity 19–2
- Section Quiz 19–2
- Reteaching Activity 19–2
- Enrichment Activity 19–2

Transparencies
- Section Focus Transparency 19–2

Multimedia
- Vocabulary PuzzleMaker
- Chapter Challenger Interactive Review
- Testmaker
- GTV: A Geographic Perspective on American History
- ABCNews InterActive™ Historic America Electronic Field Trips

process. After several unsuccessful attempts, Field managed to lay a telegraph cable across the Atlantic Ocean in 1866. The new transatlantic telegraph carried messages in a matter of seconds, bringing the United States and Europe closer together.

Inventions of the Late 1800s

Inventor	Date	Invention
Elisha Otis	1852	elevator brake
Henry Bessemer	1856	Bessemer process
George Pullman	1864	rail sleeping car
Thaddeus Lowe	1865	ice machine
George Westinghouse	1868	air brake
Stephen Dudley Field	1874	electric streetcar
Alexander Graham Bell	1876	telephone
Thomas Alva Edison	1877	phonograph
Anna Baldwin	1878	milking machine
Thomas Alva Edison	1879	incandescent lightbulb
James Ritty	1879	cash register
Lewis Howard Latimer	1882	improved lightbulb filament
Jan E. Matzeliger	1883	shoemaking machine
Sarah E. Goode	1885	folding cabinet bed
Granville T. Woods	1887	automatic air brake
Charles and J. Frank Duryea	1893	gasoline-powered car
John Thurman	1899	vacuum cleaner

Chart Study

Inventions helped the American economy prosper and expand in the late 1800s.

1. Which of the above inventions still affects your life today?
2. **Comparing** How many of the inventions listed above were used outside of the home?

Biography

The Telephone Rings In

Alexander Graham Bell invented a device that revolutionized communications even more than Morse's telegraph. Born and educated in Scotland, Bell moved to the United States, where he studied ways of teaching people who were hearing impaired to speak. At the same time, he experimented with sending voices through electrical wires.

By 1876 Bell developed a device that transmitted speech—the telephone. While Bell was preparing to test the device, he accidentally spilled some battery acid on his clothes. In panic Bell called out to his assistant in another room: "Mr. Watson, come here. I want you!" Watson heard Bell's voice coming through the telephone. The invention was a success.

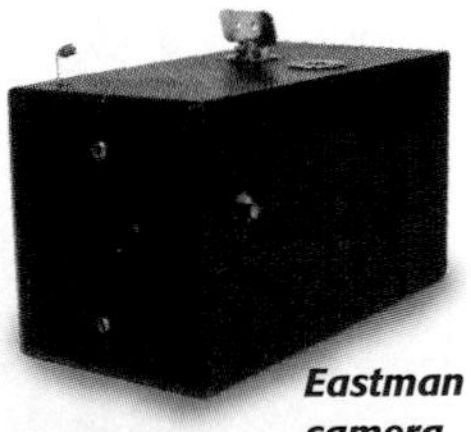

Eastman camera

Bell's phone transmitter

Bell formed the Bell Telephone Company in 1877. By the 1890s he had sold nearly 500,000 phones. Most early telephone customers were businesses. Before long, though, telephones became common in homes.

The Genius of Invention

The late 1800s saw a burst of inventiveness in the United States. Between 1860 and 1890, the United States government granted more than 400,000 patents for new inventions.

Many of the inventions helped businesses operate more efficiently. Among these were Christopher Sholes's typewriter (1868) and William Burroughs's adding machine (1888).

Other inventions affected everyday life. In 1888 **George Eastman** invented a small camera

Cooperative Learning Activity

Writing a Newspaper Article Have students work in pairs and choose an appliance, a toy or game, or a machine that they like or use often. Students should imagine that it is a new invention and that they are newspaper journalists describing the invention to other people. Students' articles should not name the product, but explain what it does, how it works, and what it looks like. After planning the article together, one student should write it and the other should act as editor to correct spelling and so on. Encourage students to make their writing reflect the excitement that people in the late 1880s must have felt when they learned about a new invention. Have pairs swap articles with other pairs and try to guess each other's inventions.

2 TEACH

L1, ELL Ranking Inventions Have students choose from the section five inventions or improvements and rank them in importance. Have volunteers read their lists aloud and ask the other students to challenge the volunteers' choices/rankings.

Chart Study

Answers

1. Have students explain their answers.
2. 10

Guided Reading Activity 19–2

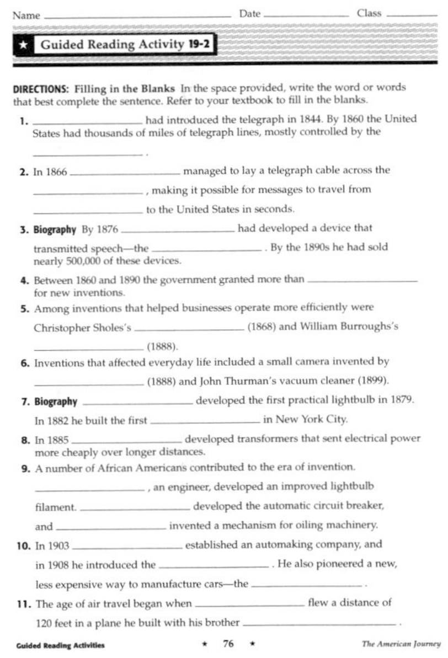

Name ______ Date ______ Class ______

★ Guided Reading Activity 19-2

DIRECTIONS: Filling in the Blanks In the space provided, write the word or words that best complete the sentence. Refer to your textbook to fill in the blanks.

1. ______ had introduced the telegraph in 1844. By 1860 the United States had thousands of miles of telegraph lines, mostly controlled by the ______.
2. In 1866 ______ managed to lay a telegraph cable across the ______, making it possible for messages to travel from ______ to the United States in seconds.
3. **Biography** By 1876 ______ had developed a device that transmitted speech—the ______. By the 1890s he had sold nearly 500,000 of these devices.
4. Between 1860 and 1890 the government granted more than ______ for new inventions.
5. Among inventions that helped businesses operate more efficiently were Christopher Sholes's ______ (1868) and William Burroughs's ______ (1888).
6. Inventions that affected everyday life included a small camera invented by ______ (1888) and John Thurman's vacuum cleaner (1899).
7. **Biography** ______ developed the first practical lightbulb in 1879. In 1882 he built the first ______ in New York City.
8. In 1885 ______ developed transformers that sent electrical power more cheaply over longer distances.
9. A number of African Americans contributed to the era of invention. ______, an engineer, developed an improved lightbulb filament. ______ developed the automatic circuit breaker, and ______ invented a mechanism for oiling machinery.
10. In 1903 ______ established an automaking company, and in 1908 he introduced the ______. He also pioneered a new, less expensive way to manufacture cars—the ______.
11. The age of air travel began when ______ flew a distance of 120 feet in a plane he built with his brother ______.

Guided Reading Activities ★ 76 ★ *The American Journey*

NATIONAL GEOGRAPHIC SOCIETY

VIDEODISC
GTV: A Geographic Perspective on American History

Side 4, Chapter 1

Title: *Modern Times*
Ask: What technology changed lifestyles in the early 1900s? *(airplanes, automobiles, telephones, and electric lights)*

ABCNEWS INTERACTIVE™

VIDEODISC
Historic America Electronic Field Trips

Side 2, Chapter 5

Title: *Thomas Edison's Lab*
Ask: **What are at least three inventions of Edison's?** *(movie camera, alkaline battery, lightbulb, phonograph)*

Also available in VHS.

3 ASSESS

Assign Section 2 Review as homework or as an in-class activity.

Use **Chapter Challenger Interactive Review Software** to review Section 2.

Section Quiz 19–2

Name ______________ Date ________ Class ________

★ Chapter 19

Score

Section Quiz 19-2

DIRECTIONS: Matching Match each item in Column A with the items in Column B. Write the correct letters in the blanks. *(10 points each)*

Column A	Column B
____ **1.** Jan E. Matzeliger	**A.** developed improved lightbulb filament
____ **2.** Alexander Graham Bell	**B.** invented shoemaking machine
____ **3.** Lewis Howard Latimer	**C.** introduced Model T
____ **4.** Henry Ford	**D.** built engine-powered airplane
____ **5.** Orville and Wilbur Wright	**E.** developed the telephone

DIRECTIONS: Multiple Choice In the blank at the left, write the letter of the choice that best completes the statement or answers the question. *(10 points each)*

____ **6.** This man laid a telegraph cable across the Atlantic Ocean in 1866.
A. George Westinghouse **C.** George Pullman
B. Cyrus Field **D.** John Thurman

____ **7.** The inventor of the typewriter was
A. Alexander Graham Bell. **C.** William Burroughs.
B. Thomas Alva Edison. **D.** Christopher Sholes.

____ **8.** Thomas Alva Edison's most important invention was the
A. electric lightbulb. **C.** camera.
B. vacuum cleaner. **D.** automatic circuit breakers.

____ **9.** This man was responsible for creating the assembly line.
A. George Westinghouse **C.** Henry Ford
B. Granville Woods **D.** Charles Sorenson

____ **10.** With brother Wilbur watching, Orville Wright took off in the first engine-powered plane and flew
A. 10 feet. **C.** 12 feet.
B. 120 feet. **D.** 100 feet.

Section Quizzes ★ 76 ★ *The American Journey*

Thomas Edison displays his phonograph

that made it easier and less costly to take photographs. **John Thurman** developed a vacuum cleaner in 1899 that simplified housework.

Biography

Thomas Alva Edison

Thomas Alva Edison was born in Ohio in 1847. While still in his 20s, Edison decided to go into the "invention business." In 1876, Edison set up a workshop in **Menlo Park, New Jersey.** His goal was to produce "a minor invention every ten days and a big thing every six months or so." Edison usually had 30 or 40 projects under way at one time. His workshop was the country's first industrial research laboratory.

Edison received more than 1,000 patents in his lifetime. Out of his laboratory came the phonograph, the motion picture projector, the telephone transmitter, the storage battery, and the dictating machine. Edison's most important invention was the electric lightbulb.

Edison developed the first practical lightbulb in 1879. He then designed power plants that could produce electric power and distribute it to lightbulbs. For Christmas 1880, Edison used 40 bulbs to light up Menlo Park. Visitors flocked to see the "light of the future." He built the first central electric power plant in 1882 in New York City—illuminating 85 buildings.

Electricity Transforms the Nation

Inventor **George Westinghouse** took Edison's work a step further. In 1885 Westinghouse developed and built transformers that could send electric power more cheaply over longer distances. Soon electricity powered factories, trolleys, streetlights, and lamps all over America.

African American Inventors

A number of African Americans contributed to the era of invention. **Lewis Howard Latimer,** an engineer, developed an improved filament for the lightbulb and joined Thomas Edison's company. **Granville Woods,** an electrical and mechanical engineer from Ohio, patented 35 inventions. Among them were an electric incubator and railroad improvements such as an electromagnetic brake and an automatic circuit breaker. **Elijah McCoy** invented a mechanism for oiling machinery.

Jan E. Matzeliger, another African American inventor, developed a shoemaking machine that performed many steps previously done by hand.

Lewis Howard Latimer and his patent drawing of a lamp fixture

MULTIPLE LEARNING STYLES

Interpersonal Have each student make a list of all the electrical equipment in his or her home (refrigerator, TV, computer, radio, washing machine, and so forth). Then have students ask their parents to check off the ones that were in their homes when they were growing up. Finally, have students ask their grandparents or older friends to do the same. Have students discuss the answer to this question: **What do the lists tell you about the explosion of inventions in the recent past?** **L1, ELL**

His device, which revolutionized the shoe industry, was adopted in shoe factories in the United States and overseas.

Transportation Changes

In the 1900s two inventions ushered in a new era of transportation. After a period of experimentation, the automobile became a practical method of getting from place to place. Then the airplane forever changed long-distance travel.

Henry Ford's Automobiles

Henry Ford wanted to build an inexpensive car that would last a lifetime. While working as an engineer in **Detroit, Michigan,** in the 1890s, Ford had experimented with an automobile engine powered by gasoline. In 1903 he established an automaking company and began designing cars.

In 1906 Ford had an idea for a new type of car. He told Charles Sorenson, later Ford's general superintendent, "We're going to get a car now that we can make in great volume and get the prices way down." For the next year, Ford and Sorenson worked on the **Model T**, building the car and testing it on rough roads. In 1908 Ford introduced the Model T to the public. Sorenson described the sturdy black vehicle as

Model T Ford

> "... a car which anyone could afford to buy, which anyone could drive anywhere, and which almost anyone could keep in repair."

These qualities made the Model T immensely popular. During the next 18 years, Ford's company sold 15 million Model T's. Henry Ford also pioneered a new, less expensive way to manufacture cars—the **assembly line.** On the assembly line, each worker performed an assigned task again and again at a certain stage in the production of the automobile. The assembly line revolutionized industry, enabling manufacturers to produce large quantities of goods more quickly. This **mass production** of goods decreased manufacturing costs, so products could be sold more cheaply.

Taking to the Air

Inventors experimented with engine-powered aircraft in the 1800s, but the age of air travel did not begin until 1903 at **Kitty Hawk, North Carolina. Orville** and **Wilbur Wright,** brothers and bicycle mechanics, built a wood-and-canvas plane with a 12-horsepower engine. On the morning of December 17, Orville Wright took off in their plane and flew a distance of 120 feet.

Section 2 Review

Checking for Understanding

1. ***Identify*** Cyrus Field, Alexander Graham Bell, Thomas Alva Edison, Granville Woods, Henry Ford, Orville and Wilbur Wright.
2. ***Define*** assembly line, mass production.
3. ***Name*** two inventions that changed the way people communicated in the 1800s.

Reviewing Themes

4. **Science and Technology** How was transportation improved during the early 1900s?

Critical Thinking

5. **Determining Relevance** Which invention do you think brought about the most dramatic change in people's lives? Explain.

Activity

Making a Chart Design a chart of inventors discussed in this section. Your chart should include inventors' names, what each invented and when, and a drawing of each of their inventions.

Section 2 Review Answers

1. Field, 556; Bell, 557; Edison, 558; Woods, 558; Ford, 559; Wright brothers, 559
2. The words are defined in the Glossary.
3. Any two: telegraph, telephone, phonograph, camera, motion picture projector, dictating machine
4. Transportation was improved by the following inventions: gasoline-powered car, airplane, electromagnetic train brake, automatic circuit breaker for railroads.
5. Answers will vary but should be well supported.

Activity Charts should be designed appropriately.

Reteaching Activity 19–2

Name ______ Date ______ Class ______

★ Reteaching Activity **19-2**

DIRECTIONS: Completing a Chart Use the chart below to review the inventions and developments of the mid-1800s to early 1900s. For each item listed in the chart, write the name of the inventor associated with it and briefly describe the result or impact of it. A few examples have been provided.

Inventions, 1840–1920

telegraph	telephone	typewriter
Samuel F.B. Morse—Reporters used it to send newspaper stories.		
adding machine	**small camera**	**vacuum cleaner**
electric lightbulb	**power plant**	**long-distance transformer**
	Thomas A. Edison—Electric power could be distributed to many lightbulbs at once.	
lightbulb filament	**electromagnetic break and automatic circuit breaker**	**shoemaking machine**
Lewis Howard Latimer—Bulbs lasted longer and were brighter and more reliable.		
Model T automobile	**assembly line**	**airplane with 12-horsepower engine**

Reteaching Activities ★ 76 ★ *The American Journey*

Enrichment Activity 19–2

Name ______ Date ______ Class ______

★ Enrichment Activity **19-2** ★

Inventions

During the late 1800s the government granted many patents for new inventions to inventors. One of the most famous inventors was Thomas Alva Edison. Elias Howe was another inventor of note. The pictures below show inventions made in the mid-1800s. Study each picture. Then do research about these two men to determine what each invention is and which man invented which machine.

DIRECTIONS: Drawing Conclusions On the lines provided, identify the invention and explain how it operated. Give the inventor and the year of the invention.

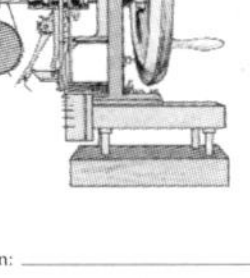

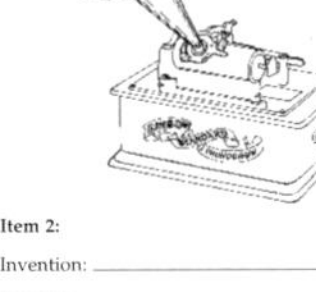

Item 1:
Invention: ______
Inventor: ______
Date: ______
How It Worked: ______

Item 2:
Invention: ______
Inventor: ______
Date: ______
How It Worked: ______

Activity **DIRECTIONS:** Choose one of the inventions above and, on a separate sheet of paper, draw a picture of its modern counterpart. Then write an advertisement for your machine that explains its special features and why someone would want to purchase it.

Enrichment Activities ★ 76 ★ *The American Journey*

4 CLOSE

In 1878 a newspaper printed a headline that read: "Edison Invents a Machine That Will Feed the Human Race—Manufacturing Biscuits, Meat, Vegetables, and Wind out of Air, Water, and Common Earth." **Ask:** **What does this April Fool's headline suggest about Edison?**

1859	1870	1890	1900
Oil discovered in Titusville, Pennsylvania	Rockefeller organizes the Standard Oil Company	Sherman Antitrust Act prohibits monopolies	Andrew Carnegie rules the steel industry

Section 3

An Age of Big Business

1 FOCUS

BELLRINGER
Motivational Activity

Before taking roll at the beginning of the class period, project Section Focus Transparency 19–3 and have students answer the questions. Discuss students' responses.

This activity is also available as a blackline master.

Section Focus Transparency 19–3

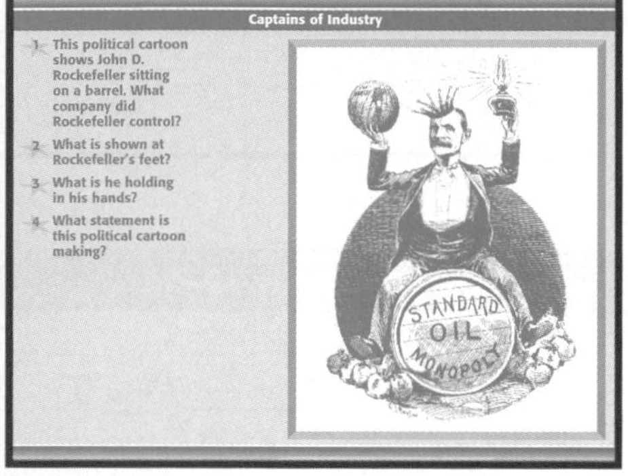

Vocabulary Precheck
Ask volunteers to define the **Terms to Learn** that they know. Have students find the definitions for the remaining terms and use each term in a sentence.

Use the **Vocabulary PuzzleMaker** to create crossword and word search puzzles.

Section Theme
Economic Factors

One of the major economic developments of the late 1800s was the growth of corporations, particularly in oil and steel.

Activity Have students find what discoveries led to the growth of the steel industry. *(Bessemer and open-hearth processes)*

READ TO DISCOVER . . .
- how new discoveries and inventions helped the steel and oil industries grow.
- why the development of large corporations brought both benefits and problems.

TERMS TO LEARN
corporation	trust
stock	monopoly
shareholder	vertical integration
dividend	philanthropy
horizontal integration	merger

The Storyteller

John D. Rockefeller, a young oil man, never tired until he got what he wanted. One person commented: "The only time I ever saw John Rockefeller enthusiastic was when a report came in . . . that his buyer had secured a cargo of oil at a figure much below the market price. He bounded from his chair with a shout of joy, danced up and down, hugged me, threw up his hat, acted so like a madman that I have never forgotten it. . . ."

John D. Rockefeller

In the hills of western Pennsylvania, a sticky black substance—petroleum—seeped from the ground. For a while promoters sold the oil as medicine. Then in the 1850s researchers found they could burn petroleum to produce heat and smoke-free light. It could also be used to lubricate machinery. Suddenly oil became valuable.

A former railroad conductor named Edwin L. Drake believed that he could find petroleum by digging a well—just as he might dig a well for water. People thought Drake was wrong. Few people knew that pools of oil did indeed exist underground.

In 1859 Drake decided to test his belief. He drilled a well in **Titusville, Pennsylvania,** and struck oil. This led to the creation of a multimillion-dollar petroleum industry.

With the economy growing after the Civil War, many railroads and other businesses looked for ways to expand. To do so they had to raise capital, or money. They needed capital to buy raw materials and equipment, to pay workers, and to cover shipping and advertising costs.

Economics

The Corporation

One way a company could raise capital was by becoming a **corporation**—a company that sold shares, or **stock,** of its business to the public. The people who invested in the corporation by buying stock were its **shareholders,** or partial owners.

SECTION RESOURCES

Reproducible Masters
- Political Cartoons
- Section Quiz 19–3
- Enrichment Activity 19–3
- Reteaching Activity 19–3

Transparencies
- Section Focus Transparency 19–3
- U.S. History & Art, Transparency 14

Multimedia
- Vocabulary PuzzleMaker
- Chapter Challenger Interactive Review
- Testmaker
- GTV: A Geographic Perspective on American History
- Facts On File: Landmark Documents in American History

In good times shareholders earned **dividends**—cash payments from the corporation's profits—on the stock they owned. If the company prospered, its stock rose in value, and the shareholders could sell it for a profit. If the company failed, however, the shareholders lost their investment. Hundreds of thousands of people shared in corporate profits by buying and selling stocks in special markets known as **stock exchanges.**

Growth of Corporations

Railroads were the first businesses to form corporations, or incorporate. Soon manufacturing firms and other businesses were incorporating as well. The growth of corporations helped fuel America's industrial expansion in the years following the Civil War.

Banks played a major role in this period of economic growth. Businesses borrowed money from banks to start or expand their operations. The banks, in turn, made profits on the loans.

The Oil Business

The oil industry grew rapidly in the late 1800s. Edwin Drake's Titusville well produced 15 barrels of petroleum a day. As word of his success spread, prospectors and investors hurried to western Pennsylvania. "Oil rush" towns with names such as Oil City and Petroleum Center sprang up overnight. The oil boom expanded as prospectors struck oil in Ohio and West Virginia.

Biography

John D. Rockefeller

Born in Richford, New York, in 1839, **John D. Rockefeller** made his fortune from oil. When Rockefeller was 26 years old, he and four partners set up an oil refinery—a plant to process oil—in **Cleveland, Ohio.**

Picturing HISTORY Cartoons of the day often portrayed Standard Oil as a "monopoly monster," with its arms reaching out to control government and suppliers.
How did Standard Oil gain a monopoly of the oil industry?

COOPERATIVE LEARNING ACTIVITY

Making a Flowchart Have students work together in small groups to make a flowchart showing how steel is made. Charts should begin with the raw materials (iron ore, limestone, and coal) and end with the finished products that are made from the slabs, blooms, and billets of steel that are produced by the steel mill. Some students may do the research, while others design and execute the chart. The finished charts may be displayed on the bulletin board.

2 TEACH

L1 Making Comparisons Have students compare the game Monopoly with the monopolies built by Carnegie, Rockefeller, and the other magnates. **Ask:** **What are the similarities?** *(To win, you need large amounts of property and control of railroads and utilities.)*

Guided Reading Activity 19–3

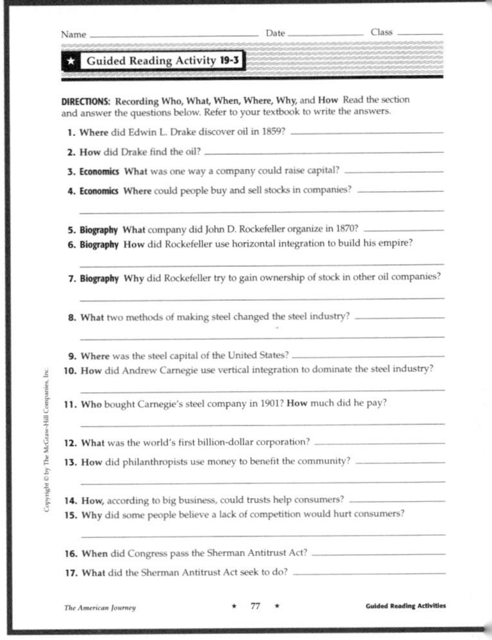
Name ______ Date ______ Class ______

Guided Reading Activity 19-3

DIRECTIONS: Recording Who, What, When, Where, Why, and **How** Read the section and answer the questions below. Refer to your textbook to write the answers.

1. **Where** did Edwin L. Drake discover oil in 1859? ______
2. **How** did Drake find the oil? ______
3. **Economics What** was one way a company could raise capital? ______
4. **Economics Where** could people buy and sell stocks in companies? ______
5. **Biography What** company did John D. Rockefeller organize in 1870? ______
6. **Biography How** did Rockefeller use horizontal integration to build his empire? ______
7. **Biography Why** did Rockefeller try to gain ownership of stock in other oil companies? ______
8. **What** two methods of making steel changed the steel industry? ______
9. **Where** was the steel capital of the United States? ______
10. **How** did Andrew Carnegie use vertical integration to dominate the steel industry? ______
11. **Who** bought Carnegie's steel company in 1901? **How** much did he pay? ______
12. **What** was the world's first billion-dollar corporation? ______
13. **How** did philanthropists use money to benefit the community? ______
14. **How,** according to big business, could trusts help consumers? ______
15. **Why** did some people believe a lack of competition would hurt consumers? ______
16. **When** did Congress pass the Sherman Antitrust Act? ______
17. **What** did the Sherman Antitrust Act seek to do? ______

The American Journey ★ 77 ★ **Guided Reading Activities**

Picturing HISTORY Rockefeller and Carnegie believed that competition was wasteful. **Answer:** *bought most refineries, produced its own supplies and equipment, lowered prices to drive competition out of business, pressured customers not to deal with competition, got rebates from railroads, formed trust to gain stock of remaining competing firms*

Facts On File

CD-ROM
Landmark Documents in American History

Title: *The Gospels of Wealth, Andrew Carnegie, 1889*
Have students read Carnegie's "Wealth" and "The Best Friends for Philanthropy" essays and summarize their findings.

American Memories

The Gilded Age

The name *Gilded Age* comes from the title of a novel written by Mark Twain and Charles Dudley Warner. The two writers felt that the flashy, get-rich-quick society of the post–Civil War times in which they were living was like a gilded object—attractive on the surface, but cheap underneath.
Answer: *opera*

NATIONAL GEOGRAPHIC SOCIETY

VIDEODISC
GTV: A Geographic Perspective on American History

Side 3, Chapter 8
Title: *The March of Industry*
Subject: Growth of American industry (1875–1900)
Ask: **What resources were required to operate industries in 1900?** *(coal, oil, iron ore, steel)*

Who?What?Where?When?

Gustavus Swift Among the tremendously wealthy magnates of the late 1800s was Gustavus Swift (1839–1903). At the age of 16, Swift borrowed $25, bought a cow, slaughtered it, and sold the meat at a $10 profit. He devoted his life to making money from meat.

History *and the* Humanities

- U.S. History and Art, Transparency 14, *Smoking Room*
- The Spirit of American Art and Music, Richard Morris Hunt

American Memories: *The Gilded Age*

What Was It Like? Well-to-do industrial leaders lived in elegant luxury. **What cultural activity—as shown in the artifacts here—did wealthy Americans enjoy during this period?**

In 1870 Rockefeller organized the Standard Oil Company of Ohio and set out to dominate the oil industry. He acquired most of the oil refineries in Cleveland and other cities.

One method Rockefeller used to build his empire was **horizontal integration**—the combining of competing firms into one corporation. The corporation produced and used its own tank cars, pipelines, and even its own wooden barrels—made from forests owned by Standard Oil. Standard Oil grew in wealth and power, becoming the most famous corporate empire of the day.

The Standard Oil Trust

To strengthen Standard Oil's position in the oil industry, Rockefeller lowered his prices to drive his competitors out of business. In addition he pressured customers not to deal with rival oil companies, and he persuaded the railroads to grant him rebates in exchange for his business.

Rockefeller increased his control of the oil industry in 1882 by forming a **trust,** a group of companies managed by the same board of directors. First he acquired stock in many different oil companies. Then the shareholders of these companies traded their stock for Standard Oil stock, which paid higher dividends. This gave Standard Oil's board of directors ownership of the other companies' stock and the right to manage those companies. Rockefeller had created a **monopoly**—total control by a single producer—of the oil industry.

The Steel Business

Steel also became a huge business in the late 1800s. A form of iron treated with carbon, steel is strong and long-lasting—the ideal material for railroad tracks, bridges, and many other products. Before the 1860s, however, steel was not widely used because of the high cost of manufacturing it. The development of new manufacturing techniques helped to overcome this problem.

MULTIPLE LEARNING STYLES

Kinesthetic Have students use library or Internet resources to find drawings and diagrams of Edwin Drake's oil well. Then have students make a model of the well, using 1-inch by 1-inch pine wood trim and 1½-inch flat pine molding. The model may be constructed on a plywood base and should have labels explaining the parts and how they worked. Some students may prefer to use similar materials to make a labeled model of a modern oil well. **L3,** ELL

Steel Industry Growth

Two new methods of making steel—the Bessemer process, developed by Henry Bessemer of England, and the open-hearth process—changed the industry. With the new methods, mills could produce steel at affordable prices and in large quantities.

In the 1870s large steel mills emerged in western Pennsylvania and eastern Ohio, close to sources of iron ore. **Pittsburgh, Pennsylvania,** became the steel capital of the United States. Cleveland, Chicago, Detroit, and Birmingham, Alabama, also became centers of steel production.

Andrew Carnegie

The leading figure in the early years of the American steel industry was **Andrew Carnegie,** son of a Scottish immigrant. Starting as a telegraph operator, Carnegie worked his way up to become manager of the Pennsylvania Railroad. In 1865 he left that job to invest in the growing iron industry.

Carnegie soon realized that steel would have an enormous market. After learning about the Bessemer process, he built a steel plant near Pittsburgh that used the new process. Carnegie named the plant the J. Edgar Thompson Steel Works, after the president of the Pennsylvania Railroad—his biggest customer.

Vertical Integration

By 1890 Andrew Carnegie dominated the steel industry. His company became powerful through **vertical integration,** acquiring companies that provided the equipment and services he needed. Carnegie bought iron and coal mines, warehouses, ore ships, and railroads to gain control of all parts of the business of making and selling steel. When Carnegie combined all his holdings into the Carnegie Steel Company in 1900, he was producing one-third of the nation's steel.

In 1901 Carnegie sold his steel company to banker **J. Pierpont Morgan** for $450 million. Morgan combined the Carnegie company with other businesses to form the United States Steel Corporation, the world's first billion-dollar corporation.

Philanthropists

Andrew Carnegie, John D. Rockefeller, and other industrial millionaires of the time grew interested in **philanthropy**—the use of money to benefit the community. The philanthropists founded schools, universities, and other civic institutions across the United States.

Carnegie donated $350 million to various organizations. He built Carnegie Hall in New York City, one of the world's most celebrated concert halls; the Carnegie Foundation for the Advancement of Teaching; and more than 2,000 libraries worldwide. Rockefeller used his fortune to establish the University of Chicago in 1892 and New York's Rockefeller Institute for Medical Research.

Corporations Grow Larger

In 1889 New Jersey encouraged the trend toward business monopolies by allowing holding companies to obtain charters, a practice

Andrew Carnegie

CHAPTER 19
Section 3, 560–564

Political Cartoons, *Battle Against the Trusts*

Who?What?Where?When?

Andrew Carnegie When Carnegie entered the iron business, he invested in one company that made rails and another that made locomotives. His shrewdest move, however, was to buy the Keystone Bridge Company, which soon became the leading maker of iron bridges. "I saw," Carnegie said later, ". . . that it would never do to depend further upon wooden bridges for permanent railway structures." Carnegie was very pleased with the bridges his company made—other bridges had given way under wind pressure, but not Keystone bridges. As Carnegie observed, "We were our own severest inspectors, and would build a safe structure or none at all."

3 ASSESS

Assign Section 3 Review as homework or as an in-class activity.

Use **Chapter Challenger Interactive Review Software** to review Section 3.

Section Quiz 19–3

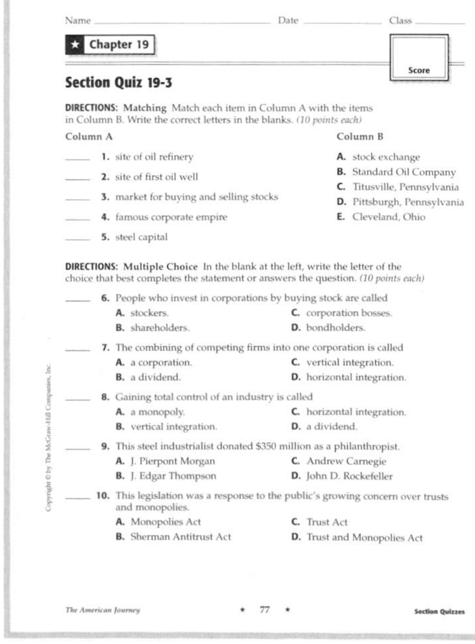

Name ______ Date ______ Class ______

★ Chapter 19 — Score

Section Quiz 19-3

DIRECTIONS: Matching Match each item in Column A with the items in Column B. Write the correct letters in the blanks. *(10 points each)*

Column A	Column B
____ 1. site of oil refinery	A. stock exchange
____ 2. site of first oil well	B. Standard Oil Company
____ 3. market for buying and selling stocks	C. Titusville, Pennsylvania
____ 4. famous corporate empire	D. Pittsburgh, Pennsylvania
____ 5. steel capital	E. Cleveland, Ohio

DIRECTIONS: Multiple Choice In the blank at the left, write the letter of the choice that best completes the statement or answers the question. *(10 points each)*

____ 6. People who invest in corporations by buying stock are called
A. stockers. C. corporation bosses.
B. shareholders. D. bondholders.

____ 7. The combining of competing firms into one corporation is called
A. a corporation. C. vertical integration.
B. a dividend. D. horizontal integration.

____ 8. Gaining total control of an industry is called
A. a monopoly. C. horizontal integration.
B. vertical integration. D. a dividend.

____ 9. This steel industrialist donated $350 million as a philanthropist.
A. J. Pierpont Morgan C. Andrew Carnegie
B. J. Edgar Thompson D. John D. Rockefeller

____ 10. This legislation was a response to the public's growing concern over trusts and monopolies.
A. Monopolies Act C. Trust Act
B. Sherman Antitrust Act D. Trust and Monopolies Act

The American Journey ★ 77 ★ Section Quizzes

MAKING CONNECTIONS ACTIVITY

Architecture The Gilded Age saw the construction of huge and elaborate mansions by industrial millionaires; some of them were "cottages" used only in the summer. Newport, Rhode Island, has preserved many such mansions, which are open to the public from spring through fall. Biltmore House in Asheville, North Carolina—constructed by Cornelius Vanderbilt's grandson George W. Vanderbilt—is another example of a Gilded Age mansion. If such mansions are geographically accessible and open to the public, take your class on a field trip to one of them. If not, perhaps there is a building constructed during this time period in your local area that can be visited by your class. If a field trip is impossible, have students find illustrated books about the Gilded Age mansions and sketch pictures of their favorite mansion. **L1, ELL**

Reteaching Activity 19–3

Name ______________ Date ________ Class ________

★ Reteaching Activity 19-3

DIRECTIONS: Completing a Venn Diagram The items in the Fact Bank are associated with John D. Rockefeller, Andrew Carnegie, or both. Write the letter of each item in the correct section of the diagram.

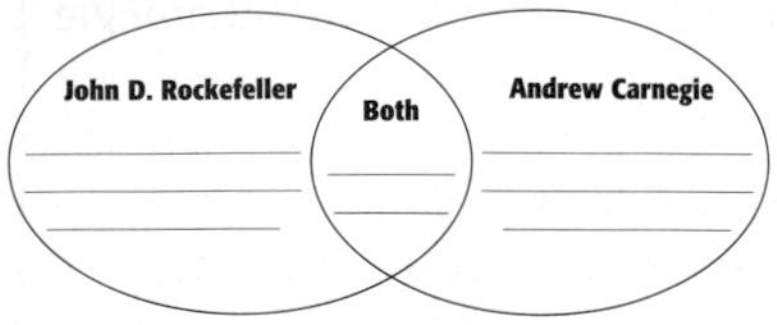

★FACT BANK

A. son of Scottish immigrant
B. formed a trust
C. dominated industry
D. sold his business to J. Pierpont Morgan
E. horizontal integration
F. worked with the railroad
G. steel plant
H. J. Edgar Thompson Steel Works
I. Bessemer process
J. Standard Oil
K. vertical integration
L. philanthropist
M. oil refineries
N. born in Richford, New York, 1839

DIRECTIONS: Essay On a separate sheet of paper, answer the questions below.

1. Explain how shareholders could make or lose money by investing in a corporation.
2. What are corporate mergers? What were the effects of corporate mergers on the American economy by 1900?

The American Journey ★ 77 ★ **Reteaching Activities**

Enrichment Activity 19–3

Name ______________ Date ________ Class ________

★ Enrichment Activity 19-3 ★

A Whale of a Party

Researchers in the 1850s found that petroleum produced heat and light and lubricated machinery. The oil industry, which began with the success of the first oil well in 1859 in Pennsylvania, grew explosively. During the late 1800s whale oil, which had been an important source of oil for oil lamps, was replaced by petroleum. Study this historical cartoon that shows a grand ball given by the whales in honor of the discovery of the first oil well.

SOURCE: Culver Pictures.

DIRECTIONS: Interpreting Information Imagine that you want to turn this cartoon into a short animated cartoon. On a separate sheet of paper, use the following categories to complete a planning sheet with as much detail as you can.

1. **Setting: Time and Place**
2. **Characters and Their Appearance**
3. **Actions**

Activity **DIRECTIONS:** After you have decided on time and place, and identified and described your characters, create a storyboard to illustrate the action of your cartoon. Include drawings of the main characters and captions that show what will happen in your cartoon. Share your storyboard with your classmates. How were your settings, characters, and storylines similar? How were they different?

The American Journey ★ 77 ★ **Enrichment Activities**

that some states prohibited. A holding company buys controlling interests in the stock of other companies instead of purchasing the companies outright. Rockefeller formed Standard Oil of New Jersey so the corporation could expand its holdings. Other states also passed laws that made corporate **mergers**—the combining of companies—easier.

Corporate Mergers

Mergers concentrated economic power in a few giant corporations and a few powerful individuals, such as Rockefeller and banker J. Pierpont Morgan. By 1900 one-third of all American manufacturing was controlled by just 1 percent of the country's corporations. These giant corporations were the driving force behind the great economic growth of the period, but they also posed problems.

Opposition to Big Business

Defenders of big business claimed that monopolies and trusts benefited society because they reduced competition and brought greater economic stability. According to this view, competition ruined many small businesses and threw great numbers of people out of work. Trusts helped consumers because large corporations could sell goods for lower prices than could smaller companies.

However, a growing number of Americans opposed trusts and monopolies. These people argued that a lack of competition hurt consumers. Without competition, corporations had no reason to keep their prices low or to improve their goods and services.

Government Regulation

State governments responded to the growing opposition to trusts and monopolies. During the 1880s, 15 states passed laws restricting business combinations that limited competition. Corporations, however, avoided these laws by incorporating in states that had no such laws.

Public pressure for a federal law to prohibit trusts and monopolies led Congress to pass the **Sherman Antitrust Act** in 1890. The law sought "to protect trade and commerce against unlawful restraint and monopoly." The act did not clearly define either "trusts" or "monopolies," however.

In its early years, the Sherman Antitrust Act did little to curb the power of big business. By contrast, in the 1890s the government did use the act to stop a strike by railroad workers that threatened to "restrain" the nation's mail delivery.

Section 3 Review

Checking for Understanding

1. ***Identify*** John D. Rockefeller, Andrew Carnegie, J. Pierpont Morgan, Sherman Antitrust Act.
2. ***Define*** corporation, stock, shareholder, dividend, horizontal integration, trust, monopoly, vertical integration, philanthropy, merger.
3. ***List*** three reasons railroads and other businesses needed to raise capital after the Civil War.

Reviewing Themes

4. **Economic Factors** Summarize the steps that John D. Rockefeller took to gain total control of the oil industry.

Critical Thinking

5. **Determining Cause and Effect** Why is competition among businesses beneficial to consumers?

Activity

Researching Local Philanthropists Research to find a philanthropist who has provided benefits to the community in which you live—in the past or present. Share your findings with the class.

4 CLOSE

John D. Rockefeller claimed that consolidation protected business from "wasteful conditions." He insisted that "individualism has gone, never to return." Ask students whether they agree. Have them support their opinions.

Section 3 Review Answers

1. John D. Rockefeller, 561; Andrew Carnegie, 563; J. Pierpont Morgan, 563; Sherman Antitrust Act, 564
2. The words are defined in the Glossary.
3. to buy raw materials and equipment, pay workers, cover shipping/advertising costs
4. bought most refineries, produced own supplies and equipment, lowered prices to drive competition out of business, pressured customers not to deal with competitors, got rebates from railroads, formed trust to gain stock of remaining competing firms
5. Without it, corporations have no reason to keep prices low or to improve their goods and services.

Activity Students should research to find a local philanthropist.

INTERDISCIPLINARY

Activities

Inventions of the Late 1800s

In the late 1800s, changes in industry and the growth of cities marked the beginning of the modern world. Experience some of these changes as you build, design, and write about developments in that fast-changing world.

Language Arts

Writing an Advertisement Americans in the late 1800s had a dazzling array of new inventions to buy for their homes and businesses. Imagine that you are an advertising manager selling one of these products: sewing machine, telephone, typewriter, telegraph, or phonograph (gramophone or talking machine). Remember that these products are new to your customers. Write and illustrate your advertisement. Display it in class.

Science

Engineering the Panama Canal The Panama Canal, opened in 1914, was an amazing feat of science and technology. Research the engineering design of the canal, and draw a cross-section diagram illustrating how ships are raised and lowered through locks in order to cross the mountains. Then make a map of the canal's path across Panama. Use your diagram and map to explain the canal system to the class.

School-to-Work

Starting a Small Business Some inventions of the late 1800s were the basis for new businesses. Choose a popular invention of this period—the bicycle, sewing machine, or typewriter, for example—and think of a business that uses the new technology. Make a business plan that includes the number and kind of machines and employees you would need, the kinds of services or products you would offer, and the prices you would charge. Think of a name and symbol for your company and make a small display to introduce it in class.

Speech

Reporting a Sports Event By the 1890s both amateur and professional sports—football, baseball, bicycling, and the new game of basketball—were immensely popular. Although radio had not yet been invented in the 1890s, imagine that you are a radio sportscaster. Choose a sport, research its history, and prepare a short broadcast in which you report from a game or race. Tape it for the class or present it as a "live" broadcast.

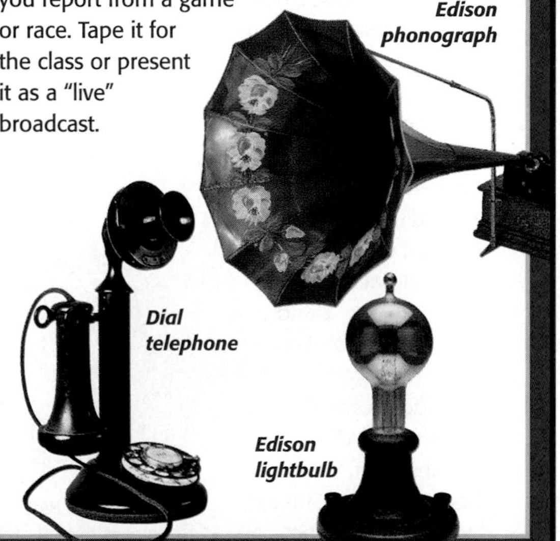

INTERDISCIPLINARY

Activities

TEACH

Background

Both the postal service and railroads expanded and became more efficient during the late 1800s and early 1900s. They allowed merchants to send goods across the country nearly as easily as across town. Some firms (notably Sears, Roebuck and Co. and Montgomery Ward) developed mail-order businesses, publishing catalogs that offered a wide variety of goods. Chain stores, which first appeared in the 1850s, also expanded. F.W. Woolworth's chain of "five and tens" sold inexpensive items, while elegant department stores served the urban upper and middle classes.

As the number and variety of stores increased, businesses used advertising to compete for customers. At first manufacturers did their own advertising. Then in 1869, Francis Wayland Ayer started an agency to produce advertising for other businesses. Other such advertising agencies soon appeared.

Have students work together in groups to complete the **Language Arts** activity, Writing an Advertisement, on this page.

Team Teaching

These Interdisciplinary Activities provide an excellent opportunity for you to employ Team Teaching and collaboration in your classroom.

School TO WORK

Entrepreneur Have students contact the local office of the Small Business Association to learn more about how to set up and operate their own business.

Multiple Learning Styles

The activities included in the feature on this student edition page are ideally suited to meet the different learning styles of your students. These include:

- Language Arts — **Writing an Advertisement** verbal/linguistic learners
- Science — **Engineering the Panama Canal** visual/spatial learners
- School-to-Work — **Starting a Small Business** interpersonal learners
- Speech — **Reporting a Sports Event** auditory/musical learners

1870 1880 1890

1869 Knights of Labor organized

1877 Railroad workers on strike

1881 National trade unions form the AFL

1886 Riots erupt in Haymarket Square

Section 4

Industrial Workers

1 FOCUS

BELLRINGER
Motivational Activity

Before taking roll at the beginning of the class period, project Section Focus Transparency 19–4 and have students answer the questions. Discuss students' responses.

This activity is also available as a blackline master.

Section Focus Transparency 19–4

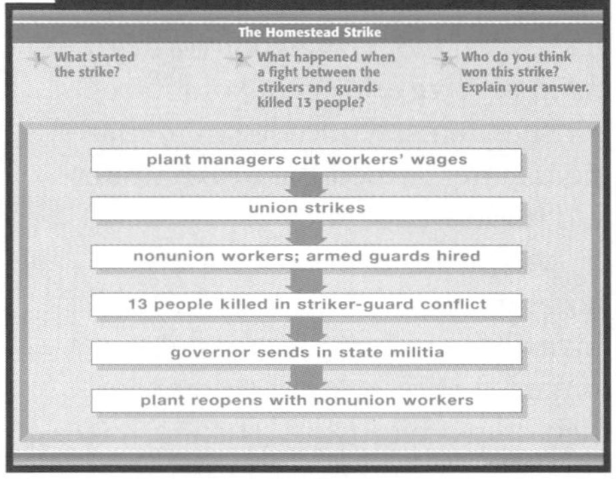

Vocabulary Precheck
Have students speculate on the meaning of each word in **Terms to Learn** and then check their guesses in the textbook glossary.

Use the **Vocabulary PuzzleMaker** to create crossword and word search puzzles.

Section Theme
Groups and Institutions

In the late 1800s and early 1900s, most industrial workers labored long hours for low pay in conditions that put their health and safety, even their lives, at risk.

Activity Have students find out how workers tried to better their working conditions. *(joined unions, such as the Knights of Labor and the AFL)*

READ TO DISCOVER . . .
- why workers demanded changes in their working conditions and wages.
- how labor unions helped workers gain economic and political power.

TERMS TO LEARN
- sweatshop
- trade union
- collective bargaining
- strikebreaker
- injunction

The Storyteller

On a spring day in 1886, about 12,000 workers in a Chicago manufacturing district were on strike. Nearly all were immigrants, and many wore small red ribbons on their jackets. At 2 o'clock a man climbed up on an empty freight car near the crowd. He moved to the edge of the roof and waved frantically at the crowd below. "Stand firm," he yelled. "Let every man stand shoulder to shoulder and we will win this fight. We must have our rights. Strike while the iron is hot. . . ."

Haymarket Riot news report

Industrial growth in the late 1800s created new jobs and raised the standard of living for many American workers. Yet workers paid a price for economic progress. Factories had once been small workplaces where employers and employees knew one another and often worked side by side. As mass production spread, however, factories became larger and less personal.

Industrial laborers worked for 10 or 12 hours a day, 6 days a week. They could be fired at any time for any reason. Many lost their jobs during business downturns or were replaced by immigrants who were willing to work for lower pay.

Working Conditions

Factories and mines were noisy, unhealthy, and unsafe. Accidents were common. Steel workers suffered burns from spills of hot steel. Coal miners died in cave-ins and from the effects of gas and coal dust. Textile workers' lungs were damaged by airborne lint. Garment workers toiled in crowded urban factories called **sweatshops**, where they ruined their eyesight by sewing for hours in poor light. Filled with flammable materials, the sweatshops were also terrible firetraps.

Women Workers

Although the majority of working women in the late 1800s had jobs as domestic servants, women also joined the industrial workforce, especially the textile industry. By 1900 more than 1 million women worked in industry. However,

SECTION RESOURCES

Reproducible Masters
- Reproducible Lesson Plan 19–4
- Guided Reading Activity 19–4
- Section Quiz 19–4
- Reteaching Activity 19–4
- Enrichment Activity 19–4

Transparencies
- Section Focus Transparency 19–4

Multimedia
- Vocabulary PuzzleMaker
- Chapter Challenger Interactive Review Software
- Testmaker
- Facts On File: Landmark Documents in American History

because no laws regulated workers' salaries, women generally received about half of what men earned for the same work.

Child Labor

Industries also hired children. In 1900 hundreds of thousands of children under 16 years of age worked in factories. Concerned groups brought child labor to the attention of their state legislatures. As a result many states passed child-labor laws. These laws stated that children working in factories had to be at least 12 years old and should not work more than 10 hours a day. Employers widely ignored child-labor laws, however. Also, the laws did not apply to agriculture, which employed about 1 million children.

Labor Unions Form

Dissatisfied workers organized into groups—labor unions—to demand better pay and working conditions from their employers. Earlier in the 1800s, skilled workers had formed unions to represent workers in certain crafts or trades, such as carpentry. These **trade unions** had little influence because each represented only one trade. By the mid-1800s labor leaders looked to expand their unions.

The Knights of Labor

In 1869 garment cutters in Philadelphia founded the Noble and Holy Order of the **Knights of Labor.** Employers fired workers who joined labor organizations, so the Knights met secretly and used special handshakes to identify each other. Under the leadership of **Terence V. Powderly,** the Knights of Labor became a national labor organization in the 1880s. Unlike most unions, the Knights recruited people who had been kept out of trade unions, including women, African Americans, immigrants, and unskilled laborers.

The Knights of Labor grew rapidly, boasting more than 700,000 members by 1886. However, a wave of strikes turned public opinion against the union, and it lost members and power in the 1890s.

The American Federation of Labor

In 1881 a group of national trade unions formed a federation that 5 years later became known as the **American Federation of Labor** (AFL). The AFL represented skilled workers in various crafts. In 1886 the AFL consisted of 12 national unions with a membership of about 150,000.

The AFL was led by **Samuel Gompers,** the tough, practical-minded president of the Cigar Makers' Union. The organization pressed for higher wages, shorter hours, better working conditions, and the right to bargain collectively with employers. In **collective bargaining,** unions represent workers in bargaining with management.

Although violent strikes turned public feeling against workers and unions in the late 1880s, the AFL survived and grew. By 1904 the AFL claimed more than 1.6 million members.

Women and the Unions

Many unions would not admit women workers, so some women formed their own unions. **Mary Harris Jones,** better known as Mother Jones, spent 50 years fighting for workers' rights.

In 1911 a fire broke out at the **Triangle Shirtwaist Company** factory, a crowded sweatshop

Young coal miners in Kingston, Pennsylvania

COOPERATIVE LEARNING ACTIVITY

Presenting Plays Organize the class into small groups. Have each group write a play about pre-strike negotiations of a company representative, two union workers, and a union representative. The dialogue should reflect the attitudes of the characters and should include appropriate vocabulary from this section. Some group members should write the dialogue, others may make or gather necessary props, and others do the acting. Have each group present its play to the class.

2 TEACH

L1 Finding Details Have students write the section's three main subheads and then, for each subhead, list at least three details that support and explain the subhead. Call on volunteers to supply details for a class list for each subhead.

Guided Reading Activity 19–4

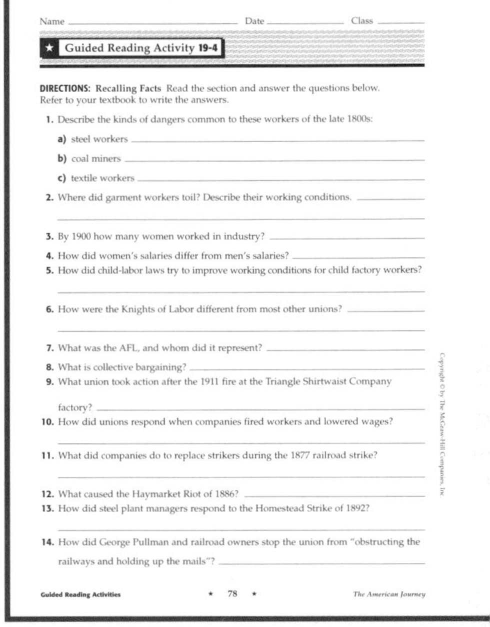

Name ______ Date ______ Class ______

★ Guided Reading Activity **19-4**

DIRECTIONS: Recalling Facts Read the section and answer the questions below. Refer to your textbook to write the answers.

1. Describe the kinds of dangers common to these workers of the late 1800s:
   a) steel workers ______
   b) coal miners ______
   c) textile workers ______
2. Where did garment workers toil? Describe their working conditions. ______
3. By 1900 how many women worked in industry? ______
4. How did women's salaries differ from men's salaries? ______
5. How did child-labor laws try to improve working conditions for child factory workers? ______
6. How were the Knights of Labor different from most other unions? ______
7. What was the AFL, and whom did it represent? ______
8. What is collective bargaining? ______
9. What union took action after the 1911 fire at the Triangle Shirtwaist Company factory? ______
10. How did unions respond when companies fired workers and lowered wages? ______
11. What did companies do to replace strikers during the 1877 railroad strike? ______
12. What caused the Haymarket Riot of 1886? ______
13. How did steel plant managers respond to the Homestead Strike of 1892? ______
14. How did George Pullman and railroad owners stop the union from "obstructing the railways and holding up the mails"? ______

Guided Reading Activities ★ 78 ★ *The American Journey*

Facts On File

CD-ROM
Landmark Documents in American History

Title: *Constitution of the American Federation of Labor, 1886*
Have students make a list of this union's goals.

you don't say...

"Strike while the iron is hot" is a metaphor from the blacksmith shop. In order to form horseshoes or other products, the blacksmith had to place pieces of iron in the forge until they were very hot. While it was still hot, the iron was malleable enough to be shaped by striking it with a hammer.

CHAPTER 19
Section 4, 566–569

When?Who?What?Where?

Labor Day In 1894 Labor Day became a national holiday through the efforts of the AFL.

3 ASSESS

Assign Section 4 Review as homework or as an in-class activity.

Use **Chapter Challenger Interactive Review Software** to review Section 4.

Section Quiz 19–4

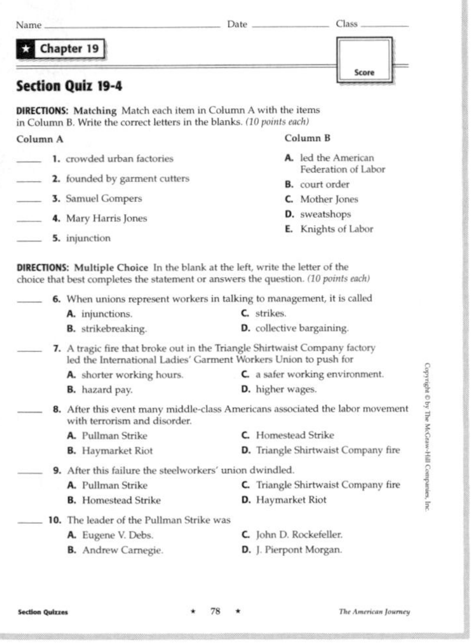
Name ______ Date ______ Class ______

Chapter 19 | Score

Section Quiz 19-4

DIRECTIONS: Matching Match each item in Column A with the items in Column B. Write the correct letters in the blanks. *(10 points each)*

Column A	Column B
____ 1. crowded urban factories	A. led the American Federation of Labor
____ 2. founded by garment cutters	B. court order
____ 3. Samuel Gompers	C. Mother Jones
____ 4. Mary Harris Jones	D. sweatshops
____ 5. injunction	E. Knights of Labor

DIRECTIONS: Multiple Choice In the blank at the left, write the letter of the choice that best completes the statement or answers the question. *(10 points each)*

____ 6. When unions represent workers in talking to management, it is called
A. injunctions. C. strikes.
B. strikebreaking. D. collective bargaining.

____ 7. A tragic fire that broke out in the Triangle Shirtwaist Company factory led the International Ladies' Garment Workers Union to push for
A. shorter working hours. C. a safer working environment.
B. hazard pay. D. higher wages.

____ 8. After this event many middle-class Americans associated the labor movement with terrorism and disorder.
A. Pullman Strike C. Homestead Strike
B. Haymarket Riot D. Triangle Shirtwaist Company fire

____ 9. After this failure the steelworkers' union dwindled.
A. Pullman Strike C. Triangle Shirtwaist Company fire
B. Homestead Strike D. Haymarket Riot

____ 10. The leader of the Pullman Strike was
A. Eugene V. Debs. C. John D. Rockefeller.
B. Andrew Carnegie. D. J. Pierpont Morgan.

Section Quizzes ★ 78 ★ *The American Journey*

Map Study

Answers
1. Anthracite coal strike
2. Surgarcane workers strike

Who?What?Where?When?

Pullman Workers One worker described life as an employee of the company: "We are born in a Pullman house, fed from the Pullman shop, taught in the Pullman school, catechized in the Pullman church, and when we die we shall be buried in the Pullman cemetery."

in New York City. The workers, mostly young immigrant women, could not escape from the building because the company had locked the doors to prevent employees from leaving early. Nearly 150 workers died in the fire. The disaster led the **International Ladies' Garment Workers Union** (ILGWU) to push for a safer working environment.

The Unions Act

Economic depressions in the 1870s and the 1890s led companies to fire workers and lower wages. Unions responded with large strikes that sometimes sparked violence.

Railroad Strike of 1877

Economic depression hit the nation following the Panic of 1873. To cut costs, companies forced their workers to take pay cuts. In July 1877 angry strikers burned rail yards, ripped up track, and destroyed railroad property.

The companies hired **strikebreakers** to replace the striking workers. After weeks of riots, federal troops restored order.

Haymarket Riot of 1886

Antilabor feeling grew stronger after a bloody clash between police and strikers in **Chicago's Haymarket Square** on May 4, 1886. Striking

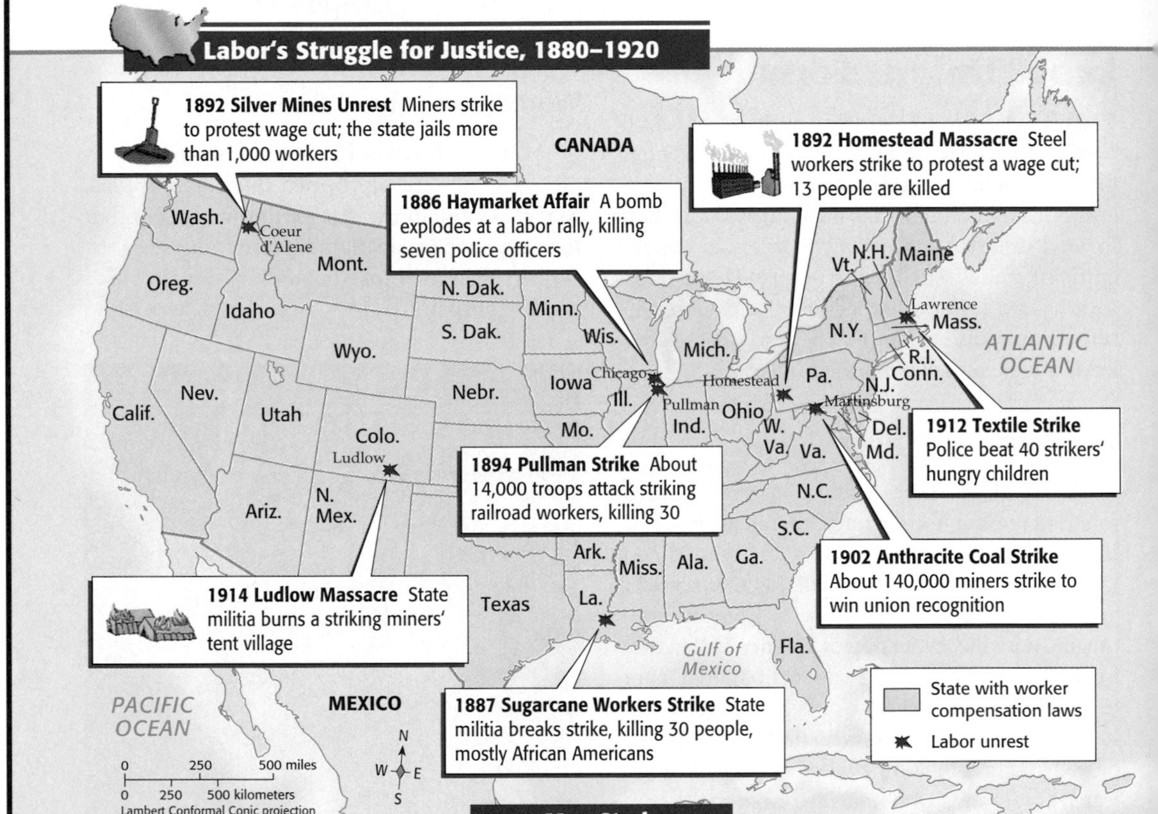

Map Study

The major weapon for workers against management was the strike.

1. **Location** Which strike involved about 140,000 miners?
2. **Analyzing Information** Which strike involved workers in agriculture?

MULTIPLE LEARNING STYLES

Intrapersonal Have students, in the role of laborers, write a description of one week of their lives. Roles may be that of a man, woman, or child. If students wish, they may write the descriptions in the form of diary entries. Before students begin, suggest that they do some further reading to find out more about a worker's daily life. Note that some people worked for companies that paid them in scrip and forced them to live in housing owned by the company. The scrip was good only at the company store, which charged higher prices than did other stores. In these ways, companies made virtual slaves of their workers. **L2**

workers from the McCormick Harvester Company gathered to protest the killings of four strikers the previous day. When police ordered the crowd to break up, an unidentified person threw a bomb that killed seven police officers. Following the **Haymarket Riot,** many middle-class Americans associated the labor movement with terrorism and disorder.

Homestead Strike of 1892

In 1892 workers went on strike at Andrew Carnegie's steel plant in **Homestead, Pennsylvania**. Plant managers had cut workers' wages, hoping to weaken the steelworkers' union. When the union called a strike, Homestead managers hired nonunion workers and brought in 300 armed guards to protect them. A fierce battle left at least 13 people dead.

Pennsylvania's governor sent the state's militia to Homestead to restore order. The plant reopened with nonunion workers, protected by the troops. After the failure of the **Homestead Strike,** the steelworkers' union dwindled.

Pullman Strike of 1894

The employees of George Pullman's railway-car plant near Chicago went on strike in May 1894, when the company cut wages. Pullman responded by closing the plant. One month later, workers in the American Railway Union supported the strikers by refusing to handle Pullman cars, paralyzing rail traffic.

National railroad strike of 1877

Pullman and the railroad owners fought back. They persuaded U.S. Attorney General Richard Olney to obtain an **injunction,** or court order, to stop the union from "obstructing the railways and holding up the mails." The workers and their leader, **Eugene V. Debs,** refused to end the strike. Debs was sent to jail.

President **Grover Cleveland** sent federal troops to Chicago, and within a month the strike was over. The failure of the **Pullman Strike** dealt another major blow to the labor union movement.

Section 4 Review

Checking for Understanding

1. ***Identify*** Terence V. Powderly, Samuel Gompers, Eugene V. Debs, Pullman Strike.
2. ***Define*** sweatshop, trade union, collective bargaining, strikebreaker, injunction.
3. ***Summarize*** the reasons that workers wanted to organize into unions.

Reviewing Themes

4. **Groups and Institutions** What were the goals of the American Federation of Labor?

Critical Thinking

5. **Drawing Conclusions** Why do you think many Americans did not immediately support the labor unions?

Activity

Designing a Board Game Design a board game in which players can experience the ups and downs of factory work in the late 1800s. Include spaces such as "Workday extended to 12 hours. Miss a turn," and "Your union wins a pay hike. Collect $5."

Section 4 Review Answers

1. Terence V. Powderly, 567; Samuel Gompers, 567; Eugene V. Debs, 569; Pullman Strike, 569
2. The words are defined in the Glossary.
3. unhealthy and unsafe working conditions, low wages, long hours, no job security
4. better wages and hours, improved working conditions, right to collective bargaining with employers
5. Students should recognize that strikes and their accompanying violence played a major role in negative public opinion against unions.

Activity Board games should show that students understand the section.

Reteaching Activity 19–4

Name ______ Date ______ Class ______

★ Reteaching Activity 19-4

DIRECTIONS: Completing a Flowchart The flowchart shows what happened as industry grew in the late 1800s. Write the letter of each item in the section of the chart where it belongs. Some items belong in more than one place.

★FACT BANK

A. at least 13 people killed
B. Federal troops restore order.
C. airborne lint
D. Terence V. Powderly
E. cave-ins
F. Pullman employees strike.
G. pushed for a safer working environment
H. Attorney general grants an injunction.
I. Strikers destroy railroad property.
J. Samuel Gompers
K. Eugene V. Debs goes to jail.
L. State militia restores order.
M. pressed for collective bargaining
N. pressed for action after Triangle Shirtwaist Company factory fire
O. Homestead, Pennsylvania steel plant
P. women's salaries not equal to men's
Q. recruited women and African Americans
R. Haymarket Riot
S. a blow to labor union movement
T. Three hundred armed guards protect nonunion workers.
U. Four strikers and seven police officers are killed.
V. McCormick Harvester Company
W. crowded, poorly lit sweatshops
X. Strikebreakers are hired.

POOR WORKING CONDITIONS AND UNFAIR WAGES

______

(led to the formation of)

LABOR UNIONS

Knights of Labor ______
AFL ______
ILGWU ______

(companies fire workers and lower wages, leading to)

STRIKES

1877 ______
1886 ______
1892 ______
1894 ______

DIRECTIONS: Essay Describe working conditions for men, women, and children in the early years of the Industrial Revolution. Write your answer on a separate sheet of paper.

Reteaching Activities ★ 78 ★ *The American Journey*

Enrichment Activity 19–4

Name ______ Date ______ Class ______

★ Enrichment Activity 19-4 ★ ★

A Range of Wages

The gap between the rich and the poor widened as business and industry grew in the late 1800s. Entries from the payroll for Lyman Cotton Mills in Holyoke, Massachusetts, for November 9, 1889, show a range of wages.

Lyman Cotton Mills Payroll, Holyoke, Massachusetts, November 9, 1889

Names	Total Hours	Hourly Wage	Weekly Wage Earned	Names	Total Hours	Hourly Wage	Weekly Wage Earned
Overseer	60	$ .40	$24.00	Picker Men			
Second Hands				Worker 8	60	$ .10	$6.00
Worker 1	60	$ .18	$10.80	Worker 9	60	$ .09	$5.40
Worker 2	60	$ .20	$12.00	Grinders			
Third Oilers and Roving Hands				Worker 10	60	$ .15	$9.00
				Worker 11	60	$ .15	$9.00
Worker 3	60	$ .12	$7.20	Railways and Drawing			
Worker 4	60	$ .10	$6.00				
Worker 5	15	$ .08	$1.20	Worker 12	60	$ .07	$4.20
Worker 6	60	$ .07	$4.20	Worker 13	60	$ .08	$4.80
Scrubber							
Worker 7	60	$ .05	$3.00				

DIRECTIONS: Using Facts Answer the following questions about the chart.

1. Who is the highest paid employee at the mill, and what were the weekly wages? ______
2. How much does the scrubber make an hour? ______
3. Why did Worker 5 earn a lower weekly wage than other workers in the same job category? ______

CRITICAL THINKING

4. How many hours are there in an average work week? ______
5. Which two jobs besides overseer probably require the most skill? Explain your answer. ______
6. Why might Worker 1 be paid less than Worker 2 when they are in the same job category? ______
7. Which job probably requires little or no skill? Explain your answer. ______

Enrichment Activities ★ 78 ★ *The American Journey*

4 CLOSE

When Mother Jones appeared before a judge, he asked her who had given her a permit to speak on the streets. She replied, "Patrick Henry, Thomas Jefferson, and John Adams." Discuss her response with students.

GLENCOE TECHNOLOGY

VIDEODISC
MindJogger Videoquiz

Use MindJogger to review the Chapter 19 content.

Chapter 19
Disc 3, Side A

Also available in VHS.

Reviewing Key Terms

Students' crossword puzzles will vary. The key terms used in this activity can be found in the textbook glossary on pages A26–A35.

Reviewing Key Facts

1. air brakes, car couplers, refrigerated cars, sleeping cars, dining cars
2. any four: phonograph, movie projector, telephone transmitter, storage battery, dictating machine, electric lightbulb, power plants
3. Assembly line allowed workers to produce large quantities of automobiles more quickly; mass production decreased manufacturing costs.
4. Congress passed the Sherman Antitrust Act.
5. Violence weakened the unions and turned public opinion against the labor movement.

Critical Thinking

1. Messages were carried in seconds via telegraph and telephone. The transatlantic cable linked the United States and Europe.
2. lowered costs of goods so more people could afford them

Chapter 19 Review and Activities

Reviewing Key Terms

On a sheet of paper, create a crossword puzzle using the following terms. Use the terms' definitions as your clues.

consolidation
standard gauge
rebate
pool
assembly line
mass production
corporation
stock
shareholder
dividend
horizontal integration
trust
monopoly
vertical integration
philanthropy
merger
sweatshop
trade union
collective bargaining
strikebreaker
injunction

Reviewing Key Facts

1. What improvements in railway transportation were brought about by new technology?
2. What were four of Thomas Edison's inventions?
3. What manufacturing methods did Henry Ford use to make his new automobile affordable?
4. What did the government do to control trusts and monopolies in response to pressure from the public?
5. What were the results of the Haymarket Riot of 1886?

Critical Thinking

Making Inferences

New transportation and communication technologies transformed the lives of the American people in the late 1800s and early 1900s.

1. How did improved communication "shrink" the country and the world?
2. How did more efficient manufacturing processes affect the average American buyer?

Time Line Activity

Create a time line on which you place the following events in chronological order.

- Henry Ford introduces the Model T
- Thomas Edison develops the first practical lightbulb
- Wright brothers make their first machine-powered flight
- Alexander Graham Bell invents the telephone
- Congress passes the Sherman Antitrust Act
- Rally at Haymarket ends in violence

Reviewing Themes

1. **Geography and History** How did the growing railroad network help American industry?
2. **Science and Technology** Describe the contributions of African American inventors in the late 1800s.
3. **Economic Factors** How did horizontal integration differ from vertical integration?
4. **Groups and Institutions** Why did workers think that forming organized labor unions would help them get what they wanted from employers?

Time Line Activity

Events should be placed in this order: Alexander Graham Bell invents the telephone, Thomas Edison develops the first practical lightbulb, Rally at Haymarket ends in violence, Congress passes the Sherman Antitrust Act, Wright brothers make their first machine-powered flight, Henry Ford introduces the Model T

Reviewing Themes

1. carried raw materials to factories and manufactured goods and farm produce to markets; encouraged growth of iron, steel, lumber, coal, railroad-car manufacturing, and railroad-equipment manufacturing industries
2. Latimer: improved lightbulb filament; Woods: invented electric incubator and

Geography Activity

Study the map below and answer the questions that follow.

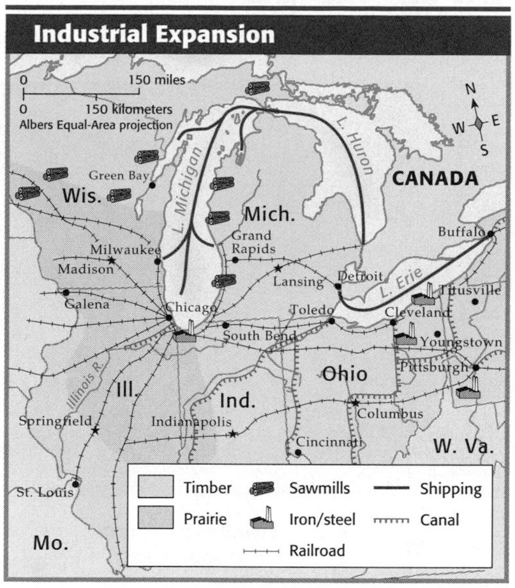

1. **Movement** What forms of transportation moved goods into and out of this region?
2. **Human/Environment Interaction** What industry grew in the timbered regions of Wisconsin and Michigan?
3. **Location** Identify the major iron/steel manufacturing centers shown on the map.

Skill Practice

Reading a Time Zones Map

Study the time zones map on page 555. Use the map to answer the following questions.

1. If you traveled from Florida to California, what time zones would you cross?
2. If it is 6:00 A.M. in Maine, what time is it in Hawaii?
3. If it is 3:00 P.M. in Texas, what time is it in Alaska?

Cooperative Activity

History and Economics Today's corporations often control many smaller companies. With a partner choose one large corporation and research to find out what other companies are under its control. On poster board make a flowchart to show the relationship and links among some of the companies. Also include the major service or product that each company provides. Display your charts for viewing by the rest of the class.

Technology Activity

Using a Spreadsheet Become an imaginary shareholder in a corporation. Search for stock market data in a daily newspaper. Choose one stock to follow for a two-week period. Track the performance of the stock on a spreadsheet by marking its daily increases and decreases. Compare your spreadsheet with classmates' results and decide if you made a good investment.

Portfolio Activity **History Journal** Review the chapter for information about the four major union strikes between 1877 and 1894. Write a headline for each that might have appeared in newspapers following the strikes.

electromagnetic railroad brake, automatic circuit breaker, and other railroad improvements; McCoy: invented mechanism for oiling machinery; Matzeliger: invented shoe making machine

3. Horizontal integration combines competing firms into one organization; vertical integration involves the acquisition of companies that provide the equipment and services needed by an industry.
4. By uniting they had more influence and a better chance of being heard. Strikes could adversely affect employers and give workers more leverage in negotiations.

Geography Activity

1. railroads, canals, and ships
2. sawmills (lumber industry)
3. Chicago, Cleveland, Youngstown, Pittsburgh

CHAPTER 19
Review and Activities

Skill Practice Activity

1. Eastern, Central, Mountain, Pacific
2. 1:00 A.M.
3. 12:00 P.M.

Cooperative Activity

Students should research to find the name of a large corporation that has control of many other companies. They should present their findings in the form of a flowchart to show the connections and relationships of some of the businesses.

Technology Activity

Students should track a stock for two weeks and present their results on a spreadsheet.

Portfolio Activity Students should refer to Section 4 for information on the major strikes of the period. They should produce one newspaper headline for each of the strikes.

Chapter Bonus Test Question

Ask: **What was the name of the man who designed and began the building of the Brooklyn Bridge, the modern world's first suspension bridge?** *(John Augustus Roebling. His son Washington took over supervision of construction after his death. Completed in 1883, it took 14 years to build. At the time it was the world's longest and highest bridge.)*

Hands-On HISTORY Lab Activity

Block Schedule

This activity may be implemented within either a traditional class period or a block scheduling framework.

FOCUS

Ask students to name petroleum products that are used today. After class members have named as many as they know, interested students can research to find others. *(Products include gasoline; fuels for trucks, trains, and planes; kerosene; asphalt; heating fuels; solvents; lubricants; and petrochemicals, from which come medicines, fertilizers, foods, plastics, paints, clothing, and soaps.)*

TEACH

L2 Petroleum Jargon Like other industries, the oil industry has its own vocabulary, which includes some terms that are part of our everyday language. Have students define as many of the following terms as they can and then look up the rest: *crude, barrel, kerosene, refinery, derrick, Christmas tree, bit, casing, rig, distillation, kelly, roughneck, pipeline, royalty, dry well.*

Hands-On HISTORY Lab Activity

Retrieving Oil

United States industrial production in 1900 depended on abundant oil reserves. How did the oil barons retrieve oil from the earth? In this lab activity, imagine you are an oil driller who must pump as much oil as possible from a particular site.

Spindletop Hill near Beaumont, Texas

The Way It Was

In 1543 the survivors of the De Soto expedition stopped on the Texas coast to caulk—make watertight—the seams of their leaking boats. On the shores they found a black sticky material—tar—which worked quite well. Native Americans used oil-based tar to waterproof bowls and utensils and probably used oil products for medical purposes. Pioneers used oil to grease the axles on their wagons.

In the 1840s a Canadian scientist discovered kerosene, a fuel that could be made from coal or oil. Kerosene became widely used for lamps and lanterns. People started to use oil to lubricate machinery. As the demand grew, operators eagerly began to drill for oil.

Believe It Or Not! On January 10, 1901, an oil well on Spindletop Hill in Texas began spewing mud. Then, with an explosive roar, the mud turned first to gas and then to oil. The gusher roared out nearly one-half million barrels of oil for six days before being capped.

1 Materials

- clear plastic bottle with spray pump
- clear plastic tubing
- 100-ml graduated cylinder
- 1–2 cups of small, clean pebbles
- liquid detergent
- 100 ml vegetable oil
- 100 ml hot water
- 50 ml cold water
- eyedropper

CURRICULUM CONNECTION

Economics Similar to the Standard Oil monopoly, OPEC (Organization of Petroleum Exporting Countries) tries to maintain stability in the oil industry to ensure profits. Since 1970 OPEC has controlled approximately one-third to one-half of the world's oil supply. In 1996 member nations were Algeria, Gabon, Indonesia, Iran, Iraq, Kuwait, Libya, Nigeria, Qatar, Saudi Arabia, United Arab Emirates, and Venezuela. The organization's headquarters are in Vienna.

2 What To Do

1. The spray bottle will be your well. Place the pebbles inside the spray bottle. Insert the plastic tubing deep into the pebbles and through the opening of the spray bottle. Keep several inches of the tubing protruding out of the sprayer.
2. Pour 100 ml of oil into your well. Seal your well. Pump as much oil as you can get out of your well into a graduated cylinder. Measure the amount.
3. Empty the oil back into your well. Rinse your cylinder thoroughly. Pour 50 ml of cold water into your well. Observe what happens in the bottle.
4. Again, pump out as much oil as you can. Give the oil and water time to separate in the graduated cylinder, then record the amount of oil you recovered. Empty the cylinder into a separate container.
5. Using 50 ml of hot water, repeat Step 4.
6. Using 50 ml of hot water and 8 drops of liquid detergent, repeat Step 4.

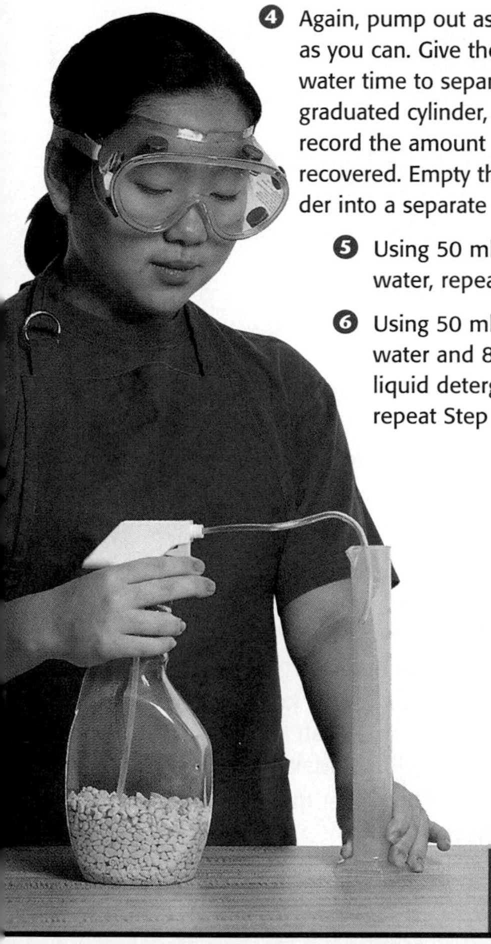

Step 6

3 Lab Report

1. How many milliliters of oil did you retrieve by pumping alone?
2. What did the oil do when you added the cold water to your well? How much oil did you pump out?
3. How much oil did you pump out using hot water?
4. How much oil did you pump out using hot water and detergent?
5. **Analyzing Information** What method of pumping oil would you recommend to an oil well owner—pumping just oil or pumping using added materials such as hot or cold water? Explain.

Go a Step Further

What do you think the results would be if you used detergent alone in your well? Make a prediction.

CURRICULUM CONNECTION

SCIENCE
Show students that oil on water can be broken up by detergent. Have students fill a beaker three-quarters full of water. Tell them to add several drops of vegetable oil to the water. What does the oil do? *(floats)* Have students drop a small amount of detergent in the middle of the oil "slick." What does the oil do? *(The oil clears out in a circle toward the edges of the beaker.)* What does detergent do to oil? *(breaks it up)*

ASSESS

Have students answer the **Lab Report** questions on this page.

CLOSE

Have students predict the results of the **Go a Step Further** activity. Then check the predictions by having a volunteer do the activity.

ANSWERS

Lab Report

1. Answers will depend on the depth to which the plastic tubing is placed.
2. The cold water made the level of the oil rise, in some cases above the end of the plastic tube.
3. The oil may mix slightly with the hot water, so more oil—mixed with water—will be pumped out.
4. Detergent will break up the oil and allow it to be pumped out more easily.
5. Recommendations should state that some material must be added to the well to increase the pressure within the well.

Go a Step Further Detergent should break up the oil and make it easier to pump out.

Chapter 20 Planning Guide

A complete, 1-page lesson plan is provided for each section in the *Reproducible Lesson Plans* booklet.

Section Resources

Daily Objectives	Reproducible Resources	Multimedia Resources
Section 1 **The New Immigrants** Evaluate the impact of the "old" and the "new" immigrants on American society.	Reproducible Lesson Plan 20–1 Guided Reading Activity 20–1* Political Cartoons, *A Nation of Immigrants* Section Quiz 20–1* Reteaching Activity 20–1 Enrichment Activity 20–1	Section Focus Transparency 20–1 Vocabulary PuzzleMaker Chapter Challenger Interactive Review Software Testmaker GTV: A Geographic Perspective on American History GTV: The American People: Fabric of a Nation ABCNews InterActive™ Historic America Electronic Field Trips
Section 2 **Moving to the City** Analyze the positive and negative effects of city life.	Reproducible Lesson Plan 20–2 Guided Reading Activity 20–2* Section Quiz 20–2* Reteaching Activity 20–2 Enrichment Activity 20–2	Section Focus Transparency 20–2 Vocabulary PuzzleMaker Chapter Challenger Interactive Review Software Testmaker GTV: A Geographic Perspective on American History GTV: The American People: Fabric of a Nation
Section 3 **A Changing Culture** Describe the changes in American culture at the beginning of the twentieth century.	Reproducible Lesson Plan 20–3 Guided Reading Activity 20–3* Section Quiz 20–3* Reteaching Activity 20–3 Enrichment Activity 20–3	Section Focus Transparency 20–3 U.S. History & Art, Transparencies 11, *A Rainy Day in Camp;* 16, *In the Garden;* 18, *The Stampede* Focus on American Art Prints, *The Gulf Stream* by Winslow Homer; *The Boating Party* by Mary Cassatt Vocabulary PuzzleMaker Chapter Challenger Interactive Review Software Testmaker American Music Cultural Traditions

** Also available in Spanish*

Poster — Transparency — CD-ROM — Software
Blackline Master — Videodisc — Audiocassette — Music Program

0:00 **OUT OF TIME?**
Assign the Chapter 20 Digest and the corresponding Chapter Digests Audiocassettes with activities and tests.

Activity

From the Classroom of...

Katherine Sweet
Rooftop K–8 School
San Francisco, CA

In-Class Pen Pals

Create in-class pen pals by first organizing the class into pairs. You may want to have students draw numbers with two sets of each number placed in a container. The two "1s" would be pen pals, two "2s," and so on. The student who draws the first "1" will write the first letter as an immigrant who has recently arrived in the United States, and the student that selects the second "1" will write a response letter, playing the role of someone still living in the immigrant's home country.

The first letter writer could write about topics such as poverty, crime, inadequate housing, and poor working conditions that are encountered in the new country. The responder could provide sympathy, understanding, and advice to the immigrant friend on how to cope with the situation. The letter exchanges should be shared with the rest of the class. Some students may want to do additional research before composing their letters. Photocopies of pictures from research materials could also be included to illustrate conditions in early America.

Block Schedule

Block scheduling differs from traditional class scheduling in the amount of time allotted to each period. The extended time frame provided by block scheduling affords you the opportunity to implement a greater number of research-oriented and activity-intense projects to motivate and involve your students. Activities that are particularly suited to use within the block scheduling framework are identified throughout this chapter by the following designation:

National Geographic Society — Teacher's Corner

Index to National Geographic Magazine

The following articles may be used for research relating to this chapter:

- "Central Park: Oasis in the City," by Joel L. Swerdlow, May 1993.
- "Miami," by Charles E. Cobb, Jr., January 1992.
- "Chicago: Welcome to the Neighborhood," by Richard Conniff, May 1991.
- "New Life for Ellis Island," by Alice J. Hall, September 1990.
- "Broadway, Street of Dreams," by Rick Gore, September 1990.
- "Immigration Today: New York's New Immigrants," by Alice J. Hall, September 1990.

National Geographic Society Products Available from Glencoe

To order the following products for use with this chapter, contact your local Glencoe sales representative, or call Glencoe at 1-800-334-7344:

- *GTV: A Geographic Perspective on American History* (Videodisc)
- *GTV: The American People: Fabric of a Nation* (Videodisc)
- *The Presidents: A Picture History of Our Nation* (CD-ROM)
- *PictureShow: Native Americans, 1 and 2* (CD-ROM, Transparencies)

Additional National Geographic Society Products

To order the following products for use with this chapter, call National Geographic Society at 1-800-368-2728:

- *Immigration: The Triumph of Hope* (Video)
- *Historical Atlas of the United States* (Atlas)

KEY TO ABILITY LEVELS

Teaching strategies have been coded for varying learning styles and abilities.

L1 **BASIC** activities for all students
L2 **AVERAGE** activities for average to above-average students
L3 **CHALLENGING** activities for above-average students
ELL **ENGLISH LANGUAGE LEARNER** activities

Chapter 20 Resource Guide

Home Involvement

Home Involvement Activity 20

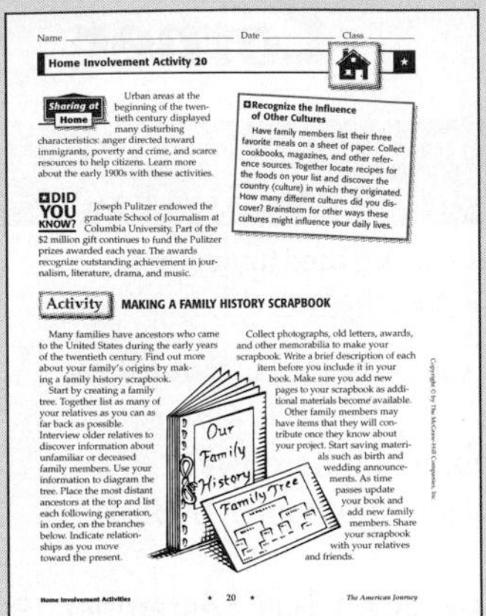

Review Activities

Chapter Summary 20

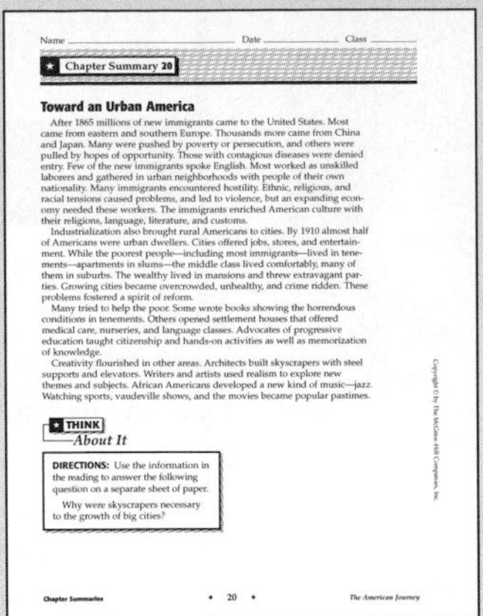

Workbook Activity 20

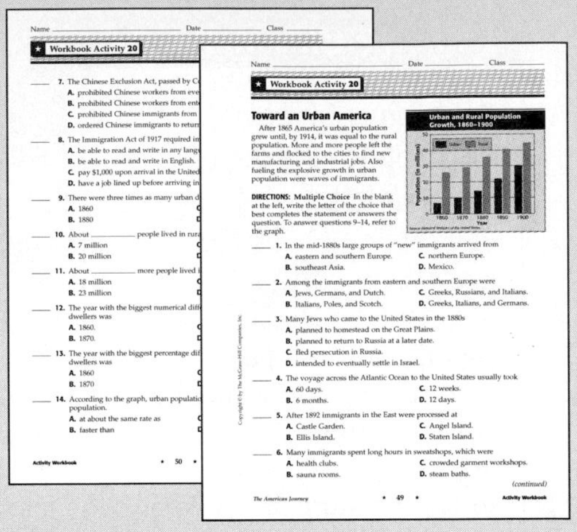

Reinforcement Activities

Time Line Activity 20

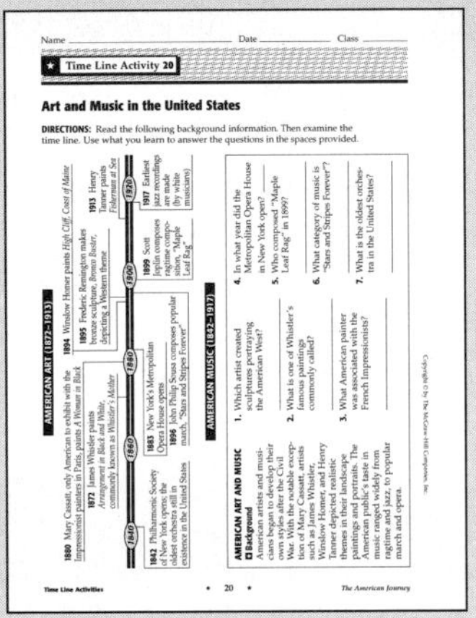

Vocabulary Activity 20

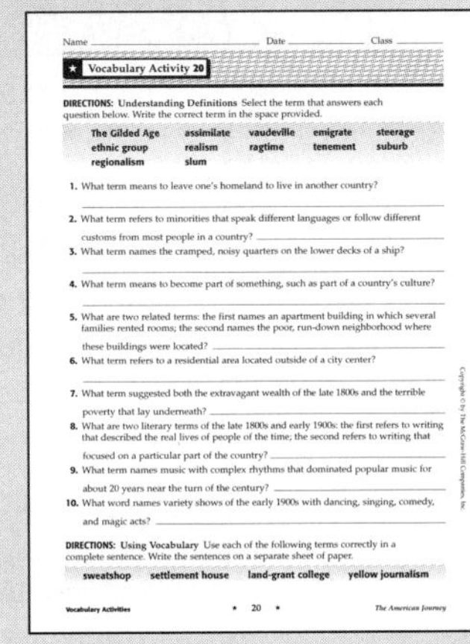

Chapter Skills Activity 20

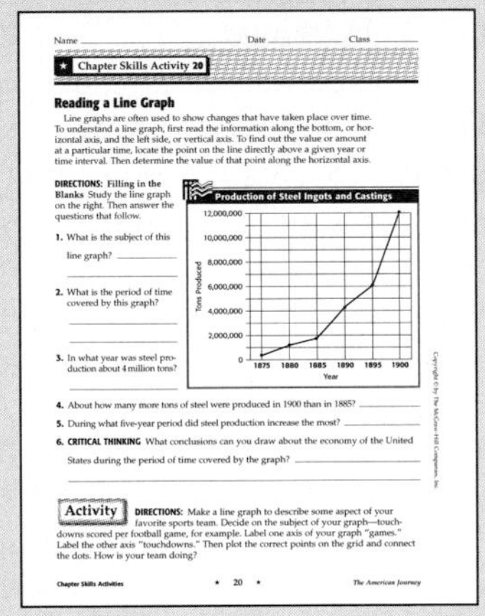

Enrichment Activities

Linking Past and Present Activity 20

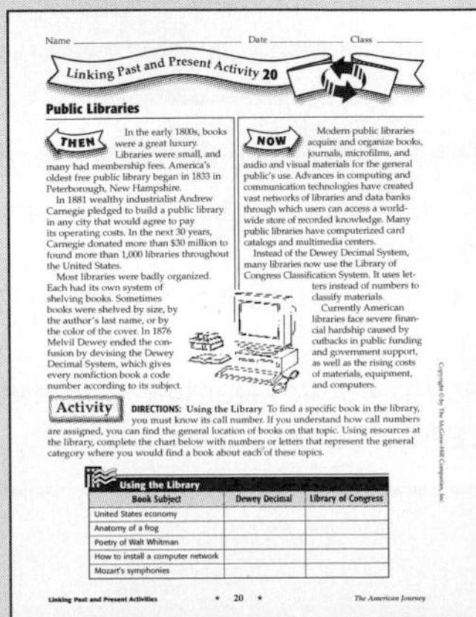

Primary Source Reading 20

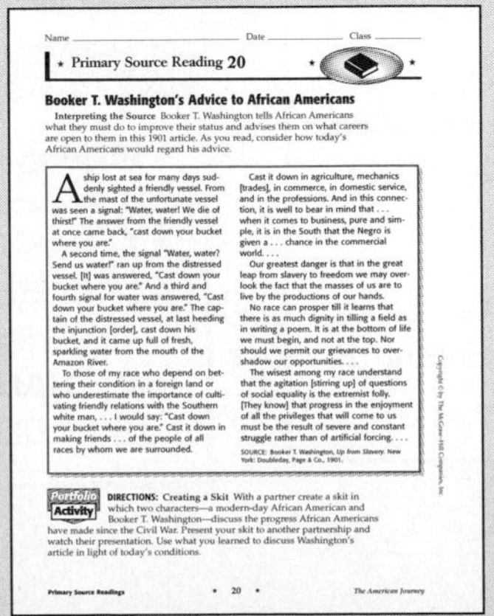

Geography Activities

Mapping History Activity 20

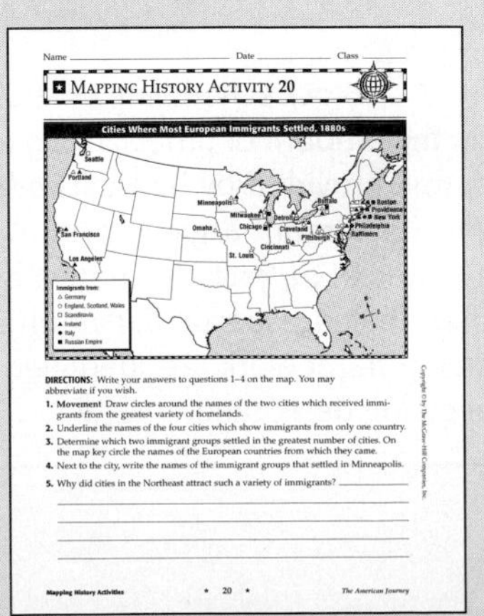

Chapter 20 Resource Guide

Assessment

Chapter 20 Test, Form A

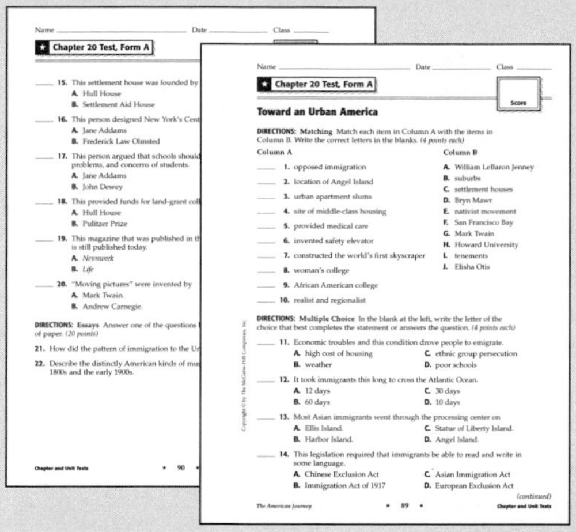

Chapter 20 Test, Form B

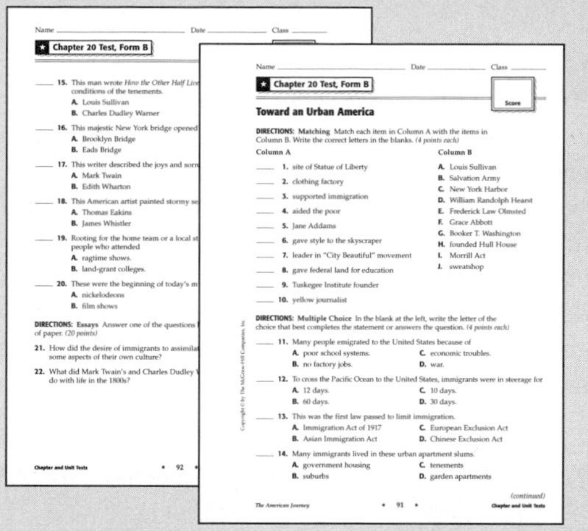

Performance Assessment Activity 20

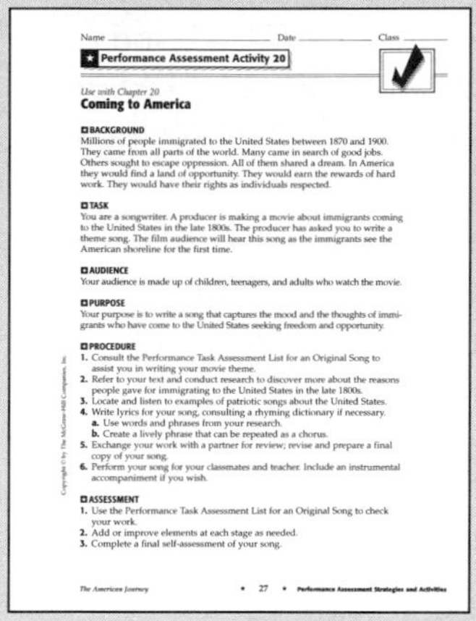

Spanish Resources

The following Spanish language materials are available in the Spanish Resources binder:

- **Spanish Chapter Summary 20**
- **Spanish Vocabulary Activity 20**
- **Spanish Guided Reading Activities, Chapter 20**
- **Spanish Section Quizzes, Chapter 20**
- **Spanish Home Involvement Activity 20**
- **Spanish Chapter 20 Digests Audiocassette Activity and Test**

Activity Manipulatives

Help students learn more about America's cultural history with:

- **American Crafts Hands-On Activities**
- **American Games Hands-On Activities**
- **American History Flash Cards**

Additional Resources From Glencoe

- **The Spirit of American Art and Music,** Lewis Hine, Thomas Eakins, Louis Sullivan, John Philip Sousa, Henry Ossawa Tanner
- **U.S. History & Art,** Transparency 11, *A Rainy Day in Camp;* Transparency 16, *In the Garden;* Transparency 18, *The Stampede*
- **American Music Cultural Traditions,** Lesson 7: "Maple Leaf Rag" and "St. Louis Tickle"
- **Political Cartoons,** *A Nation of Immigrants*
- **Focus on American Art Prints,** *The Gulf Stream* by Winslow Homer, *The Boating Party* by Mary Cassatt

A&E HOME VIDEO. Biography. THE HISTORY CHANNEL.

The following videotape programs are available from Glencoe as supplements to Chapter 20:

- **Andrew Carnegie** (ISBN 1-56501-741-2)
- **The Statue of Liberty** (ISBN 1-56501-468-5)

To order, call Glencoe at 1-800-334-7344. To find classroom resources to accompany many of these videos, check the following home pages:
A&E Television: http://www.aetv.com
The History Channel: http://www.historychannel.com

Introducing CHAPTER 20

Chapter Themes

Chapter Themes are listed by section on this chapter opening page of the Student Edition. A corresponding theme-based activity is available under "FOCUS," and a theme-based question is asked in the Section and Chapter Reviews.

Performance Assessment

Refer to Activity 20 in the *Performance Assessment Strategies and Activities* booklet.

GLENCOE TECHNOLOGY

VIDEODISC
MindJogger Videoquiz

Use MindJogger to preview the Chapter 20 content.

Chapter 20
Disc 3, Side A

Also available in VHS.

HISTORY AND ART The Bowery is a street in New York City. The term is sometimes used to describe the district around this street characterized by poor social conditions. **Ask:** What forms of transportation are shown in this illustration? *(horse and buggy, train, trolley)*

1865–1914

Toward an Urban America

Why It's Important

The modern urban nation we live in started to take shape between 1865 and 1914. By 1914 as many Americans lived in cities as in rural areas. The cities faced many of the same problems that American cities face today—poverty, crime, inadequate housing, and conflicts among people of different backgrounds. During these years of urban growth, many aspects of modern life emerged in the cities, including daily newspapers, spectator sports, public parks, and libraries.

Chapter Themes

- *Section 1,* Culture and Traditions
- *Section 2,* Science and Technology
- *Section 3,* Continuity and Change

HISTORY AND ART ***The Bowery at Night*** **by W. Louis Sonntag, Jr.** As the United States became a nation of cities, public services expanded to serve the needs of the people.

EXTRA CREDIT PROJECT

Writing a Speech Immigration to the United States peaked in 1907. Some Americans favored immigration and others opposed it. Have students scan the chapter to read about these differing viewpoints. Then ask them to decide whether they are for or against open immigration. Have students write a two-minute speech supporting their viewpoint. Ask volunteers to give their speeches to the class.

1880 — 1900 — 1920

1882 Chinese Exclusion Act is passed

1886 Statue of Liberty is erected

1892 Ellis Island starts processing immigrants

1917 Immigration Act of 1917 requires literacy

Section 1

The New Immigrants

READ TO DISCOVER . . .

- what opportunities and difficulties immigrants found in the United States.
- how the arrival of new immigrants in the 1880s changed American society.

TERMS TO LEARN

emigrate
ethnic group
steerage
sweatshop
assimilate

The Storyteller

In the 1870s two young brothers left Italy for America. "We were so long on the water that we began to think we should never get to America. . . . We were all landed on an island and the bosses there said that Francisco and I must go back because we had not enough money, but a man named Bartolo came up and told them that . . . he was our uncle and would take care of us. . . . We came to Brooklyn to a wooden house on Adams Street that was full of Italians from Naples. Bartolo had a room on the third floor and there were fifteen men in the room, all boarding with Bartolo. . . . It was very hot in the room, but we were soon asleep, for we were very tired."

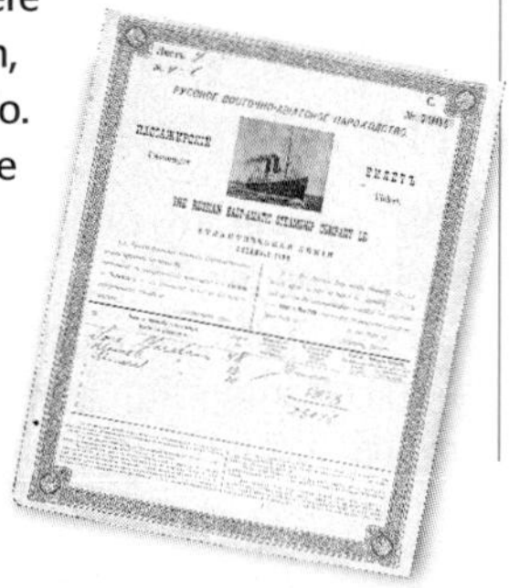

Immigrant's ticket

Before 1865 most immigrants to the United States—except for enslaved African Americans—came from northern and western Europe. The greater part of these "old" immigrants were Protestant, spoke English, and blended readily into American society.

A Flood of Immigrants

After the Civil War, growing numbers of immigrants made the journey to the United States. The tide of newcomers reached a peak in 1907, when nearly 1.3 million people came to America.

Geography

New Immigration

In the mid-1880s the pattern of immigration started to change. Large groups of "new" immigrants arrived from eastern and southern Europe. Greeks, Russians, Hungarians, Italians, Turks, and Poles were among the newcomers. At the same time, the number of "old" immigrants started to decrease. By 1907 only about 20 percent of the immigrants came from northern and western Europe, while 80 percent came from southern and eastern Europe.

Many of the newcomers from eastern and southern Europe were Catholics or Jews. Few spoke English. Because of this, they did not blend into American society as easily as the "old"

SECTION RESOURCES

Reproducible Masters
- Guided Reading Activity 20–1
- Political Cartoons
- Section Quiz 20–1
- Reteaching Activity 20–1
- Enrichment Activity 20–1

Transparencies
- Section Focus Transparency 20–1

Multimedia
- Chapter Challenger Interactive Review
- ABCNews InterActive™ Historic America Electronic Field Trips
- GTV: A Geographic Perspective on American History
- GTV: The American People: Fabric of a Nation

1 FOCUS

BELLRINGER
Motivational Activity

Before taking roll at the beginning of the class period, project Section Focus Transparency 20–1 and have students answer the questions. Discuss students' responses.

This activity is also available as a blackline master.

Section Focus Transparency 20–1

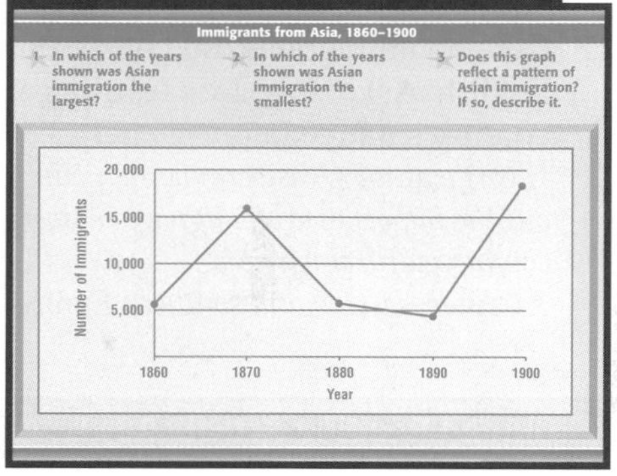

Vocabulary Precheck

Call on a volunteer to read aloud the definition of the term *emigrate.* Compare this term with *immigrate.* Explain to students that an easy way to remember these terms is to associate the first letter of each term with its definition. *Emigrate* means to exit a country and *immigrate* means to come into a country.

Section Theme
Culture and Traditions

In the mid-1800s the pattern of immigration changed from "old" to "new" immigrant groups. The "old" blended readily into American society, but the "new" held on to cultural differences.

Activity Ask students to imagine how they might feel if they moved to a new country where they did not understand the language or the customs.

2 TEACH

L1 Writing About Motivation Ask students to scan this section to find reasons for emigrating and immigrating. Then have them choose what they consider to be the most important reason and write a paragraph describing why that reason would motivate them to either emigrate or immigrate.

Picturing HISTORY Between 1815 and 1915, 7 million Germans immigrated to the United States. By 1930 only 3 percent of German immigrants did not speak English. **Ask: How does learning a country's native language help immigrants?** *(Answers should point out the importance of language in overcoming cultural barriers.)*
Answer: *eastern and southern Europe*

Guided Reading Activity 20–1

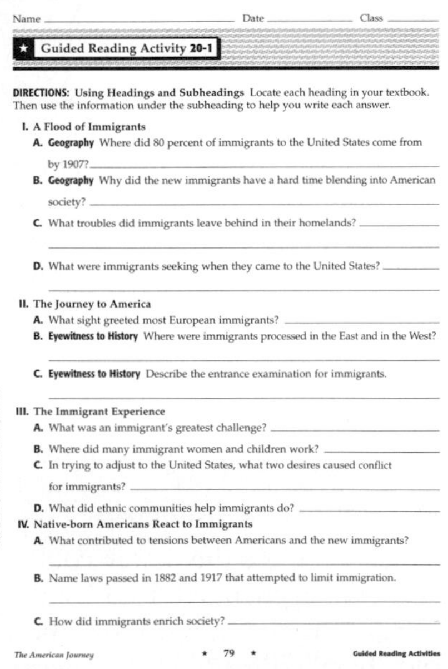
Name ______ Date ______ Class ______

★ Guided Reading Activity **20-1**

DIRECTIONS: Using Headings and Subheadings Locate each heading in your textbook. Then use the information under the subheading to help you write each answer.

I. A Flood of Immigrants
- **A. Geography** Where did 80 percent of immigrants to the United States come from by 1907? ______
- **B. Geography** Why did the new immigrants have a hard time blending into American society? ______
- **C.** What troubles did immigrants leave behind in their homelands? ______
- **D.** What were immigrants seeking when they came to the United States? ______

II. The Journey to America
- **A.** What sight greeted most European immigrants? ______
- **B. Eyewitness to History** Where were immigrants processed in the East and in the West? ______
- **C. Eyewitness to History** Describe the entrance examination for immigrants. ______

III. The Immigrant Experience
- **A.** What was an immigrant's greatest challenge? ______
- **B.** Where did many immigrant women and children work? ______
- **C.** In trying to adjust to the United States, what two desires caused conflict for immigrants? ______
- **D.** What did ethnic communities help immigrants do? ______

IV. Native-born Americans React to Immigrants
- **A.** What contributed to tensions between Americans and the new immigrants? ______
- **B.** Name laws passed in 1882 and 1917 that attempted to limit immigration. ______
- **C.** How did immigrants enrich society? ______

Copyright © by The McGraw-Hill Companies, Inc.

The American Journey ★ 79 ★ **Guided Reading Activities**

History *and the* Humanities

- The Spirit of American Art and Music, Lewis Hine
- Political Cartoons, *A Nation of Immigrants*

Picturing HISTORY Immigrants arrive in New York from Hamburg, Germany, in 1906. **Where did most immigrants to America come from after 1880?**

immigrants had. Many felt like outsiders, and they clustered together in urban neighborhoods made up of people of the same nationality.

After 1900 immigration from Mexico also increased. In addition many people came to the United States from China and Japan. They, too, brought unfamiliar languages and religious beliefs and had difficulty blending into American society.

Leaving Troubles Behind

Why did so many people leave their homelands for the United States in the late 1800s and early 1900s? They were "pushed" away by difficult conditions at home and "pulled" to the United States by new opportunities.

Many people **emigrated,** or left their homelands, because of economic troubles. In Italy and Hungary, overcrowding and poverty made jobs scarce. Farmers in Croatia and Serbia could not own enough land to support their families. Sweden suffered major crop failures. New machines such as looms put many craft workers out of work.

Persecution also drove people from their homelands. In some countries the government passed laws or followed policies against certain **ethnic groups**—minorities that spoke different languages or followed different customs from most people in a country. Members of these ethnic groups often emigrated to escape discrimination or unfair laws. Many Jews fled persecution in Russia in the 1880s and came to the United States.

Seeking Opportunity

Immigrants saw the United States as a land of opportunity and jobs, plentiful and affordable land, and a chance for a better life. Although some immigrants returned to their homelands after a few years, most came to America to stay.

Footnotes to History

The Price Is Right By the mid-1800s, a one-way ticket in steerage cost as little as $12 from Liverpool, England, to New York City. It cost less than $10 from Dublin, Ireland.

The Journey to America

Immigrants often had a difficult journey to America. Many had to first travel to a seaport to board a ship. Often they traveled for hundreds of miles on foot or on horseback and through foreign countries to get to the port cities.

Cooperative Learning Activity

Plays Organize students into groups of three to role-play an immigrant family's arrival in America. Encourage students to choose different nationalities and different points of entry into America. Have group members choose from the following roles: father, mother, uncle, aunt, son, or daughter. Allow groups either to videotape their plays to show to the class or to perform their plays live. Discuss specific problems different nationalities faced as they settled in America.

Then came the long ocean voyage to America—12 days across the Atlantic or 60 days across the Pacific. Immigrants usually could afford only the cheapest tickets, and they traveled in steerage, cramped, noisy quarters on the lower decks.

The Statue of Liberty

Most European immigrants landed at New York City. After 1886 the magnificent sight of the **Statue of Liberty** greeted the immigrants as they sailed into **New York Harbor.** The statue, a gift from France, seemed to promise hope for a better life in the new country. On the base of the statue, the stirring words of **Emma Lazarus,** an American poet, welcomed immigrants from Europe:

> "Give me your tired, your poor,
> Your huddled masses yearning to
> breathe free,
> The wretched refuse of your teeming shore.
> Send these, the homeless, tempest-
> tossed to me,
> I lift my lamp beside the golden door!"

Eyewitness to HISTORY

Entering America

Bianca De Carli arrived from Italy in 1913 as a young girl. Many years later she remembered how she felt as her ship reached New York City:

> "We all trembled because of the strangeness and the confusion and the unknownness. Some were weak from no movement and exercise, and some were sick because of the smells and the unfresh air. But somehow this did not matter because we now knew it was almost over."

Before the new arrivals could actually pass through the "golden door" to America, they had to register at government reception centers. In the East immigrants were processed at Castle Garden, a former fort on Manhattan Island, and after 1892 at **Ellis Island** in New York Harbor. Most Asian immigrants arrived in America on the West Coast and went through the processing center on **Angel Island** in **San Francisco Bay.**

Entrance Examinations

Examiners at the centers recorded the immigrants' names—sometimes shortening or simplifying a name they found too difficult to write. The examiners asked the immigrants where they came from, their occupation, and whether they had relatives in the United States. The examiners also gave health examinations. Immigrants with contagious illnesses could be refused permission to enter the United States.

The new arrivals often found this process bewildering. Nina Goodenov, who came from Russia in 1911, later wrote:

> "It was a nightmare. After all, none of us spoke English. We had no idea where we were going and no idea what was to be done to us. . . . There were hundreds and hundreds of people and they were treated exactly like sheep. . . . It took a day and a night. . . . You had to sleep on the benches, just sitting up."

Arriving at Ellis Island

Multiple Learning Styles

Verbal/Linguistic Many immigrants' experiences are preserved through oral history. Suggest that students interview a person who immigrated to the United States. Make sure students include the following in their interviews: reasons for emigrating; reasons for choosing the United States; a description of the journey; feelings upon entering the United States; and problems faced including finding a job, finding housing, and overcoming a language barrier and other cultural differences. Encourage students to present their interviews using different media such as videotape, computer multimedia, oral, written, and so on. **L2, ELL**

CURRICULUM CONNECTION

HEALTH
By 1830 about 1,000 ships carried cotton from the United States to England annually. Merchants tried to find cargo to fill the empty ships returning to the United States and stumbled on an unusual cargo—people. These ships were unsanitary and poorly ventilated and were a breeding ground for diseases such as trachoma and malignant typhus—dubbed *ship fever.*

ABCNEWS INTERACTIVE™

VIDEODISC
Historic America Electronic Field Trips

Side 2, Chapter 7

Title: *Ellis Island*
Subject: Immigration center tour
Ask: **What was Ellis Island?** *(the first and largest immigration station in the United States)*

Also available in VHS.

NATIONAL GEOGRAPHIC SOCIETY

VIDEODISC
GTV: A Geographic Perspective on American History

Side 3, Chapter 5
Title: *Making a Mark*
Subject: The impact of immigration (1870–1910)
Ask: **What made the United States desirable to immigrants?** *(freedom, land, opportunity*

Picturing HISTORY Schools emphasized reading, writing, arithmetic, American history and geography, penmanship, and spelling. Students memorized long lists of names and dates. They recited to the teacher while standing at attention.
Answer: *supplied industries with workers for economic growth; enriched society with customs, foods, languages, and literature*

Where?When?Who?What?

Ellis Island Named for its owner Samuel Ellis, Ellis Island was not the drab place one might imagine immigrants passed through. *The New Yorker* called it "the grandest single space in New York." It was a beautiful, richly decorated complex with first-class health facilities, a roof garden with inspiring views of Lower Manhattan and the Statue of Liberty, and good food for the few who were detained. Brass chandeliers and a vaulted ceiling with 29,000 handset tiles adorned its Registration Hall.

NATIONAL GEOGRAPHIC SOCIETY

VIDEODISC
GTV: The American People: Fabric of a Nation

Side 3, Chapter 1
Title: *The Golden Door*
Subject: The flood of immigration between 1880 and 1920
Ask: **Where did the immigrants to America come from after 1880?** *(Italy, Russia, Poland, other eastern European countries, Japan, Mexico, Canada, and Scandinavia)*

Picturing HISTORY Jacob Riis photographed many aspects of immigrant life in New York City. The classroom was the major place where the immigrants' children learned American ways. **How did immigrants contribute to American society?**

The Immigrant Experience

After passing through the reception centers, most immigrants entered the United States. Where would they go? How would they live? Some had relatives or friends to stay with and to help them find jobs. Others knew no one and would have to strike out on their own.

Finding Work

An immigrant's greatest challenge was finding work. Sometimes organizations in his or her homeland recruited workers for jobs in the United States. The organization supplied American employers with unskilled workers who worked at unloading cargo or digging ditches.

Some of America's fastest-growing industries hired immigrant workers. In the steel mills of Pittsburgh, for example, most of the common laborers in the early 1900s were immigrant men. They might work 12 hours a day, 7 days a week.

Women and Children at Work

Many immigrants, including women and children, worked in **sweatshops** in the garment industry. These were dark, crowded workshops where workers made clothing. The work was repetitious and hazardous, the pay low, and the hours long.

Pauline Newman, who later became an official in the International Ladies' Garment Workers Union, worked in a New York sweatshop as a child. She recalled:

> "We started work at seven-thirty in the morning, and during the busy season we worked until nine in the evening. They didn't pay you any overtime and they didn't give you anything for supper money. Sometimes they'd give you a little apple pie if you had to work very late."

Adjusting to America

In their new homes, immigrants tried to preserve some aspects of their own cultures. At the same time, most wanted to **assimilate,** or become part of the American culture. These two desires sometimes came into conflict.

Tensions arose between parents and children or between men and women. Some immigrants found that their American-born children had little interest in the culture of their European or Asian

MAKING CONNECTIONS ACTIVITY

Cultural Life Explain to students that immigrants sought to re-create the cultural heritage they left behind by establishing family traditions. Ask students to choose one of their family's traditions to illustrate on a poster. Have them portray the following on their posters: description of the tradition, how the tradition reflects and preserves cultural heritage, how the tradition has changed through the years. Encourage students to include photographs, illustrations, essays, poems, and so on. **L1, ELL**

homeland. Most children wanted to assimilate as quickly as possible.

Language highlighted the differences between generations of families. Many immigrant parents continued to speak their original languages at home. Their children spoke English at school and with friends, but they, too, spoke their original language at home. On the other hand, many immigrants' grandchildren spoke only English.

The role of immigrant women also changed in the United States, where women generally had more freedom than women in European and Asian countries. New lifestyles conflicted with traditional ways and sometimes produced friction. Immigrant women who worked in factories and at other jobs made friends and developed interests that their families did not always understand.

Building Communities

Most of the new immigrants were from rural areas. Because they lacked the money to buy farmland in America, however, they often settled in industrial cities. With little or no education, they usually worked as unskilled laborers.

Relatives who had immigrated earlier helped new arrivals get settled, and people of the same ethnic group naturally tended to form communities. As a result neighborhoods of Jewish, Italian, Polish, Chinese, and other groups quickly developed in New York, Chicago, San Francisco, and other large cities.

The immigrants sought to re-create some of the life they had left behind. The communities they established revolved around a number of traditional institutions. Most important were the houses of worship—the churches and synagogues—where worship was conducted and holidays were celebrated as they had been in their homelands. Priests and rabbis often acted as community leaders.

The immigrants published newspapers in their native languages, opened stores and theaters, and organized social clubs. Ethnic communities and institutions helped the immigrants preserve their cultural heritage.

Native-born Americans React to Immigrants

Assimilation was also slowed by the attitudes of many native-born Americans. Although employers were happy to hire immigrant workers at low wages, some American-born workers resented the immigrants. These Americans feared that the immigrants would take away their jobs or drive down everyone's wages by accepting lower pay.

Anti-Immigrant Sentiment

Ethnic, religious, and racial differences contributed to tensions between Americans and the new immigrants. Some Americans argued that the new immigrants—with their foreign languages, unfamiliar religions, and distinctive customs—did not fit into American society.

People found it easy to blame immigrants for increasing crime, unemployment, and other problems in American society. The **nativist** movement, for example, had opposed immigration since the 1830s. Nativism gained strength in the late 1800s. Some Americans formed groups to restrict the rights of immigrants. Some communities passed

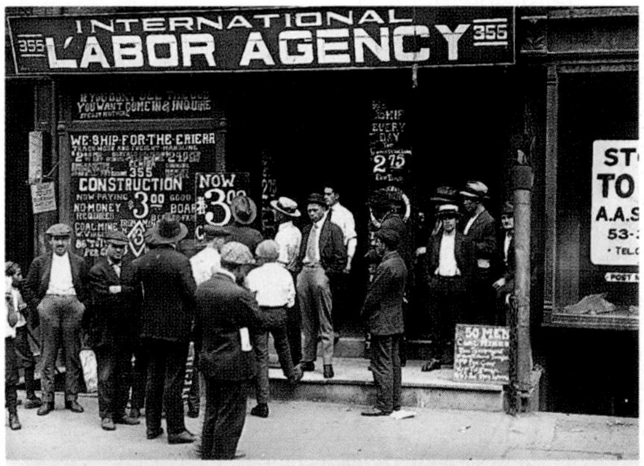

Picturing HISTORY An employment agency in New York City attracts immigrants with its advertisements for jobs. **What kinds of jobs did most immigrants hold?**

CHAPTER 20
Section 1, 575–580

3 ASSESS

Assign Section 1 Review as homework or as an in-class activity.

Use **Chapter Challenger Interactive Review Software** to review Section 1.

Section Quiz 20–1

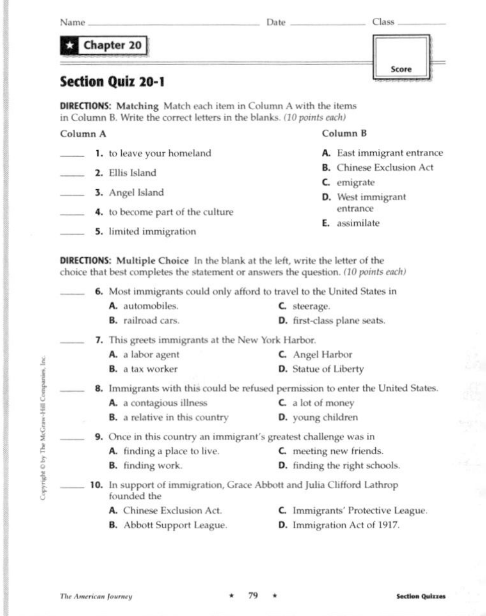
Name ______ Date ______ Class ______

Chapter 20 — Score

Section Quiz 20-1

DIRECTIONS: Matching Match each item in Column A with the items in Column B. Write the correct letters in the blanks. *(10 points each)*

Column A	Column B
____ **1.** to leave your homeland	**A.** East immigrant entrance
____ **2.** Ellis Island	**B.** Chinese Exclusion Act
____ **3.** Angel Island	**C.** emigrate
____ **4.** to become part of the culture	**D.** West immigrant entrance
____ **5.** limited immigration	**E.** assimilate

DIRECTIONS: Multiple Choice In the blank at the left, write the letter of the choice that best completes the statement or answers the question. *(10 points each)*

____ **6.** Most immigrants could only afford to travel to the United States in
A. automobiles. **C.** steerage.
B. railroad cars. **D.** first-class plane seats.

____ **7.** This greets immigrants at the New York Harbor.
A. a labor agent **C.** Angel Harbor
B. a tax worker **D.** Statue of Liberty

____ **8.** Immigrants with this could be refused permission to enter the United States.
A. a contagious illness **C.** a lot of money
B. a relative in this country **D.** young children

____ **9.** Once in this country an immigrant's greatest challenge was in
A. finding a place to live. **C.** meeting new friends.
B. finding work. **D.** finding the right schools.

____ **10.** In support of immigration, Grace Abbott and Julia Clifford Lathrop founded the
A. Chinese Exclusion Act. **C.** Immigrants' Protective League.
B. Abbott Support League. **D.** Immigration Act of 1917.

The American Journey ★ 79 ★ **Section Quizzes**

Picturing HISTORY Less than 10 percent of immigrants to America in the late nineteenth and early twentieth centuries had a trade or specific work skill. These immigrants provided much of the physical labor that built America. One immigrant upon arriving in America wrote, ". . . the streets were not paved with gold; . . . the streets were not paved at all; (immigrant workers) were expected to pave them."
Answer: *physical labor, unskilled and low-paying jobs*

CRITICAL THINKING ACTIVITY

Identifying Assumptions Explain the origin of the term *melting pot,* which comes from Israel Zangwill's 1909 play *The Melting Pot.* The play coined the term to describe America's mixture of nationalities and ethnic groups. Describe melting pot as a theory in which immigrants of various nationalities are assimilated into one culture. Also explain that many sociologists disagree with this theory. James Banks, a noted multicultural author, describes America as a patchwork quilt in which ethnic groups maintain their cultural identity while forming a part of the main culture. Discuss the underlying assumptions that form the basis of these two theories. Challenge students to choose which theory they think accurately describes America and illustrate that theory using a graphic organizer. **L3**

CHAPTER 20
Section 1, 575–580

Reteaching Activity 20–1

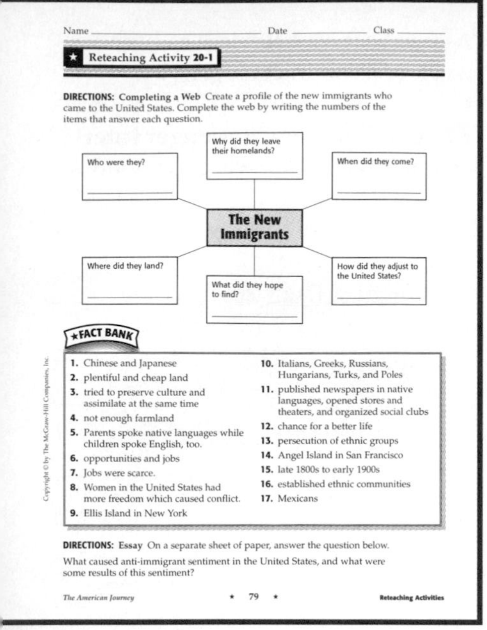
Name ______ Date ______ Class ______

★ Reteaching Activity 20-1

DIRECTIONS: Completing a Web Create a profile of the new immigrants who came to the United States. Complete the web by writing the numbers of the items that answer each question.

★FACT BANK

1. Chinese and Japanese
2. plentiful and cheap land
3. tried to preserve culture and assimilate at the same time
4. not enough farmland
5. Parents spoke native languages while children spoke English, too.
6. opportunities and jobs
7. Jobs were scarce.
8. Women in the United States had more freedom which caused conflict.
9. Ellis Island in New York
10. Italians, Greeks, Russians, Hungarians, Turks, and Poles
11. published newspapers in native languages, opened stores and theaters, and organized social clubs
12. chance for a better life
13. persecution of ethnic groups
14. Angel Island in San Francisco
15. late 1800s to early 1900s
16. established ethnic communities
17. Mexicans

DIRECTIONS: Essay On a separate sheet of paper, answer the question below.

What caused anti-immigrant sentiment in the United States, and what were some results of this sentiment?

Copyright © by The McGraw-Hill Companies, Inc.

The American Journey ★ 79 ★ Reteaching Activities

Enrichment Activity 20–1

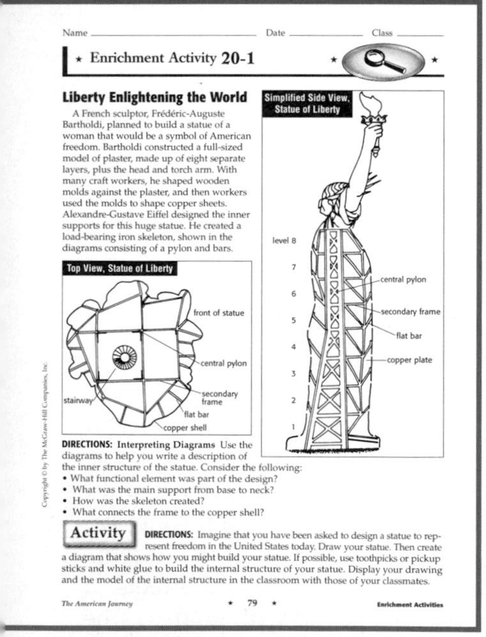
Name ______ Date ______ Class ______

★ Enrichment Activity 20-1

Liberty Enlightening the World

A French sculptor, Frédéric-Auguste Bartholdi, planned to build a statue of a woman that would be a symbol of American freedom. Bartholdi constructed a full-sized model of plaster, made up of eight separate layers, plus the head and torch arm. With many craft workers, he shaped wooden molds against the plaster, and then workers used the molds to shape copper sheets. Alexandre-Gustave Eiffel designed the inner supports for this huge statue. He created a load-bearing iron skeleton, shown in the diagrams consisting of a pylon and bars.

DIRECTIONS: Interpreting Diagrams Use the diagrams to help you write a description of the inner structure of the statue. Consider the following:
- What functional element was part of the design?
- What was the main support from base to neck?
- How was the skeleton created?
- What connects the frame to the copper shell?

Activity **DIRECTIONS:** Imagine that you have been asked to design a statue to represent freedom in the United States today. Draw your statue. Then create a diagram that shows how you might build your statue. If possible, use toothpicks or pickup sticks and white glue to build the internal structure of your statue. Display your drawing and the model of the internal structure in the classroom with those of your classmates.

Copyright © by The McGraw-Hill Companies, Inc.

The American Journey ★ 79 ★ Enrichment Activities

4 CLOSE

Brainstorm the effect immigrants' cultures have on a society and how the society's culture affects immigrants.

laws banning immigrants from holding certain jobs and denying them other rights. Jewish immigrants, for example, were denied admission to certain universities. In addition, immigrants faced physical attack. In 1880, for example, white citizens of Denver, Colorado, attacked Chinese residents and destroyed many of their homes and businesses. Calls for restrictions on immigration mounted.

New Immigration Laws

Lawmakers responded quickly to the tide of anti-immigrant feeling. In 1882 Congress passed the first law to limit immigration—the **Chinese Exclusion Act.** This law prohibited Chinese workers from entering the United States for 10 years. Congress extended the law in 1892 and again in 1902.

In 1908 the federal government and Japan came to a "gentleman's agreement." The Japanese agreed to limit the number of immigrants to the United States, while the Americans pledged fair treatment for Japanese Americans already in the United States.

Other immigration laws affected immigrants from all nations. An 1882 law made each immigrant pay a tax and also barred criminals from entering the country. In 1897 Congress passed a bill requiring immigrants to be able to read and write in some language. Although President Cleveland vetoed the bill as unfair, some years later Congress passed the **Immigration Act of 1917,** which included a similar literacy requirement.

Immigrants' Contributions

Despite some anti-immigrant sentiment, many Americans—including **Grace Abbott** and **Julia Clifford Lathrop,** who helped found the Immigrants' Protective League—spoke out in support of immigration. These Americans recognized that the United States was a nation of immigrants and that the newcomers made lasting contributions to their new society.

The new immigrants supplied the country's growing industries with the workers that were necessary for economic growth. At the same time, the new immigrants and their children—like the old immigrants before them—helped shape American life. They gave the nation its major religious groups—Protestants, Catholics, and Jews. While becoming part of the society around them, they enriched that society with their own customs and cultures, language and literature.

The effects of immigration were most visible in the cities, with their fast-growing ethnic neighborhoods. The flow of immigrants was one of the factors that transformed America's cities in the late 1800s and the early 1900s.

Section 1 Review

Checking for Understanding

1. ***Identify*** Emma Lazarus, Ellis Island, Angel Island, Chinese Exclusion Act, Immigration Act of 1917.
2. ***Define*** emigrate, ethnic group, steerage, sweatshop, assimilate.
3. ***Explain*** how the pattern of immigration changed in the 1880s.

Reviewing Themes

4. **Culture and Traditions** What were some of the cultural differences that immigrants had to adjust to in the United States?

Critical Thinking

5. **Identifying Central Issues** Why do you think some Americans blamed the "new" immigrants for many of society's problems?

Activity

Making a Collage Create a collage illustrating the origins of immigrants who came to the United States after 1880. Clip photographs from advertisements and newsmagazines to make your collage.

Section 1 Review Answers

1. Emma Lazarus, 577; Ellis Island, 577; Angel Island, 577; Chinese Exclusion Act, 580; Immigration Act of 1917, 580
2. The words are defined in the Glossary.
3. Before 1880: mostly from northern and western Europe, Protestant, English-speaking. After 1880: mostly from southern and eastern Europe, many were Catholic or Jewish, few spoke English
4. different language, lifestyles (especially women's roles), and religions
5. Answers will vary but may mention fear, anger, immigrants' differences, and the ease of blaming someone else.

Activity Collages should show images that represent people and customs of immigrants mainly from southern and eastern Europe.

Reading a Line Graph

Graphs are a way of showing numbers visually, making them easier to read and understand. Graphs are often used to compare changes over time or differences between places, groups of people, or related events.

Learning the Skill

On a line graph, numbers usually appear along the left side of the graph, or the vertical axis. Time is usually shown along the bottom of the graph, or the horizontal axis. A line on the graph shows whether the numbers go up or down over time.

Sometimes a graph contains more than one line, recording two or more related quantities. For example, you and a friend might both record your running speeds for footraces over a period of time on one graph, using two lines of different colors to represent each of your running times.

To read a line graph, follow these steps:

- Read the title of the graph.
- Read the information on the horizontal axis and the vertical axis.
- Study the points where the line intersects the grid on the line graph. This step tells you what amount existed at a given time.
- Study the changes over time that the line on the graph illustrates. Look for increases, decreases, and sudden shifts.
- Draw conclusions from the statistics presented. What trends or patterns appear?

Practicing the Skill

Study the line graph on this page and answer the following questions.

1. What is the subject of this line graph?
2. What information is presented on the horizontal axis? On the vertical axis?

Immigration to the United States, 1860–1920

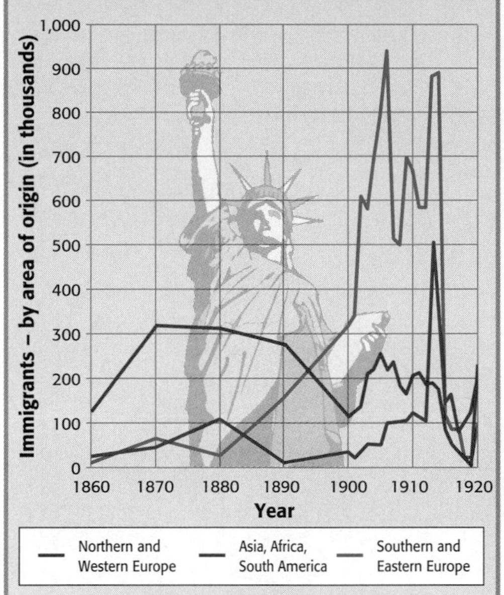

Source: U.S. Bureau of the Census; *Historical Statistics of the United States, Colonial Times to 1970,* Bicentennial Edition, Washington, D.C.

3. In about what year did immigration from northern and western Europe peak?
4. In about what year was immigration from Asia, Africa, and South America the lowest?
5. During what two decades did immigration from southern and eastern Europe peak?

Applying the Skill

Making a Line Graph Keep track of the number of hours you spend on homework each day for a one-week period. Chart the information on a line graph.

Social Studies
SKILL BUILDER

TEACH

Reading a Line Graph

This skill illustrates how line graphs are used to compare changes over time by presenting 3 different groups of immigrants over a 60-year period. By reading the line graph, students will see how data is easily compared.

Explain to students that line graphs show changes over time. Have students work in groups to use the same information on the line graph and present it on a bar graph. Have students apply the steps listed in this skill to reading a bar graph. Ask them to compare how information is presented on the two graphs and choose which type of graph they prefer.

Additional Practice

Chapter Skills Activity 20

ANSWERS TO PRACTICING THE SKILL

1. immigration to the United States from 1860 to 1920
2. time, specifically decades; thousands of immigrants by area of origin
3. 1870
4. 1890
5. 1900–1910, 1910–1920

Applying the Skill Graphs should include the hours spent on homework.

NATIONAL GEOGRAPHIC *Journeys*

NATIONAL GEOGRAPHIC SOCIETY

VIDEODISC
GTV: A Geographic Perspective on American History

Side 3, Chapter 5
Title: *Making a Mark*
Subject: The impact of immigration (1870–1910)
Ask: What was the effect of immigration on cities? *(Cities grew as immigrant population increased.)* How was immigration advantageous to the United States? *(more workers for industries, fresh mix of ideas, more demand for products)*

you don't say...

Steerage People were willing to endure almost any hardship to immigrate to America if the price was right. By packing passengers on board ships and giving them almost nothing in the way of civilizing comforts, the fares offered to passengers were not just low but irresistible. The most inexpensive ticket, steerage, was so called because accommodations were near the ship's steering mechanism and, thus, were noisy.

1 Chinese bound for the United States crowded the decks of steamships after the discovery of gold in California in 1848. Like many seeking their fortunes, 16-year-old Lee Chew left his farm in China and booked passage on a steamer about 1880. When he and other Chinese immigrants arrived in San Francisco, they confronted a great wave of anti-Asian feeling.

2 In San Francisco's Chinese quarter, immigrants ran markets, laundries, and other small shops. Chew worked for an American family and saved his earnings for two years. "Chinese laundrymen [like me] were taught by American women," he said. "There are no laundries in China."

3 With his savings Lee Chew and a partner opened a laundry serving railroad crews "in a town about 500 miles" from San Francisco. For three years the partners followed Chinese and Irish immigrants, like those above, who built the early railroads. Then the two moved on to the mines, where rough miners "came into our [laundry] to shoot and steal shirts...."

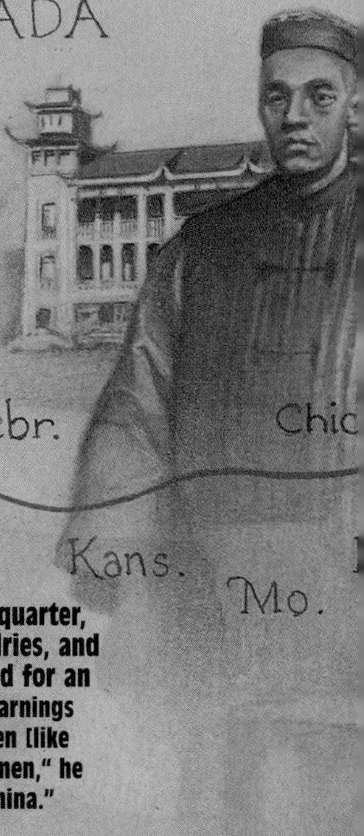

4 In 1890 Lee Chew (below) headed for Chicago. Here he stands in front of the Chinese Merchants Association, which later became the Chinatown City Hall. "I had a laundry for three years," he wrote, and "increased my capital to $2,500. After that I was four years in Detroit." In 1897 he returned to China for a year.

TEACHER'S NOTES

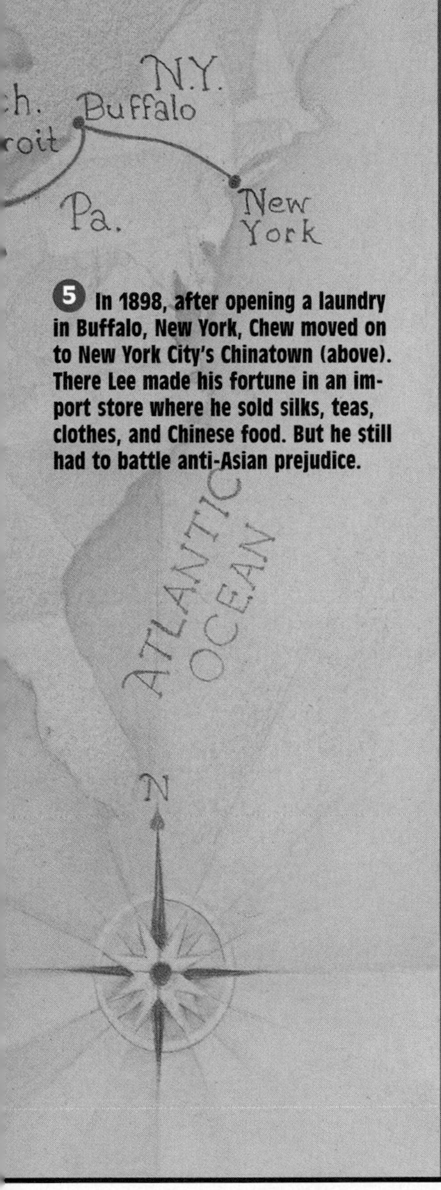

5 In 1898, after opening a laundry in Buffalo, New York, Chew moved on to New York City's Chinatown (above). There Lee made his fortune in an import store where he sold silks, teas, clothes, and Chinese food. But he still had to battle anti-Asian prejudice.

NATIONAL GEOGRAPHIC

Journeys

An Immigrant's Journey

"My father gave me $100, and I ... got steerage passage on a steamer.... I did not like [the food] at all.... The thought of what [it] might be made of, by the wicked wizards of the ship, made me ill. Of the great power of these people I saw many signs. The engines that moved the ship were wonderful monsters, strong enough to lift mountains. When I got to San Francisco ... I was half-starved, because I was afraid to eat the provisions of the barbarians.... A man got me work as a house servant ... and my start was the same as that of almost all the Chinese in this country."

—*From recollections of Lee Chew, published in* Plain Folk: The Life Stories of Undistinguished Americans *by David Katzman and William Tuttle, 1982.*

NATIONAL GEOGRAPHIC SOCIETY

VIDEODISC
GTV: The American People: Fabric of a Nation

Side 3, Chapter 3
Title: *Home Sweet Home?*
Subject: The urban immigration experience
Ask: **What did immigrants do to make themselves feel more at home?** *(They developed their own communities with their own shops, newspapers, and so on.)*

What?Where?When?Who?

Bibliography The excerpt at left was taken from *Plain Folk: The Life Stories of Undistinguished Americans* by David Katzman and William Tuttle, Jr. (University of Illinois Press, 1982).

TEACHER'S NOTES

CHAPTER 20
Section 2, 584–589

1 FOCUS

BELLRINGER
Motivational Activity

Before taking roll at the beginning of the class period, project Section Focus Transparency 20–2 and have students answer the questions. Discuss students' responses.

This activity is also available as a blackline master.

Section Focus Transparency 20–2

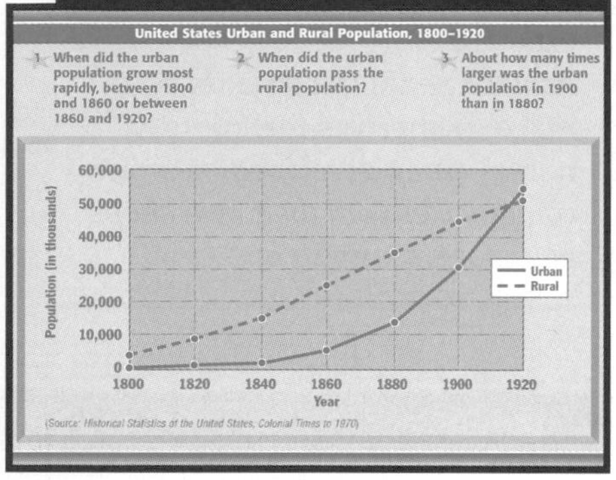

Vocabulary Precheck

Have students read the definition of *The Gilded Age* on p. 586. Ask them to define *gilded*. Lead them to understand that *gilded* means to cover up something with an appearance of value. Ask what was being covered up. *(poverty)*

Use the **Vocabulary PuzzleMaker** to create crossword and word search puzzles.

Section Theme
Science and Technology

After the Civil War, the United States changed from a rural to an urban nation. Developments in science and technology helped push Americans off the farms and pull them to the cities.

Activity Brainstorm developments in technology on the farm and in the city that would motivate people to leave the farm and move to the city.

1870 — 1880 — 1890

1873 Twain's *The Gilded Age* is published

1879 The Salvation Army originates

1883 The Brooklyn Bridge opens

1884 First skyscraper constructed in Chicago

Section 2

Moving to the City

READ TO DISCOVER . . .
- how American cities grew and changed.
- what life was like in the cities.
- what problems cities faced and how people tried to solve them.

TERMS TO LEARN

tenement
slum
suburb
The Gilded Age
settlement house

The Storyteller

A train pulling into Chicago in 1884 carried a young passenger named Hamlin Garland. For Garland, who had grown up on a farm, the big city was a bewildering sight. Garland later became famous for his stories about the Midwest. In one novel he described his feeling of dismay when he first saw Chicago. "The mere thought of a million people stunned my imagination." Garland wondered, "How can so many people find a living in one place?"

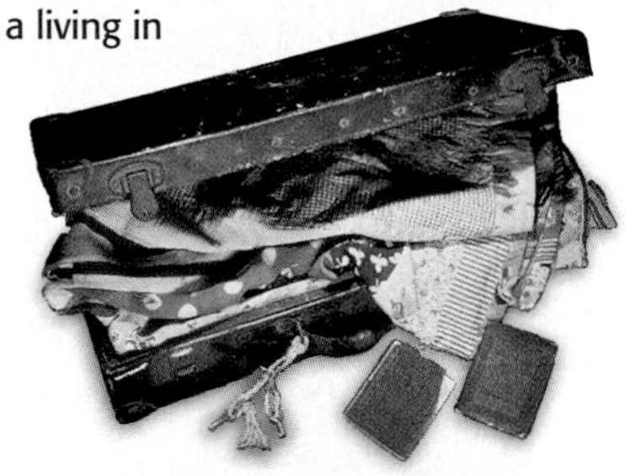

Migrant's suitcase and Bibles

American cities grew rapidly after the Civil War. In 1870, 1 American in 4 lived in cities with 2,500 or more people. By 1910 nearly half of the American population were city dwellers. The United States was changing from a rural to an urban nation.

Geography

Growth of Cities

Immigrants played an enormous part in the growth of cities. In major urban centers such as New York, Detroit, and Chicago, immigrants and their children made up 80 percent or more of the population in 1890.

Native-born Americans also contributed to urban growth. Americans moved in huge numbers from farming areas to cities, looking for jobs.

The industrialization of America had changed work on farms. New farm machinery made it possible to produce crops using fewer farmworkers. In addition women in rural areas no longer had to make clothing and household goods. These items, made by machine, could now be bought in stores or from catalogs. Freed from such chores, many women left farms to look for jobs in the cities.

African Americans also migrated to cities in large numbers. The vast majority of the country's African American population lived in the rural South in great poverty. Many African Americans began moving to Southern cities in search of jobs and to escape debt, injustice, or discrimination.

SECTION RESOURCES

Reproducible Masters
- Reproducible Lesson Plan 20–2
- Guided Reading Activity 20–2
- Section Quiz 20–2
- Reteaching Activity 20–2
- Enrichment Activity 20–2

Transparencies
- Section Focus Transparency 20–2

Multimedia
- Vocabulary PuzzleMaker
- Chapter Challenger Interactive Review Software
- Testmaker
- GTV: A Geographic Perspective on American History
- GTV: The American People: Fabric of a Nation

★ ★ ★ ★ ★ ★ ★ ★ ★ ★ ★ ★ ★ ★ ★ ★ ★

After 1914 a large number of African Americans moved to Northern cities, which offered more jobs in industry and manufacturing than Southern cities did. Many African Americans also hoped to find less discrimination and violence in the North.

★ Picturing HISTORY These children lived in a Pittsburgh neighborhood. An advertisement (inset) promotes the sale of a middle-class home in the Chicago suburbs. **How did the dwellings of poor and middle-class Americans differ during the industrial age?**

Transportation and Resources

America's expanding railroad network fed the growth of the cities. Railroads helped people move to the cities and transported the raw materials for industry. Trains carried cattle to Chicago and **Kansas City,** making these cities great meatpacking centers.

Some cities flourished because of nearby resources. **Pittsburgh** developed rapidly as a center for iron and steel manufacturing because both iron ore and coal—to fuel the industry's huge furnaces—were found in the area.

Seaports such as **New York** and **San Francisco** developed as American trade with the rest of the world increased. In addition the immigrant population of these cities provided a large pool of workers who were available for low wages.

City Life

★ Cities were exciting places that offered jobs, stores, and entertainment. But there was also substandard housing and desperate poverty. The gap between the rich and the poor was staggering.

Tenement Living

People poured into the cities faster than housing could be built to accomodate them. In the biggest, most crowded cities, the poorest residents—including most immigrants—lived in **tenements.** Originally a tenement was simply a building in which several families rented rooms. By the late 1800s, however, a tenement had come to mean an apartment building in the **slums**—poor, run-down urban neighborhoods.

Tenements had many small, dark rooms. One young immigrant from Poland spoke of living in the dimly lit rooms in the back of a New York City tenement:

Footnotes to History

A Cosmopolitan City By 1900, New York City had more Italians than the cities of Florence, Genoa, and Venice, Italy, put together. Almost as many Irish lived there as in Dublin, Ireland. And more Russians lived in New York City than in Kiev, Russia.

CHAPTER 20
Section 2, 584–589

2 TEACH

L1, ELL Making a Poster Ask students to work in small groups to create posters illustrating the new technology that aided the growth of cities.

★ Picturing HISTORY From 1870 to 1920, the population of the United States increased from about 39 million to about 106 million. During that same period of time, the urban population increased from 26 percent of the total to 51 percent of the total. **Ask:** **What was life in a tenement like?** *(dark, dirty, noisy, crowded, stifling, unsanitary)* **Answer:** *Poor: lived in run-down, overcrowded urban tenements, many without hot water or bathtubs. Middle class: lived in suburbs, had hot water, indoor toilets, and–by 1900–electricity.*

Guided Reading Activity 20–2

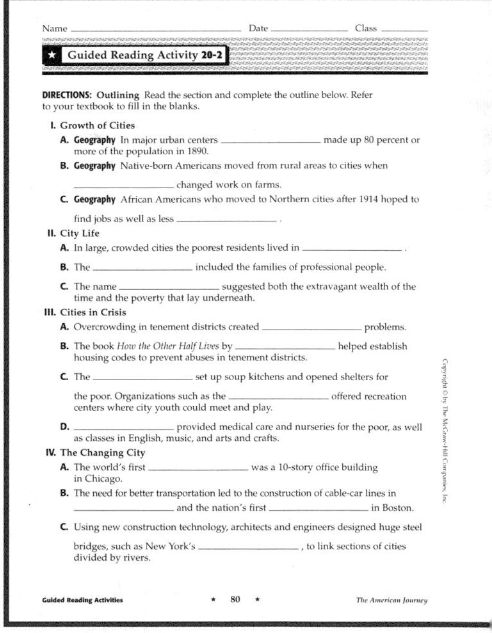

Name ______ Date ______ Class ______

★ Guided Reading Activity **20-2**

DIRECTIONS: Outlining Read the section and complete the outline below. Refer to your textbook to fill in the blanks.

I. Growth of Cities
  A. **Geography** In major urban centers ______ made up 80 percent or more of the population in 1890.
  B. **Geography** Native-born Americans moved from rural areas to cities when ______ changed work on farms.
  C. **Geography** African Americans who moved to Northern cities after 1914 hoped to find jobs as well as less ______.

II. City Life
  A. In large, crowded cities the poorest residents lived in ______.
  B. The ______ included the families of professional people.
  C. The name ______ suggested both the extravagant wealth of the time and the poverty that lay underneath.

III. Cities in Crisis
  A. Overcrowding in tenement districts created ______ problems.
  B. The book *How the Other Half Lives* by ______ helped establish housing codes to prevent abuses in tenement districts.
  C. The ______ set up soup kitchens and opened shelters for the poor. Organizations such as the ______ offered recreation centers where city youth could meet and play.
  D. ______ provided medical care and nurseries for the poor, as well as classes in English, music, and arts and crafts.

IV. The Changing City
  A. The world's first ______ was a 10-story office building in Chicago.
  B. The need for better transportation led to the construction of cable-car lines in ______ and the nation's first ______ in Boston.
  C. Using new construction technology, architects and engineers designed huge steel bridges, such as New York's ______, to link sections of cities divided by rivers.

Guided Reading Activities ★ 80 ★ *The American Journey*

Cooperative Learning Activity

Creating a Documentary of City Life Organize students into groups of five to create a videotaped documentary of city life in the late 1800s. Ask group members to choose from the following topics to portray on the videotape: transportation, housing, social services, social problems, and architecture. Encourage groups to film their textbook's photos and photos from other sources as they narrate their documentary. Have students title their documentaries *Life in the Big City.* Spend a day viewing and critiquing each other's documentaries.

Graph Study

Answers
1. about 18–20 million more
2. about 24 million more

Graph Skills Practice

Reading a Graph During which decade was there the greatest difference between rural and urban population? *(1880s)*

NATIONAL GEOGRAPHIC SOCIETY

VIDEODISC
GTV: A Geographic Perspective on American History

Side 3, Chapter 12
Title: *The Price of Progress*
Subject: Effects of the early industrial age (1890–1920)
Ask: **What problems arose in the cities as a result of industrial progress?** (overcrowding, disease, sewage problems, and pollution)

CURRICULUM CONNECTION

ECONOMICS
In the 1870s people thought that typing was physically too strenuous and intellectually too complicated for women. As a result, most secretaries were men. America's Young Women's Christian Association (YWCA) sought to change that. The YWCA's goal was to assist working-class girls who came to the city seeking education and jobs. The YWCA did a survey and found that stenography was the most lucrative of all professions and started offering shorthand and, later, typing classes for women.

Urban and Rural Population Growth, 1860–1900

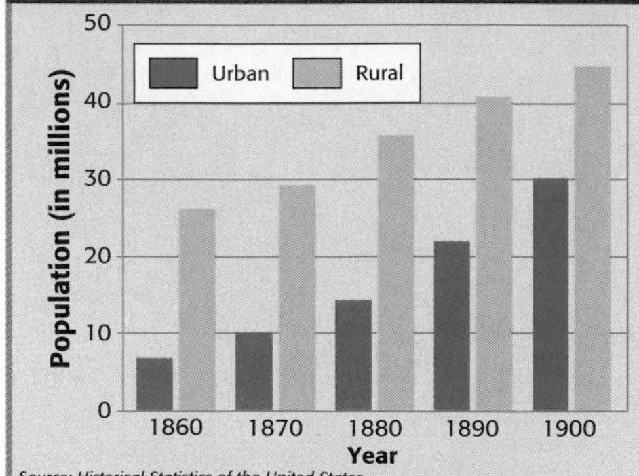

Source: *Historical Statistics of the United States.*

Graph Study

The gap between the urban and rural populations narrowed in the late 1800s.
1. About how many more people lived in rural than in urban areas in 1860?
2. **Comparing** About how many more people lived in urban areas in 1900 than in 1860?

"We would so like to live in the front, but we can't pay the rent. . . . Why, they have the sun in there. When the door is opened the light comes right in your face."

Three, four, or more people lived in each room. Usually several families had to share a cold-water tap and a toilet. Few tenement houses had hot water or bathtubs. A government inspector wrote of the "filthy and rotten tenements" of the Chicago slums in 1896, where children filled "every nook, eating and sleeping in every windowsill, pouring in and out of every door."

Middle-Class Comfort

The cities also had a growing middle class. The middle class included the families of professional people such as doctors, lawyers, and ministers. An increasing number of managers and salaried office clerks also became part of the middle class.

The middle class enjoyed a comfortable life. Many families moved from cities to the **suburbs,** residential areas that sprang up outside of city centers as a result of improvements in transportation. There they lived in houses with hot water, indoor toilets, and—by 1900—electricity. Middle-class families might have one or two servants and the leisure time to enjoy music, art, and literature.

The Gilded Age

At the top of the economic and social ladder stood the very rich. The wealthy lived very different lives from most Americans. They built enormous mansions in the cities and huge estates in the country. Some homes, such as those of J.P. Morgan and Henry Clay Frick in New York City, are now museums.

In these mansions, the rich lived lives of extreme luxury, throwing enormous parties and dinners. In 1883 Alva and William Kissam Vanderbilt gave a party for more than 1,000 guests at their New York mansion. The party was estimated to have cost $250,000—equal to about $3 million today.

Mark Twain and Charles Dudley Warner published a novel in 1873 called *The Gilded Age.* The name—which refers to something covered with a thin layer of gold—became associated with America of the late 1800s. **The Gilded Age** suggested both the extravagant wealth of the time and the terrible poverty that lay underneath.

Cities in Crisis

The rapid growth of the cities produced serious problems. Among these were overcrowding, public health dangers, and crime.

Living Conditions

The terrible overcrowding in tenement districts created sanitation and health problems. Garbage and horse manure accumulated in city streets, and the sewers could not handle the flow of human waste. Filth created a breeding ground for disease.

MULTIPLE LEARNING STYLES

Logical/Mathematical Ask students to find the height of the two tallest buildings in the United States. Have them create a double bar graph comparing these two buildings with the two tallest buildings noted in this section. Discuss past and present technological developments that enabled architects to continually design taller buildings. **L2, ELL**

Diseases spread rapidly through the crowded districts. In a poor Chicago neighborhood in 1900, many babies died—of whooping cough, diphtheria, or measles—before their first birthday. A section of New York was called the "lung block" because so many residents had tuberculosis.

In an effort to control disease, New York City began to screen schoolchildren for contagious diseases and to provide visiting nurses to mothers with young children. The city also established public health clinics for those who could not pay for medical care.

Urban Crime

The poverty in the cities inevitably led to crime. Orphaned and homeless children sometimes resorted to picking pockets and other minor crimes to survive. Gangs roaming the poor neighborhoods committed more serious crimes. **Jacob Riis,** a New York journalist, reported:

> "The gang is an institution in New York. The police deny its existence while nursing the bruises received in nightly battles with it. . . . The gang is the ripe fruit of tenement-house growth. It was born there."

Seeking Solutions

The problems of the cities did not go unnoticed. Many dedicated people worked to improve urban life and help the poor.

In 1890 Jacob Riis wrote *How the Other Half Lives.* With words and photographs, Riis's book showed the terrible conditions of the tenements. His book helped establish housing codes to prevent the worst abuses.

Religious groups aided the poor. The **Salvation Army,** started in the United States in 1879, set up soup kitchens to feed the hungry and opened shelters for homeless people. Some religious

American Memories: The New American City

What Was It Like? The growth of American cities during the late 1800s and early 1900s changed the way people lived. **How do each of the items pictured here reflect American life during this period?**

you don't say...

Gang was originally used to mean "journey." It is related to the word "go." *Gang* literally means "a group of people who go together." Gangs with names like Plug Uglies, Dead Rabbits, and Bowery B'hoys roamed the streets during the late 1800s.

NATIONAL GEOGRAPHIC SOCIETY

VIDEODISC
GTV: The American People: Fabric of a Nation

Side 3, Chapter 2
Title: *Going to Town!*
Subject: Migration to cities
Ask: **Why did people move from farms to the cities?** *(for more jobs and opportunities)*

American Memories

The New American City
Many writers focused on the problems in the new American city. Jacob A. Riis, an immigrant from Denmark, became a newspaper reporter in New York City. He focused on the problems of the city such as corruption, scandals, and life on the impoverished Lower East Side. His book, *How the Other Half Lives,* helped resolve the tenement housing problems. The sequel to that book, *The Battle with the Slum,* was one of the first social commentaries on the cycle of poverty and its effect on the home, family, community, employment, and education.
Answer: *dress and handbag: women's fashion, doll: child's play*

Making Connections Activity

Literature Have students obtain a copy of Jacob A. Riis's book *How the Other Half Lives* and investigate the legislation that Riis secured to improve slum conditions. Have them research how he went about securing this legislation. Ask students to present their findings as if they were asking Congress to pass a law to protect urban dwellers. **L3**

CHAPTER 20
Section 2, 584–589

HISTORY AND ART Frederick Law Olmsted was appointed superintendent of the construction of Central Park. He found the park filled with hog farms, bone-boiling works, and squatters' shacks. He called it "a pestilential spot where rank vegetation and miasmatic [poisonous] odors taint every breath of air."
Answer: *so city dwellers could enjoy the beauties of nature*

3 ASSESS

Assign Section 2 Review as homework or as an in-class activity.

Use **Chapter Challenger Interactive Review Software** to review Section 2.

Section Quiz 20–2

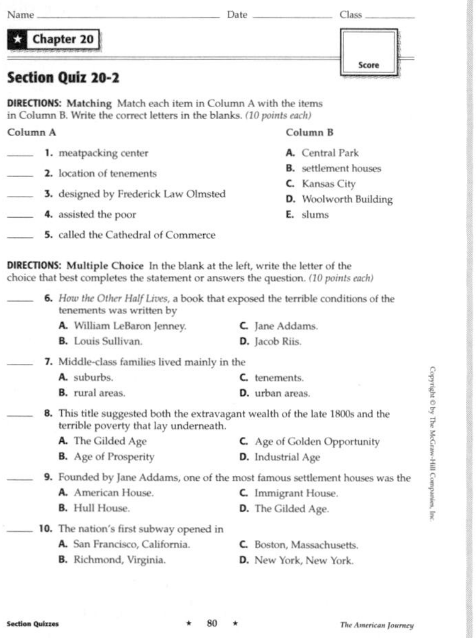
Name ______ Date ______ Class ______

★ Chapter 20 — Score

Section Quiz 20-2

DIRECTIONS: Matching Match each item in Column A with the items in Column B. Write the correct letters in the blanks. *(10 points each)*

Column A	Column B
____ 1. meatpacking center	A. Central Park
____ 2. location of tenements	B. settlement houses
____ 3. designed by Frederick Law Olmsted	C. Kansas City
____ 4. assisted the poor	D. Woolworth Building
____ 5. called the Cathedral of Commerce	E. slums

DIRECTIONS: Multiple Choice In the blank at the left, write the letter of the choice that best completes the statement or answers the question. *(10 points each)*

____ 6. *How the Other Half Lives*, a book that exposed the terrible conditions of the tenements was written by
A. William LeBaron Jenney. C. Jane Addams.
B. Louis Sullivan. D. Jacob Riis.

____ 7. Middle-class families lived mainly in the
A. suburbs. C. tenements.
B. rural areas. D. urban areas.

____ 8. This title suggested both the extravagant wealth of the late 1800s and the terrible poverty that lay underneath.
A. The Gilded Age C. Age of Golden Opportunity
B. Age of Prosperity D. Industrial Age

____ 9. Founded by Jane Addams, one of the most famous settlement houses was the
A. American House. C. Immigrant House.
B. Hull House. D. The Gilded Age.

____ 10. The nation's first subway opened in
A. San Francisco, California. C. Boston, Massachusetts.
B. Richmond, Virginia. D. New York, New York.

Section Quizzes ★ 80 ★ *The American Journey*

What? Where? When? Who?

The Brooklyn Bridge John Augustus Roebling designed this bridge with a steel web truss to keep it from swaying in the wind. Roebling's son, Washington Augustus, completed the bridge after Roebling died of a tetanus infection in 1869 after a ferryboat crushed his leg while working on the bridge.

HISTORY AND ART

***Concert in Central Park* by Jerome Myers** Central Park in New York City opened in 1859. It soon became a popular place for recreational activities. **Why were public parks designed and built in American cities during the late 1800s?**

orders helped the poor in orphanages, prisons, and hospitals. Organizations such as the **YMCA** (Young Men's Christian Association) and **YWCA** (Young Women's Christian Association) offered recreation centers where city youngsters could meet and play.

Settlement Houses

The poor also received assistance from establishments called **settlement houses.** The settlement house movement had spread to the United States from Britain. Located in poor neighborhoods, settlement houses provided medical care, playgrounds, nurseries, and libraries as well as classes in English, music, and arts and crafts. Settlement workers—mostly women—also tried to get better police protection, garbage removal, and public parks for poor districts.

One of the most famous settlement houses was Chicago's **Hull House,** founded by **Jane Addams** in 1889. Addams explained:

Jane Addams

> "We were ready to perform the humblest neighborhood services. We were asked to wash the new-born babies, and to prepare the dead for burial, to nurse the sick, and to 'mind the children.'"

The Changing City

Urban growth led to important, new developments. In the late 1800s, cities saw the introduction of a new type of building, new kinds of public transportation, and public parks.

Building Up—Not Out

Because of the limited space in cities, imaginative architects began building upward rather than outward. In the 1860s architects started to use iron frames to strengthen the walls of buildings. Iron supports—together with the safety elevator that **Elisha Otis** invented in 1852—made taller buildings possible.

In 1884 **William LeBaron Jenney** constructed a 10-story office building in Chicago. Supported by an iron-and-steel frame, it was the world's first **skyscraper.** Architect **Louis Sullivan** gave style to the skyscraper. "It must be every inch a proud and soaring thing, rising in sheer exultation," he said. Sullivan and his colleagues changed the face of America's cities.

CRITICAL THINKING ACTIVITY

Identifying Alternatives Organize students into small groups to create a three-column table illustrating social problems, solutions, and alternatives. Ask groups to identify in the first column the social problems described in this section. In the second column, students should describe the solutions that were used. Students should explain their alternative solutions in the third column. **L2**

Soon people built even higher structures. New York's **Woolworth Building,** completed in 1913, soared an incredible 55 stories—nearly 800 feet (273 m) high. People called the building the Cathedral of Commerce.

Some people looked to reshape the urban landscape. A group known as the "City Beautiful" movement believed city dwellers should be able to enjoy the beauties of nature. **Frederick Law Olmsted,** a leader in this movement, designed New York's Central Park as well as several parks in Boston.

New Forms of Transportation

As cities grew, people needed new means of transportation. Mark Twain complained in 1867 that

> "New York is too large. You cannot accomplish anything . . . without devoting a whole day to it. . . . The distances are too great."

Streetcars, which horses pulled on tracks, provided public transportation at the time. Horses were slow, however, and left piles of manure. In 1873 San Francisco began construction of cable-car lines. A large underground cable powered by a motor at one end of the rail line moved passengers along. In 1888 Richmond, Virginia, pioneered the use of the trolley car, a motorized train that was powered by electricity supplied through overhead cables. In 1897 Boston opened the nation's first subway, or underground railway.

Building Bridges

Bridge construction provided another improvement in urban transportation. Many American cities were divided or bounded by rivers. Using new construction technology, architects and engineers designed huge steel bridges to link sections of cities. The 520-foot (156-m) **Eads Bridge** across the Mississippi River in St. Louis opened in 1873. Ten years later New York's majestic **Brooklyn Bridge,** 1,600 feet (488 m) long, connected Manhattan and Brooklyn. Both bridges remain in use today.

The new forms of transportation not only helped people travel within the cities, but they also helped the cities grow. Middle-class suburbs developed along train or trolley lines stretching away from city centers. People who moved out of the city centers could easily travel downtown to work or shop.

The increase in immigration and the growth of the cities went hand in hand with other changes in American life. Education, culture, and recreation were changing too.

Section 2 Review

Checking for Understanding

1. ***Identify*** Jacob Riis, Jane Addams, Elisha Otis, Louis Sullivan, Frederick Law Olmsted.
2. ***Define*** tenement, slum, suburb, The Gilded Age, settlement house.
3. ***List*** three serious problems facing American cities in the late 1800s.

Reviewing Themes

4. **Science and Technology** What improvements in transportation in the late 1800s helped cities and suburbs to grow?

Critical Thinking

5. **Analyzing Information** How did the efforts of religious groups help those living in poverty?

Activity

Creating a Postcard Imagine that you were an immigrant living in New York City in the early 1900s. Draw the front of a postcard that shows a scene of the city.

Section 2 Review Answers

1. Jacob Riis, 587; Jane Addams, 588; Elisha Otis, 588; Louis Sullivan, 588; Frederick Law Olmsted, 589
2. The words are defined in the Glossary.
3. overcrowding, public health dangers, crime
4. railroads, trolley cars, subways, steel bridges, cable cars
5. opened soup kitchens to feed the hungry; opened shelters for homeless people; organized orphanages, prisons, and hospitals

Activity Postcard illustrations should accurately portray New York City in the early 1900s and may include skyscrapers, bridges, tenements, Central Park, and so on.

Reteaching Activity 20–2

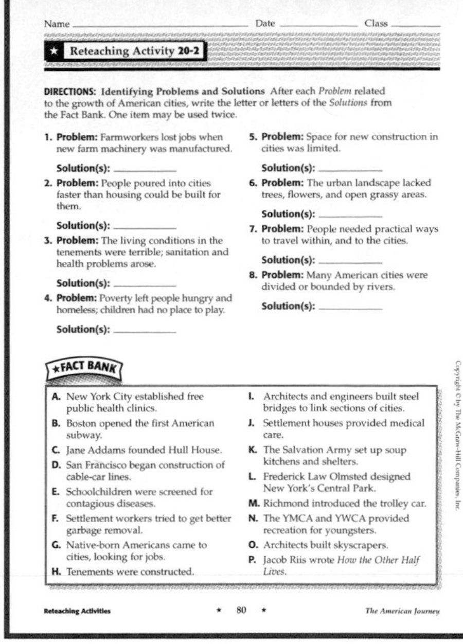
Name ______ Date ______ Class ______

★ Reteaching Activity **20-2**

DIRECTIONS: Identifying Problems and Solutions After each *Problem* related to the growth of American cities, write the letter or letters of the *Solutions* from the Fact Bank. One item may be used twice.

1. **Problem:** Farmworkers lost jobs when new farm machinery was manufactured.
   Solution(s): ______
2. **Problem:** People poured into cities faster than housing could be built for them.
   Solution(s): ______
3. **Problem:** The living conditions in the tenements were terrible; sanitation and health problems arose.
   Solution(s): ______
4. **Problem:** Poverty left people hungry and homeless; children had no place to play.
   Solution(s): ______
5. **Problem:** Space for new construction in cities was limited.
   Solution(s): ______
6. **Problem:** The urban landscape lacked trees, flowers, and open grassy areas.
   Solution(s): ______
7. **Problem:** People needed practical ways to travel within, and to the cities.
   Solution(s): ______
8. **Problem:** Many American cities were divided or bounded by rivers.
   Solution(s): ______

★FACT BANK

A. New York City established free public health clinics.
B. Boston opened the first American subway.
C. Jane Addams founded Hull House.
D. San Francisco began construction of cable-car lines.
E. Schoolchildren were screened for contagious diseases.
F. Settlement workers tried to get better garbage removal.
G. Native-born Americans came to cities, looking for jobs.
H. Tenements were constructed.
I. Architects and engineers built steel bridges to link sections of cities.
J. Settlement houses provided medical care.
K. The Salvation Army set up soup kitchens and shelters.
L. Frederick Law Olmsted designed New York's Central Park.
M. Richmond introduced the trolley car.
N. The YMCA and YWCA provided recreation for youngsters.
O. Architects built skyscrapers.
P. Jacob Riis wrote *How the Other Half Lives*.

Reteaching Activities ★ 80 ★ *The American Journey*

Enrichment Activity 20–2

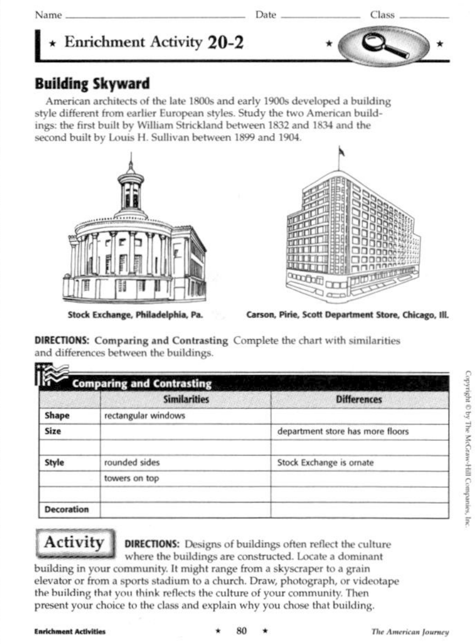
Name ______ Date ______ Class ______

★ Enrichment Activity **20-2**

Building Skyward

American architects of the late 1800s and early 1900s developed a building style different from earlier European styles. Study the two American buildings: the first built by William Strickland between 1832 and 1834 and the second built by Louis H. Sullivan between 1899 and 1904.

Stock Exchange, Philadelphia, Pa.

Carson, Pirie, Scott Department Store, Chicago, Ill.

DIRECTIONS: Comparing and Contrasting Complete the chart with similarities and differences between the buildings.

Comparing and Contrasting

	Similarities	Differences
Shape	rectangular windows	
Size		department store has more floors
Style	rounded sides	Stock Exchange is ornate
	towers on top	
Decoration		

Activity **DIRECTIONS:** Designs of buildings often reflect the culture where the buildings are constructed. Locate a dominant building in your community. It might range from a skyscraper to a grain elevator or from a sports stadium to a church. Draw, photograph, or videotape the building that you think reflects the culture of your community. Then present your choice to the class and explain why you chose that building.

Enrichment Activities ★ 80 ★ *The American Journey*

4 CLOSE

Ask students to explain which technological development they think had the most impact on the growth of American cities.

CHAPTER 20
Section 3, 590–595

1 FOCUS

BELLRINGER
Motivational Activity

Before taking roll at the beginning of the class period, project Section Focus Transparency 20–3 and have students answer the questions. Discuss students' responses.

This activity is also available as a blackline master.

Section Focus Transparency 20–3

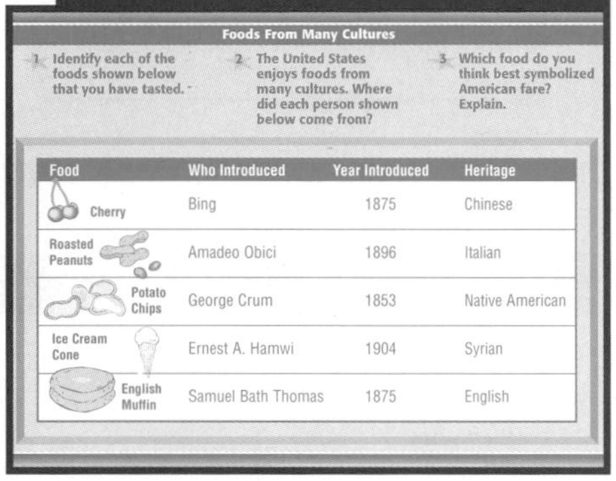

Foods From Many Cultures

1. Identify each of the foods shown below that you have tasted.
2. The United States enjoys foods from many cultures. Where did each person shown below come from?
3. Which food do you think best symbolized American fare? Explain.

Food	Who Introduced	Year Introduced	Heritage
Cherry	Bing	1875	Chinese
Roasted Peanuts	Amadeo Obici	1896	Italian
Potato Chips	George Crum	1853	Native American
Ice Cream Cone	Ernest A. Hamwi	1904	Syrian
English Muffin	Samuel Bath Thomas	1875	English

Vocabulary Precheck

Ask students to write the vocabulary words on a sheet of paper and categorize each word according to the specific cultural area it represents.

Use the **Vocabulary PuzzleMaker** to create crossword and word search puzzles.

Section Theme
Continuity and Change

By the turn of the century, a unique American culture had developed, affecting all aspects of American life.

Activity Direct students' attention to the quote by Mary Antin in **The Storyteller** on this page. Ask volunteers to explain her viewpoint on education and decide whether it applies to present-day society.

1860 — 1870 — 1880 — 1890

1862 Morrill Act is passed

1879 Carlisle Indian Industrial School is founded

1881 Booker T. Washington opens the Tuskegee Institute

1883 Joseph Pulitzer purchases the New York *World*

Section 3

A Changing Culture

READ TO DISCOVER . . .

- how education became more widely available to Americans.
- what new trends shaped American literature.
- how Americans spent their hours of leisure time.

TERMS TO LEARN

land-grant college	regionalism
yellow journalism	ragtime
realism	vaudeville

The Storyteller

Mary Antin, a young girl who came to the United States from Russia in 1894, never forgot her first day of school. "Father himself conducted us to school. He would not have delegated that mission to the president of the United States." For her father, Mary explained, education was "the essence of American opportunity, the treasure no thief could touch, not even misfortune or poverty. . . . The door stood open for every one of us."

A student's award

Most Americans in 1865 had attended school for an average of only four years. Government and business leaders and reformers believed that for the nation to progress, the people needed more schooling. Toward the end of the 1800s, the "treasure" of education became more widely available to Americans.

Expanding Education

By 1914 nearly every state required children to have at least some schooling. More than 80 percent of all children between the ages of 5 and 17 were enrolled in elementary and secondary schools.

Public Schools

The expansion of public education was particularly notable in high schools. The number of public high schools increased from 100 in 1860 to 6,000 in 1900 to 12,000 in 1914. Despite this huge increase, however, only a small percentage of teenagers attended high schools. Boys often went to work to help their families instead of attending school. The majority of high school students were girls.

The benefits of a public school education were not shared equally by everyone. In the South many African Americans received little or no education. In many parts of the country, African American children had no choice but to attend segregated elementary and secondary schools.

SECTION RESOURCES

Reproducible Masters
- Guided Reading Activity 20–3
- Section Quiz 20–3
- Reteaching Activity 20–3
- Enrichment Activity 20–3

Transparencies
- Section Focus Transparency 20–3
- U.S. History & Art, Transparencies 11, 16, 18

Multimedia
- Vocabulary PuzzleMaker
- Chapter Challenger Interactive Review Software
- Testmaker
- Focus on American Art Prints
- American Music Cultural Traditions

Around 1900 a new philosophy of education emerged in the United States. Supporters of this "progressive education" wanted to shape students' characters and teach them good citizenship as well as facts. They also believed children should learn through the use of "hands-on" activities. These ideas had the greatest effect in elementary schools. **John Dewey,** the leading spokesperson for progressive education, criticized schools for overemphasizing memorization of knowledge. Instead, Dewey argued, schools should relate learning to the interests, problems, and concerns of students.

Higher Education

Colleges and universities also changed and expanded. An 1862 law called the **Morrill Act** gave the states large amounts of federal land that could be sold to raise money for education. The states used these funds to start dozens of schools called land-grant colleges. Wealthy individuals also established and supported colleges and universities. Some schools were named for the donors—for example, Cornell University for Ezra Cornell and Stanford University for Leland Stanford.

Women and Higher Education

In 1865 only a handful of American colleges admitted women. The new land-grant schools admitted women students, as did new women's colleges—Vassar, Smith, Wellesley, and Bryn Mawr—founded in the late 1800s. By 1890 women could attend a wide range of schools, and by 1910 almost 40 percent of all American college students were women.

Minorities and Higher Education

Some new colleges, such as Hampton Institute in Virginia, provided higher education for African Americans and Native Americans. Howard University in Washington, D.C., founded shortly after the Civil War, had a largely African American student body.

One Hampton Institute student, **Booker T. Washington,** became an educator. In 1881 Washington founded the Tuskegee Institute in Alabama to train teachers and to provide practical education for African Americans.

Schools for Native Americans

Reservation schools and boarding schools also opened to train Native Americans for jobs. The Carlisle Indian Industrial School in Pennsylvania was founded in 1879, and similar schools opened in the West. Although these schools provided Native Americans with training for jobs in industry, they also isolated Native Americans from their tribal traditions. Sometimes, boarding schools were located hundreds of miles away from a student's family.

Picturing HISTORY Scientist George Washington Carver (center) supervises students at Tuskegee Institute. In 1974 Congress established the Tuskegee Institute National Historical Site, which includes the George Washington Carver Museum. The school became Tuskegee University in 1985. **What was the goal of the Tuskegee Institute?**

COOPERATIVE LEARNING ACTIVITY

Creating a Magazine Organize students into groups of four to create a magazine that would appeal to the national public in the late 1800s. Each group should first choose their target market, the type of magazine to meet that target market's needs, and the title of the magazine. Allow group members to choose from the following roles: create the cover, write an advertisement, write a short fiction story, and write a feature article. Encourage students to use a variety of media, especially computers, if available. Have groups exchange completed magazines and identify the target market.

2 TEACH

L1 Outlining Cultural Changes Ask students to create a graphic organizer showing the cultural areas discussed in this section. Have them illustrate each area to identify what made it uniquely American.

Guided Reading Activity 20–3

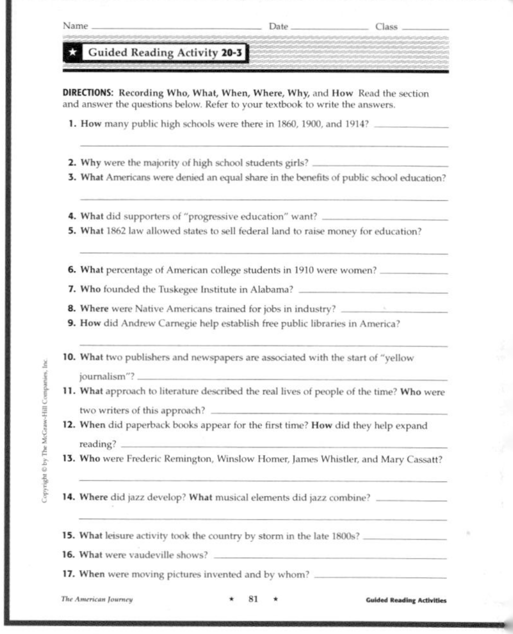

Name ________ Date ________ Class ________

★ Guided Reading Activity **20-3**

DIRECTIONS: Recording Who, What, When, Where, Why, and **How** Read the section and answer the questions below. Refer to your textbook to write the answers.

1. **How** many public high schools were there in 1860, 1900, and 1914?
2. **Why** were the majority of high school students girls?
3. **What** Americans were denied an equal share in the benefits of public school education?
4. **What** did supporters of "progressive education" want?
5. **What** 1862 law allowed states to sell federal land to raise money for education?
6. **What** percentage of American college students in 1910 were women?
7. **Who** founded the Tuskegee Institute in Alabama?
8. **Where** were Native Americans trained for jobs in industry?
9. **How** did Andrew Carnegie help establish free public libraries in America?
10. **What** two publishers and newspapers are associated with the start of "yellow journalism"?
11. **What** approach to literature described the real lives of people of the time? **Who** were two writers of this approach?
12. **When** did paperback books appear for the first time? **How** did they help expand reading?
13. **Who** were Frederic Remington, Winslow Homer, James Whistler, and Mary Cassatt?
14. **Where** did jazz develop? **What** musical elements did jazz combine?
15. **What** leisure activity took the country by storm in the late 1800s?
16. **What** were vaudeville shows?
17. **When** were moving pictures invented and by whom?

The American Journey ★ 81 ★ **Guided Reading Activities**

Picturing HISTORY George Washington Carver headed the agricultural department at Tuskegee Institute from 1896 to 1915. He set up innovative educational extension programs to encourage farmers to use the available resources to replace expensive commodities. **Ask:** What type of class is Carver teaching? *(Answers should reflect some type of lab-related science class such as chemistry, botany, and so on.)*
Answer: *to train teachers and to provide practical education for African Americans*

What?Where?When?Who?

Magazine Advertising The Woodbury soap ads of 1911 pictured a man and a woman locked in an embrace with the words "The skin you love to touch." This advertising scandalized readers of *The Ladies' Home Journal.* Some readers canceled their subscriptions, but even more readers signed on because of the ads.

CURRICULUM CONNECTION

JOURNALISM
Immigrant groups had their own theaters, libraries, and newspapers. By 1850 Germans could choose from 133 German-language newspapers. Yiddish-speaking New Yorkers had a choice of a dozen daily newspapers by the 1930s, one of which had a circulation of 125,000. Norwegians had 40 national newspapers in their own language.

Picturing HISTORY The *Woman's Home Companion,* which was first published as the *Ladies' Home Companion,* was published continuously between 1873 and 1957. Four other women's magazines established in the 1880s are still being published today. They are *McCall's Magazine* (1876), *Ladies' Home Journal* (1883), *Good Housekeeping* (1885), and *Vogue* (1892). **Ask:** **What image of women is portrayed by this magazine cover?** *(athletic, self-sufficient)*
Answer: *printing improvements, mass circulation techniques*

A Nation of Readers

As opportunities for education grew, a growing number of Americans became interested in reading. Public libraries opened across the nation, and new magazines and newspapers were created for the reading public.

Public Libraries

In 1881 **Andrew Carnegie,** the wealthy steel industrialist, made an extraordinary announcement. He pledged to build a public library in any city that would agree to pay its operating costs. In the next 30 years, Carnegie donated more than $30 million to found more than 2,000 libraries throughout the world. With gifts from Carnegie and others and the efforts of state and local governments, every state in the Union established free public libraries.

Spreading the News

Technological advances in printing, paper making, and communications made it possible to publish a daily paper for a large number of readers. The growing cities provided readers for the newspapers.

In 1883 **Joseph Pulitzer** purchased the New York *World* and created a new kind of newspaper. The paper grabbed the reader's attention with illustrations, cartoons, and sensational stories with huge, scary headlines—such as "ANOTHER MURDERER TO HANG." Under Pulitzer's management, the *World* built up its circulation to more than 1 million readers every day.

Other newspapers soon imitated Pulitzer's style. **William Randolph Hearst's** New York *Morning Journal* became even more successful than the *World,* attracting readers by exaggerating the dramatic or gruesome aspects of stories. This style of sensational writing became known as **yellow journalism**—a name that came from the paper's popular comic strip, "The Yellow Kid."

Ethnic and minority newspapers thrived as well. By 1900 there were 6 daily Jewish-language newspapers operating in New York City. African Americans started more than 1,000 newspapers between 1865 and 1900.

More magazines took advantage of printing improvements and mass circulation techniques to reach a national market. Between 1865 and 1900, the number of magazines in the United States rose from about 700 to 5,000. Some magazines of that era—the *Atlantic Monthly, Harper's,* and *Ladies' Home Journal*—are still published today.

Picturing HISTORY Glossy magazines, such as the *Woman's Home Companion,* combined stories and feature articles with appealing advertisements. **How were magazines able to reach a national market?**

Changes in Literature

Many writers of the late 1800s and the early 1900s explored new themes and subjects. Their approach to literature was called **realism** because they sought to describe the real lives of people of the time. Related to realism was **regionalism,** writing that focused on a particular region of the country.

Mark Twain was a realist and a regionalist. Many of his books, including *Adventures of Huckleberry Finn* and *The Adventures of Tom Sawyer,* are set along the Mississippi River, where Twain grew up. In *Life on the Mississippi,* Twain described the excitement created

MULTIPLE LEARNING STYLES

Interpersonal Ask students to choose a sport mentioned in this section and describe how that sport is played. Pair students to teach one another how to play that sport using verbal cues only. As a class, discuss the problems in teaching an activity without visual aids or written directions. **L2, ELL**

by the arrival of a steamboat in Hannibal, Missouri, his hometown:

> “Assembled there, the people fasten their eyes upon the coming boat as upon a wonder they are seeing for the first time. And the boat *is* rather a handsome sight, too. She is long and sharp and trim and pretty. . . . The captain lifts his hand, a bell rings, the wheels stop; then they turn back, churning the water to foam, and the steamer is at rest.”

Stephen Crane wrote about city slums in *Maggie* and about the Civil War in *The Red Badge of Courage.* In books such as *The Call of the Wild* and *The Sea Wolf,* **Jack London** portrayed the lives of miners and hunters in the far Northwest. **Edith Wharton** described the joys and sorrows of the upper-class Easterners in *The House of Mirth* and *The Age of Innocence.*

Paul Laurence Dunbar, the son of former slaves, wrote poetry and novels that used the dialects and folktales of Southern African Americans. Dunbar was one of the first African American writers to gain fame worldwide.

Paperback Books

Paperback books appeared for the first time in the late 1800s, and these inexpensive books helped expand the reading public. Many paperbacks featured lively adventure tales or stories of athletic boys and girls.

Horatio Alger wrote a successful series of young adult books with such titles as *Work and Win* and *Luck and Pluck.* Based on the idea that hard work and honesty brought success, Alger's books sold about 40 million copies.

Art and Music

For most of the 1800s, the work of American artists and musicians reflected a European influence. After the Civil War, Americans began to develop a uniquely American style.

Linking PAST & PRESENT

Vaudeville to Virtual Reality

From the 1880s to the 1930s, vaudeville was the most popular form of entertainment in the United States. Most vaudeville shows included about 10 acts, with magicians, acrobats, comedians, trained animals, jugglers, singers, and dancers.

In the 1980s, a new form of entertainment emerged—virtual reality (VR). Wearing a special helmet, gloves, and even a bodysuit, the user enters a world where everything is created by a computer. In this computerized world, or cyberspace, a user could travel back to the past and perform in a vaudeville show! **What type of present-day entertainment compares to a vaudeville show?**

Virtual reality helmet

American Artists

Some American painters pursued realist themes. **Thomas Eakins** painted the human anatomy and surgical operations. One of Eakins's students, **Henry Tanner,** depicted warm family scenes of African Americans in the South. **Frederic Remington** portrayed the American West, focusing on subjects such as cowhands and Native Americans. **Winslow Homer** painted Southern farmers, Adirondack campers, and stormy sea scenes. **James Whistler**'s *Arrangement in Grey and Black,* commonly known as *Whistler's Mother,* is one of the best-known American paintings. **Mary**

CHAPTER 20
Section 3, 590–595

Linking PAST & PRESENT

Vaudeville to Virtual Reality The term *virtual reality* (VR) was introduced into the English language in 1985. VR is a realistic simulation of an environment through high-speed, three-dimensional computer graphics. VR provides a three-dimensional effect as if the viewer is truly experiencing the action.
Answer: *variety shows or circuses*

History *and the* Humanities

U.S. History & Art, Transparency 11, *A Rainy Day in Camp;* Transparency 16, *In the Garden;* Transparency 18, *The Stampede*

Focus on American Art Prints, *The Gulf Stream* by Winslow Homer; *The Boating Party* by Mary Cassatt

The Spirit of American Art and Music, Thomas Eakins, Louis Sullivan, John Philip Sousa, Henry Ossawa Tanner

American Music Cultural Traditions, Lesson 7: “Maple Leaf Rag” and “St. Louis Tickle”

MAKING CONNECTIONS ACTIVITY

The Arts Organize students into small groups to create a fine arts trivia game showcasing the artists mentioned in this section. Have each group create five flash cards with the title of a song, painting, or book written on the front of each card and the artist's name on the back. Then have each group hold up their cards and have the other groups guess the artist. The first group to correctly identify the artist gets a point. Rotate until all groups have presented their cards. The group with the most points wins. **L1**

HISTORY AND ART Winslow Homer belonged to the group of American painters called the Ash Can School. These painters drew on their experiences as journalists, finding realistic themes for art in backyards and city streets. **Answer:** *realistic themes of people, places, and events*

CURRICULUM CONNECTION

DRAMA
Billboard magazine debuted in 1894 as an eight-page entertainment monthly. Cincinnati publishers James Hennegan and W.H. Donaldson introduced theater notes in late 1901 and a motion-picture section in 1907. Today *Billboard* is a show-business weekly.

3 ASSESS

Assign Section 3 Review as homework or as an in-class activity.

Use **Chapter Challenger Interactive Review Software** to review Section 3.

Section Quiz 20–3

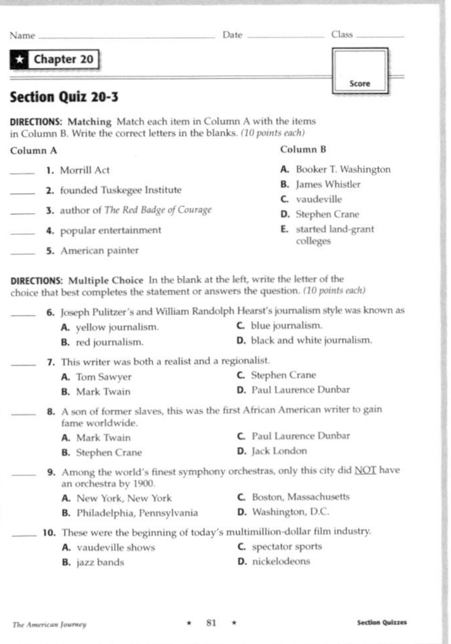
Name ______ Date ______ Class ______

Chapter 20

Score

Section Quiz 20-3

DIRECTIONS: Matching Match each item in Column A with the items in Column B. Write the correct letters in the blanks. *(10 points each)*

Column A	Column B
____ **1.** Morrill Act	**A.** Booker T. Washington
____ **2.** founded Tuskegee Institute	**B.** James Whistler
____ **3.** author of *The Red Badge of Courage*	**C.** vaudeville
____ **4.** popular entertainment	**D.** Stephen Crane
____ **5.** American painter	**E.** started land-grant colleges

DIRECTIONS: Multiple Choice In the blank at the left, write the letter of the choice that best completes the statement or answers the question. *(10 points each)*

____ **6.** Joseph Pulitzer's and William Randolph Hearst's journalism style was known as
A. yellow journalism. **C.** blue journalism.
B. red journalism. **D.** black and white journalism.

____ **7.** This writer was both a realist and a regionalist.
A. Tom Sawyer **C.** Stephen Crane
B. Mark Twain **D.** Paul Laurence Dunbar

____ **8.** A son of former slaves, this was the first African American writer to gain fame worldwide.
A. Mark Twain **C.** Paul Laurence Dunbar
B. Stephen Crane **D.** Jack London

____ **9.** Among the world's finest symphony orchestras, only this city did NOT have an orchestra by 1900.
A. New York, New York **C.** Boston, Massachusetts
B. Philadelphia, Pennsylvania **D.** Washington, D.C.

____ **10.** These were the beginning of today's multimillion-dollar film industry.
A. vaudeville shows **C.** spectator sports
B. jazz bands **D.** nickelodeons

The American Journey ★ 81 ★ **Section Quizzes**

HISTORY AND ART ***Girls with Lobster*** **by Winslow Homer** Homer painted scenes of people enjoying the New Jersey and New England seashores. **What themes did American painters pursue in their works?**

Cassatt was influential in the French Impressionist school of painting. Impressionists tried to capture the play of light, color, and patterns as they made immediate impressions on the senses.

Music in America

More distinctively American kinds of music were also becoming popular. Bandleader **John Philip Sousa** composed many rousing marches, including "The Stars and Stripes Forever." African American musicians in **New Orleans** in the late 1800s developed an entirely new kind of music—jazz. **Jazz** combined elements of work songs, gospel music, spirituals, and African rhythms. Related to jazz was ragtime music. For about 20 years, beginning around the turn of the century, ragtime—with its complex rhythms—was the dominant force in popular music. One of the best-known ragtime composers is **Scott Joplin.** He wrote "Maple Leaf Rag" and many other well-known works.

The symphony orchestras of New York, Boston, and Philadelphia—all founded before 1900—were among the world's finest. Great singers and conductors came from all over the world to perform at New York's Metropolitan Opera House.

Leisure Time

Although sweatshop workers labored long hours for six or even seven days a week, middle-class people and even some factory workers enjoyed increasing amounts of leisure time. Unlike round-the-clock farmwork, professional and industrial jobs gave people hours and even days of free time. Americans developed new forms of recreation for their leisure time.

Footnotes to History

The Olympics The first Olympics were held in 776 B.C. to celebrate amateur sports. In 1896, the first modern games were held in Athens, Greece. Women first competed in the Olympics in 1900.

CRITICAL THINKING ACTIVITY

Making Comparisons Ask students to reread the subsection *Public Schools.* Then have them write an essay comparing progressive education with the philosophy of education used in their school today. Tell students to end their essays with a description of their own philosophy of education. **L2**

The World of Sports

A version of baseball was played as early as the 1830s. After the Civil War, baseball and other sports—including football, basketball, and boxing—gained popularity. Leagues of sports teams were organized in the late 1800s, and they drew large audiences for the time. Attending these **spectator sports** and rooting for the home team or a local star became a favorite pastime.

Improvements in the bicycle in the late 1800s helped bicycle riding take the country by storm. One romantic song celebrated the bicycle:

> "It won't be a stylish marriage,
> I can't afford a carriage,
> But you'll look sweet on the seat of a
> bicycle built for two."

Theatrical Entertainment

Large cities had many theaters. Plays performed ranged from serious dramas by Shakespeare to **vaudeville** shows, variety shows with dancing, singing, comedy, and magic acts. Many people could afford the price of a ticket, and in the early 1900s, vaudeville offered the most popular shows in town. The circus also attracted large crowds. In 1910 the United States had about 80 traveling circuses.

Picturing HISTORY

Interest in sports soared. By 1900 the two major leagues in baseball had formed, and bicycling was very popular. **What development made new forms of recreation and entertainment possible?**

Baseball glove and ball, 1890s

Early Movies

Thomas Edison invented "moving pictures" in the 1880s. The "movies" soon became enormously popular. Some theaters, called nickelodeons, charged 5 cents to see short films. The nickelodeons were the beginning of today's multimillion-dollar film industry, one of the most influential forms of mass communication in history.

Section 3 Review

Checking for Understanding

1. ***Identify*** Booker T. Washington, Andrew Carnegie, Joseph Pulitzer, Paul Laurence Dunbar, Mary Cassatt.
2. ***Define*** land-grant college, yellow journalism, realism, regionalism, ragtime, vaudeville.
3. ***Summarize*** the new philosophy of education that emerged around 1900.

Reviewing Themes

4. **Continuity and Change** What sparked an increase in the number of newspapers, magazines, and books in the late 1800s?

Critical Thinking

5. **Determining Cause and Effect** Explain the connection between leisure time and development of the arts.

Activity

Making a Motion Picture Create your own moving picture by making a series of drawings on 2-inch by 4-inch slips of paper. Staple the slips of paper together on one side, then flip through them slowly to view your motion picture.

Section 3 Review Answers

1. Booker T. Washington, 591; Andrew Carnegie, 592; Joseph Pulitzer, 592; Paul Laurence Dunbar, 593; Mary Cassatt, 593–94
2. The words are defined in the Glossary.
3. progressive education: shaped character and taught citizenship; used "hands-on" activities; made learning relevant to students' interests, problems, and concerns
4. technological advances in printing, paper making, and communications and improvements in mass circulation techniques
5. With more free time, Americans had more time to enjoy and support the arts.

Activity Students should make a series of sequential drawings to create a "motion-picture" flipbook.

Picturing HISTORY At the height of the bicycle craze in 1896, there were 4 million cyclists. Brakes were introduced two years later.

Answer: *increased leisure time*

Reteaching Activity 20–3

Name ______ Date ______ Class ______

★ Reteaching Activity **20-3**

DIRECTIONS: Crossword Puzzle Complete the crossword puzzle about cultural changes in the United States in the late 1800s by writing the term that matches each clue.

land-grant colleges	**jazz**	**Mark Twain**	**Sousa**
ragtime	**Joseph Pulitzer**	**spectator sports**	**Horatio Alger**
Andrew Carnegie	**Mary Cassatt**	**Tuskegee Institute**	**Paul Laurence Dunbar**
John Dewey			

Across
1. football, baseball, basketball
4. schools started after the Morrill Act passes
5. leading spokesperson for progressive education
10. Alabama school founded by Booker T. Washington
11. African American musical form started in New Orleans
12. *Luck and Pluck* author

Down
2. donated money for free public libraries
3. one of the first African American writers to gain fame
5. published *World*
6. a realist and a regionalist
7. American impressionist painter
8. dominant force in popular music for about 20 years
9. last name of composer of "The Stars and Stripes Forever"

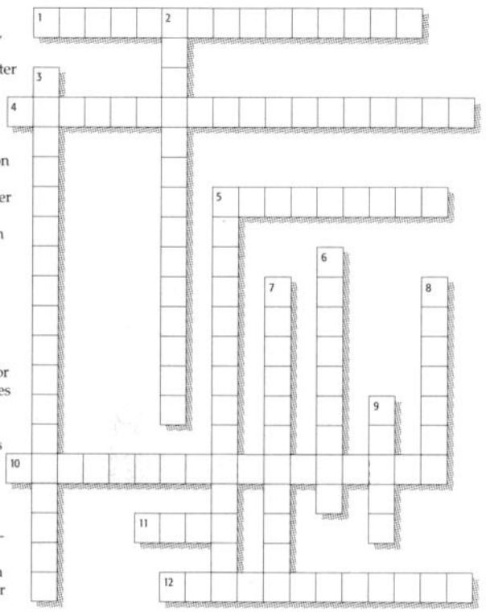

The American Journey ★ 81 ★ **Reteaching Activities**

Enrichment Activity 20–3

Name ______ Date ______ Class ______

★ Enrichment Activity **20-3** ★

Lights!

In the early 1900s large cities had many theaters. Producer David Belasco, who lived from 1859 to 1931, brought new ideas to the American theater as shown below in the excerpt from his writing.

> *. . . Lights are to drama what music is to the lyrics of a song. No other factor that enters into the production of a play is so effective in conveying its moods and feeling. They are as essential to every work of dramatic art as blood is to life. The greatest part of my success in the theatre I attribute to my feeling for colors, translated into effects of light. . . .*
>
> *The lighting effects on my stages have been secured only after years of experiment and at an expense which many other producers would consider ridiculous. . . .*
>
> *These experiments have always been the most interesting part of my work as a producer, although they have also been the most perplexing and sometimes the most baffling. It is no easy matter, for instance, to indicate the difference between the moon and stars of a Japanese night and the fanciful moon and stars of fairyland. But there is, nevertheless, a difference which an audience must be made to feel, without detecting the mechanism, just as one is conscious of heat, yet does not see it, on entering a warm room.*
>
> SOURCE: Nagler, A.M. *A Source Book in Theatrical History.* Dover Publications, Inc., New York.

DIRECTIONS: Interpreting Information Answer the following questions on a separate sheet of paper.

1. What does Belasco mean when he says "They are as essential to every work of dramatic art as blood is to life"?
2. According to Belasco, how is good lighting like heat?
3. What does Belasco think of other producers of his time?
4. Belasco and his electrician spent night after night lighting miniature models of sets in different ways. What part of Belasco's theory does this procedure support?

Activity **DIRECTIONS:** You can experiment with the effects of light using a shoebox, a flashlight, construction paper, and several different colored balloons. Build a scene inside your shoebox, much like a stage set. Then experiment to see how different colors of light change the mood of the scene. Cut the neck off one of the colored balloons and stretch the remaining piece over the flashlight. Dim the room lights, turn on the flashlight, and shine the colored light on your scene. Repeat with different colored balloons. Does the mood change with the color of light? Share your best lighting effect with your class.

The American Journey ★ 81 ★ **Enrichment Activities**

4 CLOSE

Using the graphic organizer students created in the "TEACH" activity, have students choose which cultural area they believe is most "American."

GLENCOE TECHNOLOGY

VIDEODISC
MindJogger Videoquiz

Use MindJogger to review the Chapter 20 content.

Chapter 20
Disc 3, Side A

Also available in VHS.

Chapter 20
Review and Activities

Reviewing Key Terms

On a sheet of paper, define the following terms:
ethnic group
assimilate
tenement
suburb
The Gilded Age
settlement house
land-grant college
yellow journalism
realism
ragtime
vaudeville

Reviewing Key Facts

1. Why did so many people want to leave their homelands to immigrate to the United States in the late 1800s and early 1900s?
2. How did overcrowding in the cities affect public health?
3. Describe some of the ways in which reformers tried to help the urban poor.
4. What was the purpose of the Morrill Act?
5. What new forms of music emerged during the late 1800s and early 1900s?

Critical Thinking

Synthesizing Information

The flood of immigrants who came to the United States during the late 1800s and early 1900s were searching for new opportunities.

1. Do you think the United States government should have allowed so many immigrants into the country at that time? Why or why not?
2. What advice would you have given to a person who wanted to come to America at that time?

Time Line Activity

Create a time line on which you place the following events in chronological order.

- Jane Addams founds Hull House
- Ellis Island opens as immigrant center
- Salvation Army established
- World's first skyscraper completed
- First subway built
- Joseph Pulitzer purchases New York *World*

Skill Practice Activity

Reading a Line Graph

Study the line graph below, then answer the questions that follow.

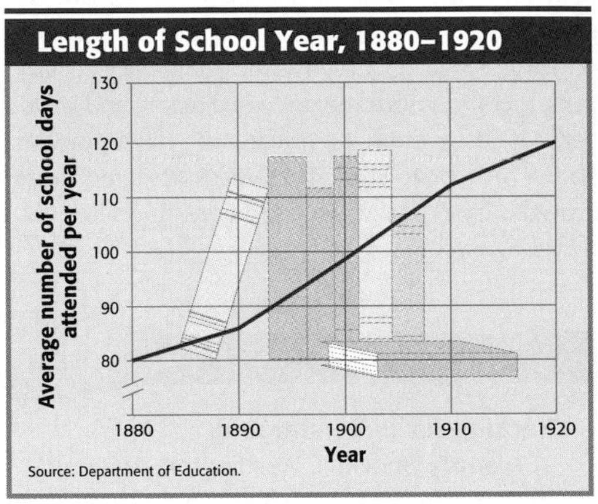

1. What is the subject of this line graph?
2. What information is presented on the horizontal axis? On the vertical axis?
3. How many years does this graph cover?
4. What are the time intervals on the horizontal axis?
5. About how many days were students in school in 1880?
6. What was the average number of school days in 1920?
7. What trend is shown in this line graph?

Reviewing Key Terms

The words used in this activity are defined in the textbook glossary on pages A26–A35.

Reviewing Key Facts

1. economic troubles, to escape persecution, new opportunities
2. Unsanitary conditions created breeding grounds for disease.
3. Journalists exposed problems; religious groups provided basic services; settlement houses provided medical services, arts, education, protection, child care; YMCA and YWCA provided place for children to meet and play.
4. gave states large amounts of federal land to be sold to raise money for education
5. jazz and ragtime

Critical Thinking

1. Answers will vary, but students should defend their responses by stating the positive or negative aspects of immigration.
2. Answers will vary but may include to learn to speak English, learn a craft or job skill before arriving to get a higher-paying job, stay away from large cities, and so on.

Time Line Activity

Events should be placed in this order: Salvation Army established, Joseph Pulitzer purchases New York *World,* World's first skyscraper completed, Jane Addams founds Hull House, Ellis Island opens as immigrant center, First subway built

Skill Practice Activity

1. Length of School Year, 1880–1920
2. time, specifically decades; average number of school days attended per year
3. 40
4. 10 years
5. 80
6. 120
7. increase in average number of school days attended per year

Technology Activity

Using a Word Processor Research the life of one of the writers, artists, or musicians discussed in Section 3. Using your word processor, prepare a one-page biography of that person to share with the class.

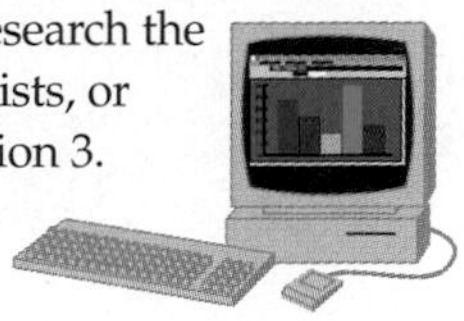

Geography Activity

Study this map and answer the questions below.

Largest Eastern Cities in 1900

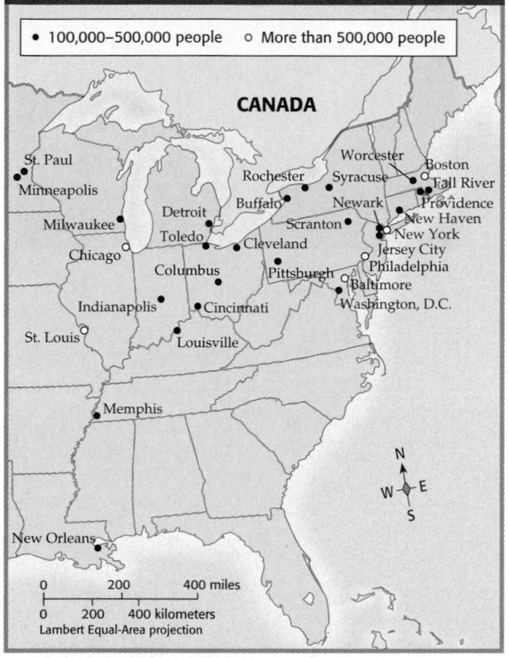

1. **Location** Which cities had more than 500,000 people in 1900?
2. **Place** About how many people lived in Washington, D.C., in 1900?
3. **Location** What is similar about the location of the cities with more than 500,000 people?

Reviewing Themes

1. **Culture and Traditions** How did immigrants try to preserve their cultural heritage?
2. **Science and Technology** Why did so many people move from farms to cities in the late 1800s and early 1900s?
3. **Continuity and Change** What new styles of writing did American authors adopt during this period?

Cooperative Activity

History and Citizenship Immigrants who want to become United States citizens today must pass a written test to qualify. Many of the questions on the test deal with United States history and customs. Work with members of your group to design a 15-question test that you think prospective citizens should be required to pass. After completing your test, exchange it with another group. Have each member of the group take the test. Score each test and report the results to the class.

Portfolio Activity History Journal Suppose you are a reformer trying to help the urban poor during this period. Make a list of the problems that exist in the cities. Choose one problem and describe what you would do to help correct it.

CHAPTER 20

Review and Activities

Reviewing Themes

1. maintained native language; formed ethnic communities; published own newspapers; founded churches, stores, theaters, and social organizations
2. Industrialization freed up farmers and their wives, made transportation to cities easier, and created jobs in the cities.
3. realism and regionalism

Cooperative Activity

Each group should prepare a 15-question citizenship test and exchange it with another group. Each group member should take the test. Students should score the tests and report the results to the class.

Portfolio Activity Students should create a list of the problems that plague the cities. Then assume the role of a reformer and write a solution to correct one of the problems.

Chapter Bonus Test Question

Ask: **What was the title of the first motion picture that told a complete story, setting a pattern of suspense drama that future moviemakers followed?** *(The Great Train Robbery)*

Technology Activity

Students should find information about one of the writers, artists, or musicians discussed in Section 3 and prepare a one-page biography to share with the class.

Geography Activity

1. Chicago, Boston, New York City, Philadelphia, Baltimore, St. Louis
2. between 100,000 and 500,000
3. located on or near water

Unit 8 Resource Guide

These Glencoe resources may be used to teach, reteach, or enrich the concepts presented in this unit of study.

Teaching Transparencies

Map Transparency 8 with Overlays A, B, C, D

Cause-and-Effect Transparency 8

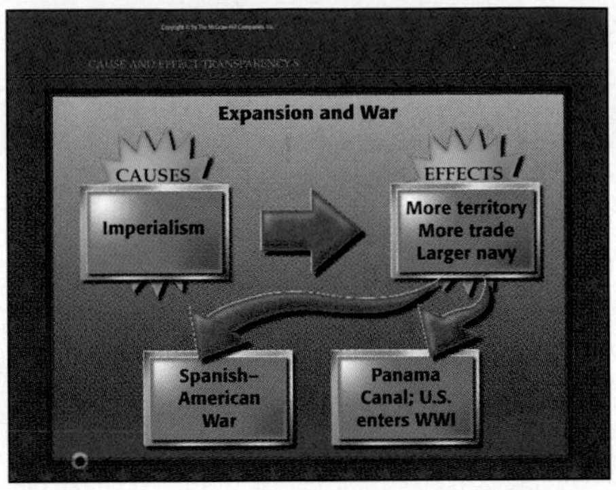

BIBLIOGRAPHY

Readings for the Student

Marrin, Albert. ***The Yanks Are Coming: The United States in the First World War.*** New York: Atheneum, 1986. Describes entry of United States into World War I and its impact on the Allies.

McKissack, Patricia and Frederick. ***W.E.B. Du Bois.*** New York: Franklin Watts, 1990. Traces the life and accomplishments of the great African American leader.

Readings for the Teacher

Jeffers, H. Paul. ***Colonel Roosevelt: Theodore Roosevelt Goes to War, 1897–1898.*** New York: John Wiley & Sons, Inc., 1996. Focuses on Roosevelt's influence on U.S. imperialistic policies.

Schneider, Dorothy and Carl J. ***American Women in the Progressive Era, 1900–1920.*** New York: Anchor Books, 1994. Discusses woman suffrage movement.

Multimedia Resources

Videocassette ***Elizabeth Cady Stanton & Susan B. Anthony.*** Princeton: Films for the Humanities, 1988. Profiles two leaders in the woman suffrage movement.

Computer Software ***American Foreign Policy.*** Garden City, NY: Focus Media, Inc., 1988 (Apple and DOS). Includes a section on Manifest Destiny.

interNET CONNECTIONS

Early 20th-century resources on the World Wide Web

Susan B. Anthony House: http://www.frontiernet.net/~lhurst/sbahouse/sbahome.htm

World War I and related links: http://www.cfcsc.dnd.ca/links/milhist/wwi.html

Resource Guide Unit 8

INTERDISCIPLINARY ACTIVITIES

American Literature Reading 8

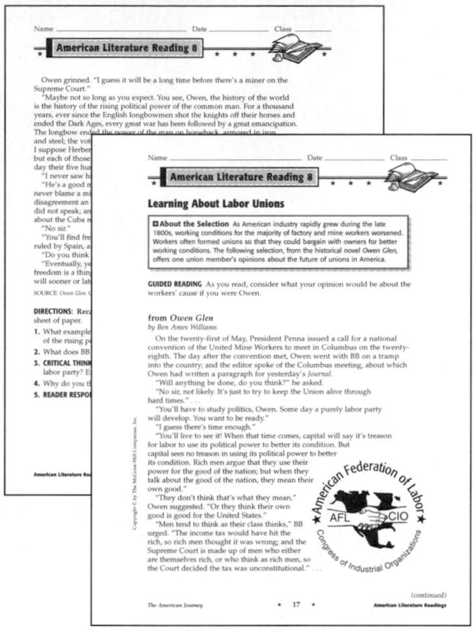

Interdisciplinary Connection 8

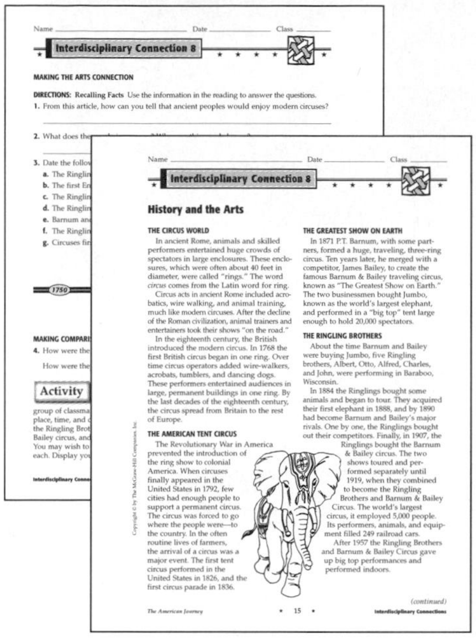

ENRICHMENT ACTIVITIES

Cooperative Learning Activity 8

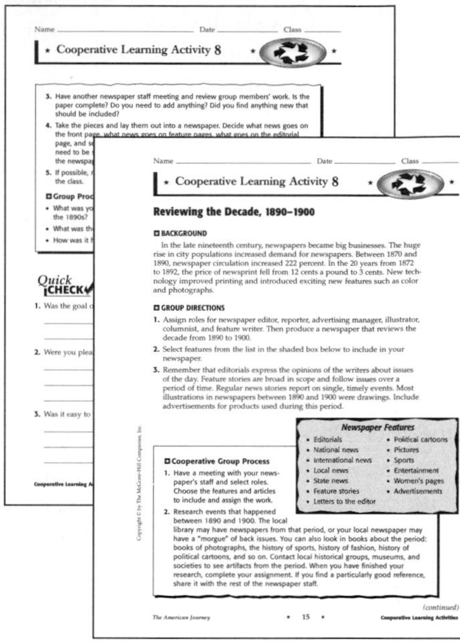

HANDS-ON ACTIVITIES

Hands-On History Lab Activity 8

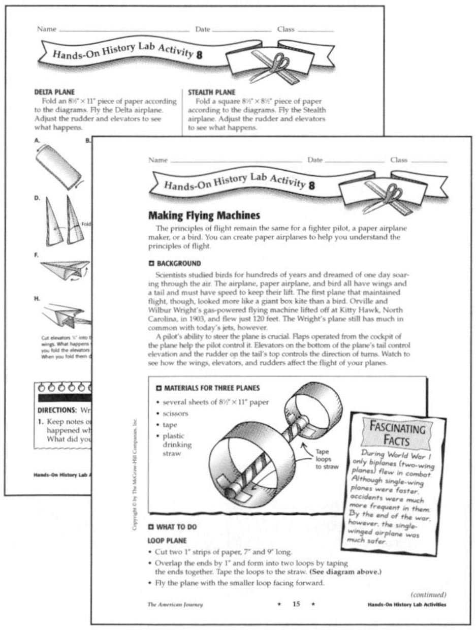

History Simulation 8

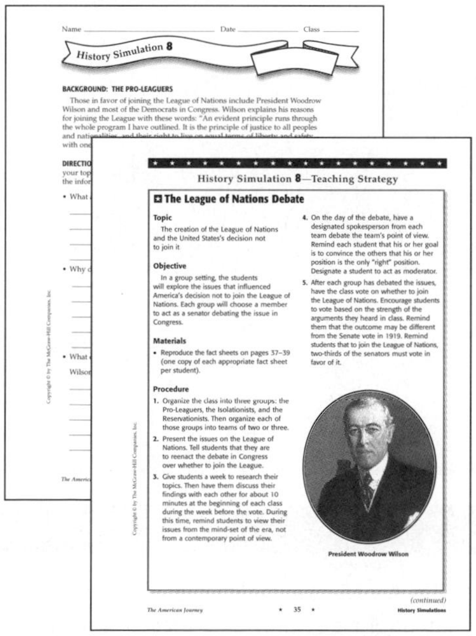

ASSESSMENT

Unit 8 Test

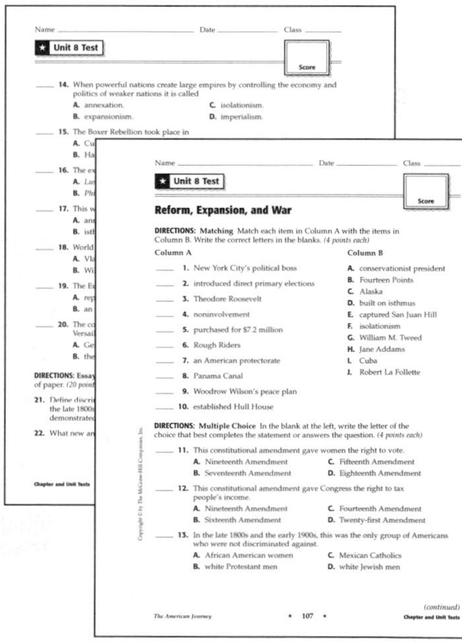

Introducing
UNIT 8

0:00 OUT OF TIME?

If your teaching time is limited, you may use the *Chapter Summaries* blackline master found in the TCR with the *Chapter Digests Audiocassette Activities and Tests* to condense individual chapters into a one-day lesson.

Introducing the Unit

Activity Discuss the following question: What makes a nation powerful? Allow a variety of interpretations of *powerful.* Then introduce this unit by asking these questions: Does greater land ownership mean greater power? Does becoming involved in other nations' problems prove a nation's power? Can a nation that doesn't correct its own problems remain powerful?

Unit Objectives

Upon completing this unit, students will be able to:

1. Discuss the need for and attempts at governmental and social reform during the late 1800s and early 1900s.
2. Explain how and why the United States expanded its economic and political influence in the Pacific and in Latin America.
3. Describe the causes, course, and outcome of World War I.

Hands-On HISTORY

Hands-On History Lab Activity 8, "Making Flying Machines," is a high-interest ***constructivist approach*** activity directly related to the main topic of the unit.

Unit 8

Reform, Expansion, and War

1865–1920

"Speak softly and carry a big stick; you will go far."
—THEODORE ROOSEVELT, 1901

MAPPING America

Portfolio Activity Trace a map of the world onto a piece of paper. As you read this unit about expansion and war, draw and shade in the boundaries of the countries discussed. Add the names of the countries mentioned, then label the events that occurred there.

World War I enlistment poster

Woodrow Wilson campaign pennant

United States

1893 Queen Liliuokalani of Hawaii is overthrown

1880 — 1890

World

1889 Brazil becomes a republic

1893 New Zealand becomes first nation to grant woman suffrage

598

TEAM TEACHING STRATEGIES

Art Have the Art teacher host a special presentation on the nature and impact of political cartoons. The teacher might begin with a discussion of artistic symbolism (for example, a dove to represent peace or Uncle Sam to represent the federal government). The presentation then could focus on cartoons of the era. Examine the works of cartoonist Thomas Nast, for example, or cartoons of such topics as the woman suffrage movement and World War I. The Art teacher also might guide the class through a project in which students locate or draw and then discuss cartoons relating to current events.

Theodore Roosevelt tin tray

HISTORY AND ART ***Regimental Band and U.S. Infantry Marching, Paris* by J. F. Boucher** Americans provided soldiers, weapons, and the moral support that the Allies needed to win World War I.

1898 Spanish-American War begins

1900 Boxer Rebellion occurs in China

1901 Theodore Roosevelt becomes president

1908 Belgium establishes control over the Congo

1909 National Association for the Advancement of Colored People (NAACP) is formed

1914 World War I begins

1917 U.S. declares war on Germany

1917 Russian Revolution begins

1919 Treaty of Versailles signed

1920 Prohibition begins nationwide; ratification of woman suffrage

1900 — *1910* — *1920*

TEAM TEACHING STRATEGIES

Science/Health Work with the Science or Health teacher to help students better understand some of the toxins discussed in this unit. When studying Chapter 21, for example, the Health teacher might explain the scientific studies the temperance movement conducted, which revealed physical and psychological effects of alcohol. He or she may provide additional information about the importance of national standards of purity in the preparation and sale of food and drugs. The Science teacher may provide more information about the effects of poison gas as a weapon of war, which is covered in Chapter 23. In both chapters, encourage students to consider how such toxins are dealt with today. Do these toxins still present dangers?

NATIONAL GEOGRAPHIC SOCIETY

VIDEODISC
GTV: A Geographic Perspective on American History

Side 4, Chapter 1
Title: *Modern Times*
Subject: Before and after World War I (1900–1925)
Ask: **What kinds of technology developed that changed lifestyles in the early 1900s?** *(airplanes, automobiles, telephones, and electric lights)*

HISTORY AND ART By the time the United States entered World War I and the American Expeditionary Force (AEF) arrived in Paris, the French had been at war for almost three years. Their country was staggering under the latest German offensive, and an Allied victory was by no means certain. **Ask:** **Given this information, how do you think the French felt about the Americans' arrival? Explain.** *(Students may suggest that the arrival gave the French new hope, for the Americans were a fresh and well-supplied fighting force.)*

Linking PAST & PRESENT

Activity The era of expansion between 1865 and 1917 saw a rise in the influence of journalists upon Americans. Sometimes journalists informed the public; sometimes they helped shape public opinion. Have students look for and share ways in which today's journalists do the same.

Block Schedule

Team Teaching These patriotic songs may be implemented in a team-teaching context, in conjunction with English/Language Arts.

Reinforcing Vocabulary

Review the **Reader's Dictionary** terms with students to be sure they understand any unfamiliar terms.

Historical Connection

Although the United States took an official position of neutrality when World War I broke out, the government offered financial support to the Allies. Such actions incurred the wrath of the Central Powers. Eventually the United States was drawn into the war. By the time President Wilson issued a formal declaration of war, most Americans eagerly expressed the sentiments found in these two songs.

Background Information

Setting Both songs are set against the entry of the United States into World War I and the arrival of American troops in Europe.

Characters In "Over There," the Germans are called "the Hun" whereas the American fighting force is called "Johnnie," "the Yanks," and "Yankees." Reference is also made to each soldier's parents and sweetheart.

The title character of "Uncle Sam" is the United States. The enemy is "the Kaiser and his crew."

Plot The lyrics offer a warning to America's enemy. "Over There" promises that the United States will not give up. "Uncle Sam" promises to "fight till tyrants quake."

America's Literature

Patriotic Songs

George M. Cohan

As the United States entered World War I, rousing songs helped bolster the spirits of soldiers and civilians alike. Composer George M. Cohan wrote "Over There"*—the most popular patriotic song of the war—in 1917. He was later awarded the Congressional Medal of Honor for writing it and for writing* "You're a Grand Old Flag," *another enthusiastic war song. Edward Bushnell, who wrote* "Uncle Sam!" *in 1917, also touched the hearts and spirits of war-torn America with his patriotic lyrics.*

Read to Discover

As you read the lyrics for the following songs, think about their purpose. How might they have helped the country's war effort? What words used by the composers are especially patriotic?

Reader's Dictionary

pine: suffer
Hun: a negative word for a German
tyrant: an absolute ruler
Kaiser: German emperor

Over There

by George M. Cohan

Johnnie get your gun, get your gun,
get your gun,
Take it on the run, on the run, on the run;
Hear them calling you and me;
Ev'ry son of liberty.
Hurry right away, no delay, go today,
Make your daddy glad, to have had such
a lad,
Tell your sweetheart not to pine,
To be proud her boy's in line.

CHORUS
Over there, over there,
Send the word, send the word over there
That the Yanks are coming, the Yanks
are coming,
The drums rum-tumming ev'rywhere
So prepare, say a pray'r,
Send the word, send the word to beware,
We'll be over, we're coming over,
And we won't come back till it's over
over there.

Johnnie get your gun, get your gun,
get your gun,
Johnnie show the Hun, you're a son
of a gun,
Hoist the flag and let her fly,
Like true heroes do or die.
Pack your little kit, show your grit,
do your bit,
Soldiers to the ranks from the towns and
the tanks,
Make your mother proud of you,
And to liberty be true.

Additional Literary Works of the Period

You may want to refer students to the following:

Hull, Robert, ed. ***A Prose Anthology of the First World War.*** Brookfield, CT: Millbrook Press, 1993. A collection of personal narratives of the war.

Du Bois, W.E.B. ***The Souls of Black Folk.*** New York: Bantam Books, 1994. Addresses African Americans at the turn of the century.

Michener, James. ***Hawaii.*** New York: Random House, 1959. Novel tracing the history of Hawaii.

Sinclair, Upton. ***The Jungle.*** New York: NAL-Dutton, 1960. Traces the lives and misfortunes of Lithuanian immigrants in Chicago at the turn of the century.

American soldiers eating at mess call, 1918

Uncle Sam

by Edward Bushnell

So you've drawn your sword again, Uncle Sam!
You're lined up with fighting men, Uncle Sam!
For when freedom is at stake,
You will fight for honor's sake,
And you'll fight till tyrants quake, Uncle Sam!

We know war is not your game, Uncle Sam!
'Twas at peace you made your fame, Uncle
Sam!
And 'tis always with regret
That you make a war-like threat;
But they've never whipped you yet, Uncle Sam!

We will sail on all the seas, Uncle Sam!
Without saying "if" or "please," Uncle Sam!
We'll not wear the Kaiser's tag,
And we'll fly no checkered rag,
For Old Glory is our flag, Uncle Sam!

Let the Eagle flap his wings, Uncle Sam!
These are sorry days for kings, Uncle Sam!
And the Kaiser and his crew
Will be missing when they're through
With the old Red, White and Blue, Uncle Sam!

Responding to Literature

1. According to Cohan, who waiting at home will be proud of the soldiers?
2. What does Bushnell's song say about the willingness of the United States to go to war?

Activity

Writing a Patriotic Song What are some issues facing the United States today that need public support? Choose an issue you believe in and write the lyrics for a song that will encourage people to support that issue. Your song can be brief, but should be enthusiastic, patriotic, and easy for people to learn and remember. You can choose a familiar tune or write a new tune for your song. Then present your composition to the class.

Answers to Responding to Literature

1. the soldiers' parents and sweethearts
2. It says that the United States would rather have peace than war—but that when "freedom is at stake," it will "fight till tyrants quake."

Activity Songs should make clear reference to a present-day issue and should encourage the listener's support. The best lyrics will follow a rhyme scheme, fit the song's rhythm and melody, and follow a logical progression. Allow ample class time for presentation of the completed songs.

History *and the* Humanities

- U.S. History & Art, Transparency 20, *I Want You for the U.S. Army;* Transparency 21, *Allies Day, May 1917*
- American Music Cultural Traditions, Lesson 8: "For Your Country and My Country," "Good Bye Broadway, Hello France," "I Don't Know Where I'm Going But I'm On My Way," "Over There"
- The Spirit of American Art and Music, John Philip Sousa

Portfolio Activity Have students locate and read letters, diaries, or other first-hand accounts by World War I veterans. Ask students to include brief synopses of these accounts in their portfolios. They should note how the accounts shed light upon the song lyrics here and upon the historical facts in this unit.

At the Movies

The film *Yankee Doodle Dandy* (1942) starring James Cagney is a biography of George M. Cohan. Other films relating to World War I include *All Quiet on the Western Front* (1930 and 1979), *A Farewell to Arms* (1932), *Paths of Glory* (1957), and *Gallipoli* (1981). All are available on videocassette.

Who? What? Where? When?

George M. Cohan wrote about 20 plays and musicals, greatly shaping the Broadway scene of that era. (A statue of Cohan stands in Times Square today.) He produced and acted in many shows, too, including *Forty-Five Minutes from Broadway* (1905), *George Washington, Jr.* (1906), and *American Born* (1925).

Chapter 21 Planning Guide

A complete, 1-page lesson plan is provided for each section in the *Reproducible Lesson Plans* booklet.

Section Resources

Daily Objectives	Reproducible Resources	Multimedia Resources
Section 1 Progressive Movement Analyze the methods and effects of progressivism in governmental and business practices.	Reproducible Lesson Plan 21–1 Guided Reading Activity 21–1* Political Cartoons, *Urban Corruption, Battle Against the Trusts* Section Quiz 21–1* Reteaching Activity 21–1 Enrichment Activity 21–1	Section Focus Transparency 21–1 Vocabulary PuzzleMaker Chapter Challenger Interactive Review Testmaker Facts On File: Landmark Documents in American History The Presidents: A Picture History of Our Nation ABCNews InterActive™ Historic America Electronic Field Trips
Section 2 Women and Progressives Identify signs of change in the roles of American women and ways in which they participated in various reform movements, especially the movement for woman suffrage.	Reproducible Lesson Plan 21–2 Guided Reading Activity 21–2* Section Quiz 21–2* Reteaching Activity 21–2 Enrichment Activity 21–2	Section Focus Transparency 21–2 Vocabulary PuzzleMaker Chapter Challenger Interactive Review Testmaker GTV: The American People: Fabric of a Nation
Section 3 Progressive Presidents Discuss reforms made by Theodore Roosevelt, William Howard Taft, and Woodrow Wilson as well as the rise of the Progressive Party.	Reproducible Lesson Plan 21–3 Guided Reading Activity 21–3* Political Cartoons, *A Third Party* Section Quiz 21–3* Reteaching Activity 21–3 Enrichment Activity 21–3	Section Focus Transparency 21–3 Vocabulary PuzzleMaker Chapter Challenger Interactive Review Testmaker GTV: A Geographic Perspective on American History Facts On File: Landmark Documents in American History The Presidents: A Picture History of Our Nation
Section 4 Excluded From Reform Contrast the era's spirit of reform with the lack of change in the treatment of America's minorities.	Reproducible Lesson Plan 21–4 Guided Reading Activity 21–4* Section Quiz 21–4* Reteaching Activity 21–4 Enrichment Activity 21–4	Section Focus Transparency 21–4 Vocabulary PuzzleMaker Chapter Challenger Interactive Review Testmaker GTV: The American People: Fabric of a Nation

** Also available in Spanish*

Blackline Master | Videodisc | Audiocassette | Music Program | Transparency | CD-ROM | Software

0:00 **OUT OF TIME?**
Assign the Chapter 21 Digest and the corresponding Chapter Digests Audiocassettes with activities and tests.

Activity

From the Classroom of...

Robyn Smith
Pointe South
Middle School
Jonesboro, GA

Women and the Progressive Movement–A Time Line

Organize students into pairs and give each pair a two-foot-long piece of blank adding machine paper. Review the format for time lines by preparing a sample horizontal time line on the chalkboard, using 25-year increments. Have students review the chapter's information about the influential women of the Progressive movement and make a list of key events or activities associated with each person. Then ask students to prepare their own time lines on the strip of paper, using 25-year increments. They should start with the year 1800 on the left and end with 1950 on the right. Have them fill in names—such as Jane Addams—and events—such as the establishment of Hull House—in chronological order. Ask students to do additional biographical research to fill in the time lines and add variety to the class collection. Students may also add prominent women from their own states or regions who have been politically influential. Display the time lines by taping one above the other, aligning the dates so that they match.

NATIONAL GEOGRAPHIC SOCIETY Teacher's Corner

INDEX TO NATIONAL GEOGRAPHIC MAGAZINE

The following articles may be used for research relating to this chapter:

- "Central Park: Oasis in the City," by Joel L. Swerdlow, May 1993.
- "Miami," by Charles E. Cobb, Jr., January 1992.
- "Chicago: Welcome to the Neighborhood," by Richard Conniff, May 1991.
- "New Life for Ellis Island," by Alice J. Hall, September 1990.
- "Broadway, Street of Dreams," by Rick Gore, September 1990.

NATIONAL GEOGRAPHIC SOCIETY PRODUCTS AVAILABLE FROM GLENCOE

To order the following products for use with this chapter, contact your local Glencoe sales representative, or call Glencoe at 1-800-334-7344:

- *GTV: A Geographic Perspective on American History* (Videodisc)
- *GTV: The American People: Fabric of a Nation* (Videodisc)
- *The Presidents: A Picture History of Our Nation* (CD-ROM)
- *PictureShow: Native Americans, 1 and 2* (CD-ROM, Transparencies)

ADDITIONAL NATIONAL GEOGRAPHIC SOCIETY PRODUCTS

To order the following products for use with this chapter, call National Geographic Society at 1-800-368-2728:

- *Immigration: The Triumph of Hope* (Video)
- *Historical Atlas of the United States* (Atlas)

Block Schedule

Block scheduling differs from traditional class scheduling in the amount of time allotted to each period. The extended time frame provided by block scheduling affords you the opportunity to implement a greater number of research-oriented and activity-intense projects to motivate and involve your students. Activities that are particularly suited to use within the block scheduling framework are identified throughout this chapter by the following designation:

KEY TO ABILITY LEVELS

Teaching strategies have been coded for varying learning styles and abilities.

L1 **BASIC** activities for all students
L2 **AVERAGE** activities for average to above-average students
L3 **CHALLENGING** activities for above-average students
ELL **ENGLISH LANGUAGE LEARNER** activities

Chapter 21 Resource Guide

HOME INVOLVEMENT

Home Involvement Activity 21

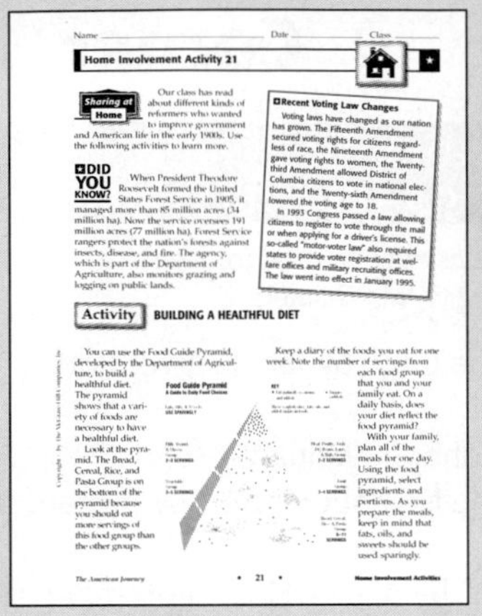

REVIEW ACTIVITIES

Chapter Summary 21

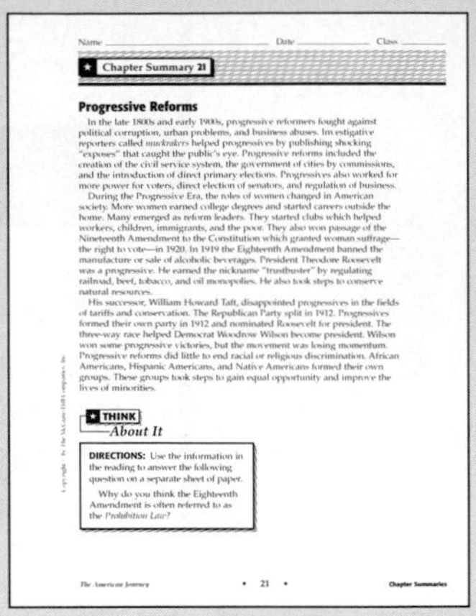

Workbook Activity 21

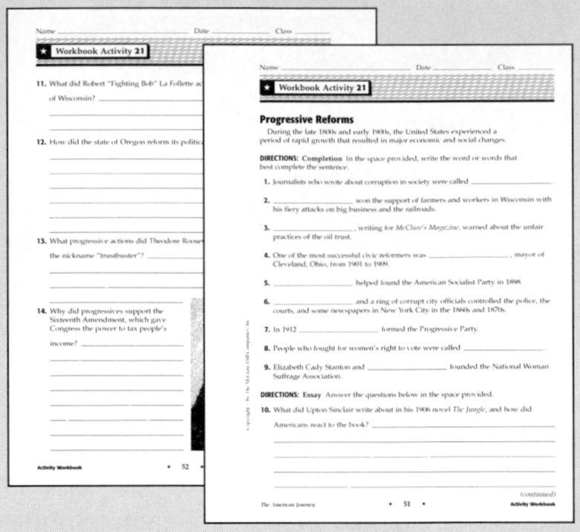

REINFORCEMENT ACTIVITIES

Time Line Activity 21

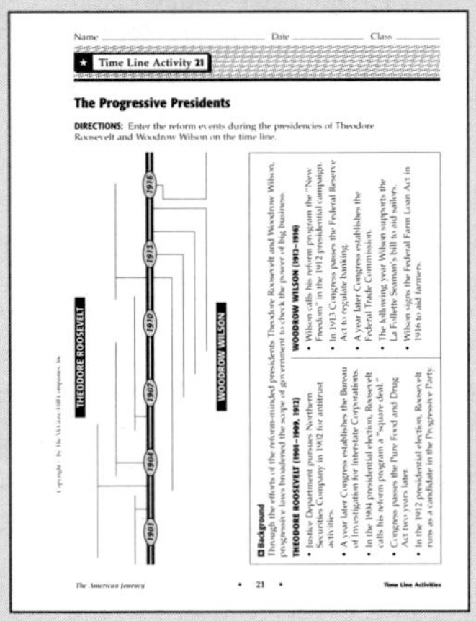

Vocabulary Activity 21

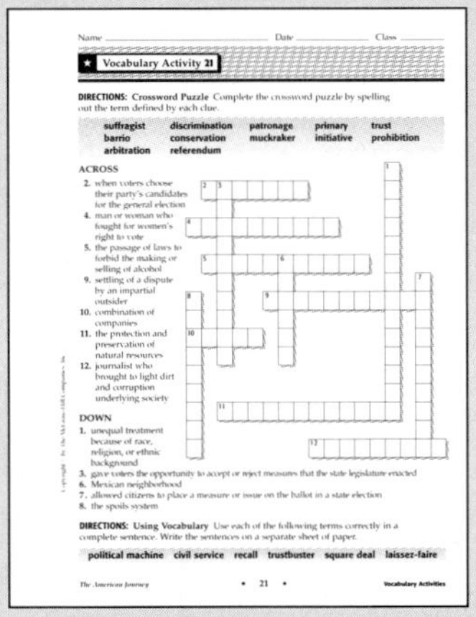

Chapter Skills Activity 21

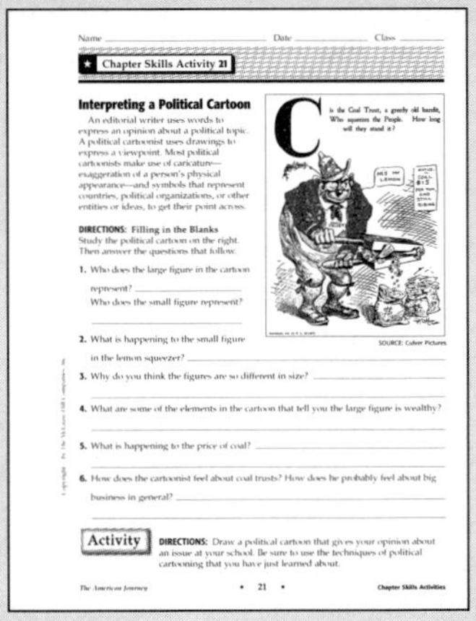

ENRICHMENT ACTIVITIES

Linking Past and Present Activity 21

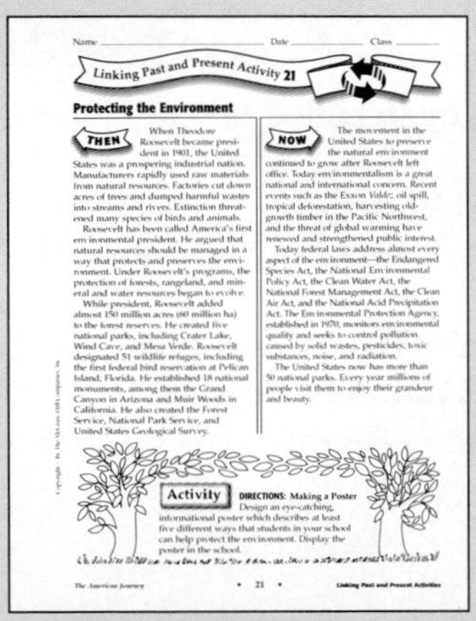

Primary Source Reading 21

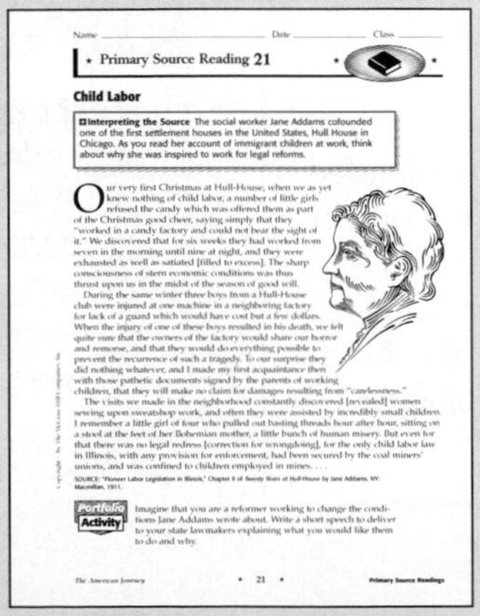

GEOGRAPHY ACTIVITIES

Mapping History Activity 21

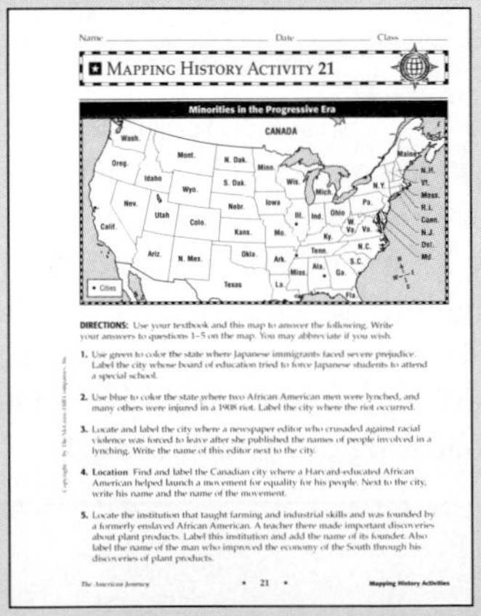

ASSESSMENT

Chapter 21 Test, Form A

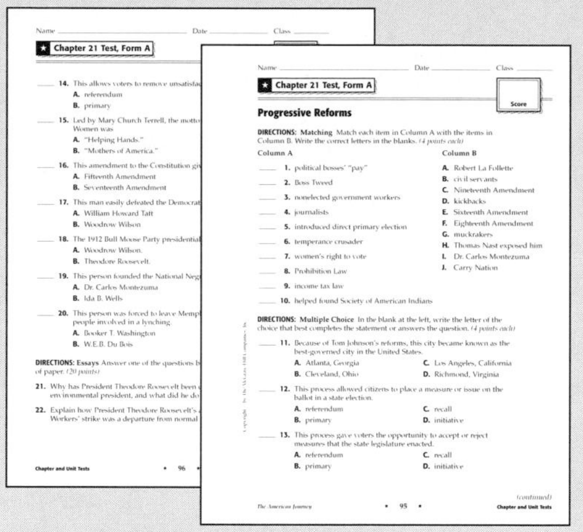

Chapter 21 Test, Form B

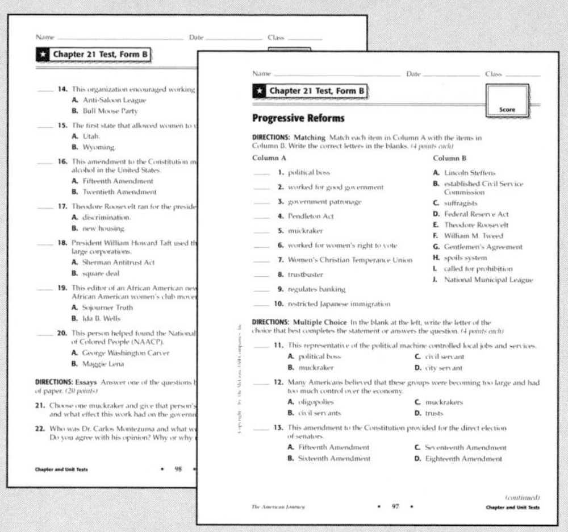

Performance Assessment Activity 21

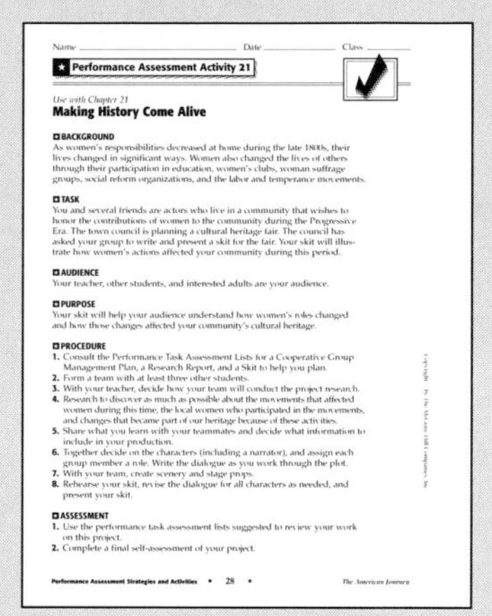

SPANISH RESOURCES

The following Spanish language materials are available in the Spanish Resources binder:

- **Spanish Chapter Summary 21**
- **Spanish Vocabulary Activity 21**
- **Spanish Guided Reading Activities, Chapter 21**
- **Spanish Section Quizzes, Chapter 21**
- **Spanish Home Involvement Activity 21**
- **Spanish Chapter 21 Digests Audiocassette Activity and Test**

ACTIVITY MANIPULATIVES

Help students learn more about America's cultural history with:

- **American Crafts Hands-On Activities**
- **American Games Hands-On Activities**
- **American History Flash Cards**

ADDITIONAL RESOURCES FROM GLENCOE

- **The Spirit of American Art and Music,** William Henry Jackson
- **Political Cartoons,** *Urban Corruption, Battle Against the Trusts, A Third Party*
- **Outline Map Resource Book**
- **U.S. Desk Map**
- **The American History Videodisc and CD-ROM,** *The Progressive Era and the First World War, 1901–1920*

A&E HOME VIDEO. Biography THE HISTORY CHANNEL.

The following videotape programs are available from Glencoe as supplements to Chapter 21:

- **Theodore Roosevelt: Roughrider to Rushmore** (ISBN 1-56501-806-0)

To order, call Glencoe at 1-800-334-7344. To find classroom resources to accompany many of these videos, check the following home pages:
A&E Television: http://www.aetv.com
The History Channel: http://www.historychannel.com

Introducing CHAPTER 21

Chapter Themes

Chapter Themes are listed by section on this chapter opening page of the Student Edition. A corresponding theme-based activity is available under "FOCUS," and a theme-based question is asked in the Section and Chapter Reviews.

Performance Assessment

Refer to Activity 21 in the *Performance Assessment Strategies and Activities* booklet.

GLENCOE TECHNOLOGY

VIDEODISC
MindJogger Videoquiz

Use MindJogger to preview the Chapter 21 content.

Chapter 21
Disc 3, Side B

Also available in VHS.

HISTORY AND ART George Luks (1867–1933) was one of "The Eight," a group of American painters who focused on real-life scenes in their work. Such scenes, like that in *Hester Street,* are typical of the group's work.

Chapter 21

1877–1920

Progressive Reforms

Why It's Important

The reform spirit gained strength during the late 1800s and flourished during the early 1900s. Some reformers believed that rapid social and economic change had resulted in a disordered and corrupt society. These reformers, called *progressives,* believed that the efforts of individuals and government could make society better and more fair. As progressive leaders reached positions of power in government, they passed laws affecting government employees, business practices, and public health. These progressive laws form the basis for modern ideas of the role of government.

Chapter Themes

- *Section 1,* Government and Democracy
- *Section 2,* Groups and Institutions
- *Section 3,* Economic Factors
- *Section 4,* Civic Rights and Responsibilities

HISTORY AND ART ***Hester Street* by George Luks** Hester Street in New York City was part of a Jewish immigrant community in the early 1900s.

EXTRA CREDIT PROJECT

Writing a Protest Poem This era saw the exposure of a wide variety of political abuses and social needs as well as the call for reform. Writing about injustice and the need for change is an American tradition. Have students choose one of the areas of reform discussed in this chapter—tenement life, corruption in city government, the power of the trusts, the struggle for woman suffrage, or problems in race relations. Then have them write a poem that describes the problem and offers a solution.

1885 | 1895 | 1905 | 1915

1887 Interstate Commerce Commission is set up

1890 Congress passes Sherman Antitrust Act

1906 Upton Sinclair writes *The Jungle*

1912 Congress passes the Seventeenth Amendment

Section 1

Progressive Movement

READ TO DISCOVER . . .

- how journalists helped shape the progressives' reform movement.
- how cities, states, and Congress answered the call for reform of the government.

TERMS TO LEARN

political machine
patronage
civil service
trust
muckraker
primary
initiative
referendum
recall

The Storyteller

Newspaper reporter Jacob Riis shocked Americans in 1890 with his book *How the Other Half Lives.* With words and powerful photographs, Riis vividly portrayed immigrant life in New York City's crowded tenements. Said Riis: "We used to go in the small hours of the morning into the worst tenements to count noses and see if the law against overcrowding was violated and the sights I saw there gripped my heart until I felt that I must tell of them, or burst."

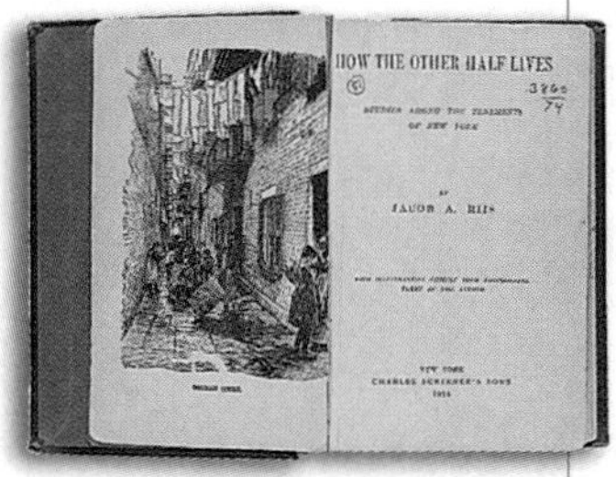

Book on urban life by Jacob Riis

Many Americans called for reform in the late 1800s. The reformers had many different goals. Progressive reformers focused on urban problems, government, and business. They claimed that government and big business were taking advantage of the American people rather than serving them.

Fighting Corruption

Political machines—powerful organizations linked to political parties—controlled local government in many cities. In each ward, or political district, within a city, a machine representative controlled jobs and services. This representative was the **political boss.** The bosses gained votes for their parties by doing favors for people such as offering turkey dinners and summer boat rides, providing jobs for immigrants, and helping needy families. A political boss was often a citizen's closest link with local government. Although they did help people, many bosses were dishonest.

Corrupt politicians found numerous ways to make money. They accepted bribes from tenement landlords in return for overlooking violations of city housing codes. They received campaign contributions from contractors hoping to do business with the city. They also accepted kickbacks. A **kickback** was an arrangement in which contractors padded the amount of their bill for city work and paid, or "kicked back," a percentage of that amount to the bosses.

Some politicians used their knowledge of city business for personal profit. A person who knew

SECTION RESOURCES

Reproducible Masters

- Guided Reading Activity 21–1
- Political Cartoons
- Section Quiz 21–1
- Reteaching Activity 21–1
- Enrichment Activity 21–1

Transparencies

- Section Focus Transparency 21–1

Multimedia

- Vocabulary PuzzleMaker
- Chapter Challenger Interactive Review
- Facts On File: Landmark Documents in American History
- The Presidents: A Picture History of Our Nation
- ABCNews InterActive™ Historic America Electronic Field Trips

1 FOCUS

BELLRINGER
Motivational Activity

Before taking roll at the beginning of the class period, project Section Focus Transparency 21–1 and have students answer the questions. Discuss students' responses.

This activity is also available as a blackline master.

Section Focus Transparency 21–1

Vocabulary Precheck

Call on volunteers to explain how each of the **Terms to Learn** relates to the reforming spirit that marked the Progressive movement.

Use the **Vocabulary PuzzleMaker** to create crossword and word search puzzles.

Section Theme
Government and Democracy

Americans took action against corruption in business and in government on both the local and national levels.

Activity Have students think about how a government practice would qualify as "corrupt." **Ask:** How might you try to change a corrupt practice? *(Answers might include contact with the media and with government officials.)*

2 TEACH

L1, ELL Recognizing Issues Ask students to complete this statement: The first step in solving a problem is ____. *(recognizing a problem exists)* Then have them list ways in which progressives helped the American people see the need for reform in the late 1800s.

Guided Reading Activity 21–1

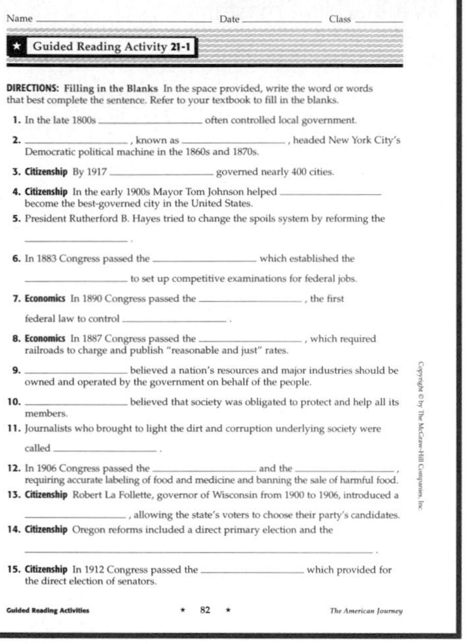
Name ______ Date ______ Class ______

★ Guided Reading Activity **21-1**

DIRECTIONS: Filling in the Blanks In the space provided, write the word or words that best complete the sentence. Refer to your textbook to fill in the blanks.

1. In the late 1800s ______ often controlled local government.
2. ______, known as ______, headed New York City's Democratic political machine in the 1860s and 1870s.
3. **Citizenship** By 1917 ______ governed nearly 400 cities.
4. **Citizenship** In the early 1900s Mayor Tom Johnson helped ______ become the best-governed city in the United States.
5. President Rutherford B. Hayes tried to change the spoils system by reforming the ______.
6. In 1883 Congress passed the ______ which established the ______ to set up competitive examinations for federal jobs.
7. **Economics** In 1890 Congress passed the ______, the first federal law to control ______.
8. **Economics** In 1887 Congress passed the ______, which required railroads to charge and publish "reasonable and just" rates.
9. ______ believed a nation's resources and major industries should be owned and operated by the government on behalf of the people.
10. ______ believed that society was obligated to protect and help all its members.
11. Journalists who brought to light the dirt and corruption underlying society were called ______.
12. In 1906 Congress passed the ______ and the ______, requiring accurate labeling of food and medicine and banning the sale of harmful food.
13. **Citizenship** Robert La Follette, governor of Wisconsin from 1900 to 1906, introduced a ______, allowing the state's voters to choose their party's candidates.
14. **Citizenship** Oregon reforms included a direct primary election and the ______.
15. **Citizenship** In 1912 Congress passed the ______ which provided for the direct election of senators.

Copyright © by The McGraw-Hill Companies, Inc.

Guided Reading Activities ★ 82 ★ *The American Journey*

Picturing HISTORY Thomas Nast (1840–1902) helped bring Tweed to justice. Although Tweed fled to Spain, authorities used one of Nast's cartoons to identify and apprehend him there in 1871. Nast's cartoons also popularized the Democratic donkey and created the Republican elephant. **Answer:** *New York City*

Where? When? Who? What?

Cities of Reform Two other Midwestern cities saw notable reforms during this time. In Toledo, Ohio, Mayor Samuel "Golden Rule" Jones established municipal ownership of public utilities and tackled police corruption. In Detroit, Michigan, Mayor Hazen Pingree set up new schools, parks, and work programs.

where the city planned to build a road could buy land there before the route became public knowledge. Later the land could be sold for a huge profit.

Boss Tweed

One of the most corrupt city bosses, William M. Tweed, known as **Boss Tweed,** headed New York City's Democratic political machine in the 1860s and 1870s. Tweed and a network of city officials—the Tweed ring—controlled the police, the courts, and some newspapers. They collected millions of dollars in illegal payments from companies doing business with the city. Political cartoonist Thomas Nast exposed the Tweed ring's operations in his cartoons for *Harper's Weekly.* Tweed went to prison in 1872.

Citizenship

New Ways to Govern Cities

To break the power of political bosses, reformers founded organizations such as the National Municipal League, formed in Philadelphia. These groups worked to make city governments more honest and efficient

Cities troubled by poor management or corruption tried new forms of government. After the tidal wave of a hurricane devastated **Galveston, Texas,** in 1900, the task of rebuilding the city overwhelmed the mayor and city council. Galveston's citizens persuaded the Texas state legislature to approve a new charter that placed the city government in the hands of five commissioners. The new commission efficiently rebuilt the city. By 1917 commissions governed nearly 400 cities. Many other cities, mostly small ones, hired professional city managers.

One successful civic reformer was **Tom Johnson,** mayor of **Cleveland, Ohio,** from 1901 to 1909. He battled corporations and party bosses to lower streetcar fares, improve food inspections, and build parks. Because of Johnson's reforms, Cleveland became known as the best-governed city in the United States.

Fighting the Spoils System

The spoils system—rewarding political supporters with jobs and favors—had been common practice since the time of Andrew Jackson. Whenever a new president came to power, job seekers flooded the nation's capital.

The spoils system—also called patronage—existed at all levels of government and led to numerous abuses. Many who received government jobs were not qualified. Some were dishonest.

Picturing HISTORY Cartoonist Thomas Nast criticized William "Boss" Tweed (left foreground) and his corrupt Democratic political machine. **What city did Tweed's political machine control?**

Tammany savings bank

COOPERATIVE LEARNING ACTIVITY

Charting Reforms Organize the class into groups of five students each, and supply each group with chart paper. Then ask each group to make a chart about the reforms discussed in the chapter. Within each group, one student can record information; the others can specialize in looking for information about the following: (1) the area of reform; (2) names of reformers; (3) suggested reforms; (4) success of the suggestions. Have students compare their information before completing the chart. When charts are completed, take a class vote on the reform or reformer that students consider the most important.

Presidents **Rutherford B. Hayes** (1877–1881) and **James Garfield** (1881) wanted to change the spoils system. Hayes tried to do this by reforming the civil service—the body of nonelected government workers—but neither the Democratic nor the Republican Party supported his efforts.

Garfield also hoped to reform the civil service. He believed that people should be appointed to government jobs not as a reward for political support but because of their qualifications. Garfield took office in 1881 but was assassinated by an unsuccessful office seeker before he could launch his reforms.

When Vice President **Chester A. Arthur** succeeded Garfield, he tried to end the spoils system. In 1883 Congress passed the **Pendleton Act,** which established the **Civil Service Commission** to set up competitive examinations for federal jobs. Applicants had to demonstrate their abilities in this examination. By 1900 the commission controlled the hiring of more than half of all federal employees.

Picturing HISTORY This political cartoon blames the government for allowing the trusts to benefit from high tariffs at the expense of the American people. **How did high tariffs affect American shoppers?**

Economics

Controlling Business

During the late 1800s, many Americans came to believe that trusts, or combinations of companies, were becoming too large. They believed these trusts had too much control over the economy and the government. This public concern led to new laws regulating big business.

A National Antitrust Law

In 1890 Congress passed the **Sherman Antitrust Act,** the first federal law to control trusts and monopolies. Supporters of the law hoped it would keep trusts from limiting competition. During the 1890s, however, the government rarely used the Sherman Act to curb business. Instead, it applied the act against labor unions, claiming that union strikes interfered with trade. Not until the early 1900s did the government win cases against trusts with the Sherman Act.

Reining in the Railroads

The railroads functioned as an **oligopoly**—a market structure in which a few large companies control the prices of the industry. Reformers called for regulations on railroad rates, but the Supreme Court ruled that only Congress could enact legislation to regulate commerce that crossed state lines.

So in 1887 Congress passed the **Interstate Commerce Act,** which required railroads to charge "reasonable and just" rates and to publish those rates. The act also created the **Interstate Commerce Commission** (ICC) to supervise the railroad industry and, later, the trucking industry.

Lowering Tariffs

The reform movement also wanted to lower tariffs. Many people believed that high tariffs led to higher prices for goods. In 1890 the Republicans raised tariffs sharply to protect American businesses from international competition. Voters showed their opposition to high tariffs by sending many Democrats to Congress. When **Grover Cleveland** became president in 1893, he also supported lower tariffs.

MULTIPLE LEARNING STYLES

Visual/Spatial Socialists were progressives, but not all progressives were socialists. Ask students to create a drawing or more technical diagram that helps show the difference between socialism and progressivism—what followers believed and how those beliefs were demonstrated in their activities—based on information in Section 1. Call on volunteers to share their final artwork with the class. **L3**

Picturing HISTORY By portraying the government as a carnival barker, the cartoon suggests that the tariff system was "rigged" and perhaps that the trusts took a rather evil pleasure in seeing Americans suffer. **Ask: Which figure in this illustration is representative of the government?** *(Uncle Sam)* **Answer:** *High tariffs made the goods they needed more expensive.*

Political Cartoons, *Urban Corruption, Battle Against the Trusts*

NATIONAL GEOGRAPHIC SOCIETY

CD-ROM
The Presidents: A Picture History of Our Nation

Have students select President Taft from the main menu and the category GAME. Suggest they learn more about Taft by playing the presidential game with a partner.

Who?What?Where?When?

Garfield's Assassin was Charles J. Guiteau, a frustrated patronage seeker who shot President Garfield. The assassination probably was the single most powerful symbol of the need for the reforms finally achieved in the Pendleton Act.

Facts On File

CD-ROM
Landmark Documents in American History

Title: *Pendleton Act (Pendleton Civil Service Act, 1883); Interstate Commerce Act, 1887 (Cullom Act); Pure Food and Drug Act, 1906; Meat Inspection Act, 1906*
Have students read and compare the provisions of the acts listed above.

Picturing HISTORY Tarbell ("that misguided woman," as John D. Rockefeller called her) extensively researched her subject. Besides studying court records of lawsuits against Standard Oil, she interviewed former colleagues of Rockefeller and businesspeople whom his oil trust had crushed. Tarbell was not against big business but against its abuses; she later wrote much in praise of Henry Ford's "Golden Rule in Industry."
Answer: *Lincoln Steffens*

3 ASSESS

Assign Section 1 Review as homework or as an in-class activity.

Use **Chapter Challenger Interactive Review Software** to review Section 1.

Section Quiz 21–1

Name ______________ Date ________ Class ________

Chapter 21 Score

Section Quiz 21-1

DIRECTIONS: Matching Match each item in Column A with the items in Column B. Write the correct letters in the blanks. *(10 points each)*

Column A	Column B
____ **1.** corrupt politicians	**A.** Cleveland, Ohio's, Tom Johnson
____ **2.** New York City's political boss	**B.** spoils system
____ **3.** successful civic reformer	**C.** accepted kickbacks
____ **4.** patronage	**D.** Eugene V. Debs
____ **5.** Socialist Party leader	**E.** William M. Tweed

DIRECTIONS: Multiple Choice In the blank at the left, write the letter of the choice that best completes the statement or answers the question. *(10 points each)*

____ **6.** In many cities local governments were controlled by
A. the federal government. **C.** patronage.
B. political machines. **D.** civil servants.

____ **7.** This organization supervised the railroad and trucking industry.
A. Civil Service Commission **C.** Interstate Commerce Commission
B. spoils system **D.** Pendleton Act

____ **8.** This group supported the government efforts to regulate industry.
A. muckrakers **C.** socialists
B. civil servants **D.** progressives

____ **9.** This writer's book led Congress to pass the Meat Inspection Act.
A. Upton Sinclair **C.** Lincoln Steffens
B. Ida Tarbell **D.** James Garfield

____ **10.** This man introduced the direct primary election.
A. Robert La Follette **C.** Boss Tweed
B. Grover Cleveland **D.** Eugene V. Debs

Section Quizzes ★ 82 ★ *The American Journey*

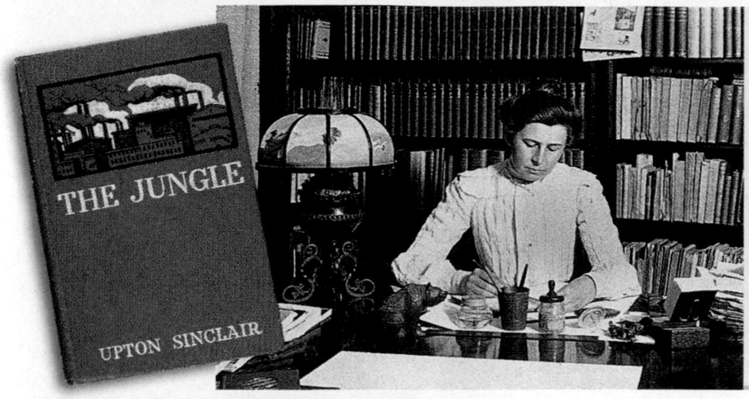

Picturing HISTORY Writing for *McClure's,* Ida Tarbell revealed the unfair practices of the oil trust. In *The Jungle,* Upton Sinclair described horrible conditions in Chicago's meatpacking plants. **What muckraker exposed corrupt practices in government?**

The New Reformers

In the early 1900s, new ideas for correcting injustice and solving social problems emerged among American reformers. Socialism and progressivism were two such ideas.

The Socialists and Progressives

Socialists believed a nation's resources and major industries should be owned and operated by the government on behalf of all the people—not by individuals and private companies for their own profit. **Eugene V. Debs** helped found the American Socialist Party in 1898. Under Debs's leadership the party won some support in the early 1900s. Debs ran for president five times but never received more than 6 percent of the popular vote.

During the same period, progressives brought new energy to the reform movement. Progressivism was not a single organization, goal, or outlook. It represented several overlapping beliefs and ideas. Like the socialists, many progressives were alarmed by the concentration of wealth and power in the hands of a few. Progressives rejected the socialist idea of government ownership of industries. Instead, they supported government efforts to regulate industry.

They also sought to reform government, to make it more efficient and better able to resist the influence of powerful business interests. Progressives also believed that society had an obligation to protect and help all its members. Many progressive reforms aimed to help those who lacked wealth and influence.

Muckrakers Expose Problems

Journalists aided the reformers by exposing injustices, corruption, and political favors. Investigative reporters wrote shocking newspaper and magazine stories that brought problems to the attention of the public—and gained readers. These journalists were called **muckrakers** because they "raked" (brought to light) the "muck" (dirt and corruption) underlying society.

One of the most effective muckrakers, **Lincoln Steffens,** reported for *McClure's Magazine.* Steffens exposed corrupt machine politics in New York, **Chicago,** and other cities. His articles, collected in a book called *The Shame of the Cities* (1904), strengthened the demand for urban reform.

Focus on Industry

Ida Tarbell, also writing for *McClure's,* laid bare the unfair practices of the oil trust. Her articles led to public pressure for more government control over big business. In her 1904 book, *The History of the Standard Oil Company,* she warned of the giant corporation's power.

In his novel *The Jungle* (1906), **Upton Sinclair** described the horrors of the meatpacking industry in Chicago. Although Sinclair's aim was to arouse sympathy for the workers, his vivid descriptions shocked Americans. The uproar caused by Sinclair's book helped persuade Congress to pass the **Meat Inspection Act** in 1906. That same year Congress also passed the **Pure Food and Drug Act,** requiring accurate labeling of food and medicine and banning the sale of harmful food.

MAKING CONNECTIONS ACTIVITY

The Arts This chapter begins by noting the power of photojournalism. Point out that in 1900 the Eastman Kodak Company introduced the Brownie camera. This point-and-shoot technology made every camera owner a potential photojournalist. Have students complete one of the following activities:

- Locate and display photographs by influential photojournalists of this era, such as Dorothea Lange and Margaret Bourke-White.
- Document a modern social situation with photographs of their own.

Set up a "gallery walk" in which students can present their photographs. **L2, ELL**

Citizenship

Expanding Democracy

In the early 1900s, progressives backed a number of reforms designed to increase the people's direct control of the government. These reforms changed the nature of American democracy.

The Wisconsin Idea

Robert La Follette led Wisconsin's reform-minded Republicans. "Fighting Bob," as he was called, won the support of farmers and workers with his fiery attacks on big business and the railroads. He served as Wisconsin's governor from 1900 until 1906 and then served four terms in Washington, D.C., as one of Wisconsin's senators.

While governor, La Follette brought about significant reforms—raising taxes for corporations and improving the civil service. "Fighting Bob's" greatest achievement, however, was reforming the state electoral system. Candidates for general elections in Wisconsin had been chosen at state conventions run by party bosses. La Follette introduced a direct primary election, allowing the state's voters to choose their party's candidates. Reformers in other states copied this "Wisconsin idea."

The Oregon System

Oregon also made changes in the political process to give voters more power and to limit the influence of political parties. The reforms included a direct primary election and the initiative, the referendum, and the recall.

The initiative allowed citizens to place a measure or issue on the ballot in a state election. The referendum gave voters the opportunity to accept or reject measures that the state legislature enacted. The recall enabled voters to remove unsatisfactory elected officials from their jobs. These reforms were called the **Oregon System.** Other western states soon adopted the reforms.

The Seventeenth Amendment

Progressives also changed the way United States senators are elected. The Constitution had given state legislatures the responsibility for choosing senators, but party bosses and business interests often controlled the selection process. Progressives wanted to give the people an opportunity to vote for their senators directly. Support for this idea grew. In 1912 Congress passed the **Seventeenth Amendment** to the Constitution to provide for the direct election of senators. Ratified in 1913, the amendment gave the people a voice in selecting their representatives.

Section 1 Review

Checking for Understanding

1. ***Identify*** Boss Tweed, James Garfield, Pendleton Act, Grover Cleveland, Ida Tarbell, Upton Sinclair, Robert La Follette.
2. ***Define*** political machine, patronage, civil service, trust, muckraker, primary, initiative, referendum, recall.
3. ***Explain*** how the Civil Service Commission helped to eliminate the spoils system.

Reviewing Themes

4. **Government and Democracy** What five reforms gave the American people more direct control of the government?

Critical Thinking

5. **Making Comparisons** Compare socialist and progressive views on industry.

Activity

Making a Campaign Poster Come up with a slogan for a progressive candidate for a local, state, or federal office. Use the slogan to create a campaign poster.

Section 1 Review Answers

1. Boss Tweed, 604; James Garfield, 605; Pendleton Act, 605; Grover Cleveland, 605; Ida Tarbell, 606; Upton Sinclair, 606; Robert La Follette, 607
2. The words are defined in the Glossary.
3. Applicants for government jobs had to take tests to prove that they were qualified. Political influence no longer guaranteed someone a job.
4. direct primary elections, direct election of senators (Seventeenth Amendment), initiative, referendum, recall
5. Socialists: industry should be owned and operated by the government; Progressives: industries should be regulated but not controlled by the government

Activity Posters should include a slogan that is in keeping with Progressive views of the day.

Reteaching Activity 21–1

Name ______ Date ______ Class ______

★ Reteaching Activity 21-1

DIRECTIONS: Completing an Outline Fill in the outline below by writing the letters of three items that would belong in each area.

Progressive Movement

I. Corrupting the Government ______
II. Finding New Ways to Govern ______
III. Fighting the Spoils System ______
IV. Controlling Big Business ______
V. Solving and Exposing Social Problems ______
VI. Increasing People's Control of Government ______

★FACT BANK

A. Wisconsin led the way in allowing voters to choose their party's candidates.
B. The National Municipal League formed in Philadelphia.
C. Mayor Tom Johnson reformed the city government of Cleveland.
D. Eugene V. Debs helped found the American Socialist Party in 1898.
E. Presidents Hayes, Garfield, and Arthur tried to reform the civil service.
F. The Oregon system helped limit the influence of political parties.
G. Political machines controlled local government in many cities.
H. Writers alerted the public to the dirt and corruption underlying society.
I. Five commissioners rebuilt Galveston, Texas, after a devastating hurricane.
J. Congress passed the Sherman Anti-trust Act (1890) to control monopolies.
K. Politicians, such as Boss Tweed, accepted bribes and kickbacks.
L. Voters elected Democrats to Congress in 1890s to show opposition to high tariffs.
M. Congress passed the Pendleton Act (1883).
N. Political bosses gained votes by doing favors for people.
O. The Seventeenth Amendment (1912) provided for the direct election of senators.
P. Progressive reforms aimed to help those who lacked wealth and influence.
Q. The Civil Service Commission set up examinations for federal job applicants.
R. Congress passed the Interstate Commerce Act (1887) to control the railroads.

Reteaching Activities ★ 82 ★ *The American Journey*

Enrichment Activity 21–1

Name ______ Date ______ Class ______

★ Enrichment Activity 21-1 ★ ★

An "Unspoiled" President?

President James A. Garfield was killed by an office seeker who was disappointed at not having received a government position. During his presidency, Garfield tried to eliminate the spoils system, which had become common political practice. In this system, political supporters expected to be rewarded with jobs. Garfield believed that people should be appointed to government jobs because they qualified, not as a reward for support.

Chester A. Arthur, who had received his political experience because of the spoils system, became the new president after Garfield was killed. Before Arthur was president, he had profited from the spoils system, but after he became president, he tried to follow Garfield's lead. Contemporary cartoons pointed out Arthur's position on this issue. The sign below was part of a cartoon that was written about Arthur after he became president.

HIS EXCELLENCY
CHESTER A. ARTHUR
THAT IS.
NOT
CHET ARTHUR
THAT WAS.
LOCAL POLITICIANS
PLEASE
TAKE NOTICE

DIRECTIONS: Recalling Facts Answer the following questions on a separate sheet of paper.

1. How did Chester A. Arthur gain experience in government?
2. What contrast was the cartoonist trying to point out?
3. Why do you think the cartoonist warns, "Local politicians, please take notice"?

Activity **DIRECTIONS:** With two of your classmates create a script for a skit in which one of you takes the role of office seeker, and the other two take the role of the president. One should interview the office seeker as President "Chet Arthur" and the other should interview the office seeker as President Chester A. Arthur. Your skit should illustrate the differences in the spoils system and the merit system of choosing government employees.

Enrichment Activities ★ 82 ★ *The American Journey*

4 CLOSE

Review the political and business reforms discussed in this section. Have students name and defend the reform that they consider the most important in each category.

Multimedia Activities

ABCNEWS INTERACTIVE™

VIDEODISC
Historic America
Electronic Field Trips

Side 2, Chapter 6
Title: *Seneca Falls*

If you do not have access to a videodisc player, the **Historic America Electronic Field Trips** are also available in VHS.

Internet Sites
The following are possible sites for completing the "Net" activity:

The Susan B. Anthony House
http://www.frontiernet.net/~lhurst/sbahouse/sbahome.htm

The Smithsonian Home Page
http://www.si.edu/

The League of Women Voters
http://www.lwv.org/

Not on the "Net" . . .
If students have limited or no access to the Internet, have them complete the activity "Women and the Progressive Movement" by using the electronic card catalog at their school or local library. At the *s:* prompt, students should type in the words *suffrage, women's rights,* or *Seneca Falls convention.* Using the books' call numbers, students should find and skim the books for significant events in the women's rights movement from 1848 to 1920. Have students photocopy illustrations from the books to include on their time lines.

Multimedia Activities

ABCNEWS INTERACTIVE™ Historic America Electronic Field Trips

Field Trip to Seneca Falls

Setting up the Video

Work with a group of your classmates to view "Seneca Falls" on the videodisc ***Historic America: Electronic Field Trips***. In 1848 hundreds of women attended the Seneca Falls Convention, which met to improve women's rights. Many women felt that equality started with the right to vote. This program discusses the importance of voting today and what women's lives were like before the Nineteenth Amendment was ratified.

Side 2,
Chapter 6

View the video by scanning the bar code or by entering the chapter number on your keypad and pressing Search.

Hands-On Activity

Go to your public library and research current salaries earned by women in various occupations. Compare these numbers with men's salaries in the same occupations. Create a line graph showing the comparison and share your results with the class.

Surfing the "Net"

Women and the Progressive Movement

The first women's rights convention took place in Seneca Falls, New York, in 1848. The result of this meeting was a written document—modeled after the Declaration of Independence—claiming that "all men and women are created equal." To find out more information about women, their struggle for equality, and the Progressive movement, search the Internet.

Getting There

Follow these steps to gather information about the Progressive movement.

1. Use a search engine. Type in the phrase *Progressive movement.*
2. After typing that phrase, enter words like the following to focus your search: *suffrage, women's rights, history.*
3. The search engine will provide you with a number of links to follow.

What to Do When You Are There

Click on the links to navigate through the pages of information and gather your findings. Then, using large poster paper, create a time line that highlights significant events that took place for the cause of women's rights from 1848 to 1920. Include illustrations and written captions for all important events. You should also include a map of the United States that pinpoints where these events took place.

TEACHER'S NOTES

1890 — 1900 — 1910 — 1920

1890 National American Woman Suffrage Association emerges

1896 National Association of Colored Women is formed

1919 The Eighteenth Amendment is ratified

1920 The Nineteenth Amendment is ratified

Section 2

Women and Progressives

READ TO DISCOVER . . .

- how the role of women in American society changed during the Progressive Era.
- how women fought for the right to vote.
- why the manufacture and sale of alcohol became illegal.

TERMS TO LEARN

suffragist
prohibition

The Storyteller

Nurse Lillian Wald followed a young girl up a rickety staircase in a filthy tenement house on New York City's Lower East Side. The girl had begged Wald to help her mother who had just given birth to a baby. A doctor had refused to treat the girl's mother because she could not pay his fee. The sight of the desperate mother and her baby was a turning point in Wald's life. Wald dedicated herself to helping poor people and educating them about health care. Eventually Wald became a national reform leader who liked to say, "The whole world is my neighborhood."

Lillian D. Wald

The situation of middle-class women changed during the late 1800s. Their responsibilities at home lessened as families became smaller, more children spent the day at school, and men worked away from home. These women also had more free time as technology made housework easier.

Women's Roles Change

Many more middle-class women were gaining higher education. About 40 percent of all college students in 1910 were women. Women were also starting professional careers—mostly in teaching but also in nursing, medicine, and other fields. Between 1890 and 1910, the number of women working outside the home increased from 4 million to nearly 7.5 million.

These changes created the "new woman"—a popular term for educated, up-to-date women who pursued interests outside their homes. Many such women became role models.

As you read in Chapter 20, **Jane Addams** established Hull House, a settlement house, in **Chicago.** Working there gave Addams an outlet for her energy and intelligence, as well as a sense of satisfaction in helping poor people.

Settlement workers such as Addams gained notice as writers, public speakers, fund-raisers, and reformers. Many young women followed the example of these talented public figures. Others found inspiration in the life of **Mother Cabrini,** an Italian nun who came to the United States to work with the poor.

1 FOCUS

BELLRINGER
Motivational Activity

Before taking roll at the beginning of the class period, project Section Focus Transparency 21–2 and have students answer the questions. Discuss students' responses.

This activity is also available as a blackline master.

Section Focus Transparency 21–2

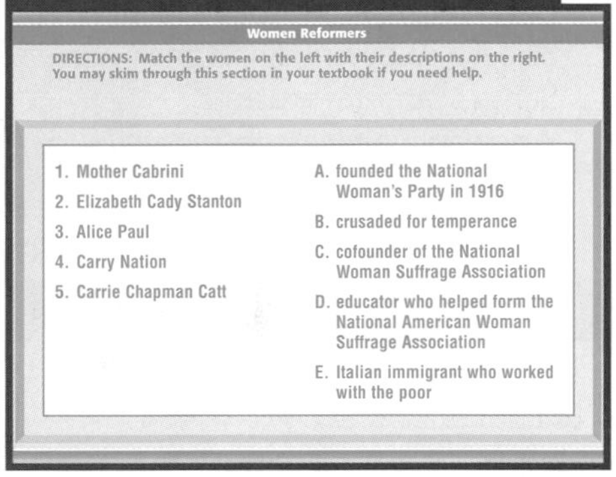

Women Reformers

DIRECTIONS: Match the women on the left with their descriptions on the right. You may skim through this section in your textbook if you need help.

1. Mother Cabrini
2. Elizabeth Cady Stanton
3. Alice Paul
4. Carry Nation
5. Carrie Chapman Catt

A. founded the National Woman's Party in 1916
B. crusaded for temperance
C. cofounder of the National Woman Suffrage Association
D. educator who helped form the National American Woman Suffrage Association
E. Italian immigrant who worked with the poor

Vocabulary Precheck

Ask a student to read aloud the definition of the term *prohibition* from the textbook glossary. Have another student use the term in a sentence.

Use the **Vocabulary PuzzleMaker** to create crossword and word search puzzles.

Section Theme
Groups and Institutions

Women banded together to work for suffrage and other social reforms.

Activity Have students list characteristics of the role of women in American society today. Volunteers may compare and contrast their responses with what they read in the text about American women in the late 1800s.

SECTION RESOURCES

Reproducible Masters
- Reproducible Lesson Plan 21–2
- Guided Reading Activity 21–2
- Section Quiz 21–2
- Reteaching Activity 21–2
- Enrichment Activity 21–2

Transparencies
- Section Focus Transparency 21–2

Multimedia
- Vocabulary PuzzleMaker
- Chapter Challenger Interactive Review Software
- Testmaker
- GTV: The American People: Fabric of a Nation

2 TEACH

L1 Charting Problems Have students create a problem/solution chart. In the left column, they should list political and/or social problems that American women addressed during this era. In the right column, they should note the accomplishments and/or solutions in each case.

Picturing HISTORY In addition to Hull House in Chicago, well-known settlement houses included Boston's South End House, New York's Henry Street Settlement, and Cincinnati's Santa Maria Institute.
Answer: *teaching, nursing, and medicine*

Guided Reading Activity 21–2

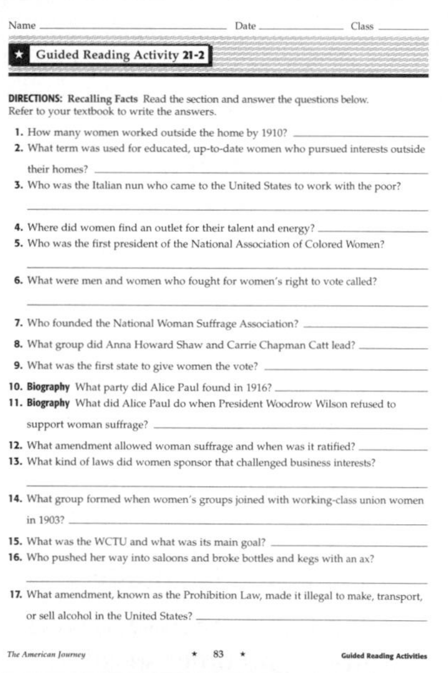

Name ______ Date ______ Class ______

★ Guided Reading Activity **21-2**

DIRECTIONS: Recalling Facts Read the section and answer the questions below. Refer to your textbook to write the answers.

1. How many women worked outside the home by 1910? ______
2. What term was used for educated, up-to-date women who pursued interests outside their homes? ______
3. Who was the Italian nun who came to the United States to work with the poor? ______
4. Where did women find an outlet for their talent and energy? ______
5. Who was the first president of the National Association of Colored Women? ______
6. What were men and women who fought for women's right to vote called? ______
7. Who founded the National Woman Suffrage Association? ______
8. What group did Anna Howard Shaw and Carrie Chapman Catt lead? ______
9. What was the first state to give women the vote? ______
10. **Biography** What party did Alice Paul found in 1916? ______
11. **Biography** What did Alice Paul do when President Woodrow Wilson refused to support woman suffrage? ______
12. What amendment allowed woman suffrage and when was it ratified? ______
13. What kind of laws did women sponsor that challenged business interests? ______
14. What group formed when women's groups joined with working-class union women in 1903? ______
15. What was the WCTU and what was its main goal? ______
16. Who pushed her way into saloons and broke bottles and kegs with an ax? ______
17. What amendment, known as the Prohibition Law, made it illegal to make, transport, or sell alcohol in the United States? ______

The American Journey ★ 83 ★ **Guided Reading Activities**

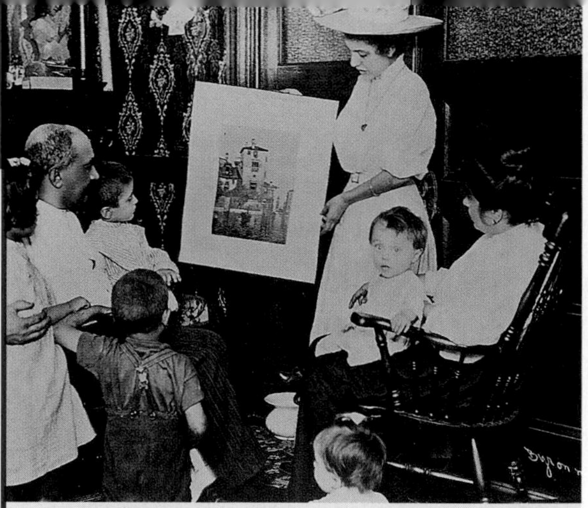

Picturing HISTORY A worker from a New York charity organization discusses health care with an Italian family. **In what two fields did women of the early 1900s increasingly find work?**

Women's Clubs

Women found another outlet for their talent and energy in women's clubs, which rapidly increased in number. At first the clubs focused on such cultural activities as music and painting. Many clubs gradually became more concerned with social problems. Middle-class clubwomen tried to help working-class women and children.

Women's clubs offered many opportunities for self-improvement. A club in Buffalo, New York, ran a library and held classes in typing and bookkeeping. The clubs also gave their members a chance to continue their education and to develop new skills.

When some clubs refused to admit African Americans, African American women established their own network of clubs. Clubs such as the Phyllis Wheatley Club of New Orleans organized classes, recreation activities, and social services. In 1896 women from these clubs formed the **National Association of Colored Women.** Its first president, **Mary Church Terrell,** was an active leader for women's rights. The association established homes for orphans, founded hospitals, and worked for woman suffrage, fulfilling their motto, "Lifting As We Climb."

The Fight for Suffrage

Women at the Seneca Falls Convention in 1848 had called for the right to vote. After the Civil War, Congress passed the Fifteenth Amendment, giving voting rights to freed men—but not to women. Some leading abolitionists became **suffragists,** men and women who fought for woman suffrage, or women's right to vote.

Like other reformers the suffragists formed organizations to promote their cause. **Elizabeth Cady Stanton** and **Susan B. Anthony** founded the **National Woman Suffrage Association,** which called for a constitutional amendment allowing women to vote in national elections. A second organization, the American Woman Suffrage Association, focused on winning woman suffrage in state elections.

In 1890 the two groups merged to form the National American Woman Suffrage Association. Led by **Anna Howard Shaw,** a minister and doctor, and **Carrie Chapman Catt,** an educator and newspaper editor, this organization grew to more than 2 million members by 1917. In a speech to the association in 1902, Catt declared:

> "The whole aim of the [women's] movement has been to destroy the idea that obedience is necessary to women; to train women to such self-respect that they would not grant obedience and to train men to such comprehension of equity [fairness] they would not exact [demand] it."

Opposition to Woman Suffrage

Groups formed to protest the idea of giving women the vote. These organizations—supported by some women as well as by men—claimed that woman suffrage would upset society's "natural" balance and lead to divorce and neglected children.

The suffrage movement gained strength, however, when respected public figures such as Jane Addams spoke out in support of the vote for women. Alice Duer Miller brought humor to the struggle for the right to vote:

COOPERATIVE LEARNING ACTIVITY

Preparing a News Report Have students portray television reporters covering a woman suffrage demonstration or rally. In their reports, have them focus on what women want and what progress women feel they are making. Coverage could include the following:
- Background material about the woman suffrage movement
- A description of the event itself
- An interview with an organizer of the event
- Reactions (pro and con) by onlookers

Various roles to be assigned or selected by students include writers, interviewers, demonstrators, onlookers, news directors, and so on.

“Said Mr. Jones in 1910:
'Women, subject yourselves to men.'
Nineteen-Eleven heard him quote:
'They rule the world without the vote.'

. . . .

By Nineteen-Thirteen, looking glum,
He said that it was bound to come.

. . . .

By Nineteen-Fifteen, he'll insist
He's always been a suffragist.”

First Suffrage Victories

The suffragists won their early victories in the West. First as a territory in 1869 and then as a state in 1890, **Wyoming** led the nation in giving women the vote. Between 1910 and 1913, six other states adopted woman suffrage. By 1919 women could vote in at least some elections in 39 of the 48 states.

Biography

Continuing the Fight

In the meantime suffragists continued their struggle to win the vote everywhere. **Alice Paul,** a Quaker who founded the National Woman's Party in 1916, was a forceful leader of the suffragist movement. She sought greater economic and legal equality as well as suffrage for women.

During a visit to Great Britain, Paul saw suffragists use protest marches and hunger strikes to call attention to their cause. When she returned to the United States, she, too, used these methods in the fight for suffrage.

In 1917 Alice Paul met with President **Woodrow Wilson** but failed to win his support for woman suffrage. Paul responded by leading women protestors in front of the White House. Day after day they marched carrying banners demanding votes for women. When Paul and other

Voting Rights for Women, 1919

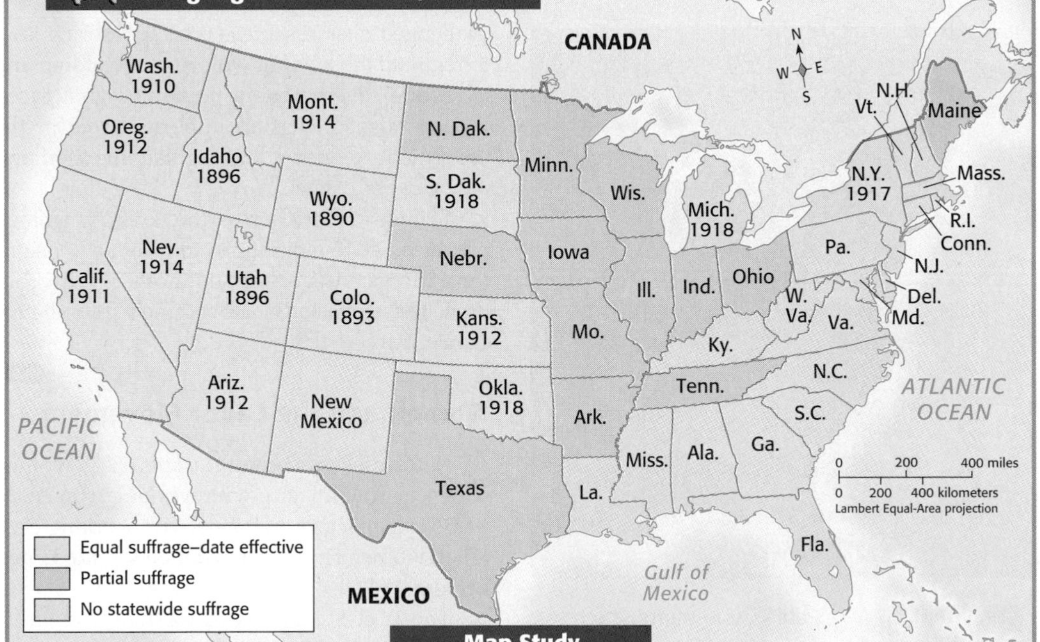

Map Study

By 1919 a total of 15 states allowed women to vote in all elections.

1. **Place** What state was the first to grant women equal suffrage?
2. **Comparing** What was the status of woman suffrage in your state by 1919?

Who? What? Where? When?

Western Women In addition to being allowed to own and run their own ranches and farms, Western women were the first to win the right to vote. The first seven states to grant woman suffrage were in the West, beginning with Wyoming in 1869. At that time, however, women could vote only in local elections. It was not until 1890 that women in Wyoming had equal suffrage and could also vote on state and national issues.

Map Study

Answers

1. Wyoming (1890)
2. Answers will vary depending upon your location.

Map Skills Practice

Reading a Map In general, why do you think the percentage of states allowing woman suffrage was so much higher in the West than in the East? *(Students may suggest that Western society was less structured, that Western states needed the votes of women to gain a stronger voice in national affairs, and so on.)*

Who? What? Where? When?

Mary Church Terrell, born in 1863, was the most prominent African American in the suffrage movement, but she also led a lifelong campaign against racial injustice. She encouraged picketing and sit-ins years before the civil rights movement adopted those strategies. She also was a cofounder of the NAACP. Fittingly, Terrell lived long enough to see the Supreme Court's landmark ruling in *Brown* v. *Board of Education.*

MULTIPLE LEARNING STYLES

Interpersonal American women who sought reform during this era needed to be persuasive. Have students portray that reforming spirit by putting themselves in the “shoes” of one of the following women:

- Jane Addams or Lillian Wald arguing for better opportunities for the poor
- Carrie Chapman Catt or Alice Paul arguing for woman suffrage
- Frances Willard or Carry Nation arguing for temperance

Ask students to speak or write what they think the reformer would have told a crowd. Interested students might enjoy turning this activity into a skit for classroom performance. **L1**

CHAPTER 21
Section 2, 609–613

3 ASSESS

Assign Section 2 Review as homework or as an in-class activity.

Use **Chapter Challenger Interactive Review Software** to review Section 2.

Section Quiz 21–2

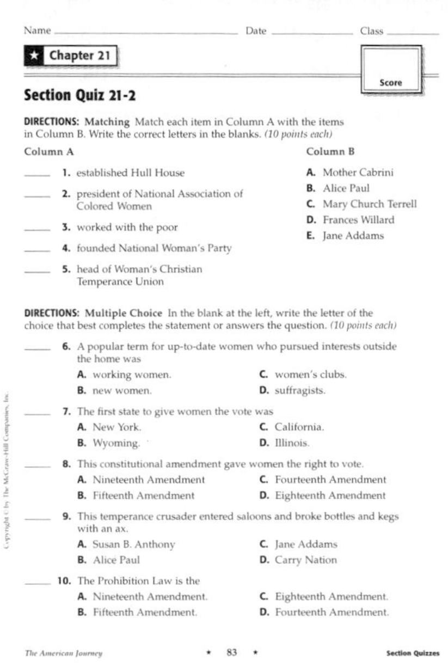

Name ______ Date ______ Class ______

Chapter 21

Score

Section Quiz 21-2

DIRECTIONS: Matching Match each item in Column A with the items in Column B. Write the correct letters in the blanks. *(10 points each)*

Column A	Column B
____ 1. established Hull House	A. Mother Cabrini
____ 2. president of National Association of Colored Women	B. Alice Paul
____ 3. worked with the poor	C. Mary Church Terrell
____ 4. founded National Woman's Party	D. Frances Willard
____ 5. head of Woman's Christian Temperance Union	E. Jane Addams

DIRECTIONS: Multiple Choice In the blank at the left, write the letter of the choice that best completes the statement or answers the question. *(10 points each)*

____ 6. A popular term for up-to-date women who pursued interests outside the home was
A. working women. C. women's clubs.
B. new women. D. suffragists.

____ 7. The first state to give women the vote was
A. New York. C. California.
B. Wyoming. D. Illinois.

____ 8. This constitutional amendment gave women the right to vote.
A. Nineteenth Amendment C. Fourteenth Amendment
B. Fifteenth Amendment D. Eighteenth Amendment

____ 9. This temperance crusader entered saloons and broke bottles and kegs with an ax.
A. Susan B. Anthony C. Jane Addams
B. Alice Paul D. Carry Nation

____ 10. The Prohibition Law is the
A. Nineteenth Amendment. C. Eighteenth Amendment.
B. Fifteenth Amendment. D. Fourteenth Amendment.

The American Journey ★ 83 ★ Section Quizzes

Picturing HISTORY As a graduate student in England, Alice Paul (1885–1977) became a militant suffragist. Her frank words and some of her methods later would isolate her from the mainstream of the woman suffrage movement. Paul also was the primary writer of the Equal Rights Amendment, which was first introduced in Congress in 1923. **Ask:** **Why do you think the National Woman's Party designed its own flag?** *(as a symbol of its unity, as a rallying point, as an advertising reminder of its existence)*
Answer: *It gave women the right to vote.*

protestors were arrested for blocking the sidewalk, they started a much-publicized hunger strike. Alva Belmont, one of the protestors, proudly declared that all the women had done was to stand there "quietly, peacefully, lawfully, and gloriously."

Women Vote Nationally

By 1917 the national tide was turning in favor of woman suffrage. Two states with large populations—New York and Illinois—gave women the vote that year. Meanwhile Congress began debating the issue, and President Wilson agreed to support an amendment to the Constitution.

In 1919 Congress voted in favor of the **Nineteenth Amendment,** which allowed woman suffrage. The amendment was ratified in 1920, in time for women to vote in that year's presidential election. For the first time, American women were able to participate in the election of their national leaders.

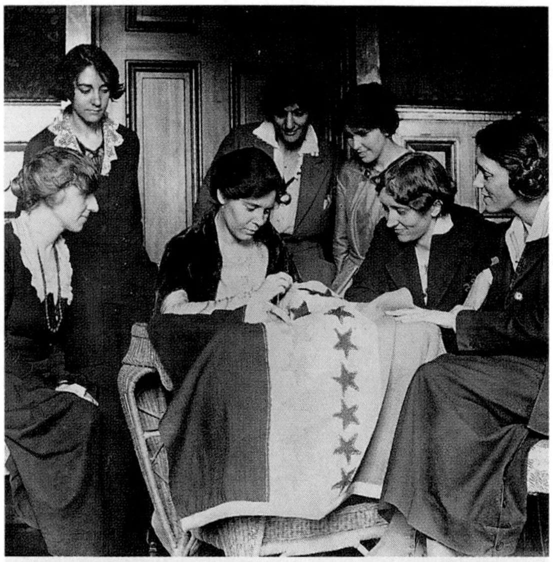

Picturing HISTORY Alice Paul sews a star on the flag of the National Woman's Party in celebration of the ratification of the Nineteenth Amendment in 1920. **What did this amendment achieve?**

Women and Social Reform

During the Progressive Era, women involved themselves in many reform movements besides woman suffrage. In 1912, for example, pressure from women's clubs helped persuade Congress to create the Children's Bureau in the Labor Department. The bureau's task was to develop federal policies that would protect children.

Working for a Better Life

While they struggled to gain rights for themselves, middle-class women of the Progressive Era also worked to improve the lives of working-class people, immigrants, and society as a whole. They supported and staffed libraries, schools, and settlement houses and raised money for hospitals and parks.

Some women promoted other causes. They challenged business interests by sponsoring laws to regulate the labor of women and children and to require government inspection of workplaces. Women also played an important role in the movement to reform and regulate the food and medicine industries.

In many states across the country, women pressured state legislatures to provide pensions for widows and abandoned mothers with children. These pensions later became part of the Social Security system.

Women and the Labor Movement

Reform efforts brought upper-class women reformers into alliance with working women. In 1903 women's groups joined with working-class union women to form the **Women's Trade Union League** (WTUL).

The WTUL encouraged working women to form women's labor unions. It also supported laws to protect the rights of women factory workers. WTUL members raised money to help striking workers and to pay bail for women who were arrested for participating in strikes.

MAKING CONNECTIONS ACTIVITY

Daily Life Through education, work opportunities, technology, and social involvement, the appearance of the "new woman" meant changes in American life. Have students explore how these changes were perceived by writing two letters for a newspaper's editorial page. The first letter should be from a "new woman" who describes how her everyday life has improved in recent years. The second letter should be from the perspective of a man or woman who resents the changes in daily life that have occurred as more women enter the workplace and classroom. Both letters should cite specific examples to support their main ideas. Interested students might present the letters as paired dramatic readings. **L3**

The Temperance Crusade

Temperance poster

A crusade against the use of alcohol had begun in New England and the Midwest in the early 1800s. The movement continued throughout the late 1800s. Protestant churches strongly supported the antialcohol movement.

Two driving forces in the crusade were the **Woman's Christian Temperance Union** (WCTU), established in 1873, and the **Anti-Saloon League,** founded 20 years later. They called for temperance, urging individuals to stop drinking, and **prohibition,** the passing of laws to prohibit the making or selling of alcohol.

Leaders of the Crusade

In 1879 **Frances Willard** became head of the WCTU. Willard led a campaign to educate the public about the links between alcohol abuse and violence, poverty, and unemployment. She turned the WCTU into a powerful organization with chapters in every state. By 1911 it was the largest women's organization the United States had yet known, with 245,000 members.

The WCTU's main goal was prohibition. However, the WCTU also supported other causes, including prison reform, woman suffrage, improved working conditions, and world peace. Through WCTU chapters, thousands of women combined their traditional role as guardians of the family and home with social activism.

Carry Nation was an especially colorful crusader for temperance. Nation began lecturing first in Kansas, then in other states, about the evils of "demon rum" and singing hymns outside saloons. Her most dramatic protests occurred when she pushed her way into saloons and broke bottles and kegs with an ax.

The Prohibition Amendment

The antialcohol movement grew steadily during the early 1900s. By 1916, 19 states had adopted prohibition laws.

Progressive reformers who wanted to ban alcohol for social reasons were joined by Americans who opposed alcohol for religious or moral reasons. In 1917 they persuaded Congress to pass a constitutional amendment making it illegal to make, transport, or sell alcohol in the United States. The **Eighteenth Amendment,** known as the Prohibition Law, was ratified in 1919.

Section 2 Review

Checking for Understanding

1. ***Identify*** Jane Addams, Mary Church Terrell, Susan B. Anthony, Carrie Chapman Catt, Alice Paul, Woodrow Wilson, Nineteenth Amendment, Frances Willard, Carry Nation, Eighteenth Amendment.
2. ***Define*** suffragist, prohibition.
3. ***Summarize*** the reasons middle-class women had more free time in the 1800s.

Reviewing Themes

4. **Groups and Institutions** How did women's clubs help to change the role of women?

Critical Thinking

5. **Drawing Conclusions** Why do you think the right to vote was important to women?

Activity

Current Events Find a newspaper article that deals with the role of women in today's society. Rewrite the article to reflect how this information might have been presented in the late 1800s and early 1900s.

Section 2 Review Answers

1. Addams, 609; Terrell, 610; Anthony, 610; Catt, 610; Paul, 611; Wilson, 611; 19th Amendment, 612; Willard, 613; Nation, 613; 18th Amendment, 613
2. The words are defined in the Glossary.
3. Home responsibilities decreased, families became smaller, more children spent the day at school, men worked away from home, technology made housework easier.
4. Many of the clubs got involved with social problems and encouraged their members to learn new skills and continue their education.
5. Without the vote, women had little influence over the laws that were made and the people who were elected to make these laws.

Activity Rewritten articles should reflect the attitudes toward women and the limited rights of women in the late 1800s and early 1900s.

CHAPTER 21
Section 2, 609–613

Reteaching Activity 21–2

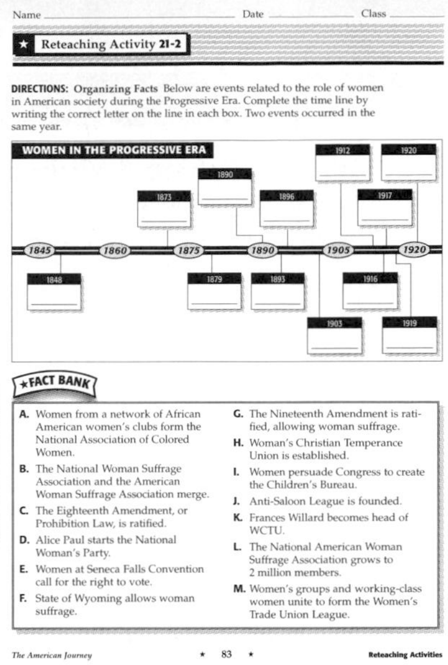
Name ______ Date ______ Class ______

★ Reteaching Activity 21-2

DIRECTIONS: Organizing Facts Below are events related to the role of women in American society during the Progressive Era. Complete the time line by writing the correct letter on the line in each box. Two events occurred in the same year.

★FACT BANK

- **A.** Women from a network of African American women's clubs form the National Association of Colored Women.
- **B.** The National Woman Suffrage Association and the American Woman Suffrage Association merge.
- **C.** The Eighteenth Amendment, or Prohibition Law, is ratified.
- **D.** Alice Paul starts the National Woman's Party.
- **E.** Women at Seneca Falls Convention call for the right to vote.
- **F.** State of Wyoming allows woman suffrage.
- **G.** The Nineteenth Amendment is ratified, allowing woman suffrage.
- **H.** Woman's Christian Temperance Union is established.
- **I.** Women persuade Congress to create the Children's Bureau.
- **J.** Anti-Saloon League is founded.
- **K.** Frances Willard becomes head of WCTU.
- **L.** The National American Woman Suffrage Association grows to 2 million members.
- **M.** Women's groups and working-class women unite to form the Women's Trade Union League.

The American Journey ★ 83 ★ **Reteaching Activities**

Enrichment Activity 21–2

Name ______ Date ______ Class ______

★ Enrichment Activity 21-2 ★ ★

March on Washington

This news article appeared in a Baltimore newspaper on March 3, 1913.

8,000 WOMEN MARCH IN WASHINGTON, D.C.

Eight thousand women, marching in the woman suffrage pageant today, practically fought their way foot by foot up Pennsylvania Avenue, through a surging throng that completely defied Washington police, swamped the marchers, and broke their procession into little companies. The women, trudging stoutly along under great difficulties, were able to complete their march only when troops of cavalry from Fort Myers were rushed into Washington to take charge of Pennsylvania Avenue. No inauguration has ever produced such scenes, which in many instances amounted to nothing less than riots.

SOURCE: Stevens, Doris. *Jailed for Freedom, American Women Win the Vote.* NewSage Press.

DIRECTIONS: Classifying Information Newspaper articles often provide information to answer the questions *Who?, What?, When?, Where?,* and *Why?* Based on this article and what you know, complete the information below with as much detail as you can about the incident.

Who? ______

What? ______

When? ______

Where? ______

Why? ______

Activity **DIRECTIONS:** Many women in the march carried signs with slogans. On a separate sheet of paper, design a sign that the writer of the article might have held while viewing the march. Be ready to explain your slogan. Did the writer of the original news story support woman suffrage, the right to peaceful marches, or the crowd's actions? How can you tell?

The American Journey ★ 83 ★ **Enrichment Activities**

4 CLOSE

Call on volunteers to suggest how women's clubs, the woman suffrage movement, the WTUL, and the temperance movement each reflected the ideals of progressivism.

NATIONAL GEOGRAPHIC

Journeys

What? Where? When? Who?

A Separate Sphere From the mid-1800s to the early 1900s, women were expected to live in a "separate sphere" of society, one in which they remained apart from political issues of the day.

Allen Marshall, an Ohio farmer, could not understand why women would want to leave their "sphere." In 1910 he wrote, "And why is it that a few women over in the state of Ohio have become so masculine in their conceptions of their divine place and sphere in the divine economy of creation that they want to make a fatal leap from the highest pinnacle of the pedestal of creation down to its base, alighting in the seething cauldron of political corruption?"

Ironically, this question had already been answered by women about 75 years earlier. At the Salem Women's Rights convention held in 1850, a woman spoke: "You ask, would you have women, by engaging in political party bickerings and noisy strife, sacrifice their integrity and purity? No, neither would we have men do it. . . . We hold that whatever is essentially wrong for a woman to do, cannot be right for man. If deception and intrigue (the elements of political craft) be degrading to women, can they be ennobling to man? . . . Nothing can be morally right for man that is morally wrong for woman."

1 Jeannette Rankin launched her political journey when she joined the suffragists. As a student she became actively involved in the campaign for voting rights for women. Later she traveled to several states to help women win the vote and eventually sought a national platform. As a representative from Montana from 1917 to 1919, Jeannette Rankin was the first woman to serve in Congress.

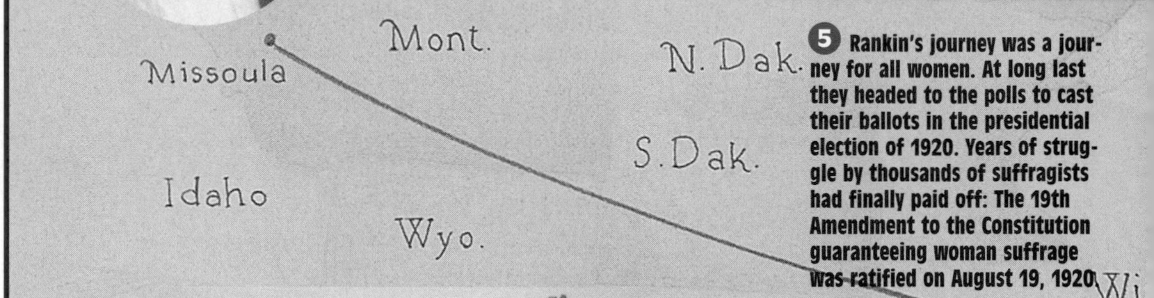

5 Rankin's journey was a journey for all women. At long last they headed to the polls to cast their ballots in the presidential election of 1920. Years of struggle by thousands of suffragists had finally paid off: The 19th Amendment to the Constitution guaranteeing woman suffrage was ratified on August 19, 1920.

3 These women from St. Louis, Missouri, joined a demonstration in 1916 to demand representation. In 1916 the tide turned—the public was beginning to agree with the suffragists. When Rankin joined the suffragists, women composed more than one-fifth of the nation's workforce but could vote in only four states.

Linking PAST & PRESENT

Protests To publicize their cause, British suffragists went to extraordinary lengths, including arson, bombing of monuments, window smashing, and hunger strikes. Some of these tactics were also used by Vietnam War protesters in the 1960s and the Sons of Liberty 200 years earlier.

TEACHER'S NOTES

NATIONAL GEOGRAPHIC

Journeys

2 In 1912 suffragists took to the streets of New York City to demand their rights. Rankin traveled to New York and 15 other states to help promote voting rights for women.

4 Jeannette Rankin addresses fellow representatives in her first speech before Congress in May 1917. Rankin served two terms in Congress—from 1917 to 1919 and again from 1941 to 1943. In her first term she worked on a committee that drafted a woman suffrage amendment to the Constitution.

A Suffragist's Journey

"[My aunt] who had been active nationally in the movement came home to Montana to head a ... drive for woman suffrage in 1911.... The details differed from Butte to Broadus, but in essence the ladies moved in on a town tacking up notices of a public meeting.... They generally chose the street corner ... across from the most popular saloon in town. At the advertised hour, a speaker would mount a real soapbox. There would be a gaggle of children, a sprinkling of housewives ... and gradually the men ... would move out of the saloon to see what the commotion was all about."

—From a reminiscence written by Mackey Brown, a niece of Jeannette Rankin, in Montana Business Quarterly, *Autumn 1971.*

615

NATIONAL GEOGRAPHIC SOCIETY

VIDEODISC
GTV: The American People: Fabric of a Nation

Side 3, Chapter 5
Title: *Sending a Message*
Subject: Citizenship and voting rights
Ask: When was the first constitutional amendment giving women the right to vote introduced in Congress? *(1878)*

What? Where? When? Who?

Bibliography The excerpt at left was taken from the article "Montana's First Woman Politician—A Recollection of Jeannette Rankin Campaigning," in *Montana Business Quarterly,* Autumn 1971.

CURRICULUM CONNECTION

CIVICS
When women first lobbied for voting rights, some critics feared that if women won the vote, men would become their servants. Political cartoons appeared that showed sour-faced men caring for babies and wringing out dirty laundry, while women happily rode around in carriages or talked excitedly around the ballot box. Other opponents claimed that if women won the vote, they would spend all their time at the polls. One poster nicknamed a woman who ran for office "Susan Sharp-Tongue, the Celebrated Man Tamer."

Teacher's Notes

CHAPTER 21
Section 3, 616–620

1 FOCUS

BELLRINGER
Motivational Activity

Before taking roll at the beginning of the class period, project Section Focus Transparency 21–3 and have students answer the questions. Discuss students' responses.

This activity is also available as a blackline master.

Section Focus Transparency 21–3

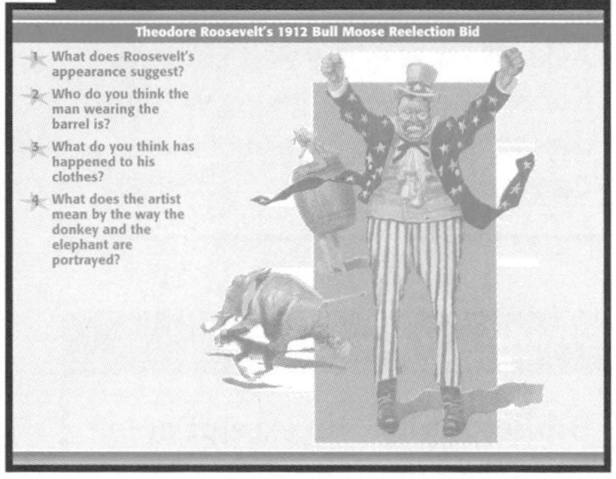

Vocabulary Precheck
Encourage students to think of a symbol or other visual to illustrate *trustbuster, arbitration,* or *conservation.*

Use the **Vocabulary PuzzleMaker** to create crossword and word search puzzles.

Section Theme
Economic Factors

Presidents Roosevelt, Taft, and Wilson sought economic reform by regulating big business and improving relations with organized labor.

Activity Have students share what they know about the opportunities and limits that presidents face in encouraging laws that promote change. *(Students may suggest that a president can support a law but cannot enact a law singlehandedly.)*

1900 — 1910 — 1920

1901 President McKinley is assassinated

1905 Roosevelt proposes the U.S. Forest Service

1913 Federal Reserve Act creates 12 regional banks

1914 Congress establishes the Federal Trade Commission

Section 3

Progressive Presidents

READ TO DISCOVER . . .
- how President Theodore Roosevelt took on big business and became a "trustbuster."
- why the progressives formed their own political party.

TERMS TO LEARN
trustbuster
arbitration
square deal
laissez-faire
conservation

The Storyteller

"We were still under a heavy fire and I got together a mixed lot of men and pushed on from the trenches and ranch houses which we had just taken, driving the Spaniards through a line of palm-trees, and over the crest of a chain of hills. . . ." With these words, a young lieutenant colonel named Theodore Roosevelt described his military adventures in Cuba during the Spanish-American War. Known for his vigor, enthusiasm, and a colorful personality, Roosevelt became president in 1901 upon the assassination of President William McKinley.

Theodore Roosevelt board game

The wave of progressive reform that began to sweep across the United States in the late 1800s eventually reached the level of presidential politics. When a young, energetic, reform-minded president named **Theodore Roosevelt** moved into the White House in 1901, he brought progressivism with him.

Biography

Theodore Roosevelt

Theodore Roosevelt came from a prosperous **New York** family. Once a sickly child, Roosevelt set out to improve his health with exercise and personal discipline. As an adult he was proud of his strength and stamina.

After studying law, young Theodore Roosevelt entered politics. He served in the New York State assembly, headed New York City's police commission, and became assistant secretary of the navy. In 1898 Roosevelt organized the **Rough Riders,** a volunteer cavalry regiment that fought in the Spanish-American War. He gained fame for leading his regiment in a charge at the Battle of San Juan Hill. A few months later, Roosevelt the war hero was elected governor of New York.

Roosevelt's efforts to clean up corruption in New York State politics did not make him popular with local Republican bosses. So to remove him as governor, they promoted Roosevelt's nomination for vice president in 1900, to run with President **William McKinley.**

SECTION RESOURCES

Reproducible Masters
- Guided Reading Activity 21–3
- Political Cartoons, *A Third Party*
- Section Quiz 21–3
- Reteaching Activity 21–3
- Enrichment Activity 21–3

Transparencies
- Section Focus Transparency 21–3

Multimedia
- Vocabulary PuzzleMaker
- GTV: A Geographic Perspective on American History
- Facts On File: Landmark Documents in American History
- The Presidents: A Picture History of Our Nation

Ohio senator Mark Hanna, chairman of McKinley's reelection campaign did not approve. Hanna considered Roosevelt too impulsive for national offices. When Hanna heard of the Roosevelt nomination he shouted, "Don't any of you realize that there's only one life between that madman and the presidency?"

McKinley and Roosevelt won the election in November 1900. Less than a year later, President McKinley was assassinated. Suddenly, 42-year-old Theodore Roosevelt became president—the youngest president in the nation's history.

Tackling Big Business

President McKinley had favored big business, but President Roosevelt was known to support business regulation and other progressive reforms. In a speech to Congress, Roosevelt declared, "There is a widespread conviction in the minds of the American people that the great corporations known as trusts are . . . hurtful to the general welfare."

In 1902 Roosevelt ordered the Justice Department to take legal action against certain trusts that had violated the Sherman Antitrust Act. His first target was the **Northern Securities Company,** a railroad monopoly formed by financiers J.P. Morgan and James J. Hill to control transportation in the Northwest. Northern Securities fought the government's accusations of illegal activity all the way to the Supreme Court. Finally, in 1904 the Justice Department won its case. The Supreme Court decided that Northern Securities had illegally limited trade and ordered the trust to be taken apart.

The "Trustbuster"

The Northern Securities case was a victory for the Progressive movement and earned Roosevelt the nickname **trustbuster.** During his presidency, Roosevelt directed the Justice Department to act against a number of trusts, including the beef trust, the tobacco trust, and Standard Oil—a petroleum trust.

Roosevelt wanted to prove that the federal government had authority over big business. Unlike some reformers who dreamed of returning to the days before big business, however, Roosevelt knew that large corporations had become a permanent part of America's economy. "We do not wish to destroy corporations," he said, "but we do wish to make them [serve] the public good."

Labor Crisis

In 1902 Roosevelt faced a major labor crisis. More than 100,000 Pennsylvania coal miners, members of the **United Mine Workers,** went on strike. They demanded better pay, an 8-hour workday, and recognition of the union's right to represent its members in discussions with mine owners.

The mine owners refused to negotiate with the workers. The **coal strike** dragged on for months. As winter approached, coal supplies dwindled. Public opinion began to turn against the owners. As public pressure mounted, Roosevelt invited representatives of the owners and miners to a meeting at the White House. Roosevelt was outraged when the owners refused to negotiate. He threatened to send federal troops to work in the mines and produce the coal. The owners finally agreed to **arbitration**—settling the dispute by

McKinley/Roosevelt glass canteen, 1900

*F*ootnotes to History

Teddy Bears Once when President Theodore Roosevelt was hunting, he supposedly refused to shoot a bear cub. A *Washington Post* cartoonist drew a cartoon of Roosevelt turning away from the helpless cub. Seeing the cartoon, Morris Michtom began to make toy bear cubs in 1903, naming them "Teddy Bears."

CHAPTER 21
Section 3, 616–620

2 TEACH

L1, ELL Applying Ideas Have students brainstorm a list of functions that a United States president performs. **Ask:** **Which functions seem to provide the best opportunity for a president to promote change?** *(Students probably will refer to functions that relate to a president's power to help shape or enact laws.)*

Guided Reading Activity 21–3

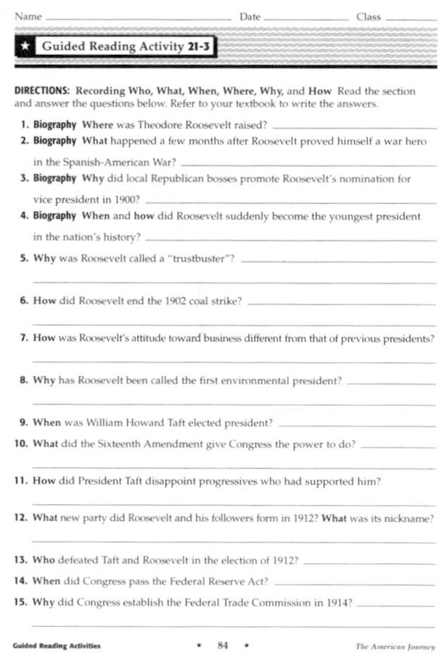

Name ______ Date ______ Class ______

Guided Reading Activity 21-3

DIRECTIONS: Recording Who, What, When, Where, Why, and **How** Read the section and answer the questions below. Refer to your textbook to write the answers.

1. **Biography** **Where** was Theodore Roosevelt raised? ______
2. **Biography** **What** happened a few months after Roosevelt proved himself a war hero in the Spanish-American War? ______
3. **Biography** **Why** did local Republican bosses promote Roosevelt's nomination for vice president in 1900? ______
4. **Biography** **When** and **how** did Roosevelt suddenly become the youngest president in the nation's history? ______
5. **Why** was Roosevelt called a "trustbuster"? ______
6. **How** did Roosevelt end the 1902 coal strike? ______
7. **How** was Roosevelt's attitude toward business different from that of previous presidents? ______
8. **Why** has Roosevelt been called the first environmental president? ______
9. **When** was William Howard Taft elected president? ______
10. **What** did the Sixteenth Amendment give Congress the power to do? ______
11. **How** did President Taft disappoint progressives who had supported him? ______
12. **What** new party did Roosevelt and his followers form in 1912? **What** was its nickname? ______
13. **Who** defeated Taft and Roosevelt in the election of 1912? ______
14. **When** did Congress pass the Federal Reserve Act? ______
15. **Why** did Congress establish the Federal Trade Commission in 1914? ______

Guided Reading Activities • 84 • *The American Journey*

History *and the* Humanities

The Spirit of American Art and Music, William Henry Jackson

Political Cartoons, *A Third Party*

COOPERATIVE LEARNING ACTIVITY

Holding a Presidential Debate Organize the class into two teams–one to represent Theodore Roosevelt, the other to represent William Howard Taft. Have students present a debate between these candidates for president. Ask groups to accomplish the following tasks, all of which might influence what is said during the debate:

- Review the candidate's accomplishments as president
- Summarize the candidate's vision of the United States's role in the world of 1912
- Confront issues that voters would care about the most

"Speechwriters" can help prepare each team's "candidate." After the debate, hold a class election.

What?Where?When?Who?

Teddy Bears Roosevelt's hunt took place on the Mississippi Delta in 1902, and Clifford Berryman was the cartoonist who captured the scene.

NATIONAL GEOGRAPHIC SOCIETY

VIDEODISC
GTV: A Geographic Perspective on American History

Side 3, Chapter 15

Title: *A Progress Report*
Subject: Early environmental reforms
Ask: **What was the major goal of conservationists?** *(to conserve the land)*

CD-ROM
The Presidents: A Picture History of Our Nation

Have students select Presidents Roosevelt, Taft, and Wilson from the main menu. Suggest they compare the lives of these leaders.

CURRICULUM CONNECTION

GEOGRAPHY
The National Park System is one of the best symbols of Roosevelt's conservation philosophy. Today there are 50 national parks, covering every kind of land and climate type in North America—from the rugged coast of Maine's Arcadia National Park to the volcanic crater of Hawaii's Halekala National Park, and from the frigid valleys of Alaska's Gates of the Arctic National Park to the subtropical wilderness of Florida's Everglades National Park.

Picturing HISTORY Created by Congress in 1890, Yosemite was one of America's first national parks. The first was Yellowstone in 1872.
Answer: *He proposed the U.S. Forest Service and formed the National Conservation Commission. He pressured Congress to preserve millions of acres of national forests and created the nation's first wildlife sanctuaries.*

agreeing to accept the decision of an impartial outsider. Mine workers won a pay increase and a reduction in hours, but they did not gain recognition for the union.

Roosevelt's action marked a departure from normal patterns of labor relations at the time. Earlier presidents had used troops against strikers, but Roosevelt had used the power of the federal government to force the company owners to negotiate. In other labor actions, however, Roosevelt supported employers in disputes with workers.

Roosevelt's Square Deal

Roosevelt ran for the presidency in 1904, promising the people a **square deal**—fair and equal treatment for all. He was elected with more than 57 percent of the popular vote.

Roosevelt's "square deal" called for a considerable amount of government regulation of business. This contrasted with an attitude toward business that dated back to the presidency of Thomas Jefferson, which was summed up in the phrase **laissez-faire** (LEH•say FEHR). This French term means, generally, "let people do as they choose."

Roosevelt introduced a new era of government regulation. He supported the **Meat Inspection** and **Pure Food and Drug acts** that gave the Department of Agriculture and the Food and Drug Administration the power to visit businesses and inspect their products. Roosevelt also supported new laws giving the Interstate Commerce Commission more power to regulate the railroads.

Conserving the Wilderness

Roosevelt held a lifelong enthusiasm for the great outdoors and the wilderness. He believed in the need for **conservation,** the protection and preservation of natural resources.

As president, Roosevelt took steps to conserve the country's forests, mineral deposits, and water resources. In 1905 he proposed the **U.S. Forest Service.** He pressured Congress to set aside millions of acres of national forests and created the nation's first wildlife sanctuaries. Roosevelt also formed the National Conservation Commission, which produced the first survey of the country's natural resources.

Roosevelt has been called America's first environmental president. While he made conservation an important public issue, Roosevelt also recognized the need for economic growth and development. He tried to strike a balance between business interests and conservation.

William Howard Taft

No president before had ever served more than two terms. Roosevelt decided not to run for reelection in 1908. Wanting to continue his progressive programs, he persuaded the Republican Party to nominate his secretary of war, **William Howard Taft,** for president. In the election of 1908, Taft easily defeated Democrat William Jennings Bryan. Taft failed to win the public affection that Roosevelt had enjoyed, however. A quiet, cautious man, Taft seemed timid in comparison with the lively, outspoken Roosevelt.

Picturing HISTORY President Theodore Roosevelt (fourth from left) visits California's Yosemite National Park in 1903. **What steps did Roosevelt take to conserve the country's natural resources?**

Roosevelt campaign button, 1904

MULTIPLE LEARNING STYLES

Kinesthetic Bring a game of Monopoly to class. Display the board and, if necessary, outline the basic rules of the game. Then have volunteers, working individually or with partners, present a lesson based upon the game. For example, they might demonstrate the acquisition of houses or buying up of railroads to explain what trusts were, how they operated in this era, and how President Theodore Roosevelt tried to "bust" them. **L2, ELL**

Continuing Progressive Reform

Although he had none of Roosevelt's flair, Taft carried out—and went beyond—many of Roosevelt's policies. Taft used the Sherman Antitrust Act to file lawsuits against dozens of large corporations. The Taft administration won more antitrust cases in four years than Roosevelt had won in seven. Taft also favored the introduction of safety standards for mines and railroads.

Taft supported the **Sixteenth Amendment,** which gave Congress the power to tax people's incomes to generate revenue for the federal government. Progressives hoped the income tax would enable the government to lower tariffs. In their view high tariffs led to higher prices for goods, which caused hardship for the poor. Progressives believed that taxes based on income were fairer. The Sixteenth Amendment, added to the Constitution in 1913, did not specify how income would be taxed. Congress passed additional laws so that higher incomes were taxed at a higher rate than lower incomes.

Taft Loses Support

Despite his progressive reforms, President Taft disappointed progressives in two important areas—tariffs and conservation. He failed to fight for a lower tariff, and he modified some conservation policies so that they favored business.

In 1910 Roosevelt returned from a long trip to Africa to find that progressives were disappointed with Taft. Roosevelt claimed that Taft had "completely twisted around" his own policies. In the congressional elections of 1910, Roosevelt campaigned for progressive Republicans. In a speech in Kansas, Roosevelt set forth his own progressive principles, declaring that social justice was possible only with a strong federal government to act as "steward [manager] of the public welfare."

The Bull Moose Party

Everywhere he went, Roosevelt was greeted by cheering crowds. This encouraged him to return to politics, and in 1912 he challenged Taft for the Republican presidential nomination.

Progressive Party banner

Picturing HISTORY Theodore Roosevelt was a vigorous campaigner. **Who were the candidates in the 1912 election?**

The showdown between Roosevelt and Taft came at the Republican national convention in Chicago in June. Although Roosevelt won every primary and had many supporters, Taft had the backing of Republican Party leaders and influential business interests who controlled the party machinery. In disputes over seating rival delegations, Taft received the votes of all but 19 of the 254 contested delegates.

A fiery Roosevelt led his supporters out of the convention hall. He and his followers formed a new party, the **Progressive Party.** In August the Progressives held their own convention in Chicago and nominated Roosevelt for president.

When a reporter asked Roosevelt about his health, the candidate thumped himself on the chest and declared, "I feel as strong as a bull moose!" From then on, the Progressive Party was known as the **Bull Moose Party.**

The Election of 1912

The split in the Republican Party hurt both Taft and Roosevelt. While Republicans and Progressives battled each other at the polls, Democrat **Woodrow Wilson** gathered enough support to defeat them in the election. Wilson had acquired a reputation as a progressive reformer while serv-

Making Connections Activity

The Environment Inspired by a conservationist president, some Americans joined early environmental causes. For example, the American Bison Society (ABS) was founded in 1905, to save an animal that had been hunted almost to extinction. The ABS was one of the first groups ever to mount a campaign for the protection of an endangered species, and it saved the American bison. Have students find and share information about how this tradition continues today. For example, students might secure a speaker from a local zoo to discuss the role of zoos in conservation efforts, or they might organize a display of materials from a national or international environmental organization. **L2**

Picturing HISTORY Roosevelt's campaign vigor was amply demonstrated in his reaction to an assassination attempt. On October 14, 1912, John N. Schrank shot Roosevelt, who was on his way to speak in Milwaukee. Although the bullet penetrated his chest and fractured a rib, Roosevelt spoke, as planned, before seeking treatment. **Answer:** *Taft (Republican), Wilson (Democrat), and Roosevelt (Progressive)*

Facts On File

CD-ROM
Landmark Documents in American History

Title: *Federal Reserve Act, 1913 (Glass-Own Act)*
Have students research the need for the Federal Reserve banking system.

3 ASSESS

Assign Section 3 Review as homework or as an in-class activity.

Use **Chapter Challenger Interactive Review Software** to review Section 3.

Section Quiz 21–3

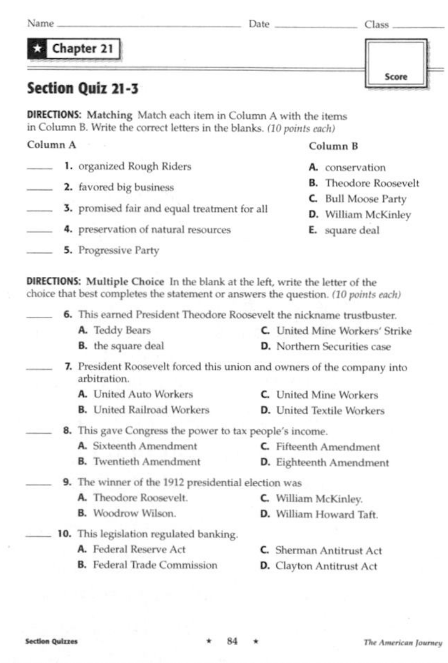

Name ________ Date ________ Class ________

Chapter 21 Score

Section Quiz 21-3

DIRECTIONS: Matching Match each item in Column A with the items in Column B. Write the correct letters in the blanks. *(10 points each)*

Column A	Column B
____ 1. organized Rough Riders	A. conservation
____ 2. favored big business	B. Theodore Roosevelt
____ 3. promised fair and equal treatment for all	C. Bull Moose Party
____ 4. preservation of natural resources	D. William McKinley
____ 5. Progressive Party	E. square deal

DIRECTIONS: Multiple Choice In the blank at the left, write the letter of the choice that best completes the statement or answers the question. *(10 points each)*

____ 6. This earned President Theodore Roosevelt the nickname trustbuster.
A. Teddy Bears C. United Mine Workers' Strike
B. the square deal D. Northern Securities case

____ 7. President Roosevelt forced this union and owners of the company into arbitration.
A. United Auto Workers C. United Mine Workers
B. United Railroad Workers D. United Textile Workers

____ 8. This gave Congress the power to tax people's income.
A. Sixteenth Amendment C. Fifteenth Amendment
B. Twentieth Amendment D. Eighteenth Amendment

____ 9. The winner of the 1912 presidential election was
A. Theodore Roosevelt. C. William McKinley.
B. Woodrow Wilson. D. William Howard Taft.

____ 10. This legislation regulated banking.
A. Federal Reserve Act C. Sherman Antitrust Act
B. Federal Trade Commission D. Clayton Antitrust Act

Section Quizzes ★ 84 ★ *The American Journey*

CHAPTER 21
Section 3, 616–620

Reteaching Activity 21–3

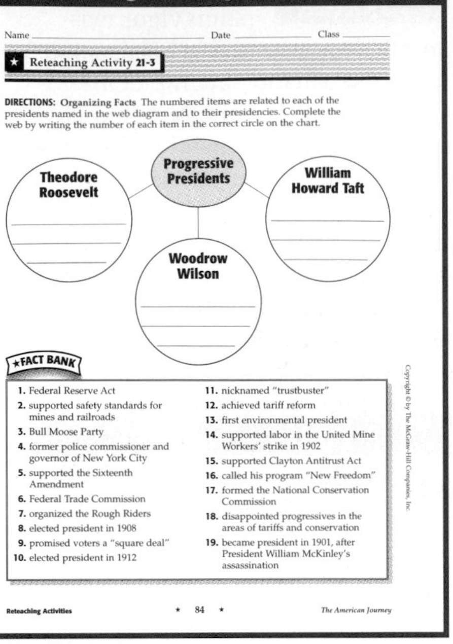
Name ________ Date ________ Class ________

★ Reteaching Activity 21-3

DIRECTIONS: Organizing Facts The numbered items are related to each of the presidents named in the web diagram and to their presidencies. Complete the web by writing the number of each item in the correct circle on the chart.

★FACT BANK

1. Federal Reserve Act
2. supported safety standards for mines and railroads
3. Bull Moose Party
4. former police commissioner and governor of New York City
5. supported the Sixteenth Amendment
6. Federal Trade Commission
7. organized the Rough Riders
8. elected president in 1908
9. promised voters a "square deal"
10. elected president in 1912
11. nicknamed "trustbuster"
12. achieved tariff reform
13. first environmental president
14. supported labor in the United Mine Workers' strike in 1902
15. supported Clayton Antitrust Act
16. called his program "New Freedom"
17. formed the National Conservation Commission
18. disappointed progressives in the areas of tariffs and conservation
19. became president in 1901, after President William McKinley's assassination

Reteaching Activities ★ 84 ★ *The American Journey*

Enrichment Activity 21–3

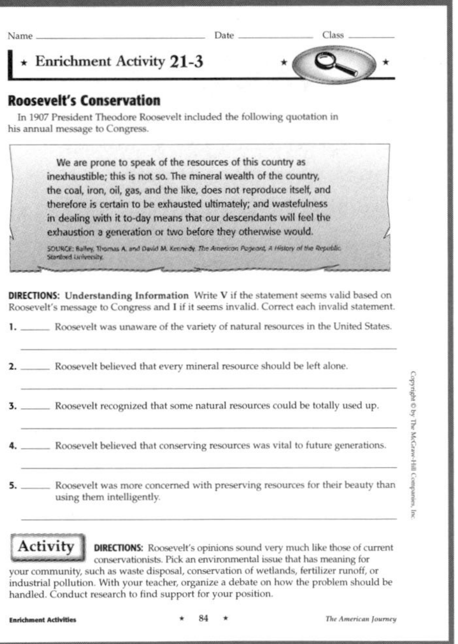
Name ________ Date ________ Class ________

★ Enrichment Activity 21-3 ★

Roosevelt's Conservation

In 1907 President Theodore Roosevelt included the following quotation in his annual message to Congress.

> We are prone to speak of the resources of this country as inexhaustible; this is not so. The mineral wealth of the country, the coal, iron, oil, gas, and the like, does not reproduce itself, and therefore is certain to be exhausted ultimately; and wastefulness in dealing with it to-day means that our descendants will feel the exhaustion a generation or two before they otherwise would.
>
> SOURCE: Bailey, Thomas A. and David M. Kennedy. *The American Pageant, A History of the Republic.* Stanford University.

DIRECTIONS: Understanding Information Write **V** if the statement seems valid based on Roosevelt's message to Congress and **I** if it seems invalid. Correct each invalid statement.

1. ______ Roosevelt was unaware of the variety of natural resources in the United States.
2. ______ Roosevelt believed that every mineral resource should be left alone.
3. ______ Roosevelt recognized that some natural resources could be totally used up.
4. ______ Roosevelt believed that conserving resources was vital to future generations.
5. ______ Roosevelt was more concerned with preserving resources for their beauty than using them intelligently.

Activity **DIRECTIONS:** Roosevelt's opinions sound very much like those of current conservationists. Pick an environmental issue that has meaning for your community, such as waste disposal, conservation of wetlands, fertilizer runoff, or industrial pollution. With your teacher, organize a debate on how the problem should be handled. Conduct research to find support for your position.

Enrichment Activities ★ 84 ★ *The American Journey*

4 CLOSE

Review Roosevelt's account of his Rough Rider experiences on page 616. Have students explain how he showed the same kind of aggressiveness as president.

America's FLAGS

Twenty-fifth Flag, 1912 Statehood for Arizona and New Mexico increased the number of stars to 48 in 1912. This flag served from 1912 to 1959, more years than any other flag.

ing as president of Princeton University and governor of New Jersey.

Wilson gained only 42 percent of the popular vote, with Roosevelt receiving 27 percent and Taft 23 percent. However, Wilson won the presidency by the largest electoral majority up to that time, sweeping 435 of the 531 electoral votes.

Wilson's Reforms

During his campaign Woodrow Wilson had criticized big government as well as big business. Wilson called his program the "New Freedom."

In 1913 Wilson achieved a long-awaited progressive goal—tariff reform. He persuaded the Democrat-controlled Congress to adopt a lower tariff on imported goods such as sugar, wool, steel, and farm equipment. Wilson believed that the pressure of foreign competition would lead American manufacturers to improve their products and lower their prices. The government income lost by lowering tariffs would be replaced by the new income tax.

That same year Congress also passed the **Federal Reserve Act** to regulate banking. By creating 12 regional banks supervised by a central board in **Washington, D.C.,** the act gave the government more control over banking activities. Banks that operated nationally were required to join the Federal Reserve System and abide by its regulations.

Regulating Business

Wilson also worked toward strengthening government control over business. In 1914 Congress established the **Federal Trade Commission** (FTC) to investigate corporations for unfair trade practices. Wilson also supported the **Clayton Antitrust Act** of 1914, which joined the Sherman Antitrust Act as one of the government's chief weapons against trusts.

By the end of Wilson's first term, progressives had won many victories. The Progressive movement lost some of its momentum as Americans turned their attention to world affairs—especially the war that had broken out in Europe in 1914.

Section 3 Review

Checking for Understanding

1. ***Identify*** Theodore Roosevelt, William McKinley, William Howard Taft, Sixteenth Amendment, Woodrow Wilson.
2. ***Define*** trustbuster, arbitration, square deal, laissez-faire, conservation.
3. ***Describe*** two progressive ideas that Roosevelt supported.

Reviewing Themes

4. **Economic Factors** Why did progressives support an income tax?

Critical Thinking

5. **Media Literacy** If you were creating a 30-second television commercial to recruit volunteers for Roosevelt's Rough Riders, what would you say and show?

Activity

Drawing a Political Cartoon Draw a political cartoon that supports Theodore Roosevelt's actions as a "trustbuster."

Section 3 Review Answers

1. Theodore Roosevelt, 616; William McKinley, 616; William Howard Taft, 618; Sixteenth Amendment, 619; Woodrow Wilson, 619
2. The words are defined in the Glossary.
3. government regulation of business such as trust-busting and labor regulations; conservation of natural resources
4. They hoped it would enable the government to lower tariffs, which, in turn, would lower prices on goods.
5. Commercials should reflect Roosevelt's ambitious and courageous spirit.

Activity Political cartoons should show support for Roosevelt's trust-busting activities.

Social Studies
SKILL BUILDER

Interpreting a Political Cartoon

You've probably heard the saying, "A picture is worth a thousand words." For more than 200 years, political cartoonists have drawn pictures to present their opinions about a person or event. Learning to interpret political cartoons can help you understand issues of both the past and present.

Learning the Skill

Political cartoons state opinions about particular subjects. To illustrate those opinions, cartoonists provide clues using several different techniques. They often exaggerate a person's physical features or appearance in a special effect called *caricature.* A person who talks a great deal, for example, might have a caricature that shows him or her with a very large mouth. A caricature can be positive or negative, depending on the artist's point of view.

Cartoonists also use symbols to represent something else. The bald eagle is often shown in political cartoons as a symbol of the United States. Sometimes cartoonists help readers interpret their message by adding labels or captions.

To interpret a political cartoon, follow these steps:

- Read the caption and any other words printed in the cartoon.
- Analyze each element in the cartoon.
- Identify the clues: What is happening in the cartoon? Who or what is represented by each part of the drawing? What or whom do the figures represent? To what do the symbols refer?
- Study all these elements to decide the point the cartoonist is making.

Practicing the Skill

The cartoon on this page shows Theodore Roosevelt looking in a window at President Taft. Analyze the cartoon, then answer the following questions.

1. What is going on in this picture?
2. What caricatures are included in this cartoon?
3. What symbols are depicted? What do these symbols represent?
4. What point is the cartoonist making?

Applying the Skill

Interpreting a Political Cartoon Bring to class a copy of a political cartoon from a recent newspaper or magazine. Explain the cartoonist's point of view and the tools used to make the point.

ANSWERS TO PRACTICING THE SKILL

1. Roosevelt is outside, watching as Taft—helplessly entangled—allows unruly pets (Congress and special-interest groups) to unravel all of Roosevelt's reforms.
2. President Taft is caricatured as an inept old woman.
3. Yarn is the symbol of Taft's entanglement; cats are representative of Republican Party leaders who supported Taft; Capitol "basket" holding the yarn is representative of Congress.
4. The cartoonist expresses concern that Taft is unable to effectively control Congress and continue Roosevelt's "Square Deal" reforms.

Applying the Skill Work with students to create a classroom display of the political cartoons they find.

Social Studies
SKILL BUILDER

TEACH

Interpreting a Political Cartoon

This skill demonstrates how political cartoons can express opinions. Begin by mentioning that political cartoons can be valuable primary sources, for they reflect the issues and feelings of a certain time and point of view.

Students probably associate cartoons with humor and entertainment. Point out that because the primary purpose of political cartoons is to comment on a situation and, at times, to suggest a course of action, the humor (if it exists at all) is understated or barbed.

Make sure that students distinguish between a caricature and a symbol. In general, a caricature is an unrealistic drawing of a real person, while a symbol is a real drawing of a concept. In a brief activity, ask students to share political symbols with which they are familiar. *(Answers may include Uncle Sam as a symbol of the federal government and the elephant and donkey as respective symbols of the Democrats and Republicans.)*

Additional Practice

Chapter Skills Activity 21

1 FOCUS

BELLRINGER
Motivational Activity

Before taking roll at the beginning of the class period, project Section Focus Transparency 21–4 and have students answer the questions. Discuss students' responses.

This activity is also available as a blackline master.

Section Focus Transparency 21–4

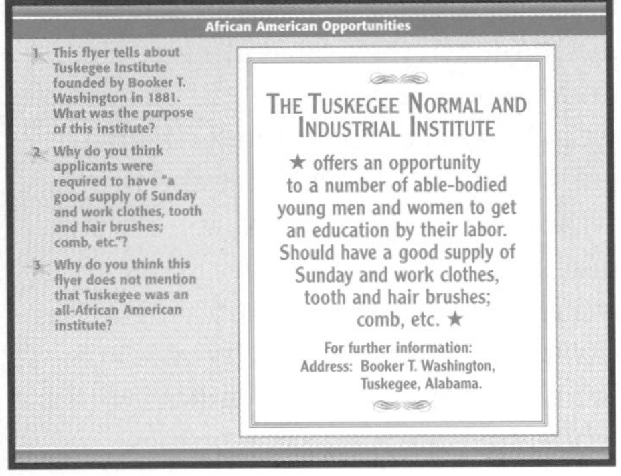
African American Opportunities

1. This flyer tells about Tuskegee Institute founded by Booker T. Washington in 1881. What was the purpose of this institute?
2. Why do you think applicants were required to have "a good supply of Sunday and work clothes, tooth and hair brushes; comb, etc."?
3. Why do you think this flyer does not mention that Tuskegee was an all-African American institute?

THE TUSKEGEE NORMAL AND INDUSTRIAL INSTITUTE

★ offers an opportunity to a number of able-bodied young men and women to get an education by their labor. Should have a good supply of Sunday and work clothes, tooth and hair brushes; comb, etc. ★

For further information:
Address: Booker T. Washington,
Tuskegee, Alabama.

Vocabulary Precheck

Point out that *discrimination* literally means "recognizing a difference (between things)." Discuss why the word has a negative connotation.

Use the **Vocabulary PuzzleMaker** to create crossword and word search puzzles.

Section Theme
Civic Rights and Responsibilities

African Americans and other minorities found that Progressive reforms did little to advance their own rights and opportunities.

Activity As students look at the pictures on page 624, ask: **Given what you know about this era, why does this scene seem out of place?** *(Students should suggest that reform and racism seem incompatible.)*

1880 — 1900 — 1920

1887 American Protective Association targets Catholics

1907 Gentlemen's Agreement restricts Japanese immigration

1909 W.E.B. Du Bois helps form the NAACP

1915 Ku Klux Klan reappears

Section 4

Excluded From Reform

READ TO DISCOVER . . .

- why progressive reforms did little to help African Americans and other minorities.
- how minorities worked to combat prejudice and move toward greater equality.

TERMS TO LEARN

discrimination — barrio

The Storyteller

Prejudice against Asians and African Americans ran deep in the early 1900s. Many Asian immigrants were detained upon arrival in the United States. Held at an immigration station in San Francisco Bay, a Chinese immigrant carved the following poem on the wall of the barracks:

I used to admire the land of the Flowery
  Flag as a country of abundance.
I immediately raised money and started
  my journey.
For over a month, I have experienced
  enough wind and waves. . . .
I look up and see Oakland so
  close by. . . .
Discontent fills
  my belly and
  it is difficult
  for me to
  sleep. . . .

Chinese shopkeeper in California

In 1908 violence erupted in **Springfield, Illinois,** when a white woman claimed to have been attacked by an African American man. Authorities jailed the man. The woman then admitted that her accusation was untrue. By that time, white townspeople had formed an angry mob.

Armed with axes and guns, the mob stormed through African American neighborhoods, destroying businesses and driving people from their homes. Rioters lynched two African American men and injured dozens more. Yet no one was ever punished for these violent crimes.

The Springfield riot shocked the nation and highlighted the deep racial divisions in American life. The riot took place in the hometown of Abraham Lincoln, the president who signed the Emancipation Proclamation. African Americans were no longer enslaved—but they were still pursued by prejudice and racial hatred.

Prejudice and Discrimination in America

During the 1800s the overwhelming majority of Americans were white, Protestant, and had been born in the United States. Many Americans believed that the United States should remain a white, Protestant nation. Nonwhite, non-Protestant, and non-native residents often faced **discrimination**—unequal treatment because of their race, religion, ethnic background, or place of birth. The government rarely interfered with this discrimination.

SECTION RESOURCES

Reproducible Masters
- Reproducible Lesson Plan 21–4
- Guided Reading Activity 21–4
- Section Quiz 21–4
- Reteaching Activity 21–4
- Enrichment Activity 21–4

Transparencies
- Section Focus Transparency 21–4

Multimedia
- Vocabulary PuzzleMaker
- Chapter Challenger Interactive Review Software
- Testmaker
- GTV: The American People: Fabric of a Nation

American Memories

Chinese Immigrant Life

Padded robe

Hat made of black silk

Pair of children's shoes

What Was It Like? By the late 1800s, busy shops and restaurants dotted the streets of San Francisco's Chinatown. **What parts of Chinese culture shown here are included in your life today?**

Anti-Catholicism

Some Americans faced discrimination because of their religion. America's largely Protestant population feared that Catholic immigrants threatened the "American" way of life. Anti-Catholic Iowans formed the American Protective Association (APA) in 1887. By the mid-1890s, the APA claimed a membership of 2 million across the nation. Among other activities, the APA spread rumors that Catholics were preparing to take over the country.

Anti-Semitism

Many Jewish immigrants came to the United States to escape prejudice in their homelands. Some of them found the same anti-Semitic attitudes in America. Landlords, employers, and schools discriminated against Jews. Eastern European Jews faced prejudice both as Jews and as eastern Europeans, whom many Americans regarded as more "foreign" than western Europeans.

Anti-Asian Policies

Discrimination was also based on race. In California and other western states, Asians struggled against prejudice and resentment. White Americans claimed that Chinese immigrants, who worked for lower wages, took away jobs. Congress passed the Chinese Exclusion Act in 1882 to prevent Chinese immigrants from entering the United States.

America's westward expansion created opportunities for thousands of Japanese immigrants who came to the United States to work as railroad or farm laborers. Like the Chinese before them, Japanese immigrants encountered prejudice. California would not allow them to become citizens. In 1906 in **San Francisco,** the school board tried to make Japanese children attend a separate school for Asians until President Roosevelt stepped in to prevent such segregation.

Roosevelt yielded to a rising tide of anti-Japanese feeling, however, and authorized the **Gentlemen's Agreement** with Japan in 1907. This

American Memories

Chinese Immigrant Life

The years 1871–1880 saw the peak of Chinese immigration to the United States, a destination the Chinese often called *Mei Kwok* ("the Beautiful Land") or *Gum Shan* ("the Mountain of Gold"). The first Chinese newspaper in the United States was printed in San Francisco (1854), as was the first Chinese/English bilingual newspaper (1891). Today San Francisco has the largest Chinese population of any American city.

Answer: *Answers will vary but may include markets and robes. Most students also are familiar with Chinese foods (not shown).*

2 TEACH

L1, ELL Making Inferences Direct students' attention to the time line at the top of page 622. Invite them to speculate about the relationship between the facts noted there and the title of the section—"Excluded From Reform."

COOPERATIVE LEARNING ACTIVITY

Comparing Viewpoints Organize the class into groups and assign each group one of the following roles: a newly arrived Asian immigrant, a progressive reformer, a political boss, a labor union leader. Direct students to formulate the views of each of these people concerning immigration and reform. Ask each group to present its viewpoint to the class and answer questions. You might suggest that students write a summary of each of the viewpoints presented and discuss the merits of each.

Guided Reading Activity 21–4

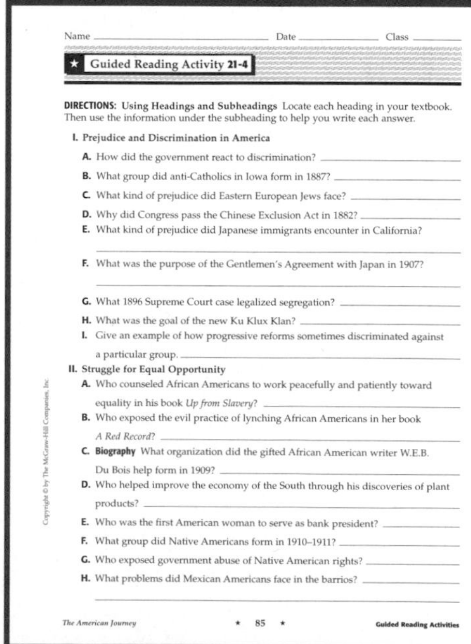

Name ________ Date ________ Class ________

★ Guided Reading Activity 21-4

DIRECTIONS: Using Headings and Subheadings Locate each heading in your textbook. Then use the information under the subheading to help you write each answer.

I. Prejudice and Discrimination in America

A. How did the government react to discrimination? ________

B. What group did anti-Catholics in Iowa form in 1887? ________

C. What kind of prejudice did Eastern European Jews face? ________

D. Why did Congress pass the Chinese Exclusion Act in 1882? ________

E. What kind of prejudice did Japanese immigrants encounter in California? ________

F. What was the purpose of the Gentlemen's Agreement with Japan in 1907? ________

G. What 1896 Supreme Court case legalized segregation? ________

H. What was the goal of the new Ku Klux Klan? ________

I. Give an example of how progressive reforms sometimes discriminated against a particular group. ________

II. Struggle for Equal Opportunity

A. Who counseled African Americans to work peacefully and patiently toward equality in his book *Up from Slavery*? ________

B. Who exposed the evil practice of lynching African Americans in her book *A Red Record*? ________

C. Biography What organization did the gifted African American writer W.E.B. Du Bois help form in 1909? ________

D. Who helped improve the economy of the South through his discoveries of plant products? ________

E. Who was the first American woman to serve as bank president? ________

F. What group did Native Americans form in 1910–1911? ________

G. Who exposed government abuse of Native American rights? ________

H. What problems did Mexican Americans face in the barrios? ________

The American Journey ★ 85 ★ **Guided Reading Activities**

NATIONAL GEOGRAPHIC SOCIETY

VIDEODISC
GTV: The American People: Fabric of a Nation

Side 3, Chapter 7
Title: *Enter the Klan*
Subject: Prejudice and intolerance in America
Ask: **What groups faced discrimination in the 1920s?** *(Asians, southern and eastern Europeans, African Americans, Catholics, Jews, Mexican Americans)*

Picturing HISTORY The revived Klan was most active from 1915 until 1924. By 1925, newspaper reports of Klan activities caused a decline in membership. Here are the reported number of lynchings of African Americans during those years:

1915: 69	1920: 61
1916: 54	1921: 64
1917: 38	1922: 57
1918: 64	1923: 33
1919: 83	1924: 16

Ask: **Why did Klan members wear white hoods?** *(to keep their identity secret and to frighten their victims)*
Answer: *African Americans and Chinese immigrants*

accord restricted Japanese immigration to the United States, but it did not bring an end to anti-Japanese feeling. In 1913 California made it illegal for Japanese immigrants to buy land. Other Western states passed similar laws.

Discrimination Against African Americans

African Americans faced discrimination in both the North and the South. Although officially free, African Americans were systematically denied basic rights and restricted to second-class citizenship.

Four-fifths of the nation's African Americans lived in the South. Most worked as rural sharecroppers or in low-paying jobs in the cities. They were separated from white society in their own neighborhoods, schools, parks, restaurants, theaters, and even cemeteries. In 1896 the Supreme Court legalized segregation in the case of *Plessy* v. *Ferguson,* which recognized "separate but equal" facilities.

The **Ku Klux Klan,** which had terrorized African Americans during Reconstruction, was reborn in Georgia in 1915. The new Klan wanted to restore white Protestant America. The Klan lashed out against minorities—Catholics, Jews, and immigrants, as well as African Americans. Calling for "100 percent Americanism," the Klan kept growing and claimed more than 2 million members by 1924, many of them in Northern cities and towns.

Racial Violence

People who lost their jobs during the economic depressions of 1893 and 1907 sometimes unleashed their anger against African Americans and other minorities. More than 2,600 African Americans were lynched between 1886 and 1916, mostly in the South. Lynchings were also used to terrorize Chinese immigrants in the West.

Progressivism and Prejudice

In the late 1800s and the early 1900s, many Americans held biased views. They believed that white, male, native-born Americans had the right to make decisions for all of society.

Most of the progressive reformers came from the middle and upper classes. They saw themselves as moral leaders working to improve the lives of people less fortunate than themselves. The reforms they supported often discriminated against one group as they tried to help another group, however.

Trade unions often prohibited African Americans, women, and immigrants from joining. Skilled laborers, these unions argued, could

Picturing HISTORY
A Ku Klux Klan pamphlet (right) promotes the Klan's hate campaign against immigrants. Meanwhile, opponents of lynching called for an end to racial murders. **What two groups experienced the terror of lynching?**

MULTIPLE LEARNING STYLES

Verbal/Linguistic W.E.B. Du Bois wrote and spoke eloquently on behalf of African Americans. Have students read his classic *The Souls of Black Folk,* then complete one of the following activities:

- Choose a selection from his book to analyze. For example, how does Du Bois state his main ideas? What comparisons does he make to illustrate those ideas? Which words or figures of speech would cause an emotional reaction in his audience?
- Study the style in a selection from his book. Then write a persuasive argument about a topic that means much to you. See if you can use some of the same techniques that Du Bois used in his argument. **L3**

Picturing HISTORY

Booker T. Washington (seated, second from left) founded the National Negro Business League. **Why did Washington stress economic power among African Americans?**

obtain better working conditions for themselves if they did not demand improved conditions for all workers.

Sometimes reforms instituted by the progressives were efforts to control a particular group. The temperance movement, for example, was partly an attempt to control the behavior of Irish Catholic immigrants. Civil service reforms required job applicants to be educated—this reduced the political influence that immigrants had begun to have in some cities. In spite of their contradictions, progressive reforms did succeed in improving conditions for many Americans.

Struggle for Equal Opportunity

Often excluded from progressive organizations because of prejudice, minorities battled for justice and opportunity on their own. African Americans, Hispanics, and Native Americans took steps to improve their lives.

African American Response

African Americans rose to the challenge of achieving equality. **Booker T. Washington,** who had been born enslaved and taught himself to read, founded the Tuskegee Institute in 1881. The institute taught African Americans farming and industrial skills.

Washington believed that if African Americans had more economic power, they would be in a better position to demand social equality and civil rights. Washington founded the **National Negro Business League** to promote business development among African Americans. In Washington's autobiography, *Up from Slavery,* he counseled African Americans to work slowly, patiently, and peacefully toward equality.

Equality Through Separation

Some African Americans thought that they would be better off in separate societies, either in the United States or in Africa. They founded organizations to establish African American towns and promoted a back-to-Africa movement. These movements were not popular, however, and their goals gained few supporters.

African American Women Take Action

African American women worked together through groups such as the National Association of Colored Women to fight the practice of lynching and other forms of racial violence. **Ida B. Wells,** the editor of an African American newspaper in Memphis, Tennessee, was forced to leave town after publishing the names of people involved in a lynching. The incident started Wells on a national crusade against the terrible practice of lynching.

Making Connections Activity

Health The National Association of Colored Women (NACW), founded in 1896, not only fought racial violence and laws that discriminated against African Americans but also worked to improve the health of African Americans. Ask students how each of these NACW programs could be seen as an effort to achieve that goal:

- Establishing a training school for nurses in New Orleans
- Buying land in Memphis to build a home for the elderly
- Sending teams into communities to teach the poor about hygiene
- Offering "Mothers' Congresses" that provided information about methods of child rearing. **L2**

Picturing HISTORY Some 400 delegates from 34 states gathered for the founding of the National Negro Business League in 1900. They elected Booker T. Washington (whose autobiography, *Up from Slavery,* was published that same year) as its president. Out of the organization grew the National Negro Finance Corporation, which encouraged investment in and expansion of African American businesses. **Ask:** **What "minority" group is missing from this photograph?** *(African American women)*
Answer: *He believed that economic power would put African Americans in a better position for demanding social equality and civil rights.*

Who?What?Where?When?

Marcus Garvey Among those who encouraged the back-to-Africa movement, no one was better known—or more outspoken—than Marcus Garvey (1887–1940). Garvey came to the United States from his native Jamaica in 1916. He believed that only through complete independence from whites could blacks achieve equality. He gathered followers and funds into his Universal Negro Improvement Association and formed the Black Star Line, a steamship company. He also began negotiations with Liberia as a new home for African Americans, but Liberia backed out. Convicted of mail fraud, Garvey was jailed from 1925 to 1927 and then deported to Jamaica. He was never able to regain his early support.

3 ASSESS

Assign Section 4 Review as homework or as an in-class activity.

Use **Chapter Challenger Interactive Review Software** to review Section 4.

CHAPTER 21

Section 4, 622–627

Picturing HISTORY Ida B. Wells (1862–1931) became a journalist after she was fired from a teaching job for daring to sue for the right to sit in a "whites only" railroad car. In 1891 she became the co-owner and editor of *Free Speech,* a Memphis weekly. In that newspaper and her later writings, she targeted lynching as her special cause.

Answer: *the National Association for the Advancement of Colored People (NAACP)*

Section Quiz 21–4

Name ______ Date ______ Class ______

★ Chapter 21 — Score

Section Quiz 21-4

DIRECTIONS: Matching Match each item in Column A with the items in Column B. Write the correct letters in the blanks. *(10 points each)*

Column A	Column B
____ 1. Anti-Catholic Iowans	A. newspaper editor
____ 2. restricted Japanese immigration	B. first female bank president
____ 3. Booker T. Washington	C. formed American Protective Association
____ 4. Ida B. Wells	D. founded National Negro Business League
____ 5. Maggie Lena	E. Gentlemen's Agreement

DIRECTIONS: Multiple Choice In the blank at the left, write the letter of the choice that best completes the statement or answers the question. *(10 points each)*

____ 6. This shocked the nation and highlighted the deep racial divisions in American life.
A. Atlanta lynching C. Richmond trial
B. New York mob D. Springfield riot

____ 7. This was the only group of Americans who did not face discrimination.
A. white Protestants C. Catholics
B. Asian Americans D. Jews

____ 8. W.E.B. Du Bois helped form this organization for legal and economic equality for African Americans.
A. Women's Clubs C. National Negro Business League
B. NAACP D. National Association of Colored Women

____ 9. This person was one of the founding members of the Society of American Indians.
A. W.E.B. Du Bois C. Dr. Carlos Montezuma
B. Ida B. Wells D. Booker T. Washington

____ 10. Mexican American neighborhoods are called
A. ghettos. C. barrios.
B. rancheros. D. suburbs.

The American Journey ★ 85 ★ Section Quizzes

Who?What?Where?When?

Carlos Montezuma stated that "The Indian Bureau system is wrong," in an address at the society's 1916 conference. "The only way to adjust wrong is to abolish it, and the only reform is to let my people go. After freeing the Indian from the shackles of government repression, what is the Indian going to do? Leave that with the Indian, and it is none of your business."

Ida B. Wells

W.E.B. Du Bois

Picturing HISTORY Journalist Ida B. Wells and educator W.E.B. Du Bois urged African Americans to speak out for their civil rights. **What interracial group was formed to promote legal and economic equality for African Americans?**

In her 1894 book, *A Red Record,* Wells showed that lynching was used primarily against African Americans who had become prosperous or who competed with white businesses. "Can you remain silent and inactive when such things are done in your own community and country?" she asked. As she traveled the country lecturing, Wells inspired the growth of the African American women's club movement.

Biography

Equality for African Americans

W.E.B. Du Bois was one of the most important African American leaders of the time. Born in Great Barrington, Massachusetts, Du Bois proved to be a gifted debater and writer. At 15, he wrote a regular column for the *New York Globe.* Du Bois graduated from Fisk University at Nashville with honors and received a Ph.D. from Harvard University.

Du Bois urged African Americans to fight for civil rights. Under no circumstances, he said, should they accept segregation. He disagreed with Booker T. Washington's approach to improving the lives of African Americans. In *The Souls of Black Folk* (1903), Du Bois wrote:

> "So far as Mr. Washington preaches Thrift, Patience, and Industrial Training . . . we must hold up his hands and strive with him. . . . But so far as Mr. Washington apologizes for injustice, North or South, does not rightly value the privilege and duty of voting, belittles the [devastating] effect of caste distinctions, and opposes the higher training and ambition of our brighter minds . . . we must unceasingly and firmly oppose [Washington's ideas]."

In 1905 Du Bois helped organize a meeting of African American teachers, writers, and business leaders in the Canadian town of **Niagara, Ontario.** The meeting launched the **Niagara Movement,** which called for immediate economic and political equality for African Americans.

Four years later Du Bois and members of the Niagara Movement combined with other African Americans and some whites to form the **National Association for the Advancement of Colored People** (NAACP). For much of the century, this interracial group has remained at the forefront of efforts to gain legal and economic equality for African Americans.

Other Successes

During the early 1900s African Americans achieved success in a variety of professions. Chemist **George Washington Carver,** director of agricultural research at Tuskegee Institute, helped improve the economy of the South through his discoveries of plant products. **Maggie Lena** founded the St. Luke Penny Savings Bank in Richmond, Virginia. She was the first American woman to serve as a bank president.

CRITICAL THINKING ACTIVITY

Identifying Alternatives By the time the NAACP was founded, the Niagara Movement was in tatters. Share these reasons for its failure:

- It could not attract broad support from whites or African Americans.
- It faced constant opposition from Booker T. Washington.
- It had financial problems and a weak internal organization.
- It lost the Boston *Guardian* as a vehicle for publicity when the paper's editor and Du Bois had a falling-out in 1907.

Ask: **Did these factors make failure inevitable? What could have been done to prevent or turn around any of these problems?** Discuss. **L2, ELL**

Native Americans Seek Justice

The federal government's efforts to assimilate Native Americans into white society threatened to break down traditional native cultures. In 1910–1911 Native American leaders from around the country formed the **Society of American Indians** to seek justice for Native Americans, to improve their living conditions, and to educate white Americans about different Native American cultures.

One of the society's founding members was **Dr. Carlos Montezuma,** an Apache who had been raised by whites. After graduating from medical school, Montezuma worked for the United States Indian Service.

Convinced that federal policies were hurting Native Americans, Montezuma turned to activism, exposing government abuse of Indian rights. Montezuma believed that Native Americans should leave the reservations and make their own way in white society.

Mexican Americans Work Together

Immigrants from Mexico had long come to the United States as laborers, especially in the West and Southwest. Between 1900 and 1914, the Mexican American population grew dramatically as people crossed the border to escape revolution and economic troubles in Mexico.

Picturing HISTORY Mexican Americans found work in the mines of the American Southwest during the 1890s. **How did Mexican Americans deal with the challenges they faced?**

Like the Japanese and other immigrant groups, Mexican Americans encountered discrimination and violence. Relying on themselves to solve their problems, they formed *mutualistas*—self-defense associations—to raise money for insurance and legal help. In labor camps and Mexican neighborhoods called barrios, they organized self-help groups to deal with overcrowding, poor sanitation, and inadequate public services.

Widespread prejudice excluded Mexican Americans and other minorities from many reform groups. Yet these groups produced dynamic leaders and created organizations to improve their circumstances and fight for justice.

Section 4 Review

Checking for Understanding

1. ***Identify*** Gentlemen's Agreement, Booker T. Washington, Ida B. Wells, W.E.B. Du Bois, Dr. Carlos Montezuma.
2. ***Define*** discrimination, barrio.
3. ***Name*** five groups of people who were the targets of discrimination in the late 1800s and early 1900s.

Reviewing Themes

4. **Civic Rights and Responsibilities** Give an example of a progressive reform that resulted in discrimination.

Critical Thinking

5. **Making Comparisons** If you had been an African American in the early 1900s, would you have supported the ideas of Booker T. Washington or W.E.B. Du Bois? Why?

Activity

Designing a Book Cover Create a title and cover design for a book about discrimination that might have been written during this time.

CHAPTER 21
Section 4, 622–627

Picturing HISTORY **Answer:** *They formed self-defense associations (mutualistas).*

Reteaching Activity 21–4

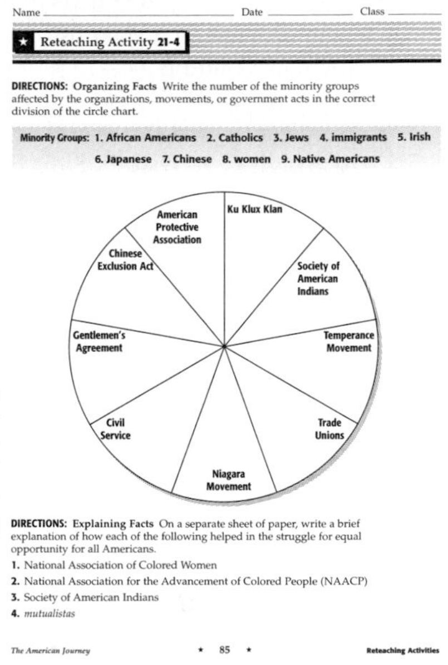

Name ______ Date ______ Class ______

★ Reteaching Activity 21-4

DIRECTIONS: Organizing Facts Write the number of the minority groups affected by the organizations, movements, or government acts in the correct division of the circle chart.

Minority Groups: 1. African Americans 2. Catholics 3. Jews 4. immigrants 5. Irish 6. Japanese 7. Chinese 8. women 9. Native Americans

DIRECTIONS: Explaining Facts On a separate sheet of paper, write a brief explanation of how each of the following helped in the struggle for equal opportunity for all Americans.

1. National Association of Colored Women
2. National Association for the Advancement of Colored People (NAACP)
3. Society of American Indians
4. *mutualistas*

The American Journey ★ 85 ★ Reteaching Activities

Enrichment Activity 21–4

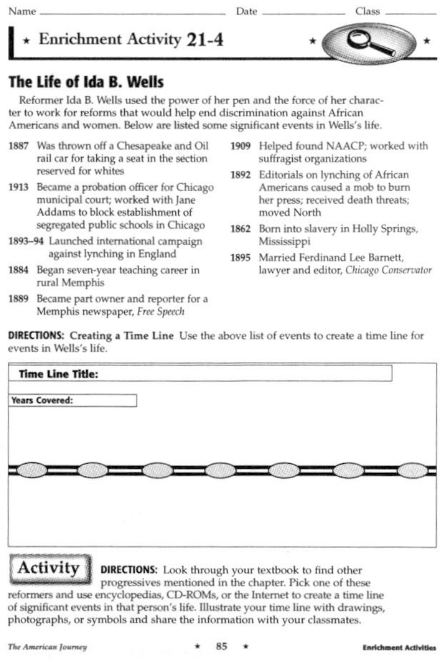

Name ______ Date ______ Class ______

★ Enrichment Activity 21-4 ★

The Life of Ida B. Wells

Reformer Ida B. Wells used the power of her pen and the force of her character to work for reforms that would help end discrimination against African Americans and women. Below are listed some significant events in Wells's life.

1887 Was thrown off a Chesapeake and Oil rail car for taking a seat in the section reserved for whites

1913 Became a probation officer for Chicago municipal court; worked with Jane Addams to block establishment of segregated public schools in Chicago

1893–94 Launched international campaign against lynching in England

1884 Began seven-year teaching career in rural Memphis

1889 Became part owner and reporter for a Memphis newspaper, *Free Speech*

1909 Helped found NAACP; worked with suffragist organizations

1892 Editorials on lynching of African Americans caused a mob to burn her press; received death threats; moved North

1862 Born into slavery in Holly Springs, Mississippi

1895 Married Ferdinand Lee Barnett, lawyer and editor, *Chicago Conservator*

DIRECTIONS: Creating a Time Line Use the above list of events to create a time line for events in Wells's life.

Activity **DIRECTIONS:** Look through your textbook to find other progressives mentioned in the chapter. Pick one of these reformers and use encyclopedias, CD-ROMs, or the Internet to create a time line of significant events in that person's life. Illustrate your time line with drawings, photographs, or symbols and share the information with your classmates.

The American Journey ★ 85 ★ Enrichment Activities

Section 4 Review Answers

1. Gentlemen's Agreement, 623; Booker T. Washington, 625; Ida B. Wells, 625; W.E.B. Du Bois, 626; Dr. Carlos Montezuma, 627
2. The words are defined in the Glossary.
3. Any five: African Americans, Native Americans, Mexican Americans, Catholics, Jews, eastern Europeans, Chinese, Japanese
4. trade unions' exclusion of minorities; the temperance movement's attempt to control Irish Catholics; civil service reforms that hampered immigrants' efforts
5. Answers should support either Washington's beliefs about increasing economic power or Du Bois's beliefs about standing up for one's rights.

Activity Titles should summarize the mood of the country at this time as it applied to the treatment of minorities.

4 CLOSE

Discuss how specific people and organizations addressed the need for reform.

GLENCOE TECHNOLOGY

VIDEODISC
MindJogger Videoquiz

Use MindJogger to review the Chapter 21 content.

Chapter 21
Disc 3, Side B

Also available in VHS.

Review and Activities

Reviewing Key Terms

On a sheet of paper, use each of the following terms in a sentence.

political machine
patronage
civil service
trust
muckraker
primary
initiative
referendum
recall
suffragist
arbitration
laissez-faire
conservation
discrimination
barrio

Reviewing Key Facts

1. How did corrupt political bosses get voters for their parties?
2. Why were journalists important to the reform movement?
3. What was the Eighteenth Amendment?
4. Why did progressives form their own political party?
5. What did Dr. Carlos Montezuma think about Native American reservations?

Critical Thinking

Determining Cause and Effect

Corruption in politics and business eventually led to stronger government regulation.

1. What conditions brought about the passage of the Meat Inspection Act?
2. Why was the railroad industry subject to so many government regulations?

Time Line Activity

Create a time line on which you place the following events in chronological order.

- Woodrow Wilson is elected president
- American Socialist Party is formed
- Women earn the right to vote
- Congress passes the Pendleton Act
- Theodore Roosevelt becomes president
- Congress passes the Meat Inspection and Pure Food and Drug acts

Reviewing Themes

1. **Government and Democracy** How did the Seventeenth Amendment give people a greater voice in government?
2. **Groups and Institutions** What did upper-class women and working women accomplish when they joined forces in the labor movement?
3. **Economic Factors** What was the purpose of the Federal Reserve Act?
4. **Civic Rights and Responsibilities** Why was the NAACP formed?

Geography Activity

The Federal Reserve System divided the nation into 12 districts. Each district served as a single "bank for bankers." Study the map on page 629 and answer the questions below.

1. **Location** Where is the Federal Reserve Bank in District 1?
2. **Location** Where is the Federal Reserve Bank in District 11?
3. **Place** How many states make up the largest Federal District?
4. **Region** In which Federal District do you live? In what city is the Federal Reserve Bank closest to you?

Reviewing Key Terms

The key terms used in this activity are defined in the textbook glossary on pages A26–A35.

Reviewing Key Facts

1. by doing favors for people in return for their votes
2. They exposed injustices, corruption, and political favors and brought them to the attention of the public.
3. It made the manufacture, transport, and sale of alcohol illegal.
4. Roosevelt wanted to run for president, but Taft had the backing of the Republican Party. Roosevelt urged Progressive Republicans to form a new party and to make him its presidential candidate.
5. He believed that Native Americans should leave the reservations and make their own way in society. He felt the policies were hurting Native Americans.

Critical Thinking

1. exposure of the horrible conditions in the meatpacking industry
2. The railroad industry abused its power in setting rates, building trusts, and other unfair business practices. As a result, the government was forced to pass laws to try to control its activities.

Time Line Activity

Events should be placed in this order: Congress passes the Pendleton Act, American Socialist Party is formed, Theodore Roosevelt becomes president, Congress passes the Meat Inspection and Pure Food and Drug Act, Woodrow Wilson is elected president, Women earn the right to vote.

Reviewing Themes

1. It provided for the direct election of senators by the people.
2. They formed the WTUL, which encouraged women to join labor unions and supported laws to protect women workers.
3. to give the government more control over banking activities
4. to gain legal and economic equality for African Americans

Regions of the Federal Reserve System

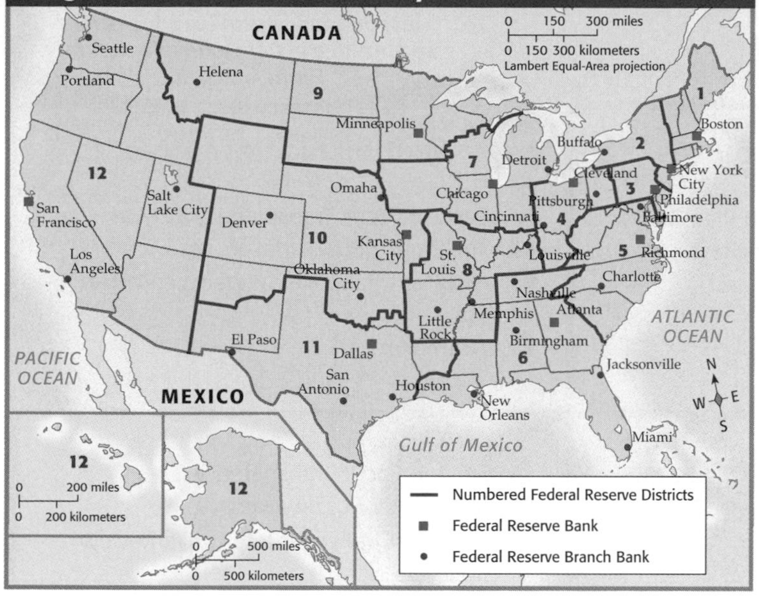

Cooperative Activity

History and Geography Work with members of a group to research another country that is currently dealing with problems generated by discrimination and prejudice. Present an oral report to the class that describes specific incidents that have occurred in the country and the groups of people who are involved. Explain what is at the root of the prejudices that exist and compare it to prejudice and discrimination that exists in the United States. Use maps and other visual aids to make your presentation interesting and informative.

Skill Practice Activity

Interpreting a Political Cartoon

Study the cartoon on page 605, then answer the following questions.

1. What figures are shown in the cartoon?
2. Is symbolism or caricature used in this cartoon? Explain.
3. What does the cartoon suggest about big business?
4. What title would you give this cartoon?

Technology Activity

Using E-Mail Research the names of five modern organizations that have some of the same goals as the progressive reformers of the late 1800s and early 1900s. Choose one organization that interests you and make contact through E-mail to get more information about the group.

Portfolio Activity **History Journal** Scan the chapter and make a list of the constitutional amendments that were passed during the Progressive Era. Make a cause-and-effect chart to show what needs, actions, or abuses led to the passage of each.

3. They are raising tariffs at the expense of the average American buyer.
4. Answers will vary but may suggest that the government is doing nothing to stop big business from hurting Americans.

Technology Activity

Students should locate the names of five modern organizations that have some of the same goals as the progressive reformers. They should select one organization from that file to contact through E-mail for more information.

Cooperative Activity

Each group should present an oral report on another country that is currently experiencing problems with discrimination and prejudice among its people. Reports should cite specific incidents, what groups of people are involved, and what is at the root of the prejudice. Each group should compare its findings to the situation that exists today in the United States. Students should use maps and other visual aids to make their reports more interesting and informative.

Portfolio Activity Students should create a cause-and-effect chart that shows the motivation behind each of the amendments discussed in this chapter.

Chapter Bonus Test Question

Ask: When Theodore Roosevelt coined the term *muckraker,* he was comparing some journalists to a character in a famous book. What book was it? *(Pilgrim's Progress)*

Geography Activity

1. Boston
2. Dallas
3. nine
4. Answers will vary depending upon your location; check for accuracy.

Skill Practice Activity

1. Uncle Sam, three strong men, and a person who looks like a wooden peg.
2. Both. The monopolies are caricatured as beefy bullies. The U.S. government is symbolized by Uncle Sam as a carnival barker. The American citizen is symbolized as a wooden peg getting knocked deeper into the ground by the strong monopolies.

Chapter 22 Planning Guide

A complete, 1-page lesson plan is provided for each section in the *Reproducible Lesson Plans* booklet.

Section Resources

Daily Objectives	Reproducible Resources	Multimedia Resources
Section 1 Expanding Horizons Explain why American imperialism grew in the nineteenth century and how imperialism shaped the foreign policy of the United States.	Reproducible Lesson Plan 22–1 Guided Reading Activity 22–1* Section Quiz 22–1* Reteaching Activity 22–1 Enrichment Activity 22–1	Section Focus Transparency 22–1 Vocabulary PuzzleMaker Chapter Challenger Interactive Review Software Testmaker
Section 2 Imperialism in the Pacific Relate the expansionist impulse to the United States's dealings with Hawaii, Samoa, China, and Japan in the late 1800s.	Reproducible Lesson Plan 22–2 Guided Reading Activity 22–2* Section Quiz 22–2* Reteaching Activity 22–2 Enrichment Activity 22–2	Section Focus Transparency 22–2 Vocabulary PuzzleMaker Chapter Challenger Interactive Review Software Testmaker The Presidents: A Picture History of Our Nation Picture Atlas of the World
Section 3 Spanish-American War Identify causes, key events, and results of the Spanish-American War.	Reproducible Lesson Plan 22–3 Guided Reading Activity 22–3* Section Quiz 22–3* Reteaching Activity 22–3 Enrichment Activity 22–3	Section Focus Transparency 22–3 Vocabulary PuzzleMaker Chapter Challenger Interactive Review Testmaker GTV: A Geographic Perspective on American History Facts On File: Landmark Documents in American History American Music Cultural Traditions, Lesson 7: "Battleship of Maine"
Section 4 Latin American Policies Discuss the building of the Panama Canal and relations with Mexico in light of the diplomatic ideas of Presidents Roosevelt, Taft, and Wilson.	Reproducible Lesson Plan 22–4 Guided Reading Activity 22–4* Political Cartoons, *Big Stick Diplomacy in the Western Hemisphere* Section Quiz 22–4* Reteaching Activity 22–4 Enrichment Activity 22–4	Section Focus Transparency 22–4 Vocabulary PuzzleMaker Chapter Challenger Interactive Review Software Testmaker The Presidents: A Picture History of Our Nation American Music Cultural Traditions, Lesson 7: "Whitehouse Blues"

** Also available in Spanish*

Blackline Master · Videodisc · Audiocassette · Music Program · Transparency · CD-ROM · Software

0:00 **OUT OF TIME?**
Assign the Chapter 22 Digest and the corresponding Chapter Digests Audiocassettes with activities and tests.

Chapter 22 Planning Guide

Activity
From the Classroom of...

Diana Dermody
Kiser Middle School
Dayton, OH

"I Was There" Radio Reports

Explain to students that before television, radio broadcasts played a major role in supplying current information about events around the world. The radio was invented in the time period covered in this chapter. Many public libraries have tapes of famous broadcasts. If possible, share an old radio news broadcast by Edward R. Murrow, Walter Cronkite, or another radio journalist.

Have students pick an area of the world to research, paying particular attention to issues in this chapter. For example, the American Planters' Revolt in Hawaii, the international tensions in the Samoa Islands, or the Boxer Rebellion in China all would be good subjects to investigate. Then have students prepare their own "I Was There" news reports to present orally to the class. Encourage students to dress up as journalists and remind them that descriptive language is important in radio because words have to paint visual images for listeners.

NATIONAL GEOGRAPHIC SOCIETY — Teacher's Corner

INDEX TO NATIONAL GEOGRAPHIC MAGAZINE

The following articles may be used for research relating to this chapter:

- "Wrangell-St. Elias: Alaska's Sky-High Wilderness," by Noel Grove, May 1994.
- "Kodiak, Alaska's Island Refuge," by John L. Elliot, November 1993.
- "Alone Across the Arctic Crown," by Keith Nyitray, April 1993.

NATIONAL GEOGRAPHIC SOCIETY PRODUCTS AVAILABLE FROM GLENCOE

To order the following products for use with this chapter, contact your local Glencoe sales representative, or call Glencoe at 1-800-334-7344:

- *GTV: A Geographic Perspective on American History* (Videodisc)
- *GTV: The American People: Fabric of a Nation* (Videodisc)
- *The Presidents: A Picture History of Our Nation* (CD-ROM)
- *Picture Atlas of the World* (CD-ROM)

ADDITIONAL NATIONAL GEOGRAPHIC SOCIETY PRODUCTS

To order the following products for use with this chapter, call National Geographic Society at 1-800-368-2728:

- *Hawaii: Strangers in Paradise* (Video)
- *Historical Atlas of the United States* (Atlas)

Block Schedule

Block scheduling differs from traditional class scheduling in the amount of time allotted to each period. The extended time frame provided by block scheduling affords you the opportunity to implement a greater number of research-oriented and activity-intense projects to motivate and involve your students. Activities that are particularly suited to use within the block scheduling framework are identified throughout this chapter by the following designation:

KEY TO ABILITY LEVELS

Teaching strategies have been coded for varying learning styles and abilities.

L1 **BASIC** activities for all students
L2 **AVERAGE** activities for average to above-average students
L3 **CHALLENGING** activities for above-average students
ELL **ENGLISH LANGUAGE LEARNER** activities

Chapter 22 Resource Guide

Home Involvement

Home Involvement Activity 22

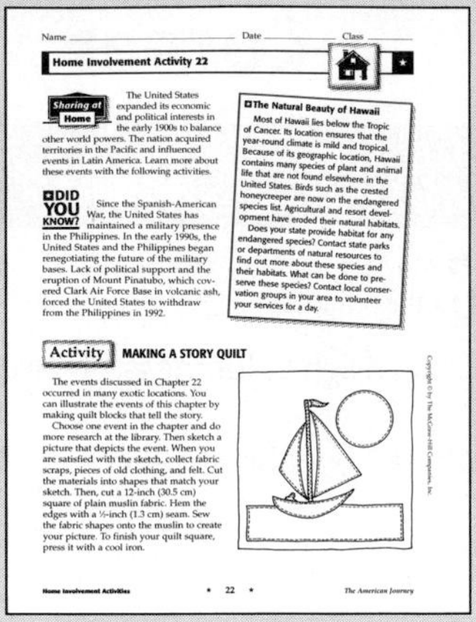

Review Activities

Chapter Summary 22

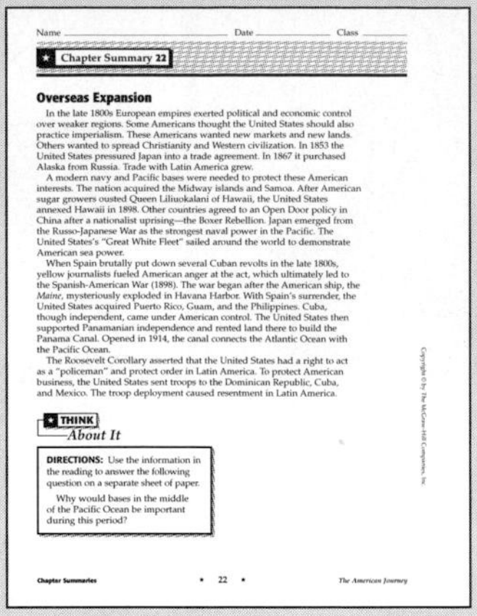

Workbook Activity 22

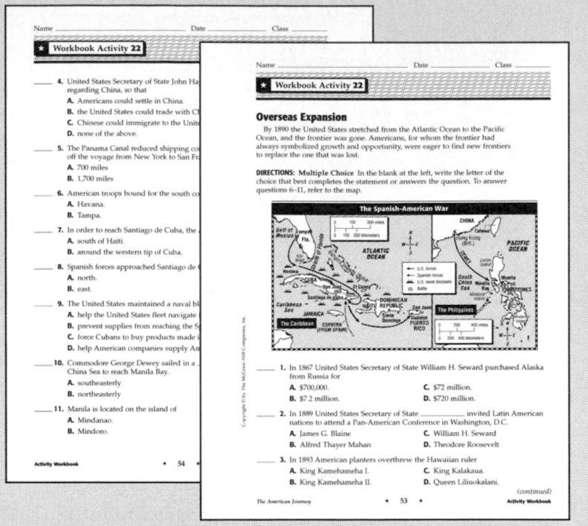

Reinforcement Activities

Time Line Activity 22

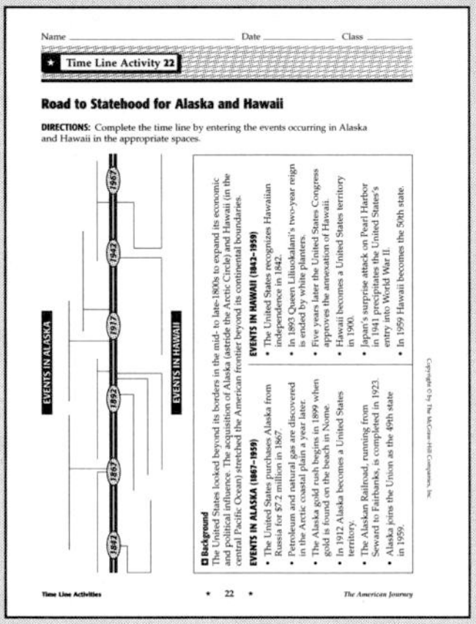

Vocabulary Activity 22

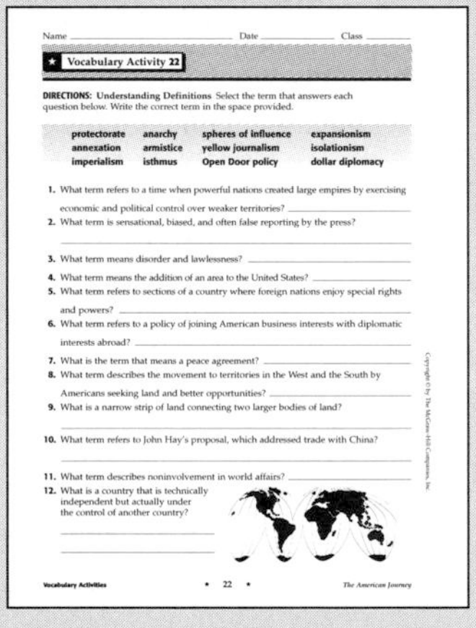

Chapter Skills Activity 22

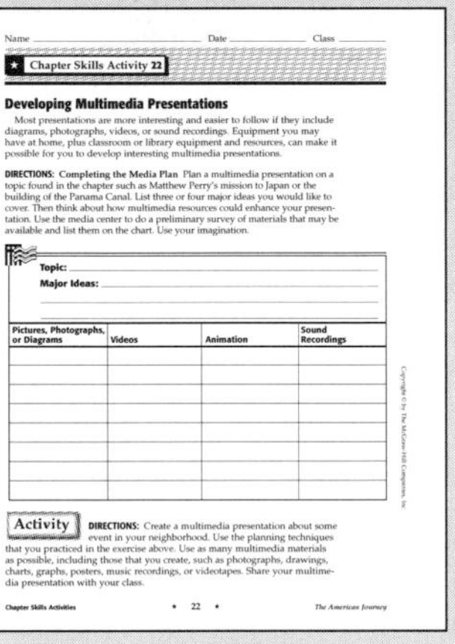

Enrichment Activities

Linking Past and Present Activity 22

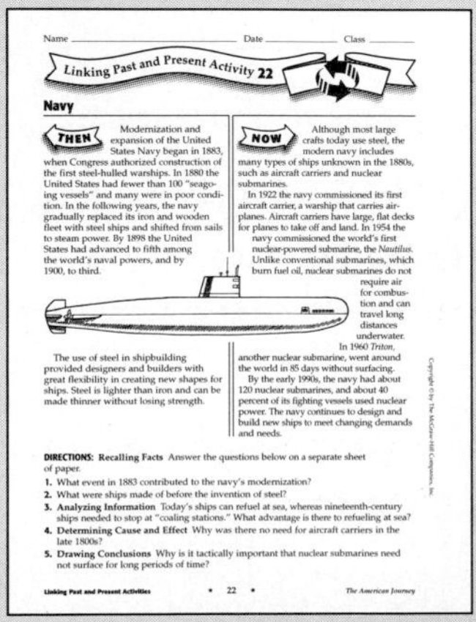

Primary Source Reading 22

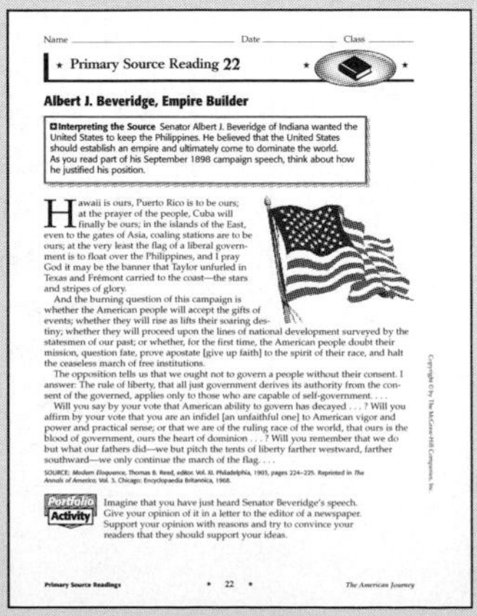

Geography Activities

Mapping History Activity 22

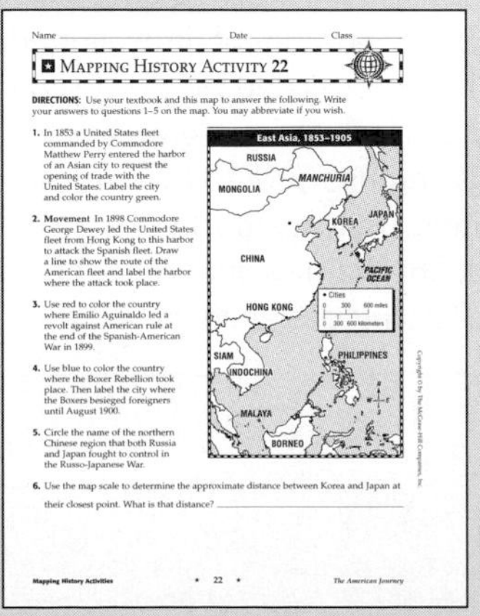

Chapter 22 Resource Guide

Assessment

Chapter 22 Test, Form A

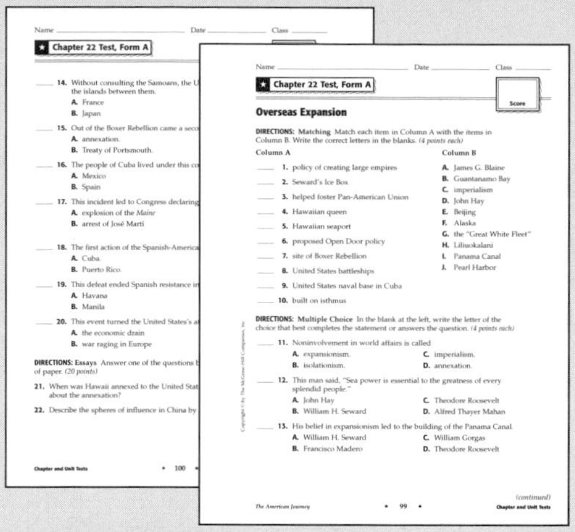

Chapter 22 Test, Form B

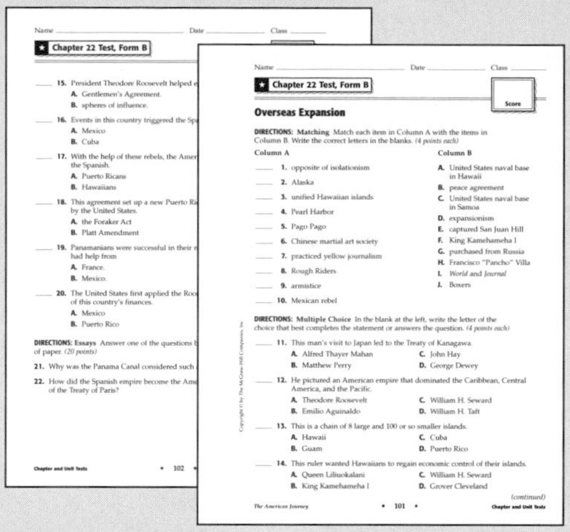

Performance Assessment Activity 22

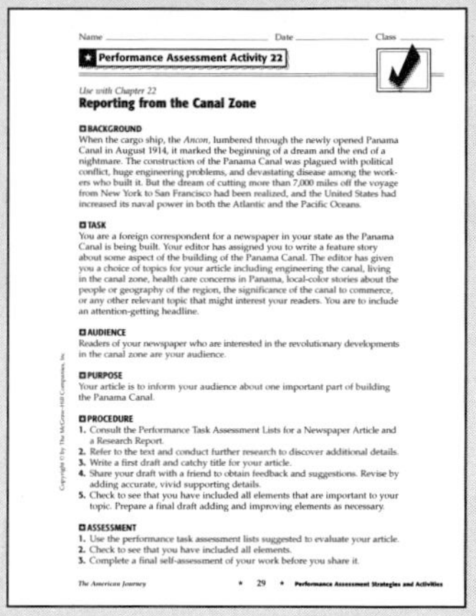

Spanish Resources

The following Spanish language materials are available in the Spanish Resources binder:

- **Spanish Chapter Summary 22**
- **Spanish Vocabulary Activity 22**
- **Spanish Guided Reading Activities, Chapter 22**
- **Spanish Section Quizzes, Chapter 22**
- **Spanish Home Involvement Activity 22**
- **Spanish Chapter 22 Digests Audiocassette Activity and Test**

Activity Manipulatives

Help students learn more about America's cultural history with:

- **American Crafts Hands-On Activities**
- **American Games Hands-On Activities**
- **American History Flash Cards**

Additional Resources From Glencoe

- **The Spirit of American Art and Music,** John Philip Sousa
- **Political Cartoons,** *Big Stick Diplomacy in the Western Hemisphere*
- **The American History Videodisc and CD-ROM,** *The Progressive Era and the First World War, 1901–1920*
- **Outline Map Resource Book**
- **U.S. Desk Map**

A&E HOME VIDEO. Biography THE HISTORY CHANNEL.

The following videotape programs are available from Glencoe as supplements to Chapter 22:

- **Theodore Roosevelt: Roughrider to Rushmore** (ISBN 1-56501-806-0)
- **The Panama Canal** (ISBN 1-56501-243-7)

To order, call Glencoe at 1-800-334-7344. To find classroom resources to accompany many of these videos, check the following home pages:
A&E Television: http://www.aetv.com
The History Channel: http://www.historychannel.com

Introducing
CHAPTER 22

Chapter Themes

Chapter Themes are listed by section on this chapter opening page of the Student Edition. A corresponding theme-based activity is available under "FOCUS," and a theme-based question is asked in the Section and Chapter Reviews.

Performance Assessment

Refer to Activity 22 in the *Performance Assessment Strategies and Activities* booklet.

GLENCOE TECHNOLOGY

VIDEODISC
MindJogger Videoquiz

Use MindJogger to preview the Chapter 22 content.

Chapter 22
Disc 3, Side B

Also available in VHS.

HISTORY AND ART A writer as well as an artist and illustrator, James Gale Tyler (1855–1931) specialized in marine studies. Some of his artwork appeared in *Harper's* and other popular magazines.

Chapter 22

1865–1917

Overseas Expansion

Why It's Important

Some of the territories that the United States acquired in the late 1800s and early 1900s have now gained their independence, and Hawaii and Alaska have joined the United States. Today United States overseas possessions include the Commonwealth of Puerto Rico and the U.S. Virgin Islands in the Caribbean, and Guam and American Samoa in the Pacific. Each of them sends a nonvoting delegate to the United States House of Representatives.

Chapter Themes

- *Section 1,* Economic Factors
- *Section 2,* Geography and History
- *Section 3,* Continuity and Change
- *Section 4,* Global Connections

HISTORY AND ART ***Battle of Santiago de Cuba* by James G. Tyler** In 1898 Tyler painted a dramatic moment in the final sea battle of the Spanish-American War. The painting focuses on the newest weapon of war, the battleship.

630

EXTRA CREDIT PROJECT

Evaluating American Influence In the late 1800s, the United States became involved in the affairs of several other countries. Have students select one of the countries listed below. Ask students to summarize the United States's involvement in that country during the years 1877–1919. Then have students research to learn (1) how the relationship between the two countries has changed in the years since World War I, and (2) what the present relationship is between the two countries. Provide a format for sharing this information.

- Japan
- Puerto Rico
- Nicaragua
- Cuba
- China
- Panama
- Hawaii
- Mexico
- the Philippines

1850 — 1870 — 1890

1853 Matthew Perry steams into Tokyo Bay

1854 Japan signs Treaty of Kanagawa

1867 William Seward signs treaty to buy Alaska

1889 Pan-American Union established

Section 1

Expanding Horizons

READ TO DISCOVER . . .

- what factors contributed to the growth of American imperialism.
- how the United States expanded its economic and political influence in the late 1800s.

TERMS TO LEARN

isolationism
expansionism
imperialism

The Storyteller

In the late 1800s and early 1900s, Americans looked beyond their borders and yearned for an empire. Merchants desired overseas markets, and adventurers wanted another frontier to conquer. Senator Albert Beveridge voiced the feelings of many when he proclaimed in 1900: "The Philippines are ours forever. . . . And just beyond the Philippines are China's illimitable markets. We will not retreat from either. . . . The Pacific is our ocean."

Patriotic song sheet, 1898

When President George Washington published his Farewell Address in 1796, he advised Americans to increase trade with other countries but to have "as little political connection as possible." Above all else, he warned Americans to "steer clear of permanent alliances with any portion of the foreign world."

These principles guided American foreign policy for about 100 years. However, various people interpreted Washington's words in different ways. Some believed he meant that the United States should follow a policy of **isolationism,** or noninvolvement, in world affairs. Others pointed out that Washington supported commercial ties and was not proposing complete isolation from the world.

American Foreign Policy

Americans have always had mixed feelings about their nation's role in world affairs. While striving to maintain their independence, merchants, farmers, and business leaders in the early United States relied on trade with other countries to obtain needed goods and to sell their own products.

American Expansionism

For many years Americans were absorbed in the dream of expanding their territory from ocean to ocean. Seeking land and better opportunities, many Americans moved to territories in the West

SECTION RESOURCES

Reproducible Masters

- Reproducible Lesson Plan 22–1
- Guided Reading Activity 22–1
- Section Quiz 22–1
- Reteaching Activity 22–1
- Enrichment Activity 22–1

Transparencies

- Section Focus Transparency 22–1

Multimedia

- Vocabulary PuzzleMaker
- Chapter Challenger Interactive Review Software
- Testmaker

1 FOCUS

BELLRINGER
Motivational Activity

Before taking roll at the beginning of the class period, project Section Focus Transparency 22–1 and have students answer the questions. Discuss students' responses.

This activity is also available as a blackline master.

Section Focus Transparency 22–1

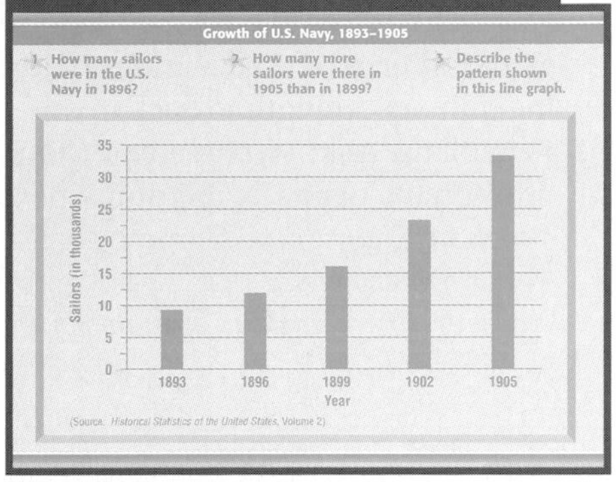

Vocabulary Precheck

Point out that all of the **Terms to Learn** end in *-ism.* Ask students to explain how each term suggests an *"ism"*—a theory that usually results in political or social action.

Use the **Vocabulary PuzzleMaker** to create crossword and word search puzzles.

Section Theme
Economic Factors

In the mid-1800s, Americans began to look beyond the nation's borders to overseas frontiers where they could expand trade and compete for political influence.

Activity Have students examine the song sheet pictured on this page. **Ask:** How did Americans feel about their country at this time? *(Answers may include a love for their country and perhaps a feeling that America was better than any other country.)*

CHAPTER 22
Section 1, 631–634

2 TEACH

L1 Responding to a Quote Have a volunteer read aloud the comments from George Washington's Farewell Address on page 631. Discuss what actions might constitute "political connection" and "permanent alliances with any portion of the foreign world."

HISTORY AND ART At first, Japanese officials ordered Perry's ships, including the frigates *Mississippi* and *Susquehanna,* to Nagasaki, the only port open to foreigners. Perry refused—and he had the military strength to back up his own plans. **Ask:** What do you think might have been the job of the person standing next to Commodore Perry? *(interpreter)*
Answer: *to ask Japan to open its ports to American ships*

Guided Reading Activity 22–1

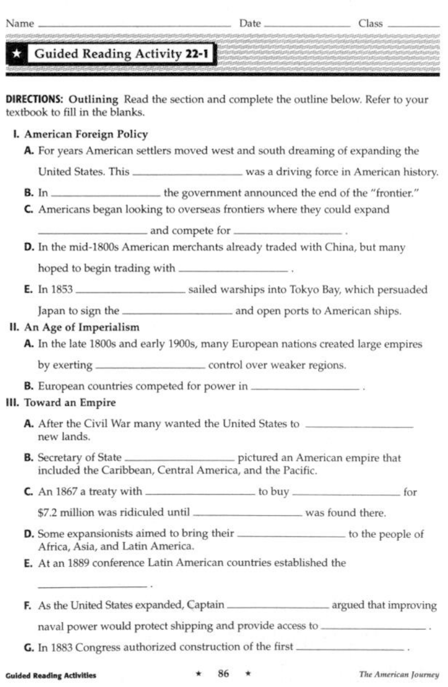
Name ______ Date ______ Class ______

★ Guided Reading Activity 22-1

DIRECTIONS: Outlining Read the section and complete the outline below. Refer to your textbook to fill in the blanks.

I. American Foreign Policy
- **A.** For years American settlers moved west and south dreaming of expanding the United States. This ______ was a driving force in American history.
- **B.** In ______ the government announced the end of the "frontier."
- **C.** Americans began looking to overseas frontiers where they could expand ______ and compete for ______.
- **D.** In the mid-1800s American merchants already traded with China, but many hoped to begin trading with ______.
- **E.** In 1853 ______ sailed warships into Tokyo Bay, which persuaded Japan to sign the ______ and open ports to American ships.

II. An Age of Imperialism
- **A.** In the late 1800s and early 1900s, many European nations created large empires by exerting ______ control over weaker regions.
- **B.** European countries competed for power in ______.

III. Toward an Empire
- **A.** After the Civil War many wanted the United States to ______ new lands.
- **B.** Secretary of State ______ pictured an American empire that included the Caribbean, Central America, and the Pacific.
- **C.** An 1867 a treaty with ______ to buy ______ for $7.2 million was ridiculed until ______ was found there.
- **D.** Some expansionists aimed to bring their ______ to the people of Africa, Asia, and Latin America.
- **E.** At an 1889 conference Latin American countries established the ______.
- **F.** As the United States expanded, Captain ______ argued that improving naval power would protect shipping and provide access to ______.
- **G.** In 1883 Congress authorized construction of the first ______.

Guided Reading Activities ★ 86 ★ *The American Journey*

HISTORY AND ART ***Perry's First Landing in Japan at Kurihama* by Gessan Ogata** A Japanese artist depicts Commodore Matthew Perry's 1853 arrival in Japan. **Why was Perry sent on a mission to Japan?**

and the South. This **expansionism** was a driving force in American history. While the nation was being torn apart during the Civil War, expansion came to a halt. After the war the United States began rebuilding and expanding again.

Americans settled the vast Great Plains, built railroads, and created large cities booming with people and busy factories. In 1890, as the nation spanned the North American continent from the Atlantic Ocean to the Pacific Ocean, the government issued a report announcing the end of the "frontier." Although areas of empty land remained, settlements could now be found from coast to coast.

To many Americans the frontier meant growth and opportunity. The idea that the frontier was no more was alarming. Americans began to look beyond the nation's borders to frontiers overseas where they could expand trade and compete for political influence.

Foreign Trade

In the mid-1800s, American merchants carried on a profitable trade with China and hoped to expand trade in other areas of the world. Many wanted to open trading relations with **Japan,** which had long been isolated from the West.

In 1853 President Millard Fillmore sent Commodore **Matthew Perry** on a mission to Japan. After steaming into Tokyo Bay with four warships, Perry asked the Japanese to open up their ports to U.S. ships. He told them he would return in several months for their answer.

The American show of force alarmed the Japanese. When Perry returned in 1854, the Japanese signed the **Treaty of Kanagawa** and opened two ports to American ships. Perry's successful mission began a period of trade between Japan and the United States. It also marked the start of greater American involvement in Asia.

An Age of Imperialism

The United States was not the only Western nation expanding its trade and influence in Asia and other parts of the world. The late 1800s and the early 1900s were called an age of **imperialism,** a time when powerful European nations created large empires by exercising economic and political control over weaker regions.

The search for materials and markets drove imperialism. The industrial nations of Europe needed raw materials from Asia and Africa. The

Linking PAST & PRESENT

Trade with Japan

The amount of goods exchanged between Japan and the United States has grown tremendously since the 1850s. By the mid-1990s, trade between the two nations totaled about $175 billion a year. After Canada, Japan is America's most important trading partner.

COOPERATIVE LEARNING ACTIVITY

Explaining Key Terms The words *isolationism, expansionism,* and *imperialism* are vital to this section, but they are rather abstract. Have groups choose various ways of making any two of these words more concrete for the rest of the class. For example, one group might create a painting to symbolize *isolationism* and perform a skit to illustrate *imperialism;* another group might present a choral reading about *expansionism* and plan a class game to demonstrate *imperialism.*

Europeans also sought new markets for the goods they manufactured. In their drive for raw materials and new markets, European powers competed with one another for power and influence in Asia and Africa.

Toward an Empire

American interest in political as well as economic expansion developed after the Civil War. Some Americans wanted the nation to build an empire. By annexing new lands, they argued, the United States would join the ranks of the world's great powers and take its rightful place at the center of power.

Secretary of State **William H. Seward,** appointed by Abraham Lincoln, supported this view. Seward pictured an American empire that dominated the Caribbean, Central America, and the Pacific. Holding this empire together would be a canal across Central America linking the Atlantic and Pacific Oceans, a thriving transcontinental railroad system, and rapid communication by means of the telegraph.

The Purchase of Alaska

Seward took a major step toward making his vision a reality with the purchase of **Alaska.** In 1867 Seward signed a treaty with Russia to buy the Russian colony for $7.2 million—an extraordinary bargain for a territory that was twice the size of Texas.

At the time many people ridiculed Seward's purchase. They regarded Alaska as a barren, icebound land. Newspapers mocked the purchase as "Seward's Ice Box" and a "polar bear garden." After gold was discovered in Alaska in the 1890s, however, Seward's "folly" began to seem more like a wise purchase. In 1912 Alaska became a territory of the United States.

A Sense of Mission

Some Americans had another reason for imperialist expansion. They had a sense of mission—a belief that they could "lift up" people they considered "uncivilized" by sharing Christianity and Western civilization with the rest of the world. **Josiah Strong,** a Congregational minister, proposed an "imperialism of righteousness," with Americans bringing their religion and their culture to the peoples of Africa, Asia, and the United States's closest neighbor, Latin America.

American Interest in Latin America

Since colonial times, the United States had carried on a flourishing trade with Latin America, including the Caribbean region. Fear of European influence in the region was a factor that led to the Monroe Doctrine in 1823, when President James

Picturing HISTORY Secretary of State William Seward (second from left) oversees the signing of the Alaska Purchase Treaty on March 30, 1867. **What country sold Alaska to the United States?**

Footnotes to History

Seward's Revenge At about 2 cents an acre, the purchase of Alaska has paid for itself many times over with the gold, copper, and oil resources discovered there. The "polar bear garden" became a literal "gold mine."

CHAPTER 22
Section 1, 631–634

3 ASSESS

Assign Section 1 Review as homework or as an in-class activity.

Use **Chapter Challenger Interactive Review Software** to review Section 1.

Section Quiz 22–1

Name ________ Date ________ Class ________

Chapter 22

Score

Section Quiz 22-1

DIRECTIONS: Matching Match each item in Column A with the items in Column B. Write the correct letters in the blanks. *(10 points each)*

Column A	Column B
____ 1. noninvolvement in world affairs	A. called for enlargement of navy
____ 2. began American involvement in Asia	B. isolationism
____ 3. Seward's "folly"	C. proposed an "imperialism of righteous"
____ 4. Josiah Strong	D. Treaty of Kanagawa
____ 5. Alfred Thayer Mahan	E. Alaska

DIRECTIONS: Multiple Choice In the blank at the left, write the letter of the choice that best completes the statement or answers the question. *(10 points each)*

____ 6. Powerful nations creating large empires by exercising economic and political control over weaker regions is called
A. expansionism. C. isolationism.
B. civilization. D. imperialism.

____ 7. Imperialism was driven by the search for
A. land. C. materials and markets.
B. gold. D. new trade routes.

____ 8. This man pictured a canal across Central America linking the Atlantic Ocean and the Pacific Ocean.
A. Matthew Perry C. James G. Blaine
B. William H. Seward D. Alfred Thayer Mahan

____ 9. The United States purchased Alaska from Russia for
A. $100 million. C. $3.5 million.
B. $10. D. $7.2 million.

____ 10. This man was responsible for establishing the Pan-American Union.
A. James G. Blaine C. Alfred Thayer Mahan
B. William H. Seward D. Matthew Perry

Section Quizzes ★ 86 ★ *The American Journey*

Picturing HISTORY The Senate approved the purchase of Alaska—whose other nicknames at the time included "Polaria," "Walrussia," and "Icebergia"—by only one vote.
Answer: *Russia*

MULTIPLE LEARNING STYLES

Visual/Spatial Use a map of the world to help students understand Seward's vision of an American empire. Call on volunteers to locate the Caribbean Sea, Central America, and the Pacific Ocean. Allow students to share what they know about countries in these areas. Remind them that Seward also envisioned a canal that would cross Central America, linking the Atlantic and Pacific Oceans. Ask students to look closely at Central America and point out one or more practical routes for the canal. (Students will read of the actual location of the canal in Section 4.) **L1, ELL**

CHAPTER 22
Section 1, 631–634

Reteaching Activity 22–1

Name ____________ Date ________ Class ________

★ Reteaching Activity 22-1

DIRECTIONS: Putting Events in Sequence Number the events in the order in which they occurred.

____ **A.** Alaska becomes a territory of the United States.
____ **B.** The Japanese sign the Treaty of Kanagawa and open two ports to American ships.
____ **C.** The Pan-American Union is established.
____ **D.** American expansion comes to a temporary halt.
____ **E.** In a response to a plea from Captain Alfred Thayer Mahan for improving and enlarging the navy, Congress authorizes construction of the first steel-hulled warships.
____ **F.** Commodore Matthew Perry, sent by President Millard Fillmore, steams into Tokyo Bay with four warships.
____ **G.** Secretary of State James G. Blaine invites Latin American countries to attend a Pan-American Conference in Washington, D.C.
____ **H.** George Washington publishes his Farewell Address, which is interpreted by many Americans to support a policy of isolationism.
____ **I.** Secretary of State William H. Seward signs a treaty with Russia, purchasing Alaska for $7.2 million.
____ **J.** With settlements spanning the United States from coast to coast, the government issues a report announcing the end of the frontier.

DIRECTIONS: Essay On a separate sheet of paper, answer the questions below.

1. What drove imperialism in the late 1800s and the early 1900s?
2. Describe the American empire envisioned by William H. Seward.
3. Why was Seward's purchase of Alaska viewed as a "folly" by many Americans? What changed their minds?
4. Describe another reason, held by Josiah Strong and other Americans, for imperialist expansion.

Reteaching Activities ★ 86 ★ *The American Journey*

Enrichment Activity 22–1

Name ____________ Date ________ Class ________

★ Enrichment Activity 22-1 ★

Opening Japanese Trade

In 1853 President Millard Fillmore sent a public letter with Commodore Matthew C. Perry to His Imperial Majesty, the Emperor of Japan. Fillmore was interested in opening trade relations with Japan. Read the following excerpts from this letter, paying attention to the techniques the president used to try to influence the Japanese.

> . . . Our great state of California produces about sixty millions of dollars in gold, every year, besides silver, quicksilver, precious stones, and many other valuable articles. Japan is also a rich and fertile country, and produces many very valuable articles. Your Imperial Majesty's subjects are skilled in many of the arts. . . .(1)
>
> . . . Many of our ships pass every year from California to China; and great numbers of our people pursue the whale fishery near the shores of Japan. It sometimes happens in stormy weather that one of our ships is wrecked on your Imperial Majesty's shores. . . . (2)
>
> Commodore Perry is also directed by me to represent to your Imperial Majesty that we understand there is a great abundance of coal and provisions in the empire of Japan. Our steam-ships, in crossing the great ocean, burn a great deal of coal, and it is not convenient to bring it all the way from America. . . . (3)
>
> SOURCE: Reynolds, Robert L. *Perry in Japan.* American Heritage Publishing Company, Inc., New York.

Activity **DIRECTIONS:** The president continued each of the paragraphs above with a description of what he expected from Japan. On the lines below, finish each paragraph with the words that you think President Fillmore might have used. Then practice saying each paragraph in a speech that President Fillmore might have given if he had visited Japan and delivered his message in person. Give your speech in front of a group of classmates. Whose speech was the most persuasive? Why?

(1) ____________
(2) ____________
(3) ____________

Enrichment Activities ★ 86 ★ *The American Journey*

Monroe warned European nations not to attempt to establish new colonies in North or South America.

United States merchants used the Monroe Doctrine to their advantage. In 1884 **James G. Blaine,** then the Republican nominee for president, declared:

> "While the great powers of Europe are steadily enlarging their colonial domination in Asia and Africa, it is the [particular] province of this country to improve and expand its trade with the nations of America."

Meanwhile, the United States signed treaties with a number of Latin American countries, allowing American businesses to influence those nations' economies.

As secretary of state in 1889, Blaine invited Latin American countries to attend a Pan-American Conference held in Washington, D.C. Blaine hoped to develop economic and political ties among the nations of the region. Although many Latin American countries worried about American domination, they decided to attend the meeting. The conference did establish the **Pan-American Union** to share information among member nations.

Building Sea Power

As the United States looked to expand its horizons, Captain **Alfred Thayer Mahan,** president of the Naval War College, called for improving and enlarging the navy. Mahan argued that sea power would protect shipping and provide access to world markets. "Sea power is essential to the greatness of every splendid people," Mahan declared. To maintain a powerful navy, the United States would need overseas colonies where ships could be refueled.

Transforming and expanding the navy began in 1883, when Congress authorized construction of the first steel-hulled warships. In the following years, the navy gradually shifted from sails to steam power and from wood to steel hulls. By the early 1900s, the United States had the naval power it needed to back up an expanded role in foreign affairs.

Senator Albert Beveridge of Indiana summed up the feeling of many American expansionists:

> "We will establish trading posts throughout the world as distributing points for American products. We will cover the ocean with our merchant marine. We will build a navy to the measure of our greatness. . . ."

Section 1 Review

Checking for Understanding

1. ***Identify*** Matthew Perry, William H. Seward, James G. Blaine, Pan-American Union, Alfred Thayer Mahan.
2. ***Define*** isolationism, expansionism, imperialism.
3. ***Discuss*** the main points of the Monroe Doctrine.

Reviewing Themes

4. **Economic Factors** What two economic needs drove American imperialism?

Critical Thinking

5. **Identifying Assumptions** Some Americans who favored imperialist expansion believed it was their mission to "civilize" the "uncivilized" people of the world. What do you think these people meant by the term *uncivilized?*

Activity

Making a Resource Map Research the natural resources of Alaska. Draw a map of the state and use symbols to represent each resource and show its location in the state.

Section 1 Review Answers

1. Matthew Perry, 632; William H. Seward, 633; James G. Blaine, 634; Pan-American Union, 634; Alfred Thayer Mahan, 634
2. The words are defined in the Glossary.
3. It was a warning to European nations to keep them from establishing colonies in North and South America.
4. the need for raw materials and new markets
5. Students should recognize that "uncivilized" essentially meant "not conforming to the American way of life" and/or "not practicing an 'acceptable' religion (that is, in the Judeo-Christian tradition)."

Activity Maps should include symbols to represent Alaska's main resources: oil, gas, forests, and fish.

4 CLOSE

Have students complete these sentences and discuss their responses. The United States became imperialistic because _____. Because the United States became imperialistic, _____.

1890 | 1900 | 1910

1893 American planters overthrow Queen Liliuokalani

1899 U.S., Britain, and Germany divide Samoa

1900 Hawaii becomes a U.S. territory

1907 The Great White Fleet begins its voyage

Section 2

Imperialism in the Pacific

READ TO DISCOVER . . .

- how the United States gained control of Hawaii and Samoa.
- how competition for influence in China and the Pacific region led to new policies.

TERMS TO LEARN

annexation
spheres of influence
Open Door policy

The Storyteller

As more Americans arrived in Honolulu, many Hawaiians feared that time was running out for their people. Kaona, a local judge in Honolulu, had visions that the end of the world was near. When volcanoes erupted and earth tremors plagued the island, his visions seemed to be coming true. Kaona and his followers prepared for the end. They dressed in flowing white robes and prayed loudly. Kaona had indeed been correct. The world that he and native Hawaiians had known would soon end.

Hawaiian stamp

Secretary of State **William H. Seward** believed the United States could build its empire through peaceful means, with American trade leading the way. The Pacific region played a key part in Seward's plan for expansion. In 1867—the same year he bought Alaska—Seward acquired the two small Pacific islands of **Midway.** He thought that these islands, more than 3,000 miles (4,800 km) west of California, would serve as an important stopping place for American ships en route to China.

American merchants and the United States Navy would need more than two small islands, however, to establish a secure foothold in the vast stretches of the Pacific. Seward believed the United States should also acquire **Hawaii.**

Geography

Hawaii

The lush Hawaiian Islands, a chain of 8 large and 100 or so smaller islands, lay about 2,000 miles (3,200 km) west of California. The Hawaiian people dwelled in independent communities, each with its own chieftain, and lived by farming and fishing. American trading ships and whalers often stopped at the islands to take on supplies and fresh water.

In the 1790s Americans began trading with the Hawaiians for local resources such as sandalwood, which the Americans traded in China. About that same time, King Kamehameha I unified the islands. Villages with good ports such as

SECTION RESOURCES

Reproducible Masters
- Reproducible Lesson Plan 22–2
- Guided Reading Activity 22–2
- Section Quiz 22–2
- Reteaching Activity 22–2
- Enrichment Activity 22–2

Transparencies
- Section Focus Transparency 22–2

Multimedia
- Vocabulary PuzzleMaker
- Chapter Challenger Interactive Review Software
- Testmaker
- The Presidents: A Picture History of Our Nation
- Picture Atlas of the World

1 FOCUS

BELLRINGER
Motivational Activity

Before taking roll at the beginning of the class period, project Section Focus Transparency 22–2 and have students answer the questions. Discuss students' responses.

This activity is also available as a blackline master.

Section Focus Transparency 22–2

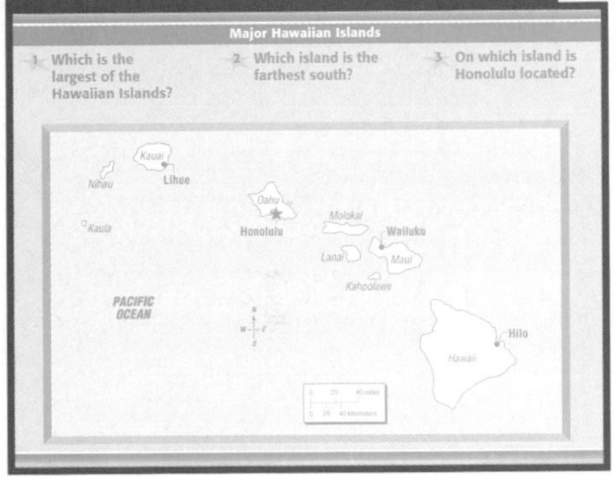

Vocabulary Precheck

Have students speculate on the meaning of each item in **Terms to Learn.** Have them check their answers by finding the terms in the textbook glossary.

Use the **Vocabulary PuzzleMaker** to create crossword and word search puzzles.

Section Theme
Geography and History

Imperialistic impulses moved the United States to exert its influence in China and the Pacific region.

Activity Have students list some nonmilitary reasons for one country to forge a relationship with another. *(Students should suggest economic reasons—that is, one country has a resource that another country wants.)*

2 TEACH

L1, ELL Evaluating Issues Have students locate Samoa and China on a world map. Discuss why people in the United States care about what happens in these parts of the world.

Guided Reading Activity 22–2

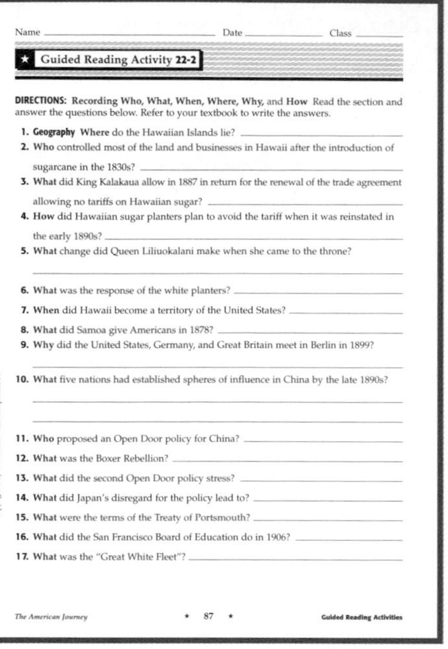
Name ______ Date ______ Class ______

★ Guided Reading Activity 22-2

DIRECTIONS: Recording Who, What, When, Where, Why, and How Read the section and answer the questions below. Refer to your textbook to write the answers.

1. **Geography Where** do the Hawaiian Islands lie? ______
2. **Who** controlled most of the land and businesses in Hawaii after the introduction of sugarcane in the 1830s? ______
3. **What** did King Kalakaua allow in 1887 in return for the renewal of the trade agreement allowing no tariffs on Hawaiian sugar? ______
4. **How** did Hawaiian sugar planters plan to avoid the tariff when it was reinstated in the early 1890s? ______
5. **What** change did Queen Liliuokalani make when she came to the throne? ______
6. **What** was the response of the white planters? ______
7. **When** did Hawaii become a territory of the United States? ______
8. **What** did Samoa give Americans in 1878? ______
9. **Why** did the United States, Germany, and Great Britain meet in Berlin in 1899? ______
10. **What** five nations had established spheres of influence in China by the late 1890s? ______
11. **Who** proposed an Open Door policy for China? ______
12. **What** was the Boxer Rebellion? ______
13. **What** did the second Open Door policy stress? ______
14. **What** did Japan's disregard for the policy lead to? ______
15. **What** were the terms of the Treaty of Portsmouth? ______
16. **What** did the San Francisco Board of Education do in 1906? ______
17. **What** was the "Great White Fleet"? ______

The American Journey ★ 87 ★ **Guided Reading Activities**

★ Picturing HISTORY Because Japan did not allow emigration until 1885, the number of Japanese workers in Hawaii was relatively small. After the ban was lifted, however, Hawaii saw a rapid increase in the number of Japanese contract workers.
Answer: *Hawaii became a territory of the United States.*

NATIONAL GEOGRAPHIC SOCIETY

CD-ROM
The Presidents: A Picture History of Our Nation

Have students click on Grover Cleveland's second term to see what was happening in the world when the Hawaiian monarchy was overthrown.

Honolulu and **Lahaina** (luh•HY•nuh) began to grow in importance, and trade increased. However, American and European ships also brought infectious diseases to the islands. These diseases devastated the island population just as they had once devastated the Native Americans.

Missionaries and Sugar Growers

In 1820 Christian missionaries from the United States began arriving in Hawaii. They established schools, created a written Hawaiian alphabet, and translated the Bible into Hawaiian. Increasing numbers of American merchants in the whaling trade came to settle there, too.

An American firm introduced sugarcane in Hawaii in the 1830s, and the missionaries and traders began buying land and establishing sugar plantations. The sugar industry grew quickly, and plantation owners brought in thousands of immigrants from Japan, China, and other Pacific lands to work in the fields. Gradually the Americans took control of most of the land and businesses. They also exerted strong influence in Hawaiian politics, serving as advisers to the Hawaiian ruling family. Although the United States recognized Hawaiian independence in 1842, the islands came increasingly under American influence.

In 1875 the United States agreed to allow Hawaiian sugar to enter the country without tariffs. As sugar exports to the United States soared, American planters in Hawaii reaped enormous profits. In 1887, in return for renewal of the trade agreement, the United States pressured King Kalakaua (kah•LAH•KAH•u•ah) to allow it to establish a naval base at **Pearl Harbor,** the best seaport in the islands.

In the early 1890s, under pressure from American sugar producers, Congress revised the tariff laws and eliminated the exemption for Hawaiian sugar. As a result, Hawaiian sugar planters had to drop their prices drastically in order to sell any sugar. Sugar exports to the United States dropped sharply. Facing financial ruin, the planters plotted a way to avoid the new tariff. They decided to make Hawaii a territory of the United States.

American Planters' Revolt

The Hawaiians, meanwhile, had begun to resist the growing influence of Americans. In 1891 Queen **Liliuokalani** (lih•LEE•uh•woh•kuh•LAH•nee) came to the throne. The new ruler wanted Hawaiians to regain economic control of their islands, and she took away powers that the American sugar planters had held. In response, the white planters overthrew Liliuokalani and set up their own **provisional,** or temporary,

Queen Liliuokalani

★ Picturing HISTORY Japanese workers tended the boiler furnaces of Hawaii's American-run sugar industry. **What happened to Hawaii in 1900?**

Cooperative Learning Activity

Debating Organize students into two groups. Ask one group to take the view that overseas expansion is in the best interest of the nation. Have the other group take the opposite viewpoint. Both groups should prepare arguments supporting their views. When students have prepared their arguments, have the debate and encourage students to ask questions. Then have the class vote *yes* or *no* for expansion based on the most convincing arguments.

government in 1893. The queen left under protest: "Now, to avoid any collision of armed forces and perhaps the loss of life, I . . . yield my authority."

Annexation

The success of the planters' revolt stemmed in part from the support of the chief American diplomat in Hawaii, **John Stevens,** who arranged for marines from the warship *Boston* to assist in the uprising. Stevens immediately recognized the new government, which sent a delegation to Washington to seek a treaty of **annexation** that would add Hawaii to the United States. President Benjamin Harrison signed the treaty during the final days of his administration and forwarded it to the Senate for approval.

However, the Senate did not act quickly enough. It failed to ratify the treaty before Harrison left office. The new president, **Grover Cleveland,** opposed annexation and withdrew the treaty from the Senate after discovering that Hawaiians did not support the revolt. Cleveland called American interference in the Hawaiian revolution "disgraceful."

Although most of the Hawaiians and the Asian immigrants in Hawaii opposed annexation, their opposition made no difference. A small, powerful group of American sugar growers, traders, and missionaries—and their Hawaiian allies, along with influential people in the United States—had the final word. Congress approved the annexation of Hawaii in 1898, after William McKinley became president. In 1900 Hawaii became a territory of the United States.

United States Overseas Possessions, 1900

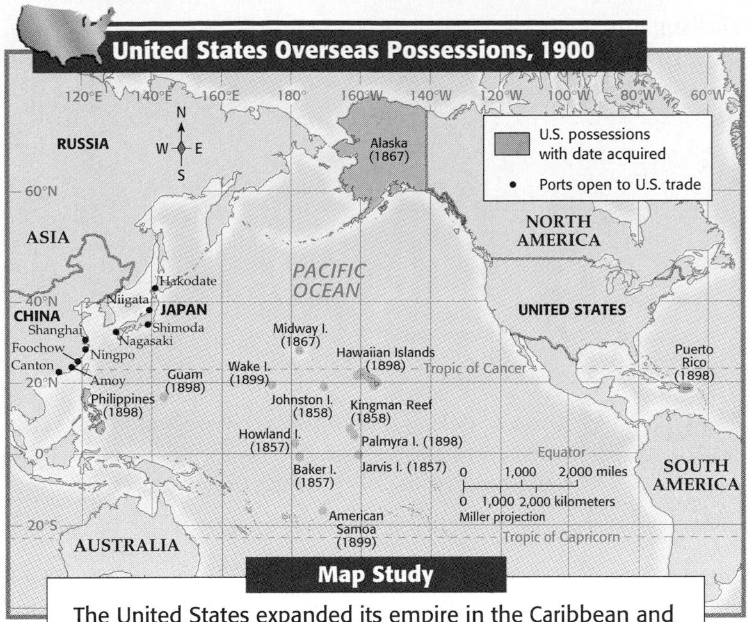

Map Study

The United States expanded its empire in the Caribbean and the Pacific from the 1850s to 1900.

1. **Location** Locate Puerto Rico, Guam, and the Philippines. Which of these is the farthest from the continental United States?
2. **Analyzing Information** When were the Hawaiian Islands acquired?

The Islands of Samoa

About 3,000 miles (4,800 km) south of Hawaii lay the **Samoa Islands,** directly on the trade route linking Australia and the United States. As early as the 1830s, missionaries from the United States landed in Samoa and began converting the people to Christianity.

In 1878 Samoa agreed to give Americans special trading rights and permission to build a naval station at the port of **Pago Pago.** Great Britain and Germany also wanted a stake in the Samoa Islands, and they secured trading rights, too. During the 1880s, tensions mounted as the three rivals competed for power in Samoa.

In 1899 the United States, Great Britain, and Germany met in Berlin and—without consulting the Samoans—decided to divide up the islands. The United States and Germany split Samoa between them, while Great Britain agreed to

L2, ELL Making a Time Line Have students create and illustrate a time line (using poster paints or markers) showing the relationship between the United States and Hawaii. Students may divide the time line according to different stages of that relationship.

Map Study

Answers

1. the Philippines
2. 1898

Map Skills Practice

Reading a Map What territories had the United States already acquired before the Civil War? *(Howland Island, Baker Island, Jarvis Island, Johnston Island, and Kingman Reef)*

you don't say...

Annexation The word *annex* comes from Latin and literally means "to bind to."

NATIONAL GEOGRAPHIC SOCIETY

CD-ROM
NGS PictureShow: Picture Atlas of the World

Students can view Oceania by clicking on the media button of various islands in the region.

MULTIPLE LEARNING STYLES

Auditory/Musical To help keep students' attention from wandering during classroom discussion, interrupt the discussion occasionally with the announcement of a "pop listening quiz." Award "listening points" to students who have been paying attention and answer the quiz questions correctly. For example, if the class is discussing the annexation of Hawaii, pop the question, "Who pushed for the annexation of Hawaii—President Grover Cleveland, American sugar growers, or the Hawaiian people themselves? Why?" **L1**

What?Where?When?Who?

Spheres of Influence In China each sphere of influence centered on a port city known as a "leasehold." John Hay's Open Door policy, discussed on page 638, was a specific request that the leaseholds controlled by various countries be kept open to vessels from all nations.

HISTORY AND ART The Boxers' violent rebellion was sparked by a rumor that Westerners were planning to dismantle a Chinese monument. Most of the foreigners who died in the uprising were Christian missionaries and their families. **Ask:** **Why did the Boxers rebel?** *(to try to stop the influence of Westerners—"foreign devils"—in China)* **Answer:** *an open door policy under which each foreign nation in China could trade freely in the other nations' spheres of influence*

3 ASSESS

Assign Section 2 Review as homework or as an in-class activity.

Use **Chapter Challenger Interactive Review Software** to review Section 2.

Section Quiz 22–2

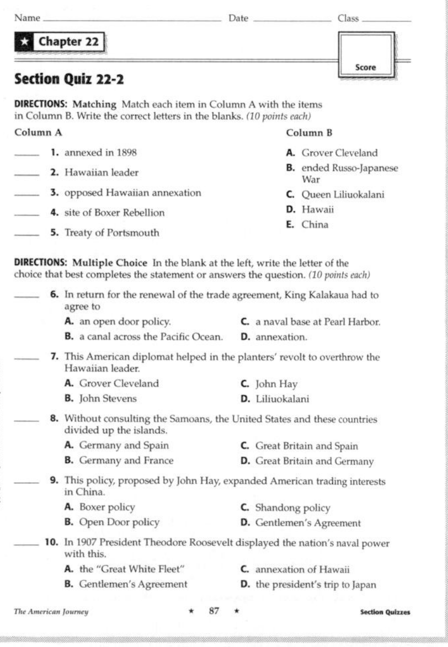

Name ________ Date ________ Class ________

Chapter 22

Score

Section Quiz 22-2

DIRECTIONS: Matching Match each item in Column A with the items in Column B. Write the correct letters in the blanks. *(10 points each)*

Column A	Column B
____ 1. annexed in 1898	A. Grover Cleveland
____ 2. Hawaiian leader	B. ended Russo-Japanese War
____ 3. opposed Hawaiian annexation	C. Queen Liliuokalani
____ 4. site of Boxer Rebellion	D. Hawaii
____ 5. Treaty of Portsmouth	E. China

DIRECTIONS: Multiple Choice In the blank at the left, write the letter of the choice that best completes the statement or answers the question. *(10 points each)*

____ 6. In return for the renewal of the trade agreement, King Kalakaua had to agree to
A. an open door policy. C. a naval base at Pearl Harbor.
B. a canal across the Pacific Ocean. D. annexation.

____ 7. This American diplomat helped in the planters' revolt to overthrow the Hawaiian leader.
A. Grover Cleveland C. John Hay
B. John Stevens D. Liliuokalani

____ 8. Without consulting the Samoans, the United States and these countries divided up the islands.
A. Germany and Spain C. Great Britain and Spain
B. Germany and France D. Great Britain and Germany

____ 9. This policy, proposed by John Hay, expanded American trading interests in China.
A. Boxer policy C. Shandong policy
B. Open Door policy D. Gentlemen's Agreement

____ 10. In 1907 President Theodore Roosevelt displayed the nation's naval power with this.
A. the "Great White Fleet" C. annexation of Hawaii
B. Gentlemen's Agreement D. the president's trip to Japan

Copyright © by The McGraw-Hill Companies, Inc.

The American Journey ★ 87 ★ Section Quizzes

Who?What?Where?When?

Roosevelt Firsts In 1904 Roosevelt won the Nobel Peace Prize—the first American to do so—for his work in ending the Russo-Japanese War. Roosevelt also was the first president to ride in an automobile and travel outside the United States.

HISTORY AND ART ***View of Peking After the Boxer Rebellion* by Yoshikazu Ichikawa** American soldiers march through the Chinese capital after the Boxer Rebellion. **What policy did the United States want for China?**

withdraw from the area in return for rights on other Pacific islands. The Americans annexed their portion of Samoa the same year.

China and the Open Door

For Americans the island territories in the Pacific, while important in themselves, represented stepping-stones to a larger prize—**China.** Torn apart by warring factions and lacking industry, China was too weak to resist the efforts of foreign powers that wanted to exploit its vast resources and markets.

Rivalries in China

By the late 1890s, Japan and the leading European powers had carved out **spheres of influence** in China—sections of the country where each of the foreign nations enjoyed special rights and powers. Japan held the island of Formosa and parts of the Chinese mainland. Germany controlled the Shandong area in east-central China. Great Britain and France held a number of Chinese provinces, and Russia moved into **Manchuria** and other areas in northern China.

In the United States, some government and business leaders worried about being squeezed out of the profitable China trade. Although the United States could not force the other foreign powers out of China, Secretary of State **John Hay** wanted to protect and expand American trading interests in the country. Hay proposed an **Open Door policy** under which each foreign nation in China could trade freely in the other nations' spheres of influence.

The Boxer Rebellion

The other major powers were reluctant to accept a policy that would benefit the United States most of all. The situation soon changed, however. By late 1899 a secret Chinese martial art society, known as the **Boxers,** led a violent uprising against the "foreign devils" in China. About 200 foreigners died in the **Boxer Rebellion;** for nearly 2 months, hundreds more were trapped in the besieged capital city of **Beijing.** Finally, in August 1900, foreign troops broke the siege and defeated the Boxers.

Out of the Boxer Rebellion came a second Open Door proposal, which stressed the importance of maintaining China's independence and respecting its borders. Alarmed by the rebellion, the other foreign powers accepted Hay's policy. They also forced China to sign new commercial treaties as compensation for the rebellion's damage.

MAKING CONNECTIONS ACTIVITY

Cultural Life The islands of Hawaii were a source of fascination for many Americans. The food, music, dance, and clothing of Hawaiians were displayed at fairs and expositions. What was shown to the public, however, was *not* indigenous to Hawaii's culture. Ask interested students to research just how "Hawaiian" the following items are:

- muumuus (actually based on a style of dress introduced to Hawaiian women by missionaries)
- pineapples (transplanted from the West Indies)
- ukuleles (brought to Hawaii by workers from Portugal) **L2**

★ ★

Japan

Eager to expand its power in Asia, Japan began to ignore the Open Door policy. Japan's actions led to war with Russia and conflict with the United States.

Russo-Japanese War

In the early 1900s, Japan and Russia clashed over their interest in Manchuria, a Chinese province rich in natural resources. On February 8, 1904, Japan launched an attack on the Russian fleet at **Port Arthur** in southern Manchuria, starting the **Russo-Japanese War.** The Japanese scored a series of victories, destroying the Russian fleet. By the spring of 1905, both Japan's and Russia's resources were nearly exhausted, and both countries were eager to make peace. President **Theodore Roosevelt** offered to meet with their leaders in **Portsmouth, New Hampshire,** to help settle the conflict. In September 1905, Japan and Russia signed the **Treaty of Portsmouth,** which recognized Japan's control of Korea in return for a pledge by Japan to halt its expansion.

Roosevelt hoped the treaty would preserve a balance of power in Asia, but it failed to do so. Japan emerged from the war as the strongest naval power in the Pacific, and it challenged the United States for influence in the region. Relations between the two nations deteriorated steadily.

Strained Relations

During the Russo-Japanese War, Japanese immigration to the United States—especially to California—increased. Many Americans resented the Japanese newcomers, claiming that they took jobs from Americans. Anti-Asian feeling mounted.

As you read in Chapter 21, in 1906 the San Francisco Board of Education ordered that all Asian students attend separate schools. The Japanese government protested. An 1894 treaty had guaranteed that Japanese living in the United States would be treated well. The Japanese felt that the treaty had been broken.

President Roosevelt forced the San Francisco school board to change its policies. In return, he persuaded Japan to consent to a **gentlemen's agreement,** promising to restrict emigration. The Japanese resented the Gentlemen's Agreement and relations between the two nations worsened. Some Americans called for war.

The "Great White Fleet"

Although President Roosevelt had no plan for war, in 1907 he sent 16 gleaming white battleships on a cruise around the world to display the nation's naval power. The **"Great White Fleet"** greatly impressed the Japanese. By the time the fleet returned to America in 1909, the United States and Japan had resolved many of their differences.

Section 2 Review

Checking for Understanding

1. ***Identify*** Liliuokalani, John Hay, Gentlemen's Agreement, Great White Fleet.
2. ***Define*** annexation, spheres of influence, Open Door policy.
3. ***Name*** three Pacific islands that the United States acquired in the late 1800s and early 1900s.

Reviewing Themes

4. **Geography and History** Why were American political leaders so interested in the Pacific islands in the late 1800s?

Critical Thinking

5. **Making Inferences** Why do you think Roosevelt considered the cruise of the Great White Fleet to be "the most important service [he] rendered for peace"?

Activity

Making a Diagram Research the process of turning sugarcane into refined sugar. Draw a diagram showing the steps involved.

CHAPTER 22
Section 2, 635–639

Reteaching Activity 22–2

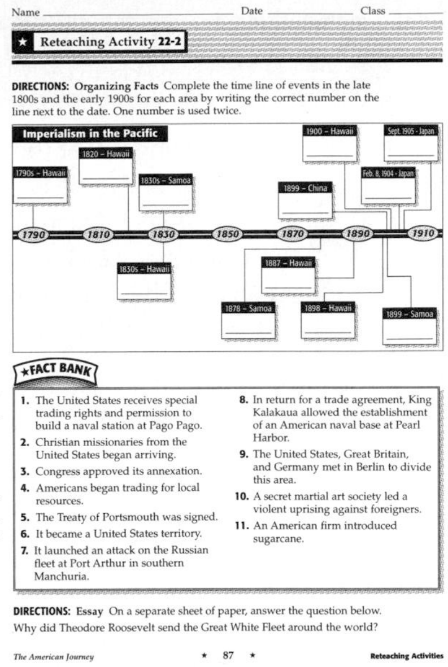
Name ______ Date ______ Class ______

★ Reteaching Activity 22-2

DIRECTIONS: Organizing Facts Complete the time line of events in the late 1800s and the early 1900s for each area by writing the correct number on the line next to the date. One number is used twice.

★FACT BANK

1. The United States receives special trading rights and permission to build a naval station at Pago Pago.
2. Christian missionaries from the United States began arriving.
3. Congress approved its annexation.
4. Americans began trading for local resources.
5. The Treaty of Portsmouth was signed.
6. It became a United States territory.
7. It launched an attack on the Russian fleet at Port Arthur in southern Manchuria.
8. In return for a trade agreement, King Kalakaua allowed the establishment of an American naval base at Pearl Harbor.
9. The United States, Great Britain, and Germany met in Berlin to divide this area.
10. A secret martial art society led a violent uprising against foreigners.
11. An American firm introduced sugarcane.

DIRECTIONS: Essay On a separate sheet of paper, answer the question below.
Why did Theodore Roosevelt send the Great White Fleet around the world?

The American Journey ★ 87 ★ **Reteaching Activities**

Enrichment Activity 22–2

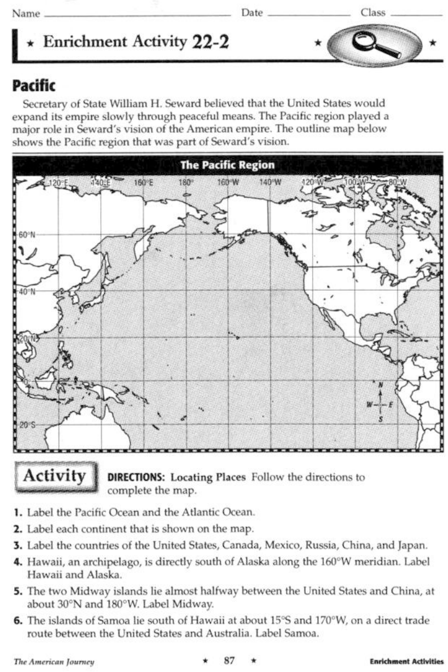
Name ______ Date ______ Class ______

★ Enrichment Activity 22-2 ★ ★

Pacific

Secretary of State William H. Seward believed that the United States would expand its empire slowly through peaceful means. The Pacific region played a major role in Seward's vision of the American empire. The outline map below shows the Pacific region that was part of Seward's vision.

Activity **DIRECTIONS: Locating Places** Follow the directions to complete the map.

1. Label the Pacific Ocean and the Atlantic Ocean.
2. Label each continent that is shown on the map.
3. Label the countries of the United States, Canada, Mexico, Russia, China, and Japan.
4. Hawaii, an archipelago, is directly south of Alaska along the 160°W meridian. Label Hawaii and Alaska.
5. The two Midway islands lie almost halfway between the United States and China, at about 30°N and 180°W. Label Midway.
6. The islands of Samoa lie south of Hawaii at about 15°S and 170°W, on a direct trade route between the United States and Australia. Label Samoa.

The American Journey ★ 87 ★ **Enrichment Activities**

Section 2 Review Answers

1. Liliuokalani, 636; John Hay, 638; Gentlemen's Agreement, 639; Great White Fleet, 639
2. The words are defined in the Glossary.
3. Midway, Hawaii, Samoa
4. The islands were stepping-stones to Asian nations and links for increasing trade.
5. It was a display of naval power that convinced many nations, especially Japan, that the United States was powerful and that challenging it in war would be unwise.

Activity Diagrams should clearly show the steps involved in turning sugarcane into refined sugar and should give evidence of student research.

4 CLOSE

Have students use this section to brainstorm reasons for and against imperialism.

CHAPTER 22
Section 3, 640–644

1 FOCUS

BELLRINGER
Motivational Activity

Before taking roll at the beginning of the class period, project Section Focus Transparency 22–3 and have students answer the questions. Discuss students' responses.

This activity is also available as a blackline master.

Section Focus Transparency 22–3

Vocabulary Precheck

Discuss the term *yellow journalism*. Ask for examples of reporting that students consider present-day yellow journalism.

Use the **Vocabulary PuzzleMaker** to create crossword and word search puzzles.

Section Theme
Continuity and Change

Through the Spanish-American War, an American empire had become a reality, and with the empire came new responsibilities.

Activity Have students look at the map on page 642 and comment on the two fronts of the Spanish-American War. Discuss why the United States found both fronts important to its own interests.

1894 — 1896 — 1898 — 1900

1895 José Martí leads revolt in Cuba

1897 William McKinley becomes president

1898 The *Maine* explodes; the Spanish-American War takes place

1900 Foraker Act sets up new government in Puerto Rico

Section 3

Spanish-American War

READ TO DISCOVER . . .

- why the Spanish-American War began.
- what territory the United States gained in the war.
- how the United States's role in the world expanded after the Spanish-American War.

TERMS TO LEARN

yellow journalism
protectorate
armistice

The Storyteller

Spanish authorities arrested José, a young Cuban teenager, for supporting Cuban independence. They sentenced him to hard labor in Havana's stone quarry. At the stone quarry, an angry guard struck José with a heavy iron chain, causing him to walk with a limp for the rest of his life. But young José wrote a play in which the main character stated: "I will be the one to free my anguished country." José Martí would, indeed, be the one to lead his people to independence from Spain.

Cuban patriot José Martí

The people of **Cuba** had lived under Spanish rule for centuries. Several times in the late 1800s, the Cubans rebelled. But each time, the Spanish overpowered them and smashed their dreams of independence. **José Martí,** one of the heroes of the Cuban independence movement, fled to the United States to gather money, arms, and troops. In 1895, as economic conditions in Cuba worsened, Martí returned to Cuba to lead his people in a new revolt.

The Cuban Rebellion

Martí's revolution led to terrible losses in human life and property. The rebels burned sugarcane fields and destroyed buildings in hopes of forcing the Spaniards to leave. In retaliation Spanish troops herded more than 300,000 Cubans into fortified towns and camps to separate them from the rebels and to break their morale. Thousands of Cubans died of starvation and disease.

War Fever

The Cuban people's struggle against Spain attracted much sympathy in the United States. Businesspeople worried about the destruction of trade and their loss of investments in Cuba. Government leaders were concerned about a rebellion so close to the United States. Finally, many Americans were horrified by the atrocities against Cuban citizens and called for the government to do something about it.

SECTION RESOURCES

Reproducible Masters
- Reproducible Lesson Plan 22–3
- Guided Reading Activity 22–3
- Section Quiz 22–3
- Reteaching Activity 22–3
- Enrichment Activity 22–3

Transparencies
- Section Focus Transparency 22–3

Multimedia
- Vocabulary PuzzleMaker
- Chapter Challenger Interactive Review
- Testmaker
- GTV: A Geographic Perspective on American History
- Facts On File: Landmark Documents in American History
- American Music Cultural Traditions

President Grover Cleveland opposed any American involvement in Cuba. In March 1897, **William McKinley** became president. He, too, hoped the conflict could be settled peacefully.

The American press reported the unfolding tragedy in Cuba in graphic detail, and its coverage intensified the debate over America's role in the crisis. Newspapers, including **Joseph Pulitzer's** *World* and **William Randolph Hearst's** *Journal,* tried to outdo each other with shocking reports on the revolution. Hearst supposedly told an artist who was illustrating a story on Cuba, "You furnish the pictures, and I'll furnish the war." This type of sensational, biased, and often false reporting—known as **yellow journalism**—played a major role in fanning the flames of prowar sentiment in the United States.

"Remember the *Maine*"

The pressure on President McKinley to take action seemed to grow by the hour. After rioting broke out in the Cuban capital of Havana in January 1898, McKinley sent the battleship *Maine* to protect the lives and property of American citizens.

The ship remained quietly at anchor in Havana Harbor for 3 weeks. Then, on the night of February 15, 1898, an enormous explosion shattered the *Maine,* killing about 260 officers and crew members. American newspapers immediately blamed the Spanish, and the slogan "Remember the *Maine*" became a rallying cry for revenge. Spain denied responsibility for the explosion. Much later, evidence indicated that the explosion may have been accidental, but at the time, Americans clamored for war with Spain.

After the *Maine* incident, President McKinley sent the Spanish a strong note demanding a truce and an end to brutality against the Cubans. The Spanish agreed to some American demands, but not enough to satisfy McKinley or Congress. On April 19 Congress recognized Cuban independence. It also demanded the withdrawal of Spanish forces and authorized the president to use the army and navy to enforce American aims. On April 25, 1898, Congress declared war on Spain.

War in the Philippines

Although events in Cuba triggered the Spanish-American War, the war's first military actions happened thousands of miles away in the Spanish colony of the **Philippines.** These islands served as a base for part of the Spanish fleet. In late February 1898, Assistant Secretary of the Navy **Theodore Roosevelt** had wired Commodore **George Dewey** and his squadron of navy vessels to prepare for action in the Philippines "in the event of declaration of war." In the early morning hours of May 1, Dewey launched a surprise attack on the Spanish fleet in Manila Bay, destroying most of the ships.

American troops arrived in July. With the help of Filipino rebels led by **Emilio Aguinaldo** (AH•gee•NAHL•doh), the Americans captured

Picturing HISTORY Yellow journalism helped build American public support for war with Spain. **What two publishers presented shocking reports of the Cuban revolt?**

Cooperative Learning Activity

Discussing the War Use a panel-discussion format to help students focus on varying views of the Spanish-American War and its connection to imperialism. Organize students into groups, with each group portraying one of the following: José Martí, William Randolph Hearst, George Dewey, Emilio Aguinaldo, Theodore Roosevelt, John Hay, Andrew Carnegie, Mark Twain. Groups should prepare questions about the causes of the war, the war's results, and their view about the wisdom of the United States's involvement in other countries. Have groups ask and answer the questions from the perspective of the person they are portraying.

2 TEACH

L1 Identifying Key Details Have pairs of students list key events in the Spanish-American War. Next to each one, have them write a comment about the significance of that event. Encourage pairs of students to meet with other pairs, sharing and commenting upon their responses.

History *and the* Humanities

- The Spirit of American Art and Music, John Philip Sousa
- American Music Cultural Traditions, Lesson 7: "Battleship of Maine"

Guided Reading Activity 22–3

Name ______ Date ______ Class ______

★ Guided Reading Activity **22-3**

DIRECTIONS: Recalling Facts Read the section and answer the questions below. Refer to your textbook to write the answers.

1. Who led a revolt against Spanish rule in Cuba in 1895? ______
2. How did the Spaniards retaliate? ______
3. For each group of Americans, tell why they had sympathy for the Cubans.
a) Businesspeople ______
b) Government leaders ______
c) Other Americans ______
4. How did the press increase prowar feelings in the United States? ______
5. Why did William McKinley send the battleship *Maine* to Havana Harbor in 1898?
6. Explain the events behind and the significance of the slogan "Remember the *Maine.*"
7. What three things did Congress do on April 19, 1898? ______
8. When did Congress declare war on Spain? ______
9. What happened early on May 1, 1898? ______
10. What happened at San Juan Hill on July 1, 1898? ______
11. Where did the United States turn its attention after Cuba? ______
12. When did the war end? ______
13. Why did John Hay call the war "a splendid little war"? ______
14. When did the United States and Spain sign the Treaty of Paris? ______
15. What were the terms of the treaty? ______
16. What was the Platt Amendment? ______
17. Who led the revolt against American rule in the Philippines? ______

Guided Reading Activities ★ 88 ★ *The American Journey*

Picturing HISTORY Joseph Pulitzer was one of the first publishers to use scare headlines such as "Baptized in Blood" and "Death Rides the Rails." He also introduced the colorized Sunday supplement and the serialized comic strip. From the yellow ink he used in his comics came the term "yellow journalism."
Answer: *Joseph Pulitzer and William Randolph Hearst*

Map Study

Answers

1. the Caribbean
2. Cuba and Puerto Rico

Map Skills Practice

Reading a Map Why was no blockade established around the Philippines? *(The Spanish forces in the Philippines were quickly defeated, so there was no reason for a blockade.)*

NATIONAL GEOGRAPHIC SOCIETY

VIDEODISC
GTV: A Geographic Perspective on American History

Side 3, Chapter 7
Title: *The Limits of Power*
Subject: The Spanish-American War
Ask: **What did the United States gain from winning the Spanish-American War?** *(dominance in Cuba and Puerto Rico; access to trade markets in Central America, South America, and the Pacific)*

CURRICULUM CONNECTION

MUSIC
The rise in patriotic feeling in the United States found musical expression in the compositions of "march king" John Philip Sousa. Lyrics to "The Stars and Stripes Forever" (1897) seemed especially appropriate to the growing war fever:

"The emblem of the brave
and true,
Its folds protect no tyrant crew,
The red and white and starry blue,
Is Freedom's shield and hope."

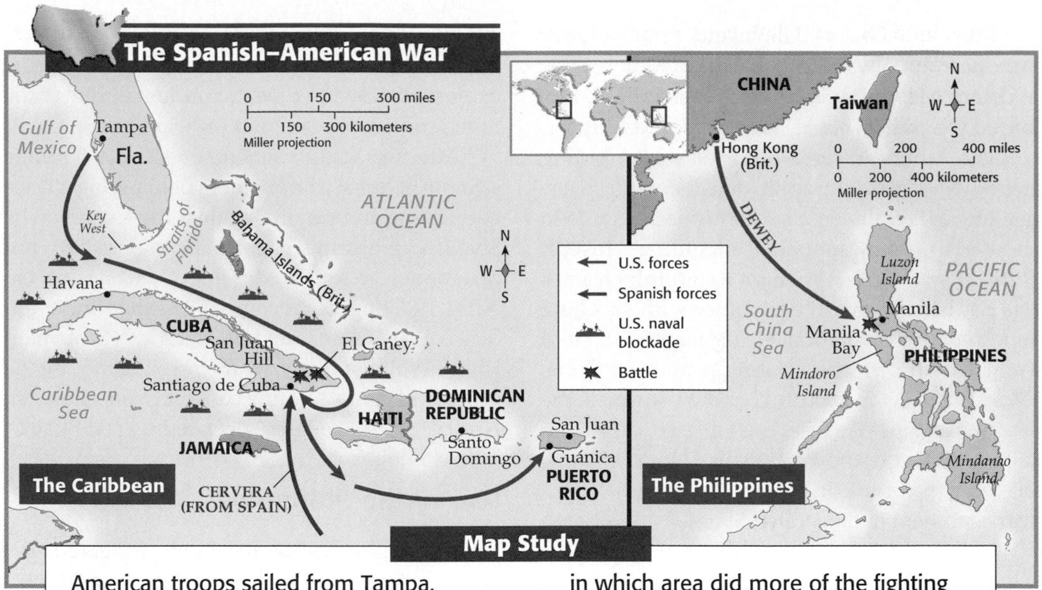

Map Study

American troops sailed from Tampa, Florida, to the south coast of Cuba in June 1898. Admiral Dewey had already sailed from Hong Kong to Manila.

1. **Movement** According to the two maps, in which area did more of the fighting take place?
2. **Analyzing Information** On what two Caribbean islands did United States forces land?

the city of Manila. As in Cuba, the Filipino rebels had struggled for years to win independence from Spain. Using American-supplied arms, they seized the main island of **Luzon,** declared independence, and created a democratic republic. The rebels expected the United States to support their independence. However, the United States debated what to do with the islands.

Fighting in Cuba

Meanwhile in the Caribbean, a Spanish fleet entered the harbor of **Santiago** on the southeastern shore of Cuba on May 19. Several days later, an American naval force blockaded the coast, trapping the Spanish in the harbor.

An American land force of about 17,000—nearly a quarter of them African American—landed near the city of Santiago. The inexperienced, ill-equipped Americans disembarked while forces under Cuban general Calixto García drove off the Spanish soldiers. When the Cuban and American forces advanced, wrote Sergeant Major Frank W. Pullen, Jr., they faced "a perfect hailstorm of bullets, which, thanks to the poor marksmanship of the Spaniards, 'went high.'" Heavy fighting followed, however.

The Rough Riders

Theodore Roosevelt resigned his position as assistant secretary of the navy to join the fighting in Cuba. He led the First Regiment of U.S. Cavalry Volunteers, an assorted group of former cowhands and college students, popularly known as the **Rough Riders.** On July 1 the Rough Riders, with African American soldiers of the Ninth and Tenth Cavalries, joined the **Battle of San Juan Hill.** "I waved my hat and we went up the hill with a rush," Roosevelt wrote later.

The Americans captured San Juan Hill after intense fighting. Two days later the Spanish fleet attempted to break out of Santiago. In a battle that lasted about four hours, the Spanish fleet was completely destroyed. This defeat ended Spanish resistance in Cuba.

MULTIPLE LEARNING STYLES

Verbal/Linguistic The zeal for selling newspapers caused some reporters of the era to twist facts or to base assumptions on slim evidence. Ask pairs or small groups of students to put their analytical skills to work by reporting a news story in two ways. Have them first give the facts in a straightforward, objective manner. Then have them try reporting the same basic story in a "yellow journalism" style. Share and lead the class in a comparison of the resulting news stories. Class discussion could lead to a discussion of this question: Can both styles be found in modern news sources? **L2**

The United States then turned its attention to the Spanish colony of **Puerto Rico,** east of Cuba. American troops landed on Puerto Rico in late July and quickly took control of the island. Then on August 12 the Spanish signed an armistice—a peace agreement—ending the war.

"A Splendid Little War"

Secretary of State **John Hay** called the **Spanish-American War** "a splendid little war." The war lasted fewer than 4 months, and only 460 Americans were killed in battle or died from wounds received in the fighting.

Yet the war had other aspects that were not at all "splendid." More than 5,000 Americans died of diseases such as yellow fever, malaria, and other diseases contracted in the tropical climate. The 10,000 African Americans who served faced the additional burden of discrimination. Serving in segregated units, African Americans battled alongside the Cuban rebel army, in which black and white troops fought as equals.

In the Caribbean

The United States and Spain signed the Treaty of Paris on December 10, 1898, marking the official end of the war. The treaty dissolved most of the Spanish empire. Cuba became an American protectorate, a country that is technically independent but actually under the control of another country. Puerto Rico and the Pacific island of **Guam** became territories of the United States. Spain also surrendered the Philippines to the United States in exchange for $20 million. The American empire had become a reality, and with the empire came new responsibilities.

Cuban Protectorate

Americans debated what to do about Cuba. Many congressional leaders believed that the Cubans were not ready for complete self-government. American business leaders feared that leaving Cuba might weaken the political stability of Cuba and jeopardize American interests there.

While Congress considered the matter, American troops remained in Cuba. Finally in 1901 the United States agreed to grant Cubans full independence, but only if their new constitution included clauses giving the United States certain rights. Known as the **Platt Amendment,** these clauses prohibited Cuba from making treaties with other nations and gave America control of a naval base at **Guantanamo Bay.** The Platt Amendment also gave the United States the right to intervene in Cuban affairs if the country's independence was threatened.

Major Charles Young

HISTORY AND ART ***Charge of the Rough Riders at San Juan Hill*** **by Frederic Remington** Rough Riders, led by Theodore Roosevelt (on horseback), fight the Battle of San Juan Hill. Major Charles Young, the highest-ranking African American officer, commanded four units of African American troops in Cuba. **What was the outcome of the Cuban campaign?**

CHAPTER 22
Section 3, 640–644

Facts On File

CD-ROM
Landmark Documents in American History

Title: *Platt Amendment, 1901*
Have students list the provisions of the Platt Amendment. What provisions, if any, are still in effect?

3 ASSESS

Assign Section 3 Review as homework or as an in-class activity.

Use **Chapter Challenger Interactive Review Software** to review Section 3.

HISTORY AND ART Frederic Remington (1861–1909) is best known for his paintings and sculptures relating to the American West. During this war, however, he worked as a correspondent, submitting his reports in both words and illustrations.
Answer: *The intervention of the Americans put down the Spanish resistance and made Cuba a protectorate of the United States.*

Section Quiz 22–3

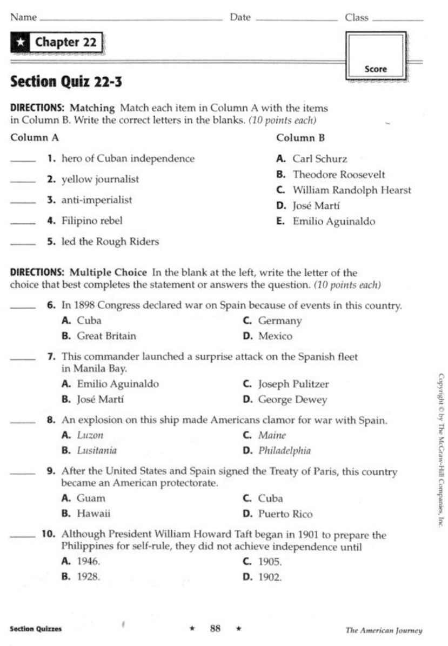

Name ____ Date ____ Class ____

Chapter 22 | Score

Section Quiz 22-3

DIRECTIONS: Matching Match each item in Column A with the items in Column B. Write the correct letters in the blanks. *(10 points each)*

Column A	Column B
____ **1.** hero of Cuban independence	**A.** Carl Schurz
____ **2.** yellow journalist	**B.** Theodore Roosevelt
____ **3.** anti-imperialist	**C.** William Randolph Hearst
____ **4.** Filipino rebel	**D.** José Martí
____ **5.** led the Rough Riders	**E.** Emilio Aguinaldo

DIRECTIONS: Multiple Choice In the blank at the left, write the letter of the choice that best completes the statement or answers the question. *(10 points each)*

____ **6.** In 1898 Congress declared war on Spain because of events in this country.
A. Cuba **C.** Germany
B. Great Britain **D.** Mexico

____ **7.** This commander launched a surprise attack on the Spanish fleet in Manila Bay.
A. Emilio Aguinaldo **C.** Joseph Pulitzer
B. José Martí **D.** George Dewey

____ **8.** An explosion on this ship made Americans clamor for war with Spain.
A. *Luzon* **C.** *Maine*
B. *Lusitania* **D.** *Philadelphia*

____ **9.** After the United States and Spain signed the Treaty of Paris, this country became an American protectorate.
A. Guam **C.** Cuba
B. Hawaii **D.** Puerto Rico

____ **10.** Although President William Howard Taft began in 1901 to prepare the Philippines for self-rule, they did not achieve independence until
A. 1946. **C.** 1905.
B. 1928. **D.** 1902.

Section Quizzes ★ 88 ★ *The American Journey*

Making Connections Activity

Geography The commitment of an American fighting force in Cuba required special geographical considerations. Have students use maps to figure out some of the problems involved in transporting troops from various parts of the United States to Cuba, as well as fighting in a tropical location. Explain that American troops endured bad food, inadequate medical care and supplies, and shortages of weapons and ammunition. Because summer gear was in short supply, many soldiers wore heavy woolen uniforms—unbearable in Cuba's heat and humidity. **L2, ELL**

CHAPTER 22
Section 3, 640–644

Reteaching Activity 22–3

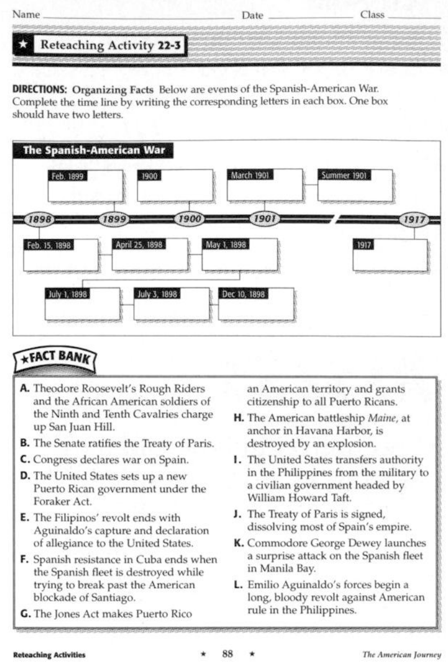

Name ______ Date ______ Class ______

★ Reteaching Activity 22-3

DIRECTIONS: Organizing Facts Below are events of the Spanish-American War. Complete the time line by writing the corresponding letters in each box. One box should have two letters.

★FACT BANK

A. Theodore Roosevelt's Rough Riders and the African American soldiers of the Ninth and Tenth Cavalries charge up San Juan Hill.
B. The Senate ratifies the Treaty of Paris.
C. Congress declares war on Spain.
D. The United States sets up a new Puerto Rican government under the Foraker Act.
E. The Filipinos' revolt ends with Aguinaldo's capture and declaration of allegiance to the United States.
F. Spanish resistance in Cuba ends when the Spanish fleet is destroyed while trying to break past the American blockade of Santiago.
G. The Jones Act makes Puerto Rico an American territory and grants citizenship to all Puerto Ricans.
H. The American battleship *Maine*, at anchor in Havana Harbor, is destroyed by an explosion.
I. The United States transfers authority in the Philippines from the military to a civilian government headed by William Howard Taft.
J. The Treaty of Paris is signed, dissolving most of Spain's empire.
K. Commodore George Dewey launches a surprise attack on the Spanish fleet in Manila Bay.
L. Emilio Aguinaldo's forces begin a long, bloody revolt against American rule in the Philippines.

Enrichment Activity 22–3

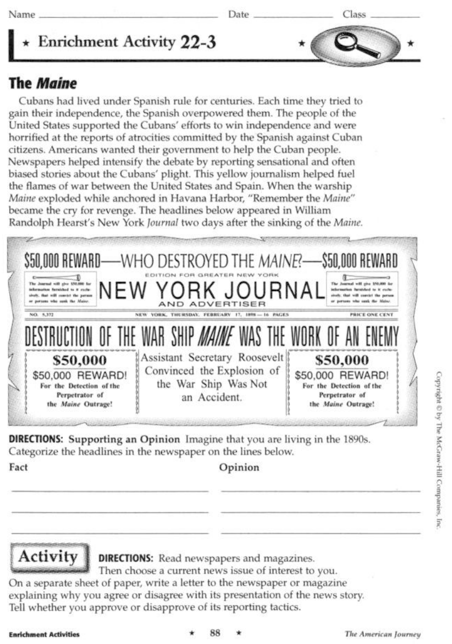

Name ______ Date ______ Class ______

★ Enrichment Activity 22-3 ★ ★

The *Maine*

Cubans had lived under Spanish rule for centuries. Each time they tried to gain their independence, the Spanish overpowered them. The people of the United States supported the Cubans' efforts to win independence and were horrified at the reports of atrocities committed by the Spanish against Cuban citizens. Americans wanted their government to help the Cuban people. Newspapers helped intensify the debate by reporting sensational and often biased stories about the Cubans' plight. This yellow journalism helped fuel the flames of war between the United States and Spain. When the warship *Maine* exploded while anchored in Havana Harbor, "Remember the *Maine*" became the cry for revenge. The headlines below appeared in William Randolph Hearst's New York *Journal* two days after the sinking of the *Maine*.

DIRECTIONS: Supporting an Opinion Imagine that you are living in the 1890s. Categorize the headlines in the newspaper on the lines below.

Fact ______ Opinion ______

Activity **DIRECTIONS:** Read newspapers and magazines. Then choose a current news issue of interest to you. On a separate sheet of paper, write a letter to the newspaper or magazine explaining why you agree or disagree with its presentation of the news story. Tell whether you approve or disapprove of its reporting tactics.

New Government for Puerto Rico

After the war, Puerto Rico remained under direct military rule. Then in 1900 the United States set up a new Puerto Rican government under the **Foraker Act.** The American government controlled the new administration. In 1917 the Jones Act made Puerto Rico a territory of the United States and granted American citizenship to all Puerto Ricans. However, many Puerto Ricans still wanted independence.

Acquiring the Philippines

★ The United States gained possession of the Philippines in the treaty that ended the Spanish-American War. But acquisition of the Philippines aroused fierce debate.

American Anti-Imperialism

During the 1890s some people—**anti-imperialists**—opposed the American enthusiasm for foreign expansion and the Spanish-American War. After the war the anti-imperialists fought approval of the treaty. Some argued that American rule of the Philippines contradicted the principles on which the United States was founded. Others opposed the large standing army that would be necessary to control the Philippines. Still others feared competition from Filipino laborers.

Many Americans—including Carl Schurz, Andrew Carnegie, and Mark Twain—joined the anti-imperialist campaign. The imperialists, led by Senators Henry Cabot Lodge and Albert Beveridge, eventually won out, however. The Senate ratified the Treaty of Paris on February 6, 1899.

Resistance to Takeover

In February 1899, Emilio Aguinaldo's forces began a long, bloody revolt against American rule. This conflict became a mammoth undertaking for the United States. More than 4,000 Americans died. Filipinos suffered far greater casualties—at least 50,000 died.

Except for sporadic fighting, the rebellion ended in March 1901 with the capture of Aguinaldo. He declared his allegiance to the United States and urged his followers to stop fighting.

In the summer of 1901, the United States transferred authority in the Philippines from the military to a civilian government headed by **William Howard Taft.** Taft set out to prepare the islands for eventual self-rule. However, the Philippines did not achieve full independence until 1946.

Section 3 Review

Checking for Understanding

1. ***Identify*** José Martí, Emilio Aguinaldo, Rough Riders, Platt Amendment.
2. ***Define*** yellow journalism, armistice, protectorate.
3. ***Summarize*** how yellow journalism influenced Americans' views of going to war with Spain.

Reviewing Themes

4. **Continuity and Change** How did the United States govern Puerto Rico and the Philippines?

Critical Thinking

5. **Making Critical Judgments** Do you think the United States should have taken permanent control of Cuba and made it part of its empire? Why or why not?

Activity

Creating a News Report Write a 45-second television news report to convince viewers that they should pressure the United States president to get involved in a war with Spain over Cuba. Use "yellow journalism" to help sway your listeners. Present your report to the class.

4 CLOSE

Have students summarize how the United States used the Spanish-American War to expand its interests in the Caribbean and in the Pacific.

Section 3 Review Answers

1. José Martí, 640; Emilio Aguinaldo, 641; Rough Riders, 642; Platt Amendment, 643
2. The words are defined in the Glossary.
3. Shocking reports of brutality and falsified information riled the American people to the point where they were ready for the United States government to take action.
4. Puerto Rico and Guam
5. Yes: the United States should have taken control of Cuba when it had the chance; it is a constant threat to United States security. No: the United States promised Cuba its independence and it had to fulfill that promise or risk having the Cuban people rebel.

Activity Television reports should rely on shocking information and distorted facts that appeal to the emotions of listeners.

Technology
SKILL BUILDER

Developing Multimedia Presentations

You want to present a research report to the rest of your class, and you want to really hold their attention. How do you do it? Your presentation can be exciting if you use various media.

Learning the Skill

At its most basic, a multimedia presentation involves using several types of media. To discuss life in the Philippines, for example, you might show photographs of the country. You could also play a recording of the country's language and music, or present a video showing the Filipino people at work and at play.

You can also develop a multimedia presentation on a computer. Multimedia as it relates to computer technology is the combination of text, video, audio, and animation in an interactive computer program.

In order to create multimedia productions or presentations on a computer, you need to have certain tools. These may include traditional computer graphic tools and draw programs, animation programs that make still images move, and authoring systems that tie everything together. Your computer manual will tell you which tools your computer can support.

Practicing the Skill

This chapter focuses on the overseas expansion of the United States in the late 1800s and early 1900s. Ask yourself questions like the following to develop a multimedia presentation on the people, politics, and industries of that era:

- Which forms of media do I want to include? Video? Sound? Animation? Photographs? Graphics? Other?
- Which of these media forms does my computer support?
- What kind of software programs or systems do I need? A paint program? A draw program? An animation program? A program to create interactive, or two-way, communication? An authoring system that will allow me to change images, sound, and motion?
- Is there a "do-it-all" program I can use to develop the kind of presentation I want?

Applying the Skill

Developing Multimedia Presentations Keeping in mind the four guidelines given above, write a plan describing a multimedia presentation you would like to develop. Indicate what tools you will need and what steps you must take to make the presentation a reality.

Technology
SKILL BUILDER

TEACH

Developing Multimedia Presentations

This skill helps students develop the ability to create multimedia presentations. Encourage students to look at this skill as an adventure rather than as "homework." Point out that this ability will do more than make for interesting classes. It might also prove helpful to them as they enter the workplace.

Discuss the technologies pictured in the photograph, but also be prepared to demonstrate some of the media appliances. For example, you might play a recording of patriotic music or show a piece of newsreel footage on a videocassette recorder. Have students brainstorm a list of possible forms of media that could be used in a multimedia presentation. Even suggestions that seem quite unusual may yield interesting possibilities.

You also may want to bring in a team teacher or guest speaker to discuss and demonstrate the development of multimedia presentations on a computer. If necessary, try to schedule computer lab time so that students can sample software and begin to build their own presentations.

Additional Practice

Chapter Skills Activity 22

ANSWERS TO PRACTICING THE SKILL

Answers will vary, depending on students' imaginations, the aspects of the topic they want to present, and the hardware and software available. Make sure that students have checked their computers' capabilities and the available software. You might give students the option of working in groups for **Practicing the Skill** and then independently for **Applying the Skill.**

Applying the Skill Presentations should be related to a social studies topic, although not necessarily about the content in this chapter. Students may wish to develop a presentation on the Civil War or the Vietnam War, for example. Be sure to arrange class time for the multimedia presentations that result.

1 FOCUS

BELLRINGER
Motivational Activity

Before taking roll at the beginning of the class period, project Section Focus Transparency 22–4 and have students answer the questions. Discuss students' responses.

This activity is also available as a blackline master.

Section Focus Transparency 22–4

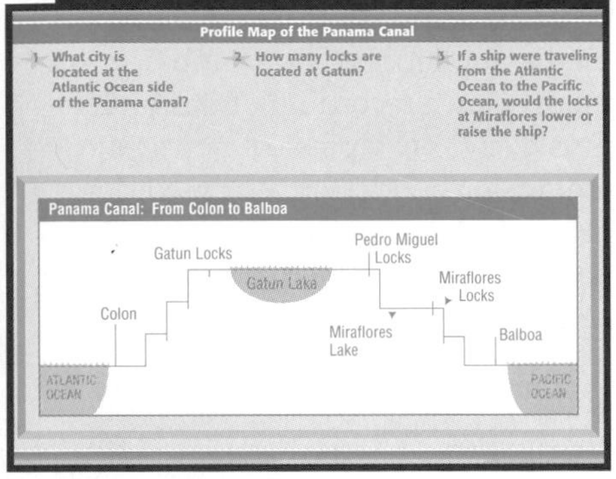

Vocabulary Precheck

Point out that the *arch* in *anarchy* is a Greek root meaning "rulership." Encourage students to think of other words with this root. *(monarch, patriarchal)*

Use the **Vocabulary PuzzleMaker** to create crossword and word search puzzles.

Section Theme
Global Connections

American investments in Latin America grew dramatically in the early 1900s and helped to build roads, railroads, and harbors. This stimulated trade and brought benefits to both Latin America and the United States.

Activity Have students discuss the word *diplomacy,* commenting on its importance in personal and governmental relationships.

1900 — 1910 — 1920

1904 Roosevelt Corollary is issued

1911 Revolution occurs in Mexico

1914 Panama Canal opens

1916 Francisco "Pancho" Villa launches uprising in Mexico

Section 4

Latin American Policies

READ TO DISCOVER . . .

- what shaped the policies the United States followed in Latin America.
- where and how the United States intervened in Latin America.

TERMS TO LEARN

isthmus
dollar diplomacy
anarchy

The Storyteller

On August 15, 1914, something described as the "greatest liberty that Man has taken with Nature" occurred. On that day, the first ship, the *Ancon,* traveled through the newly built Panama Canal. The world barely noticed, however. Most eyes were watching Europe, where World War I was gearing up. As the ship passed the words on the great seal of the Panama Canal Zone—THE LAND DIVIDED, THE WORLD UNITED—the world was setting out to tear itself to pieces.

Canal brochure

Americans and Europeans had long dreamed of building a canal across Central America to connect the Atlantic and Pacific Oceans and to eliminate the long and hazardous sea voyage around South America. Now that the United States controlled territory in both oceans, a canal that would allow faster and easier access to American interests overseas became increasingly important.

In 1879 a French company had acquired a 25-year lease from the government of Colombia to construct a canal across its province of **Panama.** Panama was an **isthmus**—a narrow strip of land connecting two larger bodies of land—about 50 miles (80 km) wide. Wedged between the Caribbean Sea and the Pacific Ocean, Panama seemed like the perfect site for the canal.

The United States in Panama

French efforts to build a canal ended in financial disaster, and in 1901 the United States bought the lease from the French for $40 million. In 1903 Secretary of State John Hay negotiated a treaty with Colombia that granted the United States a 99-year lease on a strip of land across Panama in return for a payment of $10 million and an annual rent of $250,000.

In Colombia, widespread opposition to the low price offered by the Americans led the Colombian senate to reject the treaty. In a fit of anger, President Roosevelt referred to the Colombians

SECTION RESOURCES

Reproducible Masters
- Guided Reading Activity 22–4
- Political Cartoons
- Section Quiz 22–4
- Reteaching Activity 22–4
- Enrichment Activity 22–4

Transparencies
- Section Focus Transparency 22–4

Multimedia
- Vocabulary PuzzleMaker
- Chapter Challenger Interactive Review Software
- Testmaker
- The Presidents: A Picture History of Our Nation
- American Music Cultural Traditions, Lesson 7: "Whitehouse Blues"

who rejected the treaty as "inefficient bandits." He believed the canal was essential to America's national defense.

Revolution in Panama

Roosevelt began looking for other ways to get land for the canal, and he wrote that he would "be delighted if Panama were an independent state." The Panamanians had staged revolts against Colombia in the past, but never with success. This time, however, the Panamanians had reason to believe that the Americans would support them in a revolt against Colombia.

On November 2, 1903, the American warship *Nashville* steamed into the port of Colón on the Caribbean coast of Panama. Encouraged by this show of support, the Panamanians revolted the next day and declared their independence. When Colombia sent forces to stop the revolt, the United States intervened and turned them back.

The Panama Canal

On November 6, the United States recognized Panama's independence. Less than two weeks later, Hay signed a treaty with the new nation of Panama. It gave the United States a 10-mile (16-km) strip of land across the country for the same amount offered earlier to Colombia. The United States now had land to build a canal.

Roosevelt's actions in Panama horrified many Latin Americans and angered some members of Congress and other Americans. The president, however, took great pride in his accomplishment. "I took the canal zone and let Congress debate," he said later, "and while the debate goes on, the canal does also."

Building the Canal

The United States could now start work on the canal—not an easy undertaking. Disease ran rampant among the workers. An English writer described Panama as "a damp, tropical jungle, intensely hot, swarming with mosquitoes." These mosquitoes carried two deadly diseases—yellow fever and malaria.

Colonel **William Gorgas,** an army physician who had helped eliminate yellow fever in Cuba, went to Panama to fight the diseases. Gorgas instructed workers to drain swamps, spray insecticides, spread oil on stagnant pools of water, and cut grassy marshes in order to kill mosquito eggs and destroy mosquito breeding places. By 1906 these measures had eliminated yellow fever and greatly reduced the number of malaria

Workers building the Panama Canal

HISTORY AND ART

***Work Trains, Miraflores* by Alson Skinner Clark** The building of the Panama Canal was a tribute to the skill of American engineers. **What challenges did American engineers face in building the canal?**

Cooperative Learning Activity

Comparing Policies Help students focus on this section by reviewing three important foreign policies. Organize students into three groups, one each for the Roosevelt Corollary, Dollar Diplomacy, and "moral diplomacy." Make sure that each group summarizes the policy; creates a visual symbol for the policy; names at least one leader who promoted the policy; analyzes whom the policy affected and how; and suggests how the policy changed the United States's self-perception. Have each group present its work in a format of its own choosing.

CHAPTER 22

Section 4, 646–650

2 TEACH

L1 Applying Information Call on volunteers to share what they know about situations, either recent or in past decades, when the United States has become involved in another country's disputes. Help students see how the policies forged by Theodore Roosevelt apply to such situations.

Guided Reading Activity 22–4

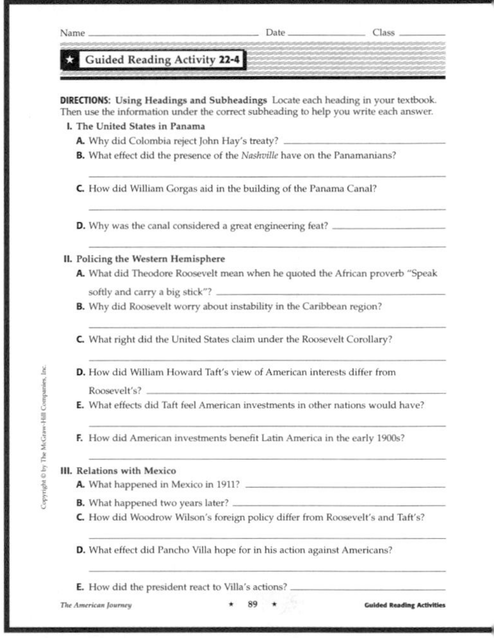

Name ____________ Date ________ Class ______

Guided Reading Activity 22-4

DIRECTIONS: Using Headings and Subheadings Locate each heading in your textbook. Then use the information under the correct subheading to help you write each answer.

I. The United States in Panama

A. Why did Colombia reject John Hay's treaty? ____________

B. What effect did the presence of the *Nashville* have on the Panamanians? ____________

C. How did William Gorgas aid in the building of the Panama Canal? ____________

D. Why was the canal considered a great engineering feat? ____________

II. Policing the Western Hemisphere

A. What did Theodore Roosevelt mean when he quoted the African proverb "Speak softly and carry a big stick"? ____________

B. Why did Roosevelt worry about instability in the Caribbean region? ____________

C. What right did the United States claim under the Roosevelt Corollary? ____________

D. How did William Howard Taft's view of American interests differ from Roosevelt's? ____________

E. What effects did Taft feel American investments in other nations would have? ____________

F. How did American investments benefit Latin America in the early 1900s? ____________

III. Relations with Mexico

A. What happened in Mexico in 1911? ____________

B. What happened two years later? ____________

C. How did Woodrow Wilson's foreign policy differ from Roosevelt's and Taft's? ____________

D. What effect did Pancho Villa hope for in his action against Americans? ____________

E. How did the president react to Villa's actions? ____________

Copyright © by The McGraw-Hill Companies, Inc.

The American Journey ★ 89 ★ **Guided Reading Activities**

HISTORY AND ART An impressionist, Alson Skinner Clark (1876–1949) studied in Paris and then in New York, but many of his paintings reflect his years in California and the Southwest. He painted a wide range of subjects but often chose Latin American scenes. **Ask:** Describe the land in this part of the Panama Canal. *(mountainous)* **Answer:** *carving a route through jungles and mountains, building a dam and a system of locks, and fighting the diseases of yellow fever and malaria*

Picturing HISTORY The cartoon illustrates what James Monroe had said in 1823: "[W]ith the governments who have declared their independence and maintained it, . . . we could not view any interposition for the purpose of oppressing them, or controlling in any other manner their destiny, by any European power in any other light than as the manifestation of an unfriendly disposition toward the United States."
Answer: *to declare the right of the United States to intervene in the affairs of Latin American nations when those nations seem unable to maintain order by themselves*

History *and the* Humanities

American Music Cultural Traditions, Lesson 7: "Whitehouse Blues"

Political Cartoons, *Big Stick Diplomacy in the Western Hemisphere*

NATIONAL GEOGRAPHIC SOCIETY

CD-ROM
The Presidents: A Picture History of Our Nation

Have students select Presidents Theodore Roosevelt, Taft, and Wilson from the main menu and the category GAME. Suggest they learn more about these presidents by playing the presidential game with a partner.

Picturing HISTORY The United States used the Monroe Doctrine to warn Great Britain and other European powers not to intervene in Latin America. **What was the purpose of the Roosevelt Corollary?**

cases. Without controlling disease, the United States could not have built the canal.

The Panama Canal was regarded as one of the great engineering feats of the time. About 40,000 workers, including many African Americans from the West Indies, struggled to carve a path through the dense jungle and over mountains. They dug out enormous amounts of earth and rock and used them to build a dam. They created a huge lake and constructed giant locks to raise and lower ships from sea level over the mountains and then back to sea level again on the other side of the isthmus.

The Grand Opening

The Panama Canal opened on August 15, 1914, and a cargo ship, the *Ancon,* made the first trip through the canal. A great success from the start, the canal reduced shipping costs by cutting more than 7,000 miles off the voyage from New York to San Francisco. The canal also helped increase and extend American naval power by allowing the United States fleet to move freely between the Atlantic and Pacific Oceans.

In the long run, the canal guaranteed a strong American presence in Latin America, where the United States now had a valuable property it intended to protect. Yet many Latin Americans remained bitter over how the Canal Zone was acquired. This resentment helped sour relations between the United States and Latin America for years.

Policing the Western Hemisphere

When Theodore Roosevelt became president in 1901, one of his major goals was to consolidate America's territorial gains in the Pacific and the Caribbean. In Roosevelt's view, the United States had both a duty and a right to intervene in these and other regions that fell under its influence.

The president often quoted an African proverb, "Speak softly and carry a big stick." He believed the United States should respond to foreign crises not by threats but by military action. Roosevelt became known for his "big stick" approach to foreign affairs. America must exercise "an international police power," he maintained, to preserve order and prevent the world from falling into **anarchy**—disorder and lawlessness.

Roosevelt Corollary

Roosevelt worried that instability in the Caribbean region would lead European powers to intervene. Two incidents confirmed his fears. In 1902, when **Venezuela** failed to meet payments on its loans, European nations imposed a blockade. The following year a revolution in the **Dominican Republic** toppled the government, causing concern that European powers would step in to protect their financial interests there.

MULTIPLE LEARNING STYLES

Intrapersonal The construction of the Panama Canal was a monumental achievement. To help students understand what the canal project meant to the United States, ask them to remember a time when they achieved some sort of personal accomplishment. **Ask:** **What obstacles stood in your way? How hard was it to reach the goal you had set?** Students need not necessarily share their answers, but have them draw upon their personal responses as they discuss how the opening of the canal affected the way the United States looked at itself and its role in world affairs. **L1, ELL**

The president responded to these incidents in 1904 by asserting America's right to act as a "policeman" in Latin America, intervening "however reluctantly . . . in cases of wrongdoing." This policy, known as the **Roosevelt Corollary,** was a significant addition to the Monroe Doctrine. Up to that time, the United States had used the Monroe Doctrine only to prevent European intervention in Latin America. Under the Roosevelt Corollary, the United States now claimed the right to intervene in the domestic affairs of Latin American nations whenever those nations seemed unstable.

The United States first applied the Roosevelt Corollary in 1905, when it took control of the Dominican Republic's finances. This arrangement continued for more than 30 years. The United States used the policy again in 1906, when troops were sent to Cuba to stop a revolution there.

Dollar Diplomacy

Theodore Roosevelt thought of American power primarily in military terms. His successor in the White House, **William Howard Taft,** took a more commercial view of American interests. Taft hoped to modify American foreign policy by "substituting dollars for bullets."

President Taft was willing to intervene in other nations whenever American prosperity and business interests were threatened. He believed that American investments would bring stability to troubled areas of the world, as well as profit and power to the United States, without the need for force. Taft's policy of linking American business interests to diplomatic interests abroad was known as dollar diplomacy.

Encouraged by dollar diplomacy, American investments in Latin America grew dramatically in the early 1900s. American investments helped build roads, railroads, and harbors, which stimulated trade and brought benefits to both Latin American countries and the United States.

Dollar diplomacy also resulted in greater United States involvement overseas. Large American companies gained great power in Latin America and controlled the politics of some nations in the region. Furthermore, when American business interests were endangered, military intervention often followed. In 1912, when a revolution in Nicaragua threatened American business interests, the United States quickly sent marines to restore peace. Such interference led to increased anti-American feelings throughout Latin America.

Relations with Mexico

In the early 1900s, **Mexico** was a poor country run by a tiny group of rich landholders. Investors in the United States poured more than $2 billion into Mexican oil wells and other businesses. Then, in 1911, Mexico entered a turbulent period in its history—one that threatened American investments, revealed the weaknesses of dollar diplomacy, and led to military intervention by the United States.

Mexican revolutionary

War in Mexico

In 1911 a popular Mexican reformer named **Francisco Madero** (muh•DEHR •oh) led a revolution to overthrow Mexico's brutal dictator **Porfirio Díaz** (DEE•AHS). Although foreign business and some Mexican politicians and landowners had prospered under the rule of Díaz, the lives of most Mexicans had grown worse.

Two years after taking power, Madero was overthrown and killed by General **Victoriano Huerta** (WEHR•tuh), who—like Díaz—favored the wealthy and foreign interests. President **Woodrow Wilson,** who had just taken office, refused to recognize Huerta's "government of butchers."

Wilson's "Moral Diplomacy"

A sincere believer in the ideals of democracy, Wilson thought the United States had a duty "to teach the South American republics to elect good men." Like Roosevelt and Taft, Wilson recognized

CHAPTER 22
Section 4, 646–650

What?Where?When?Who?

Political Humor Like many government policies, Taft's dollar diplomacy became a target for humor. American humorist Will Rogers was talking about this style of diplomacy when he said in 1923, "There's the one thing no Nation can ever accuse us of and that is Secret Diplomacy. Our Foreign dealings are an Open Book, generally a Check Book."

3 ASSESS

Assign Section 4 Review as homework or as an in-class activity.

Use **Chapter Challenger Interactive Review Software** to review Section 4.

Section Quiz 22–4

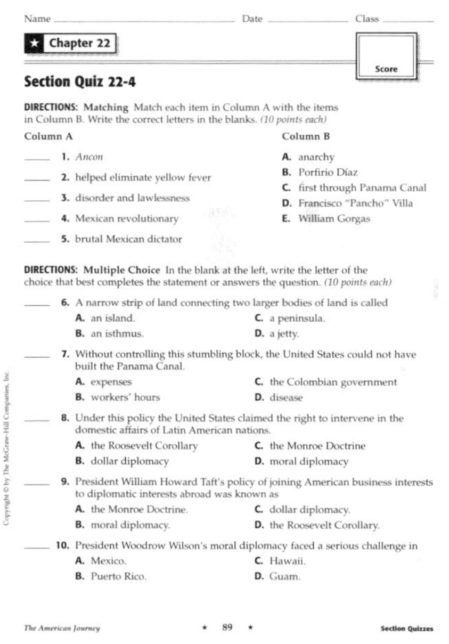

Name ____ Date ____ Class ____

★ Chapter 22

Score

Section Quiz 22-4

DIRECTIONS: Matching Match each item in Column A with the items in Column B. Write the correct letters in the blanks. *(10 points each)*

Column A

____ **1.** *Ancon*
____ **2.** helped eliminate yellow fever
____ **3.** disorder and lawlessness
____ **4.** Mexican revolutionary
____ **5.** brutal Mexican dictator

Column B

A. anarchy
B. Porfirio Díaz
C. first through Panama Canal
D. Francisco "Pancho" Villa
E. William Gorgas

DIRECTIONS: Multiple Choice In the blank at the left, write the letter of the choice that best completes the statement or answers the question. *(10 points each)*

____ **6.** A narrow strip of land connecting two larger bodies of land is called
A. an island. **C.** a peninsula.
B. an isthmus. **D.** a jetty.

____ **7.** Without controlling this stumbling block, the United States could not have built the Panama Canal.
A. expenses **C.** the Colombian government
B. workers' hours **D.** disease

____ **8.** Under this policy the United States claimed the right to intervene in the domestic affairs of Latin American nations.
A. the Roosevelt Corollary **C.** the Monroe Doctrine
B. dollar diplomacy **D.** moral diplomacy

____ **9.** President William Howard Taft's policy of joining American business interests to diplomatic interests abroad was known as
A. the Monroe Doctrine. **C.** dollar diplomacy.
B. moral diplomacy. **D.** the Roosevelt Corollary.

____ **10.** President Woodrow Wilson's moral diplomacy faced a serious challenge in
A. Mexico. **C.** Hawaii.
B. Puerto Rico. **D.** Guam.

The American Journey ★ 89 ★ **Section Quizzes**

MAKING CONNECTIONS ACTIVITY

Daily Life As the United States established a system for administering the Panama Canal, it needed personnel to make the system work. To that end, American civil servants and their families moved into the Panama Canal Zone. Setting up their own schools, stores, medical facilities, and so on, they quickly established a society that differed markedly from that of the national Panamanians. Ask interested students to research daily life in the Canal Zone and use the information to respond to these questions:

- How does one establish an "American" culture in a foreign land?
- What are the advantages and disadvantages of such isolationism? **L2**

CHAPTER 22
Section 4, 646–650

Reteaching Activity 22–4

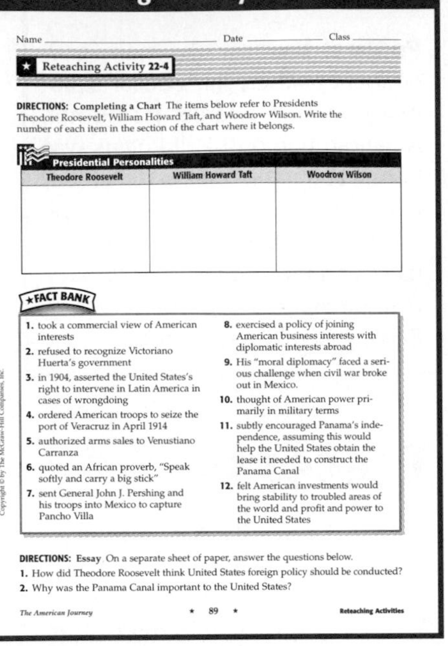
Name ______ Date ______ Class ______

★ Reteaching Activity 22-4

DIRECTIONS: Completing a Chart The items below refer to Presidents Theodore Roosevelt, William Howard Taft, and Woodrow Wilson. Write the number of each item in the section of the chart where it belongs.

Presidential Personalities

Theodore Roosevelt	William Howard Taft	Woodrow Wilson

★FACT BANK

1. took a commercial view of American interests
2. refused to recognize Victoriano Huerta's government
3. in 1904, asserted the United States's right to intervene in Latin America in cases of wrongdoing
4. ordered American troops to seize the port of Veracruz in April 1914
5. authorized arms sales to Venustiano Carranza
6. quoted an African proverb, "Speak softly and carry a big stick"
7. sent General John J. Pershing and his troops into Mexico to capture Pancho Villa
8. exercised a policy of joining American business interests with diplomatic interests abroad
9. His "moral diplomacy" faced a serious challenge when civil war broke out in Mexico.
10. thought of American power primarily in military terms
11. subtly encouraged Panama's independence, assuming this would help the United States obtain the lease it needed to construct the Panama Canal
12. felt American investments would bring stability to troubled areas of the world and profit and power to the United States

DIRECTIONS: Essay On a separate sheet of paper, answer the questions below.

1. How did Theodore Roosevelt think United States foreign policy should be conducted?
2. Why was the Panama Canal important to the United States?

The American Journey ★ 89 ★ Reteaching Activities

Enrichment Activity 22–4

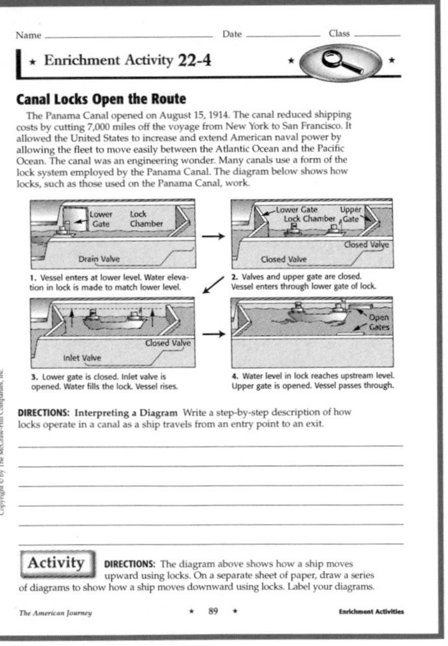
Name ______ Date ______ Class ______

★ Enrichment Activity 22-4

Canal Locks Open the Route

The Panama Canal opened on August 15, 1914. The canal reduced shipping costs by cutting 7,000 miles off the voyage from New York to San Francisco. It allowed the United States to increase and extend American naval power by allowing the fleet to move easily between the Atlantic Ocean and the Pacific Ocean. The canal was an engineering wonder. Many canals use a form of the lock system employed by the Panama Canal. The diagram below shows how locks, such as those used on the Panama Canal, work.

1. Vessel enters at lower level. Water elevation in lock is made to match lower level.
2. Valves and upper gate are closed. Vessel enters through lower gate of lock.
3. Lower gate is closed. Inlet valve is opened. Water fills the lock. Vessel rises.
4. Water level in lock reaches upstream level. Upper gate is opened. Vessel passes through.

DIRECTIONS: Interpreting a Diagram Write a step-by-step description of how locks operate in a canal as a ship travels from an entry point to an exit.

Activity **DIRECTIONS:** The diagram above shows how a ship moves upward using locks. On a separate sheet of paper, draw a series of diagrams to show how a ship moves downward using locks. Label your diagrams.

The American Journey ★ 89 ★ Enrichment Activities

4 CLOSE

Ask students to explain various meanings of the term *diplomacy* as it applied to American foreign policy under Presidents Roosevelt, Taft, and Wilson.

the importance of military power and economic interests. Yet Wilson also attempted to follow a foreign policy based on moral principles.

Wilson's "moral diplomacy" faced a serious challenge in Mexico. After Huerta took power, a civil war broke out in Mexico. Wilson hoped that the Huerta government, without American support, would fall. When that did not happen, Wilson authorized arms sales to Huerta's rival, **Venustiano Carranza** (kuh•RAN•ZUH).

In April 1914, after Huerta's troops arrested some American sailors, Wilson ordered United States troops to seize the port of **Veracruz.** This show of force strengthened Carranza's position and forced Huerta to flee in August. Carranza took power, and American troops withdrew.

Footnotes to History

Hollywood Revolution In 1914 Mexican revolutionary Francisco "Pancho" Villa made a deal with a Hollywood film company to film his battles in exchange for a $25,000 advance and 50 percent of the profits. He agreed to carry out his major raids during daylight so that the film crew could gather good footage.

Francisco "Pancho" Villa

Huerta's resignation did not end civil war in Mexico. Rebel leader **Francisco "Pancho" Villa** launched an uprising against Carranza. In January 1916, Villa seized and shot 16 Americans because of United States support for the Carranza government. Villa hoped his action would damage relations between the United States and the Carranza government, but the United States did not take steps against Mexico. Then Villa and his rebels crossed the border into **New Mexico** and burned the town of Columbus, killing 19 Americans there.

Villa's actions outraged the American public. The president sent General **John J. Pershing** with a large force of troops across the border into Mexico to capture Pancho Villa. For almost a year, Pershing's troops pursued Villa across Mexico, but the Mexican people protected Villa.

In 1917, when America's attention turned to the war raging in Europe, President Wilson withdrew the troops from Mexico. Mexico and the United States had come close to war, and American actions had caused great resentment in Mexico. America's experience in Mexico, like its policies in the Caribbean, showed that the nation would willingly use its power when it believed its interests or honor was threatened.

Section 4 Review

Checking for Understanding

1. ***Identify*** William Gorgas, Roosevelt Corollary, William Howard Taft, Francisco "Pancho" Villa, John J. Pershing.
2. ***Define*** isthmus, anarchy, dollar diplomacy.
3. ***Describe*** how the United States used Panama's desire for independence to its advantage.

Reviewing Themes

4. **Global Connections** Compare the different diplomacy styles of Presidents Roosevelt, Taft, and Wilson.

Critical Thinking

5. **Making Generalizations** Do you think our government follows Roosevelt's, Taft's, or Wilson's diplomatic ideas in setting foreign policy today? Explain.

Activity

Making a Protest Poster Create a poster that a person from Mexico might have used to protest American involvement in Mexico in the early 1900s.

Section 4 Review Answers

1. Gorgas, 647; Roosevelt Corollary, 649; Taft, 649; Villa, 650; Pershing, 650
2. The words are defined in the Glossary.
3. By supporting Panama's break with Colombia, the United States was ensured of receiving the land needed to complete the Panama Canal.
4. Roosevelt's "big stick" diplomacy relied on military power to influence other nations; Taft's "dollar" diplomacy put economic interests first and used business and trade as a bargaining tool; Wilson's "moral" diplomacy relied on moral principles and democratic ideals for its foundation.
5. Students should give specific examples to support their answers.

Activity Posters should reflect the anti-American feelings of most Mexicans at the time.

Social Studies Connections

World History | Economics | Citizenship

Geography

The Panama Canal Locks

How The Panama Canal Works

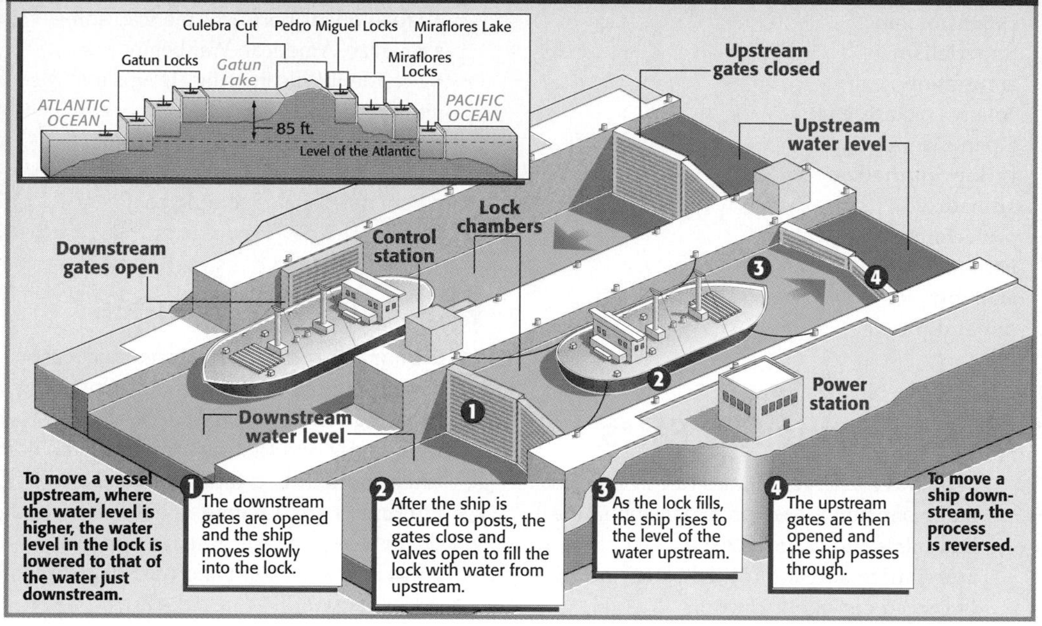

Still considered one of the greatest engineering feats in the world, the Panama Canal cuts more than 50 miles through the Isthmus of Panama. An average of 34 oceangoing vessels travel through the Panama Canal each day—about 12,500 ships every year. How do the canal locks work?

The three sets of locks in the Panama Canal are rectangular chambers, the largest concrete structures on the earth. They enable ships to move from one water level to another by changing the amount of water in the locks. Because water flows in and out of the locks by gravity, no pumps are needed. The locks are capable of raising and lowering vessels about 85 feet—the height of a 7-story building.

The locks are operated by 700-ton watertight doors or gates situated at both ends. The gates are 7 feet thick, 65 feet long, and from 47 to 82 feet high. They weigh up to 730 tons.

A ship maneuvers through the canal in about 8 hours. Before the canal was built, a ship had to travel 60 days around South America.

Activity

Canal Technology Using modeling clay, plastic containers, and toy ships, build a model canal. Present your model to the class and explain how the water levels change as you open the gates.

Social Studies Connections

Geography

TEACH

The Panama Canal Locks
Introduce this feature by sharing the famous palindrome (a number, word, or phrase that reads the same backward or forward), A MAN, A PLAN, A CANAL—PANAMA.

Building a dam and the locks for the Panama Canal was an engineering challenge. The greatest hurdle that engineers faced, however, was carving out the route through the isthmus —the 300-foot-wide Galliard Cut. The hills through which the Galliard Cut runs consist of soft volcanic material; so when workers dug a hole, more rock and earth would slide into the space or push up from below.

If students complete the **Activity** and make a model canal, explain that it must be able to show how locks enable a ship to adjust to changes in sea level. The plastic containers represent the concrete chambers that form the actual locks. Since they are to show raised and lowered levels of water, the containers must have gates at each end.

Before students work on the models, check their understanding by calling on volunteers to explain the workings of locks. Be sure to set aside time for presentation of the model canals, perhaps awarding extra credit for the most realistic model.

More About . . .

Canal Planning The French plan was to build a sea-level canal across the isthmus of Panama. In the United States, however, engineers advised that a canal with locks could be built more quickly and economically than could a sea-level canal; they also felt that locks would be a better way to deal with the variations in Panama's terrain and the changes caused by ocean tides. Members of the commission that Roosevelt appointed to take charge of the canal project were slow to agree. As a result, it was not until 1906 that Congress gave its approval to a canal plan that called for the use of locks. Additional delays kept the Panama Canal from opening until 1914, during the Wilson administration–an irony that frustrated Roosevelt.

GLENCOE TECHNOLOGY

VIDEODISC
MindJogger Videoquiz

Use MindJogger to review the Chapter 22 content.

Chapter 22
Disc 3, Side B

Also available in VHS.

Reviewing Key Terms

The words used in this activity can be found in the textbook glossary on pages A26–A35.

Reviewing Key Facts

1. America's frontiers had been settled from coast to coast, so Americans had to expand trade and compete for political influence with other nations.
2. American missionaries, merchants, and sugar growers began moving to Hawaii in the 1800s. Eventually Americans took control of almost all the land and businesses there and served as advisers to the Hawaiian royal family. After several failed attempts, the United States succeeded in annexing Hawaii in 1898.
3. Boxer Rebellion raised fear in Europe, which led to Europeans' acceptance of Secretary of State Hay's Open Door policy.
4. Cuba became an American protectorate; Puerto Rico and Guam became United States territories; Spain gave the Philippines to the United States in exchange for $20 million.
5. United States claimed the right to intervene in domestic affairs of Latin American nations whenever those nations seemed unstable.

Chapter 22

Review and Activities

Reviewing Key Terms

On a sheet of paper, define the following terms:

isolationism
expansionism
imperialism
annexation
spheres of influence
Open Door policy
yellow journalism
armistice
protectorate
isthmus
anarchy
dollar diplomacy

Reviewing Key Facts

1. Why did the United States turn from internal expansion to foreign expansion in the late 1800s and early 1900s?
2. Summarize how the United States gradually gained control of Hawaii.
3. How did the United States gain access to trade in China?
4. What were the terms of the Treaty of Paris?
5. What was the purpose of the Roosevelt Corollary?

Critical Thinking

Drawing Conclusions

Presidents Roosevelt, Taft, and Wilson had different opinions on how the United States should handle foreign policy.

1. Which type of diplomacy—"big stick," "dollar," or "moral"—do you think was most effective during this period? Why?
2. Which type of diplomacy do you think would be the least popular with foreign nations? Why?

Time Line Activity

Create a time line on which you place the following events in chronological order.

- Japan opens ports to American ships
- Spanish-American War begins
- President Wilson orders troops into Mexico to capture Pancho Villa
- Seward buys Alaska from Russia
- Hawaii becomes United States territory
- Panama Canal is completed

Reviewing Themes

1. **Economic Factors** What economic reasons did the United States have for expanding its foreign interests?
2. **Geography and History** What was the main cause of the Russo-Japanese War?
3. **Continuity and Change** What reasons did the anti-imperialists give for opposing American expansion and the Spanish-American War?
4. **Global Connections** Name two actions taken by the United States in Latin America that would damage future relations in this area.

Skill Practice Activity

Developing Multimedia Presentations

Study the list of topics below. Choose one of the topics and explain how you would use at least three types of media in a presentation to best teach the topic to your class.

1. Matthew Perry's mission to Japan
2. The development of the American navy
3. How the United States changed Hawaii forever
4. The Battle of San Juan Hill
5. Building the Panama Canal

Critical Thinking

1. Answers will vary, but students should select one type of diplomacy and explain why it would be more effective than the others.
2. Students should defend their responses with logical examples.

Time Line Activity

Events should be placed in this order: Japan opens ports to American ships, Seward buys Alaska from Russia, Spanish-American War begins, Hawaii becomes United States territory, Panama Canal is completed, President Wilson orders troops into Mexico to capture Pancho Villa

Geography Activity

The building of the Panama Canal was regarded as a great engineering feat. Study the map of the canal below, then answer the questions that follow.

The Panama Canal

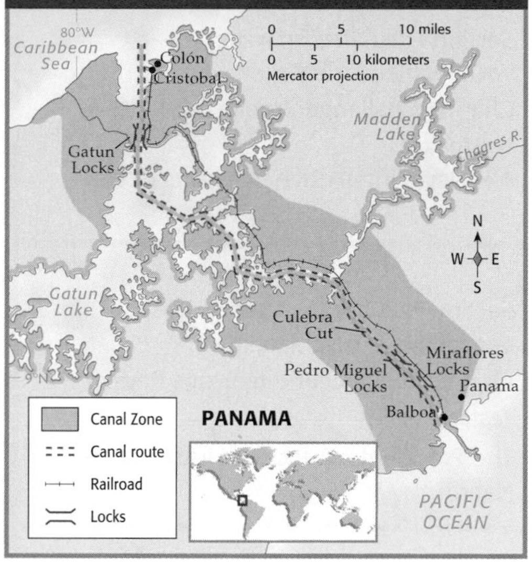

1. **Location** What cities are located near the path of the canal?
2. **Movement** In which direction would a ship en route to Cristobal from Balboa travel?
3. **Human/Environment Interaction** What does the location of Panama tell you about the climatic conditions the canal workers faced?

Now compare the map above with the diagram of the Panama Canal locks on page 651. Use this comparison to answer these questions.

4. **Location** Which of the locks are located at the highest elevation, or height above sea level?
5. **Place** Which natural waterway, of those shown on the diagram, is located at the highest elevation? Which is at the lowest elevation?

Cooperative Activity

History and Economics Work with a partner to create a map showing all of the areas acquired by the United States during the late 1800s and early 1900s. Research to find out about the natural resources that existed in each area and the importance of the area's location in world trade. Then, based on these two factors, rank each of the areas on your map as to their economic value to the United States. The area ranked number "1" should be the most valuable. Compare your maps and rankings with other members of the class and create a chart of the overall ratings.

Technology Activity

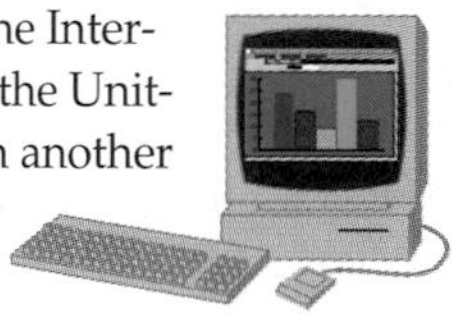

Using the Internet Search the Internet for a news report about the United States that was written in another nation. Decide if the article expresses a positive, negative, or neutral view of the United States. Print the article and underline passages that support your opinion. Think about why this nation might have formed this opinion.

Portfolio Activity **History Journal** Review the chapter for information about treaties and agreements between various nations during this period. Make a list of the agreements and draw a picture or symbol next to each that will help you recall its terms.

CHAPTER 22
Review and Activities

Skill Practice Activity

Answers will vary but may include:
1. Japanese music; art prints of Perry; animated reenactment
2. video of naval history; recording of "Anchors Aweigh"; naval uniforms
3. video of Hawaii's natural beauty; photographs of plantations; animated time line
4. reading of firsthand and/or newspaper accounts; animated reenactment; photographs
5. photographs or newsreel footage; map overlays on transparencies; reading of firsthand accounts

Geography Activity

1. Colón, Cristobal, Balboa
2. northwest
3. With the canal located at around 9°N latitude, the workers faced hot, humid, tropical conditions.
4. Pedro Miguel Locks and the highest of the Gatun Locks
5. Gatun Lake; Atlantic Ocean

Cooperative Activity

Maps should show territory acquired by the United States during this period and rank each area's potential economic value.

Technology Activity

Students should print out their articles with highlighted passages verifying their opinions.

Portfolio Activity Students should create a drawing or symbol to help recall the terms of treaties.

Reviewing Themes

1. to increase trade, to establish new markets, to find new supplies of raw materials
2. Japan and Russia both wanted Manchuria, which was rich in natural resources.
3. They called upon the tradition of isolationism that George Washington had established; they felt that such involvement violated the principle of self-determination; they did not want to see the commitment of lives and supplies to a war that did not directly involve the interests of the United States.
4. Any two: support of Panamanian drive for independence; United States troops sent to Nicaraguan revolution in 1912 to protect business interests; Wilson's military support of Mexico's overthrow of Huerta; the pursuit of Pancho Villa.

? Chapter Bonus Test Question

Ask: To what did General Pershing compare his assignment of pursuing Pancho Villa? *("looking for a needle in a haystack")*

Chapter 23 Planning Guide

A complete, 1-page lesson plan is provided for each section in the *Reproducible Lesson Plans* booklet.

Section Resources

Daily Objectives	Reproducible Resources	Multimedia Resources
Section 1 War in Europe Discuss the factors that led to large-scale war in Europe and the new technology that made the war so devastating.	Reproducible Lesson Plan 23–1 Guided Reading Activity 23–1* Section Quiz 23–1* Reteaching Activity 23–1 Enrichment Activity 23–1	Section Focus Transparency 23–1 Vocabulary PuzzleMaker Chapter Challenger Interactive Review Testmaker ABCNews InterActive™ Lessons of War
Section 2 America's Road to War Explain how the United States moved from a position of neutrality to a declaration of war and commitment of troops to the conflict.	Reproducible Lesson Plan 23–2 Guided Reading Activity 23–2* Section Quiz 23–2* Reteaching Activity 23–2 Enrichment Activity 23–2	Section Focus Transparency 23–2 Vocabulary PuzzleMaker Chapter Challenger Interactive Review Testmaker The Presidents: A Picture History of Our Nation
Section 3 Americans Join the Allies Relate the active participation of the United States in the war to Germany's request for an armistice and the cessation of hostilities.	Reproducible Lesson Plan 23–3 Guided Reading Activity 23–3* Section Quiz 23–3* Reteaching Activity 23–3 Enrichment Activity 23–3	Section Focus Transparency 23–3 Vocabulary PuzzleMaker Chapter Challenger Interactive Review Testmaker Facts On File: Landmark Documents in American History
Section 4 The War at Home Recall steps that American civilians took to pay for the war, supply the Allied forces, increase the workforce, and control public opinion.	Reproducible Lesson Plan 23–4 Guided Reading Activity 23–4* Section Quiz 23–4* Reteaching Activity 23–4 Enrichment Activity 23–4	Section Focus Transparency 23–4 U.S. History & Art, Transparencies 20, 21 Vocabulary PuzzleMaker Chapter Challenger Interactive Review GTV: A Geographic Perspective on American History American Music Cultural Traditions
Section 5 Searching for Peace Discuss the terms of and response to President Wilson's peace plan and to the Treaty of Versailles.	Reproducible Lesson Plan 23–5 Guided Reading Activity 23–5* Section Quiz 23–5* Reteaching Activity 23–5 Enrichment Activity 23–5	Section Focus Transparency 23–5 Vocabulary PuzzleMaker Chapter Challenger Interactive Review GTV: A Geographic Perspective on American History Facts On File: Landmark Documents in American History

* *Also available in Spanish*

Blackline Master · Videodisc · Audiocassette · Music Program · Transparency · CD-ROM · Software

0:00 **OUT OF TIME?**
Assign the Chapter 23 Digest and the corresponding Chapter Digests Audiocassettes with activities and tests.

ACTIVITY

From the Classroom of...

Andre Anselme
Regis High School
New York, NY

Cause and Effect—War and Change

World War I contributed to many changes that occurred in the relatively short period of 1914 to 1920. Organize students into small groups and have them prepare cause-and-effect charts showing some of the ways the war brought about change in the United States. Caution students that cause-and-effect relationships can become quite complicated. Many causes can contribute to one or more effects. Encourage students to be creative in showing this complexity. Explain that the war, for example, caused (1) the need for vital war supplies, (2) fewer American men being available to work in factories, (3) fewer immigrants to come to this country to work in factories, (4) more women needed to replace men in factories, and so on. Have groups compare their charts and discuss as a class how the charts illustrate the significant amount of change that occurred during World War I.

NATIONAL GEOGRAPHIC SOCIETY

Teacher's Corner

INDEX TO NATIONAL GEOGRAPHIC MAGAZINE

The following articles may be used for research relating to this chapter:

- "Riddle of the *Lusitania,*" by Robert D. Ballard, April 1994.
- "The Wings of War," by Thomas B. Allen, March 1994.
- "St. Petersburg, Capital of the Tsars," by Steve Raymer, December 1993.
- "The Bolshevik Revolution," by Dusko Doder, October 1992.

NATIONAL GEOGRAPHIC SOCIETY PRODUCTS AVAILABLE FROM GLENCOE

To order the following products for use with this chapter, contact your local Glencoe sales representative, or call Glencoe at 1-800-334-7344:

- *GTV: A Geographic Perspective on American History* (Videodisc)
- *GTV: The American People: Fabric of a Nation* (Videodisc)
- *The Presidents: A Picture History of Our Nation* (CD-ROM)

ADDITIONAL NATIONAL GEOGRAPHIC SOCIETY PRODUCTS

To order the following products for use with this chapter, call National Geographic Society at 1-800-368-2728:

- *1914–1918: World War I* (Video)
- *Last Voyage of the* Lusitania (Video)
- *1917: Revolution in Russia* (Video)
- *Historical Atlas of the United States* (Atlas)

Block Schedule

Block scheduling differs from traditional class scheduling in the amount of time allotted to each period. The extended time frame provided by block scheduling affords you the opportunity to implement a greater number of research-oriented and activity-intense projects to motivate and involve your students. Activities that are particularly suited to use within the block scheduling framework are identified throughout this chapter by the following designation:

KEY TO ABILITY LEVELS

Teaching strategies have been coded for varying learning styles and abilities.

L1 **BASIC** activities for all students
L2 **AVERAGE** activities for average to above-average students
L3 **CHALLENGING** activities for above-average students
ELL **ENGLISH LANGUAGE LEARNER** activities

Chapter 23 Resource Guide

Home Involvement

Home Involvement Activity 23

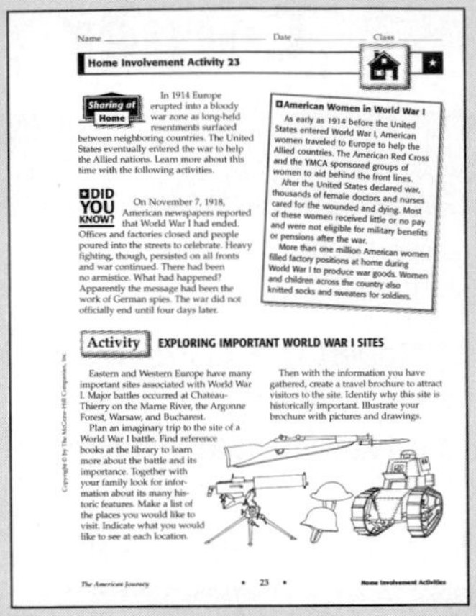

Review Activities

Chapter Summary 23

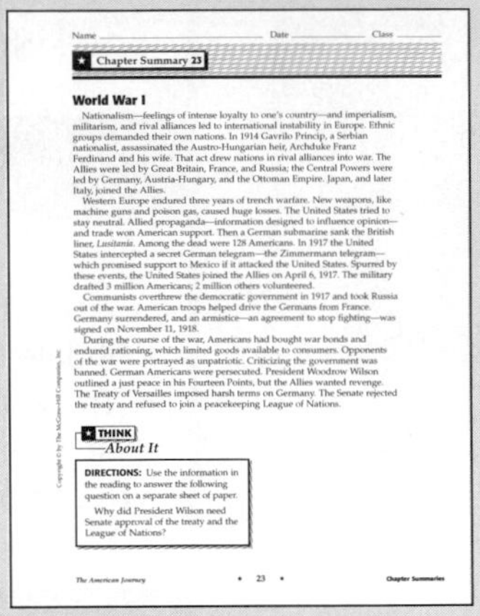

Workbook Activity 23

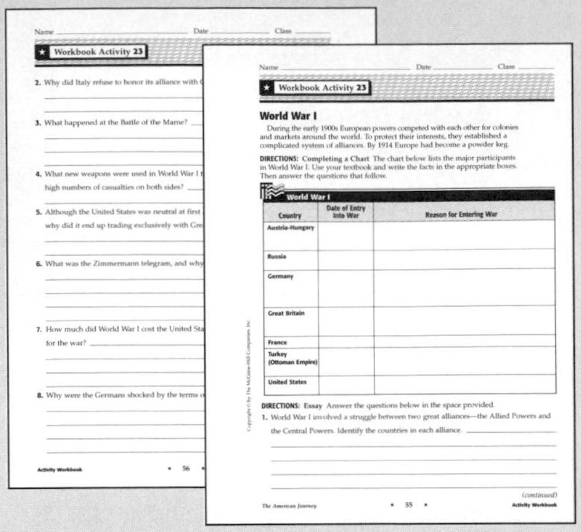

Reinforcement Activities

Time Line Activity 23

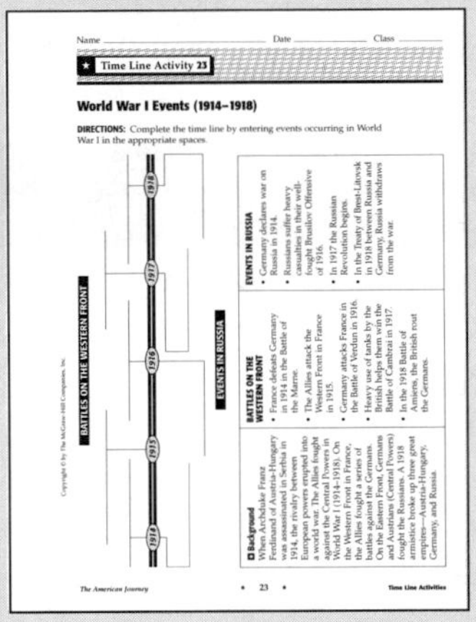

Vocabulary Activity 23

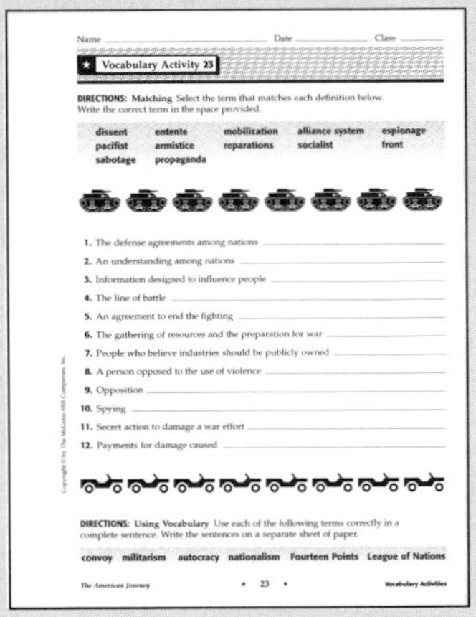

Chapter Skills Activity 23

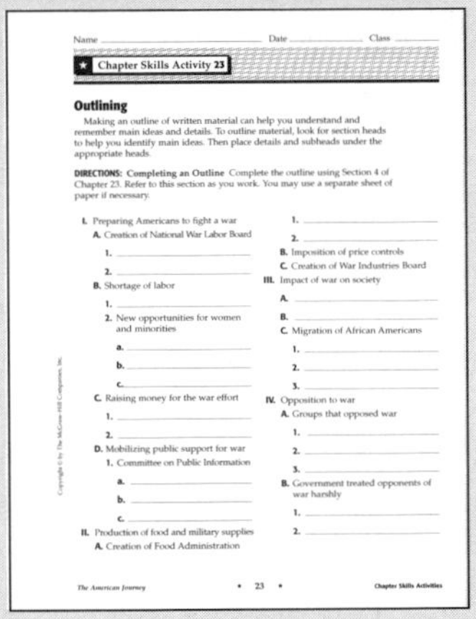

Enrichment Activities

Linking Past and Present Activity 23

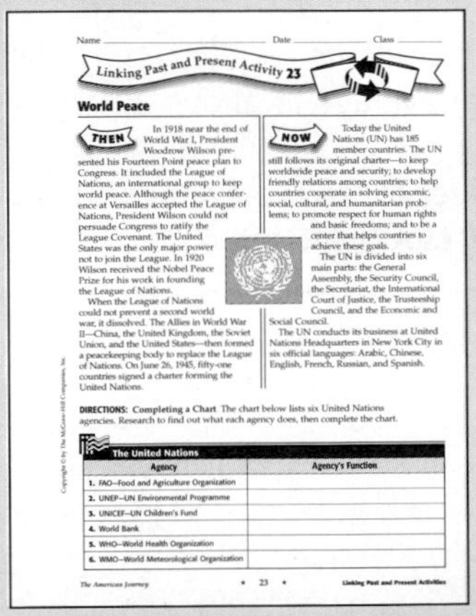

Primary Source Reading 23

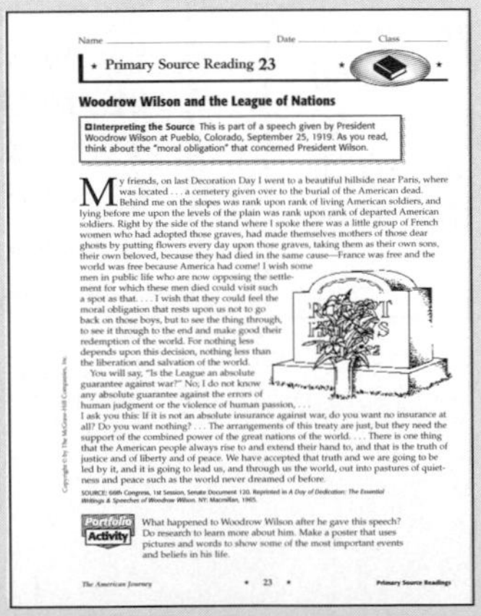

Geography Activities

Mapping History Activity 23

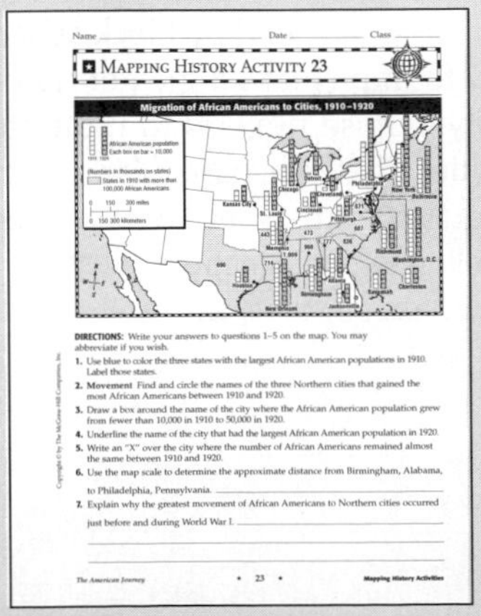

Chapter 23 Resource Guide

Assessment

Chapter 23 Test, Form A

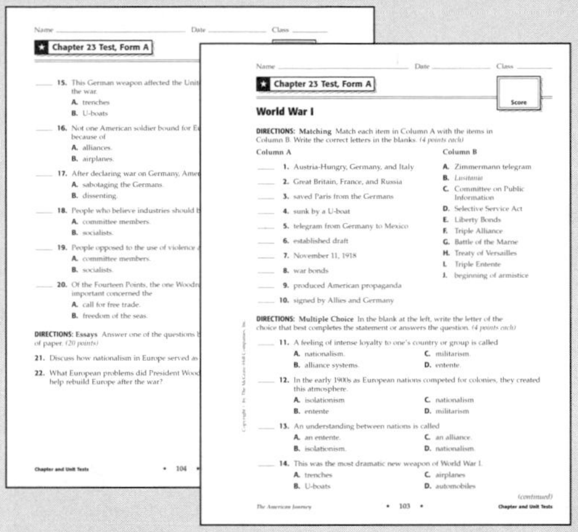
Chapter 23 Test, Form A

World War I

Chapter 23 Test, Form B

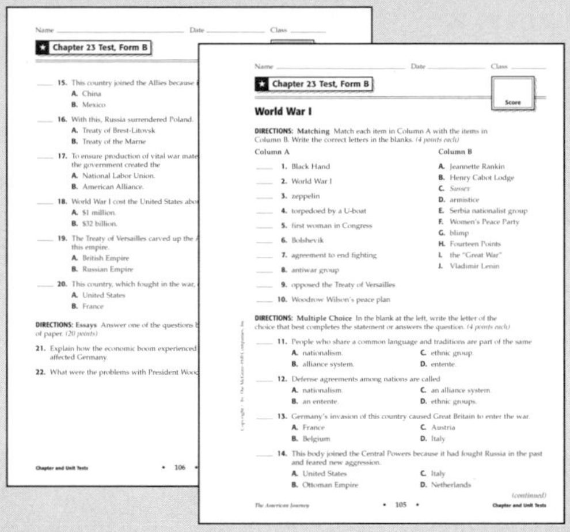
Chapter 23 Test, Form B

World War I

Performance Assessment Activity 23

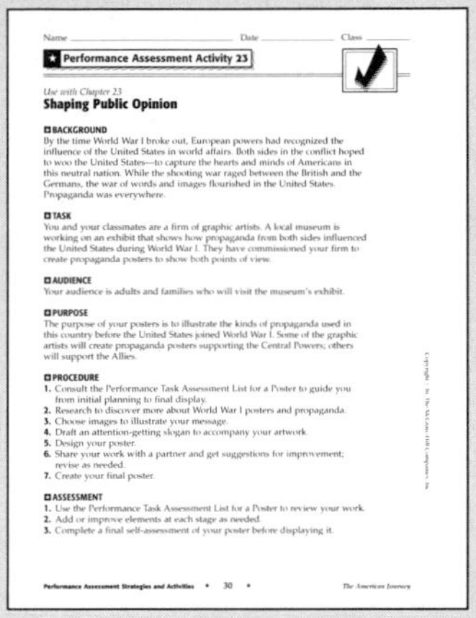
Performance Assessment Activity 23

Shaping Public Opinion

Spanish Resources

The following Spanish language materials are available in the Spanish Resources binder:

- **Spanish Chapter Summary 23**
- **Spanish Vocabulary Activity 23**
- **Spanish Guided Reading Activities, Chapter 23**
- **Spanish Section Quizzes, Chapter 23**
- **Spanish Home Involvement Activity 23**
- **Spanish Chapter 23 Digests Audiocassette Activity and Test**

Activity Manipulatives

Help students learn more about America's cultural history with:

- **American Crafts Hands-On Activities**
- **American Games Hands-On Activities**
- **American History Flash Cards**

Additional Resources From Glencoe

- **U.S. History & Art,** Transparency 20, *I Want You for the U.S. Army;* Transparency 21, *Allies Day, May 1917*
- **American Music Cultural Traditions,** Lesson 8: "War Song Hits"
- **The American History Videodisc and CD-ROM,** *The Progressive Era and the First World War, 1901–1920*
- **Outline Map Resource Book**
- **U.S. Desk Map**

A&E HOME VIDEO. Biography THE HISTORY CHANNEL.

The following videotape programs are available from Glencoe as supplements to Chapter 23:

- **The Red Baron: Master of the Air** (ISBN 1-56501-582-7)
- **Nicholas & Alexandra** (ISBN 1-56501-514-2)

To order, call Glencoe at 1-800-334-7344. To find classroom resources to accompany many of these videos, check the following home pages:
A&E Television: http://www.aetv.com
The History Channel: http://www.historychannel.com

Introducing CHAPTER 23

Chapter Themes

Chapter Themes are listed by section on this chapter opening page of the Student Edition. A corresponding theme-based activity is available under "FOCUS," and a theme-based question is asked in the Section and Chapter Reviews.

Performance Assessment

Refer to Activity 23 in the *Performance Assessment Strategies and Activities* booklet.

GLENCOE TECHNOLOGY

VIDEODISC
MindJogger Videoquiz

Use MindJogger to preview the Chapter 23 content.

Chapter 23
Disc 3, Side B

Also available in VHS.

HISTORY AND ART The Committee on Public Information, headed by journalist George Creel, commissioned and distributed posters like this one. **Ask:** What message is the poster trying to convey? *(Soldiers cannot succeed without the supplies produced by civilians back home.)*

Chapter 23

1914–1919

World War I

Why It's Important

World War I changed the world. The people of the time called the conflict the Great War, and they believed that never again would there be another like it. Although the United States tried to remain neutral, it was drawn into the conflict. The war had a profound effect on the nation, touching on all aspects of life. When the fighting was over, the United States emerged as one of the greatest powers in the world.

Chapter Themes

- *Section 1*, Science and Technology
- *Section 2*, Government and Democracy
- *Section 3*, Geography and History
- *Section 4*, Economic Factors
- *Section 5*, Global Connections

HISTORY AND ART ***On the Job for Victory*** During World War I, artists created colorful posters to encourage public support for the war effort.

654

EXTRA CREDIT PROJECT

Charting a Changing Role Have students trace United States involvement in World War I and its aftermath on a chart. The title should be *The United States and World War I* and its three columns labeled as follows: "As an Onlooker," "As a Participant," and "As a Peacemaker." As students read this chapter, they can write phrases in each column, noting how the United States reacted to the outbreak of war in Europe; how the United States became involved in the war; how its forces helped secure an Allied victory; and how President Wilson faced conflict at home as he attempted to negotiate a lasting peace at the end of the war. The resulting charts might serve as outlines for a chapter review.

1914 — 1915 — 1916

June 1914 Franz Ferdinand is assassinated

July 1914 Austria-Hungary declares war on Serbia

August 1914 Germany declares war on Russia and France

1916 France and Germany fight the Battle of Verdun

Section 1

War in Europe

READ TO DISCOVER . . .

- what factors led to World War I.
- how the early fighting progressed in Europe.
- what new weapons were used in the war.

TERMS TO LEARN

nationalism
militarism
alliance system
entente

The Storyteller

On June 28, 1914, Gavrilo Princip went to great lengths to secure Bosnia's freedom from Austria. His friend described Princip's actions: "As the [Archduke's] car came abreast he [Princip] stepped forward from the curb, drew his automatic pistol from his coat and fired two shots. The first struck the wife of the Archduke, the Archduchess Sofia, in the abdomen. . . . She died instantly. The second bullet struck the Archduke close to the heart.

He uttered only one word, 'Sofia'—a call to his stricken wife. Then his head fell back and he collapsed. He died almost instantly. . . .

The next day they put chains on Princip's feet, which he wore till his death."

Archduke Franz Ferdinand

The people of **Sarajevo** crowded the streets of their city on the morning of June 28, 1914. They wanted to see **Archduke Franz Ferdinand,** the heir to the throne of the **Austro-Hungarian Empire,** as he drove by with his wife in an open car. The royal couple had come on a state visit to **Bosnia,** an Austrian province.

Suddenly shots rang out. The archduke and his wife were hit and died soon after. The assassination destroyed the delicate balance of European stability. Within weeks Europe was at war.

Troubles in Europe

★ The tensions that led to World War I had roots that went back many years. The conflicts grew as European nations pursued dreams of empire, built up their armies, and formed alliances.

Nationalism

Nationalism, a feeling of intense loyalty to one's country or group, caused much of the tension in Europe. In the late 1800s and the early 1900s, nationalism served as both a unifying and a disruptive force. On the one hand, nationalism encouraged new nations, such as **Italy** and **Germany,** to unify and to establish their power in the world. Italy had become a kingdom in the 1860s, and the German states had united in the 1870s. Their actions challenged the position of older nations such as **Great Britain** and **France.**

On the other hand, nationalism inspired certain groups of people to break away from existing

SECTION RESOURCES

Reproducible Masters
- Reproducible Lesson Plan 23–1
- Guided Reading Activity 23–1
- Section Quiz 23–1
- Reteaching Activity 23–1
- Enrichment Activity 23–1

Transparencies
- Section Focus Transparency 23–1

Multimedia
- Vocabulary PuzzleMaker
- Chapter Challenger Interactive Review Software
- Testmaker
- ABCNews InterActive™ Lessons of War

1 FOCUS

BELLRINGER
Motivational Activity

Before taking roll at the beginning of the class period, project Section Focus Transparency 23–1 and have students answer the questions. Discuss students' responses.

This activity is also available as a blackline master.

Section Focus Transparency 23–1

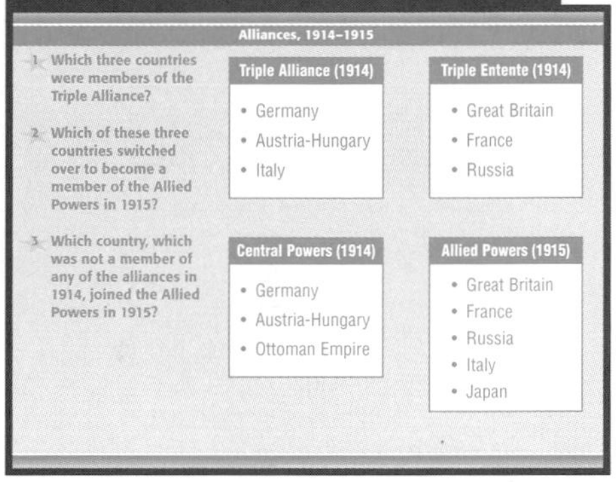

Vocabulary Precheck
Refer students to **Terms to Learn.** Have them write questions for which each listed term is an answer.

Use the **Vocabulary PuzzleMaker** to create crossword and word search puzzles.

Section Theme
Science and Technology

As new weapons and other technologies were developed, European powers scrambled to keep up with their rivals, to form alliances, and to grab colonies.

Activity Have students skim the headings in this section. **Ask:** What can you infer about the issues in this war? *(Answers include imperialistic disputes, competing alliances, and militarism.)*

CHAPTER 23
Section 1, 655–659

2 TEACH

L1 Recognizing Issues Ask students to complete this statement: A country that wants to improve its position in world affairs should _____. Look for responses that suggest alliances, militarism, or territorial expansion. Relate students' responses to the turn-of-the-century situation in Europe.

Guided Reading Activity 23–1

Name ______ Date ______ Class ______

Guided Reading Activity 23-1

DIRECTIONS: Recording Who, What, When, Where, Why, and How Read the section and answer the questions below. Refer to your textbook to write the answers.

1. **What** served as both a unifying and disruptive force in the late 1800s and early 1900s? ______
2. **Why** did the desire to increase colonial holdings create conflict between imperial powers? ______
3. **What** caused the bitter rivalry between Great Britain and Germany in the early 1900s? **What** was the result of this rivalry? ______
4. **What** nations banded together to form **a)** the Triple Alliance ______; **b)** the Triple Entente ______
5. **How** did the alliances aim to keep peace? ______
6. **Where** did a hotbed of nationalist and ethnic rivalries exist in the early 1900s? ______
7. **When** was Archduke Franz Ferdinand assassinated? ______
8. **Who** murdered Ferdinand and **why**? ______
9. **When** did World War I begin? ______
10. **Why** did Great Britain declare war on Germany? ______
11. **What** countries made up the Central Powers? ______
12. **What** countries made up the Allied Powers by 1915? ______
13. **Where** did the British and French stop the German advance on Paris? ______
14. **What** two 1916 battles resulted in huge numbers of casualties but little gains for either side? ______
15. **Who** were the first to use poison gas in warfare? ______
16. **What** other technological advances accounted for heavy casualties in battle? ______

Linking PAST & PRESENT

Nationalism Of all of Yugoslavia's breakaway republics, none has been as troubled as Bosnia-Herzegovina. Continued civil warfare and "ethnic cleansing" campaigns among Muslims, Croats, and Serbs led to NATO intervention in the 1990s. An agreement signed in December 1995 called for a cease-fire and a division of the country into two federations—one controlled by the Bosnian Serbs and the other controlled jointly by the Muslims and Croats.

nations. Some of these **ethnic groups**—people who share a common language and traditions—demanded independent nations of their own.

Imperial Expansion

Tension in Europe also grew out of the desire of nations to expand their empires. **Imperialism** led to competition for colonies in Africa, Asia, and other parts of the world. These colonies not only brought new markets and raw materials; they also added to a nation's prestige.

Great Britain and France already possessed large overseas empires, but they wanted to expand them even more. Germany, Italy, and **Russia** wanted to increase their colonial holdings as well. Because few areas were left to colonize, however, expansion by one European nation often brought it into conflict with another imperial power.

Military Buildup

As European nations competed for colonies, they strengthened their armies and navies to protect their interests. If one nation increased its military strength, its rivals felt threatened and built up their own military in response. In this atmosphere of **militarism,** Germany, France, and Russia developed huge armies in the early 1900s.

Great Britain, an island nation, had the world's largest and strongest navy. When Germany began to challenge British naval supremacy in the early 1900s, a bitter rivalry developed between the two nations. The rivalry led to an arms race that threatened European stability.

Linking PAST & PRESENT
Nationalism

Nationalism remains a strong force in the world today. Nationalist movements were a factor that led to the collapse of the Soviet Union in 1991. Soon after, Yugoslavia split because its ethnic groups–Slovenes, Croatians, and Bosnians–desired independence.

Forming Alliances

Along with militarism came a strengthening of the **alliance system,** or the defense agreements among nations. By 1914 two major alliances had been established. Germany, Austria-Hungary, and Italy banded together in the **Triple Alliance,** while Great Britain, France, and Russia joined in the **Triple Entente.** An **entente** is an understanding between nations.

The members of each alliance pledged to go to each other's aid in times of crisis. Some also agreed to protect smaller countries allied to them. The alliances aimed to keep peace by creating a **balance of power**—a system that prevents any one country from dominating the others. Yet the alliance system actually posed a great danger. An attack on one nation was all that was needed to trigger a war involving many countries.

Europe was like a powder keg. One American diplomat noted that it would take "only a spark to set the whole thing off." That spark was ignited in the **Balkans.**

Crisis in the Balkans

The Balkan Peninsula in southeastern Europe was a hotbed of nationalist and ethnic rivalries in the early 1900s. The nations of Greece, Albania, Romania, and Bulgaria argued over territory, while Slavic nationalists hoped to unite all the Slavic peoples in the region. Especially bitter was the dispute between Austria-Hungary, whose Slavic people desired independence, and the neighboring nation of Serbia, which supported the Slavs and opposed the empire.

An Assassination Leads to War

On June 28, 1914, Archduke Franz Ferdinand, heir to the throne of Austria-Hungary, was assassinated while on a goodwill visit to **Sarajevo,** the capital of the Balkan kingdom of Bosnia. The assassin, **Gavrilo Princip,** was a member of a Serbian nationalist group, the Black Hand. Princip and other terrorists had plotted the murder to advance the cause of the unification of Slavic peoples.

COOPERATIVE LEARNING ACTIVITY

Preparing a Front Page Have students imagine how the outbreak of war in Europe might have been covered on the front page of a newspaper. Articles and features could include the following:
- Headline and lead article about the assassination in Sarajevo
- Background information about the rise of European nationalism
- Map to review the European alliances
- Comments from American politicians and European diplomats (perhaps including predictions about what this war will mean to the world)

Various roles to be assigned include layout editor, illustrators, and writers. Students can paste up the finished page or use desktop publishing software to prepare it.

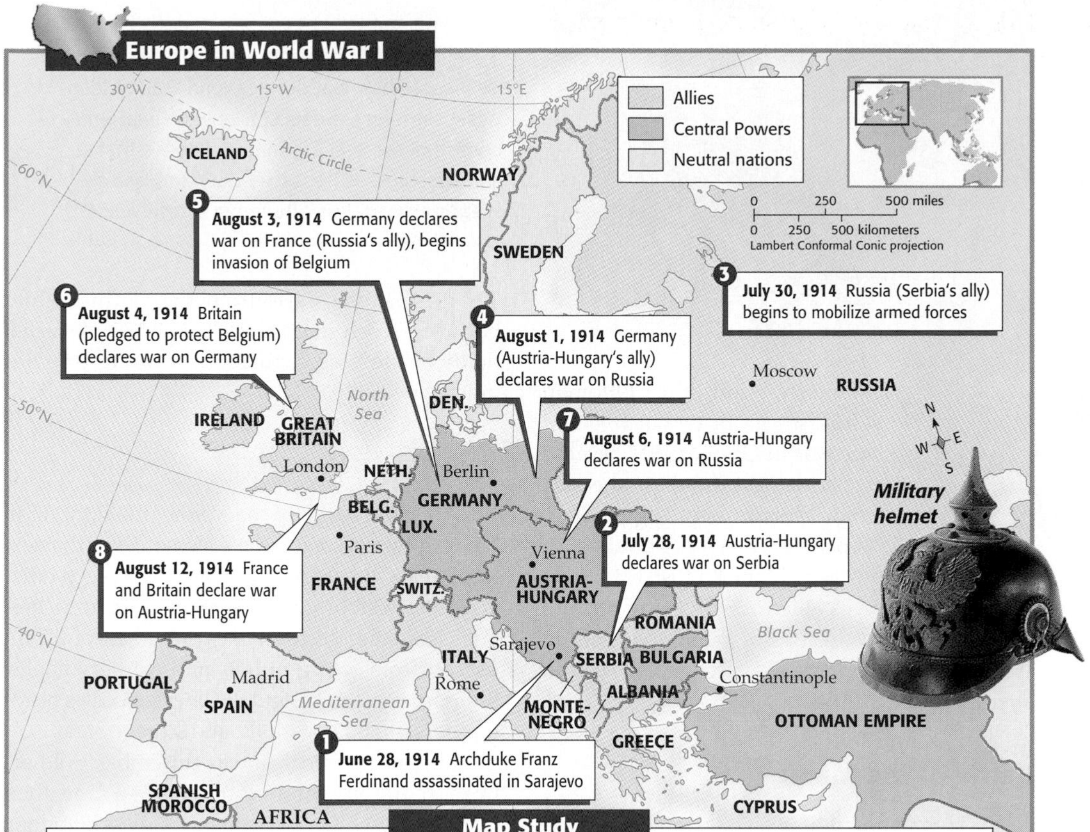

Map Study

World War I initially pitted Germany, Austria-Hungary, and the Ottoman Empire against Great Britain, France, and Russia.

1. **Region** What other country would later join the Central Powers?
2. **Analyzing Information** What incident sparked World War I?

The rulers of Austria-Hungary blamed the Serbian government for the assassination and moved to crush the Serbian nationalist movement. After making sure its ally, Germany, supported its decision, Austria-Hungary delivered a letter to Serbia listing harsh demands. When Serbia refused the conditions, Austria-Hungary declared war on Serbia on July 28, 1914.

Europe's system of alliances caused the war to spread. Russia, which had agreed to protect Serbia, prepared for war. This brought Germany to the side of its ally, Austria-Hungary. Germany declared war on Russia on August 1, 1914. Knowing France was an ally of Russia, Germany declared war on France on August 3.

A day later, Germany invaded **Belgium** as part of a plan to sweep across eastern and northern France. In doing so, Germany violated a treaty signed in 1839 guaranteeing Belgium's neutrality. The invasion of Belgium prompted Great Britain to honor its pledge to protect Belgium, and Britain declared war on Germany.

A World War Begins

The "Great War" had begun. On one side were the **Allied Powers,** or the Allies—Great Britain, France, and Russia. On the other were the **Central Powers**—Germany, Austria-

CHAPTER 23

Section 1, 655–659

ABCNEWS INTERACTIVE™

VIDEODISC
Lessons of War

Side 1, Chapter 5
Title: *How Wars Begin—World War I*
Subject: Exploration of the reasons behind war, specifically World War I
Ask: **What changed the way wars were fought during World War I?** *(New weapons; Tanks, poisonous gases, and machine guns were involved in combat.)*

Map Study

Answers

1. Bulgaria
2. the assassination of Archduke Franz Ferdinand of Austria-Hungary

Map Skills Practice

Reading a Map How much time passed between the assassination of Archduke Franz Ferdinand and France's and Britain's declaration of war on Austria-Hungary? *(45 days)*

MULTIPLE LEARNING STYLES

Visual/Spatial Have students use a map in the text or an outline map that you provide to locate the members of the Triple Alliance and the Triple Entente. Ask students to measure the distances between the capitals of the countries within the two groups. Then discuss the relative size and proximity of these groupings. **Ask:** **Why might it be beneficial for allied nations to be located near each other (as was the case of the Triple Alliance nations)? Does distance from your allies matter if your allies are large and strong (as was the case of the Triple Entente)? Why is it beneficial to have allies at all? L2, ELL**

CURRICULUM CONNECTION

LITERATURE
In his novel *All Quiet on the Western Front,* German author Erich Maria Remarque told of life in the trenches:

"The sun goes down, night comes, the shells whine, life is at an end.

"Still the little piece of convulsed earth in which we lie is held. We have yielded no more than a few hundred yards of it as a prize to the enemy. But on every yard there lies a dead man."

CHAPTER 23
Section 1, 655–659

Picturing HISTORY World War I aviators and their dogfights were a main subject of *Wings* (1927). This silent film, which included actual combat footage, won the first Academy Award for Best Picture. **Ask:** What are at least two differences between these airplanes and present-day air force airplanes? *(Airplanes shown have double wings; most fighter aircraft today do not have propellers.)*
Answer: *improved cannons and other artillery, better rifles and machine guns, poison gas, armored tanks, zeppelins, and submarines*

3 ASSESS

Assign Section 1 Review as homework or as an in-class activity.

Use **Chapter Challenger Interactive Review Software** to review Section 1.

Section Quiz 23–1

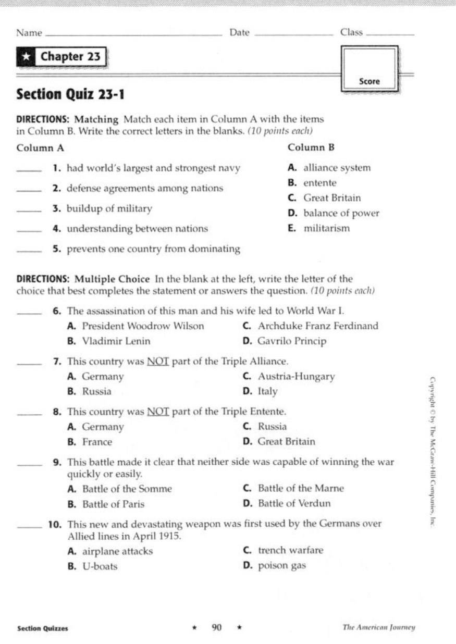
Name ______ Date ______ Class ______

★ Chapter 23 — Score

Section Quiz 23-1

DIRECTIONS: Matching Match each item in Column A with the items in Column B. Write the correct letters in the blanks. *(10 points each)*

Column A	Column B
____ 1. had world's largest and strongest navy	A. alliance system
____ 2. defense agreements among nations	B. entente
____ 3. buildup of military	C. Great Britain
____ 4. understanding between nations	D. balance of power
____ 5. prevents one country from dominating	E. militarism

DIRECTIONS: Multiple Choice In the blank at the left, write the letter of the choice that best completes the statement or answers the question. *(10 points each)*

____ 6. The assassination of this man and his wife led to World War I.
A. President Woodrow Wilson C. Archduke Franz Ferdinand
B. Vladimir Lenin D. Gavrilo Princip

____ 7. This country was NOT part of the Triple Alliance.
A. Germany C. Austria-Hungary
B. Russia D. Italy

____ 8. This country was NOT part of the Triple Entente.
A. Germany C. Russia
B. France D. Great Britain

____ 9. This battle made it clear that neither side was capable of winning the war quickly or easily.
A. Battle of the Somme C. Battle of the Marne
B. Battle of Paris D. Battle of Verdun

____ 10. This new and devastating weapon was first used by the Germans over Allied lines in April 1915.
A. airplane attacks C. trench warfare
B. U-boats D. poison gas

Section Quizzes ★ 90 ★ *The American Journey*

Copyright © by The McGraw-Hill Companies, Inc.

Picturing HISTORY Airplanes were first used in combat during World War I. Meanwhile German U-boats challenged Great Britain's control of the seas by firing torpedoes that sank surface ships. **What other new and deadly weapons were introduced in World War I?**

Hungary, and the Ottoman (Turkish) Empire, which joined the war in October 1914 because it had fought Russia in the past and feared new aggression. **Japan,** a rival of Germany in Asia, joined the Allies in late August 1914. Italy refused to honor its alliance with Germany and Austria-Hungary. Instead, it joined the Allies in 1915 after being promised territory in Austria after the war.

Battle of the Marne

In launching an offensive through Belgium, Germany hoped to defeat France quickly and destroy the French armies. This would allow Germany to move troops east against Russia.

The plan almost succeeded. The Belgians, however, held out heroically for nearly three weeks against the powerful German army. This delay gave the French and British time to mobilize their forces.

After defeating the Belgians, the Germans marched into France and advanced to within 15 miles of **Paris.** The British and French finally managed to stop the German advance at the **Marne River** just a few miles east of the city. The **Battle of the Marne,** fought between September 5 and 12, 1914, saved Paris from the Germans and boosted French morale. It also made it clear that neither side was capable of winning the war quickly or easily.

Trench Warfare

After the Battle of the Marne, the fighting in western Europe reached a stalemate. For the next three years, the opposing armies faced each other across an elaborate network of deep trenches. Trenches along the front lines provided some protection from flying bullets and artillery shells. Support trenches behind the lines served as headquarters, first-aid stations, and storage areas.

Life in the trenches was miserable. Soldiers lived in dirt and mud for months at a time, their lives filled with terrible fear and endless boredom. Between the enemy lines lay a "no-man's-land" of barbed wire and land mines. Endless days of shelling the enemy might sometimes be interrupted by an attempt to "break out" of the trenches and advance into enemy territory.

Verdun and the Somme

In 1916 both sides attempted to break the deadlock of trench warfare by launching major offensives. The German offensive, the **Battle of Verdun** in northeastern France, began in February and continued on and off until December. At first the Germans made small gains, but these

Footnotes to History

Holiday Truce On Christmas Day 1914, fighting stopped, and British and German soldiers met in no-man's-land to chat, play soccer, and pose for photographs. Officers quickly ended these goodwill meetings, and the soldiers returned to war.

MAKING CONNECTIONS ACTIVITY

Music Few things stir feelings of nationalism as does the sound of one's national anthem. Have students learn the words to one of the following:

- Our national anthem
- The national anthem of a country of their ancestry
- The national anthem of the country in which they were born, if other than the United States
- The national anthem of one of the countries mentioned in Section 1

As students share the national anthems, ask them to comment on how pride in one's country, expressed positively in national anthems, could eventually lead to war. **L2**

CHAPTER 23
Section 1, 655–659

were lost after the French counterattacked. Verdun was one of the longest and bloodiest battles of the war. When it was over, more than 750,000 French and German soldiers had lost their lives.

While the Battle of Verdun raged, the British and French launched their own offensive in northern France in July—the **Battle of the Somme**. Again the number of casualties was extremely high. The Allies gained only about 7 miles (11.2 km) in the offensive.

Deadly Technology

New and more deadly weapons accounted for the terrible slaughter during these battles. Improved cannons and other artillery fired larger shells greater distances than ever before. Better rifles enabled soldiers to hit targets with greater accuracy. A new, improved machine gun fired a burst of bullets in just a few seconds.

Poison gas, another new and devastating weapon, was first used by the Germans over Allied lines in April 1915. The gas could kill or seriously injure anyone who breathed it. "They fought with terror, running blindly in the gas cloud, and dropping . . . in agony," wrote a British officer of troops overcome by poison gas. The Allies began to use poison gas also, and gas masks became necessary equipment in the trenches.

The armored tank, invented by the British, proved effective for crossing battle lines to fire on the enemy at close range. Tanks also could crush barbed wire, providing an easier route for advancing troops. After the Germans saw the effectiveness of tanks, they produced them too.

The most dramatic new weapon—the airplane—added a new dimension to fighting in World War I. Both sides used airplanes for watching troop movements and bombing enemy targets. Daring pilots waged duels in the skies called "dogfights." The most famous pilots included Germany's "Red Baron," **Baron von Richthofen,** and America's **Eddie Rickenbacker,** who served in the French air force. The Germans used the **zeppelin,** or blimp, to bomb Allied cities.

On the Seas

With their land armies deadlocked in western Europe, both sides looked to the sea to gain an advantage in the war. Great Britain blockaded all ports under German control, eventually causing serious shortages. Many Germans suffered from malnutrition and illness because of lack of food and other supplies.

Germany had an effective naval weapon of its own: the submarine. Known as **U-boats**—from the German word for submarine, *Unterseeboot*—submarines prevented supplies, including food, from reaching Great Britain. U-boat attacks on ships at sea eventually affected the United States and changed the course of the war.

★ ★ ★ ★ ★ ★ Section 1 Review ★ ★ ★ ★ ★ ★

Checking for Understanding

1. ***Identify*** Archduke Franz Ferdinand, Allied Powers, Central Powers.
2. ***Define*** nationalism, militarism, alliance system, entente.
3. ***Discuss*** how militarism led Europe into World War I.

Reviewing Themes

4. **Science and Technology** Why were casualties so high in World War I?

Critical Thinking

5. **Identifying Central Issues** How did forming alliances increase the likelihood of war in Europe?

Activity

Building a Model Research the inventions that were developed in World War I. Using clay, papier-mâché, or other materials, build a model of the invention you researched.

Reteaching Activity 23–1

Name ________ Date ________ Class ________

★ Reteaching Activity 23-1

DIRECTIONS: Putting Events in Sequence Number the events in the order in which they occurred.

____ **A.** The Triple Alliance and the Triple Entente are established.
____ **B.** Germany invades Belgium, violating a treaty guaranteeing Belgium's neutrality.
____ **C.** The Ottoman Empire joins the Central Powers in war.
____ **D.** Great Britain declares war on Germany.
____ **E.** Germans first use poison gas, a new and devastating weapon, against Allied forces.
____ **F.** The French launch a major offensive—the Battle of the Somme.
____ **G.** Gavrilo Princip and the nationalist group, the Black Hand, plot to advance the cause of the unification of Slavic peoples.
____ **H.** The British and the French armies stop the German advance on Paris at the Marne River, just a few miles east of the city.
____ **I.** Austria-Hungary declares war on Serbia.
____ **J.** Archduke Franz Ferdinand, heir to the throne of Austria-Hungary, is assassinated.
____ **K.** The Germans launch a major offensive—the Battle of Verdun.
____ **L.** Germany declares war on Russia.
____ **M.** Germany challenges British naval supremacy in Europe.
____ **N.** Japan, a rival of Germany in Asia, joins the Allies in war.
____ **O.** Germany declares war on France.

DIRECTIONS: Essay On a separate sheet of paper, answer the questions below.

1. How did nationalism and imperialism lead to tension and conflict in Europe?
2. Describe World War I trench warfare and explain why it was so miserable for soldiers.

Reteaching Activities ★ 90 ★ *The American Journey*

Enrichment Activity 23–1

Name ________ Date ________ Class ________

★ Enrichment Activity 23-1 ★ ★

Battles in the Air

World War I began only 11 years after the Wright Brothers' first flight, yet both the Allied Powers and the Central Powers rushed warplanes into the skies.

Comparing Military Aircraft

	Fokker Dr. 1	Spad S. 13	
Description	Triplane fighter	Biplane fighter	
Length	18.93 ft. (5.8 m)	20.33 ft. (6.2 m)	
Wingspan	23.52 ft. (7.2 m)	26.3 ft. (8 m)	
Weight	1,289 lb. (585 kg)	1,801 lb. (818 kg)	
Maximum speed	115 mph at sea level (185 kph)	138 mph at sea level (222 kph)	
Armament	Two machine guns	Two machine guns	

Fokker Dr. 1

Spad S. 13

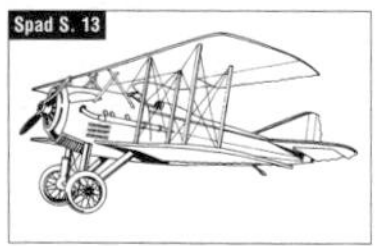

Activity **DIRECTIONS:** Research a model of a modern military aircraft, complete the third column of the chart above with that model's specifications, and draw a picture of the plane.

DIRECTIONS: Applying Facts Use the facts in the completed chart to answer the following questions on a separate sheet of paper.

1. How much more does the modern military aircraft weigh than the Spad S. 13?
2. How many times longer is the modern military aircraft than the Fokker Dr. 1?
3. Draw a bar graph that compares the speeds of modern military aircraft with the Spad and the Fokker.

Enrichment Activities ★ 90 ★ *The American Journey*

★ ★ ★ ★ ★ ★ ★ Section 1 Review Answers ★ ★ ★ ★ ★ ★ ★

1. Archduke Franz Ferdinand, 655; Allied Powers, 657; Central Powers, 657
2. The words are defined in the Glossary.
3. European nations increased their armies and navies to protect their colonial interests. This led to an arms race that threatened European stability.
4. Improved weapons, poison gas, armored tanks, airplanes, and submarines increased the number of soldiers wounded or killed.
5. Forming alliances fueled national rivalries. The greatest danger was that when conflict erupted between two rival nations, all nations allied to each side in the conflict would become involved.

Activity Models should be accurate representations of the inventions chosen.

4 CLOSE

Ask students which factor they think was most responsible for the outbreak of war in Europe and to explain their choice.

1 FOCUS

BELLRINGER
Motivational Activity

Before taking roll at the beginning of the class period, project Section Focus Transparency 23–2 and have students answer the questions. Discuss students' responses.

This activity is also available as a blackline master.

Section Focus Transparency 23–2

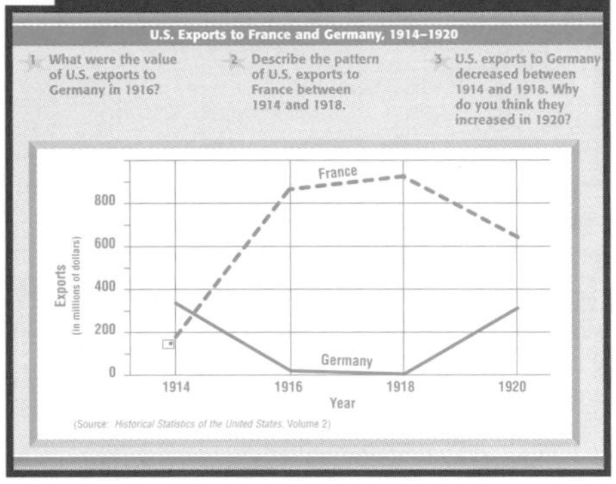

Vocabulary Precheck

Point out that *propaganda* is a Latin term derived from *Congregatio de propaganda fide* or "Congregation for propagating the faith," an organization established by Pope Gregory XV. Ask students to speculate on the connection between its derivation and present-day usage.

Use the **Vocabulary PuzzleMaker** to create crossword and word search puzzles.

Section Theme
Government and Democracy

A variety of events in war-torn Europe caused the United States, officially neutral at first, to enter the conflict on the side of the Allied Powers.

Activity Have students speculate on why it is difficult for a person—or a government—to remain neutral in a conflict.

1914 — 1916 — 1918

August 1914 Europe goes to war

May 1915 Germany torpedoes the *Lusitania*

March 1917 Zimmermann telegram angers U.S.

April 1917 U.S. declares war on Germany

Section 2

America's Road to War

READ TO DISCOVER . . .

- how Americans responded to the war in Europe.
- what led to American involvement in the war.
- how America raised an army to fight.

TERMS TO LEARN

propaganda — autocracy

The Storyteller

President Wilson struggled to remain neutral, even after Americans had been killed at the outbreak of World War I. Others felt differently. An American businessman cabled the president after the *Laconia* was sunk by Germans: "My beloved mother and sister . . . have been foully murdered on the high seas. . . . I call upon my government to preserve its citizens' self-respect and save others of my countrymen from such deep grief as I now feel. I am of military age, able to fight. If my country can use me against these brutal assassins, I am at its call. If it . . . [remains] passive under outrage, I shall seek a man's chance under another flag." Remaining neutral grew more and more difficult.

Magazine cover, 1914

When Europe went to war in August 1914, most Americans believed that the war did not concern them. Many shared the view expressed in an editorial in the *New York Sun*:

> "There is nothing reasonable in such a war, and it would be folly for the country to sacrifice itself to the frenzy of dynastic policies and the clash of ancient hatreds which is urging the Old World to destruction."

President Wilson agreed. He declared that the United States would be neutral in the war and called on Americans to be "neutral in fact as well as in name, impartial in thought as well as in action."

American Neutrality

Despite Wilson's plea to remain neutral, Americans soon began to take sides. More than one-third of the nation's 92 million people were either foreign-born or the children of immigrants. Many of these people naturally sympathized with their countries of origin. Some of the 8 million Americans of German or Austrian descent and the 4.5 million Irish Americans—who hated the British because they ruled Ireland—favored the Central Powers.

Even more Americans, however, including President Wilson, felt sympathetic to the Allies. Ties of language, customs, and traditions linked the United States to Great Britain, and many

SECTION RESOURCES

Reproducible Masters
- Reproducible Lesson Plan 23–2
- Guided Reading Activity 23–2
- Section Quiz 23–2
- Reteaching Activity 23–2
- Enrichment Activity 23–2

Transparencies
- Section Focus Transparency 23–2

Multimedia
- Vocabulary PuzzleMaker
- Chapter Challenger Interactive Review Software
- Testmaker
- The Presidents: A Picture History of Our Nation

Picturing HISTORY The *Lusitania* left New York for England on May 1, 1915. Germany had placed a warning notice in American newspapers, but few people took it seriously. **How did the United States respond to German U-boat attacks?**

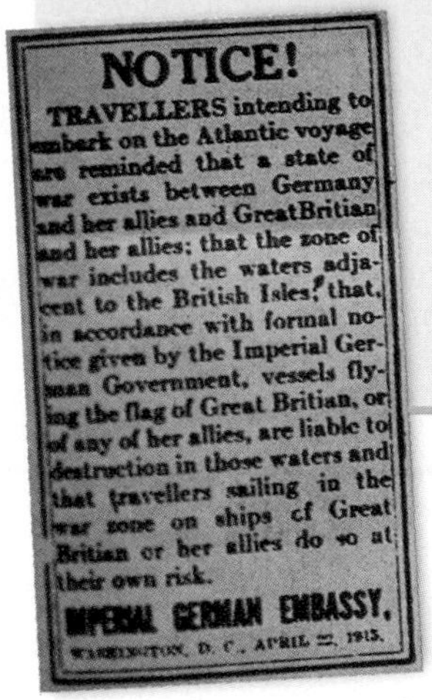

NOTICE!

TRAVELLERS intending to embark on the Atlantic voyage are reminded that a state of war exists between Germany and her allies and GreatBritian and her allies; that the zone of war includes the waters adjacent to the British Isles; that, in accordance with formal notice given by the Imperial German Government, vessels flying the flag of Great Britian, or of any of her allies, are liable to destruction in those waters and that travellers sailing in the war zone on ships of Great Britian or her allies do so at their own risk.

IMPERIAL GERMAN EMBASSY,
WASHINGTON, D. C., APRIL [illegible], 1915.

Americans were of British descent. President Wilson told the British ambassador: "Everything I love most in the world is at stake." A German victory "would be fatal to our form of government and American ideals."

Using Propaganda

To gain the support of Americans, both sides in the war used propaganda—information designed to influence opinion. Allied propaganda emphasized the German invasion of neutral Belgium and included horror stories of German atrocities. It called the Germans "Huns" and pictured them as savage barbarians.

The propaganda from the Central Powers was equally horrible, but because of British sympathies, the Allied propaganda was more effective in influencing Americans.

America's Early Involvement

Trade between the United States and the Allies helped build support for the Allied cause. As a neutral nation, America sought to trade with both sides, but Britain's blockade of Germany made this difficult.

The British navy stopped and searched American ships headed for German ports, often seizing the ships' goods. The United States protested that its ships should be able to pass without interference. The British responded with the defense that they were fighting for their survival. "If the American shipper grumbles," wrote a London paper, "our reply is that this war is not being conducted for his pleasure or profit." The United States government could do nothing about the blockade. Barred from trading with Germany, it continued trading with Britain.

Indeed, American trade with the Allies soared—from about $825 million in 1914 to about $3.2 billion in 1916. In addition Great Britain and France borrowed billions of dollars from American banks to help pay for their war efforts. All this business caused an economic boom in the United States. It also upset the Germans, who watched the United States—supposedly a neutral nation—become the arsenal of the Allies.

Submarine Warfare

To stop American economic assistance to Britain, Germany announced in February 1915 that it would use its U-boats to sink any vessels that entered or left British ports.

The United States protested the policy. President Wilson warned that America would hold

Picturing HISTORY William Jennings Bryan, Wilson's first secretary of state, strongly supported neutrality. After the sinking of the *Lusitania,* it was with great reluctance that he signed Wilson's first note of protest to Germany. When Wilson prepared a second and stronger protest, Bryan refused to sign it. Instead, he quit his cabinet position. **Ask:** **According to this notice, where were vessels warned not to travel?** *(waters adjacent to the British Isles)*
Answer: *Americans were outraged, and President Wilson denounced the attack and threatened to end diplomatic relations with Germany.*

2 TEACH

L1 Evaluating Language Call on volunteers to locate loaded words and phrases in the editorial excerpted on page 660. *(nothing reasonable, folly, sacrifice, frenzy, clash, ancient hatreds,* and *destruction.)* Discuss how the words support a stance of neutrality.

Guided Reading Activity 23–2

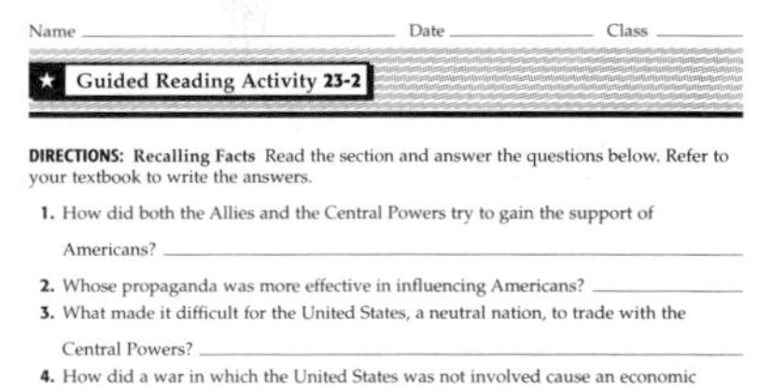

Name ______ Date ______ Class ______

★ Guided Reading Activity 23-2

DIRECTIONS: Recalling Facts Read the section and answer the questions below. Refer to your textbook to write the answers.

1. How did both the Allies and the Central Powers try to gain the support of Americans? ______
2. Whose propaganda was more effective in influencing Americans? ______
3. What made it difficult for the United States, a neutral nation, to trade with the Central Powers? ______
4. How did a war in which the United States was not involved cause an economic boom for Americans? ______
5. What did Germany do in February 1915 to stop American economic assistance to Great Britain? ______
6. Name the British passenger liner sunk by a German U-boat on May 7, 1915. ______
7. Why did Germany offer to compensate Americans injured when a German U-boat torpedoed the French passenger ship *Sussex*? ______
8. In 1916 what did some Americans see as a major step toward involvement in the war? ______
9. Why did President Woodrow Wilson break off diplomatic relations with Germany in January 1917? ______
10. What did newspapers publish on March 1, 1917, that set off a new wave of anti-German feeling in the United States? ______
11. What event in Russia led Wilson to claim that the Allies were fighting a war of democracy against autocracy? ______
12. When and why did Wilson ask Congress for a declaration of war against Germany? ______
13. Why did Congress pass the Selective Service Act on May 18, 1917? ______
14. Who was Henry Johnson? ______

The American Journey ★ 91 ★ **Guided Reading Activities**

Cooperative Learning Activity

Exploring Propaganda Organize students into two teams—one to represent Americans who wanted to support the Allied cause, the other to represent Americans who wanted to remain neutral. Have each team choose a leader and decide how to accomplish the following tasks:

- Prepare a slogan to express the team's opinion
- Create posters that express the same point of view
- Prepare spokespeople to summarize that point of view
- Write an editorial about the wisdom of the team's position

Have each team leader guide group members in the presentation of the finished material. Follow up with a class discussion.

CHAPTER 23

Section 2, 660–664

NATIONAL GEOGRAPHIC SOCIETY

CD-ROM
The Presidents: A Picture History of Our Nation

Have students click on "Woodrow Wilson" to learn more about his actions during World War I.

TECHNOLOGY AND HISTORY

More About . . .

Submarines The first German U-boat (U1) was built in 1906. During World War I, Germany was able to put several types of U-boats into service. The Desiderata class (U5-U18), for example, saw much of the frontline action. In one 1914 encounter, U9 sank three British cruisers, killing 3,600 men. The Mittel-U submarines used deck guns more often than torpedoes. The UB and UC classes specialized in coastal missions, especially minelaying, while the UE class laid mines farther out to sea. The UA class, a merchant submarine that was built late in the war, was a huge, heavily armed cruiser.
Answer to Caption: *the diving rudders*

Germany responsible for any American lives lost in submarine attacks. Determined to cut off supplies to Great Britain, the Germans ignored this threat.

On May 7, 1915, a German U-boat torpedoed the British passenger liner ***Lusitania*** off the coast of Ireland. W.T. Turner, the ship's captain, reported:

> "I saw the torpedo speeding towards us. Immediately I tried to change our course, but was unable to maneuver out of its way. There was a terrible impact as the torpedo struck the starboard side of the vessel. . . . It was cold-blooded murder."

The *Lusitania* sank in about 15 minutes. More than 1,000 people died, including 128 United States citizens. Americans were outraged, and President Wilson denounced the attack. Later it was learned that the ship carried war materials.

Several months later a German U-boat torpedoed the unarmed French passenger ship *Sussex,* injuring several Americans. The United States denounced the attack as a violation of international law, and Wilson threatened to end diplomatic relations with Germany. Fearing that the Americans might enter the war, Germany offered to compensate Americans injured on the *Sussex* and promised to warn neutral ships and passenger vessels before attacking. The Sussex Pledge, as it was called, seemed to resolve the issue.

TECHNOLOGY AND HISTORY

Submarine

During World War I, German U-boats, *or submarines, became the terror of the seas.*
What part of the craft guided the submarine up and down?

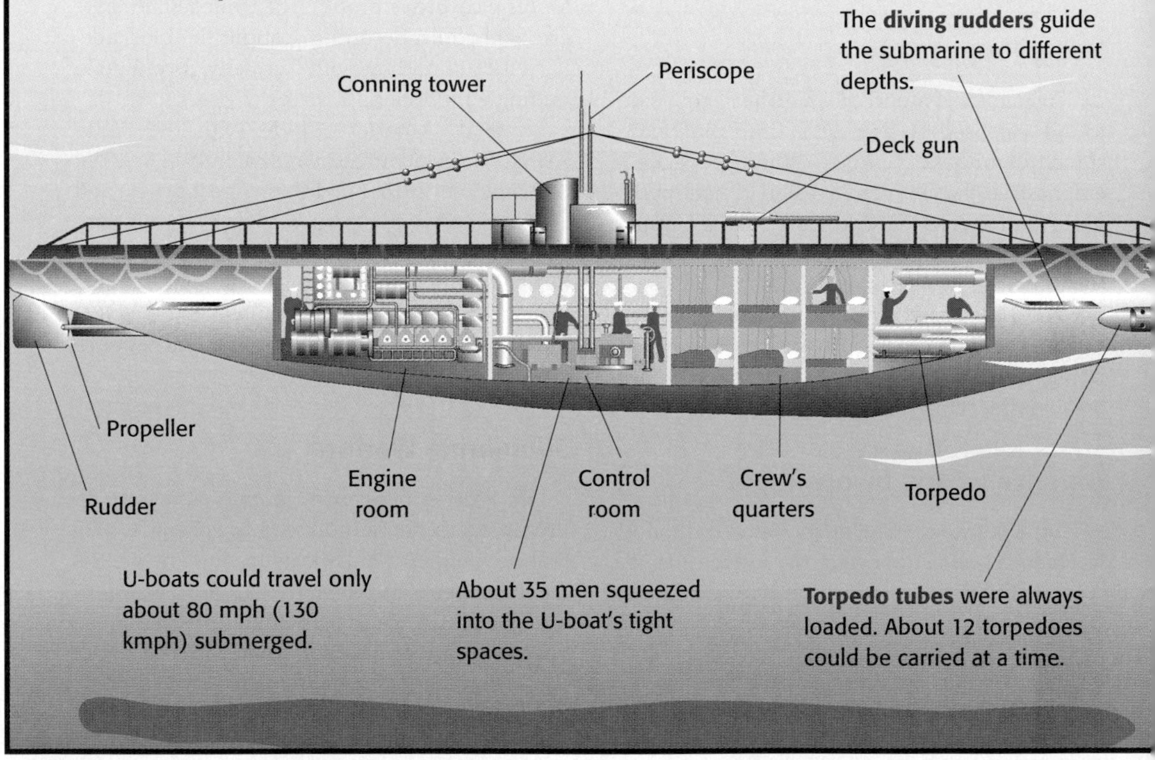

MULTIPLE LEARNING STYLES

Logical/Mathematical Why would the United States want to become involved in a conflict between European nations? Review this section by asking students who enjoy analytical questions to make up a list of Pro and Con statements that President Wilson, his advisers, and members of Congress might have made as they considered the move from neutrality to war. Encourage students to consider political, economic, and social reasons as well as personal feelings about this war and/or the countries involved in it. Interested students might use this activity as the springboard for a debate on the United States's entry into the war. **L2**

The End of Neutrality

The crisis over submarine warfare prompted the United States to take steps to strengthen its military forces. In the summer of 1916, Congress passed legislation that doubled the size of the army and provided funds to build new warships. President Wilson still hoped, however, to stay out of the war.

Antiwar sentiment remained very strong. Some Americans criticized the nation's military buildup, seeing it as a major step toward involvement in the war. A popular song in 1915 expressed this opposition:

> "I didn't raise my boy to be a soldier,
> I brought him up to be my pride and joy.
> Who dares place a musket on his shoulder,
> To shoot some other mother's
> darling boy?"

The 1916 Election

Antiwar sentiment was strong at the 1916 Democratic national convention, where all references to the president's efforts to keep the country out of war brought wild applause. After Wilson was nominated for a second term, the phrase "He Kept Us Out of War" became the Democrats' slogan. Wilson narrowly defeated the Republican presidential candidate, Charles Evans Hughes. The question of neutrality divided the Republicans, and Hughes avoided discussing the issue.

On the Brink of War

In January 1917, Germany reversed its policy on submarine warfare. It announced that it would sink on sight all merchant vessels, armed or unarmed, sailing to Allied ports. While realizing that their policy might bring the Americans into the war, the Germans believed they could defeat the Allies before the United States became heavily involved. An angry President Wilson broke off diplomatic relations with Germany.

A few weeks later, a secret telegram—intercepted by the British government—set off a new wave of anti-German feeling. In late February the German foreign minister, Arthur Zimmermann, sent a telegram to **Mexico** with an offer to the Mexican government:

> "MAKE WAR TOGETHER, MAKE PEACE TOGETHER, GENEROUS FINANCIAL SUPPORT, AND AN UNDERSTANDING ON OUR PART THAT MEXICO IS TO RECONQUER THE LOST TERRITORY IN TEXAS, NEW MEXICO, AND ARIZONA."

Newspapers published the secret **Zimmermann telegram** on March 1, and Americans reacted angrily to the German action.

Linking PAST & PRESENT

The Draft

The United States used a military draft in both world wars, the Korean War, the cold war, and the Vietnam War. In 1973 Congress ended the draft, but since 1981 men have still been required to register for military service at age 18.

Revolution in Russia

In the weeks following publication of the Zimmermann telegram, dramatic events pushed the United States to the brink of war. First, a revolution took place in **Russia.** Following a period of rioting and strikes, the Russian people overthrew the monarchy. In its place they established a provisional democratic government.

Many Americans believed that the new Russian government, which vowed to defeat Germany, would help the Allies. With Russia's change to a democratic form of government, Wilson could now claim that the Allies were fighting a war of democracy against autocracy—rule by one person with unlimited power.

Other critical events took place at sea. On March 18, German U-boats sank three American merchant ships without warning and with heavy loss of life. President Wilson concluded that the United States could no longer remain neutral.

CHAPTER 23

Section 2, 660–664

Who? What? Where? When?

Charles Evans Hughes As a Supreme Court justice since 1910, Hughes had kept quiet about public issues—yet he was the front-runner at the 1916 Republican convention. As the candidate, Hughes represented a platform that urged "a strict and honest neutrality"—yet he won the endorsement of the prowar Theodore Roosevelt. Hughes was considered the favorite in the race and came close to winning the election, taking 46 percent of the popular vote and 254 electoral votes, as opposed to Wilson's 49 percent of the popular vote and 277 electoral votes.

3 ASSESS

Assign Section 2 Review as homework or as an in-class activity.

Use **Chapter Challenger Interactive Review Software** to review Section 2.

Section Quiz 23–2

Name ______ Date ______ Class ______

Chapter 23 — Score

Section Quiz 23-2

DIRECTIONS: Matching Match each item in Column A with the items in Column B. Write the correct letters in the blanks. *(10 points each)*

Column A	Column B
____ 1. German U-boats	A. Charles Evans Hughes
____ 2. sunk by Germans	B. "He Kept Us Out of War"
____ 3. Democrats' slogan	C. *Lusitania*
____ 4. 1916 Republican candidate	D. Jeannette Rankin
____ 5. voted against war	E. submarines

DIRECTIONS: Multiple Choice In the blank at the left, write the letter of the choice that best completes the statement or answers the question. *(10 points each)*

____ 6. To gain support of Americans, both the Allies and the Central Powers used
A. nationalism. C. autocracy.
B. propaganda. D. militarism.

____ 7. With this Germany agreed to warn neutral ships and passenger vessels before attacking.
A. armistice C. sinking of the *Lusitania*
B. Zimmermann telegram D. the Sussex Pledge

____ 8. Intercepted by the British government, this caused Americans to react angrily to the Germans.
A. U-boat in the Atlantic Ocean C. Zimmermann telegram
B. the Sussex Pledge D. Selective Service Act

____ 9. Woodrow Wilson claimed that the Allies were fighting a war of democracy against
A. slavery. C. evil.
B. dictatorships. D. autocracy.

____ 10. This person was the first American to receive the French Croix de Guerre for bravery.
A. Henry Johnson C. Jeannette Rankin
B. Woodrow Wilson D. Charles Evans Hughes

The American Journey ★ 91 ★ **Section Quizzes**

MAKING CONNECTIONS ACTIVITY

Politics Share these quotations from political leaders who were active speakers during the war years:

". . . loans by American bankers to any foreign nation at war are inconsistent with the true spirit of neutrality." —William Jennings Bryan, 1914

"Germany has become a menace to the whole world. She is the most dangerous enemy of liberty now existing." —Theodore Roosevelt, 1917

"Our whole duty . . . is summed up in this motto: *America first.*" —Woodrow Wilson, 1915

Have students discuss the meaning of each comment, noting especially whether it supports neutrality or involvement in the war. **L1**

CHAPTER 23
Section 2, 660–664

Who?What?Where?When?

Jeannette Rankin Have students learn more about Jeannette Rankin by turning to pages 614–615.

Reteaching Activity 23–2

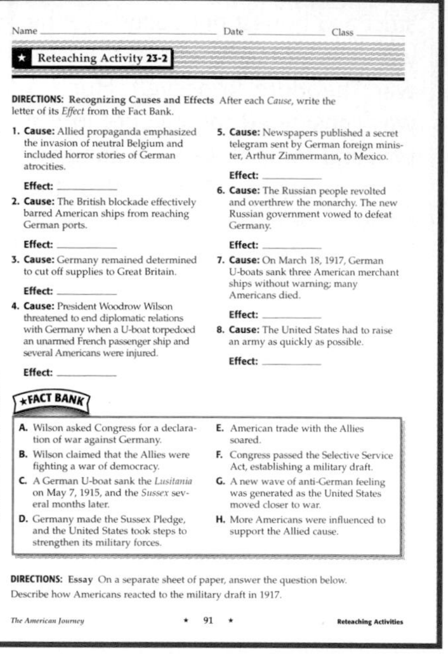
Name ________ Date ________ Class ________

★ Reteaching Activity 23-2

DIRECTIONS: Recognizing Causes and Effects After each *Cause,* write the letter of its *Effect* from the Fact Bank.

1. **Cause:** Allied propaganda emphasized the invasion of neutral Belgium and included horror stories of German atrocities.
   Effect: ________
2. **Cause:** The British blockade effectively barred American ships from reaching German ports.
   Effect: ________
3. **Cause:** Germany remained determined to cut off supplies to Great Britain.
   Effect: ________
4. **Cause:** President Woodrow Wilson threatened to end diplomatic relations with Germany when a U-boat torpedoed an unarmed French passenger ship and several Americans were injured.
   Effect: ________
5. **Cause:** Newspapers published a secret telegram sent by German foreign minister, Arthur Zimmermann, to Mexico.
   Effect: ________
6. **Cause:** The Russian people revolted and overthrew the monarchy. The new Russian government vowed to defeat Germany.
   Effect: ________
7. **Cause:** On March 18, 1917, German U-boats sank three American merchant ships without warning; many Americans died.
   Effect: ________
8. **Cause:** The United States had to raise an army as quickly as possible.
   Effect: ________

★FACT BANK

A. Wilson asked Congress for a declaration of war against Germany.
B. Wilson claimed that the Allies were fighting a war of democracy.
C. A German U-boat sank the *Lusitania* on May 7, 1915, and the *Sussex* several months later.
D. Germany made the Sussex Pledge, and the United States took steps to strengthen its military forces.
E. American trade with the Allies soared.
F. Congress passed the Selective Service Act, establishing a military draft.
G. A new wave of anti-German feeling was generated as the United States moved closer to war.
H. More Americans were influenced to support the Allied cause.

DIRECTIONS: Essay On a separate sheet of paper, answer the question below. Describe how Americans reacted to the military draft in 1917.

The American Journey ★ 91 ★ **Reteaching Activities**

Enrichment Activity 23–2

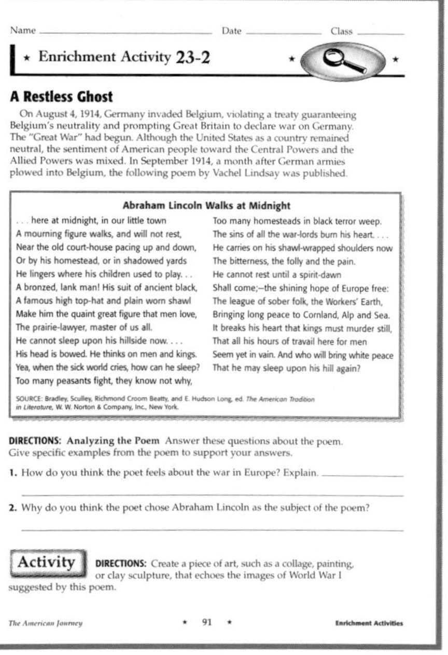
Name ________ Date ________ Class ________

★ Enrichment Activity 23-2

A Restless Ghost

On August 4, 1914, Germany invaded Belgium, violating a treaty guaranteeing Belgium's neutrality and prompting Great Britain to declare war on Germany. The "Great War" had begun. Although the United States as a country remained neutral, the sentiment of American people toward the Central Powers and the Allied Powers was mixed. In September 1914, a month after German armies plowed into Belgium, the following poem by Vachel Lindsay was published.

Abraham Lincoln Walks at Midnight

. . . here at midnight, in our little town
A mourning figure walks, and will not rest,
Near the old court-house pacing up and down,
Or by his homestead, or in shadowed yards
He lingers where his children used to play. . .
A bronzed, lank man! His suit of ancient black,
A famous high top-hat and plain worn shawl
Make him the quaint great figure that men love,
The prairie-lawyer, master of us all.
He cannot sleep upon his hillside now. . . .
His head is bowed. He thinks on men and kings.
Yea, when the sick world cries, how can he sleep?
Too many peasants fight, they know not why,
Too many homesteads in black terror weep.
The sins of all the war-lords burn his heart. . . .
He carries on his shawl-wrapped shoulders now
The bitterness, the folly and the pain.
He cannot rest until a spirit-dawn
Shall come;–the shining hope of Europe free:
The league of sober folk, the Workers' Earth,
Bringing long peace to Cornland, Alp and Sea.
It breaks his heart that kings must murder still,
That all his hours of travail here for men
Seem yet in vain. And who will bring white peace
That he may sleep upon his hill again?

SOURCE: Bradley, Sculley, Richmond Croom Beatty, and E. Hudson Long, ed. *The American Tradition in Literature,* W. W. Norton & Company, Inc., New York.

DIRECTIONS: Analyzing the Poem Answer these questions about the poem. Give specific examples from the poem to support your answers.

1. How do you think the poet feels about the war in Europe? Explain. ________
2. Why do you think the poet chose Abraham Lincoln as the subject of the poem? ________

Activity **DIRECTIONS:** Create a piece of art, such as a collage, painting, or clay sculpture, that echoes the images of World War I suggested by this poem.

The American Journey ★ 91 ★ **Enrichment Activities**

4 CLOSE

Have students use the time line on page 660 to explain why it became difficult for the United States to remain neutral about the war.

America Enters the War

On the cold, rainy evening of April 2, 1917, President Wilson stood before a special session of Congress to ask for a declaration of war against Germany.

> "The world must be made safe for democracy. . . . It is a fearful thing to lead this great peaceful people into war, into the most terrible and disastrous of all wars. . . . But the right is more precious than peace, and we shall fight for the things which we have always carried nearest our hearts—for democracy."

Jeannette Rankin

Congress passed a declaration of war, and Wilson signed it on April 6. Fifty-six members of the House and Senate voted against war, including Representative Jeannette Rankin of Montana—the first woman to serve in Congress.

Raising an Army

The United States had to raise an army quickly. On May 18, Congress passed the **Selective Service Act,** establishing a military draft. Unlike the draft during the Civil War that led to riots, this draft had the support of most of the American public.

Men aged 21 to 30 (later the draft age was extended from 18 to 45) registered by the millions. By the end of the war, some 24 million men had registered. Of those, about 3 million were called to serve; another 2 million joined the armed forces voluntarily.

In addition thousands of women enlisted in the armed forces—the first time they were allowed to do so. All the women did noncombat work, serving as radio operators, clerks, and nurses.

Many African Americans also wanted to serve their country. More than 300,000 joined the army and navy—the marines would not accept them. African Americans faced discrimination and racism in the armed forces just as they did in civilian life. Most held low-level jobs on military bases in the United States. Among the 140,000 African American soldiers sent to Europe, 40,000 saw actual combat. Many served with distinction. An African American regiment received medals for bravery from the French government. One of its members, Henry Johnson, was the first American to receive the French Croix de Guerre [Cross of War] for bravery.

Section 2 Review

Checking for Understanding

1. ***Identify*** *Lusitania,* Zimmermann telegram, Selective Service Act.
2. ***Define*** propaganda, autocracy.
3. ***Explain*** how the war in Europe brought about an economic boom in the United States.

Reviewing Themes

4. **Government and Democracy** What steps did President Wilson have to take to make an official declaration of war?

Critical Thinking

5. **Drawing Conclusions** Why was it difficult for many Americans to remain neutral during the war?

Activity

Making a List Imagine you enlisted in the World War I army. List the four things you would miss most about civilian life.

Section 2 Review Answers

1. *Lusitania,* 662; Zimmerman telegram, 663; Selective Service Act, 664
2. The words are defined in the Glossary.
3. Trade with the Allies increased dramatically, and Great Britain and France borrowed billions of dollars from American banks to help finance their war efforts.
4. He had to ask Congress in a special session for a declaration of war; Congress had to pass the declaration; and President Wilson had to sign it.
5. Many Americans were immigrants who had ties to the European countries involved in the war.

Activity Lists should reflect aspects of civilian life that were popular during that time period.

1917 — 1918 — 1919

June 1917
American troops land in France

March 1918
Russia withdraws from the war

June 1918
American Expeditionary Force begins to fight

November 1918
Armistice ends World War I

Section 3

Americans Join the Allies

READ TO DISCOVER . . .

- what was happening in Europe when the United States entered the war.
- what role American troops played in the fighting.

TERMS TO LEARN

convoy
front
armistice

The Storyteller

Drafted into the United States Army in 1917, Alvin York was reluctant to serve. "I was worried clean through," he said. "I didn't want to go and kill." York had grown up in the mountains of Tennessee, where he learned to shoot while hunting wild turkeys. Applying his sharpshooting skills in World War I, York killed 17 German soldiers with 17 shots. He also took 132 Germans prisoner and captured 35 enemy machine guns. For his actions and bravery in combat, Sergeant York received the Congressional Medal of Honor.

Congressional Medal of Honor

In 1917 the Allies desperately needed the help of American soldiers. Years of trench warfare had exhausted the Allied armies, and some French troops refused to continue fighting after a failed offensive in 1917. The British had started to run out of war supplies and food; their people were starving. Furthermore, German submarines were taking a deadly toll on Allied shipping—sinking one of every four ships that left British ports.

Supplying the Allies

The American entry into the war made an immediate difference. To ensure that needed supplies reached Great Britain, the United States Navy took two steps. First, it helped the British find and destroy German submarines. Then convoys—teams—of navy destroyers escorted groups of merchant ships across the Atlantic. The convoy system worked well. In one year it reduced Allied shipping losses from 900,000 to 300,000 tons a month. With the convoy system, not one American soldier bound for Europe was lost to submarine attack.

Russian Withdrawal

The Allies needed more troops because of a second revolution in Russia. In November 1917, the **Bolsheviks,** a group of communists, overthrew the democratic Russian government established in March 1917.

Led by **Vladimir Lenin,** the Bolsheviks wanted to end Russia's participation in the war so they

1 FOCUS

BELLRINGER
Motivational Activity

Before taking roll at the beginning of the class period, project Section Focus Transparency 23–3 and have students answer the questions. Discuss students' responses.

This activity is also available as a blackline master.

Section Focus Transparency 23–3

Medal of Honor Winners

1. In which war was the greatest number of Medals of Honor awarded?
2. How many Medals of Honor were awarded in the Korean War?
3. How many more Medals of Honor were awarded in World War II than in the Vietnam War?

War	Medals Awarded
World War I	96
World War II	432
Korean War	131
Vietnam War	238

(Source: *World Almanac*)

Vocabulary Precheck

Have students read the textbook glossary definition of each term listed in **Terms to Learn.** Then call on volunteers to restate each definition in their own words.

Use the **Vocabulary PuzzleMaker** to create crossword and word search puzzles.

Section Theme
Geography and History

The entry of the United States into the war made an immediate difference, eventually leading to Germany's request to President Wilson for an armistice.

Activity Have students complete these sentences. Use the results as a springboard for class discussion. **(1) In the war at sea, the United States ______. (2) In the land war, the United States ______.**

SECTION RESOURCES

Reproducible Masters
- Reproducible Lesson Plan 23–3
- Guided Reading Activity 23–3
- Section Quiz 23–3
- Reteaching Activity 23–3
- Enrichment Activity 23–3

Transparencies
- Section Focus Transparency 23–3

Multimedia
- Vocabulary PuzzleMaker
- Chapter Challenger Interactive Review Software
- Testmaker
- Facts On File: Landmark Documents in American History

CHAPTER 23
Section 3, 665–668

2 TEACH

L1 Reviewing Facts Ask students to recall the statements on page 661 about "America's Early Involvement." **Ask:** How was the United States already helping the Allies? *(by trading with them and lending them money)* Use that answer to introduce the additional help that came with America's official entry into the war.

Map Study

Answers

1. about 50 miles
2. France

you don't say...

Stalemate is a term from the game of chess. It describes a situation in which one player cannot make any move without putting his or her king in a position to be captured (and, as a result, losing the game). It is an apt term for the draw that was taking place along the Western Front.

Guided Reading Activity 23–3

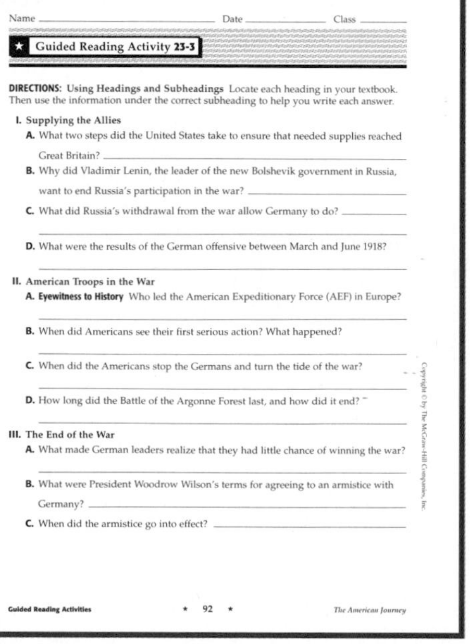
Name ______ Date ______ Class ______

★ Guided Reading Activity **23-3**

DIRECTIONS: Using Headings and Subheadings Locate each heading in your textbook. Then use the information under the correct subheading to help you write each answer.

I. Supplying the Allies
- **A.** What two steps did the United States take to ensure that needed supplies reached Great Britain? ______
- **B.** Why did Vladimir Lenin, the leader of the new Bolshevik government in Russia, want to end Russia's participation in the war? ______
- **C.** What did Russia's withdrawal from the war allow Germany to do? ______
- **D.** What were the results of the German offensive between March and June 1918? ______

II. American Troops in the War
- **A. Eyewitness to History** Who led the American Expeditionary Force (AEF) in Europe? ______
- **B.** When did Americans see their first serious action? What happened? ______
- **C.** When did the Americans stop the Germans and turn the tide of the war? ______
- **D.** How long did the Battle of the Argonne Forest last, and how did it end? ______

III. The End of the War
- **A.** What made German leaders realize that they had little chance of winning the war? ______
- **B.** What were President Woodrow Wilson's terms for agreeing to an armistice with Germany? ______
- **C.** When did the armistice go into effect? ______

The Western Front

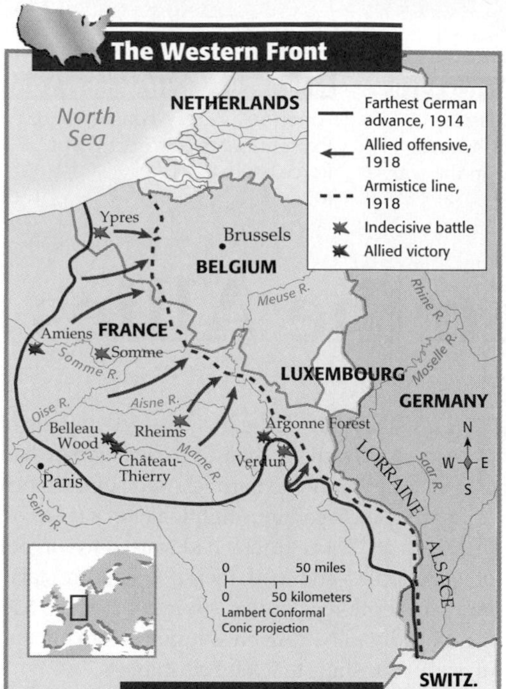

Map Study

The arrival of fresh American troops in Europe in 1917 helped turn the Allies toward victory.

1. **Location** About how close to Paris was the battle of Château-Thierry?
2. **Analyzing Information** What country was the site of most Western Front battles?

could focus their energies and resources on setting up a new Communist state. Lenin took Russia out of the war in December. In March 1918, he signed the **Treaty of Brest-Litovsk** with Germany, surrendering Poland, the Ukraine, and other territory to the Germans. Russia's withdrawal from the war allowed the Germans to move hundreds of thousands of troops from the Eastern Front—line of battle—to the Western Front in France.

New German Offensive

Reinforced by the transfer of troops, the Germans now launched a powerful offensive against the Allies. Between March and June 1918, they hammered at Allied lines, pushing them back to within 50 miles (80 km) of Paris. After years of stalemate along the Western Front—the area along the French-German border—it suddenly looked as if Germany might win the war.

American Troops in the War

★ Although the first American soldiers had reached France in June 1917, many months passed before they were ready for battle. When they finally began to fight, the Americans helped turn the war around.

Eyewitness to HISTORY

The American Expeditionary Force

General **John J. Pershing** led the American troops in Europe, the **American Expeditionary Force** (AEF). American correspondent Floyd Gibbons described the tremendous welcome the French gave Pershing and his troops in Paris:

> "The sooty girders of the Gare du Nord [railroad station] shook with cheers when the special train pulled in. . . . A minute later, there was a terrific roar from beyond the walls of the station. The crowds outside had heard the cheering within. . . . Paris took Pershing by storm."

The AEF reached full strength in Europe in the spring of 1918. The French and British wanted to use the American soldiers to build up their own troops, but General Pershing refused. He preferred to keep the AEF a separate force.

Americans Go into Action

The American Expeditionary Force saw its first serious fighting in early June 1918. It helped turn back a German offensive at **Château-Thierry** on the **Marne River** east of Paris. The American

Cooperative Learning Activity

Tracing the War's Conclusion The United States's military presence in Europe was brief but decisive. To reinforce the information in the text, organize students into an even number of groups. Half of the groups should focus on the summer of 1918 (the battles of Château-Thierry and Belleau Wood). The other half should focus on the fall of 1918 (the battles of Saint Mihiel and the Argonne Forest). Each group can prepare maps, diagrams, charts, reports, poems, and so on to review the facts of the battles and express opinions about their importance.

American Memories

In the Trenches

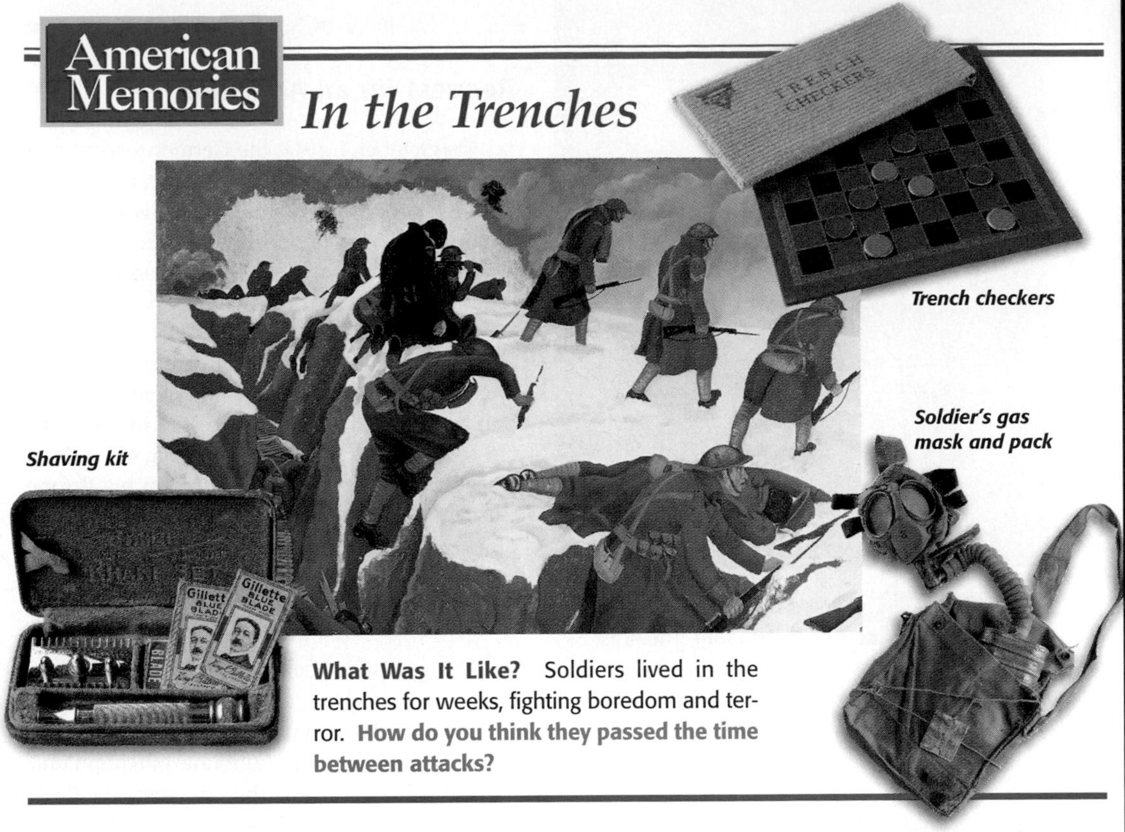

Trench checkers

Soldier's gas mask and pack

Shaving kit

What Was It Like? Soldiers lived in the trenches for weeks, fighting boredom and terror. **How do you think they passed the time between attacks?**

troops then advanced to nearby **Belleau Wood.** For 24 hours a day for the next 3 weeks, American forces fought their way through the forest against a solid wall of German machine-gun fire. In July the Americans and the French fought back German attacks on Allied forces along the Marne and the Somme Rivers.

By the middle of July, the Allies had stopped the German offensive. The battles, General Pershing wrote, had "turned the tide of war." The Allies now began an offensive of their own. In mid-September 550,000 "doughboys"—the nickname given to American soldiers—fighting alone, defeated the Germans at Saint Mihiel, east of **Verdun.** Later in the month, more than 1 million American troops joined the Allies in the **Battle of the Argonne Forest,** west of Verdun.

The Battle of the Argonne Forest raged for nearly seven weeks, with soldiers struggling over the rugged, heavily forested ground. Rain, mud, barbed wire, and withering fire from German machine guns hindered the Allies' advance, and many lives were lost.

American lieutenant Elden Betts wondered if he would survive the battle and wrote home—in case "I get mine tomorrow." He said he hoped his family would be proud of him, ending with "Now good-bye, and thank you Pop, Edie and Margie." Four days later Betts was killed.

The Battle of the Argonne Forest ended in early November, when the Allies finally pushed back the Germans and broke through the enemy lines. The Germans now were faced with an invasion of their own country.

Footnotes to History

Repaying a Debt The AEF marched through Paris to the grave of the Marquis de Lafayette, the Frenchman who had helped the Patriots win the American Revolution. An American officer, Colonel Charles Stanton, heard a great cheer from the Paris crowd when he stated, "Lafayette, we are here!" Indeed, it was time to repay the debt.

American Memories

In the Trenches

To relieve the monotony of the war, soldiers organized musicals and variety shows, betting pools, and holiday celebrations.

Answer: *Answers will vary but may include napping, writing letters, cleaning weapons, and playing games.*

Facts On File

CD-ROM
Landmark Documents in American History

Title: *Declaration of War Against Germany ("Make the World Safe for Democracy"), Woodrow Wilson, 1917*

Have students draw a propaganda poster after reading Wilson's message.

3 ASSESS

Assign Section 3 Review as homework or as an in-class activity.

Use **Chapter Challenger Interactive Review Software** to review Section 3.

Section Quiz 23–3

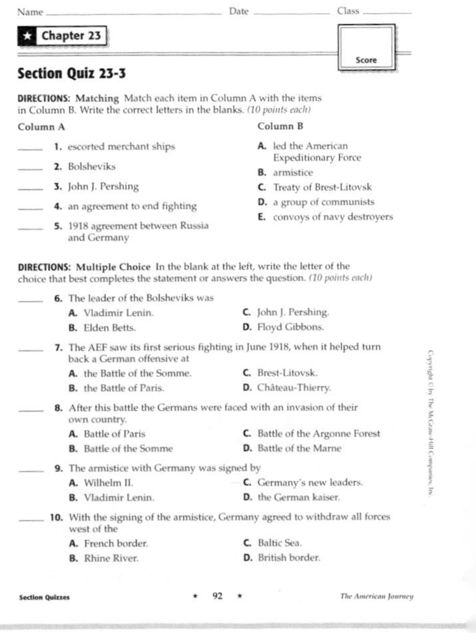

Name ______ Date ______ Class ______

★ Chapter 23

Score

Section Quiz 23-3

DIRECTIONS: Matching Match each item in Column A with the items in Column B. Write the correct letters in the blanks. *(10 points each)*

Column A	Column B
____ 1. escorted merchant ships	A. led the American Expeditionary Force
____ 2. Bolsheviks	B. armistice
____ 3. John J. Pershing	C. Treaty of Brest-Litovsk
____ 4. an agreement to end fighting	D. a group of communists
____ 5. 1918 agreement between Russia and Germany	E. convoys of navy destroyers

DIRECTIONS: Multiple Choice In the blank at the left, write the letter of the choice that best completes the statement or answers the question. *(10 points each)*

____ 6. The leader of the Bolsheviks was
A. Vladimir Lenin. C. John J. Pershing.
B. Elden Betts. D. Floyd Gibbons.

____ 7. The AEF saw its first serious fighting in June 1918, when it helped turn back a German offensive at
A. the Battle of the Somme. C. Brest-Litovsk.
B. the Battle of Paris. D. Château-Thierry.

____ 8. After this battle the Germans were faced with an invasion of their own country.
A. Battle of Paris C. Battle of the Argonne Forest
B. Battle of the Somme D. Battle of the Marne

____ 9. The armistice with Germany was signed by
A. Wilhelm II. C. Germany's new leaders.
B. Vladimir Lenin. D. the German kaiser.

____ 10. With the signing of the armistice, Germany agreed to withdraw all forces west of the
A. French border. C. Baltic Sea.
B. Rhine River. D. British border.

Section Quizzes ★ 92 ★ *The American Journey*

Multiple Learning Styles

Auditory/Musical Have students brainstorm for sounds that they associate with patriotism (for example, melodies of specific patriotic songs, a trumpet fanfare, a 21-gun salute, the flapping of a flag in the wind, or even the laughter of children). Ask students which sounds might provide an effective setting for a patriotic song about the Allied cause in World War I or for a brief speech by an American politician. Interested students might extend this activity by writing and presenting a song or promotional speech based upon their choice of setting. **L2, ELL**

CHAPTER 23
Section 3, 665–668

HISTORY AND ART Hassam (1859–1935) is famous for the flag-filled street views he created during World War I. **Answer:** *November 11, 1918*

Reteaching Activity 23–3

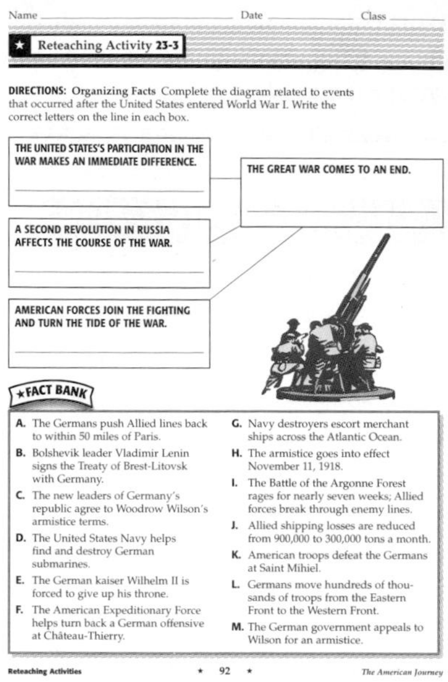
Name ______ Date ______ Class ______

★ Reteaching Activity **23-3**

DIRECTIONS: Organizing Facts Complete the diagram related to events that occurred after the United States entered World War I. Write the correct letters on the line in each box.

THE UNITED STATES'S PARTICIPATION IN THE WAR MAKES AN IMMEDIATE DIFFERENCE. ______

A SECOND REVOLUTION IN RUSSIA AFFECTS THE COURSE OF THE WAR. ______

AMERICAN FORCES JOIN THE FIGHTING AND TURN THE TIDE OF THE WAR. ______

THE GREAT WAR COMES TO AN END. ______

★FACT BANK

A. The Germans push Allied lines back to within 50 miles of Paris.
B. Bolshevik leader Vladimir Lenin signs the Treaty of Brest-Litovsk with Germany.
C. The new leaders of Germany's republic agree to Woodrow Wilson's armistice terms.
D. The United States Navy helps find and destroy German submarines.
E. The German kaiser Wilhelm II is forced to give up his throne.
F. The American Expeditionary Force helps turn back a German offensive at Château-Thierry.
G. Navy destroyers escort merchant ships across the Atlantic Ocean.
H. The armistice goes into effect November 11, 1918.
I. The Battle of the Argonne Forest rages for nearly seven weeks; Allied forces break through enemy lines.
J. Allied shipping losses are reduced from 900,000 to 300,000 tons a month.
K. American troops defeat the Germans at Saint Mihiel.
L. Germans move hundreds of thousands of troops from the Eastern Front to the Western Front.
M. The German government appeals to Wilson for an armistice.

Reteaching Activities ★ 92 ★ *The American Journey*

Enrichment Activity 23–3

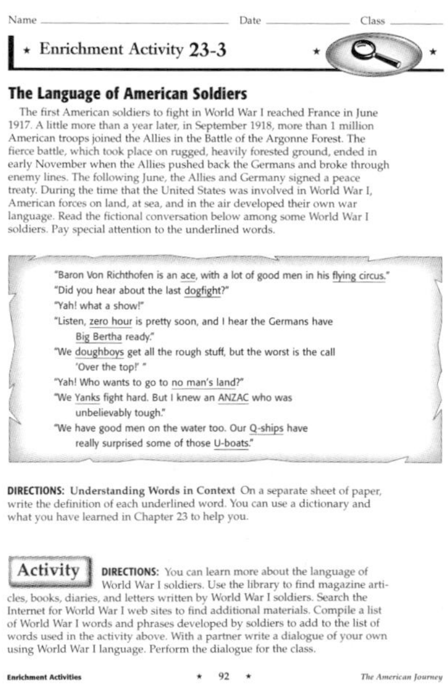
Name ______ Date ______ Class ______

★ Enrichment Activity **23-3** ★

The Language of American Soldiers

The first American soldiers to fight in World War I reached France in June 1917. A little more than a year later, in September 1918, more than 1 million American troops joined the Allies in the Battle of the Argonne Forest. The fierce battle, which took place on rugged, heavily forested ground, ended in early November when the Allies pushed back the Germans and broke through enemy lines. The following June, the Allies and Germany signed a peace treaty. During the time that the United States was involved in World War I, American forces on land, at sea, and in the air developed their own war language. Read the fictional conversation below among some World War I soldiers. Pay special attention to the underlined words.

"Baron Von Richthofen is an ace, with a lot of good men in his flying circus."
"Did you hear about the last dogfight?"
"Yah! what a show!"
"Listen, zero hour is pretty soon, and I hear the Germans have Big Bertha ready."
"We doughboys get all the rough stuff, but the worst is the call 'Over the top!' "
"Yah! Who wants to go to no man's land?"
"We Yanks fight hard. But I knew an ANZAC who was unbelievably tough."
"We have good men on the water too. Our Q-ships have really surprised some of those U-boats."

DIRECTIONS: Understanding Words in Context On a separate sheet of paper, write the definition of each underlined word. You can use a dictionary and what you have learned in Chapter 23 to help you.

Activity **DIRECTIONS:** You can learn more about the language of World War I soldiers. Use the library to find magazine articles, books, diaries, and letters written by World War I soldiers. Search the Internet for World War I web sites to find additional materials. Compile a list of World War I words and phrases developed by soldiers to add to the list of words used in the activity above. With a partner write a dialogue of your own using World War I language. Perform the dialogue for the class.

Enrichment Activities ★ 92 ★ *The American Journey*

4 CLOSE

Have students name ways in which the American entry into the war made a decisive difference.

HISTORY AND ART *Allies Day, May 1917* by **Childe Hassam** The artist captured the flags of Allied nations during a New York City celebration in 1917. **When did the armistice go into effect?**

The End of the War

With their troops in retreat, German military leaders realized they had little chance of winning the war. The Allied forces were now fortified by the Americans. In addition, the Germans suffered from severe shortages of food and other essential supplies.

Request for an Armistice

On October 4, 1918, the German government appealed to President Wilson for an armistice—an agreement to end the fighting. Wilson consented under certain conditions. Germany must accept his plan for peace and promise not to renew hostilities. All German troops must leave Belgium and France. Finally, Wilson would deal only with civilian leaders, not with the military.

While German leaders considered Wilson's demands, political unrest erupted in Germany. On November 9, the German **kaiser,** or emperor, **Wilhelm II,** was forced to give up his throne. Germany became a republic, and its new leaders quickly agreed to Wilson's terms for the armistice.

Peace Begins

The armistice began on November 11, 1918. Germany agreed to withdraw all land forces west of the **Rhine River,** withdraw its fleet to the Baltic Sea, and surrender huge amounts of equipment.

With the signing of the armistice, the Great War ended. President Wilson announced:

> "Everything for which America fought has been accomplished. It will now be our duty to assist by example, by sober, friendly counsel, and by material aid in the establishment of just democracy throughout the world."

Section 3 Review

Checking for Understanding

1. ***Identify*** Bolsheviks, Vladimir Lenin, Treaty of Brest-Litovsk, Wilhelm II.
2. ***Define*** convoy, front, armistice.
3. ***List*** three reasons the Allies needed the help of the American forces by 1917.

Reviewing Themes

4. **Geography and History** What terms did Germany agree to in the armistice?

Critical Thinking

5. **Predicting Consequences** Do you think the Allies would have won the war if the United States had not intervened? Why or why not?

Activity

Preparing a Radio Broadcast Write the text for a French radio broadcast announcing the arrival of American soldiers in Paris in 1917.

Section 3 Review Answers

1. Bolsheviks, 665; Vladimir Lenin, 665; Treaty of Brest-Litovsk, 666; Wilhelm II, 668
2. The words are defined in the Glossary.
3. Any three: Allied armies were exhausted; some French troops refused to fight; Allies were running out of war supplies and food; Russia withdrew.
4. Germany agreed to withdraw all forces west of the Rhine River and from the Baltic Sea; it also agreed to surrender military equipment.
5. Students who say *yes* may note that the Allies would never have surrendered. Students who say *no* may point out Germany's advantages and that Allied armies were tired and short on military supplies and food.

Activity Broadcasts should express the excitement and relief at the Americans' arrival.

INTERDISCIPLINARY

Activities

The Great War

Although other major wars have been fought since 1918, World War I is still known as "the Great War" because of the overwhelming destruction and change it brought. Experience what people did and thought during that period as you complete these activities.

Art

Designing a Propaganda Poster Dramatic posters did a great deal to win people's support for wartime efforts. Study posters of the era and notice their style. Then design your own poster about one of these themes: Buy Liberty Bonds; Join the Army (or Navy); Conserve Resources (steel, textiles, fuel); Promote Patriotism; Take a Factory Job; Observe Meatless (or Wheatless) Days; Plant a Victory Garden.

Science

Studying War Technology Partly because of new technology, World War I caused a horrifying number of casualties. Research one of the following technologies and prepare a report on its development, wartime use, and effects: poison gas, tanks, airplanes, dirigibles, machine guns, or submarines. Photocopy pictures from books and encyclopedias to illustrate your report, and present it in class.

Mathematics

Charting War Casualties Millions of soldiers—mostly Europeans—were killed in World War I. Use an encyclopedia or almanac to supply statistics for a double bar graph in which you compare the number of troops mobilized by a given country with the number of dead and wounded. Include these nations: Austria-Hungary, Belgium, the British Empire, France, Germany, Italy, Russia, Turkey, and the United States. Which countries had, proportionately, the greatest losses? Display your graph in the classroom.

Language Arts

Writing a Poem World War I produced a number of soldier-poets. Read some poems by Rupert Brooke or Stephen Spender. Then imagine that you were fighting in World War I as a soldier, or nurse, or ambulance driver. Write a poem giving your feelings and impressions. You may want to put your poem in the form of a letter home. Share your poetry with the class.

World War I helmet

World War I infantry boots

MULTIPLE LEARNING STYLES

The activities included in the feature on this student edition page are ideally suited to meet the different learning styles of your students. These include:

- **Art** — **Designing a Propaganda Poster** visual/spatial learners
- **Science** — **Studying War Technology** verbal/linguistic learners
- **Mathematics** — **Charting War Casualties** logical/mathematical learners
- **Language Arts** — **Writing a Poem** intrapersonal learners

INTERDISCIPLINARY

Activities

TEACH

Background

As was the case with all wars that our nation has fought, Americans of all races and ethnic backgrounds participated in World War I. The all–African American 369th Infantry Regiment—the "Harlem Hell Fighters"—saw longer continuous combat than any other American unit and was one of the most decorated units of the war. 370,000 African Americans served in the military during the war. Almost 20,000 Puerto Ricans (who were granted citizenship in 1917) served in America's armed forces, and Puerto Ricans bought more than $10 million in war bonds. Native Americans bought some $25 million in war bonds. Although they were not granted citizenship until 1924, many fought in the war—at first by going north and joining the Canadian forces, and then (when the United States declared war) by volunteering to serve in the army and navy.

Have students use this background information about minority soldiers in the **Language Arts** activity, Writing a Poem.

Team Teaching

These Interdisciplinary Activities provide an excellent opportunity for you to employ Team Teaching and collaboration in your classroom.

Block Schedule

These activities may be implemented within either a traditional class period or a block scheduling framework.

CHAPTER 23
Section 4, 670–673

1 FOCUS

BELLRINGER
Motivational Activity

Before taking roll at the beginning of the class period, project Section Focus Transparency 23–4 and have students answer the questions. Discuss students' responses.

This activity is also available as a blackline master.

Section Focus Transparency 23–4

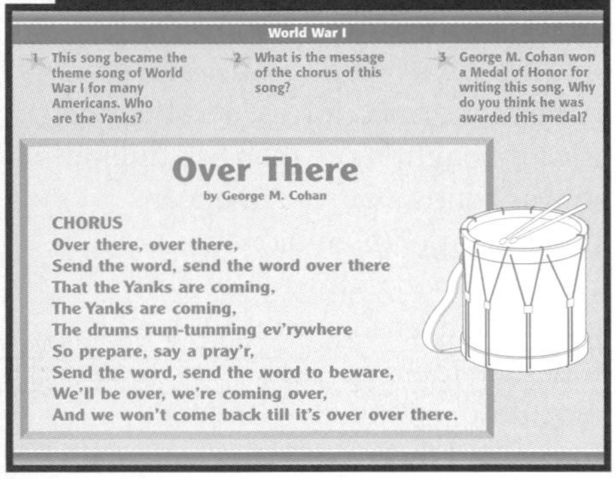
World War I

1 This song became the theme song of World War I for many Americans. Who are the Yanks?

2 What is the message of the chorus of this song?

3 George M. Cohan won a Medal of Honor for writing this song. Why do you think he was awarded this medal?

Over There
by George M. Cohan

CHORUS
Over there, over there,
Send the word, send the word over there
That the Yanks are coming,
The Yanks are coming,
The drums rum-tumming ev'rywhere
So prepare, say a pray'r,
Send the word, send the word to beware,
We'll be over, we're coming over,
And we won't come back till it's over over there.

Vocabulary Precheck

Point out that *mobilization* need not refer just to warfare. Have students think of ways in which they mobilize for a school project or social event.

Use the **Vocabulary Puzzle-Maker** to create crossword and word search puzzles.

Section Theme
Economic Factors

America's involvement in the war in Europe resulted in economic challenges and opportunities at home.

Activity Have students list needs that must be met as a nation prepares to go to war. Ask them to rank their responses in order of importance and to defend their choices.

1917 — **1918** — **1919**

July 1917 Race riots occur in East St. Louis

April 1918 National War Labor Board is set up

June 1918 Congress passes Sabotage and Sedition acts

Section 4

The War at Home

READ TO DISCOVER . . .
- what steps the United States took to organize and prepare for World War I.
- how the war affected the American people.
- how Americans treated opponents of the war.

TERMS TO LEARN

mobilization	pacifist
dissent	espionage
socialist	sabotage

The Storyteller

"Over there, over there,
Send the word, send the word over there
That the Yanks are coming, the Yanks are coming,
The drums rum-tumming ev'rywhere
So prepare, say a pray'r,
Send the word, send the word to beware,
We'll be over, we're coming over,
And we won't come back till it's over over there."

George M. Cohan wrote this rousing song to help create enthusiasm for America's participation in World War I. "Over There" was performed at rallies to raise money for the war.

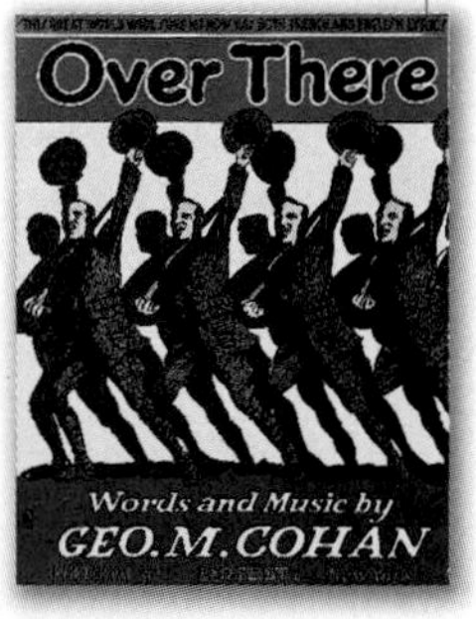

"Over There" sheet music

After declaring war on Germany in 1917, Americans immediately focused their energies on getting ready to fight a war. **Mobilization**—the gathering of resources and the preparation for war—affected almost every part of American life.

Mobilizing the Nation

To ensure production of vital war materials and to resolve labor disputes, the government created the **National War Labor Board** in April 1918. Made up of representatives of business, labor, and the public, the board pressured businesses to grant some of the workers' pressing demands. As a result workers won an 8-hour working day, extra pay for overtime, equal pay for women, and the right to form unions. In return workers agreed not to go on strike.

Workers during the War

The American participation in the war led the nation's industry to expand to meet the need for supplies and weapons. At the same time, however, the workforce grew smaller, creating a labor shortage. Millions of men left their jobs in industry to serve in the armed forces, and few European immigrants—who might have taken these jobs—came to the United States during the war.

The labor shortage provided new job opportunities for women and minorities. Many women joined the workforce for the first time. Women were hired for jobs previously held by men.

SECTION RESOURCES

Reproducible Masters
- Guided Reading Activity 23–4
- Section Quiz 23–4
- Reteaching Activity 23–4
- Enrichment Activity 23–4

Transparencies
- Section Focus Transparency 23–4
- U.S. History & Art, Transparencies 20, 21

Multimedia
- Vocabulary PuzzleMaker
- Chapter Challenger Interactive Review Software
- Testmaker
- GTV: A Geographic Perspective on American History
- American Music Cultural Traditions

The prospect of finding good jobs also brought hundreds of thousands of African Americans to Northern cities from the rural South. In addition thousands of Mexicans migrated to the United States in search of jobs.

Paying for the War

World War I cost the United States an enormous amount of money—about $32 billion. Two-thirds of this money was raised by selling the American people war bonds, or **Liberty Bonds.** To persuade people to buy the bonds, the government created colorful posters advertising the bonds and organized public events featuring actors and popular celebrities. George M. Cohan wrote his song "Over There" for a Liberty Bond rally. Children bought more than $1 billion worth of "thrift stamps," which they could paste into books and exchange for a war bond.

The federal government also raised money for the war by increasing taxes and requiring a greater number of Americans to pay income taxes. It taxed wealthy Americans at rates as high as 70 percent of their income. The government also imposed steep taxes on business profits.

Economics

Producing Supplies

The United States had to produce food not only for its own needs but also for the Allies. President Wilson appointed **Herbert Hoover,** who had helped organize food for war refugees in Europe, to head a new **Food Administration.** This agency launched a campaign to encourage American farmers to produce more and to persuade the public to eat less. The agency urged people to observe "Wheatless Mondays," "Meatless Tuesdays," and "Porkless Thursdays," and to add to their own store of food by planting "victory gardens." With slogans such as "Serve Just Enough" and "Use All Leftovers," it reminded Americans to conserve food.

The Food Administration also imposed price controls on various agricultural products to encourage voluntary **rationing**—limitation of use. As a result of such efforts, Americans consumed less food, expanded food production, and increased food exports.

Another government agency, the **War Industries Board,** headed by Bernard Baruch, supervised and coordinated the nation's industrial production. The board's responsibilities included distributing raw materials to industries, converting factories to the production of war-related goods, and setting prices for key products.

Mobilizing Support

The federal government also needed to mobilize public support for the war because antiwar sentiment remained strong even after the United States entered the war. President Wilson appointed journalist **George Creel** to head the **Committee on Public Information.** Its mission was to persuade Americans that the war represented a battle for democracy and freedom.

The Committee on Public Information distributed millions of pro-war pamphlets, posters, articles, and books. It provided newspapers with government accounts of the war and

These women workers replaced males on the Great Northern Railway

Cooperative Learning Activity

Giving Four-Minute Speeches As the text points out, Four-Minute Speeches were one means of encouraging Americans to support the war effort. Have pairs of students try writing and giving a Four-Minute Speech that presents one of the following patriotic messages:

- Buy Liberty Bonds
- Conserve food
- Don't strike
- (To women) Find a job
- (To African Americans) Come work in the North
- Remember the importance of our cause

Students can divide writing and editing tasks. Then one student can give the speech while his or her partner provides music or artwork.

2 TEACH

L1 Solving Problems Ask groups of students to brainstorm actions that Americans could take to make more supplies available for its armed forces. As groups read and discuss Section 4, have them see which solutions actually were used.

you don't say...

Hooverizing The Food Administration's campaign changed Americans' eating habits—and gave them a new word. To observe such practices as serving just enough and having Meatless Tuesdays was to "Hooverize" (after Herbert Hoover, head of the Food Administration).

Guided Reading Activity 23–4

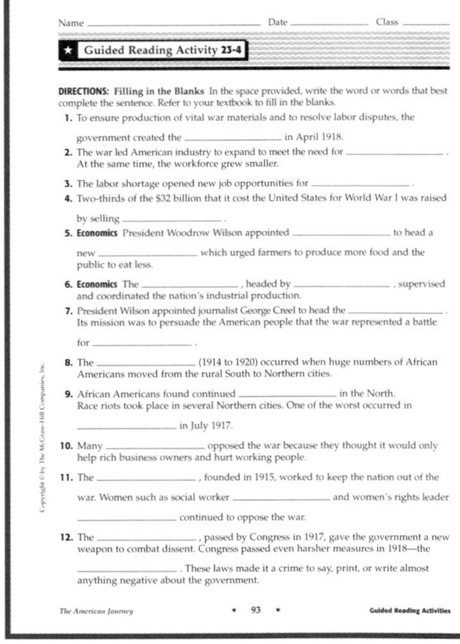

Name ______ Date ______ Class ______

★ Guided Reading Activity 23-4

DIRECTIONS: Filling in the Blanks In the space provided, write the word or words that best complete the sentence. Refer to your textbook to fill in the blanks.

1. To ensure production of vital war materials and to resolve labor disputes, the government created the ______ in April 1918.
2. The war led American industry to expand to meet the need for ______. At the same time, the workforce grew smaller.
3. The labor shortage opened new job opportunities for ______.
4. Two-thirds of the $32 billion that it cost the United States for World War I was raised by selling ______.
5. **Economics** President Woodrow Wilson appointed ______ to head a new ______ which urged farmers to produce more food and the public to eat less.
6. **Economics** The ______, headed by ______, supervised and coordinated the nation's industrial production.
7. President Wilson appointed journalist George Creel to head the ______. Its mission was to persuade the American people that the war represented a battle for ______.
8. The ______ (1914 to 1920) occurred when huge numbers of African Americans moved from the rural South to Northern cities.
9. African Americans found continued ______ in the North. Race riots took place in several Northern cities. One of the worst occurred in ______ in July 1917.
10. Many ______ opposed the war because they thought it would only help rich business owners and hurt working people.
11. The ______, founded in 1915, worked to keep the nation out of the war. Women such as social worker ______ and women's rights leader ______ continued to oppose the war.
12. The ______, passed by Congress in 1917, gave the government a new weapon to combat dissent. Congress passed even harsher measures in 1918—the ______. These laws made it a crime to say, print, or write almost anything negative about the government.

The American Journey ★ 93 ★ **Guided Reading Activities**

History *and the* Humanities

U.S. History & Art, Transparency 20, *I Want You for the U.S. Army;* Transparency 21, *Allies Day, May 1917*

American Music Cultural Traditions, Lesson 8: "War Song Hits"

CHAPTER 23

Section 4, 670–673

NATIONAL GEOGRAPHIC SOCIETY

VIDEODISC
GTV: A Geographic Perspective on American History

Side 4, Chapter 2

Title: *On the Move*
Subject: The mobile population
Ask: **What was the migration pattern that began during World War I? Why did it take place?** *(People from the South moved to the North to work in factories. Workers were needed because of the loss of immigrants and soldiers.)*

Chart Study

Answer Woodrow Wilson

3 ASSESS

Assign Section 4 Review as homework or as an in-class activity.

Use **Chapter Challenger Interactive Review Software** to review Section 4.

Section Quiz 23–4

Name ____________ Date ________ Class ______

★ Chapter 23

Score

Section Quiz 23-4

DIRECTIONS: Matching Match each item in Column A with the items in Column B. Write the correct letters in the blanks. *(10 points each)*

Column A	Column B
____ 1. helped pay for war	A. victory gardens
____ 2. headed Food Administration	B. rationing
____ 3. conservation of food	C. Liberty Bonds
____ 4. limitation of use	D. Bernard Baruch
____ 5. headed War Industries Board	E. Herbert Hoover

DIRECTIONS: Multiple Choice In the blank at the left, write the letter of the choice that best completes the statement or answers the question. *(10 points each)*

____ 6. The gathering of resources and the preparation for war is called
A. dissent. C. sabotage.
B. mobilization. D. espionage.

____ 7. This man headed the Committee on Public Information.
A. Herbert Hoover C. George Creel
B. Bernard Baruch D. Elden Betts

____ 8. From 1914 to 1920 when about 500,000 African Americans left the South and moved to the North, the migration was called the
A. Great Migration. C. Northern Migration.
B. Black Migration. D. African American Migration.

____ 9. People opposed to the use of violence are called
A. socialists. C. dissenters.
B. War Hawks. D. pacifists.

____ 10. This was one of the laws the United States government used to stifle opposition to the war.
A. Sabotage Act C. Dissenters Act
B. Socialists Act D. War Hawks Act

The American Journey ★ 93 ★ **Section Quizzes**

advertisements. It arranged for short patriotic talks, called Four-Minute Speeches, to be presented before plays and movies. The committee hired speakers, writers, artists, and actors to build support for the war. It was the greatest propaganda campaign in the history of the nation.

Americans and the War

★ World War I provided a boost for the American economy. Yet the war had harmful effects on American society as well. In the interest of national unity, the government stifled voices of **dissent,** or opposition. Racial and other tensions remained, and many Americans became intolerant of those who were "different."

Causes and Effects

CAUSES
- ★ Nationalistic pride
- ★ Competition for colonies
- ★ Military buildup
- ★ Tangled web of alliances
- ★ Assassination of Franz Ferdinand

World War I

EFFECTS
- ★ Destruction in Europe
- ★ Boom in the American economy
- ★ Suppression of dissent in U.S.
- ★ Allied victory
- ★ Defeated empires lose their colonies

Chart Study

After World War I, the United States was established as a world leader and an economic giant.
Analyzing Information How did World War I affect the economy of the United States?

African American Migration

From 1914 to 1920, between 300,000 and 500,000 African Americans left their homes in the rural South to seek jobs and settle in Northern cities. Known as the **Great Migration,** this tremendous population movement continued the northward migration begun in the late 1800s.

African Americans headed north for several reasons. Many wanted to escape the harsh economic and political conditions they faced in the South. They saw advertisements in their local papers for jobs in the North, and they listened eagerly to the stories of African Americans who had already moved there. Some Northern factory owners even sent recruiting agents to promote jobs and to encourage African Americans to come to work for them.

Many African American workers who traveled north—"Bound for the Promised Land" as they wrote on the sides of railroad cars—did find jobs. Their new lives were not easy. Often they lived in tiny, crowded apartments in segregated neighborhoods, and they found that racial prejudice continued to haunt their lives in the North. When expanding African American neighborhoods pushed up against white neighborhoods, racial hostility sometimes erupted in violence.

Terrible race riots took place in several Northern cities during the war years. One of the worst occurred in **East St. Louis, Illinois.** In July 1917, a white mob attacked an African American neighborhood, burning houses and firing on residents as they tried to escape. During the riot, as many as 40 African Americans died and thousands lost their homes.

Controlling Public Opinion

When the war began, a majority of Americans thought the United States should stay out of it. Even after America entered the war, opposition to it remained strong. Some German Americans and Irish Americans sympathized with the Central Powers. Many **socialists**—people who believe industries should be publicly owned—opposed the war because they thought it would only help rich business owners and hurt working people. Also

MULTIPLE LEARNING STYLES

Interpersonal Many Americans demonstrated an intolerance of those who opposed the war. Bring this problem to life by having groups of students prepare and present skits on one or more of the following situations:
- A crowd's reaction to a speech given by a member of the Women's Peace Party
- A socialist's reaction to an anti-dissenter newspaper ad from the Committee on Public Information
- A man caught opening the mail of a German neighbor
- A labor activist arrested under the Sedition Act

Follow up the presentation of the skits with class discussion. **L3** against the war were pacifists—people opposed to the use of violence.

Some of the strongest antiwar sentiment came from women's groups. The **Women's Peace Party,** founded in 1915, worked to keep the nation out of the war. Some women—including social worker Jane Addams and women's rights leader Alice Paul—continued to voice their opposition after America entered the war.

During the course of the war, the Committee on Public Information began trying to silence dissent and portrayed people who were against the war as unpatriotic. The **Espionage Act** that Congress passed in 1917 gave the government a new weapon to combat dissent to the war. The law provided stiff penalties for espionage, or spying, as well as for aiding the enemy or interfering with army recruiting. Congress passed even harsher measures in 1918—the **Sabotage Act** and the **Sedition Act.** These laws made it a crime to say, print, or write almost anything perceived as negative about the government. Such acts would be considered sabotage—secret action to damage the war effort.

The government used the laws to stifle all political opposition. Thousands of people—especially immigrants, socialists, pacifists, and labor activists—were convicted under the laws.

Suspicion of disloyalty led to spying on neighbors, opening mail, and even outbreaks of violence by vigilante groups. People became suspicious of German Americans and persecuted them. A few communities prohibited such activities as performing German music and teaching the German language in schools. As a result some German Americans concealed their ancestry. They even gave patriotic names—such as "liberty cabbage" and "liberty sausage"—to German-sounding words such as *sauerkraut* and *frankfurter.*

Some people spoke out against these laws and the intolerance they produced. Most Americans, however, believed that, in wartime, no measure can be "too drastic" toward traitors and disloyal Americans.

Picturing HISTORY African American soldiers served in segregated regiments, commanded for the most part by white officers. **What major change affected African Americans at home during the war years?**

Section 4 Review

Checking for Understanding

1. ***Identify*** Herbert Hoover, Great Migration.
2. ***Define*** mobilization, dissent, socialist, pacifist, espionage, sabotage.
3. ***Describe*** the role of the Committee on Public Information.

Reviewing Themes

4. **Economic Factors** Where did the United States government get most of the money to finance the war?

Critical Thinking

5. **Analyzing Information** Do you think it was necessary for the government to take such extreme measures against people who opposed the war? Explain.

Activity

Writing an Advertisement Design an advertisement that a Northern industry might have placed in a Southern newspaper to attract job applicants.

Section 4 Review Answers

1. Herbert Hoover, 671; Great Migration, 672
2. The words are defined in the Glossary.
3. The committee's job was to convince Americans that the war was a battle for democracy and freedom.
4. by selling war bonds to the American people
5. Students who feel it necessary may suggest that some Americans might have interfered with industry, raising money, or rationing food—hurting war efforts abroad. Students who feel government overstepped its bounds may note that it was unconstitutional to prohibit free speech and stifle political opposition.

Activity Advertisements should make the jobs and salaries available in the North sound attractive to Southerners.

Picturing HISTORY Some 1,400 African Americans served as officers during the war.
Answer: *the Great Migration; About half a million African Americans from the rural South relocated to cities in the North.*

Reteaching Activity 23–4

Name ______ Date ______ Class ______

Reteaching Activity 23-4

DIRECTIONS: Identifying Problems and Solutions The United States's involvement in World War I caused some problems for Americans at home. After each *Problem,* write the letters of the *Solutions* from the Fact Bank.

1. **Problem:** The government had to ensure the production of vital war materials and solve labor disputes at the same time.
   Solutions: ______
2. **Problem:** At a time when the nation's industry had to expand to meet the need for supplies and weapons, the workforce grew smaller, creating a labor shortage.
   Solutions: ______
3. **Problem:** World War I was extremely costly for the United States.
   Solutions: ______
4. **Problem:** The United States had to produce food not only for its own needs but also for the Allies.
   Solutions: ______
5. **Problem:** The federal government had to mobilize public support for the war.
   Solutions: ______
6. **Problem:** The government had to combat dissent voiced by people who continued to oppose the United States's involvement in the war.
   Solutions: ______

FACT BANK AUTO-RIFLE MACHINE GUN CARBINE TANK WEAPONS AUTO-RIFLE

A. People planted "victory gardens."
B. Americans began spying on and reporting neighbors suspected of being disloyal.
C. The federal government increased taxes, required more citizens to pay income taxes, and imposed steep taxes on business profits.
D. The government created the National War Labor Board.
E. People were urged to observe "Meatless Tuesdays."
F. Women were hired for jobs previously held by men.
G. Farmers were encouraged to produce more.
H. George Creel headed the Committee on Public Information.
I. The government agreed to a series of workers' demands.
J. The United States raised money by selling Liberty Bonds.
K. The greatest propaganda campaign in American history was launched.
L. Herbert Hoover headed the new Food Administration.
M. The prospect of finding good jobs brought many African Americans to Northern cities from the rural South.
N. Congress passed the Espionage Act, the Sabotage Act, and the Sedition Act.

The American Journey ★ 93 ★ **Reteaching Activities**

Enrichment Activity 23–4

Name ______ Date ______ Class ______

Enrichment Activity 23-4

You Have a Choice

Once the United States became involved in World War I, the country worked quickly to prepare for fighting. The nation's industry expanded to supply weapons. Women and minorities replaced men who had left their jobs in industry to join the armed forces. The government worked to resolve labor disputes, and workers agreed not to strike so production of vital war materials would not be interrupted. In order to supply food for the Allied war refugees, the government encouraged farmers to produce more food, and the public to eat less. The Committee on Public Information hired speakers, writers, artists, and actors to build support for the war by convincing Americans that the war represented a battle for democracy and freedom. The political cartoon to the right, appeared in 1917.

SOURCE: Bailey, Thomas A. and David M. Kennedy. *The American Pageant, A History of the Republic.* Stanford University.

DIRECTIONS: Analyzing the Cartoon The cartoon presents a clear message about what was expected of Americans. List the symbols and words that the cartoonist used to persuade Americans to support the war. Tell the meaning of each.

Symbol/Words	Meaning
______	______
______	______
______	______
______	______
______	______

Activity **DIRECTIONS:** On a separate sheet of paper, draw your own political cartoon supporting a current issue of importance. Use an approach similar to the one in the 1917 cartoon.

The American Journey ★ 93 ★ **Enrichment Activities**

4 CLOSE

Ask students which "at home" actions they consider positive or negative, and why.

1 FOCUS

BELLRINGER
Motivational Activity

Before taking roll at the beginning of the class period, project Section Focus Transparency 23–5 and have students answer the questions. Discuss students' responses.

This activity is also available as a blackline master.

Section Focus Transparency 23–5

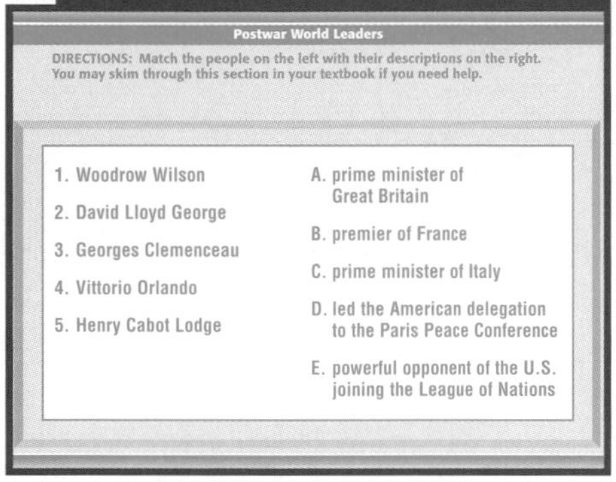
Postwar World Leaders

DIRECTIONS: Match the people on the left with their descriptions on the right. You may skim through this section in your textbook if you need help.

1. Woodrow Wilson
2. David Lloyd George
3. Georges Clemenceau
4. Vittorio Orlando
5. Henry Cabot Lodge

A. prime minister of Great Britain
B. premier of France
C. prime minister of Italy
D. led the American delegation to the Paris Peace Conference
E. powerful opponent of the U.S. joining the League of Nations

Vocabulary Precheck
Have students write a brief description of the settlement of World War I using the terms listed in **Terms to Learn.**

Use the **Vocabulary PuzzleMaker** to create crossword and word search puzzles.

Section Theme
Global Connections
The end of the war brought changes to many parts of the world and an attempt to establish world peace.

Activity Have students examine the chart on page 675. **Ask:** **How do these statistics help you understand Wilson's desire to establish a lasting peace?** *(Students should suggest that he wanted the world never again to suffer such tremendous casualties.)*

1919 — 1920 — 1921

1919 Paris Peace Conference begins; Treaty of Versailles is signed

1920 Senate rejects the League of Nations

1921 U.S. signs separate peace treaty with Central Powers

Section 5

Searching for Peace

READ TO DISCOVER . . .
- what principles Woodrow Wilson proposed as the basis for world peace.
- what terms were included in the peace treaty.
- why some Americans opposed the Treaty of Versailles.

TERMS TO LEARN
Fourteen Points
League of Nations
reparations

The Storyteller

The most brutal war of history had ended. As jubilant crowds celebrated in front of London's Buckingham Palace, British general Henry Wilson spotted an elderly woman sobbing. Wilson asked, "Is there anything that I can do for you?" The distressed woman replied, "Thank you. No. I am crying, but I am happy, for now I know that all my three sons who have been killed in the war have not died in vain." It was up to the Allied leaders and President Woodrow Wilson to make sure that the woman's words were true—that so many soldiers and civilians had not died in vain.

Peace song honoring Wilson

In January 1919, world leaders met in **Paris,** France, to try to resolve the complicated issues arising from World War I. President **Woodrow Wilson** led the American delegation to the Paris Peace Conference. When Wilson arrived in the city, enormous crowds cheered him. Well-wishers threw flowers in his path and unfurled banners that read "Long Live Wilson!" With great hope, Europeans looked to Wilson to help build a better postwar world. Yet enormous problems lay ahead.

After the War

In the aftermath of the war, Europe lay in ruins. Much of its landscape was devastated, its farms and towns destroyed. The human losses were terrible. Great Britain, France, Russia, Germany, and Austria-Hungary each lost between 1 and 2 million people in the fighting. Millions more were wounded. More than 50,000 Americans were killed in battle, while another 60,000 soldiers died from disease. Estimates for the whole war placed the number of soldiers and civilians killed worldwide at 10 million and those wounded at 20 million.

Europe also faced social and political turmoil. Millions of people found themselves homeless and hungry. Civil war raged in Russia. Poles, Czechs, and other peoples struggled to form independent nations out of the collapsed empires of Turkey, Russia, and Austria-Hungary. The overseas colonies of some European nations also sought independence. These problems complicated the search for peace and stability.

SECTION RESOURCES

Reproducible Masters
- Reproducible Lesson Plan 23–5
- Guided Reading Activity 23–5
- Section Quiz 23–5
- Reteaching Activity 23–5
- Enrichment Activity 23–5

Transparencies
- Section Focus Transparency 23–5

Multimedia
- Vocabulary PuzzleMaker
- Chapter Challenger Interactive Review Software
- Testmaker
- GTV: A Geographic Perspective on American History
- Facts On File: Landmark Documents in American History

War-torn Europe

World War I Casualties*

Country	Killed	Wounded
Allied Powers		
Russia	1,700,000	4,950,000
France	1,358,000	4,266,000
British Empire	908,400	2,090,000
Italy	650,000	947,000
Romania	335,700	120,000
United States	116,500	234,400
Central Powers		
Germany	1,773,000	4,216,000
Austria-Hungary	1,200,000	3,620,000
Turkey	325,000	400,000
Bulgaria	87,500	152,400

*Figures are approximate. Not all countries are listed.

Chart Study

World War I devastated many countries.

1. Which two countries suffered most of the casualties?
2. **Analyzing Information** Which side—the Allied or Central Powers—had more people killed?

A Vision of Peace

Woodrow Wilson had a vision of a just and lasting peace. A reformer and scholar, Wilson had served as the president of Princeton University and as governor of New Jersey before being elected U.S. president in 1912.

Wilson's Fourteen Points

Wilson outlined his peace plan in a proposal known as the **Fourteen Points.** Several of the points concerned the adjustment of boundaries in Europe and the creation of new nations. These points reflected Wilson's belief in the right of peoples to **"national self-determination"**—the right to decide how to be governed.

Wilson also proposed a number of principles for conducting international relations. These included calls for free trade, freedom of the seas, an end to secret treaties or agreements, reductions and limits on arms, and the peaceful settlement of disputes over colonies.

League of Nations

Wilson's final point, the one he considered most important, concerned the creation of a "general association of nations." This **League of Nations** would meet regularly to resolve international disputes. The League's member nations would help preserve peace and prevent future wars by pledging to respect and protect each other's territory and political independence.

Wilson's Fourteen Points reflected his strong—and perhaps unrealistic—faith in the ability of governments to resolve their problems fairly. At first many Europeans welcomed Wilson's ideas. Then problems arose when the plan interfered with the competing interests of the individual nations—in determining how to divide up territory. Also, some of Wilson's points were vague. They did not propose concrete solutions to difficult questions—such as how to achieve self-determination in regions where many different ethnic groups lived closely together.

The Peace Conference

The victorious Allies dominated the talks at the Paris Peace Conference. The Allies did not invite either Germany or Russia—now ruled by the Bolsheviks—to participate. The major figures in the negotiations were the Big Four—President Wilson, Prime Minister **David Lloyd George** of Great Britain, Premier **Georges Clemenceau** of France, and Prime Minister **Vittorio Orlando** of Italy.

Cooperative Learning Activity

Writing Interview Questions Organize students into four groups, and have each group draw up a list of interview questions for one of the principal people at the Versailles peace conference: David Lloyd George of Great Britain, Vittorio Orlando of Italy, Georges Clemenceau of France, and Woodrow Wilson of the United States. When students have completed their lists, have them compare questions. Which questions would remain the same or similar from leader to leader? Which would change depending upon the person being interviewed? Have a reporter from each group summarize the main ideas of the interview questions.

2 TEACH

L1 Supporting Key Ideas Write the following statement on the chalkboard: *The way that peace in Europe came about made it likely that peace would not last long.* Have students work together to locate details that support this statement. *(Details include Germany's severe punishment and disputed new national boundaries.)*

Chart Study

Answers

1. Russia and Germany
2. the Allied Powers

Guided Reading Activity 23-5

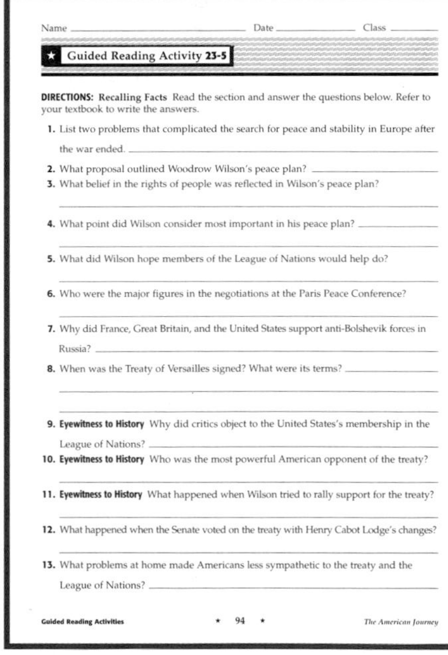

Name ______ Date ______ Class ______

Guided Reading Activity 23-5

DIRECTIONS: Recalling Facts Read the section and answer the questions below. Refer to your textbook to write the answers.

1. List two problems that complicated the search for peace and stability in Europe after the war ended. ______
2. What proposal outlined Woodrow Wilson's peace plan? ______
3. What belief in the rights of people was reflected in Wilson's peace plan? ______
4. What point did Wilson consider most important in his peace plan? ______
5. What did Wilson hope members of the League of Nations would help do? ______
6. Who were the major figures in the negotiations at the Paris Peace Conference? ______
7. Why did France, Great Britain, and the United States support anti-Bolshevik forces in Russia? ______
8. When was the Treaty of Versailles signed? What were its terms? ______
9. **Eyewitness to History** Why did critics object to the United States's membership in the League of Nations? ______
10. **Eyewitness to History** Who was the most powerful American opponent of the treaty? ______
11. **Eyewitness to History** What happened when Wilson tried to rally support for the treaty? ______
12. What happened when the Senate voted on the treaty with Henry Cabot Lodge's changes? ______
13. What problems at home made Americans less sympathetic to the treaty and the League of Nations? ______

Guided Reading Activities • 94 • *The American Journey*

Copyright © by The McGraw-Hill Companies, Inc.

Facts On File

CD-ROM
Landmark Documents in American History

Title: *Fourteen Points, Woodrow Wilson, 1918*

Have students read and summarize or paraphrase each point. Which points do they feel are the most likely to succeed, and why?

NATIONAL GEOGRAPHIC SOCIETY

VIDEODISC
GTV: A Geographic Perspective on American History

Side 4, Chapter 1
Title: *Modern Times*
Subject: World War I, before and after
Ask: **Why did most Americans oppose becoming involved in the League of Nations?** *(They wanted to isolate the United States from world conflicts and concentrate on domestic problems.)*

Map Study

Answers

1. Lithuania, Poland, Czechoslovakia, and Austria
2. Czechoslovakia, Austria, and Hungary

Map Skills Practice

Reading a Map Which nation was split into two separate parts? *(Germany)*

Who?What?Where?When?

Mrs. President Some historians say that no other First Lady had more influence on the presidency than did Mrs. Wilson, which angered some members of Congress. One senator said, "We have a petticoat government! Mrs. Wilson is President!"

The Allies Disagree

Wilson faced a difficult task. Although Europeans cheered him, their leaders showed little enthusiasm for the Fourteen Points. The European leaders were more concerned with the narrow interests of their own countries than with Wilson's call for a "peace without victory."

While Wilson opposed punishing the defeated nations, the European Allies sought revenge. Clemenceau wanted to make sure that Germany, which had invaded France twice in his lifetime, could never invade his country again. He believed that Germany should be broken up into smaller countries. Both he and Lloyd George demanded that Germany make large **reparations,** or payments, for the damage Germans caused in the war.

At the same time, the Allies had to decide how to deal with the new Bolshevik government of Russia. Fearing the spread of communism, France, Britain, and the United States supported anti-Bolshevik forces fighting for control of Russia. All three countries sent troops to Russia.

Lenin, the Bolshevik leader, had issued a statement of goals for the end of the war. Wilson's Fourteen Points came partly as a response to the Russian proposal. Although Wilson struggled to uphold the principles of his Fourteen Points at the Paris meeting, he was forced again and again to compromise or give in to the demands of the other Allies.

Europe After World War I

Map Study

The outcome of World War I brought great changes to Europe and the Middle East as new nations and colonies were created.

1. **Region** What new nations bordered on Germany?
2. **Analyzing Information** Which new nations lacked access to a major sea or ocean?

The Treaty of Versailles

On June 28, 1919, after months of difficult negotiations, the Allies and Germany signed a treaty at the Palace of Versailles outside Paris. The harsh terms of the **Treaty of Versailles** shocked the Germans. In defeat, however, they had no choice but to sign.

Under the terms of the treaty, Germany had to accept full responsibility for the war and to pay billions of dollars in reparations to the Allies. Germany also had to disarm completely and give up all its overseas colonies and some territory in Europe.

The treaty carved up the Austro-Hungarian and Russian Empires to create or restore the nations of **Austria, Hungary, Czechoslovakia,**

MULTIPLE LEARNING STYLES

Kinesthetic To help students identify with the effects of the Treaty of Versailles, ask half the students to represent the Allied nations and the other half to represent Germany. Bring a representative of each group before the class. Have the two students exchange common classroom objects to symbolize what German "rights" were taken away and what "burdens" were added because of the treaty. **Ask:** **Was this a fair treaty? Why or why not? How did the treaty leave Germany feeling? How might the German people react to a leader who promised to make things right for Germany again? L2, ELL**

Henry Cabot Lodge

Woodrow Wilson on tour

Yugoslavia, Poland, Finland, Estonia, Lithuania, and **Latvia.** The emergence of these nations fulfilled part of Wilson's vision of "national self-determination." Many of the borders of the new countries were disputed, however, and this led to future conflicts.

Though deeply disappointed by the rejection of much of his Fourteen Points, Wilson did succeed in having the League of Nations included in the peace treaty. He believed that the League would be able to correct any mistakes in the rest of the treaty.

Eyewitness to HISTORY

Opposition at Home

Wilson presented the Treaty of Versailles to the United States Senate for ratification on July 10, 1919. "Dare we reject it and break the heart of the world?" he asked. In spite of his eloquent plea, a difficult struggle lay ahead.

Many Americans had doubts about the treaty. Some, German Americans in particular, thought the treaty dealt too harshly with Germany. A great many Americans worried about participation in the League of Nations, which marked a permanent American commitment to international affairs. Critics charged that membership in the League would prevent the nation from setting its own foreign policy.

Debate over the Treaty

In 1919 the Republicans controlled the Senate, which had to ratify the treaty. Some Republican senators saw the ratification issue as a chance to embarrass President Wilson, a Democrat, and to weaken the Democratic Party before the upcoming elections of 1920. The fact that Wilson had not included any Republicans in the negotiating team he took to Paris cost him some Republican support. Other senators had sincere concerns about the treaty, particularly the League of Nations. A few senators opposed signing any treaty.

The most powerful opponent of the treaty was **Henry Cabot Lodge** of Massachusetts, head of the Senate Foreign Relations Committee. Lodge, a longtime foe of President Wilson, claimed that membership in the League would mean that

> "American troops and American ships may be ordered to any part of the world by nations other than the United States, and that is a proposition to which I for one can never assent."

Lodge delayed a vote on the treaty so that opponents could present their cases. He then proposed a number of reservations that would limit America's obligations under the treaty. One reservation, for example, stated that the League would have no say about situations arising from the

CURRICULUM CONNECTION

POLITICS
The delegation that accompanied President Wilson to Paris did not include any Republicans. Some Republicans were sympathetic to Wilson's aims, but he decided not to invite them. His lack of tact toward Republicans made many of them angry and resentful.

3 ASSESS

Assign Section 5 Review as homework or as an in-class activity.

Use **Chapter Challenger Interactive Review Software** to review Section 5.

Section Quiz 23–5

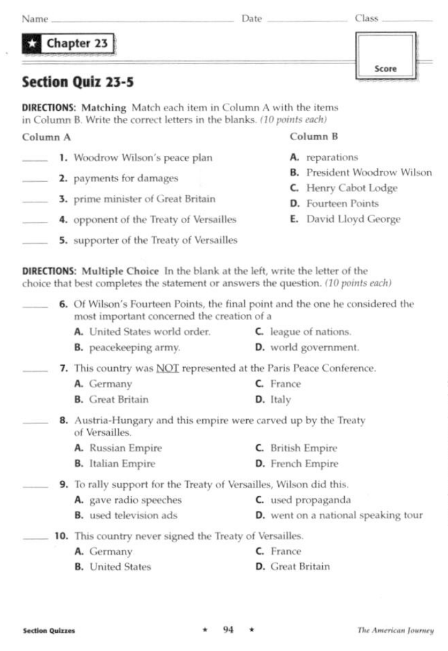

Name ______ Date ______ Class ______

Chapter 23

Score

Section Quiz 23-5

DIRECTIONS: Matching Match each item in Column A with the items in Column B. Write the correct letters in the blanks. *(10 points each)*

Column A	Column B
____ **1.** Woodrow Wilson's peace plan	**A.** reparations
____ **2.** payments for damages	**B.** President Woodrow Wilson
____ **3.** prime minister of Great Britain	**C.** Henry Cabot Lodge
____ **4.** opponent of the Treaty of Versailles	**D.** Fourteen Points
____ **5.** supporter of the Treaty of Versailles	**E.** David Lloyd George

DIRECTIONS: Multiple Choice In the blank at the left, write the letter of the choice that best completes the statement or answers the question. *(10 points each)*

____ **6.** Of Wilson's Fourteen Points, the final point and the one he considered the most important concerned the creation of a
A. United States world order. **C.** league of nations.
B. peacekeeping army. **D.** world government.

____ **7.** This country was NOT represented at the Paris Peace Conference.
A. Germany **C.** France
B. Great Britain **D.** Italy

____ **8.** Austria-Hungary and this empire were carved up by the Treaty of Versailles.
A. Russian Empire **C.** British Empire
B. Italian Empire **D.** French Empire

____ **9.** To rally support for the Treaty of Versailles, Wilson did this.
A. gave radio speeches **C.** used propaganda
B. used television ads **D.** went on a national speaking tour

____ **10.** This country never signed the Treaty of Versailles.
A. Germany **C.** France
B. United States **D.** Great Britain

Section Quizzes ★ 94 ★ *The American Journey*

MAKING CONNECTIONS ACTIVITY

Architecture The choice of the Palace of Versailles for the signing of the peace treaty implied much. Bring to class some pictures of this opulent building (or have students locate and bring in the pictures). After you display the pictures and allow students to comment upon them, **ask:** **How does this building symbolize the pride of the French (and the Allies)? Is it an appropriate place to sign a peace treaty? Why or why not? Do you think that the Germans understood what this choice of place suggested? How might they have felt about it? L1**

Reteaching Activity 23–5

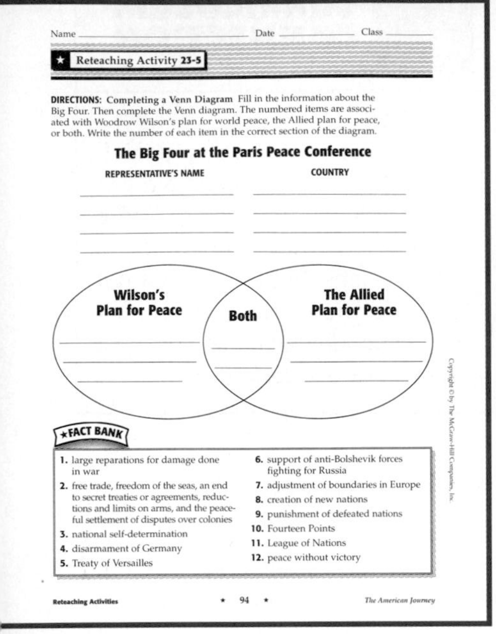
Name ______ Date ______ Class ______

★ Reteaching Activity 23-5

DIRECTIONS: Completing a Venn Diagram Fill in the information about the Big Four. Then complete the Venn diagram. The numbered items are associated with Woodrow Wilson's plan for world peace, the Allied plan for peace, or both. Write the number of each item in the correct section of the diagram.

The Big Four at the Paris Peace Conference

REPRESENTATIVE'S NAME	COUNTRY
______	______
______	______
______	______
______	______

★FACT BANK

1. large reparations for damage done in war
2. free trade, freedom of the seas, an end to secret treaties or agreements, reductions and limits on arms, and the peaceful settlement of disputes over colonies
3. national self-determination
4. disarmament of Germany
5. Treaty of Versailles
6. support of anti-Bolshevik forces fighting for Russia
7. adjustment of boundaries in Europe
8. creation of new nations
9. punishment of defeated nations
10. Fourteen Points
11. League of Nations
12. peace without victory

Reteaching Activities ★ 94 ★ *The American Journey*

Enrichment Activity 23–5

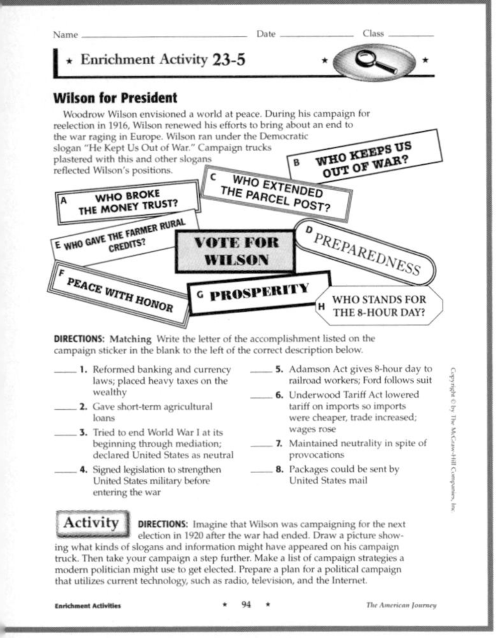
Name ______ Date ______ Class ______

★ Enrichment Activity 23-5 ★

Wilson for President

Woodrow Wilson envisioned a world at peace. During his campaign for reelection in 1916, Wilson renewed his efforts to bring about an end to the war raging in Europe. Wilson ran under the Democratic slogan "He Kept Us Out of War." Campaign trucks plastered with this and other slogans reflected Wilson's positions.

DIRECTIONS: Matching Write the letter of the accomplishment listed on the campaign sticker in the blank to the left of the correct description below.

_____ 1. Reformed banking and currency laws; placed heavy taxes on the wealthy
_____ 2. Gave short-term agricultural loans
_____ 3. Tried to end World War I at its beginning through mediation; declared United States as neutral
_____ 4. Signed legislation to strengthen United States military before entering the war
_____ 5. Adamson Act gives 8-hour day to railroad workers; Ford follows suit
_____ 6. Underwood Tariff Act lowered tariff on imports so imports were cheaper, trade increased; wages rose
_____ 7. Maintained neutrality in spite of provocations
_____ 8. Packages could be sent by United States mail

Activity **DIRECTIONS:** Imagine that Wilson was campaigning for the next election in 1920 after the war had ended. Draw a picture showing what kinds of slogans and information might have appeared on his campaign truck. Then take your campaign a step further. Make a list of campaign strategies a modern politician might use to get elected. Prepare a plan for a political campaign that utilizes current technology, such as radio, television, and the Internet.

Enrichment Activities ★ 94 ★ *The American Journey*

4 CLOSE

Call on volunteers to suggest reasons for (Pros) and reasons against (Cons) United States ratification of the Treaty of Versailles.

Monroe Doctrine. Wilson refused to accept these changes and described Senate opponents of the League as "contemptible, narrow, selfish, poor little minds that never get anywhere."

In September, Wilson went on a national speaking tour to rally support for the treaty and the League of Nations. Traveling 8,000 miles in 22 days, Wilson pleaded for his vision and warned that the League could not be effective without American participation. If the United States did not join, he believed a terrible war would come again.

On September 25, Wilson collapsed after giving a speech. The rest of his tour was canceled. Back in Washington Wilson suffered a stroke that left him partially paralyzed. During the president's illness, his wife, Edith Wilson, tried to shield him from the pressures of responsibility and took a leading role in deciding which issues were important enough to raise with him.

The Treaty Is Rejected

In the months following Wilson's stroke, opposition to the treaty grew. Yet Wilson remained unwilling to compromise. In March 1920, when the Senate voted on the treaty with Lodge's changes, Wilson ordered loyal Democrats to vote against it. He told his wife:

> "Better a thousand times to go down fighting than to dip your colours to dishonourable compromise."

Opposed by most Republicans and deserted by former supporters, the Treaty of Versailles—along with the League of Nations—was rejected in the Senate. Wilson hoped the 1920 election would be a "great and solemn referendum" on the League. He even considered running for a third term. In the end, however, Wilson did not run. In 1921 the United States signed a separate peace treaty with each of the Central Powers, and it never joined the League of Nations.

A Society in Turmoil

While the nation argued over the treaty, other issues were causing turmoil in American society. Relations between African Americans and whites turned increasingly violent, with lynchings in the South and race riots in the North. Economic problems led to labor disputes, which contributed to another source of turmoil—a fear of radicals.

President Wilson, concerned with the peace treaty and then seriously ill, never gave much attention to these problems. However, the troubles at home made Americans less sympathetic to the treaty and the League of Nations.

Section 5 Review

Checking for Understanding

1. ***Identify*** Woodrow Wilson, David Lloyd George, Georges Clemenceau, Vittorio Orlando, Treaty of Versailles, Henry Cabot Lodge.
2. ***Define*** Fourteen Points, League of Nations, reparations.
3. ***Summarize*** the provisions of the Treaty of Versailles.

Reviewing Themes

4. **Global Connections** How did President Wilson think that the League of Nations would help maintain world peace?

Critical Thinking

5. **Determining Relevance** Some Americans thought the Treaty of Versailles was too hard on Germany. What terms would you have proposed for Germany?

Activity

Comparing Maps Compare a map of Europe after World War I to a map of Europe today. Make a list of the significant border changes that have occurred since that time.

Section 5 Review Answers

1. Wilson, 674; George, 675; Clemenceau, 675; Orlando, 675; Treaty of Versailles, 676; Lodge, 677
2. The words are defined in the Glossary.
3. Germany had to accept full responsibility for the war, pay reparations to the Allies, disarm completely, and give up all overseas colonies and some European territory.
4. Wilson thought that by pledging respect and protecting each other's territory, member nations could resolve disputes without resorting to war.
5. Answers may include reducing the amount of reparations or keeping Allied forces in Germany temporarily.

Activity Lists should include the former Soviet Union, Czechoslovakia, East and West Germany, and Yugoslavia.

Study and Writing
SKILL BUILDER

Outlining

To sketch a scene, you first draw the rough shape, or outline, of the picture. Then you fill in this rough shape with details. Outlining written material is a similar process. You begin with the rough shape of the material and gradually fill in the details.

Learning the Skill

There are two kinds of outlines—formal and informal. An informal outline is similar to taking notes. You write only words and phrases needed to remember main ideas.

A formal outline has a standard format. In a formal outline, label main heads with Roman numbers, subheads with capital letters, and details with Arabic numerals and lowercase letters. Each level should have at least two entries and should be indented from the level above. All entries use the same grammatical form. If one entry is a complete sentence, all other entries at that level must also be complete sentences.

When outlining written material, first read the material to identify the main ideas. In textbooks, section heads provide clues to main topics. Then identify the subheads. Place supporting details under the appropriate head.

Practicing the Skill

Study this partial outline of Section 3. Then answer the questions that follow.

I. European Allies need help.
  A. Allied armies are exhausted.
    1. Trench warfare depleted supplies.
    2. Morale is low.
  B. Civilians are in trouble.
    1. People are starving.
    2. Supply ships are sunk by Germans.

Soldiers in the trenches

II. Americans enter the war.
  A. United States Navy patrols seas.
    1. German U-boats are destroyed.
    2. Convoys protect Allied ships.
      a. Losses are reduced by two-thirds.
      b. No American soldiers are killed.
  B. American Expeditionary Force (AEF) lands in Europe.
    1. Germans lose at Château-Thierry.
    2. Germans are defeated at Belleau Wood.
III. Allies take the offensive.
  A. Battle of Argonne Forest is fought.
  B. President Wilson lists conditions for armistice.

1. Is this a formal or an informal outline?
2. What are the three main topics?
3. If you wanted to add two facts about the AEF, where would you put them in the outline? Would you use numbers or letters to label the facts?

Applying the Skill

Outlining Following the guidelines above, prepare an outline for Section 2 of Chapter 23.

ANSWERS TO PRACTICING THE SKILL

1. formal
2. "European Allies need help." "Americans enter the war." and "Allies take the offensive."
3. They would be identified as "3" and "4" under Roman numeral II, capital letter B; numbers

Applying the Skill The outline should use section heads (e.g., "American Neutrality") as Roman numeral heads; subheads (e.g., "Using Propaganda") as heads identified by capital letters. Students might also identify at least two statements, identified by Arabic numerals, under each "capital letter head."

Study and Writing
SKILL BUILDER

TEACH

Outlining

Whether studying classroom material or preparing to do original writing, students will find that outlining helps them organize material and see relationships among details. Point out that the "standard format" of an outline includes the following considerations:

- An outline may be in topic form (with all points stated as key words and phrases) or in sentence form (with all points stated and punctuated as complete sentences). A point should not be divided unless at least two subpoints can be made. In other words, do not include an (A) if there is no (B); or a (1) if there is no (2).
- In addition to using the same grammatical form, students should try to maintain parallelism in their outlines. For example, if point (A) is expressed as a noun followed by a prepositional phrase, points (B), (C), and so on should be expressed that way as well.

Additional Practice

Chapter Skills Activity 23

What? Where? When? Who?

No Tin Soldiers During World War I, Americans observed Daylight Saving Time, established in Europe, to save electricity. Factories cut back production of women's corsets to save steel. Toymakers reduced the manufacture of many toys to save tin.

Chapter 23

Review and Activities

Reviewing Key Terms

On a sheet of paper, define the following terms:

nationalism
militarism
entente
propaganda
convoy
front
armistice
mobilization
dissent
socialist
pacifist
espionage
sabotage
Fourteen Points
League of Nations
reparations

Reviewing Key Facts

1. Why did European nations form alliances?
2. Why did the Zimmermann telegram push the United States toward war?
3. How did Russia's withdrawal affect World War I?
4. In what ways did the war help improve conditions for American workers?
5. What was Henry Cabot Lodge's greatest concern about the League of Nations?

Critical Thinking

Making Inferences

Many Americans wanted the United States to remain neutral during the war.

1. Why do you think many Americans feared war?
2. How did economic interests affect the United States's inability to remain neutral?

Skill Practice Activity

Outlining

On a separate sheet of paper, add supporting details to the outline of Section 1 below.

Steps Leading to World War I

I. Nationalism
  A. As a unifying force
  B. As a disruptive force
II. Imperial Expansion
III. Military Buildups
IV. Forming Alliances
  A. Triple Alliance members
  B. Triple Entente members

Reviewing Themes

1. **Science and Technology** What advantages did airplanes provide in the war?
2. **Government and Democracy** How did President Wilson use Russia's democratic revolution to gain support for the war?
3. **Geography and History** How did the Treaty of Brest-Litovsk affect the war?
4. **Economic Factors** What caused the labor shortage in the United States during the war?
5. **Global Connections** What four nations dominated the Paris Peace Conference?

Technology Activity

Using the Internet Search the Internet to find out more details about the "Great War"—World War I. Use the information you find to create a chart titled "World War I—A Closer Look." Focus on causes of the war, methods of warfare, and the outcome of the war for various countries. Include numbers of casualties and costs of rebuilding.

GLENCOE TECHNOLOGY

VIDEODISC
MindJogger Videoquiz

Use MindJogger to review the Chapter 23 content.

Chapter 23
Disc 3, Side B

Also available in VHS.

Reviewing Key Terms

The key terms used in this activity can be found in the textbook glossary on pages A26–A35.

Reviewing Key Facts

1. to increase their strength and protect themselves
2. Germany promised that it would help Mexico reclaim parts of Texas, New Mexico, and Arizona if Mexico would join the Central Powers. This threatened the stability of the U.S. and raised anti-German feelings.
3. It allowed Germany to move more troops to the Western Front in France.
4. To prevent strikes the National War Labor Board granted workers an eight-hour work day, overtime pay, equal pay for women, and the right to form unions.
5. that it would force the United States to intervene in too many international disputes

Critical Thinking

1. Answers will vary but might include loss of life, fear of fighting on United States soil, fear that the United States would lose power, and fear that our democratic government would be threatened if the United States were defeated in war.
2. The Allies' demand for supplies boosted industry in the United States. The United States also had an interest in protecting its international trade.

Skill Practice Activity

Students should add at least two statements for each capital-letter head. These statements should be identified by Arabic numerals.

Reviewing Themes

1. Airplanes could track troop movements and bomb enemy targets.
2. When Russia changed to a democratic form of government, many people thought that Russia would join the Allies. Wilson used Russia's new democracy to claim that the Allies were now fighting a war to save democracy.

Geography Activity

Study the map below, then answer the questions that follow.

The Eastern Front

1. **Location** Which Central Powers victories took place in East Prussia?
2. **Place** When was Warsaw, Poland, defeated by the Central Powers?
3. **Movement** Which line gave the Central Powers more territory—the armistice line of 1917 or the treaty line of Brest-Litovsk, 1918?

Time Line Activity

Create a time line on which you place the following events in chronological order.

- U.S. declares war against Germany
- Archduke Ferdinand is assassinated
- Battle of Verdun begins
- *Lusitania* torpedoed
- Treaty of Versailles signed

Cooperative Activity

History and Music With members of your group, research the life of George M. Cohan. Get copies of the lyrics to his songs, as well as recordings of the music if possible. Then find excerpts such as the following from soldiers who fought in World War I:

> "As far as the eye could see was a mass of black mud with shell holes filled with water. . . . [H]ere and there a horse's carcase [carcass] sticking out of the water; here and there a corpse. The only sign of life was a rat or two swimming about to find food and a patch of ground. At night a yellow mist hung over the mud; the stench was almost unbearable. When gas shells came over the mist turned to brown. It smelt like violets. The smell of violets was the sign of danger."
>
> —Private H. Jeary, British forces

Use Cohan's music as well as words and pictures from actual soldiers to create a multimedia presentation of "The Great War."

Portfolio Activity **History Journal** Review the chapter for names of committees and organizations created by the United States government to handle war-related concerns. Make a list that describes the responsibilities of each committee or organization.

CHAPTER 23
Review and Activities

Geography Activity

1. Tannenburg, Masurian Lakes, Masuria
2. August 1915
3. the treaty line of Brest-Litovsk, 1918

Time Line Activity

Events should be placed in this order: Archduke Ferdinand is assassinated, *Lusitania* torpedoed, Battle of Verdun begins, U. S. declares war against Germany, Treaty of Versailles signed

Cooperative Activity

Each group should prepare an interesting, informative presentation that makes use of various media.

Portfolio Activity Students should create a list of the government organizations formed during World War I to handle war-related concerns, such as the Committee on Public Information and the Food Administration, and list the responsibilities of each.

Chapter Bonus Test Question

Ask: By what nickname were the members of the American Expeditionary Force known? *(doughboys)*

3. It gave Germany an advantage by allowing it to move its troops farther west into Europe because Germans no longer had to worry about Russian interference.
4. Millions of men left their jobs to serve in the military, and fewer European immigrants were coming to the United States.
5. United States, Great Britain, France, Italy

Technology Activity

Students should use the Internet to gather information on World War I. Charts should list causes of the war, methods of warfare, casualties, bombs used, and costs of rebuilding for at least three countries.

Hands-On HISTORY Lab Activity

Block Schedule

This activity may be implemented within either a traditional class period or a block scheduling framework.

FOCUS

Brainstorm with students a list of their favorite candies. **Ask:** **Where can you get these candies?** *(supermarkets, vending machines, movie theaters, and so on)* Point out that because it is so easy to buy delicious candies of many types, students may not have thought much about the days when candy was made primarily at home. Have students name some of the ingredients that go into candy *(e.g., sugar, butter, chocolate, vanilla, and salt)*. Discuss the fact that most people of this era could get such ingredients, but that the main challenge in candy making then was finding the time to do it.

TEACH

L2 Synthesizing Information

Explain that the engraving on page 682 shows a taffy pull in a Boston home, and that its original caption describes a taffy pull as "a delightful diversion for the Fall and Winter months." After students scan the materials and instructions for a taffy pull, ask: **Why do you think the caption described this as a "Fall and Winter" activity?** (*Students may suggest that the warm, sugary mixture would be uncomfortable to work with and would attract insects during the warmer months.)*

Have students work in groups as they have their own taffy pull. Urge them to wear old clothes or aprons, because the procedure may become messy. You may wish to have a member of each group document the steps with photographs or videotape and present the group's comments in the form of a video report.

Hands-On HISTORY Lab Activity

Taffy Pull

Making candy was often a social event in the 1800s and early 1900s. Young people would gather and, as a group, make candy to be enjoyed for the evening. Try to recreate a taffy pull.

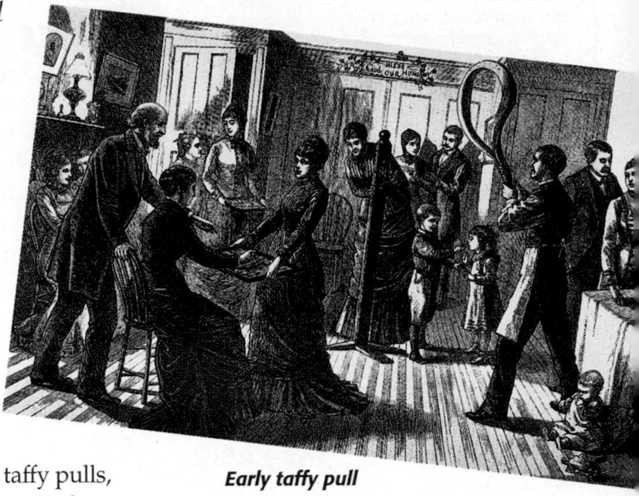
Early taffy pull

The Way It Was

Because candy was a luxury that was rarely available in the stores, taffy pulls were a popular gathering for young people. Guests would pull the golden, warm taffy into ropes and then cut the candy and eat it. Candy making, especially taffy pulls, became a family or social event because it required constant attention and many hands to stir and pull the taffy.

1 Materials

- 2 cups sugar
- 1 cup light corn syrup
- 1 cup water
- 1 1/2 teaspoons salt
- 2 tablespoons butter or margarine, softened
- 2 teaspoons vanilla
- food coloring (optional)
- extra butter
- large flat pan or cookie sheet
- 2-quart saucepan
- candy thermometer
- kitchen scissors
- waxed paper
- stove

Believe It Or Not! The average American eats 18 pounds of candy annually. More than 2,000 different kinds of candy are manufactured in the United States, and more than half of these candies are made with chocolate!

CURRICULUM CONNECTION

World History Candy making is an ancient activity, practiced around the world. We know that perhaps as many as 4,000 years ago, Egyptians made a candy by mixing honey with fruits, nuts, seeds, or sweet herbs. The Persians enjoyed a sweet reed covered with spices and honey. They called it *kand*—possibly the origin of our word *candy.* Sugar-based candies were first developed in India. Cacao beans, however, come from Central America. The Maya and the Aztec used the beans as money and ground them to make a bitter drink. Explorer Hernán Cortés took cacao beans back to Spain. From there, European cooks learned to make sweetened chocolate in the form we enjoy today.

2 What To Do

1. Butter the cookie sheet. In the saucepan combine the sugar, corn syrup, water, and salt. Heat the mixture to boiling over medium heat. Carefully stir until the sugar is dissolved.
2. Place the candy thermometer in the pan and heat the mixture until the temperature reaches 262°F. SAFETY NOTE: HANDLE HOT MATERIALS CAREFULLY. Remove the pan from the heat. Stir in the butter, vanilla, and food coloring (if desired).
3. Pour the mixture onto the cookie sheet and let it cool 10 to 15 minutes until the taffy is cool enough to handle.
4. Wash your hands very well and coat your hands with butter. Divide the mixture in half with your hands.
5. With a partner pull and twist each half until the candy holds its shape. Pull the taffy into long ropes about 3/4 inch in diameter.
6. Butter the blades of kitchen scissors and cut the rope into 1 inch pieces. Wrap each piece of candy in waxed paper.

Hardened taffy pieces

3 Lab Report

1. Why do you think it was necessary to pull the taffy instead of just letting it cool on the cookie sheet?
2. Was making taffy easier or more difficult than you thought it would be? Explain your answer.
3. **Drawing Conclusions** How long did it take to make the taffy? How often do you think making candy would occur today if it took this long to make?

Go a Step Further

Find out more about the making of candy. Research the techniques that the Swiss, Germans, and Dutch used to make their famous chocolates. Draw a diagram showing the various steps involved in turning cacao beans into chocolate candy bars.

What? Where? When? Who?

Toothaches Perhaps it was a good thing that making candy was not a frequent activity. Until about 1840, Americans suffered through horrible toothaches or, worse yet, tooth extraction without anesthesia. Many people lost about half their teeth by the time they were 20 years old. It was not until the 1950s—after World War I and World War II—that fluoride was added to water supplies and toothpastes. Fluoride has greatly reduced tooth decay.

ASSESS

Have students answer the **Lab Report** questions on page 683.

CLOSE

Encourage students to complete the **Go a Step Further** activity. If there is a *chocolatier* in your community, you may wish to add some variety to the assignment by arranging for students to visit the site and create a diagram of the candy making process there. As students display and explain the finished diagrams, discuss how the various techniques affect the prices of candy bars.

ANSWERS

Lab Report

1. Pulling taffy introduces air into the mixture and makes the taffy more pliable.
2. Students will probably find that it was more difficult than they thought.
3. Answers will vary but should be at least one hour. Most students will conclude that candy making would continue to be an occasional treat.

Go a Step Further

Diagrams should show the various steps involved in turning cacao beans into chocolate candy bars. They may include roasting and grinding the cacao beans, possibly adding milk solids (for milk chocolate), adding sugar and other ingredients, the forming of the candy bar, and perhaps the wrapping and packaging processes.

Unit 9 Resource Guide

These Glencoe resources may be used to teach, reteach, or enrich the concepts presented in this unit of study.

Teaching Transparencies

Map Transparency 9 with Overlays A, B, C, D, E

Cause-and-Effect Transparency 9

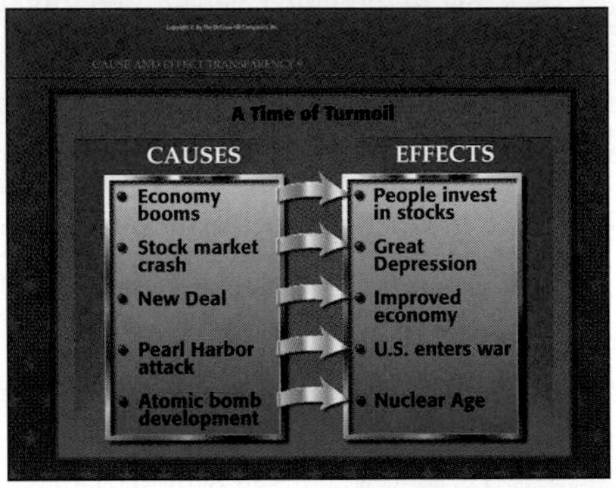

BIBLIOGRAPHY

Readings for the Student

Freedman, Russell. ***Immigrant Kids.*** New York: E. P. Dutton, 1980. Chronicles the lives of immigrant children in the late 1800s and early 1900s.

Migneco, Ronald and Timothy Levi Biel. ***The Crash of 1929.*** San Diego: Lucent Books, Inc., 1989. Describes how the 1929 stock market crash brought an end to the Roaring Twenties.

Reading for the Teacher

Rubel, David. ***The United States in the 20th Century.*** New York: Scholastic, 1995. Illustrated time lines of events.

Multimedia Resources

Videotape. ***Carnegie Hall Salutes the Jazz Masters.*** New York: Polygram, 1994. 115 minutes. A minitour of jazz music.

Videotape. ***The Road to War: BBC.*** New York: Arts & Entertainment Network, 1989. Eight videotapes document the outbreak of World War II.

Compact Disc. Guthrie, Woody. ***Dust Bowl Ballads.*** Cambridge: Rounder Records, 1988. Ballads, blues, and popular songs performed by Woody Guthrie.

interNET CONNECTIONS

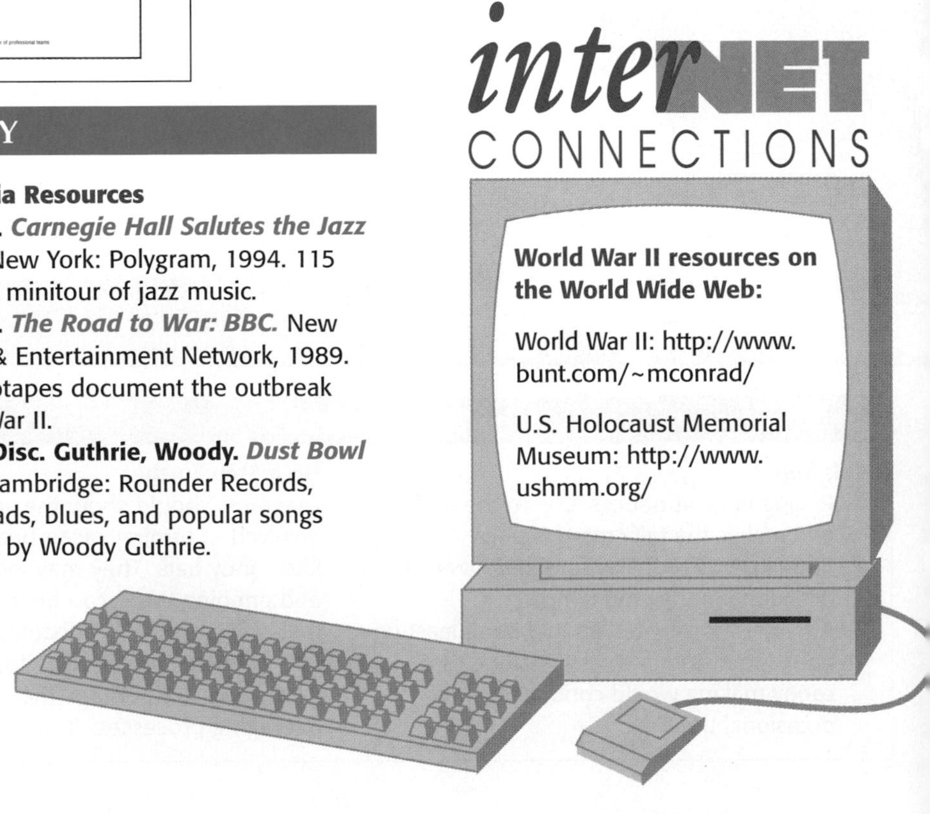

World War II resources on the World Wide Web:

World War II: http://www.bunt.com/~mconrad/

U.S. Holocaust Memorial Museum: http://www.ushmm.org/

Resource Guide Unit 9

Interdisciplinary Activities

American Literature Reading 9

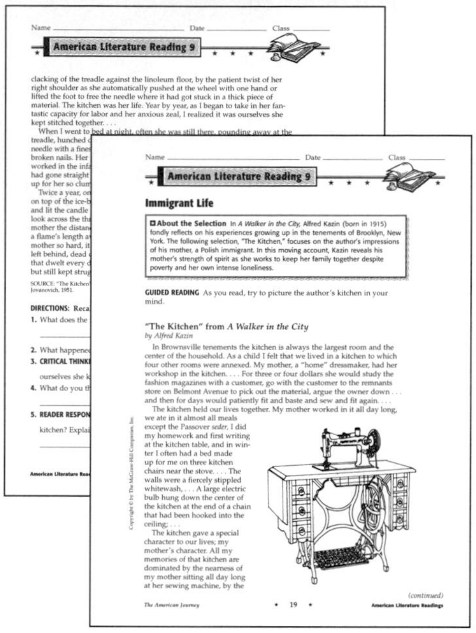

Interdisciplinary Connection 9

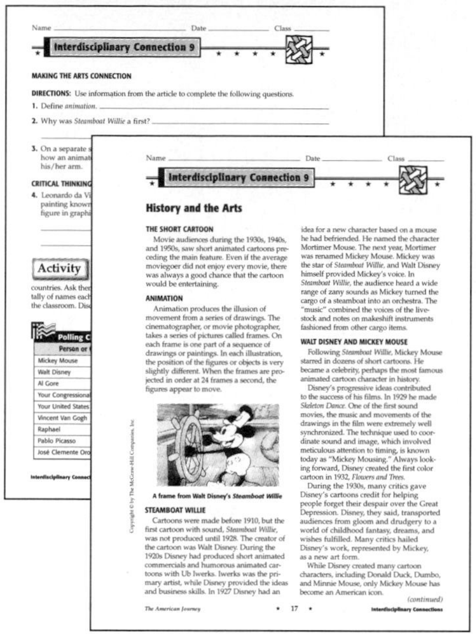

Enrichment Activities

Cooperative Learning Activity 9

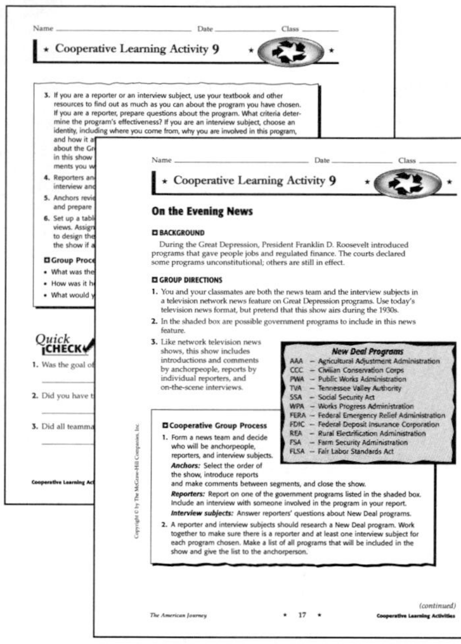

Hands-On Activities

Hands-On History Lab Activity 9

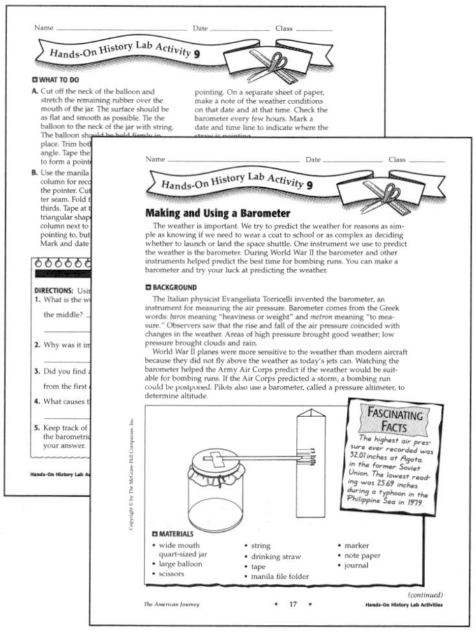

History Simulation 9

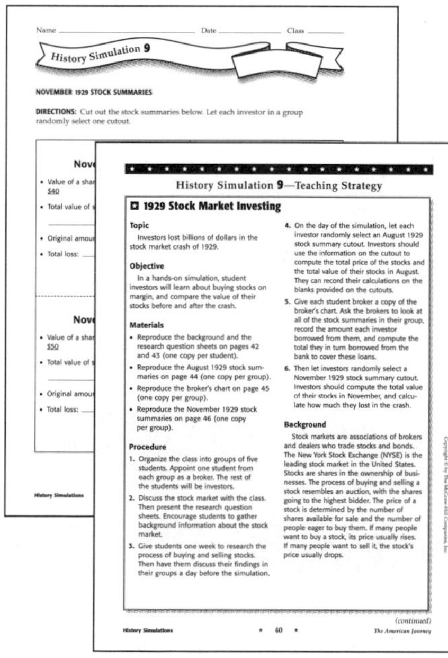

Assessment

Unit 9 Test

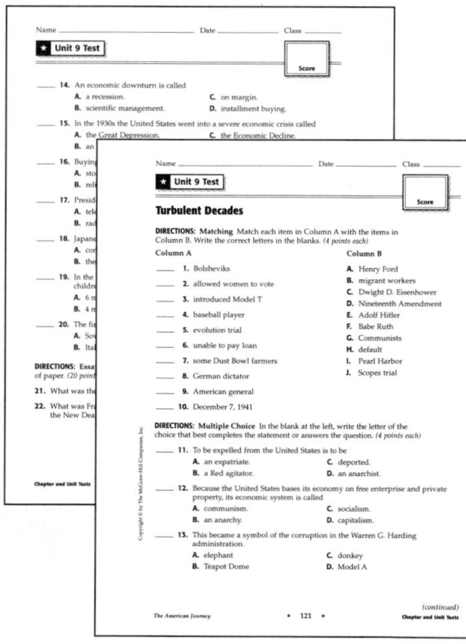

Introducing
UNIT 9

0:00 OUT OF TIME?

If your teaching time is limited, you may use the *Chapter Summaries* blackline master found in the TCR with the *Chapter Digests Audiocassette Activities and Tests* to condense individual chapters into a one-day lesson.

Introducing the Unit

Activity Ask students to review the unit time line. Then have them write a phrase to characterize each decade. Ask volunteers to share their phrases with the class. Explain to students that this unit covers three decades—the 1920s, or the Roaring Twenties; the 1930s, or the Depression years; and the 1940s, or the World War II years.

Unit Objectives

Upon completing this unit, students will be able to:

1. Evaluate the effects the events of the 1920s had on American culture.
2. Analyze the causes of the Great Depression.
3. Detail the ways in which the New Deal changed the American economy and society.
4. Investigate the causes of World War II.
5. Summarize the United States's role in World War II.

Hands-On HISTORY

Hands-On History Lab Activity 9, "Making and Using a Barometer," is a high-interest **constructivist approach** activity directly related to the main topic of the unit.

Unit 9

Turbulent Decades

1919–1945

"The only thing we have to fear is fear itself."

—Franklin Delano Roosevelt, 1933

MAPPING *America*

Portfolio Activity Draw a freehand outline map of the United States. Sketch the state borders, including Hawaii. As you read this unit about turbulent decades in American history, note major events. Include sites of labor and racial disputes, the extent of the drought that caused the "Dust Bowl," and the bombing of Pearl Harbor. Plot the location of these events on your map and label them.

684

General George A. Patton's helmet

WPA poster, mid-1930s

United States

1920 Prohibition begins

1923 Teapot Dome oil scandal erupts

1925 Scopes trial captures national attention

1920 — 1925

World

1922 Mussolini takes power in Italy

1928 Chiang Kai-shek wins control of China

TEAM TEACHING STRATEGIES

Language Arts After World War I, Americans had more leisure time to enjoy the arts and entertainment. Explain to students that during the Harlem Renaissance, a number of important writers explored the African American experience in novels, poems, and short stories. Have the Language Arts teacher help students write a three-stanza poem—one stanza for each chapter in this unit—about the African American experience during the time period covered. Ask volunteers to perform a dramatic reading of their poems for the class.

Life *magazine cover, 1926*

HISTORY AND ART ***Betio's Red Beach Three* by Tom Lovell** American marines plunge into the sea for the assault on Japanese-held islands in 1943.

1929 Stock market crashes, triggering Great Depression

1930 Uruguay wins soccer's first World Cup

1933 President Franklin D. Roosevelt launches New Deal

1933 Hitler becomes chancellor of Germany

1935 Pope Pius XI condemns Nazi atrocities

1937 Dust Bowl develops in Great Plains

1939 World War II begins in Europe

1941 Japanese attack Pearl Harbor; U.S. enters World War II

1944 Allies storm Normandy beaches

1945 Atomic bombs level Hiroshima and Nagasaki

1930 — 1935 — 1940 — 1945

TEAM TEACHING STRATEGIES

Math Discuss the impact the stock market has on the American economy. Ask students to choose a stock listed in the business section of their local newspaper. Have them "purchase" one share of the stock by recording its price. Then have them track the stock and twice a week record the stock's price. At the unit's completion, have students "sell" their stock and record the "sale" price. Work with the Math teacher to show students how to create a line or bar graph depicting changes in stock prices over time. They should also include the total amount made or lost from the "purchase" and "sale" of their stock. As a class, discuss which kinds of stocks performed best and worst.

NATIONAL GEOGRAPHIC SOCIETY

VIDEODISC
GTV: A Geographic Perspective on American History

Side 4, Chapter 1

Title: *Modern Times*
Subject: Before and after World War I
Ask: **What kinds of technology changed lifestyles in the early 1900s?** *(airplanes, automobiles, telephones, and electric lights)*

VIDEODISC
GTV: A Geographic Perspective on American History

Side 4, Chapter 6

Title: *Echoes of War*
Subject: Effects of World War II
Ask: **What effect did World War II have on the economy of the United States?** *(It brought the U.S. out of the Depression.)*

HISTORY AND ART Paintings like *Betio's Red Beach Three* captured the emotion, urgency, and excitement of World War II battles in a realistic way.

Linking PAST & PRESENT

Activity Fads and crazes dominated the social life of many Americans in the 1920s. During this decade the Charleston craze swept the nation. This dance step takes its name from Charleston, South Carolina, where the fast, flailing step first appeared. It became widely popular in 1923 after it appeared in the all–African American Broadway show *Running Wild*. Discuss current crazes and fads and how they became popular.

Block Schedule

Team Teaching This selection from *The Invisible Thread* may be implemented in a team-teaching context, in conjunction with English/Language Arts.

Reinforcing Vocabulary
Review the **Reader's Dictionary** terms with students to be sure they understand any unfamiliar terms.

Historical Connection
After the Japanese bombed Pearl Harbor in 1941, some Americans questioned Japanese Americans' loyalty to the United States. At that time about two-thirds of Japanese Americans actually were native-born, United States citizens. Nevertheless, military and political leaders worried about a Japanese invasion of the United States and which side Japanese Americans would support. President Franklin Roosevelt responded to these fears by directing the army to relocate more than 100,000 West Coast Japanese Americans to detention centers. With only days to prepare for the move, most Japanese Americans were forced to hastily abandon their homes and businesses.

Background Information
Setting This excerpt takes place in Tanforan, a horse racing park used as an internment camp for Japanese Americans during World War II.

Characters The main characters in this excerpt are two young Japanese American women—the author, Yoshiko Uchida, and her sister, Kay.

Plot Yoshiko and her sister face the daily strain of life in an internment camp.

America's Literature

The Invisible Thread

by Yoshiko Uchida

Yoshiko Uchida (1921–1992) grew up in California in the 1930s. As a Japanese American, she sometimes felt very different from the people around her. She wanted to be a "typical" American and often resented the Japanese ways of her family. Eventually Uchida learned to value the "invisible thread" that linked her to her heritage.

Read to Discover
Yoshiko Uchida's family, like many Japanese Americans, were patriotic citizens during World War II. Many Japanese Americans, however, were treated as enemies because of their heritage. During the war, the American government relocated to camps those Japanese people living in the West. How did Yoshiko and her sister, Kay, spend their time in the internment camp?

Reader's Dictionary
Tanforan: horse racing park used as a camp for Japanese Americans
mess hall: military-style dining area
canteen: a general store at a military camp
contraband: forbidden items
diversion: entertainment

Gradually we became accustomed to life in Tanforan, especially to standing in long lines for everything. We lined up to get into the mess hall or to use a laundry tub or to buy something at the canteen (finding only shoelaces when we got in) or to get into the occasional movies that were shown.

We got used to rushing back to our stall after dinner for the 6:00 P.M. head count (we were still in bed for the morning count), and to the sudden unexpected campwide searches for contraband by the FBI when we were confined to our stalls for several hours.

For diversion we could also go to talent shows, recorded concerts, discussion groups, Saturday night dances, softball games, art classes, and hobby shows exhibiting beautiful handicraft made by resourceful residents from scrap material.

Soon visitors from the outside were allowed to come in as far as the grandstand, and many of our friends came laden with cakes, fruit, candy, cookies, and news from the outside.

Representatives from the university, the YMCA and YWCA, and various church groups also came to give us their support and help. They were working on arrangements to get students out of camp and back into schools as soon as possible.

One day our neighbor Mrs. Harpainter came to see us, bringing all sorts of snacks along with flowers from her garden for Mama. Her boys, however, were not allowed inside because they were under sixteen.

When Kay and I heard they were waiting outside the gate, we hurried to the fence to talk to them.

Additional Literary Works of the Period

You may want to refer to students to the following:

Brimner, Larry Dane. ***Voices from the Camps: Internment of Japanese Americans during World War II.*** New York: Franklin Watts, 1994. Young adult literature that includes personal accounts.

Steinbeck, John. ***The Grapes of Wrath.*** New York: The Viking Press, 1939. Novel based on author's observations while traveling with migrant farm families from the Oklahoma Dust Bowl.

Tunnell, Michael O. ***The Children of Topaz: The Story of a Japanese-American Internment Camp.*** New York: Holiday House, 1996. Based on the diary of a third-grade class of Japanese American children in an internment camp during World War II.

Japanese Americans unload supplies at an internment camp during World War II.

"Teddy! Bobby!"

We ran to greet them, squeezing our fingers through the chain links to touch their hands.

But an armed guard quickly shouted, "Hey, you two! Get away from the fence!"

Kay and I stepped back immediately. We didn't want to tangle with anyone holding a gun. Bobby and Teddy watched us in total horror, and told us later that they thought we were going to be shot right before their eyes.

When my mother's good friend, Eleanor Knight, came to see us, we asked her to see how Laddie was getting along. Each day we wondered about him, but the boy who had promised to write hadn't even sent us a postcard. And then we learned why he had not written.

"I'm so sorry," Eleanor wrote, "but your dear Laddie died just a few weeks after you left Berkeley."

I was sure he had died of a broken heart, thinking we had abandoned him. I ran outside to find a place to cry, but there were people wherever I turned. I didn't want to see anybody, but there was no place to hide. There was no place to be alone—not in the latrine or the showers or anywhere in the entire camp.

Responding to Literature

1. Why were Teddy and Bobby not allowed inside the camp?
2. Why did representatives from churches and other groups visit the camp?
3. How do you think you would feel in Uchida's place in the internment camp?

Activity

Designing a Memorial Draw plans for a community memorial suitable for remembering Japanese Americans treated unfairly during World War II.

Answers to Responding to Literature

1. They were under 16 years old.
2. They wanted to get students out of the camp and back to school. They also wanted to provide support and help.
3. Answers will vary but should demonstrate an understanding of the conditions in an internment camp.

Activity Students' plans for a community memorial should reflect Japanese Americans' treatment during World War II.

Portfolio Activity Instruct students to study the photograph on this page. Then ask them to write a short story about the people pictured.

At the Movies

The film *Come See the Paradise* is a love story about an Irish American man and a Japanese American woman. The story unfolds during the controversial period of Japanese American internment during World War II. The 1951 film *Go For Broke!* deals with the historic record of the famed 442nd Regimental Combat Team, which was composed mostly of second-generation Japanese Americans called *Nisei*.

Curriculum Connection

CIVICS

In May 1942, Gordon Hirabayashi, an American-born Quaker and senior at the University of Washington, refused to register for evacuation to a detention camp. Instead he appeared at an FBI office with his lawyer to protest. He was ordered to stay indoors until his case was heard. He defied this order and was jailed for five months before his trial. Hirabayashi was found guilty of refusing to register and of breaking curfew. He appealed his case to the Supreme Court and remained in jail without bail during the three months it took for the Supreme Court to hear his case. In *Hirabayashi* v. *United States*, the Court admitted that the internment orders were racially motivated and the curfew sat on the edge of constitutionality, but upheld Hirabayashi's conviction anyway.

Chapter 24 Planning Guide

A complete, 1-page lesson plan is provided for each section in the *Reproducible Lesson Plans* booklet.

Section Resources

Daily Objectives	Reproducible Resources	Multimedia Resources
Section 1 Time of Turmoil Discuss the effects of antiforeign and antiradical sentiments on American society in the 1920s.	Reproducible Lesson Plan 24–1 Guided Reading Activity 24–1* Section Quiz 24–1* Reteaching Activity 24–1 Enrichment Activity 24–1	Section Focus Transparency 24–1 Vocabulary PuzzleMaker Chapter Challenger Interactive Review Testmaker The Presidents: A Picture History of Our Nation
Section 2 Desire for Normalcy Describe Presidents Harding's and Coolidge's attempts to return the United States to normalcy.	Reproducible Lesson Plan 24–2 Guided Reading Activity 24–2* Section Quiz 24–2* Political Cartoons, *The Teapot Dome Boils Over* Reteaching Activity 24–2 Enrichment Activity 24–2	Section Focus Transparency 24–2 Vocabulary PuzzleMaker Chapter Challenger Interactive Review Software Testmaker The Presidents: A Picture History of Our Nation
Section 3 A Booming Economy Evaluate how economic prosperity during the 1920s affected American society and culture.	Reproducible Lesson Plan 24–3 Guided Reading Activity 24–3* Section Quiz 24–3* Reteaching Activity 24–3 Enrichment Activity 24–3	Section Focus Transparency 24–3 Vocabulary PuzzleMaker Chapter Challenger Interactive Review Software Testmaker
Section 4 The Roaring Twenties Summarize the changes in American lifestyles and culture during the 1920s.	Reproducible Lesson Plan 24–4 Guided Reading Activity 24–4* Section Quiz 24–4* Reteaching Activity 24–4 Enrichment Activity 24–4	Section Focus Transparency 24–4 Vocabulary PuzzleMaker Chapter Challenger Interactive Review Software Testmaker GTV: A Geographic Perspective on American History American Music Cultural Traditions
Section 5 Clashing Cultures Analyze the causes of cultural upheaval in the 1920s.	Reproducible Lesson Plan 24–5 Guided Reading Activity 24–5* Section Quiz 24–5* Reteaching Activity 24–5 Enrichment Activity 24–5	Section Focus Transparency 24–5 Vocabulary PuzzleMaker Chapter Challenger Interactive Review Testmaker GTV: The American People: Fabric of a Nation Facts On File: Landmark Documents in American History

** Also available in Spanish*

Blackline Master · Videodisc · Audiocassette · Music Program · Transparency · CD-ROM · Software

0:00 OUT OF TIME?
Assign the Chapter 24 Digest and the corresponding Chapter Digests Audiocassettes with activities and tests.

Activity

From the Classroom of...

Abby Moquino
Bernalillo High School
Bernalillo, NM

A "Roaring Twenties" Fad Magazine

Organize students into groups of three or four. Have each group look through several current magazines that focus on popular cultural trends. Ask students to select a magazine section or component that they want to duplicate in their "Roaring Twenties" magazine. For example, one group might want to write and design advertisements to place in the magazine, paying careful attention to popular products of the time. Other groups could write stories, reviews, or interviews dealing with sports, movies, music, or fads of the period. Have students use reference materials, books, or the Internet to collect information for their sections. Encourage students to use copies of photos or to create illustrations depicting the clothes and conveniences of the time. Student material can be presented either in a binder or displayed in sections on a bulletin board.

Block Schedule

Block scheduling differs from traditional class scheduling in the amount of time allotted to each period. The extended time frame provided by block scheduling affords you the opportunity to implement a greater number of research-oriented and activity-intense projects to motivate and involve your students. Activities that are particularly suited to use within the block scheduling framework are identified throughout this chapter by the following designation:

NATIONAL GEOGRAPHIC SOCIETY Teacher's Corner

INDEX TO NATIONAL GEOGRAPHIC MAGAZINE

The following articles may be used for research relating to this chapter:

- "Offbeat New Orleans," by Priit Vesilind, January 1995.

NATIONAL GEOGRAPHIC SOCIETY PRODUCTS AVAILABLE FROM GLENCOE

To order the following products for use with this chapter, contact your local Glencoe sales representative, or call Glencoe at 1-800-334-7344:

- *GTV: A Geographic Perspective on American History* (Videodisc)
- *GTV: The American People: Fabric of a Nation* (Videodisc)
- *The Presidents: A Picture History of Our Nation* (CD-ROM)

ADDITIONAL NATIONAL GEOGRAPHIC SOCIETY PRODUCTS

To order the following products for use with this chapter, call National Geographic Society at 1-800-368-2728:

- *Historical Atlas of the United States* (Atlas)

KEY TO ABILITY LEVELS

Teaching strategies have been coded for varying learning styles and abilities.

L1 **BASIC** activities for all students
L2 **AVERAGE** activities for average to above-average students
L3 **CHALLENGING** activities for above-average students
ELL **ENGLISH LANGUAGE LEARNER** activities

Chapter 24 Resource Guide

Home Involvement

Home Involvement Activity 24

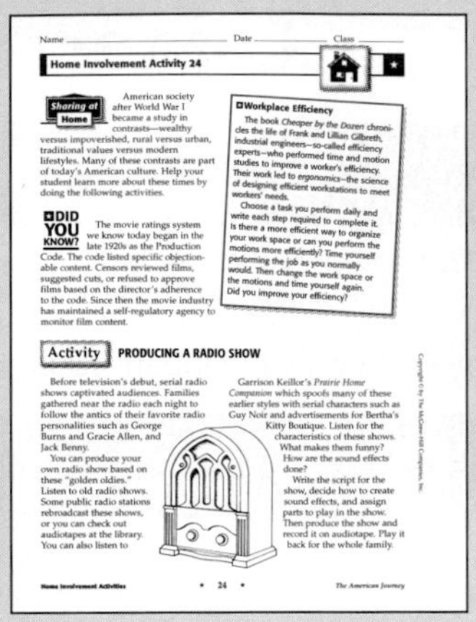

Review Activities

Chapter Summary 24

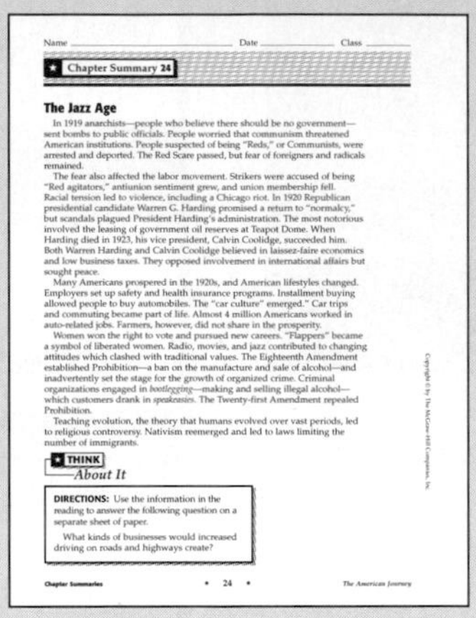

Workbook Activity 24

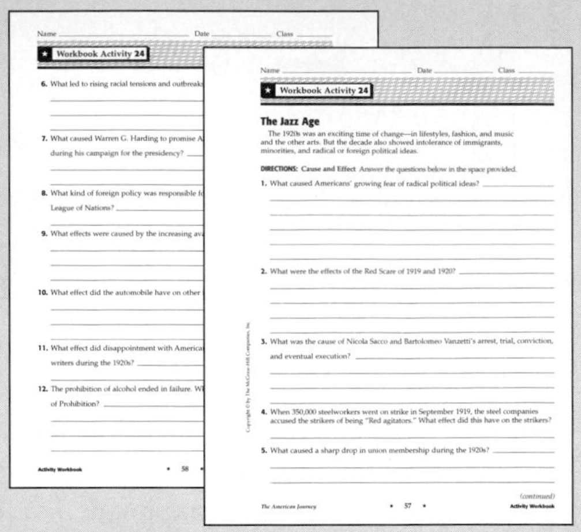

Reinforcement Activities

Time Line Activity 24

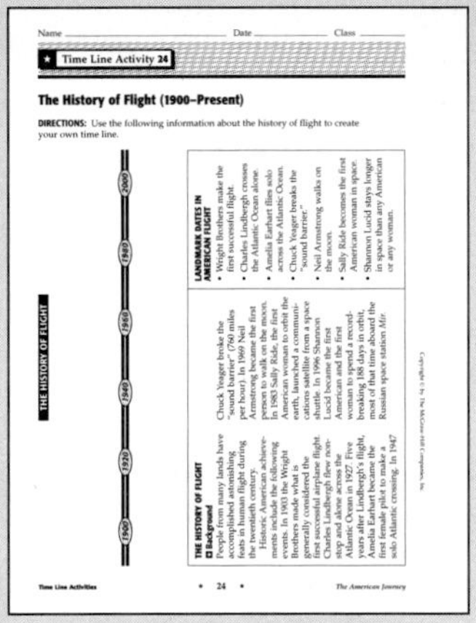

Vocabulary Activity 24

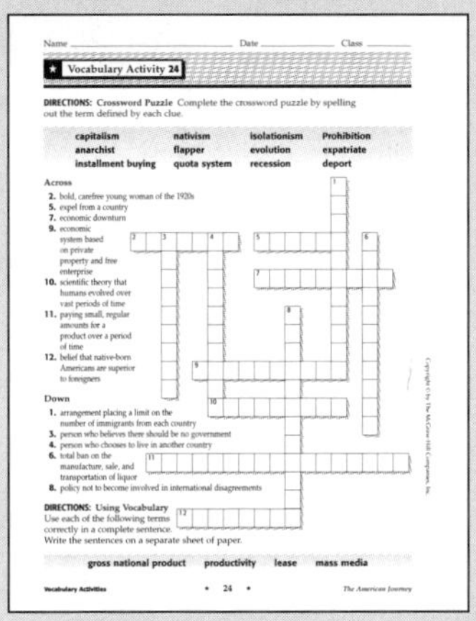

Chapter Skills Activity 24

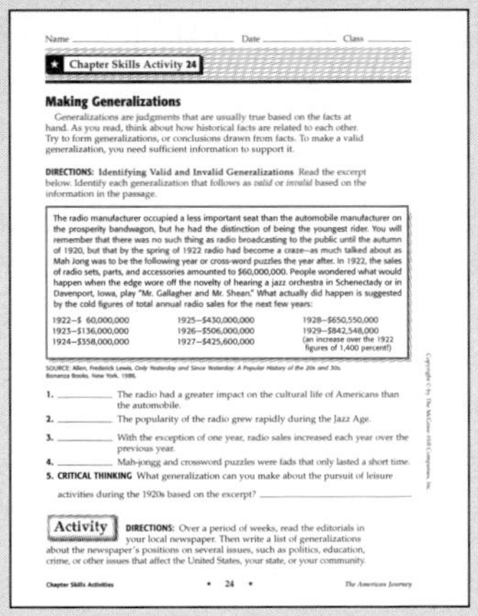

Enrichment Activities

Linking Past and Present Activity 24

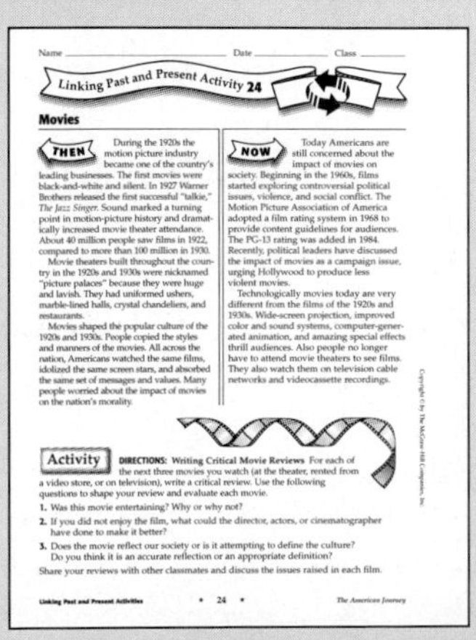

Primary Source Reading 24

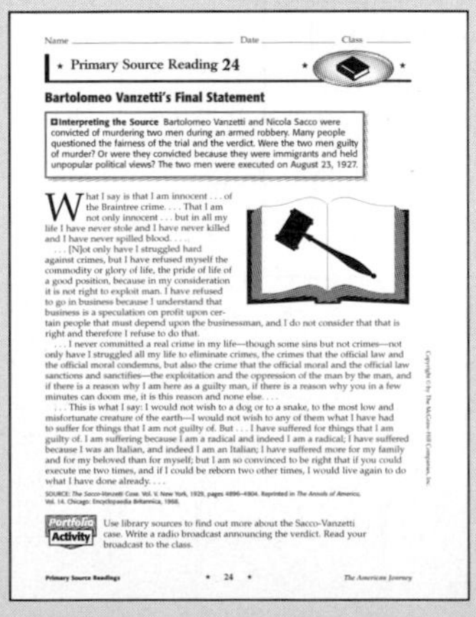

Geography Activities

Mapping History Activity 24

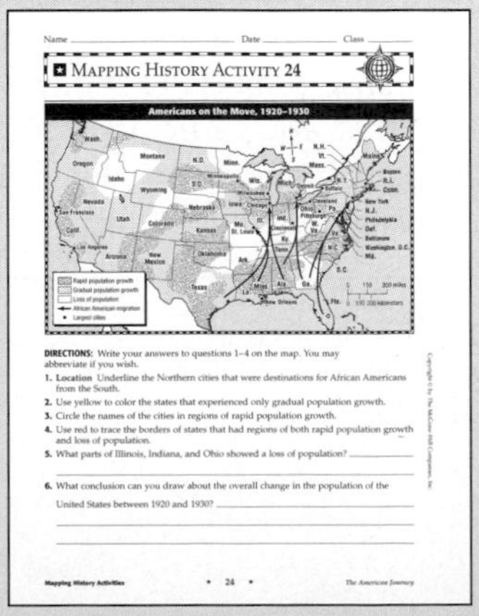

Chapter 24 Resource Guide

ASSESSMENT

Chapter 24 Test, Form A

Chapter 24 Test, Form B

Performance Assessment Activity 24

SPANISH RESOURCES

The following Spanish language materials are available in the Spanish Resources binder:

- **Spanish Chapter Summary 24**
- **Spanish Vocabulary Activity 24**
- **Spanish Guided Reading Activities, Chapter 24**
- **Spanish Section Quizzes, Chapter 24**
- **Spanish Home Involvement Activity 24**
- **Spanish Chapter 24 Digests Audiocassette Activity and Test**

ACTIVITY MANIPULATIVES

Help students learn more about America's cultural history with:

- **American Crafts Hands-On Activities**
- **American Games Hands-On Activities**
- **American History Flash Cards**

ADDITIONAL RESOURCES FROM GLENCOE

- **Political Cartoons,** *The Teapot Dome Boils Over*
- **American Music Cultural Traditions,** Lesson 8: "Muskrat Ramble" and "Downhearted Blues"
- **The Spirit of American Art and Music,** Duke Ellington, George Gershwin
- **U.S. Desk Map**
- **Outline Map Resource Book**
- **The American History Videodisc and CD-ROM,** *The Twenties and the Great Depression, 1920–1940*

A&E HOME VIDEO. Biography™ THE HISTORY CHANNEL.

The following videotape programs are available from Glencoe as supplements to Chapter 24:

- **Henry Ford: Tin Lizzy Tycoon** (ISBN 1-56501-380-8)
- **Lucky: The Charles Lindbergh Story** (ISBN 1-56501-501-0)
- **Babe Ruth** (ISBN 1-56501-422-7)

To order, call Glencoe at 1-800-334-7344. To find classroom resources to accompany many of these videos, check the following home pages:
A&E Television: http://www.aetv.com
The History Channel: http://www.historychannel.com

Chapter Themes

Chapter Themes are listed by section on this chapter opening page of the Student Edition. A corresponding theme-based activity is available under "FOCUS," and a theme-based question is asked in the Section and Chapter Reviews.

Performance Assessment

Refer to Activity 24 in the *Performance Assessment Strategies and Activities* booklet.

GLENCOE TECHNOLOGY

VIDEODISC
MindJogger Videoquiz

Use MindJogger to preview the Chapter 24 content.

Chapter 24
Disc 3, Side B

Also available in VHS.

HISTORY AND ART Jazz music was characterized by the excitement, energy, and pleasure that was a hallmark of the 1920s.

Chapter 24

1919–1929

The Jazz Age

Why It's Important

People called the 1920s the Jazz Age—in part because of the popular new music, but also because of the restless, carefree spirit of the time. The economy boomed and many Americans prospered. Not all Americans benefited from the economic progress, however. The 1920s saw a growth in racial unrest and intolerance toward foreigners. During these years, the traditional values of an older, predominately rural society clashed with the new values of a modern, urban nation.

Chapter Themes

- *Section 1,* Groups and Institutions
- *Section 2,* Global Connections
- *Section 3,* Economic Factors
- *Section 4,* Science and Technology
- *Section 5,* Culture and Traditions

HISTORY AND ART ***Music in the Plaza* by John Sloan** A crowd of evening strollers enjoy band music in the main square of Santa Fe, New Mexico, during the 1920s.

EXTRA CREDIT PROJECT

Making a Jazz Instrument Tell students to read the quote about jazz by J.A. Rogers on page 713. Ask students to use this description as a guide for them to create their own jazz instruments. Brainstorm with students a list of materials to use to make their instruments. For example, fasten strings over a circular hole in a hollow box for a stringed instrument, cut drinking straws at different lengths for a wind instrument, or fill a container with beads, seeds, or water for a percussion instrument. Ask volunteers to play their instruments for the class.

1910 1915 1920 1925

1914 Marcus Garvey founds Universal Negro Improvement Association

1917 Bolsheviks seize control of Russia

1920 Thousands arrested during Palmer raids

1921 Sacco and Vanzetti declared guilty

Section 1

Time of Turmoil

READ TO DISCOVER . . .

- what factors contributed to a fear of foreigners in the 1920s.
- how labor and racial unrest in the 1920s affected the nation.

TERMS TO LEARN

capitalism
anarchist
deport

The Storyteller

On a hot summer day in 1920, about 50,000 African Americans marched through the streets of Harlem in New York City. Thousands more lined the sidewalks, cheering the marchers. Their leader, Marcus Garvey, stirred new hope in African Americans, saying: "We are descendants of a people determined to suffer no longer." A participant at the march later recalled, "It was the greatest demonstration of [African American unity] in American history. . . ." Most of the 1920s were anything but unified, however.

Marcus Garvey

After World War I ended, President Woodrow Wilson went to Paris to try to carry through his vision of world peace. In 1919 Wilson and the world leaders attending the peace conference signed the **Treaty of Versailles.** Despite Wilson's efforts, however, the Senate refused to ratify the treaty. A great many Americans hardly seemed to notice. Tired of war and world responsibilities, Americans were eager to return to normal life. They grew more and more suspicious of foreigners and of foreign ideas, as well as of those who held views very different from their own.

Fear of Radicalism

During World War I, the United States government had taken away some of the liberties of American citizens. Many people who opposed the war were arrested. After the war an atmosphere of distrust remained.

At about the same time, the Russian Revolution deeply disturbed some Americans. As you have read in Chapter 23, the Bolsheviks took control of Russia in November 1917 and began establishing a Communist state. They encouraged workers around the world to overthrow capitalism—an economic system based on private property and free enterprise—anywhere it existed. Many Americans feared that "bolshevism" threatened American government and institutions.

Fanning those fears were the actions of anarchists—people who believe there should be no

SECTION RESOURCES

Reproducible Masters
- Reproducible Lesson Plan 24–1
- Guided Reading Activity 24–1
- Section Quiz 24–1
- Reteaching Activity 24–1
- Enrichment Activity 24–1

Transparencies
- Section Focus Transparency 24–1

Multimedia
- Vocabulary PuzzleMaker
- Chapter Challenger Interactive Review Software
- Testmaker
- The Presidents: A Picture History of Our Nation

1 FOCUS

BELLRINGER
Motivational Activity

Before taking roll at the beginning of the class period, project Section Focus Transparency 24–1 and have students answer the questions. Discuss students' responses.

This activity is also available as a blackline master.

Section Focus Transparency 24–1

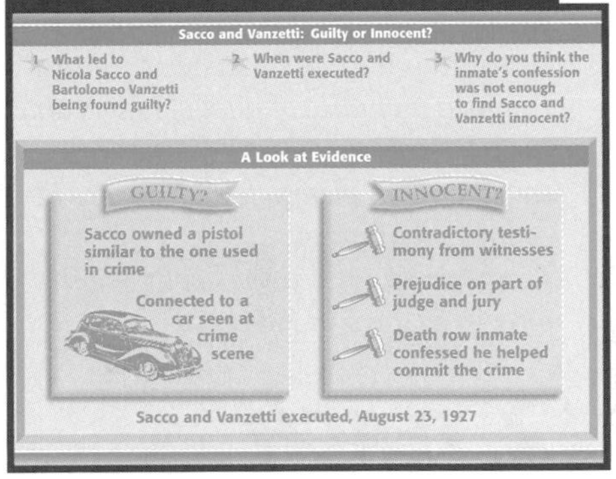

Vocabulary Precheck

Discuss with students what being *deported* from the United States meant to families during the Red Scare.

Use the **Vocabulary PuzzleMaker** to create crossword and word search puzzles.

Section Theme
Groups and Institutions

In the post–World War I era, Americans were eager to return to normal life. They grew more and more suspicious of foreigners.

Activity Compare the definitions of *capitalism* and *anarchism*. Point out that *capitalism* is "hands off" the economy and *anarchism* is "hands off" the government. Brainstorm with students why the majority of Americans in the 1920s feared anarchists but not capitalists.

CHAPTER 24
Section 1, 689–692

Picturing HISTORY Police first brought in Sacco and Vanzetti as suspects after finding them with Mike Boda, originally the main suspect in the case. Police later arrested Sacco and Vanzetti because the two men gave suspicious answers to police questions. This may have been caused by the fact that they were unskilled in English. In 1925 another man on death row confessed to having been part of the team that committed the crime, but the appeals panel chose not to believe this confession. **Ask:** What problems might two foreigners on trial have had at this time? *(limited English; prejudice of public, judge, and jury; lack of knowledge of American court system; insufficient money to hire competent attorney)*
Answer: *suggested the depth of antiforeign feelings in America*

2 TEACH

L1 Charting Information Ask students to create a cause-and-effect chart using Section 1 subheads, such as "The Red Scare." On their charts have students explain why the events were volatile and what effect each had on American society.

Guided Reading Activity 24–1

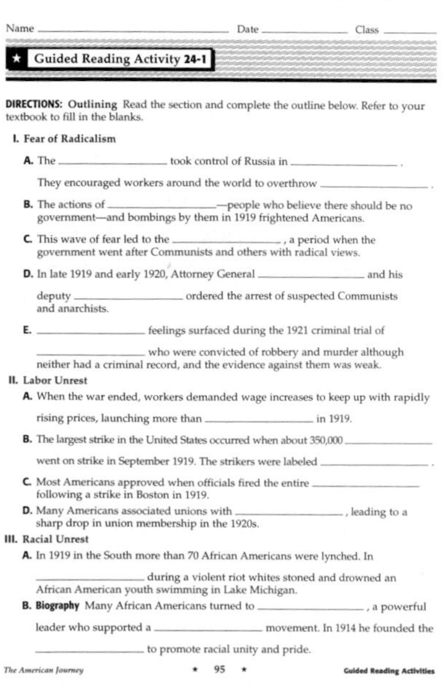
Name ______ Date ______ Class ______

★ Guided Reading Activity **24-1**

DIRECTIONS: Outlining Read the section and complete the outline below. Refer to your textbook to fill in the blanks.

I. Fear of Radicalism

A. The ______ took control of Russia in ______. They encouraged workers around the world to overthrow ______.

B. The actions of ______—people who believe there should be no government—and bombings by them in 1919 frightened Americans.

C. This wave of fear led to the ______, a period when the government went after Communists and others with radical views.

D. In late 1919 and early 1920, Attorney General ______ and his deputy ______ ordered the arrest of suspected Communists and anarchists.

E. ______ feelings surfaced during the 1921 criminal trial of ______ who were convicted of robbery and murder although neither had a criminal record, and the evidence against them was weak.

II. Labor Unrest

A. When the war ended, workers demanded wage increases to keep up with rapidly rising prices, launching more than ______ in 1919.

B. The largest strike in the United States occurred when about 350,000 ______ went on strike in September 1919. The strikers were labeled ______.

C. Most Americans approved when officials fired the entire ______ following a strike in Boston in 1919.

D. Many Americans associated unions with ______, leading to a sharp drop in union membership in the 1920s.

III. Racial Unrest

A. In 1919 in the South more than 70 African Americans were lynched. In ______ during a violent riot whites stoned and drowned an African American youth swimming in Lake Michigan.

B. Biography Many African Americans turned to ______, a powerful leader who supported a ______ movement. In 1914 he founded the ______ to promote racial unity and pride.

Picturing HISTORY Nicola Sacco and Bartolomeo Vanzetti enter a Massachusetts courtroom, while immigrant protesters in New York City demand the freedom of the two men. **What did the Sacco and Vanzetti case reveal about the feelings of many Americans?**

government. A series of anarchist bombings in 1919 frightened Americans. A number of public officials—mayors, judges, and the United States attorney general—received packages containing bombs. One bomb blew off the hands of the maid of a United States senator. Many of the anarchists were foreign-born, which contributed to the fear of foreigners that was sweeping the country.

The Red Scare

This wave of fear led to the **Red Scare,** a period when the government went after "Reds"—as Communists were known—and others with radical views. In late 1919 and early 1920, Attorney General **A. Mitchell Palmer** and his deputy J. Edgar Hoover ordered the arrest of people suspected of being Communists and anarchists. Palmer and Hoover also staged raids on the headquarters of various "suspicious" groups. In the raids, the government arrested more than 4,000 people, ransacked homes and offices, and seized records. They did not find the large stockpiles of weapons and dynamite they claimed they were seeking.

Palmer said the raids were justified. "The blaze of revolution was sweeping over every American institution of law and order," he declared, "burning up the foundations of society." The government deported—expelled from the United States—about 500 of the aliens it had arrested but quickly released many others for lack of evidence. In time people realized that the danger of revolution was greatly exaggerated. The Red Scare passed—but the fear underlying it remained.

Sacco and Vanzetti

Antiforeign and antiradical feelings surfaced in a criminal case in Massachusetts in 1920. Two men robbed a shoe factory in South Braintree, Massachusetts, shooting and killing a guard and paymaster. Soon afterward the police arrested Italian immigrants **Nicola Sacco** and **Bartolomeo Vanzetti** for the crime. Tried and convicted in July 1921, the two were sentenced to death.

The Sacco and Vanzetti case created a furor. Both men were anarchists, and Sacco owned a pistol similar to the murder weapon. Neither had a criminal record, however, and the evidence against them was weak. Future Supreme Court justice Felix Frankfurter wrote a defense of the two men. William Howard Taft, chief justice of the United States, attacked Frankfurter for "vicious propaganda."

Caught up in antiforeign fever, many Americans demanded that the death sentence be carried out. In 1927 a special commission appointed by the governor of Massachusetts upheld the verdict. Sacco and Vanzetti—still proclaiming their innocence—were executed. While historians continue to debate the verdict, the case suggested the depth of antiforeign and antiradical feelings in the United States in the 1920s.

Labor Unrest

★ Antiforeign and antiradical sentiment also affected American workers and the labor movement. During the war years, labor and man-

Cooperative Learning Activity

Writing a Song Organize the class into groups of three to write a song describing the turmoil of the early 1900s. Ask each group to choose a popular melody for the song. Then have group members write a verse on one of the following topics: fear of radicalism, racial unrest, and labor unrest. Encourage students to include names of people, places, and events mentioned in this section. Have groups combine the three verses into a song and write a chorus describing the organizations that formed from the turmoil to promote unity. Groups should perform the songs for the class.

agement had put aside their differences. A sense of patriotism, high wages, and wartime laws kept conflict to a minimum. When the war ended, conflict flared anew. American workers demanded increases in wages to keep up with rapidly rising prices, launching more than 2,500 strikes in 1919. The wave of strikes fueled American fears of Bolsheviks and radicals, whom many considered to be the cause of the labor unrest.

Workers on Strike

A long and bitter strike—the largest in American history to that point—occurred in the steel industry. Demanding higher wages and an 8-hour workday, about 350,000 steelworkers went on strike in September 1919. Using propaganda techniques learned during the war, the steel companies started a campaign against the strikers. In newspaper ads they accused the strikers of being "Red agitators." The Communist label cost the strikers public support and helped force them to end the strike—but not before violence had occurred on both sides. Eighteen strikers had died in a riot in Gary, Indiana.

In September 1919, police officers in **Boston** went on strike, demanding the right to form a union. This strike by public employees angered many Americans, and they applauded the strong stand Massachusetts governor **Calvin Coolidge** took against the strikers. Coolidge said, "There is no right to strike against the public safety by anybody, anywhere, any time." When the strike collapsed, officials fired the entire Boston police force. Most Americans approved.

Antiunion Feelings Grow

Workers found themselves deeper in debt because of rising prices and unchanged wages. Still labor unions failed to win wide support among working families. Many Americans connected unions with radicalism and bolshevism. A growing feeling against unions, together with strong pressure from employers and the government not to join unions, led to a sharp drop in union membership in the 1920s.

A. Philip Randolph

A. Philip Randolph

During this period of union decline, a dynamic African American, **A. Philip Randolph,** started the Brotherhood of Sleeping Car Porters. Made up mostly of African Americans, this union of railroad workers struggled during its early years but began to grow in the 1930s, when government policy encouraged unions. In the 1950s and the 1960s, Randolph would emerge as a leader of the civil rights movement.

Racial Unrest

★ During World War I, more than 500,000 African Americans had left the South for new jobs in the North. Many Northern whites resented African American competition for jobs.

★ Picturing HISTORY Strikes, such as the 1919 Chicago steel strike, lessened public support for labor unions. Labor leader A. Philip Randolph, however, was able to found the Brotherhood of Sleeping Car Porters. **How did unions fare during the 1920s?**

Multiple Learning Styles

Intrapersonal Ask students to assume the role of a person accused of being a Communist during the Red Scare. Have them write five diary entries describing their feelings and experiences. Tell them to explain in their entries whether they have been rightly or wrongly accused. **L1, ELL**

CHAPTER 24
Section 1, 689–692

NATIONAL GEOGRAPHIC SOCIETY

CD-ROM
The Presidents: A Picture History of Our Nation

Have students select TIME LINE from the main menu. Suggest they write headlines noting major events during President Coolidge's term in office.

3 ASSESS

Assign Section 1 Review as homework or as an in-class activity.

Use **Chapter Challenger Interactive Review Software** to review Section 1.

Section Quiz 24–1

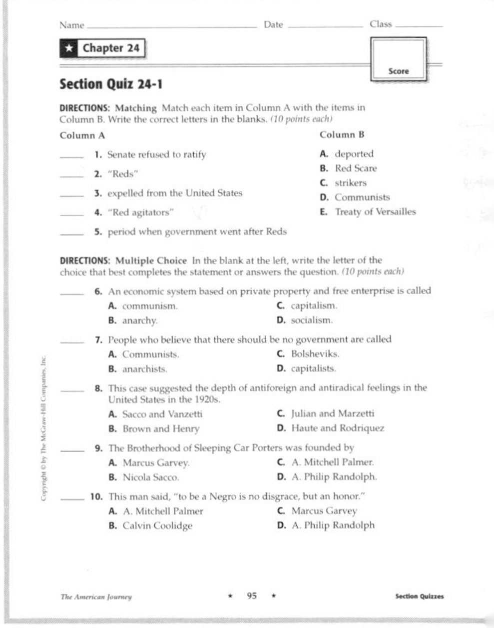

Name ______ Date ______ Class ______

★ Chapter 24

Score

Section Quiz 24-1

DIRECTIONS: Matching Match each item in Column A with the items in Column B. Write the correct letters in the blanks. *(10 points each)*

Column A	Column B
____ 1. Senate refused to ratify	A. deported
____ 2. "Reds"	B. Red Scare
____ 3. expelled from the United States	C. strikers
____ 4. "Red agitators"	D. Communists
____ 5. period when government went after Reds	E. Treaty of Versailles

DIRECTIONS: Multiple Choice In the blank at the left, write the letter of the choice that best completes the statement or answers the question. *(10 points each)*

____ 6. An economic system based on private property and free enterprise is called
A. communism. C. capitalism.
B. anarchy. D. socialism.

____ 7. People who believe that there should be no government are called
A. Communists. C. Bolsheviks.
B. anarchists. D. capitalists.

____ 8. This case suggested the depth of antiforeign and antiradical feelings in the United States in the 1920s.
A. Sacco and Vanzetti C. Julian and Marzetti
B. Brown and Henry D. Haute and Rodriquez

____ 9. The Brotherhood of Sleeping Car Porters was founded by
A. Marcus Garvey. C. A. Mitchell Palmer.
B. Nicola Sacco. D. A. Philip Randolph.

____ 10. This man said, "to be a Negro is no disgrace, but an honor."
A. A. Mitchell Palmer C. Marcus Garvey
B. Calvin Coolidge D. A. Philip Randolph

The American Journey ★ 95 ★ **Section Quizzes**

★ Picturing HISTORY In 1925, A. Philip Randolph succeeded in getting sleeping car porters' monthly wages raised $40. **Answer:** *Not well; Many Americans associated unions with radicalism and bolshevism, and many workers felt pressure from employers and the government not to join unions.*

CHAPTER 24
Section 1, 689–692

Reteaching Activity 24–1

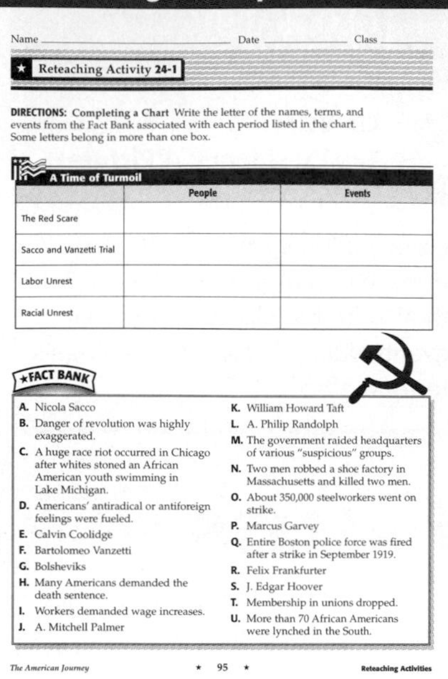

Name ______ Date ______ Class ______

★ Reteaching Activity 24-1

DIRECTIONS: Completing a Chart Write the letter of the names, terms, and events from the Fact Bank associated with each period listed in the chart. Some letters belong in more than one box.

A Time of Turmoil

	People	Events
The Red Scare		
Sacco and Vanzetti Trial		
Labor Unrest		
Racial Unrest		

★FACT BANK

- **A.** Nicola Sacco
- **B.** Danger of revolution was highly exaggerated.
- **C.** A huge race riot occurred in Chicago after whites stoned an African American youth swimming in Lake Michigan.
- **D.** Americans' antiradical or antiforeign feelings were fueled.
- **E.** Calvin Coolidge
- **F.** Bartolomeo Vanzetti
- **G.** Bolsheviks
- **H.** Many Americans demanded the death sentence.
- **I.** Workers demanded wage increases.
- **J.** A. Mitchell Palmer
- **K.** William Howard Taft
- **L.** A. Philip Randolph
- **M.** The government raided headquarters of various "suspicious" groups.
- **N.** Two men robbed a shoe factory in Massachusetts and killed two men.
- **O.** About 350,000 steelworkers went on strike.
- **P.** Marcus Garvey
- **Q.** Entire Boston police force was fired after a strike in September 1919.
- **R.** Felix Frankfurter
- **S.** J. Edgar Hoover
- **T.** Membership in unions dropped.
- **U.** More than 70 African Americans were lynched in the South.

The American Journey ★ 95 ★ Reteaching Activities

Enrichment Activity 24–1

Name ______ Date ______ Class ______

★ Enrichment Activity 24-1

Join the League?

Woodrow Wilson's plan for world peace was not supported by many Americans, who wanted to remain free of foreign entanglements. Tired of war and world responsibilities, Americans were eager to return to normal life. They grew more and more suspicious of foreigners and of foreign ideas. Many regarded the plan for the League of Nations as hopelessly unrealistic. Some critics charged that membership in the League would prevent the nation from setting its own foreign policy. During this time period, numerous political cartoons commenting on the League of Nations were published. Study the cartoon to the left.

SOURCE: Bailey, Thomas A. and David M. Kennedy. *The American Pageant, A History of the Republic.* Stanford University.

DIRECTIONS: Interpreting Intent Write a few sentences explaining the meaning of the cartoon.

Activity **DIRECTIONS:** If you had lived at the time, would you have supported or opposed the League of Nations? Draw your own political cartoon to show your viewpoint on this issue.

The American Journey ★ 95 ★ Enrichment Activities

4 CLOSE

Ask students to evaluate which event in this section created the most turmoil.

Violent Reactions

In 1919 rising racial tensions erupted in outbreaks of violence across the country. In the South more than 70 African Americans were lynched. In Chicago a violent riot broke out after a group of whites stoned an African American youth who was swimming in Lake Michigan. The youth drowned, and the incident set off rioting in the city's African American neighborhoods. For two weeks African American and white gangs roamed city streets, attacking each other and burning buildings. The riot left 15 whites and 23 African Americans dead and more than 500 people injured.

Biography

Marcus Garvey

Many African Americans turned to **Marcus Garvey** for answers. Marcus Garvey was born to a poor family in Jamaica, the youngest of 11 children. He worked a variety of jobs growing up, including as a printer's apprentice and on plantations. Educated as a journalist and filled with ambition, Garvey arrived in New York City at the age of 28. A powerful leader with a magnetic personality, Garvey opposed integration. Instead he supported a "back-to-Africa" movement, urging African Americans to establish their own country in Africa. Garvey founded the **Universal Negro Improvement Association** (UNIA) in 1914 to promote racial unity and pride.

During the 1920s Garvey gained an enormous following and great influence, especially among the urban poor. Garvey told audiences that "to be a Negro is no disgrace, but an honor." With branches in many states, the UNIA organized rallies and parades to build pride and confidence among African Americans. It helped African Americans start businesses. One African American newspaper summed up Garvey's achievements: "He taught [African Americans] to admire and praise black things and black people."

Hoping for Peace

For Americans the years following World War I were unsettling. Increasing racial tensions, the wave of strikes, and worries about the growing influence of radicals and foreigners in the United States disturbed many Americans. Most longed for an end to the turmoil.

Section 1 Review

Checking for Understanding

1. ***Identify*** Red Scare, A. Mitchell Palmer, Nicola Sacco, Bartolomeo Vanzetti, Calvin Coolidge, A. Philip Randolph, Marcus Garvey, Universal Negro Improvement Association.
2. ***Define*** capitalism, anarchist, deport.
3. ***Explain*** how the fear of radicals and foreigners affected the outcome of the Sacco and Vanzetti trial.

Reviewing Themes

4. **Groups and Institutions** Why was there a sharp drop in union membership during the 1920s?

Critical Thinking

5. **Media Literacy** Imagine you were making a video about the life of Marcus Garvey. If he could speak to American youth today, what statement might he make?

Activity

Describing an Era Make a list of five to seven adjectives that you think describe the mood of the country during the 1920s. Draw or paint these adjectives on poster board in a way that conveys the words' meanings.

Section 1 Review Answers

1. Red Scare, 690; A. Mitchell Palmer, 690; Nicola Sacco, 690; Bartolomeo Vanzetti, 690; Calvin Coolidge, 691; A. Philip Randolph, 691; Marcus Garvey, 692; Universal Negro Improvement Association, 692
2. The words are defined in the Glossary.
3. Some Americans wanted them to receive the harshest punishment, although there was no solid evidence.
4. Many Americans distrusted them. Unions were linked to radicalism and bolshevism. Employees were pressured not to join.
5. Statements should reflect Garvey's belief that African Americans should take pride in their heritage.

Activity Adjectives should describe the fears and distrust that existed during the 1920s.

1920 1925 1930

1920
Warren G. Harding is elected president

1922
Senate investigates Teapot Dome lease

1923
Calvin Coolidge becomes president

1928
Kellogg-Briand Pact aims to outlaw war

Section 2

Desire for Normalcy

READ TO DISCOVER . . .

- what problems President Harding and his administration faced.
- what policies Presidents Harding and Coolidge followed toward business and foreign affairs.

TERMS TO LEARN

lease | isolationism

The Storyteller

Warren G. Harding attracted attention with his friendly personality, fine voice, and handsome appearance. These glowing assets could easily make Harding president, thought political strategist Harry Daugherty. As Harding's campaign manager, Daugherty took credit for prodding Harding into the 1920 presidential race: "I found him sunning himself, like a turtle on a log, and I pushed him into the water."

Harding/ Coolidge decal, 1920

In the summer of 1920, the Republicans gathered in Chicago to nominate a candidate for president. Although confident of victory in the upcoming election, they had no outstanding leaders to head the party ticket. As one Republican noted, "There ain't any first raters this year." So party bosses chose "the best of the second raters" as their presidential candidate—Senator **Warren G. Harding** of Ohio. Harding had earned a reputation as a loyal Republican, and Ohio political boss Harry Daugherty pushed through his nomination.

The Harding Presidency

Sensing Americans' longing for calm and stability after decades of progressive reform and world war, Harding declared in his campaign that "America's present need is not heroics, but healing." He promised a return to "normalcy." What Harding meant by *normalcy* was not really clear, but the word sounded reassuring to those Americans who wanted an end to foreign involvement and domestic turmoil.

As Harding's running mate, the Republicans nominated Massachusetts governor **Calvin Coolidge,** celebrated for his firm stand in the Boston police strike. The Harding-Coolidge ticket won a landslide victory in November 1920—the first presidential election in which women could vote. The Republicans defeated the Democratic candidate, Governor **James Cox** of Ohio, and his young running mate, **Franklin Delano Roosevelt** of New York. The Republicans also made large gains in Congress.

CHAPTER 24
Section 2, 693–696

1 FOCUS

BELLRINGER
Motivational Activity

Before taking roll at the beginning of the class period, project Section Focus Transparency 24–2 and have students answer the questions. Discuss students' responses.

This activity is also available as a blackline master.

Section Focus Transparency 24–2

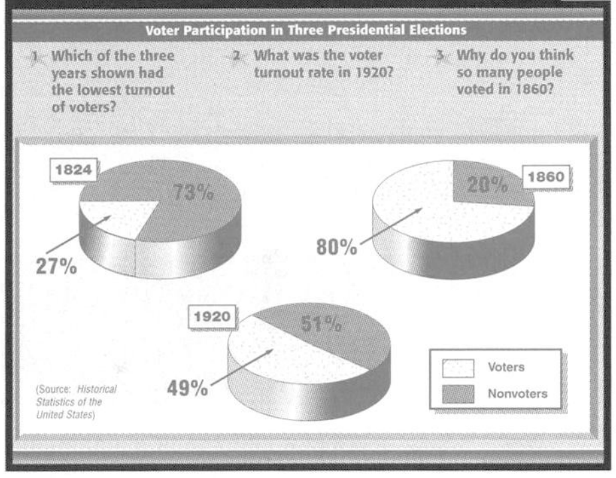

Vocabulary Precheck

Ask a volunteer to read the description on this page of how the word *normalcy* became part of the English language.

Use the **Vocabulary PuzzleMaker** to create crossword and word search puzzles.

Section Theme
Global Connections

Spurred by the desire to return to normalcy, many Americans favored isolationism.

Activity Have students assume the role of an isolationist. Ask volunteers to tell what types of global activities they would support, if any.

SECTION RESOURCES

Reproducible Masters

- Reproducible Lesson Plan 24–2
- Guided Reading Activity 24–2
- Political Cartoons, *The Teapot Dome Boils Over*
- Section Quiz 24–2
- Reteaching Activity 24–2
- Enrichment Activity 24–2

Transparencies

- Section Focus Transparency 24–2

Multimedia

- Vocabulary PuzzleMaker
- Chapter Challenger Interactive Review
- Testmaker
- The Presidents: A Picture History of Our Nation

CHAPTER 24
Section 2, 693–696

2 TEACH

L2 Writing an Essay Ask students to scan the section to find ways in which Presidents Harding and Coolidge tried to return the United States to normalcy. Have students write a four-paragraph essay. The first paragraph should describe the term *normalcy*. The second and third paragraphs should discuss Harding's and Coolidge's efforts to restore normalcy. In the final paragraph, have students imagine that they were president at the time and tell about the steps they would have taken to return America to normalcy.

Political Cartoons, *The Teapot Dome Boils Over*

NATIONAL GEOGRAPHIC SOCIETY

CD-ROM
The Presidents: A Picture History of Our Nation

Have students select President Harding from the main menu and the category GAME. Suggest they learn more about Harding by playing the presidential game with a partner.

Guided Reading Activity 24–2

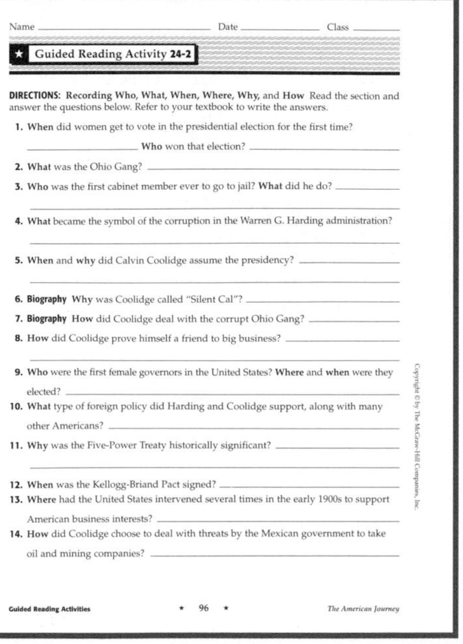
Name ______ Date ______ Class ______

★ Guided Reading Activity **24-2**

DIRECTIONS: Recording Who, What, When, Where, Why, and **How** Read the section and answer the questions below. Refer to your textbook to write the answers.

1. **When** did women get to vote in the presidential election for the first time? ______ **Who** won that election? ______
2. **What** was the Ohio Gang? ______
3. **Who** was the first cabinet member ever to go to jail? **What** did he do? ______
4. **What** became the symbol of the corruption in the Warren G. Harding administration? ______
5. **When** and **why** did Calvin Coolidge assume the presidency? ______
6. **Biography** **Why** was Coolidge called "Silent Cal"? ______
7. **Biography** **How** did Coolidge deal with the corrupt Ohio Gang? ______
8. **How** did Coolidge prove himself a friend to big business? ______
9. **Who** were the first female governors in the United States? **Where** and **when** were they elected? ______
10. **What** type of foreign policy did Harding and Coolidge support, along with many other Americans? ______
11. **Why** was the Five-Power Treaty historically significant? ______
12. **When** was the Kellogg-Briand Pact signed? ______
13. **Where** had the United States intervened several times in the early 1900s to support American business interests? ______
14. **How** did Coolidge choose to deal with threats by the Mexican government to take oil and mining companies? ______

Guided Reading Activities ★ 96 ★ *The American Journey*

Harding admitted having doubts about his qualifications for the presidency. He reportedly told a friend, "I knew that this job would be too much for me." He tried to compensate by appointing several talented people to the cabinet—**Charles Evans Hughes,** a former Supreme Court justice, as secretary of state; **Andrew Mellon,** a prominent Pittsburgh banker and financier, to head the Treasury Department; and **Herbert Hoover,** a talented organizer, as secretary of commerce.

The "Ohio Gang"

President Harding also gave jobs in government to many of his friends and political supporters—the so-called **Ohio Gang.** He appointed **Harry Daugherty** attorney general. He named Senator **Albert Fall** of New Mexico, a close friend, secretary of the interior. **Charles Forbes,** another friend, became head of the Veterans Bureau. Other friends of Harding filled offices throughout the administration.

Many of these appointees were unqualified; some turned out to be corrupt. By 1922 Washington buzzed with rumors of scandals within the Harding administration. Forbes, convicted of stealing funds from the Veterans Bureau, fled to avoid imprisonment. Daugherty was accused of receiving bribes but refused to resign.

1924 recording of a Coolidge speech

Teapot Dome Scandal

The biggest scandal of the Harding administration involved Albert Fall. In 1922 Fall secretly **leased,** or rented, government oil reserves in Elk Hills, California, and Teapot Dome, Wyoming, to the owners of two oil companies. In exchange Fall received more than $400,000. After the scandal became public, Fall was convicted of bribery and sent to prison—the first cabinet officer ever to go to jail. **Teapot Dome** became a symbol of the corruption in the Harding administration and of government corruption and scandal in general.

Harding himself was not directly involved in any scandals, but as the rumors spread, he grew increasingly distressed. "I have no trouble with my enemies," he said. "But my friends . . . they're the ones that keep me walking the floor nights!"

In the summer of 1923, before the full story of the scandals came out, Harding escaped the stresses of Washington, D.C., by taking a trip west. During the trip he became ill, suffered a heart attack, and died.

Calvin Coolidge

Vice President Calvin Coolidge was visiting his father in Vermont when he was awakened in the early morning hours of August 3, 1923, with the news of President Harding's death. Coolidge's father, a justice of the peace, administered the presidential oath of office. Then the new president—in characteristic Coolidge fashion—calmly turned off the lights and went back to bed.

Biography

Honesty Returns to the White House

Calvin Coolidge was in many ways the complete opposite of Harding. While Harding loved to talk and meet people, Coolidge said very little and earned the name "Silent Cal." In addition, Coolidge had a reputation for honesty. After becoming president, he allowed the

COOPERATIVE LEARNING ACTIVITY

Covering a News Story Organize the class into groups of four to create a newspaper that could have appeared during the Harding administration. Allow each group to name the newspaper and choose a publication date. Have group members select from the following roles: write an article on a scandal or on the corruption within the administration, write an interview with a member of Harding's cabinet, draw a political cartoon of an issue covered in this section, design an advertisement that could have been seen during this period. Group members should cooperate in laying out their articles on the newspaper. Display newspaper pages and discuss the topics covered.

investigations into the Harding scandals to proceed without interference. He fired Daugherty and replaced the remaining members of the Ohio Gang with honest officials.

Although Coolidge and Harding differed in style, they held similar political views. Coolidge believed that the best government was the least government and that government should not interfere in the life of the nation. He once said approvingly, "If the federal government should go out of existence, the common run of the people would not detect the difference for a considerable length of time."

A Friend to Business

Under President Coolidge the government took an active role in supporting business. As the president explained, "The chief business of the American people is business. . . . The man who builds a factory builds a temple."

Coolidge and the Republican-dominated Congress aimed to create a favorable climate for business to promote the nation's economic prosperity. The government lowered income tax rates on the wealthiest Americans and on corporate profits and cut government spending. It also raised tariffs protecting American business while overturning laws regulating child labor and wages for women.

Coolidge Is Reelected

Coolidge seemed to be exactly what the country wanted. At the Republican national convention in 1924, the president was nominated without opposition for a term of his own. The Democrats, deeply divided, took more than 100 ballots to nominate a little-known lawyer, John W. Davis of West Virginia, as their presidential candidate. Wisconsin senator Robert La Follette led a third party, the Progressives, in the race. Coolidge swept the 1924 presidential election with 54 percent of the popular vote. For the first time in America's history, women won governors' races—**Nellie Taylor Ross** in Wyoming and **Miriam Ferguson** in Texas.

Picturing HISTORY The Coolidge administration had close ties with business. **How did Coolidge and Congress create a favorable climate for business?**

Foreign Policy

Harding and Coolidge both favored a limited role for the nation in world affairs. They desired world peace but did not want the nation to join the League of Nations or become involved in international disagreements. Harding had promised the American people that he would not lead them into the League "by the side door, back door, or cellar door." Many Americans supported this policy of **isolationism.**

Footnotes to History

Silent Cal Calvin Coolidge did not believe in wasting money or words. Once a young lady sitting next to him at a White House dinner said, "Mr. President, I have made a bet I can get more than three words out of you during the meal." Without even looking at her he said, "You lose."

CHAPTER 24
Section 2, 693–696

Picturing HISTORY A sober and calm Coolidge stayed cool in any crisis. Theodore Roosevelt's daughter, Alice Roosevelt Longworth, once described Coolidge as a man who looked as if he "had been weaned on a dill pickle."

Answer: *lowered income tax rates, raised tariffs, overturned laws regulating child labor and wages for women*

Who?What?Where?When?

The Black Sox Scandals in the White House followed a scandal on the baseball field. In 1919, eight members of the Chicago White Sox were accused of taking mob money to lose the World Series to the Cincinnati Reds. The players, called the Black Sox, were acquitted in court but were banned from professional baseball for life.

3 ASSESS

Assign Section 2 Review as homework or as an in-class activity.

Use **Chapter Challenger Interactive Review Software** to review Section 2.

Section Quiz 24–2

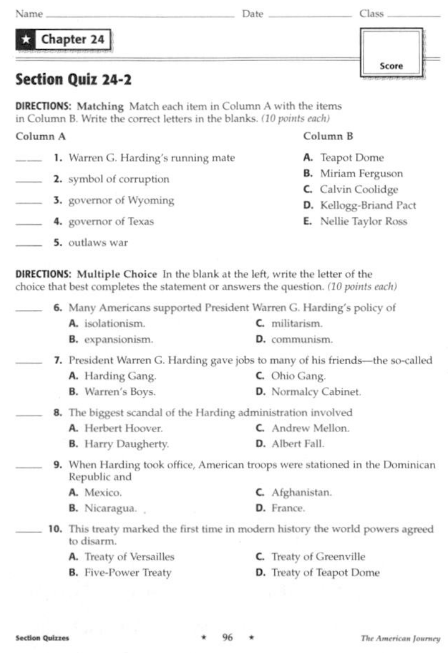

Name ______ Date ______ Class ______

Chapter 24

Score

Section Quiz 24-2

DIRECTIONS: Matching Match each item in Column A with the items in Column B. Write the correct letters in the blanks. *(10 points each)*

Column A	Column B
____ 1. Warren G. Harding's running mate	A. Teapot Dome
____ 2. symbol of corruption	B. Miriam Ferguson
____ 3. governor of Wyoming	C. Calvin Coolidge
____ 4. governor of Texas	D. Kellogg-Briand Pact
____ 5. outlaws war	E. Nellie Taylor Ross

DIRECTIONS: Multiple Choice In the blank at the left, write the letter of the choice that best completes the statement or answers the question. *(10 points each)*

____ 6. Many Americans supported President Warren G. Harding's policy of
A. isolationism. C. militarism.
B. expansionism. D. communism.

____ 7. President Warren G. Harding gave jobs to many of his friends—the so-called
A. Harding Gang. C. Ohio Gang.
B. Warren's Boys. D. Normalcy Cabinet.

____ 8. The biggest scandal of the Harding administration involved
A. Herbert Hoover. C. Andrew Mellon.
B. Harry Daugherty. D. Albert Fall.

____ 9. When Harding took office, American troops were stationed in the Dominican Republic and
A. Mexico. C. Afghanistan.
B. Nicaragua. D. France.

____ 10. This treaty marked the first time in modern history the world powers agreed to disarm.
A. Treaty of Versailles C. Treaty of Greenville
B. Five-Power Treaty D. Treaty of Teapot Dome

Section Quizzes ★ 96 ★ *The American Journey*

MULTIPLE LEARNING STYLES

Verbal/Linguistic Organize the class into small groups to write campaign slogans for the 1920 presidential election. Have each group write four slogans, two for Harding and two for Coolidge, reflecting the candidates' stands on big business and foreign affairs. **L2, ELL**

CHAPTER 24

Section 2, 693–696

Picturing HISTORY On May 10, 1927, Coolidge sent 5,000 marines to Nicaragua to quell a rebellion against its government. **Answer:** *to support American business interests*

Reteaching Activity 24–2

Name ______ Date ______ Class ______

★ Reteaching Activity 24-2

DIRECTIONS: Comparing and Contrasting Complete the comparison chart by putting a check mark next to quotes, beliefs, events, and terms associated with Warren G. Harding and his presidency, Calvin Coolidge and his presidency, or both.

Comparing Harding and Coolidge

	Harding	Coolidge
1. He had a reputation for honesty.		
2. "America's present need is not heroics, but healing."		
3. He took a firm stand in the Boston police strike.		
4. He doubted his own qualifications.		
5. He desired world peace but did not want to join the League of Nations.		
6. He appointed the Ohio Gang, a group of unqualified, corrupt individuals.		
7. He fired the Ohio Gang and replaced them with honest officials.		
8. "The man who builds a factory builds a temple."		
9. He said very little and was called "Silent."		
10. He loved to talk and meet people.		
11. He took an active role in supporting big business.		
12. He was associated with the Teapot Dome scandal.		
13. He did not want to get involved in international disagreements.		
14. He believed that the best government was the least government.		
15. During his administration, the Five-Power Treaty was signed.		
16. During his administration, the Kellogg-Briand Pact was signed.		
17. He favored a limited role for the nation in world affairs.		

DIRECTIONS: Essay On a separate sheet of paper, answer the question below.

What were the main differences and similarities in the personalities and presidencies of Harding and Coolidge?

Reteaching Activities ★ 96 ★ *The American Journey*

Enrichment Activity 24–2

Name ______ Date ______ Class ______

★ Enrichment Activity 24-2

Money Talks!

President Calvin Coolidge strongly supported business. As you read in the textbook, during Coolidge's presidency, tax rates on corporate profits and on wealthy Americans were lowered, tariffs were raised, and labor laws were overturned to support businesses over individuals. The political cartoon to the right appeared in September 1924, before the November presidential elections.

The Cash Register Chorus

SOURCE: Bailey, Thomas A. and David M. Kennedy. *The American Pageant, A History of the Republic.* Stanford University.

DIRECTIONS: Interpreting Intent Answer the questions on the lines below.

1. Who do you think the figures represent?
2. What are they doing?
3. The words to the song the chorus is singing are a paraphrase of a religious hymn of praise. What do you think this cartoonist believes this chorus worships?

Activity **DIRECTIONS: Applying Ideas** Several nicknames and phrases were applied to Calvin Coolidge based on his temperament and approach to economic policies. Research to find Calvin Coolidge's nicknames and phrases. Make a list of the nicknames and explain why they were used. Then research the economic views of any two presidents, listed below, that served after Coolidge. Based on a president's economic views and practices, write nicknames applied to that president or create nicknames of your own. Briefly explain the meaning behind each nickname. Then make a poster entitled *Presidential Images* and display the nicknames for the presidents you choose.

- Harry S Truman
- John F. Kennedy
- Dwight D. Eisenhower
- Franklin D. Roosevelt
- Richard M. Nixon
- Ronald Reagan

Enrichment Activities ★ 96 ★ *The American Journey*

4 CLOSE

Ask students to evaluate whether Presidents Harding and Coolidge succeeded in returning America to normalcy.

Picturing HISTORY United States Marines in Nicaragua display a skull-and-crossbones flag captured from Nicaraguan revolutionaries. **Why did the United States intervene in Latin America during the early 1900s?**

Promoting Peace

The Harding administration made serious efforts to promote peace. After the war the United States, Great Britain, and Japan began a naval arms race. In 1921 Secretary of State Hughes invited Japan and Britain to Washington, D.C., to discuss the problem. In February 1922 the three nations, along with France and Italy, signed the **Five-Power Treaty** to limit the size of the nations' navies. The treaty marked the first time in modern history that world powers agreed to disarm.

The United States continued working for peace. In August 1928, it joined 14 other nations in signing the **Kellogg-Briand Pact,** which called for outlawing war. Within a few years, 48 other nations had signed the pact, but it lacked any means of enforcing peace.

A More Friendly Neighbor

In the early 1900s, the United States had intervened in Latin American countries several times to support American business interests. When Harding took office, American troops were stationed in Haiti, the **Dominican Republic,** and **Nicaragua,** and relations with Mexico were tense.

After the Dominican Republic and Nicaragua held elections in the mid-1920s, the United States withdrew its troops from those countries.

At about the same time, American investors asked President Coolidge to send troops into Mexico after its government threatened to take over foreign-owned oil and mining companies. Coolidge chose to negotiate instead, and the United States reached a settlement with Mexico.

Section 2 Review

Checking for Understanding

1. ***Identify*** Warren G. Harding, Ohio Gang, Teapot Dome, Kellogg-Briand Pact.
2. ***Define*** lease, isolationism.
3. ***Discuss*** the factors that led to Harding's election to the presidency in 1920.

Reviewing Themes

4. **Global Connections** What actions did the United States take to promote world peace in the 1920s?

Critical Thinking

5. **Making Comparisons** What role did Harding and Coolidge think the government should play in people's lives?

Activity

Drawing a Political Cartoon Draw a political cartoon that illustrates an example of the corruption that took place during Warren G. Harding's administration.

Section 2 Review Answers

1. Warren G. Harding, 693; Ohio Gang, 694; Teapot Dome, 694; Kellogg-Briand Pact, 696
2. The words are defined in the Glossary.
3. Americans wanted a president who would help the nation heal, put an end to foreign involvement, and deal effectively with domestic turmoil.
4. signed Five-Power Treaty to limit the size of navies, signed Kellogg-Briand Pact to outlaw war; agreed to intervene less in Latin America
5. Both believed that the government should have a very limited role in people's lives.

Activity Cartoons should focus on one example of corruption or on a scandal that occurred during the Harding administration.

Critical Thinking
SKILL BUILDER

Making Generalizations

If you say, "We have a great football team," you are making a generalization, or general statement, about your team. If you go on to say that your team was last year's top-ranked team and has not lost a game this season, you are providing evidence to support your generalization. When studying history, it is often necessary to put together bits and pieces of information—supporting statements—to arrive at a complete picture.

Learning the Skill

In some cases, authors provide only supporting statements and you will need to make the generalizations on your own.

To make generalizations, follow these steps:

- Identify the subject matter.
- Gather facts and examples related to it.
- Identify similarities or patterns among these facts.
- Use these similarities or patterns to form some general ideas about the subject.

Traffic jam, 1920s

Practicing the Skill

Read the passage and the generalizations about the automobile on this page. Then answer the questions that follow.

By 1927, 4 out of 5 cars had closed tops, compared with only 1 in 10 in 1919. Now protected from the weather, many families hopped into their cars for short day trips. With "auto-mobility," many city workers moved to houses in the new suburbs. Car owners now traveled easily to once distant places, bringing far-flung Americans together for the first time.

Generalizations about the Automobile

a. Automobiles were too expensive to buy.
b. The automobile changed American culture in many ways.
c. Many businesses grew from the need to service the newly mobile nation.
d. Suburbs grew as a result of the automobile.

1. Which of the generalizations above are supported by the details in this passage?
2. Write one or two statements that support each of these generalizations.
3. Which of the generalizations are not supported by the passage? Explain.

Applying the Skill

Making Generalizations Make a general statement about your class that describes it. Then write three or four supporting details for that generalization.

Answers to Practicing the Skill

1. b, d
2. b: "Many families hopped into their cars for short day trips." "Many city workers moved to houses in the new suburbs." Far-flung Americans were brought together for the first time.
   d: "With auto-mobility, many city workers moved to houses in the new suburbs." "Car owners now traveled easily to once distant places."
3. a, c; not supported by facts or examples from the passage

Applying the Skill Students should write a generalization with three or four supporting details about the class.

Critical Thinking
SKILL BUILDER

TEACH

Making Generalizations

This skill teaches students how to identify and write generalizations. Students are asked to make generalizations about a passage by applying four steps. Then they are challenged to support their generalizations with evidence from the passage.

Ask students to reread **The Storyteller** at the beginning of Section 2. Then organize the class into small groups to write one generalization about the passage. Have volunteers from each group read the generalization to the class and state its supporting evidence. Have other groups either challenge or support the group's generalization.

Additional Practice

Chapter Skills Activity 24

1 FOCUS

BELLRINGER
Motivational Activity

Before taking roll at the beginning of the class period, project Section Focus Transparency 24–3 and have students answer the questions. Discuss students' responses.

This activity is also available as a blackline master.

Section Focus Transparency 24–3

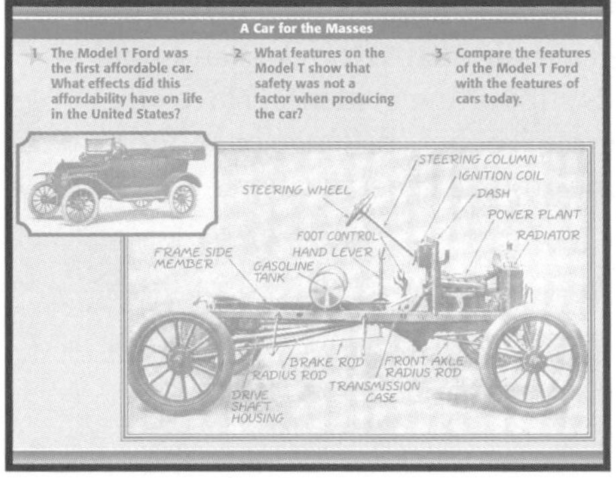
A Car for the Masses

1. The Model T Ford was the first affordable car. What effects did this affordability have on life in the United States?
2. What features on the Model T show that safety was not a factor when producing the car?
3. Compare the features of the Model T Ford with the features of cars today.

Vocabulary Precheck

Ask volunteers to define *productivity* and *installment buying*. Brainstorm with students how installment buying and productivity fueled American economic development in the 1920s.

Use the **Vocabulary PuzzleMaker** to create crossword and word search puzzles.

Section Theme
Economic Factors

After a brief postwar recession, the American economy began a steady growth that lasted for most of the 1920s.

Activity Have students create a graphic organizer illustrating the economic factors that fueled the American economy in the 1920s. Then ask them to analyze whether an economy fueled by these factors can maintain its growth.

1920 — 1925 — 1930

1920s Stock market booms

1922 GNP reaches $70 billion

1924 Model T sells for less than $300

1929 Electricity runs 70 percent of factories

Section 3

A Booming Economy

READ TO DISCOVER . . .

- how the prosperity of the 1920s affected the nation and the American people.
- what impact the automobile had on American life.

TERMS TO LEARN

recession
gross national product
productivity
installment buying

The Storyteller

During the "golden age of the automobile" in the 1920s, the car became a vital part of many Americans' lives. A mother of nine children said that her family "would rather do without clothes than give up the car." In the past, they had wanted to visit her sister-in-law, but by the time the children were "shoed and dressed" there wasn't any money left to pay for trolley fare. "Now no matter how [the children] look, we just poke 'em in the car and take 'em along."

1920s gas pump

After World War I, the American economy experienced problems readjusting to peacetime. Millions of soldiers returned, entering the labor force and competing for jobs. Government orders for wartime goods came to a halt, forcing many companies to lay off workers. Other companies went bankrupt. Prices rose, making it hard for workers to make ends meet.

This economic downturn, or **recession,** lasted about 2 years. Then the economy began a steady growth that lasted most of the decade. In 1922 the nation's **gross national product** (GNP)—the total value of all goods and services produced—was $70 billion. By 1929 it had risen to $100 billion!

Growth in the 1920s

Technology made rapid industrial growth possible, and electricity powered American industry. Before World War I, only 30 percent of factories were run by electricity. By 1929 this figure had risen to 70 percent. Electricity was cheaper than steam power. By cutting costs, businesses could lower prices and increase profits.

Scientific Management

New ways of managing operations contributed to economic growth as well. Many employers used **scientific management**—hiring experts to study how goods could be produced more quickly. By adopting new work methods, businesses sought to lower costs and increase **productivity**—how much work each worker could do.

SECTION RESOURCES

Reproducible Masters
- Reproducible Lesson Plan 24–3
- Guided Reading Activity 24–3
- Section Quiz 24–3
- Reteaching Activity 24–3
- Enrichment Activity 24–3

Transparencies
- Section Focus Transparency 24–3

Multimedia
- Vocabulary PuzzleMaker
- Chapter Challenger Interactive Review Software
- Testmaker

Many businesses adopted mass production techniques using the **assembly line,** first introduced in Henry Ford's automobile factories. Assembly line methods increased productivity and cut production costs.

Worker Relations

Businesses tried to build better relations with workers. Many companies set up safety programs that lowered the risk of death or injury on the job. Some began to provide health and accident insurance. Many companies encouraged workers to buy stock in the company. These steps—known as **welfare capitalism**—were designed to link workers more closely to the company they worked for. Business also adopted these steps to discourage workers from joining independent unions.

The Consumer Economy

American industry changed in another way as well. As electricity became more available, demand grew for appliances using electric power. By the 1920s, more than 60 percent of American households had electricity. Consumers eagerly acquired refrigerators, stoves, vacuum cleaners, fans, and radios. As demand for these items grew, more and more of them were produced, leading to reduced production costs and lower prices. Between 1920 and 1929, for example, the cost of a refrigerator dropped from $600 to $300.

These appliances transformed daily life. People did not have to spend as much time on household chores. Now they had more leisure time.

National Brands and Advertising

In the 1920s successful companies joined with or purchased competitors. Three companies—Ford, General Motors, and Chrysler—dominated the auto industry. One grocery chain—the Great Atlantic and Pacific Tea Company (A&P)—had more than 15,000 stores across the country. Businesses became national as many products of local companies were replaced by national brands.

To market those national brands, businesses spent more and more money on advertising. Propaganda techniques learned during World War I now persuaded consumers to buy a particular brand of toothpaste, clothing, or soap. Newspapers and magazines were filled with ads, and with the spread of radio a new advertising form—the commercial announcement—was born.

Buy Now, Pay Later

Spurred by ads to buy more and more, consumers gained a new way to make those purchases—**installment buying.** Consumers could now buy products by promising to pay small, regular amounts over a period of time. One critic of installment buying called the system "a dollar down and a dollar a week forever." The plan boosted consumer spending.

Auto Sales, 1920–1929

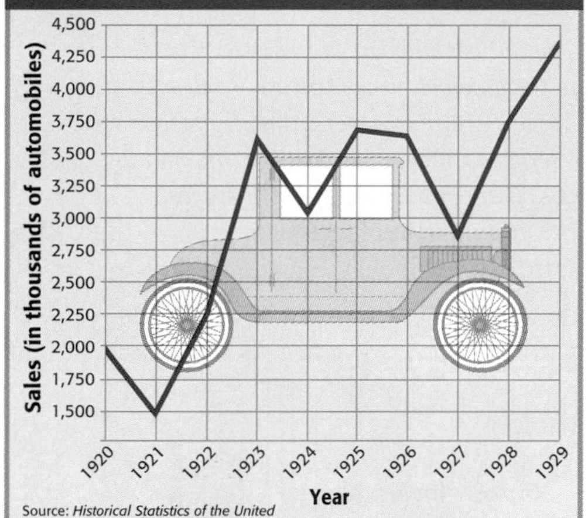

Source: *Historical Statistics of the United States from Colonial Times to 1970.*

Graph Study

A drop in auto sales occurred in 1927 when Ford stopped producing the Model T. Six months later his new Model A was produced.

1. About how many autos were sold in 1921?
2. **Comparing** About how many more autos were sold in 1928 than in 1924?

COOPERATIVE LEARNING ACTIVITY

Creating an Advertising Campaign Organize the class into groups of three to create an advertising campaign for new technology mentioned in this section. Ask groups to choose a technology and identify the target audience. Then have members choose from the following roles: write a jingle, design a magazine advertisement, or write a radio advertisement. Ask each group to pitch its campaign to the class. Have the class vote on the most effective campaign.

CHAPTER 24
Section 3, 698–701

2 TEACH

L1, ELL Creating a Visual Dictionary Ask students to scan the section to list all economic terms mentioned. Allow students to work in pairs to create a visual dictionary describing these terms. Have volunteers present their dictionaries to the class and discuss how each term positively or negatively affects the economy.

Guided Reading Activity 24–3

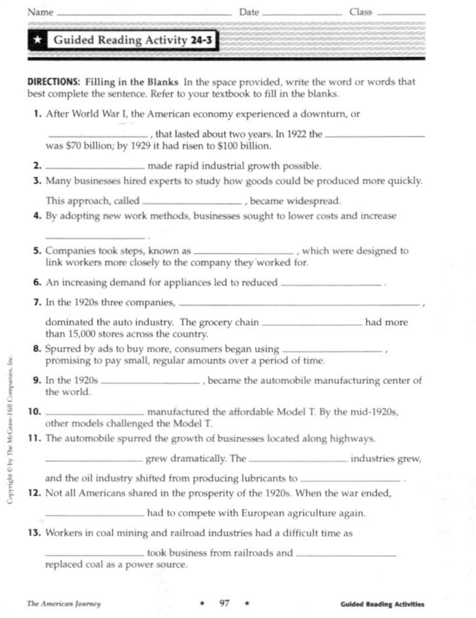

Name ______ Date ______ Class ______

★ Guided Reading Activity **24-3**

DIRECTIONS: Filling in the Blanks In the space provided, write the word or words that best complete the sentence. Refer to your textbook to fill in the blanks.

1. After World War I, the American economy experienced a downturn, or ______, that lasted about two years. In 1922 the ______ was $70 billion; by 1929 it had risen to $100 billion.
2. ______ made rapid industrial growth possible.
3. Many businesses hired experts to study how goods could be produced more quickly. This approach, called ______, became widespread.
4. By adopting new work methods, businesses sought to lower costs and increase ______.
5. Companies took steps, known as ______, which were designed to link workers more closely to the company they worked for.
6. An increasing demand for appliances led to reduced ______.
7. In the 1920s three companies, ______, dominated the auto industry. The grocery chain ______ had more than 15,000 stores across the country.
8. Spurred by ads to buy more, consumers began using ______, promising to pay small, regular amounts over a period of time.
9. In the 1920s ______, became the automobile manufacturing center of the world.
10. ______ manufactured the affordable Model T. By the mid-1920s, other models challenged the Model T.
11. The automobile spurred the growth of businesses located along highways. ______ grew dramatically. The ______ industries grew, and the oil industry shifted from producing lubricants to ______.
12. Not all Americans shared in the prosperity of the 1920s. When the war ended, ______ had to compete with European agriculture again.
13. Workers in coal mining and railroad industries had a difficult time as ______ took business from railroads and ______ replaced coal as a power source.

Copyright © by The McGraw-Hill Companies, Inc.

The American Journey ★ 97 ★ **Guided Reading Activities**

Graph Study

Answers

1. 1,500
2. 750

Graph Skills Practice

Reading a Graph In which years did auto sales drop? *(1920–1921, 1923–1924, 1925–1926, 1926–1927)*

3 ASSESS

Assign Section 3 Review as homework or as an in-class activity.

Use **Chapter Challenger Interactive Review Software** to review Section 3.

Section Quiz 24–3

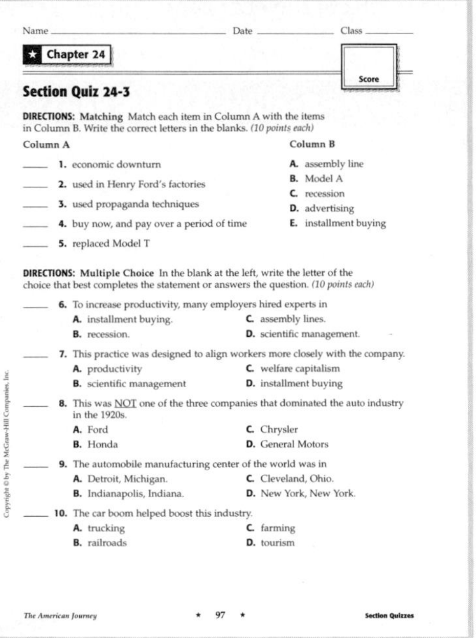

Name ______ Date ______ Class ______

★ Chapter 24 | Score

Section Quiz 24-3

DIRECTIONS: Matching Match each item in Column A with the items in Column B. Write the correct letters in the blanks. *(10 points each)*

Column A	Column B
____ **1.** economic downturn	**A.** assembly line
____ **2.** used in Henry Ford's factories	**B.** Model A
____ **3.** used propaganda techniques	**C.** recession
____ **4.** buy now, and pay over a period of time	**D.** advertising
____ **5.** replaced Model T	**E.** installment buying

DIRECTIONS: Multiple Choice In the blank at the left, write the letter of the choice that best completes the statement or answers the question. *(10 points each)*

____ **6.** To increase productivity, many employers hired experts in
A. installment buying. **C.** assembly lines.
B. recession. **D.** scientific management.

____ **7.** This practice was designed to align workers more closely with the company.
A. productivity **C.** welfare capitalism
B. scientific management **D.** installment buying

____ **8.** This was NOT one of the three companies that dominated the auto industry in the 1920s.
A. Ford **C.** Chrysler
B. Honda **D.** General Motors

____ **9.** The automobile manufacturing center of the world was in
A. Detroit, Michigan. **C.** Cleveland, Ohio.
B. Indianapolis, Indiana. **D.** New York, New York.

____ **10.** The car boom helped boost this industry.
A. trucking **C.** farming
B. railroads **D.** tourism

Copyright © by The McGraw-Hill Companies, Inc.

The American Journey ★ 97 ★ **Section Quizzes**

TECHNOLOGY AND HISTORY

More About . . .
Henry Ford's Assembly Line

Committed to large-volume production of the Model T, Henry Ford innovated mass-production techniques at his Highland Park, Michigan, plant. The plant opened in 1910, but Ford did not introduce the moving assembly line until 1913–1914. Ford stated, "The step forward in assembly came when we began taking the work to the men instead of the men to the work." **Ask:** On which floor were the engines built? *(third)*

Answer to Caption: *60-acre factory*

The Automobile Age

More often than not, people used the installment plan to buy a new car. During the 1920s, automobile registrations jumped from 8 million to 23 million. America quickly became a "car culture," in which people's lives revolved around the automobile. The nation's economy, too, revolved around the automobile. Almost 4 million Americans worked for auto companies or in related jobs. **Detroit, Michigan,** became the automobile manufacturing center of the world.

Cheaper Cars

Henry Ford was a pioneer in the manufacture of affordable automobiles with his **Model T,** built using assembly line methods. The car was sturdy, reliable, inexpensive, and available only in black. In 1914 Ford had stunned the auto industry—and all corporate leaders, for that matter—by announcing that he would pay his workers the high wage of $5 per day. Workers were happy, and Ford had more potential customers as he steadily dropped the price of his Model T. By 1924 the car sold for less than $300. With the average industrial worker earning about $1,300 a year, many families could afford to buy a Model T.

By the mid-1920s, other automobile models challenged the Model T. General Motors cut into Ford's sales by offering a line of cars in a range of colors and with features to improve passenger comfort. In 1927 Ford responded with the **Model A,** which had better engineering and came in several colors. Out of this competition came the practice of introducing new car models each year.

TECHNOLOGY AND HISTORY

Henry Ford's Assembly Line

The industrial boom of the 1920s owed much to the assembly line Henry Ford first used in 1913–1914. Parts moved on a conveyor belt. Workers attached the parts to cars moving past them at a steady speed of six feet per minute. **How large was Ford's plant?**

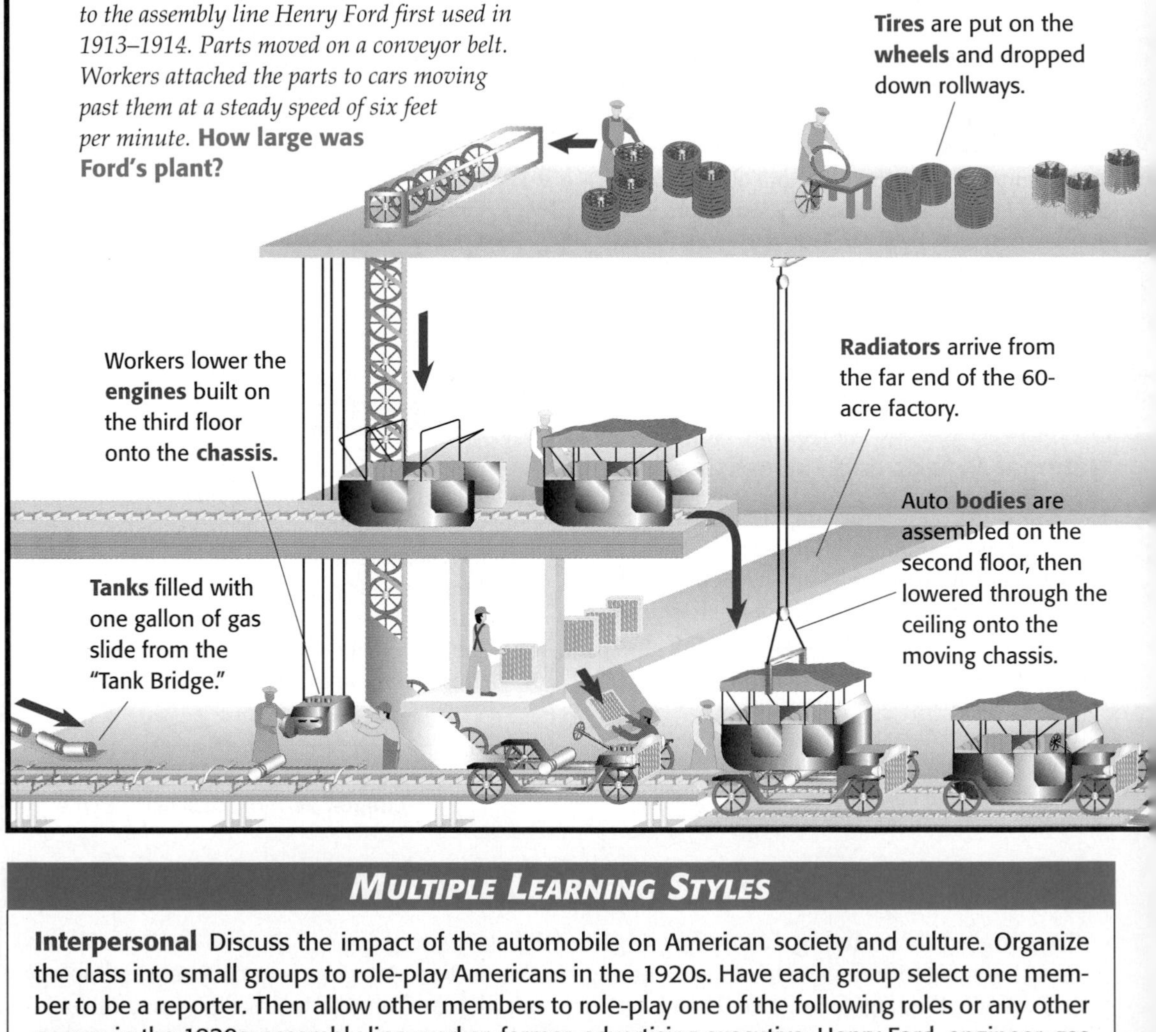

MULTIPLE LEARNING STYLES

Interpersonal Discuss the impact of the automobile on American society and culture. Organize the class into small groups to role-play Americans in the 1920s. Have each group select one member to be a reporter. Then allow other members to role-play one of the following roles or any other person in the 1920s: assembly line worker, farmer, advertising executive, Henry Ford, engineer, gas station attendant. Have all members create a list of interview questions. Then have the reporter interview the members as they play their chosen roles. Encourage groups to videotape their role plays to present to the class. **L2**

Effect on Other Industries

The automobile had a tremendous impact on other American industries. Americans' love of driving called for new roads and highways. Highways, in turn, needed gas stations and rest stops. Businesses along major roads profited from the millions of people now traveling around the country by car. Tourism grew dramatically.

The car boom affected industries that made products used in cars. The steel, rubber, and glass industries grew. During the 1920s the oil industry shifted from producing lubricants to refining gasoline for automobiles.

Picturing HISTORY During the 1920s, an increasing number of Americans used their automobiles to take trips away from home. **How did the automobile affect where people lived?**

Car Culture

The automobile dramatically changed the lives of many Americans. Travel for pleasure became a regular part of American life. People could now get into their cars and go wherever they wished. Cars also contributed to the spread of suburbs. Because people could now drive to work, they could live in a suburb and still hold a job in the city.

Those Left Behind

Despite all the signs of prosperity and the mood of optimism, many Americans did not share in the boom of the 1920s. Farmers had an especially difficult time. During the war, the federal government had purchased wheat, corn, and other products, and farmers had prospered from higher prices. When the war ended, farmers had to compete with European agriculture again. Food prices fell, and farm income plummeted. Unable to pay their debts, many farmers lost their farms.

Not all industrial workers shared in the prosperity of the 1920s. Those who worked in the coal mining and railroad industries had a difficult time as trucks took business from railroads and electricity replaced coal as a power source. Wages rose slightly for most workers, but the cost of living rose more. By 1929 nearly three-fourths of families had incomes below $2,500, the accepted level necessary for a comfortable life.

Section 3 Review

Checking for Understanding

1. ***Identify*** scientific management, assembly line, welfare capitalism, Henry Ford.
2. ***Define*** recession, gross national product, productivity, installment buying.
3. ***Describe*** the economic problems that existed in America after World War I.

Reviewing Themes

4. **Economic Factors** How did the auto industry help boost other industries?

Critical Thinking

5. **Drawing Conclusions** How did welfare capitalism discourage people from joining unions?

Activity

Tracking Progress Compare a photograph or drawing of Ford's Model T to a modern car and describe the major differences you see.

Section 3 Review Answers

1. scientific management, 698; assembly line, 699; welfare capitalism, 699; Henry Ford, 700
2. The words are defined in the Glossary.
3. Answers may include returning soldiers competing for jobs, end of government's need for war goods, bankruptcies, and rising prices.
4. demand for secondary industries such as highways and roads; travel-related businesses such as gas stations and rest stops; tourism; oil; car-related products such as steel, rubber, and glass
5. Businesses gave more benefits to employees who were less likely to join a union.

Activity Students should compare the Model T to a modern automobile and describe some of the major differences.

Picturing HISTORY The automobile brought better services and more consumer goods to rural America.
Answer: *The car allowed people to move to suburbs.*

Reteaching Activity 24–3

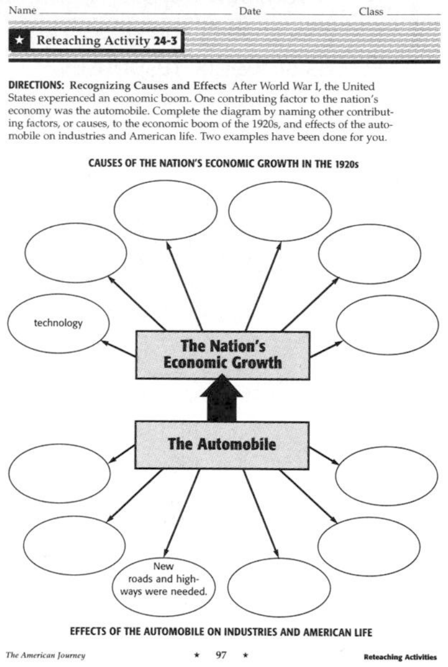
Name ______ Date ______ Class ______

Reteaching Activity 24-3

DIRECTIONS: Recognizing Causes and Effects After World War I, the United States experienced an economic boom. One contributing factor to the nation's economy was the automobile. Complete the diagram by naming other contributing factors, or causes, to the economic boom of the 1920s, and effects of the automobile on industries and American life. Two examples have been done for you.

The American Journey ★ 97 ★ Reteaching Activities

Enrichment Activity 24–3

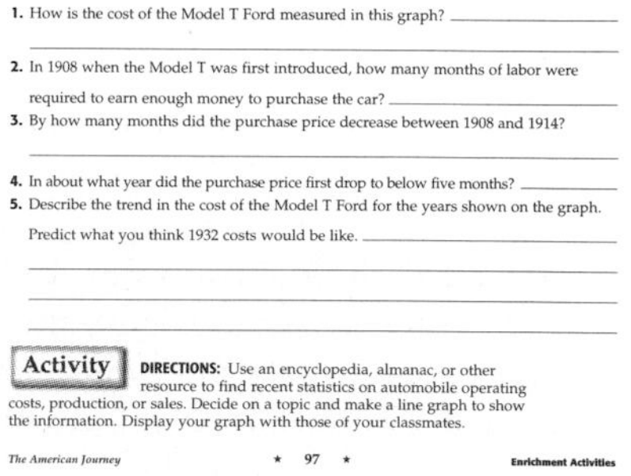
Name ______ Date ______ Class ______

Enrichment Activity 24-3

Buying a New Car

The mass production techniques that Henry Ford introduced in his factory brought the price of the Model T Ford within reach of American workers. Study the graph that shows the cost of a Model T Ford from 1908 to 1926.

SOURCE: Bailey, Thomas A. and David M. Kennedy. *The American Pageant, A History of the Republic.* Stanford University.

DIRECTIONS: Reading a Line Graph Answer the following questions.

1. How is the cost of the Model T Ford measured in this graph? ______
2. In 1908 when the Model T was first introduced, how many months of labor were required to earn enough money to purchase the car? ______
3. By how many months did the purchase price decrease between 1908 and 1914? ______
4. In about what year did the purchase price first drop to below five months? ______
5. Describe the trend in the cost of the Model T Ford for the years shown on the graph. Predict what you think 1932 costs would be like. ______

Activity **DIRECTIONS:** Use an encyclopedia, almanac, or other resource to find recent statistics on automobile operating costs, production, or sales. Decide on a topic and make a line graph to show the information. Display your graph with those of your classmates.

The American Journey ★ 97 ★ Enrichment Activities

4 CLOSE

Ask students to speculate how the American economy would have developed without mass production of automobiles.

1 FOCUS

BELLRINGER
Motivational Activity

Before taking roll at the beginning of the class period, project Section Focus Transparency 24–4 and have students answer the questions. Discuss students' responses.

This activity is also available as a blackline master.

Section Focus Transparency 24–4

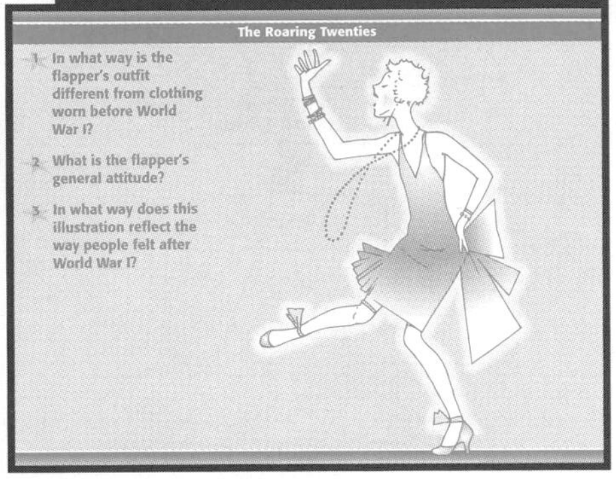

Vocabulary Precheck

Ask volunteers to describe how the term *flapper* symbolized the "liberated" woman in the 1920s.

Use the **Vocabulary PuzzleMaker** to create crossword and word search puzzles.

Section Theme
Science and Technology

Technological developments provided Americans with more leisure time for entertainment and the arts.

Activity Brainstorm with students why an increase in leisure time in the 1920s caused a boom in the arts and entertainment industries.

1920 — 1925 — 1930

1920 Nineteenth Amendment grants woman suffrage

1924 Crossword puzzles are a popular activity

1927 Charles Lindbergh flies solo across the Atlantic; Babe Ruth hits 60 home runs

Section 4

The Roaring Twenties

READ TO DISCOVER . . .

- how lifestyles in America changed in the 1920s.
- what features characterized the music and literature of the Jazz Age.

TERMS TO LEARN

flapper
mass media
expatriate

The Storyteller

On the evening of May 19, 1927, a young pilot named Charles Lindbergh learned that, although it was drizzling on Long Island, the weather reports predicted fair skies for his miraculous trip. He decided to get ready. Throughout a sleepless night, Lindbergh made the final preparations for takeoff. Shortly before 8:00 A.M., Lindbergh climbed into his aircraft and took off for Paris. With the news of his departure "flashing along the wires," the American people were united in "the exaltation of a common emotion." All minds and hearts were focused on the brave pilot who was crossing the vast Atlantic Ocean.

Song sheet honoring Lindbergh

In May 1927, aviator **Charles Lindbergh** became the first person to fly alone across the Atlantic Ocean. He did so in a tiny, single-engine plane, the *Spirit of St. Louis*. Americans went wild and hailed a new hero. Cities across the nation held parades to honor Lindbergh—in New York City well-wishers threw 1,800 tons of paper streamers—and newspapers reported on his every move. The national embrace of Lindbergh showed what one historian called a "delighted concern over things that were exciting but didn't matter profoundly."

Changes for Women

The 1920s did bring profound changes for women. One important change took place with the ratification of the **Nineteenth Amendment** in 1920. The amendment guaranteed women in all states the right to vote. Women also ran for election to political offices.

In the Workplace

Throughout the 1920s the number of women holding jobs outside the home continued to grow. Most women had to take jobs considered "women's" work, such as teaching and working in offices as clerks and typists. At the same time, increasing numbers of college-educated women started professional careers, and more women worked after marriage. But the vast majority of married women remained within the home, working as homemakers and mothers.

SECTION RESOURCES

Reproducible Masters
- Reproducible Lesson Plan 24–4
- Guided Reading Activity 24–4
- Section Quiz 24–4
- Reteaching Activity 24–4
- Enrichment Activity 24–4

Transparencies
- Section Focus Transparency 24–4

Multimedia
- Vocabulary PuzzleMaker
- Chapter Challenger Interactive Review
- Testmaker
- GTV: A Geographic Perspective on American History
- American Music Cultural Traditions

The Flapper

Symbolizing the new "liberated" woman of the 1920s was the flapper. Pictures of flappers—carefree young women with short, "bobbed" hair, heavy makeup, and short skirts—appeared in magazines. Many people saw the bold, boyish look and shocking behavior of flappers as a sign of changing morals. Though hardly typical of American women, the flapper image reinforced the idea that women now had more freedom. Prewar values had shifted, and many people were beginning to challenge traditional ways.

Flappers

Entertainment

Changes in attitudes spread quickly because of the growth of mass media—forms of communication, such as newspapers and radio, that reach millions of people. Laborsaving devices and fewer working hours gave Americans more leisure time. In those nonworking hours, they enjoyed tabloid-style newspapers, large-circulation magazines, phonograph records, the radio, and the movies.

The Movies

In the 1920s the motion picture industry in **Hollywood,** California, became one of the country's leading businesses. For millions of Americans, the movies offered entertainment and escape.

The first movies were black and white and silent, with the actors' dialog printed on the screen and a pianist playing music to accompany the action. In 1927 Hollywood introduced movies with sound. The first "talkie," *The Jazz Singer,* created a sensation.

As the popularity of movies increased, Americans became fascinated with the people who appeared in them. Adoring fans idolized stars such as Douglas Fairbanks, Gloria Swanson, Clara Bow, Charlie Chaplin, and Rudolph Valentino. Enthusiastic fans read movie magazines filled with stories about the stars' personal lives. Scandals revealed some of those lives to be less than ideal. Many Americans worried about the impact of movies on the nation's morality. The movie industry responded by creating an office to inspect the content of films and to keep out material that might offend people.

Poster for a Valentino movie

Radio

The radio brought entertainment to people's homes in the 1920s. In 1920 the first commercial radio broadcast, which carried the presidential election returns, was transmitted by station KDKA in Pittsburgh. In the next 3 years nearly 600 stations joined the airwaves. Soon stations began to combine into powerful national networks.

CHAPTER 24
Section 4, 702–706

2 TEACH

L1, ELL Expressing Individuality Ask students which of the following experiences make them feel part of a crowd and which make them aware of their individuality: reading a book, watching television, viewing a film in a theater. Discuss students' responses and explain that developments during the 1920s changed the lives of individuals and groups of Americans in many ways.

CURRICULUM CONNECTION

SCIENCE

Charles Lindbergh's trip from New York City to Paris took 33 hours, 29 minutes, and 30 seconds. The 25-year-old former stunt-show pilot landed his single-engine monoplane, *The Spirit of St. Louis,* at Le Bourget airfield outside Paris, France, on May 21, 1927. This event brought acclaim to Lindbergh and sparked immense interest in the possibilities of commercial aviation.

Guided Reading Activity 24–4

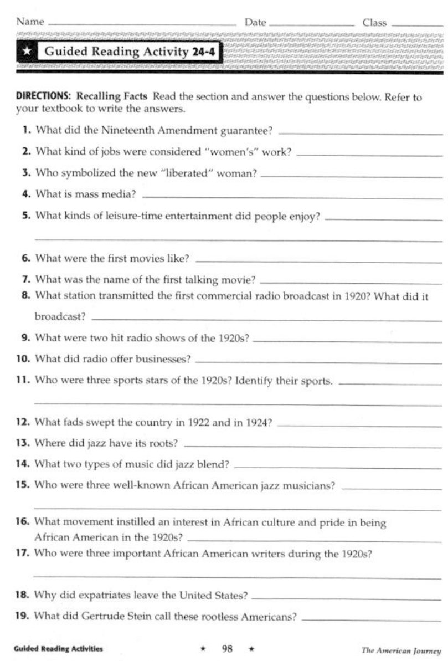
Name ______ Date ______ Class ______

★ Guided Reading Activity 24-4

DIRECTIONS: Recalling Facts Read the section and answer the questions below. Refer to your textbook to write the answers.

1. What did the Nineteenth Amendment guarantee?
2. What kind of jobs were considered "women's" work?
3. Who symbolized the new "liberated" woman?
4. What is mass media?
5. What kinds of leisure-time entertainment did people enjoy?
6. What were the first movies like?
7. What was the name of the first talking movie?
8. What station transmitted the first commercial radio broadcast in 1920? What did it broadcast?
9. What were two hit radio shows of the 1920s?
10. What did radio offer businesses?
11. Who were three sports stars of the 1920s? Identify their sports.
12. What fads swept the country in 1922 and in 1924?
13. Where did jazz have its roots?
14. What two types of music did jazz blend?
15. Who were three well-known African American jazz musicians?
16. What movement instilled an interest in African culture and pride in being African American in the 1920s?
17. Who were three important African American writers during the 1920s?
18. Why did expatriates leave the United States?
19. What did Gertrude Stein call these rootless Americans?

Guided Reading Activities ★ 98 ★ *The American Journey*

COOPERATIVE LEARNING ACTIVITY

Creating a Board Game Explain to students that board games were a popular form of entertainment in the 1920s. Organize the class into groups of three to create a board game that would have appealed to Americans in the 1920s. Have each group choose a name for the game and determine how the game will be played. Then allow members to choose from the following roles: design game board, make playing pieces or cards, or write instructions. Groups should play the game they created to fine-tune the instructions. Then have groups exchange games to play and critique.

What? Where? When? Who?

Mah-jongg is a Chinese game played with carved bone tiles with elaborate markings. The game caught the fancy of Americans in the 1920s. By 1923 more than 16 million sets had been sold. A deluxe set cost up to $500, which was more than a Model T Ford!

Graph Study

Answers

1. about 500,000
2. About 2 million more people had radios in 1929 than in 1928.

Graph Skills Practice

Reading a Graph About how many families could listen to Babe Ruth hit 60 home runs in 1927? *(about 6.75 million)*

NATIONAL GEOGRAPHIC SOCIETY

VIDEODISC
GTV: A Geographic Perspective on American History

Side 4, Chapter 4
Title: *Getting to Know You*
Subject: The information age (1915–1945)
Ask: How were motion pictures instrumental in Americans' lives? *(They provided entertainment, sources of national and international news, and served to unify American culture.)*

Families With Radios, 1922–1929

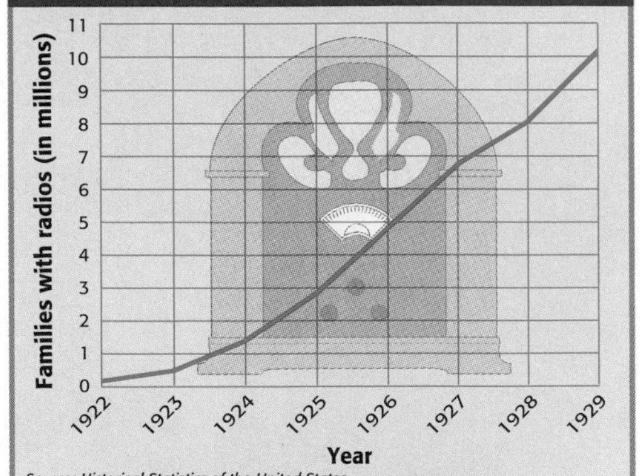

Source: *Historical Statistics of the United States.*

Graph Study

In their newfound leisure time, Americans in the 1920s listened to the radio or their phonographs.

1. About how many families had radios in 1923?
2. **Comparing** About how many more families had radios in 1929 than in 1928?

The networks broadcast popular programs across the nation. The evening lineup of programs included something for everyone—news, concerts, sporting events, and comedies. Radio offered listeners a wide range of music—opera, classical, country and western, blues, and jazz. *Amos 'n' Andy* and the *Grand Ole Opry* were among the hit shows of the 1920s. Families sat down to listen to the radio together.

Businesses soon realized that the radio offered an enormous audience for messages about their products, so they began to help finance radio programs. Radio stations sold spot advertisements, or commercials, to companies.

Sports and Fads

Among the favorite radio broadcasts of the 1920s were athletic events. Americans became fascinated with sports and sports figures. Baseball, football, and boxing soared in popularity. Americans flocked to sporting events, and more people participated in sports activities as well.

Babe Ruth

Sports stars became larger-than-life heroes. Baseball fans idolized **Babe Ruth,** the great outfielder, who hit 60 home runs in 1927—a record that would stand for 34 years. Football star Red Grange, who once scored 4 touchdowns in 12 minutes, became a national hero, too, as did boxer Jack Dempsey. Golfer Bobby Jones and Gertrude Ederle, the first woman to swim the English Channel, became household names.

In the 1920s Americans took up new activities with enthusiasm, turning them into fads. A craze for the Chinese board game mah-jongg (mah•ZHAHNG) swept the country in 1922, and in 1924 crossword puzzles were all the rage. Contests such as flagpole sitting—Alvin "Shipwreck" Kelly set the record of 23 days, 7 hours—and dance marathons—often lasting 3 or 4 days—made headlines. Americans also loved the Miss America Pageant, first held in 1921.

The Jazz Age

During the 1920s people danced to the beat of a new kind of music called jazz. Jazz captured the spirit of the era so well that the 1920s is often referred to as the **Jazz Age.**

Jazz had its roots in the South in African American work songs and in African music. A blend of ragtime and blues, it used dynamic rhythms and **improvisation**—new rhythms and melodies created during a performance. Among the best-known African American jazz musicians were trumpeter **Louis Armstrong,** pianist and composer **Duke Ellington,** and singer **Bessie Smith.** White musicians such as Paul Whiteman and Bix Biederbecke also played jazz and helped bring it to a wider audience.

Interest in jazz spread via radio and phonograph records. Jazz helped

MULTIPLE LEARNING STYLES

Kinesthetic Discuss with the class the types of fads popular in the 1920s such as mah-jongg, Ping-Pong, Bingo, Kewpie dolls, dance marathons, and so on. Explain that these fads paint a picture of 1920s culture. Ask students to work in pairs to create their own fad they think would have swept 1920s Americans off their feet. Then call on pairs to demonstrate their fad to the class. Hold a vote on which fad students think would have been the most popular in the 1920s. Discuss how the winning fad best matched the 1920s culture. **L2**

American Memories

An American Music

Jazz record label

Clarinet

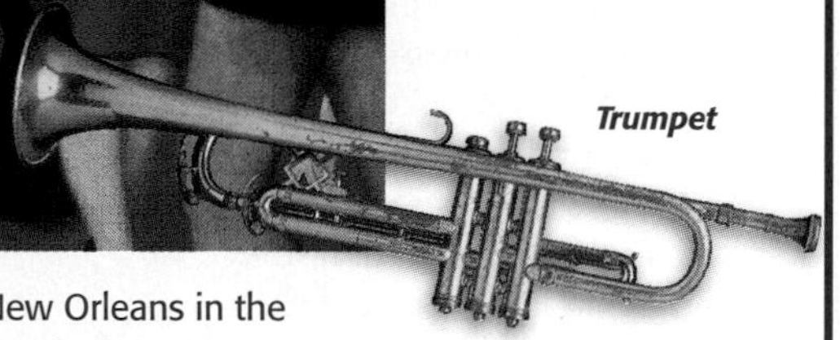

Trumpet

What Was It Like? Jazz music probably began in New Orleans in the early 1900s and soon spread to Chicago, New York, and other cities. **What instruments are associated with jazz music?**

create a unique African American recording industry. Equally important, jazz gave America one of its most distinctive art forms.

Harlem Renaissance

The rhythm and themes of jazz inspired the poetry of **Langston Hughes,** an African American writer. In the 1920s, Hughes joined the growing number of African American writers and artists who gathered in **Harlem,** an African American section of New York City. Hughes described his arrival in Harlem:

> "I can never put on paper the thrill of the underground ride to Harlem. I went up the steps and out into the bright September sunlight. Harlem! I stood there, dropped my bags, took a deep breath and felt happy again."

Harlem witnessed a burst of creativity in the 1920s—a flowering of African American culture called the **Harlem Renaissance.** This movement instilled an interest in African culture and pride in being African American.

During the Harlem Renaissance, a number of important writers explored the African American experience in novels, poems, and short stories. Along with Hughes were poets **James Weldon Johnson, Claude McKay, Countee Cullen,** and the short story writer **Zora Neale Hurston.** African American theater also blossomed during the Harlem Renaissance. Stars included actor and singer **Paul Robeson** and one of the first women in musical comedy, **Florence Mills.**

Langston Hughes

MAKING CONNECTIONS ACTIVITY

The Arts Write the following on the chalkboard: *Authors/Artists, Works*. Invite volunteers to come to the board and fill in entries under *Authors/Artists* and their *Works.* Then discuss with the class whether any of the themes expressed in the literature and art of the 1920s—such as disappointment with American values, the "fear of poverty and worship of success," small-town life, underlying clashes in American society, changes in American culture—are important in society today. **L2**

American Memories

An American Music

The origin of the term *jazz* is one of the hottest disputes in American English. It may have come from the word *Chaz*, the nickname of an early ragtime drummer named Charles Washington, or from *chasse*, a kind of dance step. It also could have originated from African or Creole sources. Regardless of its origin, *jazz* was first used after World War I to describe a type of music.

Answer: *trumpet and clarinet are shown; also piano, trombone, saxophone, flute, and so on*

3 ASSESS

Assign Section 4 Review as homework or as an in-class activity.

Use **Chapter Challenger Interactive Review Software** to review Section 4.

Section Quiz 24–4

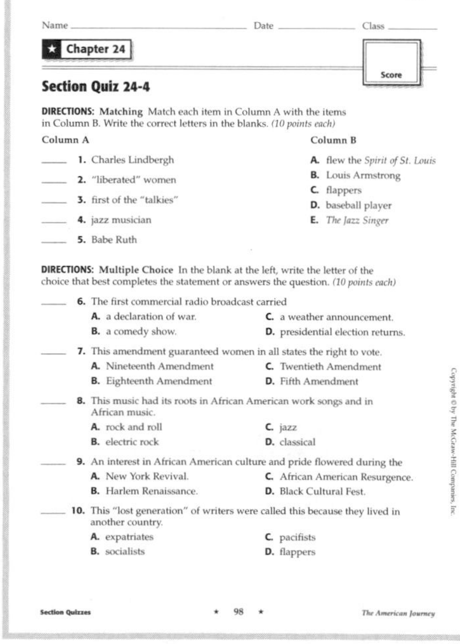

Name ______ Date ______ Class ______

★ Chapter 24

Score

Section Quiz 24-4

DIRECTIONS: Matching Match each item in Column A with the items in Column B. Write the correct letters in the blanks. *(10 points each)*

Column A

____ **1.** Charles Lindbergh
____ **2.** "liberated" women
____ **3.** first of the "talkies"
____ **4.** jazz musician
____ **5.** Babe Ruth

Column B

A. flew the *Spirit of St. Louis*
B. Louis Armstrong
C. flappers
D. baseball player
E. *The Jazz Singer*

DIRECTIONS: Multiple Choice In the blank at the left, write the letter of the choice that best completes the statement or answers the question. *(10 points each)*

____ **6.** The first commercial radio broadcast carried
A. a declaration of war. **C.** a weather announcement.
B. a comedy show. **D.** presidential election returns.

____ **7.** This amendment guaranteed women in all states the right to vote.
A. Nineteenth Amendment **C.** Twentieth Amendment
B. Eighteenth Amendment **D.** Fifth Amendment

____ **8.** This music had its roots in African American work songs and in African music.
A. rock and roll **C.** jazz
B. electric rock **D.** classical

____ **9.** An interest in African American culture and pride flowered during the
A. New York Revival. **C.** African American Resurgence.
B. Harlem Renaissance. **D.** Black Cultural Fest.

____ **10.** This "lost generation" of writers were called this because they lived in another country.
A. expatriates **C.** pacifists
B. socialists **D.** flappers

Section Quizzes ★ 98 ★ *The American Journey*

Reteaching Activity 24–4

Name ______ Date ______ Class ______

★ Reteaching Activity 24-4

DIRECTIONS: Organizing Facts Below are facts, people, and titles associated with different aspects of the Roaring Twenties. Complete the chart by writing the correct letters in each box.

The Roaring Twenties

"Liberated" Women	Mass Media	Movies	Radio
Sports & Fads	**Jazz**	**Harlem Renaissance**	**The Lost Generation**

★FACT BANK

A. Duke Ellington, Louis Armstrong, Bessie Smith, Paul Whiteman, and Bix Biederbecke
B. newspapers
C. KDKA, Pittsburgh
D. *Grand Ole Opry*
E. flappers
F. Langston Hughes, Zora Neale Hurston, Paul Robeson, and Florence Mills
G. expatriates
H. sold commercials to companies
I. *The Sun Also Rises*
J. *The Jazz Singer*
K. a blend of ragtime and blues
L. large-circulation magazines
M. *Amos 'n' Andy*
N. Babe Ruth and Gertrude Ederle
O. bold, carefree
P. flowering of African American culture
Q. *Main Street*
R. Ernest Hemingway, Gertrude Stein, and F. Scott Fitzgerald
S. flagpole-sitting and dance marathons
T. Douglas Fairbanks, Gloria Swanson, and Charlie Chaplin
U. forms of communication that reach millions of people

Reteaching Activities ★ 98 ★ *The American Journey*

Enrichment Activity 24–4

Name ______ Date ______ Class ______

★ Enrichment Activity 24-4 ★

Ballad of the Landlord

In the 1920s Harlem—an African American section of New York City—witnessed a burst of creativity from the growing number of African American writers and artists who gathered there. Writer Langston Hughes was among those who joined this flowering of African American culture which became known as the Harlem Renaissance. The movement encouraged writers like Hughes to examine the problems African Americans faced in the city and to record their observations in stories and poems such as the one below by Langston Hughes.

Ballad of the Landlord

Landlord, landlord,
My roof has sprung a leak.
Don't you 'member I told you about it
Way last week?
Landlord, landlord,
These steps is broken down.
When you come up yourself
It's a wonder you don't fall down.
Ten Bucks you say I owe you?
Ten Bucks you say is due?
Well, that's Ten Buck more'n I'll pay you
Till you fix this house up new.
What? You gonna get eviction orders?
You gonna cut off my heat?
You gonna take my
furniture and
Throw it in the street?
Um-huh! You talking high and mighty.
Talk on—till you get through.
You ain't gonna be able to say a word
If I land my fist on you.
Police! Police!
Come and get this man!
He's trying to ruin the government
And overturn the land!
Copper's whistle!
Patrol bell!
Arrest.
Precinct Station.
Iron cell.
Headlines in press:
MAN THREATENS LANDLORD
TENANT HELD NO BAIL
JUDGE GIVES NEGRO 90 DAYS IN COUNTY JAIL

SOURCE: Pichaske, David R., ed. *Beowulf to Beatles, Approaches to Poetry.* The Free Press, New York.

Activity **DIRECTIONS:** On a separate sheet of paper, rewrite the events Hughes describes in the poem as a short dramatic skit. Then assign the roles of the characters in your skit and perform the skit for the class. After the performance, ask students to compare the impact of the poem to that of your skit. Which do they believe conveys the injustice of the situation more vividly?

Enrichment Activities ★ 98 ★ *The American Journey*

4 CLOSE

Have students list on the chalkboard words or phrases that symbolize "The Roaring Twenties." Then direct them to write a paragraph explaining the terms in their own words.

Zora Neale Hurston

The Harlem Renaissance faded in the 1930s with the Great Depression. Its influence, however, lived on and affected the work of later generations of African American artists.

A Lost Generation of Writers

At the same time the Harlem Renaissance blossomed, other writers were questioning American ideals. Disappointed with American values and in search of inspiration, they settled in Paris. These writers were called **expatriates**—people who choose to live in another country. Writer **Gertrude Stein** called these rootless Americans "the lost generation."

Novelist **F. Scott Fitzgerald** and his wife, Zelda, joined the expatriates in Europe. In *Tender Is the Night,* Fitzgerald wrote of people who had been damaged emotionally by World War I. They were dedicated, he said, "to the fear of poverty and the worship of success." Another famous American expatriate was novelist **Ernest Hemingway,** whose books *The Sun Also Rises* and *A Farewell to Arms* reflected the mood of Americans in postwar Europe.

While some artists fled the United States, others stayed home and wrote about life in America. Novelist **Sinclair Lewis** presented a critical view of American culture in such books as *Main Street* and *Babbitt.* Another influential American writer was **Sherwood Anderson.** In his most famous book, *Winesburg, Ohio,* Anderson explored small-town life in the Midwest.

Throughout the 1920s America's writers and intellectuals continued to examine and criticize the changing culture of the United States. Their work revealed the underlying clashes in American society during this time of great upheaval.

Ernest Hemingway

Section 4 Review

Checking for Understanding

1. ***Identify*** Charles Lindbergh, Nineteenth Amendment, Jazz Age, Langston Hughes, Harlem Renaissance, F. Scott Fitzgerald.
2. ***Define*** flapper, mass media, expatriate.
3. ***Summarize*** the changes in women's personal and economic status during the 1920s.

Reviewing Themes

4. **Science and Technology** How did the growth of mass media affect society?

Critical Thinking

5. **Making Generalizations** Why do you think Gertrude Stein referred to many American writers as "the lost generation"?

Activity

Illustrating a Poem Read a poem by one of the writers associated with the Harlem Renaissance. Find illustrations and photographs that help to communicate the meaning of the poem. Display the poem and illustrations on a piece of poster board.

Section 4 Review Answers

1. Charles Lindbergh, 702; Nineteenth Amendment, 702; Jazz Age, 704; Langston Hughes, 705; Harlem Renaissance, 705; F. Scott Fitzgerald, 706
2. The words are defined in the Glossary.
3. more jobs open to them; more were college-educated professionals; gained the right to vote; their fashions and behavior expressed new independence; more leisure time
4. It helped to quickly spread changes in attitude throughout the country.
5. Answers should describe how writers, disappointed with American values, left the United States in search of inspiration elsewhere.

Activity Students should select a poem written by a Harlem Renaissance writer and mount it on poster board with illustrations to convey the meaning of the poem.

INTERDISCIPLINARY

Activities

All That Jazz

Almost 80 years after the Jazz Age, its music and moods are still at the heart of American culture. Read about the changes that people experienced as they moved to cities and experimented with new forms of art, music, and literature. Then become part of the Jazz Age yourself as you complete these activities.

Drama

Staging a Play Imagine that you have been asked to produce a play or musical set in the Roaring Twenties. Research the background of the 1920s, then design a series of costumes for men and women or make sketches for several different scenes. These may include a city street or a nightclub. If possible, make costumes for your classmates who perform the music of the Jazz Age.

Music

Writing a '20s Musical Listen to recordings of jazz and performances by popular musicians from the 1920s, such as Duke Ellington and George Gershwin. Choose a selection of songs you like and write a script that brings them together in a one-act musical comedy. Use the songs' original words or write new ones and add them to your script. With a group of classmates, memorize the songs and script to put on a performance for the class.

Art

Painting a Mural With a group, make a list of people and events that represent the Jazz Age. Include musicians, writers, sports figures, and other entertainers. Use a roll of brown paper to make a wall mural in the classroom. First make small sketches on a sheet of paper. Then transfer the sketches to the mural paper using chalk or pencil. Fill in color and patterns with markers or acrylics.

School-to-Work

Designing a Skyscraper By the 1920s skyscrapers were becoming part of the skyline of American cities. Research a well-known building of this period, such as the Chrysler Building in New York City. Construct a cardboard or wooden model of or sketch your own plans for a 1920s skyscraper.

Duke Ellington song sheet (left) and blues singer Bessie Smith (right)

MULTIPLE LEARNING STYLES

The activities included in the feature on this student edition page are ideally suited to meet the different learning styles of your students. These include:

- Drama — **Staging a Play** kinesthetic learners
- Art — **Painting a Mural** visual/spatial learners
- Music — **Writing a '20s Musical** auditory/musical learners
- School-to-Work — **Designing a Skyscraper** kinesthetic learners

INTERDISCIPLINARY

Activities

TEACH

Background

These activities provide students with an opportunity to experience the Jazz Age. Americans at this time had just won a war. Many felt it was time for a party. It may seem strange that this party took place during Prohibition, which actually spurred carefree and sometimes lawless activities. Americans craved adventure, and a series of frivolous fads captured their attention. This atmosphere formed the heart and soul of American culture of the 1920s.

History *and the* Humanities

- The Spirit of American Art and Music, Duke Ellington, George Gershwin
- American Music Cultural Traditions, Lesson 8: "Muskrat Ramble" and "Downhearted Blues"

School TO WORK

Architect If students are interested in learning more about architecture as a career, have them volunteer to serve as an "apprentice" for a day with a local architectural firm. You may wish to invite both an architect and a mechanical engineer to class to discuss how their professions work together.

1 FOCUS

BELLRINGER
Motivational Activity

Before taking roll at the beginning of the class period, project Section Focus Transparency 24–5 and have students answer the questions. Discuss students' responses.

This activity is also available as a blackline master.

Section Focus Transparency 24–5

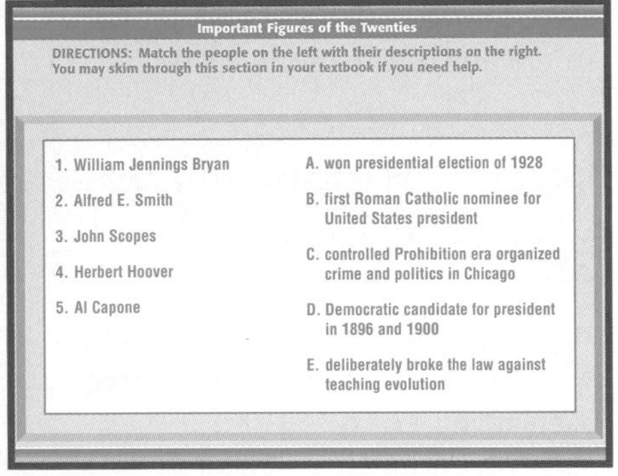
Important Figures of the Twenties

DIRECTIONS: Match the people on the left with their descriptions on the right. You may skim through this section in your textbook if you need help.

1. William Jennings Bryan	A. won presidential election of 1928
2. Alfred E. Smith	B. first Roman Catholic nominee for United States president
3. John Scopes	C. controlled Prohibition era organized crime and politics in Chicago
4. Herbert Hoover	D. Democratic candidate for president in 1896 and 1900
5. Al Capone	E. deliberately broke the law against teaching evolution

Vocabulary Precheck
Ask volunteers to discuss how the idea behind each of the **Terms to Learn** affected American culture. Point out how each idea created tension in American society.

Use the **Vocabulary Puzzle-Maker** to create crossword and word search puzzles.

Section Theme
Culture and Traditions

The clash between Americans who defended traditional beliefs and those who welcomed new ideas and lifestyles created cultural tension in the 1920s.

Activity Ask volunteers to describe traditional beliefs of the 1920s. Ask other volunteers to describe new ideas and lifestyles of the 1920s. Discuss why these different beliefs clashed.

1915 1920 1925 1930

- **1915** Second Ku Klux Klan is organized
- **1920** Eighteenth Amendment establishes Prohibition
- **1924** Congress passes National Origins Act
- **1925** Scopes trial tests teaching of evolution
- **1928** Herbert Hoover is elected president

Section 5

Clashing Cultures

READ TO DISCOVER . . .
- how Prohibition affected American society.
- what cultural clashes occurred in the United States in the 1920s.
- why Americans closed the door to new immigrants.

TERMS TO LEARN

Prohibition
nativism
quota system
evolution

The Storyteller

During the 1920s many Americans called for limits on immigration. "Refuse the refuse!" was the popular cry of those who cherished "100 percent Americanism." The secretary of the St. Petersburg, Florida, Chamber of Commerce spoke for many uninformed citizens when he declared: "The time has come to make this a hundred percent American . . . city as free from foreigners as from slums."

Anti-immigrant song sheet

During the 1920s the number of people living in cities swelled, and a modern industrial society came of age. Outside of the cities, many Americans identified this new, urban society with crime, corruption, immoral behavior, and foreign influences. They felt that the America they knew and valued—based on family, church, and tradition—was under attack.

Those most distressed by the changing society reacted with fear and anger. A series of battles erupted between two clashing cultures, between those who defended traditional beliefs and those who welcomed new ideas and lifestyles.

Prohibition

The clash of cultures during the 1920s affected many aspects of American life, particularly the use of alcoholic beverages. The temperance movement, the campaign against alcohol use, had begun in the 1800s. The movement was rooted both in religious objections to drinking alcohol and in the belief that society would benefit if alcohol were unavailable.

The movement finally achieved its goal in 1920 with the ratification of the **Eighteenth Amendment** to the Constitution. This amendment established Prohibition—a total ban on the manufacture, sale, and transportation of liquor throughout the United States. Congress passed the **Volstead Act** to provide the means of enforcing the ban.

Much of the support for Prohibition came from middle-class women, who considered it a

SECTION RESOURCES

Reproducible Masters
- Reproducible Lesson Plan 24–5
- Guided Reading Activity 24–5
- Section Quiz 24–5
- Reteaching Activity 24–5
- Enrichment Activity 24–5

Transparencies
- Section Focus Transparency 24–5

Multimedia
- Vocabulary PuzzleMaker
- Chapter Challenger Interactive Review Software
- Testmaker
- GTV: The American People: Fabric of a Nation
- Facts On File: Landmark Documents in American History

progressive social reform, and from rural Protestants, who saw it as a moral crusade. Its supporters hailed Prohibition as a "noble experiment" that would help solve such problems as poverty, unemployment, and domestic violence.

Prohibition Breaks Down

In rural areas in the South and the Midwest, where the temperance movement was strong, Prohibition generally succeeded. In the cities, however, Prohibition had little support. The nation divided into two camps: the "drys"—those who supported Prohibition—and the "wets"—those who opposed it.

A continuing demand for alcohol led to widespread lawbreaking. Some people began making wine or "bathtub gin" in their homes. Illegal bars and clubs, known as speakeasies, sprang up in cities. Hidden from view, these clubs could be entered only by saying a secret password.

With only about 1,500 agents to cover the whole country, the federal government could do little to enforce the Prohibition laws. By the early 1920s, many states in the East stopped trying to enforce the law.

Organized Crime

Prohibition contributed to the rise of organized crime. Recognizing that millions of dollars could be made from **bootlegging**—making and selling illegal alcohol—members of organized crime moved in quickly and took control. They used their profits to gain influence in businesses, labor unions, and governments.

Al "Scarface" Capone, a famous crime lord of the day, controlled organized crime and local politics in Chicago. Defending his involvement in illegal alcohol, Capone said, "I make my money by supplying a popular demand. If I break the law, my customers are as guilty as I am." Eventually, Capone was arrested and sent to prison—for income tax evasion.

Over time many Americans realized that the "noble experiment" had failed. Prohibition was repealed in 1933 with the passage of the **Twenty-first Amendment.**

Nativism

The anxieties many native-born Americans felt about the rapid changes in society contributed to an upsurge of **nativism**—the belief that native-born Americans are superior to foreigners. With this renewed nativism came a revival of the **Ku Klux Klan.**

As you read in Chapter 17, the first Klan had been founded in the 1860s in the South to control newly freed African Americans by the use of threats and violence. The second Klan, organized in 1915, still preyed on African Americans, but it had other targets as well—Catholics, Jews, immigrants, and other groups believed to represent "un-American" values.

In the 1920s the new Klan spread from the South to other areas of the country, gaining considerable power in such states as Indiana and Oregon and in many large cities. For the most part, the Klan used pressure and scare tactics to get its way, but sometimes Klan members whipped or lynched people or burned property. By 1924 the Klan claimed more than 4 million members—about 3.5 percent of the nation's population.

The Klan began to decline in the late 1920s, however, largely as a result of scandals and power struggles involving Klan leaders. Membership shrank, and politicians who had been supported by the Klan were voted out of office.

Fear of Foreigners

The concerns of the Red Scare days had not completely disappeared. Some Americans feared foreign radicals would overthrow the government. Others believed foreigners would take away their jobs. This anti-immigrant prejudice was directed mainly at southern and eastern Europeans and Asians.

New Laws

In 1921 Congress responded to nativist fears by passing the **Emergency Quota Act.** This law established a **quota system,** an arrangement placing a limit on the number of immigrants from each country. According to the act, only 3 percent

CHAPTER 24
Section 5, 708–711

2 TEACH

L2 Debating Ask students to debate the following cultural differences of the 1920s: rural versus urban life, nativism versus foreign influences, "wets" versus "drys," and traditional values versus modern values.

you don't say...

Prohibition expanded Americans' vocabulary. *Bootlegger, speakeasy,* and *hip flask* became part of common speech.

NATIONAL GEOGRAPHIC SOCIETY

VIDEODISC
GTV: The American People: Fabric of a Nation

Side 3, Chapter 7

Title: *Enter the Klan*
Subject: Prejudice in the 1920s
Ask: **What groups faced discrimination in the 1920s?** *(immigrants, African Americans, Catholics, Jews, Mexican Americans)*

Guided Reading Activity 24–5

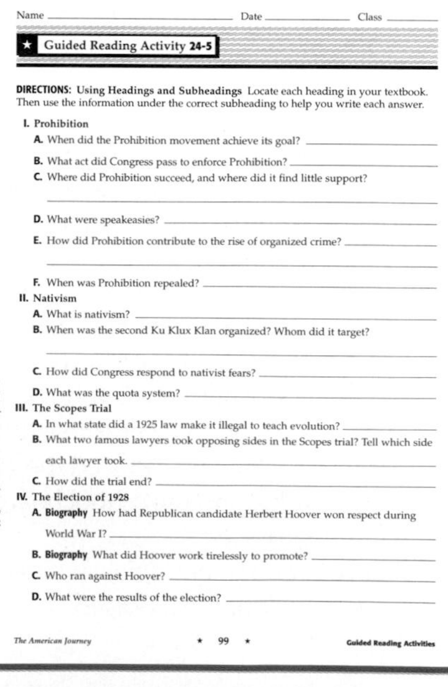

Name ______ Date ______ Class ______

★ Guided Reading Activity **24-5**

DIRECTIONS: Using Headings and Subheadings Locate each heading in your textbook. Then use the information under the correct subheading to help you write each answer.

I. Prohibition
A. When did the Prohibition movement achieve its goal? ______
B. What act did Congress pass to enforce Prohibition? ______
C. Where did Prohibition succeed, and where did it find little support? ______
D. What were speakeasies? ______
E. How did Prohibition contribute to the rise of organized crime? ______
F. When was Prohibition repealed? ______

II. Nativism
A. What is nativism? ______
B. When was the second Ku Klux Klan organized? Whom did it target? ______
C. How did Congress respond to nativist fears? ______
D. What was the quota system? ______

III. The Scopes Trial
A. In what state did a 1925 law make it illegal to teach evolution? ______
B. What two famous lawyers took opposing sides in the Scopes trial? Tell which side each lawyer took. ______
C. How did the trial end? ______

IV. The Election of 1928
A. Biography How had Republican candidate Herbert Hoover won respect during World War I? ______
B. Biography What did Hoover work tirelessly to promote? ______
C. Who ran against Hoover? ______
D. What were the results of the election? ______

The American Journey ★ 99 ★ **Guided Reading Activities**

MORE ABOUT . . .

Agents of Prohibition Isador Einstein, known as Izzy, and his partner, Moe Smith, worked as a team to trap lawbreakers during Prohibition. Masters of disguise, they were a flamboyant pair who used any number of methods to enforce the law. Izzy was particularly adept at going through any neighborhood, for he spoke five languages. He once nabbed an unsuspecting speakeasy owner by disguising himself as a pickle salesman. Together Izzy and Moe made some 4,000 arrests and hauled in about $15 million worth of alcohol.

CHAPTER 24
Section 5, 708–711

Facts On File

CD-ROM
Landmark Documents in American History

Title: *Emergency Quota Act, 1921*
Ask students if any of them would have been prevented from entering the U.S. under the act's limitations.

3 ASSESS

Assign Section 5 Review as homework or as an in-class activity.

Use **Chapter Challenger Interactive Review Software** to review Section 5.

Section Quiz 24–5

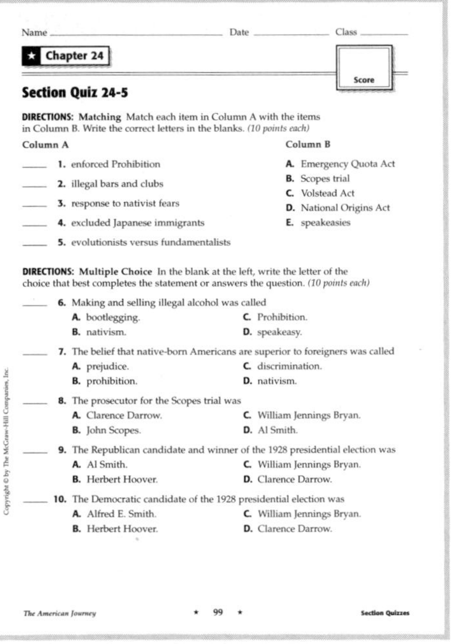
Name ______ Date ______ Class ______

★ Chapter 24

Score

Section Quiz 24-5

DIRECTIONS: Matching Match each item in Column A with the items in Column B. Write the correct letters in the blanks. *(10 points each)*

Column A	Column B
____ **1.** enforced Prohibition	**A.** Emergency Quota Act
____ **2.** illegal bars and clubs	**B.** Scopes trial
____ **3.** response to nativist fears	**C.** Volstead Act
____ **4.** excluded Japanese immigrants	**D.** National Origins Act
____ **5.** evolutionists versus fundamentalists	**E.** speakeasies

DIRECTIONS: Multiple Choice In the blank at the left, write the letter of the choice that best completes the statement or answers the question. *(10 points each)*

____ **6.** Making and selling illegal alcohol was called
A. bootlegging. **C.** Prohibition.
B. nativism. **D.** speakeasy.

____ **7.** The belief that native-born Americans are superior to foreigners was called
A. prejudice. **C.** discrimination.
B. prohibition. **D.** nativism.

____ **8.** The prosecutor for the Scopes trial was
A. Clarence Darrow. **C.** William Jennings Bryan.
B. John Scopes. **D.** Al Smith.

____ **9.** The Republican candidate and winner of the 1928 presidential election was
A. Al Smith. **C.** William Jennings Bryan.
B. Herbert Hoover. **D.** Clarence Darrow.

____ **10.** The Democratic candidate of the 1928 presidential election was
A. Alfred E. Smith. **C.** William Jennings Bryan.
B. Herbert Hoover. **D.** Clarence Darrow.

The American Journey • 99 • **Section Quizzes**

Picturing HISTORY In May 1925 the American Civil Liberties Union (ACLU) placed an advertisement in the *Chattanooga Times* seeking a biology teacher who would test the Tennessee law forbidding teachers to teach evolution. Two entrepreneurs set out to find a biology teacher. They found John Scopes. He volunteered to tutor three high-school boys and introduced the subject of evolution. The school board had him arrested.
Answer: *the role of religion in society, or fundamentalism versus science*

of the total number of people in any national group already living in the United States would be admitted during a single year. Because there had been fewer immigrants from southern and eastern Europe than from northern and western Europe at that time, the law favored northern and western European immigrants.

Congress revised the immigration law in 1924. The **National Origins Act** reduced the annual country quota from 3 to 2 percent and based it on the census of 1890—when even fewer people from southern or eastern Europe lived in America. The law excluded Japanese immigrants completely. An earlier law, passed in 1890, had already excluded the Chinese.

These quota laws did not apply to countries in the Western Hemisphere. As a result, immigration of Canadians and Mexicans increased. By 1930 more than 1 million Mexicans had come to live in the United States.

The Scopes Trial

Another cultural clash in the 1920s involved the role of religion in society. This conflict gained national attention in 1925 in one of the most famous trials of the era.

Picturing HISTORY Opposing attorneys Clarence Darrow (left) and William Jennings Bryan pose during the Scopes trial. **What basic clash of values in 1920s society did the trial represent?**

Opposing Evolution

In 1925 the state of **Tennessee** passed a law making it illegal to teach **evolution**—the scientific theory that humans evolved over vast periods of time. The law was supported by Christian fundamentalists, who accepted the biblical story of creation. The fundamentalists saw evolution as a challenge to their values and their religious beliefs.

A young high school teacher named **John Scopes** deliberately broke the law against teaching evolution so that a trial could test its legality. Scopes acted with the support of the American Civil Liberties Union (ACLU). During the sweltering summer of 1925, the nation followed day-to-day developments in the **Scopes trial** with great interest. More than a hundred journalists from around the country descended on Dayton, Tennessee, to report on the trial.

Darrow Versus Bryan

Two famous lawyers took opposing sides in the trial. **William Jennings Bryan,** Democratic candidate for president in 1896, 1900, and 1908 and a strong opponent of evolution, led the prosecution. **Clarence Darrow,** who had defended many radicals and labor union members, spoke for Scopes. The turning point of the Scopes trial came when Darrow called Bryan to the stand as an expert on the Bible. Darrow's clever questions confused Bryan, and the press ridiculed him.

Although Scopes was convicted of breaking the law and fined $100, the fundamentalists lost the larger battle. Darrow's defense made it appear that Bryan wanted to impose his religious beliefs on the entire nation. The Tennessee Supreme Court overturned Scopes's conviction, and other states decided not to prosecute similar cases.

The Scopes case may have dealt a blow to fundamentalism, but the movement continued to thrive. Rural people, especially in the South and Midwest, remained faithful to their religious beliefs. When large numbers of farmers migrated to cities during the 1920s, they brought fundamentalism with them.

MULTIPLE LEARNING STYLES

Visual/Spatial Review how nativism and fear of foreigners led to cultural clashes during the 1920s. Ask students to make a snowflake out of a coffee filter by following these steps: (a) Fold the filter in half. (b) Fold the filter in half two more times until it is wedge shaped. (c) Cut shapes into the folded edges. (d) Unfold the filter to show the snowflake's design. Discuss with students how each snowflake is different but still a snowflake. Have them write on the edges of the snowflake what makes people different or unique. Then in the center of the snowflake, ask students to write what makes people the same. Relate this activity to how Americans are different but the same. **L3, ELL**

The Election of 1928

The cultural clashes of the 1920s were played out in the 1928 presidential election. The election featured two candidates who represented very different views of American life.

Al Smith campaign button

Hoover campaign poster

Biography

Herbert Hoover

In 1927 President Coolidge shocked everyone by announcing that he would not run for a second full term. **Herbert Hoover** declared his candidacy for the Republican nomination.

Born in Iowa and trained as a mining engineer, Hoover had made millions of dollars in private business and then turned to public service. During World War I, Hoover had won respect as the head of a committee providing food relief for Europe. He showed such a gift in the role that "to Hooverize" came to mean "to economize, to save and share." Later, Hoover ably served Presidents Harding and Coolidge as secretary of commerce.

Hoover worked tirelessly to promote cooperation between government and business. A symbol of the forward-looking middle class, he easily won the Republican nomination.

The Democratic Candidate

The Democrats chose a far different kind of candidate—**Alfred E. Smith,** governor of New York. The son of immigrants and a man of the city, Smith opposed Prohibition and championed the poor and the working class. Many Americans found his strong New York accent jarring. As the first Roman Catholic nominee for president, Smith was the target of anti-Catholic feeling. Hoover won the election by a landslide due to both the Republican prosperity of the 1920s and the prejudice against Smith. The contest reflected many of the tensions in American society—rural versus urban life, nativism versus foreign influences, "wets" versus "drys," Protestants versus Catholics, traditional values versus modern values.

Section 5 Review

Checking for Understanding

1. ***Identify*** Eighteenth Amendment, Twenty-first Amendment, Ku Klux Klan, National Origins Act, Scopes trial, William Jennings Bryan, Clarence Darrow, Herbert Hoover, Alfred E. Smith.
2. ***Define*** Prohibition, nativism, quota system, evolution.
3. ***Discuss*** how Prohibition led to a rise in organized crime.

Reviewing Themes

4. **Culture and Traditions** How did the Scopes trial reflect the desire of many Americans to return to traditional values?

Critical Thinking

5. **Making Inferences** If a presidential election were held today, do you think Herbert Hoover or Alfred E. Smith would be most likely to win? Explain.

Activity

Composing a Song Write a humorous song that someone might have written during the 1920s that pokes fun at the fads of the era.

Reteaching Activity 24–5

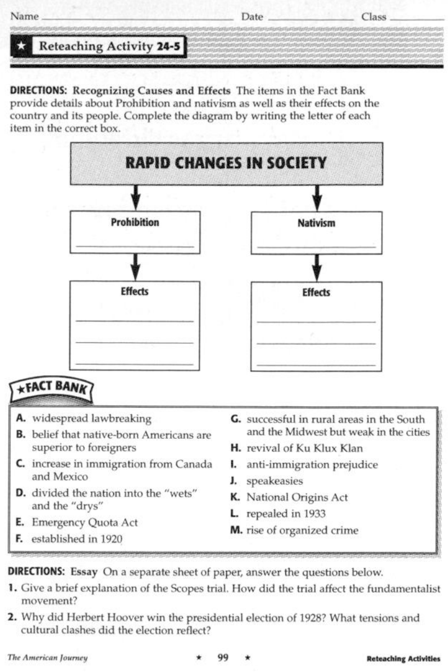

Name ____ Date ____ Class ____

★ Reteaching Activity 24-5

DIRECTIONS: Recognizing Causes and Effects The items in the Fact Bank provide details about Prohibition and nativism as well as their effects on the country and its people. Complete the diagram by writing the letter of each item in the correct box.

RAPID CHANGES IN SOCIETY
Prohibition — Effects
Nativism — Effects

★FACT BANK

A. widespread lawbreaking
B. belief that native-born Americans are superior to foreigners
C. increase in immigration from Canada and Mexico
D. divided the nation into the "wets" and the "drys"
E. Emergency Quota Act
F. established in 1920
G. successful in rural areas in the South and the Midwest but weak in the cities
H. revival of Ku Klux Klan
I. anti-immigration prejudice
J. speakeasies
K. National Origins Act
L. repealed in 1933
M. rise of organized crime

DIRECTIONS: Essay On a separate sheet of paper, answer the questions below.

1. Give a brief explanation of the Scopes trial. How did the trial affect the fundamentalist movement?
2. Why did Herbert Hoover win the presidential election of 1928? What tensions and cultural clashes did the election reflect?

Copyright © by The McGraw-Hill Companies, Inc.

The American Journey ★ 99 ★ Reteaching Activities

Enrichment Activity 24–5

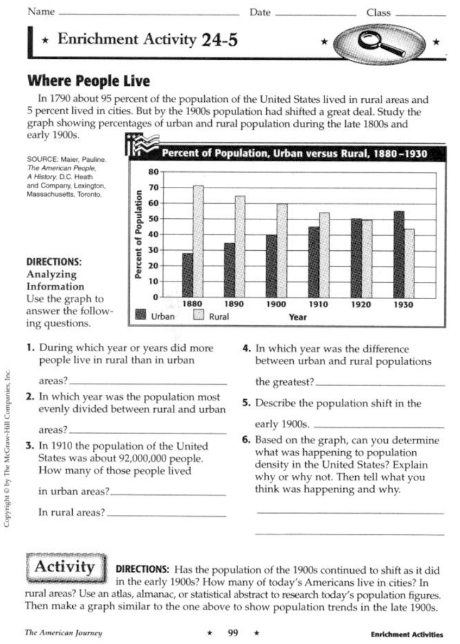

Name ____ Date ____ Class ____

★ Enrichment Activity 24-5

Where People Live

In 1790 about 95 percent of the population of the United States lived in rural areas and 5 percent lived in cities. But by the 1900s population had shifted a great deal. Study the graph showing percentages of urban and rural population during the late 1800s and early 1900s.

SOURCE: Maier, Pauline. *The American People, A History.* D.C. Heath and Company, Lexington, Massachusetts, Toronto.

Percent of Population, Urban versus Rural, 1880–1930
Percent of Population: 0, 10, 20, 30, 40, 50, 60, 70, 80
Year: 1880, 1890, 1900, 1910, 1920, 1930
Urban, Rural

DIRECTIONS: Analyzing Information Use the graph to answer the following questions.

1. During which year or years did more people live in rural than in urban areas? ____
2. In which year was the population most evenly divided between rural and urban areas? ____
3. In 1910 the population of the United States was about 92,000,000 people. How many of those people lived in urban areas? ____ In rural areas? ____
4. In which year was the difference between urban and rural populations the greatest? ____
5. Describe the population shift in the early 1900s. ____
6. Based on the graph, can you determine what was happening to population density in the United States? Explain why or why not. Then tell what you think was happening and why.

Activity **DIRECTIONS:** Has the population of the 1900s continued to shift as it did in the early 1900s? How many of today's Americans live in cities? In rural areas? Use an atlas, almanac, or statistical abstract to research today's population figures. Then make a graph similar to the one above to show population trends in the late 1900s.

Copyright © by The McGraw-Hill Companies, Inc.

The American Journey ★ 99 ★ Enrichment Activities

Section 5 Review Answers

1. Eighteenth Amendment, 708; Twenty-first Amendment, 709; Ku Klux Klan, 709; National Origins Act, 710; Scopes trial, 710; Bryan, 710; Darrow, 710; Hoover, 711; Smith, 711
2. The words are defined in the Glossary.
3. It made bootlegging profitable; members of organized crime controlled bootlegging and used profits to gain influence in business, unions, and the government.
4. Many Americans opposed teaching evolution, which challenged traditional values.
5. Students may note that voters today may admire a candidate like Alfred E. Smith who has an immigrant background and works for the rights of the poor.

Activity Songs should be humorous, poking fun at a 1920s fad.

4 CLOSE

Lead a class discussion on how differences can exist within the mainstream American culture.

GLENCOE TECHNOLOGY

VIDEODISC
MindJogger Videoquiz

Use MindJogger to review the Chapter 24 content.

Chapter 24
Disc 3, Side B

Also available in VHS.

Chapter 24 Review and Activities

Reviewing Key Terms

On a sheet of paper, use the following vocabulary words to write two paragraphs about the "turbulent decade" of the 1920s.

anarchist	**flapper**
deport	**mass media**
lease	**expatriate**
isolationism	**Prohibition**
recession	**nativism**
gross national product	**quota system**
productivity	**evolution**
installment buying	

Reviewing Key Facts

1. Describe the attitude of many Americans toward foreigners and radicals after the war.
2. What role did Presidents Harding and Coolidge think that the United States should play in world affairs?
3. How did electricity change the lives of American consumers?
4. How did African Americans benefit from the Harlem Renaissance?
5. What two laws did Congress pass to control immigration?

Critical Thinking

Making Inferences

Although the 1920s was a prosperous time for many Americans, corruption and scandal were widespread.

1. Why do you think the new prosperity made corruption more tempting?
2. Novelist F. Scott Fitzgerald said that after World War I many people were dedicated "to the fear of poverty and the worship of success." What do you think he meant?

Time Line Activity

Create a time line on which you place the following events in chronological order.

- First movie with sound is released
- Thousands arrested in Red Scare
- Prohibition repealed
- Teapot Dome scandal
- Scopes trial
- Herbert Hoover takes office as president

Reviewing Themes

1. **Groups and Institutions** How did some companies use the Red Scare to turn the public against unions?
2. **Global Connections** How did Presidents Harding and Coolidge feel about the League of Nations?
3. **Economic Factors** What were the advantages of scientific management? Can you think of any disadvantages? What are they?
4. **Science and Technology** What new forms of entertainment were available to the American people in the 1920s as a result of new technology?
5. **Culture and Traditions** Discuss the cultural and political differences between the two major-party candidates in the presidential election of 1928.

Cooperative Activity

History and the Arts With a partner select an American writer or artist of the 1920s. Find and copy examples of his or her work that illustrate some of the turmoil in the United States during this period. Combine your examples with those of your classmates in a booklet entitled "The 1920s through the Eyes of Its Artists and Writers."

Reviewing Key Terms

The key terms used in this activity can be found in the textbook glossary on pages A26–A35. Students' paragraphs should focus on the Roaring Twenties.

Reviewing Key Facts

1. fear and distrust, which led to the Red Scare, racial tension, and a suspicion of unions
2. have a limited role and practice a policy of isolationism, while maintaining world peace
3. Affordable electrical appliances made household chores easier and less time-consuming, which resulted in more leisure time.
4. increased awareness and interest in African culture and pride in being African American
5. Emergency Quota Act and National Origins Act

Critical Thinking

1. Answers will vary but may address the disparity in the distribution of wealth.
2. Answers will vary but should point out that Americans were motivated by both the fear of poverty and the quest for success.

Time Line Activity

Events should be placed in this order: Thousands arrested in Red Scare, Teapot Dome scandal, Scopes trial, First movie with sound is released, Herbert Hoover takes office as president, Prohibition repealed

Reviewing Themes

1. They accused striking workers of being "Red agitators." They turned opinion against strikers by labeling them "Communists."
2. Both were against joining it.
3. Advantages: It made work more efficient, lowered costs, increased productivity. Possible disadvantages: Workers lost independence and pride in their work.

Geography Activity

Study the chart below, then answer the questions that follow.

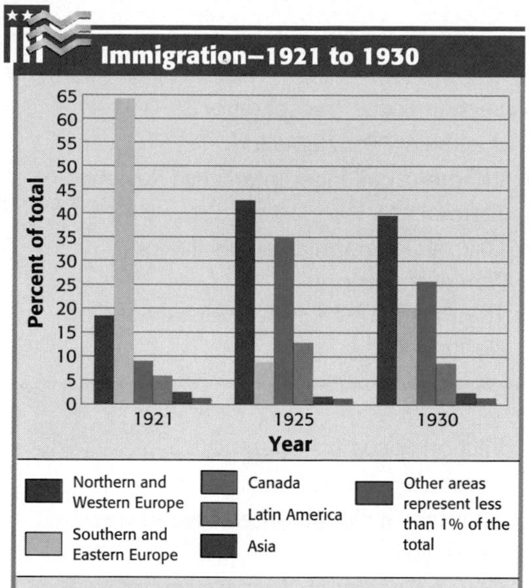

Source: *Historical Statistics of the United States: Colonial Times to 1970.*

1. **Movement** What percentage of immigrants came from Asia in 1925?
2. **Movement** During which year shown was immigration from Canada the highest?
3. **Place** From what region was immigration the highest in 1921?

Technology Activity

Using a Word Processor The 1920s was a time of fads. Look through current store catalogs and magazines for fads of today. Choose one that you think is particularly interesting. On your word processor, write a one-paragraph explanation of why you think this fad developed.

Skill Practice Activity

Making Generalizations

Read the two paragraphs that follow. Then write a generalization about each paragraph that is supported by statements in the passage.

A. Before World War I, women had been arrested for smoking or using profanity in public. Appearing at the beach without stockings was considered indecent exposure, even in cities as large and sophisticated as Chicago.

B. Singing of joy in the face of oppression, jazz contains strands of music from many European countries. Nevertheless, jazz is above all an African American creation, and it could have developed only in the United States. Jazz drew upon field work songs, spirituals, and special funeral music. Other influences were the blues and ragtime. In 1925 J.A. Rogers wrote, "With its cowbells, auto horns, calliopes, rattles, dinner gongs, kitchen utensils, cymbals, screams, crashes, clankings and monotonous rhythm [jazz] bears all the marks of a [noisy, excitable] civilization."

Portfolio Activity History Journal For an entire day record how and when you and the people who live in your household make use of automobiles. Review Section 3 to compare your use of the automobile to that of people who lived in the 1920s.

Geography Activity

1. about 2 percent
2. 1925
3. southern and eastern Europe

Technology Activity

Students should find an example of a current fad and write a one-paragraph explanation of why they think it developed.

Skill Practice Activity

A. Generalizations should reflect the evidence that before World War I it was illegal for women to perform certain activities in public.

B. Generalizations may reflect the origins of jazz and the instruments used.

Portfolio Activity Journal entries should describe today's use of automobiles and compare it to use in the 1920s.

Chapter Bonus Test Question

Ask: What was the title and the author of the first piece of jazz written for the concert hall? *("Rhapsody in Blue" by George Gershwin)*

4. radio, movies, phonographs, tourism, tabloid-style newspapers, large-circulation magazines
5. Differences should include rural versus urban life, nativism versus foreign influences, people for and against Prohibition, Protestants versus Catholics, traditional values versus modern values.

Cooperative Activity

Partners should select one writer or artist from the 1920s and find one or more examples of his or her work that illustrates the turmoil of the 1920s. As a class, students should combine their examples in a booklet titled "The 1920s through the Eyes of Its Artists and Writers."

Chapter 25 Planning Guide

A complete, 1-page lesson plan is provided for each section in the *Reproducible Lesson Plans* booklet.

Section Resources

Daily Objectives	Reproducible Resources	Multimedia Resources
Section 1 **The Great Depression** Examine the causes and effects of the Great Depression.	Reproducible Lesson Plan 25–1 Guided Reading Activity 25–1* Section Quiz 25–1* Reteaching Activity 25–1 Enrichment Activity 25–1	Section Focus Transparency 25–1 Vocabulary PuzzleMaker Chapter Challenger Interactive Review Testmaker GTV: A Geographic Perspective on American History The Presidents: A Picture History of Our Nation
Section 2 **Roosevelt's New Deal** Summarize the programs passed during the Hundred Days.	Reproducible Lesson Plan 25–2 Guided Reading Activity 25–2* Political Cartoons, *New Deal Policies* Section Quiz 25–2* Reteaching Activity 25–2 Enrichment Activity 25–2	Section Focus Transparency 25–2 Vocabulary PuzzleMaker Chapter Challenger Interactive Review Testmaker GTV: A Geographic Perspective on American History Facts On File: Landmark Documents in American History The Presidents: A Picture History of Our Nation
Section 3 **Life During the Depression** Describe how the Great Depression affected American society.	Reproducible Lesson Plan 25–3 Guided Reading Activity 25–3* Section Quiz 25–3* Reteaching Activity 25–3 Enrichment Activity 25–3	Section Focus Transparency 25–3 U.S. History & Art, Transparency 24 Vocabulary PuzzleMaker Chapter Challenger Interactive Review Testmaker GTV: A Geographic Perspective on American History American Music Cultural Traditions
Section 4 **Effects of the New Deal** Evaluate how President Roosevelt's Second New Deal affected the American economy and society.	Reproducible Lesson Plan 25–4 Guided Reading Activity 25–4* Section Quiz 25–4* Reteaching Activity 25–4 Enrichment Activity 25–4	Section Focus Transparency 25–4 Vocabulary PuzzleMaker Chapter Challenger Interactive Review Testmaker GTV: The American People: Fabric of a Nation The Presidents: A Picture History of Our Nation

** Also available in Spanish*

Blackline Master · Videodisc · Audiocassette · Music Program · Transparency · CD-ROM · Software

0:00 **OUT OF TIME?**
Assign the Chapter 25 Digest and the corresponding Chapter Digests Audiocassettes with activities and tests.

ACTIVITY

From the Classroom of...

Corbett Mullins
Hindman City Schools
Hindman, KY

Playing the Stock Market

To illustrate how unpredictable stock investments are and how the crash of 1929 happened, set up a mini stock market in your classroom. Before introducing the activity, create four fictitious companies by making up humorous names to go along with their products or services. For example, an airline could be called "For the Birds Airline." Next, prepare five brief daily reports for each company, including the price of the company's stock for that day. Stock prices should fluctuate depending on the reports. For example, one day the report could announce record ticket sales for the airline with stock at $29 a share; the next day the report could indicate a potential pilots' strike with the stock dipping to $19. Stock performance during the week should fluctuate widely to show how unpredictable the stock market can be.

Organize students into groups of four. Give each group $2,000 in play money. Let groups buy and sell stock in these companies over a five-day period. See which group earns the most money. It is more challenging for students if one company's stock at the end of the week has gone up, one has gone down, and two have stayed roughly the same.

Block Schedule

Block scheduling differs from traditional class scheduling in the amount of time allotted to each period. The extended time frame provided by block scheduling affords you the opportunity to implement a greater number of research-oriented and activity-intense projects to motivate and involve your students. Activities that are particularly suited to use within the block scheduling framework are identified throughout this chapter by the following designation:

NATIONAL GEOGRAPHIC SOCIETY

Teacher's Corner

INDEX TO NATIONAL GEOGRAPHIC MAGAZINE

The following articles may be used for research relating to this chapter:

- "The Okies—Beyond the Dust Bowl," by William Howarth, September 1984.

NATIONAL GEOGRAPHIC SOCIETY PRODUCTS AVAILABLE FROM GLENCOE

To order the following products for use with this chapter, contact your local Glencoe sales representative, or call Glencoe at 1-800-334-7344:

- *GTV: A Geographic Perspective on American History* (Videodisc)
- *GTV: The American People: Fabric of a Nation* (Videodisc)
- *The Presidents: A Picture History of Our Nation* (CD-ROM)

ADDITIONAL NATIONAL GEOGRAPHIC SOCIETY PRODUCTS

To order the following products for use with this chapter, call National Geographic Society at 1-800-368-2728:

- *1929–1941: The Great Depression* (Video)
- *Historical Atlas of the United States* (Atlas)

KEY TO ABILITY LEVELS

Teaching strategies have been coded for varying learning styles and abilities.

L1 BASIC activities for all students
L2 AVERAGE activities for average to above-average students
L3 CHALLENGING activities for above-average students
ELL ENGLISH LANGUAGE LEARNER activities

Chapter 25 Resource Guide

Home Involvement

Home Involvement Activity 25

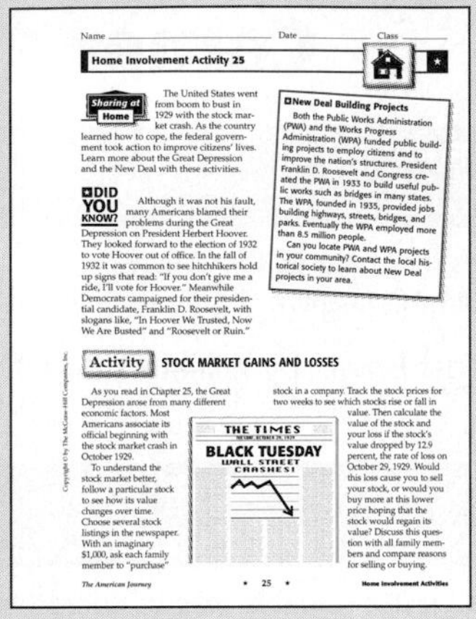

Review Activities

Chapter Summary 25

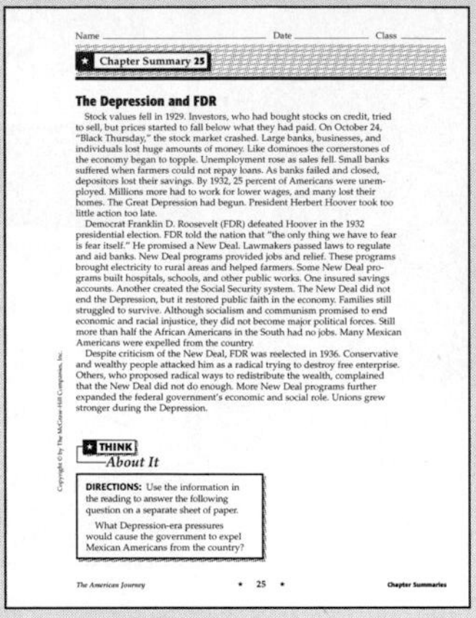

Workbook Activity 25

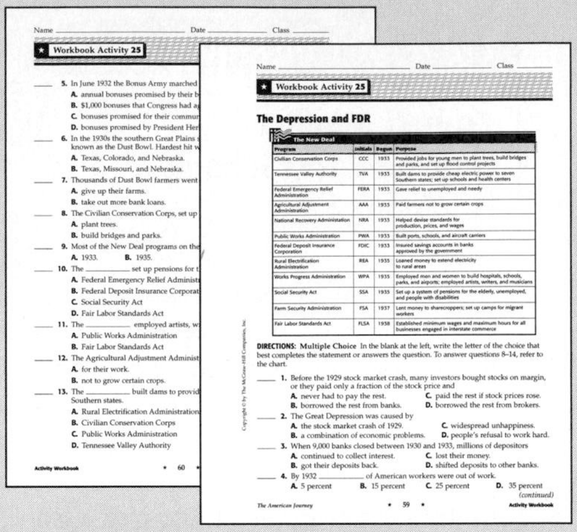

Reinforcement Activities

Time Line Activity 25

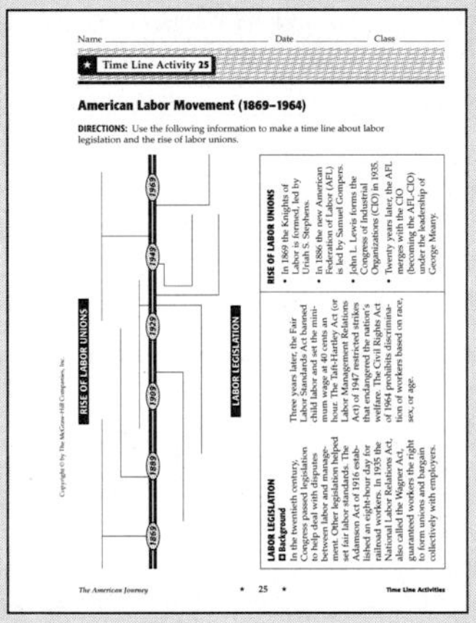

Vocabulary Activity 25

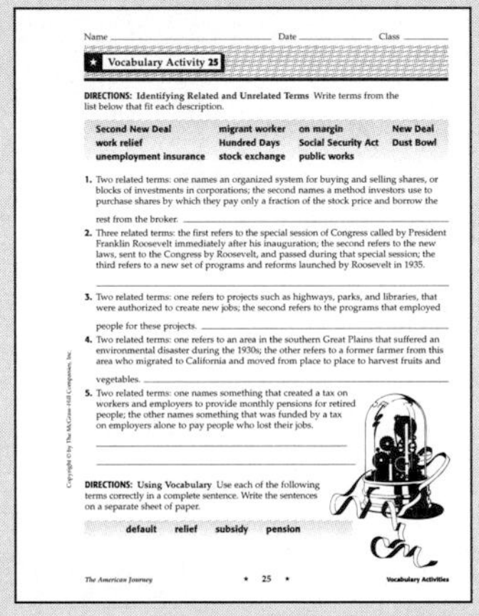

Chapter Skills Activity 25

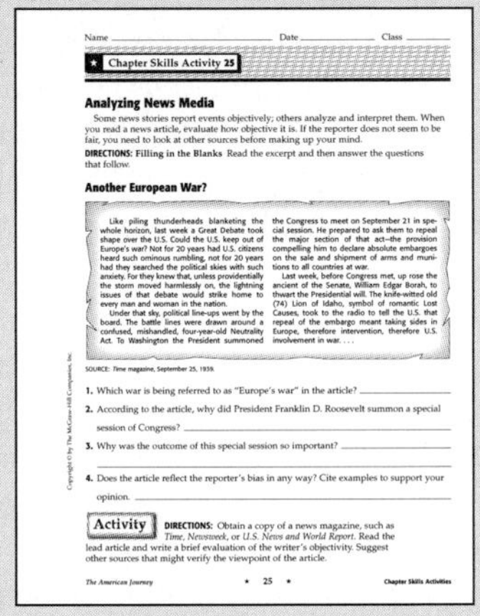

Enrichment Activities

Linking Past and Present Activity 25

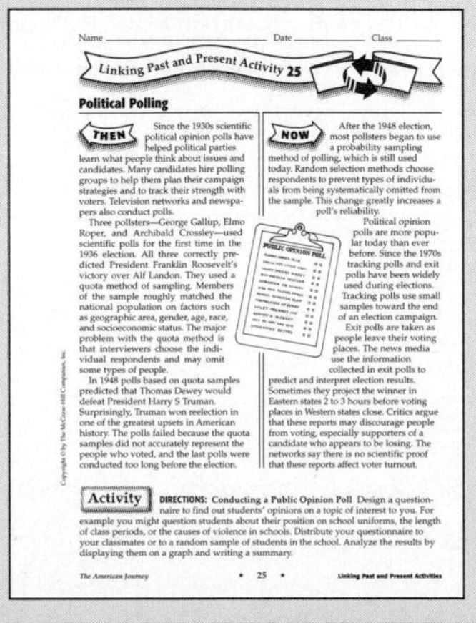

Primary Source Reading 25

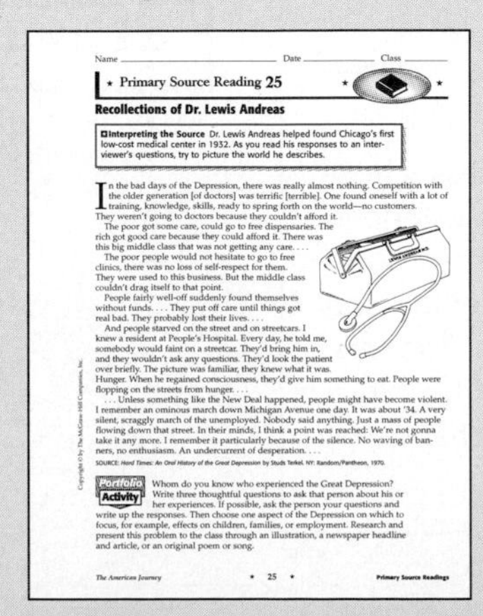

Geography Activities

Mapping History Activity 25

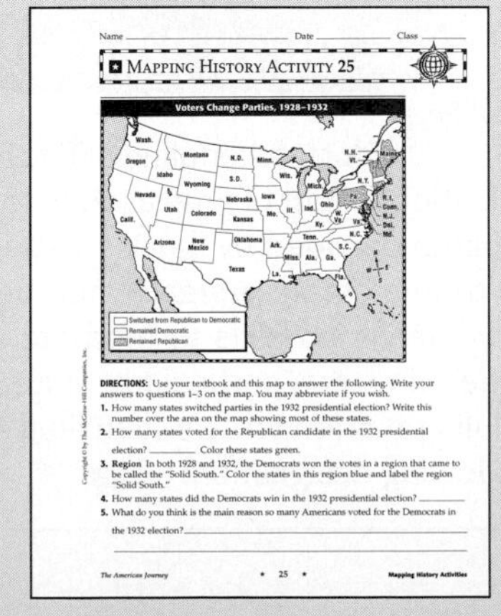

Chapter 25 Resource Guide

Assessment

Chapter 25 Test, Form A

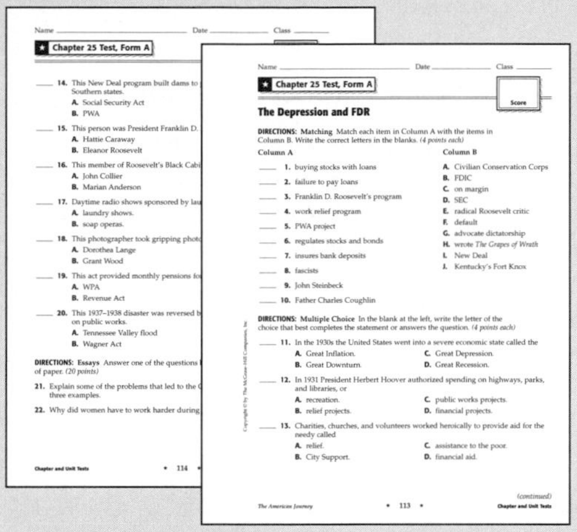

Chapter 25 Test, Form B

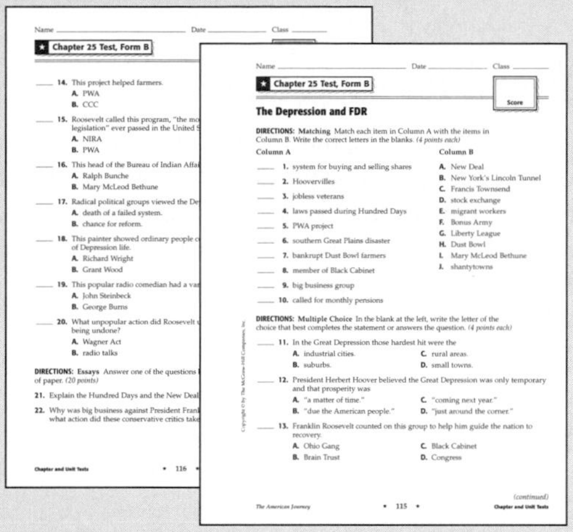

Performance Assessment Activity 25

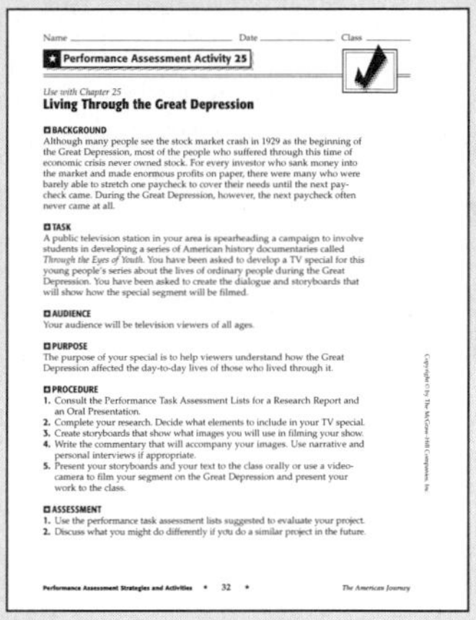

Spanish Resources

The following Spanish language materials are available in the Spanish Resources binder:

- **Spanish Chapter Summary 25**
- **Spanish Vocabulary Activity 25**
- **Spanish Guided Reading Activities, Chapter 25**
- **Spanish Section Quizzes, Chapter 25**
- **Spanish Home Involvement Activity 25**
- **Spanish Chapter 25 Digests Audiocassette Activity and Test**

Activity Manipulatives

Help students learn more about America's cultural history with:

- **American Crafts Hands-On Activities**
- **American Games Hands-On Activities**
- **American History Flash Cards**

Additional Resources From Glencoe

- **U.S. History & Art,** Transparency 24, *Migrant Mother*
- **American Music Cultural Traditions,** Lesson 9: "Talking Dust Bowl" and "Franklin D. Roosevelt's Back Again"
- **Political Cartoons,** *New Deal Policies*
- **The American History Videodisc and CD-ROM,** *The Twenties and the Great Depression, 1920–1940*
- **U.S. Desk Map**
- **Outline Map Resource Book**

A&E HOME VIDEO. Biography THE HISTORY CHANNEL.

The following videotape programs are available from Glencoe as supplements to Chapter 25:

- **FDR: The Years of Crisis** (ISBN 1-56501-511-8)
- **Eleanor Roosevelt: A Restless Spirit** (ISBN 1-56501-405-7)
- **Huey Long** (ISBN 1-56501-534-7)

To order, call Glencoe at 1-800-334-7344. To find classroom resources to accompany many of these videos, check the following home pages:
A&E Television: http://www.aetv.com
The History Channel: http://www.historychannel.com

Introducing CHAPTER 25

Chapter Themes

Chapter Themes are listed by section on this chapter opening page of the Student Edition. A corresponding theme-based activity is available under "FOCUS," and a theme-based question is asked in the Section and Chapter Reviews.

Performance Assessment

Refer to Activity 25 in the *Performance Assessment Strategies and Activities* booklet.

GLENCOE TECHNOLOGY

VIDEODISC
MindJogger Videoquiz

Use MindJogger to preview the Chapter 25 content.

Chapter 25
Disc 4, Side A

Also available in VHS.

HISTORY AND ART Homeless men of the Depression era were often called hoboes. They crisscrossed the country on trains, jumping on the slow-moving freights when railroad guards were off duty or had their backs turned. Wherever hoboes got off the trains, they looked for work and food before moving on again.

Chapter 25

1929–1941

The Depression and FDR

Why It's Important

The boom years of the 1920s had hidden problems. Those problems became visible in 1929, when the nation's economy shifted into a downward slide. The New Deal, created in the midst of the Depression, changed the way Americans viewed government. Before the New Deal, the government usually took little responsibility for the economy's health. The New Deal actively involved the government in social and economic concerns and created the Social Security system, which still affects us all.

Chapter Themes

- *Section 1,* Economic Factors
- *Section 2,* Individual Action
- *Section 3,* Geography and History
- *Section 4,* Government and Democracy

HISTORY AND ART ***Private Cars* by LeConte Stewart** During the Depression, many unemployed workers in search of jobs traveled around the country by hitchhiking on trains.

EXTRA CREDIT PROJECT

Creating a Mobile Invite interested students to create a chapter mobile. First have them scan the chapter for the major events and dates covered. Then have them cut a sheet of poster board into various shapes and sizes. Ask students to depict the events through illustrations or photographs on the pieces of poster board. Instruct students to number the pieces in the order in which the events occurred. Have them attach the completed pieces to a wire hanger with yarn or string. Hang completed mobiles throughout the classroom.

1928 Herbert Hoover is elected president

1929 Stock market crashes

1930s The Great Depression engulfs country

1932 Bonus Army marches on Washington, D.C.

Section 1

The Great Depression

READ TO DISCOVER . . .

- what caused the stock market crash.
- how the Great Depression plunged many Americans into poverty and misery.
- how Hoover reacted to the Depression.

TERMS TO LEARN

stock exchange
on margin
default
relief
public works

The Storyteller

The bubble of American prosperity burst when the New York stock market collapsed in October 1929. Thousands of investors lost all their savings. Wall Street—the nation's financial center—was in a state of shock. Many Americans suddenly found themselves out of work. In 1932 the popular actor and humorist Will Rogers remarked: "We'll hold the distinction of being the only nation in the history of the world that ever went to the poorhouse in an automobile."

STAGE BROADWAY SCREEN
VARIETY 25¢
WALL ST. LAYS AN EGG
DROP IN STOCKS RIPES SHOWMEN
FILTHY SHOW OF SHUBERTS GOOD FOR SCREEN

Stock market crash headline

In the booming economy of the 1920s confident business and government leaders said the nation had entered a new era of prosperity for all. The chairman of General Motors advised people to invest money in the stock market every month—and many followed his advice. "Grocers, motormen, plumbers, seamstresses, and . . . waiters were in the market," reported writer Frederick Lewis Allen. The "market had become a national mania."

Suddenly, in October 1929, the picture changed. Almost overnight the value of stocks plunged. Millionaires lost fortunes, and thousands of less wealthy investors lost their savings. The United States was about to enter its worst domestic crisis since the Civil War.

The Stock Market Boom

A **stock exchange** is an organized system for buying and selling shares, or blocks of investments, in corporations. In the late 1920s, the value of stocks on the New York Stock Exchange climbed to dizzying heights, reaching record levels in September 1929. Because many investors lacked the money to continue purchasing stock, they bought **on margin.** This means they paid only a fraction of the stock price and borrowed the rest from their brokers. Brokers, in turn, borrowed their money from banks. As long as the value of stocks continued to rise, the buyer could sell later, pay back what had been borrowed, and make a profit. If that value fell, though, investors and brokers would not have enough cash to pay off the loans.

SECTION RESOURCES

Reproducible Masters
- Reproducible Lesson Plan 25–1
- Guided Reading Activity 25–1
- Section Quiz 25–1
- Reteaching Activity 25–1
- Enrichment Activity 25–1

Transparencies
- Section Focus Transparency 25–1

Multimedia
- Vocabulary PuzzleMaker
- Chapter Challenger Interactive Review Software
- Testmaker
- GTV: A Geographic Perspective on American History
- The Presidents: A Picture History of Our Nation

1 FOCUS

BELLRINGER
Motivational Activity

Before taking roll at the beginning of the class period, project Section Focus Transparency 25–1 and have students answer the questions. Discuss students' responses.

This activity is also available as a blackline master.

Section Focus Transparency 25–1

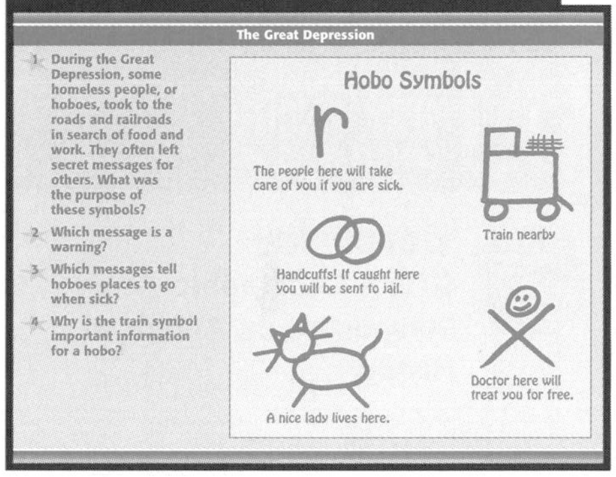

Vocabulary Precheck

Ask students to use the **Terms to Learn** in sentences.

Use the **Vocabulary Puzzle-Maker** to create crossword and word search puzzles.

Section Theme
Economic Factors

The problems that led to the Great Depression began to give warning signals in the early 1920s.

Activity Read the following quote by Herbert Hoover in 1928: "We in America today are nearer to the final triumph over poverty than ever before in the history of any land. The poorhouse is vanishing from among us." Then tell students that in 1929 about 75 percent of Americans lived in poverty or on the very edge of it. Discuss the discrepancies between Hoover's statement and the facts.

CHAPTER 25

Section 1, 715–718

2 TEACH

L1 Creating a Graphic Organizer Ask students to scan the section to find the factors that fueled the Great Depression. Then have them create a graphic organizer illustrating these factors.

Graph Study

Answers

1. 1929
2. 1927, 1928, 1929, 1930, 1931

NATIONAL GEOGRAPHIC SOCIETY

VIDEODISC
GTV: A Geographic Perspective on American History

Side 4, Chapter 3

Title: *Thinking Big*
Subject: The Great Depression
Ask: **What kinds of hardships did Americans face in the 1930s?** *(unemployment, loss of businesses)*

Guided Reading Activity 25–1

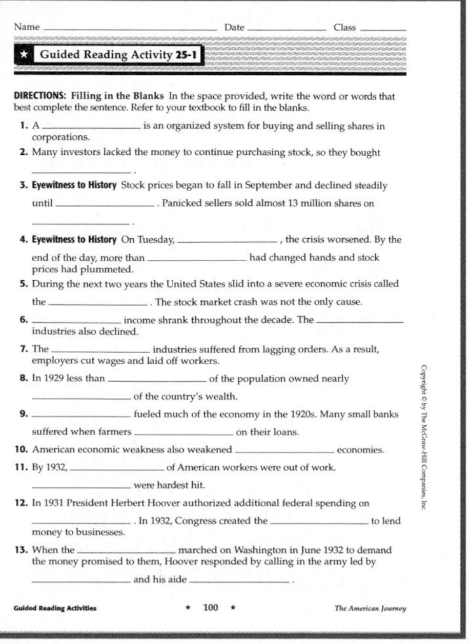

Name ______ Date ______ Class ______

★ Guided Reading Activity **25-1**

DIRECTIONS: Filling in the Blanks In the space provided, write the word or words that best complete the sentence. Refer to your textbook to fill in the blanks.

1. A ______ is an organized system for buying and selling shares in corporations.
2. Many investors lacked the money to continue purchasing stock, so they bought ______.
3. **Eyewitness to History** Stock prices began to fall in September and declined steadily until ______. Panicked sellers sold almost 13 million shares on ______.
4. **Eyewitness to History** On Tuesday, ______, the crisis worsened. By the end of the day, more than ______ had changed hands and stock prices had plummeted.
5. During the next two years the United States slid into a severe economic crisis called the ______. The stock market crash was not the only cause.
6. ______ income shrank throughout the decade. The ______ industries also declined.
7. The ______ industries suffered from lagging orders. As a result, employers cut wages and laid off workers.
8. In 1929 less than ______ of the population owned nearly ______ of the country's wealth.
9. ______ fueled much of the economy in the 1920s. Many small banks suffered when farmers ______ on their loans.
10. American economic weakness also weakened ______ economies.
11. By 1932, ______ of American workers were out of work. ______ were hardest hit.
12. In 1931 President Herbert Hoover authorized additional federal spending on ______. In 1932, Congress created the ______ to lend money to businesses.
13. When the ______ marched on Washington in June 1932 to demand the money promised to them, Hoover responded by calling in the army led by ______ and his aide ______.

Guided Reading Activities ★ 100 ★ *The American Journey*

Stock Prices, 1920–1932

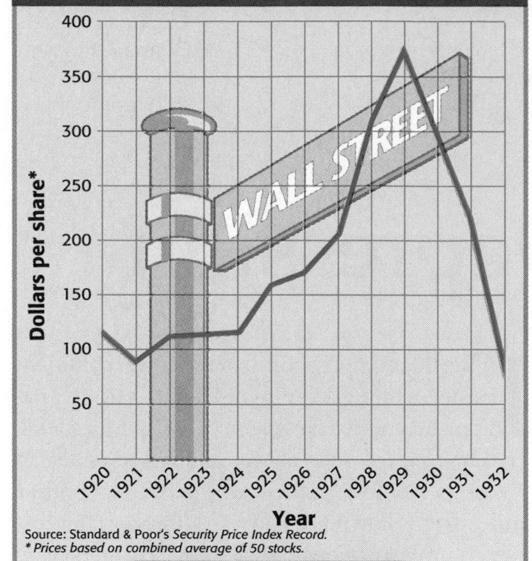

Source: Standard & Poor's *Security Price Index Record.*
** Prices based on combined average of 50 stocks.*

Graph Study

Stock prices rose dramatically in the mid-1920s.

1. In what year did the average share of stock reach its highest price?
2. **Comparing** During what years did stock prices pass $200 per share?

Eyewitness to HISTORY

The Crash

Fearing that the boom market would end, some investors began selling their stocks in late September. Their selling made stock prices fall. Brokers began to demand repayment of loans, forcing investors who had bought on margin to sell their stock.

Prices declined steadily until October 21, but most financial experts thought the market was experiencing nothing more than a "period of readjustment." Then, for 3 straight days, stock prices plunged as investors sold millions of shares a day. Panicked traders sold almost 13 million shares on **"Black Thursday,"** October 24.

Following a few days of calm, the decline and confusion continued on Monday. On Tuesday, October 29, the crisis worsened. By the end of the day, more than 16 million shares had changed hands and stock prices had plummeted. Journalist Jonathan Norton Leonard described the scene:

> "The selling pressure was . . . coming from everywhere. The wires to other cities were jammed with frantic orders to sell. So were the cables, radio, and telephones to Europe and the rest of the world. Buyers were few, sometimes wholly absent."

The New York Stock Exchange closed for a few days to prevent more panic selling. Shock spread across the country.

The Great Depression

During the next two years, the United States slid into a severe economic crisis called the **Great Depression.** The nation's total economic output dropped 43 percent in 3 years, from $104 billion in 1929 to $58 billion in 1932.

While the stock market crash shook people's confidence in the economy, it did not cause the Depression. Other factors, working together, sent the economy into a long tailspin.

An Unbalanced Economy

The problems that led to the Great Depression began to give out warning signals in the early 1920s. Farm income shrank throughout the decade. The textile, lumber, mining, and railroad industries also declined. In the months before the stock market crash, the automobile and construction industries suffered from lagging orders. As a result, employers cut wages and laid off workers. With their incomes slashed, many Americans could no longer afford the consumer goods that the nation's industries had been churning out.

Another factor that fueled the Depression was the growing gap in wealth between rich people and most Americans. The prosperity of the 1920s did not help all Americans equally. In 1929

COOPERATIVE LEARNING ACTIVITY

Organizing Events Organize the class into groups of three to create an illustrated time line. Ask group members to scan the section to gather dates and events leading up to and through the Great Depression. This information should be included on the time lines. Have group members choose from the following tasks: design time line, illustrate each event, and write a caption describing each event. Ask groups to construct the illustrated time lines on a bulletin board or on poster board.

less than 1 percent of the population owned nearly one-third of the country's wealth. At the same time, about 75 percent of American families lived in poverty or on the very edge of it.

Credit Crisis

Borrowed money fueled much of the economy in the 1920s. Farmers, plagued by low prices since the end of World War I, bought land, equipment, and supplies on credit. Consumers used credit to buy cars. Investors borrowed to buy stocks. Many small banks suffered when farmers **defaulted,** or failed to meet loan payments. Large banks, which had bought stocks as an investment, suffered huge losses in the stock market crash. These losses forced 9,000 banks across the nation to close between 1930 and 1933, and millions of depositors lost their money.

International Depression

Weaknesses in the American economy also sapped the strength of foreign economies. European countries needed to borrow money from American banks and to sell goods to American consumers in order to repay their World War I debts to the United States. During the late 1920s, bank funds for loans dried up. International trade slowed down because, without American loans, other nations had less money to spend.

Joblessness and Poverty

As the Depression tightened its grip on the United States, millions lost their jobs. By 1932, 25 percent of American workers were out of work. The unemployment rate remained near 20 percent throughout the decade. Industrial cities were hardest hit. Workers who managed to keep their jobs worked only part-time or for reduced wages.

The newly unemployed felt devastated. New Yorker Sidney Lens, who lost his job, wrote about developing "a feeling of worthlessness—and loneliness; I began to think of myself as a freak and misfit." Long lines of hungry people snaked through the streets of the nation's cities. They waited for hours to receive a slice of bread, a cup

Panic hits the stock market

of coffee, or a bowl of soup from soup kitchens run by local government or charities.

Unemployed people tried to earn a few cents by shining shoes or selling apples on street corners. Those who had lost their homes built shelters out of old boxes and other debris, sometimes grouped together in pitiful shantytowns. Some referred bitterly to the shantytowns as **Hoovervilles** because of President Hoover's failure to act. Across the country Americans wondered why the president did nothing to end the suffering.

Hoover and the Crisis

★ President Hoover thought the economic crisis was only temporary, that prosperity was "just around the corner." He also believed that the "depression cannot be cured by legislative action or executive pronouncement." Instead, Hoover called on business leaders not to cut wages or production of goods and on charities to do their best for the needy. Voluntary action by private citizens and local governments, Hoover said, would pull the nation through tough times.

Charities, churches, and volunteers worked heroically to provide **relief**—aid for the needy. So did state and local governments. Some cities

CHAPTER 25
Section 1, 715–718

you don't say...

Bulls and Bears When the stock market rises, it is called a *bull market.* If prices drop, it is called a *bear market.* These terms come from the way the two animals attack. A bull throws its victims up in the air and a bear knocks its victims down.

NATIONAL GEOGRAPHIC SOCIETY

CD-ROM
The Presidents: A Picture History of Our Nation

Have students select the category Presidents' Birthplaces. Suggest they find whether President Hoover carried his home state in the 1928 and 1932 elections.

3 ASSESS

Assign Section 1 Review as homework or as an in-class activity.

Use **Chapter Challenger Interactive Review Software** to review Section 1.

Section Quiz 25–1

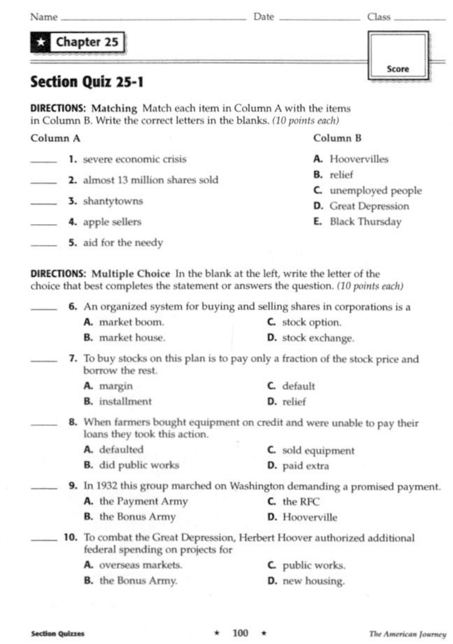

Name ______ Date ______ Class ______

★ Chapter 25

Score

Section Quiz 25-1

DIRECTIONS: Matching Match each item in Column A with the items in Column B. Write the correct letters in the blanks. *(10 points each)*

Column A	Column B
____ 1. severe economic crisis	A. Hoovervilles
____ 2. almost 13 million shares sold	B. relief
____ 3. shantytowns	C. unemployed people
____ 4. apple sellers	D. Great Depression
____ 5. aid for the needy	E. Black Thursday

DIRECTIONS: Multiple Choice In the blank at the left, write the letter of the choice that best completes the statement or answers the question. *(10 points each)*

____ 6. An organized system for buying and selling shares in corporations is a
A. market boom. C. stock option.
B. market house. D. stock exchange.

____ 7. To buy stocks on this plan is to pay only a fraction of the stock price and borrow the rest.
A. margin C. default
B. installment D. relief

____ 8. When farmers bought equipment on credit and were unable to pay their loans they took this action.
A. defaulted C. sold equipment
B. did public works D. paid extra

____ 9. In 1932 this group marched on Washington demanding a promised payment.
A. the Payment Army C. the RFC
B. the Bonus Army D. Hooverville

____ 10. To combat the Great Depression, Herbert Hoover authorized additional federal spending on projects for
A. overseas markets. C. public works.
B. the Bonus Army. D. new housing.

Section Quizzes ★ 100 ★ *The American Journey*

MULTIPLE LEARNING STYLES

Visual/Spatial Explain to students that hoboes left secret messages for each other telling where they might get food, where they could be treated by a doctor, or places they should try to avoid to prevent being sent to jail. Tell students that hoboes used a special kind of picture writing to display these messages. Have students create pictorial messages that might have been helpful to hoboes during the Depression. Ask students to show their messages to the class and have others decipher each message. Discuss how hoboes' secret sign language helped them survive. **L2, ELL**

CHAPTER 25
Section 1, 715–718

Reteaching Activity 25–1

Name ____________ Date ________ Class ________

★ Reteaching Activity **25-1**

DIRECTIONS: Completing an Outline Fill in the outline below by writing the letters of items that could belong under each topic.

The Great Depression

I. The Stock Market Crash
____

II. Other Problems Leading to the Depression
____

III. Credit Problems and the Banks
____

IV. Effects of the Depression on Americans and the World
____

V. The President Calls for Action
____

VI. The President Takes Action
____

★FACT BANK

A. On Tuesday, October 29, 1929, more than 16 million shares changed hands.
B. Charities, churches, and volunteers provided relief.
C. The demand for consumer goods decreased.
D. Unemployment rose to 25 percent in 1932.
E. Farmers defaulted on bank loans.
F. Businesses were asked not to cut wages or production of goods.
G. Large banks suffered huge losses in the stock market crash.
H. Stock market prices plunged.
I. Congress created the Reconstruction Finance Corporation (RFC).
J. Panicked traders sold almost 13 million shares of stock.
K. International trade slowed.
L. Some cities used part of city workers' wages to fund soup kitchens.
M. Automobile orders declined.
N. People lived in box shelters in shantytowns called Hoovervilles.
O. Federal spending on public works was authorized.
P. The gap between the rich and most Americans grew.
Q. Nine thousand banks closed between 1930 and 1933.

Enrichment Activity 25–1

Name ____________ Date ________ Class ________

★ Enrichment Activity **25-1** ★ ★

The Economy

In the 1920s confidence in the American economy was at an all-time high. During the Roaring Twenties people invested in the stock market at a dizzying speed, sometimes investing their whole life savings. Then, in October 1929, the United States's golden era of prosperity came to a disastrous halt when the stock market crashed. Investors lost billions as the value of stocks plummeted. For the next two years, the economic decline continued as the country slid into the era known as the Great Depression. The three line graphs on the right show different aspects of the economy from 1929 to 1937.

SOURCE: Historical Statistics of the United States.

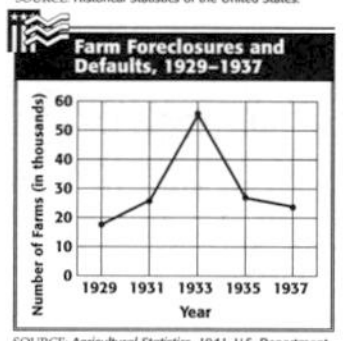

SOURCE: *Agricultural Statistics, 1941*. U.S. Department of Agriculture.

DIRECTIONS: Reading Line Graphs Use the line graphs to answer the following questions.

1. How many people were not employed in 1931? ________ In 1937? ________
2. By about how much did farm foreclosures drop between 1933 and 1935? ________
3. In the same year that about 8 million people were unemployed, what was the rate of farm foreclosures and defaults? ________
4. How many more people were unemployed in 1937 than in 1929? ________
5. Based on the graphs, what was the worst year of the Great Depression? ________
6. Which years showed the sharpest rise in unemployment? ________ In farm foreclosures and defaults? ________

Activity **DIRECTIONS:** Choose one area of the economy from a recent 10-year time period. Draw a line graph to show the changes that occurred during this period. Use the graphs shown on the right as models. Then create two or three questions to accompany your graph and exchange graphs and questions with a partner.

Bonus Army camp, June 1932

withheld part of city workers' wages—already reduced—to fund soup kitchens. But the masses who needed help were simply overwhelming.

Government Action

Eventually Hoover recognized that the federal government had to take steps to combat the Depression. In 1931 he authorized additional federal spending on **public works**—projects such as highways, parks, and libraries—to create new jobs. State and local governments ran out of money, however, and the combined spending by all three levels of government declined.

Hoover tried a different measure in January 1932, when he asked Congress to create the **Reconstruction Finance Corporation** (RFC). The RFC lent money to businesses. It also provided funds for state and local programs providing relief. However, the RFC's directors were reluctant to make risky loans, and much of its budget remained unspent.

The Bonus Army

The march on Washington by the **Bonus Army** turned many Americans, who were already blaming Hoover for the Depression, firmly against the president. Congress had agreed to give each veteran of World War I a $1,000 bonus in 1945. Jobless veterans wanted the bonuses right away. In June 1932, they formed the Bonus Army and marched to **Washington, D.C.,** to demand their money. At its peak the Bonus Army included about 20,000 veterans. Congress and the president turned the veterans down. Most of the veterans left, but about 2,000, joined by their families, vowed to remain until the bonuses were paid. When the police tried to disband the veterans' camp, conflict broke out and two people were killed.

Hoover responded by calling in the army. With tanks, machine guns, and cavalry, troops led by Army chief of staff General **Douglas MacArthur** and his aide **Dwight D. Eisenhower** entered the protesters' camp. Veterans and their families fled in terror as the troops burned their camp.

Hoover announced that "a challenge to the authority of the United States government has been met." Many Americans were horrified that the government had attacked its own citizens, particularly war veterans. Hoover seemed cold, distant, and out of touch with ordinary people. Many people thought the time had come for a change in government.

Section 1 Review

Checking for Understanding

1. ***Identify*** Great Depression, Bonus Army.
2. ***Define*** stock exchange, on margin, default, relief, public works.
3. ***List*** four factors that led to the Depression.

Reviewing Themes

4. **Economic Factors** How did buying stocks on margin contribute to the stock market crash?

Critical Thinking

5. **Making Critical Judgments** Do you think President Hoover followed the proper course in his handling of the Depression?

Activity

Tracking the Economy For one week keep track of references in the media to unemployment. Indicate whether the information was, in your view, positive or negative.

4 CLOSE

Pair students to create a cause-and-effect diagram illustrating causes of the 1929 stock market crash. Ask pairs to explain their diagrams to the class and speculate on how the crash might have been prevented.

Section 1 Review Answers

1. Great Depression, 716; Bonus Army, 718
2. The words are defined in the Glossary.
3. any four: stock market crash, increase in unemployment, large gap between wealthy and poor, decline in consumer spending, reliance on credit, international depression
4. Investors borrowed to buy stock; brokers borrowed from banks; many investors sold stock and prices fell; brokers demanded repayment of loans, forcing investors who bought on margin to sell stock at a loss, often defaulting on loans.
5. Answers will vary but should demonstrate an understanding of Hoover's view that the Depression was temporary.

Activity Students should track references in the media and judge whether the information was generally positive or negative.

Social Studies Connections

Citizenship | Geography | World History | **Economics**

Brother Can You Spare a Dime?

The Great Depression saw "Hoovervilles," such as this one in New York City, and unemployed workers standing on street corners pleading for jobs.

Brother Can You Spare a Dime?" was a popular song in the 1930s during the Great Depression. In those days, prices were so low that if you were lucky enough to have a dime, you could actually buy something with it.

When the stock market crashed in 1929, the economy fell sharply. One quarter of the workforce was unemployed, and those who kept their jobs faced salary cuts. Hourly wages dropped as much as 60 percent. This meant that someone who previously earned 1 dollar an hour was now making only 40 cents an hour.

Few people could afford meat or fresh vegetables, so they lived on beans and soup. To cut down on heating bills, many families heated only one room of their homes. They stopped going to doctors and dentists, and patched their shoes with rubber from tires. People in one Iowa county burned corn to heat the courthouse because corn was cheaper than coal.

Listed below are Depression-era prices for selected foods. Read the list to see how far that "dime" from your "brother" would last.

Prices During 1932–1934	
Sirloin steak (per pound)	$0.29
Chicken (per pound)	.22
Bread (20-ounce loaf)	.05
Potatoes (per pound)	.02
Bananas (per pound)	.07
Milk (per quart)	.10
Cheese (per pound)	.29
Tomatoes (16-ounce can)	.09
Oranges (per dozen)	.27
Cornflakes (8 ounces)	.08

Activity

Budgeting Using the food prices from 1932 to 1934, make a grocery list of what you could buy on a budget of $3.00 a week. Make another list of what you could buy today if you only had $3.00 a week.

More About . . .

Music "Brother Can You Spare a Dime?" with lyrics by E.Y. Harburg and music by Jay Gorney, became the anthem of the Depression. They wrote the song for a musical revue, *Americana,* which opened on October 5, 1932, at the Shubert Theater in New York City. The musical ran for 77 performances and is remembered mainly for this popular song. Americans could relate to the song because it described what had happened to many of them who had worked hard to build a dream only to end up begging for a dime.

Social Studies Connections

Economics

TEACH

Brother Can You Spare a Dime?

Explain to students that budgeting is a way of tracking income and expenses. In this activity students prepare a household budget for the early 1930s and one for today, using $3.00 as weekly income. Discuss what they discovered about a budget based on a $3-a-week income.

Ask students to copy the price list on this page onto a sheet of paper. Have them add another column to the list and go to a local grocery store to record current prices for each item.

CURRICULUM CONNECTION

MUSIC

E.Y. Harburg wrote the song that captured the desperation of the unemployed:

They used to tell me I was
building a dream.
And so I followed the mob
When there was earth to plough
or guns to bear
I was always there right there on
the job.
They used to tell me I was
building a dream
With peace and glory ahead
Why should I be standing in line
Just waiting for bread?

Once I built a railroad, made it run,
Made it race against time.
Once I built a railroad,
Now it's done
Brother, can you spare a dime?

Once I built a tower, to the sun.
Brick and rivet and lime,
Once I built a tower,
Now it's done,
Brother, can you spare a dime?

1 FOCUS

BELLRINGER
Motivational Activity

Before taking roll at the beginning of the class period, project Section Focus Transparency 25–2 and have students answer the questions. Discuss students' responses.

This activity is also available as a blackline master.

Section Focus Transparency 25–2

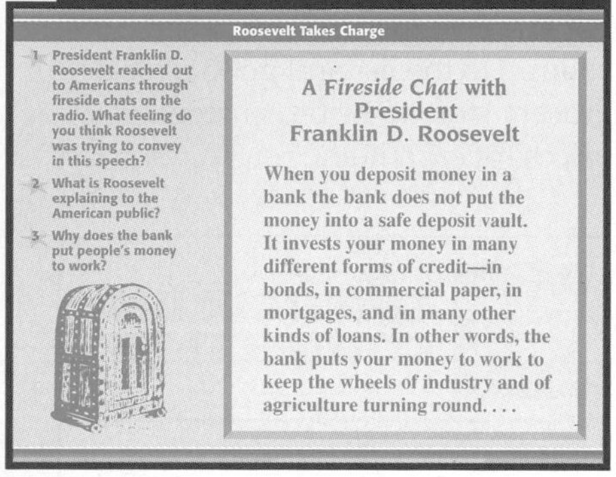
Roosevelt Takes Charge

1. President Franklin D. Roosevelt reached out to Americans through fireside chats on the radio. What feeling do you think Roosevelt was trying to convey in this speech?
2. What is Roosevelt explaining to the American public?
3. Why does the bank put people's money to work?

A *Fireside Chat* with President Franklin D. Roosevelt

When you deposit money in a bank the bank does not put the money into a safe deposit vault. It invests your money in many different forms of credit—in bonds, in commercial paper, in mortgages, and in many other kinds of loans. In other words, the bank puts your money to work to keep the wheels of industry and of agriculture turning round. . . .

Vocabulary Precheck

Ask students to read the definitions of *Hundred Days* and *New Deal.* Discuss why President Roosevelt's name is synonymous with these terms.

Use the **Vocabulary PuzzleMaker** to create crossword and word search puzzles.

Section Theme
Individual Action

Under President Franklin D. Roosevelt's leadership, Americans began to grow optimistic again, as New Deal legislation affected banking, the stock market, industry, agriculture, public works, welfare, and conservation.

Activity Ask a volunteer to read aloud the quote on page 723 by Thomas Stokes describing the Hundred Days. Evaluate whether one person, such as a president, can have such a dramatic effect on a country.

1932 | 1933 | 1934

1932 Franklin Roosevelt is elected president

1933 Programs during the Hundred Days improve the economy

1934 Securities and Exchange Commission is created

Section 2

Roosevelt's New Deal

READ TO DISCOVER . . .

- how Roosevelt reassured the American people.
- what New Deal programs were created in Roosevelt's first 100 days.

TERMS TO LEARN

Hundred Days	work relief
New Deal	subsidy

The Storyteller

Washington, D.C., was dark and dreary on March 4, 1933. President Franklin D. Roosevelt stood bareheaded in the chilly wind, tightly gripping the sides of the reading stand in front of him. His face was stern as he began his Inaugural Address. "This nation asks for action and action now!" he cried.

As Roosevelt spoke, his voice had an electric effect on the masses of people before him. The crowd shouted back its approval. To millions of despairing Americans, Roosevelt's voice was the symbol of hope. It seemed that the gloom was starting to lift.

Roosevelt inaugural button, 1933

With the nation's economy crumbling, the Democrats believed they had a good chance of winning the presidency. Meeting in Chicago in June 1932, the Democrats chose Governor **Franklin D. Roosevelt** of New York as their candidate. Roosevelt—or FDR, as he was called—seemed to bring a fresh approach to politics.

When Roosevelt learned that he had been nominated, he flew to Chicago to deliver the first acceptance speech ever made at a convention. He told the Democrats—and the nation—"I pledge you, I pledge myself, to a new deal for the American people."

Biography

Franklin D. Roosevelt

As the Republicans and Democrats held their conventions in 1932, the Depression grew worse. The Republicans met in Chicago and nominated President Hoover for reelection. With the country's economy in trouble, Hoover's chances for winning reelection looked poor.

Early Years of Promise

Franklin D. Roosevelt, a distant cousin of former president Theodore Roosevelt, came from a wealthy family. Ambitious and charming, FDR decided on a career in politics. In 1904 he married Theodore Roosevelt's niece, **Eleanor Roosevelt,** and she became a tireless partner in his public life.

SECTION RESOURCES

Reproducible Masters
- Guided Reading Activity 25–2
- Political Cartoons
- Section Quiz 25–2
- Reteaching Activity 25–2
- Enrichment Activity 25–2

Transparencies
- Section Focus Transparency 25–2

Multimedia
- Vocabulary PuzzleMaker
- Chapter Challenger Interactive Review
- GTV: A Geographic Perspective on American History
- Facts On File: Landmark Documents in American History
- The Presidents: A Picture History of Our Nation

Picturing HISTORY President Roosevelt explained his policies directly to the people in his "fireside chats" over the radio. **What effect did Roosevelt's radio talks have on the American people?**

FDR's political career began with his election to the New York state senate in 1910. In 1913 he became assistant secretary of the navy, and in 1920 the Democrats chose him as their candidate for vice president. The Democrats lost the election to Warren G. Harding, but Franklin Roosevelt's political future seemed bright.

Then in 1921 polio struck Roosevelt, paralyzing both his legs. Yet FDR's will remained strong. "Once I spent two years lying in bed trying to move my big toe," he said later. "After that, anything else seems easy."

Return to Politics

After a few years, FDR decided to return to politics. He never publicly mentioned his paralyzed legs, and he asked journalists not to photograph his leg braces or wheelchair. Elected governor of New York in 1928 and reelected in 1930, Roosevelt won a national reputation as a reformer. He drew on the advice of a group of progressive lawyers, economists, and social workers—known as the **Brain Trust**—to develop relief programs for the state. When he decided to run for president, he counted on the Brain Trust to help him guide the nation to recovery.

During the 1932 campaign, Roosevelt declared that "the country needs and . . . demands bold, persistent experimentation." He also spoke of trying to help "the forgotten man at the bottom of the economic pyramid."

FDR Takes Charge

The American people were charmed by Roosevelt's confidence and his promise of action. On November 8, they went to the polls and elected Roosevelt in a landslide. He captured all but 6 states and received 472 of the 531 electoral votes. Democrats won important victories in Congress, also. People clearly wanted a change.

In the months before Roosevelt took office, the economy worsened. Protests in some cities erupted into violence. Meanwhile the banking system was collapsing. As more people rushed to withdraw their deposits, more and more banks went out of business. People became desperately afraid.

At his inauguration on March 4, 1933, Roosevelt told the nation that "the only thing we have to fear is fear itself—nameless, unreasoning, unjustified terror." He reassured people and pointed

Footnotes to History

A Presidential Family Theodore Roosevelt was Franklin Roosevelt's fifth cousin. Franklin was also distantly related to 10 other presidents: Washington, both Adamses, Madison, Van Buren, both Harrisons, Taylor, Grant, and Taft.

2 TEACH

L1, ELL Keeping Score Ask students to work in small groups to review the section for information about President Roosevelt's and Congress's actions in the Hundred Days. Then have groups create a scorecard listing when, what, and why action was taken. Encourage groups to graphically illustrate their scorecards.

Picturing HISTORY Roosevelt gave his first fireside chat on March 12, 1933. He announced the reopening of banks.
Answer: *restored confidence*

Facts On File

CD-ROM
Landmark Documents in American History

Title: *First Inaugural Address ("Nothing to Fear But Fear Itself")* Have students read the address and write a paragraph describing how FDR's words affected them.

Political Cartoons, *New Deal Policies*

Guided Reading Activity 25–2

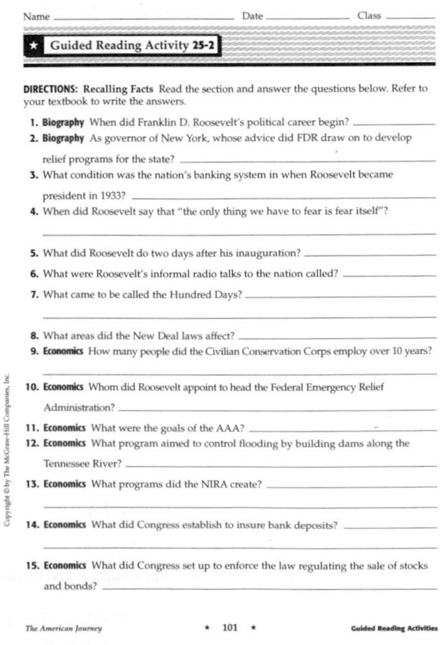

Name ________ Date ________ Class ________

Guided Reading Activity 25-2

DIRECTIONS: Recalling Facts Read the section and answer the questions below. Refer to your textbook to write the answers.

1. **Biography** When did Franklin D. Roosevelt's political career begin? ________
2. **Biography** As governor of New York, whose advice did FDR draw on to develop relief programs for the state? ________
3. What condition was the nation's banking system in when Roosevelt became president in 1933? ________
4. When did Roosevelt say that "the only thing we have to fear is fear itself"? ________
5. What did Roosevelt do two days after his inauguration? ________
6. What were Roosevelt's informal radio talks to the nation called? ________
7. What came to be called the Hundred Days? ________
8. What areas did the New Deal laws affect? ________
9. **Economics** How many people did the Civilian Conservation Corps employ over 10 years? ________
10. **Economics** Whom did Roosevelt appoint to head the Federal Emergency Relief Administration? ________
11. **Economics** What were the goals of the AAA? ________
12. **Economics** What program aimed to control flooding by building dams along the Tennessee River? ________
13. **Economics** What programs did the NIRA create? ________
14. **Economics** What did Congress establish to insure bank deposits? ________
15. **Economics** What did Congress set up to enforce the law regulating the sale of stocks and bonds? ________

The American Journey ★ 101 ★ **Guided Reading Activities**

Cooperative Learning Activity

Creating an Illustrated Chart Organize the class into groups of three to create an illustrated, poster-sized, three-column chart of the New Deal programs. Ask groups to scan the section to list all the New Deal programs mentioned. Then have them create charts with the categories *Agricultural Relief, Industrial Relief,* and *Help for the Unemployed,* listing each program in the appropriate category. Allow members to choose a category to illustrate on the chart. Post charts around the classroom and compare how each group categorized the programs.

CURRICULUM CONNECTION

CIVICS
In 1933 the Twentieth Amendment to the Constitution changed the inauguration date of the president from March 4 to January 20. This change reflects the swifter means of communication and transportation of the twentieth century. The amendment shortens the lame-duck period from the election to the beginning of the president's term. Franklin D. Roosevelt was the last president to have a March inauguration.

NATIONAL GEOGRAPHIC SOCIETY

VIDEODISC
GTV: A Geographic Perspective on American History

Side 4, Chapter 3
Title: *Thinking Big*
Subject: New Deal
Ask: **What did President Franklin D. Roosevelt attempt to do through the TVA program?** *(provide jobs while building dams to use for power, and to prevent floods)*

Chart Study

Answers
1. CCC, TVA, AAA, REA, FSA
2. It safeguarded savings accounts.

Chart Skills Practice

Reading a Chart Which program supported the painting of public murals? *(WPA)*

out that the "greatest primary task is to put people to work." He also promised immediate action on the banking crisis.

Restoring Confidence in Banks

Two days after the inauguration, Roosevelt ordered all banks closed for four days. He also called Congress to a special session, at which he presented the administration's plan for handling the banking problem. About seven hours later, Congress had passed and Roosevelt had signed the **Emergency Banking Relief Act.** The act proposed a wide range of presidential powers over banking and set up a system by which banks would open again or be reorganized. By mid-March half of the nation's banks had reopened.

At the end of his first week in office, FDR assured Americans "that it is safer to keep your money in a reopened bank than under the mattress." The next day deposits far exceeded withdrawals. The banking crisis had ended.

The New Deal

Program	Initials	Begun	Purpose
Civilian Conservation Corps	CCC	1933	Provided jobs for young men to plant trees, build bridges and parks, and set up flood control projects
Tennessee Valley Authority	TVA	1933	Built dams to provide cheap electric power to seven Southern states; set up schools and health centers
Federal Emergency Relief Administration	FERA	1933	Gave relief to unemployed and needy
Agricultural Adjustment Administration	AAA	1933	Paid farmers not to grow certain crops
National Recovery Administration	NRA	1933	Helped devise standards for production, prices, and wages
Public Works Administration	PWA	1933	Built ports, schools, and aircraft carriers
Federal Deposit Insurance Corporation	FDIC	1933	Insured savings accounts in banks approved by the government
Rural Electrification Administration	REA	1935	Loaned money to extend electricity to rural areas
Works Progress Administration	WPA	1935	Employed men and women to build hospitals, schools, parks, and airports; employed artists, writers, and musicians
Social Security Act	SSA	1935	Set up a system of pensions for the elderly, unemployed, and people with disabilities
Farm Security Administration	FSA	1937	Lent money to sharecroppers; set up camps for migrant workers
Fair Labor Standards Act	FLSA	1938	Established minimum wages and maximum hours for all businesses engaged in interstate commerce

Chart Study

Under the Roosevelt New Deal during the 1930s, the federal government assumed responsibility for the welfare of many citizens.

1. Which programs listed above improved the lives of farmers?
2. **Analyzing Information** Why did setting up the FDIC help all Americans?

MULTIPLE LEARNING STYLES

Auditory/Musical Brainstorm with students what makes a folk song popular. If your library has recordings of music by Woody Guthrie or other folk singers of the era, you could play these for students. Ask students to write two verses and a chorus to a folk song about any aspect of the Great Depression. Hold a contest to judge the completed songs. **L3**

American Memories: A 1930s Kitchen

Teapot

Cookbook, 1930s

Coal bucket

What Was It Like? In 1939 President Roosevelt set the next-to-last Thursday in November as Thanksgiving Day. **How do you think Americans celebrated Thanksgiving during the 1930s?**

The president's radio talk was the first of many. He called these informal talks **fireside chats** because he sat next to a fireplace in the White House as he spoke. These fireside chats, which often began with "My friends," helped FDR gain the public's confidence.

The Hundred Days

After solving the banking crisis, FDR quickly tackled other areas of concern. He sent Congress a stack of proposals for new programs to deal with the nation's economic problems. In all Roosevelt sent 15 proposals to Congress, and Congress approved every one of them.

Lasting about three months, the special session of Congress came to be called the **Hundred Days.** It was an amazingly productive time. Optimism swept through the capital. Journalist Thomas Stokes recalled, "The gloom, the tenseness, the fear of the closing months of the Hoover administration had vanished."

The New Deal Takes Shape

The new laws that Congress passed during the Hundred Days—and in the months and years that followed—came to be called the **New Deal.** New Deal laws and regulations affected banking, the stock market, industry, agriculture, public works, relief for the poor, and conservation of resources. These laws changed the face of America dramatically.

Frances Perkins, Roosevelt's secretary of labor, later recalled those early, exciting days of the New Deal:

> "In March 1933, the New Deal was not a plan. . . . It was a happy phrase [FDR] had coined during the campaign. . . . It made people feel better, and in that terrible period of depression they needed to feel better."

Making Connections Activity

Daily Life Discuss how oral history can paint a vivid picture of what life was really like during the Great Depression. Ask students to work in small groups to prepare a list of 10 questions they will use to interview a person who lived through the Great Depression. After groups have interviewed at least one person, have them prepare a two-minute, oral segment using the information from the interview to describe daily life during the Great Depression. **L2**

American Memories

A 1930s Kitchen

Favorite snacks eaten in the 1930s were Eskimo Pies, Popsicles, and Twinkies. The most famous snack eaten in a 1930s kitchen was the Dagwood sandwich named after the cartoon character, Dagwood Bumstead, who first slapped together his famous snack on April 16, 1936.

Ask: How was coal used in a 1930s kitchen? *(fuel for stove)*

Answer: *frugally*

Who? What? Where? When?

Frances Perkins is a woman who has many "firsts" associated with her name. She blazed a trail for other women in government. Perkins was the first woman to be named to the New York State Industrial Commission. In that position in 1919, she became the highest-paid state employee, commanding an annual salary of $8,000. When Governor Franklin Roosevelt, who had named her to that position, became president in 1933, he appointed Perkins secretary of labor and the first woman cabinet member.

Curriculum Connection

ECONOMICS

Because of a surplus of apples, the International Shippers Association set up a system for unemployed people to sell apples. A person could get credit for $1.75 to buy 100 to 120 apples. The person would then sell each apple for 5 cents, making a small profit.

HISTORY AND ART The TVA became one of the nation's largest and cheapest suppliers of power. It also enabled federal and state governments to determine how costly electrical power was, allowing them to better regulate private power companies. **Describe the area in which this power line is being built.** *(rural, open)*
Answer: *controlled flooding, promoted conservation and development, set up schools and health centers*

you don't say...

The Philadelphia Eagles
The owner of Philadelphia's professional football team showed his patriotic spirit in 1933 by naming his club the Eagles, after the symbol of the National Recovery Administration (NRA).

3 ASSESS

Assign Section 2 Review as homework or as an in-class activity.

Use **Chapter Challenger Interactive Review Software** to review Section 2.

Section Quiz 25–2

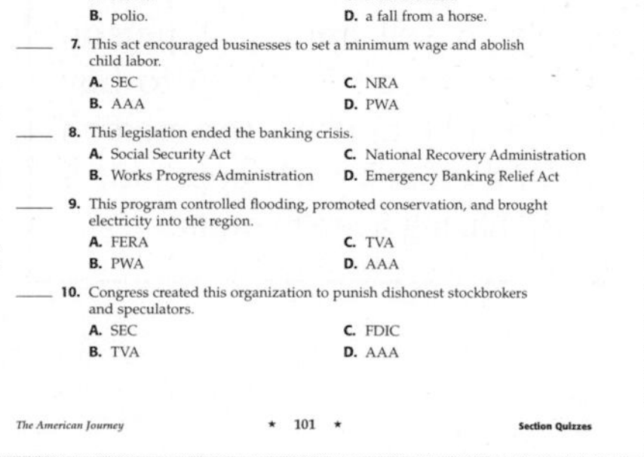

Name ______ Date ______ Class ______

Chapter 25 Score

Section Quiz 25-2

DIRECTIONS: Matching Match each item in Column A with the items in Column B. Write the correct letters in the blanks. *(10 points each)*

Column A	Column B
____ 1. FDR's group	A. radio talks
____ 2. president's fireside chats	B. FDIC
____ 3. laws passed during Hundred Days	C. work relief program
____ 4. Civilian Conservation Corps	D. New Deal
____ 5. insures bank deposits	E. Brain Trust

DIRECTIONS: Multiple Choice In the blank at the left, write the letter of the choice that best completes the statement or answers the question. *(10 points each)*

____ 6. President Franklin Roosevelt's legs were paralyzed when he had
A. the flu. C. a car accident.
B. polio. D. a fall from a horse.

____ 7. This act encouraged businesses to set a minimum wage and abolish child labor.
A. SEC C. NRA
B. AAA D. PWA

____ 8. This legislation ended the banking crisis.
A. Social Security Act C. National Recovery Administration
B. Works Progress Administration D. Emergency Banking Relief Act

____ 9. This program controlled flooding, promoted conservation, and brought electricity into the region.
A. FERA C. TVA
B. PWA D. AAA

____ 10. Congress created this organization to punish dishonest stockbrokers and speculators.
A. SEC C. FDIC
B. TVA D. AAA

The American Journey ★ 101 ★ Section Quizzes

HISTORY AND ART ***Electrification*** **by David Stone Martin** Workers install power lines that will bring electricity to an area of Tennessee. **What other activities were carried out by the Tennessee Valley Authority (TVA)?**

Economics

Jobs and Relief

Roosevelt gave high priority to creating jobs. He planned to help the unemployed with **work relief** programs, giving needy people government jobs. During his first month in office, FDR asked Congress to create the **Civilian Conservation Corps** (CCC). Over the next 10 years, the CCC employed about 2.5 million young men to work on projects that benefited the public, planting trees to reforest areas, building levees for flood control, and improving national parks.

Roosevelt made aid to the poor and suffering another priority. FDR established the **Federal Emergency Relief Administration** (FERA) to give money to the states for use in helping people in need. Roosevelt appointed **Harry Hopkins,** a New York social worker, to lead the FERA. Hopkins became one of FDR's closest advisers and got involved in several other New Deal programs.

Roosevelt did not forget agriculture. On May 12, Congress passed the **Agricultural Adjustment Act** (AAA). The act had two goals—to raise farm prices quickly and to control production so that farm prices would stay up over the long term.

In the AAA's first year, though, the supply of food outstripped demand. The AAA could raise prices only by paying farmers to destroy crops, milk, and livestock. To many it seemed shocking to throw food away when millions of people went hungry. The New Dealers claimed the action was necessary to bring prices up.

To control production and farm prices, the AAA paid farmers to leave some of their land uncultivated. If market prices of key farm products such as wheat and cotton fell below a certain level, the AAA would pay farmers **subsidies**—grants of money—to make up the difference. In the first three years of the New Deal, farmers' incomes rose by about 50 percent. The Supreme Court ruled that the AAA was unconstitutional in *United States* v. *Butler* (1936).

Rebuilding a Region

One of the boldest programs launched during the Hundred Days was the **Tennessee Valley Authority** (TVA), an experiment in regional planning. The TVA aimed to control flooding, promote conservation and development, and bring electricity to rural areas along the **Tennessee River.** By building 5 dams and improving 20 others, the TVA ended the region's disastrous floods. And with hydroelectric power generating affordable electricity, thousands of farms and homes in 6 Southern states were wired for electricity for the first time.

Some critics charged that funds for the TVA should be used to support programs nationwide. Power companies also attacked the program as unfair and communistic. When the spring rains came in 1937, however, the system worked—the dams prevented the Tennessee River from flooding. In the end, most observers agreed that the TVA was an example of successful social and economic planning.

CRITICAL THINKING ACTIVITY

Formulating Questions Have students work in three groups to create and play a *Jeopardy!*-style game called Alphabet Soup. Assign each group one of the following categories to create game cards: New Deal program name, program initials, and program purpose. Using the chart on page 722 as a guide, have groups use a separate index card to write the information about each New Deal program. Collect completed cards to play Alphabet Soup. Rotating groups select the top card and create a question that can be answered by the information on the selected card. Allow other groups to challenge the accuracy of the question. **L3**

★ ★ ★ ★ ★ ★ ★ ★ ★ ★ ★ ★ ★ ★ ★

Helping Business and Labor

On the last day of the Hundred Days, Congress passed the **National Industrial Recovery Act** (NIRA), which Roosevelt called "the most important and far-reaching legislation" ever passed in the United States. The NIRA aimed to boost the economy by helping business regulate itself.

The NIRA created the **National Recovery Administration** (NRA), which encouraged businesses to set a minimum wage and abolish child labor. In addition the NRA tried to set up codes governing pricing and other practices for every industry. **Hugh Johnson,** a former general named to head the NRA, launched a campaign to promote the agency. Before long, the agency's blue eagle symbol and slogan—"We Do Our Part"—appeared everywhere.

Another program that the NIRA launched was the **Public Works Administration** (PWA). Its goal was to stimulate the economy through the building of huge public works projects that needed large numbers of workers. The agency employed people to work on the construction of roads, shipyards, hospitals, city halls, and schools. Many PWA projects—such as New York City's Lincoln Tunnel and Kentucky's Fort Knox—still stand. The PWA spent its funds slowly, though, and did not have much immediate impact on unemployment.

Quilt displaying NRA emblem

To avoid future banking crises, Roosevelt called for reform of the nation's financial system. Congress established the **Federal Deposit Insurance Corporation** (FDIC) to insure bank deposits. The government guaranteed that money placed in a bank insured by the FDIC would not be lost if the bank failed.

Congress also passed a law regulating the sale of stocks and bonds and created the **Securities and Exchange Commission** (SEC). This 1934 law gave the SEC the power to punish dishonest stockbrokers and speculators.

Assessing the Early New Deal

The New Deal did not cure the nation's ills. The Depression dragged on, bringing continued hardship. Farmers continued to lose their land. Unemployment remained at high levels. Many people still struggled to survive and to make ends meet.

Yet the darkest days had passed. The panic of 1932 and 1933 had receded, and the flurry of activity from the nation's capital had restored some measure of confidence.

★ ★ ★ ★ ★ ★ Section 2 Review ★ ★ ★ ★ ★ ★

Checking for Understanding

1. ***Identify*** Franklin D. Roosevelt, Civilian Conservation Corps, Harry Hopkins, Tennessee Valley Authority, National Recovery Administration.
2. ***Define*** Hundred Days, New Deal, work relief, subsidy.
3. ***Discuss*** actions that President Roosevelt took to restore public confidence in banks and in the stock exchange.

Reviewing Themes

4. **Individual Action** What programs did Roosevelt create to provide work relief?

Critical Thinking

5. **Making Comparisons** Compare Hoover's and Roosevelt's programs to combat the Depression.

Activity

Making a Table Create a table that lists the positive and negative aspects of the New Deal farm program.

★ ★ ★ ★ ★ ★ ★ Section 2 Review Answers ★ ★ ★ ★ ★ ★ ★

1. Franklin D. Roosevelt, 720; Civilian Conservation Corps, 724; Harry Hopkins, 724; Tennessee Valley Authority, 724; National Recovery Administration, 725
2. The words are defined in the Glossary.
3. signed the Emergency Banking Relief Act, fireside chats, created FDIC and SEC
4. FERA, CCC, WPA, PWA
5. Hoover: programs involving businesses, private citizens, and local governments—not federal government; Roosevelt: wide range of federal programs

Activity Tables should show how the AAA, FSA, and REA affected farmers both positively and negatively.

CHAPTER 25
Section 2, 720–725

Reteaching Activity 25–2

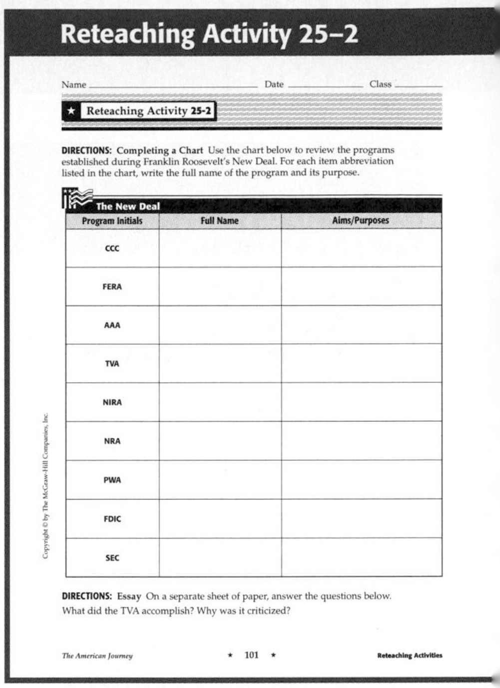

Name ______ Date ______ Class ______

★ Reteaching Activity **25-2**

DIRECTIONS: Completing a Chart Use the chart below to review the programs established during Franklin Roosevelt's New Deal. For each item abbreviation listed in the chart, write the full name of the program and its purpose.

The New Deal

Program Initials	Full Name	Aims/Purposes
CCC		
FERA		
AAA		
TVA		
NIRA		
NRA		
PWA		
FDIC		
SEC		

DIRECTIONS: Essay On a separate sheet of paper, answer the questions below.
What did the TVA accomplish? Why was it criticized?

The American Journey ★ 101 ★ **Reteaching Activities**

Enrichment Activity 25–2

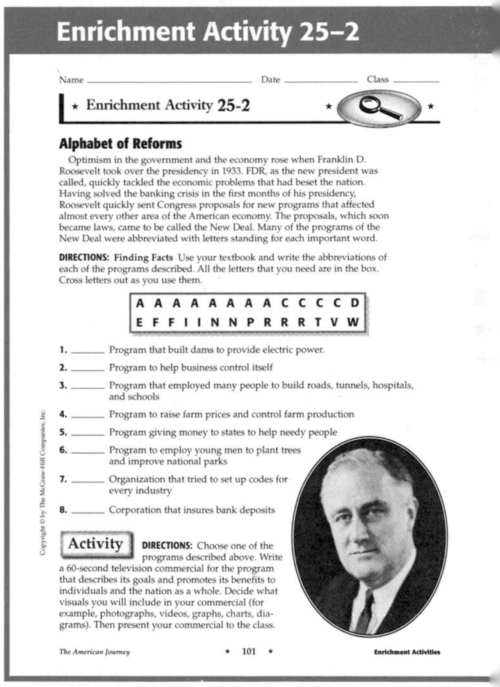

Name ______ Date ______ Class ______

★ Enrichment Activity 25-2 ★ ★

Alphabet of Reforms

Optimism in the government and the economy rose when Franklin D. Roosevelt took over the presidency in 1933. FDR, as the new president was called, quickly tackled the economic problems that had beset the nation. Having solved the banking crisis in the first months of his presidency, Roosevelt quickly sent Congress proposals for new programs that affected almost every other area of the American economy. The proposals, which soon became laws, came to be called the New Deal. Many of the programs of the New Deal were abbreviated with letters standing for each important word.

DIRECTIONS: Finding Facts Use your textbook and write the abbreviations of each of the programs described. All the letters that you need are in the box. Cross letters out as you use them.

A	A	A	A	A	A	A	A	C	C	C	C	D
E	F	F	I	I	N	N	P	R	R	R	T	V	W

1. ______ Program that built dams to provide electric power.
2. ______ Program to help business control itself
3. ______ Program that employed many people to build roads, tunnels, hospitals, and schools
4. ______ Program to raise farm prices and control farm production
5. ______ Program giving money to states to help needy people
6. ______ Program to employ young men to plant trees and improve national parks
7. ______ Organization that tried to set up codes for every industry
8. ______ Corporation that insures bank deposits

Activity **DIRECTIONS:** Choose one of the programs described above. Write a 60-second television commercial for the program that describes its goals and promotes its benefits to individuals and the nation as a whole. Decide what visuals you will include in your commercial (for example, photographs, videos, graphs, charts, diagrams). Then present your commercial to the class.

The American Journey ★ 101 ★ **Enrichment Activities**

4 CLOSE

Have students review the scorecards they created in the "TEACH" activity. Ask them to evaluate which act they think had the greatest effect on correcting the American economy.

NATIONAL GEOGRAPHIC

Journeys

NATIONAL GEOGRAPHIC SOCIETY

VIDEODISC
GTV: A Geographic Perspective on American History

Side 4, Chapter 2

Title: *On the Move*
Subject: U.S. migration patterns
Ask: **Identify the three migration patterns that took place in the first 30 years of the twentieth century.** *(migration from South to North during World War I, migration from farm to factory, and migration from the Great Plains to the West in the 1930s)*

Who?What?Where?When?

Woody Guthrie is a legendary folk singer and folk song writer. He wrote more than 1,000 songs, mostly about the struggles of the common people during the Great Depression. You may wish to play some of Guthrie's songs such as "Union Maid," "So Long, It's Been Good to Know Yuh (Dusty Old Dust)," and "This Land Is Your Land."

CURRICULUM CONNECTION

HEALTH
"Black blizzards," with winds gusting up to 60 miles per hour, engulfed entire towns in the Dust Bowl. People caught outside covered their faces with cloth, terrified that the air would become too thick to breathe. Some without protection died of suffocation. Others caught "dust pneumonia," or the slow accumulation of dust in the lungs.

2 **Tough times show in the faces of this migrant family traveling west in 1936. Like many looking for seasonal jobs, this family hoped to pick cotton in the fields south of Needles, California.**

4 **Determined to find a better life, these Dust Bowl refugees trudge down the highway toward Los Angeles, California, in March 1937.**

3 **Some families' autos stalled on the road. But most kept going and—in folk-singer Woody Guthrie's words—"rattled down that highway/To never come back again." Homesteaders and sharecroppers had depleted the dry, sandy soil back home and most migrants never returned to the land that could no longer feed them.**

TEACHER'S NOTES

NATIONAL GEOGRAPHIC

Journeys

1 **Depression and drought drove half a million migrants west during the 1930s. Abandoning the Dust Bowl states of the Great Plains, many of the migrants headed across Route 66 bound for California, the land of opportunity and hope.**

A Hard Times Road

“Highway 66 is the path of a people in flight, refugees from the dust and shrinking land, from the thunder of tractors and shrinking ownership... from the twisting winds that howl up out of Texas, from the floods that ... steal what richness is there.... They come into 66 from the tributary side roads, from the wagon tracks and the rutted country roads. 66 is the mother road, the road of flight.”

—*From* The Grapes of Wrath *by John Steinbeck, published in 1939.*

727

NATIONAL GEOGRAPHIC SOCIETY

CD-ROM
The Presidents: A Picture History of Our Nation

Have students select Time Line from the main menu. Suggest they write headlines noting major events during President Franklin D. Roosevelt's terms in office.

you don't say...

Dust Bowl The term *dust bowl* was first used by Associated Press reporter Robert Geiger in a story published in April 1935.

What? Where? When? Who?

Bibliography The excerpt at left is taken from John Steinbeck's *The Grapes of Wrath,* published in 1939. Reprint New York: Penguin Books, 1981.

CURRICULUM CONNECTION

GEOGRAPHY
The first of the great dust storms began on November 11, 1933. In South Dakota the sky was pitch dark by noon. Historian William Manchester wrote that by the time the sun reappeared, “fields had been replaced by sand while roads, trees, sheds, fences, and machinery had disappeared beneath great hanging dunes of soil. By then the wind was headed for Texas. A towering pall darkened Chicago and was visible as far east as Albany.” The dust storms continued on and off for 10 years. The westerly winds carried the dust as much as 300 miles into the Atlantic, depositing it on ships that plied the ocean.

TEACHER'S NOTES

CHAPTER 25
Section 3, 728–732

1 FOCUS

BELLRINGER
Motivational Activity

Before taking roll at the beginning of the class period, project Section Focus Transparency 25–3 and have students answer the questions. Discuss students' responses.

This activity is also available as a blackline master.

Section Focus Transparency 25–3

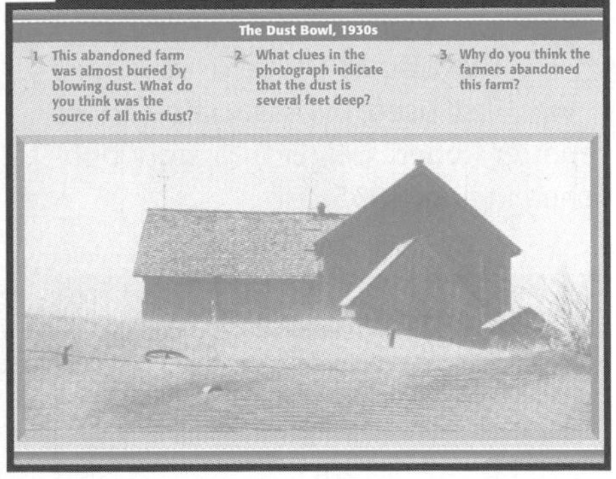

Vocabulary Precheck

Ask volunteers to use both terms in one cause-and-effect sentence.

Use the **Vocabulary PuzzleMaker** to create crossword and word search puzzles.

Section Theme
Geography and History

The southern Great Plains suffered an environmental disaster during the Great Depression, resulting in a large migration of people from the region.

Activity Discuss how the Depression affected the different geographic regions of the United States and how Americans in those regions reacted. Brainstorm ways in which the present-day economy affects different regions.

1930 — 1935 — 1940

1932 Hattie Caraway is elected first woman senator

1934 Indian Reorganization Act is passed

1939 *Gone With the Wind* film is released

Section 3

Life During the Depression

READ TO DISCOVER . . .
- how the Depression affected minority groups.
- what radical political movements gained influence during the Depression.

TERMS TO LEARN

Dust Bowl
migrant worker

The Storyteller

"They hung around street corners and in groups. . . . They felt despised, they were ashamed of themselves. They cringed, they comforted one another. They avoided home." With these words, a social worker described unemployed Pennsylvania coal miners. Their pain was echoed across America by countless men, women, and children whose hopes were being crushed by the Depression.

Soup kitchen

Not every worker lost a job during the Depression. Not every family needed aid. Most Americans, however, had to make do with less—less income, less food, and less security.

Hard Times in America

Some families survived the Depression by pulling together. Parents and children shared homes with grandparents or other relatives to save money. Although the birthrate had decreased, school enrollment actually increased; because fewer young people could find work, they remained in school.

The strain shattered other families, however. Nearly 2 million men—and a much smaller number of women—abandoned their homes. They took to the road, drifting to warm places such as Florida and California.

Women Go to Work

Many people thought that women should not hold jobs as long as men were unemployed. Despite such prejudices, desperation drove a large number of women into the workforce. Many families survived on a woman's income—even though American women earned less than men.

Women also worked harder at home to make ends meet. Instead of buying clothes or groceries,

---

SECTION RESOURCES

Reproducible Masters
- Guided Reading Activity 25–3
- Section Quiz 25–3
- Reteaching Activity 25–3
- Enrichment Activity 25–3

Transparencies
- Section Focus Transparency 25–3
- U.S. History & Art, Transparency 24

Multimedia
- Vocabulary PuzzleMaker
- Chapter Challenger Interactive Review
- Testmaker
- GTV: A Geographic Perspective on American History
- American Music Cultural Traditions, Lesson 9: "Talking Dust Bowl" and "Franklin D. Roosevelt's Back Again"

they sewed their own clothing, baked their own bread, and canned their own vegetables. Some women started home businesses such as laundries or boardinghouses.

The New Deal era opened doors for women in public life. President Roosevelt appointed the first woman ever to serve in the cabinet, **Frances Perkins.** He also named more than 100 other women to federal posts. One—Ellen Sullivan Woodward—started a program to give jobs to women. In 1932 **Hattie Caraway** of Arkansas became the first woman to be elected to the United States Senate.

The best-known woman in American public life was **Eleanor Roosevelt,** who often acted as her husband's "eyes and ears." She made many fact-finding trips for the president because polio had limited his mobility. Mrs. Roosevelt campaigned vigorously for women and minorities and other humanitarian concerns. She wrote a daily newspaper column and used her boundless energy to meet people all over the country.

Eyewitness to HISTORY

The Dust Bowl

The southern Great Plains suffered an environmental disaster during the 1930s. Hardest hit were western Kansas and Oklahoma, northern Texas, and eastern Colorado and New Mexico—the region dubbed the **Dust Bowl.**

Dust Bowl Migration

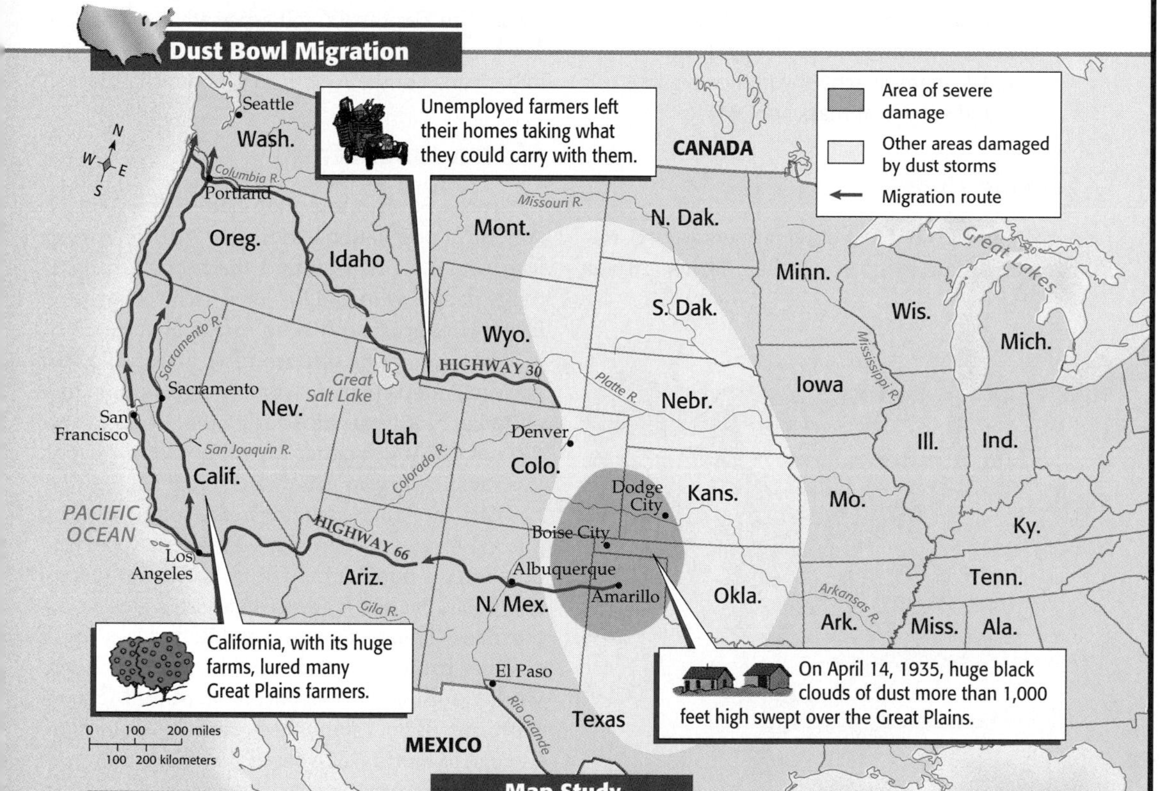

Map Study

During the Dust Bowl years of the 1930s, farmers from the Great Plains headed west in search of a better life.

1. **Movement** Along what two routes did the farmers travel?
2. **Analyzing Information** What states were severely affected by the dust storms?

Cooperative Learning Activity

Creating a Booklet Organize the class into groups of five to create a booklet depicting how the Great Depression affected these groups of Americans: women, children, African Americans, Native Americans, and Hispanic Americans. Ask students to choose one of these groups and write a one-page account describing the hardships this group faced. Then have members paste each account on a separate sheet of construction paper and create a cover for the booklet. Ask groups to illustrate each page and bind the sheets together to form a booklet.

2 TEACH

L1, ELL Illustrating Agriculture Ask students to locate photographs that show modern methods of irrigation and agricultural practices. At the conclusion of this section, ask students to write a paragraph in which they argue whether another dust bowl in the United States is possible today.

History *and the* Humanities

U.S. History & Art, Transparency 24, *Migrant Mother*

American Music Cultural Traditions, Lesson 9: "Talking Dust Bowl" and "Franklin D. Roosevelt's Back Again"

Guided Reading Activity 25–3

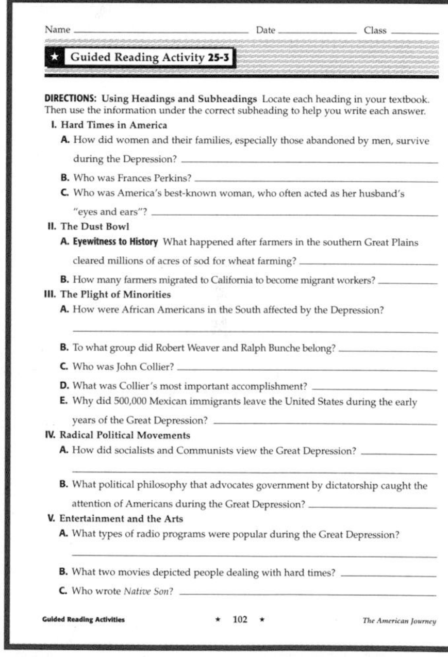
Name ______ Date ______ Class ______

Guided Reading Activity 25-3

DIRECTIONS: Using Headings and Subheadings Locate each heading in your textbook. Then use the information under the correct subheading to help you write each answer.

I. Hard Times in America
A. How did women and their families, especially those abandoned by men, survive during the Depression? ______
B. Who was Frances Perkins? ______
C. Who was America's best-known woman, who often acted as her husband's "eyes and ears"? ______

II. The Dust Bowl
A. Eyewitness to History What happened after farmers in the southern Great Plains cleared millions of acres of sod for wheat farming? ______
B. How many farmers migrated to California to become migrant workers? ______

III. The Plight of Minorities
A. How were African Americans in the South affected by the Depression? ______
B. To what group did Robert Weaver and Ralph Bunche belong? ______
C. Who was John Collier? ______
D. What was Collier's most important accomplishment? ______
E. Why did 500,000 Mexican immigrants leave the United States during the early years of the Great Depression? ______

IV. Radical Political Movements
A. How did socialists and Communists view the Great Depression? ______
B. What political philosophy that advocates government by dictatorship caught the attention of Americans during the Great Depression? ______

V. Entertainment and the Arts
A. What types of radio programs were popular during the Great Depression? ______
B. What two movies depicted people dealing with hard times? ______
C. Who wrote *Native Son*? ______

Guided Reading Activities ★ 102 ★ *The American Journey*

Copyright © by The McGraw-Hill Companies, Inc.

Map Study

Answers

1. Highways 66 and 30
2. Colorado, Kansas, Oklahoma, Texas, New Mexico

Map Skills Practice

Reading a Map In what directions did farmers move? *(northwest and west)*

NATIONAL GEOGRAPHIC SOCIETY

VIDEODISC
GTV: A Geographic Perspective on American History

Side 4, Chapter 3
Title: *Thinking Big*
Subject: Dust Bowl
Ask: **What role did people play in causing the Dust Bowl disaster?** *(They had plowed up and grazed livestock on the grasslands. This led to soil erosion.)*

What?Where?When?Who?

The War of the Worlds On October 30, 1938, Orson Welles announced at the beginning of his radio show that he was about to present an adaptation of H.G. Wells's book, *The War of the Worlds.* Many Americans tuned in late, however, only to hear "news flashes" reporting the invasion of armed Martians. Terror-stricken Americans panicked, calling the police, packing their bags, or simply huddling in their homes. Welles issued an apology and WCBS announced repeatedly that it had been a hoax. Nevertheless, stunned Americans recognized the power of live radio.

Picturing HISTORY Dorothea Lange ran a portrait business in San Francisco for 10 years. When the Depression struck, Lange became a documentary photographer. By the mid-1930s her photographs earned her a position with the Farm Security Administration. Lange later traveled through the Dust Bowl states, capturing people's suffering in a book called *An American Exodus, A Record of Human Erosion.*
Answer: *They migrated to California.*

What Caused the Dust Bowl?

Using new technology such as tractors and disc plows, farmers had cleared millions of acres of sod for wheat farming. They did not realize that the roots of the grass had held the soil in place. When a severe drought struck in 1931, crops died and the soil dried out. Strong prairie winds simply blew the soil away.

Each storm stripped away more soil. One storm in 1934 carried about 300 million tons of soil, depositing some of it on ships 300 miles out in the Atlantic Ocean. The drought—and the storms—continued for years.

People called the storms "black blizzards." A Texas boy wrote:

> "These storms were like rolling black smoke. We had to keep the lights on all day. We went to school with headlights on, and with dust masks on."

Leaving Home

Thousands of Dust Bowl farmers went bankrupt and had to give up their farms. About 300,000 farmers migrated to California and became **migrant workers,** moving from place to place to harvest fruits and vegetables. So many came from Oklahoma that people called them "Okies." One observer described their arrival:

> "They came in decrepit [broken-down], square-shouldered [cars] . . . that looked like relics of some antique culture . . . piled high with mattresses and cooking utensils and children, with suitcases, jugs and sacks strapped to the running boards."

Picturing HISTORY Dorothea Lange photographed a homeless Oklahoma family during Dust Bowl days. **How did Dust Bowl farmers survive?**

The Plight of Minorities

The Depression fell especially hard on the minority groups who were already on the lower rungs of the American economic ladder.

African Americans

In the South more than half of the African American population had no jobs. African American urban workers found their jobs taken by white people who had lost theirs. The collapse of farm prices crushed African American farmers.

Seeking more opportunity, about 400,000 African American men, women, and children migrated to Northern cities during the decade. They did not fare much better there, however. The jobless rate for African Americans remained high.

African Americans did make some political gains during the Depression. President Roosevelt appointed a number of African Americans to federal posts. He had a group of advisers, known as the Black Cabinet, that included Robert Weaver, a college professor, and **Ralph Bunche,** who worked for the State Department. **Mary McLeod Bethune,** who established Bethune-Cookman College in Florida, also served as an adviser.

African Americans continued to fight against prejudice. In 1939 opera singer Marian Anderson was denied permission to sing in Constitution Hall because she was black. Mrs. Roosevelt helped arrange for Anderson to give a historic concert at the Lincoln Memorial.

MULTIPLE LEARNING STYLES

Interpersonal Ask students to imagine they are looking for work during the Great Depression. Instruct them to write a two-minute oral description highlighting their skills and experiences that would entice a prospective employer to hire them. Pair students to role-play employer and employee during a job interview in which the employee uses his or her prepared description. **L2,** ELL

Native Americans

The 1930s did bring some benefits to Native Americans. The new head of the Bureau of Indian Affairs, **John Collier,** introduced a set of reforms known as the Indian New Deal.

Collier halted the sale of reservation land, got jobs for 77,000 Native Americans in the Civilian Conservation Corps, and obtained Public Works Administration funds to build new reservation schools. Most important, he pushed Congress to pass the Indian Reorganization Act of 1934. This law restored traditional tribal government and provided money for land purchases to enlarge some reservations.

Hispanics

At the beginning of the 1930s, about 2 million people of Hispanic descent lived in the United States, mostly in California and the Southwest. Many had emigrated from Mexico. They worked as farmers, migrant workers, and laborers. As the Great Depression deepened, resentment against Mexican Americans grew. Many lost their jobs. Politicians and labor unions demanded that Mexicans be forced to leave the United States.

The government encouraged Mexican immigrants to return to Mexico. Authorities gave them one-way train tickets to Mexico or simply rounded them up and shipped them south across the border. More than 500,000 Mexican Americans left the United States during the early years of the Depression, often involuntarily.

Radical Political Movements

Hard times helped **radical** political groups gain ground in the United States during the 1930s. Radical groups advocate extreme and immediate change. Socialists and Communists viewed the Depression not as a temporary economic problem but as the death of a failed system. They proposed sweeping changes.

Picturing HISTORY Mary McLeod Bethune worked to improve educational opportunities for African Americans. **What other African Americans advised President Roosevelt?**

Communism attracted workers, minority-rights activists, and intellectuals with promises to end economic and racial injustice. Although both socialism and communism had significant influence, neither became a major political force in the United States.

Another political development that caught the attention of many Americans was the rise of **fascists** in Germany and Italy. Fascism is a political philosophy that holds the individual second to the nation and advocates government by dictatorship. In 1936 the **Spanish Civil War** began. Germany and Italy supported fascists who were trying to take over the Spanish government. Although the United States remained neutral, more than 3,000 Americans went to Spain to fight the fascists.

Footnotes to History

Monopoly Each player's goal in the board game Monopoly is to make money while forcing opponents into bankruptcy. Oddly enough, the game was invented during the height of the Great Depression. Charles Darrow was an unemployed Philadelphia engineer when he designed the game in 1931.

CHAPTER 25
Section 3, 728–732

Picturing HISTORY After being turned down by the Presbyterian Mission to be a missionary because she was African American, Mary McLeod Bethune became a teacher. In 1904 she opened the Daytona Normal and Industrial Institute with her own six children as the first students. By 1923 the faculty and staff had grown to 25 and students to 300.

Answer: *Ralph Bunche and Robert Weaver*

3 ASSESS

Assign Section 3 Review as homework or as an in-class activity.

Use **Chapter Challenger Interactive Review Software** to review Section 3.

Section Quiz 25–3

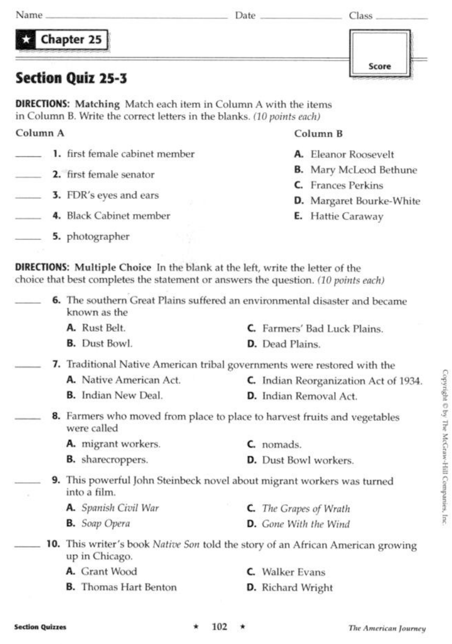

Name ______ Date ______ Class ______

Chapter 25 — Score

Section Quiz 25-3

DIRECTIONS: Matching Match each item in Column A with the items in Column B. Write the correct letters in the blanks. *(10 points each)*

Column A	Column B
____ 1. first female cabinet member	A. Eleanor Roosevelt
____ 2. first female senator	B. Mary McLeod Bethune
____ 3. FDR's eyes and ears	C. Frances Perkins
____ 4. Black Cabinet member	D. Margaret Bourke-White
____ 5. photographer	E. Hattie Caraway

DIRECTIONS: Multiple Choice In the blank at the left, write the letter of the choice that best completes the statement or answers the question. *(10 points each)*

____ 6. The southern Great Plains suffered an environmental disaster and became known as the
A. Rust Belt. C. Farmers' Bad Luck Plains.
B. Dust Bowl. D. Dead Plains.

____ 7. Traditional Native American tribal governments were restored with the
A. Native American Act. C. Indian Reorganization Act of 1934.
B. Indian New Deal. D. Indian Removal Act.

____ 8. Farmers who moved from place to place to harvest fruits and vegetables were called
A. migrant workers. C. nomads.
B. sharecroppers. D. Dust Bowl workers.

____ 9. This powerful John Steinbeck novel about migrant workers was turned into a film.
A. *Spanish Civil War* C. *The Grapes of Wrath*
B. *Soap Opera* D. *Gone With the Wind*

____ 10. This writer's book *Native Son* told the story of an African American growing up in Chicago.
A. Grant Wood C. Walker Evans
B. Thomas Hart Benton D. Richard Wright

Section Quizzes ★ 102 ★ *The American Journey*

Making Connections Activity

The Environment The Dust Bowl emerged from 300,000 square miles of Great Plains territory that had been stripped of its protective buffalo grass. "Black blizzards" swept the region, carrying off much-needed topsoil. One "blizzard" blew away 300 million tons of topsoil, roughly the amount of earth dredged from the Panama Canal. It was an ecological disaster that provided important lessons to a later, more environmentally aware, generation. Direct students to scan the section to find the causes and effects of the Dust Bowl, using this information to create a cause-and-effect chart. Discuss the environmental lessons learned from the Dust Bowl. **L2, ELL**

Reteaching Activity 25–3

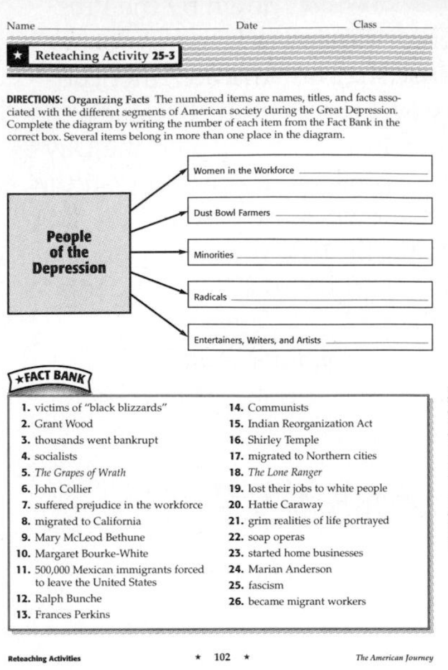

Name ______ Date ______ Class ______

★ Reteaching Activity 25-3

DIRECTIONS: Organizing Facts The numbered items are names, titles, and facts associated with the different segments of American society during the Great Depression. Complete the diagram by writing the number of each item from the Fact Bank in the correct box. Several items belong in more than one place in the diagram.

People of the Depression
- Women in the Workforce ______
- Dust Bowl Farmers ______
- Minorities ______
- Radicals ______
- Entertainers, Writers, and Artists ______

★FACT BANK

1. victims of "black blizzards"
2. Grant Wood
3. thousands went bankrupt
4. socialists
5. *The Grapes of Wrath*
6. John Collier
7. suffered prejudice in the workforce
8. migrated to California
9. Mary McLeod Bethune
10. Margaret Bourke-White
11. 500,000 Mexican immigrants forced to leave the United States
12. Ralph Bunche
13. Frances Perkins
14. Communists
15. Indian Reorganization Act
16. Shirley Temple
17. migrated to Northern cities
18. *The Lone Ranger*
19. lost their jobs to white people
20. Hattie Caraway
21. grim realities of life portrayed
22. soap operas
23. started home businesses
24. Marian Anderson
25. fascism
26. became migrant workers

Reteaching Activities ★ 102 ★ *The American Journey*

Enrichment Activity 25–3

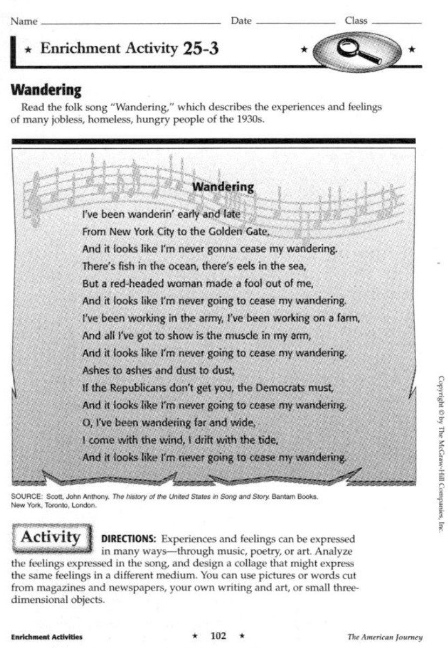

Name ______ Date ______ Class ______

★ Enrichment Activity 25-3

Wandering

Read the folk song "Wandering," which describes the experiences and feelings of many jobless, homeless, hungry people of the 1930s.

Wandering

I've been wanderin' early and late
From New York City to the Golden Gate,
And it looks like I'm never gonna cease my wandering.
There's fish in the ocean, there's eels in the sea,
But a red-headed woman made a fool out of me,
And it looks like I'm never going to cease my wandering.
I've been working in the army, I've been working on a farm,
And all I've got to show is the muscle in my arm,
And it looks like I'm never going to cease my wandering.
Ashes to ashes and dust to dust,
If the Republicans don't get you, the Democrats must,
And it looks like I'm never going to cease my wandering.
O, I've been wandering far and wide,
I come with the wind, I drift with the tide,
And it looks like I'm never going to cease my wandering.

SOURCE: Scott, John Anthony. *The history of the United States in Song and Story.* Bantam Books. New York, Toronto, London.

Activity **DIRECTIONS:** Experiences and feelings can be expressed in many ways—through music, poetry, or art. Analyze the feelings expressed in the song, and design a collage that might express the same feelings in a different medium. You can use pictures or words cut from magazines and newspapers, your own writing and art, or small three-dimensional objects.

Enrichment Activities ★ 102 ★ *The American Journey*

***Movie poster advertising* The Grapes of Wrath**

Entertainment and the Arts

The Depression produced two separate trends in entertainment and the arts. One was escapism—light or romantic entertainment that helped people forget about their problems. The other was social criticism—portraits of the suffering and injustice of Depression America.

Escaping Troubled Times

Radio became enormously popular during the 1930s. Daytime dramas sponsored by laundry detergents earned the nickname "soap operas." Adventure programs such as *Dick Tracy, The Lone Ranger,* and *Superman* had millions of listeners, as did variety shows featuring comedians George Burns and Gracie Allen and Jack Benny.

Every week about 85 million people went to movie theaters, usually to escape their cares and worries. Shirley Temple, a blond, curly-haired child star, became Hollywood's top box-office draw.

Some movies did explore serious topics. For example, *The Grapes of Wrath* (1940) was a screen version of **John Steinbeck's** powerful novel about Okies fleeing the Dust Bowl. The 1939 film of Margaret Mitchell's novel, *Gone With the Wind,* set in the Civil War era, also portrayed people coping with hard times.

Images of Despair

Many writers and painters portrayed the grim realities of Depression life. **Richard Wright's** novel *Native Son* told the story of an African American man growing up in Chicago. Writer **James Agee** and photographer **Walker Evans** depicted poor Southern farm families in *Let Us Now Praise Famous Men.*

Photographer **Margaret Bourke-White** also recorded the plight of American farmers, and **Dorothea Lange** took gripping photographs of migrant workers. Painters such as **Grant Wood** and **Thomas Hart Benton** showed ordinary people confronting the hardships of Depression life.

Section 3 Review

Checking for Understanding

1. ***Identify*** Frances Perkins, Eleanor Roosevelt, Ralph Bunche, Mary McLeod Bethune, John Collier.
2. ***Define*** Dust Bowl, migrant worker.
3. ***List*** three benefits that Native Americans received from the Indian New Deal.

Reviewing Themes

4. **Geography and History** What caused the Dust Bowl?

Critical Thinking

5. **Determining Cause and Effect** Why did radical political movements gain popularity during the 1930s?

Activity

Writing a Screenplay Think of a modern story idea that would be considered social criticism. Using the outline of the story, write a play in which the characters point out a flaw in their society.

Section 3 Review Answers

1. Frances Perkins, 729; Eleanor Roosevelt, 729; Ralph Bunche, 730; Mary McLeod Bethune, 730; John Collier, 731
2. The words are defined in the Glossary.
3. Any three: halted sale of reservation land, created jobs, provided funds to build new reservation schools, helped to pass the Indian Reorganization Act
4. Farmers used new technology to clear millions of acres of sod, which held the soil in place. Drought and high winds blew the soil away.
5. Radicals viewed the Depression as evidence of a failed system, and they promised to end racial and economic injustice.

Activity Students should write an outline and use it to write a play in which the characters point out a flaw in society.

4 CLOSE

The movie *The Wizard of Oz* debuted in the 1930s. Play the song "Somewhere Over the Rainbow" from the movie. Discuss how it relates to the mood of the 1930s.

1934 John L. Lewis forms the CIO

1935 FDR launches the Second New Deal

1936 FDR wins reelection

1937 Sit-down strike occurs in Flint, Michigan

Section 4

Effects of the New Deal

READ TO DISCOVER . . .

- why people criticized Roosevelt and the New Deal.
- how the Second New Deal created new economic and social roles for government.

TERMS TO LEARN

pension
Second New Deal
Social Security Act
unemployment insurance

The Storyteller

Support for Franklin D. Roosevelt's efforts to end the Great Depression was far from unanimous. Many wealthy and conservative people attacked the president's "radical" policies. A political cartoon of the 1930s showed a boy writing the word *ROOSEVELT* on the sidewalk in front of his rich family's house. His sister calls out, "Mother, Wilfred wrote a bad word!"

Anti-New Deal button

In the early days of his presidency, FDR counted on big business to support his efforts to revive the economy. The National Recovery Administration, for example, invited participation from the business community. In general, however, the business world opposed the New Deal.

New Deal Opponents

Business leaders accused Roosevelt of spending too much government money and of trying to destroy free enterprise. In 1934 some of these conservative critics formed the Liberty League. The League wanted government to let business alone and play a less active role in the economy. Although the Liberty League did not win widespread support, its existence convinced FDR that big business was against him.

Demanding More Reform

At the same time, Roosevelt drew fire from liberal and radical critics. They wanted a more active government. Three men gained wide popularity with schemes to help the average American.

One of Roosevelt's critics was Father **Charles Coughlin,** a Detroit priest who reached millions of listeners through his weekly radio program. Coughlin, once a Roosevelt supporter, attacked FDR for not dealing firmly enough with big business, calling him "Franklin Double-Crossing Roosevelt." Coughlin used his radio show to attack bankers, Jews, Communists, and labor unions, as

1 FOCUS

BELLRINGER
Motivational Activity

Before taking roll at the beginning of the class period, project Section Focus Transparency 25–4 and have students answer the questions. Discuss students' responses.

This activity is also available as a blackline master.

Section Focus Transparency 25–4

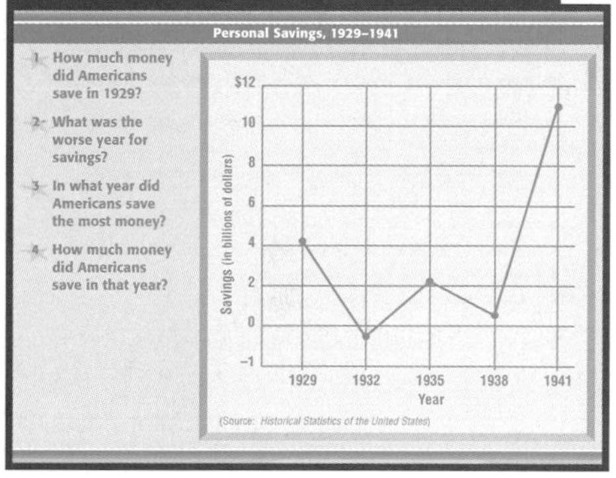

Vocabulary Precheck

Ask students to speculate on how the changes initiated by each of the **Terms to Learn** changed the future of the American economy and society.

Use the **Vocabulary PuzzleMaker** to create crossword and word search puzzles.

Section Theme
Government and Democracy

In 1935 President Franklin Roosevelt launched a new set of programs and reforms, often called the Second New Deal.

Activity Ask students to create a two-column chart with the headings "New Deal Supporters" and "New Deal Opponents." Have students scan the section to complete the chart.

SECTION RESOURCES

Reproducible Masters
- Reproducible Lesson Plan 25–4
- Guided Reading Activity 25–4
- Section Quiz 25–4
- Reteaching Activity 25–4
- Enrichment Activity 25–4

Transparencies
- Section Focus Transparency 25–4

Multimedia
- Vocabulary PuzzleMaker
- Chapter Challenger Interactive Review Software
- Testmaker
- GTV: The American People: Fabric of a Nation
- The Presidents: A Picture History of Our Nation

2 TEACH

L1 Drawing a Political Cartoon Direct students to reread **The Storyteller** on page 733. Instruct them to assume the role of an American during the Great Depression. Challenge them to decide whether they would have been for or against the New Deal programs. Then ask students to draw a political cartoon expressing their opinion about the New Deal.

Guided Reading Activity 25–4

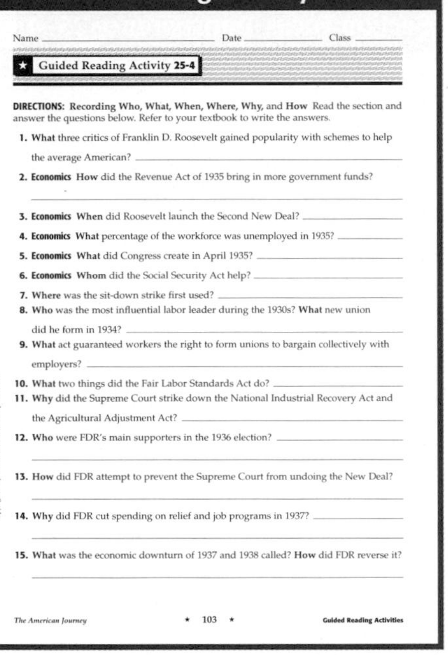
Name ______ Date ______ Class ______

Guided Reading Activity 25-4

DIRECTIONS: Recording Who, What, When, Where, Why, and How Read the section and answer the questions below. Refer to your textbook to write the answers.

1. What three critics of Franklin D. Roosevelt gained popularity with schemes to help the average American? ______
2. **Economics** How did the Revenue Act of 1935 bring in more government funds? ______
3. **Economics** When did Roosevelt launch the Second New Deal? ______
4. **Economics** What percentage of the workforce was unemployed in 1935? ______
5. **Economics** What did Congress create in April 1935? ______
6. **Economics** Whom did the Social Security Act help? ______
7. Where was the sit-down strike first used? ______
8. Who was the most influential labor leader during the 1930s? What new union did he form in 1934? ______
9. What act guaranteed workers the right to form unions to bargain collectively with employers? ______
10. What two things did the Fair Labor Standards Act do? ______
11. Why did the Supreme Court strike down the National Industrial Recovery Act and the Agricultural Adjustment Act? ______
12. Who were FDR's main supporters in the 1936 election? ______
13. How did FDR attempt to prevent the Supreme Court from undoing the New Deal? ______
14. Why did FDR cut spending on relief and job programs in 1937? ______
15. What was the economic downturn of 1937 and 1938 called? How did FDR reverse it? ______

The American Journey • 103 • Guided Reading Activities

NATIONAL GEOGRAPHIC SOCIETY

CD-ROM
The Presidents: A Picture History of Our Nation

Have students view "Franklin D. Roosevelt" and use the information to write a brief biography of the president.

well as the New Deal. In time Coughlin lost support because of his extreme views.

Francis Townsend, a California doctor, rose to fame with his plan for a monthly **pension,** or payment, for older people. Older workers who quit their jobs, making them available to younger people, would receive a pension. Townsend's plan received little support from Congress. It did, however, force many Americans to think about the plight of the elderly poor and the needs of retired people.

Of greatest concern to Roosevelt, however, was Senator **Huey Long** of Louisiana. Long had won wide support when he was governor of Louisiana with public works projects and attacks on big businesses.

In 1932 Long supported FDR, but within a year, the two men had split. One of Long's major complaints against the president was that he had not taken steps to redistribute wealth in the United States. By 1934 Long had developed his own plan for doing so. His "Share Our Wealth Plan" called for taxing the rich heavily, then using that money to give every American a home and $2,500 a year. As his appeal spread, Long became a threat to Roosevelt. Polls indicated that he might receive as many as 4 million votes on a third-party ticket in 1936. But in 1935 he was assassinated.

Father Coughlin emblem

Economics

The Second New Deal

By the mid-1930s the economy had improved slightly, but the Depression was far from over. FDR took bolder steps.

To bring in more government funds, Roosevelt pushed Congress to pass the **Revenue Act** of 1935. The act raised taxes on wealthy people and corporations. Critics accused him of "soaking the rich" to pay for his programs, but many Americans cheered.

In 1935 President Roosevelt launched a new set of programs and reforms, often called the **Second New Deal.** The laws passed at this time changed American life even more than the Hundred Days had done.

Creating Jobs

Millions of people—20 percent of the workforce—were still unemployed in 1935. In April Congress created the **Works Progress Administration** (WPA). Led by Harry Hopkins, the WPA kept about 2 million people employed between 1935 and 1941. WPA workers built or repaired about 600 airports, 110,000 public buildings, 100,000 bridges, and 500,000 miles of roads.

The WPA also found work for unemployed writers, artists, and musicians. WPA painters decorated the new public buildings with murals. Writers and photographers documented life throughout America. The writers produced *Life in America,* 150 volumes that recorded folktales and songs, African American narratives, and Native American traditions.

Help for Those in Need

Before the Second New Deal, America was the only advanced industrial nation without a national government program to help the needy. In August 1935 Congress passed the Social Security Act.

The **Social Security Act** created a tax on workers and employers. That money provided monthly pensions for retired people. Another tax, on employers alone, funded **unemployment insurance** payments to people who lost their jobs. In addition, Social Security helped people with disabilities, the elderly poor, and children of parents who could not support them.

With the Social Security Act, the federal government took responsibility for the welfare of all citizens. It launched the American welfare system.

COOPERATIVE LEARNING ACTIVITY

Creating a Guidebook The Works Progress Administration (WPA) set up a federal writers' program for unemployed writers, who created a series of state guidebooks. The series was so well written that several guides have remained in print. Ask students to work in groups of three to create a community guidebook. As a group, have students choose what points of interest to include. Then allow group members to choose from the following roles: photographer, writer, and cartographer. After members have completed their tasks, have them cooperatively design a cover and assemble the guidebook. Have groups exchange guidebooks to critique.

The Labor Movement

Labor unions grew stronger as workers battled the Depression. In 1937 workers at the General Motors plant in **Flint, Michigan,** used a new technique—the sit-down strike. Strikers occupied the plant and refused to work until management agreed to negotiate their demands. For 44 days families and friends of the Flint strikers brought them food. Finally, the strikers won the right to organize their union.

The most influential labor leader during the 1930s was **John L. Lewis,** head of the United Mine Workers. To increase labor's power, Lewis strived to unite workers in every industry in a single union. Most unions in the American Federation of Labor (AFL) represented only skilled workers. Lewis called for industrial unions to include unskilled workers—the largest group in the labor force—as well as skilled workers.

In 1935 Lewis formed a new union called the **Congress of Industrial Organizations** (CIO), which helped create industrial unions. By 1938 the CIO had 4 million members, including large numbers of women and African Americans.

Unions found support in the New Deal. The 1935 **National Labor Relations Ac**t—also called the **Wagner Act** after its sponsor, Senator Robert Wagner of New York—guaranteed workers the right to form unions to bargain collectively with employers. The act also created the National Labor Relations Board to enforce its provisions. In 1938 Congress passed the **Fair Labor Standards Act** (FLSA), which banned child labor and set a minimum wage of 40 cents an hour. The FLSA and the Wagner Act form the basis of American labor rights today.

Picturing HISTORY This glass sign was hand-painted by a member of the United Mine Workers union. **How did workers benefit from the New Deal?**

The Supreme Court

Those who opposed the New Deal challenged many of its laws in the courts, claiming that they were unconstitutional. Several important cases reached the Supreme Court.

In May 1935, the Supreme Court ruled that the National Industrial Recovery Act was unconstitutional. In the opinion of the Court, Congress had exceeded its lawful power to regulate interstate commerce. In January 1936, the Supreme Court struck down the Agricultural Adjustment Act. Cases were also pending against the Wagner Act, the Social Security Act, and the Tennessee Valley Authority. It seemed as though the Supreme Court might destroy the New Deal.

A Second Term

The presidential campaign of 1936 was based on a single issue: Did the American people support FDR and the New Deal?

To run against Roosevelt, the Republicans nominated **Alfred M. Landon,** governor of Kansas. Landon attracted dissatisfied Democrats as well as Republicans. FDR campaigned as the champion of the average American. He denounced big business and the rich, who "are unanimous in their hate for me—and I welcome their hatred."

On Election Day FDR received 61 percent of the popular vote, the biggest landslide in an American presidential election to that time. Roosevelt's support came from progressives and liberals, the poor and unemployed, urban workers, and African Americans. These groups would form the core of the Democratic Party for decades to come.

CHAPTER 25
Section 4, 733–736

Picturing HISTORY During the 1930s union membership, helped by New Deal legislation, increased from less than 3.5 million to nearly 9 million.
Answer: *gained right to form unions, right to collective bargaining, child labor ban, minimum wage of 40 cents an hour*

NATIONAL GEOGRAPHIC SOCIETY

VIDEODISC
GTV: The American People: Fabric of a Nation

Side 3, Chapter 8

Title: *Shoulder to Shoulder*
Subject: Diversity during the Depression
Ask: Who does the narrator blame for the Depression? *(big-business owners)*

3 ASSESS

Assign Section 4 Review as homework or as an in-class activity.

Use **Chapter Challenger Interactive Review Software** to review Section 4.

Section Quiz 25–4

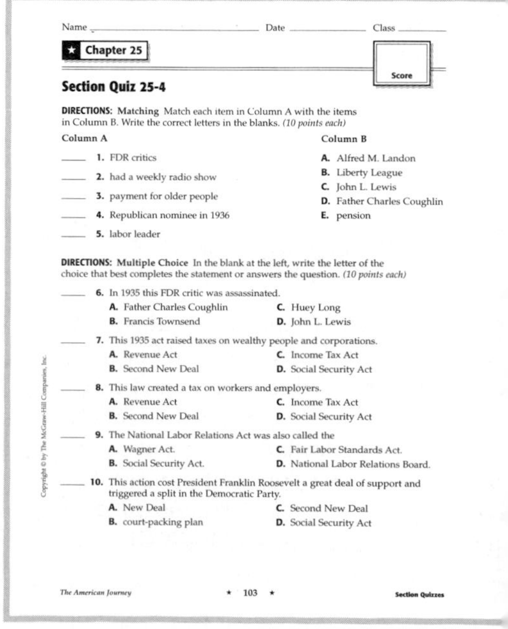
Name ______ Date ______ Class ______

Chapter 25

Score

Section Quiz 25-4

DIRECTIONS: Matching Match each item in Column A with the items in Column B. Write the correct letters in the blanks. *(10 points each)*

Column A	Column B
____ 1. FDR critics	A. Alfred M. Landon
____ 2. had a weekly radio show	B. Liberty League
____ 3. payment for older people	C. John L. Lewis
____ 4. Republican nominee in 1936	D. Father Charles Coughlin
____ 5. labor leader	E. pension

DIRECTIONS: Multiple Choice In the blank at the left, write the letter of the choice that best completes the statement or answers the question. *(10 points each)*

____ 6. In 1935 this FDR critic was assassinated.
A. Father Charles Coughlin   C. Huey Long
B. Francis Townsend   D. John L. Lewis

____ 7. This 1935 act raised taxes on wealthy people and corporations.
A. Revenue Act   C. Income Tax Act
B. Second New Deal   D. Social Security Act

____ 8. This law created a tax on workers and employers.
A. Revenue Act   C. Income Tax Act
B. Second New Deal   D. Social Security Act

____ 9. The National Labor Relations Act was also called the
A. Wagner Act.   C. Fair Labor Standards Act.
B. Social Security Act.   D. National Labor Relations Board.

____ 10. This action cost President Franklin Roosevelt a great deal of support and triggered a split in the Democratic Party.
A. New Deal   C. Second New Deal
B. court-packing plan   D. Social Security Act

The American Journey ★ 103 ★ Section Quizzes

MULTIPLE LEARNING STYLES

Verbal/Linguistic Brainstorm with students how a person can use the media to communicate a specific point of view. Lead a discussion on current talk radio hosts, their points of view, and their audiences. Organize the class into three groups. Assign each group one of the following people: Father Charles Coughlin, President Franklin Roosevelt, and Senator Huey Long. Ask each group to role-play the assigned person by holding an open-line, radio talk show. Have other groups "call in" questions to the radio-host group. Ask each group to respond to the questions from the point of view of the assigned person. **L3**

CHAPTER 25
Section 4, 733–736

Reteaching Activity 25–4

Name ________ Date ________ Class ________

Reteaching Activity 25-4

DIRECTIONS: Crossword Puzzle Complete the crossword puzzle about the New Deal.

Wagner Act **Revenue Act** **CIO** **Alfred M. Landon**
Huey Long **Coughlin** **Liberty League** **Social Security Act**
John L. Lewis **Second New Deal** **child labor** **WPA**

Across
2. FDR's opponent in the 1936 election
3. head of United Mine Workers
5. banned by the 1938 Fair Labor Standards Act
6. wanted government to let business alone
7. 1935 act that raised taxes on wealthy people and corporations
10. created a tax on workers and employers to provide a pension for retired people
11. senator who developed the "Share Our Wealth Plan"
12. initials of new union formed in 1934 by John L. Lewis

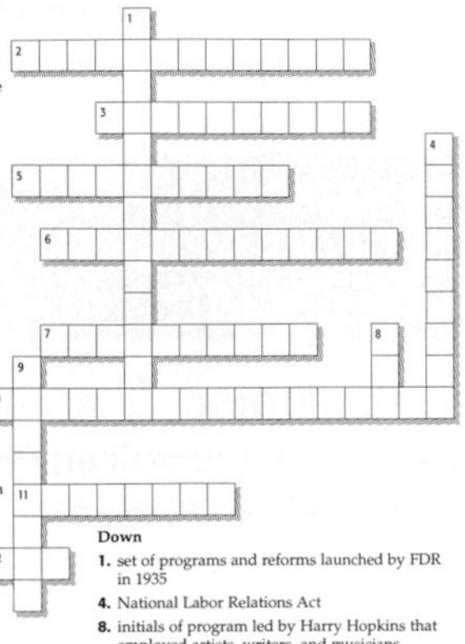

Down
1. set of programs and reforms launched by FDR in 1935
4. National Labor Relations Act
8. initials of program led by Harry Hopkins that employed artists, writers, and musicians
9. Detroit priest who attacked FDR on the radio for not dealing firmly with big business

Enrichment Activity 25–4

Name ________ Date ________ Class ________

★ Enrichment Activity **25-4** ★ ★

Paychecks

DIRECTIONS: Reading a Table Use the information on the table to fill in the blanks and answer the questions.

1. Average hourly wage in 1936: ________

Change in average hourly wage between 1933 and 1940: ________

2. Average hours worked by men in 1931: ________

Lowest average hourly wage for men between 1929 and 1941: ________

Wages and Hours for Production Workers, 1929–1941

Year	All Production Workers		Male Workers		Female Workers	
	Av. wage per hr.	Av. hrs. per wk.	Av. wage per hr.	Av. hrs. per wk.	Av. wage per hr.	Av. hrs. per wk.
1929	$ .59	48.3	$ .63	49.1	$ .40	44.2
1930	.59	43.9	.62	44.5	.40	40.5
1931	.56	40.4	.60	40.4	.37	39.8
1932	.50	34.8	.53	34.4	.33	36.3
1933	.49	36.4	.52	36.3	.34	36.6
1934	.58	34.7	.61	34.8	.43	34.0
1935	.60	37.2	.63	37.5	.44	35.2
1936	.62	39.5	.65	40.1	.43	36.2
1937	.70	38.7	.74	39.3	.47	36.1
1938	.72	34.3	.76	34.6	.48	32.6
1939	.72	37.6	.77	38.0	.48	35.8
1940	.74	38.6	.78	39.2	.49	35.5
1941	.81	41.2	.87	41.8	.53	38.0

SOURCE: *Historical Statistics of the United States*

3. Highest average hours worked by women between 1929 and 1941: ________

Highest average hourly wage for women between 1929 and 1941: ________

4. If a man worked an average week at average pay, how much more would he earn in 1929 than a woman who worked an average week at average pay? ________

Activity **DIRECTIONS:** Are there still differences in wages for men and women in the United States? What has been the trend over the past 20 years? Find data in the media center for the 1970s and the 1990s. Use the data to draw a double line graph showing the difference in wages for men and women for each decade.

4 CLOSE

Ask students to speculate on the possible bankruptcy of Social Security, which originated during the New Deal. Have students brainstorm alternative ways of providing pensions for retired persons.

Packing the Court cartoon, 1937

Roosevelt's "Court-Packing" Plan

Soon after his reelection, FDR took action to prevent the Supreme Court from undoing the New Deal. He asked Congress to increase the number of justices on the Court from 9 to 15, saying that the 9 justices were overworked and needed additional help. FDR would appoint the 6 new justices—selecting, of course, justices who would uphold the New Deal.

The proposal aroused bitter opposition. Critics accused the president of trying to "pack" the Court and ruin the system of checks and balances set up in the Constitution. The issue died when the Court ruled in favor of the Wagner Act and the Social Security Act. The New Deal was no longer in serious danger from the Court. The unpopularity of the court-packing plan, however, cost Roosevelt a great deal of support and triggered a split in the Democratic Party.

The Roosevelt Recession

By the summer of 1937, the national income had nearly returned to its 1929 level. Believing that the Depression was finally over, Roosevelt tried to reduce the government's debt by cutting spending on relief and job programs.

The economy faltered immediately. Farm prices dropped. Four million people lost their jobs. Times nearly as hard as 1932–1933 returned. The new economic downturn, known to some as the **Roosevelt Recession,** lasted into 1938. Roosevelt helped to reverse it with a flood of government spending on public works.

The End of the New Deal

The court-packing fight and the Roosevelt Recession cost FDR support in Congress. The economy had not fully recovered, in spite of the wide-ranging New Deal programs. As the 1930s drew to a close, however, world events caused Americans to turn their attention from domestic to foreign affairs. Dangerous forces were on the rise in Asia and Europe.

Section 4 Review

Checking for Understanding

1. ***Identify*** Charles Coughlin, Huey Long, Works Progress Administration, John L. Lewis, Wagner Act, Roosevelt Recession.
2. ***Define*** pension, Second New Deal, Social Security Act, unemployment insurance.
3. ***Summarize*** the economic plans of Huey Long and Francis Townsend.

Reviewing Themes

4. **Government and Democracy** What was the aim of Social Security?

Critical Thinking

5. **Identifying Central Issues** Why did many business leaders oppose Roosevelt's New Deal programs?

Activity

Doing Community Research Research the effect of the New Deal in your community. Find out if the federal government in the 1930s supported any local projects in conservation, construction, or the arts.

Section 4 Review Answers

1. Charles Coughlin, 733; Huey Long, 734; Works Progress Administration, 734; John L. Lewis, 735; Wagner Act, 735; Roosevelt Recession, 736
2. The words are defined in the Glossary.
3. Long: redistribute wealth by taxing rich; Townsend: monthly pension for older people
4. Federal government took responsibility for the welfare of all citizens.
5. Answers will vary but should point out that most business leaders did not want the federal government to intervene in the economy.

Activity Students should research to find out about any local New Deal projects.

Social Studies
SKILL BUILDER

Analyzing News Media

Every citizen needs to be aware of current issues and events to make good decisions when exercising citizenship rights. To stay informed, people use a variety of news sources—from broadcast media (television and radio) to print media (newspapers and news-magazines).

Learning the Skill

To get an accurate profile of current events, you must learn to think critically about the news you hear or read. The steps below will help you think critically.

- First, think about the source of the news story. Reports that reveal sources are more reliable than those that do not. If you know the sources, you can evaluate them. Can all facts be verified?
- Many news stories also analyze and interpret events. Such analyses may be more detailed than other reports, but they also reflect a reporter's biases. See if you can identify biases as you read or listen to news stories.
- Ask yourself whether the news is even-handed and thorough. Is it reported on the scene or secondhand? Does it fairly represent both sides of an issue? How many sources are used? The more sources cited for a fact, the more reliable the fact usually is.

Practicing the Skill

Following is an excerpt from the *New York Times* newspaper on February 6, 1937. Read the excerpt, then answer the questions that follow.

AIM TO PACK COURT, DECLARES HOOVER

President Roosevelt's message to Congress asking for authority to appoint new Federal judges whenever existing ones were over 70 years old was characterized last night by Herbert Hoover, his predecessor in the White House, as a proposal for "packing" the Supreme Court to get through New Deal measures. . . .

"The Supreme Court has proved many of the New Deal proposals as unconstitutional. Instead of the ample alternatives of the Constitution by which these proposals could be submitted to the people through constitutional amendment, it is now proposed to make changes by 'packing' the Supreme Court. It has the implication of subordination of the court to the personal power of the Executive."

1. What point is the article trying to make?
2. Is the article reported on the scene or secondhand?
3. Does the article reflect bias?
4. Is only one side of the issue presented?

Applying the Skill

Analyzing News Media Think of an issue in your community on which public opinion is divided. Read newspaper features and editorials about the issue and listen to television reports. Can you identify biases? Which reports more fairly represent the issue and the solutions? Which reports are the most reliable?

Social Studies
SKILL BUILDER

TEACH

Analyzing News Media

This skill emphasizes that citizens need to stay informed about current events and issues and be able to think critically about the news they read or hear. While applying the steps for critically evaluating news media, students interpret an excerpt from the *New York Times* about President Roosevelt and his attempt to "pack" the Supreme Court.

Explain to students that in addition to detecting a reporter's biases, they should be aware of a publisher's or station's biases. For example, some papers like the *New York Times* have a liberal bias, whereas others like the *Wall Street Journal* have a conservative bias. Have students use the reports from **Applying the Skill** to identify the bias of a newspaper or television station.

Additional Practice

Chapter Skills Activity 25

Answers to Practicing the Skill

1. President Roosevelt is using personal power to subordinate the Supreme Court.
2. secondhand
3. yes
4. yes

Applying the Skill Students will study an issue in their community on which public opinion is divided. They should identify biases and identify which reports are most fair and most reliable.

GLENCOE TECHNOLOGY

VIDEODISC
MindJogger Videoquiz

Use MindJogger to review the Chapter 25 content.

Chapter 25
Disc 4, Side A

Also available in VHS.

Chapter 25
Review and Activities

Reviewing Key Terms

On a sheet of paper, use at least six of the following terms to write a paragraph on the Great Depression or New Deal.

on margin	**migrant worker**
default	**pension**
relief	**Second New Deal**
public works	**Social Security Act**
Hundred Days	**subsidy**
New Deal	**unemployment insurance**
Dust Bowl	

Reviewing Key Facts

1. Why did a rise in unemployment during the Depression cause a decrease in consumer spending?
2. How did the CCC benefit the unemployed as well as the nation?
3. What was the purpose of the Tennessee Valley Authority project?
4. Summarize the advances made by African Americans and women during the Great Depression.
5. Describe the two laws passed during the Second New Deal that helped workers and unions.

Critical Thinking

Making Generalizations

President Roosevelt's leadership abilities and personality helped him push through his New Deal policies and made him popular with the public.

1. What personality traits and leadership abilities helped Roosevelt manage the country during the Great Depression?
2. How did Hoover's and Roosevelt's personalities and styles of leadership differ?

Time Line Activity

Create a time line on which you place the following events in chronological order.

- Roosevelt wins second term
- Stock market crashes
- Congress passes Social Security Act
- President Hoover loses reelection bid
- Indian Reorganization Act passed

Reviewing Themes

1. **Economic Factors** How did the trend of buying on credit in the 1920s affect banks during the Depression?
2. **Individual Action** In what way did FDR's fireside chats raise public confidence?
3. **Geography and History** How did new technology help cause the Dust Bowl disaster?
4. **Government and Democracy** How did the role of the federal government change during Roosevelt's administration?

Skill Practice Activity

Analyzing News Media

Find two articles, one in a current newspaper and the other in a newsmagazine, on a topic involving welfare reform. Read the articles, then answer the following questions.

1. Which article provided more in-depth coverage?
2. What points were the articles trying to make? Were the articles successful? Can the facts be verified?
3. Did either of the articles reflect bias? List any unsupported statements.
4. Was the news reported on the scene or secondhand? Do the articles seem to represent both sides fairly?

Reviewing Key Terms

The key terms used in this activity can be found in the textbook glossary on pages A26–A35. Students' paragraphs will vary.

Reviewing Key Facts

1. Without jobs people had less money to purchase consumer goods.
2. It created jobs by employing workers on government projects that benefited the nation.
3. built dams to control flooding and to provide cheap electric power to rural areas, set up schools and health centers, promoted conservation and development
4. Many African Americans and women held government offices for the first time or served as advisers to the president.
5. Wagner Act: guaranteed the right to form unions and bargain collectively; Fair Labor Standards Act: banned child labor and set minimum wage

Critical Thinking

1. Answers may include optimistic, risk taker, self-confident, persistent, sympathetic, and so on.
2. Answers will vary but may describe Hoover as slow to act and aloof and Roosevelt as responsive and understanding.

Time Line Activity

Events should be placed in this order: Stock market crashes, President Hoover loses reelection bid, Indian Reorganization Act passed, Congress passes Social Security Act, Roosevelt wins second term

Reviewing Themes

1. Borrowers defaulted on loans, and banks closed. Depositors lost their money.
2. His informal talks brought him into people's homes. People believed he cared about their problems.
3. New kinds of tractors and disc plows enabled farmers to clear large amounts of sod, leaving soil vulnerable to erosion.

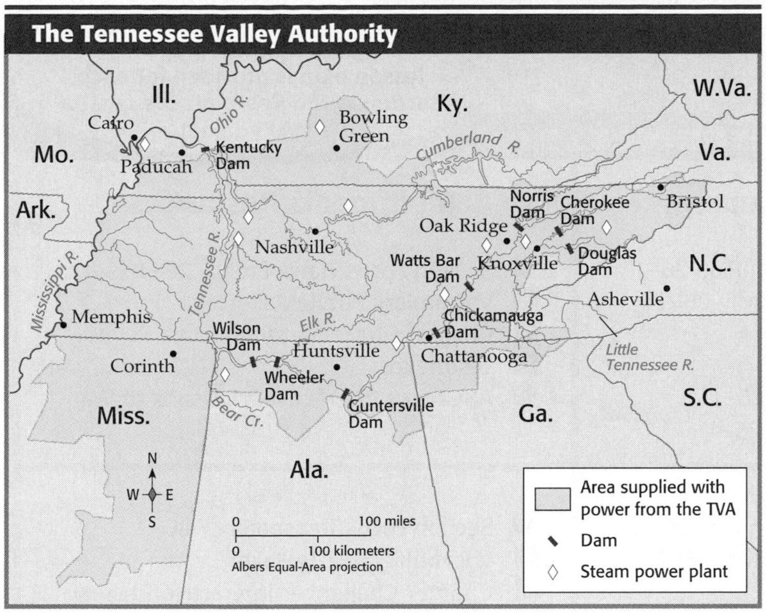

Cooperative Activity

History and Art Work with members of your group to prepare a photo essay to document the hardships of the Depression. Research to find out the names of photographers who documented the plight of Americans during this time. Photocopy some of their photos and display them in an interesting way on a sheet of cardboard. Write captions for each photo, provide photo credits, and write a title for your essay. Then with the rest of the class, create a walk-through gallery to display all the photo essays.

Geography Activity

Study the map above and answer these questions.

1. **Place** What physical feature made Tennessee particularly suited for the Tennessee Valley Authority project?
2. **Region** Which states were supplied with power from the TVA?
3. **Location** On the map, what seven dams are located along the Tennessee River?

Technology Activity

Using an Electronic Card Catalog Use the electronic card catalog at your school or community library to find information about the current Social Security Administration and its activities. Type in the words *Social Security* at the "subject" prompt. Note the call numbers of the books listed, and find these books in the library. Prepare a list of benefits and services that this organization provides to Americans today.

Portfolio Activity **History Journal** Both Eleanor and Franklin Roosevelt received many letters from the public during the Depression asking for jobs, money, food, and clothing. Write a letter from either of the Roosevelts responding to a plea for help. Explain in your letter what you can or cannot do for this person. Use what you have learned about the Roosevelts' personalities to make your letters realistic.

CHAPTER 25

Review and Activities

Geography Activity

1. a network of rivers
2. Kentucky, Virginia, North Carolina, Georgia, Alabama, Mississippi, and Tennessee
3. Kentucky, Wilson, Wheeler Guntersville, Chickamauga, Watts Bar, and Norris Dams

Technology Activity

Students should use the electronic card catalog to find books on the Social Security Administration and prepare a list of benefits and services it provides.

Cooperative Activity

Each group should prepare a photo essay using copies of photographs taken by Great Depression photographers. Essays should include captions, photo credits, and a title. The whole class should create a walk-through gallery to display its work.

Portfolio Activity Students should use their knowledge of Franklin and Eleanor Roosevelt's personalities to help them answer a letter from a person asking the government for help during the Depression.

Chapter Bonus Test Question

Ask: What was the first full-length animated movie that premiered in 1937? *(Walt Disney's* Snow White and the Seven Dwarfs*)*

4. It became actively involved in welfare of people and helped solve social and economic problems.

Skill Practice Activity

1. Students should choose the article with more in-depth coverage.
2. Students should identify the points made in each article, evaluate whether the points were successfully made, and state whether the facts could be verified.
3. Students should note bias in either article and list any unsupported statements.
4. Students should note whether each article is based on first- or secondhand news and determine whether the articles fairly represent both sides.

Chapter 26 Planning Guide

A complete, 1-page lesson plan is provided for each section in the *Reproducible Lesson Plans* booklet.

Section Resources

Daily Objectives	Reproducible Resources	Multimedia Resources
Section 1 Road to War Describe the political climate of the world before World War II.	Reproducible Lesson Plan 26–1 Guided Reading Activity 26–1* Political Cartoons Section Quiz 26–1* Reteaching Activity 26–1 Enrichment Activity 26–1	Section Focus Transparency 26–1 Vocabulary PuzzleMaker Chapter Challenger Interactive Review Testmaker ABCNews InterActive™ Lessons of War
Section 2 War Begins Identify the countries Germany invaded at the start of the war, describe American involvement in the war, and explain why America entered the war.	Reproducible Lesson Plan 26–2 Guided Reading Activity 26–2* Section Quiz 26–2* Reteaching Activity 26–2 Enrichment Activity 26–2	Section Focus Transparency 26–2 Vocabulary PuzzleMaker Chapter Challenger Interactive Review Testmaker GTV: A Geographic Perspective on American History American Music Cultural Traditions
Section 3 On the Home Front Summarize changes in the United States economy and the adaptations the American people made during World War II.	Reproducible Lesson Plan 26–3 Guided Reading Activity 26–3* Section Quiz 26–3* Reteaching Activity 26–3 Enrichment Activity 26–3	Section Focus Transparency 26–3 Vocabulary PuzzleMaker Chapter Challenger Interactive Review Testmaker GTV: The American People: Fabric of a Nation
Section 4 War in Europe and Africa Name some of the important battles and tactics that led to Allied victory in Africa and Europe.	Reproducible Lesson Plan 26–4 Guided Reading Activity 26–4* Political Cartoons Section Quiz 26–4* Reteaching Activity 26–4 Enrichment Activity 26–4	Section Focus Transparency 26–4 U.S. History & Art, Transparency 25 Vocabulary PuzzleMaker Chapter Challenger Interactive Review Testmaker ABCNews InterActive™ Lessons of War ABCNews InterActive™ Field Trips
Section 5 War in the Pacific Explain how the Allies won the war in the Pacific.	Reproducible Lesson Plan 26–5 Guided Reading Activity 26–5* Section Quiz 26–5* Reteaching Activity 26–5 Enrichment Activity 26–5	Section Focus Transparency 26–5 Chapter Challenger Interactive Review Testmaker ABCNews InterActive™ Lessons of War ABCNews InterActive™ Communism and the Cold War

* *Also available in Spanish*

Blackline Master · Videodisc · Audiocassette · Music Program · Transparency · CD-ROM · Software

0:00 **OUT OF TIME?**
Assign the Chapter 26 Digest and the corresponding Chapter Digests Audiocassettes with activities and tests.

Chapter 26 Planning Guide

ACTIVITY

From the Classroom of...

Alfonso Saldaña
Horace Mann Middle School
San Antonio, TX

Interviews on Isolationism

To help students understand how internally isolated most Americans felt prior to World War II, have them interview a relative or older friend who remembers the beginning of World War II.

Before the interviews, have students draft at least four questions to ask, such as, "Had you heard of Pearl Harbor before it was bombed by the Japanese?" or "How many places did you learn about during the war that you did not know about before?" The goal is to have students discover how isolated from the rest of the world Americans were at that time compared to now. Students' interviews should also reveal how the lack of television and other modern communication devices prior to the war contributed to this isolationism. Have students present their findings in oral reports to the class.

Block Schedule

Block scheduling differs from traditional class scheduling in the amount of time allotted to each period. The extended time frame provided by block scheduling affords you the opportunity to implement a greater number of research-oriented and activity-intense projects to motivate and involve your students. Activities that are particularly suited to use within the block scheduling framework are identified throughout this chapter by the following designation:

NATIONAL GEOGRAPHIC SOCIETY Teacher's Corner

INDEX TO NATIONAL GEOGRAPHIC MAGAZINE

The following articles may be used for research relating to this chapter:

- "Hiroshima," by Ted Gup, August 1995.
- "Blueprints for Victory," by John F. Shupe, May 1995.
- "Douglas MacArthur: An American Soldier," by Geoffrey C. Ward, March 1992.
- "Pearl Harbor: A Return to the Day of Infamy," by Thomas B. Allen, December 1991.
- "Remembering the Blitz," by Cameron Thomas, July 1991.
- "The Bismarck Found," by Robert D. Ballard, November 1989.
- "Living With Radiation," by Charles E. Cobb, Jr., April 1989.

NATIONAL GEOGRAPHIC SOCIETY PRODUCTS AVAILABLE FROM GLENCOE

To order the following products for use with this chapter, contact your local Glencoe sales representative, or call Glencoe at 1-800-334-7344:

- *GTV: A Geographic Perspective on American History* (Videodisc)
- *GTV: The American People: Fabric of a Nation* (Videodisc)
- *The Presidents: A Picture History of Our Nation* (CD-ROM)

ADDITIONAL NATIONAL GEOGRAPHIC SOCIETY PRODUCTS

To order the following products for use with this chapter, call National Geographic Society at 1-800-368-2728:

- *Lost Fleet of Guadalcanal* (Video)
- *Historical Atlas of the United States* (Atlas)

KEY TO ABILITY LEVELS

Teaching strategies have been coded for varying learning styles and abilities.

L1 BASIC activities for all students
L2 AVERAGE activities for average to above-average students
L3 CHALLENGING activities for above-average students
ELL ENGLISH LANGUAGE LEARNER activities

Chapter 26 Resource Guide

Home Involvement

Home Involvement Activity 26

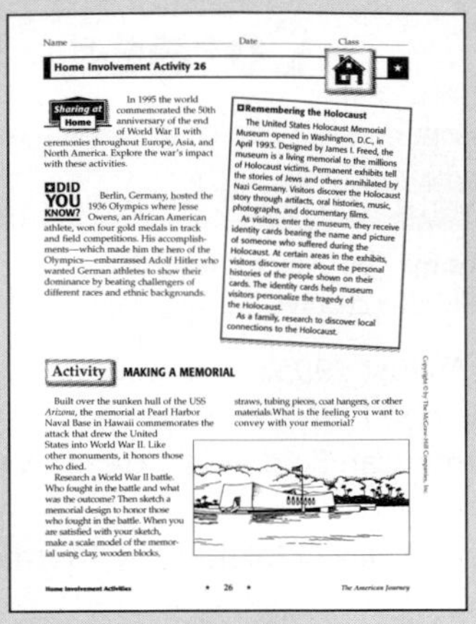

Home Involvement Activity 26

Remembering the Holocaust

Activity MAKING A MEMORIAL

Review Activities

Chapter Summary 26

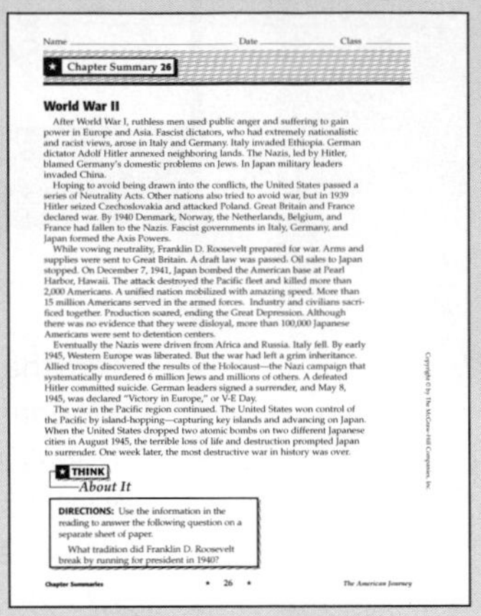

Chapter Summary 26

World War II

Workbook Activity 26

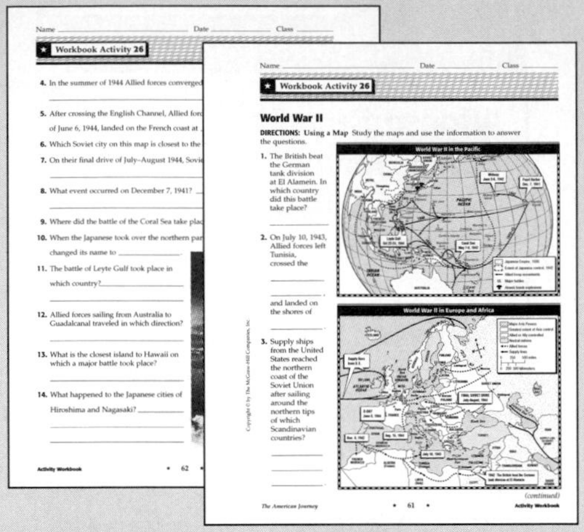

Workbook Activity 26

World War II

Reinforcement Activities

Time Line Activity 26

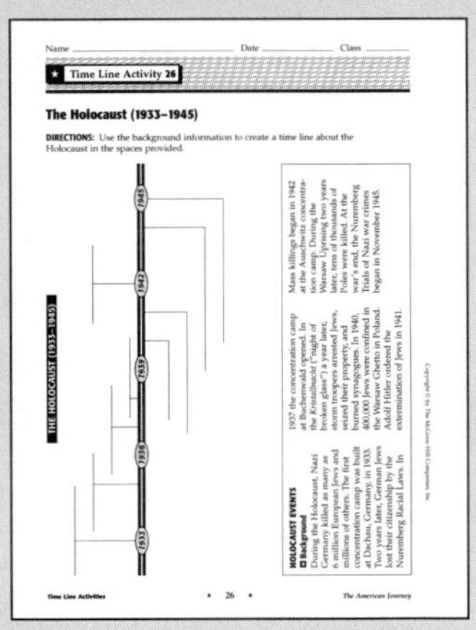

Time Line Activity 26

The Holocaust (1933–1945)

Vocabulary Activity 26

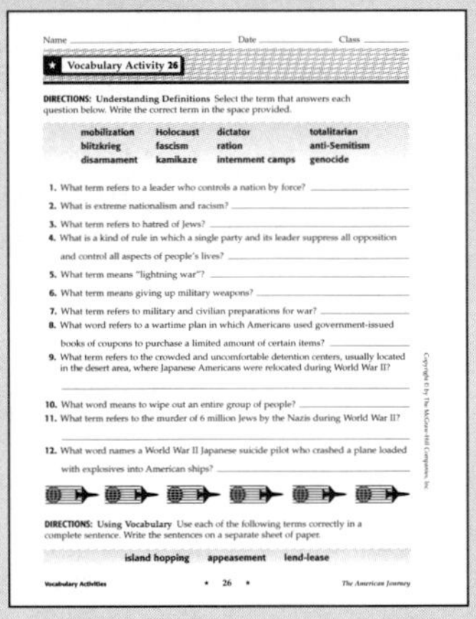

Vocabulary Activity 26

Chapter Skills Activity 26

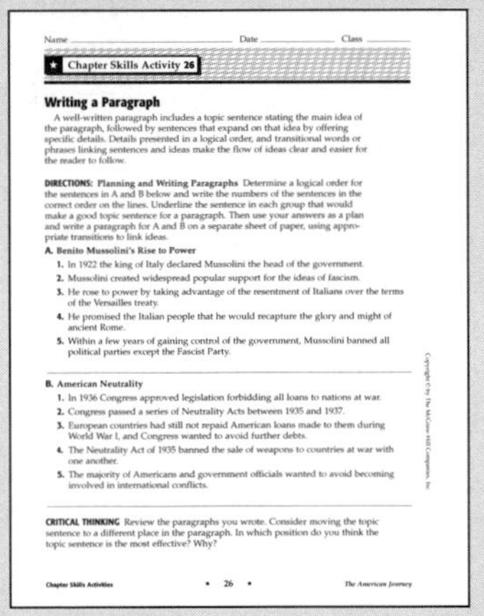

Chapter Skills Activity 26

Writing a Paragraph

Enrichment Activities

Linking Past and Present Activity 26

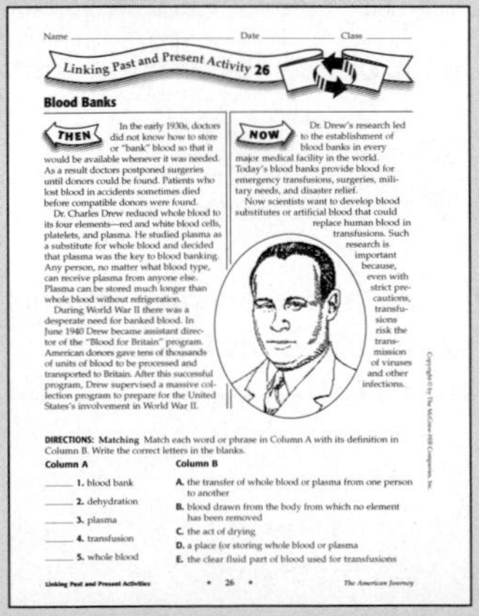

Linking Past and Present Activity 26

Blood Banks

Primary Source Reading 26

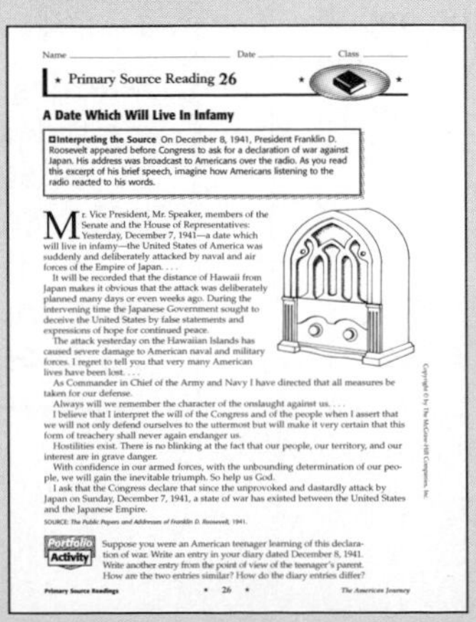

Primary Source Reading 26

A Date Which Will Live In Infamy

Geography Activities

Mapping History Activity 26

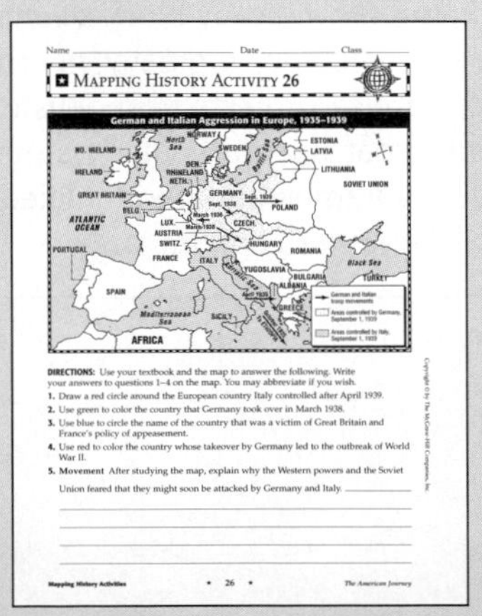

Mapping History Activity 26

German and Italian Aggression in Europe, 1935–1939

Chapter 26 Resource Guide

Assessment

Chapter 26 Test, Form A

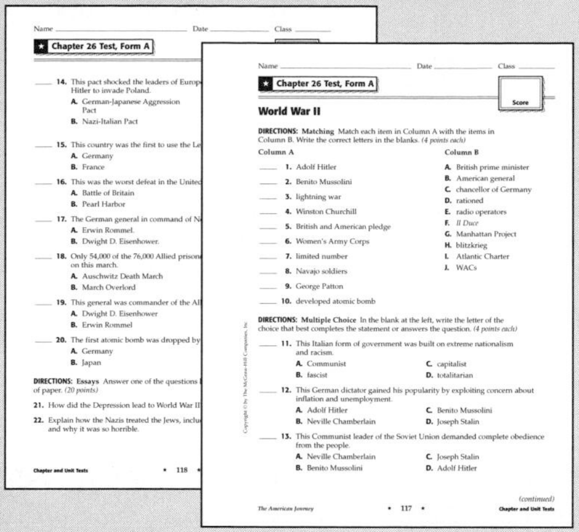
Name ______ Date ______ Class ______

Chapter 26 Test, Form A

World War II

DIRECTIONS: Matching Match each item in Column A with the items in Column B. Write the correct letters in the blanks. (4 points each)

Column A	Column B
___ 1. Adolf Hitler	A. British prime minister
___ 2. Benito Mussolini	B. American general
___ 3. lightning war	C. chancellor of Germany
___ 4. Winston Churchill	D. rationed
___ 5. British and American pledge	E. radio operators
___ 6. Women's Army Corps	F. Il Duce
___ 7. limited number	G. Manhattan Project
___ 8. Navajo soldiers	H. blitzkrieg
___ 9. George Patton	I. Atlantic Charter
___ 10. developed atomic bomb	J. WACs

DIRECTIONS: Multiple Choice In the blank at the left, write the letter of the choice that best completes the statement or answers the question. (4 points each)

___ 11. This Italian form of government was built on extreme nationalism and racism.
A. Communist C. capitalist
B. fascist D. totalitarian

___ 12. This German dictator gained his popularity by exploiting concern about inflation and unemployment.
A. Adolf Hitler C. Benito Mussolini
B. Neville Chamberlain D. Joseph Stalin

___ 13. This Communist leader of the Soviet Union demanded complete obedience from the people.
A. Neville Chamberlain C. Joseph Stalin
B. Benito Mussolini D. Adolf Hitler

(continued)

The American Journey • 117 • Chapter and Unit Tests

Chapter 26 Test, Form B

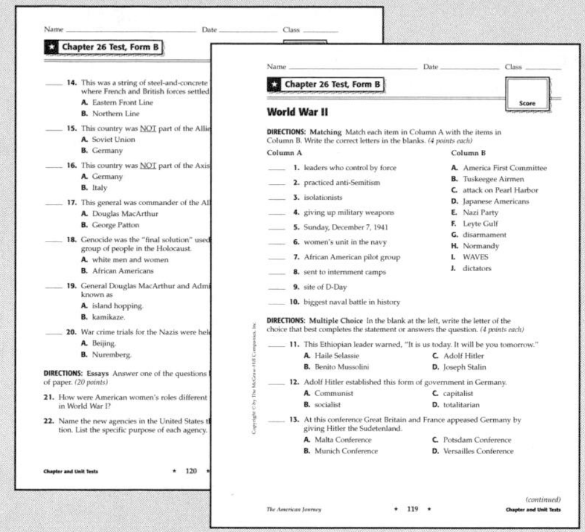
Name ______ Date ______ Class ______

Chapter 26 Test, Form B

World War II

DIRECTIONS: Matching Match each item in Column A with the items in Column B. Write the correct letters in the blanks. (4 points each)

Column A	Column B
___ 1. leaders who control by force	A. America First Committee
___ 2. practiced anti-Semitism	B. Tuskegee Airmen
___ 3. isolationists	C. attack on Pearl Harbor
___ 4. giving up military weapons	D. Japanese Americans
___ 5. Sunday, December 7, 1941	E. Nazi Party
___ 6. women's unit in the navy	F. Leyte Gulf
___ 7. African American pilot group	G. disarmament
___ 8. sent to internment camps	H. Normandy
___ 9. site of D-Day	I. WAVES
___ 10. biggest naval battle in history	J. dictators

DIRECTIONS: Multiple Choice In the blank at the left, write the letter of the choice that best completes the statement or answers the question. (4 points each)

___ 11. This Ethiopian leader warned, "It is us today. It will be you tomorrow."
A. Haile Selassie C. Adolf Hitler
B. Benito Mussolini D. Joseph Stalin

___ 12. Adolf Hitler established this form of government in Germany.
A. Communist C. capitalist
B. socialist D. totalitarian

___ 13. At this conference Great Britain and France appeased Germany by giving Hitler the Sudetenland.
A. Malta Conference C. Potsdam Conference
B. Munich Conference D. Versailles Conference

(continued)

The American Journey • 119 • Chapter and Unit Tests

Performance Assessment Activity 26

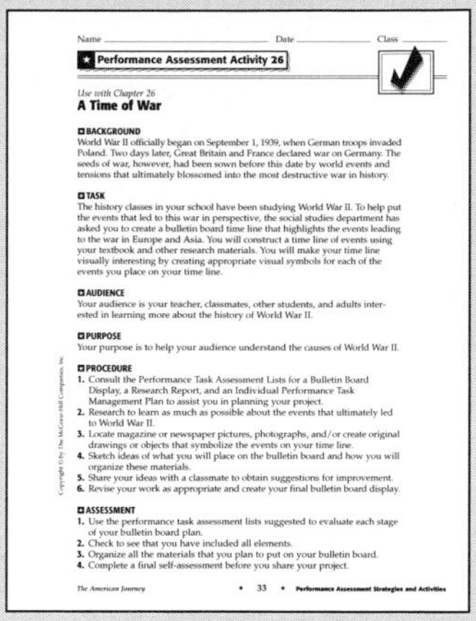
Name ______ Date ______ Class ______

Performance Assessment Activity 26

Use with Chapter 26

A Time of War

BACKGROUND
World War II officially began on September 1, 1939, when German troops invaded Poland. Two days later, Great Britain and France declared war on Germany. The seeds of war, however, had been sown before this date by world events and tensions that ultimately blossomed into the most destructive war in history.

TASK
The history classes in your school have been studying World War II. To help put the events that led to this war in perspective, the social studies department has asked you to create a bulletin board time line that highlights the events leading to the war in Europe and Asia. You will construct a time line of events using your textbook and other research materials. You will make your time line visually interesting by creating appropriate visual symbols for each of the events you place on your time line.

AUDIENCE
Your audience is your teacher, classmates, other students, and adults interested in learning more about the history of World War II.

PURPOSE
Your purpose is to help your audience understand the causes of World War II.

PROCEDURE
1. Consult the Performance Task Assessment Lists for a Bulletin Board Display, a Research Report, and an Individual Performance Task Management Plan to assist you in planning your project.
2. Research to learn as much as possible about the events that ultimately led to World War II.
3. Locate magazine or newspaper pictures, photographs, and/or create original drawings or objects that symbolize the events on your time line.
4. Sketch ideas of what you will place on the bulletin board and how you will organize these materials.
5. Share your ideas with a classmate to obtain suggestions for improvement.
6. Revise your work as appropriate and create your final bulletin board display.

ASSESSMENT
1. Use the performance task assessment lists suggested to evaluate each stage of your bulletin board plan.
2. Check to see that you have included all elements.
3. Organize all the materials that you plan to put on your bulletin board.
4. Complete a final self-assessment before you share your project.

The American Journey • 33 • Performance Assessment Strategies and Activities

Spanish Resources

The following Spanish language materials are available in the Spanish Resources binder:

- **Spanish Chapter Summary 26**
- **Spanish Vocabulary Activity 26**
- **Spanish Guided Reading Activities, Chapter 26**
- **Spanish Section Quizzes, Chapter 26**
- **Spanish Home Involvement Activity 26**
- **Spanish Chapter 26 Digests Audiocassette Activity and Test**

Activity Manipulatives

Help students learn more about America's cultural history with:

- **American Crafts Hands-On Activities**
- **American Games Hands-On Activities**
- **American History Flash Cards**

Additional Resources From Glencoe

- **U.S. History & Art,** Transparency 25, *The Red Stairway*
- **American Music Cultural Traditions,** Lesson 9: "Take Me Back to Tulsa," "Boogie Woogie Bugle Boy," "Jersey Bounce"
- **The American History Videodisc and CD-ROM,** *World War II and the Beginning of the Cold War, 1941–1960*
- **Political Cartoons,** *The Path of Appeasement, World War II Winds Down*
- **U.S. Desk Map**
- **Outline Map Resource Book**

A&E HOME VIDEO. Biography THE HISTORY CHANNEL.

The following videotape programs are available from Glencoe as supplements to Chapter 26:

- **World War II: The War Chronicles (Seven-Video Set)** (ISBN 1-56501-484-7)
- **The Last Days of World War II (Set)** (ISBN 1-56501-536-3)
- **FDR: The War Years** (ISBN 1-56501-458-8)
- **The Complete Churchill: BIOGRAPHY® Set** (ISBN 1-56501-091-4)
- **Patton: A Genius for War** (ISBN 1-56501-580-0)
- **Mussolini: Italy's Nightmare** (ISBN 1-56501-818-4)
- **Hirohito** (ISBN 1-56501-461-8)
- **Enola Gay and the Atomic Bombing of Japan** (ISBN 1-56501-598-3)

To order, call Glencoe at 1-800-334-7344. To find classroom resources to accompany many of these videos, check the following home pages:
A&E Television: http://www.aetv.com
The History Channel: http://www.historychannel.com

Introducing CHAPTER 26

Chapter Themes

Chapter Themes are listed by section on this chapter opening page of the Student Edition. A corresponding theme-based activity is available under "FOCUS," and a theme-based question is asked in the Section and Chapter Reviews.

Performance Assessment

Refer to Activity 26 in the *Performance Assessment Strategies and Activities* booklet.

GLENCOE TECHNOLOGY

VIDEODISC
MindJogger Videoquiz

Use MindJogger to preview the Chapter 26 content.

Chapter 26
Disc 4, Side A

Also available in VHS.

HISTORY AND ART In his message to Congress on January 6, 1941, President Roosevelt said, "We look forward to a world founded upon four essential human freedoms." **Ask:** **Which freedoms might you add to the four noted by President Roosevelt?** *(Students' answers will vary.)*

Chapter 26

1939–1945

World War II

Why It's Important

World War II, the most destructive war in history, resulted in the deaths of more than 40 million people. More than half of them were civilians, including about 6 million Jews and many others killed in the Holocaust. At the end of the war, the United States emerged as the strongest nation in the world and the sole possessor of a powerful weapon—the atomic bomb. This marked the beginning of the nation's role as a superpower. It brought the United States new responsibilities in almost every area of the world.

Chapter Themes

- *Section 1,* Continuity and Change
- *Section 2,* Global Connections
- *Section 3,* Economic Factors
- *Section 4,* Geography and History
- *Section 5,* Individual Action

HISTORY AND ART ***Embarkation, San Francisco, California*** **by Barse Miller** World War II American soldiers believed they were fighting for what President Roosevelt called the Four Freedoms: freedom of speech and expression, freedom of worship, freedom from want, and freedom from fear.

EXTRA CREDIT PROJECT

The National Mood Before Franklin Roosevelt took office, many Americans feared that the country would soon erupt in revolution. They believed that the nation's social fabric was weakened by the Great Depression. Ask interested students to interview someone who lived through the early 1930s. Interviewers should encourage their subjects to recall what people were talking about at the time. What were their concerns? Expectations? Hopes for the future? If an interviewee is not available, have students find answers to these questions in Studs Terkel's *Hard Times.* Ask students to share their findings with the class.

1930 | 1935 | 1940

1931 Japan invades Manchuria

1933 Hitler becomes chancellor of Germany

1935 Italian forces invade Ethiopia

1939 Germany seizes Czechoslovakia

Section 1

Road to War

READ TO DISCOVER . . .

- why dictators came to power around the world.
- what foreign policy the United States pursued in the 1930s.
- what actions led to the outbreak of World War II.

TERMS TO LEARN

dictator	totalitarian
fascism	appeasement
anti-Semitism	

The Storyteller

Many people underestimated Adolf Hitler's influence, but not American journalist William Shirer. He described a rally for Hitler at Nuremberg in September 1934: "Like a Roman emperor Hitler rode into this medieval town. . . . The streets, hardly wider than alleys, are a sea of brown and black uniforms. . . . [W]hen Hitler finally appeared on the balcony for a moment . . . [people] looked up at him as if he were a Messiah, their faces transformed into something positively inhuman." The passion of the Nazis shocked Shirer, and soon it would shock the rest of the world.

Hitler's *Mein Kampf*

In the late 1920s, **Adolf Hitler** achieved wide popularity in Germany. In his book *Mein Kampf* (My Struggle), Hitler set forth his political views.

> "He who wants to live must fight, and he who does not want to fight in this world, where eternal struggle is the law of life, has no right to exist."

When Hitler became the leader of Germany, he put his strong words into action.

The Rise of Dictators

A number of ruthless men—such as Adolf Hitler—rose to power in the 1920s and 1930s by taking advantage of people's anger and suffering. Some Europeans resented the terms of the Treaty of Versailles, signed in 1919, which ended World War I. When a worldwide depression hit in the 1930s, frustration and fear added to this anger.

Hitler and other leaders promised a better life. They described a glorious future to people humiliated by losing a war. Once they gained political power, these men became **dictators,** leaders who control their nations by force.

Italy

Benito Mussolini rose to power by appealing to the resentment of many Italians who felt they had not won enough in the Versailles treaty.

SECTION RESOURCES

Reproducible Masters
- Reproducible Lesson Plan 26–1
- Guided Reading Activity 26–1
- Political Cartoons, *The Path of Appeasement*
- Section Quiz 26–1
- Reteaching Activity 26–1
- Enrichment Activity 26–1

Transparencies
- Section Focus Transparency 26–1

Multimedia
- Vocabulary PuzzleMaker
- Chapter Challenger Interactive Review Software
- Testmaker
- ABCNews InterActive™ Lessons of War

1 FOCUS

BELLRINGER
Motivational Activity

Before taking roll at the beginning of the class period, project Section Focus Transparency 26–1 and have students answer the questions. Discuss students' responses.

This activity is also available as a blackline master.

Section Focus Transparency 26–1

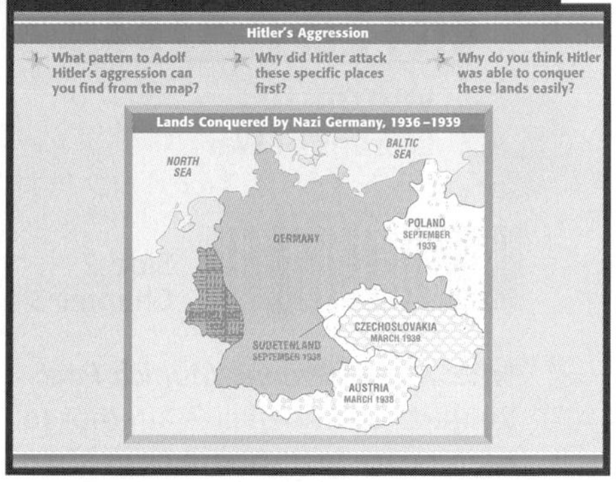

Vocabulary Precheck

Call on students to read aloud from the textbook glossary the definitions of the **Terms to Learn.** Then have volunteers use each term in a sentence.

Use the **Vocabulary PuzzleMaker** to create crossword and word search puzzles.

Section Theme
Continuity and Change

As dictators threatened world peace, the United States tried to follow a policy of neutrality, while Europe tried to avoid war by a policy of appeasement.

Activity Have students find the actions that made it impossible for the United States and Europe to continue those policies. *(Hitler invaded Poland; Japan invaded more and more Asian territories.)*

2 TEACH

L1 Comparing Have students draw a chart with three columns. In the first column students should list the leaders of Japan *(General Tōjō)*, Germany *(Hitler)*, and Italy *(Mussolini)*. In the second column, list reasons for each leader's aggressive policies in the early to mid-1930s. In the last column, name the countries each leader's armies invaded.

ABCNEWS INTERACTIVE™

VIDEODISC
Lessons of War

Side 2
Chapter 3

Title: *Appeasement: Munich Pact*
Subject: Chamberlain's attempt to keep peace with Germany in 1938
Ask: **What happened to the Munich Pact?** *(It failed.)*

Picturing HISTORY Hitler's stiff-armed Nazi salute was the required salute for Germans and the peoples they conquered.
Answer: *the Jews*

Guided Reading Activity 26–1

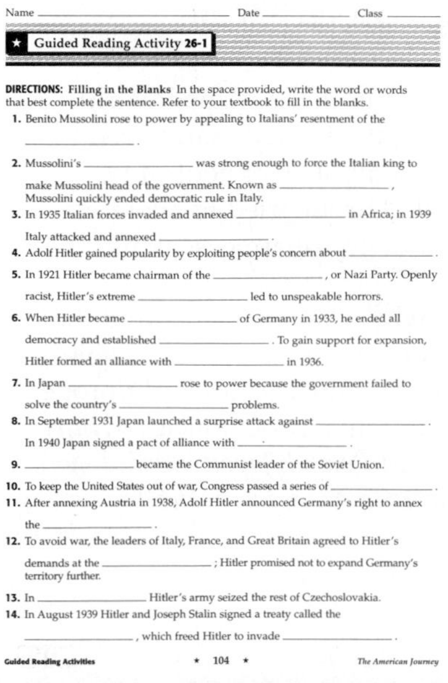
Name ________ Date ________ Class ________

★ Guided Reading Activity **26-1**

DIRECTIONS: Filling in the Blanks In the space provided, write the word or words that best complete the sentence. Refer to your textbook to fill in the blanks.

1. Benito Mussolini rose to power by appealing to Italians' resentment of the ________ .
2. Mussolini's ________ was strong enough to force the Italian king to make Mussolini head of the government. Known as ________ , Mussolini quickly ended democratic rule in Italy.
3. In 1935 Italian forces invaded and annexed ________ in Africa; in 1939 Italy attacked and annexed ________ .
4. Adolf Hitler gained popularity by exploiting people's concern about ________ .
5. In 1921 Hitler became chairman of the ________ , or Nazi Party. Openly racist, Hitler's extreme ________ led to unspeakable horrors.
6. When Hitler became ________ of Germany in 1933, he ended all democracy and established ________ . To gain support for expansion, Hitler formed an alliance with ________ in 1936.
7. In Japan ________ rose to power because the government failed to solve the country's ________ problems.
8. In September 1931 Japan launched a surprise attack against ________ . In 1940 Japan signed a pact of alliance with ________ .
9. ________ became the Communist leader of the Soviet Union.
10. To keep the United States out of war, Congress passed a series of ________ .
11. After annexing Austria in 1938, Adolf Hitler announced Germany's right to annex the ________ .
12. To avoid war, the leaders of Italy, France, and Great Britain agreed to Hitler's demands at the ________ ; Hitler promised not to expand Germany's territory further.
13. In ________ Hitler's army seized the rest of Czechoslovakia.
14. In August 1939 Hitler and Joseph Stalin signed a treaty called the ________ , which freed Hitler to invade ________ .

American cartoon of Mussolini

Mussolini made **fascism**—extreme nationalism and racism—popular in Italy. By 1922 his **Fascist Party** had gained enough strength to force the king of Italy to declare Mussolini the head of the government. Within a few years, Mussolini had banned all political parties except his Fascist Party.

Known as *Il Duce*—the leader—Mussolini quickly put an end to democratic rule in Italy. Civil liberties and the free press ceased to exist. Boys and girls of all ages were enrolled in military organizations that taught them loyalty to the regime. Mussolini built up Italy's military and vowed to recapture the glory of the ancient Romans.

In 1935 Mussolini sent Italian forces to invade the African nation of **Ethiopia,** which it annexed—took over as its own territory. Ethiopian emperor Haile Selassie appealed to the League of Nations for help: "God and history will remember your judgment. It is us today. It will be you tomorrow." The League responded by banning trade in weapons and certain other materials with Italy, but it lacked the power to enforce the ban. Italy withdrew from the League and continued its aggressive policies, attacking and annexing its neighbor Albania in 1939.

Germany

The Great Depression had hit Germany extremely hard. Millions of people had lost their jobs, and its economy teetered on the edge of collapse. Germans rallied around Adolf Hitler, a shrewd politician and a spellbinding speaker. Hitler gained popularity by exploiting people's concern about unchecked inflation and severe unemployment. Hitler also played upon bitterness over the Versailles treaty. The treaty had forced Germany to give up some of its territory and to make heavy payments to the victors for war damages.

In 1921 Hitler became chairman of the National Socialist German Workers' Party, or the **Nazi Party.** Openly racist, Hitler and the Nazis portrayed the German people as superior to all others. They directed much of their anger against Jews, whom Hitler blamed for Germany's problems. His extreme **anti-Semitism**—hatred of the Jews—would later lead to unspeakable horrors.

Soon after he became chancellor, or chief minister, of Germany in 1933, Hitler ended all democracy and established totalitarian rule. In a **totalitarian** state, a single party and its leader suppress all opposition and control all aspects of people's lives.

Hitler claimed that Germany had a right to expand its territory. The country needed *lebensraum*—living space—he said. Germany's neighbors watched uneasily as he rebuilt Germany's military strength in defiance of the Versailles treaty. To gain support in his expansion plans, Hitler formed an alliance with Italy in 1936.

Picturing HISTORY Hitler salutes German troops at a Nazi rally in 1938. **What group especially suffered from the Nazis?**

COOPERATIVE LEARNING ACTIVITY

Integrating a Map and Chart Organize the class into groups to create a map for the bulletin board showing the nations involved in World War II. Have students make a chart beside the map, identifying each country and giving pertinent data about it, such as key geographical features, major products, and involvement in World War II. As students complete Sections 2, 4, and 5 of this chapter, they may add more countries. Assign some students to do the necessary research and others to draw and label the map. Capital cities and major battle sites may be included as space permits.

Japan

During the Depression many Japanese grew frustrated with their government's failure to solve economic problems. As a result, military leaders rose to power in the early 1930s. These leaders thought they would solve Japan's problems by expanding Japanese power in Asia.

In September 1931, Japan launched an attack on the province of **Manchuria** in northeastern China. Henry Stimson, the American secretary of state, and the League of Nations condemned the attack—but took no action to halt the aggression.

Left unchallenged, Japan set up a government in Manchuria. In 1937 Japan took further steps to expand its power, invading northern China and moving southward until it occupied most of the country. Three years later Japan signed a pact of alliance, known as the "Axis," with Germany and Italy.

Picturing HISTORY Victorious Japanese soldiers celebrate their capture of the Chinese port of Hankou in October 1938. **Why did military leaders rise to power in Japan during the 1930s?**

Soviet Union

In the late 1920s, **Joseph Stalin** rose to power as the Communist leader of the Soviet Union. Stalin demanded complete obedience from the people he ruled and got it through the use of force. Stalin executed his rivals, ordered the death of thousands suspected of supporting his rivals, and sent millions of Russians to labor camps. He also reorganized the nation's economy, forcing millions onto government-owned farms.

American Neutrality

While dramatic changes were taking place in the world in the 1920s and the 1930s, most Americans wanted to avoid involvement in international crises and conflicts. To keep the nation out of future wars, Congress passed a series of **Neutrality Acts** between 1935 and 1937 that banned the sale of weapons to nations at war. The laws also restricted trade to nations that could pay cash for goods and transport the goods in their own ships. Many American loans to European countries from World War I remained unpaid, and Congress wanted to prevent more debts.

Germany on the March

In Germany, Hitler began moving forward with his plans for expansion. In March 1936, he ordered troops into the **Rhineland.** The Treaty of Versailles had declared the Rhineland, a German territory west of the Rhine River, a neutral zone and had prohibited German soldiers in the area. France and Britain protested the German action—but did little else.

Hitler's next victim was **Austria.** Hitler insisted that Germany should be unified with Austria, a German-speaking nation. In March 1938, he sent troops into Austria and annexed it.

Hitler turned next to the **Sudetenland,** an area of Czechoslovakia where many German-speaking people lived. Falsely claiming that these people were being persecuted, Hitler announced Germany's right to annex the Sudetenland.

Czechoslovakia was prepared to fight to keep the Sudetenland. Britain and France, fearing a full-fledged war in the region, sought a peaceful solution to the crisis. In September 1938, the leaders of Germany, Italy, France, and Great Britain met in Munich, Germany, to discuss the Sudetenland.

Picturing HISTORY In 1950 Hankou, along with the cities of Wuchang and Hanyang, were combined to form one city called Wuhan, which is an inland port located at the confluence of the Han Shui and Chang Jiang.
Ask: **How long had Japanese forces been in China when this picture was taken?** *(7 years—September 1931 to October 1938)*
Answer: *Unhappy with their government's failure to solve economic problems, the Japanese looked to military leaders to solve those problems.*

Political Cartoons, *The Path of Appeasement*

3 ASSESS

Assign Section 1 Review as homework or as an in-class activity.

Use **Chapter Challenger Interactive Review Software** to review Section 1.

Section Quiz 26–1

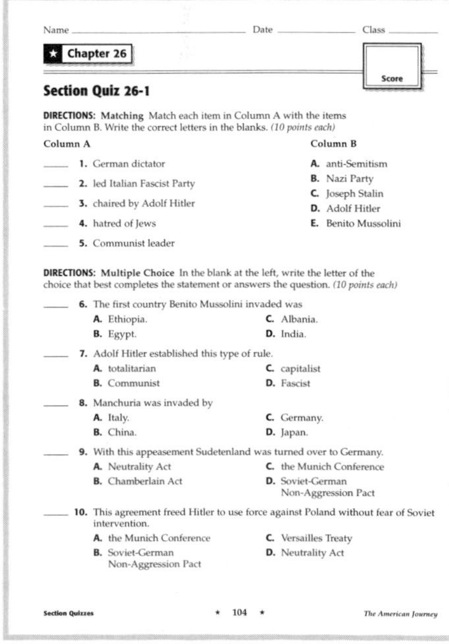

Name ______ Date ______ Class ______

★ Chapter 26 | Score

Section Quiz 26-1

DIRECTIONS: Matching Match each item in Column A with the items in Column B. Write the correct letters in the blanks. *(10 points each)*

Column A	Column B
____ **1.** German dictator	**A.** anti-Semitism
____ **2.** led Italian Fascist Party	**B.** Nazi Party
____ **3.** chaired by Adolf Hitler	**C.** Joseph Stalin
____ **4.** hatred of Jews	**D.** Adolf Hitler
____ **5.** Communist leader	**E.** Benito Mussolini

DIRECTIONS: Multiple Choice In the blank at the left, write the letter of the choice that best completes the statement or answers the question. *(10 points each)*

____ **6.** The first country Benito Mussolini invaded was
A. Ethiopia. **C.** Albania.
B. Egypt. **D.** India.

____ **7.** Adolf Hitler established this type of rule.
A. totalitarian **C.** capitalist
B. Communist **D.** Fascist

____ **8.** Manchuria was invaded by
A. Italy. **C.** Germany.
B. China. **D.** Japan.

____ **9.** With this appeasement Sudetenland was turned over to Germany.
A. Neutrality Act **C.** the Munich Conference
B. Chamberlain Act **D.** Soviet-German Non-Aggression Pact

____ **10.** This agreement freed Hitler to use force against Poland without fear of Soviet intervention.
A. the Munich Conference **C.** Versailles Treaty
B. Soviet-German Non-Aggression Pact **D.** Neutrality Act

Section Quizzes ★ 104 ★ *The American Journey*

Multiple Learning Styles

Intrapersonal Although he was considered a ruthless dictator, Benito Mussolini was much admired as someone who had streamlined Italy's institutions and made them more efficient. In the popular phrase of the day, Mussolini finally "made the trains run on time." Have students write a justification of support for Mussolini from the point of view of Italian citizens of the time. Then have students rebut that position with the hindsight of citizens of today. **L1**

CHAPTER 26
Section 1, 741–744

Picturing HISTORY After Munich, Churchill observed, "Britain and France had to choose between war and dishonor. They chose dishonor. They will have war." **Answer:** *It was given to Germany.*

Reteaching Activity 26–1

Name ______________ Date ______________ Class ______________

★ Reteaching Activity **26-1**

DIRECTIONS: Organizing Facts Create profiles of the dictators whose actions led the world into war in the early 1930s. In the blanks on the chart, write the letter of each item below in the correct category. Some items may fit in more than one place.

Axis Leaders

Leader	Country	Party/ Political Beliefs	Actions/Events
Adolf Hitler			
Benito Mussolini			
Joseph Stalin			
Many Military Leaders			

★**FACT BANK**

A. Fascist Party
B. Soviet Union
C. Germany
D. Communist
E. Japan
F. Nazi
G. Italy
H. extreme anti-Semitism
I. believed it could solve the country's economic problems by expansion
J. vowed to recapture the glory of ancient Romans
K. annexed Ethiopia and Albania
L. put an end to democratic rule
M. occupied most of China by 1941
N. rose to power by appealing to resentment over Treaty of Versailles
O. formed alliance with other dictators
P. annexed the Rhineland, Austria, and the Sudetenland
Q. tolerated no other political parties or rivals
R. exploited economic concerns
S. believed the country needed *lebensraum*—living space
T. invaded Manchuria in 1931
U. violated the Munich Pact
V. sent millions of Russians to labor camps

Reteaching Activities ★ 104 ★ *The American Journey*

Enrichment Activity 26–1

Name ______________ Date ______________ Class ______________

★ Enrichment Activity **26-1** ★

Our Place in the World

As Europe approached World War II, American policy remained isolationist. Most Americans sympathized with the Allies but were determined to avoid international entanglements. Nevertheless, President Franklin D. Roosevelt, while promising to keep American forces at home, took steps to prepare for war. He requested that Congress enlarge the navy and enacted the first peacetime draft in United States history. As the war in Europe continued, the struggle to keep the United States out of the conflict became more and more difficult to maintain.

SOURCE: *Washington Star*, Washington, D.C.

DIRECTIONS: Drawing Conclusions Study the political cartoon. Then write a one-sentence caption that explains the United States's international position during the early wartime years, according to the cartoon.

____

____

Activity **DIRECTIONS:** Consider the position of the United States in the world today. Create a scrapbook of political cartoons that represent ideas related to United States international policies. Collect a variety of cartoons from newspapers and magazines. You may also draw cartoons of your own. Share your scrapbook with a group of classmates. Discuss the positions illustrated in the cartoons.

Enrichment Activities ★ 104 ★ *The American Journey*

4 CLOSE

Ask: Could a Hitler or Mussolini ever again rise to such power? Explain.

Picturing HISTORY A deeply saddened woman (left) gives a forced Nazi salute as German troops enter the Sudetenland. Neville Chamberlain greets Hitler at the Munich Conference (right). **What happened to the Sudetenland as a result of the Munich agreement?**

The Munich Pact

Britain and France thought that they could avoid war by accepting Germany's demands—a policy later known as appeasement. At the **Munich Conference,** the leaders agreed to turn the Sudetenland over to Germany. Hitler, in turn, promised not to expand Germany's territory further. The British prime minister, **Neville Chamberlain,** returned home to cheering crowds, declaring that the agreement had preserved "peace for our time."

Hopes for peace were shattered the following spring. In March 1939, Hitler's army seized the rest of Czechoslovakia. Now even Chamberlain realized that Hitler could not be trusted.

The Nazi-Soviet Pact

Meanwhile, Hitler was making plans to invade **Poland.** He worried, however, that such an attack would anger Stalin because Poland bordered the Soviet Union. Though bitter enemies, Hitler and Stalin signed a treaty called the **Soviet-German Non-Aggression Pact** in August 1939.

The two leaders pledged not to attack one another. They also secretly agreed to divide Poland and other eastern European countries between them. The pact freed Hitler to use force against Poland without fear of Soviet intervention. Stalin wanted to delay the day the Soviet Union would have to fight Germany. The Nazi-Soviet pact shocked the leaders of Europe.

Section 1 Review

Checking for Understanding

1. ***Identify*** Adolf Hitler, Benito Mussolini, Joseph Stalin, Neutrality Acts, Rhineland.
2. ***Define*** dictator, fascism, anti-Semitism, totalitarian, appeasement.
3. ***Explain*** how Hitler gained popularity in Germany.

Reviewing Themes

4. **Continuity and Change** What was the aim of U.S. foreign policy in the 1930s?

Critical Thinking

5. **Making Comparisons** What goals did the dictators and military leaders of the nations of Germany, Italy, and Japan share in the 1930s?

Activity

Making a Time Line Create a time line tracing the major events in Hitler's rise to power in Germany before World War II.

Section 1 Review Answers

1. Adolf Hitler, 741; Benito Mussolini, 741; Joseph Stalin, 743; Neutrality Acts, 743; Rhineland, 743
2. The words are defined in the Glossary.
3. A spellbinding speaker, Hitler exploited people's concerns about the failing German economy and their bitterness over the Versailles treaty.
4. remain neutral, adopt a policy of isolation
5. to expand their political power and add to their nations' territory

Activity Time lines should include: chairman of Nazi Party (1921), chancellor of Germany (1933), alliance with Italy (1936), occupation of Rhineland (1936), annexation of Austria and Sudetenland (1938), invasion of Czechoslovakia, and Soviet-German non-aggression pact (1939).

1939 1940 1941 1942

September 1939 Germany invades Poland

August 1940 Britain is bombed by Germany

June 1941 Hitler attacks the Soviet Union

December 1941 Japan bombs Pearl Harbor

Section 2

War Begins

Read to Discover . . .

- which European countries fell to Germany in 1939 and 1940.
- how America responded to the war in Europe.
- what effect Japan's actions had on America.

Terms to Learn

blitzkrieg
lend-lease
disarmament

The Storyteller

Sixteen-year-old John Garcia, like others who witnessed the attack on Pearl Harbor, never forgot it: "My grandmother . . . informed me that the Japanese were bombing Pearl Harbor. I said, 'They're just practicing.' She said, no, it was real and the announcer is requesting that all Pearl Harbor workers report to work. . . . I was asked . . . to go into the water and get sailors out that had been blown off the ships. Some were unconscious, some were dead. So I spent the rest of the day swimming inside the harbor, along with some other Hawaiians. . . . We worked all day at that."

United States poster after Pearl Harbor bombing

In a speech in 1937, President Franklin Roosevelt expressed the feeling of many Americans toward the growing "epidemic of world lawlessness":

> "We are determined to keep out of war, yet we cannot insure ourselves against the disastrous effects of war and the dangers of involvement."

Within two years the nations of Europe were at war again. Two years after that, a surprise attack by Japan on Pearl Harbor plunged America deep into the terrible conflict.

War in Europe

On September 1, 1939, Hitler sent his armies into **Poland.** Two days later Great Britain and France declared war on Germany. World War II had begun.

The German attack on Poland was swift and fierce. German planes bombed and machine-gunned targets, German tanks blasted holes in Polish defenses, and thousands of soldiers poured into Poland. The Germans called the offensive a blitzkrieg, or "lightning war." Then Soviet troops moved into and occupied eastern Poland, acting on the Soviet agreement with Germany to divide Poland.

Great Britain and France could do little to help Poland because its defeat came so quickly. In late September 1939, the conquered country was split in half by Hitler and Stalin. Stalin also forced

Section Resources

Reproducible Masters

- Reproducible Lesson Plan 26–2
- Guided Reading Activity 26–2
- Section Quiz 26–2
- Reteaching Activity 26–2
- Enrichment Activity 26–2

Transparencies

- Section Focus Transparency 26–2

Multimedia

- Vocabulary PuzzleMaker
- Chapter Challenger Interactive Review Software
- Testmaker
- GTV: A Geographic Perspective on American History
- American Music Cultural Traditions, Lesson 9

1 FOCUS

BELLRINGER
Motivational Activity

Before taking roll at the beginning of the class period, project Section Focus Transparency 26–2 and have students answer the questions. Discuss students' responses.

This activity is also available as a blackline master.

Section Focus Transparency 26–2

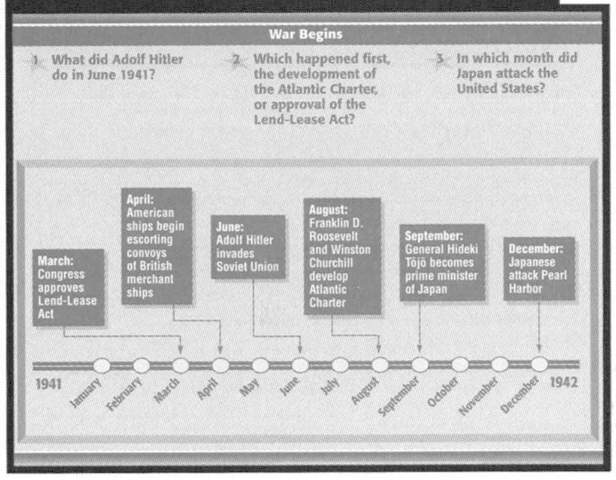

Vocabulary Precheck

Ask why the Germans called their attack on Poland a *blitzkrieg* (lightning war). *(because of the speed with which it was carried out)*

Use the **Vocabulary PuzzleMaker** to create crossword and word search puzzles.

Section Theme
Global Connections

Despite their efforts to avoid war, nations all over the globe were drawn into the conflict, largely because of political alliances and economic interdependence.

Activity Have students find out what Japan did after America applied economic pressure on that nation. *(Japan attacked Pearl Harbor.)*

2 TEACH

L1 Completing Ideas Have students explain the importance of the following five events: the fall of Poland, the Allied retreat to Dunkirk, the Battle of Britain, the passage of the Lend-Lease Act, and the bombing of Pearl Harbor. Students should complete five short paragraphs, beginning with the words "[The fall of Poland] was important because. . . ."

Guided Reading Activity 26–2

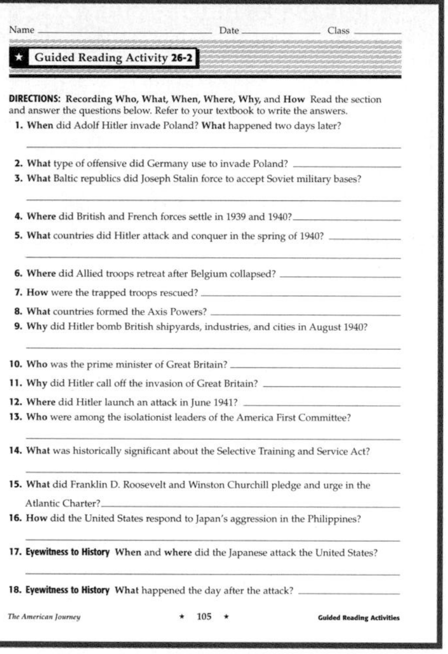
Name ______ Date ______ Class ______

★ Guided Reading Activity **26-2**

DIRECTIONS: Recording Who, What, When, Where, Why, and **How** Read the section and answer the questions below. Refer to your textbook to write the answers.

1. **When** did Adolf Hitler invade Poland? **What** happened two days later?
2. **What** type of offensive did Germany use to invade Poland?
3. **What** Baltic republics did Joseph Stalin force to accept Soviet military bases?
4. **Where** did British and French forces settle in 1939 and 1940?
5. **What** countries did Hitler attack and conquer in the spring of 1940?
6. **Where** did Allied troops retreat after Belgium collapsed?
7. **How** were the trapped troops rescued?
8. **What** countries formed the Axis Powers?
9. **Why** did Hitler bomb British shipyards, industries, and cities in August 1940?
10. **Who** was the prime minister of Great Britain?
11. **Why** did Hitler call off the invasion of Great Britain?
12. **Where** did Hitler launch an attack in June 1941?
13. **Who** were among the isolationist leaders of the America First Committee?
14. **What** was historically significant about the Selective Training and Service Act?
15. **What** did Franklin D. Roosevelt and Winston Churchill pledge and urge in the Atlantic Charter?
16. **How** did the United States respond to Japan's aggression in the Philippines?
17. **Eyewitness to History** **When** and **where** did the Japanese attack the United States?
18. **Eyewitness to History** **What** happened the day after the attack?

Copyright © by The McGraw-Hill Companies, Inc.

The American Journey ★ 105 ★ **Guided Reading Activities**

HISTORY AND ART This painting highlights the drama of the Dunkirk rescue by focusing on the many small boats that evacuated the soldiers. Despite the success of the evacuation (which took eight days), Churchill warned Parliament, "Wars are not won by evacuations." **Ask:** What did he mean? *(You need to win battles, not just save soldiers.)*
Answer: *The collapse of Belgium forced the Allies to retreat and trapped them between the advancing Germans and the French coast.*

the **Baltic** republics of Latvia, Lithuania, and Estonia to accept Soviet military bases. When he tried to do the same with **Finland,** war broke out. The Finns held out heroically until March 1940 before the Soviets forced them to surrender.

The War Expands

All through the winter of 1939–40, the western front was quiet. British and French forces settled in at the **Maginot Line,** a string of steel-and-concrete bunkers along the German border from Belgium to Switzerland. In the spring the fighting began again. Hitler attacked **Denmark** and **Norway** to the north in April, and the following month he turned west to invade the **Netherlands** and **Belgium.** The Netherlands and Belgium immediately asked for help from Great Britain and France—the **Allies.** After terrible bombing raids, the Dutch surrendered. The Belgians fought courageously, but they too were overwhelmed.

With the collapse of Belgium, Allied troops retreated to the port of **Dunkirk** in the northwest corner of France on the **English Channel.** They were now trapped between the advancing Germans and the French coast. In a daring move, more than 800 British ships—warships, ferries, and fishing boats—joined an operation to rescue the troops. Crossing the Channel again and again, the boats evacuated more than 300,000 French and British troops to safety.

In June the Germans crossed the Somme River and continued their sweep into France. Italy joined the war on the side of Germany and attacked France from the southeast. Germany and Italy—and later Japan—formed the **Axis Powers.** On June 14, 1940, German troops marched victoriously into Paris. The French surrendered a week later, stunned by the German blitzkrieg.

The Battle of Britain

All that stood between Hitler's domination of western Europe was Great Britain. In August 1940, the Germans bombed British shipyards, industries, and cities, destroying entire neighborhoods of London and killing many civilians. Hitler's goal was to break British morale before invading Britain. The British people endured, however, in part because of the inspiration of Prime Minister **Winston Churchill.** When Hitler called for Britain to surrender, Churchill responded defiantly:

> "We shall defend our island, whatever the cost may be. We shall fight on the beaches, we shall fight on the landing grounds, we shall fight in the fields and in the streets, we shall fight in the hills; we shall never surrender."

Although the **Battle of Britain** continued until October, the Germans never gained control

HISTORY AND ART

***The Withdrawal from Dunkirk, June 1940* by Charles R.A. Cundall** Boats of every size crossed the English Channel to bring Allied troops from France to safety in England. **Why did Allied forces retreat?**

COOPERATIVE LEARNING ACTIVITY

Making Models and Drawings Have students work together in small groups to illustrate some of the weapons and equipment used in World War II. Have the group choose the subjects to illustrate. Then ask individuals to do the necessary research and others to make labeled drawings or diagrams of tanks, airplanes, bombs, or artillery. Some World War II buffs may choose to make models rather than drawings. **L2, ELL**

The Nation Gears Up for Conflict

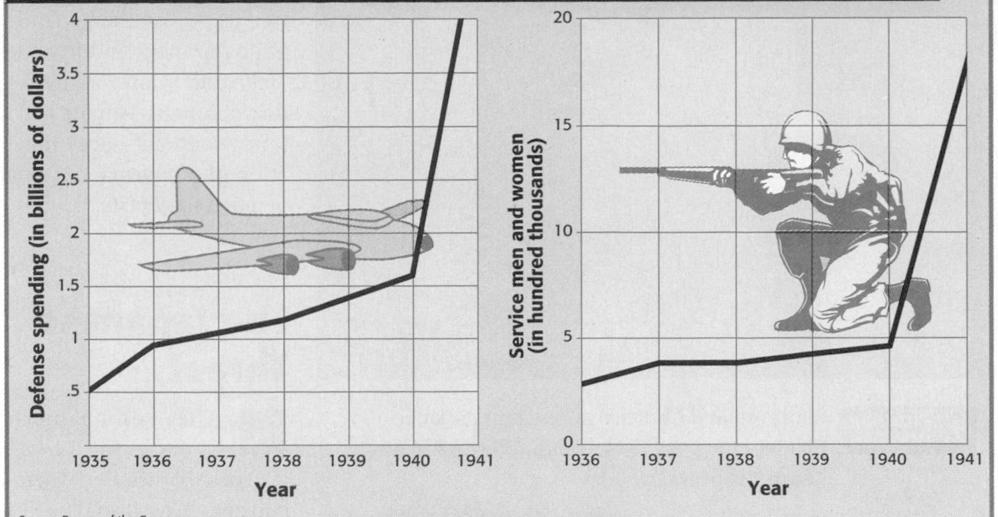

Source: Bureau of the Census.

Graph Study

As early as 1938 American factories planned for producing war equipment. Military personnel also increased.

1. About how many Americans served in the military in 1941?
2. **Analyzing Information** About how much more money was spent on defense in 1940 than in 1938?

of the skies over Britain. The British Royal Air Force (RAF) mounted a heroic defense and inflicted heavy losses on the German air force. Finally, Hitler ended the air attacks and called off the invasion of Britain.

Germany Turns East

Frustrated by his failure in Britain, Hitler decided to realize one of his oldest dreams—to destroy the Soviet Union. Ignoring the pact he had made with Stalin, Hitler launched an attack on the Soviet Union in June 1941. Within months German armies had moved into Soviet territory.

America and the War

The United States watched the war in Europe with growing concern. Although most Americans sympathized with the Allies, they were determined to avoid war. Isolationists banded together to form the **America First Committee.** Its members thought the United States should keep out of Europe's business. Among those who led this group were aviation hero Charles Lindbergh and automaker Henry Ford.

While vowing to remain neutral, Roosevelt took steps to prepare for war. In 1938, at his request, Congress voted to strengthen the navy. In 1939 the president asked Congress to pass a new Neutrality Act that allowed the United States to sell weapons to other countries on a "cash and carry" basis. In 1940 FDR signed the Selective Training and Service Act, the first peacetime draft in United States history. The law applied to American men between the ages of 21 and 35.

The 1940 Election

With the world in crisis, President Roosevelt decided to run for a third term, breaking the tradition set by George Washington. His Republican opponent was **Wendell Willkie.** Public sentiment to stay out of the war was so strong that Roosevelt promised the American people, "Your boys are not going to be sent into any foreign wars." Roosevelt won an easy victory.

Multiple Learning Styles

Visual/Spatial In addition to the hundreds of documentaries about the war, there are several good feature films. Students might get a flavor of the period from any of the following award-winning films: *The Bridge on the River Kwai*—drama about the battle of wills between commanders over the construction of a bridge (1957, 161 minutes); *A Bridge Too Far*—re-creation of the Allied defeat at Arnhem in 1944 (1977, 175 minutes); *Guns of Navarone*—an epic about six men sent to destroy German guns on an Aegean island (1961, 159 minutes); *Summer of My German Soldier*—a Jewish girl befriends an escaped German POW in a small town in Georgia (U.S.) (1978, 98 minutes); *They Were Expendable*—two Americans pit their PT boats against the Japanese fleet (1945, 135 minutes). **L1**

Graph Study

Answers

1. 1,800,000
2. $0.4 billion ($400 million)

Graph Skills Practice

Reading a Graph What general statement can you make about these graphs? *(Defense spending and the number of military personnel gradually increased during the 1930s, then spiked sharply in 1940.)*

NATIONAL GEOGRAPHIC SOCIETY

VIDEODISC
GTV: A Geographic Perspective on American History

Side 4, Chapter 6
Title: *Echoes of War*
Subject: Effects of World War II
Ask: **What effect did World War II have on the economy of the United States?** *(War industries helped to bring the U.S. economy out of the Great Depression.)*

Linking PAST & PRESENT

Poland's military was valiant but old-fashioned. It still included cavalry units, which were demolished by German tanks. The slaughter marked the end of mounted soldiers in a major war.

History *and the* Humanities

American Music Cultural Traditions, Lesson 9: "Take Me Back to Tulsa," "Boogie Woogie Bugle Boy," "Jersey Bounce"

CHAPTER 26
Section 2, 745–749

Picturing HISTORY Churchill and Roosevelt formed a strong working partnership in the early years of the war.

Answer: *It set the goals for the world after the Nazis were destroyed: every nation free to choose its government and live free of "fear and want," disarmament, creation of a "permanent system of general security."*

Who?What?Where?When?

Jeannette Rankin, the first woman elected to Congress, was the only member of the House to cast a dissenting vote against American entry into both World War I and World War II. A statue of Rankin now stands in the Capitol in Washington, D.C., bearing the motto: "I cannot vote for war."

3 ASSESS

Assign Section 2 Review as homework or as an in-class activity.

Use **Chapter Challenger Interactive Review Software** to review Section 2.

Section Quiz 26–2

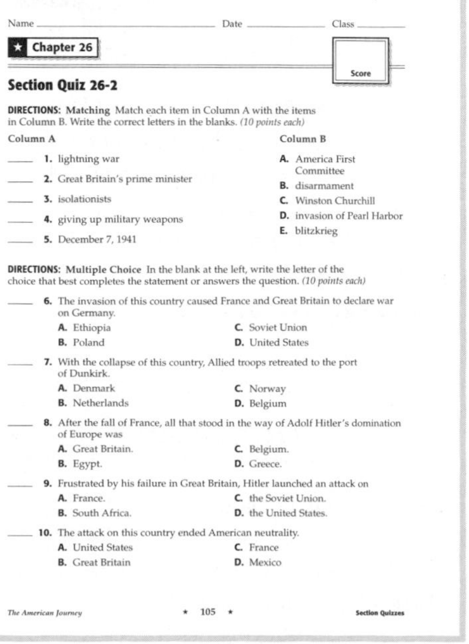

Name ______ Date ______ Class ______

★ Chapter 26 — Score

Section Quiz 26-2

DIRECTIONS: Matching Match each item in Column A with the items in Column B. Write the correct letters in the blanks. *(10 points each)*

Column A	Column B
____ **1.** lightning war	**A.** America First Committee
____ **2.** Great Britain's prime minister	**B.** disarmament
____ **3.** isolationists	**C.** Winston Churchill
____ **4.** giving up military weapons	**D.** invasion of Pearl Harbor
____ **5.** December 7, 1941	**E.** blitzkrieg

DIRECTIONS: Multiple Choice In the blank at the left, write the letter of the choice that best completes the statement or answers the question. *(10 points each)*

____ **6.** The invasion of this country caused France and Great Britain to declare war on Germany.
A. Ethiopia **C.** Soviet Union
B. Poland **D.** United States

____ **7.** With the collapse of this country, Allied troops retreated to the port of Dunkirk.
A. Denmark **C.** Norway
B. Netherlands **D.** Belgium

____ **8.** After the fall of France, all that stood in the way of Adolf Hitler's domination of Europe was
A. Great Britain. **C.** Belgium.
B. Egypt. **D.** Greece.

____ **9.** Frustrated by his failure in Great Britain, Hitler launched an attack on
A. France. **C.** the Soviet Union.
B. South Africa. **D.** the United States.

____ **10.** The attack on this country ended American neutrality.
A. United States **C.** France
B. Great Britain **D.** Mexico

The American Journey ★ 105 ★ Section Quizzes

Picturing HISTORY Roosevelt and Churchill adopted the Atlantic Charter in August 1941. **What did the Atlantic Charter express?**

Growing Involvement

With the election won, Roosevelt moved to support the Allies openly. At Roosevelt's urging, Congress approved the **Lend-Lease** Act in March 1941. The Lend-Lease Act allowed America to sell, lend, or lease arms or other war supplies to any nation considered "vital to the defense of the United States." Britain, which was running out of cash, was the first to use lend-lease. Isolationists opposed the Lend-Lease Act, arguing that it would increase American involvement in the war.

German submarines in the Atlantic Ocean had been sinking British ships, including those carrying supplies from the United States. In April 1941, American ships began escorting convoys of British merchant ships. After the Germans began firing on American destroyers, Roosevelt issued a "shoot-on-sight" order to American naval vessels that found German and Italian ships in certain areas.

The Atlantic Charter

In August 1941, President Roosevelt and British prime minister Churchill met and drew up the **Atlantic Charter.** While Roosevelt made no military commitments, he joined Churchill in setting goals for a world after "the final destruction of the Nazi tyranny." The two nations pledged that the people of every nation would be free to choose their own form of government and live free of "fear and want." They urged **disarmament**—giving up military weapons—and the creation of a "permanent system of general security."

The Japanese Threat

After seizing much of China in the 1930s, the Japanese continued their expansion. After the fall of France in 1940, they seized the French colony of **Indochina** in Southeast Asia. Japan also planned to take the Dutch East Indies, British Malaya, and the American territory of the Philippines, primarily to acquire badly needed rubber and oil.

The United States Responds

The United States responded to Japan's aggression by applying economic pressure. Roosevelt froze all Japanese assets in American banks, preventing the Japanese from obtaining funds they had in the United States. He also stopped the sale of oil, gasoline, and other natural resources that Japan lacked. The action outraged the Japanese.

In September 1941, General **Hideki Tōjō** became prime minister of Japan. Desperate for resources and confident of Japan's military might, the Tōjō government began planning an attack on the United States.

Eyewitness to HISTORY

Attack on Pearl Harbor

At 7:55 A.M. on Sunday, December 7, 1941, Japanese warplanes attacked the American military base at **Pearl Harbor,** Hawaii, putting an end to American neutrality. Rear Admiral William R. Furlong reported:

MAKING CONNECTIONS ACTIVITY

Foreign Affairs Have students prepare a *Who's Who?* of military leaders in World War II. In addition to those mentioned in the text (Patton, Eisenhower, Rommel, MacArthur, Nimitz), students may include Omar Bradley, Mark Clark, Claire Chennault, Curtis LeMay, William F. Halsey, and Isoroku Yamamoto. Have students write a paragraph on each person, giving birth and death dates, the country for which each fought, the branch of the armed forces in which each served, key battles and accomplishments, and other pertinent or interesting data, such as nicknames. **L2**

> “I was on the deck of my flagship and saw the first enemy bomb fall. . . . Plumes over one hundred feet high went up from bombs that hit close alongside of battleships.”

The attack devastated the American fleet, destroying 8 battleships, 3 cruisers, and 4 other vessels. Hundreds of planes were destroyed on the ground. More than 2,400 soldiers, sailors, and civilians were killed.

Fortunately, at the time of the attack, the navy's three aircraft carriers were at sea. Their escape from destruction provided the only good news that day.

Grace Tully, one of the president's secretaries, received an urgent call to report to the White House. She later recalled:

> “Most of the news on the . . . attack was then coming to the White House by telephone from Admiral Stark, Chief of Naval Operations, at the Navy Department . . . each report more terrible than the last, and I could hear the shocked unbelief in Admiral Stark's voice.”

Pearl Harbor was the worst defeat in United States military history. Yet Pearl Harbor also united Americans. All debate about involvement in the war ended. On the day after Pearl Harbor, President Roosevelt asked Congress for a declaration of war, calling December 7 “a date which will live in infamy [shame].” Congress quickly approved the president's request to declare war on Japan.

Three days later Germany and Italy, Japan's allies, declared war on the United States. Congress then declared war on them as well. The United States had joined the Allied nations—including Great Britain, France, and the Soviet Union—against the Axis Powers—Germany, Italy, and Japan—in World War II.

Picturing HISTORY Japan's surprise attack on Pearl Harbor severely damaged the United States Pacific Fleet. **How did the attack affect American neutrality?**

Section 2 Review

Checking for Understanding

1. ***Identify*** Allies, Axis Powers, Winston Churchill, Atlantic Charter, Pearl Harbor.
2. ***Define*** blitzkrieg, lend-lease, disarmament.
3. ***Describe*** the action that started World War II.

Reviewing Themes

4. **Global Connections** What actions did the United States take to prevent Japan from taking over nations in Asia?

Critical Thinking

5. **Predicting Consequences** Do you think the United States would have eventually joined the war even if the Japanese had not bombed Pearl Harbor? Explain.

Activity

Media Literacy Write and record a 15-second radio news bulletin announcing the Japanese bombing of Pearl Harbor.

Section 2 Review Answers

1. Allies, 746; Axis powers, 746; Winston Churchill, 746; Atlantic Charter, 748; Pearl Harbor, 748
2. The words are defined in the Glossary.
3. Germany invaded Poland on September 1, 1939.
4. froze all Japanese assets in United States banks and stopped the sale of many resources to Japan
5. Answers may include: *Yes,* the U.S. was closely allied to Britain and would have stepped in to help. Also, the U.S. might have been forced to stop Japan from taking over the Philippines. *No,* without a direct attack, the U.S. would have stayed out of war.

Activity Students' news bulletins should capture the drama of the event.

Picturing HISTORY In 1924, General William Mitchell predicted planes from aircraft carriers would strike Pearl Harbor some morning at about 7:30.
Answer: *It ended American neutrality.*

Reteaching Activity 26–2

Name ______ Date ______ Class ______

★ Reteaching Activity 26-2

DIRECTIONS: Putting Events in Sequence For each section, number the events in the order in which they occurred.

Section I. War in Europe

____ **A.** Adolf Hitler attacks Denmark and Norway.
____ **B.** Hitler launches an attack on the Soviet Union.
____ **C.** Great Britain and France declare war on Germany.
____ **D.** German troops march victoriously into Paris.
____ **E.** Hitler's army uses the blitzkrieg to attack Poland.
____ **F.** More than 800 British ships rescue more than 300,000 British and French soldiers trapped at Dunkirk.
____ **G.** Hitler calls off the invasion of Great Britain.
____ **H.** The Finns surrender to the Soviet Union after a heroic battle.
____ **I.** The Germans bomb and destroy entire London neighborhoods in an attempt to weaken British morale.
____ **J.** The Netherlands and Belgium ask the Allies (Great Britain and France) for help when Hitler invades these countries.

Section II. America and the War

____ **A.** Germany and Italy declare war on the United States.
____ **B.** Franklin Roosevelt signs the Selective Training and Service Act.
____ **C.** General Hideki Tōjō becomes prime minister of Japan.
____ **D.** Roosevelt asks Congress for a declaration of war.
____ **E.** Roosevelt and Winston Churchill draw up the Atlantic Charter.
____ **F.** Congress votes to enlarge and strengthen the navy.
____ **G.** The Lend-Lease Act allows the United States to sell, lend, or lease arms or other war supplies to any nation considered “vital” to American defense.
____ **H.** Japanese warplanes attack the American military base at Pearl Harbor, Hawaii.

The American Journey ★ 105 ★ Reteaching Activities

Enrichment Activity 26–2

Name ______ Date ______ Class ______

★ Enrichment Activity 26-2

The Four Freedoms Speech

In 1941 President Franklin D. Roosevelt made this speech:

> In the future days which we seek to make secure, we look forward to a world founded upon four essential human freedoms.
>
> The first is freedom of speech and expression—everywhere in the world.
>
> The second is freedom of every person to worship God in his own way—everywhere in the world.
>
> The third is freedom from want—which translated into world terms, means economic understandings which will secure to every nation a healthy peacetime life for its inhabitants—everywhere in the world.
>
> The fourth is freedom from fear, which, translated into world terms, means a world-wide reduction of armaments to such a point and in such a thorough manner that no nation will be in a position to commit an act of . . . aggression against any neighbor—anywhere in the world.

1. What phrase did Roosevelt repeat after he identified each freedom?
2. Why do you think Roosevelt repeated that phrase?
3. How many of Roosevelt's freedoms do you think have been accomplished? Explain.

Activity **DIRECTIONS:** Think about what freedom meant to Americans at the time of the Revolutionary War and what freedom means today. How do the ideas Roosevelt expressed compare to earlier and later ideas of freedom? Are his four freedoms the most important ones? On a separate sheet of paper, write an essay to answer these questions. In your essay, be sure to tell what freedom means to you.

The American Journey ★ 105 ★ Enrichment Activities

4 CLOSE

Ask students to discuss ways in which the United States became “the great arsenal of democracy.”

CHAPTER 26
Section 3, 750–754

1 FOCUS

BELLRINGER
Motivational Activity

Before taking roll at the beginning of the class period, project Section Focus Transparency 26-3 and have students answer the questions. Discuss students' responses.

This activity is also available as a blackline master.

Section Focus Transparency 26-3

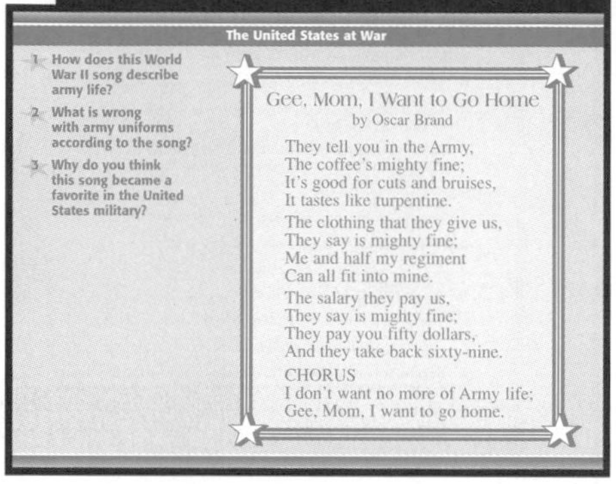

Vocabulary Precheck

Ask students to say the root word of *mobilization. (mobile)* Then have them define *mobilization.*

Use the **Vocabulary PuzzleMaker** to create crossword and word search puzzles.

Section Theme
Economic Factors

The United States had to switch rapidly from a peacetime economy to a wartime economy—providing arms and other supplies for thousands of troops.

Activity Have students speculate on why some consumer goods were in short supply during the war. *(Factories were making war materials instead of consumer goods.)*

1941 FDR establishes Fair Employment Practices Commission

1942 Revenue Act raises taxes to finance the war; Office of War Information promotes patriotism

1943 Navajo soldiers develop unbreakable radio code

Section 3

On the Home Front

READ TO DISCOVER . . .

- what steps the United States took to prepare for fighting World War II.
- how the war affected the American people.

TERMS TO LEARN

mobilization
ration
internment camp

The Storyteller

Despite the serious nature of war, Americans tried to keep their morale high during World War II through cooperation and humor. People bought war bonds, ate less butter, made war jokes, and became air raid wardens. In *Yank,* the Army weekly magazine, one writer had this to say about the rationing of foods such as butter and sugar:

"Roses are red,
Violets are blue,
Sugar is sweet—
remember?"

U.S. sailor, World War II

World War II required commitment and sacrifice from all Americans. While American soldiers risked their lives in combat overseas, people at home worked hard and learned to do without goods and services they had taken for granted.

America Prepares

The Japanese attack on Pearl Harbor united the American people as nothing else could. With astonishing speed the nation's economy and its people prepared to fight the war.

Raising an Army

Even before Pearl Harbor, the United States had begun raising an army under the Selective Service acts of 1940 and 1941. More than 15 million Americans joined the armed forces during the war, both as draftees and as volunteers.

For the first time, large numbers of women served in the military. About 350,000 women served in the **WACs** (Women's Army Corps), the **WAVES** (Women Appointed for Volunteer Emergency Service in the Navy), and women's units in the marines, Coast Guard, and army air corps. These women did not fight in combat—most performed clerical tasks or worked as nurses—but they played important roles in the war effort.

Equipping the troops and providing arms and other war materials required changes in the nation's economy. To speed up **mobilization**—military and civilian preparations for war—the

SECTION RESOURCES

Reproducible Masters
- Reproducible Lesson Plan 26-3
- Guided Reading Activity 26-3
- Section Quiz 26-3
- Reteaching Activity 26-3
- Enrichment Activity 26-3

Transparencies
- Section Focus Transparency 26-3

Multimedia
- Vocabulary PuzzleMaker
- Chapter Challenger Interactive Review Software
- Testmaker
- GTV: The American People: Fabric of a Nation

American government created a number of new government agencies.

The **War Production Board** supervised the conversion of industries to war production. Under its guidance, automakers shifted from building cars to producing trucks and tanks. The **Office of Price Administration** set limits on consumer prices and rents to prevent inflation. The **National War Labor Board** helped resolve labor disputes that might slow down war production. Later, the **Office of War Mobilization** was established to help these agencies operate efficiently.

Financing the War

From 1941 to the end of World War II, the United States spent more than $320 billion on the war effort—10 times the amount spent in World War I. Much of this money was raised through taxes. The Revenue Act of 1942 raised corporate taxes and required nearly all Americans to pay income taxes. Congress approved a system for withholding taxes from workers' paychecks—a practice still in effect.

The government also borrowed money to finance the war. As in World War I, the government sold war bonds. Movie stars and other celebrities urged people to buy bonds to support the war.

Wartime America

During the war, industry soared. Factories produced more than 70,000 ships, almost 100,000 tanks and airplanes, and millions of guns. Production speed increased as well. Some cargo ships were built in only 17 days.

Wartime production helped restore prosperity to the nation after the long years of the Depression. Incomes rose and prices remained fairly stable.

Ration coupons

WAC hat

Picturing HISTORY More than 25,000 women applied to become members of the Women's Airforce Service Pilots (WASPs). About 2,000 were accepted, and 1,074 won their wings. **What were the responsibilities of women in the service?**

Making Sacrifices

With the war effort came sacrifices. For millions of American families, the war meant separation from loved ones serving overseas. Those at home lived in dread of receiving a telegram announcing that a family member had been killed, wounded, or captured.

With industries making war materials, Americans faced shortages of many consumer goods. After 1942, for example, automakers stopped making new cars and turned instead to making tanks, planes, and trucks. Women could not buy stockings—silk imports from war-torn Asia had halted, and nylon was needed to make parachutes.

In addition many resources and goods needed for the war effort were **rationed**—consumers could buy only limited numbers of them. Americans used government-issued books of ration coupons to purchase certain items, such as shoes, gasoline, tires, sugar, and meat. When people ran out of coupons, they did without the rationed items. But because Americans overwhelmingly supported the war effort, they generally accepted inconveniences and shortages with good spirits.

CHAPTER 26
Section 3, 750–754

Picturing HISTORY The Women's Airforce Service Pilots tested new and rebuilt fighter planes and flew military aircraft from factories to bases in the United States and Europe. Despite their outstanding service, they did not receive recognition or veterans benefits until 1979. **Ask: What were other women's units?** *(WACs, WAVES, and units in marines, Coast Guard, and army air corps)*
Answer: *Most performed clerical tasks or worked as nurses.*

2 TEACH

L1 Summarizing Work with students to write summary statements for each subsection in Section 3. Remind students that a summary statement must be detailed.

Guided Reading Activity 26–3

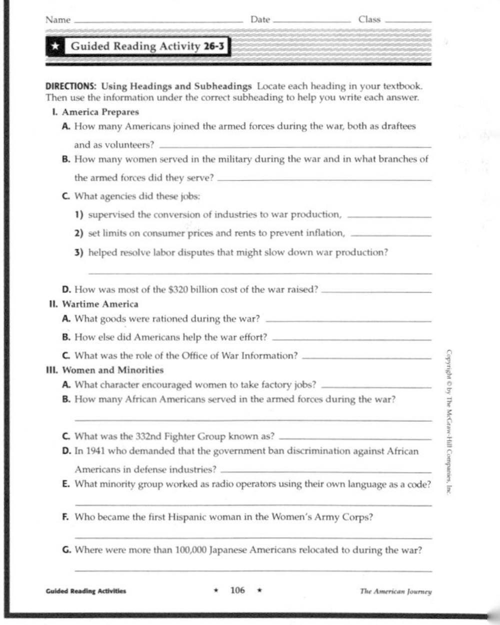

Name ________ Date ________ Class ________

Guided Reading Activity 26-3

DIRECTIONS: Using Headings and Subheadings Locate each heading in your textbook. Then use the information under the correct subheading to help you write each answer.

I. America Prepares

A. How many Americans joined the armed forces during the war, both as draftees and as volunteers? ________

B. How many women served in the military during the war and in what branches of the armed forces did they serve? ________

C. What agencies did these jobs:

1) supervised the conversion of industries to war production, ________

2) set limits on consumer prices and rents to prevent inflation, ________

3) helped resolve labor disputes that might slow down war production? ________

D. How was most of the $320 billion cost of the war raised? ________

II. Wartime America

A. What goods were rationed during the war? ________

B. How else did Americans help the war effort? ________

C. What was the role of the Office of War Information? ________

III. Women and Minorities

A. What character encouraged women to take factory jobs? ________

B. How many African Americans served in the armed forces during the war? ________

C. What was the 332nd Fighter Group known as? ________

D. In 1941 who demanded that the government ban discrimination against African Americans in defense industries? ________

E. What minority group worked as radio operators using their own language as a code? ________

F. Who became the first Hispanic woman in the Women's Army Corps? ________

G. Where were more than 100,000 Japanese Americans relocated to during the war? ________

Guided Reading Activities • 106 • *The American Journey*

COOPERATIVE LEARNING ACTIVITY

Finding Slogans During the war, posters with catchy slogans encouraged people to perform various patriotic acts. For example, slogans urging women to enlist in the WAACs (Women's Army Auxiliary Corps) included, "Speed Them Back, Join the WAAC" and "I'd Rather Be with Them—Than Waiting for Them." Have students find other examples of World War II slogans and/or propaganda and work in small groups to either reproduce the posters on which the slogans originally appeared or to create new posters with students' own slogans and designs.

Graph Study

Answers
1. 1910
2. 24 percent

Graph Skills Practice

Reading a Graph How can the percentage of women in the labor force be the same in 1910 and 1920, even though more women were employed in 1920? *(The total population of the labor force was higher in 1920.)*

Who?What?Where?When?

Women's Airforce Service Pilots (WASPs) Although women were not allowed to serve in combat, they were pilots. Members of the WASPs flew warplanes to the places where they were needed, freeing men for combat duty. The obstacles women faced were enormous. Resentful males often refused to fly with them, and in one case a male pilot may have sabotaged a plane, killing a female pilot. WASPs flew more than 60 million miles in all types of planes, and 38 WASPs died while on duty.

NATIONAL GEOGRAPHIC SOCIETY

VIDEODISC
GTV: The American People: Fabric of a Nation

Side 4, Chapter 2
Title: *United We Stand?*
Subject: World War II at home
Ask: What two minority groups gained job opportunities during World War II? *(African Americans and women)*

U.S. Women in the Labor Force, 1900–1950

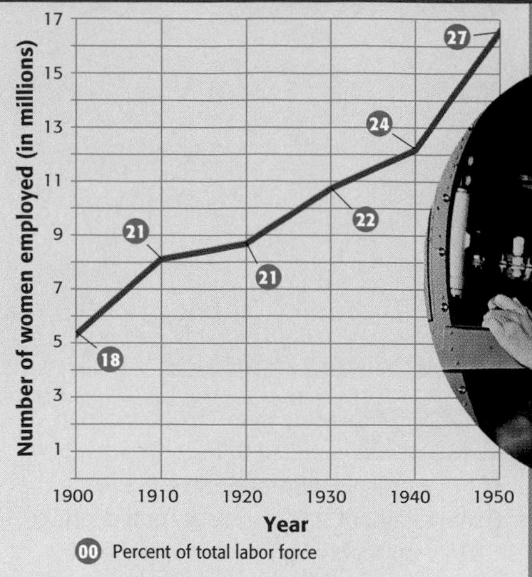

(00) Percent of total labor force

Source: *Historical Statistics of the United States: Colonial Times to 1970.*

Graph Study

During World War II, the American workforce took on a whole new look.
1. During what year were there about 8 million women in the labor force?
2. **Analyzing Information** In 1940 what percent of the labor force was made up of women?

Helping the War Effort

People found other ways to help the war effort. Many planted "victory gardens" to grow vegetables, which were in short supply. Children collected scrap metal for use in industry.

Many people joined in **civil defense**—protective measures in case of attack. For example, volunteer spotters scanned the skies for enemy aircraft that might try to approach America. Coastal cities enforced blackouts at night so that lights could not serve as beacons for enemy pilots.

The **Office of War Information,** established by the government, promoted patriotism and helped keep Americans united behind the war effort. It also broadcast messages all over the world.

Women and Minorities

The war had a tremendous impact on the lives of women and minorities. It brought opportunity for new jobs and a new role in society. Yet for some, unfair treatment left lasting scars.

Wartime worker

As millions of men joined the armed forces, more women than ever before entered the labor force. In factories women worked as welders and riveters and in other jobs held previously by men. An advertising campaign featuring a character called **Rosie the Riveter** encouraged women to take factory jobs. For many women it was their first opportunity to work outside the home.

Although women had new job opportunities, they usually earned less than men. Moreover, when the war ended and the troops returned home, most women would lose their jobs. Still, the war opened new fields to women and changed public opinion about women's right to work.

African Americans During the War

About 700,000 African Americans served in the armed forces during the war. At first most were given low-level assignments and kept in segregated units. Gradually, military leaders assigned them to integrated units. In 1942 the army began training whites and African Americans together in officer candidate school. Finally, African Americans were allowed to take combat assignments. The 332nd Fighter Group, known as the **Tuskegee Airmen,** shot down more than 200 enemy planes. **Benjamin Davis, Jr.,** who trained at the Tuskegee flying school, became the first African American general in the United States Air Force. His father, Benjamin Davis, Sr., had been the first African American general in the army.

In civilian life African Americans sought change. In the summer of 1941, labor leader **A. Philip Randolph** demanded that the

MULTIPLE LEARNING STYLES

Verbal/Linguistic Have students research the American home front during World War II and present their findings to the class. They may either expand on a topic covered in the section or choose a new one. One good source is *The Home Front: U.S.A.* (New York: Time-Life Books, 1977). Students may find the section on the efforts of children (pages 120–127) and the section on scientific and technological advances (page 185) particularly interesting. **L2**

government ban discrimination against African Americans in defense industries. He planned a large demonstration in Washington in support of his demands. President Roosevelt persuaded Randolph to call off the march by establishing the Fair Employment Practices Commission to combat discrimination in industries that held government contracts. The president announced that

> "... there shall be no discrimination in the employment of workers in defense industries or government because of race, creed, color, or national origin."

Picturing HISTORY Doris Miller, World War II's first recognized African American hero, won the Navy Cross for bravery for defending a battleship during the Japanese attack at Pearl Harbor. **How did the position of African Americans in the armed forces change during World War II?**

The war accelerated the population shift that had begun during World War I. Large numbers of African Americans moved from the rural South to industrialized cities in the North and the West in search of work. In some cities, racial tensions erupted in violence. The violence sometimes resulted in death. The riots inspired the African American poet **Langston Hughes** to write:

> "Yet you say we're fightin'
> for democracy.
> Then why don't democracy
> Include me?"

Picturing HISTORY In 1943 the United States Marines recruited Navajo soldiers to develop a military code that the Japanese could not break. **In what other ways did Native Americans contribute to the war effort?**

Native Americans

Thousands of Native Americans served in the armed forces. **Ira Hayes** became a hero in the battle for Iwo Jima in the Pacific. Navajo soldiers worked as radio operators, using their own language as a code. Many Native Americans left reservations to work in defense industries.

Hispanic Americans

Approximately 500,000 Hispanic Americans served in the armed forces. The Congressional Medal of Honor, the nation's highest military medal, was awarded to 17 Mexican Americans. **Mercedes Cubría** of Cuba became the first Hispanic woman officer in the Women's Army Corps. **Horacio Rivero** of Puerto Rico became the first Hispanic four-star admiral since David Farragut to serve in the United States Navy.

Prompted by the wartime need for labor, United States labor agents recruited thousands of farm and railroad workers from Mexico. This program, called the **bracero** program, stimulated emigration from Mexico during the war years.

Like African Americans, Mexican Americans suffered from discrimination, and their presence

Making Connections Activity

Literature John J. McCloy, assistant secretary of the army, in 1942 described the relocation of Japanese Americans as skillful, speedy, and humane, saying that "extreme care . . . has been taken to protect the persons and goods and even the comforts of each individual." Evaluate the statement with students. Then have them read the excerpt from *The Invisible Thread* on pages 686–687.

An internment camp in Santa Anita was formerly a racetrack, and detainees had to live in horse stalls along with the stench of manure and the biting of horseflies. In a camp in Puyallup, Washington, the detainees were supplied with only one washroom for every 100 families. Compare McCloy's statement with the true conditions of the internment camps. **L2**

CHAPTER 26
Section 3, 750–754

Picturing HISTORY Miller worked in the ship's mess aboard the U.S.S. *Arizona.* Despite his "noncombatant" status, he voluntarily manned a machine gun and brought down four Japanese planes. He was cited for "distinguished devotion to duty, extreme courage, and disregard of his personal safety during attack."
Answer: *at first given low-level assignments and kept in segregated units, gradually integrated and allowed combat assignments*

3 ASSESS

Assign Section 3 Review as homework or as an in-class activity.

Use **Chapter Challenger Interactive Review Software** to review Section 3.

Section Quiz 26–3

Name ________ Date ________ Class ________

★ Chapter 26 | Score

Section Quiz 26-3

DIRECTIONS: Matching Match each item in Column A with the items in Column B. Write the correct letters in the blanks. *(10 points each)*

Column A	Column B
____ **1.** preparations for war	**A.** mobilization
____ **2.** promoted patriotism	**B.** Rosie the Riveter
____ **3.** recruited Mexican workers	**C.** civil defense
____ **4.** protective measures	**D.** Office of War Information
____ **5.** star of advertising campaign	**E.** bracero program

DIRECTIONS: Multiple Choice In the blank at the left, write the letter of the choice that best completes the statement or answers the question. *(10 points each)*

____ **6.** WACs and WAVES were military personnel who were all
A. African Americans. **C.** non-native Americans.
B. specialty trained men. **D.** women.

____ **7.** Because of rationing, many people
A. died of starvation. **C.** stole food.
B. ate in restaurants. **D.** planted victory gardens.

____ **8.** This 332nd Fighter Group, the Tuskeegee Airmen, was made up of all
A. African American men. **C.** women.
B. African American women. **D.** white men.

____ **9.** Many Navajo soldiers worked as this, using their own language as a code.
A. infantry men **C.** radio operators
B. tank drivers **D.** pilots

____ **10.** During the war Japanese Americans were forced into
A. retirement camps. **C.** the army.
B. internment camps. **D.** labor camps.

Section Quizzes ★ 106 ★ *The American Journey*

Picturing HISTORY The Navajo name for Hitler was *Daghailchiih* (mustache smeller). Bombers were *jaysho* (buzzards), and bombs were *ayeshi* (eggs).
Answer: *served in armed forces and worked in defense industries*

CHAPTER 26
Section 3, 750–754

Picturing HISTORY The forced movement of persons of Japanese ancestry from the West Coast continued until 1945.
Answer: *relocated to internment camps, lost homes and businesses*

Reteaching Activity 26–3

Name ____________ Date ________ Class ______

★ Reteaching Activity 26-3

DIRECTIONS: Recognizing Supporting Details Each main idea is related to the topic given. Complete the chart by writing the letter of the items that support each main idea.

Wartime Commitment

Topic: World War II required committment from all Americans in almost every aspect of their lives.	
1. Main Idea: More than 15 million Americans joined the armed forces. **Supporting Details:**	**2. Main Idea:** Americans made personal sacrifices to support the war effort. **Supporting Details:**
3. Main Idea: Women and minorities contributed to the wartime need for labor at home. **Supporting Details:**	**4. Main Idea:** Americans contributed financially to the war effort. **Supporting Details:**

★FACT BANK

A. Women could not buy nylon stockings.
B. Americans had taxes withheld from their paychecks.
C. Ira Hayes, one of the thousands of Native Americans who served, became a hero at Iwo Jima.
D. About 350,000 women served in the WACs, the WAVES, and women's units of the marines, Coast Guard, and army air corps.
E. Celebrities urged people to buy war bonds.
F. Americans used government-issued ration coupons to buy shoes, gasoline, tires, sugar, and meat.
G. Women worked as welders and riveters in factories.
H. About 700,000 African Americans served in the armed forces.
I. Many Native Americans left reservations to work in defense industries.
J. People planted "victory gardens" to grow vegetables.
K. Agents recruited farm and railroad workers from Mexico.
L. Of the approximately 500,000 Hispanic Americans who served in the war, 17 received the Medal of Honor.

Reteaching Activities ★ 106 ★ *The American Journey*

Enrichment Activity 26–3

Name ____________ Date ________ Class ______

★ Enrichment Activity 26-3

Unbreakable Code

Sending coded messages that cannot be easily decoded is vital to the secrecy of military operations. During World War II the United States Marine Corps enlisted more than 400 Navajo volunteers to be Code Talkers. The Code Talkers sent military messages in their own language in a code that was never broken, or decoded, by the Japanese. For military terms that had no Navajo equivalents, the Code Talkers invented names using words they knew.

DIRECTIONS: Understanding Imagery Read the military terms and Navajo words below. The meanings of the Navajo words are in the word bank. Try to match the Navajo words with the translated meaning that suggests the military term. Make your best guess. Write the matching meaning on the line. Then verify your answers with your teacher.

Word Bank

bird carrier **short big gun** **light streak** **iron fish**
potatoes **owl** **whale** **hummingbird** **eggs**

Military term	Navajo word	Meaning
1. fighter plane	*da-he-tih-hi*	________
2. submarine	*besh-lo*	________
3. flare	*wo-chi*	________
4. battleship	*lo-tso*	________
5. observation plane	*ne-as-jah*	________
6. bombs	*a-ye-shi*	________
7. howitzer	*be-el-ton-tso-quodi*	________
8. aircraft carrier	*tsidi-ney-ye-hi*	________
9. grenades	*ni-ma-si*	________

Activity **DIRECTIONS:** With a partner, develop your own code. Create a codebook of code words and their meanings. Then write several messages using the code and challenge classmates to break the code.

Enrichment Activities ★ 106 ★ *The American Journey*

4 CLOSE

Have students speculate how they might have felt toward the American government if they had been sent to an internment camp.

Picturing HISTORY A distressed Japanese American family watches an FBI agent search their family albums for evidence of disloyalty to the United States. **What major hardship did West Coast Japanese Americans face during World War II?**

created tensions in some cities. In 1943, for example, a four-day riot started in **Los Angeles** when white sailors attacked Mexican American teens.

Japanese Americans

After the Japanese bombed Pearl Harbor, Japanese Americans were feared and hated by many other Americans. About two-thirds of Japanese Americans were **Nisei**—American citizens who had been born in the United States. But this fact made little difference to some who questioned the loyalty of Japanese Americans.

Japanese Americans Relocated

Military and political leaders worried about the loyalty of Japanese Americans if Japanese forces invaded the United States. The president directed the army to relocate more than 100,000 West Coast Japanese Americans to detention centers. Located mostly in desert areas, these **internment camps** were crowded and uncomfortable. Conditions were harsh.

With only days to prepare for the move, most Japanese Americans left valuable possessions behind. Many abandoned their homes and businesses or sold them at a loss. Most had to stay in internment camps for the next three years.

Peter Ota and his family were sent to a camp in Colorado. His father had come to California in 1904 and built up a successful fruit and vegetable business. After the war Ota remembered how his father had suffered.

> "After all those years, having worked his whole life to build a dream—having it all taken away. . . . He died a broken man."

In 1988 Americans acknowledged the injustice of relocation. Congress issued a formal apology and agreed to give each survivor $20,000, a token of the nation's regret.

Section 3 Review

Checking for Understanding

1. ***Identify*** WACs, WAVES, Benjamin Davis, Jr., A. Philip Randolph.
2. ***Define*** mobilization, ration, internment camp.
3. ***List*** two ways the United States financed the war effort.

Reviewing Themes

4. **Economic Factors** How did wartime industrial production help the American economy recover from the Depression?

Critical Thinking

5. **Making Critical Judgments** Do you think the United States government was justified in sending Japanese Americans to internment camps? Explain.

Activity

Writing a Journal Entry Imagine you are a woman working in a defense factory during the war. This is the first job you have ever had away from home. Write a journal entry describing your first day on the job.

Section 3 Review Answers

1. WACs, 750; WAVES, 750; Benjamin Davis, Jr., 752; A. Philip Randolph, 752
2. The words are defined in the Glossary.
3. taxes and war bonds
4. Unemployment dropped, incomes rose, and prices remained fairly stable.
5. Students should recognize that internment was unjustified; it was a clear violation of the constitutional rights of Japanese American citizens.

Activity Journal entries may reflect excitement, eagerness to do a good job, and anxiety that she might not.

January 1942
U.S. joins Allies

June 1944
Allied ships land at Normandy

December 1944
Battle of the Bulge takes 75,000 lives

May 1945
Germany surrenders

1942 · 1944 · 1946

Section 4

War in Europe and Africa

READ TO DISCOVER . . .

- what important battles took place in North Africa, Italy, and the Soviet Union between 1942 and 1944.
- what factors contributed to the Allied victory in Europe.

TERMS TO LEARN

genocide

Holocaust

The Storyteller

Ernie Pyle, a war correspondent, described the life of the World War II American soldier: "In the magazines war seemed romantic and exciting, full of heroics and vitality. . . . I saw instead men suffering and wishing they were somewhere else. . . . All of them desperately hungry for somebody to talk to besides themselves . . . cold and fairly dirty, just toiling from day to day in a world full of insecurity, discomfort, homesickness and a dulled sense of danger."

World War II GI work uniform

On January 1, 1942—three weeks after Pearl Harbor—the United States joined Britain, the Soviet Union, and 23 other Allied nations in vowing to defeat the Axis Powers. Although the Japanese were conquering vast areas in the Pacific, the Allied leaders decided to concentrate first on defeating Hitler before dealing with Japan. The situation in Europe was desperate. German forces occupied almost all of Europe and much of **North Africa.** If the Germans defeated the Soviets, Germany might prove unstoppable.

North African Campaign

Stalin and many American military leaders wanted the Allies to launch a major attack on continental Europe across the English Channel. Such an attack would force the Germans to defend the heart of their own empire. Churchill, however, argued that such an assault would be too difficult because of the German military presence in the area. FDR concluded that Churchill was right. The Allies made plans to attack North Africa instead. The Axis forces there were under the command of German general **Erwin Rommel,** known as the "Desert Fox" because of his success in desert warfare.

In November 1942, the British turned Rommel back at El Alamein in Egypt. The victory prevented the Germans from capturing the **Suez Canal,** a vital sea link between Europe and Asia.

Landing in Algeria and Morocco on November 8, American, British, and Canadian troops

SECTION RESOURCES

Reproducible Masters
- Guided Reading Activity 26–4
- Political Cartoons, *World War II Winds Down*
- Section Quiz 26–4
- Reteaching Activity 26–4
- Enrichment Activity 26–4

Transparencies
- Section Focus Transparency 26–4
- U.S. History & Art, Transparency 25, *The Red Stairway*

Multimedia
- Vocabulary PuzzleMaker
- Chapter Challenger Interactive Review Software
- Testmaker
- ABCNews InterActive™ Lessons of War
- ABCNews InterActive™ Electronic Field Trips

1 FOCUS

BELLRINGER
Motivational Activity

Before taking roll at the beginning of the class period, project Section Focus Transparency 26–4 and have students answer the questions. Discuss students' responses.

This activity is also available as a blackline master.

Section Focus Transparency 26–4

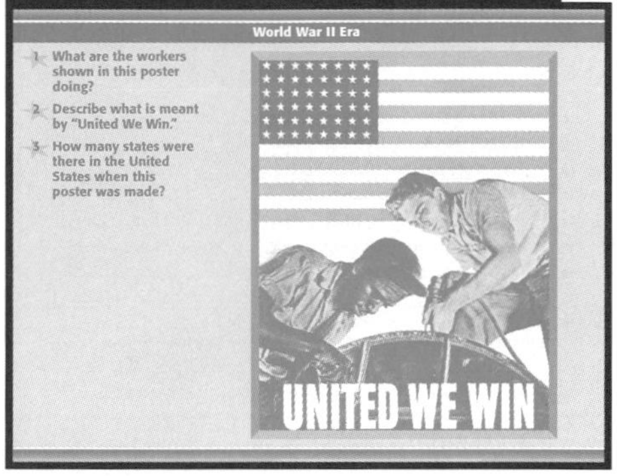

Vocabulary Precheck

Note that *genocide* comes from the Greek *genos* (race) and the word part *-cide* (to kill). Ask students whether they can think of other words with the element *-cide. (homicide, suicide, insecticide, herbicide, and so on)* Have students research their meanings.

Use the **Vocabulary PuzzleMaker** to create crossword and word search puzzles.

Section Theme
Geography and History

To win the war, the Allies had to regain control of North Africa and most of Europe.

Activity Have students read to learn why conquering North Africa was important for the Allies. *(North Africa was used as a base for attacking southern Europe, and gave control of the Suez Canal to Allies.)*

2 TEACH

L1, ELL Identifying Battle Sites Have students describe each of the following battles: El Alamein, Sicily, Monte Cassino, Anzio, Leningrad, Moscow, Stalingrad.

Guided Reading Activity 26–4

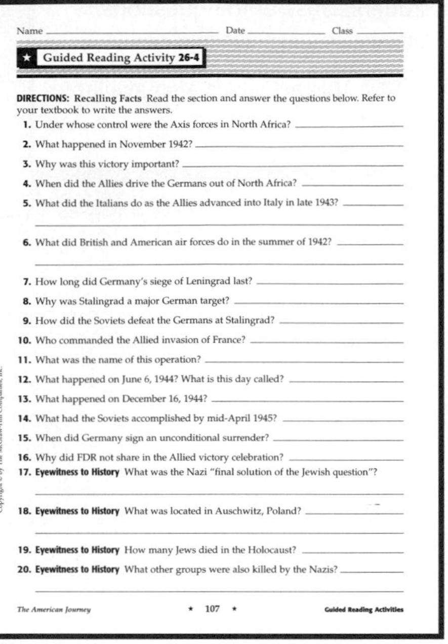
Name ____ Date ____ Class ____

Guided Reading Activity 26-4

DIRECTIONS: Recalling Facts Read the section and answer the questions below. Refer to your textbook to write the answers.

1. Under whose control were the Axis forces in North Africa?
2. What happened in November 1942?
3. Why was this victory important?
4. When did the Allies drive the Germans out of North Africa?
5. What did the Italians do as the Allies advanced into Italy in late 1943?
6. What did British and American air forces do in the summer of 1942?
7. How long did Germany's siege of Leningrad last?
8. Why was Stalingrad a major German target?
9. How did the Soviets defeat the Germans at Stalingrad?
10. Who commanded the Allied invasion of France?
11. What was the name of this operation?
12. What happened on June 6, 1944? What is this day called?
13. What happened on December 16, 1944?
14. What had the Soviets accomplished by mid-April 1945?
15. When did Germany sign an unconditional surrender?
16. Why did FDR not share in the Allied victory celebration?
17. Eyewitness to History What was the Nazi "final solution of the Jewish question"?
18. Eyewitness to History What was located in Auschwitz, Poland?
19. Eyewitness to History How many Jews died in the Holocaust?
20. Eyewitness to History What other groups were also killed by the Nazis?

Copyright © by The McGraw-Hill Companies, Inc.

The American Journey • 107 • Guided Reading Activities

Map Study

Answers

1. Normandy (France)
2. July 10, 1943

ABCNEWS INTERACTIVE™

VIDEODISC
Lessons of War

Side 1
Chapter 12

Title: *Laws of War*
Subject: Rules that place limits on the types of weapons used in war
Ask: **How did Germany break laws of war?** *(exterminated about 12 million people, 6 million of whom were Jews)*

under American general **Dwight D. Eisenhower** advanced eastward swiftly. The inexperienced Americans met defeat in Tunisia. With the backing of British air and naval power, however, American general **George Patton** closed in on Rommel. The Allies drove the Germans out of North Africa in May 1943.

The Invasion of Italy

The Allies used bases in North Africa to launch an invasion of southern Europe. They took the island of **Sicily** in the summer of 1943 and landed on the Italian mainland in September. As the Allies advanced, the Italians overthrew dictator Benito Mussolini and surrendered. However, German forces in Italy continued to fight.

In the winter of 1943, the Allies met fierce resistance at the monastery town of **Monte Cassino** in central Italy, and their advance faltered. The next January the Allies landed farther north at **Anzio,** a seaport near Rome. German forces kept the Allies pinned down on the beaches at Anzio for four months. The Allies finally broke through the German lines in May and advanced toward **Rome.** They liberated Rome in June 1944.

World War II in Europe and Africa

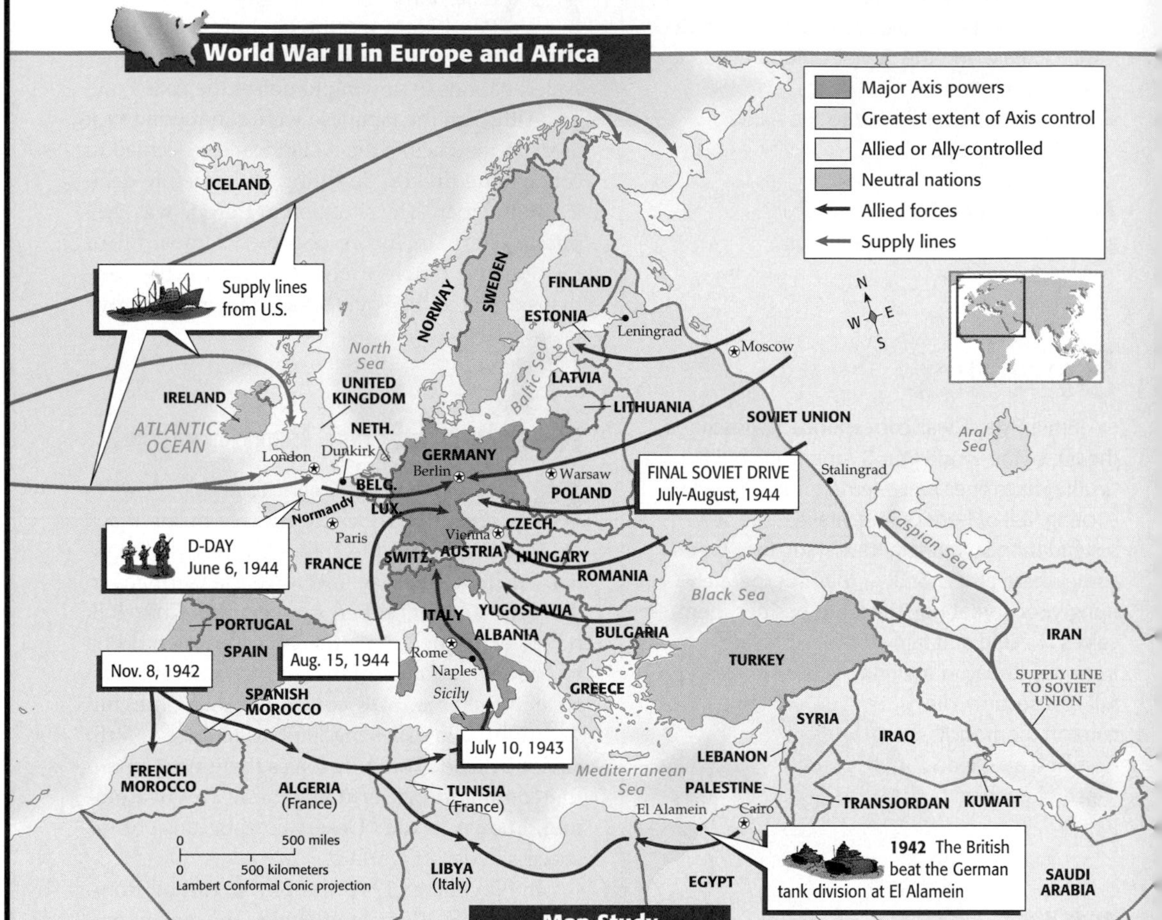

Map Study

Churchill and Roosevelt delayed an attack in Europe to first fight in North Africa.

1. **Location** Where did the Allied forces land on D-Day?
2. **Analyzing Information** When did Allied forces invade Sicily?

COOPERATIVE LEARNING ACTIVITY

Video Presentation Organize the class into 7 groups to create a 15-minute video documentary about military offensives during World War II. Assign each group one of the following countries to research: Great Britain, France, United States, Germany, Italy, Japan, Russia. Suggest that students use pictures of events and people, sound effects, "interviews," speeches, and songs in their films. Each group should choose a narrator for its segment. When the documentaries are completed, have students present them to other groups.

Air War over Germany

While fighting raged in North Africa and Italy, the Allies launched an air war against Germany. In the summer of 1942, British and American air forces began a massive bombing campaign against Germany. Each day hundreds of American bombers pounded German factories and cities. Each night British bombers battered the same targets. The bombing caused massive destruction in many German cities and killed thousands of German civilians. Yet the attacks failed to crack Germany's determination to win the war.

Homeless woman in Cologne, Germany

The Tide Turns in Europe

Meanwhile, the Soviets and the Germans were locked in ferocious combat. For months the Soviet Union bore the main force of Germany's European war effort.

The Eastern Front

After invading the Soviet Union in June 1941, German troops had moved quickly into the nation's interior. By September the Germans surrounded **Leningrad** and began a **siege,** or military blockade, that lasted nearly 900 days. The German attack continued, but Leningrad did not fall. As food ran out, the people of the city ate horses, cats, and dogs—even bread made from wallpaper paste. Thousands died. The Germans could not take the city, however, and in early 1944 the siege was broken.

German forces also attacked other Soviet cities. In 1941 the Germans tried to capture the Soviet capital of **Moscow.** Heavy losses and bad weather slowed their advance, but the Germans reached Moscow's outskirts by December. When all seemed lost, the Soviets staged a counterattack and forced a German retreat.

In the spring of 1942, Germany launched another powerful offensive. A major German target was the city of **Stalingrad,** key to oil-rich lands to the south. To take the city, the Germans had to fight street by street and house by house. No sooner had the Germans won Stalingrad than Soviet forces surrounded the city, cutting off the German supply lines. Cold and starving, the German troops fought on until February 2, 1943, when the tattered remains of their army finally surrendered. German losses exceeded 300,000.

After Stalingrad, a major Soviet offensive drove the Germans back hundreds of miles. The Germans mounted a counteroffensive in the summer of 1943, but their defeat at Stalingrad marked a major turning point in the war.

Invasion of France

As the Soviets pushed toward Germany from the east, the Allies were planning a massive invasion of France from the west. General Eisenhower, the commander of Allied forces in Europe, directed this invasion, known as **Operation Overlord.**

Eisenhower planned to land his troops on the French coast of **Normandy** on June 5, but rough seas forced him to delay the landing. Finally, on June 6, 1944—**D-Day**—the Allied ships landed on the coast of Normandy. After wading ashore the troops faced land mines and fierce fire from the Germans. Many Allied troops were hit as they stormed across the beaches to establish a foothold on high ground. Within a few weeks, the Allies had landed a million troops, 566,648 tons of supplies, and 171,532 vehicles in France.

From Normandy the Allies pushed across France. On August 25 French and American soldiers marched through joyful crowds and liberated Paris.

MULTIPLE LEARNING STYLES

Verbal/Linguistic Assign small groups of students to research one of the following topics: *Kristallnacht,* the Warsaw ghetto, German use of slave labor, artworks stolen by Germany from occupied countries. Have each group present a panel discussion based on their research. After all panels have been presented, have the class discuss how Hitler's "New Order" was carried out through these various places and activities. **L2**

Linking PAST & PRESENT

Napoleon's Defeat in Russia
An attempt by French emperor Napoleon to conquer Russia in 1812 also ended in disaster. More than 500,000 French soldiers died during the campaign—in battle, from hunger, and from the bitterly cold Russian winter.

Political Cartoons, *World War II Winds Down*

you don't say...

GI In World War II, American enlisted men called themselves GIs from an abbreviation of *government issue.* Since they wore GI shirts, slept under GI blankets, ate GI rations, and so on, the soldiers began applying the term to themselves.

ABCNEWS INTERACTIVE™

VIDEODISC
Historic America
Electronic Field Trips

Side 2, Chapter 9

Title: *The Holocaust Museum*
Subject: Tour of the museum in Washington, D.C.
Ask: **Why were Jews ordered to wear a yellow star on their clothes?** *(to separate them from others)*

Also available in VHS.

Picturing HISTORY Eisenhower described the armed forces waiting for the invasion as a "mighty host . . . tense as a coiled spring." The first wave of the attack included 4,000 ships, 12,000 planes, and 1,500 tanks. **Ask:** **Where is Normandy?** *(northwest coast of France)* **Answer:** *land mines, fierce enemy fire from the Germans*

History *and the* Humanities

U.S. History & Art, Transparency 25, *The Red Stairway*

3 ASSESS

Assign Section 4 Review as homework or as an in-class activity.

Use **Chapter Challenger Interactive Review Software** to review Section 4.

Section Quiz 26–4

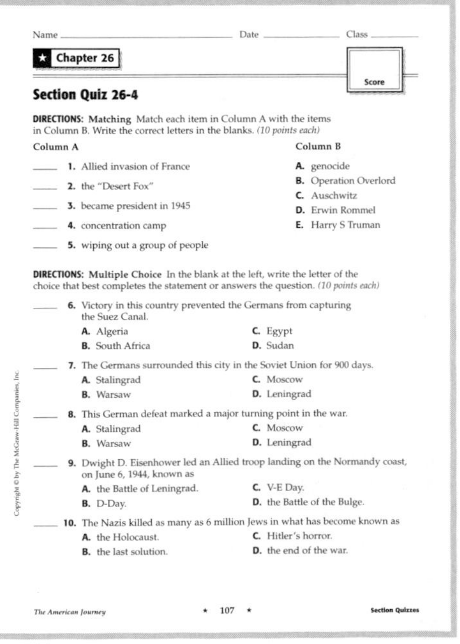
Name ______ Date ______ Class ______

Chapter 26 Score

Section Quiz 26-4

DIRECTIONS: Matching Match each item in Column A with the items in Column B. Write the correct letters in the blanks. *(10 points each)*

Column A	Column B
____ 1. Allied invasion of France	A. genocide
____ 2. the "Desert Fox"	B. Operation Overlord
____ 3. became president in 1945	C. Auschwitz
____ 4. concentration camp	D. Erwin Rommel
____ 5. wiping out a group of people	E. Harry S Truman

DIRECTIONS: Multiple Choice In the blank at the left, write the letter of the choice that best completes the statement or answers the question. *(10 points each)*

____ 6. Victory in this country prevented the Germans from capturing the Suez Canal.
A. Algeria C. Egypt
B. South Africa D. Sudan

____ 7. The Germans surrounded this city in the Soviet Union for 900 days.
A. Stalingrad C. Moscow
B. Warsaw D. Leningrad

____ 8. This German defeat marked a major turning point in the war.
A. Stalingrad C. Moscow
B. Warsaw D. Leningrad

____ 9. Dwight D. Eisenhower led an Allied troop landing on the Normandy coast, on June 6, 1944, known as
A. the Battle of Leningrad. C. V-E Day.
B. D-Day. D. the Battle of the Bulge.

____ 10. The Nazis killed as many as 6 million Jews in what has become known as
A. the Holocaust. C. Hitler's horror.
B. the last solution. D. the end of the war.

Copyright © by The McGraw-Hill Companies, Inc.

The American Journey ★ 107 ★ Section Quizzes

Picturing HISTORY American, British, Canadian, and French troops took part in the D-Day invasion, making it the largest invasion force ever assembled. **What dangers did the Allied soldiers face when landing on the Normandy beaches?**

Victory in Europe

Germany fought for survival on two fronts. In the east the Soviets pushed the Germans out of eastern Europe. In the west the British and Americans approached the German border.

The Advance on Germany

The Allied advance across France moved so rapidly that some people thought the war would be over by the end of the year. In late 1944, however, the drive came to a halt at the Rhine River, stalled by German defenses and cold weather.

In mid-December the Germans mounted a last, desperate offensive. On December 16, 1944, they launched a surprise attack along a 50-mile front in Belgium. In the **Battle of the Bulge,** the Germans at first drove troops and artillery deep into a bulge in the Allied lines. After several weeks, however, the Allies pushed the Germans back. The battle, which resulted in more than 75,000 casualties, marked the end of serious German resistance.

The final phase of the war in Europe now began. By mid-April 1945, the Soviets had surrounded **Berlin,** the German capital. Hitler, who had spent the final months of the war in an underground bunker there, realized that the situation was hopeless and committed suicide on April 30. Germany signed an unconditional surrender on May 7, ending the war in Europe. The Allies declared May 8 **V-E Day** for "Victory in Europe."

General Dwight D. Eisenhower

Death of a President

President Roosevelt did not share in the Allied victory celebration. In February 1945, he had traveled to Yalta in the Soviet Union to meet with Churchill and Stalin. After returning home Roosevelt had gone to Warm Springs, Georgia, for a vacation. He died there suddenly on April 12, 1945.

Americans were saddened by the death of the man who had led them for 12 difficult years. When Vice President **Harry S Truman** heard the news, he asked Eleanor Roosevelt if there was anything he could do for her. She replied, "Is there anything *we* can do for *you?* You are the one in trouble now."

Eyewitness to HISTORY

The Holocaust

As the Allies liberated areas that had been under German control, they found horrifying evidence of Nazi brutality. Hitler had warned in 1939 that another war would result in "the destruction of the Jews in Europe." Nazi leaders developed what they called "the final solution of the Jewish question." Their "solution" was **genocide**—wiping out an entire group of people.

Ever since Hitler had gained power in 1933, the Nazis persecuted Jews. This persecution became more deadly as German power spread through Europe. Once the war began, Nazis

MAKING CONNECTIONS ACTIVITY

Science Have students investigate and write several paragraphs about the life and work of Charles Drew, an African American physician who conducted pioneering research on blood plasma in the 1930s. During World War II, Drew was asked to head the United States military's blood plasma program. By collecting, storing, transporting, and transfusing donated blood plasma, this program saved the lives of countless soldiers. Some believe that Drew bled to death after being refused treatment at a white hospital for injuries sustained in a car accident. This story is not true, but it is true that the military refused to accept blood donations from African Americans unless their blood was segregated and given only to black soldiers. **L2**

rounded up thousands of Jews, shooting them and throwing them into mass graves. One man who witnessed a massacre of Russian Jews wrote:

> "I watched a family of about eight persons. . . . [A soldier] instructed them to go behind the earth mound. . . . They went down into the pit, lined themselves up against the previous victims and were shot."

Nazi troops crammed thousands more into railroad cars like cattle, depositing them in **concentration camps**—prison camps for civilians. Guards took the prisoners' belongings, shaved their heads, and tattooed camp numbers on their arms. Forced to live in horrible conditions, the prisoners often had only a crust of bread or watery soup to eat. Thousands became sick and died.

In the early 1940s, the Nazis embarked on their "final solution" to destroy the Jews. They built death camps where they killed thousands of people a day in gas chambers, then burned their bodies in ovens. At the largest camp—**Auschwitz** in Poland—the Nazis killed between 1 and 2 million people. As many as 6 million Jews died in what has become known as the **Holocaust.** Millions of others—Soviet prisoners of war, Poles, Gypsies, and people with handicaps—were also ruthlessly killed.

As Allied forces moved through Germany and Poland after V-E Day, they saw firsthand the unspeakable horrors of the camps. R.W. Thompson, a British reporter, wrote about one such camp:

Starved survivors at the concentration camp at Evensee, Austria

> "Across the sandy clearing is the incinerator, but it ran out of [fuel]. A rough record by the chief burner of bodies records 17,000 burned last month. They say each body was roughly clubbed as it went in."

People around the world were stunned by this terrible result of Nazi tyranny.

Section 4 Review

Checking for Understanding

1. ***Identify*** Erwin Rommel, Dwight D. Eisenhower, George Patton, D-Day, V-E Day.
2. ***Define*** genocide, Holocaust.
3. ***Trace*** the path of Allied forces through Africa and Europe from 1942 to D-Day.

Reviewing Themes

4. **Geography and History** Which large Allied countries defended the eastern front in Europe in 1944? The western front?

Critical Thinking

5. **Drawing Conclusions** Why do you think Hitler felt threatened by Jews and other minorities?

Activity

Making a Map Make a map of the former Soviet Union and use symbols to show the outcome of battles between the Germans and the Soviets during World War II.

Section 4 Review Answers

1. Erwin Rommel, 755; Dwight D. Eisenhower, 756; George Patton, 756; D-Day, 757; V-E Day, 758
2. The words are defined in the Glossary.
3. Allied forces moved from North Africa to Sicily to Italy's mainland to air war in Germany and then to France.
4. eastern: Soviet Union; western: Great Britain and the United States
5. Students should recognize that Hitler's formula for power included convincing Germans that they were superior to everyone else. Anyone who did not fall under his definition of the "superior race" became a threat to his power.

Activity Maps should show battles between Germany and the Soviet Union and use symbols to indicate the outcome of each.

Ask students: **Who, in addition to Jews, were victims of the Holocaust?** *(Soviet prisoners of war, Poles, Gypsies, people with disabilities)*

Reteaching Activity 26–4

Name ______ Date ______ Class ______

★ Reteaching Activity **26-4**

DIRECTIONS: Organizing Facts Below are events that took place along the way to an Allied victory in Europe. Complete the time line by writing the corresponding letters in each box. Two boxes will have two letters.

ALONG THE ROAD TO VICTORY IN EUROPE

1941 — 1942 — 1943 — 1944 — 1945 — 1946

June 1941 ____ | Summer 1942 ____ | Nov. 1942 ____ | Winter 1943 ____ | May 1943 ____ | May 1944 ____ | June 6, 1944 ____ | Aug. 25, 1944 ____ | Dec. 16, 1944 ____ | April 12, 1945 ____ | May 7, 1945 ____

★FACT BANK

- **A.** The British turn Erwin Rommel back in Egypt, preventing the Germans from capturing the Suez Canal.
- **B.** The Allies drive the Germans out of North Africa.
- **C.** D-Day—Allied ships land on the coast of Normandy.
- **D.** After a four-month battle at Anzio, the Allies break through German lines and advance toward Rome.
- **E.** Allied advance falters in Monte Cassino in central Italy.
- **F.** Franklin Roosevelt dies suddenly.
- **G.** The inexperienced Americans meet with defeat in Tunisia.
- **H.** Germany signs an unconditional surrender.
- **I.** Allies bombard German factories and cities day and night.
- **J.** German troops surrender in Stalingrad.
- **K.** Germans surround Leningrad to begin a 900-day siege.
- **L.** Germans launch the Battle of the Bulge.
- **M.** French and American soldiers liberate Paris.

DIRECTIONS: Essay On a separate sheet of paper, answer the question below.
What terrible result of the Nazi tyranny did the world discover after Germany surrendered?

The American Journey ★ 107 ★ **Reteaching Activities**

Enrichment Activity 26–4

Name ______ Date ______ Class ______

★ Enrichment Activity **26-4** ★ ★

Military Leadership

In May 1943 the Allies drove the Germans out of North Africa. The commander of American troops in that decisive World War II victory was General George Patton. Field Marshall Erwin Rommel commanded the Axis forces. Study the Venn diagram that compares these two great generals.

DIRECTIONS: Reading a Venn Diagram Use the Venn diagram to answer the following questions.

General George Patton "Old Blood and Guts"
- Born in 1885
- Dyslexic
- Graduated from West Point
- Colorful, charismatic, combative, and outspoken
- Fearless in battle
- Slapped two hospitalized soldiers when he thought they were faking illness
- Compared the Nazis to losers in an election
- Died in car accident in 1945

Both
- Served in World War I
- Lead by example
- Proponent of mobile tactics
- Adored by his men
- Wounded in battle
- Lost command of troops when he voiced his opinions

Field Marshall Erwin Rommel "The Desert Fox"
- Born in 1891
- War college instructor
- Chivalrous, decent, dedicated, and clever
- Daring and ferocious in battle
- Resourceful in desert warfare
- Told Hitler the war was futile
- Implicated in a plot to kill Hitler
- Committed suicide in 1944 when given the choice of suicide or a trial

1. What disability did Patton have to overcome to graduate from West Point? ______
2. What were two personality traits of Patton? ______
3. What were two personality traits of Rommel? ______
4. How did Rommel lose favor with Hitler? ______
5. In what ways were Patton and Rommel alike? ______
6. Why do you think Patton was called "Old Blood and Guts"? ______

Activity **DIRECTIONS: Applying Ideas** Choose two other military leaders from the past or present. When you have researched your choices, use a Venn diagram, chart, or another graphic organizer to compare the two leaders.

The American Journey ★ 107 ★ **Enrichment Activities**

4 CLOSE

When Vice President Truman heard that FDR had died, he said that he felt "like the moon, the stars, and all the planets have fallen on me." Have students explain why.

ABCNEWS INTERACTIVE™

VIDEODISC
Historic America
Electronic Field Trips

Side 2, Chapter 8
Title: *The U.S.S.* Arizona *Memorial*

If you do not have access to a videodisc player, the **Historic America Electronic Field Trips** are also available in VHS.

Internet Sites

The following are possible sites for completing the "Net" activities:

United States Holocaust Memorial Museum
http://www.ushmm.org/

L'Chaim: A Holocaust Web Project
http://www.charm.net/~rbennett/l'chaim.html

The Central Intelligence Agency-World Fact Book 1996
http://www.odci.gov/cia/publications/nsolo/wfb-all.htm

Not on the "Net" . . .

If students have limited or no access to the Internet, have them complete the activity "The Holocaust" by using the computerized card catalog at their school or local library. At the *s:* prompt, have students type in the word *Holocaust.* Have students use the call numbers to find resources describing Holocaust survivors' memoirs. From these resources, students may complete their own booklets. Have students discuss the experiences of the Holocaust survivors with parents or older adults.

Multimedia Activities

ABCNEWS INTERACTIVE™ Historic America Electronic Field Trips

Field Trip to the U.S.S. *Arizona* Memorial

Setting up the Video

Work with a group of your classmates to view the videodisc "The U.S.S. *Arizona* Memorial" on the videodisc ***Historic America: Electronic Field Trips***. This program gives detailed accounts of the December 7, 1941, bombing of Pearl Harbor, which caused the United States to join the Allied cause in World War II. The program ends with scenes of the U.S.S. *Arizona* Memorial.

Side 2, Chapter 8

View the video by scanning the bar code or by entering the chapter number on your keypad and pressing Search.

Hands-On Activity

As a nation we have built many memorials to Americans who have lost their lives during war. On large drawing paper, create a sketch of a monument for a patriotic cause. Then use your sketch to make a three-dimensional monument out of papier-mâché or modeling clay.

Surfing the "Net"

The Holocaust

During World War II the Nazis murdered 12 million people, 6 million of whom were Jews. This mass murder of Jewish people has come to be known as the Holocaust. As Allied forces moved through Germany and Poland after V-E Day, they saw the horrors of the concentration camps. To learn more about the Holocaust, use the Internet.

Getting There

Follow these steps to gather information about the Holocaust experience.

1. Use a search engine. Type in the phrase *Holocaust Survivors.*
2. After typing in this phrase, enter words such as the following to focus your search: *stories, experiences, oral history.*
3. The search engine should provide you with a number of links to follow. Links are "pointers" to different sites on the Internet.

What to Do When You Are There

Click on the links to navigate through the pages of information. Print your findings. Work with a partner or group to create a booklet of Holocaust survivors' memoirs. Design each memoir as a separate page of your book. Show your booklet to your parents or older adults and discuss the experiences of the Holocaust survivors. If possible, interview a person who lived during the World War II era. Ask what he or she remembers about the public's response when the existence of concentration camps became known.

TEACHER'S NOTES

1942 — 1944 — 1946

April 1942 Allies surrender Bataan

March 1945 Americans seize Iwo Jima

August 1945 Atomic bomb is dropped on Hiroshima

September 1945 Japan surrenders; World War II ends

Section 5

War in the Pacific

READ TO DISCOVER . . .

- how the United States planned to gain control in the Pacific region.
- what role the atomic bomb played in ending the war.

TERMS TO LEARN

island hopping   kamikaze

The Storyteller

Bob Krell, a soldier in World War II, felt a need to describe his life in the war: "At night before a big airborne operation you crawl deeper in your sack, but you can't get away from the noise. Over the roar of engines, somebody is shouting a bunch of names. . . . [W]e will climb into our parachutes as dawn breaks. We will trudge out to the planes and climb in, not saying much of anything about anything. . . ." Bob Krell was killed in action 12 hours after he wrote these words.

Silver Star, awarded for gallantry in action

On December 7, 1941, the same day the Japanese attacked Pearl Harbor, Japanese bombers struck American airfields in the **Philippines** and on the islands of **Wake** and **Guam**—key American bases in the Pacific. In the following days, the Japanese intensified their campaign in the Pacific. They invaded Thailand and Malaya and captured Guam, Wake Island, and the British colony of Hong Kong.

The Pacific Front

★ Japanese troops had landed in the Philippines in mid-December and quickly taken the capital of Manila. The defending forces—Filipino and American troops commanded by American general **Douglas MacArthur**—were forced to retreat to the rugged **Bataan** Peninsula west of Manila and the small island fortress of **Corregidor.**

Eyewitness to HISTORY

The Philippines Fall

After months of fierce fighting, the exhausted Allied troops defending Bataan surrendered on April 9, 1942. The forces on Corregidor held out for another month. The Japanese forced their Bataan prisoners—many sick and near starvation—to march to a prison camp more than 60 miles away. Only much later did the public learn what these prisoners endured. About 76,000

SECTION RESOURCES

Reproducible Masters
- Reproducible Lesson Plan 26–5
- Guided Reading Activity 26–5
- Section Quiz 26–5
- Reteaching Activity 26–5
- Enrichment Activity 26–5

Transparencies
- Section Focus Transparency 26–5

Multimedia
- Vocabulary PuzzleMaker
- Chapter Challenger Interactive Review Software
- Testmaker
- ABCNews InterActive™ Lessons of War
- ABCNews InterActive™ Communism and the Cold War

1 FOCUS

BELLRINGER
Motivational Activity

Before taking roll at the beginning of the class period, project Section Focus Transparency 26–5 and have students answer the questions. Discuss students' responses.

This activity is also available as a blackline master.

Section Focus Transparency 26–5

Vocabulary Precheck

Ask for a volunteer to define *kamikaze.*

Use the **Vocabulary PuzzleMaker** to create crossword and word search puzzles.

Section Theme
Individual Action

The war in the Pacific was won not only by the valiant efforts of the troops but also by the actions, strategies, and decisions of military and civilian leaders.

Activity Have students identify the decision made by President Truman that led the Japanese to surrender. *(decision to use atomic bomb)*

2 TEACH

L1 Matching Have students make quizzes matching places and people in the section with brief identifications. Then have them answer each other's quizzes.

Guided Reading Activity 26–5

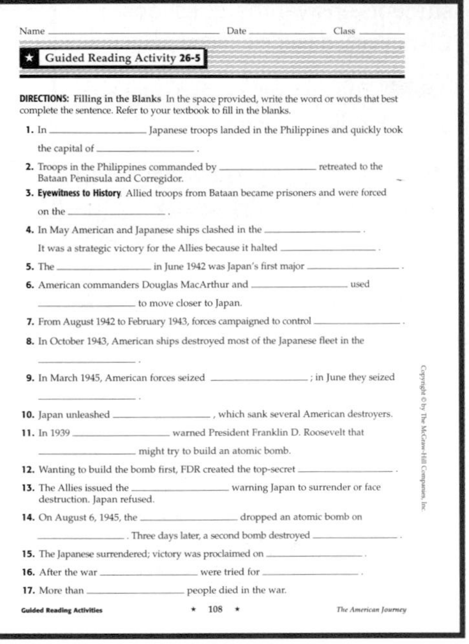
Name ________ Date ________ Class ________

★ Guided Reading Activity **26-5**

DIRECTIONS: Filling in the Blanks In the space provided, write the word or words that best complete the sentence. Refer to your textbook to fill in the blanks.

1. In ________ Japanese troops landed in the Philippines and quickly took the capital of ________ .
2. Troops in the Philippines commanded by ________ retreated to the Bataan Peninsula and Corregidor.
3. **Eyewitness to History** Allied troops from Bataan became prisoners and were forced on the ________ .
4. In May American and Japanese ships clashed in the ________ . It was a strategic victory for the Allies because it halted ________ .
5. The ________ in June 1942 was Japan's first major ________ .
6. American commanders Douglas MacArthur and ________ used ________ to move closer to Japan.
7. From August 1942 to February 1943, forces campaigned to control ________ .
8. In October 1943, American ships destroyed most of the Japanese fleet in the ________ .
9. In March 1945, American forces seized ________ ; in June they seized ________ .
10. Japan unleashed ________ , which sank several American destroyers.
11. In 1939 ________ warned President Franklin D. Roosevelt that ________ might try to build an atomic bomb.
12. Wanting to build the bomb first, FDR created the top-secret ________ .
13. The Allies issued the ________ warning Japan to surrender or face destruction. Japan refused.
14. On August 6, 1945, the ________ dropped an atomic bomb on ________ . Three days later, a second bomb destroyed ________ .
15. The Japanese surrendered; victory was proclaimed on ________ .
16. After the war ________ were tried for ________ .
17. More than ________ people died in the war.

Guided Reading Activities ★ 108 ★ *The American Journey*

Copyright © by The McGraw-Hill Companies, Inc.

you don't say...

Kamikaze is a Japanese word that means "divine wind." The first divine wind was a typhoon that saved Japan by destroying an invading Mongol fleet in 1281. The Japanese were hoping for a similar miracle with their kamikaze pilots.

Map Study

Answers

1. Manchuria, a large part of the northeast, and the coast
2. Hiroshima, Nagasaki

Map Skills Practice

Reading a Map Which Pacific island was the site of a battle that lasted from June 3 to June 6 in 1942? *(Midway)*

prisoners started out, but only about 54,000 of those on the **Bataan Death March** reached the camp. As one survivor recalled:

> "Anybody that could walk, they forced 'em into line. . . . If you fell out to the side, you were either shot by the guards or you were bayoneted [stabbed] and left there."

Two months before the surrender, General MacArthur had left for Australia to take command of Allied forces in the Pacific. MacArthur promised the Filipinos, "I shall return."

General Douglas MacArthur

World War II in the Pacific

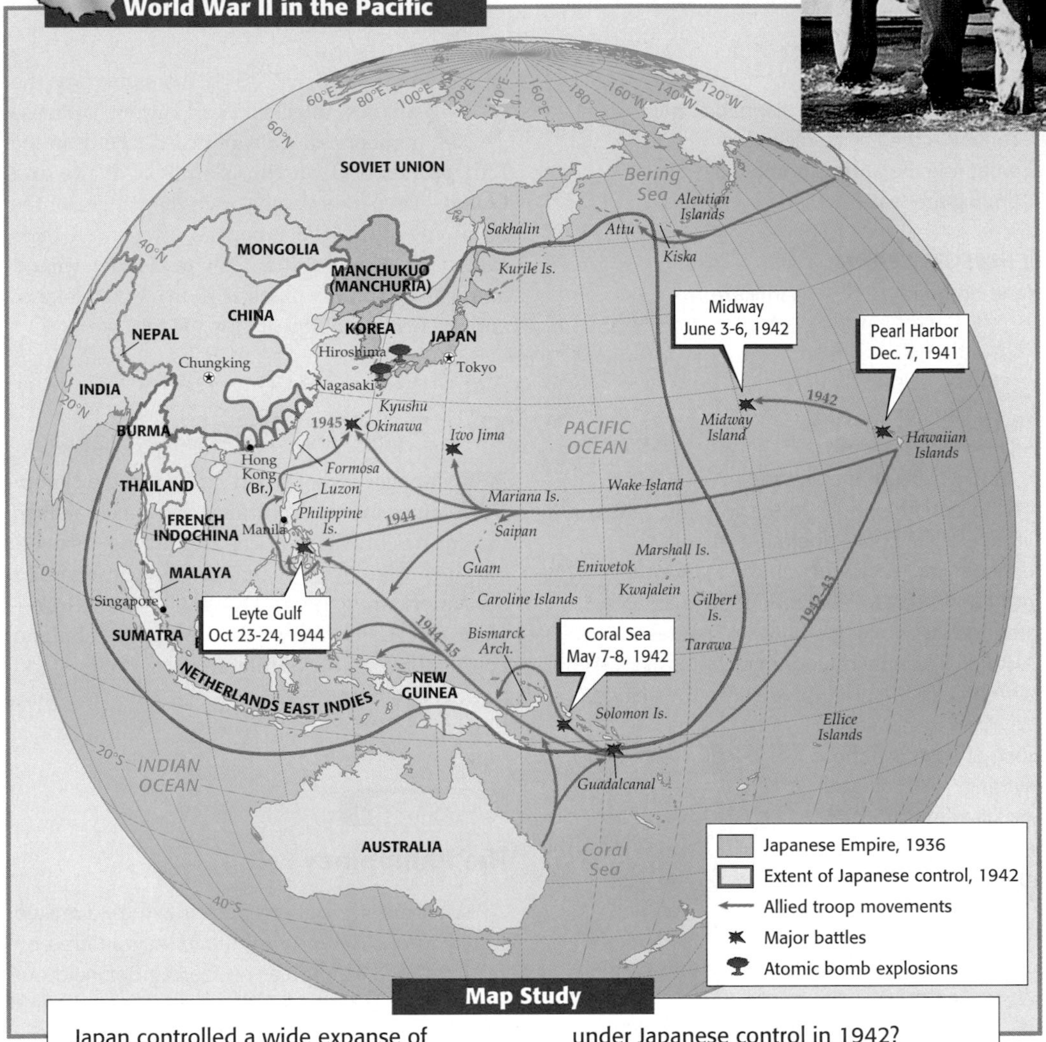

Map Study

Japan controlled a wide expanse of territory in Asia and the Pacific.

1. **Location** What parts of China were under Japanese control in 1942?
2. **Analyzing Information** What two cities were destroyed by atomic bombs?

COOPERATIVE LEARNING ACTIVITY

Making a Class Museum Have students work together to make a class museum of World War II artifacts. Students should search their homes and community for memorabilia and memorials or monuments. In some cases, actual artifacts may be brought to class. In other cases, students will need to make drawings or photographs of the items. Caution students that they need the owner's permission to use any actual artifacts. Some students may wish to tape-record interviews with older relatives or friends who remember the war. Artifacts, drawings, and photographs should have labels explaining their significance. **L1, ELL**

Island Hopping

With Japan's string of quick victories, American morale was low. Then in mid-April, 16 American B-25 twin-engine bombers, launched from an aircraft carrier in the Pacific, bombed **Tokyo.** This daring raid led by James Doolittle had little military importance, but it lifted Americans' spirits.

In May, American and Japanese fleets clashed in the Coral Sea northeast of Australia. American ships were heavily damaged, but the Japanese suffered crippling losses. The **Battle of the Coral Sea** was a strategic victory because it halted the Japanese advance on Australia.

An even greater victory followed in June 1942. In the **Battle of Midway,** northwest of Hawaii, the navy destroyed four Japanese aircraft carriers and hundreds of airplanes. This was the first major Japanese defeat.

The United States was now ready to go on the offensive against Japan. The commanders—General MacArthur and Admiral **Chester Nimitz**—adopted a strategy known as **island hopping.** This called for attacking and capturing certain key islands. The United States then used these islands as bases for leapfrogging to others, moving ever closer to the Philippines—and to Japan.

Between August 1942 and February 1943, American forces engaged in one of the most vicious campaigns of the war for the control of **Guadalcanal,** one of the Solomon Islands. The Japanese put up fierce resistance; however, with superior air and naval power, the Americans finally secured the island.

In June 1944, American forces captured Guam and other islands nearby. Guam provided a base for launching bombing strikes on Japan. In October, American ships destroyed most of the Japanese fleet at the **Battle of Leyte Gulf** in the Philippines, the biggest naval battle in history—in all, 282 ships took part. MacArthur had fulfilled his promise to return to the Philippines.

The Advance on Japan

American forces now closed in on Japan itself. In March 1945, they seized the island of **Iwo Jima** and in June the island of **Okinawa.** The Japanese fought fiercely to defend these islands so near to Japan. Thousands of Americans died in the battles, and many thousands more were wounded.

With most of Japan's air force and navy destroyed, American B-29 bombers pounded Tokyo and other Japanese cities. The raids killed thousands of civilians and crippled Japan's economy.

In desperation, the Japanese unleashed a corps of suicide pilots known as **kamikazes.** They crashed planes loaded with explosives into American ships. Kamikaze pilots sank several destroyers during the battle for Okinawa.

Linking PAST & PRESENT

Aerial Warfare

Flying Grumman Wildcat Fighter, 1942

Germany introduced jet planes late in World War II. The German jets could fly almost 550 miles per hour. By the 1960s American and Soviet jets roared through the skies at 1,000 miles per hour. Today United States military aircraft includes the F-117 stealth fighter. A winglike shape and flat surfaces that absorb radar energy make it difficult for enemy radar to detect it. **How do World War II planes differ from modern stealth bombers?**

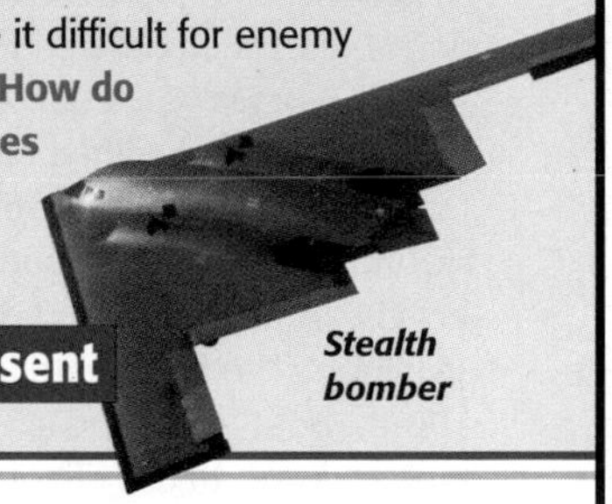

Stealth bomber

The Atomic Bomb

Although the Japanese faced certain defeat, they continued to fight. Their refusal to surrender led the United States to use a powerful new weapon: the atomic bomb.

In 1939 the German-born physicist **Albert Einstein** had written to President Roosevelt warning him that the Nazis might try to use the energy of the atom to build "extremely powerful bombs of a new type." Wanting to develop such

Linking PAST & PRESENT

Answer: *Stealth bombers are faster, use computers and other high-tech equipment, are difficult to track by radar, have more aerodynamic shape.*

ABCNEWS INTERACTIVE™

VIDEODISC
Lessons of War

Side 1
Chapter 6

Title: *Can a Battle Change History?*
Subject: The Battle of Midway
Ask: **Why was the Battle of Midway a turning point in World War II history?** *(Midway was a strategic attempt by Japan to shut off U.S. supply lines. The U.S. stopped the Japanese and changed the direction of the war.)*

3 ASSESS

Assign Section 5 Review as homework or as an in-class activity.

Section Quiz 26–5

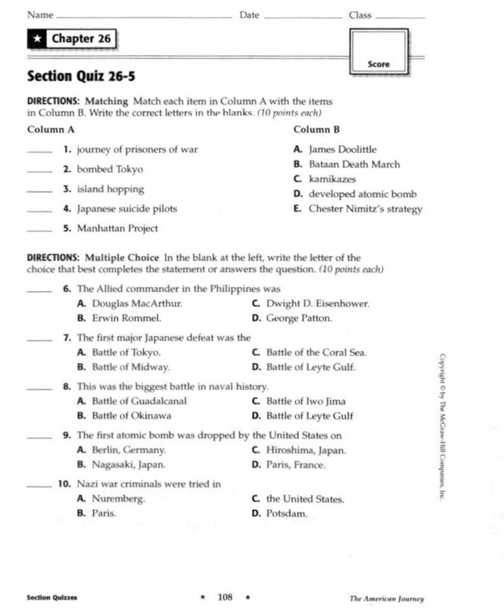
Name ______ Date ______ Class ______

Chapter 26

Score

Section Quiz 26-5

DIRECTIONS: Matching Match each item in Column A with the items in Column B. Write the correct letters in the blanks. *(10 points each)*

Column A	Column B
____ 1. journey of prisoners of war	A. James Doolittle
____ 2. bombed Tokyo	B. Bataan Death March
____ 3. island hopping	C. kamikazes
____ 4. Japanese suicide pilots	D. developed atomic bomb
____ 5. Manhattan Project	E. Chester Nimitz's strategy

DIRECTIONS: Multiple Choice In the blank at the left, write the letter of the choice that best completes the statement or answers the question. *(10 points each)*

____ 6. The Allied commander in the Philippines was
A. Douglas MacArthur. C. Dwight D. Eisenhower.
B. Erwin Rommel. D. George Patton.

____ 7. The first major Japanese defeat was the
A. Battle of Tokyo. C. Battle of the Coral Sea.
B. Battle of Midway. D. Battle of Leyte Gulf.

____ 8. This was the biggest battle in naval history.
A. Battle of Guadalcanal C. Battle of Iwo Jima
B. Battle of Okinawa D. Battle of Leyte Gulf

____ 9. The first atomic bomb was dropped by the United States on
A. Berlin, Germany. C. Hiroshima, Japan.
B. Nagasaki, Japan. D. Paris, France.

____ 10. Nazi war criminals were tried in
A. Nuremberg. C. the United States.
B. Paris. D. Potsdam.

Section Quizzes ★ 108 ★ *The American Journey*

MULTIPLE LEARNING STYLES

Logical/Mathematical Have students use the Internet or library resources to compare World War I with World War II. The comparison should include the number of nations participating and their names, the number of soldiers mobilized, the number of lives lost, and the amount of money spent. Students might present their information as an oral report. The report should be accompanied by charts and graphs illustrating the statistics. **L3**

CHAPTER 26
Section 5, 761–764

Use **Chapter Challenger Interactive Review Software** to review Section 5.

Reteaching Activity 26–5

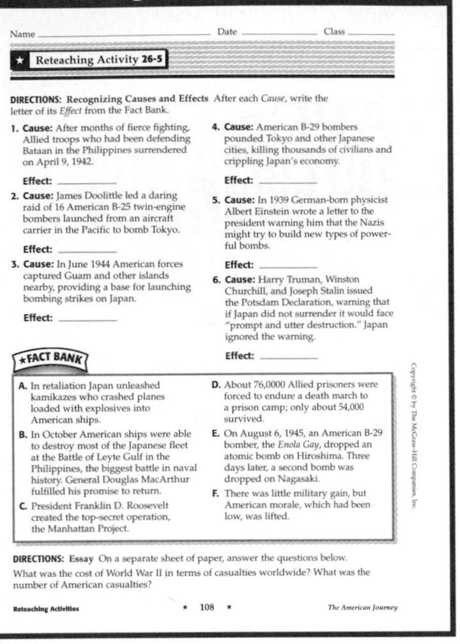

Name ____________ Date ________ Class ________

★ Reteaching Activity 26-5

DIRECTIONS: Recognizing Causes and Effects After each *Cause*, write the letter of its *Effect* from the Fact Bank.

1. **Cause:** After months of fierce fighting, Allied troops who had been defending Bataan in the Philippines surrendered on April 9, 1942.

   Effect: ________

2. **Cause:** James Doolittle led a daring raid of 16 American B-25 twin-engine bombers launched from an aircraft carrier in the Pacific to bomb Tokyo.

   Effect: ________

3. **Cause:** In June 1944 American forces captured Guam and other islands nearby, providing a base for launching bombing strikes on Japan.

   Effect: ________

4. **Cause:** American B-29 bombers pounded Tokyo and other Japanese cities, killing thousands of civilians and crippling Japan's economy.

   Effect: ________

5. **Cause:** In 1939 German-born physicist Albert Einstein wrote a letter to the president warning him that the Nazis might try to build new types of powerful bombs.

   Effect: ________

6. **Cause:** Harry Truman, Winston Churchill, and Joseph Stalin issued the Potsdam Declaration, warning that if Japan did not surrender it would face "prompt and utter destruction." Japan ignored the warning.

   Effect: ________

★FACT BANK

A. In retaliation Japan unleashed kamikazes who crashed planes loaded with explosives into American ships.

B. In October American ships were able to destroy most of the Japanese fleet at the Battle of Leyte Gulf in the Philippines, the biggest battle in naval history. General Douglas MacArthur fulfilled his promise to return.

C. President Franklin D. Roosevelt created the top-secret operation, the Manhattan Project.

D. About 76,0000 Allied prisoners were forced to endure a death march to a prison camp; only about 54,000 survived.

E. On August 6, 1945, an American B-29 bomber, the *Enola Gay*, dropped an atomic bomb on Hiroshima. Three days later, a second bomb was dropped on Nagasaki.

F. There was little military gain, but American morale, which had been low, was lifted.

DIRECTIONS: Essay On a separate sheet of paper, answer the questions below.

What was the cost of World War II in terms of casualties worldwide? What was the number of American casualties?

Enrichment Activity 26–5

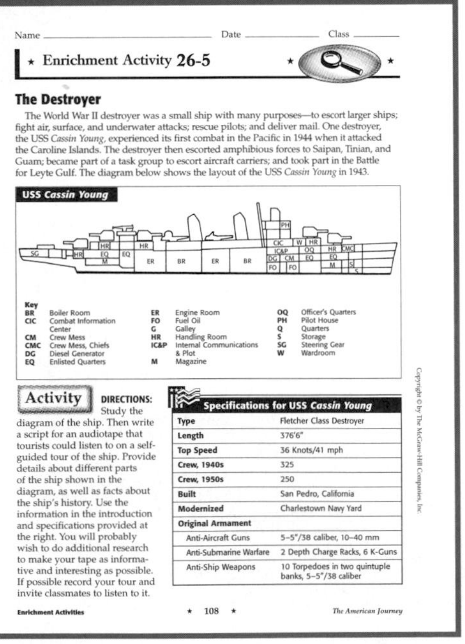

Name ____________ Date ________ Class ________

★ Enrichment Activity 26-5

The Destroyer

The World War II destroyer was a small ship with many purposes—to escort larger ships; fight air, surface, and underwater attacks; rescue pilots; and deliver mail. One destroyer, the USS *Cassin Young*, experienced its first combat in the Pacific in 1944 when it attacked the Caroline Islands. The destroyer then escorted amphibious forces to Saipan, Tinian, and Guam; became part of a task group to escort aircraft carriers; and took part in the Battle for Leyte Gulf. The diagram below shows the layout of the USS *Cassin Young* in 1943.

USS *Cassin Young*

Key
BR Boiler Room
CIC Combat Information Center
CM Crew Mess
CMC Crew Mess, Chiefs
DG Diesel Generator
EQ Enlisted Quarters
ER Engine Room
FO Fuel Oil
G Galley
HR Handling Room
IC&P Internal Communications & Plot
M Magazine
OQ Officer's Quarters
PH Pilot House
Q Quarters
S Storage
SG Steering Gear
W Wardroom

Activity **DIRECTIONS:** Study the diagram of the ship. Then write a script for an audiotape that tourists could listen to on a self-guided tour of the ship. Provide details about different parts of the ship shown in the diagram, as well as facts about the ship's history. Use the information in the introduction and specifications provided at the right. You will probably wish to do additional research to make your tape as informative and interesting as possible. If possible record your tour and invite classmates to listen to it.

Specifications for USS *Cassin Young*

Type	Fletcher Class Destroyer
Length	376'6"
Top Speed	36 Knots/41 mph
Crew, 1940s	325
Crew, 1950s	250
Built	San Pedro, California
Modernized	Charlestown Navy Yard
Original Armament	
Anti-Aircraft Guns	5–5"/38 caliber, 10–40 mm
Anti-Submarine Warfare	2 Depth Charge Racks, 6 K-Guns
Anti-Ship Weapons	10 Torpedoes in two quintuple banks, 5–5"/38 caliber

4 CLOSE

Have students write an epitaph or design a memorial for a marine killed in the Pacific.

weapons first, Roosevelt created a top-secret operation, the **Manhattan Project.** After years of work, scientists tested the atomic bomb in the New Mexico desert on July 16, 1945. Truman now had to decide whether to use the bomb against Japan.

Raising the U.S. flag at Iwo Jima

The Allies issued the **Potsdam Declaration,** warning that if Japan did not surrender, it faced "prompt and utter destruction." The Japanese leaders did not surrender, and Truman ordered the use of the bomb.

On August 6, 1945, an American B-29 bomber, the *Enola Gay,* dropped an atomic bomb on the Japanese city of **Hiroshima.** Three days later, a second bomb was dropped on the city of **Nagasaki.** The atomic bombs caused unimaginable destruction. The first bomb leveled Hiroshima and killed about 70,000 people; the Nagasaki bomb killed about 40,000. Thousands more were injured, and many died later from radiation.

The War Ends

★ After the bombings, the Japanese government agreed to surrender. August 15, 1945, was proclaimed **V-J Day,** for "Victory over Japan." All around America, people expressed happiness and relief. Japan signed the formal surrender on September 2 aboard the battleship the U.S.S. *Missouri.* World War II had finally ended.

The War Trials

In the years immediately after the war, Allied authorities put the top Nazi and Japanese leaders on trial. Those brought to trial were accused of war crimes and crimes against humanity. The Allies held the trials in Nuremberg, Germany, and in Tokyo, eventually convicting and executing 24 Nazis and 7 Japanese for their crimes. Hundreds more were imprisoned.

The Cost of the War

World War II was the most destructive conflict in history. More than 40 million people died during the war; more than half of these were civilians killed by bombing, starvation, disease, torture, and murder. American casualties—about 322,000 dead and 800,000 injured—were high, but light compared with those of other nations. The Soviet Union suffered more than 20 million deaths. Those who survived faced the daunting task of trying to rebuild their lives and their countries. Nationalist movements grew, particularly in colonial nations that had suffered invasions by the warring powers. Many colonies began to seek independence in the postwar years.

Section 5 Review

Checking for Understanding

1. ***Identify*** Douglas MacArthur, Chester Nimitz, Manhattan Project, V-J Day.
2. ***Define*** island hopping, kamikaze.
3. ***Explain*** the significance of the Battle of Leyte Gulf.

Reviewing Themes

4. **Individual Action** What did Japan's use of kamikazes illustrate about its desire to win the war?

Critical Thinking

5. **Identifying Central Issues** If you had been President Truman, would you have allowed the United States to drop the atomic bomb on Japan? Why or why not?

Activity

Creating a Graph Make a line graph that compares the number of people killed during the war in the major Axis and Allied countries.

Section 5 Review Answers

1. Douglas MacArthur, 761; Chester Nimitz, 763; Manhattan Project, 764; V-J Day, 764
2. The words are defined in the Glossary.
3. U.S. ships destroyed most of the Japanese fleet in this battle—the largest naval battle in history. After the battle the Japanese fleet no longer posed a serious threat to the U.S.
4. Students may answer that the Japanese were desperate to win the war at all costs.
5. Answers may include: *Yes,* Japan refused to surrender, so extreme measures were necessary. *No,* this type of warfare results in horrendous suffering and death. The United States should have relied on other means to get Japan to surrender.

Activity Graphs should show the number of war-related deaths in major Axis and Allied nations.

Study and Writing
SKILL BUILDER

Writing a Paragraph

Paragraphs are the building blocks of an essay or other composition. Each paragraph is a unit, a group of sentences about a single topic or idea.

Learning the Skill

Most well-written paragraphs share four characteristics.

- First, a paragraph expresses one main idea or is about one subject. A topic sentence states that main idea. The topic sentence may be located at the beginning, the middle, or the end of a paragraph.
- Second, the rest of the sentences in a paragraph support the main idea. The main idea may be developed by facts, examples, or reasons.
- Third, the sentences are arranged in a logical order.
- Fourth, transitional words link sentences within the paragraph. These words can also link one paragraph with the next. Examples include *next, then, finally, also, because, however,* and *as a result*.

Practicing the Skill

Use the following sentences to build a paragraph containing a topic sentence and other sentences that give supporting details. Arrange the sentences in a logical order and add transitional words if you need to. Underline your topic sentence.

1. Three days later an American plane dropped another bomb on Nagasaki.
2. The bomb killed between 70,000 and 100,000 people.
3. This second bomb killed nearly 40,000 people instantly and many more later.
4. On August 6, 1945, the United States dropped an atomic bomb on Hiroshima, Japan.
5. About 100,000 others died later from the effects of radiation.
6. When the bomb exploded, a sheet of flame spread over the city.

Hiroshima after the atomic bomb

Applying the Skill

Writing a Paragraph Choose another topic from the World War II era and write an explanatory paragraph about it. Rewrite the paragraph with its sentences out of order. Then exchange papers with a classmate. Can he or she find the topic sentence in your paragraph? Does it work logically?

ANSWERS TO PRACTICING THE SKILL

Sentence order should be as follows: 4, 6, 2, 5, 1, 3. Transitional words will vary.

Applying the Skill Students should exchange their out-of-order sentences with classmates. Have them arrange the sentences logically and explain their decisions.

Study and Writing
SKILL BUILDER

TEACH

Writing a Paragraph

This skill teaches students to write paragraphs correctly. Have students study some of the paragraphs in the chapter, identifying the main idea and topic sentence; the type of supporting sentences (facts, examples, reasons); and transitional words.

Note that some paragraphs have a fifth characteristic—a clincher, or wrap-up sentence, at the end. An example is the last sentence of the first paragraph under the heading "War Ends" on page 764—"World War II had finally ended."

Additional Practice

Chapter Skills Activity 26

ABCNEWS INTERACTIVE™

VIDEODISC
Lessons of War

Side 1
Chapter 11

Title: *Weapons of War*
Subject: Quest to find technological advantage over enemies
Ask: **How is technology important to war?** *(leads to the development of new weapons and methods of attack)*

VIDEODISC
Communism and the Cold War

Side 1
Chapter 5

Title: *The Bomb*
Subject: Bombing of Hiroshima and Nagasaki
Ask: **How did dropping the atomic bombs change the world?** *(It began a new era of the most deadly weapons.)*

GLENCOE TECHNOLOGY

VIDEODISC
MindJogger Videoquiz

Use MindJogger to review the Chapter 26 content.

Chapter 26
Disc 4, Side A

Also available in VHS.

Reviewing Key Terms

The key terms used in this activity are defined in the textbook glossary on pages A26–A35. Students' sentences will vary.

Reviewing Key Facts

1. appeasement, signed the Munich Pact
2. enlarged and strengthened the navy, supported passage of the Neutrality Acts and Lend-Lease Act, signed the Selective Training and Service Act (peacetime draft), stopped selling resources to Japan and froze their assets, drew up Atlantic Charter with Churchill
3. Office of War Mobilization coordinated the following activities: converted industries to war production, set limits on consumer prices and rents to prevent inflation, and resolved labor disputes that might slow down war production.
4. the massive invasion of Europe that began with the D-Day landing at Normandy, France; Soviets pushed from the east while British and Americans came from the west (France)
5. Japan continued to fight and refused to surrender even though it faced certain defeat.

Review and Activities

Reviewing Key Terms

On a sheet of paper, use each of the following terms in a sentence:

dictator
fascism
anti-Semitism
appeasement
blitzkrieg
lend-lease
ration
internment camp
genocide
Holocaust
island hopping
kamikaze

Reviewing Key Facts

1. How did Britain and France try to prevent war with Germany?
2. What steps did President Roosevelt take to prepare for war even though he vowed to remain neutral?
3. What did the government do to keep the American economy stable and to ensure that industries produced enough war materials?
4. What was Operation Overlord?
5. What actions by the Japanese convinced the United States to use the atomic bomb?

Critical Thinking

Analyzing Information

Despite having to deal with continuing racial tension, African Americans gained new opportunities during the war.

1. What advances did African Americans make in the military?
2. What rights did A. Philip Randolph win for civilian African Americans?

Time Line Activity

Create a time line on which you place the following events in chronological order.

- Congress passes Lend-Lease Act
- World War II begins
- Hitler and Stalin sign nonaggression pact
- V-E Day
- Hitler becomes German chancellor
- Japan bombs Pearl Harbor

Reviewing Themes

1. **Continuity and Change** Why did most Americans want to avoid involvement in international conflicts after World War I?
2. **Global Connections** What was Japan's main reason for wanting to take over the Dutch East Indies, British Malaya, and the Philippines?
3. **Economic Factors** Why did the government require rationing during the war?
4. **Geography and History** Despite the fact that Japan was conquering areas in the Pacific, why did the Allies focus first on the war in Europe?
5. **Individual Action** What was the significance of the bombing raid on Tokyo led by American James Doolittle?

Technology Activity

Using the Internet Search the Internet for a World War II site that includes memoirs or excerpts from veterans and/or civilians. Copy or print a part of the memoirs that you find interesting. Post the excerpts on the classroom bulletin board under the heading "Voices of World War II."

Critical Thinking

1. Units were no longer segregated. They were allowed to attend officers training school and to take combat assignments.
2. His pressuring of the president to ban discrimination in defense industries resulted in the establishment of the Fair Employment Practices Commission.

Time Line Activity

Events should be placed in this order: Hitler becomes German chancellor, Hitler and Stalin sign nonaggression pact, World War II begins, Congress passes Lend-Lease Act, Japan bombs Pearl Harbor, V-E Day

Geography Activity

The map below shows the Allied invasion routes from Great Britain to Normandy beginning on June 6, 1944. Utah, Omaha, Gold, Juno, *and* Sword *were code names for the Normandy beaches. Study the map below, then answer the questions that follow.*

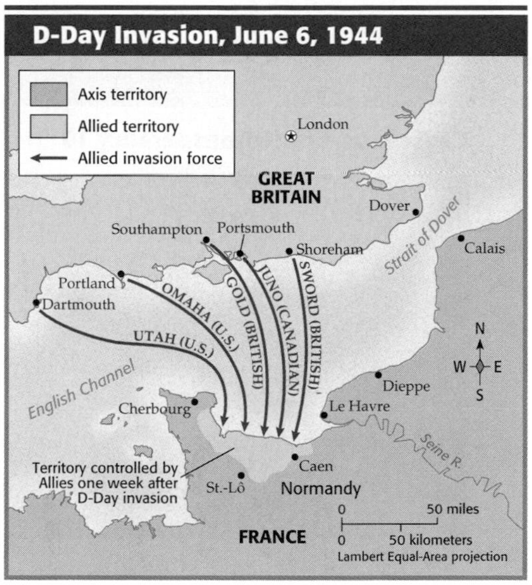

1. **Location** From where did the United States forces leave Great Britain?
2. **Movement** Why do you think the invasion was launched from five sites?
3. **Location** The Nazis were fooled into thinking the invasion would come near Calais. Why do you think the Allies chose to land on the Normandy peninsula instead?

Skill Practice Activity

Writing a Paragraph

Write a short paragraph for each of the topic sentences that follow. Each paragraph must have at least three sentences supporting the topic and arranged in a logical way. Use transitional words or phrases to connect your ideas smoothly.

1. The leaders of Italy, Germany, and Japan attempted to restore their nations to their former greatness through the use of the military.
2. Minority groups played vital roles in World War II, both in the armed forces and at home.
3. During World War II, Americans at home made many sacrifices.

Cooperative Activity

History and Law As a class create a courtroom with students role-playing a panel of judges, a three-member prosecution team, three defense attorneys, a jury, three defendants, and an audience. Put the following people on trial for crimes against humanity: Adolf Hitler—for beginning World War II and establishing the Nazi death camps; a German military officer—for carrying out orders to execute Jews in a death camp; General Hideki Tōjō—for ordering kamikaze attacks against Allied forces in the Pacific. Try each case separately, decide on a verdict, and recommend a punishment.

Portfolio Activity **History Journal** Review the chapter to find information on the major battles of World War II. Use your notes to make a chart that lists the names of the battles or their locations, and the outcome of each.

CHAPTER 26
Review and Activities

Technology Activity

You may wish to discuss with students the reasons they chose the memoirs they did.

Geography Activity

1. Dartmouth and Portland
2. Students may note that multiple attacks would hurt German resistance.
3. Hitler expected Allies to land at Calais, so it was more heavily fortified than Normandy; Eisenhower wanted to have the element of surprise. In addition, the Normandy beachheads were closer to Paris and to the main ports of departure.

Skill Practice Activity

Paragraphs will vary but should be arranged in logical order and include a topic sentence, supporting details, and transitional words.

Cooperative Activity

Students should volunteer to play the roles suggested. The goals of the activity are to present the facts on both sides, come up with verdicts, and recommend punishments.

Portfolio Activity Students should use their notes about each of the major battles of World War II to make a study chart.

Chapter Bonus Test Question

Ask: What were the names of the three aircraft carriers that escaped destruction at Pearl Harbor because they were at sea? *(Saratoga, Lexington, Enterprise)*

Reviewing Themes

1. Most Americans wanted to focus on their own problems. Many loans made to European countries remained unpaid and Congress wanted to prevent more debt.
2. to get rubber and oil
3. The government had to make sure that Allied armies had the resources and supplies they needed. American industries also had to focus on making war materials, which meant a shortage of consumer goods.
4. German forces had taken almost all of Europe and large areas of North Africa. The Allies feared that if the Soviets were defeated by the Germans, there would be no stopping them.
5. It had little military significance, but it boosted morale.

Unit 10 Resource Guide

These Glencoe resources may be used to teach, reteach, or enrich the concepts presented in this unit of study.

Teaching Transparencies

Map Transparency 10 with Overlays A, B, C

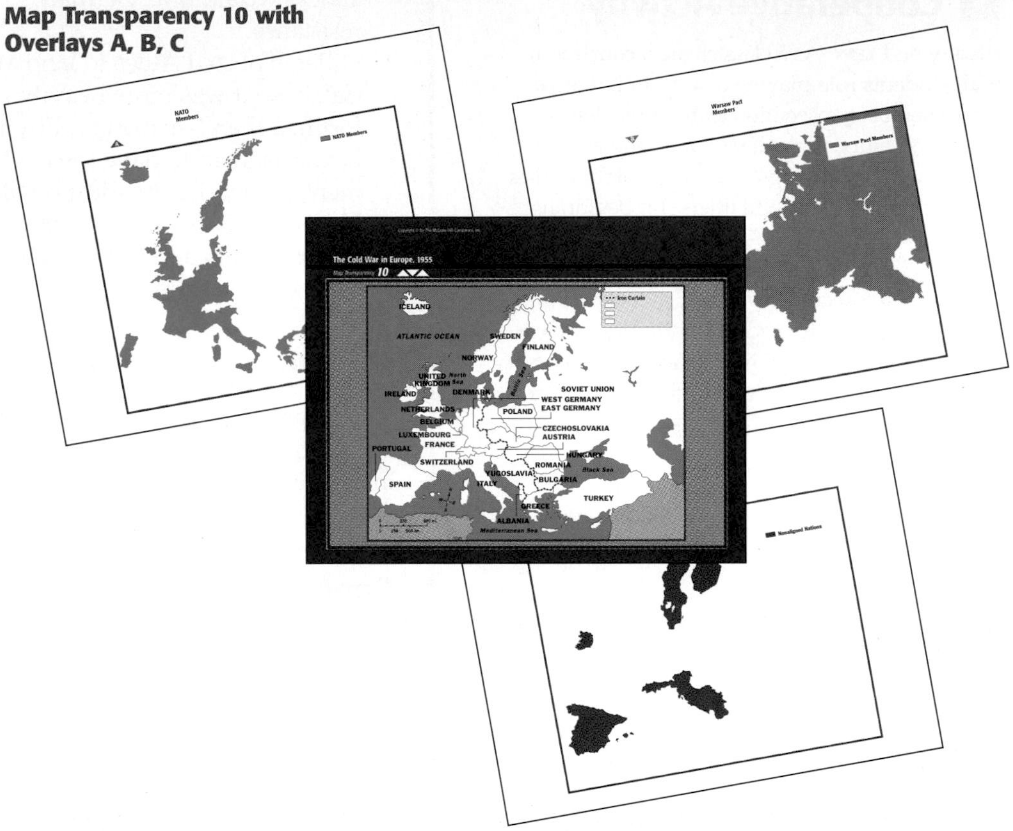

Cause-and-Effect Transparency 10

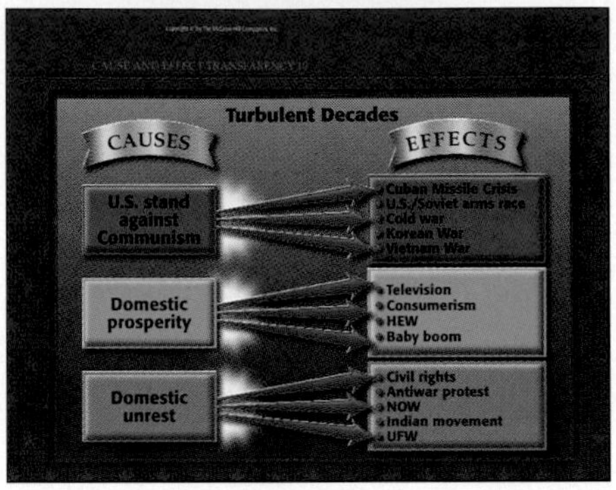

BIBLIOGRAPHY

Readings for the Student

Archer, Jules. ***Incredible Sixties: The Stormy Years That Changed America.*** New York: Harcourt Brace Jovanovich, 1986. Covers political, social, and other issues of the era.

Hauptly, Denis J. ***In Vietnam.*** New York: Atheneum, 1985. Includes background and issues related to the Vietnam War.

Readings for the Teacher

Hampton, Henry, and Steve Fayer. ***Voices of Freedom: An Oral History of the Civil Rights Movement from the 1950s Through the 1980s.*** New York: Bantam Books, 1990. Participants of the civil rights movement.

Kaldin, Eugenia. ***Mothers and More: American Women in the 1950s.*** New York: Hall, 1984. Important women of the era and the seeds of feminism.

Multimedia Resources

Videodisc ***Struggles for Justice, Volume I: African Americans, Native Americans, Latinos.*** Jefferson City, MO: Scholastic New Media, 1993. Depicts civil rights issues of the era through various media.

CD-ROM ***The USA Wars—Korea*** **and** ***The USA Wars—Vietnam.*** Minneapolis: Quanta Press, Inc., 1994. IBM and Macintosh. Examines the causes, major issues, and military history of these two wars.

interNET CONNECTIONS

World Wide Web resources

Cold war links:
http://www.stmartin.edu/~dprice/cold.war.html

National Civil Rights Museum:
http://www.mecca.org/~crights/ncrm.html

Vietnam Veterans home page:
http://www.vietvet.org/

Interdisciplinary Activities

American Literature Reading 10

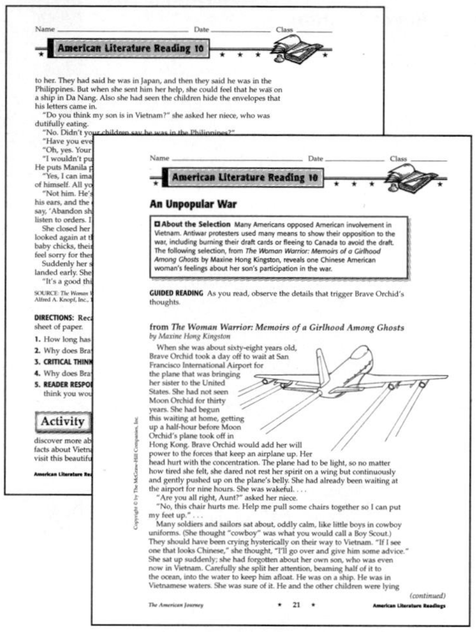
Name ______ Date ______ Class ______
American Literature Reading 10
An Unpopular War
from *The Woman Warrior: Memoirs of a Girlhood Among Ghosts* by Maxine Hong Kingston

Interdisciplinary Connection 10

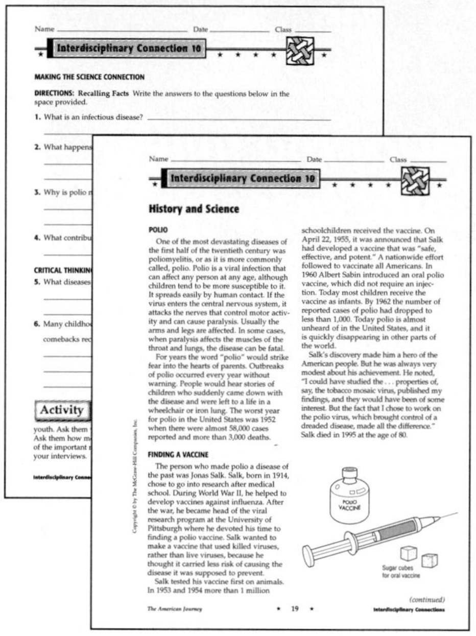
Name ______ Date ______ Class ______
Interdisciplinary Connection 10
History and Science
POLIO
FINDING A VACCINE

Enrichment Activities

Cooperative Learning Activity 10

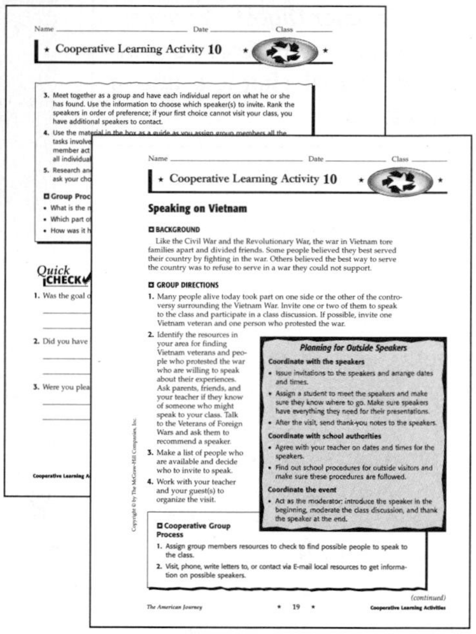
Name ______ Date ______ Class ______
Cooperative Learning Activity 10
Speaking on Vietnam

Hands-On Activities

Hands-On History Lab Activity 10

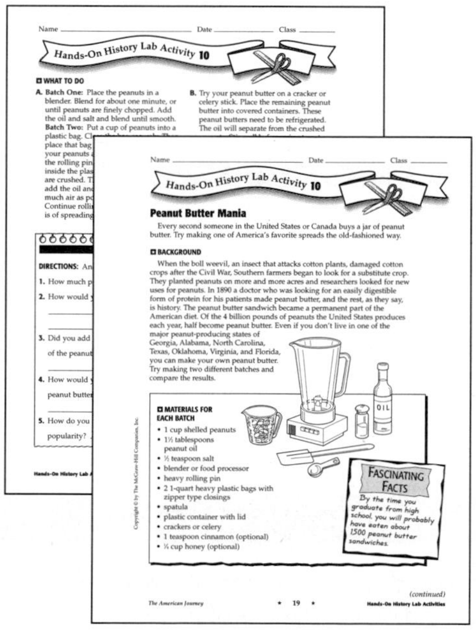
Name ______ Date ______ Class ______
Hands-On History Lab Activity 10
Peanut Butter Mania

History Simulation 10

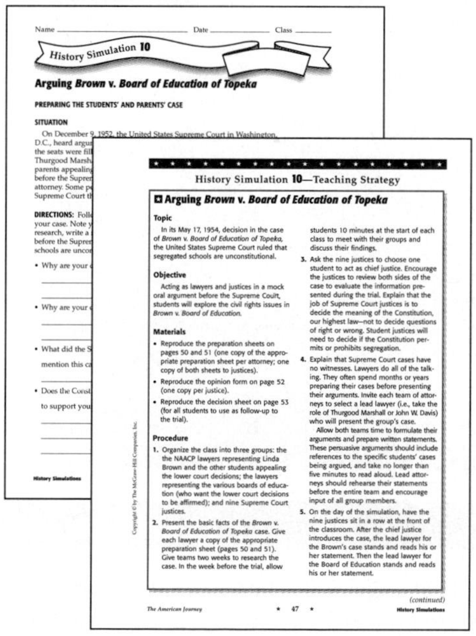
History Simulation 10—Teaching Strategy
Arguing *Brown v. Board of Education of Topeka*

Assessment

Unit 10 Test

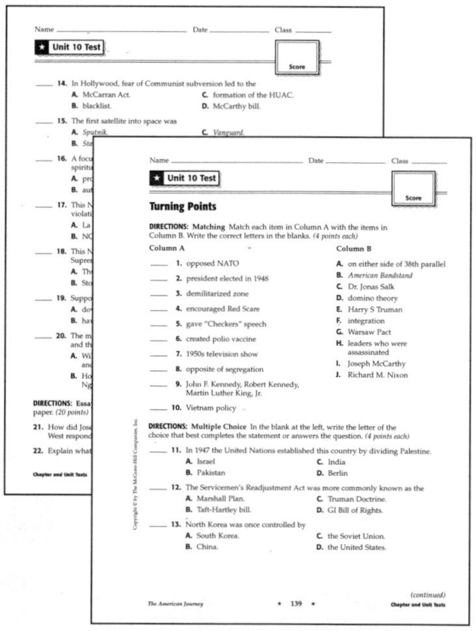
Name ______ Date ______ Class ______
Unit 10 Test
Turning Points

0:00 OUT OF TIME?

If your teaching time is limited, you may use the *Chapter Summaries* blackline master found in the TCR with the *Chapter Digests Audiocassette Activities and Tests* to condense individual chapters into a one-day lesson.

Introducing the Unit

Activity Have students interview people who were adolescents or teenagers during the 1960s. Have them ask, **When you were my age, what events did you think were important? How did the world seem to be changing?** Call on volunteers to share some of the responses. Point out that these responses may help students understand what the United States was like during the 1960s and how events of that decade have shaped Americans' attitudes today.

Unit Objectives

Upon completing this unit, students will be able to:

1. Analyze causes and results of the increased tensions between the United States and the Soviet Union after World War II.
2. Relate the economic, social, and cultural distinctions of the United States during the 1950s.
3. Discuss the rise of the civil rights movement in the United States, including its leaders and its influence on other groups of disadvantaged Americans.
4. Describe the causes, course, and effects of the Vietnam War.

Hands-On HISTORY

Hands-On History Lab Activity 10, "Peanut Butter Mania," is a high-interest **constructivist approach** activity directly related to the main topic of the unit.

Unit 10

Turning Points

1945–1975

"Justice too long delayed is justice denied."

—Martin Luther King, Jr., 1963

MAPPING America

Portfolio Activity Draw a freehand outline map of China, Korea, and the former Soviet Union. As you read this unit about turning points in postwar America, note major events. Plot the location of these events on your map and label them.

768

Boycott button

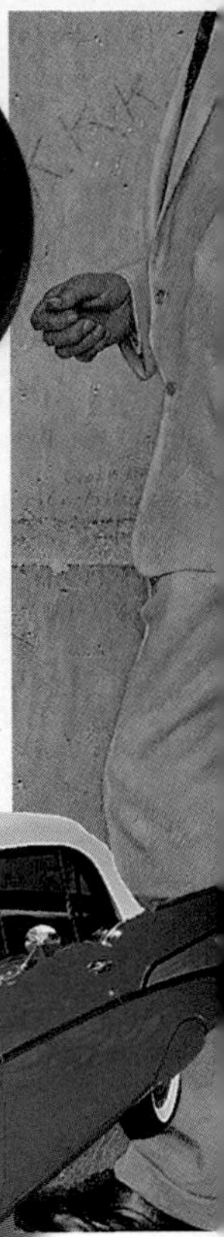

1957 Chevrolet

United States

1947 Jackie Robinson first plays for Brooklyn Dodgers

1953 McCarthyism stirs nation

1940 — 1950

World

1947 Truman Doctrine is announced

1949 Communist forces take China

1950 North Korea invades South Korea

Team Teaching Strategies

Civics Have a Civics teacher provide background information on protest as part of American life. This information may include an overview of civil disobedience and other methods of protest, legal restrictions upon protest, recent examples of protest, and so on. It also may include quotations from the speeches, writings, and songs of protesters for various causes.

Vietnam veteran's hat

HISTORY AND ART ***Problem We All Live With* by Norman Rockwell** Postwar America faced increasing tension over racial discrimination—a critical situation that affected all Americans, young and old alike.

1954 *Brown* v. *Board of Education* decision

1955 Rosa Parks inspires Montgomery bus boycott

1959 Alaska and Hawaii become states

1965 Freedom Marchers journey from Selma to Montgomery

1973 U.S. ends role in Vietnam

1960 — 1970 — 1980

1959 Fidel Castro takes over Cuba

1961 Berlin Wall is built

1966 China's Cultural Revolution begins

1973 Arab oil embargo intensifies energy crisis

TEAM TEACHING STRATEGIES

Math Ask a Math teacher to explain to students how to draw the following circle or bar graphs. The first graph should show the ethnic makeup of the nation, your state, or your community, circa 1940. The second graph should show it at present. Encourage comparisons of the graphs and explanations for any changes.

Science Amazing advances in technology have taken place in the past few decades. Invite the Science teacher to discuss advances in one or more of the following:

- sound recording
- computers
- space flight
- nuclear power
- ocean exploration
- medical research

Introducing UNIT 10

ABCNEWS INTERACTIVE™

VIDEODISC
Communism and the Cold War

Side 2
Chapter 5

Title: *How We Saw Them*
Subject: U.S. perspective on the Soviet Union during the cold war
Ask: **How did the United States view the Soviet Union?** *(as a country that wanted to convert the whole world to communism)*

Side 2
Chapter 6

Title: *How They Saw Us*
Subject: Soviet perspective on the United States during the cold war
Ask: **What did the Soviets identify as the reason happiness could not exist in a capitalist society?** *(They believed competition led to unhappiness and a large gap between the rich and the poor.)*

HISTORY AND ART Norman Rockwell (1894–1978) was best known for his paintings that covered the *Saturday Evening Post* and other magazines. He usually painted middle-class Americans, often in small-town settings, to comment upon Americans' values.

Linking PAST & PRESENT

Activity As students read Chapters 27–30, have them note how events of the recent past are remembered today. For example, has a current news story made reference to the civil rights movement? How do people feel now about the war in Vietnam? Help students see that these events continue to influence Americans today.

America's Literature

Block Schedule

Team Teaching This selection from *I Know Why the Caged Bird Sings* may be implemented in a team-teaching context, in conjunction with English/Language Arts.

Reinforcing Vocabulary

Review the **Reader's Dictionary** terms with students to be sure they understand any unfamiliar terms.

Historical Connection

The 1950s saw the rise of the civil rights movement in the United States—a movement that challenged all Americans to rethink their views on racial issues. Although this scene from *I Know Why the Caged Bird Sings* takes place shortly before that time, it captures the innate dignity upon which African Americans soon would build their campaign.

Background Information

Setting This scene takes place around 1940 in the African American community in the town of Stamps, Arkansas.

Characters The main characters are "Momma" (the narrator's grandmother) and Mrs. Bertha Flowers, whom the narrator describes as "the aristocrat of Black Stamps." The narrator, Marguerite, also is a character in the scene.

Plot Marguerite comments upon the differences she once observed between Momma and Mrs. Flowers, noting that she now realizes they were very similar. As a child, however, Marguerite was embarrassed by Momma's common ways but took personal pride in the example set by Mrs. Flowers's refinement.

America's Literature

I Know Why the Caged Bird Sings

by Maya Angelou

Maya Angelou (1928–) has written poetry, fiction, and plays. She worked on a newspaper in Egypt, lectured at the University of Ghana, and directed a film in Hollywood. Born Marguerite Johnson, Angelou and her brother, Bailey, were raised by their grandmother, Annie Henderson (whom they called "Momma"), the owner of a general store in the black area of Stamps, Arkansas.

Read to Discover

In the following excerpt from Angelou's autobiography, she is about 10 years old. Bright but painfully self-conscious, she has become withdrawn and refuses to speak to anyone. As you read, notice the influence that Mrs. Flowers has on Marguerite.

Reader's Dictionary

voile: lightweight, sheer fabric
benign: showing kindness and gentleness
bungalow: one-story house with a low roof
moors: also called "heath"; open, wild land
scones: pastries
crumpets: muffins
morocco: soft leather

For nearly a year, I sopped around the house, the store, the school and the church, like an old biscuit, dirty and inedible. Then I met, or rather got to know, the lady who threw me my first life line.

Mrs. Bertha Flowers was the aristocrat of Black Stamps. She had the grace of control to appear warm in the coldest weather, and on the Arkansas summer days it seemed she had a private breeze which swirled around, cooling her. She was thin without the taut look of wiry people, and her printed voile dresses and flowered hat were as right for her as denim overalls for a farmer. She was our side's answer to the richest white women in town.

Her skin was a rich black that would have peeled like a plum if snagged, but then no one would have thought of getting close enough to Mrs. Flowers to ruffle her dress, let alone snag her skin. She didn't encourage familiarity. She wore gloves too.

I don't think I ever saw Mrs. Flowers laugh, but she smiled often. A slow widening of her thin black lips to show even, small white teeth, then the slow effortless closing. When she chose to smile on me, I always wanted to thank her. The action was so graceful and inclusively benign.

She was one of the few gentlewomen I have ever known, and has remained throughout my life the measure of what a human being can be.

Momma had a strange relationship with her. Most often when she passed on the road in front of the Store, she spoke to Momma in that soft yet carrying voice, "Good day, Mrs. Henderson." Momma responded with "How you, Sister Flowers?"

Mrs. Flowers didn't belong to our church, nor was she Momma's familiar.

Additional Literary Works About the Period

You may refer students to the following:

Berry, Henry. ***Hey, Mac, Where Ya Been? Living Memories of the U.S. Marines in the Korean War.*** New York: St. Martin's Press, 1988. Recollections of Marines in Korea.

Haskins, James. ***The 60s Reader.*** New York: Viking, 1988. Chronicle of this decade, told through speeches, songs, and other documents of the day.

Washington, James M., ed. ***Testament of Hope: The Essential Writings of Martin Luther King, Jr.*** New York: Harper & Row, 1986. Collection of the civil rights leader's speeches, sermons, and interviews.

Willenson, Kim. ***Bad War: An Oral History of the Vietnam War.*** New York: New American Library, 1987. Provides views on both sides of the controversial Vietnam conflict.

Why on earth did she insist on calling her Sister Flowers? Shame made me want to hide my face. Mrs. Flowers deserved better than to be called Sister. Then, Momma left out the verb. Why not ask, "How *are* you, *Mrs.* Flowers?" With the unbalanced passion of the young, I hated her for showing her ignorance to Mrs. Flowers. It didn't occur to me for many years that they were as alike as sisters, separated only by formal education.

Although I was upset, neither of the women was in the least shaken by what I thought an unceremonious greeting. Mrs. Flowers would continue her easy gait up the hill to her little bungalow, and Momma kept on shelling peas or doing whatever had brought her to the front porch.

Occasionally, though, Mrs. Flowers would drift off the road and down to the Store and Momma would say to me, "Sister, you go on and play." As I left I would hear the beginning of an intimate conversation. Momma persistently using the wrong verb, or none at all.

"Brother and Sister Wilcox is sho'ly the meanest—" "Is," Momma? "Is"? Oh, please, not "is," Momma, for two or more. But they talked, and from the side of the building where I waited for the ground to open up and swallow me, I heard the soft-voiced Mrs. Flowers and the textured voice of my grandmother merging and melting. They were interrupted from time to time by giggles that must have come from Mrs. Flowers (Momma never giggled in her life). Then she was gone.

She appealed to me because she was like people I had never met personally. Like women in English novels who walked the moors

Her World *by Philip Evergood*

(whatever they were) with their loyal dogs racing at a respectful distance. Like the women who sat in front of roaring fireplaces, drinking tea incessantly from silver trays full of scones and crumpets. Women who walked over the "heath" and read morocco-bound books and had two last names divided by a hyphen. It would be safe to say that she made me proud to be Negro, just by being herself.

She acted just as refined as whitefolks in the movies and books and she was more beautiful, for none of them could have come near that warm color without looking gray by comparison.

Responding to Literature

1. How does the author describe Mrs. Flowers's attitude toward familiarity?
2. Does this attitude make you like or dislike Mrs. Flowers? Explain.
3. In what way does Marguerite think her grandmother's relationship with Mrs. Flowers is strange?

Activity

Writing a Sketch Write a one-page sketch describing an encounter you had with a person who influenced your life in a positive way. Explain the changes that occurred as a result of the encounter.

Answers to Responding to Literature

1. "She didn't encourage familiarity," Marguerite says, but it becomes apparent that Mrs. Flowers is gracious when others act familiarly toward her.
2. Answers will vary. Some students may find her too aloof; others may like her because of Marguerite's vivid descriptions and Mrs. Flowers's own graciousness toward Momma.
3. Although the two women seem to have little in common, they occasionally and easily fall into intimate conversation.

Activity Sketches should provide a setting and basic plot, but characterization should make the strongest impact. The more effective sketches may imply the character's importance (through dialogue or choice of plot details, for example) rather than state it directly.

History *and the* Humanities

Spirit of American Art and Music, Elizabeth Catlett, Gordon Parks, Maya Angelou

Focus on American Art Prints, *Children at Play* by Jacob Lawrence

U.S. History & Art, Transparency 30, *Forward*

Portfolio Activity Have students locate and read memoirs or speeches by people involved in the civil rights movement. Ask them to relate issues raised by these people to Maya Angelou's circumstances in this excerpt from her autobiography.

At the Movies

The film *I Know Why the Caged Bird Sings,* a 1979 made-for-television adaptation of this novel, is available on videocassette. Other films relating to race relations of the recent past include *The Autobiography of Miss Jane Pittman* (1974), *Driving Miss Daisy* (1989), and *Words by Heart* (1984), all of which also are available on videocassette.

Curriculum Connection

LANGUAGE ARTS

Maya Angelou has excelled in many forms of writing—autobiography, poetry, fiction, plays, songs, newspaper reports, and television programs. President Bill Clinton honored her achievements as a writer by asking her to read her work at his 1993 inauguration. Angelou wrote and read the poem, "On the Pulse of the Morning," at the inauguration.

Chapter 27 Planning Guide

A complete, 1-page lesson plan is provided for each section in the *Reproducible Lesson Plans* booklet.

Section Resources

Daily Objectives	Reproducible Resources	Multimedia Resources
Section 1 Cold War Origins Explain why United States foreign policy changed after World War II, especially in regard to communism.	Reproducible Lesson Plan 27–1 Guided Reading Activity 27–1* Section Quiz 27–1* Reteaching Activity 27–1 Enrichment Activity 27–1	Section Focus Transparency 27–1 Vocabulary PuzzleMaker Chapter Challenger Interactive Review Testmaker ABCNews InterActive™ Communism and the Cold War GTV: A Geographic Perspective on American History Facts On File: Landmark Documents in American History
Section 2 Postwar Politics Discuss how President Truman attempted to deal with economic problems as well as problems in race relations.	Reproducible Lesson Plan 27–2 Guided Reading Activity 27–2* Political Cartoons, *President Truman and the Fair Deal* Section Quiz 27–2* Reteaching Activity 27–2 Enrichment Activity 27–2	Section Focus Transparency 27–2 Vocabulary PuzzleMaker Chapter Challenger Interactive Review Testmaker Facts On File: Landmark Documents in American History The Presidents: A Picture History of Our Nation
Section 3 The Korean War Interpret changes in the views of American leaders toward Korea and the struggle against communism itself in light of key events in the Korean War.	Reproducible Lesson Plan 27–3 Guided Reading Activity 27–3* Political Cartoons, *Chinese Checkers in the Korean War* Section Quiz 27–3* Reteaching Activity 27–3 Enrichment Activity 27–3	Section Focus Transparency 27–3 Vocabulary PuzzleMaker Chapter Challenger Interactive Review Testmaker ABCNews InterActive™ Communism and the Cold War ABCNews InterActive™ Lessons of War
Section 4 The Red Scare Analyze McCarthyism and other signs of fears about communism that marked American society at this time.	Reproducible Lesson Plan 27–4 Guided Reading Activity 27–4* Political Cartoons, *Joseph McCarthy and the Communist Scare* Section Quiz 27–4* Reteaching Activity 27–4 Enrichment Activity 27–4	Section Focus Transparency 27–4 Vocabulary PuzzleMaker Chapter Challenger Interactive Review Testmaker ABCNews InterActive™ Communism and the Cold War Facts On File: Landmark Documents in American History

** Also available in Spanish*

Poster — Transparency — CD-ROM — Software
Blackline Master — Videodisc — Audiocassette — Music Program

0:00 **OUT OF TIME?**
Assign the Chapter 27 Digest and the corresponding Chapter Digests Audiocassettes with activities and tests.

Activity

From the Classroom of...

Kay Selah
Landmark Middle School
Jacksonville, FL

A Press Conference After Yalta

Organize the class into six groups to hold a press conference after the meeting at Yalta. Two groups are responsible for researching and collecting information on Franklin D. Roosevelt; two groups are assigned to Winston Churchill; and two groups will research Joseph Stalin. One group assigned to each individual is responsible for representing that person in a news conference; the corresponding group will role-play reporters and be responsible for asking informed questions of that person. Three separate news conferences can be held, or the whole class can have a joint news conference. Have students focus particular attention on the meeting in Yalta in 1945. Reporters should prepare questions concerning the conference, and those being interviewed should anticipate the types of questions that may be asked. Encourage students to dress in character and use props.

Block Schedule

Block scheduling differs from traditional class scheduling in the amount of time allotted to each period. The extended time frame provided by block scheduling affords you the opportunity to implement a greater number of research-oriented and activity-intense projects to motivate and involve your students. Activities that are particularly suited to use within the block scheduling framework are identified throughout this chapter by the following designation:

National Geographic Society Teacher's Corner

INDEX TO NATIONAL GEOGRAPHIC MAGAZINE

The following articles may be used for research relating to this chapter:

- "St. Petersburg, Capital of the Tsars," by Steve Raymer, December 1993.

NATIONAL GEOGRAPHIC SOCIETY PRODUCTS AVAILABLE FROM GLENCOE

To order the following products for use with this chapter, contact your local Glencoe sales representative, or call Glencoe at 1-800-334-7344:

- *The Presidents: A Picture History of Our Nation* (CD-ROM)
- *GTV: A Geographic Perspective on American History* (Videodisc)
- *GTV: The American People: Fabric of a Nation* (Videodisc)

ADDITIONAL NATIONAL GEOGRAPHIC SOCIETY PRODUCTS

To order the following products for use with this chapter, call National Geographic Society at 1-800-368-2728:

- *The Rise and Fall of the Soviet Union* (Video)
- *1945–1989: The Cold War* (Video)
- *Historical Atlas of the United States* (Atlas)

KEY TO ABILITY LEVELS

Teaching strategies have been coded for varying learning styles and abilities.

L1 **BASIC** activities for all students
L2 **AVERAGE** activities for average to above-average students
L3 **CHALLENGING** activities for above-average students
ELL **ENGLISH LANGUAGE LEARNER** activities

Chapter 27 Resource Guide

HOME INVOLVEMENT

Home Involvement Activity 27

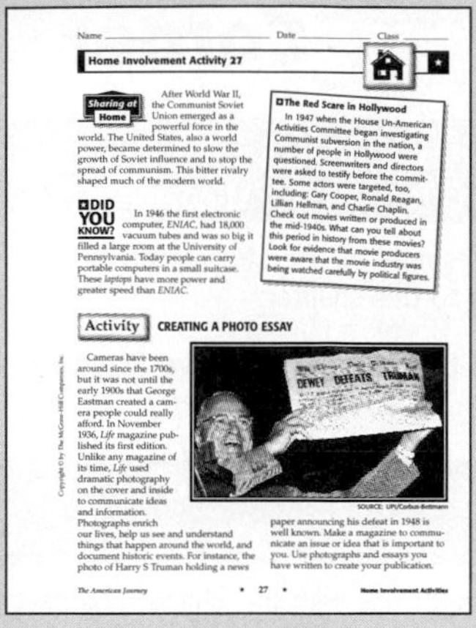

REVIEW ACTIVITIES

Chapter Summary 27

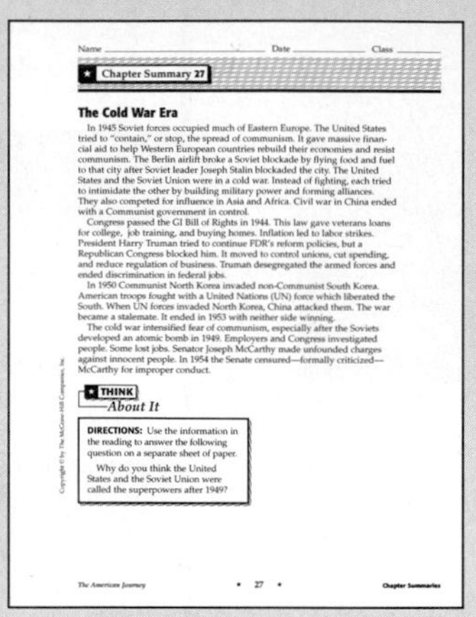

Workbook Activity 27

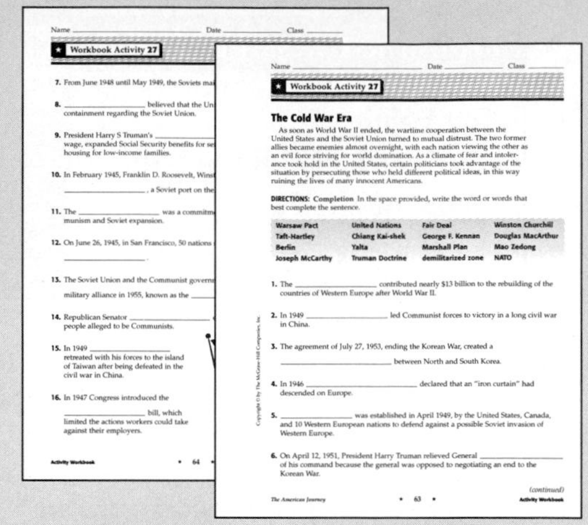

REINFORCEMENT ACTIVITIES

Time Line Activity 27

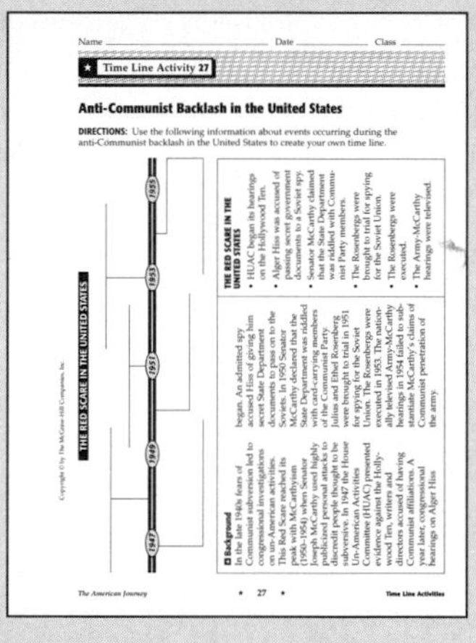

Vocabulary Activity 27

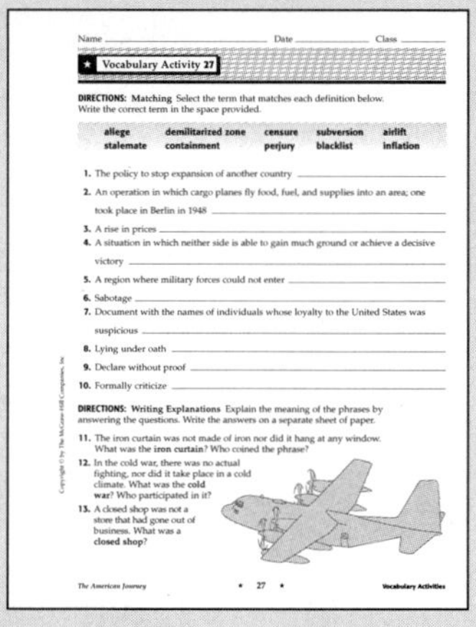

Chapter Skills Activity 27

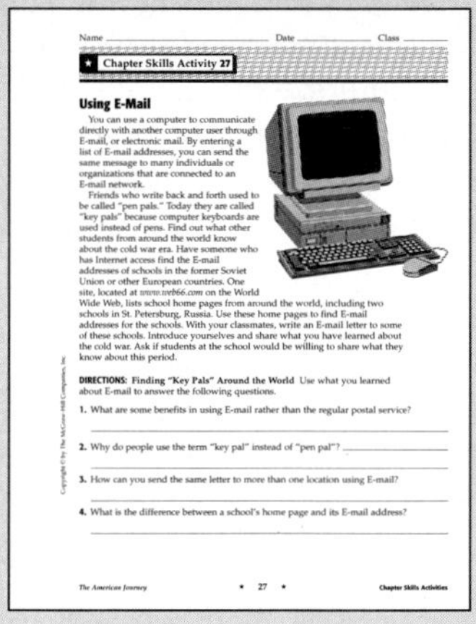

ENRICHMENT ACTIVITIES

Linking Past and Present Activity 27

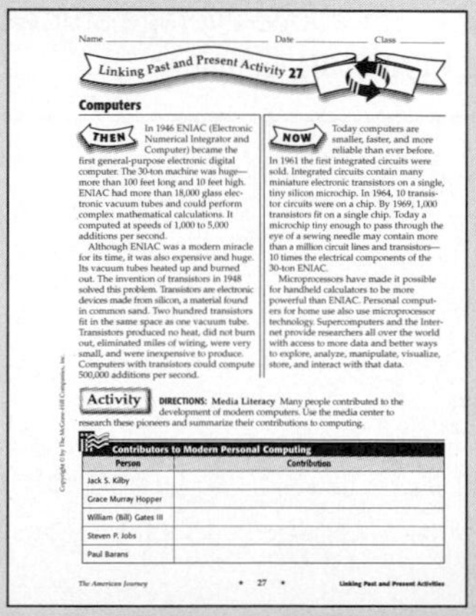

Primary Source Reading 27

GEOGRAPHY ACTIVITIES

Mapping History Activity 27

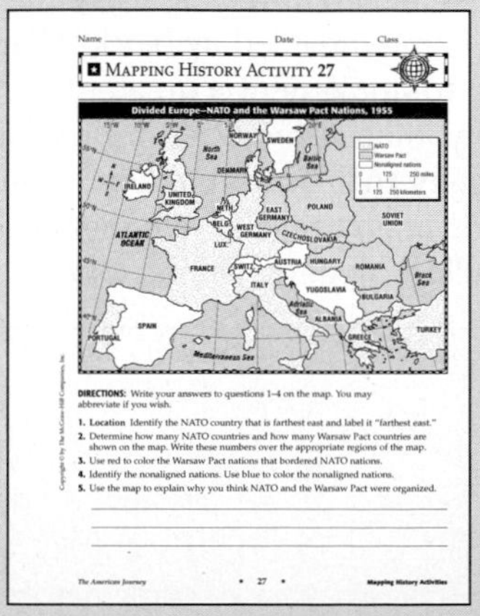

Chapter 27 Resource Guide

Assessment

Chapter 27 Test, Form A

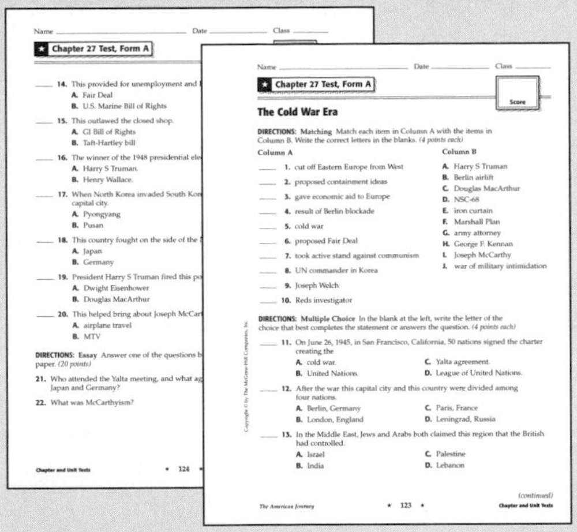

Chapter 27 Test, Form B

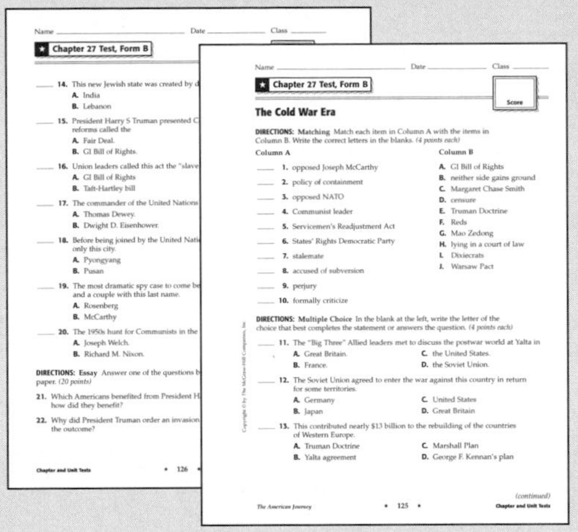

Performance Assessment Activity 27

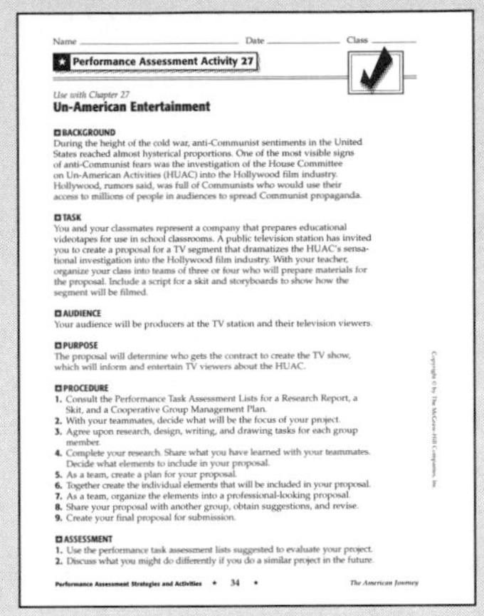

Spanish Resources

The following Spanish language materials are available in the Spanish Resources binder:

- **Spanish Chapter Summary 27**
- **Spanish Vocabulary Activity 27**
- **Spanish Guided Reading Activities, Chapter 27**
- **Spanish Section Quizzes, Chapter 27**
- **Spanish Home Involvement Activity 27**
- **Spanish Chapter 27 Digests Audiocassette Activity and Test**

Activity Manipulatives

Help students learn more about America's cultural history with:

- **American Crafts Hands-On Activities**
- **American Games Hands-On Activities**
- **American History Flash Cards**

Additional Resources From Glencoe

- **Political Cartoons,** *President Truman and the Fair Deal, Chinese Checkers in the Korean War, Joseph McCarthy and the Communist Scare*
- **The American History Videodisc and CD-ROM,** *World War II and the Beginning of the Cold War, 1941–1960*
- **U.S. Desk Map**
- **Outline Map Resource Book**

A&E HOME VIDEO. Biography THE HISTORY CHANNEL.

The following videotape programs are available from Glencoe as supplements to Chapter 27:

- **Harry S Truman: A New View** (ISBN 1-56501-449-9)
- **The Complete Churchill: BIOGRAPHY® Set** (ISBN 1-56501-091-4)
- **Joseph Stalin** (ISBN 1-56501-820-6)
- **General Douglas MacArthur: Return of a Legend** (ISBN 1-56501-609-2)
- **Senator Joseph McCarthy: An American Inquisitor** (ISBN 1-56501-610-6)

To order, call Glencoe at 1-800-334-7344. To find classroom resources to accompany many of these videos, check the following home pages:
A&E Television: http://www.aetv.com
The History Channel: http://www.historychannel.com

Chapter Themes

Chapter Themes are listed by section on this chapter opening page of the Student Edition. A corresponding theme-based activity is available under "FOCUS," and a theme-based question is asked in the Section and Chapter Reviews.

Performance Assessment

Refer to Activity 27 in the *Performance Assessment Strategies and Activities* booklet.

GLENCOE TECHNOLOGY

VIDEODISC
MindJogger Videoquiz

Use MindJogger to preview the Chapter 27 content.

Chapter 27
Disc 4, Side A

Also available in VHS.

HISTORY AND ART Because Congress never declared war, the United States involvement in the Korean struggle has never been officially called a "war," but rather a "conflict."

Chapter 27

1945–1954

The Cold War Era

Why It's Important

The bitter rivalry between the United States and the Soviet Union after World War II shaped much of the modern world. Each side sought to gain allies and to prove that its system—democracy and free enterprise or communism—was better. At times their rivalry and hostile relations threatened to turn into open warfare. The collapse of the Soviet Union in 1991 marked the end of the cold war era.

Chapter Themes

- *Section 1,* Global Connections
- *Section 2,* Economic Factors
- *Section 3,* Government and Democracy
- *Section 4,* Individual Action

HISTORY AND ART ***Korea* by T.H. Jackson** The Korean War began in June 1950 when North Korean forces invaded South Korea. For three years UN troops and Communist forces battled up and down the Korean peninsula.

EXTRA CREDIT PROJECT

Charting Cold War Influences The growing power—and seeming threat—of the Soviet Union after World War II affected Americans' attitudes about many topics. In some cases, it made people rethink their own politics; in others, it caused a change in priorities. As students read Chapter 27, ask them to write a brief paragraph that describes how Americans felt about at least three of the following topics: foreign policy, economics, the arts, political leadership, race relations. Were Americans' opinions on these topics influenced by the cold war with the Soviet Union? Have students review their paragraphs as they continue into Chapter 28.

1945 — 1947 — 1949

February 1945 Conference at Yalta is held

April 1945 Harry S Truman succeeds FDR

May 1948 Jewish leaders proclaim new state of Israel

June 1948 Soviets blockade West Berlin

October 1949 Mao Zedong forms Communist China

Section 1

Cold War Origins

READ TO DISCOVER . . .

- how the United States attempted to stop the spread of communism.
- how postwar foreign policy changed as a result of the cold war.

TERMS TO LEARN

iron curtain	airlift
containment	cold war

The Storyteller

The three most powerful men in the world met around a conference table in Yalta to discuss the fate of the postwar world. President Roosevelt hoped to promote his vision of postwar cooperation. Prime Minister Churchill spoke elegantly and forcefully. Soviet leader Stalin remained stubbornly opposed to much of what was proposed. Stalin stated to his aides: "They want to force us to accept their plans on Europe and the world. Well, that's not going to happen." As the Allies discovered, Stalin had his own plans.

The Big Three at Yalta

As the Allies moved toward victory in 1945, questions about the organization of the postwar world arose. Soviet forces had pushed back German armies and occupied much of Eastern and Central Europe. Should these areas—including Poland, Hungary, and Czechoslovakia—remain in Soviet hands?

Wartime Diplomacy

In February 1945, the "Big Three" Allied leaders—**Franklin D. Roosevelt, Winston Churchill,** and **Joseph Stalin**—met at **Yalta,** a Soviet port on the Black Sea. They came to discuss issues affecting the postwar world. Out of this meeting came the Yalta agreement, in which the Soviet Union agreed to enter the war against Japan. In return, the Soviets received some territories in Asia.

Reaching an agreement on postwar arrangements proved more difficult. Roosevelt and Churchill feared the Soviet domination of Eastern Europe and the spread of communism. Stalin, on the other hand, wanted to keep a large area of land between the Soviet Union and its potential enemies in the West.

Germany presented a special problem. The Allies finally agreed to divide Germany into four zones until elections could be held to determine its future. The Soviet Union, the United States, Britain, and France would each control a zone.

Stalin agreed to allow free elections in occupied Eastern Europe and to cooperate in planning for the new international organization proposed

SECTION RESOURCES

Reproducible Masters
- Reproducible Lesson Plan 27–1
- Guided Reading Activity 27–1
- Section Quiz 27–1
- Reteaching Activity 27–1
- Enrichment Activity 27–1

Transparencies
- Section Focus Transparency 27–1

Multimedia
- Vocabulary PuzzleMaker
- Chapter Challenger Interactive Review
- Testmaker
- ABCNews InterActive™ Communism and the Cold War
- GTV: A Geographic Perspective on American History
- Landmark Documents in American History

1 FOCUS

BELLRINGER
Motivational Activity

Before taking roll at the beginning of the class period, project Section Focus Transparency 27–1 and have students answer the questions. Discuss students' responses.

This activity is also available as a blackline master.

Section Focus Transparency 27–1

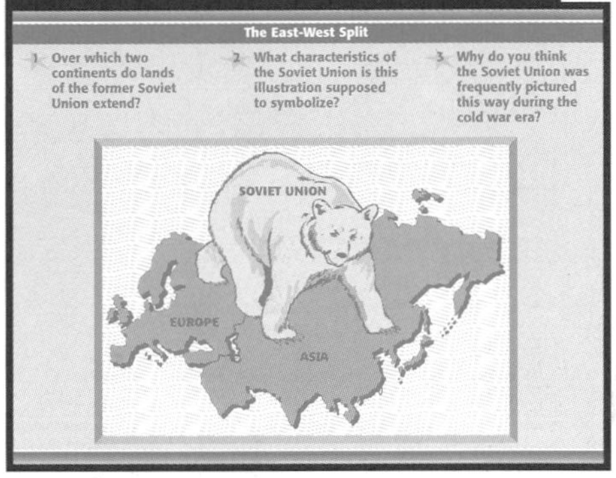

Vocabulary Precheck

Have students find the **Terms to Learn** in the text and read the sentence in which each term is used. Then have students write their own sentences, using each term correctly.

Use the **Vocabulary PuzzleMaker** to create crossword and word search puzzles.

Section Theme
Global Connections

The challenges of ending World War II gave way to the challenges presented by Soviet expansionism in Europe.

Activity Have students summarize the conference at Yalta. **Ask: Why were the Allies nervous about the Soviet Union, which had joined them in fighting the Axis Powers?** *(The Soviet Union's political ideals and goals were very different from those of its temporary allies.)*

2 TEACH

L1 Responding to a Quote Share with students this statement from President Truman: "History will remember my term of office as the years when the cold war began to overshadow our lives." Discuss the effectiveness of his words in describing the United States's postwar concerns about the Soviet Union.

Guided Reading Activity 27–1

Name ______ Date ______ Class ______

★ Guided Reading Activity 27-1

DIRECTIONS: Recording Who, What, When, Where, Why, and How Answer the questions below. Refer to your textbook to write the answers.

1. Who were the Big Three leaders?
2. Where did the Big Three meet in February 1945?
3. What were the terms of the agreement that came out of that meeting?
4. How was Germany to be divided and controlled?
5. When and where was the charter signed forming the United Nations?
6. Geography What two camps did Europe split into?
7. Geography Who first used the term "iron curtain?" What did he mean?
8. What policy did George F. Kennan's ideas about Soviet expansion lead to?
9. What was the Truman Doctrine?
10. Who proposed a plan to provide massive economic aid to Europe? What was this plan called?
11. Why did Joseph Stalin create the Berlin blockade on June 24, 1948?
12. How did President Harry Truman save West Berlin?
13. What two nations did Germany become in October 1949?
14. What did the crisis in Berlin confirm?
15. What divided Europe into two armed camps?
16. How did the UN propose to settle the dispute over Palestine?
17. Who led the opposing forces in China's civil war? How did the war end?

Copyright © by The McGraw-Hill Companies, Inc.

The American Journey • 109 • Guided Reading Activities

Map Study

Answers
1. Austria
2. Berlin and Vienna

What?Where?When?Who?

Truman's Middle Initial The "S" in "Harry S Truman" was his legal middle name and not an initial. Truman's parents chose the unusual name because they could not decide whether to name him after his father's father, Anderson Shippe Truman, or his mother's father, Solomon Young.

by the United States and Britain. Roosevelt and Churchill felt encouraged about a peaceful postwar world. Their hopes went unfulfilled.

The United Nations

President Roosevelt died suddenly on April 12, 1945. Vice President **Harry S Truman** succeeded him. Facing the enormous responsibilities of the presidency, Truman told reporters, "When they told me yesterday [of Roosevelt's death], I felt like the moon, the stars, and all the planets had fallen on me."

One of Truman's first decisions as president was to go ahead with the meeting to form the new international organization discussed at Yalta. On June 26, in San Francisco, California, 50 nations—including the Soviet Union—signed the charter creating the **United Nations** (UN). The members hoped the UN could settle disputes between nations and prevent future wars.

UN flag

Europe After World War II

Map Study

After World War II, the Allies agreed to divide and occupy Germany.

1. **Place** What other nation was divided after the war?
2. **Analyzing Information** What two cities were jointly occupied by both the Allies and the Soviet Union?

Cooperative Learning Activity

Mapping "Hot Spots" Greece, Turkey, and Czechoslovakia were troubled by Soviet influence during this time, which concerned American leaders. Organize students into at least three groups. Supply each group with an outline map of the world. Give group members the responsibility of locating, coloring, and labeling the troubled countries named in this section. Ask students to compare their finished maps. Point out that these countries—the "hot spots"—are far away from the United States. Discuss why American leaders felt threatened by communism nevertheless.

Geography

Soviet Expansion in Europe

The uneasy wartime alliance between the Western nations and the Soviet Union did not last. Stalin did not keep his promise to hold free elections in Eastern Europe. Instead the Soviets set up Communist governments in these countries, and Soviet forces remained in the region.

Developments in Eastern Europe led to a growing distrust between the Soviet Union and Western nations. Europe split into two camps—the Soviet-controlled Communist governments of the East and the capitalist democracies.

Picturing HISTORY James Byrne, President Truman's secretary of state, tried to get along with the Soviets. But Winston Churchill (left), who coined the phrase "iron curtain," foresaw troubles with the Soviet Union. **What did Churchill mean by this phrase?**

The Iron Curtain

Winston Churchill believed that the division between East and West was permanent. In 1946 he declared in a speech in Fulton, Missouri, that an **"iron curtain"** had descended on Europe. Churchill meant that the Soviets had cut off Eastern Europe from the West. Behind this iron curtain, he said, lay the countries of Eastern Europe "in what I must call the Soviet sphere, and all are subject to a very high . . . measure of control from Moscow."

Churchill warned that the Soviets would eventually look beyond Eastern Europe and try to gain control of other parts of the world. This idea alarmed Americans, who had feared the spread of communism ever since the Russian Revolution in 1917.

In **Greece,** as Communist rebels armed by the Soviet Union attempted to overthrow the Greek king and his pro-Western government, civil war raged in the country. At the same time, the Soviets put enormous pressure on **Turkey** to give them naval bases on the straits leading to the Mediterranean Sea.

Containing the Soviets

Seeking ways to counter Soviet expansion, President Truman drew from the ideas of **George F. Kennan,** an American diplomat and an expert on Soviet history and culture. Kennan argued that the United States and the Soviet Union could not cooperate and that the United States must take forceful steps to stop Soviet expansion. His ideas led to the policy of **containment.** The United States would try to "contain" Soviet expansion through limited military means and nonmilitary means in areas of the world that were of strategic importance to the United States. Kennan defined these areas narrowly—mostly Western Europe and Japan. But other United States officials gradually expanded their view of what was of strategic importance to the country and its future.

Multiple Learning Styles

Verbal/Linguistic Winston Churchill's metaphor of an iron curtain to describe Soviet control in Eastern Europe is very evocative. Have students work individually or with partners to brainstorm words and images they associate with *iron* (for example, its seeming invulnerability, its use in the making of weapons) and *curtain* (for example, its ability to cut off contact with others or to hide what lies behind it). Allow students to draw as well as list the images that come to mind. Call on volunteers to share responses as you introduce or review this section. **L1, ELL**

ABC NEWS INTERACTIVE™

VIDEODISC
Communism and the Cold War

Side 1, Chapter 3
Title: *End of Alliance*
Subject: Summary of events near the end of World War II that led to the cold war
Ask: Why did the United States view the Soviet Union as a threat? *(The U.S. believed the Soviet Union was trying to spread communism.)* **Why did the Soviet Union view the United States as a threat?** *(The Soviet Union believed the U.S. was an imperialistic power that wanted to destroy communism.)*

Picturing HISTORY Churchill described the "iron curtain" as stretching "from Stettin in the Baltic to Trieste in the Adriatic" and as taking in "all the capitals of the ancient states of central and eastern Europe." **Ask: What is Churchill's hand signal meant to represent?** *(It is a sign of victory—in this context, victory over Soviet expansionism.)*
Answer: *He meant that the Soviet Union had cut off Eastern Europe from the West.*

CURRICULUM CONNECTION

WORLD HISTORY
The only two superpowers after World War II were the United States and the Soviet Union. They possessed as much productive capacity as the rest of the world combined. Throughout the cold war era, the two superpowers would vie for the loyalty and support of the rest of the world.

NATIONAL GEOGRAPHIC SOCIETY

VIDEODISC
GTV: A Geographic Perspective on American History

Side 4, Chapter 6
Title: *Echoes of War*
Subject: Effects of World War II on America
Ask: **What happened to American isolationism as a result of World War II and the United Nations?** *(Isolationism was no longer possible because America had become too involved in the international scene.)*

Facts On File

CD-ROM
Landmark Documents in American History

Title: *"Iron Curtain" speech, Sir Winston Churchill, 1946*
Title: *Truman Doctrine, 1947*
Have students read both documents, then rewrite one in their own words.

Picturing HISTORY Senator Robert A. Taft of Ohio was one American who did not agree with the Marshall Plan. He called it a "global . . . give-away" program and worried that it would bankrupt the United States. **Ask:** **What event in Europe made congressional approval of the Marshall Plan a surety?** *(In 1948 Communists took over the government of Czechoslovakia.)* **Answer:** *It provided nearly $13 billion for the rebuilding of Western European countries.*

The Truman Doctrine

The policy of containment soon went into effect. Speaking to Congress in March 1947, the president proposed a policy that became known as the **Truman Doctrine,** a commitment to help nations threatened by communism and Soviet expansion.

> "I believe that it must be the policy of the United States to support free peoples who are resisting attempted subjugation [conquest] by armed minorities or by outside pressures."

Congress voted to give military and economic assistance to Greece and Turkey to hold back the Soviets.

The Marshall Plan

At the end of World War II, much of Europe lay in ruins. Bombing had destroyed countless houses, factories, bridges, and roads. Many people lacked homes, jobs, and often enough food to eat. Their war-ravaged societies provided fertile ground for communism with its promises of housing and employment for all.

George Marshall, the United States secretary of state, saw Western Europe as strategically important to the United States. He believed that the best way to keep the countries of Western Europe free of communism would be to help restore their economies. In June 1947, Marshall proposed a plan to provide massive economic aid to Europe. At first his plan met some resistance in Congress. After Soviet-supported Communists took over the government of **Czechoslovakia** in February 1948, however, this resistance disappeared.

Congress approved the program of economic aid for Europe, the **Marshall Plan,** which became a vital part of the policy of containment. Between 1948 and 1951, the Marshall Plan contributed nearly $13 billion to the rebuilding of the countries of Western Europe. As Marshall had predicted, no Western government in the region fell to a Communist revolution.

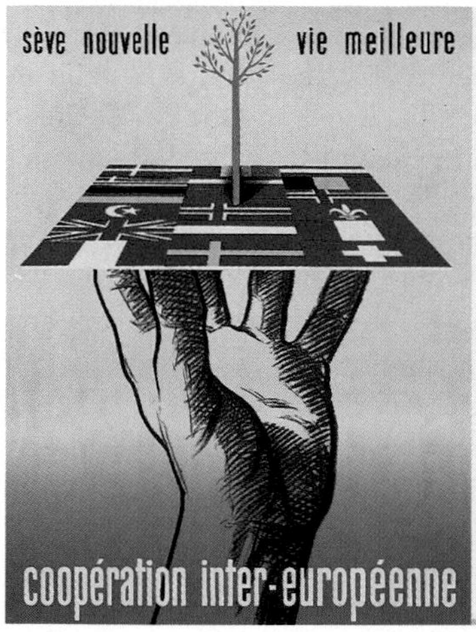

Picturing HISTORY A poster urges European cooperation with the Marshall Plan. **How did the Marshall Plan affect Western Europe?**

Crisis in Berlin

The Allied leaders at Yalta had divided Germany into four occupation zones. The Soviet Union controlled the eastern part of the country, while the United States, Britain, and France divided the western part. The German capital of **Berlin,** located deep within Soviet-controlled East Germany, was also divided among the four nations.

President Truman believed that a reunited Germany was essential to the future of Europe. Stalin, on the other hand, feared that a reunited Germany would once again pose a threat to the Soviet Union. He sought to maintain Soviet influence in a divided Germany. Tensions over the German issue led to a serious crisis in 1948.

The Berlin Blockade

On June 7, 1948, the United States, Britain, and France announced that they were uniting their zones to form a new West German republic. Each nation's section of Berlin would be included in this republic as well, even though the city lay within Soviet-held East Germany.

The **Berlin blockade** was Stalin's answer to the West's plans for West Germany. On June 24, 1948, Soviet troops rushed into position around the

MAKING CONNECTIONS ACTIVITY

Global Issues Remind students that the Soviet Union no longer exists, but communism does. Have interested students research communism and whether it is still a threat. Use the following questions to help refine their research:

- **How strong is the Communist movement within the former Soviet Union? How likely is it for Russia or its former republics to regain a Communist government?**
- **What Communist influences does China exert in Asia or elsewhere?**
- **What Communist influences does Cuba exert in Latin America or elsewhere?**
- **Locate some countries where civil strife is intense right now. In which places are Communist movements active? L3**

Picturing HISTORY During the 1948 blockade, Berlin children, standing in the rubble of their shattered city, watch an American bomber fly in with supplies. **What effect did the airlift have on the Soviet blockade?**

edge of West Berlin. Almost overnight they created a blockade, stopping traffic on all highway, railroad, and water routes through East Germany to West Berlin. As a result, West Berlin and its 2 million citizens were cut off from vital supplies. The Soviets hoped this blockade would drive the West out of Berlin.

The Berlin Airlift

President Truman refused to give in to the Soviets. "We stay in Berlin, period," he declared, but he did not want to risk war by using military force to end the blockade. Instead he organized a massive airlift to save the city.

American and British cargo planes began flying food, fuel, and other supplies into West Berlin. The **Berlin airlift** continued day and night for more than 10 months, delivering about 2.5 million tons of supplies to West Berlin. A West Berlin taxi driver told a visiting journalist about how the airlift boosted Berliners' morale:

> "We lost all our faith at first. . . . We thought the West would pull out. Now we have it back. There. You hear? There is another plane. And there's another. Our faith doesn't come from our hearts or our brains any more. It comes through the ears."

Realizing that the Western powers intended to stay in the city, Stalin ended the Berlin blockade in May 1949.

Despite the success of the airlift, Berlin and Germany remained divided. In October 1949, the division of Germany into two nations—the **Federal Republic of Germany,** or West Germany, and the **German Democratic Republic,** or East Germany—became official.

Two Armed Camps

The crisis in Berlin confirmed that the United States and the Soviet Union were locked in a cold war—a war in which the two enemies

Linking PAST & PRESENT

German Reunification

On October 3, 1990, the two parts of Germany finally reunited, and Berlin—rejoined as one city—again became the nation's official capital. The German government's move to Berlin from the West German capital of Bonn is scheduled to be completed in the year 2003.

Picturing HISTORY The airlift plan called for cargo planes to be in and out of Berlin every three minutes. At times, a plane was landing every minute. The cost of the airlift is estimated to have surpassed $200 million. **Ask:** How long did the Berlin airlift last? *(It lasted for more than 10 months.)*
Answer: *The airlift made the Soviet blockade ineffective and ultimately brought the blockade to an end.*

ABCNEWS INTERACTIVE™

VIDEODISC
Communism and the Cold War

Side 1
Chapter 15

Title: *Berlin Wall*
Subject: Newsreel reports of the building of the Berlin Wall
Ask: **How did East Berlin's people try to escape during the blockade?** *(They jumped from windows and broke through barbed wire fences.)*

Side 1
Chapter 4

Title: *Spheres of Influence: NATO and the Warsaw Pact*
Subject: Creation of alliances
Ask: **What organization did the Soviet Union create in response to NATO?** *(the Warsaw Pact)*

CRITICAL THINKING ACTIVITY

Determining Relevance The policy of containment was open to much interpretation. For example, what determined a "strategic" area for United States and Soviet interests? What "nonmilitary means" of challenge would be used? What limits would be placed upon "limited military means"? To realize the challenges that this policy posed, ask students to suggest hypothetical situations and places in which United States officials might be concerned about Soviet "expansion" (military, economic, philosophical). In each case, discuss the strategic quality of the area, reasons that the United States might be concerned, and possible military and nonmilitary responses. In which cases do students find containment a relevant policy? **L3**

you don't say...

Cold war Walter Lippmann, writer of the syndicated column "Today and Tomorrow," published some of his columns in a book entitled *The Cold War.* That title brought the term *cold war* into the American vocabulary.

Picturing HISTORY When Arab nations attacked the new nation of Israel, the UN sent Count Folke Bernadotte of Sweden to mediate. When he was assassinated, the UN sent in Ralph Bunche, an African American diplomat. Through Bunche, a temporary peace was negotiated. In 1950 Bunche was awarded the Nobel Peace Prize for his work. **Ask:** **Which European nation previously had governed Palestine?** *(Great Britain)*
Answer: *hostility from its Arab neighbors, who did not accept the UN's partition plan*

3 ASSESS

Assign Section 1 Review as homework or as an in-class activity.

Use **Chapter Challenger Interactive Review Software** to review Section 1.

Section Quiz 27–1

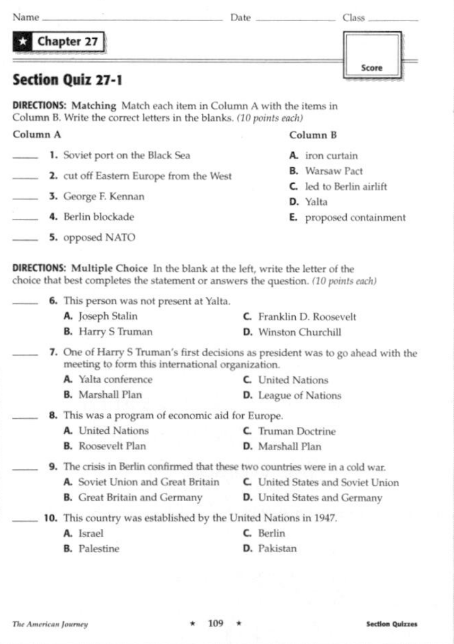
Name ______ Date ______ Class ______

★ Chapter 27

Score

Section Quiz 27-1

DIRECTIONS: Matching Match each item in Column A with the items in Column B. Write the correct letters in the blanks. *(10 points each)*

Column A

____ **1.** Soviet port on the Black Sea
____ **2.** cut off Eastern Europe from the West
____ **3.** George F. Kennan
____ **4.** Berlin blockade
____ **5.** opposed NATO

Column B

A. iron curtain
B. Warsaw Pact
C. led to Berlin airlift
D. Yalta
E. proposed containment

DIRECTIONS: Multiple Choice In the blank at the left, write the letter of the choice that best completes the statement or answers the question. *(10 points each)*

____ **6.** This person was not present at Yalta.
A. Joseph Stalin **C.** Franklin D. Roosevelt
B. Harry S Truman **D.** Winston Churchill

____ **7.** One of Harry S Truman's first decisions as president was to go ahead with the meeting to form this international organization.
A. Yalta conference **C.** United Nations
B. Marshall Plan **D.** League of Nations

____ **8.** This was a program of economic aid for Europe.
A. United Nations **C.** Truman Doctrine
B. Roosevelt Plan **D.** Marshall Plan

____ **9.** The crisis in Berlin confirmed that these two countries were in a cold war.
A. Soviet Union and Great Britain **C.** United States and Soviet Union
B. Great Britain and Germany **D.** United States and Germany

____ **10.** This country was established by the United Nations in 1947.
A. Israel **C.** Berlin
B. Palestine **D.** Pakistan

The American Journey ★ 109 ★ **Section Quizzes**

Picturing HISTORY
After World War II, many Jewish refugees from the Holocaust settled in Palestine. In 1948 part of Palestine became the Jewish state of Israel. **What major challenge did Israel face?**

Declaration of the State of Israel

did not actually fight each other. Instead each nation began building up its military forces and arms in an attempt to intimidate the other. European nations began to take sides in this mounting cold war.

NATO

The United States and the countries of Western Europe agreed that the best way to contain the Soviets was through mutual defense. In April 1949, the United States, Canada, and 10 Western European nations signed a pact establishing the **North Atlantic Treaty Organization** (NATO). The agreement stated that "an armed attack against one or more of [the member nations] shall be considered an attack against all." To defend against a possible Soviet invasion of Western Europe, the NATO countries created a large military force composed of troops from all the member nations.

The Warsaw Pact

In response to NATO, the Soviet Union created an alliance of its own with the Communist governments of Eastern Europe. The alliance, established in 1955 by mutual defense treaties known as the **Warsaw Pact,** had a military force that the Soviet Union controlled. The formation of NATO and the Warsaw Pact divided Europe into two armed camps.

The United States Rearms

After World War II, some of President Truman's foreign policy advisers in the **National Security Council** (NSC) argued that America could not rely on other nations to contain the Soviets and resist the spread of communism. Unlike George Kennan and the supporters of the containment policy, the NSC advisers believed the United States needed to take a more active stand against communism everywhere—not just in strategic locations.

In 1950 the NSC released a report, known as **NSC-68,** which said that the United States must actively "foster the seeds of destruction within the Soviet Union" and fight Communist movements wherever they arose. Within several years of this report, the United States had built the largest military force in history and was committed to combating Communist expansion everywhere in the world.

MORE ABOUT . . .

George F. Kennan wrote an article called "The Sources of Soviet Conduct." In this article he noted, "It is clear that the main element of any United States policy towards the Soviet Union must be that of a long-term, patient but firm and vigilant containment of Russian expansive tendencies. . . . Soviet pressure against the free institutions of the Western world is something that can be contained by the adroit and vigilant application of counter-force at a series of constantly shifting geographical and political points."

Postwar Developments

As the cold war grew more bitter in Europe, nations in other parts of the world were undergoing dramatic changes. Many states broke free of colonial rule and established independence. Others suffered strife.

Independence Movements

The Philippines gained independence from the United States in 1946. For years afterward Filipinos struggled with terrible poverty, government corruption, and civil war. In the late 1940s, Asian countries such as India, Pakistan, and Burma broke away from the British Empire to form new nations. During the 1950s and the early 1960s, more than 25 African nations gained independence from European colonial powers. As these new nations struggled with political and economic problems, the United States and the Soviet Union competed for influence in Africa and Asia.

In the Middle East, Jews and Arabs both claimed the region of **Palestine,** an area the British had controlled. In 1947 the United Nations proposed dividing Palestine into independent Jewish and Arab states with Jerusalem as an international city. The Jews accepted the plan, but the Arab states did not. After Israel declared its independence Arab armies attacked the new Jewish state of **Israel** in the first of six major wars in the region between the Arabs and Israel.

Mao Zedong

Communism in China

Perhaps the most threatening change of the postwar period occurred in **China,** the largest country in Asia. In 1949 a long civil war ended with the victory of Chinese Communist forces led by **Mao Zedong** (MAU ZUH•DUNG) over the armies commanded by **Chiang Kai-shek** (JEE•AHNG KY•SHEHK), the head of the Chinese government. Mao Zedong formed a new Communist state, the People's Republic of China, while Chiang Kai-shek retreated with his forces to the island of **Taiwan** off the southeastern coast of China. The United States recognized the government in Taiwan as the legitimate government of all China.

With Communists in control of mainland China, the Soviet Union had a powerful ally in Asia. It appeared to many people that the entire continent of Asia was in danger of turning to communism.

Section 1 Review

Checking for Understanding

1. ***Identify*** Winston Churchill, Joseph Stalin, Harry S Truman, Mao Zedong, Chiang Kai-shek.
2. ***Define*** iron curtain, containment, airlift, cold war.
3. ***Explain*** how the Marshall Plan helped to contain the spread of communism in Western Europe.

Reviewing Themes

4. **Global Connections** Summarize Truman's postwar foreign policy.

Critical Thinking

5. **Synthesizing Information** Explain why the United States's actions against the Soviet Union in the Berlin blockade were considered part of a "cold war."

Activity

Comparing Maps Compare a map of Africa after World War II to a map of Africa today. Photocopy or draw a modern map and indicate five countries that have changed their names or boundaries during this 50-year period.

Reteaching Activity 27–1

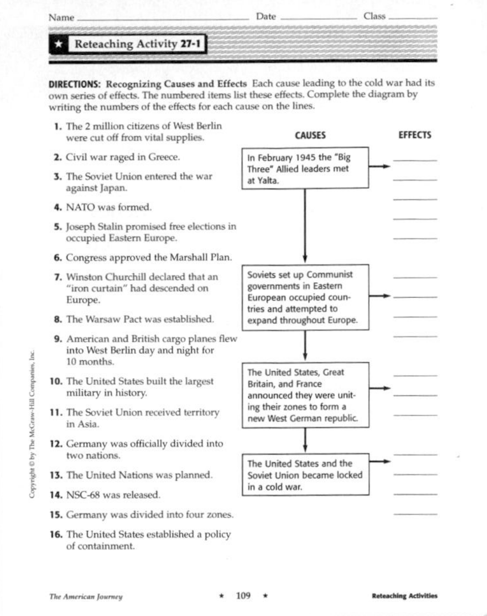

Name ____________ Date ________ Class ________

★ Reteaching Activity 27-1

DIRECTIONS: Recognizing Causes and Effects Each cause leading to the cold war had its own series of effects. The numbered items list these effects. Complete the diagram by writing the numbers of the effects for each cause on the lines.

1. The 2 million citizens of West Berlin were cut off from vital supplies.
2. Civil war raged in Greece.
3. The Soviet Union entered the war against Japan.
4. NATO was formed.
5. Joseph Stalin promised free elections in occupied Eastern Europe.
6. Congress approved the Marshall Plan.
7. Winston Churchill declared that an "iron curtain" had descended on Europe.
8. The Warsaw Pact was established.
9. American and British cargo planes flew into West Berlin day and night for 10 months.
10. The United States built the largest military in history.
11. The Soviet Union received territory in Asia.
12. Germany was officially divided into two nations.
13. The United Nations was planned.
14. NSC-68 was released.
15. Germany was divided into four zones.
16. The United States established a policy of containment.

CAUSES / EFFECTS

In February 1945 the "Big Three" Allied leaders met at Yalta.

Soviets set up Communist governments in Eastern European occupied countries and attempted to expand throughout Europe.

The United States, Great Britain, and France announced they were uniting their zones to form a new West German republic.

The United States and the Soviet Union became locked in a cold war.

Copyright © by The McGraw-Hill Companies, Inc.

The American Journey ★ 109 ★ **Reteaching Activities**

Enrichment Activity 27–1

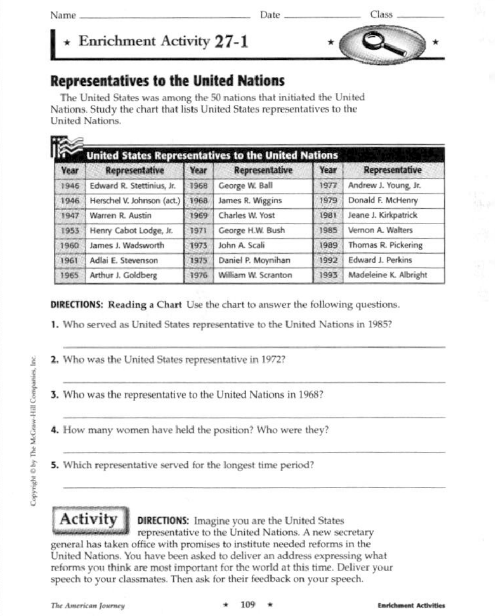

Name ____________ Date ________ Class ________

★ Enrichment Activity 27-1 ★ ★

Representatives to the United Nations

The United States was among the 50 nations that initiated the United Nations. Study the chart that lists United States representatives to the United Nations.

United States Representatives to the United Nations

Year	Representative	Year	Representative	Year	Representative
1946	Edward R. Stettinius, Jr.	1968	George W. Ball	1977	Andrew J. Young, Jr.
1946	Herschel V. Johnson (act.)	1968	James R. Wiggins	1979	Donald F. McHenry
1947	Warren R. Austin	1969	Charles W. Yost	1981	Jeane J. Kirkpatrick
1953	Henry Cabot Lodge, Jr.	1971	George H.W. Bush	1985	Vernon A. Walters
1960	James J. Wadsworth	1973	John A. Scali	1989	Thomas R. Pickering
1961	Adlai E. Stevenson	1975	Daniel P. Moynihan	1992	Edward J. Perkins
1965	Arthur J. Goldberg	1976	William W. Scranton	1993	Madeleine K. Albright

DIRECTIONS: Reading a Chart Use the chart to answer the following questions.

1. Who served as United States representative to the United Nations in 1985?
2. Who was the United States representative in 1972?
3. Who was the representative to the United Nations in 1968?
4. How many women have held the position? Who were they?
5. Which representative served for the longest time period?

Activity **DIRECTIONS:** Imagine you are the United States representative to the United Nations. A new secretary general has taken office with promises to institute needed reforms in the United Nations. You have been asked to deliver an address expressing what reforms you think are most important for the world at this time. Deliver your speech to your classmates. Then ask for their feedback on your speech.

Copyright © by The McGraw-Hill Companies, Inc.

The American Journey ★ 109 ★ **Enrichment Activities**

Section 1 Review Answers

1. Winston Churchill, 773; Joseph Stalin, 773; Harry S Truman, 774; Mao Zedong, 779; Chiang Kai-shek, 779
2. The words are defined in the Glossary.
3. It provided economic aid to Western European countries to keep them from being tempted by the Communists' offer of housing and employment for all.
4. Truman's policy focused on the containment of communism throughout the world.
5. Ending the blockade did not require military action; rather, the United States employed a massive airlift of supplies to render the blockade ineffectual. The two sides tried to intimidate each other.

Activity Maps should highlight countries in Africa whose names or boundaries have changed since World War II.

4 CLOSE

Ask students to comment on what was common to the Truman Doctrine, Marshall Plan, NATO, and the Berlin Airlift. *(They were all part of the policy of containment.)*

CHAPTER 27
Section 2, 780–784

1 FOCUS

BELLRINGER
Motivational Activity

Before taking roll at the beginning of the class period, project Section Focus Transparency 27–2 and have students answer the questions. Discuss students' responses.

This activity is also available as a blackline master.

Section Focus Transparency 27–2

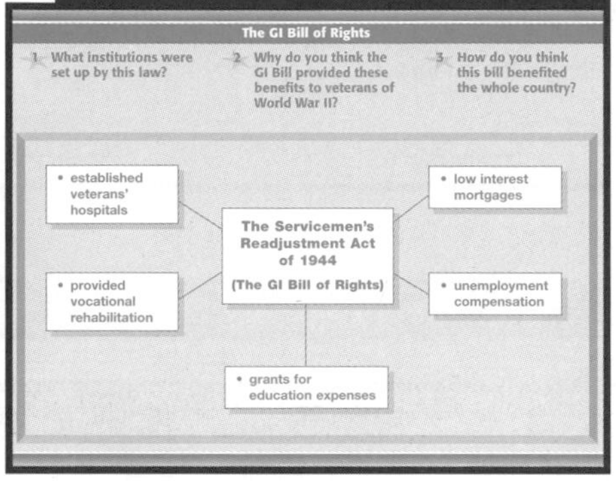

Vocabulary Precheck
Ask students to get a mental picture of balloons or items that can be inflated. Then discuss *inflation* in its economic context, relating the "blowing up" of prices to students' images.

Use the **Vocabulary PuzzleMaker** to create crossword and word search puzzles.

Section Theme
Economic Factors

Moving from a wartime economy to a peacetime economy required President Truman to solve a number of problems.

Activity Read aloud President Truman's views about a free society: "I think small business, the small farmer, the small corporation are the backbone of any free society, and when there are too many people at the top who control the wealth of the country, then we must look out." Ask students to paraphrase this statement.

1944 — 1946 — 1948

1944 Congress approves the GI Bill of Rights

1946 Miners and railroad workers strike

1947 Taft-Hartley Act limits unions

1948 Truman wins the presidency

Section 2

Postwar Politics

READ TO DISCOVER . . .
- what economic problems Americans faced in the immediate postwar years.
- how President Truman and the Republican-controlled Congress proposed to deal with the nation's problems.

TERMS TO LEARN
inflation
closed shop

The Storyteller

When soldiers returned home after World War II, they came back to a nation facing the difficult task of changing from wartime to peacetime. Would the economy collapse again and another depression sweep the country? President Truman was optimistic: "We are having our little troubles now. Just a blowup after a little let-down from war." Public concern, however, forced the nation's political leaders into a heated debate over the best way to deal with America's economic problems.

Truman campaign button

After World War II, the nation and its economy had to adjust to peacetime life. Industries had to shift from producing war materials to making **consumer goods.** Defense workers had to be retrained to work in consumer industries, and returning soldiers needed jobs.

Economics

The Postwar Economy

In 1944 Congress passed the Servicemen's Readjustment Act, better known as the **GI Bill of Rights.** This law provided billions of dollars in loans to help returning GIs—soldiers, sailors, and marines—attend college, receive special training, set up businesses, or buy homes. It also provided unemployment and health benefits for the GIs as they looked for jobs.

This flood of money to GIs helped reduce unemployment in the postwar years and boosted the economy. At the same time, though, it contributed to one of the major problems of the period—rapidly increasing prices.

Threat of Inflation

During the war, government price controls had kept the cost of consumer goods such as food and clothing quite stable. When the government removed these controls, prices began to surge. This rise in prices, or **inflation,** also resulted from a huge increase in consumer demand and

SECTION RESOURCES

Reproducible Masters
- Guided Reading Activity 27–2
- Political Cartoons
- Section Quiz 27–2
- Reteaching Activity 27–2
- Enrichment Activity 27–2

Transparencies
- Section Focus Transparency 27–2

Multimedia
- Vocabulary PuzzleMaker
- Chapter Challenger Interactive Review Software
- Testmaker
- Facts On File: Landmark Documents in American History
- The Presidents: A Picture History of Our Nation

spending. During the war years, Americans had saved their money because many consumer goods were unavailable or rationed. Now they were eager to spend this money on new consumer products and services.

Workers Seek Higher Wages

As a result of inflation, consumer prices rose at a much faster rate than wages. During the war, workers had accepted government controls on wages and agreed not to strike. Now they would no longer be put off. When employers refused to raise wages, labor unions called strikes. In 1945 and 1946, millions of steelworkers, railroad workers, and others walked off their jobs, demanding higher wages and better conditions.

Labor unrest and strikes disrupted the nation's economy. When miners went on strike in 1946, many Americans feared that dwindling coal supplies would cause the economy to grind to a halt. At about the same time, a strike by railroad workers caused a total shutdown of the nation's railroads, which were vital to the economy.

Truman Takes Action

Alarmed by the labor unrest, President Truman pressured the striking miners and railroad workers to go back to their jobs. In May 1946, he threatened to draft them into the army if they did not return to work. The president insisted he had the right to take such steps to keep vital industries operating.

President Truman finally forced striking miners back on the job by having the government take over the mines. At the same time, however, he persuaded the mine owners to grant many of the workers' demands. Truman also pressured railroad workers to return to work.

Picturing HISTORY Enthusiastic military veterans at Indiana University clutch admission papers. **What benefits did the GI Bill of Rights provide to veterans?**

Truman Faces the Republicans

In September 1945, President Truman, a Democrat, presented Congress with a plan of domestic reforms aimed at solving some of the nation's economic problems. Truman later called this program the **Fair Deal.**

Truman proposed to raise the minimum wage, expand Social Security benefits, increase federal spending to create jobs, build new public housing, and create a system of national health insurance. But because of opposition by a coalition of Republicans and Southern Democrats, these measures failed to pass in Congress.

Footnotes to History

A Young Scholar By the time Harry Truman was 8 years old, he had to wear glasses. Afraid that he might break them, he spent his time reading instead of playing sports. Truman did not go to college, but by the time he was 14 he had read every book in the Independence, Missouri, library.

2 TEACH

L2 Solving Problems Have groups of students create a problem/solution chart. In the left column, they should list economic and social problems that Truman addressed. In the right column, they should note what he did to solve each problem.

Picturing HISTORY Signing the GI Bill of Rights, President Roosevelt declared, "It gives emphatic notice to the men and women in the armed forces that the American people do not intend to let them down." **Ask:** **What was the official name of the GI Bill of Rights?** *(It was passed as the Servicemen's Readjustment Act.)* **Answer:** *It provided loans to help GIs attend college, get special training, set up businesses, and buy homes.*

Guided Reading Activity 27–2

Name ______ Date ______ Class ______

Guided Reading Activity 27-2

DIRECTIONS: Using Headings and Subheadings Locate each heading in your textbook. Then use the information to help you write each answer.

I. The Postwar Economy
- **A. Economics** What is another name for the Servicemen's Readjustment Act? ______
- **B. Economics** How did this law help returning GIs? ______
- **C. Economics** In what way did this law threaten the economy? ______
- **D. Economics** What caused prices to surge after the war? ______
- **E. Economics** What happened when employers refused to raise wages? ______
- **F. Economics** How did President Harry Truman force striking miners back to work and help them at the same time? ______

II. Truman Faces the Republicans
- **A.** What slogan helped the Republicans win control of Congress in 1946? ______
- **B.** What bill did Congress introduce in 1947 to limit the power of labor unions? ______
- **C.** Why was Truman the underdog in the election of 1948? ______
- **D.** How did Truman campaign against Thomas Dewey, who was leading in the polls? ______
- **E.** What newspaper wrongly declared Dewey as the winner of the 1948 election? ______

III. A Fair Deal for Americans
- **A.** What laws from Truman's Fair Deal did Congress pass after the election? ______
- **B. Citizenship** What steps did Harry Truman take to advance the civil rights of African Americans? ______

Cooperative Learning Activity

Holding a Workers' Debate Organize the class into two teams. Ask both teams to imagine themselves as workers considering Harry S Truman as a presidential candidate in 1948. Have teams prepare and present a debate—one team praising Truman's labor reforms and promises to improve the lives of working Americans; the other criticizing his "interference" with organized labor and blaming him for the nation's economic problems. Some team members can do research, others can prepare key statements, others will defend the team's position in the debate. Afterward, hold a class election. Do students agree or disagree with Truman's treatment of workers?

CHAPTER 27
Section 2, 780–784

Facts On File

CD-ROM
Landmark Documents in American History

Title: *Taft-Hartley Act, (Labor-Management Relations Act), 1947* Have students read the act twice. The first time they should read it from the perspective of a Republican business owner; the second time as an underpaid and overworked employee. Have students note how their attitude toward the act changes.

What?Where?When?Who?

Taft-Hartley Act Despite the Taft-Hartley Act, union membership rose from 14.3 million people in 1945 to more than 18 million people by 1955.

Map Study

Answers
1. the South
2. 114 electoral votes over Dewey

Map Skills Practice

Reading a Map Why are Alaska and Hawaii not represented on this map? *(They had not yet been granted statehood.)*

NATIONAL GEOGRAPHIC SOCIETY

CD-ROM
The Presidents: A Picture History of Our Nation

Have students view "Harry S Truman" and use the information to write a brief biography to include in their portfolios.

Republicans Control Congress

Many Americans blamed Truman and the Democratic Party for the nation's economic problems. In the congressional elections of 1946, the slogan "Had Enough?" helped Republicans win control of both houses of Congress.

The new Republican Congress moved quickly to create its own plans for the nation. Having rejected Truman's program for reform, the Republicans now set up proposals to enact a program that would limit government spending, control labor unions, reduce government regulation of the economy, and reverse policies adopted in the 1930s under FDR's New Deal.

For many Republicans in Congress, the most important problem facing the nation was labor unrest and the growing power of labor unions. Conservative Republicans favored big business and wanted to limit the power of unions. In the spring of 1947, Congress introduced the **Taft-Hartley bill.** This bill limited the actions workers could take against their employers. It outlawed the **closed shop,** a workplace that hires only union members. It also allowed the government to temporarily stop any strike that endangered public health or safety. This provision aimed to prevent any future strikes like those of the miners and the railroad workers the year before. Union members and their leaders sharply criticized the Taft-Hartley Act, calling it a "slave labor bill." Although President Truman opposed recent strikes, he also knew that the Democrats needed the support of labor. Truman vetoed the act, but the Republican-controlled Congress overrode his veto.

The Election of 1948

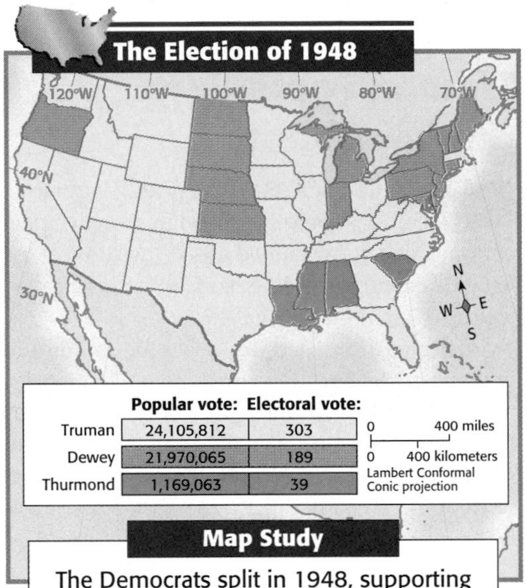

Map Study

The Democrats split in 1948, supporting both Truman and Thurmond.

1. **Region** From which region did Thurmond receive support?
2. **Analyzing Information** By how many electoral votes did Truman win over Dewey?

The Election of 1948

As the 1948 presidential election approached, Truman appeared to be the underdog. Continuing economic problems made the president unpopular with many Americans, and his lack of success in winning passage of domestic reforms made his administration look weak and ineffective.

Divisions within the Democratic Party also increased the chances of an easy Republican victory. At the party's national convention, a group of Southern Democrats walked out to protest Truman's support for civil rights legislation. The Southern Democrats formed the States' Rights Democratic Party, or Dixiecrats, and nominated Governor **Strom Thurmond** of South Carolina for president. At the same time, some liberal members of the Democratic Party left to form the Progressive Party, with **Henry Wallace** as their nominee for president. Wallace opposed Truman's foreign policy and called for closer ties between the United States and the Soviet Union.

Dewey Leads Polls

With the Democrats badly divided, it looked as though Governor **Thomas Dewey** of New York, the Republican nominee, would surely win the election. Opinion polls showed Dewey with a huge lead. One pollster remarked: "Mr. Dewey is still so clearly ahead that we might just as well get ready to listen to his inaugural."

Multiple Learning Styles

Kinesthetic Meeting and talking with people—punctuated by shaking hands—is an important part of election campaigns. Ask each student to choose to represent Harry S Truman, Thomas Dewey, Strom Thurmond, or Henry Wallace. Then have students interact by shaking hands with each other and making some kind of campaign statement—for example, a reminder of past government service or a promise of what the candidate will do as president. Follow up with these questions:

- **As a candidate, what could you say about yourself in such a brief meeting?**
- **As a voter, which statements meant the most to you, and why?** **ELL, L3**

Picturing HISTORY President Truman displays a newspaper headline that wrongly declared Thomas E. Dewey as the winner of the 1948 presidential race. **Why was Truman expected to lose the election?**

Truman campaigned aggressively. Traveling more than 30,000 miles by train on a "whistle-stop" tour of the country, he gave some 350 speeches along the way. In town after town, he sharply attacked what he called "that do-nothing, good-for-nothing, worst Congress" for rejecting his Fair Deal legislation.

Truman Stages an Upset

On Election Day experts still expected Dewey to win. Expectations for a Republican victory were so great that on the evening of the election—before many votes were counted—the *Chicago Daily Tribune* newspaper issued a special edition announcing "Dewey Defeats Truman."

The nation was in for a great surprise. When all the ballots were counted, Truman had edged out Dewey by more than 2 million votes in a narrow upset victory. Democrats also regained control of both the House of Representatives and the Senate in the election.

A Fair Deal for Americans

Truman took the election results as a sign that Americans wanted reform. He quickly reintroduced the **Fair Deal** legislation he had presented to Congress in 1945. Some of these reform measures passed, but his plan lacked broad support among the American people, and Congress responded by defeating most of the measures. Congress did pass laws to raise the minimum wage, expand Social Security benefits for senior citizens, and provide funds for housing for low-income families.

Citizenship

A Stand on Civil Rights

In a message to Congress in 1948, President Truman declared:

> "We shall not, however, finally achieve the ideals for which this nation was founded so long as any American suffers discrimination as a result of his race, or religion, or color, or the land of origin of his forefathers."

Although Truman championed ending such discrimination, he was unable to persuade Congress to pass legislation that would protect the voting rights of African Americans, abolish the poll tax, and make lynching a federal crime. Still, President Truman did take serious steps to

Making Connections Activity

Daily Life President Truman wanted to see a rise in the minimum wage, and his hope finally was realized. In 1949 the minimum wage went from 40 cents to 70 cents per hour; in 1955 the hourly rate reached $1. Brainstorm with students to list positive results of a raised minimum wage (for example, the ability to buy new products and enjoy an overall higher standard of living). Then discuss some possible drawbacks (such as employee cutbacks or a rise in the cost of products to offset the higher payouts in wages). Ask students how understanding the possible negative as well as positive results of increased wages affects their view of their own employment. **L2**

Picturing HISTORY This famous photograph was taken in St. Louis, as Truman made his way back from Missouri to Washington, D.C. A sign in front of the *Washington Post* greeted Truman with this apology: "Mr. President, we are ready to eat crow whenever you are ready to serve it." **Ask: What political office did Thomas Dewey, Truman's chief opponent, hold?** *(He was governor of New York.)* **Answer:** *It was thought that the Democrats were too badly divided to overcome the Republicans.*

Political Cartoons, *President Truman and the Fair Deal*

3 ASSESS

Assign Section 2 Review as homework or as an in-class activity.

Use **Chapter Challenger Interactive Review Software** to review Section 2.

Section Quiz 27–2

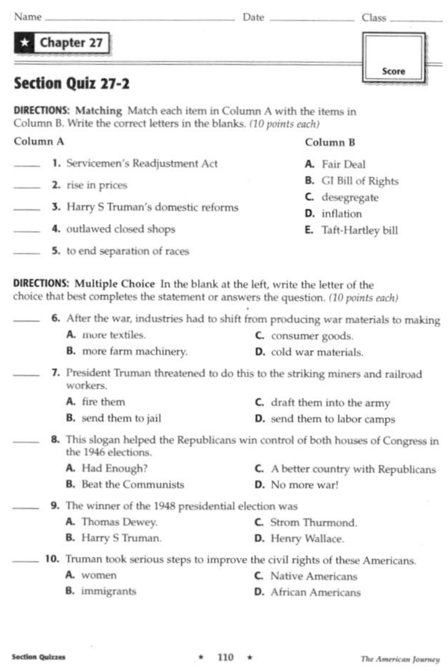
Name ____ Date ____ Class ____

Chapter 27 Score

Section Quiz 27-2

DIRECTIONS: Matching Match each item in Column A with the items in Column B. Write the correct letters in the blanks. *(10 points each)*

Column A	Column B
____ 1. Servicemen's Readjustment Act	A. Fair Deal
____ 2. rise in prices	B. GI Bill of Rights
____ 3. Harry S Truman's domestic reforms	C. desegregate
____ 4. outlawed closed shops	D. inflation
____ 5. to end separation of races	E. Taft-Hartley bill

DIRECTIONS: Multiple Choice In the blank at the left, write the letter of the choice that best completes the statement or answers the question. *(10 points each)*

____ 6. After the war, industries had to shift from producing war materials to making
A. more textiles. C. consumer goods.
B. more farm machinery. D. cold war materials.

____ 7. President Truman threatened to do this to the striking miners and railroad workers.
A. fire them C. draft them into the army
B. send them to jail D. send them to labor camps

____ 8. This slogan helped the Republicans win control of both houses of Congress in the 1946 elections.
A. Had Enough? C. A better country with Republicans
B. Beat the Communists D. No more war!

____ 9. The winner of the 1948 presidential election was
A. Thomas Dewey. C. Strom Thurmond.
B. Harry S Truman. D. Henry Wallace.

____ 10. Truman took serious steps to improve the civil rights of these Americans.
A. women C. Native Americans
B. immigrants D. African Americans

Section Quizzes ★ 110 ★ *The American Journey*

CHAPTER 27
Section 2, 780–784

Picturing HISTORY Truman gained support from African Americans through his association with the NAACP. **Answer:** *He ordered an end to segregation in the armed forces; made reforms in many parts of the federal government.*

Reteaching Activity 27–2

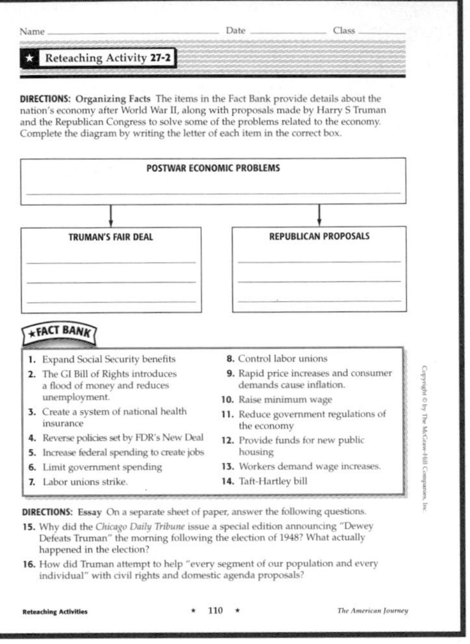
Name ____________ Date ________ Class ______

★ Reteaching Activity **27-2**

DIRECTIONS: Organizing Facts The items in the Fact Bank provide details about the nation's economy after World War II, along with proposals made by Harry S Truman and the Republican Congress to solve some of the problems related to the economy. Complete the diagram by writing the letter of each item in the correct box.

POSTWAR ECONOMIC PROBLEMS

TRUMAN'S FAIR DEAL

REPUBLICAN PROPOSALS

★FACT BANK

1. Expand Social Security benefits
2. The GI Bill of Rights introduces a flood of money and reduces unemployment.
3. Create a system of national health insurance
4. Reverse policies set by FDR's New Deal
5. Increase federal spending to create jobs
6. Limit government spending
7. Labor unions strike.
8. Control labor unions
9. Rapid price increases and consumer demands cause inflation.
10. Raise minimum wage
11. Reduce government regulations of the economy
12. Provide funds for new public housing
13. Workers demand wage increases.
14. Taft-Hartley bill

DIRECTIONS: Essay On a separate sheet of paper, answer the following questions.

15. Why did the *Chicago Daily Tribune* issue a special edition announcing "Dewey Defeats Truman" the morning following the election of 1948? What actually happened in the election?
16. How did Truman attempt to help "every segment of our population and every individual" with civil rights and domestic agenda proposals?

Reteaching Activities ★ 110 ★ *The American Journey*

Enrichment Activity 27–2

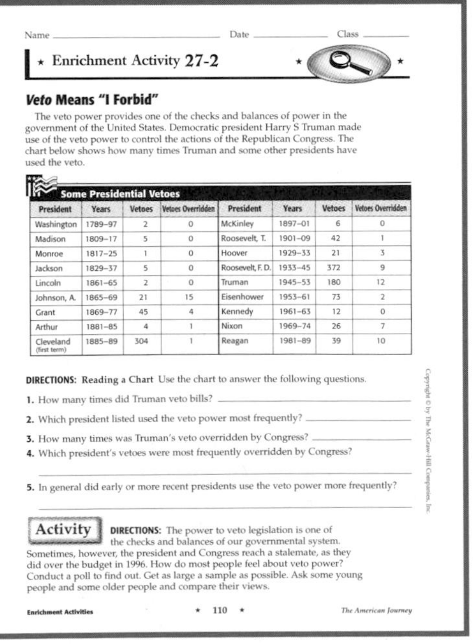
Name ____________ Date ________ Class ______

★ Enrichment Activity **27-2** ★ ★

Veto Means "I Forbid"

The veto power provides one of the checks and balances of power in the government of the United States. Democratic president Harry S Truman made use of the veto power to control the actions of the Republican Congress. The chart below shows how many times Truman and some other presidents have used the veto.

Some Presidential Vetoes

President	Years	Vetoes	Vetoes Overridden	President	Years	Vetoes	Vetoes Overridden
Washington	1789–97	2	0	McKinley	1897–01	6	0
Madison	1809–17	5	0	Roosevelt, T.	1901–09	42	1
Monroe	1817–25	1	0	Hoover	1929–33	21	3
Jackson	1829–37	5	0	Roosevelt, F. D.	1933–45	372	9
Lincoln	1861–65	2	0	Truman	1945–53	180	12
Johnson, A.	1865–69	21	15	Eisenhower	1953–61	73	2
Grant	1869–77	45	4	Kennedy	1961–63	12	0
Arthur	1881–85	4	1	Nixon	1969–74	26	7
Cleveland (first term)	1885–89	304	1	Reagan	1981–89	39	10

DIRECTIONS: Reading a Chart Use the chart to answer the following questions.

1. How many times did Truman veto bills? ____________
2. Which president listed used the veto power most frequently? ____________
3. How many times was Truman's veto overridden by Congress? ____________
4. Which president's vetoes were most frequently overridden by Congress? ____________
5. In general did early or more recent presidents use the veto power more frequently? ____________

Activity **DIRECTIONS:** The power to veto legislation is one of the checks and balances of our governmental system. Sometimes, however, the president and Congress reach a stalemate, as they did over the budget in 1996. How do most people feel about veto power? Conduct a poll to find out. Get as large a sample as possible. Ask some young people and some older people and compare their views.

Enrichment Activities ★ 110 ★ *The American Journey*

4 CLOSE

Ask which of Truman's achievements students consider most influential, and why.

1948 civil rights button

Picturing HISTORY African Americans welcome Truman to Harlem during his 1948 presidential campaign. **How was Truman successful in advancing civil rights?**

advance the civil rights of African Americans. He ordered federal departments and agencies to end job discrimination against African Americans and ordered the armed forces to **desegregate**—to end the separation of races. The president also instructed the Justice Department to actively enforce existing civil rights laws.

When Truman proposed his domestic agenda to Congress in 1949, he proclaimed that "every segment of our population and every individual has a right to expect from our government a fair deal." Truman asked for the clearance of slums, government-backed medical insurance, higher minimum wages, and more federal money for public schools. Although much of the president's Fair Deal vision went unfulfilled, he made an important start toward improving the lives of millions of Americans.

Section 2 Review

Checking for Understanding

1. ***Identify*** GI Bill of Rights, Taft-Hartley bill, Strom Thurmond, Henry Wallace, Thomas Dewey.
2. ***Define*** inflation, closed shop.
3. ***Describe*** the adjustments made in the United States after World War II to convert from a wartime to a peacetime economy.

Reviewing Themes

4. **Economic Factors** What caused inflation after World War II?

Critical Thinking

5. **Determining Cause and Effect** How was the Republican Congress's view of big business reflected in the Taft-Hartley bill?

Activity

Tracking Inflation At your school or public library, ask to see copies of newspapers published 5–10 years ago. Compare the prices of items advertised at that time to the same items today. Calculate the percent of increase in price for each of the products to determine an inflation rate.

Section 2 Review Answers

1. GI Bill of Rights, 780; Taft-Hartley bill, 782; Strom Thurmond, 782; Henry Wallace, 782; Thomas Dewey, 782
2. The words are defined in the Glossary.
3. Production shifted from war materials to consumer goods; defense workers were retrained for consumer industries; jobs had to be made available to returning soldiers.
4. GIs had extra money; price controls were removed; there was an increase in consumer demand and spending.
5. Many Republicans favored big business and wanted to limit the power of unions, which they did by passing the Taft-Hartley bill.

Activity Students should calculate the inflation rate by comparing the prices of similar products at different points in time.

1950 — 1952 — 1954

June 1950 North Korea invades South Korea; Truman sends "police action" to help South Korea

April 1951 Truman fires General MacArthur

July 1953 Cease-fire agreement is signed

Section 3

The Korean War

READ TO DISCOVER . . .

- what events led to the Korean War.
- how America's war aims changed during the course of the Korean War.
- how the war ended.

TERMS TO LEARN

stalemate demilitarized zone

The Storyteller

The bitter wind stung the raw faces of 12 U.S. Marine officers. They had just fought for 5 bloody days to lead their troops out of a Chinese trap in the icy wastes of northeast Korea. Now they listened to the words of their commander: "We are going to come out of this as Marines, not as stragglers. We're going to bring out our wounded and our equipment. We're coming out . . . as Marines or not at all." Two more days of fighting followed, as the tired but determined Marines held off fierce enemy attacks. With the arrival of air cover on the third day, the Marines were able to push back the Chinese and make their escape.

Korean service medal

On June 24, 1950, President Truman flew to his home in Independence, Missouri, for a brief vacation. While sitting on his porch on a hot summer night, the president received a telephone call from Secretary of State Dean Acheson. "Mr. President," Acheson said in a grim tone, "I have very serious news. The North Koreans have invaded South Korea." Truman knew this meant only one thing: the United States soon would be involved in military action in Asia.

The Conflict Begins

Before June 1950, few Americans knew much about **Korea,** a small east Asian country located on the Korean Peninsula west of Japan. In 1945 the country was a colony of Japan. At the end of World War II, the United States and the Soviet Union both sent troops into Korea and agreed to occupy it temporarily. They divided the peninsula in half along the **38th parallel** of latitude, with the Soviets controlling North Korea and the Americans controlling South Korea.

The Soviet Union and the United States could not agree on how to unify Korea. When these two nations removed their forces in 1949, Korea remained divided. Tensions between the two Koreas were high.

The Invasion of South Korea

After the American troops pulled out of South Korea, North Korea decided to unify the country by force. On June 25, 1950, the armies of North

SECTION RESOURCES

Reproducible Masters
- Guided Reading Activity 27–3
- Political Cartoons
- Section Quiz 27–3
- Reteaching Activity 27–3
- Enrichment Activity 27–3

Transparencies
- Section Focus Transparency 27–3

Multimedia
- Vocabulary PuzzleMaker
- Chapter Challenger Interactive Review Software
- Testmaker
- ABCNews InterActive™ Lessons of War
- ABCNews InterActive™ Communism and the Cold War

1 FOCUS

BELLRINGER
Motivational Activity

Before taking roll at the beginning of the class period, project Section Focus Transparency 27–3 and have students answer the questions. Discuss students' responses.

This activity is also available as a blackline master.

Section Focus Transparency 27–3

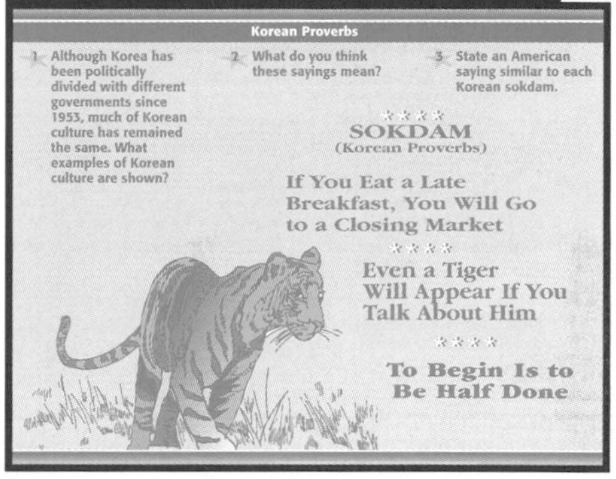

Vocabulary Precheck

Discuss the term *stalemate.* Ask students to suggest situations, both military and nonmilitary, for which *stalemate* would be an appropriate description.

Use the **Vocabulary PuzzleMaker** to create crossword and word search puzzles.

Section Theme
Government and Democracy

America's involvement in the Korean War told the Soviet Union and China that the United States was committed to fighting Communist expansion with money, weapons, and even lives.

Activity Have students look at Korea on the inset map on page 786. **Ask:** Why might two world powers feel that such a small country was worth a war? *(Students should suggest that a small country might be a stepping-stone to subsequent conquest.)*

CHAPTER 27
Section 3, 785–788

2 TEACH

L1 Identifying Key Events Have pairs of students list key events in the Korean War and a comment about the significance of each event. Encourage students to meet with other pairs, sharing and commenting upon their responses.

Political Cartoons, *Chinese Checkers in the Korean War*

Guided Reading Activity 27–3

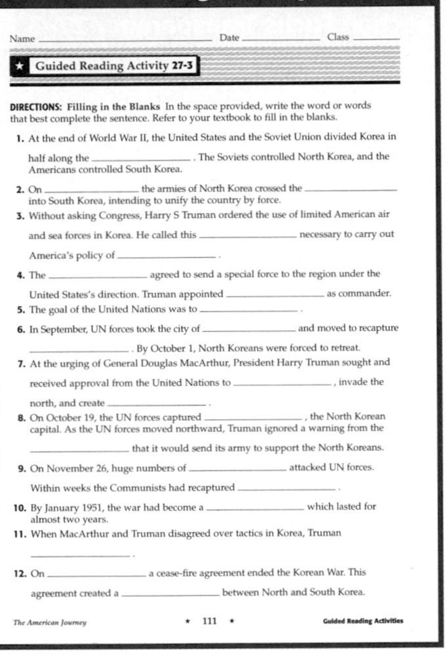
Name ________ Date ________ Class ________

★ Guided Reading Activity 27-3

DIRECTIONS: Filling in the Blanks In the space provided, write the word or words that best complete the sentence. Refer to your textbook to fill in the blanks.

1. At the end of World War II, the United States and the Soviet Union divided Korea in half along the ________. The Soviets controlled North Korea, and the Americans controlled South Korea.
2. On ________ the armies of North Korea crossed the ________ into South Korea, intending to unify the country by force.
3. Without asking Congress, Harry S Truman ordered the use of limited American air and sea forces in Korea. He called this ________ necessary to carry out America's policy of ________.
4. The ________ agreed to send a special force to the region under the United States's direction. Truman appointed ________ as commander.
5. The goal of the United Nations was to ________.
6. In September, UN forces took the city of ________ and moved to recapture ________. By October 1, North Koreans were forced to retreat.
7. At the urging of General Douglas MacArthur, President Harry Truman sought and received approval from the United Nations to ________, invade the north, and create ________.
8. On October 19, the UN forces captured ________, the North Korean capital. As the UN forces moved northward, Truman ignored a warning from the ________ that it would send its army to support the North Koreans.
9. On November 26, huge numbers of ________ attacked UN forces. Within weeks the Communists had recaptured ________.
10. By January 1951, the war had become a ________ which lasted for almost two years.
11. When MacArthur and Truman disagreed over tactics in Korea, Truman ________.
12. On ________ a cease-fire agreement ended the Korean War. This agreement created a ________ between North and South Korea.

The American Journey ★ 111 ★ Guided Reading Activities

Map Study

Answers
1. Panmunjom
2. UN forces

Map Skills Practice

Reading a Map What river separates North Korea from China? *(Yalu River)*

Who?What?Where?When?

Leaders in Agreement Truman and MacArthur would clash about how to fight the war, but they agreed about its importance. MacArthur said, "Our first line of defense for Western Europe is not the Elbe, it is not the Rhine—it is the Yalu."

Korea crossed the 38th parallel into South Korea. Poorly armed, the South Koreans were no match for the North. Within days the Communist forces had gained control over much of South Korea, including **Seoul,** the capital city.

President Truman reacted quickly to the Korean invasion, which he believed was supported by the Soviet Union. Without asking Congress to actually declare war, Truman ordered the use of limited American air and sea forces in Korea. He called this "police action" necessary to carry out America's policy of containment. Truman said:

> "Korea is the Greece of the Far East. If we are tough enough now, if we stand up to them like we did in Greece three years ago, they won't take any next steps."

The Korean War, 1950–53

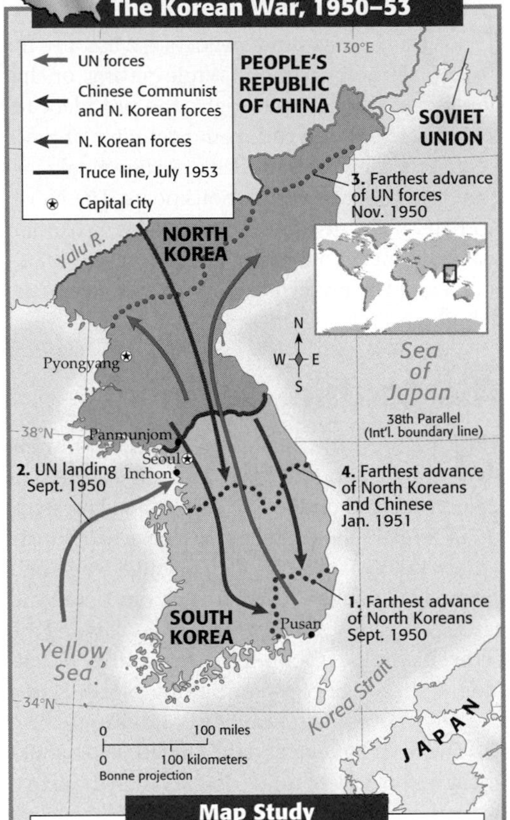

Map Study

The Korean War raged along the Korean Peninsula.

1. **Location** What city is located along the 38th parallel?
2. **Analyzing Information** Whose forces landed at Inchon in September 1950?

United Nations Responds

At the same time, President Truman asked the UN to send forces to defend the South Koreans. The United Nations condemned the invasion of South Korea and agreed to send a special force to the region under the United States's direction. President Truman quickly appointed General **Douglas MacArthur,** a hero of World War II, to command the UN forces.

On June 30, just days after the North Korean invasion, General MacArthur led American troops into Korea to stop the Communist advance. By the end of 1950, 20 nations were supplying troops or other assistance to the American-led war effort. Even so, Americans made up the majority of troops throughout the Korean War.

The Korean War

★ The United Nations had a clear but difficult goal: push the North Koreans back across the 38th parallel. During the course of the war, this goal changed as China intervened in the conflict, and Truman and MacArthur clashed over military strategy.

Early Phases of the War

By September 1950, North Korean forces had pushed all the way to the southern tip of the Korean Peninsula. Only a small area in the southeast around the port city of **Pusan** was still held by the South Korean army.

After joining the South Koreans, General MacArthur designed a bold counterattack against North Korea. In September, United Nations forces

Cooperative Learning Activity

Discussing the War Use a panel-discussion format to help students focus on the issues of the Korean War. Call on volunteers to portray President Truman, Douglas MacArthur, a representative from the United Nations, a Chinese diplomat, a South Korean civilian, and a North Korean civilian. Then invite other students to ask this panel questions about why there is a war in Korea, why United States forces are fighting there, and how the fighting can be ended. Work with students to compile a list of memorable statements from the discussion for review purposes.

made a daring landing midway on the Korean Peninsula near the port of **Inchon.** They took that strategic city and moved on to recapture Seoul.

Meanwhile American and UN troops began pushing north from Pusan. By October 1 the North Koreans, caught between UN forces advancing from both Seoul and Pusan, were forced to retreat north across the 38th parallel. South Korea now came under the control of the United Nations forces.

Taking the Offensive

Encouraged by this success, General MacArthur urged President Truman to order an invasion of North Korea. He assured Truman that neither **China** nor the Soviet Union would enter the war to help North Korea, and he promised to have troops "home by Christmas." Truman sought and received approval from the United Nations to cross the 38th parallel, invade the North, and create "a unified, independent and democratic Korea"—a new goal for the war.

After receiving the new orders from Truman, MacArthur moved his forces swiftly northward. The UN forces captured **Pyongyang,** the North Korean capital, on October 19, and then moved north toward the **Yalu River,** part of North Korea's border with China. Total victory seemed just days away.

As the United Nations forces advanced northward, the United States Department of State received a serious warning from the Chinese. If the invasion of North Korea continued, China would send in its army to support the North Koreans. Believing the Chinese warning was a bluff, President Truman allowed MacArthur to continue moving north.

Picturing HISTORY American troops move forward to the battlefield, while South Korean women and children flee from the Communists. **What was the state of the Korean conflict in 1951?**

The Chinese were not bluffing, however. By late October, thousands of Chinese troops began massing along the border, and some crossed the Yalu River southward into North Korea. On November 26, huge numbers of Chinese troops launched an attack on United Nations forces. Badly outnumbered, the UN forces retreated south back across the 38th parallel. Within weeks, the Communists had recaptured Seoul.

American Leadership Divided

By January 1951, United Nations forces managed to stop their retreat. Launching a counteroffensive, they retook Seoul and pushed the Communists back across the 38th parallel. The war now became a **stalemate,** a situation in which neither side was able to gain much ground or achieve a decisive victory. The stalemate lasted for almost two years, with much bitter fighting along the 38th parallel.

Footnotes to History

Like Father, Like Son Douglas MacArthur and his father are the only father and son to have both received the Congressional Medal of Honor. This medal is given only to people who perform extraordinary acts of heroism.

CHAPTER 27
Section 3, 785–788

Picturing HISTORY **Answer:** *a stalemate*

ABCNEWS INTERACTIVE™

VIDEODISC
Lessons of War

Side 1
Chapter 9

Title: *The United States Goes to War*
Ask: **Who has the power to declare war?** *(Congress)*

VIDEODISC
Communism and the Cold War

Side 2
Chapter 7

Title: *Korean War*
Ask: **How did the Soviet Union view U.S. involvement in Korea?** *(imperialist tactic to gain land)*

3 ASSESS

Assign Section 3 Review as homework or as an in-class activity.

Section Quiz 27–3

Name ________ Date ________ Class ________

Chapter 27

Score

Section Quiz 27-3

DIRECTIONS: Matching Match each item in Column A with the items in Column B. Write the correct letters in the blanks. *(10 points each)*

Column A	Column B
____ 1. President Harry S Truman's home	A. Soviet Union
____ 2. once controlled North Korea	B. Douglas MacArthur
____ 3. once controlled South Korea	C. United States
____ 4. commander of UN forces in Korea	D. China
____ 5. attacked UN forces in North Korea	E. Independence, Missouri

DIRECTIONS: Multiple Choice In the blank at the left, write the letter of the choice that best completes the statement or answers the question. *(10 points each)*

____ 6. The original goal of the United Nations forces in Korea was to push the North Koreans back across the
A. 29th parallel. C. 32nd parallel.
B. 38th parallel. D. 42nd parallel.

____ 7. The capital of South Korea is
A. Pyongyang. C. Pusan.
B. Inchon. D. Seoul.

____ 8. After the goal of pushing the North Koreans back, this became a new goal for the war.
A. a democratic Korea C. a Communist Korea
B. a fascist Korea D. a socialist Korea

____ 9. The capital of North Korea is
A. Pyongyang. C. Pusan.
B. Inchon. D. Seoul.

____ 10. The agreement ending the Korean War created
A. another war. C. a demilitarized zone.
B. a unified Korea. D. a 42nd parallel.

The American Journey ★ 111 ★ Section Quizzes

MULTIPLE LEARNING STYLES

Visual/Spatial Help students trace the progress of the war by providing them with four outline maps of Korea or having them draw their own. (If students trace the map on page 786, make sure that they trace only the outline of Korea.) As students follow the text's discussion of the war, have them use colored pencils or markers to show (1) North Korean control of the peninsula in August 1950; (2) UN forces along the Yalu River in October 1950; (3) the Communist recapture of Seoul in late 1950; and (4) the stalemate at the 38th parallel. As students compare the maps, invite comments about the strength of the opposing forces and the frustrations of the conflict. **L1, ELL**

CHAPTER 27
Section 3, 785–788

Use **Chapter Challenger Interactive Review Software** to review Section 3.

Reteaching Activity 27–3

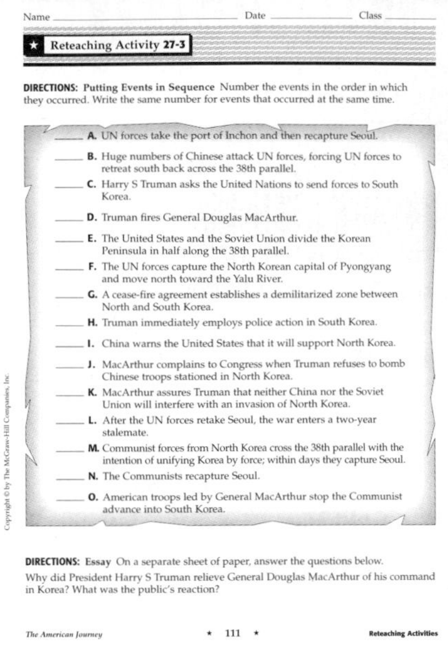
Name ______ Date ______ Class ______

Reteaching Activity 27-3

DIRECTIONS: Putting Events in Sequence Number the events in the order in which they occurred. Write the same number for events that occurred at the same time.

____ A. UN forces take the port of Inchon and then recapture Seoul.
____ B. Huge numbers of Chinese attack UN forces, forcing UN forces to retreat south back across the 38th parallel.
____ C. Harry S Truman asks the United Nations to send forces to South Korea.
____ D. Truman fires General Douglas MacArthur.
____ E. The United States and the Soviet Union divide the Korean Peninsula in half along the 38th parallel.
____ F. The UN forces capture the North Korean capital of Pyongyang and move north toward the Yalu River.
____ G. A cease-fire agreement establishes a demilitarized zone between North and South Korea.
____ H. Truman immediately employs police action in South Korea.
____ I. China warns the United States that it will support North Korea.
____ J. MacArthur complains to Congress when Truman refuses to bomb Chinese troops stationed in North Korea.
____ K. MacArthur assures Truman that neither China nor the Soviet Union will interfere with an invasion of North Korea.
____ L. After the UN forces retake Seoul, the war enters a two-year stalemate.
____ M. Communist forces from North Korea cross the 38th parallel with the intention of unifying Korea by force; within days they capture Seoul.
____ N. The Communists recapture Seoul.
____ O. American troops led by General MacArthur stop the Communist advance into South Korea.

DIRECTIONS: Essay On a separate sheet of paper, answer the questions below.
Why did President Harry S Truman relieve General Douglas MacArthur of his command in Korea? What was the public's reaction?

The American Journey • 111 • Reteaching Activities

Enrichment Activity 27–3

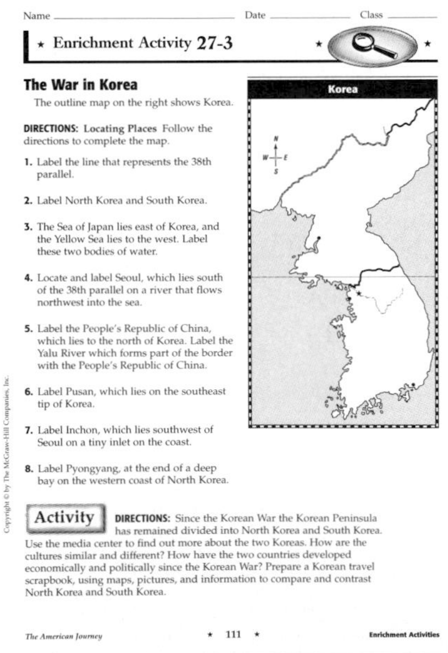
Name ______ Date ______ Class ______

Enrichment Activity 27-3

The War in Korea

The outline map on the right shows Korea.

DIRECTIONS: Locating Places Follow the directions to complete the map.

1. Label the line that represents the 38th parallel.
2. Label North Korea and South Korea.
3. The Sea of Japan lies east of Korea, and the Yellow Sea lies to the west. Label these two bodies of water.
4. Locate and label Seoul, which lies south of the 38th parallel on a river that flows northwest into the sea.
5. Label the People's Republic of China, which lies to the north of Korea. Label the Yalu River which forms part of the border with the People's Republic of China.
6. Label Pusan, which lies on the southeast tip of Korea.
7. Label Inchon, which lies southwest of Seoul on a tiny inlet on the coast.
8. Label Pyongyang, at the end of a deep bay on the western coast of North Korea.

Activity DIRECTIONS: Since the Korean War the Korean Peninsula has remained divided into North Korea and South Korea. Use the media center to find out more about the two Koreas. How are the cultures similar and different? How have the two countries developed economically and politically since the Korean War? Prepare a Korean travel scrapbook, using maps, pictures, and information to compare and contrast North Korea and South Korea.

The American Journey • 111 • Enrichment Activities

4 CLOSE

Ask each student to write a paragraph explaining reasons for United States involvement in Korea.

Truman and MacArthur Disagree

As the stalemate dragged on, President Truman began to consider negotiating an end to the fighting. General MacArthur, however, argued that the UN forces should now attack China, either by invading the country or by bombing Chinese troops stationed in North Korea. Truman opposed MacArthur's plan, fearing that such actions would lead to a larger war with China or escalate into another world war.

In a letter to a member of Congress, MacArthur complained that he was being kept from doing his job. "We must win," he wrote. "There is no substitute for victory."

MacArthur Fired

On April 12, 1951, President Truman relieved General MacArthur of his command in Korea. "I could do nothing else and still be president of the United States," Truman concluded. He later wrote:

> "If I allowed him to defy the civil authorities in this manner, I myself would be violating my oath to uphold and defend the Constitution."

MacArthur's firing created a storm of protest in the United States. The general was extremely popular, and polls showed that a majority of Americans supported him against the president. Moreover, MacArthur did not go quietly. After receiving a hero's welcome on his return to the United States, he delivered a farewell speech to Congress. "Old soldiers never die," he said, "they just fade away."

Ending the Conflict

The two sides in the Korean War began negotiations in July 1951. The talks lasted for two years before a cease-fire agreement was signed on July 27, 1953, during the presidency of Dwight Eisenhower. This agreement ending the war created a **demilitarized zone**—a region where military forces could not enter—between North and South Korea. The zone extended roughly a mile and a half on either side of the 38th parallel.

The Korean War ended with neither side achieving victory and almost no change in territory. Losses had been great. More than 54,000 Americans died in the war, and another 103,000 were wounded. Nearly 2 million Koreans and Chinese lost their lives, and large portions of North and South Korea were devastated.

America's involvement in the Korean War sent a clear message to the Soviet Union: The United States was committed to fighting Communist expansion with money, arms, and even lives.

Section 3 Review

Checking for Understanding

1. ***Identify*** 38th parallel, Seoul, Douglas MacArthur, Pyongyang.
2. ***Define*** stalemate, demilitarized zone.
3. ***Summarize*** Truman's actions after he heard that South Korea had been invaded.

Reviewing Themes

4. **Government and Democracy** How did American goals change during the course of the Korean War?

Critical Thinking

5. **Making Critical Judgments** Do you think Truman should have allowed MacArthur to attack China? Why or why not?

Activity

Writing an Editorial Write a one-page editorial in which you argue whether a United States military leader should or should not be able to override a president's decision.

Section 3 Review Answers

1. 38th parallel, 785; Seoul, 786; Douglas MacArthur, 786; Pyongyang, 787
2. The words are defined in the Glossary.
3. Truman immediately ordered the American military to South Korea as a "police action" to contain the spread of communism and asked the UN to send forces, which were commanded by General Douglas MacArthur.
4. First goal was to contain communism in North Korea. Then U.S. decided to take over all of Korea to make it "unified, independent and democratic." With China's invasion, policy of containment returned.
5. Students should provide reasons for their responses.

Activity Editorials should examine the constitutional power that grants the president authority over the armed forces.

1945 | 1950 | 1955

1947 House Un-American Activities Committee holds hearings

1950 Congress passes the McCarran Act

1953 The Rosenbergs are executed as spies

1954 McCarthy is censured

Section 4

The Red Scare

READ TO DISCOVER . . .

- what effect cold war fears had on domestic politics.
- how McCarthyism affected the country.

TERMS TO LEARN

subversion
blacklist
perjury
allege
censure

The Storyteller

In 1947, a congressional committee held public hearings on the alleged Communist influence in the Hollywood film industry. Many witnesses called before the committee were asked the same questions: "Are you now or have you ever been a member of the Communist Party?" Two witnesses denied having Communist ties, but 10 others refused to give a straight "yes" or "no" answer. In dramatic moments worthy of the movies, these "Hollywood Ten" challenged the committee's right to ask about their political beliefs. One of the accused yelled, "This is the beginning of an American concentration camp!"

"Red Scare" literature

The cold war intensified Americans' fears of Communist **subversion,** or sabotage. Stories of stolen government documents and spy rings gripped the country in the late 1940s. Then in 1949 Americans learned that the Soviet Union had built its own atomic bomb.

Many Americans worried that Communist spies and sympathizers—people friendly to Communists, or "Reds" as they were known—had penetrated all levels of American society and were attempting to weaken the government. This **Red Scare** dominated the nation's politics for years and led to a massive hunt to uncover Communists across the country. In this climate of fear, few Americans were safe from accusations of disloyalty—not even the president.

Cold War Fears

Republican critics began accusing President Truman of being too easy on Communists. In 1947 Truman responded by ordering an investigation into the loyalty of all federal employees. More than 6 million government workers had to undergo security checks, and 14,000 were investigated by the FBI. Although the investigations found little evidence of espionage, many federal employees lost their jobs.

Loyalty Oaths

Many state and local governments, colleges and universities, businesses, and other institutions began similar campaigns to uncover Communist

SECTION RESOURCES

Reproducible Masters
- Guided Reading Activity 27–4
- Political Cartoons
- Section Quiz 27–4
- Reteaching Activity 27–4
- Enrichment Activity 27–4

Transparencies
- Section Focus Transparency 27–4

Multimedia
- Vocabulary PuzzleMaker
- Chapter Challenger Interactive Review Software
- Testmaker
- ABCNews InterActive™ Communism and the Cold War
- Facts On File: Landmark Documents in American History

1 FOCUS

BELLRINGER
Motivational Activity

Before taking roll at the beginning of the class period, project Section Focus Transparency 27–4 and have students answer the questions. Discuss students' responses.

This activity is also available as a blackline master.

Section Focus Transparency 27–4

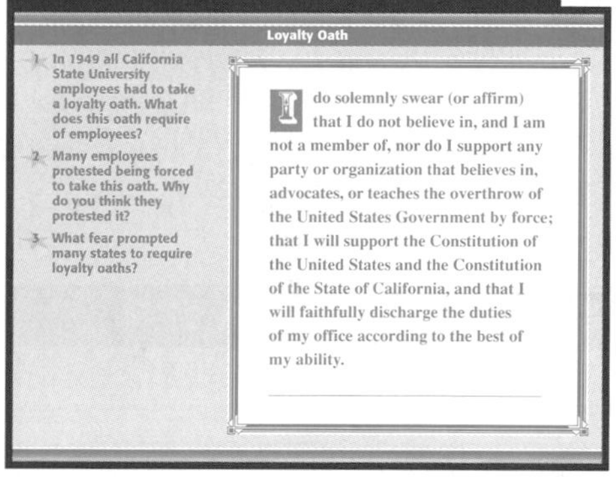
Loyalty Oath

1. In 1949 all California State University employees had to take a loyalty oath. What does this oath require of employees?
2. Many employees protested being forced to take this oath. Why do you think they protested it?
3. What fear prompted many states to require loyalty oaths?

I do solemnly swear (or affirm) that I do not believe in, and I am not a member of, nor do I support any party or organization that believes in, advocates, or teaches the overthrow of the United States Government by force; that I will support the Constitution of the United States and the Constitution of the State of California, and that I will faithfully discharge the duties of my office according to the best of my ability.

Vocabulary Precheck

Point out that *subversion* comes from a Latin prefix and root meaning "to turn from beneath." Discuss what Americans of the 1950s feared was "beneath" and what they feared it might "turn."

Use the **Vocabulary PuzzleMaker** to create crossword and word search puzzles.

Section Theme
Individual Action

As personified in Senator Joseph McCarthy, Americans of the postwar era took steps to combat the spread of communism within the United States.

Activity Have students brainstorm words and images that they associate with the word *communism.* Have them compare their responses to the responses that are suggested in this section.

CHAPTER 27
Section 4, 789–792

2 TEACH

L1 Analyzing Bias Direct students' attention to **The Storyteller** on page 789. Discuss the images that *concentration camp* is meant to produce and why those images seem all the more horrifying when *concentration camp* is linked with *American.*

Picturing HISTORY The Rosenbergs had been accused by David Greenglass, a worker at Los Alamos—and Ethel's brother. **Answer:** *They conducted investigations and often required participants to sign loyalty oaths. Furthermore, all Communist organizations had to register with the government, and the HUAC conducted its own investigations.*

Guided Reading Activity 27–4

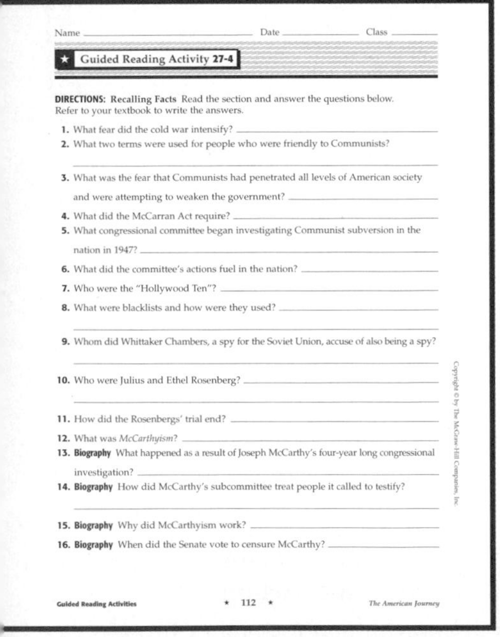
Name ______ Date ______ Class ______

★ Guided Reading Activity 27-4

DIRECTIONS: Recalling Facts Read the section and answer the questions below. Refer to your textbook to write the answers.

1. What fear did the cold war intensify? ______
2. What two terms were used for people who were friendly to Communists? ______
3. What was the fear that Communists had penetrated all levels of American society and were attempting to weaken the government? ______
4. What did the McCarran Act require? ______
5. What congressional committee began investigating Communist subversion in the nation in 1947? ______
6. What did the committee's actions fuel in the nation? ______
7. Who were the "Hollywood Ten"? ______
8. What were blacklists and how were they used? ______
9. Whom did Whittaker Chambers, a spy for the Soviet Union, accuse of also being a spy? ______
10. Who were Julius and Ethel Rosenberg? ______
11. How did the Rosenbergs' trial end? ______
12. What was *McCarthyism*? ______
13. **Biography** What happened as a result of Joseph McCarthy's four-year long congressional investigation? ______
14. **Biography** How did McCarthy's subcommittee treat people it called to testify? ______
15. **Biography** Why did McCarthyism work? ______
16. **Biography** When did the Senate vote to censure McCarthy? ______

Facts On File

CD-ROM
Landmark Documents in American History

Title: *McCarran Act (Subversive Activities Control Act), 1950*
Have students outline the provisions of this act.

Picturing HISTORY On April 5, 1951, Ethel and Julius Rosenberg were convicted of spying for the Soviet Union. **How did the government, universities, and businesses try to uncover Communist subversion?**

subversion. Some organizations required individuals to sign oaths swearing their loyalty to the United States. Those who refused risked losing their jobs.

In 1950 Congress passed the **McCarran Act,** which required all Communist organizations to register with the government and to provide lists of members. President Truman vetoed the act. "In a free country, we punish men for crimes they commit," he said, "but never for the opinions they hold." Congress overrode his veto.

Un-American Activities

In 1947 a congressional committee, the **House Un-American Activities Committee** (HUAC), began investigating Communist subversion in the nation. In widely publicized hearings, the committee questioned people about their knowledge of Communists or Communist sympathizers. Individuals came under suspicion because of the beliefs of their friends or coworkers—guilt by association. The committee's activities fueled an anti-Communist hysteria in the nation.

Footnotes to History

"Witch" Trials In his 1953 play *The Crucible,* playwright Arthur Miller wrote about the witch trials in Salem, Massachusetts, in the 1600s. Despite its seventeenth-century setting, the play was widely recognized as referring to the anti-Communist fervor of the McCarthy era.

HUAC launched a sensational investigation of the Hollywood film industry, rumored to be full of Communists. A number of those who were summoned refused to testify, and several screenwriters and directors—the "Hollywood Ten"—went to jail for refusing to answer questions about their political beliefs or those of their colleagues. Reacting to public and government pressure, film companies created **blacklists**—lists of individuals whose loyalty was suspicious—that barred people from working in Hollywood.

American Spies Revealed

In 1948 **Whittaker Chambers,** a magazine editor, volunteered to testify before HUAC. After admitting that he had spied for the Soviet Union in the 1930s, Chambers accused **Alger Hiss,** a former State Department official, of giving him secret government documents in 1937 and 1938 to pass on to the Soviets.

Hiss denied the charges. Chambers produced secret State Department papers he claimed were written by Hiss and microfilm of other secret documents. Chambers swore that he had received the microfilm (which was hidden in a pumpkin in his garden) from Hiss. Investigators could not prosecute Hiss for spying because too much time had passed since the events in the case had occurred. However, he was found guilty of **perjury,** or lying, and sent to prison.

The most dramatic spy case to come before HUAC involved the atomic bomb. **Julius and Ethel Rosenberg,** a New York couple who were members of the Communist Party, were accused

COOPERATIVE LEARNING ACTIVITY

Enacting the Red Scare To dramatize cold war fears, have groups of students prepare and present skits on any of the following situations:

- A history teacher finding out that she is being investigated by the FBI
- A blacklisted actor at an audition
- Coworkers in an office discussing the case of Alger Hiss or Julius and Ethel Rosenberg
- A parent trying to explain communism to a child
- A family talking about building a bomb shelter

Each group should choose a director and a secretary. Encourage the actors to try different roles in the skit before choosing the characters whom they will portray.

of plotting to pass secret information about the atomic bomb to the Soviet Union. Brought to trial in 1951, the Rosenbergs were convicted and sentenced to death. The judge in the case declared their crime "worse than murder."

Groups around the world protested the sentence as a gross injustice, but higher courts upheld the death sentence decision. Executed in 1953, the Rosenbergs maintained their innocence to the end and claimed that they were persecuted because of their political beliefs.

McCarthyism

★ From 1950 to 1954, the hunt for Communists in America was dominated by Senator **Joseph McCarthy** of Wisconsin. During those years, McCarthy publicly attacked many people alleged—declared without proof—to be Communists. His unfounded accusations destroyed the careers of numerous innocent Americans and heightened the atmosphere of anti-Communist hysteria in the country. A new word was coined, ***McCarthyism,*** which meant the use of unproved accusations against political opponents.

Biography

The Rise of McCarthy

Joseph McCarthy rose to national attention almost overnight. In a speech in Wheeling, West Virginia, in February 1950, he announced that America had been betrayed by the "traitorous actions" of certain individuals. Raising a sheet of paper, he claimed to have in his hand "a list of 205 State Department employees who were members of the Communist Party." Millions of Americans believed McCarthy's charges.

Over the next four years, McCarthy continued to accuse government officials and others of being Communists. His congressional subcommittee attacked and bullied the people it called to testify. Many federal employees resigned or were dismissed as a result of McCarthy's investigations. Even the most powerful government officials hesitated to oppose him. Senator **Margaret Chase Smith** of Maine did speak up, however. In an attack on McCarthy's tactics in June 1950, she declared:

> "Those of us who shout the loudest about Americanism in making character assassinations are all too frequently those who . . . ignore some of the basic principles of Americanism: the right to criticize, the right to hold unpopular beliefs, the right to protest, the right of independent thought."

Causes and Effects

CAUSES

- ★ The Soviet Union expands into Eastern Europe.
- ★ Communism extends into Western Europe, the Middle East, and Asia.
- ★ Western governments fear Soviet aggression.

The Cold War

EFFECTS

- ★ United States aids anti-Communist forces in Greece, Turkey, and Western Europe.
- ★ Berlin airlift ends Soviet blockade.
- ★ Western powers form NATO. Communist nations form the Warsaw Pact.
- ★ Korean War erupts.
- ★ Americans fear Communist influence at home.
- ★ U.S.–Soviet arms race develops.

Chart Study

The cold war pitted the Soviet Union and its satellites against the United States and its allies.

Analyzing Information What organization did Western powers form?

CHAPTER 27

Section 4, 789–792

ABC NEWS INTERACTIVE™

VIDEODISC
Communism and the Cold War

Side 1
Chapter 11

Title: *Communists in Our Midst: McCarthyism*
Ask: **How were Americans who believed in Communist ideas treated?** *(investigated, shunned, and considered treasonous)*

Chart Study

Answer: NATO

3 ASSESS

Assign Section 4 Review as homework or as an in-class activity.

Use **Chapter Challenger Interactive Review Software** to review Section 4.

Section Quiz 27–4

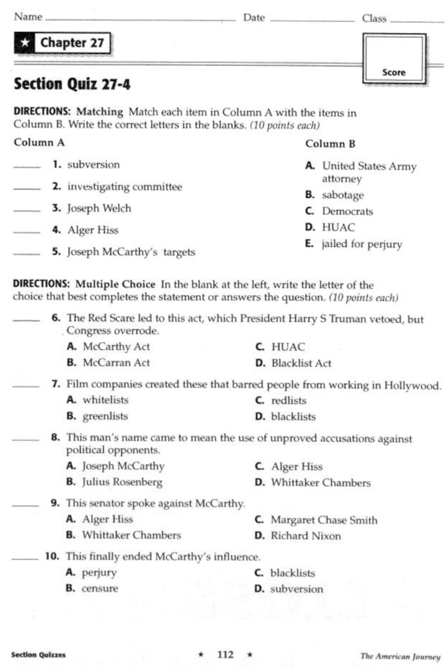
Name ______ Date ______ Class ______

★ Chapter 27

Score

Section Quiz 27-4

DIRECTIONS: Matching Match each item in Column A with the items in Column B. Write the correct letters in the blanks. *(10 points each)*

Column A	Column B
____ 1. subversion	A. United States Army attorney
____ 2. investigating committee	B. sabotage
____ 3. Joseph Welch	C. Democrats
____ 4. Alger Hiss	D. HUAC
____ 5. Joseph McCarthy's targets	E. jailed for perjury

DIRECTIONS: Multiple Choice In the blank at the left, write the letter of the choice that best completes the statement or answers the question. *(10 points each)*

____ 6. The Red Scare led to this act, which President Harry S Truman vetoed, but Congress overrode.
A. McCarthy Act C. HUAC
B. McCarran Act D. Blacklist Act

____ 7. Film companies created these that barred people from working in Hollywood.
A. whitelists C. redlists
B. greenlists D. blacklists

____ 8. This man's name came to mean the use of unproved accusations against political opponents.
A. Joseph McCarthy C. Alger Hiss
B. Julius Rosenberg D. Whittaker Chambers

____ 9. This senator spoke against McCarthy.
A. Alger Hiss C. Margaret Chase Smith
B. Whittaker Chambers D. Richard Nixon

____ 10. This finally ended McCarthy's influence.
A. perjury C. blacklists
B. censure D. subversion

Section Quizzes ★ 112 ★ *The American Journey*

MULTIPLE LEARNING STYLES

Interpersonal Why was McCarthyism a traumatic experience for some? To illustrate, call on two volunteers—one to portray a member of the House Un-American Activities Committee, the other to portray an average American who is testifying before the committee. Have the HUAC member question the witness for several minutes, pressing for knowledge of Communist influence in his or her workplace, among his or her friends, and so on. Afterward, ask both participants to share their feelings about the questioning. Then ask the listeners: **For which person did you feel more sympathy—the HUAC member or the witness? Why? L2**

CHAPTER 27

Section 4, 789–792

Picturing HISTORY McCarthy's theatrics made him the object of ridicule. **Answer:** *televising of the Army-McCarthy Hearings, which brought his fanaticism to a wide audience*

Reteaching Activity 27–4

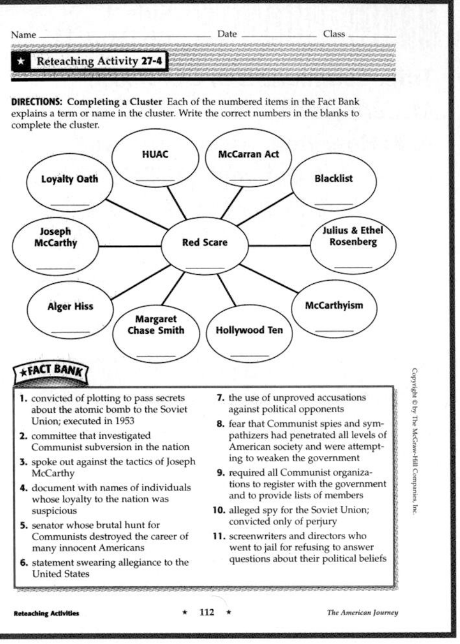
Name ______ Date ______ Class ______

★ Reteaching Activity 27-4

DIRECTIONS: Completing a Cluster Each of the numbered items in the Fact Bank explains a term or name in the cluster. Write the correct numbers in the blanks to complete the cluster.

★FACT BANK

1. convicted of plotting to pass secrets about the atomic bomb to the Soviet Union; executed in 1953
2. committee that investigated Communist subversion in the nation
3. spoke out against the tactics of Joseph McCarthy
4. document with names of individuals whose loyalty to the nation was suspicious
5. senator whose brutal hunt for Communists destroyed the career of many innocent Americans
6. statement swearing allegiance to the United States
7. the use of unproved accusations against political opponents
8. fear that Communist spies and sympathizers had penetrated all levels of American society and were attempting to weaken the government
9. required all Communist organizations to register with the government and to provide lists of members
10. alleged spy for the Soviet Union; convicted only of perjury
11. screenwriters and directors who went to jail for refusing to answer questions about their political beliefs

Reteaching Activities ★ 112 ★ *The American Journey*

Enrichment Activity 27–4

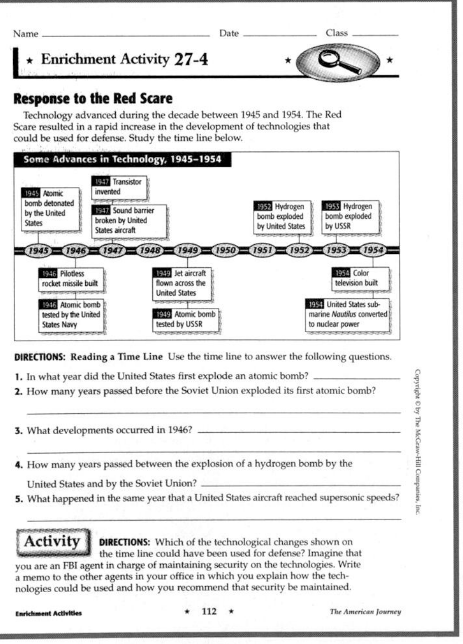
Name ______ Date ______ Class ______

★ Enrichment Activity 27-4

Response to the Red Scare

Technology advanced during the decade between 1945 and 1954. The Red Scare resulted in a rapid increase in the development of technologies that could be used for defense. Study the time line below.

DIRECTIONS: Reading a Time Line Use the time line to answer the following questions.

1. In what year did the United States first explode an atomic bomb? ______
2. How many years passed before the Soviet Union exploded its first atomic bomb? ______
3. What developments occurred in 1946? ______
4. How many years passed between the explosion of a hydrogen bomb by the United States and by the Soviet Union? ______
5. What happened in the same year that a United States aircraft reached supersonic speeds? ______

Activity **DIRECTIONS:** Which of the technological changes shown on the time line could have been used for defense? Imagine that you are an FBI agent in charge of maintaining security on the technologies. Write a memo to the other agents in your office in which you explain how the technologies could be used and how you recommend that security be maintained.

Enrichment Activities ★ 112 ★ *The American Journey*

4 CLOSE

Discuss with students their completion of the following statements: (1) The Red Scare began because ____. (2) Because of the Red Scare, ____.

McCarthy often targeted Democrats. He and his Republican colleagues in Congress saw anti-communism as an important issue to use against the Democratic Party. Some Republican candidates for Congress, including **Richard Nixon,** successfully smeared their opponents with charges of being soft on communism. Such tactics worked because so many Americans were terrified of the Soviet Union and the threat of communism.

McCarthy's Downfall

In 1954 McCarthy launched an investigation of the United States Army. He made alarming claims that Communists had infiltrated the military. In a series of televised hearings, watched by millions of Americans, McCarthy hurled wild accusations at highly respected army officials.

The televised Army-McCarthy Hearings proved the turning point in the McCarthy investigations. For weeks Americans witnessed McCarthy's sneering and cruel attacks. Toward the end of the hearings, **Joseph Welch,** an attorney for the army, said to McCarthy:

> "Until this moment, Senator, I think I never really gauged your cruelty or your recklessness. . . . Have you left no sense of decency?"

Many Americans now came to view McCarthy as a cruel bully who had little basis for his accusations. Congress also turned against McCarthy. In December 1954, the Senate voted to **censure,** or formally criticize, him for "conduct unbecoming a senator." Censure and the loss of public support ended McCarthy's influence. Yet during the years when fears of communism had raged in the country, McCarthyism had damaged the lives of many innocent people.

Picturing HISTORY This 1950 political cartoon shows McCarthy spreading charges of disloyalty and damaging American ideals. **What event brought about McCarthy's downfall?**

Section 4 Review

Checking for Understanding

1. ***Identify*** Red Scare, Whittaker Chambers, Alger Hiss, Julius and Ethel Rosenberg, Joseph McCarthy, Richard Nixon.
2. ***Define*** subversion, blacklist, perjury, allege, censure.
3. ***Describe*** the aim of loyalty oaths.

Reviewing Themes

4. **Individual Action** What negative effects did McCarthy's anti-Communist actions have on American society?

Critical Thinking

5. **Drawing Conclusions** What part of the Constitution is supposed to protect Americans from laws such as the McCarran Act?

Activity

Drawing a Political Cartoon Draw a political cartoon that focuses on the effect Senator Joseph McCarthy had on the American people.

Section 4 Review Answers

1. Red Scare, 789; Whittaker Chambers, 790; Alger Hiss, 790; Julius and Ethel Rosenberg, 790; Joseph McCarthy, 791; Richard Nixon, 792
2. The words are defined in the Glossary.
3. Loyalty oaths were meant to quiet fears about Communist activity in local governments, schools, businesses, and so on.
4. It destroyed the careers of many Americans and caused anti-Communist hysteria.
5. the First Amendment

Activity Political cartoons should focus on the effects of anti-Communist hysteria upon Americans.

Technology
SKILL BUILDER

Using E-Mail

When people share information, thoughts, and feelings with others, they are communicating. *Telecommunication* refers to communicating at a distance through the use of a telephone, video, or computer. How can you get your own computer to "talk" with other computers?

Learning the Skill

A computer is ready for telecommunication after two parts are added to it. The first is a piece of hardware called a *modem.* A modem is a device that enables computers to communicate with each other through telephone lines.

The second part is *communications software,* which lets your computer prepare and send information to the modem. It also lets your computer receive and understand the information it receives from the modem.

Electronic mail, or "E-mail" for short, is one way of sending and receiving messages electronically. Anyone who is part of an E-mail network can send and receive private messages.

If you are on an E-mail network you have a specific address. This address identifies the location of your electronic "mailbox"—the place where you receive your E-mail. To send an E-mail message to another person you must include that person's E-mail address, just as you might address an envelope.

Many corporations are using E-mail communications, which makes some environmentalists happier. More electronic communication means less use of paper and more saved trees.

Practicing the Skill

To send a message to a friend on an E-mail network, complete the following steps.

- Select the "message" function from your communications software.
- Type in your message—and proofread it for errors.
- Type in an E-mail address and select the "send" button.

The E-mail system places the message in the receiver's "mailbox." He or she can read the message at any time—and then send you a return message.

Applying the Skill

Using E-Mail Many intriguing spy novels were written during the Red Scare. Use E-mail to contact a librarian. Ask for recommendations of young adult books related to the Red Scare or the cold war era.

ANSWERS TO PRACTICING THE SKILL

If possible, have students who are familiar with E-mail help you guide novices through the process of sending a message. Because of computer availability, you may find it more practical to have groups of students work together on the activity.

Applying the Skill Students may also ask their librarians for more recently written spy novels. Encourage students to report on any E-mail responses they received from librarians, as well as what novels they actually read.

Technology
SKILL BUILDER

TEACH

Using E-Mail

As electronic communication becomes an ever-greater part of our daily lives, students almost inevitably will find that they must know how to send and receive E-mail. You might begin discussion of this feature by taking a class survey to find out if anyone frequently corresponds in this fashion.

In discussing components of an E-mail system, mention that it is possible to attach documents and other kinds of files to E-mail messages. For example, a student can send an essay to a friend without typing it again as part of the message itself.

Demonstrate sending a message and opening and printing a received message. If necessary, schedule time in the computer lab so that students can send E-mail on their own.

Additional Practice

Chapter Skills Activity 27

ABCNEWS INTERACTIVE™

VIDEODISC
Communism and the Cold War

Side 1, Chapter 12
Title: *Espionage*
Subject: Various espionage cases that occurred during the cold war
Ask: **What is espionage?** *(spying to uncover secrets of other countries)* **What were the Rosenbergs convicted of?** *(giving U.S. atomic secrets to the Soviet Union)*

GLENCOE TECHNOLOGY

VIDEODISC
MindJogger Videoquiz

Use MindJogger to review the Chapter 27 content.

Chapter 27
Disc 4, Side A

Also available in VHS.

Review and Activities

Reviewing Key Terms

On graph paper, create a word search puzzle using the following terms. Crisscross the terms vertically and horizontally, then fill in the remaining squares with extra letters. Use the terms' definitions as clues to find the words in the puzzle. Share your puzzle with a classmate.

iron curtain
containment
airlift
cold war
inflation
closed shop
demilitarized zone
stalemate
subversion
blacklist
perjury
allege
censure

Reviewing Key Facts

1. Why was communism attractive to some European countries after the war?
2. Why did many labor unions strike after the war?
3. Which of Truman's Fair Deal reforms were approved by Congress?
4. What was the outcome of the conflict in Korea?
5. What was the purpose of the House Un-American Activities Committee?

Critical Thinking

Identifying Central Issues

After World War II, Joseph Stalin, leader of the Soviet Union, began to cut his ties with the West.

1. What was the first sign that Stalin was not going to cooperate with Western nations after the war?
2. According to most Americans, what was the Soviet Union's main ambition after the war?

Time Line Activity

Create a time line on which you place the following events in chronological order.

- The Taft-Hartley bill is passed
- Berlin blockade stops traffic through East Germany to West Berlin
- United Nations is established
- Communists take control of China
- Korean War begins
- Senate censures Joseph McCarthy

Reviewing Themes

1. **Global Connections** What was the purpose of the Truman Doctrine?
2. **Economic Factors** How did the GI Bill of Rights affect inflation?
3. **Government and Democracy** How did Truman exercise his power as commander in chief of the United States military during the Korean War?
4. **Individual Action** In addition to a fear of communism, what other motivation did Senator McCarthy have for his actions?

Skill Practice Activity

Using E-Mail

Using your communications software, type a message asking people who grew up during the 1950s for their memories of Harry S Truman, Douglas MacArthur, or the Korean War.

1. What do the people remember?
2. How did people feel about American involvement in the war between North and South Korea?
3. How did civilians feel about Truman firing MacArthur?
4. How did soldiers feel about it? Share your responses with the rest of the class.

Reviewing Key Terms

The key terms used in this activity can be found in the textbook glossary on pages A26–A35. Students' word search puzzles will vary.

Reviewing Key Facts

1. World War II left many Europeans homeless and unemployed. Communism promised homes and jobs.
2. Wages were not keeping up with rising prices. With the war over, unions no longer had to accept government control of their wages.
3. Congress approved raising the minimum wage, expanding Social Security benefits for senior citizens, and funding low-income housing.
4. Neither side won the war, and boundaries changed only slightly. A demilitarized zone was created between North and South Korea.
5. It investigated Americans charged with subversion.

Critical Thinking

1. He did not hold free elections in Eastern Europe; instead, he took over these countries by setting up Communist governments whose leaders were loyal to the Soviet Union.
2. to spread communism throughout the world by taking over other nations

Time Line Activity

Events should be placed in this order: United Nations is established, The Taft-Hartley bill is passed, Berlin blockade stops traffic through East Germany to West Berlin, Communists take control of China, Korean War begins, Senate censures Joseph McCarthy

Reviewing Themes

1. It was meant to help nations threatened by communism and Soviet expansionism.
2. It gave returning soldiers more money to spend, which increased consumer spending and contributed to rising prices.
3. He ordered the use of limited American air and sea forces in Korea; later he fired General MacArthur.

Geography Activity

Study the map below, then answer the questions that follow.

The Occupation of Berlin

1. **Region** Among what four countries was Berlin divided?
2. **Place** What country or countries occupied East Berlin?
3. **Place** What country or countries occupied West Berlin?
4. **Location** What is unusual about the location of the airports in Berlin? Explain your reasoning.

Technology Activity

Using the Internet Search the Internet for information about how the United Nations is organized. Design a flowchart or graphic organizer that shows the names of each of the main bodies of the UN and how they are related to each other.

Cooperative Activity

History and Citizenship The GI Bill provided many benefits to soldiers returning from World War II. Through these benefits Americans who thought they could never go to college or own their own homes could now achieve these goals. Organize into four groups to explore the incentives offered today for people who join the United States Army, Navy, Marines, and Coast Guard. Use the list of questions that follow to guide your group's research.

- Is attending college or another institution of extended learning still an option?
- What kinds of economic incentives are offered to recruits?
- What advantages are awarded to those joining the armed services today that were not available at the end of World War II?

Use your information to design a recruitment plan to attract people to a particular branch of the service. Include all forms of media in your plan such as billboards, newspaper ads, radio, and television.

Portfolio Activity **History Journal** The United States government was anxious to avoid military conflict after World War II. Review the chapter and make a list of examples of how the United States government used negotiation and other nonviolent means to resolve international problems without resorting to war.

CHAPTER 27
Review and Activities

Technology Activity

Students should use the Internet to find information about the United Nations and then create a flowchart showing how the main bodies of the UN are organized.

Cooperative Activity

Each group should research the incentives offered by a branch of the armed forces today and create a recruitment plan for that branch.

Portfolio Activity Students should find examples of how the United States used negotiation and other nonviolent tactics to avoid war after World War II.

Chapter Bonus Test Question

Ask: What Asian nation came under Communist control when Chinese troops invaded it in 1950? *(Tibet)*

4. As a Republican, he used suspicions of communism to discredit Democrats.

Skill Practice Activity

Have students share and comment upon their responses, which will vary.

Geography Activity

1. Great Britain, the United States, France, and the Soviet Union
2. the Soviet Union
3. Great Britain, the United States, and France
4. All of the airports are in West Berlin, probably a reflection of travel restrictions that Soviet-controlled East Berlin put upon its people.

Chapter 28 Planning Guide

A complete, 1-page lesson plan is provided for each section in the *Reproducible Lesson Plans* booklet.

Section Resources

Daily Objectives	Reproducible Resources	Multimedia Resources
Section 1 Eisenhower's Domestic Policy Identify government programs President Eisenhower proposed to improve life in the United States.	Reproducible Lesson Plan 28–1 Guided Reading Activity 28–1* Section Quiz 28–1* Reteaching Activity 28–1 Enrichment Activity 28–1	Section Focus Transparency 28–1 Vocabulary PuzzleMaker Chapter Challenger Interactive Review Software Testmaker The Presidents: A Picture History of Our Nation
Section 2 Eisenhower and the Cold War Discuss foreign policy challenges faced by the Eisenhower administration.	Reproducible Lesson Plan 28–2 Guided Reading Activity 28–2* Political Cartoons, *Two Views of the Atom Bomb, Twists and Turns in the Cold War* Section Quiz 28–2* Reteaching Activity 28–2 Enrichment Activity 28–2	Section Focus Transparency 28–2 Vocabulary PuzzleMaker Chapter Challenger Interactive Review Software Testmaker ABCNews InterActive™ Communism and the Cold War
Section 3 1950s Prosperity Describe the growth of suburbs and other characteristics of the improved lifestyle that many Americans of this era enjoyed.	Reproducible Lesson Plan 28–3 Guided Reading Activity 28–3* Section Quiz 28–3* Reteaching Activity 28–3 Enrichment Activity 28–3	Section Focus Transparency 28–3 U.S. History & Art Transparencies Vocabulary PuzzleMaker Chapter Challenger Interactive Review Testmaker GTV: The American People: Fabric of a Nation GTV: A Geographic Perspective on American History American Music Cultural Traditions Focus on American Art Prints
Section 4 Problems in a Time of Plenty Contrast the seeming prosperity of the 1950s with the plight of America's poor and the rise of dissenters.	Reproducible Lesson Plan 28–4 Guided Reading Activity 28–4* Section Quiz 28–4* Reteaching Activity 28–4 Enrichment Activity 28–4	Section Focus Transparency 28–4 Vocabulary PuzzleMaker Chapter Challenger Interactive Review Software Testmaker GTV: The American People: Fabric of a Nation

** Also available in Spanish*

Poster | Blackline Master | Videodisc | Audiocassette | Music Program | Transparency | CD-ROM | Software

0:00 **OUT OF TIME?**
Assign the Chapter 28 Digest and the corresponding Chapter Digests Audiocassettes with activities and tests.

ACTIVITY
From the Classroom of…

Anne Thomas
Forest Trail Junior High
Park Forest, IL

Welcoming the 49th and 50th States

Organize the class into small groups. Have half the groups research Hawaii and the other half research Alaska. Groups may use their research findings either to create posters about these states or to construct dioramas. Students should address the following question as they work on these projects: "What do these states contribute to the rest of the country?"

Make sure students collect information concerning natural resources, economic activities, and culture. This information should be reflected in the groups' final projects. In addition, have students interview relatives or friends who have visited these states or who remember when the states were admitted to the Union. Have members of each group compile a report to deliver to the class while they are presenting their posters or dioramas.

NATIONAL GEOGRAPHIC SOCIETY Teacher's Corner

INDEX TO NATIONAL GEOGRAPHIC MAGAZINE

The following articles may be used for research relating to this chapter:

- "Wrangell—St. Elias: Alaska's Sky-High Wilderness," by Noel Grove, May 1994.
- "Kodiak, Alaska's Island Refuge," by John L. Elliott, November 1993.
- "Alone Across the Arctic Crown," by Keith Nyitray, April 1993.

NATIONAL GEOGRAPHIC SOCIETY PRODUCTS AVAILABLE FROM GLENCOE

To order the following products for use with this chapter, contact your local Glencoe sales representative, or call Glencoe at 1-800-334-7344:

- *GTV: A Geographic Perspective on American History* (Videodisc)
- *GTV: The American People: Fabric of a Nation* (Videodisc)
- *The Presidents: A Picture History of Our Nation* (CD-ROM)

ADDITIONAL NATIONAL GEOGRAPHIC SOCIETY PRODUCTS

To order the following products for use with this chapter, call National Geographic Society at 1-800-368-2728:

- *Hawaii: Strangers in Paradise* (Video)
- *1945–1989: The Cold War* (Video)
- *Historical Atlas of the United States* (Atlas)

Block Schedule

Block scheduling differs from traditional class scheduling in the amount of time allotted to each period. The extended time frame provided by block scheduling affords you the opportunity to implement a greater number of research-oriented and activity-intense projects to motivate and involve your students. Activities that are particularly suited to use within the block scheduling framework are identified throughout this chapter by the following designation:

KEY TO ABILITY LEVELS

Teaching strategies have been coded for varying learning styles and abilities.

L1 **BASIC** activities for all students
L2 **AVERAGE** activities for average to above-average students
L3 **CHALLENGING** activities for above-average students
ELL **ENGLISH LANGUAGE LEARNER** activities

Chapter 28 Resource Guide

Home Involvement

Home Involvement Activity 28

Review Activities

Chapter Summary 28

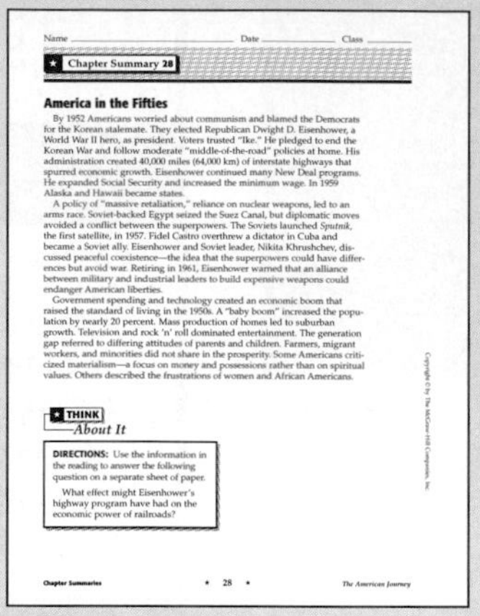

Workbook Activity 28

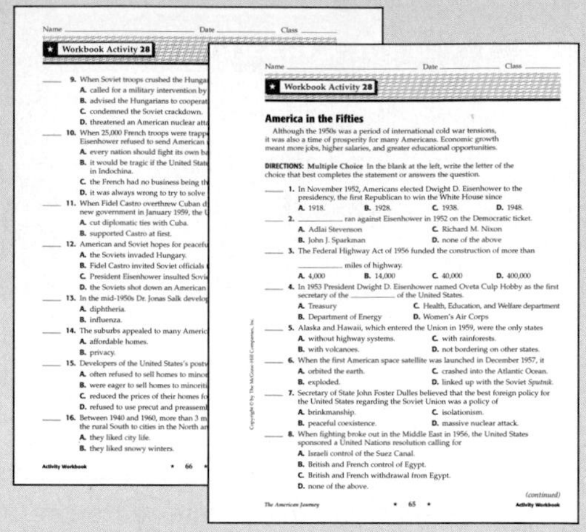

Reinforcement Activities

Time Line Activity 28

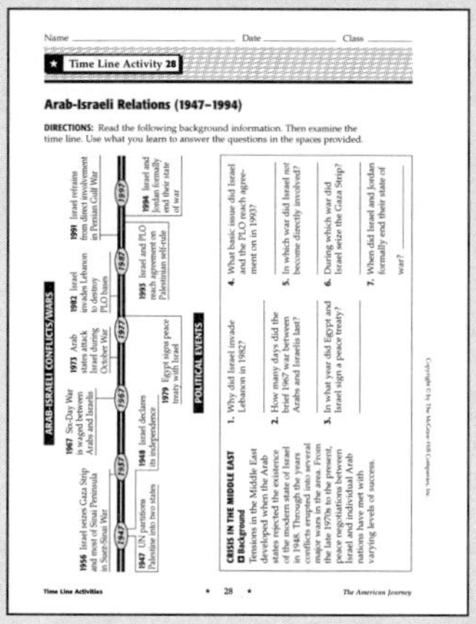

Vocabulary Activity 28

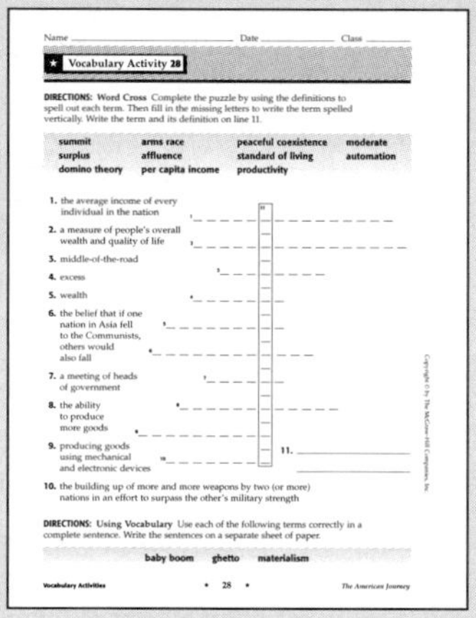

Chapter Skills Activity 28

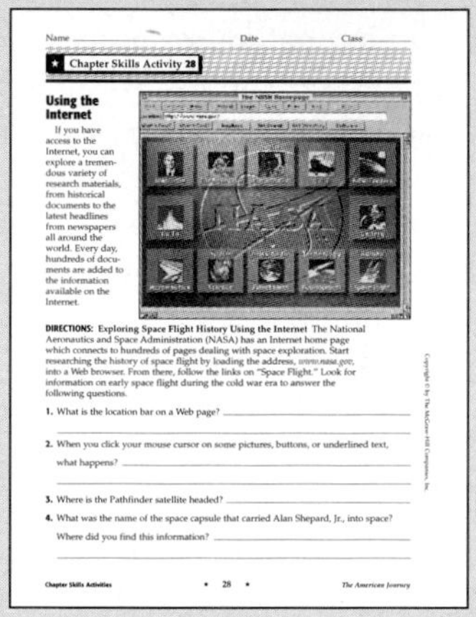

Enrichment Activities

Linking Past and Present Activity 28

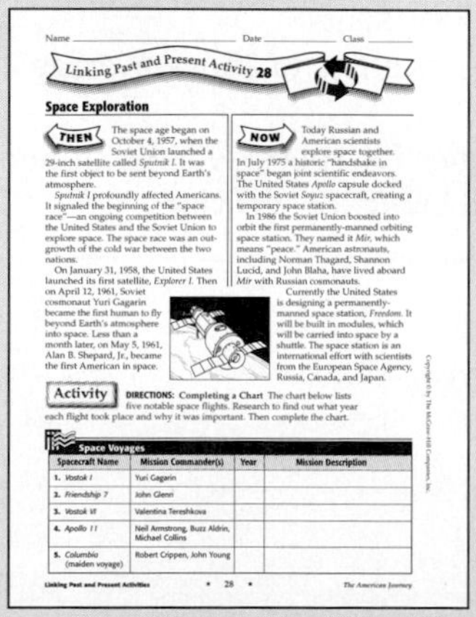

Primary Source Reading 28

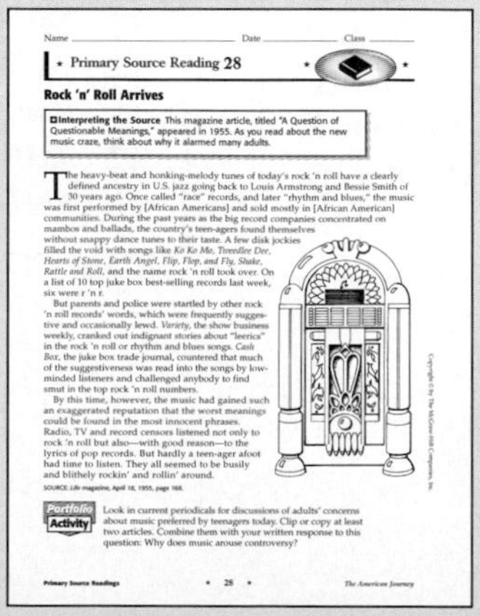

Geography Activities

Mapping History Activity 28

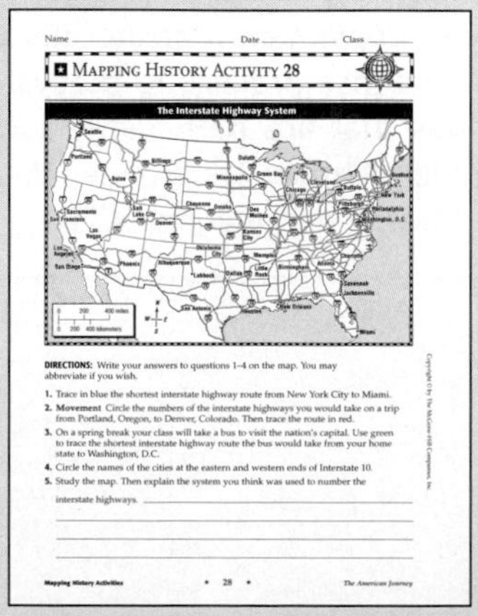

Assessment

Chapter 28 Test, Form A

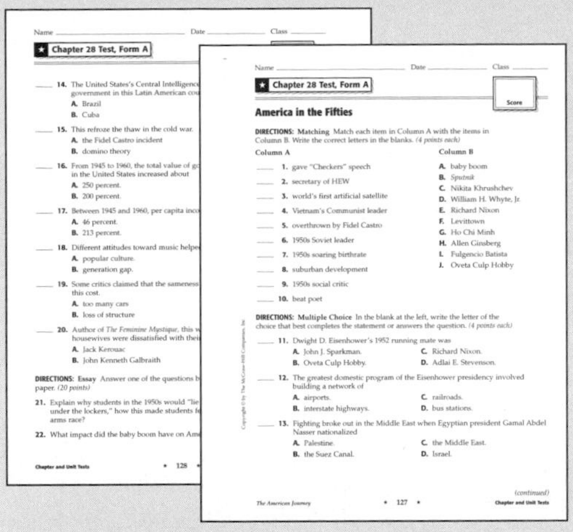
Chapter 28 Test, Form A
America in the Fifties

Chapter 28 Test, Form B

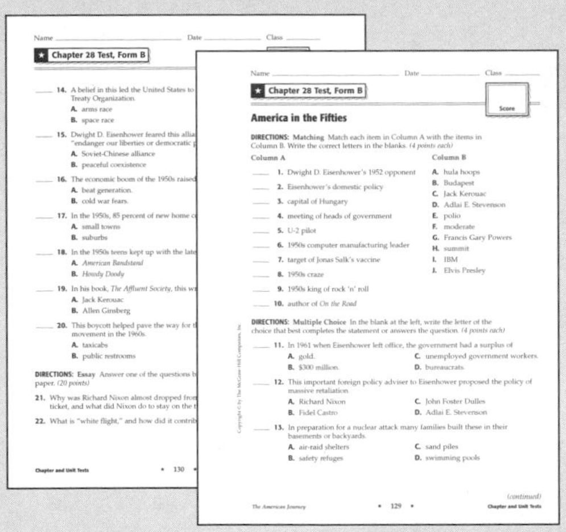
Chapter 28 Test, Form B
America in the Fifties

Performance Assessment Activity 28

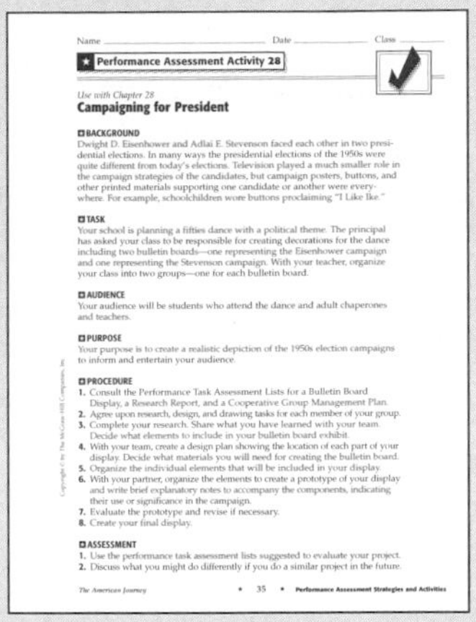
Performance Assessment Activity 28
Campaigning for President

Spanish Resources

The following Spanish language materials are available in the Spanish Resources binder:

- **Spanish Chapter Summary 28**
- **Spanish Vocabulary Activity 28**
- **Spanish Guided Reading Activities, Chapter 28**
- **Spanish Section Quizzes, Chapter 28**
- **Spanish Home Involvement Activity 28**
- **Spanish Chapter 28 Digests Audiocassette Activity and Test**

Activity Manipulatives

Help students learn more about America's cultural history with:

- **American Crafts Hands-On Activities**
- **American Games Hands-On Activities**
- **American History Flash Cards**

Additional Resources From Glencoe

- **Focus on American Art Prints,** *New York, New Haven and Hartford* by Edward Hopper
- **American Music Cultural Traditions,** Lesson 9: "Old Man Atom," "Rocket 88," "Rock Around the Clock"
- **U.S. History & Art,** Transparency 26, *Map;* Transparency 27, *Dawn;* Transparency 28, *The Family*
- **Political Cartoons,** *Two Views of the Atom Bomb, Twists and Turns in the Cold War*
- **U.S. Desk Map**
- **Outline Map Resource Book**
- **The American History Videodisc and CD-ROM,** *World War II and the Beginning of the Cold War, 1941–1960*

A&E HOME VIDEO. Biography™ THE HISTORY CHANNEL.

The following videotape programs are available from Glencoe as supplements to Chapter 28:

- **Dwight D. Eisenhower: Commander-in-Chief** (ISBN 1-56501-807-9)

To order, call Glencoe at 1-800-334-7344. To find classroom resources to accompany many of these videos, check the following home pages:
A&E Television: http://www.aetv.com
The History Channel: http://www.historychannel.com

Introducing CHAPTER 28

Chapter Themes

Chapter Themes are listed by section on this chapter opening page of the Student Edition. A corresponding theme-based activity is available under "FOCUS," and a theme-based question is asked in the Section and Chapter Reviews.

Performance Assessment

Refer to Activity 28 in the *Performance Assessment Strategies and Activities* booklet.

GLENCOE TECHNOLOGY

VIDEODISC
MindJogger Videoquiz

Use MindJogger to preview the Chapter 28 content.

Chapter 28
Disc 4, Side A

Also available in VHS.

HISTORY AND ART Have students analyze this painting, then ask them the following: **What is this girl doing?** *(babysitting on New Year's Eve)* **What articles of her clothing reveal that it is the 1950s?** *(bobby socks, saddle shoes, and so on)*

Chapter 28

1953–1960

America in the Fifties

Why It's Important

The prosperity of the 1950s raised questions that remain important in American society today. First, can a period of economic growth bring benefits to all Americans—or are some groups likely to be excluded? Second, can the nation's economic growth be guided by cultural and social values—or does growth occur at the expense of those values? Americans in the 1950s discussed these issues and still debate them today.

Chapter Themes

- *Section 1,* Economic Factors
- *Section 2,* Science and Technology
- *Section 3,* Continuity and Change
- *Section 4,* Groups and Institutions

HISTORY AND ART ***Happy New Year* by Ben Prins** The 1950s was a unique period in American life. Steady economic growth and new technology gave birth to new forms of leisure for many Americans.

EXTRA CREDIT PROJECT

Evaluating Reporting It is one thing to read, in retrospect, about events of this era—but how were these events reported in their day? As students read Chapter 28, have them use the microfilm/microfiche resources of the library to look for newspaper or magazine articles from this time. Topics may include (but are not limited to) the following:

- the defeat of Stevenson in 1952
- *Sputnik's* launch
- Castro's rise to power in Cuba
- the growth of urban ghettos
- the creation of SEATO
- school desegregation
- the building of Levittown
- rock 'n' roll music

Ask students to comment upon the attitudes revealed in the coverage.

1950 — 1955 — 1960

1952 Eisenhower is elected president

1953 Oveta Culp Hobby heads HEW

1956 Congress passes the Federal Highway Act

1959 Alaska and Hawaii enter the Union

Section 1

Eisenhower's Domestic Policy

READ TO DISCOVER . . .

- why Republicans won the election of 1952.
- what beliefs and policies characterized Eisenhower Republicanism.

TERMS TO LEARN

moderate

surplus

The Storyteller

"He merely has to smile at you, and you trust him at once." These words were used to describe Dwight D. Eisenhower, Republican presidential candidate in 1952. Eisenhower had an appeal that went far beyond his party label. His performance in World War II had made him an unquestioned hero in the eyes of almost every American. Above all, his personality and political style made many people feel safe, comfortable, and confident.

Campaign button and woman's compact

By 1952 Harry S Truman faced widespread dissatisfaction with his presidency. Many Americans were frustrated over the stalemated war in Korea and worried about reports of Communist subversion in government. As Truman's popularity sank, Republicans saw a chance to recapture the White House.

Republican Revival

To the Democrats' relief, Truman decided not to run for reelection. The Democrats nominated the respected governor of Illinois, **Adlai E. Stevenson,** for president and Senator John J. Sparkman of Alabama as his running mate.

To head their presidential ticket, the Republicans chose General **Dwight D. Eisenhower**—the popular World War II hero. For vice president, the Republicans selected **Richard M. Nixon,** a young senator from California who had won fame as a tough opponent of communism.

Biography

Soldier Turned Politician

Born in Texas and raised in rural Kansas, Dwight D. Eisenhower graduated from the United States Military Academy at West Point. He rose steadily through the army to become supreme

SECTION RESOURCES

Reproducible Masters

- Reproducible Lesson Plan 28–1
- Guided Reading Activity 28–1
- Section Quiz 28–1
- Reteaching Activity 28–1
- Enrichment Activity 28–1

Transparencies

- Section Focus Transparency 28–1

Multimedia

- Vocabulary PuzzleMaker
- Chapter Challenger Interactive Review Software
- Testmaker
- The Presidents: A Picture History of Our Nation

1 FOCUS

BELLRINGER
Motivational Activity

Before taking roll at the beginning of the class period, project Section Focus Transparency 28–1 and have students answer the questions. Discuss students' responses.

This activity is also available as a blackline master.

Section Focus Transparency 28–1

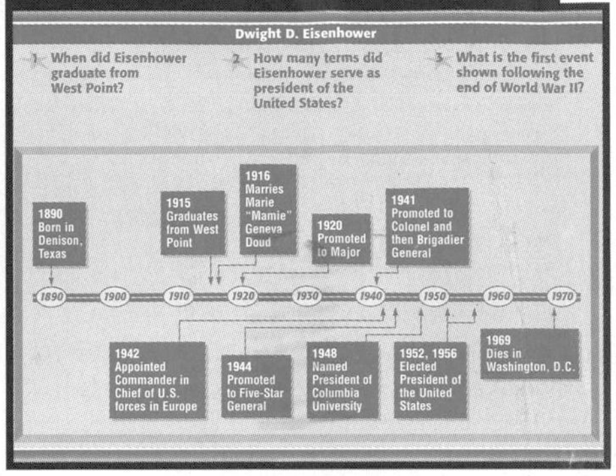

Vocabulary Precheck

Point out that *moderate* comes from the Latin for "measurement." Discuss how being politically moderate requires keeping a measured distance from left-wing and right-wing extremes.

Use the **Vocabulary PuzzleMaker** to create crossword and word search puzzles.

Section Theme
Economic Factors

President Eisenhower followed a conservative domestic economic policy but also promoted the largest public works program in America's history.

Activity Have students share what they know or feel about today's national debt. Then introduce Section 1 by pointing out that there was a time, not so long ago, when the government actually had a surplus.

2 TEACH

L1 Selecting a President Ask students what kind of president they think Americans wanted in the early 1950s. *(someone who would make the country stable and secure)* As students read this section, tell them to focus on the type of leadership Americans received from President Eisenhower.

Guided Reading Activity 28–1

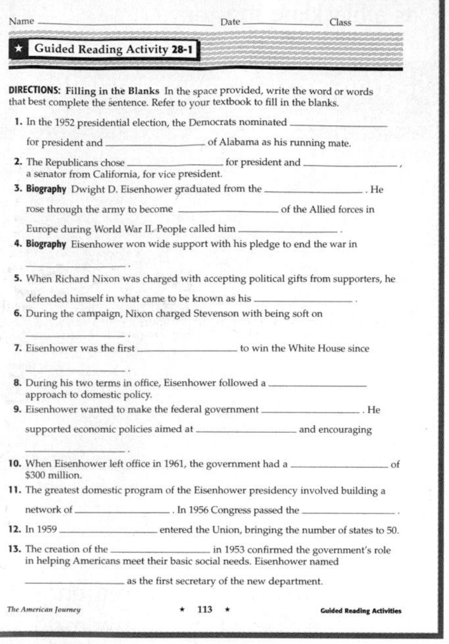

Name _____ Date _____ Class _____

Guided Reading Activity 28-1

DIRECTIONS: Filling in the Blanks In the space provided, write the word or words that best complete the sentence. Refer to your textbook to fill in the blanks.

1. In the 1952 presidential election, the Democrats nominated _____ for president and _____ of Alabama as his running mate.
2. The Republicans chose _____ for president and _____, a senator from California, for vice president.
3. **Biography** Dwight D. Eisenhower graduated from the _____. He rose through the army to become _____ of the Allied forces in Europe during World War II. People called him _____.
4. **Biography** Eisenhower won wide support with his pledge to end the war in _____.
5. When Richard Nixon was charged with accepting political gifts from supporters, he defended himself in what came to be known as his _____.
6. During the campaign, Nixon charged Stevenson with being soft on _____.
7. Eisenhower was the first _____ to win the White House since _____.
8. During his two terms in office, Eisenhower followed a _____ approach to domestic policy.
9. Eisenhower wanted to make the federal government _____. He supported economic policies aimed at _____ and encouraging _____.
10. When Eisenhower left office in 1961, the government had a _____ of $300 million.
11. The greatest domestic program of the Eisenhower presidency involved building a network of _____. In 1956 Congress passed the _____.
12. In 1959 _____ entered the Union, bringing the number of states to 50.
13. The creation of the _____ in 1953 confirmed the government's role in helping Americans meet their basic social needs. Eisenhower named _____ as the first secretary of the new department.

Copyright © by The McGraw-Hill Companies, Inc.

The American Journey ★ 113 ★ **Guided Reading Activities**

NATIONAL GEOGRAPHIC SOCIETY

CD-ROM
The Presidents: A Picture History of Our Nation

Have students select President Eisenhower from the main menu and the category Game. Suggest students play the presidential game with a partner.

3 ASSESS

Assign Section 1 Review as homework or as an in-class activity.

Use **Chapter Challenger Interactive Review Software** to review Section 1.

Republican and Democratic presidential candidates, 1952

commander of the Allied forces in Europe during World War II. People called him Ike—and they trusted him. His warmth and sincerity attracted many voters.

Eisenhower's steadiness made Americans feel secure. He won wide support with his pledge to "bring the Korean War to an early and honorable end. If that job requires a personal trip to Korea," he declared, "I shall make that trip."

A Brief Crisis

The Republicans faced a brief crisis during the presidential campaign when the story broke that Richard Nixon had accepted political gifts from supporters. Nixon went on television to defend himself in what came to be known as the "Checkers" speech. He proclaimed that he had done nothing wrong and had kept only one gift—his family dog, Checkers. The speech won broad support for Nixon, persuading Eisenhower to keep him on the ticket.

The Democratic Candidate

Intelligent and often witty, Adlai Stevenson became a target of the Republican Party. Nixon unleashed harsh attacks on Stevenson, charging him with being "soft" on communism. Republicans claimed Stevenson was more concerned with intellectual matters than with practical matters. They said that he questioned too many things and lacked the decisiveness needed to combat communism.

Landslide Republican Victory

In November 1952, Americans elected Eisenhower to the presidency in a landslide victory—the first Republican to win the White House since 1928. Far more people voted in 1952 than in any previous presidential election. Eisenhower collected more than 6 million more popular votes than Stevenson and carried the electoral college 442 to 89. The Republicans also won control of Congress. The election seemed to usher in a new era in national politics.

Eisenhower in Office

Although Eisenhower had little political experience, he proved to be an effective politician. During his two terms in office, Eisenhower followed a **moderate,** or middle-of-the-road, approach to domestic policy. He described himself as "conservative when it comes to money and liberal when it comes to human beings."

Eisenhower helped steer the country on a steady course. He avoided ambitious new government programs but resisted the pressure to abolish popular older ones and sometimes even expanded them. As he once told reporters:

> "I feel pretty good when I'm attacked from both sides. It makes me more certain I'm on the right track."

Economic Policy

President Eisenhower wanted to make the federal government "smaller rather than bigger." He supported economic policies aimed at limiting government spending and encouraging private enterprise. With the support of Republicans and conservative Democrats in Congress, the president removed the wage and price controls that the Truman administration had established during the Korean War. He also managed to transfer some authority in financial matters to the states and to make some cuts in government spending. When he left office in 1961, the federal budget had a **surplus,** or excess, of $300 million.

COOPERATIVE LEARNING ACTIVITY

Analyzing Moderation President Eisenhower was a political moderate. Help students examine how moderate views were reflected in his presidency. Organize the class into groups of six students—three sets of partners—each. As all members of each group review Section 1, have one set of partners look for ways in which Eisenhower cut back on programs or policies, another set of partners look for ways in which he expanded upon programs or policies or introduced new ones, and the third set of partners look for programs or policies that he left unchanged. As groups compare their answers, ask them if they agree with Eisenhower's comment that he was "conservative when it comes to money and liberal when it comes to human beings."

The Nation Expands

The greatest domestic program of the Eisenhower presidency involved building a network of interstate highways. In June 1956 Congress passed the **Federal Highway Act** to provide easy transportation for military forces in case of an attack. The law funded the construction of more than 40,000 miles (64,000 km) of highways that tied the nation together. The highway program—the largest public works program in the nation's history—also spurred growth in many areas of the nation's economy, including the automobile and oil industries.

The nation itself also grew during Eisenhower's presidency. In 1959 **Alaska** and **Hawaii** entered the Union, bringing the number of states to 50. Alaska and Hawaii became the only states not bordering on the other states.

Social Programs

Eisenhower believed that government should protect the basic welfare of Americans. He refused to tamper with Social Security and other New Deal social programs. During his presidency, Eisenhower agreed to extend Social Security benefits to 10 million more people and to provide unemployment insurance to 4 million more Americans. He also approved greater funding for public housing and, in 1955, Eisenhower agreed to an increase in the minimum wage from 75 cents an hour to $1.00.

The creation of the **Department of Health, Education, and Welfare** (HEW) in 1953 confirmed the government's role in helping Americans meet their basic social needs. Eisenhower named **Oveta Culp Hobby** as the first secretary of the new department. Hobby was only the second woman in American history to hold a cabinet post.

Eisenhower's moderation and leadership won the approval of a majority of Americans. In the 1956 presidential election, he ran against Democrat Adlai Stevenson again. This time Eisenhower won by an even bigger margin, receiving more than 57 percent of the popular vote.

America's FLAGS

Stars and Stripes Today Statehood for Alaska and Hawaii brought the number of stars to 50 (its current number) in the flag of 1960.

Section 1 Review

Checking for Understanding

1. ***Identify*** Adlai E. Stevenson, Dwight D. Eisenhower, Richard M. Nixon, Federal Highway Act, Oveta Culp Hobby.
2. ***Define*** moderate, surplus.
3. ***Name*** the two states added to the Union while Eisenhower was president.

Reviewing Themes

4. **Economic Factors** What public works program spurred growth in the automotive and oil industries?

Critical Thinking

5. **Analyzing Primary Sources** How did Eisenhower's domestic policy reflect his belief that he was "conservative when it comes to money and liberal when it comes to human beings"?

Activity

Drawing a Cartoon Draw a cartoon describing the phrase *middle-of-the-road* as it applies to politics.

Section 1 Review Answers

1. Adlai E. Stevenson, 797; Dwight D. Eisenhower, 797; Richard M. Nixon, 797; Federal Highway Act, 799; Oveta Culp Hobby, 799
2. The words are defined in the Glossary.
3. Hawaii and Alaska
4. the Federal Highway Act
5. Students should mention that Eisenhower was very careful when it came to spending government money on new programs, but he was willing to keep and expand existing social programs to ensure the welfare of American citizens.

Activity Cartoon definitions should describe someone who takes the middle ground in politics—not too conservative and not too liberal.

CHAPTER 28
Section 1, 797–799

Section Quiz 28-1

Name ______ Date ______ Class ______

★ Chapter 28 — Score

Section Quiz 28-1

DIRECTIONS: Matching Match each item in Column A with the items in Column B. Write the correct letters in the blanks. *(10 points each)*

Column A	Column B
____ 1. Dwight D. Eisenhower's running mate	A. Adlai E. Stevenson
____ 2. 1952 Democratic presidential candidate	B. Federal Highway Act
____ 3. excess	C. Oveta Culp Hobby
____ 4. funded 40,000 miles of roads	D. surplus
____ 5. HEW secretary	E. Richard Nixon

DIRECTIONS: Multiple Choice In the blank at the left, write the letter of the choice that best completes the statement or answers the question. *(10 points each)*

____ 6. This kept Richard Nixon on the Republican ticket in 1952.
A. end of the war C. the "Checkers" speech
B. television commercials D. his work for Joseph McCarthy

____ 7. During his two terms in office, Dwight D. Eisenhower followed this approach to domestic policy.
A. moderate C. radical
B. conservative D. reactionary

____ 8. President Eisenhower supported economic policies aimed at
A. limiting government spending. C. discouraging private enterprise.

Reteaching Activity 28-1

Name ______ Date ______ Class ______

★ Reteaching Activity 28-1

DIRECTIONS: Organizing Facts Follow the directions in the chart to create a profile of Dwight D. Eisenhower and his presidency.

Dwight D. Eisenhower	
I. Fill in the information for each of these items related to Eisenhower.	
Education	
Military Experience	
Nickname	
Political Party	
Vice President	
Election Opponent	
II. Make a check next to Eisenhower's policies, beliefs, and actions.	
A. Followed a moderate approach to domestic policy	
B. Avoided ambitious new government programs	
C. Abolished popular old programs	
D. Wanted to make the federal government bigger	
E. Removed wage and price controls	
F. Believed the government should protect the basic welfare of Americans	
G. Made drastic changes in Social Security and other New Deal programs to reduce their effectiveness	
H. Approved an increase in minimum wage	
III. Answer the following questions about major events and accomplishments of the Eisenhower administration.	
A. The Department of Health, Education, and Welfare (1953)	

Enrichment Activity 28-1

Name ______ Date ______ Class ______

★ Enrichment Activity 28-1 ★

Names of States

State names have many different origins that reflect the variety of people and cultures that make up the United States.

DIRECTIONS: Using Context Clues Match each origin of a state name with one of the state names in the box.

Georgia	Nevada	Tennessee	Indiana	Louisiana
Pennsylvania	Arizona	Alaska	Hawaii	Michigan

1. ______ After a Cherokee village called *tanasi*
2. ______ From its people's native word *hawaiki* or *owhyhee*, which means "homeland"
3. ______ From an Aztec word, *arizuma*, which means "having silver"
4. ______ For King George II of England, who granted a charter for the founding of the colony
5. ______ Adopted by the Russians from an Aleutian word *alakshak*, or "land that is not an island"
6. ______ From a Chippewa word *micigama*, meaning "great water"
7. ______ For the French King Louis XIV

4 CLOSE

Have students brainstorm a list of ways in which the United States and its people prospered during the Eisenhower administration.

1 FOCUS

BELLRINGER
Motivational Activity

Before taking roll at the beginning of the class period, project Section Focus Transparency 28–2 and have students answer the questions. Discuss students' responses.

This activity is also available as a blackline master.

Section Focus Transparency 28–2

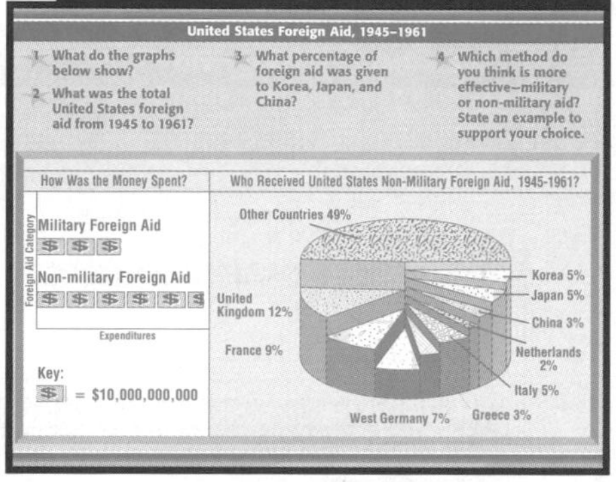

Vocabulary Precheck

Write the entries listed in **Terms to Learn** on the chalkboard. Call on volunteers to restate each definition in their own words.

Use the **Vocabulary PuzzleMaker** to create crossword and word search puzzles.

Section Theme
Science and Technology

During the Eisenhower administration, tensions between the United States and the Soviet Union were demonstrated in competing technologies as well as in political conflicts.

Activity Have students discuss the term *peaceful coexistence,* suggesting situations that call for the need for it and ways to tell that it is working.

1957 The Soviets launch *Sputnik*

1958 NASA launches the *Explorer*

1959 Fidel Castro takes over Cuba

1960 Soviets shoot down U.S. U-2 plane

Section 2

Eisenhower and the Cold War

READ TO DISCOVER . . .

- what characterized American foreign policy under President Eisenhower.
- what foreign policy challenges the Eisenhower administration faced.

TERMS TO LEARN

arms race
domino theory
summit
peaceful coexistence

The Storyteller

On October 4, 1957, millions of Americans heard startling news: the Soviets had launched a satellite known as *Sputnik.* That evening, Lyndon B. Johnson took a walk on his Texas ranch. His eyes focused on the clear night sky for any sign of the Soviet spacecraft. "In the Open West you learn to live closely with the sky," Johnson wrote later. "It is a part of your life. But now, somehow, in some new way, the sky seemed almost alien. . . ."

Card game

On October 4, 1957, the Soviet Union stunned the world with an announcement that it had sent into space the world's first artificial satellite—called *Sputnik.* A month later, the Soviets successfully launched a second satellite.

Americans read the news with horror and awe. They feared that the United States was lagging behind the Soviets in scientific knowledge. They also feared that the Soviets could launch atomic weapons against America from space.

Worry turned to embarrassment in December 1957, when the United States tried to launch its own space satellite—*Vanguard.* Hundreds of reporters and spectators watched the rocket rise a few feet off the launching pad—and then explode. The foreign press made fun of the launch, calling it "Flopnik" and "Stayputnik." American prestige declined.

United States–Soviet Rivalry

During the 1950s the United States–Soviet rivalry kept the cold war at the center of American foreign policy. The Eisenhower administration continued to oppose the spread of communism. At the same time, the president looked for ways to keep American-Soviet tensions from erupting into open conflict.

SECTION RESOURCES

Reproducible Masters
- Reproducible Lesson Plan 28–2
- Guided Reading Activity 28–2
- Political Cartoons, *Two Views of the Atom Bomb, Twists and Turns in the Cold War*
- Section Quiz 28–2
- Reteaching Activity 28–2
- Enrichment Activity 28–2

Transparencies
- Section Focus Transparency 28–2

Multimedia
- Vocabulary PuzzleMaker
- Chapter Challenger Interactive Review
- Testmaker
- ABCNews Interactive™ Communism and the Cold War

New Foreign Policy

Secretary of State **John Foster Dulles** became Eisenhower's most important foreign policy adviser. Dulles condemned the containment policy of the Truman administration. Eisenhower and Dulles proposed a new, bolder policy. If the Soviet Union attacked any nation, the United States would launch **massive retaliation**—an instant nuclear attack. Vice President Nixon explained:

> "Rather than let the Communists nibble us to death all over the world in little wars, we will rely in the future on massive mobile retaliatory [attacking] powers."

Dulles believed that the United States had to use threats to push the Soviets to the brink of war before they would agree to anything. Critics called this tough stance "brinkmanship." The more cautious Eisenhower, however, almost always avoided taking crises to "the brink."

By relying more on nuclear weapons, the Eisenhower administration could reduce other areas of defense, such as the size of the army and the arsenal of **conventional,** or non-nuclear, weapons. These reductions would allow Eisenhower to cut the military budget. As Secretary of Defense Charles Wilson explained, nuclear weapons gave the United States "more bang for the buck."

The Arms Race

Despite Eisenhower's intentions, defense spending increased again. The policy of massive retaliation—and Soviet efforts to counter it—produced a nuclear **arms race.** Both the United States and the Soviet Union built more and more weapons in an effort to surpass the other's military strength.

The superpowers built immensely destructive hydrogen bombs—nuclear weapons that were many times more powerful than atomic bombs. They developed a variety of guided missiles capable of delivering nuclear warheads. The **intermediate-range ballistic missile** (IRBM) could reach targets up to 1,500 miles (2,414 km) away. The **intercontinental ballistic missile** (ICBM) had a range of many thousands of miles. Soon both sides had massive nuclear arsenals capable of destroying the other side many times over.

Picturing HISTORY During the 1950s, the intercontinental ballistic missile (ICBM) became part of the arsenals of the United States and the Soviet Union. **Why were missiles developed?**

As the arms race continued, Americans began preparing for a nuclear attack. The federal **Civil Defense Administration** educated the public with pamphlets and radio and television messages. Some families built air-raid shelters in their basements or backyards. Schools held air-raid drills. One student described his school's air-raid drill: "Students lie on the floor and stick their heads under the lockers." He later recalled that he believed this would make him safe during a nuclear attack.

Competing in Space

The Soviet launch of *Sputnik* and the *Vanguard* failure led America to develop its own space program. Federal money poured into the **National Aeronautics and Space Administration (NASA),**

COOPERATIVE LEARNING ACTIVITY

Preparing a News Report Have students prepare a hypothetical television news special about the 1956 crisis in the Suez. Ask students to focus on Arab-Israeli tensions. Coverage could include the following:

- Background information about the founding of Israel and its effect upon the Arab states
- Maps showing the countries involved and the invasion of the Sinai Peninsula
- Interviews with spokespersons for the Egyptian and United States governments
- A commentary about this conflict's effects upon United States–Soviet tensions

Students may serve in their groups as researchers and writers, interviewers, artists, program hosts, and so on.

2 TEACH

L1 Reviewing Policies Remind students that the policy of containment began during Truman's administration. **Ask: What was the policy of containment?** *(It was the plan for the United States to do whatever was necessary to keep communism from spreading.)* Have students look for ways that President Eisenhower also tried to contain communism.

Picturing HISTORY While the United States delayed its missile program until a smaller warhead was devised, the Soviet Union developed a huge rocket capable of delivering a large warhead. The Soviets first tested an ICBM in September 1957, more than a year before the Americans did.
Answer: *to deliver nuclear warheads to their targets*

Guided Reading Activity 28–2

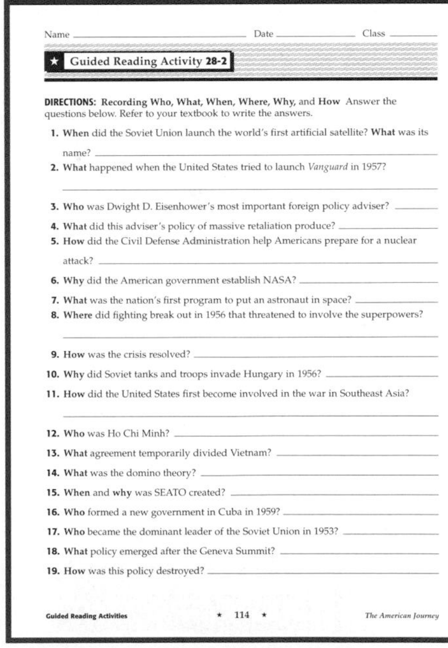

Name ________ Date ________ Class ________

Guided Reading Activity 28-2

DIRECTIONS: Recording Who, What, When, Where, Why, and **How** Answer the questions below. Refer to your textbook to write the answers.

1. **When** did the Soviet Union launch the world's first artificial satellite? **What** was its name? ________
2. **What** happened when the United States tried to launch *Vanguard* in 1957? ________
3. **Who** was Dwight D. Eisenhower's most important foreign policy adviser? ________
4. **What** did this adviser's policy of massive retaliation produce? ________
5. **How** did the Civil Defense Administration help Americans prepare for a nuclear attack? ________
6. **Why** did the American government establish NASA? ________
7. **What** was the nation's first program to put an astronaut in space? ________
8. **Where** did fighting break out in 1956 that threatened to involve the superpowers? ________
9. **How** was the crisis resolved? ________
10. **Why** did Soviet tanks and troops invade Hungary in 1956? ________
11. **How** did the United States first become involved in the war in Southeast Asia? ________
12. **Who** was Ho Chi Minh? ________
13. **What** agreement temporarily divided Vietnam? ________
14. **What** was the domino theory? ________
15. **When** and **why** was SEATO created? ________
16. **Who** formed a new government in Cuba in 1959? ________
17. **Who** became the dominant leader of the Soviet Union in 1953? ________
18. **What** policy emerged after the Geneva Summit? ________
19. **How** was this policy destroyed? ________

Guided Reading Activities ★ 114 ★ *The American Journey*

When? Who? What? Where?

A Decade of Stockpiling In 1950 the United States had 350 nuclear warheads and the Soviet Union had 5. By 1960 the United States had 18,700 nuclear weapons and the Soviet Union had 1,700.

CHAPTER 28
Section 2, 800–805

ABCNEWS INTERACTIVE™

VIDEODISC
Communism and the Cold War

Side 1, Chapter 14
Title: Sputnik *Launches the Space Race*
Subject: The beginning of the space race
Ask: **Why did the United States panic when the Soviet Union unveiled *Sputnik?*** *(because the U.S. feared that the enemy was more technologically advanced)*

Political Cartoons, *Two Views of the Atom Bomb, Twists and Turns in the Cold War*

Map Study

Answers
1. East Germany, Czechoslovakia, Bulgaria, and Albania
2. the Soviet Union

Map Skills Practice

Reading a Map Which nonaligned countries bordered on both a NATO nation and a Warsaw Pact nation? *(Austria, Yugoslavia, and Finland)*

Linking PAST & PRESENT

H-Bomb Comment Edward Teller, the chief developer of the hydrogen bomb, advocated more testing of such weapons. He said, "It won't be until the bombs get so big that they can annihilate everything that people will really become terrified and begin to take a reasonable line in politics."

the new government agency in charge of the space program. When the United States succeeded in launching the *Explorer* satellite in January 1958, the Associated Press reported:

> "The missile took off in a beautiful launching. It rose slowly at first in a huge splash of flame with a roar that could be heard for miles. . . ."

The **space race** had begun, and the United States soon began pulling ahead. **Project Mercury** was the nation's first program to put an astronaut in space. Along with its commitment to space exploration and scientific research, the government also encouraged science education by providing more funds for the teaching of science and technology in the nation's schools.

Foreign Policy Challenges

With the stakes in the nuclear arms race so high, the United States and the Soviet Union had to act carefully. A minor crisis, badly managed, could lead to all-out war.

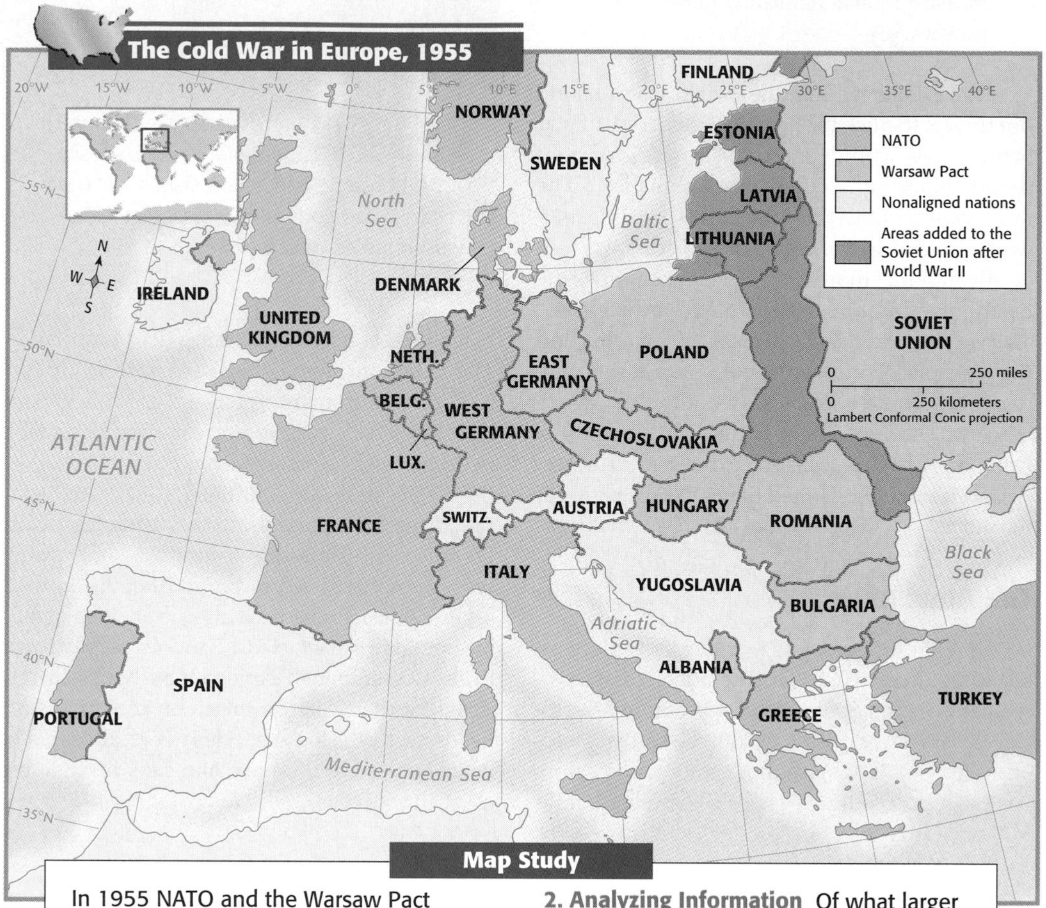

Map Study

In 1955 NATO and the Warsaw Pact divided Europe.

1. **Location** Which Warsaw Pact nations bordered NATO nations?
2. **Analyzing Information** Of what larger nation were Estonia, Latvia, and Lithuania a part?

MULTIPLE LEARNING STYLES

Kinesthetic According to the domino theory, if one nation in Asia was taken over by communism, other nations could be next. Ask students to demonstrate the domino theory by first labeling real dominoes with names of countries in Asia, Europe, and Africa. Students should then set up a display of the dominoes in the order that American leaders thought communism would take hold. Knock over one domino that will topple them all. Encourage students to be creative and make sure that they explain the meaning of the domino theory in their own words. **L1**

★ ★ ★ ★ ★ ★ ★ ★ ★ ★ ★ ★ ★ ★ ★ ★

Crisis in the Middle East

Trouble arose first in the Middle East. Tensions there had remained high ever since Arab states attacked Israel soon after its founding in 1948. Because the United States backed Israel while the Soviet Union maintained ties with the Arab states, a Middle East conflict threatened to involve the superpowers.

Fighting did break out in the Middle East in 1956, when Egyptian president **Gamal Abdel Nasser** nationalized, or brought under government control, the **Suez Canal** from British control. Great Britain and France feared that Nasser might close the canal and cut off shipments of oil between the Middle East and Western Europe. In October, the two European powers invaded Egypt. Great Britain and France hoped to overthrow Nasser and seize the canal. Israel, angered by repeated Arab attacks along its borders, agreed to help by invading Egypt.

The United States immediately sponsored a United Nations resolution calling for British and French withdrawal from Egypt. The Soviets threatened rocket attacks on British and French cities. In the face of this pressure, the three nations pulled out of Egypt. United Nations forces were sent to patrol the Egyptian-Israeli border.

Uprising in Hungary

Another crisis erupted that fall in Europe. In October 1956, students and workers demonstrated in **Budapest,** the capital of **Hungary,** for changes in the government. Strikes and riots soon spread throughout the country. A new government came to power and demanded withdrawal of all Soviet troops from Hungary. Early in

Picturing HISTORY Hungarians topple a statue of Soviet dictator Joseph Stalin during demonstrations in 1956. **How did the Hungarian uprising end?**

November, Soviet tanks and troops poured into Hungary and crushed the revolt. Hungarian rebels appealed to the United States for help. President Eisenhower condemned the Soviet crackdown and aided Hungarian refugees but did not intervene.

War in Southeast Asia

Another trouble spot appeared in Southeast Asia, in France's former colony of **Vietnam.** In the early 1950s, the United States gave France billions of dollars in military aid to help it fight the **Vietminh,** nationalist rebels led by Communist leader **Ho Chi Minh.**

In spite of American aid, the French soon faced defeat. In March 1954, Vietminh forces trapped 25,000 French troops at the French base of **Dien Bien Phu.** The French pleaded with the United States to send American forces, but Eisenhower refused. The Korean War was still fresh in his memory. "I can conceive of no greater tragedy," he said, "than for the United States to become engaged in all-out war in Indochina."

Without American troops, the French were forced to surrender in May. Soon after, French and Vietminh representatives in **Geneva,** Switzerland, negotiated a cease-fire agreement. The agreement, known as the **Geneva Accords,** temporarily divided Vietnam. The Vietminh

Footnotes to History

Bomb Goes Airborne On May 21, 1956, the world's first airborne hydrogen bomb was exploded. This explosion was part of a new series of nuclear tests in the Pacific conducted by the U.S. Atomic Energy Commission.

Picturing HISTORY The Hungarian protesters took up arms against their government and had a very brief victory. On October 30, 1956, Budapest radio told the Hungarians, "You have won!" For five days the capital was free—and then the Soviet tanks came. **Ask:** **How did the United States assist the Hungarians?** *(The United States gave aid to refugees from Hungary but nothing more.)*
Answer: *The Soviet military came in and crushed the Hungarian revolt.*

you don't say...

Accord The root of *accord* is the Latin word for "heart." Political accords, then, assume that the participants share the same "heart" for reaching their goal—an assumption that, unfortunately, sometimes proves not to be true.

ABCNEWS INTERACTIVE™

VIDEODISC
Communism and the Cold War

Side 1, Chapter 6
Title: *The Arms Race*
Subject: Development of the arms race between the United States and the Soviet Union
Ask: **What was the "arms race"?** *(a competition between the United States and the Soviet Union in the development of high-tech weaponry)*

MAKING CONNECTIONS ACTIVITY

Technology The term *arms race* brings pictures of bombs and bullets to mind. During this era, however, the concept also included technological advances in weapons *delivery* systems—in particular, airplanes and submarines. Ask interested students to research and report on several of these advances (for example, increases in air speed, transpolar submarine voyages, and the ability of both planes and submarines to travel longer distances without stopping to refuel). As students present their findings (with illustrations, if they wish), encourage them to explain how these advances gave an edge to the superpower that achieved them first. **L3**

Picturing HISTORY This exchange between Nixon and Khrushchev became most heated in a model American kitchen—and before television cameras. A casual conversation quickly escalated to the possibility of war over the situation in Berlin. Khrushchev complained, "You don't know anything about Communism except fear of it." Nixon cautioned the Soviet leader that "if war comes, we both lose." **Ask: Who was Khrushchev's predecessor?** *(Joseph Stalin)*
Answer: *The Soviet downing of an American U-2 spy plane and capture of its pilot ended the "thaw."*

3 ASSESS

Assign Section 2 Review as homework or as an in-class activity.

Use **Chapter Challenger Interactive Review Software** to review Section 2.

Section Quiz 28–2

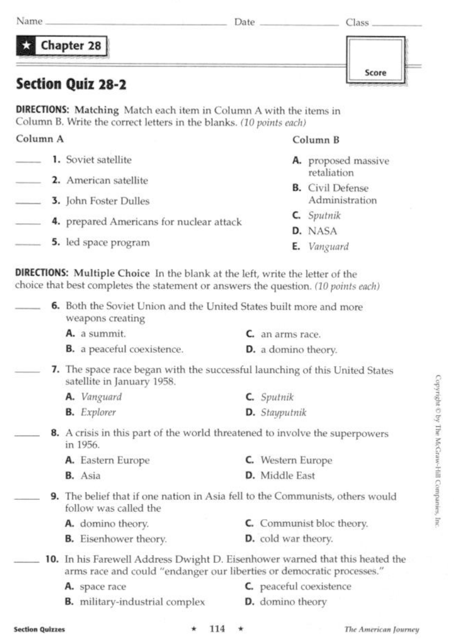

Name ______ Date ______ Class ______

Chapter 28 — Score

Section Quiz 28-2

DIRECTIONS: Matching Match each item in Column A with the items in Column B. Write the correct letters in the blanks. *(10 points each)*

Column A	Column B
____ **1.** Soviet satellite	**A.** proposed massive retaliation
____ **2.** American satellite	**B.** Civil Defense Administration
____ **3.** John Foster Dulles	**C.** *Sputnik*
____ **4.** prepared Americans for nuclear attack	**D.** NASA
____ **5.** led space program	**E.** *Vanguard*

DIRECTIONS: Multiple Choice In the blank at the left, write the letter of the choice that best completes the statement or answers the question. *(10 points each)*

____ **6.** Both the Soviet Union and the United States built more and more weapons creating
A. a summit. **C.** an arms race.
B. a peaceful coexistence. **D.** a domino theory.

____ **7.** The space race began with the successful launching of this United States satellite in January 1958.
A. *Vanguard* **C.** *Sputnik*
B. *Explorer* **D.** *Stayputnik*

____ **8.** A crisis in this part of the world threatened to involve the superpowers in 1956.
A. Eastern Europe **C.** Western Europe
B. Asia **D.** Middle East

____ **9.** The belief that if one nation in Asia fell to the Communists, others would follow was called the
A. domino theory. **C.** Communist bloc theory.
B. Eisenhower theory. **D.** cold war theory.

____ **10.** In his Farewell Address Dwight D. Eisenhower warned that this heated the arms race and could "endanger our liberties or democratic processes."
A. space race **C.** peaceful coexistence
B. military-industrial complex **D.** domino theory

Section Quizzes ★ 114 ★ *The American Journey*

Copyright © by The McGraw-Hill Companies, Inc.

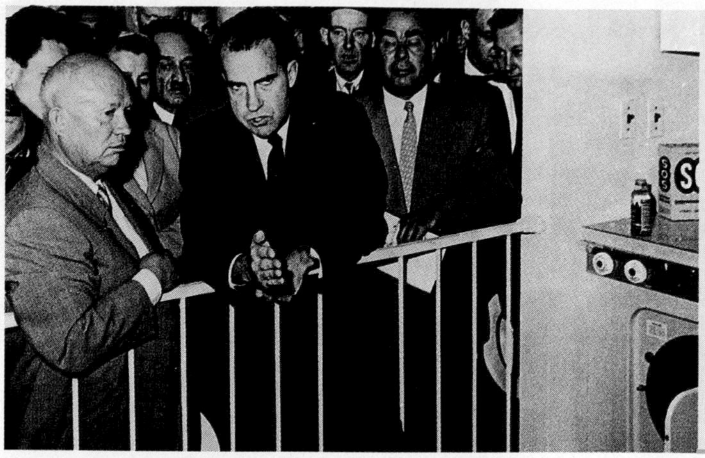

Picturing HISTORY During a 1959 visit to the Soviet Union, Vice President Nixon (center) debates issues with Soviet premier Khrushchev (left front) at the American Exhibition in Moscow. **What incident in 1960 ended hopes for a "thaw" between the two superpowers?**

controlled the north, while other Vietnamese—more friendly to the French—held the south. The accords also arranged for the withdrawal of all French troops and called for free elections in a reunited Vietnam in 1956.

Eisenhower believed that if one nation in Asia fell to the Communists, others would also fall, one after the other. He described the danger in what came to be called the **domino theory:**

> "You have a row of dominoes set up. You knock over the first one, and what will happen to the last one is that it will go over very quickly."

To keep South Vietnam from becoming the first domino, the United States aided its anti-Communist government, even though the rulers had little support among the people. In another step to defend against Communist aggression, the United States helped to create the **Southeast Asia Treaty Organization** (SEATO) in 1954. The United States, Great Britain, France, New Zealand, Australia, the Philippines, Pakistan, and Thailand made up the alliance. The nations pledged joint action against any aggressor.

Troubles in Latin America

The Eisenhower administration also faced Communist challenges in Latin America. In 1954 the **Central Intelligence Agency** (CIA) helped overthrow the government of Jacobo Arbenz in **Guatemala,** which some American leaders feared was leaning toward communism. Latin Americans resented the intervention in Guatemala, criticizing what they considered "Yankee imperialism." Growing anti-American feelings began to erode the Good Neighbor Policy established in the 1930s.

Anti-American feeling became a part of the growing revolutionary movement in **Cuba.** Following the overthrow of dictator Fulgencio Batista (buh•TEES•tuh), rebel leader **Fidel Castro** formed a new government in January 1959. The United States supported Castro at first and welcomed his promise of democratic reforms. But Castro angered Americans when he seized foreign-owned property. His government became a dictatorship and formed close ties with the Soviet Union. During the last days of his presidency in 1961, Eisenhower cut diplomatic ties with Cuba. Relations between the two nations have remained strained ever since.

Cold War "Thaws"

When Soviet dictator Joseph Stalin died in 1953, **Nikita Khrushchev** (krush•CHAWF) emerged as the dominant leader. By the mid-1950s, both American and Soviet leaders were interested in easing cold war tensions and improving relations.

CRITICAL THINKING ACTIVITY

Determining Cause and Effect To help students better grasp the world crises during the Eisenhower administration, have pairs or small groups of students select various events discussed in this section (for example, the anti-Communist uprising in Hungary, the nationalist rebellion in Vietnam, Castro's rise to power in Cuba, or the U-2 incident). For each event, have them create a diagram or flowchart that presents the event, some of its causes, and some of its results. Encourage comparisons of the finished diagrams, asking students to look for common threads in the events. **L2, ELL**

The Geneva Summit

In July 1955, Eisenhower, NATO leaders, and Soviet officials met at a summit conference in Geneva, Switzerland. A **summit** is a meeting of heads of government. The leaders discussed disarmament and German reunification. The meeting produced no specific agreements, but the friendly atmosphere, promptly called the "Spirit of Geneva," renewed hopes for peace.

Peaceful Coexistence

After the Geneva summit, a policy of **peaceful coexistence** began to emerge. This meant that the two superpowers would compete with one another but would avoid war. Khrushchev proposed to Eisenhower that the two leaders visit each other's country and attend another summit in **Paris** in 1960. Eisenhower agreed.

Khrushchev's 10-day trip to the United States in 1959 captured world headlines. As the leaders made plans for their next meeting in Paris, Eisenhower hoped to reach agreements on arms control and nuclear test bans.

The U-2 Incident

Hopes of peace fell to earth with an American plane. For years American pilots had flown high-altitude spy planes—**U-2s**—over Soviet territory to photograph Soviet nuclear sites and military bases. As the Paris summit approached, Eisenhower ordered a final U-2 flight over an area of the Soviet Union that had not been inspected for missile sites.

The Soviets shot down the plane on May 1, 1960 and captured its pilot, Francis Gary Powers. Khrushchev denounced the United States for invading Soviet airspace. Although the Paris summit began as scheduled on May 16, the mood had changed. Hauling along part of the wreckage of the U-2 plane, Khrushchev attacked the United States for the spy flights and called off Eisenhower's trip to the Soviet Union. The summit broke up the next day. The brief "thaw" in the cold war had ended.

Eisenhower's Warning

In his January 1961 Farewell Address to the nation, President Eisenhower issued a warning about the growing influence of the military. The military budget had grown dramatically, he said, and military leaders had allied with business to seek bigger and more expensive weapons. Eisenhower feared that this alliance—a **"military-industrial complex"**—heated the arms race and could "endanger our liberties or democratic processes." In a twist of history, this former army general warned the nation of the growing influence of the military.

Section 2 Review

Checking for Understanding

1. ***Identify*** Gamal Abdel Nasser, Ho Chi Minh, Dien Bien Phu, Geneva Accords, Fidel Castro, Nikita Khrushchev.
2. ***Define*** arms race, domino theory, summit, peaceful coexistence.
3. ***Explain*** why President Eisenhower was willing to send massive aid to Vietnam.

Reviewing Themes

4. **Science and Technology** How did the Soviet launch of *Sputnik* affect science and technology in the United States?

Critical Thinking

5. **Making Comparisons** How did the Eisenhower administration differ with Truman's view of foreign policy?

Activity

Making a Time Line Make a two-level time line tracking the achievements of the United States and Soviet Union in space from 1957 to 1967.

Section 2 Review Answers

1. Nasser, 803; Ho Chi Minh, 803; Dien Bien Phu, 803; Geneva Accords, 803; Castro, 804; Khrushchev, 804
2. The words are defined in the Glossary.
3. If Vietnam fell to Communists, Eisenhower thought other nations would follow.
4. It forced the United States to engage the Soviet Union in a "space race" and to do more scientific research. The U.S. also made a greater commitment to science and technology education in schools.
5. Eisenhower was rather cautious, but his policy was bolder than Truman's had been. Instead of containment, the policy included threats of massive nuclear retaliation to stop Soviet aggression.

Activity Time lines should show achievements in space between 1957 and 1967.

Reteaching Activity 28–2

Name ________ Date ________ Class ________

★ Reteaching Activity **28-2**

DIRECTIONS: Recognizing Causes and Effects After each *Cause,* write the letter of its *Effect* from the Fact Bank.

1. **Cause:** John Foster Dulles proposed a policy of massive retaliation.
   Effect: ________
2. **Cause:** The superpowers built immensely powerful hydrogen bombs.
   Effect: ________
3. **Cause:** The Soviet Union successfully launched the first artificial satellite.
   Effect: ________
4. **Cause:** President Gamal Abdel Nasser nationalized the Suez Canal.
   Effect: ________
5. **Cause:** Students and workers demonstrated in Budapest for changes in the government.
   Effect: ________
6. **Cause:** Dwight D. Eisenhower vividly recalled the tragedies of the Korean War.
   Effect: ________
7. **Cause:** The domino theory created fear among nations around the world.
   Effect: ________
8. **Cause:** Rebel leader Fidel Castro formed close ties to the Soviet Union.
   Effect: ________
9. **Cause:** Soviets shot down a U-2 plane and captured its pilot.
   Effect: ________
10. **Cause:** Military leaders allied with business to seek bigger, costlier weapons.
    Effect: ________

★FACT BANK

- **A.** Great Britain, France, and Israel invaded Egypt.
- **B.** SEATO was formed.
- **C.** Hungarian rebels appealed to the United States for help when the Soviets invaded the country.
- **D.** The president refused to send American troops to aid the French in Vietnam.
- **E.** The United States and the Soviet Union became involved in a nuclear arms race.
- **F.** Eisenhower warned the nation of a growing military influence.
- **G.** Eisenhower cut diplomatic ties to Cuba.
- **H.** Families built air-raid shelters and schools held air-raid drills as fear of a nuclear attack grew.
- **I.** Hopes of peaceful coexistence were destroyed.
- **J.** Funding for teaching of science and technology increased.

Enrichment Activity 28–2

Name ________ Date ________ Class ________

★ Enrichment Activity **28-2** ★ ★

Racing for Space

The space race resulted in the launching of many satellites in a short period of time. The time line shows the major launches made between 1957 and 1960 by the United States and the Soviet Union.

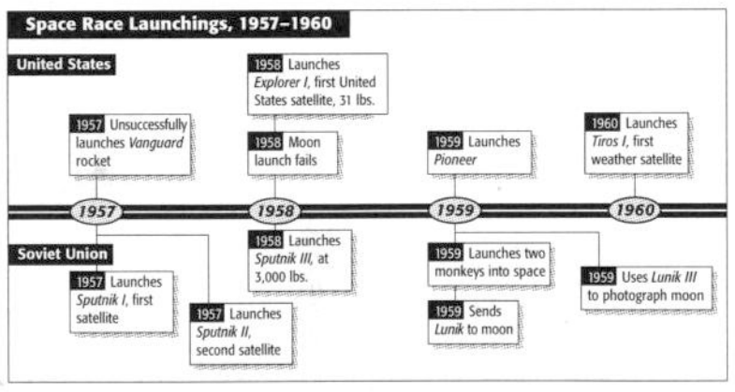

DIRECTIONS: Reading a Time Line Answer the following questions in the space provided.

1. How much heavier was the Soviet Union's 1958 satellite than the United States's satellite launched in the same year? ________
2. What were the first living things to be launched into space, and when did the launch take place? ________
3. When was the first United States weather satellite launched? ________
4. Which happened first, the successful launch of the first United States satellite or the launch of the second Soviet satellite? ________

Activity **DIRECTIONS:** Imagine that you are a newspaper reporter in 1960. Design a special feature on the space race, including drawings or photos, with captions; headlines; and text for the article. If possible, use the Internet or media center to locate information on the time line topics.

4 CLOSE

Have students use a map to locate the places named in this section.

Ask: Why was Eisenhower's administration on worldwide alert? *(Crises erupted in Europe, the Middle East, Southeast Asia, and Latin America.)*

INTERDISCIPLINARY

Activities

TEACH

Background

"I believe that this nation should commit itself to achieving a goal, before the decade is out, of landing a man on the moon and returning him safely to the earth." So said President John F. Kennedy in a 1961 message to Congress. In fact, he made that statement on the day that Alan B. Shepard, Jr., became the first American in space—just less than one month after the Soviet Union had put a cosmonaut into space. With Kennedy's declaration, the space race gathered momentum.

In the early 1960s, the Soviet Union consistently reached its milestones first (including first woman in space, first flight with more than one passenger, and first space walk). The United States reached Kennedy's goal first, however, achieving something in the Apollo 11 flight in 1969 that the Soviet Union never did.

In 1975 the two countries had their first joint mission, the Apollo-Soyuz Test Project. The two programs have continued to work together on occasion.

Have your students work individually or in groups to list "space goals" (for example, a mission to Mars or robots on Pluto) they would like to see met in the 21st century.

Team Teaching

These Interdisciplinary Activities provide an excellent opportunity for you to employ Team Teaching and collaboration in your classroom.

INTERDISCIPLINARY

Activities

The Space Race

When the first humans stood on the moon in 1969, it was a high point in the exploration of space and in the space race between the United States and the Soviet Union. Learn more about the early days of space flight as you complete these out-of-the-world activities.

Art

Picturing Other Worlds Movies and television have given us many pictures of space journeys and alien worlds. Use your imagination to paint a scene from outer space—the sun (or suns) rising on the surface of a distant planet, an alien civilization, or a space station. Use any medium you like—acrylics, watercolor, markers. Give your painting a title and display it in class.

Science

Designing a Science Experiment Most space flights today carry various experiments that test how organisms or machines work in space. Design a biology experiment for astronauts to take into space. Specify the kinds of organisms—plant or animal—that the experiment will involve and the information you hope to gain from it. How will these results be important on Earth? Write a description of your experiment to share with the rest of the class.

Astronaut in space

Language Arts

Writing Science Fiction Write a science fiction story whose central figure is traveling in space. Your story should focus on this character, not on space aliens or monsters, and explain the purpose of his or her space voyage. Remember to set your story in a specific location and time. Read your story to the class.

School-to-Work

Showing How Rockets Work What propels a rocket? You can demonstrate rocket propulsion with a balloon, a drinking straw, and a long cord. Push the cord through the straw, then anchor both ends of the cord on either side of the room. Blow up the balloon part way, holding the end tightly so air does not escape. Have another person use two pieces of tape to hang the balloon securely from the straw. Blow the balloon up all the way, then let go. Notice how far and how fast it travels along the cord.

School to WORK

Astronaut Students can learn more about rocket propulsion, space suits, and how to think like an astronaut. Have them contact the U.S. Space Camp®, U.S. Space & Rocket Center at One Tranquility Base, Huntsville, Alabama 35805.

MULTIPLE LEARNING STYLES

The activities included in the feature on this student edition page are ideally suited to meet the different learning styles of your students. These include:

- Art — **Picturing Other Worlds** visual/spatial learners
- Language Arts — **Writing Science Fiction** verbal/linguistic learners
- Science — **Designing a Science Experiment** logical/mathematical learners
- School-to-Work — **Showing How Rockets Work** kinesthetic learners

1945 1950 1955 1960

1947 William Levitt starts first suburban development

1955 Polio vaccine given to school children

1956 Elvis Presley gains national popularity

Section 3

1950s Prosperity

READ TO DISCOVER . . .

- what factors contributed to the booming economy of the 1950s.
- what effect the prosperity of the 1950s had on American society and culture.

TERMS TO LEARN

productivity
standard of living
per capita income
affluence
baby boom

The Storyteller

During the prosperous 1950s, many Americans left the cities to settle in the suburbs, hoping for a better life for themselves and their children. "Suburbia"—with its great distances between home, school, shopping area, and downtown—gradually became not only a place but also a lifestyle. One suburban resident observed: "Before we came here, we used to live pretty much to ourselves. . . . Now we stop around and visit people or they visit us. I really think [suburban living] has broadened us."

1950s children's board game

After World War II, many experts predicted America's economy would level off or decline as production of war goods decreased. Instead, after a few years of adjustment, the economy began to grow rapidly and steadily.

A Booming Economy

From 1945 to 1960, the total value of goods and services produced each year in the United States increased about 250 percent. Some of this amazing growth resulted from the burst of military spending during the Korean War. Government spending on housing, schools, welfare, highways, and veteran benefits also spurred the rapid economic expansion.

Technological advances contributed to economic growth as well. Business, industry, and agriculture adopted new technology and new production methods, resulting in greater **productivity**—the ability to produce more goods with the same amount of labor. The demand for new technology led to greater investment in research and in the education and training of scientists, engineers, and technicians.

The **computer** represented one of the 1950s' important technological advances. Unlike today's small personal computers, early computers were immense, weighing tons and filling whole rooms. Although first used only by the military and the government, computers soon appeared in large corporations. By 1955 International Business Machines (IBM) was the leader in the field, with orders for 129 of its big computers.

SECTION RESOURCES

Reproducible Masters

- Guided Reading Activity 28–3
- Section Quiz 28–3
- Reteaching Activity 28–3
- Enrichment Activity 28–3

Transparencies

- Section Focus Transparency 28–3
- U.S. History & Art, Transparencies 26, 27, 28

Multimedia

- Vocabulary PuzzleMaker
- Chapter Challenger Interactive Review
- Testmaker
- GTV: American People: Fabric of a Nation
- GTV: A Geographic Perspective on American History
- American Music Cultural Traditions
- Focus on American Art Prints

CHAPTER 28
Section 3, 807–812

1 FOCUS

BELLRINGER
Motivational Activity

Before taking roll at the beginning of the class period, project Section Focus Transparency 28–3 and have students answer the questions. Discuss students' responses.

This activity is also available as a blackline master.

Section Focus Transparency 28–3

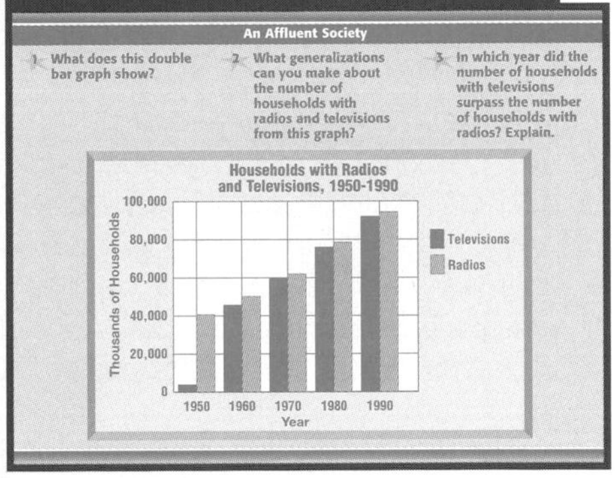

Vocabulary Precheck

Encourage students to think of symbols or other visuals to illustrate the **Terms to Learn,** such as a sack of money and a sports car to represent *affluence.*

Use the **Vocabulary Puzzle-Maker** to create crossword and word search puzzles.

Section Theme
Continuity and Change

The economic growth and prosperity of the 1950s transformed the social and cultural life of Americans.

Activity Ask students to list 10 things that make them happy. Then ask them to count how many things on their lists are material goods. As students read this section, have them focus on the ways that affluence affected American life during the 1950s.

CHAPTER 28

Section 3, 807–812

2 TEACH

L1 Discussing Key Terms Have students share what they know about the terms *baby boomers, suburbs, credit cards, television,* and *rock 'n' roll.*

Guided Reading Activity 28–3

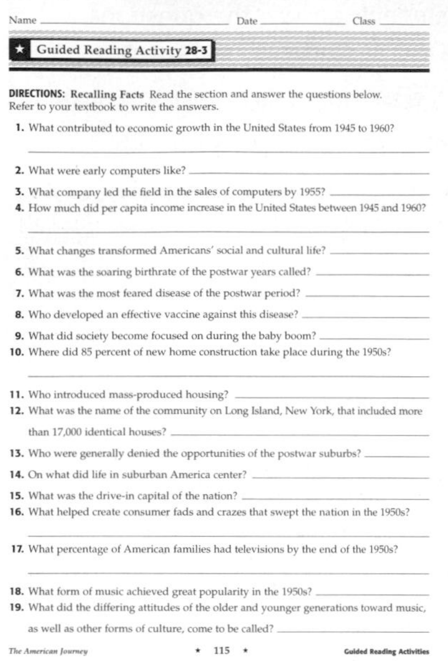

Name ____________ Date ________ Class ______

Guided Reading Activity 28-3

DIRECTIONS: Recalling Facts Read the section and answer the questions below. Refer to your textbook to write the answers.

1. What contributed to economic growth in the United States from 1945 to 1960?
2. What were early computers like?
3. What company led the field in the sales of computers by 1955?
4. How much did per capita income increase in the United States between 1945 and 1960?
5. What changes transformed Americans' social and cultural life?
6. What was the soaring birthrate of the postwar years called?
7. What was the most feared disease of the postwar period?
8. Who developed an effective vaccine against this disease?
9. What did society become focused on during the baby boom?
10. Where did 85 percent of new home construction take place during the 1950s?
11. Who introduced mass-produced housing?
12. What was the name of the community on Long Island, New York, that included more than 17,000 identical houses?
13. Who were generally denied the opportunities of the postwar suburbs?
14. On what did life in suburban America center?
15. What was the drive-in capital of the nation?
16. What helped create consumer fads and crazes that swept the nation in the 1950s?
17. What percentage of American families had televisions by the end of the 1950s?
18. What form of music achieved great popularity in the 1950s?
19. What did the differing attitudes of the older and younger generations toward music, as well as other forms of culture, come to be called?

The American Journey • 115 • **Guided Reading Activities**

CURRICULUM CONNECTION

SCIENCE

Between April and September 1955, approximately 6.5 million American children received the polio vaccine. Its success was so great that the American Medical Association called Salk's discovery "one of the greatest events in the history of medicine."

Graph Study

Answers

1. 20 percent
2. Suburban growth exploded, going from about 20 percent to about 65 percent.

Higher Incomes

The economic boom of the 1950s raised the **standard of living**—a measure of people's overall wealth and quality of life—of millions of Americans. Between 1945 and 1960, **per capita income**—the average income of every individual in the nation—increased 46 percent, from $1,515 to $2,219. By the end of the 1950s, Americans had the highest standard of living in the world.

A Rosy Future

Prosperity and steady economic growth also led to new optimism. Economists began to think it was possible to maintain prosperity and growth permanently. Americans felt confident that the government could, when necessary, take steps to avoid serious **recessions,** or downturns in the economy.

Where Americans Lived, 1901–1960

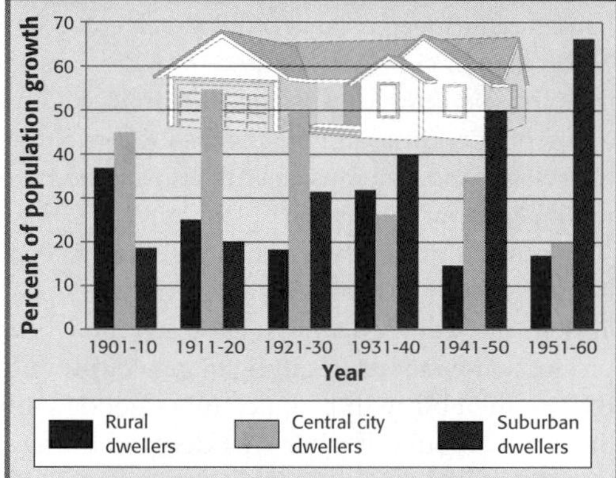

Source: *Bureau of the Census.*

Graph Study

Many Americans moved to the suburbs during the 1950s.

1. Between 1951 and 1960, what percentage of population growth was in the central cities?
2. **Comparing** How did the percentage of suburban dwellers change from 1920 to 1960?

A Changing Nation

Economic growth and prosperity brought many changes to America. These included a growth in population, increased **affluence,** or wealth, suburban expansion, and a greater demand for consumer goods.

The Baby Boom

Like the economy, the family enjoyed great growth during the postwar years. During the 1950s the nation's population rose from 150 million to 179 million, an increase of nearly 20 percent. People called the nation's soaring birthrate a **baby boom.**

Several factors encouraged the baby boom. Couples who had postponed having children during the Depression and World War II started having families. With higher incomes, couples felt they could afford to have more children. In addition, better health care for women and babies, improved nutrition, and medical advances against disease helped reduce the infant death rate.

The baby boom had a powerful impact on society. Many women left the workforce to stay home and raise their children. The demand for baby products and services grew, stimulating the economy. School enrollment soared as the "baby boomers" reached school age, putting a great strain on the educational system.

Medical Advances

By the early 1950s, medical science had made great strides toward combating childhood diseases. Antibiotics and vaccines helped control diseases such as diphtheria, influenza, and typhoid fever. **Polio,** however, continued to baffle the medical profession. Polio became the most feared disease of the postwar period because the disease left many of its victims paralyzed for life. In the mid-1950s, Dr. **Jonas Salk,** an American physician, developed an effective vaccine against polio. After the vaccine was tested, the Salk vaccine was administered to school children beginning in 1955. The threat of polio was almost completely eliminated.

COOPERATIVE LEARNING ACTIVITY

Depicting a Culture Ask one or more groups of students to create a mural that illustrates the broad theme "America in the 1950s." The mural should depict the expansion and prosperity of middle-class Americans during this era. Have students divide the work so that everyone brainstorms and chooses what to show. Some students can work on layout; some students can research for artistic accuracy; some students can provide sketches and lettering; and everyone should color and provide finishing touches. As group representatives explain their finished murals, invite comments from the class—both about the details depicted and (as you continue into Section 4) about Americans who were not part of this culture.

American Memories

Life in the Suburbs

Traveler's suitcase

Tricycle, 1950s model

Milk delivered to homes

What Was It Like? With greater affluence, everyday life in the 1950s became easier and more comfortable for Americans living in the suburbs. **What leisure activities do you think were popular in 1950s suburban America?**

Expanding Suburbs

During the 1950s, 85 percent of new home construction took place in the **suburbs.** The new suburbs were usually located on the fringes of major cities.

William Levitt introduced mass-produced housing, based on experience he had gained building houses for the navy. He started his first suburban development, called **Levittown,** on Long Island, New York, in 1947. Levittown included more than 17,000 identical houses, built from materials precut and preassembled at a factory and then erected quickly on designated lots. Other builders adopted Levitt's methods or used their own techniques for rapid construction, creating a massive house-building boom.

Suburban housing developments appealed to many Americans. In addition to affordable homes, they offered privacy, isolation from urban problems, space for cars, and a sense of belonging to a community formed by people similar in age, social background, and race.

Though affordable, the suburbs did not offer opportunities for home ownership to everyone. Many American cities had growing populations of middle-class minorities, particularly African American and Hispanic American, who longed to escape the noise and the crime of the cities. However, the developers of the nation's postwar suburbs often refused to sell homes to minorities.

A Nation on Wheels

The car made suburban escape possible. People needed cars to get to work, to go shopping, and to run errands. For suburban families cars were not a luxury but a necessity.

The construction of thousands of miles of new highways in the 1950s encouraged the spread of suburbs. Suburban America became a "car culture" in which life centered on the automobile. Southern California came to symbolize suburban life and this car culture. In California, the drive-in capital of the nation, a person could go to the movies, eat fast food, do banking,

MULTIPLE LEARNING STYLES

Interpersonal The 1950s often are looked back upon, nostalgically, as a time of strong families and friendships. Ask students to think about TV shows that present such an image of the decade. Then review some of the topics covered in the text–the baby boom, the growth of the suburbs, increased consumerism, the rise of TV, and the emergence of rock 'n' roll. Ask students to write some thoughts about the possible effects of each topic. Allow them to use their notes as you lead them in a discussion of this question: **Did these trends of the 1950s set an ideal for Americans, or did they help drive people apart? L2**

American Memories

Life in the Suburbs

Many new products and innovations contributed to the easy, affluent lifestyle linked with suburbia. Some are still used today, including Minute Rice and Corn Pops (both 1950), Tupperware and power steering in automobiles (both 1951), sugar-free soft drinks (1952), *TV Guide* (1953), McDonald's and Kentucky Fried Chicken fast-food restaurants (both 1955), Frisbees (1957; originally called "Pluto Platters"), and the Barbie doll and panty hose (both 1959).

Answer: *Leisure activities included playing in the neighborhood and going on family vacations.*

NATIONAL GEOGRAPHIC SOCIETY

VIDEODISC
GTV: The American People: Fabric of a Nation

Side 4, Chapter 4
Title: *Greener Pastures*
Subject: Development and impact of suburbs
Ask: **Where are suburbs usually located?** *(on the fringes of major cities)*

History ***and the*** **Humanities**

U.S. History & Art, Transparency 26, *Map;* Transparency 27, *Dawn*; Transparency 28, *The Family*

American Music Cultural Traditions, Lesson 9: "Old Man Atom," "Rocket 88," "Rock Around the Clock"

Focus on American Art Prints, *New York, New Haven and Hartford* by Edward Hopper

Picturing HISTORY Diaper services were one way to avoid washing diapers; another was disposable diapers. In 1951 Marion Donovan used a cut-up shower curtain to make disposable diapers. She later took the idea into production and eventually sold her company for $1 million. **Ask:** **How did the baby boom affect working women?** *(Many women left the workforce so they could stay at home and raise their children.)*
Answer: *Factors that spurred the baby boom included higher family incomes, a good economic climate, and better health care.*

What?Where?When?Who?

TV Dinners As Americans spent more and more time watching TV, many ate their meals in front of the television set. The food industry encouraged the trend. In 1952 the Swanson Company created frozen "TV dinners" so that people could dine and watch television at the same time.

NATIONAL GEOGRAPHIC SOCIETY

VIDEODISC
GTV: A Geographic Perspective on American History

Side 4, Chapter 10
Title: *Where the Action Is*
Subject: A new look at American cities (1950–1990)
Ask: **What is the trend regarding cities?** *(Cities are growing up and out.)*

Picturing HISTORY This fleet of diaper service trucks in front of new homes represents two major social trends of the period: the baby boom and the growth of the suburbs. **What factors encouraged the baby boom?**

Cereal ad, 1950s

and even attend religious services without leaving the car. One suburban California woman explained the need for a car:

> "I live in Garden Grove, work in Irvine, shop in Santa Ana, go to the dentist in Anaheim, my husband works in Long Beach, and I used to be the president of the League of Women Voters in Fullerton."

Air Travel

Americans were also finding it easier to travel by air. The jet engine was perfected in the 1950s, and the first jet-powered commercial aircraft began operation. By the early 1950s, the airliner was on the way to replacing the railroad train and the ocean liner as the preferred transportation for long-distance travel.

A Consumer Society

Americans of the 1950s went on a buying spree. Affluence, the growing variety and quantity of products available, and expanded advertising all played a role in the increased demand for consumer goods. Buying goods became easier, too, with the use of credit cards, charge accounts, and easy-payment plans.

Consumers eagerly sought the latest products—dishwashers, washing machines, television sets, stereos, and clothes made from synthetic fabrics. The growing market for bigger and better cars prompted automakers to outdo one another by manufacturing bigger, faster, and flashier cars. They came out with new models every year, adding stylish features such as chrome-plated bumpers and soaring tail fins.

The advertising and marketing of products on television, on radio, and in magazines created consumer fads and crazes that swept the nation. In the late 1950s, Americans bought millions of hula hoops—large plastic rings they twirled around their waists. Other popular fads included crew cuts for boys, poodle skirts for girls, and a new snack—pizza.

An American Culture

The transformation of America into an affluent suburban society brought significant changes in popular culture. Television came to dominate entertainment, and a new form of popular music burst on the American scene.

Television

In the late 1940s, about 17,000 Americans owned television sets. These large wooden cabinets had small screens that displayed grainy

MAKING CONNECTIONS ACTIVITY

Music One way to trace the beginnings of the generation gap is to review the top-selling records during the 1950s. In 1952, for example, the pop charts were dominated by such hits as "Blue Tango" and "I Saw Mommy Kissing Santa Claus." By 1956 "Whatever Will Be, Will Be (Que Sera, Sera)" competed with Elvis Presley's "Hound Dog." By 1959 rock 'n' roll was pushing for ever-greater dominance on the charts. Bring to class (or have students bring in) recordings that illustrate these various pop styles. Discuss how the changing music reflected a changing American society. **L1, ELL**

black-and-white images. During the 1950s Americans bought 6 or 7 million sets a year. By the end of the decade, nearly 90 percent of American families had television.

Television profoundly changed American life. It became the main form of entertainment for many people as well as an important source of news and information.

Millions of Americans watched the same programs. Families gathered to watch quiz shows such as *The $64,000 Question.* Children tuned in to programs such as *The Mickey Mouse Club* and *Howdy Doody.* Teens kept up with the latest hit songs on *American Bandstand.* Families followed weekly episodes of *I Love Lucy, Leave It to Beaver,* and *Father Knows Best.* The images shown in many programs—of happy middle-class families in neat middle-class homes—helped shape Americans' expectations for their own lives.

Finally, television had an important effect on the consumer culture. The Davy Crockett stories shown on television led to a national craze for Davy Crockett hats, lunch boxes, and other goods. Television advertising helped create a vast national market for new products and fashions. Some shows—such as the *Philco Television Playhouse*—adopted the names of their sponsors, which brought the sponsors prestige.

Rock 'n' Roll

A new form of music—rock 'n' roll—achieved great popularity in the 1950s. A blending of African American rhythm and blues with country,

TECHNOLOGY AND HISTORY

Jet Travel

The first commercial jet transport, the Boeing 707, made aviation history with its maiden flight July 15, 1954. It could carry more passengers for longer distances than any previous aircraft. **In what ways do you think jet aircraft affected the American economy?**

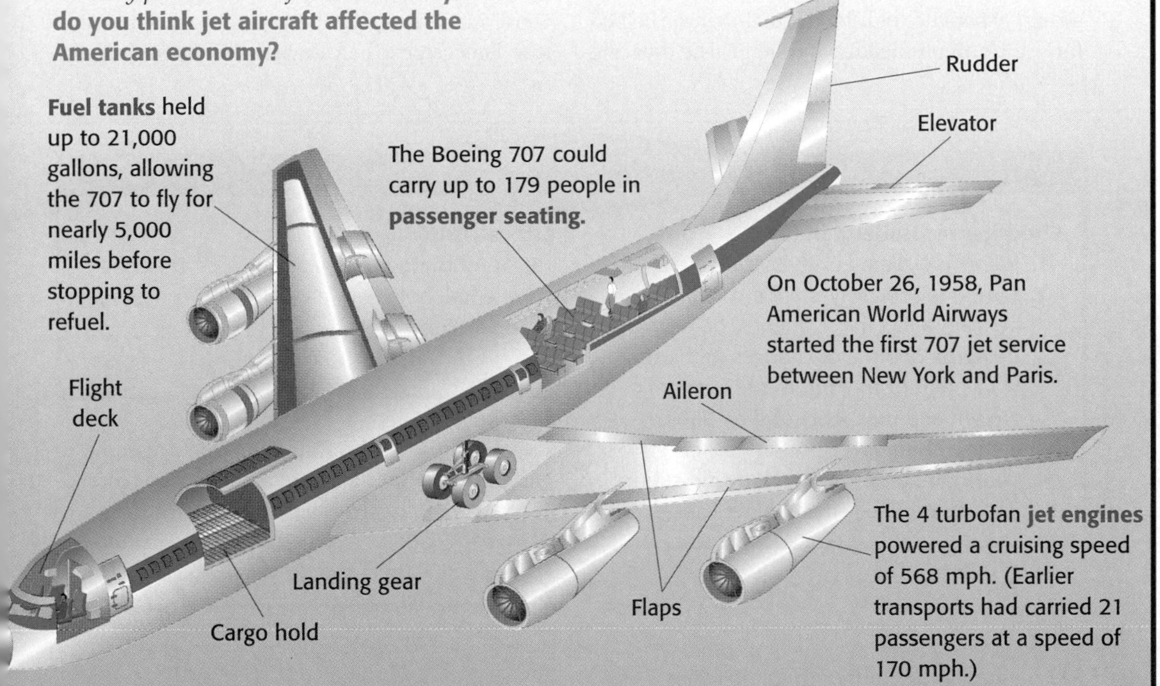

CRITICAL THINKING ACTIVITY

Identifying Assumptions Increased spending and the use of consumer credit are trends of the 1950s that suggest several assumptions–that Americans deserved the latest and best products and that the economy would continue to prosper. Ask students to review Section 3, identifying other assumptions they can link with specific trends and developments. The following topics can guide their thinking:

- the baby boom
- the suburban lifestyle
- the "car culture"
- fads and crazes
- the popularity of television
- the popularity of rock 'n' roll **L2**

CHAPTER 28
Section 3, 807–812

3 ASSESS

Assign Section 3 Review as homework or as an in-class activity.

Use **Chapter Challenger Interactive Review Software** to review Section 3.

Section Quiz 28–3

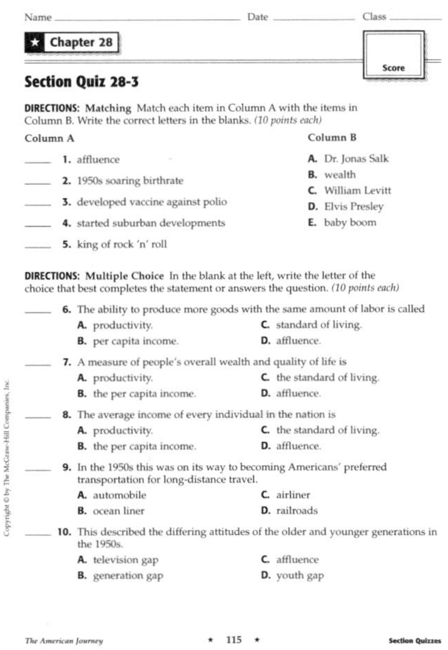
Name ________ Date ________ Class ________

★ Chapter 28 — Score

Section Quiz 28-3

DIRECTIONS: Matching Match each item in Column A with the items in Column B. Write the correct letters in the blanks. *(10 points each)*

Column A	Column B
____ 1. affluence	A. Dr. Jonas Salk
____ 2. 1950s soaring birthrate	B. wealth
____ 3. developed vaccine against polio	C. William Levitt
____ 4. started suburban developments	D. Elvis Presley
____ 5. king of rock 'n' roll	E. baby boom

DIRECTIONS: Multiple Choice In the blank at the left, write the letter of the choice that best completes the statement or answers the question. *(10 points each)*

____ 6. The ability to produce more goods with the same amount of labor is called
A. productivity. C. standard of living.
B. per capita income. D. affluence.

____ 7. A measure of people's overall wealth and quality of life is
A. productivity. C. the standard of living.
B. the per capita income. D. affluence.

____ 8. The average income of every individual in the nation is
A. productivity. C. the standard of living.
B. the per capita income. D. affluence.

____ 9. In the 1950s this was on its way to becoming Americans' preferred transportation for long-distance travel.
A. automobile C. airliner
B. ocean liner D. railroads

____ 10. This described the differing attitudes of the older and younger generations in the 1950s.
A. television gap C. affluence
B. generation gap D. youth gap

The American Journey ★ 115 ★ Section Quizzes

TECHNOLOGY AND HISTORY

More About . . .

Jet Travel The Boeing 707's jet engine was meant to replace the piston engine. On March 12, 1957, a National Airlines Boeing 707 flew from Seattle to Baltimore in 3 hours, 48 minutes—a speed record for transcontinental commercial passenger flight. The 707 quickly became the standard for commercial long-distance flights.

Answer to Caption: *more efficient business transactions, more Americans spent money to fly on jets, and so on*

CHAPTER 28
Section 3, 807–812

Graph Study

Answers

1. about 4 million homes
2. about 20 million more homes

Reteaching Activity 28-3

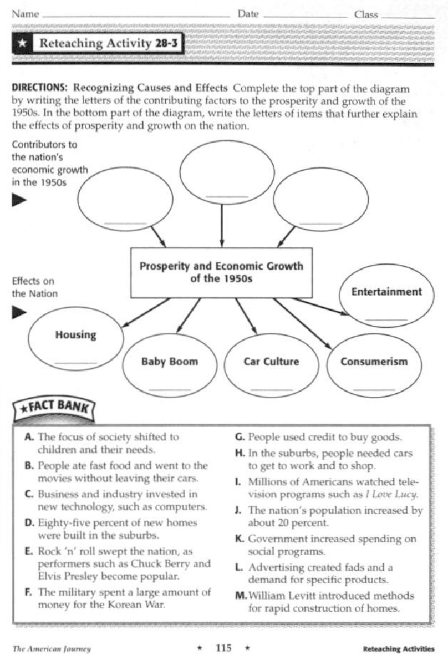

Name ______ Date ______ Class ______

Reteaching Activity 28-3

DIRECTIONS: Recognizing Causes and Effects Complete the top part of the diagram by writing the letters of the contributing factors to the prosperity and growth of the 1950s. In the bottom part of the diagram, write the letters of items that further explain the effects of prosperity and growth on the nation.

FACT BANK

A. The focus of society shifted to children and their needs.
B. People ate fast food and went to the movies without leaving their cars.
C. Business and industry invested in new technology, such as computers.
D. Eighty-five percent of new homes were built in the suburbs.
E. Rock 'n' roll swept the nation, as performers such as Chuck Berry and Elvis Presley become popular.
F. The military spent a large amount of money for the Korean War.
G. People used credit to buy goods.
H. In the suburbs, people needed cars to get to work and to shop.
I. Millions of Americans watched television programs such as *I Love Lucy.*
J. The nation's population increased by about 20 percent.
K. Government increased spending on social programs.
L. Advertising created fads and a demand for specific products.
M. William Levitt introduced methods for rapid construction of homes.

Enrichment Activity 28-3

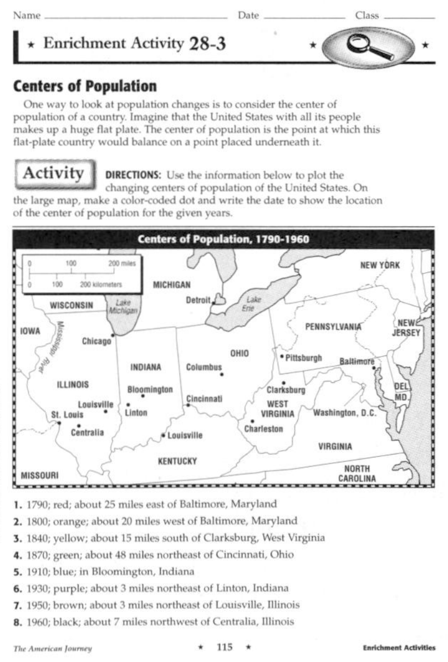

Name ______ Date ______ Class ______

Enrichment Activity 28-3

Centers of Population

One way to look at population changes is to consider the center of population of a country. Imagine that the United States with all its people makes up a huge flat plate. The center of population is the point at which this flat-plate country would balance on a point placed underneath it.

Activity **DIRECTIONS:** Use the information below to plot the changing centers of population of the United States. On the large map, make a color-coded dot and write the date to show the location of the center of population for the given years.

1. 1790; red; about 25 miles east of Baltimore, Maryland
2. 1800; orange; about 20 miles west of Baltimore, Maryland
3. 1840; yellow; about 15 miles south of Clarksburg, West Virginia
4. 1870; green; about 48 miles northeast of Cincinnati, Ohio
5. 1910; blue; in Bloomington, Indiana
6. 1930; purple; about 3 miles northeast of Linton, Indiana
7. 1950; brown; about 3 miles northeast of Louisville, Illinois
8. 1960; black; about 7 miles northwest of Centralia, Illinois

4 CLOSE

Ask students to list the changes in 1950s American society. Have them vote for the one they feel has had the most influence upon their lives.

gospel, and other forms of popular music, rock 'n' roll found a ready audience among teenagers.

Rock 'n' roll grew from the rhythm and blues music that African American musicians had created years before. It often had some elements of country music. In rock 'n' roll, the tempo was quicker and electrically amplified instruments—mostly guitars—were used.

One of the first rock hits, recorded in 1955, was Bill Haley and the Comets' *Rock Around the Clock,* which sold 17 million copies. Adapting the style of African American performers such as Chuck Berry and Little Richard, **Elvis Presley** burst on the national scene in 1956. Presley quickly became known as the king of rock 'n' roll and an idol to millions of young Americans. Many young men copied his ducktail haircut and swaggering manner.

1950s TV

For teenagers, the shared experience of listening to the music helped forge a common identity and bond. The differing attitudes of the older and younger generations toward music, as well as other forms of popular culture, later came to be known as the **generation gap.**

Homes With Television Sets

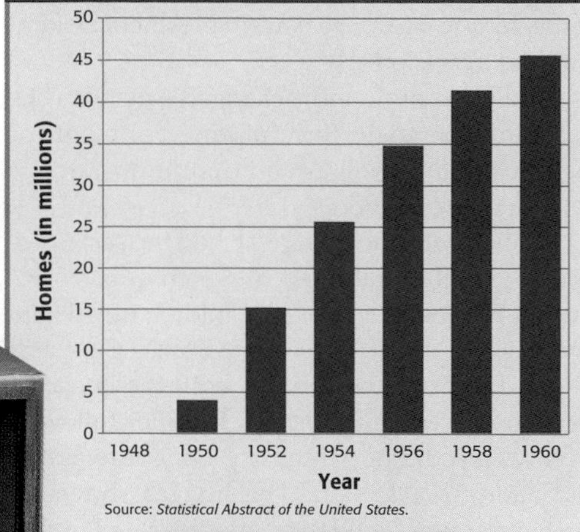

Source: *Statistical Abstract of the United States.*

Graph Study

During the 1950s electricity consumption more than doubled as Americans purchased more electrical appliances.

1. About how many homes had television sets in 1950?
2. **Comparing** How many more homes had sets in 1960 than in 1954?

Section 3 Review

Checking for Understanding

1. ***Identify*** William Levitt, Elvis Presley.
2. ***Define*** productivity, standard of living, per capita income, affluence, baby boom.
3. ***Describe*** two major changes in the United States that resulted from the economic growth and prosperity of the 1950s.

Reviewing Themes

4. **Continuity and Change** Why did suburban life appeal to many Americans?

Critical Thinking

5. **Determining Cause and Effect** Describe the link between television and consumer spending in the 1950s.

Activity

Defining Rock 'n' Roll Paste photographs or drawings on poster board of the musician or musical group that you think represents the best of modern rock 'n' roll. Write captions that include your definition of rock 'n' roll.

Section 3 Review Answers

1. William Levitt, 809; Elvis Presley, 812
2. The words are defined in the Glossary.
3. Any two: population growth, increased affluence, suburban expansion, greater demand for consumer goods
4. Homes were affordable. The suburbs offered a sense of community, more privacy, isolation from urban problems, and space for cars.
5. Popular television created a desire for program-related products; television advertising reached millions of viewers; corporate-sponsored programs brought the names of companies into peoples' homes.

Activity Students should create a display showing their favorite rock group or rock musician and write a caption that includes their own definition of rock 'n' roll.

1950 — 1955 — 1960

1950s More than 20 percent of Americans live in poverty

1950s "Beat" writers influence nonconformists

1950s Women and African Americans question their roles in society

Section 4

Problems in a Time of Plenty

READ TO DISCOVER . . .

- what groups of Americans did not share in the prosperity of the 1950s.
- why some people criticized American values of the 1950s.

TERMS TO LEARN

ghetto
automation
materialism

The Storyteller

Picture postcards of New York City in the 1950s showed soaring skyscrapers, sleek passenger jets, and the Statue of Liberty offering promises of a good life. Hidden behind the tall buildings was a very different United States, however. It was a nation of crumbling streets and rat-infested tenements, hungry and, sometimes, homeless people. The "invisible poor" lived in a nation not of affluence and plenty but of desperate need.

Study of the changing American society

In the 1950s more than 20 percent of Americans lived in poverty. Millions more struggled to survive on incomes only slightly above the poverty level. Such poverty marred the landscape of the affluent society.

Rural Poverty

Many farmers did not share in the prosperity of the 1950s. Huge crop surpluses during those years caused the prices of farm products—and thus farm income—to decline dramatically.

Large business enterprises bought vast areas of available farmland. They used large sums of money to transform agriculture into a thriving business. New machines and chemicals helped produce an abundance of food for American and foreign consumers.

While some farmers benefited from these changes, others suffered. Because small farms could not compete with large farms, many small-farm families sold their land and migrated to urban areas. Thousands of small farmers who remained in agriculture struggled to stay out of poverty.

Farmworkers suffered as well. In the South, African American sharecroppers and tenant farmers had always struggled to survive. Their problems increased when mechanized cotton pickers replaced workers. The popularity of synthetic

SECTION RESOURCES

Reproducible Masters
- Reproducible Lesson Plan 28–4
- Guided Reading Activity 28–4
- Section Quiz 28–4
- Reteaching Activity 28–4
- Enrichment Activity 28–4

Transparencies
- Section Focus Transparency 28–4

Multimedia
- Vocabulary PuzzleMaker
- Chapter Challenger Interactive Review Software
- Testmaker
- GTV: The American People: Fabric of a Nation

1 FOCUS

BELLRINGER
Motivational Activity

Before taking roll at the beginning of the class period, project Section Focus Transparency 28–4 and have students answer the questions. Discuss students' responses.

This activity is also available as a blackline master.

Section Focus Transparency 28–4

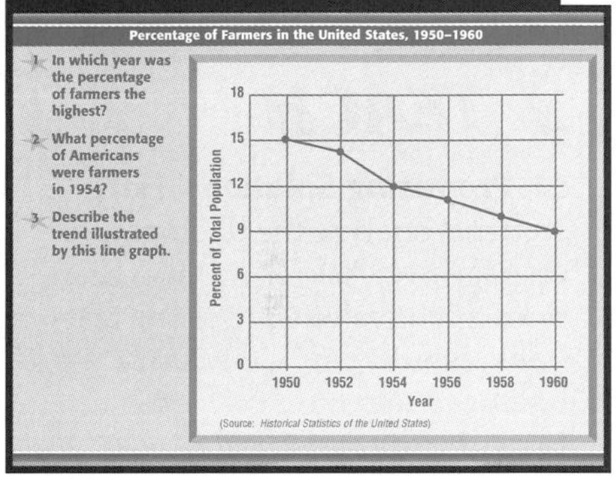

Vocabulary Precheck

Explain that *ghetto* is a term first used in Europe, where it referred to a segregated area in which Jews were forced to live. Have students relate that background to the slightly different meaning they learn about in this section.

Use the **Vocabulary Puzzle-Maker** to create crossword and word search puzzles.

Section Theme
Groups and Institutions

The prosperity that many Americans enjoyed in the 1950s was not shared by the rural and urban poor, and rising voices of dissent questioned Americans' values.

Activity Have students skim the headings in this section. **Ask: What social problems can you infer were part of the 1950s?** *(Answers include poverty, unemployment, and restrictions upon civil rights.)*

Picturing HISTORY Many Americans thought that the New Deal programs of the 1930s and the economic boom created by World War II and its aftermath had more or less done away with poverty. It was not until the Kennedy and Johnson administrations of the 1960s that poverty would receive focused national attention. **Ask:** **How did poverty add to the problem of "white flight"?** *(As poor members of minority groups moved into the cities looking for work, many white people moved out of the cities into the suburbs.)* **Answer:** *more than 20 percent*

2 TEACH

L1 Proposing Solutions Have students analyze the photographs on page 814. **Ask:** **If you had seen these pictures outside of the textbook, would you know that they had been taken in the 1950s? Explain.** *(Students should suggest that the scenes are a surprising contrast to what has been said about the prosperity of the 1950s.)* Have students propose several solutions to reduce or eradicate poverty in the United States.

Guided Reading Activity 28–4

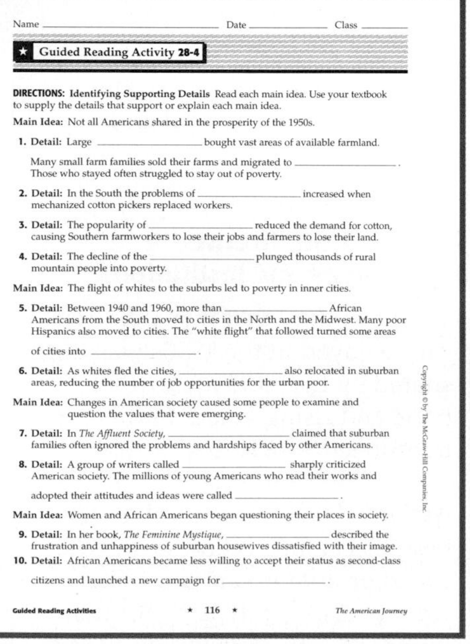

Name ______ Date ______ Class ______

★ Guided Reading Activity 28-4

DIRECTIONS: Identifying Supporting Details Read each main idea. Use your textbook to supply the details that support or explain each main idea.

Main Idea: Not all Americans shared in the prosperity of the 1950s.

1. **Detail:** Large ______ bought vast areas of available farmland. Many small farm families sold their farms and migrated to ______. Those who stayed often struggled to stay out of poverty.
2. **Detail:** In the South the problems of ______ increased when mechanized cotton pickers replaced workers.
3. **Detail:** The popularity of ______ reduced the demand for cotton, causing Southern farmworkers to lose their jobs and farmers to lose their land.
4. **Detail:** The decline of the ______ plunged thousands of rural mountain people into poverty.

Main Idea: The flight of whites to the suburbs led to poverty in inner cities.

5. **Detail:** Between 1940 and 1960, more than ______ African Americans from the South moved to cities in the North and the Midwest. Many poor Hispanics also moved to cities. The "white flight" that followed turned some areas of cities into ______.
6. **Detail:** As whites fled the cities, ______ also relocated in suburban areas, reducing the number of job opportunities for the urban poor.

Main Idea: Changes in American society caused some people to examine and question the values that were emerging.

7. **Detail:** In *The Affluent Society*, ______ claimed that suburban families often ignored the problems and hardships faced by other Americans.
8. **Detail:** A group of writers called ______ sharply criticized American society. The millions of young Americans who read their works and adopted their attitudes and ideas were called ______.

Main Idea: Women and African Americans began questioning their places in society.

9. **Detail:** In her book, *The Feminine Mystique*, ______ described the frustration and unhappiness of suburban housewives dissatisfied with their image.
10. **Detail:** African Americans became less willing to accept their status as second-class citizens and launched a new campaign for ______.

Guided Reading Activities ★ 116 ★ *The American Journey*

Picturing HISTORY Poverty affected families in urban and rural America. Families like the Sturgills of Mayking, Kentucky, (right) worked hard but struggled to make ends meet. Children play in the streets of a Washington, D.C., ghetto, not far from the Capitol (far left). **About what percentage of Americans in the 1950s lived in poverty?**

fibers reduced the demand for cotton. Southern farmworkers lost their jobs, cotton production fell, and thousands of farmers lost their land. Migrant farmworkers in the West and the Southwest—mostly Mexican Americans and Asian Americans—also suffered. They toiled long hours for very low wages and lived in substandard housing.

Rural poverty did not always come from agricultural problems. In **Appalachia,** a region stretching along the Appalachian Mountains through several states, the decline of the coal industry plunged thousands of rural mountain people into desperate poverty.

Urban Poverty

As increasing numbers of middle-class Americans moved to the suburbs in the 1950s, they left the poor behind. The inner cities became islands of poverty. To these islands people still came looking for work. Continuing their migration from rural areas of the South, more than 3 million African Americans moved to cities in the North and the Midwest between 1940 and 1960. Many poor Hispanics—Puerto Ricans in the East and Mexicans in the Southwest and the West—also moved to American cities.

The migration of poor African Americans and Hispanics to Northern cities hastened the departure of whites to the suburbs. This "white flight" turned some areas of cities into **ghettos**—neighborhoods inhabited mainly by poor minority groups.

Urban Unemployment

Few good job opportunities existed for the growing numbers of urban poor. As whites fled cities, factories and businesses also relocated in suburban areas. With a declining population, cities faced growing financial problems. Taxes could no longer keep up with the demands for such services as public transportation and police protection. Moreover, **automation**—producing goods using mechanical and electronic devices—reduced jobs in the industries that remained. It became more and more difficult for the urban poor to rise from poverty and improve their lives.

The urban poor struggled not only with poverty but also with racial discrimination in employment, housing, and education. Crime and violence often grew out of inner-city poverty, especially among young people who saw no hope for escape from life in the ghetto.

COOPERATIVE LEARNING ACTIVITY

Comparing Images of the Fifties Sections 3 and 4 of this chapter present different images of American society in the 1950s. Both images are correct, but neither can stand alone. To review these sections, organize the class into two teams. Have one team list the positive factors discussed in Section 3. Have the other list the negative factors discussed in Section 4. Within each team, have some students specialize in economic matters, others in interpersonal relationships, others in technology, and so on. As teams compare their lists, help them look for connections. (For example, the rise of affordable housing in the suburbs left many urban neighborhoods hurting economically—a condition that contributed to the growth of ghettos.)

Voices of Dissent

Changes in American society in the 1950s caused some people to question the values that were emerging. Some critics charged that the sameness of suburban and corporate life had a cost—the loss of individuality. Others condemned American materialism—a focus on accumulating money and possessions rather than an interest in spiritual matters.

Social Critics

During the 1950s, leading social critics examined the complexity of modern society. Many wrote about its effects on individual behavior. **William H. Whyte, Jr.**, in *The Organization Man*, studied American business life. He concluded that young executives who abandoned their own views to "get along" were the most likely to succeed. He drew a somber picture of "organization men" who "have left home spiritually as well as physically."

In his book *The Affluent Society*, economist **John Kenneth Galbraith** wrote of the prosperous American society of the 1950s. Not all Americans shared in this prosperity, however. Galbraith described a suburban family, comfortably installed in an "air-conditioned, power-steered and power-braked automobile," driving "through cities that are badly paved, made hideous by litter, blighted buildings, billboards." Prosperous Americans, he claimed, often ignored the problems and hardships faced by other Americans.

The Beat Generation

A group of writers called the Beats had even sharper criticism of American society. The term *Beat*, invented by novelist **Jack Kerouac** in 1948, meant "weariness with all forms of the modern industrial state." Kerouac, poet **Allen Ginsberg**, and other Beats rebelled against American culture for its conformity, blind faith in technology, and materialism.

Kerouac's novel *On the Road*, the most influential book of the Beats, described the wild adventures of friends who drove aimlessly around the country. Its main character was "mad to live, mad to talk, mad to be saved, desirous of everything at the same time." The novel made Kerouac an instant celebrity.

Millions of young Americans read the works of Beat writers. Some adopted Beat attitudes of rebellion and isolation from society. Dressed in black and wearing sunglasses and berets, they were called **beatniks.** The Beat writers and their followers put forth ideas and attitudes that contributed to the youth rebellion of the 1960s.

Writer Jack Kerouac

Picturing HISTORY A crowd of similarly dressed suburban residents returns home from working in the city. **What criticisms did writers such as Jack Kerouac make about American middle-class society of the 1950s?**

CHAPTER 28
Section 4, 813–816

NATIONAL GEOGRAPHIC SOCIETY

VIDEODISC
GTV: The American People: Fabric of a Nation

Side 4, Chapter 3

Title: *Up and Out*
Subject: Moving North
Ask: **What caused African Americans to move North?** *(more opportunities, less rural poverty)*

Picturing HISTORY The photo illustrates *The Man in the Gray Flannel Suit*, a 1956 novel: "It seemed as though all I could see was a lot of bright young men in gray flannel suits rushing around New York in a frantic parade to go nowhere. They seemed to be pursuing neither ideals nor happiness—they were pursuing a routine."
Answer: *criticized conformity, materialism, and blind faith in technology*

3 ASSESS

Assign Section 4 Review as homework or as an in-class activity.

Section Quiz 28–4

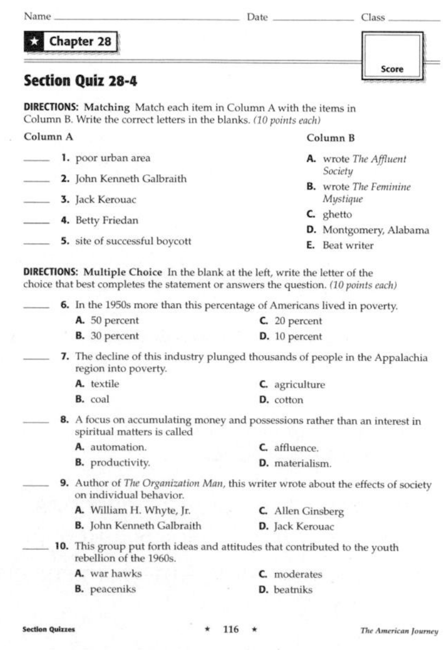

Name ______ Date ______ Class ______

Chapter 28

Score

Section Quiz 28-4

DIRECTIONS: Matching Match each item in Column A with the items in Column B. Write the correct letters in the blanks. *(10 points each)*

Column A	Column B
____ 1. poor urban area	A. wrote *The Affluent Society*
____ 2. John Kenneth Galbraith	B. wrote *The Feminine Mystique*
____ 3. Jack Kerouac	C. ghetto
____ 4. Betty Friedan	D. Montgomery, Alabama
____ 5. site of successful boycott	E. Beat writer

DIRECTIONS: Multiple Choice In the blank at the left, write the letter of the choice that best completes the statement or answers the question. *(10 points each)*

____ 6. In the 1950s more than this percentage of Americans lived in poverty.
A. 50 percent C. 20 percent
B. 30 percent D. 10 percent

____ 7. The decline of this industry plunged thousands of people in the Appalachia region into poverty.
A. textile C. agriculture
B. coal D. cotton

____ 8. A focus on accumulating money and possessions rather than an interest in spiritual matters is called
A. automation. C. affluence.
B. productivity. D. materialism.

____ 9. Author of *The Organization Man*, this writer wrote about the effects of society on individual behavior.
A. William H. Whyte, Jr. C. Allen Ginsberg
B. John Kenneth Galbraith D. Jack Kerouac

____ 10. This group put forth ideas and attitudes that contributed to the youth rebellion of the 1960s.
A. war hawks C. moderates
B. peaceniks D. beatniks

Section Quizzes ★ 116 ★ *The American Journey*

MULTIPLE LEARNING STYLES

Verbal/Linguistic Exploring the word *affluent* (as in the title of Galbraith's *The Affluent Society*) can help students review the social factors of the 1950s. Have students use brainstorming or word-webbing to analyze the word's meaning at that time. These questions can spur students' thinking:

- **Why did Galbraith feel that *affluent* was a good way to describe America at that time?**
- **How could an American of the 1950s tell if he or she were affluent?**
- **Which Americans of that time could not be described as affluent? Why not?**

Have students share their thoughts in small-group or whole-class discussion. **L2**

Use **Chapter Challenger Interactive Review Software** to review Section 4.

Reteaching Activity 28–4

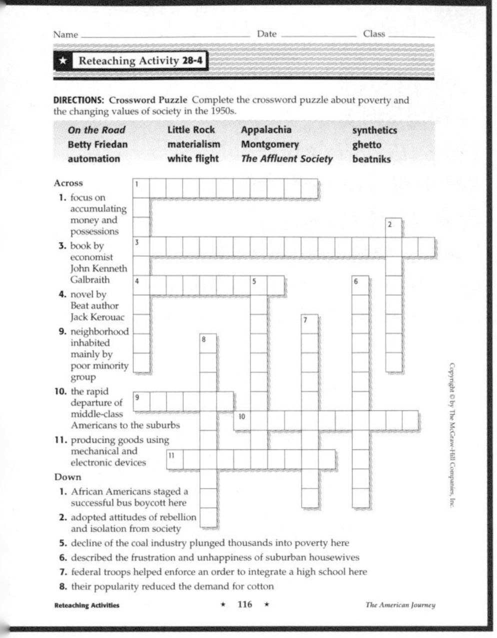
Name ______ Date ______ Class ______

★ Reteaching Activity **28-4**

DIRECTIONS: Crossword Puzzle Complete the crossword puzzle about poverty and the changing values of society in the 1950s.

On the Road	**Little Rock**	**Appalachia**	**synthetics**
Betty Friedan	**materialism**	**Montgomery**	**ghetto**
automation	**white flight**	***The Affluent Society***	**beatniks**

Across
1. focus on accumulating money and possessions
3. book by economist John Kenneth Galbraith
4. novel by Beat author Jack Kerouac
9. neighborhood inhabited mainly by poor minority group
10. the rapid departure of middle-class Americans to the suburbs
11. producing goods using mechanical and electronic devices

Down
1. African Americans staged a successful bus boycott here
2. adopted attitudes of rebellion and isolation from society
5. decline of the coal industry plunged thousands into poverty here
6. described the frustration and unhappiness of suburban housewives
7. federal troops helped enforce an order to integrate a high school here
8. their popularity reduced the demand for cotton

Enrichment Activity 28–4

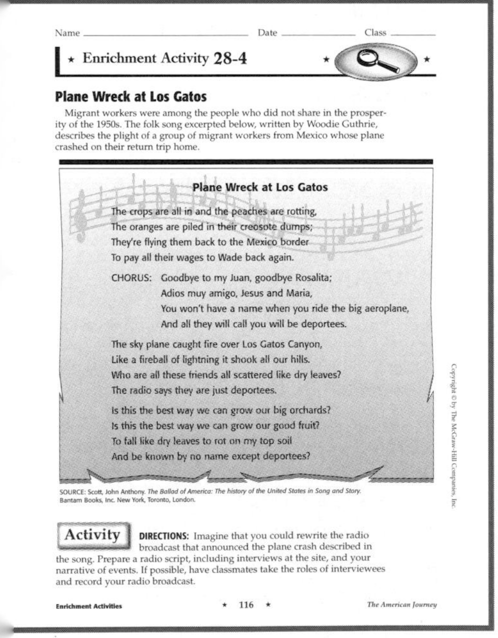
Name ______ Date ______ Class ______

★ Enrichment Activity 28-4

Plane Wreck at Los Gatos

Migrant workers were among the people who did not share in the prosperity of the 1950s. The folk song excerpted below, written by Woodie Guthrie, describes the plight of a group of migrant workers from Mexico whose plane crashed on their return trip home.

Plane Wreck at Los Gatos

The crops are all in and the peaches are rotting,
The oranges are piled in their creosote dumps;
They're flying them back to the Mexico border
To pay all their wages to Wade back again.

CHORUS: Goodbye to my Juan, goodbye Rosalita;
Adios muy amigo, Jesus and Maria,
You won't have a name when you ride the big aeroplane,
And all they will call you will be deportees.

The sky plane caught fire over Los Gatos Canyon,
Like a fireball of lightning it shook all our hills.
Who are all these friends all scattered like dry leaves?
The radio says they are just deportees.

Is this the best way we can grow our big orchards?
Is this the best way we can grow our good fruit?
To fall like dry leaves to rot on my top soil
And be known by no name except deportees?

SOURCE: Scott, John Anthony. *The Ballad of America: The history of the United States in Song and Story.* Bantam Books, Inc. New York, Toronto, London.

Activity **DIRECTIONS:** Imagine that you could rewrite the radio broadcast that announced the plane crash described in the song. Prepare a radio script, including interviews at the site, and your narrative of events. If possible, have classmates take the roles of interviewees and record your radio broadcast.

4 CLOSE

Have students suggest questions that critics of the 1950s might ask about the problems American society faces today.

Linking PAST & PRESENT

Political Power

The growing African American population in the cities laid the foundation for political power in the 1950s and beyond. In 1950 no American city had an African American mayor. By the early 1990s, African Americans served as mayors of 30 major cities and held more than 10,000 other city and county offices across the nation.

Questioning Roles

With society changing, women and African Americans began questioning their roles. In the 1950s African Americans fought to end segregation and to gain greater freedom and equality.

The Suburban Housewife

"The suburban housewife was the dream image of the young American woman," wrote **Betty Friedan,** herself a suburban wife and mother. "She was healthy, beautiful, educated, [and] concerned only about her husband, her children, and her home." Television, advertising, and magazines reinforced this image of women as perfect wives and mothers and suburban life as the path to a full and happy life.

As Friedan discovered, however, many suburban housewives were dissatisfied with this role. Her book, *The Feminine Mystique,* became one of the first works to describe the frustration and unhappiness of these women.

African Americans

African Americans also questioned their place in society in the 1950s. After years of struggling for their rights, African Americans became increasingly impatient for change and less willing to accept their status as second-class citizens. They launched a new campaign for full civil rights.

Three events in the 1950s proved especially important for African Americans. First came the Supreme Court decision in *Brown* v. *Topeka Board of Education* (1954), which declared racial segregation in public schools to be unconstitutional. Second, African Americans staged a successful boycott of segregated public buses in **Montgomery, Alabama.** Third, President Eisenhower sent federal troops to **Little Rock, Arkansas,** to enforce a court order to integrate a high school. These three events, which you will learn more about in Chapter 29, helped pave the way for the successes of the civil rights movement in the 1960s.

Section 4 Review

Checking for Understanding

1. ***Identify*** Jack Kerouac, Allen Ginsberg, Betty Friedan.
2. ***Define*** ghetto, automation, materialism.
3. ***Summarize*** the reasons most farmers did not share in the prosperity of the 1950s.

Reviewing Themes

4. **Groups and Institutions** What did the Beats dislike about American society?

Critical Thinking

5. **Drawing Conclusions** Why do you think some suburban housewives were dissatisfied with their roles in life during the 1950s?

Activity

Writing a Poem Write a poem at least 12 lines long that might have been written by a social critic of the 1950s.

Section 4 Review Answers

1. Jack Kerouac, 815; Allen Ginsberg, 815; Betty Friedan, 816
2. The words are defined in the Glossary.
3. Huge crop surpluses caused farm prices to decline dramatically, reducing their income. When many farmers quit farming and moved to urban areas, they were faced with high prices on consumer products and had a difficult time staying above the poverty level.
4. They disliked Americans' conformity, blind faith in technology, and materialism.
5. Answers may include that many women wanted to contribute more to society, and were frustrated by their lack of power and in their attempts to live up to the ideal of the perfect housewife.

Activity Poems should express some of the sentiments of social critics in the 1950s.

Technology
SKILL BUILDER

Using the Internet

Are you one of the many people worldwide who would like to surf the Net? Using the Internet can give you the chance to find information on many subjects.

Learning the Skill

The Internet is a global computer network that offers many features, including electronic mail, information, and on-line shopping. Before you can connect to the Internet and use the services it offers, however, you must have three things: a computer, a modem (the device that lets your computer send and receive data over a telephone line), and a service provider. A service provider is a company that, for a fee, gives you entry to the Internet.

Once you are connected, the easiest and fastest way to access sites and information is to use a "Web browser," a program that lets you view and explore information on the World Wide Web. The Web consists of many documents called "Web pages," each of which has its own address, or Uniform Resource Locator (URL). Many URLs start with the keystrokes *http://*

Practicing the Skill

This chapter focuses on the 1950s, when Elvis Presley became popular. Surf the Internet to learn about the king of rock 'n' roll.

1. Log on to the Internet and access one of the World Wide Web search tools, such as Yahoo, Lycos, or WebCrawler.
2. Search by category or by name. If you search by category in Yahoo, for example, click on *Entertainment* or *Business and Economy.* To search by name, type in *Elvis* or *Elvis Presley.*
3. Scroll the list of Web pages that appears when the search is complete. Select a page to bring up and read or print. Repeat the process until you have enough information you can use to develop a short report on Elvis and his music during the 1950s.

Elvis Presley

Applying the Skill

Using the Internet Go through the steps just described to search the Internet for information on automobiles of the 1950s or baseball in the 1950s. Based on the information, write an article for your school newspaper or magazine about your topic.

Technology
SKILL BUILDER

TEACH

Using the Internet

Students who are familiar with the Internet have an interactive way to learn. The Internet, a powerful research tool, often can provide students with more recent information than would appear in books or magazines. The Internet offers access to a world of resources that might not be available in students' local libraries. The feature on page 793 provides an introduction to the Internet using E-mail.

Discuss the need for an Internet provider. Students probably have heard of such providers as America Online and CompuServe. Use the Yellow Pages to mention a few local providers as well. If possible, ask a representative from a local provider to speak to the class about the Internet. Discuss various World Wide Web browsers. If you have access to the Internet at school, demonstrate and supervise its use.

As you talk about URLs—Web page addresses—point out that although they all start with *http://*, that prefix is not always followed by *www.* Finally, mention some of the domain designations that may end a URL—*.com* for a commercial organization, *.org* for a nonprofit organization, *.edu* for an educational organization, and *.gov* for government organization.

Additional Practice

Chapter Skills Activity 28

ANSWERS TO PRACTICING THE SKILL

Some report details about Elvis and his music during the 1950s will vary and will arise from varying information. You might have groups of students use different search tools and later discuss the helpfulness of each one. Have students provide a rough bibliography along with their finished report.

Applying the Skill Students should search the Internet for information about automobiles or baseball during the 1950s and write an article based on the information. Be sure to have them name their sources. If time permits, lead a class discussion in which students can share their experiences in doing research for this assignment.

GLENCOE TECHNOLOGY

VIDEODISC
MindJogger Videoquiz

Use MindJogger to review the Chapter 28 content.

Chapter 28
Disc 4, Side A

Also available in VHS.

Reviewing Key Terms

The key terms used in this activity can be found in the textbook glossary on pages A26–A35. Students' paragraphs will vary.

Reviewing Key Facts

1. Although he believed in limiting government power and encouraging private enterprise, he often expanded programs that involved social welfare.
2. Any three: Soviet–U.S. arms race and space race; seizure of Suez Canal by Egypt; uprising in Hungary; Vietnam conflict; CIA overthrow in Guatemala; cutting diplomatic ties with Castro in Cuba
3. The United States and the Soviet Union agreed on a policy of peaceful coexistence.
4. Answers may include the computer, medical advances such as antibiotics and vaccines, jet-powered commercial aircraft, dishwashers, washing machines, television, stereos, synthetic fabrics.
5. They began to deteriorate. Many people who lived in these areas were unemployed and recently had emigrated from other areas of the country. There were few job opportunities, and many people faced racial discrimination. Violence often erupted from the poverty.

Chapter 28
Review and Activities

Reviewing Key Terms

On a sheet of paper, use the following words in two paragraphs that describe life in America in the 1950s.

moderate
arms race
domino theory
summit
peaceful coexistence
productivity
standard of living
per capita income
affluence
baby boom
ghetto
automation
materialism

Reviewing Key Facts

1. Summarize President Eisenhower's domestic policy.
2. Name three foreign policy challenges the Eisenhower administration faced.
3. How did the Geneva summit help to ease cold war tensions?
4. Identify technological advances of the 1950s.
5. How did the mass movement to the suburbs affect inner cities?

Critical Thinking

Making Inferences

The social critics of the 1950s criticized American culture for its conformity, blind faith in technology, and materialism.

1. Give an example of the conformity that these critics might have been referring to.
2. Why do you think a blind faith in technology might be harmful?

Time Line Activity

Create a time line on which you place the following events in chronological order.

- SEATO formed
- Alaska and Hawaii enter Union
- Federal Highway Act passed
- Nixon gives "Checkers" speech
- Soviets launch *Sputnik*
- President Eisenhower is elected to first term
- Strikes spread through Hungary
- *Explorer* satellite is launched
- Salk vaccine first given to school children

Reviewing Themes

1. **Economic Factors** What general economic policies did the Eisenhower administration support?
2. **Science and Technology** Why did the development of nuclear weapons allow Eisenhower to cut the military budget?
3. **Continuity and Change** Why was there such a great demand for automobiles in the 1950s?
4. **Groups and Institutions** Discuss two problems farmers faced in the 1950s.

Skill Practice Activity

Using the Internet

Go through the steps described on page 817 to search the Internet for information on the beatniks or fads—such as telephone booth stuffing or the hula hoop—of the 1950s. Write an article for the school newspaper or magazine based on the information you retrieve about your topic.

Critical Thinking

1. Answers may include the middle-class movement to the suburbs, adopting of similar suburban values, and the race to acquire new technological gadgets and appliances.
2. Answers may note that when people blindly rely on technology to solve problems, there is no watchdog to monitor the effects that the technology might have on the environment, jobs, and other areas of our lives.

Time Line Activity

Events should be placed in this order: Nixon gives "Checkers" speech, President Eisenhower is elected to first term, SEATO formed, Salk vaccine first given to school children, Federal Highway Act passed, Strikes spread through Hungary, Soviets launch *Sputnik, Explorer* satellite is launched, Alaska and Hawaii enter Union

Geography Activity

Coal mining is a crucial part of Appalachia's economy. The introduction of new machine technology after World War II had a drastic effect on employment. Study the map below, then answer the questions that follow.

The Appalachia Region, 1950s

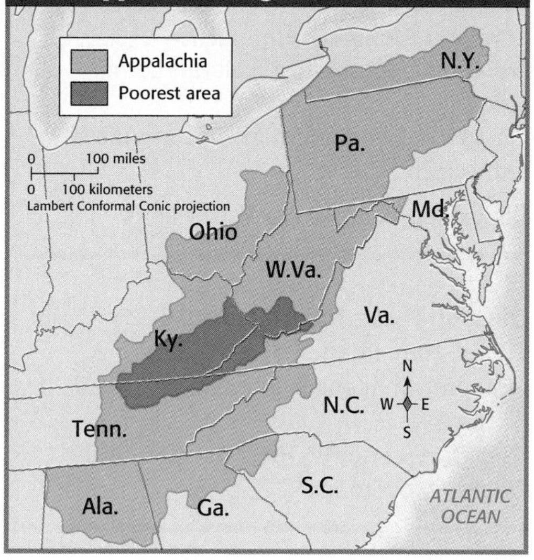

1. **Region** How many states are included in the Appalachia region?
2. **Location** In what states did poverty strike the hardest?
3. **Human/Environment Interaction** Why do you think unemployed miners did not turn to farming or ranching to make a living?

Cooperative Activity

History and Literature Throughout history social critics have tried to draw attention to the ills of society. With members of your group, research to find three poems written by modern poets that deal with current social problems. Social problems might include, for example, poverty, prejudice, and the prevalence of violence. Mount each of your poems on an 8 ½" x 11" sheet of paper and use photographs or drawings to illustrate each. Your group might also want to include short descriptions or captions to identify your photographs or drawings. Combine your poems with those of other groups to create a poetry collection book titled "A Decade of Dissent."

Technology Activity

Using E-Mail In the 1950s it would have been hard to imagine the role computers would play in our lives today. One by-product of the computer revolution is the hundreds of new computer-related words we have added to our language. Words such as *surfing* and *megabyte* describe computers and how we use them. Using E-mail, send a message asking for a list of words that probably did not exist before computers were invented in the 1950s. Share your findings with the class.

Portfolio Activity History Journal Review Section 2 and create a world map that shows the hot spots of foreign policy during Eisenhower's administration. Use a different symbol to represent the activities in each area, and create a map key to explain your symbols.

Skill Practice Activity

Students should search the Internet for information on beatniks or on fads of the 1950s and write an article based upon the information found.

Geography Activity

1. 12 states
2. West Virginia, Virginia, Tennessee, and Kentucky
3. Miners lived in mountainous areas—land that was not conducive to farming or ranching.

Cooperative Activity

Each group should research to find three modern poems that deal with social criticism. Groups should compile their poems and illustrations in a class booklet.

Technology Activity

Students should use E-mail to help them find examples of new words that entered the English language as a result of the increased use of computers.

Portfolio Activity Students should create a map showing each of the hot spots described in Section 2. They should use symbols to describe the activity that took place in each location.

Chapter Bonus Test Question

Ask: Who brought the term *rock 'n' roll* into mainstream American vocabulary? *(The term was popularized by Cleveland disc jockey Alan Freed, through his radio programs and live music shows.)*

Reviewing Themes

1. He supported limiting government spending and encouraging private enterprise.
2. By relying on nuclear weapons, the United States could reduce other areas of defense, such as the size of the army and the number of conventional weapons.
3. More people were moving to the suburbs and needed cars to get to work, to shop, and to run errands.
4. Any two: Crop surpluses drove down income; small farms could not compete with large business-run farms; machines replaced some work done by hand; synthetics replaced some farm-grown products.

Chapter 29 Planning Guide

A complete, 1-page lesson plan is provided for each section in the *Reproducible Lesson Plans* booklet.

Section Resources

Daily Objectives	Reproducible Resources	Multimedia Resources
Section 1 The Civil Rights Movement Recall key events in the rise of the civil rights movement in the United States during the 1950s.	Reproducible Lesson Plan 29–1 Guided Reading Activity 29–1* Supreme Court Case Studies, *Brown v. Board of Education of Topeka, Kansas* Section Quiz 29–1* Reteaching Activity 29–1 Enrichment Activity 29–1	Section Focus Transparency 29–1 Vocabulary PuzzleMaker Chapter Challenger Interactive Review ABCNews InterActive™ Martin Luther King, Jr. Facts On File: Landmark Documents in American History American Music Cultural Traditions
Section 2 Kennedy and Johnson Discuss the nature and effects of the domestic policies promoted by Presidents Kennedy and Johnson.	Reproducible Lesson Plan 29–2 Guided Reading Activity 29–2* Section Quiz 29–2* Reteaching Activity 29–2 Enrichment Activity 29–2	Section Focus Transparency 29–2 Vocabulary PuzzleMaker Chapter Challenger Interactive Review Testmaker Set On Freedom™ The American Civil Rights Movement
Section 3 The Struggle Continues Describe how the civil rights movement in the United States changed in the 1960s.	Reproducible Lesson Plan 29–3 Guided Reading Activity 29–3* Section Quiz 29–3* Reteaching Activity 29–3 Enrichment Activity 29–3	Section Focus Transparency 29–3 U.S. History & Art, Transparencies 29, 30 Vocabulary PuzzleMaker Chapter Challenger Interactive Review Testmaker Set On Freedom™ The American Civil Rights Movement ABCNews InterActive™ Martin Luther King, Jr. GTV: The American People: Fabric of a Nation
Section 4 Other Groups Seek Rights Recall ways in which women, Hispanic Americans, Native Americans, and disabled Americans took action to improve their lives in the 1960s and 1970s.	Reproducible Lesson Plan 29–4 Guided Reading Activity 29–4* Section Quiz 29–4* Reteaching Activity 29–4 Enrichment Activity 29–4	Section Focus Transparency 29–4 U.S. History & Art, Transparency 28 Vocabulary PuzzleMaker Chapter Challenger Interactive Review Testmaker Set On Freedom™ The American Civil Rights Movement ABCNews InterActive™ Martin Luther King, Jr.

** Also available in Spanish*

Blackline Master · Videodisc · Audiocassette · Music Program · Transparency · CD-ROM · Software

0:00 **OUT OF TIME?**
Assign the Chapter 29 Digest and the corresponding Chapter Digests Audiocassettes with activities and tests.

Activity

From the Classroom of...

Cheryl Smith-Fountain
Sidney Lanier School
Montgomery, AL

A Civil Rights Tour

Explain to students that Montgomery, Alabama, is considered by some historians to be the birthplace of the civil rights movement. Supply students with a Montgomery city map. (This map can be obtained from reference material at the local library, or there are several map resources on the Internet that can easily be printed out.) Have pairs of students research the Chapter 29 contents and other reference materials to find sites in Montgomery that have historical connections with the civil rights movement, such as the Parsonage and the state capitol. After each pair has a list of sites, have them write a description of a tour through the city, giving brief histories of their sites. Each group can present its tour to the class, using maps to show how to travel from one site to the next and explaining the significance of each site.

National Geographic Society Teacher's Corner

Index to National Geographic Magazine

The following articles may be used for research relating to this chapter:

- "Philadelphia's African Americans," by Roland L. Freeman, August 1990.
- "I Dream a World: America's Black Women," by Brian Lanker, August 1989.

National Geographic Society Products Available from Glencoe

To order the following products for use with this chapter, contact your local Glencoe sales representative, or call Glencoe at 1-800-334-7344:

- *The Presidents: A Picture History of Our Nation* (CD-ROM)
- *GTV: A Geographic Perspective on American History* (Videodisc)
- *GTV: The American People: Fabric of a Nation* (Videodisc)

Additional National Geographic Society Products

To order the following products for use with this chapter, call National Geographic Society at 1-800-368-2728:

- *Historical Atlas of the United States* (Atlas)

Block Schedule

Block scheduling differs from traditional class scheduling in the amount of time allotted to each period. The extended time frame provided by block scheduling affords you the opportunity to implement a greater number of research-oriented and activity-intense projects to motivate and involve your students. Activities that are particularly suited to use within the block scheduling framework are identified throughout this chapter by the following designation: [block schedule icon]

KEY TO ABILITY LEVELS

Teaching strategies have been coded for varying learning styles and abilities.

L1 **BASIC** activities for all students
L2 **AVERAGE** activities for average to above-average students
L3 **CHALLENGING** activities for above-average students
ELL **ENGLISH LANGUAGE LEARNER** activities

Chapter 29 Resource Guide

Home Involvement

Home Involvement Activity 29

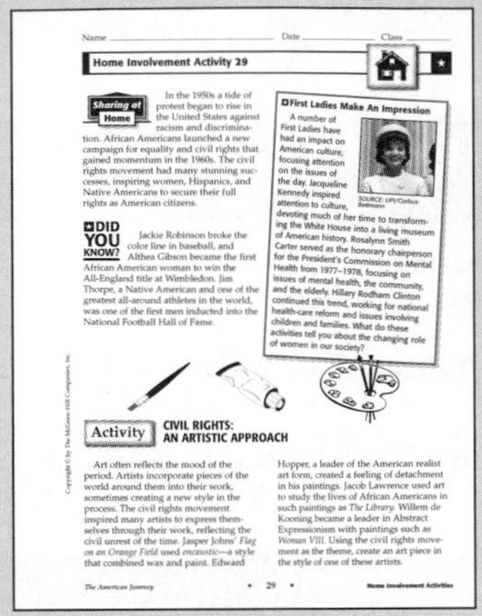

Review Activities

Chapter Summary 29

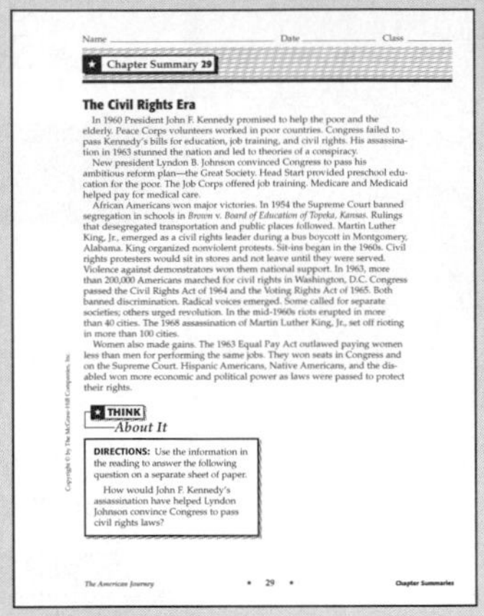

Workbook Activity 29

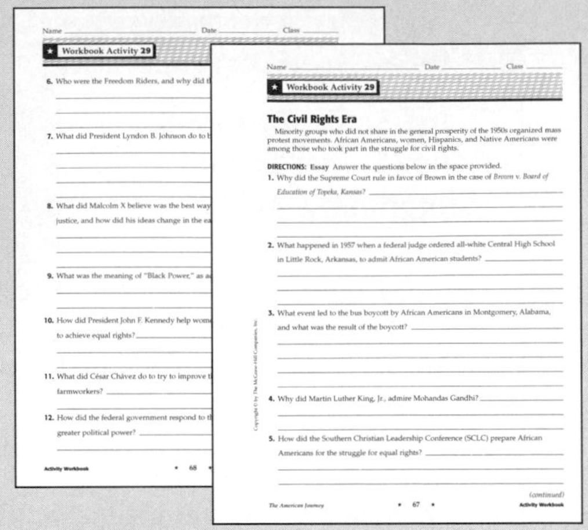

Reinforcement Activities

Time Line Activity 29

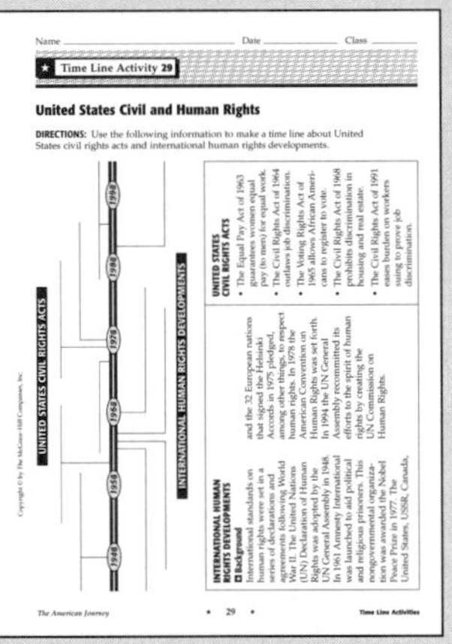

Vocabulary Activity 29

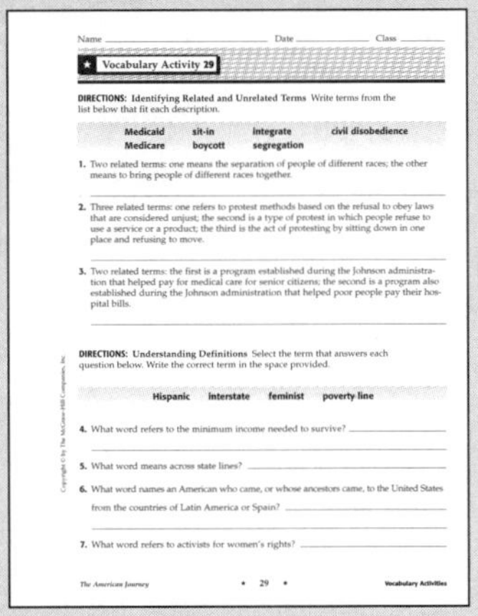

Chapter Skills Activity 29

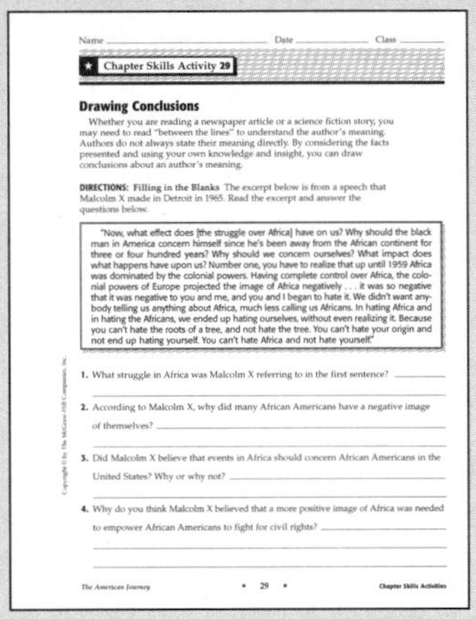

Enrichment Activities

Linking Past and Present Activity 29

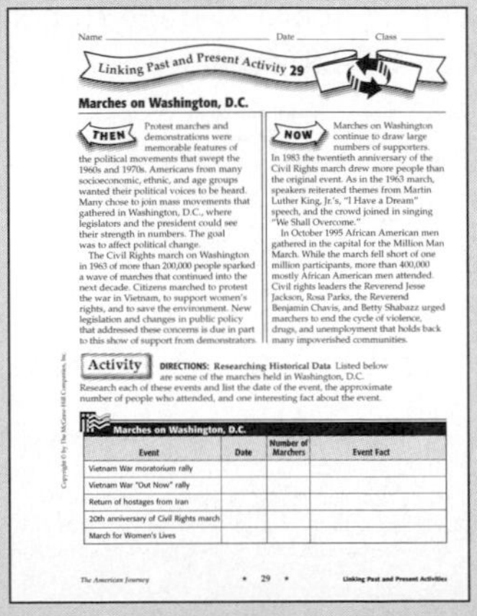

Primary Source Reading 29

Geography Activities

Mapping History Activity 29

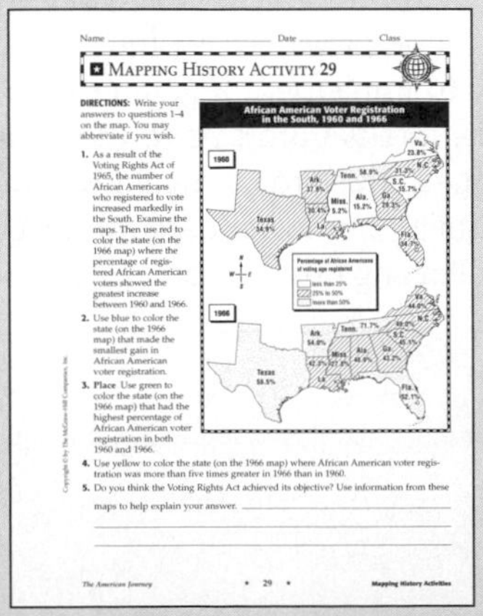

Chapter 29 Resource Guide

ASSESSMENT

Chapter 29 Test, Form A

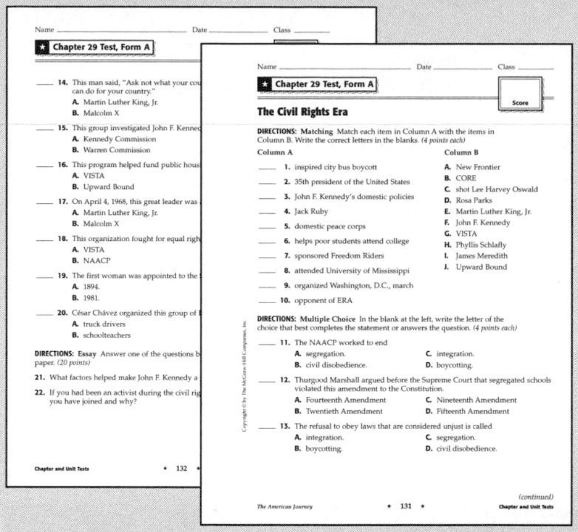
Chapter 29 Test, Form A

The Civil Rights Era

DIRECTIONS: Matching Match each item in Column A with the items in Column B. Write the correct letters in the blanks. (4 points each)

Column A	Column B
1. inspired city bus boycott	A. New Frontier
2. 35th president of the United States	B. CORE
3. John F. Kennedy's domestic policies	C. shot Lee Harvey Oswald
4. Jack Ruby	D. Rosa Parks
5. domestic peace corps	E. Martin Luther King, Jr.
6. helps poor students attend college	F. John F. Kennedy
7. sponsored Freedom Riders	G. VISTA
8. attended University of Mississippi	H. Phyllis Schlafly
9. organized Washington, D.C., march	I. James Meredith
10. opponent of ERA	J. Upward Bound

DIRECTIONS: Multiple Choice In the blank at the left, write the letter of the choice that best completes the statement or answers the question. (4 points each)

11. The NAACP worked to end
A. segregation. C. integration.
B. civil disobedience. D. boycotting.

12. Thurgood Marshall argued before the Supreme Court that segregated schools violated this amendment to the Constitution.
A. Fourteenth Amendment C. Nineteenth Amendment
B. Twentieth Amendment D. Fifteenth Amendment

13. The refusal to obey laws that are considered unjust is called
A. integration. C. segregation.
B. boycotting. D. civil disobedience.

Chapter 29 Test, Form B

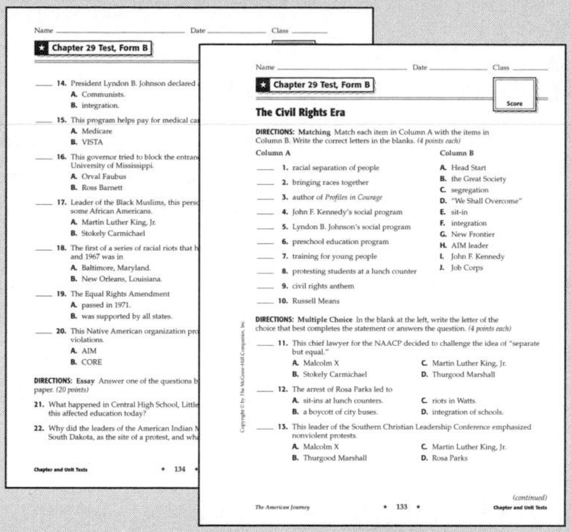
Chapter 29 Test, Form B

The Civil Rights Era

DIRECTIONS: Matching Match each item in Column A with the items in Column B. Write the correct letters in the blanks. (4 points each)

Column A	Column B
1. racial separation of people	A. Head Start
2. bringing races together	B. the Great Society
3. author of *Profiles in Courage*	C. segregation
4. John F. Kennedy's social program	D. "We Shall Overcome"
5. Lyndon B. Johnson's social program	E. sit-in
6. preschool education program	F. integration
7. training for young people	G. New Frontier
8. protesting students at a lunch counter	H. AIM leader
9. civil rights anthem	I. John F. Kennedy
10. Russell Means	J. Job Corps

DIRECTIONS: Multiple Choice In the blank at the left, write the letter of the choice that best completes the statement or answers the question. (4 points each)

11. This chief lawyer for the NAACP decided to challenge the idea of "separate but equal."
A. Malcolm X C. Martin Luther King, Jr.
B. Stokely Carmichael D. Thurgood Marshall

12. The arrest of Rosa Parks led to
A. sit-ins at lunch counters. C. riots in Watts.
B. a boycott of city buses. D. integration of schools.

13. This leader of the Southern Christian Leadership Conference emphasized nonviolent protests.
A. Malcolm X C. Martin Luther King, Jr.
B. Thurgood Marshall D. Rosa Parks

Performance Assessment Activity 29

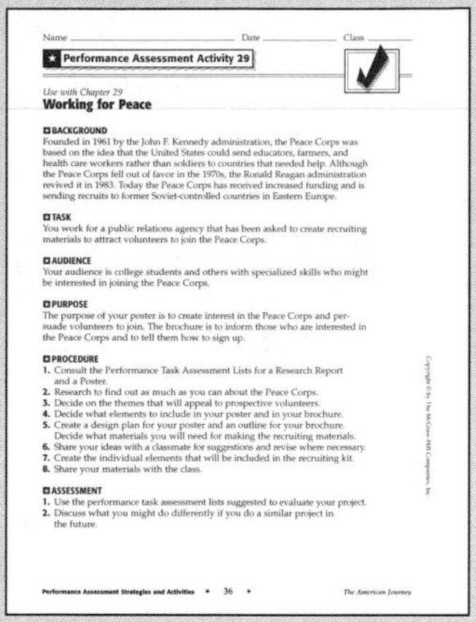
Performance Assessment Activity 29

Working for Peace

BACKGROUND
Founded in 1961 by the John F. Kennedy administration, the Peace Corps was based on the idea that the United States could send educators, farmers, and health care workers rather than soldiers to countries that needed help. Although the Peace Corps fell out of favor in the 1970s, the Ronald Reagan administration revived it in 1983. Today the Peace Corps has received increased funding and is sending recruits to former Soviet-controlled countries in Eastern Europe.

TASK
You work for a public relations agency that has been asked to create recruiting materials to attract volunteers to join the Peace Corps.

AUDIENCE
Your audience is college students and others with specialized skills who might be interested in joining the Peace Corps.

PURPOSE
The purpose of your poster is to create interest in the Peace Corps and persuade volunteers to join. The brochure is to inform those who are interested in the Peace Corps and to tell them how to sign up.

PROCEDURE
1. Consult the Performance Task Assessment Lists for a Research Report and a Poster.
2. Research to find out as much as you can about the Peace Corps.
3. Decide on the themes that will appeal to prospective volunteers.
4. Decide what elements to include in your poster and in your brochure.
5. Create a design plan for your poster and an outline for your brochure.
6. Share your ideas with a classmate for suggestions and revise where necessary.
7. Create the individual elements that will be included in the recruiting kit.
8. Share your materials with the class.

ASSESSMENT
1. Use the performance task assessment lists suggested to evaluate your project.
2. Discuss what you might do differently if you do a similar project in the future.

SPANISH RESOURCES

The following Spanish language materials are available in the Spanish Resources binder:

- **Spanish Chapter Summary 29**
- **Spanish Vocabulary Activity 29**
- **Spanish Guided Reading Activities, Chapter 29**
- **Spanish Section Quizzes, Chapter 29**
- **Spanish Home Involvement Activity 29**
- **Spanish Chapter 29 Digests Audiocassette Activity and Test**

ACTIVITY MANIPULATIVES

Help students learn more about America's cultural history with:

- **American Crafts Hands-On Activities**
- **American Games Hands-On Activities**
- **American History Flash Cards**

ADDITIONAL RESOURCES FROM GLENCOE

- **American Music Cultural Traditions,** Lesson 10: "We Shall Not Be Moved"
- **The Spirit of American Art and Music,** Gordon Parks, Maya Angelou, Diana Ross, Mary Brave Bird, Joan Baez
- **U.S. History & Art,** Transparency 28, *The Family;* Transparency 29, *Day of the Fair;* Transparency 30, *Forward*
- **Supreme Court Case Studies,** *Brown* v. *Board of Education of Topeka, Kansas*
- **U.S. Desk Map**
- **Outline Map Resource Book**
- **The American History Videodisc and CD-ROM,** *Contemporary America, 1960–1990s*

A&E HOME VIDEO. Biography THE HISTORY CHANNEL.

The following videotape programs are available from Glencoe as supplements to Chapter 29:

- **Jackie Robinson** (ISBN 1-56501-154-6)
- **Lee Harvey Oswald: An American Tragedy** (ISBN 1-56501-716-1)
- **Malcolm X** (ISBN 1-56501-674-2)

To order, call Glencoe at 1-800-334-7344. To find classroom resources to accompany many of these videos, check the following home pages:
A&E Television: http://www.aetv.com
The History Channel: http://www.historychannel.com

Introducing
CHAPTER 29

Chapter Themes

Chapter Themes are listed by section on this chapter opening page of the Student Edition. A corresponding theme-based activity is available under "FOCUS," and a theme-based question is asked in the Section and Chapter Reviews.

Performance Assessment

Refer to Activity 29 in the *Performance Assessment Strategies and Activities* booklet.

GLENCOE TECHNOLOGY

VIDEODISC
MindJogger Videoquiz

Use MindJogger to preview the Chapter 29 content.

Chapter 29
Disc 4, Side B

Also available in VHS.

HISTORY AND ART Hundreds of peaceful civil rights marches, protests, and demonstrations took place across the nation in the 1950s and 1960s.

Chapter 29

1954–1973

The Civil Rights Era

Why It's Important

In the 1950s a tide of protest began to rise in America against deeply rooted attitudes of racism and discrimination. The campaign for equality expanded and gained momentum in the 1960s. Although the civil rights movement could not overcome all the obstacles that stood in the way of full citizenship, it achieved some stunning successes. Inspired by those victories, women, Hispanics, Native Americans, and others intensified their efforts to secure their full rights as citizens.

Chapter Themes

- *Section 1,* Civic Rights and Responsibilities
- *Section 2,* Individual Action
- *Section 3,* Groups and Institutions
- *Section 4,* Continuity and Change

HISTORY AND ART ***March on Detroit*** **by Stephen Hall** Demonstrations brought thousands together in the demand for social justice and equal opportunity.

EXTRA CREDIT PROJECT

Memorializing Equal Rights United States postage stamps often commemorate historical events, leaders, or milestones. The civil rights movement events described in Chapter 29 offer many possibilities for such tribute. As students read, ask them to propose a series of postage stamps that memorialize moments in the struggle for more equitable rights for various groups of Americans. Encourage students to suggest stamps relating to rights for women, African Americans, Hispanics, Native Americans, and the disabled. If they choose to draw their suggested stamps, work with them to create an appropriate display.

1954 · 1955 · 1956 · 1957

1954
Supreme Court strikes down segregation in education

1955
Rosa Parks is arrested; Montgomery bus boycott begins

1957
Martin Luther King, Jr., heads SCLC; Federal troops help integrate a Little Rock high school

Section 1

The Civil Rights Movement

READ TO DISCOVER . . .

- how a Supreme Court decision helped African Americans in their struggle for equal rights.
- why Martin Luther King, Jr., emerged as a leader of the civil rights movement.

TERMS TO LEARN

segregation	boycott
integrate	civil disobedience

The Storyteller

Jackie Robinson could do everything on a baseball field—hit singles, slam home runs, and speed from base to base. Robinson was the first African American to play major league baseball. When his team, the Brooklyn Dodgers, reached the World Series in 1947, Robinson recalled: "I experienced a completely new emotion when the National Anthem was played. This time, I thought, it is being played for me, as much as for anyone else. . . . I am standing here with all the others; and everything that takes place includes me."

Jackie Robinson baseball card

African Americans had suffered from racism and discrimination in the United States since colonial times. As the nation entered the second half of the twentieth century, many African Americans believed that the time had come for them to enjoy an equal place in American life. They fought for equal opportunities in jobs, housing, and education. They also fought against **segregation**—the separation of people of different races.

Equality in Education

★ During the 1950s and the early 1960s, African Americans boldly rejected the humiliating practice of forced separation. The **NAACP** (National Association for the Advancement of Colored People) had worked on behalf of African Americans since its founding in 1909, attacking discrimination and segregation. In the 1950s, NAACP lawyers searched for cases they could use to challenge the laws allowing the segregation of public education.

The Supreme Court had upheld segregation laws in the past. In 1896 in ***Plessy* v. *Ferguson,*** it had ruled that "separate but equal" public facilities were legal. **Thurgood Marshall,** the chief lawyer for the NAACP, decided to challenge the idea of "separate but equal." Then the NAACP began to decide which among the nation's segregated school districts to bring before the Court.

SECTION RESOURCES

Reproducible Masters
- Guided Reading Activity 29–1
- Supreme Court Case Studies
- Section Quiz 29–1
- Reteaching Activity 29–1
- Enrichment Activity 29–1

Transparencies
- Section Focus Transparency 29–1

Multimedia
- Vocabulary PuzzleMaker
- Chapter Challenger Interactive Review
- Testmaker
- ABCNews InterActive™ Martin Luther King, Jr.
- Landmark Documents in American History
- American Music Cultural Traditions

1 FOCUS

BELLRINGER
Motivational Activity

Before taking roll at the beginning of the class period, project Section Focus Transparency 29–1 and have students answer the questions. Discuss students' responses.

This activity is also available as a blackline master.

Section Focus Transparency 29–1

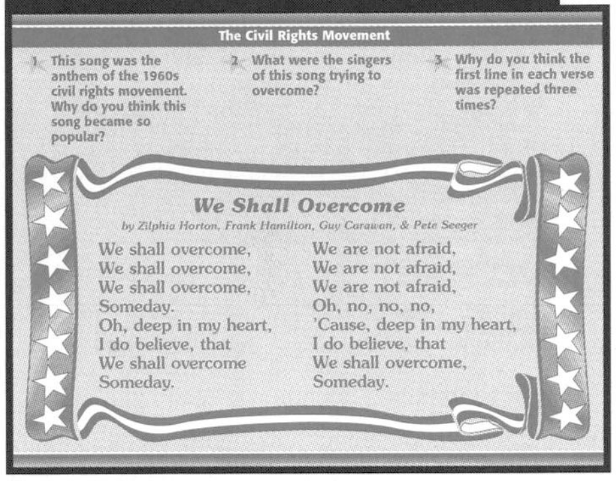

Vocabulary Precheck

After discussing the **Terms to Learn,** have students write and share sentences using the terms. Each sentence should contain two of the terms and should show the relationship between the two.

Use the **Vocabulary PuzzleMaker** to create crossword and word search puzzles.

Section Theme
Civic Rights and Responsibilities

In the 1950s African American activism became more intense and organized in an effort to secure equal rights in education and other areas.

Activity Ask: How would you feel if you were not allowed to go into a restaurant or sit on certain seats in a bus, or if people tried to stop you from going to school? Discuss students' responses.

2 TEACH

L1 Exploring Key Ideas Work with students to construct a concept web around the word *equality.* Discuss which responses were or were not generally true for African Americans of the early 1950s.

Guided Reading Activity 29–1

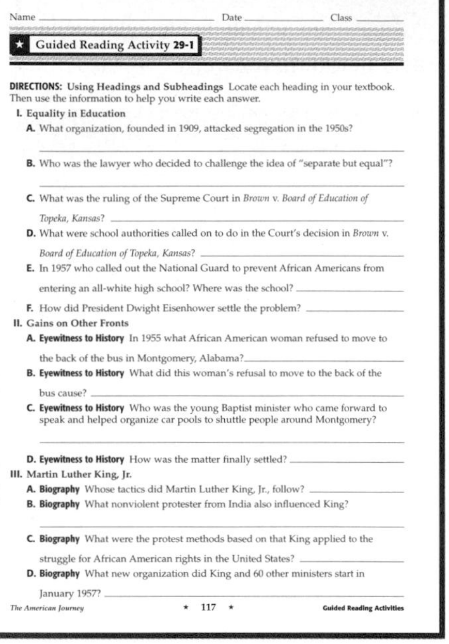
Name ____ Date ____ Class ____

★ Guided Reading Activity 29-1

DIRECTIONS: Using Headings and Subheadings Locate each heading in your textbook. Then use the information to help you write each answer.

I. Equality in Education

A. What organization, founded in 1909, attacked segregation in the 1950s? ____

B. Who was the lawyer who decided to challenge the idea of "separate but equal"? ____

C. What was the ruling of the Supreme Court in *Brown* v. *Board of Education of Topeka, Kansas*? ____

D. What were school authorities called on to do in the Court's decision in *Brown* v. *Board of Education of Topeka, Kansas*? ____

E. In 1957 who called out the National Guard to prevent African Americans from entering an all-white high school? Where was the school? ____

F. How did President Dwight Eisenhower settle the problem? ____

II. Gains on Other Fronts

A. Eyewitness to History In 1955 what African American woman refused to move to the back of the bus in Montgomery, Alabama? ____

B. Eyewitness to History What did this woman's refusal to move to the back of the bus cause? ____

C. Eyewitness to History Who was the young Baptist minister who came forward to speak and helped organize car pools to shuttle people around Montgomery? ____

D. Eyewitness to History How was the matter finally settled? ____

III. Martin Luther King, Jr.

A. Biography Whose tactics did Martin Luther King, Jr., follow? ____

B. Biography What nonviolent protester from India also influenced King? ____

C. Biography What were the protest methods based on that King applied to the struggle for African American rights in the United States? ____

D. Biography What new organization did King and 60 other ministers start in January 1957? ____

The American Journey ★ 117 ★ **Guided Reading Activities**

Copyright © by The McGraw-Hill Companies, Inc.

Linking PAST & PRESENT

***Brown,* Reopened** In 1989 Linda Brown (now Linda Brown Smith) was concerned that integration was not happening quickly enough. To make sure that her grandson received an equal education, she attempted to reopen the *Brown* case. It did not get to the courts because she and her local board of education resolved their differences.

Map Study

Answers

1. 17 states
2. the South

The *Brown* Decision

Seven-year-old African American Linda Brown was not permitted to attend an all-white elementary school just blocks from her house. To get to the segregated elementary school she was assigned to, Brown had to cross railroad tracks and take a bus for several miles. The Brown family sued the school system but lost. Marshall and the NAACP appealed the case all the way to the Supreme Court.

The case of ***Brown* v. *Board of Education of Topeka, Kansas,*** combined with several similar cases, reached the Supreme Court in December 1952. Thurgood Marshall argued that segregated schools were not and could not be equal to white schools. For that reason segregated schools violated the Fourteenth Amendment to the Constitution.

On May 17, 1954, the Court delivered its opinion. Quiet filled the Supreme Court chamber when the ruling was announced. All nine justices sat at the long bench. Nobody knew what the Court would say. Contrary to its usual practice, the Court had not released the text of the decision beforehand.

The Supreme Court ruled in *Brown* v. *Board of Education of Topeka, Kansas* that it was unconstitutional to separate schoolchildren by race. The *Brown* decision reversed the Court's decision in *Plessy* v. *Ferguson.*

Integrating the Schools

The Court's decision in *Brown* v. *Board of Education* called on school authorities to make plans for **integrating**—bringing races together in—public schools. The Court also ordered that

Segregation in United States Schools, 1950

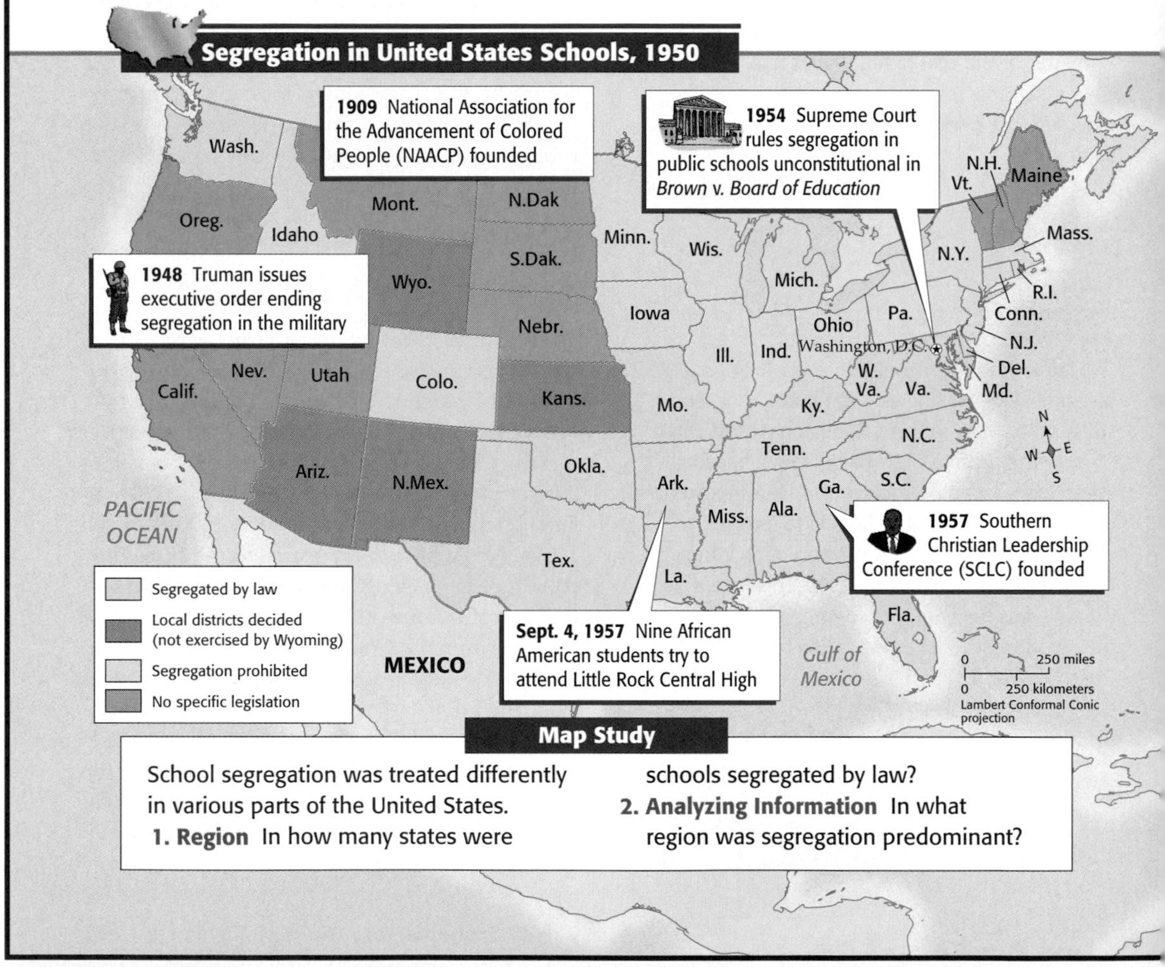

Map Study

School segregation was treated differently in various parts of the United States.

1. **Region** In how many states were schools segregated by law?
2. **Analyzing Information** In what region was segregation predominant?

COOPERATIVE LEARNING ACTIVITY

Preparing a Choral Reading In this section, students learn about the Montgomery bus boycott and the rising visibility of Martin Luther King, Jr., in the civil rights movement. Ask groups of students to prepare choral readings that pay tribute to those events. Offer *One day in Montgomery* as a starting point or recurring phrase. In each group, have some students work as writers, fact-checkers, and editors; have others take the speaking parts. In each group, advise a student director to assign parts and organize rehearsals. Follow up the groups' readings with class review of the details and importance of these events.

Picturing HISTORY Elizabeth Eckford (center) braves the insults of white citizens to enter Central High School in Little Rock, Arkansas. *NAACP button*

How did President Eisenhower respond to the crisis in Little Rock?

integration was to be carried out "with all deliberate speed"—as fast as reasonably possible.

Some school systems across the country integrated quickly. However, in parts of the South, local leaders vowed to keep African American children out of white schools. Some people formed organizations to fight integration. A clash between the federal government and these states seemed unavoidable.

Confrontation in Little Rock

In 1957 a federal judge ordered Central High School in **Little Rock, Arkansas,** an all-white school, to admit African American students. Arkansas governor **Orval Faubus** opposed integration. He called out the state's National Guard to prevent African Americans from entering the high school.

On the day the students were scheduled to begin school, armed members of the National Guard blocked the school's entrance and turned away nine African American students. One of them, 15-year-old **Elizabeth Eckford,** recalled that when she tried to squeeze past a member of the guard, "He raised his bayonet, and then the other guards moved in and raised their bayonets."

For the first time since the Civil War, a Southern state had defied the authority of the federal government. Although Eisenhower had some doubts about the *Brown* decision, he believed it was his duty to enforce the law. The president warned Faubus that if the governor did not admit the students, the federal government would act.

When a federal judge ruled that the governor had violated federal law, Faubus finally removed the National Guard. Eisenhower sent hundreds of soldiers to Little Rock to protect the students. Shielded by the federal troops, the nine African American students finally entered the school.

Footnotes to History

Thurgood Marshall In 1967 Thurgood Marshall—the great-grandson of an enslaved person—became the first African American justice on the Supreme Court.

Gains on Other Fronts

While school integration continued, African Americans made other advances in securing their rights. More and more took part in a movement dedicated to securing fair and equal treatment.

CHAPTER 29
Section 1, 821–825

Picturing HISTORY Have students analyze the facial expressions of the people.
Answer: *warned Faubus that the government would intervene to force integration, sent federal troops to protect the students*

History *and the* Humanities

- American Music Cultural Traditions, Lesson 10: "We Shall Not Be Moved"
- The Spirit of American Art and Music, Gordon Parks
- Supreme Court Case Studies, *Brown v. Board of Education of Topeka, Kansas*

ABCNEWS INTERACTIVE™

VIDEODISC
Martin Luther King, Jr.

Side 1, Chapter 10
Title: *1956 Montgomery Bus Boycott: Rosa Parks*
Subject: Rosa Parks describes what happened
Ask: **Was Rosa Parks right in refusing to give up her seat although it meant breaking the law? Explain.**

Side 1, Chapter 11
Title: *1956 Montgomery Bus Boycott: Street Scenes*
Subject: Film of Montgomery during bus boycott
Ask: **If you had lived in Montgomery, would you have joined the boycott? Explain.**

Multiple Learning Styles

Intrapersonal Have students try to identify with Linda Brown, Elizabeth Eckford, and others who were the first few African Americans to attend all-white schools. Give students a few minutes to write private journal notes about how it might have felt to be such an obvious "outsider" and why a student would be willing to go through the stress of entering a school where he or she was, for the most part, unwanted. Then ask students to use art (such as a watercolor painting), writing (a poem, for example), or drama (read or enacted) to present the imagined thoughts of one of these "outsiders." Encourage students to be creative but also to include some of the factual details from the text. Work with students to present the results. **L1, ELL**

CHAPTER 29
Section 1, 821–825

Facts On File

CD-ROM
Landmark Documents in American History

Title: *Statements by Eisenhower concerning Little Rock, 1957*
Have students read and summarize Eisenhower's position on developments at Central High School.

3 ASSESS

Assign Section 1 Review as homework or as an in-class activity.

Use **Chapter Challenger Interactive Review Software** to review Section 1.

Section Quiz 29–1

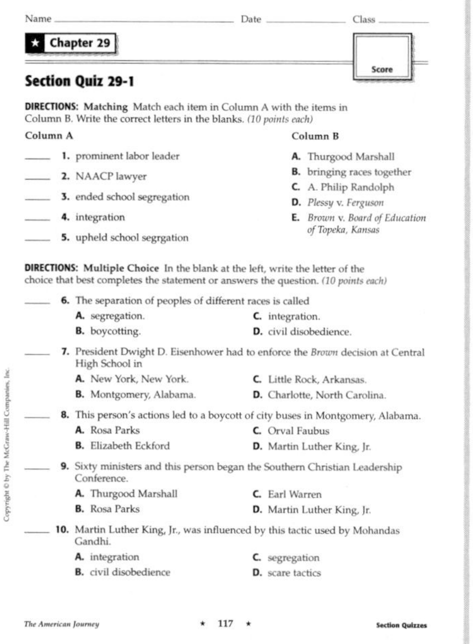
Name ____________ Date ________ Class ________

★ Chapter 29

Score

Section Quiz 29-1

DIRECTIONS: Matching Match each item in Column A with the items in Column B. Write the correct letters in the blanks. *(10 points each)*

Column A	Column B
____ **1.** prominent labor leader	**A.** Thurgood Marshall
____ **2.** NAACP lawyer	**B.** bringing races together
____ **3.** ended school segregation	**C.** A. Philip Randolph
____ **4.** integration	**D.** *Plessy* v. *Ferguson*
____ **5.** upheld school segrgation	**E.** *Brown* v. *Board of Education of Topeka, Kansas*

DIRECTIONS: Multiple Choice In the blank at the left, write the letter of the choice that best completes the statement or answers the question. *(10 points each)*

____ **6.** The separation of peoples of different races is called
A. segregation. **C.** integration.
B. boycotting. **D.** civil disobedience.

____ **7.** President Dwight D. Eisenhower had to enforce the *Brown* decision at Central High School in
A. New York, New York. **C.** Little Rock, Arkansas.
B. Montgomery, Alabama. **D.** Charlotte, North Carolina.

____ **8.** This person's actions led to a boycott of city buses in Montgomery, Alabama.
A. Rosa Parks **C.** Orval Faubus
B. Elizabeth Eckford **D.** Martin Luther King, Jr.

____ **9.** Sixty ministers and this person began the Southern Christian Leadership Conference.
A. Thurgood Marshall **C.** Earl Warren
B. Rosa Parks **D.** Martin Luther King, Jr.

____ **10.** Martin Luther King, Jr., was influenced by this tactic used by Mohandas Gandhi.
A. integration **C.** segregation
B. civil disobedience **D.** scare tactics

Copyright © by The McGraw-Hill Companies, Inc.

The American Journey ★ 117 ★ **Section Quizzes**

Chart Study

Answer the Montgomery bus boycott

Chart Skills Practice

Reading a Chart Which cause do you think is most directly related to James Meredith's attendance at the University of Mississippi? *(Students may suggest the conflict at Little Rock, also about school desegregation.)*

Eyewitness to HISTORY

The Montgomery Bus Boycott

On the evening of December 1, 1955, **Rosa Parks** boarded a bus in downtown **Montgomery, Alabama.** Parks, a seamstress, was secretary of the local chapter of the NAACP. She found an empty seat in the section reserved for whites.

When white passengers entered the bus, the driver told Parks, an African American, to move to the rear of the bus. Parks refused. At the next bus stop, she was taken off the bus by police, arrested for breaking the law, and fined $10. The episode could have ended there—but it did not.

Causes and Effects

CAUSES
- ★ 1955 Rosa Parks is arrested
- ★ 1955 Montgomery bus boycott begins
- ★ 1957 Conflict at Little Rock
- ★ 1957 SCLC is organized
- ★ 1960 Students stage sit-ins
- ★ 1963 March on Washington, D.C.

Move Toward Equality

EFFECTS
- ★ 1962 James Meredith enrolls at University of Mississippi
- ★ 1967 Thurgood Marshall appointed to Supreme Court
- ★ 1968 Shirley Chisholm elected to House
- ★ 1972 Barbara Jordan first African American woman from a Southern state to serve in Congress

Chart Study

African Americans faced many obstacles in their struggle for equal rights. **Analyzing Information** What protest followed the arrest of Rosa Parks?

Rosa Parks's arrest led African Americans in Montgomery to put into effect plans to **boycott**—refuse to use—the city's buses. The boycott organizers hoped to hurt the city financially and force it to alter its policies. They had strength in numbers—almost 75 percent of the bus company's riders were African American.

At a boycott meeting, a young Baptist minister came forward to speak. Not widely known at the time, **Martin Luther King, Jr.,** made an impact on the crowd. He declared:

> "We're here because first and foremost, we are American citizens, and we are determined to acquire our citizenship to the fullness of its meaning. We are tired—tired of being segregated and humiliated, tired of being kicked about by the brutal feet of oppression."

The boycott upset many people's daily lives, but the African Americans of Montgomery pulled together to make it work. Students hitchhiked to school; workers walked or rode bikes to their jobs. King helped organize car pools to shuttle people from place to place.

Rosa Parks on the Montgomery bus

Some white people in Montgomery struck back. Old laws were dug up to arrest the boycott's leaders. In January 1956, extremists exploded a bomb at King's house, causing damage but no injuries. The attack was only one of several violent incidents.

The bus boycott lasted for more than a year. City officials arrested King and other leaders at different times, but African Americans held firm. The local bus company lost thousands of dollars in fares, and downtown businesses lost many of their African American customers. Finally, the Supreme Court settled the matter by ruling that the Montgomery bus segregation law was unconstitutional. In December, the boycott ended.

MAKING CONNECTIONS ACTIVITY

Sports In 1947 Jackie Robinson became the first African American to play major-league baseball. Other professional sports integrated at different times. Professional football, for example, had its first African American player (Charles W. Follis) in 1904, and African American prize fighters and jockeys had been successful before that. On the other hand, it was not until 1950 that an African American was signed to play on a National Basketball Association team (Charles "Chuck" Cooper on the Boston Celtics). Have students research and share more about these and other milestones (such as Olympic triumphs) for African Americans in sports. **L3**

Biography

Martin Luther King, Jr.

With the victory in Montgomery, King became a leader of the civil rights movement. He followed the tactics of **A. Philip Randolph,** the nation's most prominent African American labor leader. King was also strongly influenced by **Mohandas Gandhi,** who had used nonviolent protest to help free the nation of India from Great Britain. In keeping with his beliefs, Gandhi used protest methods based on **civil disobedience,** or the refusal to obey laws that are considered unjust. King applied the same techniques to the struggle for African American rights in the United States.

In January 1957, King and 60 other ministers started a new organization called the **Southern Christian Leadership Conference** (SCLC). The SCLC elected King as president.

The SCLC leaders emphasized nonviolent protest. They suggested ways to react to taunts and jeers and showed civil rights workers how to protect themselves from violent attacks. The SCLC also discussed how to identify targets for protests and how to organize people for support. In taking these steps, the SCLC prepared African Americans for the struggle for equal rights.

Picturing HISTORY Martin Luther King, Jr., stands in his office near a portrait of the Indian independence leader, Mohandas Gandhi. **How was King influenced by Gandhi?**

Section 1 Review

Checking for Understanding

1. ***Identify*** NAACP, *Brown* v. *Board of Education,* Rosa Parks, Martin Luther King, Jr., SCLC.
2. ***Define*** segregation, integrate, boycott, civil disobedience.
3. ***Name*** the Supreme Court decision that banned segregation in education.

Reviewing Themes

4. **Civic Rights and Responsibilities** How did the Montgomery bus boycott end?

Critical Thinking

5. **Demonstrating Reasoned Judgment** Why do you suppose Martin Luther King, Jr., thought nonviolent protest would be the most effective way to work toward civil rights?

Activity

Composing Lyrics Write song lyrics to be sung at a civil rights march. Base your lyrics on the story of Rosa Parks and her courage the night of her arrest.

Section 1 Review Answers

1. NAACP, 821; *Brown* case, 822; Rosa Parks, 824; Martin Luther King, Jr., 824; SCLC, 825
2. The words are defined in the Glossary.
3. *Brown* v. *Board of Education of Topeka, Kansas*
4. In 1956 the Supreme Court ruled that segregation in public transportation was unconstitutional, and the boycott ended.
5. Answers will vary, but students might refer to Gandhi's success in India or the likelihood that violent protests would have turned most people against the civil rights movement.

Activity Song lyrics may convey Rosa Parks's feelings on the night of her arrest and might predict the importance her action would have for the civil rights movement as a whole.

Picturing HISTORY Gandhi called his philosophy of nonviolent civil resistance *Satyagraha* (Sanskrit for "truth and firmness"). **Answer:** *adopted Gandhi's ideas of nonviolent protest and civil disobedience*

Reteaching Activity 29–1

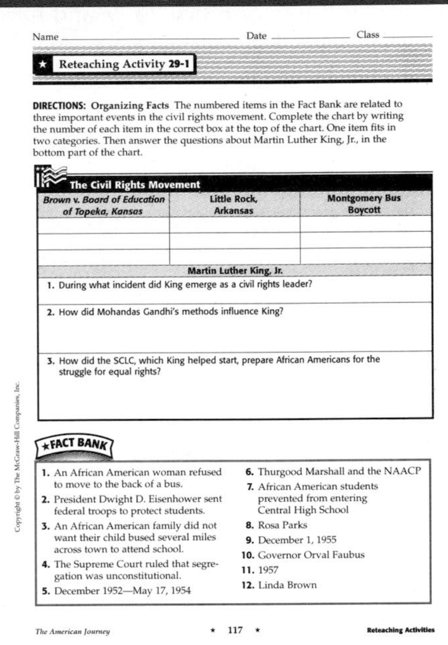

Name ______ Date ______ Class ______

★ Reteaching Activity 29-1

DIRECTIONS: Organizing Facts The numbered items in the Fact Bank are related to three important events in the civil rights movement. Complete the chart by writing the number of each item in the correct box at the top of the chart. One item fits in two categories. Then answer the questions about Martin Luther King, Jr., in the bottom part of the chart.

The Civil Rights Movement

Brown v. Board of Education of Topeka, Kansas	Little Rock, Arkansas	Montgomery Bus Boycott

Martin Luther King, Jr.

1. During what incident did King emerge as a civil rights leader?
2. How did Mohandas Gandhi's methods influence King?
3. How did the SCLC, which King helped start, prepare African Americans for the struggle for equal rights?

★FACT BANK

1. An African American woman refused to move to the back of a bus.
2. President Dwight D. Eisenhower sent federal troops to protect students.
3. An African American family did not want their child bused several miles across town to attend school.
4. The Supreme Court ruled that segregation was unconstitutional.
5. December 1952—May 17, 1954
6. Thurgood Marshall and the NAACP
7. African American students prevented from entering Central High School
8. Rosa Parks
9. December 1, 1955
10. Governor Orval Faubus
11. 1957
12. Linda Brown

The American Journey ★ 117 ★ Reteaching Activities

Enrichment Activity 29–1

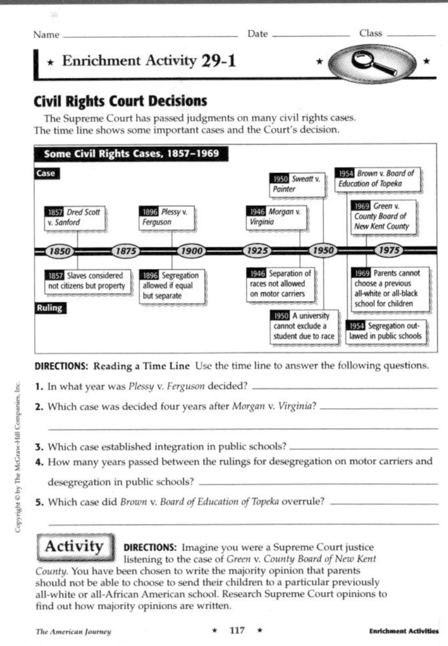

Name ______ Date ______ Class ______

★ Enrichment Activity 29-1

Civil Rights Court Decisions

The Supreme Court has passed judgments on many civil rights cases. The time line shows some important cases and the Court's decision.

DIRECTIONS: Reading a Time Line Use the time line to answer the following questions.

1. In what year was *Plessy* v. *Ferguson* decided? ______
2. Which case was decided four years after *Morgan* v. *Virginia*? ______
3. Which case established integration in public schools? ______
4. How many years passed between the rulings for desegregation on motor carriers and desegregation in public schools? ______
5. Which case did *Brown* v. *Board of Education of Topeka* overrule? ______

Activity **DIRECTIONS:** Imagine you were a Supreme Court justice listening to the case of *Green* v. *County Board of New Kent County.* You have been chosen to write the majority opinion that parents should not be able to choose to send their children to a particular previously all-white or all-African American school. Research Supreme Court opinions to find out how majority opinions are written.

The American Journey ★ 117 ★ Enrichment Activities

4 CLOSE

Have students use the time line on page 821 to describe the first steps of the civil rights movement.

1 FOCUS

BELLRINGER
Motivational Activity

Before taking roll at the beginning of the class period, project Section Focus Transparency 29–2 and have students answer the questions. Discuss students' responses.

This activity is also available as a blackline master.

Section Focus Transparency 29–2

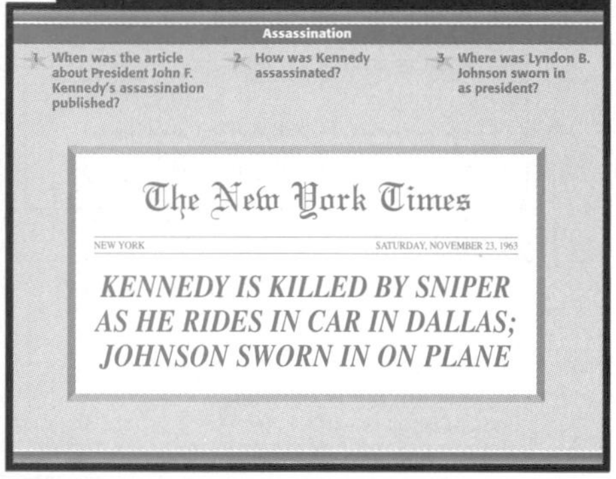

Vocabulary Precheck

Encourage students to write a brief description of the social programs of Presidents Kennedy and Johnson using the terms *poverty line, Medicare,* and *Medicaid.*

Use the **Vocabulary Puzzle-Maker** to create crossword and word search puzzles.

Section Theme
Individual Action

Presidents Kennedy and Johnson each encouraged civil rights reform, declared a war on poverty, and dealt with urban decay.

Activity Write the terms *New Frontier* and *Great Society* on the chalkboard. **Ask: How do you think these terms are meant to make Americans feel about their country?** *(Answers should suggest optimism, goodwill, and a sense of adventure.)*

1960 — 1962 — 1964 — 1966

1961 John F. Kennedy takes office as president

1963 Kennedy is assassinated

1964 President Johnson announces war on poverty

July 1964 Civil Rights Act of 1964 is passed

Section 2

Kennedy and Johnson

READ TO DISCOVER . . .

- what John F. Kennedy planned for America.
- how the nation responded to Kennedy's assassination.
- what new programs were created as part of the "Great Society."

TERMS TO LEARN

poverty line
Medicare
Medicaid

The Storyteller

They stood together on the inaugural platform: 43-year-old John F. Kennedy, tanned, vigorous, and coatless despite the subfreezing weather, and 70-year-old Dwight D. Eisenhower, wearing a muffler, looking like a tired general. The appearances of the two men, a generation apart in age, symbolized the change of leadership. Kennedy's speech promised so much: "Let every nation know . . . that we shall pay any price, bear any burden, meet any hardship, support any friend, oppose any foe to assure the survival and the success of liberty. . . ."

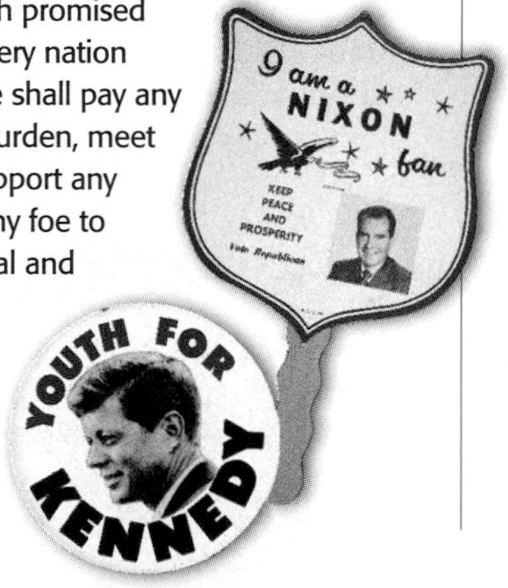

1960 presidential campaign items

By 1960, the crusade for civil rights had become a national movement. Against this background, the nation prepared for a presidential election.

The Republican candidate, Vice President **Richard M. Nixon,** pledged to continue the policies of President Eisenhower. The Democratic candidate, **John F. Kennedy,** promised new programs to help the poor and the elderly. He vowed to "get the country moving again."

Election of 1960

For much of the campaign, polls showed Nixon in the lead. One reason for this was the fact that Kennedy was Roman Catholic. No Catholic had ever been president, and many Americans feared that if Kennedy won he might show more loyalty to his church than to his country. Kennedy answered by stressing his belief in the separation of church and state.

Biography

John F. Kennedy

Kennedy came from one of the country's wealthiest and most powerful families. His father, Joseph P. Kennedy, was a successful business leader and the American ambassador to Britain during World War II.

John Kennedy joined the United States Navy during World War II and was assigned to active

SECTION RESOURCES

Reproducible Masters
- Reproducible Lesson Plan 29–2
- Guided Reading Activity 29–2
- Section Quiz 29–2
- Reteaching Activity 29–2
- Enrichment Activity 29–2

Transparencies
- Section Focus Transparency 29–2

Multimedia
- Vocabulary PuzzleMaker
- Chapter Challenger Interactive Review Software
- Testmaker
- Set On Freedom™ The American Civil Rights Movement

duty in the Pacific. When the Japanese sank the PT (patrol torpedo) boat he commanded, Kennedy saved the life of a crew member by swimming to shore with the injured man on his back. The rescue effort led to navy and marine medals for Kennedy but also aggravated an old back injury he had. The story of the rescue was later described in Robert Donovan's book *PT 109.*

Kennedy's political career began in 1946 when he won a seat in Congress from Massachusetts. Six years later, he was elected to the United States Senate. The young senator wrote a book, *Profiles in Courage,* which described difficult political decisions made by past United States senators. The book became a best-seller and received a Pulitzer Prize. After easily winning reelection to the Senate in 1958, Kennedy began campaigning for the presidency in 1960.

President John F. Kennedy

A New President

The turning point in the 1960 election came when the candidates took part in the first televised presidential debates. Kennedy appeared handsome and youthful. Nixon, who was recovering from an illness, looked tired and sick. Kennedy spoke with confidence about the future. Many viewers thought that Kennedy made a better impression.

In November, nearly 70 million voters turned out to choose between Nixon and Kennedy. For the first time, the people of Alaska and Hawaii took part in a presidential election. The results were extremely close. In the popular vote, Kennedy won 49.9 percent, while Nixon received 49.6 percent. In the electoral vote, Kennedy gained a greater margin over Nixon—303 to 219 votes.

The New Frontier

On January 20, 1961, snow covered Washington, D.C., and icy winds whipped through the city. Still, thousands of people streamed to the Capitol to see John Fitzgerald Kennedy become the thirty-fifth president of the United States. He offered the nation youth, energy, and hope. In his Inaugural Address, Kennedy spoke of a new era:

> "Let the word go forth from this time and place . . . that the torch has been passed to a new generation of Americans."

The young president promised to face the nation's challenges with determination. In closing, Kennedy roused the American people to action:

> "And so, my fellow Americans: ask not what your country can do for you—ask what you can do for your country."

Domestic Policies

Kennedy drew up plans for the **New Frontier,** a group of proposals involving increased government spending on social programs. One bill he sent to Congress called for more federal funds for education. Another bill aimed to help poor people get jobs. Reluctant to commit to Kennedy's expensive, untried programs, Congress failed to pass most of these bills.

2 TEACH

L1, ELL Solving Problems Ask students to complete this statement: **A president who believes in the need for reform can ____.** *(Answers include encourage Congress to make laws to achieve reform* and *reassure the people by talking about reform.)* Discuss students' responses.

CURRICULUM CONNECTION

CIVICS

The 1960 vote was so close that Nixon considered demanding a recount, but he then decided against it. He explained that if there were a recount, "the organization of the new administration and the orderly transfer of responsibility from the old to the new might be delayed for months. The situation within the entire federal government would be chaotic." For similar reasons he urged New York journalist Earl Mazo to stop writing a series of investigative reports about possible voting fraud.

COOPERATIVE LEARNING ACTIVITY

Reviewing the Kennedy Assassination Help students assess the profound effect that President Kennedy's death had on the United States. Organize them into three groups, each group working together to accomplish one of the following tasks:

- Locating video recordings or still photos of the assassination and its aftermath
- Outlining the "lone gunman" and various conspiracy theories
- Interviewing people they know for personal recollections of the event

When these tasks are finished, form new groups, making sure that at least two members from each of the previous groups are included in each new group. Have new group members share what they have learned.

Guided Reading Activity 29–2

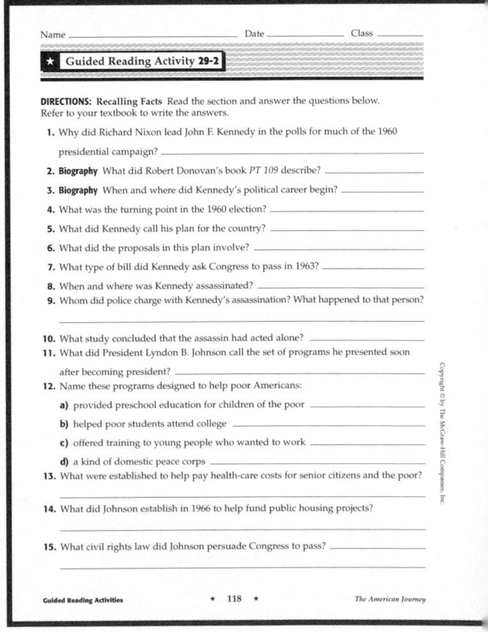

Name ____ Date ____ Class ____

★ Guided Reading Activity **29-2**

DIRECTIONS: Recalling Facts Read the section and answer the questions below. Refer to your textbook to write the answers.

1. Why did Richard Nixon lead John F. Kennedy in the polls for much of the 1960 presidential campaign? ____
2. **Biography** What did Robert Donovan's book *PT 109* describe? ____
3. **Biography** When and where did Kennedy's political career begin? ____
4. What was the turning point in the 1960 election? ____
5. What did Kennedy call his plan for the country? ____
6. What did the proposals in this plan involve? ____
7. What type of bill did Kennedy ask Congress to pass in 1963? ____
8. When and where was Kennedy assassinated? ____
9. Whom did police charge with Kennedy's assassination? What happened to that person? ____
10. What study concluded that the assassin had acted alone? ____
11. What did President Lyndon B. Johnson call the set of programs he presented soon after becoming president? ____
12. Name these programs designed to help poor Americans:
    a) provided preschool education for children of the poor ____
    b) helped poor students attend college ____
    c) offered training to young people who wanted to work ____
    d) a kind of domestic peace corps ____
13. What were established to help pay health-care costs for senior citizens and the poor? ____
14. What did Johnson establish in 1966 to help fund public housing projects? ____
15. What civil rights law did Johnson persuade Congress to pass? ____

Guided Reading Activities ★ 118 ★ *The American Journey*

CHAPTER 29
Section 2, 826–829

GLENCOE TECHNOLOGY

VIDEODISC
Set On Freedom™
The American Civil Rights Movement

Side A
Chapter 22

Title: *The Civil Rights Act of 1964*
Subject: Events surrounding this landmark legislation
Ask: **What did President Johnson say the purpose of this act was?** *(to eliminate injustice)*

What?Where?When?Who?

A World in Mourning The shock of Kennedy's death reached far. In the Soviet Union, people wept openly in the streets of Moscow.

3 ASSESS

Assign Section 2 Review as homework or as an in-class activity.

Use **Chapter Challenger Interactive Review Software** to review Section 2.

Section Quiz 29–2

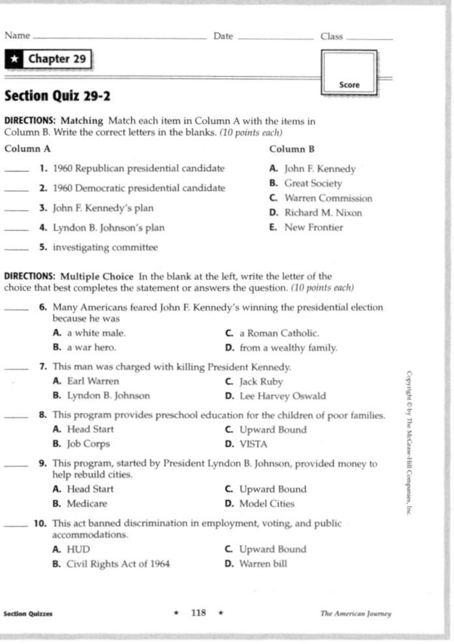
Name ______ Date ______ Class ______

Chapter 29 — Score

Section Quiz 29-2

DIRECTIONS: Matching Match each item in Column A with the items in Column B. Write the correct letters in the blanks. *(10 points each)*

Column A	Column B
____ 1. 1960 Republican presidential candidate	A. John F. Kennedy
____ 2. 1960 Democratic presidential candidate	B. Great Society
____ 3. John F. Kennedy's plan	C. Warren Commission
____ 4. Lyndon B. Johnson's plan	D. Richard M. Nixon
____ 5. investigating committee	E. New Frontier

DIRECTIONS: Multiple Choice In the blank at the left, write the letter of the choice that best completes the statement or answers the question. *(10 points each)*

____ 6. Many Americans feared John F. Kennedy's winning the presidential election because he was
A. a white male. C. a Roman Catholic.
B. a war hero. D. from a wealthy family.

____ 7. This man was charged with killing President Kennedy.
A. Earl Warren C. Jack Ruby
B. Lyndon B. Johnson D. Lee Harvey Oswald

____ 8. This program provides preschool education for the children of poor families.
A. Head Start C. Upward Bound
B. Job Corps D. VISTA

____ 9. This program, started by President Lyndon B. Johnson, provided money to help rebuild cities.
A. Head Start C. Upward Bound
B. Medicare D. Model Cities

____ 10. This act banned discrimination in employment, voting, and public accommodations.
A. HUD C. Upward Bound
B. Civil Rights Act of 1964 D. Warren bill

Another area of concern for Kennedy was civil rights. The president wished to help African Americans in their fight for equal rights. At the same time, he worried that moving too quickly would anger Southern Democrats in Congress whose support he needed to enact legislation.

In 1963 Kennedy decided to ask Congress to pass a bill guaranteeing civil rights. The House approved the measure, but it stalled in the Senate. Meanwhile, the president left on a campaign trip for **Dallas, Texas.**

Kennedy Assassinated

On November 22, 1963, Kennedy arrived in Dallas with his wife, Jacqueline. As the president and the First Lady rode through the streets in an open car, several shots rang out. Kennedy slumped against his wife. The car sped to a hospital, but the president was dead. Shortly afterward, Vice President **Lyndon B. Johnson** took the oath of office as president.

The assassination stunned the nation. Television networks broadcast the news almost without interruption for the next few days. Millions of Americans numbly watched the funeral.

In the midst of the grief came another shock. The day of Kennedy's shooting, Dallas police had arrested **Lee Harvey Oswald** and charged him with killing the president. Two days later, as police moved Oswald from one jail to another, Jack Ruby jumped through the circle of police officers and journalists and shot and killed Oswald.

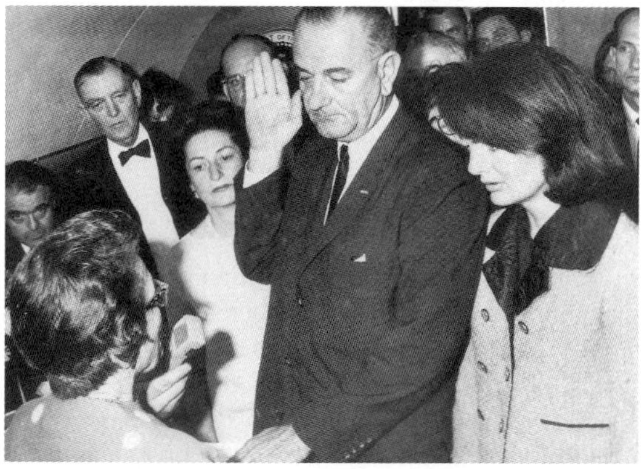
Lyndon Johnson takes the oath of office after the assassination of President Kennedy

Rumors that a group of enemies had plotted the assassination swirled around the country. Soon afterward, President Johnson appointed **Earl Warren,** chief justice of the United States, to head a commission to investigate the Kennedy shooting. After months of study, the **Warren Commission** issued its report. Oswald had acted on his own, it said. The report did not satisfy everyone, however. Many people believed the assassination was a conspiracy, or secret plot.

The "Great Society"

Soon after becoming president, Lyndon B. Johnson outlined a set of programs even more ambitious than Kennedy's New Frontier. He called his proposals the **"Great Society."** In a speech he explained his vision of America:

> "In a land of great wealth, families must not live in hopeless poverty. In a land rich in harvest, children must not go hungry. . . . In a great land of learning and scholars, young people must be taught to read and write."

Johnson had acquired great skill as a legislator during his 22 years in Congress. He used this skill to persuade Congress to launch programs that would make the Great Society real.

The War on Poverty

In January 1964, President Johnson declared "an unconditional war on poverty in America." The first part of his plan for a Great Society consisted of programs to help Americans who lived below the **poverty line**—the minimum income needed to survive. A program called **Head Start** provided preschool education for the children of poor families. **Upward Bound** helped poor students attend college. The **Job Corps** offered training to young people who wanted to work. **Volunteers in Service to America** (VISTA)

MULTIPLE LEARNING STYLES

Visual/Spatial Americans found inspiration in Kennedy's idealism, grieved at his death, and recaptured some hope for their country in President Johnson's determination. Ask students to create a poster that they feel captures the essence of President Kennedy's "New Frontier," or of President Johnson's "Great Society." Work with students to prepare a "gallery walk," in which the posters are grouped thematically and artists can explain their work to onlookers. **L1, ELL**

was a kind of domestic peace corps of citizens working in poor neighborhoods.

Among the most important laws passed under Johnson were those establishing **Medicare** and **Medicaid.** Medicare helped pay for medical care for senior citizens. Medicaid helped poor people pay their hospital bills.

Helping Cities and Schools

Other parts of the Great Society targeted the nation's crumbling cities. In 1966 President Johnson established the **Department of Housing and Urban Development** (HUD), which helped fund public housing projects. Another program, Model Cities, provided money to help rebuild cities.

Schools received a boost from the Elementary and Secondary Education Act of 1965, which greatly increased spending for education. Under Johnson, the amount of federal money spent on education more than doubled.

Civil Rights

Although raised in the South, Lyndon Johnson was not a segregationist. He believed that the nation must protect the rights of all American citizens.

When Johnson took office, he vowed to turn the civil rights bill Kennedy had proposed into law. In early 1964 he warned Congress that he would accept nothing but success: "We are going to pass a civil rights bill if it takes all summer."

Congress passed the **Civil Rights Act of 1964** in July. The act prohibited discrimination against African Americans in employment, voting, and public accommodations. It banned discrimination not only by race and color, but also by sex, religion, or national origin.

A major force leading to its passage came from outside the nation's capital in the form of growing support for the goals of the civil rights movement.

Picturing HISTORY President Johnson passes out Medicare checks to senior citizens in Beaumont, Texas. **What was the purpose of Medicare?**

"Thank you" gift to LBJ for Medicare

Section 2 Review

Checking for Understanding

1. ***Identify*** John F. Kennedy, New Frontier, Lyndon B. Johnson.
2. ***Define*** poverty line, Medicare, Medicaid.
3. ***List*** the new government programs that Johnson created in his "War on Poverty."

Reviewing Themes

4. **Individual Action** Describe Johnson's policies regarding equal rights.

Critical Thinking

5. **Making Comparisons** If Nixon had won the 1960 presidential election, do you think he would have created his own Great Society? Explain.

Activity

Creating a Poster Choose one of President Kennedy's or Johnson's programs and make a poster supporting or opposing it.

Section 2 Review Answers

1. John F. Kennedy, 826; New Frontier, 827; Lyndon B. Johnson, 828
2. The words are defined in the Glossary.
3. Head Start, Upward Bound, Job Corps, VISTA, Medicare, and Medicaid
4. Johnson persuaded Congress to pass the Civil Rights Act of 1964, which prohibited discrimination in employment, voting, and public accommodations.
5. Answers will vary. Students should recognize that Nixon, as a Republican, was inclined to believe that the government's role should be limited. During his campaign, Nixon vowed to continue Eisenhower's policies, which supported existing social programs but not new ones.

Activity Posters should make clear why students support or oppose the program.

Picturing HISTORY Before becoming president, Johnson had represented Texas in both houses of Congress.

Answer: *It helped pay for medical care for senior citizens.*

Reteaching Activity 29–2

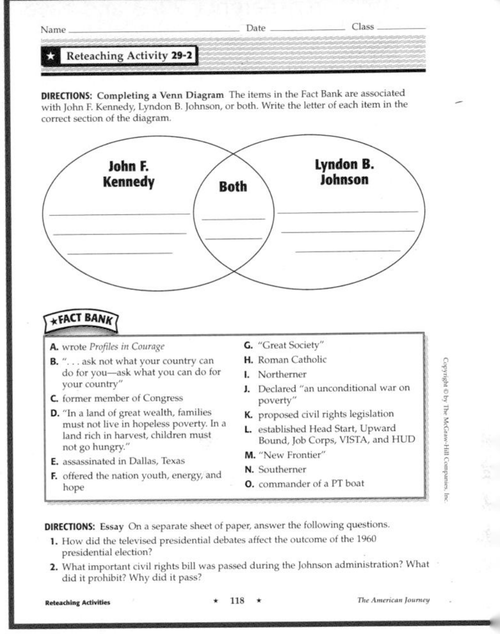

Name ____________ Date ________ Class ________

Reteaching Activity 29-2

DIRECTIONS: Completing a Venn Diagram The items in the Fact Bank are associated with John F. Kennedy, Lyndon B. Johnson, or both. Write the letter of each item in the correct section of the diagram.

FACT BANK

- **A.** wrote *Profiles in Courage*
- **B.** ". . . ask not what your country can do for you—ask what you can do for your country"
- **C.** former member of Congress
- **D.** "In a land of great wealth, families must not live in hopeless poverty. In a land rich in harvest, children must not go hungry."
- **E.** assassinated in Dallas, Texas
- **F.** offered the nation youth, energy, and hope
- **G.** "Great Society"
- **H.** Roman Catholic
- **I.** Northerner
- **J.** Declared "an unconditional war on poverty"
- **K.** proposed civil rights legislation
- **L.** established Head Start, Upward Bound, Job Corps, VISTA, and HUD
- **M.** "New Frontier"
- **N.** Southerner
- **O.** commander of a PT boat

DIRECTIONS: Essay On a separate sheet of paper, answer the following questions.

1. How did the televised presidential debates affect the outcome of the 1960 presidential election?
2. What important civil rights bill was passed during the Johnson administration? What did it prohibit? Why did it pass?

Reteaching Activities ★ 118 ★ *The American Journey*

Enrichment Activity 29–2

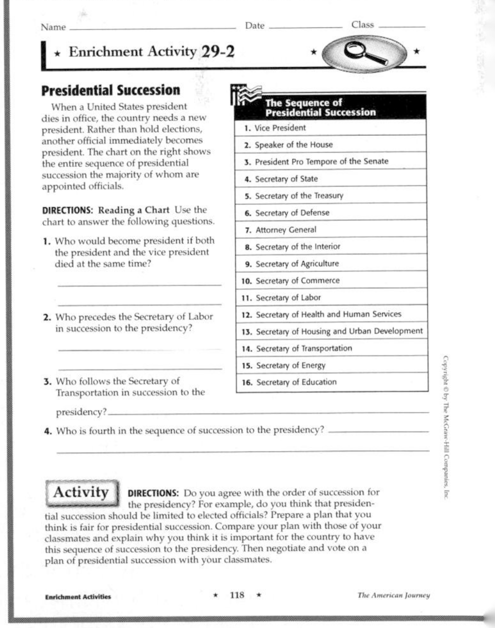

Name ____________ Date ________ Class ________

★ Enrichment Activity 29-2

Presidential Succession

When a United States president dies in office, the country needs a new president. Rather than hold elections, another official immediately becomes president. The chart on the right shows the entire sequence of presidential succession the majority of whom are appointed officials.

The Sequence of Presidential Succession
1. Vice President
2. Speaker of the House
3. President Pro Tempore of the Senate
4. Secretary of State
5. Secretary of the Treasury
6. Secretary of Defense
7. Attorney General
8. Secretary of the Interior
9. Secretary of Agriculture
10. Secretary of Commerce
11. Secretary of Labor
12. Secretary of Health and Human Services
13. Secretary of Housing and Urban Development
14. Secretary of Transportation
15. Secretary of Energy
16. Secretary of Education

DIRECTIONS: Reading a Chart Use the chart to answer the following questions.

1. Who would become president if both the president and the vice president died at the same time?
2. Who precedes the Secretary of Labor in succession to the presidency?
3. Who follows the Secretary of Transportation in succession to the presidency?
4. Who is fourth in the sequence of succession to the presidency?

Activity **DIRECTIONS:** Do you agree with the order of succession for the presidency? For example, do you think that presidential succession should be limited to elected officials? Prepare a plan that you think is fair for presidential succession. Compare your plan with those of your classmates and explain why you think it is important for the country to have this sequence of succession to the presidency. Then negotiate and vote on a plan of presidential succession with your classmates.

Enrichment Activities ★ 118 ★ *The American Journey*

4 CLOSE

Have students list the reforms that occurred during the Kennedy and early Johnson administrations.

CHAPTER 29
Section 3, 830–835

1 FOCUS

BELLRINGER
Motivational Activity

Before taking roll at the beginning of the class period, project Section Focus Transparency 29–3 and have students answer the questions. Discuss students' responses.

This activity is also available as a blackline master.

Section Focus Transparency 29–3

Civil Rights Organizations

DIRECTIONS: Match the organizations on the left with their descriptions on the right. You may skim through this section in your textbook if you need help.

1. Congress of Racial Equality (CORE)
2. Student Nonviolent Coordinating Committee (SNCC)
3. Southern Christian Leadership Conference (SCLC)
4. Black Panthers
5. Nation of Islam

A. demanded reforms and opposed the police
B. organized Freedom Riders in 1961
C. advocated separation of races
D. organized major demonstration in Selma, Alabama
E. organized nonviolent marches in Birmingham, Alabama

Vocabulary Precheck

Point out that the prefix *inter-* in *interstate* means "between." Call on volunteers to name and define other words with the same prefix.

Use the **Vocabulary Puzzle-Maker** to create crossword and word search puzzles.

Section Theme
Groups and Institutions

A new wave of civil rights activity swept across the nation in the 1960s as more radical groups became involved in the movement.

Activity On the chalkboard, write *I HAVE A DREAM.* Ask students to share what they know about the "dream" of Martin Luther King, Jr., and the effect of his leadership.

1960 — 1965 — 1970

1961 Freedom Riders move through the South

1962 James Meredith enrolls at University of Mississippi

1963 More than 200,000 people march in Washington, D.C.

1968 Martin Luther King, Jr., is assassinated

Section 3

The Struggle Continues

READ TO DISCOVER . . .
- what actions African Americans took in the early 1960s to secure their rights.
- how radical voices emerged in the civil rights movement.
- why riots erupted in some cities.

TERMS TO LEARN

sit-in   interstate

The Storyteller

On February 1, 1960, four African American students walked into a store in Greensboro, North Carolina. After buying a few items, they sat down at a "whites-only" lunch counter. When a waitress questioned what they were doing, one of the students replied, "We believe since we buy books and papers in the other part of the store, we should get served in this part." They were refused service, and the four sat at the counter until the store closed. By the end of the week, hundreds of students had joined the protest. Angry whites jeered at the students and dumped food on them. The protesters refused to leave or strike back.

Supporting the sit-ins

A new wave of civil rights activity swept across the nation in the 1960s. Early actions targeted segregation in the South. Segregation existed in the North as well, but social patterns rather than laws provided the main obstacle to integration there. In Northern cities and suburbs, African Americans and whites often lived in different neighborhoods; as a result, their children often attended different schools. Soon African Americans expanded their goal to fighting discrimination and racism in the North as well as in the South.

Growing Protests

What four students began in Greensboro in February 1960 quickly spread. High school and college students staged sit-ins in nearly 80 cities. A **sit-in** is the act of protesting by sitting down. By the summer of 1961, more than 70,000 activists—African American and white—had taken part in sit-ins. Sit-ins were staged throughout the nation against stores that practiced segregation. Store managers wanted to end the disturbances and the loss of business. Gradually many stores agreed to desegregate.

The sit-ins helped launch a new civil rights group, the **Student Nonviolent Coordinating Committee** (SNCC). Civil rights activist **Ella Baker** was a guiding spirit behind SNCC and one of its organizers. Earlier, Baker had played important roles in both the NAACP and the SCLC. SNCC was a key player in the civil rights movement for several years.

SECTION RESOURCES

Reproducible Masters
- Guided Reading Activity 29–3
- Section Quiz 29–3
- Reteaching Activity 29–3
- Enrichment Activity 29–3

Transparencies
- Section Focus Transparency 29–3
- U.S. History & Art, Transparencies 29, 30

Multimedia
- Vocabulary PuzzleMaker
- Chapter Challenger Interactive Review
- Testmaker
- Set On Freedom™ The American Civil Rights Movement
- ABCNews InterActive™ Martin Luther King, Jr.
- GTV: American People: Fabric of a Nation

Freedom Rides

The Supreme Court had ruled in 1960 against segregated bus facilities. Another civil rights group, the **Congress of Racial Equality** (CORE), decided to see whether the ruling was being enforced.

On May 4, 1961, a group of African American and white CORE members left Washington, D.C., on two buses bound for New Orleans. They called themselves **Freedom Riders.** The bus trip went smoothly until it reached Alabama, where angry whites stoned and beat the Freedom Riders.

Television and newspapers broadcast reports of the beatings. **Robert Kennedy**, the United States attorney general, asked CORE to stop the Freedom Rides for a "cooling-off period." CORE leader **James Farmer** responded: "We have been cooling off for 350 years. If we cool off any more, we will be in a deep freeze."

Violence and Arrests

The Freedom Riders pressed on, only to meet more violence in Birmingham and Montgomery, Alabama. There were no mobs waiting for the Freedom Riders in Jackson, Mississippi. However, police, state troopers, and Mississippi National Guard units were everywhere. As the Riders stepped off the bus and tried to enter the whites-only waiting room at the bus station, they were arrested for trespassing and jailed.

Despite the violence and the jail sentences, more Freedom Riders kept coming all summer. In the fall the Interstate Commerce Commission took steps to enforce the Supreme Court ruling, issuing new regulations that banned segregation on interstate buses—those that crossed state lines—and in bus stations.

Gaining Momentum

African Americans continued to apply pressure to secure their civil rights. Their actions came during John Kennedy's presidency. They spurred the president to take a more active role in the civil rights struggle.

Integrating Universities

In 1962 a federal court ordered the University of Mississippi to enroll its first African American student, **James Meredith.** However, Mississippi governor **Ross Barnett,** with the aid of state police, prevented Meredith from registering. When President Kennedy sent federal marshals to escort Meredith to the campus, riots erupted. A mob stormed the administration building armed with guns and rocks. The marshals fought back with tear gas and nightsticks. Two people were killed, but Meredith succeeded in registering. Federal troops were stationed at the university to protect him until he graduated in 1963.

Another confrontation between state and federal power took place in June 1963—this time in Alabama. Governor **George Wallace** vowed he would "stand in the schoolhouse door" to block the integration of the University of Alabama in Tuscaloosa. President Kennedy, acting on the advice of his brother, sent the Alabama National Guard to ensure the entry of African Americans to the university. As a result, Wallace backed down.

Picturing HISTORY James Meredith (center) became the first African American to attend the University of Mississippi. **What action did the federal government take to make sure that Meredith could enroll?**

COOPERATIVE LEARNING ACTIVITY

Discussing Forms of Protest To review the civil rights movement as it progressed into the 1960s, ask students to count off from 1 to 5 to determine which of the following topic groups they will join: (1) student sit-ins; (2) SCLC marches; (3) speeches by Stokely Carmichael; (4) Freedom Rides; (5) speeches by Malcolm X. Within each group, ask volunteers to take on the tasks of explaining the form of protest, why it was chosen, where it was used (if known), and what results it had. Conclude by taking a class vote on the most conservative, most radical, and most effective forms of protest.

2 TEACH

L1 Reviewing Facts Have students recall the civil rights concerns of Presidents Kennedy and Johnson. **Ask: How could people who were *not* in the government express their concerns about civil rights?** *(Answers include demonstrating, giving speeches, writing letters, and petitioning lawmakers.)*

Guided Reading Activity 29–3

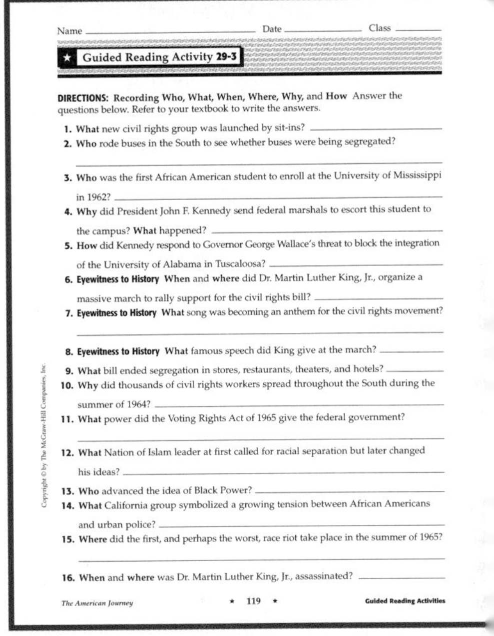

Name ______ Date ______ Class ______

★ Guided Reading Activity **29-3**

DIRECTIONS: Recording Who, What, When, Where, Why, and **How** Answer the questions below. Refer to your textbook to write the answers.

1. **What** new civil rights group was launched by sit-ins? ______
2. **Who** rode buses in the South to see whether buses were being segregated? ______
3. **Who** was the first African American student to enroll at the University of Mississippi in 1962? ______
4. **Why** did President John F. Kennedy send federal marshals to escort this student to the campus? **What** happened? ______
5. **How** did Kennedy respond to Governor George Wallace's threat to block the integration of the University of Alabama in Tuscaloosa? ______
6. **Eyewitness to History When** and **where** did Dr. Martin Luther King, Jr., organize a massive march to rally support for the civil rights bill? ______
7. **Eyewitness to History What** song was becoming an anthem for the civil rights movement? ______
8. **Eyewitness to History What** famous speech did King give at the march? ______
9. **What** bill ended segregation in stores, restaurants, theaters, and hotels? ______
10. **Why** did thousands of civil rights workers spread throughout the South during the summer of 1964? ______
11. **What** power did the Voting Rights Act of 1965 give the federal government? ______
12. **What** Nation of Islam leader at first called for racial separation but later changed his ideas? ______
13. **Who** advanced the idea of Black Power? ______
14. **What** California group symbolized a growing tension between African Americans and urban police? ______
15. **Where** did the first, and perhaps the worst, race riot take place in the summer of 1965? ______
16. **When** and **where** was Dr. Martin Luther King, Jr., assassinated? ______

The American Journey ★ 119 ★ **Guided Reading Activities**

Picturing HISTORY Constance Baker Motley, the NAACP attorney who represented Meredith, later noted, "Under our system, the federal court is supreme to any state government, and the South was not agreeing to that proposition when it came to the rights for Black Americans. So our Constitution was put to the test and survived. Our country is stronger now for having had that demonstration of what the Constitution means in practical application." **Ask: Who led the movement to keep Meredith out of the university?** *(Mississippi governor Ross Barnett)* **Answer:** *President Kennedy sent in federal marshals to make sure that Meredith registered and kept troops stationed at the university until Meredith graduated.*

CHAPTER 29
Section 3, 830–835

Picturing HISTORY Page 843 has excerpts of King's "Letter From a Birmingham Jail." **Answer:** *brought the reality of the civil rights struggle into Americans' homes*

GLENCOE TECHNOLOGY

VIDEODISC
Set On Freedom™
The American Civil Rights Movement

Side A
Chapter 9

Title: *The Sit-In Movement, 1960*
Subject: Contributions of SNCC
Ask: **Do you think you would have had the courage of these young people? Explain.**

Side A
Chapter 11

Title: *Freedom Rides, 1961*
Subject: Role of Freedom Riders in ending interstate travel segregation
Ask: **In what state did the Riders encounter the most violence?** *(Alabama)*

Side A
Chapter 24

Title: *The Assassination of Malcolm X, 1965*
Subject: Malcolm X
Ask: **What did Malcolm X say would solve African Americans' problems?** *(for African Americans to be loyal among themselves)*

Linking PAST & PRESENT

An Unhappy Enemy FBI director J. Edgar Hoover was no supporter of King. He compiled information to use against the civil rights leader. When King's Nobel award was announced, Hoover redoubled his efforts to discredit King and turn government leaders against him.

Picturing HISTORY Police in Birmingham, Alabama, used high-pressure water hoses against civil rights marchers. **What role did television have in advancing the civil rights cause?**

Poster advertising 1963 March on Washington

Birmingham

In the spring of 1963, Martin Luther King, Jr., and the SCLC targeted **Birmingham, Alabama,** for a desegregation protest. Police arrested hundreds of demonstrators, including King, but the demonstrations continued. National television carried vivid pictures of police setting snarling police dogs on unarmed demonstrators and washing small children across streets with the powerful impact of fire hoses. President Kennedy sent 3,000 troops to restore peace. Then, in June, he proposed a new civil rights bill that would outlaw segregation throughout the nation.

Eyewitness to HISTORY

March on Washington

To rally support for the civil rights bill, Martin Luther King, Jr., and the SCLC organized a massive march in Washington, D.C., on August 28, 1963. More than 200,000 people, of all colors and from all over the country, arrived to take part. Emily Rock, a 15-year-old African American, described how she felt at the march:

> "There was this sense of hope for the future—the belief that this march was the big step in the right direction. It could be heard in the voices of the people singing and seen in the way they walked. It poured out into smiles."

About 6,000 police officers stood nearby, but they had nothing to do but direct traffic. There was no trouble. Proceeding with great dignity and joy, the marchers carried signs urging Congress to act. They sang songs, including one that was becoming the anthem of the civil rights movement: "We Shall Overcome."

Late in the afternoon, Martin Luther King, Jr., spoke to the crowd in ringing words of his desire to see America transformed:

> "I have a dream that one day this nation will rise up and live out the true meaning of its creed: 'We hold these truths to be self-evident; that all men are created equal.' . . . When we let freedom ring, . . . we will be able to speed up that day when all of God's children . . . [will] join hands and sing in the words of the old . . . spiritual, 'Free at last! Free at last! Thank God Almighty, we are free at last!'"

Footnotes to History

The Prize For his nonviolent pursuit of equal rights, Martin Luther King, Jr., won the Nobel Peace Prize in 1964.

MULTIPLE LEARNING STYLES

Auditory/Musical Locate a recording of King's "I Have a Dream" speech. Have students listen to it twice. The first time, discourage them from taking notes; rather, let them focus on the tone and cadence of King's voice. Then have them pause to make a few notes about the "sound" of the speech. The second time, students can write freely as they listen. Discuss with students any phrasing and ideas in the speech that they found memorable. Ask them to comment about the inspiration they heard in those ideas—and in the sound of King's voice. **L2**

Freedom Summer

Congress did not pass Kennedy's civil rights bill until after his death. President **Lyndon B. Johnson,** who succeeded Kennedy, finally persuaded Congress to pass the bill. The **Civil Rights Act of 1964** outlawed discrimination in hiring and ended segregation in stores, restaurants, theaters, and hotels. Yet in many states, African Americans still could not vote. Poll taxes and other discriminatory laws prevented them from exercising this right.

During the summer of 1964, thousands of civil rights workers spread throughout the South to help African Americans register to vote. They called the campaign **Freedom Summer,** but the workers faced strong, sometimes violent, opposition.

The Right to Vote

The next year SNCC organized a major demonstration in **Selma, Alabama,** to protest the continued denial of African Americans' right to vote. Police attacks on the marchers again dramatized the cause.

President Johnson stepped in. On March 15, 1965, in a televised speech, the president urged passage of a voting rights bill. "About this there can be no argument," he said. "Every American citizen must have an equal right to vote." Three months later Johnson signed the **Voting Rights Act of 1965** into law. The act gave the federal government the power to force local officials to allow African Americans to register to vote.

The act led to dramatic changes in political life in the South. In 1966 about 100 African Americans held elective office in the South. By 1972 that number had increased 10 times.

Other Voices

By the mid-1960s, the civil rights movement had won numerous victories. Yet a growing number of African Americans grew tired of the slow pace of change and bitter over white attacks.

American Memories

March on Washington, 1963

Button celebrating the March on Washington

Button honoring the march

NAACP hat

What Was It Like? On August 28, 1963, more than 200,000 gathered at the Lincoln Memorial to call for civil rights reform. **What was the theme of Martin Luther King, Jr.'s, address?**

MAKING CONNECTIONS ACTIVITY

Civic Issues Does discrimination—racial or otherwise—still exist in the United States? Have students support an answer to this question by providing an illustration or photo. Students may draw or photograph a scene, or they may find an appropriate visual. If students believe that discrimination continues today, their illustration or photo should show a commonplace setting (for example, a school lunchroom) in which someone is being "segregated" in some fashion. Students who believe that discrimination is a thing of the past should show an everyday example of cooperation between people with obvious differences. Work with students to prepare a display of the visuals; follow up with class discussion. **L1, ELL**

ABCNEWS INTERACTIVE™

VIDEODISC
Martin Luther King, Jr.

Side 2, Chapters 4–28
Title: *The Speech, August 28, 1963*
Subject: "I Have a Dream"
Ask: **How were you affected by the speech?**

History *and the* Humanities

U.S. History & Art, Transparency 29, *Day of the Fair;* Transparency 30, *Forward*

The Spirit of American Art and Music, Maya Angelou, Diana Ross

American Memories

March on Washington, 1963
Because of racial violence in June, President Kennedy urged King not to hold the march, but King and his colleagues held firm. March organizer Bayard Rustin later said, "What made the march was that black people voted that day with their feet. They came from every state, they came in jalopies, on trains, buses, anything they could get—some walked. . . . And after [members of Congress] came and saw that it was very orderly, that there was fantastic determination, that there were all kinds of people there other than black people, they knew there was a consensus in this country for the civil rights bill."
Answer: *King's theme was his dream of an America in which all people were free and equal.*

CHAPTER 29
Section 3, 830–835

Picturing HISTORY Refer students to Malcolm X's quote on page 844.
Answer: *He started off supporting the separation of blacks and whites, but by 1965 he had changed to an idea of "white-black brotherhood."*

Who? What? Where? When?

Black Panthers The name *Black Panthers* reflected the group's militant stand. Members dressed in black from their berets to their black leather boots. Eldridge Cleaver, cofounder of the Black Panthers, noted the aims of the organization in his book *Soul on Ice* (1967): "What the white man must be brought to understand is that the black man . . . does not intend to be tricked again into another hundred-year forfeit of freedom. Not for a single moment or for any price will the black men now rising up in America settle for anything less than their full . . . share . . . in the sovereignty of America."

3 ASSESS

Assign Section 3 Review as homework or as an in-class activity.

Section Quiz 29–3

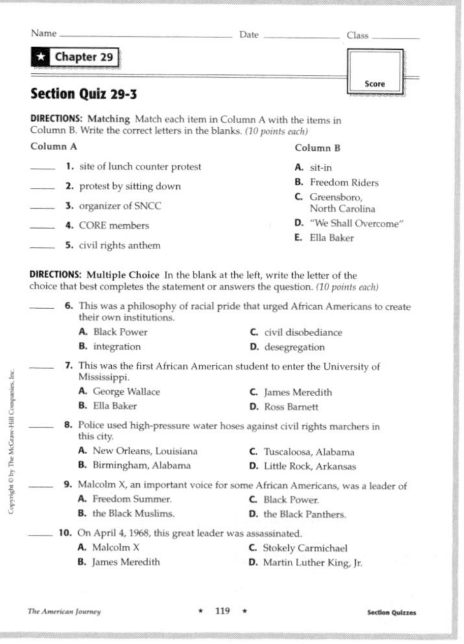

Name ______ Date ______ Class ______

Chapter 29

Score

Section Quiz 29-3

DIRECTIONS: Matching Match each item in Column A with the items in Column B. Write the correct letters in the blanks. *(10 points each)*

Column A	Column B
____ **1.** site of lunch counter protest	**A.** sit-in
____ **2.** protest by sitting down	**B.** Freedom Riders
____ **3.** organizer of SNCC	**C.** Greensboro, North Carolina
____ **4.** CORE members	**D.** "We Shall Overcome"
____ **5.** civil rights anthem	**E.** Ella Baker

DIRECTIONS: Multiple Choice In the blank at the left, write the letter of the choice that best completes the statement or answers the question. *(10 points each)*

____ **6.** This was a philosophy of racial pride that urged African Americans to create their own institutions.
A. Black Power **C.** civil disobediance
B. integration **D.** desegregation

____ **7.** This was the first African American student to enter the University of Mississippi.
A. George Wallace **C.** James Meredith
B. Ella Baker **D.** Ross Barnett

____ **8.** Police used high-pressure water hoses against civil rights marchers in this city.
A. New Orleans, Louisiana **C.** Tuscaloosa, Alabama
B. Birmingham, Alabama **D.** Little Rock, Arkansas

____ **9.** Malcolm X, an important voice for some African Americans, was a leader of
A. Freedom Summer. **C.** Black Power.
B. the Black Muslims. **D.** the Black Panthers.

____ **10.** On April 4, 1968, this great leader was assassinated.
A. Malcolm X **C.** Stokely Carmichael
B. James Meredith **D.** Martin Luther King, Jr.

The American Journey ★ 119 ★ **Section Quizzes**

Picturing HISTORY In 1964, after a lengthy trip to Africa and the Middle East, Malcolm X called for closer ties between African Americans and African people in other parts of the world. **How did Malcolm X's ideas change during the early 1960s?**

Separatism

Malcolm X, a leader in the Nation of Islam (or Black Muslims), emerged as an important new voice for some African Americans. Malcolm X criticized the civil rights goal of integration, declaring that the best way for African Americans to achieve justice was to separate themselves from whites.

Malcolm X gained increasing support. By 1965, however, he had begun to change his ideas. Instead of racial separation, he called for "a society in which there could exist honest white-black brotherhood." Soon afterwards, he was killed by an assassin from a rival group among the Black Muslims.

His fiery words and passionate ideas, contained in his autobiography and other writings, continued to influence the civil rights movement after his death.

Black Power

Other African American leaders embraced more radical approaches. **Stokely Carmichael,** who became the leader of SNCC, advanced the idea of **Black Power.** This was a philosophy of racial pride that said African Americans should create their own culture and political institutions. Carmichael and other radicals called at times for revolution, a complete transformation of society. Although rejected by such groups as the NAACP, which saw it as a threat to law and order, the idea of Black Power had a great impact on the civil rights movement.

Violence Erupts

★ In Oakland, California, a group of young radicals formed the **Black Panther Party.** A chief goal of the group was to protect the African American community from police actions that Panther leaders considered brutality.

The Black Panthers symbolized a growing tension between African Americans and urban police. Large numbers of African Americans in urban areas felt frustrated over poverty and unemployment. The Panthers demanded reforms and armed themselves in opposition to the police. Several armed clashes with the police occurred.

Cities Burn

The first major urban riots since the 1940s took place in the summer of 1965 in the **Watts** section of **Los Angeles.** In a week of rioting, 34 people died and much of Watts burned to the ground. National Guard troops were called in to end the

Linking PAST & PRESENT

Honoring King

In 1983 Congress made the birthday of Martin Luther King, Jr., a national holiday. It is celebrated on the third Monday in January.

CRITICAL THINKING ACTIVITY

Formulating Questions Have students prepare questions to interview someone who lived through the civil rights movement. Help students prepare questions that encourage more than a "yes" or "no" answer, such as the following:

- **When were you first aware that "civil rights" was a movement and not just a need?**
- **Which forms of protest most impressed you? In which, if any, did you participate?**
- **How did your life change as a result of the civil rights movement?**
- **How do you think the civil rights movement should be remembered today?**

If possible, arrange for at least one in-class interview. Discuss how responses to the questions compare with information in the text. **L2** uprising. The Watts riot was the first of a series of racial disorders that hit cities in the summers of 1965, 1966, and 1967.

In 1966 rioting broke out in more than 40 Northern cities, including San Francisco, Chicago, and Cleveland. In July 1967, 5 days of protests, looting, and burning of buildings in Newark, New Jersey, ended with the deaths of 23 people and more than $10 million in damage. The next week, a massive uprising in **Detroit** shut the city down for several days until the National Guard and the army could restore order.

President Johnson named a commission of officials and scholars to study the causes of the riots and to suggest steps to improve conditions. The report of this group, the Kerner Commission, warned that "our nation is moving toward two societies, one black, one white—separate and unequal."

The wave of urban riots devastated many African American neighborhoods. The riots ended—but not before one last burst of rage.

Family and friends mourn at the funeral of Martin Luther King, Jr.

King Is Assassinated

On April 4, 1968, racial tension in the United States took another tragic turn. On that night in Memphis, Tennessee, an assassin shot and killed Dr. Martin Luther King, Jr. King's assassination set off angry rioting in more than 100 cities. Fires burned in the nation's capital, just blocks from the Capitol and the White House.

Thousands of people attended King's funeral in Atlanta. Millions more watched on television. All mourned the death of an American hero who, the night before his death, had said God "has allowed me to go up to the mountain, and I've seen the promised land. I may not get there with you. But I want you to know tonight, that we, as a people, will get to the promised land!"

Section 3 Review

Checking for Understanding

1. ***Identify*** Freedom Riders, James Meredith, Civil Rights Act of 1964, Voting Rights Act of 1965, Malcolm X, Stokely Carmichael.
2. ***Define*** sit-in, interstate.
3. ***Describe*** actions taken by African Americans to secure the right to vote.

Reviewing Themes

4. **Groups and Institutions** How did the philosophy of radical groups such as the Black Panthers differ from that of Martin Luther King, Jr.?

Critical Thinking

5. **Drawing Conclusions** Why did riots take place in so many of the nation's cities during the 1960s?

Activity

Creating a Visual Biography Use photographs and drawings to illustrate a poster on the life and accomplishments of Martin Luther King, Jr.

Section 3 Review Answers

1. Freedom Riders, 831; James Meredith, 831; Civil Rights Act of 1964, 833; Voting Rights Act of 1965, 833; Malcolm X, 834; Stokely Carmichael, 834
2. The words are defined in the Glossary.
3. Answers may include marches and other demonstrations like the one held in Selma.
4. King believed in nonviolent tactics to gain equal rights. The more radical groups urged African Americans to separate from whites and create their own culture and political institutions, even if it meant a revolution.
5. Riots resulted from growing tensions between African Americans and police, from poverty and unemployment, and from the slowness of change.

Activity Students should create a poster to illustrate King's life and accomplishments.

Use **Chapter Challenger Interactive Review Software** to review Section 3.

Reteaching Activity 29–3

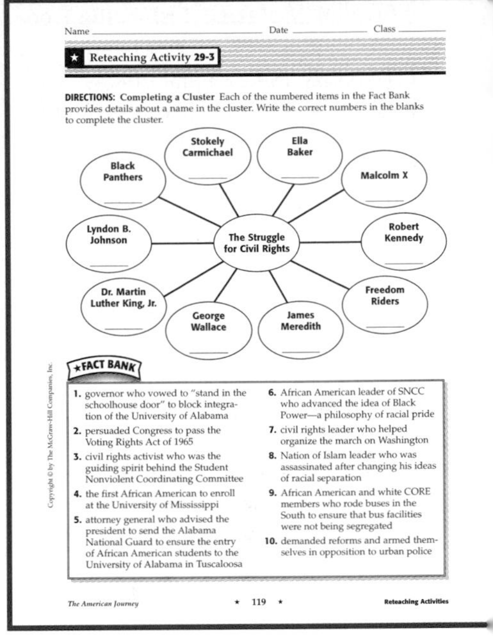

Name ______ Date ______ Class ______

★ Reteaching Activity 29-3

DIRECTIONS: Completing a Cluster Each of the numbered items in the Fact Bank provides details about a name in the cluster. Write the correct numbers in the blanks to complete the cluster.

★FACT BANK

1. governor who vowed to "stand in the schoolhouse door" to block integration of the University of Alabama
2. persuaded Congress to pass the Voting Rights Act of 1965
3. civil rights activist who was the guiding spirit behind the Student Nonviolent Coordinating Committee
4. the first African American to enroll at the University of Mississippi
5. attorney general who advised the president to send the Alabama National Guard to ensure the entry of African American students to the University of Alabama in Tuscaloosa
6. African American leader of SNCC who advanced the idea of Black Power—a philosophy of racial pride
7. civil rights leader who helped organize the march on Washington
8. Nation of Islam leader who was assassinated after changing his ideas of racial separation
9. African American and white CORE members who rode buses in the South to ensure that bus facilities were not being segregated
10. demanded reforms and armed themselves in opposition to urban police

Enrichment Activity 29–3

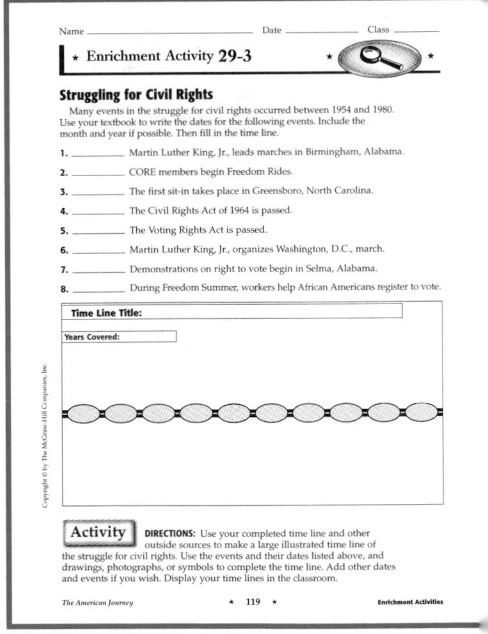

Name ______ Date ______ Class ______

★ Enrichment Activity 29-3 ★

Struggling for Civil Rights

Many events in the struggle for civil rights occurred between 1954 and 1980. Use your textbook to write the dates for the following events. Include the month and year if possible. Then fill in the time line.

1. ______ Martin Luther King, Jr., leads marches in Birmingham, Alabama.
2. ______ CORE members begin Freedom Rides.
3. ______ The first sit-in takes place in Greensboro, North Carolina.
4. ______ The Civil Rights Act of 1964 is passed.
5. ______ The Voting Rights Act is passed.
6. ______ Martin Luther King, Jr., organizes Washington, D.C., march.
7. ______ Demonstrations on right to vote begin in Selma, Alabama.
8. ______ During Freedom Summer, workers help African Americans register to vote.

Activity **DIRECTIONS:** Use your completed time line and other outside sources to make a large illustrated time line of the struggle for civil rights. Use the events and their dates listed above, and drawings, photographs, or symbols to complete the time line. Add other dates and events if you wish. Display your time lines in the classroom.

4 CLOSE

Have students read the excerpt of King's "I Have a Dream" speech (page A20) and then comment upon the events discussed in this section.

NATIONAL GEOGRAPHIC

Journeys

What? Where? When? Who?

Similar Violence Just as the Freedom Riders faced violence in Alabama, Melba Patillo Beals faced violence in school. She was another student brought in to Central High School under guard in 1957. She recalls some of the challenges: "We'd be showering in gym and someone would turn your shower on to scalding. You'd be walking out to the volleyball court and someone would break a bottle and trip you on the bottle . . . first you're in pain, then you're angry, then you try to fight back, . . . And then you mellow out and just realize that survival is day-to-day and you start to grasp the depth of the human spirit, you start to understand your own ability to cope no matter what. That is the greatest lesson I learned."

NATIONAL GEOGRAPHIC SOCIETY

VIDEODISC
GTV: The American People: Fabric of a Nation

Side 4, Chapter 5
Title: *The War at Home*
Subject: The civil rights movement
Ask: What strategies does the narrator say were used in the civil rights movement? *(legal case battles, boycotts, sit-ins, public demonstrations)*

2 On May 14th, a white mob ambushed the bus in Anniston, Alabama. They stoned the bus, slashed tires, ripped luggage, and threw a firebomb into the bus. The angry whites tried to block the doors, but officers waved their guns and finally dispersed the mob, allowing the Freedom Riders to stumble out.

4 The eyes of the nation focused on James Farmer, a principal organizer, and other Freedom Riders as they filed into police vehicles in Jackson, Mississippi. The Freedom Riders were arrested for "disobeying an officer" when they refused to leave the whites-only waiting room in the bus station. Busloads of black and white civil rights workers continued to pour into Jackson until the facilities were finally desegregated.

3 Attorney General Robert Kennedy struggled to stop the racial violence when mobs attacked the Freedom Riders in Birmingham and Montgomery, Alabama. To restore order, Kennedy sent out hundreds of federal marshals, and the governor of Alabama called out the National Guard.

5 Tired of violence and fearing more delays, the original group of Freedom Riders completed the last leg of the journey—from Jackson to New Orleans—by plane.

TEACHER'S NOTES

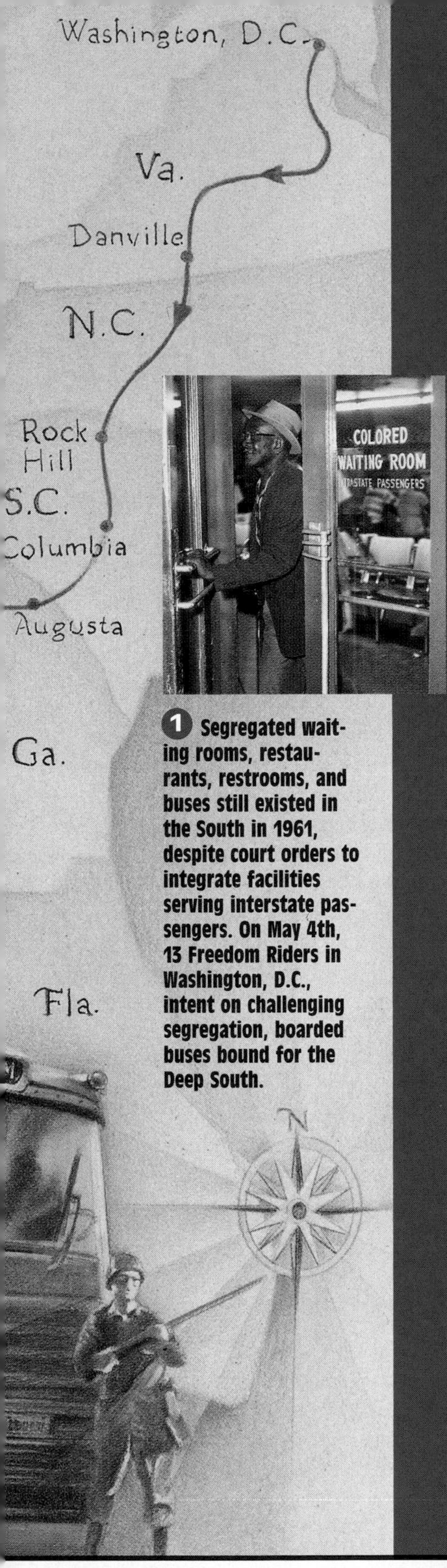

1 Segregated waiting rooms, restaurants, restrooms, and buses still existed in the South in 1961, despite court orders to integrate facilities serving interstate passengers. On May 4th, 13 Freedom Riders in Washington, D.C., intent on challenging segregation, boarded buses bound for the Deep South.

NATIONAL GEOGRAPHIC

Journeys

The Freedom Riders

"[Martin Luther] King emerged from the office looking very weary. He called me to him and said, 'Jim, the attorney general asks that you halt the Freedom Rides and have a cooling-off period to give him time to work things out.'

'No, Martin,' I replied. 'I won't stop it now.... We will continue the Ride until people can sit wherever they wish on buses and use the facilities in any waiting room available to the public. Please tell the attorney general that we have been cooling off for 350 years. If we cool off any more, we will be in a deep freeze. The Freedom Ride will go on.'"

—*James Farmer in* Lay Bare the Heart: An Autobiography of the Civil Rights Movement, *published 1985*

837

Teacher's Notes

NATIONAL GEOGRAPHIC SOCIETY

VIDEODISC
GTV: The American People: Fabric of a Nation

Side 1, Chapter 1
Title: *Living in the Promiseland*
Subject: America: people, promises, problems
Ask: What was the significance of this video segment? *(It showed the diversity of people in the United States.)* What was one reason for the race riots in the 1960s? *(frustration over the slow pace of civil rights changes)*

you don't say...

Bombingham Many cities in the South had histories of active intolerance—particularly Birmingham. The KKK chapter there was thought to be one of the most violent in the South. Since World War II, the city had seen some 50 bombings, including those of many black churches and two synagogues, and had earned the nickname "Bombingham." In 1979, however, the city elected Richard Arlington as its first African American mayor.

What? Where? When? Who?

Bibliography The excerpt at left was taken from *Lay Bare the Heart: An Autobiography of the Civil Rights Movement* by James Farmer (New York: Arbor House ©1985).

1 FOCUS

BELLRINGER
Motivational Activity

Before taking roll at the beginning of the class period, project Section Focus Transparency 29–4 and have students answer the questions. Discuss students' responses.

This activity is also available as a blackline master.

Section Focus Transparency 29–4

The Roles of Women

1. Do you think Betty Friedan accepted the traditional role of women as housewives? Explain.
2. Do you think Friedan believed that women who wanted to be poets, physicians, or presidents were unfeminine and unhappy? Explain your answer.

"Over and over women heard in voices of tradition . . . that they could desire no greater destiny than to glory in their own femininity (and) to pity the neurotic, unfeminine, unhappy women who wanted to be poets or physicians or presidents."

—Betty Friedan, from *The Feminine Mystique*

Vocabulary Precheck

Encourage students to write definitions of the terms *feminist* and *Hispanic.* Then have them find the terms in the text to check the accuracy of their definitions.

Use the **Vocabulary PuzzleMaker** to create crossword and word search puzzles.

Section Theme
Continuity and Change

In the 1960s and 1970s, women, Hispanic Americans, Native Americans, and disabled Americans used political action to shatter stereotypes and improve their lives.

Activity Have students list what they feel are some basic civil rights. As they read through Section 4, have them comment about ways in which minority groups felt they were being denied such rights.

1960 | 1965 | 1970 | 1975

1963 Congress passes Equal Pay Act; *The Feminine Mystique* is published

1966 National Organization for Women is created

1973 American Indian Movement protests at Wounded Knee, South Dakota

Section 4

Other Groups Seek Rights

READ TO DISCOVER . . .
- what steps women took to claim their civil rights.
- how Hispanic American groups organized in the 1960s and the 1970s.
- why Native Americans took action to improve their lives.

TERMS TO LEARN

feminist
Hispanic

The Storyteller

Mexican American farmworker Jesse Lopez de la Cruz had labored for decades in the grape and cotton fields of the Southwest. In 1972 she began working for the United Farm Workers Union. Cruz made speaking tours, trying to bring women into the union. "Women can no longer be taken for granted—that we're just going to stay home and do the cooking and cleaning," she told her listeners. "It's way past the time when our husbands could say, 'You stay home! You have to take care of the children! You have to do as I say!'"

Women's rights button

The effects of the civil rights movement reached well beyond the African American community. Women, Hispanics, Native Americans, and people with disabilities all found inspiration in the struggles of African Americans.

Women's Rights

In 1961 President John F. Kennedy created the Commission on the Status of Women. It reported that women—an ever growing part of the workforce—received lower pay than men, even for performing the same jobs. In 1963 Kennedy convinced Congress to pass the **Equal Pay Act,** which prohibited employers from paying women less than men for the same work.

Voices of Change

In a book called *The Feminine Mystique,* **Betty Friedan** gave voice to the frustration that a growing number of women experienced. Friedan's book described how many women felt disappointed in a society that expected them to be wives and mothers but did not support women in other roles.

Uniting for Action

In 1966 Friedan and other **feminists**—activists for women's rights—created the **National Organization for Women** (NOW). NOW fought for equal rights for women in all aspects of life—in jobs, education, and marriage.

SECTION RESOURCES

Reproducible Masters
- Guided Reading Activity 29–4
- Section Quiz 29–4
- Reteaching Activity 29–4
- Enrichment Activity 29–4

Transparencies
- Section Focus Transparency 29–4
- U.S. History & Art, Transparency 28

Multimedia
- Vocabulary PuzzleMaker
- Chapter Challenger Interactive Review
- Testmaker
- Set On Freedom™ The American Civil Rights Movement
- ABCNews InterActive™ Martin Luther King, Jr.

NOW launched a campaign for an **Equal Rights Amendment** (ERA) to the Constitution. The amendment stated that "equality of rights under the law shall not be denied or abridged by the United States or by any state on account of sex." **Phyllis Schlafly** and other opponents of the ERA warned that the amendment would upset the traditional roles of society and lead to the breakdown of the family. Some people argued that the amendment was unnecessary because the Constitution already provided women with adequate protection. In the end, not enough states ratified the amendment to make it law.

Women Gain Opportunities

Despite the defeat of the Equal Rights Amendment, women progressed in a number of areas in the 1970s. In 1971 the federal government outlawed discrimination against women in the workplace. This law, along with the efforts of many businesses, helped women begin to make advances in the world of work. Women gained more job opportunities, and more women rose to higher-level jobs in their companies.

Changes in education benefited women as well. Most of the nation's all-male colleges and universities began admitting women. More women than ever before entered medical school and law school to become doctors and lawyers.

Women also made progress in the political arena. Many women gained local and state offices. Several women won seats in the Senate and the House of Representatives and appointments to the president's cabinet. In 1981 President Ronald Reagan appointed **Sandra Day O'Connor** as the first female justice of the Supreme Court.

ERA opponent Phyllis Schlafly

Women march for equal rights

Linking PAST & PRESENT

Women and Sports

In the 1950s and early 1960s, American physical educators still argued that women's competitive sports were "unfeminine." An athlete such as Babe Didrickson Zaharias was unusual. By 1990, however, nearly 2 million females were active in sports—an increase of 600 percent in a 20-year span! **Besides female athletes, what other groups faced discrimination in the early 1960s?**

Past

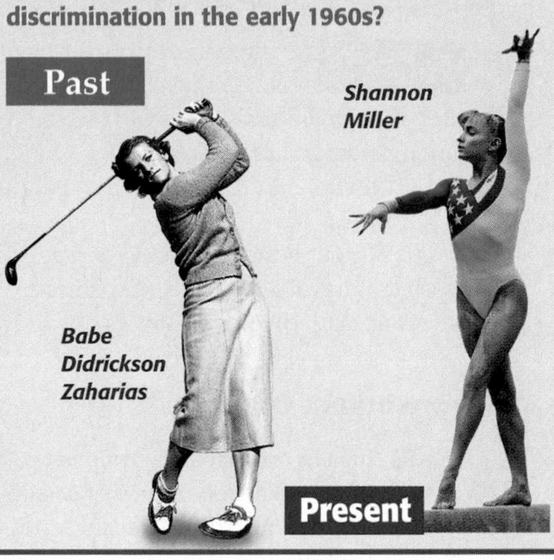

Babe Didrickson Zaharias

Shannon Miller

Present

Hispanic Americans

In the 1960s the rapidly growing **Hispanic** population sought equal rights. The term *Hispanic American* refers to those Americans who have come, or are descended from others who have come to the United States, from the countries of Latin America and Spain. From 3 million in 1960, the Hispanic population in the United States rose to 9 million in 1970 and to 15 million

Cooperative Learning Activity

Creating Concept Webs Section 4 focuses on the inspiration that the civil rights movement gave to other groups of Americans who experienced discrimination. To review the section, organize students into four teams. Supply each team with posterboard and markers. Within each team, have some students specialize in rights for women, others in rights for Hispanic Americans, others in rights for Native Americans, and others in rights for the disabled. Ask each team to create a concept web relating to this section. Have teams begin with the phrase *My Rights* in the center of the page, branch out to show the kinds of rights sought, and note a few details about each group discussed. Encourage teams to compare and discuss their webs.

2 TEACH

L1, ELL Drawing Conclusions Ask students to recall the activism and some of the successes of the civil rights movement. Have them draw conclusions about its inspirational impact upon other groups of Americans.

Linking PAST & PRESENT

Women and Sports Babe Didrickson Zaharias became famous during the Great Depression, winning track events, Olympic medals, and golf tournaments. She also won prizes for diving and tennis and was excellent at basketball, baseball, and bowling. Her popularity continued in the 1940s and 1950s, but her career was ended by cancer. She died in 1956.

Answer: *Women in general faced discrimination in some areas, as did African Americans, Hispanic Americans, Native Americans, and the disabled.*

Guided Reading Activity 29–4

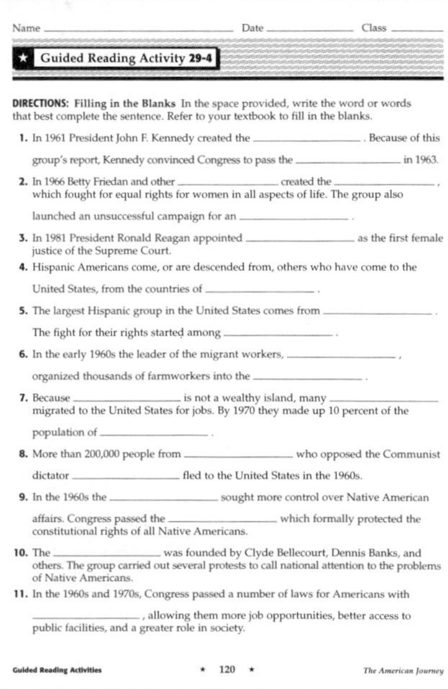

Name ______ Date ______ Class ______

★ Guided Reading Activity 29-4

DIRECTIONS: Filling in the Blanks In the space provided, write the word or words that best complete the sentence. Refer to your textbook to fill in the blanks.

1. In 1961 President John F. Kennedy created the ______. Because of this group's report, Kennedy convinced Congress to pass the ______ in 1963.
2. In 1966 Betty Friedan and other ______ created the ______, which fought for equal rights for women in all aspects of life. The group also launched an unsuccessful campaign for an ______.
3. In 1981 President Ronald Reagan appointed ______ as the first female justice of the Supreme Court.
4. Hispanic Americans come, or are descended from, others who have come to the United States, from the countries of ______.
5. The largest Hispanic group in the United States comes from ______. The fight for their rights started among ______.
6. In the early 1960s the leader of the migrant workers, ______, organized thousands of farmworkers into the ______.
7. Because ______ is not a wealthy island, many ______ migrated to the United States for jobs. By 1970 they made up 10 percent of the population of ______.
8. More than 200,000 people from ______ who opposed the Communist dictator ______ fled to the United States in the 1960s.
9. In the 1960s the ______ sought more control over Native American affairs. Congress passed the ______ which formally protected the constitutional rights of all Native Americans.
10. The ______ was founded by Clyde Bellecourt, Dennis Banks, and others. The group carried out several protests to call national attention to the problems of Native Americans.
11. In the 1960s and 1970s, Congress passed a number of laws for Americans with ______, allowing them more job opportunities, better access to public facilities, and a greater role in society.

Guided Reading Activities ★ 120 ★ *The American Journey*

Picturing HISTORY Robert F. Kennedy once called Chávez "one of the heroic figures of our time." The strike that Chávez led lasted for five years (1965–1970). The support that it gathered from around the country cost California grape growers millions of dollars.
Ask: What long-term effects did the UFW have? *(It improved the lives of migrant workers and encouraged Hispanic Americans to participate more in politics.)*
Answer: *By striking and organizing nationwide boycotts, the UFW won better wages and working conditions for its members.*

you don't say...

Hispanic Words Many words we use today come from Spanish. Some of the most common ones are *alligator, buffalo, cafeteria, canyon, mosquito, patio, pronto,* and *tornado.*

GLENCOE TECHNOLOGY

VIDEODISC
Set On Freedom™
The American Civil Rights Movement

Side A, Chapter 42
Title: *The Poor People's Campaign, 1968*
Subject: Publicizing the problem of poverty in the United States
Ask: What did Ralph Abernathy say The Poor People's Campaign wanted to accomplish? *(to plague the government until the poor were provided with meaningful jobs and guaranteed annual incomes)*

Picturing HISTORY César Chávez led the United Farm Workers during the 1960s. **How did the UFW help Mexican American migrant farmworkers?**

by 1980. Although they share the heritage of the Spanish culture and language, Hispanics are a diverse group with different histories.

Farmworkers Organize

By far, the largest Hispanic group in the United States comes from the country of Mexico. By 1980 more than 8 million Mexican Americans were living in the United States.

The fight for rights started among Mexican American migrant farmworkers. These people, who planted and harvested a large share of the nation's food supply, faced great hardships. The migrant farmers did backbreaking work, laboring from dawn until dusk for low wages. When one job ended, they had to travel from farm to farm in search of the next job.

In the early 1960s, migrant workers formed unions to fight for better wages and working conditions. Their leader, **César Chávez,** organized thousands of farmworkers into the United Farm Workers (UFW).

The union went on strike and organized nationwide boycotts. Consumers across the country supported the UFW by refusing to buy grapes, lettuce, and other farm produce under boycott. The success of the boycotts enabled the UFW to win higher wages and shorter work hours for many farmworkers.

The union boycott was followed by emerging political power among Hispanic Americans. In the years that followed, Hispanic Americans would join together in an organization called **La Raza Unida** to fight discrimination and to elect Hispanics to government posts. **The League of United Latin American Citizens** (LULAC) won suits in federal court to guarantee Hispanic Americans the right to serve on juries and to send their children to unsegregated schools.

Puerto Ricans

Puerto Ricans, another major group of Hispanics, come from the island of Puerto Rico, a commonwealth of the United States. They are American citizens who have made major contributions to the United States.

In 1970 the first representative to Congress of Puerto Rican origin, **Herman Badillo,** was elected from New York City. After four terms, Badillo served as the city's deputy mayor. Baseball all-time great **Roberto Clemente** performed heroically both on and off the baseball diamond. In 1972 Clemente died in a plane crash while delivering relief supplies to earthquake victims in Nicaragua.

Because Puerto Rico is not a wealthy island, many Puerto Ricans have migrated to American cities in search of jobs. By 1970 they made up 10 percent of the population of New York City. As with African Americans, though, they often faced discrimination in their job search, leading to no work or work for low pay. Many of the children and grandchildren of the Puerto Ricans who arrived in New York in the 1960s migrated to neighboring states, but many Puerto Ricans remained centered in New York City.

Cubans Arrive

After the Cuban Revolution of 1959, dictator Fidel Castro established a Communist government and seized the property of many Cubans. More than 200,000 people opposed to Castro fled to the United States in the 1960s. Thousands more came in the 1980s.

MULTIPLE LEARNING STYLES

Logical/Mathematical Students may struggle to understand the attitudes (attitudes that largely have changed over time) that made laws such as the Equal Pay Act and the extension of the Voting Rights Act necessary. Help students to understand the frustrations of minority groups by asking them to analyze questions such as the following:

- **In a company, who would benefit if women were paid less than men?**
- **On a farm, who would benefit if migrant workers received low wages?**
- **On a Native American reservation, who would benefit from limited tribal government? L2**

These immigrants settled all over the United States. The largest number of Cubans settled in south Florida, where they have established a thriving community.

In 1975 Hispanic people and other groups won a victory with the extension of voting rights. The new law required that registration and voting be carried out in other languages as well as in English. This was designed to help those citizens who might not read or speak English. Election materials, for example, are available in Spanish and English in many states.

Native Americans

The years after World War II were a time of transition for Native Americans. Starting in the early 1950s, the federal government urged Native Americans to leave the reservations for work in cities. Federal policy also tried to weaken the power of tribal government.

This policy did not improve the lives of Native Americans. Many could not find jobs in the cities. Those still crowded on reservations enjoyed few jobs or other opportunities. More than one-third of Native Americans lived below the poverty line. Unemployment was widespread—as high as 50 percent in some areas. A 1966 study revealed that Native Americans suffered so much from malnutrition and disease that their life expectancy was only 46 years.

Efforts to Organize

In the 1960s Native Americans organized to combat these problems. They demanded political power and independence from the United States government. Native Americans also increasingly emphasized their own history, language, and culture in their schools. The **National Congress of American Indians** (NCAI) sought more control over Native American affairs.

In 1961 more than 400 members of 67 Native American nations gathered in Chicago. In a Declaration of Indian Purpose, these delegates asserted that Native Americans have the "right to choose our own way of life."

The federal government recognized the Native Americans' issues. Congress passed the **Indian Civil Rights Act of 1968,** which formally protected the constitutional rights of all Native Americans. At the same time, the new law recognized the right of Native American nations to make laws on their reservations.

A Supreme Court decision in the 1970s reaffirmed the independence of tribal governments. Other court decisions confirmed Native Americans' rights to land granted in treaties.

American Indian Movement

Believing the process of change too slow, some younger Native Americans began taking stronger actions. In 1968 a group established the

Picturing HISTORY In the 1973 AIM takeover of Wounded Knee, Native American leaders Russell Means (left) and Dennis Banks (right) protested broken treaties and civil rights violations. **Why was Wounded Knee chosen as the place for the AIM protest?**

***Wounded Knee* button**

Making Connections Activity

Architecture The Americans With Disabilities Act grew out of the momentum for civil and equal rights during the 1960s and 1970s. Offer a choice of these activities relating to this law:

- Find out how the design of your school provides access for people with physical disabilities. Was such access part of the original plan for the building or were changes recently incorporated?
- Imagine that you, an architect, have been asked to submit a design for a new library. Sketch a floor plan for the library. Be sure to include features that provide easy access for the disabled as well as resources and equipment to accommodate hearing and visually impaired citizens. **L3**

History *and the* Humanities

U.S. History & Art, Transparency 28, *The Family*

The Spirit of American Art and Music, Mary Brave Bird, Joan Baez

3 ASSESS

Assign Section 4 Review as homework or as an in-class activity.

Use **Chapter Challenger Interactive Review Software** to review Section 4.

Picturing HISTORY Increased Native American activism led to several important court decisions. In one, the Pueblo people of Taos, New Mexico, regained Blue Lake, a place sacred to their religious life. In 1975 a federal court declared that the Passamaquoddy and Penobscot nations had a valid claim to more than half the state of Maine—and to $25 billion in damages and unpaid rents.
Answer: *Wounded Knee was the site of an 1890 massacre of Sioux by federal troops.*

Section Quiz 29–4

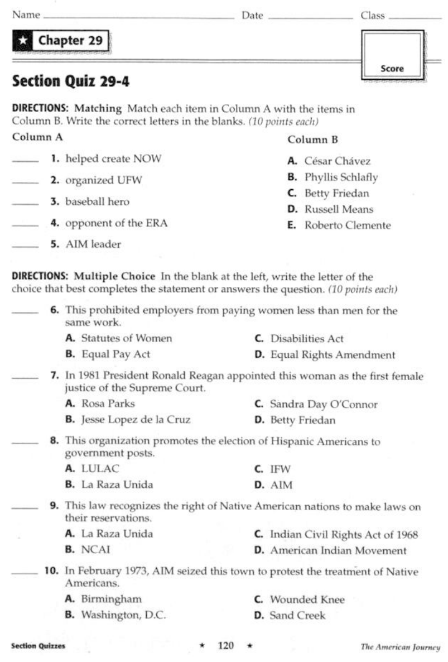

Name ________ Date ________ Class ________

Chapter 29 — Score

Section Quiz 29-4

DIRECTIONS: Matching Match each item in Column A with the items in Column B. Write the correct letters in the blanks. *(10 points each)*

Column A	Column B
____ 1. helped create NOW	A. César Chávez
____ 2. organized UFW	B. Phyllis Schlafly
____ 3. baseball hero	C. Betty Friedan
____ 4. opponent of the ERA	D. Russell Means
____ 5. AIM leader	E. Roberto Clemente

DIRECTIONS: Multiple Choice In the blank at the left, write the letter of the choice that best completes the statement or answers the question. *(10 points each)*

____ 6. This prohibited employers from paying women less than men for the same work.
A. Statutes of Women C. Disabilities Act
B. Equal Pay Act D. Equal Rights Amendment

____ 7. In 1981 President Ronald Reagan appointed this woman as the first female justice of the Supreme Court.
A. Rosa Parks C. Sandra Day O'Connor
B. Jesse Lopez de la Cruz D. Betty Friedan

____ 8. This organization promotes the election of Hispanic Americans to government posts.
A. LULAC C. IFW
B. La Raza Unida D. AIM

____ 9. This law recognizes the right of Native American nations to make laws on their reservations.
A. La Raza Unida C. Indian Civil Rights Act of 1968
B. NCAI D. American Indian Movement

____ 10. In February 1973, AIM seized this town to protest the treatment of Native Americans.
A. Birmingham C. Wounded Knee
B. Washington, D.C. D. Sand Creek

Section Quizzes ★ 120 ★ *The American Journey*

CHAPTER 29
Section 4, 838–842

Picturing HISTORY In 1990 Congress passed the Americans With Disabilities Act.
Answer: *passed laws to ensure equal access to public places, require more employment opportunities, and guarantee equal educational opportunities*

Reteaching Activity 29–4

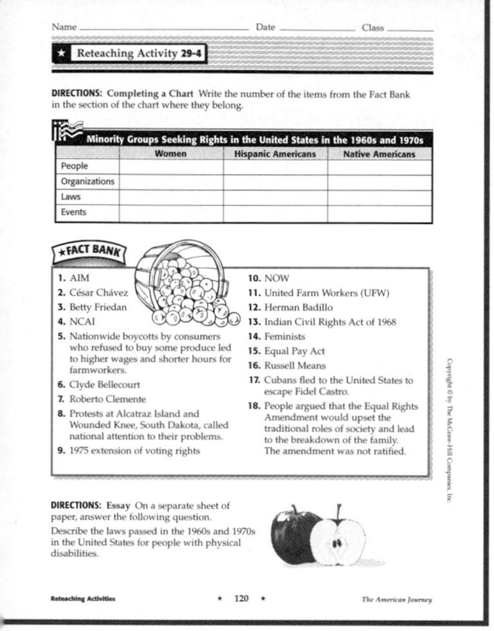
Name ______ Date ______ Class ______

★ Reteaching Activity 29-4

DIRECTIONS: Completing a Chart Write the number of the items from the Fact Bank in the section of the chart where they belong.

Minority Groups Seeking Rights in the United States in the 1960s and 1970s

	Women	Hispanic Americans	Native Americans
People			
Organizations			
Laws			
Events			

★FACT BANK

1. AIM
2. César Chávez
3. Betty Friedan
4. NCAI
5. Nationwide boycotts by consumers who refused to buy some produce led to higher wages and shorter hours for farmworkers.
6. Clyde Bellecourt
7. Roberto Clemente
8. Protests at Alcatraz Island and Wounded Knee, South Dakota, called national attention to their problems.
9. 1975 extension of voting rights
10. NOW
11. United Farm Workers (UFW)
12. Herman Badillo
13. Indian Civil Rights Act of 1968
14. Feminists
15. Equal Pay Act
16. Russell Means
17. Cubans fled to the United States to escape Fidel Castro.
18. People argued that the Equal Rights Amendment would upset the traditional roles of society and lead to the breakdown of the family. The amendment was not ratified.

DIRECTIONS: Essay On a separate sheet of paper, answer the following question.
Describe the laws passed in the 1960s and 1970s in the United States for people with physical disabilities.

Reteaching Activities ★ 120 ★ *The American Journey*

Enrichment Activity 29–4

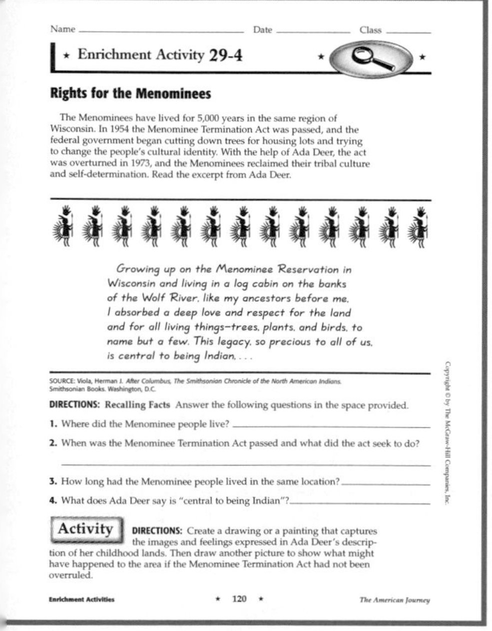
Name ______ Date ______ Class ______

★ Enrichment Activity 29-4

Rights for the Menominees

The Menominees have lived for 5,000 years in the same region of Wisconsin. In 1954 the Menominee Termination Act was passed, and the federal government began cutting down trees for housing lots and trying to change the people's cultural identity. With the help of Ada Deer, the act was overturned in 1973, and the Menominees reclaimed their tribal culture and self-determination. Read the excerpt from Ada Deer.

Growing up on the Menominee Reservation in Wisconsin and living in a log cabin on the banks of the Wolf River, like my ancestors before me, I absorbed a deep love and respect for the land and for all living things—trees, plants, and birds, to name but a few. This legacy, so precious to all of us, is central to being Indian. . . .

SOURCE: Viola, Herman J. *After Columbus, The Smithsonian Chronicle of the North American Indians.* Smithsonian Books. Washington, D.C.

DIRECTIONS: Recalling Facts Answer the following questions in the space provided.

1. Where did the Menominee people live? ______
2. When was the Menominee Termination Act passed and what did the act seek to do? ______
3. How long had the Menominee people lived in the same location? ______
4. What does Ada Deer say is "central to being Indian"? ______

Activity **DIRECTIONS:** Create a drawing or a painting that captures the images and feelings expressed in Ada Deer's description of her childhood lands. Then draw another picture to show what might have happened to the area if the Menominee Termination Act had not been overruled.

Enrichment Activities ★ 120 ★ *The American Journey*

4 CLOSE

Ask students to summarize the political activism of women, Hispanics, Native Americans, and the disabled in the 1960s and 1970s.

American Indian Movement (AIM), which worked for equal rights and improvement of living conditions. AIM was founded by Clyde Bellecourt, Dennis Banks, and others. Later, Russell Means became a leader.

AIM carried out several protests. In November 1969, for example, AIM was one of the Native American groups that took over Alcatraz Island, a former federal prison in San Francisco Bay. AIM wanted the island to serve as a cultural center. The incident ended in June 1971 when the groups surrendered to United States marshals.

In the fall of 1972, AIM members occupied the Bureau of Indian Affairs in Washington, D.C. They demanded the lands and rights guaranteed Indians under treaties with the United States. They surrendered the building after the government agreed to review their complaints.

In February 1973, AIM seized the town of **Wounded Knee, South Dakota,** the site of the 1890 massacre of Sioux by federal troops. In the early 1970s, Wounded Knee was part of a large Sioux reservation. The people there suffered from terrible poverty and ill health.

AIM leaders vowed to stay until the government met demands for change and investigated the treatment of Native Americans. The siege ended on May 8, but it focused national attention on the terrible conditions of Native Americans.

Picturing HISTORY Since the 1960s, people with physical disabilities have demanded better access to stadiums, restaurants, and other public buildings. **How has Congress responded to their protests?**

Americans With Disabilities

People with physical disabilities also sought equal treatment in the 1960s and the 1970s. Congress responded by passing a number of laws.

One law concerned the removal of barriers that prevented some people from gaining access to public facilities. Another required employers to offer more opportunities for disabled people in the workplace. Yet another asserted the right of children with disabilities to equal educational opportunities. As a result of these actions, people with disabilities enjoyed more job opportunities, better access to public facilities, and a greater role in society.

Section 4 Review

Checking for Understanding

1. ***Identify*** Betty Friedan, National Organization for Women, Equal Rights Amendment, César Chávez.
2. ***Define*** feminist, Hispanic.
3. ***Explain*** what migrant farmworkers did to earn more rights.

Reviewing Themes

4. **Continuity and Change** What rights did Native Americans gain in the 1960s?

Critical Thinking

5. **Stating Problems Clearly** Why do you think people with disabilities felt the need to work for equal treatment in the 1960s and 1970s?

Activity

Making a Protest Sign Create a sign that you might carry in a protest march to either support or oppose the ERA.

Section 4 Review Answers

1. Betty Friedan, 838; NOW, 838; ERA, 839; César Chávez, 840
2. The words are defined in the Glossary.
3. They formed unions and went on strike to fight for better wages and working conditions. They organized national boycotts.
4. The Indian Civil Rights Act of 1968 protected Native Americans' constitutional rights and recognized their right to make laws on their reservations.
5. Students should recognize that people with disabilities also can be targets of discrimination and that, at this time, they were not protected by government laws guaranteeing equal treatment.

Activity Students should create a protest sign either in favor of or opposing the ERA.

Critical Thinking
SKILL BUILDER

Drawing Conclusions

"Elementary, my dear Watson." Detective Sherlock Holmes often said these words to his assistant when he unlocked the key to a mystery. Holmes would examine all the available evidence, or facts, and draw conclusions to solve the case.

Learning the Skill

Drawing conclusions allows you to understand ideas that are not stated directly. Follow these steps in learning to draw conclusions:

- Review the facts that are stated directly.
- Use your knowledge and insight to develop some conclusions about these facts.
- Look for information to check the accuracy of your conclusions.

Practicing the Skill

Read the excerpt that follows, written by Martin Luther King, Jr., after he was arrested in Birmingham, Alabama, for peaceably demonstrating against segregation. King began writing this letter in response to a newspaper ad in which a group of white ministers called for an end to the demonstrations. King's words attempt to explain to the white ministers his use of civil disobedience. After reading the excerpt, answer the questions, which require you to draw conclusions.

Martin Luther King, Jr.

"We know through painful experience that freedom is never voluntarily given by the oppressor; it must be demanded by the oppressed. . . . For years now I have heard the word 'Wait!' It rings in the ear of every Negro with piercing familiarity. This 'Wait' has almost always meant 'Never.' We must come to see, with one of our distinguished jurists, that 'justice too long delayed is justice denied.'"

—Martin Luther King, Jr.
"Letter from Birmingham Jail," 1963

1. How does King say that freedom is earned?
2. What were the African Americans "waiting" for?
3. What happens to justice if it is delayed?
4. What conclusions can you draw from King's overall tone in his letter?
5. What evidence could help prove your conclusions?

Applying the Skill

Drawing Conclusions Read a newspaper article about a criminal court case. Use the facts in the article to draw a conclusion about the innocence or guilt of the accused.

Answers to Practicing the Skill

1. He says that freedom must be demanded and that it sometimes may come only after a time of pain.
2. They were waiting for freedom and justice.
3. If justice is delayed too long, it is, in effect, denied altogether.
4. Students may suggest that King fully identified with all African Americans and that the need for freedom and justice was increasing in urgency.
5. Evidence might include the use of the words *painful, piercing, we,* and *our* and the repetition of *"Wait!"*

Applying the Skill You might have students who choose the same case work together. Have students make a copy of the article and mark the details that they use for evidence.

Critical Thinking
SKILL BUILDER

TEACH

Drawing Conclusions

Point out to students that a conclusion is an inference, or reasoned final judgment, based on information presented.

Discuss the steps for drawing a conclusion. Note that factual information provides the most reliable source on which to draw a conclusion, but a stated opinion also can help support a conclusion. For example, the quotation from "one of our distinguished jurists" lends credibility to King's "Letter from Birmingham Jail."

Before students answer the questions that follow the excerpt, have them read the introduction to the quote. **Ask:** What conclusions might you draw from it? *(Students may suggest that the ministers who had run the ad did not understand the long history of suffering endured by African Americans or the nonviolent origins of the civil rights movement.)*

Additional Practice

Chapter Skills Activity 29

ABCNEWS INTERACTIVE™

VIDEODISC
Martin Luther King, Jr.

Side 1
Chapter 17

Title: *1963 Birmingham: King's Letter from Jail*
Subject: King reads a portion of his letter, written while serving time for marching in a civil rights protest.
Ask: **How did the Alabama clergy believe African Americans should obtain their rights?** *(by negotiating with local leaders or filing complaints in the courts)*

GLENCOE TECHNOLOGY

VIDEODISC
MindJogger Videoquiz

Use MindJogger to review the Chapter 29 content.

Chapter 29
Disc 4, Side B

Also available in VHS.

Chapter 29
Review and Activities

Reviewing Key Terms

On graph paper, create a word search puzzle using the following terms. Crisscross the terms vertically and horizontally, then fill in the remaining squares with extra letters. Use the terms' definitions as clues to find the words in the puzzle. Share your puzzle with a classmate.

poverty line	**integrate**
Medicare	**boycott**
Medicaid	**sit-in**
segregation	**Hispanic**

Reviewing Key Facts

1. What Supreme Court case abolished segregation in schools?
2. What was the main goal of President Kennedy's New Frontier program?
3. Summarize the philosophy and goals of Martin Luther King, Jr.

Critical Thinking

Making Generalizations

During the 1950s and 1960s, many African Americans worked for equal rights.

1. Why do you think the civil rights movement gained momentum during this era?
2. How did television affect the struggle for civil rights?

Time Line Activity

Create a time line on which you place the following events in chronological order.

- President Johnson signs Civil Rights Act
- Supreme Court bans segregation in schools
- President Kennedy is assassinated
- Montgomery bus boycott begins

Reviewing Themes

1. **Civic Rights and Responsibilities** According to Thurgood Marshall, what constitutional amendment was violated by allowing segregation in schools?
2. **Individual Action** Summarize the goals of Johnson's Great Society.
3. **Groups and Institutions** How did the idea of Black Power differ from Martin Luther King's goals for the civil rights movement?
4. **Continuity and Change** Summarize the impact that the African American civil rights movement had on other minorities.

Skill Practice Activity

Drawing Conclusions

Read the passage below and answer the questions that follow. Remember to review the information and add your own knowledge before drawing any conclusions.

Malcolm X, a strong African American leader, bitterly and regretfully recalled his youthful efforts at straightening his hair in order to look more like a white person:

> "This was my first big step toward self-degradation: when I endured all of that pain, literally burning my flesh to have it look like a white man's hair. I had joined that multitude of Negro men and women in America who are brainwashed into believing that the black people are 'inferior'—and white people 'superior.'"
>
> —Malcolm X, *Autobiography of Malcolm X*, 1965

1. What reason does Malcolm X give for straightening his hair?
2. As an adult, how did he view his youthful actions?

Reviewing Key Terms

The key terms used in this activity can be found in the textbook glossary on pages A26–A35. Students' word search puzzles will vary.

Reviewing Key Facts

1. *Brown* v. *Board of Education of Topeka, Kansas*
2. to increase spending on social programs, especially for the poor and elderly
3. To win equal rights for African Americans. His goal was to use nonviolent means to draw attention to the inequalities that existed for them.

Critical Thinking

1. Answers will vary but might indicate that the presidents during this period supported civil rights, that the affluence of the white middle class made the inequalities more visible, and that several strong African American leaders emerged at this time.
2. People around the nation were able to see how African Americans were being treated in response to their protests for equal rights.

Time Line Activity

Events should be placed in this order: Supreme Court bans segregation in schools, Montgomery bus boycott begins, President Kennedy is assassinated, President Johnson signs Civil Rights Act

Reviewing Themes

1. the Fourteenth Amendment
2. to pass laws giving more advantages to poor and elderly Americans, to rebuild cities, to increase spending for education, and to support civil rights
3. Black Power supporters urged African Americans to adopt a policy of racial separation rather than to focus on integration into white society. They were not opposed to using violence if they felt it necessary. King wanted to gain equal rights by nonviolent means.
4. The movement inspired others who were fighting for equal rights to become active in their own movements.

3. What conclusion can you draw about the views of many African American people toward white people at that time?
4. What statement from the passage supports your conclusion?

Geography Activity

The map below shows the route that the Freedom Riders took in 1961. Study the map, then answer the questions that follow.

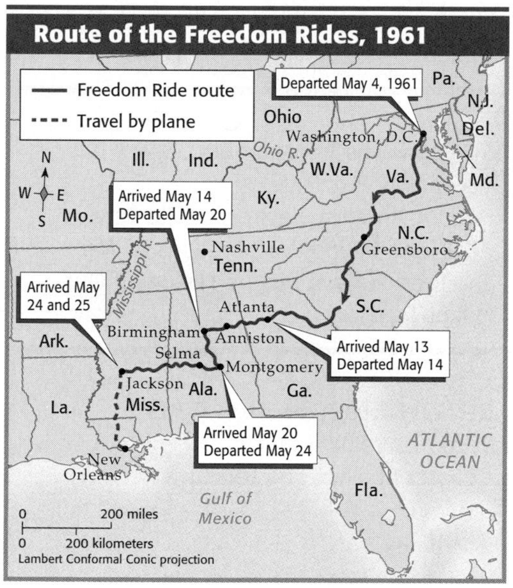

1. **Movement** What direction did the route follow from Atlanta to Montgomery?
2. **Location** Where did the Freedom Rides begin?
3. **Location** In what city did the entire route end?
4. **Movement** About how many miles did the Freedom Riders go by bus?
5. **Movement** About how many miles did the Freedom Riders travel by airplane?
6. **Region** Through what states did the Freedom Riders journey?

Cooperative Activity

History and Citizenship With members of your group research to find out how many people of different ethnic backgrounds live in your county. Make a graph to illustrate your findings. Then choose one of the minority ethnic groups to research. Prepare a written report with illustrations to provide more information about this particular ethnic group in your county. You may want to find out if members of this ethnic group have settled in one particular area of the county, if they have formed special clubs or organizations, or if they observe any special holidays.

Technology Activity

Using the Internet The United Farm Workers are still active today. Search the Internet for information about this organization and create a brochure that explains its goals.

Portfolio Activity History Journal Review the chapter for dates important to minority groups. Create a time line that traces the progress of African Americans, Hispanics, Native Americans, and women in their struggle for equal rights during the 1950s and 1960s.

Skill Practice Activity

1. to look more like a white person
2. According to the introduction, he regretted it. Malcolm X also called it an act of self-degradation and said that he had been brainwashed into believing whites were better than blacks.
3. Many African Americans must have felt that they would not be accepted unless they hid their distinctiveness and looked more like people who considered themselves "superior."
4. He states that this was the view of a "multitude of Negro men and women" whom he describes as "brainwashed."

CHAPTER 29
Review and Activities

Geography Activity

1. west to Birmingham and then south to Montgomery
2. Washington, D.C.
3. New Orleans
4. They traveled only by bus, for about 1,200 miles.
5. about 200 miles
6. Virginia, North Carolina, South Carolina, Georgia, Alabama, Mississippi, and Louisiana

Cooperative Activity

Each group should research to find out how many people in your county come from different ethnic backgrounds. Each group should use its figures to create a population graph. Each group then should write a report on one of the ethnic groups, including specific information about that group's culture and some of its activities in your county.

Technology Activity

Students should use the Internet to gather information about the United Farm Workers and use the information to create a brochure that outlines the organization's goals.

Portfolio Activity Students should create a time line tracing the progress of African Americans, Hispanics, Native Americans, and women in their struggle for equal rights during the 1950s and 1960s.

Chapter Bonus Test Question

Ask: How did Martin Luther King, Jr., hope his children (people) would be judged? *(not by the color of their skin, but by the content of their character)*

Chapter 30 Planning Guide

A complete, 1-page lesson plan is provided for each section in the *Reproducible Lesson Plans* booklet.

Section Resources

Daily Objectives	Reproducible Resources	Multimedia Resources
Section 1 Kennedy's Foreign Policy Discuss President Kennedy's general foreign policy goals and his responses to actions by the Soviet Union in Cuba, in Berlin, and in space.	Reproducible Lesson Plan 30–1 Guided Reading Activity 30–1* Section Quiz 30–1* Reteaching Activity 30–1 Enrichment Activity 30–1	Section Focus Transparency 30–1 Vocabulary PuzzleMaker Testmaker ABCNews InterActive™ Communism and the Cold War The Presidents: A Picture History of Our Nation
Section 2 War in Vietnam Recall the origins of civil strife in Vietnam and the escalating participation of American forces in that conflict.	Reproducible Lesson Plan 30–2 Guided Reading Activity 30–2* Section Quiz 30–2* Reteaching Activity 30–2 Enrichment Activity 30–2	Section Focus Transparency 30–2 Vocabulary PuzzleMaker Historic America Electronic Field Trips ABCNews InterActive™ Lessons of War The Presidents: A Picture History of Our Nation
Section 3 The Vietnam Years at Home Analyze the viewpoints and actions that indicated how Americans in various segments of society felt about the Vietnam War.	Reproducible Lesson Plan 30–3 Guided Reading Activity 30–3* Political Cartoons, *Uproar Over Vietnam* Section Quiz 30–3* Reteaching Activity 30–3 Enrichment Activity 30–3	Section Focus Transparency 30–3 Vocabulary PuzzleMaker Chapter Challenger Interactive Review Software Testmaker American Music Cultural Traditions
Section 4 1968—Year of Crises Summarize the changes in the Vietnam War in 1968 and key events at home that indicated a growing distaste for that war.	Reproducible Lesson Plan 30–4 Guided Reading Activity 30–4* Section Quiz 30–4* Reteaching Activity 30–4 Enrichment Activity 30–4	Section Focus Transparency 30–4 Vocabulary PuzzleMaker Chapter Challenger Interactive Review Testmaker ABCNews InterActive™ Martin Luther King, Jr.
Section 5 Nixon and Vietnam Describe President Nixon's change of strategy in the Vietnam War, the reaction it received at home, and the ultimate conclusion of the war.	Reproducible Lesson Plan 30–5 Guided Reading Activity 30–5* Section Quiz 30–5* Reteaching Activity 30–5 Enrichment Activity 30–5	Section Focus Transparency 30–5 Chapter Challenger Interactive Review Testmaker Communism and the Cold War ABCNews InterActive™ Lessons of War Historic America Electronic Field Trips The Presidents: A Picture History of Our Nation Focus on American Art Prints

** Also available in Spanish*

Poster · Blackline Master · Videodisc · Audiocassette · Music Program · Transparency · CD-ROM · Software

0:00 **OUT OF TIME?**
Assign the Chapter 30 Digest and the corresponding Chapter Digests Audiocassettes with activities and tests.

Activity

From the Classroom of…

Renee Trufant Hannen
Brevard Middle School
Brevard, NC

An Assignment Menu

Students usually appreciate the opportunity to pick and choose from a variety of assignments. Give students an assignment "menu" in the form of a tic-tac-toe grid, with one assignment in each of the nine boxes. Students can then pick three assignments that cover three boxes in a vertical, horizontal, or diagonal row.

Use the following assignments along with two of your own to complete the grid. (1) Research and present an oral report on the Alliance for Progress. (2) Construct a mobile illustrating the Apollo Project. (3) Write a brief report explaining the roles of Ho Chi Minh, Ngo Dinh Diem, and President Lyndon Johnson. (4) Make a time line covering the presidencies between 1960 and 1975. (5) Write a letter to the editor from the viewpoint of a high school student in the year 1972. (6) Research and write a brief biography of an important figure during this time period, such as Fidel Castro, George McGovern, Martin Luther King, Jr., or Henry Kissinger. (7) Make a chart or diagram that contrasts and compares the Korean and Vietnam Wars.

Block Schedule

Block scheduling differs from traditional class scheduling in the amount of time allotted to each period. The extended time frame provided by block scheduling affords you the opportunity to implement a greater number of research-oriented and activity-intense projects to motivate and involve your students. Activities that are particularly suited to use within the block scheduling framework are identified throughout this chapter by the following designation:

NATIONAL GEOGRAPHIC SOCIETY Teacher's Corner

INDEX TO NATIONAL GEOGRAPHIC MAGAZINE

The following articles may be used for research relating to this chapter:

- "The New Saigon," by Tracy Dahlby, April 1995.
- "The Mekong," by Thomas O'Neill, February 1993.
- "Hong Kong—Plight of the Boat People," by Larry Kohl, February 1991.
- *Vietnam: The Hard Road to Peace,* (A Special Edition), November 1989.

NATIONAL GEOGRAPHIC SOCIETY PRODUCTS AVAILABLE FROM GLENCOE

To order the following products for use with this chapter, contact your local Glencoe sales representative, or call Glencoe at 1-800-334-7344:

- *The Presidents: A Picture History of Our Nation* (CD-ROM)
- *Picture Atlas of the World* (CD-ROM)
- *GTV: A Geographic Perspective on American History* (Videodisc)
- *GTV: The American People: Fabric of a Nation* (Videodisc)

ADDITIONAL NATIONAL GEOGRAPHIC SOCIETY PRODUCTS

To order the following products for use with this chapter, call National Geographic Society at 1-800-368-2728:

- *Historical Atlas of the United States* (Atlas)
- *Historical Atlas of the World* (Atlas)

KEY TO ABILITY LEVELS

Teaching strategies have been coded for varying learning styles and abilities.

L1 **BASIC** activities for all students
L2 **AVERAGE** activities for average to above-average students
L3 **CHALLENGING** activities for above-average students
ELL **ENGLISH LANGUAGE LEARNER** activities

Chapter 30 Resource Guide

Home Involvement

Home Involvement Activity 30

Review Activities

Chapter Summary 30

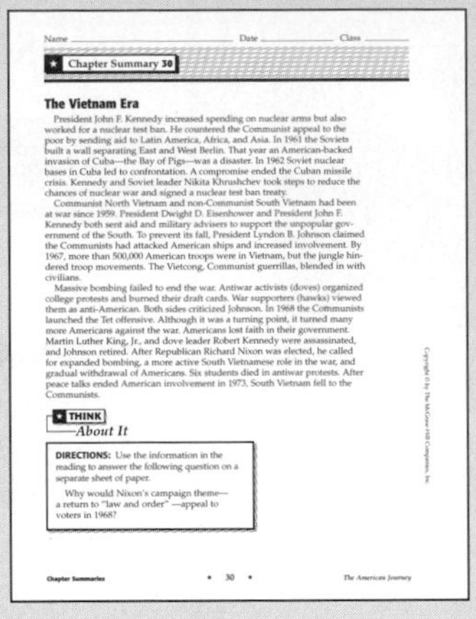

Workbook Activity 30

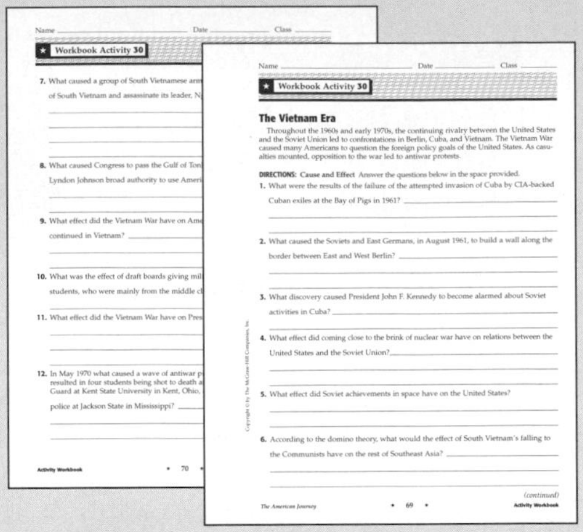

Reinforcement Activities

Time Line Activity 30

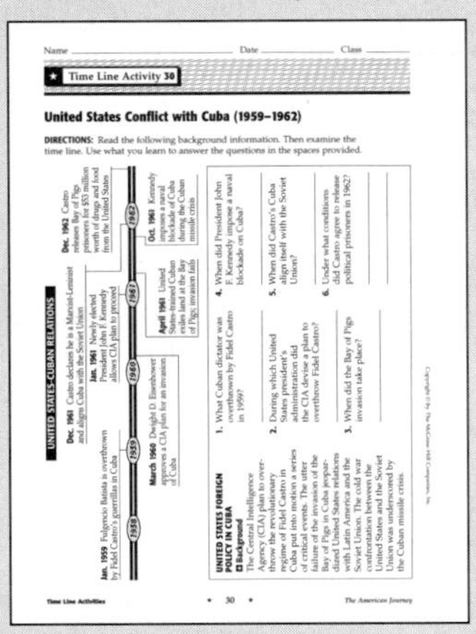

Vocabulary Activity 30

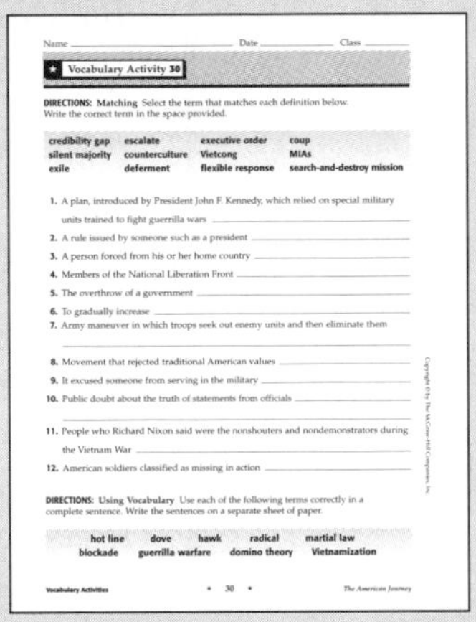

Chapter Skills Activity 30

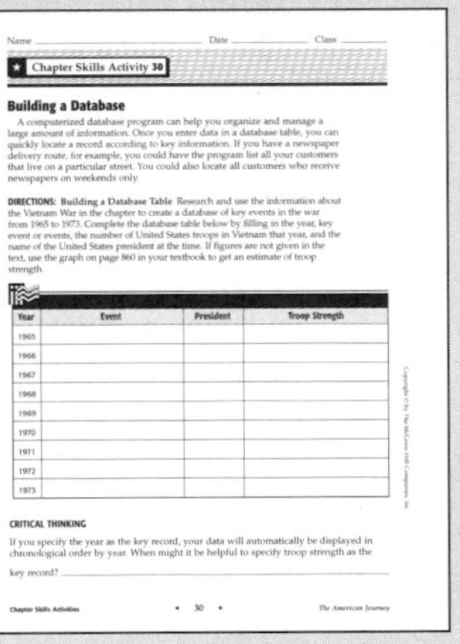

Enrichment Activities

Linking Past and Present Activity 30

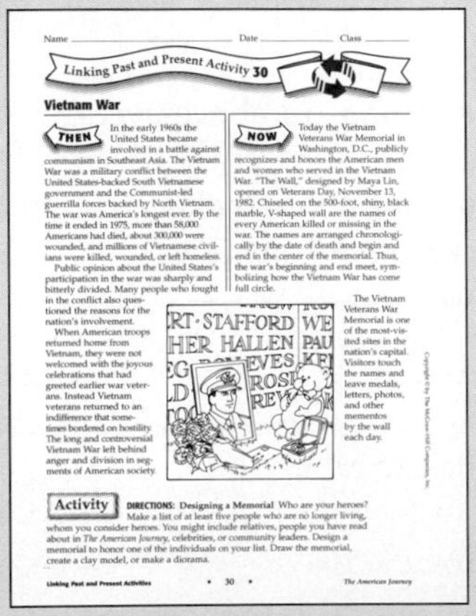

Primary Source Reading 30

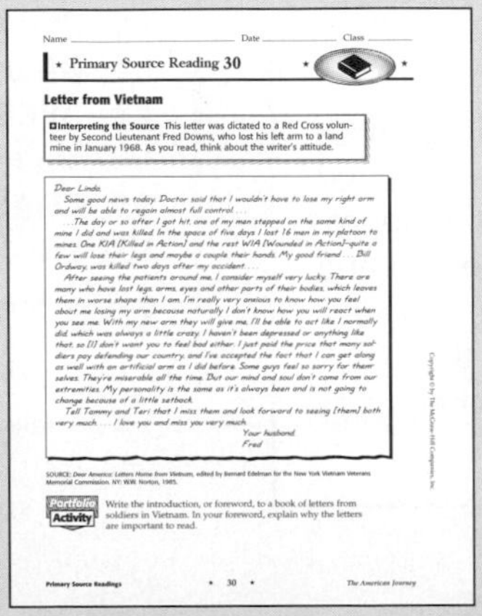

Geography Activities

Mapping History Activity 30

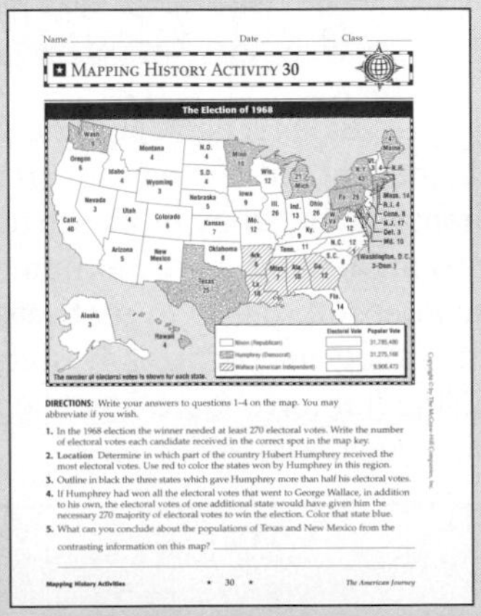

Chapter 30 Resource Guide

ASSESSMENT

Chapter 30 Test, Form A

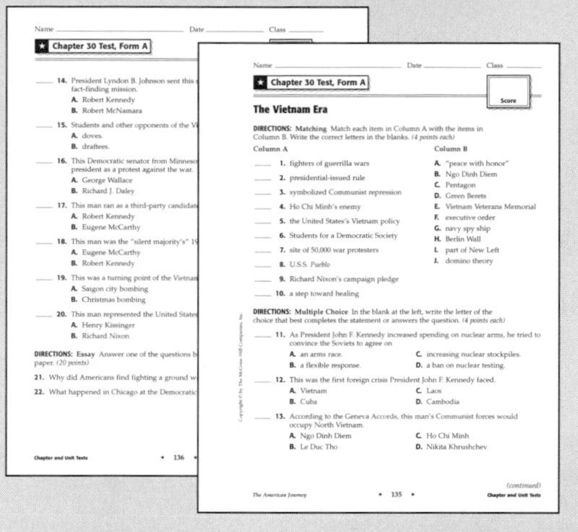
Chapter 30 Test, Form A
The Vietnam Era

Chapter 30 Test, Form B

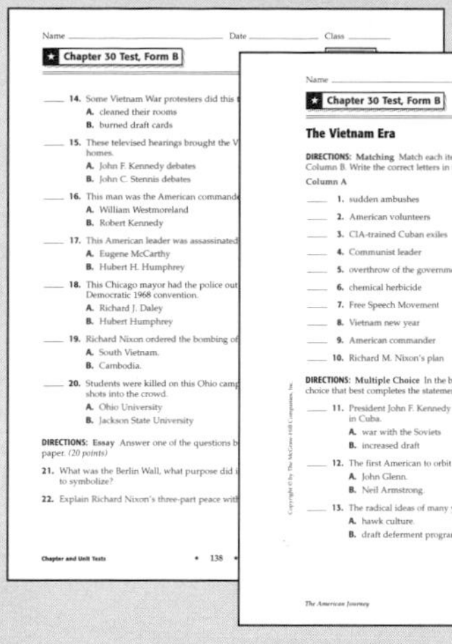
Chapter 30 Test, Form B
The Vietnam Era

Performance Assessment Activity 30

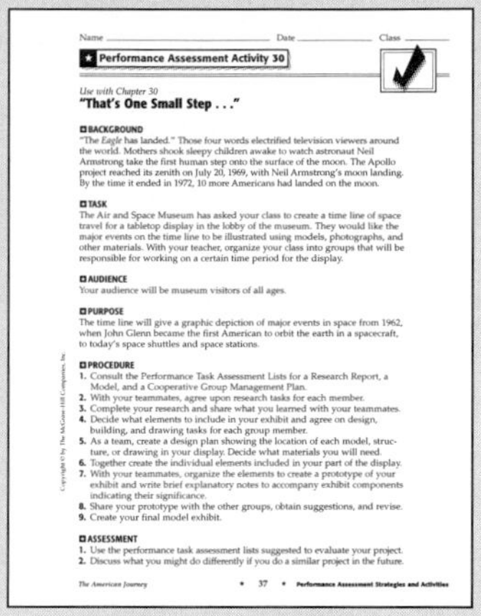
Performance Assessment Activity 30
"That's One Small Step . . ."

SPANISH RESOURCES

The following Spanish language materials are available in the Spanish Resources binder:

- **Spanish Chapter Summary 30**
- **Spanish Vocabulary Activity 30**
- **Spanish Guided Reading Activities, Chapter 30**
- **Spanish Section Quizzes, Chapter 30**
- **Spanish Home Involvement Activity 30**
- **Spanish Chapter 30 Digests Audiocassette Activity and Test**

ACTIVITY MANIPULATIVES

Help students learn more about America's cultural history with:

- **American Crafts Hands-On Activities**
- **American Games Hands-On Activities**
- **American History Flash Cards**

ADDITIONAL RESOURCES FROM GLENCOE

- **The Spirit of American Art and Music,** Joan Baez, Maya Lin
- **American Music Cultural Traditions,** Lesson 10: "Waist Deep in the Big Muddy" and "Okie from Muskogee"
- **Focus on American Art Prints,** *Vietnam Veterans Memorial* by Maya Ying Lin
- **The American History Videodisc and CD-ROM,** *Contemporary America, 1960–1990s*
- **U.S. Desk Map**
- **Outline Map Resource Book**

A&E HOME VIDEO. Biography. THE HISTORY CHANNEL.

The following videotape programs are available from Glencoe as supplements to Chapter 30:

- **Lee Harvey Oswald: An American Tragedy** (ISBN 1-56501-716-1)
- **Great American Monuments: The War Memorials** (ISBN 1-56501-642-4)
- **The Secret Service (Set)** (ISBN 1-56501-521-5)

To order, call Glencoe at 1-800-334-7344. To find classroom resources to accompany many of these videos, check the following home pages:
A&E Television: http://www.aetv.com
The History Channel: http://www.historychannel.com

Introducing
CHAPTER 30

Chapter Themes

Chapter Themes are listed by section on this chapter opening page of the Student Edition. A corresponding theme-based activity is available under "FOCUS," and a theme-based question is asked in the Section and Chapter Reviews.

Performance Assessment

Refer to Activity 30 in the *Performance Assessment Strategies and Activities* booklet.

GLENCOE TECHNOLOGY

VIDEODISC
MindJogger Videoquiz

Use MindJogger to preview the Chapter 30 content.

Chapter 30
Disc 4, Side B

Also available in VHS.

HISTORY AND ART GI slang referred to helicopters as the *TWA*—teenie-weenie airline. With gas turbine replacing piston engines, the HU-1A helicopter (also called the "Huey") had remarkable range and maneuverability. It could carry eight soldiers for combat or four stretchers for medical evacuation, plus two pilots.

Chapter 30

1960–1975

The Vietnam Era

Why It's Important

The Vietnam era left scars on America. More than 58,000 United States troops died in Vietnam, and thousands more were wounded. The war damaged people's confidence in their government. The American people became more willing to challenge the president on military and foreign policy issues after Vietnam. The war also became a yardstick to gauge whether to involve American troops in later crises in other countries.

Chapter Themes

- *Section 1,* Geography and History
- *Section 2,* Government and Democracy
- *Section 3,* Continuity and Change
- *Section 4,* Civic Rights and Responsibilities
- *Section 5,* Individual Action

HISTORY AND ART ***Chopper Pick-Up* by Brian H. Clark** Helicopters in combat were first used on a large scale by United States forces during the Vietnam War. Helicopters served on rescue missions and for aerial observation.

EXTRA CREDIT PROJECT

Applying Song Lyrics The troubles of the United States, abroad and at home, during the Vietnam era were touched upon by several songs of the time. Have students locate a recording of one of the following songs and consider its lyrics:

- "Abraham, Martin, and John"
- "Blowin' in the Wind"
- "Eve of Destruction"
- "If I Had a Hammer"
- "One Tin Soldier"
- "Revolution"
- "What's Going On?"
- "Where Have All the Flowers Gone?"

Ask students to summarize the song and comment about its application to the foreign or domestic problems discussed in Chapter 30.

1960		1965		1970

1961 Bay of Pigs invasion fails

1962 Cuban missile crisis occurs

1963 Telephone hot line links U.S., Soviet leaders

1969 Neil Armstrong walks on the moon

Section 1

Kennedy's Foreign Policy

READ TO DISCOVER . . .

- what course President Kennedy planned to follow in foreign policy.
- how the Kennedy administration handled foreign policy crises in its first year.
- what happened in the Cuban missile crisis.

TERMS TO LEARN

guerrilla warfare	exile
flexible response	blockade
executive order	hot line

The Storyteller

"In the long history of the world, only a few generations have been granted the role of defending freedom in its hour of maximum danger. I do not shrink from this responsibility—I welcome it." So spoke John F. Kennedy in his Inaugural Address. Although Kennedy talked of approaching this responsibility with "energy" and "devotion," events unfolding around the world—in Cuba, Eastern Europe, and Vietnam—would challenge his determination. The new president and nation soon faced a series of crises.

Kennedy inaugural ribbon

President Kennedy continued the anti-Communist foreign policy begun under Presidents Truman and Eisenhower. In pursuing that policy, though, Kennedy tried some new approaches.

New Directions

During the presidential campaign, Kennedy led Americans to believe that the nation had fewer nuclear missiles than the Soviet Union. As president, Kennedy increased spending on nuclear arms. At the same time, he tried to convince **Nikita Khrushchev,** the Soviet leader, to agree to a ban on nuclear testing.

Strength Through Flexibility

Kennedy also worked to improve America's ability to respond to threats abroad. In certain areas of the world, Communist groups fought to take control of their nation's government. Many of these groups received aid from the Soviet Union. They employed **guerrilla warfare,** or fighting by small bands using tactics such as sudden ambushes.

The United States needed a new approach for fighting guerrilla wars. Kennedy introduced a plan called **flexible response,** which relied on special military units trained to fight guerrilla wars. One of these units was the Special Forces, known as the **Green Berets.** The Special Forces provided the president with troops ready to fight guerrilla wars anywhere around the world.

SECTION RESOURCES

Reproducible Masters
- Reproducible Lesson Plan 30–1
- Guided Reading Activity 30–1
- Section Quiz 30–1
- Reteaching Activity 30–1
- Enrichment Activity 30–1

Transparencies
- Section Focus Transparency 30–1

Multimedia
- Vocabulary PuzzleMaker
- Chapter Challenger Interactive Review Software
- Testmaker
- ABCNews InterActive™ Communism and the Cold War
- The Presidents: A Picture History of Our Nation

1 FOCUS

BELLRINGER
Motivational Activity

Before taking roll at the beginning of the class period, project Section Focus Transparency 30–1 and have students answer the questions. Discuss students' responses.

This activity is also available as a blackline master.

Section Focus Transparency 30–1

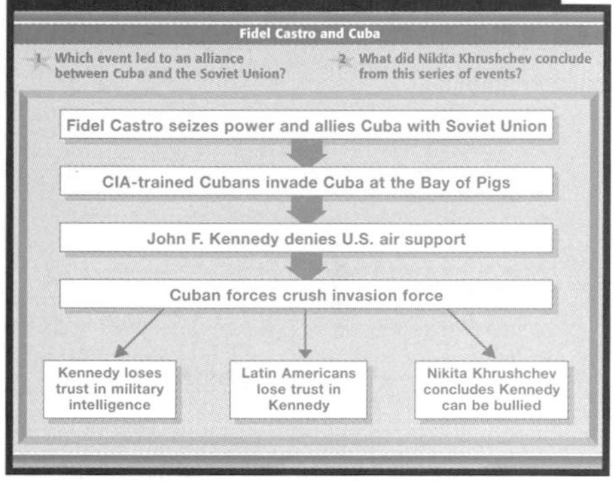

Vocabulary Precheck

Have students demonstrate their understanding of the **Terms to Learn** by writing and sharing questions to which the terms are the answers.

Use the **Vocabulary PuzzleMaker** to create crossword and word search puzzles.

Section Theme
Geography and History

During the Kennedy administration, the United States faced Soviet threats relating to Cuba, to Berlin, and even to outer space.

Activity Ask: Do you think that a nuclear war is likely to happen today? Why or why not? Relate students' responses to the international tensions discussed in this section.

2 TEACH

L1, ELL Solving Problems Ask students how they think most Americans would react upon learning that another country was pointing missiles at the United States. Also ask students how they think the United States should respond. Compare their responses with Kennedy's response to the Cuban missile crisis.

Guided Reading Activity 30–1

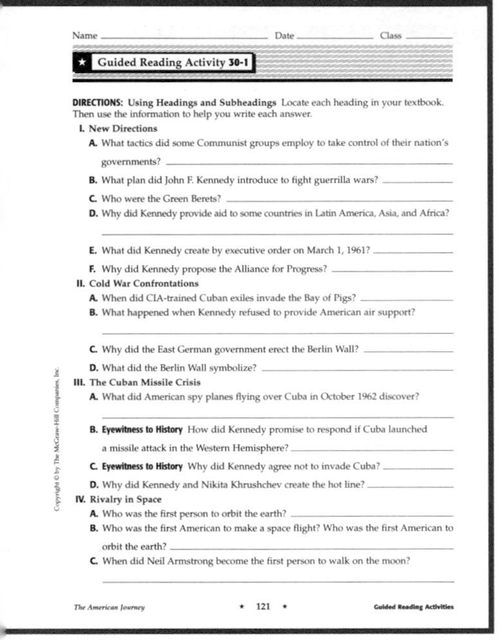
Name ______ Date ______ Class ______

★ Guided Reading Activity 30-1

DIRECTIONS: Using Headings and Subheadings Locate each heading in your textbook. Then use the information to help you write each answer.

I. New Directions
A. What tactics did some Communist groups employ to take control of their nation's governments? ______
B. What plan did John F. Kennedy introduce to fight guerrilla wars? ______
C. Who were the Green Berets? ______
D. Why did Kennedy provide aid to some countries in Latin America, Asia, and Africa? ______
E. What did Kennedy create by executive order on March 1, 1961? ______
F. Why did Kennedy propose the Alliance for Progress? ______

II. Cold War Confrontations
A. When did CIA-trained Cuban exiles invade the Bay of Pigs? ______
B. What happened when Kennedy refused to provide American air support? ______
C. Why did the East German government erect the Berlin Wall? ______
D. What did the Berlin Wall symbolize? ______

III. The Cuban Missile Crisis
A. What did American spy planes flying over Cuba in October 1962 discover? ______
B. Eyewitness to History How did Kennedy promise to respond if Cuba launched a missile attack in the Western Hemisphere? ______
C. Eyewitness to History Why did Kennedy agree not to invade Cuba? ______
D. Why did Kennedy and Nikita Khrushchev create the hot line? ______

IV. Rivalry in Space
A. Who was the first person to orbit the earth? ______
B. Who was the first American to make a space flight? Who was the first American to orbit the earth? ______
C. When did Neil Armstrong become the first person to walk on the moon? ______

Copyright © by The McGraw-Hill Companies, Inc.

The American Journey ★ 121 ★ **Guided Reading Activities**

HISTORY AND ART In 1963 Norman Rockwell left the *Saturday Evening Post* to work for *Look* magazine. The paintings he created for *Look* focused on world events and leaders and on important issues of the day, but they maintain the personal touch for which Rockwell was known. **Ask:** What is this Peace Corps worker teaching? *(agricultural skills—in this case, the use of a plow)*
Answer: *the Alliance for Progress*

Strength Through Aid

President Kennedy understood that the poverty in Latin America, Asia, and Africa made the Communist promises of economic equality seem attractive. He decided to provide aid to countries in those areas to counteract the appeal of communism. On March 1, 1961, the president signed an **executive order** creating the **Peace Corps.** An executive order is a rule issued by the Chief Executive.

Americans who volunteered for the Peace Corps worked in other countries as teachers, health workers, and advisers in farming, industry, and government. By 1963 some 5,000 Peace Corps volunteers worked in more than 40 countries.

To promote Latin America's growth, Kennedy proposed a 10-year development plan for the region called the **Alliance for Progress.** In his Inaugural Address, Kennedy promised Latin American leaders that the United States would "assist free men and free governments in casting off the chains of poverty." He hoped as well to prevent the rise of Communist states in the region.

Cold War Confrontations

★ In 1961, just a few months after taking office, President Kennedy faced a foreign policy crisis in **Cuba.** That same year, the United States and the Soviet Union clashed in Europe.

The Bay of Pigs

As you read in Chapter 28, **Fidel Castro** had seized power in Cuba in 1959. When Castro formed an alliance with the Soviet Union, Americans felt threatened because Cuba lay only 90 miles (144 km) south of Florida. In the final months of Eisenhower's presidency, officials in the Central Intelligence Agency (CIA) forged a plan to overthrow Castro.

The CIA recruited a military force from the refugees who had fled Castro's Cuba and settled in the United States. The plan called for these **exiles,** or persons forced from their homes, to land in Cuba, spark an uprising, and overthrow Castro. Although Kennedy had doubts about the plan, he accepted the advice of military advisers and the CIA and allowed it to go forward.

On April 17, 1961, 1,500 CIA-trained Cuban exiles landed at the **Bay of Pigs** in southern Cuba. Many blunders occurred, and at a crucial moment, Kennedy refused to provide American air support. Within days Cuban forces crushed the invasion and captured the survivors.

The Bay of Pigs embarrassed Kennedy, who took the blame for the failure. The disaster had three consequences. First, Kennedy never again completely trusted military and intelligence advice. Second, other nations in Latin America lost trust in Kennedy. Third, Soviet premier Khrushchev concluded that Kennedy was not a strong leader and could be bullied.

HISTORY AND ART

***The Peace Corps in Ethiopia, 1966* by Norman Rockwell** Volunteers worked in many developing countries. **Which Kennedy program dealt with Latin America's economy?**

COOPERATIVE LEARNING ACTIVITY

Surveying the Country's Mood To review this section, ask the class to imagine that it is December 1962. Organize one group of students to take an end-of-year survey. Have members of that group approach their classmates, asking these questions: **Are you optimistic about the future? Why or why not?** As students respond, encourage them to not be swayed by others' answers but to come up with their own reasons for replying yes or no. Have the surveyors pool their responses and present them to the class, drawing special attention to answers that touch upon the foreign policy crises discussed in Section 1.

Picturing HISTORY In the early 1960s, some East Germans tried to escape their Communist-ruled homeland by building tunnels (shown below) under the Berlin Wall. **What did the Berlin Wall come to symbolize?**

The Berlin Wall

Though 16 years had passed since the end of World War II, the wartime Allies had still not settled the status of Germany. West Germany gained complete independence in 1949, but the Soviet Union continued to control East Germany.

The location of **Berlin**—fully within Soviet-controlled East Germany—posed special problems. American, British, and French troops still remained in the western part of the city, and they sometimes had difficulty getting into West Berlin and maintaining control there. Meanwhile a steady flow of people fled to West Berlin from Communist East Berlin, hoping to escape economic hardship and find freedom.

At a June 1961 summit conference in **Vienna, Austria,** Premier Khrushchev told President Kennedy that the West must move out of Berlin, and he insisted on an agreement by the end of the year. Kennedy rejected Khrushchev's demand. To emphasize the West's right to stay in West Berlin, the United States later sent more troops to protect the city.

Later that summer, a large number of East Germans fled to the West. On August 13, the East German government, with Soviet backing, closed the border between East and West Berlin and built a wall of concrete blocks and barbed wire along it. The Soviets posted armed guards along the wall to stop more East Germans from fleeing to the West. The **Berlin Wall** cut communications between the two parts of the city.

The Western Allies continued to support the freedom and independence of West Berlin. They could do little, however, to stop the building of the wall, which came to symbolize Communist repression.

The Cuban Missile Crisis

The most dangerous cold war dispute between the Americans and Soviets came in 1962. Once again the dispute involved Cuba.

Missiles in Cuba

In mid-October 1962, an American spy plane flying over Cuba made a disturbing discovery. Photographs revealed that the Soviets were building launching sites for nuclear missiles. These missiles could easily reach the United States in a matter of minutes.

Picturing HISTORY Soon after the Berlin Wall was constructed, stories emerged about *wall-jumpers*—people who regularly crossed the wall. One story told of three East Berliners who sneaked into West Berlin every weekend, watched the latest Hollywood movies, and sneaked back into East Berlin in time for work on Monday.
Answer: *Communist repression*

ABCNEWS INTERACTIVE™

VIDEODISC
Communism and the Cold War

Side 2
Chapter 13

Title: *Bay of Pigs*
Subject: 1961 invasion of Cuba
Ask: **Why did the United States want to overthrow Castro?** *(because he had allied Cuba with the Soviet Union)*

Side 1
Chapter 16

Title: *Cuban Missile Crisis*
Subject: Summary of the crisis
Ask: **Why did the United States panic when the Soviet Union put missiles in Cuba?** *(It felt threatened because Cuba was located so close to its borders.)*

Where?When?Who?What?

West Berlin In June 1963, Kennedy visited West Berlin. A vast, cheering crowd gathered to hear him at the city hall. The president told them: "Freedom has many difficulties and democracy is not perfect, but we have never had to put up a wall to keep our people in. . . . All free men, wherever they may live, are citizens of Berlin, and therefore, as a free man I take pride in the words, 'Ich bin ein (I am a) Berliner.'"

MULTIPLE LEARNING STYLES

Visual/Spatial To help students better understand Americans' fears of nuclear war, ask them to view one of these films (available on videocassette):
The Atomic Cafe (1982), a collection of government films and newsreel footage that shows how Americans worried about "the bomb" and tried to prepare for nuclear attack.
The Missiles of October (1974), a made-for-television dramatization of the Cuban missile crisis that focuses on the responsibilities placed upon Kennedy and Khrushchev.
Have students report on the films, commenting upon memorable scenes and describing how the films capture the fear of the time. **L1**

CHAPTER 30
Section 1, 847–851

NATIONAL GEOGRAPHIC SOCIETY

CD-ROM
The Presidents: A Picture History of Our Nation

Have students view "John F. Kennedy" and write a brief biography about him.

Map Study

Answers
1. Guantanamo Bay
2. aircraft carriers to form a blockade

Map Skills Practice

Reading a Map What Caribbean island southeast of Cuba was the site of a U.S. base? *(Puerto Rico)*

3 ASSESS

Assign Section 1 Review as homework or as an in-class activity.

Use **Chapter Challenger Interactive Review Software** to review Section 1.

Section Quiz 30–1

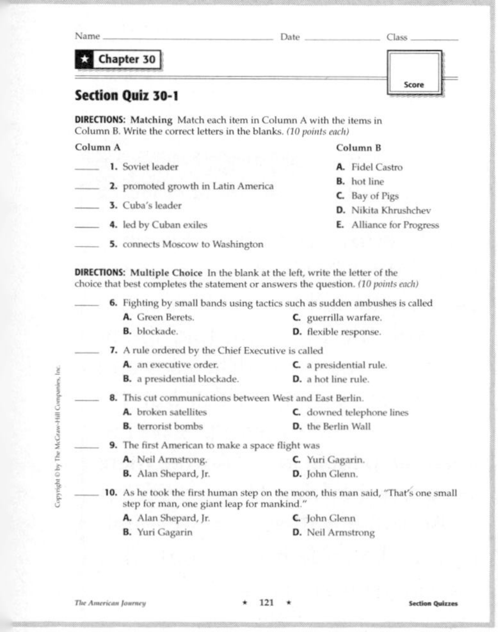

Name ______ Date ______ Class ______

Chapter 30 | Score

Section Quiz 30-1

DIRECTIONS: Matching Match each item in Column A with the items in Column B. Write the correct letters in the blanks. *(10 points each)*

Column A	Column B
____ 1. Soviet leader	A. Fidel Castro
____ 2. promoted growth in Latin America	B. hot line
____ 3. Cuba's leader	C. Bay of Pigs
____ 4. led by Cuban exiles	D. Nikita Khrushchev
____ 5. connects Moscow to Washington	E. Alliance for Progress

DIRECTIONS: Multiple Choice In the blank at the left, write the letter of the choice that best completes the statement or answers the question. *(10 points each)*

____ 6. Fighting by small bands using tactics such as sudden ambushes is called
A. Green Berets. C. guerrilla warfare.
B. blockade. D. flexible response.

____ 7. A rule ordered by the Chief Executive is called
A. an executive order. C. a presidential rule.
B. a presidential blockade. D. a hot line rule.

____ 8. This cut communications between West and East Berlin.
A. broken satellites C. downed telephone lines
B. terrorist bombs D. the Berlin Wall

____ 9. The first American to make a space flight was
A. Neil Armstrong. C. Yuri Gagarin.
B. Alan Shepard, Jr. D. John Glenn.

____ 10. As he took the first human step on the moon, this man said, "That's one small step for man, one giant leap for mankind."
A. Alan Shepard, Jr. C. John Glenn
B. Yuri Gagarin D. Neil Armstrong

The American Journey ★ 121 ★ **Section Quizzes**

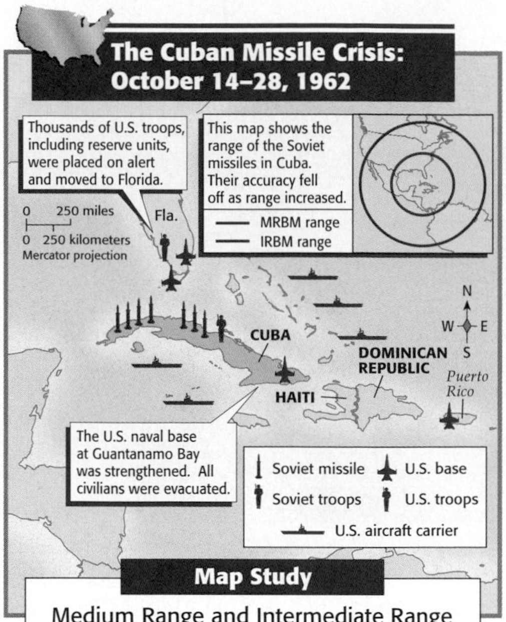

Map Study

Medium Range and Intermediate Range Ballistic Missiles (MRBMs and IRBMs) in Cuba posed an immediate danger to the United States.

1. **Location** Where was the major U.S. naval base on Cuba located?
2. **Analyzing Information** What military equipment did the United States use to answer the Soviet threat in Cuba?

For the next week, President Kennedy met secretly with advisers to determine how to deal with the **Cuban missile crisis.** They explored several options, including invading Cuba and bombing the missile sites. New spy photographs showed the bases nearing completion faster than expected. A decision had to be made.

Eyewitness to HISTORY

"Eyeball to Eyeball"

On October 22, President Kennedy, speaking on national television, revealed the "secret, swift, and extraordinary buildup" of missiles in Cuba. Kennedy ordered the navy to **blockade,** or close off, Cuba until the Soviets removed the missiles. He promised to destroy any Soviet ship that tried to break through the blockade. The president also declared:

> "It shall be the policy of this nation to regard any nuclear missile launched from Cuba against any nation in the Western Hemisphere as an attack by the Soviet Union on the United States."

The United States would respond, he warned, with a nuclear attack against the Soviet Union.

As the two superpowers neared the brink of nuclear war, people all over the world waited nervously. However, Khrushchev was not ready to back down, and Soviet ships—some carrying missiles—continued to approach Cuba.

Two days after Kennedy's announcement, a breakthrough occurred. Some Soviet ships nearing the blockade turned back. One American official announced, "We're eyeball to eyeball, and I think the other fellow just blinked."

Khrushchev sent a message, saying that the two countries

> ". . . ought not to pull on the ends of the rope in which you have tied the knot of war. . . . Let us take measures to untie that knot."

However, some Soviet ships still headed toward Cuba, and work on the missile bases continued. The president's advisers worked on plans for an air attack on the missile sites—just in case.

Fears grew on the fifth day, when Cuba shot down an American spy plane. At the same time, Kennedy and Khrushchev neared an agreement. Finally, after a week of tension, the Soviets announced they would "dismantle the arms which you describe as offensive, and . . . crate and return them to the Soviet Union." In return, Kennedy agreed not to invade Cuba. He also gave private assurances that the United States would remove some missiles—aimed at the Soviet Union—from Turkey and Italy after the Soviet Union removed the missiles from Cuba.

MAKING CONNECTIONS ACTIVITY

Foreign Affairs Through the Peace Corps, American volunteers offered help to developing nations around the world. Ask students to imagine that they want to join the Peace Corps today. Have them choose a developing nation and research its current needs. Then have them write a letter of application to the Peace Corps. In the letter they should discuss the needs of the country in which they would like to serve and identify the skills (real or imaginary) that would qualify them to be of help. If time permits, have a panel of student judges evaluate the letters and choose three students to "go abroad." **L2**

The Aftermath

Having come so close to nuclear disaster, the superpowers worked to establish a better relationship. In the summer of 1963, Kennedy and Khrushchev created a direct telephone link, called the **hot line,** between Moscow and Washington to allow the leaders to communicate instantly in times of crisis.

That same summer, the two nations signed a treaty banning nuclear tests above ground and underwater.

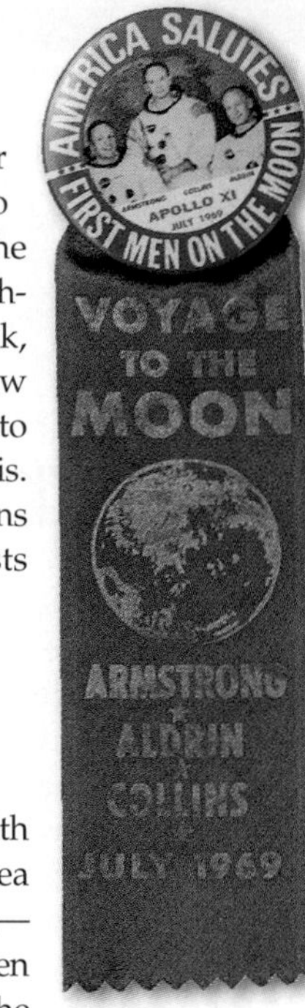

Apollo *button*

Rivalry in Space

The United States competed with the Soviet Union in another area during the Kennedy administration—outer space. The space race began when the Soviet Union launched *Sputnik,* the world's first successful satellite, in 1957. In April 1961, Soviet cosmonaut **Yuri Gagarin** (guh•GAHR•uhn) became the first person to orbit the earth. One month later, **Alan Shepard, Jr.,** became the first American to make a spaceflight.

Shortly after Shepard's flight, Kennedy challenged the nation to a great undertaking. In a speech to Congress, he said:

> "I believe that this nation should commit itself to achieving the goal, before this decade is out, of landing a man on the moon and returning him safely to the earth."

The president asked Congress for more money for **NASA** (the National Aeronautics and Space Administration), which ran the space program. NASA expanded its launching facility in Florida and built a control center in Houston, Texas.

Astronaut **John Glenn** thrilled the country in February 1962 when he orbited the earth in a spacecraft, the first American to do so. An even greater triumph for the space program came on July 20, 1969, with the **Apollo project.** Awestruck television viewers around the world watched the spacecraft *Eagle* land on the surface of the moon. Hours later, with millions still watching, astronaut **Neil Armstrong** took the first human step on the moon and announced: "That's one small step for man, one giant leap for mankind." By the end of the Apollo project in 1972, 10 more Americans had landed on the moon.

Section 1 Review

Checking for Understanding

1. ***Identify*** John F. Kennedy, Nikita Khrushchev, Alliance for Progress, Fidel Castro, Bay of Pigs, Berlin, Cuban missile crisis, Apollo project.
2. ***Define*** guerrilla warfare, flexible response, executive order, exile, blockade, hot line.
3. ***Cite*** three consequences that President Kennedy faced as a result of the failure of the Bay of Pigs invasion.

Reviewing Themes

4. **Geography and History** Why did West Berlin's location make it difficult for the United States and its allies to defend it?

Critical Thinking

5. **Making Inferences** Why do you think Khrushchev sent missiles to Cuba?

Activity

Writing a Speech Write a speech that President Kennedy might have written to defend his actions during the Cuban missile crisis.

Section 1 Review Answers

1. John F. Kennedy, 847; Nikita Khrushchev, 847; Alliance for Progress, 848; Fidel Castro, 848; Bay of Pigs, 848; Berlin, 849; Cuban missile crisis, 850; Apollo project, 851
2. The words are defined in the Glossary.
3. Kennedy never again completely trusted military or intelligence advice. Latin American nations lost trust in Kennedy. Khrushchev viewed him as a weak leader.
4. Berlin was fully contained within Soviet-controlled East Germany.
5. Students may conclude that the Soviet Union was planning to attack the United States at some point or that the missiles were a defense against any future American attacks against Cuba or the Soviet Union.

Activity Speeches should reflect some of Kennedy's motivations for his actions.

Reteaching Activity 30–1

Name ________ Date ________ Class ________

★ Reteaching Activity **30-1**

DIRECTIONS: Identifying Problems and Solutions The pursuit of anti-Communist foreign policy caused problems for both the United States and the Soviet Union during the Kennedy administration. The solutions to some of these problems did not always work and occasionally caused other problems. After each *Problem,* write the letters of the *Solutions* from the Fact Bank.

1. **Problem:** In certain areas of the world, Communist groups used guerrilla tactics to take control of their nation's government.
   Solutions: ________
2. **Problem:** The free governments of poverty-stricken countries in Latin America, Asia, and Africa were vulnerable to Communist overthrow.
   Solutions: ________
3. **Problem:** Fidel Castro formed an alliance with the Soviet Union.
   Solutions: ________
4. **Problem:** The Soviet Union wanted to assert its position in East Germany and stop the flow of East Germans to the West.
   Solutions: ________
5. **Problem:** The Soviets built launching sites for nuclear missiles in Cuba.
   Solutions: ________
6. **Problem:** The buildup and testing of nuclear weapons by the superpowers created a potential for a nuclear disaster.
   Solutions: ________

★FACT BANK

A. The CIA recruited a military force from Cuban exiles who had settled in the United States.
B. John F. Kennedy proposed the Alliance for Progress.
C. Kennedy warned the Soviets that an attack against any nation in the Western Hemisphere would be seen as an attack on the United States.
D. Kennedy created the Peace Corps.
E. The Berlin Wall was erected.
F. Kennedy and Nikita Khrushchev created a hot line between Moscow and Washington.
G. The United States and the Soviet Union signed a treaty, banning nuclear tests above ground and underwater.
H. Kennedy introduced a plan called flexible response.
I. Khrushchev told Kennedy that the West must move out of Berlin.
J. American-trained forces invaded Cuba to try to spark an uprising.
K. Kennedy ordered the navy to blockade Cuba.
L. Special military units such as the Green Berets were created.

The American Journey ★ 121 ★ **Reteaching Activities**

Enrichment Activity 30–1

Name ________ Date ________ Class ________

★ Enrichment Activity **30-1** ★ ★

The Peace Corps

Between 1961 and 1989 Peace Corps volunteers served in many countries of the world. Most of the countries were located in South America, Central America, Africa, and Asia. The map on the right shows countries in the region called *Inter-America* by the Peace Corps.

Countries with Peace Corps Workers, 1961-1989

DIRECTIONS: Reading a Map Use the map to answer the following questions.

1. Name four Central American countries that had Peace Corps workers.
   ____
   ____
   ____
   ____
2. How many countries in South America had Peace Corps workers? ________
3. About what percentage of all the countries of South America had Peace Corps help?
   ____
4. Which South American countries did not have Peace Corps help? (You may need to use another map to find the names.) ________

Activity **DIRECTIONS:** Imagine it is the 1960s and you are a Peace Corps volunteer who will work in the Inter-American Region. Choose the country you want to work in. In order for you to become familiar with the tasks, language, and culture, begin assembling materials about that country. Try to identify the needs of the country and to include information about the culture. Present the information that you have collected to the class.

The American Journey ★ 121 ★ **Enrichment Activities**

4 CLOSE

Tell students that President Kennedy once said that the United States "cannot right every wrong or reverse every adversity." Ask them to apply that statement to the events in this section.

1 FOCUS

BELLRINGER
Motivational Activity

Before taking roll at the beginning of the class period, project Section Focus Transparency 30–2 and have students answer the questions. Discuss students' responses.

This activity is also available as a blackline master.

Section Focus Transparency 30–2

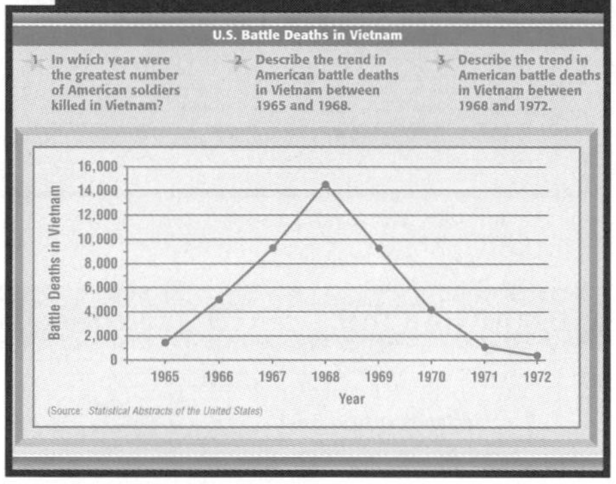

Vocabulary Precheck

Point out that *coup* is short for *coup d'etat*, a French term meaning "stroke of state"—a major political blow. Call on volunteers to name situations (not necessarily political ones) that they think could be described by the word *coup*.

Use the **Vocabulary PuzzleMaker** to create crossword and word search puzzles.

Section Theme
Government and Democracy

United States military involvement in Vietnam steadily increased from a few hundred advisers during the Eisenhower administration to more than 500,000 soldiers during the Johnson administration.

Activity Call on volunteers to share what they have heard about Vietnam. Use their responses to begin an examination of the war's origins.

1950 — 1960 — 1970

1954 Geneva Accords divide Vietnam

1959 Civil war in Vietnam begins

1964 Gulf of Tonkin Resolution passed

1967 More than 500,000 U.S. troops are in Vietnam

Section 2

War in Vietnam

READ TO DISCOVER . . .

- how Vietnam became a divided country.
- how the United States first became involved in Vietnam.
- why America increased its involvement in the Vietnam War.

TERMS TO LEARN

Vietcong	escalate
domino theory	search-and-destroy mission
coup	

The Storyteller

In March 1967 David Parks, an African American soldier serving in Vietnam, described an enemy attack on his camp: "I was asleep when the first shell exploded. The earth shook and I rolled to the ground as someone hollered, 'Incoming!' . . . I shook like jelly as the shrapnel burst all around our bunker. . . . All we could do was open up with our 50-caliber and small arms. . . . I'm not sure the native people are with us. They smile at us in the daytime and their sons shoot at us at night. It's hard to spot the real enemy."

Soldier's boots, Vietnam War

In the early 1960s, the United States became involved in a fight against communism in Southeast Asia. The war in **Vietnam** did not unfold as Americans had hoped, however. General Maxwell Taylor, who served as American ambassador to Vietnam, reflected on the war in Vietnam years after it had ended:

> "First, we didn't know ourselves. We thought we were going into another Korean war, but this was a different country. Secondly, we didn't know our South Vietnamese allies. We never understood them, and that was another surprise. And we knew even less about North Vietnam."

Origins of the War

The roots of the Vietnam conflict can be traced back to World War II, when Japanese forces captured the French colony of Indochina in Southeast Asia. Vietnamese forces led by Communist **Ho Chi Minh** (HOH CHEE MIHN) fought against the Japanese.

When Japan surrendered at the end of World War II, Ho declared Vietnam's independence. The French, however, were unwilling to give up their empire. Their Indochina colony—the present-day nations of Cambodia, Laos, and Vietnam—was among the richest of France's colonies, supplying such valuable resources as rice, rubber, and tin. Ho and his forces fought the French in a long, bloody war, finally defeating the French in 1954.

SECTION RESOURCES

Reproducible Masters
- Reproducible Lesson Plan 30–2
- Guided Reading Activity 30–2
- Section Quiz 30–2
- Reteaching Activity 30–2
- Enrichment Activity 30–2

Transparencies
- Section Focus Transparency 30–2

Multimedia
- Vocabulary PuzzleMaker
- Chapter Challenger Interactive Review
- Testmaker
- ABCNews InterActive™ Historic America Electronic Field Trips
- ABCNews InterActive™ Lessons of War
- The Presidents: A Picture History of Our Nation

The Geneva Accords

That same year, diplomats from the United States, France, Great Britain, the Soviet Union, Communist China, and Vietnam met in Geneva, Switzerland, to hammer out a peace agreement. According to the **Geneva Accords,** Vietnam would be divided temporarily. Ho Chi Minh's Communist nationalists would control the North. Non-Communist forces—supported by the United States—would control the South. Vietnam would be unified in 1956 after national elections.

Neither the United States nor South Vietnam signed the agreement, but they did not oppose its provisions. At the same time, an American representative warned that the United States reserved the right to step in if Communist North Vietnam moved aggressively against the South.

Renewed Conflict

In 1955 **Ngo Dinh Diem** (NOH DIHN deh •EHM), French-educated Vietnamese leader, gained control of the government of South Vietnam. The following year, Diem, with American support, refused to hold the elections promised by the Geneva Accords. Diem's brutal policies and his refusal to hold elections angered many Vietnamese.

Communist supporters of Ho Chi Minh remained in the South after Vietnam was divided. They challenged Diem's efforts to gain control of the country. In the late 1950s, Diem launched a campaign to destroy the power of the Communists. In response, the Communists organized themselves as the **National Liberation Front** (NLF)—better known to Americans as the **Vietcong**. In 1959 the Vietcong, on orders from Ho Chi Minh, began a war against the Diem regime.

A Growing American Role

The United States had replaced the French as the dominant foreign power in the South in 1955. If Communists took South Vietnam, President Eisenhower once said, the other countries of Southeast Asia would fall to communism like a row of dominoes—one right after the other. This **domino theory** helped shape American policy in Vietnam for the next 20 years.

To support South Vietnam, the Eisenhower administration sent the country billions of dollars in aid. It also dispatched a few hundred soldiers, who acted as advisers to the South Vietnamese government and army.

The Kennedy Years

Like Eisenhower, President Kennedy saw Vietnam as part of the global struggle in the fight against communism. Kennedy sent more Special Forces troops—the Green Berets—to train and advise South Vietnamese troops. Kennedy also pressured Diem to make political and economic reforms to

Ho Chi Minh

Picturing HISTORY Buddhist monks often led protests against unpopular South Vietnamese governments. **Why did Vietnam's Buddhists protest against the Diem government?**

Cooperative Learning Activity

Creating Headlines Students can trace the events in Section 2 by writing imaginary newspaper headlines for the events. Organize the class into two teams. On each team, have one or two students examine present-day newspapers and report to the team about headline "style." About half the students on each team should work together to outline the events discussed in this section, from the Geneva Accords of 1954 through the disagreements in the White House in 1968. The remaining students should write two headlines for each event, with the team as a whole voting for the preferred headline in each case. Discuss both teams' headlines with the class as an outline for review.

2 TEACH

L1 Organizing Information Have students draw a time line of events leading to the United States involvement in Vietnam. Have them add more information to the time line after studying Sections 4 and 5.

Guided Reading Activity 30–2

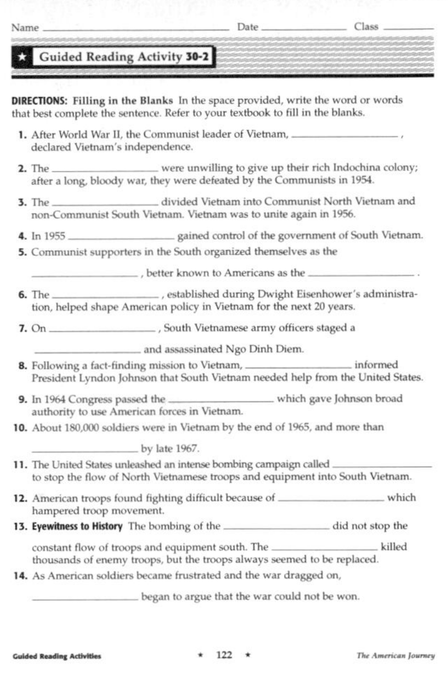

Name ______ Date ______ Class ______

Guided Reading Activity 30-2

DIRECTIONS: Filling in the Blanks In the space provided, write the word or words that best complete the sentence. Refer to your textbook to fill in the blanks.

1. After World War II, the Communist leader of Vietnam, ______, declared Vietnam's independence.
2. The ______ were unwilling to give up their rich Indochina colony; after a long, bloody war, they were defeated by the Communists in 1954.
3. The ______ divided Vietnam into Communist North Vietnam and non-Communist South Vietnam. Vietnam was to unite again in 1956.
4. In 1955 ______ gained control of the government of South Vietnam.
5. Communist supporters in the South organized themselves as the ______, better known to Americans as the ______.
6. The ______, established during Dwight Eisenhower's administration, helped shape American policy in Vietnam for the next 20 years.
7. On ______, South Vietnamese army officers staged a ______ and assassinated Ngo Dinh Diem.
8. Following a fact-finding mission to Vietnam, ______ informed President Lyndon Johnson that South Vietnam needed help from the United States.
9. In 1964 Congress passed the ______ which gave Johnson broad authority to use American forces in Vietnam.
10. About 180,000 soldiers were in Vietnam by the end of 1965, and more than ______ by late 1967.
11. The United States unleashed an intense bombing campaign called ______ to stop the flow of North Vietnamese troops and equipment into South Vietnam.
12. American troops found fighting difficult because of ______ which hampered troop movement.
13. **Eyewitness to History** The bombing of the ______ did not stop the constant flow of troops and equipment south. The ______ killed thousands of enemy troops, but the troops always seemed to be replaced.
14. As American soldiers became frustrated and the war dragged on, ______ began to argue that the war could not be won.

Guided Reading Activities • 122 • *The American Journey*

Picturing HISTORY Buddhists followed the Eightfold Path—know the truth, resist evil, say nothing to hurt others, respect life, work for the good of others, free your minds of evil, control your thoughts, and practice meditation. **Answer:** *Diem refused to hold elections, took away Buddhists' rights*

ABCNEWS INTERACTIVE™

VIDEODISC
Historic America Electronic Field Trips

Side 2, Chapter 10

Title: *The Vietnam Veterans Memorial*
Subject: Steps leading to war

Also available in VHS.

Picturing HISTORY Lt. Gary B. Roush, a helicopter pilot in Vietnam, said, "Flying has been described as hours and hours of boredom interrupted by moments of terror. In Vietnam, flying helicopters in combat was hours and hours of excitement interrupted by intense periods of extreme terror." **Ask:** **Why do you think helicopters were used extensively in Vietnam?** *(They were effective at pinpointing enemy positions, and they provided the quickest possible response.)*
Answer: *in 1965 after the Gulf of Tonkin Resolution*

ABCNEWS INTERACTIVE™

VIDEODISC
Lessons of War

Side 1, Chapter 8
Title: *"The First Casualty"*
Subject: The relationship between journalists and the military in times of war
Ask: **How was television instrumental in shaping public response during the Vietnam conflict?** *(For the first time, vivid images of war were brought into every family's living room through the television. As people watched media coverage portraying the suffering and reality of bloodshed and death, some began to oppose the Vietnam conflict.)*

Picturing HISTORY American soldiers leap from a helicopter during a mission in South Vietnam. **When did President Johnson begin to escalate American involvement in Vietnam?**

eliminate the conditions that had allowed communism to take root in the first place. But Diem refused to comply. Instead of paying for new schools, health clinics, or land reform, American funds often ended up in the pockets of corrupt South Vietnamese officials. At the same time, North Vietnam sent aid and troops to the South to help the Vietcong in a guerrilla war against Diem that began in 1959.

The Diem government lost support throughout the country. His government took rights away from **Buddhists**—the majority of the people in South Vietnam—and favored Catholics, like himself. Buddhists responded with protests, some of which ended in bloodshed when government troops fired into the crowds.

In early 1963 Buddhist monks showed their opposition to Diem's rule by setting themselves on fire on busy streets. Horrifying photographs of monks engulfed in flames appeared in newspapers and on television screens around the world. The Kennedy administration found it difficult to continue to support Diem.

On November 1, 1963, a group of South Vietnamese army officers staged a **coup**—overthrew the government—and assassinated Diem. The Kennedy administration had supported the coup, but not the assassination. After President Kennedy was assassinated later that same month, the question of what to do in Vietnam fell on the shoulders of President **Lyndon B. Johnson.**

The Conflict Deepens

At the time of Kennedy's death, the United States had nearly 15,000 American troops in Vietnam as advisers. President Johnson sent Secretary of Defense **Robert McNamara** to Vietnam on a fact-finding mission.

McNamara told the president that South Vietnam could not resist the Vietcong rebels without more help from the United States. In a May 1964 conversation, taped but not made public until 1997, Johnson himself expressed doubts about American commitment. "I don't think it's worth

MULTIPLE LEARNING STYLES

Intrapersonal The increased military commitment to Vietnam touched virtually every neighborhood in the United States. As a result, almost every American was challenged to consider the United States's involvement in this war. Capture that challenge by asking students to imagine that they have just been drafted for military service in Vietnam. Have them write diary entries or letters in which they share their thoughts—their fears, hopes, and questions about being part of the United States presence in Vietnam. Work with students to create a format for sharing their writing. **L2**

Linking PAST & PRESENT

From War to Tourism

Ho Chi Minh City (formerly Saigon) proclaimed 1990 its "Year of Tourism." Tunnels once used by the Vietcong guerrillas—a network of 200 miles—were one of the featured tourist attractions.

fighting for," he said, "but I don't think we can get out." Nevertheless, as Vietcong attacks continued, the United States moved toward deeper involvement.

Gulf of Tonkin Resolution

President Johnson wanted congressional support for expanding the American role in Vietnam. The opportunity to get that support came in August 1964, when North Vietnamese patrol boats allegedly attacked American destroyers in the **Gulf of Tonkin** near North Vietnam. Congress quickly passed a resolution that allowed the president to "take all necessary measures to repel any armed attack against the forces of the United States." The **Gulf of Tonkin Resolution** gave Johnson broad authority to use American forces in Vietnam.

Military Buildup

In 1965 Johnson began to escalate—gradually increase—United States involvement in Vietnam. The buildup included both ground troops and an air campaign.

United States Marines landed near **Da Nang,** South Vietnam, on March 8, 1965. During the next three years, the number of American troops in Vietnam increased sharply. About 180,000 soldiers were in Vietnam by the end of 1965, almost 400,000 by the end of 1966, and more than 500,000 by late 1967.

The United States also unleashed an intense bombing campaign called Operation Rolling Thunder. Some planes attacked the **Ho Chi Minh Trail,** a network of roads, paths, and bridges that snaked from North Vietnam through **Cambodia** and **Laos** into South Vietnam. North Vietnamese troops used this route to bring equipment south. Other planes targeted bridges, docks, factories, and military bases in the North.

The bombing increased in intensity from 1965 through 1968. By then American planes had dropped more bombs on North Vietnam than they had dropped on Germany, Italy, and Japan during World War II.

Fighting the War

The American troops found fighting a ground war in Vietnam difficult. Dense jungles, muddy trails, and swampy rice paddies

Picturing HISTORY Villagers believed to be Vietcong supporters are watched by South Vietnamese soldiers. **How did the North Vietnamese send supplies to the Vietcong in South Vietnam?**

Making Connections Activity

Technology The United States used a variety of strategies in its attempt to cut off North Vietnamese supply routes and locate the ground units of the North Vietnamese and Vietcong. Ask interested students to research and report on some of these strategies, including saturation bombing and the use of napalm and chemical defoliants. Have students explain how each strategy worked and the kind of damage it did (sometimes including damage to civilians and to American troops). As students present their information, discuss why such firepower failed to bring the Communist forces to the point of surrender. **L3**

Who? What? Where? When?

Army nurses had to be brave in front of the wounded, but true feelings came through in the nurses' letters home. Lynda Van Devanter, for example, wrote to her family late in 1969, "I'm sick of facing, every day, a new bunch of children ripped to pieces. They're just kids—eighteen, nineteen years old! It stinks! Whole lives ahead of them—cut off. I'm sick to death of it. . . . "

NATIONAL GEOGRAPHIC SOCIETY

CD-ROM
The Presidents: A Picture History of Our Nation

Tell students that some political scientists and critics believe that had it not been for the Vietnam War, President Johnson might have been viewed as the greatest president of the century. Ask students to research the biography of LBJ to find evidence to support or refute this hypothesis.

Picturing HISTORY The Vietcong used hit-and-run tactics. Not as well equipped as the Americans, the Vietcong and North Vietnamese used ambushes, boobytraps (which ultimately caused 11 percent of U.S. combat deaths during the war), and small-scale attacks. They moved swiftly by night and by day hid in the jungles or in friendly villages. Using terrorism against civilians, the Vietcong controlled much of the countryside. **Ask:** **What kind of mission placed finding Vietcong as its goal?** *(the search-and-destroy mission)*
Answer: *Supplies traveled along the Ho Chi Minh Trail.*

3 ASSESS

Assign Section 2 Review as homework or as an in-class activity.

Use **Chapter Challenger Interactive Review Software** to review Section 2.

Section Quiz 30–2

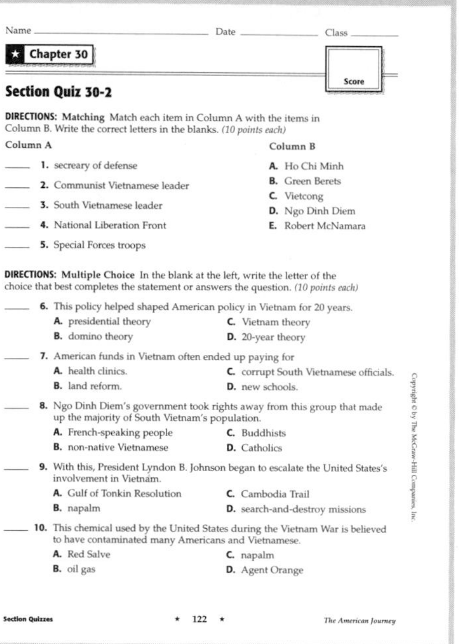
Name ____________ Date ________ Class ______

Chapter 30

Score

Section Quiz 30-2

DIRECTIONS: Matching Match each item in Column A with the items in Column B. Write the correct letters in the blanks. *(10 points each)*

Column A	Column B
____ 1. secreary of defense	A. Ho Chi Minh
____ 2. Communist Vietnamese leader	B. Green Berets
____ 3. South Vietnamese leader	C. Vietcong
____ 4. National Liberation Front	D. Ngo Dinh Diem
____ 5. Special Forces troops	E. Robert McNamara

DIRECTIONS: Multiple Choice In the blank at the left, write the letter of the choice that best completes the statement or answers the question. *(10 points each)*

____ 6. This policy helped shaped American policy in Vietnam for 20 years.
A. presidential theory C. Vietnam theory
B. domino theory D. 20-year theory

____ 7. American funds in Vietnam often ended up paying for
A. health clinics. C. corrupt South Vietnamese officials.
B. land reform. D. new schools.

____ 8. Ngo Dinh Diem's government took rights away from this group that made up the majority of South Vietnam's population.
A. French-speaking people C. Buddhists
B. non-native Vietnamese D. Catholics

____ 9. With this, President Lyndon B. Johnson began to escalate the United States's involvement in Vietnam.
A. Gulf of Tonkin Resolution C. Cambodia Trail
B. napalm D. search-and-destroy missions

____ 10. This chemical used by the United States during the Vietnam War is believed to have contaminated many Americans and Vietnamese.
A. Red Salve C. napalm
B. oil gas D. Agent Orange

Section Quizzes ★ 122 ★ *The American Journey*

Picturing HISTORY Capt. Michael O'Donnell, who later was killed in action, wrote of American casualties in Vietnam:

each of us
is a can of tomato paste
and though we may not
all have the same label
as we spin thru the air,
when we land too hard
or get torn,
from the outside or within,
we spill out and
stain the hands of everyone
who knew us.

Ask: In what two ways did the war begin to escalate in 1965? *(More American troops were sent to Vietnam, and the intensity of the bombing campaign increased.)*
Answer: *more than 500,000 soldiers*

hampered troop movement. The South Vietnamese army did not always fight effectively. As the Vietcong guerrillas blended with the population, American soldiers found it hard to tell friends and enemies apart.

On the Ground

The American forces began to conduct **search-and-destroy missions.** The goal was to seek out Vietcong or North Vietnamese units and destroy them. The Americans hoped to eventually defeat the Communists or force them to negotiate.

Ground troops coordinated their moves with air support. Patrols on the ground radioed their location, and helicopter gunships roared to the scene to blast the enemy with cannon and machine-gun fire.

Planes bombed areas of South Vietnam in an effort to drive guerrillas from their jungle cover. Both sides used planes to drop **napalm,** an explosive that burned intensely, to destroy jungle growth. North Vietnamese and Vietcong forces also used napalm in flamethrowers, devices that expel fuel or a burning stream of liquids. To improve visibility, chemical herbicides were sprayed in Vietnam to clear out forests and tall grasses. One herbicide, **Agent Orange,** is believed to have contaminated many Americans and Vietnamese, causing serious health problems.

Eyewitness to HISTORY

Frustration Grows

The bombing of the Ho Chi Minh Trail and the North did not stop the constant flow of troops and equipment south. Neither did it break the morale of the North Vietnamese. As one of their leaders later said,

> "The Americans thought that the more bombs they dropped, the quicker we would fall to our knees and surrender. But the bombs heightened, rather than dampened, our spirit."

The search-and-destroy missions killed thousands of North Vietnamese and Vietcong

Picturing HISTORY A wounded American soldier reaches for a fallen comrade (above). **How many American troops were in Vietnam by the end of 1967?**

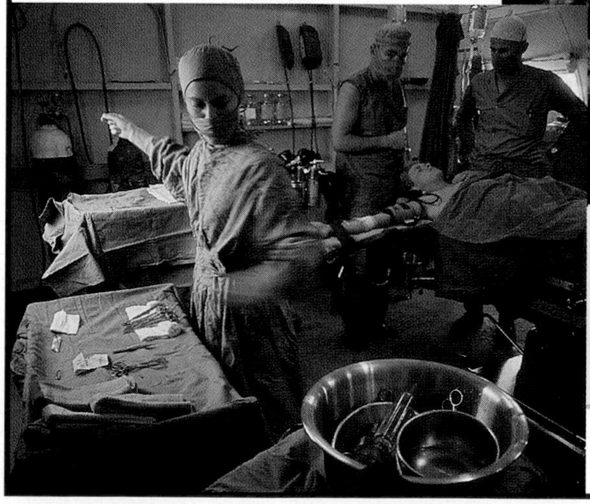

More than 7,500 American nurses (below) served during the Vietnam conflict.

CRITICAL THINKING ACTIVITY

Analyzing Information Have students, working individually or with partners, research and write a report about the importance of the Gulf of Tonkin Resolution. Ask them to address these questions in their analysis:

- **What happened in the Gulf of Tonkin incident?**
- **What information about the incident did President Johnson withhold from Congress and the American people?**
- **What might have been done to prevent the spreading of misinformation?**
- **How did the resolution affect the future of U.S. involvement in Vietnam?**

Have students share their findings and conclusions, perhaps in panel-discussion format. **L3**

★ ★ ★ ★ ★ ★ ★ ★ ★ ★ ★ ★ ★ ★ ★

troops—but the troops always seemed to be replaced. What Ho Chi Minh had said to the French became true again:

> "You can kill ten of my men for every one I kill of yours. But even at those odds, you will lose and I will win."

American troops advanced into rice paddies, jungles, and small villages and killed scores of Vietcong. Yet the next day, the same area had to be attacked again.

American soldiers grew frustrated. Philip Caputo, a young marine lieutenant, recalled the changing attitude:

> "When we marched into the rice paddies on that damp March afternoon, we carried, along with our packs and rifles, the implicit convictions that the Vietcong could be quickly beaten. We kept the packs and rifles; the convictions, we lost."

American soldiers on patrol

Debate in the White House

Officials in the Johnson administration saw the mounting Communist losses and believed at first that the United States could succeed. As the war dragged on, however, some government officials saw a gloomier situation. Secretary of Defense McNamara began to argue that the ground war and the air attacks had failed and that the war could not be won. Outside the nation's capital, opposition to the war grew. Soon it swelled to anger.

Section 2 Review

Checking for Understanding

1. ***Identify*** Ho Chi Minh, Ngo Dinh Diem, Lyndon B. Johnson, Gulf of Tonkin Resolution.
2. ***Define*** Vietcong, domino theory, coup, escalate, search-and-destroy mission.
3. ***Describe*** the agreement reached at the Geneva Accords.

Reviewing Themes

4. **Government and Democracy** How did President Johnson gain the approval from Congress to use American forces in Vietnam?

Critical Thinking

5. **Analyzing Information** What signs existed during the mid-1960s that indicated the United States would have a difficult time winning the Vietnam War?

Activity

Creating a Cartoon Draw a cartoon illustrating the domino theory as it applied to the spread of communism in Southeast Asia.

Section 2 Review Answers

1. Ho Chi Minh, 852; Diem, 853; Johnson, 854; Gulf of Tonkin Resolution, 855
2. The words are defined in the Glossary.
3. The agreement divided Vietnam temporarily, with Ho Chi Minh controlling Communist North Vietnam and non-Communist forces controlling South Vietnam. Vietnam was set to be unified in 1956.
4. The alleged attack of an American destroyer in the Gulf of Tonkin caused Congress to pass the Gulf of Tonkin Resolution, granting the U.S. permission to defend itself.
5. The North Vietnamese seemed to have an unlimited number of soldiers. The Vietcong were indistinguishable from the South Vietnamese. Soldier morale was low.

Activity Students should draw a cartoon to explain the domino theory.

CHAPTER 30

Section 2, 852–857

Reteaching Activity 30–2

Name ______ Date ______ Class ______

★ Reteaching Activity **30-2**

DIRECTIONS: Putting Events in Sequence Number the events in the order in which they occurred. Use the same number for events that happened at the same time.

____ **A.** Robert McNamara travels to Vietnam on a fact-finding mission.
____ **B.** Vietnamese forces defeat the French in a long, bloody war.
____ **C.** Ngo Dinh Diem refuses to hold elections in South Vietnam.
____ **D.** South Vietnamese army officers stage a coup and assassinate Diem.
____ **E.** The terms of the Geneva Accords divide Vietnam temporarily into Communist North Vietnam and non-Communist South Vietnam.
____ **F.** American ground forces conduct search-and-destroy missions to seek out Vietcong; in the air, planes deliver napalm to destroy the jungle growth where the Vietcong hide.
____ **G.** Ngo Dinh Diem gains control of South Vietnam.
____ **H.** John F. Kennedy sends Special Forces troops to South Vietnam.
____ **I.** Congress passes the Gulf of Tonkin Resolution.
____ **J.** Japanese forces capture the French colony of Indochina.
____ **K.** Diem launches a campaign to destroy the power of the Communist supporters in South Vietnam.
____ **L.** Robert McNamara begins to argue that the war cannot be won.
____ **M.** The Vietcong begin a war against the Diem regime.
____ **N.** The United States becomes the dominant foreign power in South Vietnam.
____ **O.** United States Marines land near Da Nang as Lyndon B. Johnson begins to escalate United States involvement in Vietnam.
____ **P.** Ho Chi Minh declares Vietnam's independence.
____ **Q.** Buddhist monks set themselves on fire on busy South Vietnam streets to show their opposition to the government.

DIRECTIONS: Essay On a separate sheet of paper, answer the following question. Why was the ground war in Vietnam difficult for American troops?

Reteaching Activities ★ 122 ★ *The American Journey*

Enrichment Activity 30–2

Name ______ Date ______ Class ______

★ Enrichment Activity **30-2** ★

The War in Vietnam

The outline map to the right shows Vietnam. Study the map. Use your textbook or other atlas to complete the activity that follows.

Activity DIRECTIONS: Follow the directions to complete the map.

1. Label North Vietnam and South Vietnam.
2. The Gulf of Tonkin lies to the east of North Vietnam, and the South China Sea lies to the east of South Vietnam. Label these two bodies of water.
3. The Ho Chi Minh Trail ran approximately north-south from Vinh in North Vietnam through Laos to Kontum and Can Ranh Bay in South Vietnam. Label the Ho Chi Minh Trail and Laos.
4. Label Da Nang, which lies on the northeast coast of South Vietnam.
5. Label Saigon, which lies along the east coast of northern South Vietnam in a large bay.
6. Label Hanoi, which lies inland on the Red River in North Vietnam.
7. The Mekong River forms the border between Laos and Thailand and flows through Cambodia into the Mekong Delta at the southern tip of South Vietnam. Label the Mekong River, Thailand, Cambodia, and the Mekong Delta.

Enrichment Activities ★ 122 ★ *The American Journey*

4 CLOSE

Have students list the decisions made by President Johnson regarding the war in Vietnam. Discuss which one they feel had the most far-reaching effect.

1 FOCUS

BELLRINGER
Motivational Activity

Before taking roll at the beginning of the class period, project Section Focus Transparency 30–3 and have students answer the questions. Discuss students' responses.

This activity is also available as a blackline master.

Section Focus Transparency 30–3

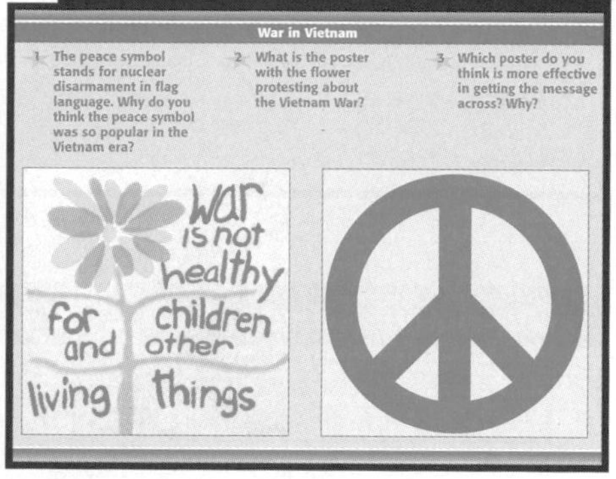

Vocabulary Precheck

Point out that *defer* in *deferment* means "to put off" or "to be different." Ask students to relate that meaning to the word's use in relation to the military draft.

Use the **Vocabulary Puzzle-Maker** to create crossword and word search puzzles.

Section Theme
Continuity and Change

Opinions about United States participation in the Vietnam War brought Americans into sharp disagreement with one another.

Activity Have students think of a government action—factual or fictional—that might be unpopular (though not illegal). **Ask:** **How could people show their unhappiness with that action?** *(Students may suggest peaceful protests, information campaigns, contacting officials, and so on.)*

1962 1964 1966 1968

1962 Students for a Democratic Society organize

1964 Free Speech Movement protests at Berkeley

1967 War protesters march on Pentagon

Section 3

The Vietnam Years at Home

READ TO DISCOVER . . .
- what factors contributed to the rise of the counterculture.
- how Americans at home responded to the war in Vietnam.

TERMS TO LEARN

radical
counterculture
deferment
dove
hawk

The Storyteller

As the Vietnam War dragged on, Americans became divided—usually by age—over the U.S. presence in that country. Even reporters showed their biases when they covered the antiwar demonstrations at the Pentagon in 1967. On one hand, older reporters who stood behind the police wrote about radicals storming the Pentagon. On the other side of the police barricade, younger reporters wrote about the brutality of the U.S. marshals. Each side of the generation gap firmly believed that its version of the story was correct.

Antiwar button

While fighting raged in Vietnam, the American people disagreed sharply over the war. Prowar and antiwar groups attacked each other with mounting anger. Antiwar demonstrators called President Johnson and his supporters "killers." Supporters of the war referred to the protesters as "traitors."

Americans watched these deep divisions with increasing alarm. The war seemed to split America—and much of the division resulted from what people called the **generation gap.**

The Youth Protest

The protest movement against the Vietnam War grew in part out of a broader dissatisfaction with American society. Inspired by the ideals of the civil rights movement, many high school and college students criticized the United States for its racial discrimination and its overemphasis on material values. The desire of these young people to change society came to be focused on the war in Vietnam. The Students for a Democratic Society and the Free Speech Movement were two influential groups.

The New Left

In 1962, at a meeting in Port Huron, Michigan, students from across the country organized **Students for a Democratic Society** (SDS). The

SECTION RESOURCES

Reproducible Masters
- Guided Reading Activity 30–3
- Political Cartoons, *Uproar Over Vietnam*
- Section Quiz 30–3
- Reteaching Activity 30–3
- Enrichment Activity 30–3

Transparencies
- Section Focus Transparency 30–3

Multimedia
- Vocabulary PuzzleMaker
- Chapter Challenger Interactive Review
- Testmaker
- American Music Cultural Traditions, Lesson 10: "Waist Deep in the Big Muddy" and "Okie from Muskogee"

group had broad goals and "an agenda for a generation," which condemned racism, poverty, and nuclear weapons. Rejecting efforts at reform, the students in SDS called for a radical transformation of American society.

Another movement emerged in California two years later. Officials of the University of California at Berkeley had taken steps to limit the recruiting efforts of protest groups on campus. Angered by the restrictions, students launched what they called the **Free Speech Movement,** staging a protest that paralyzed the university for several days.

These new ideas and protests spread to other campuses around the country. Although not part of a single movement, the activists who shared these ideas came to be called the **New Left.**

The Counterculture

The radical ideas of the New Left, which challenged the values and institutions of American society, reached only a minority of students. Yet many young people did rebel against their parents' world, and they expressed their opposition in colorful ways.

In the counterculture, a movement that rejected traditional American values, the students sought to create a new lifestyle. Some common symbols of the counterculture—torn blue jeans and long hair for males—aroused opposition from parents. Popular music played a role in communicating the ideas of the counterculture. Many 1960s songs, such as this one by Bob Dylan, expressed a longing for peace and justice:

> "Yes, 'n' how many times must the cannon balls fly
> Before they're forever banned?
> The answer, my friend, is blowin' in the wind,
> The answer is blowin' in the wind."

Other parts of the counterculture represented a more serious challenge to traditional middle-class values. Some young people refused to follow customary social roles of study, work, and family. They aimed to reject aspects of American society they criticized—the competition for material goods and personal success.

As the 1960s progressed, the New Left, the counterculture, and other movements shared one common element. They all expressed growing opposition to the war in Vietnam.

Opposition to the Draft

Student protests targeted the selective service system—the **draft** that supplied soldiers for the war. The law required all men to register for the

Picturing HISTORY An antiwar protester places flowers in the rifles of soldiers guarding the Pentagon near Washington, D.C. **What were common symbols of the counterculture?**

Cooperative Learning Activity

Dramatizing Division Feelings about the war in Vietnam increasingly divided Americans. Ask groups of students to prepare and present skits that reveal divided feelings through the following situations:

- A group of friends deciding whether to participate in an antiwar rally
- A draft-card burner being confronted by police
- A member of the SDS speaking at a meeting of university officials
- A college student trying to explain the counterculture to her parents

Each group should choose a director and a secretary. Encourage the actors to try different roles in the skit before choosing the characters whom they will portray.

2 TEACH

L1 Conducting a Debate Tell students that television and newspapers brought the Vietnam War into Americans' homes and contributed to their divided opinions. Organize the class into two groups. Have the first group advocate the "hawk" viewpoint. Have the second group advocate the "dove" viewpoint. Have a moderator try to reconcile the differences between the groups.

Guided Reading Activity 30–3

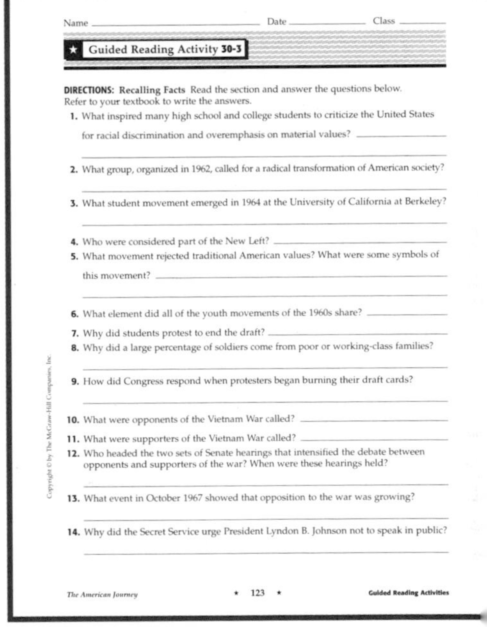

Name ______ Date ______ Class ______

★ Guided Reading Activity **30-3**

DIRECTIONS: Recalling Facts Read the section and answer the questions below. Refer to your textbook to write the answers.

1. What inspired many high school and college students to criticize the United States for racial discrimination and overemphasis on material values?
2. What group, organized in 1962, called for a radical transformation of American society?
3. What student movement emerged in 1964 at the University of California at Berkeley?
4. Who were considered part of the New Left?
5. What movement rejected traditional American values? What were some symbols of this movement?
6. What element did all of the youth movements of the 1960s share?
7. Why did students protest to end the draft?
8. Why did a large percentage of soldiers come from poor or working-class families?
9. How did Congress respond when protesters began burning their draft cards?
10. What were opponents of the Vietnam War called?
11. What were supporters of the Vietnam War called?
12. Who headed the two sets of Senate hearings that intensified the debate between opponents and supporters of the war? When were these hearings held?
13. What event in October 1967 showed that opposition to the war was growing?
14. Why did the Secret Service urge President Lyndon B. Johnson not to speak in public?

The American Journey ★ 123 ★ **Guided Reading Activities**

Picturing HISTORY Many members of the counterculture held liberal views, but the movement as a whole was not very active politically—a fact that drew criticism from New Left activists. The difference was seen clearly in the summer of 1967. The SDS had called for it to be a "summer of protest" against the Vietnam War, but the counterculture proclaimed it a "summer of love."

Answer: *torn blue jeans and long hair for males*

CHAPTER 30
Section 3, 858–861

Graph Study

Answers
1. 1971
2. about 150,000 soldiers

Graph Skills Practice

Reading a Graph In general terms, how did the American people react to the Tet offensive? *(Greater numbers of Americans opposed the war.)*

History *and the* Humanities

- The Spirit of American Art and Music, Joan Baez
- American Music Cultural Traditions, Lesson 10: "Waist Deep in the Big Muddy" and "Okie from Muskogee"
- Political Cartoons, *Uproar Over Vietnam*

3 ASSESS

Assign Section 3 Review as homework or as an in-class activity.

Use **Chapter Challenger Interactive Review Software** to review Section 3.

Section Quiz 30–3

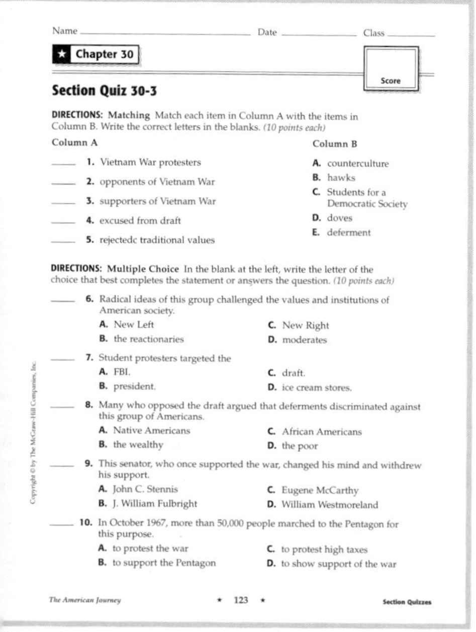
Name ______ Date ______ Class ______

★ Chapter 30

Score

Section Quiz 30-3

DIRECTIONS: Matching Match each item in Column A with the items in Column B. Write the correct letters in the blanks. *(10 points each)*

Column A	Column B
____ 1. Vietnam War protesters	A. counterculture
____ 2. opponents of Vietnam War	B. hawks
____ 3. supporters of Vietnam War	C. Students for a Democratic Society
____ 4. excused from draft	D. doves
____ 5. rejectedc traditional values	E. deferment

DIRECTIONS: Multiple Choice In the blank at the left, write the letter of the choice that best completes the statement or answers the question. *(10 points each)*

____ 6. Radical ideas of this group challenged the values and institutions of American society.
A. New Left C. New Right
B. the reactionaries D. moderates

____ 7. Student protesters targeted the
A. FBI. C. draft.
B. president. D. ice cream stores.

____ 8. Many who opposed the draft argued that deferments discriminated against this group of Americans.
A. Native Americans C. African Americans
B. the wealthy D. the poor

____ 9. This senator, who once supported the war, changed his mind and withdrew his support.
A. John C. Stennis C. Eugene McCarthy
B. J. William Fulbright D. William Westmoreland

____ 10. In October 1967, more than 50,000 people marched to the Pentagon for this purpose.
A. to protest the war C. to protest high taxes
B. to support the Pentagon D. to show support of the war

Copyright © by The McGraw-Hill Companies, Inc.

The American Journey ★ 123 ★ Section Quizzes

United States in the Vietnam War

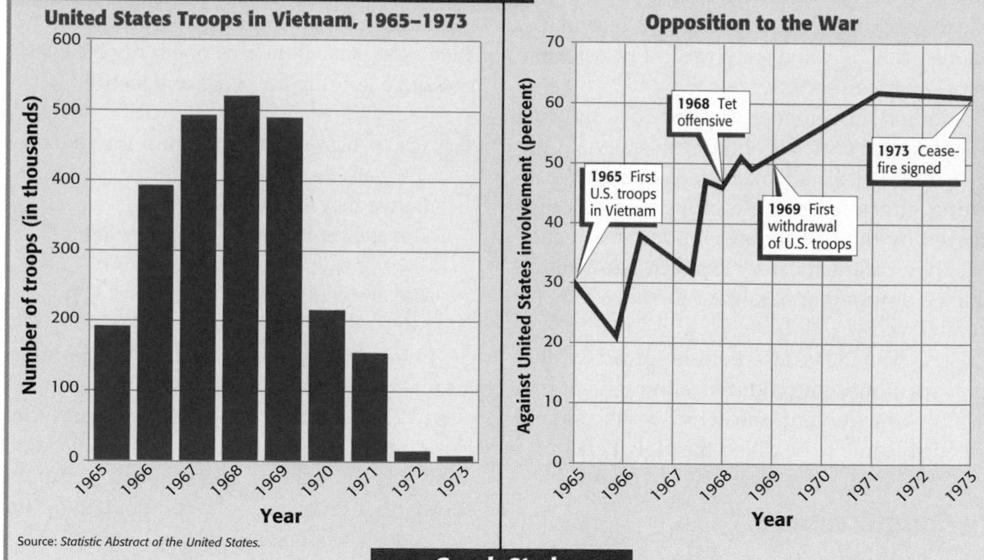

Source: *Statistic Abstract of the United States.*

Graph Study

The Vietnam War never had complete public support, but as the war dragged on, opposition increased.
1. In what year was there the most opposition to the war?
2. **Analyzing Information** About how many U.S. troops were in Vietnam in that year?

draft when they reached age 18. Opposition to the draft had two sources.

Those strongly opposed to American involvement in Vietnam believed that by forcing an end to the draft they could halt the supply of soldiers needed to fight there. Others called the draft unfair. Draft boards could give people **deferments** that excused them from the draft for various reasons. Full-time college students—mostly from the middle class—received such deferments. As a result an increasing percentage of soldiers came from poor or working-class families. Many who opposed the draft argued that deferments discriminated against the poor.

Some protesters became **conscientious objectors,** claiming that their moral or religious beliefs prevented them from fighting in the war. Other protesters showed their opposition by burning their draft cards, their military registration forms. Congress responded with a law making draft-card burning a crime.

Debating the War

Students and other opponents of the Vietnam War came to be called **doves.** Supporters of the war became known as **hawks.**

Doves and Hawks

Opposition to the war grew within the government. Two sets of Senate hearings intensified the debate between the doves and hawks.

In 1966 Senator **J. William Fulbright,** head of the Senate Foreign Relations Committee, held hearings on the war in Vietnam. Some of the government officials who testified thought the war was a mistake. The televised hearings brought the debate into Americans' homes. Fulbright, who had once supported the war, now doubted "the ability of the United States to achieve [its] aims."

Senator **John C. Stennis** of Mississippi held another round of hearings in 1967. At these

MULTIPLE LEARNING STYLES

Verbal/Linguistic As the text points out, *hawk* and *dove* became part of the slang of the Vietnam era (though both had been used during the Cuban missile crisis). Ask students to locate and share with the class information about these and other words and phrases associated with the protests of the era: *draft dodger, draft evader, moratorium, peacenik, Yippie.* To extend the activity, have students write dialogue that includes some of this slang. **L2**

hearings of the Senate Armed Services Committee, officials made a case for continuing the war. A report from the Stennis hearings concluded that the United States should "do whatever is necessary . . . and apply the force that is required to see the job through."

Congress was of two minds on the Vietnam War. The same could be said of the American people.

America Divided

Across the nation more and more Americans came to view the war unfavorably. Some thought the United States should not be fighting in Vietnam. Others opposed the way the government conducted the war. Both hawks and doves criticized President Johnson for his handling of the war in Vietnam, and his approval rating declined dramatically.

The War Loses Support

As opposition to the war mounted, the opponents staged larger demonstrations. In October 1967, more than 50,000 people marched to the **Pentagon**—headquarters of the Defense Department—to protest the war.

Attacks by opponents of the war grew sharper and more bitter. The Secret Service, charged with guarding President Johnson, feared for his safety and urged him not to speak in public. He began to appear only before crowds known to be sympathetic.

The president had often urged people to come together to discuss issues calmly. "Let us reason together," he had said. By 1968 Americans showed less willingness to talk reasonably, and violent events often overtook discussion.

Picturing HISTORY Antiwar demonstrations, such as this gathering in Washington, D.C., were held throughout the nation in the late 1960s. **What government practice affecting young men was often targeted by antiwar protesters?**

Section 3 Review

Checking for Understanding

1. ***Identify*** New Left, J. William Fulbright, John C. Stennis, Pentagon.
2. ***Define*** radical, counterculture, deferment, dove, hawk.
3. ***List*** two reasons some Americans began to oppose involvement in Vietnam.

Reviewing Themes

4. **Continuity and Change** Besides the Vietnam War, what other parts of American society did the counterculture of the 1960s condemn?

Critical Thinking

5. **Synthesizing Information** How would you define the "generation gap"?

Activity

Conducting an Interview Interview friends and relatives who lived during the Vietnam War era to see how people in your community reacted to the conflict. Present an oral report of your findings.

Section 3 Review Answers

1. New Left, 859; J. William Fulbright, 860; John C. Stennis, 860; Pentagon, 861
2. The words are defined in the Glossary.
3. Any two: the draft, draft deferments, belief that the United States could not win the war, political leaders' disunity on the issue
4. racial discrimination and overemphasis on material values and goods
5. Answers may refer to the gap that opened or widened between the younger and older generations as a result of their different values.

Activity Students should conduct interviews with several people who lived during the Vietnam War era to find out community reactions to the conflict.

CHAPTER 30
Section 3, 858–861

Picturing HISTORY About 500,000 men refused to report when they were drafted. About 3,000 went to prison rather than fight. **Answer:** *the draft*

Reteaching Activity 30–3

Name ______ Date ______ Class ______

Reteaching Activity 30-3

DIRECTIONS: Crossword Puzzle Complete the crossword puzzle about poverty and the changing values of society in the 1950s.

Stennis	**doves**	**Free Speech Movement**	**radical**	**draft**
New Left	**deferments**	**SDS**	**Fulbright**	**draft cards**
counterculture	**hawks**	**Pentagon**		

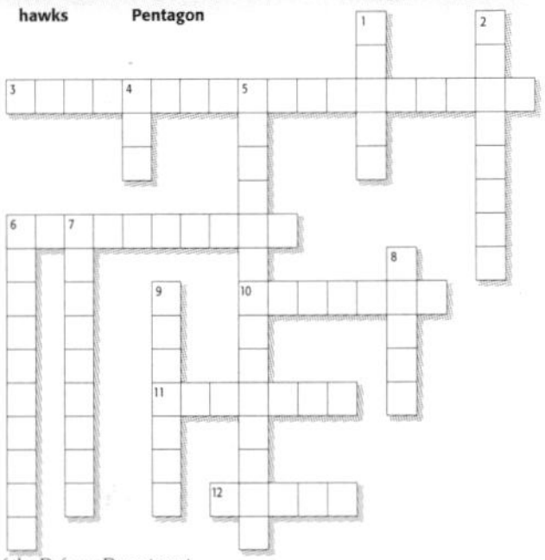

Across

3. launched at University of California at Berkeley
6. given to excuse college students from serving in the military
10. revolutionary or new
11. name given to Americans who embraced the new ideas of the 1960s
12. the selective service system

Down

1. opponents of the Vietnam War
2. headquarters of the Defense Department
4. student group, founded in 1962, that called for a radical transformation of American society
5. movement that rejected traditional American values
6. military registration forms burned by protesters in the 1960s
7. senator who headed 1966 hearings on Vietnam War; he doubted that the United States could "achieve its aims" in Vietnam
8. supporters of the Vietnam War
9. senator who headed 1967 hearings which concluded that the United States should stay in Vietnam

The American Journey ★ 123 ★ Reteaching Activities

Enrichment Activity 30–3

Name ______ Date ______ Class ______

★ Enrichment Activity 30-3 ★

Opposed to War

As the Vietnam War dragged on, opposition to America's continued participation in the war grew. Read the quotes that illustrate the conflicted feelings and actions generated by the Vietnam War, even among our nation's leaders.

> "I have had advice to load our planes with bombs and to drop them on certain areas that I think would enlarge the war and escalate the war, and result in our committing a good many American boys to fighting a war that I think ought to be fought by the boys of Asia to help protect their own lands."
>
> —President Lyndon B. Johnson, campaign speech, August 29, 1964

> "We want no part of a war of extermination. We oppose the criminal waste of American lives and resources. We refuse to go to Vietnam."
>
> —from a joint statement of three soldiers who refused to go to Vietnam, July 1966

> "I spend my professional life with American youth of draft age. And while I will not use the classroom for such purposes, I will make clear that from now on my concerns about Vietnam will be explicitly focused on counseling, aiding and abetting all students who declare that out of moral conviction they will not fight in Vietnam. . . . I will continue to do this until I am arrested. As long as I am not arrested, I will do it with increasing intensity, for I am no longer willing that 18- or 19-year old boys should pay with their lives for the initially bumbling but now deliberate folly of our national leaders."
>
> —a professor of religion at Stanford University, 1967

> "We wish to express our sincere thanks to the Congress of the United States for their continuing inactivity in regard to their Constitutional responsibilities regarding the Vietnam war. Because of your inactivity towards stopping our participation in this useless and senseless war, we have lost our only son, and only child, to a Vietnam contracted disease."
>
> —from an open letter to Congress from the father of a Marine who had died in Vietnam

> "As I have walked among the desperate and rejected and angry young men, I have told them Molotov cocktails and rifles would not solve their problems. . . . But, they have asked, what about Vietnam?. . . Their questions hit home, and I knew that I could never again raise my voice against the violence of the oppressed in the ghettos without having first spoken clearly to the greatest purveyor of violence in the world today—my own government."
>
> —Martin Luther King, Jr., "Declaration of Independence from the War in Vietnam," speech delivered April 4, 1967

Activity **DIRECTIONS: Applying Ideas** On a separate sheet of paper, write other quotes from the late 1960s and early 1970s that show America's conflicted feelings toward the Vietnam War. Then use the quotes in a dramatic reading. You may wish to collect photographs and videos of news clips to display during your reading. Invite listeners to share their reactions to your presentation.

The American Journey ★ 123 ★ Enrichment Activities

4 CLOSE

Ask students what was achieved by student protesters and counterculture members.

CHAPTER 30
Section 4, 862–865

1 FOCUS

BELLRINGER
Motivational Activity

Before taking roll at the beginning of the class period, project Section Focus Transparency 30–4 and have students answer the questions. Discuss students' responses.

This activity is also available as a blackline master.

Section Focus Transparency 30–4

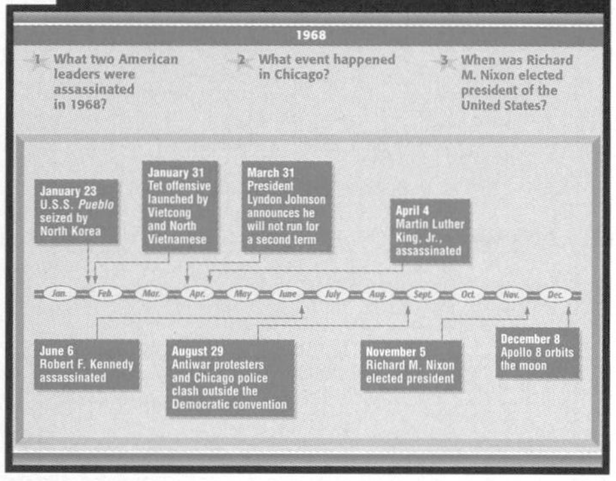

Vocabulary Precheck

Have students speculate about the meanings of the terms *credibility gap* and *silent majority*. Then compare their responses with the meanings given in the text.

Use the **Vocabulary Puzzle-Maker** to create crossword and

Section Theme
Civic Rights and Responsibilities

Opposition to the Vietnam War played a major role in the selection of candidates for the presidential election of 1968.

Activity Have students look at the photograph on page 864. Point out that the barbed wire is being used to keep people out of a meeting that relates to the election of a president. **Ask:** Does that photo encourage you to trust the government? Explain.

1968 — **January** North Korea captures U.S.S. *Pueblo* — **April** Martin Luther King, Jr., is assassinated — **June** Robert Kennedy is assassinated — **August** Violence erupts at Democratic convention in Chicago — **November** Richard Nixon wins presidency — **1969**

Section 4

1968–Year of Crises

READ TO DISCOVER . . .
- how the Tet offensive affected the war in Vietnam and politics in the United States.
- which political leaders ran for president in 1968 and what they stood for.

TERMS TO LEARN
credibility gap
silent majority

The Storyteller

In January 1968, about 10,000 U.S. Marines fought fiercely to hold their position in the hills at Khe Sanh, Vietnam, north of Saigon. North Vietnamese troops had surrounded Khe Sanh and opened fire on the Americans. The marines held Khe Sanh. Corporal James Hebron later explained what it was like to be there for 77 days: "All you saw was the air being ripped apart and the ground shaking underneath you—and you bouncing into the air. . . . [T]he trenches would shake."

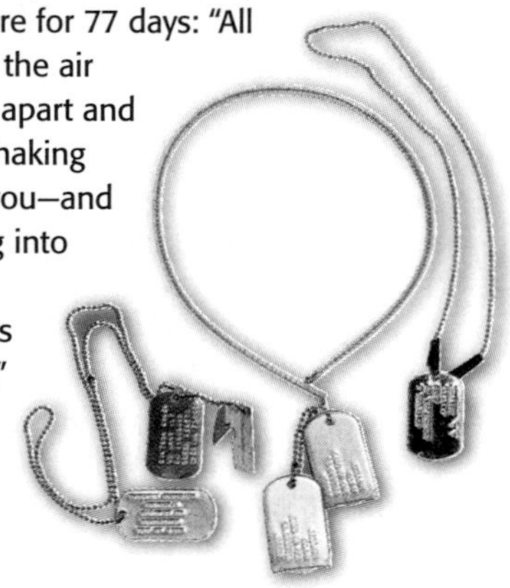
Dog tags—military identification tags

The year 1968 opened with a shock for the American people. On January 23, North Korean boats seized the **U.S.S. *Pueblo,*** a navy spy ship cruising in international waters off the coast of Korea. The news that a foreign country had captured an American ship and its crew shocked the nation.

The next week brought another staggering blow as North Vietnam launched a major series of attacks in South Vietnam. As Americans soon learned, 1968 would be a long, dramatic, and very difficult year.

The Tet Offensive

On January 31, 1968, the North Vietnamese and Vietcong launched a series of attacks throughout South Vietnam. The attacks, which began on the Vietnamese new year—Tet—became known as the **Tet offensive.** Tet marked a turning point in the Vietnam War.

Attacks in South Vietnam

The Tet offensive targeted American military bases and South Vietnam's major cities. Vietcong troops raided the United States embassy in **Saigon,** the capital. The Vietcong also struck in **Hue,** the ancient capital of Vietnam, and fought for almost a month.

All across South Vietnam, Americans and South Vietnamese troops fought bravely to retake the cities. They finally drove the Vietcong back and inflicted thousands of casualties. The

SECTION RESOURCES

Reproducible Masters
- Reproducible Lesson Plan 30–4
- Guided Reading Activity 30–4
- Section Quiz 30–4
- Reteaching Activity 30–4
- Enrichment Activity 30–4

Transparencies
- Section Focus Transparency 30–4

Multimedia
- Vocabulary PuzzleMaker
- Chapter Challenger Interactive Review Software
- Testmaker
- ABCNews InterActive™ Martin Luther King, Jr.

enormous losses that the Vietcong suffered forced North Vietnam to take over a larger share of the fighting. In military terms, the Americans and the South Vietnamese won the battle.

Impact Back Home

In the United States, however, the Tet offensive turned many more Americans against the war—and against President Johnson. The sight of Vietcong guerrillas killing Americans in the embassy shocked television viewers. The many days needed to defeat the assault on Hue undermined the army's statements about the United States winning the war.

Major newspapers and magazines openly criticized the Johnson administration's conduct of the war. The *Wall Street Journal* wrote, "The American people should be getting ready to accept . . . the prospect that the whole Vietnam effort may be doomed."

Most Americans seemed to agree. Fewer people believed that the army was making progress in the war. More people believed that the army was losing ground. The Johnson administration developed a **credibility gap**—fewer people trusted its statements about the war.

Challenges to the President

As opposition to the war grew, President Johnson faced challenges in his own party. In late 1967, Democratic senator **Eugene McCarthy** of Minnesota had announced that he would run for the party's nomination for the presidency as a protest against the war. Not well known, McCarthy seemed to have little chance of winning. In the March 12 primary in New Hampshire, however, McCarthy surprised everyone by taking 42 percent of the popular vote. Although Johnson won the primary, McCarthy's strong showing indicated widespread opposition to the war.

Later, another antiwar candidate entered the race. **Robert F. Kennedy,** attorney general during his brother's presidency and now a senator from New York, announced that he, too, would seek the Democratic nomination.

Picturing HISTORY During the Tet offensive, United States Marines climb a mound of rubble that was once a tower of the fortress of Hue. **Why was the Tet offensive a turning point in the Vietnam War?**

President Lyndon Johnson

The President Responds

Events in Vietnam and the growing antiwar movement disturbed President Johnson. Following the Tet offensive, the American commander in Vietnam, General **William Westmoreland,** had requested still more troops. Instead of agreeing, the president ordered a reevaluation of the war. He also reevaluated his own campaign for reelection in 1968.

On March 31, 1968, after consulting advisers, President Johnson appeared on television to announce a "new step toward peace"—he would halt the bombing of North Vietnam's cities. He asked North Vietnam for a comparable action so that peace negotiations could begin.

The president concluded his speech with a startling announcement. He said, "I shall not seek, and I will not accept, the nomination of my party for another term as your president."

CHAPTER 30
Section 4, 862–865

2 TEACH

L1 Reporting the News Stage an event in your classroom. Ask students to write an account of the event. The accounts should be purely objective, answering who was involved, what happened, where the event took place, when the event took place, and why it took place. Have students compare their accounts, noting any variances in the stories. Point out that any news—just like news during the Vietnam era—is often slanted to support a particular bias.

Picturing HISTORY The Americans killed by a 15-person Vietcong suicide squad at the Saigon embassy included military police and a marine. The Vietcong were all killed by American troops airlifted to the site. Partly because of initially erroneous news reports and partly because the embassy had been raided, more Americans began to believe that President Johnson's reports about the war could not be trusted.

Answer: *It turned more Americans against President Johnson and the war itself.*

Guided Reading Activity 30–4

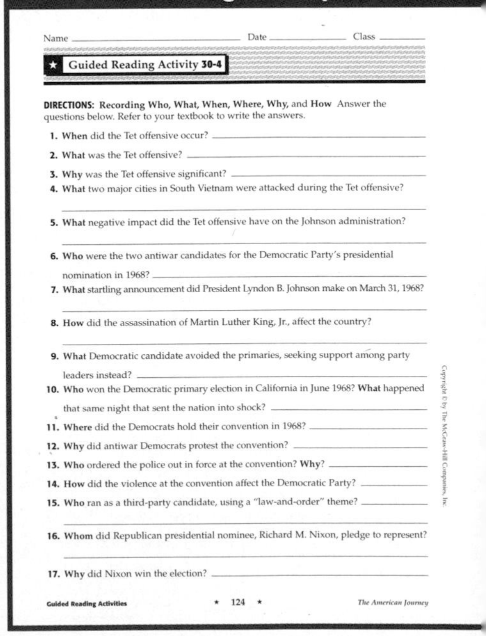

Name ______ Date ______ Class ______

★ Guided Reading Activity **30-4**

DIRECTIONS: Recording Who, What, When, Where, Why, and **How** Answer the questions below. Refer to your textbook to write the answers.

1. **When** did the Tet offensive occur? ______
2. **What** was the Tet offensive? ______
3. **Why** was the Tet offensive significant? ______
4. **What** two major cities in South Vietnam were attacked during the Tet offensive? ______
5. **What** negative impact did the Tet offensive have on the Johnson administration? ______
6. **Who** were the two antiwar candidates for the Democratic Party's presidential nomination in 1968? ______
7. **What** startling announcement did President Lyndon B. Johnson make on March 31, 1968? ______
8. **How** did the assassination of Martin Luther King, Jr., affect the country? ______
9. **What** Democratic candidate avoided the primaries, seeking support among party leaders instead? ______
10. **Who** won the Democratic primary election in California in June 1968? **What** happened that same night that sent the nation into shock? ______
11. **Where** did the Democrats hold their convention in 1968? ______
12. **Why** did antiwar Democrats protest the convention? ______
13. **Who** ordered the police out in force at the convention? **Why**? ______
14. **How** did the violence at the convention affect the Democratic Party? ______
15. **Who** ran as a third-party candidate, using a "law-and-order" theme? ______
16. **Whom** did Republican presidential nominee, Richard M. Nixon, pledge to represent? ______
17. **Why** did Nixon win the election? ______

Guided Reading Activities ★ 124 ★ *The American Journey*

Cooperative Learning Activity

Symbolizing a Campaign A wide variety of hopefuls sought the presidency in 1968. To illustrate their differences, organize students into five groups: one each for Eugene McCarthy, Robert F. Kennedy, Hubert H. Humphrey, George C. Wallace, and Richard M. Nixon. Have members of each group write three words that describe their candidate and one sentence about their candidate's political views. They should then work together to create a campaign button, banner, or logo for their candidate. Have groups share and discuss their ideas.

Picturing HISTORY **Answer:** *Many Americans believed the Democrats could not control their own convention. People were ready for a return to "law and order."*

ABCNEWS INTERACTIVE™

VIDEODISC
Martin Luther King, Jr.

Side 1
Chapter 36

Title: *Beyond Civil Rights: Vietnam*
Subject: Dr. King's involvement in the anti–Vietnam war movement
Ask: **How did King respond to allegations that he was hurting the civil rights movement by joining in the anti-war effort?** *(He stated that he had fought hard against segregation, therefore he would not "segregate his moral concerns.")*

3 ASSESS

Assign Section 4 Review as homework or as an in-class activity.

Section Quiz 30–4

Name ______ Date ______ Class ______

★ Chapter 30

Score

Section Quiz 30-4

DIRECTIONS: Matching Match each item in Column A with the items in Column B. Write the correct letters in the blanks. *(10 points each)*

Column A

____ **1.** seized by North Korea
____ **2.** capital of South Vietnam
____ **3.** ancient capital of Vietnam
____ **4.** site of antiwar protest
____ **5.** law and order candidate

Column B

A. Hue
B. George C. Wallace
C. Chicago
D. USS *Pueblo*
E. Saigon

DIRECTIONS: Multiple Choice In the blank at the left, write the letter of the choice that best completes the statement or answers the question. *(10 points each)*

____ **6.** These attacks, which began on the Vietnamese new year, marked a turning point in the war.
A. Tet offensive **C.** USS *Pueblo* attacks
B. Gulf of Tonkin attacks **D.** attacks on Saigon

____ **7.** After the Tet offensive, the Lyndon Johnson administration developed a
A. silent majority. **C.** credibility gap.
B. new offensive. **D.** generation gap.

____ **8.** The American commander in Vietnam was
A. Richard J. Daley. **C.** Hubert H. Humphrey.
B. Eugene McCarthy. **D.** William Westmoreland.

____ **9.** This person was NOT a presidential hopeful in 1968.
A. Eugene McCarthy **C.** Lyndon B. Johnson
B. Robert F. Kennedy **D.** Hubert H. Humphrey

____ **10.** This presidential candidate claimed to represent the silent majority.
A. George C. Wallace **C.** Eugene McCarthy
B. Richard M. Nixon **D.** Robert F. Kennedy

Section Quizzes ★ 124 ★ *The American Journey*

Picturing HISTORY After Robert Kennedy's death in June 1968, a divided Democratic convention met in Chicago. Chicago mayor Richard Daley had barbed wire set up at the convention hall to keep out antiwar protesters. **How did most Americans react to the violence in Chicago?**

Violence Erupts

A few days after Johnson's withdrawal from the presidential race, tragedy struck the nation. A sniper in Memphis, Tennessee, shot and killed **Martin Luther King, Jr.,** the leading activist in the civil rights movement.

The King assassination triggered a rash of riots across the country. Army troops were called on to control unruly crowds in various cities. Already saddened by King's death, Americans worried about the renewed urban violence.

Another Kennedy Assassination

While the nation agonized over unrest at home and war abroad, the presidential race picked up speed. Vice President **Hubert H. Humphrey** joined Eugene McCarthy and Robert Kennedy in seeking the Democratic nomination. Kennedy edged out McCarthy in a number of primary elections, but McCarthy rebounded and scored a primary victory in Oregon. Humphrey, meanwhile, avoided the primaries. He gathered support among Democratic Party leaders, who in some states chose the delegates.

In early June 1968, Kennedy and McCarthy faced each other in the primary election in California, the state with the most delegates. That night, after Kennedy won, an assassin shot and killed him—and the nation reeled with the shock of yet another assassination.

The Democratic Convention

By the time the Democrats held their convention in **Chicago,** Humphrey appeared to have enough votes to win the nomination. As a longtime supporter of civil rights and labor causes, Humphrey had considerable backing in his party. As a supporter of Johnson's Vietnam policy, however, Humphrey was linked to the prowar faction of the party.

Antiwar Democrats felt angry and excluded from the convention. Tension filled the air. When trouble broke out, though, it did not occur as much in the convention hall as in the city's streets.

Frustrated by the almost certain victory of Humphrey, thousands of antiwar activists flocked to Chicago to protest. Chicago's mayor, **Richard J. Daley,** feared violence from the demonstrators and had the police out in force. The police made some arrests the first two nights, but no major problems developed.

On the third day, the antiwar protesters planned to march to the convention site to protest Humphrey's nomination. Police blocked the marchers at the hall. When the marchers headed in another direction, the police stopped them again. The protesters began to pelt the police with sticks and bottles. The police threw tear gas and charged in, wielding nightsticks. They pursued those who fled, beating some and arresting many.

Humphrey won the Democratic nomination, but the violence outside and the anger within the hall—all shown on television—had damaged his candidacy. The Democrats appeared unable to control their own convention. Humphrey admitted, "Chicago was a catastrophe."

MULTIPLE LEARNING STYLES

Interpersonal The 1968 Democratic convention was perhaps the most dramatic illustration of the divisive spirit in the United States in the late 1960s. Ask students with strong interpersonal skills to review the text's coverage of this event and write a paragraph stating why it was so hard for Americans to come together at this troubled time. Conclude with this comment from Robert McNamara's *In Retrospect: The Tragedy and Lessons of Vietnam:* "A nation's deepest strength lies not in its military prowess but, rather, in the unity of its people." **L3**

Election of 1968

A majority of Americans disapproved of the police action in Chicago but, at the same time, strongly opposed the actions of the protesters. The years of protest and dissent had taken their toll, and a backlash had set in. Most Americans fervently wished for a return to "law and order."

The Wallace Candidacy

One presidential candidate who used the "law and order" theme was Governor **George C. Wallace** of Alabama. Running as a third-party candidate, Wallace promised to crack down on "long-hair . . . draft card-burning youth." In addition, he criticized efforts to integrate schools by busing students and ridiculed "pointy-headed" bureaucrats in Washington for telling people how to run their lives.

Wallace's tough stand on law and order and his appeal to racial fears attracted many voters. Some political reporters predicted Wallace could win as much as 20 percent of the vote.

The "Silent Majority"

The Republican presidential nominee, former vice president **Richard M. Nixon,** also tried to tap into voters' growing conservative sentiment. Nixon pledged to represent the "quiet voice" of the "great majority of Americans, the non-shouters, the nondemonstrators." He called these people the **"silent majority."** Declaring that the "first civil right of every American is to be free from domestic violence," Nixon promised a return to law and order.

On Vietnam Nixon remained vague. He promised that he would achieve "peace with honor," but he would not provide details of his plan.

During the election campaign, Nixon sought to win some of the traditionally Democratic Southern states with the law-and-order issue. This "Southern strategy" paid off. Although Wallace did take 5 Southern states, Nixon won 7 Southern states and their 78 electoral votes.

Nixon Wins

The popular vote was close. Nixon edged out Humphrey by about 500,000 votes—a difference of less than 1 percent. In the electoral vote, however, Nixon won a solid majority—301 votes to Humphrey's 191.

Nixon entered the presidency with the votes of only 43.4 percent of the people. Nixon and Wallace together, however, had won almost 57 percent of the vote. It seemed that a substantial majority of Americans wanted the government to restore order.

Section 4 Review

Checking for Understanding

1. ***Identify*** Tet offensive, Eugene McCarthy, Robert F. Kennedy, William Westmoreland, Hubert H. Humphrey, Richard M. Nixon.
2. ***Define*** credibility gap, silent majority.
3. ***Discuss*** the effect of the Tet offensive.

Reviewing Themes

4. **Civic Rights and Responsibilities** What was the result of the 1968 election?

Critical Thinking

5. **Making Inferences** How did a credibility gap affect Johnson's effectiveness as president?

Activity

Making Headlines Write a headline that might have appeared in a January 1, 1969, newspaper article summing up the mood of the country after surviving the turmoil of 1968.

Section 4 Review Answers

1. Tet offensive, 862; Eugene McCarthy, 863; Robert F. Kennedy, 863; William Westmoreland, 863; Hubert H. Humphrey, 864; Richard M. Nixon, 865
2. The words are defined in the Glossary.
3. Because of the Tet offensive, North Vietnam took over a larger share of the fighting from the Vietcong. More Americans also became more critical of President Johnson and began to doubt that the war could be won.
4. Richard M. Nixon became president of the United States.
5. Because a large portion of the public no longer trusted what he said about the war, he lost public support.

Activity Headlines should express the sentiments that might have existed in the nation after surviving a year of turmoil.

CHAPTER 30
Section 4, 862–865

Use **Chapter Challenger Interactive Review Software** to review Section 4.

Reteaching Activity 30–4

Name ____ Date ____ Class ____

★ Reteaching Activity 30-4

DIRECTIONS: Organizing Facts Below are events that took place in 1968. Complete the time line by writing the corresponding letters from the Fact Bank in each box.

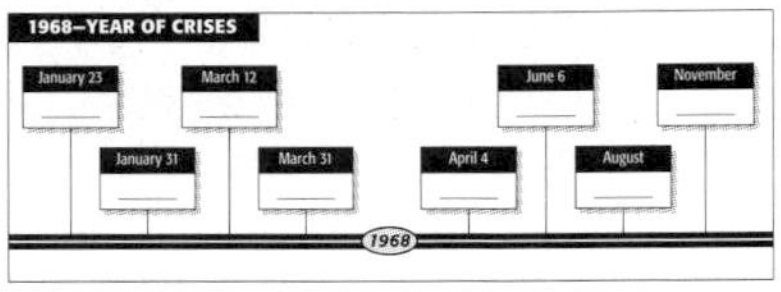

★FACT BANK

A. In a television appearance, President Lyndon B. Johnson announces a "new step toward peace"; he also shocks the nation by announcing that he will not run for another term as president.
B. The silent majority elects Richard M. Nixon for president.
C. After winning the California primary earlier in the day, Robert F. Kennedy is assassinated.
D. Little-known candidate Eugene McCarthy, a Democratic senator from Minnesota who opposes the Vietnam War, takes 42 percent of the vote in the New Hampshire primary.
E. North Korean boats seize the U.S.S. *Pueblo,* a navy spy ship.
F. Violence outside the Democratic convention hall and anger within turn the Democratic candidacy into a catastrophe.
G. Martin Luther King, Jr., is shot and killed in Tennessee, setting off a wave of riots across the country.
H. The North Vietnamese and Vietcong launch the Tet offensive, a series of attacks throughout South Vietnam.

DIRECTIONS: Essay On a separate sheet of paper, answer the following question.
If you had lived during the Vietnam War era, what position would you have taken about the war? Support your ideas with specific reasons.

Reteaching Activities ★ 124 ★ *The American Journey*

Enrichment Activity 30–4

Name ____ Date ____ Class ____

★ Enrichment Activity 30-4

A Different War

The year 1968 was important in NASA's Apollo program, which was racing to send United States astronauts to the moon. *Apollo-Saturn 7* accomplished the first piloted flight of the command-service module. The event was shown on public television in October 1968. *Apollo-Saturn 8,* in December 1968, made the first lunar orbit by United States astronauts. Television viewers got their first live close-up glimpse of the moon on television. Study the diagram of the Apollo rocket on the right.

DIRECTIONS: Recalling Facts Use the information provided and the diagram to answer the following questions.

1. What event was shown on public television in October of 1968? ____
2. Which United States spacecraft made the first lunar orbit? ____
3. How many stages did that rocket have? ____
4. What fuel combinations did each stage use? ____

Activity **DIRECTIONS:** On a separate sheet of paper, redraw the rocket from the diagram provided. Then make a poster entitled "Space Exploration" by developing a collage of space exploration images around your drawing. Use the media center to find newspaper accounts from the period. Include important dates, images, and interesting bits of information in your collage.

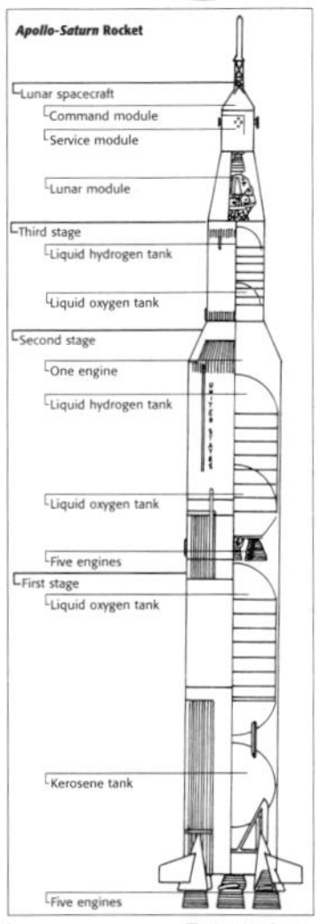

Enrichment Activities ★ 124 ★ *The American Journey*

4 CLOSE

Review Humphrey's comment: "Chicago was a catastrophe." Ask students to list several areas in which 1968 could be said to have been a "catastrophe."

Technology
SKILL BUILDER

TEACH

Building a Database

Students who know how to construct and use a database will have the special confidence that arises from access to information. They also may save themselves time in locating specific facts and figuring out relationships among facts. You might begin discussion of this page by taking a class survey to find out if any students have done computer database searches. (Students who have used a computerized card catalog at the library have used a database.)

In discussing the construction of a database, give some examples of *fields*—for example, the year that an event takes place, the name of the event, or people connected with the event. Then explain that all of the data fields related to the same subject make up a record, and that a collection of records is a data file. If possible, show students examples of data files, records, and fields on a computer as well as the use of a database management system.

Additional Practice

Chapter Skills Activity 30

Technology
SKILL BUILDER

Building a Database

Have you ever collected baseball cards or cataloged the CDs in your collection? Have you ever kept a list of the names and addresses of your friends and relatives? If you have collected information and kept some sort of list or file, then you have created a database.

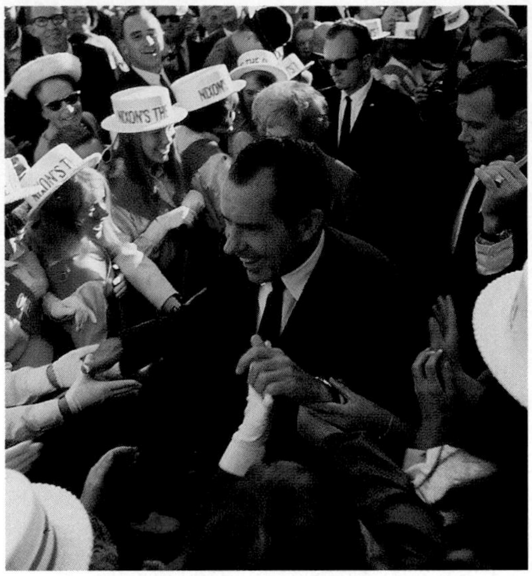
Nixon greets well-wishers at a campaign rally

Learning the Skill

An electronic database is a collection of facts that are stored in files on the computer. The information is organized in fields.

A database can be organized and reorganized in any way that is useful to you. By using a database management system (DBMS)—special software developed for record keeping—you can easily add, delete, change, or update information. You give commands to the computer telling it what to do with the information, and it follows your commands. When you want to retrieve information, the computer searches through the files, finds the information, and displays it on the screen.

Practicing the Skill

Richard M. Nixon is one of the presidents discussed in this chapter. Follow these steps to build a database of the political and cultural events that took place during his presidency.

1. Determine what facts you want to include in your database.
2. Follow instructions in the DBMS you are using to set up fields. Then enter each item of data in its assigned field.
3. Determine how you want to organize the facts in the database—chronologically by the date of the event, or alphabetically by the name of the event.
4. Follow the instructions in your computer program to place the information in order of importance.
5. Check that the information in your database is all correct. If necessary, add, delete, or change information or fields.

Applying the Skill

Building a Database Bring to class current newspapers. Using the steps just described, build a database of political figures mentioned in the newspapers. Explain to a partner why the database is organized the way it is and how it might be used in this class.

ANSWERS TO PRACTICING THE SKILL

Have students review Chapter 30, noting the references to Richard M. Nixon, before they choose their facts. If students work at school computers, spot-check their progress, offering advice as requested. Invite students to share information about their completed databases. Point out the fields that are used most often, as well as ideas that are original and practical.

Applying the Skill Students may prefer to build their databases in pairs. Again, have students share information about the organization and use of their databases. Point out notable similarities and differences.

1968 1970 1972 1974

June 1969 Nixon begins to withdraw troops from Vietnam

April 1970 Nixon sends troops to Cambodia

May 1970 Six students killed at Kent State and Jackson State

January 1973 Paris peace accords end U.S. involvement in Vietnam

Section 5

Nixon and Vietnam

READ TO DISCOVER . . .
- what new strategy President Nixon followed in Vietnam.
- how protests against the war continued.
- how the fighting in Vietnam ended.

TERMS TO LEARN

Vietnamization
MIAs
martial law

The Storyteller

President Nixon's inauguration in January 1969 took place on a cold, gloomy day. Along Pennsylvania Avenue in Washington, D.C., stood hundreds of demonstrators chanting antiwar slogans and holding anti-Nixon posters. At one point Nixon's limousine was pelted with sticks, stones, and bottles. Offended by this behavior, World War II veterans shouted at the demonstrators, labeling the protesters "Communists" and "traitors." This marked the first time an inaugural parade was disrupted in the 180 years of the presidency.

Nixon inaugural button

In his Inaugural Address in January 1969, **Richard M. Nixon** appealed to the American people for calm:

> "We cannot learn from one another until we stop shouting at one another—until we speak quietly enough so that our words can be heard as well as our voices."

In the early days of Nixon's presidency, the level of anger and confrontation decreased. Still, as Nixon said, Vietnam remained a "bone in the nation's throat." The war created divisions among Americans, and those divisions could rise to the surface at any time.

A New Strategy

The new president had campaigned on a pledge of "peace with honor" in Vietnam. He wanted to pull American forces out of Vietnam, but he did not want American withdrawal to be seen as a sign of defeat. Nixon's strategy of peace with honor had three parts—reform of the selective service system, giving South Vietnam more responsibility in fighting the war, and intense bombing.

Draft Reform

Under President Nixon the selective service system changed. College students could no longer obtain draft deferments; only 19-year-olds could

SECTION RESOURCES

Reproducible Masters
- Reproducible Lesson Plan 30–5
- Guided Reading Activity 30–5
- Section Quiz 30–5
- Reteaching Activity 30–5
- Enrichment Activity 30–5

Transparencies
- Section Focus Transparency 30–5

Multimedia
- Chapter Challenger Interactive Review
- Testmaker
- Communism and the Cold War
- Lessons of War
- Historic America Electronic Field Trips
- The Presidents: A Picture History of Our Nation
- Focus on American Art Prints

1 FOCUS

BELLRINGER
Motivational Activity

Before taking roll at the beginning of the class period, project Section Focus Transparency 30–5 and have students answer the questions. Discuss students' responses.

This activity is also available as a blackline master.

Section Focus Transparency 30–5

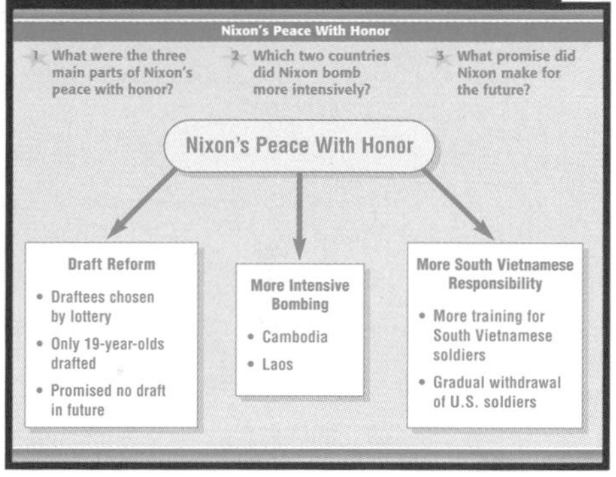

Vocabulary Precheck

Point out that *MIAs* is the plural form of an abbreviated phrase. Call on volunteers to find the unabbreviated phrase in the textbook.

Use the **Vocabulary PuzzleMaker** to create crossword and word search puzzles.

Section Theme
Individual Action

President Nixon's pledge of "peace with honor" in Vietnam included draft reform, intense bombing, and Vietnamization of the war.

Activity Read aloud the Nixon quotation that begins this section. Ask students to speculate about what would have to change in the United States at that time to stop the "shouting at one another."

CHAPTER 30
Section 5, 867–872

2 TEACH

L1 Solving conflict Ask students to suggest a variety of ways in which the Vietnam War might have been concluded, such as total victory by one side, nationwide elections, third party arbitration, and so on.

Guided Reading Activity 30–5

Name ________ Date ________ Class ________

★ Guided Reading Activity **30-5**

DIRECTIONS: Outlining Read the section and complete the outline below. Refer to your textbook to fill in the blanks.

I. A New Strategy
- **A.** Richard Nixon's strategy of "peace with honor" had three parts—________
- **B.** Under President Nixon, college students could no longer obtain ________; only 19-year-olds could be called for service in Vietnam; and draftees would be chosen by ________.
- **C.** By the end of 1969, Nixon had developed his plan of ________, which called for the ________ to be more active in the fighting.
- **D.** The bombing of enemy supply routes and hideouts in ________ was kept secret from the American people.

II. Renewed Opposition at Home
- **A.** In October 1969, more than 300,000 people took part in an ________ in Washington, D.C.
- **B.** ________ represented the United States in the Paris peace talks.
- **C.** The North Vietnamese believed that the ________ in the United States would force the Americans to withdraw.
- **D.** Nixon's decision to attack ________ in April 1970 outraged Congress.
- **E.** **Eyewitness to History** In May at a campus protest at ________, the National Guard fired on student protesters, killing four.
- **F.** Violence flared again on May 14 at ________ in Mississippi, where two students were shot and killed.

III. "Peace Is at Hand"
- **A.** In the fall of 1972, North Vietnam and the United States reached a tentative peace agreement. Negotiators signed a peace agreement on ________.
- **B.** In early 1975 North Vietnamese forces closed in on ________. The city finally fell to the Communists in the early hours of ________.

IV. Legacy of the War
- **A.** More than ________ Americans died in the Vietnam War.
- **B.** The construction of the ________ in Washington, D.C., helped heal the country's wounds.

The American Journey ★ 125 ★ **Guided Reading Activities**

Map Study

Answers
1. North Vietnam, Laos, Cambodia, and South Vietnam
2. the 17°N latitude line

Map Skills Practice

Reading a Map Where did most of the United States bases lie? *(along the coast of South Vietnam)* Why do you think those sites were chosen? *(Coastal bases provide access for transporting troops and supplies.)*

History *and the* Humanities

The Spirit of American Art and Music, Maya Lin

Focus on American Art Prints, *Vietnam Veterans Memorial* by Maya Ying Lin

The Vietnam War

December 1972 Giant B-52 bombers, powered by jet engines, were among the aircraft used to fly more than 2,000 missions against North Vietnam in the "Christmas" bombing. It was the most concentrated bombing of the war—and in history.

Map Study

Throughout the war United States troops and the government of South Vietnam controlled the major cities.
1. **Movement** Through which countries did the Ho Chi Minh Trail run?
2. **Analyzing Information** Along what line of latitude did the demilitarized zone run?

be called for service in Vietnam; and draftees would be chosen by lottery on the basis of their birth date. Protests against the draft faded because of these reforms, because the government began calling up fewer young men, and because President Nixon promised to eliminate the selective service in the future.

Vietnamization

President Nixon started withdrawing American troops from Vietnam in June 1969. He did not, however, want to abandon South Vietnam to the Communists.

By the end of the year, Nixon had developed his plan of Vietnamization and announced it to the American people. **Vietnamization** called for the army of South Vietnam to take a more active role in fighting the war—and for Americans to become less involved. While stepping up the training of South Vietnamese soldiers, American ground troops would gradually withdraw from the country.

When Nixon took office in January 1969, more than 540,000 American troops were in Vietnam. By the end of 1970, the number had fallen to 334,000 and by 1971 to about 60,000.

Intensified Bombing

In the third part of his Vietnam policy, Nixon expanded the bombing campaign. Hoping to relieve pressure on troops in South Vietnam, the president ordered the bombing of enemy supply routes and hideouts in neighboring **Cambodia** and **Laos.** Although the Nixon administration sought publicity for changes to the draft and the withdrawal of troops, it kept the bombing of Cambodia secret.

Renewed Opposition at Home

A new round of antiwar demonstrations began in late 1969, reflecting the growing sentiment for ending the war. In October more than 300,000 people took part in an antiwar protest in Washington, D.C.

Appeal for Support

The government also tried to end the war through peace talks with North Vietnam. **Henry Kissinger,** the president's national security

COOPERATIVE LEARNING ACTIVITY

Round-Robin Wrap-Up Organize the class into groups of 5–7 students each. Have the groups consider this fill-in-the-blank statement: *The war in Vietnam was tragic because* ____. Ask everyone in the group to provide one original answer—perhaps relating to military or political reasons, or social or personal reasons. Assign a secretary in each group to present the responses to the class. As a class, look for common elements in the responses.

adviser, represented the United States in the Paris talks. The United States had launched the bombing campaign to persuade the North Vietnamese to agree to settlement terms, but the North Vietnamese adopted a wait-and-see attitude. They believed that the strength of the antiwar movement in the United States would force the Americans to withdraw.

The new antiwar protests and North Vietnam's unyielding attitude alarmed President Nixon. In his speech on Vietnamization in November, he appealed to the "silent majority" of Americans for support for his policy. "North Vietnam cannot defeat or humiliate the United States," he said. "Only Americans can do that."

Expanding the War

Further conflict gripped Southeast Asia when Cambodia plunged into a civil war between Communist and non-Communist forces. Nixon decided in April 1970 to send American troops to destroy Communist bases in Cambodia.

On April 30, President Nixon told the nation of the attack on Cambodia, saying, "We shall not be defeated in Vietnam. . . . The world's most powerful nation [will not act] like a pitiful helpless giant." Yet the attack aroused outrage in Congress and elsewhere. By sending American troops to Cambodia, critics charged, Nixon invaded a neutral country and overstepped his constitutional authority as president.

Eyewitness to HISTORY

Kent State

The Cambodian invasion provoked a storm of antiwar protests on campuses across the nation. Most proceeded peacefully. But two protests ended in tragedy.

At a protest at Kent State University in **Kent, Ohio,** students burned a military building on campus. Ohio's governor declared martial law—emergency military rule—on the campus and ordered 3,000 National Guard troops to Kent.

On May 4 armed troops arrived on campus. Eighteen-year-old Leone Keegan, a freshman, remembered going to class that morning:

> "I saw all these young men in uniforms standing on the street corners with their rifles, and I was thinking, What is this?"

At noon students gathered for a protest rally on the campus lawn. The National Guard members—young, inexperienced, and nervous—told

Picturing HISTORY President Nixon (left) and national security adviser Henry Kissinger discuss foreign policy strategy. **In what three ways did Nixon plan to achieve "peace with honor" in Vietnam?**

MULTIPLE LEARNING STYLES

Auditory/Musical Bring to class a recording of Bob Dylan's song "Blowin' In the Wind." As you play the recording, have students do one of the following:
- Paint a picture or make a collage to pay tribute to someone who served in Vietnam
- Write a poem or song highlighting the fact that more than 58,000 Americans died fighting a war that many Americans felt was unjustified
- Write an editorial offering ideas about how to keep such a war from happening again

Students may keep their drawings or writings private, but ask students to discuss the third option aloud in class. **L1, ELL**

ABCNEWS INTERACTIVE™

VIDEODISC
Communism and the Cold War

Side 2, Chapter 8
Title: *Vietnam War*
Subject: Summary and different perspectives of the Vietnam War
Ask: **Why did Gennadi Gerasimov refer to Vietnam as a "folly of the cold war"?** *(because the war was a result of the animosity between U.S. capitalism and Soviet communism)*

NATIONAL GEOGRAPHIC SOCIETY

CD-ROM
The Presidents: A Picture History of Our Nation

Have students view "Richard M. Nixon" and use the information to write a summary of the president's Vietnam War years.

Picturing HISTORY Kissinger, a German immigrant and former Harvard professor of government, helped Nixon develop a policy of *détente,* or relaxed tensions, between the United States and Communist nations. Under the Nixon Doctrine (announced in 1969), the United States would provide aid but not troops to allies that were experiencing civil strife. **Ask:** Where were the peace talks for the Vietnam War held? *(Paris)*
Answer: *The strategy included draft reform, giving more responsibility to South Vietnam, and intense bombing.*

CHAPTER 30
Section 5, 867–872

Picturing HISTORY Attorney General John Mitchell originally refused to have the Justice Department investigate what came to be called the "Kent State Massacre." It took five years before any of the National Guard troops were indicted in the incident (for violation of the students' civil rights), and those eight guardsmen were acquitted. **Ask:** Why were National Guard troops on the campus? *(They had been ordered there by James Rhodes, the governor of Ohio.)*
Answer: *The unrest was a response to the American invasion of Cambodia.*

ABCNEWS INTERACTIVE™

VIDEODISC
Lessons of War

Side 2
Chapter 6

Title: *Philosophy of Nonviolence*
Subject: How Ghandi's and King's philosophies are used in protests
Ask: How effective were the protests by Americans during the Vietnam conflict? *(The protests showed the unpopularity of the conflict and eventually resulted in a withdrawal of American troops.)*

What?Where?When?Who?

Student Protests Some college students showed their unhappiness over the Vietnam War by staging teach-ins, or all-night sessions in which students, faculty, and guest speakers denounced the war. Other students occupied college administration buildings, held school officials captive, and then used the media attention to state their cases.

3 ASSESS

Assign Section 5 Review as homework or as an in-class activity.

Picturing HISTORY A stunned woman kneels beside the body of a student killed at Kent State. **What event sparked the student unrest at Kent State?**

the protesting students to leave. "Evacuate the area. You have no right to assemble," they shouted through bullhorns. The students shouted back, "We don't want your war." Some students threw stones.

The troops shot tear gas toward the students; many students ran. One National Guard unit chased some students between two buildings. Then—for reasons that are unclear—the troops opened fire. ". . . [T]hey're killing us," screamed one student in disbelief. Four students were dead and 13 more were wounded.

Jackson State

Violence flared again on May 14 at the nearly all-African American college of **Jackson State** in Mississippi. Following a night of campus violence, two students were shot and killed. Witnesses charged that the police had recklessly blasted the residence hall with shotguns. The police claimed they were protecting themselves from sniper fire.

Footnotes to History

Peace Prize In 1973 Henry Kissinger of the United States shared the Nobel Peace Prize with Le Duc Tho of North Vietnam for negotiating a cease-fire in the Vietnam War.

Reactions

A wave of student strikes followed the tragedies at Kent State and Jackson State. Hundreds of colleges and universities suspended classes or closed down completely.

The president took a hard line. The Kent State shootings, he said, "should remind us once again that when dissent turns to violence it invites tragedy." A commission that investigated events at Kent State found that the shootings were unjustified. A majority of Americans, however, seemed to agree with the president.

"Peace Is at Hand"

Meanwhile, the Nixon administration continued to negotiate with representatives of the North Vietnamese government. These talks stalled, however.

A Peace Agreement Fails

In March 1972, the North Vietnamese launched another major offensive in the south. Because the United States had few troops left in Vietnam, Nixon responded to the attacks with renewed bombing. He also ordered the navy to plant mines in North Vietnamese harbors.

The president stopped insisting that North Vietnam remove all its troops from South Vietnam before a full American withdrawal. Nixon sent Henry Kissinger to meet in private with the North Vietnamese foreign minister. In the fall of 1972—just before the presidential

MAKING CONNECTIONS ACTIVITY

Architecture Maya Ying Lin's design for the Vietnam Veterans Memorial was praised as having an "extraordinary sense of dignity and nobility." It was also condemned as being "unheroic" and "a black gash of shame." Construction did not begin until it was agreed that a statue and an American flag would be added. Nevertheless, there is no question that most visitors to the monument today are quite moved by what they see. Use this information to open a discussion about what makes a monument moving and memorable. Extend the discussion by inviting interested students to submit sketches for a memorial to a person or cause that they consider noteworthy. **L2, ELL**

election in the United States—they reached a tentative agreement. "Peace is at hand," Kissinger announced.

His statement came too soon. The agreement collapsed because the South Vietnamese president objected to allowing North Vietnamese forces to remain in South Vietnam.

Peace Finally Comes

After his reelection, Nixon unleashed American airpower against North Vietnam. In December 1972, the heaviest bombardment of the war fell on North Vietnam's cities, provoking outrage in the United States and abroad.

Nixon stood firm, and North Vietnam returned to the peace talks. The Americans pressured the South Vietnamese to accept the peace terms. On January 27, 1973, the negotiators signed the peace agreement.

The United States agreed to pull its remaining troops out of the country. The North Vietnamese agreed to return all American prisoners of war. While the Paris peace accords ended American involvement in Vietnam, they did not end the conflict.

The War Ends

The North Vietnamese never abandoned their goal of unifying Vietnam under their control. In early 1975 they launched a final major offensive. The weakened South Vietnamese army collapsed suddenly on all fronts. Within a few weeks, North Vietnamese tanks reached the outskirts of Saigon.

The Fall of Saigon

As North Vietnamese forces closed in on Saigon, the last Americans scrambled to escape the country, some by helicopter from the roof of the American embassy. Thousands of Vietnamese citizens who had supported or worked for the Americans also fled to the United States. Many more could not escape. In the early hours of April 30, 1975, Saigon fell to the Communists. Soon after, South Vietnam surrendered. The long war was over.

Legacy of the War

The Vietnam War took a staggering toll of life and suffering. An estimated 1.4 million Vietnamese—civilians as well as soldiers on one side or the other—died between 1965 and 1975. Vietnam lay in ruins, with many villages destroyed.

More than 58,000 Americans were dead; 300,000 were wounded, many of them permanently disabled. The United States had poured more than $150 billion into the war.

About 2.7 million Americans had served in Vietnam. Unlike the veterans of World War II, they found no hero's welcome when they returned home. Many Americans simply wanted to forget the war. They paid little attention to those who had fought and sacrificed in Vietnam.

The relatives of the American soldiers who had been classified as missing in action, or as **MIAs**, continued to demand that the government press the Vietnamese for information. The Vietnamese did allow a number of American groups to scour the countryside looking for MIAs. As the years passed, however, the likelihood of finding anyone alive faded.

Picturing HISTORY On April 29, 1975, an American helicopter evacuated Americans and South Vietnamese from the roof of the American embassy in Saigon. **Why were these people fleeing the city?**

CHAPTER 30
Section 5, 867–872

Use **Chapter Challenger Interactive Review Software** to review Section 5.

Section Quiz 30–5

Name ______ Date ______ Class ______

Chapter 30

Score

Section Quiz 30-5

DIRECTIONS: Matching Match each item in Column A with the items in Column B. Write the correct letters in the blanks. *(10 points each)*

Column A	Column B
____ 1. Paris talks representative	A. Kent State University
____ 2. site where National Guard killed students	B. MIAs
____ 3. site where police killed students	C. Henry Kissinger
____ 4. soldiers missing in action	D. Maya Ying Lin
____ 5. designed Vietnam Veterans Memorial	E. Jackson State

DIRECTIONS: Multiple Choice In the blank at the left, write the letter of the choice that best completes the statement or answers the question. *(10 points each)*

____ 6. The third part of President Richard M. Nixon's strategy for peace with honor called for
A. pulling out of the war. C. intense bombing.
B. decreased bombing. D. draft reform.

____ 7. President Richard Nixon changed the draft so that draftees would be chosen from
A. Social Security numbers. C. Selective Service numbers.
B. a lottery. D. volunteers.

____ 8. When Nixon secretly sent American troops into this country, his critics charged that he overstepped his authority as president.
A. Cambodia C. Japan
B. China D. Southeast Asia

____ 9. The Paris peace talks
A. punished North Vietnam. C. ended the Vietnam War.
B. punished South Vietnam. D. ended American involvement in Vietnam.

____ 10. The conflict in Vietnam ended this way.
A. Paris peace accords C. Communist capture of Saigon
B. agreement to stop bombing D. in an American victory

The American Journey • 125 • **Section Quizzes**

Reteaching Activity 30–5

Name ______ Date ______ Class ______

Reteaching Activity 30-5

DIRECTIONS: Organizing Facts Complete the top part of the chart by writing the number of each item from the Fact Bank related to Richard Nixon's peace with honor strategy. Then complete the time lines related to the invasion of Cambodia and the end of the Vietnam War by writing the number of the item that matches each date given.

Nixon's Peace with Honor Strategy

Draft Reform	Vietnamization	Intense Bombing

The Invasion of Cambodia	The War Ends
April 30, 1970	Fall 1972
May 4, 1970	December 1972
May 14, 1970	January 27, 1973
	Early 1975
	April 30, 1975

FACT BANK

1. The mission would be a secret.
2. Nixon unleashes the heaviest bombardment of the war on North Vietnam.
3. Protests against the draft fade.
4. College students could no longer obtain draft deferments.
5. Enemy supply routes in Cambodia and Laos would be attacked.
6. Saigon falls to the Communists.
7. Police shoot and kill two students at a protest at Jackson State in Mississippi.
8. Nixon informs the nation that he sent troops to attack Cambodia.
9. Negotiators at the Paris peace talks sign an agreement.
10. Only 19-year-olds could be called for service in Vietnam.
11. The army of South Vietnam would take a more active role in fighting the war.
12. A protest at Kent State turns violent; four students are killed by National Guard members.
13. The last Americans scramble to escape Vietnam.
14. Draftees would be chosen by lottery on the basis of birth date.
15. American ground troops would gradually withdraw, lowering their number to 60,000 by 1971.
16. Henry Kissinger announces "Peace is at hand."

The American Journey • 125 • **Reteaching Activities**

Picturing HISTORY In 18 hours, U.S. helicopters removed 1,373 Americans and 6,422 non-Americans from Saigon.
Answer: *Saigon was falling to the Communists.*

CRITICAL THINKING ACTIVITY

Making Generalizations To review the Vietnam War and the events associated with it, ask students to make a list of generalizations about the war. The following generalizations might stir student thinking:

- The Vietnam War grew out of political repression in South Vietnam.
- The U.S. government covered up some of the truth about the war.
- Not only the American people but their leaders were divided over the proper course of action in Vietnam.

When their list is finished, have students choose various generalizations and try to find facts in the chapter that support or expand upon them. **L2**

CHAPTER 30
Section 5, 867–872

American Memories

Healing the Wounds

Part of the veterans' pain came immediately upon their return, as they faced a civilian population that praised draft evaders and often looked at veterans as pawns of the government. Some veterans continue to suffer from post-traumatic stress disorder, and some claim disabling conditions due to the use of "Agent Orange" in Vietnam.
Answer: *These items represent patriotism, honor, and death.*

Enrichment Activity 30–5

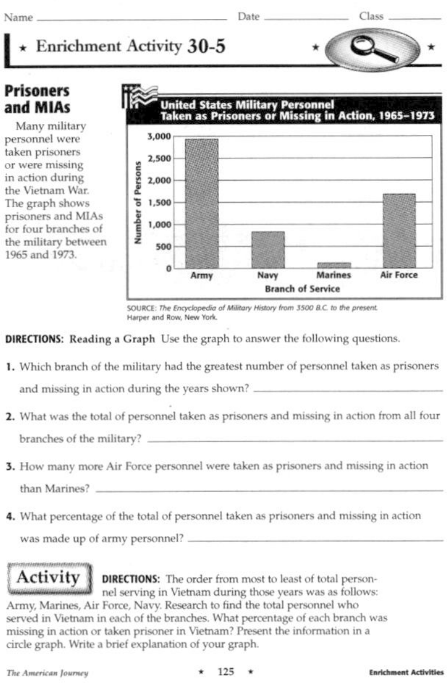

Name ________ Date ________ Class ________

★ Enrichment Activity **30-5** ★

Prisoners and MIAs

Many military personnel were taken prisoners or were missing in action during the Vietnam War. The graph shows prisoners and MIAs for four branches of the military between 1965 and 1973.

SOURCE: *The Encyclopedia of Military History from 3500 B.C. to the present.* Harper and Row, New York.

DIRECTIONS: Reading a Graph Use the graph to answer the following questions.

1. Which branch of the military had the greatest number of personnel taken as prisoners and missing in action during the years shown? ________
2. What was the total of personnel taken as prisoners and missing in action from all four branches of the military? ________
3. How many more Air Force personnel were taken as prisoners and missing in action than Marines? ________
4. What percentage of the total of personnel taken as prisoners and missing in action was made up of army personnel? ________

Activity **DIRECTIONS:** The order from most to least of total personnel serving in Vietnam during those years was as follows: Army, Marines, Air Force, Navy. Research to find the total personnel who served in Vietnam in each of the branches. What percentage of each branch was missing in action or taken prisoner in Vietnam? Present the information in a circle graph. Write a brief explanation of your graph.

The American Journey ★ 125 ★ **Enrichment Activities**

4 CLOSE

Ask students if they think the Vietnam War could have been ended before the spring of 1975. Discuss their responses.

American Memories

Healing the Wounds

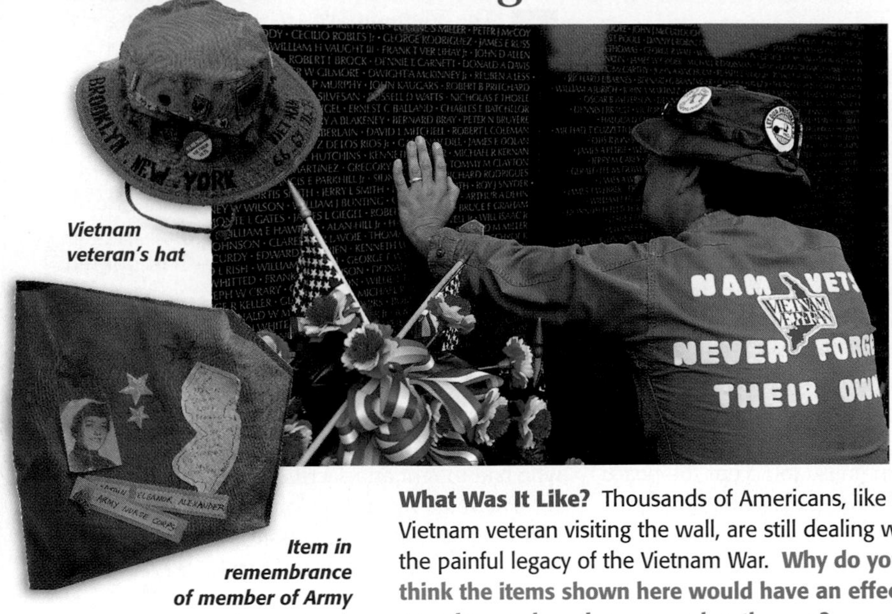

Vietnam veteran's hat

Item in remembrance of member of Army Nurses Corps

Wreath left on Memorial Day, 1989

What Was It Like? Thousands of Americans, like this Vietnam veteran visiting the wall, are still dealing with the painful legacy of the Vietnam War. **Why do you think the items shown here would have an effect on Americans when they remember the war?**

A Step Toward Healing

The construction of the **Vietnam Veterans Memorial** in Washington, D.C., provided a step toward healing the country's wounds. Designed by **Maya Ying Lin,** the striking memorial is a polished black granite wall in the shape of a private's stripes. It bears the names of all the Americans who died or were missing in action in the conflict.

When they visit the wall, families, friends, and comrades in war seek out the names of those who fought in Vietnam and did not return. Since the memorial was dedicated in 1982, visitors have left thousands of keepsakes and remembrances there. The flowers, letters, poems, and pictures left at the wall pay a proud and moving tribute to the Americans who died in the service of their country.

★ ★ ★ Section 5 Review ★ ★ ★

Checking for Understanding

1. ***Identify*** Richard M. Nixon, Henry Kissinger.
2. ***Define*** Vietnamization, martial law, MIAs.
3. ***Describe*** Nixon's three-part strategy for ending the war.

Reviewing Themes

4. **Individual Action** Why did Nixon's actions in Cambodia anger many people?

Critical Thinking

5. **Demonstrating Reasoned Judgment** Do you think Nixon succeeded in attaining "peace with honor"? Explain.

Activity

Creating a Memorial Design a memorial to the students who died at Kent State in Ohio.

★ ★ ★ Section 5 Review Answers ★ ★ ★

1. Richard M. Nixon, 867; Henry Kissinger, 868
2. The words are defined in the Glossary.
3. reform of the selective service system, giving South Vietnam more responsibility in fighting the war, intensive bombing
4. Critics charged that Nixon had invaded a neutral country and had overstepped his constitutional authority as president.
5. Many students probably will answer no. The war dragged on with large American losses. Soon after the United States pulled out, South Vietnam crumbled. A yes answer is also acceptable if backed up with evidence.

Activity Students should design a memorial for those who died at Kent State.

Multimedia Activities

ABCNEWS INTERACTIVE™

Historic America Electronic Field Trips

Field Trip to the Vietnam Veterans War Memorial

Setting up the Video

With a group of your classmates, view "The Vietnam Veterans War Memorial" on the videodisc ***Historic America: Electronic Field Trips***. On November 13, 1982, a monument for Americans who served during the Vietnam War was dedicated in Washington, D.C. This program gives a short overview of United States involvement in the Vietnam War, and the conflict it created among the American people.

Side 2, Chapter 8

View the video by scanning the bar code or by entering the chapter number on your keypad and pressing Search.

Hands-On Activity

After the Vietnam War, many veterans suffered from what is today called post-traumatic stress disorder. This is a condition in which a person who has experienced a traumatic event feels severe and long-lasting aftereffects. Using your school or local library, write a minireport on how this disorder is treated.

Surfing the "Net"

The Vietnam War

The Vietnam War left a profound mark on many Americans. Most deeply affected were the 2.7 million men and women who fought in the war and their families. Veterans who returned home did not receive a hero's welcome. Bitter memories of the war still remain with many veterans today. The war left many with physical and psychological problems. To learn more about experiences of soldiers of the Vietnam War, look on the Internet.

Getting There

Follow these steps to gather information about the Vietnam experience for American military veterans.

1. Go to a search engine.
2. Type in the word *Vietnam.* Following this word, enter words like these to focus your search: *oral history, stories, history.*
3. The search engine should provide you with a number of links to follow. Links are "pointers" to different sites on the Internet.

What to Do When You Are There

Click on the links to navigate through the pages of information. Gather your findings. Using the information from the Internet, interview a Vietnam veteran about his or her experiences during the war. Record your interview and share your findings with the class.

TEACHER'S NOTES

Multimedia Activities

ABCNEWS INTERACTIVE™

VIDEODISC
Historic America
Electronic Field Trips

Side 2, Chapter 10
Title: *The Vietnam Veterans Memorial*

If you do not have access to a videodisc player, the **Historic America Electronic Field Trips** are also available in VHS.

Internet Sites

The following are possible sites for completing the "Net" activities:

How to Do an Oral History About the Impact of the Vietnam Era
http://www.pbs.org/pov/stories/vietnam/curriculum.html

Vietnam Veterans Memorial
http://milkman.cac.psu.edu/~cooper/Tour Of DC/monuments/viet-nam-memorial.html

Vietnam Veterans Home Page
http://www.vietvet.org/

Not on the "Net" . . .

If your students do not have access to the Internet, have them complete the activity "The Vietnam War" by using the computerized card catalog at their school or local library. At the *s:* prompt, have students type in *Vietnam* or *veterans.* An excellent source of Vietnam veterans' stories is Bill McCloud's *What Should We Tell Our Children About Vietnam?* (Copyright ©1989 by Bill McCloud. Norman, OK: University of Oklahoma Press).

GLENCOE TECHNOLOGY

VIDEODISC
MindJogger Videoquiz

Use MindJogger to review the Chapter 30 content.

Chapter 30
Disc 4, Side B

Also available in VHS.

Reviewing Key Terms

The key terms used in this activity can be found in the textbook glossary on pages A26–A35.

Reviewing Key Facts

1. to overthrow Castro
2. After a temporary division of North and South Vietnam, elections were to be held in 1956 to select a government to rule the reunited nation.
3. Some Americans agreed with and supported the United States's efforts in Vietnam; others believed the United States should not be fighting there.
4. The war escalated as the United States tried to regain the cities taken by North Vietnam. This caused increased antiwar sentiment and led to a distrust of Johnson and his running of the war.
5. North Vietnam took over South Vietnam, unifying the two countries under Communist rule.

Chapter 30 Review and Activities

Reviewing Key Terms

On a sheet of paper, define the following terms:

flexible response	**escalate**
hot line	**deferment**
Vietcong	**Vietnamization**
domino theory	**MIAs**

Reviewing Key Facts

1. What was the main purpose of the Bay of Pigs invasion?
2. How did the Geneva Accords plan to unite North and South Vietnam?
3. Why were the American people divided over the Vietnam War?
4. How did the Tet offensive affect the war?
5. What happened in Vietnam after the United States withdrew?

Critical Thinking

Making Comparisons

World War II and the Vietnam War had very different outcomes.

1. Why do you think most Americans supported World War II but did not support the Vietnam War?
2. How did the American people's attitudes toward both wars affect the way Americans treated returning soldiers?

Time Line Activity

Create a time line on which you place the following events in chronological order.

- Neil Armstrong walks on moon
- Berlin Wall constructed
- United States pulls out of Vietnam
- Cuban missile crisis erupts

Reviewing Themes

1. **Geography and History** Why was the Berlin Wall built?
2. **Government and Democracy** What actions did President Eisenhower take regarding the conflict in Vietnam?
3. **Continuity and Change** How did members of the antiwar movement demonstrate against the war?
4. **Civic Rights and Responsibilities** How did American voters express their discontent with the direction the country was taking in the election of 1968?
5. **Individual Action** Why did Nixon order the bombing of Cambodia and Laos?

Skill Practice Activity

Using a Database Prepare a database of the major battles of the Vietnam War involving United States troops. At your local library, research to find information about the sites of the battles, who the commanding officer was, how many American soldiers were killed or wounded at the sites, and how many North Vietnamese were killed or wounded. Share your database with the rest of your class.

Cooperative Activity

History and Global Issues One of the hardest decisions a president has to make is when to intervene in an international crisis. With members of your group brainstorm to create a list of international situations in which you think the United States would be justified in intervening and using military force if necessary. Combine your list with those of the other groups and then have all the groups vote to narrow your list down to three situations.

Critical Thinking

1. Students may suggest that World War II directly affected the well-being of Americans but the Vietnam War did not. In addition, during World War II the government spent large amounts of money to raise public support for the war, unlike the Vietnam War.
2. World War II soldiers returned as heroes. Americans were eager to forget Vietnam, so returning soldiers were largely ignored.

Time Line Activity

Events should be placed in this order: Berlin Wall constructed, Cuban missile crisis erupts, Neil Armstrong walks on moon, United States pulls out of Vietnam

Reviewing Themes

1. to prevent East Germans from escaping to West Berlin and to cut communications and other links between East and West Germany
2. Eisenhower sent American diplomats to work out the Geneva Accords. He also sent financial aid and a few hundred American military advisers to South Vietnam.

Geography Activity

Study the two maps on this page, then answer the questions that follow.

The Election of 1960

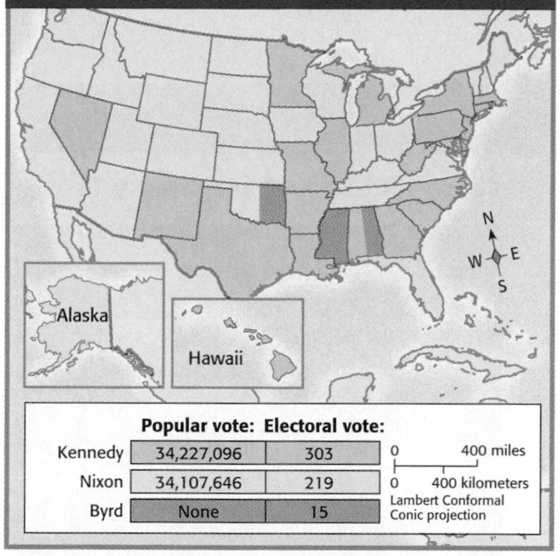

The Election of 1968

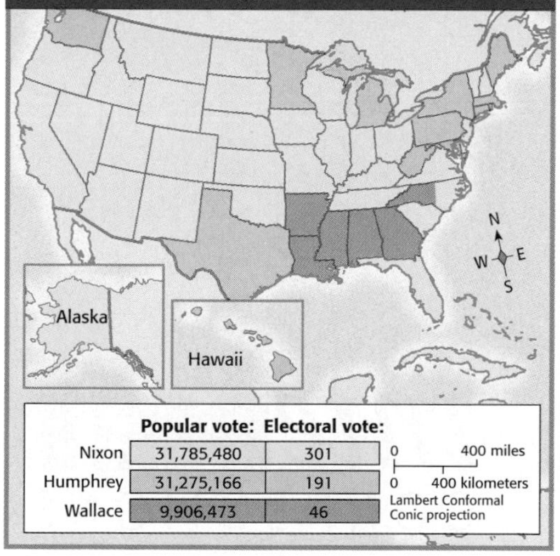

1. **Place** Which candidate won Florida's electoral votes in 1960? In 1968?
2. **Place** Which candidate won Alaska's electoral votes in 1968?
3. **Location** How many states voted for Nixon in 1960?
4. **Region** In what regions of the country did Kennedy receive the strongest support in the 1960 election? In which regions was support for Kennedy weakest?
5. **Region** What regions supported Nixon in 1960? In 1968?
6. **Region** Explain why you agree or disagree with the following: The Northeast was Nixon's strongest region in 1968.

Technology Activity

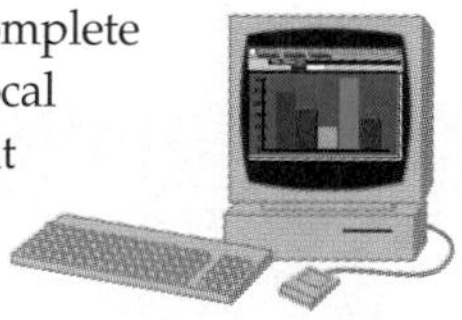

Using a Word Processor Complete research at your school or local library for information about the assassinations of John F. Kennedy, Martin Luther King, Jr., and Robert Kennedy. Use the information you find and your word processor to compose a ballad-type song honoring their memory. Add graphics and a border around your printed song sheet.

Portfolio Activity **History Journal** Review the chapter for examples of the United States's efforts to stop the spread of communism and record them in your journal. Rank each of the examples according to how effective you think each action was.

CHAPTER 30
Review and Activities

Cooperative Activity

Each group should brainstorm a list of international situations in which it thinks the United States would be justified in intervening.

Geography Activity

1. Nixon; Nixon
2. Nixon
3. 25 plus part of Oklahoma
4. Kennedy was strongest in the East and South and weakest in the West.
5. In 1960 the West was almost solidly for Nixon. Except in the Northeast, Nixon virtually swept the nation in 1968.
6. Disagree; the Northeast was Wallace's strongest region.

Technology Activity

Students should find information on the assassinations of John F. Kennedy, Martin Luther King, Jr., and Robert Kennedy. They should use their information to write a ballad honoring the memories of these leaders.

Portfolio Activity Students should review the chapter and record examples of how the United States tried to stop the spread of communism. They should rank their examples based on the perceived effectiveness of each action.

Chapter Bonus Test Question

Ask: What was the My Lai incident, and how did it affect American public opinion about the war? *(A platoon led by Lt. William Calley was ordered to destroy the village of My Lai, which was suspected of being a Vietcong stronghold. The platoon wiped out more than 200 people. Americans were horrified by news of My Lai. Calley was convicted in 1971 of war crimes.)*

3. They marched to protest the United States's involvement in the war and protested in other ways, sometimes violently.
4. Many voters supported candidates, such as Richard Nixon and George Wallace,who promised a return to law and order.
5. because they contained part of the enemy supply routes and hideouts

Skill Practice Activity

Students should prepare a database of the major Vietnam battles in which U.S. troops took part. Finished databases should indicate an adequate amount of library research and should be easy to access.

Unit 11 Resource Guide

These Glencoe resources may be used to teach, reteach, or enrich the concepts presented in this unit of study.

Teaching Transparencies

Map Transparency 11 with Overlays A, B, C

Cause-and-Effect Transparency 11

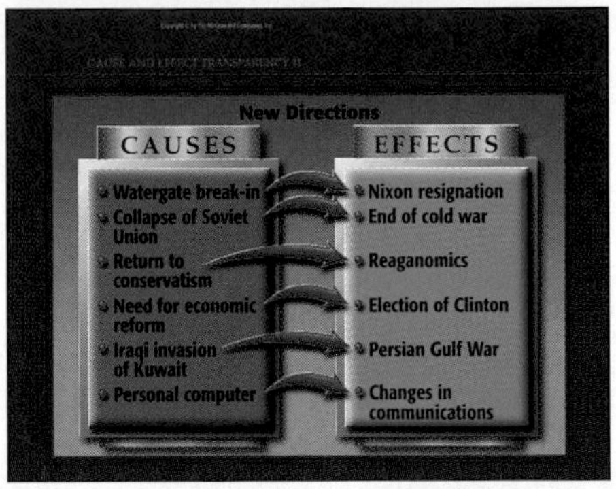

BIBLIOGRAPHY

Readings for the Student

Goldberg, Judy, ed. ***Dear Chelsea: Letters from Kids.*** New York: Scholastic, 1994. A compilation of letters to President Clinton's daughter, Chelsea.

Lillegard, Dee. ***Richard Nixon: Thirty-seventh President of the United States.*** Describes Richard Nixon's life and career. Chicago: Children's Press, 1988.

Readings for the Teacher

Maraniss, David. ***First in His Class: A Biography of Bill Clinton.*** New York: Simon & Schuster, 1995. Bill Clinton's rise to power.

Witcover, Jules. ***Marathon: The Pursuit of the Presidency 1972–1976.*** New York: The Viking Press, 1977. A Washington correspondent tells Jimmy Carter's story.

Multimedia Resources

Videodisc. ***The Haldeman Diaries: Inside the Nixon White House.*** Santa Monica: Sony, 1994. Haldeman's private daily diary with 700 still images and 45 minutes of video. User guide.

Videotape. ***Richard Nixon Reflects.*** Oak Forest: MPI Home Video, 1990. A 90-minute, candid memoir by former president Nixon giving his personal thoughts on Kennedy, Bush, Reagan, Gorbachev, and Watergate.

interNET CONNECTIONS

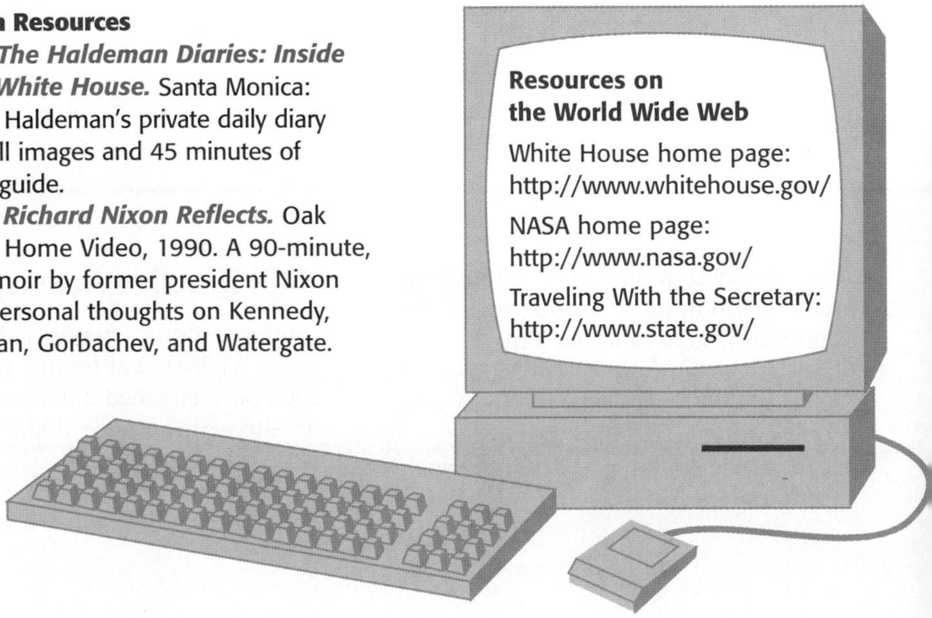

Resources on the World Wide Web

White House home page:
http://www.whitehouse.gov/

NASA home page:
http://www.nasa.gov/

Traveling With the Secretary:
http://www.state.gov/

★ ★ ★ ★ ★ ★ ★ ★ ★ ★ ★ ★ ★ ★ ★ **Resource Guide** Unit 11

INTERDISCIPLINARY ACTIVITIES

American Literature Reading 11

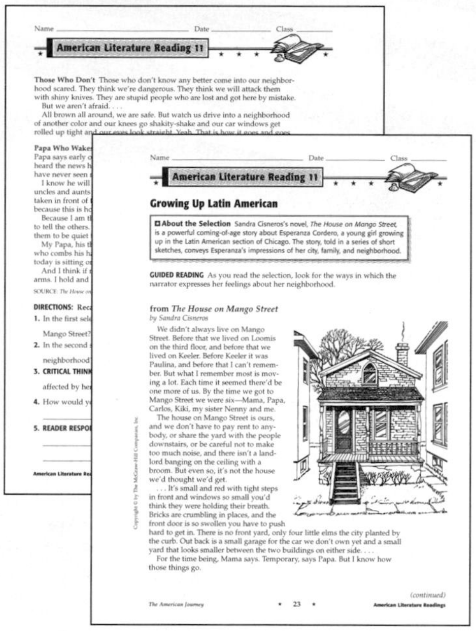

Interdisciplinary Connection 11

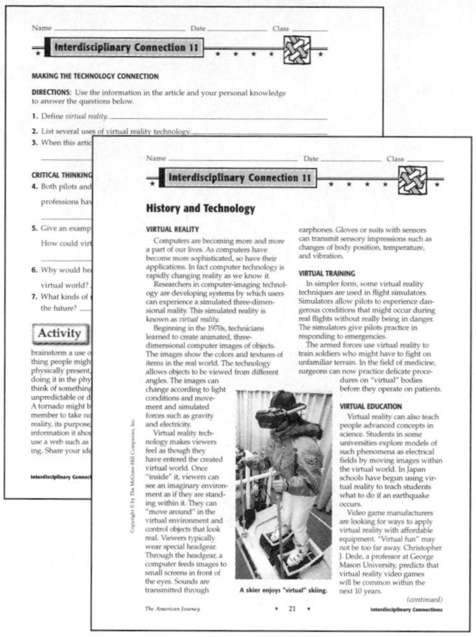

ENRICHMENT ACTIVITIES

Cooperative Learning Activity 11

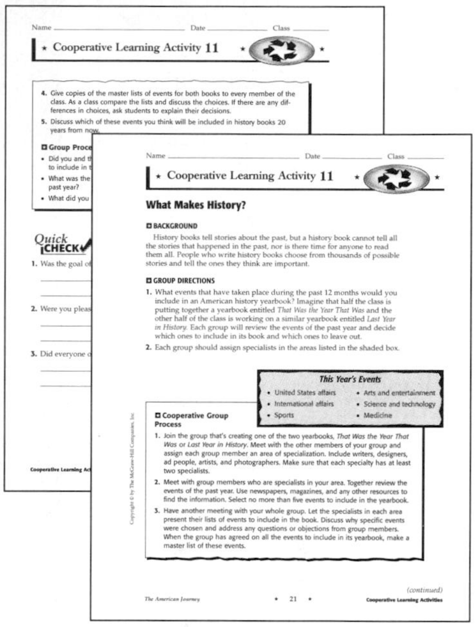

HANDS-ON ACTIVITIES

Hands-On History Lab Activity 11

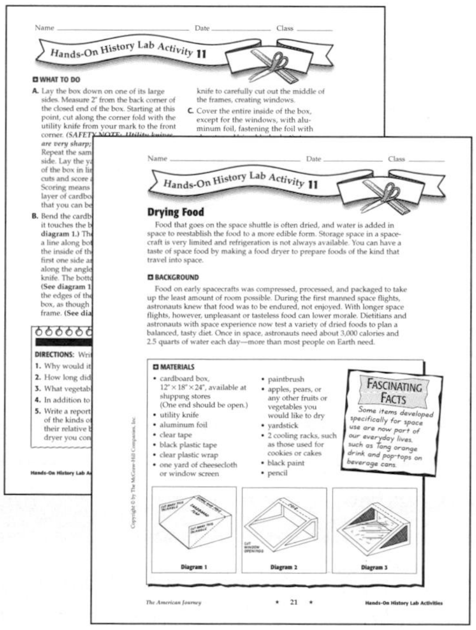

History Simulation 11

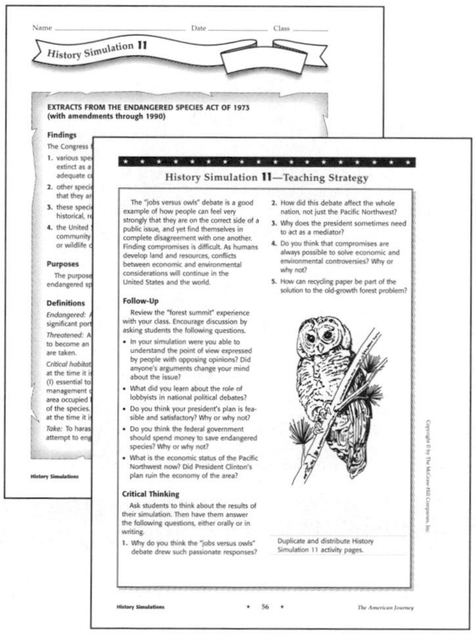

ASSESSMENT

Unit 11 Test

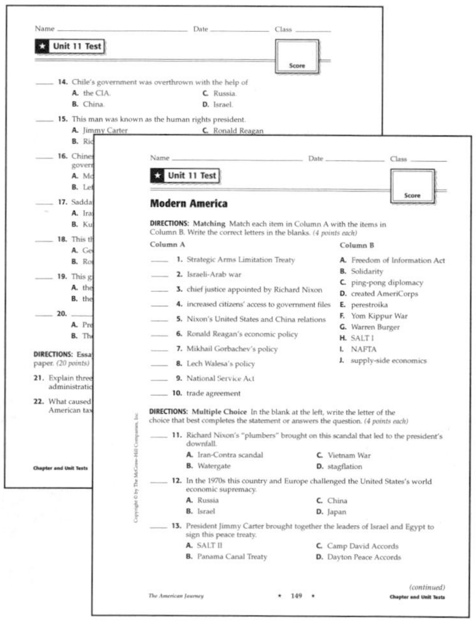

Introducing UNIT 11

0:00 OUT OF TIME?

If your teaching time is limited, you may use the *Chapter Summaries* blackline master found in the TCR with the *Chapter Digests Audiocassette Activities and Tests* to condense individual chapters into a one-day lesson.

Introducing the Unit

Activity Direct students' attention to the *World* section of the time line and have them note events that reflect changes around the world. Conduct a class discussion about how these changes might affect policies of the United States.

Unit Objectives

Upon completing this unit, students will be able to:

1. Describe domestic and foreign policies that characterized the 1970s, 1980s, and 1990s.
2. Evaluate the impact of the Nixon, Ford, Carter, Reagan, Bush, and Clinton administrations on American politics.

Hands-On HISTORY

Hands-On History Lab Activity 11, "Drying Food," is a high-interest **constructivist approach** activity directly related to the main topic of the unit.

Unit 11

Modern America

1968–present

"Let us set our sights upon a land of new promise."

—President Bill Clinton, 1997 Inaugural Address

MAPPING America

Portfolio Activity Trace an outline map of the world. As you read this unit about modern America, note the countries involved in U.S. foreign policy issues during the 1970s, 1980s, and 1990s. Mark the location of these countries on your map, with a short caption explaining the reasons for their involvement with the United States.

Decorative flag, computer art

AIDS awareness ribbon

United States

1974 President Nixon resigns from office

1983 American troops invade Grenada

1975 — 1980

1981 AIDS identified by medical experts

1982 Argentina invades Falkland Islands

World

Team Teaching Strategies

Speech Invite the Speech teacher to explain to the class the meaning of *sound bite*, a brief statement excerpted from a taped speech used in a broadcast news story. *Bite* implies a small section of soundtrack taken from a longer piece and includes undertones of the high-tech description of units of information (bytes). Have students select a presidential election described in this unit and work with the Speech teacher to write a sound bite for the candidate of their choice. Encourage students to audiotape or videotape their sound bite as if it were part of a broadcast on a news program. Have students either perform or show their sound bites to the class.

American marine in Persian Gulf

HISTORY AND ART ***Telecommunications Network, United States*** As it enters a new century, the world is undergoing a technological revolution as significant as the Industrial Revolution of the early 1800s.

1985 · 1990 · 1995 · 2000

- **1986** Space shuttle *Challenger* explodes
- **1987** INF Treaty signed
- **1989** Exxon *Valdez* oil spill occurs in Alaska
- **1989** Communism crumbles in Eastern Europe
- **1990** Operation Desert Shield begins
- **1993** Israel–PLO treaty signed
- **1994** Nelson Mandela elected president of South Africa
- **1996** President Bill Clinton wins second term
- **1997** Colin Powell heads summit on community service

Team Teaching Strategies

Science Many new areas of study have developed as a result of the environmental movement of the 1970s. Invite the Science teacher to discuss recycling techniques, solid waste management, and water and soil conservation methods. Have students discuss how they think recycling works and ask what other alternatives to waste disposal they can think of.

Introducing
UNIT 11

ABCNEWS INTERACTIVE™

VIDEODISC
Communism and the Cold War

Side 2, Chapter 21
Title: *Changing Images*
Subject: Changes in American perceptions of the Soviet Union
Ask: **What do the commercials shown on this video segment reveal about the changes in the former Soviet bloc?** *(that those nations formerly under Soviet control now have more choices)*

HISTORY AND ART On January 2, 1969, the United States government launched the Internet, a telecommunications superhighway, by forming teams of scientists to research computer networking. The Internet's original goal was to keep military communications open during war. **Ask:** What special type of photograph is shown? *(a satellite photograph)*

Linking PAST & PRESENT

Activity Have students work in small groups to create a time line detailing the history of communications technology, starting with the invention of the telegraph in 1844 and ending with computer-based communication today.

Block Schedule

Team Teaching This selection from *Barrio Boy* may be implemented in a team-teaching context, in conjunction with English/Language Arts.

Reinforcing Vocabulary

Review the **Reader's Dictionary** terms with students to be sure they understand any unfamiliar terms.

Historical Connection

Explain to students that the word *Hispanic* first appeared as a census term as recently as 1980. Today Hispanics are the fastest growing ethnic group in the United States. The term *Hispanic* is an imposed label and is more convenient than precise. It includes Mexicans, Cubans, Puerto Ricans, Central and South Americans, and other Spanish-speaking people of many races.

Background Information

Setting The characters in this excerpt ride on a train across the border from Mexico to the United States; get a hotel in Tucson, Arizona; and take a train to Sacramento, California.

Characters The major characters in this excerpt are the author, Ernesto Galarza, and his mother. They describe their experience immigrating to the United States from Mexico.

Plot As young Galarza travels from Mexico to Sacramento, California, he describes his first impressions of America and Americans. Point out the first thing Ernesto noticed as he entered the United States from the Mexican border—how close the two countries are. The only things that look different are the American and Mexican flags.

America's Literature

Barrio Boy

by Ernesto Galarza

Like many immigrants who come continually to the United States, Ernesto Galarza (1905–1984) arrived facing the challenge of adjusting to his adopted country. This excerpt from his autobiography, Barrio Boy, *tells the story of how Galarza and his mother traveled from Mexico to Sacramento, California, to meet his uncles, Gustavo and José. His story describes common experiences of those arriving in the United States then and now.*

Read to Discover

Unable to speak English and unfamiliar with the customs in the United States, 6-year-old Galarza and his mother embarked on a new life. Their trip was a journey into another world for young Ernesto. As you read, notice what is frightening and what is amusing about moving to a new community.

Reader's Dictionary

barrio: Spanish word for "neighborhood"
Jalcocotán: a mountain village in western Mexico
mesón: Spanish word for "inn"
Mazatlán: a city on the west coast of central Mexico
Sacramento: a city in central California; the capital of the state
Tucson: a city in southeastern Arizona
centavo, tostón, peso: Mexican money; the peso is the monetary unit and contains 100 centavos; a tostón is a 50-centavo piece

In the sunny morning of the next day we walked back to the station. Our train was still there, the flats and boxcars and coaches deserted, Mexican and American soldiers walking back and forth. "Look, the American flag," my mother said. It was flying over a building near us. Down the street, beyond the depot, there was a Mexican flag on a staff. "We are in the United States. Mexico is over there."

It took further explaining to clear up certain points to my satisfaction. The North was the same place as the United States, and we had finally arrived. The Americans never drew an eagle on their flag. The red and white were the same as on ours but why they liked blue better than green was just one of those peculiar things about Americans. Where did Mexico begin? Just beyond the railway station. How far did it go? "A long way," said Doña Henriqueta, "far down the track, farther than Jalcocotán." It was the closest thing we did to saying good-bye to our country.

That evening at the mesón, José and my mother and I reread Gustavo's letter, the last we had received in Mazatlán. José was to work his way on the railroad to a place called Sacramento. My mother and I were to go to another city called Tucson and wait there until another pass and money could be obtained.

José then explained a remarkable thing about our money. Mexican centavos and tostones and pesos were good for nothing in the United States. He had already exchanged some of our Mexican currency for dollars. "Listen carefully," he told us. "You have to give two pesos for one dollar. For one tostón you get one

Additional Literary Works of the Period

You may want to refer students to the following:

Bandon, Alexandra. ***Mexican Americans.*** New York: New Discovery Books, 1993. Recent historical and first-person narrative accounts of Mexican immigrants.

Migrants to the United States. Tucson: University of Arizona Press, 1995. Artwork of Mexican Americans.

Strom, Yale. ***Quilted Landscapes: Conversations with Young Immigrants.*** New York: Simon & Schuster, 1996. Includes illustrations and maps as well as interviews with immigrant youth.

quarter. For ten centavos you get one nickel." On the table he laid out the coins in rows two for one.

. . . In Tucson we found our way to the address Gustavo had sent. It was a small hotel where the clerk spoke Spanish. He took us down a long, dark hall to a room, where I immediately began to explore the remarkable inventions of the Americans.

Young Hispanic dancers perform at a festival

Hanging from a cord attached to the middle of the ceiling there was an electric bulb, low enough for an adult to reach and turn the black switch. I realized that this was our own electric light for us to turn on and off as we pleased. I pushed a chair under it and after some instruction from my mother proceeded to create lightening in the room by turning the switch as fast as I could.

. . . Regularly we went to the hotel to ask for mail from Gustavo. Almost always there was a letter with money, but it was many weeks before we received the most important one of all, the one that had the pass and the instructions for the trip. We were to take the train to Sacramento, go to the Hotel Español and stay there until Gustavo and José came for us.

. . . And from what I saw in the coach on that long ride, the Americans were indeed different. They ate the repulsive sandwiches with relish. They put their feet, shoes and all, on the seats in front of them. When the men laughed it seemed more like a roar, and if they were close by it scared me. Doña Henriqueta frowned and admonished me. "Be careful I never hear you braying like that." Many of them kept their hats on as if they didn't know that the inside of a coach was like the inside of a house, and wearing your hat in either a sure sign of being *mal educado* [ill-mannered].

Responding to Literature

1. What does Ernesto do with the electric light switch? Why do you think he is so excited about it?
2. What observations do Ernesto and his mother make about Americans?
3. What parts of Ernesto's story are probably shared by all people coming to a new place?

Activity

Writing a Postcard Imagine that you are Ernesto writing a postcard to a friend in Mazatlán. Describe the "modern" conveniences that you have seen, and explain their functions in a comical way.

Answers to Responding to Literature

1. turned the light on and off to create "lightening" in the room; because he probably did not have electricity or electric lighting in Mexico
2. had remarkable inventions, were different, ate repulsive sandwiches, put feet up on seats, roared with laughter, wore hats inside, were rude and ill-mannered in general
3. Answers may include problems with money exchange and language, and observations of American inventions and people.

Activity Postcards should be addressed to a friend in Mazatlán and should describe "modern" conveniences and their functions in a comical way.

America's Literature

Portfolio Activity Ask students to write in their journals about a time when they found themselves in an unfamiliar place. Ask them to describe how they felt and to tell what was frightening and amusing about being in that new place.

At the Movies

Sparked by the civil rights movement, ethnic awareness and pride surged during the 1970s, 1980s, and 1990s—the time period covered in this unit. Fueled by this trend, an estimated 130 million viewers watched *Roots* on television January 23–30, 1977. Based on the best-selling book by Alex Haley, this 12-hour miniseries told the story of Haley's family history from slavery to modern times.

Curriculum Connection

CIVICS

Write the following information on the chalkboard for students to use to create a circle graph showing projected percentages of ethnic group population in the United States in the year 2050:

- Anglo American, 52 percent
- Hispanic American, 21 percent
- African American, 16 percent
- Asian American, 10 percent
- Native American, 1 percent

Discuss the concept of *minority group* and whether it can be applied to any ethnic group in 2050. Invite interested students to research current census data on ethnic populations and to create a circle graph showing current percentages. Have these students share their findings with the class. Compare current data with projected data.

Chapter 31 Planning Guide

A complete, 1-page lesson plan is provided for each section in the *Reproducible Lesson Plans* booklet.

Section Resources

Daily Objectives	Reproducible Resources	Multimedia Resources
Section 1 Nixon's Foreign Policy Describe President Nixon's foreign policy.	Reproducible Lesson Plan 31–1 Guided Reading Activity 31–1* Section Quiz 31–1* Reteaching Activity 31–1 Enrichment Activity 31–1	Section Focus Transparency 31–1 Vocabulary PuzzleMaker Chapter Challenger Interactive Review Software Testmaker ABCNews InterActive™ Communism and the Cold War
Section 2 Nixon and Watergate Summarize Nixon's domestic policies and the actions that led to his resignation.	Reproducible Lesson Plan 31–2 Guided Reading Activity 31–2* Section Quiz 31–2* Reteaching Activity 31–2 Enrichment Activity 31–2	Section Focus Transparency 31–2 Vocabulary PuzzleMaker Chapter Challenger Interactive Review Software Testmaker The Presidents: A Picture History of Our Nation Facts On File: Landmark Documents in American History
Section 3 A Time for Healing Evaluate Ford's response to controversies, foreign affairs, and economic problems.	Reproducible Lesson Plan 31–3 Guided Reading Activity 31–3* Section Quiz 31–3* Reteaching Activity 31–3 Enrichment Activity 31–3	Section Focus Transparency 31–3 Vocabulary PuzzleMaker Chapter Challenger Interactive Review Software Testmaker Facts On File: Landmark Documents in American History GTV: A Geographic Perspective on American History
Section 4 The Carter Presidency Analyze how Carter's goal to create a more informal, moral presidency affected his reelection.	Reproducible Lesson Plan 31–4 Guided Reading Activity 31–4* Section Quiz 31–4* Reteaching Activity 31–4 Enrichment Activity 31–4	Section Focus Transparency 31–4 Vocabulary PuzzleMaker Chapter Challenger Interactive Review Software Testmaker ABCNews InterActive™ Communism and the Cold War ABCNews InterActive™ Lessons of War

** Also available in Spanish*

Poster — Transparency — CD-ROM — Software
Blackline Master — Videodisc — Audiocassette — Music Program

0:00 OUT OF TIME?
Assign the Chapter 31 Digest and the corresponding Chapter Digests Audiocassettes with activities and tests.

Activity

From the Classroom of...

Sonya Weaver
Greencastle-Antrim
Middle School
Greencastle, PA

A 1970s Living History Day

Reserve the gym or another large school room to hold an open house highlighting the 1970s. Have students research topics dealing with the 1970s and set up booths in which they can re-create events and people of that era. For example, some students can role-play Nixon campaigners and distribute election materials. Another group can represent Alaskan pipeline workers, and the group next to them can act as environmental protesters. A news conference can be staged showing Nixon's resignation. Use photographs from the period to show students how to dress in character for the event. Research should include interviews with people in the community, who can be invited to attend the event. Also invite other classes to participate. Science classes, for example, could have a display explaining scientific advancements made during this time.

Block Schedule

Block scheduling differs from traditional class scheduling in the amount of time allotted to each period. The extended time frame provided by block scheduling affords you the opportunity to implement a greater number of research-oriented and activity-intense projects to motivate and involve your students. Activities that are particularly suited to use within the block scheduling framework are identified throughout this chapter by the following designation:

NATIONAL GEOGRAPHIC SOCIETY Teacher's Corner

NATIONAL GEOGRAPHIC SOCIETY PRODUCTS AVAILABLE FROM GLENCOE

To order the following products for use with this chapter, contact your local Glencoe sales representative, or call Glencoe at 1-800-334-7344:

- *GTV: A Geographic Perspective on American History* (Videodisc)
- *GTV: The American People: Fabric of a Nation* (Videodisc)
- *The Presidents: A Picture History of Our Nation* (CD-ROM)

ADDITIONAL NATIONAL GEOGRAPHIC SOCIETY PRODUCTS

To order the following products for use with this chapter, call National Geographic Society at 1-800-368-2728:

- *Branches of Government Series* (Video)
- *Democratic Government Series: The United States* (Video)
- *Historical Atlas of the United States* (Atlas)

KEY TO ABILITY LEVELS

Teaching strategies have been coded for varying learning styles and abilities.

L1 **BASIC** activities for all students
L2 **AVERAGE** activities for average to above-average students
L3 **CHALLENGING** activities for above-average students
ELL **ENGLISH LANGUAGE LEARNER** activities

Chapter 31 Resource Guide

Home Involvement

Home Involvement Activity 31

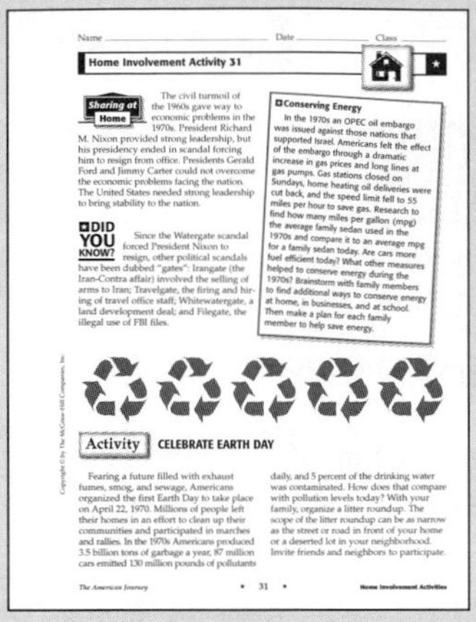

Review Activities

Chapter Summary 31

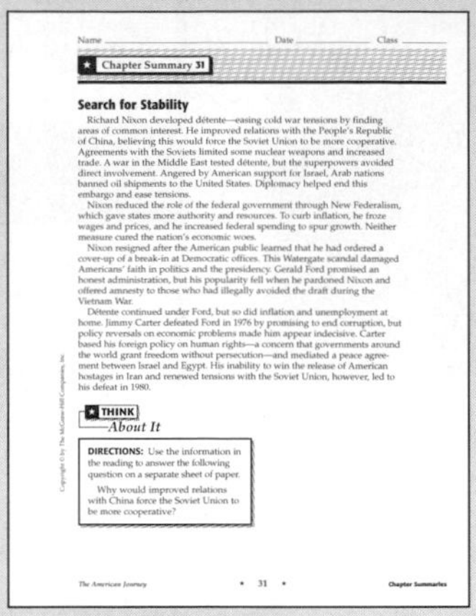

Workbook Activity 31

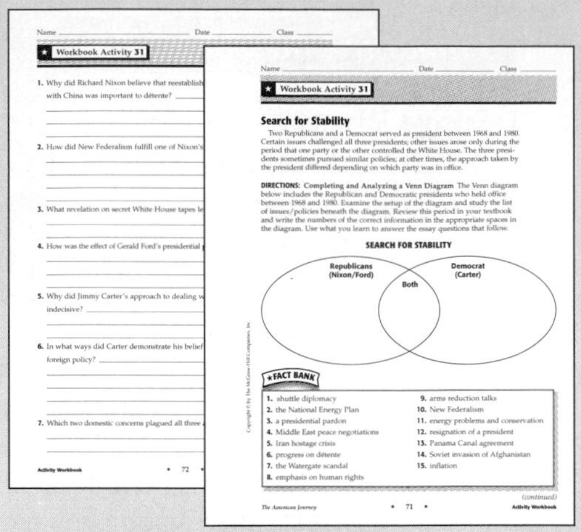

Reinforcement Activities

Time Line Activity 31

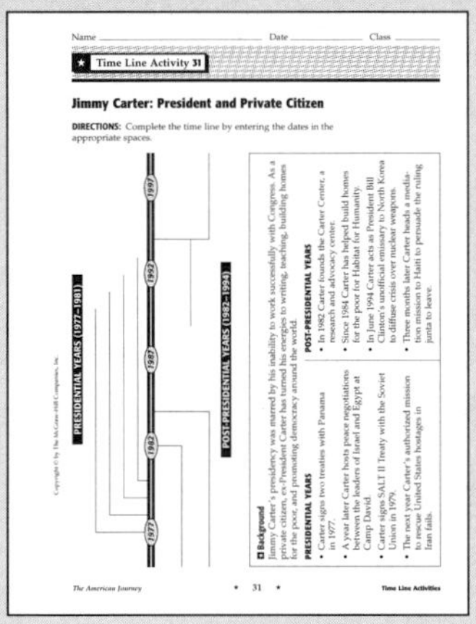

Vocabulary Activity 31

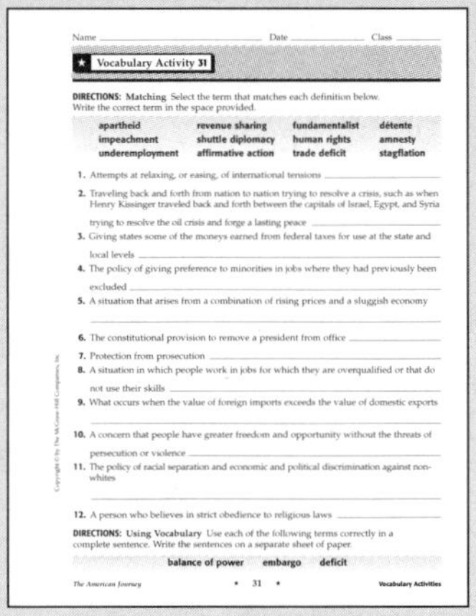

Chapter Skills Activity 31

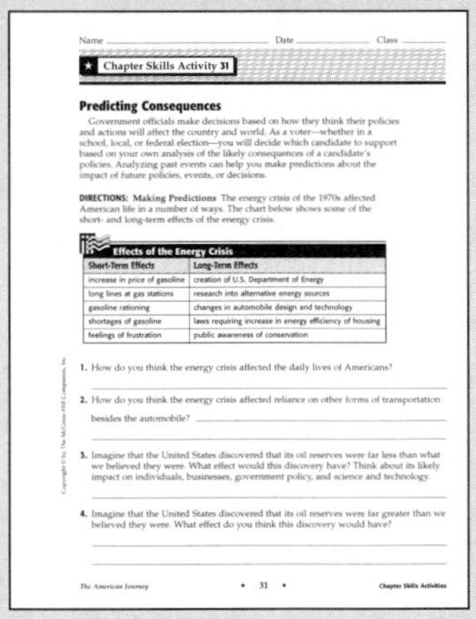

Enrichment Activities

Linking Past and Present Activity 31

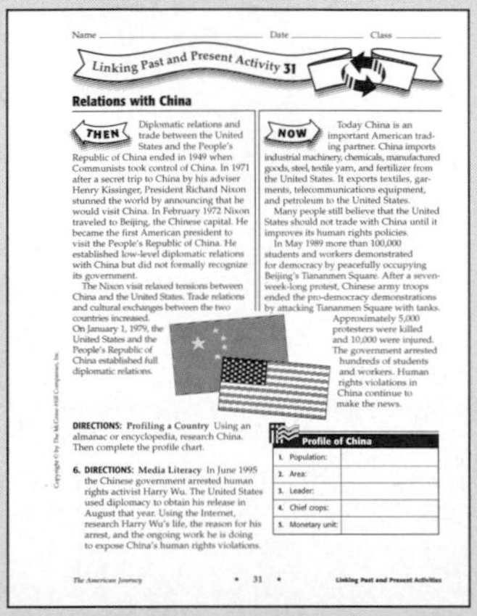

Primary Source Reading 31

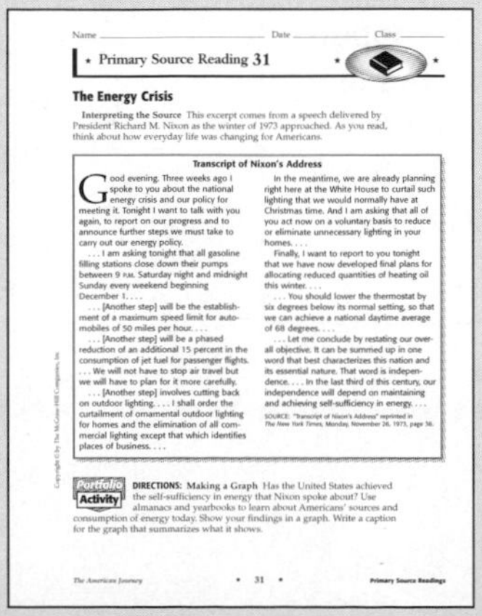

Geography Activities

Mapping History Activity 31

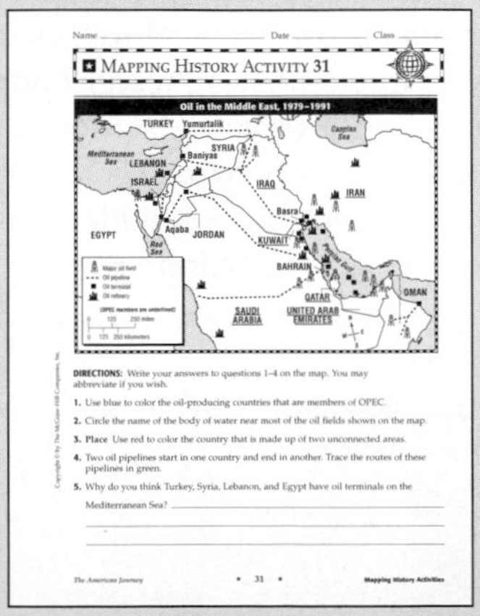

Assessment

Chapter 31 Test, Form A

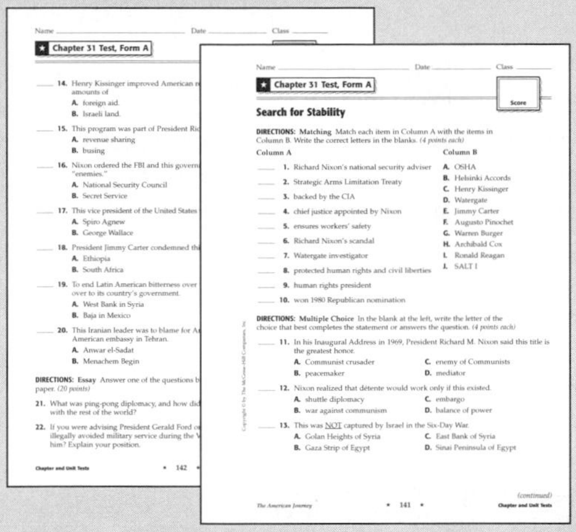

Chapter 31 Test, Form B

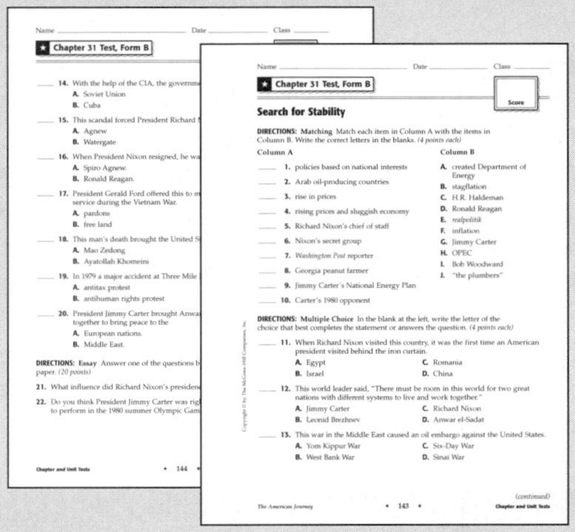

Performance Assessment Activity 31

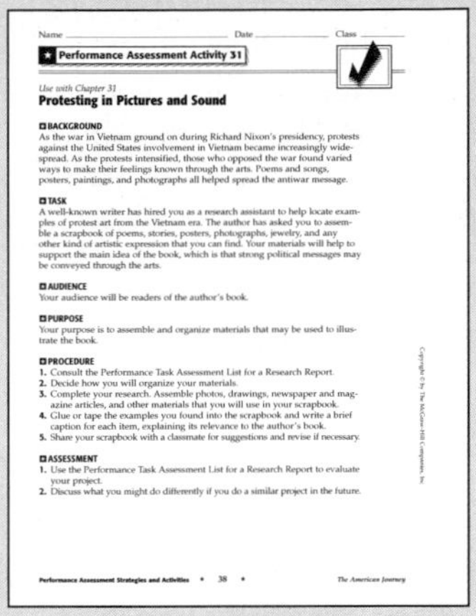

Spanish Resources

The following Spanish language materials are available in the Spanish Resources binder:

- **Spanish Chapter Summary 31**
- **Spanish Vocabulary Activity 31**
- **Spanish Guided Reading Activities, Chapter 31**
- **Spanish Section Quizzes, Chapter 31**
- **Spanish Home Involvement Activity 31**
- **Spanish Chapter 31 Digests Audiocassette Activity and Test**

Activity Manipulatives

Help students learn more about America's cultural history with:

- **American Crafts Hands-On Activities**
- **American Games Hands-On Activities**
- **American History Flash Cards**

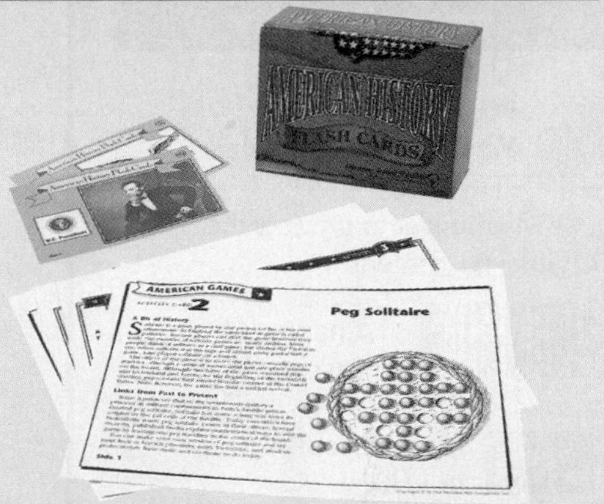

Additional Resources From Glencoe

- **The American History Videodisc and CD-ROM,** *Contemporary America, 1960–1990s*
- **U.S. Desk Map**
- **Outline Map Resource Book**

A&E HOME VIDEO. Biography THE HISTORY CHANNEL.

The following videotape programs are available from Glencoe as supplements to Chapter 31:

- **Richard Nixon: Man and President** (ISBN 1-56501-742-0)
- **Jimmy Carter** (ISBN 1-56501-530-4)

To order, call Glencoe at 1-800-334-7344. To find classroom resources to accompany many of these videos, check the following home pages:
A&E Television: http://www.aetv.com
The History Channel: http://www.historychannel.com

Chapter Themes

Chapter Themes are listed by section on this chapter opening page of the Student Edition. A corresponding theme-based activity is available under "FOCUS," and a theme-based question is asked in the Section and Chapter Reviews.

Performance Assessment

Refer to Activity 31 in the *Performance Assessment Strategies and Activities* booklet.

GLENCOE TECHNOLOGY

VIDEODISC
MindJogger Videoquiz

Use MindJogger to preview the Chapter 31 content.

Chapter 31
Disc 4, Side B

Also available in VHS.

HISTORY AND ART As part of the Bicentennial celebration, tall ships sailed into New York harbor from around the world. Tall ships signify inventors' finest efforts in mastering and utilizing the forces of nature.

Chapter 31

1968–1981

Search for Stability

Why It's Important

During the 1960s and 1970s, the American people's view of the nation and the government changed. Some believed that the United States had lost its position as the economic and political leader of the free world. Many grew distrustful of politics and political leaders. Today many Americans continue to express doubts about the political system. Mistrust of politicians, especially "Washington insiders," has reduced voter turnout in elections. It has also spurred the creation of political movements outside the two major parties.

Chapter Themes

- *Section 1,* Global Connections
- *Section 2,* Economic Factors
- *Section 3,* Continuity and Change
- *Section 4,* Civic Rights and Responsibilities

HISTORY AND ART ***America's Bicentennial, 1976*** On July 4, 1976, Americans celebrated the Bicentennial, the nation's 200th birthday. These Bicentennial fireworks explode over New York Harbor and the Statue of Liberty.

880

EXTRA CREDIT PROJECT

Creating a Photo Album Invite interested students to create a photo album of the key players of the Watergate break-in and cover-up. Explain to students that instead of using photographs for their albums, they should draw caricatures of each person involved in Watergate. Instruct students to place caricatures in the album in the order in which their originals are mentioned in the chapter and to create a cover for their albums.

1970 — 1972 — 1974

April 1971
American ping-pong team visits Communist China

February 1972
President Nixon visits Beijing

May 1972
Nixon and Brezhnev sign the first Strategic Arms Limitation Treaty

October 1973
Arab countries impose oil embargo on the U.S.

Section 1

Nixon's Foreign Policy

READ TO DISCOVER . . .
- how Nixon attempted to ease cold war tensions.
- what policies the United States pursued in the Middle East and Latin America.

TERMS TO LEARN

détente
balance of power
embargo
shuttle diplomacy

The Storyteller

To improve relations with the Communist world, President Richard Nixon made a historic visit to China in February 1972. Nixon later described how he felt upon his arrival in Beijing, the Chinese capital: ". . . 'The Star Spangled Banner' had never sounded so stirring to me as on that windswept runway in the heart of Communist China. . . . As we left the airport, [Chinese leader Chou En-lai] said, 'Your handshake came over the vastest ocean in the world—twenty-five years of no communication.' "

1972 button

In his Inaugural Address on January 20, 1969, President Richard M. Nixon told the American people, "The greatest honor . . . is the title of peacemaker." Many Americans wondered whether Nixon fit the role of peacemaker. During his years in Congress, he had gained a reputation as a fierce enemy of communism. Few people imagined that Nixon, the anti-Communist crusader, would introduce policies to improve America's relations with the Communist world.

Easing the Cold War

President Nixon intended to leave his mark on foreign policy. He hoped to build a more stable, peaceful world by reaching out to the Soviet Union and the People's Republic of China. In the summer of 1969, Nixon visited several countries, including Romania—the first time an American president had gone behind the iron curtain. Nixon wanted to find areas of common interest and cooperation with these cold war opponents.

Changes in Foreign Policy

To help him in this ambitious task, Nixon appointed **Henry Kissinger,** a Harvard University professor, as his national security adviser. Kissinger and Nixon shared a belief in *realpolitik*—policies based on national interests rather than political ideology. They believed that peace among nations would come through negotiation rather than through threats or force.

CHAPTER 31
Section 1, 881–885

1 FOCUS

BELLRINGER
Motivational Activity

Before taking roll at the beginning of the class period, project Section Focus Transparency 31–1 and have students answer the questions. Discuss students' responses.

This activity is also available as a blackline master.

Section Focus Transparency 31–1

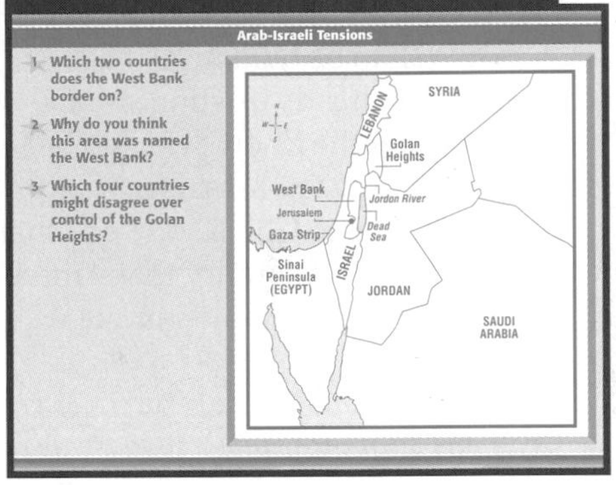

Vocabulary Precheck
Have pairs of students look up the **Terms to Learn** in the textbook glossary. Then have them restate each definition in their own words.

Use the **Vocabulary PuzzleMaker** to create crossword and word search puzzles.

Section Theme
Global Connections
President Richard Nixon introduced foreign policies that improved America's relations with the Communist world.

Activity Review with students the effects of the Red Scare. Discuss why it took someone like Richard Nixon, an ardent anti-Communist, to mend relations between the United States and Communist countries.

SECTION RESOURCES

Reproducible Masters
- Reproducible Lesson Plan 31–1
- Guided Reading Activity 31–1
- Section Quiz 31–1
- Reteaching Activity 31–1
- Enrichment Activity 31–1

Transparencies
- Section Focus Transparency 31–1

Multimedia
- Vocabulary PuzzleMaker
- Chapter Challenger Interactive Review Software
- Testmaker
- ABCNews InterActive™ Communism and the Cold War

2 TEACH

L1 Creating a Time Line Assign students to work in small groups to create poster-size, illustrated time lines of the Nixon administration's foreign policy events. Discuss the events on the completed time lines and how each event served as a building block for other events.

Picturing HISTORY Built mainly of earth and stone, the Great Wall stretches 1,400 miles (2,253 km). Emperor Qin Shihuangdi Ti ordered additional sections of the Great Wall to be built in 221–206 B.C. to connect already existing sections built during the Zhou dynasty. Television coverage of Kissinger's and Nixon's visits to China showed what life was like in a country that Americans previously had little or no knowledge about.
Answer: *Nixon wanted to forge closer relations with the Chinese to make the Soviets more cooperative.*

Guided Reading Activity 31–1

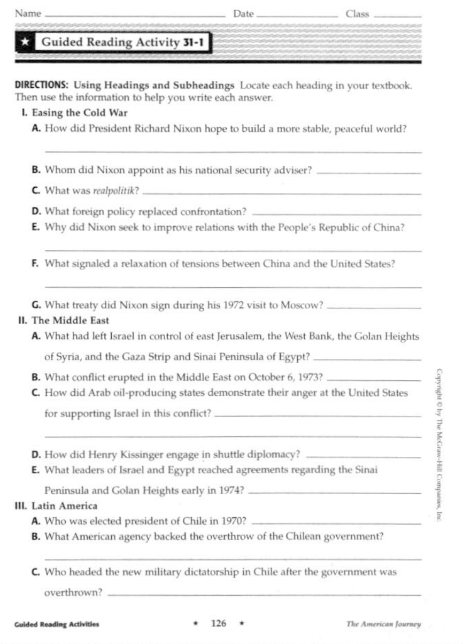

Name ______ Date ______ Class ______

★ Guided Reading Activity 31-1

DIRECTIONS: Using Headings and Subheadings Locate each heading in your textbook. Then use the information to help you write each answer.

I. Easing the Cold War

A. How did President Richard Nixon hope to build a more stable, peaceful world? ______

B. Whom did Nixon appoint as his national security adviser? ______

C. What was *realpolitik*? ______

D. What foreign policy replaced confrontation? ______

E. Why did Nixon seek to improve relations with the People's Republic of China? ______

F. What signaled a relaxation of tensions between China and the United States? ______

G. What treaty did Nixon sign during his 1972 visit to Moscow? ______

II. The Middle East

A. What had left Israel in control of east Jerusalem, the West Bank, the Golan Heights of Syria, and the Gaza Strip and Sinai Peninsula of Egypt? ______

B. What conflict erupted in the Middle East on October 6, 1973? ______

C. How did Arab oil-producing states demonstrate their anger at the United States for supporting Israel in this conflict? ______

D. How did Henry Kissinger engage in shuttle diplomacy? ______

E. What leaders of Israel and Egypt reached agreements regarding the Sinai Peninsula and Golan Heights early in 1974? ______

III. Latin America

A. Who was elected president of Chile in 1970? ______

B. What American agency backed the overthrow of the Chilean government? ______

C. Who headed the new military dictatorship in Chile after the government was overthrown? ______

Guided Reading Activities • 126 • *The American Journey*

Picturing HISTORY Secretary of State Henry Kissinger (center) and Chinese officials walk across part of the Great Wall, one of China's historic structures. **Why did President Nixon seek to improve relations with China?**

Détente

President Nixon formulated a foreign policy plan of **détente**—attempts at relaxing, or easing, international tensions. As détente replaced confrontation, the United States and Communist states could begin working together to resolve issues that divided them.

Nixon realized that détente would work only if a **balance of power** existed. A balance of power is a distribution of power among nations to prevent any one nation from becoming too powerful. "It will be a safer world and a better world," he declared, "if we have a strong, healthy United States, Europe, Soviet Union, China, Japan—each balancing the other, not playing one against the other."

China

The **People's Republic of China** played a key role in Nixon's plan for achieving a balance of power. Diplomatic relations and trade between the United States and China had been severed after the Communists took control of mainland China in 1949.

If the United States could improve relations with the People's Republic, Nixon reasoned, the Soviets might become more cooperative. Nixon knew that the Soviets would fear a Chinese-American alliance.

In the fall of 1970, Nixon hinted at a new China policy. "If there is anything I want to do before I die," he told a reporter, "it is to go to China." He also stopped referring to China as "Red China," a negative term used by U.S. presidents since Truman. Noting this change in tone, the Chinese responded by inviting an American table-tennis team to visit the country in April 1971. A week later the United States announced the opening of trade with China.

"Ping-pong diplomacy" was accompanied by secret talks between U.S. and Chinese officials about forging closer ties between the two nations. After Kissinger made a secret trip to China in June 1971, President Nixon announced that he would visit **Beijing,** the Chinese capital, "to seek the normalization of relations."

Accompanied by his wife, Pat, government officials, and reporters, Nixon arrived in Beijing in February 1972. "While we cannot close the gulf between us," Nixon told the Chinese leaders, "we can try to bridge it so that we may be able to talk across it." Pictures of the American president visiting the Great Wall of China and toasting Chinese Communist leaders at lavish banquets made news all over the world.

Another seven years passed, however, before China and the United States established full diplomatic relations. In the meantime, trade

Footnotes to History

No More Red The term *Red,* referring to communism, came from the main color in the Communist flag–red.

COOPERATIVE LEARNING ACTIVITY

Analyzing Foreign Policy Organize students into small groups to review Nixon's foreign policy. Have students in each group read the section to review Nixon's contributions and setbacks in foreign policy. Ask them to take notes as they read. Then have students meet in their groups to create a chart based on the information in their notes and on their reading. Have each group select a spokesperson to report the group's analysis.

relations and cultural exchanges between the two countries increased. The Nixon visit signaled a relaxation of tensions between China and the United States.

The Soviet Union

Nixon followed his history-making trip to China with a visit to **Moscow,** the Soviet capital, in May 1972. The Soviets eagerly welcomed the thaw in cold-war politics. They wanted to prevent a Chinese-American alliance and to slow the costly arms race. They also hoped to gain access to United States technology and to buy badly needed American grain. Soviet leader **Leonid Brezhnev** remarked, "There must be room in this world for two great nations with different systems to live together and work together."

Pictures of Nixon in Moscow, talking and smiling with Brezhnev in the halls of the Kremlin, gave the impression of a new era in Soviet-American relations. While in Moscow, President Nixon signed the Strategic Arms Limitation Treaty, or **SALT I.** This landmark treaty, the result of talks begun in 1969, restricted the number of certain types of nuclear missiles in U.S. and Soviet arsenals. Although SALT I did not end the arms race, it greatly reduced tensions between the United States and the Soviet Union.

The United States and the Soviet Union also agreed to work together in trade and science. Nixon—and the world—hoped that a new era of cooperation between the United States and the Soviet Union would bring greater stability to world affairs.

Picturing HISTORY Soviet leader Brezhnev and President Nixon sign the SALT I agreement during Nixon's visit to Moscow in 1972. **What was the goal of the SALT I treaty?**

Linking PAST & PRESENT

China's Leaders

China under Mao Zedong underwent dramatic changes. After Mao's death in 1976, new Communist leaders, led by Deng Xiaoping, allowed Western-style economic reforms while maintaining tight political control over the country. With Deng's death in 1997 came political change. A group of leaders—rather than one individual like Mao or Deng—is expected to hold governing authority.

The Middle East

President Nixon's foreign policy aimed to maintain world stability without being drawn into regional disputes. The president wanted to avoid any involvement that might lead to another situation like Vietnam. Nixon stated that the United States would help in "the defense and development of allies and friends" but not take "basic responsibility" for the future of those nations. A crisis soon arose in the Middle East that tested this policy.

Arab-Israeli Tensions

Since the founding of the Jewish state of Israel in 1948, the United States had supported Israel in its struggles against its Arab neighbors. Tensions between Israel and the Arab states had erupted in war in 1948, 1956, and 1967. The Six-Day War of 1967 left Israel in control of east Jerusalem, the **West Bank**, the **Golan Heights** of Syria, and the

CURRICULUM CONNECTION

Biology In 1972, as a gesture to normalize relations between the two countries, China gave two giant pandas to the United States. These two pandas, named Ling-Ling (the female) and Hsing-Hsing (the male), were placed in the National Zoological Park in Washington, D.C. Giant pandas live in bamboo forests on upper mountain slopes of western and southwestern China. They are rare and protected by law in China. The female panda twice gave birth to cubs, but each cub died shortly after birth.

Picturing HISTORY SALT culminated with a May 1972 Moscow summit. In addition to signing the SALT agreement, Nixon and Brezhnev also agreed to increase trade, exchange scientific information, and cooperate in preventing pollution.
Answer: *to restrict the number of certain types of nuclear missiles in American and Soviet arsenals*

ABCNEWS INTERACTIVE™

VIDEODISC
Communism and the Cold War

Side 1, Chapter 20
Title: *Détente*
Subject: Overview of détente between the United States and the Soviet Union
Ask: Why did it suddenly seem necessary to end the arms race in the early 1970s? *(Both sides had enough weapons to destroy the other several times.)*

Side 2, Chapter 10
Title: *Middle East*
Subject: The U.S. decision to assist Israel in the 1973 Yom Kippur War
Ask: How did the Yom Kippur War almost become a war between the U.S. and U.S.S.R.? *(The countries represented different sides in the war, and there was the risk of nuclear war between the superpowers.)*

Picturing HISTORY For 20 years after the 1967 war, Arabs and Israelis could not agree on the future of the Israeli-occupied territories. Since the early 1990s, the Israelis and Palestinians (PLO) have recognized each other and agreed to eventual self-government for Palestinians in the West Bank and Gaza Strip. In January 1996, the Palestinians chose Yassar Arafat as their first president.
Answer: *Egypt and Syria attempted to regain territory lost during the Six-Day War.*

3 ASSESS

Assign Section 1 Review as homework or as an in-class activity.

Use **Chapter Challenger Interactive Review Software** to review Section 1.

Section Quiz 31–1

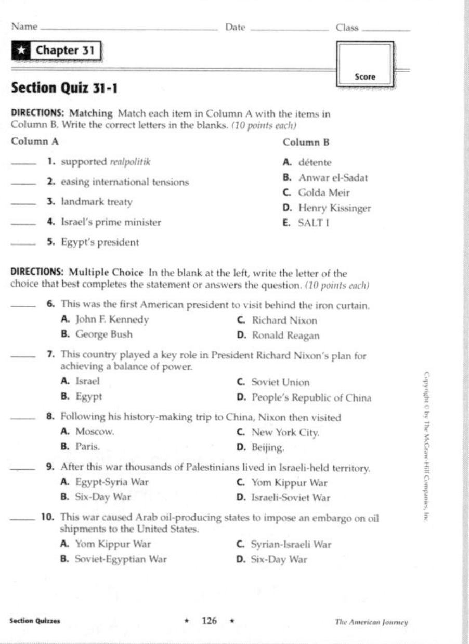
Name ______ Date ______ Class ______

★ Chapter 31

Score

Section Quiz 31-1

DIRECTIONS: Matching Match each item in Column A with the items in Column B. Write the correct letters in the blanks. *(10 points each)*

Column A	Column B
____ 1. supported *realpolitik*	A. détente
____ 2. easing international tensions	B. Anwar el-Sadat
____ 3. landmark treaty	C. Golda Meir
____ 4. Israel's prime minister	D. Henry Kissinger
____ 5. Egypt's president	E. SALT I

DIRECTIONS: Multiple Choice In the blank at the left, write the letter of the choice that best completes the statement or answers the question. *(10 points each)*

____ 6. This was the first American president to visit behind the iron curtain.
A. John F. Kennedy C. Richard Nixon
B. George Bush D. Ronald Reagan

____ 7. This country played a key role in President Richard Nixon's plan for achieving a balance of power.
A. Israel C. Soviet Union
B. Egypt D. People's Republic of China

____ 8. Following his history-making trip to China, Nixon then visited
A. Moscow. C. New York City.
B. Paris. D. Beijing.

____ 9. After this war thousands of Palestinians lived in Israeli-held territory.
A. Egypt-Syria War C. Yom Kippur War
B. Six-Day War D. Israeli-Soviet War

____ 10. This war caused Arab oil-producing states to impose an embargo on oil shipments to the United States.
A. Yom Kippur War C. Syrian-Israeli War
B. Soviet-Egyptian War D. Six-Day War

Copyright © by The McGraw-Hill Companies, Inc.

Section Quizzes ★ 126 ★ *The American Journey*

Picturing HISTORY Many Palestinians lived in exile, scattered throughout the Middle East, North Africa, and Europe. **What was the cause of the Yom Kippur War?**

Gaza Strip and **Sinai Peninsula** of Egypt. The 1967 war also increased the number of Arab refugees. Thousands of Palestinians now lived in Israeli-held territory, and thousands more lived in neighboring Arab states. The Palestinians' demand for their own homeland became another source of instability in the region.

Yom Kippur War

War erupted again on October 6, 1973. Egypt and Syria attacked Israel in an attempt to regain territory lost in the Six-Day War. Because the attack occurred on Yom Kippur, a major Jewish holiday, the conflict became known as the **Yom Kippur War.**

Caught off guard, the Israelis struggled at first to stop the Arab advance before launching a counteroffensive. The United States helped by rushing ammunition to Israel. Meanwhile, the Soviets supplied arms to Egypt and Syria.

The war tested the United States–Soviet détente. The Soviet Union threatened to send airborne troops to the Middle East. The United States responded by putting its nuclear forces on global alert for the first time since the Cuban missile crisis in 1962. Both sides backed down.

In the end the United States pressured Israel to accept a cease-fire. But not before the Israelis had regained most of the territory lost in the initial Arab advance and had taken additional territory from Syria and Egypt.

Angry at the United States for supporting Israel, Arab oil-producing states imposed an **embargo**—a ban on shipments—of oil to the United States and to other nations not seen as "friendly." The embargo caused an oil shortage in the United States. Long lines of cars formed at gas pumps, and Americans became angry as gas prices skyrocketed.

Shuttle Diplomacy

President Nixon sent Kissinger, now secretary of state, to the region to gain the trust of Arab leaders and to negotiate some type of agreement

MAKING CONNECTIONS ACTIVITY

Yom Kippur Explain to students that Yom Kippur, or the Day of Atonement, is the last of the Ten Days of Penitence in the Jewish religion. Like Rosh Hashanah, it is one of the two High Holydays of Judaism. This day is marked by 24 hours of prayer and fasting. On the eve of this day as the sun sets, the family gathers for a festive meal. The family lights candles, and members ask forgiveness of one another for the wrongs they have committed so they can enter the sacred day with a clean slate. Have students write an essay explaining why the Arabs—in the Yom Kippur War—would attack the Israelis on this particular day. Ask volunteers to read their essays to the class. **L2**

between Israel and its Arab neighbors. During the next two years, Kissinger engaged in **shuttle diplomacy**—traveling back and forth between the capitals of Israel, Egypt, and Syria trying to resolve the oil crisis and forge a lasting peace.

Early in 1974, **Golda Meir,** the prime minister of Israel, and **Anwar el-Sadat,** the president of Egypt, reached agreements that separated Israeli and Arab forces in the Sinai Peninsula and Golan Heights. Then in March 1974, Kissinger persuaded the Arab nations to end the oil embargo. Kissinger also improved U.S. relations with Egypt, the largest and most powerful Arab state, by promising large amounts of foreign aid.

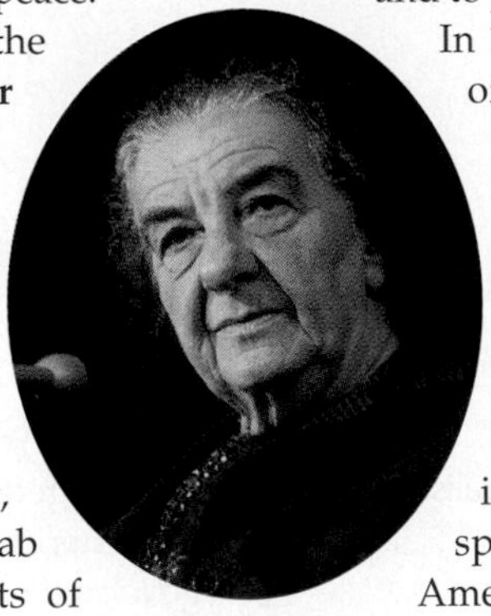

Golda Meir

Latin America

The Nixon administration sought to protect U.S. interests in Latin America and to prevent the spread of communism. In 1970 the South American country of **Chile** elected **Salvador Allende** president. Allende was a follower of **Karl Marx,** the founder of communism. When the new Chilean government took over U.S. businesses in Chile, the United States protested. Nixon and his foreign-policy advisers feared an increase in Soviet influence in Chile and the spread of communism in Latin America.

With the backing of the CIA (Central Intelligence Agency), a small group of Chilean military leaders under General **Augusto Pinochet** overthrew the government and killed Allende. The United States immediately recognized the new military dictatorship and restored foreign aid to Chile.

The situation in Chile reflected another aspect of Nixon's foreign policy. Although willing to pursue détente with China and the Soviet Union, the president was still determined to contain the spread of communism—and Soviet influence—in the world.

Footnotes to History

Young Leader Golda Meir showed remarkable leadership while growing up in Milwaukee, Wisconsin. Realizing that many of the students in her school could not afford the fees for books, Meir rented a large hall for a fund-raiser featuring refreshments and speeches. Eleven-year-old Golda herself presented the main speech.

Section 1 Review

Checking for Understanding

1. ***Identify*** Henry Kissinger, Leonid Brezhnev, SALT I, Yom Kippur War, Golda Meir, Anwar el-Sadat, Salvador Allende.
2. ***Define*** détente, balance of power, embargo, shuttle diplomacy.
3. ***Summarize*** Nixon's main foreign policy goal.

Reviewing Themes

4. **Global Connections** Why did Nixon think that improving relations with China would make the Soviet Union more cooperative?

Critical Thinking

5. **Identifying Central Issues** How did Nixon show that he was still devoted to containing the spread of communism?

Activity

Studying Current Events Find a newspaper article that discusses the Israeli-Arab relationship today and compare it to the relationship that existed in the 1960s and 1970s.

CHAPTER 31
Section 1, 881–885

Reteaching Activity 31–1

Name ________ Date ________ Class ________

★ Reteaching Activity 31-1

DIRECTIONS: Recognizing Supporting Details Each main idea is related to the topic given. Complete the chart by writing the letter of the items from the Fact Bank that support each main idea.

Topic: President Nixon's foreign policy reflected his commitment to building a more stable, peaceful world while containing the spread of communism.

1. **Main Idea:** Richard Nixon sought to ease tensions among nations by changing foreign policy.
Supporting Details: ________
2. **Main Idea:** Nixon hoped to improve relations with the People's Republic of China and the Soviet Union.
Supporting Details: ________
3. **Main Idea:** The Yom Kippur War tested Nixon's resolve to avoid American involvement in regional disputes.
Supporting Details: ________
4. **Main Idea:** Nixon aimed to protect American interests in Latin America while halting the spread of communism there.
Supporting Details: ________

★FACT BANK

A. The United States put its nuclear forces on global alert when the Soviet Union threatened to send airborne troops to the Middle East.
B. "Ping-pong diplomacy" was accompanied by secret talks.
C. The United States protested when the Chilean government took over American businesses in Chile.
D. Nixon went to Beijing "to seek the normalization of relations."
E. Nixon formulated a policy plan of détente.
F. The United States rushed ammunition to Israel.
G. Nixon strove to achieve a balance of power among nations.
H. The CIA backed Augusto Pinochet in the overthrow of Salvador Allende.
I. Nixon appointed Henry Kissinger as his national security adviser.
J. Kissinger engaged in shuttle diplomacy.
K. Nixon visited Moscow and signed SALT I.
L. Nixon stopped referring to China as "Red China."

Reteaching Activities ★ 126 ★ *The American Journey*

Enrichment Activity 31–1

Name ________ Date ________ Class ________

★ Enrichment Activity 31-1 ★ ★

Foreign Oil

Every year the United States imports large amounts of petroleum from members of the Organization of Petroleum Exporting Countries (OPEC). When relations with countries are strained, as they were in 1973, imports can decrease considerably. Study the table that shows United States net imports of petroleum (imports minus exports) for 1973–1983.

United States Net Imports of Petroleum, 1973–1983

	Average Annual Rate In Thousands of Barrels per Day		
Year	**From Arab OPEC***	**From OPEC****	**From All Countries**
1973	914	2,991	6,025
1974	752	3,277	5,892
1975	1,382	3,599	5,846
1976	2,423	5,063	7,090
1977	3,184	6,190	8,565
1978	2,962	5,747	8,002
1979	3,054	5,633	7,985
1980	2,549	4,293	6,365
1981	1,844	3,315	5,401
1982	852	2,136	4,298
1983	630	1,843	4,312

*Arab OPEC members include Algeria, Iraq, Kuwait, Libya, Qatar, Saudi Arabia, and United Arab Emirates.
**OPEC members include Arab OPEC countries and Gabon, Indonesia, Iran, Nigeria, and Venezuela.

DIRECTIONS: Reading a Table Use the table to answer the following questions.

1. List the two years imports from Arab OPEC countries were lowest. ________
2. Each day how many thousands of barrels of oil imported from OPEC countries in 1977 were from the so-called non-Arab OPEC countries? ________
3. Each day how many barrels of oil were imported from non-OPEC countries in 1973 and in 1983? ________
4. About what percentage of the total oil imports for 1978 came from Arab OPEC countries? ________
5. What was the total for imported oil from Arab OPEC countries during the entire year of 1979? ________

Activity **DIRECTIONS:** Pick one of the years from the chart above and use the information to make a circle graph for that year. Your graph should have the following segments: imports from Arab OPEC countries, imports from other OPEC countries, and imports from non-OPEC countries.

Enrichment Activities ★ 126 ★ *The American Journey*

Section 1 Review Answers

1. Henry Kissinger, 881; Leonid Brezhnev, 883; SALT I, 883; Yom Kippur War, 884; Golda Meir, 885; Anwar el-Sadat, 885; Salvador Allende, 885
2. The words are defined in the Glossary.
3. to stabilize relations with the Soviet Union and China
4. He knew the Soviets would fear a Chinese-American alliance.
5. With the backing of the CIA, Chilean military leaders overthrew the Chilean government and killed the Communist Chilean leader. The United States then recognized the new military dictatorship and restored aid to Chile.

Activity Students should find a newspaper article about the current Israeli-Arab relationship and compare it to the relationship that existed in the 1960s and 1970s.

4 CLOSE

Ask students to review the time lines they created in the *TEACH* activity and choose the most and least successful events. Ask volunteers to explain their choices.

1 FOCUS

BELLRINGER
Motivational Activity

Before taking roll at the beginning of the class period, project Section Focus Transparency 31–2 and have students answer the questions. Discuss students' responses.

This activity is also available as a blackline master.

Section Focus Transparency 31–2

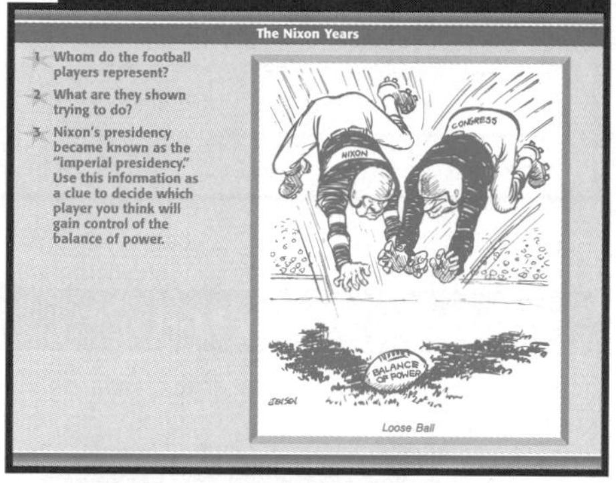

Vocabulary Precheck

Discuss the definitions of *stagnation* and *inflation*. Tell students that these two terms form the term *stagflation*.

Use the **Vocabulary PuzzleMaker** to create crossword and word search puzzles.

Section Theme
Economic Factors

President Nixon called for a reduction in federal spending and the federal government's involvement in people's lives. At the same time he had to deal with serious economic problems that required the federal government's attention.

Activity Brainstorm with students how much impact a president actually has on the economy. Discuss why the economy has such a great effect on voters' choices of presidential candidates.

1972 — 1973 — 1974

June 1972 Break-in at Watergate occurs

November 1972 Nixon wins reelection

1973 OPEC oil embargo reduces U.S. supplies

August 1974 Nixon resigns the presidency

Section 2

Nixon and Watergate

READ TO DISCOVER . . .
- why Nixon called for a "New Federalism."
- how Nixon dealt with the nation's economic problems.
- how the Watergate scandal affected the nation.

TERMS TO LEARN
revenue sharing
affirmative action
stagflation
deficit
impeachment

The Storyteller

President Nixon had grave concerns about the state of American society. "We live in a deeply troubled and profoundly unsettled time. Drugs, crime, campus revolts, racial discord, draft resistance—on every hand we find old standards violated, old values discarded." Nixon believed that a "silent majority" of middle-class Americans shared his concerns about increasing crime and social disorder. In an ironic twist of events, however, the Nixon administration itself would get caught up in a web of illegal activities.

1968 Republican campaign button

In his 1968 presidential campaign, Nixon had pledged to bring "law and order" back to American society. He also vowed to reduce government's role in people's lives.

Domestic Goals

Nixon's drive to restore law and order involved "cracking down on crime" and imposing stiffer penalties on lawbreakers. To strengthen the power of the police Nixon used federal funds to help state and city police forces.

The Courts

Nixon thought the federal courts should be tougher on criminals. "As a judicial conservative," he said, "I believe some Court decisions have gone too far in weakening the peace forces against the criminal forces in our society." During his presidency, four vacancies arose on the Supreme Court. Nixon hoped that the justices he appointed—**Warren Burger** as chief justice, and **Harry Blackmun, Lewis Powell,** and **William Rehnquist**—would shift the Court to a more conservative position. The decisions of the new justices did not fully meet the president's conservative goals, however.

New Federalism

Nixon wanted to reduce federal involvement in people's lives and to cut federal spending. He pledged to "reverse the flow of power and resources from the states and communities to

SECTION RESOURCES

Reproducible Masters
- Reproducible Lesson Plan 31–2
- Guided Reading Activity 31–2
- Section Quiz 31–2
- Reteaching Activity 31–2
- Enrichment Activity 31–2

Transparencies
- Section Focus Transparency 31–2

Multimedia
- Vocabulary PuzzleMaker
- Chapter Challenger Interactive Review Software
- Testmaker
- The Presidents: A Picture History of Our Nation
- Facts On File: Landmark Documents in American History

Washington and start power and resources flowing back . . . to the people." To accomplish this goal, he introduced a program called the **New Federalism.**

One part of the New Federalism called for giving the states some of the revenue earned from federal taxes for use at the state and local levels. This **revenue sharing** became law in 1972.

Nixon also sought to end or scale back many Great Society programs begun under President Johnson. He promised to "quit pouring billions of dollars into programs that have failed." He abolished the Office of Economic Opportunity, the agency that had led Johnson's War on Poverty.

On civil rights issues, Nixon took a conservative position aimed at appealing to white voters. For example, Nixon opposed **busing.** Busing was used to promote racial integration by transporting students from mostly white or African American neighborhoods to racially mixed schools. At the same time, however, his administration worked to carry out federal court orders to integrate schools. The Nixon administration also promoted **affirmative action,** or preference to minorities in jobs where they had previously been excluded.

A practical politician, President Nixon did accept new government programs that had popular support. He approved the creation of two new agencies—the **Occupational Safety and Health Administration** (OSHA) to ensure workers' safety and the **Environmental Protection Agency** (EPA) to protect the environment.

$ Economics

Economic Problems

While attempting to change the direction of government, President Nixon had to deal with serious economic problems. Industry and manufacturing were declining because of foreign competition. Businesses and consumers struggled with **inflation**—a general rise in the prices of goods and services—fueled by international competition for raw materials and the increasing cost of oil. The United States also faced slow economic growth and high unemployment.

Seeking Economic Stability

President Nixon tried a number of approaches to reduce inflation. He began by cutting federal spending. At the same time, he called for a **tight money policy.** Interest rates were raised so that people would borrow less and spend less. With less money in circulation, prices dropped. However, as demand slowed, business began to cut back and output fell. These steps slowed economic growth and brought on **stagflation**—a combination of rising prices and a sluggish economy.

Nixon then switched tactics. He temporarily froze wages and prices and issued guidelines for any future increases. This put a brake on inflation, but the economy remained in a recession.

Late in 1971, Nixon tried a third approach—increasing federal spending to stimulate the economy. Although this policy helped revive the economy for a short time, it also created a budget

Picturing HISTORY This cartoon reflects how the value of the American dollar declined during the early 1970s. **What other economic problems did Americans face during this period?**

CHAPTER 31
Section 2, 886–891

2 TEACH

L1 Reporting Instruct students to assume the role of a newspaper reporter like Bob Woodward or Carl Bernstein. Ask students to write a newspaper account of the event during Nixon's presidency they think had the greatest effect on American society. Ask volunteers to read their news stories to the class.

Guided Reading Activity 31–2

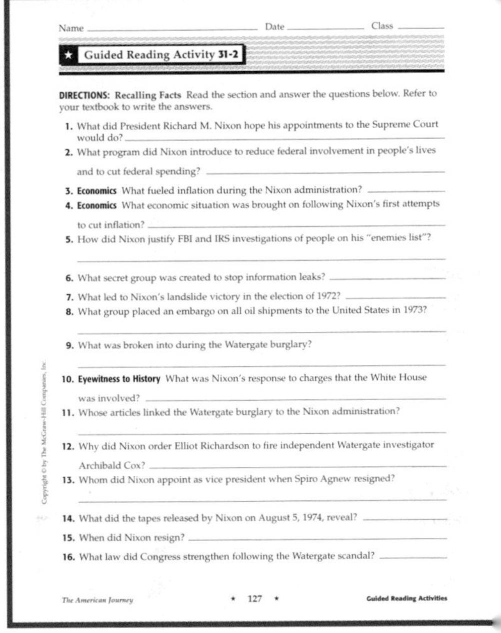

Name ________ Date ________ Class ________

★ Guided Reading Activity 31-2

DIRECTIONS: Recalling Facts Read the section and answer the questions below. Refer to your textbook to write the answers.

1. What did President Richard M. Nixon hope his appointments to the Supreme Court would do? ________
2. What program did Nixon introduce to reduce federal involvement in people's lives and to cut federal spending? ________
3. **Economics** What fueled inflation during the Nixon administration? ________
4. **Economics** What economic situation was brought on following Nixon's first attempts to cut inflation? ________
5. How did Nixon justify FBI and IRS investigations of people on his "enemies list"? ________
6. What secret group was created to stop information leaks? ________
7. What led to Nixon's landslide victory in the election of 1972? ________
8. What group placed an embargo on all oil shipments to the United States in 1973? ________
9. What was broken into during the Watergate burglary? ________
10. **Eyewitness to History** What was Nixon's response to charges that the White House was involved? ________
11. Whose articles linked the Watergate burglary to the Nixon administration? ________
12. Why did Nixon order Elliot Richardson to fire independent Watergate investigator Archibald Cox? ________
13. Whom did Nixon appoint as vice president when Spiro Agnew resigned? ________
14. What did the tapes released by Nixon on August 5, 1974, reveal? ________
15. When did Nixon resign? ________
16. What law did Congress strengthen following the Watergate scandal? ________

The American Journey ★ 127 ★ **Guided Reading Activities**

Picturing HISTORY Inflation is usually measured by using price indexes. The consumer price index (CPI) is a number used to compare the average level of prices for a number of typical items bought by urban families.
Answer: *inflation, increasing costs of oil, high interest rates, stagflation, recession, wage and price freezes, federal budget deficit*

COOPERATIVE LEARNING ACTIVITY

Creating Election Paraphernalia Organize the class into groups of four to create paraphernalia for the 1972 presidential election. Have each group choose one of the presidential candidates and develop a campaign platform and slogan. Allow group members to choose which of the following they would like to create: bumper sticker, placard, button, or hat. Ask groups to present their campaign platform, slogan, and paraphernalia to the class. Allow the class to vote on the most persuasive campaign.

CURRICULUM CONNECTION

CIVICS
After Richard Nixon was defeated in the 1960 presidential race and in the 1962 governor's race for California, he blamed the press for his losses. He told reporters, "You won't have Nixon to kick around anymore, because, gentlemen, this is my last press conference." Nixon said he would never run for office again.

What? Where? When? Who?

Doonesbury In 1969, 20-year-old Yale student Garry Trudeau debuted his antiwar comic strip "Doonesbury" in 25 newspapers nationwide. After 1972, when Trudeau satirized the growing Watergate scandal, "Doonesbury" became a household word.

NATIONAL GEOGRAPHIC SOCIETY

CD-ROM
The Presidents: A Picture History of Our Nation

Have students view "Richard M. Nixon" and use the information to write a brief biographical report.

Facts On File

CD-ROM
Landmark Documents in American History

Title: *Articles of Impeachment for Richard Nixon, 1974*
Have students read the document and paraphrase the charges in their own words.

deficit in which government spending was greater than government revenue. None of Nixon's policies managed to restore the economy to its previous strength, and economic problems continued to trouble his administration.

The Election of 1972

Looking ahead in 1971 to the presidential campaign of 1972, Nixon had doubts about his chances for reelection. The war in Vietnam had not yet ended, and the easing of tensions with China had not yet occurred. Businesses and consumers had to struggle with the effects of inflation. The president and his supporters wanted to ensure his reelection.

A Campaign Against Enemies

To help plan campaign strategy, Nixon relied on a small group of loyal aides. The aides closest to the president were **John Ehrlichman,** his chief domestic adviser, and **H.R. Haldeman,** his chief of staff.

In their drive to win reelection, the president and his closest advisers, it was later revealed, stretched, and sometimes crossed, the boundaries of the law. In 1971, for example, Nixon asked his aides for an "enemies list" of people considered unfriendly to the administration. He then ordered the FBI and the Internal Revenue Service (IRS) to investigate some of these people. Nixon justified such actions as necessary to maintain national security, arguing that those who challenged government policies posed a serious danger to the nation.

Nixon button and McGovern tie

Nixon's campaign committee collected millions of dollars. It used some of this money to create a secret group—nicknamed "the plumbers"—to stop leaks of information that might hurt the administration. Some campaign money also went to pay for dirty tricks against Nixon's Democratic foes, but that party had many problems of its own.

Democratic Disunity

The Democratic Party was split. Four candidates competed for the nomination: former vice president **Hubert Humphrey,** Senators **Edmund Muskie** of Maine and **George McGovern** of South Dakota, and former governor of Alabama **George Wallace.** Muskie and Humphrey could not gain enough support. Wallace's campaign was cut short in May 1972 by a would-be assassin's bullet that left him paralyzed.

McGovern, the most liberal of the four candidates, won the nomination. Many voters found some of his views disturbing.

A Landslide Victory

The Democrats' lack of unity as well as an upsurge in the economy and the prospect of peace in Vietnam led to a landslide victory for Nixon. He won 60.7 percent of the popular vote. The Republican victory in the electoral college was even more lopsided—520 to 17.

The Energy Crisis

During Nixon's second term as president, severe economic problems confronted the nation. One of the most critical problems was the cost of fuel, especially imported oil.

The U.S. economy depended heavily on oil. Much of this oil came from the Middle East. Arab oil-producing countries belonged to **OPEC,** the Organization of Petroleum Exporting Countries. In 1973 these countries placed an embargo on all oil shipments to the United States. At the same time, they raised their prices. Between 1971 and 1974, the price of light crude oil jumped from \$1.80 to \$11.65 a barrel (42 gallons).

MULTIPLE LEARNING STYLES

Visual/Spatial Have students draw pictures illustrating each of the **Terms to Learn** for this section: revenue sharing, affirmative action, stagflation, deficit, impeachment. Have students exchange completed pictures to identify which term each picture describes. Motivated students may use their drawings as a base for a political cartoon that makes a statement about one of the terms. **L2, ELL**

The sharp price increases and the six-month embargo damaged the nation's economy. Many companies had to lay off workers, while others raised their prices. Angry consumers complained about the high prices and the long lines at gas stations.

The president imposed emergency measures to conserve oil. Nixon also urged Americans to conserve energy voluntarily. Congress reduced speed limits on highways because a vehicle burns less fuel at lower speeds.

To deal with the long-range problem of dependence on imported oil, Nixon urged development of domestic oil, especially in **Alaska,** which possessed vast, untapped oil reserves.

Sign of the times

Picturing HISTORY Motorists line up outside a Virginia gas station. **Why did Americans face higher fuel prices and gas shortages?**

The Watergate Crisis

During Nixon's second term, what seemed like a small scandal turned into a presidential crisis. The scandal began with the president's reelection campaign. In June 1972, his reelection committee had wanted information about the Democrats' campaign plans. Members of the Nixon campaign ordered "the plumbers" to break into the headquarters of the Democratic National Committee to install telephone listening devices—bugs. This break-in set in motion events that would rock the presidency and the nation.

Eyewitness to HISTORY

A Third-Rate Burglary

Sometime after midnight on June 17, 1972, Frank Wills, a security guard at the **Watergate** office-apartment complex in Washington, D.C., noticed tape covering the locks on doors leading to an underground parking garage. "I took the tape off," he later recalled, "but I didn't think anything of it." About an hour later, he found that someone had retaped the locks. Wills decided to call the police.

Frank Wills's discovery led to the arrest of five men who had broken into Democratic Committee headquarters in the Watergate complex. The arrests of "plumbers" Gordon Liddy and E. Howard Hunt followed soon afterward. Investigations revealed that Liddy and Hunt were connected to the Nixon campaign and were paid from White House funds.

The White House denied any involvement. Nixon's press secretary, Ronald Ziegler, dismissed the break-in as a "third-rate burglary." The president declared that "no one in the White House staff, no one in the administration . . . was involved in this bizarre incident."

A Scandal Unravels

Meanwhile, two newspaper reporters for the *Washington Post,* **Bob Woodward** and **Carl Bernstein,** began publishing a series of articles that linked the burglary to the Nixon campaign. As the election approached, however, fewer than half of the American people had even heard of the Watergate break-in.

John Sirica, the federal district court judge presiding over the trial of the Watergate burglars, resolved to uncover the truth. Eventually, one of the burglars, James McCord, admitted that White House aides had lied about their involvement and had pressured the burglars "to plead guilty and remain silent."

Picturing HISTORY In reaction to the Arab oil embargo, Americans rallied to save energy. Motorists dropped their speed to 55 mph (89 kmph), abiding first by state and then federal regulations. Gas stations closed on Sundays. Commuters took up carpooling, mass transit, and other means of transportation such as walking and bicycling. To conserve energy the nation went on year-round daylight saving time. Many Americans lowered their thermostats to 68°F (20° C) or less. **Ask:** What conservation measure is shown? *(rationing)* **Answer:** *The United States economy was dependent on oil imports. In 1973 oil-producing Arab countries placed an embargo on all oil shipments to the United States and raised oil prices.*

At the MOVIES

In 1972 two young writers for the *Washington Post*, Carl Bernstein and Bob Woodward, realized the implications of the Watergate break-in while they pursued the story. After working 12–18 hours a day, seven days a week, they published their findings in 1974 in a best-selling book, *All the President's Men*. In 1976 it debuted as a film with Robert Redford, Dustin Hoffman, and Jason Robards. The movie is available on videotape from Warner Home Video. This 139-minute video dramatizes the early days of the Watergate investigation.

MAKING CONNECTIONS ACTIVITY

Politics Explain to students that they are going to create a story map of the Watergate crisis. Review the following basic parts of a story map: description of objective, roadblocks to objective, high point, and objective attained or lost. Have students draw a story map labeling the four parts. Then ask them to fill in the information to map out the plot of the Watergate crisis. **L2**

CHAPTER 31
Section 2, 886–891

Picturing HISTORY On February 7, 1973, the Senate voted 70–0 to establish a seven-person Select Committee on Presidential Campaign Activities. In addition to the appointment of Sam J. Ervin, Jr., as chairman, the committee selected Professor Samuel Dash as chief counsel. **Answer:** *taped White House conversations*

When?Who?What?Where?

August 8, 1974 This date marks President Richard Nixon's resignation. By historic coincidence, on the same day in 1815, Napoleon Bonaparte sailed for Saint Helena to spend the rest of his life in exile.

3 ASSESS

Assign Section 2 Review as homework or as an in-class activity.

Use **Chapter Challenger Interactive Review Software** to review Section 2.

Section Quiz 31–2

Name ______ Date ______ Class ______

★ Chapter 31

Score

Section Quiz 31-2

DIRECTIONS: Matching Match each item in Column A with the items in Column B. Write the correct letters in the blanks. *(10 points each)*

Column A	Column B
____ 1. Richard Nixon's secret group	A. New Federalism
____ 2. called for revenue sharing	B. EPA
____ 3. ensures workers' safety	C. OPEC
____ 4. protects the environment	D. OSHA
____ 5. Arab oil-producing countries	E. "the plumbers"

DIRECTIONS: Multiple Choice In the blank at the left, write the letter of the choice that best completes the statement or answers the question. *(10 points each)*

____ 6. Showing a preference to minorities in jobs where they had previously been excluded is called
- A. affirmative action.
- B. stagflation.
- C. revenue sharing.
- D. impeachment.

____ 7. A combination of rising prices and a sluggish economy is called
- A. inflation.
- B. recession.
- C. stagflation.
- D. depression.

____ 8. Nixon appointed this person chief justice of the Supreme Court.
- A. Harry Blackmun
- B. Warren Burger
- C. Lewis Powell
- D. William Rehnquist

____ 9. This "third-rate burglary" eventually forced President Nixon to resign.
- A. Watergate
- B. Stargate
- C. CREEP
- D. White House break-in

____ 10. This gives citizens more access to government files.
- A. affirmative action
- B. Impeachment Act
- C. Freedom of Information Act
- D. Watergate Information Reform

The American Journey ★ 127 ★ **Section Quizzes**

Picturing HISTORY The Senate Watergate Committee hears testimony. **What evidence later revealed that President Nixon had been involved in a cover-up?**

Early in 1973 the Senate voted to hold hearings on Watergate. As pressures mounted, Nixon shook up the White House staff. He fired the White House counsel, **John Dean,** and forced aides H.R. Haldeman and John Ehrlichman to resign. He also declared that he would take responsibility for the mistakes of others because "there can be no whitewash at the White House." Nixon also agreed to Senate demands to appoint a special prosecutor—someone independent of the Justice Department—to investigate Watergate. **Archibald Cox** took the job.

The Senate Watergate hearings began in May 1973. Chaired by Senator **Sam Ervin** of North Carolina, the hearings slowly revealed the inner workings of the Nixon White House. The most damaging testimony came from John Dean. Dean testified that there had been a cover-up and that Nixon himself directed it, but he produced no evidence to confirm his account.

Then in July investigators learned that a secret taping system had recorded all conversations in the president's office. Ervin and Cox demanded the tapes. President Nixon refused and claimed **executive privilege,** insisting that release of the tapes would endanger national security.

When Cox requested a court order to get the tapes in October, Nixon ordered his attorney general, Elliot Richardson, to fire Cox. Richardson refused—and then resigned. Deputy Attorney General William Ruckelshaus also refused to carry out the order and resigned. Finally, Nixon found a Justice Department official willing to fire Cox. This **Saturday Night Massacre,** as the resignations and firing became known, resulted in a storm of public protest.

A New Vice President

In the middle of this turmoil, another scandal struck the administration. The Justice Department charged Vice President **Spiro Agnew** with taking bribes while governor of Maryland. On October 10, 1973, he resigned. Nixon appointed Representative **Gerald R. Ford** of Michigan, the Republican leader of the House, to succeed Agnew. Congress quickly confirmed the nomination.

The Crisis Deepens

Public outrage over the Saturday Night Massacre forced Nixon to appoint a new special prosecutor, **Leon Jaworski.** Meanwhile, the House of Representatives began considering **impeachment**—the constitutional provision to remove a president from office. If the House charged Nixon with committing "high crimes and misdemeanors," he would then be tried in the Senate. If a two-thirds majority of senators found him guilty, he would no longer be president.

In April 1974, Nixon decided to release printed copies of some of the tapes. These transcripts, heavily edited and missing significant portions, led to new protests. Nixon refused court orders to hand over the unedited tapes. Appeals reached the Supreme Court, which ruled on July 24 that the president had to surrender the tapes.

Footnotes to History

Watergate Statistics A total of 56 men were convicted of Watergate-related offenses, including 20 members of the cabinet, the White House staff, and the Committee to Re-Elect the President (CREEP).

CRITICAL THINKING ACTIVITY

Evaluating Information Ask students to work in pairs to draw an outline map of Alaska. Then have students research the location of the pipeline and sketch it on the map. Have one student in each pair list the benefits and the other list the liabilities of the Alaskan pipeline. Each pair should put a plus sign next to each benefit and a minus sign next to each liability. Then ask students to total the positive and negative signs and conclude whether the pipeline was a benefit or a liability. **L3**

At the end of July, after weeks of closed hearings, the House Judiciary Committee adopted three articles of impeachment, charging the president with obstruction of justice, abuse of power, and contempt of Congress. Nixon released the tapes on August 5. A conversation on one tape revealed that the president had ordered a cover-up of the Watergate break-in just a few days after it happened. The conversation provided the crucial piece of evidence that linked Nixon to Watergate.

President Nixon leaves the White House

Nixon Resigns

Public reaction and the prospect of an impeachment trial forced Nixon to resign. On the evening of August 8, 1974, he went on national television to announce his decision.

The next morning a tearful Richard Nixon said good-bye to his staff and then left the White House by helicopter. He was succeeded by Gerald Ford, who became the first U.S. president never elected to the office of president or vice president.

Impact of Watergate

★ The Watergate crisis revealed that a powerful president could abuse his power and violate the Constitution. Yet the system of checks and balances had worked, and the president who had abused his oath of office lost his power.

Congress passed laws to correct abuses, including a law limiting campaign spending. Congress also strengthened the **Freedom of Information Act** of 1972, giving citizens more access to government files containing information about them and others.

The Watergate scandal damaged the public's faith in their political institutions and leaders and tarnished the image of the presidency. It would take time for this faith to be restored.

Section 2 Review

Checking for Understanding

1. ***Identify*** John Ehrlichman, H.R. Haldeman, Watergate, Spiro Agnew, Gerald R. Ford.
2. ***Define*** revenue sharing, affirmative action, stagflation, deficit, impeachment.
3. ***List*** three actions that Nixon took to restore law and order.

Reviewing Themes

4. **Economic Factors** What role did the oil embargo play in America's economic crisis?

Critical Thinking

5. **Synthesizing Information** Explain how the government's checks and balances system worked when Nixon abused his power as president.

Activity

Preparing a Résumé Research one of the persons involved in the Watergate scandal. Prepare a résumé of that person's career since Watergate.

Reteaching Activity 31–2

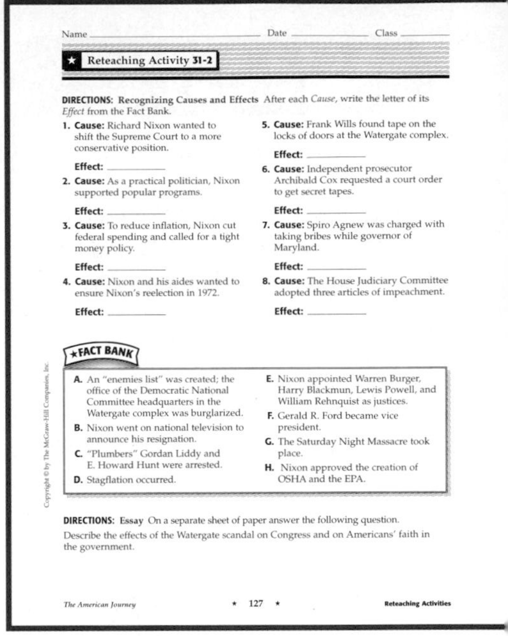
Name ______ Date ______ Class ______

★ Reteaching Activity **31-2**

DIRECTIONS: Recognizing Causes and Effects After each *Cause*, write the letter of its *Effect* from the Fact Bank.

1. **Cause:** Richard Nixon wanted to shift the Supreme Court to a more conservative position.
   Effect: ______
2. **Cause:** As a practical politician, Nixon supported popular programs.
   Effect: ______
3. **Cause:** To reduce inflation, Nixon cut federal spending and called for a tight money policy.
   Effect: ______
4. **Cause:** Nixon and his aides wanted to ensure Nixon's reelection in 1972.
   Effect: ______
5. **Cause:** Frank Wills found tape on the locks of doors at the Watergate complex.
   Effect: ______
6. **Cause:** Independent prosecutor Archibald Cox requested a court order to get secret tapes.
   Effect: ______
7. **Cause:** Spiro Agnew was charged with taking bribes while governor of Maryland.
   Effect: ______
8. **Cause:** The House Judiciary Committee adopted three articles of impeachment.
   Effect: ______

★FACT BANK

A. An "enemies list" was created; the office of the Democratic National Committee headquarters in the Watergate complex was burglarized.
B. Nixon went on national television to announce his resignation.
C. "Plumbers" Gordan Liddy and E. Howard Hunt were arrested.
D. Stagflation occurred.
E. Nixon appointed Warren Burger, Harry Blackmun, Lewis Powell, and William Rehnquist as justices.
F. Gerald R. Ford became vice president.
G. The Saturday Night Massacre took place.
H. Nixon approved the creation of OSHA and the EPA.

DIRECTIONS: Essay On a separate sheet of paper answer the following question.
Describe the effects of the Watergate scandal on Congress and on Americans' faith in the government.

The American Journey ★ 127 ★ **Reteaching Activities**

Enrichment Activity 31–2

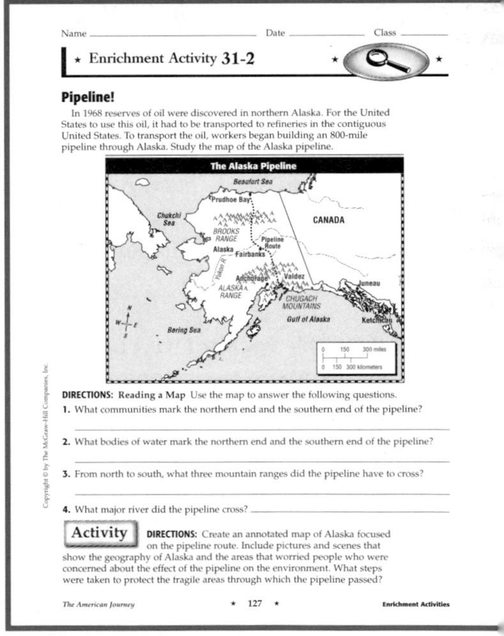
Name ______ Date ______ Class ______

★ Enrichment Activity **31-2** ★ ★

Pipeline!

In 1968 reserves of oil were discovered in northern Alaska. For the United States to use this oil, it had to be transported to refineries in the contiguous United States. To transport the oil, workers began building an 800-mile pipeline through Alaska. Study the map of the Alaska pipeline.

The Alaska Pipeline

DIRECTIONS: Reading a Map Use the map to answer the following questions.

1. What communities mark the northern end and the southern end of the pipeline?
2. What bodies of water mark the northern end and the southern end of the pipeline?
3. From north to south, what three mountain ranges did the pipeline have to cross?
4. What major river did the pipeline cross? ______

Activity **DIRECTIONS:** Create an annotated map of Alaska focused on the pipeline route. Include pictures and scenes that show the geography of Alaska and the areas that worried people who were concerned about the effect of the pipeline on the environment. What steps were taken to protect the fragile areas through which the pipeline passed?

The American Journey ★ 127 ★ **Enrichment Activities**

Section 2 Review Answers

1. John Ehrlichman, 888; H. R. Haldeman, 888; Watergate, 889; Spiro Agnew, 890; Gerald R. Ford, 890
2. The words are defined in the Glossary.
3. He imposed stiffer penalties for criminals, strengthened the power of the police, and appointed conservative Supreme Court justices.
4. It caused fuel costs to rise, and oil-dependent companies laid off workers and raised prices on their products.
5. Students should demonstrate an understanding of Congress's power to launch an investigation of the president's actions and its constitutional power to impeach him.

Activity Students should choose one of the people involved in Watergate and prepare a résumé of that person's career since Watergate.

4 CLOSE

Assign students to write an essay entitled *It Was the Best of Times, It Was the Worst of Times* describing Richard Nixon's presidency. Instruct them to write one paragraph explaining the best of his presidency and one detailing the worst.

CHAPTER 31
Section 3, 892–895

1 FOCUS

BELLRINGER
Motivational Activity

Before taking roll at the beginning of the class period, project Section Focus Transparency 31–3 and have students answer the questions. Discuss students' responses.

This activity is also available as a blackline master.

Section Focus Transparency 31–3

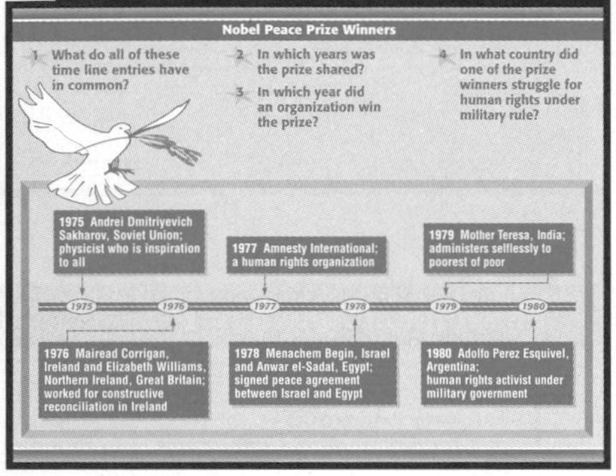

Vocabulary Precheck

Ask students to cite examples of *underemployment*. Discuss the differences between this term and *unemployment*.

Use the **Vocabulary PuzzleMaker** to create crossword and word search puzzles.

Section Theme
Continuity and Change

President Ford continued some of the Nixon administration policies, but he also had to deal with new problems regarding the economy and foreign affairs.

Activity Tell students that after Gerald Ford assumed the presidency and pardoned Richard Nixon, the stock market plunged and Ford's popularity rating dropped from 71 percent to 50 percent. Ask students how they would have handled the charges against Richard Nixon.

1974 — 1975 — 1976

August 1974
Gerald Ford becomes president

September 1974
Ford pardons Nixon

December 1974
CIA's secret files revealed

July 1975
Helsinki Accords signed

Section 3

A Time for Healing

READ TO DISCOVER . . .
- what controversies arose during Ford's presidency.
- what policies Ford followed in foreign affairs.
- how Ford tried to solve economic problems.

TERMS TO LEARN

amnesty
underemployment

The Storyteller

Millions watched on television as the helicopter carrying Richard Nixon rose into the sky. Vice President Gerald Ford and his wife, Betty, turned and walked back to the White House. There, in the East Room, 61-year-old Ford took the oath to become the thirty-eighth president of the United States. Ford assured Americans, "Our long national nightmare is over." Relieved to put the Watergate crisis behind them, most Americans welcomed the new president and a fresh start for the nation.

Time *magazine, August 19, 1974*

President Gerald Ford promised the American people that he would be open and honest as president and would work with Congress to solve the nation's problems. To fill the office of vice president, Ford selected **Nelson Rockefeller,** a highly respected Republican and former governor of New York. *Time* magazine remarked on "a mood of good feeling and even exhilaration in Washington that the city has not experienced for many years."

Ford Faces Controversy

Ford's reputation for honesty and his sincere desire to put the Watergate crisis behind brought the promise of stability to the American nation. One of Ford's first acts, however, destroyed much of this confidence. On September 8, 1974, only a month after taking office, Ford granted Richard Nixon a **pardon** for any crimes he may have committed as president.

This meant that the former president could not be prosecuted for his part in the cover-up. Ford hoped that the pardon would help heal the wounds of Watergate. Instead, the pardon stirred controversy. Many Americans questioned why Nixon should escape punishment when others involved in the Watergate scandal went to jail. Some even accused Ford of striking a bargain with Nixon in advance—the promise of a pardon in exchange for Nixon's resignation. Although Ford defended his action, the new president never fully regained the trust and popularity he had enjoyed in his first weeks in office.

SECTION RESOURCES

Reproducible Masters
- Reproducible Lesson Plan 31–3
- Guided Reading Activity 31–3
- Section Quiz 31–3
- Reteaching Activity 31–3
- Enrichment Activity 31–3

Transparencies
- Section Focus Transparency 31–3

Multimedia
- Vocabulary PuzzleMaker
- Chapter Challenger Interactive Review Software
- Testmaker
- Facts On File: Landmark Documents in American History
- GTV: A Geographic Perspective on American History

Spying on American Citizens

In December 1974, Americans were startled to learn that the CIA had spied and kept secret files on some U.S. citizens. A few months later, they discovered that the FBI also had secret files. President Ford appointed a special commission to investigate CIA and FBI misconduct. He and Congress began working on new laws to regulate the activities of the two agencies.

Vietnam Amnesty

Yet another controversy arose when President Ford offered **amnesty,** or protection from prosecution, to men who had illegally avoided military service during the Vietnam War. Ford promised that these people would not be punished if they pledged loyalty to the United States and performed some type of national service. While many people approved of amnesty, others thought it was too lenient. Supporters of the Vietnam War argued that draft dodgers and deserters should be punished.

Picturing HISTORY The changing of presidents on August 9, 1974, is symbolized in this replacement of former president Nixon's official portrait by one of the new president, Gerald Ford. **What position did Ford hold before becoming president?**

Ford and Foreign Affairs

With little experience in foreign affairs, Ford relied on Henry Kissinger, his secretary of state, and continued the policies of the Nixon administration. Ford extended the policy of détente with the Soviet Union. In late 1974, he met with Soviet leader **Leonid Brezhnev** to discuss arms control. The two leaders reached a preliminary agreement on limiting nuclear weapons.

In July 1975, Ford traveled to Helsinki, Finland, where he signed the **Helsinki Accords** with the Soviet Union and various Western nations. The countries pledged to respect the human rights and civil liberties of their citizens.

The Ford administration also worked to improve relations with China. When Chinese premier **Mao Zedong** died in 1976, a more moderate government came to power. The new Chinese leaders wanted to expand economic and political ties to the United States, and the two nations moved a little closer.

Footnotes to History

Twenty-fifth Amendment Ratified in 1967, the Twenty-fifth Amendment deals with presidential succession if the president dies, becomes disabled, or leaves office. It also establishes a procedure for selecting a new vice president.

Domestic Affairs

The economic problems that the Nixon administration faced continued to plague President Ford. Inflation remained high and unemployment rose.

2 TEACH

L1 Outlining Instruct students to use the heads and subheads to outline the section. Discuss how President Ford's actions described under each head affected his presidency.

Picturing HISTORY Gerald Ford is the only person in United States history to serve as both president and vice president without being elected.

Ford's name at birth was Leslie King, Jr., but when he was 2 years old, his mother divorced his father and soon married Gerald Ford, Sr., who adopted the boy and gave him his new name.

Answer: *vice president*

Guided Reading Activity 31–3

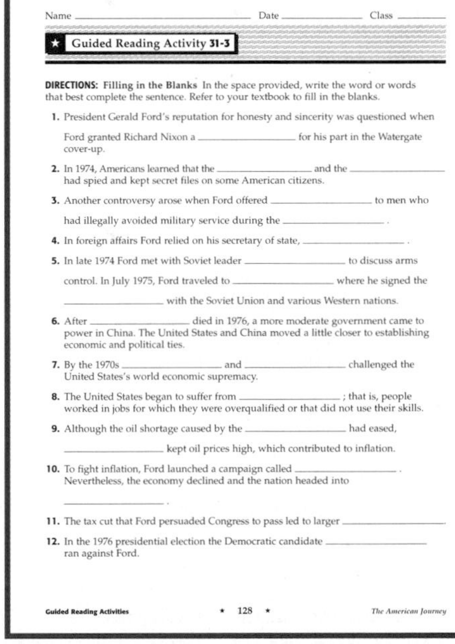

Name ________ Date ________ Class ________

Guided Reading Activity 31-3

DIRECTIONS: Filling in the Blanks In the space provided, write the word or words that best complete the sentence. Refer to your textbook to fill in the blanks.

1. President Gerald Ford's reputation for honesty and sincerity was questioned when Ford granted Richard Nixon a ________ for his part in the Watergate cover-up.
2. In 1974, Americans learned that the ________ and the ________ had spied and kept secret files on some American citizens.
3. Another controversy arose when Ford offered ________ to men who had illegally avoided military service during the ________ .
4. In foreign affairs Ford relied on his secretary of state, ________ .
5. In late 1974 Ford met with Soviet leader ________ to discuss arms control. In July 1975, Ford traveled to ________ where he signed the ________ with the Soviet Union and various Western nations.
6. After ________ died in 1976, a more moderate government came to power in China. The United States and China moved a little closer to establishing economic and political ties.
7. By the 1970s ________ and ________ challenged the United States's world economic supremacy.
8. The United States began to suffer from ________ ; that is, people worked in jobs for which they were overqualified or that did not use their skills.
9. Although the oil shortage caused by the ________ had eased, ________ kept oil prices high, which contributed to inflation.
10. To fight inflation, Ford launched a campaign called ________ . Nevertheless, the economy declined and the nation headed into ________ .
11. The tax cut that Ford persuaded Congress to pass led to larger ________.
12. In the 1976 presidential election the Democratic candidate ________ ran against Ford.

Guided Reading Activities ★ 128 ★ *The American Journey*

Copyright © by The McGraw-Hill Companies, Inc.

Cooperative Learning Activity

Creating a Chart Organize the class into groups of three to create a poster-size chart illustrating the Ford administration. Instruct groups to create the chart with the following four headings: *Controversies, Foreign Policies, Economic Problems,* and *Effects*. Allow group members to choose which of the first three headings they would like to complete on the chart with the appropriate information. Then as a group, have students evaluate the effects each action had on Americans and fill in this information in the fourth column.

Facts On File

CD-ROM
Landmark Documents in American History

Title: *Helsinki Accord, 1975*
Have students read the document, then write their own pledge to respect human rights and civil liberties.

CHAPTER 31
Section 3, 892–895

3 ASSESS

Assign Section 3 Review as homework or as an in-class activity.

Use **Chapter Challenger Interactive Review Software** to review Section 3.

Section Quiz 31–3

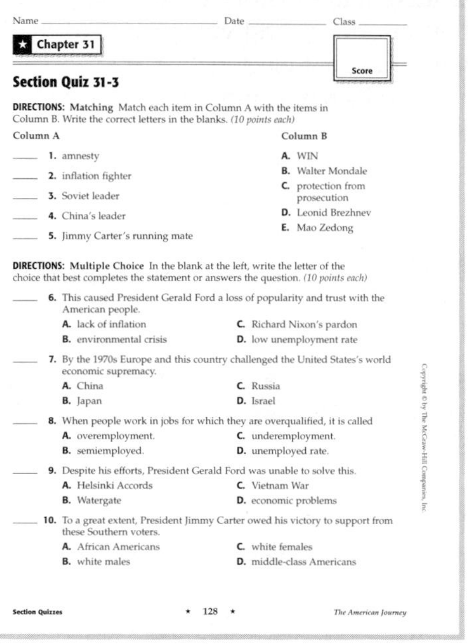
Name ________ Date ________ Class ________

★ Chapter 31 — Score

Section Quiz 31-3

DIRECTIONS: Matching Match each item in Column A with the items in Column B. Write the correct letters in the blanks. *(10 points each)*

Column A	Column B
____ 1. amnesty	A. WIN
____ 2. inflation fighter	B. Walter Mondale
____ 3. Soviet leader	C. protection from prosecution
____ 4. China's leader	D. Leonid Brezhnev
____ 5. Jimmy Carter's running mate	E. Mao Zedong

DIRECTIONS: Multiple Choice In the blank at the left, write the letter of the choice that best completes the statement or answers the question. *(10 points each)*

____ 6. This caused President Gerald Ford a loss of popularity and trust with the American people.
A. lack of inflation — C. Richard Nixon's pardon
B. environmental crisis — D. low unemployment rate

____ 7. By the 1970s Europe and this country challenged the United States's world economic supremacy.
A. China — C. Russia
B. Japan — D. Israel

____ 8. When people work in jobs for which they are overqualified, it is called
A. overemployment. — C. underemployment.
B. semiemployed. — D. unemployed rate.

____ 9. Despite his efforts, President Gerald Ford was unable to solve this.
A. Helsinki Accords — C. Vietnam War
B. Watergate — D. economic problems

____ 10. To a great extent, President Jimmy Carter owed his victory to support from these Southern voters.
A. African Americans — C. white females
B. white males — D. middle-class Americans

Copyright © by The McGraw-Hill Companies, Inc.

Section Quizzes ★ 128 ★ *The American Journey*

American Memories

Teens of the '70s
Fashions for teenagers of the 1970s included hot pants, designer jeans, slogan-printed or tie-dyed T-shirts, and elephant bell-bottoms. Lava lamps, black lights, and posters adorned teenagers' bedrooms. Music ranged from soft rock to hard rock, funk to punk, and glitter to disco.
Answer: *Answers will vary but should point out the differences between clothing styles of teens in the 1970s and teens today.*

A Troubled Economy

By the 1970s Europe and Japan challenged America's world economic supremacy. Inexpensive and efficient Japanese cars flooded the American market. European products also provided strong competition to American-made goods.

This foreign competition led to factory closings in the United States and massive layoffs of U.S. workers. America began to suffer from **underemployment;** that is, people worked in jobs for which they were overqualified or that did not use their skills. Underemployment resulted, in part, from the loss of jobs to foreign competition.

The actions of OPEC continued to influence the American economy, also. Although the oil shortage caused by the embargo of 1973–1974 had eased, OPEC kept oil prices high, and the high prices contributed to inflation. The American economy seemed to be crumbling, and Ford struggled for a solution.

Ford's Response

To fight inflation Ford launched a campaign called Whip Inflation Now (WIN), a voluntary program of wage and price controls. He called on Americans to save their money rather than spend it and to plant their own gardens to counter rising food prices. Although the effort led to a small drop in inflation, the economy declined and the nation headed into recession.

Another approach Ford urged for controlling inflation was to cut government spending. However, the Democratic-controlled Congress wanted to maintain or increase spending for social programs. Ford vetoed several congressional spending bills in an attempt to control spending, but his actions did not curb inflation.

To stimulate the economy and encourage economic growth, Ford persuaded Congress to pass a tax cut. Although the cut did bring some improvement in the economy, it led to larger budget

American Memories
Teens of the '70s

Popular album, 1972

Bell-bottom jeans

Acoustic guitar

What Was It Like? Teenagers of the 1970s had a lifestyle that set them apart from older generations. **How do teenagers today differ from teens of the 1970s in dress and style?**

MULTIPLE LEARNING STYLES

Interpersonal Ask students to work in groups of four to conduct a television talk show. Instruct each group to choose a current talk show to use as a model. Have one student play the role of the talk show host and the other three play Nixon, Ford, and Carter. Ask each group to prepare a 10-minute talk show segment to role-play before the class. **L3**

deficits as government revenue declined and spending remained the same or increased. Despite his efforts, President Ford was unable to solve the nation's economic problems.

Caricature of Gerald Ford

Picturing HISTORY Gerald Ford and Jimmy Carter were the major party candidates for president in 1976. **Who won the election?**

The Election of 1976

As the 1976 elections approached, President Ford hoped to win the election outright. But Ford's prospects did not look particularly good. Although he had helped to restore confidence in government, Watergate was still fresh in the minds of the American people.

In early 1976, **Jimmy Carter** ran as a Democratic candidate in the presidential primary election in New Hampshire. Few voters knew who Carter was. Then Carter began winning key primary elections. Stressing his integrity, religious faith, and his standing as an outsider, Carter gathered enough delegates to win the Democratic nomination. Senator **Walter Mondale** of Minnesota ran as vice president.

Meanwhile President Ford had struggled to gain the Republican nomination. He faced a strong challenge from the former governor of California, **Ronald Reagan,** who was favored by party conservatives. Ford chose Senator **Robert Dole** of Kansas as his running mate.

During the campaign, Ford tried to stress his achievements as president. Carter promised to clean up the government and ran as much against the memory of Nixon and government corruption as against Ford. Carter won in a very close election, gaining 50 percent of the popular vote to Ford's 47.9 percent. To a great extent, Carter owed his margin of victory to support from African American Southern voters.

Section 3 Review

Checking for Understanding

1. ***Identify*** Leonid Brezhnev, Helsinki Accords, Mao Zedong, Jimmy Carter.
2. ***Define*** amnesty, underemployment.
3. ***Cite*** two of Ford's actions early in his presidency that angered many citizens.

Reviewing Themes

4. **Continuity and Change** Explain why the Democrats regained the presidency in 1976.

Critical Thinking

5. **Determining Cause and Effect** How did strong competition from Europe and Japan in the 1970s affect the economy of the United States?

Activity

Creating a Bumper Sticker Create a bumper sticker that supports or opposes Ford's pardon of President Nixon in the Watergate scandal.

Section 3 Review Answers

1. Leonid Brezhnev, 893; Helsinki Accords, 893; Mao Zedong, 893; Jimmy Carter, 895
2. The words are defined in the Glossary.
3. pardoning Nixon and granting amnesty to Vietnam draft dodgers
4. Although Ford had helped to restore confidence in government, Watergate was still fresh in the minds of Americans; Carter received strong support from African American Southern voters.
5. Many domestic factories that produced American goods had to close when American consumers began buying more goods from other countries. These buying trends caused a loss of jobs and a rise in underemployment.

Activity Students should create a bumper sticker supporting or opposing Ford's pardon of Nixon.

Picturing HISTORY Ford, a former star football player, lost the election but boasted that after 25 years in government, "I don't have a single enemy."
Answer: *Jimmy Carter*

Reteaching Activity 31–3

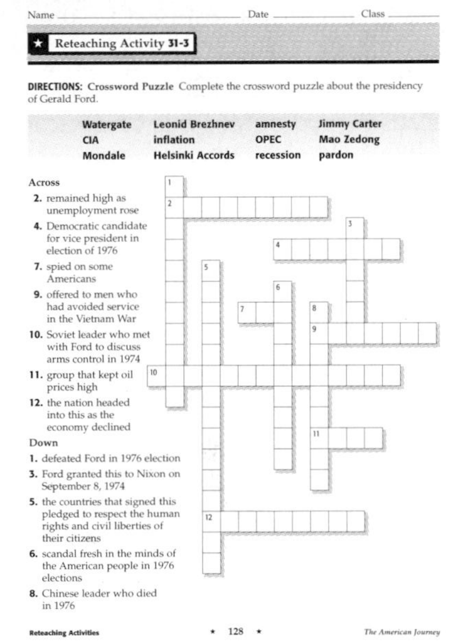
Name ______ Date ______ Class ______

★ Reteaching Activity 31-3

DIRECTIONS: Crossword Puzzle Complete the crossword puzzle about the presidency of Gerald Ford.

Watergate, CIA, Mondale, Leonid Brezhnev, inflation, Helsinki Accords, amnesty, OPEC, recession, Jimmy Carter, Mao Zedong, pardon

Across
2. remained high as unemployment rose
4. Democratic candidate for vice president in election of 1976
7. spied on some Americans
9. offered to men who had avoided service in the Vietnam War
10. Soviet leader who met with Ford to discuss arms control in 1974
11. group that kept oil prices high
12. the nation headed into this as the economy declined

Down
1. defeated Ford in 1976 election
3. Ford granted this to Nixon on September 8, 1974
5. the countries that signed this pledged to respect the human rights and civil liberties of their citizens
6. scandal fresh in the minds of the American people in 1976 elections
8. Chinese leader who died in 1976

Reteaching Activities ★ 128 ★ *The American Journey*

Copyright © by The McGraw-Hill Companies, Inc.

Enrichment Activity 31–3

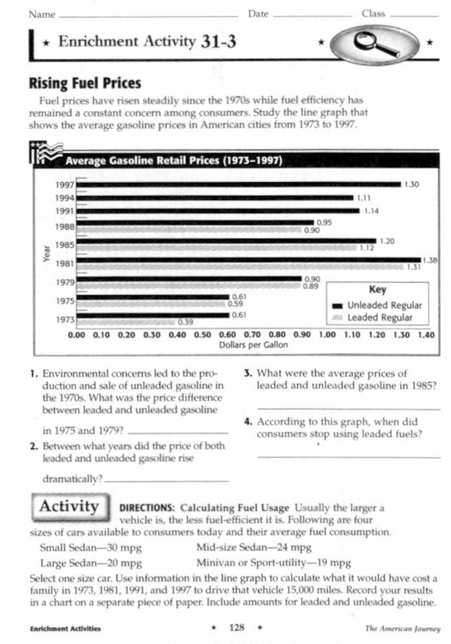
Name ______ Date ______ Class ______

★ Enrichment Activity 31-3 ★

Rising Fuel Prices

Fuel prices have risen steadily since the 1970s while fuel efficiency has remained a constant concern among consumers. Study the line graph that shows the average gasoline prices in American cities from 1973 to 1997.

1. Environmental concerns led to the production and sale of unleaded gasoline in the 1970s. What was the price difference between leaded and unleaded gasoline in 1975 and 1979? ______
2. Between what years did the price of both leaded and unleaded gasoline rise dramatically? ______
3. What were the average prices of leaded and unleaded gasoline in 1985? ______
4. According to this graph, when did consumers stop using leaded fuels? ______

Activity **DIRECTIONS: Calculating Fuel Usage** Usually the larger a vehicle is, the less fuel-efficient it is. Following are four sizes of cars available to consumers today and their average fuel consumption.

Small Sedan—30 mpg Mid-size Sedan—24 mpg
Large Sedan—20 mpg Minivan or Sport-utility—19 mpg

Select one size car. Use information in the line graph to calculate what it would have cost a family in 1973, 1981, 1991, and 1997 to drive that vehicle 15,000 miles. Record your results in a chart on a separate piece of paper. Include amounts for leaded and unleaded gasoline.

Enrichment Activities ★ 128 ★ *The American Journey*

Copyright © by The McGraw-Hill Companies, Inc.

4 CLOSE

Ask students to review the outlines they created in the *TEACH* activity. Then have them evaluate why they think Ford lost the election.

INTERDISCIPLINARY **Activities**

TEACH

Our Fragile Planet

By the early 1970s, 70 percent of Americans ranked the environment as the nation's most pressing domestic problem. This concern was apparent in Americans' support for the first Earth Day held on April 22, 1970. An estimated 20 million Americans turned out for this ecological rally to improve the environment. It was the largest, most upbeat public demonstration since the end of World War II. More than 14,000 schools, colleges, and community groups held workshops, teach-ins, "trash-ins," and other events. New York City barred automobiles from Fifth Avenue so 100,000 people could take an exhaust-free stroll on the street. In Washington, D.C., crowds gathered at the Washington Monument to listen to rock music and speeches. Have students work together to plan events for their own community Earth Day.

Team Teaching

These Interdisciplinary Activities provide an excellent opportunity for you to employ Team Teaching and collaboration in your classroom.

NATIONAL GEOGRAPHIC SOCIETY

VIDEODISC
GTV: A Geographic Perspective on American History

Side 4, Chapter 12

Title: *What Goes Around, Comes Around*
Subject: An environmental statement (1950–1990s)
Ask: **Identify the mentioned environmental pollutants.** *(transportation exhaust, pesticides, fertilizers, and industrial waste)*

INTERDISCIPLINARY **Activities**

Our Fragile Planet

In the 1970s, people around the world became increasingly aware that Planet Earth's environment might be in danger. Increase your environmental awareness by completing these activities.

Science

Testing for Acid Rain Acid rain, caused by pollution in the air, damages forests and kills wildlife. This experiment demonstrates that damage. Label one glass jar "Water," another, "Vinegar." Dig up two clumps of sod and grass; put one clump in each jar. Add 1/4 cup of water to one jar and 1/4 cup of vinegar to the other. Observe the two clumps of grass for 4 to 6 days. Keep a record of the changes you see. If the jars dry out, add water to both. Explain the results of your experiment to the class.

Mathematics

Measuring Wasted Water Water shortages threaten the environment in many places. How much water do people waste? Take a survey based on the following figures. If you leave the faucet running (as most people do), you use these amounts of water: 15-25 gallons per shower, 36 gallons for a tub bath, 2 gallons for washing hands, 10 gallons for brushing teeth. How much water does your family use on an average morning? How much water does your class use every morning? Chart your results.

School-to-Work

Planning a Recycling Program Plan a program in which students and teachers in your school recycle paper, glass, and plastic. Before starting, check with local community programs to see what materials are being collected. Then, with your school administrator, prepare a plan that explains where to place bins in the collection areas of your school, who will collect the materials, and how often recyclable materials will be collected.

Art

Making an Earth Day Poster Since 1970 people have observed Earth Day as a reminder to take care of the environment. Design a poster with original artwork or a collage encouraging people to observe this environmental holiday and respect the earth and its ecology. Hang your posters in the classroom.

Celebrating Earth Day

MULTIPLE LEARNING STYLES

The activities included in the feature on this student edition page are ideally suited to meet the different learning styles of your students. These include:

- Science — **Testing for Acid Rain** logical/mathematical learners
- Mathematics — **Measuring Wasted Water** logical/mathematical learners
- School-to-Work — **Planning a Recycling Program** interpersonal learners
- Art — **Making an Earth Day Poster** visual/spatial learners

1976 Jimmy Carter wins the presidency

1977 Panama Canal treaties signed

1978 Camp David Accords lead toward Arab-Israeli peace

1979 Iranians take 52 Americans hostage

Section 4

The Carter Presidency

READ TO DISCOVER . . .

- how Carter differed from Nixon and Ford.
- how Carter dealt with economic problems.
- how Carter changed the nation's foreign policy.
- why Carter failed to win reelection.

TERMS TO LEARN

trade deficit	apartheid
human rights	fundamentalist

The Storyteller

Jimmy Carter brought a simple lifestyle to the White House. For example, to save money President Carter once planned to visit his hometown of Plains, Georgia, by car instead of by helicopter. He soon discovered that it was much less expensive to go by helicopter. Carter later stated about going by car: "A good portion of the Georgia State Patrol had been marshaled to block every country crossroads for more than 60 miles! It was obvious that I was not simply one of the people anymore."

Papier-mâché peanut with Jimmy Carter grin

Carter, an "outsider" with no experience in national politics, did not fit the image of a typical politician. A former governor of Georgia, Carter liked to say he was just a peanut farmer from a small town called Plains who wanted to serve his country.

An Informal Presidency

From the beginning, Carter set a down-to-earth tone. At his inauguration he wore an ordinary business suit rather than formal clothing. After the ceremony, Carter and his family walked up Pennsylvania Avenue from the Capitol to the White House instead of riding in the traditional limousine. These gestures symbolized Carter's desire to create a more informal presidency. Carter wanted to be seen as an average American.

Struggling with the Economy

When Carter took office, the nation still suffered from high inflation and unemployment. Carter tried to jolt the economy out of recession by increasing federal spending and cutting taxes. Both measures were meant to stimulate economic growth. Unemployment came down, but inflation took off. Carter then reversed course and proposed spending cuts and a delayed tax cut.

Carter's reversals on economic policies made him seem weak and uncertain. As an outsider, the president had trouble gaining support for his programs in Congress. Although Carter needed the backing of congressional Democrats, his administration made little effort to work with them.

CHAPTER 31
Section 4, 897–900

1 FOCUS

BELLRINGER
Motivational Activity

Before taking roll at the beginning of the class period, project Section Focus Transparency 31–4 and have students answer the questions. Discuss students' responses.

This activity is also available as a blackline master.

Section Focus Transparency 31–4

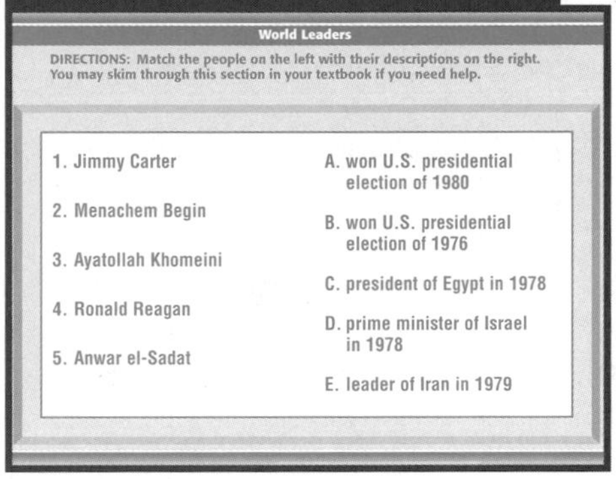

World Leaders

DIRECTIONS: Match the people on the left with their descriptions on the right. You may skim through this section in your textbook if you need help.

1. Jimmy Carter	A. won U.S. presidential election of 1980
2. Menachem Begin	B. won U.S. presidential election of 1976
3. Ayatollah Khomeini	C. president of Egypt in 1978
4. Ronald Reagan	D. prime minister of Israel in 1978
5. Anwar el-Sadat	E. leader of Iran in 1979

Vocabulary Precheck

Ask students to rewrite the definitions of the **Terms to Learn** in their own words.

Use the **Vocabulary PuzzleMaker** to create crossword and word search puzzles.

Section Theme
Civic Rights and Responsibilities

President Carter wanted to create an informal, moral presidency. He based his foreign policy on human rights.

Activity Tell students that in the mid-1970s many Americans resented presidential authority. President Carter tried to develop a more informal approach to government, a style sometimes characterized as "Jacksonian." Ask students what they think this means. *("man of the people" or "folksy" manner)*

SECTION RESOURCES

Reproducible Masters
- Reproducible Lesson Plan 31–4
- Guided Reading Activity 31–4
- Section Quiz 31–4
- Reteaching Activity 31–4
- Enrichment Activity 31–4

Transparencies
- Section Focus Transparency 31–4

Multimedia
- Vocabulary PuzzleMaker
- Chapter Challenger Interactive Review Software
- Testmaker
- ABCNews InterActive™ Communism and the Cold War
- ABCNews InterActive™ Lessons of War

2 TEACH

L1 Creating a Graphic Organizer Have students create a graphic organizer illustrating Carter's domestic and foreign policies. Then ask them to circle the most important policy, and check the one they think led to Carter's failed reelection.

Guided Reading Activity 31-4

Name ____ Date ____ Class ____

★ Guided Reading Activity 31-4

DIRECTIONS: Recording Who, What, When, Where, Why, and How Answer the questions below. Refer to your textbook to write the answers.

1. **Why** did Jimmy Carter wear an ordinary business suit to his inauguration and walk to the White House instead of riding in a limousine? ____
2. **How** did Carter try to jolt the economy out of recession? ____
3. **What** happened to Carter's image when he reversed his economic policies? ____
4. **What** did the nation face as American money flowed overseas to purchase oil? ____
5. **What** did Carter present in April 1977, that aimed at resolving the energy crisis? ____
6. **Where** did a major nuclear accident occur in March 1979? ____
7. **What** was the basis of Carter's foreign policy? ____
8. **Why** did Carter condemn South Africa? ____
9. **How** many Cuban refugees entered the United States in 1980? ____
10. **Why** did Carter agree to turn the Panama Canal over to Panama by the year 2000? ____
11. **Who** participated in the Camp David Accords? ____
12. **When** were the Camp David Accords announced? ____
13. **What** did the Camp David Accords lead to? ____
14. **Why** did Carter impose an embargo on grain exports to the Soviet Union and refuse to let American athletes participate in the 1980 summer Olympics? ____
15. **Who** used American aid to build up military forces in Iran? ____
16. **Who** became ruler of Iran after Islamic fundamentalists forced the shah to flee? ____
17. **When** and **where** did Iranian students take 52 Americans hostage? ____
18. **How** did the hostage crisis affect the presidential election of 1980? ____

The American Journey ★ 129 ★ **Guided Reading Activities**

Picturing HISTORY President Carter, devout in his religion, was a born-again Baptist. **Answer:** *He condemned South Africa for its policy of apartheid.*

ABCNEWS INTERACTIVE™

VIDEODISC
Communism and the Cold War

Side 2
Chapter 9

Title: *Afghanistan*
Ask: Why did the Soviet Union invade Afghanistan? *(They could not allow a border country to hold anti-Communist views.)*

Energy Crisis

Carter made energy policy a priority. The high costs of energy added to inflation. In addition, as American money flowed overseas to purchase oil, the nation faced a growing **trade deficit**—the value of foreign imports exceeded the value of American exports.

In April 1977, Carter presented the **National Energy Plan,** aimed at resolving the energy crisis. To stress the need to reduce energy use, for example, the president turned down the thermostat in the White House.

Carter's plan included the creation of a Department of Energy to coordinate energy policy, research funds to explore alternative sources of energy, and tax policies to encourage domestic oil production and energy conservation. Congress enacted a weakened version of the plan in 1978.

Nuclear Power

In the late 1970s, Americans became more concerned about the threats of nuclear power. In March 1979 a major accident occurred at the **Three Mile Island** nuclear power plant near Harrisburg, Pennsylvania.

An anti-nuclear protest movement soon spread. President Carter, however, was unwilling to halt the nuclear energy program, which provided more than 10 percent of the nation's energy needs. At the same time, supporters of nuclear power argued that, with proper safeguards, there was no danger to the environment.

Foreign Affairs

Carter based his foreign policy on **human rights**—a concern that governments around the world grant greater freedom and opportunity without the threat of persecution or violence. He proposed that any nation that violated human rights should not receive U.S. aid and support.

Carter withdrew economic and military aid from such countries as Argentina, Uruguay, and Ethiopia because of human rights violations. He condemned South Africa for its policy of **apartheid,** racial separation and economic and political discrimination against non-whites.

Carter's human rights diplomacy sometimes caused problems in the United States. In 1980 Cuban dictator Fidel Castro allowed thousands of Cubans, including criminals and political prisoners, to leave Cuba.

Beginning in April, Cuban refugees began leaving from **Mariel Harbor;** most were en route to Florida. The United States, however, had trouble absorbing such large numbers of people. Some of the emigrants were detained in refugee camps. In June, President Carter ordered other Cubans be moved to federal prisons to await removal hearings. Then, in September, Castro sealed off the boatlift. About 125,000 Cuban refugees had entered the United States.

Picturing HISTORY Jimmy Carter and his wife, Rosalynn, worship with African American leaders, including Coretta Scott King, widow of Martin Luther King, Jr. **What stand did Carter take against South Africa once he became president?**

COOPERATIVE LEARNING ACTIVITY

Creating a News Script Organize students into small groups to develop scripts for a newsmagazine program about one of the major events, issues, or policies of the Carter administration. Suggest that the groups use the following structure for their programs: a statement on the subject of the program, a brief report providing background information on the subject, and a discussion involving a moderator and at least two people with differing views on the subject. Have groups perform their scripts for the rest of the class.

Carter had learned that a foreign policy based on a single issue, human rights, had many limitations. Even so, the president continued to speak out on the issue.

The Panama Canal

Carter also acted to end Latin American bitterness over the Panama Canal. Over the years, U.S. ownership of the canal and its control of the Canal Zone had caused friction between the United States and **Panama.** Carter signed two treaties with Panama in 1977. The treaties turned the U.S.-controlled Panama Canal over to Panama by the year 2000 but guaranteed that the canal would remain a neutral waterway open to all shipping. Some Republicans in the Senate tried to block ratification of the treaties, charging that Carter was giving away U.S. property. The Senate approved the treaties in 1978, however.

Picturing HISTORY President Carter meets with Egyptian president Anwar el-Sadat (left) and Israeli prime minister Menachem Begin (right). **Why were the Camp David Accords important?**

The Middle East

President Carter sought to bring peace to the Middle East. When peace talks between Israel and Egypt stalled in 1978, Carter invited Israeli prime minister **Menachem Begin** and Egyptian president **Anwar el-Sadat** to Camp David, Maryland, for a summit meeting.

For two weeks, the three leaders discussed issues dividing Israel and Egypt. On September 17, 1978, they announced an agreement to work toward peace. Known as the **Camp David Accords,** the agreement led to an Egyptian-Israeli peace treaty signed at the White House in March 1979. The treaty marked the first time that Israel and an Arab nation had reached a peace agreement.

The Soviet Union

Carter hoped to continue détente with the Soviet Union. At the same time, he strongly criticized Soviet human-rights violations—which broke promises Soviet leaders had made in the Helsinki Accords. At the same time, he continued negotiations on arms control. In June 1979, the president signed a second Strategic Arms Limitation Treaty, or **SALT II.** Critics in the Senate charged that the treaty gave the Soviets an advantage, and the Senate delayed ratification.

Any hope of the Senate approving SALT II disappeared in December 1979, when Soviet troops invaded **Afghanistan,** a country in southwestern Asia bordering the Soviet Union. Responding to the invasion, Carter imposed an embargo on U.S. grain exports to the Soviet Union. In addition, the United States and 61 other nations refused to send athletes to the 1980 summer Olympic Games in Moscow. Soviet actions cast a dark cloud over Soviet-U.S. relations, and the cold war began to heat up again.

Crisis in Iran

In the 1970s, **Iran** was one of the strongest U.S. allies in the Persian Gulf region, an area vital to Western oil needs. Shah Mohammed Reza Pahlavi, the ruler of Iran, used U.S. aid to build up a powerful military force. Many Iranians, however, complained about corruption in the government. Others objected to Western influence in the country, which they felt weakened traditional Muslim values.

MULTIPLE LEARNING STYLES

Logical/Mathematical Ask students to work in small groups to create a computerized database of the presidents in this chapter. Instruct groups to create the following four fields: *president, action, characteristic,* and *strengths/weaknesses*. Have groups enter data about each president in the appropriate fields. Instruct groups to create a query or filter and a report, using the count function to find which president has the most strengths. Then ask each group to reveal the results to the class. Discuss the discrepancies in each group's results and whether data can truly be unbiased. If computers are not available, have students create a paper-and-pencil database and tally the strengths. **L3**

CHAPTER 31
Section 4, 897–900

Picturing HISTORY El-Sadat and Begin were awarded the 1978 Nobel Peace Prize.
Answer: *first time Israel and an Arab nation agreed to peace*

ABCNEWS INTERACTIVE™

VIDEODISC
Lessons of War

Side 2
Chapter 4

Title: *Diplomacy: Camp David Accords*
Subject: 1978 meeting between Carter, Begin, and el-Sadat
Ask: **What caused the three men to continue the talks after reaching a standstill?** *(the thought of a future without peace for their grandchildren)*

3 ASSESS

Assign Section 4 Review as homework or as an in-class activity.

Use **Chapter Challenger Interactive Review Software** to review Section 4.

Section Quiz 31–4

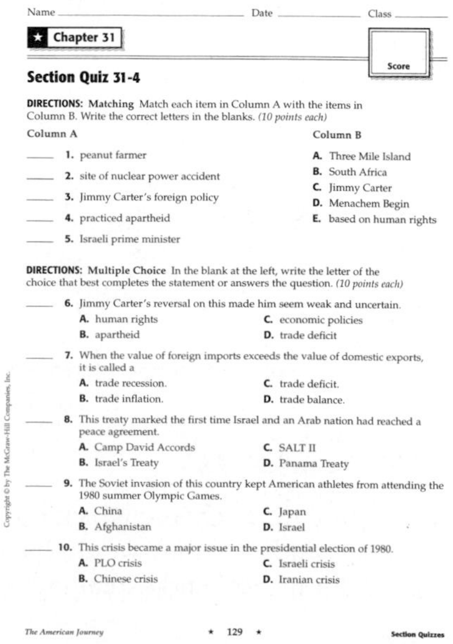

Name ________ Date ________ Class ________

Chapter 31

Score

Section Quiz 31-4

DIRECTIONS: Matching Match each item in Column A with the items in Column B. Write the correct letters in the blanks. *(10 points each)*

Column A

____ **1.** peanut farmer
____ **2.** site of nuclear power accident
____ **3.** Jimmy Carter's foreign policy
____ **4.** practiced apartheid
____ **5.** Israeli prime minister

Column B

A. Three Mile Island
B. South Africa
C. Jimmy Carter
D. Menachem Begin
E. based on human rights

DIRECTIONS: Multiple Choice In the blank at the left, write the letter of the choice that best completes the statement or answers the question. *(10 points each)*

____ **6.** Jimmy Carter's reversal on this made him seem weak and uncertain.
A. human rights **C.** economic policies
B. apartheid **D.** trade deficit

____ **7.** When the value of foreign imports exceeds the value of domestic exports, it is called a
A. trade recession. **C.** trade deficit.
B. trade inflation. **D.** trade balance.

____ **8.** This treaty marked the first time Israel and an Arab nation had reached a peace agreement.
A. Camp David Accords **C.** SALT II
B. Israel's Treaty **D.** Panama Treaty

____ **9.** The Soviet invasion of this country kept American athletes from attending the 1980 summer Olympic Games.
A. China **C.** Japan
B. Afghanistan **D.** Israel

____ **10.** This crisis became a major issue in the presidential election of 1980.
A. PLO crisis **C.** Israeli crisis
B. Chinese crisis **D.** Iranian crisis

The American Journey ★ 129 ★ **Section Quizzes**

CHAPTER 31

Section 4, 897–900

★ Picturing HISTORY The American hostages spent 444 days in Iranian captivity.
Answer: *led to a dramatic decline in his popularity*

Reteaching Activity 31–4

Name ________ Date ________ Class ________

★ Reteaching Activity **31-4**

DIRECTIONS: Putting Events in Sequence Number the events in the order in which they occurred. Use the same number for events that happened at the same time.

_____ **A.** Fidel Castro seals off the boatlift after about 125,000 Cuban refugees had entered the United States.
_____ **B.** A major accident occurs at Three Mile Island nuclear power plant near Harrisburg, Pennsylvania.
_____ **C.** Soviet troops invade Afghanistan.
_____ **D.** President Jimmy Carter, Menachem Begin, and Anwar el-Sadat announce the Camp David Accords.
_____ **E.** The American hostages in Iran are released.
_____ **F.** Iranian students storm the American embassy in Tehran and take 52 Americans hostage.
_____ **G.** Carter presents the National Energy Plan, aimed at resolving the energy crisis.
_____ **H.** An Egyptian-Israeli peace treaty is signed at the White House.
_____ **I.** Ronald Reagan takes the oath of office.
_____ **J.** Carter orders Cuban refugees moved to federal prisons to await removal hearings.
_____ **K.** Islamic fundamentalists force Shah Mohammed Reza Pahlavi to flee Iran.
_____ **L.** Cuban refugees begin leaving from Mariel Harbor, en route to Florida.
_____ **M.** Carter signs second Strategic Arms Limitation Treaty.

DIRECTIONS: Essay On a separate sheet of paper, answer the following questions.
1. Explain the basis of Carter's foreign policy. Give at least two examples of how Carter carried out his foreign policy.
2. How did Carter act to end Latin American bitterness over the Panama Canal?

The American Journey ★ 129 ★ **Reteaching Activities**

Enrichment Activity 31–4

Name ________ Date ________ Class ________

★ Enrichment Activity **31-4** ★ ★

Energy Sources

In the early 1970s Americans depended heavily on fossil fuels, or nonrenewable energy sources. Leaders recognized that Americans needed to conserve energy and find new sources of energy that would not be used up. Study the circle graph of energy sources in 1970.

DIRECTIONS: Reading a Circle Graph Use the graph to answer the following questions.
1. What are the fossil fuels shown on the graph? ________
2. What percentage of the total energy sources was oil? ________
3. Was the amount of natural gas about one-tenth, one-half, or one-third the amount of oil? ________

United States Energy Sources, 1970

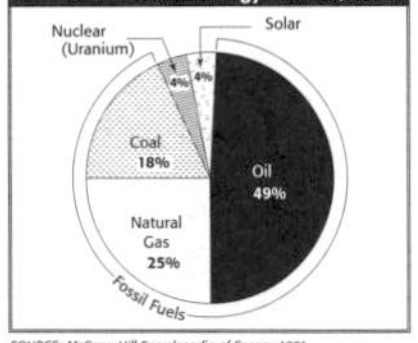

SOURCE: *McGraw-Hill Encyclopedia of Energy*, 1981

4. Which two sources provided an equal amount of energy? ________
5. What percentage of energy was not supplied by fossil fuels? ________
6. Why do you think leaders in the United States urged Americans to conserve energy in the 1970s? ________
7. Do you think energy conservation is still important in the 1990s? Why or why not?

Activity **DIRECTIONS:** Use the media center to find out more about renewable energy resources. Then prepare a scrapbook of materials about one of the renewable sources that interest you, such as geothermal energy, solar energy, wind energy, and so on. With your teacher, find classmates who have researched different renewable energy sources and combine your materials to make a renewable energy resources handbook.

The American Journey ★ 129 ★ **Enrichment Activities**

4 CLOSE

Ask students to choose which presidential candidate they would have voted for in 1980 and explain why.

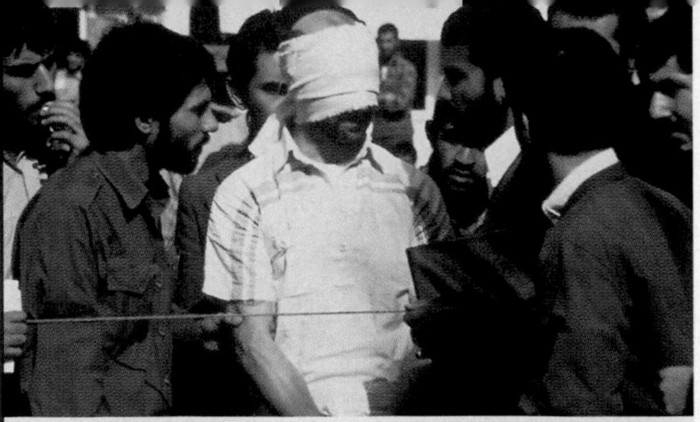

★ Picturing HISTORY Iranians present blindfolded and handcuffed American hostages. **How did the hostage crisis affect Carter's presidency?**

In January 1979, Islamic **fundamentalists**—people who believe in strict obedience to religious laws—forced the shah to flee Iran. The new ruler, Muslim leader **Ayatollah Khomeini,** was hostile to the United States because of its support of the shah.

In November 1979, Iranian students, with the support of fundamentalists in the government, stormed the American embassy in **Tehran,** the capital of Iran, and took 52 Americans hostage. The United States was outraged. Attempts to negotiate the release of the hostages failed, and a daring desert rescue attempt ended in tragedy with the death of 8 American soldiers. The hostage crisis dragged on and became a major issue in the presidential election of 1980.

The Election of 1980

★ The Iranian crisis, together with increased cold war tensions and continuing economic problems, damaged the president politically. By the time the election campaign began, Carter's popularity among the public had declined dramatically.

The Republicans nominated **Ronald Reagan** for president in 1980. In marked contrast to Carter, Reagan radiated charm, confidence, and optimism. His conservative message of lower taxes, reduced spending, stronger defense, and a restoration of American pride found an eager reception among Americans weary of government and economic problems. When Reagan asked, "Are you better off now than you were four years ago?" most Americans answered, "No!"

Reagan swept to victory, with 51 percent of the popular vote and an electoral vote margin of 489 to 49. Republicans also gained control of the Senate for the first time since 1952. The election resulted in a bitter defeat for Jimmy Carter, who only 4 years earlier had promised a new era in American politics.

A final disappointment for Carter came in January 1981. During the closing weeks of his administration, he worked tirelessly to obtain the release of the hostages. The Iranians finally did release them—after Ronald Reagan took the oath of office.

Section 4 Review

Checking for Understanding
1. ***Identify*** Menachem Begin, Anwar el-Sadat, Ayatollah Khomeini.
2. ***Define*** trade deficit, human rights, apartheid, fundamentalist.
3. ***Explain*** how Jimmy Carter's manner differed from many other president's.

Reviewing Themes
4. **Civic Rights and Responsibilities** What issue guided Carter's foreign policy?

Critical Thinking
5. **Drawing Conclusions** Which of Carter's actions do you think did the greatest damage to his chances for reelection? Explain.

Activity

Creating a Poster Divide a sheet of paper into two vertical columns. Label one column "Successes" and the other "Failures." Create a poster that lists each of President Carter's domestic and foreign policy efforts in the appropriate column.

Section 4 Review Answers

1. Menachem Begin, 899; Anwar el-Sadat, 899; Ayatollah Khomeini, 900
2. The words are defined in the Glossary.
3. Carter was much more informal in his approach to politics, brought a simpler lifestyle to the White House, and was a political outsider.
4. human rights
5. Answers will vary. Students should select an issue and explain how Carter's handling of this issue damaged his chances for reelection.

Activity Posters should list the successes and failures of Carter's domestic and foreign policies.

Critical Thinking
SKILL BUILDER

Predicting Consequences

Did you ever wish you could see into the future? Predicting future events is very difficult. You can, however, develop skills that will help you identify the logical consequences of decisions or actions.

Learning the Skill

Follow these steps to help you accurately predict consequences.

- Review what you already know about a situation by listing facts, events, and people's responses. The list will help you recall events and how they affected people.
- Analyze patterns. Try to determine what the patterns show.
- Use your knowledge and observations of similar situations. In other words, ask yourself, "What were the consequences of a similar decision or action that occured in the past?"
- Analyze each of the potential consequences by asking, "How likely is it that this will occur?"
- Make a prediction.

Practicing the Skill

Candidates for public office often make campaign promises based on how they think voters will respond. Use the information in the chart below to help you predict what type of candidate would be elected in 1980. Answer the questions that follow.

1. Review the facts and events listed on the chart. Do you notice any patterns? What do the facts tell you about the 1970s?
2. Recall similar situations in which voters faced hard times. What kind of president do you think Americans would want?

Applying the Skill

Predicting Consequences Read newspapers for articles about an event that affects your community, such as tearing down a historic landmark or building a new shopping mall. Make an educated prediction about what will happen. Explain your reasoning.

Events of the 1970s	Results and Reactions
OPEC oil embargo causes a shortage of fuel.	Americans feel helpless and angry.
President Ford vetoes programs in health, housing, and education to reduce government spending.	Many people lose jobs, and the nation suffers the worst recession in 40 years.
President Carter asks the public to conserve energy.	Americans feel frustrated.
To conserve energy, Americans buy smaller, imported cars.	American workers suffer unemployment as several automobile plants closed.
U.S. citizens are taken hostage by Iranians. The hostages are released after 14 months.	Americans see their leaders forced to give in to terrorists' demands.

Critical Thinking
SKILL BUILDER

TEACH

Predicting Consequences

This skill teaches students to predict consequences using a five-step process. By using the information in a chart about the 1970s, students apply the five steps to predict the winner of the 1980 presidential election. Then in **Applying the Skill,** students choose a community event and follow the same process to predict how that event will affect their community.

Ask students to work in small groups to create a collage. Tell groups to divide a sheet of poster board into two sections, one for the 1970s and one for the 1980s. Have group members use the information in this chapter to create the collage on one section for the 1970s. Then have members evaluate the 1970s collage and apply the five steps for predicting consequences to create a collage predicting what the 1980s will bring.

Additional Practice

Chapter Skills Activity 31

ANSWERS TO PRACTICING THE SKILL

1. In the 1970s many people felt helpless, angry, and frustrated because they had lost jobs, inflation rose dramatically, and overseas nations seemed to be pushing the U.S. around. Conclusions about the 1970s should describe domestic changes, such as conservation, and foreign policy changes, such as a more defensive posture.
2. During the Great Depression and the early postwar years, Americans struggled. They wanted a leader to restore the nation's strength. This usually means wanting a change from the current president or political party.

Applying the Skill Students should choose a local event and use the five steps for predicting consequences to predict the effects the event will have on their community.

GLENCOE TECHNOLOGY

VIDEODISC
MindJogger Videoquiz

Use MindJogger to review the Chapter 31 content.

Chapter 31
Disc 4, Side B

Also available in VHS.

Reviewing Key Terms

The key terms used in this activity can be found in the textbook glossary on pages A26–A35. Students' word search puzzles will vary.

Reviewing Key Facts

1. Soviet Union and China
2. Congressional investigations revealed that he had been aware of the Watergate incident and had ordered a cover-up.
3. Answers may include increased competition from European and Japanese products, inflation, devalued dollar, Arab oil embargo, and so on.
4. Carter developed a National Energy Plan that created the Department of Energy, set aside research funds to explore alternative energy sources, and created tax policies to encourage domestic oil production and energy conservation. Congress passed only a weakened version of this policy, however.
5. He invited Israeli prime minister Begin and Egyptian president el-Sadat to the United States to work on a peace agreement. The Camp David Accords resulted in an Egyptian-Israeli treaty in 1979.

Review and Activities

Reviewing Key Terms

On graph paper, create a word search puzzle using the following terms. Crisscross the terms vertically and horizontally, then fill in the remaining squares with extra letters. Use the terms' definitions as clues to find the words in the puzzle. Share your puzzle with a classmate.

détente
embargo
shuttle diplomacy
revenue sharing
stagflation
deficit
impeachment
amnesty
underemployment
trade deficit
human rights
apartheid
fundamentalist

Reviewing Key Facts

1. Which two nations were the focus of Nixon's attempt to ease cold war tensions?
2. Explain why President Nixon was forced to resign.
3. Why did the United States lose its place as a world economic leader in the 1970s?
4. What did President Carter do to resolve the energy crisis?
5. How did Carter bring temporary peace to the Middle East?

Critical Thinking

Drawing Conclusions

Using human rights as the primary basis for foreign policy caused many problems for President Carter.

1. How did Carter's support of the shah of Iran ignore the interest of Islamic fundamentalists in that country?
2. Do you think our government can fairly judge when other nations are violating human rights? Explain.

Time Line Activity

Create a time line on which you place the following events in chronological order.

- Camp David Accords are signed
- Yom Kippur War occurs
- Nixon resigns
- Carter is elected president
- Nixon signs SALT I
- Iranians seize 52 U.S. hostages
- Watergate hearings begin
- Ford meets with Brezhnev
- Carter proposes National Energy Plan

Reviewing Themes

1. **Global Connections** What was Nixon's main reason for establishing friendly relations with the Soviet Union?
2. **Economic Factors** What did Nixon do to create a New Federalism?
3. **Continuity and Change** How were the foreign policies of Ford and Nixon alike?
4. **Civic Rights and Responsibilities** What did Carter think the United States should do to any nation that violated human rights?

Skill Practice Activity

Predicting Consequences

Review the skill on predicting consequences on page 901. Then read the following statements and predict three consequences for each. Rank the three consequences in order of most likely to occur to least likely to occur.

1. If a person in a public office, including the president, commits a crime, he or she should not be pardoned.
2. Engineers develop an effective, efficient electric-powered automobile.
3. The school year is lengthened by 30 days.

Critical Thinking

1. By supporting the shah, Carter aided the shah's efforts to modernize and westernize the nation, which many Muslims believed weakened their traditional Islamic values.
2. Answers will vary. *Yes;* when people in other nations are suffering as a result of their nation's policies, the United States has a moral obligation to intervene. *No;* our government's views of human rights may differ from another nation's views of human rights based on differences in culture, religion, and other factors.

Time Line Activity

Events should be placed in this order: Nixon signs SALT I, Watergate hearings begin, Yom Kippur War occurs, Nixon resigns, Ford meets

Geography Activity

In 1973 Saudi Arabia imposed an embargo, or a restriction of trade, on oil shipped to Israel's allies including the United States. At the same time, other OPEC countries raised their prices. Although the embargo was lifted in 1974, its economic effects continued through the end of the decade. Study the chart below, then answer the questions that follow.

Gasoline Consumption and Prices

Year	Consumption (billions of gallons)	Cost per Gallon Reg.	Prem.	No lead
1973	110.5	$.40	.45	NA
1974	106.3	.53	.57	.55
1975	109.0	.57	.61	.60
1976	115.7	.59	.64	.61
1977	119.6	.62	.67	.66
1978	125.1	.63	.69	.67
1979	122.1	.86	.92	.90
1980	115.0	1.19	1.28	1.25

Source: *Statistical Abstract of the United States.*

1. **Movement** In what year did consumption first exceed 120 billion gallons?
2. **Movement** How much more did a gallon of regular gasoline cost in 1980 than in 1973?
3. **Human/Environment Interaction** Based on billions of gallons consumed, in which year shown on the chart was the environment most polluted with automobile fumes?

Cooperative Activity

History and Economics Since the 1930s the United States has had deficit, or unbalanced, federal budgets most of the time. This policy of deficit spending led to increasingly large budgets and a growing national debt. The United States entered World War II with a national debt of about $40 billion. The government emerged from the war owing nearly $259 billion. By 1996 the national debt surpassed $5 trillion. With a partner, research to find the dollar figure of the national debt from 1950 to today. Use the figures to construct a line graph. Then answer these questions: What definite patterns or directions can be seen on the graph? What could be some underlying causes of the trends shown on the graph?

Technology Activity

Using a Word Processor The Freedom of Information Act of 1974 allowed public access to many government records. Before 1974 and prior to the abuses of the CIA and FBI in the 1970s, those records were kept secret. Research information on how to use the Freedom of Information Act to get government records. Then using your word processor, write a step-by-step guide explaining the procedure.

Portfolio Activity **History Journal** Review the chapter and make a list of the successes and failures of Presidents Nixon, Ford, and Carter. Based on your list, which of the three would you vote for in a presidential election today? Explain your choice.

CHAPTER 31
Review and Activities

Skill Practice Activity

The following are listed from most likely to least likely to occur:

1. possible three consequences: brought to trial, removed from public office, publicly disgraced
2. possible three consequences: air pollution is reduced, gasoline prices drop, gas-powered automobiles become obsolete
3. possible three consequences: students become more intelligent, school operating costs increase, family vacations disrupted

Geography Activity

1. 1978
2. $ 0.79
3. 1978

Cooperative Activity

Each pair should find the annual federal government deficit or surplus from 1950 to today. They should create a line graph and use it to answer the questions.

Technology Activity

Students may use the Internet to help them find guidelines on how to retrieve information using the Freedom of Information Act of 1974.

Portfolio Activity Students should review the chapter and record the successes and failures of Presidents Nixon, Ford, and Carter. They should decide which one they would vote for if a presidential election were held today.

with Brezhnev, Carter is elected president, Carter proposes National Energy Plan, Camp David Accords are signed, Iranians seize 52 U.S. hostages

Reviewing Themes

1. to ease cold war tensions and create a balance of power
2. revenue sharing between federal and state governments, reduced Great Society programs, took a conservative position on civil rights
3. both relied on Kissinger, both worked to improve relations with the Soviet Union and China
4. bar that nation from American aid and support

Chapter Bonus Test Question

Ask: **What is the length of the trans-Alaska pipeline, which was built on stanchions above the permafrost from Prudhoe Bay to the port of Valdez?** *(800 miles [1,287 kilometers])*

Chapter 32 Planning Guide

A complete, 1-page lesson plan is provided for each section in the *Reproducible Lesson Plans* booklet.

Section Resources

Daily Objectives	Reproducible Resources	Multimedia Resources
Section 1 **The Reagan Presidency** Describe Reagan's presidency in regard to his views on government size, government spending, and communism.	Reproducible Lesson Plan 32–1 Guided Reading Activity 32–1* Political Cartoons, *Government in Our Lives* Section Quiz 32–1* Reteaching Activity 32–1 Enrichment Activity 32–1	Section Focus Transparency 32–1 Vocabulary PuzzleMaker Chapter Challenger Interactive Review ABCNews InterActive™ Communism and the Cold War The Presidents: A Picture History of Our Nation
Section 2 **The Bush Presidency** Summarize events in Eastern Europe and the Soviet Union that led to the end of the cold war and the breakup of the Soviet Union. Compare Bush's foreign policy toward Iraq and China.	Reproducible Lesson Plan 32–2 Guided Reading Activity 32–2* Section Quiz 32–2* Reteaching Activity 32–2 Enrichment Activity 32–2	Section Focus Transparency 32–2 Vocabulary PuzzleMaker Chapter Challenger Interactive Review ABCNews InterActive™ Communism and the Cold War ABCNews InterActive™ Lessons of War The Presidents: A Picture History of Our Nation American Music Cultural Traditions
Section 3 **The Clinton Presidency** Discuss the domestic and foreign issues facing the president and Congress during Clinton's presidency.	Reproducible Lesson Plan 32–3 Guided Reading Activity 32–3* Section Quiz 32–3* Reteaching Activity 32–3 Enrichment Activity 32–3	Section Focus Transparency 32–3 Vocabulary PuzzleMaker Chapter Challenger Interactive Review Testmaker GTV: The American People: Fabric of a Nation GTV: A Geographic Perspective on American History
Section 4 **Toward the 21st Century** Describe the domestic political, economic, and social climate of the late 1990s. List domestic and global challenges of the next century.	Reproducible Lesson Plan 32–4 Guided Reading Activity 32–4* Section Quiz 32–4* Reteaching Activity 32–4 Enrichment Activity 32–4	Section Focus Transparency 32–4 U.S. History & Art, Transparencies 28, 29 Chapter Challenger Interactive Review Testmaker GTV: The American People: Fabric of a Nation GTV: A Geographic Perspective on American History The Presidents: A Picture History of Our Nation Focus on American Art Prints

* *Also available in Spanish*

Poster · Blackline Master · Videodisc · Music Program · Transparency · CD-ROM · Software

0:00 **OUT OF TIME?**
Assign the Chapter 32 Digest and the corresponding Chapter Digests Audiocassettes with activities and tests.

ACTIVITY

From the Classroom of...

Rosa Dominguez
Poe Middle School
San Antonio, TX

Adopt a Country

Have students either individually or in groups draw a country's name out of a hat. The countries should include those listed in Chapter 32, such as Iran, Iraq, a few of the 14 former Soviet republics, Nicaragua, and so on. Have each student or group research their country, looking specifically for information on the Reagan, Bush, and Clinton administrations' policies toward that country. Policies regarding economics, trade, tariffs, and military intervention should all be examined. Have students compile their information for an oral report to the class. Ask students to imagine that they are from their selected country and to present their reports from that country's point of view.

Block Schedule

Block scheduling differs from traditional class scheduling in the amount of time allotted to each period. The extended time frame provided by block scheduling affords you the opportunity to implement a greater number of research-oriented and activity-intense projects to motivate and involve your students. Activities that are particularly suited to use within the block scheduling framework are identified throughout this chapter by the following designation:

NATIONAL GEOGRAPHIC SOCIETY Teacher's Corner

INDEX TO NATIONAL GEOGRAPHIC MAGAZINE

The following articles may be used for research relating to this chapter:

- "A Broken Empire," by Mike Edwards, March 1993.
- "Mother Russia on a New Course," by Mike Edwards, February 1991.
- "Berlin's Ode to Joy," by Priit Vesilind, April 1990.
- "Inside the Kremlin," by Jon Thompson, January 1990.

NATIONAL GEOGRAPHIC SOCIETY PRODUCTS AVAILABLE FROM GLENCOE

To order the following products for use with this chapter, contact your local Glencoe sales representative, or call Glencoe at 1-800-334-7344:

- *GTV: A Geographic Perspective on American History* (Videodisc)
- *GTV: The American People: Fabric of a Nation* (Videodisc)
- *The Presidents: A Picture History of Our Nation* (CD-ROM)

ADDITIONAL NATIONAL GEOGRAPHIC SOCIETY PRODUCTS

To order the following products for use with this chapter, call National Geographic Society at 1-800-368-2728:

- *Branches of Government Series* (Video)
- *Democratic Government Series: The United States* (Video)
- *Democratic Government Series: Germany* (Video)
- *The Rise and Fall of the Soviet Union* (Video)
- *Russia: After the U.S.S.R.* (Video)
- *Historical Atlas of the United States* (Atlas)

KEY TO ABILITY LEVELS

Teaching strategies have been coded for varying learning styles and abilities.

L1 **BASIC** activities for all students
L2 **AVERAGE** activities for average to above-average students
L3 **CHALLENGING** activities for above-average students
ELL **ENGLISH LANGUAGE LEARNER** activities

Chapter 32 Resource Guide

Home Involvement

Home Involvement Activity 32

Review Activities

Chapter Summary 32

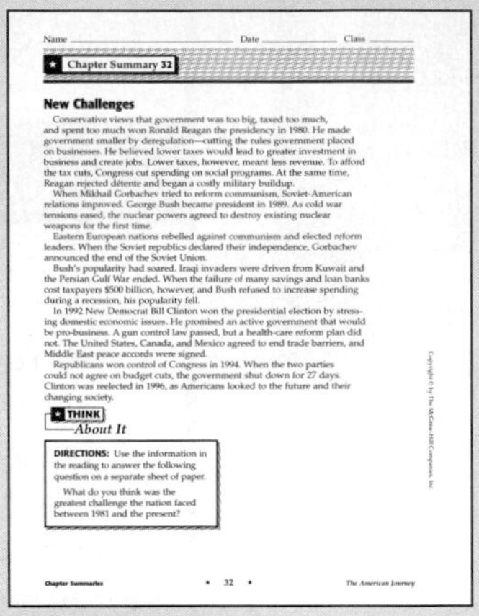

Workbook Activity 32

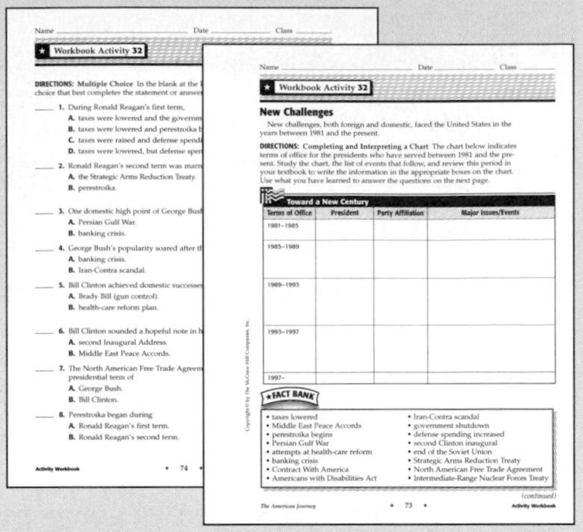

Reinforcement Activities

Time Line Activity 32

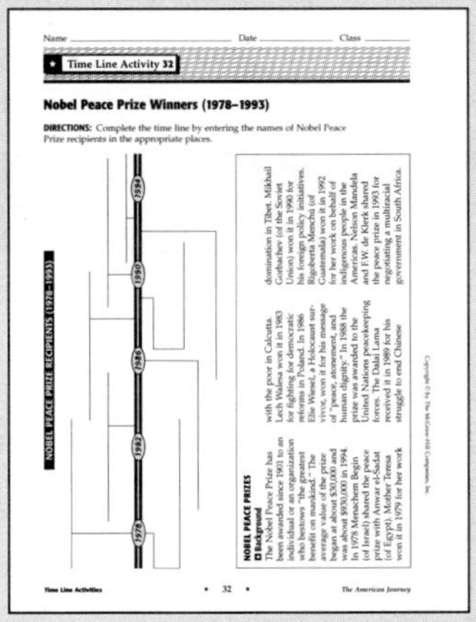

Vocabulary Activity 32

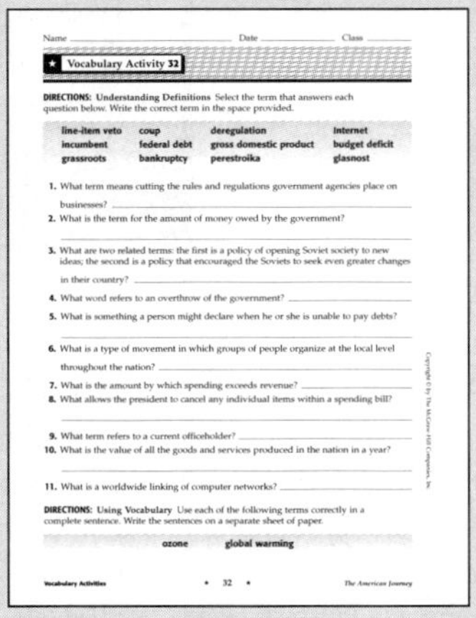

Chapter Skills Activity 32

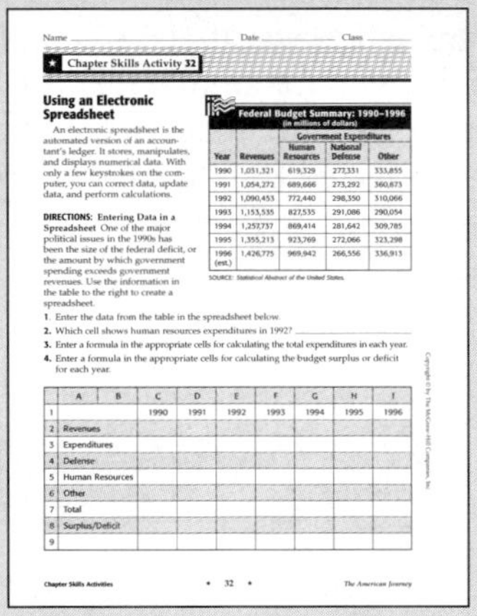

Enrichment Activities

Linking Past and Present Activity 32

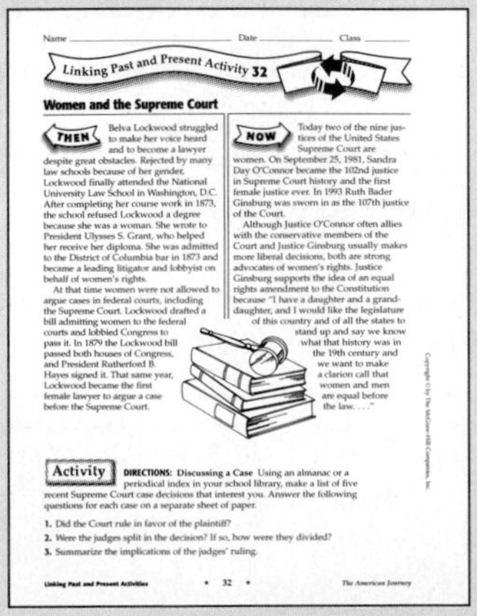

Primary Source Reading 32

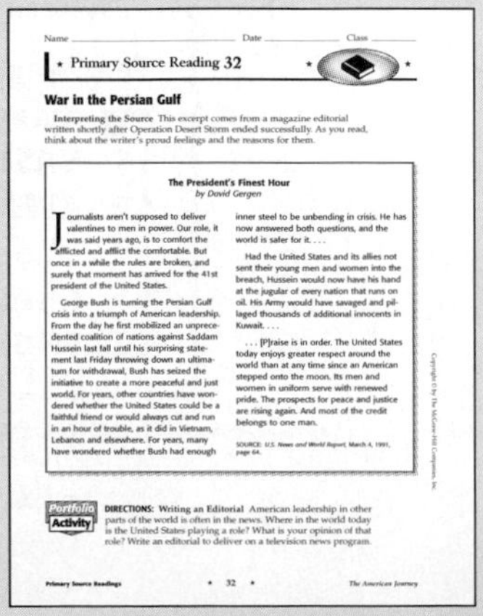

Geography Activities

Mapping History Activity 32

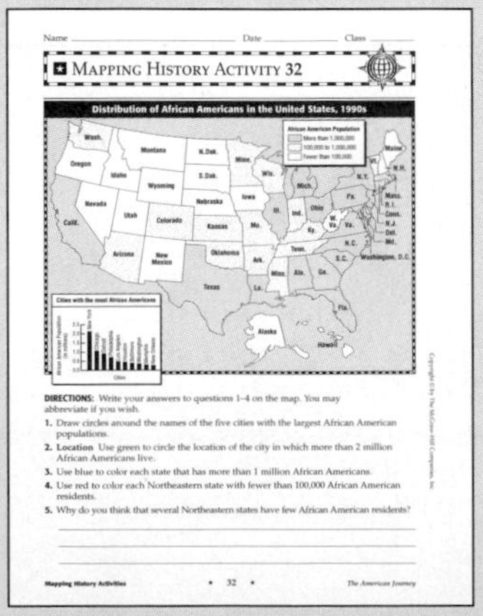

Chapter 32 Resource Guide

Assessment

Chapter 32 Test, Form A

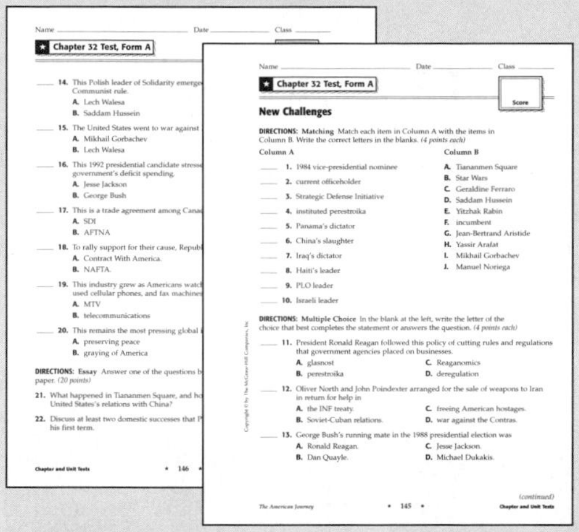

Chapter 32 Test, Form B

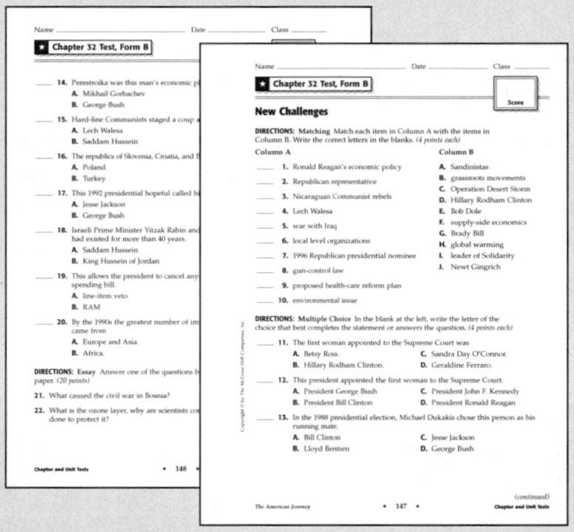

Performance Assessment Activity 32

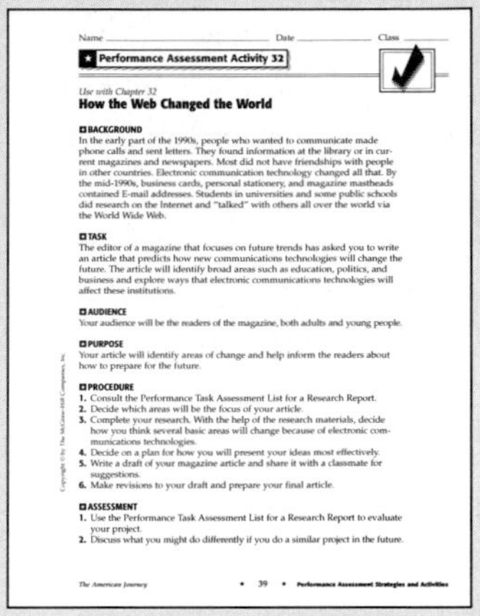

Spanish Resources

The following Spanish language materials are available in the Spanish Resources binder:

- **Spanish Chapter Summary 32**
- **Spanish Vocabulary Activity 32**
- **Spanish Guided Reading Activities, Chapter 32**
- **Spanish Section Quizzes, Chapter 32**
- **Spanish Home Involvement Activity 32**
- **Spanish Chapter 32 Digests Audiocassette Activity and Test**

Activity Manipulatives

Help students learn more about America's cultural history with:

- **American Crafts Hands-On Activities**
- **American Games Hands-On Activities**
- **American History Flash Cards**

Additional Resources From Glencoe

- **American Music Cultural Traditions,** Lesson 10: "Crossfire"
- **Political Cartoons,** *Government In Our Lives*
- **U.S. History & Art,** Transparency 28, *The Family;* Transparency 29, *Still Life With Red Car*
- **Focus on American Art Prints,** *Springtime on the Pedernales* by Porfirio Salinas
- **The American History Videodisc and CD-ROM,** *Contemporary America, 1960–1990s*
- **U.S. Desk Map**
- **Outline Map Resource Book**

THE HISTORY CHANNEL.

The following videotape programs are available from Glencoe as supplements to Chapter 32:

- **Ronald Reagan: The Role of a Lifetime** (ISBN 1-56501-808-7)
- **George Bush: A Sense of Duty** (ISBN 1-56505-809-5)
- **Norman Schwarzkopf** (ISBN 1-56501-787-0)
- **Jesse Jackson: I Am Somebody** (ISBN 1-56501-497-9)
- **Colin Powell: A Soldier's Campaign** (ISBN 1-56501-701-3)
- **Yitzhak Rabin** (ISBN 1-56501-714-5)

To order, call Glencoe at 1-800-334-7344. To find classroom resources to accompany many of these videos, check the following home pages:
A&E Television: http://www.aetv.com
The History Channel: http://www.historychannel.com

Introducing CHAPTER 32

Chapter Themes

Chapter Themes are listed by section on this chapter opening page of the Student Edition. A corresponding theme-based activity is available under "FOCUS," and a theme-based question is asked in the Section and Chapter Reviews.

Performance Assessment

Refer to Activity 32 in the *Performance Assessment Strategies and Activities* booklet.

GLENCOE TECHNOLOGY

VIDEODISC
MindJogger Videoquiz

Use MindJogger to preview the Chapter 32 content.

Chapter 32
Disc 4, Side B

Also available in VHS.

Picturing HISTORY Clinton was the first Democrat to win reelection since FDR. However, between FDR and Clinton, two Democrats served a partial term upon the death of a president and then were elected in their own right. **Ask:** Who were those two Democrats? *(Truman, on the death of FDR, and Johnson, on the death of JFK)*

Chapter 32

1981–Present

New Challenges

Why It's Important

The 1980s and 1990s ushered in a period of great change. With the collapse of communism in Europe, relations between East and West changed dramatically. Former foes sought closer ties. At home, new advances in technology, medicine, and industry helped the nation move forward.

Chapter Themes

- *Section 1,* Economic Factors
- *Section 2,* Global Connections
- *Section 3,* Groups and Institutions
- *Section 4,* Science and Technology

Picturing HISTORY **The 1996 Democratic National Convention** Bill Clinton; his wife, Hillary; and daughter, Chelsea, celebrate Clinton's second nomination as president.

EXTRA CREDIT PROJECT

Making a Time Capsule Have students choose articles to place in a time capsule to show future generations what the students' world was like. Encourage them to choose items, drawings, cultural phenomena, news articles and photographs of political or environmental issues, and pictures showing clothing and hairstyles. Possible items include a favorite book, video, or CD; a popular toy or game; magazines; a television program guide; and so forth.

1980 | 1985 | 1990

1981 Sandra Day O'Connor appointed to Supreme Court

1985 Mikhail Gorbachev becomes leader of Soviet Union

1987 Reagan and Gorbachev sign INF Treaty

Section 1

The Reagan Presidency

Read to Discover . . .

- what factors contributed to the growth of conservatism.
- what economic policies Ronald Reagan followed.
- what approach President Reagan took toward communism.

Terms to Learn

deregulation
federal debt
glasnost
perestroika

The Storyteller

On March 30, 1981, President Reagan gave a speech at the Washington Hilton. As he walked to his car, gunshots rang out. The president was hit in the chest. Also injured were two security officers and the president's press secretary, James Brady. The assassin, John Hinckley, Jr., was quickly subdued. Despite the attempt on his life, the president never lost his sense of humor. In the operating room, he told the surgeons, "Please tell me you're Republicans."

1980 Reagan campaign poster

Ronald Reagan's election to the presidency in 1980 marked a significant conservative shift in America. The conservative movement grew across the country, particularly in the South and Southwest, a region known as the **Sunbelt.** When the Sunbelt's population increased during the 1970s, the conservative movement gained political power.

The Reagan Revolution

Many Americans wanted a return to what President Ronald Reagan called "traditional American values"—an emphasis on family life, hard work, respect for law, and patriotism. They shared the conservative view that the federal government made too many rules, collected too much in taxes, and spent too much money on social programs.

Air Traffic Controllers' Strike

A few months after Ronald Reagan became president, the nation's air traffic controllers went on strike. They refused to go back to work despite the president's orders to do so. President Reagan acted at once, firing the controllers and ordering military staff to oversee air traffic while new controllers were trained to do the work.

President Carter had been criticized for his lack of leadership and indecision. With this action, Ronald Reagan showed that he would stand firm and use his position as president to carry out the policies in which he believed.

Section Resources

Reproducible Masters

- Guided Reading Activity 32–1
- Political Cartoons, *Government in Our Lives*
- Section Quiz 32–1
- Enrichment Activity 32–1
- Reteaching Activity 32–1

Transparencies

- Section Focus Transparency 32–1

Multimedia

- Vocabulary PuzzleMaker
- Chapter Challenger Interactive Review Software
- Testmaker
- ABCNews InterActive™ Communism and the Cold War
- The Presidents: A Picture History of Our Nation

1 FOCUS

BELLRINGER
Motivational Activity

Before taking roll at the beginning of the class period, project Section Focus Transparency 32–1 and have students answer the questions. Discuss students' responses.

This activity is also available as a blackline master.

Section Focus Transparency 32–1

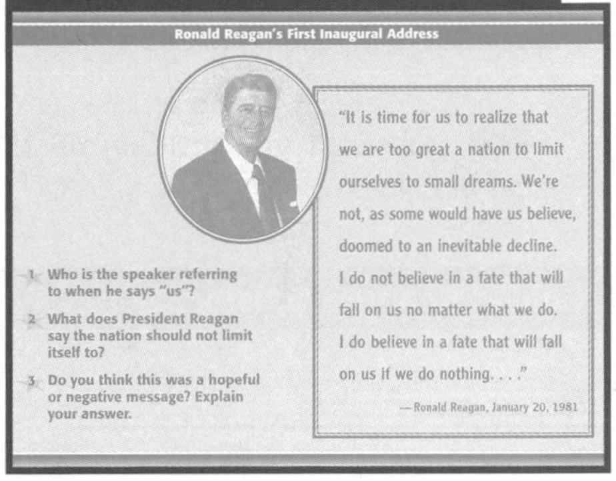

Vocabulary Precheck

Have students analyze the term *deregulation*—prefix *de-* indicates reversal or undoing, root word *regulate,* and suffix *-ion* indicates act, process, outcome, state of being.

Use the **Vocabulary PuzzleMaker** to create crossword and word search puzzles.

Section Theme
Economic Factors

Economic conservatism was a mainstay of Reagan's presidency, showing itself in spending cuts, deregulation, tax cuts, and Reagan's approach to communism.

Activity Have students find one area in which Reagan favored increased spending. *(military)*

CHAPTER 32
Section 1, 905–909

2 TEACH

L1 Defending a Point of View Have students choose one of Reagan's policies (deregulation, spending cuts to federal programs, increased military spending, SDI, fighting communism) and state whether they agree or disagree with it and why.

Picturing HISTORY Since the founding of the Supreme Court in 1789, there have been 17 Chief Justices.
Answer: *She was the first woman appointed to the Supreme Court.*

Political Cartoons, *Government in Our Lives*

Guided Reading Activity 32–1

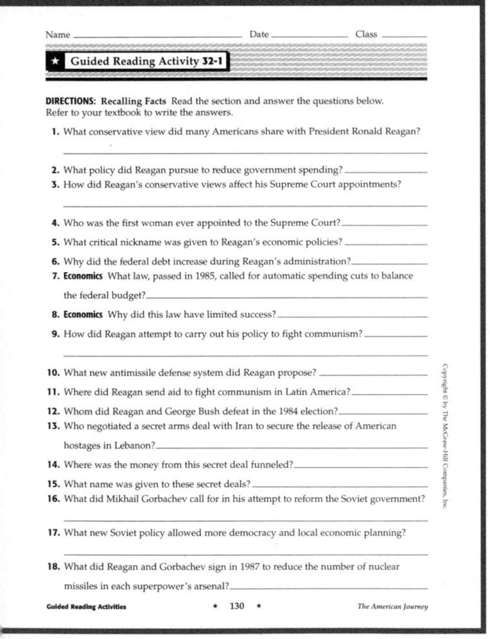

Name ________ Date ________ Class ________

★ Guided Reading Activity **32-1**

DIRECTIONS: Recalling Facts Read the section and answer the questions below. Refer to your textbook to write the answers.

1. What conservative view did many Americans share with President Ronald Reagan?
2. What policy did Reagan pursue to reduce government spending? ________
3. How did Reagan's conservative views affect his Supreme Court appointments?
4. Who was the first woman ever appointed to the Supreme Court? ________
5. What critical nickname was given to Reagan's economic policies? ________
6. Why did the federal debt increase during Reagan's administration? ________
7. **Economics** What law, passed in 1985, called for automatic spending cuts to balance the federal budget? ________
8. **Economics** Why did this law have limited success? ________
9. How did Reagan attempt to carry out his policy to fight communism? ________
10. What new antimissile defense system did Reagan propose? ________
11. Where did Reagan send aid to fight communism in Latin America? ________
12. Whom did Reagan and George Bush defeat in the 1984 election? ________
13. Who negotiated a secret arms deal with Iran to secure the release of American hostages in Lebanon? ________
14. Where was the money from this secret deal funneled? ________
15. What name was given to these secret deals? ________
16. What did Mikhail Gorbachev call for in his attempt to reform the Soviet government?
17. What new Soviet policy allowed more democracy and local economic planning?
18. What did Reagan and Gorbachev sign in 1987 to reduce the number of nuclear missiles in each superpower's arsenal? ________

Guided Reading Activities ★ 130 ★ *The American Journey*

What? Where? When? Who?

The Federal Aviation Administration is an agency of the United States Department of Transportation. Its primary responsibility is to promote safety standards for air flights. It regulates air commerce and provides guidance and regulations for operation of air traffic controls for both civilian and military aircraft.

Picturing HISTORY Sandra Day O'Connor appears with Supreme Court Chief Justice Warren Burger on the steps of the Supreme Court building. **Why was O'Connor's appointment significant?**

Deregulation

As part of his promise to reduce government and "get the government off the backs of the American people," President Reagan pursued a policy of **deregulation.** This meant cutting the rules and regulations government agencies placed on businesses. Under President Reagan, for example, the Department of Transportation wrote new rules for automobile exhaust systems and safety measures that were easier for car manufacturers to meet.

Footnotes to History

Oldest President Ronald Reagan was 69 years old when he was elected—the oldest man to be elected president. A professional actor most of his life, Reagan made such convincing speeches that the media called him the "Great Communicator."

The Supreme Court

Reagan also put a conservative stamp on the Supreme Court by naming justices to the Court who shared his views. He appointed **Sandra Day O'Connor** in 1981, the first woman ever appointed to the Supreme Court. He later appointed **Antonin Scalia** and **Anthony Kennedy.**

Reaganomics

Deregulation and his court appointments showed President Reagan's commitment to a conservative view of government. It was his economic policies, however, that formed the core of the "Reagan Revolution." Reagan believed that lower taxes would allow individuals and corporations to invest in new businesses. Because a tax cut would mean less income, Reagan also called for less government spending. Supporters called Reagan's economic policy **supply-side economics** because it proposed to stimulate the economy by increasing the supply of goods and services. The president's critics ridiculed the policy as "Reaganomics."

In 1981 Congress lowered taxes and slashed nearly $40 billion from federal programs such as school lunches, student aid, welfare, low-income housing, and food stamps. Critics charged that these cuts hurt both the working poor and unemployed people. Supporters argued that Reaganomics would boost the economy, helping everybody in the long run.

While Reagan cut domestic programs, he pushed for sharp increases in military spending. The president declared that the Soviet threat made it necessary to build up the military.

Government Debt

With higher defense spending and lower taxes, the government spent more money than it collected in revenue. It had to borrow money to make up the difference. This borrowing increased the **federal debt**—the amount of money owed by the government. Between 1970 and 1980, the federal debt had grown from $381 to $909 billion. By 1990 the debt had jumped to $3.2 trillion.

COOPERATIVE LEARNING ACTIVITY

Evaluating Policies Have students reread the subsection *Reaganomics.* Then organize the class into three groups and ask group members to prepare for a panel discussion on the impact of President Reagan's economic policies. One group should represent business owners; another should represent workers in manufacturing industries; and the third group should represent people on fixed incomes, such as senior citizens or welfare recipients. Each group should research the positive and negative aspects of supply-side economics in order to defend or negate the other groups' comments.

Economics

Recession and Recovery

President Reagan's new economic policies seemed to falter when a serious recession began early in his first term. However, the economy recovered a year later and began to boom.

In 1983 the economy began a long, steady rise. Businesses expanded, and the high jobless rate of 1982 declined. Investors showed confidence in the economy with a boom in stock trading.

The federal debt continued to grow as well. In 1985 Congress tried to halt growth of the debt by passing the **Gramm-Rudman-Hollings Act.** The act set a series of targets for eliminating the federal budget deficit by October 1990. If Congress and the president could not agree on *voluntary* spending cuts, the law called for *automatic* spending cuts to balance the budget. The provision for automatic cuts did not apply to all areas of the budget, however, so it had limited success.

Reagan's Foreign Policy

Ronald Reagan pledged in his campaign to wage a tough fight against communism. To carry out his policy, President Reagan launched a massive buildup of the military. He expanded the American arsenal of tanks, ships, aircraft, and nuclear missiles. He defended these actions by quoting George Washington's advice: "To be prepared for war is one of the most effective means of preserving peace."

Reagan also proposed a new antimissile defense system, the **Strategic Defense Initiative** (SDI). Nicknamed "Star Wars," the SDI would consist of a land- and space-based defensive shield against enemy missiles. However, scientists were unable to develop the necessary technology.

Latin America

Besides building up the nation's military strength, Reagan also committed American forces and aid to the fight against communism, especially in nearby Latin America.

Late in the Carter presidency, Communist rebels in **Nicaragua**—called **Sandinistas**—had overthrown the government. After becoming president, Reagan sent aid to the **contras,** a group battling the Sandinistas. The fighting in Nicaragua continued for many years and became a source of disagreement between President Reagan and Congress.

In October 1983, President Reagan took direct military action in the Caribbean. Rebels on the tiny Caribbean island of Grenada staged an uprising. Concerned about the fate of 800 American medical students on the island, Reagan dispatched troops to rescue the Americans and establish a prodemocracy government. Reagan's action won widespread approval at home.

The Middle East

President Reagan was less successful with peace efforts in the Middle East. In 1982, he sent a force of marines to help keep the peace in the war-torn nation of Lebanon. The Americans soon were caught in a web of violence. A car bomb blast

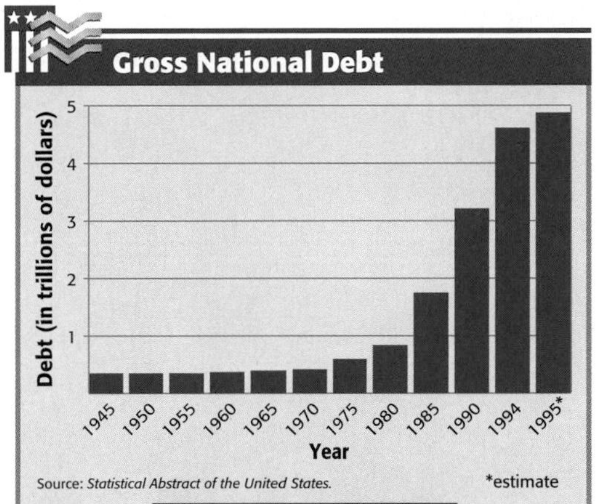

Graph Study

Some economists fear the increasing national debt will never stop growing.

1. When did the gross national debt first pass $1 trillion?
2. **Analyzing Information** During what 5-year period shown on the graph did the national debt increase the most?

Multiple Learning Styles

Visual/Spatial Ask students to research the following events in El Salvador, Granada, and Nicaragua during the Reagan era: major factions in each country, interrelationships with the United States, major events, and important leaders. Have them present their findings in chart form. Charts should be accompanied by a map of Central America with hot spots labeled. Have volunteers give a brief oral explanation of their chart and map. **L3**

CHAPTER 32
Section 1, 905–909

ABCNEWS INTERACTIVE™

VIDEODISC
Communism and the Cold War

Side 2, Chapter 15
Title: *Nicaragua*
Subject: Sandinista-Contra struggle
Ask: Why did Nicaraguan contras rebel? *(because they believed a Communist regime was taking over Nicaragua)*

NATIONAL GEOGRAPHIC SOCIETY

CD-ROM
The Presidents: A Picture History of Our Nation

Have students view "Ronald Reagan" and use the information to write a brief biography of him.

Graph Study

Answers

1. between 1980 and 1985
2. 1985–1990

Graph Skills Practice

Reading a Graph How large was the national debt in 1990? *(about $3 trillion)*

Who?What?Where?When?

Geraldine Ferraro A 1990 magazine interview reported Ferraro's belief that by running for vice president in 1984 she had made the path easier for future female candidates. Said Ferraro in that interview, "We have a real shot at having a woman president in this . . . decade."

CHAPTER 32

Section 1, 905–909

3 ASSESS

Assign Section 1 Review as homework or as an in-class activity.

Use **Chapter Challenger Interactive Review Software** to review Section 1.

Section Quiz 32–1

Name ______ Date ______ Class ______

★ Chapter 32

Score

Section Quiz 32-1

DIRECTIONS: Matching Match each item in Column A with the items in Column B. Write the correct letters in the blanks. *(10 points each)*

Column A	Column B
____ 1. supported traditional American values	A. Star Wars
____ 2. Ronald Reagan's policy	B. Oliver North
____ 3. opening Soviet society to new ideas	C. Ronald Reagan
____ 4. Strategic Defense Initiative	D. glasnost
____ 5. involved in Iran-Contra scandal	E. deregulation

DIRECTIONS: Multiple Choice In the blank at the left, write the letter of the choice that best completes the statement or answers the question. *(10 points each)*

____ 6. Critics ridiculed President Ronald Reagan's economic policy, calling it
A. Ergonomics. C. Reaganomics.
B. Ron's economics. D. Ron's Revolution.

____ 7. The fighting in this country became a source of disagreement between Ronald Reagan and Congress.
A. Contras C. Sandinistas
B. Nicaragua D. Mexico

____ 8. The 1984 Democratic vice-presidential candidate was
A. Ronald Reagan. C. Walter Mondale.
B. George Bush. D. Geraldine Ferraro.

____ 9. Mikhail Gorbachev's new policy for the Soviet Union was called
A. perestroika. C. Reaganomics.
B. Gorby's Revolution. D. Gorbachnomics.

____ 10. This treaty between the United States and the Soviet Union helped reduce the threat of nuclear war.
A. Star Wars Treaty C. perestroika treaty
B. INF Treaty D. Reagan's Treaty

Section Quizzes ★ 130 ★ *The American Journey*

Picturing HISTORY At the public hearings investigating the Iran-Contra affair, North claimed that he believed all his activities were authorized by his superiors.

Answer: *The arms sales to Iran contradicted American policies of not dealing with Iran or negotiating with terrorists. Critics charged that these activities also violated federal laws barring officials from aiding the contras and interfered with Congress's role in making foreign policy.*

killed more than 50 people at the U.S. embassy in Beirut in April 1983. Then in October, 241 Americans and 58 French died in attacks on U.S. and French military headquarters. Rather than become more deeply involved in the struggle, President Reagan withdrew all American forces from Lebanon.

Reagan's Second Term

By 1984 the American economy was booming. In his State of the Union Address, President Reagan declared: "America is back—standing tall, looking [toward the future] with courage, confidence and hope."

President Reagan and Vice President **George Bush** continued using this optimistic theme in their campaign for reelection. The Democrats chose **Walter Mondale,** vice president under Jimmy Carter, and **Geraldine Ferraro,** a member of Congress from New York. Ferraro became the first woman to run for vice president on a major political party ticket.

Picturing HISTORY Marine lieutenant colonel Oliver North (center) takes the oath before the joint congressional committee investigating the Iran-Contra affair. **Why did the Iran-Contra dealings create an uproar?**

Reagan won the electoral votes of 49 out of 50 states. It was one of the most lopsided presidential elections in American history. Spurred on by high employment, a strong economy, and low interest rates, Reagan enjoyed high popularity ratings early in his second term.

The Iran-Contra Scandal

Despite his popularity, a scandal cast a shadow over part of President Reagan's second term. Terrorists, with ties to the Iranian government, held U.S. citizens hostage in Lebanon. Hoping to secure the release of the hostages, Reagan officials made a deal with Iran.

Marine lieutenant colonel **Oliver North** and Navy vice admiral John Poindexter, both assigned to the White House National Security Council, arranged for the sale of weapons to Iran in return for help in freeing American hostages. North and Poindexter decided to funnel money from this secret arms sale to help the Nicaraguan contras.

News of these secret deals—which came to be known as the **Iran-Contra scandal**—created an uproar in the United States. Critics charged that these activities violated federal laws barring officials from aiding the contras. They also said that the deals violated the Constitution by interfering with Congress's role in making foreign policy. Congress held hearings to determine whether President Reagan had participated in breaking the law. But there was never any proof of the president's involvement.

A Changing Soviet Policy

A remarkable shift in Soviet-American relations began to take shape at the beginning of Reagan's second term as president. Changes in Soviet leadership helped trigger the change. In 1985 Communist Party leaders of the Soviet Union chose a new general secretary, or leader—**Mikhail Gorbachev**. To the surprise of people all around the world, Gorbachev was committed to reforming the Soviet government. He called for a policy of **glasnost**—opening Soviet society to new ideas.

MAKING CONNECTIONS ACTIVITY

Drama Organize the class into groups of four to five students each. Ask each group to reenact its interpretation of how events discussed in the section might have taken place. For example one group might role-play Reagan, Gorbachev, and their advisers discussing nuclear arms reduction. Another group might hypothesize about discussions Gorbachev had with his staff leading up to his call for glasnost. **L2**

Picturing HISTORY President Reagan and Soviet leader Gorbachev shake hands at their June 1988 summit meeting in Moscow. **What major step did both leaders take earlier toward ending the threat of nuclear war?**

Soviet button celebrating summit

Gorbachev also tried to change the way his country was governed. Moving away from the government's near-total control of the economy, he allowed more democracy and local economic planning. This new policy, **perestroika,** encouraged the Soviets to seek even greater changes.

Gorbachev also wanted to establish productive ties with the United States. With the Soviet economy in shambles, Gorbachev knew that the Soviet Union could not afford to build nuclear weapons. At several meetings he tried to convince President Reagan that he wanted to end the nuclear arms race. These early meetings accomplished little.

In 1987, however, President Reagan and Premier Gorbachev signed an agreement, the **Intermediate-Range Nuclear Forces (INF) Treaty.** The treaty aimed to reduce the number of nuclear missiles in each superpower's arsenal. Reagan explained the agreement by quoting what he said was a Russian proverb: "Trust, but verify." While both nations still held vast nuclear arsenals, they had taken a major step toward reducing the threat of nuclear war.

★ ★ ★ ★ ★ ★ Section 1 Review ★ ★ ★ ★ ★ ★

Checking for Understanding

1. ***Identify*** Sandra Day O'Connor, George Bush, Geraldine Ferraro, Oliver North, Mikhail Gorbachev.
2. ***Define*** deregulation, federal debt, glasnost, perestroika.
3. ***List*** two of President Reagan's actions that proved he was committed to creating a more conservative government.

Reviewing Themes

4. **Economic Factors** Why did Reagan think that lower taxes would aid the economy?

Critical Thinking

5. **Demonstrating Reasoned Judgment** Do you think Reagan administration officials were justified in violating policies and laws in the Iran-Contra incident? Explain.

Activity

Analyzing Language Research to find the literal meaning of the terms *contras* (Spanish) and *perestroika* (Russian). Then find an English word or phrase that has the same meaning.

★ ★ ★ ★ ★ ★ ★ Section 1 Review Answers ★ ★ ★ ★ ★ ★ ★

1. Sandra Day O'Connor, 906; George Bush, 908; Geraldine Ferraro, 908; Oliver North, 908; Mikhail Gorbachev, 908
2. The words are defined in the Glossary.
3. deregulation, Supreme court appointments, lowering taxes, spending cuts
4. He believed that it would allow individuals and corporations to invest in new businesses.
5. Most students will probably say that these actions were not justified. Congress should have been involved in making these important decisions. Reagan officials violated American policy in dealing with terrorists and unlawfully decided to channel funds to the contras.

Activity *contra*—against; *perestroika*—restructuring

Picturing HISTORY **Answer:** *They signed the INF treaty, which banned intermediate-range nuclear missiles.*

Reteaching Activity 32–1

Name ______ Date ______ Class ______

★ Reteaching Activity 32-1

DIRECTIONS: Recognizing Causes and Effects After each *Cause,* write the letter of its *Effect* from the Fact Bank.

1. **Cause:** Ronald Reagan wanted to reduce government spending.
   Effect: ______
2. **Cause:** The federal debt grew at a rapid pace because of higher defense spending and lower taxes during the Reagan years.
   Effect: ______
3. **Cause:** Reagan vowed to wage a tough fight against communism.
   Effect: ______
4. **Cause:** In 1984 the economy was booming and interest rates were low.
   Effect: ______
5. **Cause:** In 1985 Mikhail Gorbachev was committed to reforming the Soviet style of government.
   Effect: ______
6. **Cause:** The Soviet economy was in shambles.
   Effect: ______

★FACT BANK

A. Mikhail Gorbachev introduced the policies of glasnost and perestroika in the Soviet Union.
B. Nearly $40 billion dollars were slashed from federal programs such as school lunches, student aid, and welfare.
C. Congress passed the Gramm-Rudman-Hollings Act to balance the budget.
D. Mikhail Gorbachev tried to convince Ronald Reagan to end the nuclear arms race.
E. President Ronald Reagan expanded the American arsenal of tanks, ships, and nuclear missiles; he initiated "Star Wars"; and he sent aid to the contras in Nicaragua.
F. President Ronald Reagan enjoyed high popularity ratings with the American people.

DIRECTIONS: Essay On a separate sheet of paper answer the following questions.

1. What was the Iran-Contra scandal, who was involved, and what did critics say it violated?
2. What actions did Ronald Reagan take that resulted in an enormous increase in the national debt?

Reteaching Activities ★ 130 ★ *The American Journey*

Enrichment Activity 32–1

Name ______ Date ______ Class ______

★ Enrichment Activity 32-1 ★ ★

Military Buildup

President Ronald Reagan strengthened the United States military with a buildup of machinery and weapons. The table to the right shows national defense spending in the years just before and during Reagan's presidency. The first column shows the actual amount of money spent on national defense between 1978 and 1989. The numbers in the second column show by what percentage a given year's defense spending increased over defense spending in the preceding year.

National Defense Spending, 1978–1989

Year	Defense Spending (in billions of dollars)	Annual Percentage Change in Defense Spending
1978	104.5	7.5
1979	116.3	11.3
1980	134.0	15.2
1981	157.5	17.6
1982	185.3	17.6
1983	209.9	13.3
1984	227.4	8.3
1985	252.7	11.1
1986	273.4	8.2
1987	282.0	3.1
1988	290.4	3.0
1989	303.6	4.5

DIRECTIONS: Reading a Table Use the table to answer the questions.

1. Which year shows the greatest amount of defense spending? Which year shows the least amount? ______
2. How much money was spent on defense in 1981, the first year of Reagan's administration? ______
3. How did the amount spent in 1989 compare with defense spending in 1981? ______
4. In what two years was the annual percentage change in defense spending the greatest? ______
5. What trend in the annual percentage change in defense spending started in 1985? ______

Activity **DIRECTIONS:** Use the data from the table to create a line graph to show how defense spending increased between 1978 and 1989. Give your graph a title. The horizontal axis should be labeled **Year** and should have marks for the years 1978 to 1989. The vertical axis should be labeled **Dollars (in billions)**. The dollar amounts should range from zero to 310 (billion). Study the table to see what happened to the annual percentage change in defense spending after 1986. In what way does your graph show the same trend in defense spending?

Enrichment Activities ★ 130 ★ *The American Journey*

4 CLOSE

Have students describe Reagan's presidency in one paragraph. Include events they consider both successful and unsuccessful.

1 FOCUS

BELLRINGER
Motivational Activity

Before taking roll at the beginning of the class period, project Section Focus Transparency 32–2 and have students answer the questions. Discuss students' responses.

This activity is also available as a blackline master.

Section Focus Transparency 32–2

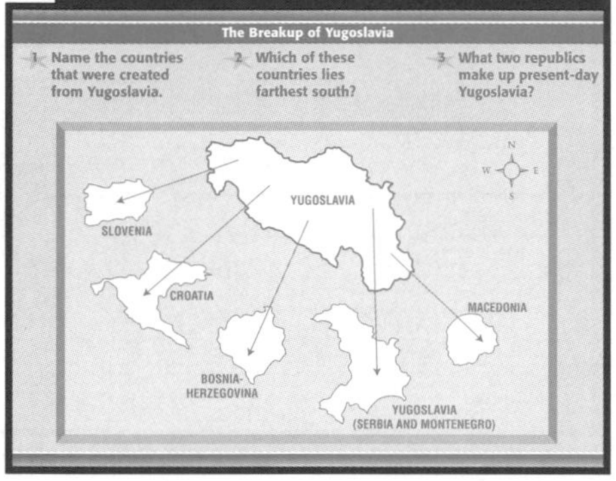

Vocabulary Precheck

Make sure students know that the *p* in *coup* is silent. Then have a volunteer read aloud the textbook glossary definition of each term.

Use the **Vocabulary PuzzleMaker** to create crossword and word search puzzles.

Section Theme
Global Connections

Conflicts and great political changes characterized the global situation during Bush's presidency.

Activity Have students skim the section to find the places where conflict and great political change were occurring. *(Soviet Union; Eastern Europe, including Poland, East Germany, and Yugoslavia; Panama; China; Persian Gulf countries)*

1988 1990 1992

1988 George Bush is elected president

June 1989 Chinese students protest in Tiananmen Square

November 1989 The Berlin Wall is torn down

January 1991 Allies launch Operation Desert Storm

December 1991 The Soviet Union is dismantled

Section 2

The Bush Presidency

READ TO DISCOVER . . .

- how the cold war ended.
- why the Soviet Union broke apart.
- what President Bush's foreign policy was.
- why President Bush began few new domestic programs.

TERMS TO LEARN

coup
bankruptcy

The Storyteller

On September 2, 1944, a young pilot took part in a bombing mission against Japanese bases. World War II was raging. His jet—launched from an aircraft carrier—suffered a direct hit from a Japanese anti-aircraft gun. The pilot and his two crew members bailed out into the Pacific Ocean. A U.S. submarine rescued the pilot from a life raft, but the other two men were never found. For his heroism, the pilot—George Bush—was awarded the Distinguished Flying Cross. More than 40 years later, Bush would become the forty-first president of the United States.

1992 Bush campaign button

As Ronald Reagan's second term drew to a close, the election campaign for his successor heated up. Vice President **George Bush** swept through the 1988 primaries to win the Republican presidential nomination. Bush chose Indiana senator **Dan Quayle** as his running mate.

Election of 1988

Many Democrats vied for their party's nomination, but the field quickly narrowed to two candidates—civil rights leader **Jesse Jackson** and Massachusetts governor **Michael Dukakis.** Dukakis, who ran the most effective primary campaign, won the nomination and chose Senator **Lloyd Bentsen** of Texas as his running mate.

On Election Day, Bush carried 40 states, giving him 426 electoral votes to 112 for Dukakis. However, Bush's victory did not extend to Congress. The Democrats retained control of the House and the Senate.

With much experience in foreign affairs, newly elected president George Bush was called upon to steer the United States through a time of sweeping change facing the world. Many important changes dealt with the Soviet Union.

A New World Order

In December 1988, Soviet leader Mikhail Gorbachev stood before the United Nations to describe the "new world order" to come.

SECTION RESOURCES

Reproducible Masters
- Reproducible Lesson Plan 32–2
- Guided Reading Activity 32–2
- Section Quiz 32–2
- Enrichment Activity 32–2
- Reteaching Activity 32–2

Transparencies
- Section Focus Transparency 32–2

Multimedia
- Vocabulary PuzzleMaker
- Testmaker
- ABCNews InterActive™ Communism and the Cold War
- ABCNews InterActive™ Lessons of War
- The Presidents: A Picture History of Our Nation
- American Music Cultural Traditions

Gorbachev stressed that people throughout the world wanted "independence, democracy, and social justice."

Achieving Arms Cuts

Gorbachev wanted to end the arms race so he could focus on reforms within the Soviet Union. He sought to continue the progress on arms control begun with President Reagan.

In 1990 Gorbachev and President Bush agreed with European leaders to destroy tanks and other conventional weapons deployed in Europe. In 1991, with the **Strategic Arms Reduction Treaty** (START), they achieved a breakthrough. For the first time, two nuclear powers agreed to destroy existing nuclear weapons.

Unrest in the Soviet Union

Most Soviet citizens, however, were more concerned about their own problems than about arms control. For years they had endured shortages of food and basic items such as shoes and soap because of government mismanagement and heavy defense spending.

Gorbachev's policies aimed to solve the economic problems, but changes came slowly. The shortages continued, and people grew impatient with the conditions.

With Gorbachev's policy of glasnost, Soviet citizens began to express their dissatisfaction openly. Thousands of people marched through Moscow in February 1990, demanding an end to Communist rule. Unrest and calls for democracy had also spread throughout the Soviet Union. Many of the republics that made up the Soviet Union demanded independence.

Eastern Europe

While events were unfolding in the Soviet Union, the people of Eastern Europe also grew restless. Many people sensing change occurring in the Soviet Union under Gorbachev's leadership felt freer to demand change in their countries as well.

A Rising Tide of Freedom

The first democratic moves outside of the Soviet Union occurred in **Poland,** where shipyard workers had won the right to form an independent labor union—called **Solidarity**—in October 1980. **Lech Walesa,** the leader of Solidarity, emerged as a symbol of resistance to Communist rule. He led the Poles in calling for reforms. Although the government cracked down on the democratic movement in the mid-1980s, the movement gained strength and forced the government to hold open elections in June 1989.

The democratic cause spread to neighboring countries. Across Eastern Europe, demonstrators filled the streets of major cities. As a result of a relaxation of Soviet control and public pressure, long-sealed national borders were opened and Communist governments toppled. In the last 3 months of 1989, the Iron Curtain that had separated Eastern and Western Europe for more than 40 years began to crumble. Throughout 1989, Gorbachev not only refused to intervene, but he encouraged reform.

Picturing HISTORY Lech Walesa served as Poland's president from 1990 to 1995. **What role did Walesa have in Polish affairs during the 1980s?**

COOPERATIVE LEARNING ACTIVITY

Mapping the Former Soviet Union Have students work together in small groups to make a large map of the countries that were once republics of the Soviet Union. Have students use library or Internet resources to find out what has been happening in those nations and place an important fact in a balloon caption for each country. The groups should also create a time line of important events to accompany the map. Some group members should do the research, some should draw the map, and others should create the time line.

CHAPTER 32
Section 2, 910–916

2 TEACH

L1, ELL Making a Chart Have students make a chart listing the countries in the section and describing important events in each place.

Guided Reading Activity 32–2

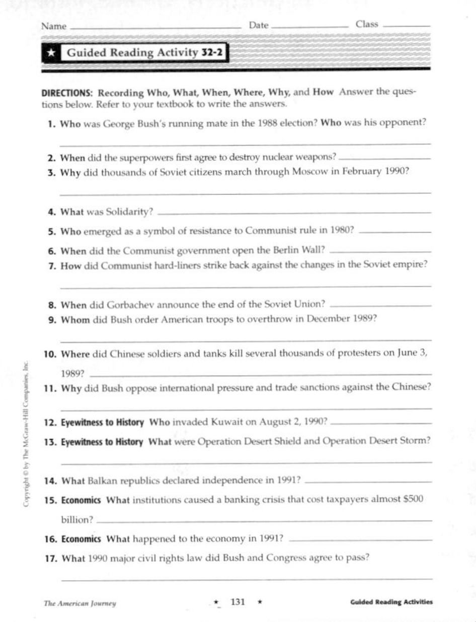

Name ______ Date ______ Class ______

★ Guided Reading Activity 32-2

DIRECTIONS: Recording Who, What, When, Where, Why, and **How** Answer the questions below. Refer to your textbook to write the answers.

1. **Who** was George Bush's running mate in the 1988 election? **Who** was his opponent?
2. **When** did the superpowers first agree to destroy nuclear weapons?
3. **Why** did thousands of Soviet citizens march through Moscow in February 1990?
4. **What** was Solidarity?
5. **Who** emerged as a symbol of resistance to Communist rule in 1980?
6. **When** did the Communist government open the Berlin Wall?
7. **How** did Communist hard-liners strike back against the changes in the Soviet empire?
8. **When** did Gorbachev announce the end of the Soviet Union?
9. **Whom** did Bush order American troops to overthrow in December 1989?
10. **Where** did Chinese soldiers and tanks kill several thousands of protesters on June 3, 1989?
11. **Why** did Bush oppose international pressure and trade sanctions against the Chinese?
12. **Eyewitness to History** **Who** invaded Kuwait on August 2, 1990?
13. **Eyewitness to History** **What** were Operation Desert Shield and Operation Desert Storm?
14. **What** Balkan republics declared independence in 1991?
15. **Economics** **What** institutions caused a banking crisis that cost taxpayers almost $500 billion?
16. **Economics** **What** happened to the economy in 1991?
17. **What** 1990 major civil rights law did Bush and Congress agree to pass?

Copyright © by The McGraw-Hill Companies, Inc.

The American Journey ★ 131 ★ **Guided Reading Activities**

Picturing HISTORY Walesa changed the centralized economy to a free market.
Answer: *led independent labor union Solidarity, became symbol of resistance to Communist rule*

ABCNEWS INTERACTIVE™

VIDEODISC
Communism and the Cold War

Side 1
Chapter 21

Title: *A New Soviet Union: Communist Rule Ends*
Subject: Rise of Gorbachev
Ask: **What changes were made by Gorbachev's reforms?** *(People were allowed to vote, political prisoners were set free, and the ruling party was not required to be Communist.)*

Map Study

Answers

1. Estonia, Latvia, Lithuania, Belarus, Ukraine, Moldova, Georgia, Armenia, Azerbaijan, Russia, Turkmenistan, Uzbekistan, Kazakstan
2. Austria, Belgium, Denmark, Finland, France, Germany, Greece, Ireland, Italy, Luxembourg, Netherlands, Portugal, Spain, Sweden, United Kingdom

Map Skills Practice

Reading a Map Which countries rejected membership in the European Union? *(Norway, Switzerland)*

What?Where?When?Who?

The European Union was known as the European Community until 1992. The European Union's goals are to integrate the economies, coordinate social developments, and bring about political union of the democratic states of Europe. As a result of its efforts, the movement of goods, services, capital, workers, and tourists is unrestricted within the member nations. The EU hopes to establish a common currency for at least some of its member nations by 1999. Plans are to include Cyprus and Malta as full members.

ABCNEWS INTERACTIVE™

VIDEODISC
Communism and the Cold War

Side 1
Chapter 24

Title: *Germany: United Once More*
Subject: Reunification of Germany
Ask: How did the end of Communist control affect Germany? *(It was once again a unified country.)*

Europe, 1997

Map Study

Political and economic changes swept the former Soviet Union and its allies in Eastern Europe after 1989.

1. **Region** Which countries shown above used to be part of the Soviet Union?
2. **Analyzing Information** Which countries joined the European Union?

The Wall Comes Tumbling Down

Freedom also came to East Germany—the focus of so much cold war tension. With protests raging and thousands of citizens fleeing to West Germany, the Communist government opened the Berlin Wall on November 9, 1989.

Germans brought hammers and chisels to chop away at the Berlin Wall, long the symbol of the barrier to the West. In 1990 East Germany voted to reunite with West Germany.

Russian soldier after coup failed

Collapse of the Soviet Union

As Europe was changing, Gorbachev faced mounting opposition from political rivals within the Soviet Union. Some reformers demanded that he move more quickly. Hard-line Communists in the military and secret police resisted his changes and feared the collapse of the Soviet empire.

In August 1991, the hard-liners struck back. A group of Communist officials and army generals staged a **coup**, an overthrow of the government. They held Gorbachev captive and ordered soldiers to seize the parliament building.

As the world waited anxiously, about 50,000 Russians surrounded the parliament building to protect it from the soldiers. **Boris Yeltsin,** president of the Russian Republic and a reformer, stood on top of a tank and declared, "Democracy will win!" President Bush telephoned Yeltsin to express America's support. On August 22 the coup collapsed. Freed, Gorbachev returned to Moscow.

MULTIPLE LEARNING STYLES

Verbal/Linguistic Have students use library resources to research the conflict in Yugoslavia from the nation's formation in 1918 through Tito's long rule (1943–1980), to the current situation. Students may present their findings in a format of their own choosing—tape recorded or live oral report, written report, or storyboard for a "documentary." **L2, ELL**

The defeat of the coup turned the tide of democracy into a tidal wave. Soon all 15 republics had declared their independence from the Soviet Union. Yeltsin outlawed the Communist Party in Russia. On December 25, 1991, Gorbachev announced the end of the Soviet Union, and the Soviet flag that flew over the Kremlin was lowered for the last time.

The End of the Cold War

President Bush responded quickly to the new situation. In the spring of 1992, Bush and other world leaders pledged $24 billion in assistance to the former Soviet republics. President Bush declared:

> "For over 40 years, the United States led the West in the struggle against communism and the threat it posed to our most precious values. That confrontation is over."

A New Foreign Policy

With the end of the cold war came both renewed hope and new challenges to maintaining world peace. While trying to redefine the goals of American foreign policy, President Bush had to deal with crises in Central America, China, the Middle East, and the Balkans.

Panama

In the eyes of the United States, **Manuel Noriega,** the military dictator of Panama, had two strikes against him. First, Noriega had been charged with drug trafficking by an American court. Second, he had refused to yield power to the newly elected president of Panama, Guillermo Endara. In December 1989, Bush ordered U.S. troops to the Central American nation to overthrow Noriega. When the troops gained control of the country, Noriega surrendered. Endara became Panama's new president, and the U.S. troops left Panama. In 1992 Noriega was tried and convicted in the United States.

China

George Bush had served as the first U.S. **envoy**—diplomatic representative—to China, when the two countries reopened relations in 1974. He took a special interest in China, claiming, "I know the Chinese." During the 1980s, China's Communist government began to reform the economy, but it refused to make political reforms. In May 1989, students and workers in China held demonstrations calling for more democracy. As the protests spread, the country seemed on the verge of revolution.

The Chinese government sent troops to crush the uprising. On June 3, 1989, soldiers and tanks killed several thousand protesters gathered in

Picturing HISTORY In the spring of 1989, about 100,000 students demanding democratic reform gathered in the main square of Beijing, China's capital. **How did the Chinese government respond to the demonstrations?**

CHAPTER 32
Section 2, 910–916

What? Where? When? Who?

Commonwealth of Independent States (CIS) After the fall of the Soviet Union, 11 of the former republics joined Russia in a loose alliance called the CIS. As the largest and most powerful republic, Russia dominated the organization. With Yeltsin as its president, the CIS played a key role in reshaping the governments and economic systems of the newly independent nations.

ABCNEWS INTERACTIVE™

VIDEODISC
Communism and the Cold War

Side 2, Chapter 19
Title: *Tiananmen Square*
Subject: The 1989 student-led demonstrations in China
Ask: **What were the protests in Tiananmen Square about?** *(Students and others protested for democratic reform in China.)*

Picturing HISTORY During the demonstration, protesters put up a 30-foot (9-m) statue, which they named the Goddess of Democracy and which was quite similar to the Statue of Liberty. The slogan on the sign in the photograph resembles a statement by an American Patriot of the Revolutionary War era: ". . . give me liberty or give me death." **Ask:** **Who spoke those famous words?** *(Patrick Henry)*
Answer: *sent soldiers and tanks to crush the uprising, killing several thousand protesters*

MAKING CONNECTIONS ACTIVITY

The Environment A major test of Gorbachev's glasnost policy involved the explosion of a reactor at the Chernobyl nuclear power plant on April 26, 1986. In the long tradition of Soviet communism, there was a deafening silence from Soviet officials after the explosion. Finally, moved by criticism that his call for glasnost was a sham, Gorbachev allowed Soviet and Western reporters to investigate the disaster. Have students find out what happened at Chernobyl and what the consequences have been and will continue to be. **L2**

you don't say...

Saddam Iraqi leader Saddam Hussein liked to be called by his first name. When pronounced correctly, with the emphasis on the second syllable, *Saddam* means "leader," "learned one," or "he who confronts." President Bush insisted on pronouncing the name with the emphasis on the first syllable, however. When spoken this way, *Saddam* means "a boy who fixes or cleans shoes"—a grave insult in many Arab countries.

ABCNEWS INTERACTIVE™

VIDEODISC
Lessons of War

Side 2
Chapter 7

Title: *Who Fights Wars?*
Subject: Soldiers who fought in the Persian Gulf conflict
Ask: **How old must one be to enlist in the armed services in the U.S.?** *(18 years old)*

Picturing HISTORY The Persian Gulf War was probably more thoroughly covered by the media than any previous war. At times the reporters and camera crews were a threat to security and to troop safety.
Answer: *Iraq had invaded oil-rich Kuwait, and some feared Iraq would also invade Saudi Arabia.*

History *and the* Humanities

American Music Cultural Traditions, Lesson 10: "Crossfire"

Tiananmen Square in the center of Beijing. World leaders condemned the slaughter. Although President Bush disapproved of the Chinese leaders' use of force, he carefully avoided words or actions that might lead the Chinese to break off relations with the United States. He did not believe that international pressure or trade sanctions would result in a change in Chinese policies. Although Bush's policy met opposition, it permitted U.S. trade with China to continue to grow.

Eyewitness to HISTORY

The Persian Gulf War

The Bush administration—and the world—faced a serious challenge to stability in 1990. On August 2 Iraq's dictator, **Saddam Hussein** (hoo•SAYN), sent his army into **Kuwait,** a small neighboring country rich in oil. Kuwait was quickly overwhelmed. Nations around the world feared that Iraq would also invade Saudi Arabia.

Vowing to "draw a line in the sand," President Bush persuaded other nations to join what he called **Operation Desert Shield.** Hundreds of thousands of troops moved to Saudi Arabia to prevent an invasion of that country. The coalition forces were under the command of United States general **Norman Schwarzkopf.** Hussein was ordered to withdraw his troops from Kuwait—but the Iraqi troops did not leave and tension mounted. The United Nations set a deadline. Iraq must withdraw by January 15, 1991, or the allies would use force to remove them. Congress voted to support military action if Iraq did not withdraw.

Operation Desert Storm

Iraq refused to budge, and on January 16 the allies launched **Operation Desert Storm.** Laser-guided missiles and thousands of tons of bombs fell on Iraq, destroying its air defenses and other military targets, and damaging many civilian sites as well. President Bush explained the attack:

> "The world could wait no longer. . . . While the world waited, Saddam Hussein met every overture of peace with open contempt."

After six weeks of round-the-clock bombardment, Hussein's forces still refused to leave Kuwait. In late February the allies opened the second phase of Desert Storm—a ground war in which they attacked Iraqi troops from the side and rear. At the same time, planes bombarded Iraqi positions.

Kuwait is Liberated

Thousands of Iraqi soldiers died. Thousands more surrendered. Just 100 hours after the ground war began, President Bush suspended military action. "Kuwait is liberated," he announced. "America and the world have kept their word."

Picturing HISTORY Customers in an Illinois cafe eagerly search newspapers for details about allied air strikes in Iraq. **Why did the United States go to war?**

CRITICAL THINKING ACTIVITY

Synthesizing Information In the debate over whether to use force against Saddam Hussein, some who favored military action used the example of Hitler to justify their stance. Those who opposed action used the example of Vietnam. Have students (a) explain how each of these examples applies to the situation in Kuwait, and (b) decide whether the outcome of the war means that one historical example was more fitting than the other. **L3**

Iraq accepted the allied cease-fire terms, and Saddam Hussein's troops finally left Kuwait.

Americans celebrated the sudden victory. They hailed the leaders of Desert Storm, Norman Schwarzkopf and General **Colin Powell,** chairman of the Joint Chiefs of Staff, and held parades for the troops. President Bush's approval rating in opinion polls soared above 90 percent. After the war, the United States helped rebuild Kuwait. It took 9 months to extinguish the hundreds of oil well fires set by fleeing Iraqi troops.

Picturing HISTORY Women serving in the military made up about 10 percent of the U.S. forces involved in the Persian Gulf War. **What was the outcome of the Persian Gulf War?**

War in the Balkans

Another challenge to world peace arose in Yugoslavia. Yugoslavia had been composed of several republics. After the collapse of Yugoslavia's government, the republics of **Slovenia, Croatia,** and **Bosnia-Herzegovina** declared independence in 1991. The population of Croatia and Bosnia included many Serbs—people from the Yugoslav republic of Serbia. These Serbs, backed by the Serbian republic, fought to hold on to certain areas of Croatia and Bosnia. In the terrible civil war that followed, thousands died.

Reports of atrocities committed by the Serbs outraged world leaders. In 1992 the UN passed a resolution that placed a boycott on trade with Serbia until the fighting stopped.

Economics

Domestic Issues

At home the Bush administration faced great difficulties. Like Reagan, Bush opposed an active government role in domestic affairs. The few proposals Bush did introduce faced determined opposition in the Democratic Congress. Most important, though, the federal debt and a banking crisis required substantial government funds, leaving little money for new programs.

Banking Crisis

Early in his presidency, Bush faced a banking crisis. During the 1980s, the Reagan administration had cut regulations in many industries. New laws eased restrictions on savings and loan associations (S&Ls)—financial institutions that specialized in making loans to buy homes.

The new laws allowed managers of S&Ls to become more aggressive in offering attractive returns to savers—and in making far more risky loans. When many borrowers could not repay their loans and real estate values declined, S&Ls began to lose millions of dollars. Many failed completely and closed their doors. Individual deposits in S&Ls were insured by the government, which now had to pay out billions of dollars to the customers of the failed institutions. To prevent the crisis from spreading, the government bailed out other struggling S&Ls. This policy eventually cost taxpayers almost $500 billion.

Economic Downturn

The heavy borrowing of the 1980s loomed as another source of trouble for the economy. As the federal debt continued to reach new highs, business and personal debt grew as well. In 1991, when the economy slowed to a recession, many

TEACHER'S NOTES

CHAPTER 32
Section 2, 910–916

Picturing HISTORY Since 1993 women have been allowed to fly combat aircraft and to serve aboard warships but not allowed to serve in ground combat units.
Answer: *Allied forces liberated Kuwait; Iraq withdrew its forces and accepted allied cease-fire terms.*

NATIONAL GEOGRAPHIC SOCIETY

CD-ROM
The Presidents: A Picture History of Our Nation

Have students research George Bush's experience in foreign affairs. Ask them to identify how the positions he held would be helpful in the presidency.

3 ASSESS

Assign Section 2 Review as homework or as an in-class activity.

Use **Chapter Challenger Interactive Review Software** to review Section 2.

Section Quiz 32–2

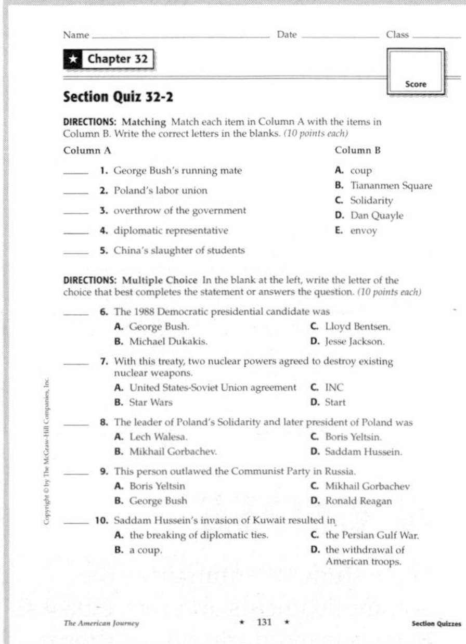

Name ______ Date ______ Class ______

Chapter 32

Score

Section Quiz 32-2

DIRECTIONS: Matching Match each item in Column A with the items in Column B. Write the correct letters in the blanks. *(10 points each)*

Column A	Column B
____ 1. George Bush's running mate	A. coup
____ 2. Poland's labor union	B. Tiananmen Square
____ 3. overthrow of the government	C. Solidarity
____ 4. diplomatic representative	D. Dan Quayle
____ 5. China's slaughter of students	E. envoy

DIRECTIONS: Multiple Choice In the blank at the left, write the letter of the choice that best completes the statement or answers the question. *(10 points each)*

____ 6. The 1988 Democratic presidential candidate was
A. George Bush. C. Lloyd Bentsen.
B. Michael Dukakis. D. Jesse Jackson.

____ 7. With this treaty, two nuclear powers agreed to destroy existing nuclear weapons.
A. United States-Soviet Union agreement C. INC
B. Star Wars D. Start

____ 8. The leader of Poland's Solidarity and later president of Poland was
A. Lech Walesa. C. Boris Yeltsin.
B. Mikhail Gorbachev. D. Saddam Hussein.

____ 9. This person outlawed the Communist Party in Russia.
A. Boris Yeltsin C. Mikhail Gorbachev
B. George Bush D. Ronald Reagan

____ 10. Saddam Hussein's invasion of Kuwait resulted in
A. the breaking of diplomatic ties. C. the Persian Gulf War.
B. a coup. D. the withdrawal of American troops.

The American Journey ★ 131 ★ Section Quizzes

CHAPTER 32
Section 2, 910–916

Picturing HISTORY Accessibility includes providing ramps, elevators, and wheelchair lifts. **Answer:** *outlaws job discrimination against people with disabilities*

Reteaching Activity 32–2

Name ______ Date ______ Class ______

★ Reteaching Activity 32-2

DIRECTIONS: Organizing Facts The items in the Fact Bank name people, places, groups, dates, and events associated with the places listed in the circle chart. Write the letters of the items that go with each place in the appropriate section of the chart. One item belongs in two sections.

★FACT BANK

A. December 25, 1991
B. Clean Air Act
C. Boris Yeltsin
D. Solidarity
E. Berlin Wall
F. Kuwait is invaded.
G. Operation Desert Shield
H. Manuel Noriega
I. Lech Walesa
J. June 3, 1989
K. Serbia
L. S&L banking crisis
M. Tiananmen Square
N. Mikhail Gorbachev
O. Guillermo Endara
P. Saddam Hussein
Q. November 9, 1989
R. Operation Desert Storm
S. January 15, 1991
T. Strategic Arms Reduction Treaty
U. The economy slows to a recession.
V. Norman Schwarzkopf and Colin Powell
W. Slovenia, Croatia, and Bosnia-Herzegovina
X. Americans with Disabilities Act of 1990

The American Journey ★ 131 ★ **Reteaching Activities**

Enrichment Activity 32–2

Name ______ Date ______ Class ______

★ Enrichment Activity 32-2

Changes Around the World

During the presidency of George Bush, many dramatic changes took place around the world. The time line below shows some of these changes.

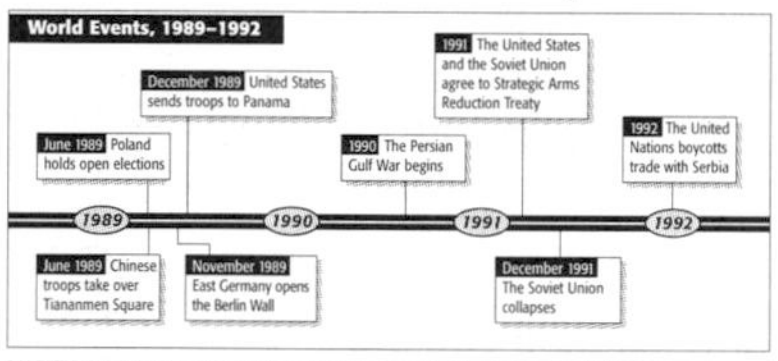

DIRECTIONS: Reading a Time Line Use the time line to answer the following questions.

1. In what year did Poland first hold democratic elections? ______
2. Which event occurred first, the opening of the Berlin Wall or the uprising in Tiananmen Square? ______
3. Which events occurred after the Persian Gulf War? ______
4. How many years passed between the opening of the Berlin Wall and the end of the Soviet Union? ______
5. Which Soviet block country achieved its goal of a democratic government first? ______

Activity **DIRECTIONS:** Imagine you were living in one of the foreign countries or regions mentioned on the time line when one of the events took place. Create a scrapbook of items that will help you remember that important event. Collect photographs, make drawings, and write short descriptions of what happened. Add items that might have been a part of that time and place. Include appropriate captions. Share your scrapbook with your classmates.

The American Journey ★ 131 ★ **Enrichment Activities**

4 CLOSE

Have students summarize the accomplishments and the setbacks that occurred during Bush's term.

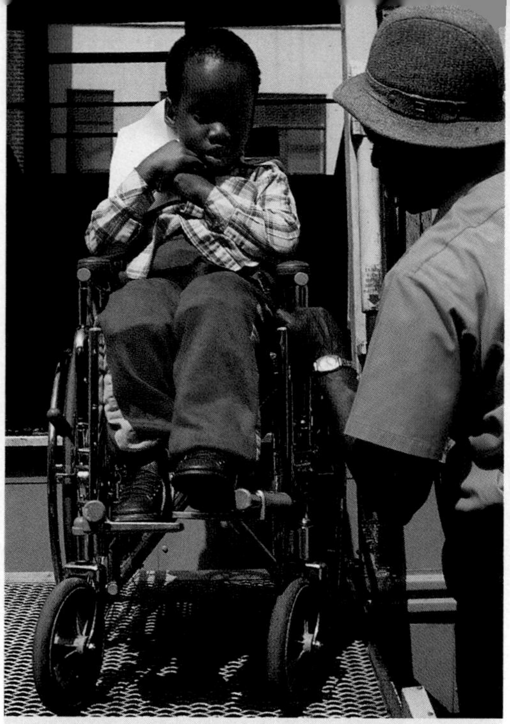

Picturing HISTORY The Americans with Disabilities Act of 1990 requires institutions to provide disabled people with easier access to public transportation. **What other protection does the act provide?**

people and businesses could not meet loan payments. Some had to declare **bankruptcy,** selling off everything they owned to pay debts. Across the country businesses closed. Cuts in military spending, made possible by the end of the cold war, led to additional job losses.

Many people called for the government to step in to stimulate the economy. President Bush refused to increase federal spending. He did agree to extend unemployment benefits for people who had lost their jobs, but he opposed further government involvement. The nation had to wait out the recession.

Accomplishments

While the president and Congress disagreed on many issues, they cooperated on some legislation. In 1990, for example, the president signed a law updating the Clean Air Act. The next year he signed a law combating job discrimination.

Bush and Congress agreed on a major civil rights law as well. The Americans with Disabilities Act of 1990 outlawed job discrimination against people with disabilities. It also required institutions to provide disabled people with easier access to workplaces, communications, transportation, and housing.

Another important part of the president's domestic agenda was the war on illegal drugs. In 1989 President Bush created the Office of National Drug Control Policy. This department coordinates the activities of more than 50 federal agencies involved in the war on drugs.

Section 2 Review

Checking for Understanding

1. ***Identify*** George Bush, Jesse Jackson, Lech Walesa, Boris Yeltsin, Saddam Hussein.
2. ***Define*** coup, bankruptcy.
3. ***Explain*** why the people of Eastern Europe abandoned communism.

Reviewing Themes

4. **Global Connections** Compare President Bush's handling of the Tiananmen Square incident in China to his handling of Iraq's invasion of Kuwait.

Critical Thinking

5. **Determining Cause and Effect** What economic issues reduced Bush's popularity?

Activity

Drawing a Map Illustrate a world map showing the cities and regions discussed in the section.

Section 2 Review Answers

1. George Bush, 910; Jesse Jackson, 910; Lech Walesa, 911; Boris Yeltsin, 912; Saddam Hussein, 914
2. The words are defined in the Glossary.
3. People sensing change in the Soviet Union felt freer to demand change in their countries.
4. Bush took no action against China because he thought international pressure would be ineffective. In contrast, he strongly supported the allies in military action against Iraq.
5. savings and loan failures, rise in federal debt, recession, his refusal to involve federal government in stimulating the economy

Activity Maps should show former Soviet Union, Poland, former East Germany, former Yugoslav republics, Panama, China, Iraq, Kuwait, and Saudi Arabia.

Social Studies Connections World History

Economics | Citizenship | Geography

The Berlin Wall

On the night of August 12, 1961, all of the trains between East Berlin and West Berlin screeched to a halt. The passengers were told to get off and walk home. As people watched in disbelief, Soviet troops unloaded trucks filled with barbed wire, cement, and steel posts. The sound of jackhammers rang throughout the night as the army began building a wall that would separate East and West Berlin.

A joyful crowd celebrates the destruction of the Berlin Wall in November 1989.

Built to prevent East Germans from escaping to West Berlin, the "Wall of Shame" cut through backyards and neighborhoods, dividing families in its wake. About 13 feet high and 97 miles long, the wall looped around West Berlin and cut the city off from East Berlin and East Germany.

Hundreds of people died trying to escape across the wall to West Berlin. Guards with searchlights and machine guns were stationed along the wall in its 300 towers. Some people who tried to escape hid under cars or in coffins. Others swam canals or scaled the wall with grappling hooks. One person even built a submarine and made his escape underwater. About 5,000 people escaped to West Berlin.

For 28 years the wall divided Berlin and its people. With the reunification of the two Germanys in 1990, the wall was destroyed. Today only one section remains as a memorial to its history and the people who died in their attempts to escape.

Activity

"Walling" Your State Make a photocopy of your state map. Draw a line that runs from north to south down the middle of your state to represent a wall. If you were prevented from crossing this wall, which large cities would you be cut off from? What friends and relatives would you never see again? What parks, recreation areas, and bodies of water would be off-limits?

Social Studies Connections World History

TEACH

The Berlin Wall

Egon Krenz was the East German leader who opened the Berlin Wall. He did so in response to the growing unrest in his country, hoping that the gesture would satisfy the people and calm the situation. His strategy backfired, however, as thousands of East Germans poured through the wall.

As one welcoming gesture, each visiting East German had been given 100 marks ($50) in "greeting money" by the West German government. Many chose to spend their money on fresh fruits and vegetables, which showed how poor the East German economy was.

Have students try to imagine how the East Germans felt as they viewed stores filled with modern appliances, beautiful clothing, electronics, and an abundance of groceries. Ask each student to tell how he or she might have spent the $50.

ABC NEWS INTERACTIVE™

VIDEODISC
Communism and the Cold War

Side 1, Chapter 23
Title: *Fall of the Wall*
Subject: Tearing down the wall
Ask: **What did the fall of the Berlin Wall symbolize?** *(the end of Soviet control)*

MORE ABOUT . . .

Erich Honecker was the East German leader before Egon Krenz. A hard-liner, he was vehemently opposed to Gorbachev's reforms. He pledged to use a "Chinese solution" to restore order after massive demonstrations for freedom and democracy took place in East Germany. In early October 1989, he ordered a security force of soldiers, police, and secret-police agents carrying weapons with live ammunition to be prepared to break up a demonstration in Leipzig. However, Honecker faced opposition from Krenz and other Politburo members, who disliked the idea of using force against their own people. Krenz flew to Leipzig and canceled Honecker's orders, and Honecker resigned a few days later.

CHAPTER 32
Section 3, 918–921

1 FOCUS

BELLRINGER
Motivational Activity

Before taking roll at the beginning of the class period, project Section Focus Transparency 32–3 and have students answer the questions. Discuss students' responses.

This activity is also available as a blackline master.

Section Focus Transparency 32–3

North American Trade Balances

1. What was the United States balance of trade with Canada in 1993?
2. What was the United States balance of trade with Mexico in 1991?
3. Describe the trend shown in the United States balance of trade with Canada.

U.S. Trade with Canada and Mexico

Year	Balance of Trade with Canada	Balance of Trade with Mexico
1991	–$5,914,000	+$2,147,000
1992	–$8,036,000	+$5,381,000
1993	–$10,772,000	+$1,664,000
1994	–$14,506,000	+$1,348,000
1995	–$18,232,000	–$15,393,000

(Source: *Statistical Abstracts of the United States*)

(–) negative numbers show a trade deficit
(+) positive numbers show a trade surplus

Vocabulary Precheck
Have students use each **Term to Learn** in a sentence.

Use the **Vocabulary PuzzleMaker** to create crossword and word search puzzles.

Section Theme
Groups and Institutions

Although the president and Congress disagreed on many issues, Clinton was able to implement some of his "New Democrat" programs, while at the same time, the Congress passed some of its Contract with America.

Activity Have students skim the section to find legislation that was passed in Clinton's first term. *(Brady Bill, Family Medical Leave Act of 1993, National Service Act, "Motor Voter" law, increase in minimum wage, Congressional Accountability Act)*

1992 | 1994 | 1996

1992 Bill Clinton is elected president

1993 Congress passes the Brady Bill; NAFTA eliminates trade barriers

1995 Serbs, Croats, and Bosnian Muslims sign a peace plan

1996 Legislation reverses New Deal social welfare

Section 3

The Clinton Presidency

READ TO DISCOVER . . .
- what policies Clinton pursued as president.
- what happened after the Republicans gained control of Congress in 1994.

TERMS TO LEARN
grassroots
budget deficit
line-item veto

The Storyteller

A president appears on MTV. Politicians perform rock music on talk shows. What would George Washington have thought about such events? In 1991 polls showed that voters were turned off by politics. So the 1992 presidential candidates found new ways to reach the public—especially young people. President Bush and challenger Bill Clinton appeared on TV and radio talk shows. On the late evening Arsenio Hall show, Clinton put on sunglasses, and played saxophone. Both he and running mate Al Gore appeared on MTV. By the end of the campaign, even President Bush wanted his time on the music network—and got it!

Clinton inaugural button

After victory in the Persian Gulf War, President Bush seemed assured of winning a second term of office. A lengthening recession, however, raised doubts about his leadership and encouraged challengers to enter the race.

The 1992 Election

In 1992 the Republicans supported President Bush in his bid for reelection. The Democrats nominated Arkansas governor **Bill Clinton** as their candidate. Clinton chose Senator **Al Gore** of Tennessee as his running mate.

During the campaign Clinton promised to overhaul America's current health-care system and to reform welfare. He called himself a New Democrat—favoring an active government that promoted pro-business policies. Above all, Clinton stressed Americans' concerns about the economy.

A third-party candidate, billionaire Texas businessman **H. Ross Perot,** fashioned a strong challenge. Perot stressed the need to end the federal government's deficit spending—spending more money than it takes in. Much of Perot's support came from a grassroots movement—groups of people organizing at the local level throughout the nation.

Bill Clinton won the election with only 43 percent of the popular vote but with 370 of the 538 electoral votes. Bush won 38 percent of the popular vote; Perot received 19 percent—the best showing for a third-party candidate since 1912—but no electoral votes.

SECTION RESOURCES

Reproducible Masters
- Reproducible Lesson Plan 32–3
- Guided Reading Activity 32–3
- Section Quiz 32–3
- Reteaching Activity 32–3
- Enrichment Activity 32–3

Transparencies
- Section Focus Transparency 32–3

Multimedia
- Vocabulary PuzzleMaker
- Chapter Challenger Interactive Review Software
- Testmaker
- GTV: The American People: Fabric of a Nation
- GTV: A Geographic Perspective on American History

Clinton's Agenda

The new president put forth an ambitious domestic program. President Clinton also tried to reduce the **budget deficit**—the amount by which spending exceeds revenue—while ending the recession. His first budget cut government spending, increased taxes on the wealthiest Americans, and gave tax credits to the poorest.

Health Care

During the election campaign, Clinton had promised to reform America's health-care system. High costs were only part of the problem. Across the nation, an estimated 39 million people had no health insurance. His goal was to provide health care for every American and control rising health-care costs.

To prepare the plan, the president appointed a task force headed by his wife, **Hillary Rodham Clinton.** Never before had a First Lady taken such a major role in public policy.

Critics soon attacked the Clinton plan. They called it too complex, too expensive, and too reliant on government control. In the end, Congress never voted on the plan, and the Clinton administration's health-care reform effort died.

Domestic Legislation

During his first term, President Clinton achieved some success. Despite strong opposition, the president succeeded in passing the **Brady Bill** of 1993. The bill required a waiting period before people could buy handguns. The 1994 crime bill banned 19 kinds of assault weapons and provided for 100,000 new police officers.

President George Bush, H. Ross Perot, and Bill Clinton debate during the 1992 campaign.

Another bill on the Clinton agenda to pass Congress was the Family Medical Leave Act of 1993. It permitted workers to take time off from their jobs for special family situations. The National Service Act created AmeriCorps, which enabled college students to repay government education loans by performing community service. The "Motor Voter Law" of 1993 allowed citizens to register to vote when getting a driver's license.

Foreign Policy

President Clinton took office at a time when the nation's attention had shifted from foreign to domestic affairs. With the Soviet Union gone, the concern of many centered on the nation's position in the global economy.

NAFTA

In 1993 Clinton persuaded Congress to ratify the North American Free Trade Agreement, or **NAFTA,** despite strong opposition from labor unions and others who feared the treaty would mean a loss of U.S. jobs. In NAFTA the United States, Canada, and Mexico agreed to eliminate trade barriers among the three nations. NAFTA supporters hoped the treaty would lower costs for U.S. consumers and expand markets.

*F*ootnotes to History

The Brady Bill Legislators named the gun-control bill after James Brady, the White House press secretary who had been severely wounded in the 1981 shooting of President Reagan. Brady and his wife, Sarah, actively worked for passage of the law.

COOPERATIVE LEARNING ACTIVITY

Making a Time Line Have students work together in small groups to make an illustrated time line of events in the history of conflict in Israel, beginning with the conflict over the post-war formation of the country. After the time line is completed, have each group choose one event and prepare a brief talk about the event. Presentations should be accompanied by appropriate visuals. ELL

2 TEACH

L1 Making Summaries Have students create two- or three-sentence summaries for each of the major parts of this section. Have volunteers read their summaries and have the class compare their responses.

When? Who? What? Where?

In 1992, Carol Mosely-Braun of Illinois became the first African American woman elected to the United States Senate, and Ben Nighthorse Campbell of Colorado became the first Native American senator.

Guided Reading Activity 32–3

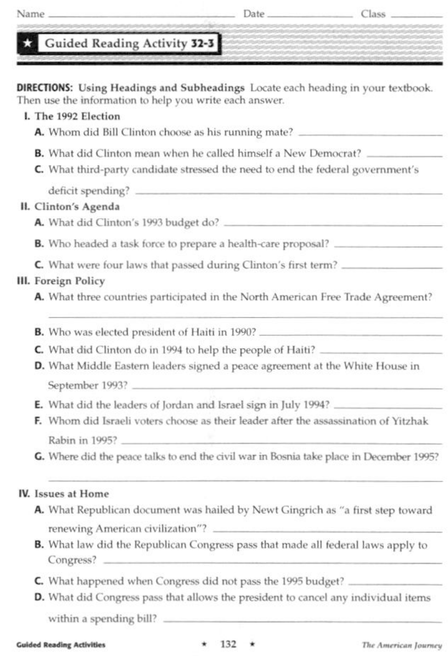

Name ________ Date ________ Class ________

★ Guided Reading Activity **32-3**

DIRECTIONS: Using Headings and Subheadings Locate each heading in your textbook. Then use the information to help you write each answer.

I. The 1992 Election
A. Whom did Bill Clinton choose as his running mate? ________
B. What did Clinton mean when he called himself a New Democrat? ________
C. What third-party candidate stressed the need to end the federal government's deficit spending? ________

II. Clinton's Agenda
A. What did Clinton's 1993 budget do? ________
B. Who headed a task force to prepare a health-care proposal? ________
C. What were four laws that passed during Clinton's first term? ________

III. Foreign Policy
A. What three countries participated in the North American Free Trade Agreement? ________
B. Who was elected president of Haiti in 1990? ________
C. What did Clinton do in 1994 to help the people of Haiti? ________
D. What Middle Eastern leaders signed a peace agreement at the White House in September 1993? ________
E. What did the leaders of Jordan and Israel sign in July 1994? ________
F. Whom did Israeli voters choose as their leader after the assassination of Yitzhak Rabin in 1995? ________
G. Where did the peace talks to end the civil war in Bosnia take place in December 1995? ________

IV. Issues at Home
A. What Republican document was hailed by Newt Gingrich as "a first step toward renewing American civilization"? ________
B. What law did the Republican Congress pass that made all federal laws apply to Congress? ________
C. What happened when Congress did not pass the 1995 budget? ________
D. What did Congress pass that allows the president to cancel any individual items within a spending bill? ________

Guided Reading Activities ★ 132 ★ *The American Journey*

Copyright © by The McGraw-Hill Companies, Inc.

NATIONAL GEOGRAPHIC SOCIETY

VIDEODISC
GTV: The American People: Fabric of a Nation

Side 4, Chapter 6

Title: *Look Again*
Subject: Hispanic American diversity
Ask: **By how much is the Hispanic population expected to jump in the next 40 years?** *(by 187 percent)*

3 ASSESS

Assign Section 3 Review as homework or as an in-class activity.

Use **Chapter Challenger Interactive Review Software** to review Section 3.

Section Quiz 32–3

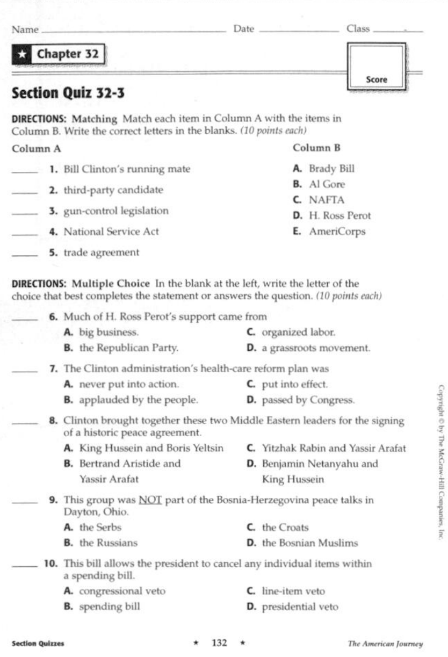

Name ________ Date ________ Class ________

★ Chapter 32

Score

Section Quiz 32-3

DIRECTIONS: Matching Match each item in Column A with the items in Column B. Write the correct letters in the blanks. *(10 points each)*

Column A	Column B
____ **1.** Bill Clinton's running mate	**A.** Brady Bill
____ **2.** third-party candidate	**B.** Al Gore
____ **3.** gun-control legislation	**C.** NAFTA
____ **4.** National Service Act	**D.** H. Ross Perot
____ **5.** trade agreement	**E.** AmeriCorps

DIRECTIONS: Multiple Choice In the blank at the left, write the letter of the choice that best completes the statement or answers the question. *(10 points each)*

____ **6.** Much of H. Ross Perot's support came from
A. big business. **C.** organized labor.
B. the Republican Party. **D.** a grassroots movement.

____ **7.** The Clinton administration's health-care reform plan was
A. never put into action. **C.** put into effect.
B. applauded by the people. **D.** passed by Congress.

____ **8.** Clinton brought together these two Middle Eastern leaders for the signing of a historic peace agreement.
A. King Hussein and Boris Yeltsin **C.** Yitzhak Rabin and Yassir Arafat
B. Bertrand Aristide and Yassir Arafat **D.** Benjamin Netanyahu and King Hussein

____ **9.** This group was NOT part of the Bosnia-Herzegovina peace talks in Dayton, Ohio.
A. the Serbs **C.** the Croats
B. the Russians **D.** the Bosnian Muslims

____ **10.** This bill allows the president to cancel any individual items within a spending bill.
A. congressional veto **C.** line-item veto
B. spending bill **D.** presidential veto

Section Quizzes ★ 132 ★ *The American Journey*

Picturing HISTORY Haiti's secret police, the dreaded Tontons Macoutes, used murder and torture to quash the opposition. **Ask:** Why were Haitians glad to see U.S. troops? *(Haitians hoped they would restore order.)*
Answer: *to enforce an agreement ending rule by Haiti's military and restoring the government of President Jean-Bertrand Aristide*

Democracy in Haiti

Unrest in the Caribbean nation of **Haiti** posed difficult challenges for the United States. Haiti had been ruled by dictators during much of its recent history, but a popular reform-minded priest, **Jean-Bertrand Aristide,** was elected president in 1990. In 1991 military leaders overthrew the Aristide government. The new rulers used violence to put down opposition, causing many Haitians to flee to the United States.

In September 1994, President Clinton readied a U.S. force to invade Haiti and topple the military rulers. After former President Jimmy Carter interceded, the Haitian rulers agreed to step down peacefully. U.S. troops landed to enforce the agreement and oversee the return of President Aristide.

Middle East Peace Accords

In September 1993, President Clinton invited Israeli prime minister **Yitzhak Rabin** and **Yassir Arafat,** head of the Palestine Liberation Organization (PLO), to the White House for the signing of a historic agreement between the two Middle Eastern leaders. Israel recognized the PLO as the representative of the Palestinian people, and the PLO recognized Israel's right to exist.

Picturing HISTORY United States troops met welcoming crowds of Haitians in Port-au-Prince in the fall of 1994. **Why did American troops land in Haiti?**

In July 1994 came another step toward peace in the Middle East. In Washington, D.C., **King Hussein** of **Jordan** and Prime Minister Rabin of Israel signed a declaration ending a state of war that had existed for more than 40 years. The road to peace was anything but smooth, however. The assassination of Prime Minister Rabin in 1995 led to a change in policy in Israel. When Israeli voters chose **Benjamin Netanyahu,** a leader who emphasized security over peace, the future of the peace agreement seemed uncertain.

Civil War in Bosnia

As you read earlier, in 1991 ethnic and religious tensions had erupted in a civil war in the small nation of **Bosnia-Herzegovina** in southeastern Europe. After nearly four years of fighting, the Clinton administration arranged peace talks in Dayton, Ohio. Under pressure from around the world, the Serbs, the Croats, and the Bosnian Muslims accepted a peace plan and signed an agreement in December 1995. However, the peace was unstable, and President Clinton announced that U.S. troops would remain in Bosnia-Herzegovina until 1998.

Issues at Home

★ President Clinton's achievements in foreign policy did not increase his popularity at home. With scandals that touched the Clintons further weakening the president, Republicans hoped to gain ground in the 1994 elections.

The "Contract With America"

To rally support for their cause, the Republicans created a document called the Contract With America. Representative **Newt Gingrich** of Georgia hailed the contract as "a first step toward renewing American civilization."

In the contract, Republicans promised to cut back the size of the federal government, balance the budget, lower taxes, and reform Congress. They also pledged to pass laws to reduce crime, reform welfare, and strengthen the family.

MULTIPLE LEARNING STYLES

Intrapersonal Have students choose one of the following topics: Bloodshed in the Balkans, Unrest in Haiti, Moves Toward Peace in the Middle East. Ask each student to write a feature article evaluating the policies of the Clinton administration in one of these areas. Each article should define the policy and assess its success. What problems still remain? What speculations can be made about the future in these areas? Have students share their articles and discuss the strengths and weaknesses of Clinton's foreign policy. **L3**

A Republican Congress

The Republicans won a major victory, and for the first time since 1954 they controlled both houses of Congress. Now the Republicans appeared to have enough power to push through their programs.

The new Congress opened with a bustle of activity. As part of its promise to reduce the size of government, the House cut the number of committees and reduced the power of committee chairs. They also passed the Congressional Accountability Act, which made all federal laws apply to Congress. A farm bill, enacted in 1996, cut farm subsidies—a program of government payments to farmers that had started in the 1930s.

After the first flush of victory, however, the Republican program slowed. While Republicans in the House eagerly followed Speaker Gingrich's lead, those in the Senate moved more cautiously, and Democrats opposed most of the Republican program. Moreover, President Clinton used his veto to kill several Republican bills on welfare reform and the budget.

Budget Battles

The fiercest battles between the Republican-controlled Congress and President Clinton concerned the budget. Republicans wanted to cut taxes and balance the budget by the year 2002. Clinton and the Democrats balked at making tax cuts that they believed would damage education programs, environmental regulation, and Medicare.

The dispute blocked passage of the 1996 budget, causing the federal government to run out of money. The federal government shut down nonessential services twice for a total of 27 days. Finally, in April 1996, President Clinton and Congress reached a compromise. They also pledged to balance the budget by 2002.

Bipartisan Action

In the final months before the 1996 election, Democrats and Republicans came together to pass sweeping legislation. Congress passed and the president signed a **line-item veto** bill that allows the president to cancel any individual items within a spending bill. In August 1996, the president signed a bill that reversed social welfare policy introduced during the New Deal.

Congress also approved a bill to protect health insurance. While not the major health-care reform the president wanted, the bill assured health coverage for people who changed or lost jobs. Both Democrats and Republicans claimed credit for the legislation as they prepared to campaign to win the White House and Congress.

Section 3 Review

Checking for Understanding

1. ***Identify*** Bill Clinton, Al Gore, H. Ross Perot, Hillary Rodham Clinton, Brady Bill.
2. ***Define*** grassroots, budget deficit, line-item veto.
3. ***Describe*** the goals of NAFTA.

Reviewing Themes

4. **Groups and Institutions** How did the 1994 election affect the balance of parties in Congress?

Critical Thinking

5. **Drawing Conclusions** Why do you think the Republicans and Democrats agreed to cooperate on budget issues in the final months before the 1996 election?

Activity

Prioritizing Events Make a list of Clinton's foreign policy achievements. Then use your own judgment to rank them in order, with the most important achievement as number one. Explain your reasons for your first and last choices.

Section 3 Review Answers

1. Bill Clinton, 918; Al Gore, 918; H. Ross Perot, 918; Hillary Rodham Clinton, 919; Brady Bill, 919
2. The words are defined in the Glossary.
3. to eliminate trade barriers among the United States, Canada, and Mexico with the hope that the treaty would lower costs for American consumers and expand markets for American businesses
4. Republicans gained control of both houses.
5. Both parties wanted to win public support before the election.

Activity Students should rank Clinton's foreign policy achievements from most important to least important. Students should justify their choices for first and last place.

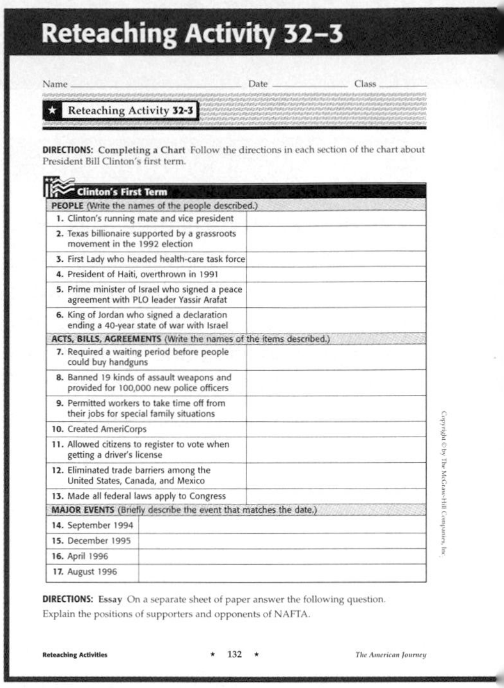
Reteaching Activity 32–3

Name ________ Date ________ Class ________

★ Reteaching Activity 32-3

DIRECTIONS: Completing a Chart Follow the directions in each section of the chart about President Bill Clinton's first term.

Clinton's First Term	
PEOPLE (Write the names of the people described.)	
1. Clinton's running mate and vice president	
2. Texas billionaire supported by a grassroots movement in the 1992 election	
3. First Lady who headed health-care task force	
4. President of Haiti, overthrown in 1991	
5. Prime minister of Israel who signed a peace agreement with PLO leader Yassir Arafat	
6. King of Jordan who signed a declaration ending a 40-year state of war with Israel	
ACTS, BILLS, AGREEMENTS (Write the names of the items described.)	
7. Required a waiting period before people could buy handguns	
8. Banned 19 kinds of assault weapons and provided for 100,000 new police officers	
9. Permitted workers to take time off from their jobs for special family situations	
10. Created AmeriCorps	
11. Allowed citizens to register to vote when getting a driver's license	
12. Eliminated trade barriers among the United States, Canada, and Mexico	
13. Made all federal laws apply to Congress	
MAJOR EVENTS (Briefly describe the event that matches the date.)	
14. September 1994	
15. December 1995	
16. April 1996	
17. August 1996	

DIRECTIONS: Essay On a separate sheet of paper answer the following question. Explain the positions of supporters and opponents of NAFTA.

Reteaching Activities ★ 132 ★ *The American Journey*

Copyright © by The McGraw-Hill Companies, Inc.

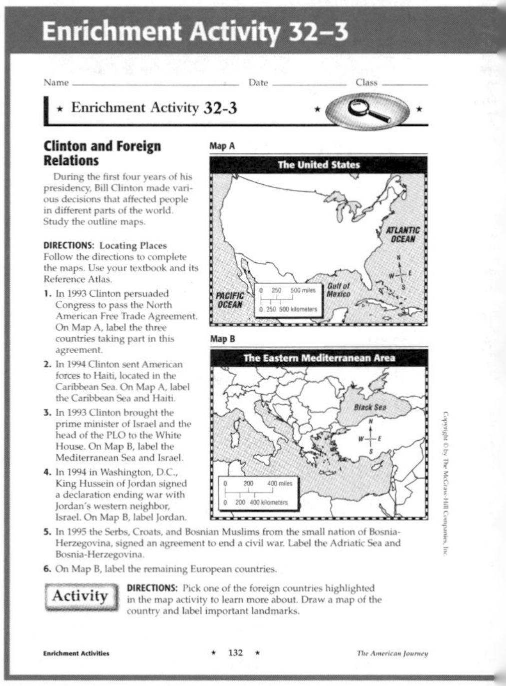

Enrichment Activity 32–3

Name ________ Date ________ Class ________

★ Enrichment Activity 32-3 ★

Clinton and Foreign Relations

During the first four years of his presidency, Bill Clinton made various decisions that affected people in different parts of the world. Study the outline maps.

DIRECTIONS: Locating Places Follow the directions to complete the maps. Use your textbook and its Reference Atlas.

1. In 1993 Clinton persuaded Congress to pass the North American Free Trade Agreement. On Map A, label the three countries taking part in this agreement.
2. In 1994 Clinton sent American forces to Haiti, located in the Caribbean Sea. On Map A, label the Caribbean Sea and Haiti.
3. In 1993 Clinton brought the prime minister of Israel and the head of the PLO to the White House. On Map B, label the Mediterranean Sea and Israel.
4. In 1994 in Washington, D.C., King Hussein of Jordan signed a declaration ending war with Jordan's western neighbor, Israel. On Map B, label Jordan.
5. In 1995 the Serbs, Croats, and Bosnian Muslims from the small nation of Bosnia-Herzegovina, signed an agreement to end a civil war. Label the Adriatic Sea and Bosnia-Herzegovina.
6. On Map B, label the remaining European countries.

Map A

Map B

Activity **DIRECTIONS:** Pick one of the foreign countries highlighted in the map activity to learn more about. Draw a map of the country and label important landmarks.

Enrichment Activities ★ 132 ★ *The American Journey*

Copyright © by The McGraw-Hill Companies, Inc.

4 CLOSE

Discuss why having the line-item veto is an important power for the president.

NATIONAL GEOGRAPHIC

Journeys

What? Where? When? Who?

Calculators The first true calculating machines were developed in the 1600s. Blaise Pascal invented the first automatic calculator in 1642. It performed addition and subtraction by means of a set of wheels linked by gears. The first wheel represented the numbers 1 to 10; the second wheel represented the 10s; the third, the 100s; and so on. When the first wheel was turned 10 notches, a gear moved the second wheel forward one notch.

CURRICULUM CONNECTION

TECHNOLOGY

In the 1830s Charles Babbage developed the idea for a mechanical computer, an idea that he refined for almost 40 years. When performing calculations, Babbage's machine could store completed sets of punched cards for use in later operations. This machine contained all the elements of a modern computer: storage, a working memory, a system for moving between the two, and an input device. The technology of Babbage's time, however, was not sophisticated enough to create the precision parts he needed to construct his machine, and Babbage lacked funding for his project. In addition, Babbage, like others of his time, did not understand electricity.

Computer chips and fiber-optic cables (in background) have changed the way we live and work. Introduced in the 1970s, the computer chip went inside machines, cars, and appliances. Fiber-optic cables—sending messages as pulses of light through glass in the cables—enabled computers to communicate at lightning speeds. Everywhere, people hooked up computers and shared information.

2 In 1903 the Wright brothers coaxed an airplane (above left) into the air for a 12-second flight. Today the space shuttle (above), guided by scientists and computers, carries people and experiments hundreds of miles beyond the planet.

1 Invented in 1876, the telephone quickly gained popularity. By the mid-20th century, the world was using it for business and pleasure. Today a computer chip in a portable cellular phone (above right) processes radio signals so that a caller can make a call from virtually anywhere.

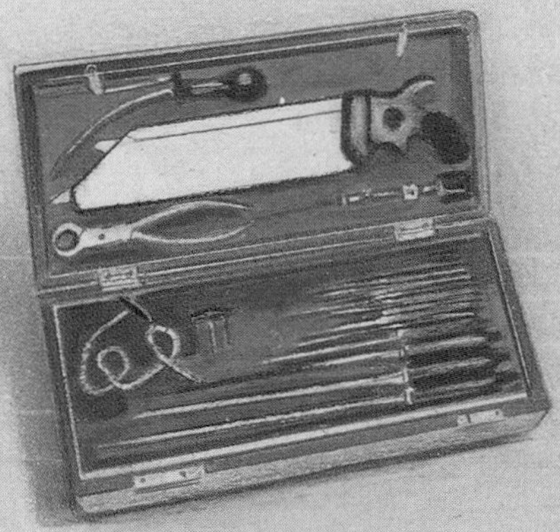

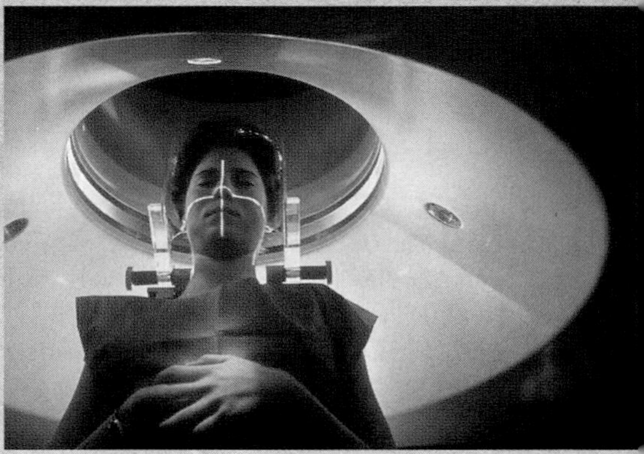

3 Surgeons once operated with crude equipment, such as the implements at left, with no idea that germs cause infection. Today's doctors are armed with greater knowledge and sophisticated machinery. The patient above gets a CT (computer tomography) scan, which will give her doctor a 3-D image of her brain before—or perhaps even instead of—an operation.

TEACHER'S NOTES

NATIONAL GEOGRAPHIC
Journeys

4 A century ago students learned to read and write in one-room schoolhouses. Today students can sit in class and roam the planet. Computers and telephones collaborate to bring information, images, and sound from all corners of the world. In the photo above, a student, using a computer at National Geographic Society headquarters in Washington, D.C., interacts with members of a scientific expedition in Hawaii.

Technology's Journey

"Futurist Alvin Toffler has written about three 'waves' of civilization. [The first two waves were agricultural and industrial.] According to Toffler, a Third Wave has begun in which computing and telecommunications technologies will transform the global economy and [profoundly alter our society]. The Third Wave began almost 50 years ago with ENIAC ... the first all-electronic computer.... Yet the computer ... will be dwarfed by the impact of new digital telecommunications technologies ... [which will] forever change the way we live, learn, work, and communicate."

—From "The Information Superhighway: What It Will Mean" by Vice President Al Gore, Jr., published in The World Almanac, *1995.*

NATIONAL GEOGRAPHIC SOCIETY

VIDEODISC
GTV: A Geographic Perspective on American History

Side 4, Chapter 14
Title: *You've Grown Accustomed to My Face*
Subject: Coming of age in the Information Age
Ask: **Which development—the television, computer, telephone, or something else—do you think has had the greatest impact on the world?** *(Have students justify their responses.)*

Linking PAST & *PRESENT*

Early Computers In 1946 ENIAC, the first general-purpose electronic digital computer, filled a huge room. It weighed 30 tons.

The first personal computer, the Altair, was introduced in 1975. It cost $400, and came in a hard-to-assemble kit. Only hobbyists bought this computer, which did not work that well. It had no external memory, no printer, and no keyboard. Limited programming and data entry could be done by flipping toggle switches on the front. Despite this, the Altair was a big hit with hobbyists, who sensed that they were on the front line of a technological revolution.

In 1977 Steven Jobs and Stephen Wozniak founded the Apple Computer Company. They introduced the Apple II personal computer. It was much less expensive than a mainframe, and so, for the first time, computers became available to people other than technicians and computer specialists.

TEACHER'S NOTES

CHAPTER 32
Section 4, 924–928

1 FOCUS

BELLRINGER
Motivational Activity

Before taking roll at the beginning of the class period, project Section Focus Transparency 32–4 and have students answer the questions. Discuss students' responses.

This activity is also available as a blackline master.

Section Focus Transparency 32–4

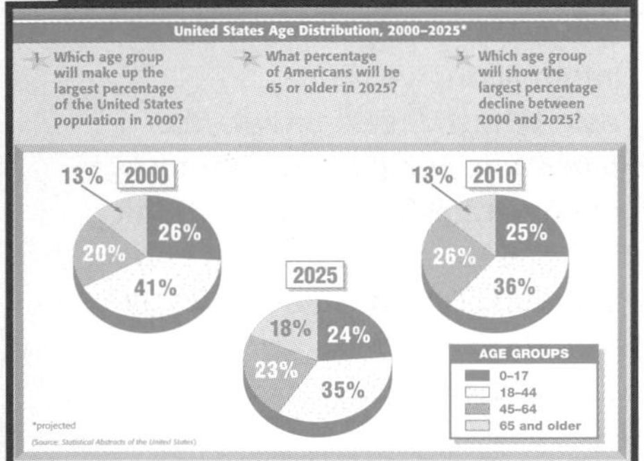

Vocabulary Precheck
Call on volunteers to skim the section to find the terms and read them in context.

Use the **Vocabulary PuzzleMaker** to create crossword and word search puzzles.

Section Theme
Science and Technology
By the mid-1900s a new telecommunications revolution had spread throughout our nation as Americans used computers in homes, schools, offices, and factories, and watched television by cable or satellite, spoke on cellular phones, and exchanged messages by fax.

Activity Have students give examples of how they use some of this technology.

1994 — 1996 — 1998 — 2000

1995
Computers are an essential part of American life

1996
UN environmental agencies meet to discuss ozone problem

November 1996
Bill Clinton wins reelection

2000
People over age 65 make up 20 percent of the population

Section 4

Toward the 21st Century

READ TO DISCOVER . . .
- what candidates and issues were involved in the 1996 elections.
- how American society is changing.

TERMS TO LEARN
incumbent
gross domestic product
Internet
ozone
global warming

The Storyteller

Poet Robert Frost wrote "The Road Not Taken" in 1915. As the 21st century approaches, what will your own journey be like?

Two roads diverged in a yellow wood,
And sorry I could not travel both
And be one traveler, long I stood
And looked down one as far as I could
To where it bent in the undergrowth; . . .

I shall be telling this with a sigh
Somewhere ages and ages hence;
Two roads diverged in a wood, and I—
I took the one less traveled by,
And that has made all the difference.

Earth *by David Laurence*

The 1996 presidential election pitted a president whom many Americans mistrusted against a Republican challenger whom many voters associated with the unpopular 104th Congress.

The 1996 Elections

Early in 1995, the Republicans had high hopes of winning the White House in the next election. However, the political climate changed during the budget battles of 1995–1996. Clinton and the Democrats gained support by defending government-funded health care for the elderly and educational and environmental programs. They claimed that Republican cuts would wreck Medicare and ruin the environment.

The Candidates

By early 1996 a number of prominent Republicans had entered the presidential race. Senator **Bob Dole** of Kansas, the Republican leader in the Senate, eventually won his party's nomination. A war hero wounded in World War II, the 72-year-old Dole had served in Congress since 1961.

Senator Dole chose **Jack Kemp** as his running mate. Kemp, a former representative from New York, had served as secretary of housing and urban development under President Reagan.

On the Democratic side, President Clinton and Vice President **Al Gore** easily won renomination. Clinton sought to portray himself as the best leader for America's future. In his acceptance

SECTION RESOURCES

Reproducible Masters
- Guided Reading Activity 32–4
- Section Quiz 32–4
- Reteaching Activity 32–4
- Enrichment Activity 32–4

Transparencies
- Section Focus Transparency 32–4
- U.S. History & Art, Transparencies 28, 29

Multimedia
- Chapter Challenger Interactive Review
- Testmaker
- GTV: American People: Fabric of a Nation
- GTV: A Geographic Perspective on American History
- The Presidents: A Picture History of Our Nation
- Focus on American Art Prints

speech at the Democratic national convention, Clinton used a phrase that would become the slogan of his campaign: "I want to build a bridge to the twenty-first century."

In August, **H. Ross Perot,** who had received 19 percent of the popular vote in the 1992 election, entered the presidential race. This time he ran as the candidate of the Reform Party, which he had created. Perot named **Pat Choate,** a conservative economist, as his running mate.

The Campaign

All three candidates proclaimed their dedication to balancing the budget, reducing crime, supporting basic family values, and improving education. Many Americans expressed a lack of enthusiasm for any of the candidates.

Early in the campaign, Dole announced plans for a 15 percent tax cut. He promised to reduce taxes and still balance the federal budget. "The federal government is too big and takes too much of your money," Dole told voters.

Dole raised other issues as well. He favored measures to stop illegal immigration. He accused Clinton of being a big spender. He also raised doubts about the ethics of the Clinton administration. Dole assured Americans, "I will never compromise ethics or violate the public trust."

Clinton ran on his record as president. Declaring the nation to be "on the right track," he asked Americans to consider whether they were better off than they had been in 1992. He also took credit for "10.5 million more jobs, rising incomes, falling crime rates and welfare rolls, a strong America at peace."

Ross Perot made few campaign appearances. As in 1992, he relied heavily on television "infomercials." He declared that neither the Republican nor the Democratic Party could solve the nation's problems and attacked Clinton on the ethics issue. "Shouldn't the occupant of the White House," Perot asked, "be honest, trustworthy and loyal?"

Bob and Elizabeth Dole during the campaign

Clinton Is Reelected

Fewer than half the nation's eligible voters went to the polls on Election Day—the lowest turnout for a presidential election since 1924. Those who did vote seemed to agree with Clinton that the country was doing fairly well. The president won reelection.

The Election of 1996

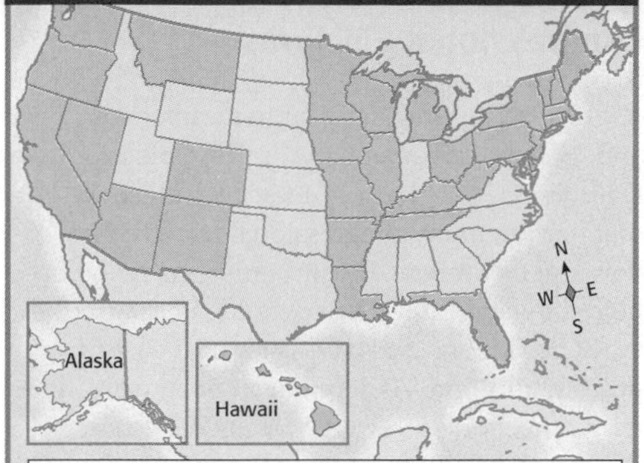

	Popular vote:	Electoral vote:
Clinton	45,628,667	379
Dole	37,869,435	159
Perot	7,874,283	0

Map Study

Bill Clinton's victory in 1996 marked the first time a Democratic president had won reelection in more than 50 years.

1. **Place** Which candidate won the electoral votes in your state?
2. **Analyzing Information** How many electoral votes did Clinton receive?

*F*ootnotes to History

Madeleine Albright President Clinton named Madeleine K. Albright secretary of state. She was the first woman to serve in that post and the highest-ranking woman ever in the federal government. Previously, Albright served as UN ambassador.

COOPERATIVE LEARNING ACTIVITY

Making a Survey Organize the class into groups of five. Have the groups create a questionnaire on the major issues confronting the United States today. Point out that the objective of the questionnaire is to discover what Americans think will be the greatest challenges for the nation as the twenty-first century begins. Have groups give the questionnaire to friends and family members and present their findings to the class. Ask groups to combine their results to find the five most important issues.

2 TEACH

L1 Formulating Questions Have students turn the **Read to Discover** items into questions and write a one- or two-paragraph answer to each.

Map Study

Answers

1. Answer depends on student's state.
2. 379

Guided Reading Activity 32–4

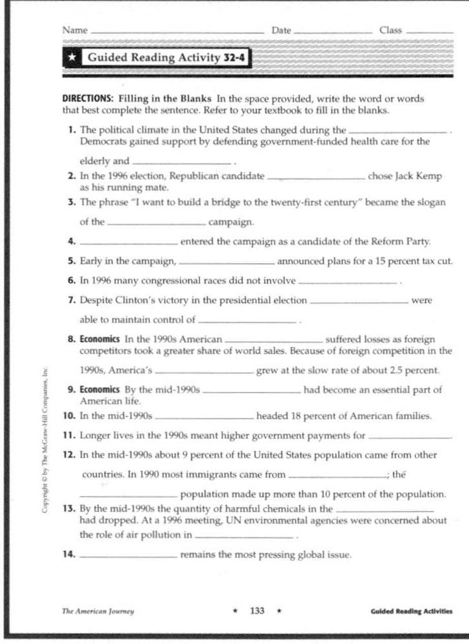
Name Date Class

★ Guided Reading Activity 32-4

DIRECTIONS: Filling in the Blanks In the space provided, write the word or words that best complete the sentence. Refer to your textbook to fill in the blanks.

1. The political climate in the United States changed during the ________. Democrats gained support by defending government-funded health care for the elderly and ________.
2. In the 1996 election, Republican candidate ________ chose Jack Kemp as his running mate.
3. The phrase "I want to build a bridge to the twenty-first century" became the slogan of the ________ campaign.
4. ________ entered the campaign as a candidate of the Reform Party.
5. Early in the campaign, ________ announced plans for a 15 percent tax cut.
6. In 1996 many congressional races did not involve ________.
7. Despite Clinton's victory in the presidential election ________ were able to maintain control of ________.
8. **Economics** In the 1990s American ________ suffered losses as foreign competitors took a greater share of world sales. Because of foreign competition in the 1990s, America's ________ grew at the slow rate of about 2.5 percent.
9. **Economics** By the mid-1990s ________ had become an essential part of American life.
10. In the mid-1990s ________ headed 18 percent of American families.
11. Longer lives in the 1990s meant higher government payments for ________.
12. In the mid-1990s about 9 percent of the United States population came from other countries. In 1990 most immigrants came from ________; the ________ population made up more than 10 percent of the population.
13. By the mid-1990s the quantity of harmful chemicals in the ________ had dropped. At a 1996 meeting, UN environmental agencies were concerned about the role of air pollution in ________.
14. ________ remains the most pressing global issue.

The American Journey ★ 133 ★ **Guided Reading Activities**

Who? What? Where? When?

The Candidate's Wives Elizabeth Hanford Dole was appointed secretary of transportation by President Reagan in 1983. In 1989 she was appointed secretary of labor by President Bush. Since 1990 she has been the director of the American Red Cross. In 1977 Hillary Rodham Clinton founded the Arkansas Advocates for Children and Families. In that same year, she joined a law firm where she specialized in patent infringement and intellectual property. She was twice named one of the 100 most influential lawyers in America by the *National Law Journal.*

NATIONAL GEOGRAPHIC SOCIETY

VIDEODISC
GTV: The American People: Fabric of a Nation

Side 4, Chapter 8

Title: *The Center Cannot Hold?*
Subject: Diversity and unity
Ask: **Who said "A big part of . . . having people . . . solve their own problems is getting people to believe they can"?** *(Chief Wilma Mankiller)*

CD-ROM
The Presidents: A Picture History of Our Nation

Suggest that students select "Political Parties" from the main menu and the subcategory THIRD PARTIES. Have students identify elections in which third-party candidates had a significant impact.

History *and the* Humanities

U.S. History & Art, Transparency 28, *The Family;* 29, *Still Life With Red Car*

Focus on American Art Prints, *Springtime on the Pedernales* by Porfirio Salinas

TECHNOLOGY AND HISTORY

More About . . .
Computer Software Software for the first computers was written by people who built the machines. By the early 1970s, nearly half the cost of a computer was in the software. Companies then decided to start charging for the software separately. Soon separate software companies developed, and the number of software programs exploded.
Answer to Caption: *the central processing unit (CPU)*

Congressional Elections

In 1996 an unusually large number of House and Senate members, both Republicans and Democrats, decided not to seek reelection. For that reason, many congressional races did not involve an incumbent. **Incumbents**—current officeholders—often have an advantage because they are better known and have built up a base of support. In addition, 70 Republican freshmen—first-term officeholders—were seeking reelection.

Despite Clinton's victory in the presidential race, Republicans were able to maintain control of both houses of Congress. In the Senate, Republicans gained 2 seats. They now held 55 seats, while the Democrats held 45. In addition, 10 of the 20 incumbent senators seeking reelection were returned to office. In the House, Democrats gained 11 seats but still trailed the Republicans 226 to 207. Two seats were held by independents.

Looking to the Future

As Americans prepared to enter a new century, many questioned what lay ahead. In his 1997 Inaugural Address, President Bill Clinton sounded a hopeful note:

> "At the dawn of the twenty-first century, a free people must choose to shape the forces of the information age and the

TECHNOLOGY AND HISTORY

Personal Computer

The first computers were 8 feet high and 50 feet long. Today some personal computers can fit in your lap! **What part of the computer does the "thinking"?**

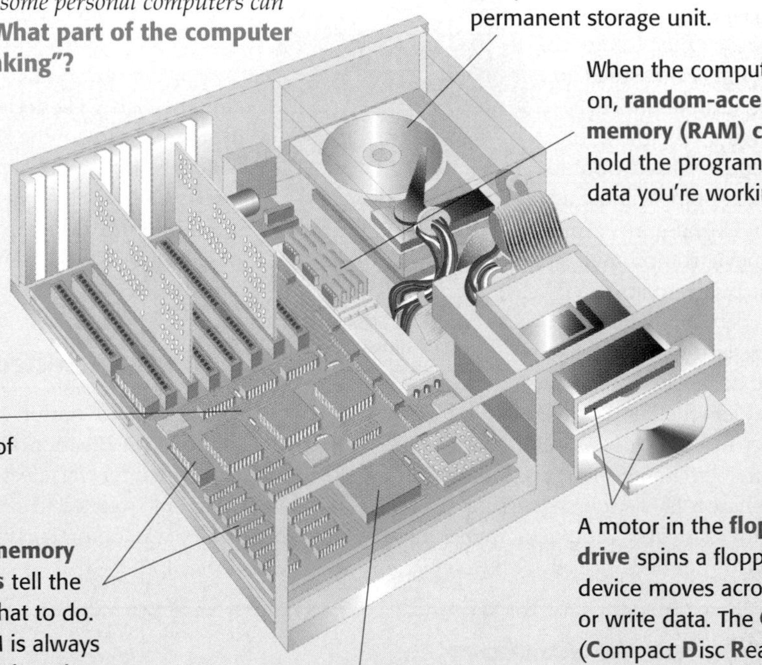

The **hard disk drive** is the computer's main permanent storage unit.

When the computer is on, **random-access memory (RAM) chips** hold the program and data you're working on.

Thin metal lines on the fiberglass **motherboard** connect all the electronic parts of the computer.

Read-only memory (ROM) chips tell the computer what to do. Data in ROM is always there, even when the computer is turned off.

The **central processing unit (CPU)** does all of the computer's thinking and runs all of its programs.

A motor in the **floppy disk drive** spins a floppy disk as a device moves across it to read or write data. The **CD-ROM** (**C**ompact **D**isc **R**ead-**O**nly **M**emory) drive reads information from a compact disc.

MULTIPLE LEARNING STYLES

Logical/Mathematical Have students choose a subject appropriate to the section, such as the incidence of AIDS and HIV infection in various nations, the growth of the national debt, the percentage of the United States population at various age levels, or the gross domestic product over a period of years. Have students find information for making tables and graphs on those subjects. Display the finished products on the bulletin board. Some students may wish to prepare their tables and graphs on the computer (see Technology Skill Builder on page 929). **L2**

global society, to unleash the limitless potential of all our people and form a more perfect union. ❞

Economics

The Changing Economy

Although the United States still ranked as the world's largest economy in the 1990s, the nation faced tough competition from other nations. U.S. steel, auto, and electronics industries, in particular, suffered losses as foreign competitors took a greater share of world sales.

The impact of increased foreign competition on the United States could be measured in its rate of growth, or **gross domestic product** (GDP). GDP is the value of all the goods and services produced in the nation in a year. In the post–World War II boom, the nation's GDP grew by nearly 4 percent a year. In the 1990s, the GDP continued to grow but at a slower rate—about 2.5 percent.

Impact of Technology

Certain industries did expand in the 1990s. Telecommunications grew rapidly as Americans watched television by cable or satellite, spoke on cellular phones, and exchanged messages by fax. By the mid-1990s computers held an important place in homes, schools, offices, and factories. Through the **Internet**, a worldwide linking of computer networks, American students could communicate with students in countries halfway around the world.

Picturing HISTORY A Missouri farmer uses a laptop computer to obtain information vital to raising his crops. **How have computers transformed American life?**

A Changing Society

Continuing a trend that began in the 1970s, more and more two-parent families saw both parents working. At the same time, economic pressures and other factors pushed up divorce rates; two-parent families became less typical than before. In the mid-1990s single women headed 18 percent of the families in the country. Working mothers, whether single or married, often found it difficult to juggle a job and a family.

An Aging Population

Because Americans were living longer than in the past, elderly people formed a larger portion of the population. In 1970, 8 percent of all Americans were over 65 years old. By 1990 the figure had risen to 12 percent, and experts predicted that by the year 2000 people over 65 would make up 20 percent of the population.

This "graying" of the American people had consequences for society at large. As more people lived longer, government payments for Social Security and Medicare increased. Analysts feared that these increased payments would put a burden on a shrinking workforce.

Filipino woman sworn in as new citizen

Changes in Immigration

The composition of the American people changed in another way as the proportion of immigrants increased. In the mid-1990s about 9 percent of the population came from other countries—the highest level since 1940. In earlier years, the largest groups of immigrants had come from Europe. By the 1990s Asia and Latin America

CHAPTER 32
Section 4, 924–928

Picturing HISTORY The small laptop computer is made possible by microchips, one of which can hold 10 times the electrical circuits of the old room-sized computers of the 1940s.
Answer: *Communication has increased with the use of computers in homes, schools, offices, stores, and factories.*

NATIONAL GEOGRAPHIC SOCIETY

VIDEODISC
GTV: A Geographic Perspective on American History

Side 4, Chapter 21

Title: *What Goes Around, Comes Around*
Subject: Environmental statement
Ask: **How much trash do Americans throw away annually?**
(6 billion tons)

3 ASSESS

Assign Section 4 Review as homework or as an in-class activity.

Section Quiz 32–4

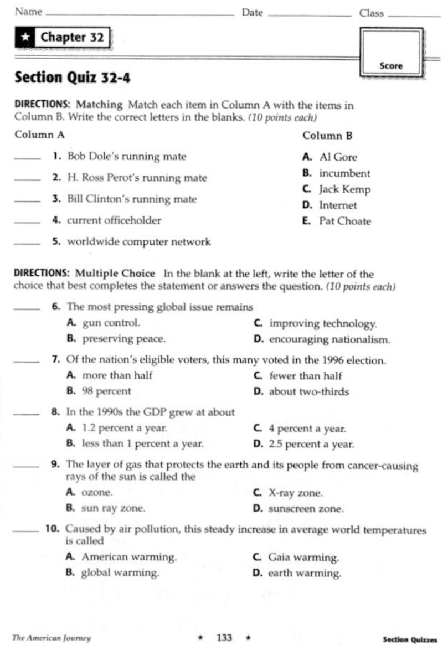

Name ______ Date ______ Class ______

★ Chapter 32   Score

Section Quiz 32-4

DIRECTIONS: Matching Match each item in Column A with the items in Column B. Write the correct letters in the blanks. *(10 points each)*

Column A	Column B
____ 1. Bob Dole's running mate	A. Al Gore
____ 2. H. Ross Perot's running mate	B. incumbent
____ 3. Bill Clinton's running mate	C. Jack Kemp
____ 4. current officeholder	D. Internet
____ 5. worldwide computer network	E. Pat Choate

DIRECTIONS: Multiple Choice In the blank at the left, write the letter of the choice that best completes the statement or answers the question. *(10 points each)*

____ 6. The most pressing global issue remains
A. gun control. C. improving technology.
B. preserving peace. D. encouraging nationalism.

____ 7. Of the nation's eligible voters, this many voted in the 1996 election.
A. more than half C. fewer than half
B. 98 percent D. about two-thirds

____ 8. In the 1990s the GDP grew at about
A. 1.2 percent a year. C. 4 percent a year.
B. less than 1 percent a year. D. 2.5 percent a year.

____ 9. The layer of gas that protects the earth and its people from cancer-causing rays of the sun is called the
A. ozone. C. X-ray zone.
B. sun ray zone. D. sunscreen zone.

____ 10. Caused by air pollution, this steady increase in average world temperatures is called
A. American warming. C. Gaia warming.
B. global warming. D. earth warming.

The American Journey ★ 133 ★ Section Quizzes

MAKING CONNECTIONS ACTIVITY

Global Issues Some of the issues addressed in Section 4 unite the world because they create common concerns, goals, and needs. Point out that students will be involved in the search for solutions to these issues in their adult years. Hold a roundtable discussion on an issue selected by the class. Then organize the class into a number of committees to investigate various aspects of the issue. Have groups report their findings to the class. Ask students to suggest ways in which they as adults would attempt to resolve the issue. **L3**

CHAPTER 32
Section 4, 924–928

Use **Chapter Challenger Interactive Review Software** to review Section 4.

Reteaching Activity 32–4

Name ______ Date ______ Class ______

★ Reteaching Activity 32-4

DIRECTIONS: Word Cross Complete the puzzle by using the clues to spell out each term. Then fill in the missing letters to write the term spelled vertically. Write the term and its definition on line 11.

Bob Dole	**ozone**	**H. Ross Perot**	**Internet**
telecommunications	**Bill Clinton**	**gross domestic product**	**Al Gore**
global warming	**incumbents**	**Hispanic**	

1. Democratic candidate for vice president in 1996 election
2. candidate who relied on television infomercials in 1996 election
3. ethnic group that made up more than 10 percent of the population by 1995
4. layer of gas that protects the earth's people from cancer-causing sun rays
5. a worldwide linking of computer networks
6. many of these current officeholders did not run for reelection in 1996
7. candidate in 1996 election who took credit for millions of new jobs, rising incomes, and falling crime rates
8. a steady increase in average world temperatures
9. Republican candidate for president in 1996 election
10. one of the industries that grew rapidly in the United States in the 1990s

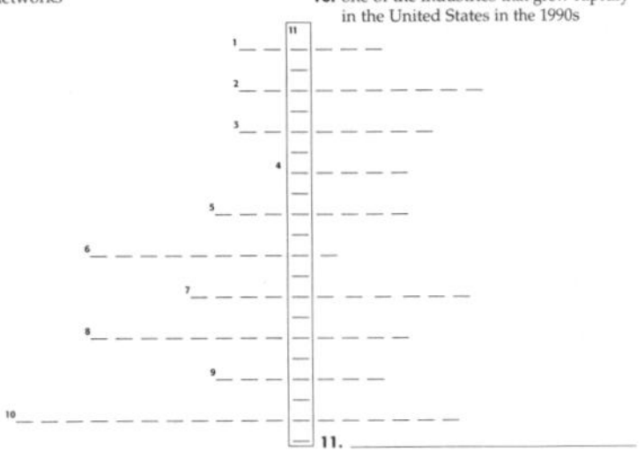

11. ______

The American Journey ★ 133 ★ **Reteaching Activities**

Enrichment Activity 32–4

Name ______ Date ______ Class ______

★ Enrichment Activity 32-4 ★

Words for a New World

In his 1997 State of the Union speech, President Bill Clinton discussed the changes ahead. As these kinds of changes in technology and lifestyle occur, new words are added to the language to accommodate the changes.

DIRECTIONS: Defining Words The box below contains some recent words added to our language. Write the word that matches each definition.

cyberspace	**fax**	**Internet**	**ecotourist**
infomercial	**hot button**	**infotainment**	**cocooning**

1. ______ Spending free time at home, not going out
2. ______ Person who travels to view natural habitats in a way that avoids harming or changing them
3. ______ Online world of computer networks
4. ______ Television news program presented in an entertaining way
5. ______ Issue that triggers instant response
6. ______ Television program, with discussions and demonstrations, that is a long advertisement
7. ______ Worldwide linking of computer networks
8. ______ Exact copy of a document sent over telephone lines

Activity **DIRECTIONS:** What things do you think will be invented in the future? Think of an item, make up a word for it, and write a definition of your future invention. Draw a picture to go with your definition. Then describe how your invention will work, who will manufacture it, who will buy it, and what benefits the purchaser will receive from your invention. Finally, explain how you will promote and sell your invention.

The American Journey ★ 133 ★ **Enrichment Activities**

4 CLOSE

In 1996 President Clinton said that America should not try to be the world's police [officer] but rather its peacemaker. **Ask: How is being the world's police [officer] different from being its peacemaker?**

provided the greatest number of immigrants. The Hispanic population in the United States had grown quickly and by 1995 made up more than 10 percent of the nation's population.

Global Challenges

Today more than ever, the countries and peoples of the world depend on each other. Goals such as preserving the world's environment and maintaining peace cannot be accomplished by any one country alone.

Protecting the Environment

For years scientists noted that the earth's atmosphere was losing **ozone.** This layer of gas protects the earth and its people from cancer-causing rays of the sun. Certain chemicals cause reactions that decrease ozone. In 1987, 23 nations agreed to take steps to reduce the manufacture and use of ozone-destroying chemicals. In the mid-1990s, researchers announced that the quantity of these chemicals had dropped. While scientists predicted it would still take years for the ozone to be restored, they agreed a first step had been taken.

Scientists continue to debate the seriousness of another important environmental issue: **global warming**—a steady increase in average world temperatures. A 1996 meeting of UN environmental agencies expressed concern over the possible role of air pollution in global warming. Their report urged stronger enforcement of a 1992 treaty signed by 159 nations to reduce industrial pollution, noting that "a wait-and-see approach would be imprudent [unwise]."

World Peace

Preserving peace remains the most pressing global issue. The United States has taken steps toward removing a major threat to peace by negotiating agreements to control nuclear weapons with Russia and Ukraine. Another major threat to world peace comes from ethnic conflict. Mistrust between ethnic and religious groups boiled to the surface in the 1990s in Europe, Africa, and the Middle East. The United States has tried to convince warring groups to settle differences peacefully.

In his 1997 State of the Union Address, President Clinton explained his view of the role of the United States in world affairs:

> "America must continue to be an unrelenting force for peace—from the Middle East to Haiti, from Northern Ireland to Africa. . . . We are the world's most diverse democracy, and the world looks to us to show that it is possible to live and advance together across those kinds of differences."

Section 4 Review

Checking for Understanding

1. ***Identify*** Bob Dole, Jack Kemp, Al Gore, H. Ross Perot.
2. ***Define*** incumbent, gross domestic product, Internet, ozone, global warming.
3. ***Name*** three American industries that suffered from foreign competition.

Reviewing Themes

4. **Science and Technology** What American industries have prospered as a result of recent technology?

Critical Thinking

5. **Predicting Consequences** Why might an aging population place a burden on younger people in the workforce?

Activity

Creating a Diagram Draw a diagram that illustrates the process of global warming.

Section 4 Review Answers

1. Bob Dole, 924; Jack Kemp, 924
2. The words are defined in the Glossary.
3. steel, auto, and electronics industries
4. telecommunications and computer industries
5. The government will probably raise taxes to provide more money for Social Security and Medicare, and younger people in the workforce will be the ones to pay those taxes.

Activity Students' diagrams should show that they understand the process of global warming.

Technology
SKILL BUILDER

Using an Electronic Spreadsheet

People use electronic spreadsheets to manage numbers quickly and easily. You can use a spreadsheet any time a problem involves numbers that you can arrange in rows and columns.

Students working on a computer spreadsheet

Learning the Skill

A spreadsheet is an electronic worksheet. All spreadsheets follow a basic design of rows and columns. Each column (vertical) is assigned a letter or a number. Each row (horizontal) is assigned a number. Each point where a column and row intersect is called a *cell.* The cell's position on the spreadsheet is labeled according to its corresponding column and row—Column A, Row 1 (A1); Column B, Row 2 (B2), etc.

Spreadsheets use *standard formulas* to calculate the numbers. You create a simple mathematical equation that uses these standard formulas and the computer does the calculations for you.

Practicing the Skill

Suppose you want to know how many votes the Republican, Democratic, and Independent candidates received across six states in the 1996 presidential election. Use these steps to create a spreadsheet that will provide this information:

1. In cells B1, C1, and D1 respectively, type a candidate's name or political party. In cell E1, type the term *total.*
2. In cells A2–A7, type the name of a state. In cell A8, type the word *total.*
3. In row 2, enter the number of votes each candidate received in the state named in cell A2. Repeat this process in rows 3–7.
4. Create a formula to calculate the votes. The formula for the equation tells what cells (2B + 2C + 2D) to add together.
5. Copy the formula down in the cells for the other five states.
6. Use the process in steps 4 and 5 to create and copy a formula to calculate the total number of votes each candidate received.

Applying the Skill

Using a Spreadsheet Use a spreadsheet to enter your test scores and your homework grades. At the end of the grading period, the spreadsheet will calculate your average grade.

ANSWERS TO PRACTICING THE SKILL

Students will use a spreadsheet to keep track of their class grade during the grading period. Spreadsheets will vary according to students' grades.

Technology
SKILL BUILDER

TEACH

Using an Electronic Spreadsheet

This skill teaches students to work with a spreadsheet program on the computer. Review **Practicing the Skill** with students, and then allow them computer time to apply the directions. Ask volunteers for suggestions of types of information that could be placed on spreadsheets. *(budgets, grades, schedules, and so forth)* Some students may wish to use the application as they do the **Multiple Learning Styles** activity on page 926.

Additional Practice

Chapter Skills Activity 32

GLENCOE TECHNOLOGY

VIDEODISC
MindJogger Videoquiz

Use MindJogger to review the Chapter 32 content.

Chapter 32
Disc 4, Side B

Also available in VHS.

Reviewing Key Terms

The key terms used in this activity can be found in the textbook glossary on pages A26–A35.

Reviewing Key Facts

1. Reagan's economic policy, which was based on increasing the supply of goods and services in order to stimulate the economy, and by lowering taxes and reducing government spending
2. Gorbachev called for more honesty and openness in government, allowed more democracy and local economic planning, and reduced military spending.
3. Polish shipyard workers formed Solidarity—the first independent labor union in Poland. Under Lech Walesa, the union called for reforms. By June 1989, Solidarity had forced the government to hold open elections and other eastern European governments followed their example.
4. Iraq's invasion of Kuwait and refusal to withdraw by the UN deadline
5. high costs, 39 million people without coverage
6. The accords were an important step toward peace in an area that had seen years of violence.
7. The GDP is still growing but at a slower rate of 2.5% a year, versus 4% during the post-World War II boom.
8. Asia, Latin America

Critical Thinking

1. made it harder to get support for his policies
2. Students should convey that voters were not satisfied with Democratic candidates and were looking for change.

Time Line Activity

Events should be placed in this order: Sandra Day O'Connor named to Supreme Court; Geraldine Ferraro is first woman from a major party to run for vice president; Ronald Reagan is reelected president; Iraq invades Kuwait; Soviet Union dissolves; Bill Clinton is elected to first term as president; Serbs, Croats, and Bosnian Muslims sign peace agreement to end civil war

---

Chapter 32

Review and Activities

Reviewing Key Terms

On a sheet of paper, define the following terms:

deregulation	**budget deficit**
federal debt	**incumbent**
glasnost	**gross domestic product**
perestroika	**Internet**
coup	**ozone**
bankruptcy	**global warming**
grassroots	**line-item veto**

Reviewing Key Facts

1. What is supply-side economics?
2. How did Mikhail Gorbachev try to reform the Soviet government?
3. How did Poland lead the way in toppling communism in Eastern Europe?
4. What event triggered the Persian Gulf War?
5. Why was health care an important issue in the 1990s?
6. What was the significance of the Middle East Peace Accords?
7. How did the growth rate of the gross domestic product during the 1990s compare to the rate after World War II?
8. What world regions contributed the largest number of immigrants during the 1990s?

Critical Thinking

Making Inferences

Republicans gained control of both houses of Congress in the 1994 election.

1. How did this affect Clinton's effectiveness as president?
2. What message do you think voters were trying to convey by electing a majority of Republicans to both houses of Congress?

Time Line Activity

Create a time line on which you place the following events in chronological order.

- Serbs, Croats, and Bosnian Muslims sign peace agreement to end civil war
- Soviet Union dissolves
- Bill Clinton is elected to first term as president
- Geraldine Ferraro is first woman from a major party to run for vice president
- Iraq invades Kuwait
- Sandra Day O'Connor named to Supreme Court
- Ronald Reagan is reelected president

Reviewing Themes

1. **Economic Factors** What was the goal of President Reagan's policy of deregulation?
2. **Global Connections** What event marked the end of the cold war?
3. **Groups and Institutions** Why did the federal government run out of money in 1995?
4. **Science and Technology** What is the connection between technology and global warming?

Skill Practice Activity

Using an Electronic Spreadsheet

Use a spreadsheet to enter the daily high, average, and low temperatures for your community for four weeks. At the end of this period, calculate your average local temperature. Then use the spreadsheet to make line graphs showing the monthly high temperatures, average temperatures, and low temperatures for your community.

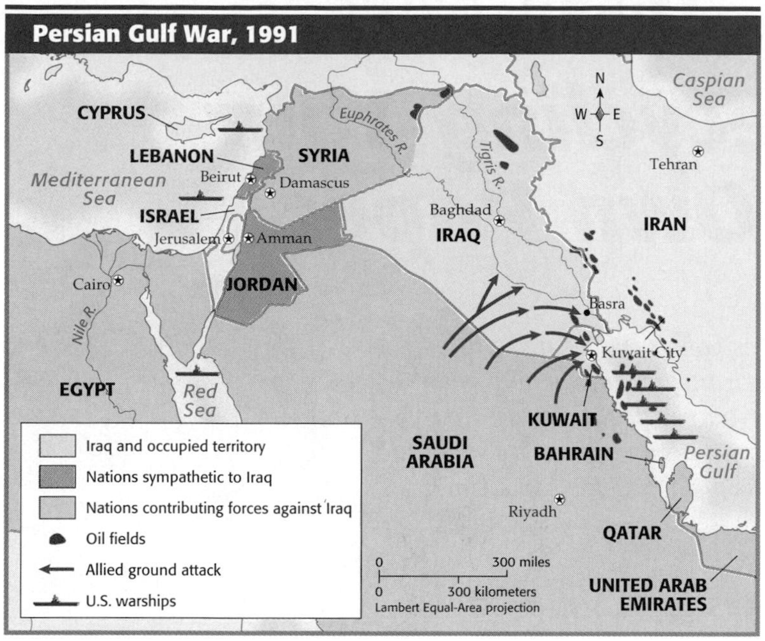

Geography Activity

Study the map on this page, then answer the questions that follow.

1. **Region** Which countries were sympathetic to Iraq?
2. **Location** In what countries did the allied ground attack take place?
3. **Movement** Which nations helped in the allied invasion?
4. **Location** In what three bodies of water did U.S. warships show their presence?

Technology Activity

Using the Internet

Use a browser to search the Internet for information about Kuwait. Write a short description of what a traveler visiting this nation might expect to find.

Cooperative Activity

History and Music What do you think the United States will be like in 100 years? Will everyday life be vastly different or much like it is today? What challenges will the nation face? Work with a group of classmates to write lyrics for a song about the future. You may want to focus on one specific issue such as the environment, or you might fashion your lyrics to express your thoughts about several issues. Use the music from an existing song to accompany your lyrics. Type or write down your lyrics and share them with the other students.

Portfolio Activity **History Journal** Review the chapter for information about how the three presidents in office from 1980 to 2000 viewed the role of the federal government. Record the information in your journal. Use your notes to summarize each president's view in a single sentence.

CHAPTER 32
Review and Activities

Geography Activity

1. Jordan, Lebanon
2. Iraq, Kuwait
3. Syria, Egypt, Saudi Arabia, Bahrain, Qatar, United Arab Emirates
4. Mediterranean Sea, Red Sea, Persian Gulf

Technology Activity

Students should use the Internet to help them find information about Kuwait to create short descriptions for someone who will be traveling there.

Cooperative Activity

Students should use their knowledge of the past and the information in this chapter to write a song about what the United States might be like in 100 years.

Portfolio Activity Students should review the chapter and record how Presidents Reagan, Bush, and Clinton viewed the role of the federal government. They should summarize each president's view in a single sentence.

Chapter Bonus Test Question

Ask: **In 1989 Virginia elected the nation's first African American governor since Reconstruction. Who was he?** *(L. Douglas Wilder)*

Reviewing Themes

1. It cut rules and regulations that were placed on businesses by the government. Deregulation made it easier and cheaper for manufacturers to meet government requirements.
2. the breakup of the Soviet Union
3. The dispute between Republicans and Democrats over balancing the federal budget blocked passage of the 1996 budget.
4. Air pollution generated by vehicles and industries plays a role in global warming.

Skill Practice Activity

Students should enter on their spreadsheets daily high, average, and low temperatures for four weeks and then calculate the average local temperature. They should use the application to make line graphs showing high, average, and low temperatures.

Hands-On HISTORY Lab Activity

Block Schedule

This activity may be implemented within either a traditional class period or a block scheduling framework.

FOCUS

To illustrate the importance of paper in everyday life, have students note the ways in which they have used paper today. Their responses might include reading newspapers and books, taking notes during lessons, writing letters to friends, using paper napkins at lunch. Ask students to discuss what their lives would be like without paper.

TEACH

L1 Analyzing Significance Point out that Cai Lun, a Chinese court official, is credited with inventing paper in A.D. 105. He noticed that a thin wet layer of interlaced fibers—made from tree bark, rags, or fish netting—dried to form paper. The Chinese kept this knowledge to themselves for more than 500 years. Ask students to discuss why they think paper development was an important hallmark of civilization. Some may be interested in researching other Chinese inventions, or "firsts."

Refer students to the March 1997 issue of *National Geographic* for an article about paper.

Hands-On HISTORY Lab Activity

Recycling Your Own Paper

One of the challenges facing the United States today is TRASH. Americans generate about four pounds of trash per person per day. One way to reduce the amount of trash is to recycle. Try making your own paper—and recycle it at the same time!

The Way It Was

People have been writing for centuries. But what did they write *on* throughout history? Ancient Egyptians learned how to make paper from papyrus reeds, which they flattened and pressed together. The American colonists wrote government documents on parchment; newspapers, pamphlets, and personal letters were written on paper of lesser quality. Fibers from linen and cotton rags were pounded and pressed together to make this paper. Modern paper is made from wood pulp.

Believe It Or Not! The garbage thrown away each year in the United States could fill garbage trucks lined up bumper-to-bumper on a four-lane highway circling the earth.

1 Materials

- wire clothes hanger
- 1 woman's nylon stocking
- 2 full pages of newspaper torn into small pieces
- 2-3 cups of water
- a blender (a kitchen mixer or similar hand tool will also work)
- dishpan
- 2 tablespoons of school glue

CURRICULUM CONNECTION

Science Inform students that the recycling of old newspapers involves more than simply combining the papers with water to make pulp. Before the old paper can be used, it must be washed with special chemicals to remove the ink. In one cleaning process, the paper is placed on screens and the chemicals are run through until the ink is washed out. In another process, the paper is placed with the chemicals in a large container, or flotation cell. The ink floats to the top of the mixture and is then skimmed off.

Hands-On HISTORY Lab Activity

2 What To Do

❶ Untwist the clothes hanger and form it into a 6-inch square.

❷ Carefully slip the nylon stocking around the wire square. Pull the nylon tight so it fits snugly. Tie a knot on both sides to keep it in place.

❸ Put some torn newspaper into the blender. Close the lid and turn the blender on high. Slowly add the rest of the paper and small amounts of water until the paper disappears and the mixture turns into a large ball of pulp. Put 4 inches of water into the dishpan. Add the glue and pulp mixture and stir.

❹ While stirring the mixture, quickly slip the wire frame under the pulp and rest it on the bottom of the dishpan. Then lift the frame slowly as you count to 20. Your wire frame should be covered with pulp mixture.

❺ Place the wire frame on paper towels or another flat surface to dry completely. When the paper is completely dry, gently peel it off the frame.

❻ If possible, use a hot iron to steam your paper as flat as possible. Your paper is ready to use!

tep 3

Step 5

3 Lab Report

1. About how long did you have to mix the paper and water for it to form a ball of pulp?
2. Describe the texture of the pulp before you added it to the dishpan.
3. How easy or difficult was it to write on your paper?
4. **Drawing Conclusions** How do you think your paper compares to the paper made out of cloth rags by the colonists? Which type of paper would be easier to use?

Go a Step Further

A ton of recycled paper saves more than 4,000 kilowatt-hours of energy, 7,000 gallons of water, and 17 trees. Research solutions to the trash crisis facing the United States that you can support or implement.

L2, ELL Identifying Alternatives Note that parchment was made from goat skin or sheep skin. Discuss other surfaces that people have used for writing. *(vellum, which is fine parchment made from the skin of calf, lamb, or kid; clay tablets; stone; cotton; bamboo; and jute)* **Ask:** **What are the advantages of paper over clay or stone?** *(less bulky, easier to carry)* **Disadvantages?** *(less permanent)*

ASSESS

Have students answer the **Lab Report** questions on this page.

CLOSE

Encourage students to complete the **Go A Step Further** activity. Ask volunteers to share their findings with the class.

ANSWERS

Lab Report

1. Answers will vary, but students should note that about 5 minutes or less was needed.
2. The pulp will be a thick, gooey substance.
3. Students might indicate that writing was difficult because of the texture of their paper.
4. The colonists' paper was of a higher quality because their procedures were more refined.

Go a Step Further

Students' findings should include reusing materials, avoiding buying products with excess packaging, buying in bulk rather than in individual- or small-sized packages, recycling, avoidance of packaging that cannot be recycled, and buying products made from recycled materials.

Appendix Contents

Presidents of the United States	**A1**
The White House	**A8**
Documents of America's Heritage	**A9**
Gazetteer	**A21**
Glossary	**A26**
Index	**A36**
Spanish Glossary	**A59**
Credits and Acknowledgments	**A70**

Flag Etiquette

Over the years, Americans have developed rules and customs concerning the use and display of the flag. One of the most important things every American should remember is to treat the flag with respect:

- ★ The flag should be raised and lowered by hand and displayed only from sunrise to sunset. On special occasions, it may be displayed at night.
- ★ The flag may be displayed on all days, weather permitting, particularly on national and state holidays and on historic and special occasions.
- ★ No flag should be flown above the American flag or to the right of it at the same height.
- ★ The flag may be flown at half-mast to mourn the death of public officials.
- ★ The flag should never touch the ground or floor beneath it.
- ★ The flag may be flown upside down only to signal distress.
- ★ When the flag becomes old and tattered, it should be destroyed by burning. According to an approved custom, the Union (the white stars on the blue field) is first cut from the flag; then the two pieces, which no longer form a flag, are burned.

Presidents of the United States

** The Republican Party during this period developed into today's Democratic Party. Today's Republican Party originated in 1854.

George Washington

1

1789–1797

Born: 1732
Died: 1799
Born in: Virginia
Elected from: Virginia
Age when elected: 56
Occupations: Planter, Soldier
Party: None
Vice President: John Adams

John Adams

2

1797–1801

Born: 1735
Died: 1826
Born in: Massachusetts
Elected from: Massachusetts
Age when elected: 61
Occupations: Teacher, Lawyer
Party: Federalist
Vice President: Thomas Jefferson

Thomas Jefferson

3

1801–1809

Born: 1743
Died: 1826
Born in: Virginia
Elected from: Virginia
Age when elected: 57
Occupations: Planter, Lawyer
Party: Republican**
Vice Presidents: Aaron Burr, George Clinton

James Madison

4

1809–1817

Born: 1751
Died: 1836
Born in: Virginia
Elected from: Virginia
Age when elected: 57
Occupation: Planter
Party: Republican**
Vice Presidents: George Clinton, Elbridge Gerry

James Monroe

5

1817–1825

Born: 1758
Died: 1831
Born in: Virginia
Elected from: Virginia
Age when elected: 58
Occupation: Lawyer
Party: Republican**
Vice President: Daniel D. Tompkins

John Quincy Adams

6

1825–1829

Born: 1767
Died: 1848
Born in: Massachusetts
Elected from: Massachusetts
Age when elected: 57
Occupation: Lawyer
Party: Republican**
Vice President: John C. Calhoun

Andrew Jackson

7

1829–1837

Born: 1767
Died: 1845
Born in: South Carolina
Elected from: Tennessee
Age when elected: 61
Occupations: Lawyer, Soldier
Party: Democratic
Vice Presidents: John C. Calhoun, Martin Van Buren

Martin Van Buren

8

1837–1841

Born: 1782
Died: 1862
Born in: New York
Elected from: New York
Age when elected: 54
Occupation: Lawyer
Party: Democratic
Vice President: Richard M. Johnson

William H. Harrison

9

1841

Born: 1773
Died: 1841
Born in: Virginia
Elected from: Ohio
Age when elected: 67
Occupations: Soldier, Planter
Party: Whig
Vice President: John Tyler

John Tyler

10

1841–1845

Born: 1790
Died: 1862
Born in: Virginia
Elected as V.P. from: Virginia
Succeeded Harrison
Age when became President: 51
Occupation: Lawyer
Party: Whig
Vice President: None

James K. Polk

11

1845–1849

Born: 1795
Died: 1849
Born in: North Carolina
Elected from: Tennessee
Age when elected: 49
Occupation: Lawyer
Party: Democratic
Vice President: George M. Dallas

Zachary Taylor

12

1849–1850

Born: 1784
Died: 1850
Born in: Virginia
Elected from: Louisiana
Age when elected: 63
Occupation: Soldier
Party: Whig
Vice President: Millard Fillmore

Millard Fillmore

13

1850–1853

Born: 1800
Died: 1874
Born in: New York
Elected as V.P. from: New York
Succeeded Taylor
Age when became President: 50
Occupation: Lawyer
Party: Whig
Vice President: None

Franklin Pierce

14

1853–1857

Born: 1804
Died: 1869
Born in: New Hampshire
Elected from: New Hampshire
Age when elected: 47
Occupation: Lawyer
Party: Democratic
Vice President: William R. King

James Buchanan

15

1857–1861

Born: 1791
Died: 1868
Born in: Pennsylvania
Elected from: Pennsylvania
Age when elected: 65
Occupation: Lawyer
Party: Democratic
Vice President: John C. Breckinridge

Abraham Lincoln

16

1861–1865

Born: 1809
Died: 1865
Born in: Kentucky
Elected from: Illinois
Age when elected: 51
Occupation: Lawyer
Party: Republican
Vice Presidents: Hannibal Hamlin, Andrew Johnson

Andrew Johnson

17

1865–1869

Born: 1808
Died: 1875
Born in: North Carolina
Elected as V.P. from: Tennessee
Age when became President: 56
Succeeded Lincoln
Occupation: Tailor
Party: Republican
Vice President: None

Ulysses S. Grant

18

1869–1877

Born: 1822
Died: 1885
Born in: Ohio
Elected from: Illinois
Age when elected: 46
Occupations: Farmer, Soldier
Party: Republican
Vice Presidents: Schuyler Colfax, Henry Wilson

Rutherford B. Hayes

19

1877–1881

Born: 1822
Died: 1893
Born in: Ohio
Elected from: Ohio
Age when elected: 54
Occupation: Lawyer
Party: Republican
Vice President: William A. Wheeler

James A. Garfield

20

1881

Born: 1831
Died: 1881
Born in: Ohio
Elected from: Ohio
Age when elected: 49
Occupations: Laborer, Professor
Party: Republican
Vice President: Chester A. Arthur

Chester A. Arthur

21

1881–1885

Born: 1830
Died: 1886
Born in: Vermont
Elected as V.P. from: New York
Succeeded Garfield
Age when became President: 50
Occupations: Teacher, Lawyer
Party: Republican
Vice President: None

Grover Cleveland

22 24

1885–89, 1893–97

Born: 1837
Died: 1908
Born in: New Jersey
Elected from: New York
Age when elected: 47; 55
Occupation: Lawyer
Party: Democratic
Vice Presidents: Thomas A. Hendricks, Adlai E. Stevenson

Benjamin Harrison

23

1889–1893

Born: 1833
Died: 1901
Born in: Ohio
Elected from: Indiana
Age when elected: 55
Occupation: Lawyer
Party: Republican
Vice President: Levi P. Morton

William McKinley

25

1897–1901

Born: 1843
Died: 1901
Born in: Ohio
Elected from: Ohio
Age when elected: 53
Occupations: Teacher, Lawyer
Party: Republican
Vice Presidents: Garret Hobart, Theodore Roosevelt

Theodore Roosevelt

26

1901–1909

Born: 1858
Died: 1919
Born in: New York
Elected as V.P. from: New York
Succeeded McKinley
Age when became President: 42
Occupations: Historian, Rancher
Party: Republican
Vice President: Charles W. Fairbanks

William H. Taft

27

1909–1913

Born: 1857
Died: 1930
Born in: Ohio
Elected from: Ohio
Age when elected: 51
Occupation: Lawyer
Party: Republican
Vice President: James S. Sherman

Woodrow Wilson

28

1913–1921

Born: 1856
Died: 1924
Born in: Virginia
Elected from: New Jersey
Age when elected: 55
Occupation: College Professor
Party: Democratic
Vice President: Thomas R. Marshall

Warren G. Harding

29

1921–1923

Born: 1865
Died: 1923
Born in: Ohio
Elected from: Ohio
Age when elected: 55
Occupations: Newspaper Editor, Publisher
Party: Republican
Vice President: Calvin Coolidge

Calvin Coolidge

30

1923–1929

Born: 1872
Died: 1933
Born in: Vermont
Elected as V.P. from: Massachusetts
Succeeded Harding
Age when became President: 51
Occupation: Lawyer
Party: Republican
Vice President: Charles G. Dawes

Herbert C. Hoover

31

1929–1933

Born: 1874
Died: 1964
Born in: Iowa
Elected from: California
Age when elected: 54
Occupation: Engineer
Party: Republican
Vice President: Charles Curtis

Franklin D. Roosevelt

32

1933–1945

Born: 1882
Died: 1945
Born in: New York
Elected from: New York
Age when elected: 50
Occupation: Lawyer
Party: Democratic
Vice Presidents: John N. Garner, Henry A. Wallace, Harry S Truman

Harry S Truman

33

1945–1953

Born: 1884
Died: 1972
Born in: Missouri
Elected as V.P. from: Missouri
Succeeded Roosevelt
Age when became President: 60
Occupations: Clerk, Farmer
Party: Democratic
Vice President: Alben W. Barkley

Dwight D. Eisenhower

34

1953–1961

Born: 1890
Died: 1969
Born in: Texas
Elected from: New York
Age when elected: 62
Occupation: Soldier
Party: Republican
Vice President: Richard M. Nixon

John F. Kennedy

35

1961–1963

Born: 1917
Died: 1963
Born in: Massachusetts
Elected from: Massachusetts
Age when elected: 43
Occupations: Author, Reporter
Party: Democratic
Vice President: Lyndon B. Johnson

Lyndon B. Johnson

36

1963–1969

Born: 1908
Died: 1973
Born in: Texas
Elected as V.P. from: Texas
Succeeded Kennedy
Age when became President: 55
Occupation: Teacher
Party: Democratic
Vice President: Hubert H. Humphrey

Richard M. Nixon

37

1969–1974

Born: 1913
Died: 1994
Born in: California
Elected from: New York
Age when elected: 55
Occupation: Lawyer
Party: Republican
Vice Presidents: Spiro T. Agnew, Gerald R. Ford

Gerald R. Ford

38

1974–1977

Born: 1913
Born in: Nebraska
Appointed by Nixon as V.P. upon Agnew's resignation; assumed presidency upon Nixon's resignation
Age when became President: 61
Occupation: Lawyer
Party: Republican
Vice President: Nelson A. Rockefeller

James E. Carter, Jr.

39

1977–1981

Born: 1924
Born in: Georgia
Elected from: Georgia
Age when elected: 52
Occupations: Business, Farmer
Party: Democratic
Vice President: Walter F. Mondale

Ronald W. Reagan

40

1981–1989

Born: 1911
Born in: Illinois
Elected from: California
Age when elected: 69
Occupations: Actor, Lecturer
Party: Republican
Vice President: George H.W. Bush

George H.W. Bush

41

1989–1993

Born: 1924
Born in: Massachusetts
Elected from: Texas
Age when elected: 64
Occupation: Business
Party: Republican
Vice President: J. Danforth Quayle

William J. Clinton

1993–

Born: 1946
Born in: Arkansas
Elected from: Arkansas
Age when elected: 46
Occupation: Lawyer
Party: Democratic
Vice President: Albert Gore, Jr.

THE WHITE HOUSE . . .
The President's Home

White House Statistics

3 Elevators
5 Major Floors with:
2 Basements
7 Staircases
12 Chimneys
32 Bathrooms
132 Rooms
160 Windows
412 Doors

White House Technology Firsts

1834 Indoor Plumbing
1845 Central Heating
1848 Gas Lighting
1866 Telegraph
1877 Telephone
1891 Electricity
1921 Radio
1926 Electric Refrigerator
1933 Air Conditioning
1942 Bomb Shelter
1947 Television
1979 Computer

Did You Know?

- ***The first baby born in the White House*** was Thomas Jefferson's grandson in 1806.
- ***The first White House wedding held*** was for Dolley Madison's sister in 1812.
- ***General Lafayette visited the White House in 1825 with his pet alligator,*** which he kept in the East Room.
- ***Cows grazed on the front lawn of the White House*** up until 1913.
- ***The only president married in the White House*** was Grover Cleveland, in 1886.

Documents of America's Heritage

The Magna Carta

The Magna Carta, signed by King John in 1215, marked a decisive step forward in the development of constitutional government in England. Later, it became a model for colonists who carried the Magna Carta's guarantees of legal and political rights to America.

1. That the English church shall be free, and shall have her rights entire, and her liberties inviolate; . . .

2. We also have granted to all the freemen of our kingdom, for us and for our heirs forever, all the underwritten liberties, to be had and holden by them and their heirs, of us and our heirs forever. . . .

39. No freeman shall be taken or imprisoned, or diseased, or outlawed, or banished, or in any way destroyed, nor will we pass upon him, nor will we send upon him, unless by the lawful judgment of his peers, or by the law of the land.

40. We will sell to no man, we will not deny to any man, either justice or right.

41. All merchants shall have safe and secure conduct to go out of, and to come into, England, and to stay there and to pass as well by land as by water, for buying and selling by the ancient and allowed customs, without any unjust tolls, except in time of war, or when they are of any nation at war with us. . . .

42. It shall be lawful, for the time to come, for any one to go out of our kingdom and return safely and securely by land or by water, saving his allegiance to us (unless in time of war, by some short space, for the common benefit of the realm).

60. All the aforesaid customs and liberties, which we have granted to be holden in our kingdom, as much as it belongs to us, all people of our kingdom, as well clergy as laity, shall observe, as far as they are concerned, towards their dependents.

63. . . . It is also sworn, as well on our part as on the part of the barons, that all the things aforesaid shall be observed in good faith, and without evil duplicity. Given under our hand, in the presence of the witnesses above named, and many others, in the meadow called Runnymede, between Windsor and Staines, the 15th day of June, in the 17th year of our reign.

Illuminated manuscript, Middle Ages

The Mayflower Compact

On November 21, 1620, 41 colonists aboard the Mayflower drafted this agreement. The Mayflower Compact was the first plan of self-government ever put in force in the English colonies.

In ye name of God Amen. We whose names are underwritten, the loyall subjects of our dread soveraigne Lord King James, by ye grace of God, of Great Britaine, Franc, & Ireland king, defender of ye faith, &c. Haveing undertaken, for ye glorie of God, and advancemente of ye Christian faith and honour of our king & countrie, a voyage to plant ye first colonie in ye Northerne parts of Virginia, doe by these presents solemnly & mutualy in ye presence of God, and one of another, covenant, & combine ourselves togeather into a Civill body politick; for our better ordering, & preservation & furtherance of ye ends aforesaid; and by vertue hereof to enacte, constitute, and frame such just & equall Lawes, ordinances, Acts, constitutions, & offices, from time to time, as shall be thought most meete & convenient for ye generall good of ye colonie: unto which we promise all due submission and obedience. In witnes whereof we have hereunder subscribed our names at Cap-Codd ye -11- of November, in ye year of ye raigne of our soveraigne Lord King James of England, Franc, & Ireland ye eighteenth, and of Scotland ye fiftie fourth. Ano Dom. 1620.

The Federalist, No. 10

James Madison wrote several articles supporting ratification of the Constitution for a New York newspaper. In the excerpt below, Madison argues for the idea of a federal republic.

By a faction, I understand a number of citizens . . . who are united and actuated by some common impulse . . . adverse to the rights of other citizens. . . .

The inference to which we are brought is that the causes of faction cannot be removed and that relief is only to be sought in the means of controlling its effects. . . .

A republic, by which I mean a government in which the scheme of representation takes place . . . promises the cure for which we are seeking. . . .

The two great points of difference between a democracy and a republic are: first, the delegation of the government, in the latter, to a small number of citizens elected by the rest; secondly, the greater number of citizens, and greater sphere of country, over which the latter may be extended.

The effect of the first difference is . . . to refine and enlarge the public views by passing them through the medium of a chosen body of citizens, whose wisdom may best discern the true interest of their country, and whose patriotism and love of justice will be least likely to sacrifice it to temporary or partial considerations. . . .

James Madison

Washington's Farewell Address

At the end of his second term as president, George Washington spoke of the dangers facing the young nation. He warned against the dangers of political parties and sectionalism, and he advised the nation against permanent alliances with other nations.

George Washington

Citizens by birth or choice of a common country, that country has a right to concentrate your affections. The name of American, which belongs to you, in your national capacity, must always exalt the just pride of patriotism more than any appellation derived from local discriminations. With slight shades of difference, you have the same religion, manners, habits, and political principles. You have in a common cause fought and triumphed together. . . .

In contemplating the causes which may disturb our Union, it occurs as matter of serious concern that any ground should have been furnished for characterizing parties by geographical discriminations. . . .

No alliances, however strict between the parts, can be an adequate substitute. They must inevitably experience the infractions and interruptions which all alliances in all times have experienced. . . .

The great rule of conduct for us, in regard to foreign nations, is in extending our commercial relations to have with them as little political connection as possible. . . .

. . . I anticipate with pleasing expectations that retreat in which I promise myself to realize . . . the sweet enjoyment of partaking, in the midst of my fellow citizens, the benign influence of good laws under a free government, the ever favorite object of my heart, and the happy reward, as I trust, of our mutual cares, labors, and dangers.

The Star-Spangled Banner

During the British bombardment of Fort McHenry during the War of 1812, a young Baltimore lawyer named Francis Scott Key was inspired to write the words to "The Star-Spangled Banner." Although it became popular immediately, it was not until 1931 that Congress officially declared "The Star-Spangled Banner" as our national anthem.

O! say can you see, by the dawn's early light,
What so proudly we hail'd at the twilight's last gleaming,
Whose broad stripes and bright stars through the perilous fight,
O'er the ramparts we watched, were so gallantly streaming?
And the Rockets' red glare, the Bombs bursting in air,
Gave proof through the night that our Flag was still there;
O! say, does that star-spangled banner yet wave
O'er the Land of the free and the home of the brave!

The Monroe Doctrine

In an 1823 address to Congress, President James Monroe proclaimed the Monroe Doctrine. Designed to end European influence in the Western Hemisphere, it became a cornerstone of United States foreign policy.

. . . With the existing colonies or dependencies of any European power we have not interfered and shall not interfere. But with the governments who have declared their independence and maintained it, and whose independence we have, on great consideration and on just principles, acknowledged, we could not view any interposition for the purpose of oppressing them, or controlling in any other manner their destiny, by any European power in any other light than as the manifestation of any unfriendly disposition toward the United States. . . .

Our policy in regard to Europe, which was adopted at an early stage of the wars which have so long agitated that quarter of the globe, nevertheless remains the same, which is not to interfere in the internal concerns of any of its powers; to consider the government de facto as the legitimate government for us; to cultivate friendly relations with it, and to preserve those relations by a frank, firm, and manly policy, meeting in all instances the just claims of every power, submitting to injuries from none. . . .

James Monroe

Memorial and Protest of the Cherokee Nation

While Native Americans were being forced from their homeland, Cherokee leaders put their protest before the United States Senate. Their call for justice went unheard.

It cannot be concealed that the situation of the Cherokees is peculiarly distressing. In adverting to that situation it is not done to arouse, at this late day, a useless sympathy, but only as matter of history, and from necessity in giving a fair and impartial illustration of their difficulties. It is well known to those who have paid any attention to their history for the last five years, that they have been contending for the faithful execution of treaties between their nation and the United States, and that their distresses have not been mitigated; their efforts seem to have increased their difficulties. It remains for them to seek an adjustment by treaty, and an equitable acknowledgement of their rights and claims, so far as circumstances will permit.

For this purpose, this delegation has been deputed, as the proper organ of the Cherokee people, to settle, by treaty, their difficulties; and they wish, in sincerity, to have them settled, for the good, peace, and harmony of the whole nation.

Beaded shoulder bag, Cherokee people

The Seneca Falls Declaration

One of the first documents to express the desire for equal rights for women is the Declaration of Sentiments and Resolutions, issued in 1848 at the Seneca Falls Convention in Seneca Falls, New York. Led by Lucretia Mott and Elizabeth Cady Stanton, the delegates adopted a set of resolutions that called for woman suffrage and opportunities for women in employment and education. Excerpts from the Declaration follow.

When, in the course of human events, it becomes necessary for one portion of the family of man to assume among the people of the earth a position different from that which they have hitherto occupied, but one to which the laws of nature and of nature's God entitle them, a decent respect to the opinions of mankind requires that they should declare the causes that impel them to such a course.

We hold these truths to be self-evident: that all men and women are created equal; that they are endowed by their Creator with certain inalienable rights; that among these are life, liberty, and the pursuit of happiness; that to secure these rights governments are instituted, deriving their just powers from the consent of the governed. Whenever any form of government becomes destructive of these ends, it is the right of those who suffer from it to refuse allegiance to it, and to insist upon the institution of a new government, laying its foundation on such principles, and organizing its powers in such form, as to them shall seem most likely to effect their safety and happiness. Prudence, indeed, will dictate that governments long established should not be changed for light and transient causes; . . . But when a long train of abuses and usurpations, pursuing invariably the same object, evinces a design to reduce them under absolute despotism, it is their duty to throw off such government and to provide new guards for their future security. . . .

The history of mankind is a history of repeated injuries and usurpations on the part of man toward woman, having in direct object the establishment of an absolute tyranny over her. To prove this, let facts be submitted to a candid world. . . .

Now, in view of the entire disfranchisement of one-half the people of this country, their social and religious degradation, in view of the unjust laws above mentioned, and because women do feel themselves aggrieved, oppressed, and fraudulently deprived of their most sacred rights, we insist that they have immediate admission to all the rights and privileges which belong to them as citizens of the United States. . . .

Elizabeth Cady Stanton

The Emancipation Proclamation

On January 1, 1863, President Abraham Lincoln issued the Emancipation Proclamation, which freed all slaves in states under Confederate control. The Proclamation was a significant step toward the Thirteenth Amendment (1865) that ended slavery in all of the United States.

. . . That on the 1st day of January, in the year of our Lord 1863, all persons held as slaves within any state or designated part of a state, the people whereof shall then be in rebellion against the United States, shall be then, thenceforward, and forever free; and the executive government of the United States, including the military and naval authority thereof, will recognize and maintain the freedom of such persons and will do no act or acts to repress such persons, or any of them, in any efforts they may make for their actual freedom.

That the executive will, on the 1st day of January aforesaid, by proclamation, designate the states and parts of states, if any, in which the people thereof, respectively, shall then be in rebellion against the United States; and the fact that any state or the people thereof shall on that day be in good faith represented in the Congress of the United States by members chosen thereto at elections wherein a majority of the qualified voters of such states shall have participated shall, in the absence of strong countervailing testimony, be deemed conclusive evidence that such state and the people thereof are not then in rebellion against the United States. . . .

And, by virtue of the power and for the purpose aforesaid, I do order and declare that all persons held as slaves within said designated states and parts of states are, and henceforward shall be, free; and that the executive government of the United States, including the military and naval authorities thereof, will recognize and maintain the freedom of said persons.

And I hereby enjoin upon the people so declared to be free to abstain from all violence, unless in necessary self-defense; and I recommend to them that, in all cases when allowed, they labor faithfully for reasonable wages.

And I further declare and make known that such persons of suitable condition will be received into the armed service of the United States. . . .

Abraham Lincoln

Members of 4th U.S. Infantry

The Gettysburg Address

On November 19, 1863, President Abraham Lincoln gave a short speech at the dedication of a national cemetery on the battlefield of Gettysburg. His simple yet eloquent words expressed his hopes for a nation divided by civil war.

Four score and seven years ago our fathers brought forth on this continent a new nation, conceived in liberty, and dedicated to the proposition that all men are created equal.

Now we are engaged in a great civil war, testing whether that nation or any nation so conceived and so dedicated can long endure. We are met on a great battlefield of that war. We have come to dedicate a portion of that field as a final resting place for those who here gave their lives that that nation might live. It is altogether fitting and proper that we should do this.

But, in a larger sense, we can not dedicate—we can not consecrate—we can not hallow—this ground. The brave men, living and dead, who struggled here have consecrated it far beyond our poor power to add or detract. The world will little note nor long remember what we say here, but it can never forget what they did here. It is for us, the living, rather, to be dedicated here to the unfinished work which they who fought here have thus far so nobly advanced.

It is rather for us to be here dedicated to the great task remaining before us—that from these honored dead we take increased devotion to that cause for which they gave the last full measure of devotion; that we here highly resolve that these dead shall not have died in vain; that this nation, under God, shall have a new birth of freedom; and that government of the people, by the people, and for the people, shall not perish from the earth.

Soldier's kit, Civil War

Gettysburg Memorial

I Will Fight No More

In 1877 the Nez Perce fought the government's attempt to move them to a smaller reservation. After a remarkable attempt to escape to Canada, Chief Joseph realized that resistance was hopeless and advised his people to surrender.

Tell General Howard I know his heart. What he told me before I have in my heart. I am tired of fighting. Our chiefs are killed. Looking Glass is dead. It is the young men who say yes or no. He who led the young men is dead. It is cold and we have no blankets. The little children are freezing to death. My people, some of them have run away to the hills and have no blankets, no food; no one knows where they are—perhaps freezing to death. I want to have time to look for my children and see how many I can find. Maybe I shall find them among the dead. Hear me my chiefs. I am tired; my heart is sick and sad. From where the sun now stands, I will fight no more forever.

Shield made of buffalo hide

The Pledge of Allegiance

In 1892 the nation celebrated the 400th anniversary of Columbus's landing in America. In connection with this celebration, Francis Bellamy, a magazine editor, wrote and published the Pledge of Allegiance. The words "under God" were added by Congress in 1954 at the urging of President Dwight D. Eisenhower.

I pledge allegiance to the Flag of the United States of America and to the Republic for which it stands, one Nation under God, indivisible, with liberty and justice for all.

Students in a New York City school recite the Pledge of Allegiance

The Fourteen Points

On January 8, 1918, President Woodrow Wilson went before Congress to offer a statement of aims called the Fourteen Points. Wilson's plan called for freedom of the seas in peace and war, an end to secret alliances, and equal trading rights for all countries. The excerpt that follows is taken from the President's message.

. . . We entered this war because violations of right had occurred which touched us to the quick and made the life of our own people impossible unless they were corrected and the world secured once for all against their recurrence. What we demand in this war, therefore, is nothing peculiar to ourselves. It is that the world be made fit and safe to live in; and particularly that it be made safe for every peace-loving nation which, like our own, wishes to live its own life, determine its own institutions, be assured of justice and fair dealings by the other peoples of the world, as against force and selfish aggression. All the peoples of the world are in effect partners in this interest, and for our own part we see very clearly that unless justice be done to others it will not be done to us.

The program of the world's peace, therefore, is our program, and that program, the only possible program, as we see it, is this:

I. Open covenants of peace, openly arrived at, after which there shall be no private international understandings of any kind, but diplomacy shall proceed always frankly and in the public view.

II. Absolute freedom of navigation upon the seas, outside territorial waters, alike in peace and in war, except as the seas may be closed in whole or in part by international action for the enforcement of international covenants.

III. The removal, so far as possible, of all economic barriers and the establishment of an equality of trade conditions among all the nations consenting to the peace and associating themselves for its maintenance.

IV. Adequate guarantees given and taken that national armaments will be reduced to the lowest point consistent with domestic safety.

V. Free, open-minded, and absolutely impartial adjustment of all colonial claims, based upon a strict observance of the principle that in determining all such questions of sovereignty the interests of the population concerned must have equal weight with the equitable claims of the Government whose title is to be determined. . . .

XIV. A general association of nations must be formed under specific covenants for the purpose of affording mutual guarantees of political independence and territorial integrity to great and small states alike. . . .

Leaders (left to right) David Lloyd George of Great Britain, Vittorio Orlando of Italy, Georges Clemenceau of France, and Woodrow Wilson of the United States

Brown v. *Board of Education*

On May 17, 1954, the Supreme Court ruled in Brown *v.* Board of Education *that racial segregation in public schools was unconstitutional. This decision provided the legal basis for court challenges to segregation in every aspect of American life.*

The plaintiffs contend that segregated public schools are not "equal" and cannot be made "equal," and that hence they are deprived of the equal protection of the laws. Because of the obvious importance of the question presented, the Court took jurisdiction. . . .

Our decision . . . cannot turn on merely a comparison of these tangible factors in the Negro and white schools involved in each of the cases. We must look instead to the effect of segregation itself on public education.

In approaching this problem, we cannot turn the clock back to 1868 when the Amendment was adopted, or even to 1896 when *Plessy* v. *Ferguson* was written. We must consider public education in the light of its full development and its present place in American life throughout the nation. Only in this way can it be determined if segregation in public schools deprives these plaintiffs of the equal protection of the laws.

Today, education is perhaps the most important function of state and local governments. Compulsory school attendance laws and the great expenditures for education both demonstrate our recognition of the importance of education to our democratic society. . . . In these days, it is doubtful that any child may reasonably be expected to succeed in life if he is denied the opportunity of an education. Such an opportunity, where the state has undertaken to provide it, is a right which must be made available to all on equal terms.

Troops escort students to newly integrated school.

We come then to the question presented: Does segregation of children in public schools solely on the basis of race, even though the physical facilities and other "tangible" factors may be equal, deprive the children of the minority group of equal educational opportunities? We believe that it does.

. . . We conclude that in the field of public education the doctrine of "separate but equal" has no place. Separate educational facilities are inherently unequal. Therefore, we hold that the plaintiffs and others similarly situated for whom the actions have been brought are, by reason of the segregation complained of, deprived of the equal protection of the laws guaranteed by the Fourteenth Amendment. . . .

John F. Kennedy's Inaugural Address

President Kennedy's Inaugural Address on January 20, 1961, set the tone for his administration. In his address Kennedy stirred the nation by calling for "a grand and global alliance" to fight tyranny, poverty, disease, and war.

We observe today not a victory of party but a celebration of freedom—symbolizing an end as well as a beginning—signifying renewal as well as change. For I have sworn before you and Almighty God the same solemn oath our forebears prescribed nearly a century and three-quarters ago.

The world is very different now. For man holds in his mortal hands the power to abolish all forms of human poverty and all forms of human life. And yet the same revolutionary beliefs for which our forebears fought are still at issue around the globe—the belief that the rights of man come not from the generosity of the state but from the hand of God.

We dare not forget today that we are the heirs of that first revolution. Let the word go forth from this time and place, to friend and foe alike, that the torch has been passed to a new generation of Americans born in this century, tempered by war, disciplined by a hard and bitter peace, proud of our ancient heritage—and unwilling to witness or permit the slow undoing of those human rights to which this nation has always been committed, and to which we are committed today at home and around the world.

Let every nation know, whether it wishes us well or ill, that we shall pay any price, bear any burden, meet any hardship, support any friend, oppose any foe to assure the survival and the success of liberty.

This much we pledge—and more.

To those old allies whose cultural and spiritual origins we share, we pledge the loyalty of faithful friends. United, there is little we cannot do in a host of cooperative ventures. Divided, there is little we can do. . . .

Let us never negotiate out of fear. But let us never fear to negotiate. . . . Let both sides explore what problems unite us instead of belaboring those problems which divide us. . . . Let both sides seek to invoke the wonders of science instead of its terrors. Together let us explore the stars, conquer the deserts, eradicate disease, tap the ocean depths, and encourage the arts and commerce. . . .

And so, my fellow Americans—ask not what your country can do for you—ask what you can do for your country.

My fellow citizens of the world—ask not what America will do for you but what together we can do for the freedom of man.

President Kennedy speaking at his inauguration

I Have a Dream

On August 28, 1963, while Congress debated wide-ranging civil rights legislation, Martin Luther King, Jr., led more than 200,000 people in a march on Washington, D.C. On the steps of the Lincoln Memorial he gave a stirring speech in which he eloquently spoke of his dreams for African Americans and for the United States. Excerpts of the speech follow.

. . . There are those who are asking the devotees of civil rights, "When will you be satisfied?"

We can never be satisfied as long as the Negro is the victim of the unspeakable horrors of police brutality. . . .We cannot be satisfied as long as the Negro's basic mobility is from a smaller ghetto to a larger one. We can never be satisfied as long as a Negro in Mississippi cannot vote and a Negro in New York believes he has nothing for which to vote. . . .

Martin Luther King, Jr.

I say to you today, my friends, that in spite of the difficulties and frustrations of the moment I still have a dream. It is a dream deeply rooted in the American dream.

I have a dream that one day this nation will rise up and live out the true meaning of its creed, "We hold these truths to be self-evident, that all men are created equal."

I have a dream that one day on the red hills of Georgia the sons of former slaves and the sons of former slaveowners will be able to sit down together at the table of brotherhood.

I have a dream that one day even the state of Mississippi, a desert state sweltering with the heat of injustice and oppression, will be transformed into an oasis of freedom and justice.

I have a dream that my four little children will one day live in a nation where they will not be judged by the color of their skin, but by the content of their character. . . .

. . . When we let freedom ring, when we let it ring from every village and every hamlet, from every state and every city, we will be able to speed up that day when all of God's children, black men and white men, Jews and Gentiles, Protestants and Catholics, will be able to join hands and sing in the words of the old Negro spiritual: "Free at last! Free at last! Thank God Almighty, we are free at last!"

The March on Washington

The gazetteer is a geographical dictionary that lists political divisions, natural features, and other places and locations. Following each entry is a description, its latitude and longitude, and a page reference that indicates where each entry may be found in this text.

A

Abilene city in Kansas (39°N/97°W) 531

Africa continent of the Eastern Hemisphere south of the Mediterranean Sea and adjoining Asia on its northeastern border (10°N/22°E) 40

Alabama state in the southeastern United States; 22nd state to enter the Union (33°N/87°W) 314

Alamo Texas mission captured by Mexican forces in 1836 (29°N/98°W) 364

Alaska state in the United States, located in northwestern North America (64°N/150°W) 633

Albany capital of New York State located in the Hudson Valley; site where Albany Congress proposed first formal plan to unite the 13 colonies (42°N/74°W) 85

Allegheny River river in western Pennsylvania uniting with the Monongahela River at Pittsburgh to form the Ohio River (41°N/79°W) 122

Andes Mountains mountain system extending along western coast of South America (13°S/75°W) 26

Antietam Civil War battle site in western Maryland (40°N/77°W) 471

Appalachian Mountains chief mountain system in eastern North America extending from Quebec and New Brunswick to central Alabama (37°N/82°W) 60

Appomattox Court House site in central Virginia where Confederate forces surrendered ending the Civil War (37°N/78°W) 488

Arizona state in the southwestern United States; 48th state to enter the Union (34°N/113°W) 27

Arkansas state in the south central U.S.; acquired as part of Louisiana Purchase (35°N/94°W) 314

Asia continent of the Eastern Hemisphere forming a single landmass with Europe (50°N/100°E) 42

Atlanta capital of Georgia located in the northwest central part of the state (34°N/84°W) 419

Atlantic Ocean ocean separating North and South America from Europe and Africa (5°S/25°W) RA14

Australia continent and country southeast of Asia (25°S/125°E) 42

Austria-Hungary former monarchy in central Europe (47°N/12°E) 656

B

Baltimore city on the Chesapeake Bay in central Maryland (39°N/77°W) 89

Barbary Coast north coast of Africa between Morocco and Tunisia (35°N/3°E) 289

Bay of Pigs site of 1961 invasion of Cuba by U.S.-trained Cuban exiles (22°N/79°W) 848

Beijing capital of China located in the northeastern part of the country (40°N/116°E) 638

Belgium country in northwest Europe (51°N/3°E) 657

Bering Strait waterway between North America and Asia where a land bridge once existed (65°N/170°W) 18

Beringia land bridge that linked Asia and North America during the last Ice Age (65°N/170°W) 17

Berlin city in east central Germany; former capital divided into sectors after World War II (53°N/13°E) 758

Birmingham city in north central Alabama; scene of several civil rights protests (33°N/86°W) 832

Black Hills mountains in southwestern South Dakota; site of conflict between the Sioux and white settlers during 1870s (44°N/104°W) 541

Boston capital of Massachusetts located in the eastern part of the state; founded by English Puritans in 1630 (42°N/71°W) 80

Brazil country in eastern South America (9°S/53°W) 47

Breed's Hill site near Boston where the Battle of Bunker Hill took place (42°N/71°W) 146

Buffalo industrial city and rail center in New York State (43°N/79°W) 313

Bull Run site of two Civil War battles in northern Virginia; also called Manassas (39°N/77°W) 466

C

Cahokia fur trading post in Illinois during the Revolution (39°N/90°W) 29

California state in the western United States; attracted thousands of miners during gold rush of 1849 (38°N/121°W) 369

Cambodia country in Southeastern Asia bordering Gulf of Siam; official name Democratic Kampuchea (12°N/105°E) 855

Canada country in northern North America (50°N/100°W) 62

Cape of Good Hope southern tip of Africa (34°S/18°E) 44

Caribbean Sea tropical sea in the Western Hemisphere (15°N/75°W) 19

Central America area of North America between Mexico and South America (11°N/86°W) 19

Chancellorsville site of 1863 Confederate victory (38°N/78°W) 483

Charleston city in South Carolina on the Atlantic coast; original name Charles Town (33°N/80°W) 90

Chesapeake Bay inlet of the Atlantic Ocean in Virginia and Maryland (38°N/76°W) 72

Chicago largest city in Illinois; located in northeastern part of the state along Lake Michigan (42°N/88°W) 314

Chile South American country (35°S/72°W) 885

China country in eastern Asia; mainland (People's Republic of China) under communist control since 1949 (37°N/93°E) 638

Chisholm Trail pioneer cattle trail from Texas to Kansas (34°N/98°W) 532

Cincinnati city in southern Ohio on the Ohio River; grew as a result of increasing steamship traffic during the mid-1800s (39°N/84°W) 264

Cleveland city in northern Ohio on Lake Erie (41°N/82°W) 419

Colombia country in South America (4°N/73°W) 24

Colorado state in the western United States (39°N/107°W) 510

Colorado River river that flows from the Colorado Rockies to the Gulf of California (36°N/113°W) 52

Columbia River river flowing through southwest Canada and northwestern United States into the Pacific Ocean (46°N/120°W) 284

Concord village northwest of Boston, Massachusetts; site of early battle of the American Revolution (42°N/71°W) 144

Connecticut state in the northeastern United States; one of the original 13 states (42°N/73°W) 81

Cuba country in the West Indies, North America (22°N/79°W) 52

Czechoslovakia former country in central Europe; now two countries, the Czech Republic and Slovakia (49°N/16°E) 676

D

Dallas a leading city in Texas (33°N/97°W) 828

Delaware state in the northeastern United States; one of the original 13 states (39°N/75°W) 85

Detroit city in southeastern Michigan; site of significant battles during the French and Indian War and the War of 1812; center of automobile industry (42°N/83°W) 296

Dien Bien Phu site in northwestern Vietnam where French troops were defeated by Vietminh troops in 1954 (21°N/102°E) 868

Dodge City Kansas cattle town during the 19th century (37°N/100°W) 531

Dominican Republic country in the West Indies on the eastern part of Hispaniola Island (19°N/71°W) 47

Dust Bowl area of the Great Plains where the drought of the 1930s turned the soil to wind-borne dust (37°N/98°W) 729

E

East Germany country in central Europe; reunified with West Germany in 1990 (52°N/12°E) 776

Egypt country in northeastern Africa (27°N/27°E) 756

England division of the United Kingdom of Great Britain and Northern Ireland (52°N/2°W) 48

Erie Canal the waterway connecting the Hudson River with Lake Erie through New York State (43°N/76°W) 316

Ethiopia country in eastern Africa, north of Somalia and Kenya (8°N/38°E) 742

Europe continent of the northern part of the Eastern Hemisphere between Asia and the Atlantic Ocean (50°N/15°E) 48

F

Florida state in the southeastern United States (30°N/85°W) 322

Fort McHenry fort in Baltimore harbor; inspired poem that later became "The Star-Spangled Banner" (39°N/76°W) 298

Fort Necessity Pennsylvania fort built by George Washington's troops in 1754 (40°N/80°W) 119

Fort Sumter Union fort during the Civil War located on island near Charleston, South Carolina; site of first military engagement of Civil War (33°N/80°W) 457

Fort Ticonderoga British fort on Lake Champlain (44°N/73°W) 147, 166

France country in western Europe (50°N/1°E) 48

Fredericksburg city and Civil War battle site in northeast Virginia (38°N/77°W) 482

Freeport city in northern Illinois; site of 1858 Lincoln-Douglas campaign debate (42°N/89°W) 451

G

Gadsden Purchase portion of present-day Arizona and New Mexico; area purchased from Mexico in 1853 (32°N/111°W) 375

Galveston city on the Gulf of Mexico coast in Texas; created nation's first commission form of city government (29°N/95°W) 604

Gaza Strip narrow coastal strip along the Mediterranean (31°N/34°E) 884

Georgia state in the southeastern United States (33°N/84°W) 92

Germany country in central Europe; divided after World War II into East Germany and West Germany; unified in 1990 (50°N/10°E) 655

Gettysburg city and Civil War battle site in south central Pennsylvania; site where Lincoln delivered the Gettysburg Address (40°N/77°W) 483

Great Britain commonwealth comprising England, Scotland, and Wales (56°N/2°W) 655

Great Lakes chain of five lakes, Superior, Erie, Michigan, Ontario, and Huron, in central North America (45°N/87°W) 61

Great Plains flat grassland in the central United States (45°N/104°W) 389

Great Salt Lake lake in northern Utah with no outlet and strongly saline waters (41°N/113°W) 379

Greece country in southeastern Europe (39°N/21°E) 775

Greensboro northern North Carolina city; scene of sit-ins to protest segregation (36°N/80°W) 830

Grenada country in the Caribbean (12°N/61°W) 907

Guadalcanal island in the Solomons east of Australia (10°S/159°E) 763

Guam U.S. possession in the western Pacific Ocean (14°N/143°E) 643

Guatemala country in Central America, south of Mexico (16°N/92°W) 21

Gulf of Mexico gulf on the southeast coast of North America (25°N/94°W) 26

Gulf of Tonkin gulf in South China Sea east of northern Vietnam (20°N/108°E) 855

H

Haiti country on Hispaniola Island in the West Indies (19°N/72°W) 47

Hanoi capital of Vietnam (21°N/106°E) 868

Harlem northern section of Manhattan in New York City; cultural center of African Americans in the early and mid-1900s (41°N/74°W) 705

Harpers Ferry town in northern West Virginia on the Potomac River (39°N/78°W) 452

Hartford capital of Connecticut located along the Connecticut River (42°N/73°W) 81

Hawaii state in the United States located in the Pacific Ocean (20°N/157°W) 635

Hiroshima city in southern Japan; site of first military use of atomic bomb, August 6, 1945 (34°N/132°E) 764

Hispaniola island in the West Indies in North America (17°N/73°W) 52

Horseshoe Bend Alabama site where Creek-U.S. battled in 1814 (33°N/86°W) 297

Hudson Bay large bay in northern Canada (60°N/86°W) 62

Hudson River river flowing through New York State (53°N/ 74°W) 315

Hungary country in central Europe (47°N/20°E) 676

I

Idaho state in the northwestern U.S.; ranks among top states in silver production (44°N/115°W) 537

Illinois state in the north central United States; one of the states formed in the Northwest Territory (40°N/91°W) 193

Indian Territory land reserved by the United States government for Native Americans, now the state of Oklahoma (36°N/98°W) 342

Indiana state in the north central United States; one of the states formed in the Northwest Territory (40°N/87°W) 193

Indochina region in Southeast Asia (17°N/105°E) 748

Iowa state in the north central U.S. acquired as part of the Louisiana Purchase (42°N/94°W) 419

Iran country in southwestern Asia (31°N/53°E) 756

Iraq country in southwestern Asia (32°N/42°E) 756

Ireland island west of England, occupied by the Republic of Ireland and by Northern Ireland (54°N/8°W) 756

Israel country of the Middle East in southwestern Asia along the Mediterranean Sea (33°N/34°E) 779

Italy country in southern Europe along the Mediterranean (44°N/11°E) 655

J

Jackson Mississippi capital (32°N/90°W) 831

Jamestown first permanent English settlement in North America; located in southeastern Virginia (37°N/77°W) 72

Japan island country in eastern Asia (36°N/133°E) 632

K

Kansas state in the central United States; fighting over slavery issue in 1850s gave territory the name "Bleeding Kansas" (38°N/99°W) 400

Kentucky state in the south central United States; border state that sided with the Union during the Civil War (37°N/87°W) 283

Korea peninsula in eastern Asia between China, Russia, and the Sea of Japan, on which are located the countries North Korea and South Korea (38°N/127°E) 785

Kuwait country of the Middle East in southwestern Asia between Iraq and Saudi Arabia (29°N/49°E) 916

L

Lake Erie one of the five Great Lakes between Canada and the U.S. (42°N/81°W) 60

Lake Huron one of the five Great Lakes between Canada and the U.S. (45°N/83°W) 60

Lake Michigan one of the five Great Lakes between Canada and the U.S. (43°N/87°W) 60

Lake Ontario the smallest of the five Great Lakes (43°N/79°W) 60

Lake Superior the largest of the five Great Lakes (48°N/89°W) 60

Laos southeast Asian country, south of China and west of Vietnam (20°N/102°E) 852

Latin America Central and South America; settled by Spain and Portugal (14°N/90°W) 848

Lexington Revolutionary War battle site in eastern Massachusetts; site of first clash between colonists and British, April 19, 1775 (42°N/71°W) 144

Leyte island of the east central Philippines, north of Mindanao (10°N/125°E) 763

Little Rock capital of Arkansas located in the center of the state; site of 1957 conflict over public school integration (35°N/92°W) 419

London capital of United Kingdom located in the southeastern part of England (51°N/0°) 72

Los Angeles city along Pacific coast in southern California; industrial, financial, and trade center of western United States (34°N/118°W) 358

Louisiana state in the south central United States (31°N/93°W) 298

Louisiana Territory region of west central United States between the Mississippi River and the Rocky Mountains purchased from France in 1803 (40°N/95°W) 134

Lowell city in Massachusetts (43°N/83°W) 390

M

Maine state in the northeastern United States; 23rd state to enter the Union (45°N/70°W) 320

Mali country in Western Africa (16°N/0°) 40

Manchuria region of northeast China; invaded by Japan in 1931 (48°N/125°E) 743

Manila capital and largest city of the Philippines located on southwest Luzon Island and Manila Bay (14°N/121°E) 642

Maryland state in the eastern United States; one of the original 13 states (39°N/76°W) 88

Massachusetts state in the northeastern United States; one of the original 13 states (42°N/72°W) 73

Massachusetts Bay Colony Pilgrim settlements along the Charles River (42°N/71°W) 80

Mediterranean Sea sea between Europe and Africa (36°N/13°E) 38

Memphis Tennessee city on the Mississippi River near the Mississippi border (35°N/90°W) 484

Mexican Cession territory gained by the United States after war with Mexico in 1848 (37°N/111°W) 375

Mexico country in North America south of the United States (24°N/104°W) 21

Mexico City capital and most populous city of Mexico (19°N/99°W) 23

Michigan state in the north central United States; one of the states formed in the Northwest Territory (45°N/85°W) 193

Midway Islands U.S. possession in the central Pacific Ocean (28°N/179°W) 763

Milwaukee city in eastern Wisconsin (43°N/88°W) 597

Minnesota state in the north central United States; fur trade, good soil, and lumber attracted early settlers (46°N/96°W) 408

Mississippi state in the southeastern United States; became English territory after French and Indian War (32°N/90°W) 314

Mississippi River river flowing through the United States from Minnesota to the Gulf of Mexico; explored by French in 1600s (29°N/ 89°W) 53

Missouri state in the south central U.S.; petition for statehood resulted in sectional conflict and the Missouri Compromise (41°N/93°W) 314

Missouri River river flowing through the United States from the Rocky Mountains to the Mississippi River near St. Louis (39°N/90°W) 117

Montana state in the northwestern United States; cattle industry grew during 1850s (47°N/112°W) 527

Montgomery capital of Alabama located in the central part of the state; site of 1955 bus boycott to protest segregation (32°N/86°W) 824

Montreal city along the St. Lawrence River in southern Quebec, Canada (45°N/73°W) 60

Moscow capital of former Soviet Union and capital of Russia (56°N/37°E) 757

N

Nagasaki Japanese city; site of the second atom-bombing in 1945, ending World War II (32°N/130°E) 764

Nashville capital of Tennessee located in the north central part of the state (36°N/87°W) 419

Natchez city in western Mississippi along the Mississippi River (32°N/91°W) 314

National Road road from Baltimore, Maryland, to Vandalia, Illinois (40°N/81°W) 314

Nebraska state in the central United States (42°N/101°W) 400

Netherlands country in northwestern Europe (53°N/4°E) 48

Nevada state in the western United States (39°N/117°W) 510

New Amsterdam town founded on Manhattan Island by Dutch settlers in 1625; renamed New York by British settlers (41°N/74°W) 84

New England region in northeastern United States (42°N/72°W) 79

New France French land claims stretching from Quebec to Louisiana (39°N/85°W) 94

New Hampshire state in the northeastern United States; one of the original 13 states (44°N/72°W) 81

New Jersey state in the northeastern United States; one of the original 13 states (40°N/75°W) 86

New Mexico state in the southwestern United States; ceded to the United States by Mexico in 1848 (34°N/107°W) 368

New Netherland Dutch Hudson River colony (42°N/72°W) 84

New Orleans city in Louisiana in the Mississippi Delta (30°N/90°W) 95

New Spain part of Spain's empire in the Western Hemisphere (35°N/110°W) 95

New York state in the northeastern United States; one of the original 13 states (43°N/78°W) 85

New York City city in southeastern New York State at the mouth of the Hudson River; first capital of nation (41°N/74°W) 86

Newfoundland province in eastern Canada (48°N/56°W) 46

Nicaragua country in Central America (13°N/86°W) 696

Normandy region along French coast and site of D-Day invasion, June 6, 1944 (48°N/2°W) 757

North America continent in the northern part of the Western Hemisphere between the Atlantic and Pacific oceans (45°N/100°W) 19

North Carolina state in the southeastern United States; one of the original 13 states (36°N/81°W) 89

North Dakota state in the north central U.S.; Congress created Dakota Territory in 1861 (47°N/102°W) 284

North Korea Asian country on the northern Korean Peninsula (40°N/127°E) 785

North Vietnam communist nation in Southeast Asia; unified with South Vietnam (21°N/106°E) 853

Northwest Territory territory north of the Ohio River and east of the Mississippi River (47°N/87°W) 193

O

Ohio state in the north central United States; first state in the Northwest Territory (40°N/83°W) 193

Ohio River river flowing from Allegheny and Monongahela rivers in western Pennsylvania into the Mississippi River (37°N/85°W) 117

Oklahoma state in the south central United States; Five Civilized Tribes moved to territory in the period 1830–1842 (36°N/98°W) 400

Oregon state in the northwestern United States; adopted woman suffrage in 1912 (44°N/124°W) 355

Oregon Trail pioneer trail from Independence, Missouri, to the Oregon Territory (42°N/110°W) 357

P

Pacific Ocean world's largest ocean located between Asia and the Americas (0°/175°W) 19

Palestine region or country in southwest Asia between the Mediterranean Sea and the Jordan River; area sometimes called the Holy Land (32°N/35°E) 779

Panama country in the southern part of Central America, occupying the Isthmus of Panama (8°N/81°W) 646

Panama Canal canal built across the Isthmus of Panama through Panama to connect the Caribbean Sea and the Pacific Ocean (9°N/80°W) 647

Pearl Harbor naval base at Honolulu, Hawaii; site of 1941 Japanese attack, leading to United States entry into World War II (21°N/158°W) 636

Pennsylvania state in the northeastern United States (41°N/78°W) 85

Persian Gulf gulf in southwestern Asia between Iran and the Arabian Peninsula (28°N/50°E) 916

Peru country in South America, south of Ecuador and Colombia (10°S/75°W) 26

Philadelphia city in eastern Pennsylvania on the Delaware River; Declaration of Independence and the Constitution both adopted in city's Independence Hall (40°N/75°W) 85

Philippines island country in southeast Asia (14°N/125°E) 641

Pikes Peak mountain in Rocky Mountains in central Colorado (38°N/105°W) 283

Pittsburgh city in western Pennsylvania; one of the great steelmaking centers of the world (40°N/80°W) 563

Plymouth town in eastern Massachusetts, first successful English colony in New England (42°N/71°W) 78

Poland country on the Baltic Sea in Eastern Europe (52°N/18°E) 744

Portugal country in southwestern Europe (38°N/8°W) 48

Potomac River river flowing from West Virginia into Chesapeake Bay (38°N/77°W) 89

Providence capital of Rhode Island; site of first English settlement in Rhode Island (42°N/71°W) 81

Puerto Rico United States possession in the West Indies (18°N/67°W) 52

Pullman a company town south of Chicago; site of 1897 railroad strike (42°N/87°W) 568

Q

Quebec city in Canada, capital of Quebec Province, on the St. Lawrence River; first settlement in New France (47°N/71°W) 94

R

Rhode Island state in the northeastern United States; one of the original 13 states (41°N/72°W) 81

Richmond capital of Virginia located in the central part of the state; capital of the Confederacy during the Civil War (37°N/77°W) 406

Rio Grande river between the United States and Mexico in north America; forms the boundary between Texas and Mexico (26°N/97°W) 52

Roanoke island off the coast of present-day North Carolina that was site of early British colonizing efforts (35°N/76°W) 72

Rocky Mountains mountain range in western United States and Canada in North America (50°N/114°W) 284

Russia name of republic; former empire of eastern Europe and northern Asia-coinciding with Soviet Union (60°N/64°E) 633

S

Sacramento capital of California located in the north central part of the state (38°N/121°W) 358

Saigon present-day Ho Chi Minh City; former capital of South Vietnam (11°N/106°E) 862

Salt Lake City capital of Utah located in the northern part of the state; founded by Mormons in 1847 (41°N/112°W) 379

San Antonio city in south central Texas (29°N/98°W) 365

San Diego city in southern California (33°N/117°W) 96

San Francisco city in northern California on the Pacific coast (38°N/122°W) 358

Santa Fe capital of New Mexico located in the north central part of the state (36°N/106°W) 358

Santa Fe Trail cattle trail from Independence, Missouri, to Santa Fe, New Mexico (36°N/106°W) 358

Saratoga Revolutionary War battle site in the Hudson Valley of eastern New York State (43°N/74°W) 169

Savannah city in far eastern Georgia (32°N/81°W) 89
Seattle Washington city bordered by Puget Sound and Lake Washington (47°N/122°W) RA6
Selma Alabama city; site of a 1965 voter-registration drive (32°N/87°W) 833
Seneca Falls town in New York State; site of women's rights convention in 1848 (43°N/77°W) 425
Shiloh site of 1862 Union victory in Tennessee (35°N/88°W) 469
Sicily Italian island in the Mediterranean (37°N/13°E) 756
Sierra Nevada mountain range in eastern California (39°N/120°W) 358
Sinai Peninsula peninsula in the Middle East separating Egypt from Israel (29°N/34°E) 884
South America continent in the southern part of the Western Hemisphere lying between the Atlantic and Pacific oceans (15°S/60°W) 19
South Carolina state in the southeastern United States; one of the original 13 states (34°N/81°W) 89
South Dakota state in the north central United States; acquired through the Louisiana Purchase (44°N/102°W) 527
South Korea country in Asia on the Korean Peninsula (36°N/128°E) 785
South Vietnam country in Southeast Asia united in 1976 with North Vietnam to form Vietnam (11°N/107°E) 853
Soviet Union former country in northern Europe and Asia (60°N/64°E) 743
Spain country in southwestern Europe (40°N/4°W) 48
St. Augustine city in northeastern Florida on the Atlantic coast; oldest permanent existing European settlement in North America, founded in 1565 (30°N/81°W) 52
St. Lawrence River river flowing from Lake Ontario, between Canada and the United States, through parts of Canada to the Atlantic Ocean (48°N/69°W) 60
Stalingrad city in the former Soviet Union on the Volga River; present name Volgograd (49°N/42°E) 757
Sudetenland region in northwest Czechoslovakia; taken by Hitler's forces in 1938 (50°N/18°E) 743
Suez Canal canal built between the Mediterranean Sea and the Red Sea through northeastern Egypt (31°N/32°E) 755
Switzerland European country in the Alps (47°N/8°E) 93

T

Taiwan island country off the southeast coast of China; seat of the Chinese Nationalist government (24°N/122°E) 779
Tehran capital of Iran (36°N/52°E) 900
Tennessee state in the south central United States; first state readmitted to the Union after the Civil War (36°N/88°W) 283
Tenochtitlán Aztec capital on the site of present-day Mexico City (19°N/99°W) 23
Texas state in the south central United States; Mexican colony that became a republic before joining the United States (31°N/101°W) 365
Tokyo capital of Japan located on the eastern coast of Honshu Island (36°N/140°E) 763
Toronto city in Canada on Lake Ontario; capital of the province of Ontario (44°N/79°W) RA12
Trenton capital of New Jersey located on the Delaware River in the central part of the state; site of Revolutionary War battle in December 1776 (40°N/75°W) 167

U

Union of Soviet Socialist Republics *See* Soviet Union.
United Kingdom country in northwestern Europe made up of England, Scotland, Wales, and Northern Ireland (56°N/2°W) 774
United States country in central North America; fourth largest country in the world in both area and population (38°N/110°W) RA6
Utah state in the western United States; settled by Mormons in 1840s (39°N/113°W) 379

V

Valley Forge Revolutionary War winter camp northwest of Philadelphia (40°N/75°W) 172
Venezuela South American country on the Caribbean Sea (8°N/65°W) 648
Vermont state in the northeastern United States; 14th state to enter the Union (44°N/73°W) 191
Vicksburg city and Civil War battle site in western Mississippi on the Mississippi River (42°N/85°W) 484
Vietnam country in southeastern Asia (16°N/108°E) 852
Virginia state in the eastern United States; colony of first permanent English settlement in the Americas (37°N/ 80°W) 73

W

Wake Island island in the central Pacific Ocean; annexed by United States in 1898 (19°N/167°E) 761
Washington state in the northwestern United States; territory reached by Lewis and Clark in 1805 (47°N/121°W) 527
Washington, D.C. capital of the United States located on the Potomac River at its confluence with the Anacostia River, between Maryland and Virginia coinciding with the District of Columbia (39°N/77°W) 260
West Indies islands in the Caribbean Sea, between North America and South America (19°N/79°W) 47
West Virginia state in the east central United States (39°N/81°W) 462
Willamette Valley valley of the Willamette River in western Oregon (45°N/123°W) 359
Wisconsin state in the north central United States; passed first state unemployment compensation act, 1932 (44°N/91°W) 193
Wounded Knee site of battle between settlers and Native Americans in southern South Dakota in 1890 and of Native American movement protest in 1973 (43°N/102°W) 543
Wyoming state in the western United States; territory provided women the right to vote, 1869 (43°N/108°W) 531

Y

Yalu River river in eastern Asia, between China and North Korea (41°N/126°E) 787
Yorktown town in southeastern Virginia and site of final battle of Revolutionary War (37°N/76°W) 182
Yugoslavia country in southeast Europe, on the Adriatic Sea (44°N/20°E) 677

Glossary

A

abolitionist a person who strongly favors doing away with slavery (p. 416)
abstain to not take part in some activity, such as voting (p. 440)
adobe a sun-dried mud brick used to build the homes of Native Americans (p. 31)
affirmative action an active effort to improve educational and employment opportunities for minority groups and women (p. 887)
affluence the state of having much wealth (p. 808)
airlift a system of transporting food and supplies by aircraft into an area otherwise impossible to reach (p. 777)
alien an immigrant living in a country in which he or she is not a citizen (p. 271)
alleged stated as a fact but without proof (p. 791)
alliance system defense agreements among nations (p. 656)
ambush a surprise attack (p. 185)
amendment an addition to a formal document such as the Constitution (pp. 211, 219)
American System policies devised by Henry Clay to stimulate the growth of industry (p. 320)
amnesty the granting of pardon to a large number of persons; protection from prosecution for an illegal act (pp. 496, 893)
anarchist person who believes that there should be no government (p. 689)
anarchy disorder and lawlessness (p. 648)
annex to add a territory to one's own territory (p. 366)
annexation bringing an area under the control of a larger country (p. 637)
anti-Semitism hostility toward or discrimination against Jews (p. 742)
apartheid racial separation and economic and political discrimination against nonwhites, a policy formerly practiced in the Republic of South Africa (p. 898)
appeasement accepting demands in order to avoid conflict (p. 744)
apprentice assistant who is assigned to learn the trade of a skilled craftsman (p. 113)
appropriate to set aside for a particular purpose, especially funds (p. 221)
arbitration settling a dispute by agreeing to accept the decision of an impartial outsider (p. 617)
archaeology the study of ancient peoples (p. 17)
armistice a temporary peace agreement to end fighting (pp. 643, 668)
arms race the competition between the United States and the Soviet Union to build more and more weapons in an effort to surpass the other's military strength (p. 801)
arsenal a storage place for weapons and ammunition (p. 452)
article a part of a document, such as the Constitution, that deals with a single subject (p. 206)
artifact an item left behind by early people that represents their culture (p. 17)
assembly line a production system with machines and workers arranged so that each person performs an assigned task again and again as the item passes before him or her (p. 559)
assimilate to absorb a group into the culture of a larger population (p. 578)
astrolabe an instrument used by sailors to observe positions of stars (p. 39)
autocracy government in which one person has unlimited power (p. 663)
automation a system or process that uses mechanical or electronic devices that replace human workers (p. 814)

B

baby boom a marked increase in the birthrate, especially in the United States immediately following World War II (p. 808)
backcountry a region of hills and forests west of the Tidewater (p. 108)
balance of power the distribution of power among nations so that no single nation can dominate or interfere with another (p. 882)
bankruptcy the condition of being unable to pay one's debts; one's property is managed or sold to pay those to whom one owes money (p. 916)
barrio a Spanish-speaking neighborhood in a city, especially in the southwest U.S. (p. 627)
bicameral consisting of two houses, or chambers, especially in a legislature (p. 190)
black codes laws passed in the South just after the Civil War aimed at controlling freedmen and enabling plantation owners to exploit African American workers (p. 499)
blacklist list of persons who are disapproved of and are punished, such as by being refused jobs (p. 790)
blitzkrieg name given to the sudden, violent offensive attacks the Germans used during World War II; "lightning war" (p. 745)
blockade cut off an area by means of troops or warships to stop supplies or people from coming in or going out; to close off a country's ports (pp. 177, 463, 850)
blockade runner ship that sails into and out of a blockaded area (p. 467)
bond a note issued by the government, which promises to pay off a loan with interest (p. 259)
boomtown a community experiencing a sudden growth in business or population (p. 377)

border ruffians Missourians who traveled in armed groups to vote in Kansas's election during the mid-1850s (p. 444)
border states the states between the North and the South that were divided over whether to stay in the Union or join the Confederacy (p. 461)
bounty money given as a reward, as to encourage enlistment in the army (p. 479)
boycott to refuse to buy items from a particular country (p. 135); to refuse to use in order to show disapproval or force acceptance of one's terms (p. 824)
brand a symbol burned into an animal's hide to show ownership (p. 531)
budget deficit the amount by which spending exceeds revenue, especially in reference to the government (p. 919)
bureaucracy system in which nonelected officials carry out laws and policies (p. 337)
burgesses elected representatives to an assembly (p. 74)

C

cabinet a group of advisers to the president (p. 258)
Californios Mexicans who lived in California (p. 374)
canal an artificial waterway (p. 315)
capital money for investment (pp. 306, 399)
capitalism an economic system based on private property and free enterprise (p. 689)
caravel small, fast ship with a broad bow (p. 40)
carbon dating a scientific method used to determine the age of an artifact (p. 20)
carpetbaggers name given to Northern whites who moved South after the war and supported the Republicans (p. 505)
cash crop farm crop raised to be sold for money (pp. 106, 515)
casualty a military person killed, wounded, or captured (p. 469)
caucus a meeting held by a political party to choose their party's candidate for president or decide policy (pp. 269, 337)
cede to give up by treaty (p. 375)
censure to express formal disapproval of some action (p. 792)
census official count of a population (p. 313)
charter a document that gives the holder the right to organize settlements in an area (p. 72)
charter colony colony established by a group of settlers who had been given a formal document allowing them to settle (p. 111)
checks and balances the system in which each branch of government has a check on the other two branches so that no one branch becomes too powerful (pp. 207, 218)
circumnavigate to sail around the world (p. 49)
civil disobedience refusal to obey laws that are considered unjust as a nonviolent way to press for changes (p. 825)
civil service the body of nonelected government workers (p. 605)
civil war conflict between opposing groups of citizens of the same country (p. 445)
civilization a highly developed culture, usually with organized religions and laws (p. 21)
classical relating to ancient Greece and Rome (p. 38)
clipper ship a fast sailing ship with slender lines, tall masts, and large square sails (p. 386)
closed shop a workplace in which the employer by agreement hires only union members (p. 782)
coeducation the teaching of male and female students together (p. 426)
cold war a struggle over political differences between nations carried on by methods short of war (p. 777)
collective bargaining discussion between an employer and union representatives of workers over wages, hours, and working conditions (p. 567)
Columbian Exchange exchange of goods, ideas, and people between Europe and the Americas (p. 55)
commission a group of persons directed to perform some duty (p. 511)
committee of correspondence an organization that used meetings, letters, and pamphlets to spread political ideas through the colonies (p. 139)
compromise agreement between two or more sides in which each side gives up some of what it wants (p. 201)
concurrent powers powers shared by the states and the federal government (p. 218)
Conestoga wagon sturdy vehicle topped with white canvas and used by pioneers to move west (p. 281)
conquistador Spanish explorer in the Americas in the 1500s (p. 50)
conservation the protection and preservation of natural resources (p. 618)
consolidation the practice of combining separate companies into one (p. 551)
constituents people that members of Congress represent (p. 221)
constitution a formal plan of government (pp. 90, 189)
containment the policy or process of preventing the expansion of a hostile power (p. 775)
convoy a group that travels with something, such as a ship, to protect it (p. 665)
cooperative store where farmers bought products from each other; an enterprise owned and operated by those who use its services (p. 545)
corporation a group that is authorized by law to carry on an activity but having the rights and duties of a single person (p. 560)
corruption dishonest or illegal actions (p. 505)

cotton gin a machine that removed seeds from cotton fiber (pp. 306, 397)
counterculture a social movement whose values go against those of established society (p. 859)
coup a sudden overthrow of a government by a small group (pp. 854, 912)
coureur de bois French trapper living among Native Americans (p. 62)
court-martial to try by a military court (p. 323)
credibility gap lack of belief; a term used to describe the lack of trust in the Johnson administration's statements about the Vietnam War (p. 863)
credit a form of loan; ability to buy goods based on future payment (p. 402)
culture a way of life of a group of people who share similar beliefs and customs (p. 20)
customs duties taxes on foreign imported goods (p. 279)

D

debtor person or country that owes money (p. 92)
decree an order or decision given by one in authority (p. 363)
default to fail to meet an obligation, especially a financial one (p. 717)
deferment an excuse, issued by the draft board, that lets a person be excused from military service for various reasons (p. 860)
deficit the shortage that occurs when spending is greater than income (p. 888)
demilitarize to remove armed forces from an area (p. 322)
demilitarized zone a region where no military forces or weapons are permitted (p. 788)
deport to send out of a country aliens who are considered dangerous (pp. 271, 690)
depreciate to fall in value (p. 194)
depression a period of low economic activity and widespread unemployment (pp. 196, 349)
deregulation the act of cutting the restrictions and regulations that government places on business (p. 906)
desert to leave without permission (p. 172)
deserter soldier who runs away from battle or war (p. 167)
détente a policy which attempts to relax or ease tensions between nations (p. 882)
dictator a leader who rules with total authority, often in a cruel or brutal manner (p. 741)
disarmament removal of weapons (pp. 322, 748)
discrimination unfair treatment of a group; unequal treatment because of a person's race, religion, ethnic background, or place of birth (pp. 391, 622)
dissent disagreement with or opposition to an opinion (pp. 78, 672)
diversity variety or difference (p. 107)
dividend a stockholder's share of a company's profits, usually as a cash payment (p. 561)
dollar diplomacy a policy of joining the business interests of a country with its diplomatic interests abroad (p. 649)
domestic tranquility maintaining peace within the nation (p. 215)
domino theory the belief that if one nation in Asia fell to the Communists, neighboring countries would follow (pp. 804, 853)
dove a person who opposes war or warlike policies, such as one who opposed the Vietnam War (p. 860)
draft the selection of persons for required military service (p. 478)
drought a long period of time with little rainfall (p. 28)
dry farming a way of farming dry land in which seeds are planted deep in ground where there is some moisture (p. 535)
due process of law idea that the government must follow procedures established by law and guaranteed by the Constitution (p. 226)
Dust Bowl the name given to the area of the southern Great Plains severely damaged by droughts and dust storms during the 1930s (p. 729)

E

effigy rag figure representing an unpopular individual (p. 135)
Electoral College a special group of voters selected by their state legislatures to vote for the president and vice president (p. 206)
emancipate to free from slavery (p. 473)
embargo an order prohibiting trade with another country (pp. 291, 884)
emigrant a person who leaves a country or region to live elsewhere (p. 357)
emigrate to leave one's homeland to live elsewhere (p. 576)
empresario a person who arranged for the settlement of land in Texas during the 1800s (p. 363)
encomienda system of rewarding conquistadors with tracts of land and the right to tax and demand labor from Native Americans who lived on the land (p. 54)
Enlightenment movement during the 1700s that spread the idea that knowledge, reason, and science could improve society (p. 205)
entente an understanding between nations (p. 656)
entrenched occupying a strong defensive position (p. 482)
enumerated powers powers belonging only to the federal government (p. 217)
escalate to increase or expand (p. 855)

espionage spying (p. 673)
ethnic group a minority that speaks a different language or follows different customs than the majority of people in a country (p. 576)
evolution the scientific theory that humans and other living things have evolved over time (p. 710)
executive branch the branch of government, headed by the president, that carries out the nation's laws and policies (pp. 206, 218)
executive order a rule issued by a chief executive that has the force of law (p. 848)
exile a person forced to leave his or her country (p. 848)
expansionism a policy that calls for expanding a nation's boundaries (p. 632)
expatriate a person who gives up his or her home country and chooses to live in another country (p. 706)
export a good sold abroad (p. 111)

F

factory system system bringing manufacturing steps together in one place to increase efficiency (p. 307)
famine an extreme shortage of food (p. 392)
fascism a political system, headed by a dictator, that calls for extreme nationalism and racism and no tolerance of opposition (p. 742)
favorite son candidate that receives the backing of his home state rather than of the national party (p. 333)
federal debt the amount of money owed by the government (p. 906)
federalism the sharing of power between federal and state governments (pp. 205, 217)
Federalists supporters of the Constitution (p. 209)
federation a type of government that links different groups together (p. 32)
feminist a person who advocates or is active in promoting women's rights (pp. 425, 838)
fixed costs regular expenses such as housing or maintaining equipment that remain about the same year after year (p. 402)
flapper a young woman of the 1920s who defied conventions in her behavior and dress (p. 703)
flexible response a plan that used special military units to fight guerrilla wars (p. 847)
forty-niners people who went to California during the gold rush of 1849 (p. 376)
Fourteen Points the peace plan to end World War I and restructure the countries of Europe, proposed by Woodrow Wilson (p. 675)
free silver the unlimited production of silver coins (p. 546)
freedman a person freed from slavery (p. 497)
frigate warship (p. 297)
front a region where warfare is taking place (p. 666)
fugitive runaway or trying to run away (p. 439)
fundamentalist a person who believes in the literal meaning of religious texts and strict obedience to religious laws (p. 900)

G

genocide the deliberate destruction of a racial, political, or cultural group (p. 758)
ghetto a part of a city in which a minority group lives because of social or economic pressure (p. 814)
ghost town former mining town that became deserted (p. 526)
Gilded Age the name associated with America in the late 1800s, referring to the extravagant wealth and the terrible poverty that lay underneath (p. 586)
glasnost a Soviet policy allowing more open discussion of political and social issues, as well as more widespread news and information (p. 908)
global warming a steady increase in average world temperatures (p. 928)
grandfather clause a clause that allowed individuals who did not pass the literacy test to vote if their fathers or grandfathers had voted before Reconstruction began; an exception to a law based on preexisting circumstances (p. 515)
grassroots society at the local and popular level away from political or cultural centers (p. 918)
greenback a piece of U.S. paper money first issued by the North during the Civil War (p. 480)
gross domestic product the value of all the goods and services produced in a nation during a one-year period (p. 927)
gross national product the total value of all goods and services produced by a nation's residents during a year, regardless of where production takes place (p. 698)
guerrilla referring to surprise attacks or raids rather than organized warfare (p. 346)
guerrilla warfare a hit-and-run technique used in fighting a war; fighting by small bands of warriors using tactics such as sudden ambushes (pp. 179, 847)

H

habeas corpus a legal order for an inquiry to determine whether a person has been lawfully imprisoned (p. 478)
hawk a person who advocates war or warlike policies, such as a supporter of the Vietnam War (p. 860)
hieroglyphics an ancient form of writing using symbols and pictures to represent words, sounds, and concepts (p. 23)
Hispanic a person from or descended from people who came from the countries of Latin America or Spain (p. 839)

Holocaust the name given to the mass slaughter of Jews and other groups by the Nazis during World War II (p. 759)
homestead to acquire a piece of U.S. public land by living on and cultivating it (p. 534)
horizontal integration the combining of competing firms into one corporation (p. 562)
hot line a direct telephone line for emergency use (p. 851)
human rights rights such as freedom from unlawful imprisonment, torture, and execution regarded as belonging to all persons (p. 898)
Hundred Days a special session of Congress that dealt with problems of the Depression (p. 723)

I

Ice Age a period of extremely cold temperatures when part of the planet's surface was covered with massive ice sheets (p. 17)
impeach to formally charge a public official with misconduct in office (pp. 221, 502)
impeachment charging a public official with misconduct in office; if proven guilty before a designated court, the official is removed from office (p. 890)
imperialism the actions used by one nation to exercise political or economic control over smaller or weaker nations (p. 632)
implied powers powers not specifically mentioned in the Constitution (pp. 220, 268)
import a good bought from foreign markets (p. 111)
impressment forcing people into service, as in the navy (pp. 264, 290)
inauguration the ceremony in which the president takes the oath of office (p. 257)
incumbent someone who currently holds an office or position (p. 926)
indentured servant laborer who agreed to work without pay for a certain period of time in exchange for passage to America (p. 88)
Industrial Revolution the change from an agrarian society to one based on industry which began in Great Britain and spread to the United States around 1800 (p. 306)
inflation a continuous rise in the price of goods and services (pp. 174, 480, 780)
initiative the right of citizens to place a measure or issue before the voters or the legislature for approval (p. 607)
injunction a court order to stop an action, such as a strike (p. 569)
installment buying a system of paying for goods in which customers promise to pay small, regular amounts over a period of time (p. 699)
integrate to end separation of different races and bring into equal membership in society (pp. 507, 822)
interchangeable parts uniform pieces that can be made in large quantities to replace other identical pieces (p. 309)
internal improvements federal projects, such as canals and roads, to develop the nation's transportation system (p. 319)
Internet a worldwide linking of computer networks (p. 927)
internment camps the detention centers where Japanese Americans were moved to and confined during World War II (p. 754)
interstate across state lines; connecting or existing between two or more states (p. 831)
iron curtain the political and military barrier that isolated Soviet-controlled countries of Eastern Europe after World War II (p. 775)
ironclad armored naval vessel (p. 468)
Iroquois Confederacy a powerful group of Native Americans in the eastern part of the United States made up of five nations: the Mohawk, Seneca, Cayuga, Onondaga, and Oneida (p. 117)
island hopping a strategy used during World War II that called for attacking and capturing certain key islands and using these islands as bases to leapfrog to others (p. 763)
isolationism a national policy of avoiding involvement in world affairs (pp. 631, 695)
isthmus a narrow strip of land connecting two larger land areas (p. 646)

J

joint occupation the possession and settling of an area shared by two or more countries (p. 356)
joint-stock company a company in which investors buy stock in the company in return for a share of its future profits (p. 72)
judicial branch the branch of government, including the federal court system, that interprets the nation's laws (pp. 206, 218)
judicial review the right of the Supreme Court to determine if a law violates the Constitution (pp. 220, 280)

K

kamikaze during World War II, a Japanese suicide pilot whose mission was to crash into his target (p. 763)

L

laissez-faire policy that government should interfere as little as possible in the nation's economy (pp. 278, 350, 618)

land-grant college originally, an agricultural college established as a result of the 1862 Morrill Act that gave states large amounts of federal land that could be sold to raise money for education (p. 591)
landslide an overwhelming victory (p. 335)
League of Nations an association of nations to preserve peace and resolve international disputes proposed in Wilson's Fourteen Points (p. 675)
lease to hand over property in return for rent (p. 694)
legislative branch the branch of government that makes the nation's laws (pp. 206, 218)
lend-lease the act passed during World War II allowing the United States to sell, lend, or lease arms or other war supplies to any nation considered "vital to the defense of the United States" (p. 748)
line of demarcation an imaginary line running down the middle of the Atlantic Ocean from the North Pole to the South Pole dividing the Americas between Spain and Portugal (p. 47)
line-item veto the power that allows the president to cancel individual spending items in a budget or bill (p. 921)
literacy the ability to read and write (p. 114)
literacy test a method used to prevent African Americans from voting by requiring prospective voters to read and write at a specified level (p. 515)
lock in a canal, an enclosure with gates at each end used in raising or lowering boats as they pass from level to level (p. 316)
lode a mass or strip of ore sandwiched between layers of rock (p. 525)
log cabin campaign name given to William Henry Harrison's campaign for the presidency in 1840, from the Whigs' use of a log cabin as their symbol (p. 350)
Loyalists American colonists who remained loyal to Britain and opposed the war for independence (pp. 146, 164)
lynching putting to death a person by the illegal action of a mob (p. 516)

M

maize an early form of corn grown by Native Americans (p. 20)
majority more than half (p. 334)
Manifest Destiny the idea popular in the United States during the 1800s that the country must expand its boundaries to the Pacific (p. 359)
manumission the freeing of some enslaved persons (p. 198)
martial law the law applied by military forces in occupied territory or in an emergency (p. 869)
martyr a person who sacrifices his or her life for a principle or cause (p. 452)
mass media types of communication that reach large numbers of people, such as newspapers, radio, and television (p. 703)
mass production the production of large quantities of goods using machinery and often an assembly line (p. 559)
materialism attaching too much importance to physical possessions and comforts (p. 815)
Mayflower Compact a formal document, written in 1620, that provided law and order to the Plymouth colony (p. 79)
Medicaid a social program that gives the states money to help those who cannot afford to pay for their hospital bills (p. 829)
Medicare a social program that helps pay for medical care for the elderly (p. 829)
mercantilism the theory that a state's or nation's power depended on its wealth (pp. 59, 110)
mercenary paid soldier who serves in the army of a foreign country (p. 164)
merger the combining of two or more businesses into one (p. 564)
MIAs soldiers classified as missing in action (p. 871)
migrant worker a person who moves from place to place to find work harvesting fruits and vegetables (p. 730)
migration a movement of a large number of people into a new homeland (p. 18)
militarism a buildup of military strength within a country (p. 656)
militia a group of civilians trained to fight in emergencies (pp. 118, 143)
minutemen companies of civilian soldiers who boasted that they were ready to fight on a minute's notice (p. 143)
mission religious settlement (pp. 54, 96)
mobilization gathering resources and preparing for war (pp. 670, 750)
moderate opposed to major social change or extreme political ideas (p. 798)
monopoly total control of a type of industry by one person or one company (p. 562)
Morse code a system for transmitting messages that uses a series of dots and dashes to represent the letters of the alphabet, numbers, and punctuation (p. 388)
mosque a Muslim house of worship (p. 41)
mountain man a frontiersman living in the wilderness, as in the Rocky Mountains (p. 356)
muckraker a journalist who uncovers abuses and corruption in a society (p. 606)
mudslinging attempt to ruin an opponent's reputation with insults (p. 335)

N

national debt the amount of money a national government owes to other governments or its people (p. 259)

National Grange the first farmers' organization in the United States (p. 545)

nationalism loyalty to a nation and promotion of its interests above all others (pp. 294, 655)

nativism the belief that those born in a country are superior to immigrants (p. 709)

nativist a person who favors those born in his country and is opposed to immigrants (p. 393)

neutral taking no side in a conflict (p. 163)

neutral rights the right to sail the seas and not take sides in a war (p. 290)

neutrality a position of not taking sides in a conflict (p. 264)

New Deal the name given to the new laws aimed at relieving the Depression, which were passed by Congress during the Hundred Days and the months that followed (p. 723)

nomadic moving from place to place with no permanent home (p. 538)

nomads people who move from place to place, usually in search of food or grazing land (p. 18)

nominating convention system in which delegates from the states selected the party's presidential candidate (p. 337)

nonimportation an agreement not to import or use certain goods (p. 135)

normal school a two-year school for training high school graduates as teachers (p. 413)

Northwest Passage water route to Asia through North America sought by European explorers (p. 59)

nullify to cancel or make ineffective (pp. 272, 338)

O

offensive position of attacking or the attack itself (p. 464)

on margin to buy stock by paying only a fraction of the stock price and borrowing the rest (p. 715)

Open Door policy a policy that allowed each foreign nation in China to trade freely in the other nations' spheres of influence (p. 638)

open range land not fenced or divided into lots (p. 531)

ordinance a law or regulation (p. 192)

ore a mineral mined for the valuable substance it contains, such as silver (p. 525)

override to overturn or defeat, as a bill proposed in Congress (p. 500)

overseer person who supervises a large operation or its workers (pp. 108, 403)

ozone the layer of gas composed of a form of oxygen that protects the earth and its people from cancer-causing sun rays (p. 928)

P

pacifist person opposed to the use of war or violence to settle disputes (pp. 87, 673)

partisan favoring one side of an issue (p. 267)

patent a document that gives an inventor the sole legal right to an invention for a period of time (p. 307)

Patriots American colonists who were determined to fight the British until American independence was won (pp. 146, 163)

patronage another name for the spoils system, in which government jobs or favors are given out to political allies and friends (p. 604)

patroon landowner in the Dutch colonies who ruled like a king over large areas of land (p. 85)

peaceful coexistence agreement between opposing countries that they will compete with one another but will avoid war (p. 805)

pension a sum paid regularly to a person, usually after retirement (p. 734)

per capita income average income of each person in the nation (p. 808)

perestroika a policy of government and economic reform in the Soviet Union in the mid-1980s (p. 909)

perjury lying when one has sworn an oath to tell the truth (p. 790)

persecute to treat someone harshly because of that person's beliefs or practices (p. 78)

petition a formal request (pp. 149, 192)

philanthropy charitable acts or gifts of money to benefit the community (p. 563)

pilgrimage a journey to a holy place (p. 41)

Pilgrims Separatists who journeyed to the colonies during the 1600s for a religious purpose (p. 79)

plantation a large estate run by an owner or manager and farmed by laborers who lived there (p. 55)

plurality largest single share (p. 334)

political machine an organization linked to a political party that often controlled local government (p. 603)

poll tax a tax of a fixed amount per person that had to be paid before the person could vote (p. 515)

pool a group sharing in some activity, for example, among railroad barons who made secret agreements and set rates among themselves (p. 554)

popular sovereignty political theory that government is subject to the will of the people (p. 216); before the Civil War, the idea that people living in a territory had the right to decide by voting if slavery would be allowed there (p. 443)

Populist Party U.S. political party formed in 1892 representing mainly farmers, favoring free coinage of silver and government control of railroads and other monopolies (p. 546)
poverty line a level of personal or family income below which one is classified as poor according to government standards (p. 828)
preamble the introduction to a formal document, especially the Constitution (pp. 152, 215)
precedent a tradition (p. 257)
prejudice an unfair opinion not based on facts (p. 391)
presidio Spanish fort in the Americas built to protect mission settlements (p. 54)
primary an election in which voters choose their party's candidate (p. 607)
privateer armed private ship (pp. 177, 297)
productivity how much work each worker does (pp. 698, 807)
prohibition the forbidding by law of the making or selling of alcoholic beverages (p. 613)
Prohibition the nationwide ban on the manufacture, sale, and transportation of liquor in the United States that went into effect when the Eighteenth Amendment was ratified in 1920 (p. 708)
propaganda ideas or information designed and spread to influence opinion (pp. 139, 661)
proportional to be the same as or corresponding to (p. 200)
proprietary colony colony run by individuals or groups to whom land was granted (pp. 85, 112)
protectorate a country that is technically independent, but is actually under the control of another country (p. 643)
public works projects such as highways, parks, and libraries built with public funds for public use (p. 718)
pueblo home or community of homes built by Native Americans (pp. 28, 54)
Puritans Protestants who, during the 1600s, wanted to reform the Anglican Church (p. 78)

Q

quota system an arrangement placing a limit on the number of immigrants from each country (p. 709)

R

radical extreme (p. 496); referring to one who favors making extreme changes to the government or society, such as the New Left (p. 859)
ragtime a type of music with a strong rhythm and a lively melody with accented notes, which was popular in early 1900s (p. 594)
ranchero Mexican ranch owner (p. 370)
rancho huge properties for raising livestock set up by Mexican settlers in California (p. 370)
ratify to give official approval to (pp. 184, 209, 474)
ration to give out scarce items on a limited basis (p. 751)
realism an approach to literature, art, and theater that shows things as they really are (p. 592)
rebate discount or return of part of a payment (p. 553)
Rebel Confederate soldier, so called because of opposition to the established government (p. 465)
recall the right that enables voters to remove unsatisfactory elected officials from office (p. 607)
recession a downward turn in business activity (p. 698)
reconciliation settling by agreement or coming together again (p. 509)
Reconstruction the reorganization and rebuilding of the former Confederate states after the Civil War (p. 495)
recruit to enlist soldiers in the army (p. 165)
referendum the practice of letting voters accept or reject measures proposed by the legislature (p. 607)
regionalism in art or literature, the practice of focusing on a particular region of the country (p. 592)
relief aid for the needy; welfare (p. 717)
relocate to force a person or group of people to move (p. 342)
Renaissance a period of intellectual and artistic creativity, c. 1300–1600 (p. 38)
rendezvous a meeting (p. 356)
reparations payment by the losing country in a war to the winner for the damages caused by the war (p. 676)
repeal to cancel an act or law (p. 135)
republic a government in which citizens rule through elected representatives (p. 190)
reservation an area of public lands set aside for Native Americans (p. 540)
reserved powers powers retained by the states (p. 217)
resolution a formal expression of opinion (p. 135)
revenue incoming money (p. 134)
revenue sharing money raised from federal taxes and given to the states for use at the state and local levels (p. 887)
revival a series of meetings conducted by a preacher to arouse religious emotions (p. 411)

S

sabotage secret action by enemy agents or sympathizers to damage a nation's war effort (p. 673)
scalawags name given by former Confederates to Southern whites who supported Republican Reconstruction of the South (p. 505)
search-and-destroy mission a strategy used in Vietnam in which American forces sought Vietcong and North Vietnamese units to destroy them (p. 856)

secede to leave or withdraw (pp. 285, 338, 439)
secession withdrawal from the Union (p. 454)
Second New Deal a new set of programs and reforms launched by Franklin D. Roosevelt in 1935 (p. 734)
sectionalism loyalty to a region (pp. 319, 437)
sedition activities aimed at weakening established government (p. 271)
segregation the separation or isolation of a race, class, or group (pp. 516, 821)
Separatists Protestants who, during the 1600s, wanted to leave the Anglican Church in order to found their own churches (p. 78)
settlement house institution located in a poor neighborhood that provided numerous community services such as medical care, child care, libraries, and classes in English (p. 588)
sharecropping system of farming in which a farmer works land for an owner who provides equipment and seeds and receives a share of the crop (p. 507)
shareholder a person who invests in a corporation by buying stock and is a partial owner (p. 560)
shuttle diplomacy negotiations between nations carried on by a person who travels back and forth between them (p. 885)
silent majority the phrase used by Nixon to describe the majority of Americans, those who did not protest or demonstrate (p. 865)
sit-in the act of occupying seats or sitting down on the floor of an establishment as a form of organized protest (p. 830)
slave code the laws passed in the Southern states that controlled and restricted enslaved people (p. 405)
slum poor, crowded, and run-down urban neighborhoods (p. 585)
smuggling trading illegally with other nations (p. 111)
Social Security Act a law requiring workers and employers to pay a tax; the money provides a monthly pension for retired people (p. 734)
socialist person who believes industries should be publicly owned and run by the government rather than by private individuals (p. 672)
sodbuster a name given to the Plains farmer (p. 535)
speculator person who risks money in order to make a large profit (pp. 124, 260)
sphere of influence section of a country where one foreign nation enjoys special rights and powers (p. 638)
spiritual an African American religious folk song (p. 405)
spoils system practice of handing out government jobs to supporters; replacing government employees with the winning candidate's supporters (p. 337)
square deal Theodore Roosevelt's promise of fair and equal treatment for all (p. 618)
stagflation a combination of rising prices and a sluggish economy with relatively high unemployment (p. 887)
stalemate a situation during a conflict when action stops because both sides are equally powerful and neither will give in (p. 787)
standard gauge the uniform width of 4 feet, 8.5 inches for railroad tracks, adopted during the 1880s (p. 552)
standard of living a measure of people's overall wealth and quality of life; a minimum of necessities and luxuries that a group is accustomed to (p. 808)
states' rights rights and powers independent of the federal government that are reserved for the states by the Constitution; the belief that states' rights supersede federal rights and law (pp. 272, 338, 455)
steerage cramped quarters on a ship's lower decks for passengers paying the lowest fares (p. 577)
stock shares of ownership a company sells in its business which often carry voting power (p. 560)
stock exchange a place where shares in corporations are bought and sold through an organized system (p. 715)
strait a narrow passageway connecting two larger bodies of water (p. 49)
strike a stopping of work by workers to force an employer to meet demands (p. 391)
strikebreaker person hired to replace a striking worker in order to break up a strike (p. 568)
subsidy grant of money from the government to a person or a company for an action intended to benefit the public (pp. 527, 724)
subsistence farming farming in which only enough food to feed one's family is produced (p. 104)
suburbs residential areas that sprang up close to or surrounding cities as a result of improvements in transportation (p. 586)
subversion an attempt to overthrow a government by persons working secretly from within (p. 789)
suffrage the right to vote (pp. 336, 426)
suffragist a man or woman who fought for a woman's right to vote (p. 610)
summit a meeting of heads of government (p. 805)
surplus excess; amount left over after necessary expenses are paid (p. 798)
sweatshop a shop or factory where workers work long hours at low wages under unhealthy conditions (pp. 566, 578)

T

tariff a tax on imports or exports (pp. 261, 338)
technology the application of scientific discoveries to practical use (pp. 39, 306)

Tejano a Mexican who claims Texas as his home (p. 362)
telegraph a device or system that uses electric signals to transmit messages by a code over wires (p. 388)
temperance the use of little or no alcoholic drink (p. 412)
tenant farmer farmer who works land owned by another and pays rent either in cash or crops (pp. 95, 401)
tenement a building in which several families rent rooms or apartments, often with little sanitation or safety (p. 585)
terrace a raised piece of land with the top leveled off to promote farming (p. 25)
theocracy a form of government in which the society is ruled by religious leaders (p. 22)
Tidewater a region of flat, low-lying plains along the seacoast (p. 107)
toleration the acceptance of different beliefs (p. 81)
total war war on all aspects of the enemy's life (p. 487)
totalitarian a political system in which the government suppresses all opposition and controls most aspects of people's lives (p. 742)
trade deficit the situation when the value of a country's foreign imports exceeds the value of its exports (p. 898)
trade union organization of workers with the same trade or skill (pp. 391, 567)
Transcendentalist any of a group of New England writers who stressed the relationship between human beings and nature, spiritual things over material things, and the importance of the individual conscience (p. 414)
transcontinental extending across a continent (p. 527)
triangular trade a trade route that exchanged goods between the West Indies, the American colonies, and West Africa (p. 105)
tribute money paid for protection (pp. 51, 289)
trust a combination of firms or corporations formed by a legal agreement, especially to reduce competition (pp. 562, 605)
trustbuster someone who breaks up a trust into smaller companies (p. 617)
turnpike a road that one must pay to use; the money is used to pay for the road (p. 314)

U

unconstitutional not agreeing or consistent with the Constitution (p. 260)
underemployment the condition when people work at jobs for which they are overqualified or that do not utilize their skills (p. 894)
Underground Railroad a system that helped enslaved African Americans follow a network of escape routes out of the South to freedom in the North (p. 420)
unemployment insurance payments by the government for a limited period of time to people who have lost their jobs (p. 734)
utopia community based on a vision of a perfect society sought by reformers (p. 411)

V

vaquero Hispanic ranch hand (p. 532)
vaudeville stage entertainment made up of various acts, such as dancing, singing, comedy, and magic shows (p. 595)
vertical integration the combining of companies that supply equipment and services needed for a particular industry (p. 563)
veto to reject a bill and prevent it from becoming a law (p. 349)
viceroy person who rules a country or province as the representative of the monarch (p. 54)
Vietcong the guerrilla soldiers of the Communist faction in Vietnam, also known as the National Liberation Front (p. 853)
Vietnamization Nixon's policy that called for South Vietnam to take a more active role in fighting the war and for Americans to become less involved (p. 868)
vigilantes people who take the law into their own hands (pp. 377, 526)

W

War Hawks Republicans during Madison's presidency who pressed for war with Britain (p. 294)
warrant an official order (p. 226)
work relief programs that gave needy people government jobs (p. 724)
writ of assistance legal document that enabled officers to search homes and warehouses for goods that might be smuggled (p. 134)

Y

Yankee Union soldier (p. 465)
yellow journalism writing which exaggerates sensational, dramatic, and gruesome events to attract readers, named for stories that were popular during the late 1800s (p. 592); a type of sensational, biased, and often false reporting (p. 641)
yeoman Southern owner of a small farm who did not have slaves (p. 401)

Index

Italicized page numbers refer to illustrations. The following abbreviations are used in the index:
m = map, *c* = chart, *p* = photograph or picture, *g* = graph, *crt* = cartoon, *ptg* = painting, *q* = quote

A

Abilene, Kansas, 531, 532, 533
abolitionists, 407, 416–22, 424–25, 446; African American, 416, 418–20; John Brown and, 444–45, 452; leaders, 416–420; Abraham Lincoln's attitude toward, 472; violence against, 422. *See also* antislavery movement
Acadians, 123
acid rain, 896
Act of Toleration, 89–90
Adams, Abigail, *ptg151, q151,* 271, *q322;* on women's rights, *q151,* 174–75, *q175*
Adams, John, *q163,* A1; Continental Congresses, 142, 148, 149, 153, 155; criticism of, 270; Declaration of Independence, 148, 150, 152–156; as defense attorney, 140; election, 269–70; 1796 election, 268; 1800 election, 272, 277–78; France, relations with, 270–71, 272; judicial appointments of, 279–80; Treaty of Paris 1783, 184, 195; U.S. representative in London, 195; as vice president, 257, 258
Adams, John Quincy, *ptg334, q437,* A2; Adams-Onís Treaty, 355; election, 333–34, *c334;* 1828 election, *c334,* 334–35; and Manifest Destiny, 359; as secretary of state, 322, 323, 356
Adams, Samuel, 135, 139, 140, 142, 144; Continental Congresses, 142, 148
Adams-Onís Treaty, 323, 362
Addams, Jane, *p588, q588,* 588, 609, 610, 673
affirmative action, 887
Afghanistan, 899
AFL. *See* American Federation of Labor
Africa: back-to-Africa movement, 692; Barbary Coast states, 289–90, *m290;* Cape of Good Hope, 44; colonial trade, 105; Egypt's relations with Israel, 803, 884, 885, 899; Egypt's relations with Soviet Union, 803, 884; Ethiopia, 898; Ghana, 40; Gold Coast, 44, 45; trading kingdoms of, *m40,* 40–41
African Americans: abolitionists, 416–22; after Civil War, 497, 499–500, 507; after Reconstruction, *q513,* 515–16; black codes, 499–500; boycott, use of, 136, 816, 824; citizenship granted to, 500; civil rights movement, 821–25, 830–37; in the Civil War, 465, 473, 474–75; colonial population of, *g83,* 103, *m127;* cowhands, 532, 533; culture of, 109, 705–06; education, 405, 413, 497, 507, 590, 591, 625; in English colonies, 88; first, in America, 75; free, in the North, 391–92, 418–20, 442–43, 473–74; free, in the South, 406; in government, 504–05; during Great Depression, 730; hopes for equality, 175, 625, 626; inventors, 558–59; leaders, 419–20, 505, 610, 625–26, 691, 692, 824, 825, 830, 834; literature of, 68–69; Middle Passage, 105; migration, 584–85, 814, 671, 672, 730, 753; music, 405, 594, 704–05; political power of, 816; during Reconstruction, *p494,* 499–500, 505–06, *p506,* 507, 516; in Seminole wars, 346; settlements in the West, 534; as soldiers, 164, *ptg167,* 167, *ptg183,* 475, 642, 643, 664, *p673,* 752, *q852;* in Spanish colonies, 54–55; violence against, 499, 501, 506, 509, *q512,* 516, 622, 624, 625–26, 692; voting rights, 190, 337, 391, 833; voting rights, loss of, *crt512, q512,* 515, 546; voting rights, during Reconstruction, 496, 502, 503; Washington, D.C., city planning, 260; white reaction to freedom, 505–06, 512, 515–16; during World War II, 752–53; as workers, 391–92, 528, 648; in World War I mobilization, 671, 672; writers, 593, 705–06
Agent Orange, 856
Agnew, Spiro, *p886,* 890
Agricultural Adjustment Act, 735
Agricultural Adjustment Administration (AAA), *c722,* 724
agriculture, *m400;* after Revolutionary War, 196; cash crops, 106, 107, 396, 397–08, 398; colonial, 73, 79–80, 89, 90–91, 104, 106, 107–08; decline in products prices, 1950s, 813; electrification, 724; expansion of, 1800s, 309–10; in Great Depression, 716, *c722,* 724, 730; Great Plains, 535–36; of Native Americans, 20, 21, 25, 27, 32, 79–80; revolution in, 388–89; sharecropping, 507, 515, 813–14; in the South (mid-1800s), 396–98, *m400;* subsistence farming, 104; tenant farming, 95, 401–02, 515, 813–15
Aguinaldo, Emilio, 641–42, 644
AIDS, 876
airplanes, 559; technology in, 810, *p811,* 811; in World War I, *p658,* 659; in World War II, 746, 748–49, 757, 761, *p763,* 763, 764
Alabama, *mRA6, cRA4;* civil rights movement, 824, 831, 836; readmission to Union, 502; secession, 455; statehood, 316
Alamo, Battle of the, 364–65
Alaska, , *mRA6, cRA4;* 355; Beringia and, 18; oil supply, 889; purchase of, 633, 635; statehood, 630, 799
Albania, 656, *m657;* annexation by Italy, 742
Albany, New York, 119, 123, 168, 169
Albany Plan of Union, 119
Albright, Madeleine, 925
alcohol: antialcohol movement, 412, 613, 708–09. *See also* prohibition
Alger, Horatio, 593
Allen, Ethan, 145
Allende, Salvador, 885
Alliance for Progress, 848
Allied Powers. *See* Allies, World War I
Allies, World War I, 660, 661; attitudes during peace conference, 675–77; members, 657–58; supplies for, 661, 665
Allies, World War II, 746, 749, 755–58
Amendment(s), 219, 242–51; proposing and ratifying process, *c218,* 219, 240. *See also* Constitution of the United States. *See also* specific amendments, by number
America First Committee, 747
American Antislavery Society, 418
American Civil Liberties Union (ACLU): Scopes trial, 710
American colonies. *See* English colonies
American Federation of Labor (AFL), 567, 735
American Indian Movement (AIM), 841–42
American Party. *See* Know-Nothing Party
American Red Cross, 478
American Revolution, 152, 162–85; beginnings of, 143–46; causes and effects, *c143, c173;* Continental Congress, First, 142–43; Continental Congress, Second, 148–49; Declaration of Independence, 150–52, 154-55, 156–59; Dutch support for, 172; early years, 163–69; events leading to, 133–41, 142–44; French support for, 171; Spanish support for, 171–72; Treaty of Paris, 184. *See also* Revolutionary War
Americans with Disabilities Act, 916
American Woman Suffrage Association, 610
AmeriCorps, 919
amnesty: during Reconstruction, 496, 498, 509; Vietnam, 893
Anderson, Marian, 730

Angelou, Maya, *p770,* 770–71
Anglican Church, 80, 114; dissent from, 78–79; Loyalists and, 164
Anthony, Susan B., *p426,* 426, 610
anticommunism: after World War II, 789–90, 791; 1952 election, 797, 798; Reagan administration, 907
Antietam, Battle of, 471, 473
Antifederalists, 210–11
anti-immigrant sentiment, 393–94, 449, 579–80, 582, 583, 622, 623, 639, 708, 709–10; during the Red Scare, 690; effect on labor strikes, 690–91; Klu Klux Klan, 709
anti-Semitism, 623, 709; in Germany, 742, 758–59
antislavery movement, 416–22, 424–25, 443; free African American colony, 417; Northern reaction to, 422; of Quakers, 197; roots of, 109; Southern reaction to, 421–22. *See also* abolitionists
antiwar sentiments: Vietnam War protests, 858, *p859, p861,* 861, 864, 868, 869–70, *p870;* World War I, 663, 671, 672–73
Apache, the, 31, 538, 542
apartheid, 898
Apollo Project, 851
Appalachian Mountains, 4, 108; as colonial western boundary, 124, 133
Appomattox Court House, Virginia, 487, 488
Arab-Israeli conflict(s): in Egypt, 803; in Israel, 779, 883–85
Arafat, Yassir, 920
Arapaho, the, 538, 541
Argentina, 898
Aristide, Jean-Bertrand, 920
Arizona, *mRA6, cRA4;* statehood, 620
Arkansas, *mRA6, cRA4;* civil rights movement, 823; denied readmission, 496; readmission to Union, 502; secession, 457
armed forces, *p696;* desegregation of, 784; draft during Civil War, 478–79; draft during World War I, 663, 664; enlistment during Civil War, 464–65, 467, 474–75, 478–79; integration of, 752, *p753;* segregation in, 643, 673, 752; women in, 664, 750, *p751, p915,* 915. *See also* military
arms race, 801, 802-03, 883, 893; efforts to end, 911
Armstrong, Louis, 704
Armstrong, Neil, *q851,* 851
Army, United States: buildup of, 663, 664; creation of, 235; reduction of, under Thomas Jefferson, 279; in World War I, 666–68
Army of Northern Virginia, 482
Army of the Potomac, 467, 469–70, 471, 479, 485
Arnold, Benedict, 149, 168
art: American style of, 593–94; Aztec, *p23;* colonial needlework, *p104;* of early Native Americans, *ptg16,* 33, *p51;* trends in, 414–15
Arthur, Chester A., 605, A4
Articles of Confederation, 189–95, *p190;* America's first constitution, 190–91, approving the, 191–92; central government under, 190–91; Constitution, compared to, *c203;* reform of, 198–202; state government under, 192, 215; weaknesses of, 192, 215
Asia: European interest in, 37–38, 42, 44, 45, 48–49; land bridge from, 17, 18, 19
Asian Americans, 814. *See also* individual country of origin
assembly line, 559, 699, *p700,* 700
Astor, John Jacob, 356
astronauts, 802, *p806,* 851
Atlanta, Georgia, 485, 486, 487
Atlanta Constitution, 514
Atlanta University, 497, 507
Atlantic Charter, 748
Atlantic Coastal Plains, 3
Atlantic Monthly, 592
atomic bomb, 740, 763–64; in Soviet Union, 789, 790–91
Attucks, Crispus, 139
Audubon, John James, 414
Auschwitz, Poland, 759
Austin, Moses, 363
Austin, Stephen F., *ptg363,* 363
Australia: in SEATO, 804
Austria, *m676,* 676; annexation by Germany, 743
Austria-Hungary, 655, *m657,* 656–57, 676; in Central Powers, 657–58; declaration of war, 657; treaty terms, 676
automation, 814
automobile, 559; effect on other industries, 701; increase in productivity, 699, 700; sales in, *g699,* 700
Axis Powers: membership, 742, 743, 746, 749, *m756*
Aztec Empire, 21, 23–24, *m26;* homes in, *p51;* religion in, 24; Spain, conquering of, 50–51, 52

B

baby boom, 808
Bacon, Nathaniel, 90
Bacon's Rebellion, 90
Badillo, Herman, 840
Baker, Ella, 830
balance of power, 656, 882
Balboa, Vasco Núñez de, 48
Balkans, 656–57, 915
Baltimore, Maryland, 89; Democratic-Republican first national convention, 337; War of 1812, 299
banking: during Great Depression, 717, 721, *c722,* 722, 725; regulation of, 620, savings and loan crisis, 915
Bank of the United States, First, 260–61, 268, 310
Bank of the United States, Second, 310, 319-20, 321; Andrew Jackson, action against, 348–49, *crt350,* 351
Banks, Dennis, *p841,* 842
Banneker, Benjamin, 260
Baptist Church, 412
Barbados: immigrants, 91–92
Barbary Coast states, 289–90, *m290*
Barnett, Ross, 831
Barrio Boy, 878–79
Barton, Clara, 478
baseball, 594
Bataan, Philippines, 761–62; Death March, *q762,* 762
Batista, Fulgencio, 804
Baumfree, Isabella. *See* Truth, Sojourner
Bay of Pigs invasion, 848
Beauregard, P.G.T., 466, 469
Beecher, Catharine, 427
Beecher, Lyman, 412
Begin, Menachem, *p899,* 899
Beijing, China, 638, 881, 882
Belgium, *m657,* 657, 658; invasion of Germany, 746
Belize: early civilization of, 21
Bell, Alexander Graham, *c577,* 557
Belleau Wood, France, 667
Bellecourt, Clyde, 842
Bellows, George, 521
Benton, Thomas Hart, 732
Bentsen, Lloyd, 910
Bering Strait, 18
Beringia, 17, 18, 19
Berkeley, Lord John, 86
Berkeley, Sir William, 90
Berlin, Germany, 758, 776–77
Berlin airlift, *p777, q777,* 777
Berlin Wall, *p849,* 849, 912, *p917,* 917
Bernstein, Carl, 889
Bessemer, Henry, *c557,* 563
Bethune, Mary McLeod, 730, *p731*
bicycle, *p595,* 595
Biddle, Nicholas, 348, *ptg349,* 349
Biederbecke, Bix, 704
big business, age of, 560–64; opposition to, 564. *See also* business
Bill of Rights, 201, 202, 210, 219, 242–43; Constitution, addition to the, 211; ratified by states, 259; rights of citizens, 226
Bill of Rights, English, 110, 205
Bingham, George Caleb, 332, 414
Bingham, Hiram, 21, 25
Birmingham, Alabama, 831, 832, 836
Black Americans, *See* African Americans
Black Cabinet, 730
black codes, 499–500
Black Hawk, chief, *q342,* 345, *ptg346*
Black Hills, 541
Black Moccasin, chief, *ptg286*
Blackmun, Harry, 886
Black Muslims, 834
Black Panther Party, 834
Black Power, 834
Blackwell, Elizabeth, 427–28
Blaine, James G., *q643*
blitzkrieg, 745, 746
blockade, 177; British, of German ports, 659, 661; British, in War of 1812, 297; of Cuba, 850; national economy, effect on, 310; Union, of Southern ports, 463–64, 467–68, 480; of Tripoli, 290; of Venezuela, 648
Blue Jacket, chief, 263
Bolívar, Simón, 324
Bolivia: independence from Spain, 324
Bolsheviks, 665–66, 675, 676; fear of, 689, 691

Bonaparte, Napoleon, 298, 299; James Madison, relations with, 293; plans for American empire, 282
bonds: after American Revolution, 259–60; in Civil War, 480
Bonhomme Richard, 177
Bonus Army, *p718,* 718
Booth, John Wilkes, 497
bootlegging, 709
border states: in Civil War, 461–62, 472
Bosnia, 655, 656
Bosnia-Herzegovina, *m912,* 915, 920
Boston, Massachusetts, *ptg70,* 80, 135, 141; American Revolution, 138–41, 144, 149
Boston Massacre, 139
Boston Tea Party, 130–31, *ptg131,* 140, 141
Bourke-White, Margaret, 732
Bowie, Jim, 364, 365
Boxer Rebellion, 638
boycotts: African American, 816, 824; colonial, 135, 136, 140, 142, 143; United Farm Workers, 840
Boyd, Belle, 477
bracero program, 753
Braddock, Edward, 120–21, 122
Bradford, William, 79
Brady Bill, 919
Brady, Mathew, 479
Braille, Louis, 413
Brant, Joseph, 176
Brazil, 47; independence from Portugal, 324
Brazos River: settlement of, 363
Breckinridge, John, 454
Breed's Hill, 146
Brezhnev, Leonid, *p883, q883,* 883, 893
Bridger, Jim, 356
Broker, Ignatia, *p254,* 254–55
Brown, Henry, 421
Brown, John, 448; Kansas, 444–45; raid on Harpers Ferry, 452
Brown, Linda, 822
Brown, Mackey, *q615*
Brown* v. *Board of Education of Topeka, Kansas, 816, 822–23, A18
Bruce, Blanche K., *p505,* 505
Bryan, William Jennings, 547, 618, *p710,* 710
Bryn Mawr College, 591
Buchanan, James, 394, 449, 456, A3
Budapest, Hungary, 803
Buddhists, *p853,* 854
budget deficit. *See* deficit, budget
Buena Vista, Mexico, 373
buffalo, 538–39, 540, 542
Buffalo Bill. *See* Cody, William
Bulgaria, 656, *m676*
Bulge, Battle of the, 758
Bull Moose Party. *See* Progressive Party
Bull Run, First Battle of, 466–67, *p467,* 487
Bull Run, Second Battle of, 471
Bunche, Ralph, 730
Bunker Hill, 165; Battle of, 146, 149, *m170*
Bureau of Indian Affairs, 540–41, 731, 842
Burger, Warren, 886, *p906*
Burma, 779
Burns, Anthony, *p442,* 442
Burnside, Ambrose, 471, 482
Burr, Aaron: 1796 election, 269; 1800 election, 277–78; Hamilton, duel with, 285
Bush, George, 908, A7; domestic policies, 915–16; election, *p910,* 910, 918, *p919;* foreign policy, 910, 911, *q913,* 913–15, *q914;* relations with Congress, 915, 916; in World War II, 910
Bushnell, Edward, 600, 601
business: competition in, 553–54, 562, 564, 605; government regulation of, 564, 567, 605, 617, 618, 620; during Great Depression, 716, 725, 733
busing, 887
Butler, Andrew P., 445

C

Cabeza de Vaca, Àlvar Núñez, 53
cabinet, 224; of Thomas Jefferson, 279; of George Washington, *ptg258,* 258
Cabot, John, 59, *c61*
Cabral, Pedro, 47, *c61*
Cahokia, 29, *p29*
Calhoun, John C., 295, 319–20, *q441;* 1828 election, 335; on protecting slavery, 438, 440; as secretary of war, 323; states' rights, support of, 338, 339
California, *mRA6, cRA4;* anti-Asian sentiments, 623–24; Bear Flag Republic, 374; Gold Rush, 376–78, 382, 525; Mexico, control of, 370, 372-73, 375, 438; Mexican War, 373–75; migration to, 726–27, 730; missions of, 96, 369, 370; settlement of, 369, 370, 372, 376; slavery, 439, 440; statehood, 378, 439
Californios, 374
Call of the Wild, The, 593
Calvert, Cecilius, 88–89. *See also* Baltimore, Lord
Calvert, Sir George, 88
Calvin, John, 58
Cambodia, 855, 868, 869
Camden, South Carolina, 178–79
camera: Civil War, *p479,* 479; Eastman, *p557,* 557–58
Camp David Accords, 899
Canada, 123; American invasion of, 296–97; American Revolution, 149; British control of, 123; exploration in, 60, 62; French/English conflicts in, 116–17; French settlement of, 95, 96; in NAFTA, 919; Native American flight to, 542; in NATO, 778; Rush-Bagot Treaty, 322; War of 1812, campaign in, 296, 297; in World War II, 755, 758
canals, 315–16, *m316,* 317, 386, 387–88
Canary Islands, 44, 46
capital, 306, 310, 399; raising, for business expansion, 560–61
capitalism, 689. *See also* business; ecomomy; industry; workers
Capone, Al "Scarface," 709
Caputo, Philip, *p857*
Caraway, Hattie, 729
Caribbean Islands, 47
Carlisle Indian Industrial School, 591
Carmichael, Stokely, 834
Carnegie, Andrew, *p563,* 563, 569, 592, 644
Carolinas: settling the, 90–92
carpetbaggers, 505
Carranza, Venustiano, 650
Carson, Kit, 356, 374
Carter, Jimmy, *p898,* A7; domestic policy, 897–98; election, *p895,* 895; energy crisis, 898; foreign policy, 898–900, *p899;* Iran hostage crisis, *p900,* 900
Carteret, Sir George, 86
Cartier, Jacques, 60, *c61*
cartoons: caricature, *crt895;* Andrew Jackson, *crt338, crt350;* interpreting political, *crt621,* 621; political, *crt604, crt605, crt648, crt695, crt792;* Sedition Act, *crt271;* Standard Oil, *crt561;* yellow journalism, *crt641*
Carver, George Washington, *p591,* 626
cash crops, 106, 107, 389, *m400;* cotton, 396, 397–98, 515
Cass, Lewis, 438–39
Cassatt, Mary, 593–94
Castro, Fidel, 840; effect on U.S. foreign policy, 804; Mariel boatlift, 898; takeover of Cuba, 804, 848
Catholic Church, 37, 58, 59; in England, 78; in English colonies, 78, 88, 89–90; immigrants, members of, 393; Native Americans, missions, 56–57, 96, 369; Protestant Reformation and, 58–59; role in conflict between England and Spain, 71
Catholics: immigrants, 575, 623; Ku Klux Klan, 709
Catlin, George, 286, 414, 523
Catt, Carrie Chapman, *q610,* 610
cattle industry, 531–33
Cavelier, Robert. *See* La Salle, Sieur de
CD-ROM: using, 481
census, 313; 1790, 313; 1820, 313
Central High School, Little Rock, Arkansas, 823
Central Intelligence Agency (CIA), 804, 848, 893; involvement in Chile, 885
Central Powers, 660, 661, 678; members of, 657–58
Chamberlain, Neville, *p744,* 744
Chambers, Whittaker, 790
Champlain, Samuel de, *c61,* 62
Chancellorsville, Virginia: Battle of, 483
Chaplin, Charlie, 703
Charles I, king of England, 80, 84, 88
Charles II, king of England, 84, 85, 87, 90, 110
Charleston, South Carolina, 90, 91, 92, *ptg93,* 178, 184
charter colonies, 111
Charter of Liberties, 87
Château-Thierry, France, 666
Chattanooga, Tennessee, 485

Chávez, César, *p840,* 840
checks and balances, 207–08, 218–19, *c222,* 243
Cherokee, the, 32, 342, 365; alphabet, 344; Trail of Tears, 340–41, 343–45; *Worchester v. Georgia,* 343
Chesapeake, 291
Chesapeake Bay, 72, 76, 77
Cheyenne, the, 538, 541–42
Chiang Kai-shek, 779
Chicago Daily Tribune, 783
Chicago, Illinois: civil rights movement, 835; 1968 Democratic convention, *p864,* 864; race riot, 692
Chichén Itzá, 22, *p33*
Chickasaw, the, 32, 342
child labor, 308–09, *p390, p567,* 567, 578; overturn of laws regulating, 695
Chile, 885; independence from Spain, 324
China: Boxer Rebellion, 638; Communist control of, 779; immigration, 376, 526, 528, 576, 579, *p582, p583,* 582–83, *p623,* 623, 624; immigration to Hawaii, 636; Japanese occupation of, 743; in Korea, 786, 787, 788; Nixon visit, *p881, q881,* 881; Open Door policy, 638–39; trade with U.S., 632, 638, 882–83. *See also* People's Republic of China
Chinese Exclusion Act, 580, 623
Chinook, the, 31, 286
Chisholm Trail, 532
Choate, Pat, 925
Choctaw, the, 342
Chou En-lai, *p881, q881,* 881
Christianity: Hawaiians' conversion to, 636; Samoans' conversion to, 637; Native Americans' conversion to, 56–57, 95, 96, 369; missions, 357. *See also* religion; individual churches
Churchill, Winston, *q746,* 746, *p748,* 758, *p733, p775;* iron curtain speech, *q775,* 775; post-World War II goals, 748; World War II diplomacy, 773–74; World War II strategy, 755
Church of England, 58–59. *See also* Anglican Church
Church of Jesus Christ of the Latter-day Saints. *See* Mormons
CIA. *See* Central Intelligence Agency
cities: Aztec, 23–24; crisis in, 586–87; 1870–1910, growth of, 584–85; Industrial Revolution, growth of, 310–11; life in industrial, 311, 392, *ptg574, p578, p585,* 585–87, *p587, ptg588,* 588; Mayan, 22; Moundbuilders, *p29;* of Native Americans, early, 21, 25; Northern, growth of in mid-1800s, 392; population growth in, 310, *g311,* 392; poverty in, 813, 814; Southern, in mid-1800s, 406; unemployment in, 814
citizenship: defined, 245; responsibilities of, 208, 227–28; rights of, 226–27
city government: corruption in, 603–04; reform of, 604
civics: citizen duties, 227–28; citizen responsibilities, 228; citizen rights, 226–27
civil disobedience, 825
"Civil Disobedience," 407
Civilian Conservation Corps (CCC), *c722,* 724, 731
civil rights, 206, 226–27; Bill of Rights, 219, 226, 242–43; Declaration of Independence, 152, 154-55, 156, 226; Fourteenth Amendment, 245; march for, *p228;* types of, 226; Truman advancement of, *q783, q784, p784,* 783–84
Civil Rights Act of 1866, 500
Civil Rights Act of 1964, 829, 833
civil rights movement, 820–43, *ptg820;* African Americans, 821–25, 830–37; beginnings of, 816; Hispanic Americans, *q838,* 838, 839–40; legislation, 829, 833, 838, 841; Little Rock confrontation, 823; move toward equality, causes and effects, *c824;* Native Americans, 841–42; organizations, 821–22, 825, 830, 831, 841; protests, *ptg820,* 830–31, *p832,* 832, *p833,* 836–37, 842; radicals, 834–35; school integration, 822–23; school segregation, 821–23, 831; separatism, 834; Supreme Court rulings, 516, 624, 821, 822–23, 824, 831, 841; violence, 824, 831, 834–35, 836; voting rights, 833; white activists, 830, 831, 832, 836; white reaction to protests, 830, 831, 836; white reaction to school integration, 823; women, 838–39
civil service: reform of, 605, 607, 625
Civil War, 460–89: abolitionists, 472; African American involvement, 465, 473, 474–75; border states, 461–62, 472; defined, 445; early years, 466–71; in the East, *m468,* 469–70; events leading to, 436–57; final battles of, 485–88, *m486;* invasion of the North, 483–84; life during, 476–80, *p477;* in literature, 434–35; medical care, 477–78; military leadership, 467, 469, 470, 471, 483–84; opposition to, 478–79; raising armies, 464–65, 467, 470, 474–75, 478–79; results of, 488; soldier identification tags, 474; suspension of constitutional rights, 462, 478; taxation, 480; the two sides, 461–65; in the West, 469, *m484;* women, 474, 477–78
Clark, George Rogers, 176–77, 189
Clark, William, 283–84
Clay, Henry, *ptg321;* American System, 320–21; Bank of the United States, 348–49; compromise tariff bill, 339; 1824 election, 333–34, *c334;* 1840 election, 351; 1844 election, *p360,* 360, 367; Missouri Compromise, 438, *p439;* new compromise, 439–40; as War Hawk, 295
Clayton Antitrust Act, 620
Clean Air Act, 916
Clemenceau, Georges, 675, 676, *pA17*
Clemens, Samuel Langhorne. *See* Twain, Mark
Clermont, 315, *p325,* 325
Cleveland, Grover: A4; Cuba, opposition to involvement in, 641; election, 546: free silver, opposition to, 547; Hawaii, opposition to annexation of, 637; and Pullman Strike, 569; tariffs, lowering of, 605
Cleveland, Ohio: civic reform, 604; civil rights movement, 835; oil industry, 561–62
climate(s), 5–6; U.S. climate regions, *m5*
Clinton, Bill, *p224, q876, p904, q928,* A8; domestic policy, 919; election, *p918,* 918, *p919;* foreign policy, 919–20; Inaugural Address, *q926–27;* reelection, 924–25; relations with Congress, 919, 921
Clinton, De Witt, 315–16
Clinton, Henry, 178, 180, 182, 183
Clinton, Hillary Rodham, *p904,* 919
clipper ships, *ptg386,* 386
coal industry, 552, 701, 814; strike of 1902, 617–18
Cody, William (Buffalo Bill), 539
Coercive Acts, 141. *See also* Intolerable Acts
Cohan, George M., 600, 670, 671
cold war, 772–93; causes and effects, *c791;* confrontations, 848–50; Eisenhower and, 800–805; end of, 913; in Europe, *m802;* increase in fears of communism, 789, 791; origins, 773–77; thaws in, 804–05, 881; U.S.-Soviet rivalry, 800–802
collective bargaining, 567
Colombia: control of Panama, 646–47; independence from Spain, 324
colonies. *See* English colonies
Colorado, *mRA6, cRA4;* mining industry, 526–27; Pike's expedition, 285; statehood, 526
Colored Farmers' National Alliance, 545
Columbian Exchange, 55
Columbia River: and claims on Oregon country, 355; Lewis and Clark expedition, 284, 355
Columbus, Christopher, *q12,* 14–15, *ptg15,* 37, 43, *c61;* first voyages of, 46–47
Comanche, the, 538, 541
Committee on Public Information, 671–72, 673
committees of correspondence, 139–40, 142
Committee to Re-Elect the President (CREEP), 890
Common Sense, 150, 154, 167
communication: of early Native Americans, 24–25; improvements in, 388, 556–57; mass media, 703–04
communism: Allies' fear of spread of, 676; in Chile, 885; in China, 779; during Great

Depression, 731; in Eastern Europe, 775; Eisenhower policy toward, 800–01, 804; fear of international spread of, 774, 775, 779; in Russia, 665–66, 689; in Southeast Asia, 852, 853–54, 869; U.S. public opinion of, 689, 690, 691, 789, 791
competition, 564; in business, 605; foreign business, 620; in railroad industry, 553–54
Compromise of 1850, 440, 442, 443, *m444*
Compromise of 1877, 511
computer(s), 807, 922–23, *p926,* 926, 927
Comstock Lode, 526
concentration camps, *p759, q759,* 759
Concord, Massachusetts, *m144,* 144, *ptg145,* 145, 147, 148
"Concord Hymn, The," 145
Conestoga wagons, *ptg281,* 281, *p294,* 294
Confederacy: army, 464–65, 469, 474, 476–77; before the Civil War, 463; economy, 473, 480; formation of, 455; goals, 464; reactions to, 455–56; resources, *g463,* 463, 467, 477
Confederate Battle Flag, 483
Confederate States of America. *See* Confederacy
Confederation Congress: attempt to stop spread of slavery, 193; responsibilities of, 190–91; weaknesses of, 192, 193–95
Congregationalists, 113
Congress; checks and balances, 207, 221; committees, 221–23; composition of, 206; constitutional authority, 191, 206, 234, 246, 248; the first, 258–59; declaration of war, 224, 234; functions of, 221–23, 233–34; legislative branch, 218, 221–23; powers of, 206, 218, 220, 234–235; powers denied, 233. *See also* House of Representatives. *See also* Senate
Congressional Medal of Honor, *p665,* 665, 753, 787
Congress of Industrial Organizations (CIO), 735
Congress of Racial Equality (CORE), 831
Connecticut, *mRA6, cRA4;* as charter colony, 111; English settlement, 81
conquistadors, 50–55
conservation, 618, 619
constitution: the first, written in America, 81; Iroquois, 32; state. *See* state government
***Constitution* (Old Ironsides),** 297
Constitutional Convention, 199–202; approving the Constitution; the Great Compromise, 200–01; New Jersey Plan, 200; Three-Fifths Compromise, 201; Virginia Plan, 199–200
Constitution of the United States, *p214,* 215–20, 230–251; amendment process, *c218,* 219; *See also* specific amendments, by number; Bill of Rights, 201, 202, 210, 211, 219, 226, 242–43, 259; branches of government, 206–07, 221–25; checks and balances, 207–08, 218–19; commerce clause, 220; compared to Articles of Confederation, *c203;* elastic clause, 220; federal government powers, 221–25; the federal system, 205, *c217;* goals of, 215–16; government powers, 217–19; implied powers, 220, 268; limited government, 217; popular sovereignty, 216; Preamble, 215, 231; ratification of the, 209–11; roots of the, 204–05; strict interpretation of, 268; underlying principles of, 216–17
Continental Army, 149; African Americans in, 167; early battles of, 165–66; early victories of, 167–69; establishment of, 149, 165; struggles in the South, 178–79, *ptg179,* 180; at Valley Forge, 172–73; winning the war, 182–84
Continental Colors flag, 149
Continental Congress, First: delegates to, 142–43, 148; decisions of, 143
Continental Congress, Second, 154, 169, 171, 185; approves Articles of Confederation, 191–92; approves the Constitution, 202; delegates to, 148–49; establishes an army, 149, 165, 167; plans for new government, 190–91; prints paper money, 174; votes for independence, 151, 155
Continental Divide, 4
Contract With America, 920
Convention of 1818, 322
conventions, national party: Democratic-Republican, 337; 1968 Democratic National Convention, 864
Coolidge, Calvin, *p693,* 693, *crt695, q695,* A6; becoming president, 694; business, support of, 695; foreign policy, 695–96; reelection, 695; strikes, opposition to, *q691,* 691
Cooper, James Fenimore, 414
Coral Sea, Battle of the, *m762,* 763
Corbin, Margaret, 165
Corinth, Mississippi, 469
Cornell University, 591
Cornish, Samuel, 392, 418
Cornwallis, Charles, 168, 178–79, 180, 182; surrender at Yorktown, 183, *ptg184*
Coronado, Francisco Vásquez, 53
corporations, 560–61; growth of, 561, 562, 563–64; use of Sherman Antitrust Act on, 619
Corregidor, 761
corruption: city governments, 603–04; Grant administration, 508–09; Harding administration, 694; Reconstruction governments, 505; state governments, 616
Cortés, Hernán, *q24,* 24, 50–51, 52
cotton gin, *p106,* 306–07, 309; *p397,* 397, 398
cotton industry, expansion of, 309; Southern, 396–400
Coughlin, Charles, 733–34, *p734*
court system, federal, 206–07, 220, 224–25, *c225;* creation of, 224, 258–59
cowhands, 532–33
Cowpens, South Carolina, *ptg179,* 180
Cox, Archibald, 890
Crane, Stephen, *p434,* 434–35, 593
Crawford, William H., 333, *c334*
Crazy Horse, chief, 538, 541–42
credit, 402; defaults in, 717; increase in, 810
Creek, the, 32, 297, 336, 342, 347, 365
Creel, George, 671
crime: in cities, 579, 586–87; organized crime, 709
Crisis, The, 167
Crittenden, John, 454, 464
Croatia, 576, 915
Croatoan, 72
Crockett, Davy, *ptg362, q362,* 362; and Texas war for independence, 364, *q365,* 365
Cromwell, Oliver, 84
Crow, the, 538
Crucible, The, 790
Cruz, Jesse Lopez de la, *q838,* 838
Cruz, Juana Inés de la, *ptg54,* 54
Cuba, 122, 123, 324; as American protectorate, 643; Castro takeover, 804, 848; communism in, 840; immigrants, 840–41; independence, 641, 643; rebellion against Spain, 640–41, 642–43; relations with Soviet Union, 804, 848, 849–50; Spanish-American War, 640–43, *m642;* Spanish control of, 640–41, 642; U.S. relations with, 804, 848, 849–50
Cullen, Countee, 706
culture(s): African American, 108, 705–06; American, changing of, 393, 590–95, 706, 707, 810–12; clashes of different, 708–11; emerging, of colonial America, 102, 113–14; enslaved persons, 403, 404–05; growth of, 20; of immigrants, 578–79; Native Americans, *m30,* 538–39, 542, 543, 627
currency. *See* money
Currier and Ives, 9
Custer, George Armstrong, 541–42
Cuzco, 24, 25
cyberspace, 593
Czechoslovakia, *m676,* 676; Communist takeover, 776; invasion by Germany, 743–44

D

Da Gama, Vasco, 44, *c61*
Dakota people, the, 31
Dakota Territory, 540–41
Daley, Richard, 864
Dallas, Texas, *m549,* 828
Da Nang, South Vietnam, 855
Dare, Virginia, 72
Darrow, Clarence, *p710,* 710

database: building a, 866
Daugherty, Harry, 693, 694, 695
Daughters of Liberty, 137, 140
Daughters of Temperance, 426
Davis, Benjamin, Jr., 752
Davis, Benjamin, Sr., 752
Davis, Jefferson, 455, *p457,* 457, 463, 464; capture of, 488; commander in chief, 471; suspension of civil rights, 279
Davis, John W., 695
Dawes, William, 144, 145
Dawes Act, 543
D-Day invasion, 757, *p758*
Dean, John, 890
Debs, Eugene V., 569, 606
debt. *See* national debt
Decatur, Stephen, 290
Declaration of Independence, 156–59; writing of the, 148, 150–51, 152, 154-55; signed, 151, 155, *ptg157*
Declaration of Indian Purpose, 841
Declaratory Act of 1766, 136
Deerslayer, The, 414
deficit, budget: effort to end, 907; Nixon administration, 887–88; Ford administration, 894–95
Degas, Edgar, 515
De Grasse, François, 183
Delaware, *mRA6, cRA4;* in the Civil War, 461; as proprietary colony, 112; ratification of Constitution, 210–11
Delaware, the, 293
Democratic Party: division of, 448, 453–54; during Reconstruction, 509, 510; Mexican War, support for, 373; Oregon, support for taking by force, 360, 367
Democratic-Republican Party: campaign tactics, 277; Constitution, view of, 268; 1796 election, 268–69; 1800 election, 277–78; 1824 election, 333; 1828 election, 334–35; emergence of, 267, *c269;* Federalists, differences between, *c268,* 268; France, support of, 267, 271; National Republicans, split from, 334; nominating convention, 337; Sedition Act, 271–72; states' rights, 272; War of 1812, support of, 294–95, 300
Deng Xiaoping, 883
Denmark, *m676;* invasion by Germany, 746
Department of Energy, 898
Department of Health, Education, and Welfare (HEW), 799
Department of Housing and Urban Development (HUD), 829
Department of Transportation, 906
depression, 624; of 1837, 349–50; after the Revolution, 196–97. *See also* Great Depression
deregulation, 906
De Soto, Hernando, 53, *c61*
détente, 882–83, 884, 893, 899
Detroit, Michigan, 123–24; automobile industry of, 559, 700; civil rights movement, 835; in War of 1812, 296
Dewey, George, 641
Dewey, John, 591
Dewey, Thomas, 782–83
Dias, Bartholomeu, 44, *c61*
Díaz, Porfirio, 649
Dickens, Charles, *q385*
Dickinson, Emily, 415
Diem, Ngo Dinh, 853–54
disabled, rights of, 842
disarmament, 322, 748
Discovery, 72
discrimination, 821, 830; African Americans, 391–92, *q512,* 512, 584–85, 664, 753; ethnic groups, 576, 623–24, 627; female workers, 392; Hispanic Americans, 840; Mexican Americans, 753–54; defined, 622; progressivism attitude toward, 624–25; racial, 624, 814; religious, 623; in the West, 533, 623–24
disease(s): of city dwellers, 311, 586–87; early settlers, effect on, 72, 73, 79; Hawaiians, effect on, 636; medical advances to combat, 808; Mexican War, men lost to, 375; Native Americans, effect on, 52, 55, 82, 357; Panama Canal, effect on workers, 647–48; Spanish-American War, men lost to, 643; World War I, men lost to, 674
district courts, 224–25
District of Columbia: slavery, 439–40. *See also* Washington, D.C.
Dix, Dorothea, 414, 478
Dodge City, Kansas, 531, 533
Dole, Robert: 1976 election, 895; 1996 election, 924, *p925, q925,* 925
Dominican Republic, 648; intervention in, 696
domino theory, 804, 853
Doolittle, James, 763
Dorris, Michael, *p14,* 14–15
Douglas, Stephen A.: Compromise of 1850, 440; 1860 election, 453–54, *p454;* Kansas-Nebraska Act, 443; Lincoln-Douglas debates, *p451, q451,* 451; popular sovereignty, 450, 451, 452
Douglass, Charles, *p474*
Douglass, Frederick, 373, 405, *p406,* 416, 418, *q419,* 419–20, 423, 450, *q474, q475, p505, q512*
draft: in Civil War, 478–79; defined, 28; end of the, 663; opposition to, 859–60; reform of, 867–68; resistance to, 479; in World War I, 663, 664
Drake, Sir Francis, 71
***Dred Scott* decision,** 449–50, 500; effect on popular sovereignty, 450
drought, 535, 730; defined, 28
Du Bois, W.E.B., *q517, p626, q626,* 626
due process, 226–27; Fifth Amendment, 242
Dukakis, Michael, 910
Dulles, John Foster, 801
Dunbar, Paul Laurence, 593
Dunkirk, France, *p746,* 746, *m756*
Duryea, Charles and J. Frank, *c557*
Dust Bowl, 726–27; causes of, 729–30; migration from, 726–27, *m729,* 730
Dutch West Indies Company, 84–85
Dylan, Bob, 589

E

Eagle, 851
Eakins, Thomas, 593
Earth Day, 896
East Germany, 776, 777. *See also* Germany
Eastman, George, 557–58
Eckford, Elizabeth, *p823, q823,* 823
economics: corporations, 560–61; of financing war, 174, 367, 375; financing World War II, 751; free silver currency system, 546–47; mining, 525–26; in New England colonies, 104–05; of plantations, 402–03; producing supplies for World War I, 671; railroads effect on, 529, 552; in Southern colonies, 107; theory of mercantilism, 59
economy: after American Revolution, 194, 196; after World War I, 698–701; after World War II, 780–81; building up of, 260–61; Carter administration, 897–98; during depressions, 196–97, 349–50; effect of foreign competition on, 894, 927; Great Depression, 716–17, 725, 734, 735; Industrial Revolution, 310; of Jefferson administration, 279; 1950s prosperity, 807–12; Nixon administration, 887–89; Reagan administration, 907, 908; of the South, late 1800s, 513–15
Ecuador: independence from Spain, 324
Ederle, Gertrude, 704
Edison, Thomas Alva, *c557, p558,* 558, 595
education, 412–13; African Americans, 405, 413, 497, 507, 590; in the colonies, 113–14; colleges, 114, 413, 425, 427, 428, 497, 507, 563, 591, 869, 870; integrating schools, 822–23; Johnson administration and, 829; Native Americans, 591; normal schools, 413; philosophy of, 591; for people with disabilities, 413, 414; public schools, 507, 590–91; reform of, 412–13; segregation in schools, 590, 623, 624, 639, 821–23; women, 413, 425, 427–28, 591, 609, 839
Edwards, Jonathan, 113
Egypt: relations with Israel, 803, 884, 885, 899; relations with Soviet Union, 803, 884
Ehrlichman, John, 888, 890
Eighteenth Amendment, 219, 247, 613, 708
Eighth Amendment, 243
Einstein, Albert, 763
Eisenhower, Dwight D., 718, 826, A6; and cold war, 800–805; domestic policy, 797–99, *q798;* economic policy, 798; election, 797, *p798,* 798; Farewell Address, 805; foreign policy, 800–805,

Index

q803, q804, 848, 853; Korean War cease-fire agreement, 788; prepresidential experience, 797–98; social programs, 799; World War II role, 756, 757, *p758*
elastic clause, 220, 234
El Camino Real, 96
elderly: effect on social and medical programs, 927; pension plan for, 734
Elections of: 1796, 268–69; **1800,** 277–78, *m278;* **1804,** 290; **1808,** 292; **1816,** 318; **1824,** 333–34, *c334;* **1828,** 333, 334–35; campaign tactics in, 335; **1832,** 348, 349; **1836,** 349; **1840,** 350; **1844,** 351, 438; **1848,** 438–39; **1856,** 449; **1860,** 453–54; **1864,** 486; **1868,** 503; **1876,** *m510,* 510–11; **1912,** 619–20; **1916,** 663; **1920,** 614; **1928,** 711; **1948,** *m782,* 782; **1960,** 826, 827; **1968,** 865; **1972,** 888; **1992,** 918; **1996,** 924–26, *m925*
Electoral College: 277–78; majority and plurality of votes, 334; selection of electors, 206
electricity, 558, 698, 724
Elementary and Secondary Education Act of 1965, 829
Eleventh Amendment, 243
Elizabeth I, queen of England, 71–72
Ellington, Duke, 704, *p707*
Ellis Island, *p577,* 577
Emancipation Proclamation, 472, 473–74, A14
embargo, 291–92; 310; oil, 884–85, 888–89
Emerson, Ralph Waldo, *q145,* 411, 414, 452
Endara, Guillermo, 913
England: exploration by, 59, 61–62, 71–72; North American colonies, trade with, 110–11; Protestant Reformation in, 58–59; religious persecution in, 78, 80; Spain, war with, 71. *See also* Great Britain
English Civil War, 110
English colonies, 71–75; agriculture in, 73, 79–80, 89, 90–91, 104, 106, 107–08; culture of, 102, 113–14; economies of, 104–05; education in, 113–14; government in, 74, 79, 80, 81, 86, 87, 111–41, 149; manufacturing in, 104, 106–07; Middle, 84–87; Native Americans, relations with 72, 73, 75, 76, 79–80, 82, 87, 90; New England, 78–82, 103–06; populations, *g83,* 85–86, 87, 93, 102, 103, *m127;* religious freedom in, 79, 81, 85, 88, 89–90; slavery in, 75, 89, 91–92, 107, 108, 109; Southern, 88–93, 107–08; taxation, 134–37; trade, *g98, g139,* 104–05, 110–11, 134; wars in, with Native Americans, 82
English settlements, the first, *m73*
Enlightenment, the, 114; influence on the Constitution, 205
Enola Gay, 764
enslaved persons: in the Civil War, 473–75; cotton industry, 396, 397, 398, *ptg399, q401,* 401, 402, 403–06; Emancipation Proclamation, 473–74; families, 404; as fugitives, 421, 439, 442–43; life of, on plantations, 108, 109, *p403,* 403–04, *p404;* music, 405; Native American, 24, 54–55; religion of, 405: revolts in the U.S., 405, 452. *See also* slavery
enumerated powers, 217
environment: Earth's, 896; protecting the, 928. *See also* conservation, global warming, ozone
Environmental Protection Agency (EPA), 887
Equal Pay Act, 838
Equal Rights Amendment (ERA), 839
Equator, 361; defined, 10
Equino, Olaudah, 68–69, *q105*
Era of Good Feelings, 318–19
Erie, Lake, 315; War of 1812, 297
Erie Canal, 316, 387
Eriksson, Leif, 46
Ervin, Sam, 890
Espionage Act, 673
Estevanico, 53
Estonia, *m676,* 677, 746
Ethiopia, 898; annexation by Italy, 742
Europe: 1997, *m912;* Asia, trade with, 38, 39, 42, 44; early exploration by, *m48, c61,* 43–49, 60–62; Monroe Doctrine, 324; U.S. trade with, 338; during World War I, *m657;* after World War I, 674, *p675, m676,* 676–77; after World War II, *m774,* 776; during World War II, 745–47, *m756,* 756–58
Europe, Eastern: end of communism, 911–13; immigrants, 575–76; Soviet occupation of, 773, 774
Europe, Southern: immigrants, 575–76
Europe, Western: U.S. economic aid to, 776
Evans, Oliver, 306
Evans, Walker, 732
evolution, 710
executive branch, 223–24; checks and balances, 221; constitutional authority, 206, 220; departments of, 224, 258; powers of, 206, 218, 220. *See also* presidency
executive departments, 224, 258; creation of Navy Department, 270–71
Executive Office of the President (EOP), 224
executive privilege, 890
Exodusters, *p534,* 534
expansionism. *See* Manifest Destiny
exploration: of the Americas, 36–62; by the English, 59, 61–62, 71–72; European voyages of, *m48;* by the French, 59–60; motives for, 42; of North America, 58–62
Explorer, 802
explorers, European, *m60, c60*
exports. *See* trade

F

factories: conditions favoring development of, 306; in the North (mid-1800s), 390–92; source of power for, 306, 308; in the South (mid-1800s), 399–400; textile, 307, *p308,* 308–09, 312; working conditions in, 308–09, 312, 390–91, 566
factory system, 307–08, 390–91
Fair Deal, 781–82, 783–84
Fair Labor Standards Act (FLSA), *c722,* 735
Fallen Timbers, Battle of, 263, *m264,* 264
families: enslaved persons, 404; extended, 404, 539; Great Plains farmers, *p535,* 535; mid-1900s, 927; Native American, *ptg345,* 538–39; role of, in colonies, 113
Family Medical Leave Act, 919
Farewell to Arms, A, 706
Farmer, James, *q831,* 831, *p836, q837,* 836–37
farmers: armed protest of, 262; in Dust Bowl, 730; Great Plains, 533–36; migration to cities, 813–14; organizations of, 545; poverty of, 813–14, *p814;* problems of, 1920s, 701; problems with railroads, 544, 545, 546; protests of, 544–47; revolt of, 196–97; sharecroppers, 507, 515, 813–14; as soldiers, in Civil War, 465; tenant farmers, 95, 515, 813–14; on western frontier, 262
Farmers' Alliances, 545, 546
Farm Security Administration, *c723*
Farragut, David, 469, 486, 753
fascism: rise of, 731, 742
Federal Bureau of Investigation (FBI), 686, 754, 789, 888, 893
federal debt. *See* national debt
Federal Deposit Insurance Corporation (FDIC), *c722,* 725
Federal Emergency Relief Administration (FERA), *c722,* 724
federal government: branches of, 218, 221–25; formation of, 257–59; land policy of, 534; limits of, 207–08, 217; Native Americans, conflicts with, 541–43; Native Americans, policy, 263, *m264,* 342–45, 540–41, 543; people's role in, 216, 226–28; powers of, 217–18; regulation of business, 605, 617, 618, 620; role in social welfare, 724, 734, 783; separation of powers, 218–19; state government, sharing powers with, 205, 217–18, *c217*
Federal Highway Act, 799
federalism, 205, *c217,* 217
Federalist, The, 210; No. 10, A10
Federalist Party: Alien and Sedition acts, 271–72; Aaron Burr, support for, 285; campaign tactics of, 269, 277; Constitution, views on, 268; Democratic-Republican Party, differences between, *c268;* division of, 272; Embargo Act, opposition to,

291–92; emergence of, 267; Great Britain, support of, 267; Louisiana Purchase, opposition to, 285; Naturalization Act, 271; policies of, 267; and representative government, 268; secession plans of, 285: War of 1812, opposition to, 295, 297, 300
Federal Republic of Germany (West Germany), 777
Federal Reserve Act, 620
Federal Trade Commission (FTC), 620
Feminine Mystique, The, 816, 838
feminists, 425, 838–39
Ferdinand, Franz, archduke, *p655,* 655, 656–57
Ferguson, Miriam, 695
Ferraro, Geraldine, 908
Field, Cyrus, 556–57
Fifteenth Amendment, 246, 503, 512, 515, 610
Fifth Amendment, 226, 242, 450
Fifty-fourth Massachusetts, 475
Fillmore, Millard, 394, 449, A3; as president, 379, 440, 632
Finland, 677, 746
First Amendment, 227, 242
First Virginia Infantry flag, 466
Fisk University, 497, 626
Fitzgerald, F. Scott, 706
Fitzgerald, Zelda, 706
Five-Power Treaty, 696
flag etiquette, 934
flags: American protest banner, *p138;* American Revolutionary War, *p128;* Betsy Ross flag, 261; Continental Colors, 149; Confederate Battle Flag, 483; of England (British Union), 81; First Stars and Stripes, 169; First Star-Spangled Banner, 300; 1st Virginia Infantry flag, *p466;* Flag of 1818, 319; Great Star flag, 319; Seventeenth Flag of the Union, 483; of Spain, 1492, 47; Stars and Stripes, 1960, 799; Texas Republic, 1839, 366; 37-Star flag, 500; Twentieth Flag of the Union, 526; Twenty-fifth Flag, 620
Florida, , *mRA6, cRA4;* Adams-Onís Treaty, 323; British control, 123; East Florida invasion, 322–23; Native American resistance to removal, 345–46; Ponce de León in, 53; readmission to Union, 502; secession, 455; Spanish control in, 195, 322–23
Forbes, Charles, 694
Forbes, Esther, 130–31
Ford, Gerald R., *crt895,* A7; becomes president, 891, *p892,* 892, *p893;* becomes vice president, 890; domestic policy, 893–95; foreign policy, 893; Nixon pardon, 892; Vietnam amnesty, 893
Ford, Henry, *q559,* 559, 700, 747
Ford Motor Company, 699, 700
foreign policy: and American expansionism, 631–32; Monroe Doctrine, 324; presidential role in, 224; George Washington's views on, 265
Fort Detroit, 124
Fort Donelson, 469
Fort Duquesne, 118, 119, 121, 123
Fort Frontenac, 123
Fort Gibson, 340
Fort Henry, 469
Fort Knox, 293
Fort McHenry, 299, 300
Fort Necessity, 119
Fort Pitt, 124
Fort Stanwix, 168, 169
Fort Sumter, 453, 457
Fort Ticonderoga, 145, 149, 150, 169
forty-niners, 376, 377, 379, *p382,* 382
Fourteen Points, 675, 676, 677, A17
Fourteenth Amendment, 227, 245–46, 500–501, 502, 512, 822
Fourth Amendment, 226, 242
Fox people, the, 342, 345
France: John Adams administration, relations with, 270–71, 272; appeasement of Germany, 743–44; in China, 638; Civil War, involvement in, 474; division of Germany, 773, 776; explorations by, 59–60, *m60,* 62, 95–96; Great Britain, 1793 war with, 264; Thomas Jefferson, relations with, 282; Louisiana Territory, possession of, 282; James Madison, relations with, 292–93; Native Americans, relations with, 96, 117, 120, 121; naval reduction, 694; Panama Canal, efforts to build, 646; Revolution, 264, 267; role of, in Revolutionary War, 171, *c173;* 173, 174, 182, 183, 184, 185; role in Suez crisis, 803; Santo Domingo rebellion, 282; in SEATO, 804; in Vietnam, 803–04, 852; George Washington, relations with, 264; West Indies, control of, 123; in World War I, 657, 658–59, 667; in World War II, 745, 746, *m756,* 757; XYZ Affair, 270. *See also* French and Indian War. *See* Seven Years' War
Frankfurter, Felix, 690
Franklin, Benjamin, 110, 164, 171, *q204, q219;* Albany Plan of Union, *q119,* 119, 123; Constitution, support for, 209–10; Constitutional Convention, 199, 200; Continental Congress, Second, 150; contributions of, 114; Declaration of Independence, 152; France, seeking support from, 171; Treaty of Paris, 184
Fredericksburg, Virginia: Battle of, 482
Free African Society, 197, 198
Freedmen's Bureau, 496–97, 500, 507
Freedom of Information Act, 891
freedom of speech: Bill of Rights, 219, 242–43
Freedom Riders, 831, *p836,* 836–37
Freeport Doctrine, 451
Free-Soil Party, 438–39, 448
Free Speech Movement, 858, 859
Frémont, John C., 370, 374, 449
French-American alliance, 1778: causes and effects, *c173*
French and Indian War, 119, 120–24, *m122,* 133, 134; events leading to, 116–19; land claims after, 123; Native Americans and, 123–24
French Revolution, 264, 267
Friedan, Betty, *q816,* 816, 838
Frost, Robert, 924
Fugitive Slave Act, 442–43, 446
Fulbright, J. William, 860
Fuller, Margaret, 414
Fulton, Robert, 315, 386
fundamentalists: Islamic, 900
Fundamental Orders of Connecticut, 81
fur trade, 62, 94, 95, *ptg96;* 116, 117, 356

G

Gadsden Purchase, 375
Galarza, Ernesto, *p878,* 878–79
Galbraith, John Kenneth, 815
Gallaudet, Thomas, 413
Galveston, Texas, 604
Gálvez, Bernardo de, 172
Gandhi, Mohandas, *p825,* 825
García, Calixto, 642
Garfield, James: A4; assassination, 605; spoils system, opposition to, 605
Garland, Hamlin, 330–31, *q584,* 584
Garrison, William Lloyd, 416, *p417,* 417–18, 422, 426
Garvey, Marcus, *p689,* 689, 692
Gates, Horatio, 169, 178, 180
Gaza Strip, 884
General Motors Company, 699, 700, 735
Genêt, Edmond, 264
Geneva Accords, 803, 853
Geneva College, 428
Geneva Summit, 805
genocide, 758
geography: five themes of, 2; handbook, 1–11
George, David Lloyd, 675, 676
George III, king of Great Britain, *ptg132, ptg141;* American independence, agrees to, 184; Boston Tea Party, response to, 141; establishes boundary for colonies, 124; Olive Branch Petition, response to, 149; prepares for war, 144, 149; punishes colonies, 141, 154
Georgia, *mRA6, cRA4;* Cherokee Nation of, 343; in the Civil War, 485, 486, 487, 488; colony, 92–93; readmission to Union, 502; royal colony, 112; secession, 455
German Americans, 660, 672, 673, 677
German Democratic Republic (East Germany), 777
Germany: armistice terms, 1918, 668; in China, 638; fascism, support of, 731; immigrants, 107, 393, *p575;* naval strength, 656, 661–62, 663; peace treaty terms, 1918,

676; post-World War II division of, 773, 776–77; reunification of, 777, 912; in Samoa Islands, 637–38; unification of, 1870s, 655; under Hitler, 742; in World War I, *m657,* 657–59, 661–62, 663, 666–67; in World War II, 743–47, *m756,* 755–58
Geronimo, 542
Gerry, Elbridge, 202
Gettysburg, Pennsylvania: Battle of, *ptg460,* 483–84, 489
Gettysburg Address, 484–85, *q485,* A15
Ghana, 40
Ghost Dance, 543
GI Bill of Rights, 780
Gilded Age, *p562,* 586
Gingrich, Newt, 920, 921
Ginsberg, Allen, 815
glasnost, 908, 911
Glenn, John, 851
global warming, 928
Glorious Revolution, 110
Godey's Lady's Book, 428
Golan Heights, 883, 885
gold: in Alaska, 633; Black Hills, 541; in California, 376–78, 382, 525; as a form of payment, 50; mining of, 525–26, 527; standard of currency, 546, 547; trade of, 40, 42, 43, 44; for wealth, 53, 54, 59
Goliad, Texas, *m365,* 365
Gompers, Samuel, 567
Gone With the Wind, 732
Gonzales, Texas, 364, *m365,* 365
Good Hope, Cape of, 44
Goodnight-Loving Trail, 532
Gorbachev, Mikhail, 908–09, *p909,* 910–11, 912
Gore, Al, Jr., 918, *p919,* 923, 924
Gorgas, William, 647
government: Articles of Confederation, 190–95; branches of, 218–19, 221–25; colonial, 74, 79, 80–81, 86, 87, 110–12, 149, 133–41; constitutional powers of, 217–19; Fundamental Orders of Connecticut, 81; limited, 207–08, 217; military rule, 74; Native American, 32; public's role in, 216, 268; after Reconstruction, 513; in South during Reconstruction, 499–500, 502, 504–05. *See also* city government; federal government; state government
governors, state: limited powers of, 190
GPS. *See* NAVSTAR Global Positioning System
Gramm-Rudman-Hollings Act, 907
Grand Ole Opry, 704
Grange, Red, 704
Grange, the, 545
Grant, Ulysses S., *p485, p503, crt509,* A4; background, 485; Battle of Shiloh, 469; Battle of Vicksburg, 484; corruption in administration, 508–10; election, 503; Mississippi violence, reaction to, 508; plan to crush Confederacy, 485–86; surrender terms to Lee, 488; total war plan, 487–88
Grapes of Wrath, The, *q727, p732,* 732
Great Awakening, 113
Great Awakening, Second, 411–12
Great Britain: colonies, 133–41; American Civil War, 474; appeasement of Germany, 743–44; in China, 638; Canada, control of, 123; division of Germany, 773, 776; Florida, control of, 123, 322; France, 1793 war with, 264; French and Indian War, role in, 120–23; Industrial Revolution, 305–06, 307; Native Americans, relations with, 123–24, 133, 176, 263, 293–94; naval reduction, 696; naval strength, 656, 661; Oregon, land claims in, 355–56, 360; role in Suez crisis, 803; in Samoa Islands, 637–38; in SEATO, 804; trade policy of, 195; U.S., relations with, 189, 195, 310, 322; War of 1812, 296–300; in World War I, 657–58; in World War II, 745, 746–47. *See also* England. *See also* Seven Years' War
Great Compromise, the, 200–01
Great Depression, 706, 714, 715–18; causes, 716–17; economy, 716–17, 725, 734; food prices, 719; Hoover's handling of, 717–18; international, 717, 741, 742, 743; life during, *p728,* 728–32; plight of minorities, 730–31; stock market crash, 715, 716; works projects, 718, 724, 725
Great Migration: African Americans in early 1900s, 672; Puritans, 80
Great Northern Railroad, 552, *p671*
Great Plains, 4; climate, 535; Native Americans, 538–43; white settlement of, 533–36
Great Salt Lake, 379
Great Star flag, 319
Great Wall of China, *p882,* 882
Great White Fleet, 639
Greece, 656, *m676;* civil war, 775, 776; immigration, 575
Greeley, Horace, 509
Green Berets, 853
Greenhow, Rose O'Neal, 479
Green Mountain Boys, 145, 169
Greensboro, North Carolina, 830
Grenada, 907
Grenville, George, 134
Grimké, Angelina, 418, 425
Grimké, Sarah, 418, 425
gross domestic product (GDP), 927
gross national product (GNP), 698
Guadalcanal, Battle of, 763
Guam, 630; American territory, 643; in World War II, 761, 763
Guantanamo Bay, 643
Guatemala: early civilization of, 21, 22; U.S. intervention in, 804
Guerrière, 297
guerrilla warfare, 179, 180, 346, 847, 854, 856, 863
Gulf of Mexico, 95
Gulf of Tonkin Resolution, 855
Guthrie, Woody, 726

H

habeas corpus, 478
Haiti: intervention in, 690; restoration of Aristide, *p920,* 920
Haldeman, H.R., 888, 890
Hale, Nathan, *q166,* 166
Hamilton, Alexander, *ptg200, q257, ptg258;* Aaron Burr, duel with, 285; Constitution, support of, 209–10; Constitutional Convention, 198, 199; Federalists, support of, 209–10, 267, 268; Thomas Jefferson, conflicts with, 266–67, 268; as secretary of the treasury, 258, 259–61, 268; George Washington, relations with, 261, 266–67, 268
Hampton Institute, 591
Hancock, John, 104, 138, 144, 148, 151
Harding, Warren G., *q695,* A5; corruption in administration, 694; death of, 694; election, *p693, q693,* 693; peace effort of, 696
Harlem Renaissance, 705–06
Harpers Ferry, Virginia, *ptg436,* 452
Harrison, Benjamin, 637, A5
Harrison, William Henry, 293–94, 296, 297, 350, *ptg 351,* A2
Hartford, Connecticut, 81
Hartford Convention, 300
Harvard University, 114, 626
Hawaii, *mRA6, cRA4;* annexation, 637; planters revolt, 636–37; republic, 635–37; statehood, 630, 799
Hawthorne, Nathaniel, *p414,* 414
Hay, John, 638, 643, 646, 647
Hayes, Ira, 753
Hayes, Rutherford B., 510–11, *p511,* A4; Inaugural Address, *q511,* 511; spoils system, opposition to, 605
Haymarket Riot, 566, *m568,* 568–69
Hayne, Robert: Daniel Webster, debate with, 338
Hays, Mary, 176
Head Start, 828
hearing impaired, 413, 557
Hearst, William Randolph, 592, 641
Helsinki Accords, 893
Hemingway, Ernest, *p706,* 706
Henry, Patrick, *q128,* 135, *ptg136;* Constitution, opposition to, *q209,* 209, 211; Continental Congress, 142, *q143,* 148
Henry VIII, king of England, 58–59
Henry the Navigator, 43–44
Hickok, Wild Bill, 553
Hidalgo, Miguel, 324
hieroglyphics, 23
highland, 6, 10
Hill, James J., 552, 617
Hinckley, John, Jr., 905
Hiroshima, Japan, 764, *p765*
Hispanics: in the Civil War, 465; defined, 839; migration to cities, 814; vaqueros, 532, 533

Hispanic Americans: civil rights, 839–40; population, 839–40. *See also* Cuba; Latin America; Mexico; Puerto Rico; Spain
Hiss, Alger, 790
Hitler, Adolf, *q741, p742, p744;* death of, 758; political philosophy, 742, 743–44; rise to power, 741, 742
Hobby, Oveta Culp, 799
Ho Chi Minh, 803, 852, *p853,* 853, *q857*
Hohokam, the, 27
Holmes, Emma, 453
Holocaust, the, 740, *p759,* 758–59, 760
Homer, Winslow, 410, 494, 593, 594
Homestead Act, 534
Homestead Strike, *m568,* 569
Honduras: early civilization of, 21
Hong Kong, 761
Honolulu, Hawaii, 635, 636
Hooker, Joseph, 482–83
Hooker, Thomas, 81
Hoover, Herbert, 671, A6; election, *p711,* 711; Great Depression, handling of, 717–18; on Supreme Court packing, *q737*
Hoover, J. Edgar, 690
Hoovervilles, 717, *p719*
Hopewell, the, 28–29
Hopi, the, 31
Hopkins, Harry, 724, 734
Horseshoe Bend, Battle of, 297, 336
hostages, *p900,* 900, 908
House of Burgesses, 74, 134, 149
House of Representatives: creation of, 201; checks and balances, 207; constitutional authority, 206; functions of, 221–23; number of representatives in, 221; selection of president, 334; states' representation in, 206
House Un-American Activities Committee (HUAC), 790
Houston, Sam, 365, 366, *ptg367, q444*
Houston, Texas, 851
Howard University, 497, 591
Howe, Elias, 385
Howe, Samuel Gridley, 413
Howe, Sir William, 149, 165, 168, 169, 172
How the Other Half Lives, 587, *p603,* 603
Hudson, Henry, 60, *c61,* 62
Hudson Bay, 62, 116
Hudson River School, 414
Hue, South Vietnam, 862–63
Huerta, Victoriano, 649, 650
Hughes, Charles Evans, 663, 694, 696
Hughes, Langston, *p705, q705,* 705, 706, *q753*
Hull House, 588, 609
human/environment interaction: defined, 2
human rights, 898
humid climate: continental, 5; subtropical, 6
Humphrey, Hubert H., 864, 880
Hundred Days, 723–25
Hungary, 676; immigration, 575, 576; revolt against Soviet Union, *p803,* 803
Hunt, E. Howard, 889
Hurston, Zora Neale, 705, *p706*
Hussein, king of Jordan, 920
Hussein, Saddam, 914–15
Hutchinson, Anne, 81–82
hydrogen bomb, 801

I

Ice Age, 17–18, 19
Idaho, *mRA6, cRA4;* statehood, 527
I Know Why the Caged Bird Sings, 770–71
ILGWU. *See* International Ladies' Garment Workers Union
Illinois, *mRA6, cRA4;* 316
immigrants, 566, 567, *p577,* 575–80, 582–83; Asian, in Hawaii, *p636,* 636, 637; building communities, 579; contributions of, 580; discrimination against, 623–25, 627; education, *p578;* entrance examinations for, 577; finding work, 578, *p579,* 582–83; and growth of cities, 584, 585; homelands of, 575–76; Ku Klux Klan, 709; laws to limit, 580, 623, 709–10; lives of, 578–79, 582–83, 585–86, 603, *p623;* religions of, 575–76, 579, 580, 623. *See also* anti-immigrant sentiment
Immigrants' Protective League, 580
immigration, *g394,* 530, *p533,* 534; Alien and Sedition acts, 271–72; changes in, in mid-1900s, 927–28; Chinese Exclusion Act, 580, 623; to English colonies, 103, 107, *m127;* gentlemen's agreement, 580, 623–24, 639; impact of, mid-1800s, 392–94; Mexican effort to control, 363. *See also* individual nations
impeachment, 221; Andrew Johnson, 502–03; Nixon, 890
imperialism: age of, 632–34; European, 632–33, 656; in the Pacific, 635–39
implied powers, 220, 268
imports. *See* trade
impressment, 264, 265, 290–91, *ptg291*
Inaugural Address: Bill Clinton, 876; Rutherford B. Hayes, 511; Andrew Jackson, 336; Thomas Jefferson, 278; John F. Kennedy, A19; Abraham Lincoln, 456, 487, 495; James Monroe, 318
Inca Empire, 21, 24–25, *m26,* 51–52
income tax, 546, 547; after World War I, 695; in World War I, 671; in World War II, 751
indentured servants, 75, 88, 89, 107, 112, 113
independence: causes and effects, *c143;* colonists declare, 150–52
Independence Hall, *ptg199, ptg202, ptg253*
India, 122, 123, 779
Indiana, *mRA6, cRA4;* settlement of, 317; statehood, 316
Indian Civil Rights Act of 1968, 841
Indian New Deal, 731
Indian Peace Commission, 540, 541
Indian Removal Act, 342
Indian Reorganization Act, 731
Indians. *See* Native Americans; *see also* individual Native American nations
Indian Territory, 340, 342, 536, 540–41
Indochina: Japanese invasion of, 748
Industrial Revolution: American economy, effect on, 310; cities, growth of, 310–11; Great Britain, started in, 305–06, 307; in New England, 306–09; technology of, 306–07, 309
industry: after Civil War, 514; cattle, 531–33; during Great Depression, 716; during World War II, 751; growth of, 305–07; mining, 525–27; North, development of, 385–86; growth of, 550–69; South, after Civil War, 514; textile, 305–06, 307–09, 514
inflation: Carter administration, 897–98; Civil War, 480; Nixon administration, 887–88; Revolutionary War, 174; post-World War II, 780–81
Information Superhighway, *q923*
initiative, 607
integration, 507, 822–23
interchangeable parts, 309
Interior Plains, *p4,* 4
Intermountain region, 4
internal improvements, 319, 320–21; regional disagreements over, 319–20
International Date Line, 361
International Ladies' Garment Workers Union (ILGWU), 568, 578
Internet, 927; using, 817
internment of Japanese Americans, 686–87, *p687, p754,* 754
Interstate Commerce Commission (ICC), 605, 618, 831
Intolerable Acts, 141, 142, 143. *See also* Coercive Acts
Inuit, the, 29–31
inventions, 556–59, 565; of African Americans, 558–59; communications, 388, 556–57; farm machinery, 389; manufacturing, 385–86; railroads, 553, 558; textile industry, 305–06; transportation, 314–15, 559
Invisible Thread, The, 686–87
Iowa, , *mRA6, cRA4;* 345
Iran-Contra scandal, 908
Iran hostage crisis, 899–900, *p900*
Iraq, 914
Ireland, *m676,* immigrants, 316, 392–93, *p393,* 528, 585
Irish Americans, 660, 672
iron curtain, 775, 911
Iroquois, the, 32
Iroquois League, the, 32, 117–18, 119
irrigation: Mormons, use of, 379; Native Americans, use of, 27

Index

IRS. *See* Internal Revenue Service
Irving, Washington, 414
Isabella, queen of Spain, 46, 47
Islam. 40, 41, 42, 46, 803, 883–84, 885, 889, 900, 920
Israel, *p778,* 778, 779; relations with Egypt, 803, 884, 885, *p899,* 899; U.S. relations with, 803, 884, 885; wars with Arab states, 883–84
Italy: fascism, support of, 731; immigration, 575, 576, 577, 579, 585; naval reduction, 696; under Mussolini, 741–42; unification of, 656; in World War I, 658; in World War II, 746, *m756,* 756
"I Will Fight No More," A16
Iwo Jima, 753, 763, *p764*

J

Jackson, Andrew, *crt338, ptg341, q348, q349, crt350,* 365, 604, A2; Bank of the United States, opposition to, 348–49; election, 333, 334–35, *c334;* 1824 election, 333–34; era of, 332–35, 336–39, 348–51; inauguration reception, *ptg337;* Native Americans, relocation of, 341, 342–45; reelection, 349; Spanish forts, capture of, 322–23; states' rights, view on, 339; Texas annexation, opposition to, 366–67; in War of 1812, 297, 299–300, 336
Jackson, Helen Hunt, *q543,* 543
Jackson, Jesse, 910
Jackson, Thomas "Stonewall," 466, *p467,* 470; death of, 483
Jackson, Mississippi, 831, 836
Jackson State University, 870
James I, king of England, 72, 73, 75
James II, king of England, 110
Jamestown settlement, 72–75, *ptg74,* 77, 90
Japan: China, occupation of, *p743,* 743; expansionism, 743, 748, 852; immigration, 576, 580, 623–24, 627; immigration to Hawaii, *p636,* 636; Korea, control of, 638; Manchuria, invasion of, 743; naval reduction, 696; Marco Polo's travels to, 43; trade with U.S., 632; war with Russia, 639; in World War I, 658; in World War II, 748–49, 761–64, *m762*
Japanese Americans: internment of, 686–87, *p754,* 754; in World War II, 754
Jaworski, Leon, 890
Jay, John, 142, 184, *q195;* as chief justice, *ptg259,* 259; Constitution, support of 209–10; Jay's Treaty, 264–65, 270
Jay's Treaty, 264–65, 270
jazz, 594; age of, 688, 704–06, 707
Jazz Singer, The, 703
Jefferson, Thomas, 147, *q151, q152,* 154-55, *ptg258, q282, q437,* A1; American System, opposition to, 321; Bank of the United States, opposition to, 260–61; cabinet of, 279; Continental Congress, 149, 154-55; Declaration of Independence, 148, 150–51, 152, 154-55, 156; Democratic-Republicans, support of, 267, 268; on education, 412; election, 277–78; embargo, use of, 291; on federal courts, 280; France, relations with, 282; Alexander Hamilton, conflicts with, 266–67, 268; Inaugural Address, 278; Lewis and Clark expedition, 283–84; Louisiana Purchase, 282; plan for division of territories, 192; reelection, 290; as secretary of state, 258, 260–61, 268; as vice president, 269; Virginia Plan, 198; George Washington, relations with, 261, 266–67, 268
Jerusalem, 883
Jews/Jewish Americans, 70, 81, 93; Holocaust, 740, *p758,* 758–759, 760; immigrants, 575–76, 579, 580, 623, *ptg602;* Ku Klux Klan, 709; Nazi persecution, 758–59, 760
Jim Crow laws, 516
Johnny Tremain, 130–31
Johnson, Andrew, 449, 497, A4; African Americans, attitude toward, 498; commander in chief, 502; impeachment proceedings, 502–03; Reconstruction plan, 498
Johnson, James Weldon, 706
Johnson, Lyndon B., *q800, p863,* A7; becomes president, *p828,* 828; civil rights movement, 829, *q833,* 833, 835; criticism of, 863; domestic policy, 828–29, *p829;* Great Society, *q828,* 828–29; relations with Congress, 855, 860–61; Vietnam policy, *q854–55,* 854–55, 863; withdrawal from 1968 election, *q863,* 863
Johnson, Tom, 604
Johnston, Albert Sidney, 469
joint-stock company, 72
Joliet, Louis, 94–95
Jones, Absalom, *ptg198*
Jones, Bobby, 704
Jones, John Paul, 177
Jones, Mary Harris (Mother Jones), 567
Joplin, Scott, 594
Jordan, Barbara, *q220*
Jordan, 920
Joseph, Chief, *p542, q542,* 542
judicial branch, 224–25; constitutional authority, 206–07, 220, 238–39; creation of, 258–59; powers of, 206–07, 218–19, 220
judicial review, 220, 225, 280
Judiciary Act of 1789, 224, 258–59, 280
Judiciary Act of 1801, 279–80
Jungle, The, 606

K

Kalakaua, king of Hawaii, 636
Kamehameha, king of Hawaii, 635–36
kamikazes, 763
Kansas, *mRA6, cRA4;* Bleeding Kansas, 444–45; slavery, 444–45
Kansas-Nebraska Act, 443–44, *m444,* 448
Kansas Pacific Railroad, 539
Kearny, Stephen Watts, 373–74
Kemp, Jack, 924
Kennedy, Anthony, 906
Kennedy, Jacqueline, *p828,* 828
Kennedy, John F., *ptg827,* A6; assassination, 828; attitude toward communism, 847, 848, 854; in Berlin, 849; civil rights movement, 828, 831, 832, 838; Cuban missile crisis, 850; domestic policy, 827–28; election, *p826,* 826, 827; foreign policy, 847–51; Inaugural Address, *q826, q827, q847, p847, q848,* A19; New Frontier, 827–28; Peace Corps, *p848;* prepresidential experience, 826–27; relations with Congress, 827–28; relations with Khrushchev, 847, 848–51, *q850;* space program, *q851,* 851; Vietnam policy, 853–54
Kennedy, Robert: assassination, 864; as attorney general, 831, *p836,* 836; 1968 election, 863, *p864,* 864
Kent State University, 869–70, *p870*
Kentucky, *mRA6, cRA4;* in the Civil War, 461, 462, 469; statehood, 300
Kentucky Resolution, 272
Kerner Commission, 835
Kerouac, Jack, *p815,* 815
Key, Francis Scott, 299, 300
Khan, Kublai, 37
Khomeini, Ayatollah, 900
Khrushchev, Nikita, *p804;* cold war thaw, 804–05; Cuban missile crisis, 849–51; relations with John Kennedy, 847, 848–51, *q850*
"Kidnapped Prince, The," 68–69, *ptg69*
King, Coretta Scott, *p835, p898*
King, Martin Luther, Jr., *q768,* 837, *p843, q843;* assassination, *p835, q835,* 835, 864; Congress honors, 834; I Have a Dream speech, *q832, p833,* A20; leadership, *q824,* 824, *p825,* 825, 832; philosophy, 825, 832
King Philip. *See* Metacomet
King Philip's War, 82
Kings Mountain, North Carolina, 179–80
Kino, Father Francisco Eusebio, 56–57, *q57*
Kiowa, the, 541
Kissinger, Henry: Ford administration, 893; Nixon administration, 868–69, *p870,* 870–71
Knights of Labor, 567
Know-Nothing Party, 394, 449
Knox, Henry, *ptg258*
Korea: controlled by Japan, 638; North Korean invasion, 785–86
Korean War, *p772,* 785–88, *m786, p787;* casualities, 788; effect on U.S. economy, 807; events leading to, 785–86; peace negotiations, 788; United Nations in, 786–87
Kosciuszko, Thaddeus, 173
Kuwait, 914–15

Ku Klux Klan: in the 1920s, *p624,* 624, 709; during Reconstruction, 506, 509

L

Labor Department: Children's Bureau, 612
labor unions, 292; after World War II, 781, 782; anti-immigrant sentiments, 691; discrimination in, 624–25; formation of, 567–68; migrant farmworkers, 840; New Deal effect on, 735; public opinion of, 567, 568, 691; Theodore Roosevelt administration, 617–18; Sherman Antitrust Act effect on, 605; strikes of, *m568,* 568–69, 617–18, 691, 781; and women, 567–68, 612–13
Ladies' Home Journal, 592
Lafayette, Marquis de, 173, 180, 182, *ptg183,* 667
La Follette, Robert, 607, 695
land claims: in North America, 1783, *m187;* of the original states, *m191*
land-grant colleges, 591
land policies: after the Revolution, 192–93
Langdon, Alfred M., 735
Lange, Dorothea, 730, 732
Laos, 855, 868
La Raza Unida, 840
La Salle, Sieur de, 95
Las Casas, Bartolomé de, 54–55
Latimer, Lewis Howard, *c557, p558,* 558
Latin America: American influence in, 633–34; anti-American feelings in, 647, 648, 649, 650, 804; dollar diplomacy, 649; Monroe Doctrine, 624, 649; moral diplomacy, 649–50; Roosevelt Corollary, 648–49; Spain, conquests in, 50–52; Spanish empire in, 324; U.S. intervention in Guatemala, 804; U.S. anticommunist actions in, 804, 907; U.S. policies toward, 646–50, 848, 885, 913, 919. *See also* specific country
latitude: defined, 10; understanding, 361
Latvia, 677, 746
law: due process of, 226, 500; duty to obey, 227; equal protection of, 226–27, 500
Lazarus, Emma, *q577*
League of Nations, 675, 677–78, 742, 743; congressional opposition to, 677–78; presidential opposition to, 695; Wilson support of, 677, 678
League of United Latin American Citizens (LULAC), 840
Leaves of Grass, 415
Lebanon, 907–08
Lee, Richard Henry, 142, 148, *q150,* 150, 151, 154; on property rights, 192–93
Lee, Robert E., *q455,* 464, *p470,* 474; Battle of Antietam, 471; Battle of Fredericksburg, 482–83; capture of John Brown, 452; defense of Richmond, 470; invasion of the North and Gettysburg, 483–84; surrender to Grant, 488
Lee Chew, *p582 q583,* 582–83
"Legend of Sleepy Hollow, The," 414
legislation: presidential role in, 224; process of, 221–23; Supreme Court role in, 225
legislative branch. *See* Congress
leisure time, 586, *ptg587,* 593, *ptg594,* 594–95; fads, 704; increase of, 703–04; sports, 704
Lend-Lease Act, 748
L'Enfant, Pierre-Charles, 260
Lenin, Vladimir, 665–66, 676
Leningrad, Soviet Union, *m756,* 757
Let Us Now Praise Famous Men, 732
Levittown, 809
Lewis, John L., 735
Lewis, Meriwether, 283–84, 286, *q287,* 288
Lewis, Sinclair, 706
Lewis and Clark expedition, *m283,* 283, 355; journals of, *q287,* 288, 301; Native Americans, relations with, 284, 286; scientific discoveries, 288
Lexington, Massachusetts, 144–45, *m144:* Battle of, 147
Leyte Gulf, 763
Liberator, The, 417, 418
Liberia, 417
Liddy, Gordon, 889
Life on the Mississippi, 522–23, 592–93
Liliuokalani, queen of Hawaii, *p636,* 636–37, *q637*
limited government, 217, 272; under Thomas Jefferson, 279
Lin, Maya Ying, 872
Lincoln, Abraham, 373, *q432, p454, q455, ptg472,* 489, A3; abolition, attitude toward, *q472;* assassination, 497–98; commander in chief, 461, 467, 470, 471, 483, 484, 485; elections, 450–52, 454; Emancipation Proclamation, *ptg473,* 473–74, Gettysburg Address, 484–85, *q485;* Inaugural Address, *q487;* Lincoln-Douglas debates, *p451, q451,* 451, 452; Reconstruction plan, 495–96; reelection 486, 487; secession, response to, *q456,* 455–56, *q457,* 457; slavery, attitude toward, 451, *q472,* 473; suspension of constitutional rights, 462, 478; visit to Richmond, 487
Lincoln, Mary Todd, 464
Lindbergh, Charles, 702, 747
line-item veto, 921
literacy tests, 515, 580
literature, 130–31, 414–15, 434–35, 522–23; African American, 68–69, 770–71; changes in American, 592–93; Mexican American, 878–79; Native American, 14–15; Japanese American, 686–87
Lithuania, 677, 746
Little Bighorn, 541–42
Little Rock, Arkansas, 816, 833
Livingston, Robert, 150, 282, 315
location: absolute, 2, 10; relative, 2
Locke, John, 90, *ptg205;* influence on Constitution, 205
Lodge, Henry Cabot, 644, *p677, q677,* 677–78
London, Jack, 593
Lone Star flag, 366
Long, Huey, 734
Long Drive, 532, 533
Longfellow, Henry Wadsworth, *q143,* 415
Long Island, New York: Battle of, 165–66
longitude, 555; defined, 10; understanding, 361
Los Angeles, California: race riot, 754
Louisbourg, 117, 122
Louis XIV, king of France, 94, 95, 173
Louis XVI, king of France, 264
Louisiana, *mRA6, cRA4;* in Civil War, 469, 484; denied readmission, 496; readmission to Union, 502; secession, 455; statehood, 316
Louisiana Purchase, 281–85; France, possession of, 282; Spain, possession of, 281–82; and western exploration, *m283*
Louisiana Territory, 95, 123, 362; slavery agreement in, 320
Lovejoy, Elijah, 422
Lovell, Tom, 685
Lowell, Francis Cabot, 307–08
Lowell girls, 308–09
Loyalists, 146, 164, 184; British dependence on, 178, 179; treatment of, 175
loyalty oaths, 789–90
Lucas, Eliza, 91
lumber industry, 552
Lundy, Benjamin, 416–17
Lusitania, *p661,* 662
Luther, Martin, *ptg58,* 58
lynchings, 516, 622, 624, 625–26, 692
Lyon, Mary, 413, *p427,* 427
Lyon, Matthew, *crt271,* 272

M

MacArthur, Douglas, 787; breakup of Bonus Army, 718; in Korean War, 786–87; in Philippines, 761, *p762, q762,* 762, 763; relations with Truman, 786, 787, *p788,* 788
Machu Picchu, *p25*
Madero, Francisco, 649
Madison, Dolley, 298
Madison, James, *ptg199, q296,* A1; Bank of the United States, First, opposition to, 260–61; Bank of the United States, Second, support for, 310; and the Bill of Rights, 259; Constitution, support of, 209–10, 211; Constitutional Convention, 198–99; Democratic-Republicans, support of, 267, 268; election, 292; France, relations with, 292–93; as president, 292–93, 294, 295; as secretary of state, 280, 291; and the Virginia Plan, 199, 200; writing the Constitution, 205
Magellan, Ferdinand, *ptg49,* 49, *c61,* 63

Index

Maginot Line, 746
Magna Carta, The, A9
Maine, *mRA6, cRA4;* Missouri Compromise, 320
***Maine,* the,** 641
Makkah (Mecca), 41
Malaya, 761
Malcolm X, *p834,* 834
Mali, 40–41
Manassas, Virginia, 466
Manchuria, 638, 639; Japanese occupation of, 743
Mandan, the, 284, 286
Manhattan Island, New York, 84–85
Manhattan Project, 764
Manifest Destiny, 359–60, 367, 524; and California, 370, 372; causes and effects, *c378;* expansion overseas, 631–32; and New Mexico, 369, 372
Manila, Philippines, 642
Mann, Horace, 412–13, *q413*
manufacturing: British inventions for, 306; of cloth, 307–08; capital for, 306; machines for, 305, 307, 385–86; mass production, 385–86; in New England, 307–09; South, limited role of, 398–99
Mao Zedong, *p779,* 779, 883, 893
Marbury* v. *Madison, 220, 280
March on Washington, 832, *p833,* 833
Marina, Doña, 51
Marion, Francis, 179, *ptg180,* 180
Marne, Battle of the, 658
Marquette, Jacques, 94–95
Marshall, James, 376, 382
Marshall, John, 220, *q280;* as chief justice, 279–80, 321, 343; judicial review, 280
Marshall, Thurgood: NAACP lawyer, 821–22; Supreme Court, 823
Marshall Plan, 776
Martí, José, *p640,* 640
martial law, 869
Marx, Karl, 885
Mary, queen of England, 110
Maryland, *mRA6, cRA4;* in the Civil War, 461–62, 471; *McCulloch* v. *Maryland,* 321; as proprietary colony, 88–89, 112; tobacco industry of, 89, 107
Mason, Charles, 89
Mason, George, 199, 202
Massachusetts, *mRA6, cRA4;* in American Revolution, 142, 143; constitution of, 190; as royal colony, 112
Massachusetts Antislavery Society, 419
Massachusetts Bay Colony, 80–81, 82
mass media, 703–04; analyzing, 737
mass production, 385–86, 559, 566, 699; *See also* manufacturing
Maya Empire, 21–23, *m26*
Mayflower, 78, 79
Mayflower Compact, *ptg67,* 79, A10
McCarran Act, 790
McCarthy, Eugene, 863, 864
McCarthy, Joseph, 791–92, *crt792*
McClellan, George B., 464, 467, 469–70, 471
McClure's Magazine, 606
McCord, James, 889
McCormick, Cyrus, 389
McCulloch* v. *Maryland, 321
McDowell, Irvin, 466
McGovern, George, 888
McKay, Claude, 706
McKinley, William: A5; assassination, 616, 617; election, 547, 617; Hawaii, approval of annexation, 637; role in Spanish-American War, 641
McNamara, Robert, 854–55, 857
Meade, George, 483, 484
Means, Russell, *p841,* 842
Meat Inspection Act, 606, 618
Medicaid, 829
Medicare, 829
medicine; in the Civil War, 477–78; in mid-1800s, 317; 1950s advances in, 808; during the Revolutionary War, 179
***Mein Kampf* (My Struggle),** 741, *q741*
Meir, Golda, *p885,* 885
Melville, Herman, 415
Memphis, Tennessee, 469, 499, 501, 835, 864
"Memorial and Protest of the Cherokee Nation", A12
Mennonites, 109
mental illness, 414
mercantilism, 59, 110–11
Meredith, James, *p831,* 831
meridian(s), 361; defined, 11. *See also* longitude
Merrimack, 468
Mesa Verde, 28
Metacomet, 82
Methodist Church, 412
Mexican Americans, 362, 370, 374, *p627,* 814; civil rights movement, *q838,* 838, 840; discrimination against, 627; during Great Depression, 731; migrant farmworkers, 840; migration to cities, 814; in World War II, 753
Mexican Cession, 375, 379
Mexican War, 373–75, *m374;* disputes leading to, 372–73
Mexico: California, control of, 370, 372, 373, 374–75; early civilizations of, 21, 22, 23, 50–51, 52; immigration, 526, 576, *p627,* 627, 753; independence from Spain, 363; migration to U.S., 671; in NAFTA, 919; New Mexico, control of, 368, 369, 370, 372, 373; provinces of Spain, 53, 54; rebellion in, 323, 324; Texas, conflict over, 362–66; war in, 649–50; Wilson, relations with, 649–50; in World War I, 663
Mexico City, Mexico, 23, 373, 375
Miami, the, 116, 263, 293
MIAs, 871
Michigan, *mRA6, cRA4;* settlement, 317
middle class, 585, 586; women of, 609, 610, 612, 708–09
Middle Colonies, *m85,* 84–87; agriculture in, 106; education in, 114; government in, 86, 87; industries of, 106–07; population, 85–86, 87; religious freedom in, 85; religious revival in, 113. *See also* individual colonies
Middle East, the: Arab-Israeli conflicts, 803, 883–85; U.S. peace efforts for, 883–85, 884–86, 899, 907–08, 920
Middle Passage, 105
Midway Islands, 635, 763
migrant farmworkers, *p726, p727,* 726–27, *m729, p730,* 730, 814
militarism: European, 656
military: Aztec, 24; Inca, 34; Spanish, 52
military, U.S.: cold war buildup of, 778; constitutional authority for, 215–16; president as commander in chief, 224; roles in civil rights movement, 823, 831, 832
militias; at Bunker Hill, 146; at Concord, 144, 145; forming of, for Revolutionary War, 143; forts built by, 118; in French and Indian War, 121; Green Mountain Boys, 169; New York State, *p435;* Patriot membership in, 163, 165; and Shays's Rebellion, *ptg197,* 197; in War of 1812, 296, 299; in the West, 541
Miller, Alice Duer, 610–11, *q611*
Miller, Arthur, 790
Miller, Doris, *p753,* 753
minimum wage, 781, 783
mining industry, 525–27; expansion of, 552
Minnesota, *mRA6, cRA4;* 534
minutemen, 143, 145
Miralles, Juan de, 173
missile crisis, Cuban, 849–50
missionaries: American, overseas, 636, 637
missions: abolishment of, 370: California, 96, 369, 370; defined, 96; Oregon country, 357; Spanish, 54, 56–57, 95–96
Mississippi: *mRA6, cRA4;* civil rights movement, 831; in the Civil War, 469, 484; political violence in, 508; readmission to Union, 502; statehood, 316; secession, 455
Mississippi, University of, 831
Mississippians, the, 29
Mississippi River, 53, 123; American shipping rights on, 195, 265, 281, 282; in the Civil War, 461, 464, 469, 484; French exploration of, 94–95; in literature, 522–23; as national boundary, 281; Spanish exploration of, 96
Missouri: *mRA6, cRA4;* cattle industry, 531; in the Civil War, 461, 462; secession, 455; slavery, 437–38; statehood, 316, 437
Missouri Compromise, *m320,* 320, 437–38, 443, 450
Missouri River, 284
Mitchell, Maria, *p428,* 428
Moby Dick, 415
Mohawk, the, 32, 82, 117
Mondale, Walter, *p895,* 895, 908
money: Continentals, 173, paper notes, *p174,* 174; printing of, by governments during wars, 194, 480; shortage of, after the Revolution, 196–97; value of the dollar, 887
Monitor, 468
Monroe, James: A2; election, 318; France, special representative to, 282; Monroe Doctrine, 324, 633–34; reelection to presidency, 319; tour of nation, *ptg318,* 318–19

Monroe Doctrine, 324, 633–34, A12; and Roosevelt Corollary, 649
Montana: *mRA6, cRA4;* statehood, 527
Montcalm, Marquis de, 123
Montesquieu, Baron de, 205, 206
Montezuma, 51
Montezuma, Carlos, 627
Montgomery, Alabama, 831, 836; bus boycott in, 136, 816, 824
Monticello, 154
Montreal, Canada, 60, 94, 123, 149
Morehouse College, 507
Morgan, Daniel, 180
Morgan, J. Pierpont, 563, 564, 586, 617
Mormons, *p378,* 378–79, *p379,* 411
Morning Girl, 14–15
Morrill Act, 591
Morris, Gouverneur, 199
Morris, Robert, *ptg194;* Constitutional Convention, 199; head of department of finance, 194
Morse, Samuel, 388, 492, 556
Morse code, 388, *p492,* 492, 556
Moscow, Soviet Union, 757, 883
Mother Cabrini, 609
motion pictures, 595; during Great Depression, 732; invention of, 558; of the 1920s, 703
Mott, Lucretia, 425–26, *p426*
Mound Builders, the, 28–29
muckrakers, 606
Muhammad, Askia, 41
Munich Conference, 744
Musa, Mansa, *ptg41,* 41
music: American style, 594; jazz, 594, 688, 704–05; Native American, 33; patriotic songs, 600–601, 670, 671; rock 'n' roll, 811–12; spiritual, 405
Muskie, Edmund, 888
Muslims. *See* Islam
Mussolini, Benito (Il Duce), *crt742,* 756; political philosophy, 742
mutualistas, 627

N

NAACP. *See* National Association for the Advancement of Colored People
NAFTA. *See* **North American Free Trade Agreement**
Nagasaki, Japan, 764
napalm, 856
Napoleon. *See* Bonaparte, Napoleon
Narragansett, the, 81, 82
NASA. *See* National Aeronautics and Space Administration
Nasser, Gamal Abdel, 803
Nast, Thomas, 604
Nation, Carry, 613
National Aeronautics and Space Administration (NASA), 801–02, 851
National American Woman Suffrage Association, 610
National Anti-Slavery Convention, 418
National Association for the Advancement of Colored People (NAACP), 626, 821, 822, 824, 830, *p833,* 834
National Association of Colored Women, 610, 625
National Congress of American Indians (NCAI), 841
National Conservation Commission, 618
National Convention of Colored Men, 512
national debt, *g907;* after American Revolution, 194, 259–60, *g260;* Bush administration, 915–16; defense spending, 909; of Thomas Jefferson administration, 279; Reagan administration, 906, 907
National Energy Plan, 898
National Gazette, 267
National Grange, 545
National Guard: role in civil rights riots, 834–35; role in Kent State protest, 869–70; role in Little Rock, 823; role in University of Mississippi desegregation, 831
National Industrial Recovery Act (NIRA), 725, 735
National Labor Relations Act, 735
National Liberation Front (NLF), 853. *See also* Vietcong
National Negro Business League, 625
National Organization for Women (NOW), 838–39
National Origins Act, 710
National Recovery Administration (NRA), *c722,* 725
National Road, 314
National Security Council (NSC), 778
National Socialist German Workers' Party. *See* Nazi Party
National War Labor Board, 670, 751
National Woman's Party, 611, 612
National Woman Suffrage Association, 610
Nation of Islam. *See* Black Muslims
Native Americans, 16–35; agriculture of, 20, 21, 25, 79–80; buffalo, dependence on, 538–39; Christianity, conversions to, 59, 95, 357, 369; civil rights, 841–42; culture, 538–39, 542, 543; diseases, effect on, 55, 82, 357, 841; early civilizations, 17–32; economic conditions, 841; education, 591; English colonists, relations with, 72, 73, 75, 76, 79–80, 82, 87, 90, 123–24; federal government, conflicts with, 541–43; federal government, policies, 263, *m264,* 342–45, 540–41, 543, 627, 841; France, relations with, 117, 120, 121; French colonists, relations with, 95; fur trade, 62, 356; Great Britain, relations with, 133, 176, 293–94; Great Plains, 538–43; land ownership, *m343,* 342–44, 345–46, *m540,* 541, 542; land taken from, *m302,* 340–45, 342–45; Lewis and Clark expedition, 284, 286; New Deal benefits, 731; Pontiac's War, 123–24; population, 82, 133, *g542;* religions of early, 22–23, 24, 25; relocation of, 342–45, *m343,* 540–42; resistance to relocation, 345–46, 541–42; role in French and Indian War, 120, 121, 122; in Spanish colonies, 54–55, 95, 370; Trail of Tears, 340–41, 344–45; voting rights of, 337; in War of 1812, 296, 297; white settlers, conflicts with, 293–94; in World War II, *p753,* 753. *See also* individual Native American Nations
Native Son, 732
nativists, 393–94, 579–80, 709–10
NATO. *See* North Atlantic Treaty Organization
naturalization, 530
Naturalization Act, 271, 279
natural resources, United States, *m7*
Navajo, the, 31; in World War II, *p753,* 753
NAVSTAR Global Positioning System (GPS), *p39,* 39
navy, 270–271, *ptg276;* American, role of in Revolutionary War, 177; in the Civil War, 463–64, 467–68, 469, 474, 486; Great Britain, in War of 1812, 296, 297; expansion of, 634; in Mexican War, 374; reduction of, 696; in War of 1812, 297; in World War I, 665; in World War II, 748, 763
Nazi Party, 742, 758–59
Nebraska: *mRA6, cRA4;* statehood, 500
Netanyahu, Benjamin, 920
Netherlands, the: colonies of, 84–85; explorations by, 62; invasion by Germany, 746; as religious refuge, 78–79; support of American Revolution, 171–72
Neugin, Rebecca, *p340,* 340–41, *q341*
neutrality, 163–64; George Washington, proclaimed by, 264; in World War I, 660, 663; in World War II, 743
Nevada, *mRA6, cRA4;* 526
New Amsterdam, 84–85
Newark, New Jersey: civil rights movement, 835
New Deal, 714, 720–25, *c722;* agriculture, effect on, 724; banking, *c722,* 725; effects of, 733–36; end of, 736; labor unions, effect on, 735; legislation, *c722,* 722, 724, 725, 731; opponents to, 733–34; Second, 734; support for the elderly, 734, 735; Supreme Court rulings, 724, 735, 736, 737; taxation, 734; unemployment relief, 718, 724, 725, 734
New England: education, 412; Industrial Revolution in, 306–09
New England Antislavery Society, 418
New England colonies, 78–82, *m79,* 84, 85; agriculture in, 104; attempts to end slavery, 175; and colonists' resistance movement, 143–46; commerce in, 104; education

in, 114; government in, 79, 80, 81; life in, 103–06; Native Americans, relations with, 79–80, 82; religious freedom in, 79, 81; religious revival in, 113; trade in, 104. *See also* individual colonies
New England Primer, the, 114
New Federalism, 886–87
New France, 94–95, 116; the fall of, 123; growth of, 95; trading posts in, 94
New Frontier, 827–28
New Hampshire, *mRA6, cRA4;* ratification of Constitution, 211; as royal colony, 112; settlement of, 81
New Harmony, Indiana, 411
New Jersey, *mRA6, cRA4;* colonial, 86; American victories in, 167–68
New Jersey Plan, the, 200
New Mexico, *mRA6, cRA4;* Mexican War, 373–74, 375; Mexico, control of, 368, 369, 372, 375, 438; and Pancho Villa, 650; statehood, 620; Texas border dispute, 439–40
New Netherland colony, 84–85
New Orleans, Louisiana, 95, 120, 123; Battle of, 299–300; in the Civil War, 469; Spain, possession of, 281–82
New Spain colony, 95–96; missions in, *m64*
newspapers, 388; ethnic and minority, 592; immigrants, 579; increase in, 592; investigative reporters, 606; Joseph Pulitzer's effect on, 592
New York (state), *mRA6, cRA4;* ratification of Constitution, 211; Revolutionary War fighting in, 165–66, 167, 168–69
New York Central Railroad, 552
New York City, *ptg102,* 106, *p2;* British occupation of, 165–66, *ptg168,* 184, 185; growth of, 85–86; immigrant settlement, 575, *p576,* 577, *p578,* 579, 583, 585–86, *ptg602,* 603
New York Globe, 626
New York Sun, *q660*
New York Times, *q737*
New York World, 592, 641
Nez Perce, the, 31, 542, A16
Ngo Dinh Diem. *See* Diem, Ngo Dinh
Niagara Movement, 626
Nicaragua, 649; communism in, 907; intervention in, *p696,* 696
Night Flying Woman, 254–55
Nimitz, Chester, 763
Nineteenth Amendment, 247, 608, *p612,* 612, 614–15, 702
Ninth Amendment, 227, 243
Nisei, 754
Nixon, Richard M., 792, *q886,* A7; anticommunism, 797, 885; Checkers speech, 798; China visit, *p881,* 881, 882; détente, *q882,* 882–83, *p883,* 884; domestic policy, 886–88; election, 865, *p866, p888,* 888; 1952 election, 797, *p798;* 1960 election, *p826,* 826, 827; foreign policy, 881–85; impeachment proceedings, 890, 891; Inaugural Address, *q867, p867,* 867, *q881;* Middle East policy, 883–85; New Federalism, 886–87; pardon, 892; reelection, *p886, 887,* 887; resignation, *p891,* 891, *p893;* Supreme Court appointments, 886; as vice president, *q801, p804;* Vietnam War policy, 867–69, *q869, p869,* 870–71; Watergate crisis, 889–891
nomadic life, 538, 539, 543
Norfolk, Virginia, 468
Noriega, Manuel, 913
Normandy, France, *m756,* 757, *m767*
North, Oliver, *p908,* 908
North America: England, trade with, *g98,* 110–11; land claims (1783), *m187;* Monroe Doctrine, 324; Native Americans, early cultures in, *m30;* settlement of, 17–18, *m19,* 71–73
North American Free Trade Agreement (NAFTA), 919
North Atlantic Treaty Organization (NATO), 174, 778; U.S. role in, 778
North Carolina, *mRA6, cRA4;* Constitution, ratification of, 211; English settlement, 90–92; readmission to Union, 502; Roanoke Island, 71–72; as royal colony, 112; secession, 457
North Dakota, *mRA6, cRA4;* statehood, 527
North Korea, 785–87, 862
North Vietnam, 853, 855, 862–63; peace negotiations, 868–69, 870–71
Northwest Ordinance, 193, 449
Northwest Passage, 59–60, 62
Northwest Territory, *m193,* 193; conflicts between Native Americans and white settlers in, 263; Native American campaigns, *m264;* restoring order in, 263; white settlement of, 281
Norway: immigration, 534; invasion by Germany, 746
nuclear weapons: cold war threats, 801; in Cuba, 849–50, *m850;* destruction agreement, 911; increase of, 847; limiting number of, 883, 893; reducing number of, 909; treaty to ban testing, 851
Nueces River, 373
nullification, 272, 338, 339
Nuremberg, Germany, 764

O

Oberlin College, 413, 428
Occupational Safety and Health Administration (OSHA), 887
O'Connor, Sandra Day, *p906,* 906
Office of National Drug Control Policy, 916
Oglethorpe, James, 92, 93
Ohio, *mRA6, cRA4;* early villages, *m35;* National Road, 314; population growth, 316; settlement of, 263, 293; statehood, 293, 314, 316
Ohio River valley, 116, 120, 123
oil: embargo, 884–85, 888–89; importing of, 888; Middle East, 888; uses for, products, 560, 572
oil industry, 561–62, *p572,* 572; John D. Rockefeller's effect on, 561–62; trusts, 606, 617
Ojibway, the, 254–55
Okinawa, 763
Oklahoma, *mRA6, cRA4;* Indian Territory, 340, 342, 536, 540–41; land rush, *p536,* 536; Trail of Tears, 340
Olive Branch Petition, 149
Olmec Empire, 21
Olympics, 594
Omaha, Nebraska, 528, 546
Oñate, Juan de, 53–54
Oneida, the, 32, 117
Onondaga, the, 32, 117
OPEC. *See* Organization of Petroleum Exporting Countries
Open Door policy, 638–39
Operation Desert Shield, 914
Operation Desert Storm, 914–15
Operation Overlord, 757
Ordinance of 1785, 192–93
Oregon, *mRA6, cRA4;* Oregon System, 607
Oregon Country, 322, 355–60, 367; disputes over land claims, 355–56; division of, 359–60
Oregon Trail, 370, 376, 357–59, *m358*
Organization of Petroleum Exporting Countries (OPEC), 888, 894
Orlando, Vittorio, 675
Osceola, chief, *ptg345,* 345–46, *ptg346*
Oswald, Lee Harvey, 828
Otis, Elisha, *c557,* 588
Otis, Hannah, 104
Otis, James, 135
Ottawa, the, 123
Ottoman Empire, *m657,* 658
"Over There," 600, *q670,* 670, 671
Owen, Robert, 411
ozone, 928

P

Pachacuti, Inca Yupanqui, 24
Pacific Northwest: Adams-Onís Treaty, 323
Pacific Ocean: claimed for Spain, 48; Lewis and Clark expedition, 284; naming of, 49
pacifists, 87, 163–64, 673
Pahlavi, Mohammed Reza (shah of Iran), 899–900
Paine, Thomas, 150, 154, *q167,* 167; opposition to Constitution, 210
Pakistan, 779; in SEATO, 804
Palestine, *p778,* 779
Palestine Liberation Organization (PLO), 920
Palestinians, *p884,* 884
Panama: Carter's treaties with, 899; independence from Colombia, 647; independence from Spain, 324; as site for a canal, 646; U.S. overthrow of Noriega, 913
Panama Canal, 565, 646, *p647, ptg647;* building of, 647–48; locks of, *p651,* 651
parallel(s), 361; defined, 11. *See also* latitude

Paris, France: in World War I, 658, 666, 674; in World War II, 757
Parks, Rosa, *p824,* 824
parks: public, *ptg588,* 588, 589
Parliament, 84, 110, 112; laws limiting freedom of colonists, 133–34, 141, 143, 144, 152; powers of the British, 204–05; tax laws passed by, 134–37, 138, 139, 140
patents, 307, 557–58
Paterson, William, 200
Patriots, *ptg132,* 146, 163; advantages of, in war, 164–65, 185; war victories of, 167–69, 176–77, 179–80, 183, 185
Patton, George, 756
Paul, Alice, 611–12, *p612,* 673
Pawnee, the, 538
Peace Corps, *ptg848,* 848
peaceful coexistence, 805
Pearl Harbor: attack on, *p745,* 745, 748–49, *p749,* 750, 761; naval base established, 636
Pendleton Act, 605
Penn, William, *ptg86,* 87, 89
Pennsylvania, *mRA6, cRA4;* in the Civil War, 483–84; settling of, *m85,* 87, 89; proprietary colony, 112
Pennsylvania State House. *See* Independence Hall
Pentagon, 858, *p859,* 859, 861
People's Party of the U.S.A. *See* Populist Party
People's Republic of China, 779, 881, 882
Pequot, the, 82
per capita income, 808
perestroika, 909
Perkins, Frances, *q723,* 729
Perot, H. Ross, 918, *q925,* 925
Perry, Matthew, *ptg632,* 632
Perry, Oliver Hazard, 297
Pershing, John J., 650, 666–67
Persian Gulf War, *p877,* 914–15
Peru, 21; conquered by Spain, 51, 52, 53, 54; independence from Spain, 324
Petersburg, Virginia, 486, 487
petroleum. *See* oil
Philadelphia, 290
Philadelphia, Pennsylvania: British occupation of, 168, 169; building of, 87; as capital of United States, 266; colonial population of, 106; site of Continental Congresses, 142, 148, 150, 152, 154–55; site of Constitutional Convention, 198–99, 200
Philadelphia Female Anti-Slavery Society, 425
Philippines: debate over possession of, 649; independence, 779; revolt against American rule, 644; in SEATO, 804; war in the, 641–42, 643; in World War II, 761–62, 763
phonograph, 558, *p565*
Pickens, Francis, 457
Pickett's Charge, 484
Pierce, Franklin, 443, 444, 449, A3
Pikes Peak, Colorado, 285, 525
Pilgrims, 79–80
Pinckney, Charles, 269; 1800 election, 277; 1804 election, 290; 1808 election, 292
Pinochet, Augusto, 885
Pitcairn, John, 144
Pitcher, Molly. *See* Hays, Mary
Pitt, William, 122
Pittsburgh, Pennsylvania: steel industry of, 563
Pizarro, Francisco, 51–52
plantations, *p92;* cotton, 309, *p402,* 402–03; labor needed for, 89, 91–92, 403; in Spanish colonies, 55; tobacco, 107–08
Platt Amendment, 643
Plattsburgh, Battle of, 299
Pledge of Allegiance, The, A16
Plessy* v. *Ferguson, 516, 624, 821, 822
Plymouth, Massachusetts: colony, 78, 79
Pocahontas, *ptg73,* 73, 76
Poe, Edgar Allan, 415
Poindexter, John, 908
Poland: end of Communist rule, 911, *m912;* German invasion of, 744, 745, *m756;* immigration, 575, 579, 585; in World War I, 666, *m676,* 677
police: roles in civil rights movement, 831, *p832,* 832, 833, 834; role in 1968 Democratic convention, 864; role in Jackson State protest, 870
polio, 721, 808
political machines, 603–04, 607
political parties, *c269;* differences between, *c268;* the first American, 266–69; George Washington, opposition to, 265, 266
politics: corruption and, 505; disputed votes, 510–11; Reconstruction and, 501, 502, 504, 508–11; sectionalism, 319–20, 321, 437
Polk, James, 351, *p360,* A3; election, 438; Manifest Destiny, support of, 360, 367, 370, 372; and Mexican War, 372–373, 375
Polo, Marco, *p37,* 37, *ptg38,* 43
Pomo, the, 31
Ponce de León, Juan, 53, *c61*
Pontiac, chief, *q120,* 123–24, *ptg124*
Poor Richard's Almanack, 97, *p110,* 114, 177
Pope, John, 470–71
popular sovereignty, 216, 443, 450, 451
population: California (1848–1852), 378; English colonies, 103, 163; Great Britain in 1776, 163; growth of, in cities, 310, *g311;* Hispanic Americans, 839–40; in late 1900s, 1; Native American, 82, 133, *g542;* Northern cities (1800s), 392; Ohio (1800–1820), 316; redistribution of, 554; shifts in, *m8;* Southern cities (mid-1800s), 405; urban and rural growth, *g586;* western settlers, 192. *See also* census
Populist Party, 546–47
Portolá, Gaspar de, 369
Portugal: explorers, 43–45, 47; independence from Brazil, 324; trade, 40, 43, 44
Potomac River, 89
Potsdam Declaration, 764
poverty: Native American, 841; rural, 813–14, *p814;* urban, *p814,* 814; war on poverty, 828–29
Powderly, Terence V., 567
Powell, Colin, 915
Powell, Lewis, 886
powers: concurrent, 218; of Congress, 206, 221–23; enumerated, 217; implied, 220, 268; national government, limited, 207–08, 217, 235–36, 243; of presidency, 206, 220; reserved, 217–18; separation of, 205, 207–08, *c217,* 218–19; shared between federal and state governments, *c217,* 205, 218; states, Articles of Confederation, 189–92
Powers, Francis Gary, 805
Powhatan, the, 73, 76, 82
Preamble to the Constitution, *q152,* 152, 156, 215, 231
prejudice: against African Americans, 391–92, 730; against immigrants, 393–94, 622, 623; against women, 424–25, 738; progressivism attitude toward, 624–25
Prescott, William, 146
presidency: bill approval, 223, 234; commander in chief, 224; constitutional authority, 206, 220, 238; election to, 206, 236–37, 244, 247–48, 337; executive branch, authority over, 258; oath of office, 237; powers of, 220; qualifications, 237; replacing, 250–51; roles of, 223–24, 238; salary, 237; term of office, 236, 249; vacancies, 237; George Washington's precedents, 256, 257–61, 262, 268
Presley, Elvis, 812, *p817*
press, freedom of. *See* freedom of speech
Prime Meridian, 361, 555; defined, 11
Princeton, New Jersey, 167–68
Princeton University, 620, 675
Princip, Gavrilo, 655, 656
Proclamation of Neutrality, 264
Proclamation of 1763, 124, 133–34, *m134*
Profiles in Courage, 827
progressivism: business reforms, 620; in education, 591; governmental reforms, 604, 607; immigrants, attitude toward, 624–25; journalism support of, 606; race, attitudes toward, 625; reforms, 602–27; women's involvement in, 609–13
prohibition, 613; Prohibition, 708–09
Project Mercury, 802
Promontory Point, Utah, 528
propaganda, 139, 661, 669, 671–72; advertising techniques, 699; used by steel companies, 691
Prophet, the, 293
proprietary colonies, 85, 112
protective tariff, 261; Tariff of 1816, 310, 320; of 1828, 338, 339
Protestant Reformation, the, 58–59
Protestants, 59; in English colonies, 78, 89–90; immigrants, 575

Index

Ptolemy, 45
PT 109, 827
public health: in cities, 586–87
public housing: Eisenhower administration funding, 799; Johnson administration funding, 829
Public Works Administration (PWA), *c722,* 725, 731
Pueblo, the, 54
pueblos, *p28,* 28, 54
Puerto Rico, 630; immigration, 840; Spain, possession of, 324, 643; U.S. territory, 643, 644
Pulaski, Casimir, 173
Pulitzer, Joseph, 592, 641
Pullman, George M., 553, *c557,* 569
Pullman Strike, *m568,* 569
Pure Food and Drug Act, 606, 618
Puritans, 78, 80, 81–82, 84, 109, 113–14
Pyle, Ernie, *q755*
pyramids, 21, *p22,* 22, *p29, p33*

Q

Quadruple Alliance, 324
Quakers, 87, 109, 114, 163; antislavery movement, 416–17, 425; antislavery society of, 197
Quayle, Dan, 910
Quebec, Canada, 62, 94, 149–50; Battle of, 123
Quechua, 25
quipus, 25
quota system, 709

R

Rabin, Yitzhak, *p224,* 920
racism, 422, 513, 515, 821, 830; Ku Klux Klan, 506, 709; in World War I armed forces, 664, 672
radicalism: during Great Depression, fear of, 689–91; demands for reform, 733–34; increase in, 731
Radical Republicans, 496, 498; conflicts with Andrew Johnson, 500, 501, 502–03; Reconstruction plan, 496
radio, 703–04, *g704;* during Great Depression, 732; fireside chats, 723
railroads, 386–88, *m387,* 400, 551–54, *m553;* after the Civil War, 514; competition between, 553–54; consolidation of, 551–52; corporations, 561; economic effects of, 529, 552; effect of, on buffalo, 539; effect of, on cattle industry, 531–32; expansion of, 527–29, 551–52; farmers' problems with, 544, 545, 546; government aid to, 527; impact of, on western settlement, 529, 534; improving, 552–53; rate setting, 544, 545, 553–54, 605; schedules of, 529; strike of 1877, 568, *p569;* transcontinental lines, 527–29, 551
Raleigh, Sir Walter, 71–72
Randolph, A. Philip, *p691,* 691, 752–53, 825
Randolph, Edmund, 199, 200, 202, 211; as attorney general, *ptg258,* 258
Rankin, Jeannette, *p614,* 614–15, *p615, p664,* 664
rationing, 671, 751
Reagan, Ronald, 839, A7; anticommunism, 907; appeal, 900, 906; assassination attempt, 905; defense policy, 907; domestic policy, 905–07; election, 900, *p905,* 905; 1976 election, 895; foreign policy, 907–08, *p909,* 909; Iran hostage release, 900; presidential style, 905; reelection, *q908,* 908; relations with Congress, 906, 907, 908; Supreme Court appointments, *p906,* 906
realism: in art, 593–94; in literature, 592
Rebels, 465. *See also* Confederacy
recall of elected officials, 607
recession: after World War I, 698; Bush administration, 915–16; defined, 698; Nixon administration, 887; Reagan administration, 907; Roosevelt Recession, 736
Reconstruction, 494–513; African Americans, 504–06; aftermath of, 513–16; conflict between president and Congress, 496, 500, 501, 502–03; Congressional plan, 500–01; end of, 508–11; impact of, 516; Andrew Johnson's plan, 498; Lincoln's plan, 495–96; military districts, *m501,* 502; politics during, 501, 504, 508–10; Radical, 501–02; Radical Republican plan, 496; resistance to, 505–06; state governments affected by, 495–96, 498, 502
Reconstruction Finance Corporation (RFC), 718
recycling, 932
Red Badge of Courage, The, 434–35, 593
Red Cloud, chief, *q538*
Red Scare, 690, 709, 789–92
referendum, 607
reforms, 410–28; alcohol, 412; business, 620; education, 412–13; governmental, 604, 607; labor, 546, 547; political, 546, 547; progressivism, 602–27; slavery, 416–22; social, 411–15, 603–13; women's rights and, 424–28
region, 21; U.S. physical regions, *m3*
Rehnquist, William, 886
religion(s): of enslaved persons, 405; freedom of, 78, 79, 81, 85, 86, 219; effect of Great Awakening on, 113; of immigrants, 575, 576, 579, 580; of early Native Americans, 22–23, 24, 25; in the Netherlands, 78; reform of, 80, 411–12; toleration of, 81, 89–90. *See also* individual religions
religious intolerance, 78, 80–81, 88, 576, 758–59, *q759*
Remington, Frederic, 593, 643
Renaissance, the, 38
Republican Leader, The, *q441*
Republican Party: beginnings of, 448–49; during Reconstruction, 504, 508–10; slavery, opposition to, 448, 451, 454–55
reservations, *m343,* 540–41, 542, 543
reserved powers, 217–18
resolution, 135
responsibilities, citizen's, 227–28
Restoration, the, 84
Revels, Hiram, *p505,* 505
revenue sharing, 887
Revere, Paul, 139; midnight ride, 143, 144, 145, *ptg181*
revivals, 411–12, *p412*
Revolutionary War, *m166;* African Americans in, 164, *ptg167,* 167, *ptg183;* American advantages, 164–65, 185; British advantages, 163–64; campaigns in, 165–66, 167–68; colonies taking sides, 146, 151, 163–64; financing, American, 174; first battles in, 144–46; Native Americans and, 176; role of European allies, 171–72; in the South, 178–80, *m178;* Valley Forge, 172–73; in the West, 176–77, *m177;* women fighting in, 165. *See also* American Revolution
Rhode Island, *mRA6, cRA4;* charter colony, 111; English settlement, 81–82; opposition to Constitution, 209, 211; ratification of Constitution, 211
Richardson, Elliot, 890
Richmond, Virginia: in the Civil War, 470, *p487,* 487; Confederate capital, 461, 464, 487
Richthofen, Baron von, 659
Rickenbacker, Eddie, 659
rights of citizens, 226–27; basic, 152, 156; bearing arms, 242; equal treatment, 226–27, 242–43; freedom of assembly, 219, 242; freedom of religion, 78–79, 81, 85, 88, 89–90, 219, 242; freedom of speech, 219, 242; limits on, 227; search and seizure, 226, 242; voting rights, 112, 190, 227, 228, 246, 247, 249, 336–37. *See also* civil rights
Riis, Jacob, *p578, q587,* 587, *q603,* 603
Rio Grande: Texas/Mexican border dispute, 372–73, 375
Rivero, Horacio, 753
river travel, 314–15, 386
"Road Not Taken, The," 924
roads, 386; to the West, 313–14, *m314*
Roanoke Island, North Carolina, *m72,* 72
Roaring Twenties, 702–06
Robeson, Paul, 706
Robinson, Jackie, *p821, q821,* 821
Rochambeau, Jean Baptiste de, *ptg182,* 182–83
Rock, Emily, *q832*
Rockefeller, John D., *p560,* 560, 561–62, 563, 564
Rockefeller, Nelson, 892
rock 'n' roll, 811–12
Rockwell, Norman, 769, 848
Rocky Mountains, *p2,* 4; Lewis and Clark expedition, 284; and mountain men, 356; and Oregon Trail, 357

Rogers, Francis, *q289*
Rogers, Will, *q715*
Rolfe, John, 73
Roman Catholic Church. *See* Catholic Church
Romania, 656, *m657, m676, m756,* 881, *m912*
Rome, Italy, 756
Rommel, Erwin, 755–56
Roosevelt, Eleanor, 720, 729, *q758*
Roosevelt, Franklin Delano, *q684,* 693, *p721, q745, p748, q753,* 755, 763–64, *p773,* A6; advisers, 721, 730; banking crisis, 722; death of, 758; 1932 election, *q720,* 720, *q721,* 721; inauguration, 720, *q721,* 721; neutrality efforts, 747, 748; polio, *q721,* 721; post-World War II goals, 748, 773; presidential years, 720–21; reelection, *q735,* 735; Supreme Court packing plan, 736, 737; third term, 747–48; wartime diplomacy, 773–74. *See also* New Deal
Roosevelt, Theodore, *q598, q616,* 616–18, *q617, p618, p619, crt621, ptg643,* A5; anti-Asian policies, 623–24, 639; conservationism, 618; election, 618; 1912 election, 619–20; labor crisis, 617–18; progressive reforms, attitude toward, 617; Roosevelt Corollary, 648–49; Russo-Japanese War, role in ending, 639; as secretary of the navy, 641; in Spanish-American War, 616, 642; square deal, 618; Taft, relations with, 619; as trustbuster, 617
Rosenberg, Ethel, *p790,* 790–91
Rosenberg, Julius, *p790,* 790–91
Ross, Betsy, 174, 261
Ross, John, chief, *ptg341*
Ross, Nellie Taylor, 695
Rough Riders, 616, 642, *p643*
royal colonies, 112
Ruby, Jack, 828
Ruckelshaus, William, 890
Rush-Bagot Treaty, 322
Russell, Charles, 532
Russia: *m912;* Alaska, sale of, 633; immigration, 575, 576, 577, 585, 590; in Manchuria, 638; Oregon country, claim on, 355; revolutions, 1917, 663, 665–66, 689; treaty terms for, 676; war with Japan, 639; in World War I, 657, *m657,* 658, 665–66, *m676. See also* Soviet Union
Russo-Japanese War, 639
Russwurm, John B., 392, 418
Ruth, Babe, *p704,* 704

S

Sabotage Act, 673
Sacagawea, 284, *ptg286*
Sacco, Nicola, *p690,* 690
Sacramento, California, 528
Sadat, Anwar el-, 885, *p899,* 899
Saigon, South Vietnam: fall of, *p871,* 871; Tet offensive, 862–63
St. Augustine, Florida, 53, 97
St. Lawrence River, 95, 120, 123
St. Louis, Missouri, 284
Salem, Peter, 167
Salk, Jonas, 808
Salt Lake City, Utah, 379
SALT I treaty, 883
SALT II treaty, 899
Salvation Army, 587
Samoa Islands, 630, 637–38
Samoset, 79–80
Sampson, Deborah, 165
San Antonio, Texas, 96, *ptg366;* and Texas war for independence, 364
San Diego, California, 96, 374
Sandinistas, 907
San Francisco, California, 376, 377; civil rights movement, 835; immigrant settlement, 577, 579, 582, 583, 585, *p623,* 623
San Jacinto, Battle of, 366
San Juan Hill, Battle of, 616, 642, *ptg643*
San Martín, José de, 324
San Salvador, 47
Santa Anna, Antonio López de, 363–67
Santa Fe, New Mexico, 96, 368, 373, *ptg688*
Santa Fe Trail, 368–69, 376
Santo Domingo: revolution in, 282
Sarajevo, Bosnia, 655, 656
Saratoga, New York, 169, 171, 185; Battle of, 169
Saturday Night Massacre, 890
Saudi Arabia, 914
Sauk, the, 342, 345
Savannah, Georgia, 92, 178, 184; capture of, by Union forces, 487
Scalia, Antonin, 906
Scarlet Letter, The, 414
Schlafly, Phyllis, *p839,* 839
school. *See* education
Schurz, Carl, *q505,* 644
Schwarzkopf, Norman, 914, 915
science. *See* technology
Scopes trial, 710
Scott, Dred, 449–50, *p450*
Scott, Winfield, 340, 344, 375
SEATO. *See* Southeast Asia Treaty Organization
secession, 453–57; defined, 285, 439; Federalists' plan for, 285; reactions to, 454–56, 462; Southern states vote for, 454, 455, *m456,* 457; states' rights, basis for, 338, 339, 455
Second Amendment, 242
Securities and Exchange Commission (SEC), 725
sedition, 319
Sedition Act: 1798, 271–72, 279; 1918, 673
segregation: of African Americans, 391–92, 475, 516, 624, 626; in armed forces, 643, 673, 752–53; in schools, 590, 623, 624, 639, 821–23; Supreme Court rulings, 516, 624, 816, 821, 822–23, 824, 831; in the U.S., *m822*
Selassie, Haile, *q742*
Selective Service Act, 664
Selective Training and Service Act, 747, 750
Seminole, the, 323, 342, 345–46
Senate: checks and balances, 207; creation of, 201; election of, 206, 246, 607; functions of, 221–23; number of representatives, 206, 221; *See also* Congress
Seneca, the, 32, 117
Seneca Falls Convention, 425–26, 608, 610
Seneca Falls Declaration, The, A13
Seoul, Korea, 786, 787
separate but equal, 516, 624, 821
separation of powers, 205, 206, 207–08, *c217;* 218–19. *See also* checks and balances
Separatists: in England, 78; in the Netherlands, 78–79
Sequoya, 344
Serbia, 576, 656–57, *m657, m912,* 915
Serra, Junípero, *ptg96,* 96, 369
Servicemen's Readjustment Act, 780
Seven Days battles, *m468,* 470
Seventeenth Amendment, 206, 246, 607
Seventeenth Flag of the Union, 483
Seventh Amendment, 243
Seven Years' War, 121–22
Seward, William, 454, 497, *p633,* 633, 635
Seymour, Horatio, 503
Shakers, 411
sharecroppers, 507, 515, 624, 813–14
shares. *See* stocks
Shawnee, the, *ptg263,* 263, 293
Shays, Daniel, 197
Shays's Rebellion, 197, 198, 215
Shenandoah Valley, 487
Shepard, Alan, Jr., 851
Sheridan, Philip, 487
Sherman, Roger, 150, *ptg200,* 201
Sherman, William Tecumseh, 464, *q465,* 485, *q487,* 487, 488
Sherman Antitrust Act, 564, 605, 617, 619, 620
Shiloh, Battle of, 469, 477, *m484*
shipbuilding, 104, 105, *ptg292,* 292
ships: clippers, 386; galleons, *p45;* merchant, 289; privateers, 177, 297; Renaissance, 40
Sholes, Christopher, 557
Shoshone, the, 31, 284
shuttle diplomacy, 884–85
Sicily, 756
Sierra Nevada, 4, 376, 377
silver mining, 526, 527
Sinai Peninsula, 884, 885
Sinclair, Upton, 606
Sioux, the, 538–39, 540–42, 543, 842
Sirica, John, 889
sit-ins, *p830,* 830
Sitting Bull, 538, *p541, q541,* 541–42, 543
Six-Day War, 883, 884
Sixteenth Amendment, 246, 619
Sixth Amendment, 243
skyscrapers, 588–89
Slater, Samuel, 307
slavery: abolition of, in Eastern states, 197; abolition of, in Northern states, 197–98; in Africa, 40, 41, 44; attempt to stop spread of, 193; California, issue of, 378, 439, 440; criticism of, 109, 175, 197–98; effect on Civil War, 436, 448–52, 454–55; Emancipation Proclamation, 473–74; in English colonies,

Index

75, 89, 91–92, 93, 108–09; free and slave states, 449, 438; freedom from, 405–06; in literature, 68, 415; Missouri Compromise, 320; of Native Americans, 24, 54–55, 369; population counts of, 201; resistance to, 405–06; slave codes, 108, 405; in the South (mid-1800s), 396, 397, 398, *ptg399*; in Southern colonies, 107, 108; in Spanish colonies, 54–55; states' rights, 319; in the territories, 437–39, 443–45, 448, 449–50; in Texas, 363, 366, 367, 438; in the West, 437–40. *See also* antislavery movement. *See also* enslaved persons

slave trade, 40, 44, 55, 105, 201, 405, 439–40

Slidell, John, 373

Slovenia, 915

Smith, Alfred E., *p711,* 711

Smith, Bessie, 704, *p707*

Smith, Jedediah, 356, 369, 370

Smith, John, 73, 76–77, *ptg77,* 78

Smith, Joseph, 379

Smith, Margaret Chase, *q791*

Smith College, 591

smuggling, 111, 134, 138, 291–92

socialism, 606; during Great Depression, 731

socialists: antiwar sentiments, 672

social reform: in cities, 578, 588, 603, 609; journalism influence on, 606; progressivism, 603–13; temperance movement, 412, 426, 613, 708; women's involvement in, 612–13, 708

Social Security: Eisenhower expansion of, 799; Truman's attempts to expand, 781, 783

Social Security Act, *c722,* 734, 735

Society of American Indians, 627

Solidarity, 911

Somme, Battle of the, 659

Songhai, *m40,* 41

Son of the Middle Border, A, 330–31

Sons of Liberty, 135, 140, 144, 148

Sorenson, Charles, *q559,* 559

Souls of Black Folk, The, 626

Sousa, John Philip, 594

South (region): agriculture, 309, *g514,* 514–15; after the Civil War, 495; economy of (mid-1800s), 398–400; economy after Reconstruction, 513–15; education, 497, 507; Embargo Act, 291; industry after Civil War, 514; during Reconstruction, 504–07; social structure, 401–03; tariff debate, 1828, 338, 339; support of Texas annexation, 367

South Africa: apartheid, 898

South America: ancient cities of, 21; Monroe Doctrine, 324; settlement of, 17, *m19;* Spain, conquests in, 50–52; Spain, independence from, 324

South Carolina, *mRA6, cRA4;* in the Civil War, 487, 488; English settlement in, 90–92; Nullification Act, 339; readmission to Union, 502; secession, 454

South Dakota, *mRA6, cRA4;* statehood, 527

Southeast Asia Treaty Organization (SEATO), 804

Southern Alliance, 545

Southern Christian Leadership Conference (SCLC), 825, 830, 832

Southern Colonies, 88–93, *m89,* 107–08; agriculture in, 89, 90–91, 107–08; economics in, 107; population counts of, 93; religious freedom in, 88, 89–90; slavery in, 107, 108. *See also* individual colonies

South Korea, 785–87

South Pacific Railroad, 527

South Vietnam, 853; surrender of, 871; unstable government, 853–54. *See also* Vietnam War

Soviet-German Non-Aggression Act, 744

Soviet Union: atomic bomb, 789, 790–91; attack by Germany, 747, 757; breakup of, 656, 911–13; Berlin blockade, 776–77; Communist coup, *p912,* 912–13; defeat of Germany, 757, 758; division of Germany, 773, 776–77; human rights, 893, 899; Hungarian revolt, *p803,* 803; in Korea, 786; Middle East policy, 803, 884; nuclear weapons, 801; occupation of Eastern Europe, 775; in post-World War II East Germany, 848; relations with Cuba, 804, 848, 849–50; relations with Nazi Germany, 744; under Stalin, 743; U.S. relations with, 775–79, 801, 803–05, 848–51, 883, 884, 899, 908–09; in World World II, 745–46, 747, 758; Yalta agreement, 758, 773. *See also* Russia

space exploration, 802, 806, 851, 922

Spain: Adams-Onís Treaty, 323; in America, 50–55; early explorers of, 46–49, *m52;* California, control of, 355, 369; civil war, 731; Cuba, control of, 640–41, 642; England, war against, 71; Florida, control of, 195, 322–23; Latin American empire, 324; Louisiana Territory, possession of, 123, 281–82; Mexico, control of, 368; role of, in Revolutionary War, 171–72, 173, 185; settlements of, on the Pacific coast, 96; settlements of, 95–96; Seven Years' War, involvement in, 122; South America, independence from, 324; Texas, control of, 362–63; George Washington, relations with, 265

Spanish-American War, 616, *ptg630,* 640–44, *m642;* African American involvement, 642, 643; declaration of, 641; events leading to, 640–41

Spanish Armada, 71

Sparkman, John J., 797, *p798*

Special Forces. *See* Green Berets

Speckled Snake, *q347*

spheres of influence, 638

Spirit of Laws, The, 205

Spirit of St. Louis, 702

spoils system, 337, 604–05

sports, spectator, 594; popularity of, 1920s, 704

Springfield, Illinois: riot, 622

Springfield, Massachusetts, 197

Sputnik, 800, 801, 851

Squanto, 79–80

Stalin, Joseph, 744, *p773, q773;* actions in Eastern Europe, 744, 745–46, 775; death of, 804; division of Germany, 776–77; post-World War II plans, 773; rise to power, 743

Stalingrad, Soviet Union, 757

Stamp Act, 135–36, *ptg137,* 140, 148

standard of living, 566, 808

Standard Oil Company, *crt561,* 562, 564, 617

Stanford, Leland, 528–29, 552, 591

Stanford University, 591

Stanton, Edwin, 502

Stanton, Elizabeth Cady, 425–26, *q426,* 610

Stars and Stripes flag, 1960, 799

"Stars and Stripes Forever, The," 594

"Star-Spangled Banner, The," 299, 300, A11

State, Department of, 224; creation of, 258

state government: challenges faced by new, 190; child-labor laws, 567; constitutional authority, 239–40; constitutions, adoption of, 1776–1780, 189–90; constitutions, changes in, 337, 502; corruption in, 616; federal government, sharing powers with, 205, 217–18, *c217;* powers of 217–18; primary elections, 607; railroad rates, 545; reforms in, 607

statehood: requirements for admission to the Union, 192, 193

states' rights, 278, 463; Democratic-Republicans, support of, 334–35; Kentucky Resolution, 272; regional conflicts over, 319–20, 321; secession, 338–39, 455; Virginia Resolution, 272; Webster–Hayne debate, 338

States' Rights Democratic Party (Dixiecrats), 782

Statue of Liberty, 577

stealth bomber, *p763,* 763

steamboats, 314–15, 316, *p325,* 325, 386, 522–23, *ptg523*

steam engine, 306, 314–15

steel industry, 552, 562–63; Andrew Carnegie's effect on, 563; workers' strike, 1919, 691

Steffens, Lincoln, 606

Stein, Gertrude, 706

Steinbeck, John, 727, 732

Stennis, John C., 860–61

Stephens, Alexander, 499

Steuben, Friedrich von, 173, 180

Stevens, Thaddeus, *q496*

Stevenson, Adlai E., 797, *p798,* 798, 799
stock(s), 560, 562, 564; buying on margin, 715; prices, *g716*
stock market, 561; boom, 715; crash of, 715, 716, *p717,* 719
Stone, Lucy, 428
Stowe, Harriet Beecher, 415, *p443,* 443
Strategic Arms Limitation Treaty. *See* SALT I and SALT II
Strategic Arms Reduction Treaty (START), 911
Strategic Defense Initiative (SDI), 907
strikes, 391, 567, *m568;* Boston police, 691; coal strike, 1902, 617–18; General Motors, 735; Haymarket Square, 566, 568–69; post-World War II, 781; public opinion of, 567, 568–69, 617, 691; Pullman Strike, 569; steel workers, 691
Strong, Josiah, 633
Stuart, James E.B., 470
Student Nonviolent Coordinating Committee (SNCC), 830, 834
student protests, 858–60, *p859,* 869–70
Stuyvesant, Peter, *ptg85,* 85
submarine warfare: in World War I, *p658,* 659, 661–62, *p662,* 663, 665; in World War II, 748
suburbs, 585, 586, 589, 700; effect of expansion on cities, 814; 1950s expansion of, 807, *g808, p809,* 809, *p810;* housewives in, 816; minorities and, 809
Sudetenland, 743–44
Suez Canal, 755, 803
suffrage, 336–37, 426–27, 610–12. *See also* voting rights
Sugar Act, 134
Sullivan, Louis, *q588,* 588
Sumner, Charles, 445, *q502–03*
Sun Belt, *m8,* 905
supply-side economics, 906
Supreme Court, *p208,* 225; cases to be heard by, 207; checks and balances, 208, 218–19; constitutional authority, 207, 225, 239; creation of, 224; *Dred Scott* decision, 449–50; expanded powers of, 220; the first, 259; *Marbury* v. *Madison,* 220; John Marshall's effect on, 280; *McCulloch* v. *Maryland,* 321; Northern Securities trust, 617; *Plessy* v. *Ferguson,* 516, 624; ruling on Watergate tapes, 890; rulings on New Deal legislation, 724, 735; rulings on segregation, 516, 624, 816, 821, 822–23, 824, 831; *Worchester* v. *Georgia,* 343
Supreme Court justices, *p208,* 823, 839, 886, *p906,* 906
Sussex, 662
Sussex Pledge, 662
Sutter, John, 376, 382, 530
sweatshops, 566, 567–68, 578
Sweden: immigration, 534, 576
Swift, Gustavus, 553
symphony orchestras, 594
Syria: shuttle diplomacy, 885; war with Israel, 883, 884

T

Taft, William Howard, *crt621,* A5; as chief justice, 690; dollar diplomacy, 649; election, 618; head of Philippines government, 644; progressivism, 619
Taft-Hartley Act, 782
Taino, the, 14–15, *ptg15*
Taiwan, 779
Talleyrand, Charles de, 270, 282
Taney, Roger B., 450
Tanner, Henry, 593
Tarbell, Ida, *p606,* 606
Tariff of Abominations, 338, 339
tariffs, *crt605;* of Jackson administration, 338, 339; of Coolidge administration, 695; lowering of, 605, 619, 620; protective, 261, 320–21, 338, 339; regional disagreements over, 319–20; on sugar, 636; Tariff of 1816, 310, 320
taxation: after the American Revolution, 194; on business, 734, 751; in the Civil War, 480; on colonists, 114, 122, 134–37; income tax, 619, 620, 671, 734, 751; levied by states, 196, 197; of Jefferson administration, 279; poll tax, 515; Social Security, 734; unemployment insurance, 734; on whiskey, 261, 279; without representation, 133–37. *See also* excise tax; *see also* tariffs
Taylor, Maxwell, *q852*
Taylor, Zachary, *p372,* 372, 373, 378, A3; death of, 440; 1848 election, 438–39
Tea Act of 1773, 140
Teapot Dome scandal, 694
technology, 112; advances in (1400s), 39–40; aircraft, *p811,* 811; computers, 922–23, 926; construction, 588–89; contributions of Benjamin Franklin to, 114; effect on economy, 807; electric appliances, 810; electronics, 807, 810–11; and industrial growth, 1920s, 698–99; farm, 388–89; Industrial Revolution, 306–07, 309; machinery, 385–86; printing improvements, 592; railroad, 553; steam locomotive, 386, *p388, p528,* 528; weapons, 658, 659, 662, 669
Tecumseh, *q293,* 293–94, *ptg295,* 296, 297, 350
Tehran, Iran, 899
Tejanos, 362, 364, 365
telecommunications, 927
telegraph, *p385,* 388, *p492,* 492, 556–57
telephone, 557, *p565*
television, *p796,* 810–11, *g812, p812;* impact on culture, 810–11, 827
"Tell-Tale Heart, The," 415
temperance movement, 412, 426, 613, 625, 708
tenant farmers, 95, 401–02, 515, 813–14
Tender Is the Night, 706
tenements, 585–86, 587, 603
Tennessee, *mRA6, cRA4;* in the Civil War, 462, 469, 485; denied readmission, 496; ratification of Fourteenth Amendment, 501; readmission to Union, 502; secession, 457; statehood, 316
Tennessee River, 724; in the Civil War, 469
Tennessee Valley Authority (TVA), *c722,* 724, 735, *m739*
Tenochtitlán, 23–24, 50, 51
Ten Percent Plan, 495–96
Tenth Amendment, 218, 243
Tenure of Office Act, 502
Terrell, Mary Church, 610
Tet offensive, 862–63, *p863*
Texas, *mRA6, cRA4;* border disputes over, 372–73, 375; cattle industry, 531–32; conflicts over, 362–63; land grants in, 362–63; New Mexico, border dispute, 439–40; oil industry, *p572;* readmission to Union, 502; Spain, control of, 96, 323, 362–63; secession, 455; slavery in, 363, 366, 367, 438; statehood, 366, 367, 438; war for independence, 363–66, *m365*
Texas, Republic of: debate over annexation of, 366–67; independence declared, 365; recognition of, 366–67
textile industry: British inventions for, 305–06, 307; cotton gin, *p306,* 306–07, *p397,* 397, 398; mass production in, 385–86; New England factories, 307–09
Thailand, 761; in SEATO, 804
Thames, Battle of the, 297
Thanksgiving, 53, 80, 723
Third Amendment, 242
thirteen colonies, founding the, *c91*
Thirteenth Amendment, 244, 474, 498, 512
37-Star Flag, 500
Thoreau, Henry David, *p407, q407,* 407, *q411,* 414
Three-Fifths Compromise, the, 201
Three Mile Island, 898
Thurmond, Strom, 782
Tiananmen Square slaughter, *p913,* 913–14
Tidewater, the, 107–08
Tilden, Samuel J., 502, 510–11, *p511*
Timbuktu, *m40,* 41
time zones, *m555;* creation of, 529, 554; reading, 555
Tippecanoe, Battle of, 293–94, 350
Tlingit, the, 31
tobacco: as a cash crop, 107, 396; importance of, in English colonies, 73, 75, 76, 89, 90, 107
Tōjō, Hideki, 748
Tokyo, Japan, 763, 764
Tompkins, Sally, 478
Tories. *See* Loyalists
Toronto, Canada, 297
totalitarian state, 742
Toussaint-Louverture, *ptg282,* 282
town meetings, 103, *p226*
Townsend, Francis, 734
Townshend, Charles, 136
Townshend Acts, 136–37, 139
trade: American, expansion of, 289, 387–88; with Asia, 632; between Europe and Africa,

40, 44; colonial, *g99,* 104–05, 110–11, 134, *g139;* Embargo Act, effect on, 291–92; and exchange of ideas and customs, 39, 40; of fur, 62, 94, 95, *ptg96,* 116, 117; growth of, 38, 39; with Hawaii, 635–36; Native Americans, 23; Nonintercourse Act, 292; restrictions on, 111, *c139,* 143; by ship, 38, 40, 104–05, 289; of slaves, 40, 44, 55, 105, 201, 405, 439–40; triangular, 104–05, *m106*
trade deficit, 898
trade goods: from Africa, 40, 44, 105; from the colonies, 73, 94, 105; from the East, 38, 39; of early Native Americans, 23; from the West Indies, 105
trade routes: Santa Fe Trail, *m358,* 369, 373; triangular, 104–05, *m106*
trade unions, 391, 567. *See also* labor unions
Trail of Tears, 340–41, *ptg344,* 344–45
transcendentalists, 414
transportation: air travel, 810, *p811,* 811; automobiles, *p701,* 701, 809–10; canals, 315–16; Conestoga wagons, 294; fashion and, *p315;* improvements in, 386–88; early Native American, 23, 24–25; public, 586, 588, 589; on rivers, 314–15; roads, 313–14; in the South (mid-1800s), 400; ships, 386
Travis, William B., *q363,* 363–64, 365
Treasury, Department of: creation of, 258
Treaty of Brest-Litovsk, 666
Treaty of Ghent, 299
Treaty of Greenville, 263, *m264*
Treaty of Guadalupe Hidalgo, 375
Treaty of Kanagawa, 632
Treaty of Paris, 1763, 123, 124
Treaty of Paris, 1783, 184, 189, 195
Treaty of Paris, 1898, 643, 644
Treaty of Portsmouth, 639
Treaty of Tordesillas, 47, 59
Treaty of Versailles, 676–78, 689, 741, 742, 743
trench warfare, 477; in World War I, 658, 665, *p667, p679*
Trenton, New Jersey, 167–68
trial by jury, 134; Bill of Rights, 219, 243
Triangle Shirtwaist Company, 567–68
Triple Alliance, 656, *m657*
Triple Entente, 656, *m657*
Tripoli: United States, conflict with, 289–90
Truman, Harry S, *q774,* 774, *p780,* 781, 797, A6; becoming president, 758; Berlin airlift, 777; criticism of, 801; domestic policies, 781, *q783,* 783–84; Korean War, *q786,* 786, 788; policy of containment, 775–76; *q776,* 786; policy toward communism, 789, *q790,* 790; reelection, 782–83, *p783;* relations with Congress, 781–82, 783; relations with MacArthur, 786, 787, *q788,* 788; role in World War II, 764
Truman Doctrine, 776
Trumbull, John, 157, 183
trusts, 562, 564, *crt605;* regulation of, 605, 617, 620; oil trust, 606, 617; Theodore Roosevelt, attitude toward, 617; William Howard Taft's antitrust efforts, 619
Truth, Sojourner, *q420,* 420, 421, *p425, q425,* 425
Tubman, Harriet, 405, *p421, q421,* 421, *p446, q446,* 446; in the Civil War, 474, 477
Turkey, 775, 776; immigration, 575
Turner, Nat, 405
turnpikes, 313–14
Tuskegee Airmen, 752
Tuskegee Institute, *p591,* 591, 625, 626
Twain, Mark, *p522,* 522–23, 586, *q589,* 592–93, *q593,* 644
Tweed, William M. "Boss," *crt604,* 604
Twelfth Amendment, 278, 334
Twentieth Amendment, 247–48
Twentieth Flag of the Union, 526
Twenty-first Amendment, 219, 248, 709
Twenty-second Amendment, 249
Twenty-third Amendment, 249
Twenty-fourth Amendment, 250
Twenty-fifth Amendment, 250–51, 893
Twenty-fifth Flag, 620
Twenty-sixth Amendment, 227, 251
Twenty-seventh Amendment, 219, 251
Two Treatises on Civil Government, 205
Tyler, John, 350–51, 367, A2

U

U-boats. *See* submarine warfare
Uchida, Yoshiko, 686–87
Ukraine, 666
Uncle Tom's Cabin, 415, 443
Underground Railroad, 405–06, 407, *m419, ptg420,* 420–21, 423, 442, 446–47
unemployment, 714, 715; in cities, 814; Native Americans, 841; New Deal work programs, 718, 724, 725, 734
unemployment insurance, 799, 916
Union (North before Civil War): before the Civil War, 437, 462–63, abolition and, 452, 455, politics, 448, 449; during the Civil War, economy, 480; goals, 463–64, 469, 472, politics, 478, resources, 462, *g463. See also* Civil War
Union Pacific Company, 528, *p529,* 551
unions. *See* labor unions
United Farm Workers (UFW), 838
United Mine Workers, 617–18, 735
United Nations, 774, 779; in Korea, 786; in the Middle East, 803; in Persian Gulf War, 914
United States: boundary of, after Revolutionary War, 184; boundary of, in 1824, *m323;* geographic facts about, *c1;* total land area of, RA16
United States Forest Service, 618
United States Military Academy at West Point, 463, 464, 797
United States Steel Corporation, 563
United States* v. *Butler, 724
Universal Negro Improvement Association (UNIA), 692
Up from Slavery, 625
Upward Bound, 828
Uruguay, 898
U.S.S. *Arizona,* Memorial, 760
U.S.S. *Missouri,* 764
U.S.S. *Pueblo,* 862
Utah, *mRA6, cRA4;* settlement of, 378–79; statehood, 379
Ute, the, 31
utopias, 411
U-2 incident, 804

V

Valentino, Rudolph, *p703,* 703
valley: defined, 11
Valley Forge, Pennsylvania, 172–73
Van Buren, Martin: A2; economic depression, 349–50; election, 349; 1840 election, 350; 1848 election, 439; opposition to Texas annexation, 367
Vanderbilt, Cornelius, 552
Vanderbilt, William Kissam and Alva, 586
Vanguard, 800, 801
Vanzetti, Bartolomeo, *p690,* 690
vaqueros, *ptg369,* 532
Vassar College, 428, 591
vaudeville shows, 593, 594
V-E Day, 758
Velázquez, Loretta Janeta, 477
Venezuela: blockade of, 648; independence from Spain, 324
Veracruz, Mexico, 375, 650
Verdun, France, 667; Battle of, 658–59
Vermont: statehood, *mRA6, cRA4;* 300, 316
Verrazano, Giovanni da, 59, *c61*
veto, 208, *c223,* 234, 349
vice presidency: election to, 206, 236–37, 244, 247–48, 269; term of office, 236; vacancies, 237
Vicksburg, Mississippi: Battle of, 484
Vietnam: French involvement, 803–04; Geneva Accords, 803
Vietnam Veterans Memorial, *p872,* 872, 873
Vietnam War, *p846, q852,* 852–57, *p854, p855, p856, p858,* 862–63, *p863, m868,* 869, 870–71; American withdrawal, 868; casualties, 871; Congressional involvement, 855, 860–61; demonstrations against, 858, *p859, p861,* 861, 864, 868, 869–70, *p870;* eco-

nomic aspects, 871; end of, 871; escalation, 855, 869; events leading to, 852–55; Johnson administration, 854–55; Kennedy administration, 853–54; Nixon administration, 867–71; peace negotiations, 868–69, 870–71; public opinion, 858, *g860,* 861, 863; Tet offensive, 862–63; veterans, 871, 873
Vikings, 45–46
Villa, Francisco "Pancho," 650
Virginia, *mRA6, cRA4;* and the Declaration of Independence, 155; in the Civil War, 462, 466–67, 468, 470–71, 482–83, 485–86, 487; ratification of Constitution, 211; growth of, 90; Jamestown, 72–75; readmission, 502; as royal colony, 84, 112; secession, 457; settlement of, 79, 84, 90; tobacco industry of, 73, 107
Virginia City, Nevada, 526
Virginia Company of London, the, 72–73, 74, 79
Virginia House of Burgesses, 135, 149
Virginia Plan, 199–200
Virginia Resolution, 272
Virgin Islands, United States, 630
virtual reality, 593
visually impaired, 413
V-J Day, 764
Volstead Act, 708
Volunteers in Service to America (VISTA), 828–29
voting rights, 112, 113; of African Americans, 190, 337, 391, 496, 502, 503, *crt512, q512,* 515, 546, 833; after American Revolution, 190; colonial, 112; District of Columbia, 249; expansion of (1800s), 336–37; Fifteenth Amendment, 246; property requirements for, 336–37; struggle for, 332; Twenty-sixth Amendment, 227, 251; of women, 247, 337, 426–27; women, leadership, 610, 611–12, 614–15; women, in the West, 426–27, *m611,* 611
Voting Rights Act of 1965, 833

W

Wade-Davis Bill, 496
Wagner Act, 735, 736
Wake Island, 761
Wald, Lillian, *p609,* 609
Walesa, Lech, *p911,* 911
Wallace, George C., 831, *q865,* 865, 888
Wallace, Henry, 782
Wall Street Journal, *q863*
Wampanoag, the, 79, 82
War, Department of: creation of, 258
War Hawks, 294–95, 296, 300
War Industries Board, 671
War of 1812, 296–300, *m298;* America, unprepared for, 296; blockade of American ports, 310; British attack on Washington, D.C., 298–99, *ptg299, q301;* Canadian campaign, 296–97; Native Americans and, 296, 297; naval battles, 297; Treaty of Ghent, 299
War Production Board, 751
Warren, Earl, 828
Warren, Joseph, 144
Warren, Mercy Otis, *ptg210, q210*
Warren Commission, 828
Warsaw Pact, 778
Washington, *mRA6, cRA4;* statehood, 527
Washington, Booker T., 591, *p625,* 625, 626
Washington, D.C., *q301;* becoming capital, 260; British capture of, 298–99, *ptg299, q301;* in the Civil War, 461, 462, 466; life in (early 1800s), 277, *ptg279. See also* District of Columbia
Washington, George, *ptg118, ptg129, ptg162, ptg196, q252, ptg256, ptg258, q631, q907,* A1; cabinet of, 258; Constitution, support for, 209–10, 211; Constitutional Convention, 196, 198, 199; Continental Army, chosen commander of, 149; Continental Army leadership, 154, 164–66, 167, 168, 172–73, 182–83; Continental Congresses, 142, 148; Farewell Address, A11, 265; farewell to troops, 185; first command, 118–19, 120; on foreign relations, 256, 265; France, relations with, 264; Great Britain, relations with, 264, 265; Alexander Hamilton, relations with, 261, 266–67, 268; inauguration, 257; Thomas Jefferson, relations with, 261, 266–67, 268; political parties, opposition to, 265, 266; precedents set, 256, 257–61, 262, 265; pre-French and Indian War, 121; Spain, relations with, 265; Whiskey Rebellion, 262
Washington, Martha, 173, *ptg256*
Washington Post, 889
Watergate scandal, 889–91, 892; break-in, 889; Saturday Night Massacre, 890; Senate hearings, *p890,* 890; tape recordings, 890–91
Watts, California, 834–35
Wayne, Anthony, 183, 263, 264
weapons: of early explorers, 40, 52; of early Native Americans, 24, 31, *p66;* of World War I, 658, 659, 662, 669
Weaver, James B., 546
Weaver, Robert, 730
Webster, Daniel, 320, *q328, q440;* Bank of the United States, 348–49; Robert Hayne, debate with, 338
Welch, Joseph, *q792*
Weld, Theodore, 418
welfare: government, 717–18, 724, 734; private, 717–18
Wellesley College, 591
Wells, Ida B., 625–26, *p626, q626*
"We Shall Overcome," 832
West (region): agricultural expansion (1800s), 310; anti-Asian sentiments, 580, 623–24; cattle industry, 531–33; Embargo Act, 291; farming life, 262; land use, *m537;* mining industry, 376–77, 525–27; railroads, 527–29; slavery, 437–40; social life, 317; territorial divisions in, 192–93. *See also* western settlers
West, Benjamin, 86
West Africa: and triangular trade route, 105, *m106*
West Bank, 883
western frontier, 524–47
western land claims, original states, *m191*
western settlers, 176, 263, 313–17, 526, 529; African Americans, 532, 533, 534; California (1840s), 370, 376–77, *c378;* communities of, 317; education, 413; Great Plains, 531–36; life of, 313, 358–59, *ptg359;* in literature, 330–31; Mormons, 378–79; Native Americans, conflicts with, 263, 293–94; Oregon Country, 322, 357–59; population of, in 1780s, 192; railroads, effect on, 529; travel routes, *m314,* 314, 357, *m358*
Western Union Telegraph Company, 556
West Germany, 776, 777
West Indies, 46, 91, 122, 123; and the triangular trade route, 105, *m106*
Westinghouse, George, 553, *c557,* 558
Westmoreland, William, 863
West Point, 463, 464
West Virginia, *mRA6, cRA4;* statehood, 462
Wharton, Edith, 593
Wheelwright, John, 81
Whig Party, 349, 350–51; destruction of, 448, 449; 1844 election, 360, 367; 1848 election, 439–40; Mexican War, opposition to, 373
Whip Inflation Now (WIN), 894
Whiskey Rebellion, 262
Whistler's Mother, 593
White, John, 72
Whitefield, George, 113
White House, 271, 319, A8
Whiteman, Paul, 704
Whitman, Marcus, 357
Whitman, Narcissa, 357
Whitman, Walt, 415
Whitney, Eli, *ptg306,* 306–07, 309, 397
Wilhelm II, kaiser, 668
Willard, Emma, 427
Willard, Frances, 613
William and Mary College, 114
William of Orange, king of England, 110
Williams, Roger, 81
Willkie, Wendell, 747
Wills, Frank, 889
Wilmot Proviso, 438, 439
Wilson, Charles, 801
Wilson, Edith, 678
Wilson, James, 199
Wilson, Woodrow, *q664, q668,* A5; administration, suspension of civil liberties, 673, 689; big government and big business, opposition to, 620; conduct of World War I, 664, 668, 671; election, 619–20, 663; Fourteen Points, 675, 676, 677; moral diplomacy, 649–50; national speaking tour, *p677,* 678; on neutrality, *q660,* 660, 663; peace propos-

als, 674, 675–77, 689; relations with Congress, 677–78, 689; woman suffrage, attitude toward, 611–12
Winesburg, Ohio, 706
Winthrop, John, 80, 81
Wisconsin, *mRA6, cRA4;* reform of electoral system, 607
Wolfe, James, 122–23
Woman's Christian Temperance Union (WCTU), 613
Woman's Home Companion, *p592*
women: in antislavery movement, 418, 420, 421, 424–25; in armed forces, 664, 750, *p751, p915,* 915; in Civil War, 474, 477–78; clothing, 426; as colonial protesters, 137; education, 413, 425, 427–28, 591, 702, 839; in government, 614–15, 664, 695, 729, 799, 839, 906, 908, 925; homesteaders, 534; in Jamestown, 74–75; and labor unions, 567–68, 612; "liberated" in 1920s, 702–03; in mining towns, 377, 526; on plantations, duties of, 402–03; progressivism, role in, 609–13; Revolutionary War, impact on, 174–75; role of, in Iroquois society, 32; roles of, in colonies, 103, 113, 114; and social reform, 609, 612–13, 708–09; in Spanish colonies, 54; voting rights of, 247, 337, 426–27, *m611,* 612, 702; voting rights, leadership, 610, 611–12, 614–15; voting rights, in the West, 426–27, 611; in war, 165, 176, *p915,* 915; as workers, 308–09, 391, 392, 566–67, 578, 702, 728, *g752, p752,* 752; in World War I mobilization, 670, *p671;* in World War II mobilization, *p752,* 752. *See also* women's rights movement
Women Appointed for Volunteer Emergency Service in the Navy (WAVES), 750
Women's Airforce Service Pilots (WASPS), *p751,* 751
Women's Army Corps (WACs), 750, 753
women's clubs, 610
Women's Peace Party, 673
women's rights movement, 424–28; leaders, 425–28, 608, 610, 838; in the 1960s, 838–39, *p839;* Seneca Falls Convention, 425–26, 608, 610
Women's Trade Union League (WTUL), 612
Wood, Grant, 732
Woods, Granville T., *c557,* 558
Woodward, Bob, 889
Woodward, Ellen Sullivan, 729
Woolworth Building, 589
Worchester* v. *Georgia, 343
Work and Win, 593
workers: African Americans, 391–92; agricultural and nonagricultural, *g395;* immigrants, 566, 567, 578, *p579,* 582–83; industrial, 566–69; on plantations, 403; unemployment of, 1930s, *p714,* 715, 717, 718, *p719,* 719, 724, *p728;* wages, 308, 391, 566, 567, 578, 691, 700, 719; women, 308–09, 391, 392, 566–67, 578, 728, *g752, p752,* 752; working hours, 308, 312, 391, 566, 567, 568, 578, 691; during World War I, 670–71
working conditions, 308–09, 312, 390–91, 566, 578
Works Progress Administration, *c722,* 734
"World Turned Upside Down, The," 184
World War I, 654–78; armistice, 668; casualties, 659, 669, 674, *c675;* causes and effects, *c672;* events leading to, 655–57; outbreak of, 657–58; peace process, 674–78; public opinion, *q660,* 660–61, 662, 663, 671, 672–73; technology of, *p658,* 659, 662, 669; veterans, 718; Western Front, *m666;* women in, 664
World War I, U.S. involvement: declaration of war, 664; military involvement, 665, 666–68; mobilization, 670–72; neutrality, *q660,* 660–63; peace mediation, 674, 675–77; social change, 672, 678; suspension of civil liberties during, 673, 689–90; trade with Allies, 661; workforce, 670–71
World War II, 740–65; African Americans, 752–53; on the Atlantic, 748–49; Battle of Britain, 746–47; bombing, 746, 748–49, 757, 761, 763, 764; casualties, 740, 749, 757, 758, 759, 763, 764; events leading to, 741–44; Holocaust, 740, 758–59, 760; invasion of Czechoslovakia, 744; in Europe, 745–47, *m756,* 756–58; in France, 746, 757; German surrender, 758; in Italy, 756; Japanese surrender, 764; Mexican Americans, 753; Native Americans, *p753,* 753; Normandy invasion, 757; in North Africa, 755–56, *m756;* outbreak, 745; in the Pacific, 761–64, *m762;* invasion of Poland, 745; in Soviet Union, 747, 757; submarine warfare, 748; war trials, 764; women in, 750
World War II, U.S. involvement: declaration of war, 749; economic involvement, *g747,* 748, 751; military involvement, 755–58, 761–64; neutrality, 743, 747, 748; mobilization, 750–51; preparation for, *g747,* 747, 748, 750–51; social changes, 750–54; strategy, 755, 757, 763
Wounded Knee, South Dakota, 543, 842
Wovoka, 543
Wright, Orville, 559
Wright, Richard, 732
Wright, Wilbur, 559
writs of assistance, 134
Wyoming, *mRA6, cRA4;* statehood, 527; voting rights, 426–27, 611

XYZ

XYZ Affair, 270
Yakima, the, 31
Yalta conference, 758, 773, 776
Yalu River, *m786,* 787
Yankee, 465. *See also* Union
"Yankee Doodle," 169, 184
Yeardley, Sir George, 74
yellow fever, 643, 647–48
yellow journalism, 592, *crt641,* 641
Yeltsin, Boris, 912, 913
Yom Kippur War, 884
York, Alvin, 665
York, Duke of, 85, 86
Yorktown, **745**
Yorktown, Virginia, 180, 184, 185; Battle of, 182–83
Yosemite National Park, *p618*
Young, Brigham, 379
Young, Charles, *p643,* 643
Young Men's Christian Association (YMCA), 588, 686
Young Women's Christian Association (YWCA), 588, 686
"You're a Grand Old Flag," 600
Yugoslavia, 656, 677, *m774, m912,* 915
Zaharias, Babe Didrickson, *p839,* 839
zeppelin, 659
Ziegler, Ronald, 889
Zimmermann, Arthur, 663
Zuni, the, 31

A

abolitionist/abolicionista una persona que favorece firmemente suprimir la esclavitud (p. 416)
abstain/abstenerse no tomar parte de una actividad, como de votar (p. 440)
adobe/adobe un ladrillo de lodo, seco al sol, usado para construir las casas de los Nativos Americanos (p. 31)
affirmative action/acción afirmativa un esfuerzo activo para mejorar las oportunidades de educación y empleo para grupos de minorías y de la mujer (p. 887)
affluence/afluencia la condición de tener mucha riqueza (p. 808)
airlift/puente aéreo un sistema de transportar comida y abastos por vehículos aéreos hasta una área que no se puede alcanzar de otras maneras (p. 777)
alien/extranjero una persona inmigrante que vive en un país en el cual no es ciudadano (p. 271)
alleged/alegado dicho como un hecho pero sin pruebas (p. 791)
alliance system/sistema de alianza acuerdos de defensa entre naciones (p. 656)
ambush/emboscada un ataque por sorpresa (p. 185)
amendment/enmienda una adición a un documento formal tal como la Constitución (pp. 211, 219)
American System/Sistema Americano políticas ideadas por Henry Clay para estimular el crecimiento de la industria (p. 320)
amnesty/amnistía el otorgar perdón a un número grande de personas; la protección del proceso a causa de una acción ilegal (pp. 496, 893)
anarchist/anarquista una persona que cree que no debe de haber ningún gobierno (p. 689)
anarchy/anarquía desorden y sin ley (p. 648)
annex/anexar añadir un territorio a su propio territorio (p. 366)
annexation/anexión traer una área bajo el control de un país más grande (p. 637)
anti-Semitism/antisemitismo hostilidad hacia o discriminación en contra de los judíos (p. 742)
apartheid/*apartheid* la separación racial y discriminación económica y política en contra de la gente no blanca, una política anteriormente practicada en la República de África del Sur (p. 898)
appeasement/apaciguamiento aceptar demandas para evitar conflictos (p. 744)
apprentice/aprendiz asistente asignado para aprender el oficio de un artesano experto (p. 113)
appropriate/destinar apartar para un propósito en particular, dicho especialmente de fondos (p. 221)
arbitration/arbitraje arreglo de una disputa por medio de un acuerdo para aceptar la decisión de una persona imparcial (p. 617)
archaeology/arqueología el estudio de pueblos antiguos (p. 17)
armistice/armisticio un acuerdo temporal de paz para suprimir combates (pp. 643, 668)
arms race/carrera de armas la competición entre los Estados Unidos y la Unión Soviética para construir más y más armas, cada uno con el propósito de sobrepasar el poder militar del otro (p. 801)
arsenal/arsenal un lugar para el almacenaje de armas y municiones (p. 452)
article/artículo una parte de un documento tal como la Constitución que trata de un solo tema (p. 206)
artifact/artefacto un artículo dejado por pueblos antiguos que representa su cultura (p. 17)
assembly line/línea de montaje un sistema de producción arreglado con máquinas y trabajadores para que cada persona haga vez tras vez su trabajo designado mientras el artículo pasa por en frente de él (p. 559)
assimilate/asimilar introducir a un grupo dentro de la cultura de una población más grande (p. 578)
astrolabe/astrolabio un instrumento usado por los marineros para observar las posiciones de las estrellas (p. 39)
autocracy/autocracia gobierno en el cual una persona lleva el poder sin límite (p. 663)
automation/automatización un sistema o proceso que usa aparatos mecánicos o electrónicos para reemplazar a los trabajadores humanos (p. 814)

B

baby boom/auge de nacimientos un aumento marcado de la proporción de nacimientos, como el de los Estados Unidos inmediatamente después de terminar la Segunda Guerra Mundial (p. 808)
backcountry/monte una región de colinas y bosques al oeste de la orilla del mar (p. 108)
balance of power/balance de poder la distribución de poder entre naciones para que ninguna nación en particular pueda dominar o interferir con otra (p. 882)
bankruptcy/bancarrota la condición de no poder pagar sus deudas; la propiedad de uno es manejada o vendida para pagar a las personas a las cuales uno debe dinero (p. 916)
barrio/barrio una vecindad hispanoparlante de una ciudad, especialmente en el sudoeste de los EE.UU. (p. 627)
bicameral/*bicameral* que consiste de dos cámaras, especialmente dicho en una legislatura (p. 190)
black codes/códigos negros leyes establecidas en el Sur al terminar la Guerra Civil para controlar a los libertos y permitir a los dueños de plantaciones la explotación de los trabajadores afroamericanos (p. 499)
blacklist/lista negra una lista de personas que son desaprobadas y castigadas, tal como rehusar a darles trabajo (p. 790)
blitzkrieg/*blitzkrieg* nombre dado a los ataques ofensivos súbitos y violentos usados por los alemanes durante la Segunda Guerra Mundial; "guerra relámpago" (p. 745)
blockade/bloqueo el cerrar una área por medio de tropas o de buques de guerra para prohibir el entrar y el salir de abastos y de personas; cerrar los puertos de un país (pp. 177, 463, 850)

English/Spanish Glossary

blockade runner/forzador de bloqueo un buque que navega adentro de y afuera de una área bloqueada (p. 467)

bond/bono una obligación hecha por el gobierno la cual promete pagar un préstamo con interés (p. 259)

boomtown/pueblo en bonanza una comunidad experimentando un auge repentino de comercio o población (p. 377)

border ruffians/rufianes fronterizos hombres de Missouri que viajaban en grupos armados a votar en la elección de Kansas a mediados de los años 1850 (p. 444)

border states/estados fronterizos los estados entre el Norte y el Sur que fueron divididos sobre el problema de quedarse en la Unión o de unirse a la Confederación (p. 461)

bounty/gratificación dinero dado como recompensa, como para animar el alistamiento en el ejército (p. 479)

boycott/boicotear rehusar comprar artículos de un país en particular (p. 135); rehusar usar (p. 824)

brand/marca a fuego un símbolo quemado en la piel de un animal para mostrar título de propiedad (p. 531)

budget deficit/déficit del presupuesto la cantidad por la cual los gastos exceden las rentas, especialmente referente al gobierno (p. 919)

bureaucracy/burocracia sistema en el cual oficiales no elegidos administran las leyes y políticas (p. 337)

burgesses/burgueses representantes elegidos para una asamblea (p. 74)

C

cabinet/gabinete un grupo de consejeros del presidente (p. 258)

Californios/californios mexicanos que vivían en California (p. 374)

canal/*canal* vía de agua artificial (p. 315)

capital/capital dinero para inversión (pp. 306, 399)

capitalism/capitalismo un sistema económico basado en la propiedad particular y la empresa libre (p. 689)

caravel/carabela un buque pequeño y veloz con una proa ancha (p. 40)

carbon dating/datar con carbón un método científico usado para determinar la edad de un artefacto (p. 20)

carpetbaggers/*carpetbaggers* nombre dado a los blancos norteños que se trasladaban al Sur después de la guerra y apoyaban a los republicanos (p. 505)

cash crop/cultivo comercial cosecha cultivada para vender por dinero (pp. 106, 515)

casualty/baja un miliciano muerto, herido, o capturado (p. 469)

caucus/junta electoral una reunión llevada a cabo por un partido político para escoger el candidato a la presidencia de su partido o para decidir políticas (pp. 269, 337)

cede/ceder abandonar por tratado (p. 375)

censure/censurar expresar desaprobación formal de alguna acción (p. 792)

census/censo registro oficial de una población (p. 313)

charter/carta de privilegio un documento que otorga los derechos de organizar establecimientos en una área (p. 72)

charter colony/colonia a carta colonia establecida por un grupo de colonizadores a quienes se les había dado un documento formal permitiéndoles colonizar (p. 111)

checks and balances/inspecciones y balances el sistema en el cual cada rama de gobierno refrena las otras dos ramas para que ninguna rama vuelva a ser demasiado poderosa (pp. 207, 218)

circumnavigate/circunnavegar navegar alrededor del mundo (p. 49)

civil disobedience/desobediencia civil el rehusar obedecer las leyes que uno considera injustas como una manera pacífica para inisistir en cambios (p. 825)

civil service/servicio civil el cuerpo de trabajadores gubernamentales no elegidos (p. 605)

civil war/guerra civil conflicto entre grupos opuestos de ciudadanos del mismo país (p. 445)

civilization/civilización una cultura sumamente desarrollada, generalmente con religiones y leyes organizadas (p. 21)

classical/clásico relacionado a Grecia y Roma antigua (p. 38)

clipper ship/buque clíper un buque veloz con líneas delgadas, mástiles altos, y grandes velas cuadradas (p. 386)

closed shop/taller cerrado un lugar de trabajo en el cual, por acuerdo, el empresario contrata sólo a los miembros del sindicato (p. 782)

coeducation/coeducación la enseñanza conjunta de estudiantes hombres y mujeres (p. 426)

cold war/guerra fría una lucha sobre diferencias políticas entre naciones llevada a cabo por métodos fuera de guerra (p. 777)

collective bargaining/negociaciones colectivas discusión entre el empresario y los representantes sindicales de los trabajadores sobre salario, horas, y condiciones del taller (p. 567)

Columbian Exchange/Cambio Colombiano el cambio de productos, ideas, y personas entre Europa y las Américas (p. 55)

commission/comisión un grupo de personas dirigidas a hacer algún deber (p. 511)

committee of correspondence/comité de correspondencia una organización que usaba reuniones, cartas, y panfletos para propagar ideas políticas para las colonias (p. 139)

compromise/compromiso un acuerdo entre dos o más partidos en el cual cada partido abandona algo de lo que quiere (p. 201)

concurrent powers/poderes concurrentes poderes compartidos por los estados y el gobierno federal (p. 218)

Conestoga wagon/conestoga vehículo firme cubierto de lona blanca usado por los pioneros para moverse hacia el oeste (p. 281)

conquistador/conquistador explorador español en las Américas en los años 1500 (p. 50)

conservation/conservación la protección y preservación de recursos naturales (p. 618)

consolidation/consolidación la práctica de juntar compañías particulares en una (p. 551)

constituents/constituyentes personas representadas por miembros del Congreso (p. 221)

constitution/constitución un plan formal de gobierno (pp. 90, 189)

containment/contención la política o proceso de prohibir la expansión de un poder hostil (p. 775)

convoy/*convoy* un grupo que viaja con algo, tal como un buque, para protegerlo (p. 665)

cooperative/cooperativa una tienda donde los granjeros compraban productos uno al otro; una empresa poseída y operada por los que usan sus servicios (p. 545)

corporation/sociedad anónima un grupo autorizado por ley a montar una actividad pero con los derechos y deberes de una persona particular (p. 560)

corruption/corrupción acciones deshonestas o ilegales (p. 505)

cotton gin/despepitadora de algodón una máquina que sacaba las semillas de las fibras de algodón (pp. 306, 397)

counterculture/contracultura un movimiento social cuyos valores están en contra de los de la sociedad establecida (p. 859)

coup/*coup* derrocamiento súbito de un gobierno por un grupo pequeño (pp. 854, 912)

coureur de bois/*coureur de bois* cazador de pieles francés viviendo entre los Nativos Americanos (p. 62)

court-martial/consejo de guerra someter a juicio por un tribunal militar (p. 323)

credibility gap/resquicio de credibilidad falta de creencia; un término usado para describir la falta de confianza en los anuncios de la administración de Johnson referente a la Guerra en Viet Nam (p. 863)

credit/crédito una forma de préstamo; la capacidad de comprar productos basada en pagos futuros (p. 402)

culture/cultura la manera de vivir de un grupo de personas que tienen en común sus creencias y costumbres (p. 20)

customs duties/derechos de aduana impuestos sobre productos importados del extranjero (p. 279)

D

debtor/deudor persona o país que debe dinero (p. 92)

decree/decreto una orden o decisión dada por alguién de autoridad (p. 363)

default/incumplimiento de pago fallar en hacer una obligación, especialmente una financiera (p. 717)

deferment/aplazamiento un perdón, aprobado por la junta de reclutamiento, que permite que sea perdonado una persona del servicio militar por varias razones (p. 860)

deficit/déficit escasez que ocurre cuando los gastos son más que los ingresos (p. 888)

demilitarize/desmilitarizar quitar fuerzas armadas de una área (p. 322)

demilitarized zone/zona desmilitarizada una región donde no se permite ninguna fuerza militar ni armas (p. 788)

deport/deportar mandar afuera de un país a los extranjeros que se consideran peligrosos (pp. 271, 690)

depreciate/depreciar caer en valor (p. 194)

depression/depresión un período de poca actividad económica y de desempleo extenso (pp. 196, 349)

deregulation/deregulación el acto de quitar las limitaciones y reglamentos que el gobierno había puesto en el comercio (p. 906)

desert/desertar salir sin permiso (p. 172)

deserter/desertor soldado que huye de la batalla o la guerra (p. 167)

détente/*détente* una política que intenta relajar o aliviar tensiones entre naciones (p. 882)

dictator/dictador un líder que manda con plena autoridad, a menudo de una manera cruel o brutal (p. 741)

disarmament/desarme el quitar armas (pp. 322, 748)

discrimination/discriminación trato injusto de un grupo; trato parcial a causa de la raza, la religión, los antecedentes étnicos, o lugar de nacimiento de alguién (pp. 391, 622)

dissent/disensión desacuerdo con u oposición a una opinión (pp. 78, 672)

diversity/diversidad variedad o diferencia (p. 107)

dividend/dividendo cheque que se paga a los accionistas, por lo general trimestralmente, representa una porción de las ganancias de la corporación (p. 561)

dollar diplomacy/diplomacia del dólar una política de unir los intereses comerciales de un país con sus intereses diplomáticos al extranjero (p. 649)

domestic tranquility/tranquilidad doméstica mantener la paz dentro de la nación (p. 215)

domino theory/teoría dominó la creencia de que si una nación de Asia hubiera caído a los comunistas los países vecinos la habrían seguido (pp. 804, 853)

dove/paloma una persona que se opone a la guerra y las políticas de guerra, tal como una persona que se oponía a la Guerra en Viet Nam (p. 860)

draft/reclutamiento la selección de personas a servicio militar requirido (p. 478)

drought/sequía un largo período con poca lluvia (p. 28)

dry farming/agricultura seca una manera de cultivar tierra seca en la cual las semillas se plantan al fondo de la tierra donde hay un poco de humedad (p. 535)

due process of law/proceso justo de ley idea de que el gobierno debe de seguir los procesos establecidos por ley y garantizados por la Constitución (p. 226)

Dust Bowl/Cuenca de Polvo el nombre dado al área del sur de las Grandes Llanuras extensivamente dañada por las sequías y las tempestades del polvo durante los años 1930 (p. 729)

E

effigy/efigie una figura rellenada de trapos que representa una persona impopular (p. 135)

Electoral College/Colegio Electoral un grupo especial de votantes escogidos por sus legislaturas estatales para elegir al presidente y al vicepresidente (p. 206)
emancipate/emancipar liberar de la esclavitud (p. 473)
embargo/embargo una orden que prohibe el comercio con otro país (pp. 291, 884)
emigrant/emigrante una persona que sale de un país o una región para vivir en otras partes (p. 357)
emigrate/emigrar dejar su patria para vivir en otras partes (p. 576)
empresario/empresario una persona que arregló la colonización de tierra en Texas durante los años 1800 (p. 363)
encomienda/encomienda sistema de recompensar a los conquistadores con extensiones de tierra y el derecho de recaudar impuestos y exigir mano de obra a los Nativos Americanos que vivían en la tierra (p. 54)
Enlightenment/Siglo de las Luces movimiento durante los años 1700 que propagaba la idea de que el conocimiento, la razón, y la ciencia podrían mejorar la sociedad (p. 205)
entente/convenio un acuerdo entre naciones (p. 656)
entrenched/atrincherado que ocupa una posición fuerte defensiva (p. 482)
enumerated powers/poderes enumerados poderes que pertenecen solamente al gobierno federal (p. 217)
escalate/intensificar aumentar o extender (p. 855)
espionage/espionaje espiar (p. 673)
ethnic group/grupo étnico una minoría que habla un idioma diferente o que sigue costumbres diferentes que la mayoría de la gente de un país (p. 576)
evolution/evolución la teoría científica de que los seres humanos y otros seres vivos se han desarrollado tras largos períodos de tiempo (p. 710)
executive branch/rama ejecutiva la rama de gobierno, dirigida por el presidente, que administra las leyes y la política de una nación (pp. 206, 218)
executive order/orden ejecutiva una regla emitida por un jefe ejecutivo que lleva la fuerza de ley (p. 848)
exile/exilio una persona forzada a abandonar su patria (p. 848)
expansionism/expansionismo una política que demanda el extender las fronteras de una nación (p. 632)
expatriate/expatriado una persona que abandona su patria y decide vivir en otro país (p. 706)
export/exportación un producto vendido en el extranjero (p. 111)

F

factory system/sistema de fábrica sistema que junta en un solo lugar las categorías de fabricación para aumentar la eficiencia (p. 307)
famine/hambre una escasez extrema de comida (p. 392)
fascism/fascismo un sistema político, dirigido por un dictador, que demanda nacionalismo y racismo extremo, y ninguna tolerancia de oposición (p. 742)
favorite son/hijo favorito candidato que recibe el apoyo de su estado natal en lugar del partido nacional (p. 333)
federal debt/deuda federal la cantidad de dinero debido por el gobierno (p. 906)
federalism/federalismo el compartir el poder entre el gobierno federal y los gobiernos estatales (pp. 205, 217)
Federalists/federalistas apoyadores de la Constitución (p. 209)
federation/federación una forma de gobierno que une grupos diferentes (p. 32)
feminist/feminista una persona que aboga por o está activa en promulgar los derechos de la mujer (pp. 425, 838)
fixed costs/costos fijos gastos regulares tal como de vivienda o mantenimiento de equipo que se quedan casi iguales año tras año (p. 402)
flapper/*flapper* una jovencita de los años 1920 que retaba las costumbres de comportamiento e indumentaria (p. 703)
flexible response/respuesta flexible un plan que usaba unidades militares especiales para montar guerras al estilo guerrilla (p. 847)
forty-niners/*forty-niners* personas que fueron a California durante la fiebre del oro en 1849 (p. 376)
Fourteen Points/Catorce Puntos el plan de paz para suprimir la Primera Guerra Mundial y reestructurar los países de Europa, propuesto por Woodrow Wilson (p. 675)
free silver/plata libre la producción sin límite de monedas de plata (p. 546)
freedman/liberto una persona liberada de la esclavitud (p. 497)
frigate/fragata buque de guerra (p. 297)
front/frente una región donde la guerra activa se lleva a cabo (p. 666)
fugitive/fugitivo evadido que trata de huir (p. 439)
fundamentalist/fundamentalista una persona que cree en el sentido literal de escrituras religiosas y la obediencia estricta a leyes religiosas (p. 900)

G

genocide/genocidio el eradicar un grupo racial, político, o cultural (p. 758)
ghetto/*ghetto* una parte de una ciudad en la cual vive un grupo de minoría a causa de presión económica o social (p. 814)
ghost town/pueblo de espectros pueblo anterior de mineros que se dejó (p. 526)
Gilded Age/la Época Dorada el nombre asociado con América al final de los años 1800, referente a la gran riqueza de los tiempos y la terrible pobreza que estaba debajo (p. 586)
glasnost/*glasnost* una política soviética que permitía discusión más abierta de cuestiones políticas y sociales, y la promulgación más amplia de noticias e información (p. 908)

global warming/calentamiento mundial un aumento contínuo del promedio de temperaturas mundiales (p. 928)

grandfather clause/cláusula de abuelo una cláusula que permitía votar a las personas que no aprobaron el examen de alfabetismo si sus padres o sus abuelos habían votado antes de que empezó la Reconstrucción; una excepción a una ley basada en circunstancias preexistentes (p. 515)

grassroots/la gente común la sociedad al nivel local y popular afuera de los centros políticos y culturales (p. 918)

greenback/billete de dorso verde un billete de la moneda de EE.UU. expedido primeramente por el Norte durante la Guerra Civil (p. 480)

gross domestic product/producto interno bruto valor de todos los productos dentro de las fronteras nacionales de un país en un año (p. 927)

gross national product/producto nacional bruto valor total de todos los productos producidos en un año con la mano de obra y la propiedad suplidas por los residentes de un país, sin importar donde toma lugar la producción (p. 698)

guerrilla/guerrilla referente a ataques sorpresas o incursiones en lugar de la guerra organizada (p. 346)

guerrilla warfare/contienda a guerrilleros una técnica de tirar y darse a la huída usada en combates de guerra (pp. 179, 847)

H

habeas corpus/hábeas corpus una orden legal para una encuesta para determinar si una persona ha sido encarcelada legalmente (p. 478)

hawk/halcón una persona que aboga por la guerra y las políticas de guerra, tal como un apoyador de la Guerra en Viet Nam (p. 860)

hieroglyphics/jeroglíficos una forma antigua de escribir usando símbolos y dibujos para representar palabras, sonidos, y conceptos (p. 23)

Hispanic/hispánico una persona de o descendiente de la gente que vinieron de los países de Latinoamérica o de España (p. 839)

Holocaust/Holocausto el nombre dado a la matanza extensa de judíos y otros grupos por los nazis durante la Segunda Guerra Mundial (p. 759)

homestead/*homestead* adquirir una pieza de tierra pública de los EE.UU. por medio de vivir en ella y cultivarla (p. 534)

horizontal integration/integración horizontal la asociación de firmas competitivas en una sociedad anónima (p. 562)

hot line/línea de emergencia una línea telefónica directa para uso en caso de emergencia (p. 851)

human rights/derechos humanos derechos, tal como la libertad de encarcelamiento ilegal, tortura, y ejecución, considerados como pertenecientes a todas las personas (p. 898)

Hundred Days/Cien Días una sesión especial del Congreso llamada por Franklin D. Roosevelt para tratar los problemas de la Depresión (p. 723)

I

Ice Age/Época Glacial un período de temperaturas extremadamente frías cuando parte de la superficie del planeta estaba cubierta de extensiones masivas de hielo (p. 17)

impeach/residenciar acusación formal a un oficial público de mala conducta en la oficina (pp. 221, 502)

impeachment/residenciamiento el acusar a un oficial público de mala conducta en la oficina; si se le prueba culpable ante una corte designada, se le despide de la oficina (p. 890)

imperialism/imperialismo las acciones usadas por una nación para ejercer control político o económico sobre naciones más pequeñas y débiles (p. 632)

implied powers/poderes implícitos poderes no mencionados específicamente en la Constitución (pp. 220, 268)

import/importación un producto comprado de mercados extrajeros (p. 111)

impressment/requisición captura de marineros para forzarlos a servir en una marina extranjera (pp. 264, 290)

inauguration/inauguración la ceremonia en la cual el presidente presta el juramento de la oficina (p. 257)

incumbent/titular alguién que actualmente tiene un oficio o posición (p. 926)

indentured servant/sirviente contratado trabajador que consiente trabajar sin pago durante un cierto período de tiempo a cambio del pasaje a América (p. 88)

Industrial Revolution/Revolución Industrial el cambio de una sociedad agraria en una basada en la industria que empezó en la Gran Bretaña y se promulgó a los Estados Unidos alrededor del año 1800 (p. 306)

inflation/inflación aumento contínuo del precio de productos y servicios (pp. 174, 480, 780)

initiative/iniciativa el derecho de los ciudadanos de poner una medida o tema ante los votantes o la legislatura para aprobación (p. 607)

injunction/amonestación una orden judicial para terminar una acción, tal como una huelga (p. 569)

installment buying/compra a plazos un sistema de comprar productos en el cual los clientes prometen hacer pagos pequeños y regulares a través de un período de tiempo (p. 699)

integrate/integrar suprimir la segregación de las razas diferentes e introducir a membrecía igual y común en la sociedad (pp. 507, 822)

interchangeable parts/partes intercambiables piezas uniformes que pueden ser hechas en grandes cantidades para reemplazar otras piezas idénticas (p. 309)

internal improvements/mejoramientos internos proyectos federales, tal como canales y carreteras, para desarrollar el sistema de transportación de una nación (p. 319)

Internet/*Internet* enlaze a través de todo el mundo de redes de computadoras (p. 927)

internment camps/campos de internamiento los centros de detención adonde los americanos japoneses fueron trasladados y allí encerrados durante la Segunda Guerra Mundial (p. 754)

interstate/interestatal a través de fronteras estatales; que conecta o existe entre dos o más estados (p. 831)

iron curtain/cortina de hierro la barrera política y militar para los países de Europa Oriental controlados por los soviéticos que los aislaba después de la Segunda Guerra Mundial (p. 775)

ironclad/acorazado buque armado (p. 468)

Iroquois Confederacy/Confederación Iroquesa un grupo poderoso de Nativos Americanos de la región oriental de los Estados Unidos compuesto de cinco naciones: los pueblos mohawk, séneca, cayuga, onondaga y oneida (p. 117)

island hopping/saltar islas una estrategia usada durante la Segunda Guerra Mundial que demandó el atacar y capturar ciertas islas importantes para usarlas como bases para saltar por encima de otras (p. 763)

isolationism/aislacionismo una política nacional de evitar el involucramiento en asuntos mundiales (pp. 631, 695)

isthmus/istmo una faja estrecha de tierra que conecta dos áreas de tierra más grandes (p. 646)

J

joint occupation/ocupación en común la posesión y colonización de una área como esfuerzo compartido por dos o más países (p. 356)

joint-stock company/compañía por acciones una compañía en la cual los inversionistas compran acciones de la compañia a cambio de una porción de las ganancias en el futuro (p. 72)

judicial branch/rama judicial la rama de gobierno, incluyendo el sistema de tribunales federales, que interpreta las leyes de una nación (pp. 206, 218)

judicial review/repaso judicial el derecho del Tribunal Supremo para determinar si una ley viola la Constitución (pp. 220, 280)

K

kamikaze/kamikase durante la Segunda Guerra Mundial, un piloto suicida japonés cuya misión era chocar con el blanco (p. 763)

L

laissez-faire/*laissez-faire* la creencia de que el gobierno no debe de involucrarse en los asuntos comerciales y económicos del país (pp. 278, 350, 618)

land-grant college/colegio de tierras donadas originalmente, un colegio agrícola establecido como resultado del Decreto Morrill de 1862 que dio a los estados, grandes cantidades de tierras federales que podrían ser vendidas para recaudar dinero para la educación (p. 591)

landslide/victoria arrolladora una victoria abrumadora (p. 335)

League of Nations/Liga de Naciones una asociación de naciones para mantener la paz y resolver disputas internacionales propuesta en los Catorce Puntos de Wilson (p. 675)

lease/arrendar entregar propiedad en cambio de renta (p. 694)

legislative branch/rama legislativa la rama de gobierno que redacta las leyes de una nación (pp. 206, 218)

lend-lease/prestar-arrendar el decreto aprobado durante la Segunda Guerra Mundial que permitía a los Estados Unidos que vendiera, prestara, o arrendara armas u otros abastos de guerra a cualquier nación considerada "vital para la defensa de los Estados Unidos" (p. 748)

line of demarcation/línea de demarcación una línea imaginaria a lo largo del medio del Océano Atlántico desde el Polo Norte hasta el Polo Sur para dividir las Américas entre España y Portugal (p. 47)

line-item veto/veto de partida el poder que permite al presidente que cancele partidas particulares de gastos de un presupuesto o proyecto de ley (p. 921)

literacy/alfabetismo la capacidad de leer y escribir (p. 114)

literacy test/examen de alfabetismo un método usado para prohibir a los afroamericanos a votar por requerir a presuntos votantes que pudieran leer y escribir a niveles especificados (p. 515)

lock/esclusa en un canal un recinto con puertas en cada extremo y usado para levantar y bajar los buques mientras pasan de un nivel al otro (p. 316)

lode/filón una faja o venero de mena intercalada entre estratos de piedra (p. 525)

log cabin campaign/campaña de cabaña rústica el nombre dado a la campaña para la presidencia de William Henry Harrison en 1840, debido al uso de una cabaña rústica de troncos como su símbolo por los whigs (p. 350)

Loyalists/lealistas colonizadores americanos que quedaron leales a la Bretaña y se opusieron a la guerra para la independencia (pp. 146, 164)

lynching/linchamiento matar a una persona a través de la acción ilegal de una muchedumbre airada (p. 516)

M

maize/maíz una forma antigua de elote cultivado por los Nativos Americanos (p. 20)

majority/mayoría más de la mitad (p. 334)

Manifest Destiny/Destino Manifiesto la idea popular en los Estados Unidos durante los años 1800 de que el país debería de extender sus fronteras hasta el Pacífico (p. 359)

manumission/manumisión el liberar a unas personas esclavizadas (p. 198)

martial law/ley marcial ley administrada por las autoridades civiles en una situación de emergencia (p. 869)

martyr/mártir una persona que sacrifica su vida por un principio o una causa (p. 452)

mass media/difusoras de información formas de comunicación que alcanzan a grandes números de personas, tal como periódicos, radio, y televisión (p. 703)

mass production/fabricación en serie la producción de grandes cantidades de productos usando máquinas y muchas veces una línea de montaje (p. 559)

materialism/materialismo atribuir demasiada importancia a las posesiones y comodidades físicas (p. 815)

Mayflower Compact/Convenio del Mayflower un documento formal escrito en 1620 que proporcionó leyes para el mantimiento del orden público en la colonia de Plymouth (p. 79)

Medicaid/*Medicaid* un programa social que da dinero a los estados para ayudar a las personas que no pueden pagar la factura del hospital (p. 829)

Medicare/*Medicare* un programa social que ayuda en pagar el esmero médico para los ancianos (p. 829)

mercantilism/mercantilismo idea de que el poder de una nación dependía de ampliar su comercio y aumentar sus reservas de oro (pp. 59, 110)

mercenary/mercenario soldado remunerado para servir en el ejército de un país extranjero (p. 164)

merger/fusión de empresas la asociación de dos o más negocios en uno (p. 564)

MIAs/*MIAs* soldados clasificados como extraviados en la guerra, inglés *missing in action* (p. 871)

migrant worker/obrero migrante una persona que se mueve de un lugar a otro para buscar trabajo en la cosecha de frutas y vegetales (p. 730)

migration/migración el movimiento de un gran número de personas hacia una nueva patria (p. 18)

militarism/militarismo un desarrollo de poder militar dentro de un país (p. 656)

militia/milicia un grupo de civiles entrenados para luchar durante emergencias (pp. 118, 143)

minutemen/*minutemen* compañías de soldados civiles que se jactaban de que podrían estar listos para tomar armas en sólo un minuto (p. 143)

mission/misión una comunidad religiosa (pp. 54, 96)

mobilization/mobilización juntar recursos y preparar para la guerra (pp. 670, 750)

moderate/moderado opuesto a gran cambio social o ideas políticas extremas (p. 798)

monopoly/monopolio control total de una industria por una persona o una compañía (p. 562)

Morse code/código Morse un sistema para transmitir mensajes que usa una serie de puntos y rayas para representar las letras del abecedario, los números, y la puntuación (p. 388)

mosque/mezquita una casa de alabanza musulmana (p. 41)

mountain man/hombre montañés colonizador que vivía en el monte, como en las Montañas Rocosas (p. 356)

muckraker/expositor de corrupción periodista que descubre abusos y corrupción en una sociedad (p. 606)

mudslinging/detractar intentar arruinar la reputación de un adversario con insultos (p. 335)

N

national debt/deuda nacional la cantidad de dinero que un gobierno debe a otros gobiernos o a su pueblo (p. 259)

National Grange/Granja Nacional la primera organización de granjeros de los Estados Unidos (p. 545)

nationalism/nacionalismo lealtad a una nación y promoción de sus intereses sobre todos los demás (pp. 294, 655)

nativism/nativismo la creencia de que aquellos que nacieron en un país son mejores que los inmigrantes (p. 709)

nativist/nativista una persona que favorece a los nacidos en su patria y se opone a los inmigrantes (p. 393)

neutral/neutral que no toma partido a ninguna persona ni a ningún país en un conflicto (p. 163)

neutral rights/derechos neutrales el derecho para navegar en el mar sin tomar partido en una guerra (p. 290)

neutrality/neutralidad una posición de no tomar partido en un conflicto (p. 264)

New Deal/Nuevo Trato el nombre dado a las leyes nuevas con la meta de aliviar la Depresión que fueron estatuidas por el Congreso durante los Cien Días y los meses siguientes (p. 723)

nomadic/nómada que se mueve de un lugar a otro sin hogar permanente (p. 538)

nomads/nómadas personas que se mueven de lugar a lugar, generalmente en busca de comida o de tierras para pastar (p. 18)

nominating convention/convención nominadora sistema en el cual los diputados estatales escogieron al candidato para la presidencia de su partido (p. 337)

nonimportation/no importación un acuerdo de no importar ni usar ciertos productos (p. 135)

normal school/escuela normal una escuela con programa de dos años para entrenar a los graduados de preparatoria para ser maestros (p. 413)

Northwest Passage/Paso Noroeste ruta acuática para Asia por América del Norte buscada por exploradores europeos (p. 59)

nullify/anular cancelar o hacer sin efecto (pp. 272, 338)

O

offensive/ofensiva la posición de atacar o el mismo ataque (p. 464)

on margin/al margen comprar acciones por pagar sólo una fracción del precio del valor y el resto del préstamo recibido a un corredor (p. 715)

Open Door policy/política de Puerta Abierta una política que permitía a cada nación extranjera en China que comerciara libremente en las esferas de influencia de las otras naciones (p. 638)

open range/terreno abierto tierra sin cercas ni dividida en solares (p. 531)
ordinance/ordenanza una ley o regulación (p. 192)
ore/mena un mineral minado por la sustancia valorable que contiene, tal como plata (p. 525)
override/vencer rechazar o derrotar, como un proyecto de ley propuesto en el Congreso (p. 500)
overseer/capataz persona que supervisa una operación grande o a sus trabajadores (pp. 108, 403)
ozone/ozono el estrato de gas compuesto de una forma de oxígeno que protege la tierra y a su gente de los rayos del sol que causan el cáncer (p. 928)

P

pacifist/pacifista persona opuesta al uso de guerra o violencia para arreglar disputas (pp. 87, 673)
partisan/partidario a favor de una parte de un asunto (p. 267)
patent/patente un documento que da al inventor el derecho exclusivo legal de una invención durante un período de tiempo (p. 307)
Patriots/patriotas colonizadores americanos que estaban determinados para luchar en contra de los británicos hasta que se ganara la independencia americana (pp. 146, 163)
patronage/patronazgo otro nombre del sistema de recompensa política en el cual puestos y favores gubernamentales se dan a aliados políticos y a amigos (p. 604)
patroon/*patroon* terrateniente de las colonias holandesas que gobernaba áreas grandes de tierra como un rey (p. 85)
peaceful coexistence/coexistencia pacífica acuerdo entre países opuestos de que competirán uno con el otro pero evitarán la guerra (p. 805)
pension/pensión una cantidad pagada a una persona, generalmente después de la jubilación (p. 734)
per capita income/ingresos por persona el promedio de ingresos de cada persona de la nación (p. 808)
perestroika/*perestroika* una política de gobierno y economía empezada por Gorbachev en la Unión Soviética a mediados de los años 1980 (p. 909)
perjury/perjurio el mentir después de haber jurado decir la verdad (p. 790)
persecute/perseguir tratar cruelmente a alguién a causa de sus creencias o prácticas (p. 78)
petition/petición una solicitud formal (pp. 149, 192)
philanthropy/filantropía acciones caritativas o donaciones de dinero para beneficiar a la comunidad (p. 563)
pilgrimage/peregrinación un viaje a un sitio sagrado (p. 41)
Pilgrims/peregrinos separatistas que viajaron a las colonias durante los años 1600 por un propósito religioso (p. 79)
plantation/plantación una finca grande manejada por el dueño o un gerente y cultivada por trabajadores que vivían allí (p. 55)
plurality/pluralidad el mayor número de individuos (p. 334)
political machine/máquina política una organización aliada con un partido político que muchas veces controlaba el gobierno local (p. 603)
poll tax/impuesto de capitación un impuesto de una cantidad fija por cada persona que tenía que ser pagada antes de que pudiera votar la persona (p. 515)
pool/consorcio un grupo compartiendo de una actividad, por ejemplo, entre barones ferrocarrileros que hacían acuerdos secretos y fijaban tipos entre ellos mismos (p. 554)
popular sovereignty/soberanía popular la teoría política de que el gobierno está sujeto a la voluntad del pueblo (p. 216); antes de la Guerra Civil, la idea de que la gente que vivía en un territorio tenía el derecho de decidir por votar si allí sería permitida la esclavitud (p. 443)
Populist Party/Partido Populista partido político de los EE.UU. formado en 1892 que representaba principalmente a los granjeros, que favorecía la acuñación libre de plata y el control gubernamental de ferrocarriles y otros monopolios (p. 546)
poverty line/línea de pobreza el nivel de ingresos personales o familiares clasificado de pobre según la norma del gobierno (p. 828)
preamble/preámbulo la introducción de un documento formal, especialmente la Constitución (pp. 152, 215)
precedent/precedente una tradición (p. 257)
prejudice/prejuicio una opinión injusta no basada en los hechos (p. 391)
presidio/presidio un fuerte español en las Américas construido para proteger las colonias misioneras (p. 54)
primary/elección preliminar una elección en la cual los votantes escogen al candidato de su partido (p. 607)
privateer/buque corsario buque armado privado (pp. 177, 297)
productivity/productividad la cantidad de trabajo que hace cada trabajador (pp. 698, 807)
prohibition/prohibición leyes que prohiben el hacer o vender de bebidas alcohólicas (p. 613)
Prohibition/Prohibición entredicho contra la fabricación, transportación, y venta de bebidas alcohólicas por todo los Estados Unidos (p. 708)
propaganda/propaganda ideas o información diseñadas para influenciar la opinión (pp. 139, 661)
proportional/proporcional que son iguales o que corresponden (p. 200)
proprietary colony/colonia propietaria colonia dirigida por personas o grupos a quienes se les había otorgado la tierra (pp. 85, 112)
protectorate/protectorado un país que es técnicamente independiente, pero que en realidad está bajo el control de otro país (p. 643)
public works/proyectos públicos proyectos tal como carreteras, parques, y bibliotecas construidos con fondos públicos para el uso del público (p. 718)

pueblo/pueblo una casa o una comunidad de casas construidas por Nativos Americanos (pp. 28, 54)
Puritans/puritanos protestantes que, durante los años 1600, querían reformar la Iglesia anglicana (p. 78)

Q

quota system/sistema de cuotas un arreglo que pone un límite en el número de inmigrantes de cada país (p. 709)

R

radical/radical extremo (p. 496); referente a alguién que favorece hacer cambios extremos al gobierno o a la sociedad, como la Nueva Izquierda (p. 859)
ragtime/*ragtime* una clase de música con un ritmo fuerte y una melodía animada con notas acentuadas que era popular al principio del siglo XX (p. 594)
ranchero/ranchero dueño de rancho mexicano (p. 370)
rancho/rancho propiedades grandísimas para producir ganado establecidas por colonizadores mexicanos en California (p. 370)
ratify/ratificar dar aprobación oficial para (pp. 184, 209, 474)
ration/racionar distribuir los artículos escasos sobre una base limitada (p. 751)
realism/realismo una perspectiva de literatura, arte, y teatro que representa las cosas tal como son (p. 592)
rebate/rebaja descuento o devolución de una porción de un pago (p. 553)
Rebel/rebelde soldado confederado, así nombrado a causa de su oposición al gobierno establecido (p. 465)
recall/elección de revocación el derecho que permite a los votantes que despidan de la oficina a los oficiales elegidos que son inadecuados (p. 607)
recession/recesión un deslizamiento en actividades comerciales (p. 698)
reconciliation/reconciliación arreglar por acuerdo o por reunirse de nuevo (p. 509)
Reconstruction/Reconstrucción la reorganización y la reconstrucción de los anteriores estados confederados después de la Guerra Civil (p. 495)
recruit/reclutar enlistar a soldados para el ejército (p. 165)
referendum/referéndum la práctica de permitir a los votantes que acepten o rechazen medidas propuestas por la legislatura (p. 607)
regionalism/regionalismo en arte o literatura, la práctica de enfocar en una región en particular del país (p. 592)
relief/ayuda social ayuda para los pobres; asistencia pública (p. 717)
relocate/reubicar forzar a una persona o a un grupo de personas a trasladarse (p. 342)
Renaissance/Renacimiento un período de creatividad intelectual y artística, alrededor de los años 1300–1600 (p. 38)
rendezvous/*rendezvous* una reunión (p. 356)
reparations/reparaciones pago por el país que pierde una guerra al país que gana por los daños causados por la guerra (p. 676)
repeal/revocar cancelar un decreto o ley (p. 135)
republic/república un gobierno en el cual ciudadanos gobiernan por medio de representantes elegidos (p. 190)
reservation/reservación una área de tierra pública apartada para los Nativos Americanos (p. 540)
reserved powers/poderes reservados poderes retenidos por los estados (p. 217)
resolution/resolución una expresión formal de opinión (p. 135)
revenue/ingresos entrada de dinero (p. 134)
revenue sharing/ingreso compartido dinero recaudado de impuestos federales y dado a los estados para uso a los niveles estatales y locales (p. 887)
revival/renacimiento religioso una serie de reuniones dirigidas por un predicador para animar emociones religiosas (p. 411)

S

sabotage/sabotaje acción secreta por agentes del enemigo o los que compadecen para dañar el esfuerzo de guerra de una nación (p. 673)
scalawags/*scalawags* nombre dado por los confederados anteriores a los blancos sureños que apoyaban la Reconstrucción republicana del Sur (p. 505)
search-and-destroy mission/misión de buscar y destruir una estrategia usada en Viet Nam en la cual las fuerzas americanas buscarían las unidades norteviet-nameses y vietconenses para destruirlas (p. 856)
secede/separarse abandonar o retirar (pp. 285, 338, 439)
secession/secesión retiro de la Unión (p. 454)
Second New Deal/Segundo Nuevo Trato un nuevo juego de programas y reformas lanzados por Franklin D. Roosevelt en 1935 (p. 734)
sectionalism/regionalismo lealtad a una región (pp. 319, 437)
sedition/sedición actividades con el propósito de debilitar un gobierno establecido (p. 271)
segregation/segregación la separación o aislamiento de una raza, una clase, o un grupo (pp. 516, 821)
Separatists/separatistas protestantes que, durante los años 1600, querían dejar la Iglesia anglicana para fundar sus propias iglesias (p. 78)
settlement house/casa de beneficencia institución colocada en una vecindad pobre que proveía numerosos servicios a la comunidad tal como cuidado médico, cuidado de niños, bibliotecas, y clases de inglés (p. 588)
sharecropping/aparcería sistema de agricultura en el cual un granjero labra la tierra para un dueño que provee equipo y semillas y recibe una porción de la cosecha (p. 507)

shareholder/accionista una persona que invierte en una sociedad anónima por comprar acciones y que es un dueño parcial (p. 560)
shuttle diplomacy/diplomacia de lanzadera negociaciones entre naciones llevada a cabo por una persona que viaja entre ellas yendo y viniendo (p. 885)
silent majority/mayoría callada la frase usada por Nixon para describir la mayoría de los americanos, los que no protestaban ni demostraban (p. 865)
sit-in/plantón el acto de ocupar asientos o de sentarse en el suelo de un establecimiento como una forma de protesta organizada (p. 830)
slave code/código de esclavos las leyes aprobadas en los estados sureños que controlaban y restringían a la gente esclavizada (p. 405)
slum/barrio bajo vecindad pobre, superpoblada, y de de vecindades ruinosas (p. 585)
smuggling/contrabandear cambiar ilegalmente con otras naciones (p. 111)
Social Security Act/Decreto de Seguro Social una ley que exige a los empleados y a los empresarios que paguen un impuesto; el dinero provee una pensión mensual para personas jubiladas (p. 734)
socialist/socialista una persona que cree que las industrias deben de ser poseídas por el público y manejadas por el gobierno en lugar de personas particulares (p. 672)
sodbuster/rompedor de césped nombre dado al granjero de las Llanuras (p. 535)
speculator/especulador persona que arriesga dinero para hacer una ganancia grande (pp. 124, 260)
sphere of influence/esfera de influencia sección de un país donde una nación extranjera tiene derechos y poderes especiales (p. 638)
spiritual/espiritual una canción popular religiosa afroamericana (p. 405)
spoils system/sistema de despojos la práctica de dar puestos gubernamentales a los partidarios; reemplazar a los empleados del gobierno con los partidarios del candidato victorioso (p. 337)
square deal/trato justo la promesa de Theodore Roosevelt para el trato justo e igual para todos (p. 618)
stagflation/stagflación una combinación del alza de precios y una economía estancada con una tasa alta de desempleo (p. 887)
stalemate/estancamiento una situación durante un conflicto cuando la acción se para debido a que ambos partidos son igualmente poderosos y ningún de los dos lo abandonará (p. 787)
standard gauge/medida normal la anchura uniforme de 4 pies, 8.5 pulgadas de las vías ferroviarias, adoptada durante los años 1880 (p. 552)
standard of living/norma de vivir una medida de calidad comprensiva de vida y riqueza de la gente; el mínimo de las necesidades y lujos a los cuales un grupo está acostumbrado (p. 808)
states' rights/derechos estatales derechos y poderes independientes del gobierno federal que son reservados a los estados por la Constitución (pp. 272, 338, 455)
steerage/entrepuente los cuarteles apretados de las cubiertas bajas de un barco para los pasajeros que pagan los pasajes más bajos (p. 577)
stock/acciones valores de propiedad de comercio que vende una compañía que llevan muchas veces el poder de votar (p. 560)
stock exchange/mercado de acciones un lugar donde acciones de sociedades anónimas se venden y se compran a través de un sistema organizado (p. 715)
strait/estrecho un paso angosto que conecta dos extensiones más grandes de agua (p. 49)
strike/huelga un paro de trabajo por los trabajadores para forzar al empresario a satisfacer demandas (p. 391)
strikebreaker/esquirol una persona contratada para reemplazar a un huelguista para suprimir una huelga (p. 568)
subsidy/subsidio donación de dinero del gobierno a una persona o una compañía para una acción con el propósito de beneficiar al público (pp. 527, 724)
subsistence farming/agricultura para subsistencia labranza que produce solamente la comida que se necesita para dar de comer a la familia del trabajador (p. 104)
suburbs/suburbios áreas residenciales que brotaron cerca de o alrededor de ciudades como resultado de mejoramientos de transportación (p. 586)
subversion/subversión un esfuerzo para derrocar un gobierno montado por personas trabajando secretamente desde adentro (p. 789)
suffrage/sufragio el derecho al voto (pp. 336, 426)
suffragist/sufragista un hombre o mujer que luchaba para el derecho al voto de la mujer (p. 610)
summit/conferencia cumbre una reunión de altos jefes de gobierno (p. 805)
surplus/superávit exceso; la cantidad que sobra después de pagar los gastos necesarios (p. 798)
sweatshop/fábrica-opresora un taller o fábrica donde se explota a los trabajadores, trabajándolos muchas horas por poco pago y en condiciones malsanas (pp. 566, 578)

T

tariff/tarifa impuesto sobre productos importados o exportados (pp. 261, 338)
technology/tecnología el uso de conocimientos científicos para propósitos prácticos (pp. 39, 306)
Tejano/tejano un mexicano que reclama Texas como su patria (p. 362)
telegraph/telégrafo un aparato o sistema que usa señales eléctricas para transmitir mensajes a códigos a través de alambres (p. 388)
temperance/templanza el uso de poca o de ninguna bebida alcohólica (p. 412)

tenant farmer/granjero arrendatario un granjero que labra la tierra de otro dueño y paga renta ya sea con la cosecha o al contado (pp. 95, 401)

tenement/casa de vecindad un edificio en el cual varias familias alquilan cuartos o apartamentos, a menudo con pocas medidas sanitarias o seguridad (p. 585)

terrace/terraza una parcela de tierra elevada y allanada para fomentar la agricultura (p. 25)

theocracy/teocracia una forma de gobierno en la cual la sociedad está gobernada por líderes religiosos (p. 22)

Tidewater/Orilla del Mar una región de llanuras planas y bajas alrededor de la costa del mar (p. 107)

toleration/tolerancia el aceptar creencias diferentes (p. 81)

total war/guerra total la guerra en todo aspecto de la vida del enemigo (p. 487)

totalitarian/totalitario un sistema político en el cual el gobierno suprime toda oposición y controla muchos aspectos de la vida de la gente (p. 742)

trade deficit/déficit de cambio la situación cuando el valor de las importaciones de un país excede el valor de las exportaciones (p. 898)

trade union/gremio una organización de artesanos con el mismo oficio o destreza (pp. 391, 567)

Transcendentalist/transcendentalista uno de un grupo de escritores de Nueva Inglaterra que acentuaban la relación entre los seres humanos y la naturaleza, asuntos espirituales sobre asuntos materiales, y la importancia de la conciencia particular (p. 414)

transcontinental/*transcontinental* que se extiende a través del continente (p. 527)

triangular trade/trato triangular una ruta de comercio para cambiar productos entre las Antillas, las colonias americanas, y África del Oeste (p. 105)

tribute/tributo dinero pagado para protección (pp. 51, 289)

trust/cártel una combinación de firmas o sociedades anónimas formada por un acuerdo legal, especialmente para reducir la competición (pp. 562, 605)

trustbuster/rompedor de cárteles alguién que divide un cártel en compañías más pequeñas (p. 617)

turnpike/autopista una carretera que uno debe de pagar para usar; el dinero se usa para pagar el costo de la carretera (p. 314)

U

unconstitutional/anticonstitucional no de acuerdo ni consistente con la Constitución (p. 260)

underemployment/empleo insuficiente la condición cuando la gente trabaja en puestos para los cuales están sobrecalificados o que no utilizan sus destrezas (p. 894)

Underground Railroad/Ferrocarril Subterráneo un sistema que ayudó a los afroamericanos esclavizados a seguir una red de rutas de escape afuera del Sur hacia la libertad del Norte (p. 420)

unemployment insurance/seguro de desempleo pagos por el gobierno durante un cierto período limitado de tiempo a las personas que han perdido sus trabajos (p. 734)

utopia/utopía una comunidad basada en una visión de la sociedad perfecta buscada por los reformistas (p. 411)

V

vaquero/vaquero trabajador ranchero hispánico (p. 532)

vaudeville/teatro de variedades entretenimiento compuesto de varios actos, tal como baile, canción, comedia, y espectáculos de mágica (p. 595)

vertical integration/integración vertical la asociación de compañías que abastecen con equipo y servicios necesarios para una industria particular (p. 563)

veto/vetar rechazar un proyecto de ley y prevenir que vuelva a ser una ley (p. 349)

viceroy/virrey persona que gobierna un país o una provincia como el representante del monarca (p. 54)

Vietcong/*Vietcong* los soldados guerrillistas de la facción comunista en Viet Nam, también conocidos por el Frente Nacional para Liberación (p. 853)

Vietnamization/vietnamización la política de Nixon que demandó que Viet Nam del Sur tomara un papel más activo en luchar la guerra y que los americanos se involucraran menos (p. 868)

vigilantes/vigilantes gente que toman la ley en sus propias manos (pp. 377, 526)

W

War Hawks/halcones de guerra republicanos durante la presidencia de Madison que insistían en la guerra con la Bretaña (p. 294)

warrant/citación una orden oficial (p. 226)

work relief/ayuda de trabajo programas que dieron trabajos gubernamentales a los pobres (p. 724)

writ of assistance/escrito de asistencia documento legal que permitía a los oficiales que exploraran las casas y bodegas en busca de productos que tal vez pudieran ser de contrabandeado (p. 134)

XYZ

Yankee/yanqui soldado de la Unión (p. 465)

yellow journalism/periodismo amarillista escritura que exageraba acontecimientos sensacionales, dramáticos, y repulsivos para atraer a los lectores, citando historias que fueron populares durante los fines de los años 1800 (p. 592); una clase de reportaje sensacional, prejuzgado, y a menudo falso (p. 641)

yeoman/terrateniente menor dueño sureño de una granja pequeña que no tenía esclavos (p. 401)

Credits and Acknowledgments

Acknowledgments

741 Excerpt from *Mein Kampf* by Adolf Hitler, translated by Ralph Manheim. Copyright © 1943, renewed 1971 by Houghton Mifflin Co. Reprinted by permission of Houghton Mifflin Co. All rights reserved.
753 From *Collected Poems* by Langston Hughes. Copyright © 1944 by the Estate of Langston Hughes. Reprinted by permission of Alfred A. Knopf Inc.
832, A20 Reprinted by arrangement with the Heirs to the Estate of Martin Luther King, Jr., c/o Writers House, Inc. as agent for the proprietor. Copyright © 1963 by Martin Luther King, Jr., copyright renewed 1991 by Coretta Scott King.
859 From *Blowin' in the Wind* by Bob Dylan. Copyright © 1962 by Warner Bros. Music, copyright renewed 1990 by Special Rider Music. All rights reserved. International copyright secured. Reprinted by permission.

Photo Credits

Cover, title page, back cover Jim Barber Studio; **iii** Collection of David J. & Janice L. Frent; **iv** Chicago Historical Society; **v** Copyright, Virginia Historical Society, 1996, All rights reserved; **vi** The Historical Society of Pennsylvania; **vii** Kari Haavisto; **viii** (t)Museum of Ethnology (b)Library of Congress; **ix** (t)Musee de L'Homme. Photo M. Delaplanche, (b)Chicago Historical Society; **x** (t)Minute Man National Historical Park, (bl)Concord Museum, Concord, MA., (br)Smithsonian Institution; **xi** (l)Indiana Historical Society, (r)Smithsonian Institution; **xii** (t)Picture Research Consultants, Inc., (b)Collection of Nancy Gewirz, Antique Textile Resource; **xvi** (t)Stanford University Museum of Art, (c)Collection of David J. and Janice L. Frent, (b)North Carolina Museum of Art, Raleigh. Purchased with funds from the State of North Carolina; **xvii** (t)Jerry Jacka/courtesy Arizona State Museum, University of Arizona, (bl)Mercantile Money Museum, (br)collection of Michael Barson; **xviii** Larry Kunkel/FPG; **Geo. Handbook title page** © James Randklev/AllStock; **2** (t)Robert W. Madden/ National Geographic Society, (b)Rich Buzzelli/Tom Stack & Assoc.; **4** (t)David M. Dennis, (b)Walter Meayers Edwards/National Geographic Society; **6** (l)Eliot Cohn, (r)Johnny Johnson; **9** Scala/Art Resource; **12** (binocular, compass)H. Armstrong Roberts, (Viking head)University Museum of National Antiquities Oslo, Norway, photo Erik Irgens Johnsen; **12-13** courtesy, John Carter Brown Library, Brown University; **13** Musee de L'Homme, Paris, photo M. Delaplanche; **15** Private Collection; **16** Doug Stern & Enrico Ferorelli/National Geographic Image Collection; **17** file photo; **21** Boltin Picture Library; **22** (l) © Richard Alexander Cooke III, (r)David Hiser/Tony Stone Images; **23** (l)Michel Zabé/Museo Templo Major, (r)Museum of Ethnology; **25** (l)Ed Simpson/Tony Stone Images, (r)Heye Foundation, National Museum of American Indian/ Smithsonian Institution; **27** Jerry Jacka/courtesy, Arizona State Museum, Arizona University; **28** (l,c)David Muench, (r) © Richard Alexander Cooke III; **29** Cahokia Mounds State Historic Site/Painting by L.K. Townsend; **30** courtesy Morning Star Gallery, Santa Fe, NM. photo by Addison Doty; **33** © Richard Alexander Cooke III; **36** U.S. Architect of the Capitol, Washington, DC; **37** Brown Brothers; **38** Bodleian Library, Oxford; **39** National Maritime Museum, London; **41** (l)Giraudon/Art Resource, NY, (r)National Museum of African Art/photo by Jeffrey Ploskonka; **43** Peabody Essex Museum, Salem, MA; **46** (l)Giraudon/Art Resource, NY, (r)Archivio Fotografico del Museo Preistorico Etnografico L. Pigorini, Roma; **49** Maritime Museum, Seville/Artephot/Oronoz; **50** courtesy of The Oakland Museum of California; **51** (tl, r,bl)Michel Zabé, (c)e.t. archive; **54** Museo de Historia, Chapultepec, photo by Bob Schalkwijk; **56** (t)Brian Lanker, (b)Bill Ballenberg; **56-57** Kevin Chadwick; **57** Lowell Georgia; **58** SuperStock; **59** "Catherine Tekakwitha" by Father Claude Chauchetiere, photo by Jacques Turcot, Mission Saint-François-Xavier, Caughnawaga, Quebec.; **61** courtesy of The Oakland Museum of California; **66** (t)Dedham Historical Society, (c)Colonial Williamsburg Foundation, (b)Peabody Museum, Harvard University. Photo by Hillel Burger; **66-67** Private Collection; **67** Plimoth Plantation; **68** Royal Albert Memorial Museum, Exeter, England; **69** National Maritime Museum, London; **70** Child's Gallery; **71** Jamestown-Yorktown Foundation; **72** Princeton University Libraries; **73** National Portrait Gallery, Smithsonian Institution/Art Resource, NY; **74** Colonial National Historic Park; **75** (l)Collection of the New-York Historical Society, (r)Bill Pugliano/Black Star; **76** (t)Ashmolean Museum, (b)Farrell Grehan; **76-77** Kevin Chadwick; **77** National Portrait Gallery, Smithsonian Institution/Art Resource, NY; **78** Plimoth Plantation; **80** courtesy of the Pilgrim Society, Plymouth, Massachusetts; **82** courtesy of the Haffenreffer Museum of Anthropology, Brown University; **84** courtesy, Winterthur Museum; **85** Collection of the New-York Historical Society; **86** courtesy of the Museum of American Art of the Pennsylvania Academy of the Fine Arts, Philadelphia. Gift of Mrs. Sarah Harrison (The Joseph Harrison, Jr. Collection); **88** British Museum; **90** The Association for the Preservation of Virginia Antiquities, Bacon's Castle. Library of Virginia; **92** (l, rb, rt)courtesy of the Rice Museum from VOICES OF TRIUMPH: PERSEVERANCE photo by Craig Moran © 1993 Time-Life Books, Inc., (c)Gibbes Museum of Art; **93** Colonial Williamsburg Foundation; **94** National Archives of Canada; **95** Paul Harris Art Selections, Scotland/photo courtesy of Joslyn Art Museum; **96** Historical Picture Collection/Stock Montage, Inc.; **100** Library of Congress; **101** Doug Martin; **102** Old John Street United Methodist Church; **103** Colonial Williamsburg Foundation; **104** courtesy, Museum of Fine Arts, Boston; **105** (l)Peabody Essex Museum, Salem, MA, (r)file photo; **107** (l)Botany Library, Harvard University, (r)Peabody Essex Museum, Salem, MA. Photo by Mark Sexton; **108** Colonial Williamsburg Foundation; **109** courtesy, American Antiquarian Society; **110** Yale University Art Gallery; **111** (l,tr,br)courtesy of Historic Deerfield, Inc. Photography by Amanda Merullo, (c)Addison Gallery; **113** Yale University Art Gallery; **115** Collection of the Blue Ridge Institute & Museums/Ferrum College; **116** courtesy, American Antiquarian Society; **118** (l)Washington and Lee University, (tr,br)Chicago Historical Society; **119** Library of Congress; **120** Musee de L'Homme. Photo by M. Delaplanche ; **121** State Historical Society of Wisconsin Museum Collection; **124** Culver Pictures; **128** (t)David A. Schorsch, NYC, (b)Reza Estakhrian/Tony Stone Images; **128-129** The Metropolitan Museum of Art, Gift of John S. Kennedy, 1897. (97.34); **129** Peabody Essex Museum, Salem, MA; **130** Corbis-Bettmann; **131** Library of Congress; **132** Lafayette College Art Collection, Easton, PA; **133** Crown copyright. Historic Royal Palaces. Photo: David Chalmers; **135** Massachusetts Historical Society; **136** "Patrick Henry Before the Virginia House of Burgesses" (1851) by Peter F. Rothermel.; The Patrick Henry National Memorial, Brookneal, VA; **137** Library of Congress; **138** file photo; **140** (l)DAR Museum on loan from Boston Tea Party Chapter, (r)courtesy, American Antiquarian Society; **141** The Royal Collection © Her Majesty Queen Elizabeth II; **142** (l)Lexington Historical Society, (r)Fort Ticonderoga Museum; **145** Photograph courtesy of the Concord Museum, Concord, MA; **146** Chicago Historical Society; **148** Smithsonian Institution; **150** Virginia Historical Society; **151** Massachusetts Historical Society; **154** (t)Yale University Art Gallery, (c)John Lewis Stage, (b)The Thomas Gilcrease Institute of American History and Art, Tulsa, Oklahoma; **154-155** Kevin Chadwick; **156** Raza Estakhrian/Tony Stone Images; **157** (l)Architect of the Capitol, Washington, DC, (r)The National Gallery of Art, Washington, DC; **162** Library of Congress; **163** West Point Museum, U.S. Military Academy, West Point, NY; **164** Library of Congress; **165** Corbis-Bettmann; **167** Collection of A. A. McBurney; **168** Collection of the New-York Historical Society; **171** Chicago Historical Society; **172** The Valley Forge Historical Society; **174** Eric P. Newman, Numismatic Education Society; **176** Collection of Mark Nichipor; **179** (tl,tr)Minuteman National Historical Park, (c)Collection of the State of South Carolina, (br)Massachusetts Historical Society; **180** William T. Ranney, MARION CROSSING THE PEDEE, 1850, o/c, 1983.126; Amon Carter Museum, Fort Worth, Texas; **181** Private Collection; **182** Chicago Historical Society; **183** Lafayette College Art Collection, Easton, PA. Gift of Mrs. John Hubbard; **184** Trumbull Collection, Yale University Art Gallery; **188** Fraunces Tavern Museum; **189** The Metropolitan Museum of Art, Gift of J.H. Grenville Gilbert, 1939 (39.87ab); **190** Picture Research Consultants, Inc.; **192** Chicago Historical Society; **194** (l)Independence National Historic Park, (r)Chicago Historical Society; **196** Independence National Historic Park; **197** Corbis-Bettmann; **198** (l)Gift of Absalom Jones School, Wilmington/Delaware Art Museum, (r)Howard University Gallery; **199** (l)Historical Society of Pennsylvania, (r)Library of Congress; **200** Columbiana Collection, Columbia University; **201** Yale University Art Gallery; **202-204** Independence National Historic Park; **205** courtesy of The National Portrait Gallery, London; **206** Fred Maroon/Smithsonian Institution; **207** (tr)Peabody Essex Museum, Salem, MA. Photo by Mark Sexton, (c)Ellen Kelleran Gardner Fund. courtesy, Museum of Fine Arts. Boston, (br, l)Colonial Williamsburg Foundation; **208** Collection, The Supreme Court Historical Society; **209** Scotchtown/photo by Katherine Wetzel; **210** Bequest of Winslow Warren. courtesy, Museum of Fine Arts, Boston; **211** Collection of The New-York Historical Society; **214** Michael Evans/Time Magazine; **215** Independence National Historic Park; **216** Picture Research Consultants, Inc.; **220** Massachusetts Historical Society; **221** SuperStock; **224** Colburn/PhotoReporters; **226** Bob Daemmrich/Tony Stone Images; **228** Sylvain Grandadam/Tony Stone Images; **230** Mark Burnett; **244** Boltin Picture Library; **249** Cobalt Productions; **251** Paul Conklin; **252** (t)Smithsonian Institution, (b)Museum of American Textile History; **252-253** courtesy, Winterthur Museum; **253** Smithsonian Institution; **254** © 1996 STAR TRIBUNE/Minneapolis-St. Paul; **255** Robert M. Friedman/Frozen Images; **256** The Brooklyn Museum. Gift of the Crescent-Hamilton Club; **257** Frank & Marie-Therese Wood Print Collection, Alexandria, VA ; **258** Library of Congress; **259** Yale University Art Gallery; **262** Atwater Kent Museum; **263** Chicago Historical Society; **266** Independence National Historic Park/photo by Joseph Painter; **267** courtesy, American Antiquarian Society; **270** Collection of David J. & Janice L. Frent; **271** Stock Montage; **276** Peabody Essex Museum, Salem, MA. Photo by Mark Sexton; **277** Boltin Picture Library; **279** SuperStock/Huntington Library, San Marino, CA; **280** Duke University Archives; **281** Colonial Williamsburg Foundation; **282** courtesy, American Antiquarian Society; **284** Chicago Historical Society; **285** Collection of The New-York Historical Society; **286** (tl)Royal Ontario Museum, Toronto, (tr,br)National Museum of American Art, Washington, DC/Art Resource, NY, (bl)Montana Historical Society; **286-287** Kevin Chadwick; **287** Peabody Museum, Harvard University; **288** Missouri Historical Society; **289** Peabody Essex Museum, Salem, MA. Photo by Mark Sexton; **291** Library of Congress; **292** (tr,br)Colonial Williamsburg Foundation, (c)Prints Collection, Miriam & Ira Wallach Division of Art, Prints & Photography, New York Public Library, Astor, Lenox and Tilden Foundation, (l)Peabody Essex Museum, Salem, MA. Photo by Jeffrey Dykes; **295** (l)Library of Congress, (r)"Tecumseh". Field Museum of Natural History FMNH Neg # A993851; **296** Princeton University Library; **297** New-York State Historical Association, Cooperstown; **299** Anne S K Brown Military Collection, Brown University; **301** Missouri Historical Society; **304** Jacob Edwards Library, Southbridge, MA/Photo by Clive Russ; **305** Bob Mullenix; **306** (l)Smithsonian Institution, (r)Yale University Art Gallery, Gift of George Hoadley, B.A. 1801.; **307** (l)Slater Mill Historic Site, (r)Museum of American Textile History; **309** Frank Wheelock's Farm , oil on canvas, .641x1.22 by Francis Alexander, c. 1822. Gift of Edgar and Bernice Chrysler Garbisch, ©

1996 Board of Trustees, National Gallery of Art, Washington, DC; **310** (l)courtesy Samuel Herrup Antiques, (r)Library Company of Philadelphia; **313** Smithsonian Institution; **315** (tr)Valentine Museum, (c)The Metropolitan Museum of Art, Rogers fund. 1942. (2.95.11), (br)Old Sturbridge Village/Thomas Neill 12.14.69 a-b, (l)Smithsonian Institution; **316** Collection of The New-York Historical Society; **317** (t)Henry Groskinsky, (b)Peter Menzel; **318** James Monroe Museum; **321** Collection of the New-York Historical Society; **322** The Historic New Orleans Collection, 1955.57; **328** (l)Private Collection/ Photo by Craig McDougal, (r)Photo by Anthony Richardson, courtesy Kit Carson Historic Museum; **328-329** The Saint Louis Art Museum; **329** courtesy, The Charleston Museum; **330** Corbis-Bettmann; **331** Library of Congress; **332** From the Art Collection of the Boatmen's National Bank of St. Louis; **333-334** Collection of David J. & Janice L. Frent; **335** Collection of the New-York Historical Society; **336** Collection of David J. & Janice L. Frent; **337** Library of Congress; **338** Library Company of Philadelphia; **340** Archives & Manuscript Division of the Oklahoma Historical Society; **340-341** Kevin Chadwick; **341** (l)White House Historical Assn., (r)Archives & Manuscript Division of the Oklahoma Historical Society; **342** National Museum of American Indian/Smithsonian Institution; **344** SuperStock; **345** (t)National Museum of American Art, Smithsonian Institution. Gift of Mrs. Joseph Harrison, Jr./Art Resource, NY, (bc)Tippecanoe County Historical Society, Lafayette, Indiana. Gift of Mrs. Cable A. Ball, (bl,br,btr)Fulton County Historical Society/photo by Mike Kenny; **346** The Thomas Gilcrease Institute of American History and Art, Tulsa, Oklahoma; **348** Corbis-Bettmann; **349** Historical Society of Pennsylvania; **350** Collection of the New-York Historical Society; **351** (l)National Portrait Gallery, Smithsonian Institution/Art Resource, NY, (r)Smithsonian Institution; **354** Collection of Mrs. J. Maxwell Moran ; **355** Nikki Pahl; **356** courtesy, Colorado Historical Society; **357** Joslyn Art Museum, Omaha, Nebraska; **358** Henry Groskinsky; **359** (l)Henry Groskinsky, (r)Mongerson-Wunderlich; **360** Collection of David J. & Janice L. Frent; **362-363** Archives Division-Texas State Library; **364** Friends of the Governor's Mansion, Austin, Texas; **366** courtesy of Bexar County and The Witte Museum, San Antonio, Texas; **367** Archives Division - Texas State Library; **368** Panhandle-Plains Historical Museum; **369** (tr,bl)courtesy of the Oakland Museum of California, (c)The Thomas Gilcrease Institute of American History and Art, Tulsa, Oklahoma, (br)Panhandle-Plains Historical Museum; **371** Collection Matthew R. Isenburg; **372** Collection of David J. & Janice L. Frent; **373** Collection of Michael Bremer; **375** California State Library, Sacramento, CA; **376** courtesy of The Oakland Museum of California; **377** (l)Levi Strauss & Company, (r)Doug Martin; **378** International Society Daughters of Utah Pioneers; **379** Denver Public Library Western History Department; **382** California State Library, Sacramento, CA; **383** Doug Martin; **384** Louisiana State University Museum of Art, Baton Rouge. Gift: Friends of the Museum and Mrs. Ben C. Hamilton in memory of her mother, Mrs. Tela Hamilton Meier; **385** Smithsonian Institution/Charles Phillips; **386** Peabody Essex Museum, Salem, MA. Photo by Mark Sexton; **388** The Chessie System, B&O Railroad Museum Archives; **390** Jack Naylor Collection; **391** M. & M. Karolik Collection, courtesy, Museum of Fine Arts, Boston; **393** (l)Museum of the City of New York, Gift of Mrs. Robert M. Littlejohn, (r)Bostonian Society Photo by Mark Sexton; **396** Grant Heilman, Grant Heilman Photography; **399** Corbis-Bettmann; **401** John Deere Museum; **402** Collection of the J. Paul Getty Museum, Los Angeles, CA; **403** Collection of The New-York Historical Society; **404** (tr)Collection of the Blue Ridge Institute & Museums/Ferrum College, (c)T.W. Wood Gallery and Arts Center, (l)Louisiana State Museum, New Orleans, (br)Valentine Museum; **406** Chester County Historical Society, Westchester, PA. Gift of Albert Cook Myers; **407** (l)National Portrait Gallery, Smithsonian Institution, Washington, DC, (r)Picture Research Consultants, Inc.; **410** SuperStock; **411** Corbis-Bettmann; **412** Collection of The New-York Historical Society; **413** Oberlin College Archives; **414** Peabody Essex Museum, Salem, MA. Photo by Mark Sexton; **415** From the Collection of Edith Hariton/Antique Textile Resource, Bethesda; **416** Massachusetts Historical Society; **417** Peabody Essex Museum, Salem, MA. Photo by Mark Sexton; **418** courtesy, American Antiquarian Society; **420** Cincinnati Art Museum; **421** Library of Congress; **424** Daughters of the American Revolution Museum, Washington, DC (Gift of Mrs. Erwin L. Broecker); **425** William Gladstone; **426** (l)Chicago Historical Society, (r)courtesy Meserve-Kunhardt Collection; **427** Joseph Goodhue Chandler (American, 1813-84), Mary Lyon, oil on canvas, 1844. Mount Holyoke College Art Museum, South Hadley, Massachusetts; **428** Maria Mitchell Assoc.; **429** Corbis-Bettmann; **432** (t)Larry Sherer, (b)Photo Network; **432-433** Frank & Marie-Therese Wood Print Collection, Alexandria, VA; **433** Mark Burnett; **434** Corbis-Bettmann; **435** Medford Historical Society; **436** courtesy Robert M. Hicklin, Jr. Inc; **437** Frank & Marie-Therese Wood Print Collection, Alexandria, VA; **438** Collection of David J. & Janice L. Frent; **439** National Portrait Gallery, Smithsonian Institution; **442** Library of Congress; **443** Schlesinger Library, Radcliffe College; **445** The State House, Topeka, Kansas/Photo courtesy of Photo One; **446** (b,r)Schomburg Center for Research in Black Culture, The New York Public Library, (l)Jim Gensheimer; **446-447** Kevin Chadwick; **448** North Wind Picture Archive; **449** (l)Collection of David J. & Janice L. Frent, (r)Museum of American Political Life/Sally Anderson Bruce; **450** Missouri State Historical Society; **451** courtesy of the Illinois State Historical Library; **453** Chicago Historical Society; **454** Collection of David J. & Janice L. Frent; **455** (t)Picture Research Consultants, Inc., (b)Matt Meadows; **457** National Portrait Gallery, Smithsonian Institution. Gift of Joel A.H. Webb and Mrs. Varina Webb Stewart/Art Resource, NY; **460** Painting by Don Troiani, Photo courtesy of Historical Art Prints, Ltd.; **461** Stamatelos Brothers Collection, Cambridge/photo Larry Sherer; **462** Seventh Regiment Fund, New York City; **464** Library of Congress; **465** Picture Research Consultants, Inc.; **466** Museum of the Confederacy; **467** (l)U.S. Naval Academy Museum, Beverly R. Robinson Collection, (r)courtesy of Stonewall Jackson Foundation, Lexington, VA; **468** Photo Larry Sherer; **469** Library of Congress; **470** Museum of the Confederacy; **472** McLellan Lincoln Collection, The John Hay Library, Brown University; **473** U.S. Capitol Historical Society; **474** Moorland-Spingarn Research Center, Howard University; **476** Collection of Larry Williford; **477** Library of Congress; **478** Museum of the Confederacy; **481** Doug Martin; **482** Manassas National Battlefield Park/photo by Larry Sherer; **485** (l)U.S. Army Center of Military History, (r)Brown Brothers; **487** Library of Congress; **488** West Point Museum/photo by Henry Groskinsky; **490** Cincinnati Historical Society; **492** © 1985 Time-Life Books Inc./Smithsonian Institution/photo by Peter Harholdt; **493** Aaron Haupt; **494** Cincinnati Art Museum, John J. Emory Fund acc. #1924.247; **495** Smithsonian Institution; **496** Gettysburg National Military Park; **497** (l) © 1986 Time-Life Books, Inc., from the series "Civil War"/ Edward Owen/Photographer, (r)Illinois State Historical Library; **499** Chicago Historical Society; **500** Tennessee Botanical Gardens & Museum of Art; **502** file photo; **503** Collection of David J. & Janice L. Frent; **504** courtesy Peter Hill, Inc.; **505** Library of Congress; **506** (tr)The State Museum of Pennsylvania, Pennsylvania Historical and Museum Commission, (l)Collection of the Blue Ridge Institute & Museums/Ferrum College, (c)Richard Norris Brooke, "A Pastoral Visit, Virginia" 1881 oil on canvas, 47 3/4 x 65 3/4 inches. In the Collection of The Corcoran Gallery of Art, Washington, DC. Museum Purchase, Gallery Fund, (br)Anacostia Museum; **507** National Museum of American History, Smithsonian Institution/photo by Rudolf Eickmeyer; **508** The American Numismatic Society; **509** Stock Montage; **511** Collection of David J. & Janice L. Frent; **512** Museum of American Political Life; **513** Smithsonian Institution; **515** Erich Lessing/Art Resource, NY; **517** courtesy Babcock Galleries, New York; **518** North Wind Picture Archive; **520** (t) courtesy Morning Star Gallery, Santa Fe, NM. photo by Addison Doty, (b)From the Collections of the Dallas Historical Society; **520-521** Collection of Mr. and Mrs. Paul Mellon, © 1996 Board of Trustees, National Gallery of Art, Washington, DC ; **521** National Park Service Collection; **522** National Portrait Gallery, Smithsonian Institution/Art Resource, NY; **523** National Museum of American Art, Washington, DC/Art Resource, NY; **524** Stark Museum of Art, Orange, Texas; **525** courtesy of the Oakland Museum of California; **527** Colorado Historical Society; **529** The Andrew J. Russell Collection, The Oakland Museum of California; **531** The Beinecke Rare Book and Manuscript Library; **532** (l)courtesy of the Arizona Historical Society, (r)The Thomas Gilcrease Institute of American History and Art, Tulsa, Oklahoma; **533** Kansas Collection, University of Kansas Libraries; **534** Library of Congress; **535** Montana Historical Society, Helena; **536** courtesy of the Oklahoma Historical Society, #10605; **538** Museum of the American Indian/Smithsonian Institution; **539** (tl, bl, r) courtesy Morning Star Gallery, Santa Fe, NM. photo by Addison Doty, (c)#1540(3), courtesy Department of Library Services, American Museum of Natural History; **541** (l)Smithsonian Institution, (r)Denver Public Library Western History Department; **544** Collection of the New-York Historical Society; **545** courtesy, American Antiquarian Society; **546** (l)Collection of David J. & Janice L. Frent, (r)Kansas State Historical Society, Topeka, Kansas; **550** Collection of Westmoreland Museum of American Art. Gift of Anthony Picadio, Pittsburgh; **551-552** Picture Research Consultants, Inc.; **556** W.H. Clark/Armstrong Jones; **557** (t)courtesy George Eastman House, (b)Smithsonian Institution; **558** (t)Library of Congress, (bl)Picture Research Consultants, Inc., (br)Queens Borough Public Library; Latimer-Noroman Family Collection; **559** courtesy Ford Motor Company; **560** courtesy of the Rockefeller Archive Center; **561** Library of Congress; **562** (tr, c)courtesy of Biltmore Estate, Asheville, North Carolina, (l)courtesy of the Oakland Museum of California, (br)Museum of the City of New York, Gift of Mary & Charles Ogden; **563** National Portrait Gallery/Smithsonian Institution/Art Resource, NY; **565** (tr)Picture Research Consultants, Inc., (bl)courtesy of AT&T Archives, (br)Michael Freeman; **566-567** Library of Congress; **569** Carnegie Library of Pittsburgh; **572** Archives Division-Texas State Library; **573** Doug Martin; **574** Museum of the City of New York, 32.275.3 Gift of Mrs. William B. Miles; **575** Photography by Karen Yamauchi for Chermayeff & Geismar Inc./Metaform Inc.; **576** (l)Library of Congress, (r)Photography by Karen Yamauchi for Chermayeff & Geismar Inc./Metaform Inc.; **577** Corbis-Bettmann; **578** Museum of the City of New York; **579** Photo by Lewis W. Hine, courtesy the New York Public Library; **582** (t)Culver Pictures, Inc., (c)courtesy of the California History Room, California State Library, Sacramento, CA, (r)Museum of American Political History, (b)Montana Historical Society, Helena; **582-583** Kevin Chadwick; **583** Library of Congress; **584** Smithsonian Institution; **585** (l)Sears, Roebuck and Company, (r)Social Ethics Collection, Carpenter Center, Harvard University; **587** (tl)Museum of the City of New York , (c)Collection of the New-York Historical Society, (r)Museum of the City of New York, Gift of Mrs. Andrew J. Miller, (bl)Museum of the City of New York, Gift of Phelps Warren; **588** (t)Kennedy Galleries, Inc, (b)University of Illinois at Chicago. The University Library. Jane Addams Memorial Collection; **590** Collection of Sue and Lars Hotham ; **591** Library of Congress; **592** Picture Research Consultants, Inc.; **593** (t)Collection of Mr. & Mrs. Arthur G. Altschul, (b)John Evans; **594** Winslow Homer, American, 1836-1910. Girls with Lobster, 1873. Watercolor, 134.3 x 33.0 cm © The Cleveland Museum of Art, 1996, Purchase from the J.H. Wade Fund, 1943.660; **595** (l)Smithsonian Institution, (r)Library of Congress; **598** (t)National Archives, (b)Collection of David J. & Janice L. Frent; **598-599** West Point Museum, U.S. Military Academy, West Point, NY; **599** Collection of David J. & Janice L. Frent; **600** Archive Photos; **601**

Credits and Acknowledgments

National Archives; **602** The Brooklyn Museum, Dick S. Ramsay Fund; **603** Doug Martin; **604** (l)Library of Congress, (r)Picture Research Consultants, Inc.; **605** Culver Pictures, Inc.; **606** (l)By permission of the Houghton Library, Harvard University, (r)Pelletier Library, Allegheny College; **609** Museum of the City of New York; **610** Museum of the City of New York. The Byron Collection; **612** Schlesinger Library, Radcliffe College; **613** Picture Research Consultants, Inc.; **614** (tl)Library of Congress, (tr)Brown Brothers,(bl)Missouri Historical Society; **614-615** Kevin Chadwick; **615** National Archives; **616-617** Collection of David J. & Janice L. Frent; **618** (l)Yosemite Museum/Leroy Radanovich, (r)Museum of American Political Life; **619** (l)Library of Congress, (r)file photo; **621** Theodore Roosevelt Collection, Harvard College Library by Permission of the Houghton Library; **622** Library of Congress; **623** (tr, l, br)Peabody Essex Museum, Salem, MA. Photo by Jeffrey Dykes, (c)Private Collection; **624** (l)Corbis-Bettmann, (r)Private Collection; **625** Culver Pictures, Inc.; **626** Schomburg Center for Research in Black Culture, The New York Public Library; **627** Wyoming Division of Cultural Resources; **630** Franklin D. Roosevelt Library; **631** Picture Research Consultants, Inc.; **632** courtesy U.S. Naval Academy Museum; **633** Historic Seward House/Photo by James M. Via; **635** National Postal Museum, Smithsonian Institution, Washington, DC; **636** Bishop Museum; **638** Library of Congress; **640** Brown Brothers; **641** Library of Congress; **643** (t)West Point Museum, U.S. Military Academy, West Point, NY, (b)courtesy of the Frederic Remington Art Museum, Ogdensburg, NY; **645** Aaron Haupt; **646** Picture Research Consultants, Inc.; **647** (t)Corbis-Bettmann, (b)Private Collection, photo courtesy R.H. Love Galleries, Inc., Chicago; **648** Library of Congress; **649** El Paso Public Library; **654** Library of Congress; **655** Corbis-Bettmann; **657** Collection of Colonel Stuart S. Corning; **658** (l)Corbis-Bettmann, (r)U.S. Air Force; **660** Picture Research Consultants, Inc.; **661** (l)Larry O. Nighswander/National Geographic Society Image Collection, (r)Corbis-Bettmann; **664** Corbis-Bettmann; **665** Military Records, Comm. of MA; **667** (tr, br, l)Collection of Colonel Stuart S. Corning, (c)Imperial War Museum London; **668** National Gallery of Art, Washington, DC. Gift of Ethelyn McKinney in memory of her brother, Glen Ford McKinney; **669** Collection of Colonel Stuart S. Corning; **670** Picture Research Consultants, Inc.; **671-673** National Archives; **674** Smithsonian Institution; **675** Imperial War Museum London; **677** (l)Corbis-Bettmann, (r)National Portrait Gallery, Smithsonian Institution; **679** Bayerisches, Hauptstaatsarchiv, Munich; **682** Corbis-Bettmann; **683** Doug Martin; **684** (t)Collection of Major General George S. Patton. Photograph © Rob Huntley/Lightstream, (b)Library of Congress; **684-685** United States Marine Corps Museum; **685** Picture Research Consultants, Inc.; **686** Deborah Storms/Macmillan Publication Co.; **687** Myron Davis, Life Magazine © 1977 Time Inc.; **688** Collection of the Museum of Fine Arts, Museum of New Mexico, Gift of Mrs. Cyrus McCormick, 1952; **689** Brown Brothers; **690** (l)Wide World, (r)Corbis-Bettmann; **691** (t)Chicago Historical Society, (b)Corbis-Bettmann; **693-694** Collection of David J. & Janice L. Frent; **695** Picture Research Consultants, Inc.; **696** National Archives; **697** Brown Brothers; **698** Photo by Decio Grassi; **701** Library of Congress; **702** Picture Research Consultants, Inc.; **703** (t)Schomburg Center for Research in Black Culture, The New York Public Library, (b)The New York Public Library at Lincoln Center; **704** The Museum of Modern Art, New York. Gift of Mrs. Nickolas Muray; **705** (tl)Frank Driggs Collection, (tr,rc)The Historic New Orleans Collection, 92-48-L, (tc)Archibald John Motley, Jr., American, 1891-1981, Blues, oil on canvas, 1929, 80x100.3 cm, Lent by Archie Motley and Valerie Gerrard Browne, 2.1993 © 1996, The Art Institute of Chicago. All Rights Reserved., (bl, br)The Beinecke Rare Book & Manuscript Library, Yale University; **706** National Archives; **707** (l)Private Collection, (r)Frank Driggs Collection; **708** Library of Congress; **710** Brown Brothers; **711** Collection of David J. & Janice L. Frent; **714** "Private Car" by Leconte Stewart © The Church of Jesus Christ of Latter-Day Saints courtesy of The Museum of Church History & Art. Used by Permission; **715** Corbis-Bettmann; **717** Collection of John P. Axelrod; **718** Library of Congress; **719** (l)Photo by Berenice Abbot, neg. #35 Federal Arts Project "Changing New York" Museum of the City of New York, (r)Detroit Publishing Company; **720** Collection of David J. & Janice L. Frent; **721** Franklin D. Roosevelt Library; **722** Library of Congress; **723** (l, tr)Collection of Mr. & Mrs. Edmund Berry/Picture Research Consultants, Inc., (c)Doris Lee, American, 1905-1983, Thanksgiving, oil on canvas, 1935, 71.4x101.6cm, Mr. & Mrs. Frank G. Logan Prize Fund, 1935.313 © 1996, The Art Institute of Chicago. All Rights Reserved., (br)Collection of Fay Kyle/Picture Research Consultants, Inc.; **724** courtesy of the General Services Administration's Public Buildings Service, on loan to the National Gallery of Art, Washington, DC; **725** Franklin D. Roosevelt Library; **726** (tl)Corbis-Bettmann, (tr)Library of Congress; **726-727** Kevin Chadwick; **727** Library of Congress; **728** Corbis-Bettmann; **730** Library of Congress; **731** Corbis-Bettmann; **732** Everett Collection; **733, 734, 735** Collection of David J. & Janice L. Frent; **736** Franklin D. Roosevelt Library; **740** U.S. Army Center of Military History; **741** By permission of the Houghton Library, Harvard University; **742** (t)Manezh, Moscow, (b)Hugo Jaeger, Life Magazine © Time Inc.; **743** Paul Dorsey, Life Magazine © Time Inc. ; **744** (l)National Archives, (r)Wide World; **745** National Archives; **746** Imperial War Museum London; **748** Franklin D. Roosevelt Library; **749** U.S. Army photo; **750** Private Collection; **751** (tl)Private Collection, (tr)United States Air Force Museum, (b)Picture Research Consultants, Inc.; **752** Franklin D. Roosevelt Library; **753** (t)Picture Research Consultants, Inc., (b)National Archives; **754** Los Angeles Daily News Morgue, Department of Special Collections, University Research Library, UCLA; **755** Picture Research Consultants, Inc.; **757** Johnny Florea, Life Magazine © Time Inc.; **758** (l)Combat Art Division, U.S. Navy, (r)Department of the Army; **759** Corbis-Bettmann; **761** Warren Motts Photographic Center; **762** Carl Mydans, Life Magazine © Time Inc.; **763** (t)SuperStock, (b)Corbis-Bettmann; **764** Library of Congress; **765** National Geographic Society Image Collection; **768** (t)Ralph J. Brunke, (b)Robert Reiff/FPG, Int.; **768-769** Photo courtesy of The Norman Rockwell Museum at Stockbridge/Norman Rockwell Family Trust; **769** David J. Sams/Stock Boston; **770** Don Perdue/Gamma Liaison; **771** The Metropolitan Museum of Art, Arthur Hoppock Hearn Fund, 1950. (50.29); **772** U.S. Army Center of Military History; **773** U.S. Army; **774** Glencoe Photo; **775** (l)Wide World, (r)Reprinted from the Des Moines Register. Jay N. Darling 1946; **776** George C. Marshall Foundation; **777** Corbis-Bettmann; **778** (t)Wide World, (b)Collection of Haya Gordin; **779** Wide World; **780** Collection of David J. & Janice L. Frent; **781** Indiana University Photo Services; **783** Corbis-Bettmann; **784** (l)Cornell Capa, Life Magazine © Time Inc., (r)Collection of David J. & Janice L. Frent; **785** Collection of Colonel Corning; **787** Corbis-Bettmann; **789** Michael Barson/Past Perfect; **790** Corbis-Bettmann; **792** Picture Research Consultants, Inc.; **793** Mark Burnett; **796** © The Curtis Publishing Company; **797** Smithsonian Institution; **798** Collection of David J. & Janice L. Frent; **800** Collection of Michael Barson; **801** Michael Barson/Past Perfect; **803** Corbis-Bettmann; **804** Wide World; **806** National Geographic Society Image Collection; **807** Picture Research Consultants, Inc.; **809** (tr)Picture Research Consultants, Inc., (l)Collection of Jim Catania, Woburn, MA, (c) © The Curtis Publishing Company, (br)Collection of Doug Sikes, Granby, CT; **810** (l)Ralph Crane, Life Magazine © Time Inc., (r)Picture Research Consultants, Inc.; **812-813** Picture Research Consultants, Inc.; **814** (l) © Martin Manger/ courtesy, Center for Creative Photography, The University of Arizona, (r)Wide World ; **815** (t)F. DeWitt, (b)Dan Weiner, courtesy Sandra Weiner; **817** Collection of Michael Barson/Past Perfect; **820** Collection of Stephen Hall/photo by Gary Newyear & Co.; **821** Collection of Michael Barson/Past Perfect; **823** (l)Frances Miller/Life Magazine © Time Inc., (r)Collection of David J. & Janice L. Frent; **824** "The Beginning" by Artis Lane; **825** Bob Fitch/Black Star; **826** Collection of David J. & Janice L. Frent; **827** Smithsonian Institution; **828** Corbis-Bettmann; **829** (t)Yoichi R. Okamoto/LBJ Library Collection, (b)Henry Groskinsky; **830** Don Uhrbroch/Life Magazine © Time Inc.; **831** Don McCoy/Black Star; **832** (l)Charles Moore/Black Star, (r)Picture Research Consultants, Inc.; **833** (tr) Collection of David J. & Janice L. Frent, (l,br)Picture Research Consultants, Inc., (c)James P. Blair/National Geographic Image Collection; **834** Corbis-Bettmann; **835** Vernon Merritt/Black Star; **836** (t)Corbis-Bettmann (l,br)Wide World; **836-837** Kevin Chadwick; **837** Corbis-Bettmann; **838** Picture Research Consultants, Inc.; **839** (tl)Corbis-Bettmann, (tr)Mike Powell/ Allsport, (bl)Steve Northrup © 1977 Time, (br)Lynda Gordon/Gamma Liaison; **840** Arthur Schatz © 1968 Time Inc.; **841** (l)Collection of David J. & Janice L. Frent, (r)Wide World; **842** Bruce Kliewe/The Picture Cube, Inc.; **843** Bob Daemmrich/Stock Boston; **846** U.S. Army Center of Military History; **847-848** Collection of David J. & Janice L. Frent; **849** (l)Wide World, (r)Black Star; **851** Collection of David J. & Janice L. Frent; **852** Private Collection; **853** (l)Wide World, (r)Corbis-Bettmann; **854** Harry Breedlove; **855** Dick Swanson, Life Magazine © Time Inc.; **856** (l)Ray Cranbourne, Empore/Black Star, (r)Larry Burrows, Life Magazine © Time Inc.; **857** Larry Burrows, Life Magazine © Time Inc.; **858** Collection of David J. & Janice L. Frent; **859** © Bernie Boston; **861** Costa Manos/Magnum Photos, Inc.; **862** Private Collection; **863** (t)John Olsen, (b)Corbis-Bettmann; **864** (l)Steve Shapiro/Black Star, (r)Corbis-Bettmann; **866** Black Star; **867** Collection of David J. & Janice L. Frent; **869** Camera Press/Retna Ltd.; **870** John Filo; **871** Corbis-Bettmann; **872** (tl)Antique Textile Resource, (r,bl)Smithsonian Institution, (c)Christopher Morris/ Black Star; **876** (t)John Sohm/Chromosohm/Stock Boston, (b)Aaron Haupt; **876-877** National Center for Supercomputing Applications; **877** Corbis-Bettmann; **878** San Jose Mercury News; **879** Bob Daemmrich; **880** Milton Bond, Private Collection; **881** Collection of David J. & Janice L. Frent; **882** Corbis-Bettmann; **883** Dirck Halstead/Gamma Liaison; **884** Corbis-Bettmann; **885** Magnum/Black Star; **886** Collection of David J. & Janice L. Frent; **887** courtesy of the Richmond Times-Dispatch; **888** Collection of David J. & Janice L. Frent; **889** (l)Mike Mazzaschi/Stock Boston, (r)Dennis Brack/Black Star; **890** Fred Ward/Black Star; **891** Alex Webb/ Magnum Photos, Inc.; **892** Picture Research Consultants, Inc.; **893** Wide World; **894** (tl)Picture Research Consultants, Inc., (c)Forum Gallery, (r)Antique Textile Resource, Bethesda, (bl)The Music Emporium, Inc.; **896** Dagmar Fabricius/ Gamma Liaison; **895** (l)Collection of David J. & Janice L. Frent, (r)Gerald R. Ford Library and Museum; **897** Henry Groskinsky; **898** Jimmy Carter Library; **899-900** Gamma Liaison; **904** Robert Kusel/Tony Stone Images; **905** Collection of David J. & Janice L. Frent; **906** Fred Ward/Black Star; **908** Terry Ashe/Time Magazine; **909** (l)Collection of David J. & Janice L. Frent, (r)David Burnett/ Contact Press Images; **910** Collection of David J. & Janice L. Frent; **911** Peter Marlow/ Magnum; **912** Sygma; **913** Sergei Guneyev/Time; **914** Steve Liss/Time Magazine; **915** Luc Delahaye/Sipa Press; **916** Marion Bernstein; **917** R. Bossu/ Sygma; **918** Mark Burnett; **919** Wide World; **920** Peter Turnley/Black Star; **922** (t)Printed from Digital Images © 1996 Corbis, (c)Frank Siteman/Tony Stone Images, (b)The Image Bank; **922-923** Kevin C. Chadwick; **923** Mark Thiessen/ National Geographic Society; **924** David Lawrence/Stock Market; **925** Steve Lehman/Tony Stone Images; **927** (t)Joe Sohm/The Stock Market, (b)David Butow/SABA; **929** Life Images; **932** RMIP/Richard Hayes; **933** Aaron Haupt; **934** Glencoe Photo; **A1-A8** White House Historical Association; **A9** North Wind Picture Archive; **A10-A11** Corbis-Bettmann; **A12** (t)Corbis-Bettmann, (b)Museum of American Indians; **A13** National Portrait Gallery/ Smithsonian Institution/Art Resource, NY; **A14** (l)Mark Burnett, (r)Smithsonian Institution; **A15** Mark Burnett; **A16** (t)Denver Art Museum, (b)Corbis-Bettmann Archive; **A17, A18, A19** Corbis-Bettmann; **A20** Flip Schulke/Black Star.